VARIETY
Film Reviews

Garland Publishing, Inc.
New York and London
1988

Contents

Film Reviews
1985–1986

VOLUME NINETEEN

Includes an Index to Titles
for 1985–1986

Garland Publishing, Inc.
New York and London
1988

Library of Congress Serial Data

Variety Film Reviews, 1985–1986
    Volume 19

ISSN 0897-4373

ISBN 0–8240–5219-6

Manufactured in the United States of America

Printed on acid-free,
250-year-life paper

Preface

The reviews contained in this volume are complete and comprehensive reproductions of the original reviews printed in *Variety*. Only full-length feature films are included. Short subjects and made for television films are not included.

User's Guide

The reviews in this collection are published in chronological order, by the date on which the review appeared. The date of each issue appears at the top of the column where the reviews for that issue begin. The reviews continue through that column and all following columns until a new date appears at the top of the page. Where blank spaces occur at the end of a column, this indicates the end of that particular week's reviews. An index to film titles for the years 1985–1986 is published in this volume.

1985

A Private Function
(BRITISH-COLOR)

London, Dec. 30.

An Island Alive release (U.S.) of a Hand-Made Films production. Produced by Mark Shivas. Executive producers, Denis O'Brien, George Harrison. Directed by Malcolm Mowbray. Stars Michael Palin, Maggie Smith. Screenplay, Alan Bennett; camera (color), Tony Pierce-Roberts; editor, Barrie Vince; music, John Du Prez; production design, Stuart Walker; costumes, Phyllis Dalton. Reviewed at the Odeon Haymarket, London, Dec. 29, 1984. (BBFC Certificate: 15.) Running time: **93 MINS.**

Gilbert Chilvers	Michael Palin
Joyce Chilvers	Maggie Smith
Mother	Liz Smith
Doctor Swaby	Denholm Elliott
Allardyce	Richard Griffiths
Lockwood	John Normington
Mr. Wormold	Bill Paterson
Mr. Sutcliff	Tony Haygarth
Mrs. Allardyce	Alison Steadman
Broadbent	Pete Postlethwaite
Inspector Noble	Jim Carter

"A Private Function" is a neat comedy rooted in uniquely English eccentricities which, nevertheless, stands a good chance of hitting home with other English-speaking audiences. That's largely credit to a perceptive and witty script from vet tv screenwriter Alan Bennett and topnotch ensemble acting.

Central characters are the husband and wife team played by Maggie Smith and Michael Palin, who previously worked together in "The Missionary," also for HandMade. She's a bullying wife anxious to reach the social highspots in the Yorkshire village where he works as a foot doctor. Their domestic crises are made more complex and amusing by the presence of a greedy mother (Liz Smith) who lives in terror of being put away.

Pic is set in 1947, at a time of national rejoicing over a royal wedding and hardship caused by food rationing. Plot evolves out of a plan hatched by a group of town notables to fatten up a secret pig for festive devouring on the wedding night.

The laughs come fast, however, after Gilbert is cajoled by his wife into stealing the unlicensed pig, thus unsettling the plans of the local dignitaries. Slightly vulgar comic situations result from the pig's unhealthy gastric situation, Gilbert's reluctance to use his chiropody tools for butchery, and the desperation of the dignitaries in their search for alternative food sources.

Malcolm Mowbray, who's a graduate from the National Film School with a handful of tv drama credits, neatly orchestrates the resulting drama, and points up the class antagonisms at play.

The humor has a broad scope from gentle irony to outright farce With excellent production design, camerawork and musical score credits, it makes for an ace eccentric pic. —*Japa.*

The Last Night Of Madam Chin
(TAIWAN-HONG KONG-COLOR)

Hong Kong, Nov. 19.

A First Film Organization Ltd. production and release. Directed by Lin Chen-ping. Stars Yao Wei, Ou Yang, Mu Su Cheng. Screenplay, Pai Chin, Music, Chen Chi Yuan; costumes, Wnag Yu Sheng; soundtrack vocals, Tsai Chin. Reviewed at Park Theater, Hong Kong, Nov. 18, 1984. Running time: **100 MINS..**

The setting is the turbulent, colorful and decadent world of the ballrooms that flourished in Shanghai before 1949.

Jolie Chan (Lin Chen-ping) is a ballroom girl (taxi dancer) at the Paramount Club in the then swinging city. She falls in love with a young student and gets pregnant. The family of the young man intervenes and she is forced to have an abortion.

Many years later, Jolie is a rich, flamboyant queen of the ballroom girl circuit (of a higher class) at the Nuits De Paris, located in the heart of Taipei's nightclub area.

In her dressing room while preparing for her grand exit, Madam Chin reflects on her youth, her first true love and her second lover.

In this First Films presentation, one can see the more relaxed treatment of the erotic sequence in Taiwan through the performers still look shy when things get intimate. The general presentation is commendable, but could have been a better film with more impact had the editor made the sequences more compact. —*Mel.*

The Mutilator
(COLOR)

Dull horror pic.

A Marvin Films release of an OK Prods. picture. Produced by Buddy Cooper. Directed by Cooper, John S. Douglass. Features entire cast. Screenplay, Cooper; camera (Movielab color), Peter Schnall; editor, Stephen Mack; music, Michael Minard; production manager, Tamara Bally; assistant directors, Richard Garber, M. Walker Pearce; sound, Larry Loewinger; special makeup effects, Mark Shostrom, Anthony Showe; add'l makeup effects, Edward Ferrell; set decoration, Stephen Davis; stunts, Art Drewyor; associate producer, Neil B. Whitford. Reviewed at RKO National 2 theater, N.Y., Jan. 5, 1984. (No MPAA Rating.) Running time: **86 MINS.**
With: Matt Mitler, Ruth Martinez, Bill Hitchcock, Frances Raines, Morley Lampley, Connie Rogers, Jack Chatham, Ben Moore, Pamela Weddle Cooper, Trace Cooper.

"The Mutilator" is a boring horror film, designed strictly for fans of explicit gore. Picture was filmed in North Carolina in 1983 as "Fall Break" (in keeping with the trend of scare films linked to seasonal holidays), a title retained in its theme song, played twice.

Weak premise has young boy Ed (Trace Cooper) accidentally shooting his mom while cleaning his dad's guns. Dad (Jack Chatham) is understandably perturbed, but no explanation is given for him becoming a grotesque, homicidal nut later. Story continues when Ed (played by Matt Mitler as an adult) is at college, taking along five friends during fall semester break to take care of dad's island condo on the beach.

There's no more story in filmmaker Buddy Cooper's arsenal, as the bulk of the picture consists of waiting for these stupid teenagers to be horribly killed by daddy and mounted on the wall as part of his trophy collection. Acting is subpar, with Bill Hitchcock providing needed comic relief.

Gore effects are exaggerated and plentiful enough to merit an X rating if the film is submitted to the MPAA; it's currently in release with a printed poster/ad warning that is equivalent to the meaning of an R rating. — *Lor.*

Other Halves
(NEW ZEALAND-COLOR)

Wellington, N.Z., Oct. 18.

An Oringham Limited production. Directed by John Laing. Produced by Tom Finlayson and Dean Hill. Screenplay, Sue McCanley, based on her novel; camera (color) Leon Narbey; production design, Robert Gilles; editor, Harley Oliver; music, Don McGlashan; sound, Graham Morris. Reviewed at a preview, Embassy theater, Wellington, Oct. 17, 1984. Running time: **102 MINS.**

Liz	Lisa Harrow
Tug	Mark Pilisi
Michael	Fraser Stephen-Smith
Ken	Paul Gittins
Audrey	Emma Piper
Irwin	Bruce Purchase
Jim	John Bach
Aileen	Clare Clifford
Tony	Temuera Morrison
Billy	Raymond Reid

The great leap forward by Kiwi filmmakers has been achieved with scripts that primarily locate their stories in the country's rural-scenic hinterland ("Sleeping Dogs," "Vigil," "Utu"), or small towns and communities ("Skin Deep," "Scarecrow," "Death Warmed Up"). The here-and-now largely has been avoided.

"Other Halves" is a breakthrough in that it is urban and contemporary. It matches Auckland, New Zealand's largest city and the world's largest city of Polynesian population, with a love story between a 32-year-old middle-class white woman and a 16-year-old Polynesian street kid. It is international in the resonances its theme will have for metropolitan audiences in Europe, North America and Japan.

Based on the novel by Sue McCauley, who wrote the screenplay, the film centers on the struggle of Liz Harvey (Lisa Harrow) and Tug Morton (Mark Pilisi) to weld a relationship across barriers of age, color and class.

The city Liz knows is secure and safe, affluent and genteel. Tug's streets are hostile and violent. The two meet at a time when both are beginning to lose control of their particular environments and lifestyles.

From this first meeting, the relationship develops fitfully as Liz leaves her husband and young son to build an independent life, while Tug starts to realize there is more to living than staying one step ahead of the police and the courts.

Harrow makes Liz' gradual switch from a life of passive acceptance to one of individual action moving and real. As Tug, Pilisi is all raw energy and restlessness. A real life street kid undertaking his first acting role, he has a natural ability for sly humor on celluloid.

However, while the turbulence of the affair is generally well-detailed, its quieter moments are sometimes missing. At times too, more shading of Harrow's performance would have helped leaven the drama.

However, director Laing knows the priorities — how to move a story imaginatively, how to get performances and how to concentrate his images.

The star of the film — even given the sterling performances of Harrow and Pilisi and Emma Piper (Audrey) and Temuera Morrison (Tony) in secondary roles — could well be Auckland. It comes through as a pulsating, vital and human metropolis. — *Nic.*

World Safari II
(AUSTRALIAN-DOCU-COLOR)

Sydney, Dec. 24.

A World Safari production. Produced and directed by Alby Mangels. Camera (color),

Steve Levitt, Don McLeod, Geoff Hall; editors, Peter Fletcher, Lyn Tunbridge, Chris Cordeaux; music, Mario Marlo, Glenn Shorrock; commentary written by Ken Ross, spoken by Roger Cardwell: Reviewed at Hoyts Warringah Theater, Sydney, Dec. 21, 1984. Running time: **120 MINS.**

As the title suggests, this is a sequel to a 1975 docu of the same name and represents the further adventures of Dutch-born Alby Mangels. The title is misleading, though, as this particular safari covers only the Southern Hemisphere, namely Australia, Papua-New Guinea and some Latin American countries.

Pic is essentially an elaborate home movie of a sometimes hazardous trip on which the intrepid Mangels was accompanied by a bewildering series of glamorous women — who come and go with hardly a comment from the narrator — and, in the beginning, by his feisty bull terrier, Sam. Mangels and his small crew initially set sail in his square-rigged sail-ship, "Gretta Marie," though he detours into the Australian outback by jeep, motorbike and light aircraft to search for opals, catch wild animals and take part in — and win — a fiercely competitive outback horse race.

During his lengthy trek, Mangels survives the fire that destroys his ship (off-screen), crocodiles, a savage wild pig and a South American car crash (also off-screen) that almost kills the tv game-show hostess who's his partner at the time. His dog, the liveliest character in the film, is shot by an unknown assailant.

This is a roughly made, amateurish affair, though in halls all over the country, Mangels mopped up with the first film, which was equally roughly made. He seems set to do the same again with this one.
— *Strat.*

Cabra Marcado Para Morrer
(A Man Labeled To Die)
(BRAZILIAN-COLOR/B&W)

Rio de Janeiro, Nov. 22.
A Mapa release of a Mapa production. Directed by Eduardo Coutinho. Camera, (color), Edgar Moura (1981), & (b&w), Fernando Duarte (1964); editor, Eduardo Escorel; music, Rogerio Rossini; direct sound, Jorge Saldanha; assistant camera, Nonato Estrela; narration, Ferreira Gullar, Tite de Lemos, Eduardo Coutinho; associate producer, Valdimir Carvalho; executive producer, Zelito Viana; produced by Produções Cinematográficas Mapa and Eduardo Coutinho. Reviewed at main screening room, Hotel Nacional, First Intl. Festival of Cinema, TV and Video of Rio de Janeiro, Nov. 31, 1984. Running time: **119 MINS.**
With Elizabeth Teixeira and her family, João Virginio Silva and the people of the village of Engenho Galiléia, state of Pernambuco, Brazil.

"Cabra Marcado Para Morrer" by Eduardo Coutinho won the Golden Tucano (principal official award) of the first Rio Festival. It also won the Intl. Critics Award, the OCIC and the Naitional Federation

of Cineclubs award.

Film is at the same time a documentary and a fictional story; a political work and an almost experimental investigation of the medium itself.

Originally, "Cabra" was conceived as a feature film based on fact: the murder in 1962 of peasant leader João Pedro Teixeira. Coutinho started shooting by 1963, in black and white and with a quasineorealistic approach, as was usual with the polticially committed Brazilian films of that time, which anticipated by a few months the explosion of the *cinema novo*. João Pedro's widow, Elizabeth Teixeira, would play her own role, as well as a number of fellow peasants.

The military coup of 1964 interrupted the work. The material was confiscated, the crew was held for a few days and the performers were forced to move to other villages.

Over the following 17 years, director Eduardo Coutinho worked as journalist at newspapers and, recently, Globo TV. In 1981, he decided to go back to the northeast to resume his work on "Cabra." Taking the equipment and a 16m print of what he had shot up to 1964, he showed the material to the original performers and characters of João Pedro's story, and documented their reactions. "Cabra" was reborn as a documentary on the fate of its own characters. It became a historical document of the revolution from the losers' viewpoint.

"Cabra" suggests the cinema's capacity to be an agent of its own creative process. It is a highly original documentary. — *Hoin.*

Akropolis Now
(SWISS-COLOR)

Zurich, Dec. 18.
A Rex Film AG Zollikon release of a Bernard Lang AG Zürich production. Written and directed by Hans Liechti. Stars Wolfram Berger, Max Rüdlinger. Based on a story by David Hoener, Ernst Spycher; screenplay collaborators, Su Kappeler, Rainer Klausmann; camera (Eastman/Fujicolor), Klausmann; sound, Hans Künzi; editor, Fee Liechti; lighting, Felix Meyer, Willy Kopp; music, Ben Jeger. Reviewed at the Movie 2, Zurich, Dec. 17, 1984. Running time: **103 MINS.**
Flo . . . . Wolfram Berger
Walti . . . . Max Rüdlinger
Camille . . . . Dominique Laffin
Erika . . . . Christine Lauterburg
Jean-Luc . . . . Roger Jendly
Helen . . . . Yvonne Kupper
Walti's Mother . . . . Alice Brüngger
Mr. Schweizer . . . . Hans Liechti
Mrs. schweizer . . . . Ursula Bischof
Xavier . . . . Michalis Janatos
Camille's Father . . Vasilis Diamantopoulos
Waiter . . . . Dimitri Poulikakas
Driver . . . . Fotini Kotrotzi
Barman . . . . Rolf Lyssy
Barman's Wife . . . . Yolanda Gambaro

"Akropolis Now" (the pun on Francis Coppola's "Apocalypse Now" is intentional), is Swiss cameraman Hans Liechti's first film

as a scripter-director. He shows a flair for lighthanded comedy rarely found in Swiss films.

Two Zurich buddies, both in their mid-30s, one a married architect and the other a bachelor owning a smalltime cabaret, decide to drive two American cars via Italy and Greece to Cairo to sell them for a big profit. They are joined by an attractive, mysterious French girl who succeeds in driving off alone in one of the cars and luring the two pals, now together in the other car, all the way to Athens. There, the whole journey is revealed as a hoax cleverly staged by the girl.

Liechti centers his attention on the psychological situation of the two friends nearing their midlife crisis. At the end of the journey which, financially, goes up into thin air, one has been softened, and the other may shake off his Swiss stolidity.

Liechti considers his film a team effort as the actors also had a say in the script. This has its advantages, such as added spontaneity and a relaxed atmosphere. On the other hand, a director's firm hand is sometimes missing, and in its lesser moments, the film just leisurely tags along.

The picture's chief asset is its cast. Austrian actor Wolfram Berger and Swiss newcomer Max Rüdlinger are an irresistible pair. The former's slightly cocky, boyish charm blends perfectly with Rüdlinger's at first sourpuss, later drily sarcastic personality. French actress Dominique Laffin is just right as the mystery woman. In the Greek sequences, shot on location, excellent cameos are contributed by local actors Michalis Janatos, Vasilis Diamantopoulos and Dimitri Poulikakas.
— *Mezo.*

Tuff Turf
(COLOR)

Compelling youth film.

Hollywood, Dec. 20.
A New World Pictures release of a Donald Borchers production. Directed by Fritz Kiersch. Produced by Borchers. Screenplay, Jette Rinck; camera (CFI Color), Willy Kurant; editor, Marc Grossman; sound, Ed White, Craig Felburg; art direction, Craig Stearns; set decorator, Anne Kuljian; music, Jonathan Elias; associate producer, Bob Manning; assistant director, James Murray, Jesse Wayne; coproducer, Pat Kehoe; casting, Linda Francis. Previewed at MGM/UA, Dec. 19, 1984. (MPAA Rating: R.) Running time: **112 MINS.**
Morgan Hiller . . . . James Spader
Frankie Croyden . . . . Kim Richards
Nick Hauser . . . . Paul Mones
Jimmy Parker . . . . Robert Downey
Stuart Hiller . . . . Matt Clark
Page Hiller . . . . Claudette Nevins
Ronnie . . . . Olivia Barash
Mickey . . . . Panchito Gomez
Eddie . . . . Michael Wyle
Feather . . . . Catya Sassoon
Brian Hiller . . . . Bill Beyers
Man at Bus Stop . . . . Frank McCarthy
Jim Carroll . . . . Himself

Like the staccato rhythm of its title, this modestly budgeted youth pic delivers sufficient street punch to lay claim to a boxoffice payoff for New World Pictures. Second-time director Fritz Kiersch ("Children Of The Corn"), producer and former New World v.p. Donald Borchers, and scenarist Jette Rinck exchange sex, nudity and foul language for a poor man's and partially musicalized "Rebel Without A Cause," with a touch of "The Warriors" thrown in.

Rebellious newcomer James Spader is the James Dean character and saucy gang moll Kim Richards is the Natalie Wood character. They go through social and romantic hell for each other and, in the process, a large slice of suburban L.A. and uncomprehending parenthood embellish a story that is deceptively compelling despite, in this case, a distracting mix of comedy and music.

Latter, which includes on-screen appearances by the L.A. band Jack Mack and the Heart Attack and rocker Jim Carroll, gives the production a socking sound (and in the case of Carroll's number, "It's Too Late," the songwriter sings the lyric his record company found too controversial to include in his first recorded album: "It's too soon/but the bullet's gonna dance/in the brain of Reverend Moon").

The on-screen music, however, lurches the film off balance, especially combined with unexpected and dramatically jarring numbers by the two stars (Spader materializing as a balladeer in a country club — with his voice dubbed by Art Carney's son, Paul Carney — and Richards whirling into an aerodynamic disco dancer.) The effect is not unlike suddenly watching James Dean in "Rebel Without A Cause" swoon a love song from a bandstand. Likeable in themselves, all these numbers flaw an otherwise taut and tension-filled youth drama. Younger kids shouldn't mind but discriminating late teeners will.

Protagonist's family situation is interesting. Hero's once successful dad (nicely essayed by durable Matt Clark) has fallen on hard times and has had to move family from the yachting club set on the East Coast to a modest home in what appears to be the nether reaches of Van Nuys. New school, new tough environment greet the intelligent, quietly focused and troubled Spader. His situation suggests Holden Caulfield meets Valley Girl.

Spader's violent and growingly crazed antagonist is played with strong bite and edge by Paul Mones. His violence, locked as it is to losing his "property" in the form of g.f. Richards, is anchored in believability. His showdown with Spader at film's climax is particularly well executed and choreographed, with a pair of nasty dobermans thrown in.

Robert Downey is a fresh surprise in a nice sidekick role, and Olivia Barash and Catya Sassoon (the daughter of Vidal Sassoon) lend able teen support. Only unpleasant performance is the young protagonist's snotty mother, played with more unappeal than necessary by Claudette Nevins. — *Loyn.*

Les Fausses Confidences
(The False Confidences)
(FRENCH-COLOR)

Paris, Dec. 5.

An Epoc Films release of a Gerland Productions film. Produced by Roger Coggio. Directed by Daniel Moosmann. Screenplay, Moosmann, Bernard G. Landry, from the Marivaux play; camera (color), Etienne Becker; art director, Michel de Broin; music, Jean Musy; makeup, Muriel Paupere; costumes, Sylvie Poulet; editors, Anna Ruiz, Christian Allanic; production manager, Jacques Schaeffer. Reviewed at the Georges V cinema, Paris, Dec. 4, 1984. Running time: **110 MINS.**

Dorante	Jean-Pierre Bouvier
Dubois	Roger Coggio
Marton	Fanny Cottençon
Araminte	Brigitte Fossey
M. Rémy	Michel Galabru
Mme Argante	Micheline Presle
Arlequin	Paul Préboist
The Count	Robert Rimbaud

"Les Fausses Confidences" is a conscientious, finely acted filming of the comedy of manners by the 18th century French playwright Marivaux. Basically this is conventional canned theater, but done with feeling, polish and the underlying belief that the classics don't need contemporary-minded facelifts to find a new audience.

It is the first in a projected series of stage- and page-to-screen theatrical films advocated by Roger Coggio, the producer-actor-director who already has filmed Molière's "Scapin" and "The Bourgeois Gentleman," both debatable but estimable efforts. For "Confidences" he's selected as helmer Daniel Moosmann, who has three theatrical features to his credit.

Marivaux' exquisite piece deals with the efforts of an impoverished young man of good family to win the hand (and fortune) of a rich young widow, into whose household he's gained admission as a possible administrator. Despite the machinations of his former valet, who has entered the widow's service to set up the plot, the protagonist encounters obstacles in a series of romantic quid pro quos and conflicting projects from the widow's mother, who's eyeing a marriage of convenience for her with a wealthy count.

The beauty of Marivaux' work is in its elegantly ironic dialog and the double-edged finesse with which the author dissects the romantic impulses and ulterior motivations of his complex characters.

Moosman, aided by co-adaptor Bernard G. Landry (who worked on Coggio's Molière films), has pre-

served these qualities in the screen transcription, which fluidly opens up the play to evolve in and about the widow's country mansion. The setting for each scene is blocked out carefully, with only one sequence misconceived (a confrontation between the young man and the widow which opens by latter surprising former stepping naked from his bath — it's a blatantly 1980s reading that jars with Marivaux' subtle classical manner).

Pic's major success is the silken ensemble performances, which set out Marivaux' glittering prose with evident relish. The women shine notably: Brigitte Fossey as the radiantly desirable widow, Fanny Cottençon as her no-less-charming waiting-maid, and Micheline Presle as Fossey's authoritative, social-minded mother. On the male side, Jean-Pierre Bouvier is quietly fine as the penniless protagonist in search of Fossey's hand, Michel Galabru is in his comic element as his uncle, and Coggio gives the manipulating valet a disquieting ambiguity.

Camerawork, art direction and costumes are first-rate, and Jean Musy's lovely music continues to pirouette in the mind after the final celluloid curtain. —*Len.*

Hong Kong 1941
(HONG KONG-COLOR)

Hong Kong, Nov. 12.

A D&B Films & Bo Ho Films production. Presented by Dickson Poon and Samo Hung. Directed by Leong Po-chi. Stars Chow Yan Fat, Cecilia Yip, Alex Man, Han Yee Sang, Sak Kin, Kuk Fung, Yu San, Paul Chun. Producer, John Sham; production designer, screenplay, Chan Koon-chung; cinematographer, Brian Lai, Chung Chi-Man; art direction, Yee Chungman; stunt coordinator, Lam Ching-Ying. Reviewed at Harbour City Mini-theater, Hong Kong, Nov. 11, 1984. Running time: **98 MINS.**
(Cantonese soundtrack with English subtitles)

London-trained film director Po Chih Leung (Leong Po-chi) redeems his erratic Hong Kong movie career with "Hong Kong 1941," a well-made romance-adventure-drama set at the start of the Japanese occupation of Hong Kong as lived by three sympathetic screen characters.

Chow Yan Fat is a wandering trainee of an opera troupe living with his relatives. Without any formal education and jobless, he takes odd jobs to make ends meet. He encounters Alex Man, a rough and ready loudmouthed coolie who is in love with rich, fragile-looking Cecilia Yip who gets occasional epileptic attacks. Yip's father is a corrupt rice merchant who is willing to hoard rice and befriend the Japanese for his own financial benefits.

When the Japanese do arrive, there is chaos, looting and killings. Man and Yip are somehow saved by Chow who turns informer collabo-

rator for patriotic reasons not known to his close friends. How these three major characters survive, love, escape torture and death amid the atrocities of the Japanese army and Chinese gangsters cum black marketeers sets the framework of a ''Jules And Jim'' type of triangular touching relationship.

The romantic bonds and camaraderie between the two men and a tomboyish child-woman, a dominant European concept, works well in this Cantonese context. Chow gives an earnest performance, his best to date, while Man, a physical actor, generates continual attention with his breezy, arresting portrayal of a common laborer, complete with a raspy voice. Yip is excellent as the fragile woman who is in love with Man but is attracted to Chow.

"Hong Kong 1941" is definitely arresting and powerful local film with fine direction, excellent acting and high production values. The dramatic ending is memorable.

"Hong King 1941" is definitely one of the best from Hong Kong this year and deserves world exposure and attention in international filmfests. It has commercial and artistic qualities that don't insult intelligent viewers — a rare treat in Cantonese filmmaking. —*Mel.*

Ankaemaul
(Village In The Mist)
(S. KOREAN-COLOR)

London, Dec. 3.

A Hwa Chun Trading Co. Production. Produced by Pak Chong-ch'an. Executive produced by Kim Chae-ung, Cho Myong-hwa. Directed by Im Kwon-t'aek. Features entire cast. Screenplay, Song Kil-han (from the book "Island without a Name," by I Mun-yol); camera (Scope, color), Chong Il-song; editor, Kim Ch'ang-sun; production design, Kim U-chun; music, Kim Chong-kil; sound, Kim Pyong-su. Reviewed at London Film Festival, Dec. 1, 1984. Running time: **89 MINS.**

Kae-ch'ol	An Song-ki
Su-ok (teacher)	Chong Yun-hui
Kwan-sop	I Ye-min
Wol-ye	Kim Chi-yong
Hwa-ch'on	Ch'oe Tong-chun

Though there's no question of this film's exceptional visual qualities, with magnificent use of the Scope screen and inventive soundtrack. It's a difficult pic to assess for Western audiences.

It opens with a traditional set-up: a pretty young schoolteacher from the city is dropped off by bus at a remote village where she's come to work. She's lonely and a bit nervous about living so far from anywhere, especially as the village is extremely in-bred (all but one of the locals are members of the same family). The one exception is a somewhat sinister, scruffy, outsider, Kae-ch'ol, who scrounges meals and even a bed for the night from the villagers, though they treat him with a strange kind of respect.

One rainy day, the teacher shelters in an old mill not realizing that Kae-ch'ol is hiding inside. He attacks and rapes her. Women viewers will be rightly distressed, not so much by the way the rape is depicted, or even by the length of the scene, but by the fact that the film makes it clear that, for the girl, it was not an unpleasurable experience. At any rate, she says nothing, and later discovers that the outsider has, in fact, slept once only with every woman in the village, with the tacit complicity of all, an that this is even considered useful because it reduces adultery and thus further in-breeding. Indeed, at fadeout, the rapist is depicted as a kind of shabby hero ("The one we long for," says the narration) and there's a new teacher innocently walking into the same situation.

Controversial stuff, the film has more than a few plot implausibilities. But there's no denying the film is superbly crafted, inventively directed, and acted with restraint. The director has apparently made 70 feature films over the years, and "Village In The Mist," for all its questionable aspects, is further evidence of the glowing qualities of the South Korean cinema. —*Strat.*

Torachianhun Milsa
(Mission Of No Return)
(NORTH KOREAN-COLOR)

London, Dec. 3.

A Shin Films Production. Produced by Shin Sang-ok. Directed by Ch'oe Un-hui. Features entire cast. Screenplay, Shin San-ok; camera, (Scope, color), Ch'oe Sung-chun, Pavel Caslavsky; music, Kim Chi-hon; sound, Won Nam-hui; editor, Kim Ryon-sun; production design, Li- To-ik, Ch'oe To-i). Reviewed at London Film Festival, Nov. 28, 1984. Running time: **125 MINS.**

Li-jun	Kim Chun-sik
Li Wi-chong	Kim Yun-hung
Li Il-chong	Kim Ok-hui
Marianna	Anna Kasanova
Homer B. Hulbert	Miroslav Homola
General Hasegawa	O Yong-hwan
Mrs. So	Mun Ye-pong
Madam O	Kim Myong-hui

On the surface, this is a pedestrian — and apparently inaccurate — tale about Japan's colonization of Korea at the beginning of this century and the fate of a patriot-hero, Li-jun, who led a tiny delegation of his countrymen to the International Peace Conference at The Hague in 1907.

According to the film, Li-jun disemboweled himself on the floor of the conference when his efforts to denounce Japan met with failure; in actuality, it seems, the poor man simply succumbed to a particularly virulent bout of influenza.

The film's writer-producer, Shin Sang-ok, was, until the mid-seventies, the best-known director in South Korea. Since mid-1978, when he was seen in Hong Kong, Shin, a critic of the South Korean government, had dropped from sight and it was even rumored that he'd been murdered. Now it transpires that he's been working for North Korea, though his production company, Shin Films, seems to be located in Vienna. In London for the screening of "Mission Of No Return" at the Film Festival, Shin averred that he, in fact, directed the film, not the credited Ch'oe Un-hui (his wife).

In any event, no-one familiar with Shin's earlier work could easily believe the same director was responsible for the turgid item under review, which makes poor use of the Scope screen format (the Shin of old was a master of Scope framing) and has no sense of pace or rhythm. The film was apparently shot entirely in Prague (apart from some brief travelog shots of Korea), and Czech actors manfully attempt to portray Americans and Dutch.

On the other hand, if this film is really to be considered North Korean (the credits don't indicate that it was a coproduction with Czechoslovakia), then it must be seen as technically far superior to the few other North Korean films seen. Students of Asian cinema will doubtless have fun sorting it all out. —*Strat.*

Fandango
(COLOR)

Rites of passage pic is a promising debut for Kevin Reynolds.

Hollywood, Jan. 18.

A Warner Bros. release from Amblin Entertainment. Produced by Tim Zinnemann. Executive producers, Frank Marshall, Kathleen Kennedy. Directed, written by Kevin Reynolds. Features entire cast. Camera (Technicolor), Thomas Del Ruth; editor, Arthur Schmidt, Stephen Semel; music, Alan Silvestri; art direction, Peter Landsdown Smith; sound (Dolby), Richard Bryce Goodman; associate producers, Barrie M. Osborne, Pat Kehoe; assistant director, Kehoe; casting, Mary Goldberg. Reviewed at The Burbank Studios, Burbank, Jan. 18, 1985. (MPAA Rating: PG.) Running time: **91 MINS.**
Gardner Barnes .... Kevin Costner
Phil Hicks .... Judd Nelson
Kenneth Waggener .... Sam Robards
Dorman .... Chuck Bush
Lester .... Brian Cesak
Truman Sparks .... Marvin J. McIntyre
The Girl .... Suzy Amis
Trelis .... Glenne Headly
Gas station mechanic .... Pepe Serna
Judy .... Elizabeth Daily
Lorna .... Robyn Rose

Cranked up prior to "Gremlins" nearly two years ago under Amblin Entertainment's Warner Bros. deal, "Fandango" emerges as a quite promising feature debut by writer-director Kevin Reynolds.

With its feet squarely within the overused boys'-coming-of-age genre but its heart betraying an appealingly anarchic, iconoclastic bent, pic seems torn at times between trying to please a mass public and fully expressing itself as the distinctive effort it aspires to be. While not the stuff of major b.o., it should be allowed to settle in, à la "Diner," for instance, and find a sympathetic audience. It opens exclusively in New York Friday (25).

Just as George Lucas' first feature, "THX 1138," was an outgrowth of a short student film, "Fandango" is an elaboration upon "Proof," a 22-minute picture Reynolds made at the USC Cinema School. Steven Spielberg saw the short and recruited Reynolds for Amblin, although unlike the case on "Gremlins," Spielberg elected not to share exec producer credit with Frank Marshall and Kathleen Kennedy on this one.

Set in 1971, when the Vietnam War and the draft were still looming factors in students' lives, tale describes the final wild fling, or fandango, of five college roommates in Texas before splitting up to face the dreaded realities of the world at large.

Kevin Costner plays the ringleader, a reckless but knowing adventurer who has extended his college stay by three years and puts off acknowledging the future as long as possible. Judd Nelson is the outcast of the group by virtue of his involvement in ROTC, Sam Robards has drunkenly called off his wedding to Costner's former flame at the last moment, Chuck Bush is a hulking, silent giant given to reading Jean-Paul Sartre and Kahlil Gibran, while Brian Cesak remains a drunken package just along for the ride.

Costner has dedicated himself and his cronies to irresponsibility as a way of life, but as the film progresses, it becomes clear that Reynolds' interest lies not in the occasional stunts and hijinx pulled by the group, but in the way the gang, and Costner in particular, are trying desperately to cling onto the youth they know is irretrievably receding.

Despite the mildly rueful tone, pic's highlight is the comic mid-section dominated by hippie pilot and certifiable space cadet Marvin J. McIntyre. Quite reminiscent of Bruce Spence's delightful gyro captain in "The Road Warrior," McIntyre presides over the abandoned Pecos Parachute School where, under the terms of a wager, Nelson skydives out of a plane over the Texas wasteland. Up for anything, McIntyre takes off again to pick up Robards' fiancee and leads the local helicopter patrol on a dizzy and beautifully filmed wild goose chase over and onto the landscape. McIntyre, the only holdover cast member from "Proof," delivers a wonderful supporting turn.

Costner, who previously starred in "Stacy's Knights" but was a cutting room floor casualty in both "The Big Chill" and "Frances," is a dynamic presence at the film's center. Charismatic enough to hold both the fictional group and the pic together, he has the sort of dangerous unpredictability that makes for topflight film performers. The others are not in his league but are up to the demands placed upon them, and Judd Nelson has come good moments as the straightest guy in the bunch.

It takes awhile to put a finger on Reynolds' style, since much of the early-going is given over to rather typical collegiate pranks. But by the time of the parachuting episode, an offbeat, individualistic personality has surfaced which, if not as surreal or off-the-wall as Alex Cox's in "Repo Man," is at least headed encouragingly in that direction. The vintage rock songs score and traditional cutting somewhat iron out and homogenize the film's inherent idiosyncracies, but there is no doubt of the new talent presenting itself here. —*Cart.*

The Party Animal
(COLOR)

Poorly-made sexploitation pic.

Hollywood, Jan. 10.

An Intl. Film Marketing release of an Alan C. Fox presentation. Executive producer, Fox. Produced by Bryan England, Mark Israel. Directed by David Beaird. Features entire cast. Screenplay, Beaird, based on a story by Fox and Beaird. Camera (Deluxe color), England; editor, Susan Jenkins; production designer, Ron Siegal sound, Bryon De Mellier; associate producer, Terrie Cohen, Charles A. Duncombe Jr.; assistant director, Gerald Michenaud. Reviewed at the Paramount theater, Jan. 9, 1984, Hollywood, California. (MPAA rating: R). Running time: **78 MINS.**
Pondo Sinatra .... Matthew Causey
Studley .... Tim Carhart
Natasha .... Robin Harlan
Miranda .... Suzanne Ashley
Elbow .... Jerry Jones
The professor .... Frank Galati
Sophia .... Luci Roucis

"The Party Animal" is a tasteless, amateurishly made exploitation pic that aims for the lowest common denominator and hits its mark. Even as these types of pictures go, this one is a cut below.

Witless story follows the exploits of one Pondo Sinatra (Matthew Causey), a college student with one thing on his mind. Problem is he has no luck with women and three-quarters of the film is spent tracking his various attempts at scoring. Character is so unappealing it's no wonder no one will go near him.

For some reason campus is stocked with a bevy of beauties to torment poor Pondo. Frustration knows no bounds and he offers his soul to the devil for a little bit of luck. His challenge apparently is taken up by the mysterious Miranda (Suzanne Ashley), who is always lurking in the background, although what is actually going on is muddled by sloppy editing and incomprehensive dream sequences.

Obviously made on shoestring, film's production values are poor. Biggest plus for the pic is an okay rock soundtrack featuring R.E.M., The Untouchables, The Buzzcocks among others. —*Jagr.*

Escape From The Bronx
(ITALIAN-COLOR)

A New Line Cinema release of a Fulvia Film S.r.l. production. Produced by Fabrizio De Angelis. Directed by Enzo G. Castellari. Features entire cast. Screenplay, Tito Carpi, Castellari, from story by Carpi; camera (Telecolor), Blasco Giurato; editor, Gianfranco Amicucci; music, Francesco De Masi; art direction-costumes, Massimo Lentini; production manager, Claudio Grassetti; assistant director, Giuseppe Giglietti; stunt coordinator, Riccardo Petrazzi; special effects, Corridori. Reviewed at Cine 42 No. 1 theater, N.Y., Jan. 19, 1985. (MPAA Rating: R.) Running time: **89 MINS.**

Trash . . . . Mark Gregory
Wangler . . . . Henry Silva
Moon . . . . Valeria D'Obici
Strike . . . . Timothy Brent
Also with: Paolo Malco, Thomas Moore, Antonio Sabáto, Alessandro Prete, Massimo Vanni, Andrea Coppola, Eva Czemerys.

"Escape From The Bronx" is a thinly plotted followup by the same Italian filmmakers who made one of Vic Morrow's last features, "1990: The Bronx Warriors." Prospects are quite limited at the nation's action houses.

Mark Gregory returns, circa the year 2000, as Trash, one of the survivors of gang warfare in this sci-fi extrapolation of New York City's problems. Story, heavily indebted to John Carpenter's "Escape From New York," has the General Construction Corp. hiring Wangler (Henry Silva) to exterminate the residents of the Bronx, while manipulating the press and public into believing that the populace is being relocated in new housing in New Mexico. Scheme is to raze the Bronx and build luxury housing there.

A crusading reporter, Moon (Valeria D'Obici, star of Ettore Scola's "Passione D'Amore") tries to help the Bronx denizens, coming up with the idea of kidnapping G.C. Corp.'s president as a bargaining chip. Master thief Strike (Timothy Brent) is recruited to pull off the caper, but the dull second half of the picture consists largely of nihilistic shootouts in place of plot twists.

Director Enzo G. Castellari's action style is overly heavy on slow motion balletics in place of the exciting chases which made "The Road Warrior" and latterly "The Terminator" hits in this genre. Cast, including a cute son to help out Strike, is merely functional, but pic is aided by acceptable post-synching of English-articulated dialog.
—*Lor.*

Walking The Edge
(COLOR)

Routine vengeance meller.

An Empire Pictures release of a Manfred Menz presentation of a Cinema Overseas Distributors picture. Produced by Sergei Goncharoff. Executive producer, Marketing Film. Directed by Norbert Meisel. Stars Robert Forster, Nancy Kwan. Screenplay, Curt Allen; camera (United color), Ernie Poulos; editor, Warren Chadwick; music, Jay Chattaway; sound, Don Summer; assistant director, David Watkinson; art direction, Dana Roth; set dresser, Kim Buckley; stunt coordinator,

Phil Fravel; special effects; Don Power; opticals, Apogee Inc. Reviewed at RKO National 2 theater, N.Y., Jan. 19, 1985. (MPAA Ratings: R.) Running time: **93 MINS.**
Jason Walk . . . . Robert Forster
Christine . . . . Nancy Kwan
Brusstar . . . . Joe Spinell
Tony . . . . A Martinez
Julia . . . . Aarika Wells
McKee . . . . Wayne Woodson
Jimmy . . . . James McIntire
Leon . . . . Russ Courtney
Delia . . . . Frankie Hill
Danny . . . . Doug Toby
Ron . . . . Howard Honig

Filmed in 1982 under the title "A Deadly Chase," "Walking The Edge" is an antiquated vengeance picture, harking back in most respects to the blaxploitation cycle of a decade earlier. Action prospects are modest for this indie acquisition released by Charles Band's Empire Pictures.

In a strong central performance (overcoming extreme deficiencies in Curt Allen's scripting and Norbert Meisel's directing), Robert Forster toplines as an L.A. cabbie and numbers runner named Jason Walk, accidentally thrown in with femme-in-trouble Christine (Nancy Kwan), whom he adopts as a protector against gangsters led by the nasty Brusstar (typecast Joe Spinell). One of several irritating plot gaps has Christine suddenly resurfacing, after a violent teaser opening which has Brusstar and cohorts kill her husband and son, to become a one-woman vengeance squad involving cabbie Walk.

While harboring Christine at his house and dully continuing his daily numbers rounds, Walk gradually catches the revenge bug himself, particularly when his garage mechanic buddy Tony (A Martinez) is brutally tortured and killed by Brusstar. Pic ends unsatisfyingly with star duo having successfully wiped out all the bad guys and facing a non-future.

Qualifying as a B-movie at least two decades after the Bs went out of fashion, "Edge" lacks the colorful casting and intriguing plot twists that made such pictures delightful. Gore is substituted for exciting action setpieces and the vulgar dialog will need considerable laundering for tv use. Apart from Forster, who inserts sly touches to take the sting out of another sadistic antihero, acting honors go to Frankie Hill, stopping the show as a feisty prostitute who first castigates Walk but later helps him out in a pinch.
—*Lor.*

Ghoulies
(COLOR)

Old-fashioned horror cheapie.

Hollywood, Jan. 18.

An Empire Pictures release, produced by Jefery Levy. Exec producer, Charles Band. Directed by Luca Bercovici. Features entire cast. Screenplay, Luca Bercovici, Jefery Levy; camera (DeLuxe color), Mac Ahlberg; editor, Ted Nicolaou; sound, Doug Arnold; Ghoulies and special effects makeup design, John Carl Buechler; assistant director, Betsy Magruder; associate producer, Debra Dion; music, Richard Band, Shirley Walker; casting, Joanna Ray. Reviewed at Hollywood Pacific, Jan. 18, 1985. (MPAA Rating: PG-13.) Running time: **84 MINS.**

Jonathan Graves . . . . Peter Liapis
Rebecca . . . . Lisa Pelikan
Malcolm Graves . . . . . Michael Des Barres
Wolfgang . . . . Jack Nance
Grizzel . . . . Peter Risch
Greedigut . . . . Tamara de Treaux
Mike . . . . Scott Thomson
Mark (Toad Boy) . . . . Ralph Seymour
Donna . . . . Mariska Hargitay
Dick . . . . Keith Joe Dick
Eddie . . . . David Dayan

The stars of "Ghoulies" are diminutive, slimy uglies in the service of Lucifer. The subject is black magic. Its environment is a bleak, grim, tattered Hollywood mansion; the tone is low camp. With an old-fashioned style, length of run for this programmer from Charles Band's Empire Pictures mill will be short.

The production, shot at the deserted Wattles Mansion in West Hollywood, has a quaint corniness about it, as if it were a cheapie horror movie from the 1950s. Shot non-DGA and non-IATSE, and repping the directorial debut of Luca Bercovici (who cowrote with producer Jefery Levy), "Ghoulies" toplines Peter Liapis as an earnest youth who falls under the devilish spell of his Satanic father, temporarily taking seven converts along with him (one of them is played by the daughter of Jayne Mansfield and Mickey Hargitay, Mariska Hargitay).

Pic is slow to take off but once the grinning little hairy, salivating creatures materialize (they were operated by puppeteers and controlled by retractable cables), the Ghoulies become the characters and the live actors recede into the creaky background.

The bewitched hero also is aided by two midget actors, Peter Risch and Tamara de Treaux (latter was the figure briefly inside E.T. during certain scenes of "E.T."). They turn in the best performances. Lisa Pelikan lends a certain human anchor as the protagonist's flustered girl friend.

Special effects and production values are mediocre, which in this case is part of the fun.—*Loyn.*

The Falcon And The Snowman
(COLOR)

Great acting in real-life espionage drama.

Hollywood, Jan. 15.

An Orion Pictures release of a Gabriel Katzka and Hemdale presentation. Produced by Katzka and John Schlesinger. Executive producer, John Daly. Directed by Schlesinger. Stars Timothy Hutton, Sean Penn. Screenplay, Steven Zaillian, based on book by Robert Lindsey; camera (Deluxe Color), Allen Daviau; editor, Richard Marden; music, Pat Metheny, Lyle Mays; sound, Rene Borisewitz; production design, James D. Bissell; production manager-coproducer, Edward Teets; associate producer, Michael Childers; assistant director, Patrick Crowley; Lyle Mays; casting, Wally Nicita. Reviewed at the Directors Guild of America, L.A., Jan. 14, 1985. (MPAA rating: R). Running time: **131 MINS.**
Christopher Boyce . . . . Timothy Hutton
Daulton Lee . . . . Sean Penn
Alex . . . . David Suchet
Lana . . . . Lori Singer
Mr. Boyce . . . . Pat Hingle
Gene . . . . Dorian Harewood
Dr. Lee . . . . Richard Dysart
Laurie . . . . Mady Kaplan
Larry . . . . Macon McCalman
Mikhael . . . . Boris Leskin
Karpov . . . . George C. Grant
Carole . . . . Jennifer Runyon
Mrs. Boyce . . . . Joyce Van Patten
Mrs. Lee . . . . Priscilla Pointer
David Lee . . . . Chris Makepeace

All the way through "The Falcon And The Snowman" director John Schlesinger and an exemplary cast grapple with a true story so oddly motivated it would be easily dismissed if fictional. Clearly, the creative team triumphs, but the final result remains more involving than satisfying.

Working backwards from a 1977 espionage trial, newspaperman Robert Lindsey wrote a book examining how an idealistic 22-year-old college dropout and a wacked-out drug pusher carried off a successful scheme to sell U.S. secrets to the Soviets. With one working with a mind confused by addled loyalties and the other with a mind confused by chemicals, it remains hard to fathom exactly what they hoped to achieve or how they managed to progress so far toward achieving it.

As the two lads, however, Timothy Hutton and Sean Penn are superb. As the one who comes into unexpected access to state secrets, Hutton has the tougher job in making treason at all sympathetic while Penn is left with the shallower part of the deteriorating druggie, to which he nonetheless adds necessary dimensions.

Helping immensely is David Suchet as the KGB agent in Mexico who receives the secrets, another cliché possibility that Suchet transcends.

In the smaller parts, Pat Hingle shines as Hutton's father and Lori Singer is solid as Hutton's girlfriend. Also good in lighter parts are Dorian Harewood and Mady Kaplan as Hutton's coworkers.

A $140-a-week clerk, Hutton has access to the top secret material at a private company where the security is so lax the film almost plays initially as a spy spoof. However, that's the way it apparently was in real life, raising the question how anyone working there could take matters as seriously as Hutton's character did.

After making the espionage business look fairly silly at the start, "Falcon" becomes increasingly somber as it proceeds to a grim conclusion. There's a lesson in there somewhere and the picture at least challenges an audience to uncover it. —*Har.*

Avenging Angel
(COLOR)

Angel's back with moderate b.o. potential.

Chicago, Jan. 11.

A New World Picture release of a Republic Entertainment Intl. presentation of a Sandy Howard production. Produced by Sandy Howard, Keith Rubinstein. Directed by Robert Vincent O'Neil. Features entire cast. Screenplay, O'Neil, Joseph M. Cala; camera (CFI color), Peter Lyons Collister; editor, John Bowey; art director, Steve Marsh; music, Chris Young; sound, Jonathan Stein; set decorator, Patti Hall; special effects, Greg Landerer, Gary Bentley; stunt coordinator, Vincent Deadrick Jr.; additional photography, Bryan England; casting Debra Rubinstein. Reviewed at the Water Town theater, Chicago, Jan. 11, 1985. (MPAA Rating: R). Running time: 93 MINS.

Angel/Molly	Betsy Russell
Kit Carson	Rory Calhoun
Detective Andrews	Robert F. Lyons
Solly	Susan Tyrrell
Captain Moradian	Ossie Davis
John Glitter	Barry Pearl
Ray Mitchell	Ross Hagen
Teddy Butts	Tim Rossovich
Cindy	Estee Chandler
Yo-Yo Charlie	Steven M. Porter
Arthur Gerrard	Paul Lambert
Miles Gerrard	Frank Doubleday
Terry	Richard DeHaven
Pat	Tracy Robert Austin
Mike	Michael A. Andrews
Janie Soon Lee	Karin Mani

When last seen, Molly Stewart was getting straight A's at high school and hustling Hollywood Boulevard most evenings. That was a year ago when "Angel" made New World Pictures a tidy sum in film rentals.

Now Molly's back as an earnest law school student and an enthusiastic "Avenging Angel," bent on mowing down the murderer of her mentor/savior-from-the-streets. The New World item, a routine action-meller with polished production values, promises moderate b.o.

The pic largely duplicates the "Angel" formula. Softcore sleaze, taut thighs, car chases and beaucoup gunplay are accompanied by a raft of "colorful" street characters who make unwanted claims on the audience's attention.

Big casting changes haven't helped. Cliff Gorman, the cop mentor who extricated the original Angel (Donna Wilkes) from the sporting life, has been succeeded by Robert F. Lyons. The character is bumped off within the first five minutes, setting up the plot premise.

Wilkes has been replaced in the lead by Betsy Russell, who plays the part with the artistic vigor of an athletic high school cheerleader. Her physical attributes, though, nicely mesh with those of her character.

Back again this time is Susan Tyrrell as a foul-mouthed cross between a low-rent landlady and pop sculptor. She wildly overacts mostly to the obligators of Kit Carson (Rory Calhoun), an aged wild west sort incarcerated in a loony bin since Angel first worked the streets under his fatherly eye.

In "Avenging Angel," she first has to extricate Calhoun — and then return to the streets to track down those responsible for killing her mentor. They include a rapacious real estate tycoon (Paul Lambert in a broadly comic turn) plus some convincing gun-toting heavies (Tim Rossovich and Ross Hagen).

All are undermined by director Robert Vincent O'Neil's feeble script (along with Joseph M. Cala) which limps along sans key exploitation elements. Violence is strictly in slow motion, softcore sex is sparse and, in the case of the nubile lead, nonexistent.

Ossie Davis, a fine actor, lends a dignity to the proceedings as a police captain. He, too, is undermined in the end, however. —*Sege.*

The Boatman
(FILIPINO-COLOR)

Manila, Dec. 20.

An AMA Communications production with support of the Film Center, U. of the Philippines. Produced by King Aguiluz. Directed by Tikoy Aguiluz. Screenplay, Joe Lacaba, Raffy Guerrero; camera (color), Jun Dalawis; music, Jaime Fabregas; editor, Miriam Medina-Bhunjun; production design, Nick de Ocampo. Reviewed at Manila Film Center, Dec. 18, 1984. Running time: 120 MINS.

Felipe	Ronnie Lazaro
Gigi	Sarsi Emmanuelle
Andy	Jonas Sebastian
Emily	Suzanna Love

"The Boatman," an erotic film drawing phenomenal queues at the censorship-free Manila Film Center, is the first Tagalog film in the genre to prove here that explicit sex and lots of bare flesh can transcend cheap pornography when handled with taste and skill.

"Boatman" is the debut of helmer Tikoy Aguiluz, whose skill in docus and photography helped put credible touches to the film although its thematic content and milieu provide nothing new. Nevertheless, it is interesting to take a trip to a local redlight district, inside a seedy den where illicit live sex plays called *toro* are staged.

Original title of film was "Boy Toro," meaning the lead stud in sex shows. Fear of ire of censors urged producer King Aguiluz of the U.S.-based AMA Communications to opt for "Boatman."

Story is about a young boatman of tourist spot Pagsanjan Falls. Felipe Angeles (Ronnie Lazaro) is one of the "bangkeros" (boatmen) hired by tourists to shoot the rapids.

Felipe is ambitious and goes to Manila to try his luck. He lands in a sex lair where he is teamed with female lead Gigi (Sarsi Emmanuelle). Duo become live-in partners and succeed in the *toro* business. They also become top stars of videocassette blue films.

However, Felipe's obsessive ambition gets him in hot water as he is hired by an American, Emily (Suzanna Love) to be her paid and kept bed-partner. Emily has an influential Filipino boyfriend surrounded by henchmen. The clandestine affair of Felipe and Emily is discovered and the story winds up in violence and gore.

"Boatman" is headed for international film festivals. It is also the first Filipino film to be taken under the wing of the Film Center of the U. of the Philippines. — *Gron.*

That's Dancing!
(COMPILATION-COLOR/B&W)

Mixed bag of old and new terping. Unlikely to attract a wide audience.

Hollywood, Jan. 5.

An MGM/UA Entertainment release of an MGM presentation. Produced by David Niven Jr., Jack Haley Jr. Written and directed by Haley. Additional camera (color), Andrew Laszlo, Paul Lohmann; supervising editor-associate producer, Bud Friedgen; editor, Michael J. Sheridan; assistant directors, Ira Halberstadt, Richard Hinds, Joel Tuber; research, Jessica Berman-Bogdan, Howard W. Hayes, Stephen Fisch; music, Henry Mancini. Reviewed at MGM Studios, Culver City, Jan. 4, 1985. (MPAA Rating: G.) Running time: 105 MINS.

Narrators: Gene Kelly, Sammy Davis Jr., Mikhail Baryshnikov, Liza Minnelli, Ray Bolger.

With "That's Dancing," MGM and Jack Haley Jr. amply demonstrate once more what audiences once liked about movies, but face the problem of what audiences like now.

Its predecessor, "That's Entertainment!" was a popular boxoffice attraction. Released in 1974, the initial collection of MGM musical clips amassed domestic rentals of $12,062,082. However, the followup of additional selections in 1976 was a flop, taking only $1,987,982. The initial effort had freshness and all of the MGM library to choose from, the second had less and the third is even farther back in quality.

For anyone who wants to see big-screen terpsichorean art at its top, "Dancing" is definitive. MGM has not only dipped into its own generous collection, but borrowed judiciously from most of the other studios that were in brisk competition during the golden years of movie musicals.

For openers from the early days, there is a lot of Busby Berkeley, plus Ruby Keeler and Dick Powell, followed by the wonderful work of Fred Astaire and Ginger Rogers and on through an absolutely complete list of the greats.

Much is made of a recently discovered Ray Bolger-Judy Garland dance number from "The Wizard Of Oz," omitted from the final cut of the original. It's interesting to see now, but also easy to see (contrary to the gushing narration) why it was left out: the technique is a bit tacky and hardly up to the quality of what was released.

As far as quality, what hurts "Dancing" is an understandable effort toward the end to add present-day appeal by including clips of recent teenthrobs (straining along the way to qualify Michael Jackson's "Beat It" music video as a "short subject").

John Travolta, to be sure, still shows some style from "Saturday Night Fever," but he will never challenge the memory of those who've been earlier displayed. The other moderns shown are embarrassingly clumsy by comparison, especially the group from "Fame" jumping up and down on cars.

Whatever that was, it wasn't dancing. —*Har.*

J'Ai Recontré le Père Noël
(Here Comes Santa Claus)
(FRENCH-COLOR)

Paris, Jan. 9.

A Distributeurs Associés release (New World Pictures in U.S.) of a Lapaca production. Produced and directed by Christian Gion. Features entire cast. Screenplay, Didier Kaminka; camera (Fujicolor), Jacques Assuerus; art director, Patrice Renault; editor, Pauline Leroy; music, Francis Lai; French lyrics, Pierre-André Dousset; costumes, Olga Pelletier; special effects, Excalibur, Ron Berkely, Grey Berkeley; production manager, Patrick Denauneux. Reviewed at the UGC Biarritz theater, Paris, Jan. 8, 1985. (MPAA Rating: G.) Running time: **83 MINS.**
Schoolteacher/the fairy . . . . . Karen Cheryl
Santa Claus . . . . Armand Meffre
Simon . . . . Eric Chapuis
Elodie . . . . Alexia Haudot
The Ogre/custodian . . . . . Dominique Hulin
Father . . . . Jean-Louis Foulquier
Mother . . . . Hélène Zidi
Grandmother . . . . Jeanne Hervialle
Bouake . . . . Baye Fall

The most noteworthy thing about "Here Comes Santa Claus" is producer-director Christian Gion's stateside distribution coup with New World Pictures (*Variety*, Nov. 14, 1984). Otherwise there is little to recommend this soporific kiddie item, which lacks the imagination and production values to make it pleasing to any but the very young.

Script by comedy writer Didier Kaminka (whose recent credits include Claude Zidi's delightful "Les Ripoux") tells of a young Paris schoolboy who decides he's going to ask Santa Claus to help find his parents, who have disappeared in Africa.

During a class outing to the airport, he and a girl classmate slip aboard a plane bound for Finland, where he has been told Santa lives. Upon arrival, they quickly lose themselves in the forest, but are soon picked up by Saint Nick in person, who takes them to his village.

When he hears the boy's Christmas request, Santa zips off to the dark continent in the company of the fairy who supervises his workshop. After a few misadventures, they manage to freee the parents from some African guerrillas, and return north in time to save the kids from the clutches of a local ogre, who's planning to have them for dinner. Santa then drops the children off at home during his Christmas eve rounds, and the next morning the boy discovers his mom and dad, safe and sound.

Despite location lensing (in Finland and Senegal) and an above-average (for France) budget, pic looks scrappy — young audiences may feel cheated by the unfancy presentation of Santa's village: a banal snowbound hamlet, peopleu by some droopy elves who man an equally unprepossessing toy assembly line.

As Father Christmas, Armand Meffre is just another actor with false beard and pillow, and it's no surprise that the two kids never seem impressed. Karen Cheryl, a local singer, brings some much-needed vivacity to her double employ as warbling schoolteacher and fairy, and Dominique Hulin has some deep-voiced allure as the ogre and the ogrous school custodian who persecutes the young protagonist. —*Len.*

Non Ci Resta Che Piangere
(Nothing Left To Do But Cry)
(ITALIAN-COLOR)

Rome, Jan. 16.

A Mario and Vittorio Cecchi Gori presentation of a Mauro Berardi/Ettore Rosbach production for Jarno Film and Best Intl. and Columbia release. Starring and directed by Massimo Troisi and Roberto Benigni; screenplay by Troisi, Benigni and Giuseppe Bertolucci; camera (color), Giuseppe Rotunno; art director, Francesco Frigeri; editor, Nino Baragli; music, Pino Donaggio. Reviewed at Quirinale Cinema, Rome, Jan. 15, 1985. Running time: **119 MINS.**
Mario . . . . Massimo Troisi
Saverio . . . . Roberto Benigni
Pia . . . . Amanda Sandrelli

When the project of putting two of Italy's funniest and most original young comics in a film together was announced, it sounded like a great idea. Roberto Benigni, the difficult "intellectual" clown from Tuscany and Neapolitan charmer Massimo Troisi ("Starting From Three") both had worked their way up from variety shows to directing their own features, and each has a special brand of humor that appeals to the more sophisticated type of young audiences.

Result of this quasi-historical partnering, which included screenplay and direction credits, leaves most of the satisfaction to pic's backers: "Nothing Left To Do But Cry" has topped the holiday release charts, surpassing not only veteran moneymakers like Alberto Sordi, but also American releases. Dyed-in-the-wool fans, however, will be disappointed to find a lack of sparkle, dash and original craziness usually associated with the two stars. A tough export.

Two friends, while driving through the country one day, accidentally stumble into the year 1492. Saverio (Benigni) instantly adapts to the new conditions, dons local garb and discusses getting a job with the local hangman. Mario (Troisi), more faint-hearted, demonstrates a fearful distaste for the new (old) life and unquenchable longing to return to the familiar 20th century, until he meets a beauteous 15-year-old (Amanda Sandrelli).

Saverio the thinker remembers the big event of 1492 when Columbus sailed to America, and a radical idea takes shape in his brain. If they stopped Columbus from going, all those Indians wouldn't be on reservations today. Dragging the romantic Mario away from his lady friend, he repairs to Spain, but is too late to alter the course of history.

This skimpy story is merely the excuse to watch the two comics at work, dividing screen time with bits of business. At times pic veers into an incoherent series of tv skits going nowhere. While Benigni excels at pun-filled nonsense monologs with social targets and Troisi is an expert at conveying insecurity and uncertainty through his rambling speech, picture doesn't give them the opportunity to exhibit these talents in a meaningful way. The duo has no real goal to reach and pic seems more like actors doing guest spots on each other's variety shows than a fully worked-out feature.

There are high points — Troisi trying to impress Amanda Sandrelli (daughter of actress Stefania) by singing "Yesterday" and other songs "of his own composition;" Benigni attempting to explain the steam engine and other small marvels to Leonardo Da Vinci. A topnotch support crew is led by cameraman Giuseppe Rotunno. — *Yung.*

Ein Film Für Bossak
Und Leacock
(A Film For Bossak And Leacock)
(WEST GERMAN-COLOR/
B&W-DOCU-16m)

Berlin, Jan. 1.

A Norddeutscher Rundfunk (NDR) Documentary by Klaus Wildenhahn. A portrait of Jerzy Bossak and Richard Leacock, featuring a compilation of both documentary filmmakers' work. Camera (color), Wolfgang Jost; sound, Wildenhahn. Reviewed at Berliner Screening Room, Dec. 30, '84. Running time: **115 MINS.**

Here we have two recognized masters of their trade, Jerzy Bossak of Poland and Richard Leacock of the U.S., discussing not only their own views on docu filming, but also being viewed in turn in portrait form by West Germany's recognized master of the documentary, Klaus Wildenhahn.

Wildenhahn went to the Oberhausen festival to film Bossak during that filmer's jury duties and in general conversation with colleagues and friends. Next, he was off to M.I.T. in Cambridge, Mass., to observe Leacock teaching film courses on the docu and during his off-hours. In both cases, Wildenhahn employed the opportunities to view clips from the filmmakers' work, and allow the respective directors room to talk about the making of those historical docus. Lastly, he made a special trip to Poland to film with a Super-8m camera additional footage (blown up to 16m), and winged off to the Toronto Film Festival in 1983 to catch both filmers as guests there for a mutual exchange on the very nature of the documentary media: Was, for instance, Robert Flaherty's "Louisiana Story" (camera work by Leacock) docu or fiction?

One of the interesting aspects of Wildenhahn's double portrait is that Bossak and especially Leacock appear to be puzzled at just what's going on in Wildenhahn's head, for there doesn't seem to be a preconceived plan or subjective attitude taken on the making of the film. Wildenhahn apparently is relying very much on the talent of both filmmakers to articulate their positions with as much refinement as they can wield a camera.

Docu buffs have a treat in store if the've never seen the clips from Bossak's masterful documentaries: the nearly destroyed "Majdanek" (1944), on the Nazi Extermination Camp near Lubin liberated by Soviet troops; "Flood" (1947), about the catastrophic flood that wiped out bridges in its path (filmed at the risk of Bossak's on life); and "Warsaw '56" (1956), on housing problems and the plight of the underprivileged as Warsaw rose again from its wartime ruins.

As for Leacock, his review of discussed film clips includes the homemade "Canary Bananas" (1935), made as a 14-year-old on the Canary Islands (where he was born and raised); "Louisiana Story" (1948), as Robert Flaherty's cameraman; and "Primary" (1960), paving the way for cinéma-vérité techniques using more portable sound-and-camera equipment. It's quite clear, in Leacock's case, that Wildenhahn also wants to anchor the Cambridge filmmaker in his historical position of a great contemporary documentarist.

"A Film For Bossak And Leacock" is the kind of production that German tv does so well in the documentary film, one that deserves broader international recognition and wider distribution. —*Holl.*

I Due Carabinieri
(The Two Cops)
(ITALIAN-COLOR)

Rome, Jan. 17.

A Columbia release, produced by Mario and Vittorio Cecchi Gori for C.G. Silver

Film. Stars Carlo Verdone and Enrico Montesano. Directed by Verdone. Screenplay by Leo Benvenuti, Piero De Bernardi and Verdone; camera (color), Danilo Desideri; editor, Antonio Siciliano; art director, Franco Velchi; music, Fabio Liberator. Reviewed at Metropolitan Cinema, Rome, Jan. 16, 1985. Running time: **96 MINS.**

Marino Spada . . . . .Carlo Verdone
Glauco . . . . .Enrico Montesano
With Massimo Boldi, Paola Onofri, Marisa Solinas.

Second on the list of Christmas grossers, outstripping many veteran competitors, "The Two Cops" owes its success to the astute partnering of its young comic leads, Carlo Verdone and Enrico Montesano, on screen together for the first time. Verdone, who also directs, has affirmed himself over the last few years as a solid humorsmith capable of tapping the youth audience. The picture itself is plodding and uneventful, interesting only for its stars' characterizations, which will be the main drawing card for any offshore market.

Pic opens with pudgy, baby-faced Marino Spada (Verdone) getting his hair cut Marine-style prior to taking an entrance test to join the carabinieri, Italy's military police corps. He is a reluctant recruit, forced into it by his uncle because he's jobless at 30.

Similar motives bring Glauco (Montesano), all Roman street slang and irresistable boyish grin, to take the exam. Both of these unlikely candidates pass; presumably everybody does.

Pic is structured around a few long sequences. In the first, Marino and Glauco are assigned to guard a crooked financier in the hospital. When he escapes, their only concern is to bring him back before anyone notices they let him get away.

Film steers a delicate course between the traditionally mocking carabinieri jokes and respect for the uniform. In two action sequences, more significant because they come at the end of the film, the corps is shown heroically routing a drug ring, and later rescuing a trainload of Boy Scouts from a gun-waving lunatic. All is interwoven with the two friends' common love interest, Rita, who is Marino's cousin and first love but who eventually marries Glauco. Their spat over her is healed at the altar.

Verdone and Montesano have fine control over this limited material and hold audience sympathy throughout. Excellent supporting work comes from Massimo Boldi, a standout as a cowardly hypochondriac, who dies a hero's death.
— *Yung.*

The Tigress
(CANADIAN-COLOR)

Winnipeg, Dec. 28.

A Cinepix release of a Mount Everest Enterprises production. Produced by Julian Parnell. Directed by Jean Lafleur. Features entire cast. Screenplay by Marven McGara. Camera (color), Richard Ciupka; editor, Debra Karjala; art direction, Claude Marchand; music, uncredited. Reviewed at the Epic Theatre, Winnipeg, Dec. 27, 1984. (MPAA Rating: R.) Running time: **89 MINS.**

With Dyanne Thorne (The Colonel), Michel Morin (Andrei Chicurin), Jean-Guy Latour, Michel Maillot, Tony Angelo, Terry Coady, Joe Mattia, Sonny Forbes, Greg Gianus, Howard Mauer, Ray Landry, Terry Haig, Henry Gamer.

"The Tigress" (a.k.a. "Ilsa, the Tigress of Siberia"), dating back to 1977, was the unofficial capper to the Ilsa dominatrix series which saw star Dyanne Thorne first offer her services to the Nazis and later a group of oil sheiks. And, like earlier efforts, the story is banal and neither performance nor direction is particularly inspired. So, it's a bit of a wonder, considering the continued appeal of the first two films, as to why "The Tigress" has failed to acquire theatrical or cassette sales in the U.S.

The usual combination of gore and sex again prevails. The opening, set in Siberia in 1953, has Ilsa (here called simply the Colonel) brutally overseeing the activities of a gulag. To keep her prisoners in line she even has a pet tiger who's regularly fed dissidents. Other social activities of the camp include spear catching, swimming in icy waters, arm wrestling over a chainsaw and a crude form of brainwashing.

So, after a hard day's work, the Colonel naturally delights in sexual games with her coworkers. However, her fun has been disrupted by one prisoner who refuses her sexual favors and will not give up his political beliefs even under the most gruelling torture. Only the news of Stalin's demise keeps him from the tiger's clutches. However, Ilsa does manage to kill all the other prisoners and most of the remaining compound as she departs.

Then, just as we are getting used to the routine, the action shifts to Montreal in 1977. The survivor is now with Soviet security as chaperone for a hockey team and the Colonel and her aides are running a prostitution ring out of a massage parlor. The passage of time on her face and body is unnoticable and she still enjoys a diet of sex and cruelty.

It doesn't take much to guess that the two will again come face to face with each other. However, the final confrontation certainly allowed the producers to continue the series. And although such projects as "Ilsa Meets Bruce Lee in the Devil's Triangle" and "Ilsa, Nanny to Royalty" were announced in the intervening years, Cinepix' John Dunning insists the series has seen its day and will not be revived.

Of course both artistic and technical credits are lackluster but this was never a detriment in previous incarnations. The sheer outrageousness of the endeavor (and total dismissal of logic and craft) should still have appeal for Ilsa's followers, so she might live yet again at least in video outlets and paycable outings.
— *Klad.*

... And When They Shall Ask
(CANADIAN-DOCU-COLOR)

Winnipeg, Dec. 18.

A David Dueck Film Production released by the Mennonite Media Society. Producer and executive producer, David Dueck; associoate producer, Toni Dueck. Direction and screenplay by John Morrow. Script and research, John Toews, Barbara Anderson; camera (color), Rene Ohashi, additional photography, Rodger Boller, Ian Elkin, Barry Lank, Richard Stringer; editor, Robert Petch; music, Victor Davies; sound, Leon Johnson. Reviewed at Towne Cinema 8, Winnipeg, Dec. 17, 1984. Running time: **83 MINS.**

One of seven entries in Canada's Genies for theatrical documentary, "And When They Shall Ask" is an awkward mixture of interviews, historic material and dramatic reconstruction. This painfully sincere study of the Russian Mennonite community from the 18th century to the present — with its numbers scattering primarily to North and South America — lacks any real focus to engage nonpartisan audiences.

While most definitely ambitious in scope, the film is unable to wed a variety of styles into a cohesive format for openers. Separately, the elements of new and archival footage have a degree of integrity. Nonetheless, such sloppy efforts as highminded narration only serve to sap the emotional nature of the story.

The film begins with a brief prehistory, dating the roots of the group to 15th-century Switzerland. Pacifist by doctrine, the Mennonites have been persecuted for centuries but found political sanctuary in Russia in 1786 and settled into an area of the Ukraine. The following century represented an era of relative peace, and economic and cultural growth for the group.

However, both World War I and the Russian 1917 Revolution finally forced them from the area. Briefly, in minimally staged vignettes, this period is recaptured and the strain on the sect's pacifist attitude explored. As pure information, the film serves as a reasonable primer.

Writer-director John Morrow has considerably less success in his use of living witnesses to the era who now live in Canada. Their stories aren't well bridged and often continue well beyond their emotional impact. One man is even seen returning to his boyhood home 50 years later for a reunion with his brother. This section occurs late in the film and one feels it was never properly conceived.

The film already has played extensively for Mennonite groups in North America and could have some life in educational and study groups. Theatrical prospects are dim owing to the picture's inability to tap the obvious emotional components of the group's struggle, and its uneven technical credits.
— *Klad.*

Der Schnüffler
(Sniffing Around)
(WEST GERMAN-COLOR)

Berlin, Jan. 1.

An UFA Film Production, Berlin, in coproduction with Second German Television (ZDF), Mainz. Directed by Ottokar Runze. Screenplay, Christian Rateuke, Hartmann Schmige; camera (color), Michael Epp; editor, Marina Runne; costumes Rotraut Braun; music, Willy Siebert; production manager, Werner Mietzner. Reviewed at Berliner Screening Room, Dec. 29, 1984. Running time: **91 MINS.**

With: Dieter (Didi) Hallervorden (Herbie Melbourne), Catherine Alric, Nikolaus Dutsch, Tilo Prückner, Manfred Lehmann, Peter Kuiper, Utl Richter, Siegfried Wischnewski, Eddie Constantine, Joachim Wichmann, Siegfried Kernen, Hans Schellbach, Anton Diffring.

Didi Hallervorden is the hottest commercial name star working presently in German cinema. In "Sniffing Around" he's a taxi driver who one day has to deliver a passenger to the other side of the Berlin Wall — a D.O.A. affair, natch. So the Russian KGB and East German Secret Police get in on the act: they want Didi to act as an agent to find out who killed their comrade. Hallervorden then suddenly finds himself in the middle of a double-agent caper, for no sooner is he back on the other side than the CIA and West German police peg him for a Russian spy and offer him double to become "Super Agent Herbie Melbourne."

The rest gets bogged down in overdone slapstick chase routines and helmer Ottokar Runze's penchant for trick camera effects. It's still highly amusing throughout when Didi's on camera trying to figure out how he ever got into this mess in the first place. The twist in the title concerns a ploy used by a femme headshrinker to get Didi to gain a measure of self-confidence to fight back on his own: she gives him a small bottle to sniff out of, thereby converting him into a take-charge superman. That gimmick, in turn, opens the way for Didi's love affair with the warmhearted psychiatrist, played with verve and finesse by Catherine Alric. —*Holl.*

Bananen Paul
(Banana Paul)
(WEST GERMAN-COLOR)

Berlin, Jan. 1.

AC & H Film, Berlin. Directed by Richard Claus. Screenplay, Claus, Manfred Weis; camera (color), Jörg Jeshel; sound, Christian Moldt; sets, Iva Rybova-Weis; production manager, Petra Haffter. Reviewed at Berliner Screening Room, Dec. 29, 1984. Running time: 84 MINS.
With: Otto Schnelling, May Buschke, Martin Lüttge, Buddy Elias, Günter Berger, Marcel Werner, Rainer Pigulla, Evelyn Lazar.

Richard Claus' "Banana Paul" was made for the growing kidpic trade in West Germany and appeared a season ago at the Berlinale in the Children's Film Festival. It's pretty drab stuff on the whole with an impersonated bear named "Banana Paul" becaue he likes to eat bananas — in the title role.

This performing circus bear has learned too much about driving a motorcycle from his trainer, so one day he slams the cage door on the keeper and is off on the bike to see the world — that is, a small provincial town. The spectacle of the bear on a motorcycle, of course, strikes fear in the hearts of all the wacky grownups, but delights a young girl who enjoys having a new companion to play with. Only she knows the bear can also talk.

It's the police and the know-it-all public officials who scurry around in panic. This is good for a couple laughs at the outset — until clichés and stereotypes take over for the rest of the plodding plot and slow-paced film. —*Holl.*

The Purple Rose Of Cairo
(COLOR/B&W)

Clever but thin Woody Allen tragicomedy; quite modest b.o. prospects.

Hollywood, Jan. 26.
An Orion release of a Jack Rollins and Charles H. Joffe production. Produced by Robert Greenhut. Executive producer, Joffe. Directed, written by Woody Allen. Features entire cast. Camera (Deluxe color/b&w), Gordon Willis; editor, Susan E. Morse; original music, Dick Hyman; production design, Stuart Wurtzel; art direction, Edward Pisoni; set decorations, Carol Joffe; costume design, Jeffrey Kurland; sound, James Sabat; associate producers, Michael Peyser, Gail Sicilia; assistant director, Thomas Reilly; casting, Juliet Taylor. Reviewed at the Orion Screening Room, L.A., Jan. 25, 1985. (MPAA Rating: PG). Running time: 82 MINS.

Cecilia	Mia Farrow
Tom Baxter/Gil Shepherd	Jeff Daniels
Monk	Danny Aiello
Emma	Dianne Wiest
Larry	Van Johnson
The Countess	Zoe Caldwell
Jason	John Wood
Father Donnelly	Milo O'Shea
Rita	Deborah Rush
Theater manager	Irving Metzman
Mr. Hirsch's lawyer	John Rothman
Cecilia's sister	Stephanie Farrow
Raoul Hirsch	Alexander H. Cohen
Olga	Camille Saviola
Kitty Haynes	Karen Akers
Gil's agent	Michael Tucker
Delilah	Annie Joe Edwards
The Communist	Peter McRobbie
Usherette	Juliana Donald
Henry	Edward Herrmann
Diner Boss	David Kieserman
Arturo	Eugene Anthony
Bandleader	Ebb Miller

Woody Allen's fascination with film trickery and the intermingling of "real" and fictional characters continues in "The Purple Rose Of Cairo," an initially appealing but frustratingly thin conceit which had its world premiere at the U.S. Film Festival last weekend. Second film, after "Interiors," directed but not starring Allen should generate only modest b.o., even in the urban centers where most of his audience resides.

Tale is a light, almost frivolous treatment of a serious theme, as Allen here confronts the unalterable fact that life just doesn't turn out the way it does (or did) in Hollywood films. For all its situational goofiness, pic is a tragedy, and it's too bad Allen didn't build up the characters and drama sufficiently to give some weight to his concerns.

Working from the same idea he used in his short story "The Kugelmass Episode," in which the leading character got his wish of actually meeting Madame Bovary, Allen introduces Depression-era waitress Mia Farrow, a hopeless film buff so consumed by motion picture gossip and fantasies she can barely hold down her job.

Her husband, Danny Aiello, is a complete boor, so she spends all her free time seeing films over and over again until Tom Baxter (Jeff Daniels), a character in a fictional RKO epic "The Purple Rose Of Cairo," stops the action, starts speaking to Farrow directly from the screen, and, fed up with repeating the same action time after time, steps out of the film and asks to be shown something of real life.

Some of the ramifications of this are very clever and genuinely amusing. Since he's had plenty of practice onscreen, Baxter is a great kisser, but when he's taken to a bordello by tart Dianne Wiest, he has no idea what to do with the girls since films always fade out before the real action begins. At the same time, Baxter's departure from the script leaves all the other "film" characters stranded; pic's funniest moments have the increasingly bored Manhattan socialites sitting around in their salon trading barbs with the cinema audience in Farrow's small town theater, awaiting Baxter's return.

Informed of this bizarre occurrence, Hollywod execs hightail it to New Jersey to see what they can do and begin receiving reports that the Baxter character is behaving oddly on other screens as well. Unfortunately, nothing much happens to Baxter and Farrow during his brief excursion into "reality;" he professes his love for her, and she prepares to leave her husband for this ideal fellow, but the film is held down by Baxter's inherent one-dimensionality. As in "Zelig," the technical wizardry and cleverness dominate over characters that barely exist.

Finally, Gil Shepherd, the "actor" who plays Baxter, shows up and proceeds to similarly sweep Farrow off her feet, forcing her to choose between the reality of Shepherd and the fantasy of Baxter. To convince her to choose him, Baxter brings Farrow momentarily into the fictional film, a device which seems like it should have been funnier than it is, but she is finally left to make her fateful decision. Ending is a rueful commentary on the question often asked by the late François Truffaut, "Are films more important than life?"

Mia Farrow is excellent again under Allen's direction, and at certain times (especially when lying to her husband) begins to sound like him. Jeff Daniels is okay as the bland 1930s adventurer come to life, although he's rather restricted by role's unavoidable thinness. Having the most fun are the characters within the fictional film (played by Edward Herrmann, Zoe Caldwell, Van Johnson, John Wood, Milo O'Shea, Deborah Rush and Annie Joe Edwards, among others).

As always with Allen, pic is technically superb and admirably concise. Gordon Willis' lensing is beautifully muted, Stuart Wurtzel's production design economically conjures up the Depression setting, and Dick Hyman's original score perfectly complements some source music of the era.—*Cart.*

Superstition
(COLOR)
Gory witchcraft thriller.

An Almi Pictures release of a Mario Kassar and Andrew Vajna presentation of a Penaria Corp. production. Executive producers, Kassar, Vajna. Produced by Ed Carlin; coproducers, John D. Schwartz, Robert L.J. Lewis. Directed by James W. Roberson. Features entire cast. Screenplay, Michael Sajbel, Bret Plate, Brad White, Donald G. Thompson, from story "The Witch" by Sajbel; camera (CFI color), Lee Madden; editor, Al Rabinowitz; music, David Gibney; sound, Ron Judkins; assistant director, Jan S. Ervin; production manager, Michael Bennett; art direction, Penny Hadfield; set decoration, Cricket Rowland; stunt coordinator, Bud Davis; special effects makeup, Bill Munns (supervisor), Steve LaPorte, David B. Miller; casting, Ruth Conforte. Reviewed at Almi screening room, N.Y., Jan. 23, 1985. (No MPAA Rating.) Running time: 84 MINS.

Rev. David Thompson	James Houghton
Insp. Sturgess	Albert Salmi
Melinda Leahy	Lynn Carlin
George Leahy	Larry Pennell

Also with: Maylo McCaslin, Heidi Bohay, Billy Jacoby, Jacquelyn Hyde, Kim Marie, Stacy Keach Sr., Joshua Cadman, Robert Symonds, Carole Goldman, John Alderman, Johnny Doran, Bennett Liss, Casey King.

"Superstition" is a poorly constructed supernatural horror film, being marketed without an MPAA rating for fans of explicit gore effects. Picture, with the alternate title of "The Witch," was filmed in 1981 by Carolco's Mario Kassar and Andy Vajna just before duo hit paydirt with "First Blood."

Falling within the familiar haunted house genre, picture concerns a piece of property owned by the church, where unsolved murders have occurred. Chief suspect is Arlen (Joshua Cadman), a mute, hulking son of weird old caretaker Elvira (Jacquelyn Hyde), who escapes from the police led by Inspector Sturgess (Albert Salmi).

Rev. Leahy (Larry Pennell) and his family move in, while Rev. David Thompson (James Houghton) investigates the house's history. He discovers a witch was tried, found guilty and drowned at a nearby pond there in 1692, but her spirit lives on to wreak bloody havoc.

Pic is hurt by grainy photography and a very confusing finale which manages to kill off the entire cast without resolving the story adequately. Post-production sound synch is also deficient. Makeup effects are the drawing card, while the appearances of a demon are disappointingly kept off camera, only its clutching, claw-like hands shown.
—*Lor.*

Witness
(COLOR)

Interesting drama betrayed by violence.

Hollywood, Jan. 24.

A Paramount Pictures release, produced by Edward S. Feldman. Directed by Peter Weir. Stars Harrison Ford. Screenplay, Earl W. Wallace, William Kelley; camera (Technicolor), John Seale; editor, Thom Noble; sound, Barry D. Thomas; coproducer. David Bombyk; production design, Stan Jolley; assistant director, David McGiffert; associate producer, Wendy Weir; music, Maurice Jarre; casting, Dianne Crittenden. Reviewed at Paramount Studios, Hollywood, Jan. 23, 1985. (MPAA rating: R). Running time: **112 MINS.**

John Book . . . . Harrison Ford
Rachel . . . . Kelly McGillis
Schaeffer . . . . Josef Sommer
Samuel . . . . Lukas Haas
Eli . . . . Jan Rubes
Daniel . . . . Alexander Godunov
McFee . . . . Danny Glover
Carter . . . . Brent Jennings
Elaine . . . . Patti LuPone

"Witness" is at times a gentle, affecting story of star-crossed lovers limited within the fascinating Amish community. Too often, however, this fragile romance is crushed by a thoroughly absurd shoot-em-up, like ketchup poured over a delicate Pennsylvania Dutch dinner.

This is Australian director Peter Weir's first film with an American setting and he is obviously awed by the Amish, the quaint agrarian sect which maintains a 17th-century lifestyle, forsaking all modern conveniences while maintaining intense religious vows, including a pacifism most pertinent here.

Venturing outside the community on a trip to see her sister, recently widowed Kelly McGillis is drawn unfortunately into the 20th century when her young son, Lukas Haas, witnesses a murder in the men's room at the train station.

Enter gruff, foul-mouthed, streetwise detective Harrison Ford, whom writers Earl W. Wallace and William Kelley must somehow get out into the countryside as soon as possible so the cross-cultural romance can begin.

Without pausing a moment for logic, the plot has young Haas identify a narcotics cop as the killer, and Ford filling in his trusted superior on what's happening, fingering himself for execution in the process. Given several obvious solutions to this problem — none of which requires him to become a lone victim on the lam — Ford ends up with a bullet wound, hiding out in McGillis' rustic bedroom where everyone accepts and protects this outsider for the sake of the boy's safety.

Forgetting such quibbles, without which there probably wouldn't have been a film at all, "Witness" warms up as the attraction builds between Ford, McGillis and Haas — all performing excellently through this portion. Admirable, too, is Ford's growing admiration for the people he's been thrown among.

Furnishing solid assistance with this aspect in his film debut is Alexander Gudonov as a quiet Amish farmer who has his eye on McGillis also and naturally resents Ford, but likes him, too. Additional help comes from Jan Rubes as McGillis' father-in-law, also liking Ford but fearful of the effect he's having on girl and grandson. His speech to McGillis about her danger of being "shunned" by the community is a beaut.

Needless to say, the growing question is whether this new love can survive, since one party or the other will have to sacrifice all and undergo a radical change in lifestyles. But Weir never really has to come to grips with the details because he still has the murderous cops lurking back in Philadelphia.

One night they show up in this peaceful rural community with shotguns and proceed to blow the whole picture to bits. But the middle parts do have their moments.

— *Har.*

El Milusos II
(The Jack-of-All-Trades, Part II)
(MEXICAN-COLOR)

Mexico City, Oct. 25.

A Televicine release of a Nuevo Cinema Producciones, S.A.-Roberto G. Rivera, S.A.-Televicine production. Directed by Roberto G. Rivera. Screenplay, Ricardo Garibay; camera (color), Raúl González; editing, Enrique Puente Portillo; sound, Nacho Ambriz; musical direction, Kiki Campos; music, Pepe Arevalo y Sus Multos and Los Tigres del Norte. Reviewed at Televicine, Mexico City, Oct. 23, 1984. Running time: **110 MINS.**

Tránsito . . . . Héctor Suáreez
El Transas . . . . Roberto (El Falco) Guzmán
Lupita . . . . Lucha Villa
Also with: José Carlos Ruiz, Roberto Cobo (Calambres), Guillermo Rivas (El Borras), Pedro Weber (Chatanuga), Manuel (Flaco) Ibañez, Gloria Mayo and Alejandra Meyer.

"El Milusos II" comes as a pleasant surprise.

Part one, which was the top-grossing national film for 1983 in Mexico, concerned the misadventures of a sympathetic country bumpkin named Tránsito, played by comedian Héctor Suárez. At the death of his father, Tránsito leaves his native Tlaxcala and ventures to Mexico City in search of work. Since he has no skills, he is labeled a "milusos" (jack-of-all-trades), doing any odd job that comes his way. Instead of finding a better life in the capital, he is taken advantage of by almost everyone he meets.

Part two is much more serious than the first installment, although its comic moments are more natural. It does not attempt to continue the storyline of the first part, but rather continues with the character of Tránsito, this time a poor widowed farmer with a young son. With the help of a passing truck, Tránsito ends up in the sprawling Mexico City slum of Nezahualcóyotl, boasting 3,000,000 inhabitants.

Director Rivera uses his "cinéma verité" style to advantage once more, shooting the entire movie on location with real people as extras. There is a type of honesty within the artifice of the film, that even though the story is fiction, the background and those who inhabit it are not.

Doing odd jobs, Tránsito sells tacos, hawks elixirs in a medicine show, becomes a waiter and an amateur boxer, and even crosses into the United States illegally. He is condemned to be a loser, never receiving the breaks or staying long enough to get ahead.

Suárez is perfect as the wide-eyed innocent. He is sympathetic, but never pathetic. As Tránsito, he is a victim of his own ignorance.

Because of its difuse and episodic form, "El Milusos II" also suffers from an uneven overall tone, but for a commercial comedy, one finds it more in keeping with its subject than in part one.

Besides moments of preaching, another problem with the film is that we never find out what becomes of Tránsito's young son. He is deserted at the beginning of the movie, and as far as we know, he has no other living relative to help him. Rather, he posed a burden on the plot and so was cast aside as soon as possible to get on with the misadventures of Tránsito. From the looks of things, these misadventures will receive a third and perhaps even a fourth installment. —*Lent.*

Heavenly Bodies
(COLOR)

Boring dance display.

Hollywood, Jan. 26.

An MGM/UA release of a Producers Sales Organization presentation of a Robert Lantos/Stephen J. Roth production. Produced by Lantos, Roth. Directed by Lawrence Dane. Features entire cast. Screenplay, Dane and Ron Base; camera (Medallion color), Thomas Burstyn; editor, Robert Lambert; production designer, Lindsey Goddard; choreography, Brian Foley; music supervisors, Irwin Mazur, Kevin Benson; costumes, Julie Ganton; associate producer, Andras Hamori; assistant director, Mac Bradden; casting, Deidre Bowen. Reviewed at MGM/UA screening room, L.A., Calif., Jan. 25, 1985. (MPAA rating: R). Running time: **89 MINS.**

Samantha . . . . Cynthia Dale
Steve . . . . Richard Rebiere
Jack . . . . Walter George Alton
Debbie . . . . Laura Henry
Joel . . . . Stuart Stone

"Heavenly Bodies" offers conclusive proof that beauty is only skin deep. Yes, the bodies are heavenly, but little else matters in this me-generation rip-off of "Flashdance." Self-absorption of this magnitude is a bore and unlikely to generate much excitement at the boxoffice.

For a film trying to cash in on the aerobic dance craze, pic is painfully static. Numerous dance sequences surrounded by like-sounding pop songs are unimaginatively shot by director Lawrence Dane. Production totally miscalculates the appeal of watching sweaty bodies in motion without a dramatic framework for them to move in.

Script by Dane and Ron Base, modeled after a Pineapple Studios-like dance club, is totally devoid of feeling or any resemblance to real life. It's an '80s fairy tale about how if you try hard you can get what you want. The problem is the only thing people seem to care about here is having a great body. People are too concerned with themselves to have believable relationships.

Cynthia Dale as the working girl with the vision to open her own dance center, Heavenly Bodies, is attractive and has a genuine screen presence, but unfortunately she is given a limited repertoire to work with. Her big romance with pro footballer Richard Rebiere is as flat and predictable as her dancing is lively. As lovers they're pretty enough, but there is no earned emotion.

Everything seems to come too easily in this film. Samantha wants to open a dance club; she finds a warehouse that looks like a million bucks went into it after only a casual clean-up. Her first dance class features a group of healthy people who look like they've been dancing together for years so perfectly choreographed are their movements. No rough edges here.

In fact, the film's heavy, Walter George Alton as the owner of a rival health club, is all bluff and bluster and can't be taken seriously despite the dramatic crisis he presents. Dance marathon instigated by Alton's jealous girlfriend (Laura Henry) to determine the survival of the dance center is treated with the seriousness usually reserved for affairs of state. When the Heavenly Bodies crew holds a demonstration to save their facility, it is interesting to note what direction '60s activism has taken in this '80s version.

These people simply don't have enough meat on the bones for the audience to care about what happens to them. It is especially unfortunate in Dale's case that the story never reveals what dancing means to her beyond a beautiful body.

Tech credits are fine all around, but can't overcome the overall stiffness and artificiality of the production. —*Jagr.*

Too Scared To Scream
(COLOR)

Uneasy mixture of slasher pic and police drama.

Hollywood, Jan. 18.
The Movie Store release. Produced by Mike Connors. Directed by Tony Lo Bianco. Executive producer, Ken Norris. Screenplay, Glenn Leopold and Neal Barbera; camera (CFI color), Larry Pizer; editor, Ed Beyer; supervising editor, Michael Economou; music, George Garvarentz; sound, Doug Holman; production design, Lilly Kilvert; assistant director, Mike Haley; associate producer, A. Kitman Ho; casting, Louis De Giaimo. Reviewed at Paramount theater, Hollywood, Calif., Jan. 17, 1985. (MPAA Rating: R.) Running time: **104 MINS.**

Lt. Dinardo	Mike Connors
Kate	Anne Archer
Frank	Leon Isaac Kennedy
Hardwick	Ian McShane
Irma	Ruth Ford
Lab Technician	John Heard
Graziella	Carrie Nye
Mother	Maureen O'Sullivan
Jack	Murray Hamilton
Mike	Ken Norris

Despite its title and ad campaign, "Too Scared To Scream" aims to be more than another slasher film, and therein lies its undoing. The idea of an intelligent cut-and-dice picture may be contradictory to the genre, but "Too Scared To Scream" gives it a try mixing elements of a psychological police drama with the usual blood letting. Result is neither fish nor fowl which is unlikely to satisfy many paying customers.

(Picture was lensed in 1982 in New York City under the title "The Doorman." — *Ed.*)

Direction by Tony Lo Bianco is competent, if obvious, with a better than average cast for this kind of fare featuring credible work by Mike Connors, Anne Archer and Ian McShane. John Heard turns up as well in one brief scene as a police lab technician.

Plot involving a series of women being murdered at a plush Manhattan apartment house doesn't supply enough thrills and chills and is not totally successful as a character study either. Screenwriters Glenn Leopold and Neal Barbera have tried to develop full-blooded characters in order to have more to spill, but results are rather flat on both counts.

Chief suspect for the murders is a Shakespeare-spouting doorman (McShane) who lives with his invalid mother (Maureen O'Sullivan) in a pathological relationship which ultimately proves to be less than meets the eye. Hard on his heels is Connors as Lt. Dinardo, the kind of dick usually seen on tv cops and robbers shows.

Connors has some kind of relationship going with undercover agent Archer who is eventually used as a decoy in the apartment house to draw out the suspected killer. Level of police work is just incompetent enough to allow plot points to pop up as needed.

As a director, Lo Bianco is better at setting up details and ambience than creating suspense and there is little tension mounted despite the supposed life and death situations. Revelation of the true killer arrives with almost no impact.

Shock value on a pure blood and guts level is also rather restrained and almost presented in a tasteful, artistic fashion.

Technical credits are professional throughout with crisp cutting supplied by Ed Beyer. — *Jagr.*

Le Septième Cible
(The Seventh Target)
(FRENCH-COLOR)

Paris, Jan. 15.
A Gaumont release of a Gaumont Intl./Production Marcel Dassault coproduction. Produced by Alain Poiré. Directed by Claude Pinoteau. Stars Lino Ventura. Screenplay, Pinoteau, Jean-Loup Dabadie; camera (Eastmancolor), Edmond Séchan; art director, Pierre-Louis Thévenet; sound, Bernard Bats; editor, Marie-Josèphe Yoyotte; music, Vladimir Cosma; production manager, Marc Goldstaub. Reviewed at the Paris theater, Paris, Jan. 14, 1985. Running time: **108 MINS.**

Bastien Grimaldy	Lino Ventura
Nelly	Lea Massari
Jean	Jean Poiret
Laura	Elisabeth Bourgine
Catherine	Béatrice Agenin
Esperanza	Jean-Pierre Bacri
Hagner	Robert Hoffmann
Inspector Buvard	Erick Desmarestz
Commissioner Paillard	Roger Planchon
Mrs. Grimaldy	Lina Volonghi
Pierre	Karol Zuber
Gabrielle	Annick Alane
Bolek	Jean-Jacques Moreau
Mrs. Bolek	Sylvie Orcier

Actor Lino Ventura is a stalwart screen presence, usually providing firm dramatic anchorage to even the most flimsy and conventional of scripts. In his new film, "The Seventh Target" he is in fine form as a successful novelist persecuted by mysterious aggressors and enigmatic threats who is edged toward a paranoid state before learning he is the victim of an international extortion racket.

Scripter Jean-Loup Dabadie and director Claude Pinoteau, who have packaged two earlier vehicles for Ventura, give polish and smooth articulation to a conventional plot that finally takes the star to Berlin for its climax.

Pic has its share of familiar suspense sequences, smartly executed by Pinoteau (who previously directed the Gaumont "La Boum" hits), and dexterously interweaves a series of seemingly banal domestic scenes that offset and aggravate Ventura's deepening anxiety. Dabadie's sense of colorful portraiture is evident in these moments of romantic insecurity and familial crises.

The quietly forceful Ventura has good company from a solid supporting cast, notably the excellent Jean Poiret (author of "La Cage Aux Folles"), playing an alcoholic ventriloquist who's unhappily married to Ventura's former girl friend (Lea Massari). Béatrice Agenin, as his current love interest, Elizabeth Bourgine, as his young ward, and Lina Volonghi, as his crusty Italian mother, make the most of their screen time.

In more episodic roles, legit director Roger Planchon again displays a remarkable screen personality as a skeptical police commissioner, and Jean-Pierre Bacri is delightful in the comic personage of a divorced inspector assigned to protect Ventura with his two school-age daughters in tow.

Tech credits (and Vladimir Cosma's dramatically functional music) are fine. — *Len.*

Witches' Brew
(COLOR)

Failed fantasy sitcom.

A Joshua Lightman Co. production. Executive producer, Jack Bean. Produced by Donna Ashbrook; supervising producer, W.L. Zeltonoga. Directed by Richard Shorr. Additional sequences directed by Herbert L. Strock. Stars Richard Benjamin, Teri Garr. Screenplay, Syd Dutton, Shorr; camera (color), Norman Gerard, for additional sequences — João Fernandes; editor, Strock; music, John Parker; sound, Mike Sabo, Gerald Wolfe; assistant directors, David Kahler, Frank Martinez; art direction, Marie Kordus; "Lucifer" demon created by David Allen; additional animation effects, Visual Concepts Engr.; stunt coordinator, Fred Lerner. Reviewed on Showtime, N.Y., Jan. 15, 1985. (MPAA Rating: PG.) Rating: **98 MINS.**

Josua Lightman	Richard Benjamin
Margaret Lightman	Teri Garr
Vivian Cross	Lana Turner
Susan Carey	Kathryn Leigh Scott
Linus Cross	James Winker
Nick Carey	Bill Sorrels
Linda Reynolds	Kelly Jean Peters
Charlie Reynolds	Jordan Charney

"Witches' Brew," a.k.a "Which Witch Is Which?" is a comedy about witchcraft filmed in 1978, revamped years later by film doctor Herbert L. Strock and finally surfacing on paycable after having been shelved for theatrical release and subjected to litigation. Review here is for the record.

An impressive toplined cast is trapped in this amateurish production, revolving around the sitcom premise (in the vein of the "Bewitched" tv series) of housewife Margaret (Teri Garr) helping her college psychology prof hubbie Joshua (Richard Benjamin) get ahead via witchcraft. His luck changes for the worse when she lifts all her benevolent spells, after Joshua mocks her aid.

Key point of historical interest is that "Brew" relies upon exactly the same premise employed years later in Carl Reiner's Steve Martin hit "All Of Me:" wicked witch Vivian (Lana Turner) is ailing, but contrives to shift her soul into pupil Margaret's body having willed her fortune to "Margaret." Even the differing mirror image gimmick is trotted out here.

Garr and Benjamin make a comfortable team, but entire cast is hurt by poor sound recording, unfunny dialog ("Bat jowls" is frequently repeated for supposed sure-fire laughs) and terrible continuity.
— *Lor.*

Bertoldo, Bertoldino E Cacasenno
(Bertoldo, Bertoldino And Cacasenno)
(ITALIAN-COLOR)

Rome, Dec. 20.
A Gaumont release, produced by Luigi and Aurelio De Laurentiis for Filmauro. Stars Ugo Tognazzi, Alberto Sordi and Lello Arena. Directed by Mario Monicelli. Screenplay by Leo Benvenuti, Suso Cecchi D'Amico, Piero De Bernardi and Mario Monicelli, freely inspired by a story by Giulio Cesare Croce. Camera (Telecolor), Camillo Bazzoni; art director, Lorenzo Baraldi; costumes, Gianna Gissi; editor, Ruggero Mastroianni; music, Nicola Piovani. Reviewed at ANICA, Rome, Dec. 18, 1984. Running time: **125 MINS.**

Bertoldo	Ugo Tognazzi
Bertoldino	Maurizio Nichetti
King Alboino	Lello Arena
Fra Cipolla	Alberto Sordi
Marcolfa	Annabella Schiavone
Queen Magonia	Pamela Denise Roberts

"Bertoldo, Bertoldino And Cacasenno" is a classy fairytale-farce with kings and peasants set in the year 1000. Veteran helmer Mario Monicelli has tackled historical comedy before to good effect in "The Brancaleone Army." Here the aim is to forge family entertainment out of folklore most familiar to the scholars. Scripters have skillfully turned their source material into imaginative fantasy dosed with bawdiness, humor and irony. Mostly it works.

Film was withheld from the Venice Fest earlier this year by producers Luigi and Aurelio De Laurentiis so it would arrive at the Christmas b.o. scramble unburned. Pic's two top stars, Ugo Tognazzi and Alberto Sordi, got it off to an okay start. They should be an important factor in off-shore sales, though the film is far less of a regional product than most Italo sitcoms.

Principal character is the rough-hewn peasant Bertoldo (Tognazzi), who uses intelligence and cunning to placate the ire of his cross-eyed tyrant, King Alboini (Lello Arena). Despite his Neanderthal looks, Bertoldo outwits the despot when he tries to tax his starving subject for smelling the succulent aromas wafting from the royal kitchen. Bertoldo pays his fine by dropping a gold ducat and letting the king hear its ring.

Less often on the screen but equally memorable is Sordi in the role of Fra Cipolla, a bearded religious fake adept at fleecing the gullible. His adventure with Bertoldo and son involves hiding gold coins in a donkey's stomach and selling the beast to some peasants who believe it is the equivalent of the goose that laid the golden egg. This escapade ends with Bertoldo being condemned to death, though the king agrees to let him choose the tree he wants to swing from. After months of searching, Bertoldo returns to the castle with a potted plant and suggests they let it grow.

The comic skill and timing of Tognazzi, Sordi and Arena (who plays the northern king with a Neapolitan accent for extra laughs) are enough to carry pic through most of its two-hour length. In supporting roles, Maurizio Nichetti and Annabella Schiavone as Bertoldo's goose-boy son and naive wife are less original. The real stars of the film are Gianni Gissi's dazzling, humorous costumes. Cameraman Camillo Bazzoni provides atmospheric visuals. — *Yung.*

Cherie
(HONG KONG-COLOR)

Hong Kong, Dec. 30.

A Brainchild Production, released by Shaw Brothers. Executive Producer, Selina Show. Directed by Patrick Tam. Stars Chung Chu-hung, Liang Chia Hui and Chu Yuen. (No other credits provided by producers.) Reviewed at Jade Theater, Hong Kong, Dec. 29, 1984. Running Time: **98 MINS.**
(Cantonese soundtrack with English subtitles)

Cherie (Chung Chu-hung) is a physical fitness instructor, a contemporary Chinese woman of Hong Kong, lively, lovely, Westernized, rather loose, but with some Oriental conservatism.

The young woman has a millionaire admirer (Chu Yuen, a Shaw Brothers director on an acting kick) who is always driving around in his Rolls Royce. The second man in her life is a photographer (Liang Chia-hua), who happens to have been trained abroad which explains his nice apartment and American ways.

They all end up at a resort and the two men fight it out and are taught a lesson while the heroine takes off alone with the desire to pursue other affairs.

The film was Shaw's Christmas presentation and the starring vehicle for the hot favorite of the year, Chung Chu-hung. The film seems to exist only to showcase her in different poses, dresses and stages of undress.

The curiosity appeal is there but

the pretentiousness in this modern comedy-drama is baffling. The situations tease a lot, but nothing much happens and picture will likely irritate filmgoers. — *Mel.*

Tomboy
(COLOR)

Subpar Crown exploitation fare.

Chicago, Jan. 24.

A Crown Intl. Pictures release of a Marimark production. Produced by Marilyn Tenser; coproducer, Michael Castle. Directed by Herb Freed. Features entire cast. Screenplay, Ben Zelig, based on Mark Tenser's original story idea; camera (Deluxe), Daniel Yarussi; second unit camera, Bryan England; editor, Richard Westover; music supervision, Michael Lloyd; art director, Randy Ser; exec producer, Mark Tenser. Reviewed at Plitt Screening Room, Chicago, Jan. 24, 1985. (MPAA Rating: R.) Running time: **92 MINS.**
Tommy Boyd	Betsy Russell
Randy Starr	Jerry Dinome
Seville Ritz	Kristi Somers
Chester	Richard Erdman
Earl Delarue	Philip Sterling
Ernie Leeds Jr.	Eric Douglas
Frankie	Paul Gunning
Harold	Toby Iland
Pimples	E. Danny Murphy
Jennifer	Rory Barish
Amanda	Cynthia Ann Thompson
Carlos	Cory Hawkins
Goodley	Shane McCabe
Tod	Aaron Butler

The Crown Intl. duo of Marilyn and Mark Tenser often have mined softcore exploitation to surprisingly good result (e.g., "My Tutor," "Weekend Pass"). With "Tomboy," Crown has taken a wrong turn that limits the pic's wicket potential to shockingly unfussy teenagers (despite the R tag).

In virtually every aspect, "Tomboy" is a loser. This plotless exercise revoles about a pretty teenage girl (Betsy Russell) doing the sorts of things (fixing cars, riding motorcycles, playing basketball) teenage girls aren't supposed to. She meets a heartthrob race car driver (Jerry Dinome) who at long last awakens the girl's romantic side.

What little dramatic tension there is comes at the finale when the femme takes on the handsome driver in a winner-take-all-racing match. He races his standard souped up model, she comes on with a sophisticated chunk of mechanical wizardry — concocted during a busy week back at the garage — worthy of James Bond. Guess who wins.

Intersticed between these less-than-riveting episodes are scenes involving a would-be actress (Kristi Somers) who strips at the blink of a false eyelash; a rich young man who appears to be a pimp (Eric Douglas, Kirk's youngest son, who here resembles a young Truman Capote); and loud Hollywood parties peopled largely by balding, middle-

aged men.

There is the standard mix of nudity (Russell is photographed taking a shower) and a soupçon of simulated coupling. All is softer than Crown's usual core, and very dull. Big problem, perhaps fatal, is the casting of Jerry Dinome as the romantic lead. A male model making his feature debut, Dinome isn't directed well and comes up woefully short as a forceful male presence.

Russell is appealingly straightforward in the title role. She looks fine and tries to convey some depth to a strictly cardboard script characterization. Somers shows a nice capacity for sexy pertness.

Veteran character actor Richard Erdman is wasted as the title character's mentor. Philip Sterling is solid as a racing car money man.

Woefully lacking are Herb Freed's direction (even car chases are a thorough yawn), Ben Zelig's script (based, it says, on Mark Tenser's story idea), and Daniel Yarussi's cinematography. "Tomboy" has a bleached-out look with sets and costumes to match. In all, nowhere near up to Crown's recent standard. — *Sege.*

Turk 182
(COLOR)

Compelling populist drama should score well.

Hollywood, Feb. 3.

A 20th Century Fox release, produced by Ted Field and Rene DuPont. Executive producers, Peter Samuelson and Robert Cort. Directed by Bob Clark. Stars Timothy Hutton. Screenplay by James Gregory Kingston, Ddenis & John Hamill, based on story by Kingston; camera (TVC color), Reginald H. Morris; editor, Stan Cole; sound, James Sabat; production design, Harry Pottle; assistant director, Ken Goeh; associate producer, Gary Goeh; art director, Paul Eads; music, Paul Zaza; casting, Mike Fenton and Jane Feinberg (L.A.) and Marcia Shulman (N.Y.). Reviewed at Avco Theatre, L.A., Feb. 2, 1985. (MPAA Rating: PG-13). Running time: **98 MINS.**
Jimmy Lynch	Timothy Hutton
Terry Lynch	Robert Urich
Danny Boudreau	Kim Cattrall
Mayor Tyler	Robert Culp
Detective Kowalski	Darren McGavin
Jockamo	Steven Keats
Detective Ryan	Peter Boyle
Himself	Paul Sorvino
Hanley	Thomas Quinn
Hooley	Norman Parker
Power House Chief	Dick O'Neill

Taking aim squarely at the popular theme of the working man's struggle against the inequities in the system, "Turk 182," a cleverly conceived story of a mystery rebel in New York City whose popularity reaches almost mythic proportions, convincingly hits its mark and could generate significant returns at the boxoffice.

The spark provided also grows increasingly appealing at a time of headline-grabbing vigilante activity because Timothy Hutton, the pic's hero, gets even with his foes and becomes a media hit by using his wits and not his gun.

Hutton plays a 20-year-old whose life doesn't become focused until it comes time for him to defend the honor of his older brother (Robert Urich), fireman who, when off-duty at a neighborhood bar, responds to a plea for help and risks his life by going into a burning building to save the life of a young girl.

Literally sent crashing through a window by the force of spraying water with the child still in his arms, Urich is severely injured but the city refuses to come to his aid, maintaining that he should not have entered the premises in his intoxicated state.

That's when Hutton takes his plea on his brother's behalf through the city bureaucracy to no avail, including a forced confrontation with the mayor (Robert Culp), during an impromptu press interview. With his election drawing near, the mayor, busy sweeping aside a potential scandal concerning an officio up on charges who skipped town, turns an emphatically unsympathetic ear on Hutton.

Director Bob Clark instills frequent doses of humor in his depiction of city government-types which sometimes makes secondary the outrageous human tragedy of Urich's character, who has become suicidal. But depicting public figures as incompetent buffoons is mostly well-advised in setting them up for their public undressing.

While the audience watches Hutton's maneuverings the media delight in telling the city of the mystery-man, "Turk 182's," one-man quest to embarrass and discredit the mayor at each of his pseudo-events aimed at assuring his reelection.

The efforts include a trip to Giants Stadium (located in New Jersey, assumedly showing that a politico will even go outside of his state to win votes) in an unusually imaginative, inventive and stirring scene which will score huge points, particularly with sports fans.

Besides its compelling storyline, "Turk 182" features outstanding performances across the board, with Hutton perfect in the role of the determined unassuming hero. He and Urich are very convincing as brothers with an unusually strong bond, and Urich draws a very accurate and sometimes moving picture, particularly during hospital scenes.

Culp delivers an on-the-mark portrayal as the mayor, with his ever-eager to please painted-on public smile, and is particularly effective when teamed with Peter Boyle, whose Detective Ryan character takes most of the heat for the force's inability to find the man who has been making his presence felt all over the city.

Kim Cattrall does a refreshing turn as social worker Danny Boudreau, who eventually becomes romantically involved with Hutton.

Also figuring nicely are Darren McGavin as the detective brought in on the case and Dick O'Neill in the brief but delicious role as the Power House Chief. Adding authenticity are a handful of w.k. New York-area newscasters.

Though it ultimately falls short of the "Rocky"-like posture struck by pic's hero during the opening titles, "Turk 182" has more than enough going for it on many levels to give filmgoers things to remember after leaving the theater. —Klyn.

House On The Edge Of The Park
(La Casa Nel Parco)
(ITALIAN-COLOR)

A Bedford Entertainment/Trio Entertainment release of an F.D. Cinematografica production. Produced by Franco Palaggi, Franco Di Nunzio. Directed by Ruggero Deodato. Stars David Hess. Screenplay, Gianfranco Clerici, Vincenzo Mannini; camera (Luciano Vittori color), Sergio D'Offizi; editor, Vincenzo Tomassi; music, Riz Ortolani; produc-

tion design-costumes, M.A. Geleng; unit manager, Vito Di Barto. Reviewed at RKO Warner 2 theater, N.Y., Feb. 2, 1985. (No MPAA Rating.) Running time: **91 MINS.**
Alex ....David Hess
Lisa ....Annie-Belle
Ricky ....John Morghen
Gloria ....Lorraine De Selle
Also with: Cristian Borromeo, Marie Claude Joseph.

———

"House On The Edge Of The Park" is an Italian-made softcore sex film, filmed in 1979 and released here regionally last summer on a campaign geared to the terror film reputation (in Wes Craven's "Last House On The Left") of lead player David Hess. It is reviewed for the record, finally arriving at Manhattan theaters.

Thin premise has two thugs (Hess and John Morghen) from New York barging in on a dinner party at a posh mansion in New Jersey and terrorizing the young men and women there for kicks. Padded running time consists of domination and submission sex games with the usual European film emphasis on class distinctions, all very reminiscent of the sexploitation import released by Group 1 a few years back under the appropriate title "Sex And Violence."

Thoroughly unconvincing plot twist has the young aristocrats turning out to be the bad guy aggressors, but little sympathy for the psychotic, low-life "heroes" has been drummed up by then, particularly given the bug-eyed overacting by Hess and Morghen. Lensing by top cameraman Sergio D'Offizi is a plus, with New York City exteriors for establishing shots and interior footage shot in Rome. Beautiful women in the cast include Annie-Belle, her short, platinum blond tresses died black for a change, and the striking young horror film actress Lorraine De Selle. Cast mainly articulates in English, but post-synching of dialog is variable in quality. —Lor.

———

Heaven Help Us
(COLOR)

———

Funny look at Catholic school may be a tough sell.

———

Hollywood, Feb. 1.
A Tri-Star Pictures release of an HBO Pictures presentation in association with Silver Screen Partners. Produced by Dan Wigutow, Mark Carliner. Directed by Michael Dinner. Features entire cast. Screenplay, Charles Purpura; camera (Technicolor/Metrocolor prints), Miroslav Ondricek; editor, Stephen A. Rotter; music, James Horner; production design, Michael Molly; art direction, Robert Guerra; set decoration, Gary J. Brink; costume design, Joseph G. Aulisi; sound, Peter A. Eliardi; associate producer, Kenneth Utt; assistant director, Peter Giuliano; casting, Howard Feuer, Jeremy Ritzer. Reviewed at the Picwood Theatre, West L.A., Jan. 31, 1985. (MPAA Rating: R.) Running time: **104 MINS.**
Brother Thadeus ......Donald Sutherland
Brother Timothy ....John Heard
Michael Dunn.........Andrew McCarthy
Danni..........Mary Stuart Masterson
Rooney ....Kevin Dillon
Caesar ....Malcolm Danare
Boo ....Jennie Dundas
Grandma ....Kate Reid
Father Abruzzi ....Wallace Shawn
Brother Constance ....Jay Patterson
Brother Paul ....Philip Bosco
Corbet ....Patrick Dempsey
Williams ....Stephen Geoffreys

———

"Heaven Help Us" represents an admirable, if not 100% successful, attempt to pull back from the excesses of the teenage comedies of the last several years. Very funny in spots and wonderfully evocative of Brooklyn, circa 1965, pic suffers somewhat by dividing its attention between outrageous pranks and realistic sketches of the Catholic school experience. Film has considerable appeal and more than enough yocks to please almost any audience, but hackneyed title and unpromising campaign in evidence don't bode well for setting the box-office on fire.

Lensed under the equally uncommercial but more descriptive title "Catholic Boys," this marks the feature directorial debut of Michael Dinner, who scored a year or so back with his adaptation of "Miss Lonelyhearts" for PBS, as well as the first produced work of screenwriter Charles Purpura. Both display considerable skill here.

High school has always provided an ideal setting for mirth and virtually universal audience identification, and Catholic schools offer their own particular targets, what with the exceptionally rigorous conduct codes and the emphasis on strenuous repression of natural bodily impulses.

"Heaven Help Us" focuses upon several boys, three in particular, who get into an increasing amount of trouble with the presiding priests. Andrew McCarthy, a new arrival at St. Basil's, instantly latches onto reigning outsider in his class, Malcolm Danare, a chubby egghead who is constantly picked on by school bully Kevin Dillon.

It's virtually inconceivable that the intelligent, sensible McCarthy or Danare would have anything to do with the likes of ne'er-do-well Dillon in real life, but Dillon intimidates them into something resembling friendship. Along with a couple of other large, silent boys, they receive their share of corporal punishment for relatively harmless offenses, wreak havoc during confession and communion and ultimately inspire some helpful changes to be made in the school heirarchy.

Domestic scenes with parents are largely avoided, but some poignancy is added via a tentative romance McCarthy has with cute but hard-boiled Mary Stuart Masterson, a

non-Catholic dropout who works at the snackshop across the street from school. This subplot is dropped quite abruptly, and any ramifications of Dillon destroying his 'father's Lincoln Continental are totally ignored.

Film benefits tremendously by astute casting all down the line. Getting the most mileage out of his appearance here, and stimulating the most hilarity, is Malcolm Danare as the tubby genius type whose dreams of going to Harvard are dashed by his involvement with the rowdy element. McCarthy is wary, sensitive and alert as the newcomer, and Masterson is just right as the cute urchin who opens up to him. Kevin Dillon, a somewhat rougher version of his brother Matt, is also ideal as the roughneck and would have been right at home as one of the Dead End kids.

Authority figures are aptly represented by Donald Sutherland as the headmaster, Jay Patterson as a horrifying disciplinarian, Wallace Shawn as a priest hung up on sex and John Heard, a new arrival who identifies more with the students than his fellow Brothers.

It is clear that, in its heart, film wants to be a bright, relatively realistic portrait of adolescence in a particular environment, but at times it goes too far in catering to the contempo youth audience accustomed to the outrageousness of "Animal House," "Porky's" and the like. By and large, however, this stands as a healthy corrective in the area of teenpix.

Technically, film is superior. Miroslav Ondricek's cinematography gives the picture a great deal of texture, Stephen A. Rotter's editing is sharp, and production designer Michael Molly and other craftsmen have managed a flawless, but not overelaborated, recreation of a period not long gone. In repertory houses down the line, this will make a nice companion piece with "The Flamingo Kid," another look at suburban New York at virtually the same time. —Cart.

———

The Dungeonmaster
(COLOR)

———

Short fantasy from seven helmers.

———

Hollywood, Feb. 2.
An Empire Pictures release of a Charles Band production. Produced by Charles Band. Directed by Rosemarie Turko, John Buechler, Charles Band, David Allen, Steve Ford Peter Manoogian, Ted Nicolaou. Screenplay, Allen Actor; camera (CFI color), Mac Ahlberg; editor, Marc Leif, Ted Nicolaou; sound, Doug Arnold. Ike Magal, Ann Krupa; production design, Julie Stroh; music, Richard Band, Shirley Walker; associate producer, Debra Dion; assistant directors, Matia Karrell, Debbie Pinthus, John Dahl, David War-

field, Michaelle Noble, Caren Singer, Betsy Magruder; costume creations, Kathie Clar; special effects makeup, John Buechler. Reviewed at Hollywood Pacific, Hollywood, Calif., Feb. 1, 1985. (MPAA Rating: PG-13.) Running time: **73 MINS.**

Paul Bradford	Jeffrey Byron
Mestema	Richard Moll
Gwen	Leslie Wing
Heavy Metal	Blackie Lawless
Slasher	Danny Dick

Right on the heels of "Ghoulies," producer Charles Band's Empire Pictures claws back with another modestly budgeted schlocky film, this one notable for the curiosity of seven credited directors who individually helm seven super-challenges facing the young hero. Will it make money? Probably, but there is one boxoffice qualification: the filmmakers have hedged on production length, giving theatergoers only 67 minutes of actual movie. The other six minutes is an endless roll of credits.

This is the shortest theatrical in memory, although that's not bad considering the old matinee and serial tone of the material. Shot at the end of 1983 under title "Ragewar," the film had its first engagement Jan. 18 in the South.

As for the use of seven directors, that's rare but not unprecedented. (Paramount's "Paramount On Parade," 1930, had 11 directors; Columbia's "Casino Royale," '67, used five; Paramount's "If I Had A Million," '32, and a British film, RKO's "Forever And A Day," '43, each had seven. They were all episodic films. "Dungeonmaster" is also episodic, although the same three characters perform throughout the movie.)

Production values are jokey, in the manner of "Ghoulies," and the acting is straight enough to be amusing. The evil one who makes the hero engage all these horrific figures is played with a certain flare by Richard Moll (the bailiff in tv's "Night Court" sitcom). The savior is played with wooden earnestness by Jeffrey Byron. And the girlfriend, held hostage by the villain, is performed by a fetching brunette, Leslie Wing, who does look distressful.

Story's running gimmick is that the hero, in real world, is a computer whiz and his confrontation with monstrous forces — one is a heavy metal band (the L.A. band W.A.S.P.) and the other a city slasher — takes on the guise of laser-beamed computer electronics vs. the power of black magic.

—*Loyn.*

Je Vous Salue, Marie
(Hail, Mary)
(FRENCH-SWISS-COLOR)

Paris, Feb. 4.

A Luna-Gérick/Gaumont release of a Pégase/JLG Films/Sara Films/SSR/Channel 4 (London) coproduction. Written and directed by Jean-Luc Godard. Camera (color), Jean-Bernard Menoud; sound, François Musy; music, Bach, Dvorak, John Coltrane. No other credits provided. Reviewed at Gaumont Colisée theater, Feb. 2, 1984. Running time: **86 MINS.**

Mary	Myriem Roussel
Joseph	Thierry Rode
The Angel	Philippe Lacoste
Juliette	Juliette Binoche
Girl	Manon Andersen
Jesus	Malachi Jara Kohan
Arthur	Dick
Professor	Johann Leysen
Eva	Anne Gauthier

The incorrigible Jean-Luc Godard has overreached the usual buff response with his new film, "Je Vous Salue, Marie," an idiosyncratic rendering of the immaculate conception in a contemporary context. It has provoked sharp protests from some parts of the French Catholic community, which have lobbied unsuccessfully to have it banned from national screens, though some religious authorities have unexpectedly sung its praises.

"Marie," which follows Godard's impertinent redo of the Carmen story ("Prenom: Carmen"), recasts the prelude to The Greatest Story Ever Told with the Virgin as a Swiss Miss who works in her father's gas station and sidelines as member of a local girl's basketball team.

Her boyfriend, Joseph, is a taxi driver, who is frustrated by his ignorance (in the biblical sense) of Mary, and is understandably upset when she is diagnosed as being pregnant, fulfilling the prophecy of a passing angel (a client of Joseph's). Marie of course swears she has never known a man, and is not yet ready for a roll in the manger hay with her betrothed.

When the child is born, Mary and Joseph finally settle down to a seemingly banal domesticated family life. Years pass and the boy, now old enough to be tart-tongued, runs away. Mary assures her husband — "He'll be back by Easter." Final image is that of the sexually standoffish Mary applying lipstick, symbolizing her return from transcendent realms.

Film will decidedly help maintain the gulf between the acolytes and the heretics who continue to consider Godard a formidably clever cinematic charlatan.

For this reviewer, admittedly not a Godard worshiper, this new film is one of his more watchable productions, though continually irritating in the filmmaker's fastidious attention to collage soundtrack effects. Godard's manner of filming his attractive leading lady, Myriem Roussel (who played a musician in "Passion") provides his most graceful study of the female body since his "A Married Woman." The fine lensing is by Swiss cameraman Jean-Bernard Menoud.

Feature is billed, by the way, with a 20-minute short by Godard's companion and collaborator, Anne-Marie Mieville: "Le Livre de Marie" (The Book Of Mary), which despite the title has no discernible connection with Godard's opus.

With some of the maestro's mannerisms evident, Mieville in her short subject tells of the reactions of a young girl to her parent's painful separation. Bruno Cremer and Aurore Clément are wooden as mom and dad, but young Rebecca Hampton is engaging as the youngster who deflects family crisis with innate energy, and curiosity. — *Len.*

Mischief
(COLOR)

Very appealing '50s teen comedy.

Hollywood, Jan. 23.

A Twentieth Century Fox release of a Jere Henshaw-Michael Nolin production. Produced by Sam Manners, Michael Nolin. Directed by Mel Damski. Features entire cast. Screenplay—executive producer, Noel Black; camera (DeLuxe color). Donald E. Thorin; editor, Nick Brown; music supervision, Barry DeVorzon; sound, Bud Alper; production designer, Paul Peters; costume designer, Mina Mittelman; set decorator, Ernie Bishop; casting, Mike Fenton, Jane Feinberg, Marci Liroff; assistant director, Yudi Bennett. Reviewed at UA Egyptian Westwood, Jan. 22, 1984. (MPAA Rating: R.) Running time: **93 MINS.**

Jonathan	Doug McKeon
Bunny	Catherine Mary Stewart
Marilyn	Kelly Preston
Gene	Chris Nash
Kenny	D.W. Brown
Rosalie	Jami Gertz
Claire Miller	Maggie Blye
Mr. Travis	Graham P. Jarvis
Claude Harbrough	Terry O'Quinn

An affectionate and sharply rendered period evocation of teenage angst in smalltown 1956 mid-America, "Mischief" is a warm winter surprise from writer Noel Black (trading on some be-bop memories), director Mel Damski (a big step forward after "Yellowbeard"), and 20th Century Fox.

Studio is opening wide, in 1,200 sites, and what will stick certainly deserves to, although tone of film appears to ask for a slow rather than fast drumroll. With a negative cost in area of $5,200,000, however, Fox has reasonable shot with moviegoers who are hungering for a youth film that's nostalgic, dramatically effective (if lightweight), and humorous.

Almost anyone who endured repressed sexual fantasies and realities in the pre-'60s Be-Bop-a-Lulu world of pegged jeans, pony tails, letter sweaters, and poodle skirts has got to give a part of his or her heart to this picture. The story is sanitized but in the spirit of a Norman Rockwell "Post" cover — if Rockwell had ever been a bit racy.

The drama in the scenario is divided between the traumas of two high school buddies (a shy Doug McKeon and troubled newcomer-to-town Chris Nash). McKeon (the young boy in "On Golden Pond") delivers a terrific portrait of a lovable, klutzy kid who wants to get laid with the campus hotshot blonde (Kelly Preston). When he finally does, the scene has to rank among the truest and funniest of its kind.

Nash, in a screen debut that has a kind of whiplash dynamic, has no trouble with girls. He roars into town on a Triumph — a nice counterpoint to McKeon's pedal bike — and his unlikely friendship with the unworldly McKeon against conformist forces is the movie's narrative anchor. Nash's drama is his edgy relationship with a struggling, widowed father, who finally kicks the boy out after one scrape too many with the town's value system.

Nash's girlfriend is essayed by Catherine Mary Stewart, whose eyes glow like a pocket torch. D.W. Brown as the snotty scion to a wealthy family and Jami Gertz as a food-spilling, smitten waitress in the local soda shop lend good support. Pop background is a treasure chest from the fab '50s.

Film is detailed with effective touches: a drive-in movie scene, which features "Rebel Without A Cause" on the screen, serves as a segue to a dangerous "chicken" car battle bewtween Nash and the bully Brown. Later, the kids carouse some distance from a theater, and "Untamed" on the marquee (both, for the record, Fox films from 1955).

But for all the baggy cuffed slacks and fluffy strapless prom dresses, the film scores for its unpretentious story of friendship. That's not an innocent subject in any period and youthful audiences — for whom the '50s now correspond to what the '20s were for the subjects of the movie — will find an appeal along with the old doo-wop and syrupy ballad crowd. —*Loyn.*

After The Fall Of New York
(ITALIAN-FRENCH-COLOR)

An Almi Pictures release of a Nuova Dania Cinematografica (Rome), Medusa Distribuzione (Rome) and Les Films du Griffon (Paris) coproduction. Produced and created by Luciano Martino. Directed by "Martin Dolman" (Sergio Martino). Features entire cast. Screenplay, Julian Berry, Gabriel Rossini, "Martin Dolman;" camera (Telecolor), Giancarlo Ferrando; editor, Eugenio Alabiso; music, Oliver Onions; art direction, Antonello Geleng; assistant director, Masimo Manasse; special effects, Paolo Ricci; stunt coordinator, Nazzareno Cardinali; dialog director, Peter Fernandez; makeup, Fabrizio Sforza, Gino Tamagnini. Reviewed at Almi screening room, N.Y., Jan. 23, 1985. (MPAA Rating: R.) Running time: **95 MINS.**

Parsifal ....Michael Sopkiw
Giaiada ....Valentine Monnier
Ania....................Anna Kanakis
Rachet ....Roman Geer
Bronx ....Vincent Scalondro
Big Ape ....George Eastman
President ....Edmund Purdom
Shorty ....Louis Ecclesia

———

"After The Fall Of New York" is a European-made pastiche of various U.S. science fiction films, notably following up John Carpenter's "Escape From New York." Picture boasts many fantasy elements (unlike chintzier trend films from Italy of late) which should appeal to genre fans, but is hurt by silly dialog and frequent reversion to conventional material such as fist fights which detracts from the intended futuristic mood.

Pic is set in the year 2019, 20 years after a nuclear war won by the Eurax. The losers (Pan American Confederation) are headquartered in Alaska, where the president (Edmund Purdom) summons Parsifal (Michael Sopkiw) to go on a mission to Eurax-held New York City and find the one fertile woman left on Earth. She is to be fetched to restart the human race, as no children have been born for 15 years.

Episodic adventures, which include photogenic location photography in Monument Valley for a nod to both westerns and biker movies, have Parsifal joined by colorful sidekicks Rachet (Roman Geer, filling the William Smith-type role here), Shorty (dwarf actor Louis Ecclesia), a hairy swashbuckler type Big Ape (George Eastman) and the lovely Giaiada (Valentine Monnier). Parsifal succeeds in the mission, finding the fertile daughter of a scientist who has kept her in suspended animation since before the war, but his comrades are killed in the process.

Film's model effects are fake-looking (no sense of scale is imparted) and when in doubt, director Sergio Martino (using a *nom de film* of "Martin Dolman") brings on the rats to presumably appease the sensation-seeking audinece. Science fiction content, particularly the plan to travel to the "planets" of the star Alpha Centauri, is ridiculous.

Acting is unnecessarily wooden, though visually the cast fits the comic strip format. Lead player Michael Sopkiw is actually a Manhattan actor, lately finding employment in Italian adventure films.
—*Lor.*

———

Vision Quest
(COLOR)

———

Diffuse teen rites of passage film.

———

Hollywood, Feb. 2.

A Warner Bros. release of a Guber-Peters Co. production. Produced by Jon Peters, Peter Guber. Executive producer, Stan Weston, Adam Fields. Directed by Harold Becker. Features entire cast. Screenplay, Darryl Poniçsan, based on a novel by Terry Davis; camera (Technicolor), Owen Roizman; editor, Maury Winetrobe; music, Tangerine Dream; production designer, Bill Malley; set decorator, Jaff Haley; sound (Dolby stereo), William Randall; costumes, Susan Becker; assistant director, Thomas Mack; casting, Nancy Klopper. Reviewed at the Bruin theater, Westwood, Calif., Feb. 1, 1985 (MPAA Rating: R.) Running time: **105 MINS.**

Louden Swain ....Matthew Modine
Carla ....Linda Fiorentino
Kuch ....Michael Schoeffling
Mr. Louden ....Ronny Cox
Tanneran ....Harold Sylvester
Coach ....Charles Hallahan
Elmo.......................J.C. Quinn
Margie Epstein ....Daphne Zuniga
Shute ....Frank Jasper

———

"Vision Quest" is an example of filmmaking by numbers, so calculated is every ingredient to elicit a specific response. Pic is a virtual catalog of cliches from recent teen hits without a true heart or center of its own. However, with so many rockets firing, "Vision Quest" is likely to hit a section of the less demanding teen audience.

The only surprises in "Vision Quest" are the implausibilities of the plot. Carla (Linda Fiorentino), a streetwise young woman from New Jersey, arrives in Spokane, Wa. just in time to stir the bursting sexuality of our hero Louden Swain (Matthew Modine). Through an obscure series of events involving a broken-down car, Carla is implanted in Louden's home to torment and distract him from his training as a high school wrestler.

Script by Darryl Poniçsan from Terry Davis' novel doesn't allow anything to develop organically out of the characters, but rather injects as many elements as possible designed to strike a chord in the youth audience. Louden is a wrestler as in "The Karate Kid," is trying to win a scholarship as in "All The Right Moves" and the picture is flooded with an array of pop music as in Guber-Peters' previous hit, "Flashdance."

Film even supplies a bit of pop philosophy. In trying to lose 10 pounds for a match-up with the state's best wrestler, Louden is on a personal "Vision Quest" (whatever that means) and in his 18th year, his time is now. As Louden, Modine is a quirky character (not unlike his role in "Birdy") meant to be unique and fascinating. With a desire to be "a doctor in outer space," instead, he comes off a bit dopey.

Louden's quest leads him everywhere except to the father, son and holy ghost. His friend Kuch (Michael Schoeffling), a mock indian with a mohawk haircut, offers the spiritual advice and a visit to his grandfather (Roberts Blossom) is a talk with the old wise man. There are supportive friends and a sympathetic father (Ronny Cox) along the way, but there is never a sense of people dealing with real human problems, even teen ones.

Dramatic build-up to the climactic wrestling scene is rather flat, although the final confrontation is nicely staged by director Harold Becker and shot by Owen Roizman. As for Louden's other climax, pic adopts a rather coy, almost teasing attitude about its inevitable sexual encounter. Less explicit than most teen fare, Fiorentino's undeniable appeal hovers around the picture without ever really giving the film its center.

In order to make sure it covers all the bases, "Vision Quest" is going off in too many directions at once. And as heavy and intrusive as the score is by Tangerine Dream, with songs by the likes of Journey and Madonna (who appears on screen as a club singer), it does not anchor the action. Try as it might, this picture goes nowhere.

Tech credits are fine with locations and production design often the most evocative part of a scene.—*Jagr.*

———

Reveillon Chez Bob
(New Year's Eve At Bob's)
(FRENCH-COLOR)

———

Paris, Dec. 26.

A Parafrance release of a Swanie Productions/TF 1 Films coproduction. Produced by Norbert Saada. Directed by Denys Granier-Deferre. Stars Jean Rochefort. Screenplay, Granier-Deferre, Jacques Audiard, Yves Stavrides; camera (color), Alain Derobe; art director, Serge Douy; music, Michel Magne; sound, Guillaume Sciama; editor, Jacques Witta; production manager, Pierre Tati; executive producers, Pierre Tati, Norbert Chalon. Reviewed at the George V cinema, Paris, Dec. 26, 1984. Running time: **100 MINS.**

Louis Alban ....Jean Rochefort
Thierry Hubert ....Guy Bedos
Florence ....Agnès Soral
Douglas ....Michel Galabru
Madeleine ....Mireille Darc
Kremeur ....Bernard Fresson
Jeremy ....Thierry Magnier

———

This second film by Denys Granier-Deferre (son of veteran helmer Pierre Granier-Deferre) confirms the young director's ambitions in tackling complicated cross-section narratives, but also shows he still lacks the directing skills necessary. His feature debut, "Que Les Gros Salaires Levent le Doigt!" examined white collar relationships in a group of office workers invited for a weekend at the boss' country home.

The group in "Reveillon Chez Bob" is smaller and centers on Jean Rochefort, a highstrung cartoonist, who receives a New Year's greeting card from his son and learns his ex-wife's new mate, Bob, has been physically abusing the boy. Incensed, he jumps in his car (he lives in Switzerland to soothe his frayed nerves) and speeds to Paris, where he plans to put a few corrective bullets into the sadistic Bob that very evening.

Unfortunately, the address is an imposing complex of apartment towers and Rochefort's son has neglected to indicate building and apartment number. For good reason: the boy has invented "Bob" (in fact, his doctor in the same complex) in order to bring about a reunion between his parents. With the complicity of the block's security guard, (Bernard Fresson) he makes sure Rochefort will lose his way in the residential labyrinth where the only signs of life are some wild New Year's parties.

In his wanderings Rochefort comes across other lone figures in the concrete landscape: Guy Bedos, an anxious garage owner invited to the party of the real Bob; Agnès Soral, his young new accountant; and Michel Galabru, a gun-toting resident who offers his madcap support. Soon all four are lost in the bowels of the building, but emerge at dawn for the final reconciliation plotted by Rochefort's son.

The script, by the director, Yves Stavrides and Jacques Audiard, never develops beyond the basic idea of assembling some disparately neurotic characters in an unusual situation and setting, and letting each unfold his tics in obviously arranged comic set pieces. The actors fail to relate to each other, and the story line (known to the spectator from the start) zigzags unimaginatively, without any helpful energy from Granier-Deferre's dully realistic direction. — *Len.*

———

The Beach Boys: An American Band
(DOCU-COLOR)

———

Lotsa music, little analysis.

———

Hollywood, Jan. 25.

A Sharp Features release of a High Ridge Production in association with Malcolm Leo Prods. Exec producers, Jon Peisinger, Michael Wiese. Produced by Leo and Bonnie Peterson. Written and directed by Leo. Camera (color), John Toll; additional photography, Fritz Roland; sound, Doug Nelson; location sound, Bruce Bisenz; editor, David Fairfield, Mark Cole. Reviewed on vidcassette at Rear View Inc., L.A., Jan. 24, 1985. (MPAA Rating: PG-13.) Running time: **103 MINS.**

———

This fond, fast-paced overview of California's Beach Boys, who've been preaching the gospel of sun, surf, cars and "girls," with varying membership, over the past 24 years, is packed with some 44 tunes, leaving little room, apparently, for any penetrating analysis of the music or the men behind it.

Writer-director-coproducer Malcolm Leo, whose music docus include "This Is Elvis," knows how to package such fare agreeably. State-of-the-art reprocessing of the music, plus some footage never before seen in this country, as well as material shot specifically for this production, offer extra treats.

Opening theatrically in Dolby stereo in 10 markets initially, Vestron Video, the production's backer, will have a homevideo version available later this year, and this is presumably where it will find its most profitable market.

Docu eschews the conventional narrator (or pontificating rock critic) approach, allowing the music and filmed sequences to do the talking.

Production follows the tale fairly chronologically, wrapping with the band's return to Washington, D.C. last year after the famous run-in in 1983 with then-Interior Secretary James Watt.

Brian Wilson's withdrawal, first from live performances with the group (he makes some appearances these with the band) and then life itself — spending years, in essence, locked away in his bedroom — makes the latter portion of the film more of a study of the individuals than a group, which may be the most telling comment of all.

Death of drummer-brother Dennis Wilson in late 1983 is also touched upon, as are his drug-alcohol problems, but the point of view is pretty protective here, as it is in discussing how the brothers' father, Murry, was fired by the band as manager.

Included are the group's performance of "Surfin' U.S.A.," shot for the "T.A.M.I. Show" feature but removed from all prints after initial release; footage shot in connection with the aborted "Smile" album, and a promo film, done for European broadcast, of "Wouldn't It Be Nice," a 1966 precursor of today's musicvid, for the "Pet Sounds" LP. Segments of the band's 1983 performance in Atlantic City — where the band played on July 4 when Watt wouldn't let them play D.C. — are also shown for the first time, and record Dennis Wilson's last filmed performance with the group.

Throughout is the more-than-infectious Beach Boys music to gladden the hearts of fans, and early performance footage to demonstrate to those too young to remember the initial incarnation why they're so appealing.—*Kirk.*

Brazil
(BRITISH-COLOR)

Paris, Feb. 10.

A Fox/Hachette release, France, (Universal Pictures-U.S.) of an Arnon Milchan production. Produced by Milchan. Directed by Terry Gilliam. Features entire cast. Screenplay, Gilliam, Tom Stoppard, Charles McKeown; camera (color), Roger Pratt; production designer, Norman Garwood; costumes, Jim Acheson; editor, Julian Doyle; sound, Bob Doyle, Rodney Glenn; special effects supervisor, George Gibbs; special effects camera, Tim Spence; models supervisor, Richard Conway; makeup and hairdo, Maggie Weston; original music, Michael Kamen; art directors, Keith Pain, John Beard; production manager, Graham Ford; coproducer, Patrick Cassavetti. Reviewed at the Gaumont screening room, Feb. 8, 1985. (No MPAA Rating.) Running time: 142 MINS.

Sam Lowry	Jonathan Pryce
Harry Tuttle	Robert De Niro
Jack Lint	Michael Palin
Jill Layton	Kim Greist
Ida Lowry	Katherine Helmond
Kurtzmann	Ian Holm
Warren	Ian Richardson
Helpmann	Peter Vaughan
Spoor	Bob Hoskins
Dowser	Derrick O'Connor
Lime	Charles McKeown
Mrs. Terrain	Barbara Hicks
Shirley	Kathryn Pogson
Dr. Jaffe	Jim Broadbent
Dr. Chapman	Jack Purvis
Spiro	Bryan Pringle
Mrs. Buttle	Sheila Reid

"Brazil" is black comedy for the Orwellian '80s, as "Dr. Strangelove" was for the Fail-Safe '60s. Terry Gilliam, one of the comic terrorists of Monty Python, hits his full directorial stride in his third solo venture (after "Jabberwocky" and "Time Bandits"), which offers a chillingly hilarious vision of the near-future, set "somewhere in the 20th Century." As with the Python films, it will not be everybody's cup of poisoned tea, but should be a piquant delight to those thirsting for darker flows of humor.

Straight and comic predictions of society-to-come, in which the human element is bled dry by technological and political oppression, are pretty much old hat in both film and literature. However, Gilliam, abetted by playwright Tom Stoppard (here curbing his linguistic pyrotechnic displays) and Charles McKeown (who also plays a harrowed bureaucrat), knows the clichés and how to transcend them, working with a palette that encompasses satire, parody, the grotesque, fantasy and tragi-comedy.

Still, "Brazil" is impressively coherent in design, usually far-removed from the anarchic nonsense of the Python assaults and the surreal abandon of Gilliam's previous pictures and cartoons. Despite its unusual length, it is for the most part rigorously constructed and vigorously sustained, with the director's talents as graphic artist and animator obviously responsible for the film's often startling visualizations.

His witty sense of architectural nightmare is on display in the all-too-credible depiction of a progressive megalopolis, in which ducts, pipes and conduits of all shapes, sizes and colors strangle conventional living space and even countryside (invisible from the exhaust-polluted highways because of the solid walls of giant billboards).

Gilliam reportedly wanted to call the film "1984-½." As in Orwell's classic, society is monitored by an insidious, tentacular ministry, and the film's protagonist, a diligent but unambitious civil servant, Sam Lowry — played with vibrant comic imagination by Jonathan Pryce — becomes a victim of his own romantic delusions, and is crushed by a system he had never before thought of questioning.

Pryce is hopelessly doped out. Though ultra-competent on the job, he otherwise lives in a dream world of adolescent fantasies, seeing himself as a winged super-hero, part-Icarus, part-Siegfried, soaring lyrically through the clouds to the tune of "Brazil," the old Xavier Cugat favorite, which as the film's ironic musical leitmotif, recurs in numerous mock variations.

The wall between dream and reality begins to crumble when he one day spots and gives pursuit to a beautiful young girl who resembles his fantasy Dulcinea. She, in fact a tomboyish truckdriver, is suspected of subversive activity connected to a terrorist network, which has been bombing public sites for years.

Another fortuitous encounter that also helps seal his fate is with a scab maintenance man and saboteur who intercepts his call for help when his air conditioning system fails. Robert De Niro shows delightful comic flair in this small, but succulent characterization of proletariat superhero, who disposes of some obnoxious rival repairmen in a disgustingly original manner, but meets a most bizarre end in the film's nightmare climax.

Gilliam has assembled a brilliant supporting cast of character actors, notably Ian Holm, as the edgy, paranoid ministry department chief hopelessly dependent on Pryce to untie bureaucratic knots; Katherine Helmond, as his beauty-conscious mother, pulling top-level strings to see her boy promoted, and having her face pulled like taffy by her plastic surgeon to get rid of wrinkles; Peter Vaughan, as the glibly paternalistic deputy minister, and Michael Palin, as the ministry's torturer, whose operating chair is in a vast, empty silo. Yank newcomer Kim Greist is perfect as the mysterious yet down-to-earth lady of the hero's dreams.

Production designer Norman Garwood and special effects and model supervisors Georges Gibbs and Richard Conway prove top-flight collaborators for Gilliam, as does lenser Roger Pratt, who skillfully adapts to the script's shifting textures and tones. Michael Kamen's original music and marvelous pastiche arrangements are part of the fun. Other tech credits are excellent. — *Len.*

Der Biss
(The Bite)
(WEST GERMAN-COLOR-16m)

Saarbrücken, Jan. 20.

A Marianne Enzenberger Film Production, West Berlin. Written and directed by Enzenberger. Features entire cast. Camera (color), Jeff Preiss, Klemens Becker; sound, Ian Charles Wright, Michael Shepard; music, Gerd Pasemann, Unlimited Systems; production manager, Renée Gundelach. Reviewed at Saarbrücken Film Fest (Max Ophüls Prize), Jan. 19, 1985. Running time: 84 MINS.

With: Marianne Enzenberger (Sylvana), Marianne Rosenberg (Sara), Ulrike Buschbauer, Michael Shepard, Jörg Pfennigwerth, Anette Humpe, Martin Sperr, Rosa von Praunheim, Friedrich Steinhauer.

The Berlin Underground scene keeps broadening in scope with new trends and styles. The latest to score at Hof and Saarbrücken is Marianne Enzenberger's "The Bite."

It begins in New York, where Sylvana gets lost in the Village and, in exhaustion, is carried into a strange brownstone housing a black vampire who sinks his teeth into her throat. After this bite, she drops her erstwhile boyfriend and wings her way back to Berlin as a woman-vampire in search of victims of her own. Nobody wants to get bitten by Sylvana, and she begins to get on everyone's nerves as she moves from commune to bourgeois family to cult culture and so on. In general the joke wears thin and the situations become too repetitive.

Enzenberger has at least proved she can film on a shoestring (pic cost about $80,000). —*Holl.*

Streetwise
(DOCU-COLOR)

Grim account of teenage outcasts, up for an Oscar.

An Angelika Films release of a film by Martin Bell, Mary Ellen Mark and Cheryl McCall. Executive producers, Angelika T. Saleh, Connie and Willie Nelson. Produced by McCall. Directed by Bell. Editor, Nancy Baker; music, Tom Waits; camera (color), Bell; sound, Keith Desmond; associate editor, Jonathan Oppenheim; assistant editor, Meredith Birdsall; sound editors, Janet Swanson, Oppenheim, Pola Rapaport, Birdsall; camera assistants, Douglas Pellegrino, Eve Pellegrino; production assistants, Diane Birdsall, Jan Stonehall; re-recording supervisor, Dick Vorisek; title design, Barbara Kurgan. Reviewed at Magno Penthouse screening room, N.Y. Feb. 7, 1985 (No MPAA Rating.) Running time: 92 MINS.

Features: Tiny, Rat, Dewayne, Shadow, Shellie, Patti, Munchkin, Kim and Lulu.

The outgrowth of an April 1983 Life magazine piece by reporter Cheryl McCall and photographer Mary Ellen Mark on the dead-end lives of teenage drifters in Seattle, this grim but detached documentary was shown there theatrically last October. Its Oscar nomination in the best documentary category will probably open the way to limited exhibition in other big cities, but the portrayal of adolescent detritus presented in "Streetwise" and its implied indictment of society's failure to remedy the consequences of family erosion in contemporary America will undoubtedly be too discomforting for a wide audience. Ultimately, the documentary might more effectively communicate its message via cable tv or PBS.

Like the street life it documents, the film has a rough, inexorable rhythm, rapidly cross-cutting among the principal young runaways and outcasts who narrate their own stories of abandonment and alienation. At first they are almost indistinguishable from one another but as the documentary unfolds, these brash, but pitiable young hookers and hustlers are brought into focus as distinct personalities whose values are based on a quotidian struggle for survival even as they nurture pathetically self-delusive American dreams of fabulous wealth and unfettered freedom.

The most charismatic of the street kids is Rat, a wiry 17-year-old skilled in scavenging and petty crime. He lives in an abandoned hotel with an older, hippie-type buddy and protector (a subtheme in the docu is the failure of the '60s Woodstock nation to create the dreamed-of "better world" for the next generation) who's instructed him in the arts of hustling and jumping trains. Rat talks of returning to school and joining the armed forces, but his intoxication with "the open road U.S.A." makes this an unlikely daydream.

Rat's best friends are 16-year-old Dewayne, whose father is in prison in California (their visitation scene is one of the film's most powerful) and Tiny, a 14-year-old prostitute whose alcoholic mother wants to believe her confused womanchild is going through "a phase." Although the kid drifters boast about being "streetwise," the naivete of tyro hookers like 16-year-old Kim and 13-year-old Shellie makes them easy prey for unsavory, young macho pimps like 18-year-old Shadow and Munchkin. Lulu, a 19-year-old lesbian, is possessed of the strongest self-image of all the street kids — she's a tough, sidewalk enforcer who's prepared to stand down any aggressor. The code of mutual self-protection is all-powerful among the tight-knit teenaged renegades of "Streetwise."

The documentary is not unsympathetic in its treatment of the agents of the outside, adult world. There are social workers, doctors, and a born-again evangelist who seem genuinely concerned with pulling these kids out of an abysmal lifecycle of drugs, disease, crime and poverty. Even the police are restrained in their efforts to keep order on the streets where the principal characters live in a tense, interracial community of skid-row derelicts, and old-before-their-time social dropouts.

But most of the feral protagonists of "Streetwise," all of whom have been alienated from or rejected by their families (in spite of sporadic attempts at reconciliation) seem disinterested in long-range help. While it's possible that some of their bravado has been laid on for the camera's eye (the tricky issue of documentary truth underlies even the most sincere attempts at objective, nonfiction filmmaking), this legion of new American social outcasts seem to have set their course in a direction that's likely to end as it does in some cases here, either in prison or an early grave. — Rich.

The Exterminators Of The Year 3000
(ITALIAN-SPANISH-COLOR)

A New Line Cinema release of a 2T Produzione Film S.r.l. (Rome)/Globe Film (Madrid) coproduction presented by Ugo Tucci and Camillo Teti. Directed by Jules Harrison. Stars Robert Jannucci, Alicia Moro. Screenplay, Elisa Briganti, Dardano Sacchetti, José Truchado Reyes; camera (Luciano Vittori color), Alejandro Ulloa; editor, Adriano Tagliavia; music, Detto Mariano; assistant director, Goffredo Unger; set design, Enrico Fiorentini; special effects, Gino De Rossi, Edmondo Natali; costume design, Luciana Marinucci. Reviewed on Thorn EMI Video cassette, N.Y., Jan. 29, 1985. (MPAA Rating: R.) Running time: **91 MINS.**
Alien .... Robert Jannucci
Trash .... Alicia Moro
Papillon .... Alan Collins
Tommy .... Luca Ventantini
John .... Venantino Venantini
Also with: Eduardo Fajardo, Fred Harris, Beryl Cunningham, Anna Orso, Sergio Mioni.

"The Exterminators Of The Year 3000" is a weak imitation of "The Road Warrior" hit. In unusual fashion, it opened simultaneously in the theatrical (on 42d St.) and homevideo market, with meager prospects in either medium.

After a plotless opening reel of old cars chasing around (though set in the year 3000, pic is populated with well-preserved models from the 1960s and 1970s), story concerns the search for water in a post-nuclear wasteland. Teamed up are the handsome hero Alien (Robert Jannucci), a pretty girl he used to know named Trash (Alicia Moro) and a cute bionic boy Tommy (Luca Ventantini). Tommy's dad was murdered by the bald baddie Crazy Bull, who leads a gang of bikers whom he tastefully calls "Mother grabbers" in the poorly-dubbed dialog when not shouting out quaint expressions such as "Let's purloin that water."

When Tommy loses a biomechanical arm, they go to an ex-astronaut Papillon (Alan Collins) to fix it. Papillon has already fixed Alien's souped-up stolen car which is called the Exterminator. Baddies are defeated and pic ends with the star trio frolicking in the first rainfall in years, though the Earth's ozone layer has been destroyed by nuclear bombs making for cloudless skies.

Pic has little to offer beyond okay stunts and action footage. Oddly anticipating "Road Warrior II's" casting of Tina Turner, veteran black actress in Continental productions Beryl Cunningham is cast as a vicious killer in Crazy Bull's gang. — Lor.

Fast Forward
(COLOR)

Weak youth dance musical from Sidney Poitier. Meager b.o. chances.

Hollywood, Feb. 7.
A Columbia Pictures release of a Verdon-Cedric production. Produced by John Patrick Veitch. Executive producer, Melville Tucker. Directed by Sidney Poitier. Features entire cast. Screenplay by Richard Wesley, from a story by Timothy March; camera (Metrocolor), Matthew F. Leonetti; editor, Harry Keller; music, Tom Scott, Jack Hayes; executive music producer, Quincy Jones; art director, Michael Baugh; set decorator, Jerry Adams; choreography, Rick Atwell; sound (Dolby stereo), Gene S. Cantamessa; costumes, Winnie D. Brown; assistant director, Candace Allen; casting, Joy Todd. Reviewed at the Academy of Motion Picture Arts & Sciences, Beverly Hills, Calif., Feb. 7, 1985. (MPAA Rating: PG.) Running time: **110 MINS.**
Matt Sherman .... John Scott Clough
Michael Stafford .... Don Franklin
June Wolsky .... Tamara Mark
Meryl Stanton .... Tracy Silver
Francine Hackett .... Cindy McGee
Valerie Thompson .... Gretchen F. Palmer
Rita Diaz .... Monique Cintron
Debbie Hughes .... Debra Varnado
Susan Granger .... Karen Kopins
Ida Sabol .... Irene Worth
Clem Friedkin .... Sam McMurray

If good intentions and sincerity translated into quality, "Fast Forward" would be a winner. As it stands, however, pic is one of the weaker entries in the recent slew of youth dance films and is hopelessly crippled by the amateurishness and naiveté of its script. Despite a likable cast of newcomers and a few good dance numbers, "Fast Forward" should be fast gone at the boxoffice.

Starting out with a high school dance act, the Adventurers Eight from Sandusky, Ohio, who want to make it in New York, is not exactly the most promising or original premise on which to base a film. The problem lies more in the treatment of the material then its inherent dreariness. Treated by scriptwriter Richard Wesley with an old-fashioned quaintness, these kids are moving backwards, not forward.

This is not to say that all teenagers in films must be super-sophisticated, precocious wiseguys, but the life situations and relationships between these kids are caricatures of an imagined innocence without a sense of what teenagers are really like. There is no ear for the way they talk and certainly no insight into the way they think.

Although director Sidney Poitier puts the Eight briskly through their paces, the dancing becomes repetitious even as the group picks up cues from the street dancing of New York and incorporates them into their act. Music by Tom Scott and Jack Hayes and an array of pop tunes don't help the story over its humps either.

Led by the fast-talking Matt (John Scott Clough), the group goes to N.Y. in hopes of getting an audition for the Big Showdown sponsored by an important management company. Unfortunately their one contact has died and the kids must come up with an alternate plan or give up their dreams. They decide to rough it out in a N.Y. that looks more like a summer camp then a big city.

Along the way they meet their share of hustlers and fakers, but the triumph of the kids is, of course, never in doubt, as if their innocence alone could defeat all obstacles.

As dancers the cast is more competent than as actors with lines often sounding wooden and unbelievable. Among the group Tamara Mark as Matt's girlfriend makes a charismatic debut as does Cindy McGee as the most streetwise of the girls. — Jagr.

Der Rekord
(The Record)
(WEST GERMAN-B&W)

Saarbrücken, Jan. 20.
A Munich Film Academy (HFF) production, in collaboration with Bayerischer Rundfunk (BR), Munich, Swiss TV (SRG), Zurich, and the German Federal Film Board, Berlin. Written and directed by Daniel Helfer. Features entire cast. Camera (b&w), Kay Gauditz; music, The Chance; sets, Leo Kloster; editing, Peter Adam; TV producers, Martin Schassmann (SRG), Axel von Hahn (BR). Reviewed at Saarbrücken Film Fest, Jan. 19, 1985. Running time: **92 MINS.**
With: Uwe Ochsenknecht (Rico), Laszlo I. Kish (Banana), Catarina Raacke (Bigi), Kurt Raab (P.K. Witrich), Andras Fricsay (TV reporter), Dietrich Mattausch (Sabo director), Vitus Zeplichal (Doctor).

After presenting "The Record" at the Hof fest last October, debuting helmer Daniel Helfer (Swiss grad of Munich Film Academy) lopped off an excess 20 minutes and was back with a tighter and better version at the Max Ophüls Competition in Saabrücken.

"The Record" is a refined mixture of black comedy and intellectual satire. Pic is aimed at the tv and video consumer. A young viewer decides to enter the Guinness Book of World Records by sitting down before a tv set to rack up a nonstop gawking record. In the beginning, it's all innocent fun; in the end, the obsession takes hold.

The in-joke works because everything's in black-and-white and a real-life attempt at tv record-breaking was observed in rather minute detail. Lensing in particular is tops, backed by able thesping.
— *Holl.*

The Breakfast Club
(COLOR)

Blame it all on mom and pop.

Hollywood, Feb. 8.
A Universal Pictures release of an A&M Film, produced by Ned Tanen and John Hughes. Written and directed by Hughes. Features entire cast. Exec producers, Gil Friesen, Andrew Meyer. Camera (Technicolor), Thomas Del Ruth; editor, Dede Allen; sound, Jim Alexander; production design, John W. Corso; coproducer, Michelle Manning; assistant director, Robert P. Cohen; music, Keith Forsey; casting, Jackie Burch. Reviewed at Universal Studios, Feb. 8, 1985. (MPAA Rating: R.) Running time: **97 MINS.**

Andrew	Emilio Estevez
John	Judd Nelson
Claire	Molly Ringwald
Brian	Anthony Michael Hall
Allison	Ally Sheedy
Vernon	Paul Gleason
Carl	John Kapelos

For those who attend, "The Breakfast Club" will probably pass as deeply profound among today's teenage audience, meaning the youngsters in the film spend most of their time talking to each other instead of dancing, dropping their drawers and throwing food. This, on the other hand, should not suggest they have anything intelligent to say.

For those who care to listen, writer-director John Hughes has come up with a wondrous message: No matter what is wrong with the individual youth of today, it is the parents' fault. What's more, if the kids just whine and complain enough, there's no limit to the deep and meaningful impact they can have on each other.

Why, right here in typical Shermer High in Chicago, there's a cross-section of five students — the jock, Miss Popularity, the ruffian, the nerd and Miss Weirdo — thrown together under adverse circumstances and able to cast aside all discord and unite under the sudden

insight that none would be such a despicable little twit if mom or dad or both weren't so rotten.

Right from the start, it's easy to sympathize with the unceasing harshness of their young lives. If the unspeakable horror can be spoken of, the querulous quintet are actually being forced to *spend the entire day at school on Saturday* for some previous infraction of the rules.

Coming together as strangers, none of the group initially likes thuggish loudmouth Judd Nelson, who taunts pretty Molly Ringwald, torments dorkish Anthony Michael Hall and challenges champ athlete Emilio Estevez while the odd lady, Ally Sheedy, looks on from a different space.

When not quarreling, the group occasionally unites in opposition to their faculty overseer, Paul Gleason, who shows up from time to time to remind them that adults are all either bullies or buffoons, and sometimes both.

Eventually, the kids come upon the universal antidote to their immediate discomfort: They get stoned. After that, it's just a matter of sharing secrets about the old folks at home and how really awful they are.

Blessedly, however, this keeps them so occupied they only rarely break into dancing and vandalism. Though romance blossoms in all the expected places, nary a real kiss is exchanged.

When the causes of the Decline of Western Civilization are finally writ, Hollywood will surely have to answer why it turned one of man's most significant art forms over to the self-gratification of high-schoolers. Or does Hughes really believe, as he writes here, that "when you grow up, your heart dies."

It may. But not unless the brain has already started to rot with films like this. — *Har.*

Parfait Amour
(DUTCH-COLOR)

Amsterdam, Jan. 8.
A Eurocentrafilm release of a De Eerste Amsterdamse Filmassociatie van 1980 production. Written and directed by Jean van de Velde. Camera (color), Jules van den Steenhoven; editor, Edgar Burcksen; music, Johanna d'Armagnac; sound, Otto Horsch, Erik Langhout. Reviewed at Cinema Intl., Amsterdam, Jan. 3, 1985. Running time: **95 MINS.**

Pavel Mosz	Onno Molenkamp
Maddy	Guusje van Tilborgh
Rudy	Peter Tuinman
Jaromir	Leen Jongewaard
Guido	Piey Kamerman
Lucien	Helmert Woudenberg

"Parfait Amour" is distinguished by the ace lensing of Jules van den Steenhoven in his feature debut. The film, three years in the making, is less notable, and b.o.

prospects are thin.

Problem lies in Jean van de Velde's approach to screenwriting. As a director, he knows how to create a brooding atmosphere and secure credible performances from actors, even when they haven't a clue what they are supposed to be thinking or feeling. As a writer, however, he is so busy being clever he leaves a set of loose ends.

Story centers on Pavel Mosz, a dissident refugee from Prague. The KGB tires to pin one murder on him and then do him in. It's a perfect plan but Pavel survives, in a state of amnesia. The ever-resourceful KGB then creates a new past for Pavel and inveigles him into another assassination.

The pic is a mass of impossibilities. The intended fusion of psychological drama and *film noir* never takes place.

It's a shame. The marvelous photography, the original score, the impish charm of Guusje van Tilborgh as Maddy and the okay performance of Onno Molenkamp as Pavel cannot prevent the viewer's attention from wandering after the first 30 minutes. — *Wall.*

Ca N'Arrive Qu'à Moi
(It Only Happens To Me)
(FRENCH-COLOR)

Paris, Feb. 6.
An AMLF release of a Sara Films/Films A2 coproduction. Produced by Alain Sarde. Starring and directed by Francis Perrin. Screenplay, Gilles Jacob, Didier Jacob, Perrin, camera (color), Didier Tarot; editor, Ghislaine Desjonquères; art director, Jean-Baptiste Poirot; music, Philippe Sarde; sound, Dominique Levert; production manager, Hubert Mérial. Reviewed at the Marignan-Concorde theater, Paris, Feb. 4, 1985. Running time: **95 MINS.**

François Pépin	Francis Perrin
Prudence Guilledou	Véronique Genest
Mr. Guilledou	Bernard Blier
Mme. Guilledou	Christiane Minazzoli
Batala	François Perrot

"Ca N'Arrive Qu'à Moi" is comedian Francis Perrin's third, and poorest, self-directed screen vehicle. He is a blithe and appealing farceur desperately in need of guidance in his film material and a good director to keep him in line. He has neither here. (Nor does he have Paul Claudon, who produced his earlier films, and had a hand in their scripting.)

Produced by Alain Sarde, this new comedy was penned by novice screenwriter Gilles Jacob, general delegate of the Cannes Film Festival, and his son Didier. Perrin collaborated with former on the final shooting script, which ostensibly betrays the comic's desire for some romantic seriousness in his characterizations. It doesn't suit him.

Nor does the style of humor — comedy adventure in a Philippe de Broca vein. Perrin plays an

accident-prone journalist who falls for the daughter of a French press baron, partly because she seems to bring him good luck. When she is kidnapped and held for ransom, he gets involved. Soon they are fleeing through the Alps pursued by the gangsters, and are eventually saved by the girl's dad.

Script offers no new twists on a predictable format, and Perrin is at a total loss behind the camera, desperately resorting to spoofing other films during the flagging climax. — *Len.*

Kolp
(WEST GERMAN-COLOR)

Saarbrücken, Jan. 21.
A Frank Röth Film Production, Munich. Features entire cast. Directed by Roland Suso Richter. Screenplay, Röth; camera (color), Ernst J. Kubitza; sound, Winfried Leyh; sets, Katharina Wöppermann; editing, Richter, Rainer Standke; music, Röth, Richter. Reviewed at Saarbrücken Film Fest (Max Ophüls Prize), Jan. 20, 1985. Running time: **106 MINS.**
With: Frank Röth (Hans Kolp), Katja Flint (Hilde), Barbara Weinzierl (Lissi), Heiner Lauterbach (Karl), Ottfried Fischer (Ekke), Charly Huber (Jack), Hans-Joachim Grau (Horst).

Young 22-year-old helmer Roland Suso Richter teamed with 24-year-old writer-producer-actor Frank Röth to make "Kolp." It preemed at Munich to strong reviews last June, then surfaced at Hof, and finally won accolades at the Max Ophüls competition in Saarbrücken. Next is the German Series at Berlin, with good chances thereafter to tour the fest circuit overseas.

This is a "zero hour" story, set in a small Bavarian town bordering the Oden Forest in 1947. It was a time of rampant black-marketing before the currency reform, when kids learned fast how to make a fast buck by impersonating personnel of the Allied Forces to steal and trade Yankee goods. Hans Kolp, a lad of about 16, learns English from his black "Ami" friend quartered in his hometown of Lützbach. In school there's nothing much more to learn with only one teacher and all the classes jammed together into a one-room-schoolhouse (the railway station, as the real school is now a barracks), so he forms a gang on the side and begins wheeling and dealing with a stolen jeep.

It works. Like a small-change Bonnie-and-Clyde gang, success breeds habit — until a larger fish enters the pond and encourages bigger blackmarket booty with stolen American Army vehicles and uniforms. Some of the kids know when enough's enough, so the last job is an affair with Kolp and his girlfriend alone. It ends in the expected shootout.

Pic's strength lies in its capturing of the atmosphere of the times: sets and costumes ring true down to details. Thesp performances are also notable, the outstanding one being Frank Roth as Kolp blessed with a knack of Yankee lingo.—*Holl.*

Phenomena
(ITALIAN-COLOR)

Rome, Feb. 8.

A Titanus release, produced by Dario Argento for Dacfilm. Written and directed by Argento. Stars Jennifer Connelly. Camera (Color), Romano Albani; editor, Franco Fraticelli; music, the Goblins and others. Reviewed at Fiamma Cinema, Rome, Feb. 8, 1985. Running time: **115 MINS.**

Jennifer Carvino	Jennifer Connelly
John McGregor	Donald Pleasence
School director	Dalila Di Lazzaro
An assistant	Daria Nicolodi
Police commissioner	Patrick Bauchau

Italo horror king specializing in Baroque floods of blood and gore, Dario Argento is one of the most popular genre auteurs with his own cult following. New entry avoids some of helmer's worst excesses and turns to more inward horror in a story crafted around the ghostly delicateness of young star Jennifer Connelly, known from Sergio Leone's "Once Upon A Time In America." Script is more logical and satisfying than usual. Good prospects for its markets.

Jennifer Corvino (Connelly) is an American girl sent to a snobbish Swiss boarding school. Sketching in the atmosphere of the "Richard Wagner School for Girls" in a few heavy strokes, pic shows Jennifer being mentally tortured by iron maiden schoolmarms Dalila Di Lazzaro and Dari Nicolodi and mercilessly teased by her classmates, who are jealous of the fact her father is a famous film idol. Revenge is sweet: Jennifer's strange power to communicate with insects and call on them for help makes the school the center of a sinister fly-storm.

Meanwhile, not for nothing do they call the scenic mountain region "the Transylvania of Switzerland." A monster is on the loose who kills young girls and makes off with their bodies. Commissioner Patrick Bauchau appears desultorily on his track, but the better detective is paralyzed entomologist John McGregor (Donald Pleasence), who puts Jennifer on the trail with a "sarcophagus fly" supposed to lead her to rotting corpses. McGregor will pay for his amateur sleuthing with his life.

Characters are haphazardly mixed with plot ends that never get completely unraveled, but Argento and his special effects team come up with some four-star images. Sleepwalking dream sequences (one of his fortés) run off into the waking nightmares of the horror genre, where insect vigilante squads vie for audience sympathy with child cannibals and slasher monkeys. Absurd as it is, this is one Argento pic that avoids self-parody and keeps story interest going to the end.

Fans will find the helmer's trademark of an ear-shattering Dolbyized rock track shamelessly amping up the terror with a flick of the sound engineer's wrist; in other respects, pic is relatively subdued. Flights of psychic weirdness take precedence over bodily torture and mutilation, seemingly out of respect for the ethereal heroine.

Connelly, a photogenic youngster with strong screen presence, brings an angelic innocence to the part that seems beyond such earthly emotions as terror or fear. Miraculously scraping through the worst adventures physically and mentally untouched, she steps out of the lake with complete composure after battling a monster underwater. Pleasence plays the crippled scientist with tongue-in-cheek seriousness, making us sure he's going to leap out of his wheelchair any moment and start creating mayhem. The clean wholesomeness of the Swiss landscape provides a perfect backdrop for spilled blood and warped minds. Top quality technical work gives a pro look. —*Yung.*

The Mean Season
(COLOR)

Potent crime drama spells a hit.

Hollywood, Feb. 8.

An Orion Pictures release of a Turman-Foster production. Produced by David Foster and Larry Turman. Directed by Philip Borsos. Stars Kurt Russell, Mariel Hemingway. Screenplay, Leon Piedmont, from the novel, "In The Heat Of The Summer" by John Katzenbach; camera (color), Frank Tidy; editor, Duwayne Dunham; music, Lalo Schifrin; sound, Bill Nelson; production designer, Philip Jefferies; associate producer, Steven Perry; assistant director, Tom Seidman; casting, Janet Hirshenson, Jane Jenkins. Reviewed at Warner Hollywood Studios, Feb. 7, 1985. (MPAA Rating: R.) Running time: **103 MINS.**

Malcolm Anderson	Kurt Russell
Christine Connelly	Mariel Hemingway
Alan Delour	Richard Jordan
Bill Nolan	Richard Masur
Andy Porter	Joe Pantoliano
Phil Wilson	Richard Bradford
Ray Martinez	Andy Garcia
Kathy Vasquez	Rose Portillo

Taut, atmospheric crime thriller featuring potent portrayals by Kurt Russell and Richard Jordan point to a green boxoffice fun for "Mean Season," the U.S. directional bow of Phillip Borsos (who helmed "The Grey Fox").

Based on the novel, "In The Heat Of The Summer," by former Miami Herald crime reporter John Katzenbach, pic establishes solid Florida heat and humidity as the "mean" background to a series of murders that perversely link together the killer (Jordan, unseen till late in the film) and a Miami police reporter (Russell) who becomes the psychopath's personal spokesman through his media clout.

Jordan is at his shrewdly crazed best, anchoring the movie with a felt terror, initially just through his off-screen voice as he manipulates the reporter over the phone and ultimately through his cunning. Feature has both a suspenseful murder plot — terrifyingly opening on a deserted beach on a young girl whom we come to realize is about to be shot — and an intriguing theme about the news media's responsibility.

Russell plays a reporter (production used the city room of the Miami Herald) who, credibly enough, gets swept away with all the national hype he's getting as the only man who can talk to the killer, whom he dubs the "Numbers Killer." But he doesn't realize the trap he's baiting for himself, or how much of a participant he's become in his own stories.

His live-in elementary school teacher g.f., essayed rather uneventfully by Mariel Hemingway, grows outraged as the reporter succumbs to his own ego, to the killer's tantalizing calls, and to his increased stature as newsmaker.

When Hemingway is kidnapped by the madman, the stage is set for the inexorable showdown between Jordan and Russell. A surprise twist in the film's final scenes doesn't quite work, logically speaking, and there are a few red herrings along the way, but the sum of the parts is solid entertainment.

The ambience of Russell at work on a story, and the teamwork he enjoys with his photographer, wonderfully etched by Joe Pantoliano (the pimp in "Risky Business"), contribute to a rich newspaper yarn. In a supporting role, Andy Garcia makes a telling imprint as a homicide detective.

Lalo Schifrin's score, Duwayne Dunham's editing, and Frank Tidy's alternately hot and cloud-dark cinematography deliver compelling rhythms.—*Loyn.*

The Lost Empire
(COLOR)

Fantasy spoof featuring undressed women warriors. Modest outlook.

A JGM Enterprises release of a Harwood Prods. presentation. Produced by Jim Wynorski. Coproducers, Alex Tabrizi, Robert Greenberg; associate producer, Raven de la Croix. Written and directed by Wynorski. Features entire cast. Camera (Deluxe color), Jacques Haitkin; editor, Larry Bock; music, Alan Howarth; sound, Mark Ulano; produc-tion design, Wayne Springfield; special animated effects, Steve Neill; production manager-second unit director, Max Bloom; assistant director, Betsy Magruder; unit manager, Jeff Folmsbee; stunt coordinator, Rick Barker; postproduction supervisor, Adam Weiss. Reviewed at 42d St. Cine Rialto theater, Feb. 8, 1985. (MPAA Rating: R.) Running time: **83 MINS.**

Angel Wolfe	Melanie Vincz
Whitestar	Raven de la Croix
Heather	Angela Aames
Rick	Paul Coufos
Koro	Bob Tessier
Dr. Sin Do	Angus Scrimm
Krager	Blackie Dammett
Cindy	Linda Shayne
Whiplash	Angelique Pettyjohn
Cop	Kenneth Tobey
Doctor	Garry Goodrow

Also with: Art Hern, Annie Gaybis, Gary Don Cox, Jason Stuart, Tom Rettig.

"The Lost Empire" is a misfired spoof of various fantasy genres, marking an overly ambitious low-budget feature directing debut for former Roger Corman publicist Jim Wynorski. Featuring numerous statuesque women in various states of undress, this entry in the yet-to-succeed Women Warriors genre (e.g., "Sheena," unreleased "She" remake) was started as a 3-D production in latter's recent 1983 boomtime, but was ultimately filmed and released "flat."

Not so flat are the bevy of heroines, three of whom go ("Enter The Dragon" style) to the Pacific island of Golgotha where Dr. Sin Do (Angus Scrimm) has a cult. Sin Do, who turns out to be the ancient Li Chuk, has a pact with the devil whereby he causes natural disasters, and currently is searching for the second jeweled Eye of the Avatar (made by the lost race of the Lemurians) to match his own and give him endless power.

Amidst much science fiction trappings including cheap mattework, and spoof of old-style serials exposition, with not enough funny gags. Fantasy fans will be intrigued, but picture is largely a skin show, spot-lighting the beauty of stripper Raven de la Croix, who also acted as associate producer and provided her own gaudy American Indian costumes. Acting is generally poor, with lead player Melanie Vincz apparently not informed of the jokes by Wynorski, while familiar baddie, bald Bob Tessier, suffers with stuck on eyebrows which vary in size and shape from shot to shot. Angus Scrimm, a sinister presence in "Phantasm" in the 1970s, is an effectively hammy villain who, courtesy of impressive makeup effects by Steve Neill, turns into a black, lizard-skin monster at the finale. —*Lor.*

De Ijssalon
(The Ice-Cream Parlor)
(DUTCH-COLOR)

Amsterdam, Jan. 22.

A Tuschinski release of a Roeland Kerbosch Filmproductie production. Produced by Roeland Kerbosch. Directed by Dimitri Frenkel Frank. Stars Gerard Thoolen, Renée Soutendijk, Bruno Ganz. Screenplay, Frenkel Frank, based on an idea by Kerbosch; camera (color), Theo van de Sande; sound, Paul Veld; editor, Edgar Burcksen. Reviewed at Tuschinski theater, Amsterdam, Jan. 22, 1985. Running time: **92 MINS.**

Otto ....Gerard Thoolen
Gustav ....Bruno Ganz
Trudi ....Renée Soutendijk
Gestapo chief ....Carol van Herwijnen
Hans ....Kees Hulst
Luuk ....Gijs de Lange

———

"De Ijssalon" is a wartime resistance pic about people rather than history. It's set in Holland in 1941, when the Nazi occupiers were still trying to win Dutch'sympathies. Although no blockbuster, this $500,-000-budgeted pic has international appeal. Thorn EMI has worldwide video rights.

Fictional story is based around an ice-cream parlor in Amsterdam which is run by a Jewish immigrant from Berlin as a center for anti-Nazi activities. Otto (Gerard Thoolen) is no hero, just a guy who tries to make good ice cream and tasty pastry from ersatz ingredients and wants to believe the war will end soon and normality reappear.

When his best friend Gustav (Bruno Ganz) comes to visit he's in uniform and gradually wins the love of Otto's friend Trudi (Renée Soutendijk). Trudi and Gustav try to help Otto when he's arrested for housing resistance meetings in his parlor. Otto is executed and Gustav returns to the war.

Pic is about the attitudes of the three protagonists towards the ever-changing moral challenges with which they are confronted. A subplot is created in the conflict between two childhood friends, Luuk, Trudi's younger brother who is virulently anti-German, and young Dutch Nazi Hans.

Writer-director Dmitri Frenkel Frank, with over 60 legit and tv credits as well as two previous features, is good at writing dialog but not so strong when it comes to telling a story with the camera.

Pic relies heavily on the main actors. Gerard Thoolen battles valiantly and in general successfully with his role as the rather soft and fun-loving extrovert who, when cornered, sticks to his human principles. Bruno Ganz, however, has too little scope. Renée Soutendijk is perfect in a smaller role. Other actors are good and technical credits are more than adequate.—*Wall.*

———

Lieber Vater
(Dear Father)
(SWISS-COLOR-16m)

———

Saarbrücken, Jan. 18.

A Heinz Bütler Film Production, Zurich. Written and directed by Bütler. Features entire cast. Camera (color), Hansueli Schenkel; music, Art Lande, First Avenue, Terje Rydal, Ralph Towner, Barre Phillips. Only credits available. Reviewed at Saarbrücken Film Fest (Max Ophüls Prize), Jan. 17, 1985. Running time: **90 MINS.**

With: Hubert Kronlachner (the baker), David Lendenmann, Renate Steiger, Hanns Zischler, Marina Wandruszka.

———

Heinz Bütler's "Dear Father" is typical of a new style of three-country film productions: it's a Swiss pic set in a small provincial town in West Germany that features a trip to Vienna across the border in Austria. This is a modest and unassuming tale of little people rendered with a light directorial hand.

Picture describes the adventures of a shy, retiring lad of 13 years, whose father is a baker with a flair for classical music and a *joie de vivre* that includes a liking for lovely ladies, elegant dining, and trips away from home to Vienna. The boy sees his father in the company of an artist's model and is fearful he will lose his closest friend as well as father, so one day he leaves school to visit his father in a family hotel in Vienna.

The boy's adventures on the trip form the narrative thread, for everyone he meets gathers why he's there and sees through the excuses he makes for the trip. When the father happens to be away, the hotel personnel care for him. A warm and human kidpic for grownups although paced a bit too slow.

—*Holl.*

———

Duo Valentianos
(Two Valentianos)
(WEST GERMAN-COLOR)

———

Saarbrücken, Jan. 21.

A Gertrud Pinkus Film Production, West Germany. Features entire cast. Written and directed by Gertrud Pinkus. Camera (color), Jörg Jeshel; music, Otto Beatus. (Only credits available.) Reviewed at Saarbrücken Film Fest (Max Ophüls Prize), Jan. 20, 1985. Running time: **90 MINS.**

With: Uli Scholz, Angelika Bartsch, Margarethe Wiedstruck, Gilles Lothe.

———

Swiss-born Gertrud Pinkus works as an independent artist, stage-designer and filmmaker. As a cine-feminist she won recognition for "The Greatest Value Of A Woman Is Her Silence" (1980), but she's also made several tv-films, a photo-novel, and cartoons and docus.

"Duo Valentianos" is her latest, a fiction-documentary that begins with shots of the life-style of two street-musicians (an elderly woman and her grown son), and then dips back into the past to investigate how a musician-juggler during the Nazi period worked for a time unnoticed in the Underground Resistance. It's these fiction scenes set in the 1930s (apparently before the war) that form the core of the film and stick to the memory, for they are handled with a feeling for story and atmosphere. The same actor-magician who interprets this role also appears as the researcher into the fate of the "Duo Valentianos" found in an old scrapbook: it seems that there really was a forgotten artistic pair who made the rounds of the variety shows back then. Fiction and documentary are thus wedded into a unified whole.

Pincus has perhaps tackled too complex a theme in the long run. Just when the research into the "Duo Valentianos" is getting interesting — for instance, there's a scene of the artist-researcher crossing Checkpoint Charlie in Berlin over to the East Sector to call on a clippings-collector for more information on the fate of the pair — then suddenly the scene switches to the 1930s or to the present without much rhyme or reason. All the same, each of the three narrative lines are cinematically striking, tied together by the mime and magician-juggling skills of Gilles Lothe.

The final shot as we come to know or suppose the fate of the "Duo Valentianos" is particularly appropriate. Over the roofs of Berlin tenement houses is stretched a tightrope, upon which one tightrope-walker after another pass over the viewer's gaze and disappear into the blue heavens. The camera angle (lensed by Jörg Jeshel) hints of an ascent to an eternal reward for, undoubtedly, many forgotten and unsung heroes of the German Resistance Movement. — *Holl.*

———

Lost In America
(COLOR)

———

Warm comedy about dropping out.

———

Hollywood, Feb. 8.

A Warner Bros. release of a David Geffen Co. production. Produced by Marty Katz. Executive producer, Herb Nanas. Directed by Albert Brooks. Screenplay, Brooks and Monica Johnson; camera (Technicolor), Eric Saarinen; editor, David Finfer; sound, Bill Nelson; production designer, Richard Sawyer; music, Arthur B. Rubinstein; casting, Barbara Claman; assistant director, Michael Daves. Reviewed at Warner Bros., Hollywood, Calif., Feb. 8, 1985. (MPAA Rating: R.) Running time: **91 MINS.**

David Howard ....Albert Brooks
Linda Howard ....Julie Hagerty
Casino manager ....Garry Marshall
Employment agent...........Art Frankel
Paul Dunn ....Michael Greene
Brad Tooley.................Tom Tarpey
Pharmacist ....Ernie Brown
Patty ....Maggie Roswell
Highway officer ....Charles Boswell
Ex-convict.................Donald Gibb

———

Finding strong and funny identification with the urban impulse to chuck the rat race and hit the open road, this sharp and modest comedy is sure to please Albert Brooks'

fans and also win converts for those who missed or failed to admire his earlier two films ("Real People" and "Modern Romance"). Film open regionally in Gotham Friday (15), a couple of weeks later in L.A., and the step-openings seem a wise move.

Word-of-mouth should particularly spread among yuppies and the upwardly mobile who secretly hanker to act on irresponsible, youthful fantasies to drop out of society.

Film opens on Brooks and wife Julie Hagerty in bed on eve of their move to a $450,000 house and also what Brooks presumes will be his promotion to a senior exec slot in a big ad agency. Brooks is a nervous mess, made worse when vaguely bored Hagerty tells him their life has become "too responsible, too controlled."

Her suppressed wish for a more dashing life comes startlingly true the next day when a confident Brooks glides into his boss' L.A. office only to hear that his expected senior v.p. stripes are going to someone else and he's being transferred to New York.

Brooks' response to his silken-toned boss, wonderfully played by Michael Greene, is probably what gets the movie its R rating. It's pure relief for Brooks, who, in turn, convinces his wife to quit her personnel job. The pair will liquidate their assets, buy a Winnebago, and head across America.

"We'll be like 'Easy Rider' — with a nestegg," chortles Brooks.

Hagerty is delicious: sweet but unbreakable, even after she sneaks out on Brooks to exercise a hidden gambling compulsion in a Vegas casino — and watches their $150,-000 nestegg melt away. This is where the real fun begins.

Brooks, who directed and cowrote with Monica Johnson, is irrepressible but always very human. When he asks the casino manager, another fine supporting turn, by producer-director-turned-actor Garry Marshall, if he would return their lost money because such a gesture would be a great public relations coup for the hotel, the hilarious moment is quintessential Brooks.

Brooks' long-supressed blowup at his wife, as they shout over a bunch of tourists at Hoover Dam, propels the comedy into a totally unexpected romantic turn.

In fact, it's director Brooks' light touch in the domestic department that gives the production its deceptive warmth. the fact that most such couples would be killing each other doesn't bother Brooks. You do believe these people, even when Brooks has to resort to a job in Stafford, Ariz., as a school crossing guard while Hagerty is slinging hamburgers.

The couple's final solution — it's sellout time! — is as inevitable as it is sobering. Everything between Arizona and Manhattan is covered with montages, but it's okay. We've been on a ride.

Brooks retained three key hands who worked on his prior two films: cinematographer Eric Saarinen, editor David Finfer and cowriter Johnson. Even the exec producer, Herb Nanas, shows up in the movie, as a leathery rich guy behind the wheel of a leathery Mercedes. —Loyn.

Nieder Mit Den Deutschen
(Down With The Germans)
(WEST GERMAN-B&W)

Saarbrücken, Jan. 17.

A Dietrich Schubert Film Production, Cologne, in collaboration with the Film Fund of Northrhine-Westphalia. Written and directed by Schubert. Features entire cast. Camera (b&w), Michael Giefer; sound, Michael Loeken; editing, Hanne Huxoll; music, Wolfgang Hamm. Reviewed at Saarbrücken Film Fest (Max Ophüls Prize), Jan. 16, 1985. Running time: 91 MINS.
With: Hans Künster (Fritz), Ruth Brück (Brigitte), Heinz Opfinger (Rio), Will Courth (Cellar guard), Andreas Würfel (Michael), Barbara Grupe (Petra), Burghart Klaussner (Sammy), Stefan Horn (Press spokesman).

Dietrich Schubert, a respected documentary filmmaker with a string of socially engaged films to his credit, was previously in the running for the Max Ophüls Prize with "Pretty Far Away" (1982), his debut feature. Now he's back in an out-of-competition slot with "Down With The Germans," which also unspooled at the Munich fest.

The title refers to a French expression scratched on the walls of a Gestapo cellar prison in downtown Cologne, the site now put aside as a monument to the Nazi Resistance movement. Schubert had previously made a docu on the subject, "Resistance And Persecution In Cologne, 1933-1945" (1976), of which this is an obvious 16m sequel (blown up later to 35m). In order to grasp its full meaning, a knowledge of the so-called "Edelweisspiraten" (Edelweiss Pirates) resistance group is also necessary. Schubert, too, happened to make a docu on this as well: "Research Into The Story Of The Edelweiss Pirates" (1980).

The Edelweiss Pirates were youth groups (some teenage gangs) with an edelweiss-flower badge as identificiation. They were active not only in Cologne, but in several cities, and their form of resistance to the Nazis as children of Socialists or Communists or other anti-Nazi parties was anything from singing forbidden songs to carrying hidden weapons for protest and demonstration purposes. In November 1944 in the Cologne suburb of Ehrenfeld, where many of these groups had grown up to roam the streets, the most active members of the group were hanged publicly without a trial.

"Down With The Germans" is a completely fictional tale about a former member of the youth group who returns from self-exile in a distant part of Germany to Cologne 30 years after the fact: he has read in the papers that the former Gestapo-cellar in Cologne has been reopened to serve as a memorial to the Resistance fighters tortured and murdered there. The protagonist, Fritz, still has nightmares of his experiences in this cellar as a member of the Edelweiss Pirates.

The return to Cologne is more painful than anticipated. During a press tour the day before the Gestapo-cellar is to be opened officially, Fritz recognizes a former cellar-guard among the spectators, and later recalls in the hotel that this was the man who beat him half to death while he was interned and questioned there. The rest is the obsession of wanting to take revenge — but how? The situation is resolved by the presence of third parties: an enquiring femme reporter and a youth about his age when he was a member of the old gang. Finally, a meeting with a former Edelweiss chum, a woman with full memories of her own, sends Fritz back home with a cleansed conscience.

"Down With The Germans" should awaken interest in the Edelweiss Pirates abroad, but Schubert's documentary on the subject is a better film. —Holl.

Er Moretto — Von Liebe Leben
(Living Off Of Love)
(SWISS-COLOR-16m)

Saarbrücken, Jan. 19.

A Simon Bischoff Film, Switzerland. Written and directed by Bischoff. Features entire cast. Camera (color), Raffaele Mertes; music, Teresa Gatta, Alberto Antinori; editing, Anerose Koop. Only credits available. Reviewed at Saarbrücken Film Fest (Max Ophüls Prize), Jan. 17, 1985. Running time: 85 MINS.
With: Alevino de Silvio, Franco Mazzieri, Vinicio Diamanti, Ciro Cascina, Rosa Di Brigida, Renato Faillaci, Francesco Gnerre, Lara Toijaclan, Irene Staub.

Simon Bischoff's "Living Off Of Love" sneaked into the Max Ophüls Prize competition in Saarbrücken via the backdoor: the original language is Italian, but the director is German-Swiss and the subtitles are in German. Further, this is more of a documentary than a fiction-documentary, for the added improvised scenes seem quite superfluous and cornball in view of the overall attempt at an honest treatment of a hot-potato subject: male youth prostitution in Rome.

Bischoff won the confidence of one of the boys hanging around the Circo Massimo, "Er Moretto," the 17-year-old Franco whom the filmmaker first met in 1980 as a 13-year-old runaway from miserable family living conditions. Photos of the face of the lad over the past five years document his life as well as "living off of love" to survive in the prostitution jungle around the coliseum. Bischoff also seems to hint in the boy's answer to interview-questions that he practices some of the trade himself as at least a potential customer, so a certain authenticity is perceived and felt throughout the film project.

Some details are of more than passing significance, particularly how the youth is picked up by a middle-aged bourgeois to become his companion. Among the fiction sequences is a rather absurd spectacle of a toothless monk in a cassock flapping around the district as though he's on the loose from a nuthouse. Further, Bischoff avoids taking any stance on the subject.

This, together with snapshots of the male organ in closeup indicates he's aiming for the commercial market to exploit the pic's controversial subject matter.

In short, one is left with a sour gut feeling that the audience is being used in a similar manner as "Er Moretto." —Holl.

Der Sprung
(The Crack In The Facade)
(WEST GERMAN-COLOR-16m)

Saarbrücken, Jan. 20.

A Thorsten Näter Film Production, Berlin. Written and directed, photographed and edited, and music by Näter. Features entire cast. Assistant director, Nino Jacusso; assistant camera, Stefan Guntli; sound assistance, Marek Vizner. Reviewed at Saarbrücken Film Fest (Max Ophüls Prize), Jan. 18, 1985. Running time: 85 MINS.
With: Christian Miaria Goebel (Michael), Jörg Biester (Max), Emilio De Marchi (Angelo), Guido Meyn (Guido), Lisa Meyn (Johanna), Stefan Beckers (Stefan), Susanne Jakob (Sabine).

Thorsten Näter came from a background in German music conservatories, then ventured into stage production, and finally ended up at the Munich Film Academy. He prefers to write, photograph, edit and compose the music for the films he directs, two features to date being "The Stone River" (1982) and now "The Crack In The Facade," which preemed at Saarbrücken.

Despite general technical qualities, and given that Näter put this feature together on a low-budget subsidy offered by the Berlin Film Fund to aspiring filmers, picture suffers from chic symbolic clichés. A down-and-out avant-garde theater troupe suddenly receives an offer from a donor to back a production of Sophocles' "Oedipus Rex," provided however that he remain anonymous save to the group's manager and have a small part in the play.

The rest of the story tells why the donor, an ex-physician, is backing the eventual flop in the first place (Sophocles is far beyond the talents of the troupe), and why a mysterious gunman is blackmailing the manager to pay his debts. Naturally, there's a moral to be found in connection with the leading palyer interpreting Oedipus, but by that time things have become pretty dull. —Holl.

Schalltot
(The Noise Kill)
(WEST GERMAN-COLOR-16m)

Saarbrücken, Jan. 19.

A Fred van der Kooij Film Production, West Germany. Written and directed by van der Kooij. Features entire cast. Camera (color), Immo Rentz; music, van der Kooij. Only credits available. Reviewed at Saarbrücken Film Fest (Max Ophüls Prize), Jan. 18, 1985. Running time: 84 MINS.
With: Peter Wyssbrod, Wolfram Berger, Henning Heers, Nicola Weisse, Eduard Saussen, Rolf Dienewald, Andreas Szerda, Eva Rollauer, Fritz Mertel.

Dutch helmer Fred van der Kooij studied painting and then music. Now that he's working as a freelance filmmaker in Germany and Switzerland, he's made his first feature on the subject of using noise as an instrument of death.

There's a twist that gives the film experiment some depth. A worn out sound-effects man who spends his hours daily in a synchronization studio creating noises appropriate to the action on the screen begins to imagine hearing things during his free moments. One evening he meets a colleague in a restaurant and they decide to have a "shootout" with their sound-and-noise gimmicks in their traveling suitcases. The irony of the whole affair is that the sounds become instruments of death, so tigers really claw and the roof really caves in while the two are having a go at each other like two modern-day noisemakers in a duel of death.

The gag has some punch, but over the long stretch it dies a quick death itself. Peter Wyssbrod in the lead role gives a finely etched performance of a burnt-out case.
— Holl.

Wiener Brut
(Vintage Vienna)
(AUSTRIAN-COLOR)

Saarbrücken, Jan. 18.

A Hans Fädler Film Production, Vienna. Written and directed by Fädler. Features entire cast. Camera (color), Peter Mazzucheli; music, Brian Cos, Wiener Art Orchestra, Nervöse Vogel. Only credits available. Reviewed at Saarbrücken Film Fest (Max Ophüls Prize), Jan. 17, '85. Running time: 97 MINS.

With: Artur Singer, Wendy Singer, Martin Wich, Johannes Weidinger, Kurt Freimüller, Peter Turrini, Hansi Lang.

Hans Fädler's "Wiener Brut" (here translated as "Vintage Vienna" for kicks) is one of those transvestite romps through the Vienna Woods and the palacial gardens of barons and baronesses, as well as church choirs and ménage-à-trois bedroom suites. The in-crowd (but few others) will find plenty here for kicks and fun-moments.

"Wiener Brut" runs all over the place in gorgeous costumes and piled-on wigs as though this were carnival time in Rio. It was awarded a Public's Prize at Saarbrücken and packed 'em in for a midnight show. — *Holl.*

Der Todesspringer
(The Death Springer)
(WEST GERMAN-COLOR)

Saarbrücken, Jan. 17.

A Lerch/Trautmann Film Production, Berlin. Features entire cast. Written, directed and edited by Benno Trautmann. Camera (color), H.G. Bücking; sound, C. Moldt. Reviewed at Saarbrücken Film Fest (Max Ophüls Prize), Jan. 16, 1985. Running time: **87 MINS.**

With: Nicole Heesters, Mathew T. Anden, Toni Lerch, Werner Rehm, Sona McDonald, Hans-Peter Korff, Peter Albers, Stefan Reck, Gerd Wameling, Tamara Navas, Irene Kugler, Ernst Stötzner.

Helmer Benno Trautmann and actress-producer Toni Lerch made the eyecatching "Evictor" (1976), on Berlin housing problems, and now after a couple tries in between they're back with "The Death Springer," an entry at Hof and one of the kudo winners at the Saarbrücken fest. -

"The Death Springer" fulfills all the requirements for cultural fodder among pseudo-intellectuals and diehard German film buffs: actors from the prestigious Schaubühne Ensemble in Berlin, "Theater of the Absurd" intertwined dialog scenes, and a backdrop of decayed diplomatic buildings in the Tiergarten section of Berlin. But it makes for empty and "in-crowd" filmfare.

Each figure that's introduced is in dialog with the camera (that old-style "I'm the camera" technique of the postwar 1950s), which is okay for an intimate art-film aud. However, all the situations are supposed to be pages out of the human comedy: a bored film director off to work each morning, test-shots with would-be actors, and a button-eyed protagonist (he failed the test) who meets a variety of Beckettian characters with neuroses as burdening as his.

New German Cinema lost in an labyrinth of turned phrases and empty gestures may be too harsh a critique on "The Death Springer," but the long and short of this film treatise are the same — there's no point to the film other than its self-indulgent intellectual mumbo-jumbo. Even the motto for the pic's promo is a headscratcher: "Through a Chain of Unfortunate Circumstances One Still Manages To Stay Alive ..."

Technical credits are mostly on the plus side. — *Holl.*

Tränen In Florenz
(Tears In Florence)
(WEST GERMAN-COLOR)

Saarbrücken, Jan. 19.

A Marianne Schäfer Film Production, West Germany. Directed by Schäfer. Features entire cast. Screenplay, Schäfer, Peter Rueben; camera (color), Jacques Steyn; music, Charles Kalmann. Only credits available. Reviewed at Saarbrücken Film Fest (Max Ophüls Prize), Jan. 18, 1985. Running time: **87 MINS.**

With: Wolfgang Joop (Rüdiger Keienburg), Violetta Sanchez (Countess Vera da Vinci), Christoph Eichhorn (Wolfram Dernbach), Rita Kail (Gerda), Yolande Gilot (Anabel), Werner Eichhorn, Ortrud Beginnin.

Marianne Schäfer's "Tears In Florence" was one of surprise hits at the Max Ophüls Prize competition in Saarbrücken. A debut feature, it draws its inspiration from a socalled "trial novel" found in droves on paperback stands of large European cities. The love story melodramas are usually set in plush settings and deal with the idle rich finding and losing and finding each other under circumstances that are suppose to stimulate the reader's emotions and tear ducts.

Film begins in San Remo on the Riviera, where a Düsseldorf fashion-king runs over a fair countess while driving his sports car too fast on curving lanes. She ends up in a hospital and needs plastic surgery to repair the scar on her face, but it's still love at first sight. Meanwhile, back at the shop, a fashion-show is rescued from a flop at the last minute by replacing the ankle-injured mannequin with a cinderella lovely who goes on to steal not only the show but the heart of young manager and clothing designer.

The fashion czar and the countess from Florence wish to marry, but a quirk of fate reveals that they're related by blood — in fact, Rüdiger is rescued in the nick of time from marrying his half-sister. Naturally, everything gets unraveled at the end to reveal more oddities in the family tree.

Everything is done tongue-in-cheek and in grand parody style: corny lines and silly costumes. The Hamburg designer Wolfgang Joop plays the couturier Rüdiger to the hilt, while the Italian countess is in real-life an Yves Saint-Laurent mannequin from Paris, Violetta Sanchez. All the other roles, too, fit their personalities like kid-gloves.

The other plus is Jacques Steyn's talent for lighting and decoration. — *Holl.*

King Kongs Faust
(King Kong's Fist)
(WEST GERMAN-COLOR)

Saarbrücken, Jan. 17.

A Katrin Seybold Film in coproduction with Norddeutscher Rundfunk (NDR) and the Independent Feature Project (New York), with support from the Kuratorium Junger Deutscher Film. Features entire cast. Directed by Heiner Stadler. Screenplay, Stadler, Ulrich Enzensberger, Lilly Targownik; camera (color), Stadler, Markus Dürr; sets, Claus Jürgen Pfeiffer, Monika Grube; sound, Toni Sulzbeck; music, Gerhard Stäbler; editing, Rolf Basedow, Angelique Fiedler; production manager, Katrin Seybold; tv producer, Eberhard Scharfenberg. Reviewed at Saarbrücken Film Fest (Max Ophüls Prize), Jan. 16, 1985. Running time: **80 MINS.**

With: Leonard Lansink (Klaus Uwe Matthies), Werner Grassmann (Fritz Ackrewa), Heinz van Nouhuys (chief editor), Wolfgang Längsfeld (colleague), Gisela Weilemann (woman in bar), Gad Klein, Volker Stollberg, Doris Dörrie, Philip Behrens, Michael Stejskal, "Ponkie," Peggy Parnass (critics), Wilm Wenders (film director), Peter Przygodda (film editor), Helmut Färber (film historian), Franz Seitz (film producer), Laslo Benedek (English collector), Johanna Eisenrieder (archivist), Burt Willis (old man in Los Angeles), Lila Waters (woman in bus), Crofton Hardester (character in coffee shop), Helga Oswald (guest), Ginger Myers (singer), Rosa Elena Lujan (B. Traven's widow), Hermann Weigel (screenwriter), Bernd Eichinger (film producer).

Everyone who's seen "King Kong" as religiously as "Casablanca" each time the classic Hollywood entertainment surfaces in a repertory house will laugh himself silly over this wild and woolly debut feature by a former grad (camera and documentary section) of the Munich Film School. Heiner Stadler's "King Kong's Fist," one of the real surprises at the Saarbrücken film fest, is a parody on the fanatic dedication of film historians, a bit overdone at times but seldom drifting too far away from the original pun to become trite or self-indulgent.

This is not to say that Stadler doesn't enjoy getting in his wacks at the German and Hollywood film scenes every chance he gets. And he certainly (like any boy wonder on the New German Cinema treadmill) is angling to get his docudrama shown at this year's Berlinale in conjunction with the special effects retrospective and exhibition.

Here is a young film critic trying to break into the ranks without much success — until he happens by chance into a retro screening at the 1984 Berlinale of an Expressionist film made in the 1920s by an unknown filmmaker (apparently an F.W. Murnau restored snippet of a lost masterpiece with beginning and end lost forever). Next, the cub reporter is in a projection booth manned by an old friend (Werner Grassmann, a prominent Hamburg film exhibitor in a delightful cameo), who feeds him a hot tip: the unknown director was Bobo Wawerka, but no one knows whatever became of him after he left for Hollywood — save that he was the maker of the monster's fist in "King Kong!"

The reporter is able to convince an editor at a film journal to back him for a research trip to London, then Hollywood, and finally Mexico. A mad collector in London (Laslo Benedek) is in possession of the monster's fist from the 1933 classic, and a photo stolen from the RKO archive reveals there was an unidentified man on the set working in Willis O'Brien's special effects crew on "King Kong." The bait is swallowed and off the film buff wings to Hollywood. It's here he discovers, however, that the unidentified technican was not Bodo Wawerka — in fact, there never was a Bobo Wawerka.

The rest is how the inquiring reporter dreams up a story to bring back to Germany and save face before his peers.

Final twist is back at the 1984 Berlinale, after a producer has swallowed the same bait again and wants to make a film on the unknown Bodo Wawerka due to the sensation the reporter's story has aroused. The joke — stretched even that far — is still quite amusing. Even filmer Wim Wenders and producer Bernd Eichinger (both Munich Film Academy chums of Heiner Stadler) contribute tongue-in-cheek cameos. —*Holl.*

Pizza Connection
(Attacco Alla Piovra)
(ITALIAN-COLOR)

Rome, Jan. 31.

A Columbia release. Produced by Mario and Vittorio Cecchi Gori for Alexandra Film and C.G. Silver productions. Directed by Damiano Damiani. Stars Michele Placido. Screenplay, Laura Toscano, Franco Marotta, Damiani; camera (color), Nino Celeste; editor, Enzo Meneconi; music, Carlo Savina. Reviewed at Metropolitan Cinema Rome, Jan. 28, 1985. Running time: **119 MINS.**

Mario	Michele Placido
Michele	Mark Chase
Cecilia	Simona Cavallario
Cecilia's mother	Ida Di Benedetto

"Pizza Connection" is a gripping, fast-paced Mafia actioner by genre master Damiano Damiani, whose "Octopus" on the same subject took last season's tv audiences by storm. Pic has the makings of a b.o. hit and the professional look of an international release. It will unspool at the Berlin Fest out of competition.

Reversing the good guy role usually accorded star Michele Placido, one of Italy's top young thesps, "Pizza Connection" cleverly upsets audience expectations right from the start. Mario, owner of a Brooklyn pizza parlor, is sent to Palermo by the Organization on a contract. Dropping in on his poor but respectable Sicilian family, Mario plays the big-shot while trying to convince his teenage brother Michele (Mark Chase) to come in on the job.

Michele, however, angelic in face and character, at first will have nothing to do with Mario's diabolic proposals. Michele has fallen for Cecilia (Simona Cavallario), a curly-haired waif of 14 who is coolly prostituted by mama Ida Di Benedetto to buy dope for her brother. Pic paints the lurid family scene with a few chilling strokes, skipping the graphic details. Michele's search for a way to buy the girl back from a life on the streets provides the motive for agreeing to shoot a bodyguard. Mario is pleased the money will remain in the family and his kid brother is finally going to amount to something.

While taking up its position firmly within its genre, "Connection" is sophisticated enough to avoid the most clichéd plot turns. Damiani and editor Enzo Meneconi show themselves masters of tight pacing and precisely timed action sequences; the scattered killings take place mostly offscreen after a long build-up, with the emphasis on creating suspense rather than ogling blood baths. When Mario finally picks off his target, an investigating magistrate, camera arrives at the scene a minute later to record bystanders' reaction. Passing on easy effects and hyped-up violence, "Connection" does well to focus on characterization and plotting — the personal effects of Mob violence rather than the political or spectacular.

Strong performances from all hands carry pic through its ridiculously literary dialog, which subtitles can be expected to downplay. Placido, an old hand at playing Southerners, is convincingly cynical when he urges his innocent sibling to kill a colt in the field — "If you can't shoot a horse, how can you shoot a man?" American thesp Mark Chase is a perfect boy growing up, his tender years — like Cecilia's — used dramatically to depict innocence in the midst of a society permeated with violence and corruption. Both Chase and newcomer Cavallario bring a total naturalness to their characters, making them believable and sympathetic. — *Yung.*

Hungarian Film Week

Oberst Redl
(Colonel Redl)
(WEST GERMAN-HUNGARIAN-AUSTRIAN-COLOR)

Budapest, Feb. 12.

A Manfred Durniok Film, West Berlin, and Hungarofilm (Mafilm-Objektiv Studio), Budapest, coproduction in collaboration with Second German Television (ZDF), Mainz, and Austrian Television (ORF), Vienna. Produced by Durniok. Directed by Istvan Szabo. Stars Klaus Maria Brandauer. Screenplay, Szabo, Peter Dobai; camera (Eastmancolor), Lajos Koltai. Only technical credits available. Reviewed at Budapest Film Fest, Feb. 11, 1985. Running time: **149 MINS.**

Alfred Redl	Klaus Maria Brandauer
The Crown Prince	Armin Müller-Stahl
Von Roden	Hans-Christian Blech
Katalin Kubinyi	Gudrun Landgrebe
Christoph Kubinyi	Jan Miklas
Clarissa	Dorottya Udvaros
Female Singer	Anthina Papadimirtriu
Dr. Sonnenschein	Andras Balint
Jaromil Schorm	Karoly Eperjes
Velocchio	Laszlo Galffi
Col. Ruzitska	Laszlo Mensaros
Baron Ullmann	Robert Rathonyi
Grandfather Kubinyi	Tamas Major
Adjutant to Crown Prince	Gyorgy Banffy
Wilhelmina	Agnes T. Katona

"Colonel Redl" — German title is "Oberst Redl" while in Hungarian it's "Redl Ezredes" — is the heralded followup to the Oscar-winning "Mephisto" made by the same team of producer Manfred Durniok (West Germany) director Istvan Szabo (Hungary), and actor Klaus Maria Brandauer (Austria). It won the Grand Prix hands-down at the Hungarian Festival of Feature Films in Budapest, should be the likely Hungarian entry at Cannes this May, and is in many ways a far better production than "Mephisto." Pic needs only proper handling to be a winner at the boxoffice as well, despite the complex historic background.

"Colonel Redl" is also inspired by John Osborne's controversial play on homosexuality, "A Patriot For Me," but only because the primary issue is the same. As for the historical background, the Alfred Redl affair can be found in most factual accounts of the times leading up to the outbreak of World War I and the fall of the Austrian-Hungarian Empire. He was an aspiring military officer who, as the son of a minor civil servant in the Ruthenian province (northeastern section bordering Russia), worked his way up from nowhere to become head of the Secret Police and commander of the Eighth Army in Prague when caught as a secret agent of the Russians and forced to commit suicide in order to smooth over the affair of his homosexuality and other indiscretions.

Naturally enough, the facts go well beyond this bare account, and some historians are still piecing together the full story from both actual and falsified documentation. It's to scripters Istvan Szabo and Peter Dobai's credit that they opt for the bare bones of history and interpret the facts as need be to sketch a panorama of the times with heavy emphasis on the atmospheric elements relating to both the military and the intrigues inside the Hapsburg court.

Pic begins with young Redl entering the military academy to make friends with another cadet, Christoph Kubinyi of a noble Hungarian family, and rising through the ranks with him. He even has an affair with his friend's sister, Katalin, and the two remain attached to each other after entering into unhappy marriages on their own. Redl also has the good fortune of being promoted to higher ranks via a high military officer, von Roden, and soon he has made several enemies through his appointment to head of the secret police. Lastly, Redl is his own worst enemy due to definite homosexual tendencies that particularly include fellow friends in the military.

Once Redl has made the acquaintance of the Crown Prince and heir-apparent to the Hapsburg throne, however, he faces a doubtful admirer of his talents for spying and intrigue. Franz Ferdinand would prefer setting Redl up for a show trial as a secret agent, the main reason being that Redl as a Ruthenian would be the perfect victim to make an example of for the rest of the military and to quell further intrigues within the decaying empire. The film shows the ambitious officer did betray his country to a Russian agent by revealing military forces guarding the eastern border and placements there too for a possible invasion of Russia. He is arrested and given a pistol to put an end to his own life. Shortly thereafter, in the film's epilog, the Crown Prince is shot in Sarajevo, and World War I breaks out to put an end to most monarchies of Europe for good.

A superb acting performance by Brandauer keeps the pic running at a taut and tense pace throughout, and he is ably supported by Hans Christian Blech as von Roden and Armin Müller-Stahl as the Crown Prince. Lensing is also a major plus, in addition to the care taken for every detail relating to the military world of the Hapsburg court and Hungarian nobility.

This is Istvan Szabo's best film to date and ample evidence he can handle epic spectacles as well as intimate stories. The only drawback is keeping the time frame clearly in mind as the years pass — until the "Redl Affair" surfaces in the press in 1913. — *Holl.*

Valaki Figyel
(The Peephole And The Key)
(HUNGARIAN-COLOR)

Budapest, Feb. 10.

A Hunnia Studio, Mafilm, production. Directed by Andras Lanyi. Features entire cast. Screenplay, Lanyi; camera (Eastmancolor), Sandor Kardos; music, Zoltan Papp; art director, Andras Gyurky; editor, Maria Nagy; sound, Janos Retl; costumes, Zsuzsa Partenyi, Nora Kovats. Reviewed at Hungarian Film Week, Budapest, Feb. 9, 1985. Running time: **103 MINS.**

Halasz	Peter Vallai
Marta	Katalin Takacs
The Tempter	Laszlo Sinko

"The Peephole And The Key" is an intriguing tale of a rather shiftless young man, separated from his nagging wife, who one day, while strolling through a city arcade, stops to watch through a window a couple getting hurriedly undressed. At the same moment he's approached by a stranger who wants to hire him as a kind of private eye to spy on the young woman in the room above.

He refuses at first, but the stranger keeps at him until he agrees. He starts to follow the girl and in doing so meets all kinds of odd people without ever quite realizing what information's he's supposed to be seeking and what will be done with it when he reports. Inevitably he finds himself involved with the girl and one day is about to make love to her when he realizes he's in the very room above the arcade where the story originally started.

Director Andras Lanyi keeps about as many secrets from the audience as he does from his bewildered hero, which makes for a sometimes confusing, sometimes tantalizing experience. A wry sense of humor alleviates this Kafkaesque tale of spying and everyday intrigue.

Technical credits are fine and the actors all slot well into their ambivalent roles. Mark this one down as an oddly amusing effort, made with a good deal of invention and charm. Original Magyar title translates as "Someone Is Watching You." — *Strat.*

Omega, Omega ...
(HUNGARIAN-DOCU-COLOR)

Budapest, Feb. 12.

A Dialog Studios, Mafilm-Magyar Television Mokep coproduction. Directed by Miklos Jancso. Screenplay, Gyula Hernadi; camera (color), Ivan Mark; choreographer, Bela Szirmai. Reviewed at Hungarian Film week, Budapest, Feb. 11, 1985. Running time: **76 MINS.**

With: Omega (Laszio Benkö, keyboard; Ferenc Debreceni, drums; Janos Kobor, lead singer; Tamas Mibaly, bass; György Molnar, guitar; György Kopecsni, guitar; Miklos Toth, keyboard).

Concert film, covering a November 1982 gig by popular Hungarian group Omega, was lensed on video and the transfer to 35m film is inadequate.

Followers of the career of Miklos Jancso, who directed, will find the helmer has somehow included his usual trademark — shots of fully naked women — in what is otherwise a conventional record of the concert. Some brief interviews with members of the group are interpolated.

Omega appear to be working in the tradition of The Rolling Stones, and lead-singer Janos Kobor struts around the stage like a younger Mick Jagger. Generally speaking, this film, which lacks the impact of last year's rock musical "Istvan The King," looks to have purely local appeal. —*Strat.*

Vörös Gröfnö
(The Red Countess)
(HUNGARIAN-COLOR)

Budapest, Feb. 9.

A Dialog Studio, Mafilm, production. Directed and written by Andras Kovacs. Features entire cast. Camera (Eastmancolor), Miklos Biro; music, Laszlo Vidovszky; art director, Vilmos Nagy; editor, Maria Szecsenyi; sound, Gabor Erdelyi; costumes, Fanni Kemenes. Reviewed at Hungarian Film Week, Budapest, Feb. 8, 1985. Running time: 153 MINS.
Katinka ....Juli Basti
Mihaly Karolyi..............Ferenc Bacs
Gyula Andrassy ....Ferenc Kallai
Mrs. Andrassy ....Hedi Temessy

"The Red Countess" is a richly mounted biopic of Count Mihaly Karolyi (1875-1955) and his feisty wife, Katinka. Katinka Karolyi is still alive and living in the South of France: the old lady introduces this tribute to her late husband herself at the beginning of the film.

The Karolyis were unusual in that, during the chaotic period during and following World War I, they, as aristocrats, sided with the people against the apparent interests of their own class. Director Andras Kovacs tells their story with lots of factual background (including much use of contemporary newsreels), but little passion. The film is academically interesting without ever being terribly involving.

The first half of the pic, presented with an intermission, depicts the courtship of young, headstrong Katinka Andrassy (Juli Basti), who has already attempted suicide over one failed love affair, for Count Karolyi, 23 years older than herself, and involved with a mistress of long-standing. This 73-minute part of the film is set against a background of lavish balls, vicious fox hunts and elegant surroundings un-

til the willful Katinka gets her man.

Part 2 (80 minutes) is more interesting as it involves the political events post World War I in Hungary, and the violent reactions against Karolyi's policies. In these, the film suggests, his wife was even more radical than he. After the Communist takeover in 1919, Karolyi stays on to advise the new government, and he and his wife only go into exile when a counter-revolution brings the old guard back into power.

No doubt the tale of a couple of aristocrats who side with the Left and even give away their estates to the people is full of potential interest. However, Kovacs tends to avoid all the climaxes, all the big scenes in the picture. The background of war and revolution is kept resolutely offscreen, making for a talky, rather stodgy pic.

It is, however, superb to look at, with imposing settings, rich photography and elegant costumes. The principal actors acquit themselves very well indeed, though some minor roles are played poorly, and it was careless to cast, as an American military man, a player whose grasp of English is so tenuous. The music score of Laszlo Vidovszky is another asset.

The newsreel footage used is impressive, and incidentally shows that actors Juli Basti and Ferenc Bacs look quite similar to their real-life counterparts. A sequel, recounting the years in exile of the 'red countess' and her husband, is promised. —*Strat.*

Competing At Berlin

Seburi Monogatari
(The Seburi Story)
(JAPANESE-COLOR)

Berlin, Feb. 19.

A Toei Co. Ltd. production. Produced by Tatsuo Honda, Masao Sato. Executive producer, Kasaku Shimizu. Directed and written by Sadao Nakajima. Features entire cast. Camera (Fujicolor), Fuminori Minami; editor, Eifu Tamaki; sound, Hideto Kuriyama; music, Takayuki Inoue, Seiji Hayami; art director, Toshiyuki Manabe. Reviewed at Berlin Film Festival (in competition), Feb. 18, 1985. Running time: 120 MINS.
Hajime Kinoshita ......Kenichi Hagiwara
Kuni ....Yumiko Fujita
Hidé ....Michiko Kawano
Kazuo ....Tsuyoshi Naito
Hana ....Ai Saotome
Jiro....................Ken Mitsuishi

As recently as the 1940s, the so-called Seburi people of western Japan lived a traditional nomadic life, rejecting any notion of living in houses or apartments, and preferring to shelter in tents, despite the often bitter weather. This handsomely made, sometimes powerful film is about a group of Seburi who come into violent conflict with hostile townspeople and with military police rounding up men for conscription into the war.

Director Sadao Nakajima takes his time in the early scenes to establish the unique rituals and customs of these people, via marriage, birth and death. He then homes in on a group of characters affected by the inevitable changes, and especially the fate of Hidé and her forbidden love affair with a non-Seburi, Jiro (sex outside marriage is strictly forbidden). When Hidé's "crime" is discovered, she's buried up to her neck in the ground and left there for days.

Shot amid majestic scenery, where winter avalanches swell streams into raging rivers impossible to cross, "The Seburi Story" has some affinities with "The Ballad Of Nayarama," winner of the Grand Prix at Cannes two years back, in that both are about primitive communities holding fast to old laws and customs despite the encroachment of modern civilization. This is a savage world, where a woman gives birth unaided, where the hardship of the elements is matched only by the emnity of people who fear the Seburi because they're so strange and different.

Impeccable production is extremely handsome, and though pacing early on is slow, it picks up midway to tell a tragedy of classical proportions. Acting is suitably earthy and uninhibited. — *Strat.*

Pehlivan
(The Wrestler)
(TURKISH-COLOR)

Berlin, Feb. 17.

A Seref Film Production. Produced by Seref Gür. Directed by Zeki Okten. Features entire cast. Screenplay, Fehmi Yasar; camera (color), Hüseyin Dzashin; editor, Nevzat Disiacik; sound, Erkan Aktas; music, Tarik Ocal; art director, Yavuzer Cetinkaya. Reviewed at Berlin Film Festival (in competition), Feb. 16, 1985. Running time: 94 MINS.
Bilal ....Tarik Akan
Senem ....Meral Orhonsay
Mestan ....Erol Günaydin
Tefvik ....Yaman Okay
Father ....Ahmet Kayiskesen

Zeki Okten is known as the nominal director of "The Herd" and "The Enemy," two films written and prepared by the late Yilmaz Güney from his prison cell. On the basis of "The Wrestler," it looks as though Okten himself is a competent craftsman much in need of a

firm script; he hasn't got it here.

Set in a small Thracian village, it's a tale of a proud man whose father and grandfather were champion wrestlers. Anxious to win substantial prize money in a provincial contest, Bilal devotes all his time to training in the traditional wrestling of the area, where the combatants are heavily oiled to make getting a grip on your opponent more difficult. About a quarter of the film (it seems) is taken up with watching wrestling bouts; the uninitiated will be bored. Predictably, Bilal loses in the end, and equally predictably the pic ends on a freeze-frame image of his defeat.

A more interesting subplot concerns the return home, after 12 years in West Germany, of Bilal's brother, sister-in-law and Westernized niece; their comments on life in Germany, and difficulties in reassimilating themselves, would make an interesting film.

Thesping is okay, with Tarik Akan suitably rugged as the hero and a lovely cameo from Ahmet Kayiskesen as his aged father. Other Turkish films have had limited distribution in the West, with Güney's "Yol" the most successful, but it's doubtful "The Wrestler" will have much luck in this direction. —*Strat.*

Wetherby
(BRITISH-COLOR)

Berlin, Feb. 19.

An MGM-UA Classics release (U.S.) of a Greenpoint Films-Film Four Intl.-Zenith Prods. coproduction. Produced by Simon Relph. Directed and written by David Hare. Stars Vanessa Redgrave. Camera (Technicolor), Stuart Harris; editor, Chris Wimble; sound, Clive Winter; music, Nick Bicât; production design, Hayden Griffin; coproducer, Patsy Pollock. Reviewed at Berlin Film Festival (in competition), Feb. 18, 1985. Running time: 97 MINS.
Jean Travers ....Vanessa Redgrave
Stanley Pilborough ....Ian Holm
Marcia Pilborough ....Judi Dench
Verity Braithwaite ....Marjorie Yates
Roger Braithwaite ....Tim Wilkinson
John Morgan...........Tim McInnerny
Karen Creasy ....Suzanna Hamilton
Mike Langdon ....Stuart Wilson
Young Jean Travers .....Joely Richardson
Jim Mortimer ....Robert Hines

After a successful and influential career in theater and television (where he wrote and directed "Licking Hitler" among others), David Hare makes an original, refreshing feature film debut as director which must rank as one of the best British films about personal relationships since the late Joseph Losey's "Accident" in the mid-'60s.

The title refers to a small town in the northeastern county of Yorkshire. Jean Travers (Vanessa Redgrave) has lived here all her life; she's a lonely schoolteacher, tormented by the memory of a teenage love affair with a boy who was senselessly murdered while on air force duty in Malaya some 35 years ago.

The film opens with a dinner party hosted by Jean in her little cottage. Present are two couples, close friends, and a young stranger, John Morgan, whom Jean assumes came with one of the couples, while they in turn assume he is her guest. They talk of politics (what Margaret Thatcher's doing to the country), make jokes about Nixon and discuss the apparent lack of ambition in today's youth. All seems perfectly normal. Next day, Morgan returns to the cottage, and while Jean is making tea, he pulls out a gun and kills himself. It is, as someone says, the ultimate practical joke.

Why did he do it? Was it because of the general malaise that seems to affect a young generation growing up under the shadow of MX missile deployments? Or was it because the girl he liked (Suzanna Hamilton, from the film "1984") rejected him so totally? The investigating policeman, Langdon (Stuart Wilson), who has personal troubles of his own, can't let the matter rest.

For the viewer, the skill of Hare's approach is that he initially allows us to assume, via normal cinema techniques, that what we saw of the dinner party was the whole story. Gradually, however, we realize we only saw a highly selected part of that evening, and as we return to it again and again, picking up moments we've seen before but discovering new clues (such as the hitherto unnoticed fact that Jean has changed her clothes at one point), the whole story takes on a different complexion.

Hare constantly is keeping the audience on its toes, confounding its expectations. The result is an immensely satisfying drama in which not a moment is wasted, not a line of dialog (some of which is very witty) superfluous. Performances are uniformly excellent, starting with Vanessa Redgrave as Jean. As the young suicide, Tim McInnerny makes a considerable impression, while Suzanna Hamilton confirms her talent with an incisive portrait of a modern teenager. Ian Holm and Judi Dench are fine as a bickering couple, while Joely Richardson (real-life daughter of Redgrave and Tony Richardson) portrays Redgrave in her youth with great conviction.

"Wetherby" is a beautifully directed film in which all the technical elements mesh to form a most satisfying and stimulating whole. Special note should be made of Hayden Griffin's impeccable production design. Pic should do well with proper handling in theaters around the world which specialize in top-quality British cinema. MGM/UA Classics has it for the U.S.
— *Strat.*

Into The Night
(COLOR)

Uneasy caper-comedy for buffs only.

Hollywood, Feb. 16.

A Universal Pictures release, produced by George Folsey Jr. and Ron Koslow. Directed by John Landis. Exec producer, Dan Allingham. Screenplay, Koslow; camera (Technicolor), Robert Paynter; editor, Malcolm Campbell; sound, William B. Kaplan; production design, John Lloyd; associate producer, David Sosna; music, Ira Newborn; casting, Michael Chinich, Jackie Burch. Reviewed at the Avco Theatre, L.A., Feb. 14, 1985. (MPAA rating: R.) Running time: **115 MINS.**
Ed Okin .... Jeff Goldblum
Diana .... Michelle Pfeiffer
Jack Caper .... Richard Farnsworth
Shaheen .... Irene Papas
Christie .... Kathryn Harrold
Bud .... Paul Mazursky
Melville .... Roger Vadim
Herb .... Dan Aykroyd
Morris .... David Bowie
Ellen .... Stacey Pickren
Larry .... Jake Steinfeld
Charlie .... Bruce McGill
Joan........................ Vera Miles
Williams.................. Carl Perkins
Agent .... Clu Gulager
Also with: Jack Arnold, Paul Bartel, David Cronenberg, Jonathan Demme, Richard Franklin, Carl Gottlieb, Amy Heckerling, Jim Henson, Colin Higgins, Lawrence Kasdan, Jonathan Kaufer, John Landis, Andrew Marton, Daniel Petrie, Don Siegel.

"Into The Night" will probably be into the ether in a hurry unless there is an extensive trivia interest beyond Hollywood in how many of his filmmaker friends director John Landis can fit into one wandering romp.

Beyond the film buffs, there is another potential audience, though even smaller in number. Thanks to a perfect portrayal by Michelle Pfeiffer, there's a pleasantly painful memory or two here for any man who has ever ventured near one of those beautiful wackos who are nothing but trouble but impossible to resist.

Make no mistake: This is not a Goldie Hawn sweet thing with a streak of bad luck. Pfeiffer's inspiration is major-league, top-of-the-line, state-of-the-art Bimboism in full bloom, the kind whose clothes are stored from one end of L.A. to the other, along with whatever morals she might have hit town with originally.

Over in the suburbs dwells quiet aerospace engineer Jeff Goldblum whose job is going nowhere while his wife goes too far with another man. Mulling all this over in the middle of the night, Goldblum ambles aimlessly out to the airport where Pfeiffer has just arrived with six smuggled emeralds.

Apparently, Pfeiffer has performed this chore for one or more boyfriends and the promise of some cash, but she is hardly prepared for the four killers awaiting her arrival. Fleeing them, she leaps into Goldblum's car and from then on, it's just one misadventure and murder after another.

In pursuit of the jewels are a series of cameo-plus parts handled by Irene Papas, Roger Vadim, David Bowie and a band of Iranian zanies that includes Landis himself. Among others on the fringes in equally small appearances are Dan Aykroyd, Richard Farnsworth, Kathryn Harrold, Paul Mazursky, Vera Miles, Carl Perkins and Clu Gulager.

And for real insiders, there are a host of well-known Hollywood names popping up as a doorman here, a waitress there, a bum, a cop, etc. Harmless enough is the best that can be said for all the trouble.

The film itself tries sometimes too hard for laughs and at other times strains for shock. Aside from Goldblum and Pfeiffer, none of the large cast has much to do, and whatever that is only serves to muddle the story. But Goldblum is nonetheless enjoyable as he constantly tries to figure out just what he's doing in all of this. And, as the answer, Pfeiffer provides all the appeal that "Night" can force.
— *Har.*

The Other Cuba
(ITALIAN-U.S.-DOCU-COLOR)

Meet the new boss, same as the old boss.

Miami, Feb. 8.

A Promovision Intl. release of an RAI/Guede production. Directed by Orlando Jimenez-Leal. Screenplay, Jorge Ulla and Jimenez-Leal; camera (color), Jimenez-Leal, Emilio Guede, Eric Kollmar, Henry Vargas, Ramon Carthy, Ramon Suarez; editor, Gloria Pineyro; music, Paquito D'Rivera. Reviewed at the Gusman theater, Miami Film Festival, Feb. 8, 1985. Running time: **110 MINS.**
With: Carlos Franqui, Valerio Riva and the people of Cuba in exile.

"The Other Cuba" begins with the same newsreel footage director Brian DePalma used to open "Scarface." Fidel Castro is seen ranting and raving about the Mariel refugees: "We don't want them. We don't need them. They cannot adapt to the spirit of the revolution."

For the following 110 minutes, Spanish director Orlando Jimenez-Leal ("Improper Conduct") teams with co-screenwriter Jorge Ulla on Carlos Franqui and Valerio Riva's story to offer a detailed account — through international interviews, phone calls, vintage film clips and newsreel footage — of how the revolution went so bad, so fast; how the one-time guerrilla hero Castro betrayed his ideals, his friends, his confidantes and, finally, his country to become so solidly aligned with the USSR.

While "The Other Cuba" is an innovative and highly interesting documentary, there's a very elementary problem in the theme.

The exiled artists, poets, writers, political prisoners and filmmakers all interviewed here have intense and agonizing stories to tell, but are never once provoked to deal with the theme of "won't get fooled again." These people all thought Bastista was so bad, so they backed Castro, only to find out he was worse. Now they think that if Castro takes a hard fall, things in Havana will go from Dante's "Inferno" to Paradisio. Jimenez-Leal makes a grievous error in never pushing these people to talk about this touchy subject — and he should have.

"The Other Cuba" also glosses over the problems the Mariel boatlift created for America, especially Miami. The narrator states how in Miami "you now hear more Spanish than English." This one sentence alone cries for a more thorough investigation.

On the plus side, the interviews provide a devastating insight into a revolution with high hopes and even higher ideals with that quickly dissolved into sheer torture, bloodshed, censorship, imprisonment and a collapsing economy. "The Other Cuba" is a good documentary (even the use of Cuban exile Paquito D'Riviera's music is a lovely touch) that should definitely be seen by everyone — not just Latin Americans — to have a better understanding of the hopes, dreams and families which people left behind to escape the Castro regime. —*Marl.*

Hearts And Diamonds
(COLOR)

Low-budget rites of passage.

Miami, Feb. 8.

An East 7th St. production. Produced, written and directed by Eleanor Gaver. Executive producer, Rufus Barkley. Camera (color), James Hayman; art directors, Gaver, Wanda Wysong, Leigh Morse; editors, Peter J. Friedman, Frank Kern. Reviewed at the Beaumont Cinema, Miami Film Festival, Feb.7, 1985. Running time: **83 MINS.**
With: Lucinda Jenney, Michael Speero, Matthew Dunne, Bonne Brown Smith, Susan Strahon, Ed Breen, Harriet Rodgers, Cheyenne Holder, Noah Gaver.

The print of American writer-director Eleanor Gaver's "Hearts And Diamonds" exhibited at the second Miami Film Festival was shown with a multi-song soundtrack with tunes selected from various Top 10 rock and country recording artists. An original score now reportedly is being composed for the film and, upon its completion, the current soundtrack will be deleted.

New music, however, is not likely to improve the film's prospects. Though Gaver shows she can stretch an ultra-low budget, "Hearts And Diamonds" is a candidate for neither a cult following nor midnight audiences.

The story opens with a group of teenagers stalking at an amusement park — all mutli-colored lights, buzzing neon, kewpie dolls and spinning merry-go-rounds. For the few seconds, "Hearts And Diamonds" has the look of a movie with some very serious rites-of-passage potential. Gaver attempts in vain to spoof those rites in a combination with a "No Nukes" theme. A newly built nuclear plant is leaking toxic waste into a seaside resort's waters, killing every fish in sight.

Coinciding with the nuclear tragedy, a young beautician shifts from lovable to obnoxious, and must decide between partnering with a wealthy wimp or a poor hulk. Gaver tries playing her self-penned script mostly for laughs, but there simply aren't any.

Making matters worse, the film constantly lapses into passé music-video-style footage. —*Marl.*

Certain Fury
(COLOR)

Good cast in standard actioner.

Hollywood, Feb. 17.

A New World Pictures release, produced by Gilbert Adler. Directed by Stephen Gyllenhaal. Stars Tatum O'Neal, Irene Cara. Exec producer, Lawrence Vanger. Screenplay, Michael Jacobs; camera (Deluxe Color), Kees Van Oostrum; editor, Todd Ramsey; sound, Ralph Parker; assistant director, Martin Walters; music, Bill Payne, Russ Kunkel, George Massenburg; casting, Sally Dennison. Reviewed at Paramount Theatre, Hollywood, Feb. 16, 1985. (MPAA Rating: R.) Running time: **87 MINS.**
Scarlet .... Tatum O'Neal
Tracy .... Irene Cara
Sniffer .... Nicholas Campbell
Lt. Spier .... George Murdock
Dr. Freeman .... Moses Gunn
Rodney .... Peter Fonda
Superman .... Rodney Gage
Barker .... Jonathon Pallone

It usually takes longer for talents like Tatum O'Neal and Irene Cara to go from the heights of Oscar attention to the depths of Boulevard action picture, but they have made the transition with "Certain Fury," which drew about half a house to a sneak preview Saturday (16).

In the beginning and for a few flickers thereafter, though, there are signs of what may have attracted O'Neal and Cara to the project. Before the shooting starts and in between stabbings, attempted rapes and assorted explosions, O'Neal makes the most of a chance to deepen her character of a street-smart tough as does Cara with her part as an upper-class, sheltered young lady thrown into terrifying circumstances.

The two meet in court, where O'Neal is a regular customer and

Cara has arrived on a first-offense, picked up the night before on a minor infraction. But they don't get much time to emote before a couple of hookers grab a cop's gun and begin to blow the place apart.

Fleeing the carnage together, they find themselves pursued by angry police who believe they were in on the shootout. Neither girl likes the other, but they stick together seeking refuge, speeding from one peril to the next until friendship blossoms at the finale.

Director Stephen Gyllenhaal and lenser Kees Van Oostrum handle the action well enough, but sacrifice none of it to linger very long over character development. It's pretty plain the girls had to struggle for what they got. — *Har.*

Water
(BRITISH-COLOR)

Hollywood, Feb. 15.

A Rank release (U.K.) of a HandMade production. Produced by Ian La Frenais. Coproduced by David Wimbury. Executive producers, George Harrison, Denis O'Brien. Directed by Dick Clement. Stars Michael Caine. Screenplay, Clement, Ian La Frenais, Bill Persky, camera (color), Douglas Slocombe; production design, Norman Garwood, costumes, Jim Acheson; editor, John Victor Smith; music, Mike Moran. Reviewed at Mann's National theater, Westwood, Calif., Feb. 15, 1985. (No MPAA Rating.) Running time: **95 MINS.**
Baxter .... Michael Caine
Pamela .... Valerie Perrine
Bianca .... Brenda Vaccaro
Delgado .... Billy Connolly
Sir Malcolm .... Leonard Rossiter
Prime minister .... Maureen Lipman
Rob .... Dennis Dugan
Eric .... Fulton Mackay
Garfield .... Chris Tummings
Pepito .... Trevor Laird
Nado .... Kevin Olmaro
Miguel .... Oscar James
Angola .... Stefan Kalipha
Jesus .... Alan Ibgon
Industrialist .... Fred Gwynne

A British satire of political muddle in Caribbean island, sneak-previewed in U.S. without a domestic distributor. "Water" is a frenetic mishmash from HandMade Films. The search for a domestic distrib should be a stiff challenge, given the anchorless script and tepid audience reaction.

Michael Caine is fine as a laidback British governor who is aptly described as "the Patty Hearst of the British diplomatic corps," but he can't salvage a production that's topheavy with multinational plots threatening the island's harmony. Those include a singing revolutionary (Billy Connolly) backed by Cubans, mindless British officials (a nice turn by the late Leonard Rossiter and a Margaret Thatcher send-up by Maureen Lipman), some fuzzy French-German intruders, and a U.S. industrialist (Fred Gwynne) who's exploiting the island's underground reserves of mineral water.

The British filmmakers, who shot

on the West Indies island of St. Lucia, obviously were targeting the invasions of Grenada and the Falkland Islands as subjects of cinematic satire. There are some funny lines and twists of humor, but the film is totally devoid of a narrative center and, without continuity and sustained imagination, it quickly becomes an overproduced cliché.

Playing Caine's hysterical South American wife, Brenda Vaccaro hits the nadir of her career in a performance that is one unrelieved shriek. Valerie Perrine, as a green environmentalist, is generally wasted. Only Caine's bemused demeanor and Rossiter's on-target stuffiness make the experience disarming.

Film doesn't even brush close to Woody Allen's 1971 political Latin satire, "Bananas." For the record, Robin Williams is set for a forthcoming and similarly themed comedy, "Island Jack," for Warner Bros.—*Loyn.*

Came A Hot Friday
(NEW ZEALAND-COLOR)

Wellington, N.Z. Feb. 15.

A Mirage Films production. Directed by Ian Mune. Produced by Larry Parr. Screenplay, Dean Parker and Ian Mune; camera (Color), Alun Bollinger; production design, Ron Highfield; editor, Ken Zemke; music, Stephen McCurdy; sound, Hammond Peek. Reviewed at National Film Unit Preview Theater, Wellington, Feb. 14, 1985. (No MPAA Rating.) Running time: **105 MINS.**
Wes Pennington .... Peter Bland
Cyril Kidman .... Philip Gordon
The Tainuia Kid .... Billy T. James
Don Jackson .... Michael Lawrence
Sel Bishop .... Marshall Napier
Esmeralda .... Marise Wipani
Dinah .... Erna Larsen
Dick .... Phillip Holder
Cray .... Don Selwyn
Claire .... Patricia Phillips
Morrie .... Michael Morrissey

"Came A Hot Friday" is a major advance in Kiwi film comedy. A barrel load of talent, nurtured during New Zealand's filmmaking renaissance and now signaling distinctive maturity, has been brought together in this Mirage Films presentation to explore a folk tale of intrigue and delight.

Director Ian Mune, who has made major creative contributions to the growth of the local industry as actor and writer (he most recently received billing as adviser to director Roger Donaldson for "The Bounty") is the catalyst.

His hand is obvious in the way a

picaresque story full of traps for the unwary is propelled with great humor and visual joy.

Of particular pleasure is the realization that, finally, a film based on the thoroughly original writing of Ronald Hugh Morrieson has done him justice. For this, further credit must go to Mune and co-screenwriter Dean Parker.

Morrieson, a provincial recluse who died in 1972, has found a niche of his own in N.Z. literature as a great folk scribe. Two of his other stories, "The Scarecrow," starring John Carradine, and "Pallet On The Floor," also have been adapted to film.

"Came A Hot Friday" is heartland New Zealand circa 1949. Wes Pennington (Peter Bland) and loyal mate Cyril (Philip Gordon), conmen and gamblers, are ripping off small-town bookmakers in one of the last great scams of horseracing. They take advantage of delayed radio broadcasts to clean out bookies in rural pubs — and move on. But snags arise at Tainuia Junction where they become involved in a tangle of events that uncovers bootlegging, arson, murder and provokes mayhem of extraordinary proportions.

The range of locals, not least the duo's apparent guardian angel, The Tainuia Kid (Billy T. James), is worthy of national preservation in a folkloric museum.

Production values are first-rate, particularly the wry charm and subtlety of Alun Bollinger's photography, the original '40s-style music of Stephen McCurdy, and the convincing and integrated production design of Ron Highfield.

There are fine performances from Bland, a kind of homely English carpetbagger, and Gordon. Erna Larsen, as the town belle Dinah, shines among the many neatly etched cameos.

But the acting standout is Polynesian Billy T. James, in what is a riveting, totally original performance as The Tainuia Kid. This Zorro-with-a-difference, who emits a schizo blend of Western cowboy hero and Mexican patriot, with Monty Pythonesque overtones, is a fine creation. This kid says more about cultural cross-breeding in small countries like New Zealand than any learned academic. —*Nic.*

Egy Kicsit En ...
Egy Kicsit Te
(A Little Bit Of You ...
A Little Bit Of Me)
(HUNGARIAN-COLOR)

Budapest, Feb. 10.

A Dialog Studio, Mafilm production. Directed by Livia Gyarmathy. Features entire cast. Screenplay, Geza Böszörmenyl, Csaba Kardos; camera (Eastmancolor), Ferenc Pap; music, György Selmeczi; art director, Tamas

Banovich; editor, Eva Karmentö; sound, Janos Reti; costumes, Ildiko Szabo. reviewed at Hungarian Film week, Budapest, Feb. 9, 1985. Running time: **92 MINS.**

Eva	Cecilia Esztergalyos
Feri	Andor Lukats
Juli	Ildiko Toth
Pali	Jozsef Toth
Eva's mother	Jirina Jiraskova
Feri's mother	Bella Tanay
Feri's uncle	Lajos Öze
Karcsi	Tamas Bartucz
Anna	Kati Sir
The Waiter	György Dörner

A charming, unaffected comedy which proved one of the best of the current crop of Hungarian films, Livia Gyarmathy's "A Little Bit Of You ... A Little Bit Of Me" is universal in application and rich in character.

Eva and Feri and a happily married couple who only fall out over one thing, their 15-year-old daughter, Juli. Eva disapproves of Juli's raffish boyfriend, while Feri is inclined to be tolerant of him. Perhaps that's because Feri teaches art and comes across plenty of modern teenagers at work, while Eva, who works in a smart hotel, expects more formal behavior. Even more disapproving than Eva is her mother, who lives with them, and who thinks the way innocent young Juli behaves is quite scandalous.

After a few bitter arguments, the frustrated Feri calls up an exgirl-griend for consolation and the furious Eva goes to bed with a hotel waiter, though first she calls her husband to let him know exactly how she's taking her revenge.

Things work out, of course, with the generations making an attempt to understand each other, but in the meantime there are plenty of good-natured jokes and a wealth of amusing characters including Feri's madcap, invalid uncle, played with considerable elan by the late Lajos Öze.

Indeed, all the performances are top-rate, and the pic would be an asset to any festival looking for a bright comedy to add to the program, or any specialized distrib with an eye for superior family sitcom, Magyar style.—*Strat.*

Szirmok, Viragok, Koszoruk
(Flowers Of Reverie)
(HUNGARIAN-COLOR)

Budapest, Feb. 10.

A Budapest Film Studio, Mafilm, production. Directed by Laszlo Lugossy. Features entire cast. Screenplay, Istvan Kardos, Lugossy; camera (Eastmancolor), Elemer Ragalyi; music, György Selmeczi; art director. Attila Kovacs; editor, Margit Galamb; sound, György Pinter; costumes, Gizella Koppany. Reviewed at Hungarian Film Week, Budapest, Feb. 9, 1985. Running time: **107 MINS.**

Ferenc Majlath	György Cserhalmi
Maria Majlath	Grazyna Szapolowska
Kornel	Boguslaw Linda
Uncle Heinrich	Jiri Adamira
Miklos	Peter Malcsiner
The Colonel	Lajos Öze

Hungary's entry to the current Berlin Film Festival is a beautifully made, pessimistic film which, though set in the mid-19th century, has obvious contemporary allusions. Downbeat theme will doubtless make it a tough bet on the international art-house circuit, but it will be worth a try.

It opens in 1849. Hungarian hussars, fighting against Austria for their country's independence, have lost the final battle (ironically, it's Austria's ally, Imperial Russia, which has assured their defeat). A Hungarian officer, unable to accept the situation, caresses his beloved horse, then shoots the animal and himself. From the first scene, director Laszio Lugossy creates an air of sadness and melancholy.

The film's protagonist is Ferenc (excellently played by György Cserhalmi). Two years after the defeat, he's trying to live a quiet life with his wife and her family. The main thing is to stay out of trouble, as the country is filled with secret police only too eager to mete out punishment to supporters of the failed rebellion. Enter Ferenc's former superior officer, the Colonel (the late Lajos Oze), who comes to the house one night with futile talk of a new revolution. Next day, the police arrest everyone, and throw Ferenc into an insane asylum. From there he's somehow able to smuggle a letter attacking the Austrian monarchy out to Switzerland, where it's printed in an influential newspaper. Austrian censors read the letter, bringing more trouble down on the beleaguered family.

There are modern parallels here, with occupied Hungary depicted as a place where dissenters are harassed by police and even placed in mental institutions. But this is presumably how it was then, proving there's nothing new under the sun.

Film's original title can be translated as "Petals, Flowers, Wreaths," which is to be preferred to the official English title. By any name, Lugossy's poetic, calm but deeply pessimistic film is worth seeing, its beauty and its sadness making for a sobering experience.
— *Strat.*

Egy Elet Muzsikaja —
Kalman Imre
(Music Of A Lifetime)
(HUNGARIAN-SOVIET--COLOR)

Budapest, Feb. 12.

A Dialog Studio, Mafilm-Mosfilm coproduction. Directed by György Palasthy. Features entire cast. Screenplay, Yuri Magibin; camera (Eastmancolor), Miklos Ilerczenik; editor, Teri Losonci; art directors, Matyas Varga, Konstantin Forostenko; sound, Oleg Zilberstein; costumes. Emöke Csengey, Alina Budnikova. Reviewed at Hungarian Film

Week, Feb. 11, 1985. Running time: **112 MINS.**

Imre Kalman	Peter Huszti
Paula	Ildiko Piros
Vera	Enikö Eszenyi
Agnes	Tatiana Plotnikova

"Music Of A Lifetime" is a poorly conceived, clumsily executed biopic of Imre Kalman, Hungarian composer of light operettas.

Kalman is first discovered as a child aged four, already a musical prodigy. He trains as a lawyer, but music is his first love, and soon he's successful and famous. His first wife is Paula, an actress, and after her death 20 years later he marries the young and talentless Vera. He's been living for years in Vienna when the Germans invade, and Hitler offers to ignore his Jewishness if he'll compose operettas for the Reich. Kalman refuses and heads for America, where Vera divorces him and marries another man, though she's soon back seeking forgiveness and they remarry. He dies in Paris in 1953.

Kalman's popularity in the Soviet Union (Khrushchev loved his music) seems to be the reason behind the coproduction status of the film, which has resulted in an unsubtle script by Russian Yuri Magibin. The whole approach is banal and hollow, the musical numbers awkwardly staged, the personal relationships unconvincing, and even the makeup (as Kalman ages) tatty. One musical sequence of German and British soldiers leaving the trenches in World War I singing cheerfully as they kill each other, really takes the cake.

Some will doubtless compare this to the less fortunate Hollywood biopics of famous composers of yesteryear, but any of those Hollywood films is better than this. They, at least, had style. — *Strat.*

Sortüz Egy Fekete Bivalyert
(Volley For A Black Buffalo)
(HUNGARIAN-FRENCH-COLOR)

Budapest, Feb. 10.

An Objektiv Studio, Mafilm-Procinex (Paris) coproduction. Directed by Laszlo Szabo. Stars Jean-Louis Trintignant, Jean Rochefort. Screenplay, Szabo, Ferenc Jell, Ferenc Andras, from a novel by Nandor Gijon; camera (Eastmancolor), Janos Kende; music, Elek Petrovics; art director, Tamas Banovich; editor, Maria Szecsenyi; sound, György Kovacs; costumes, Zsuzsa Borsi. Reviewed at Hungarian Film Week, Budapest, Feb. 9, 1985. Running time: **103 MINS.**

Mr. Fodo	Jean-Louis Trintignant
Lajos Acsi	Jean Rochefort
Mrs. Fodo	Fanny Cottençon
Elizabeth Novak	Bertha Dominguez
David	Laszlo Maté
Tamas	Laszlo Berendi
Peter Fekete	Miklos Szekely
Mrs. Fekete	Lili Monori
The Priest	Ferenc Kallai
Dukay	Istvan Bujtor

"Volley For A Black Buffalo" is a wafer-thin comedy-drama set in a small Hungarian village soon after the last war. The story is seen through the eyes of David, an orphaned Jewish lad, who is a new arrival. Characters include Fodo, the irascible schoolteacher, whose pretty blond wife runs off with the strong man from a traveling fair; Fodo's friend Acsi, who used to be the local landowner but now bums around doing little; the fiery music-teacher; the rotund priest; Dukay, the local official in charge of removing any leftover weapons and live ammunition; and sickly Fekete, whose team of two black buffalos are stronger than any vehicle in the place. There's also the monstrous cemetery-keeper, whose idea of fun is to tie a couple of sticks of dynamite to a terrified cat and light them (animal lovers will be furious at this sequence, which involves an obviously distraught animal, and is quite painful to watch).

Director Laszlo Szabo, best known for his acting roles in French and Hungarian pics, creates some sympathetic characters but doesn't do much with them. A sense of narrative structure is noticeably lacking, and key scenes (such as the unexpected return of the schoolteacher's errant wife) go for almost nothing. Lushly lensed by Janos Kende, film is strong on atmosphere, and a few individual scenes, such as an accident involving the precious buffalo, and the climax where the children find an unexploded shell and start playing with it, are quite effective. What was needed was a firmer hand in putting all the details together.

The French actors seem uncomfortable in these surroundings, though the dubbing into Hungarian is adequate. — *Strat.*

Csak Egy Mozi
(Just A Movie)
(HUNGARIAN-COLOR)

Budapest, Feb. 13.

A Hunnia Studio, Mafilm, production. Directed by Pal Sandor. Stars Jean-Pierre Léaud. Screenplay, Peter Molnar Gal, Sandor; camera (Eastmancolor), Elemer Ragalyi; music, Tchaikovsky; art director, Attila Kovacs; editors, György Kovacs, Sandor; costumes, György Szakacs. Reviewed at Hungarian Film Week, Budapest, Feb. 12, 1985. Running time: **98 MINS.**

Peter	Jean-Pierre Léaud
Judit	Deborah Javor
The Old Actor	Tamas Major
Mother	Gisela May
Wife	Denisa Kucerova

Admirers of the work of Pal Sandor, and especially his last film, the excellent "Daniel Takes A Train," are likely to be puzzled and disappointed by "Just A Movie," an indulgent, rambling non-event.

It's the old one about the movie

director who gets stumped during the making of a film. Peter, the director, is shooting a filmed ballet of Tchaikovsky's "Swan Lake" on a country location, and the elderly actor playing a key role is just not working out. Peter decides he must be replaced and shooting is halted for three days.

At the railway station with his wife, Peter's eye is caught by a beautiful young girl on the platform; impulsively, he leaps off the train without a world of explanation, and picks her up. He drives her back to the deserted film location, where there are half a dozen caravans, hoping for a tête-à-tête; but they're joined by the old actor, who missed his train, then by Peter's mother. The rest of the film explores the uninteresting relationships among this quartet.

For this kind of whimsical tale to work it has to be beautifully acted and timed. The peculiar casting of Jean-Pierre Léaud was a major miscalculation, for the French actor, who can be most effective with firm direction, just goes through his usual range of mannerisms which by now are as familiar as they are dull. Tamas Major is dignified as the oldster, Deborah Javor is attractive as the young girl, and Gisela May fine as the mother, but they really have nothing very interesting to do. The film just drifts along, without a point of view or a communicable sense of humor. — *Strat.*

Eszmejes
(To See The Light)
(HUNGARIAN-COLOR)

Budapest, Feb. 13.

A Hunnia Studio, Mafilm, production. Directed, written by Ferenc Grunwalsky. Features entire cast. Camera (Eastmancolor), Tibor Mathé; music, György Jurtag Jr., Peter Peterdi; art director, Tamas Vayer; editor. Klara Majoros; sound, Karoly Peller; costumes, Zsuzsa Vicze. Reviewed at Hungarian Film Week, Budapest, Feb. 12, 1985. Runing time: **102 MINS.**

Imre Tanyir . . . . Peter Andorai
Jozsef Banffy . . . . Jan Nowicki
Sandor Sebök . . . . György Cserhalmi
Balint Sebök . . . . Karoly Eperjes
Denes Banffy . . . . Denes Ujlaky
Gabor . . . . Janos Derzsi

An interesting tale, set in Hungary around the turn of the century, "To See The Light" is marred by rather self-conscious, pretentious direction.

A small landowner, Jozsef Banffy, leaves his house and farm to a peasant boy rather than to his family before he commits suicide. Some 16 years later, Imre, the peasant, becomes involved with a movement to educate and radicalize his fellow peasants. This brings him into conflict with the authorities, and eventually his land is confiscated by the state. He winds up in a state of acute melancholia.

The film has an exceptionally strong cast of some of Hungary's finest actors. Peter Andorai is the tormented Imre, while the charismatic György Cserhalmi is a peasant killed by a soldier during a demonstration at the farm. Karoly Eperjes, another popular thesp, plays a man tortured by the military for his political beliefs.

The trouble with the film is that director Ferenc Grunwalsky's penchant for gigantic closeups and shaky hand-held camera make the pic visually irritating and confusing.
— *Strat.*

Uramisten
(The Philadelphia Attraction)
(HUNGARIAN-COLOR)

Budapest, Feb. 11.

A Hunnia Studio, Mafilm, production. Directed by Peter Gardos. Features entire cast. Screenplay, Andras Osvat, Gardos; camera (Eastmancolor), Tibor Maté; music, Janos Novak; editor, Maria Rigo; art director, Pal Lovas; sound, Gyula Traub; costumes, Zsuzsa Pataki. Reviewed at Hungarian Film Week, Budapest, Feb. 10, 1985. Running time: **94 MINS.**

Lipot Bindor . . . . Kamill Felekl
Oszkar Sajek . . . . Karoly Eperjes
Simi . . . . György Dörner
Boldi . . . . Deszö Garas
Dudi . . . . Denes Ujlaky
Mrs. Dudi . . . . Vera Pap
The girl . . . . Juli Nyako
The mother . . . . Nora Tabori
The waiter . . . . Laszlo Csakanyi

Basically a two-hander, "The Philadelphia Attraction" is about a warm relationship between an elderly recluse and an ambitious young man. The old-timer, Lipot, was once a famous illusionist; now he locks himself away in a hotel room, seeing few people. The young man, Oszkar, is a would-be illusionist, who desperately seeks the formula for a great trick Lipot performed many years earlier.

In the end, Lipot dies without having revealed his secret — or has he? The denouement is original and touching.

This is a modest, but attractive film. Its main strength lies in the two excellent central performances, Kamill Felekl as old Lipot and Karoly Eperjes (seen last year in "Light Physical Injuries") as the go-getting Oszkar. The warm relationship of this odd couple is depicted affectionately by debuting director Peter Gardos.

The original title properly translates as "My God." — *Strat.*

Partenaires
(Partners)
(FRENCH-COLOR)

Paris, Jan. 31.

I.D. Films release of a Dedalus/FR3/Viscache Inc. coproduction. Produced by Henry Lange. Directed by Claude d'Anna. Screenplay, d'Anna, Laure Bonin. Camera (color), Pierre Dupouey; art director, Didier Sainderichin; editor, Kenout Peltier; sound, Gérard Barra, Yves Zlotnicka; makeup, Aida Carange; music; excerpts from Richard Henberger's "Der Openball," sung by Elisabeth Schwartzkopf, and Egisto Macchi's "Sognata Memoria;" production manager, Jean-Marie Bertrand, Michel Moitessier. Reviewed at the Georges V cinema, Paris, Jan. 29, 1985. Running time: **78 MINS.**

Marion Wormser . . . . Nicole Garcia
Gabriel Gallien . . . . . . Jean-Pierre Marielle
Charlie . . . . Michel Galabru
Laurent Tedesco . . . . . . Michel Duchaussoy
Marie-Lou Pasquier . . . . Elisa Servier
Marie-Lou's mother . . . . Jénny Clève
Raymond de Malleret . Alexandre Rignault
Fan . . . . Georges Montillier

"Partenaires" is an adequate telefilm posing as a theatrical feature. Directed by Claude d'Anna from an original script by himself and wife Laure Bonin, it is a conventional backstage drama about a theater couple, played by Nicole Garcia and Jean-Pierre Marielle.

Screen time and real time are the same, as the two play out their strained relationship during final half of a hit Boulevard comedy in which they are appearing. She is the costar with the piece's preeningly mediocre author (Michel Duchaussoy). He has a bit part and spends the rest of the performance nursing a bottle in their dressing room.

He seems bitter about his former glory as a tragedian and disappointed that Garcia has renounced her ambitions for tinsel commercial success. Their behind-the-scenes bickering is interrupted and mediated by their fellow players, and the theater's timid house manager (Michel Galabru).

Some well-observed scripting and dialog are marred by the injection of a Dark Secret that explains the couple's alienation, but the performances are fine (notably Marielle) while o'Anna nicely evokes the long-run blues and tension of legit celebrity. Lensing and art direction are a plus, but film's best bet is on the home screen.—*Len.*

La Terra In Due
(Land In Two)
(WEST GERMAN-DUTCH-DOCU-COLOR-B&W-16m)

Amsterdam, Jan. 21.

A Casa Film production. Produced by Rosemarie Blank and Frans van de Staak. Written and directed by Blank. Camera (color, 16m), Ali Reza Mohaved, Blank; editor, Jan Dop, Blank; sound, Karl Baumgartner; sound, Piotr van Dijk; music, Rosanna and Oliviero Barbanera. Reviewed at the Filmtheater Desmet, Amsterdam, Jan. 18, 1985. Running time: **82 MINS.**

German-Dutch Rosemarie Blank's first major docu is set in the high plain of Tuscany. Subject is the effect of technical and economic developments on the traditional peasant culture of the area. Title alludes to the conflict between landowners and peasants.

Pic, which will be of interest to ethnologists and docu film buffs, is a natural for the fest circuit and smallscreen playoff. Topnotch cinematography means it will lend itself to a 35m blowup.

Blank established contact with her Tuscan subjects some 10 years back. She incorporates early b&w super 8m material featuring family gatherings, special occasions and daily life into the movie, along with contemporary comments by the people involved.

Formal framing and editing give the pic resonance and mark "La Terra In Due" as a well-judged piece of filmmaking.—*Wall.*

Crimen en Familia
(Family Crime)
(SPANISH-COLOR)

Madrid, Feb. 9.

A Multivideo Producciones film. Directed by Santiago San Miguel. Screenplay, Gonzalo Goicoechea, San Miguel, Perla Vonasek; exec producers Isabel Mulá and José Maria Cunillés; camera (Fujicolor), José G. Galisteo; editor, José Salcedo; sets, Igancio Acarregui; direct sound, José Nogueira. Reviewed at Imagfic screening room (Madrid), Feb. 8, 1985. Running time: **92 MINS.**

Nuria . . . . Charo López
Costa . . . . Agustin González
Mariana . . . . Cristina Marsillach
Also with: Francisco Casares, Sandra Toral, Francisco Merino, Conchita Leza, Javier Garcia, José Coimenero.

Based on an incident that happened in Barcelona, "Family Crime" is a frontal attack upon a tyrannical and cruel type of paterfamilias such as is particularly associated with the years of the dictatorship. Such monsters, of course, exist in all societies, and the Hispanic model chosen here is probably no worse than that found in other countries.

Costa, the anti-hero of the yarn, is a self-made man who has risen to power and wealth by working hard and investing shrewdly in real estate and construction. He has nothing but contempt for the weak and frail, and stalks his domains, domestic and professional, like a tiger in the jungle.

On the domestic side, he has a servile wife, who nonetheless is carrying on an affair, and four children whom he brutalizes; he wants to be loved, but is only hated. His contempt, in fact, extends to his family: his wife (Charo López), useful only to sate his seemingly incessant sexual desires; and his children, weak, spineless creatures, all of whom, except one daughter, are cowed by his presence. Politically, Costa is a member of the extreme rightwing Fuerza Nueva group (now disbanded); he always carries a gun and has a bodyguard.

The family decides to take its vengeance upon the tyrant and in a somewhat anticlimactic scene, the favorite daughter gets up the courage to pull the trigger as he's sleeping. Final scene, during a fulsome Mass, indicates "terrorists" have been accused of the murder and the family has got off free, a rather unbelievable denouement. The moral? Domestic tyrants may be shot with all moral justification. Maybe the police will shut one eye — or will they?

Gonzalez and López turn in fine performances; direction is matter-of-fact, direct sound faulty and script rather too episodic. Item may do okay domestically, though criticism from conservative sectors is bound to be vociferous. —*Besa*.

The Second Spring Of Old Muo
(TAIWANESE-COLOR)

Hong Kong, Jan. 7.
A Shaw Brothers Release. Directed by Li Yu Ning. Stars Sun Yueh, Chang Shaun Fang, Chen Chen Lei, Chang Pei Hsin. Screenplay, Wu Nien Chien. (No other credits provided by producer and releasing company). Reviewed at Shaw Bros. Studios, Jan. 5, 1985. Running time: **100 MINS.**
(Mandarin soundtrack with Chinese and English subtitles.)

When Old Muo got discharged from military service after 20 years he discovered his wife and son had died in Mainland China and his foster son, whom he helped educate, is now in America with a foreign wife and no plans of returning home. Muo is lonely and alone. His only friend, also a retired military man, has decided to marry a young bride, a bought and paid for aborigine girl about 17.

Inspired by the idea that he can also find happiness in his advancing years and possibly have a son, Muo arranges for a wife, also an aborigine, called Ku. Due to a generation and cultural gap, the initial stages of the marriage are bumpy. There are many misunderstandings, petty jealousies and bitterness, but also occasional laughter.

Slowly, the link between husband and wife, despite the huge age gap, diminishes. With a baby son about to be delivered, an even stronger bond is created between Muo and Ku as the problems of domesticity are solved. They finally find true happiness and it seems Old Muo's second spring is just beginning.

This film was accorded best movie at the recent Golden Horse Awards and deserves it. Sun Yueh, an actor of great dramatic range, can express subtle changes of thoughts and feelings without seeming to do anything special. His underdog look and sympathetic movements arouse audience empathy and he is superb in his role as Old Muo

(which earned him best actor award in the Golden Horse competition).
Director Li Yu Ning has a compassionate feel for people and "Old Muo" projects true emotions and realism.—*Mel*.

Takin' It Off
(COLOR)

Mild striptease feature.

A Hansen & Gervasoni Prods. presentation. Produced by Robert T. Gervasoni. Directed by Ed Hansen. Stars Kitten Natividad. Screenplay, Bob Canning, Hansen; camera (Foto Kem color), Eric Maxwell; editor, Hansen; music arranged by Don Ralke; songs, Ralke, Hansen, Gervasoni, Casey Anderson, Billy Adems; John Thomas, The Muglestons; sound, David Ray Bould; art direction, Billy Proud; assistant director, A.C. Hyatt. Reviewed on Vestron Video cassette, N.Y., Feb. 1, 1985. (No MPAA Rating.) Running time: **89 MINS.**
With: Kitten Natividad (Betty), Angelique Pettyjohn (Anita Little), Adam Hadum, Ashley St. John, Lucia, The Velvet Odyssey, Susie Stewart, Helen Crookes, Juliet Laurel, Nancy Smalley, Luretta McCray, Leslie Liberty, Judith Marlyn, Rudy de la Mor, Robert Charles, Sam Strong, Manuel Felix, Little Joe Shaver, Will S. Raymond.

"Takin' It Off" is a throwback to the nudie-cutie films of two decades ago, showcasing several ecdysiasts doing their peeling routines. Unreleased theatrically, feature is a mildly diverting homevideo entry.
Star Kitten Natividad, well-known through her Russ Meyer films, reteams with director Ed Hansen, who piloted her somewhat satirical 1983 workout tape "Eroticise." Portraying Betty Bigwons (spelling is a guess), she has fun lampooning her image in an absurd storyline: she must lose three inches around her massive bustline in order to qualify for a spot on a tv series. This takes Betty to Dr. Buzz Raunchy's diet institute, to psychiatrist-exorcist Dr. Lucifer Chaser and ultimately to Fosdick's Fat Farm. Meanwhile, the Little Playhouse, a striptease club run by Anita Little (Angelique Pettyjohn) is carrying on minus its star attraction.

Pic features okay dancing, a variety of stripping segments (including a young woman who features a Jim Henson-style puppet in her act christened The Nookie Monster) and some rather strained burlesk-style humor. Nudity is plentiful of course, while the softcore sex content would probably qualify, just barely, for an X rating if submitted for same. The disco-style title song is played four times through during the padded running time.
—*Lor*.

Tigers In Lipstick
(Letti Selvaggi)
(ITALIAN-COLOR)

A Zodiac (Rome) production. Produced by Giorgio Salvioni. Directed by Luigi Zampa. Stars Ursula Andress, Laura Antonelli, Sylvia Kristel, Monica Vitti. Screenplay, Tonino Guerra, Salvioni; camera (color), Giuseppe Ruzzolini, Armando Nannuzzi; editor, Franco Fraticelli; music, Riz Ortolani; English dialog direction by Lewis E. Ciannelli; production manager, Ennio Onorati; art direction, Elena Poccetto Ricci. Reviewed on Monterey Home Video cassette, N.Y., Feb. 5, 1985. (No MPAA Rating.) Running time: **83 MINS.**
With: Ursula Andress, Laura Antonelli, Sylvia Kristel, Monica Vitti, Orazio Orlando, Michele Placido, Jose Sacristan, Roberto Benigni, Enrico Beruschi, Jose Luis Lopez Vasquez.

"Tigers In Lipstick," which has gone through various title changes including "Wild Beds" and "Hijinks," is a made-in-1979 Italian throwback to the multi-part sex comedies that flourished in the early 1960s. Okay film is interesting for never having obtained a U.S. theatrical distributor, instead belatedly surfacing via homevideo after rights were acquired by Julian Schlossberg's Castle Hill Prods.

Lack of U.S. theatrical release can probably be traced to the fact that Laura Antonelli, then at the peak of her U.S. popularity, does not disrobe in the film. Nudity is provided by Sylvia Kristel, but overall package tips the balance towards comedy, neglecting the obvious voyeuristic potential of the material (which remains an important factor for European imports, even those of the arthouse variety).

Seven segments of various lengths emphasize the woman as aggressor, with various Continental actors and comics playing second fiddle to the attractive leading ladies. Most effective routine is "The Pickup," in which Antonelli has a field day as a nonstop businesswoman who makes an assignation with a young orchestra conductor who approaches her on the street, but keeps putting him off and getting him into slapstick situations as she runs around wheeling and dealing with lawyers, real estate men, etc. Unfortunately, this funny seg ends abruptly, lacking a satisfying or ironic payoff.

Monica Vitti is also amusing in "The Shell Game," getting to pose as a nun and as a doddering old lady as she competes with Michele Placido in trying to steal an expensive necklace from a lady at a casino. Kristel is lovely but wooden in her turns, while Ursula Andress is the sexiest performer in the film. As with Antonelli, Andress avoids nude footage.

Vet neorealist director ("To Live In Peace," etc.) Luigi Zampa is merely marking time here, with film helped by a bouncy Riz Ortolani score.—*Lor*.

The G.I. Executioner
(Wit's End)
(COLOR)

Oddball but ingratiating B-actioner.

A Troma Team release, presented by Lloyd Kaufman and Michael Herz. A Lion City Prods. Ltd. production. Executive producer-production supervisor, Michael Renard. Produced by Marvin Farkas. Directed by Joel M. Reed. Features entire cast. Screenplay, Reed, from story by Keith Lorenz and Ian Ward; camera (Cineffects color), Farkas; editor, Victor Kanefsky; music, Elliot Chiprut, Jason Garfield; sound, Gary Leibman, Stephen Szabo; assistant director, Brian Walden; production manager, Joseph Zucchero; associate producers, Walter Hoffman, S.M. Chuan. Reviewed at 42d St. Selwyn theater, N.Y., Feb. 8, 1985. (MPAA Rating: R.) Running time: **82 MINS.**
Dave Dearborn . . . . Tom Keena
Foon Mai Lee . . . . Victoria Racimo
Bonnie . . . . Angelique Pettyjohn
Also with: Janet Wood, Brian Walden, Peter Gernert, Walter Hill, Jonathan Grant.

Though purportedly in its New York debut (hence this review for the record) "The G.I. Executioner" is actually an entertaining low-budget vault item, having been rated by the Motion Picture Assn. of America way back in 1971 under the title "Wit's End" (that title is retained in a theme song played twice). Picture was previously handled under the title "Dragon Lady" by Joseph Green Pictures for distribution, apparently quite limited, and is now a Troma pickup with new monicker.

Falling comfortably within the Far East, Soldier of Fortune format, pic toplines Tom Keena as Dave Dearborn, an ex-Marine who later excelled at undercover journalistic assignments in the 1960s in Saigon and elsewhere. Now running a restaurant aboard a junk in Singapore, he is tapped to track down a defecting Red Chinese nuclear scientist (experimenting with antimatter) who may have been kidnaped by the Triad Tong. Key suspect is gangster Lim Tok Sing, whose current Chinese concubine, Foon Mai Lee (Victoria Racimo), is an ex-girlfriend of Dearborn's. Also helping out on the case is sexy stripper Bonnie (Angelique Pettyjohn), while the oversexed Dearborn dallies with his current main squeeze (Janet Wood) whom he calls his "niece."

Nutty foreign intrigue plot (sure enough, the bad guy turns out to be Dearborn's old nemesis from Saigon) is hampered by use of stiff, nonactors in minor roles, but "Executioner" develops a certain charm with its old-fashioned B-film clichés, to which modern ultra-violence and sex have been added. Weird plot turns and melodramatic elements in later reels prove to be entertaining in campy fashion, though dance scenes, hairstyles, etc., have become dated.

Keena, who combines John Garfield's chip-on-shoulder attitude with a voice resembling that of Gene Kelly, is an interesting, tortured *film noir* hero, though he hams up his injured and death scenes laughably in the final reel. The cast's leading ladies are beautiful, in and out of clothing, but Victoria Racimo is not in the least bit Chinese in a role played straight ahead with no make-up. In an odd coincidence, statues-que costar Angelique Pettyjohn had a new film of hers "The Lost Empire" open the same day as this one in New York, nearly bookending a career which ranges from guest starring on "Star Trek" to hardcore porn.

Location lensing in Singapore offers plentiful local color, but tech credits are subpar. —*Lor.*

Mask
(COLOR)

Powerful drama from Peter Bogdanovich.

Hollywood, Feb. 22.

A Universal Pictures release of a Martin Starger production. Produced by Starger. Directed by Peter Bogdanovich. Coproducer, Howard Alston. Stars Cher. Screenplay, Anna Hamilton Phelan, based on the true story of Rocky Dennis; camera (Technicolor), Laszlo Kovacs; editor, Barbara Ford; music, songs by various artists; art director, Norman Newberry; set decorator, Richard J. deCinces; Rocky make-up designer, Michael Westmore; sound, Keith Webster, Crew Chamberlain; assistant director, Katy Emde; associate producer, George Morfogen, Peggy Robertson; casting, Michael Chinich, Jackie Burch. Reviewed at Universal screening room, Universal City, Calif., Feb. 21, 1985. (MPAA Rating: PG-13.) Running time: **120 MINS.**

Rusty Dennis	Cher
Gar	Sam Elliott
Rocky Dennis	Eric Stoltz
Evelyn	Estelle Getty
Abe	Richard Dysart
Diana	Laura Dern
Babe	Micole Mercurio
Red	Harry Carey Jr.
Dozer	Dennis Burkley
Ben	Lawrence Monoson

Anyone looking for a good uplifting cry should be well satisfied by "Mask," Peter Bogdanovich's tale of a deformed, but otherwise normal American teenager. Pic is not a weeper *per se,* but taps human feelings with a depth rarely felt in films. Beautifully acted and executed, "Mask" marks something of a comeback for Bogdanovich, who hasn't directed a film in four years. Favorable word of mouth should overcome any audience resistance and even turn the unusual subject matter to its advantage.

Based on a true story by first-time screenwriter Anna Hamilton Phelan, "Mask" is alive with the rhythms and textures of a unique life. Rocky Dennis (Eric Stoltz) is a 16-year-old afflicted with a rare bone disease which has ballooned his head to twice its normal size and cast the shadow of an early death over him.

Rocky is one of those rare individuals who has a vitality and gift for life and the emphasis here is not on dying, but living. The irony of the title is that his feelings are exposed far more than is customary and his experiences are intensified rather than dulled.

One of the accomplishments of "Mask," and a technique Bogdanovich has been developing throughout his career, is the fullness of the environment it creates. Foremost in that portrait is Rocky's mother Rusty (Cher) and her motorcycle-gang friends. Unlike "The Elephant Man," Rocky is by no means a solitary character and his unconventional relationship with his mother amplifies his humanity.

Both in the background and foreground, "Mask" draws a vivid picture of life among a particular type of lower middle class Southern California whites. Rusty is a woman who could only be described as having been around the block. Tough and brassy on the outside, she is more vulnerable than her son and, when her feelings become too painful, she resorts to drugs, which becomes a sore-point in their relationship.

Bogdanovich presents this community of outcasts with a good deal of compassion, and people who are usually dismissed in films as just weird, are shown to be warm and caring people.

The other man in Rusty's life is biker Gar. Played beautifully by Sam Elliott, he is a no-nonsense man with a weathered wisdom and rock-solid presence. With a minimum of dialog, Elliott is able to communicate his love for both Rocky and his mother. The fruit of human kindness extends to the other bikers as well, including a near-mute brute with a heart of gold (Dennis Burkley) and the patriarch of the group (Harry Carey Jr.). This is Rocky's family and he is really the center of their universe.

Rocky's positive attitude towards life despite his fate makes his attempt to have a normal life — go to school, have a girlfriend, explore the world — touching without being overly sentimental for the most part.

There are easily several points in the film when the tear ducts could start working. Extremely moving is Rocky's love affair when he goes away to summer camp for the blind and falls for Diana (Laura Dern). For her part, Dern is able to communicate her own vulnerability and longing for human contact.

It's a delicate balance between sympathy and bathos and for the most part Bogdanovich manages the trick. There are, however, isolated instances where the simple givens of the situation become too easy a way to evoke emotion, rather than earning it.

Much of the credit for keeping the film from tripping over must go to the cast, especially Stoltz, who, with only his eyes visible behind an elaborate makeup job (by Michael Westmore), brings a lively, life-affirming personality to his role without a trace of self-pity. Equally fine is Cher, who perfectly suggests a hard exterior covering a wealth of conflicting and confused feelings.

Kudos also to cinematographer Laszlo Kovacs whose deep focus photography captures the movement and pulse of this little community. Phelan's script is sharp and crisp with an ear for her people.

—*Jagr.*

Tranches de Vie
(Slices Of Life)
(FRENCH-COLOR)

Paris, Feb. 21.

An AAA release of a Films Ariane production. Produced by Alexandre Mnouchkine and Georges Dancigers. Directed by François Leterrier. Features entire cast. Screenplay, Gérard Lauzier; camera (Eastmancolor), Eduardo Serra; art director, Eric Moulard; editor, Claudine Bouché; sound, J. Charles Ruault and Jean Labussier; music, Jean-Claude Pettit. Reviewed at the Marignan-Concorde theater, Paris, Feb. 20, 1985. Running time: **93 MINS.**

With: Laura Antonelli, Michel Boujenah, Jean-Pierre Cassel, Christian Clavier, Jean-Pierre Darroussin, Gérard Jugnot, Luis Rego, Catherine Alric, Marie-Anne Chazel, Pierre Mondy, Roland Giraud, Daniel Prevost, Jean Rougerie, Josiane Balasko, Michel Galabru, Laurence Badie, Anémone, Martin Lamotte, Barbara Nielsen, Hubert Deschamps, John Levis, Constantin Kotlarow, Ginette Garcin, Pierre Richard.

Cartoonist-filmmaker Gérard Lauzier sits out his latest comedy as scripter only, leaving the directing chores to François Leterrier, whose helming is only as good as the material. Since "Slices Of Life" is a sketch film, quality of both tend to vary widely.

Lauzier's 11 playlets range from sex farce to political black comedy; a few are of blackout sketch duration, others are developed at length. Writer is more at ease sticking pins into the pretensions and prejudices of the French than in spoofing genre films or knocking military dictatorship.

There are a few nuggets in this grabbag. Funniest is "Paris Will Always Be Paris," a bright sendup of French xenophobia. A journalist on assignment in densely populated immigrant quarter of Paris interviews a young French housewife (Josiane Balasko) whose family has thoroughly assimilated the mores and manners of its neighbors. She wears traditional African garments, calls her son Mohammed (his classmates made fun of his real name, Jean-Pierre) and concludes: no racism here — the French are accepted.

Lauzier mocks France's Moral Majority in a segment in which an average provincial couple (Michel Galabru and Laurence Badie) is interviewed for tv about its sexual and social attitudes. Another amusing sketch lays into male cowardice in the tale of a young man who, weighed down with both provincial and Paris girlfriends, tries to dump one in order to marry the other, but instead gets married to both and finally bagged for bigamy. Lauzier is either less inspired or totally out of his element in most of the remaining items.

Cast, including many names from café-theater milieu, is spirited, and comic Pierre Richard drops in, rather pointlessly, for a flash cameo at the end. — *Len.*

The Sure Thing
(COLOR)

Sweetly comic coming-of-age/road pic.

Hollywood, Feb. 14.

An Embassy Pictures release of an Embassy Films Associates presentation of a Monument Pictures production. Produced by Roger Birnbaum. Executive producer, Henry Winkler. Directed by Rob Reiner. Coproduced by Andrew Scheinman. Features entire cast. Screenplay, Steven L. Bloom, Jonathan Roberts; camera (Deluxe color), Robert Elswit; editor, Robert Leighton; music, Tom Scott; production designer, Lilly Kilvert; set decorator, Lisa Fischer; costumes, Durinda Wood; sound, Bob Eber; assistant director, Thomas Lofaro; casting, Janet Jenkins, Janet Hirshenson. Reviewed at Embassy screening room, L.A., Calif. Feb. 13, 1985. (MPAA Rating: PG-13.) Running time: **94 MINS.**

Walter (Gib) Gibson	John Cusack
Alison Bradbury	Daphne Zuniga
Lance	Anthony Edwards
Jason	Boyd Gaines
Gary Cooper	Tim Robbins
Mary Ann Webster	Lisa Jane Persky
Prof. Taub	Viveca Lindfors
The Sure Thing	Nicollette Sheridan
Truck driver	Larry Hankin

Surrounded with the trappings of the omnipresent youth comedy, ''The Sure Thing'' is at heart a sweetly old fashioned look at the last lap of the coming-of-age ordeal in which the sure thing becomes less important than the real thing. Realization may not be earth shattering, but in an era of fast food and faster sex, return to the traditional is downright refreshing. Approach should prove appealing to young adults as well as more thoughtful teens.

Borrowing its form from classic road comedies like ''It Happened One Night,'' ''The Sure Thing'' uses the clash of opposites to deliver its message that love may be a more powerful force than lust. Unlike most contempo sex comedies, script by Steven L. Bloom and Jonathan Roberts takes the time to develop sympathetic and basically believable characters.

Gib (John Cusack) is a beer guzzling junk food devotee with a flair for the outrageous, but he is not having much luck with the opposite sex in his freshman year at an eastern Ivy League college. One of the women he strikes out with is Alison (Daphne Zuniga), a prim and proper coed who thinks that spontaneity is a social disease. The plot thickens as they both arrange a ride, unbeknownst to each other, with a California bound couple for the Christmas break. Gib is off to score with the sure thing (Nicollette Sheridan) while Alison is visiting her boorish boyfriend (Boyd Gaines).

Stranded together, the two travelers mix like oil and water, volatile at first and gradually realizing that their different personalities complement each other. Chemistry between Cusack and Zuniga is a plus as they change and grow together as the film progresses.

Initially given to pranks like jumping into the pool with his clothes on, Gib must learn to think of someone else besides himself. For her part Alison learns to have fun and becomes more likable as she loosens up. Both Cusack and Zuniga are fine.

While film takes some easy shots and the outcome is never in doubt, there are enough original and amusing bits to keep the audience going. Off-key serenade of showtunes from Tim Robbins and Lisa Jane Persky in the car heading west supplies the same daffy humor director Rob Reiner brought to his mock documentary, ''This Is Spinal Tap.''

Reiner also throws in some east coast jabs at California that have become stereotypes and lack the bite Woody Allen brings to the same territory. As the freewheeling Professor Taub, Viveca Lindfors is equally trite and overstated.

Technically pic looks fine and has a number of well-placed rock tunes sprinkled throughout. Cinematography by Robert Elswit is crisp despite one nagging visual inconsistency. Why do these kids travel on only the most scenic two-lane blacktops instead of super-highways? —*Jagr.*

Péril en la Demeure
(Danger In The House)
(FRENCH-COLOR)

Paris, Feb. 22.

A Gaumont release of a Gaumont/Elefilm/TF-1 Films coproduction. Produced by Emmanuel Schlumberger. Exec producer-screenplay collaborator-assistant director, Rosalinde Damamme. Written and directed by Michel Deville, based on the novel ''Sur la Terre Comme au Ciel'' by René Belletto. Camera (Eastmancolor), Martial Thury; sound, André Hervée, Alain Sempé, Claude Villand, Joel Beldent; editor, Raymonde Guyot; art director, Philippe Combastel; music, Brahms, Granados, Schubert; production manager, Franz Damamme. Reviewed at the Marignan-Concorde theater, Paris, Feb. 21, 1985. Running time: **100 MINS.**

David Aurphet	Christophe Malavoy
Julia Tombsthay	Nicole Garcia
Graham Tombsthay	Michel Piccoli
Edwige Ledieu	Anémone
Daniel Forest	Richard Bohringer
Vivianne Tombsthay	Anais Jeanneret

''Péril en la Demeure'' is a sleek drama of eroticism and murder from Michel Deville, who is finally earning the commercial success that has evaded his last few films, including ''Deep Water,'' a failed attempt to adapt a Patricia Highsmith novel.

Based on a French novel, ''Péril'' finds the tone of disturbing ambiguity and perversity missing in ''Deep Water,'' though the conventional, overexplicit denouement dilutes the overall effect. Still for most of its length, pic intrigues by its camera virtuosity, cryptic dialog and shadowy characterizations.

Christophe Malavoy is an unsuspecting guitar instructor hired by a well-heeled suburban couple (Nicole Garcia and Michel Piccoli) to give lessons to their teenage daughter. Latter is nubile and seemingly attracted to Malavoy, but mother Garcia is quicker on the sexual draw and beds the young man in no time, visiting him at his Paris loft.

Malavoy drifts on the erotic currents, not overly concerned with the apparent complicity of Garcia's husband or the prying of a voyeuristic neighbor (Anémone). Complications arise when videocassette recordings of their trysts are mailed to the lovers.

A new element in the drama comes in the form of a professional killer (Richard Bohringer), who saves Malavoy from a mugger and befriends him, apparently out of homosexual impulse. Bohringer soon admits he has a contract out on Piccoli, and warns Malavoy about his involvement.

Deville's direction is stealthy and stylish, aided by Martial Thury's gliding camera and Raymonde Guyot's sly editing, which enforce the feeling of deepening insecurity. Fine use of limpid themes by Brahms, Schubert and Granados offer contrast to the unsettling events that climax in Malavoy's apparent murder of Piccoli.

Garcia brings her own flavor to the conventional femme fatale. Her love scenes with Malavoy are quietly effective (but will disappoint voyeurs who expect their screen sex torrid and graphic).

Rest of the cast is solid, notably Bohringer, whose performance as a hired killer who engineers his own death is fascinating. His ''suicide'' recalls Alain Delon's death scene in Jean-Pierre Melville's 1967 thriller classic, ''Le Samourai.''—*Len.*

Fraternity Vacation
(COLOR)

Standard youthful hijinks.

Hollywood, Feb. 22.

A New World Pictures release. Produced by Robert C. Peters. Coproducer, Boris Malden. Executive producer, Larry Thompson. Directed by James Frawley. Features entire cast. Screenplay, Lindsay Harrison; camera (CFI color), Paul Ryan; editor, Chris Nelson; music, Brad Fiedel; production design, Roberta Neiman; set decoration, Don Elmblad; costume design, Tracy Tynan; sound, Art Names; assistant director, Bill Carroll; additional photography, Bryan England; casting, Annette Benson. Reviewed at the UA Warner Center, Woodland Hills, Calif., Feb. 22, 1985. (MPAA Rating: R.) Running time: **93 MINS.**

Wendall Tvedt	Stephen Geoffreys
Ashley Taylor	Sheree J. Wilson
Joe Gillespie	Cameron Dye
Charles Lawlor 3d	Leigh McCloskey
Mother	Tim Robbins
J.C. Springer	Matt McCoy
Chief Ferret	John Vernon
Yvette	Britt Ekland
Mrs. Ferret	Nita Talbot

It's all play and no work for the boys and girls in ''Fraternity Vacation,'' an amiable enough little sex farce from New World. Neither wildly gross nor unbearably funny, pic nevertheless maintains a cheerful attitude throughout as the singleminded teenage characters pursue the opposite sex with all the subtlety of dogs checking each other out. This should do okay biz in the expected quick playoff situations.

Film's working titles of ''Party Party Party'' and ''Beginner's Luck'' are evident on a placard brandished by a reveler and in the end-title song, respectively. Either would have been just as appropriate as the one finally chosen, as the confection sees three wide-eyed Iowa State frat boys abandon a blizzard for a Palm Springs weekend filled with t&a gazing and bikini chasing.

Nerdy Stephen Geoffreys (recently seen as the perpetually horny youth in ''Heaven Help Us'') gets into no end of trouble since the father of the nice girl he courts is none other than local police chief John Vernon. Most of the running time is given over to the strenuous efforts made by his two buddies and a pair of rival frat brothers to bed blond goddess Sherre J. Wilson. It comes as no great shock at the end that the innocent Geoffreys should be the one on whom the beauteous Wilson finally bestows her favors, to the amazement of the other fellows.

Working within the narrow parameters of the yawningly familiar genre, writer Lindsay Harrison and director James Frawley have at least made a noticeable attempt to portray some relatively companionable characters and vaguely believable human emotions here and there, and to this end they are well served by a decent young cast.

On the other hand, the Palm Springs police department won't be too pleased by what Vernon does for its reputation, as his strongarm tactics seem more appropriate to the South of ''The Phenix City Story'' or ''Walking Tall'' than to this land of jacuzzis and Mercedes. Prominently billed with a ''special appearance'' card, Britt Ekland is in for about 30 seconds as a cocktail waitress.

Little-used desert locations look good, as do the well-shaped and occasionally undraped bodies on display. The numerous pop tunes, including three from Bananarama, are all bouncy. — *Cart.*

Caught At The Berlinale

Tokyo Saiban
(The Tokyo Trial)
(JAPANESE-DOCU-B&W)

Berlin, Feb. 18.

A Kodansha Ltd. Production. Produced by Hiroshi Suto, Masaya Araki. Executive producer, Tadakatsu Mitsumori. Directed by Masaki Kobayashi. Screenplay, Kobayashi, Ryu Yasutake, Kiyoshi Ogasawara, based on original material by Shun Inagaki; editor, Kelichi Uraoka; sound, Hideo Mishizaki; music, Toru Takemitsu; narrators in English version, Stuart Atkin, Frank Rogers (original Japanese narrator, Kei Sato). Reviewed at Berlin Film Festival (out of competition), Feb. 17, 1985. Running time: **265 MINS.**

This extraordinary historical document, which makes exemplary use of archive newsreel footage, is an exhaustive account of the court proceedings held by the Intl. Military Tribunal for the Far East between May 1946 and November 1948. On trial were 28 top Japanese officials charged with war crimes, crimes against humanity, conspiracy and aggression; they were selected from 100 alleged war criminals (there was only room for 28 chairs in the courtroom, hence the actual number charged), the most famous among them being former Prime Minister Hideki Tojo.

Director Masaki Kobayashi and his team culled 30,000 reels of film and viewed 170 hours of material before settling on the trial footage included here. They have also augmented the trial scenes themselves with background historical footage, going back to the Russo-Japanese War of 1904 and lucidly explaining such little-known (in the West) events as the establishment of an "independent" Manchurian state (carved out of Chinese territory) in the mid-30s as well as events leading up to the conflict. Kobayashi completes the perspective by including key events taking place outside Asia, but always from a Japanese perspective; these include the rise of fascism and Nazism in Italy and Germany, the invasion of Poland by Germany, the Hitler-Stalin pact, and so on.

Mostly, the film concerns the trial itself, presided over by an international team of judges headed by Australian Sir William Webb, Chief Justice of the State of Queensland. Prosecution team was headed by American Joseph B. Keenan. Because the accused were unfamiliar with Anglo-American court proceedings, they were given American defense councils, who frequently clashed with the crusty Webb. Trial started off with a minor sensation when one of the accused, Okawa, suddenly caused a disturbance by hitting the prisoner in front of him; he was hauled away to a mental hospital. Three other prisoners died before the trial was completed.

Statistics are immense: it took two days to read the indictment and the reading of the final judgments took a week. Kobayashi is extremely selective in his use of material, but he makes a compulsive drama out of it all. He's no stranger to epic-length films about Japan's recent past; his extraordinary nine-hour "The Human Condition" (1959-61) ranks as one of the greatest pacifist films ever made. Here it's often the small details that impress: a Japanese official doffs his hat, and a piece of paper falls out of it onto the floor; the judges are caught napping or looking desperately bored; an MP removes a prisoner's headphone before he's finished listening to a translation, and he angrily snatches it back.

Some may feel Kobayashi is soft on the military men and politicians who led Japan into war, but as is pointed out, these things have also to be considered from an Asian perspective; there's an underlying touch of racism to the trial proceedings, probably to be expected at this time. Another problem facing the court was Gen. MacArthur's political decision not to charge Emperor Hirohito, or allow him to testify, a decision which apparently riled Webb and other judges.

The film ends with a coda reminding the viewer of other world events since World War II — of Hungary and Czechoslovakia, of Vietnam and the nuclear arms race. The point is well taken.

The film's English version runs 265 minutes (the fest program had it incorrectly at 310 minutes which may cause confusion in the future). Part 1 timed at 129 minutes and, following an interval, Part 2 came in at 136 minutes. It's a lot of film to sit through, but well worth the effort for a unique perspective on history. — *Strat*.

It Don't Pay To Be An Honest Citizen
(U.S.-COLOR-16m)

Comedy-thriller fails to thrill.

Berlin, Feb. 17.

A film by Object Prods., N.Y. Directed, photographed (color), and edited by Jacob Burckhardt. Screenplay, Burckhardt, Rochelle Kraut, Reed Bye; music, Hugh Lovick; sound, Corry Soeterboek, Ulrich Killian, John Baumann, Rene Witcentsen, Toshiko Chuma. Produced with a grant from the Jerome Foundation. Reviewed within Special Screenings, Berlin Intl. Film Festival, Feb. 16, 1985. (No MPAA Rating.) Running time: **85 MINS.**

Warren	Reed Bye
Sidney, the lawyer	Allen Ginsberg
Mafia Don	William Burroughs
Anita	Mary Tepper

This comedy — based on true events that occured to its director — should have been less faithful to its original sources and instead more inventive. Autobiographical fragments do not a feature make.

Burckhardt is making his feature debut after 17 years of low-budget amateur shorts, having secured a grant of $25,000 from the Jerome Foundation in St. Paul.

Storyline is not so much a plot as an undeveloped situation, a premise that fails to build to complication and resolution. For a crime film, this can be a deadly fault, especially if comedy is intended.

Young cinéaste Warren is mugged late one night, losing cash but also his precious can of film. Warren begins an odyssey within Brooklyn's underworld, trying to track down and retrieve the film. Police, friends, neighbors, even the muggers and their pals, variously advise, threaten, misinform and delude Warren, who by film's end, as the harassed victim, exemplifies the film's title and moral — it don't pay to be an honest citizen. Warren never gets back his film, but in a sense he has undergone an education — about crime but not punishment.

Poet Allen Ginsberg, in an engaging cameo role, performs with sly mockery as a dubious attorney. Avant-garde artist and filmmaker Rudy Burckhardt, father of the director, also appears briefly as a demented bum. In a third cameo, William Burroughs as an aging Mafia don tries to make sense of Warren's lost-film problem and finally orders him to accept the loss, quit complaining and "take it on the chin."—*Hitch*.

Screamplay
(U.S.-B&W-16m)

Indie horror-comedy tries hard but fails.

Berlin, Feb. 18.

A Boston Movie Co. Production, produced by Dennis M. Piana. Directed by Rufus Butler Seder. Screenplay by Seder and Ed Greenberg; camera (b&w, 16m), Piana; editor Seder; art director, Cheryl Hirschman; sound, Flip Johnson, Theodore Braun; music, George Cordeiro, Basil J. Bova; special effects, Johnson, Eugene Seder. Reviewed at Information Program, Berlin Intl. Film Festival, Feb. 18, 1985. Running time: **90 MINS.**

Edgar Allen	Rufus Butler Seder
Martin	George Kucher
Holly	Katy Bolger
Sgt. Joe Blatz	George Cordeiro
Tony Cassano	Basil J. Bova
Mina Ray	M. Lynda Robinson
Al Weiner	Eugene Seder

The screams of "Screamplay" are intended to be both screams of horror and screams of comic delight, in the tradition of parodies of comedy-horror for initiated audiences. The cast and crew double and triple in various functions, suggesting a small zealous production team of amateurs. They obviously try hard and enjoy their collaboration. However, the film's zany premises and sight gags soon wear thin. Screams become yawns halfway through the film.

Storyline of "Screamplay" centers on aspiring writer of murder films, Edgar Allen, acted by director/co-scenarist/editor Rufus Butler Seder. He comes to Hollywood as a naive idealist, finds employment as a janitor in the macabre Welcome Apartments, and soon is involved innocently in a series of strange comic murders, perpetrated per his own purloined movie script. Other characters are comic stereotypes from Hollywood's seamy pool of leftovers, dropouts and neverweres.

"Screamplay" may have a minor future within that specialized big-city circuit that distributes midnight cult horror-comedies. It opened, self-distributed, last November in Boston. — *Hitch*.

Parker
(BRITISH-COLOR)

Berlin, Feb. 21.

A Virgin Films Intl. release of a Moving Picture Co. production. Produced by Nigel Stafford-Clark. Directed by Jim Goddard. Stars Bryan Brown, Cherie Lunghi, Kurt Raab. Screenplay, Trevor Preston; camera (Fujicolor), Peter Jessop; editor, Ralph Sheldon; sound, Andrew McAlpine. Reviewed at Berlin Film Festival (out of competition), Feb. 20, 1985. Running time: **96 MINS.**

David Parker	Bryan Brown
Jenny Parker	Cherie Lunghi
Inspector Haag	Kurt Raab
Jillian	Hannelore Elsner
Rohl	Bob Peck
Reich	Phil Smeeton
Andrea	Gwyneth Strong
Richard Parker	Simon Rouse

A strong theatrical debut from a top British tv director ("Callan," "Kennedy," "The Black Stuff"), Jim Goddard's "Parker" is a well-crafted suspense thriller, shot on a low budget but making maximum impact.

David Parker (Bryan Brown) is an Australian businessman based in London with a lovely wife (Cheire Lunghi) and three children. On a business trip to Munich, where he has a mistress (Hannelore Elsner), he's kidnapped by three men and a woman, all masked, but after 11 days as a prisoner, he's released unexpectedly. His wife wasn't asked to pay a ransom, indeed she wasn't contacted at all; nor were his business associates. So why was he kidnapped? The suspicious German cop (Kurt Raab) heading the investigation begins to suspect that maybe he wasn't really kidnaped at all, and eventually his wife begins to suspect the same thing.

It's certainly an intriguing situation, and Parker becomes obsessed to discover the solution. He suspects, rightly, that his mistress was somehow involved, but the more he probes into the case the more mayhem follows in his wake. The mistress is murdered, and so are all the kidnapers. Eventually, the trail leads to Parker's brother, who's involved in drug-running and is in conflict with an international crime syndicate.

Thriller addicts will find this a most satisfying outing. Goddard segues to the big screen with apparent ease, and handles the sometimes complex plot with dexterity. He also packs in a lot of detail and keeps the audience guessing almost all the way.

Brown gives a solid performance as the obsessed, vengeful Parker, while Lunghi registers strongly as his disturbed wife, and Raab makes the police Inspector subtly cynical, even sinister.

Made on a tight six-week shoot (two weeks location work in Germany), "Parker" (shot under the monicker "Bones") is technically fine with fluid lensing by Peter Jessop and an unusual music score by Richard Hartley to underline the action.—*Strat.*

Competing At Berlin

After Darkness
(SWISS-BRITISH-COLOR)

Berlin, Feb. 19.

A T&C Film AG (Zurich)-Green Man Prods.-Philum Inc. coproduction. Produced by Marcel Hoehn. Executive producer, Rudolf Santschi. Directed and written by Dominique Othenin-Girard, Sergio Guerraz. Stars John Hurt. Camera (Eastmancolor), William Lubtchansky; editor, Daniela Roderer; sound, Luc Yerslu; art director, Nicolas Meylan; music, Susanne Pisieur, Giacomo Peier; costumes, Denise Fusco. Reviewed at Berlin Film Festival (in competition), Feb. 19, 1985. Running time: **104 MINS.**

Peter Huninger	John Hurt
Laurence Huninger	Julian Sands
Pascale	Victoria Abril
Elisabeth Huninger	Pamela Salem
Dr. Coles	William Jacques
Twins	Michel & Philippe Herzog

Overwrought melodrama about madness and guilt, "After Darkness" is an English-track Swiss-British coproduction whose chief distinction is yet another socko performance from the prodigious John Hurt.

He plays Peter Huninger, a professor of anthropology, who comes to Geneva where his younger brother, Laurence, has been in an insane asylum, apparently as a result of a severe childhood trauma when his twin brother was killed in a bizarre accident. Peter, against the wishes of his sensible wife, releases his brother and rents a shabby, vast apartment for them to live in.

It soon becomes clear that Peter is just as batty as Laurence, especially when a charming young student (Spanish thesp Victoria Abril) happens on the scene and takes a shine to Laurence. It all ends in murder and retribution, with none of the mystery solved.

Audiences probably won't care much, for writer-directors Dominique Othenin-Girard and Sergio Guerraz have concocted a turgid piece which has a few moments of invention and genuine drama, but which is mostly familiar and overdone dramatics. As a suspense thriller, the pic is not suspenseful or thrilling enough and as a serious psychological drama, it's just silly.

As the disturbed Laurence, Julian Sands copes quite well with an impossible part; Abril shows she can handle English-language roles with confidence and charm; but the film, such as it is, belongs to Hurt, one of the most remarkable film actors around right now and able, during the course of this otherwise unremarkable film, to turn dross into gold. The only mystery is why he accepted such a script in the first place. — *Strat.*

Les Enfants
(The Children)
(FRANCE-COLOR)

Berlin, Feb. 21.

A Ministry of Culture & Les Productions Berthemont production. Produced by Fréderic Vieille. Directed by Marguerite Duras, Jean-Marc Turin, Jean Mascolo (see note). Screenplay, Duras; camera (color), Bruno Nuytten, Pierre Novion, Idislav Kielar; editor, Françoise Belleville; art direction, Annie Senechal, Arnaud de Moleron; costumes, Christian Gasc; sound, Michel Vionnet, Jean-Pierre Fenié; music, Carlos d'Alessio. Reviewed at the Berlin Film Festival (in competition), Feb. 20, 1985. Running time: **94 MINS.**

Ernesto	Alexander Bougosslavsky
Enrico	Daniel Gelin
Natasha	Tatiana Moukhine
Nicole	Martine Chevalier
School director	André Dussolier
Journalist	Pierre Arditi

There is confusion concerning the credits for "Les Enfants:" in one program listing is an additional name, that of Yann Andrea, credited as codirector, another listing skips his name. Prior to the screening, an announcement was made that the production had deleted one credit title from the film, but the festival would show this title separately. It finally turned out to be the directing credit, which accords the honors to Duras, Turin and Mascolo. (Only Duras was credited in Berlin awards. -*Ed.*)

The film is long on static dialog and short on action, but is one of the more entertaining Marguerite Duras has made. She recently received the highly prized Goncourt literary award subsequently becoming a best-selling author.

The script deals with a strange family. The seven-year-old son (played by a 40-year-old adult), decides one day to give up school for he doesn't want to learn things he doesn't know. He has come to the conclusion that listening to pupils discuss their studies for a month or two has been sufficient for him to acquire all the knowledge there is. He strongly believes nothing matters in this godless world.

This is the basis on which Marguerite Duras elaborates her opinion on everything, from pedagogy to faith. For once she has a cast of characters who are more than just spokesmen for the author. They seem to fit quite normally in her absurd scheme, and their daily occupations reflect on human condition as if by accident while the movie focuses on weightier matters.

Acting is highly resourceful, with Daniel Gelin doing his best job in years as the befuddled father, Axel Bougousslavsky lending the grown-up child an aura of sad wisdom which fits in well with the theories he puts forward, and Tatiana Moukhine is the soulful mother who will never deny support to her child.

Technical credits are of a high standard, so is the soundtrack. It may well have strong legs in specialized houses. —*Edna.*

Die Frau und der Fremde
(The Woman And The Stranger)
(EAST GERMAN-COLOR)

Berlin, Feb. 24.

A DEFA Film Production, East Berlin. World sales, DEFA Aussenhandel, East Berlin. Written and directed by Rainer Simon. Features entire cast. Camera (color), Roland Dressel; sets, Hans Poppe; editor, Helga Gentz; music, Rainer Bredemeyer. Reviewed at Berlin Film Fest (in competition), Feb. 23, 1985. Running time: **95 MINS.**

With: Joachim Lätsch (Karl), Kathrin Waligura (Anna), Peter Zimmermann (Richard), Hans-Uwe Bauer, Siegfried Höchst, Katrin Knappe, Ulrich Mühe, Christine Schorn.

Rainer Simon's "Woman And The Stranger," the official East German entry at this year's Berlinale, is based on a short story by Leonhard Frank and comes across as a three-person kammerspiele drama of bruised emotions. The performance by Kathrin Waligura as the woman-in-between is pic's outstanding quality.

("Stranger" shared the fest's Golden Bear Grand Prix award. — *Ed.*)

The setting is towards the end of World War I on the Russian front. German POWs are consigned heavy labor duties, and two of them, Karl and Richard, become good friends — so much so that Richard reveals a wealth of details about his wife, Anna. This is later to lead to one of those weird, but comprehensible situations in which Karl is to assume the identity of Richard upon escaping from the POW camp and making his way back to Richard's home in a small town. Indeed, there is evidence enough in wartime records that this very thing happened.

The mistake in this film version is that the original was penned in 1926 under the then heavy influence of German Expressionism. The novella was then successfully adapted to the stage in 1929 and again maintained its appeal due to its expressionist weight and emotional sketch of the characters. The film is much too naturalistic to come up to par, the main drawback being that the main characters never really take on the flesh-and-blood to make the story credible.

Helmer Rainer Simon tries a couple stylistic tricks of his own to give "The Woman And The Stranger" more depth. He shifts from a sepia-like tint to warmer color hues whenever it appears Anna's hopes of finding Richard truly alive (after being pronounced dead by the war department) might come true after all. He also changes the setting to keep track of Richard's roundabout return from the dead as a repatrioted POW, thus priming the pump for the confrontation at the family hearth — a letdown that is inevitable on the narrative side (and only really possible as Expressionist, emotion-packed drama).

Oddly, the film ends on the very note where the story is beginning to get interesting. — *Holl.*

Caught At The Berlinale

Continued

Streetwalkin'
(U.S.-COLOR)

Berlin, Feb. 22.

A Rodeo production. Produced by Robert Alden. Directed by Joan Freeman. Stars

Melissa Leo, Dale Midkiff. Screenplay, Freeman, Alden; camera (Deluxe color), Steven Fierberg; editors, John K. Adams, Patrick Rand; sound, Rick Waddell; music, Matthew Ender, Doug Timm; art director, Jeffrey Robbins. Reviewed at Berlin Film Festival (out of competition), Feb. 21, 1985. (MPAA Rating: R.) Running time: **85 MINS.**

Cookie . . . . Melissa Leo
Duke . . . . Dale Midkiff
Queen Bee . . . . Julie Newmar

Also with: Antonio Fargas, Leon Robinson, Annie Golden, Randall Batinkoff, Deborah Offner, Khandi Alexander, Greg German.

A slick, sleazy thriller about a hooker and her homicidal pimp, "Streetwalkin'" is a low-budget item which delivers more than its share of sex and violence. It could mop up wherever there's an audience for this kind of thing, but it lacks the crossover potential (suggested by its Berlin Fest preem) of a "Blood Simple."

Cookie is a sweet young out-of-towner, driver from home by her spiteful mother, who arrives penniless in New York with her kid brother. At Grand Central Terminal, she meets Duke, a handsome and apparently kindly fellow, and a credit title (and little song) later she's working on the street for him, and seemingly happy with the situation.

Duke goes berserk when another of his girls threatens to quit, and savagely beats her, almost to death. Cookie gets scared, and hides out with friends, while the lovesick, demented Duke searches for her, scattering bodies in his wake. It culminates in a suspenseful and effective sequence of harrowing violence in which it's finally left to Cookie to pump her erstwhile lover full of lead.

Sex scenes, despite one involving a middle-aged masochist who begs to be whipped by Cookie and another prostie, are relatively restrained, but the scenes of violence are not. Joan Freeman apparently favors scenes in which characters, usually young women, are brutally and continually beaten. Then there are the shootings and stabbings — lots of them.

Handling is brisk and economical, but the almost comic overkill, which can work in a horror item like "Evil Dead," doesn't fit as well in these realistic settings; audiences won't know whether to laugh at the excesses or take it all at face value. Melissa Leo is a sweet heroine and her plight towards the end of the film carries with it genuine tension. Technical credits are pro considering the obviously modest budget.

Chances of cult recognition, though, seem to be dim. Despite the presence of a femme director at the helm, feminists will undoubtedly be outraged. — *Strat.*

Le Meilleur de la Vie
(The Best In Life)
(FRENCH-COLOR)

Berlin, Feb. 17.

An Abilene-Siotint coproduction. Directed by Renaud Victor. Features entire cast. Screenplay, Murielle Theodori, Sophie Rouffio, Victor, with the collaboration of Gérard Brach; camera (Eastman color), Richard Copans; editor, Jean Gargonne; sound, Antoine Ouvrier, Julien Cloquet; art director, Michel Vandestuen. Reviewed at Berlin Film Festival (out of competition), Feb. 16, 1985. Running time: **96 MINS.**

Véronique . . . . Sandrine Bonnaire
Adrien . . . . Jacques Bonnafe
V's mother . . . . . . Marie-Christine Barrault
Véronique's father . . . . . . Jean-Marc Bory
Adrien's mother . . . . Jenny Cleve
Solange . . . . Julie Jezequel
The Unknown Man . . . . Renaud Victor

For most of its length, "The Best In Life," plays as a superior and all-too-realistic drama of the trials and tribulations of a young married couple. Véronique, from a well-to-do provincial family, is very much in love with Adrien, whose humble background is faraway Brittany. She gets pregnant and they marry. For a while they're deliriously happy, but after a baby girl is born, Véronique, still a student, starts spending much of her time with her friends while the non-intellectual Adrien is literally left holding the baby. Naturally, they have quarrels, quarrels which turn into fights. They part, come together and part again.

Sandrine Bonnaire made a name for herself just over a year ago in Maurice Pialat's "A Nos Amours," and she's once again extraordinary here. Matching her all the way is Jacques Bonnafe as her tortured young husband. Their scenes together are electric, and the unabashed nudity of several sequences somehow adds to their authenticity.

Ultimately, the pic takes off in an unexpected direction. The couple separates, and one his way home from visiting his mother in Brittany, Adrien steals a car, crashes it and undergoes a kind of calvary on damp, cold moorland, aided by an ambiguous stranger (played by the director) whose motives aren't clear. Downbeat ending is rather bizarre.

Nonetheless, overall impression is of a director of talent in Renaud Victor and a most interesting film, with definite art house possibilities on its gritty contemporary updating of traditional themes. Small-town atmosphere (pic was shot in Nimes) is superbly captured, and the lensing of Richard Copans is impeccable. A music score of classical excerpts (Verdi, Brahms, Beethoven, et al.) is apt. — *Strat.*

Over The Summer
(U.S.-COLOR)

Banal rites of passage opus.

Berlin, Feb. 18.

A film by 'Shine Productions. Produced by Sara Margarat (Buffy) Queen. Written and directed by Teresa Sparks. Camera (color), Afshin Chamasmany; music, Steven Heller. No other credits provided. Presented by Filmtrans. Reviewed at Film Market, Berlin Intl. Film Festival, Feb. 17, 1985. Running time: **100 MINS.**

The two young women who directed and produced "Over The Summer" are both from the Smoky Mountains, studied film and tv separately at big universities and are serious professionals with impressive credentials. They are more interesting than their film, however, and one wonders how they could have made such a commonplace, poorly crafted and inauspicious feature debut.

Big-city punk teenager Tina is deposited for a summer with North Carolina grandparents. The countryside is idyllic, but steamy repressed passions among the North Carolina farmers and small-towners make for ugly complications. Rape, arson, beatings, attempted murder, fetishism, voyeurism, suicide — all these are part of "Over The Summer," which is structured like a summer maturation movie about teenagers on the brink.

End of "Over The Summer" finds the home once again in big-city Atlanta, no longer a virgin, but presumably safer and wiser than being down home with just plain folks.

Storyline has flaws of motivation, shallow characterizations and the usual cornpone stereotypes. Accents are a hodgepodge, with only minor characters speaking like authentic mountaineers. Performances are almost uniformly substandard, due to the banality of the film's original conception, described in press releases as "a country-punk version of coming of age in America."

"Over The Summer" perhaps can find its audience among teenagers on the threshold. The film is unlikely, however, to help them understand the transformation they are going through. — *Hitch.*

Orions Belte
(Orion's Belt)
(NORWEGIAN-COLOR)

Berlin, Feb. 17.

A Filmeffekt A/S Production. Produced by Dag Alveberg. Petter Borgli. Directed by Ola Solum. Features entire cast. Screenplay, Richard Harris, from the novel by Jon Michelet; camera (color), Harald Paalgaard; editors, Bjorn Breigutu, Yogve Refseth; music, Geir Bohren, Bent Aserud; sound, Jan Lindvik (Dolby Stereo). Reviewed at Berlin Film Festival Market, Feb. 16, 1985. Running time: **101 MINS.**

Tom Jansen . . . . Helge Jordal
Larse . . . . Sverre Anker Ousdal
Sverre . . . . Hans Ola Sorile
Eva Jelseth . . . . Kjersti Holmer

"Orion's Belt" is a crackerjack contemporary Cold War thriller which must rate as the most commercial Norwegian pic made to date, though the title could be improved upon.

The setting is Svalbard, an island off the northwest coast of Norway. Tom, Larse and Sverre own a small boat which they use to take small groups of tourists around the spectacularly beautiful, icy northern waters (giving lenser Harald Paalgaard marvelous opportunities to display some impressive images of polar bears, walruses and majestic ice floes). There isn't much money to be made, and the trio decide to smuggle a tractor across to Greenland. On the way back, a storm disables the boat and, although they make it to Svalbard, they're on the wrong side of the island. Here they unexpectedly stumble across a Russian listening post (on Norwegian territory) and suddenly are attacked by armed Russian soldiers, who wound Sverre. Fighting back, they kill a Russian and escape back to their boat, but before long a Russian helicopter attacks them, causing extensive damage. The resourceful Tom manages to destroy the chopper, but before they can reach safety another appears; this time Sverre and Larse are killed, and the boat sunk, though the injured Tom manages to escape.

Somehow he makes it through the freezing wasteland, but as soon as he reaches his village, more dead than alive, he's hauled off to Oslo to tell his story. What might have been an anti-climactic final 30 minutes suddenly develops into a different kind of suspense tale as we realize the Norwegian government doesn't want to rock the Soviet boat, and Tom will never be allowed to tell his story to the outside world.

This is a superbly mounted, convincingly told adventure thriller. Action scenes, such as the helicopter attack, are excitingly staged, and the suspense never lets up. As the rugged Tom, Helge Jordal is very good.

Pic is already a hit in Norway and could do very well anywhere in the West, though as noted a title change is indicated (Orion's Belt is the name of the part of the island where the Russian base is found). Norway's most expensive production to date, this is a picture where the money is on the screen. — *Strat.*

Deng-Byod
(The Blazing Sun)
(SOUTH KOREAN-COLOR)

Berlin, Feb. 21.

A Hwa Chun Trading Co. Ltd. production.

Produced by Chong-Chan Park. Directed by Myung-Joong Ha. Features entire case. Screenplay, Yong-Il Lee, Han-Bong Na, from a novel by Yeo-Jung Kim; camera (color), Kwang-Suk Chung; editor, Dong-Chun Hyun; sound, Kyung-Il Kim; music, Young-Dong Kim; art director, Hoon Young Kim. Reviewed at Berlin Film Festival (in competition), Feb. 20, 1985. Running time: **100 MINS.**

Choon-Ho . . . . Myung-Joong Hah
Soony . . . . Young-Won Cho
Hyang-Sim . . . . Heli-Young Lee
Mong-Tai . . . . Joo-Bong Choi

A grim tale of poverty and deprivation, set in the late 1930s, "The Blazing Sun" ranks high among South Korean films shown in the West recently as far as its magnificent visual qualities are concerned. Lighting and labwork are splendid.

At the time the film is set, Korea was occupied by Japan. Central characters are poor peasants trying to eke out a living. They arrive in a mining village, which seems at first to offer promise of work, but the Japanese close the mine. After much suffering, the pregnant wife is taken ill, but when her husband manages to get her to a Japanese hospital they're given a hostile reception. The wife eventually dies, but the husband vows to carry on.

Pic is a real downer, somewhat relieved by its handsome look. There's a good deal of violence wrought against the suffering couple as they trek through glorious mountain scenery to an uncertain future.

The director has noted the film is not anti-Japanese, but anti-oppression; indeed, Japanese characters only appear in the hospital scene, though in that situation they're thoroughly nasty. Pic could play at fests interested in showing Asian films, but commercially won't make any headway. — *Strat.*

Contar Hasta Diez
(Count To Ten)
(ARGENTINE-COLOR)

Berlin, Feb. 22.

An Oscar Barney Film production. Produced by Mario Vitali. Directed and written by Oscar Barney Finn. Features entire cast. Camera (Eastmancolor), Juan Carlos Lenardi; editor, Julio Di Risio; sound, Jorge Stavropoulos; music, Luis Maria Serra; art director, Alfredo Iglesias. Reviewed at Berlin Film Festival (in competition), Feb. 21, 1985. Running time: **109 MINS.**

Francisco Vallajos . . . . Hector Alterio
Ramon Vallajos . . . . Oscar Martinez
Pedro Vallajos . . . . Arturo Maly
Paula . . . . Julia von Grolman
Ana . . . . Maria José Demare
Federico . . . . Arturo Bonin
Lucia . . . . Selva Aleman
Grandmother . . . . Eva Franco

Set in 1979, "Count To Ten" is a somber tale of a young man who travels from his home in Patagonia (in the south of Argentina) to Buenos Aires to look for his missing brother. The expectations are that Pedro, the brother, was one of the many thousands who disappeared, presumably murdered, during the chaotic period of the mid-'70s. Ramon does, eventually, find his brother, though by then Pedro is insane and suicidal.

This is undoubtedly a film which would mean a great deal more to its domestic audience than it can ever mean abroad; it simply doesn't travel well, as it contains dozens of allusions to political figures in Argentina, plus other references, which foreigners won't pick up. In any event, the film is very sluggish, consisting almost entirely of discussions and two-way conversations, and has at its center an uncharismatic, self-pitying hero who quickly becomes a bore.

Hector Alterio, who lived and worked in Spain for many years, brings distinction to his small but pivotal role of the brothers' father, whose political allegiances are obscure yet obviously important.
— *Strat.*

Morenga
(WEST GERMAN-COLOR)

Berlin, Feb. 17.

A Provobis Film, Berlin, in coproduction with TNF-Tele Norm Film, Munich, and Westdeutscher Rundfunk, Cologne. Tv producer, Wolf-Dietrich Brucker. Features entire cast. Written and directed by Egon Günther, based on the novel with the same title by Uwe Timm. Camera (color), Gernot Roll; sets, Bernhard Henrich; editor, Ingrid Bichler; sound, Frank Schneider; costumes, Charlotte Flemming, Slvia Risa; production manager, Ike Werk. Reviewed at Berlin Film Fest (in competition), Feb. 16, 1985. Running time: **112 MINS.**

With: Jacques Breuer (Gottschalk), Edwin Noel (Wenstrup), Jürgen Holtz (von Kageneck), Manfred Seipold (von Koppy), Tobias Hösl (von Treskow), Harrison Coburn (von Schwanebach), Arnold Vosloo (von Schiller), Robert Whitehead (Haring), Vernon Dobtcheff (Lohmann), Brian O'Shaughnessy (Mr. Lüdemann), Susanne Stoll (Mrs. Lüdemann), Ken Gampu (Morenga), Gideon Camm (Jakobus), Katharina (Momsa Nenee).

"Morenga" is made by Egon Günther, a former top East German director living and working the past six years in West Germany, who adapted this tale on colonial Southwest Africa from a story by Uwe Timm.

The period is 1904 when the area was known as German Southwest Africa with the capital at Windhuk (today Windhoek), and there was a dispute between Germany and England over jurisdictional rights (particularly as cattleraising was then a profitable venture). Many settlers from Hamburg and northern Germany settled here, among them non-militarists but veterinarian-colonialists in the army like the pic's chief protagonists Gottschalk and Wenstrup. These two have learned to speak the language of the native Hottentots, are shocked by the wanton taking of innocent lives to counteract a black uprising under a local leader named Morenga and find themselves suddenly in a position that could be considered desertion, worthy of court-martial.

The inner conflict — brutal colonialism vs. humanitarian settlement — forms the crux of the story and when Günther concentrates on that element alone, he's in command of a fascinating narrative with controlled acting and sharp lensing (Gernot Roll, who worked with Edgar Reitz on his epic, "Heimat"). Unfortunately, pic quickly slips into a cowboys-and-indians affair as the German troops fall into one trap after another laid for them by the intrepid Geronimo-like Morenga. The Germans suffer heavy losses, particularly when the trusted native Christians themselves dupe the naive vets into transferring false information to the troop commander.

In the end, it's the British forces who decide to get rid of Morenga for diplomatic reasons once the black leader has crossed over to South Africa for protection.

"Morenga" might prove to be attractive for international fests, but offshore chances are slim otherwise.
— *Holl.*

Niemanns Zeit — Ein Deutscher Heimatfilm
(Niemann's Time — A German 'Heimatfilm')
(WEST GERMAN-COLOR)

Berlin, Feb. 19.

A coproduction of the Literarisches Colloquium, Berlin and Westdeutscher Rundfunk, Cologne. Features entire cast. Written and directed by Horst Kurnitzky and Marion Schmid. Camera (color), Wladimir Woitinski; editing, Christiane Fazlagic; sound, Paul Oberle; music, Jolyon Brettingham-Smith; chorus, Marcus Creed; tv producer, Martin Wiebel. Reviewed at Berlin Film Fest (out-of-competition), Feb. 18, 1985. Running time: **100 MINS.**

With: Gerd Wameling (Niemann), Elke Petri (speaker on tape recorder), Klaus Heinrich, Hansjörg Hemminger, Reinhold Messner (talk-show participants), Bruno Kurz. Sira Manopas (children), Franz Salzberger (painter on the meadow), Angela Scheider (guide in National Gallery of Art), Leonard Lorenz (guide through the Obersalzberg Bunker).

Horst Kurnitzky and Marion Schmid's "Niemann's Time — A German 'Heimatfilm' " is a combination of feature narrative, documentary, and experimental film. It all adds up to a very fine out-of-competition entry a this year's Berlinale in a late-nite slot at the Zoo Palast (this pic needing that large screen to impress).

Picture sorts through Germany's political past via an antiquarian collection of postcards issued during the Nazi period as well as many other remnants of the time in order to study German human nature.

The protagonist, Niemann, a loner, is buried up to his eyebrows in records in a factory-space studio overlooking the wasteland in West Berlin straddling the Wall that was formerly the Gestapo headquarters and torture chamber. A pile of rubble still stands before this building as landscapers prepare to turn the area into a memorial park in the near future.

This mountain of rubble takes on an image of the Nazi past, particularly when Niemann begins to reflect on the Nazi quarters in Obersalzberg, Hitler's favorite retreat that even today attracts thousands of tourists to view the bunkerlabyrinth (it also happens to be the recreational site of Allied Army officers).

As an important extra complement of this isolated and obsessive research project, Kurnitzky and Schmid examine the sheer hopelessness of bringing three "experts" together on a tv talkshow to discuss romanticism from separate viewpoints: a philosopher-theologian, a sociology analyst and a mountain climber (Reinhold Messner, who scaled Mount Everest alone from the so-called "impossible side"). One notes immediately that communication on "nature" has been reduced to absurdity.—*Holl.*

Klaani: Tarina Sammakoitten Suvusta
(The Clan: Tale Of The Frogs)
(FINNISH-COLOR)

Berlin, Feb. 21.

A Villealfa Filmproductions Oy production. Produced by Jaakko Talaskivi, Anssi Mäntaari. Directed by Mika Kaurismäki. Features entire cast. Screenplay, Aki Kaurismäki, Mika Kaurismäki, from a novel by Tauno Kaukonen; camera (color), Tomo Salminen; sound, Mikael Sieves; music, Anssi Tikanmäki; art director, Matti Jaaranen; costumes, Irma Sarjanen. Reviewed at Berlin Film Fest (Market), Feb. 20, 1985. Running time: **95 MINS.**

Alex Sammakko (Frog) . . . Markku Halme
Miriam Andersson . . . . Minna Soisalo
Samuel Sammakko . . . . Juhani Niemelä
Leevi Sammakko . . . . Karl Väänänen
Benjamin Sammakko . . . . Antti Litja
Birger Andersson . . . . . . Mikko Majanlahti

Robert Andersson . . . . Sakari Rouvinen
Crewcut (Police Inspector) . . . Lasse Pöysti

"Sammakko" means "frog" in Finnish, and the "Frog" family, a group of petty criminals and deadbeats, living in the apparently idyllic surroundings of rural Finland, are at the center of this curiously affecting thriller.

The Frogs have always been on the wrong side of the law, and consequently in and out of prison. The film begins when two of them manage to escape while being transported by guards, and head back for their home turf, pursued by the cops. Youngest member of the Frog clan is Alexander, who's seen what's happened to his alcoholic father and to other members of the family, and who wants to go straight himself. Besides, he's in love with Miriam whose family is almost as hopeless as his; the two of them want to find a new way. Naturally, Alexander comes under pressure to behave as a good Frog should, but, despite the antagonism of the local cops, who think every Frog is a bad apple, he makes it.

Shot in sumptuous locations during Finland's brief, beautiful summer, "The Clan" is distinguished by fine acting and an authentic feel. Plotting is a bit rambling, but helmer Mika Kaurismäki, making his second feature, shows a fine feel for atmosphere and character. Particularly outstanding is Juhani Niemelä as the young hero's pathetic, hopelessly alcoholic father who, though on his last legs, carries out his defiance of the authorities literally to the grave.

Outside Scandinavia, the film has some possibilities on its unusual setting and bizarre characters, though only time will tell if, commercially speaking, these Frogs have legs.

—*Strat.*

Uz Se Nebojim
(I Am Not Afraid Anymore)
(CZECHOSLOVAKIAN-COLOR)

Hungarian Film Week

Yerma
(WEST GERMAN-HUNGARIAN-CANADIAN-COLOR)

Budapest, Feb. 11.
A Coproduction of Starfilm and Macropus Film, Munich; Mafilm (Hunnia Studio) and Hungarian Television, Budapest; and Sefel Pictures Intl., Calgary. Directed by Imre Gyöngyössy and Barna Kabay. Stars Gudrun Landgrebe. Screenplay, Gyöngyössy, Kabay, Katlalin Petenyl; camera (color), Gabor Szabo; music, Zoltan Pesko. Reviewed at Hungarian Film Week, Budapest, Feb. 10, 1985. Running time: **104 MINS.**
With: Gudrun Landgrebe (Yerma), Titiusz

Berlin, Feb. 22.
A production of Filmstudio Gottwaldov-Kudlev. Directed by Otakar Kosek. Screenplay, Kosek, Petr Krenek; camera (color), Jiri Kolin; editor, A Strojsa, Ivan Matous; sound, Radomir Kontek; music, Vadim Petrov; art director, Petr Smola. Reviewed at Kinderfilmfest, Berlin Film Festival, Feb. 21, 1985. Runnin gtime: **76 MINS.**
Jozka . . . . Jiri Korytar
His mother . . . . Jana Plichtova
His father . . . . Vladimir Durdik
His teacher, Pavel . . . . Michal Pesek

Theme of "I'm Not Afraid Anymore" is expressed in its title — overcoming fear. This is a well-constructed parable film for young audiences that teaches moral and physical courage, as a rite of passage for adolescents. Film has larger relevance as well, as a family film, as instruction for parents who obtusely misunderstand their own troubled progeny. Because the film is thus keyed to psychological basics, it could fit any nation, once the language problem has been whipped.

Only child Jozka is depressed since the accidental drowning of his devoted father and has developed a phobia for swimming. He does badly in school, is abused by his peers and is slapped in public by his mother, a frustrated widow. Along comes the new schoolteacher, a young eccentric Mr. Fix-it, who works patiently with the boy, teaches him to become the school's swimming champion, punishes his tormentors, and restores him to his mother's love. By the end of the spring term, Jozka has graduated, both as a student now getting good marks, and as a boy who has triumphed over fears, having accepted his father's death by a transference of affection to his teacher.

"I'm Not Afraid Anymore" is beautifully shot in the Czech countryside of rolling hills and farmlands. Production values are first-rate, and the directing is self-assured and competent, serving the intelligent script. — *Hitch.*

Kovacs (Juan), Matthieu Carrière (Victor).

Although the team of Imre Gyöngyössy and Barna Kabay scored a success with their previous artpic, the West German-Hungarian coproduction "Job's Revolt" (Oscar Nomination 1983), the same unfortunately cannot be said of "Yerma," a German-Hungarian-Canadian coproduction whose main drawback is its calculated combo of classic literatue and stars.

"Yerma" is based on Lorca's

mystically poetic drama (penned in 1934) about a neglected, passionate, unconsummated married woman; the original is admitted by commentators as one of the few poetic tragedies of this century. That two Hungarian writer-directors would attempt to film this Spanish classic in Spain with German and Hungarian thesps in the lead is an eyebrow-raiser to begin with, but that they would miscast it so badly and then turn the whole venture into a picture-postcard tourist attraction amounts to a tragedy in itself.

Indeed, two of the main characters, Gudrun Landgrebe as Yerma and Matthieu Carrière as a desired acquaintance, go through their motions as though following rigidly the same formula for success used in their previous teaming in Robert Van Ackeren's coolly directed German artpic, "A Woman In Flames" (Oscar nominee at same time as "Job").—*Holl.*

Hany Az Ora, Vekker Ur?
(What's The Time, Mr. Clock?)
(HUNGARIAN-COLOR)

Budapest, Feb. 14.
An Objektiv Studio, Mafilm, production. Directed, written by Peter Bacso (from a short story by Geza Paskandi). Features entire cast. Camera (Eastmancolor), Tamas Andor; music, György Vukan; art director, Tamas Vayer; editor, Mihaly Morell; sound, Karoly Peller; costumes, Erzsebet Mihalkovszky. Reviewed at Hungarian Film Week, Budapest, Feb. 13, 1985. Running time: **108 MINS.**
Arpad (Mr. Clock) . . . . Tamas Jordan
Elza . . . . Ildiko Bansagi
Gestapo Chief . . . . György Melis
Priest . . . . Ferenc Kallai
Colonel . . . . Kornel Gelley
Panni . . . . Barbara Hegyi

Peter Bacso's new film is the best this prolific director has made since "The Witness" (1968). Set in the picturesque little village of Koszeg in 1943, pic expertly treads the knife-edge of making a warm and human comedy out of a grim situation.

Arpad Weiskopf, nicknamed Mr. Clock, is a Jewish watchmaker, popular in the village; he has the uncanny knack of being able to tell the exact time without consulting his watch. One day, while working on the clock-tower of the local church, Elza, his wife, who left him 10 years earlier, unexpectedly returns; Arpad is so surprised to see her he falls from his perch, but fortunately a safety rope prevents a fatal accident and the fire brigade is called to help him down. It seems Elza wants to return to him, but other, less welcome, strangers also involve the town. The Germans, dissatisfied with the loyalty of their Hungarian ally, have chosen this moment to take over.

The Gestapo chief has a valuable collection of clocks, and he appears to be friendly towards Arpad. But

when he asks the Jew to tell him a joke, to prove the Germans have a sense of humor, he doesn't find it at all funny (though it's a scene that will have the audience in stitches, thanks to the superb comic timing of György Melis as the German). Soon the local Hungarian colonel, a strict disciplinarian, is arrested along with a number of other local citizens including Arpad. Their watches are confiscated, but word comes from the outside that an escape is planned for the colonel, dependent on split-second timing. Of course, Arpad comes to the rescue — and his troubles multiply.

Although a new English title should be found, it seems certain "Mr. Clock" will have a successful international career. It had a troubled production history, with a good part of the film already in the can when the actor originally playing Arpad, Lajos Öze, died suddenly. A great many scenes had to be reshot with replacement Tamas Jordan, who's excellent in the role.
— *Strat.*

Játszani Kell
(Lily In Love)
(HUNGARIAN-U.S.-COLOR)

Budapest, Feb. 10.
A Dialog Studio, Mafilm-Robert Halmi Inc. coproduction. Directed by Karoly Makk. Stars Christopher Plummer, Maggie Smith. Screenplay, Frank Cucci; camera (Eastmancolor), Tamas Andor; music, Szabolcs Fenyes. No further credits available. Reviewed at Hungarian Film Week, Budapest, Feb. 9, 1985. Running time: **108 MINS.**
Fitz . . . . Christopher Plummer
Lily . . . . Maggie Smith
Alice . . . . Elke Sommer
Jerry . . . . Adolph Green
The Director . . . . Sandor Szabo

Karoly Makk, one of Hungary's most distinguished directors ("Love," "Another Way") has unwisely attempted a screwball, Hollywood-style comedy from another era. Tale of a husband and wife actor-writer team who bicker constantly sorely needs a Lubitsch touch, or the witty and wise handling of a Cukor. Titled "Játszani Kell" or "Lily In Love" in English, pic has gone through many earlier monikers, including "Fitz And Lily," "Players" and "Playing For Keeps."

Plot has elements of "Two-Faced Woman." Fitz, a famous Broadway star, yearns to act in a successful film (citing the actors he admires, he mentions Cagney, Bogart, Tracy and Frank Morgan); Lily, a brilliant writer, has written a marvelous movie script, but there's no part for Fitz in it — she needs a blond Italian.

No prizes for guessing that Fitz disguises himself in a blond wig and passes himself off, with phony Italian accent, as the required thesp, or that Lily (apparently) doesn't recognize him, though he still looks exactly like Christopher Plummer in a blond wig. So, they all fly off to Budapest, where the pic's to be made, accompanied by Jerry (mournful-looking Adolph Green), their friend and producer.

At least in the Hungarian version, "Lily In Love" resolutely fails to take off; audience reaction may vary from embarrassment at seeing distinguished actors laboring with such material, to sending the whole thing up. Latter is probably the better course.

Makk is surprisingly tough on his country's filmmakers: in the scenes involving the making of the film (which looks to be just as awful as "Lily In Love") the Hungarian crewmembers are derided as amateurs, and the Hungarian director falls asleep at every opportunity.

On the plus side, there are some attractive touristy images of Budapest and Lake Balaton, and one rather funny scene where a wind machine runs amok during an intimate romantic encounter.

Pic is technically tops, but the music is as schmaltzy and old fashioned as the concept. — *Strat.*

Im Damenstift
(A Home For Ladies)
(WEST GERMAN-COLOR-DOCU-16m)

Berlin, Jan. 1.
An Eberhard Fechner Film, Hamburg, in coproduction with Westdeutscher Rundfunk (WDR), Cologne. Written and directed by Fechner. Camera (color), Karsten H. Müller; sound, Hanner Reichel; assistant director, Jannet Gefken; editor, Brigitte Kirsche; production manager, Frank Roell; tv producer, Helga Poche. Reviewed at Berliner Screening Room, Dec. 30, '84. Running time: **90 MINS.**

Eberhard Fechner's forté as a German tv documentarist is his concern for questions dealing with a social history of Germany from the turn-of-the-century to the present. His latest, "A Home For Ladies," is about an unusual Old People's Home for retired unmarried ladies of the German nobility. There are 16 countesses, baronesses, and other titled ladies living today in Schloss Ehreshoven on the good graces of a wealthy benefactor who gave the home an endowment in 1920. The only requirements for entrance are a title, Catholic religious belief and a maid for a lifetime (that is, never married).

Fechner sets each of the ladies at ease — their ages are 76-88 — then lets them simply recount the past. The results are a warm and humorous historical review of Germany in the Kaiser Wilhelm era, World War I and II, and both reconstruction periods. One senses from the very beginning that life has sort of passed the entire group by,

for they were reared by their families to fit snugly into the courtly manners of the nobility, but little else. —*Holl.*

Epic
(AUSTRALIAN-ANIMATED-COLOR)

Sydney, Feb. 19.
A Yoram Gross presentation. (Cori Films Intl. outside Australia). Produced, directed and edited by Gross. Scriptwriter, John Palmer, from an original story by Gross; associate prod., Sandra Gross; director of animation, Athol Henry; camera (color), Graham Sharpe, Jan Carruthers, Ricky Vergara; production manager, Jeanette Toms; coordinator, Meg Rowed; character voices by Ross Higgins, Robyn Moore. Reviewed at Yoram Gross Film Studio, Sydney, Feb. 18, 1985. (Commonwealth Film Censor rating: G.) Runing time: **70 MINS.**
With: Benita Collings.

The seventh feature from Sydney-based producer/director Yoram Gross, "Epic" marks a departure from the format of the bulk of his earlier work, which was built around the adventures of a character named Dot and an assortment of animals ("Dot And The Kangaroo..Bunny," etc.).

This pic bears the familiar Gross trademark of animation matched over live action, but it is pitched to a slightly older age group than the "Dot" vehicles and its subject matter is more serious, without being profound.

The "Dot" series found ready markets on television and home-video in the U.S. and Europe, and "Epic" should follow the same profitable path. The producer/director intends to launch the film theatrically in Australia during the second Children's Intl. Film Festival in Sydney in May (presented under the Gross banner).

Imaginative plot follows search for the socalled secret of life by central characters Sol and Luna, who are raised by a pack of dingos (wild dogs — shades of the mythical Romulus and Remus) after being rescued from a flood which engulfed the Earth.

Pitted against the elements — fire, water and wind are typified as malevolent spirits and monsters — Sol and Luna learn that each can cause great havoc as easily as they can be harnessed with the Earth for good purposes.

In the end, the elements combine to regenerate life and Sol and Luna become the kingdom's new king and queen.

Dialog is minimal so the storytelling rests on the visuals and narration. The battle sequences are well rendered, if a little drawnout, and are likely to cause squeals of excitement among the young brigade, and there are dashes of humor, as in two cute, six-eyed cave-dwellers rejoicing in the names Wag and Pug.

Special effects, an area in which Gross has not had much involvement, are okay although some devices deployed in the opening flood scenes are clumsy. —*Dogo.*

Sauvage et Beau
(Wild And Beautiful)
(FRENCH-DOCU-COLOR)

Paris, Jan. 22.
A Parafrance Communication release of a Télé-Hachette/C.D.G./Parafrance/FR3 coproduction. Directed by Frédéric Rossif. Commentary, Jacques Tremolin, spoken by Richard Berry; camera (color), Daniel Barrau, Yves Pouffary; editor, Dominique Cazeneuve; sound, Renato Girometta, Jean Umansky; music, Vangelis; assistant director, Jean-Charles Cuttoli; production manager, Michelle Wiart. Reviewed at the Monte Carlo theater, Paris, Jan. 21, 1985. Running time: **92 MINS.**

Veteran docu filmmaker Frédéric Rossif returns to the wildlife study in this conventional feature length item, shot over an 18-month period in various climes.

With nothing new, the lack of genuine theme or organization makes this an overlong presentation. Rossif has nonetheless brought back some marvelous footage of birds and beasts from Africa, South America and Canada.

Much credit is obviously due chief lenser Daniel Barrau and his camera operator Yves Pouffary, sharp in eye and reflex in recording the predatory grace and lethal elans of their subjects. Rossif is still a glutton for slow-motion (and sometimes accelerated) photography, though it is often apt and effective.

The electronic whipped cream score is by Vangelis and Jacques Tremolin's spare commentary (spoken by actor Richard Berry) unhelpfully drags in quotations by Gustave Flaubert and Guy de Maupassant.
—*Len.*

Le Téléphone Sonne Toujours Deux Fois!!
(The Telephone Always Rings Twice)
(FRENCH-COLOR)

Paris, Feb. 6.
A UGC release of a Producteurs Associés/FR3 coproduction. Produced by André Djaoui. Directed by Jean-Pierre Vergne. Screenplay, Didier Bourdon, Bernard Campan, Seymour Brussel, with the collaboration of Pascal Legitimus and Jean-Pierre Vergne; camera (color), Robert Fraisse; art director, Daniel Budin; editor, Nicole Berckmans; sound, Daniel Olivier; music, Gabriel Yared; production manager, André Mennecier. Reviewed at the Marignan-Concorde theater, Paris, Feb. 5, 1985. Running time: **90 MINS.**
Marc Elbichon .... -.. Didier Bourdon
Franck .... Seymour Brussel
Ugo .... Bernard Campan
Momo .... Smain
Commissioner .... Jean-Claude Brialy
Marraine .... Michel Galabru
Dr. Clipps .... Henri Courseaux
Also with: Jean Yanne, Darry Cowl,

Patrick Sébastien, Michel Constantin, Clémentine Celarie.

Yet another parody of detective melodramas, "The Telephone Always Rings Twice" introduces five young performers who have gained a certain popularity in improvisational tv skits and café-theater farces. They are personable, energetic and have an irreverent sense of fun. However, their collective writing-acting debut, under the direction of another screen newcomer Jean-Pierre Vergne, is undisciplined and feeble, dragging on from one poor sketch-like scene to another. It displays little command of storytelling or comic rhythm.

Group portrays a young private eye and four cronies who want to scoop the police in capturing the dreaded "Telephone Killer," a psychotic who does away with women by beating them with a phone receiver and stomping the dial into their forehead. There are some good ideas and a few honest laughs, but most of the gag lines are wrong numbers.

Jean-Claude Brialy plays a publicity-conscious police commissioner competing with the amateur investigation, and there are cameo appearances by Michel Galabru, Jean Yanne, Darry Cowl, Michel Constantin and Patrick Sébastien which add little. — *Len.*

Smugglarkungen
(The Smuggler King)
(SWEDISH-COLOR)

Malmö, Feb. 13.
An SF release of Drakfilm production for SF, Filmhuset, S.T.C. Finans, Probo Filmfinans, the Swedish Film Institute and (from Denmark) Nordisk Film. Directed and edited by Sune Lund-Sörensen. Executive produer, Göran Lindström. Original story and script, Ake Cato, Jan Richter. Camera (Eastman color), Claus Loof; music, Stefan Nilsson; costumes, Mago; production design, Anders Barreus. Reviewed at the Royal Theater, Malmö, Feb. 13, 1985. Running time: **105 MINS.**
Albert Jansson .... Janne Carlsson
Lt. Winkel .... Björn Skifs
Grethe .... Sanne Salomonsen
Strauss .... Ernst Günther
Edvard .... Pierre Lindstedt
Sickan .... Nina Gunke
Nilla .... Lena Dahlman
The Norwegian .... Arne Bang Hansen

"The Smuggler King" is a witty backwards look at old Swedish films involving young love and lurking crime, the good and the poor, the evil and the rich, in idyllic communities by the sea. Along with the nostalgia, Denmark's Sweden-based director Sune Lund-Sörensen has fashioned a Prohibition Era comedy that verges on farce without ever daring to really take the plunge. This is unfortunate since film tends to bog down in pride of costumes and cinematography instead of allowing its silly plot to run fast enough to make its many lapses of narrative logic less obvious.

In the early 1920s, honest fisherman Jansson (played by Janne Carlsson, a beloved comedian in Sweden where the mere showing of his stubbled-bearded moon face evokes shrieks of pleasure) turns to bootlegging. In latter métier, he succeeds splendidly and even catches the amorous fancies of a banker's daughter (Nina Gunke) and vampish band singer Grethe (Denmark's ace rock performer Sanne Salomonsen).

He also runs into the rough-and-tumble methods of Strauss (the hitherto established King of Smugglers in the area) and his comic-book bullies. His potentially most formidable foe, a customs lieutenant sent down from Stockholm (a silly/charming performance by fusion music star Björn Skifs), seems from the start defeated more by the local customs force

Occasionally — at its best — "The Smuggler King" pays open tribute to Erik Balling's Danish petty thieves comedy series about "The Olsen Gang," but lacks latter's knife-sharp precision and sustained Runyonesque madness.

Janne Carlsson actually gets little chance to display the inner comedy dynamo that brought him to fame. Sanne Salomonsen is hardly an actress, but she shines as the vocalist-vamp with musicianship as well as with sly wit.

"The Smuggler King" is sure to hit the boxoffice ceiling at home and should do fair business in neighboring Scandinavian territories. Otherwise, with or without passport, it will hardly cross any borders.—*Kell.*

Les Nanas
(The Chicks)
(FRENCH-COLOR)

Paris, Feb. 22.

A UGC release of a Stand'-Art/A.F.C./-FR3 coproduction. Produced by Lise Fayolle. Coproducers, Maurice Bernart and Jean-Pierre Teyssier. Directed by Annick Lanoë. Screenplay, Lanoë, Chantal Pelletier; Camera (color), François Catonné; sound, Jean-Claude Laureux; art directors, Max Berto, Glaudie Gastine; sound, Jean-Claude Laureux, Gérard Lamps; editor, Joëlle Van Effenterre; music, Francois Valéry; production managers, Bernard Lorain, Daniel Messere. Reviewed at the Marignan-Concorde theater, Paris, Feb. 22, 1985. Running time: **90 MINS.**
With: Marie-France Pisier, Dominique Lavanant, Macha Méril, Odette Laure, Catherine Samie, Juliette Binoche, Clementine Clearie, Sophie Artur, Marilu Marini, Myriam Mézières, Anémone.

"Les Nanas" is a contemporary Paris update of Clare Boothe's "The Women," minus the bitchiness. There are no men to be seen in this first feature by Annick Lanoë. Nothing but women, talking about nothing but men. A good distaff cast makes this watchable, but it's

much too demure and well-behaved to be really fun.

Central character is Marie-France Pisier, a sales-girl whose theories about liberated relationships hit the reefs where her lover starts seeing another woman. About her move several other ladies, all representative of certain types of nonchalant modern womankind.

Coscripted by Chantal Pelletier, author of a long-running café-theater comedy about femmes, film tries to encompass all the characters in a loosely-constructed design that fails to cover up the stage-minded conception of its authors. Cinema here is little more than a mechanical expedient for scene-changing.

The roles are not caricatured, but nonetheless depend on the actresses for their credible humanity. Best of the cast are Dominique Lavanant, as Pisier's book-dealer rival, and newcomer Clementine Celarie, as the falsely enlightened actress who winds up with the man both Pisier and Lavanant have loved and lost.

Tech credits are unexceptional.
— *Len.*

Fasnacht
(Carnival)
(WEST GERMAN-SWISS-COLOR-16m)

Saarbrücken, Jan. 18.

A Munich Film Academy (HFF) Film in coproduction with Bayerischer Rundfunk (BR), Norddeutscher Rundfunk (NDR), and Swiss Television (SRG). Features entire cast. Written and directed by Bruno Kiser. Camera (color), Frank Heinig, Heiner Stadler; sets, Sabine Rieger; editing, Edith Eisenstecken, music, Norbert Jürgen Schneider, Thoms Henzen; production manager, Wolfgang Längsfeld, Uli Möller. Reviewed at Saarbrücken Film Fest (Max Ophüls Prize), Jan. 17, 1985. Running time: **83 MINS.**
With: Gerhard Dillier (Markus), Christina Ettlin (Andrea), Melinda Spitzer (Agnes), Beppi Baggenstoss (Peter), Peter Fürst (Fritz), Reudi Hinter (Martin), Jörg Niederberger (Alex), Genoveva Kiser (Frau Wagner).

Bruno Kiser's "Fasnacht" is set during carnival season in German-Switzerland, a time of gay costumes and decorated floats in the streets over a long weekend before Lenten fasting (in the old church tradition) sets in. It's also a time — as in Mardi Gras in Rio and New Orleans — for playful pranks and blowing off steam.

Swiss filmer Kiser grew up in the Obwalden Canton of German Switzerland and knows his milieu well. Indeed, it's the film's atmosphere that makes "Fasnacht" a convincing debut feature by this grad of the Munich Film Academy. And the story has an autobiographical touch. A down-on-his-luck Swiss actor can't break through in Munich, not even as an extra in a tv serial, so he decides to return home for the Fasnacht celebration in order to see mom and blow off a little steam with the old gang. But his

friends are well established in their provincial nest, his old girlfriend has a new beau (an old rival), and he feels himself more and more an outsider, with a chip on his shoulder to boot.

The distraught actor's cool arrogance gets him deeper and deeper into trouble. And just as in the Fasnacht celebrations depicting the Swiss mountaineers getting the best of the Romans, so too the provincial pals begin to needle the native stranger for coming back at all. A spat breaks out over the girlfriend, and the hero is getting the best of the affair when an accident happens: the rival falls into a ravine and is hospitalized with a concussion.

The hero, Markus, has to turn over his passport until the investigation is completed. Then comes regular harassment — punctured auto tires, ostracism by villagers, gang threats from the old buddies — and Markus makes the mistake of hitting back with a mechanic's wrench at one showdown. He hides in an abandoned shed in the woods while being hunted by police and the pals out for vigilante revenge. Then, just when blood is about to be spilled, the girlfriend stands up for his innocence and forces the issue to an open hearing. Soon, Markus is on his way back to Munich, a bit wiser for it all.

Although little more than a straightforward tale of love and rivalry, "Fasnacht" is nevertheless well acted by nonprofessionals and moves at a fast narrative pace from start to finish. The on-the-spot Fasnacht street celebrations are particularly fascinating, for they seem to be wilder and more pagan in expression than even the famous and colorful event traditionally visited by hundreds in nearby Basel.
—*Holl.*

Missing In Action 2 —
The Beginning
(COLOR)

Wobbly prequel to Chuck Norris hit.

Hollywood, March 1.

A Cannon Releasing release of a Cannon Group presentation of a Golan-Globus production. Produced by Yoram Globus and Menahem Golan. Directed by Lance Hool. Stars Chuck Norris. Screenplay, Arthur Silver, Larry Levinson, Steve Bing; camera (TVC color), Jorge Stahl Jr.; editors, Mark Conte, Marcus Nanton; music, Brian May; production designer, Michael Baugh; sound, Jakob Goldstein; assistant director, Joe Ochoa; associate producer, Christopher Pearce; casting, John Crowther. Reviewed at Hollywood Pacific, March 1, 1985. (MPAA Rating: R.) Running time: **95 MINS.**

Col. Braddock	Chuck Norris
Col. Yin	Soon-Teck Oh
Mazilli	Cosie Costa
Nester	Steven Williams
Dou Chou	David Chung
Opelka	Joe Michael Terry
Franklin	John Wesley
Col. Ho	Bennett Ohta
Lao	Prof. Toru Tanaka
Emerson	Christopher Cary
François	Pierre Issot

This prequel to last winter's box-office burst from Cannon is neither as well produced as the original "Missing In Action" nor does it have the muscle to do the same kind of business.

First pic, released Nov. 19, took off like a shot, grossing $6,100,000 the first weekend and more than $22,000,000 by year's end. Bowing Friday (1) in another saturation run, "Missing In Action 2 — The Beginning" charts what happened in Vietnam to Colonel Braddock (Chuck Norris) before his escape to the U.S. and his fiery return to find M.I.A.'s.

This time "Missing In Action" exec producer Lance Hool makes his directorial debut. Pic was shot in Mexico and West Indies island of St. Kitts, and with the exception of Norris and sound man Jakob Goldstein, all the key hands are different personnel. Aside from tradition that signals tougher challenge for followups, the scenario on this second outing is claustrophobic compared to the other venture. (This film was actually shot first last year under the title "Missing In Action," but the Joseph Zito present-day second film, lensed as "Battle Rage" was released first by Cannon and took this film's title for itself. —*Ed.*)

Action is almost entirely centered in a postwar Vietnamese prisoner of war camp, where a lunatic is running a slave labor opium operation. In contrast to the visual and geographic scope of its predecessor, the Biblical-sounding "The Beginning" telescopes its action in a steel-willed, eyeball to eyeball confrontation between Norris and his Vietnamese nemesis and crazed-cool captor (Soon-Teck Oh).

On the violent side, production is

risible for two moments: Norris is hung upside down with a maddened rat inside a guney sack that's tied around his head; he has to bite its head off to survive. And one dying American soldier is lit up like a funeral pyre. The rest is conventional torture, booby traps and napalm.

Norris has found his self-reliant niche here, but the feature reflects both the mentality and simplicity of war films made during World War II, notwithstanding its martial arts and the soldier who sells out to the enemy. This action programmer can rest a short while on its predecessor's shoulders but on its own it's wobbly. —Loyn.

Queen Kelly
(B&W-1929)

Unfinished Von Stroheim masterwork.

Hollywood, Feb. 14.

A Kino Intl. release of a Gloria (Swanson) production for United Artists. Directed, written by Erich Von Stroheim. Stars Gloria Swanson. Titles, Marian Ainslee. Camera (b&w), Gordon Pollock, Paul Ivano; editor, Viola Lawrence; art direction, Harold Miles; costumes, Max Ree; music, Adolph Tandler. Dates of production: Nov. 1, 1928-Jan. 21, 1929. Reviewed at the Los Angeles County Museum of Art, Feb. 13, 1985. (No MPAA Rating.) Running time: **96 MINS.**

Kitty Kelly . . . . Gloria Swanson
Queen Regina . . . . Seena Owen
Prince Wolfram . . . . Walter Byron
Prince's Adjutant . . Wilhelm Von Brincken
Mother Superior . . . . Madge Hunt
Valet . . . . Wilson Benge
Lackey . . . . Sidney Bracey
Maid to Prince
  Wolfram . . . . Lucille Van Lent
Maid Who Escorts Kelly
  To Altar . . . . Ann Morgan
Jan Bloehm Vryheid . . . . Tully Marshall
Kelly's Aunt . . . . Florence Gibson
Kali . . . . Mme. Sul Te Wan
Coughdrops . . . . Ray Daggett

Fifty-six years after production was shut down with only about one-third of the full script shot, Erich Von Stroheim's flamboyant epic "Queen Kelly" is entering commercial distribution in the United States in what is apparently, at 96 minutes, an as-complete-as-possible version. Released minimally in Europe and South America in an different cut in the early 1930s, shown occasionally by producer-star Gloria Swanson at museums over the years and memorably excerpted by Billy Wilder in "Sunset Boulevard," film was never reviewed by *Variety*, so is covered now as one of the great, unfinished historical curiosities of film history. Current edition complied by Dennis Doros for Kino Intl. had its U.S. premiere Friday (1) at the Los Angeles County Museum of Art and will bow in regional preems over the next couple of months before going the theatrical route and, presumably, into cable and cassette.

"Queen Kelly," which Von Stroheim originally wrote as "The Swamp," was the director's eighth silent picture and was undertaken at the behest of Swanson under the auspices of financier Joseph Kennedy (who goes uncredited) for distributor United Artists. Best guess is that Von Stroheim's full scenario would have played for at least five hours' running time. Film was in production less than three months, from Nov. 1, 1928 to Jan. 21, 1929, when Swanson, finally fed up with her director's excesses, told Kennedy to shut it down after an expenditure of $800,000. Incident ruined Von Stroheim's Hollywood directorial career, which had been stormy and littered with office battles all along, and he directed (and only partially, at that) just one further picture, "Walking Down Broadway" ("Hello, Sister"), in 1933 before being put out to pasture as an actor.

Since "Queen Kelly" was shot in sequence, what exists of it plays very smoothly and coherently up through its arbitrary, but dramatically valid, conclusion. Set in the sort of fin-de-siècle Ruritanian principality usually favored by the director, tale presents the mad young Queen Regina (Seena Owen) forcing the playboy Prince Wolfram (Walter Byron) into a royal marriage.

Far from resigned to a life of amorous inactivity, Wolfram encounters a troup of convent girls while on cavalry drill in the country and, in a legendary scene, so distresses one of them, Kitty Kelly (Gloria Swanson), with his flirtations that her underpants fall down her legs. Utterly embarrased, Kitty impulsively flings the garment at Wolfram, who is delighted to keep them as a souvenir (Von Stroheim reportedly filmed some takes of Wolfram sniffing the pants, but this bit of business is nowhere to be seen).

On the night before he is to be married, Wolfram and his adjutant sneak off to the convent and burn it down in order to smoke Kitty out. Back at the palace, Wolfram treats her to a champagne dinner and begins seducing her, but is caught in the act by the Queen, who drives Kitty away, in an ultra-Von Stroheimesque sequence, by beating her with her riding crop.

After being saved from suicide, Kitty is called for by a dying aunt and goes to join her in German East Africa, where she takes up residence in auntie's bordello and is forced into marriage with the appalingly depraved plantation owner (Tully Marshall).

Shooting ended at this point with, according to Swanson, the ceasure triggered by Von Stroheim's insistence that Marshall dribble tobacco juice on her hand as he places the wedding ring on her finger. Version of the film released in the 1930s ended with Kitty successfully committing suicide, and the African footage was not discovered until 1963.

As planned by the director, film would have continued ever-deeper into grand melodrama until, coming full circle, Kitty would have truly become Queen Kelly along with Wolfram, displacing Regina on the throne.

As with all other Von Stroheim productions, the settings are incomparably sumptuous, the detail of costume and behavior is unparalaled, and the understanding and expression of human perversity and cruelty is virtually unique in the cinema. The bare bones of the plot are melodramatic in the extreme, but, even in this truncated version, it is clear that Von Stroheim was diving so deep into his characters and the bizarre situations he created for them that "Queen Kelly" could well have been a great film.

Seen today, some of the on-location scenes, in particular, have the pristine quality of something trapped in a box and only exposed to light and air 50 years later. The sequence of Wolfram and Kitty's first meeting possesses a freshness and wit that leap off the screen, and the sexual sophistication and innuendo on display throughout are continually provocative and keep things lively even for viewers not accustomed to watching silent pictures.

Due to the great care with which Swanson maintained the original film materials, the picture, shot by Gordon Pollock and Paul Ivano, is a visual feast. An additional plus is the music score by Adolph Tandler, which was written for Swanson's abridged 1931-32 version and discovered on a nitrate soundtrack for use in the current edition. Notes by Von Stroheim for appropriate sound effects were also followed in creating this definitive version.

On the negative side, some scenes seem to go on longer, and more languorously, than they should, which can undoubtedly be attributed to the fact that the director never really finished a cut of his own, and to a desire on the part of the restoration team to err on the side of comprehensiveness and include as much footage as possible. Despite the rapid succession of startling events, the pacing is somewhat off, an excusable fault given the unique nature of what's on view.

For film buffs, the new availability of "Queen Kelly" is a tremendously welcome event, given the grandness of Von Stroheim's ambition and partial achievement and the performances of all the actors from Swanson on down to the smallest bit player. Of all the great directors who did much, or most, of their important work in the silent era, Von Stroheim's has always been among the most difficult to see in accessible locations and good prints, so it is to be hoped that further efforts will be made to preserve, restore and distribute the limited output of this fascinating artist, whose efforts continue to hold a strange, corrosive power.
—Cart.

Flashpoint Africa
(Die Rebellen)
(SOUTH AFRICAN-WEST GERMAN-COLOR)

A VCL presentation of a Samarkand/Regina/Victoria production. Produced by Barrie Saint Clair. Executive producer, John F. Hume; coproducer, James Faulkner; associate producers, Dieter Nobbe, Rafi Rafaeli. Directed by Francis Megahy. Features entire cast. Screenplay, Tom Wolsky, Rafi Rafaeli, Bernie Cooper; camera (Irene color), Vincent Co; editor, Peter Thornton; music, Eric Smith; sound, Peter Usmar; production manager, K.C. Jones; art direction, John Rosewarne; special effects, Paul Ballanger; stunt supervisor, Jannie Wienand. Reviewed on Media Home Entertainment videcassette, Jan. 30, 1985. (No MPAA Rating.) Running time: **86 MINS.**

Lisa Ford . . . . Gayle Hunnicutt
Ramon . . . . James Faulkner
Joe . . . . Siegfried Rauch
Ann Barriclough . . . . Belinda Mayne
Matari . . . . Ken Gampu
Programmes controller . . . Trevor Howard
Mrs. Barriclough . . . . Helen Cherry
Mr. Barriclough . . . . Patrick Holt
Barbara Fenton . . . . Deidre Bates
Don . . . . Graham Armitage

"Flashpoint Africa" is a very heavy-handed political thriller, filmed in 1978 under the original title "One Take Two" (which refers to a phrase recited in place of a clapperboard before a documentary scene is shot). Theatrically unreleased, film is now available on videcassette.

Gayle Hunnicutt toplines as a too-posh looking newshen Lisa Ford, who, together with her cameraman Joe (Siegfried Rauch) gets involved with rebel forces in a Black African country in the midst of a post-independence revolution. Accompanied by a camera-shy Cuban advisor Ramon (played unconvincingly with phony accent by the film's coproducer James Faulkner), they are led to Matari (Ken Gampu), the rebel leader who just happens to be an old Oxford college chum of Ford's. He has kidnapped two girls (Belinda Mayne and Deidre Bates), whose plight is focusing media attention on his rebel cause.

In trying to make a statement concerning managed news and the lack of objectivity in making news documentaries, director Francis Megahy resorts to a very awkward structure, framing "Flashpoint" with frequent cuts back to a London editing room where network programmes controller Trevor Howard is deciding which footage to be deleted and how the docu lensed by Lisa and Joe will be put together. In a ridiculous audience cheating device, Megahy presents the "Flashpoint" viewer with loads of material that Howard cannot see, in order to hammer home the point that Howard is acting as a self-serving censor.

Although gratuitous material such as the pretty kidnapped girls (who become radicalized conveniently a la Patty Hearst) is included, "Flashpoint" emerges as more of a tract than entertainment.

Cast is uninspired (Hunnicutt and Faulkner are miscast, as stated) and tech credits subpar, particularly the crude direct-sound recording. .

—Lor.

Ikite Wa Mita Keredo...
(I Live, But ...)
(JAPANESE-DOCU-COLOR/B&W)

Berlin, Feb. 17.

A Shochiku production. Directed by Kazuo Inoue. Written and edited by Inoue, Koki Takeoka; music, Kojun Saito; narrator, Tasuja Jo. Reviewed at Intl. Forum of Young Film, Berlin Intl. Film Festival, Feb. 16, 1985. Running time: **118 MINS.**

This tribute to and career-biography of Japanese director Yasujiro Ozu is an excellent survey of his films and also serves to illuminate Japanese cinema in general. Further, we learn much about Japan itself, its arts and culture, its philosophical and moral values, especially in relation to family and the status of women — Ozu's special province.

From 1929 until his death in 1962, several dozen films later, Ozu graduated from conventional silent b&w comedies and melodramas to mastery of his craft. Less well-known abroad than Akira Kurosawa, whose films were often closer to Western tastes and action themes, Ozu was insistently Japanese, emphasizing family duty, sacrifice and loyalty. A preoccupation with the passage of time, reflected in films named for the season, characterized his later work, often with the same performers growing old along with the characters, in film after film.

In this eulogy-film 23 years after Ozu's death, his relatives and former colleagues describe Ozu the man and his meticulous directorial style. Excerpts from 18 of his films are intecut with interviews, stills and sound recordings of Ozu.

Because of Ozu's enduring reputation among film scholars, and the popularity of Japanese studies on campuses and in urban centers, this Ozu film can find a secure if modest place within 16m distribution and public television.

—Hitch.

L'Arbre Sous La Mer
(The Tree Under The Sea)
(FRENCH-COLOR)

Berlin, Feb. 24.

A Synchronie-Paradise Productions production, with assistance from the French Ministry of Culture. Executive producer, Georges Pellegrin. Directed, written by Philippe Muyl, from the book "A Naked Young Girl," by Nikos Athanassiadis. Camera (Eastmancolor), Bernard Lutic; editor, Jean-François Goyet; sound, Yves Osmu; music, Luc Le Masne; art director, Nikos Meletopoulos. Reviewed at Berlin Film Festival (out of competition), Feb. 23, 1985. Running time: **94 MINS.**

Mathieu . . . . Christophe Malavoy
Eleni . . . . Eleni Dragoumi
Loucas . . . . Julien Guiomar
Thomas . . . . Yavuz Ozkan

A surly young French geologist arrives on a Greek island where, fortunately for him, everyone happens to speak French. The population consists of a boatman who commutes to the mainland, a lonely fisherman and latter's daughter. While the single-minded protagonist sets about examining the rocks, the daughter drifts around fetchingly in nothing but a man's shirt. Clearly it won't be long before they get together.

There's a mystery on the island, involving a petrified tree he wants to examine but can't get near, and he also wonders why the lovely Eleni spends so much time swimming, especially at night. Eventually it turns out that, like the heroine of an old Spike Jones song, she swims with the fishes *and* her kiss is delicious. After a rather lovely, if overlong, sequence in which the naked Eleni besports herself in the water with a cheerful and friendly dolphin, we come to realize, along with the arrogant hero, that the girl's antecedents may be very fishy. Film's ending is a replay of "Splash," but without the laughs.

It's basically a silly film, made sillier by the earnestness with which the story is told. Christophe Malavoy makes the hero a singularly unappealing guy, though Eleni Dragoumi is a convincing child of the sea. Emphasis on ethnographic details (beetles, reptiles and other assorted creepy-crawlies) doesn't do much to enliven the pic, despite attractive location-work and lensing.

—Strat.

Tarsasutazas
(Package Tour)
(HUNGARIAN-DOCU-COLOR)

Budapest, Feb. 12.

A New Yorker Films release (U.S.) of a Hungarofilm presentation of a Mafilm-Objektiv Studios production. Directed by Guyla Gazdag. Camera (Eastmancolor), Elemer Regalyi; Editor, Júlia Sivó; sound, György Kék. Reviewed at the Hungarofilm screening room, Budapest, Feb. 12, 1985. Running time: **75 MINS.**

This feature length documentary "The Decision," produced last year confirms the director's leading position among the new generation of Hungarian filmmakers and his unusually effective use of the documentary.

Without any narration, Gazdag has chosen as his subject an organized tour starting from Budapest in the direction of Auschwitz and Birkenau.

Imagining these chambers of horror as subjects of touristic attraction is already monstrous enough, and showing the proximity between normal tourist reactions and the conduit of some visitors in these hellish spots is scary.

This, however, is only the background, for the participants in this package tour are mostly old people, who have gone through the concentration camps and are returning to honor their dead and to attempt to understand in some way the enormity of the events they have survived. There are also some younger people, brought over by their parents and relatives, to remain living witnesses to the darkest episode of humanity, which should be never forgotten.

As Gazdag follows those people around, the frightening image of the Holocaust emerges again in its full impact. This, in spite of the fact that there isn't one foot of newsreel footage from that period. Everything is written in the deep furrows of these people's faces.

Gazdag intertwines the documentation of the tour with an interview of a woman who had wanted to join it, but couldn't, since she had to go through one more operation, the result of tortures she went through in the camps. It is not only her memories, but particularly her story about a man in the hospital to which she had been taken recently, who maintained Hitler wasn't such a bad man after all, it is only a pity he didn't manage to finish his job, which bookend the film.

While produced by a film studio and shot in 35m, this film may not be quite the fare for theatrical release. However, it is bound to receive plenty of attention from tv all over the world, and quite deservedly so. —Edna.

Notre Mariage
(Our Marriage)
(FRENCH-COLOR-16M)

Miami, Feb. 8.

A Les Films du Passage production. Directed by Valéria Sarmiento. Screenplay, Sarmiento Raul Ruiz from the novel "Mi Boda Contigo" by Corin Tellado; camera (color, 16m), Acacio de Almeida; art director, Isabel Branco; editors, Claudio Martinez, Martine Bouquin; music, Jorge Arriagada. Reviewed at the Arcadia theater, Miami Film Festival, Feb. 7, 1985. Running time: **90 MINS.**

With: Nicolas Silberg, Nadège Clair, Jean-Pierre Teilhade, Maud Rayer, Aurelie Chazelle.

After offering a mesmerizing documentary detailing the universal stud ("A Man When He Is A Man"), Chilean writer-director Valeria Sarmiento moves into feature films via "Our Marriage," based upon the purple-prose novel of Corin Tellado.

There are some intriguing and promising aspects here, though not enough to make "Our Marriage" a good bet. On the script's surface, cowritten by Sarmiento and Raul Ruiz, it would seem there's more than enough lust to make this an exciting and possibly even controversial film. "Our Marriage," shot in Portugal but spoken in French, is the tale of a sickly young girl who's given away by her father to a couple who can't have children. It seems the couple paid the girl's hospital bills and the father felt heavily indebted.

Twenty years later, the same girl, following the death of her adopted mother, marries the man she's been calling "father" all these years. She wants to keep their relationship platonic while tormenting her father-husband with glossy red lipstick, black-seamed stockings and bedroom eyes.

It all sounds hot. Yet, Sarmiento never ignites the fuse that will cause these people — and the film — to explode. The characters move along in a snail-paced daze, talking too much and acting too little. Rather than provide a seamy, steamy body heat — which is what Tellado's book was all about — Sarmiento opts for allegory and esoterica. For "Our Marriage" to work, passions needed to run wild, not mild.

—Marl.

Gossliwil
(SWISS-DOCU-COLOR-16m)

Berlin, Feb. 17.

Produced by Filmkollectiv Zurich. Produced by Hans Sturm; Directed by Sturm and Beatrice Leuthold. Camera (color), Sturm; still photos, Sturm, Leuthold; editors, Sturm, Leuthold; sound, Leuthold, Andre Pinkus. Narration and dialog in Swiss-German. Reviewed at Intl. Forum of Young Film, Berlin Film Festival, Feb. 16, 1985. Running time: **232 MINS.**

Gossliwil is a farming village of 160 people in German-speaking Switzerland. This four-hour film is thematically organized as five "film essays," emphasizing three families, seen in all seasons, over a three-year period.

Appreciating "Gossliwil" as a film requires caring for Gossliwil as a way of life. There are no big dramatic incidents in the film, no great heroines and heroes. These people are hard-working farmers dedicated to the cultivation of their land, the care of their animals and the continuity of their families. They regard their farming vocation as the primary basis of civilization. In a sense, theirs is a holy mission. They are at peace within themselves and prepared to die within a state of grace, to quote an axiom from the film — "Seldom does a peasant die irreconciled."

Themes of "Gossliwil" include nature, work, rural economy, ownership of land, tradition of the large patriarchal family, on being a native or an outsider, on freedom within fences and boundary stones. These themes are sensed in "Gossliwil" as common to farmers worldwide, and they reverberate to other areas of society. In "Gossliwil," one feels that the village is beleagured to some extent, as the big cities of Europe are nearby, representing a source of pressure and corrupting temptation, especially for the young.

"Gossliwil" is beautifully photographed by filmmakers who plainly loved this village and what it stands for. The film is edited to bring out small events, such as the birth of a calf, so that the audience can fully experience and participate.

Subtitled, "Gossliwil" may be of interest, to U.S. public television.
— *Hitch.*

Potomok Belogo Barssa
(The Descendant Of The Snow Leopard) (SOVIET-COLOR)

Berlin, Feb. 20.

A Kirghizfilm (Kirghizian Republic, Soviet Union) production. World rights, Sovexportfilm, Moscow. Features entire cast. Directed by Tolomush Okeyev. Screenplay, Mar Baidshijev, Okeyev, based on a Kirghizian folk legend; camera (color), Nurtal Borbijev; editor, R. Shershneva; music, M. Begalijev; costumes, M. Abdijev. Reviewed at Berlin Film Fest (in competition), Feb. 19, 1985. Running time: 134 MINS.
With: Dokdurbek Kydralijev (Koshoshash), Aliman Shankorosova (Saikal), Doskhan Sholshakssynov (Mundusbai), Guinara Alimbajeva (Aike), A. Chokubajev (Kassen), M. Shantelijev (Sajak), Sh. Seidakmatova (Begaim), G. Kadyralijeva (Sulaika), K. Akmatova (Batma), Aibek Kydryralijev (Kalygul), A. Kulanbajev (Karypbai), S. Chebodejeva-Chaptykova (Sonun), S. Kababajev (Bijaly), M. Machmadov (Sultanbek), R. Seitov (Bakass), D. Achimóv, A. Arashtajev (Merchants).

"The Descendant Of The Snow Leopard" was made by Tolomush Okeyev, a major director who helped to put Kirghizian cinema on the map in the Soviet Union. It's a ballad-film that requires a full knowledge of Kirghizian legends in order to be fully appreciated, and although impressive as a seasonal epic on a large screen, pic has only limited chances to be shown abroad save in Soviet or Kirghizan film weeks or at an offbeat film fest.

The ballad upon which the film is based is on the order of the European equivalent. "The Song Of Roland," whereby events take place that don't really connect to each other any more than a balladeer follows a precise narrative line. The hero is the hunter Koshoshash, who has to wrestle with nature's harsh weather conditions in the mountains where his tribe lives. One year, a drought in the summer followed by a harsh winter nearly brings his tribe to the brink of starvation. Nevertheless, Koshoshash finds a way to keep his people alive by respecting the laws of nature and

seeking help from neighboring tribes — but for a price.

Koshoshash is able to win renown in the area via feats of valor. However, the fatal flaw surfaces when the laws of nature are violated in killing animals coming to their traditional watering-places.

The panoramic views of mountain passes and snow avalanches are particularly of striking beauty.
— *Holl.*

Duhblyor Hatchilhaeyet Deystvquati
(The Double Start To Act) (SOVIET-COLOR)

Berlin, Feb. 17.

A Lenfilm Production. Directed by Ernest Jassan. Ualantine Tchernich, Piotr Koriakin, Jassan; Screenplay, camera (color), Vladimir Burikin; sets, Yelena Fomina; music, Vadim Bibergan; bound, Galina Golubeva. Reviewed at the Berlin Film Festival Intl. Forum of Young Film, Feb. 16, 1985. Running time: 89 MINS.
Kostin . . . . Boris Plotnikov
Zybin . . . . Michail Glujisky
Parschin . . . . Igor Gorbatschau
Seregin . . . . Alexander Udavin
Schnurkov . . . . Piotr Yurtschenkov
Kroschkin . . . . Alexander Romanzov
Olga . . . . Natalyia Danilova
Heili . . . . Rimma Korostylova
Lydia . . . . Olga Vaikova

This light romantic comedy arrived from the Soviet Union accompanied by a reputation of subversiveness dissimulated under its apparently innocuous subject. It turns out that whatever courageous statements were implied, they have been solidly covered by thick coats of sugar, to hide completely the taste of vitriol.

The plot is based on a real-life experiment in the city of Omsk, when the younger generation of leaders was allowed to take over an important industry, for a one month period, in order to put in them some more zest and prepare them for responsibilities to come. The young immediately set out to straighten all the compromises made by the previous leaders.

Which would all be a critical statement if all the young guys hadn't been presented as such hopeless, inflexible clods.

Characters are one-dimensional. Technical credits are merely okay and the ending, telling us that the young, even if they did not find a formula for a better society, hope they can somehow improve the one we live in, sounds complacent, compared with the intimations introduced in the first part of the film.
— *Edna.*

Suart 17
(Sweet 17) (NORWEGIAN-COLOR)

Berlin, Feb. 21.

A Filmgruppe 1 A/S-Norsk Film coproduction. Produced by Knut Andersen, Hans Otto

Nicolayssen. Executive producer, Kirsten Bryhni. Directed by Laila Mikkelsen. Stars Gerd Brotnow. Screenplay, Karin Sveen; camera (color), Rolv Haan; editor, Bente Kaas; sound, Svein Hovde, Peik Borud; music, Anne Grete Preus; art director, Frode Krogh. Reviewed at Berlin Film Festival (Market), Feb. 20, 1985. Running time: 72 MINS.
Marianne . . . . Gerd Brotnow
Bjorn . . . . Bjorne Johan Foss
Mother . . . . , ... Kirsten Hofseth
Father . . . . Helge Jordal
Bente . . . . : . . . . . . Ann Kristin Lepsoe
Kirsten . . . . Tove Grasaasen
Svein . . . . Runar Kristiansen

An appealing little picture about a plump, plain teenager, "Sweet 17" doesn't quite make the most of its opportunities.

First half of the film is the best, introing poor Marianne (Fatso to her friends) who never gets asked to parties or on dates; she lives a rather lonely life, but has a pen-pal (with whom she communicates by audio tape) who lives out in the sticks. When he announces he's coming to Oslo, she's terrified; maybe when he sees her, he'll reject her too. He doesn't, they have a nice weekend together, and Marianne loses her virginity.

Second half of the film is a familiar tale of a girl who finds herself pregnant and doesn't know how to tell friends and family. She opts for an abortion. It's touchingly handled, but we've been here many times before and it's a pity the writer couldn't come up with some more original ideas for Marianne's future.

As played by tubby Gerd Brotnow, who exemplifies the slogan that fat is beautiful, Marianne is a lovely character. Her modest adventures are hardly enough to fill a feature film, even one as short as this; it almost looks like a short subject that's been extended. — *Strat.*

Tasveer Apni Apni
(Their Own Faces) (INDIA-COLOR)

Berlin, Feb. 19.

A Mrinal Sen production. Written and directed by Sen. Camera (color), Sambit Bose; editor, Mrinmoy Chakraborty; sets, Nitish Roy; sound, B.K. Chatuvedi. Reviewed at Berlin Film Festival (information), Feb. 18, 1985. Running time: 66 MINS.
Employee . . . . K.K. Raina
Manager . . . . M.K. Raina
Author . . . . Shyamanand Jalan

This is one of the lesser efforts by prolific Indian filmmaker, Mrinal Sen. Produced for television, it has almost amateurish acting and photography, and never really comes to grips with the theme.

An employee in a big office is about to be sacked for negligence, and he has to act in order to preserve his position, for he is the sole support of his family. During the film's 66 minutes he tries several different approaches to get his boss to change the decision. Between these

attempts, Sen introduces dialogs in which the main character argues with the author who has created him, complaining he is nothing more than a powerless pawn in a game he does not control.

The problem is that it all takes place on a theoretical level, and the basic idea leads only to long talk sessions. —*Edna.*

Megfelelo Ember Kehyes Feladatra
(The Right Man For A Delicate Job) (HUNGARIAN-COLOR)

Budapest, Feb. 13.

A Mafilm-Objektiv Studios, Hungarian Television Budapest & Deltafilmi Oy Helsinki, production. Directed by János Kovácsi. Screenplay, Kovácsi and Juha Vakkuri, based on novel by Vakkuri; camera (color), Miklos Jancsó Jr.; editor, Eva Palotay; sets, Gabor Bachmann; costumes, Judit Szekulesz; sound, Istvan Sipos; muisc: Mátyás Várkonyi. Reviewed at the Hungarofilm screening room, Budapest, Feb. 12, 1985. Running time: 96 MINS.
The young official . . . . Boguslaw Linda
The commander . . . . Ferenc Zenthe
The unknown woman . . . . Anna Fehér
Lady in the hat . . . . Beata Tygzkiewicz
Chief of secret police . . . . . . Esho Siaminen

This political science fiction thriller uses a lot of contemporary references to forecast an image of an eventual totalitarian regime, without ever specifying time or place.

Its prolog, consisting of pseudo-documentary b&w footage of a popular uprising against a corrupt government, invites comparison with Budapest 1958, Prague 1968 or Warsaw 1982, leaving the viewer free to choose his own model.

The man responsible for the successful revolt is simply known as the Commander, but before the main story even begins, we witness the national funeral he is granted after giving his life for his ideals.

The plot itself concerns a young official (again no name), who is given the chance of his life. He is to head a jury sitting in at a historical competition whose subject is the establishment of the new order. The job turns out to be much more dangerous than it would appear at first sight, for the deeper the young official digs into the subject, the more confused and unclear it seems to be.

Director János Kovácsi adopts a light comedy thriller approach, as it flippantly follows the adventures of the "innocent" along the corridors of power and corruption.

Trying to put all of this in a coherent form and not step on any toes in the process seems to be beyond Kovácsi's reach. Indeed, it appears he did have some censorship problems which resulted in his having to delete several passages, that might have been helpful from a narrative standpoint.

Altogether, Kovácsi's political

satire is rather naive, underestimating the ruthlessness and the determined policies of governments of the kind he deals with.

The film has been selected for this year's Directors Fortnight in Cannes. — *Edna.*

Pacific Inferno
(U.S.-FILIPINO-COLOR)

A VCL presentation of a Nathaniel Prods./Arbee coproduction. Executive producer, Jim Brown. Produced by Spencer Jourdain, Cassius V. Weathersby. Associate producer, Rod Perry. Directed by Rolf Bayer. Stars Brown, Richard Jaeckel. Screenplay, Bayer; additional dialog, Roland S. Jefferson, Eric P. Jones; camera (CFI color), Mars (Nonong) Rasca; supervising editor, Richard C. Meyer; editor, Ann Mills; sound, Donald Santos; set design, Vicente Bonus; special effects, Jess Sto. Domingo; production manager-underwater camera, Kim Ramos. Reviewed on Media Home Entertainment vidcassette, N.Y., Feb. 8, 1985. (No MPAA Rating.) Running time: **89 MINS.**

Clyde Preston	Jim Brown
Dealer	Richard Jaeckel
Dawson	Tim Brown
Yamada	Tad Horino
Totoy	Dindo Fernando
Tita	Wilma Reading
Dennis	Rik von Nutter
Leroy	Jimmy Shaw

Also with: Vic Silyan, Dick Adair, Vic Diaz.

"Pacific Inferno" is actor-athlete Jim Brown's unsuccessful attempt to enter the film producer ranks, a dull lowbudgeter imitating his "The Dirty Dozen" hit. Picture was lensed in the Philippines in 1977 under titles "Ship Of Sand" and "Do They Every Cry In America?," never released domestically and now surfacing for homevideo fans.

Picture takes almost 10 minutes to get started, limning the W.W. II story of captured U.S. Navy divers forced by the Japanese to recover $16,000,000 in silver pesos dumped in Manila Bay in 1942 by orders of Gen. MacArthur (to avoid their falling into Japanese hands). Racist white Lt. Dennis (Rik von Nutter) is ranking officer among the Yanks, though Preston (Jim Brown) is their natural leader.

Preston works with Filipino prisoner Totoy (Dindo Fernando) to organize an escape, in return for getting the silver pesos to the local partisans. Pic climaxes with Brown duplicating his "Dirty Dozen" brokenfield running with explosives in hand, abetted by teammate from that earlier film, Richard Jaeckel.

Physical production is deficient, with anachronistic hairstyles and attitudes taken from the 1970s. Casting is a joke, as Filipino film regular Vic Diaz plays a nasty Japanese and busty black actress-singer Wilma Reading is introed as a Filipino partisan. Brown's thank you credits are extended to Hugh Hefner, Don Cornelius, Maurice White, Bill Russell and Richard Pryor (last-named briefly his latter-day employer at Indigo Prods.), among others.—*Lor.*

Montag — Eine Parodie
(Monday, A Parody)
(WEST GERMAN-B&W)

Saarbrücken, Jan. 18.

A Florian Prey Film Production, West Germany. Written and directed by Prey. Features entire cast. Camera (b&w), Thomas Weber; music, Thomas Lachnit. Only credits available. Reviewed at Saarbrücken Film Fest (Max Ophüls Prize), Jan. 18, 1985. Running time: **95 MINS.**

With: Christoph Naumann, Thomas Wiedenhofer, Rita Hadasch, Rudi Klaffenböck, Bernd Kretz.

Florian Prey's "Monday, A Parody" aims its darts at the venerated tradition of the German "Heimatfilm," those mountain-and-rural landscape films that rely on set formulas of melodrama and high-blown tragedy. If the viewer has examples of the genre in mind when he sits down to absorb this parody, the pic works to some extent until the in-jokes begin to wear thin.

Two half-brothers don't get along very well with each other, particularly after a mutual girlfriend was found dead in the woods and the father drowned in a lake. One brother flees to America after the other accuses him of evil misplay in the tragic accidents. America, however, is soon wiped out in an atomic war, and the brother is back in the arms of his loving mother. The spiteful brother swears revenge, and the plot bends this way and that — until it's clear it was the father who was guilty all along of the murder and drowned himself in the lake thereafter.

Prey, a disciple and assistant director to Bavaria's Herbert Achternbusch, might have hit pay dirt with a short-feature version of this parody attempt. Better still: he could have staged the whole affair on a legit stage, where takeoffs on the "Heimat" theme are rather commonplace. As it is here, the film falls apart. —*Holl.*

Der Tod Des Weissen Pferdes
(The Death Of The White Steed)
(WEST GERMAN-COLOR)

Berlin, Feb. 21.

A Basis-Film Verleih Production, Berlin, in coproduction with Westdeutscher Rundfunk (WDR), Cologne. Written and directed by Christian Ziewer. Features entire cast. Camera (color), Gerard Vandenberg; editor, Stefanie Wilke; music, Erhard Grosskopf; sets, Norbert Scherer; costumes, Haidi Schürmann. Reviewed at Berlin Film Fest (in competition), Feb. 20, 1985. Running time: **111 MINS.**

With: Thomas Anzenhofer (Veit Gall, "Oxen-Farmer"), Angela Schanelec (Anna, his wife), Udo Samel (Father Andreas, a monk), Peter Franke (Kilian Feuerbacher, small landowner), Dietmar Schönherr (Caspar von Schenkenstein, a knight), Ulrich Wildgruber (George, abbot of the Auhausen Cloiser; also his brother, a rich merchant in the city), Raimund Dummert (Poor Hans, the boy), Franz Wittich (the village shepherd), Arnulf Schumacher (Father Thomas, monk and village priest), Ellen Esser (Marie), Jürgen von Alten (Behaimhaus, the blind man), Wolfgang Liere (Bartel, his son, a merce-

nary), Helmut Krauss (Linhart, a hops-farmer), Georg Messingschlager (Simon, an old peasant).

"The Death Of The White Steed" was a project five years in the making, and it's to his credit that filmmaker Christian Ziewer has clung stubbornly to his vision despite a cut in the original budget that reduced this planned historical tableau to about $500,000 in the end. One can sense he has had to patchwork the production through to the end and possibly thereby lost the direction of his original vision somewhere along the way. Thus, his illustrated picture-book interpretation of the revolutionary Peasants' Revolt of 1525 in Germany is too naive to be convincing and yet not naive enough to be taken as some kind of "Volkslied" or folk-ballad.

The names are all fictitious and the setting is a small village in Franconia of southern Germany. References to a Thomas Münzer or Florian Geyer as a peasant leader are not to be found save in a figurative sense.

Ziewer's tale has the monks in a village cloister playing the villains in the piece. A false document turns over a promising stretch of meadowland to the cloister, thus making the lot of peasants harsher than ever. However, the good monk who forged the document clears his conscience by spilling the beans, and the peasants now look to a savior-emperor on a white steed to appear and right the wrongs. A mercenary helps them to arm themselves, and in the beginning they are victorious in plundering the cloister and capturing a knight as a hostage and potential backer. But when the wrath of the lords is felt in the blinding of an innocent shepherd, the time of reckoning has come. The white steed appears one day without a rider, and the ending is swift and ruthless for the peasant revolutionaries.

Sharp (though conventional) lensing by Gerard Vandenberg and some fine performances by thesps in key roles —*Holl.*

Wrong World
(AUSTRALIAN-COLOR)

Berlin, Feb. 19.

A Seon Film Prods., Victoria production. Produced by Bryce Menzies. Directed by Ian Pringle. Screenplay, Doug Ling; camera (color), Raymond Argall; editor, Argall; production design, Christine Johnson; sound, Bruce Emery; music, Eric Gradman. Reviewed at the Berlin Film Festival (in competition), Feb. 18, 1985. Running time: 94 MINS.

David Trueman	Richard Moir
Mary	Jo Kennedy
Rangott	Nicolas Lathouris
Robert	Robbie McGregor
Laurence	Esben Storm
Psychiatre	Tim Robinson
Old Man	Cliff Ellen

This is a rather belated addition to the self-searching films of the "Easy Rider" era, with the main

character roaming around the world to look for solace, after having all his humanistic dreams shattered.

Choosing for this character the name of Trueman already denotes in the clearest fashion the attitude he is supposed to represent. Trueman is a physician who wanted to dedicate his career to the poor, to become, as he puts it, "Dr. Schweitzer of Bolivia." But when faced with the corruption and the military juntas ruling Latin America, he takes to drugs, crosses America coast to coast to lose himself in the wide open spaces, and is finally committed to an institution. Every time he needs money, he fleeces one of his former colleagues who had not dared to fulfill lofty ideals, and consequently suffers now from a bad conscience.

He meets Mary, another dropout at odds with the entire world, and hooked on heroin. While accompanying her to her sister's home they discover a mutual interest in their respective anxieties and find a way out of their anguished solitude.

A typical road movie, moving back and forth in time, in order to substantiate Trueman's present problems through flashbacks of his past exprinces, the picture treads a path used often enough in the past, adding very little to this genre. Harsh, gritty camerawork is probably intended to suggest a semi-documentary approach, but burdened with verbose monologs by the protagonist.

Richard Moir plays the lead as in a daze, but Jo Kennedy, as the junkie he picks up, acquits herself much better. (She won Best Actress Silver Bear award. —*Ed.)* —*Edna.*

Los Motivos de Berta
(Berta's Motives)
(SPANISH-B&W)

Berlin, Feb. 19.

A Jose Luis Guerin production. Written, directed and edited by Guerin. Camera (b&w), Gerardo Gormezano; sets, Andres Sanchez Sanz; costumes, Marta and Ma. Antonia Carral Miguel Guillen; music performed by Arielle Dombasle (soprano) and Jean-Luis Valero (piano); sound, Jose Luis Mendieta. Reviewed at the Berlin Film Festival (Forum), Feb. 18, 1985. Running time: 115 MINS.

Berta	Silvia Garcia
Mabel	Arielle Dombasle
Demetrio	Inaki Aierra
Ismael	Rafael Diaz
Nino	Juan Diego Botto
Belardo	Raul Freire
Agueda	Carmen Avila
Widow	Cristina Bodelon

An amazingly controlled and well shaped film, this first feature by 25-year-old Spanish director Jose Luis Guerin was one of the nicest surprises in this year's Berlin Forum. Limited by its nature to art houses and festivals, it augurs a new talent.

Using a minimalist approach, Guerin shows the minute changes taking place in the life of Berta, in her early teens, taking her from the end of childhood to the beginning of womanhood.

The script has almost no dialog, the entire story is presented simply and even Arielle Dombasle, the luscious blond in tv's "Lace" and Eric Rohmer's "Pauline At The Beach," fits in quite naturally, lending her singing voice on and off the screen.

The black and white photography has the slightly washed-out look of nostalgic pictures from the past. The soundtrack is constructed with care for every detail. Altogether, a remarkable achievement for a first film. —Edna.

Martha Dubronski
(SWISS-COLOR)

Saarbrücken, Jan. 17.

A Gruppe Ansia and Kuert-Riesen Film Production, Zürich. Written and directed by Beat Kuert, based on Ingrid Puganigg's novel "Fasnacht." Features entire cast. Camera (color), Hansueli Schenkel, Bernhard Lehner; music, Konstantin Wecker; sound, Markus Fischer; sets, Uschi Stähli. Reviewed at Saarbrücken Film Fest (Max Ophüls Prize), Jan. 16, 1985. Running time: **96 MINS.**
With: Ingrid Puganigg (Martha Dubronski), Peter Wyssbrod (Dubronski, her husband), Barbara Freier (Pia, the painter), Konstantin Wecker (the butcher), Jörg Reichlin (Clemens), Barbara Melzl (Marion), Frank Niemöller (Peter), Nesa Gschwend (Monika), Luciano Simioni (Christian), Rüdiger Vogler (Schelling).

Swiss helmer Beat Kuert comes out of the Zurich stage and cultural-programming department of Swiss tv.

"Martha Dubronski" is an oddity because it's based on Ingrid Puganigg's novel with the authoress playing the title role. It concerns the relationship of a frail and sickly woman with an ugly scar on her face with her crippled husband, who delivers newspapers for a living. When she becomes ill at carnival time, he's left on his own and gradually deteriorates from a compassionate individual to a spiteful drunkard.

As for Martha, she recovers — only to find she must contend with men who pursue her for erotic purposes simply because her general disfigurement entices them. Once all this overlapping misery has been elucidated, however, the story meanders wearyingly into the world of mental derangement and pschological fantasies. —Holl.

Noite
(Night)
(BRAZILIAN-COLOR)

Berlin, Feb. 24.

A Morena Filmes Gavea Filmes-Embrafilme coproduction. Produced and directed by Gilberto Loureiro. Features entire cast. Screenplay, José Louzeiro, Loureiro, from a book by Erico Verissimo; camera (Eastman color), Antonio Penido; editor, Marco Antonio Cury; sound, Fred Leite; music, Sergio G. Saraceni; art director, Arturo Uranga. Reviewed at Berlin Film Festival (out of competition), Feb. 23, 1985. Running time: **81 MINS.**

With: Paulo Cesar Peréio, Aldine Muller, Eduardo Tornaghi, Christina Aché, Guará Rodrigues, Nina de Padua.

Winner of the prize for Best First Feature at last year's Rio Film Festival, "Night" is an odd mixture of black comedy and softcore porn pic.

Story centers around the investigation into the savage murder of a woman in her apartment. A couple of petty crooks run across an amnesiac in a bar; he's immaculately dressed, but has no ID and is in possession of a blood-stained handkerchief. The criminals are certain he's the murderer and set out to give him a good time, mostly with Ruiva, a redheaded prostie of endless energy.

Brazilian films have had raunchy scenes before, but this one goes about as far as it can short of hardcore. It becomes boring. There are also some basic jokes at the expense of the unintelligent cops.

It doesn't add up to much. Technically, film is rough, with ugly color detracting from visual enjoyment. Acting is okay, but the lack of much substance, or genuine humor, makes that Rio prize a real puzzler. —Strat.

Bericht Von Einem Verlassenen Planeten
(Report From An Abandoned Planet)
(WEST GERMAN-COLOR)

Saarbrücken, Jan. 18.

A Peter Krieg Film Production, West Germany. Written and directed by Krieg. Features entire cast. Camera (color), Otmar Schmid, Krieg; music, Rolf Riehm. Only credits available. Reviewed at Saarbrücken Film Fest (Max Ophüls Prize), Jan. 17, 1985. Running time: **82 MINS.**
With: Ilse Böttcher, Ernst Jünger, Ullo von Peinen.

Peter Krieg's "Report From An Abandoned Planet" is partly experimental, partly documentary, partly fiction — and all political. It deals with such sensitive questions as atomic energy plants and rockets with maximum destruction warheads, and for this reason the production has had some problems collecting its final subsidy payments from a government film agency.

"Report From An Abandoned Planet" works on the supposition that on a fictitious planet enough has taken place to warrant a research space team. When the team gets there, however, radio contact is lost, so a second team is sent out to investigate. The planet now is certified as abandoned and devoid of every form of life. As the investigations are carried out, the viewer can easily build bridges in his own imagination to what might one day happen on our own Earth given the present stockpiling of nuclear weapons. — Holl.

Irrsee
(Sea Of Errors)
(AUSTRIAN-SWISS-WEST GERMAN-B&W-16m)

Saarbrücken, Jan. 20.

A Friederike Pezold Film Production. Written and directed by Friederike Pezold. Features entire cast. Camera (b&w), Pezold, Thomas Meissner. Only credits available. Reviewed at Saarbrücken Film Fest (Max Ophüls Prize), Jan. 19, 1985. Running time: **83 MINS.**
With: Friederike Pezold, Marianne Sägebrecht, Alfonso Collorado, Tschakos Checco.

Friederike Pezold was last seen at the Intl. Forum of Young Cinema with "Canale Grande" (1983), in which she tramps through West Berlin with a tv-set on her back and a recording camera in her hand to get instant playback of the reality around her.

Now she's back again with "Irrsee" (translated roughly as "Sea Of Errors"), a late entry in the Max Ophüls Prize sweepstakes at Saarbrücken. The video-artist tramps again through the streets of a big city with nonsense rhymes on the soundtrack to summarize everything that's wrong with our daily routines — from walking the dog to visiting a pharmacy to questioning life and existence.

The results: there's a lot of rational madness floating around in the sea of social contacts. Not even love and friendship can protect the innocent, she seems to be saying. Technical credits are only so-so. —Holl.

Los Pajaros Tirandole A La Escopeta
(Birds Will Fly)
(CUBAN-COLOR)

Berlin, Feb. 21.

An I.C.A.I.C. production. Produced by Evello Delgado. Directed and written by Rolando Diaz. Features entire cast. Camera (color), Pablo Martinez; sound, Germinal Hernandez; editor, Jorge Abello; music, Juan Formell. Reviewed at Berlin Film Festival (Market), Feb. 20, 1985. Running time: **80 MINS.**
Felo Garcia . . . . Reinaldo Miravalles
Hilda Fernandez . . . . Consuelo Vidal
Emilito Fernandez . . . . Alberto Pujol
Magdalena Garcia . . . . Beatriz Valdez
Grandmother . . . . Silvia Planas
Themselves . . . . Los Van Van

"Birds Will Fly" is a brisk, genuinely funny comedy which sets out to deflate the machismo of the Latin male in much the same way Tomas Alea's "Up To A Certain Point" did last year. Obviously, the sex war is heating up in Cuba.

Emilito and Magdalena fall in love, but one day when they sneak into his apartment for a roll in the hay, they're horrified to be disturbed by Magdalena's father, Felo, a widower, and Emilito's mother, Hilda, a widow, who are having an affair of their own. This is too much

for Emilito. At the same time, Felo is enraged to find his precious daughter is no longer a virgin.

Indeed, Magdalena is pregnant, so the young couple marry, but the bitter quarrels between the two men continue until the women get sick of all the double standards involved and drive the protesting guys away. Of necessity, Felo and Emilito become allies, brothers-in-arms upholding male honor against encroaching feminism.

All of this is done with a sprightly sense of humor. The four actors are splendid, especially Reinaldo Miravalles as the overweight, posturing Felo.

A bouncy soundtrack of catchy songs is an added plus, coupled with fine location shooting on the streets of Havana. Apart from the fact that Magdalena is the union rep at her factory, overt politics remain absent from this beguiling comedy.
— Strat.

Gyakufunsha-Kazoku
(The Back-Jet Family)
(JAPAN-COLOR)

Berlin, Feb. 21.

A Directors Co., Kokusai Houei, Art Theatre Guild of Japan production. Produced by Tomoaki Takahashi. Directed by Sogo Ishii. Screenplay, Yoshinori Kobayashi; camera (color), Masashi Tamura; editor, Junichi Kikuchi; art director, Terumi Hosoishi; bound, Noboru Fukuda; music; 1984. Reviewed at the Berlin Film Festival (Forum), Feb. 20, 1985. Running time: **106 MINS.**
Father . . . . Katsuya Kobayashi
Mother . . . . Mitsuko Baisho
Son . . . . Yoshiki Arizono
Daughter . . . . Yuki Kudo
Grandfather . . . . Hitoshi Ueki

This ferocious satire on consumerist society and the Japanese middle class seems to fit in with a feeling of discontent and criticism among some of Japan's younger filmmakers (director Sogo Ishii is 28). In translation, the title refers to the particular technique used by modern airplanes to brake their speed when landing, by reversing the direction of their jets.

The film deals with a typical bourgeois family, overjoyed in the first scenes to be able to move to a new and more comfortable environment. They settle into their new house with all the gadgetry required by modern life, fully equipped to be worthy members of their social class. The only thing, however, is that the emotional balance of this family is shaky at best.

Rapid parodies of film genres, such as horror films, war pictures, samurai epics and kung fu yarns succeed each other, intentional jump-cuts all over the place add to the general turmoil, soundtrack is deafening, grotesque verges on the disgusting, and the maniacal proceedings culminate in an explosion which somehow clears the atmosphere and pulls the family together in their common destructive madness.

At the end, they resemble the survivors of a nuclear war in a science fiction film, who have to start everything all over again.

The entire thing is to be taken, of course, as an allegory of modern cramped life. Situations are obviously manipulated, and so are the characters. Acting however is effective all around. —*Edna.*

Du Sel Sur La Peau
(Salt On The Skin)
(BELGIAN-CANADIAN-FRENCH-COLOR)

Brussels, Jan. 27.

An F3/RTBF/Odessa Films (Paris)/Swan Productions (Paris)/Ciné Groupe, Inc. (Montreal) coproduction. Produced by Godefroid Courtmans. Written and directed by Jean-Marie Degesves. Camera (color), Raoul Coutard; art director, Raymond Renard; sound, Ricardo Castro; editors, Monique Rysselinck, Véronique Mahillon; music, Christian Lété; associate producers, Evelyne July, Yannick Bernard, Jacques Pettigrew. Reviewed at the Brussels Film Festival, Jan. 26, 1985. Running time: **90 MINS.**

With: Richard Bohringer, Catherine Frot, Anne Clignet, Yvette Merlin, Isabelle Glorie, Michel Galabru.

A light romantic comedy from a country (Belgium) that produces little in that vein, "Du Sel sur la Peau" is a slight but agreeable divertissement that might work in Belgian theatrical situations, but may not stand up to anything more than homescreen exposure elsewhere.

Writer-director Jean-Marie Desgesves has nonetheless tried to maximize its commercial potential (in French-speaking territories, at least) through coproduction with France and Canada, leads recruited from Paris, and one of Europe's finest lensers, Raoul Coutard, whose work here, ironically, is undistinguished.

Richard Bohringer, usually cast as inscrutable, quiet-voiced villains in French melodramas, is surprisingly effective in a more banal register as an unassuming computer operator who has sworn off women after a painful romantic liaison. Resisting the match-making efforts of his astrology-minded mom, he devotes himself to his job and his hobbies: photography and remot-controlled model planes.

A car breakdown in front of his house thrusts two women into his life: Catherine Frot, a young single mother, and her 10-year-old daughter. Bohringer, who is fond of children takes to the latter and decides to use her as subject in a shutterbug competition, while keeping his distance from Frot, who also has suffered personal disappointments and is not eager to start again.

Final destination of the story is obvious but Desgesves takes a casually roundabout route in emphasizing Bohringer's charming rapport with Frot's daughter, played with irrepressible high spirits by Anne Clignet.

French comedian Michel Galabru makes a guest appearance as a lovelorn middle-aged man who tries to pick up Frot in a restaurant and gets into an embarrassing quid pro quo for his efforts. — *Len.*

Olle Henry
(Old Henry)
(EAST GERMAN-COLOR)

Saarbrücken, Jan. 21.

A DEFA Film Production, East Berlin; world rights, DEFA Aussenhandel, East Berlin. Directed by Ulrich Weiss. Features entire cast. Screenplay, Dieter Schubert; camera (color), Roland Dressel; music, Peter Rabenalt. Only credits available. Reviewed at Saarbrücken Film Fest (Max Ophüls Prize), Jan. 20, 1985. Running time: **100 MINS.**

With: Michael Gwisdek (Henry Wolters), Aniko Safar (Xenia), Siegfried Höchst, Rolf Hoppe.

East German helmer Ulrich Weiss's "Old Henry" ran out-of-competition at the Saarbrücken fest in the sweepstakes for the Max Ophüls Prize beause the feature's production dates from 1983 instead of last year. It happened that the German Democratic Republic didn't have an appropriate feature by a newcomer, so this one was entered pretty much as a neighborly courtesy to complete the all-around German-lands representation (Austria and Switzerland, East and West Germany).

"Old Henry" scores as an atmospheric treatment of the immediate months after World War II. An aging boxer returns from the front, where he has been wounded, to pick up the lost pieces of his life, but finds himself drifting until he meets a friendly belle-of-the-night who takes him in as her free boarder in an abandoned railway car that now serves for home. The boxer gradually gets up the gumption to box once more, but the match proves harmful and leaves him punchdrunk for life.

Scripter Dieter Schubert was just such a hang-around boxer in the "zero hour" period, and that authenticity is what makes "Old Henry" memorable.

The point made in the film, to be sure, is that the war made a physical and spiritual wreck of everyone, so what was even the sense of boxing save to win back of bit of self-respect.

Ulrich Weiss has made two features, one on the prewar period, the other on the postwar aftermath. He has a refined sense of the historical and the timely. At Saarbrücken he was awarded the first "Mayor's Prize" for the films he brought with him to the festival: the 1981 pic "Your Unknown Brother" and "Olle Henry," portraits of the 1930s-1940s and 1940s-1950s.

— *Holl.*

Einmal Ku'Damm Und Zurück
(A Berlin Love Story)
(WEST GERMAN-COLOR)

Berlin, Jan. 29.

A Cinecom Film Production, Berlin, in coproduction with Sender Freies Berlin (SFB) and Neue Film produktion. Features entire cast. Directed by Herbert Ballmann. Screenplay, Jürgen Engert; camera (color), Ingo Hamer; sets, Hans-Jürgen Kiebach; music, Jürgen Knieper; costumes, Ingrid Zoré; TV producer, Franz Thies. Reviewed at Astor Theater, Berlin, Jan. 28, 1985. Running time: **92 MINS.**

With: Ursela Monn (Ulla Haferkorn), Christian Kohlund (Thomas Stauffer), Evelyn Meyka (Erika Haferkorn), Peter Schiff (Karl Haferkorn), Peter Seum (Atze Scholz), Brigitte Mira (Toilet Lady).

This year's Max Lubitsch Prize (awarded by the Assn. of Berlin Film Journalists) went deservedly to thesp Ursela Monn for her performance in Herbert Ballmann's "A Berlin Love Story," the German title literally translated being "Once To Kurfürstendamm And Back" (in reference to West Berlin's main fashion boulevard). The thematic joke is well understood by anyone living in this divided city, for most of the film is set in East Berlin and concerns the wishes of a young GDR miss to visit the Kudamm in West Berlin just once and return right away.

The story is true. The secretary of an East Berlin official fell in love with the cook at the Swiss embassy in the GDR. Being in possession of a diplomatic passport and allowed to cross the border at Checkpoint Charlie or elsewhere as often as he pleased (often to buy necessary provisions in West Berlin for state affairs like dinners and cocktail parties), the cook had but to stuff his East German girlfriend in the trunk of his car — and off they would go to the Kudamm and back.

The film version has the cook returning one day in his Mercedes to the Swiss embassy after picking up a supply of fresh fish in the country. It's raining, and he picks up too a soaking-wet miss (Monn) on the highway to bring her home to her parents' modest apartment. Of course, it's love at first sight — but such East-West connections are officially frowned upon in the German Democratic Republic, from the West as well as the East due to the tenuous nature of living in a divided city.

The heroine, Ulla (Monn), first hits on the idea of visiting the Kudamm in West Berlin on a lark when one evening Thomas, the cook, drives over the border to the other side just to pick up some pizza. The border guards are so used to seeing the cook on such "service trips" that he is simply waved through with a word of greeting. If that works without a hitch, why not fulfill a long desired dream of ogling the shops and cafes on the Kurfür-

stendamm?

It's done — and it does work like a charm. They then get up the gumption to do it more often.

The rest is how a diplomatic faux pas is resolved with the East-West Berlin love story hanging in the balance. Credits are generally a plus, the story is funny in itself, and the atmospheric East German scenes are accurate down to details.

— *Holl.*

Urgence
(Emergency)
(FRENCH-COLOR)

Paris, Feb. 25.

A Parafrance release of a Lira Elephant production. Produced by Raymond Danon. Executive producer, Ralph Baum. Associate producer, Claire Tucherer. Directed by Gilles Béhat. Stars Richard Berry. Screenplay, Béhat and Jean Herman, from the novel, "Qui Vous Parle de Mourir?" by Gérard Carré and Didier Cohen; camera (color), Pierre Lhomme; editor, Geneviève Vaury; art director, Jean-Pierre Kohut-Svelko; sound, Paul Lainé; music, Jean-Hector Drand; title song performed by Arthur Simms. Reviewed at the Paramount-City-Triomphe cinema, Paris, Feb. 25, 1985. Running time: **99 MINS.**

Jean-Pierre Mougin	Richard Berry
Lyza Forestier	Fanny Bastien
Lucas	Bernard-Pierre Donnadieu
Murneau	Jean François Balmer
Béatrice	Nathalie Courval
VIllard	Georges Géret
Martel	Jean-Jacques Moreau
Arthur Simms	Himself

Gilles Béhat, a former rock drummer turned filmmaker, made lots of francs with his "Rue Barbare" (Street Of The Lost), a noisy, self-conscious transposition of a David Goodis novel to existential France. His new film mines the same pulp vein, but comes off better because it foregoes dime-novel metaphysics for a straight action picture, preposterous in script, but handled with speed and rhythm.

Béhat's new virile, super-cool hero is Richard Berry, a sports journalist who gains possession of a videotape recording the activities of a neo-Nazi cell and its plot to bomb a pop concert organized as an anti-racism benefit. With only a few hours remaining to the dreaded incident, he drives, runs and fights his way through crooked police traps, aided by sympathetic motorcycle and street gangs and pretty young Fanny Bastien, whose brother made the incriminating film and has been eliminated.

Pic's nemesis is razor-wielding Bernard-Pierre Donnadieu, the chief nasty of "Rue Barbare," and already typecast as a stocky, laconic brute. He is good enough to deserve the chance to do something better. Foreign audiences may remember him as the real Martin Guerre in Daniel Vigne's "The Return Of Martin Guerre."

Arthur Simms plays himself as the pop singer with a message for the world, whom, ironically, Berry must shoot in order the prevent the impending castrophe.

Tech credits, dominated by Pierre Lhomme's moody lensing and Geneviève Vaury's crisp editing, are fine.—*Len.*

The Day Of The Cobra
(ITALIAN-COLOR)

A Laser Films S.r.l. production. Produced by Turi Vasile. Directed by Enzo G. Castellari. Stars Franco Nero. Screenplay, Fabio Carpi, Tito Carpi, Aldo Lado from story by Lado; camera (Technicolor), Gianni Bergamini; editor, Gianfranco Amicucci; music-production manager, Paolo Vasile; stunt sequences by Rocco Lerro; special effects, Cataldo Galiano; set design, Stefano M. Ortolani. Reviewed on Media Home Entertainment vidcassette, N.Y., Feb. 7, 1985. (No MPAA Rating.) Running time: **94 MINS.**
Larry Stanciani . . . . Franco Nero
Brenda . . . . Sybil Danning
Goldsmith . . . . William Berger
Tim . . . . Carlo Gabriel Sparanero
Also with: Mario Maranzana, Licinia Lentini, Enio Girolami, Mickey Knox, Massimo Vanni, Sasha D'Arc, Romano Puppo, Angelo Ragusa.

"The Day Of The Cobra" is a pleasant surprise: an effective Italian action film, shot in 1980 and imported as a vidcassette, bypassing U.S. theatrical release.

Picture harks back to a very fine decade-earlier opus, "Detective Belli," with star Franco Nero comfortably essaying another Bogart-styled police detective on a big narcotics case. Both features include solid acting and action sequences plus serviceable storylines.

Working as a private eye in San Francisco, Larry Stanciani (Nero) is summoned by Goldsmith (William Berger) of the narcotics bureau to go on a mission to his hometown of Genoa in search of drug king Kandinsky. Unofficial assignment holds the promise of getting Stanciani his police job back — he lost it and was sent to jail years back in a frameup engineered by Kandinsky.

Amidst a series of doublecrosses, solid fight scenes and chases, Stanciani has a run-in with glamorous disco deejay Brenda (Sybil Danning) and disco owner Lola, who turns out to be a transvestite in an effective plot twist, the clue for which is that Lola is the tallest thesp in the cast.

Nero is very good in this role, his hardboiled personality balanced by sentimental scenes with his cute young son. Both Nero and Danning do their own English dialog in a generally well-dubbed (articulation is in English) soundtrack. Pic is a welcome change of pace from director Enzo G. Castellari, who has been making numerous imitative fantasy and science fiction films lately. — *Lor.*

Les Enragés
(The Rabid Ones)
(FRENCH-COLOR)

Paris, Jan. 30.
An AMLF release of Fildebroc/Renn Productions/FR 3 Films coproduction. Produced by Michèle de Broca. Directed by Pierre-William Glenn. Features entire cast. Screenplay, Gérard Brach. Camera (Fujicolor), Jean-Claude Vicquery; art director, Willy Holt; sound, Michel Desrois; editor, Thierry Derocles; music, Vincent Gemignani, Alain Lecointe, Jacky Liot. Reviewed at the Gaumont Ambassade theater, Jan. 27, 1985. Running time: **96 MINS.**
Jessica Melrose . . . . Fanny Ardant
Marc . . . . François Cluzet
Laurent . . . . Jean-Roger Milo
Nadine . . . . Marie-Christine Rousseau

Leading French cinematographer Pierre-William Glenn, who has done memorable work with François Truffaut, Bertrand Tavernier and others, is just another neophyte trying too hard to make an impression in "Les Enragés," his first theatrical fiction feature as director. It is a shrill, obvious melodrama about two young delinquents who terrorize a movie star at her tastelessly splashy country abode. That veteran scripter Gérard Brach wrote it in no way redeems a tale that reeks of cinematic *déja vu*.

Fanny Ardant is the film star, though she is hardly the stuff of celluloid fanaticism, despite some overwrought vidclip closeups. François Cluzet, one of the most promising of a new generation of French screen actors, takes a wrong turn in his career in playing Ardant's chief antagonist, who is a uncouth fan with a taste for drag exhibitionism. Fellow mug is played by Jean-Roger Milo, whose homely features have doomed him to typecast parts as simian plug-uglies.

The repellent story, unsympathetic characterizations and pretentious turns in the *huis clos* confrontation are more than Glenn can handle, and his direction deteriorates even faster than Ardant's nerves. Tech credits, notably Jean-Claude Vicquery's lensing, are mediocre.
— *Len.*

The Land Of William Tell
(SWISS-B&W-16m)

Saarbrücken, Jan. 17.
A Hayek Film Production, Zürich. Features entire cast. Directed by G. Nicolas Hayek. Screenplay, Hayek, Carlo Mandelli; camera (b&w) Joder Macharz; music, Daniel Brunetti, Alexandre Deplats. Reviewed at Saarbrücken Film Fest (Max Ophüls Prize), Jan. 16, 1985. Running time: **75 MINS.**
With: Ettore Cella (the filmmaker), Agnes Dünneisen (the bankrobber), Teco Celio (the man in the wheelchair), Frank Hamilton (the American), Edi Huber, G. Nicolas Hayek.

This delightful first feature, a low-budget tour-de-force by a young Swiss filmer who wrote, directed, produced and acted, makes merry fun of Switzerland as a land of innocent chumps and grabby busybodies. Even the English title (instead of a German one) gets in its digs at the outset: helmer G. Nicolas Hayek has a former American bomber pilot, who crash-

landed here in a field in 1944 while on a mission over Germany, returning to a village as a guest of honor and proclaiming how delightful it is to be back in "the land of William Tell." The ceremony is soon dispersed when a non-detonated bomb is dug out of the ground on the very spot where the memorial is to be placed.

At this point, it's suddenly clear the whole story of "The Land Of William Tell" is the daydreaming creation of a struggling young filmmaker trying to write his first scenario for a possible feature film project. The hero shortly throws the plot into a stuffed wastebasket and is back again at his daily job washing cars when a lady bankrobber happens on the scene, and a real-life adventure takes place that beats anything he's yet conceived of on paper.

The erstwhile filmmaker is kidnapped by the would-be bankrobber, and taken to his own apartment, which serves as a hideout. While the police are scouring the area, who should be eyeballing the apartment but the wheelchair busybody across the way. By this time it's clear to the educated film buff that the frame of reference is Alfred Hitchcock's "Rear Window," and the whole film is a brace of scrambled Yankee-style genres (try Woody Allen comedies, to begin with). The funny part is that even the plot's filmmaker is trying to figure out what's going on about him even after the aud has been sufficiently clued.

In the end, the lady bankrobber hasn't made it to Waikiki Beach as she hoped, and all the stolen loot hasn't been recovered by the arresting police. Where are the missing Swiss francs? In the flowerpot of the filmmaker's otherwise bare apartment — but known only to the spying neighbor, who now uses a singing-telegram ploy to distract the unwary chum and get into the flat for a second run at the money! The rest has to be seen, for the end has a few more merry twists that tickle the funnybone.

"The Land Of William Tell" introduces Swiss helmer Hayek whose prior training was at the Paris Film School (IDHEC) and Swiss Television, which explains a bit where the deft directorial hand comes from. —*Holl.*

Dirty Story
(FINNISH-SWEDISH-COLOR)

Berlin, Feb. 21.
A Jörn Donner production, in association with the Finnish Film Institute, Golden Films and the Swedish Film Institute. Produced by Donner, Peter Kropenin, Tuula Söderberg. Directed and written by Donner. Stars Erland Josephson. Camera (color), Tony Forsberg; editor, Olof Oscar; sound, Thomas Samuelsson; music, Pedro Hietanen; costumes, Marjatia Missinen, Kirsi Manninen. Reviewed at

Berlin Film Festival (Market), Feb. 20, 1985. Running time: **96 MINS.**
Gabriel Berggren . . . . Erland Josephson
Camilla . . . . Charlotta Larsson
Also with: Nils Brandt, Agneta Ekmanner, Lilga Kovanko, Ake Lindman, Lasse Pöysti.

Jörn Donner's quaintly titled new film is for much of its length a tense little drama about the dilemmas of a 60-year-old company executive, played with his accustomed skill by Erland Josephson. With his marriage on the rocks, Gabriel Berggren finds himself in business difficulties too, when the chairman of his company, United Metal, dies at Berggren's desk one night. Amid the boardroom jockeying as to who'll run the company now, and the need to layoff staff and curb production, Berggren finds himself also involved with a pretty young girl, Camilla, who comes to work in the office.

Pic climaxes when he's taken ill at the wedding celebrations of an obese rival (who somehow has married a Miss Finland).

Scandinavian audiences will doubtless be well aware that Charlotta Larsson, the charming young actress who plays the teasing Camilla, is, in actuality, Erland Josephson's daughter; it's no surprise, then, that there's no more than a hint of romance between the two of them, but there's a definite charge nonetheless. Film is a bit dry, and the ending is exceptionally abrupt and unsatisfactory. — *Strat.*

Torpedonosszy
(Torpedo Planes)
(SOVIET-COLOR/B&W)

Berlin, Feb. 21.
A Lenfilm production. Directed by Semjon Aranovich. Features entire cast. Screenplay Karmalita, from stories by Juri German; camera (Sovcolor, b&w), Vladimir Iljin; sound, Galina Lukina; music, Alexander Knaifel; art editor, Isaak Kaplan. Reviewed at Berlin Film Festival (out of competition), Feb. 20, 1985. Running time: **95 MINS.**
With: Rodion Nacapetov, Vera Clagoleva, Alexei Sharkov, Vsevolod Schilowski, Andrei Boltnev, Nadeshda Lukaschevich.

Apparently based on personal reminiscences, and utilizing a good deal of impressive on-the-spot war coverage footage, "Torpedo Planes" is nonetheless a rather sentimental and familiar tale of the men who go off to fly and the women who stay at home to worry.

The year is 1944 and a Soviet squadron at a Baltic base has to hunt down German ships and submarines. Early on, we see a crippled aircraft deliberately crash into a German vessel to sink it, bringing bereavement to wives and sweethearts back home and causing grief to the dead men's comrades. Bulk of the film deals with personal relationships: Bebolrov, recently wounded, discovers his wife's infidelity; Cherepovets begins courting Maria, who works as a waitress, but she contracts TB and leaves by a ship which is later sunk by a German sub; Gavrilov is reunited with his small son, though he suspects the child, who doesn't remember him at all, may, in fact, *not* be his son.

The finale is another battle sequence and, as in the early scene, about 50% of the action seems to be stock footage, cleverly integrated and obviously shot under hazardous conditions. In fact, throughout the pic (dated 1983) there is a mixture of black and white and rather muddy Sovcolor, presumably in order to make the vintage material less obtrusive when it comes.

Performances are all adequate, though sentimentality is barely kept in check. It's an old-fashioned film, which tells us little that's new about war, but on its own modest terms it's reasonably effective. — *Strat.*

Firar
(The Escape)
(TURKISH-COLOR)

Berlin, Feb. 18.

A Gúlsah Film Production. Directed by Serif Gören. Features entire cast. Screenplay, Erdogan Túnas, from novel by Osman Sahin; camera (color), Orhan Oguz; editor, Gören; sound, Erkan Esenboga; music, Yeni Türkü Gurubu. Reviewed at Berlin Film Festival (out of competition), Feb. 17, 1985. Running time: 90 MINS.
Ayse . . . . Hülya Kocyigit
Mahmut . . . . Talat Bulut

Made by Serif (pronounced "sheriff") Gören, the nominal director of the late Yilmaz Güvey's "Yol," "The Escape" is a bit more conventional, but still a well-made pic about the plight of a woman who murders her beastly de facto husband when she discovers he's secretly been married to another woman all along. She's thrown in the slammer, but manages to seduce a guard to help her escape.

She winds up working as a cook for some miners, but soon she finds herself in bed with the mine foreman. Then the prison guard shows up and she's forced to flee. Finally, she makes it to where her two daughters are living, only to be picked up by the cops at the moment of reunion.

Hülya Kocyigit doesn't entirely convince as the put-upon heroine, but she puts plenty of energy into the role. None of the various men in the film are likeable, so this tale of a woman's plight may register with some audiences; but she does tend to make all the wrong decisions in solving her problems, starting with the stabbing of her slobbish "husband."

Gören's direction is economical and the film is well shot by Orhan Oguz, though the lab work, which gives the film a very pallid look, leaves a lot to be desired. In all, not to be placed in the top rank of recent Turkish films, but an interesting item. —*Strat.*

Holi
(Festival Of Fire)
(INDIAN-COLOR)

Berlin, Feb. 19.

A Film Unit Production. Produced by Ketan Mehta, Pradeep Uppoor. Directed by Mehta. Features entire cast. Screenplay, Mehta, Mahesh Elkunchwar, from the latter's play; camera (color), Jehangir Chaudhary; editor, Subhash Sehgal; sound, A.M. Padmanabhan; music, Rajat Dholakia; art director, Archana Shah. Reviewed at Berlin Film Festival (out of competition), Feb. 18,1985. Running time: 120 MINS.
With: Sanjeev Gandhi, Rahul Ranade, Asutosh Gowaikar, Amole Gupte, Aamir Hussain, Naseeruddin Shah, Om Puri.

The team of filmmakers responsible for this tale of student unrest and rebellion is obviously composed of film buffs. Pic is distinguished by the use of extremely long, fluid, complex takes, rather in the manner of Hungary's Miklos Jancso. However, narrative structure seems not to be the team's strong point.

Based on a play, "Festival Of Fire" is a tale of conflicts between the student body and the faculty which escalate into violent rebellion. It is slackly paced, but has plenty of visual ideas in compensation, though the shoddy lab work is a letdown.

Some name actors such as Naseeruddin Shah and Om Puri play small roles, apparently to encourage the relatively youthful director, Ketan Mehta, It's ultimately an interesting pic, which shows a talent, but one which needs more discipline and sense of structure.
—*Strat.*

La Vie de Famille
(Family Life)
(FRENCH-COLOR)

Paris, Feb. 23.

A Fox/Hachette release of a TF1/Flach Film coproduction. Produced by Charles Brabant and Jean-François Lepetit. Directed by Jacques Doillon. Stars Sami Frey. Screenplay, Doillon, Jean-François Goyet; camera (color), Michel Carre; editor, Nicole Dedieu; sound, Michel Guiffan; production manager, Jacques Pol. Reviewed at the Marignan-Concorde theater, Paris, Feb. 22, 1985. Running time: 98 MINS.
Emmanuel . . . . Sami Frey
Elise . . . . Mara Goyet
Mara . . . . Juliet Berto
Natacha . . . . Juliette Binoche
Lili . . . . Aina Walle

Good news from Jacques Doillon. After the shrill psychodramatics of his last few films — notably "La Pirate" which provided the obligatory scandal at last year's Cannes Film Festival — he now returns to the quieter, more subtle manner of his earlier work.

"La Vie de Famille" is a poignant, well-observed drama of an estranged father and daughter seeking surreptitiously to renew contact during a brief trip on the road. He (Sami Frey) lives with his second wife (Juliet Berto) and her teen daughter, but spends weekends with his 10-year old daughter from a previous marriage. This routine creates tension within Frey's new household, where his relationship with his stepdaughter is fraught with sexual ambiguity.

Story follows the incidents of one particular weekend — opening with a sequence of domestic hysteria. Once Frey has left to pick up his daughter, the film finds a more discursive, restrained tone and, barrin' several scenes, sticks to it.

Equipped with a video camera, father and daughter decide to make their way from the South of France into Spain, elaborating a film she has partially scripted. Through the home movie and other games and exchanges, a shift in their relationship takes place, climaxing in a long sequence in a Madrid hotel, where Frey, unable to speak directly, confesses his fears and inadequacies alone in front of the camera.

Film's discreet· emotion owes much to Sami Frey, a fine actor whose seductive, soft-spoken manner can convey violence and affection without melodramatics. The girl is played beautifully by Mara Goyet, daughter of Doillon's co-scripter, Jean-François Goyet, a film editor. All have helped the director make one of his most mature and affecting films.

Pic, handsomely produced, was made for the TF-1 network but shot in 35m and released in theatrical situations before its homescreen airing.—*Len.*

El Juguete Rabioso
(The Enraged Toy)
(ARGENTINE-COLOR)

Berlin, Feb. 23.

An M.R.P. Soc. production. Produced by Reynaldo Mangiaterra. Directed by José Maria Paolantonio. Features entire cast. Screenplay, Mirtha Arlt, Paolantonio, from a novel by Roberto Arlt; camera (Eastman color), Esteban Pablo Courtalon; editor, Oscar Souto; sound, Miguel Babuini; music, Luis Maria Serra; art directors, Martha Albertinazzi, Oscar Aizpeolea. Reviewed at Berlin Film Festival (out of competition), Feb. 22, 1985. Running time: 112 MINS.
With: Julio de Grazia, Cipe Lincovsky, Osvaldo Terranova, Pablo Cedron, Lucrecia Capello, Salo Vasocchi, Nicolas Frei, Aldo Braga.

A handsomely produced pic adapted from a novel by Roberto Arlt, "The Enraged Toy" is a serious study of the development of a bitter and dangerous young man.

Apparently set in the '20s, or thereabouts, it intros Silvio Astier (Julio de Grazia), an intelligent, ambitious youth from an Italian working-class immigrant family. Thrown over by his upper-class girl because he isn't good enough for her, Silvio is determined to succeed. He enrolls in an air force officer training course, but after being accepted on his merits is displaced by a (presumably less talented) youth of better social standing.

After a brief brush with a pathetic transvestite in a seedy hotel, he gets a job in a bookstore run by an eccentric Italian family who seem to have strayed from a Dickens novel. But this winds up in frustration and a misplaced act of revenge. Finally, Silvio decides to betray his best friend, an old man he knows is planning to rob a wealthy businessman; but after he sees his friend beaten by police, he can't even accept the reward money he hoped for.

It can be assumed Silvio represents a whole generation of Argentines, frustrated by the limitations placed upon them through no fault of their own, and finally reacting negatively and violently against all of life's knocks.

It's a downbeat item, but quite effectively handled, with rich and detailed production dress, fine visuals, and effective performances. It is, perhaps, too familiar in its surface treatment to make it outside Spanish-speaking territories.

The English subtitles seem to have been written by a Londoner who hasn't kept up with changes in the English language, with epithets such as "Cor blimey!" looking extemely quaint. —*Strat.*

Louise ... L'Insoumise
(Louise The Rebel)
(FRENCH-COLOR)

Berlin, Feb. 16.

A Gerland Production. Produced by Geneviève Lefebvre. Directed and written by Charlotte Silvera. Features entire cast. Camera (Fujicolor), Dominique Le Rigoleur; editor, Geneviève Louveau-Sebestik; sound, Claude Bertrand; music, Jean-Marie Senia; art director, Sylvain Chauvelot. Reviewed at Berlin Film Festival (out of competition), Feb. 15, 1985. Running time: 98 MINS.
Louise . . . . Myriam Stern
Mother . . . . Catherine Rouvel
Father . . . . Roland Bertin
Gisèle . . . . Joelle Tami
Viviane . . . . Deborah Cohen
Mme. Royer . . . . . Marie-Christine Barrault
Aunt . . . . Lucia Bensasson
Uncle . . . . Dominique Bernard

Feature debut of 29-year-old Charlotte Silvera is an accomplished, if familiar, tale of a stifled childhood in the early '60s, presumably autobiographical.

Louise, aged about 12, is the second of three daughters of a Jewish couple who came to France from Tunisia. Her problem is not anti-semitism, but rather the old-fashioned attitudes of her parents, and especially her mother, whom she detests. She yearns to be allowed to attend the birthday party of a school friend, but it's on a Saturday and her mother won't permit it. Her unresponsive, rather lazy, father won't intervene.

Acting is excellent, with Myriam Stern a find as the pugnacious Louise. Provincial setting is nicely etched in by director Charlotte Silvera, and pic is technically very good. The period (about 1961) is evoked via tv news bulletins concerning the problems in Algeria and the beginnings of terrorism in France. —*Strat.*

Bhombal Sardar
(INDIAN-B&W)

Berlin, Feb. 19.

Produced by Dept. of Information and Cultural Affairs, Government of West Bengal. Directed by Nripen Gangali. Screenplay, Khagendra Math Mitra; camera (b&w), Soumendra Ray; editor, Samaresh Bose; music, Anupam Mookerji; art director, Ashoke Bose. Reviewed at Kinderfilmfest, Berlin Film Festival, Feb. 18, 1985. Running time: 75 MINS.

Bhombal is an engaging lad of the Huck Finn stripe who leaves his village for an odyssey of adventure after being beaten by his uncle for killing a snake. During the travels, Bhombal is fortified from loneliness by his fantastic imagination. He encounters various people who test his will. On occasion, Bhombal sings to himself to pluck up his courage. By the film's end, he is reunited with his uncle, who pledges never again to beat him.

Because the film is crudely written, directed and performed, lacking even an interesting use of the Bengali landscape as background, its prospects for U.S. distribution seem doubtful. —*Hitch.*

Osslinaja Schkura
(Donkey Skin)
(SOVIET-COLOR-70M)

Berlin, Feb. 21.

A production of Studio Lenfilm, Leningrad. Directed by Madeshda Koschewerowa. Screenplay, Michael Wolpin, from a work by Charles Perrault; camera (color, 70m), Eduard Rosowski; music, Moissej Weinberg. Reviewed at Kinderfilmfest, Berlin Film Festival, Feb. 20, 1985. Running time: 85 MINS.

Unlike American cinema, East Europeans excel at theatrical films made specifically for children — emphasizing entertainment, not propaganda. This new Soviet 70m color extravaganza is in that tradition, a comedy-fantasy of non-stop visual action with big opulent sets and a large cast in fantastic costuming. Kinderfilmfest audience of tiny moppets at Berlin loved it.

Busy story concerns a royal donkey with magic powers in a long-ago make-believe monarchy. Handsome young Prince Jacques is betrothed to blond stunner Princess Theresa, who is protected by a good fairy. The Wicked Stepmother goads the weakling king into mischief, with result that the princess is forced to flee, becoming a beggar-maid. The prince wants to marry her, rags and all, meaning he renounces royal status for true love. Come to think of it, maybe that is a communist theme.

Veteran director Koschewerowa debuted with Studio Lenfilm in 1929, specializing in comedies and fairy tales. Her "Cinderella" of 1947 is regarded a children's film classic. —*Hitch.*

Una
(YUGOSLAVIAN-COLOR)

Berlin, Feb. 18.

A Film Danas-Croatia Film-Smart Egg Pictures Production. Produced and directed by Misa Radivojevic. Features entire cast. Screenplay, Nebojsa Pajkic, from the book by Momo Kapor; camera (color), Aleksander Petkovic; music, Kornelisje Kodec; editor, Vuksan Lukovas. Reviewed at Berlin Film Fest (Market), Feb. 17, 1985. Running time: 103 MINS.
Una Vojvodic ....Sonja Savic
Michel Babic ....Rade Serbedzija
Mrs. Babic ....Milena Dravic
The Other Woman ....Isabel Ines Madden
Zdravkovic...................Petar Kralj
Father ....Dusan Janicijevic

A somewhat curious mixture of softcore sex film and political drama, "Una" is a handsomely produced affair which introduces a sex star in lissome Sonja Savic. She plays a 24-year-old sociology student with ambitions to become a journalist. When her boyfriend gets thrown in the cooler, she's approached by the Powers That Be with a special assignment: to interview a controversial university professor and hopefully get him to say something incriminating, with audio tapes to be passed on to the authorities. Una complies and soon is having a steamy affair with the prof (Rade Serbedzija), a world-weary cynic with a pretty wife (Milena Dravic) and radical ideas which inflame his bosses.

For too much of its length, the film ignores the interesting aspects of the professor's alleged crimes to concentrate on a variety of energetic sex scenes. Savic is a looker in the Sylvia Kristel tradition, but enough is enough. Helmer Misa Radivojevic should have at least integrated these scenes better into the plot.

Helped by fine lensing from Aleksander Petkovic, "Una" looks handsome enough, but can't seem to decide what audience it's aiming at. —*Strat.*

Dance With A Stranger
(BRITISH-COLOR)

London, Feb. 25.

A Samuel Goldwyn Co. release (U.S.) of a First Picture Co. production for Goldcrest and the National Film Finance Corp. Produced by Roger Randall-Cutler. Directed by Mike Newell. Stars Miranda Richardson, Rupert Everett and Ian Holm. Screenplay, Shelagh Delaney; camera (color), Peter Hannan; production design, Andrew Mollo; art direction, Adrian Smith; costumes, Pip Newberry; editor, Mick Audsley; music, Richard Hartley. Reviewed at the Plaza, London, Feb. 26, 1985. (BBFC certificate; 15.) Running time: 101 MINS.
Ruth Ellis ....Miranda Richardson
David Blakeley ....Rupert Everett
Desmond Cussen ....Ian Holm
Andy ....Matthew Carroll
Anthony Findlater ....Tom Chadbon
Carole Findlater ....Jane Bertish
Cliff Davis ....David Troughton
Clive Gunnell..............Paul Mooney
Morrie Conley ....Stratford Johns

"Dance With A Stranger" is a tale of dark passions based on a true story of the London underworld during the 1950s. Pic figures to perform well in specialized houses thanks especially to a riveting performance by newcomer Miranda Richardson and taut direction by Mike Newell, whose previous features include the New Zealand-located "Bad Blood" pic and the Charlton Heston-starrer "The Awakening."

Film charts the rocky course of the relationship between Ruth Ellis, a divorcee and prostitute-turned-nightclub manageress, and the upperclass dropout David Blakeley. He's too emotionally immature to care while she's too infatuated to take the commonsense course of ending the affair. Film ends with Ellis entering mythology as the last woman to be hanged under British law, for her shooting of Blakeley.

The script by Shelagh Delaney, who last figured in theatrical film credits for "A Taste Of Honey" (1961) and "Charlie Bubbles" (1968), is densely packed with social and psychological nuances. Audiences are left largely to draw their own conclusions as to what drew the seemingly ill-matched couple together, and also to raise the judicial questions posed by Ellis' execution.

Film opens with Ellis apparently on an upward course, but Blakeley's arrival promptly puts her life on the skids. She loses her job when he throws an ugly scene in the nightclub where she works. Ellis is ejected from her new home with tame lover Desmond Cussen when he discovers that the Blakeley relationship is ongoing. Moved by Cussen into a smaller apartment, she suffers a miscarriage and takes up her old life on the streets. Tracking down the miscreant Blakeley to a country pub, she receives only bruises.

There are too few tender moments between Ellis and Blakeley to make for easy understanding of what draws the two together and why Ellis loses her marbles when she knows she's lost Blakeley for good. In terms of plot structure, however, there's compensation in low-key moments between Ruth and Desmond or her son Andy.

Miranda Richardson's performance as Ruth Ellis indicates her potential as a firstrate screen actress. With her rolling eyes and impulsive gestures, she captures the delicate nuances of an attractive girl who's both cool and coquettish, and who is caught up in emotional storms that she's little equipped to deal with.

Major flaw is Rupert Everett's inability to convey more about David Blakeley than that he's set to fail consistently in work and in life. Ian Holm is okay as the well-meaning Desmond Cussen whose human decency cannot satisfy Ruth's deeper longings.

Production design is evocative of the period. There's also an impressive jazz-oriented score that makes telling use of a handful of songs. Pic is set for U.S. release in June via the Samuel Goldwyn Co. —*Japa.*

The Aviator
(COLOR)

Dull aerial yarn.

Hollywood, March 6.

An MGM/UA Entertainment release of a Mace Neufeld production. Produced by Neufeld and Thomas H. Brodek. Directed by George Miller. Stars Christopher Reeve, Rosanna Arquette. Screenplay, Marc Norman (based on the novel, "The Aviator," by Ernest Gann); camera (Metrocolor), David Connell; editor, Duane Hartzell; production designer, Brenton Swift; music, Dominic Frontiere; sound, Patrick Mitchell; art director, Dusko Jericevic; costumes, Patricia Smith; associate producer, Dan Tana; special aerial photography, John Oaten, John Edwards; assistant director, John Powditch, Zoran Budak; casting, Joe D'Agosta. Reviewed at MGM/UA Studios, Culver City, March 6, 1985. (MPAA Rating: PG). Running time: 96 MINS.
Edgar Anscombe ......Christopher Reeve
Tillie Hansen ....Rosanna Arquette
Moravia ....Jack Warden
Bruno Hansen ....Sam Wanamaker
Jerry Stiller ....Scott Wilson
Evelyn Stiller.................Tyne Daly
Rose Stiller ....Marcia Strassman
Old Man ....Will Hare

"The Aviator" does not fly. Script is flat, costars Christopher Reeve and Rosanna Arquette fail to overcome unattractive characters, and the production's inherent flavor — 1920s' Stearman biplanes — is too quickly sacrificed for a drama of survival in a desolate wilderness. Boxoffice outlook is bleak.

Film first was test-released in Tucson and Phoenix and hit 400 theaters in a largely Midwest regional bow March 8.

Shot in Yugoslavia, and based on a novel by aviation author Ernest Gann, pic is the most claustrophobic airplane yarn in memory. Sullen and withdrawn Reeve character, who flies the Pasco, Wash.-Elko, Nev. mail route for a ragtag airmail line in 1928, meets rich, bratty Rosanna Arquette when he's forced to take her aboard as a passenger.

They're instant antagonists. Then their plane crashes in the mountains and they spend the rest of the film caring for each other and fighting off wolves. Reeve, whose emotional paralysis is accompanied by a terrible facial scar from a tragic accident that opens the film, finds his soul and will to live in the course of their survival. Arquette grows up.

Central to the soft underbelly of the feature is lack of solid characterization. Spark between Reeve and Arquette never ignites.

Meanwhile, back at the little airport, crusty Jack Warden, who runs the line, tells the missing girl's callow and angry father (Sam Wanamaker) that the boys who fly the mail are a tattered, crippled lot of open-cockpit addicts. Scott Wilson and Tyne Daly lend okay support as a pilot and his wife who are close to Reeve.

Film was directed by Australian George Miller, who does on occasion capture some of the scenic beauty suggested by his earlier film, "The Man From Snowy River;" cameraman, David Connell, is also Australian. Highlight of the production, literally, is an interlude featuring ravenous wolves.

Inexcusably, the rescue of the beleaguered Reeve and Arquette is never seen. As the rescue pilot who finds the pair, Wilson spots the victims from the air and then the film abruptly cuts to their arrival back in Elko. Point is the rough mountain terrain clearly offered no place for a plane to land but perhaps audience is supposed to imagine there was a clearing out there somewhere.
— *Loyn.*

Martin's Day
(COLOR)

Timid picture; poor outlook.

Hollywood, Feb. 27.
An MGM/UA Entertainment of a United Artists presentation of a World Film Services production. Produced by Richard F. Dalton, Roy Krost. Directed by Alan Gibson. Stars Richard Harris. Screenplay, Allan Scott, Chris Bryant. Camera (Medallion color), Frank Watts; editor, David de Wilde; music, Wilfred Josephs; production designer, Trevor Williams; set decorator, Steve Shewchuk; sound, David Lee; costumes, Lynne Mackay; assistant director, Bill Corcoran; casting, Deirdre Bowen. Reviewed at MGM/UA screening room, L.A., Feb. 26, 1985. (MPAA Rating: PG.) Running time: **98 MINS.**
Martin Steckert . . . . .Richard Harris
Dr. Mennen . . . . .Lindsay Wagner
Lt. Lardner . . . . .James Coburn
Martin . . . . .Justin Henry
Karen . . . . .Karen Black
Brewer . . . . .John Ireland

The major obstacle for family oriented fare to overcome is a blandness that immediately identifies it as a PG picture. "Martin's Day" never makes that hurdle. A Canadian-made pickup by MGM/-UA, film has been on the shelf for over a year and is only now receiving a limited test release. With kids today accustomed to flashier entertainment, film is unlikely to find a warm reception.

It is not that this friendship story between an escaped con and the young boy he kidnaps is inherently dull material. It is the flatness and simplicity of the telling that makes it unable to capture the imagination. The characters lack the complexity and depth to stimulate an audience, even a young one.

After some muddled exposition about a rejected parole, inmate Martin Steckert (Richard Harris) sets himself on fire and masterminds a prison escape. Once out he kidnaps a young boy (Justin Henry) and heads for his own boyhood lakeside hideaway.

Steckert is a dotty character who can break into song one moment and ran down a house in a police car the next. Psychiatrist Lindsay Wagner is along to explain Steckert and to supply some tea and sympathy, but fails to untangle his psyche or make much sense herself.

Also largely wasted is James Coburn as the police lieutenant chasing Steckert. Though it becomes something of a personal challenge for him, there is little passion to his obsession. Steckert's encounter with former girlfriend Karen Black is also short in the passion department.

Script by Allan Scott and Chris Bryant really doesn't flush out what the connections are between these people and director Alan Gibson leaves them stranded for the most part. Harris, in particular, is either painfully obvious or inexplicably deep.

Cinematogrpahy by Frank Watts, like the film's emotional center, seems to be in perpetual soft focus. Fall locations in Ontario are lovely, but, like a post card, unreal. —*Jagr.*

Gringo
(U.S.-DOCU-COLOR-16m)

Berlin, Feb. 21.
A presentation by Kasba Productions, Newell Media I, and Ann S. Barish, of a Tom Norman film. Executive producer, Gareth E. Newell; coproduced by Barish and Lech Kowalski; associate producer, Karen O'Toole. Directed by Kowalski. Camera (color) and editing, Raffi Kuklowsky; sound, Benoit Deswartes; music, Chuck Kentis; story consultant, John Spacely. Reviewed at Berlin Film Festival (information), Feb. 20, 1985. Running time: **85 MINS.**

British-born director Lech Kowalski, following upon his 1980

"D.O.A." about the Sex Pistols and the drug-doomed lovers, Sid Vicious and Nancy, has produced in "Gringo" a portrait of the addict as a young punk.

"Gringo" is a self-portrait of heroin addict John Spacely, credited as "story consultant." Spacely narrates and acts out for the camera, even shooting up, as do others in this strange film. This is a docudrama with controlled re-enactments, as actual people go through their own true events, using the typical day-and-night-in-the-life-of format.

Spacely-"Gringo" appears to be in his late 20s, visibly unemployed, busily hustling his daily fix. He is tall, slender, with unkempt platinum-dyed hair, earrings, a crucifix at his neck, black leather vests and a private's patch over one eye, per partial blindness caused by a gang beating. "Gringo" enjoys being the center of the film, narrates in depth about himself and a description of the how-to's of the Lower East Side drug sub-culture. He even assists the film crew to connect with junkie pals for scenes of harrowing realism.

An ugly film of nonstop brutalization of the spirit, e.g., a sewing-circle group of a half-dozen young girls all shooting up together, "Gringo" is nevertheless of interest to those who would confront and understand the American mania for narcotics. — *Hitch.*

Didi Und Die Rache Der Enterbten
(Didi And The Revenge Of The Disinherited)
(WEST GERMAN-COLOR)

Berlin, Feb. 28.
An Ufa-Film production, West Berlin, in coproduction with Second German Television (ZDF), Mainz. Directed by Christian Rateuke and Dieter Hallervorden. Stars Hallervorden. Screenplay, Hartmann Schmige, Rateuke; camera (color), Günter Marczinkowski; music, Günter Fischer, makeup, Klaus Börnert. Reviewed at Zoo Palast, Berlin, Feb. 27, 1985. Running time: **92 MINS.**
With: Dieter (Didi) Hallervorden, Wolfgang Kieling, Gerhard Wollner, Christoph Hofrichter, Karl Schulz.

Although it appears to be a b.o. winner (as all the Didi Hallervorden comedies have been up to now), "Didi And The Revenge Of The Disinherited" is down in quality from his prior "Trouble With My Double" (1984) blockbuster. This is the first occasion that Hallervorden himself has codirected — he teamed with Christian Rateuke of his usual scriptwriting duo of Rateuke & Hartmann Schmige — and the results are uneven.

This is a thinly disguised variation on the theme of getting rid of legal

inheritors before reaching the pot of gold at the end of the rainbow, previously essayed by Ealing Studios' "Kind Hearts And Coronets." The star plays not only the ancient miser who leaves $10,000,000 to the heir who never asked him for a penny during his life (he apparently didn'thave the address), one Didi Dödel, but also five other disenchanted heirs (seven roles in all). The disinherited collectively hit upon the plan of wiping Didi and each other out along the way to lay their hands on the millions, while our comic nobody doesn't even know he's being stalked for an "accidental" rub-out. Each time when it looks like Didi is in the bag, a quirk of fate leaves he goof-ball up on top — until he's finally the only one left, and now the inheritance lawyer is trying, also in vain, to turn the trick.

Some visual slapstick routines require Hallervorden's acrobatic skills, but the gags are mostly too pat and expected and the dialog lame in general. — *Holl.*

Not Quite Jerusalem
(BRITISH-COLOR)

London, March 5.
A Rank Organisation release of an Acorn Pictures production. Produced and directed by Lewis Gilbert. Executive producer, Herbert Oakes. Coproduced by William P. Cartlidge. Stars Joanna Pacula, Sam Robards. Screenplay, Paul Kember; camera (color) Tony Imi; editor, Alan Strachan; music, Gian Reverberi; production designer, John Stoll; assistant art director, Giora Porter; wardrobe, David Murphy; sound, Daniel Brisseau; assistant director, Michel Cheyko; casting, Esta Charkham; Howard Feuer. Reviewed at the Bijou theater, London, March 4, 1985. Running time: **114 MINS.**
Gila . . . . .Joanna Pacula
Mike . . . . .Sam Robards
Pete . . . . .Kevin McNally
Rothwell T. Schwartz . . . . .Todd Graff
Carrie . . . . .Selina Cadell
Dave . . . . .Bernard Strother
Angus . . . . .Ewan Stewart
Grace . . . . .Kate Ingram
Steve . . . . .Gary Cady
Yoshiko . . . . .Sawally Srinonton
Menachem . . . . .Zafrir Kochanovsky
Reuven . . . . .Shlomo Tarshish

"Not Quite Jerusalem" is basically an old-fashioned romance of the cliffhanging variety set in a kibbutz. Pic lacks the dramatic bite of Lewis Gilbert's previous "Educating Rita," but is sufficiently enriched by fine comedy, action and drama and its desert setting to ensure broad youth appeal.

Like "Educating Rita," film is based on a stage play, but Paul Kember's script has traveled much farther from its legit origins than did the earlier item. Plot has been broadened to take in Israel's landscape and terrorist activity. Also, the affair between an Israeli girl and a happy-go-lucky American volunteer for kibbutz life replaces the activities of various English characters at center stage.

A consequence of the screenplay's origin is that the four volunteers from Blighty are the best developed. At the pic's comic core are Kevin • McNally and Bernard Strother, who give fine performances as working class youths whose distaste for the mother country is combined with a fairly chauvinistic attitude to kibbutz life. There's also a girl, played by Selina Cadell, who's come to Israel from a nervous breakdown and an equally traumatized former British soldier.

By contrast, the central romance never really comes to life. Sam Robards plays a Yank who's come to fill in time before medical school, while Joanna Pacula is a kibbutznik rather fed up with the constant flow of uncommitted foreigners. Audiences will find it easier to believe in the pair's sexual chemistry than their emotional compatibility.

Pic doesn't waste time on the philosophy of kibbutz life, nor does it allot much space for Israelis other than Pacula's Gila. Other parts are mere cameos, apart from that of an awestruck American Jew rendered in a rather over-the-top performance by Todd Graff.

Film moves at a fair lick towards its triple climax conclusion. English lads Pete and Dave rescue a group of kids from the conflagration caused by the cigaret of ex-soldier Angus. When some volunteers accompanied by Gila are kidnaped by Arabs while on a sightseeing exhibition, the Israeli army turns out in force. Finally, there's the question of whether loverboy Mike will go or stay. Gilbert's directorial flair ensures the maximum emotional impact is wrought from these scenes.

Tony Imi's topnotch lensing makes fine use of landscapes familiar from Bible-related films. Score, although tilted towards the pic's soft center, is also good. —Japa.

Invitation To The Wedding
(BRITISH-COLOR)

London, March 1.

A new Realm release of a Chancery Lane production. Produced and directed by Joseph Brooks. Executive producer, Peter Alkaly. Features entire cast. Screenplay, William Fairchild; camera (color), Freddie Young; editor, Gerry Hambling; production design, Andrew Mollo; costumes, Maggie Quigley; music, Joseph Brooks. Reviewed at the Film-Centa, London, Feb. 28, 1985. (BBFC certificate: PG). Running time: **90 MINS.**
Uncle Willie . . . . Ralph Richardson
Rev. Clyde Ormiston . . . . John Gielgud
David Anderson . . . . Paul Nicholas
Lady Caroline . . . . Elizabeth Shepherd
Earl Harry . . . . John Standing
Clara & Charles Eatwell . . . . Ronald Lacey
Lady Anne . . . . Susan Brooks

This piece of tosh is a self-financed picture by composer Joseph Brooks, who earlier hit with "You Light Up My Life." Filmed over two years ago in the U.K. and released here with zero publicity, its prospects are grim.

The implausible and unamusing plot features a young American who is accidentally married to the daughter of an aristocratic English family at what is supposed to be the rehearsal for her wedding a week later. In the intervening seven days the pair ride horses, fish and picnic in the English countryside. They fall in love and the second wedding is aborted by the presiding bishop.

Performances are atrocious. Susan Brooks (the director's wife) as the bride can do nothing but smile. John Gielgud in the role of an American evangelist is too preoccupied with his Texan accent to act. Only the late Ralph Richardson as the bumbling cleric and Paul Nicholas as the bridegroom are okay.

On the technical side, Freddie Young's camerawork is fine, but Gerry Hambling's editorial skill cannot patch up the director's botched job. Print viewed sported chinagraph marks and some poor grading. —Japa.

L'Amour Braque
(Mad Love)
(FRENCH-COLOR)

Paris, Feb. 27.

An AMLF release of a Sara Films production. Produced by Alain Sarde. Directed by Andrzej Zulawski. Stars Sophie Marceau, Francis Huster. Screenplay, Zulawski and Etienne Roda-Gil (freely inspired by Fyodor Dostoyevsky's "The Idiot"); camera (color), Jean-François Robin; art director, Dominique André; editor, Marie-Sophie Dubus; sound, Guillaume Sciama; makeup, Sophie Landry; music, Stanislas Syrewicz; production manager, Antoine Gannagé. Reviewed at the Gaumont Colisée theater, Paris, Feb. 27, 1985. Running time: **100 MINS.**
Leon . . . . Francis Huster
Mickey . . . . Tcheky Karyo
Mary . . . . Sophie Marceau
Aglaé . . . . Christiane Jean
André . . . . Michel Albertini
Commissioner . . . . Roland Dubillard
Simon Venin . . . . Jean-Marc Bory
Gang leader . . . . Said Amadis
Gilbert Venin . . . : . . . . Ged Marlon
The Baron . . . . Serge Spira
Gisèle . . . . Julie Ravix

Stripping Dostoyevsky's holy fool in "The Idiot" of his essential dignity, and resetting the action to 1980s Paris, director Andrzej Zulawski offers us a penniless prince bound for France after internment in a mental institution in Hungary. On the train, where we first see him in his underwear, hanging his washroom laundered clothing up to dry in his compartment, he strikes up a friendship with a frenetic young hood, who has just knocked over a provincial bank with his mates.

The seedy aristocrat and gun-touting outlaw quickly become embroiled in a romantic rivalry over a young Parisian prostitute and are pitched into a bloody vendetta with a depraved underworld family.

The director opens his tale in a spirit of burlesque and horseplay, which soon switches into even higher gear as the screen is set ablaze with a breathless series of gunbattles, car pursuits and sexual encounters. As usual, his characters are given to ranting and frenzied gestures, which eventually tend to numb the spectator into indifference.

The "Idiot" is Francis Huster, who was the megalomaniacal director trying to film Dostoyevsky's "The Possessed" in Zulawski's "The Public Woman" last year. Here he hovers epileptically on the fringes of the bloodletting, picks his nose, throws fits, flaps his arms like a seagull (Chekhov is also dragged screaming into the melée), and occasionally beds the heroine during some rare lulls in the action. So much for Dostoyevsky's basic theme of a saintly innocent adrift in wicked, debased society.

Sophie Marceau, the chaste teen heroine of Gaumont's "La Boum" hits, has been angling for "adult" roles, and here goes whole hog for Zulawski as the coveted prostitute; if full frontal nudity and simulated performances of fellatio are requisites for a mature screen image, then Marceau has made it.

Only Tcheky Karyo, as the maddened young hood, responds skillfully to Zulawski's dramatic imperatives.

Tech credits, notably Jean-François Robin's lensing, are much less striking than in previous Zulawski epics. —Len.

Kingpin
(NEW ZEALAND-COLOR)

Wellington, N.Z., Feb. 18.

A Morrow Productions and The Film Investment Corp. of New Zealand presentation. Directed by Mike Walker. Produced by Gary Hannam, Walker. Screenplay, Walker and Mitchell Manuel; camera (color), John Toon; editor, Paul Sutorius; music, Schtung (Andrew Hagan and Morton Wilson); sound, Ken Saville. Reviewed at National Film Unit preview theater, Wellington, Feb. 15, 1985. Running time: **89 MINS.**
Riki Nathan . . . . Mitchell Manuel
Willie Hoto . . . . Junior Amigo
Karl Stevens . . . . Nicholas Rogers
Dave Adams . . . . Terence Cooper
Paul Jeffries . . . . Peter McCauley
Alison Eastwood . . . . Judith McIntosh
Mike Herewini . . . . Jim Moriarty
Mr. Nathan . . . . Wi Kuki Kaa

"Kingpin" is a story about rivalry and friendship in a boy's reform school that falls uneasily between imagined events and documentary.

Riki Nathan (Mitchell Manuel) arrives at the reform school to join its inmates, mainly Maori teenagers, who dream of home, love and escape, particularly Willie (Junior Amigo).

Riki is encouraged to challenge the institution's leading thug, and "kingpin," Karl (Nicholas Rogers). It takes a string of incidents, of varying dramatic impact, involving Willie, before Riki takes up the cudgels.

A low-budget Morrow Productions presentation, shot in 16m and blown up to 35m, "Kingpin" is not high in production values, relying heavily on the performances of its young, macho-looking, but largely inexperienced, Maori cast.

The rookie thesps are not helped by a script that suggests too much last minute improvisation and virtually no considered character motivation.

More experienced actors have been engaged as the wardens of the school and Wi Kuki Kaa, who made a strong impression in "Utu" and "The Bounty," has a cameo as Riki's alcoholic father.—Nic.

Bittere Ernte
(Bitter Harvest)
(WEST GERMAN-COLOR)

Berlin, Feb. 23.

A CCC-Filmkunst production, Berlin, ir. coproduction with Admiral Film, Munich. Produced by Artur Brauner. Directed by Agnieszka Holland. Features entier cast. Screenplay, Paul Hengge, Holland, based on material by Hermann Field; camera (color), Josef Ort-Snep; editor, Barbara Kunze; sound, Gunther Kortwich; music, Jörg Strassburger; sets, Werner Schwenke; costumes, Hanne-Lore Wessel. Reviewed at Berlin Film Fest (special screening), Feb. 22, 1985. Running time: **102 MINS.**
With: Armin Müller-Stahl (Leon), Elisabeth Trissenaar (Rosa), Käthe Jaenicke (Anna), Hans Beerhenke (Kaspar), Isa Haller (Magda), Margit Carstensen (Eugenia), Wojciech Pszioniak (Cybolowski), Gerd Baltus (Cleric), Anita Höfer (Pauline), Kurt Raab (Maslanko), Gunter Berger (Walden), Wolf Donner (Dan).

Polish femme helmer Agnieszka Holland's first West German feature, "Bitter Harvest," is loaded with talented name thesps, but the material is without dramatic high points — and apparently not even Holland herself, a gifted scriptwriter who has worked with Andrzej Wajda on most of his recent projects, could rescue it by a required feat of doctoring.

It's 1943 somewhere in occupied Poland. A rich farmer, Leon (Armin Müller-Stahl), has managed by to live in comfort by hoarding meat and produce while trading on the black-market. One day he is surprised to find a girl on the run in the woods, Rosa (Elisabeth Trissenaar), a Jewess near starvation and ill with fever. Leon takes her in, hides her in his cellar from the authorities, and nurses the girl back to health. Then he makes her his prisoner for reasons quite other than humanitarian.

Rosa gradually realizes that she has to submit to the farmer's advances in order to live, so she capitulates. Leon salves his conscience by confessing to the village priest without filling-in the important hostage details. One day, he tragically kills her, burying the corpse in the cellar. The final note of irony is that he swears to passing resistance fighters, who believes Leon to be a good man, that he has never seen Rosa although she was seen in the area while on the run.

Leon survives the war at the end, and still manages to keep up appearances with a twisted conscience in spite of everything.

Particularly disappointing is the way everything seems to have been slapped together. Neither Müller-Stahl nor Trissenaar give the least hint that they understand the nature of the complex erotic and psychological relationship that forms the hub of the story. Lensing is mostly cramped studio shooting.—*Holl.*

The Communists Are Comfortable (And Three Other Stories)
(U.S.-COLOR/B&W-16m)

Berlin, Feb. 22.
A production of Ken Kobland. Directed and edited by Kobland. Screenplay, James Stahe; narrator, Kobland. Reviewed at Berlin Film Festival (Forum), Feb. 22, 1985. Running time: 75 MINS.
With: Willem Dafoe, Spalding Gray, Lushe Sacker, Pwyton Smith, Ron Vawter.

Associated with the avant-garde Wooster Theater Group in New York, filmmaker Kobland has made this film in part as a tribute to playwright Clifford Odets, who had been almost a foster uncle to him as a child and who had testified as a friendly witness before the House Un-American Activities Committee. It is also a homage to the late experimental filmmaker Hollis Frampton and the film came to the Forum in Berlin from the Collective for Living Cinema, showcase theater in New York.

The closest that "Communists" comes to a specific statement is a sequence using Kobland's voice, speaking words that are a fictionalized equivalent of Odets, authored by Stahe, words simultaneously heard and read in bold lettering on the screen. Although the film purports politically to express a mood of post-liberal depression and resignation, little of significance is revealed.

Sequences in "Communists" include a young man closely examining his coated tongue and also his pimples, testing them and trying to decide if they're ripe enough. We also see long tracking shots within a Bronx apartment and interminable shots of a single group of leafless trees in wintry Central Park, with

traffic sounds in the background. Another sequence of about four minutes is devoted to frying an egg. Several clips from "Citizen Kane" are used, as well as news footage of World War II bombings and atrocities. A long boring monolog is witnessed in one shot, of a youngish worker having a cup of coffee while rambling autobiographically about disenchanted idealism. Other visuals in the film are similarly static.

Opening is a long orchestra tune-up over blank screen. Soundtrack also includes rock, country, Bugs Bunny, Howard Hanson's "Adagio For Strings," Bernard Herrmann's score for "Citizen Kane," the anthem "Internationale," and the sound of urinating. For one sequence of a derrick oil-fire, a laugh-track is heard. — *Hitch.*

Verführung: Die Grausame Frau
(Seduction: The Cruel Woman)
(WEST GERMAN-COLOR-16m)

Berlin, Feb. 25.
A Hyäne Film production. Written and directed by Elfi Mikesch and Monika Treut. Features entire cast. Camera (color), Mikesch; editor, Renate Merck; sound Cäsar Gremmler; sets, Manfred Blösser; costumes, Anne Jud. Reviewed at Berlin Film Fest (Forum), Feb. 24, 1985. Running time: 85 MINS.
With: Mechthild Grossmann, Udo Kier, Shelia McLaughlin, Carola Regnier, Peter Weibel, Georgette Dee.

"Seduction: The Cruel Woman," codirected by Elfi Mikesch and Monika Treut, was in the news long before the project went before the cameras. Its theme of masochism was not considered appropriate for a federal subsidy, even though some members of a selection board are reported to have supported it. Now that the film has been made, it might just as well be forgotten.

A sex tyrant named Wanda practices the profession of cruelty, particularly for those who fall within her power as either needy of sado-masochism or intrigued by her personality. Since every normal human being has sex fantasies of one sort or another, the perversions of the self (soul, psyche, whatever) have to be repressed or released as the occasion demands, Mikesch and Treut seem to be contending. Wanda comes into contact with different types and entices them all into the web of her sexual domination.

The shower of banal dialog and images leaves little or no room for intellectual reflection on the matter. —*Holl.*

Otto Klemperers Lange Reise Durch Seine Zeit
(Otto Klemperer's Long Journey Through His Times)

(WEST-GERMAN-AUSTRIAN-DOCU-B&W-16m)

Berlin, Feb. 17.
A.R.M. Productions Film, in coproduction with Westdeutscher Rundfunk (WDR) and Austrian Television (ORF). A Documentary by Philo Bregstein. Camera (b&w, 16m), Kees Colson, Anton Haakman, Jan Oonk; editor, Silvano Agosti; coordination, Otto Freudenthal; documentation, Tom van Leeuwen; adviser, Marlin Bregstein, Peter Heyworth; sound, Ed Pelster, Tom Tholen. Reviewed at Berlin Film Fest (Forum), Feb. 16, 1985. Running time: 90 MINS.

Philo Bregstein's docu, "Otto Klemperer's Long Journey Through His Times," has been updated from its earlier 1974 version by the Dutch filmmaker with support of German and Austrian tv stations. As a document on this century, the film is highly recommended, for Bregstein collects a mass of news footage to accompany a text in which not only Klemperer, one of this century's great visonary conductors, sits before the camera, but also a host of personalities from the European art and music scene.

Among those queried for commentaries on Klemperer's career are Ernst Bloch, Pierre Boulez, Paul Dessau, Walter Felsenstein, Gottfried Reinhardt and H.H. Stuckenschmidt. They talk about the conductor's untiring quest to further the musical compositions of Mahler, Stravinsky, Schönberg, and Hindemith, even in the Socialist lands following World War II, where modern music was condemned under the then current tenets of Socialist Realism. He fought this committed fight until his death in 1974 at 88.

For the record, Klemperer is worthy of this homage due in great part to his courageous fight against a brain tumor and stroke in 1939, when he was at the height of his career upon making America his home in exile from Germany. He went to Budapest after the war to raise the opera company there to world class, whereupon the Communist Party turned around and repressed the conductor's preference for Schönberg over the classics. Upon returning to America, his passport was withdrawn by over-zealous McCarthyites during the Red Scare. Klemperer's last years were spent in West Germany.

The docu is a well researched and highly recommended portrait of a remarkable music personality against the background of his times.
—*Holl.*

Noc Smaragodového Mesice
(The Night Of The Emerald Green Moon)
(CZECH-COLOR)

Berlin, Feb. 26.
A Barrandov Film Studio production. Directed by Vaclav Matejka. Features entire

cast. Screenplay, Matejka, Jiri Krenek; camera (Scope, color), Jiri Machane; music, Jiri Svoboda; art director, Vladimir Labsky. Reviewed at Berlin Film Festival (in competition), Feb. 25, 1985. Running time: 83 MINS.
Jan Kysucan ....Radoslav Brzobohaty
Cyril Kysucan ....Jerzy Trela
Vojta ....Pavol Visnovsky
Marie ....Bozidara Turzonovova
Slavka...............:.Magda Vasaryova
Jarmila.................Milena Dvorska
Old Mother ....Vera Kubankova
Young Mother ....Zlata Adamovska

The plot of this turgid, gloomy pic is said to be an idea by coscripter Jiri Krenek; possibly he'd seen the Francesco Rosi film "Three Brothers," as the basic story is identical: three brothers, who haven't seen much of each other in recent years, are reunited for a funeral, in this case that of their mother.

Any similarities between the films end there. The brothers here are singularly uninteresting characters (a scientist, a bus driver, a criminal) and their problems resolutely predictable. Flashbacks to the war are thrown in, but add little.

To make matters worse, the print shown in Berlin was so dark as to be almost incomprehensible at times. Even supposedly bright outdoor scenes are gloomy and flat. If this was intentional, it was a major miscalculation.—*Strat.*

Domina — Die Last Der Lust
(Domina — The Burden Of Lust)
(WEST GERMAN-DOCU-COLOR/B&W)

Berlin, Feb. 25.
A Tupro-Weekend-Cine Production, Berlin. A Documentary Film by Klaus Tuschen. Camera (color, b&w), Hans Rombach; editor, Stefan Beckers; sound, Michael Eiler; music, Fono Dor. Reviewed at Berlin Film Fest (information), Feb. 24, '85. Running time: 91 MINS.
With: Lady de Winter, Madame Dunja, Mademoiselle Ruth, Mis Doreen.

A pseudo artfilm, Klaus Tuschen's "Domina — The Burden Of Lust" starts out with a dubious quote from James Purdy, "Love is a violent passion."

Lady de Winter is the interesting figure in the docu. Per program notes, she's 33 years old, was raised in a provincial German town as the daughter of a civil servant, gave birth at 18 to a child, whom she left with her parents upon departing from the family, and was married and divorced before opening up her whip-and-leather trade in West Berlin some six years earlier.

The trouble is nothing is ever seen of her everyday life; the audience only plays peep-hole voyeur as she practices her trade before hidden cameras (the usual blotting-out of faces is supposed to tickle the libido a bit more). —*Holl.*

Los Chicos de la Guerra
(The Children Of The War)
(ARGENTINE-COLOR)

Berlin, Feb. 25.

A K. Films SRL production. Directed by Bebe Kamin. Screenplay, Daniel Kon, Kamin, Maria-Teresa Ferrari, from novel by Kon; camera (color), Yito Blanc; editor, Luis Mutti; art director, Maria de los Angeles Favale; costumes, Marta Albertinazzi, Nora Renan; sound, Jose-Luis Diaz; music, Luis Maria Serra. Reviewed at the Berlin Film Festival. (Forum), Feb. 24, 1985. Running time: 101 MINS.

Pablo	Gabriel Rovito
Fabian	Gustavo Belatti
Santiago	Leandro Regunaga
Marcelo	Javier Garcia
Andrea	Emilia Mazer
Pablo's father	Hector Alterio
Pablo's mother	Mirta Gonzalez
Fabian's father	Alfonso de Grazia
Fabian's mother	Tina Serrano
Bar keeper	Ulises Dumont

This is the first Argentine film to deal frontally with the Malvinas war, putting the blame squarely on the corruption and indifference of the older generation, to be paid in full by the youngsters sent to the front unprepared to fight a war they did not want.

"Children Of The War," previously shown at a Venice Fest sidebar, is the typical well-intentioned but superficial statement, too general to really bother anyone and too schematic to draw audiences in.

Script follows (through a series of flashbacks) the past of four youngsters, from their first day in school to their mobilization and final defeat. There is the expected division of traits between these four, one artistic, another headstrong; there is one rich kid, another who is poor; and there are ample reactions of grownups, ranging from the indifference of the lower middleclass, to the miltaristic elitism of the upper classes, not forgetting the ignorant nationalism of the blue collar workers.

Also present are the different stages of growing up in Argentina, with whiffs of political corruption and manipulation, of brutal and mindless terrorism, and media brainwashing.

Some sequences work well, whether a shy love scene between two teenagers or the sudden horrifying attack of two teenagers by a gang of unspecified thugs armed to the teeth. However, characters are at best sketchy and the film's construction is too mechanical.

Print sent by the Argentines for screening at Berlin was in atrocious condition.—*Edna*.

Die Schwärmer
(The Dreamers)
(WEST GERMAN-COLOR-16m)

Berlin, Feb. 22.

A Regina Ziegler Film Production, Berlin, in coproduction with Westdeutscher Rundfunk (WDR), Cologne. Written and directed by Hans Neuenfels, based on the stage play with the same title by Robert Musil. Features entire cast. Camera (color, 16m), Jürgen Jürges; music, Erik Satie (from "Gnossiennes" and "Trois Gymnopédies"); editors, Dörte Völz, Jeanette Menzel; sound, Detlev Fichtner, Uwe Griem; sets, Mark Gläser; costumes, Barbara Braun; tv editor, Gunther Witte, Volker Canaris. Reviewed at Berlin Film Fest (Forum), Feb. 21, 1985. Running time: 116 MINS.

With: Hermann Treusch (Thomas), Sabine Sinjen (Maria), Elisabeth Trissenaar (Regine), Joachim Bliese (Anselm), Lothar Blumhagen (Josef), Lieselotté Rau (Fräulein Mertens), Gottfried John (Stader), Stefan Wieland (Johannes), Hans-Eckert Eckhardt, Ulrich Hass, Jörg Holm.

Hans Neuenfels' "Dreamers" follows a tried-and-true formula already polished to perfection in this stage director's other film adaptations of dramatic works. Now he's turned to Robert Musil's autobiographical drama, "The Dreamers" (penned in 1921 at the age of 41), staged in Berlin before being programmed as a tv-film variant for WDR Cologne.

The only trouble with this formula is that it backfires as soon as the discipline of the two art forms, stage and cinema, are unhappily wed. The thesps haven't even attempted to adapt to a different art form; the voices are raised constantly to utter each syllable and reach the last row of the theater.

"The Dreamers" focuses on the problem of passing 40 years of age. Two couples (five principals in all) gather in an old Berlin villa on a wintery morning in February 1926 in this version, and the drama ends the next morn. During their stay, a dialog along the lines of Edward Albee's "Who's Afraid Of Virginia Woolf?" takes place on life, reality, relationships and downright alienation. Indeed, Neuenfels' approach is more Expressionistic in context than even Albee's emotionally charged drama, so much so that the outlines of Robert Musil's original intentions (he was an opponent of overcharged Expressionist drama) are barely visible. — *Holl.*

Cauchemar
(Nightmare)
(MOROCCAN-COLOR)

Berlin, Feb. 25.

No production company listed. Produced by Abdellatif Yachfine. Directed and written by Ahmed Yachfine. Features entire cast. Camera (color), Abdelkrim M. Derkaoui; editor, Abdelsalem Agnaw; music, Haj Younous; art director, Abdelkrim Ghattas. Reviewed at Berlin Film Festival (out of competition), Feb. 24, 1985. Running time: 102 MINS.

With: Azz El-Arab Kaghat, Ibrahim Jawhari, Rachida Azfar, Khadija Mhamdi, Charifa A. Lemrani, Maima Yusri.

The nightmare of the title is that of a rich businessman who has an unsettling experience on a trip into the hinterland. The film's opening sequence, set in his plush city home, establishes the fact that he's an uneasy sleeper, given to dreams and sleepwalking. On a long drive, his car breaks down miles from anywhere and he's forced to spend the night in a broken-down hut. He dreams he's a peasant with three wives, whom he keeps locked up in a tiny room when he's got no use for them. In his dream, one of the three is slowly poisoning him.

A background to the dream is that officials in the area are rounding up young men to serve in the military (the program note suggests the film is taking place in the '40s, but it appears timeless), bringing great distress to the people. Eventually he dies of the poison, then wakes up, manages to start his car, and goes home. In his pocket he's amazed to discover the key he used to lock the wives away in his dream.

The moral of the film is an obvious one, and the treatment is quite straightforward, but there are intriguing elements which make it watchable. Though the labwork is patchy, it's quite well shot, and there's a delightful music score. Acting is fine, with Azz El-Arab Kaghat convincing as both businessman and peasant. Pacing, however, is very slow. —*Strat.*

Die Praxis Der Liebe
(The Practice Of Love)
(AUSTRIAN-WEST GERMAN-COLOR)

Berlin, Feb. 26.

A Valie Export Film Production, Vienna in coproduction with Königsmark & Wullenweber Film, Hamburg, and in collaboration with Austrian Television (ORF), Vienna, and Second German Television (ZDF), Mainz. Written and directed by Export. Features entire cast. Camera (color), Jörg Schmidt-Reitwein; sets, Gregor Eichinger, Christian Knechtl; editing, Juno Sylva Englaender; music, Stephen Ferguson. Reviewed at Berlin Film Fest (Competition), Feb. 25, 1985. Running time: 90 MINS.

With: Adelheid Arndt (Judith), Rüdiger Vogler (Dr. Alphons Schlögel), Hagnot Elischka (Dr. Josef Fischoff), Liane Wagner (Frau Schlögel), Elisabeth Vitouch (Frau Fischoff), Paul Muller (French merchant), Günther Nenning (Chief tv editor), Wolfgang Kainz (tv editor), Walter Schreiber (news commentator), Franz Kantner (Reinhard Flegel), Traute Furthner (Flegel's mother), Regina Fritsch (Flegel's sister), Thomas de Claude (porter at hospital), Paul Mühlauser (porter in Hotel Wien), Claudia Schneider (room maid).

Valie Export (real name Waltraud Höllinger) carved a reputation out of experimental video work in the early 1970s, when the field was new and perhaps more challenging than today. Her first feature film, "The Practice Of Love," was chosen for the competition at the Berlinale, undoubtedly a step too high for this interesting but flawed sketch of the trials and tribulations, loves and misfortunes, of a femme tv reporter.

Judith (Adelheid Arndt), with a camera team, is assigned to report on the peep-show trade in Hamburg and comes back to Vienna with a report too opinionated for her boss (talk-show host Günther Nenning in a nice cameo). However, while in Hamburg, she renews an acquaintance and love affair with an old flame (Rüdiger Vogler), who also happens to be over his head in the gun-smuggling trade. Judith is having an affair with another married man, a psychiatrist who can't make up his mind between his wife and his mistress, it seems.

Along comes a murder case, which Judith feels compelled to investigate due to the involvement of her gun-smuggling boyfriend; the man who was killed is his sidekick. All along the line her dreams and fantasies mix with her own view of reality, so the viewer is challenged to piece the puzzle together as the psychological thriller winds down.

It would have been better, undoubtedly, to hold to the logic of the genres in question, either a narrative thriller or a critical thesis on preception in this fast-paced age of technology, than to jumble them both together into a potpourri of often unrelated images.

"The Practice Of Love" also suffers from its blowup from 16m to 35m. The lensing by Jörg Schmidt-Reitwein, best known for his work with Werner Herzog and Herbert Achternbusch, is particularly disappointing.—*Holl.*

Zielscheiben
(Moving Targets)
(WEST GERMAN-COLOR)

Berlin, Feb. 24.

A Studio Hamburg Film production, Hamburg. Written and directed by Volker Vogeler. Features entire cast. Camera (color), Günther Wulff; editor, Claudia Pieneck; sound, Reinhard Levin; music, Edward Aniol; production manager, Claus Schmitt-Holldack. Reviewed at Berlin Film Fest (German Series), Feb. 23, '85. Running time: 88 MINS.

With: Bernard Fresson (Flütterer), Oliver Stritzel (Zorro), William Berger (Broschat), Franz-Josef Steffens (Gotta), Dietrich Mattausch (Dr. Singer), Siegfried Kernen (Dr. Schneider), Christian Koch (States Attorney), Katharina Schütz (Blond Girl), Eva Maria Hagen (Helma), Marquard Bohm (Bertold), Ralph Richter (Strotzki).

Volker Vogeler's "Moving Targets" marks the entry of Studio Hamburg into feature-film production. It appeared in rough cut on the final day of the Hof fest last October and was programmed at the Berlinale in the German Series. Vogeler has specialized in narrative cinema, tv productions and an occasional detective thriller for tv.

"Moving Targets" follows the

formula of the tv criminal series, but adds a number of comic twists and unexpected Hitchcockian happenings along the way to make it both amusing and eye-catching.

Zorro (Oliver Stritzel), a small-time conman, is the only witness to a mafia murder and thus the police need to keep him alive as he's being transported to a gang trial to serve as a witness. The gamble is to send him along with a police detective, Fütterer (Bernard Fresson), to keep his out of sight until his testimony is needed. The old-and-tired detective and perennial loser-conman make a pair as soon as they realize some organization (mafia or police?) is out to liquidate both before they reach their destination.

Fresson and Stritzel are adept thesps in handling the material; they bounce back after every misfortune, play an amiable game of one-upsmanship and continue stubbornly on their way after each narrow scrape with death.

What particularly makes the film well worth a look-see is the manner in which Vogeler has danger lurking around the corner in broad daylight. The setting is along the northern seacoast during the tourist-hotels' out-of-season, a Hitchcock touch if there ever was one. —*Holl.*

Yamaha Yudang
(Yamaha Fish Stall)
(CHINESE-COLOR)

Berlin, Feb. 26.

A Pearl River Studio (Canton) production. Directed by Liang Zhang. Features entire cast. Screenplay, Zhang Yiwu, Dong Jinhong; camera (color) Han Xinyuan, Wang Hengli; music, Chen Qixiong. No further credits available. Reviewed at Berlin Film Festival (Out of competition), Feb. 25, 1985. Running time: **93 MINS.**
With: Tianxi Zhang, Ruiping Xu.

A film from the southern part of mainland China, close to Hong Kong, this is a lively youth pic which is admittedly naive by Western standards, but which has a good deal of a spirit and élan.

Pic is pushing the Party strategy of encouraging "small company structures," i.e., limited private enterprise, and the moral is that if you work hard you'll earn lots of money. Three young people take over a fish stall in the city's bustling market (they call it the "Yamaha" stall after the motor-bike of one of them). At first they try to get rich by cheating the customers, but they're soon discovered and humiliated. They return with better intentions, and are soon raking in the cash.

There's a romance too, involving a shy young girl and her suitor, complicated by the arrival of a rich outsider from Macao (which still has the same status as Hong Kong). Even this capitalist is so impressed

by the money to be made by China's private enterprise that he decides to stay on and work there himself.

Someone even asks the question that presumably many Chinese are asking: How long can this private enterprise continue? The answer, firmly given, is that it will continue indefinitely.

Acting is natural, pacing brisk, and the color lab-work excellent. —*Strat.*

Vybuch Bude V Pet
(The Explosion Happens At Five O'Clock)
(CZECH-COLOR)

Berlin, Feb. 26.

A Filmstudio Barrandov Film Production, Prague; world rights, Czechoslovak Film Export, Prague. Directed by Josef Pinkava. Features entire cast. Screenplay, Alena Vostra; camera (color), Karel Kopecky; editor, Ivan Matous; sound, Josef Javorik; music, Zdenek John; sets, Vladimir Labsky. Reviewed at Berlin Film Fest (children's section), Feb. 26, 1985. Running time: **78 MINS.**
With: Robert Nespor (Ludvik), Zdenek Hadrbo Icova (Mother), Oldrich Slavik (Father), Mahulena Bocanova (Ludvik's Sister), Alice Hlobilkova (Ludvik's Friend), Jiri Halek (Physics Teacher), Daniel Dite (Sports Teacher).

Josef Pinkava's latest charming kidpic, "The Explosion Happens At Five O'Clock" is about a young lad named Ludvik who's crazy about physics and particularly homemade experiments. Everything he touches goes awry: he floods the bathroom while testing the Achimedes Principle, he smashes the melon harvest to smithereens in proving the law of gravity, and the neighbor worries about his prize hares when the lad learns that electrical energy can be generated by rubbing a rod on the fur of a rabbit.

His parents, however, wish that he would take up music, particularly as the father is a musician and the mother a teacher. Ludvik's next experiment won't be with the violin (as the family hopes) but with an explosion that can be extracted from a mixture of carbide and water. The physics teacher gets into the act when a school chum squeals on the "explosion planned for five" — this happens, heard off in the distance right in the middle of a school concert that requires its own boom-boom effect. —*Holl.*

The Slugger's Wife
(COLOR)

Baseball set to rock music doesn't play.

Hollywood, March 7.

A Columbia Pictures release from Columbia-Delphi Prods. II of a Ray Stark production. Produced by Ray Stark. Executive producer, Margaret Booth. Directed by Hal Ashby. Features entire cast. Screenplay, Neil Simon. Camera (Metrocolor), Caleb Deschanel; editor, George Villasenor, Don Brochu; music, Patrick Williams; executive music producer, Quincy Jones, Tom Bahler; production design, Micheal Riva; set decorator, Bruce Weintraub; set designer, Ginny Randolph; art director, Rick Carter; sound (Dolby stereo), Jeff Wexler; costumes, Ann Roth; assistant director, Frank Bueno; casting, Pennie du Pont. Reviewed at MGM/-UA screening room, L.A., Calif., March 6, 1985. (MPAA rating: PG-13.) Running time: **105 MINS.**

Darryl Palmer	Michael O'Keefe
Debby Palmer	Rebecca DeMornay
Burly De Vito	Martin Ritt
Moose Granger	Randy Quaid
Manny Alvarado	Cleavant Derricks
Aline Cooper	Lisa Langlois
Gary	Loudon Wainwright 3d

"The Slugger's Wife" is yet another example of a soundtrack album accompanied by a film. Push to strike a contempo note actually does the material a disservice here with the modern love story between a baseball player and a musician coming out about as affecting as a rock video. Despite some decent tunes and interesting performances, elements never jell.

Baseball background is a curious setting for the overdose of music dished up in "Slugger's Wife" and probably marks the first ballgame orchestrated with a rock soundtrack. Although director Hal Ashby has previously demonstrated a talent for integrating action with music it's not a double play combination that works here.

Film opens with Atlanta Braves slugger Darryl Palmer (Michael O'Keefe) spying an aspiring rock singer (Rebecca DeMornay) at a local nightspot and falling instantly head over heels. Courting ritual is a typical cutesy collection of calamities until DeMornay is just worn out by O'Keefe's insistence that she's the girl for him.

Their romance, however, is on an obvious collision course because DeMornay has sacrificed her career to be near her husband. His love for her becomes a major charm to propel him to new batting feats and he is actually supposed to be besting Roger Maris' home run mark.

Unfortunately, the film never really catches the spirit to make this kind of wish fulfillment fairytale believable.

Second half of the picture, after the couple splits up, works slightly better since O'Keefe is faced with making some life changes. Also his

comaraderie with teammates Randy Quaid and Cleavant Derricks, as well as team manager Martin Ritt, is more believable and more fun than his romantic troubles.

In his second film role after Max Schell's "End Of The Game," director Ritt must have taken lessons from Tommy Lasorda to model his role of the unscrupulous but lovable manager. Ritt seems to be having the time of his life making life miserable for his players. Quaid, as always, turns in a totally credible job as Moose, a mediocre player robbed of his one moment of glory.

O'Keefe is energetic and does well with material that makes him essentially an unsympathetic character for half the film. Coupling of him with DeMornay, however, doesn't have the passion that the accompanying music insists that it does. Lisa Langlois generates considerably more heat of her own as another club singer. Assortment of real-life baseballers also make an appearance with cinematic stint on the mound by Mark "the Bird" Fidrych a touching irony for fans.

Script by Simon manages a few base hits, but scores few runs.

Cinematography by Caleb Deschanel and production design by Michael Riva is fine, especially for the baseball sequences which will leave fans longing for the real thing. —*Jagr.*

Sylvester
(COLOR)

Warm family film.

Hollywood, March 8.

A Columbia Pictures release of a Rastar production. Produced by Martin Jurow. Directed by Tim Hunter. Features entire cast. Screenplay, Carol Sobieski; camera (Metrocolor), Hiro Narita; production design, James W. Newport; editors, Howard Smith, Suzanne Pettit, David Garfield; music, Lee Holdridge; sound, Petur Hliddal; costume designer, Sharon Day; casting, Pennie du Pont; assistant director, Pat Crowley; equestrian consultant, Benita Allen; second unit director, Michael Moore; second unit camera, Rexford Metz. Reviewed at Samuel Goldwyn theater, March 7, 1985. (MPAA Rating: PG.) Running time: **102 MINS.**

Foster	Richard Farnsworth
Charlie	Melissa Gilbert
Matt	Michael Schoeffling
Muffy	Constance Towers
Harris	Pete Kowanko
Grant	Yankton Hatten
Seth	Shane Serwin
Red	Chris Pedersen

Tale of a teenage girl fighting to keep a dream alive while raising her young, orphaned brothers, "Sylvester" marks a respectable and warm return to the maligned genre of the family picture.

Melissa Gilbert, in a winning motion picture debut, and Richard

Farnsworth, in another one of his patented, hard-head roles, this time laced with booze and guilt, deliver solid performances. Result is a natural for family audiences, not to mention equestrian lovers.

As a test case, can a drama with decent values, quiet, steady pacing, and unadorned cinematic style capture audiences that flocked to this kind of pic two generations ago? This one has Rastar and Columbia as tub-thumpers.

Writer Carol Sobieski and director Tim ("Tex") Hunter have included contemporary elements (some four-letter words, an aborted rape sequence early in the picture), but the production works in direct proportion to its unpretentious expression of such verities as honor, loyalty, bravery.

Story should have strong appeal to young girls. Gilbert, gritty, determined, vulnerable, matches the crusty spirit of Farnsworth as the pair overcomes mutual obstacles in a Texas stockyards to turn an unmanageable, gray ex-rodeo horse into an equestrian champion at an Olympics trial in the bluegrass country of eastern Kentucky.

Yarn suffers from a certain blandness in the switch from the rugged Texas ranch country to the classy horse barns of Lexington. Also it struggles to hold interest during the formal dressage, cross-country endurance and stadium jumping sequences. However, the performances — including those of supporting love interest Michael Schoeffling and aristocratic Kentucky horse queen Constance Towers — anchor the production.

The contrast between the pic's wide-open Texas look and the haughty bluegrass world does give the material an edge of irony, and writer Sobieski (who wrote Ray Stark's "Annie" and "The Toy") occasionally lifts the dialog to a lyrical touch. —Loyn.

Les Rois du Gag
(The Gag Kings)
(FRENCH-COLOR)

Paris, March 7.

An AMLF release of a Films 7/Films A2 coproduction. Produced and directed by Claude Zidi. Stars Michel Serrault, Gérard Jugnot, Thierry Lhermitte. Screenplay, Zidi, Didier Kaminka, Michel Fabre; camera (color), Jean-Jacques Tarbes; art director, Daniel Heitz; editor, Nicole Saunier; sound, Jean-Louis Ughetto; music, Vladimir Cosma; production manager, Pierre Gauchet. Reviewed at the Ponthieu screening room, Paris, March 5, 1985. Running time: **98 MINS.**
Gaetan/Wellson . . . . Michel Serrault
Paul . . . . Gérard Jugnot
Francois . . . . Thierry Lhermitte
Jacqueline . . . . Macha Meril
Alexandra . . . . Mathilda May
Georges . . . . Coluche
René . . . . Didier Kaminka

Robert . . . . Maurice Baquet
Jean . . . . Pierre Doris

———

Director Claude Zidi seduced both critics and public with "Les Ripoux," a dramatic comedy about crooked cops that has just been consecrated with French César awards for best picture and director. His new film, "Les Rois du Gag," deals directly with the craft of low comedy that has been Zidi's specialty previously, but it is a surprisingly clumsy, and worse, pretentious affair.

Michel Serrault plays a tv comedian with a long-running show badly in need of new writing blood. When his current old-time gagsters are suddenly put out of service, he decides to recruit from the younger generation of the Paris café-theater. His choice falls on two struggling comics, Gérard Jugnot and Thierry Lhermitte, who despise Serrault's tired, conventional image, but are lured into a contract by the lucre and Serrault's pretty daughter (Mathilda May).

The talent graft promises to bear fruit when Serrault suddenly is offered the straight dramatic lead in the film of a grubby, obnoxious highbrow filmmaker (also played by Serrault, padded and madeup as a composite caricature physically modeled on Orson Welles). Serrault, prodded by his snobbish wife (Macha Meril), jumps at the chance, but the project ends in a fiasco. Deterred from suicide by his young colleagues, he returns to his former employ.

"Les Rois du Gags," is secondrate in its comedy (which includes the skits Jugnot and Lhermitte propose Serrault) and self-conscious in its theme, eventually forgetting to be funny when it starts stigmatizing intellectuals and the inferiority complex of the popular laughmaker.

Serrault tries in vain to give some substance to an inadequate role, while his young costars breeze along okay in their usual casual manner. Fellow screen comic Coluche does a special guest stint as a fleapit transvestite comedian who takes Serrault's daughter hostage in exchange for his own tv comedy slot. Sequence is a poor capsule variation on Martin Scorsese's "The King Of Comedy." —Len.

Giulia In Ottobre
(Julia In October)
(ITALIAN-COLOR-16m)

Berlin, Feb. 25.

A Bilico Films production. Directed by Silvio Soldini. Soldini, Lara Fremder; camera (color, 16m), Luca Bigazzi; editor, Claudio Cormio, Soldini; sets and costumes, Franca

Bertagnolli; sound, Pino Castellet, Roberto Mozzarelli. Reviewed at the Berlin Film Festival (Forum), Feb. 24, 1985. Running time: **60 MINS.**
With: Carla Chiarelli, Giuseppe Cederna, Daniela Morelli, Andrea Novicov, Moni Ovadia.

———

Milan filmmaker Silvio Soldini is bent on transmitting moods rather than a plot in "Julia In October." Mood is that of a girl who tries to surmount her exceeding loneliness at the end of a love affair. There is no story to speak of, just a series of encounters, all of them brief and of no consequence, each one helping her to retrieve her emotional balance.

The film's $10,000 budget probably didn't allow for more than the basic equipment, 16m and direct sound, which, considering the conditions, create adequate atmosphere.

Carla Chiarelli, who has already acted before with Soldini is probably atuned to his goals, for she exudes the sort of melancholy that is necessary to make the part believable.
—Edna.

The New Kids
(COLOR)

———

Tame thriller.

———

Hollywood, March 15.

A Columbia Pictures release. Produced by Sean S. Cunningham and Andrew Fogelson. Directed by Cunningham. Features entire cast. Screenplay, Stephen Gyllenhaal; camera (Metrocolor), Steve Poster; editor, Rita Roland; sound, Howard Warren; art direction, Pete Smith; assistant director, Brian Frankish; associate producer, Barbara De Fina; music, Lalo Schifrin; casting, Julie Hughes, Barry Moss, Pennie du Pont. Reviewed at the Metro Theatre, L.A., March 15, 1985. (MPAA Rating: R.) Running time: **90 MINS.**
Loren . . . . Shannon Presby
Abby . . . . Lori Loughlin
Dutra . . . . James Spader
Gideon . . . . John Philbin
Moonie . . . . David H. MacDonald
Joe Bob . . . . Vincent Grant
Gordon . . . . Theron Montgomery
Charlie . . . . Eddie Jones
Aunt Fay . . . . Lucy Martin
Mark . . . . Eric Stoltz
Karen . . . . Paige Lyn Price
Sheriff . . . . Court Miller

———

"The New Kids" is "Friday The 13th" director Sean S. Cunningham's latest stroll down the terror trail. Pic is well made and cast puts in credible performances, but the story spends an inordinate amount of time coming up to speed, the characters are too pat and the tension strangely minimal. Result is neither a typical slasher pic nor an edge-of-the-seat thriller. Boxoffice chances are dim.

Shannon Presby (Loren) and Lori

Loughlin (Abby) play a brother and sister who lose their parents in an accident and wind up living with relatives in a small Florida town. They quickly run afoul of some local toughs led by James Spader (Dutra), a drug-dealing borderline psychotic.

Loughlin's looks quickly trigger bets among the gang as to who will be the first to bed her, but the chaste Loughlin will have none of it and her athletic brother is a powerful defender.

Events slowly escalate from meanish pranks to rabbit killing and beyond, all of which is finally resolved in a climactic brawl where Presby and Loughlin prove tough as nails and the gang reveal themselves as horrible shots.

As a terror film, "Kids" is astonishingly tame, a fact which will undoubtedly cheer folks concerned about screen violence, but dismay the hordes of theater-going teens who relish that sort of thing.

Presby does a standup job in portraying the neat and clean Loren and the virginal Abby is equally well presented by Loughlin. Spader's evil gang leader has just the right touch of insanity and indeed, from ne'er-do-well Uncle Charlie (Eddie Jones) to lowlife Gideon (John Philbin), the actors all pitch in to glean everything possible from characters steeped in cliché.

Film was released originally by Col in Florida and Texas in January, then put into wide release in Los Angeles without the usual industry screenings. — Dani.

Baby
(COLOR)

———

Cute dinosaur pic from Disney.

———

Hollywood, March 8.

A Buena Vista release of a Touchstone Films presentation. Produced by Jonathan T. Taplin. Executive producer, Roger Spottiswoode. Directed by B.W.L. Norton. Features entire cast. Screenplay, Clifford and Ellen Green; camera (Technicolor), John Alcott; editors, Howard Smith, David Bretherton; production design, Raymond G. Storey; sound, Kirk Francis; music, Jerry Goldsmith; art directors, John B. Mansbridge, Steve Spence; associate producer, E. Darrell Hallenbeck; assistant director, Steve McEveety; casting, Bill Shepard, Rose Tobias Shaw; dinosaurs created by Isidoro Raponi, Roland Tantin. Reviewed at Walt Disney Prods., March 8, 1985. (MPAA rating: PG.) Running time: **95 MINS.**

George Loomis . . . . William Katt
Susan Matthews-Loomis . . . . . Sean Young
Dr. Eric Kiviat . . . . Patrick McGoohan
Nigel Jenkins . . . . Julian Fellowes
Cephu . . . . Kyalo Mativo
Kenge Obe . . . . Hugh Quarshie
Colonel Nsogbu . . . . Olu Jacobs
Sergeant Gambwe . . . . Eddie Tagoe

———

A huggable prehistoric hatchling discovered by a young American couple in an African rain forest will win the hearts of kids, although with a hefty negative cost Touchstone's ''Baby'' poses a family-oriented marketing challenge for the folks at Buena Vista.

At a glance, this baby dinosaur yarn seems too cartoonish for Touchstone (heretofore the launching pad for ''Splash'' and ''Country'') but, on the other hand, such contempo elements as a flash of bare breasts in an Ivory Coast parade sequence, the implied lovemaking between costars William Katt and Sean Young, and violence (to dinosaur parents and African soldiers) lifts pic beyond the conventional Disney distrib banner.

The story has an engaging performance from Katt, who plays the sportswriter husband of paleontologist Young. Latter, whose maternal and scientific instincts propel events, is rather bland (following stronger portrayals in ''Blade Runner'' and ''Young Doctors In Love'').

Evil foil is Patrick McGoohan as a rival, ruthless paleontologist who enlists the aid of a rapacious revolutionary army to capture Baby's towering brontosaurus mama, after overzealous soldiers gun down the 70-or-so-foot tall papa.

Katt and Young risk their lives to save the baby, who stretches 10 feet, has a kind of ''E.T.'' winsomeness, and once even hops like a shaggy family pooch in between the covers of Katt and Young.

Shot in the Ivory Coast, production, under the direction of B.W.L. Norton, from a scenario by Clifford and Ellen Green, is a rare dinosaur yarn insofar as the behemoths are friendly.

As Katt and Young scamper to reunite the baby with its captured mother, the filmmakers veer into a violent gun and grenade battle at an African compound. The degree of mayhem here lurches the picture unnecessarily off course and creates a confusion of tone.

Cameraman John Alcott opts for a bright look; he also uses the same widescreen Supertechniscope technique he introduced in ''Greystoke.''

Production has good support in a simpering turn by McGoohan assistant Julian Fellowes, and a wonderfully natural and humorous tribesman played by African actor Kyalo Mativo.

Dinosaur movements derive from both cable and from operators who were inside the gargantuan structures, which were created by and engineered by Isidoro Raponi and Roland Tantin. —*Loyn.*

Segreti Segreti
(Secrets Secrets)
(ITALIAN-COLOR)

Rome, March 12.
An Instituto Luce-Italnoleggio release. Produced by Gianni Minervini for A.M.A. Film, Istituto Luce and Italnoleggio. Directed by Giuseppe Bertolucci. Features entire cast. Screenplay, Bertolucci, Vincenzo Cerami; camera (color), Renato Tafuri; editor, Nino Baragli; art director, Francesco Frigeri; music, Nicola Piovani. Reviewed at Cinefonico, Rome, March 11, 1985. Running time: **94 MINS.**

Laura	Lina Sastri
Laura's mother	Léa Massari
Rosa	Giulia Boschi
Rosa's mother	Rosanna Podestà
Gina	Alida Valli
Renata	Stefania Sandrelli
Judge	Mariangela Melato

One of the most serious new works to appear this season, ''Secrets Secrets'' is a feather in the cap of younger helmer Giuseppe Bertolucci (''An Italian Woman'') and producers Gianni Minervini (''Picone Sent Me'') and Italnoleggio-Istituto Luce. Like his big brother Bernardo, Giuseppe incorporates an enthusiasm for film culture into the fabric of the picture, without resorting to homages or pastiche. In this case, pic is a virtual textbook about the Italian film actress, with an all-femme cast of seven top performers.

Though it has something of a gimmick about it, the idea works of casting one of the glories of the Italo cinema, Alida Valli, alongside current marquee lights Stefania Sandrelli and Mariangela Melato, cult favorites Léa Massari and Rosanna Podestà, and two of the brightest newcomers, Lina Sastri and Giulia Boschi. Even when the story slackens, cast serves up top performances in an almost competitive atmosphere. It emerges an art house entry that may have more b.o. chances offshore than at home, where female entertainers notoriously draw worse than their male counterparts.

Story begins in Venice, where stony-faced terrorist Laura (Sastri) shoots a judge and then finishes off a faltering member of the gang. Through her, the other women are involved. Rosa (Boschi), a pretty Southerner and sister of the dead terrorist, attends his funeral with her mother (Podestà) amid the desolation of Avellino, where people are still living in gypsy-like trailer camps after the earthquake. Gina (Valli), Laura's old nanny, guesses her ''secret'' without being told and indignantly packs her bags. Laura's mother (Massari), a rich widow, is shocked into facing reality for what seems to be the first time when she comes home and finds the house full of police waiting to arrest her daughter. Her tragic end is meas-

ured against the vanity-suicide attempt of her actress friend Renata (Sandrelli).

Last to appear on the scene in a powerfully convincing performance is Melato, the investigating judge who grills Laura after her arrest. That morning her little daughter has told her she saw daddy kissing another woman. Melato is still in shock when she listens to Laura's uncontrollable confession, a flood of terrible secrets that maybe, pic suggests, would be better left covered.

Pic is not a political thriller, but a series of character sketches and glimpses into the human heart. Thus, the episodes depend heavily on the strength of the acting. The consumate professionalism of Valli and Massari, and the rising star of young Giulia Boschi, shine in every scene, while Sastri and Podestà are too type-cast for comfort. Many act in dialect accents not their own, to uncertain effect.

Sensitive use is made of Nicola Piovani's haunting musical score, and Renato Tafuri's confident camerawork, the eye-catching sets by Francesco Frigeri and quick-paced back-and-forth cutting from editor Nina Baragli, all show the attention lavished on pic's technical side.
— *Yung.*

Hellhole
(COLOR)

Lower case women-in-stir picture.

An Arkoff International Pictures release of a Hellhole production. Produced by Billy Fine, Louis S. Arkoff. Directed by Pierre de Moro. Features entire cast. Screenplay, Vincent Mongol; additional story & new dialog, Lance Dickson; additional dialog, Mark Evan Schwartz; camera (Deluxe color), Steven Posey; editor, Steve Butler; editorial consultant, Bill Butler; music, Jeff Sturges; sound, Jerry Wolfe; assistant director, D.K. Miller; production manager, Tony Lopez; art direction, Chris Henry; set decoration, Lauren Polizzi; special effects, Dale Martin; special makeup, Donn Markel; stunt coordinator, Sandy Gimpel. Reviewed at UA Twin 1 theater, N.Y., March 15, 1985. (MPAA Rating: R.) Running time: **95 MINS.**

Silk	Ray Sharkey
Susan	Judy Landers
Dr. Fletcher	Mary Woronov
Dr. Dane	Marjoe Gortner
Vera	Edy Williams
Sidnee Hammond	Terry Moore
Brad	Robert Darcy
Ron	Rick Cox
Monroe	Martin Beck
Mom	Lynn Borden
Dr. Blum	Cliff Emmich
Chrysta	Dyanne Thorne

''Hellhole'' is a poorly-made throwback to the women in prison pictures, designed for hit and run

openings. Made by Billy Fine (whose ''The Concrete Jungle'' was a hit in the genre), pic marks another subpar entry following ''The Final Terror'' and Orion's ''Up The Creek'' from Sam Arkoff.

Nominal story has Susan (Judy Landers) getting amnesia from a fall after her mom (Lynn Borden) is killed by thug Silk (Ray Sharkey). Susan is sent to Ashland sanitarium for women, where Silk is trying to get her to remember where some valuable papers were put by her mom. Also at Ashland is mad scientist Dr. Fletcher (Mary Woronov), experimenting with the aid of naive Dr. Dane (Marjoe Gortner) to develop a chemical lobotomy formula, using the women as guinea pigs, while Ron (Rick Cox) is working undercover as an orderly trying to expose Fletcher. Experiments take place in the dingy nether-regions of a building outback, called Hellhole.

Risible dialog is not enough to make this material funny, as director Pierre de Moro relies on catfights and numerous lesbian scenes to titillate the target audience. Ironically, story only satisfies when it moves into the territory of ''The Island Of Dr. Moreau,'' the unsuccessful remake that Arkoff made when his American Intl. Pictures was unwisely upgrading its product in the late 1970s.

Landers is an inexpressive heroine who prudishly never disrobes, a defect in exploitation terms which would have been remedied had originally-cast Linda Blair made the film. Sharkey is embarrassing in an unwise emulation of the sleazy personages usually essayed on screen by Joe Spinell, while Gortner and Terry Moore walk through the picture.

Sole watchable element in ''Hellhole'' is Mary Woronov, delightfully campy doing her patented butch routine in high heels, too tight skirts, with lowered voice and too much makeup. Edy Williams, as usual, leads the nude brigade. — *Lor.*

Umi-Tori
(The Stolen Sea)
(JAPANESE-DOCU-COLOR)

Berlin, Feb. 22.
An ''Initiative Of The Sea,'' Seirinsha production. Produced by Yuzo Matsuhashi. Written and directed by Noriaki Tsuchimoto. Camera (color), Yoshio Shimizu; editor, Kunimori Fuchiwaki; sound, Koji Okamoto; narrated by Soichi Ito. Reviewed at the Berlin Film festival (Forum), Feb. 21, 1985. Running time: **103 MINS.**

''The Stolen Sea'' goes into the details concerning the efforts of a fishermen's community in the

Shimokita peninsula in Japan to prevent the invasion of an atomic power plant, which would kill off their trade.

The Japanese government, as it turns out, tries to deal with the matter fairly, by offering compensation to the inhabitants and attempting to relocate them.

The point of this documentary is to prevent such a measure being applied in the Shimokita case. The trouble is that unless one is familiar with specific aspects of the problem there, one may well get lost in the labyrinth of minute details. The film's stodgy, determined pace leaves no doubt about the serious, single-minded approach of the filmmakers, but the product is limited to students of the Japanese fishing industries, or those documenting the ecological struggle around the world. —Edna.

James Joyce's Women
(COLOR)

Powerful dramatization by Fionnula Flanagan.

Hollywood, March 14.
Universal Pictures release of a Rejoycing Co. production. Produced by Fionnula Flanagan. Executive producers, Garrett O'Connor, Flanagan. Directed by Michael Pearce. Stars Flanagan. Screenplay, Flanagan, adapted from the writings of James Joyce; camera (color), John Metcalfe; editor, Arthur Keating, Dan Perry; music, Vincent Kilduff, Keating, O'Connor; associate producer, Patrick Flanagan; assistant director, Barry Blackmore. Reviewed at the Fox Intl. Theater, Venice, Calif., March 13, 1985. (No MPAA Rating.) Running time: **91 MINS.**
Nora Barnacle Joyce, Sylvia Beach,
Molly Bloom, Gerty MacDowell,
Harriet Shaw Weaver,
Washerwoman 1 . . . . . . Fionnula Flanagan
The interviewer . . . . . Timothy E. O'Grady
James Joyce . . . . Chris O'Neill
Leopold Bloom . . . . Tony Lyons
Dubliner . . . . Gerald Fitzmahony
Dubliner . . . . Joseph Taylor
Joyce's father . . . . Martin Dempsey
Stannie Joyce . . . . Paddy Dawson

As much about Irish author James Joyce as his female creations, "James Joyce's Women" blurs the line between life and art and comes up with a unique view of one of this century's major cultural figures. Originally presented on stage and financed by Universal Pictures in England for the cable market, company is now thinking of a theatrical release for the art market where the film should be received warmly.

While not quite a one-woman show, production is clearly the inspiration of Irish actress Fionnula Flanagan who not only plays half a dozen characters, but wrote, produced and had the vision for the project. Dublin born and Abbey

Theater-trained, Flanagan obviously brings a wealth of background and total credibility to each of the women presented. In fact she duplicates her earlier incarnation as Gerty MacDowell from Joseph Strick's 1967 film of "Ulysses."

Framework of the film is an interview with the elderly Nora Joyce, the author's wife, who reminisces about their life together. A fascinating woman in her own right, she provides a good deal of insight into the life and times of her husband. Flanagan has done her homework and apparently had access to Joyce letters and memorabilia. Tone occasionally becomes a bit bookish, but never totally loses its entertainment value, especially the way Flanagan delivers Joyce's lyrical language.

Along with Nora, other historical figures brought to life by Flanagan is Sylvia Beach, owner of Shakespeare and Co. Books in Paris, the first publisher of "Ulysses." Flanagan suggests Nora was, if not the inspiration, then the source of much of Joyce's understanding of women and consequently, his writing.

Among Joyce's fictional women represented are Molly Bloom, who delivers her famous sensual soliloquy from "Ulysses," and the washerwoman from the Anna Livia Plurabelle section of "Finnegan's Wake." Although much of the language from the Anna Livia section is indecipherable the sheer music of the language does Joyce proud.

Supporting cast is adequate and occasionally striking as in the case of Chris O'Neill as the middle-aged Joyce and Gladys Sheehan and Rebecca Wilkenson as washerwomen with extraordinary faces. Direction by Michael Pearce and cinematography by John Metcalfe emphasizing closeups gives away the film's origins for the cable market, but with such expressive faces the production does not really suffer.

The heart of this film is Joyce, whose work is manifested through Flanagan's extraordinary performance. —Jagr.

L.A. Filmex Review

28 Up
(BRITISH-DOCU-COLOR)

Hollywood, March 8.
A Granada Television production. Executive producer, Steve Morrison. Produced, directed by Michael Apted. Camera (color), George Jesse Turner; editors, Oral Norrie Ottey, Kim Horton; sound, Nick Steer. Reviewed at the American Film Institute (Filmex), March 7, 1985. (No MPAA Rating.) Running time: **133 MINS.**

A fascinating, one-of-a-kind document, "28 Up" represents a visual and spoken record of the lives of 14 young Britishers as caught in four visits with each separated by seven-year gaps. Originally produced by Granada Television and the recent winner of a British Academy Award, complete work is now entering the festival circuit.

When he was a 23-year-old researcher, Michael Apted helped select the 14 seven-year-olds to be interviewed for a British tv documentary. He found and filmed them again when they were 14, 21, and, finally, 28, with an eye to discovering how their lives had progressed, how they either did, or did not, fulfill any youthful promise, and how the vestiges of the English class systems still determine the stations to which its subjects will gravitate. Entire spectacle of growing up is framed within the context of the famous dictum (originated by St. Francis Xavier and adopted by Lenin), "Give me a child until he is seven, and I will give you the man."

Aptly, the 14 represent a good cross-section of urbanites and rural inhabitants, men and women, upper classmen and East Enders. None of the group died, two emigrated (one to Australia, another to the U.S.), one dropped out of society and two of the best educated elite, claiming they had nothing further to contribute, declined to be filmed at 28.

Despite the crumbling of the empire, the evidence on display here incidates the English class system, and the strong deterministic influence of the accompanying school systems, still persists as an amazingly resilient force. Furthermore, even those individuals furthest down the economic scale seem only marginally bitter and discontent; even if they might criticize the current Thatcher government on certain points, none displays any coherent political thoughts or any sense of creative rebellion.

Typically, many of the subjects who seemed bright and bushy-tailed at seven and 14 are confused and sullen at 21, but have emerged into acceptance of conventional marriage and family, and of their lot in life, by 28. One, Neil, sadly evolved into a total misfit who wanders the countryside looking for odd jobs. A true lost soul who fell between the cracks of society, he has no prospects and is the saddest of the group.

The only black in the bunch, Simon, is, if anything, the least political of them all, as he's busily engaged in raising and supporting his large family and has little time to consider broader matters.

Michael Apted, well-known for his feature work on "Coal Miner's Daughter," "Gorky Park" and

others, was fortunate to be involved in such a project at an early age, and has capitalized on his luck superbly by so conscientiously following up on his previous work. Despite its exclusive concentration on English society, this would prove interesting to any audience, and deserves further airing at other fests and on American television. —Cart.

Before & After
(B&W-16m)

Amateur night at the bijou.

Hollywood, Feb. 28.
A Little Deer production. Produced, directed by Aziz Ghazal. Screenplay, Rebecca Ghazal, Aziz Ghazal; camera (b&w), Dan Gillman; editors, Aziz Ghazal, Gary Nelson, Roy Seeger; music, Steve Bernstein. Reviewed at the American Film Institute (Filmex), Feb. 27, 1985. (No MPAA Rating.) Running time: **83 MINS.**
With: Ken Shippy, Lynn Chaplin, Nancy Parker, Biff Yeager, Mike Alvarez.

An amateur-night production from beginning to end, "Before & After" bears all the earmarks of a bad first feature — all-embracing pretentiousness, arty editing, sloppy post-synched sound and delusions of self-importance. Made by an Israeli-born filmmaker living in the U.S. since 1975, pic looks every penny of its $10,000 budget and will perform well with masochistic audiences everywhere.

No doubt inspired by "Hiroshima, Mon Amour," director Aziz Ghazal begins by presenting the spectacle of a man shooting his daughter, wife and himself after learning of the first A-bomb blast in Japan in 1945, then cuts to the present, where a skid row denizen named Ray, son of the killer, is wracked with guilt over having survived the mini-holocaust at home as a child.

In addition, Ray has serious sexual and religious problems and acts hostile towards just about everyone who crosses his path, waving a gun in people's faces at every opportunity. In short, Ray is a total drag, and no insights except the obvious ones are offered to induce the viewer to take an interest in him.

Despite having been shot on location in L.A. in gritty, 16m black-and-white, film possesses a tremendous phoniness, especially in the way secondary characters and extras are introduced artificially to populate it.

Acting from top to bottom is broad and frequently awkward in student film fashion, and the wait for the inevitably violent ending seems virtually interminable.
—Cart.

Mark Twain
(ANIMATED-COLOR)

Generally effective Claymation feature.

Hollywood, March 15.
A Harbour Towns Films presentation of a Will Vinton Prods. film. Produced by Will Vinton. Executive producer, Hugh Kennedy Tirrell. Directed by Vinton. Screenplay, Susan Shadburne; editor, Kelley Baker, Michael Gall, Will Vinton; music, Billy Scream; character design, Barry Bruce; set design, Joan C. Gratz, Don Merkt; claypainting effects, Gratz; principal character claymation, William L. Fiesterman, Tom Gasek, Mark Gustafson, Craig Bartlett, Bruce McKean; featured voices, James Whitmore (Mark Twain), Michele Mariana (Becky Thatcher), Gary Krug (Huck Finn), Chris Ritchie (Tom Sawyer). Reviewed at the Mann Westwood Theater, L.A., March 15, 1985. (No MPAA Rating.) Running time: **90 MINS.**

"Mark Twain" is a charming homage to writer Samuel Clemens and his world on the occasion of his 150th birthday rendered through Will Vinton's claymation process of animation. Immensely imaginative on the one hand and highly fragmented on the other, claymation is both the strength and weakness of the film. Overall, however, pic is successful in capturing much of the wit and spirit of Twain and should prove entertaining to a broad audience.

Screenplay by Susan Shadburne imagines a final journey for Twain to Halley's comet in a hot air balloon which looks something like a riverboat. Stowing away on board are three figments of Twain's imagination, Huck Finn, Tom Sawyer and Becky Thatcher.

Creation, artistic and cosmic, is very much the point as Twain literally travels to meet his maker, telling his friends tales along the way. Stories include familiar Twain territory such as "The Jumping Frog Of Calaveras County" and meeting with characters such as Injun Joe. Other flights of fantasy are as diverse as a retelling of the Adam and Eve legend and an encounter with heaven and hell.

Visually, virtues of claymation are a fluidity of motion and a superior range of expressions from traditional animation. Still these are not full-blooded people and although the film almost overcomes calling attention to its technique, it never quite lets one forget. Backgrounds and sets are often quite imaginative, particularly a storm sequence, but camera range is limited to closeups much of the time and visuals too often are simply illustrations of the accompanying narration.

Twain himself, however, is a joy with the voice of James Whitmore suggesting the warmth and wisdom of the character.

Credit should go the numerous technical people who have executed the claymation technique with consumate skill, among them Barry Bruce, who designed the characters, Joan Gratz and Don Merkt, who did the set design, and William Fiesterman, Tom Gasek, Mark Gustafson, Craig Bartlett and Bruce McKean, principal claymators.
— *Jagr.*

La Vaquilla
(The Little Bull)
(SPANISH-COLOR)

Zaragoza, Feb. 28.
An Incine-Jet Films production. Directed by Luis Gacia Berlanga. Executive producer, Alfredo Matas; associate producer, Benjamin Benhamou. Screenplay, Rafael Azcona, Berlanga; camera (Eastmancolor), Carlos Suárez; production manager, Marisol Carnicero; editor, José Luis Matesanz; music, Miguel Asins Arbo; sets, Enrique Alarcón; costumes, León Revuelta. Reviewed at Cine Palafox (Zaragoza), Feb. 28, 1985. Running time: **116 MINS.**

Mariano	Guillermo Montesinos
Castro	Alfredo Landa
Broceta	José Sacristán
Priest	Carlos Velat
Guadalupe	Violeta Cela
Marquis	Adolfo Marsillach
Nationalist Commander	Agustin Gonzalez

Also with: Santiago Ramos, Juanjo Puig Corbe, Amelia de la Torre, Francisco Sala, Maria Luisa Ponce, Sergio Mendizabal, Fernando Sancho, Paco Valdivia, A.J. Leal, Luis Ciges, Pedro Beltrán.

Spain's Luis Garcia Berlanaga has pulled an old script out of his drawer written close to 20 years ago together with Rafael Azcona, and come up with one of the most youthful and entertaining comedies seen here in many a year.

Using as a backdrop a non-belligerent front during the Spanish Civl War, Berlanga limns a whimsical yarn about a group of five Republican soldiers who cross enemy lines in 1938 to try to steal a young bull during a village fiesta.

One member of the bumbling detachment happens to be from the village and has his girlfriend there; another is an amateur bullfighter who is to dispatch the bull, dismember him and bring back the meat to the hungry Republicans.

The mission is constantly thwarted as the Republican soldiers, dressed in Nationalist uniforms, become embroiled in the "running" of the bull, a religious procession, the activities of a brothel, and finally the bullfight, in which the bull manages to escape from the makeshift arena. Ultimately the five men manage to get back to their lines, but the bull dies in no man's land and is eaten by the vultures, a nice symbolic ending.

Acting by all players is memorable, as Berlanga, eschwing any political axe grinding, uses long sequences that often last five to 10 minutes each, shifting from one personage to another. Film was shot entirely in exteriors. Direct sound and Carlos Suarez' camerawork leave much to be desired. Nonetheless pic comes across as a solid and entertaining work which sould titillate audiences both in and out of Spain. —*Besa.*

Nelisita
(ANGOLAN-B&W)

Ouagadougou, Feb. 27.
An Edecine-Luanda release, produced by Laboratorio Nacional de Cinema (Luanda). Directed and written by Ruy Duarte de Carvallo. Camera (B&W), Victor Henriques; editor, Jacqueline Mepiel; sound, Orlando Rodrigues. Reviewed at the Pan-African Film Festival, Ouagadougou, Burkina Faso, Feb. 26, 1985. Running time: **90 MINS.**

A black-and-white retelling of Angolan legends combining magnificent visual simplicity with great narrative sophistications, "Nelisita" won the Seventh Art Prize at the Pan-African Film Festival and deserves a chance to be seen more widely.

Portugese-born helmer Ruy Duarte de Carvallo, now an African resident, weaves two legends from southeast Angola into a single story with clearly allegorical ramifications. A family is starving during a great famine. The man goes in search of food and stumbles across a grain deposit, jealously guarded by a group of "evil spirits" with great powers (hats and clothing symbolically identify them as Europeans, Americans, etc.). The first expedition goes okay and the man returns with enough food to feed his family and others drawn to his kitchen.

He agrees to bring his friend along on a second mission, but dazzled by the piles of wealth he sees, the friend hesitates and is caught by the evil spirits.

A child is born — Nelisita — who grows into the hero of the tale. He fights the spirits with the help of animals and other friends and delivers his people.

Camera is kept at a distance in most shots, with minimum movement; long takes give pic a slow, unhurried pace. A few titles destroy any attempt to locate the tale in time by indications like " a hundred years later." Actors walk through their roles with little direction, wearing a humorous mixture of short-sleeved plaid shirts and native garb.

Substituting imagination for production money, "Nelisita" uses a whole range of delightful ploys to circumvent technical problems. When script calls for the hero to separate a massive pile of seed and grain, he calls on his bird friends for help, with little boys appearing as the birds. Same tactic for a herd of gazelles who have to clear a field in record time: a corps of graceful maidens fills the bill. —*Yung.*

Leben In Wittstock
(Life In Wittstock)
(E. GERMAN-DOCU-B&W)

Berlin, Feb. 21.
A DEFA Studio for Documentary Film production, East Berlin, GDR. A documentary by Volker Koepp. Commentary, Annerose Richter, Volker Koepp, Wolfgang Geier; camera (b&w), Christian Lehmann; music, Rainer Böhm; sound, Eberhard Pfaff; editor, Lutz Körner. Reviewed at Berlin Film Fest (Forum), Feb. 21, 1985. Running time: **85 MINS.**
With: Stupsi, Renate and Edith, together with other workers in a textile factory.

Volker Koepp's "Life In Wittstock" scores as a documentary taking a glance over the shoulder at what has proceeded it in "Girls In Wittstock" (1975), "Again In Wittstock" (1976) and "Living And Weaving" (1981). The documentarist, well known in East Germany for his poetic approach to life and work against a peculiar background, here summarizes his thoughts and feelings on three central characters presented to the viewing public a full decade ago.

Wittstock is a small provincial city not far from the East Berlin capital, whose main contribution to the Socialist state is a large textile factory employing 2,000 girls whose average age is 21. Naturally, the overflow of working population in the small town has its repercussions both on the job and during free hours.

Koepp picked up the lifestyle of two girls, Stupsi and Edith, adding Renate along the way. In "Life In Wittstock" he sets these three against the life of the city as the population adjusts to the rhythm of women workers, mostly young but many now growing into middleage, in the course of a decade. As realistically authentic as the footage is in b&w lensing, however, the main drawback is that the whole is too much in the nature of talking heads for an inquiring camera.

All the same, outside of Winfried Junge's "Paths Of Life" (covering a gradeschool class over 20 years), this docu sketch of working life in the German Democratic Republic, 1974-1984, tells more about East Germany than what's available in the DEFA-produced fictional feature films. — *Holl.*

The Way It Is or Eurydice In The Avenues
(U.S.-B&W)

Berlin, Feb. 18.
A The Way It Is Co., Daniel Sales and Eric Mitchell Production. Written and directed by Mitchell. Camera (black and white), Bobby Bukowski; edited by Bob Gould and Sue

Graef; sound, Randal Goya; music, Vincent Gallo. Reviewed at the Berlin Film Festival (Forum), Feb. 17, 1985. Running time: **80 MINS.**
With: Kai Eric, Boris Major, Vincent Gallo, Jessica Stutchbury, Mark Boone Jr., Steve Buscemi, Rockets Redglare.

New York underground filmmaker Eric Mitchell tries in this film to mix life and fiction, using Lower Manhattan as one would use a film set, or theater decor.

A theater group is trying to produce an unconventional version of Jean Cocteau's "Orphée." When the leading actress, who is supposed to play Eurydice, is found dead, each of the other characters goes back in his own past trying to unravel the mystery. At the same time, each is suspect, which makes their testimonies ambiguous.

Made on a shoestring budget with no direct sound, the plot's twists and detours often obscure the story itself.

While the film has its moments, mostly when exploiting the natural boisterousness of its cast, Mitchell lacks rigor in constructing his picture. —*Edna.*

Artie Shaw: Time Is All You've Got
(CANADIAN-DOCU-B&W/COLOR)

Hollywood, March 15.
A Bridge Film Production. Produced, directed, and written by Brigitte Berman. Camera (color), Mark Irwin, Jim Aquila; music, Artie Shaw and his various orchestras; editors, Berman, Barry Backus. Reviewed at Filmex, L.A., March 15, 1985. (No MPAA Rating.) Running time: **114 MINS.**
With: Artie Shaw, Helen Forrest, Evelyn Keyes, Polly Haynes, John Wexley, Lee Castle, Mel Tormé.

This full-length profile of jazz great Artie Shaw, made by Toronto-based documentary filmmaker Brigitte Berman, is a riveting look back at both the big band era and one of its burning lights.

The docu has strong potential in cable, public television, and home-video markets. No distributor is set.

Berman snared Shaw's permission and lengthy on-camera interview time after Shaw viewed her earlier and impressive film on Bix Beiderbecke. Berman retained editorial control and the result is a swinging odyssey and one not always flattering of its subject. A mixture of contempo interviews and black and white clips (including scenes from Shaw playing himself in two movies, the 1939 "Dancing Co-Ed" and the 1940 "Second Chorus"), is smartly edited, capturing the notoriety of Shaw's life and also the much lesser-known intellectual and creative drive that set him apart from most of his colleagues.

Aside from the bumptious and cheery candor of Shaw's on-camera

remarks, the docu is notable for a particularly fascinating interval with Evelyn Keyes, last of Shaw's seven wives.

The picture is strongest visually on the '30s and '40s, charting in brief, telling touches Shaw's nerve and his loss of nerves: his hiring of Billie Holliday in 1937, "the first time a black singer sang with a white band and played the South," reports Shaw, and Shaw's psychological breakdown as a serviceman entertaining the troops in the South Pacific during World War II.

Marriages to such stars as Lana Turner and Ava Gardner are observed and brushed off, although next to Shaw's music, his romantic notoriety lingers in the public's mind as one of his legacies. This film puts that side of his life in its proper and comparatively unimportant perspective, and revives his musical riches. —*Loyn.*

Les Specialistes
(The Specialists)
(FRENCH-COLOR)

Paris, March 13.
A Gaumont/Fechner release of a Christian Fechner/Films A2 coproduction. Produced by Bernard Artigues. Directed by Patrice Leconte. Stars Bernard Giraudeau, Gérard Lanvin. Screenplay, Leconte, Patrick Dewolf, Michel Blanc; camera (color), Eduardo Serra; art directors, Ivan Maussion and Jacques Bufnoir; editor, Joëlle Hache; sound, Alain Lachassagne; music, Eric Demarsan; production manager, Henri Brichetti. Reviewed at the Gaumont Ambassade theater, Paris, March 13, 1985. Running time: **92 MINS.**
Paul Brandon . . . . Bernard Giraudeau
Stéphane Carella . . . . Gérard Lanvin
Laura . . . . Christiane Jean
Mazetti . . . . Bertie Cortez
Kovacs . . . . Maurice Barrier
Casino manager . . . . Daniel Jegou

"The Specialists," a so-so entry into the caper thriller genre, is producer Christian Fechner's bid to launch the French male duo of the '80s, in the mode of that created by Jean-Paul Belmondo and Alain Delon in the '60s.

Gérard Lanvin and Bernard Giraudeau are elected, cast as a pair of daredevil outlaws who engineer the burgling of a Nice casino, managed by a Mafia kingpin, in order to trigger internecine gang war.

They are discovered escaping from a police paddywagon in the mountains. Lanvin, whose term is up in a year's time, is not anxious for a getaway, but since he is handcuffed to the seemingly desperate and dangerous Giraudeau, he has no choice but to clamber up sheer rock faces and take death-defying leaps into the rapids to escape police bullets.

Later they hold up in the isolated house of a pretty young widow (Christiane Jean) where they plan the job of the century. As it turns out, Giraudeau is in fact a supercop

planted to spring Lanvin and manipulate him into doing the heist.

Despite their super-cool manner and sex appeal, Lanvin and Giraudeau don't really muster the larger-than-life panache to make their buddy-buddy exploits ignite. They are not dissimilar enough to make a genuine complementary team, and the story and direction lack the slick interlocking craftsmanship of classic heist pictures.

Pic's makers are not specialists in the genre. The director, Patrice Leconte, packaged a series of light comedies for Fechner which have made a fortune in French cinemas. The dialog writer, Michel Blanc, is the café-theater clown who has been Leconte's scripter-star and recently helmed the top-grossing local pic of 1984, "Marche à l'Ombre," also costarring with Lanvin. Working with Bruno Tardon, who wrote the original story, they apply themselves dutifully, but the effort shows too often.

Actual caper is sufficiently contrived to seem ingenious and fairly suspenseful, but surrounding scenes and action setpieces (the romantic angle with Jean seems like a reluctant afterthought by the writers) are often underwritten and predictable in development.

First-day results in France show another monster success for Fechner, who recently removed his commercial green thumb from French major Gaumont's financially weedy motion picture plot. However, "The Specialists" may not be the picture that will conquer new foreign markets for its producer's growing ambitions. — *Len.*

King David
(COLOR)

Well-produced but overly literal Biblical epic.

Hollywood, March 22.
A Paramount Pictures release. Produced by Martin Elfand. Directed by Bruce Beresford. Stars Richard Gere. Screenplay, Andrew Birkin, James Costigan, based on Samuel I and II, Chronicles I and Psalms of David; camera (Rank color), Donald McAlpine; editor, William Anderson; music, Carl Davis; sound, Brian Marshall; production design, Ken Adam; costumes, John Mollo; associate producer, Charles Orme; assistant director, David Tomblin; art direction, Terry Ackland-Snow; casting, Irene Lamb. Reviewed at Paramount Studios, Hollywood, March 21, 1985. (MPAA Rating: PG-13.) Running time: **114 MINS.**
David . . . . Richard Gere
Saul . . . . Edward Woodward
Samuel . . . . Denis Quilley
Nathan . . . . Niall Buggy
Jonathan . . . . Jack Klaff
Michal . . . . Cherie Lunghi
Bathsheba . . . . Alice Krige
Absalom . . . . Jean-Marc Barr
Young David . . . . Ian Sears
Ahimelech . . . . Hurd Hatfield
Abner . . . . John Castle
Joab . . . . Tim Woodward
Ahitophel . . . . David De Keyser

"King David" is an intensely literal telling of familiar portions of the saga of Israel's first two rulers, more historical in approach than religious. Nonetheless, it's a "Biblical" picture, once a boxoffice certainty but a big question mark now among generations unaccustomed to such material.

For better or worse, director Bruce Beresford is certainly no Cecil B. DeMille, often accused of taking certain liberties with scripture in favor of theatricality. Beresford and writers Andrew Birkin and James Costigan stay close to the Book here, but are somewhat trapped in that fidelity.

"David" thus moves from one monumental event to the next, trying to cover as much of the story as possible. The result is to minimize each step and every complex relationship (and doubtlessly confuse many of those who haven't been to Sunday School for awhile).

Though the overall problems may not be of his making, Richard Gere is of little help in the title role. Granted, he could have been truly awful (which he isn't), but he doesn't seem comfortable, either. Holding back, Gere rarely makes it felt why he loves Absalom so, or lusts after Bathsheba or tolerates Saul's persecution beyond the fact that it says so in the Bible (or in the script).

Film begins with Samuel's condemnation of Saul and the anointing of young David (played by Ian Sears, who unfortunately looks more like Barbra Streisand than Gere), proceeding through the fight with Goliath and then skipping forward until David is grown.

Gere appears in early favor with Saul (excellently played throughout by Edward Woodward), then suffers the king's jealous ire, wanders in hiding and returns to rule upon Saul's death. Then follows his sin with Bathsheba (Alice Krige).

Final chapter is Absalom and after the unhappy end to that, off-screen narration tells that David maintained until the succession of Solomon.

"David" really isn't as trifling as quick summary makes it seem. There's a lot of history here, brought to life with good period film work and performances are generally fine.

Though the rating is PG-13, the Biblical theme obviously brought lenience from the censors (as it always did). The fighting is R-level bloody, with lots of beheadings and slewing befitting the Old Testament.

Finally, Israel's God is obviously of central importance to "David," but there are no miracles here and nobody talks to the Lord directly. They talk of Him and his effect on them, as their history demands they would. Throughout, though, "David" is the story of extraordinary men, unfortunately moreso than the film ever conveys.—*Har.*

Desperately Seeking Susan
(COLOR)

Pleasant; lightweight entertainment.

Hollywood, March 18.

An Orion Pictures release. Produced by Sarah Pillsbury and Midge Sanford. Directed by Susan Seidelman. Stars Rosanna Arquette, Madonna. Exec producer, Michael Peyser. Screenplay, Leora Barish; camera (Deluxe color), Edward Lachman; editor, Andrew Mondshein; sound, Les Lazarowitz; production design, Santo Loquasto; assistant director, Joel Tuber; art direction, Speed Hopkins; production manager, Peyser; music, Thomas Newman; casting, Risa Bramon, Billy Hopkins. Reviewed at the Directors Guild of America, Hollywood, March 18, 1985. (MPAA Rating: PG-13.) Running time: **104 MINS.**

Roberta	Rosanna Arquette
Susan	Madonna
Dez	Aidan Quinn
Gary	Mark Blum
Jim	Robert Joy
Leslie	Laurie Metcalf
Crystal	Anna Levine
Nolan	Will Patton
Ian	Peter Maloney
Larry	Steven Wright
Ray	John Turturro
Victoria	Anne Carlisle
Jail matron	Shirley Stoler

"Desperately Seeking Susan" passes as a distinctly gratifying deviation, clearly female in its overall outlook, yet never feminist. For all its qualities, though, "Susan" will have to establish itself quickly or be desperately seeking an audience thereafter.

Because of Madonna's identity with "bimbo rock," there's already some resistance out in the marketplace from thinking women. Setting aside the prejudice, however, the ladies may be pleasantly surprised that Madonna not only turns in a rounded, interesting performance but the whole picture reflects the fact that none of the producers, director or writer is named Joe or Sam.

And Rosanna Arquette, as well, does more than her share in the pivotal part of a bored Yuppie housewife who follows the personal ads, wondering about the identities behind a "desperately seeking Susan" item that runs from time to time.

The ads are the way one boyfriend (Robert Joy) communicates with free-spirited Madonna between her street-life liaisons with other men, one of whom has been bumped off after stealing a pair of rare Egyptian earrings. Before his demise, Madonna has lifted the jewelry, thinking they are trinkets.

Drawn by curiosity to spy on Madonna, Arquette winds up with a bump on the head and a case of amnesia, complicated by the fact that Joy's pal Aidan Quinn thinks Arquette is Madonna and Arquette doesn't know she isn't.

Through circumstances, Madonna is wearing one earring and Arquette the other, with the killer in pursuit. Meanwhile, Arquette's insufferable husband, Mark Blum, is back home sort of worrying about her in between thoughts of his hot-tub business.

All of this is cause for consistent smiling and a few outright laughs, without ever building to complete comedy. It's not clear either, that director Susan Seidelman and writer Leora Barish ever intend for it to be funnier, so that can't be faulted.

"Susan" is simply easy entertainment with a lively cast caught up in a silly situation, with everything worked out well in the end. —*Har.*

The Last Dragon
(COLOR)

First kung fu musical.

Hollywood, March 21.

A Tri-Star Pictures release of a Motown Productions picture from Tri-Star-Delphi III Prods. Produced by Rupert Hitzig. Executive producer, Berry Gordy. Directed by Michael Schultz. Features entire cast. Screenplay, Louis Venosta; camera (Technicolor, prints by Metrocolor), James A. Contner; editor, Christopher Holmes; music, Mischa Segal; production designer, Peter Larkin; art director, William Barclay; set decorator, Thomas Tonery; costumes, Robert de Mora; choreography, Lester Wilson; sound (Dolby stereo); Dennis Maitland; stunt coordinator, Frank Ferrara; associate producer, Joseph Caracciolo; assistant director, Thomas Reilly; special visual effects, Rob Blalack, Praxis Filmworks; casting, Howard Feuer, Jeremy Ritzer. Reviewed at Picwood Theater, L.A., Calif., March 20, 1985. (MPAA Rating: PG-13.) Running time: **109 MINS.**

Leroy	Taimak
Laura	Vanity
Eddie	Chris Murney
Sho'Nuff	Julius J. Carry 3d
Angela	Faith Prince
Richie	Leo O'Brien
Rock	Mike Starr
Daddy Green	Jom Moody
Johnny Yu	Glen Eaton

"The Last Dragon" may be the first kung fu musical, but it is unlikely to generate a host of imitators. Featuring an array of cartoon-like characters, a dose of martial arts and a display of rock video visuals, "The Last Dragon" is so daffy it is unlikely a film like this could be duplicated anyway. No great work of art, pic does have its moments and is enough fun to find a following among the young.

Pic has several not terribly related stories going on at once, but logic is beside the point here and doesn't really slow things down. Leroy (Taimak) is an aspiring martial arts master who falls for music video disco jockey (Vanity) and gets tangled up in some nefarious criminal activity. At the same time he is being hunted by Sho'Nuff, the Shogun of Harlem (Julius J. Carry 3d), who wants to prove his dominance of the neighborhood.

Love story isn't much although Vanity looks great. (She previously acted in several Canadian films such as "Tanya's Island" and "Terror Train," made in 1979, using the name D.D. Winters. —*Ed.*). The film's best touch is its cast of villains inspired by Batman and Superman comics. Eddie Arkadian (Christopher Murney), a video game magnate, is, in fact reminiscent of Lex Luthor. His friends include an ex-heavyweight boxer (Mike Starr) who has a man-eating fish for a pet and a dizzy would-be rockstar girlfriend (Faith Prince).

When Eddie tries to strongarm Vanity into playing his girl's video at her hot nightspot, Leroy comes to her rescue. Along the way he encounters some formidable enemies.

In one of the film's outrageous scenes, Sho'Nuff, all six foot five of him, dressed in headdress and feathers, bursts into a theater and challenges Leroy to battle while a Bruce Lee film runs in the background. Sho'Nuff is accompanied by a crew who look something like kung fu bikers.

No match for the powers of the ancient East, Eddie recruits a group of enormous, bizarre musclemen to ambush Leroy. Final showdown at the nightclub is visually imaginative with an enormous video screen projecting images as these grotesque figures stalk their prey.

Director Michael Schultz displays a good sense of visual wit, but film is less effective with the more serious elements. Action sequences are competently filmed, but it's hard to believe or care about the hero's prowess when the villains are so much more entertaining.

Film offers a better-than-average musical score by Motown artists which could become a hit of its own. Digital sound recording is crisp and well defined. — *Jagr.*

Porky's Revenge
(COLOR)

Tame third outing.

Hollywood, March 22.

A 20th Century Fox release of a Melvin Simon and Astral Bellevue Pathé presentation. Produced by Robert L. Rosen. Executive producers, Melvin Simon, Milton Goldstein. Directed by James Komack. Features entire cast. Screenplay, Ziggy Steinberg, based on characters created by Bob Clark; camera (Deluxe color), Robert Jessup; editor, John W. Wheeler; music, Dave Edmonds; production design, Peter Wooley; set decorator, Nicholas Romanac; sound, Howard Warren; costumes, Frances Harrison Hays; assistant director, David M. Whorf; casting, Lou Digiamo. Reviewed at the Hollywood Pacific Theater, Hollywood, March 22, 1985. (MPAA Rating: R.) Running time: **91 MINS.**

Pee Wee	Dan Monahan
Tommy	Wyatt Knight
Meat	Tony Ganios
Billy	Mark Herrier
Wendy	Kaki Hunter
Brian	Scott Colomby

Ms. Balbricker . . . . .Nancy Parsons
Porky . . . . .Chuck Mitchell

By now something of the grand-daddy of the gross-out genre, time, alas, has mellowed the butt of its jokes and "Porky's Revenge," the third installment of the trilogy, has become, gasp, tame. Since its fore-bears have earned over $71,000,000 in domestic film rentals, it's a fair bet that "Porky's Revenge" will do some initial business trading off its family name. However, kids today are used to heartier stuff and this Porky simply doesn't bring home the bacon.

While most of the cast is still at Angel High, they have become a more conservative bunch. Still cap-able of a rude remark and a crude gesture, pic barely earns its R rating. Overall, territory is still adolescent wish-fullfilment where all adults are idiots and kids can get away with anything, but with original director and writer Bob Clark gone, these kids barely know what to do with themselves.

Plot, even for this type of pic, is slim, revolving around a plan to get even with Porky who humiliated the kids in their first film. After sitting out "Porky's II," Chuck Mitchell is back in the title role and indeed fits the part. The kids — Dan Mona-han, Wyatt Knight, Tony Ganios, Mark Herrier, Kaki Hunter and Scott Colomby — on the other hand, are getting a little long in tooth to be high school cutups. Why don't they get a job already?

Porky's attempt to blackmail the boy's basketball coach for gambling debts and other sordid subplots are really digressions from the one true and lasting concern here — sex. While scoring is the main motiva-tion, script by Ziggy Steinberg finds few interesting set-ups for the wild libidos. Needless to say, there is nothing in the slightest erotic here.

Direction by James Komack does little to enliven the proceedings and even a state championship basket-ball game looks as if it were shot in slow motion. Soundtrack by Dave Edmonds is one of the film's few bright spots along with a well select-ed assortment of rock numbers.
— *Jagr.*

Sanford Meisner —
The Theater's
Best Kept Secret
(DOCU-COLOR/B&W—16m)

Fascinating profile of Broad-way drama coach.

A Columbia Pictures presentation. Execu-tive Producer, Sydney Pollack. Producer, for Playhouse Repertory Company, New York, Kent Paul. Directed, photographed (color) and edited by Nick Doob; music, Skip Kennon; principal creative advisor, and interviews conducted by Stephen Harvey. Reviewed at private screening, Playhouse Repertory Play-

house, N.Y., March 23, 1985. Running time: **60 MINS.**

Veteran Broadway drama coach Sanford Meisner at 80 celebrates half a century of teaching and is the subject of this excellent career-docu-mentary, exec produced by ex-stu-dent Sydney Pollack. Director Kent Paul is a newcomer to cinema, whose background is theater and who heads the Playhouse Repertory Company in New York.

Prized at the recent Hemisfilm International Film Festival in San Antonio, Texas, a participant at Filmex, and winner of a CINE Golden Eagle for festival distribu-tion abroad, "Sanford Meisner — The Theater's Best Kept Secret" opens at Joseph Papp's Film at the Public, "Public Service" series, in New York, on April 5, for a month of weekends. A PBS airdate is not yet announced although a deal is firm.

Meisner's career began opposite Libby Holman in "The Garrick Gaities" by Richard Rodgers, whom Meisner didn't encounter again until 50 years later, when both were patients in the same hospital for the same throat surgery, a laryn-jectomy. In this film, Meisner speaks with the aid of a special voice box, his speech halting but emphat-ic. Meisner appeared with the Group Theater in New York during the 1930s, in the plays of Odets, Behrman and Laurents. Then, 50 years ago, Meisner began drama coaching and in time began to de-vote himself exclusively to teaching, with a small select group of care-fully chosen newcomers.

Among these Meisner students — and they appear in the film to priase his firm and precise method — are Sydney Pollack, Jon Voight, Bob Fosse, Gwen Verdon, Joanne Woodward, Mary Steenburgen, Tony Randall, Mark Rydell, Peter Falk, Robert Duvall, Frances Stern-hagen, Eli Wallach, Anne Jackson, Vivian Matalon, Suzanne Pleshette, David Mamet, Lee Grant and Greg-ory Peck. Film clips illustrate the careers of two other Meisner form-er students, Gracy Kelly and Steve McQueen.

Meisner himself appears in a scene from the 1960 film, "The Sto-ry On Page One," written and directed by Clifford Odets. During his career, Meisner appeared in two other films — "Mikey And Nicky," directed by Elaine May, with his ex-student Peter Falk, and "Tender Is The Night," with Jason Robards and his ex-student Jennifer Jones. Group Theater colleague Elia Kazan also appears in this documentary, disucssing Meisner's impact on two generations of Broadway and Hollywood performers.

This film will have long-range value in 16m distribution to high school and college classes in drama

and to specialized acting academies. More than that, as a profile of an in-domitable artist-teacher and a dyn-amic spirit, the film is a lesson for us all in how to live meaningfully.
— *Hitch.*

Friday The 13th — A
New Beginning
(COLOR)

Same old slice and dice picture.

Hollywood, March 22.
A Paramount Pictures release. Produced by Timothy Silver. Executive producer, Frank Mancuso Jr. Directed by Danny Steinmann. Features entire cast. Screenplay, Martin Kitrosser, David Cohen, Steinmann; camera (Metrocolor), Stephen L. Posey; editor, Bruce Green; production design, Robert Howland; music, Harry Manfredini; sound, Mark Ulano; special makeup effects, Martin Beck-er; casting, Fern Champion, Pamela Basker; assistant director, Leon Dudevoir. Reviewed at Paramount Studios, March 21, 1985. (MPAA Rating: R.) Running time: **92 MINS.**
Tommy Jarvis . . . . .John Shepard
Pam . . . . .Melanie Kinnaman
Reggie . . . . .Shavar Ross
Dr. Matthew Peters . . . . . . .Richard Young
Ethel Hubbard . . . . .Carol Lacatell
George . . . . .Vernon Washington
Joey . . . .'.Dominic Brascia
Violet . . . . .Tiffany Helm
Tina . . . . .Debbisue Voorhees
Eddie . . . . .John Robert Dixon
Junior Hubbard . . . . .Ron Sloan

The fifth "Friday The 13th" film in as many years reiterates a chroni-cle of butcherings with even less var-iation than its predecessors. Hitting more than 1,700 theaters, produc-tion's paucity of either interesting or likeable characters and its abject predictability would normally point to dismal business. However, the recorded success of these films says otherwise.

Beginning with the original model in 1980, successive domestic film rentals amounted to $17,000,000, $9,500,000, $16,500,000, and for last year's socalled "The Final Chapter," $16,000,000. Even if the imagination behind these pictures has dissipated, the end is obviously not in sight.

Director Danny Steinmann (who made his theatrical debut with last year's "Savage Streets") does a lot with rain in this film and his conclu-sion is moderately well-orchestrated for maximum effect. However, the film, which features a new Jason this time (but the same hockey mask), takes much too long to set up its litany of eviscerations.

For the record, the little boy who helped kill Jason in the last film is now a troubled teenager (John Shepard) hellbent on a crazed future of his own. — *Loyn.*

The Care Bears Movie
(CANADIAN-ANIMATED-
COLOR)

Hollywood, March 20.
A Samuel Goldwyn Co. presentation of a Nelvana Production. Produced by Michael Hirsh, Patrick Loubert, Clive Smith. Execu-tive producers, Carole Mac Gillvray, Robert Unkel, Jack Chojnacki, Lou Gioia. Directed by Arna Selznick. Screenplay, Peter Sauder; music, John Sebastian; title song, Carole King. Reviewed at the Nosseck Projection Theatre, Hollywood, Calif., March 19, 1985. (MPAA Rating: G.) Running time: **75 MINS.**
Voice of Mr. Cherrywood .Mickey Rooney
Voice of Love-a-Lot-Bear . .Georgia Engel
Voice of Brave
Heart Lion . . . . .Harry Dean Stanton

Care Bears, popular toy store items, move to 1,000 domestic screens in the first national re-lease for Toronto-based animation house, Nelvana Ltd. Boxoffice out-look is iffy for distributor Samuel Goldwyn Co., given the animated film's very specifically targeted small fry and the production's prob-able lack of crossover appeal to peo-ple more than seven or eight years old.

Animation style, although featur-ing special effects, as in Rainbow Rescue beams or the Care Bears Stare, tends toward a primer reader level. There's a colorful evil spirit (albeit rather derivative of the witch in "Snow White And The Seven Dwarfs") plotting to make children miserable but dominant flavor of the movie is pink fluffiness and bil-lowy images, associated with the magical huggable bears who live above the earth in Care-A-Lot and whose tummies are emblazoned with personal characteristics, such as a heart or a four-leaf clover or the moon.

The bears' mission is caring, "to make everyone share their feelings with someone else." Tone of the production recalls Hanna-Barbera's 1973 feature, "Charlotte's Web," but that picture had advantage of E.B. White's whimsy.

However, critical nagging does not deny the genuine entertainment here for very young children and, at 75 minutes, the length of the film is perfectly calibrated. Success of pic depends squarely on parents and grandparents taking toddlers and kindergarten-age kids to the theater.

According to press material, director Arna Selznick is only the third woman in the history of film to helm a feature-length, animated work (following Germany's Lotte Reiniger for "The Adventures Of Prince Ahmed" in 1926 and British-er Joy Batchelor for "Ruddigore" in 1966).

Mickey Rooney supplies voice of the adult narrator figure who runs an orphanage and who turns out to be the central subject of his story about a young magician's helper who sold his soul to the devil be-cause he was so desperate for friends.

Carole King wrote and sings the title song. Pic has four musical numbers but two bog down the narrative pacing. —*Loyn*.

Zuckerbaby
(Sugar Baby)
(WEST GERMAN-COLOR)

Berlin, Feb. 26.

A Pelemele Film Production, Munich. Written and directed by Percy Adlon. Features entire cast. Camera (color), Johanna Heer. Only credits available ("film surprise" showing). Reviewed at Berlin Film Fest (Forum), Feb. 25, 1985. Running time: **87 MINS.**
With: Marianne Sägebrecht (the woman from the mortuary), Eisi Gulp (the subway-train driver).

The "film surprise" at the Forum of the Berlinale, Percy Adlon's "Sugar Baby" doesn't measure up to what viewers have come to expect from this talented director, but it does have its moments and might score with proper handling on the artfilm circuit.

"Sugar Baby" is about a frustrated employee at a Munich mortuary, a heavy-set loner who has a crush on a subway-driver she sees while going to and from her job. The crush gradually becomes an obsession, to the point that she's always keeping track of him in order to ride his train and his train only.

One day, she takes her saved-up vacation time, departs from the mortuary, and now searches every angle possible to casually meet her dreamboat — or "sugar baby," taking the cue from a pop-song on the radio.

The pic's first half has to do with the lady's efforts to track down her prey on and off the job, in the process of which she learns that the young man's wife will be leaving home for a couple weeks. This allows for the set-up meeting and the pairing of the odd couple in the second part. In the end, after the acquaintance has led to an affair of the heart, the wife is back.

"Sugar Baby" has its charm. The two principals handle the thin plot and situation well, while the lensing is a sure plus. One has the feeling throughout that the same story could have been reduced to a wordless half-hour and thus been the winner this stretched out feature film is not. — *Holl.*

Palace
(FRENCH-W. GERMAN-COLOR)

Paris, Feb. 27.

A Parafrance release of a Wonderful Productions/Third Wave Productions/Rapid Films (Munich) coproduction. Produced by Jean-Pierre Labrande, Frank Lipsik, Jean-Jacques Vuillermin. Directed by Edouard Molinaro. Stars Claude Brasseur, Daniel Auteuil. Screenplay, Alain Godard, freely inspired by "Liberté Chérie" by Claude Briac; camera (color), Michael Epp; art directors, Jacques Bufnoir, Aribert Hantke; editor, Marie-Josée Audiard; sound, Philippe Lioret;

music, Michel Legrand; costumes, Krista Recker, Jacques Cottin; executive producer, Peter Hahne. Reviewed at the Paramount City Triomphe theater, Paris, Feb. 26, 1985. Running time: **95 MINS.**
Robert Morland . . . . Claude Brasseur
Lucien Morland . . . . Daniel Auteuil
Hanna . . . . Gudrun Landgrebe
Cook . . . . Jean-Pierre Castaldi
Waiter . . . . Jean-Michel Dupuis
Inge . . . . Leslie Malton

"Palace," the first theatrical film production venture of Paris homevid distribs Frank Lipsik and Jean-Jacques Vuillermin, tells of two French brothers emprisoned in Germany towards the end of World War II and attempts to dramatize their differing attitudes towards captivity and their captors.

Claude Brasseur is the hedonist elder, living the life of Riley in a German stalag. A one-time pianist, he is requisitioned by the Germans to provide entertainment at a nearby luxury hotel. As an extra bonus, he beds the establishment's attractive manager, Gudrun Landgrebe.

The snake in his garden comes in the form of his younger brother, Daniel Auteuil, who has escaped from his German escorts after being taken prisoner at the D-Day landings. Brasseur has no choice but to hide him in the prison camp, but quickly comes into conflict with him. Brasseur is not willing to give up his cozy corner in the midst of the surrounding horror, while Auteuil is anxious to escape and get back into the fight.

Alain Godard's script, based on the memoirs of a former French POW who lived in similar circumstances during the last war, fails to get beyond the surface ironies of a by-now banalized war film subgenre. Director Edouard Molinaro executes the comedy-drama (which at times recalls Jean Renoir's "The Vanishing Corporal") with professionalism, but without giving it real flavor. Performances are equally competent but unexceptional.
—*Len.*

Im Innern Des Wals
(Inside The Whale)
(WEST GERMAN-COLOR)

Berlin, Feb. 22.

A DNS-Film, Munich, in coproduction with Haro Senft Filmproduktion, Munich, and Norddeutscher Rundfunk (NDR), Hamburg. Directed by Doris Dörrie. Features entire cast. Screenplay, Dörrie, Michael Juncker: camera (color), Axel Block; editor, Raimund Barthelmes; sound, Sven Funke; music, Klaus Bantzer; sets, Jörg Neumann; production manager, Molly von Fürstenberg, Denyse Noever. Reviewed at Berlin Film Fest (information) Feb. 21, 1985. Running time: **103 MINS.**
With: Janna Marangosoff (Carla), Eisi Gulp (Rick), Silvie Reize (Marta), Peter Sattmann (Frank), Ulrike Kriener (Elli Winter), Fabietto Scanu (Sergio), Fabio Faes (Adolfo), Harry Baer (Hartmann).

"Inside The Whale" centers on a father-daughter conflict. A di-

vorced police detective is a stickler for law-and-order in his own home, particularly as his 15-year-old daughter, Carla, is beginning to take after her messy housewife mother, who left 10 years ago.

The girl runs away because she finally wants to meet her mother, whose address has been changing with her jobs over the years. She has a few clues, however, and who should pick her up while hitchhiking than Rick, an erstwhile avenger of his honor, which was bruised coincidentally by her cop father.

Rick and Carla grow to like each other. He becomes, in other words, the kind of father the girl badly desires and needs. In her euphoria she mails her father a postcard, which ultimately leads to the clue the police need to track the couple down and resolve the supposed kidnapping.

After the film goes full circle, an unresolved ending cuts against the narrative grain.

There are many amusing moments in this game of reverse hide-and-seek, with director Doris Dörrie making a cameo appearance as a pension receptionist. Lensing is also tops. — *Holl.*

Always
(COLOR)

Engaging comedy about divorce.

Hollywood, March 23.

A Jagtown Film from International Rainbow Pictures. Produced, directed, written by Henry Jaglom. Camera (Deluxe color), Hanania Baer; music consultant, Miles Kreuger; sound, Ike Magal; associate producer, Judith Wolinsky. Reviewed at the Westwood Triplex (Filmex), L.A., March 23, 1985. (No MPAA Rating.) Running time: **105 MINS.**
Judy . . . . Patrice Townsend
David . . . . Henry Jaglom
Lucy . . . . Joanna Frank
Eddie . . . . Alan Rachins
Peggy . . . . Melissa Leo
Maxwell . . . . Jonathan Kaufer
The notary . . . . Amnon Meskin
Judy's father . . . . Bud Townsend
David's neighbor . . . . Bob Rafelson
David's brother . . . . Michael Emil
Party philosopher . . . . Andre Gregory

"Always" is writer-director-producer Henry Jaglom's confessional comedy about his divorce from actress Patrice Townsend. The two star, more or less, as themselves, and are joined by two other couples who are, respectively, near the beginning and toward the middle of the marriage process for an alternately awkward, painful, loving and farcical July Fourth weekend. Pic's subject matter is at once highly personal and utterly universal. Any audience would find this an accessible film, but marketing challenge for eventual distributor will consist of surmounting the fact that this is also something of a home movie without a name cast. Film was warmly

received at its world premiere at Filmex on Saturday (23).

From the beginning, it is clear that Jaglom intends this as his "Annie Hall," a deeply felt melancholy tribute to a romance that's gone awry but that he still cherishes. A la Woody Allen, Jaglom frames the proceedings with ruminations directed straight at the viewer, then jumps into a telling of how Townsend showed up one night at Jaglom's home to sign the divorce papers and ended up staying on for a weekend of emotional confrontations, recriminations, joyful reminiscences and partial reconciliation.

Also entering into the equation are the pair's old friends, Alan Rachins and Joanna Frank, a visiting married couple with their fair share of problems, and Townsend's sister and new boyfriend (Melissa Leo and Jonathan Kaufer), a wild, sexually free girl and retiring fellow who decide to get married in the course of the weekend.

In French farce style, two unexpected flings take place, but mainly, picture is wall-to-wall talk about what went wrong between Jaglom and Townsend, about emotional happiness and lack of same, about sexual matters, and many related topics. All the characters are singlemindedly concerned about the state of their relationships and address the subject in philosophical terms that emerge as both real and sweetly comic.

As with John Cassavetes, Jaglom is interested in performance and emotional truth virtually to the exclusion of visual style and other technical niceties, something which could put off viewers accustomed to nothing but slick, professional-looking product. Hanania Baer's lensing is clean and straightforward and agreeably captures changes in the light according to the time of day, but there are many jump and mis-matched cuts and other rough edges that seem to go hand-in-hand with the director's undying allegiance to his performers.

For the most part, however, Jaglom's obsessiveness pays strong dividends, and he has come up with a rueful romantic comedy filled with plenty of memorable moments. Audience engagement with the characters is so solid that the occasional moments when improvisatory inspiration flags are quite noticeable. Whenever he drops the ball, however, Jaglom is able to quickly pick it up and get things moving. Pic is very good as it is, but might profit from some slight tightening here and there.

Entire cast is engaging and, with smart marketing, there's no reason this can't be distributed to good effect to the mid-to-upscale Yuppie market. —*Cart.*

Se Permuta
(House For Swap)
(CUBAN-COLOR)

Hollywood, March 20.

An ICAIC presentation. Directed by Juan Carlos Tabio. Screenplay, Tabio, Raul Garcia, based on an idea by T.G. Alea; camera (color), Julio Valdes; editor, Roberto Bravo; music, Juan Marquez; sound, Garcia; assistant director, Mario Crespo. Reviewed at the Mann's Westwood Triplex (Filmex), L.A., March 16, 1985. (No MPAA Rating). Running time: **98 MINS.**

With: Rosita Fornes, Isabel Santos, Mario Balmaseda, Ramoncito Veloz.

"House For Swap" is a lively, unexpectedly quirky satire on housing conditions in Cuba and the extreme lengths to which people will go to secure better digs. Wholly unpolitical on the surface, pic is a straightforward entertainment and one of the most mainstream productions from Cuba yet seen on foreign shores. Lightweight nature of the proceedings makes it a fairly dubious arthouse entry in the U.S., but it would probably be a good bet with Spanish-speaking audiences everywhere.

Mechanics of finding housing in Cuba are not explained in detail, but film indicates people can jockey in applying for houses and apartments and can even try to convince current tenants to vacate their premises. This is the central premise of the picture, as middle-aged matron Gloria Perdomo (Rosita Fornes) spends the entire running time manipulating others in her single-minded quest for better and better accommodations.

Gloria's daughter Yolanda (Isabel Santos) becomes engaged to a devil-may-care graphic designer and, thrilled, Gloria makes elaborate plans to move in with the couple and cunningly talks a lonely, elderly lady to move out of her "mansion."

Meanwhile, Yolanda takes an interest in Pepe, a serious civil engineer, who is himself engaged and is thinking of moving to a distant island construction site for career reasons. Pic flip-flops btween Yolanda's romantic travails and Gloria's frantic efforts to coordinate the housing situation of herself and countless others. Latter ends up getting so many people on a string, each dependent upon the whims of others, that only chaos can result.

Just before the climax, first-time director Juan Carlos Tabio presents a clip from a tv show about cinema called "24 X Second," in which the commentator offers the critique that the film now underway has started out funny but has become boring. Evaluation is just about on the money. Early reels are filled with off-the-wall visual and aural gags reminiscent of Frank Tashlin, and a pleasant buoyancy is maintained for some time until a certain sameness and lack of focus sets in.

Most interesting aspect of the film is the sociological spectacle Tabio presents of a materialistically oriented populace with little on its collective mind other than social climbing and status-seeking as determined by the fashionability and size of one's residence. Maybe people really are the same everywhere, but the upfront exposure of individuals' baser natures comes as something of a surprise in a Cuban picture.

Despite unevenness, this marks a reasonably auspicious debut for Tabio. Music and technical contributions are good. —Cart.

The Little Sister
(COLOR-16m)

Solid indie drama.

Hollywood, March 21.

A Little Sister Partnership production in association with American Playhouse. Produced by Steve Wax. Directed, written by Jan Egleson. Features entire cast. Camera (DuArt color), Ed Lachman; editor, Sanya Polonsky; music, Pat Metheny; set decoration, Stephen Roll; sound, Thomas Brandon; assistant directors, Kevin Dowd, Mark Silverman. Reviewed at the Westwood Triplex (Filmex), Marc 20, 1985. (No MPAA Rating.) Running time: **103 MINS.**

Tim Donovan . . . . John Savage
Nicki Davis . . . . Tracy Pollan
Sarah . . . . Roxanne Hart
Also with: Jack Kehoe, Henry Tomaszewski, Richard Jenkins.

Latest Boston indie effort from writer-director Jan Egleson is a solid, intriguing look at troubled youth on both sides of the economic tracks. Much more professionally shot and acted than his Filmex entry of four years ago, "The Dark End Of The Street," pic will receive its primary domestic exposure on American Playhouse, but is a good entry for fests elsewhere. It also serves notice that Egelson is now fully ready to make the jump into big-time filmmaking.

Lifting his title from Raymond Chandler, Egleson introduces John Savage as a conscientious probation officer whose personal interest in his young subjects sees him letting his job consume his entire life.

His immediate concern is Tracy Pollan, an 18-year-old, upper-class blond with a curious predilection for hanging out in the Combat Zone with her drug dealer boyfriend and other ne'er-do'wells. Intrigued by her attractions to the gutter and hardly uninterested in her physically, Savage tails her avidly and tries to set her straight, but is warned off by her bigshot father, who insists he knows what's best for his daughter.

Savage also becomes involved with a strip joint operator and major drug dealer, is on the scene when Pollan's b.f. is busted by the police, and is finally instrumental in dredging up the truth behind the reasons for the young lady's odd behavior.

Unfortunately, the film's big secret is quite predictable very early on, so the shocks and revelations of the final reels bear less impact than they might have. Otherwise, tale is dramatically sound and well written, with Egleson doing a good job of expressing the edginess of these people who have mixed motives for dealing with each other.

Savage is fine in the lead, and Tracy Pollan is outstanding as the troubled youngster. Also notable are Ed Lachman's superior lensing (this is one of the best-looking 16m pictures in memory), Sanya Polonsky's sharp editing and Pat Metheny's hard-edged, ominous score. —Cart.

Blue Heaven
(COLOR)

Laughably maladroit study of wifebeating.

Hollywood, Feb. 28.

A Five Point Films presentation. Produced by Elaine Sperber. Coproducers, Kathleen Dowdey, Jed Dannenbaum. Executive producer, Dannenbaum. Directed, written, edited by Dowdey. Camera (DuArt color), Kees Van Oostrum; art direction, Howard Cummings; music, Fonda Feingold; associate producer, Elaine Gilner Friedman; casting, Judy Courtney, D.L. Newton. Reviewed at the American Film Institute (Filmex), L.A., Feb. 27, 1985. (No MPAA Rating.) Running time: **111 MINS.**

Carol Sabella . . . . Leslie Denniston
Tony Sabella . . . . James Eckhouse
Also with: Lisa Sloan, Marsha Jackson, Bruce Evers, Brenda Bynum, Merwin Goldsmith.

A case study of the alleged wife-beating epidemic, "Blue Heaven" is an earnest liberal tract that becomes increasingly laughable in direct inverse ratio to how serious it becomes. If this utterly unmarketable item can find financing, there's hope for independents everywhere.

Subject matter, of course, is not laughable at all, but treatment provoked more yocks, even among women, at screening caught than many a good comedy.

Writer-director-editor Kathleen Dowdey's schematic approach begins with hubby James Eckhouse administering playful spanking to wife Leslie Denniston when she's naughty, but every 10 minutes or so, the gravity of his beatings escalates to the point where she's finally a battered wreck.

As if to prove how dumb someone can be, Denniston keeps coming back for more, until she finally seeks refuge in a home for abused women. Political slant, intentions and direction of the dramaturgy are all so predictable as to invite disbelief. Dowdey also seems to believe that the events depicted are all the more shocking because they take place in a Yuppie household, a milieu which invites even further audience derision.

Lensed in Atlanta, pic boasts an impressively professional look.

—Cart.

Blue Money
(BRITISH-COLOR-16m)

Hollywood, March 18.

A London Weekend Television/Blue Money production. Produced by June Roberts, Jo Apted. Executive producer, Nick Elliott. Directed by Colin Bucksey. Screenplay, Stewart Parker; camera (Rank color), Peter Jessop; editor, Ron Costelloe; music, Richard Hartley; production design, Mike Oxley; costume design, Brenda Fox; sound, Reg Mills; assistant director, David Brown. Reviewed at the Westwood Triplex, (Filmex), L.A., March 17, 1985. (No MPAA Rating.) Running time: **85 MINS.**

Larry Gormley . . . . Tim Curry
Pam Hodge . . . . Debby Bishop
Des . . . . Billy Connolly
Brogan . . . . Dermot Crowley
Fidelma . . . . Frances Tomelty

"Blue Money" is a generally amusing, if slightly strained, comedy of opportunism and irresponsibility. British television production gives Tim Curry his biggest chance to carry on without a leash since "The Rocky Horror Show," and his performance is an audience pleaser. Theatrical potential Stateside is limited, with better prospects seemingly lying in the vidcassette area.

Curry toplines as a crazy London cabbie whose musical and theatrical aspirations far outweigh his talent and luck. Such is misfortune that, after unsuccessfully pursuing a career for years, he finally wins a major role in a West End musical, only to have the producer promptly drop dead after casting him, blowing the whole venture out of the water.

Still seeking his break, Curry finds a cash-filled briefcase in the back of his cab and, instead of returning it to the shady businessman who left it there, makes off with it instead.

Some pretty unpredictable adventures follow. Not only the mob, but the Irish Republican Army, are quickly hot on his trail, and at different points Curry must masquerade in drag and as a nun in Dublin in order to elude his adversaries. Along the way, Curry, the perennial hapless fool, manages to lose a great deal of the dough, but it all ends up happily with Curry finally getting his moment in the spotlight.

Pic is basically an excuse for a star turn, which Curry pulls off with a nonstop display of feverish energy and manic comedy. At the same time, however, Colin Bucksey establishes himself as a director of some promise thanks to the way he adroitly keeps things moving through a multitude of locations and situations.

Music plays a considerable role in the proceedings, and Curry gets to do imitations of Elvis Presley and, much more effectively, Mick Jagger. It's all light fun, a piece of contempo fluff pulled off with appealing élan. — *Cart.*

La Segua
(COSTA RICAN-MEXICAN-COLOR)

Hollywood, March 12.

A Cinematograficia Costarricense S.A. presentation of an Oscar Castillo production in association with Conacine S.A. de C.V. Estudios Churubusco-Azteca Mexico. Produced by Castillo. Executive producer, Alvaro Sancho. Directed by Antonio Yglesias. Screenplay, Alberto Cañas, Yglesias, Castillo, Sidney Field, based on the play by Cañas. Camera (color), Mario Cardona; editor, Rafael Ceballos; production design, Jean Moulaert; music, Benjamin Gutierrez, Orlando Garcia. Reviewed at the American Film Institue (Filmex), L.A., March 11, 1985. (No MPAA Rating.) Running time: **102 MINS.**
Encarnacion Sancho . . . . Isabel Hidalgo
Petronila . . . . Blanca Guerra
Also with: Oscar Castillo, Ana Poltronieri, Fresia Astica, Rafa Rojas, Alfredo Catania, Fernando del Castillo, Ana María Barrionuevo, Luis A. Chocano, Carlos Catania, Orlando García, William Zúñiga, Marcelo Johnson, Ana Serrano, German Silesky.

An overwrought tale of superstition, witchcraft and romantic possession, "La Segua" doesn't do much for the cause of Latin American cinema. Hysterical and ponderous by turn, pic is of interest solely as a rare production from Costa Rica.

Set in the last year of Spanish colonialism, tale begins somewhat promisingly, with a handsome young lieutenant falling madly in love with Encarnacion Sancho, the most beautiful girl in the small village. Unfortunately, his mistress, tavern dancer Petronila, gets wind of this and gives the officer a potion that quickly drives him insane.

Shortly thereafter, a gentleman from foreign parts, Camila de Aguilar, arrives and announces he will undertake a expedition to unearth the gold in some jungle mines. It doesn't take him long, however, to similarly fall under the spells of both Encarnacion and Petronila, with different, but equally dire, results.

Throughout, constant mention is made of "La Segua," an untranslated phenomenon which is something along the lines of a witch, is firmly believed in by the local populace and attacks men who allow themselves to fall prey to it. Because of the manipulations of Petronila and her ugly old partner in nefariousness, Encarnacion begins to believe she is actually "La Segua," and gradually goes nuts.

Antonio Yglesias has directed the half-cocked story with considerable vigor, if little grace, and none of it makes much sense. Making this watchable, however, is a mostly attractive cast led by Isabel Hidalgo, who fully lives up to the description applied to Encarnacion, and the foxy Blanca Guerra as the jealous, scheming Petronila.

Lensed mostly on natural locations, pic boasts fine costumes and solid production values down the line.—*Cart.*

Under The Biltmore Clock
(COLOR)

Superficial Fitzgerald rendering.

Hollywood, March 19.

A Rubicon Film production in association with KTCA and American Playhouse. Produced, directed by Neal Miller. Screenplay, Ilene Cooper, Miller, based on the short story "Myra Meets His Family" by F. Scott Fitzgerald; camera (Astro color), Jeff Jur; editor, Peter C. Frank; music, Alan Barens; art direction, Jane Musky; set decoration, Linda Buchanan; costume design, Kaye Nottbush; sound, Hans Roland; assistant director, Kelly Van Horn. Reviewed at the American Film Institute (Filmex), L.A., March 7, 1985. (No MPAA Rating.) Running time: **68 MINS.**
Myra Harper . . . . Sean Young
Knowleton Whitney . . . . Lenny von Dohlen
Ludlow Whitney . . . . Barnard Hughes

"The rich are different from you and me," F. Scott Fitzgerald is supposed to have told Ernest Hemingway, who retorted, "Yes, they have more money." But in "Under The Biltmore Clock," adapted from Fitzgerald's story "Myra Meets His Family," the rich are possessed by more than just money. They are genuine loons, other-worldly creatures with ways unfathomable to mere mortals.

Made for PBS' American Playhouse series and entered in Filmex' independent film competition, Neal Miller's short feature gets by on the strength of Fitzgerald's eccentric characters and amusing plot twists, but remains a prosaic telling of a tale at once goofy and grave. Brief running time destines this for virtually exclusive exposure on television.

Myra Harper is the consummate 1920s flapper who dances and drinks the years away until realizing it's time to get married. Calculatingly, she sets her sights on the richest man of her acquaintance, who proposes and reluctantly invites her to the home of his eccentric parents.

Myra is mistreated in ways that initially seem merely innocuous but shortly become downright cruel. Then the plot twists are set into motion, and Myra emerges with her own form of character-building revenge.

On a doubtlessly tiny budget, production team has come up with a small-scale but delightful evocation of the 1920s. A great mansion was found for the principal setting, and Kaye Nottbush's costumes, in particular, seem utterly right.

Unfortunately, Miller's direction, while attractive enough, is straightforwardly dedicated to conveying only the major character and plot points and is devoid of subtext, nuance and life force. Piece is strictly one-dimensional and literal-(and literature-) minded, despite decent work by leads Sean Young and Lenny von Dohlen. — *Cart.*

Shonben Raidaa
(P.P. Rider)
(JAPANESE-COLOR)

Hollywood, March 20.

A Kitty Films production for Toho. Produced by Hidemori Naga. Directed by Shinji Somai. Screenplay, Takuya Nishioka, Chieko Schrader, based on a story by Leonard Schrader; camera (color), Masaki Tamura, Akihiro Ito; music, Mssaru Hoshi. Reviewed at the Westwood Triplex (Filmex), L.A., March 19, 1985. (No MPAA Rating.) Running time: **122 MINS.**
With: Tatsuya Fuji, Michiko Kawai, Masatoshi Nagase, Yoshikazu Suzuki, Shinobu Sakagami.

"P.P. Rider" is a talented but aggravating third feature from young Japanese director Shinji Somai. Film's style is defined by tremendously long takes often resembling those of Bertolucci and Jancso, but these as often as not contribute to an overwhelming lethargy and lack of dynamism which rob the effort of its inherent genre excitement. Pic was reportedly quite popular in its native country, but is too erratic to merit much playoff internationally.

Action-adventure tale involving young teenagers attempting to rescue a colleague kidnaped by Yokohama gangsters has a notably Western-style structure, something undoubtedly attributable to fact that Leonard Schrader, brother of Paul and his collaborator on "The Yakuza," penned the original story. Script was cowritten by Leonard's wife, Chieko, and the pair recently worked with Paul on the forthcoming Japanese production, "Mishima."

There's nothing wrong with the basic setup, which encompasses periodic confrontations, rescue attempts and shootouts, but many of the individual scenes are bewildering in the extreme. Youngsters manage to hook up with various underworld types and shady cops, but what transpires among them makes no sense and stalls, rather than advances, the clothesline of a plot.

Somai's long, mostly hand-held takes initially look intriguing and elaborate, but well before fade-out become predictable and self-defeating. Director clearly is very concerned with stylistic manners, but will have to take the next step of correctly adapting his camera style to content and dramatic expressiveness. Soundtrack is equally bizarre, as it emphasizes real background noises in conjunction with highly artificial sound effects. — *Cart.*

Crossover Dreams
(COLOR)

Tale of ambitious salsa musician.

A Crossover Films production. Produced by Manuel Arce. Directed by Leon Ichaso. Features entire cast. Screenplay, Leon Ichaso and Manuel Arce; camera (color), Claudio Chea; editor, Garry Karr; art director, Richard Karnback; production designer, Octavio Soler; associate producer, Susan Rollins; assistant director, Carl Haber; original score, Mauricio Smith. Music by Rubén Blades, Conjunto Libre, Andy Gonzales, Jerry Gonzales, Yomo Toro, Virgilio Marti, Marco Rizo and the Ballistic Kisses. Reviewed at the Museum of Modern Art Roy & Niuta Titus Theater 2 (New Directors/New Films), N.Y., March 26, 1985. (No MPAA Rating.) Running time: **86 MINS.**

Rudy Veloz	Rubén Blades
Orlando	Shawn Elliot
Lou Rose	Tom Signorelli
Liz Garcia	Elizabeth Pena
Ray Soto	Frank Robles
Neil Silver	Joel Diamond

Tracing the rise, fall and redemption of a salsa singer who yearns to hit it big in the anglo pop music business, "Crossover Dreams" presents an oldfashioned cinematic morality play with a contemporary New York latin perspective. The easygoing charisma of Panamanian *salsero* Rubén Blades, a spicy soundtrack, and the pic's ironic humor should appeal to big city audiences of assimilated Hispanics and young, musically hip non-Latin filmgoers.

Rudy Veloz (Rubén Blades), scraping by with gigs on the New York latin social club circuit, longs to "get out" of his dead-end life in Harlem's "El Barrio." Puerto Rico-born but New York-bred, Rudy's well aware of the Beatles and all that followed them, and he's determined to "cross over" to the green pastures of American rock stardom. Although Rudy is ambitious, Blades plays him with a touch of the self-effacing *campesino* bumpkin. He's reluctant to force the issue with manipulative, foul-mouthed clubowner Ray Soto (essayed with appropriate repulsiveness by Frank Robles) when his band is underpaid, then "tipped" with loose joints and cocaine.

As a favor, Soto sets Rudy up with sleazy agent Lou Rose (Tom Signorelli) — a self-proclaimed "crossover specialist" who's busted by narcotics cops in the middle of Rudy's audition! Undaunted, Rudy turns for advice to his salsa mentor (salsa veteran Virgilio Marti). A dignified purist whose Spanish-language songs celebrate the tropical homeland with images of "moonlight and honey," the older man belittles Rudy's English-language song, telling his protege not to emulate "Elvis Presley or those long-haired hippies." Soon after, the older man dies of a heart attack (appro-priately enough, during a gig) and at the funeral Rudy meets smooth-talking, silver-haired anglo record producer Neil Silver, who happened to have known the maestro.

Impressed with Rudy's song, the charmingly unctuous Silver (Joel Diamond) gives him $15,000 to make a single and life begins to change. He breaks with a furious Soto, buys a flashy yellow sportscar "on credit" and agrees to marry his loving girlfriend Liz (Elizabeth Pena) at some indeterminate time in the future.

When the English-language single becomes a modest hit, an LP contract follows. Rudy's life changes more dramatically with a new apartment downtown, good clothes, spending money, limos, photo sessions, radio interviews and even a "Scarface"-style sunk-in bathtub stocked with nubile bimbos. Obsessed with making the musical major leagues, Rudy drifts apart from Liz and, at Silver's urging, dismisses his longtime trumpet player/sidekick, Orlando, played with natural grittiness by Shawn Elliot.

Alas, the album flops and Rudy, with creditors on his heels, winds up in a Times Square flophouse. Liz marries a dentist, Silver puts him off, Soto humiliates him and Rose tempts Rudy with a devil's bargain to make a smuggling run to Colombia.

At this point, Ichaso launches Rudy's rehabilitation with an ample dose of sentimental latin emotionalism. This makes for a commercially plausible, upbeat ending, but undermines the perceptive cynicism that informs the film's better moments.

Ichaso and his capable cinematographer, Claudio Chea, opt for a poetic, rooftops & bridges vision of New York, giving the streets of Spanish Harlem little more than a quick documentary once-over. However, the nightclub scenes are intimately evocative of New York latin life, and charged with salsa's stirring, beguiling currents.—*Rich.*

Police Academy 2: Their First Assignment
(COLOR)

Out of step with the original.

Hollywood, March 30.

A Warner Bros. release of a Ladd Company presentation of a Paul Maslansky production. Produced by Maslansky. Coproducer, Leonard Kroll. Executive producer, John Goldwyn, Directed by Jerry Paris. Features entire cast. Screenplay, Barry Blaustein, David Sheffield, based on characters created by Neal Israel and Pat Proft; camera (Technicolor), James Crabe; editor, Bob Wyman; music, Robert Folk; production design, Trevor Williams; set decoration, Dennis Peeples, Bob Furginson; costumes, Bernie Pollack; sound, Bill Nelson; casting, Fern Champion, Pamela Basker. Reviewed at The Bur-bank Studios, Burbank, Calif., March 29, 1985. (MPAA Rating: PG-13.) Running time: **87 MINS.**

Carey Mahoney	Steve Guttenberg
Hightower	Bubba Smith
Tackleberry	David Graf
Larvell Jones	Michael Winslow
Doug Fackler	Bruce Mahler
Laverne Hooks	Marion Ramsey
Kirkland	Colleen Camp
Peter Lassard	Howard Hesseman
Lt. Mauser	Art Metrano
Commandant Lassard	George Gaynes

Thanks to the success ($38,500,-000 in domestic rentals) of the film that inspired it, "Police Academy 2: Their First Assignment" will undoubtedly do some quick cashing in at the boxoffice over its first weekend or two in release. Just as surely, it can be said that, if "Police Academy" had been this bad, there never would have been a sequel.

Withheld from press screening until opening day, the follow-up features much of the original's cast but none of its key behind-the-scenes creative talent, save producer Paul Maslansky. Given that the basic set-up presents almost infinite comic possibilities, it's almost amazing how unfunny this clinker is.

Only actor to get any mileage out of this one is series newcomer Art Metrano, as an ambitious lieutenant bent upon taking over the department. With the recruits assigned to saving the neighborhood from the grasp of marauding punks, Metrano does everything he can to make them fail, whereupon they exact some faintly amusing revenge upon him.

Metrano somehow manages to shine in these murkiest of circumstances, and Michael Winslow has a couple of good moments doing his patented sound effects and engaging in some kung fu, complete with unsynchronized yells and screams.

No doubt about it. It's time for this bunch to turn in their badges. — *Cart.*

The Secret Of The Sword
(ANIMATED-COLOR)

Subpar animated kiddie fantasy.

Hollywood, March 30.

An Atlantic Releasing release of a Filmation presentation. Executive producer, Lou Scheimer. Producer, Arthur Nadel. Directors, Ed Friedman, Lou Kachivas, Marsh Lamore, Bill Reed, Gwen Wetzler. Screenplay, Larry Ditillo, Robert Forward. Reviewed at UA Egyptian, Hollywood, Calif., March 29, 1985. (MPAA Rating: G.) Running time: **87 MINS.**

Voice of He-Man	John Erwin
Voice of She-Ra	Melendy Britt
Voice of Hordak	George DiCenzo
Other Voices:	Linda Gary, Ericka Scheimer, Erik Gunden, Alan Oppenheimer

He-Man, hero and champion of good, and She-Ra, princess of power, spin off highly popular He-Man Mattel toy and Group W syndie action in this sword-and-sorcery animated feature from Filmation.

She-Ra (who turns out to be the long-lost twin sister of He-Man) gets her own animated kidvid series in the fall. The pump is primed to the hilt, but the film, notwithstanding its obvious appeal to children, is visually diverting because of its optical effects rather than its animation.

The animated movements are surprisingly tv-jerky for a full-length feature and the narrative line is encumbered by an equally staccato effect. Visual variety of the good and bad guys, however, is flavorful.

Story and tone often suggest the menacing forces and breezy camaraderie of the "Star Wars" trilogy. The virtues of family, bravery and loyalty are trumpeted.

The overwhelming majority of the violence is suffered by the villains. The worst thing seen happening to the side of right is the near-lethal blow to a winged white horse (the horse is brought back to life in the same kind of palm-over movement that Jeff Bridges used on a deer in "Starman").

Weapons on view range from bow and arrow to high-tech laser zaps. The fact is, to an adult, a typically tacky Saturday a.m. music track and the flashy matted opticals distract from the animation at hand and pander in the broadest way possible. — *Loyn.*

Def-Con 4
(CANADIAN-COLOR)

Chicago, March 25.

A New World Pictures release of a Salter Street Films production. Produced by B.G. Gillian, Maura O'Connell, Paul Donovan. Directed by Paul Donovan. Exec producers, P.M. Robinson, J. William Ritchie. Features entire cast. Screenplay, uncredited (Donovan); camera (color), Doug Connell, Les Krizsan; editor, Todd Ramsay; production design, J. Walch, Emanuel Jannasch; music, Chris Young. Reviewed at Carnegie theater, Chicago, March 24, 1985. (MPAA Rating: R.) Running time: **85 MINS.**

J.J.	Lenore Zann
Vinny	Maury Chaykin
Jordan	Kate Lynch
Gideon	Kevin King
Walker	John Walsch
Howe	Tim Choate
Lacey	Jeff Pustil
Alice	Donna King
Boomer	Allan MacGillivray
Mrs. Boyd	Florence Paterson

This grim little picture, which is being booked on a regional basis by New World, slipped into Chicago two weeks ago with little advance notice and slipped out again without making much of a ripple. (Picture was lensed in Canada in 1983 under the title "Dark Eyes," renamed "Ground Zero" and finally "Def-Con 4." — *Ed.*)

There are a lot of things against

"Def-Con 4," among them a meandering script, a lack of character development and a pocketchange look to the production. At the same time, the picture accomplishes a great deal with limited resources, and the direction often cleverly distracts from the picture's shortcomings — minimal acting and not much of a plot.

It is basically another cautionary movie about the horrors of a post-nuclear-war world and it contains many of the clichés associated with what is becoming a genre: The world gets blown up and everyone is thrown back to Stone Age survival conflicts.

After an opening sequence involving a trio of scientists orbiting the earth on some kind of mission, the picture quickly evolves into a standard pursuit-escape-and-capture format. The near-term future time-frame obviates the need for expensive futuristic hardware — the weapons are ordinary automatic rifles, not expensive ray-guns, and the big instrument of destruction is not something that bleeps and blinks but one of those dirt loaders with a bucket in front.

An objection can be made that this is another of the Boogeyman nuclear war pictures, in which the potential holocaust provides a cheap chill to hype up a routine story. Maybe every other kind of fear has been exploited to the point of uselessness, and what's left is the ultimate Big Chill. — *Mor.*

Lucy
(GERMAN-DOCU-B&W-16m)

Berlin, Feb. 19.

A German Film Academy Berlin Film Production. A Documentary written, directed, photographed (b&w, 16m), sound recorded, and edited by Verena Rudolph. Reviewed at Berlin Film Fest (German Series), Feb. 18, 1985. Running time: **60 MINS.**

Verena Rudolph may be remembered as the female lead opposite Heinz Schubert in Alexander Kluge's "Strongman Ferdinand" (1975). She also starred on the stage at the Schiller-Theater in Berlin and elsewhere. Then she decided to discard her acting career by enrolling in the Berlin Film Academy, and has now completed her courses there with this eye-catching diploma film, totally self-made.

Verena is on the trail of her long-lost Aunt Lucy, who emigrated to America in 1935 from a little village in Lower Bavaria. Now, 50 years later, the niece, cum femme filmer, is in New York with a Bolex and cassette recorder. The almost legendary existence of this (perhaps ficticious) aunt is pieced together, entirely by women friends now over 90 years of age and a black adopted daughter (also named Lucy) living in Harlem.

If the tale is to be swallowed whole (and it's hard not to), Aunt Lucy was a former song-and-dance performer on Broadway who toured the world. Her downfall was the bottle, which apparently helped her to perform better; one day she disappeared from sight, even among her friends. It is found that she became a wizard at playing the stock market on Wall Street, took up residence in Harlem and became an inveterate gambler with the "Poker Ladies" in the neighborhood (where no questions were ever asked). Finally, she disappeared forever, although it is said she bought a pineapple plantation in Hawaii.

Not only is the story a delight to follow, but also the grainy 16m, b&w photography has the imprint of the existentialist 1940s stamped all over it. The soundtrack, with those crackling and fragile old voices of the eyewitnesses, plus honky-tonk musical passages, tickles the funny bone from start to finish. "Lucy" should wind up in German Film Weeks as one of the surprises of the current (and disappointing) Teutonic film season. — *Holl.*

Ladyhawke
(COLOR)

Good-looking medieval romance-adventure.

Hollywood, March 29.

A Warner Bros. release of a Warner Bros. and 20th Century Fox presentation. Produced by Richard Donner and Lauren Schuler. Directed by Richard Donner. Exec producer, Harvey Bernhard. Stars Matthew Broderick, Rutger Hauer, Michelle Pfeiffer. Screenplay, Edward Khmara, Michael Thomas, Tom Mankiewicz; camera (Technicolor), Vittorio Storaro; editor, Stuart Baird; sound, Bud Alper; production design, Wolf Kroeger; art direction, Giovanni Natallucci; costumes, Nana Cecchi; assistant director, Luciano Sacripanti; visual effects, Richard A. Greenberg; music, Andrew Powell; casting, Marion Dougherty, Mary Selway, Francesco Cinieri. Reviewed at the Wilshire Theatre, Santa Monica, Calif., March 20, 1985. (MPAA Rating: PG-13). Running time: **124 MINS.**

Phillipe	Matthew Broderick
Navarre	Rutger Hauer
Isabeau	Michelle Pfeiffer
Imperius	Leo McKern
Bishop	John Wood
Marquet	Ken Hutchison
Cezar	Alfred Molina
Fornac	Giancarlo Prete
Jehan	Loris Loddi
Pitou	Alessandro Serra

Today's young audience has yet to show an intense interest in costumers, but that problem aside, "Ladyhawke" is a very likeable, very well-made fairytale that insists on a wish for its lovers to live happily ever after.

Caught at a special screening for high-schoolers, "Ladyhawke" seemed to grab their full attention after a few restless moments.

Handsome Rutger Hauer is well-cast as the dark and moody knight who travels with a hawk by day. Lovely Michelle Pfeiffer is perfect as the enchanting beauty who appears by night, always in the vicinity of a vicious but protective wolf.

As readers of one or more variations of this legend will instantly recognize, Pfeiffer is the hawk and Hauer the wolf, each changing form as the sun rises and sets, former lovers cursed to never humanly share the clock together.

The spell was cast by an evil bishop, John Wood, when Pfeiffer spurned him for Hauer, who is now bent on revenge, with the help of young Matthew Broderick, the only one to ever escape Wood's deadly dungeon.

The remaining key figure is Leo McKern, who once betrayed the lovers to Wood, but now seeks to make amends by showing them how to undo the spell that's upon them, which they don't believe is possible.

Though simple, the saga moves amidst beautiful surroundings (filmed in Italy), with director Richard Donner receiving splendid help from lenser Vittorio Storaro, production designer Wolf Kroeger and especially costumer Nana Cecchi.

For those who care about the period at all — and have missed films like this — "Ladyhawke" is worthwhile for its extremely authentic look alone.

Given the structure of the yarn, which Donner can't avoid in an otherwise top-notch effort, it is a bit frustrating that such sex-charged characters as Hauer and Pfeiffer are kept apart until the final, fleeting clinch. Maybe chaste romance will be a welcome change for kids not used to using their imaginations.

Most importantly, Donner creates a real desire that the duo be together after the credits fade, leaving unshown what will happen next.
— *Har.*

Die Grünstein-Variante
(Grünstein's Clever Move)
(WEST GERMAN-COLOR)

Berlin, Feb. 20.

An Allianz Film Production, Berlin, in coproduction with Westdeutscher Rundfunk (WDR), Cologne, produced in the DEFA-Studios for Feature Films in Potsdam-Babelsberg (East Germany). Directed by Bernhard Wicki. Features entire cast. Screenplay, Wolfgang Kohlhaase, Wicki; camera (color), Edward Klosinki, Günter Sahr; sets, Alfred Hirschmeier; costumes, Christine Dorst, Marcel Manoury; sound, Klaus Tolstorf; music, Günter Fischer; editor, Tanja Schmidbauer, Gudrun Kieckheim; tv editor, Hartwig Schmidt. Reviewed at Berlin Film Fest (out of competition), Feb. 19, 1985. Running time: **105 MINS.**

With: Fred Düren (Grünstein), Klaus Schwarzkopf (the Greek), Jörg Godzuhn (Lodek), Rolf Ludwig (Garstecki), Rolf Hoppe (Prison Director), Arno Wyzniewski (Kaminski), Willi Schrade (1st Guard), Hubert Gleissner (Civil Servant).

"Grünstein's Clever Move," based on a radio play, is set in a Paris detention-pending-investigation cell in 1939, just prior to the outbreak of World War II. Three people of different backgrounds are brought together to while the time away until their cases are resolved. One is a German seaman (Lodek), an opponent of the Hitler regime. It is through his eyes that the story is recalled and related many years later. The second is a Jewish butcher (Grünstein) from East Poland, who happens to be in Paris due to the possibility of inheriting a sum of money from his recently deceased uncle. The third is a naive Greek cook, who met Kaiser Wilhelm 2d once on the island of Corfu and now dreams of renewing the acquaintance.

In order to pass the time, Lodek persuades the Jewish butcher to learn the game of chess. This is done simply by whittling out respective figures from dried bread and utilizing a markeshift board. After the 19th game, Grünstein suddenly hits upon his "clever move," a variation on a classic tactic, and defeats Lodek three times in a row. Many years later, Lodek is trying to figure out this same chess strategy, and thus recounts, too, the exchange of ideas, beliefs and standpoints of the three prison mates, two of whom are shortly thereafter to disappear and never be heard of again.

Dialog in itself is not the essence of a film, and nearly two hours of talking heads in an investigation cell can wear anyone down. Fred Düren as Grünstein is the standout among the three talented lead thesps.
—*Holl.*

What Sex Am I?
(DOCU-COLOR)

Transsexual surgery supplies some answers.

A Joseph Feury Production. Produced by Joseph Feury, Milton Justice, Mary Beth Yarrow. Directed and narrated by Lee Grant. Camera (color), Fred Murphy; editors, Joanne Burke, Stephanie Palewski; sound, Maryte Kavaliauskus; production coordinator, Charlayne Haynes. Produced in consultation with National Gender Counseling Referrals, Janus Information Facility, San Francisco. Reviewed at Joseph Papp's Public Theater, "Public Service" series, N.Y., March 8, 1985. Running time: **60 MINS.**

An intelligent film of dynamic understatement, compassionate yet cool, and resisting any attempt to sensationalize, Lee Grant's "What Sex Am I?" asks frank questions and collects troubling answers regarding sexual identity.

The data alone is stunning: 2,500 male and female Americans per month, in equal number, seek sex change operations. Since that young G.I. flew off to Denmark and returned as Christine Jorgensen — the film uses old b&w news shots of her press conferences, juxtaposed to a color interview of Jorgensen today — since the 1950s many thousands of Americans have followed that route.

Interviews and brief life-profiles make up much of the film. The theme throughout is the necessity for calm decision-making. Courage, integrity, the extent to which one is determined to be fully one's own true self — these are other themes of the film. Sex-change surgery and/or intensive hormone therapy, accompanied by radical changes in emotional and social behavior, create, in effect, a new life, and need proper counseling. Alas, some cases end badly, as with the young man who has undergone irreversible surgery in the film and discovers too late that for him it is a mistake.

This fascinating and valuable film, produced with taste and frankness, is set for April telecast on HBO's "America Undercover" documentary series. It can reach another audience in the years ahead in 16m distribution to colleges and to the medical/psychiatric community. — Hitch.

Signe Charlotte
(Signed Charlotte)
(FRENCH-COLOR)

Paris, March 15.
A Parafrance release of a Films de la Tour/FR3 coproduction. Produced by Adolphe Viezzi. Directed by Caroline Huppert. Screenplay, Caroline Huppert. Luc Béraud, Joëlle Goron; camera (color), Bruno de Keyzer; art director, Patrice Mercier; sound, Jean-Louis Ughetto; music, Philippe Sarde; production manager, Louis Wipf. Reviewed at the Paramount Mercury cinema, March 12, 1985. Running time: 92 MINS.

Charlotte .... Isabelle Huppert
Mathieu .... Niels Arestrup
Christine .... Christine Pascal

A minor but sympathetic theatrical debut from Caroline Huppert, who has until now written and directed for the stage and television, "Signé Charlotte" is yet another variation on that favorite Gallic romantic configuration — the triangle.

Isabelle Huppert, the director's sister, stars as a pop singer who takes refuge at the home of a former boy friend (Niels Arestrup), after her current mate is found murdered in his apartment.

Complications arise because Arestrup, a musician, is living happily with a teacher (Christine Pascal), and her young son, and they soon intend to marry. Worse, Arestrup has never gotten over the heartache Huppert caused him in their relationship and is deeply disturbed

about her sudden reappearance.

Still, he agrees to hide her in his study above the garage, but after two days she disappears. When she calls in later, desperate for help, Arestrup takes off to join her and the two become lovers again, and fugitives from justice. Pascal is wounded by the unexpected turn of events, but out of love for Arestrup, comes to their aid. Huppert and Arestrup plan to escape across to border into Spain, but she realizes the damage she has caused, and disappears without him. Years later he comes across her path at a train station with a rich Spanish husband.

Scripting is fairly conventional, but Huppert directs soundly and gets fine performances from her young trio of players; notably Arestrup, affecting as a man torn from his hard-won domesticity and emotional security by the siren call of a volatile past.

Huppert is not quite credible as a pop singer (film opens with her doing a number in a club), but then she's not especially meant to be a success. Pascal's role is lesser, but she fills it out feelingly. Tech credits are good. —Len.

Alamo Bay
(COLOR)

Failed study of racial intolerance, with slim prospects.

Hollywood, March 29.
A Tri-Star Pictures release of a Tri-Star-Delphi III production. Produced by Louis Malle, Vincent Malle. Executive producer, Ross Milloy. Directed by Louis Malle. Stars Ed Harris, Amy Madigan. Screenplay, Alice Arlen; camera (Du-Art color, Metrocolor prints), Curtis Clark; editor, James Bruce; music, Ry Cooder; production design, Trevor Williams; art direction, Rhiley Fuller; set decoration, Christian Kelly; costume design, Deirdre Williams; sound, Danny Michael; assistant director, Fred Berner; second unit camera, Constantine Makris; casting, Juliet Taylor, Ellen Chenoweth. Reviewed at the Samuel Goldwyn Theatre, Beverly Hills, Calif., March 28, 1985. (MPAA Rating: R.) Running time: 98 MINS.

Glory .... Amy Madigan
Shang .... Ed Harris
Dinh .... Ho Nguyen
Wally .... Donald Moffat
Ben .... Truyen V. Tran
Skinner .... Rudy Young
Honey .... Cynthia Carle
Luis................. Martino Lasalle
Mac .... William Frankfather
Ab Crankshaw .... Lucky Mosley
Sheriff .... Bill Thurman

"Alamo Bay" is a failed piece of social consciousness. The peripatetic Louis Malle, who in the past has provided unusual insights into such far-flung settings as Calcutta, Nazi-occupied France, turn-of-the-century New Orleans and the new Atlantic City, hasn't managed to shed any meaningful light on his current subject, that of the conflict between refugee Vietnamese and local fisherfolk around Galveston

Bay, Texas, circa 1979-1981. Commercial prospects don't look healthy.

As he frequently has before, Malle dared to place an exceedingly unsympathetic character at the center of his drama. Here it is Ed Harris, a bruising, philandering, unreflective lout who resents the intrusion of Vietnamese into his community and finally resorts to the easiest method of dealing with them, i.e., brutal, illegal violence.

Scene-setting is devoted to the native whites and newcomer Asians trying to fish the same waters, with the whites becoming increasingly irritated as the Vietnamese, in their view, horn in on their traditional territory, and work for lower wages to boot.

Attempts at mediation by religious types don't help much, and the good ole boys, led by Harris, welcome the embrace of the Ku Klux Klan in driving off the "gooks." Mixed in with this is a sort-of reignition of a romance between Harris and Amy Madigan, latter being the daughter of controversial fish factory operator Donald Moffat and now at odds politically with her former boy friend.

Situation is rife with ironies and lively sociological aspects, particularly the fact that many of these right-wing macho men a decade earlier had figuratively fought alongside these same Vietnamese they now call commies. Unfortunately, Malle and screenwriter Alice Arlen ("Silkwood") have only presented the surface of the dilemma, and have proved singularly unsuccessful in humanizing it or providing it with any galvanizing dramatic urgency.

What they have in mind is a study of intolerance and racial hatred. However, Harris, the prime focus of the interest, neither emerges as a great villain nor a flawed human being whose defects are attempted to be understood. He's just an unthinking jerk.

On the other side of the fence is new arrival Ho Nguyen, who at first wears a permanent, subservient smile in hopes of ingratiating himself, but later refuses to be intimidated along with the rest of his people and ultimately forces a showdown. Audience sympathy naturally swings to him, but he, too, remains one-dimensional, as does his eventual comrade-in-arms, the flinty Madigan.

Malle's aspirations in seeking out such unusual, obscure and upsetting material are to be admired, but his execution is entirely unsatisfactory; he hasn't even been able to avoid the usual suspense film clichés, including the last-minute rescue.

Ry Cooder delivers his customary strong score, and tech contributions are good enough. —Cart.

Dangerous Moves
(La Diagonale du Fou)
(SWISS-COLOR)

Hollywood, March 29.
An Arthur Cohn production, produced by Cohn. Directed, screenplay by Richard Dembo. Camera (color), Raoul Coutard; editor, Agnes Guillemot; music, Gabriel Yared; art design, Ivan Maussion; costumes, Pierre Albert; sound, Alix Compte; chess games created by Nicolas Giffard. Reviewed at the Westwood Triplex (Filmex), L.A., March 28, 1985. (No MPAA Rating.) Running time: 100 MINS.

Akiva Liebskind .... Michel Piccoli
Pavius Fromm .... Alexandre Arbatt
Henia .... Leslie Caron
Marina .... Liv Ullmann
Tac-Tac .... Daniel Olbrychski
Kerossian .... Michel Aumont
Fadenko .... Serge Avedikian
Yachvili .... Pierre Michael
Anton Heller .... Pierre Vial
Felton .... Wojtek Pszoniak
Miller .... Jean-Hugues Anglade
Foldes .... Hubert Saint-Macary
Puhl .... Bernhard Wicki
(In French with English subtitles)

"Dangerous Moves" is an absorbing, if not inspired, suspense drama with a great subject, that of a championship chess showdown between a Soviet title-holder and an exiled dissident challenger. This year's Oscar winner for best foreign-language film proves very conventional aesthetically, but makes the specialized arena of world-class chess accessible to the general viewer and also draws upon intriguing political issues. A U.S. distributor has yet to be set, but the Oscar will provide the stimulus for a good domestic launch.

Recalling the famous Karpov-Korchnoi match of some years back, script by first-time director Richard Dembo has the aging Russian grand old man of chess, Michel Piccoli, travel to Geneva for a long-anticipated confrontation with 30-year-old whippersnapper Alexandre Arbatt, who left his homeland five years before.

Both are surrounded by the usual aides-de-camp, but two critical people are missing from their respective entourages — Piccoli, who is seriously ailing, is denied permission for his doctor, a Jew with family in Israel, to accompany him out of the country, while Arbatt has been forced to live in the West without his wife, who has been detained in the USSR. Both parties come to be used as pawns at crucial stages in the competition.

The contrast between the two combatants could hardly be greater, with Piccoli's stately, singleminded professional standing as a model of discipline as compared to the wild, longhaired Arbatt, who persistently turns up late for matches and has little regard for protocol.

Predictably, both sides pull psychological stunts along the way, with the Russians placing an evil-looking parapsychologist in the audience to distract Arbatt and finally bringing in his wife, Liv Ullmann, to upset him emotionally. As the match pushes toward a conclusion, Piccoli's health declines precipitously, and ending is both curious and satisfactory.

An opera director and cofounder of the Directors' Fortnight at the Cannes Film Festival, Dembo orchestrates the proceedings with a fair measure of skill and brings in just enough specifics of chess strategy to grab viewer interest in the contest (although he fails at the outset to reveal how many wins are necessary to capture the championship).

On the other hand, the roles created for the women in the drama are embarrassingly one-dimensional. Leslie Caron is saddled with the responsibility of clinging steadfastly by Piccoli, but no depth in the martial relationship is suggested, while Liv Ullmann, her own desire not to harm her husband's game notwithstanding, can't help but be the irritating influence the Russians intend her to be.

Overall, pic could have done with a good deal more intensity and detail concerning the extraordinary politics involved in international chess. But subject alone makes this an engaging picture. —Cart.

In The Name Of The People
(SALVADORAN-U.S.-DOCU-COLOR-16m)

Hollywood, March 9.
A First Run Features/Icarus Films release of a Pan American Films production. Produced by Alex W. Drehsler, Frank Christopher. Directed, edited by Christopher. Written by Drehsler; camera (color), John Chapman; sound-second unit camera, Doug Bruce; music, Lanuza and El Grupo Insurecto de Guazapa; associate producer, Isaac Artenstein. Reviewed at the American Film Institute (Filmex), L.A., March 8, 1985. (No MPAA Rating.) Running time: 73 MINS.
Narrator: Martin Sheen.

Partisan but not propagandistic, humanistic but not sentimental, "In The Name Of The People" is a strong, clear-eyed look at the rebel movement in war-torn El Salvador. Oscar-nominee (it lost) this year in the best feature documentary category will find its most receptive audiences on campuses and in specialized urban houses, and will interest anyone concerned about current events in Latin America.

Lensed mainly in rebel-held territory close to San Salvador under obviously rigorous and, at times, combat conditions over a period of five weeks in early 1982, sober document reveals why many peasants have joined the anti-government forces, and shows the sacrifices, bravery and training involved in their fully committed struggle.

Unlike many "revolutionary" documentaries, this one does not preach only to the already converted. Passionately, but with measured factuality, narrator Martin Sheen briefly fills in recent history of horror, that of rampaging right-wing death squads, raping and murdering, obstruction of medical services and unendurable hunger, all of which has left 40,000 dead.

Filmmakers Frank Christopher, Alex W. Drehsler and the late lenser John Chapman concentrate on two rebel compounds, where peasant recruits begin basic training and plan for armed confrontations while still maintaining a semblance of everyday life. Children are educated, a couple gets married, food is gathered, but all under the heightened conditions of wartime.

The persistent theme running through the film, which is taken up to a great extent in conversations with individual rebels, is that repressive and increasingly hopeless conditions virtually forced them into opposition to the government. A few of the leaders can spout ideology, but the vast majority of those interviewed have personal tales of such tragedy to tell that the human motivation to take up arms becomes quite apparent and comprehensible.

Pic does not attempt to tell the whole story of what's going on in El Salvador; the "enemy" is described only in monolithic terms, rebel connections, or lack of same, to Nicaragua and other outside political forces are not explored, and, short of a military victory or a vaguely mentioned "negotiated settlement," it is unclear what kind of resolution would be acceptable to the rebels.

Nevertheless, this is a powerful, instructive document, one worthy of exposure wherever films of this sort can find distribution. It debuted domestically last November.
—Cart.

Monkey Mia
(AUSTRALIAN-COLOR-16m)

Hollywood, Feb. 28.
A Dog Star production. Produced, directed by Bill Leimbach. Camera (color), Mike Edols, Leimbach; editor, Chris Cordeaux; music, The Bahloo Music Show; sound, David Roach. Reviewed at the American Film Institute (Filmex), Feb. 28, 1985. (No MPAA Rating.) Running time: 90 MINS.
With: The Bahloo Music Show, Mukki, Shanto, Peter Shenstone.

Anyone looking for a brand-spanking new rendition of a circa 1969 hippie documentary won't want to miss "Monkey Mia." Probably the most ridiculous entry in Filmex 1985, pic charts the journey of 20-odd vagabonds across the Australian continent who are keen on meeting up with some dolphins who are rumored to communicate with humans.

Caravan travels in vans sporting paintings, not of flowers, but dolphins, and is financed by the predictably wealthy American. Long hairs on the trip are into yoga, meditation, health food and non-violence, and are given to singing folk-type songs about dolphins, the constant playing of which expands the film from its appropriate length as a short subject into an incredibly padded feature.

Whenever a disagreement among the group members comes up, somebody says that they should stop bickering because, "Dolphins don't argue, man," and the entire trip seems to have been treated as a test of their "dolphin consciousness."

Dramatic climax occurs, not when they finally reach the little bay, known as Monkey Mia, where the dolphins are frolicking, but shortly before, when one of the troupe insists that he will refuse to give his permission to be depicted in the picture if a Dolphinarium is shown on-screen.

It's that kind of film.—Cart.

Diles Que No Me Maten
(Tell Them Not To Kill Me)
(VENEZUELAN-COLOR)

Hollywood, March 18.
A Cinema Department of the University of the Andes production. Executive producer, Maria Saldvia. Directed, written, edited by Freddy Siso, based on a story by Juan Rulfo. Camera (color), Mario Robles; assistant director, Roberto Siso. Reviewed at the Westwood Triplex (Filmex), L.A., March 17, 1984. (No MPAA Rating.) Running time: 98 MINS.

The tale of the lifelong, soul-killing injustices visited upon a decent, uneducated Venezuelan peasant, "Tell Them Not To Kill Me" is an earnest, ponderous entry in consciousness-raising Latin American cinema. Produced through the auspices of the university at Merida's film department, pic is irreproachable in intent but treads familiar ground in tedious fashion. Commercial prospects outside Latin countries don't exist.

Writer-director-editor Freddy Siso relates this tragic personal saga through long flashbacks, which show how Juvencio Nava was reduced from a well-meaning peasant rancher to a fugitive from justice for the last 40 years of his life.

His fateful journey was precipitated when arrogant landowner Don Pedro refused to allow Nava to graze his 20 cows on his massive, well-irrigated holdings during a drought. Desperate, Nava sneaks his cattle onto the pasture land at night, and when Don Pedro discovers this, he has the beasts butchered. Understandably provoked, Nava kills Don Pedro, escapes a dragnet but is finally apprehended 40 years later by none other than Don Pedro's son, who unforgivingly orders him executed.

Unfortunately, Nava proves to be a pathetic, boring figure who wallows in self-pity throughout, crying and begging for a pardon. That he is a helpless victim of an evil class structure cannot be denied, but one would have hoped that political Third World cinema had gotten past the point where such matters could be examined only in the simplest, black-and-white terms.

Pacing is turgid in the extreme, and all the points Siso has to make come clear long before the inevitable conclusion. Technical credits are okay. —Cart.

Ezra Pound/American Odyssey
(DOCU-COLOR)

Okay intro to the life of a poet.

Hollywood, Feb. 26.
A New York Center For Visual History Production. Produced and directed by Lawrence Pitkethly. Camera (color), Jonathan David; editor, Variety Moszynski; program consulant, James Laughlin; narrator, Paul Hecht; voice of Pound, Sam Tsoutsouvas. Reviewed at AFI screening room (Filmex), Feb. 25, 1985, L.A. Running time: 90 MINS.

It would be difficult to make a dull documentary about the life of poet Ezra Pound, one of the seminal cultural figures of this century, and much of the fascination of Lawrence Pitkethly's film derives from the originality and controversy of Pound's life. However, "Ezra Pound/American Odyssey" serves as more of an introduction to Pound's life than a source of new insights for people already familiar with his work.

From his origins in America to his prominence in Europe and friendships with James Joyce, Ernest Hemingway and T.S. Eliot and his imprisonment after World War II for collaborating with the fascists in Italy, Pound's life is full of high drama that could hardly be imagined in a fictional film.

To his credit, Pitkethly touches all the bases, following the course of Pound's nomadic life and including interviews with many of the people who knew him, as well as scholars Alfred Kazin and Hugh Kenner. The pros and cons of Pound's choices are defended without really illuminating them or drawing conclusions, but perhaps there are no easy explanations for a man who wrote such sensitive poetry yet attacked the American government on Italian radio during World War II.

Pitkethly's attempt to give a visual context to the verse is largely successful as he frequently imposes the text over images that formed it. He fails, however, to identify the speakers after their first appearance on the screen and it becomes difficult to keep track of the personalities. It is also unclear when the poet himself is reading his work and when it is being recited by Sam Tsoutsouvas.

Included is some rare footage of Pound, particularly moving as an old man in Rapallo. All criticisms of the film seem minor when compared to the incredibly striking image of Pound, his face sculptured by time, reciting from his cantos: "Pull Down Thy Vanity." — *Jagr.*

Ranjau Sepanjang Jalan
(No Harvest But A Thorn)
(MALAYSIAN-COLOR)

Hollywood, Feb. 20.

A Kay Film SDN BHD production. Produced by Kamarul Ariffin, Sarimah. Directed, written by Jamil Sulong. Camera (color, widescreen), Johan Ibrahim; editor, Johari Ibrahim; music, Ooi Eow Jin. Reviewed at American Film Institute (Filmex), L.A., Feb. 19, 1985. (No MPAA Rating.) Running time: **101 MINS.**

Lahuma ....,.........Ahmad Mahmood
Jeha ....Sarimah
Sanah .... Puteri Salbiah
Milah ....Noraishah
Jenab ....Rohayatie
Semek ....Marlia
Liah ....Malissa
Lebar/Kiah ....Rosmawaite

"No Harvest But A Thorn" is the Malaysian entry in the farm film cycle. As in the recent American entries in the genre, the family depicted must endure no end of punishment from nature in order to get the crop in but, unlike the domestic pictures, the heroine does not persevere nobly. Instead, she goes stark, raving mad, which makes for an interesting twist in an othewise plodding saga.

Like Jessica Lange in "Country," Sarimah coproduced and stars in this handsomely mounted production, which creates a panorama of unimaginable horrors for its industrious characters.

In the early going, Sarimah is terrorized by a cobra, which initiates a series of awful fantasies which only grow worse over time. Shortly thereafter, her husband steps on a poisonous thorn, the infection from which festers and gradually overtakes the rest of his body so that he looks infinitely worse than the Elephant Man by the time he finally dies.

Bearing up under the succession of tragedies, the couple's seven young daughters continue to work the rice paddies despite the onslaught of a flood and invasions by crabs, birds and leeches. During all this, Sarimah must be carted off to the looney bin, and she eventually becomes the village idiot.

Picture presents a relentlessly grim portrait of peasant life, and matters aren't helped much by the repetitive nature of the montages of destruction and elemental havoc. The economics of the situation are not divulged, so one doesn't know quite what to make of the daughters' plight and their prospects for the future.

Film has been ambitiously made in widescreen and with Dolby sound. Writer-director Jamil Sulong is one of the veterans of the local film industry, having made some 70 features and documentaries since 1958.—*Cart.*

Morons From Outer Space
(BRITISH-COLOR)

London, March 22.

A Thorn EMI Screen Entertainment presentation. Produced by Barry Hanson. Executive producer, Verity Lambert. Directed by Michael Hodges. Stars Mel Smith, Griff Rhys Jones. Screenplay, Mel Smith and Griff Rhys Jones; camera (color), Phil Meheux; editor, Peter Boyle; sound, Chris Munro; production designer, Brian Eatwell; visual effects, David Speed; special effects, Jeff Luff; music, Peter Brewis. Reviewed at the Warner West End Theatre, London, March 22, 1985. (BBFC Rating: PG.) Running time: **91 MINS.**

Bernard ....Mel Smith
Graham Sweetley ....,Griff Rhys Jones
Julian ....Paul Bown
Sandra ....Joanne Pearce
Desmond ....Jimmy Nail
Commander Matteson ... Dinsdale Landen
Colonel Laribee ....James B. Sikking

This British sortie into the science fiction comedy genre spotlights the tv comedy writing and acting team Mel Smith and Griff Rhys Jones. Script features some witty dialog, but its basic premise is insufficient to sustain a feature-length film. Pic will have to be sold as a cultural oddity to make any impact in theatrical markets.

As the title indicates, film basically attempts to debunk the school of sf writing which suggests that visitors from another planet would be particularly intelligent or threatening. Problem is that the moronic space travellers Bernard, Desmond, Julian and Sandra are too human to be interesting beyond a single introductory scene.

Feature tries various ways to stretch out the humor, including multiple ripoffs from Steven Spielberg's "Close Encounters Of the Third Kind" and several other films, but these scenes do not really enrich the plot's central themes.

The early moments in space are promising. Ultra-idiot Desmond, played with fine wit by Jimmy Nail, sets the spaceship on its earthbound course. He leaves Bernard floating in outer space. The lecherous and cadaverous spacehopper who comes to the rescue later unloads Bernard over the U.S.

The other three land on a motorway in the U.K., where they cause multiple pileups before being taken in for investigation. The American officer, heavy-handedly played by James B. Sikking, is convinced that they are dangerous invaders. Dinsdale Landen as the British investigator unconvincingly falls head-over-heels in love with the female alien.

It falls to junior tv reporter Graham Sweetley, played by Griff Rhys Jones, to rescue the group from various lynch mobs and find them a source of income as tv talkshow stars and rock performers. Their rise to stardom via an introduction to the British aristocracy is only sketchily described.

It's a trip to the U.S. by the pop-star aliens that enables Bernard, recently escaped from the looney bin (hence gratuitous imitation of "One Flew Over the Cuckoo's Nest") to meet up with his mates. Shortly after they give him the cold shoulder, a spaceship rental company arrives to reclaim the group's vehicle and whisk the three of them back home.

"Morons From Outer Space" is nicely directed by Mike Hodges. Performances are, for the most part, nicely judged. However, apart from some splendid moments, project remains stuck on the launch pad. — *Japa.*

Du Verbe Aimer
(The Word Love)
(BELGIAN-COLOR/B&W-16m)

Berlin, Feb. 22.

A Productions de la Phalène, Centre Audio-Visuel, Perfo Studio, Lima, Peru production. Produced by Carole Courtoy. Written and directed by Mary Jimenez. Camera (color, b&w), Raymond Fromont; editor, France Duez, Suzanne Reneau; sound, Guillermo Palacios' music, Tchaikovsky's "Swan Lake." Reviewed at the Berlin Film Festival (Forum), Feb. 21, 1985. Running time: **85 MINS.**

"The Word Love" is a rather unusual 16m experimental film in which director Mary Jimenez goes back to Peru after living for many years in Belgium. This act triggers a similar emotion trip with filmmaker facing the camera, to review her entire life.

Jimenez attempts to understand her relationship with her mother and meets with people who were close to her at different stages in her past. She underwent analysis, starting at age 12 and cut off a dozen years later in worse condition than she has ever been before. This even led to her being treated with electroshock therapy, which might explain her fascination with the madmen of Lima who roam freely along the city's avenues.

Naturally, this is a highly personal film, sometimes suggesting something close to an additional analysis session. —*Edna.*

Die Kümmeltürkin Geht
(Melek Leaves)
(WEST GERMAN-DOCU-COLOR-16m)

Berlin, Feb. 22.

A Journal Film KG Klaus Volkenborn production, Berlin. A documentary by Jeanine Meerapfel. Camera (color 16m), Johann Feindt; music, Jakob Lichtmann; sound, Paul Oberle, Margit Eschenbach; editor, Klaus Volkenborn. Reviewed at Berlin Film Fest (Forum), Feb. 22, 1985. Running time: **88 MINS.**
With: Melek Tez, the Kantemir Family, Niyazi Türgay, Maksud Yilmaz, Erna Krause, Etta Czach.

Jeanine Meerapfel's "Melek Leaves" deals with a 38-year-old Turkish foreign-worker (referred to in the title as a "Kümmeltürkin" or roughly "seedy Turkish woman") living in Berlin for the past 14 years and performing one menial task after another. Now that jobs are scarce and unemployment has risen, the German government has worked out a plan to return Turkish citizens to their homeland with a receipt-of-departure payment, and Melek decides to leave.

Meerapfel has obviously, via the nature of her text and questions-and-answers, set out to find an unusual yet typical woman with a strong will for survival and natural artistic talents, and accompany her on her bureaucratic route of departure. The truth is that Melek Tez is not very exemplary of the current situation, so both director and subject have to grope for sympathy and understanding. Melek (as Pogo in the Walt Kelly comic-strip might have put it) is a dad-burned grumbler who don't be happy anywhere you put her or find her.

A socially engaged docu packed with good intentions like this breaks all the fundamental rules of the genre. In a 90-minute documentary one expects to learn enough about the individual's background in order to weigh the value and direction of her statements. Instead, along the way we discover Melek has a daughter who was raised by somebody else while she was seeking her fortune abroad, and that her reasons for coming to Germany in the first place were more romantically oriented than otherwise. Whether she can fit in either in Turkey or Germany is doubtful, so what's the point of the whole affair? — *Holl.*

Paradiset er ikke til salg
(Paradise Is Not For Sale)
(DANISH-DOCU-COLOR)

Copenhagen, Feb. 28.

A State Film Central release of Saga Video & Kortfilm production for the State Film Central. Directed by Teit Ritzau. Screenplay, Ole Henning Hansen, Ritzau; camera (Eastmancolor) Dirk Brüel; editor, Hansen; production management, Louise Kjär, Gerd

Roos. Reviewed at Saga Kortfilm screening room, Feb. 28, 1985. Running time: **60 MINS.**

With: (appearing as themselves): Christine Jorgensen, Giorgia O'Brian, Thomas Holck, Hanna Rasmussen, the High Society Duo.

"Paradise Is Not For Sale" (an English-language dubbed version will be marketed internationally) by Teit Ritzau is a docu with heart as well as art. Doing well without any voiceover narration, film takes a both warm-hearted and sober look at the world, fate and feelings of the sexual transvestite.

Christine Jorgensen, the G.I. who had a sex change operation in Copenhagen in 1950, returns to Denmark to meet the doctors, George Stürup and Christian Hamburger, who gave her the start of a new life as a showbiz performer.

Snippets are shown of the Danish Tourist Board's "This Is Denmark" docu short she did in 1952, showing herself off in feminine splendor for the first time.

Hanna Rasmussen appears at family functions with his son and his mother as a rather rotund, routine-looking elderly taxi driver, but says he lives the better part of his life in drag.

Giorgia O'Brian has appeared under that name in several Fellini films. Born in Palermo as Giorgio Montana, she never found happiness until she started doing her opera parodies in drag.

Thomas Holck, a young man with a close-cropped beard, never felt at ease as a girl in Copenhagen Catholic School. He now prides himself, after a sex change operation, to be a better lover than most "ordinary" males.

Apart from Holck, the protagonists of Ritzau's film are all men turned into women. They are in their 50s or more, thus making a lie of what one quotes to be a common superstition: that no transvestite escapes the urge to commit suicide beyond age 50.

Film also use footage from Russian and East German archives to show the fates of transvestites in Hitler's Germany, and a sequence from a 1919 UFA feature, "Different From The Others" (Anders Als Die Anderen), starring Conrad Veidt in a sexual deviate role.

Funded by the Danish State Film Central and primarily thought to be aimed for the educational circuit at home, "Paradise Is Not For Sale" has obvious international tv sales potential. A book, using the film's title and theme, and coauthored by Ritzau and Danish surgeon Preben Hertoft, will be published in the U.S. by Crown. — *Kell.*

Dars Ar Spoku
(A Ghost In The Garden)
(SOVIET-COLOR)

Berlin, Feb. 26.

A Riga Studio (Latvia) production. Directed by Olgert Dunkers. Features entire cast. Screenplay, Dunkers, Erik Lans; camera (Sovcolor), Martinjsch Kleins; sound, Viktor Lytschew; music, Juris Karlsons; art director, Gunar Balodis. Reviewed at Berlin Film Festival, (out of competition), Feb. 25, 1985. Running time: **87 MINS.**
Albin . . . . Martinjsch Kveps
Imant . . . . Andis Kveps
Linda . . . . Aquelina Livmane

Films from Latvia, the Baltic republic with its own language and customs, are not so often seen abroad. "A Ghost In The Garden" has an infectious charm in its tale of a city couple who buy a quaint cottage in the country so they can live and work there. The old lady from whom they bought the place dies (they arrive to move in during her funeral), leaving behind her great-nephew, abandoned by his parents, for whom she was caring. The couple take him in, too, though he's troubled by visions of his mother, the garden "ghost" of the title.

It's a modest film, but the Nordic setting and unfamiliar language and customs somehow bring their own appeal. Martinjsch Kveps is very good as the troubled little boy.
— *Strat.*

Blaue Blumen
(Blue Flowers)
(WEST GERMAN-COLOR)

Berlin, Feb. 27.

A Herbert Achternbusch Film Production Produced, written and directed by Achternbusch. Camera (color), Adam/Olech, Herbert Schild (super-8 sequences); sound, Marek Vizner. Reviewed at Berlin Film Fest (Forum), Feb. 26, '85. Running time: **72 MINS.**
With: Herbert Achternbusch.

Herbert Achternbusch's films are static vehicles for his loosely flowing commentary on the state of things in his native Bavaria. The more one is familiar with the world inspiring him, the easier it is to settle down on a stool and listen to his discourse.

Achternbusch bears an amiable kinship with that master of the Hollywood short, Robert Benchley. If only his diatribes could be whittled down to a consistent half-hour instead of feature-length, they might rate as jewels on the currently fruitless landscape of German cinema.

"Blue Flowers" has Achternbusch off to the People's Republic of China with a trust super-8m camera wielded by a sidekick. There he lenses children, flowers and parks while commenting on the impossibility today of making films in Germany; in fact, if he's going to die anywhere, then why not China?

Minus his usual ace lenser, Jörg Schmidt-Reitwein, pic's images are particularly lacking. This is one of those grainy-and-smeared, Super-8 to 35m blowups. — *Holl.*

L'Eté Prochain
(Next Summer)
(FRENCH-COLOR)

Paris, Feb. 28.

A Parafrance release of a Sara Films/TF 1 Films coproduction. Produced by Sara Films. Written and directed by Nadine Trintignant. Camera (color), William Lubtchansky; art director, Michèle Abbe-Vannier; editor, Marie-Josèphe Yoyotte; sound, Pierre Gamet; music, Philippe Sarde; production manager, Christine Gozland. Reviewed at the Paramount City Triomphe Theater, Paris, Feb. 26, 1985. Running time: **100 MINS.**
Edouard . . . . Philippe Noiret
Jeanne . . . . Claudia Cardinale
Paul . . . . Jean-Louis Trintignant
Dino . . . . Fanny Ardant
Sidonie . . . . Marie Trintignant
Farou . . . . Pierre-Loup Rajot
Jude . . . . Jérome Ange
Manuel . . . . Riton Liebman
Juliette . . . . Dominique Rousseau

Nadine Trintignant's "L'Eté Prochain" is a lyrical ode to the family, in part recruited from the writer-director's own clan. Husband Jean-Louis Trintignant and their daughter Marie are part of the cast, headed by Philippe Noiret and Claudia Cardinale, who play the parents of the large, disparate brood, torn apart but reunited in the sentimental end.

Noiret and Cardinale have six children together, but former's infidelities and immature behavior lead to a split.

Their eldest daughter, Fanny Ardant, is married to a struggling playwright, Jean-Louis Trintignant, and their relationship is an on-again/off-again mess.

Younger daughter Marie Trintignant is an aspiring pianist with a bad case of stage fright, so bad she devises the most drastic excuses to avoid honoring a playdate. She experiences love at first sight and marries quickly.

Fate of these three couples provides the essentials of Nadine Trintignant's script, which abounds in emotional effusions and clever audience manipulation.

Tale moves to a poignant climax when the far-flung family is gathered at a Riviera clinic where Noiret is undergoing an operation for a cerebral hemorrhage. Clan camps out in a nearby country house and has time to mull things over. Happily Noiret comes out a winner and reunites with Cardinale, and they return to the cozy mountain home where their kids grew up.

Most of this is conventional romantic syrup, but the acting is heartfelt and ingratiating, and the production is smart. It's old-fashioned, pleasant, heart-on-the-sleeve filmmaking. — *Len.*

Biberspur
(The Beaver Track)
(EAST GERMAN-COLOR)

Berlin, Feb. 21.

A DEFA Film Production, "Johannisthal" Group, East Berlin; world rights, DEFA Aussenhandel, East Berlin. Directed by Walter Beck. Features entire cast. Screenplay, Gudrun Deubener, freely adapted from Bernd Wolff's book with the same title; camera (color), Wolfgang Braumann; editor, Ilse Peters; Günther Fischer; costumes, Dorit Gründel; production manager, Hans-Erich Busch. Reviewed at Berlin Film Fest (children's section), Feb. 20, 1985. Running time: **80 MINS.**
With: Erik Schmidt (Jochen), Jana Mattukat (Corinna), Christine Jentsch (Dörte), Jörg Kleinau (Wolfram Euler), Peter Sodann (Schoolteacher Schaper), Manfred Heine (Dr. Randolf), Gunnar Helm (Erwin), Pedro Hebenstreit (Ferryman), Gerry Wolff (Dr. Bornschlüter).

Walter Beck's East German entry in the kidpic fest at the Berlinale, "The Beaver Track," carries an ecological message as well as a moral for young auds. It has a Tom Sawyer detective strain in the story, plus a few unexpected twists, to make it a standout despite a somewhat plodding narrative style.

Jochen, a 12-year-old, is entranced by his favorite storybook hero, Gordon Byk, who avenges the helpless and sets things right whenever an injury against the social fabric surfaces. One day, while out scouting, he runs across a dead beaver that had been plugged with a shotgun instead of dying a natural death. He takes the specimen to his understanding schoolteacher and sets out to catch the culprit on his own.

Naturally enough, this offers plenty of room to explore the living habits of the local beaver — and this is where the story takes on color and adventure. It turns out that this rural area is being strip-mined for brown-coal (lignite), which means that the beaver will have to be transferred from their usual habitat on a tributary of the Elbe River to somewhere further north. The time he spends at a nearby Biological Station recalls the cajun boy's quest in Robert Flaherty's "Louisiana Story."

In the end, the slaying mystery is also solved — it turns out to be his older sister's boyfriend, who loses his hunting license for six months — and young Jochen grows up to find that real life offers many more complex challenges than what he reads in books for the youngsters.
— *Holl.*

Ceremonia Pogrzebowa
(Funeral Ceremony)
(BRITISH-POLISH-COLOR)

Berlin, Feb. 27.

A Green Man presentation. Produced by Green Man Productions with Poltel Films. Produced by Kevin Attew. Written and directed by Jacek Bromski. Camera (color), Jerzy Garstecki; editor, Jadwiga Zajicek; art director, Bromski; sound, Grazyna Niwinska; music, Henri Seroka. Reviewed at the Berlin Film Festival (information), Feb. 26, 1985. Running time: **96 MINS.**
Anna . . . . Jadwiga Jankowska-Cieslak
Teresa . . . . Anna Romantowska

Stephen	Boguslaw Linda
John	Piotr Machalica
Margaret	Malgorzata Pieczynska

The premise for this plot has been used countless times: take a divided family, arrange a reason for them to live in close quarters for a short period and let them drop their masks and take each other to task.

The event here is the death of a respected and learned academician, who was a tyrant and a phony in his private life. As the film starts, the family is waiting impatiently for the prodigal elder son, who had always battled with his father's authority, to come, in order for the funeral to proceed.

There is quite a lot of nudity and lovemaking involved, before the final vengeance of the deceased on his disappointing sons is revealed. Finally, all the fooling around, dramatic clashes and strident arguments result in the conclusion that nothing changes, everything stays the same.

Boguslaw Linda leads a cast rating far above the material. Both Ann Romantowska and Malgorzata Pieczynska exude sensuality while Jadwiga Jankowska-Cieslak, who scored highly in an earlier Hungarian film, "Another Way," is less visible as the ex-wife of the painter.

While film is distributed by a British firm, Green Man Productions, it has very much the look associated with Polish productions, in atmosphere, in photography and in backgrounds. Editing is brisk throughout and music effectively highlights dramatic moments. —*Edna.*

O Magico E O Delegado
(The Magician And The Police Commissioner)
(BRAZILIAN-COLOR)

Berlin, Feb. 20.

A production of Sani Films, Embrafilme. Directed by Fernando Coni Campos. Screenplay, Campos, Mario Carneiro, from a novel by Josue Guimaraes; camera (color), Carneiro, Jaime Schwartz; sound, Roberto Leite; editor, Roberto Pires, Eunice Gutman, Regina Veiga, Watler Goulart; music, Nelson Jacobina. Reviewed at Cinema, Berlin Film Festival (Forum), Feb. 20, 1985. Running time: **108 MINS.**
With: Nelson Xavier, Luthero Luis, Tania Alves, Maria Silvia, Jurema Pena, Helber Rangel.

This film contrasts two men, two vocations, as two opposing philosophies, ideologies and ways of life, in a charming and amusing political parable stating that the meek shall inherit the earth.

It takes place in the recent past, in a remote Brazilian town where the local police commissioner has total power as sheriff, judge, jury and censor of press and theater. Although the man is a macho brute, he is funny and ultimately exposed as a harmless and clumsy windbag.

Opposite the sheriff is an itinerant magician, a quiet man of wise smiles and suave charm, who arrives to perform in town, accompanied by a beautiful woman, his lover and assistant. Appalled by the wretched poverty he sees in the town, the magician transforms the marketplace into a cornucopia of abundance. The economic order of the town, rooted in social injustice, is sabotaged by these acts of magical munificence. Naturally the magician must be jailed by the commissioner as a dangerous subversive. After the magician dies in his cell, the coffin at his funeral is revealed magically to contain only white doves, which fly away at the end, symbolic of his unconquerable spirit.

This is an entertaining film of originality and vitality, with an important theme told non-controversially. —*Hitch.*

La Présence Réele
(The Real Presence)
(FRENCH-COLOR)

Berlin, Feb. 21.

An INA, FR3, Ministry of Culture Production. Written and directed by Raul Ruiz. Camera (color), Jacques Bouquin; editor, Martine Bouquin; sound, Jean-Claude Brisson. Reviewed at the Berlin Film Festival (Forum), Feb. 20, 1985. Running time: **60 MINS.**
With: Frank Oger and the voices of Christian Rist, Nadège Clair, Camila Mora, Catherine Oudin, Louis Castel, Jean-Loup Rivière.

Raul Ruiz' presence at the Avignon Theatre Festival in 1983 was already noted by the Berlin Forum last year, in a remarkable, if outlandish, version of Racine's classical play "Berenice." This year the Forum offered a second helping of the same vintage.

While it looks like a documentary, purporting to follow one unemployed actor during the festival, Ruiz' intentions go further. Part of the film has been written and prepared beforehand, while other scenes are evidently incorporated from documentation picked up in Avignon, including selections from plays produced there.

The questions asked by the actor playing an actor in the film, lead directly towards the theatrical field of interpreting art, so close to Ruiz' heart. For example, what are the limits of the screen, what is the relation between stylized art and real life and how far can art dare attack its public by the shows it puts on? —*Edna.*

Idol
(The Idol)
(POLISH-COLOR)

Berlin, Feb. 27.

A Film Polski Production, "Perspektiwa (Perspective) Group," Warsaw; world rights, Film Polski. Warsaw. Written and directed by Feliks Falk. Features entire cast. Camera (color, Wieslaw Zdort; sets, Jerzy Sajko; music, Jan Kanty, "Perspektiwa;" editor, Miroslawa Garlicka; production manager, Jacek Szeligowski. Reviewed at Berlin Film Fest (Forum), Feb. 26, 1985. Running time: **101 MINS.**
With: Krzysztof Pieczynski, Jerzy Kamas, Witold Debicki, Krzysztof Zalewski, Ewa Zukowska, Tadeusz Huk, Zbigniew Zapasiewicz.

Feliks Falk's "The Idol" comes across as a stingless parable on the 1950s. Back in those troubled days, a well known Polish writer, the fictitous Piotr Korton, had to leave the country to live and work in exile, dying later in West Germany. Now, in 1969, a new young writer sets out to write an essay on Korton during the heady days of a cultural thaw that is nevertheless marked by a debilitating compromise with the powers that be. The young man slowly begins to assemble the character and even the exterior appearances of his idol, until his own identity tragically vanishes.

Undoubtedly, one can read into the parable a lesson of conformity and compromise, also of pushing an obsession to the point of eccentricity. However, the performances lack the sharp edge usually associated with Falk's prior work, so much so that the tale is drained of flesh-and-blood substance. —*Holl.*

Variete
(GREEK-COLOR)

Athens, Feb. 9.

A Movie Co. coproduction with the Greek Film Centre. Written and directed by Nicos Panayotopoulos. Features Vaguelis Germanoe, Olia Lazaridou, Despina Gueroulanou, Nikitas Tsakiroglou, Mimis Chryssomallis, Lefteris Vbyatzis. Camera (color), Aris Stavrou; art direction, Dionyssis Photopoulos; editor, Costas Joardanides. Reviewed at the Pallas Cinema of Athens, Feb. 9, 1985. Running time **140 MINS.**

"Variete" is the fourth picture by Nicos Panayotopoulos and has already won four state prizes including best picture. It is a pretentious art film, worth seeing, but somewhat difficult for the average filmgoer. It should find its way at festivals and in selected situations here and abroad.

Its main character is a film director who is going through an emotional crisis. After 10 years of married life his marriage is on the rocks due to his affair with another woman.

The unevenness of treatment and the absence of a strong storyline do not help in distinguishing easily between fantasy and reality. The forced philosophical dialog fails to give weight to the picture. Acting as a whole is good with no particular performance standing out.

Major assets of the picture are the stunning photography by Aris Stavrou and the musical background enriched by four waltzes by Chopin. Other technical credits are fine.—*Rena.*

Angelic Conversations
(BRITISH-COLOR)

Berlin, Feb. 18.

A British Film Institute production. Produced by James MacKay. Directed and photographed (color, super 8m), by Derek Jarman. Screenplay, Jarman; voiceover, Judi Dench, reading Shakespeare's sonnets; music, Coil (John Balance, Peter Christoffersen). Reviewed at Berlin Film Festival (special screenings), Feb. 18, 1985. Running time: **78 MINS.**

Footage by Derek Jarman in Super 8, shot last summer as an exercise film, has undergone two stages of transfer to video and finally to 35m, funded by the British Film Institute at £50,000. What emerges is "Angelic Conversations," a difficult film that is experimental in form and content.

Although "Angelic Conversations" works indirectly and symbolically, with no overt grappling, it is a gay love story between two young men, played by Paul Reynolds and Philip Williamson. Much of the film is in slow motion, with a highly painterly, grainy quality, set against industrial wastelands and abstract landscapes. Soundtrack includes a ticking clock, reinforcing theme of time and life's brief candle.

Voiceover is by Judi Dench, reading 14 of Shakespeare's sonnets, selected to emphasize homoeroticism. — *Hitch.*

Der Ruf Der Sibylla
(The Call Of Sibylla)
(SWISS-COLOR-16m)

Berlin, Feb. 21.

An Ombra Film production, Clemens Klopfenstien, Zürich. Directed by Clemens Klopfenstein. Features entire cast. Screenplay, Klopfenstein, Serena Kiefer, Max Rüdlinger, Franz Rickenbach; camera (color), Klopfenstein; editor, Rickenbach; sound, Iwan Seifert; sets, Kiefer. Reviewed at Berlin Film Fest (Forum), Feb. 21, 1985. Running time: **104 MINS.**
With: Christine Lauterburg (Clara), Max Rüdlinger (Balz), Michael Schacht.

In Clemens Klopfenstein's witty experimental feature, "The Call Of Sibylla," Balz, a Swiss painter living in Umbria, finds he can't live without his stage-actress girlfriend, Clara, who has her mind at the moment completely on a forthcoming premiere in a fictitious city called Jammers. To cure his worried state of mind, a friendly old Franciscan gives Balz a swig of herb schnapps, "Amaro Sibilla" (the liquor actually exists), whereupon he wishes Clara's premiere would be canceled.

It is, via a curse falling upon her leading man.

Next Balz wishes that Clara would make the trip to join him in Umbria, which also happens as she has nothing to do until her suddenly ailing colleague gets well. Once in Italy, the two are then forced to stay together because suddenly Clara loses her voice — again, a result of a magic spell being wielded innocently by Balz with the help of the mysterious schnapps. Soon, however, Clara/Sibylla begins to realize that the magic is entirely in her power once she has the bottle in her hands: one swig, and her voice is back again; another swig, and even the forces of nature (summer turns to winter, and vice-versa) obey her command.

Despite weaknesses along the way in the rather improvised story (which has many allusions to Greek and Roman mythology), "The Call Of Sibylla" amuses all the same.
— *Holl.*

Eszterlànc
(The Apple Of Our Eye)
(HUNGARIAN-COLOR)

Budapest, Feb. 14.
A Hungarofilm presentation of the Mafilm production. Directed by András Péterffy. Screenplay, Éva Vörös; camera (color), Sándor Kurucz; editor, Agnes Kulics; sound, János Réti; music, Zoltán Jeney. Reviewed at the Hungarofilm screening room, Budapest, Feb. 13, 1985. Running time: **85 MINS.**
Eszter . . . . Henriett Deres
Her mother . . . . Ildikó Bánsági
Grandfather . . . . Tibor Kenderesi
Teacher . . . . Irén Bordán
Dr. Teofil . . . . László Vajda

Somewhere between a children's film and adult fare, András Péterffy's first feature film focuses on the private and social life of a 12-year-old girl whose parents are divorced. She lives with her mother, who is trying very hard to compensate for the lack of a second parent at home by keeping as close as she can to the girl; she visits the father who has remarried the kind of woman Eszter does not fancy, and she has the typical experiences of her age at school, with an insensitive teacher, a pushy boyfriend, and her relations with the other girls.

Pleasant to watch, if never really involving, the film offers a believable image of everyday, middleclass life in Hungary, particularly as far as young people in their early teens are concerned.

Péterffy's record as a documentary director in the past shows in the way he approaches the sequences featuring the teenagers. He correctly chose for the lead a rather plain, but highly expressive girl, Henriett Deres, who makes no effort to appear cutesy or glamorous, and therefore lends the film an air of credibility.

Technical credits are above average and the overall result could fit in with family-type programming.
—*Edna.*

Let's Make Laugh II
(HONG KONG-COLOR)

Hong Kong, Feb. 22.
A Mobile Film production Ltd. for Shaw Brothers. Presented by Run Run Shaw. Produced by Mona Fong and Wong Ka Hee. Directed by Alfred Cheung. Designed by Chan Friend. Stars Erh Tung Sheng, Wang Chu Hsien, Chang Kuo Chu, Huo Yao Liang, Alfred Cheung, Chan Friend, Ho Chia Li. Screenplay, Alfred Cheung, Huang Hung Chi; camera (color), Chang Cheng Tung; art direction, Chen Ching Shen. Original soundtrack and lyrics by Chen Fei Lieh; music, Stephen Shing, So Chun Hou. Reviewed at Jade theater, Feb. 21, 1985, Hong Kong. Running time: **98 MINS.**
(Cantonese soundtrack with English subtitles)

Security guard Ah Ping (Erh Tung Sheng) is first shown watching the film version of his romance on screen (a creative way to segue into "Let's Make Laugh II"). His new assignment is to look after and guard the gay son (Huo Yao Liang) of a rich gang boss in a villa in Lantao Island to keep him away from his like friends. Ping later meets the woman next door (Wang Chu Hsien) who is the mistress of a married businessman called John (Chang Kuo Chu). So smitten is Ping that he makes every effort to be close to her with often disastrous slapstick consequences.

This is a poor sequel to the marvelous and heart-warming "Let's Make Laugh," a hit Cantonese hybrid of a Neil Simon-type comedy romance that brings to life contemporary Hong Kong life style, trends and 80's morality. —*Mel.*

Impiegati
(Employees)
(ITALIAN-COLOR)

Rome, April 2.
A D.M.V. release, produced by Antonio Avati for Due-A Films, National, Dania and Filmes. Features entire cast. Directed by Pupi Avati. Screenplay by Antonio Avati, Pupi Avati, Cesare Bonnazzini. Camera (color), Pasquale Rachini; art director, Giancarlo Basili; editor, Amadeo Salfa; music, Riz Ortolani. Reviewed at Quirnale Cinema, Rome, Mar. 29, 1985. Running time: **100 MINS.**
Luigi Stanzani . . . . Claudio Botosso
Enrico Silvestri . . . . Luca Barbareschi
Annalisa Silvestri . . . . Elena Sofia Ricci
Dario . . . . Dario Parisini
Dario's father . . . . Cesare Barbetti

Though title promises a good spoof, "Employees" is a far cry from it: a low-key, bittersweet comedy about young people who work upstairs in a bank. It takes a lot to squeeze some drama out of a crew like this, much less a laugh, but helmer Pupi Avati wrings out a moment here and there, valorizing his characters' everyday joys, sorrows, and foibles to the maximum.

It's a pleasant piece of entertainment that has garnered only fair onshore returns. Without any of Avati's stock players or his hallmark style of countryside naiveté. ("A School Outing," "We Three"), pic looks destined to remain outside his body of festival work.

Carrying over from the director's other films is the recognizable Bologna setting and ensemble acting from a cast of mostly unknowns. Lack of a star face in the central role hurts pic early on.

Luigi Stanzani (Claudio Botosso) is a fresh recruit at a big bank; stiff and priggish at the beginning, he gradually loosens up into a more human guy, though never a charmer. Through his eyes the little world of the little people is revealed as a miniature Sodom and Gomorrah of petty corruption, loose women (for everyone but the frustrated hero), and drunk hostesses who lose their inhibitions at parties and sing offkey. The middle-aged boss chases the office beauty. The rich snub the non-rich. Not everybody gets into the golf club, or stays there. Luigi passes through the tempest unscathed.

Acting is mostly passable, with stand-out performances from Dario Parisini as Dario, Luigi's college student roommate, and Elena Sofia Ricci as Annalisa, Luigi's dream girl who becomes Dario's lover. Dario's abrupt and totally uncalled-for death in an off-screen car accident is milked for pathos, though not very well, via grieving père Cesare Barbetti, good thesp in an embarrassing role.

Shortly thereafter the conniving schemer Enrico (Luca Barbareschi) is dispensed with following a hazy office scandal, and pic concludes with Luigi contemplating an empty office of whispered memories, with the bemused look of someone who can't believe he learned so much in such a short time. — *Yung.*

Kung Hei Fat Choy
(Happy New Year)
(HONG KONG-COLOR)

Hong Kong, Feb. 21.
A Cinema City Co. Ltd. production and presentation, released by Golden Princess. Produced by Karl Maka, Dean Shek and Raymond Wong. Directed by Shek. Stars Shek, Alan Tam, George Lam, Ben Ben, Chan Waiman, Ann Bridgewater, Yui Yau-hung. Production supervisor, Paul Lai; executive producer, Norman Chan; camera (color), Henry Chan; art direction, Wong Chong Wah; special effects consultant, Tsui Hark; music, Mahood Rumjahn. Reviewed at President theater, Hong Kong, Feb. 20, 1985. Running time: **98 MINS.**
(Cantonese soundtrack with English subtitles)

The God of Fortune (Alan Tam) descends to earth by accident in the form of a falling meteor in "Happy New Year." Getting away from the crowd, he sneaks into Dean Shek's

---

residence and befriends his sister Ann Bridgewater and son Ben Ben. Dean is greatly amazed to discover that some of his personal problems are solved. The God of Fortune further demonstrates his supernatural powers by getting the underworld boss Godfather's son Yiu Yau-hung and body-guard Chan Wai-man to change their evil ways.

The God also exposes the Godfather's (George Lam) conspiracy to run for election. In vengeance, the Godfather hires three soul-busters to fight the God of Fortune. They are overpowered and on Chinese New Year's Eve, guards from the space centre try to save the God of Fortune with their latest weapons.

Cinema City had "Merry Christmas" during the Yuletide season and they follow up with a sure-fire boxoffice attraction featuring lots of local stars. —*Mel.*

Wildschut
(DUTCH-BELGIAN-COLOR)

Amsterdam, March 13.
A Cannon Tuschinski Film Distribution release produced by Maggan Films and Cine/Vista (Holland) and Kunst & Kino (Belgium). Producers, Henk Bos, Gerrit Visscher, Jan van Raedonck. Executive producer, Henk Bos. Directed by Bobby Eerhart. Features entire cast. Screenplay, Felix Timmer, from his crime novel; camera (color), Paul van den Bos; editor, Victorine Habets; music, Alain Pierre; sound, Victor Dekker; second unit director, Hans Scheepmaker; second unit camera, Michel van Laer. Reviewed at Cinema International, Amsterdam, March 12, 1985. Running time: **92 MINS.**
Jim . . . . Hidde Maas
Charlie . . . . Jack Monkau
Lisa . . . . Annick Christians
Deleye . . . . Josse de Pauw
Sybil . . . . Chris Lomme
Hugo . . . . Marc van Eeghem
Dalsum . . . . Werther van der Sarren

This is an unusual offering from the Low Countries, delivering shocks and gore, sprinkled with some heady suggestions of sex. It may well succeed as exploitation fare. Plusses are terse editing by Victorine Habets and go-go action sequences directed by Hans Scheepmaker.

Dramatic impact, however, is lacking. Acting in general is curiously lifeless, even from such seasoned thesps as Chris Lomme and Hidde Maas.

If helmer Bobby Eerhart, directing his first feature after some acclaimed shorts, tried to assert a sense of style in the mundane context of an exploitation film, his approach misfired. Stilted framing tends to freeze actors' faces in fixed, masklike expressions, but Greek tragedy this is not.

"Wildschut" (literally: "gamekeeper") is the name of a secluded house in Belgian woodland. Poacher Josse du Pauw lives there with his wife Chris Lomme and her children from a first marriage, blond charmer Annick Christians and feeble-minded innocent Mac van Eeghem. Christians has a lively baby boy from De Paux, who lords it over the family.

Two runaway gangsters, Hidde Maas and Jack Monkau, in need of a hiding place, hold them hostage. De Pauw resists but to no avail.

When nearly all characters are dead — including the local cop and sundry soldiers from a nearby training camp — Christians escapes with her baby and Monkau, to whom she has taken a fancy.

Though the military pursue their car with helicopter and tanks the smiling blond finally proves the dark gangsters' undoing: she steers their car down a precipice. Clutching baby, she leaps to safety.

This ending (reportedly substituted for a happy lovers' escape) is ill-advised, as nothing presaged the girl's change of heart.—*Ewa.*

Satsuma Moso Biwa
(The Lute Of The Blind Monks Of Satsuma)
(JAPANESE-DOCU-COLOR)

Berlin, Feb. 20.
An Iwanami Films production. Written and directed by Atsushi Suwa. Camera (color), Kiyoshi Nishio; editor, Suwa: sound, Koji Okamoto; music, Takeo Yamashita; title song, Suwa (lyrics), Yamashita (music), performed by Mirei Katahara. Narrated by Mizuhi Suzuki. Reviewed at the Berlin Film Festival (Forum), Feb. 19, 1985. Running time: **90 MINS.**

This is a well-photographed, thoroughly researched documentary on the blind works of Satsuma, who train for a long time to play on a special lute (the "biwa"), considered to have holy powers by Buddhists. It covers the public service they render once they finish their training and hit the road, their duty being to visit the houses of as many believers as possible. In each home a monk is received as an honored guest, because the rural communities there are strong believers in the special magic contained in that lute's music.

All this is transmitted in a highly academic fashion, with narration. Since no translation was made available on the conversations between the monks, or between them and their hosts along the way, the scope is limited. Except for very few moments when all of a sudden visual imagination is fired by the shot of a "biwa" floating in the air, Magritte-style, or the use of a butterfly's wings to denote the change of seasons, all the rest is traditional, unexceptional stuff. The inclusion of Western-style music, played as background by electronic instruments, seems to be entirely out of context.

Educational television might eventually be interested in this material. —*Edna.*

'Robbery Under Arms
(AUSTRALIAN-COLOR)

Sydney, April 1.
An ITC Entertainment release of a South Australian Film Corporation production. Produced by Jock Blair. Directed by Ken Hannam, Donald Crombie. Stars Sam Neill. Screenplay, Graeme Koestveld, Tony Morphett, from the novel by Rolf Boldrewood; camera (color), Ernest Clark; music, Garry McDonald, Laurie Stone; editor, Andrew Prowse; sound, Lloyd Carrick; production design, George Liddle; costumes, Anna Senior; special effects, Brian Cox; stunts, Bill Stacey; associate producers, Pamela H. Vanneck, Bruce Moir; executive producer, John Morris. (Commonwealth Film Censor rating: PG.) Reviewed at Village theater, Mosman, March 28, 1985. Running time: **141 MINS.**

Captain Starlight	Sam Neill
Dick Marston	Steven Vidler
Jim Marston	Christopher Cummins
Gracey	Liz Newman
Kate	Deborah Coulls
Jeannie	Susie Lindeman
Warrigal	Tommy Lewis
Ben Marston	Ed Devereux
Aileen Marston	Jane Menelaus
Sir Frederick Morringer	Robert Grubb
Mary Marston	Elaine Cusick
George	Andy Anderson
Goring	David Bradshaw
Trooper Fall	John Dick
Mr. Falkland	Michael Duffield
McIntyre	Roger Ward
Mungo	Paul Chubb

Handsomely produced, but infuriatingly uninvolving, this latest production of the South Australian Film Corp. (a distribution bow for ITC in Australia) is the fifth film version of Rolf Boldrewood's rambling 1889 novel about Captain Starlight, the gentleman bushranger.

Starlight is an intriguing villain: an Englishman of noble, possibly royal, blood, with a taste for fine things, but a talent for rustling and robbing. In the colonial days before the turn of the century, when bushrangers (i.e., outlaws) plagued the Australian countryside, Starlight, though a fictional character, became as well known as Ned Kelly. The film follows the main thread of Boldrewood's book quite carefully as the headstrong Marston brothers leave their home to join up with their father, Ben, a loyal member of Starlight's gang. Their ensuing adventures culminate in the inevitable downbeat last-reel encounter with the constabulary.

As with most Australian films, this one is great to look at, with top-notch photography, costumes and sets which evoke the period with richness and style, plus a rousing music score. At the same time this is a fatally flawed production which proceeds in a series of choppy, truncated scenes without ever taking the trouble to establish the 10 or so principal characters, so that it's difficult, if not impossible, to care about any of them.

This has undoubtedly come about because of the project's initial concept; it was made, by two talented directors, as a tv mini-series (yet to be aired), and although the cinema version at almost two-and-a-half hours is inordinately long, it seems clear that much of the footage devoted to giving information about the Marstons and their sweethearts has been saved for the small-screen.

The script, by Graeme Koestveld and Tony Morphett, and the bland direction, by Ken Hannam ("Sunday Too Far Away") and Donald Crombie ("Caddie") contain flashes of inspiration, moments of humor, and vast stretches of rather dull and uninspiring action. The film scurries manically every which way, but the basic elements are missing, and without them all the surface derring-do becomes merely tedious.

Sam Neill makes the very most of his sketchy role as the aristocratic villain, while Ed Devereux is excellent as old Marston, a cynical, veteran bandit, and Robert Grubb rightly tenacious as their nemesis. There's also a winning, if tantalizingly brief, cameo from Paul Chubb as the gourmet cook attached to the elegant Starlight's gang in an early sequence (his fate, and that of other gang members, remains obscure).—*Strat.*

White Fire
(Vivre Pour Survivre)
(FRENCH-BRITISH-TURKISH-COLOR)

A Trans World Entertainment release of an A.F.M./Film Centre Intl./Les Films J.M.P. production. Executive producers, Tony Edwards, John L. Coletta, in association with Chris Davis. Produced by Jean-Marie Pallardy, Alan G. Rainer, in association with Sedat Akdemir, Ugur Terzioglu. Directed, written by Pallardy. Stars Robert Ginty. Camera (Fujicolor), Roger Fellous; editor, Bruno Zincone; musical director, Jon Lord; songs, Limelight & Vicky Browne; stunt director, Benito Stefanelli. Reviewed on TWE vidcassette, N.Y., March 20, 1985. (No MPAA Rating.) Running time: **91 MINS.**

Beau Donnelly	Robert Ginty
Noah	Fred Williamson
Ingrid	Belinda Mayne
Sam	Jess Hahn
Sophia	Mirella Banti
Yilmaz	Gordon Mitchell

"White Fire" is a crudely-made action picture, lensed in Turkey in the summer of 1983 and bowing domestically on vidcassette. With more filmmaking care, it could have had some domestic theatrical playoff on the action circuit.

Leads Robert Ginty and Belinda Mayne are cast as brother-and-sister diamond smugglers, in cahoots with crooked mines security officer Yilmaz (Gordon Mitchell). A pointless, 20-years-earlier prolog shows their parents killed by soldiers with the kids cared for by Sam (Jess Hahn), who is now a smuggling partner.

The legendary White Fire diamond (2,000 carats and emitting deadly radioactivity) is the main prize, but French filmmaker Jean-Marie Pallardy detours into absurd territory when Mayne is killed and Ginty picks up a girl in a bar, has plastic surgery convert her into a Mayne lookalike in order to continue the inside job at the mine, but then falls in love with her (incest psychological overtones stressed). Even guest star Fred Williamson, cast as a villain but predictably turning into Mr. nice guy in the final reel, fails to save this one.

Dubbing is crude, and gore make-up is emphasized over local color. —*Lor.*

Eating Your Heart Out
(AUSTRALIAN-DOCU-COLOR)

Sydney, March 21.
An Australian Film Institute release of a Trout Films (Australia) production, in association with Cinepak Investment and Management Services. Produced, written by Maureen McCarthy. Directed by Chris Warner; camera (color), Jaems Grant; editor, Denis Hunter; music, Mark McSherry; sound, Georgina Guilfoyle; narrator, Beverley Dunn. Reviewed at Chauvel Theater, Sydney, March 20, 1985. Running time: **76 MINS.**

A documentary about fatness and slimming "Eating Your Heart Out" is structured around a group therapy session involving eight women, selected by the filmmakers, from various backgrounds and of various ages, with one thing in common: they all have trouble with their dieting.

Pic begins with the statistic that 70% of Australians are, at one time or another, on "serious" diets, that 15% are having trouble with those diets, and that of these 90-95% are female. In a world where slimness and youth are sold as being the secrets of professional and sexual success, says the film, countless women embark on unnecessary and even dangerous diets, while a multi-million-dollar exercise industry has become established as another means of obtaining that slim figure.

It's an interesting subject, but this rather mundane film doesn't do much with it. The women in the group talk about their lives and their problems, but one doesn't really get to know or, unfortunately, to care too much about them. The various diet schemes and keep-fit organizations are fairly obvious targets for criticism, as are fashion editors of some influential women's magazines.

The serious conditions and disorders brought about by dieting unnecessarily are discussed, but only rather superficially. Basically this is a film of talking heads, discussing the problems but preaching to the converted, since the film seems to lack the possibilities for attracting a sizable audience. Nevertheless, it will have a brief theatrical run in Australia under the auspices of the Australian Film Institute. —*Strat.*

Almanya Aci Vatan
(Germany, Bitter Land)
(TURKISH-COLOR)

Sydney, March 21.

A Fatos Film production. Directed, edited by Serif Gören. Features. entire cast. Screenplay, Zehra Tan; camera (color), Izzet Akay; music, Rahmi Saltuk. No other credits available. Reviewed on SBS TV, Sydney, March 20, 1985. Running time: **98 MINS.**
Guldane . . . . Hulya Kocyigit
Mahmut . . . . Rahmi Saltuk
With Mine Tekgoz, Fikriye Korkmaz.

Made in 1980, immediately before he tackled direction of the Yilmaz Güney project "Yol," and reviewed for the record, Serif Gören's "Germany, Bitter Land" is an angry tale of Turkish "guest-workers" in West Germany.

In a pre-credit sequence set in a peaceful Turkish village, Mahmut enters into a marriage of convenience with Guldane, a local girl with German residency. The bulk of the film is set in West Berlin where Turkish workers suffer from poor accommodation, low pay, and racism. Guldane has a job in a factory making telex machines, while Mahmut has difficulty, at first, finding work.

When, inevitably, Guldane finds herself pregnant and is unable to go through with an abortion, the couple seems doomed to.a life of unrelieved poverty. Matters aren't helped when Mahmut's basic macho attitudes surface, and he neglects his wife for a pretty German girl he meets in a bar.

Film ends indecisively with the couple facing a bleak future. Gören manages to make some ironic and lucid comments on the plight of his fellow countrymen, and the atmosphere of the Turkish sections of the city is captured evocatively. Camerawork is good, but let down, as usual, by shaky lab work. Still, it's one of the best Turkish films of recent years.—*Strat.*

Der Schneemann
(The Snowman)
(WEST GERMANY-COLOR)

Hamburg, March 12.

A.Bavaria Atelier production in cooperation with NF Geria II and ZDF. Produced by Jörn Schröder. Executive producer, Günter Rohrbach. Directed by Peter Bringmann. Screenplay, Matthias Seelig, based on the novel by Jörg Fauser; camera (color), Helge Weindler; editor, Annette Dorn; music, Paul Vincent Gunia; costumes, Ute Schwippert; set design, Hubert Popp; sound, Karsten Ullrich. Reviewed at Streit's Haus, Hamburg, March 11, 1985. Running time: **102 MINS.**
Dorn . . . . Marius Müller-Westernhagen
Cora . . . . . . ₍ . . . . Polly Eltes
Laslo . . . . Towje Kleiner

Kiefer . . . . Donald Arthur
Habib . . . . Riad Gholmie
Roda . . . . Heinz Wanitschek
Hermes . . . . Manuela Riva
Alena . . . . Susann Winter
Cassar . . . . Tony Alleff
Herni . . . . Gert Burkard
Chung Li . . . . John Ma
Stefan . . . . Oliver Lentz

A suspense thriller with comic elements, "The Snowman" represents Bavaria Studio's bid to market solid commercial entertainment. Bavaria lined up the same team including male lead Marius Müller-Westernhagen that made the sleeper "Theo Against The Rest Of The World" which emerged as the most successful German production at the b.o. in 1980.

Shot in German on location in Malta, Frankfurt and Amsterdam on a sizable budget, film opens in Malta where perennial loser Dorn is attempting to sell 50,000 copies of 3-D porno magazines stacked in his hotel room. Police raid the room, but Dorn escapes via the balcony to a room on the floor below where he finds a dying man and ends up under arrest facing a murder rap.

Dorn escapes from the police only to become involved in drug trafficking.

The complex plot moves to Amsterdam where Dorn, acting on a tip from Cora (nicely played by London born singer Polly Eltes), unloads the cocaine to a Chinese drug king for a small fortune in dollars, which in an ironic twist he has to hand over to his pursuers to save Cora's life.

Storyline moves fast including a taut chase on the train to Amsterdam and escape sequences. The exotic Malta and Amsterdam locations provide atmosphere. Topliners Müller-Westernhagen and Eltes succeed in gaining audience sympathy giving credibility to the romantic ending despite the onus of drug trafficking.

Technical credits warrant praise. Eventual television use is a certainty, but export possibilities appear limited to Germany's European neighbors and offshore art circuits. —*Kind.*

De Prooi
(The Prey)
(DUTCH-COLOR)

Amsterdam, March 1.

A Concorde Film release of a Frans Rasker Film production. Produced by Rasker. Directed by Vivian Pieters. Features entire cast. Screenplay, Pieters, Ton Ruys, based on Catherine Aird's novel "Henrietta Who?" camera (color), Peter Brugman; editor, Ton Ruys; music, Henny Vrienten; sound, Kees Linthorst. Reviewed at Tuschinski 3 Theater, Amsterdam, Feb. 28, 1985. Running time: **92 MINS:**
Valerie . . . . Maayke Bouten
Mellema . . . . Johan Leysen
Ria de Jong . . . . Marlous Fluitsma
Paul . . . . Erik de Vries
Van Maurik . . . . . . ₎ . . . . Wim Bary
Bob . . . . Rijk de Gooijer
Wim Gerritsen . . . . Joop Doderer

Trudy . . . . Yoka Berretty
Mrs. Gerritsen . . . . Lettie Costhoek

In her first feature, young director Vivian Pieters essays an intriguing change of traditional thriller format. In the screenplay she and editor-husband Ton Ruys adapted from Catherine Aird's English detective story, the sleuth is not Aird's ubiquitous detective inspector, but schoolgirl Valerie, the potential victim of an unknown villain who murdered her mother, then stalks the daughter who started investigating.

Valerie (first appearance of 19-year-old Maayke Bouten, a comely but ingenuous leading lady) is shocked and distressed, first when her mother (Yoka Berretty) is killed by a hit-and-run driver, thereafter when she learns the dead woman cannot possibly have been her mother, that, in fact, she does not know whose offspring she is. The story of the film is the story of Valerie's quest, as she pursues one abortive clue after another, while being pursued herself.

By focusing on a teenager and her outlook on real-life problems "The Prey" found an appreciative young audience in Holland.

Tyro helmer, who had solid grounding as an assistant director before tackling her first feature, shows unmistakable talent in mounting and shaping individual scenes. However, script and editing could have done with quite some tightening up, and most of the acting is humdrum. One shining exception is Johan Leysen as the detective inspector. He has not much to do, but he engages audience interest each time he is on screen.— *Ewa.*

Special Effects
(U.S.-COLOR)

Madrid, March 28.

A New Line Cinema release of a Larco production. Produced by Paul Kurta. Written and directed by Larry Cohen. Exec producer, Carter De Haven. Features entire cast. Camera (Eastmancolor),Paul Glickman; editor, Armond Lebowitz; music, Michael Minard. Reviewed at Cine Albéniz, Madrid, March 27, 1985. (MPAA Rating: R.) Running time: **103 MINS.**
With: Zoë Tamerlis, Eric Bogosian, Brad Rijn, Kevin O'Connor, Bill Oland, Richard Greene.

Larry Cohen's new pic, shown in Madrid at the Imagfic Sci-Fi event, is an entertaining, cleverly scripted and engrossing film. Though a "small" picture in the sense of production values, script has enough twists and wry humor to keep interest riveted throughout its running time. (Film was given a limited territorial release in the U.S. last November. —*Ed.*)

Yarn involves a "snuff" strangulation in a fancy Soho loft apartment of an aspiring, talentless actress by a famous film director whose last effort, laden with special effects, has just bombed. Director's idea is to make a comeback and show his real mettle by filming and reconstructing the girl's murder. To do so he enlists not only the detective assigned to investigate the case, but also the girl's out of town husband, who had been accused of the crime and whom the director gets out on bail.

Despite the misleading title, there are no special effects in the film whatsoever. The convolutions of the plot, as the director becomes increasingly obsessed with his project, are alternately droll and gripping, as he strangles a film lab attendant with a strip of 35m film, and makes the murdered girl's husband unwittingly act out before cameras the director's own crime.

Thesping all around is excellent and Zoë Tamerlis' handling of two roles is uncannily convincing. Direction and all technical credits are up to snuff in what amounts to a pleasant evening's entertainment.
—*Besa.*

Sac de Noeuds
(All Mixed Up)
(FRENCH-COLOR)

Paris, April 2.

A Warner-Columbia release of an Oliane Productions film. Produced by Marie-Laure Reyre. Directed by Josiane Balasko. Screenplay, Balasko and Jacques Audiard; camera (color), François Catonne; editor, Catherine Kelber; sound, Alain Sempé; music, Michel Goglat; title song by Gérard Blanchar; makeup, Jean-Pierre Eychenne; production managers, Patrick Desmaretz and Daniel Chevalier. Reviewed at the UGC Biarritz Theater, Paris, April 1, 1985. Running time: **87 MINS.**

Rose-Marie . . . . Isabelle Huppert
Anita . . . . Josiane Balasko

Rico .Farid Chopel
Pharmacist . . . . .Jean Carmet
Coyotte . . . . .Coluche
Nurse. . . . . .Dominique Lavanant
Etienne . . . . .Michel Albertini
Commissioner . . . . .Jean-Pierre Coffe
André .Daniel Russo

Josiane Balasko, the plump, be-spectacled writer-comedienne from the Paris café-theater scene, darkens her comic palette for her filmmaking debut, "Sac de Noeuds," a dour tale of three social misfits, their private obsessions and their attempt to regenerate their failed lives together. None of Balasko's previous brash comedy scripts prepared one for the spleen she pours out in a mere 87 minutes. The overall result is a curious but unsatisfying mixture of black humor, farce, pathos and tragedy.

Balasko herself plays one of the losers, a sullen, shabby young woman who, in the opening scene, allows a Chinese shopkeeper to sodomize her as payment for a container of gaz with which she plans to commit suicide. Her misanthropy extends to a farewell note on her coat warning that she is not donating her body to science.

Her self-destruction is cut short by Isabelle Huppert, a pea-brained, cheap platinum blond housewife in her building, who bursts into her apartment, fleeing from her brutal policeman husband. When latter is apparently stabbed to death, the two women are forced to run.

They are soon joined by another reluctant fugitive, Farid Chopel, a jail-bird who had hoped to sit out his final months quietly but who is embroiled in another convict's murderous escape from a transit police van.

The disparate trio find temporary refuge in the home of a provincial druggist (Jean Carmet) before splitting up to come to terms with personal bugbears.

Balasko casts her story in the form of a road picture, which usually allows for a maximum of incident without straining credibility. Even so, her script seems overloaded with sordid plotlines and multiple climaxes that reflect a disparity of tone and wear the spectator's receptivity.

Of the three principals, Chopel is best. Lanky, swarthy and sad-faced, he comes closest to reconciling the contrasting moods of the story. (An imaginative stage clown, he previously had screen employ as inscrutable, menacing thugs.) Balasko's sour Chaplinesque composition is odd but unaffecting, while Huppert is amusingly vulgar as her flighty comrade.

Warner Bros. signed a pre-production distribution contract for the film in Europe last year, and has just released it in France. With its diminishing laugh returns, it will prove a hard sell as a comedy item.
—*Len.*

Fuego Eterno
(Eternal Fire)
(SPANISH-COLOR)

Madrid, March 26.
An Azkubia Films, Aiete Films and José Estéban Alenda production. Written and directed by José Angel Rebolledo. Camera (Eastmancolor), Xabier Aguirresarobe; editor, María Elena Sáenz de Rozas; music, Alberto Iglesias; sets, Cesar de Vera. Reviewed at Cine Amaya, Madrid, March 25, 1985. Running time: **92 MINS.**
With: Angela Molina, Imanol Arias, François Eric Gendron, Ovidi Montllor, Myriam Maeztu, Montserrat Salvador, Juan Llaneras.

Despite some beautiful lensing by Xabier Aguirresarobe and okay performances, this Basque-financed and produced picture comes across as a murky, ponderous and confusing story which fails to ever arouse much interest.

Set in 17th century northern Spain, most of the yarn is told as a long flashback as a priest delves into a case of love, murder and witchcraft that had been tried 20 years earlier, and in which young Gabrielle (Angela Molina) had been sentenced to life imprisonment.

Involved in the talky, static flashbacks is an intrigue during which a girl who was been jilted and left pregnant, seeks revenge upon her suitor by poisoning him after his marriage to Gabrielle and having her put away for murder and witchcraft. At the end of the fuzzy drama we learn in deadpan fashion that the investigating priest is, presumably, the illegitimate offspring of the jilted girl. He has been brought up by wealthy foster parents while his mother rotted in a nunnery.

Neophyte helmer-writer José Angel Rebolledo never really gets into his characters and little emotion is expressed by any of them. "Eternal Fire" is strictly for the domestic market, if that. — *Besa.*

L'Amour en Douce
(Love On The Quiet)
(FRENCH-COLOR)

Paris, April 3.
A Gaumont release of a Gaumont Intl./Productions Marcel Dassault/Cinéphonic coproduction. Produced by François Chavanne and Alain Poiré. Directed by Edouard Molinaro. Screenplay, Jean Sagols, Christian Watton, Molinaro, Jean-Louis Roncoroni, Chavanne; camera (color), Jean-Paul Schwartz; editors, Robert and Monique Isnardon; sound, Daniel Brisseau; production managers, Marc Goldstaub, Daniel Riché. Reviewed at the Gaumont Ambassade theater, Paris, April 2, 1985. Running time: **90 MINS.**
Marc . . . . .Daniel Auteuil
Antoine. . . . . .Jean-Pierre Marielle
Samantha . . . . .Emmanuelle Béart
Jeanne . . . . .Sophie Barjac
Ravignac. . . . . .Daniel Ceccaldi

Carl . . . . .Mathieu Carrière
Granny Odette . . . . . . .Blanchette Brunoy
Aunt Thérèse . . . . .René Faure

The busily eclectic Edouard Molinaro returns to the minor, romantic register with "L'Amour en Douce," a conventionally bitter-sweet tale about a young provincial lawyer who falls in love with a call girl after his marriage breaks up.

Daniel Auteuil, topbilled in Molinaro's last two French productions, is again the protagonist, an attorney in Aix-en-Provence whose capricious sexual escapades finally wear down the tolerance of his attractive, long suffering wife (Sophie Barjac).

She at last puts him out the door and begins a relationship with an older, more emotionally stable divorcé (Jean-Pierre Marielle), though she still loves Auteuil, who meets a beautiful young call girl (Emmanuelle Béart), and falls for her.

As one would expect to find in a French love story, the call girl is herself quite romantic and reciprocates. Soon the four main characters are living in the same apartment as one big, happy family. A misunderstanding threatens to destroy the delicate balance of emotions between Auteuil and Béart, but the thoughtful Marielle steps in to patch up the differences.

Despite the small crowd of screenwriters in the credits, film does not shine by its originality or insights, but Molinaro has a way with this kind of material and manages to give it some brittle charm. The players, of course, help immensely. The lovely Emmanuelle Béart (daughter of popular performing songwriter Guy Béart) is one of the most promising new faces of the French screen, destined for stardom if the right roles (and directors) come along. — *Len.*

Tschechow In Meinem Leben
(Chekhov In My Life)
(W. GERMAN-DOCU-COLOR-16m)

Berlin, March 29.
An Atossa Film Production, Munich, in coproduction with Sender Freies Berlin (SFB) and Westdeutscher Rundfunk (WDR), Cologne. Written and directed by Vadim Glowna. Features Vera Tschechowa. Camera (color), Martin Schäfer; sound, Martin Miller; music, Nicolas Economou; editor, Barbara von Weiterhausen; production manager, Manfred Heid; tv producers, Hans Kwiet, Joachim von Mengershausen. Reviewed at Studio am Kurfürstendamm, Berlin, March 29, 1985. Running time: **89 MINS.**
With: Vera Tschechowa, Vyacheslav Kupriyanov, Maya Turovskaya, Yevgeniya M. Chekhowa, Oleg Yefremov, Mark A. Prudkin, Oleg Fialko, Naum Kleiman, Oleg Tabakov, Andrei Knipper, Vladimir V. Knipper.

One reason for Vadim Glowna's "Chekhov In My Life" is the 125th anni this year of Anton Chekhov's birth. The film was made for First German Television (ARD stations in Berlin and Cologne) and will be aired this autumn. Another reason is that Glowna's actress wife, Vera Tschechowa (an Anglicized spelling of the Russian would be "Chekhova"), is a great-grand-niece of the writer dramatist.

The couple went to visit distant relatives in the Soviet Union and look through some archival files to trace her ancestry and investigate the Chekhovs' legacy to the Moscow theater scene. The film footage relates to Vera's grandmother-actress, Olga Tschechowa, and grandfather-actor, Michael Chekhov.

Until her death in 1980, Olga Tschechowa played 128 film roles and even directed a silent film production, "Der Narr seiner Liebe" (Fool In Love) (1929), with her ex-husband Michael in the lead before the latter's emigration to America. Michael died in 1955 in Hollywood, but during his stay from 1944 on he played several significant supporting-actor roles and founded his own theater ensemble and acting school.

Tschechowa and Glowna were not very well prepared in arranging and conducting the interviews in Moscow. They wander from place to place and person to person, while most of their interview partners seek primarily to upstage Chekhov by talking primarily about themselves. Even the 125th anni celebration at Melichovo in September 1984 is a dour, uninspired affair. (Pic is skedded for sidebar showing at upcoming Moscow fest.)—*Holl.*

The Indomitable Teddy Roosevelt
(DOCU-COLOR/B&W)

Hollywood, April 6.
A Gannett/Anacapa production. Produced, directed by Harrison Engle. Co-producer, Marilyn S. Engle. Written by Theodore Strauss; camera (color, b&w), Jeri Sopanen, Tom Baer, Robert Ipcar; associate producer, Sidney Kirkpatrick; sound, Thelma Vickroy. With the music of John Philip Sousa. Narrator, George C. Scott. Reviewed at the American Film Institute (Filmex), L.A., Feb. 27, 1985. (No MPAA Rating.) Running time: **93 MINS.**
With: Bob Boyd (Theodore Roosevelt), Philippa B. Roosevelt (Edith), Lisette Clemens (Alice), Thomas Batty (Ted), Sean Lavin (Kermit), Pippi Roosevelt (Ethel), Michael Roosevelt (Archie), Theodore Roosevelt 5th (Quentin), Harold Mark Kingsley (Young T.R.), William Kapinski (Father).

A hybrid of archival newsreel footage and newly shot dramatizations and illustrative sequences, "The Indomitable Teddy Roosevelt" emerges as a portrait of the United States' 26th president whose own enthusiasm for its subject proves quite contagious. Although the form of this impure creation can certainly be quarreled with, the quality of the vintage documentary material is, in many cases, so breathtaking, and the life story under consideration so exciting, that pic's overall impact is considerable. Already available nontheatrically and on videocassette, and recently unveiled in a theatrical print at Filmex, this certainly deserves the tv airing for which it was originally designed.

Docu's commercial appeal would seem to be all the greater in this age of Ronald Reagan, and while Roosevelt is generally remembered today, if at all, for his "big stick" approach to diplomacy, he was considerably more complex and multifaceted than that, which this film makes abundantly clear.

For one thing, the young Roosevelt's life was fraught with tragedy. His mother and first wife died on the same day, the latter in childbirth, a dual blow which sent the man into self-imposed exile in the West. This, in turn, led to his fervent passion for the conservation of nature and the wilderness, which in time eventuated in his establishment of vast national parks, forests and monuments, a cause for which anti-Reaganites have had to fight.

Most of the man's early life, from his sickly, but privileged childhood to his stint at Harvard and initial political positions, is neatly covered via still photographs and George C. Scott's narration, penned by Theodore Strauss, which is eloquent throughout.

From the time Roosevelt became William McKinley's vice president and, soon thereafter, ascended to the presidency in the wake of an assassination in 1901, producer-director Harrison Engle benefits from the fact that newsreel photography came into its own just at the time Roosevelt did.

Extraordinary footage reveals T.R. on the campaign trail, inspecting new naval vessels, heartily giving speeches and involving himself in no end of vigorous activities. Further material covers his 1906 visit to Panama to launch the canal, a post-presidency safari to Africa and subsquent visit with state leaders in Europe, his failed run for another term on the Progressive Party ticket, and a both courageous and foolhardy expedition to the Amazon to chart an unmapped river.

An experienced editor and creator of film clip sequences, Engle obviously has devoted great care to presenting the archival material in the most adventageous manner possi.'le, unifying the silent film speeds and even showing an early color film process. Any fan of old docu stock will have a field day.

To fill in the inevitable blanks, Engle chose to lens new, color footage with actors portraying Roosevelt and his family. Approach

here is respectful, even banal, but hardly offensive, and it doesn't go on long enough to interfere with an appreciation of the general thrust of the life's telling. Bob Boyd looks good in the title role.

Clearly a Roosevelt partisan, Engle in any event succeeds in his main mission, that of exciting the viewer about a larger-than-life figure who now seems to be neglected unfairly in American history. Roosevelt's tremendous stature as an energetic national leader is unmistakable here, and his accomplishments while in office, from cracking down on the monopolies to ramming through the Panama Canal and getting the world to take the U.S. seriously as a world power, come across as prodigious. Ultimately, film does what a good documentary can do — stimulate interest in its subject.
—*Cart.*

Girls Just Want To Have Fun
(COLOR)

Minor dance-a-thon with hot monicker.

Hollywood, April 2.

A New World Pictures release of a James G. Robinson presentation of a Girls production. Produced by Chuck Russell. Executive producer, Stuart Cornfeld. Directed by Alan Metter. Features entire cast. Screenplay, Amy Spies; camera (CFI color), Thomas Ackerman; supervising editor, David Rawlins; editor, Lorenzo DeStefano; production design, Jeffrey Staggs; art direction, Christopher Amy; set decoration, Greg Melton; original musical score, Thomas Newman; costume design, Betty Pecha Madden; sound (Dolby), Alvin Susumu Tokunow; choreography, Otis Sallid; associate producer, Robert F. Lyons; assistant directors, Daniel Schneider, Stan Zabka; casting, Geno Havens. Reviewed at the Westwood Triplex, L.A., April 1, 1985. (MPAA Rating: PG.) Running time: 87 MINS.
Janey Glenn . . . . Sarah Jessica Parker
Jeff Malene . . . . Lee Montgomery
J.P. Sands . . . . Morgan Woodward
Drew . . . . Jonathan Silverman
Lynne Stone . . . . Helen Hunt
Natalie Sands . . . . Holly Gagnier
Colonel Glenn . . . . Ed Lauter
Maggie Malene . . . . Shannen Doherty
Mr. Malene . . . . Biff Yeager
Zachary Glenn . . . . Ian Giatti
Mrs. Glenn . . . . Margaret Howell
Ira . . . . Terence McGovern
DTV Host . . . . Richard Blade

"Girls Just Want To Have Fun" is the latest teen epic in which the world revolves around winning a dance contest, ground covered in MGM/UA's recent flop "Heavenly Bodies." Its title could not be more commercial, which probably makes this a good spring release for New World, but pic is a virtual compendium of teeny bopper musical clichés, and a contrived, artificial one at that.

If hyped-up energy were all it took to put a film over, this would be a strong Oscar candidate; the characters here never walk anywhere, but literally run, bounce and jump throughout, even in the mid-

dle of dialog scenes. If the youth of America really has this much energy, it's too bad it can't be put to better use than cavorting on "Dance T.V.," the object of everyone's fascination here.

The gymnastic Sarah Jessica Parker plays a nice Catholic high school girl who must hide her secret passion for dancing from her General Patton of a father, Ed Lauter. Having qualified for the finals in a competition to become a new dancer on "D.T.V.," a highglitz hybrid of MTV and "American Bandstand," she skips classes to rehearse and must defy her father to appear in the finals.

Along the way, she falls in love with her partner, Lee Montgomery, and helps recruit some punks to disrupt the coming-out debutante ball of her arch rival, conniving rich princess Holly Gagnier.

Alleged Chicago setting is suggested via three or four establishing shots, while the rest has plainly been shot in L.A. With one exception, parents are once again cast as all-out bad guys, and the climactic Dance-Off looks like outtakes from the final production number of "Staying Alive."

Young cast is nothing if not spunky, and experienced music video director Alan Metter, in his feature debut, keeps things moving at the expected frantic pace. Music, however, is undistinguished at best, and perhaps Cyndi Lauper knew something when she, or her label, refused inquiries about using her recording of the title tune. Only a cover version is heard here, to lackluster effect. —*Cart.*

The Homefront
(DOCU-COLOR/B&W-16m)

Hollywood, April 6.

A Homefront Project production. Produced, directed, written by Steven Schechter. Coproducer, Mark Jonathan Harris. Executive producer, Jack Kaufman. Editor, Ron Brody; interview segments directed by Ben Shedd; associate producer, project historian, Franklin D. Mitchell. Reviewed at the American Film Institute (Filmex), L.A., March 4, 1985. (No MPAA Rating.) Running time: 89 MINS.
Narrator: Leslie Nielsen.

"The Homefront" is a solid, conventional, often illuminating look at how the domestic scene in America changed during World War II. Some of the territory covered by Steven Schechter's film is pretty familiar, but its insights into how much things changed for minorities in a very short time prove particularly valuable. A good entry for specialized theatrical venues in short runs, pic is a good bet for tv and nontheatrical outlets.

Women naturally play a large role in "The Homefront," and while some of the edge has by now

been taken off the subject thanks to some previous docus on the subject, it remains bracing to realize some 5,000,000 women entered the American work force during the first two years of the war alone.

A strong bittersweet taste is injected into the film through contempo interviews with numerous women who struggled to prove themselves on the job, ended up loving their work, but were then forced to return to the conventional roles of wife and mother once the men came home. As described here, it was women's lives that changed the most during the war, but it was also women who experienced the fewest longterm gains from the experience.

On the other hand, minorities, particularly blacks, were initially excluded from the callup of so many people into responsible jobs. But as the massive industrial buildup increased, social change became mandatory, and the film shows how many resistant whites were obliged, sometimes by government decree, to accept blacks in the workplace. Film holds that necessity provoked the greatest-ever strides in integration and that, unlike the situation with women, this was something that could not be reversed after the war.

Schechter also touches on such matters as the detention of Japanese Americans, the rise in juvenile delinquency, the sudden urbanization of the country and the upsetting of longstanding social patterns.

Director adroitly mixes archival footage, new interviews, photos, radio material and music of the era to sharply recreate a time not long gone, but one of which younger viewers might do well to be reminded. — *Cart.*

Station To Station
(U.S.-COLOR)

Telephone mystery is a wrong number.

Berlin, Feb. 22.

A Storm Blind Film Productions (Portland, Ore.) film. Produced and directed, written and edited by David Ling. Associate producers, Elinor Shanklin, Dan Adams; camera (color), Matthew Harrison; music, Wyatt Helin. Reviewed at Berlin Intl. Film Festival, Feb. 22, 1985. Running time: 90 MINS.
With: Padriac T.P. O'Caisidde, Marianne Doherty, Steve Boergadine, Paul Marcotte, Maria Errico.

"Station To Station" opens with credits during a bleak funeral, but without mourners, except for the elderly widower and the officiating priest. Returning to his tiny flat, the aged pensioner is troubled less by grief than by isolation. His tv set affords no consolation, so he pawns it for money with which to pay for the installation of a telephone.

A timid and retired electronics wizard, the widower is determined to assert himself somehow. He conceives a plan to wire up half the telephone booths of the city to his own number, in a gigantic communal partyline, motivated as a lonely person seeking human contact and as a prankster.

The great phone hoax succeeds, although this film does not. The party-line network is a novel gimmick for a film but remains undeveloped. When the old man finally is traced to his lair, one no longer cares. As the cops arrive, he has eluded them, presumably to strike again in another city.

Commercial prospects seem questionable. — *Hitch.*

Kartha Z Podrozy
(Postcard From A Journey)
(POLISH-COLOR)

Hollywood, April 6.
An Irzykowski Film Studio production. Executive producer, Jacek Szeligowski. Directed, written by Waldemar Dziki, suggested by the novel "Mr. Teodor Munstock" by Ladislav Fuks. Camera (color), Wit Dabal; art direction, Andrzej Przedworski; music, Zygmunt Konieczny; sound, Janusz Rosol, Piotr Domaradzki. Reviewed at the American Film Institute (Filmex), L.A., March 15, 1985. (No MPAA Rating.) Running time: **80 MINS.**
With: Wladyslaw Kowakski (Jacob Rosenberg), Rafal Wieczynski, Maja Komorowska, Halina Mikolajska, Janusz Michalowski, Jerzy Trela.

Although it represents an accomplished feature directorial debut by recent Lodz film school graduate Waldemar Dziki, "Postcard From A Journey" is one of those films that attempts to convey the reality of an excruciating experience by being a difficult experience itself. Painfully slow, measured and filled with long silences, Polish pic tells the horrifying story of a middle-aged Jew methodically preparing himself to be shipped off to a concentration camp. Very skillfully made, film has many qualities to be admired, but is far too grim and boring, in a conventional sense, to have commercial potential.

Lead character Jacob Rosenberg, who maintains center screen throughout, is a former industrial counselor who is forced, in the early days of the Nazi occupation, to work as a street cleaner. Entirely ill-equipped for this job, Rosenberg also knows that fate eventually holds something much worse in store for him, but he accepts his horrifying circumstances with an implacable calm.

A terrible, inescapable sense of doom looms over everything, but one of the bold strokes of the film is that the enemy is barely ever seen. Dziki effectively creates a hermetic, isolated world through which Rosenberg moves, with odd, seemingly arbitrary encounters contributing to a pervasive feeling of unreality and hopelessness.

What makes the picture strangely moving and memorable is Rosenberg's utter acceptance of his fate. Little by little, he systematically prepares for his unknown date with destiny, so that when the inevitable call to the railway yards finally comes, he is able to face it clear-eyed and, in a certain sense, satisfied with himself.

Despite the occasionally striking nightmarish images, bizarre music and overall technical accomplishment of the film, it is nevertheless not easy to sit through, and frequently proves aggravating. Dziki set a difficult, if not impossible, task for himself at the outset, and the outright tedium is not entirely compensated for by the artistry on display. —*Cart.*

Kraj Rata
(The End Of The War)
(YUGOSLAVIAN-COLOR)

Hollywood, April 5.
An Avala Film production. Directed by Dragan Kresoja. Screenplay, Gordan Mihic; camera (color), Predrag Popovic; music, Mladen and Predrag Vranjesevic; art direction, Vladislav Lasic. Reviewed at the American Film Institute (Filmex), L.A., March 6, 1985. (No MPAA Rating.) Running time: **93 MINS.**
With: Bata Zivojinovic (Bajo), Marko Ratic (Vukole), Gorica Popovic, Neda Arneric, Aleksandar Bercek.

A revenge melodrama set in the political context of World War II, "The End Of The War" was Yugoslavia's official entry for the best foreign-language film Oscar this year, and not a bad one at that. Well made and relatively engrossing despite its sordid subject matter, pic is a decent representative for festivals, but can't be said to possess b.o. potential for the domestic market.

Plot structure is identical to that of François Truffaut's "The Bride Wore Black." Flashbacks reveal that, in 1941, five local Fascists tortured and finally killed the young bride of a man named Bajo.

It's now 1944 and Bajo, along with his tough little son Vukole, is single-mindedly devoted to his search-and-destroy mission to murder each of the men responsible for the death of his wife.

Wartime conditions make the pair's journey all the more treacherous, as vigilant Nazis and their allies are ever present, and Bajo, who has only one arm, and his precocious son are highly conspicuous characters when they arrive in a new town.

Nevertheless, they succeed, over time, in exacting their revenge. Along the way, young Vukole befriends a club singer, the two receive the generosity of an outgoing race car driver, and they also witness the casual cruelty of the Fascists as they make their way across the war-torn landscape.

Tale never digs very deep, but director Dragan Kresoja and writer Gordan Mihic have structured it soundly and have created some strongly etched characters. Predrag Popovic's lensing is noteworthy. —*Cart.*

My Therapist
(COLOR)

A TPL Prods. presentation. Executive producer, Josef Shaftel. Produced by John Ward. Directed by Al Rossi. Stars Marilyn Chambers. Screenplay, Mel Goldberg; camera (video, color), Robert Dracup; editor, Estate Films Inc. and Tommy Monroe; music, Rob Walsh; sound, Nick Longhurst; associate director, Gardner Compton; second unit director, Robyn Reed; production design, James Riddle. Reviewed on VCL-Media Home Entertainment vidcassette, N.Y., March 28, 1985. (No MPAA Rating.) Running time: **82 MINS.**

Kelly	Marilyn Chambers
Mike	David Winn
Alex	Roger Newman
Rip Rider	Buck Flower
Doreen	Robbie Lee
Steve	Milt Kogan
Stella	Judith Jordan

"My Therapist" enters the domestic homevideo market after an unusual history: it was produced on videotape as a tv series titled "Love Ya, Florence Nightingale" for the Showtime pay-cable service in 1982-83, reedited to feature length and transferred to film for foreign theatrical release a year later, and is now back in tape format.

Though a few exterior transition shots were shot on film, pic's primarily hard-edged tape look resembles a daytime soap-opera. So does the plot, in which porn star Marilyn Chambers toplines as a sex surrogate, solving various guys' problems in episodic fashion.

Principal subplot has B-picture veteran Buck Flower cast as a recently impotent country music superstar whose melodramatic adventures include marrying a teenage groupie. He is finally saved (from drugs and dissipation) by Chambers, leading to his singing the original "Love Ya" title song to her on the radio at film's end.

Chambers' off-and-on romance with Mike (David Winn) is the other main thread, as pic reveals its condensed format. Other than failed comedy, its essential purpose is to display Chambers in frequent nude scenes, augmented by softcore sex simulation for her fans. Tame by homevideo standards, pic exemplifies the teasingly "adult" format typical of made for pay-cable programming. — *Lor.*

Les Amants Terribles
(The Terrible Lovers)
(FRENCH-COLOR)

Paris, April 1.
A Citevox release of a Films du Passage production. Produced by Paolo Branco. Written and directed by Danièle Dubroux. Camera (color), Richard Copans; editor, Martine Giordano; sound, Joaquim Pinto; music, Jorge Arriagada; art director, Ze Branco; production manager, Danièle Cini. Reviewed at the République cinema, Paris, March 29, 1985. Running time: **90 MINS.**
With: Stanko Molnar, Jean-Noël Picq, Danièle Dubroux, Manuela Gourary, Anna Achdian, Michele Placido, Silvana Fusacchia.

Latest local film critic to direct a theatrical feature is Danièle Dubroux, a Cahiers du Cinéma scribe, who has already made some shorts. She has solo writing credit on "Les Amants Terribles" and also plays one of the leads in this story of three estranged couples in Rome.

Dubroux is a Parisian in hot pursuit of her Slavic lover (Stanka Molnar). Another Frenchman (Jean-Noël Picq, a real-life psychotherapist who played in several of the late Jean Eustache's films) also disembarks, looking for his pleasure-seeking teen mistress; while another woman arrives to find her married Latin lover (Michele Placido).

All six end up in a small hotel in the center of Rome, where a series of crisscrossing romantic duelling takes place.

Dubroux' purpose is to juxtapose and contrast differing responses and attitudes to loving and being loved. Intellectually, the script is interesting and skillfully structured, but her lovers are not terribly intriguing in themselves, and the Roman setting does not alter a story that could just as easily be set in Paris. Dubroux' direction is conventional. — *Len.*

Cuore
(Heart)
(ITALIAN-COLOR)

Hollywood, April 6.
Radiotelevisione Italiana presentation of a RAI-2-Difilm-Antenne-2-RTSI production. Produced by Giancarlo di Fonzo. Directed by Luigi Comencini. Screenplay by Comencini, Suso Cecchi D'Amico, Christina Comencini, based on the novel by Edmondo De Amicis; camera (color), Luigi Kuveiller; editor, Sergio Buzi; music, Manuel De Sica; set design, Gianni Sbarra; costume design, Paola Comencini. Reviewed at the American Film Institue (Filmex), L.A., March 20, 1985. (No MPAA Rating.) Running time: **120 MINS.**

The teacher, Mr. Perboni	Johnny Dorelli
Mr. Bottini	Bernard Blier
Miss Penna Rossa	Giuliana De Sio
Enrico Bottini (grown up)	Laurent Malet
The old schoolmaster	Eduardo De Filippo
Franti's Mother	Valeria D'Obici
P.E. Master	Ugo Pagliai
Mrs. Bottini	Andrea Ferreol

Version of "Cuore" being shown internationally represents a two-hour condensation of the original six-hour miniseries produced for Italian television. Present edition has unsatisfying rhythm and shape and doesn't really measure up as a feature film. Commercial chances are slim.

Adapted from a perennially popular Italian novel, saga tells of the last generation of children to grow up prior to World War I. In the army, Bottini (Laurent Malet) runs into three old school chums, and the group remembers back to their idealized childhoods, when life seemed much simpler.

Hanging over everything is the grand theme of how the old society raised its youth to become fine young men, only to send them out to be slaughtered on the battlefield. Coupled with this, however, is the nostalgia the fellows feel for their earlier years and, unfortunately, vet director and cowriter Luigi Comencini has allowed his film to slip over into overly sweet sentimentality.

Long childhood flashbacks, which constitute the vast majority of the picture, are filled with largely familiar anecdotes concerning school, parental problems, relations among the boys and teacher-student interaction. While the last gasp of 19th-century attitudes is caught nicely, there is no harshness or irony here to offset the soft, rose-colored view of life offered up.

Unlike numerous European classics of childhood, which stressed the authoritarian nature of schools, virtually all the teachers here are kindly souls with ready smiles and an endless supply of encouragement. Kids of difficult parents earnestly toil against their handicaps, and almost everyone, no matter what his station, is blessed with such benign natures and noble intentions that one might imagine paradise on earth had at last been found.

It remains possible that some complexities and balance might have been lost in the elimination of four hours from the total work, but nothing in the unvarying tone of the flashbacks encourages this feeling. Thesps are all likeable, and the late Eduardo De Filippo is on view here in one of his last appearances.
— *Cart.*

1918
(COLOR)

Stagy drama of small Texas town during World War I.

A Cinecom Intl. Films release. Produced by Lillian Foote and Ross Milloy. Directed by Ken Harrison. Features entire cast. Executive producers, Lewis Allen and Peter Newman. Coproducer, Walker Stuart. Screenplay by Horton Foote, based on his play. Associate producer, Jim Crosby; production manager-assistant director, Dennis Bishop; camera (Duart color), George Tirl; art director, Michael O'Sullivan; set dresser, Becky Block; sound, John Pritchett; costume designer, Van Ramsey; editor, Leon Seith; WW I songs sung by Willie Nelson and Robert Duvall. Reviewed at Magno Preview 9 screening room, N.Y. April 10, 1985. (No MPAA Rating). Running time: **91 MINS.**
Horace Robedaux . . . . . William Converse-Roberts
Elizabeth Robedaux . . . . Hallie Foote
Mrs. Vaughn . . . . Rochelle Oliver
Brother . . . . Matthew Broderick
Bessie . . . . Jeannie McCarthy
Sam . . . . Bill McGhee
Mr. Thatcher . . . . L.T. Felty
Jessie . . . . Horton Foote Jr.
Stanley . . . . Tom Murrel
Bill . . . . Phillip Smith
Also with: Norma Allen, Margaret Spaulding, Carol Goodheart, Buffy Carrol, Betty Murphy, Frost O. Myers, Peggy Feury, Belinda Jackson, Randy Moore, Janice Woodson, Gil Glasco, Nick Jordon, Jerry Biggs, Cynthia Rogers, Anna Harrison, Lisa Howard, Nancy Harrison and Allan Alexander.

Horton Foote's screen adaptation of his play about Texas smalltown life during the last year of World War I is hobbled by stagy direction by Ken Harrison and a script that depends too much for dramatic momentum on the portentous element of a deadly influenza epidemic. Although "1918" effectively evokes the languid innocence of a lost America, the film's charming small ironies, painterly cinematography and respectable ensemble performances are smothered by an unrelieved melancholy that often drifts into bathos. Armadillo-like pacing and (with the exception of Matthew Broderick) lack of familiar names will make the pic a tough sell, and prospects for extended art house runs are not good.

While American soldiers are dying in the trenches of Europe, the virulent flu of 1918 is ravaging the somnolent town of Harrison, Texas. Small town gossip, the pic's chief expositional device, tells us people are dropping like flies. Those who haven't got the killer bug are frightened of catching it, and the town is also burdened by news of dead and wounded loved ones in the great patriotic cause "over there." Everyone's depressed, including handsome town dry cleaner Horace Robedaux (William Converse-Roberts), who assuages his guilt over remaining a civilian to care for his wife, Elizabeth (Hallie Foote), and baby daughter by investing heavily in war bonds.

Horace is also emotionally crippled, it seems, for having "married rich" into the proud Vaughn family, ruled by a well-meaning but obtuse and unbending patriarch (Michael Higgins) whose irrepressible youngest son, Brother (Matthew Broderick) is more interested in gambling, wenching, picture shows and going off to war than living up to his father's Fundamentalist work ethic. Apparently guilty over transcending his poor-boy roots, Horace is obsessed with erecting a tombstone over his father's unmarked and unidentified grave. This preoccupation is in keeping with the pic's morbid tone, but is too tiresome and symbolically evident for the significance Foote invests in it.

So fraught with foreboding are the days and lives of these fondly rendered provincials that the advent of tragedy is predictable and the ensuing flood of unleashed repressed emotions discomfiting rather than affecting. Elizabeth (shot too frequently in unflattering closeups) is in a perpetual funk, perhaps because she's still sorting out grudges with Mother Vaughn (Rochelle Oliver) over the family's prior opposition to her marriage. Only bright spot in the emotional dustbowl is the cocky, foolishly romantic Brother, who's blessed with a happy-go-lucky immunity to the consequences of his own actions.

Foote's closeness to his source material (story is based on family annals) is evident in the script's sentimentality. Potentially engrossing elements such as class and race relations are brushed over or encapsulated in clichés, and the depicted insularity of the townspeople is more an automatic function of the story's narrow focus than an outgrowth of character and dialog. The concluding promise of rebirth and renewal is telegraphed so far in advance that its consummation brings relief rather than rejoicing. — *Rich.*

Siete En La Mira
(Seven In The Viewfinder)
(MEXICAN-COLOR)

Mexico City, March 22.

A Películas Mexicanas-Películas Nacionales release of a Miura Pro production. Produced by Jesús A. Galindo. Directed by Pedro Galindo 3d. Screenplay Beatriz de Anda, based on a story by Gilberto de Anda, adapted by Pedro Galindo 3d and Carlos Valdermar; camera (color), Luis Medina; editor, Carlos Savage; music, Nacho Méndez; stunt man, Luis López; special effects, Jorge Farfan; makeup, Aurora Chavira. Reviewed at Cinema Insurgentes 70, Mexico City, March 21, 1985. Running time: **99 MINS.**
Sheriff Ventura . . . . Mario Almada
Marcos . . . . Fernando Almada
Vikingo . . . . Jorge Reynoso
Falco . . . . Eleazar García Jr.
Anibal . . . . Adalberto Arvizu
Yunke . . . . Javier García
Mazda . . . . Diana Gay
Adam . . . . Fernando Sainz
Pedrito . . . . Melchor Morán
Gitano . . . . Ernesto Rendón
Milo . . . . Luis López
Cherokee . . . . Julio Lerma

Also with: Rubén Benavidez, Fernando Benavidez, Leo Villanueva, Leonardo Noreiga, Nina Kovars, Baltaza Guzmán, Víctor Alanis, Maximo Escalante, Daniel Robles, Pedro González, Lili Soto.

"Seven In The Viewfinder" is another Galindo family production featuring violence and action along the U.S.-Mexican border region, using the Almada brothers to right wrongs and save the day.

Shot on location in Brownsville, Texas, a small hamlet is plagued by the visit of a motorcycle gang of eight "punks," led by Vikingo (Jorge Reynoso).

Though the sheriff (Mario Almada) has the right idea ("Leave them alone and they'll go away"), one of the town deputies, played by Javier García, takes it upon himself to execute one of the gang and frame a "nice guy" gas station attendant for the murder.

All hell breaks loose. The gang captures a school and poolhall, holding innocent townsfolk hostage while the Almadas hold the vigilantes at bay.

When patrolman Marco's young son Pedrito (Melchor Morán) is shot in the back escaping from the school, the final showdown begins with all the principal characters dead except Vikingo and Sheriff Ventura, who duel it out to the bloody death.

Though unnecessarily violent and graphic, low-budget pic should make money, evident at a packed house where the film was screened, accompanied by cheering at the prolonged deaths of the villains.

The corny facial makeup, blue punk hairstyles and heavy metal-style leather outfits of the bike gang are strictly for laughs, and Nacho Méndez' electronic score sounds like a bad imitation of Gary Numan, sans lyrics. — *Lent.*

Sylvia
(NEW ZEALAND-COLOR)

An MGM/UA Classics release of a Southern Light Pictures and Cinepro production. Produced by Don Reynolds and Michael Firth. Directed by Firth. Screenplay, Michele Quill, F. Fairfax and Firth; based on books by Sylvia Aston-Warner ("Teacher" & "I Passed This Way"); camera (color), Ian Paul; editor, Michael Horton; costume designer, Anne McKay; set designer, Gary Hansen; original score, Leonard Rosenman; production manager, Jane Gilbert; location manager, Chris Paulger; assistant director, Deuel Drodgan; camera operator, Peter Day; sound, Graham Morris; wardrobe, Joan Pearce; makeup, Deryck de Niese. Reviewed at MGM/UA screening room, (New Directors/New Films), N.Y., April 9, 1985. (No MPAA Rating.) Running time: **98 MINS.**
Sylvia Henderson (Ashton-Warner) . . . . Eleanor David
Aden Morris . . . . Nigel Terry
Keith Henderson . . . . Tom Wilkinson
Opal Saunders . . . . Mary Regan
Inspector Gulland . . . . . Martyn Sanderson
Inspector Bletcher . . . . Terence Cooper
Inspector Scragg . . . . David Letch
Vivian Wallop . . . . Sarah Peirse
Also with (in Sylvia's class): Joseph George, Eileen Glover, Graham Glover, Tessa

Wells, Jonathan Porteous, Cherie Nepia, Robert Nepia, Erica Edwards-Brown, Paul King, Frank Nathan, Awhina Soloman, Kristofer Hauraki, and Aaron Pako.

Adapted from the life and works of Sylvia Ashton-Warner, "Sylvia" respectfully dramatizes the pioneering educator's early adult years with a stately pace, a somber tone and introspective leading characters aimed strictly toward the art crowd interested in teaching and/or feminism. The recent New Directors/New Films series was an apt launching pad for this biopic, Auckland helmer Michael Firth's third film.

Set in the 1930s, pic begins with Sylvia's arrival in a remote poverty-stricken village. The wife of a headmaster, she teaches — or tries to teach — predominantly Maori native children. Opening sequences convey Sylvia's growing emotional crises brought about by isolation, culture shock, and the aftermath of a nervous breakdown (quoted briefly in flashbacks).

Frustrated by her young pupils, Sylvia takes refuge in her piano-playing, drawing and sculpting. Gradually, she adapts these disciplines to her teaching methods and the seemingly uneducable Maori moppets respond. Ignoring her successes, the school system chiefs frown upon her innovation, thus beginning the battle of wits and will between the imperious lady teacher and the rulebook-bound male administrators.

In "Sylvia," there are precious few moments of victory that the real Sylvia achieved in her lifetime. The bureaucrats "accidentally" burn her manuscript for a new kind of primer. The pic ends with Sylvia and her family leaving the village after her husband's transfer by those who wanted the pupils to be taught by the book once again.

The acting is pro throughout. Eleanor David ("Comfort And Joy," "Pink Floyd — The Wall") is appealing in a title role performance that is more subtle than bravura. Nigel Terry (of "Excalibur") plays the school inspector who sees value in Sylvia's work, but turns out to be of no help to her career. Despite the hint of an affair with the inspector, Sylvia remains faithful to her husband (Tom Wilkenson). Mary Regan, the only New Zealand actress among the topcast British players, is good as the school nurse who befriends Sylvia.

Firth fares less well in turning his pet project of many years into something special. Unlike "My Brilliant Career," "Sylvia" lacks the original strokes and the emotional sparks that would enliven the worthwhile but characteristically mundane subject matter. For example, the clashes between Sylvia and her stuffed-shirt superiors are handled routinely.

The real Sylvia, who died at age 76 last year just as her authorized biopic started rolling, is seen in black and white docu footage run under the opening credits. In an interview about 10 years ago, the spry, resilient lady recalls her earlier life as a "wifey" and, in a bit of a boast, says she represents all smart women.

It was fitting, then, that Sylvia's husband asks her in the film after one of his wife's monologs, "Do you think you're the only one with an original thought?" One aspect the film shows is that Sylvia Ashton-Warner may have been a difficult person to live with.

— Binn.

---

9 Deaths Of The Ninja
(COLOR)

Ridiculous actioner, for quick playoff.

A Crown International Pictures release of an Amritraj Prods. presentation of an American Leisure & Entertainment Co. production. Produced by Ashok Amritraj. Executive producers, Vijay Amritraj, Robert L. Friedman, Sidney Balkin; executives in charge of production, Robert Waters, Victor Ordoñez. Written and directed by Emmett Alston. Stars Sho Kosugi. Camera (United, Colorfilm & Nat. Media color; prints by Deluxe), Roy H. Wagner; editors, Alston, Waters, Ordonez; music, Cecile Colayco; sound, John Kovarek; production design, Rodell Cruz; fights choreographer, Sho Kosugi; assistant director, Jun Amazan; production manager, Aurelio Navarro; casting, Maria Metcalfe. Reviewed at UA Twin 1 theater, N.Y., April 13, 1985. (MPAA Rating: R.) Running time: 94 MINS.
Spike Shinobi .... Sho Kosugi
Steve Gordon .... Brent Huff
Jennifer Barnes .... Emilia Lesniak
Alby the Cruel .... Blackie Dammett
Honey Hump .... Regina Richardson
Rankin .... Vijay Amritraj
Also with: Lisa Friedman, Kane Kosugi, Shane Kosugi, Bruce Fanger, Sonny Erang, David Brass, Aiko Cownden, Jennifer Crumrine, Judy Blye.

"9 Deaths Of The Ninja," originally titled "Deadly Warriors," is a relentlessly silly martial arts picture that lampoons the genre rather than providing straight ahead action. Most customers will not be amused.

Villains Alby the Cruel (Blackie Dammett) and Honey Hump (Regina Richardson) kidnap a busload of tourists in Manila, demanding the release of a terrorist from the Middle East named Rahji (Sonny Erang). At the U.S. Embassy there, Rankin (Vijay Amritraj) calls for U.S. aid, with a three-person rescue squad sent in, made up of Japanese specialist Spike Shinobi (Sho Kosugi), macho Steve Gordon (Brent Huff) and a lovely blond Jennifer Barnes (Emilia Lesniak).

Martial arts activity and frequent shootouts are tediously interrupted by failed comedy as villains Dammett and Richardson camp it up outrageously, styled respectively as a Dr. Strangelove-type German megalomaniac and a lesbian sadist. Among the good guys, Kosugi, who previously scored in "Revenge Of The Ninja" and on tv's shortlived "The Master" series, tries lamely for laughs, sucking on a lollipop between fights. Brent Huff is once again (as in the French-made "The Perils Of Gwendoline") a handsome but bland sidekick, while Emilia Lesniak never deigns to muss up her hair or makeup in a supposedly action role. Kosugi's two kids Kane and Shane are also featured, with Kane strutting his chopsocky skills well.

Writer-director Emmett Alston, who previously served as second unit director on earlier Kosugi pics, wastes good production values with his meandering script. Tennis star Vijay Amritraj, who served as exec producer, pops up occasionally to make in-jokes, such as using a telephone shaped like tennis balls.

— Lor.

Cat's Eye
(COLOR)

Ineffectual three-parter from Stephen King.

Hollywood, April 11.
An MGM/UA Entertaiment release of a Dino De Laurentiis presentation. Produced by Martha J. Schumacher; coproducer, Milton Subotsky. Directed by Lewis Teague. Features entire cast. Screenplay, Stephen King; camera (Technicolor, J-D-C Widescreen), Jack Cardiff; editor, Scott Conrad; sound (Dolby), Donald Summer; production design, Giorgio Postiglione; creatures, Carlo Rambaldi; assistant director, Kuki Lopez Rodero; models, Emilio Ruiz; art direction, Jeoffrey Ginn; set design, E.C. Chen; casting, Howard Feuer, Jeremy Ritzer; music, Alan Silvestri; second unit director-stunt coordinator, Glenn Randall Jr.; special visual effects, Barry Nolan. Reviewed at MGM Studios, Culver City, April 10, 1985. (MPAA Rating: PG-13). Running time: 93 MINS.
Girl .... Drew Barrymore
Morrison .... James Woods
Donatti .... Alan King
Cressner .... Kenneth McMillan
Norris .... Robert Hays
Sally Ann .... Candy Clark
Hugh .... James Naughton
Junk .... Tony Munafo
Cindy .... Mary D'Arcy

"Cat's Eye" creeps in on foggy feet, another puzzler as to why Stephen King projects don't pay off on the screen like they do on the printed page.

Though the previous six films from his books have averaged a moderate success, none has ever been as frightening as his truly terrifying tomes. Unfortunately, the fact that King wrote a portion of "Eye" originally for the screen does not help much.

The idea for this film was hatched during Dino De Laurentiis' production of King's "Firestarter," which also starred little Drew Barrymore. Asked to do another script for Barrymore, King sketched out an idea about a cat who protects a young girl from a threatening troll in her bedroom wall.

Unfortunately, that idea got tacked onto two other King short stories that De Laurentiis had film rights to, "Quitters, Inc." and "The Ledge," lighting the fuse for the ultimate bomb.

The three stories just don't connect and efforts to join them never work. However, an excellent roster of talent does try its best.

At first, the cat is in New York city working unwillingly for Alan King, who runs a rather harsh facility to help people like James Woods stop smoking. Throwing the cat into an electrified room, King explains that the same will happen to Woods' wife, Mary D'Arcy the next time Woods has a cigarette and the techniques will get proceedingly more serious. The jolt isn't fatal to the feline or the female and the whole story is sort of amusing, but hardly scary. Most importantly, the cat doesn't have much to do with it.

Moving onto the next story in Atlantic City, Kenneth McMillan is a wealthy betting-man whose wife has been cheating on him with Robert Hays. After a quick series of events, the cat is wandering around McMillan's penthouse and Hays is outside on a narrow ledge trying to complete a walk around the building that will net him McMillan's wife and money.

Again, the second story is mildly gripping and sometimes funny, but the cat has little to do with it.

Finally, the cat makes it to Barrymore's bedroom in Wilmington, N.C., to take on the troll with no help and some complication provided by unknowing mom and dad, Candy Clark and James Naughton. This part is more frightening and still often amusing, but not enough of either.

This time, at least, the cat has a lot to do with it, but it doesn't help that much. —Har.

Relatives
(AUSTRALIAN-COLOR)

Sydney, April 19.

An Archer Films production. Produced by Basil Appleby, Henri Safran. Directed by Anthony Bowman. Features entire cast. Screenplay, Bowman; camera (color), Tom Cowan; music, Norman Kaye; editor, Colin Greive; sound, Bob Clayton; production design, Darrell Lass; art director, Louella Hatfield; costumes, Ann Benjamin. Reviewed at Film Australia screening room, April 18, 1985. Running time: **89 MINS.**

Grandfather . . . . Bill Kerr
Nancy Peterson . . . . Rowena Wallace
Joan Hedges . . . . Carol Raye
Geoffrey . . . . Ray Barrett
Uncle Edward . . . . Norman Kaye
Clare . . . . Alyson Best
Catherine Taylor . . . . Jeannie Drynan
Peter Peterson . . . . Michael Aitkens
Alfred Hedges . . . . Robin Bowering
Ross . . . . Brett Climo
Herb Taylor . . . . Ray Meagher
Alex . . . . Marian Dworakowski

"Relatives" is a modest, but frequently enjoyable, item about a family that gathers, somewhat reluctantly, to celebrate the 80th birthday of its patriarch. First-time director Anthony Bowman handles a large cast professionally, and shows promise for the future, though his script has inconsistencies and flat patches and could have benefited from a little fine tuning.

Grandfather, a magnificently crusty performance from Bill Kerr, is picked up from a home for the aged where he lives and taken to the spacious country home his family built last century. One of his sons, Geoffrey (Ray Barrett) has been running the farm, but, as in the U.S., these are hard times for farmers and the banks are foreclosing; Geoffrey has decided to sell out and quit. The rest of the family consists of an effeminate but cheerfully tipsy priest (Norman Kaye); a nagging wife (Carol Raye) and her quietly defiant husband (Robin Bowering); the latter's secret mistress (Jeannie Drynan) and her oafish spouse (Ray Meagher); a bored couple (Rowena Wallace, Michael Aitkens) and their snotty children; and Geoffrey's independent daughter (Alyson Best), her Czech boyfriend (Marian Dworakowski) and punk brother (Brett Climo).

Most of these characters loathe each other, and poor grandfather has to suffer a good deal of bickering as the day wears on. Apart from Kerr there are standout performances from Alyson Best, Norman Kaye (both these two were seen in Paul Cox' "Man Of Flowers"), Carol Raye, Michael Aitkens and Brett Climo.

An overly graphic hayloft sex scene between Best and Dworakowski seems out of place in this otherwise G-level fare, but generally this is a frequently amusing, if familiar, comedy-drama which looks as if it should play better on tv than in theatrical bookings. A pleasant plus is the gentle piano score, composed and performed by Norman Kaye (a musician before he was an actor).
—*Strat.*

Mr. Wrong
(NEW ZEALAND-COLOR)

Wellington, N.Z., April 1.

A Preston/Laing production. Produced by Gaylene Preston and Robin Laing. Directed by Preston. Screenplay, Gaylene Preston, Geoff Murphy and Graeme Tetley; camera (color), Thom Burstyn; editor, Simon Reece; music, Jonathan Crayford; sound, Ken Saville, Reviewed at National Film Unit preview theater, Wellington, March 31, 1985. Running time: **88 MINS.**

Meg . . . . Heather Bolton
Mr. Wrong . . . . David Letch
Samantha . . . . Margaret Umbers
Val . . . . Suzanne Lee
Bruce . . . . Gary Stalker
Wayne . . . . Danny Mulheron

Gaylene Preston's first feature, "Mr. Wrong," is a low-budget, gently whimsical thriller that stirs tongue-in-cheek memories of a '50s Doris Day under threat.

The difference is there is no handsome matinee idol into whose arms the heroine can fall at fadeout. The best help she has on hand is a young man with whom she went to school.

Based on a short story by Elizabeth Jane Howard, and with a screenplay for which Preston takes main credit, "Mr. Wrong" is about girl-next-door Meg (Heather Bolton), who unwittingly buys a used Jaguar car that is haunted. A previous owner, also a young woman, was murdered. Is Meg to be the next victim?

Inventiveness and an eye for sly comic detail mark the unraveling of events.

Not everything works. At times Preston seems more interested in the whimsy than the thrills, but, in large part, she gets away with it.

One of the reasons she does is the central performance of Bolton as Meg. Working against most conventions as a rather dumpy, Everyman's sister, Bolton injects the role with a fetching resourcefulness and resilience that is fresh and never mawkish.

David Letch is suitably sinister as the mysterious Mr. Wrong, with Danny Mulheron quirkily but not repellently wimpish as Wayne.

Elsewhere, Margaret Umbers, Gary Stalker and Philip Gordon impact in cameo roles.

Visual quality of the film, shot in 16m color for 35m blowup, has its grainy moments and the low budget shows in the effects department.
—*Nic.*

Deadly Intruder
(COLOR)

Unthrilling psycho thriller.

A Channel One production. Executive producer-postproduction supervisor, John Walton. Produced by Bruce Cook. Directed by John McCauley. Features entire cast. Screenplay-coproducer, Tony Crupi; camera (color), Thomas Jewett; editor, Cook; music, McCauley; sound, David Brownlow, John Huck; assistant director, Suzanne Benoit; production manager, Albert Barosso; art direction, Lois Shelton; special effects, Roger Kelton; stunt coordinators, Danny Bonaduce, Curt Bryant. Reviewed on Thorn EMI vidcassette, N.Y., March 12, 1985. (No MPAA Rating.) Running time: **84 MINS.**

Bob . . . . Chris Holder
Jessie . . . . Molly Cheek
Drifter . . . . Tony Crupi
Capt. Pritchett . . . . Stuart Whitman
John . . . . Danny Bonaduce
Amy . . . . Laura Melton
Carlos . . . . Santos Morales

Deadly dull sums up "Deadly Intruder," an underdeveloped horror picture made last year and too weak for theatrical use, going directly into the homevideo market.

Stale premise and predictable twist concern a psycho, escaped from an institution, on the rampage in a small town while a local cop (Stuart Whitman, in for a couple of scenes wearing a beard) and his men haplessly try to catch him. A drifter (played by screenwriter and coproducer Tony Crupi) kidnaps the heroine (Molly Cheek), and is mistaken for the real psycho, leading to the usual open ending.

Relying on the stalker formula, pic repeatedly sets up situations of gore and mayhem yet tastefully avoids showing the carnage on screen. However, homevideo fans will appreciate the inclusion of several nude scenes, including one of the main heroine which is photographed (head always out of frame) as if a body double were being utilized.

John McCauley's direction is mediocre, offering little style and relying upon a self-penned musical score heavily indebted to the repetitive keyboard figures favored by the Italian rock group Goblin and America's John Carpenter. — *Lor.*

Emoh Ruo
(AUSTRALIAN-COLOR)

Sydney, April 19.

A Greater Union (Australia) release of a U.A.A. Films presentation of a Palm Beach Picture. Produced by David Elfick. Executive producers, David Thomas, John Picton-Warlow. Directed by Denny Lawrence. Stars Joy Smithers, Martin Sacks. Screenplay, David Poltorak, Paul Leadon; camera (color), Andrew Lesnie; editor, Ted Otton; music, Cameron Allen; sound, Paul Brincat; art director, Robert Dein; costumes, Anthony Jones. Reviewed at Greater Union screening room, Sydney, April 16, 1985. Running time: **93 MINS.**

Terri Tunkley . . . . Joy Smithers
Des Tunkley . . . . Martin Sacks
Les Tunkley . . . . Philip Quast
Margaret York . . . . Genevieve Mooy
Helen Tunkley . . . . Louise Le Nay
Samson Tregardo . . . . Max Phipps
Jack Tunkley . . . . Jack Ellis
Wally Wombat . . . . Bill Young
Pat Harrison . . . . Helen McDonald
Warren Harrison . . . . Mervyn Drake
Thommo . . . . Ric Carter
Pete . . . . Noel Hodder

Producer David Elfick has adroitly packaged "Emoh Ruo" as a kind of "Mr. Blandings Builds His Dream House" for the '80s, at the same time giving a big opportunity to various first-timers, including director Denny Lawrence, writers David Poltorak and Paul Leadon and cinematographer Andrew Lesnie; all acquit themselves well.

Story involves a handsome young couple with a bright little son who live in cramped conditions in a caravan beside a spectacular surf beach. Although they both work, Des as a bus driver and Terri as a house cleaner, they can't afford to buy their own home (houses in Sydney are notoriously expensive) until the frustrated Terri decides to take a risk with a heavily advertised finance company. Before long the Tunkleys have their home, but it's miles away from the city in the far distant suburbs, and furthermore it's one of those cheaply built places where everything goes wrong. Des has to get up at 4 a.m. in order to get to work on time, young Jack has no one to play with and their only neighbors are nosy bigots. When Des loses his driving license after being booked for drunken driving, things go rapidly downhill.

There are bright comedy ideas aplenty here, but below the surface there's also an all-too-familiar everyday tragedy of a couple financially out of its depth. Much of this is played for broad humor, sometimes a little too broad, but it should have local audiences chuckling happily, and find offshore audiences too in countries where the trials of owning your first home are equally overwhelming.

The lasting impact of "Emoh Ruo" may well be in its introduction of fresh new actors. Phlip Quast is very funny as Des' go-getting brother, a tire salesman ("Rubber talks!") always on the make, and Martin Sacks makes Des a likeably human character. Also worth noting is young Jack Ellis (son of writers Bob Ellis and Anne Brooksbank), a natural child actor. Joy Smithers combined looks and charisma with deft comic timing, and she positively shines out of the screen.

As for that title, it's supposed to be Australian for "Our Home," with the letters spelt backwards. It seems a bit gimmicky and although it might just catch on, a change could be considered.

Overall, "Emoh Ruo" might just be the success the Australian film industry is looking for right now.
—*Strat.*

Pandit Nehru
(INDIAN-DOCU-COLOR/B&W)

San Francisco, April 15.
A National Film Development Corp. (of Bombay) release. Directed by Shyam Benegal and Yuri Aldokhin. Screenplay, Benegal, Aldokhin, Vladimir Zimianin and Aleksander Gorev. No other credits available. Reviewed at the Kokusai theater, San Francisco, April 14, 1985. Running time: **165 MINS.**
With English narration by Saeed Jaffrey.

This Indian-Soviet coproduction was apprently a three-part teledocu in genesis. It's informative and particularly poignant whenever footage catches Nehru's daughter Indira Gandhi, who spent much of her early adulthood as his companion. Devotees of the "Gandhi" theatrical feature should relish this newsreel look at the Mahatma.

Docu's main problem is in its point of view: Nehru's story is told first person, via intelligent, but obviously subjective narration. Recounting also gets bogged down in persistent peaks and valleys of the Gandhi-Nehru campaign for independence.

Still, directors have wisely injected passages of events elsewhere in the world to put into perspective the nati-colonialism politics of the Indian leaders. A half-century of history is implicit in these 165 minutes; it's a world political tour which should interest anyone who has affection for the linkage of events and the reshaping of maps.
—*Herb.*

Han Ye
(Chilly Nights)
(CHINESE-COLOR)

San Francisco, April 16.
A World Entertainment release of a Peking Studio production. Directed by Que Wen. Screenplay Wen, Lin Gongtong; camera (color), Luo Dan; art direction, Yao Bin, Ma Gai Jai; music, Lu Quiming. Reviewed at the Kokusai theater, San Francisco, April 14, 1985. Running time: **103 MINS.**
With: Xu Huan, Pan Hong, Lin Moyu.

This melodrama suffers from crude subtitling, flat direction and cutting, and slowpoke pacing. Its strength comes from set-art recreation of 1944-45 wartime Chunking and its interesting advocacy of feminism.

Three of the other pics shown at the San Francisco Film Festival this year could arguably, be dubbed "feminist:" this one, the opener "Camila" and another Chinese entry, "Qui Jin."

"Chilly Nights" offers up a wife who has a better job than her husband and who abhors having to live with her bothersome mother-in-law.

Yet she obviously cares deeply for her austere, terminally ill (tuberculosis perhaps) husband and endlessly ponders deserting him for a better life. There's a child who appears in only one early scene.

The yarn is adapted from a novel by Ba Jin, described as China's foremost living writer, and has a soap opera quality about it. Lin Moyu, as the mother-in-law, gives the most animated performance.

The lensing is murky, apparently in a deliberate attempt to evoke the gloom of the war and the pall it cast over these lives. — *Herb.*

Going To Cannes

Tokyo-Ga
(GERMAN/U.S.-DOCU-COLOR/B&W-16m)

A coproduction of Wim Wenders Produktion, Gary City Inc., Chris Sievernich Produktion and Westdeutscher Rundfunk. Produced by Chris Sievernich. Written and directed by Wim Wenders. Camera (color, 16m), Ed Lachman; editing, Jon Neuburger, Wim Wenders, Solveig Dommartin; mixing, Hartmut Eichgruen; music, Loorie Petitgand, Meche Mamecier, Chico Rojo Ortega; production assistants, Lilyan Sievernich, Ulla Zwicker. Reviewed at Lorimar screening room, N.Y., April 16, 1985. (No MPAA Rating). Running time; **92 MINS.**
With: Chishu Ryu, Yuharu Atsuta, Werner Herzog.

In this ruminative "filmed diary," Wim Wenders set about to reconcile his longstanding reverence for Japanese director Yasujiro Ozu, who died in 1963, with his burning curiosity about the nature of contemporary Tokyo. In Japanese the particle "ga" indicates a word is the subject of a sentence, but Wenders brings to Tokyo a philosophical conundrum posed by the "pure images" of Ozu's films: How does one bridge the gap between the perceived images of real life and those of cinematic reality?

The result is a haunting jigsaw of surreal travelog fragments, interviews with Ozu's associates and clips from his "Tokyo Story," and Wenders' reflective narrative monolog which mixes bits of self-indulgent bombast with flashes of perceptive insight. Pic will appeal mainly to the select audience that supported the recent Wenders nonfiction mini-films, "Room 666" and "Reverse Angle."

Wenders says Tokyo exists "like a dream" in his recollections, and "Tokyo-ga" invests the city's quotidian aspects with a hallucinatory air. Rather than try to capture whole the sprawling capital's overwhelming kinetic energy, Wenders' camera dwells with static penetration on slices of representative reality: picnics and baseball in a cemetery, the self-induced hypnosis of "Pachinko" pinball players, elevated trains (a central image in Ozu's pics) in the Ginza, a neon-lit alleyway in Shinjuku, subway commuters and rooftop golf driving ranges.

When Wenders reflects that the Pachinko players represent the existential consignment of the modern Japanese to loneliness in the crowd, or when he notes the driving range golfers have abandoned the game's ball-in-hole objective for the pursuit of pure form, he's illuminating essential facets of Japanese life. In other instances his grasp of the culture is less secure. An uncooperative child is not really "rebellious," but rather typical of the well-documented Japanese propensity to indulge their infants' whims. The teenage rock 'n' roll dancers in the park may appear to be copying Americana, but their group rituals and meticulous attention to details of fashion are distinctly Japanese.

Nevertheless, Wenders displays keen selectivity in an amusing investigation of one of Tokyo's ubiquitous phenomena, the wax food mockups that appear in display cases outside thousands of restaurants. His visit to a workshop where real food is transmuted into wax sushi, wax tempura, wax ham & cheese sandwiches and even wax cocktails works delightfully as tongue-in-cheek documentary while underscoring the pic's esoteric preoccupation with the issue of appearance and reality.

As he expects, Wenders' search for the ordered simplicity and universal truths he found in Ozu's cinematic Tokyo is thwarted in the frenetic jumble of the modern megapolis. However, the filmmaker is duly "impressed" by the city's vitality in spite of the sensory overkill brought on by its impersonal, bustling crowds, concrete & neon landscape and the profusion of Western-inspired junk images flickering on televisions so omnipresent they're even found in taxicabs. (Atop the Eiffel-like Tokyo Tower, Wenders permits his colleague Werner Herzog to sound off briefly on the despairing shortage of pure images in an impure modern world.)

To evoke the spirit of a vanished Japan, Wenders turns to veteran actor Chishu Ryu and Ozu's longtime cameraman Yuharu Atsuta, who provide fascinating accounts of their working relationships with the director. Beyond illuminating Ozu's technical and aesthetic doctrine, the aging film veterans movingly reveal an ethic of loyalty and ego-submission incomprehensible to Western individualists but fundamental to creating the "sacred" images that mesmerized Wenders since childhood. —*Rich.*

Ad Soff Halayla
(When Night Falls)
(ISRAELI-COLOR)

Tel Aviv, April 15.
A Tom Production of an Eitan Green-Micha Sharfstein film. Stars Assaf Dayan, Yoseph Millo and Orna Porath. Produced by Micha Sharfstein. Written and directed by Eitan Green. Camera (color), Amnon Salomon; editor, Era Lapid; art director, Eytan Levy; costumes, Ruth Davidson; sound, Danny Natovich; music, Itzhak Klepter; title song by Klepter (music), Eli Mohar (lyrics) sung by Giddi Gov. Reviewed at Tevat Noah screening room, Tel Aviv, April 14, 1985. Running time: **97 MINS.**

Giora	Assaf Dayan
Bernard	Yoseph Millo
Ruth	Orna Porath
Dodi	Dani Roth
Sari	Maya Pick-Pardo
Bruria	Irith Sheleg
Gidon	Amos Lavi
Karen	Lascha Rosenberg

The second time around, 33-year-old filmmaker Eitan Green appears to have ironed out most of the troubles that have marred his first effort. Emotions are still kept under a lid, but there is a strong undercurrent, easily identified, of the storms rocking his characters internally even if only ripples reach the apparently cool surface.

The plot of "When Night Falls" focuses on the relationship between a former army officer, erroneously cashiered from service for something he did not do, who operates a bar in Tel Aviv, and his father, a Christian physician who had married a Jewish girl back in Germany, had arrived in Israel with her and lived all his life at her side, as a full agnostic.

The encounter between father and son comes at a moment when they are both going through an acute crisis. For the son, it is the forced estrangement from a way of life he had adopted as his own, which throws him into complete disarray. His night philandering is destroying his family life and his drinking serves as some sort of buffer against everything that might hurt him. The father, on the other hand, has been suddenly abandoned by his wife, who now, past 60, has decided she will not let time go by without trying at least to experience some real feeling after a lifetime of prim respectability and cold routine.

Pic climaxes with a single note of despair, as the protagonist has to face the responsibilities of his own deeds and the repercussions they had on his surroundings.

While both in writing and in his handling of the camera, it is obvious that Green respects his characters' privacy, he nevertheless paints them with much affection.

Thanks to Amnon Salomon's highly sensitive camera work, Green manages to create a spare, highly economical visual style.

The film is crammed with numerous references to themes that might be considered topical right now, like the war in Lebanon, the crisis of the Israeli youth looking for its future, quite often, elsewhere, the generation gap or the increasingly violent aspects of Tel Aviv night life. However, it is first and foremost about people, and this is the film's strength.

This is Assaf Dayan's best film performance to date, for he manages to hint at the misery and distress hiding under what seems to be the self-assured and confident personality, of the officer turned bar owner. Yoseph Millo and Orna Porath, both better known for stage careers, underplay beautifully, as Dayan's parents and the same goes for the rest of the cast.

Technically the production is of an unusually high standard. Independently produced by Micha Sharfstein for his own company, the picture has been already picked up bution and has been selected for this year's Cannes Fest's Un Certain Regard section. —*Edna.*

Survivors, The Blues Today
(DOCU-COLOR)

Minneapolis, April 13.

A Heart Productions release and production. Conceived and produced by Cork Marcheschi. Directed by Marcheschi and Robert Schwartz. Editors, Tom DeBiaso and Kathleen Laughlin. Featuring the Gravenites-Cipollina Band, Dr. John, Archie Shepp, Ben Sidran, Corky Siegel, Baby Doo Caston, Valerie Wellington, Lady Bianca with the Mark Naftalin Band, Willie Murphy and the Bees, the Minnesota Barking Ducks, and John Lee Hooker. Reviewed at the Cedar Theater, Minneapolis, April 10, 1985. (No MPAA Rating.) Running time: **87 MINS.**

Bankrolled for $350,000 by a local venture capitalist, "Survivors, The Blues Today" salutes the enduring blues performers who make their living without having ever "made it." It's also a nod to Wilebski's Blues Saloon in St. Paul, where codirectors Marcheschi and Schwartz shot three nights' worth of footage. Their efforts are very slick on all counts technically, especially in the ultra-crisp sound recording. "Survivors'" overall . impact, though, is a little mild, and will take some deft selling to crack the specialized market.

Filmed in March 1983, "Survivors" intercuts its live performance activity with the offstage chat and observations of its players. The best

segments feature two crack black vocalists, Lady Bianca and Valerie Wellington; though far less of a singer, harmonica ace Corky Siegel turns in the best-sustained and best-filmed solo turn. Elsewhere, "Survivors" lets its over-generous use of crowd scenes and uninspired lecture/narration intrude on the performance rhythm.

A key strategic mistake was made in using Nick Gravenites (who recorded under the monicker Nick the Greek), no great shakes as a musician or vocalist, as the film's official spokesman. We get far too much of him and most of the story-telling sessions included here don't have the offhand, overheard quality they need.

Beyond that, Heart Prods.' first venture has the technical end down well enough to encourage more projects. No U.S. distribution scheme has been arranged as yet, but pending some details, New York-based Fox-Lorber will handle the worldwide video and direct broadcast rights. Blue Dolphin Films will distribute in Great Britain. — *Phil.*

Een Pak Slaag
(Mr. Slotter's Jubilee)
(DUTCH-COLOR)

Sydney, April 16.

A Bert Haanstra Filmproduktie production. Produced, Directed by Bert Haanstra. Features entire cast. Screenplay, Anton Koolhaas, from his novel; camera (color), Anton van Munster; editor, Rob Hakhoff; music, Jurre Haanstra; art director, Ruud van Dijk; saxophone solo, Stan Getz; co-director, Rimko Haanstra. Reviewed on SBS TV, Sydney, April 15, 1985. Running time: **106 MINS.**
Hein Slotter . . . . Kees Brusse
Old Slieps . . . . Paul Steenbergen
Also with: Bernhard Droog, Eric van Ingen, Jeroen Krabbé, Eric Schneider, Ellen de Thouars, Annet Nieuwenhuzjen, Jacques Commandeur, Gees Linnebank, Maria de Booy.

If it seems odd that a feature film from Bert Haanstra, one of the most celebrated Dutch directors, made six years ago, should be virtually unknown internationally, the solution is probably that "Mr. Slotter's Jubilee" is really a very odd picture indeed. It's reviewed here for the record.

Scripted from his own novel by Anton Koolhaas, pic concerns machinations among the directors of a baby carriage manufacturing company. Old Slieps (Paul Steenbergen), founder of the factory, is long retired and virtually senile, his successor as managing director being not, as originally expected, his son, but the efficient and boring Hein Slotter (Kees Brusse). Slotter is loathed by his fellow directors for reasons that are never made very clear, and they decide to humiliate him at his silver jubilee celebrations with the revelation (untrue) that a junior employee of the company

once thrashed him (the film's Dutch title means, literally, "A Thrashing").

First half of the film is pretty dull, with much ado about nothing made over this imaginary incident from the past. There's some slight drama in the second half as Slotter takes his humiliation and emerges stronger than ever. But the uncertain mood of the film, and the storm-in-a-teacup theme, ensures that finally it's no more than a curiosity.

Best sequence actually comes behind the opening credits: in the tradition of Haanstra's past documentary work, it's an amusing look at the way those baby carriages are manufactured. — *Strat.*

Tokyo Melody, A Film About Ryuichi Sakamoto
(FRENCH-JAPANESE-DOCU-COLOR-16m)

Produced by National Institute of Audiovisual Communication (I.N.A.), Paris, and Yoroshita Music Inc., Japan. Directed by Elizabeth Lennard. Camera (color), Jean Claude Pamart; sound, Jean Claude Brisson; editor, Makiko Suzuki; production consultant, Kiki Miyake. Reviewed at New Directors/New Films, Museum of Modern Art, N.Y. April 9, 1985. Running time: **62 MINS.**

"Tokyo Melody" combines two profiles, of Tokyo and of avant-garde composer-actor Ryuichi Sakamoto, already known in American specialized music circles and as costar with David Bowie in Nagisa Oshima's feature, "Merry Christmas, Mr. Lawrence," for which Sakamoto composed the score.

A workaholic musician and sound wizard who composes on giant electronic consoles, supported by a crew of technicians, Sakamoto occasionally performs live with a small combo in huge stadiums for mobs of screaming fans, using lighting effects, costuming and facial make-up.

Also a futuristic music theoretician with one ear tuned in on sociology, Sakamoto opines that music in Japan is omnipresent as background in cafes, elevators and stores and that people rushing by don't listen from beginning to end.

As a double profile of Sakamoto within modern Japan, "Tokyo Melody" conceivably could play theatrically in tandem with a companion film of similar length and congenial theme. Although perhaps too rich and exotic for ordinary teaching purposes, the film may do well in 16m educational distribution. It clearly is a candidate for public television. — *Hitch.*

Moving Violations
(COLOR)

Derivative spoof has dim prospects.

Hollywood, April 19.

A 20th Century Fox release of a James G. Robinson presentation of an Ufland-Roth/I.P.I. production. Produced by Joe Roth, Harry Ufland. Coproducer, Bob Israel. Executive producers, Pat Proft, Doug Draizin. Directed by Neal Israel. Features entire cast. Screenplay, Neal Israel, Proft, based on a story by Paul and Sharon Boorstin; camera (Deluxe color), Robert Elswit; editor, Tom Walls; music, Ralph Burns; art direction, Virginia Field; set decoration, Jerie Kelter, Robert Lucas; costume design, Darryl Levine; sound, James S. La Rue; associate producer, Richard Sawyer; assistant director, Irby Smith; second unit director, Bruce A. Block; second unit camera, James L. Carter; casting, Karen Rea. Reviewed at 20th Century Fox Studios, L.A., April 18, 1985. (MPAA Rating: PG-13.) Running time: **90 MINS.**
Dana Cannon . . . . John Murray
Amy Hopkins . . . . Jennifer Tilly
Deputy Halik . . . . ,. . James Keach
Scott Greeber . . . . Brian Backer
Wink Barnes . . . . Ned Eisenberg
Emma Jean . . . . Clara Peller
Joan Pudillo . . . . Wendie Jo Sperber
Mrs. Loretta Houk . . . . Nedra Volz
Terrence 'Doc' Williams . . . . . Fred Willard
Deputy Virginia Morris . . Lisa Hart Carroll
Stephanie McCarty . Nadine Van Der Velde
Spencer Popadophalos . . . . . Ben Mittleman
Raoul Bienveneda . . . . Victor Campos
Jeff Roth . . . . Willard Pugh
Judge Nedra Henderson . . Sally Kellerman

There's just no excuse for "Moving Violations." Certainly, out of the half-dozen producers of various kinds, not to mention the executives at Fox, someone should have been able to figure out there was something less than a wonderfully funny screenplay here. Coming off rather like "Police Academy 2½," pic plays like a series of vignettes from a very bad high school talent show. If you count friends and relatives, there's an audience even for that sort of thing, but enough laughs can't possibly be found here to keep this running at profitable speeds for long.

Socalled farce begins with the premise that traffic cops are evil eager beavers determined to slap tickets on as many undeserving victims as possible. Once the terminally unamusing exposition is dispensed with, pic commences with a depiction of a traffic school run by gestapo-like James Keach, who happens to be in league with crooked judge Sally Kellerman to fail everyone in class and then abscond with the profits derived from auctioning off the students' impounded vehicles.

Cast is headed by the younger siblings of better known thesps, not only including Keach, but John Murray (brother of Bill) and Jennifer Tilly (sister of Meg). Murray indulges in no end of self-conscious mugging, and only vaguely bright moments are supplied by Nedra Volz, who runs amok like a distaff version of Mr. Magoo, and Wendie Jo Sperber, who turns up at an auto clinic imagining that she, and not her car, will be receiving a lube job and a tune up.

Climax is set up as a lift from Buster Keaton's classic "Cops," but even this isn't played out extensively enough for much impact.

Although both films are loaded with wrecked vehicles, current entry shouldn't be confused with Julie & Roger Corman's 1976 "Moving Violation" (singular), which was also released by Fox. —*Cart.*

The Milpitas Monster
(COLOR)

Amateur creature feature from the vaults.

A Samuel Golden Ayer production. Produced and directed by Robert L. Burrill. Features entire cast. Screenplay, David E. Boston, from story by Burrill, David Kottas; camera (Technicolor), Marilyn Odello, Scot Henderson, Mike Pearl, Mike Clausen, Andrew Watts, Patricia Thorpe; editor, Burrill; music, Robert R. Berry Jr.; sound, Ted Armstrong, Henderson, Randy Knapp, Watts; assistant director, Clausen, Henderson; production manager, Sid Brown; art direction-special effects supervisor, Duane D. Walz; animation, Stephen C. Wathen; additional sound effects, Ben Burtt; narrator, Paul Frees. Reviewed on VCI vidcassette, N.Y., March 12, 1985. (No MPAA Rating.) Running time: **81 MINS.**
With: Douglas Hagdohl, Scot Henderson, Scott Parker, Daniel Birkhead, Duane Walz, Michael Pegg, Joseph House, Jeffrey Reid, John (Pop) Kennedy, Jack Wessels, William Guest 3d, Scott Wool, Priscilla House.

Reviewed for the record, "The Milpitas Monster" is an amateur horror film completed in 1976, theatrically unreleased and now available via homevideo (presented by "Le Bad Cinema"). Distrib VCI includes a disclaimer that pic "may insult your intelligence," but as usual, *caveat emptor.*

Premise is a huge monster (portrayed alternately by stopmotion animation and a guy in a felt suit) spawned by limitless garbage dumped in the little town of Milpitas, 40 miles from San Francisco. Between scenes of failed comedy relief concerning town drunk George Keister, monster attacks a dance hop at the local high school and is finally fried when it climbs up the town's tv transformer tower in emulation of "King Kong."

Nonactors and incompetent film technique reduce this one to the unwatchable category. Sole point of interest is credit for (much-needed in view of the shoddy sound recording) sound effects to young whiz Ben Burtt, later an Oscar-winner for "Star Wars" and key contributor to many other recent fantasy films. — *Lor.*

Prime Risk
(COLOR)

Creditable first effort, too late in the genre.

Kansas City, April 18.

An Almi Pictures release of a Mikas I production. Written and directed by Michael Farkas. Produced by Herman Grigsby. Executive producer, Bernard Farkas; associate James Reed. Camera (color), Mac Ahlberg; editor, Bruce Green; music, Phil Marshall; art director, Christopher Henry; costume design, Bernadette O'Brien; assistant director, John R. Woodward; sets, Greg McCullough; makeup, Don Markel; special effects, Gary F. Bentley; special electronic effects, John Pospisil. (MPAA Rating: PG-13.) Reviewed at Bannister Square theater, K.C., April 17, 1985. Runnng time: **100 MINS.**

Julie Collins	Toni Hudson
Michael Fox	Lee Montgomery
Bill Yeoman	Samuel Bottoms
Paul Minsky	Clu Gulager
Dr. Lasser	Keenan Wynn
Dr. Holt	Lois Hall
John	Rick Rakowski
Vance	John Lykes
Terry Franklin	James O'Connell

"Prime Risk" is the first effort of 23-year-old Michael Farkas, a graduate of the film production school at the U. of Southern California. He took on the whole chore, writing the original script, rounding up a limited partnership of investors and the production staff and directing the picture. What has emerged is not a bad little picture.

The trouble is, it is not a good big picture, and the story of young eggheads manipulating computers has been done recently on a bigger scale with bigger names.

This computer whiz is a girl, Toni Hudson, fresh out of college and turned down in her effort to land a job in the computer room of a big bank, where the computer expert steals some of her ideas. Lee Montgomery, a college student, turns against the bank because it won't transfer his funds from a Coast bank promptly.

Hudson has the electronic equipment to fake plastic credit cards and siphon funds from the bank's automatic teller. By chance she meets Montgomery, finds him miffed, and inveigles him into joining her to launch their reprisals against the bank. They are having great success at ripping off the automatic teller when they inadvertently discover a great international computer scam aimed at collapsing the Federal Reserve Bank.

They are discovered by the international culprits, headed by Keenan Wynn. There is a chase across country, then across Washington, D.C., to the F.B.I. where no one will believe them — little thieves ratting on big thieves. One agent is sympathetic when some of their claims jibe with facts he hears on a national newscast. They find the buried junction box that links the foreign computer system together and Hudson destroys it.

Farkas claims to have brought in the picture for around $1,200,000, and if so he has spent well because the picture does not have a cheap look.

Camerawork and special effects

---

are creditable. The story line has a couple of plot gaps that cause some confusion, but by and large it stays on course.

Almi spent a bundle giving the picture its world premiere in the K.C. exchange area the week of April 12, after much ballyhoo at Show-A-Rama and personal appearances by Wynn and Hudson there. Results are lightweight, however, possibly due to heavy stuff on most screens in the market and because the picture has been preceded by heavier releases in the computer genre.—*Quin.*

La Historia Oficial
(The Official History)
(ARGENTINE-COLOR)

Buenos Aires, April 5.

A Cinemania release of a Historias Cinematográfias-Progress Communications production. Executive producer, Marcelo Pineyro. Directed by Luis Puenzo. Stars Héctor Alterio, Norma Aleandro. Screenplay, Puenzo, Aída Bortnik; camera (Eastmancolor), Félix Monti; editor, Juan Carlos Macias; music, Atilio Stampone; art director, Abel Facello; costumes, Tiky García Estévez; assistant director, Raúl Outeda; sound, Abelardo Kushnir. Reviewed at the Monumental theater, B.A., April 4, 1985. Running time: **112 MINS.**

Robrto	Héctor Alterio
Alicia	Norma Aleandro
Sara	Chela Ruiz
Ana	Chunchuna Villafañe
Enrique	Hugo Arana
Benitz	Patricio Contreras
José	Guillermo Battaglia
Nata	María Luisa Robledo
Gabi	Analía Castro
Macci	Jorge Petraglia
General	Augusto Larreta
Father Ismael	Leal Rey

"The Official History," is a thought-provoking, indirect yet resolute approach to the greatest Argentine tragedy of the century: the degeneration into secret genocide of the so-called "dirty war" against terrorism in the mid- and late-70s. Director-scripter Luis Puenzo and cowriter Aida Bortnik leave local audiences breathless with this first native pic dealing with the desaparecidos (missing ones) although not focusing on their ordeals and fate, but rather the anguish and uncertainties of their survivors.

The story takes place during 1983 in Buenos Aires. It evolves around Alicia (Norma Aleandro) and Roberto (Héctor Alterio), a married couple with an adopted child, Gabi (Analía Castro). Aleandro teaches history at a private school adhering to the official textbooks, but eventually she is impressed by the investigative, revisionist spirit of some of her pupils. "History is written by the murderers," defiantly remarks

one of them. Aleandro soon starts to wonder whether that might be true when an old female friend just returned from exile reluctantly tells her about her past martyrdom at the

---

hands of torturers seeking information about her former lover.

Then come the rallies of the Mothers and Grandmothers of Plaza de Mayo demanding to know what happened to their loves ones. The terror of her daughter when her cousins storm into her room playing machinegun-armed soldiers, plus other significant details, lead Aleandro to suspect Analía could be the offspring of a desaparecida woman. When she asks her husband for the truth Alterio insists on a vague tale about having bought a just-born baby, then angrily reminds his wife they agreed to forget about the matter.

As many Argentines who were unaware of the mass carnage, Aleandro finds it difficult at first to reconcile her conveniences and emotional needs with the awakening of her conscience on the frightening realities of the holocaust. Then, overpowered by a moral instinct, she decides to investigate, finding out not only who the parents were and who is the grandmother of her adopted daughter, but also realizing her husband is linked with both the paramilitary and the local and foreign businessmen profiting from the corruption in power circles. She reaches a spiritual, unspoken understanding with the grandmother of Analía, endures a torturer-style beating from her husband — enraged when the losing of the child couples with the disintegration of the dictatorship — and leaves home.

Outstanding performances by Aleandro, Alterio and Chela Ruiz as the grandmother greatly help to inject "History" with credibility, human warmth and pathos without losing intellectual stature and political meaning in its almost wordless yet uncompromising stance for human rights. Moppet actress Analia Castro is a real find.

Luis Puenzo, an ace in the blurbs field, adds to his craftmanship a fine storytelling and dramatic insight, turning out a topical film of sustained tension. If properly handled, stressing its quality, entertainment values and ethical statement, it can hit offshore markets. It is scheduled to be released in 10 U.S. cities in September and it was chosen as the Argentine entry for Cannes.

Félix Monti's superb camerawork, Atilio Stampone's unobtrusive score, well-paced editing and an able supporting cast are pluses. Other technical credits are good. María Elena Walsh's biting song "In The Country Of I Don't Remember" is deftly inserted in two scenes.

—*Nubi.*

Poulet au Vinaigre
(FRENCH-COLOR)

Paris, April 22.

An MK2 production and release. Produced by Marin Karmitz. Directed by Claude Chabrol. Screenplay, Chabrol and Dominique Roulet, adapted from the latter's novel, "Une Mort de Trop;" camera (color), Jean Rabier; editor, Monique Fardoulis; art director, Françoise Benoit-Fresco; music, Matthieu Chabrol; production manager, Catherine Lapoujade. Reviewed at the UGC Danton cinema, April 20, 1985. Running time: 110 MINS.

Jean Lavardin . . . . Jean Poiret
Madame Cuno . . . . Stéphane Audran
Hubert Lavoisier . . . . Michel Bouquet
Anna Foscarie . . . . Caroline Cellier
Louis Cuno . . . . Lucas Belvaux
Philippe Morasseau . . . . Jean Topart
Henriette . . . . Pauline Lafont
Marthe . . . . Andrée Tainsy
Gérard Filiol . . . . . . Jean-Claude Bouillaud
Delphine Morasseau . . . Josephine Chaplin

"Poulet au Vinaigre," which is competing at Cannes, is a slow-paced, mostly routine murder mystery, which owes some occasional sardonic fun to a good cast and some tart dialog, but little to Claude Chabrol's sluggishly conventional direction.

Plot, adapted from a print whodunit by Chabrol and its author, Dominique Roulet, revolves conventionally around some scheming town notables, a notary, a physician and a parvenu butcher (Michel Bouquet, Jean Topart, and Jean-Claude Bouillaud), who are trying to get their hands on a piece of property for real estate speculations.

Its owner (Stéphane Audran) is a crazed, wheelchair cripple who won't sell out and keeps tabs on her persecutors by having her teenage son, the postal courier (Lucas Belvaux), sidetrack their mail and steam it open at home.

Belvaux, an introverted mama's boy who spends part of his day avoiding the advances of luscious fellow postal worker Pauline Lafont (daughter of Chabrol veteran, Bernadette Lafont), takes some personal initiative when he dumps sugar in the gas tank of the butcher's car, which fatally smashes up on the road.

That same day, the doctor's wife, who had dsiappeared some days before, turns up a charred corpse in another car accident. Soon after, one of her friends (Caroline Cellier), who is Bouquet's mistress, also vanishes.

Story suffers the fate of most screen-transposed mysteries — it lacks real suspense and plods predictably towards a denouement that offers no emotional or intellectual catharsis.

Only the performances matter, as Chabrol takes a back seat to his cast. Audran is a relishably despicable nutcase and her maternal abuse suggests Mrs. Bates in a prequel to Hitchcock's "Psycho."

More restrained, the superb Jean Poiret (author of "La Cage aux Folles") is disturbingly funny as the police inspector who makes a traditionally late entrance and promptly steals the show as he coolly brutalizes suspects and witnesses with an urbanity that hints of the psychotic. Chabrol and his producer, Marin Karmitz were rightly so pleased with Poiret that they are thinking of doing a series with his personage.

Other actors are okay, though their parts, like Bouquet's, are too episodic to really make an impression. Some roles, like the doctor's wife, portrayed fleetingly in the pre-credit sequence by Josephine Chaplin, seem to have suffered in the cutting room. —Len.

Friscofest Reviews
Continued

Patakin
(CUBAN-COLOR)

San Francisco, April 16.

A Cinema Guild release. Produced by Justo Vega. Directed by Manuel Octavio Gomez. Screenplay, Gomez and Eugenio H. Espinosa; camera (color), Luis Garcia Mesa; music, Rembert Egues Gomez; musical director, Manuel Duchesne Cuzan; sound, Jeronimo Labrada, Germinal Hernandez, Raul Garcia; choreography, Victor Cuellar; costumes, Gabriel Hierrezuelo; set design, Manuel O. Gomez, Luis Lacosta. Reviewed at the York theater, San Francisco, April 15, 1985. Running time: 108 MINS.

With: Miguel Benavides, Assenah Rodriguez, Enrique Arredondo, Litico Rodriguez, Alina Sanchez, Carlos Moctezuma, Hilda Oates, Jorge Losada.

This is a lively, silly, semi-nostalgic sendup of musicals, films and surprisingly, considering its source, of the worker state. There's more music per minute than on MTV, more bikinis than during Easter week at Ft. Lauderdale, more hoofing than "A Chorus Line."

"Patakin" means fable, and this melodious farce draws on mythology to pit an alleged god of thunder against a hard-working, simple fellow, portrayed by Miguel Benavides and Enrique Arrendondo, respectively. But Benavides' thunder is couched in macho meandering. He considers himself a sex symbol, a rooster of the beaches. His every advance elicits a song, or a dance, or a joke. Nothing is taken seriously here.

Technical aspects, often mocking Robbins and Berkeley, are nifty and the color splashily bold. All the performances are properly broad.
— Herb.

The Stand-In
(COLOR)

San Francisco, April 15.

A Stand-In Productions production. Produced, directed and written by Robert N. Zagone. Camera (color, video), Rick Butler; editor, Kenji Yammoto, Norm Levy; art director, Don De Fina; costumes, Marianna Astrom-De Fina; additional music, Don Lewis; sound editor, Yamamoto; exec producer, Gail Waldron. Reviewed at the Exploratorium theater, San Francisco, April 13, 1985. Running time: 87 MINS.

With: Danny Glover, Christa Victoria, Joe Bellan, Jane Dornacker, Marc Hayashi, Bob Sarlatte.

This "video feature" has production values beyond its $85,000 investment, funded in part by the American Film Institute and Rockefeller Foundation. But the often-amusing yarn, featuring Danny Glover as a low-budget film director who inadvertently gets involved in murder and false identity, is stretched beyond payoff limits:

This is the first feature (lensed with video camera) from longtime San Francisco tv freelancer Robert N. Zagone, and his direction, although hampered by some soft thesping, is pro. Glover is fine, as is comedienne Jane Dornacker, who scored well as an antsy nurse in "The Right Stuff." She and Marc Hayashi are used for Ersatz docu commentaries, à la "Zelig," to discuss the Glover character, a device which falls flat in this context.

Another Frisco standup comic, Bob Sarlatte, is delightful as the creep biker Glover kills in self defense and whose identity Glover then assumes. Oakland warbler Christa Victoria plays Glover's g.f.; she's nice to look at but lacks breadth of performance.

Score of jazz standards and additional music by Don Lewis is a plus.

Pic first unspooled at 1984 Mill Valley film fest.— Herb.

Qui Jin
(CHINESE-COLOR)

San Francisco, April 16.

A World Entertainment Inc. release of a Shanghai Film Co. production. Directed by Xie Jin. Screenplay, Jin, Huang Zongying. No other credits available. Reviewed at Kosukai theater, San Francisco, April 13, 1985. Running time: 144 MINS.

With: Li Xiuming, Li Zhiyu, Chen Xiguang, Zhang Chao.

Although in post-screening comments at the San Francisco Film Festival director Xie Jin indicated he wasn't "happy with the middle" of this pic, this turn-of-the-century tale about a historic woman revolutionary generally works.

The quick-cut pacing is deft and carries the lay viewer through the thicket of Chinese political history without excess confusion. Li Xiuming gives a particularly strong sense of stridency to the title role.

Production spent 17 shooting days in Japan, first time a Chinese crew has made a feature abroad, and is loaded with technical quality, especially considering the endless number of setups.

Couched in the brooding tale is a sense of doom, the fact that this intelligent woman who left her husband and two children to save her country is headed for tragic martyrdom.

Director Jin, whose latest film is "Reeds At The Foot Of The Mountain," says he hopes that "someday someone will be able to make an even better film about Qui Jin." He has no need to apologize. —Herb.

Drammen Festival Reviews

Jonny Roova
(SWEDISH-COLOR)

Drammen, April 13.

An SF release of Studio 24/TV-1 Fiction/SF production. Foreign sales: The Swedish Film Institute. Original story, screenplay and directed by John Olsson. Executive producer, Roy Andersson. Camera (Eastmancolor), Sten Holmberg; editor, Christin Lohman; music, Hans Sandin, Björn Sjöö. Reviewed in Nordic Film Festival at the Saga-2, Drammen, Norway, April 13, 1985. Running time: 85 MINS.

Jonny Roova . . . . Rolf Degerlund
Osborn . . . . Jan Dytlow-Kozlowski
Leila . . . . Sari Lilliestierna
Simo . . . . Johan Holm
Willmar . . . . Lars-Louis Strolin
Bernt . . . . Lars Hjelt
Reijo . . . . Kjell Morin
Marja . . . . Merja Niva

"Jonny Roova" is writer-helmer John Olsson's second feature. It has a lighter touch than his first one, "Life In Bloom," but a stronger undercurrent of emotional involvement with the characters.

Film is the typical road picture, following the young title figure's travels and travails when he leaves the security of his natural habitat in Northern Sweden.

Jonny hopes to find a more exciting life and much more money in Sweden's promised land, the South. On arriving there, he has all his belongings stolen from him, and work in the bottling plant where he starts out nearly costs him a thumb in an accident. His comrades from the plant are also dreaming of the fortune to be made somewhere else. A stray kid, left illegally behind by some repatriated foreign workers, attaches himself rather forcefully to Jonny until their fates seem so solidly intertwined that Jonny at the end chooses the boy over his new-found girlfriend and heads North again with the kid on the back of his motorcycle.

"Jonny Roova" has an almost cinema verité look, but is obviously very carefully crafted. This works to its advantage since the flow of events and the acting of all characters merge into something at once realistic and distinctly poetic. Film obviously belongs on the minor fest circuit and could later move into limited theatrical situations almost anywhere. — *Kell.*

Öye for Öye
(An Eye For An Eye)
(NORWEGIAN-COLOR)

Drammen, April 14.

A Kommunernes Filmcentral A/S release of a Norsk Film A/S production. Foreign sales: Norsk Film A/S (Frida Ohrvik). Original story, screenplay and directed by Gianni Lepre. Executive producer, Harald Ohrvik. Camera (Eastmancolor), Rolv Haan; editor, Lars Hagström; music, Antonio Bibalo; production design, Harld Egede-Nissen. Reviewed in Nordic Film Festival at the Saga-1, Drammen, Norway, April 14, 1985. Running time: **90 MINS.**
Bashir . . . . .Amjad Munir
Anne . . . . .Froydis Armand
Oscar . . . . .Björn Floberg
Lena . . . . .Torill Öyen.
Also with: Fazila Saber, Mohammed Alinass Kahn, Anne Krigsvoll, Mohammed Rashid, Roy Annar Hansen, Kari Simonsen, Majlis Granlund, Joachim Calmeyer.

Bashir, a not quite legally registered Pakistani, works in the kitchen of a dance restaurant down on its luck and happens to witness its owner Oscar's setting fire to the premises to collect the insurance and start a new business with Lena, who has goaded him to the crime. Bashir has struck up a random amourous acquaintance with Anne, who drinks too much to forget that she cannot pay the bank what she owes on her new home.

Thus, writer-director Gianni Lepre has set the stage for his feature "An Eye For An Eye" (possibly to be marketed abroad as "Landscape In White") to emerge as a latter-day "Double Indemnity," involving blackmail and, if not illicit then tantalizing interracial love. Anne, a fiery brunette, makes mild-mannered Bashir put the bite on the arsonist, and Lena, the arsonist's tough wife, makes her husband beat up Anne and Bashir. At the end Bashir's blood melts the Norwegian snow while Anne runs off to some kind of safety.

Generally, Lepre handles his film as a clear-cut crime thriller, and most of the time the interplay between thriller action and sketched-in racial conflict works nicely. At other times one aspect detracts from the other with detrimental effect to film's suspense. Still, "An Eye For An Eye" is a thoroughly professional job with impressive production credits and just-right acting from the four leads. The homevideo trade as well as tv programming are in the cards for this one when marketed offshore. —*Kell.*

Dödspolare
(Buddies Unto Death)
(SWEDISH-COLOR)

Drammen, April 12.

An Esselte Film Distribution release (foreign sales: The Swedish Film Institute) of an Omega Film with the Swedish Film Institute and Esselte Video production. Executive producers, Mats Arehn, Peter Kropénin. Original story and directed by Mats Arehn. Screenplay, Rolf Börjlind. Camera (Eastmancolor), Lasse Björne, Bertil Rosengren; editor, Tomas Samuelsson. Reviewed at the Saga-2, Drammen, Norway in Nordic Film Festival, April 12, 11985. Running time: **85 MINS.**
Tobbe . . . . .Gösta Ekman
Bertil . . . . .Sten Ljunggren
Also with: Gunnar Knas Lindkvist, Rolf Larsson, Karin Miller and Eva Dahlman (as the dead woman).

"Buddies Unto Death" is the near-ultimate low-budget feature film, shot in a few weeks with only two actors most of the time prowling the same one-room location. Lensed in 16m, the 35m blowup is predictably grainy. It is, however, debuting production setup Esselte Video's aim to prove that good, smart cinema entertainment could be fashioned that way and work for fast play-off/payoff before being entered in company's video distribution. Director Mats Arehn seems to have had just the right idea for the thing to move. "Buddies Unto Death" may have its dry stretches, but it is also a very funny and occasionally truly shocking comedy-of-errors crime story.

Immensely hung-over Tobbe, a jazz pianist, wakes up in his apartment to find himself not alone but in the company of a sleeping woman. His buddy Bertil turns up looking far less ravaged although he had been a guest at the night's party, too. Bertil is a doctor and pronounces the woman not sleeping but dead. Both men disclaim any knowledge of the woman, but it soon turns out, via the buddies' various slips of tongue, that she had once been pregnant by one of them and more than casually befriended by the other. Half-heartedly, the men commence their attempts to dispose of the body.

The woman's name was Gunilla, and most of the ensuing Trouble with Gunilla is baroque rather than Hitchcockian. Good fun is had with two actors who can twist dialog shadings and dramatic turns with the minutest of facial movement and tonal inflections. —*Kell.*

Niskavouri
(The Niskavouri Saga)
(FINNISH-COLOR)

Drammen, April 12.

A Skandia Filmi Oy production and release. Foreign sales: The Finnish Film Foundation. Based on the plays "The Women Of Niskavouri" and "The Bread Of Niskavouri" by Hella Wuolijoka. Written and directed by Matti Kassila. Camera (Eastmancolor), Pertti Muttanen; editor, Tepi Salukari; music, Rauno Lehtinen; production design, Matteus Marttila; costume design, Leila Jäntti; executive producer, Kaj Holmberg. Reviewed at the Saga-4, Drammen, Norway, in Nordic Film Festival, April 12, 1985. Running time: **118 MINS.**
Mother Niskavouri . . . . .Rauni Luoma
Aarne Niskavouri . . . . .Esko Salminen
Illona . . . . .Satu Silvo
Aarne's wife . . . . .Marja-Liisa Marton

Helle Wuoligoka, a one-time Berthold Brecht collaborator, endeared herself to Finns with her "Niskavouri Saga," a series of stage plays, six of them turned into feature films, about a farmer dynasty's love and money affairs between 1895 and the outbreak of World War II. Now, with "Niskavouri," veteran writer-helmer Matti Kassila has merged two of the plays into a soap opera-style piece of feature entertainment.

Film has wit and charm even if it is also quite unabashedly ridiculous now and then in its cliché-ridden spinning of the familiar tale of a rural family (here in the 1930s) confronted with the moral and political issues of the day, but held together by the firm hand and sly maneuvering of a wise, good-hearted and rather Macchiavellian widowed grandmother. Her favorite son, who has married rich to save the farm and to be able to stay home and till his beloved soil, has to seek a new life in the Big Town when local gossips find out about his affair (true love) with the new village schoolmarm.

Rest of film has to do with the tough old lady's plotting, social and financial, to have the son come back — which he does, while his whiner of a wife suddenly contents herself with a fat money settlement.

There is much healthy comedy in the telling, the production credits are handsome and all the actors in a large cast supply lively, folksy performances. There is no depth-probing of character psychology or of the diverse social strata of rural life as such, but pic has plenty of atmosphere to suggest the comfortable browsing of old Finnish family albums of the period. — *Kell.*

Gullsandur
(Golden Sands)
(ICELANDIC-COLOR)

Drammen, April 15.

An Isfilm Ltd. release of Mannamyndir and Icefilm Ltd. production. Original story, screenplay and direction, Agust Gudmundsson. Camera (Eastmancolor), Sigurdur Sverrir Palsson; production design, Halldor Thorgeirsson; music, Daryl Runswick. Stars Palmi Gestsson, Edda Björgvinsdottir. No other credits available. Reviewed at the Saga-2, Drammen, Norway, in Nordic Film Festival, April 14, 1985. Running time: **92 MINS.**

With a modest-in-the-extreme budget of $176,000, Agust Gudmundsson has managed to write, produce and direct a feature comedy that, for all its obvious technical shortcomings, should earn ":Golden Sands" some kudos as a bright effort in the warmly humanistic-imaginative story telling style of Scotland's Bill "Local Hero" Forsyth. Film is sure to gain access to tv airwaves around the world.

Story has a bunch of U.S. servicemen of mixed ranks setting up camp on a sandy stretch of remote Icelandic coast. The local population is immediately busy with either protesting the U.S. military presence or hoping for it to prove an occasion for economic gains. The community's anti-NATO activists (numbering two) subject the Americans to a nightly attack of firecrackers, occasioning something close to a national flap. Are the Yanks up to nuclear mischief? Or are they merely on a vacation, having fun with tracing down a hidden Spanish treasure of looted gold?

Director Gudmundsson too often loses narrative control of his story and plot developments, and he fails in his ambitions to interpolate deadly serious vignettes of Icelanders' reaction to a real-life natural disaster (volcanic) that befell the island nation in the mid-1700s. Most of the time, however, his film works as a mildly satiric romp. Sly, vigorous acting is displayed by the entire cast. —*Kell.*

Själen er större än världen
(The Soul Is Greater Than The World)
(SWEDISH-DOCU-COLOR)

Drammen, April 14.

A Folkets Hus release; foreign sales, The Swedish Film Institute. A Stefan Jarl Film production. Conceived, written and directed by Stefan Jarl. Camera (Eastmancolor), Per Källberg; editor, Anette Lycke-Lundberg; music, Ulf Dageby; production management, Tommy Ramhed, Suzanne Branner. Reviewed in Nordic Film Festival at the Saga-2, Drammen, Norway, April 14, 1985. Running time: **105 MINS.**

When documentarist Stefan Jarl started shooting "The Soul Is Greater Than The World" he expected his subject, Sweden's Ricky Bruch, the 1972 Olympic bronze medalist as a discus thrower, to wind up in 1984 in Los Angeles receiving another medal, this time in gold. Things were to work out differently. Bruch, always very outspoken and critical about the behind-the-scenes men of international sports, was turned down as a contender by Sweden's Olympic Committee even though he proved just before and after the L.A. Games, that he could throw his discus three meters longer in other international competitions than the eventual 1984 Olympic Gold Medalist.

Bruch's outspokenness also had to do with his self-confessed use of energy stimulants and his contention that drugs were in general use among the Swedish sport elite. Jarl shows his man — a bear of a balding, 38-year-old athlete at the top of his form swallowing daily fistfuls of vitamin pills and subjecting himself to all kinds of injections, while he seems to pursue his training round the clock. He does have a few other preoccupations: raising money to pay for a Communist Bloc athlete's escape to the West, and waxing philosophical about the world beyond borders only his soul is permitted to cross.

Bruch is never depicted as being a fanatic, but he is clearly devout in his endeavors to become — and to remain — the best in his chosen field. Documentarist Jarl does not pose questions, he has Bruch act out his own answers to everything one might like to ask. Film thus has natural drama, a built-in sadness, and mood shadings to approach the heart of what all sport is about. Apart from very specialized situations, "The Soul' ... would appear, with some editorial tightening, a natural for tv programming everywhere. — *Kell.*

Galskab
(Madness)
(NORWEGIAN-COLOR)

Drammen, April 13.

A Norsk Film A/S production and release. Original story, screenplay, directed and edited by Egil Kolsö. Executive producer, Jan Erik Düring. Camera (Eastmancolor), Erling Thurmann Andersen; production design, Sven Wickman; music, Beranek. Reviewed in Nordic Film Festival at the Saga-5, Drammen, Norway, April 13, 1985. Running time: **100 MINS.**

Marianne	Lise Fjeldstad
Karin	Pia Borgli
Erik	Ole Jörgen Nilsen
Peder	Per Görvel
Lise	Eli Dorseth

"Madness" is a vehicle for highly respected Norwegian stage and screen actress Lise Fjeldstad, 45, in a story that puts the actress through developments that strain credulity.

As Marianne, Fjeldstad is first seen to be slightly worried about her teenage daughter Karin's punk attitudes but otherwise content with a life of comparative ease as a translator of subtitles for tv films and as the wife of a solid-citizen stock exchange broker. When Karin leaves home and goes into hiding, her whereabouts seem to interest Marianne not at all. Instead, stung by her daughter's accusations that she and her generation are driven by narrow-minded consumer society ambitions and generally responsible for nuclear armament, defiling the environment, etc., she throws herself into Peace Movement activities. She ultimately finds her daughter in a punk-rock hangout, dances with her in the streets only to wind up sleeping and alone down in the city docks.

The madness of the title (or half of it, the rest is, of course, symbolic of society and the establishment in general) is inflicted on her by the policemen who pick her up out of kindness only to be rewarded with kicks across their shins and banging of her handbag on their heads. Isolated in a psychiatric ward, she is given a sedative by her husband's doctor friend, but makes her escape with the aid of her daughter. Soon after the escape, she and Karin seek refuge in their summer cottage, sanity and peace of mind restored at least as far as the two of them are concerned.

Even when he tries to be subtle writer-director Egil Kolsö is clearly with the Peace Movement and has latter's message spelled out wide enough to cover several barn doors. Worse, he has his lead actress mouth political slogan lines by the numbing dozen. Along with all this and with the director's preoccupation with Fjeldstad's facial and other (occasionally nude) physical assets, he throws her like a rag-doll through an orgy of clashing styles of writing and cinematography.
—*Kell.*

Adjö, Solidaritet
(Goodbye, Solidarity)
(NORWEGIAN-COLOR)

Drammen, April 13.

A UIP release of AS Mefisto Film production. Original story, screenplay, produced and directed by Svend Wam and Petter Venneröd. Camera (Eastmancolor), Philip R. Ogard; editor, Inge-Lise Langfeldt. Music (in Dolby stereo), Svein Gundersen with Tom Kobbel singing Leonard Cohen's "Bird On A Wire" and Lou Reed's "Vicious;" production design.Tone Skjeldfjord, Viggo Jönsberg; choreography, Inge-Lise Langfeldt; costume design, Kari Baade. Reviewed in Nordic Film Festival at the Saga-3, Drammen, Norway, April 13, 1985. Running time: **142 MINS.**

Atle	Svein Sturla Hungnes
Eigil	Knut Husebö
Astrid	Jorunn Kjellsby
Atle's mother	Wencke Foss
Fridtjof	Thomas Robsahm
Mefistoles	Björn Skagestad
Faust	Per Frisch
Margarete	Ellen Horn

For "Goodbye, Solidarity," the 10th feature in as many years from the writer-producer-director team of Svend Wam and Petter Venneröd the critics had a field-day branding it as gaudy, gross, tasteless, excessive in scope and length, overly theatrical and generally pretentious. Meanwhile audiences in Norway hastened to establish a new box-office smash.

"Goodbye, Solidarity" certainly is everything the local critics call it, but it also has an exuberance and vigor that help explain its audience appeal. Also, its topicality and subject-matter belongs sufficiently in the yesterday's news category to make its statements both familiar and entirely harmless. It states that the 1968 generation chose living well over both red and dead, and that they must now face the threats and drug-inflicted or unemployment-derived misery of their own teenage kids. How do the solid citizens face all this? According to Wam and Venneröd either by excessive drinking or by conniving and selling-out to advance their careers even further.

Atle, a professor-psychiatrist, and Eigil, a National Theatre stage director, are the two men seen approaching middle age with all signs of defeat-amidst-success. Theatrical tableaux are interpolated to illustrate the two men's plight as well as their past, and sometimes the tableaux and nightmares merge with the general action into straight Grand Guignol. At other times, the directors use so many cinematic tricks that all narrative sense and natural drama sink to the bottom.

As a post-graduate horror show with music, "Goodbye, Solidarity" has worked itself into the most bourgeois of Norwegian hearts.

It is highly doubtful, however, if this local brand of satiric firewater will travel well, if at all. —*Kell.*

Rakkauselokuva
(The Love Movie)
(FINNISH-COLOR)

Drammen, April 12.

A Reppufilmi Oy release of Reppufilmi/Anssi Mänttari. Camera (Eastmancolor), Heikki Katajisto; editor, Raija Talvio; music, F. Sor, Anssi Tikanmäki. Reviewed at the Saga-2 in Nordic Film Festival, Drammen, Norway, April 12, 1985. Running time: **85 MINS.**

Raja	Liisa Halonen
Hanno	Markku Toikka
Kalle	Antti Litja

Also with: Riitta Havukainen, Paavo Piskonen, Erkki Astala.

"The Love Movie" has a plot that would sound like dramatically-charged triangle stuff: a young married couple can have no children. So she has affair with other man, who happens to become gradually the husband's friend, too. The way writer-director Anssi Mänttari tells it, however, it comes out a rather sad and wise little comedy

Mänttari works mostly through fixed framings enlivened primarily by dialog and sharp though subdued acting in the three lead roles. While the plight of the young husband is at first viewed in a rather comical light, and while the lover enters mostly as a playboy-clown, both men soon prove sensitive as well as sensible in different, very sympathetic ways. When the woman finally gets pregnant by her lover, but discards him in favor of her husband, she too seems to have her actions redeemed by sound instincts.
—*Kell.*

Just One Of The Guys
(COLOR)

Gender bender eyes tender biz.

Hollywood, April 27.

Columbia Pictures release of a Summa Entertainment Group/Triton Ltd. production. Produced by Andrew Fogelson. Features entire cast. Executive producer, Jeff Franklin. Directed by Lisa Gottlieb. Screenplay by Dennis Feldman, Jeff Franklin, based on a story by Feldman; camera (Metrocolor), John McPherson; editor, Lou Lombardo; music, Tom Scott; production designer, Paul Peters; set decorator, Richard Reams; sound, Peter Hliddal; associate producers, Don McFarlane, Peck Prior; assistant director, Bill Scott; casting, Annette Benson. Reviewed at Columbia Pictures screening room, The Burbank Studios, April 26, 1985. (MPAA Rating: PG-13.) Running time: **100 MINS.**

Terry	Joyce Hyser
Rick	Clayton Rohner
Buddy	Billy Jacoby
Greg	William Zabka
Denise	Toni Hudson
Sandy	Sherilyn Fenn
Deborah	Deborah Goodrich
Kevin	Leigh McCloskey
Willie	Arye Gross
Phil	Robert Fieldsteel
Reptile	Stuart Charno
Coach Morrison	John Apicella
Mr. Raymaker	Kenneth Tigar

Popular and tenacious high school girl passing herself off as a boy at a rival campus serves as a deceptive cover for this comedy that's really about what it's like to be an outsider in the rigid teenage caste sysem. However, uneven nature of the film, which Columbia Pictures is unleashing wide, signals spotty business.

Newcomer Joyce Hyser, affecting a lower register, a short haircut, and a subtle swagger, is not totally convincing as a boy because she's too pretty and too chic in an array of great mod duds. But it doesn't really matter because the pic is a teen curiosity on the "switch angle" and Hyser is sufficiently winning in her masquerade to encourage willing suspension of disbelief.

The first feature of director Lisa Gottlieb and the first production of Summa Entertainment Group, company that producer Andrew Fogelson recently formed, "Just One Of The Guys" is an urban campus takeoff on "Yentl" and "Twelfth Night." The disguised heroine ultimately is compelled to bare all (well, at least her chest) to prove to another outsider, a sensitive male loner whom she (he) has befriended, that she really is a girl and is falling in love with him.

The scenario by Dennis Feldman and Jeff Franklin sets up the motivation for Hyser to act a boy when she becomes convinced that she lost a chance to win a summer intern job on the local daily newspaper because her journalism teacher considered her another pretty face instead of an intelligent writer.

But this feminist point is then abandoned when her new teacher makes it clear she didn't lose the journalism intern job because she's taken on as an airhead but because her contest entry was boring. You guessed it: she writes about what it's like to be a girl playing a boy in high school locker rooms, etc.

The locker room scenes and the men's P.E. classes offer the film's funniest scenes, and director Gottlieb (whose career was launched when she won a Student Academy Award for best film drama in 1980) gets solid supporting turns from John Apicella as the gym teacher and Kenneth Tigar as a journalism teacher.

But Gottlieb fails to make funny Hyser's first experience in a boys' restroom, and another effort at raunch humor — when Hyser's teen brother tries to help his sister affect macho poses by showing her how guys scratch their crotches — is crude and embarrassing.

As the sex-starved 15-year old brother, however, Billy Jacoby (the most experienced teen actor here although the youngest in the cast) manages to make an irrepressible horny role moderately entertaining.

Key male part of quiet outsider whom Hyser brings to life is essayed by another film newcomer, Clayton Rohner, but it was a casting miscue since Rohner looks too old to be a high school kid. Toni Hudson is fine as Hyser's bewildered and dateless girlfriend, but, in another off-center casting note, Hudson is much too cute to be a wallflower.

Class bully is well-played by William Zabka (reprising a role he did in "The Karate Kid"), and Leigh McCloskey is properly preppie-egotistical as Hyser's first boyfriend.

Film, from a slow start, builds momentum in its final half hour when relationships disassemble and assemble at prom night (shot at a man-made beach outside Scottsdale, Ariz., where production was billeted).

Scenario works in an affecting salute to soul godfather James Brown; and Rod Stewart's back-up band, The Brock-Davis Band, makes things hum at the prom. In sum, intention and results remain at variance through too much of the film. — *Loyn.*

Pumping Iron II:
The Women
(DOCU-COLOR)

A Cinecom Intl. Films release of a Pumping Iron presentation of a White Mountain film, in association with Gym Tech U.S.A. A Bar Belle Prods. production. Produced and directed by George Butler. Executive producers, Bernard Heng and Lawrence Chong; Screenplay, Charles Gaines and George Butler, based on their book, "Pumping Iron II: The Unprecedented Woman;" coordinating producer, John Hoffman; coproducer, Craig Perry; associate producers, Oliver Vaughan, Tommy Vaughan, Nick Irens. Features Lori Bowen, Carla Dunlap, Bev Francis, Rachel McLish. Camera (color), Dyanna Taylor; lighting, Rufus Standefer; editors, Paul Barnes, Susan Crutcher, Jane Kurson; sound (Dolby stereo), Eric Taylor; music, David McHugh, Michael Montes; additional photogrpahy, Tom Hurwitz, Chris Burrill, Joan Churchill, Jon Else; talent coordinator, Wayne DeMilia; musical consultant, Michael Kissel. Reviewed at Magno Preview 9 screening room, N.Y., April 15, 1985. (No MPAA rating.) Running time: **107 MINS.**

With: Lori Bowen, Carla Dunlap, Bev Francis, Rachel McLish, Kris Alexander, Lydia Cheng, Steve Michalik, Steve Weinberger, Randy Rice, Tina Plakinger.

This enjoyable, slickly conceived documentary on the burgeoning subculture of women's bodybuilding could have been better had director George Butler tempered his penchant for camera's eye detachment with some analytical and repertorial sweat. With its appealing vistas of glistening, uniquely sculpted female flesh, its wholehearted devotion to the cause of female potential and several interesting if not wholly revealed personalities, "Pumping Iron II" could do comfortable business in selective playoff.

Intent on avoiding a repeat of his 1977 docu, "Pumping Iron" (which launched superhunks Arnold Schwarzenegger and Louis Ferrigno on lucrative showbiz careers, but left the director to pick up the dumbbells), Butler has reached for a glossy mix of handy mid-'80s film conventions. He blends elements of "Flashdance"-type features (including a routine disco-pulsed theme track about "future sex") and quick-cut now-generation tv commercials with the vogue for narrator-free documentary in an attempt to fashion a razzle-dazzle hybrid.

Although he succeeds fairly well in exploiting the inherent drama of the 1983 Caesars Palace World Cup Championship for women bodybuilders (partly financed by the film's backers), Butler is too content to let the alluring amazons speak for themselves on the film's central question: What is femininity and how far may women go in liberating themselves from stereotypes before confronting immovable cultural resistance?

The question is embodied graphically by Australian power-lifter Bev Francis, whose awesome, spectacularly mannish physique will be matched in a great flex-off against the wiry, compellingly developed bodies of the best "feminine" bodybuilders. These include smug, shrewd defending champ Rachel McLish; the appealingly articulate Carla Dunlap, who's the only black woman in the group; and Lori Bowen, a humble girl from Texas who idolizes the aloof McLish and plans to use her prize money to free her boyfriend from his male go-go dancer's gig.

All the contenders are bonded by the common experience of painful, arduous training (by men who sometimes double as lovers) — the price they pay for their common determination to excel and stand out from the crowd. However, the film never addresses the obsessive narcissism that goes hand in hand with the sport's posing and body glorification. The documentary makes much of globetrotting visits to the principals' homes, but presents little more than surface insights into the contestants' personal histories. There's virtually no information on their diets, training regimens, means of support, and post-bodybuilding career plans.

Nevertheless, by the time the showdown comes, the docu's calculated sense of intimacy with its subjects has hooked audience interest in the outcome. Butler heightens the suspense by dwelling on the comic ineptness of the judges' deliberations and the ingrained prejudices of the male-dominated bodybuilding establishment. Arguably, justice is served by the contest's result, but rather than grapple with the consequences, the filmmaker walks away from them. —*Rich.*

Stick
(COLOR)

Tepid Burt Reynolds vehicle.

Hollywood, April 24.

A Universal Pictures release of a Jennings Lang production. Produced by Lang. Executive producer, Robert Daley. Directed by Burt Reynolds. Stars Reynolds, Candice Bergen, George Segal, Charles Durning. Screenplay, Elmore Leonard, Joseph C. Stinson, based on the novel by Leonard; camera (Technicolor), Nick McLean; editor, William Gordean; music, Barry De Vorzon, Joseph Conlan; production designer, James Shanahan; art director, Ed Richardson; set decorator, Philip Abramson; sound (Dolby stereo), Charles Darin Knight, Bob Gravenor; additional photography, Fred Koenekamp; associate producer, David Gershenson; assistant director, Jim Van Wyck; casting, Terry Liebling, Mary Colquhoun. Reviewed at Universal screening room, Universal City, Calif., April 23, 1985. (MPAA Rating: R.) Running time: **109 MINS.**

Stick	Burt Reynolds
Kyle	Candice Bergen
Barry	George Segal
Chucky	Charles Durning
Rainy	Jose Perez
Cornell	Richard Lawson
Nestor	Castulo Guerra
Moke	Dar Robinson
Firestone	Alex Rocco
Luis	David Reynoso
Bobbi	Sachi Parker
Katie	Tricia Leigh Fisher
Cecil	Tim Rossovich
Diane	Deanna Lund

Elmore Leonard's novel "Stick" about a hardboiled ex-con set loose in the nether world of South Florida drug traffic could have been a dream project for Burt Reynolds, but prolonged postproduction period, in which ending was reshot and character softened, has resulted in a hybrid Reynolds unlikely to totally satisfy any of his fans.

Pic starts off promisingly with a scruffy Stick (Reynolds) arriving by freight train fresh from the slammer in a Miami almost aglow in its malevòlence. Trouble soon erupts as Stick meets up with an old prison buddy who promptly gets blown away leaving Stick to find his revenge in true tough guy tradition.

Unfortunately, filmmakers have elected to water down Reynolds' single-mindedness and introduce a long lost daughter (Tricia Leigh Fisher) and an unlikely girlfriend (Candice Bergen). Directing himself, Reynolds may not have had the insight to realize his character is more sympathetic if he sticks to his guns rather than trying to tame the beast.

Plot is the convulted kind beloved by exhibitors since patrons can wander out for popcorn and come back without missing anything. Story doesn't really require a great deal of attention as an assortment of bad and worse guys try to get to Stick.

First is Charles Durning in a blond wig as a drug middleman under the thumb of mob kingpin Nestor (Castuelo Guerra). Heavies include an albino Moke (played by stunt whiz Dar Robinson) who Reynolds affectionately calls "bunny eyes."

Within this small circle of friends all roads lead to Palm Beach millionaire Barry Brahn (George Segal), who gives new meaning to the word crass. Stick takes shelter as Brahn's chaffeur until the twisted plot unravels in a climax somewhat lacking in punch.

Despite a few good action sequences, overall pic lacks the tension and suspense that could have got audiences involved instead of only mildly interested. Reynolds' direction is competent, but lacks the texture that could have fleshed out the distinctive personalities. Segal is on the verge of caricature and Durning, in his wig and enormous Hawaiian shirts, is so ludicrous he is hard to believe as a real person, not just another Durning character.

Tech credits are fine with Nick McLean's photography of Miami and environs providing a scenic backdrop to the nefarious goings-on.

As for Reynolds the actor, he's more convincing as a man of few words stalking his prey than a would-be family man who gets the girl and a Rolls Royce with a phone in the end.—*Jagr.*

Godzilla
(JAPANESE-COLOR)

Tokyo, April 9.

A Toho production. Directed by Koji Hashimoto. Features entire cast. Screenplay, Hidekazu Nagahara; camera (color), Kazutami Hara; music, Rejiro Koroku; sound, Nobuyuki Tanaka; art director, Akira Sakuragi; editor, Kuroiwa Yoshitami; special effects, Akiyoshi Nakano. Reviewed in Tokyo, December 1984. Running time: **103 MINS.**

Godzilla, Inoshiro Honda's highrise stomping saurian, first conquer-ed the world 30 years ago, and was to wobble through no fewer than 15 sequels for two decades. After a 10-year slumber, Godzilla rises again, awakened by director Koji Hashimoto and released last December, following months of trailers and promotional hype.

Despite its sophistiated cybernetic insides, Hashimoto's "Godzilla" totters around with all the terror of a papier-maché carnival float, its eyes rolling around like balls on a pool table. Huge in form and tiny in brains, Hashimoto's dinosaur seems closer to the real thing than he bargained for.

A first encounter between Godzilla and a ship sees handsome young scientist Hiroshi Okumara (Shin Takuma) the sole survivor aboard. Equally handsome young journalist Goro Maki (Ken Tanaka) comes to the rescue and, after bringing Okumura ashore, vows to warn the Japanese population of the approaching Godzilla menace. Prime Minister Mitamura (Keiju Kobayashi) unsuccessfully attempts to thwart him in order to avoid panic. Upon hearing that Godzilla is swimming towards the Japanese coast, actor Keiju Kobayashi runs the entire gamut of emotions for which he is famous in his daily antacid tv commercials. As Godzilla tramples the Tokyo skyline, Maki, Okumura and tiny team of heroic protagonists battle to save the world.

Along the way, Godzilla's rampage begins to trigger an accidental nuclear holocaust — leaving an incompetent cast of available foreign amateur actors to muddle through a hammy summit meeting.

Love interest derives from Maki's infatuation with Okumura's kid sister. This typically rotund, doe-eyed and submissive young lady is portrayed by singer-actress Yasuko Sawaguchi, the Toho company's answer to immensely popular Toei cutie-pie Hiroko Yakushimaru. Sawaguchi's crowning achievement is in the singing of the title song, her performance as uniformly flat and uninspiring as the others.

For all the hype, "Godzilla" generated less interest than expected, except among little boys, and performed sluggishly at the boxoffice. Lavishly filmed with no substance, the new "Godzilla" shows none of the makeshift inventiveness forming the campy charm of its predecessors. — *Born.*

Gotcha
(COLOR)

Teen comedy with espionage trappings.

Hollywood, April 27.

A Universal Pictures release of a Michael I. Levy Enterprises production. Produced by Paul G. Hensler. Executive producer, Levy. Directed by Jeff Kanew. Stars Anthony Edwards, Linda Fiorentino. Screenplay, Dan Gordon from a story by Hensler, Gordon; camera (Technicolor), King Baggot; editor, Michael Stevenson; music, Bill Conti; art direction, Norman Newberry; costumes, April Perry; sound, Colin Charles, Thomas Causey; supervising producer, Peter Macgregor-Scott; assistant director, Jim Simons; casting, Michael Fenton, Jane Feinberg. Reviewed at Mann's Regent Theater, Westwood, Calif., April 26, 1985. (MPAA Rating: PG-13.) Running time: **94 MINS.**

Jonathan Moore . . . . Anthony Edwards
Sacha . . . . Linda Fiorentino
Manolo . . . . Nick Corri
Father . . . . Alex Rocco
Russian agent . . . . Klaus Löwitsch

"Gotcha" is a typical adolescent lust comedy wrapped around a cover of Hitchcockian intrigue and exotic locations, a sort of "Notorious" for teens. It's an interesting attempt to pump some life into the tired and overworked teen genre with enough charm to attract the date-night crowd.

Jonathan (Anthony Edwards) and his roommate Manolo (Nick Corri) are UCLA students with two things on their mind. In addition to their usual obsession with scoring they also play a campus game in which they chase a group of mock agents around campus, zapping them with a pellet gun.

Fantasy becomes reality when the duo heads for France where the hapless Jonathan latches onto the lovely Sacha (Linda Fiorentino) who promises to teach him things European, viz, sex. Sacha's mock Czech accent fools no one but Jonathan who tags along when she tells him she is a courier and must make a delivery in East Germany.

Film takes a rather long time to pickup the espionage plot, foreshadowed with several not-very-subtle clues. Once pic does unravel it's a bit unbelievable, involving a roll of film presumably with vital secrets to be delivered to the West.

Director Jeff Kanew does little to create a real sense of menace or danger in the proceedings and chases through East Berlin seem more there for the scenery, which, in fact, is quite lovely. In pursuit is a KGB agent (Klaus Löwitsch) who somehow seems better suited for the campus game than the real thing. But the film's climax at UCLA, with the Russians chasing the kids followed by the CIA, is beyond belief.

The Hitchcock plot here is really a McGuffin for the romance, but unlike the real thing, the characters have little depth with nothing on the line except whether they'll get back in bed together or not. Despite a basically well written and witty script by Dan Gordon, "Gotcha" has still not abandoned the convention of the teen-sex comedies where the only thing that matters is scoring.

Other curiosity for an '80s campus film is how the CIA has become, if not the great guys, then at least the good guys.

Fiorentino is charming as the older woman and one wants to believe in their love affair, but its foundation, established with a montage of shots showing the couple having fun at various international settings, is not convincing enough.

Fortunately as Jonathan, Edwards is sweet and trusting enough to allow him his play things. Together he and Fiorentino are an unlikely, but appealing couple.

Tech credits are fine with location work by cinematographer King Baggot a plus. — *Jagr.*

Gymkata
(COLOR)

Routine martial arts, though it has moments.

Hollywood, May 4.

MGM/UA release of a Fred Weintraub Prod. Produced by Weintraub. Directed by Robert Clouse. Screenplay by Charles Robert Carnes, based on the novel "The Terrible Game" by Dan Tyler Moore; camera (Metrocolor), Godfrey Godar; editor, Robert A. Ferretti; production designer, Veljko Despotovic; music, Alfi Kabiljo; sound, Lee Milliner; art directors, William Maynard, Nemanja Petrovic; associate producer, Rebecca Poole; assistant director, Vladimir Spindler. Reviewed at Mann's Chinese Theatre, L.A., May 3, 1985. (MPAA Rating: R.) Running time: **90 MINS.**

Jonathan Cabot	Kurt Thomas
Princess Rubali	Tetchie Agbayani
Zamir	Richard Norton
Paley	Edward Bell
Gomez	John Barrett
Hao	Conan Lee
Thorg	Bob Schott
The Kahn	Buck Kartalian

Premiere American gymnast Kurt Thomas introduces fresh boy-next-door gloss to this martial arts programmer. His whirring legs, cutting down opponents like swords, comprise the entertainment quotient from producer Fred Weintraub and director Robert Clouse, same team who featured Bruce Lee in Warner Bros.' 1973 hit "Enter The Dragon."

Pic has quick playoff potential, spinning off renewed interest in gymnastics and the diehard martial arts market.

Featuring a former Miss Philippines (Tetchie Agbayani), the film's karate choreographer and villain Richard Norton, and capitalizing on ancient, bleak fortress backgrounds in Yugoslavia, pic can be credited for imaginative touches.

Typically for the genre, the story, dealing with a secret mission by Thomas to secure a military site in a remote and hostile country near the Caspian sea, is uninteresting and cartoon-like.

The acting is more stiff than usually encountered in such pics. One performance, by Buck Kartalian as a good-guy ruler, is laughably bad.

Near the conclusion, film has one terrific, long sequence that features Thomas overcoming hordes of crazies in a dank, narrowly walled village. — *Loyn.*

Code Of Silence
(COLOR)

Action-packed Chuck Norris policier.

Hollywood, April 30.

An Orion Pictures release. Produced by Raymond Wagner. Directed by Andy Davis. Stars Chuck Norris. Screenplay, Michael Butler, Dennis Shryack, Mike Gray; camera (Astro Color), Frank Tidy; editors, Peter Parasheles, Christopher Holmes; sound, Scott Smith; production design, Maher Ahmed; assistant director, James A. Dennett; stunts, Aaron Norris; music, David Frank; casting, Richard S. Kordos, Nan Charbonneau. Reviewed at the Directors Guild of America, Hollywood, April 29, 1985. (MPAA Rating: R.) Running time: **101 MINS.**

Eddie Cusak	Chuck Norris
Luis Comacho	Henry Silva
Commander Kates	Bert Remsen
Diana Luna	Molly Hagan
Nick Kopalas	Joseph Guzaldo
Tony Luna	Mike Genovese
Scalese	Nathan Davis
Cragie	Ralph Foody
Pirelli	Allen Hamilton
Victor	Ron Henriquez
Brennan	Ron Dean
Spider	Wilbert Bradley

With 27 stuntmen and Chuck Norris in the credits, "Code Of Silence" is a predictably cacophonous cops-and-crooks yarn that should play off extremely well in the action houses. It's actually quite good for the type.

Any semblance of reality, of course, is bent a bit, but not to the extremes of the usual kung-foolery. When Norris encounters a jillion toughs in a bar he's able to kick down a half-jillion of them before the other half-jillion beat him up, but at least he loses.

When all alone Norris takes on an army of thugs in a warehouse, he brings along a robot car armed with cannons and machine guns, picking off the stragglers with a shotgun and a large pistol. This all takes place in Chicago.

The best thing about Norris is he never gets involved in all that romance stuff. Granted, there's a pretty girl (newcomer Molly Hagan) whose life is at stake, put Norris never does more than hold her hand, lend his brawny chest for her to cry on, and — finally in a fit of passion — kiss her on the forehead.

Norris plays a police sergeant leading a raid on a drug den, who arrives a step behind anther gang which gets away with all the dope and money, leaving a bloody mess behind. This sets off a gang war between forces led by properly menacing Henry Silva on one side and less prominent Mike Genovese on the other. Norris' law-enforcement involvement is complicated by the fact that he knows one of his incompetent cops killed an innocent kid during the raid and he won't go along with a coverup.

Norris, in other words, is a bit lonely and exposed with two gangs out in front of him and no cops behind him. That's the way he likes it.

As sometimes happens in these films, there's a jewel of a scene not connected to anything else that highlights Zaid Farid and Dennis Cockrum as a couple of psyched-up robbers who make the mistake of holding up a barful of cops. The pair could have filled out another whole film.

Director Andy Davis moves the action along sprightly, though the cutting suggests some footage may have been lost or forgotten.—*Har.*

Cave Girl
(COLOR)

Crude and unfunny Stone Age comedy.

Hollywood, May 6.

A Crown Intl. Pictures release of a David Oliver production. Produced and directed by Oliver. Screenplay, Phil Groves, Oliver; camera (color), Oliver; editor, Robert Field; music, Jon St. James; sound, Ken Willingham, Bayard Craig, Walt Martin; associate producer, Reed Fenton. Reviewed at Mann Fox, Hollywood, Calif., May 5, 1985. (MPAA Rating: R.) Running time: **87 MINS.**

Rex	Daniel Roebuck
Cave Girl	Cindy Ann Thompson
Old prospector	Bill Adams
Teacher	Larry Gabriel
Argh	Jeff Chayette
Atilla	Valerie Greybe

Premise of a college nerd who goes on a field trip and is hurtled by a time warp into prehistoric times where he makes lewd advances on a comely cave girl results in an excruciatingly dull, raunchy, tacky production and a disastrous feature debut for director-producer-cinematographer-cowriter David Oliver, who normally makes his living shooting credit sequences.

First-time film comic Daniel Roebuck, who looks like a young, corpulent Eddie Bracken, and pert and shapely Cindy Ann Thompson (who made her debut in Crown Intl.'s "Tomboy"), play the odd couple, inanely cavorting in boulder country outside Bakersfield, Calif. After playing doctor with the cave girl, the nerd falls in love.

Crown Intl. may milk this dreck for a dime — company's plotting a regional campaign through May — but breakeven would amount to a marketing miracle. Tiny turnout (maybe 30 patrons) at Hollywood Boulevard venue snickered a total of three times over sexual crudity. — *Loyn.*

Movers & Shakers
(COLOR)

Lightweight view of Hollywood.

An MGM/UA Entertainment release of a United Artists presentation, produced in association with BHC (Briggle, Hennessey and Carrothers). Produced by Charles Grodin, William Asher; coproducers, Richard Carrothers, Dennis D. Hennessey. Directed by Asher. Stars Walter Matthau, Grodin. Screenplay, Grodin; camera (Metrocolor), Robbie Greenberg; editor, Tom Benko; music, Ken & Mitzie Welch; sound, Michael Evje; assistant director, Michele Ader; production manager-associate producer, Jean Higgins; art direction, Donald L. Harris; set decoration, Janice Flating; postproduction supervisor, Peter V. Ware; additional photography, Michael A. Jones, Michael Gershman; casting, Fern Champion, Pamela Basker. Reviewed at MGM/UA screening room, N.Y., April 30, 1985. (MPAA Rating: PG.) Running time: **79 MINS.**

Joe Mulholland	Walter Matthau
Herb Derman	Charles Grodin
Saul Gritz	Vincent Gardenia
Nancy Derman	Tyne Daly
Sid Spokane	Bill Macy
Livia Machado	Gilda Radner
Fabio Longio	Steve Martin
Reva	Penny Marshall
Marshall	Earl Boen
Arnie	Michael Lerner
Larry	Joe Mantell
Louis Martin	William Prince
Dorothy	Nita Talbot

Also with: Sandy Ward, Judah Katz, Peter Marc, Sam Anderson, Frances Bay, Luana Anders.

"Movers & Shakers" is an unsuccessful insider's look at the foibles of the creative end of Hollywood filmmaking. Comedy is only occasionally amusing and faces a bleak boxoffice future. Pic was lensed without announcement to the trade last spring under the more appropriate title "Dreamers."

First of twin stories concerns the production chief of a studio, Joe Mulholland (Walter Matthau), who is dedicated to making a meaningful, quality picture in tribute to his hero, ailing producer Saul Gritz (Vincent Gardenia). Buying the rights (literally, just the title) to the bestselling manual "Love In Sex" as a result of a deathbed promise to Gritz, Mulholland hires successful screenwriter Herb Derman (Charles Grodin) to try and come up with an idea for the impossible project. Meanwhile, second story is about Derman, who is having extreme personal problems with his withdrawn wife Nancy (Tyne Daly), who won't let him touch her.

Mulholland is in trouble with his boss Louis Martin (William Prince) at the studio, especially after installing a huge model dinosaur that cost $1,000,000 and "only moved a little" (for a special effects epic that never got made) as a monument to the man who dreamed it up, Gritz. As the film project goes awry, Derman's marital problems are paralleled by the slapstick-violent relationship of the film's goofy director Sid Spokane (Bill Macy) and his girlfriend, soon to be his wife, Livia (Gilda Radner).

In his original screenplay for "Movers & Shakers," Grodin takes various potshots at lamentable filmmaking trends, including in-jokes such as the dinosaur which instantly recalls the recalcitrant title figure in Dino De Laurentiis' "King Kong" remake that costarred Grodin. He scores his best points in presenting production meetings where a lot of thinking-out-loud occurs.

Unfortunately, film is overburdened with extensive voiceover narration by Grodin, which steals the spotlight from the central character expertly essayed by Matthau. What's more, we find out nothing about the personal life of Matthau's production topper persona, while the Daly-Grodin relationship remains cryptic and cannot sustain the emphasis placed upon it. Vet comedy director William Asher (who piloted the 1982 tv version of "Charley's Aunt" starring Grodin) fails to bring any visual style to this low-budget feature, whose talky format will probably play better on tv.

An unusually interesting cast has been recruited, with solid support provided by Macy, Radner and Daly. Steve Martin guests in a seven-minute cameo as a Ramon Novarro-era latin star, but it is not prime comedy material and Martin's ego-trip spoof is similar (but inferior by comparison) to Billy Crystal's patented Fernando Lamas takeoff. It's also a pleasure to see Nita Talbot as an acerbic coworker, Joe Mantell as Derman's agent and in a small role, Luana Anders, who costarred in 1964 in Grodin's first feature (for AIP), "Sex And The College Girl." — Lor.

Terminal Choice
(CANADIAN-COLOR)

An Almi Pictures release of a Magder Film Prods. production. Executive producers, Jean Ubaud, Maqbool Hameed. Produced by Gary Magder. Directed by Sheldon Larry. Features entire cast. Screenplay, Neal Bell, from story by Peter Lawrence; camera (Medallion color), Zale Magder; editor-second unit director-second unit camera, Murray Magder; music, Brian Bennett; sound, Peter Shewchuk; assistant director, Tony Lucibello; production design, David Jaquest. Reviewed at Almi screening room, N.Y., May 6, 1985. (MPAA Rating R.) Running time: **97 MINS.**

Frank Holt .... Joe Spano
Anna .... Diane Venora
Dr. Dodson .... David McCallum
Dr. Rimmer : .... Robert Joy
Chauncey Rand .... Don Francks
Henderson .... Nicholas Campbell
Mary O'Connor .... Ellen Barkin
Mrs. Dodson .... Chapelle Jaffe
Nurse Barton .... Clare Coulter

"Terminal Choice" is a dull medical thriller unlikely to stir the blood of horror fans with its clinical bloodletting. Pic was lensed in Toronto in 1982 and has gone through various name changes, including "Trauma," "Critical List" and "Death List."

Joe Spano (of tv's "Hill Street Blues") toplines as Dr. Frank Holt, known for his drunkenness, whose patients are dying at Dodson Medical Clinic. Audience is tipped off immediately that someone is tampering with the automated hospital's computer, and that the doctors and staff are engaged unethically in betting on details of the patients' diagnoses and recovery periods.

Computer whiz (and Holt's former g.f.) Anna (Diane Venora) is investigating, along with hospital's attorney Chauncey Rand (Don Francks) and there are many

suspicious-looking doctors on the premises, notably new intern Henderson (Nicholas Campbell). Several more stiffs enter the loss column, including pathologist Mary O'Connor (Ellen Barkin), before the bad guys are exposed and plot ends tied up in an awkwardly structured final reel windup.

More lowkey and ominous than suspenseful, pic elaborates far too much on what Stanley Kubrick succinctly created in his classic "Life Functions Terminated" computer display (when HAL the computer kills the sleeping crew members) scene in "2001: A Space Odyssey." Under debuting feature helmer Sheldon Larry's cool direction, violence is meted out by machine, with the human factor present (man controls machine) but out of sight. The tangible fears of powerlessness in a hospital situation are not really tapped, and a science fiction style open-ending (in which the computer is supposedly poised to self-program) doesn't work.

Acting is merely adequate by a cast far superior to the material at hand. Emphasis upon blood and vomiting is strictly a turnoff.—Lor.

Subway
(FRENCH-COLOR)

Paris, April 22.

Gaumont release of a Gaumont/Films du Loup/T.S.F./TF 1 Films coproduction. Produced by Luc Besson and François Ruggieri. Stars Isabelle Adjani and Christophe Lambert. Directed by Luc Besson. Screenplay, Luc Besson, Pierre Jolivet, Alain Le Henry, Sophie Schmit, Marc Perrier; camera (color), Carlo Varini; art director, Alexandre Trauner; editor, Sophie Schmit; sound, Harald Maury; makeup, Maud Baron; music, Eric Serra; production manager Edith Colnel. Reviewed at the Gaumont Colisée theater, Paris, April 20, 1985. Running time: **104 MINS.**

Helena .... Isabelle Adjani
Fred .... Christophe Lambert
Florist .... Richard Bohringer
Gesberg .... Michel Galabru
The Roller .... Jean-Hugues Anglade
Station master .... Jean Bouise
Drummer .... Jean Reno
Batman .... Jean-Pierre Bacri
Jean .... Pierre-Ange Le Pogam

"Subway" brings to mind Orson Welles' quip about the cinema being the greatest electric train a boy could have. Its director, Luc Besson, is only 26, and already has shown resourcefulness and a sense of filmmaking fun with his 1982 low-budget sci-fier "Le Dernier Combat." For his second feature, Gaumont (distrib of "Combat") gave him over 15,000,000 francs, Christophe Lambert and Isabelle Adjani as stars, and let him go play in the Paris Metro. Result may disappoint some for its singular lack of ambition or purpose and its ragged narrative, but still proves a charmingly cartoonish escapade, strong on humor and rock rhythms.

Pic's hero is Lambert, a dynamite-toting, punk-coiffed ec-

centric who has crashed a posh birthday party for poor little rich girl Adjani and stolen some compromising documents belonging to her influential husband. Pursued by a carful of latter's thugs, Lambert takes refuge in the subway at the moment of its early morning closing.

There he befriends some of the subterranean denizens — a young roller-skating purse-snatcher (Jean-Hugues Anglade), a shady flower-seller (Richard Bohringer) and a black muscleman who works out with spare subway car parts — and decides to realize his dream of managing a rock band, by recruiting the Metro's itinerant musicians.

In the meantime he is sought by the thugs, the Paris transport police (headed by Michel Galabru), and Adjani, who goes slumming to escape the boredom of her gilded milieu and perhaps find true love with Lambert. He pays court to her, but is really more concerned with his rock group.

Film went through heavy cutting in final editing stages, with 40 minutes shorn away to get it down to average commercial length, which explains the lapses in plot and sometimes disjointed continuity. But the roughness feels right in a film that resolutely refuses to take itself seriously.

To tip viewers off, Besson starts his film with a bright send-up of windy literary citations, and carries on nonchalantly right through to the apparently tragic climax, in which Lambert's clichéd romantic demise in Adjani's arms is deflated by an expected final close-up of the supposedly dead hero.

The casual manner doesn't exclude a sense of wonder and lyricism as Besson, aided by the invaluable eyes of veteran art director Alexandre Trauner and lenser Carlo Varini, explores the tunnels, stations and byways his characters inhabit.

Lambert is winningly offbeat with yellow hairdo and borrowed tuxedo, and Adjani seems to have had fun in a more episodic part that gently mocks her beauty-queen star image. Entire supporting cast joins in the lark. —Len.

Ein Kriegsende
(And End To The War)
(WEST GERMAN-B&W-16m)

Berlin, April 11.

A Studio Hamburg Atelier production in collaboration with Norddeutscher Rundfunk (NDR), Hamburg. Directed by Volker Vogeler. Features entire cast. Screenplay, Siegfried Lenz; camera (b&w), Günther Wulff; sound, Horst Stroemer; editing, Claudia Rieneck; sets, Gerd Staub; costumes, Renate Hanke; production manager, Rudolf Sander; tv-producer, Dieter Meichsner. Reviewed at Landesbildstelle Screening Room, Berlin, April 10, 1985. Running time: **80 MINS.**

With: Wigand Witting (Commander), Rüdiger Kirschstein (Coxswain), Christian Koch (Defense Lawyer), Michael Weckler

(Fireman), Franz Josef Steffens (Naval Attorney), Eike Gallwitz (Radio Operator), Boris Vogeler (Sailor).

Volker Vogeler's "An End To The War" makes for stimulating docu-drama, for this original and tightly narrated story is based loosely on true incidents that happened in the German marine in that twilight period at the end of the war between May 5 and May 13, 1945 (the actual German capitulation took place May 8). Things did not in fact exactly happen the way Siegfried Lenz narrates them, but the archival records (in Kornelimünster, near Aachen) show no fewer than nine cases involving 21 accused-and-executed sailors took place during the frightful week.

This is the story of a naval mutiny. The commander of a minesweeper is ordered in May 1945 to cross the Baltic Sea from a German-occupied Danish port (Sonderborg) to the Latvian port of Liepaja (Libau in German) on a suicide mission to rescue wounded and encircled (by the Soviet army) German troops. While the ship is underway with the intention of hugging the Swedish coast before making the attempt to cross the Baltic by night — a dangerous move that meant sure death in submarine-infested waters — the commander and the crew receive the news on the radio that the capitulation has taken place.

With this in mind, the question undoubtedly going through the minds of the crew was: why commit suicide for a cause that's already lost? Lenz describes the situation in sparse narration and even sparser dialog. The coxwain, a friend of the commander (they come form the same fishing village on the North Sea), decides to take over the ship with the help of the firemen and a dozen other sailors. There is no resistance, although the commander warns this is mutiny. The ship then tries to make for Kiel, but German naval boats still on patrol force a return back to the harbor at Sonderborg in Denmark.

And now comes the tragic twist: the Germans have, indeed, capitulated — but the formalities of obedience at sea are still held to be more binding than turning over all legal rights to the victorious British. Even the British navy allows the German officers to try and execute mutinous sailors, momentarily placing the weapons in their hands for carrying out the death sentence. Vogeler and Lenz, although working entirely within the bounds of a fictitious case, have recounted an incredible irony of fate.

Vogeler's direction is low-key and sketched in black-and-white documentary tones. The protagonists — a few thesps in key roles, the rest nonprofessionals — speak their lines in matter-of-fact cadences. The one emotional note comes when the commander of the ship (against whom the mutiny had originally taken place) reacts to the judgment of the naval court giving the death penalty to the coxwain and the fireman: "Madness — this is madness!"

In Lenz' version, only two sailors are condemned to death unjustly. The naval records show 11 were so executed on May 5, 1945 in much the same trial situation, while another five were executed on the same day in another case for sabotage. All this with the full permission of Britain's Royal Navy (whose commanders supplied the German POW officers with the guns to carry out the death penalties).

—*Holl.*

Bayo
(CANADIAN-COLOR)

St. John's, April 29.
A Norstar release of a Jape Film Services Inc. and National Film Board of Canada production, in association with the Canadian Broadcasting Corp. Produced by Harry Gulkin. Stars Ed McNamama, Patricia Phillips and Stephen McGrath. Directed by Mort Ransen. Screenplay, Ransen, Terry Ryan, Arbie Gelbart, based on the novel by Chipman Hall; camera (color) Georges Dufaux; editors, François Gill, Yves Langlois; music, Loreena McKennit. Reviewed at Avalon Mall Cinema, St. John's, Newfoundland, April 25, 1985. Running time: **100 MINS.**

While other Canadian filmmakers were masquerading the streets of Toronto for those of Toledo and attempting third-rate spinoffs of "Beach Blanket Bingo" and the like during the infamous Canadian tax shelter days of the late '70s, Montreal producer Harry ("Lies My Father Told Me") Gulkin stuck to Canadian cultural themes and carried the hopes of many that Canada could in fact develop its own distinct and vibrant film identity.

Aside from certain French-track filmmakers from the province of Quebec, such, unfortunately, was not to be; and Gulkin, beset by all manner of personal difficulties, disappeared from the scene.

Now, eight years later, Gulkin has returned with the sort of offering that had been the hallmark of his earlier produced pics. Almost like a Newfoundland version of the critically acclaimed "Lies My Father Told Me," Gulkin's latest, "Bayo," directed by Montrealer Mort Ransen, is as Canadian as the country's famed "goose" and its maple syrup. With its all-Canadian cast and crew, "Bayo" is an earnest, sensitive and touching account of the relationship between an impressionable, strong-minded 10-year-old and his crusty grandad.

Set in the rugged, strikingly picturesque environs of the Newfoundland coastal community of Tickle

Cove, the film introduces Stephen McGrath as Bayo, the young lad who feels he's wasting away because he has yet to set out for the sea like his granddad did when he was all of nine. Bayo is torn between his hot-tempered, voluptuous mom Sharon (Patricia Phillips), the Tickle Cove trollop who yearns to hightail it to relatively-upbeat Toronto with her son, and his eccentric granddad Philip (Ed McNamara), whose last wish is that he may walk on water.

Film has its witty, whimsical moments as well as its provocative ones, especially those revolving on issues of abandoning down-home rural roots. Both McGrath and Patricia Phillips as the mom turn in marvelously textured performances; unfortunately, Ed McNamara as the salty, mystical seaman isn't as salty or as mystical as would best befit the part.

Original Celtic-type score by Loreena McKennit is superlative, and photography by Georges Dufaux perfectly complements proceedings. Film should fill the elusive family entertainment gap on tv both in Canada and internationally, where foreign viewers are likely to be enthralled by a view of Canada all too rarely seen abroad — or at home, for that matter. — *Bro.*

Short Circuit
(DOCU-COLOR-16m)

Hollywood, April 12.
An Icarus Films release. Produced by Alan Francovich. Directed by Francovich. Associate producer, Molly Daughety; editor, Andrea Primdahl. Reivewed at Nuart Theater, L.A., April 11, 1985. (No MPAA Rating.) Running time: **70 MINS.**

It is unfortunate that "Short Circuit" is a film destined only to be seen by people with a special interest in Latin American politics, since its message is an important one about alleged U.S. involvement in the Salvadoran death squads. As a talking-head documentary, film will play basically to the converted.

Film is really an extended interview with the former director of the El Salvador intelligence agency, Col. Roberto Santivanez, who details how the U.S. has instigated and supported random political executions in his country.

Santivanez makes a strong case in what attempts to be a dispassionate, objective style. Throughout the film, Santivanez is filmed sitting at a restaurant table with a view of Washington, D.C. appropriately in the background. Francovich limits himself to two shots, medium-shot and close-up, and, consequently, the presentation loses much of its impact.

The director obviously felt that the material would speak for itself

and for a large part it does. Santivanez authoritatively documents atrocities such as the murder and rape of nuns, the assassination of San Salvador's Archbishop Romero and the execution of two American labor advisors.

While Santivanez describes the complex workings of the U.S./El Salvador relationship, the recitation of facts and details seems only the surface of a more difficult and complex reality.—*Jagr.*

Goodbye New York
(ISRAELI-COLOR)

A Castle Hill Prods. release of a Kole-Hill production. Produced, written and directed by Amos Kollek. Stars Julie Hagerty. Camera (color), Amnon Salomon; editor, Alan Heim; assistant director, Baruch Abilof; music, Michael Abene. Reviewed at Magno Preview 4, N.Y., April 1, 1985. (No MPAA Rating.) Running time: **90 MINS.**
With: Julie Hagerty, Amos Kollek, David Topaz, Aviva Ger, Shmuel Shiloh, Jennifer Babtist, Christopher Goutman.

"Goodbye New York" is a pleasant, albeit slight diversion from Israeli Amos Kollek, son of Jerusalem Mayor Teddy Kollek, and showcasing American actress Julie Hagerty. Tale of a sophisticated New Yorker who winds up in Israel with no money, friends or family teeters a little too shakily between comedy, drama and travelog, but remains an accomplished debut from writer-director-costar Kollek.

Pic's opening sequence, similar to many another, presents a contented Hagerty coming home to her apartment one day to find her husband with another woman. Understandably miffed, she promptly packs a bag and gets on a plane bound for Paris. Instead, through her own fault, she winds up in Tel Aviv, where she is quickly set upon by a wry, lovelorn cabbie (Kollek) who

offers her temporary shelter.

He takes her to a kibbutz where she is indoctrinated humorously into the ways of farm life. Subsequent portions of the film involve Hagerty's getting ripped off in a Jerusalem boutique and getting taken by a smooth-talking building contractor.

Film benefits from Kollek's performance as the lonely cabbie and part-time soldier who yearns for a night with Hagerty. He has a winning sense of humor; when asked by an American tourist how to get to the birthplace of Jesus, he retorts, "The Lord? Oh, *Him!*"

The writer, however, has not done well by Hagerty and her role is underdeveloped to the point of being Kollek's representative naive American. He seems to use her as an open book in which he can inscribe all that is wrong or misunderstood about the situation in the Middle East. Uneasy jokes about the PLO and ongoing warfare don't sit well with the conventional story of boy meets girl. Also pointless and out of character is a scene in which the thin, exercise-conscious Hagerty cheerily volunteers to take part in a banana-eating contest, eventually stuffing down 60 green ones.

Pic is well photographed and offers to the uninitiated an interesting look at the modern Holy Land, but commercial prospects Stateside appear limited. Hagerty's patented soft-spoken persona is sabotaged here by frequent and loud use of four-letter words, which further extends the uneasiness. Native Israeli support cast is fine and there's a cameo appearance by Mayor Kollek as a man on the street who advises Hagerty to "tell it to the mayor" after she has rattled off a litany of local humiliations. —*Gerz.*

Going To Cannes

Pale Rider
(COLOR)

Clint Eastwood brings back the Western in quality form.

Hollywood, May 1.
A Warner Bros. release of a Malpaso production. Produced and directed by Clint Eastwood. Stars Eastwood. Executive producer, Fritz Manes. Screenplay, Michael Butler, Dennis Shryack; camera (Technicolor, Panavision), Bruce Surtees; editor, Joel Cox; music, Lennie Niehaus; production design, Edward Carfagno; set design, Bob Sessa; set decoration, Ernie Bishop; costume supervision, Glenn Wright; sound (Dolby), C. Darin Knight; associate producer-assistant director, David Valdes; stunt coordinator, Wayne Van Horn; special effects, Chuck Gaspar; casting executive, Phyllis Huffman. Reviewed at The Burbank Studios, Burbank, April 30, 1985. (MPAA Rating: R.) Running time: **115 MINS.**

Preacher	Clint Eastwood
Hull	Michael Moriarty
Sarah Wheeler	Carrie Snodgress
Josh LaHood	Christopher Penn
Coy LaHood	Richard Dysart
Megan Wheeler	Sydney Penny
Club	Richard Kiel
Spider Conway	Doug McGrath
Stockburn	John Russell

After a long dry spell, the Western has returned in fine shape under the strong, knowing guidance of Clint Eastwood in "Pale Rider." Satisfying on all the essential levels, actor-director's first oater in nine years, since "The Outlaw Josey Wales," adroitly blends traditional story elements with some up-to-date attitudes to yield a winning audience pleaser. If Westerns are indeed to make a comeback, this is a good place to begin.

After having served his apprenticeship and become a star in Westerns, Eastwood clearly knows his way around the territory, and he has been very shrewd in selecting plot points and iconographic motifs that have proved effective over the years.

As he did in his Sergio Leone trilogy, Eastwood portrays a nameless drifter, here called ''Preacher,'' who descends into the middle of a struggle between some poor, independent gold prospectors and a big company intent upon raping the beautiful land for all it's worth.

Borrowing from ''Shane,'' ''Preacher,'' so dubbed because he initially appears wearing a clerical collar, moves in with a group consisting of earnest Michael Moriarty, his somewhat reluctant lady friend Carrie Snodgress and her pubesent daughter Sydney Penny.

Preach instantly gains a local reputation by rescuing Moriarty from some corporation thugs and roughing them up, and little by little he pulls the threatened community together and inspires them to fight for their rights to the land rather than give up.

Along the way, both Snodgress and her daughter develop heavy crushes on the mysterious stranger who, not too surprisingly, turns out not to be a preacher at all, but a former gunslinger.

When it appears that his business interests are genuinely threatened, ruthless tycoon Richard Dysart recruits some hired guns to take care of Eastwood, and these mercenaries materialize in striking longcoats similar to those worn by Henry Fonda's men in ''Once Upon A Time In The West.''

It's all been seen before, but Eastwood serves it up with authority, fine craftsmanship and a frequent sense of fun. Eastwood has continued to improve steadily as a director to the point where he is now one of the top actor-auteurs in the business.

This film is graced not only by an excellent visual look and confident storytelling, but by a few fine performances, led by Eastwood's own. For his part, Moriarty brings surprising nuance and depth to a rather standard noble pioneer role, and Christopher Penn represents a nicely offbeat choice to play Dysart's arrogant young son. Snodgress and Penny, a Phoebe Cates type, do well enough, but suffer a bit from limited screen time and the abruptness with which the script expects them to reveal their feelings for Eastwood.

Eastwood's final nemesis in the inevitable showdown in the middle of town is essayed by hawkfaced John Russell, (star of tv's ''Lawman'' series), who bears an uncanny resemblance to the star's former opposite number, Lee Van Cleef.

Lenser Bruce Surtees, shooting in the widescreen format, has made the most of the gorgeous Idaho locations, although some of the interiors are so dark one can barely make out the people within them. Production and costume design contribute a wonderful rustic look, and other craftwork is firstrate.

—*Cart.*

Le Thé au Harem d'Archimède
(FRENCH-COLOR)

Paris, May 4.

A K.G. production and release, with the participation of the Ministries of Culture and of Exterior Relations. Produced by Michèle Ray-Gavras. Written and directed by Mehdi Charef, based on his novel, ''Le Thé au Harem d'Archi Ahmed.'' Camera (Fujicolor). Dominique Chapuis; Kenout Peltier; art director, Thierry Flamand; editor, sound, Jean-Paul Mugel, Claude Villand; music, Karim Kacel. Reviewed at the Gaumont Ambassade theater, Paris, May 2, 1985. Running time: **110 MINS.**

With: Kader Boukhanef, Rémi Martin, Laure Duthilleul, Saïda Bekkouche, Nicole Hiss, Sandrine Dumas, Nathalie Jadot, Brahim Ghenaiem, Frédéric Ayivi, Pascal Dewaemre, Bouriem Guerdjou, Jean-Pierre Sobeaux, Nicolas Wostrikoff.

This is not the first film about life on the gray proletariat fringes of Paris, but it is certainly one of the best. Newcomer Mehdi Charef, who wrote and directed from his own quasi-autobiographical 1983 novel, is a 32-year-old Algerian immigrant who has worked in a factory most of his adult life — until filmmaker Constantin Costa-Gavras and his producer-wife Michèle Ray-Gavras optioned his book, and signed him as scripter-helmer.

There is nothing fundamentally new in this tale of two teens, one French, the other Arab, knocking about aimlessly in the suburban lower income housing projects that lodge a melting pot community ravaged by unemployment, loneliness and other private and social ills. However, Charef displays unusual skill in combining the personal experience of an insider with the objectivity of an interested observer.

Charef chronicles the daily lives of his two petty delinquents, intercutting them at times with those of family, friends and neighbors. Pat, the French boy, doesn't work because he doesn't want to, preferring to sponge off his barkeep mother. Madjid can't find a job, partly because he's an Arab, partly because he's not motivated. His large family is supported by the mother since a work accident reduced the father to a near-zombie state.

The two boys are inseparable buddies, hanging out together, picking up girls or prostitutes together, committing acts of pimping, burglary or muggings together. Pat is cynical about romance, dreaming only of becoming a gigolo on the Riviera, while Madjid pursues his friend's pretty sister, who now avoids him since landing a job in Paris. She, in fact, has become a streetwalker, and the discovery cruelly affects the young Arab.

Charef's handling of the digressive narrative is sober and confident, finding the right angle and distance on incidents without giving a global feeling of gratuitous sordidness. The theme of the two youth's friendship is remarkably rendered, in that it is never stressed. The implicit bond is strengthened by the fine, natural performances of Rémi Martin and Kader Boukhanef, both as new to film as their director.

Film's only disruptive effect is the silent film-style flashback sequence in which the title is explained: a classroom scene in which an ignorant student, asked to identify the Théoreme d'Archimèdes (Archimedes' Principle) on the blackboard, writes ''thè au harem d'Archi Ahmed'' (Tea in the harem of Archi Ahmed). The scene is funny, but jars the dispassionate manner of the storytelling.

Charef has had expert backing from a fine technical crew, including lenser Dominique Chapuis and editor Kenout Peltier, who helped the helmer recreate the texture and rhythms of working class suburban life (most of the film was shot in the melting pot municipalities of Gennevilliers and La Courneuve, north of Paris). Costa-Gavras, by the way, served as production stills photographer.

Film won this year's Jean Vigo Prize and was awarded a distribution aid grant by the Apple Foundation for the Cinema. In addition to its official screening at Cannes in Un Certain Regard, supplementary viewings are planned on the Croisette. —*Len.*

Otac Na Sluzbenoh Putu
(Father's On A Business Trip)
(YUGOSLAV-COLOR)

Berlin, April 30.

A Centar Film production, Belgrade. Produced by Mirza Pasic. Directed by Emir Kusturica. Features entire cast. Screenplay, Abdulla Sidran. Only credits available. Reviewed at Berliner Screening Room, April 29, 1985. Running time: **125 MINS.**

With: Mareno de Bartoli (Malik), Miki Manojlovic (Mesa, the father), Mirjana Karanovic (Sena, the mother).

Emir Kusturica, one of Yugoslavia's bright young talents, made his mark with his debut feature, ''Do You Remember Dolly Bell?'' (1981), awarded the Opera Prima at the Venice festival that year. Now his second feature, ''Father's On A Business Trip,'' has been selected for the competition at Cannes. It's another winner: even at its lengthy two hours running time it should score on the festival circuit.

''Father's On A Business Trip'' is set in Sarajevo during the troubled years following Tito's break with Stalin and the Soviet Cominform, from 1948 to 1952. The times were particularly difficult, for former partisans and wishful believers in the Communist future could be arbitrarily accused of Stalinism and (whether guilty or innocent) chucked into work-correction camps for the duration.

Pic is seen through the eyes of six-year-old Malik, and it's his rather witty commentary on the events about him that sets the tone of this finely etched tragicomedy. Malik sees his father always away on business trips, but what he doesn't know (until the final scenes) is that he's a brusque and lusty Lothario with a yen for the girls while maintaining a warm and tender affection for his family, the wife Sena and the two sons Malik and Mirza (the older brother).

The twist of fate comes when a girlfriend of the father, Mesa, turns her erstwhile lover over to the local police inspector during a fit of jealousy. Despite the fact that Sena's own brother is police commissioner, Mesa is picked up at night and packed off to the salt-mines, so to speak. No reasons are given for the arrest, but Mesa is sure of the real reason although his misguided sense of male honor prevents him from relating his suspicions to his wife. As a result, Sena has to suffer through three miserable years as a seamstress at home to make ends meet.

After the prison mandate is over, he has his revenge against the brother-in-law and former girlfriend in a quaint, brawny Yugoslav manner (the absurd twist to end the film).

''Father's On A Business Trip'' scores as a film of irony and sarcasm, imbued with ''human comedy'' tenderness — rendered much in the style of Czech comedies during the mid-1960s.—*Holl.*

Padre Nuestro
(Our Father)
(SPANISH-COLOR)

Madrid, May 1.

A Classic Films Produccion production. Executive producers, Eduardo Ducay and Julián Marcos. Directed by Francisco Regueiro. Screenplay, Regueiro, Angel Fernández Santos; camera (Eastmancolor), Juan Amorós; production manager, Emiliano Otegui; editor, Pedro del Rey; sound, Bernardo Menz; sets, Enrique Alarcón; make-up,

Adolfo Ponte, special effects, Antonio Molina; costumes, Gumersindo Andrés. Reviewed at Cine Conde Duque (Madrid), April 28, 1985. Running time: **104 MINS.**

Cardinal	Fernando Rey
Abel	Francisco Rabal
Cardenala	Victoria Abril
Maria	Emma Penella

Also with: Amelia de la Torre, Rafaela Aparicio, Lina Canalejas, José Vivo, Yolanda Cardama, Luis Barbero, Francisco Vidal, Diana Peñalver, M. Elena Flores.

An often sketchy plot and occasional clumsy editing leave "Padre Nuestro" hanging in indecision between a comedy and a drama. Often verging on caricature, the screenplay, despite some clever dialog and apposite scenes, never quite makes its point. Francisco Reeguerio's film will be shown in Un Certain Regard section at the Cannes Film Festival.

Story concerns a Spanish cardinal in Rome who discovers he has only one more year to live and decides to return to his hometown to straighten out his affairs, after an absence of 30 years. It turns out he had an illegitimate child by a servant girl who subsequently turned to prostitution; she in turn also had an illegitimate child, now living with the cardinal's wealthy family. The monsignor's brother is a freethinking doctor, the mother an eccentric dowager and the former servant has married a shepherd.

The cardinal tracks down the daughter and induces her to consent to marry his brother. Before this can be accomplished, the churchman dies a somewhat whimsical death right after talking to the Pope on the phone. Aside from the mild satire on the Church and reglion, just what the film is driving at never comes across. —*Besa*.

Dust
(BELGIAN-FRENCH-COLOR)

Paris, April 17.

A 20th Century Fox (France) release of a Man's Films (Brussels), Daska Intl. (Ghent), Flach Films (Paris), FR3 Films (Paris) coproduction, with the participation of the Communauté Française de Belgique and De Ministerie Van de Vlaamse Gemeenschap. Produced, written and directed by Marion Hansel, based on the novel, "In The Heart Of The Country" by J.M. Coetzee. Camera (Fujicolor), Walther Vanden Ende; editor, Susanna Rossberg; production designer, Pierre Thévenet; sound conception, Henri Morelle; sound, Ricardo Castro; music, Martin St. Pierre. Reviewed at the FR3 screening room, Paris, April 16, 1985. Running time: **87 MINS.**

Magda	Jane Birkin
The father	Trevor Howard
Hendrik	John Matshikiza
Klein Anna	Nadine Uwampa
Oud Anna	Lourdes Christina Sayo
Jacob	René Diaz

"Dust" is an English-language Belgian-French coproduction, adapted by its Flemish-born director from a South African novel and filmed with two British leads on locations in southern Spain. Despite the disconcerting heterogeneity of production and cultural components, Marion Hansel's second feature imposes impressive uniformity and style on this harrowing study of loneliness and sexual desperation.

Set on an isolated South African farmstead, story, drawn from novel by Jean-Marie Coetzee, focuses on the mental disintegration of a young, spinsterish white woman who murders her sullen, uncommunicative father (Trevor Howard) when he seduces the young wife of the farm's black foreman.

Burying the body with the help of the frightened Hottentot, she sets about trying to recreate an intimate community with the black couple, with racial barriers down. The foreman only grows more wary and angered in the face of Birkin's pathetic self-degradation. In a climactic confrontation he rapes his mistress and then runs away with his bride.

Hansel, a former actress who directed her first feature in 1983, is admirably in control of a difficult subject, artfully creating a hallucinatory zone of ambiguity and eroticism around the thoughts and actions of the main characters. As the final shot suggests, Birkin's patricide and rape may only be the fantasizing of a disturbed mind, whetted by atrocious solitude and emotional barrenness.

Director also deserves a special tip of the hat for guiding Birkin to the most electrifying dramatic performance of her career. She represents her character's suffering and disintegration with intensity and economy of means that weren't quite evident in the psychodramatic parts she had in her French-language films. Acting in her native tongue could also be a factor to her haunting portrayal.

Howard is effectively pathetic as the laconic father, turned in on himself and his own sexual longings, and indifferent to his daughter's hunger for love and attention. John Matshikiza and Nadine Uwampa are perfect in communicating the racial fears and sexual arrogance of the black couple.

Film is technically excellent, with Pierre Thevenet's production design and Walther Vanden Ende's lensing convincing the viewer he is in the South African veldt, and not in San Jose, Spain, where the entire picture was shot. Henri Morelle, credited for "sound conception," also deserves a nod for the vivid aural ambiance.

"Dust," which could find specialized interest internationally, was strangely refused for any of the sections at Cannes, and is betting on a market unspooling to stir up interest. —*Len*.

Partir Revenir
(Departure, Return)
(FRENCH-COLOR)

Paris, April 16.

A UGC release of a Films 13/UGC/Top 1/FR3 Films coproduction. Produced and directed by Claude Lelouch. Screenplay, Lelouch, Pierre Uytterhoeven, Jérôme Tonnerre, Julie Pavesi; camera (Eastmancolor), Bernard Lutic; art director, Jacques Bufnoir; sound, Harald Maury; music, Sergei Rachmaninoff, Michel Legrand; lyrics, Jean-Loup Dabadie, sung by Liliane Davis; editor, Hugues Darmois; costumes, Catherine Leterrier, Laurence Schneider. Production manager, Tania Zazulinsky. Reviewed at the UGC Normandie theater, Paris, April 15, 1985. Running time: **117 MINS.**

Hélène Rivière	Annie Girardot
Roland Rivière	Jean-Louis Trintignant
Vincent Rivière	Richard Anconina
Simon Lerner	Michel Piccoli
Sarah Lerner	Françoise Fabian
Salomé Lerner	Evelyne Bouix
Salomon Lerner	Erick Berchot
Tenardon	Charles Gérard
Priest	Jean Bouise
Salomé Lerner (1985)	Monique Lange
Governess	Isabelle Sadoyan
Priest's maid	Ginette Garcin
Angela	Marie-Sophie Pochat

Claude Lelouch's new film looks like a sub-plot he couldn't squeeze into his earlier monument of historical bathos, "Les Uns et les Autres" (a.k.a. "Bolero").

The central concern of "Partir Revenir" is the problems of a Jewish family during the early years of the German Occupation of France. When their Paris concierge denounces them to the Gestapo, the clan, headed by Michel Piccoli and Françoise Fabian, hides out in the provincial chateau owned by gentile friends Jean-Louis Trintignant and Annie Girardot.

They are again denounced, this time carted off to a concentration camp. Only the daughter (Evelyne Bouix, Mrs. Claude Lelouch) survives and returns to the chateau after the Liberation to find out who delivered them to the Nazis.

Lelouch cheats the audience by simply withholding all information that would lead one to suspect the true culprit. Instead he and his writers construct a mystification, notably around the personage of the chatelains' son (Richard Anconina), who had courted Bouix in vain and is thus the number one suspect. The intrigue is not nearly as puzzling as the innocent Anconina's weird indifference to being considered a heinous criminal.

On this the director superimposes a secondary theme of reincarnation, expressed in the framing present-day narrative about the Bouix character (portrayed by novelist Monique Lange), who believes her long-dead music-loving brother reborn in the person of celebrated young pianist Erik Berchot (who in fact plays himself and the brother in his screen debut).

Lelouch's dazzling array of virtuoso hand-held camerawork and sinuous single-shot sequences includes one roller-coaster scene that is a pretentious crib of the helmer's 1976 stunt short, "Le Rendezvous," with the camera slung low on the hood of a madly speeding sports car.

The name cast is competent within the severe limits of the script's superficial characterizations, but no player succeeds in being genuinely moving. Technical credits are typically first-rate, especially Bernard Lutic's lensing. —*Len*.

The Naked Country
(AUSTRALIAN-COLOR)

Sydney, May 1.

A Filmways (Australia) release of a Naked Country Prods. production, in association with the Queensland Film Corp. Executive producers, Mark Josem, Robert Ward, Bill Marshall. Produced by Ross Dimsey. Directed by Tim Burstall. Stars John Stanton, Rebecca Gilling. Ivar Kants. Screenplay, Dimsey, Burstall, from the novel by Morris West; camera (color), David Eggby; editor, Tony Paterson; music, Bruce Smeaton; art director, Philip Warner; sound, Max Bowring. Reviewed at Greater Union screening room, Sydney, April 29, 1985. Running time: **92 MINS.**

Lance Dillon	John Stanton
Mary Dillon	Rebecca Gilling
Sgt. Neil Adams	Ivar Kants
Mundara	Tommy Lewis
Mick Conrad	John Jarratt
Inspector Poole	Simon Chilvers
Menyan	Neela Dey

A rousing tale of survival against the odds, "The Naked Country" is a fast moving, gutsy adaptation of a Morris West novel. Set in a remote part of Northern Queensland in 1955, pic involves conflict between a single-minded rancher (John Stanton) and a tribe of Aboriginals who consider that his ranch occupies part of their tribal land.

Mundara (Tommy Lewis), a renegade from his own tribe because the woman (Neela Dey, Mrs. Tim Burstall) he loves is given in marriage to another man, gets into trouble by killing Stanton's prize Brahma bull, then also killing one of the rancher's men when he attempts to intervene. Stanton himself is speared in the shoulder and staggers off into the bush, pursued by Mundara and a group of hostile blacks.

Thus the stage is set for a central section of the film somewhat similar to Cornel Wilde's "The Naked Prey." Stanton's survival and eventual appreciation for the qualities of his noble enemy make up the bulk of the film. There's also a subplot involving Ivar Kants as a cop fresh home from Africa, where he fought as a mercenary; he's a man with a drinking problem and he also sets his sights for Stanton's beautiful, lonely wife (Rebecca Gilling), who responds briefly before rejecting Kants for his weakness.

Essentially this is a good old-fashioned Western relocated to Australia. Burstall, one of the pioneers of the Australian cinema, has a good story to tell, and tells it with plenty of energy and without pretension. David Eggby's lensing of the spectacular outback scenery is great, and the tight editing of Tony Paterson has brought the film in at a commendably tight 92 minutes.

Stanton is excellent as the rugged rancher who, despite his wounds, survives, while Kants is rightly weak and vacillating as the cop. Gilling has looks and style as the wife out of her element in the outback, while Tommy Lewis is rugged and strong as the hostile black. Supporting performances are all good, with special mention going to Simon Chilvers as Kants' displeased superior and John Jarratt as Stanton's foreman.

Theme of aboriginals attacking whites may stir some controversies Down Under, but pic should succeed on its entertaining story, well-handled action scenes, and exotic settings and characters.—*Strat.*

L'Attenzione
(Attention)
(ITALIAN-COLOR)

Rome, May 7.

A Belvaggia Film release, produced by Francesco Casati and Sergio Martinelli for Selvaggia Film productions. Stars Ben Cross and Stefania Sandrelli. Directed by Giovanni Soldati. Screenplay by Leone Colonna and Solidati with the collaboration of Rodolfo Sonego, based on a novel by Albert Moravia, camera (color), Silvano Ippoliti; art director Marco Dentici; editor, Nino Baragli; music, Pino Donaggio. Reviewed at Esparia Cinema, Rome, April 11, 1985. Running time: **85 MINS.**
Alberto . . . . .Ben Cross
Livia . . . . .Stefania Sandrelli
Monica . . . . .Amanda Sandrelli

"Attention" (aka "The Lie") has ingredients for a torrid drama of sexual passion and repressed emotions; unfortunately, it is just too slow, heavy-handed and unfocused to supply the kick it's supposed to. It's interesting mainly for the appearance of Ben Cross as an Italian journalist married to Stefania Sandrelli, whose unchained sex appeal is still a drawing card at the national b.o. Another oddity to pique the public's curiosity is the appearance of Sandrelli's daughter Amanda, getting her feet wet in the role of mother's rival to dad's affections. Offshore chances look misty.

All begins with the meeting of Livia (Stefania), then a lusty young barmaid, and dashing reporter Alberto (Cross) many years before. For Livia, their first passionate union has now turned into a worse than routine marriage, with Alberto off to China for six months at a time and only the distraction of her high fashion atelier to keep her mind off him. All her efforts to get him back, even for one night, prove in vain. What's wrong?

The answer is not hard to find, as Alberto visibly fights down his craving for delicious teenage daughter Monica, an urge that grows stronger by the scene. Livia decides to take desperate measures. Unbeknownst to her husband, she begins arranging rendezvous for him with young girls, while she listens in tortured frenzy in the next room, wishing it were her. Things take a wrong turn, however, when Monica lets herself be drawn into the scheme and (to mother's horror) makes an open bid to become Alberto's lover.

Apart from the kinky casting, the Sandrellis work with perfect conviction as the sultry mother-daughter rivals. Newcomer Amanda shows signs of budding talent as an actress and almost as much allure as mère Stefania, who is now much at home in the role of the irresistably mature woman. Cross seems much less certain about what he is doing in the film; between a totally passive role and Italian dubbing, not much of his charisma comes across.

One of the weakest sides of the pic is its lack of courage in confronting the brass tacks of the central incest issue: info that Monica isn't Alberto's flesh and blood is tossed in just before the going gets heavy. Similar teasing is accorded Livia's much-hinted-at lesbian attraction to the girls who work for her and the ambiguous pleasure she takes in becoming her husband's procurer. A little more directness from young helmer Giovanni Soldati would have been welcome. — *Yung.*

Creature
(COLOR)

Hollywood, April 26.

A Cardinal Film Releasing Corp. release of a Cardinal Entertainment Corp. and Trans World Entertainment, Inc. presentation. Produced by William Dunn, William Malone. Executive producer, Moshe Diamant, Ronnie Hadar. Features entire cast. Directed by Malone. Screenplay by Malone, Alan Reed; camera (Foto-Kem color), Harry Mathias; music, Thomas Chase, Steve Rucker; editor, Bette Cohen; art director, Michael Novatny; sound, Steve Nelson, Trevor Bloch; associate producer, Don Stern; special effects, L.A. Effects Group; assistant director, Gordon Boos, Steven Weaver; casting, Johanna Ray. Reviewed at Paramount Theater, Hollywood, Calif., April 26, 1985. (MPAA Rating: R.) Running time: **97 MINS.**
Davidson . . . . .Stan Ivar
Sladen . . . . .Wendy Schaal
Perkins . . . . .Lyman Ward
Pennel . . . . .Robert Jaffe
Dr. Oliver . . . . .Annette McCarthy
Bryce . . . . .Diane Salinger
Hofner . . . . .Klaus Kinski

"Creature" (originally titled "Titan Find") is living proof that you can't keep a good alien down for long. Pic tries to resurrect the premise of the hit Fox sci-fi chiller "Alien" from several seasons back, but at best comes off as an unintentional parody of the original. Playing it for laughs could have helped

but production opts for a serious tone unlikely to please fans of the genre.

All elements here are stripped down to the bare minimum. Plot immediately unravels as an American corporate ship arrives on one of Saturn's moons to investigate a doomed predecessor's discovery of mysterious life forms. Also in the race is a German competition vessel already downed at the site.

Lone survivor from the German ship is one Hans Rudy Hofner rendered by Klaus Kinski in what must have been one day's work. In a variation on the mad scientist role, Kinski is the only actor here to grasp the inherent humor of the material. Unfortunately, he's not around very long as he soon becomes fodder for the "Creature."

Crew of the good ship seems to be a mix of housewives and heavies who wander back and forth from the two ships pursued by the slimy creature, who has a trick of attaching mind control devices to his victims. Cast is competent given the stilted nature of the material but the real stars are the special effects and, of course, the creature.

Unfortunately, effects are basically routine with few thrills and chills to be found. Interiors of the space crafts look like updates from the old "Flash Gordon" serials. And the creature, really a man in a costume, is scary only on one or two occasions. — *Jagr.*

Little Treasure
(COLOR)

Slight story strips chances.

A Tri-Star Pictures release of a Vista Films/Herb Jaffe production. Produced by Jaffe. Stars Margot Kidder, Ted Danson and Burt Lancaster. Executive producers, Joanna Lancaster, Richard Wagner. Written and directed by Alan Sharp. Camera (Metrocolor), Alex Phillips; editor, Garth Craven; production designers, Jose Rodriguez, Granada & Enrique Estevez; music, Leo Kottke; sound, Claude Hitchcock; assistant director, Ramiro Jaloma; production manager, Ricardo Frera; casting, Lonka Becker. Reviewed at UA Gemini 1 theater, N.Y., May 3, 1985. (MPAA Rating: R.) Running Time: **95 MINS.**
Margo . . . . .Margot Kidder
Eugene . . . . .Ted Danson
Teschemacher . . . . .Burt Lancaster
Norman Kane . . . . .Joseph Hacker
Evangelina . . . . .Malena Doria
Joseph . . . . .John Pearce
Sadie . . . . .Gladys Holland
Charlie . . . . .Bill Zuckert
Chuck .James Hall

Shot on location in Mexico in early '84, Tri-Star's "Little Treasure" has received a one-theater booking in Manhattan, with little hope for wider exposure. Pic, though well photographed in seldom-seen locales, is painfully slight in terms of story and not likely to attract any but the curious.

Margot Kidder plays an aimless stripper who at film's start has arrived in a remote Mexican village, having been summoned by her long-departed father. As soon as she arrives she is befriended by a grizzly American expatriate (Ted Danson) who agrees to take her in his broken-down van to find the old man.

What appears to be intended as a key point in the picture, the reunion of father and daughter, is brushed off in a few brief scenes and is merely a setup for a hokey adventure in which Danson and Kidder search for stolen money. Father-daughter thing seems to have been concocted simply to showcase Burt Lancaster, who dies early on from gangrene. (Reported on-set fight between Lancaster and Kidder during shooting is not betrayed by their character's mutual admiration for each other.)

Picture is skittish at times, and especially unsettling during a sequence in which Kidder, who heretofore has only gone topless (she says) on stage, is offered increasing amounts of cash to go all the way by a shady young socialite (Joseph Hacker) who has hired her to perform at an intimate pool gathering. Long shots of the naked woman, with face indistinguishable, suggest a body-double tactic on Kidder's behalf.

Danson is the most appealing character on view, but his character's motivations aren't explained sufficiently to justify why he has abandoned civilization; he's simply too amiable to be convincing as a pessimistic outcast.

For the record, some of the pic's most loving closeups are reserved for cans of Coke, spotlighting the Tri-Star/Columbia connection.
— *Gerz.*

The Holy Robe Of The Shaolin Temple
(Mu Mien Jia Sha)
(CHINESE-COLOR)

Hong Kong, April 1.

A Golden Principal Film, released by Southern Films. Executive producer, Hon Pou Chu, Tsung Keh Ehian. Directed by Tsui Siu Ming. Screenplay, martial arts director, Ming. Stars Hsu Hsiang Dong, Lin Chiu Pyng, Yu Yung Kong. Narrator, Pai Hua, Lo Kwok Tsim, music, Joseph Koo Kai Fai with theme song sung by Ming. Reviewed at Nanyang theater, Hong Kong, March 25, 1985. Running time: **98 MINS.**
(Mandarin soundtrack with Chinese and English subtitles)

"The Holy Robe Of The Shaolin Temple" is set during the Ming Dynasty, when peasants were driven to stealing and a series of rebellions by the excessive taxes levied by the reigning monarchy.

The Shaolin Temple, known for its tradition of teaching the best martial arts, becomes, in the film, a center of this revolt. Through an imperial edict, government minister Wang Cheng sends an army to surround the temple and arrest Yuan Hui.

Facing the problem with inner strength, Yuan Hui orders his disciples, Hui Neng and Hu Chi, to escape from the siege with the Royal Robe Kapok Kasaya while he sets fire to himself to save the lives of the other monks in the temple.

The Kapok Kasaya is a patchwork outer vest worn only by the Abbot. As it is a treasure from the Shaolin Temple, anyone who has it can proclaim himself an Abbot.

However, Hu Chi is killed and the holy robe falls into the hands of the enemy. Help comes from a horse dealer and his four daughters and the robe finally gets to a man who rightfully deserves it.

Story is old hat and the filming style rather dated by Hong Kong standards, but the never-before-filmed sights of China, along with the superb Shaolin-type martial arts, are sufficient reasons to see this exotic picture.

Although there are no established names in the film with whom Hong Kong viewers will be familiar, the performers are experts in their fields and excel in their respective action roles.

Essentially a kung fu-type film, with some very human and honorable sentiments, pic clearly indicates China is learning fast in the field of commercial cinema, even to the level of distributing overseas. — Mel.

Staline
(FRENCH-COMPILATION-B&W)

Paris, April 29.

An AAA release of a Films Ariane production. Produced by Jean-José Richer. Directed by Jean Aurel, inspired by the book by Boris Souvarine. Editor, Jacqueline Lecompte; sound, Michel Fano, Jean-Paul Loublier; documentation, Frédérique Grou Radeneze. Reviewed at the Studio Cujas, Paris, April 28, 1985. Running time: 103 MINS.

Jean Aurel's film about Soviet dictator Josef Stalin is less documentary than diatribe. His tone is that of the smug political pamphleteer, not the objective historian, making this compilation feature often suspect as far as historical fact goes. The viewer tends to take the offensive against the commentary's undisguised contempt, even when sharing the same opinion.

Aurel, a screenwriter and sometime director (he coscripted François Truffaut's last two films and has helmed a number of short and feature-length docus on art and France at war) retraces, with the aid of French and German archive footage, the career of Stalin, from his unpromising debut during the October Revolution, through to his death in 1953, when most of the civilized world continued to pay him homage as a great leader.

Rather than provide a historical context for his viewpoint, Aurel is content to regurgitate what is generally known about Stalin's murderous regime and his monumental political gaffes, such as his faith in Hitler's non-aggression promise. There is no nuance to the presentation, which simplifies without analyzing, and dishonestly passes off still unproved conjectures as cold fact (like Stalin's hypothetical murder of writer Maxim Gorky). He even goes so far as to present scenes from an official Soviet biopic about the dictator, without identifying them as such.

Aurel denies Stalin even the most superficial qualities, summing him up as the most sanguinary monster the world has ever seen. Maybe so, but this irresponsible film doesn't bring us an iota nearer to understanding why, even today, the name of Stalin has nowhere near the resonance of evil as that of Hitler.
— Len.

Manchurian Avenger
(COLOR)

Oddball martial arts Western.

A Facet Film production and release. Executive producer, Timothy Stephenson. Produced by Robyn Bensinger. Directed by Ed Warnick. Features entire cast. Screenplay, Pat Hamilton, Stephenson, from story by Richard Kim; camera (Western Cine color), Rich Lerner; editor-sound, Hal Freeman; music, Paul Conly; assistant director-production manager, Don Rase; art director, Sarah Liles; stunt coordinator, Bernie Welch; casting, Meredith Mulholland; associate producer, M.J. Studer. Reviewed at Criterion 5 theater, N.Y., April 27, 1985. (MPAA Rating: R.) Running time: 81 MINS.

Joe .... Bobby Kim
Kamikaze .... Bill (Superfoot) Wallace
Diego .... Michael Stuart
Booyong .... Leila Hee
Kilo .... Jose Payo
Harry .... Bob Coulson
Maria .... Barbara Minardi
  Also with: Y. Tsuchimoto, Steven Harp, Larry Shephard, Song Padulla, Rich Occhuzzio, Karl Niccoletti, Jerry Witt, Sy Meheen.

The 1985 return of theatrical Western releases begins inauspiciously with the goofy "Manchurian Avenger" a martial arts cheapie shot in Colorado two years ago.

Bobby Kim, a diminutive, craggy-faced type, toplines as Joe, returning to his hometown to avenge the murder of his father many years ago. Racism is rampant there, with both orientals and Mexicans victmized (there are no Indians in this picture).

With everyone trying to find some hidden gold, Joe protects an attractive young woman Booyong (Leila Hee) and teams up with the kindly bartender Harry (Bob Coulson) and outlaw Diego (Michael Stuart) to fight the evil Cheng (Y. Tsuchimoto) and his many henchmen.

Hurt by choppy editing (there apparently wasn't enough coverage or transition footage shot), pic becomes absurd during the frequent chop-socky scenes, in which it is contrived (unbelievably) that Kim can kick any number of baddies before they shoot him down with pistols or rilfes. Second-billed martial arts champ Bill (Superfoot) Wallace has no dialog and little screen time to demonstrate his own fancy footwork.

Rich Lerner's auburn-filtered visuals occasionally suggest a period look, but over-reliance by director Ed Warnick on wide angle and low angle shots is distracting and amateurish. Acting is weak, with everybody having different sorts of accents and Michael Stuart extremely hammy as a stereotyped Mexican bandito.

Final reel attempt at mystical fantasy (Cheng conjuring up the wind machine with hand gestures and Kamikaze disappearing after his defeat in a cloud of smoke) is pointless and lacks special effects. —Lor.

MacArthur's Children
(Setouchi Shonen Yakyu Dan)
(JAPANESE-COLOR/B&W)

An Orion Classics release. Produced by You-No-Kai and Masato Hara. Directed by Masahiro Shinoda. Features Masako Natsume, Shima Iwashita and Hiromi Go. Screenplay, Takeshi Tamura, based on the novel by Yu Aku. Camera (color, b&w), Kazuo Miyagawa; production design, Yoshinobu Nishioka; music, Shinichiro Ikebe; lighting, Takeharu Sano; editor, Sachiko Yamaji; recording, Hideo Nishizaki. Reviewed at Orion Screening Room, N.Y., April 25, 1985 (MPAA Rating: PG.) Running time: 120 MINS.

Ryuta Ashigara .... Takaya Yamauchi
Saburo Masaki .... Yoshiyuki Omori
Mume Hatano .... Shiori Sakura
Komako Nakai .... Masako Natsume
Tadao Ashigara .... Shuji Otaki
Haru Ashigara .... Haruko Kato
Tetsuo Nakai .... Ken Watanabe
Jiro Masaki .... Shinsuke Shimada
Ginzo Nakai .... Taketoshi Naito
Yoko Masaki .... Chiharu Shukuri
Lieutenant Anderson .... Bill Jensen
Interpreter .... Takashi Tsumura
Admiral Hatano .... Jyuzo Itami
Masao Nakai .... Hiromi Go
Tome Anabuki .... Shima Iwashita
  Also with: Naomi Chiaki, Miyuki Tanigawa, Howard Mohett, Akihiro Hattori, Osamu Yamazaki, Munekatsu Mori, Takeshi Marutani, Tsutomu Tatsumi, Kuniyasu Toda and Ryuji Sawa.

Set on the rural island Awaji Shima just after the end of World War II, "MacArthur's Children" aims to treat in microcosm the traumatic adjustment of the Japanese to their nation's defeat and occupation by the American Army. Although director Masahiro Shinoda has fashioned a gorgeously lensed, appealingly acted film, "MacArthur's Children" fails to fully exploit the dramatic potential in the confluence of victorious and vanquished cultures. Instead the storyline puts a conventional Japanese emphasis on the emotionally wrenching personal life crises of several key characters, treating the larger topic of defeat and occupation with a subtlety that might be less discernible to non-Japanese audiences than to Shinoda's countrymen. Consequently, "MacArthur's Children" does not figure to be the long-awaited breakthrough film that will create an American commercial audience for Japanese cinema.

Comely schoolteacher Komako (Masako Natsume), her husband (Hiromi Go) presumably killed in action, lives with her well-off but callous in-laws who do nothing to shield her from the boorish advances of their elder son, Tetsuo (Ken Watanabe), a wastrel drug addict. By day, Komako instructs her schoolboy charges to remain proud during the (humiliating) adjustments that will follow the Emperor's surrender speech. These include rewriting textbooks to erase all references to the recent Imperial past. So, a textbook uncle who commands a batallion overseas becomes, with a brushstroke, "my uncle who works overseas."

The bitterness of defeat is particularly jarring to class leader Ryuta (Takaya Yamamuchi) and his pugnacious sidekick, bad boy Saburo (Yoshiyuki Omori) who, after a shocking confrontation with the principal, threatens to leave school and become a "baraketsu" (gangster) rather than dishonor the memory of his dead father in "warrior's heaven."

Ryuta's soon to have a new friend, spunky Mume Hatano (Shiori Sakura), who's arrived on the island with her father, Admiral Hatano. The somber, dignified admiral expects to be named a war criminal (he had failed to save English POW's aboard his ship when it was torpedoed and sunk) and wants to "cleanse my soul in natural surroundings" before his inevitable arrest by the occupation forces. Also waiting in anticipation for the Americans is resourceful, sexy war widow Tome (Shima Iwashita, Shinoda's wife), who observes all comings and goings-on from her dockside barbershop which serves as a clearinghouse for town gossip.

The differing, though intertwined, fates of these characters become the picture's main concern. The Americans are always held at a distance, compassionate conquerors who bring candy bars, Glenn Miller ("In The Mood" is pic's theme track) and something called "democracy," which none of the villagers quite knows how to define. Humorously, Awaji Shima is deemed such a backwater by the occupation that the Army sends a small detachment commanded by Lt. Anderson (one-dimensionally written and routinely essayed by Bill Jensen) whose only real scene comes when he upbraids his men for entering a Japanese home with shoes on. There's not much direct intercultural exchange between Americans and Japanese in the film, but there are an abundance of tearful reunions and partings, a drunken rape, a stunning surprise, tragedy and triumph of sorts in a climactic baseball game between the plucky schoolkids and the good-natured GIs.

While Shinoda perhaps overstresses the type of heartstring dramatics prized by Japanese audiences, he excels at capturing the riveting beauty of the island location, and in evoking the smalltown folkways of a vanished time in which traditional Japanese behavior codes were being replaced with exotic Western morality. —*Rich.*

Stranger At Home
(DUTCH-DOCU-COLOR-16m)

Amsterdam, April 18.

A Fugitive Cinema Holland release of a De Eerste Amsterdamse Filmassociatie production. Produced by Marjon van Schaik. Directed by Rudolf van den Berg. Camera (color), Theo van de Sande, Jules van Steenhoven; editor, Henk van Eeghen; sound, Menno Euwe; music, Boudewijn Tarenskeen; dubbing, Jan van Sandwijk. Reviewed at Filmtheater Desmet, Amsterdam, April 16, 1985. Running time: 93 MINS.

A chance meeting in Washington, D.C., when Dutch helmer Rudolf van den Berg presented his documentary "The Alien" three years ago, brought about this new 16m film. It tells of Washington-based Palestinian artist Kamal Boullata's first visit to his birthplace in 18 years, thanks to his American passport and an exhibition of his silkscreens in East Jerusalem.

Boullata, who had been refused re-entry by the Israeli authorities after the 1967 war, longed for Jerusalem but with much trepidation: how would his dreams and childhood memories measure up to the new realities?

Hope and anxiety, twin companions of returning exiles, forged a personal, often uneasy, bond between the Jewish filmmaker and his prospective protagonist, who at one point declares: "To be a Palestinian means to be a Jew on an existential level."

Film covers controversial ground and raises complex political and ethical issues. On the whole, it presents them clearly enough to spark discussion and will interest thoughtful audiences in non-theatrical and specialized situations.

Excellent cinematography and good technical credits help to sustain the emotional impact of this story of a gifted, intelligent and successful exile, unable to feel at home either in Washington or in Jerusalem.

"Stranger At Home" is a deliberately dramatized report and a highly emotional film that vividly shows two reactions to a harrowing, deadlocked situation. — *Ewa.*

Blues Metropolitano
(Metropolitan Blues)
(ITALIAN-COLOR)

Rome, May 7.

An Associated Artists release, produced by Claudio Bonivento for Numero Uno Cinematografica. Features entire cast. Directed by Salvatore Piscicelli. Screenplay by Piscicelli and Carla Apuzzo; camera (Eastmancolor), Giuseppe Lanci; editor, Raimondo Crociani; art director, Massimo Perna and Antonio Bosco; music, Joe Amoruso, Pino Daniele, Tony Esposito, Tullio De Piscopo, Little Italy, Anthra, Ascenn. Reviewed at Nuovo Cinema, Rome, May 4, 1985. Running time: 116 MINS.
Stella . . . . Marina Suma
Francesca . . . . Barbara d'Urso
Tony . . . . Stefano Sabelli
Elena . . . . Ida De Benedetto
With: Maurizio Capone, Paolo Bonetti.

A free-wheeling musical for the young set, shot in Naples around a big concert tent. Helmer Salvatore Piscicelli ("Immaculata And Concetta," "Rosa") brings considerable finesse to an apparently simple structure that alternates live performances by top new musicians with a jumble of characters and stories. The Associated Artists release was hurt by the long strike of the Gaumont-Cannon chain, but has undoubted youth appeal and can be expected to recoup in the provinces.

As fest fare, "Blues" has a tangential relationship to helmer's previous work. Though Naples is once more the setting and thesps recognizable denizens from their faces and accents, pic stays closer to the surface. Human sexual variety and the difficulty of partnering is the driving force behind the fragmentary stories: sex as obsession, as social leveler, as an exchange of money.

Among the dozens of sketches is a young music impresario restlessly running between concert numbers, a Mafia bid to buy him out, and a stunning girlfriend he wants to marry, Stella (Marina Suma). Stella, independent-minded owner of a beauty parlor, resists him and the mob's demand she buy "protection." Tony (Stefano Sabelli), a kind of punk-gigolo, flits between affairs with various rich women, including Elena (Ida Di Benedetto), handsome wife of a crippled professor.

Amid the groupies and atonal singers, two talented musicians, a local girl and a black American saxophonist, find themselves drawn to each other, but separated by a series of accidents. Finally there is Francesca (Barbara D'Urso), unwilling to choose between her lover and the drummer from Milan who is the father of her little girl, and aspiring to an unlikely ménage a trois.

Cameraman Giuseppe Lanci uses two long nights of concerts to paint a broiling summer-in-the-city atmosphere of nonstop music, casual sex and drugs, restless, rootless youth in a modern urban landscape.

Editor Raimondo Crociani skillfully cuts back and forth between music numbers (never too long to get boring) and snatches of life "outside" the tent. — *Yung.*

Le Cowboy
(FRENCH-COLOR)

Paris, April 28.

A SEDPA/AAA release of a SEDPA production. Produced by Jo Siritzky. Direced by Georges Lautner. Stars Aldo Maccione. Screenplay, Georges Wolinski; camera (color), Yves Rodallec; editor, Michèle David; sound, André Hervée; art director, Alain Gaudry; music, Philippe Sarde. Reviewed at the Paris theater, Paris, April 24, 1985. Running time: 95 MINS.
With: Aldo Maccione, Renée Saint-Cyr, Michel Beaune, Valérie Allain, Corinne Touzet, Michel Peyleron, Corinne Lorain, Henri Guybet.

Another dreary vehicle for the dim-witted, mock macho antics of

Aldo Maccione, "Le Cowboy" casts him as an oafish Nice detective who is transferred to the Chinese quarter in Paris to serve as an unwitting decoy for a planned drug ring bust.

Cartoonist Georges Wolinski, who adapted Maccione's previous (and equally poor) film from his own comic strip, concocted this one as an original script, though there is not a shred of original humor in it. Georges Lautner's direction is numbingly indifferent, and most of the acting is of a low order.

Despite Maccione's local popularity, film has fared poorly at the wickets. —*Len.*

Don't Call Me Girlie
(AUSTRALIAN-DOCU-COLOR/B&W)

Sydney, April 1.

A Ronin Films release of a Double L Films production. Produced by Hilary Furlong. Directed by Stewart Young, Andrée Wright. Written-researched by Wright; camera (color), Erika Addis, Geoff Burton; sound, Pat Fiske, Leo Sullivan; editor, Young; narrator, Penne Hackforth-Jones. Reviewed at Academy Twin cinema, Paddington, March 28, 1985. Running time: 70 MINS.

The title is a line from Ken G. Hall's 1938 feature "Dad And Dave Come To Town" and is spoken by Shirley Ann Richards, who plays the new owner of a fashion house who's quick to put down a patronizing traveling salesman. The aim of this entertaining documentary is to explore the role of women in the Australian film industry from the beginning until 1940.

Bulk of the picture consists of carefully selected excerpts from silent films and talkies illustrating the role of women in front of and behind the camera. In the early period, principal interest is centered around Lottie Lyell, the talented on- and off-screen partner of the industry's most celebrated pioneer, Raymond Longford. Scenes from "The Romantic Story Of Margaret Catchpole" (1911), the long-lost "The Woman Suffers (And The Man Goes Free)" (1918) and "The Sentimental Bloke" (1919) testify to Lyell's talents as an actress, while the elderly Marjorie Osborne, who starred in "The Blue Mountains Mystery" (1921), a lost film codirected by Lyell and Longford, asserts Lyell was the creative side of the team. Indeed, this film suggests Lyell's premature death in 1925 at 35 of tuberculosis marked the beginning of the end of Longford's creative talents. There doesn't seem to be, at this stage, enough evidence to support that contention.

Docu also explores the roles of women in silent films, playing either naive virgins, city vamps, or masterful countrywomen (as in "A Girl Of The Bush"). Behind the scenes women were rare in the industry, except the intrepid McDonagh Sisters, Paulette, Phyllis and Isobel, the last actress known as Marie Lorraine; the trio made four features between 1926 and 1933, three of them silent, of which "The Cheaters" (1929) survives as an enjoyable and intelligent melodrama.

In the sound period, Australia's most popular star was Cinesound's Shirley Ann Richards, who is interviewed in the film and reminisces about her half-dozen Australian features (later, as Ann Richards, she appeared in some American films, including King Vidor's 1944 "An American Romance" and William Dieterle's 1946 "The Searching Wind.")

"Don't Call Me Girlie" is a valuable documentary which should spark interest in vintage Australian cinema, and create a desire to see full versions of the films excerpted here. —*Strat.*

Night Caller
(HONG KONG-COLOR)

Hong Kong, April 29.

A Pyramid Films production distributed by D & B Films. Executive producer, John Sham; production supervisor, Melvin Wong. Directed by Philip Chan. Stars Melvin (Mel) Wong, Philip Chan, Pat Ha, Pauline Wong, Terry Wu, Stuart Ong, Deborah Sims and Lee

Pui Wai. Screenplay, Philip Chan. Camera consultant, Brian Rhodes; camera (color), Choi Wah Sing; art direction, Robert Luk; music, Romeo Diaz. Reviewed at President Theater, Hong Kong, April 25, 1985. Running time: **90 MINS.**
(Cantonese soundtrack with English subtitles)

Top fashion model Jessica (Terry Wu) is stabbed by a night caller, a strange figure in a raincoat and hat. The murder horrifies young daughter Edith who becomes speechless from shock and fear.

So begins the murder investigation, led by CID inspectors James Wong (Melvin Wong), Steve Chan (Philip Chan) and a new recruit (Pat Ha), a young girl detective constable known affectionately as "Porky." The trio forms a united and friendly team.

James eventually manages to identify the murderer when he accidentally discovers a built-in tape recorder inside a doll Edith was holding the night of the murder ... even naming the culprit. Unable to contact Steve, James moves in on the murderer alone. He thought at first that "Bobby" is a man, but it turns out to be a woman (Pauline Wong), who is as bizarre as they come these days. James is tied up and suffers from a series of torture and seduction schemes by the deranged woman in an effort to force him to reveal how he found the secret of her involvement. Bobby confesses she killed Stuart because she is being blackmailed.

This is Philip Chan's adequately inventive and valiant attempt to rehash Brian De Palma's flamboyant graphic style of murder and camped-up macabre mystery, in Cantonese terms. Interesting in parts, the storyline bogs down when forced situations are introduced.

Chan as cop is convincing while his buddy Mel Wong finally relaxes and is less wooden. The lesbian lovers are glamorous and kinkily amusing. The most laughable is newcomer Deborah Sims who was given more chances to emote than necessary. Sadly, she is incapable of projecting authentic emotive abilities during her dramatic moments. It is refreshing though to see Pat Ha in a light comedy role and with all her clothes intact for a change in screen image and role. —*Mel.*

Louie Bluie
(DOCU-COLOR)

San Francisco, April 21.
A Superior Pictures production. Produced and directed by Terry Zwigoff. Associate producer, Frank Simeone; editor, Victoria Lewis; camera (color), John Knoop, Chris Li; sound editor, Greg Bezat. Reviewed at Palace of Fine Arts theater (San Francisco Film Fest), April 20, 1985. Running time: **60 MINS.**

This delightful docu, invested with the hang-loose joy of 76-year-old Howard (Louie Bluie) Armstrong, leader of America's last black string band, was programmed at the Friscofest on a bill with "Minnie The Moocher And Many, Many More," a 50-minute guided tour of Harlem past by Cab Calloway, and a Les Blank-Alan Governar four-minute musical jab on the evils of the weed called "Cigarette Blues." All in all, a fine package which might be apt for brief bookings in selected situations.

"Bluie" himself is something else. He paints, plucks and prances and leaves the viewer smiling and happy to have met him. — *Herb.*

Le Pactole
(The Boodle)
(FRENCH-COLOR)

Paris, April 28.
A Jacques Letienne release of an M. Films/Films Jacques Leitienne/Imp. Ex. Ci coproduction. Directed by Jean-Pierre Mocky. Screenplay, Mocky, Patrick Grainier; camera (color), Edmond Richard; editor, Catherine Renault; art director, Etienne Mery; music, Roger Loubert. Reviewed at the Pathé Clichy theater, Paris, April 27, 1985. Running time: **90 MINS.**
Yves Beaulieu . . . . Richard Bohringer
Anne Beaulieu . . . . Pauline Lafont
Inspector Rousselet . . . . . Patrick Sébastien
Madam Rousselet . . . . Marie Laforêt
Anne's mother . . . . Bernadette Lafont

New film by the iconoclastic Jean-Pierre Mocky deals with a young married couple (Richard Bohringer and Pauline Lafont) who decide to take a shortcut to early retirement by robbing a supermarket. Before they can take the money and run, they are harassed by someone who is aware of their heist and is demanding the booty for himself. Their persecutor turns out to be the police inspector investigating the holdup, who also wants out of the rat race with his former beauty queen spouse.

Tale offers Mocky a typical canvas for his sardonic swipes at society and human nature, though this is one of his poorer efforts, beginning promisingly but quickly degenerating into a predictable comedy thriller, with neither much mystery nor genuine humor.

It is also the sloppiest of his recent pictures. Mocky has always been known for his artless direction, but his indifference to technical quality has rarely been so hideously obtrusive.

Worse, the actors — with the exception of the leads, and popular impersonator Patrick Sébastien, in his screen debut as the cop — do not invite comment. —*Len.*

El Otro
(The Other)
(MEXICAN-COLOR)

Mexico City, April 17.
A Pelicas Mexicanas/Películas Nacionales release of a Conacine, S.A. de C.V. production. Directed by Arturo Ripstein. Screenplay, Manuel Puig, based on a story by Silvina Ocampo; camera (color), Jorge Stahl; editor, Rafael Caballos; music, Chucho Zarzoza. Reviewed in Sala 1 of Cineteca Nacional, Mexico City, April 16, 1985. Running time: **105 MINS.**
Armando . . . . Rafael Sánchez Navarro
Luis . . . . Juan Ignacio Aranda
Girl . . . . Aline Davidoff
Tavares . . . . Ignacio López Tarso
Taxi driver's wife . . . . Patricia Rivera
Armando's father . . . . Abel Salazar

Arturo Ripstein's 16th feature, "El Otro" (The Other), stays in the viewer's mind perhaps more than it deserves. The complex storyline, further complicated by adherence to elements of surrealism (or "magic realism," as denoted in the current vogue among Latin American writers), doesn't show its hand until the end of the narrative. This tends to interest the viewer in untangling the crossed leads, misinformation and other narrative devices used.

Based on a short story by Argentine writer Silvina Ocampo, screenplay is by fellow countryman Manuel Puig, author of "Betrayed By Rita Hayworth" and "Kiss Of The Spider Woman," both novels written in dialog form. The story is complicated since it deals with the existence of a double, further confused by a misconception of the story's pivotal character. We are given story within story, within false narration.

The story concerns a man who has received a disturbing letter from his son Armando (Sánchez Navarro). The son, living at the Hacienda de los Cisnes in the village of Santa Barbara, decides he no longer wants to resume contact with his family. Unable to go himself, the father asks old family friend Tavares (López Tarso) to go and bring him news of his son.

Right away things get confused. As Tavares enters the train, he sees a woman (Davidoff) arguing with a young man (Aranda). The woman bursts into the compartment in tears. When Tavares tries to comfort her, she says "imagine I'm not here." Tavares gives up and goes to sleep. When he awakens, she is no longer in the room. He inquires about her to the conductor and is told he must be imagining things, "there was never any woman here."

In Santa Barbara he has trouble getting a taxi to the hacienda, and when he finally arrives, he is told Armando is out. He enters the boy's room and finds a diary, written by Armando's friend Luis, recounting the events of the previous weeks.

Now begins the story within a story as Tavares reads the diary. The problem is that Luis did not write the diary, Armando did, inventing a double in the character of his old school chum Luis. Tavares confuses the persons in the diary with the people seen on the train, and confusion reigns.

When things finally fall into place at the film's end, we realize some of this confusion was intended, while the rest was supplied by haphazard direction with little attention to detail. The action is set in an indeterminate country in the 1940s or '50s, yet anachronisms appear.

The acting is consistently bad by all of the principals; even Mexico's leading actor Ignacio López Tarso puts in a terrible performance.
—*Lent.*

El Telo Y La Tele
(The Tv And The Hotel)
(ARGENTINE-COLOR)

Buenos Aires, April 19.
A Cinematográfica Victoria production. Produced by Héctor Bailez. Director, Hugo Sofovich. Screenplay, Ricardo Talesnik; camera (Eastmancolor), Rodolfo Denevi; music, Mike Ribas; assistant director, Horacio Guisado. Reviewed at the Losuar theater, B.A., April 18, 1985. Running time: **106 MINS.**
Moria . . . . Moria Casán
Héctor . . . . Jorge Martínez
His Secretary . . . . Carmen Barbieri
Jorge . . . . Javier Portales
Elsa . . . . Haydée Padilla
Mario . . . . Mario Sánchez
Cockeyed . . . . Tristán
"Caputo" . . . . Mario Sapag
Actor . . . . Emilio Disi
Actress . . . . Elvia Andreoli
Adelita . . . . Luisa Albinoni
Technician . . . . Ricardo Espalter
Bus Driver . . . . Víctor Bo
Also with: Mario Castiglione, Dalma Millevos, Julio López, Adrián Martel, Amalia González, Silvia Pérez, Thelma Stefani, Guillermo Francella, Jorge Troiani, Gogo Andreu.

A softcore sex farce for undiscriminating audiences, it seems aimed at exciting the voyeurism of local tv addicts by showing topless some of the most buxom ladies of the boob tube. They are seen engaged in varied antics with popular male partners through cameras hidden in the rooms of a hot-sheets hotel for the benefit of panelists discussing sexuality at a pseudo-scientific congress.

Too clownish to be funny, it has dialog combining a thesaurus of dirty words with a catalog of insults. Writer Ricardo Talesnik and director Hugo Sofovich emphasize lewdness with unsophisticated viewers in mind. Title is formed by the Buenos Aires slang term for tv (tele) and hotel (telo).

Camerawork and direction are clumsy. Technical credits are below average.—*Nubi.*

Gwen, ou Le Livre de Sable
(Gwen, Or The Book Of Sand)
(FRENCH-ANIMATED-COLOR)

Paris, April 3.

A Gaumont release of a Films de la Demoiselle/Films A2 coproduction, in association with the Ministry of Culture. Directed by Jean-François Laguionie. Screenplay, Laguionie and Jean-Paul Gaspari; set design, Bernard Palacios; animators, Claude Luyet, Henri Heidsieck, Francine Léger, Claude Rocher; creation of characters, Nicole Dufour; editor, Hélène Arnal; music, Pierre Alrand. Reviewed at the Cinoche theater, Paris, April 2, 1985. Running time: **67 MINS.**

With voices of: Michel Robin, Lorella Di Cicco, Armand Babel, Raymond Jourdan, Saïd Amadis, Bertrand Bautheac, Jacques Bourier, Jacques Ruisseau.

Prize-winning animation artist Jean-François Laguionie makes his first feature-length cartoon one of his visual best, but is content to hang his superb images on an unsatisfactorily thin storyline.

Laguionie and his talented outfit, working out of a new animation center they created in the south of France, dream up marvelous landscape colors and forms for this tale of a nomad tribe in a desert world where it periodically rains artifacts (huge radiators, coffee pots and other domestic objects of our own consumer society) of a vanished civilization.

Plot concerns the journey made by the title character, a young orphan adopted by the tribe, and its most ancient woman member (173 years old) to find a child snatched by the dreaded Force responsible for the rain of objects and presumably imprisoned within the walls of the distant City of the Dead.

There they find a strange sect living in a labyrinth of suburban-style dwellings, involved in religious rites based on the readings of a sacred volume — in fact, a mail-order catalog.

Laguionie makes little of his personages, mere silhouettes conceived to guide us through a series of fantasy decors, each wonderful in itself, richly detailed and animated. However, the narrative and mock-epiphony climax leave one hungry for more dramatic substance. "Gwen" is admirable, but not as affecting as many of Laguionie's earlier efforts were, notably his haunting medium-length film, "La Traversée de l'Atlantique á la Rame," which won the Gold Palm short at the 1978 Cannes Film Festival. —*Len.*

Dr. Fischer Of Geneva
(BRITISH-COLOR)

San Francisco, April 22.

A Consolidated production, directed by Michael Lindsay-Hogg. Produced and written by Richard Broke, based on Graham Greene's novel; camera (color), Ken Westbury; editor, Ken Pearce; music, Trevor Jones. No other credits available. Reviewed at Palace of Fine Arts theater, San Francisco, April 20, 1985. Running time: **110 MINS.**

With: Alan Bates, James Mason, Greta Scacchi, Hugh Burden, Cyril Cusack, Clarissa Kaye, Barry Humphries, Nicholas LeProvost.

This Graham Greene parable — man playing God, complete with a "last supper" — is a dismal pic, noteworthy only because it was James Mason's final role. It may be difficult to believe a Greene yarn featuring Mason, Alan Bates and strong ensemble support could be a dud, but such is the case. The tale drags, the premise becomes redundant; there is a sloppy jump cut in the final third that confuses the continuity but at least quickens the pace.

Mason's title role figure is a wealthy fellow of contempt, sarcasm and malevolent manipulation. He surrounds himself with toadies who attend his dinner parties, where they slop cold porridge, because he rewards them with expensive gifts if they clean their plates. To a point, he controls their lives.

Uncontrolled, though, is his only child (Greta Scacchi, working well sans character motivation). She marries Bates, whose "younger man" makeup is dreadful, rendering him waxen, at best, and he becomes a Mason dinner guest.

The lengthy final scene, at which the diners can draw a gift of millions or death, runs so long the suspense element erodes. Pic has the look of having been lensed in about a week.

Scoring well on the guest list are Clarissa Kaye, as a not so grande dame, and Barry Humphries, offering a whiny matinee idol. — *Herb.*

The Stan Hasselgard Story
(SWEDISH-DOCU-COLOR)

San Francisco, April 18.

A Swedish Film Institute release of Swedish Television/SVT 1 production. Produced, directed, written and edited by Jonas Sima. Exec producer, Goran Bengston; camera (Eastmancolor), Ake Astrand; sound, Ragnar Samuelsson. Reviewed at Exploratorium theater, San Francisco, April 17, 1985. Running time: **105 MINS.**

Here's a distinct case of overkill, a Valentine made vapid by its length.

Ake (Stan) Hasselgard, a gifted Swedish clarinetist, died in 1948 in an auto accident at the age of 26. With the help of Benny Goodman, he was on his way to what might have been a major international career in jazz.

Because his life was so tragically short — and, off the info provided by this docu, rather mundane — director-writer Jonas Sima had to reach for "significance." Too often, the viewer is guided through domiciles once occupied or visited by Hasselgard, the reverence becomes cloying.

There are interviews with Goodman, who often gives the impression he can't believe what all this fuss is about, and with Patti Page and Buddy De Franco.

The attempt to thread Hasselgard into a musical version of James Dean is honorable but futile.
— *Herb.*

Ornette: Made In America
(DOCU-COLOR)

San Francisco, April 17.

A Caravan of Dreams production. Produced by Kathelin Hoffman. Directed and edited by Shirley Clarke; camera (color), Ed Lachman; additional photography, Baird Bryant, Hilary Harris, John Heller, Bob Elfstrom; music, Ornette Coleman. Reviewed at the Palace of Fine Arts theater (San Francisco Film Fest), April 17, 1985. Running time: **90 MINS.**

The combination of Shirley Clarke's ingenuity and the cool intelligence of saxman Ornette Coleman makes for a stunning theatrical docu that should do well in selected situations. It's a well-crafted piece or work which bespeaks the universality of music (and Coleman's mind) against a background of the isolated Americana of Fort Worth, Coleman's hometown.

Pic is built around the homefolks honoring, but clearly not understanding, Coleman. To Clarke's credit, she does not demean the Texans while exalting Coleman. It's a case of good reportage.

Coleman is one of those people with a natural glow, a man of considerable depth yet not intimidating. Clarke captures some fine conversations between the saxophonist and his drummer son. Other figures are introduced via a "neon bulb" crawl, an inventive method of using supers.

The fictive moments of the pic — using a child actor to portray the young Ornette — are overdone and a bit too fanciful. That's the only downside to this technically clean, commendably etched pic. — *Herb.*

Koko At 19
(ISRAELI-COLOR)

Tel Aviv, April 3.

A Cannon Films Presentation of a Koko production. Produced by Nathan Zahavi. Written and directed by Danny (Nokio) Verete. Camera (color), Yossi Wein; editor, Zohar Sela; music, Shlomo Mizrahi; songs performed by Danny Bassan. Reviewed at the Orly Cinema, Tel Aviv, April 1, 1985. Running time: **90 MINS.**

Koko .... Udi Cohen
Pini .... Meir Dadon
Liora .... Shifra Ha'Efrati
Yuval .... Gil Rosenthal

A first film that attempts to combine social protest, personal tragedy and a glimpse of the local pop scene, Danny Verete's "Koko At 19" rates higher on intentions than real achievements.

Koko, a young man from the wrong side of the tracks, which in Israel means he is from a poor, Oriental family, writes songs and plays with a rock group, hoping for the big break into the charts. Meanwhile he has to play for drinks in an ill-reputed Jerusalem night spot. When one of his songs is swiped by a pal, he allows himself to be tempted into participating in a burglary, which should supply him and his friends with funds to produce a record of their own.

The bungled job turns out to be the first step in Koko's downward spiral into a world he has been desperately trying to escape. Soon enough he is chased for things he has never done, because of his background.

Verete obviously has tried to paint an updated image of a certain type of youth living in Israel today, spiking it with critical remarks about the police and hints about the arbitrary way of moving deprived families to the West Bank territories, whether they like it or not.

The trouble is, all these asides are not worked into the fabric of the shaky script to a sufficient extent and the characters in themselves aren't interesting enough.

There is no denying the points he raises are relevant or that the problems are real and painful. Also, he has to be given credit for some nicely filmed sequences, but his inexperienced cast doesn't always manage to cope with the situations in which it is put and the tragic climax is largely forced.

Technical credits are on the whole satisfactory. Initial press reception was on the positive side, but first boxoffice results are rather disappointing. However, it may create some interest abroad, mainly for dealing with the ethnic conflict in Israel, not as a bad joke, as it is usually treated in local comedies, but in earnest fashion. —*Edna.*

Private Passions
· (Clair)
(AUSTRIAN-FRENCH-COLOR)

A Neue Delta Film and Uranium Films presentation. Executive producers, Daniel Cohen, Franz Antel, Georges Glass, Joseph Tallal Jr. Produced by Glass. Directed by Kikuo Kawasaki. Features entire cast. Screenplay, Peggy-Ann Cohen, Kawasaki; camera (Fujicolor), Ramon Suarez; editor, J.W. Kompare; music, The Performer's Band; sound, Jean Neny; art direction, Ferry Windberger; production manager, Kurt Kodal; associate producer, Jack Scherer. Reviewed on Prism Entertainment vidcassette, N.Y., April 2, 1985. (No MPAA Rating.) Running time: **86 MINS.**

Clair .... Susanne Ashley
Mark .... Gavin Brannan
Toni .... David Siegel
Katherine .... Sybil Danning
Albert .... Louis Velle

Also with: Irmgard Schüch, Ulrike Beimpold, Margot Hruby, Thomas Weidlich, Veronika Neubauer, Inge Prosel, Gilbert Petersen.

"Private Passions" is a miscalculated entry in the ongoing glut of "the first time" teenage sex pictures. Filmed in Kitzbühel, Austria, in 1983 under the title "Clair," pic offers beautiful countryside scenery and little else, accounting for its domestic debut on vidcassette with no theatrical release.

Thin story has cousin Mark (Gavin Brannan) from Canada visiting Toni (David Siegel) for the summer. Between visits to the local disco and tennis courts, Mark falls in love with Toni's beautiful stepsister Clair (Susanne Ashley), but is ultimately too timid to have sex with her. Meanwhile, Toni is pursuing the genre's "I gotta get you laid, Mark" premise, arranging assignations with local prostitutes to no effect.

There is no surprise in the final reel when Mark cries on the shoulder of Clair's mom (Sybil Danning) and she sympathetically introduces him to the European version of tea and sympathy.

Film's only drawing card is B-picture star Danning, but fans are bound to be angered by her avoidance of nudity, even during the finalé's older woman/young boy sex scene. Also disconcerting is that nearly all the women in the pic handle direct sound English dialog (even the supporting players) while the two young male leads are post-synched. Acting by Ashley and Brannan is wooden in the extreme.

Lacking comedy hijinks, romantic film has little to offer contemporary audiences. —Lor.

✳✳✳✳✳✳✳✳✳✳✳✳✳✳✳✳✳✳✳✳✳✳✳✳✳✳✳✳
✳ Competing At Cannes ✳
✳✳✳✳✳✳✳✳✳✳✳✳✳✳✳✳✳✳✳✳✳✳✳✳✳✳✳✳

Mishima
(U.S.-COLOR/B&W)

Hollywood, May 4.

A Warner Bros. release of a Francis Ford Coppola-George Lucas presentation of a Zoetrope Studios/Filmlink Intl./Lucasfilm Ltd. production. Produced by Mata Yamamoto, Tom Luddy. Executive producers, Lucas, Coppola. Directed by Paul Schrader. Stars Ken Ogata, Kenji Sawada, Yasosuke Bando, Toshiyuki Nagashima. Screenplay, Paul Schrader, Leonard Schrader, conceived in collaboration with Jun Shiragi, literary executor of the Mishima estate. Japanese script, Chieko Schrader. Script research, Akiko Hitomi. English narration read by Roy Scheider. Camera (Technicolor, b&w) John Bailey; editor, Michael Chandler; Tokyo editor, Tomoyo Oshima; music, Philip Glass; production design, Eiko Ishioka; executive art director, Kazuo Takenaka; set decoration, Kyoji Sasaki; costume design, Etsuko Yagyu; sound design (Dolby), Leslie Shatz; production sound, Shotaro Yoshida; line producer, Yosuke Mizuno; associate producers, Leonard Schrader, Chieko Schrader, Alan Mark Poul; assistant director, Koichi Nakajima; casting, Nobuaki Murooka. Reviewed at The Burbank Studios, Burbank, May 3, 1985. (In Competition at Cannes.) (No MPAA Rating.) Running time: **20 MINS.**

November 25, 1970

Yukio Mishima	Ken Ogata
Morita	Masayuki Shionoya
Cadet 1	Hiroshi Mikami
Cadet 2	Junya Fukuda
Cadet 3	Shigeto Tachihara
General Mashita	Junkichi Orimoto

Flashbacks

Mother	Naoko Otani
Mishima, age 18-19	Go Riju
Mishima, age 9-14	Masato Aizawa
Mishima, age 5	Yuki Nagahara
Literary Friend	Kyuzo Kobayashi
Dancing Friend	Yuki Kitazume
Grandmother	Haruko Kato

"Temple Of The Golden Pavilion"

Mizoguchi	Yasosuke Bando
Mariko	Hisako Manda
First Girl	Naomi Oki
Second Girl	Miki Takakura
Madame	Imari Tsuji
Kashiwagi	Koichi Sato

"Kyoko's House"

Osamu	Kenji Sawada
Kiyomi	Reisen Lee
Mitsuko	Setsuko Karasuma
Natsuo	Tadanori Yokoo
Takei	Yasuaki Kurata
Thug	Mitsuru Hirata

"Runaway Horses"

Isao	Toshiyuki Nagashima
Lt. Hori	Hiroshi Katsuno
Izutsu	Hiroki Ida
Kurahara	Jun Negami
Interrogator	Ryo Ikebe

(In Japanese; English subtitles and narration)

Destined to be as controversial as was the subject himself, Paul Schrader's film "Mishima" is a boldly conceived, intelligent and consistently absorbing study of the Japanese writer and political iconoclast's life, work and death. Seductively designed picture has serious limitations, to be sure, but combination of sensationalistic material and unusual esthetics should make this a hot item on the international art film circuit.

The most famous of contemporary Japanese novelists to Westerners, Yukio Mishima was also a film actor and director and leader of a militant right-wing cult bent upon restoring the glory of the emperor. He became forever notorious in 1970 when, accompanied by a few followers, he entered a military garrison in Tokyo, "captured" a general, delivered an impassioned speech to an assembly and then committed *seppuku*, or ritual suicide.

Although married and the father of children, Mishima was also a homosexual, and it has been over the depiction of this and other matters that the filmmakers and Mishima's widow have jousted over the past couple of years.

Instead of pretending to deliver a fully factual, detailed biopic, director Paul Schrader, his coscreenwriter and brother Leonard and other collaborators have opted to combine relatively realistic treatment of some aspects of Mishima's life, particularly his final day, with highly stylized renditions of assorted semi-autobiographical literary works in an effort to convey key points about the man's personality and credos.

Approach is forthrightly intellectual, and works surprisingly well overall. Technique admits its own restrictions going in, and although the points being made about Mishima are sometimes belabored at unnecessary length, they are appropriate and judiciously drawn from his own writings.

Opening sequence, which shows Mishima waking up on the last day of his life, grooming himself, laying out his military uniform and sealing a just-finished manuscript for delivery to his publisher, is a superior piece of work and instantly draws the viewer into both the story and the film's precise artfulness.

Final-day material, which reappears throughout the picture, is shot in an urgent, contemporary style, which contrasts significantly with scenes depicting Mishima's childhood, which are lensed in studied black-and-white and often from the *tatami*, or near-floor level, position favored by Yasujiro Ozu, the late Japanese director about whom Paul Schrader has written extensively.

These two styles then are joined by a third, one of swooping crane shots and extreme angles accomplished within deliberately artificial, New Wave-ish sets designed by Eiko Ishioka. These episodes, drawn from three Mishima novels and all featuring Mishima-like characters at different stages of development, artistically resemble nothing so much as Eric Rohmer's hermetically studio-bound "Perceval," and explicitly convey the author's attitudes toward beauty, suicide, art, role-playing, sexuality and politics.

Homosexual overtones are underplayed carefully but clear nevertheless. One of the strongest portrayals in the film is that of Toshiyuki Nagashima as the Mishima figure in the adaptation of the militaristic "Runaway Horses," but a major failing is pic's inability to fully articulate Mishima's political views.

On the other hand, a major plus is that Schrader, whose work until now has been perhaps unduly bound up with his own religious, sexual and violence-oriented hang-ups, has applied himself rigorously to his material here and excluded personal irrelevancies. Also, those fearing the director's frequent taste for explicit gore would result in a climactic bloodbath in "Mishima" are in for a pleasant surprise, as the guresome suicide is handled with relative restraint.

Pacing sometimes lags, particularly in the fictional interludes, and uninitiated audiences may be confused at times.

Production itself, however, is stunning, and performances, led by that of Ken Ogata as the adult Mishima, are authoritative and convincing.

John Bailey's cinematography is very strong in all three styles, while Philip Glass' hyperactive score ultimately proves extremely effective even as it sometimes threatens to go over the top. —Cart.

Kiss Of The Spider Woman
(U.S.-BRAZILIAN-COLOR)

Cannes, May 12.

An Island Alive (U.S.) release of an HB Filmes production in association with Sugarloaf Films. Produced by David Weisman. Executive producer, Francisco Ramalho Jr. Directed by Hector Babenco. Stars William Hurt, Raul Julia, Sonia Braga. Screenplay, Leonard Schrader, based on the novel by Manuel Puig; camera (color), Radolfo Sanchez; editor, Mauro Alice; music, John Neschling; production design, Clovis Bueno; art direction, Felipe Crescente; costume design, Patricio Bisso; assistant director, Amilcar Moneira; second unit camera, Lucio Kodato. Reviewed at Cannes (In Competition), May 12, 1985. (No MPAA Rating.) Running time: **119 MINS.**

Molina	William Hurt
Valentin	Raul Julia
Leni Lamaison/Marta/	
Spider Woman	Sonia Braga
Warden	Jose Lewgoy
Garbriel	Nuno Leal Maia
Clubfoot	Antonio Petrim
Michelle	Denise Dumont
Secret Policeman	Milton Goncalves
Greta	Patricio Bisso
Werner	Herson Capri
Butler/Resistance	
Leader	Nildon Parrente

"Kiss Of The Spider Woman" is a partially successful screen adaptation of Manuel Puig's celebrated, film-oriented novel. Pic has been opened up from the basic prison cell setting to a surprisingly satisfactory degree, and William Hurt's performance in the central homosexual role will give critics and audiences a lot to chew on, pro and con. Intellectual, literary, sexual and political orientation of the piece demands some strong notices to launch it in the marketplace, but if this happens, film could do well with up-scale, discerning audiences looking for works of substance.

Drama centers upon the relationship between cellmates in a South American prison. Molina, played by Hurt, is an effeminate gay locked up for having molested a young boy, while Valentin, played by Raul Julia, is a professional journalist in for a long term due to his radical political activities under a fascist regime.

They have literally nothing in common except their societal victimization, but to pass the time Molina periodically entertains Valentin with accounts of old motion pictures. Puig kicked his book off with a ravishing account of the 1940s horror pic "Cat People," but director Hector Babenco and scenarist Leonard Schrader have opted to concentrate on two purely imaginary films to intertwine with the narrative, the first and most important a Nazi World War II melodrama (also to be found in Puig) starring Sonia Braga as a French chanteuse in love with a German officer.

In its real-time sections, novel consists of nothing but dialog, with no description, and first half of the film is devoted to extended, eventually fatiguing, banter between the two principals intercut with the fantasy film. There's precious little dramatic tension here, and unusual nature of Hurt's characterization makes adjustment to the film a difficult matter.

A major plot revelation at the midway point intensifies matters considerably, and the movement of these two highly disparate characters toward a deeply felt relationship will certainly move some viewers. Last reel of more conventional suspense narrative is very well handled by Babenco, and there is no doubt that film improves steadily as it progresses.

Individual reactions to the work overall will depend to a great extent on feelings about Hurt's performance. Jarring at first with his long, dyed hair, an appearance of make-up and moderately swishy mannerisms, thesp speaks, and relates the film-within-the-film stories, in a soft, deliberately measured manner that falls somewhere between the hypnotic and the monotonous. By extension, some will find him mesmerizing, others artificially low-keyed.

By contrast, Julia delivers a very strong, straight and believable performance as an activist who at first has little patience with Hurt's predilection for escapism, but finally meets him halfway in a humanist transformation which sees Hurt accept certain political realities and Julia embrace a broader view of sentimental affiliations.

Brazilian actress Sonia Braga, who essays two fantasy film roles as well as Julia's girlfriend, has fun as the glamorous French cabaret star, and Denise Dumont is a standout in a brief role in the Nazi pic.

Faced with adapting a novel at once very theatrical and highly cinematic, Schrader has done an intelligent, creditable job, although he and Babenco must share responsibility for lagging in the first half. After the raw street power of "Pixote," Babenco has employed a slicker, more choreographed style here; interestingly, he is most successful with the straightforward dramatics of the Nazi meller and the climactic cat-and-mouse game, and less so with the prison-enclosed interchange.

A Yank-Brazilian coproduction flying the Brazilian flag in Cannes and shot entirely in São Paulo, film boasts fine lensing by Radolfo Sanchez and an excellent score by John Neschling. CBS Productions is handling worldwide sales outside the U.S. and U.K. — Cart.

Detective
(FRENCH-COLOR)

Cannes, May 10.
A Spectrafilm release (in U.S.) of a Sara Films-JLG Films coproduction. Produced by Alain Sarde. Directed by Jean-Luc Godard. Stars Claude Brasseur, Nathalie Baye, Johnny Hallyday. Screenplay, Sarde, Philippe Setbon, Anne-Marie Miéville, Godard; camera (color), Bruno Nuytten; sound (stereo), Pierre Gamet, François Musy; music, Schubert, Wagner, Chopin, Liszt, Honegger, Chabrier, Ornette Coleman, Jean Schwarz. Reviewed at Cannes Film Festival (In Competition), May 10, 1985. Running time: **98 MINS.**

Emile Chenal .... Claude Brasseur
Françoise Chenal .... Nathalie Baye
Jim Fox-Warner .... Johnny Hallyday
William Prospero
(Detective) .... Laurent Terzieff
Nephew .... Jean-Pierre Léaud
Old Mafioso .... Alain Cuny
Tiger Jones .... Stéphane Ferrara
Eugène (Manager) ...... Eugène Berthier
Grace Kelly (Fiancée) . Emmanuelle Seigner
Punk Groupie .... Cyril Autin
Wise Young Girl .... Julie Delpy
Bodyguard .... Xavier Saint Macary
Anne .... Anne Gisèle Glass
Ariel .... Aurèle Doazan

Jean-Luc Godard is getting to be as prodigious as he was 20 years ago; after the controversial "Hail Mary" in Berlin, he's competing in Cannes with "Detective," a quint-essential Godard pic that's more "Grand Hotel" than *film noir*.

The plot, as much as it matters, involves four groups of people, or "families," whose paths intersect in the lobbies, dining rooms and bedrooms of the Hotel Concorde at Saint Lazare in Paris (only the final scene is played outside the hotel, and that's in the street). There's the hotel detective (Laurent Terzieff) and his manic assistant (Jean-Pierre Léaud), still trying to solve the two-year-old murder of a Prince in the hotel. There's an avuncular Mafia boss (Alain Cuny), forever accompanied by a bodyguard, a young man and, incongruously, a small girl. There are also the Chenals (Claude Brasseur, Nathalie Baye) who are trying to get back a large sum of money owed them by a shady boxing promoter (Johnny Hallyday) who's apparently too broke to train his new protegé, Tiger Jones, in a gym, so is using a hotel room for the purpose.

All these people, it seems, have business with each other, none of it very clear in the film, but no matter; what counts is Godard's unique style, on display here at its most refined. The pic is chock-full of asides, jokes and anecdotes. There are comments on the French themselves ("How can France aspire to leadership when every Frenchman is a minor character?"), which may not go down well with local auds (the film was greeted with some boos at Cannes), on pornography ("Why does 'X' denote a porno movie?"), on the differences between theater and cinema, on the decline in urban standards of living (Godard lives in Switzerland and is clearly disenchanted with what's happening to Paris), on the talkiness of French films, even on whether a man should wash his hands before or after going to the toilet.

There are bursts of wonderfully imposing music (the film has a splendid stereo soundtrack), enjoyably off-center images (again, the photography of Bruno Nuytten is masterly), clips from other films (Erich Von Stroheim in George Archainbaud's "The Last Squadron" and Jean Marais in Jean Cocteau's "Beauty And The Beast"), eccentric titles, and a splendid last-minute dedication to John Cassavetes, Edgar G. Ulmer and Clint Eastwood!

In other words, most of Godard's concerns are here, including the theme of the commercialization of sex, the threat of the multinationals, and the mystery of the film image itself ("Seeing is deceiving"). Technically one of his best films, "Detective" also boasts one of his strongest casts, with everyone excellent, especially singer Johnny Hallyday as the boxing impresario.

Those expecting a neat plot will, of course, be bitterly disappointed: the final resolution, involving a shootout and several bodies, is so off-hand as to be quite obscure, but that's Godard. For the director's fans, especially those who like the films of his early period, "Detective" will seem like old times.
— Strat.

The Coca-Cola Kid
(AUSTRALIAN-COLOR)

Cannes, May 9.
A Cinecom Intl./Film Gallery release (U.S.) of a Cinema Enterprises, David Roe and Smart Egg Pictures presentation. Produced by David Roe. Executive producer, Les Lithgow. Directed by Dusan Makavejev. Stars Eric Roberts, Greta Scacchi. Screenplay, Frank Moorhouse, based on his short stories in "The Americans, Baby" and "The Electrical Experience;" camera (Eastman color), Dean Semler; editor, John Scott; music, William Motzing; original songs, Tim Finn; production design, Graham (Grace) Walker; assistant director, Bojana Marijan. Reviewed at Cannes Film Festival (competing), May 9, 1985. (No MPAA Rating.) Running time: 94 MINS.

Becker .... Eric Roberts
Terri .... Greta Scacchi
T. George McDowell .... Bill Kerr
Kim .... Chris Haywood
Juliana .... Kris McQuade
Frank .... Max Gillies
Bushman .... Tony Barry
Fred .... Paul Chubb
Waiter .... David Slingsby
Philip .... Tim Fin

A decade in preparation and two years in actual production, "The Coca-Cola Kid" emerges, in the year of Coca-Cola's much-publicized change in taste, with much of the flavor and character of Dusan Makavejev's earlier works such as "WR: Mysteries Of The Organism" (1968) and "Sweet Movie" (1974). But the mix of earthy symbolism, offbeat eroticism, the picaresque and the rough-and-tumble social, rather unpolitical satire now seems poured from a bottle that has been left uncapped overnight.

Still, hard-bitten Makavejev aficionados will take delight in the director's and scripter Frank Moorhouse's obvious delight in keeping audiences puzzled at their willful inconsistencies in portraying the characters — especially the title figure, a young whiz-kid troubleshooter out of Atlanta, sent to Australia by Coca-Cola h.q. to root out whatever trouble might have been overlooked by the local company representative.

Georgian Becker, played by Atlanta-raised Eric Roberts with drawl and drool, soon finds the Coca-Cola dry spot on Australia's map in a remote area where land baron Bill Kerr, playing a Colonel Sanders lookalike, has enforced his own soda pop monopoly on the population.

The ensuing fight between two parties, supposedly juxtaposing American and Australian attitudes, morals, etc., is complicated by a skirmish between Roberts and the local company secretary, Greta Scacchi in her first major film role since "Heat And Dust," Scacchi's ex-husband comes in to regularly and roughly seduce her on the office floor, when she is not hiding from her father in a Coke refrigerator box, her father being Kerr himself, coming to town to offer a truce and a merger.

There are also more violent dealings between Roberts and Kerr, and some intrigue between a poolside waiter and Roberts, when the former insists on believing Roberts to be working for the CIA. Confusion is understandable since Roberts at one

moment appears broadminded and sweet only to turn sourly dogmatic the next. When he finally succumbs to Scacchi's charms and strips her of a Santa Claus costume for a tumble on the bed among loose feathers, he seems pretty remote about this new chore. Scacchi is allowed more consistency and looks sweetly amorous.

Behind all its stylistic posturing, "The Coca-Cola Kid" has a generally friendly air about it, and production credits and cinematography (by Dean Semler of "The Road Warrior") are of the most handsome order. What is lacking in the brew is true punch.—*Kell.*

in the final scene.

Overall, and despite the built-in audience word-of-mouth from the various stage productions, this will need careful handling to find its audience. —*Strat.*

Monsieur de Pourceaugnac
(FRENCH-COLOR)

Paris, May 10.

A Films Epcc release of a Gerland production. Produced by Roger Coggio. Written and directed by Michel Mitrani, from the Molière play; camera (Fujicolor), Claude Lecomte; production design, Max Douy; costumes, Agnés Nègre; editor, Annick Baly; choreography, Mireille Pédauge; sound, Pierre Befve, Jean-Jacques Ferran; music, Jean-Baptiste Lulli; additional music, Pierre Jansen. Reviewed at the Georges V cinema, Paris (in Cannes Film Festival's Un Certain Regard section), May 9, 1985. Running time: **91 MINS.**
Monsieur de Pourceaugnac Michel Galabru
Sbrigani . . . . Roger Coggio
Julie . . . . Fanny Cottençon
Nérine . . . . Rosy Varte
Oronte . . . . Jean-Paul Roussillon
Eraste . . . . Mérôme Angé
Louis XIV . . . . Michel Mitrani

Second in producer-actor Roger Coggio's program of play-to-screen adaptations (after Daniel Moosman's "Les Fausses Confidences") is Molière's comedy-ballet, "Monsieur de Pourceaugnac," filmed by Michel Mitrani.

Piece is by general critical opinion a minor but amusing farce, and a sort of rough sketch for the playwright's later "Le Bourgeois Gentilhomme" (already filmed by Coggio) and "Le Malade Imaginaire," with their satires on pretentious parvenus and medical quackery.

Title character is a fatuous provincial gentleman (Michel Galabru) who has come to Paris to contract a marriage with a pretty young heiress (Fanny Cottençon). As is often the case in a Molière comedy, her heart belongs to a younger, more handsome suitor, and the two young lovers must appeal to a crafty Neopolitan (Coggio) to foil the alliance.

Latter foists a charade on the unsuspecting hick who, no sooner arrived in town, finds himself the victim of pompous doctors, phony creditors and a couple of women disputing him as their lawful husband.

The comedy calls for fast and furious performance, but Mitrani's film is slow and infuriating, providing another example — after last year's monotonously sinister "Le Tartuffe," filmed by Gérard Depardieu — of how contemporary revisions of classic French comedy morbidly devitalize their essential humor.

Mitrani gets in the way of a potentially ideal cast (notably Galabru, the quintessential Molière gull) with a pretentious welter of ponderous psychological interpolations and fussy cinema/theater gim-

mickry — the action spills back and forth between real locations and a variously stylized stage production for Louis XIV (for whom Molière hastily wrote the play).

Mitrani himself plays the king, offering an indulgent smile or nod at an occasional snatch of dialog or bit of business. Throughout the action, one clings to the vain hope that he'll have the director beheaded at final curtain.

Tech credits are excellent. The studio sets are by veteran production designer Max Douy, sadly underemployed in recent years. —*Len.*

Vivement Truffaut!
(FRENCH-DOCU-COLOR/B&W)

Cannes, May 12.

A Festival Intl. du Film de Cannes-FR-3 presentation. Excerpts and documents assembled by Claude de Givray, Martine Barraqué, Gilles Jacob. Reviewed at the Cannes Film Festival, (Non-competing official selection), May 12, 1985. Running time: **78 MINS.**

A documentary tribute to François Truffaut prepared for the Cannes Film Festival's homage to the late director and for airing on French television, "Vivement Truffaut!" represents an eloquent, if relatively elementary, look at the career of the most internationally estimed French filmmaker of the last quarter century. First motion picture ever to have been coproduced by the festival itself easily will find a niche in the specialized marketplace if rights to the many film clips utilized are cleared.

Probably 90% of the docu consists of excerpts drawn from 14 of Truffaut's films. Beginning with a log segment from "The Green Room," the director's obsessive meditation on death, pic then plausibly but unanalytically groups clips around such favorite Truffaut subjects as childhood, romantic affairs, marriage, *amour fou,* and his love for literature and cinema.

Aside from a few personal still photographs, next to nothing is offered in the way of biographical material. To American eyes, however, there is some nice, previously unseen film and tv interview footage of Truffaut at different stages of his career, as well as a clip of the director winning the César award for the "The Last Metro" and a brief interlude in which Jean Renoir sings the praises of "Jules And Jim."

What with the liberal dose of sequences on view, docu can't help but capture the charm, intelligence and poetry of Truffaut's work, and it will therefore prove a pleasure for anyone bearing affection for the director's career. Yet it is a long way from being a definitive docu-bio, despite the impeccable credentials of the three people who prepared it —

╔══════════════════════════╗

Non-Competing Entries

Steaming
(BRITISH-COLOR)

Cannes, May 12.

A Columbia pictures release (outside of U.S.) of a World Film Services production. Executive producer, Richard F. Dalton. Produced by Paul Mills. Directed by Joseph Losey. Stars Vanessa Redgrave, Sarah Miles, Diana Dors. Screenplay, Patricia Losey, from the play by Nell Dunn; camera (color), Christopher Challis; editor, Reginald Beck; music, Richard Harvey; art director, Michael Pickwood; sound, Malcolm Davis. Reviewed at Cannes Film Festival (Out of Competition), May 11, 1985. Running time: **95 MINS.**
Nancy . . . . Vanessa Redgrave
Sarah . . . . Sarah Miles
Violet . . . . Diana Dors
Josie . . . . Patti Love
Mrs. Meadows . . . . Brenda Bruce
Dawn Meadows . . . . Felicity Dean
Celia . . . . Sally Sagoe

On film, "Steaming" lacks the impact it had on stage. Somehow, in the transition, the ebullience and sheer fun of the original has mostly disappeared, and although this is by no means an earnest women's lib tract, it's a lesser experience. •

This is especially sad because this was Joseph Losey's last film. In making it, he returned to Britain (scene of some of his greatest successes) after four features in France which brought him somewhat mixed responses, and he also returned to the theater for inspiration. Nell Dunn (author of "Poor Cow" and "Up The Junction") had a worldwide success with the stage production, but Columbia may find that experience not repeated with the film.

The play has been treated respectfully in almost every way excepting mood. There's no opening out — all the action takes place in a rundown steam bath on ladies day (a setting similar to that of Jerzy Skolimowski's "Deep End"). Here we find the managers, Violet (Diana Dors, who earlier appeared in "Deep

End"), worried that the local council is going to close the place down; Josie (Patti Love), an ebullient type forever talking about her sex life; conservative Mrs. Meadows (Brenda Bruce) and her daughter, Dawn (Felicity Dean), a bit overweight and not allowed to undress in front of the others; and the upper-class Sarah (Sarah Miles) who introduces her friend, Nancy (Vanessa Redgrav) to the group.

Nancy's husband has left her recently for another woman, and she has to cope with loneliness and three children. Sarah has no kids and no husband either, but also feels a lonely future in the offing. Over a period of time (a concept only shakily denoted in the early scenes) they become close friends, pour out their troubles to each other, and find solidarity in each other's support and friendship. They're even instrumental in saving the baths from demolition.

Performances are all very strong, with Vanessa Redgrave probably making the least impact in the rather tight-lipped role of Nancy.

Sarah Miles positively glows as Sarah, while Patti Love seizes all her opportunities in the flashiest role. Felicity Dean is lovely as plump Dawn, and Brenda Bruce, a stalwart character actress in British films for many years, is fine as her fussy mother. Diana Dors, who, like Losey, died soon after the film was completed, looks very beautiful, and slimmer than in recent years, and is quietly effective as the motherly Violet.

Technically the pic is fine, but as noted it somehow misses the wonderful sense of humor that made the play such a success. It also downplays the nudity considerably, with the major characters (except Dors and Bruce) going naked only

Claude de Givray had been perhaps Truffaut's closest friend since youth, Martine Barraqué edited his most recent features, and Cannes fest director Gilles Jacob knows his work as well as anyone.

An incidental revelation of the docu stems from the sensational print quality of the clips. In their pristine form, as seen here, many of Truffaut's films rank with anyone's when it comes to visual beauty, but one would never know it from the quality of the copies currently playing in revival cinemas in the U.S. The disparity is truly shocking, and it is to be hoped that, with the current launch of Truffaut reissues domestically, some effort will be made to remedy the situation. —*Cart.*

Empty Quarter
(FRENCH-COLOR)

Cannes, May 13.
A Double D-FR 3 Films production. Executive produders, François Margolin, Pascale Dauman. Directed by Raymond Depardon. Stars Françoise Prenant. Screenplay, François Weyergans, Depardon; camera (color), Depardon; sound, Jean-Paul Andrieu; editor, Jacques Kebadian, Françoise Prenant; voice, Jean-Pierre Bertrand. Reviewed at Cannes Film Festival (Un Certain Regard), May 12, 1985. Running time: **86 MINS.**
With: Françoise Prenant.

Photo-journalist Raymond Depardon, whose 1981 documentary, "Reporters," was something of a landmark, teams with François Weyergans, himself a director and member of the editorial board of Cahiers du Cinema, for this hollow, pretentious exercise.

Pic, whose title is in English rather than French, is seen through the eyes of a self-absorbed, self-pitying journalist who meets a French girl in a hotel on the east coast of North Africa (the town of Djibouti) and invites her to share his room (he has two beds.)

Typical of the film's offhand style is the fact that this crucial first meeting is not shown, but conveyed by narration over a shot of an empty corridor. The man is strongly attracted to the girl, an off-hand, boyish type played listlessly by the film's co-editor, Françoise Prenant, but does nothing about it. They spend their time talking banalities, endlessly smoking cigarets, gazing down on the street below and venturing out to the cinema (to see a French-track version of "The Man From Snowy River"). Eventually they leave the town and head off into the bush, crossing the desert and winding up in Alexandria. About an hour into the film, the man, who is never seen, finally makes love to the woman (off-screen, of course), but makes a hash of it. It's hardly surprising.

This is the sort of ludicrously self-absorbed pic that gives the art house

end of French cinema a bad name. Doubtless it will have its followers who will read deep meanings into its empty philosophizing. The first-person style, with the narrator supposedly the eye of the camera, is not even as effective as it was when Robert Montgomery used it in "Lady In The Lake," and cheats outrageously, giving us a highly selective version of what the dreary protagonist sees.

As a travelog, pic fails thanks to its unappealing images and wayward style. When the rather dull young lady tells the narrator he's a bore, one can only agree with her wholeheartedly — and that goes for the film, too. —*Strat.*

Shoah
(FRENCH-SWISS-DOCU-COLOR)

Paris, May 10.
A Parafrance release of a Films Aleph/Historia Films, Geneva coproduction, with the participation of the French Ministry of Culture. Produced, conceived and directed by Claude Lanzmann. Camera (Fujicolor), Dominique Chapuis, Jimmy Glasberg, William Lubtchansky; editor, Ziva Postec; sound, Bernard Aubouy, Michel Vionnet (Israel). Reviewed at the Monte Carlo theater, Paris, May 6 and 7, 1985. Running time: **561 MINS.**

"Shoah" is a non-fiction feature about the Nazi extermination of Eastern European Jewry, and runs nearly 10 hours. In this decade of reconstructed movie epics and marathon historical dramas, it cannot be considered excessively long, and one would have to look hard for something substantial to cut.

It opened in Paris on the eve of the Cannes Film Festival, without publicity or morbid drumbeating. The fest, overly absorbed this year with gloss and festivities, was not interested in it. Too bad for the festival. "Shoah" won't need it to reach the hearts and minds of an international audience. It is already the subject of heated discussion beyond French borders and has quickly sparked controversy (the Polish government has asked for its ban).

Claude Lanzmann, who conceived, produced and directed, is a veteran journalist with a long history of political activism, having been a Resistance fighter during the German Occupation and an outspoken critic of France in the Algerian War. His life-long commitment to Israel led to his first filmmaking effort, the feature-length documentary "Pourquoi Israël," in 1973. A long-time friend of Simone de Beauvoir and Jean-Paul Sartre, he is still an active editor of the intellectual review they founded, "Les Temps Modernes."

"Shoah," which he began preparing in 1974, is not just one more film about the Holocaust. Despite its unusual length, it does not set out

to retrace the history of Nazi Germany's policy of racial and religious persecution and murder.

Its goal is unique, selective and single-minded: describe in ruthless detail the inhuman bureaucratic and technocratic machinery of the Final Solution during the years 1942-1944. "Shoah" untiringly demonstrates the innovative specificity of Hitler's campaign of genocide, from the early mobile gas chambers to the monumental industrial efficiency of Auschwitz.

Lanzmann refuses facility: no external commentary, and no Pavlovian recourse to period photos or archive material, all-too-familiar and often misleadingly exploited in that they have fudged the distinctions between the no-exit death camps and the more classic concentration camps. He has understood that the now banalized "Night And Fog" method finally drives a consoling wedge between the subject and the viewer.

Instead he has composed his film in the present tense with two subtly overlapping textures: that of the long, exhaustive interview, and that of the ferreting motion picture camera, which prowls the terrain around modern-day Treblinka, Auschwitz and other Polish sites of extermination.

Interviewed are several Jewish eyewitnesses, who survived in the very midst of the horror, like the Polish barber who cut the women's hair in the anteroom of the Auschwitz gas chamber, or the Czech Jew who, as member of the camp's special commando, stood 'at the disposal end.

Interviewed as well — and herein is the film's most astonishing and chilling scoop — are several Nazi officers and functionaries, who agreed to talk for the right sum, but only for an oral record destined for private archive use. Here Lanzmann threw scruples to the winds by hiding a video camera in the room, monitored from a van positioned in the street. No thick tome on the Holocaust will ever match the image of a former SS Untersharführer at Treblinka, describing with professional detachment the daily functions of the murder machine.

The film is particularly damning for the Polish peasants and townspeople who silently, and often indifferently, continued their lives while thousands were murdered daily nearby. Questioned by the often sarcastic director, many of them unwittingly lay bare an unconscious, deeply rooted anti-semitism which the Nazis undoubtly appreciated when they erected the death camps on Polish soil. Nor is the Polish Resistance spared in the memories of a government liaison officer, still haunted by his clandestine visits to the dying Warsaw

Ghetto, who recalls that the underground leaders refused to supply weapons to the ghetto Jews for their uprising.

The Warsaw Ghetto, focus of the film's last two hours, is also evoked by Holocaust historian Raul Hilberg, whose repeated interventions provide a more objective, analytical point of view.

With the faithful assistance of his editor, Ziva Postec, Lanzmann has assembled this overwhelming mass of material — he had over 350 hours of film — not only as a stubbornly devoted journalist and historian, but as a filmmaker and artist conscious of form and structure, and how they set off content. There is an unforgettably sinister beauty to the footage Lanzmann took in Poland on his various trips, and there is art in the way he has edited it with the faces and voices of his interviewees, like refrains in a terrifying epic poem.

"Shoah" (the biblical Hebrew word for "Holocaust") is being presented in Paris in two parts on alternating days. It may have its U.S. premiere at the New York Film Festival in the fall. — *Len.*

Rustlers' Rhapsody
(COLOR/B&W)

Hollywood, May 9.
A Paramount Pictures release. Produced by David Giler. Written and directed by Hugh Wilson. Exec producer, Jose Vicuna. Stars Tom Berenger. Camera (Madrid Film color), Jose Luis Alcaine; editor, John Victor Smith; sound, David Lee; production design, Gil Parrondo; costumes, Wayne Finkelman; assistant director-associate producer, Michael Green; art direction, Raul Paton; music, Steve Dorff; casting, Judith Holstra, Marcia Ross. Reviewed at the National theater, L.A., May 8, 1985. (MPAA Rating: PG.) Running time: **88 MINS.**
Rex O'Herlihan .... Tom Berenger
Peter .... G.W. Bailey
Tracy .... Marilu Henner
Col. Ticonderoga .... Andy Griffith
Railroad colonel .... Fernando Rey
Colonel's daughter .... Sela Ward
Bob Barber .... Patrick Wayne
Jim .... Brant Van Hoffman
Jud .... Christopher Malcolm
Blackie .... Jim Carter
Doctor .... Billy J. Mitchell

After laughing all the way through "Rustlers' Rhapsody," it's somewhat bewildering to expect that a great number of other people won't care for it all. However, there may be enough suckers for sendup silliness to cover the feed bill, and maybe more.

Taking on the oater, writer-director Hugh Wilson wisely realizes the best satires of the singing cowboys were the originals and he avoids a straight-on attack. Approaching obliquely, Wilson tries an almost surreal spoof that still manages to target the clichés.

He's doomed to lose two segments of the audience: (1) those too young to appreciate how really stupid the Saturday Westerns of the

1940s were; and (2) those who do remember, but grow impatient at Wilson's sometimes clumsy efforts to educate the first group so they'll know what's happening is funny.

For the remaining sympathizers, Tom Berenger makes a wonderful costumed crooner who travels the Wild West with an endless supply of spare hats, shiny boots and buckles plus enough fringed shirts and spotless tight pants to keep sidekick G.W. Bailey forever busy at the ironing board.

When not strumming one of his three guitars or adoring his dancing horse Wildlife, Berenger wonders why his life has a certain sameness to it. In every town he visits, there's a Main Street saloon with a hooker with a heart of gold, a sheriff in cahoots with a cattle baron riding roughshod over the sheepherders, a railroad rascal, a bountiful daughter, assorted bad guys, a daffy doctor and/or a town drunk.

So it is in the troubled town of Oakwood Estates and, though he doesn't really understand why, Berenger accepts that it is his duty and destiny to ride into town, shoot some guns out of the hands of the bad guys, help the sheepherders, sing a song and show off his horse while fending off the damsels without a kiss.

Bailey is terrific as the drunk who ultimately dons a checked shirt and a funny hat and paints a circle around his mule's eye to enlist in Berenger's service. Andy Griffith is also super as the cattle baron with rather fey habits who aligns with Fernando Rey, himself straight out of a different satire, the "spaghetti Western."

A word here for Wayne Finkelman's costumes, an essential part of the fun, not only because of Berenger's endless wardrobe but the wackiness of a gang composed of Griffith's men in traditional Western garb and Rey's in their raincoats.

Marilu Henner is perky as the prostitute who talks dirty for cash but goes no further, and Sela Ward is delightful as the daughter who can be dragged for miles behind a horse and emerge with no more than a smudged cheek.

Patrick Wayne provides the ultimate plot turn when Griffith decides to confuse Berenger by hiring another good guy instead of a black-hat like those Berenger is accustomed to besting before riding into the sunset.

Granted, none of this works perfectly but it's at least a welcome change from comedic foodfights, flatulence and bikinis. If nothing else, it's nice to again see a virgin male who loves his horse and writes letters home to mother. — *Har.*

At Cannes Market

Rainy Day Friends
(U.S.-COLOR)

Cannes, May 12.

A Signature Prods. film. Produced by Tomi Barrett and Walter Boxer. Written and directed by Gary Kent. Features entire cast. Camera (Eastmancolor), and production designer, Ronald Victor Garcia; art director, Russell Pyle; editor, Peter Appleton; music, Jimmie Haskell; casting, Pat Orseth. Reviewed at Cannes (Market), May 12, 1985 (No MPAA Rating.) Running time: **101 MINS.**
Neekos Valdez . . . . Esai Morales
Jack Marti . . . . Chuck Bail
Elaine Hammond . . . . Janice Rule
Margot Fisher . . . . Carrie Snodgress
Shirley Felton . . . . Tomi Barrett
Stephen Kendricks . . . . . . John Phillip Law
Barbara Marti . . . . Lelia Goldoni
Angel . . . . Kimberley Hill

If the ad-promo merchants can overcome the difficulties presented by this "Rainy Day Friends' " setting (a cancer hospital in Los Angeles, with the attendant pain, suffering and distress), Gary Kent-directed item will have a good shot at attracting a theatrical audience.

There is an inbuilt appeal to U.S. cities with large Hispanic elements through the commanding central presence of Esai Morales (who was one of the leads in Universal's "Bad Boys") as a 17-year-old Latino who faces a life-or-death struggle, and triumphs.

Also, the pic says enough about human values like compassion, friendship and inter-racial harmony to reach out to mainstream audiences.

In the opening sequences, Morales comes over as just another street kid from the barrios of L.A. who relies on petty crime to indulge his taste for drugs. Landing in the hospital after getting dragged along the road behind a pickup whose radio he was trying to steal (top-class stunt work and photography make this a memorable scene), Morales is told he has abdominal tumors. Disease may not be terminal, but he will require lengthy therapy.

How Morales copes with this interruption to his life, and how the hospital administrators, social workers and other patients cope with him, are the essence of strong, compelling drama.

Sympathies run strongly in the youth's favor when authorities discover he is the son of an illegal immigrant, and by-the-book hospital administrator John Phillip Law, goaded by callous head nurse Carrie Snodgress, decides he should be turned over for deportation.

The kid has his allies — cancer specialist Janice Rule and social worker Tomi Barrett (who doubles as the pic's coproducer) — but they

are powerless in these circumstances and instinct tells him to flee to the streets.

Salvation comes in the form of Chuck Bail (a stunt man and director as well as actor), a grizzled former boxer and flying ace whom Morales had befriended in the hospital. Bail was letting cancer beat him until the plucky youth raised his spirits and encouraged him to fight it.

Returning the favor, Bail tracks him down and forces the authorities to readmit him for treatment. It's an upbeat ending to a well-told, impressively directed and engaging story.

In a winning performance, Morales displays a touching vulnerability under the macho swagger, and the supporting cast is uniformly good.

Pic's changing moods are richly enhanced by Jimmie Haskell's soundtrack which mixes rock, ballads and blues, and several catchy tunes sung by Kimberley Hill, who appears as a drug pusher who has her own band. —*Dogo.*

She'll Be Wearing Pink Pajamas
(BRITISH-COLOR)

Cannes, May 13.

A Film Four Intl.-Pink Pajamas production. Produced by Tara Prem, Adrian Hughes. Directed by John Goldschmidt. Stars Julie Walters. Screenplay, Eva Hardy; camera (Eastmancolor), Clive Tickner; music, John du Prez; production design, Colin Pocock; sound, Paul Filby; editor, Richard Key. Reviewed at Cannes (Market), May 12, 1985. Running time: **90 MINS.**
Fran . . . . Julie Walters
Tom . . . . Anthony Higgins
Catherine . . . . Jane Evers
Lucy . . . . Janet Henfrey
Doreen . . . . Paula Jacobs
Ann . . . . Penelope Nice
Joan . . . . Maureen O'Brien
Anita . . . . Alyson Spiro
Judith . . . . Jane Wood
Diane . . . . Pauline Yates

Comparisons will inevitably be made between "She'll Be Wearing Pink Pajamas" and the late Joseph Losey's "Steaming:" both films are about a group of British women from mixed backgrounds who gather together, awkwardly at first, but eventually confide in each other and reveal their innermost secrets and problems. In both films the conversation revolves around the difficulties of relating to men, and attitudes to sex. Both films have mother-daughter characters, both include a nude shower scene, and both groups of women include a couple of uninhibited types who shock the rest.

Where "Steaming" proved overly solemn, however, "She'll Be

Wearing Pink Pajamas" is lots of fun. After a slightly off-key opening, in which the characters are introed, we're into the setting of an outdoor survival course for women only, a week-long exercise designed to push the participants physically as far as they can go. The intimate discussions that follow take place against outdoor backgrounds, filmed in England's beautiful Lake District, as the women ford streams, climb mountains, canoe, swing on ropes, or go on a marathon hike.

There's one man around (Anthony Higgins), but he's almost an intrusion, and though he gets to sleep with one of the women, it's a surprise choice. The women are a lively and well-differentiated lot, and there is a bevy of fine actresses playing them. Standout is Julie Walters, memorable in "Educating Rita," and reaffirming her talent here as a bouncy type who proves surprisingly weak in the crunch; her tearful revelation of a three-year period of celibacy is one of the film's genuinely moving moments.

The overall impression gained from the film is one of fun; it looks as though the cast had a great time making it, and their enthusiasm is infectious. Helmer John Goldschmidt fumbles a few moments, especially at the beginning and the very end, but the bulk of the film should please audiences, especially women, who go to see it. The music of John du Prez is not always appropriate, but the lensing of Clive Tickner is a major plus. Some of the scenes of mountain climbing, involving no extras, look genuinely hazardous.

The title, unfortunately, is totally misleading as to package's contents. — *Strat.*

Starchaser: The Legend Of Orin
(U.S.-ANIMATED-COLOR-3-D)

Cannes, May 12.

An Atlantic Releasing release of a Thomas Coleman-Michael Rosenblatt presentation. Produced, directed by Steven Hahn. Executive producers, Coleman, Rosenblatt. Screenplay, Jeffrey Scott. Animation directors, Mitch Rochon, Jang-Gil Kim. In 3-D, Deluxe color, widescreen; music, Andrew Belling; editor, sound design (Dolby), Donald W. Ernst; character design, Louise Zingarelli; hardware design, Thomas Warkentin; background design, Timothy Callahan, Roy Allen Smith; special visual effects, Michael Wolf; associate producers, Daniel Pia, Christine Danzo. Reviewed at the Olympia 9, Cannes (Market), May 11, 1985. (MPAA Rating: PG.) Running time: **98 MINS.**
Voice characterizations: Orin (Joe Colligan), Dagg (Carmen Argenziano), Elan/-Aviana (Noelle North), Zygon (Anthony Delongia), Arthur (Les Tremayne), Silica (Tyke Caravelli).

Being advertised incorrectly as the first animated 3-D feature, "Starchaser: The Legend Of Orin" turns out to be a moderately engaging sci-fier strongly in the "Star Wars" mold. Atlantic Releasing had great success reestablishing the kiddie market in the U.S. with "The Smurfs And The Magic Flute" and should do quite nicely with this one as well. Pic opens in its first regional engagements this week.

Made in South Korea and the U.S., pic can't be spoken of very seriously for the quality of its animation, since the characters are basically stick figures moving against flat backdrops. Nor is the 3-D used to any particularly startling effect. However the elemental story components, which borrow most heavily from the King Arthur legend and the first "Star Wars" entry, make for a fast-moving tale chock full of incident, resulting in an entertainment that will keep moppets plenty diverted.

Yarn opens in an underground world where robots enslave humans for hard labor. Finding a magical sword handle and advised in a vision that he should seek out the blade so he can free his people, handsome young Orin escapes to the surface world and meets up with swashbuckling Dagg. Aboard the latter's computerized spaceship, the two fight numerous battles with the evil empire before ultimately making the universe safe for human beings.

Each fellow has his love interest — in Dagg's case she's a sexy young "fembot" — and dialog is peppered with a surprising number of "hells" and "damns," given the target audience.

Animation method in the early going is none too impressive, as the characters walk around as if between sliding bits of scenery on a stage, but once the action reaches the futuristic world, look of the film is elaborate enough. The 3-D technique is easy on the eyes and overall quite agreeable.

Music by Andrew Belling is in the expected John Williams style, and nothing in the film is so silly as to make sitting through it an ordeal for adults. — *Cart.*

El Jardin Secreto
(The Secret Garden)
(SPANISH-COLOR)

Cannes, May 10.
An Incine-Jet Films production. Produced by Alfredo Matas. Direced by Carlos Suárez. Screenplay, Suárez, Salvador Maldonado; camera (Eastmancolor), Javier Aguir-resaroba; music, Alberto Bourbon. Reviewed at Star Cinema, Cannes (Market), May 9, 1985. Running time: **105 MINS.**
Lucia . . . . Assumpta Serna
Arturo . . . . Xabier Elorriaga
Also with: Taida Urruzola, Cecilia Roth.

Cameraman Carlos Suárez, brother of veteran Spanish helmer Gonzalo Suárez, makes an auspi-

cious directorial bow in this beautifully limned, engrossing pic involving a love story with sado-masochistic overtones.

Lucia, an office worker with a computer job, strikes up a romance with an out-of-town rep of the company. However, Lucia has a secret past, referred to as her "secret garden," while Arturo is married and has a child. They make a verbal pact not to refer to this shrouded past, but as their romance warms up, and Arturo decides to break with his wife, the kinky sexual appetites of Lucia become apparent, as well as a murky, complicated past seemingly involving a death of a husband or lover in a plane crash.

In addition to receiving mysterious letters in the mail, Lucia gets her kicks on the side by indulging in masochistic practices with a woman whose phone number she fishes out of the papers, and later reveals a sadistic side as well as she puts a former friend through an ordeal. Arturo gradually discovers the details of Lucia's "secret garden," and the relationship ends to the seeming satisfaction of both parties.

A tour-de-force performance by Assumpta Serna, solid support by Xabier Elorriaga and the rest of the cast, skillful direction and a strong storyline make this one of the most promising commercial pics to come out of Spain this year. Item could garner audience interest in all territories. —*Besa.*

Sahara
(Lost In The Sahara)
(SPANISH-COLOR)

Cannes, May 11.
A Cabal Film production. Written and directed by Antonio R. Cabal. Camera (Eastmancolor), Javier G. Salmones; editor, Eduardo Biurrum; production manager, Carlos Taillefer; music, Carlos Vizziello; assistant director, Paco Perinan. Reviewed at Palais des Festivals, Salle F, Cannes (Market), May 10, 1985. Running time: **97 MINS.**
Javier . . . . Antonio Iunco
Hafa . . . . Enrique Pérez
Florance . . . . Maru Valdiviafso

Theatrical director Antonio Cabal's first excursion into cinema has proved to be most felicitous. Rather than shooting his first pic as director in his native Spain, Cabal and his cohorts organized an excursion into the Algerian Sahara Desert, penetrating areas seldom visited by outsiders. The result is a fascinating film, part offbeat travelog, part an ebullient story of youthful love and tomfoolery, and part a reflection upon the mysteries of the desert.

Simple plot concerns two Madrid men in their 20s who decide to cross the Sahara in 1973 in a land rover, a trip of over 6,400 miles (as it was actually shot by the crew, using an

eight-car/van caravan). One, Javier, is serious-minded and interested in photographing antiquities and local color; the other, Hafa, is more interested in making it with a French girl who joins them on the expedition.

Pic traces the adventures that befall the two Spaniards and the girl as they cross the desert: these include having their land rover stolen, internal squabbles among the three, and illness and near-death from exposure to the elements, but also a lot of youthful fun and spontaneity. The final part of the film starts to go first symbolic and ultimately tragic, as the three get hopelessly lost and never find the main road to salvation.

Item is offbeat enough to appeal to select art house audiences. Despite its occasionally slow pacing, there is enough freshness and beauty in the film to make it attractive to discerning filmgoers. —*Besa.*

The Lie Of The Land
(NEW ZEALAND-COLOR)

Cannes, May 12.
A Grahame McLean and Assoc. production. Produced, directed and written by McLean. Camera (Eastmancolor), Warrick Attewell; editor, Jamie Selkirk; sound, David Newton; music, Dale Gold. Reviewed at Olympia 2, Cannes (Market), May 12, 1985. Running time: **91 MINS.**
Major Martin Hudson . . . . Marshall Napier
Alwyn . . . . Roberta Wallach
Henry . . . . Dean Moriarty
Clifford . . . . Terence Cooper
George . . . . Jim Moriarty
Doctor Max . . . . Jonathan Hardy
Jenna . . . . Ann Pacey

Grahame McLean's "The Lie Of The Land" is an offbeat, low budget feature of eccentric New Zealand flavor that may have difficulty making its way offshore.

For much of the time, it seems not sure whether to take its subject seriously (albeit with humor) or send it up totally. This leaves the viewer more than somewhat bemused.

Picture is set in New Zealand in the 1920s. Major Martin Hudson (Marshall Napier) returns from the war in Europe to find work with a young widow Alwyn (Roberta Wallach) and her son Henry (Dean Moriarty) in a small valley farm.

He finds the land threatened by a greedy land baron Clifford (Terence Cooper) and also by a *maketu* — a curse — palced on it by a Maori chief who resents the intrusion of European settlers on tribal land. Love and death result.

McLean, who wrote as well as produced and directed the film, has a keen eye for comedy and detail. There is a nice moment involving Alwyn and Henry tentatively killing a chicken — no blood — that really works. Overall, the story is labor-

iously episodic with paper-thin characters. —*Nic.*

Fran
(AUSTRALIAN-COLOR)

Cannes, May 10.
A Barron Films presentation. Produced by David Rapsey. Directed by Glenda Hambly. Stars Noni Hazlehurst. Exec producer, Paul Barron; screenplay, Hambly; camera (color), Jan Kenny; additional photography, Yuri Sokol; art director, Theo Mathews; composer, Greg Schultz; sound, Kim Lord; editor, Tai Tang Thien. Reviewed at Cannes Film Festival (Market). May 10, 1985. Running time: **94 MINS.**
Fran . . . . , ... Noni Hazlehurst
Marge . . . . Annie Byron
Jeff . . . . Alan Fletcher
Lisa . . . . Narelle Simpson
Tom . . . . Travis Ward
Cynthia . . . . Rosie Logie
Ray . . . . Danny Adcock
Carol . . . . Rosemary Harrison
Graham . . . . Colin McEwan

First feature from writer-helmer Glenda Hambly, "Fran" is a gritty, emotion-charged drama with a strong feminist streak.

Though many women are likely to empathize with the title character as the men in her life (nearly to a man, a callous, uncaring and violent bunch of low-lifes) combine with her own shortcomings and faults to bring her much grief and misery, the downbeat mood prevailing throughout and cheerless ending will probably restrict the pic to specialized art house audiences in many territories. Elsewhere, item will play better — and quite acceptably — on television.

Its primary strength is a virtuoso performance from Noni Hazlehurst as Fran, a young mother of three children whose construction worker husband splits after discovering she was having an affair with one of his workmates.

Fran started out in life behind the eight-ball. She never knew her father, her mother was an alcoholic and she was made a ward of the state at age five.

Life takes a happier turn — temporarily — when she links up with Jeff (Alan Fletcher) a moody, taciturn bartender who, she hopes, will rescue her from loneliness and insecurity. Of course it does not pan out that way: the children are placed in a welfare home after she and Jeff take an extended vacation in the outback; then she is told he'd sexually abused Lisa (Narella Simpson), her eldest daughter.

At the finale, the kids are adopted out, Jeff has hightailed it, Fran has had a blazing row with her neighbor and longtime ally Marge (Annie Byron) and she is left with nothing and, presumably, a grim future.

While the characters and events are totally credible (if not exactly original, save for that ugly child-molesting twist), the shrieking, tears and underlying pessimism (leavened slightly by the odd flash of wit and humor) will likely make "Fran" a downer for those who want cinema to yield entertainment.

Hambly's script is lucid, her direction is tight, and Hazlehurst is a standout. In a poignant portrait, she consistently enlists sympathy and understanding despite her character's glaring inadequacies as a wife, mother and all-round human being.

Lending solid support are Annie Byron, Narella Simpson and Alan Fletcher. Camerawork is by Jan Kenny, and she does a fine job in what exec producer Paul Barron says marks the first Australian feature lensed by a woman cinematographer. — *Dogo.*

Competing At Cannes

— Continued —

Adieu, Bonaparte
(FRENCH-EGYPTIAN-COLOR)

Paris, April 30.

An AMLF release of a Lyric Intl./Misr Intl. (Cairo)/TF-1 Films/Ministry of Culture (Paris)/Ministry of Culture (Cairo) coproduction. Produced by Humbert Balsan, Jean-Pierre Mahot and Marianne Khoury. Written and directed by Youssef Chahine. Script collaborators, Yousry Nasrallah, Mohsen Mohiedine, Jean-Michel Comet; camera (color), Mohsen Nasr; editor, Luc Barnier; music, Gabriel Yared; art director, Onsi Abou Seif; costumes, Yvonne Sassinot de Nesle; sound, Michel Brethez, Dominique Hennequin; makeup, Evelyne Byot, Mohsen Fahmy; production managers, Hussam Eddine Aly and Mohamed El Gohary. Reviewed at the Publicis screening room, Paris, April 29, 1985. (In competition at Cannes Film Festival.) Running time: 113 MINS.
General Cafarelli . . . . Michel Piccoli
Aly . . . . Mohsen Mohiedine
Yehia . . . . Mohamed Atef
Bonaparte . . . . Patrice Chereau
Horace . . . . Christian Patey
Also with: Mohsena Tewfik, Hassan Hussein, Claude Cernay, Gamil Ratib, Ahmad Abdel Asiz, Farid Mahmoud, Hoda Sultan, Salah Zulfikar, Hassan El Adl, Mohamed Dardiri, Abla Kamel, Dahlia Younes, Seif El Dine, Tahia Carioca, Tewfik El Dekken.

France's Socialist leaders were somewhat embarrassed by Andrzej Wajda's "Danton," partially financed by Culture Minister Jack Lang, which didn't conform to official left-wing interpretations of the French Revolution. They may have egg on their face when they take a gander at "Adieu, Bonaparte," France's first coproduction with Egypt, which again had important coin support from Lang.

Once again, a non-French director has been appointed to the task, which, in this case, is understandable: its ostensible subject — Napoleon Bonaparte's extraordinary Egyptian campaign of 1798 — concerns both nations equally.

However, Youssef Chahine's historical reconstruction is naive, biased and cinematically unexceptional. What begins as an epic apparently about culture shock, finally boils down to a banal tragedy of unconsummated pederasty. The film, which simple-mindedly ridicules the French, could have benefitted from less of the "auteur" and more of the spectacle-minded professional.

For much of the film, there is enough exotic color and lively large-scale movement to satisfy the average audience. Chahine was given ample means and extras to illustrate, however summarily, the French army's routing of the Mamelukes at the decisive Battle of the Pyramids, and the uprising incited by religious fanatics in Cairo. The helmer's own fascination with Hollywood films no doubt helped him here, though he has no fluent epic style of his own.

Yet he doesn't like Napoleon, and obviously thinks little of his expedition's civilizing mission. As played by Patrice Chereau, the stage and opera director who was Camille Desmoulins in Wajda's "Danton," the little Corsican is reduced even further to a contemptible caricature — a strutting, pop-eyed megalomaniac, seen buffoonishly taking part in a Muslim ritual, or rehearsing an "impromptu" speech for his chiefs of staff.

As for the extravagant corps of scholars, scientists and artists that accompanied Napoleon, they are pictured more like mooning adolescents in summer camp, than the progressive force they represented to the mostly poor and backward indigents oppressed by Turkish rule.

Film's overriding weakness however is in the central relationship between two young Alexandrian brothers, whose family has come to Cairo at the moment at Napoleon's embarkment, and the French general Cafarelli, a one-legged warrior and enlightened scholar, who was especially dear to Napoleon

Chahine also presents him as a mystical homosexual, whose friendship with the boys is not altogether innocent. The youths, not only firmly heterosexual, but also ardently nationalist, keep their distance, and make the most of Cafarelli's learning for the Arab cause. One of the boys dies in a stupid accident, but the other (Mohsen Mohiedine, seen in some of Chahine's previous pictures) survives and visits the soldier, mortally wounded in battle, for a spiritu-

al reconciliation.

The director fails to give the characters any depth or complexity, so they never acquire a representive resonance as individuals and members of differing cultures. Michel Piccoli is the peg-legged Cafarelli with his usual physical authority, though Chahine's script and direction bridle him from making of the character a truly exceptional personality, both pathetic and inspiring.

—*Len.*

Insignificance
(BRITISH-COLOR)

Cannes, May 11.

An Island Alive release of a Zenith production in association with the Recorded Picture Co. Produced by Jeremy Thomas. Executive producer, Alexander Stuart. Directed by Nicolas Roeg. Stars Gary Busey, Michael Emil, Theresa Russell. Screenplay, Terry Johnson; camera (color), Peter Hannan; editor, Tony Lawson; production design, David Brockhurst; costumes, Shuna Harwood; music, Stanley Myers; sound, Paul Le Mare; associate producer, Joyce Herlihy. Reviewed at the Cannes Film Festival (in competition) May 11, 1985. (No MPAA Rating.) Running time: 108 MINS.
The Ballplayer . . . . Gary Busey
The Senator . . . . Tony Curtis
The Professor . . . . Michael Emil
The Actress . . . . Theresa Russell
The Elevator Attendant . . . . Will Sampson

A comedy set in a New York hotel room over a sweaty night in 1953 might seem an odd assignment for such a serious and innovative director as Nicolas Roeg, whose last entry, "Eureka," was effectively shelved by its financier, MGM/UA. In fact, although the mainly linear narrative of "Insignificance" is laced with wit and irony, pic is as complex and sometimes profound as any of Roeg's previous films. Island Alive will release late August in the U.S. Given availability of marketing hooks, pic could have breakout potential in specialized locations.

Story concerns four celebrated American figures of the 1950s who, for legal reasons, are not specifically named. That's all to the good since pic dispenses with biographical detail to focus on the nature of celebrity in Cold War America.

Film was scripted by Terry Johnson from his stage play. Although legit text is not opened out in a traditional way, beautifully lensed views of the N.Y. landscape and flashbacks give the film a sense of scale. When, towards the end of the film, the Elevator Attendant greets the dawn Cherokee-style, the hotel room has become a microcosm of the world outside.

Central character is a blond actress whose image adorns all the city's bars. Although an opening sequence of a film crew at work on the billowing dress sequence from "The Seven Year Itch" establishes iden-

tification, Theresa Russell creates her own interpretation of the Marilyn Monroe persona. Her subtle performance skillfully counterpoints a cheery exterior to inner despair.

The Professor, played with neurotic charm by Michael Emil, has been summoned to New York to testify in the communist witch hunt hearings. As he makes clear from the beginning, he's not interested in the games of politicians.

The Actress arrives on the Professor's doorstep with a bag of toys which she uses for a very individual demonstration of the theory of relativity. Her stagey speech, which provides a major text for the film, charms the Professor. However, he's reluctant to reciprocate by providing human warmth.

What unites both characters, apart from their place in the public eye, is the burden they carry from the past. The Actress has been transformed by men from an exhibitionist brunet to a blond icon. The Professor has to live with his experience of the Nazi Holocaust and the link between scientific exploration and the Hiroshima bomb. In another respect, the pair complement each other. She has learned relativity by rote and doesn't understand a thing. He can explain the secrets of physics, but is a complete innocent in other fields.

With the stormy arrival of the Ballplayer, the complex relationship just established is contrasted to the simple quest for warmth within marriage. Gary Busey swaggers through the part of a guy made famous through baseball who has no handle on his actress wife's deeper needs. Marital breakup is the inevitable result.

As the Senator, Tony Curtis captures the raw ruthlessness and brutal sexuality of a right-wing politico. Performance carries extra emotional weight from memory of Curtis' association with Monroe in Billy Wilder's 1959 pic "Some Like It Hot," especially when the Senator fails to recognize the Actress in a brutal scene near the film's conclusion.

Those on the lookout for philosophical reflections will find plenty to think about in the pic's meditations upon relativity and the coming together of time. "Insignificance" also works on a simpler level as a depiction of four people struggling against despair.

Period feel is skillfully secured through set design, lighting and formal composition of shots. Some Roeg fans, indeed, will miss the camera and editing tricks which are the director's hallmark. Moody jazz-oriented score includes contributions from Will Jennings, Roy Orbison and Stanley Myers.

—*Japa.*

Saraba Hakobune
(Farewell To The Ark)
(JAPANESE-COLOR)

Cannes, May 9.

An Art Theater Guild-Gekidan Himawari-Jinriki Hikoki-sha coproduction. Produced by Fujio Sunaoka, Kyoko Kujo, Shiro Sasaki. Directed by Shuji Terayama. Features entire cast. Screenplay, Terayama, Rio Kishida; camera (Eastmancolor), Tatsuo Suzuki; music, J.A. Seazer; art director, Noriyoshi Ikeya; sound, Katsuhide Kimura; editor, Sachiko Yamaji. Reviewed at Cannes Film Festival (In Competition), May 8, 1985. Running time: **127 MINS.**

Sué . . . . Mayumi Ogawa
Sutekichi . . . .:. . . Tsutomu Yamazaki
Daisaku . . . . Yoshio Harada
Tsubana . . . . Keiko Niitaka
Temari . . . . Yoko Takahashi
Chigusa . . . . Hitomi Takahashi

One of two posthumous films in the official section of Cannes this year (the other is Joseph Losey's "Steaming"), "Farewell To The Ark" was shot early in 1982 in Okinawa when helmer Shuji Terayama was seriously ill; apparently he managed to complete post-production just before his death in May 1983, and the reasons for the delay in release are put down to legal complications over the source material.

What emerges is a superb visual treat, with often dazzling images and a bold use of color, but a narrative which is confused and erratic. Sué lives with her cousin, Sutekichi, a member of the junior branch of a village clan; but since it's believed that the offspring of cousins will be born with terrible deformities, Sué's father forces her to wear a huge, ugly chastity belt. The unfortunate Sutekichi becomes the laughing stock of the village, since everyone knows of his plight, and one day, driven beyond endurance, he stabs to death the head of the senior branch of the clan, Daisaku.

The couple flees, but return full circle to their home, where Sutekichi gradually loses his mind. An epilog is set on the fringe of a large city, where most of the villagers and their descendants are now living.

Terayama fills the pic with off-the-wall, magical moments, and it is frequently gripping on a purely visual level. For example, when the couple runs away after the murder, the color film suddenly changes to black and white, although the flames of a fire, which can't be extinguished, remain red. As in earlier Terayama films, much of the acting is theatrical and flamboyant, though there's a nicely controlled central performance from Mayumi Ogawa as Sué. The tragedy brought about by unfulfilled sexual desire is a powerful theme, given added potency by dozens of symbolic asides, such as an obsession with time. It all makes for a frequently fascinating pic, but one which will only find a limited art house audience outside Japan, though cult status is not out of the question.

It emerges as a typically idiosyncratic swansong for Terayama.
—Strat.

Rendezvous
(FRENCH-COLOR)

Paris, May 6.

A UGC release of a T. Films/Films A2 coproduction. Produced by Alain Terzian. Directed by André Téchiné. Features entire cast. Screenplay, Téchiné, Olivier Assayas; camera (color), Renato Berta; editor, Martine Giordano; music, Philippe Sarde; art director, Jean-Pierre Kohut-Svelko; sound, Jean-Louis Huguetot; costumes, Christian Gasc. Reviewed at the UGC screening room, Neuilly, May 5, 1985. (In competition at Cannes Film Festival). Running time: **82 MINS.**

Nina . . . . Juliette Binoche
Paulot . . . . Wadeck Stanczak
Quentin . . . . Lambert Wilson
Scrutzler . . . . Jean-Louis Trintignant
   Also with: Anne Wiazemsky, Dominique Lavanant, Jacques Nolot, Jean-Louis Vitrac, Michèle Moretti, Anie Noël.

Someone once described "Last Tango In Paris" as being about the difficulty of finding an apartment in the French capital. Same could be applied to André Téchiné's "Rendezvous," an equally morbid erotic drama triggered by the search for living space. Sarcasm aside, this is nonetheless a stylishly engrossing tale of obsessive sexuality and initiation, forcefully put across by excellent young actors.

Newcomer Juliette Binoche, fleetingly seen in recent films by Jean-Luc Godard ("Hail, Mary") and Jacques Doillon, is remarkable in her first lead role, that of a young provincial girl who has come to Paris to get into the theater and make the most of her sexual insouciance. Her extroverted, shallow nature quickly lands her a small part in a Boulevard comedy and allows her to indulge her young hedonistic impulses.

When her current bed partner bounches her out, she seeks a new pad at a real estate agency, where its young, apparently virginal employee (Wadeck Stanczak) takes acute interest in her. He goes out of his way to find her an apartment, hoping to bed her, but makes the mistake of introducing her to his seedy young roommate, Lambert Wilson, who soon forces himself on her and becomes her lover.

She is both fascinated and repelled by Wilson, on a course of self-degradation (he is an actor in a sex show) and self-destruction. Latter is fulfilled when he apparently throws himself in front of a car.

His death profoundly affects the once carefree girl, who is haunted by his memory and soon learns through his legit director father-in-law (Jean-Louis Trintignant) that Wilson found premature love and success as a stage actor, but was crushed by the sudden death of the girl who was his wife and stage partner.

Trintignant, invited to Paris to stage a new production of "Romeo & Juliet," the play in which Wilson made his name, imposes Binoche as the leading lady. Feeling unsure and desperate, she finally throws herself at the frustrated Stanczak, who violently makes love to her and then proceeds to forget about her. Distraught and utterly alone, Binoche arrives at the theater on opening night to tensely await the curtain's rise and her rendezvous with pained maturity.

Film's dramatic fullness reflects the white heat immediacy in which Téchiné wrote (in collaboration with Cahiers du Cinéma critic Olivier Assayas) and directed, though the relatively brief span between script's inception and end of shooting is not betrayed by its first-rate technical quality.

Wilson (son of veteran stage actor Georges Wilson) and Stanczak (like Binoche another recent discovery) should also get career mileage from their dramatically full but temperamentally polarized performances.
—Len.

Non-Competing Entries

Continued

Ososhiki
The Funeral)
(JAPANESE-COLOR)

Cannes, May 11.

An A.T.G. presentation of an Itami-N.C.P. production. Directed and written by Juzo Itami. Features entire cast. Camera (Fujicolor), Yonezo Maeda; editor, Akira Suzuki; music, Joji Yuasa; sound, Minoru Nobuoka; art director, Hiroshi Tokuda. Reviewed at Cannes Film Festival (Directors Fortnight), May 10, 1985. Running time: **123 Mins.**

Wabizuke Inoue . . . . . . Tsutomu Yamazaki
Chuzuko Amamiya . . . . Nobuko Miyamoto
Kikue Amamiya . . . .:Kin Sugai
Shokichi Amamiya . . . . Shuji Otaki
Satomi . . . . Ichiro Zaitsu
Ebihara . . . . Nekohachi Edoya
Shinkichi Amamiya . . Kiminobu Okumura
The Priest . . . . Chishu Ryu
Yoshiko Saito . . . . Haruna Takase

A big success on its home territory, this first feature by Juzo Itami, an actor who most recently scored as the father in "The Family Game" but who has also appeared in such international films as "55 Days At Peking" and "Lord Jim," takes a taboo subject — death — and turns it into a very black comedy.

An old man dies, ironically on the very day his doctor gave him a clean bill of health. His daughter and son-in-law are both television actors (they're introed in a scene neatly parodying the production of a tv film), and it's up to them to arrange the funeral. Ceremonies take place over three days, at great expense of course, and the family and friends gather round for extensive drinking and maudlin celebration.

One highlight involves the couple studiously watching a video made especially to teach how a proper funeral should be organized, even down to the correct things that should be said. Then there's the deceased's fussy brother, forever worrying about little details; the funeral home operator; and the priest, who arrives in a white Rolls. Indeed, a lot of money changes hands during these days, just as a lot of saki is consumed and a lot of photos taken, with the family grouped around the coffin with fixed smiles on their faces.

The formal Japanese funeral may have unique qualities, but there's enough universality here to suggest that, with tightening (the film is overlong by half an hour) "The Funeral" could find art-house success internationally. It's well made, often very funny (but not, of course, for anyone who might find the subject distasteful), and finely acted by an interesting cast. Tsutomu Yamazaki, as the son-in-law, was the young kidnaper in Akira Kurosawa's "High And Low" (1963), while Chishu Ryu, as the priest, played the lead in many a Yasujiro Ozu film. Nobuko Miyamoto, the wife, is director Itami's wife, and there appear to be some autobiographical elements here.

"The Funeral" was picked to open the Directors Fortnight at Cannes, a good choice since it got things off to a cheerful, offbeat start. — *Strat.*

Oriana
(Oriane)
(VENEZUELAN-FRENCH-COLOR)

Cannes, May 13.

A Pandora Films C.A. (Caracas) and Arion Prods. (Paris) production directed by Fina Torres. Screenplay, Torres, Antoine Lacomblez, from a short story by Marvel Moreno; camera (color), Jean-Claude Larrieu; music, Eduardo Marturet (with extracts from Bach. Beethoven and Faure). Reviewed at Cannes, (Un Certain Regard), May 12, 1985. Running time: **88 MINS.**

With: Doris Wells, Daniela Silverio, Rafael Briceõ, Mirta Borges, Maya Oloe, Claudia Venturini, Philippe Rouleau, Martha Canelón, Luis Armando Castillo, Asdrubal Melendez.

Basically a film of mood and atmosphere, "Oriane" is developed along a double level of memory. Marie, after living in France for many years, returns to Venezuela after her aunt Oriane's death, to sell the house and hacienda she inherited from her. Wandering around the dusty old mansion, she slowly remembers the period of her adolescence she spent there in Oriane's company and how, at the time, she was intrigued by her aunt's past and delved into her secrets.

Oriane lived all her life in that house, never leaving the hacienda. Remembrance of things past, now that she is an adult, brings Marie a new understanding of her aunt's life. She also discovers the missing link that explains it all.

Fina Torres studied at IDHEC in Paris and previously worked for television. This, although it could certainly not be inferred from the screen, is her first feature. Technical credits are good and the acting, satisfactory. "Oriane" is a small and delicate film that has a limited range, both in style and subject matter, but within these limitations accomplishes its objectives. It could well obtain art house exposure.
—*Hans.*

Le Soulier De Satin
(The Satin Slipper)
(FRENCH-PORTUGUESE-COLOR)

Paris, May 1.
A Films du Passage (Paris)/Metro E Tal (Lisbon) coproduction in association with I.N.A. (Paris), WDR (Cologne), SSR (Geneva), with the participation of the French and Portuguese Ministries of Culture and the Portuguese Film Institute. Produced by Paolo Branco and Arthur Castro Neves. Directed by Manoel de Oliveira. Screenplay, de Oliveira, from the play by Paul Claudel; literary adviser, Jacques Parsi; camera (color), Elso Roque; sets, Antonio Casimiro; costumes, Jasmin; makeup, Dominique De Vorges; production manager, Danièle Beraha. Reviewed at the Club 70, Paris, April 30, 1985. (In Cannes Film Festival as official non-competing selection in homage to Manoel de Oliveira.) Running time (theatrical film version): **169 MINS.**

Don Rodrigue . . . . Luis Miguel Cintra
Dona Prouhèze . . . . Anne Consigny
Dona Sept-Epées . . . . Patricia Barzyk
The king . . . . Jean-Yves Berthelot
Daibutsu . . . . Takashi Kawahara
Actress 1 . . . . Catherine Jarret
Actress 2 . . . . Anny Romand

"The Satin Slipper" is Portuguese director Manoel de Oliveira's reverential celluloid embalming of a sprawling French poetic drama by Paul Claudel, a Catholic playwright and lyric poet whose work is impregnated with a profound sense of Christian mysticism. Claudel composed the play in the early 1920s, but it was not staged until 1943, in an abridged version, by Jean-Louis Barrault. It was produced in its entirety — over seven hours of performance — in 1980, again by Barrault.

De Oliveira, at 76 his country's most distinguished filmmaker, has stage-filmed the whole piece under Franco-Portuguese coproduction

auspices, with additional coin from West German and Swiss tv webs. On view here is the theatrical cut of nearly three hours, which includes all of the final, fourth, act and important sections from the prolog and first and third acts, without which the action would be barely comprehensible.

On the basis of this version, it would be safe to say that de Oliveira has given the play as near-definitive a production as Claudel fans could hope for. Shot entirely in the studio in order to emphasize the theatrical trappings of the globe-straddling action, film is stunning in photography, set and costume design, and Claudel's complex dialog is spoken with fervent fluency by a mostly first-rate cast (mostly from France) dominated by its superb Portuguese lead, Luis Miguel Cintra.

The hitch is that "The Satin Slipper" will be an excruciating experience to non-French-speaking viewers and those unaccustomed to the slow, static cadences of classical European drama.

Difficulty is compounded by de Oliveira's direction, which underlines the stately pictorialism of each scene with a usually stationary camera, though there is an occasional change of viewpoint or slow dolly to reframe the scene. De Oliveira treats the comic elements of Claudel's work in the same ponderous manner as the rest of the material.

The film begins quite conventionally in a theater where "The Satin Slipper" is to be performed. The play's prolog is projected on a screen as the camera slowly moves in and merges the theatrical and filmic realities.

The theme of Claudel's play apparently is the transcendence of carnal love by love of God. Drama's principals are a glory-hungry Spanish conquistador and a Spanish noblewoman, both of whom have been smitten by love at first sight. The lady is a pious soul who confides her slipper to a statue of the

Virgin Mary as safeguard against sin.

The lovers never consummate their passion, of course. She eventually dies, and the warlord, after years of conquest in the Orient, renounces his wordly titles to lead a near-monastic existence on his ship, as a humble painter of religious pictures. He resists the Spanish king's subterfuge to lure him back into service and in the end finds spiritual salvation.

The complete play, cast as a tv miniseries of four 90-minute segments, will have its premiere at the Venice Film Festival. It will probably be more palatable in that episodic form than in this cinema cut, a sure-fire theater-evacuator.

The Cannon Group is selling both versions worldwide. — *Len.*

Visages De Femmes
(Faces Of Women)
(IVORY COAST-COLOR)

Cannes, May 15.
A Films de la Lagune production. Produced, written and directed by Désiré Ecaré. Features entire cast. Camera (Color), Francois Migeat; sound, Jean-Pierre Kaba; music, traditional. Reviewed at the Cannes Film Festival (Critics Week), May 9, 1985. Running time: **107 MINS.**
Koiassi . . . . Sidiki Bakaba
Brou . . . . Kouadio Brou
Fish seller . . . . Eugénie Cissé Roland
Also with: Albertine Guessan, Véronique Mahile, Alexis Leatche, Désiré Bama.

"Faces Of Women" features stories of African women today in the bush and city and their struggle to carve out a place for themselves in a changing world. After a hesitant start, film picks up interest as it goes along. While boldly pursuing its theme of female liberation, it treats the viewer to lots of local color, a clever structure with a chorus commenting on the action, and an unexpectedly frank nude scene. It's a good bet for fest and art house circuits.

Helmer Désiré Ecaré began "Faces" in 1973 (his first full-length feature) and took 12 years to finish it, producing it himself. This lengthy gestation period accounts for its odd format of two stories with different casts, blended into each other through the device of using a female chorus of dancers and singers in both parts.

In the opening sketch, a young wife allows her brother-in-law (Sidiki Bakaba) to court her. It is her husband's (Kouadio Brou) uncalled-for jealousy and possessiveness that spurs her to take Bakaba as a lover in a long, naturalistic, joyous love-making scene in a brown pond. Refusing to humble herself before her husband's threats and insults, the woman takes karate lessons in a humorous coda to defend herself against him.

Most of the thesps are obviously non-pro; even Bakaba, now a top African star, lacks charisma and screen presence in this early work. In film's second half, however, non-actress Eugénie Cissé Roland gives a warm and convincing performance as a 50-year-old matron with a small fish-vending business. Ecaré succeeds in giving a light touch to her frustrating struggles to get a bank loan. As a counterpoint to her tough determination is her daughter's contempt for men and traditional conviction that a pretty young woman can topple governments and that business is far beyond the female mind.

Pic suffers from occasional technical uncertainty, although liberal

use of hand-held camerawork contributes to a documentary atmosphere. Most dialog is in dialect, with French subtitles. —*Yung.*

Elle a Passé Tant d'Heures Sous les Sunlights
(She Spent So Many Hours Under The Sun Lamps)
(FRENCH-B&W)

Paris, May 4.
A Gerick Films release of a Philippe Garrel production. Produced, directed and edited by Garrel. Screenplay, Garrel and Brigitte Sy; camera (b&w), Pascal Laperrousaz; music, Nico; sound, Jean-Pierre Laforce. Reviewed at the CNC, Paris, May 3, 1985. (In French Perspectives section of Cannes Film Festival.) Running time: **137 MINS.**
With: Mireille Perrier, Jacques Bonnafé, Anne Wiazemsky, Lou Castel, Philippe Garrel, Chantal Akerman, Jacques Doillon.

Philippe Garrel, a buff critics' darling whose reputation is a dark mystery to the uninitiated, joins the private club of directors who have made a film about their inability to make a film.

This non-film begins rather coherently — the breaking up of a young couple — but suddenly shatters into a pretentious game of mirrors and film-within-a-film conceits. Garrel himself, no great camera subject, gets into the act and moons about with his undirected cast. He even drags in fellow helmers Chantal Akerman and Jacques Doillon to help fill the void. This drags on pitilessly for well over two hours.

Garrel at least has the benefit of fine b&w photography by Pascal Laperrousaz (his habitual lenser) and the pretty, sensitive face of young Mireille Perrier, first seen last year in "Boy Meets Girl."—*Len.*

L'Affaire des Divisions Morituri
(The Case Of The Morituri Divisions)
(FRENCH-B&W-16m)

Paris, May 14.
A Forum Distribution release of François-Jacques Ossang production. Camera (b&w, 16m), Maurice Ferlet: sound, Tucat-Naegelen; music, M.K.B. Fraction Provisoire. Reviewed at the CNC, Paris, May 3, 1985. (In French Perspectives section of Cannes Film Festival). Running time: **75 MINS.**
With: Gina Lola Benzina, Philippe Sfez, Frankie Tavezzano, Lionel Tua, Joseph Barbouth, Hell-Now.

Amateur hour in Punksville best describes this appalling piece of nonsense, produced, written, directed and edited by François-Jacques Ossang, a rock singer, who has published some books and made a short previously.

The story, or what one can make of it, deals with contemporary punk gladiators. There's a lot of agitation, decibels of dreadful pop music, and not a shred of sense of filmmaking ability to be gleaned.

Yet pic is at Cannes in the Perspectives on French Cinema sidebar, and even has an art house distributor locally.—*Len.*

Vertiges
(FRENCH-COLOR)

Cannes, May 11.

A Films du Passage-MK2 Diffusion production, with the participation of Channel 4 and the Ministry of Culture. Executive producer, Antonio Vaz Da Silva. Produced by Paulo Branco. Directed by Christine Laurent. Stars Magali Noël, Krystyna Janda. Screenplay, Christine and Patrick Laurent; camera (color), Acacio de Almeida; sound, Pierre Befve, Pierre Lorrain; editor, Francine Sandberg. Reviewed at Cannes Film Festival (Critics Week), May 11, 1985. Running time: **108 MINS.**
Constance . . . . .Magali Noël
Maria . . . . .Krystyna Janda
Eric Hardmour . . . . .Paulo Autran
Anne . . . . .Helene Lapiower
Marius Poudesoie. . . . . .Henri Serre
Frantz Kirkmayer. . . . . .Thierry Bosc
Herbert Ardown . . . . . .Luis Miguel Cintra

First feature by a former art director and costume designer for theater and opera, ‘‘Vertiges’’ is a backstage tale involving rehearsals for ‘‘The Marriage Of Figaro’’ which are overshadowed by the conductor’s infatuation with a great diva who has retired. He finds fault with his singers and spends a good deal of time listening to the diva singing ‘‘Carmen’’ when he’s not criticizing his ensemble.

One singer (Magali Noël) is past her prime while another (Krystyna Janda) completely loses her voice after a night of lovemaking. Eventually, the besotted conductor expires.

Though well lensed, in hard, bright colors, and with a crystal-clear soundtrack, this is an otherwise rather pretentious and overblown pic on behind-the-scenes machinations in a provincial world of smalltime opera. Helmer Christine Laurent shows a certain visual flair, but perhaps her own knowledge of this milieu is too intimate to allow her to step back and reveal a less hermetic and insular situation.

The relatively large number of monologs, theatrical in style, testify to a screenplay none too carefully edited before production. — *Strat.*

At The Cannes Market
Continued

The Frog Prince
(BRITISH-COLOR)

Cannes, May 10.

A Goldcrest and Warner Bros. presentation of an Enigma production. Executive producer, David Puttnam. Produced by Iain Smith. Directed by Brian Gilbert. Features entire cast. Screenplay, Posy Simmonds; camera (color), Clive Tickner; editor, Jim Clark; production design, Anton Furst; costumes, Judy Moorcroft; sound, Ken Weston. Reviewed at the Palais De Festivals, Cannes (Market), May 10, 1985. Running time: **93 MINS.**
Jenny. . . . . .Jane Snowden
Jean-Philippe . . . . .Alexandre Sterling
Madame Peroche . . . . .Jacqueline Doyen
Monsieur Peroche . . . . .Raoul Delfosse
Madame Declos . . . . .Jeanne Herviale
Ros . . . . .Diana Blackburn
Niels . . . . .Oystein Wiik
Annie . . . . .Françoise Tricottet
James . . . . .Jean-Marc Barr
Zar .Arabella Weir
Crissie . . . . .Lucy Durham-Matthews
Didier . . . . .Marc Andre Brunet
Dominique . . . . .Brigitte Chamarande

The second of three British pics to be made under a lowbudget film pact between Warner Bros. and David Puttnam’s Enigma Films, ‘‘The Frog Prince’’ is a nicely made but basically routine love story set in Paris in 1960. Enigma’s first production based on the European continent will take money in France. Prospects elsewhere are iffy.

The film’s basic proposition is that, however tight-laced an English girl may seem, what she’s really after is romance. French men — impetuous and charming — are just what’s required to break down her defenses.

Central character Jenny has a serious attitude to love which sets her apart from other English girls studying in the French capital. Although there’s never any doubt that she’s serious about the handsome Jean-Philippe, he has to jump many hurdles before finally bedding Jenny. His winning card is a recitation of speeches from ‘‘Romeo And Juliet’’ on a crowded metro platform.

Jane Snowden as Jenny effectively captures the anxieties that afflict an independent-minded girl growing up in a strange town. Her voluble and more adventurous friend Ros (Diana Blackburn) presents a contrasted approach to life. Both performances have a persuasive period feel. Alexandre Sterling, a bankable name in France since he appeared in the successful ‘‘La Boum’’ films, is okay as the rather simple loverboy.

What interests director Brian Gilbert is the dilemma confronting a girl as she tries to define a unique approach to love. However, script by English cartoonist and firsttime screenwriter Posy Simmonds doesn’t have the bite of Gilbert’s earlier self-scripted telefilm ‘‘Sharma And Beyond.’’

That’s largely because film is cluttered with incidents and characters with no bearing on this central theme. For example, scenes involving the families with whom Jenny and Ros reside provide only local color. Norwegian cinema buff Niels (Oystein Wiik) is little more than a useful plot device.

Film is shot well by lenser Clive Tickner and makes good use of Parisian locations, especially at night. Other technical credits are fine.
— *Japa.*

Mata Hari
(U.S.-COLOR)

Cannes, May 10.

A Cannon Releasing release of a Cannon Group production. Executive producers, Menahem Golan and Yoram Globus. Produced by Rony Yacov. Directed by Curtis Harrington. Stars Sylvia Kristel. Screenplay by Joel Ziskin; camera (Eastmancolor), David Gurfinkel; music, Wilfred Josephs; editor, Henry Richardson; art director, Tivadar Bertalan. Reviewed at Cannes (Market), May 10, 1985. Running time: **108 MINS.**
Mata Hari . . . . .Sylvia Kristel
Capt. Karl von
  Byerling. . . . . .Christopher Cazenove
Capt. Georges Ladoux. . . . . .Oliver Tobias
Fraulein Doktor . . . . .Gaye Brown
Herr Wolff . . . . .Gottfried John
Clunet. . . . . .William Fox
The Duke . . . . .Michael Anthony
Ybarra . . . . .Tutte Lemkow

Too silly to be taken seriously, and not silly enough for high camp, ‘‘Mata Hari,’’ which has already opened in some European territories, will need fast playoff before the word gets out.

Tale of a femme fatale involved with both a German and a French officer before and during World War I lacks freshness, thanks to a hackneyed script and tired direction. Sylvia Kristel disrobes on cue every 10 minutes or so, and that may be enough for some, but in terms of tension and intrigue, pic is sadly lacking.

Possible highlights, such as a topless saber duel between Kristel and a buxom rival, or a hayloft coupling between Kristel and Christopher Cazenove (the German) behind the French lines as war rages around them, go for surprisingly little.

Entire production was based in Hungary and, though some of the locations are splendid, it’s asking rather too much to accept the back streets of Budapest in place of Berlin, Paris *and* Madrid.

Most of the actors seem self-conscious, as well they might, but Kristel, looking great, enters into the spirit of things as far as she’s able, though she’s no rival for Greta Garbo, Marlene Dietrich or Jeanne Moreau, all of whom played Mata Hari in earlier, more memorable, variations on the story. —*Strat.*

Young Lady Chatterley II
(U.S.-COLOR)

Cannes, May 13.

A Park Lane Prods. presentation. Produced by Alan Roberts, Stanton Korey. Directed by Roberts. Stars Sybil Danning, Harlee McBride. Screenplay, Anthony Williams; camera (color), Bob Brownell, Bryan England; editor, Gregory Saunders; music, Misha Segal; art, Warren Skip Wildes; costumes, Eduart Castro. Reviewed at Cannes (Market) May 12, 1985. (No MPAA Rating.) Running time: **90 MINS.**
Cynthia Chatterley . . . . . . .Harlee McBride
Thomas . . . . .Brett Clark
Arthur Bohart Jr. . . . . .Adam West
Judith . . . . .Sybil Danning
French Count . . . . .Alex Sheaf

‘‘Young Lady Chatterley II,’’ a followup to the 1978 release, is an overplotted romp set on an English estate (but patently filmed in California), where mistress and servants dedicate themselves exclusively to the pursuit of carnal satisfaction. It will appeal only to undemanding followers of the genre.

Problem for Cynthia Chatterley (Harlee McBride, reprising her 1978 role) is how to secure respect of house rules from her frequent visitors. Her magic works magnificently on a former boyfriend-turned-celibate priest and his virgin nephew. She is less successful with others.

Also, rural tranquility is threatened by plans for a nuclear power plant on the property. Cynthia frustrates the developers by riding naked on a horse, which seemingly secures protected monument status for the Chatterley land.

Writhing is the only real talent exhibited by any member of this film’s cast. Adam West and Sybil Danning keep their clothing on for most of the film, but the simple-minded script doesn’t give them any opportunities for serious acting. The circa 15 acts of attempted or successful gratification, mostly filmed in full light and shot above the waist, are routine. — *Japa.*

Death Of An Angel
(U.S.-COLOR)

Cannes, May 13.

A 20th Century Fox release of an Angeles Entertainment Group and RDR Prods. presentation of an Inverness production in association with The Sundance Institute for Film and Television. Produced by Peter Burrell. Executive producers, Dimitri Villard, Robby Wald, Charles J. Weber. Directed, written by Petru Popescu. Stars Bonnie Bedelia, Nick Mancuso. Camera (Deluxe color), Fred Murphy; editor, Christopher Lebenzon; music, Peter Myers; production design, Linda Pearl; art direction, Dena Roth; costume design, Jack Bushler; sound, Susumu Tokonow; associate producer, Patrick Markey; assistant director, Jeffrey Sudzin; second unit camera, Oliver Wood; casting, Paul Bangston, David Cohn. Reviewed at the Ambassades 3, Cannes (Market), May 12, 1985. (MPAA Rating: PG.) Running time: **92 MINS.**
Grace . . . . .Bonnie Bedelia
Father Angel . . . . .Nick Mancuso
Vera . . . . .Pamela Ludwig

Robles ....Alex Colon
Also with: Abel Franco.

Towering peaks of absurb pretentiousness are scaled by "Death Of An Angel," a deadly serious allegorical stew in which such elements as religious martyrs, illegal immigrants, a female priest, Mexican gangsters and an assortment of cripples are combined with ungodly results. Developed at The Sundance Institute and originally set to be released under Fox' since-defunct TLC banner, pic has no imaginable commercial chances.

Bonnie Bedelia plays an upscale Los Angeles widow who is ordained as a priest in the opening scene. Before she knows it, her wheelchair-bound teenage daughter has run away to some sort of mission near the U.S.-Mexican border where self-styled savior Nick Mancuso lords it over a bedraggled group of poor Mexicans.

Given her new responsibilities back home, Bedelia's decision to get involved with the egotistical Mancuso's problems and go on the lam with him when Mexican baddies begin chasing him is unfathomable, but, so is the entire film.

All the characters are so confused and unlikeable the audience is given no inroad into the drama. Mancuso's maverick priest, in particular, has such a martyr complex that one suspects he wouldn't be happy unless he went to his fate carrying a cross on his back, which is exactly what he does.

Debuting writer-director Petru Popescu's penchant for dreadfully obvious symbolism is matched by his awkward staging of action and often laughable dialog, which includes such lines as, "Faith is the true, everlasting green card," and "You Latins make miracles, we gringos make deals."

Bedelia, so good a couple of years back in "Heart Like A Wheel," stumbles around without a clue as to what her character is about, and Mancuso acts with unvarying hot-blooded intensity. One suspects the worst when the two main characters are named Grace and Angel, and those suspicions are met in full. — *Cart.*

Hollywood Harry
(U.S.-COLOR)

Cannes, May 13.
A Shapiro Entertainment presentation of a Starquilt Co. production. Produced and directed by Robert Forster. Stars Robert Forster, Joe Spinell, Shannon Wilcox, Kathrine Forster. Screenplay, Curt Allen, camera (Eastmancolor), Gideon Parath; editor, Rich Meyer; music, Michael Lang. Reviewed at the Olympia, Cannes (Market), May 12, 1985. Running time: **96 MINS.**
Harry ....Robert Forster
Danielle ....Kathrine Forster
Max ....Joe Spinell

Candy ....Shannon Wilcox
Clapper ....Pete Shrum
Skeeter ....Redmond Gleeson
Farmer ....Reed Morgan
Fat Woman ....Mallie Jackson

The title character is a sort of poor man's Sam Spade, a boorish private eye who turns away would-be clients because they interfere with his boozing, and services a few grateful women as a stud for a nominal fee of five bucks a time. It's a lower-case entry, with limited prospects.

Hollywood Harry is finally forced to accept an assignment when a rich farmer, relying on his menacing henchmen, wants to trace his teenage daughter and the producer who starred her in a porno film.

The convoluted plot takes off in several directions; the detective's 14-year-old niece parks herself on him by implying her parents are dead; his partner tries manfully to keep him working, while his attractive secretary-assistant mysteriously shows up driving a Rolls Royce.

Robert Forster, who produced and directed as well as starring, infuses an occasional degree of menace into the proceedings when outsize henchman Pete Shrum uses weight and muscle as his method of persuasion. There are also a couple of car chases, a few fights, some agreeable dancing and a pleasant music track.

As the private eye who is galvanized into action by his precocious niece, Forster performs within a limited but adequate range. Kathrine Forster as the teenager is too worldly wise to be convincing, but that's the fault of the screenplay. Shannon Wilcox is a shapely and handsomely dressed secretary, while Joe Spinell, as Harry's partner, makes an almost avuncular character. Shrum stands out as the overweight menace. —*Myro.*

The Zoo Gang
(U.S.-COLOR)

Cannes, May 12.
A New World Pictures presentation of a Hersch Production with Insight Group Film. Produced and directed by John Watson and Pen Densham. Features entire cast. Screenplay, John Watson, Pen Densham, based on story by Watson, Densham, Stuart Birnbaum, David Dashev. Executive producer, Kerry Hersch. Camera (Eastmancolor), Bob New; editor, James Symonds; music, uncredited. Reviewed at Cannes (Market) at Olympia-5, May 12, 1985. (No MPAA Rating). Running time: **90 MINS.**
With: Ben Vereen, Jackie Earle Haley, Eric Gurry, Tiffany Helm, Jason Gedrick.

"The Zoo Gang" takes its name from a disco in an unidentified outlying district of a big city. A group of teenagers keeps having its premises threatened by a gang of uglies, young and old, there is a lot

of quite vicious fighting, but writer-directors John Watson and Pen Densham's aim has been to make a comedy feature and in this they succeed in an unpretentious way that should ensure them access to the youth market just about everywhere.

Film thus has the look of a small, safe winner with a comedy-drama blend resembling old Disney family entertainments but with the bounce of the rock generation added to it.

All young actors perform with a vigor and bubble that must rub off on audiences, and Ben Vereen puts in a fine, rhythmically precise performance as an ex-fighter-turned-bum who comes hilariously to the youngsters' rescue.

While film has no original viewpoint nor any innovation of comedy devices, it works on sly wit and gutsy dash in staging of otherwise run-of-the action sequences. —*Kell.*

Lorca And The Outlaws
(BRITISH-COLOR)

Cannes, May 13.
A VTC and Rediffusion Films presentation of a Lorca Film Production. Produced by Michael Guest. Directed by Roger Christian. Features entire cast. Screenplay, Christian, Matthew Jacobs; camera (Eastmancolor), John Metcalfe; exec producers, Charles Aperia and Guy Collins; editor, Derek Trigg; production designer, Owen Williams; original music, Tony Banks. Reviewed at the Cannes Film Festival (Market), May 12, 1985 (No MPAA Rating.) Running time: **100 MINS.**
Lorca ....John Tarrant
Abbie ....Donogh Rees
Kid ....Deep Roy
Suzi ....Cassandra Webb
Jowitt ....Ralph Cotterill
Danny ....Hugh Keays-Byrne
Lena....................Joy Smithers
Det. Droid ....Tyler Coppin
M.P. Droid ....James Steele

British produced and financed, and lensed in Australia (apart from studio footage in England) with a predominantly Aussie cast, "Lorca And The Outlaws" is a celluloid comic strip clearly inspired by "Star Wars" and other space sci-fiers of that ilk, but a thousand light years distant behind that stellar performer in its likely boxoffice path.

Weighed down by a tissue-strength plot, minimal characterization and plodding direction which fails to muster much suspense or excitement, undistinguished item probably will find its appeal limited to small groups of youngsters on rainy days. There's nothing in it for the older set.

Set in the year 2084 (which gave rise to its working title, "2084") on the desert planet Ordessa, yarn by helmer Roger Christian and Matthew Jacobs pits a band of fairly drab humans against a force of military police droids commanded by unscrupulous mercenary Ralph Cotterill (whose last name is misspelled "Cottrell" in the screen

credits).

Dialog is kept to a minimum, which may be a good thing since our 21st-century heroes and heroines mouth such 20th-century clichés as "It's our asses on the line," and "Let's get the hell out of here."

Aiding the mortal resistance fighters is a benevolently programmed, undersized droid named Kid (Deep Roy), possibly a distant cousin of C-3PO, whose oriental-accented voice is sometimes difficult to understand, with a reverb effect which is faintly annoying.

Best scenes are a tussle on a giant earth-mover between Lorca (John Tarrant) and repulsive bounty-hunter Hugh Keays-Byrne, and the Kid hurtling through a tunnel to save Lorca's g.f. Donogh Rees, but such moments are rare.

Model work and other special effects are unremarkable by "Star Wars," "Alien," and "Star Trek" standards, and acting by humans and robots alike is uniformly mechanical. The bad guys don't radiate much menace and the goodies, who naturally triumph in the end, probably won't earn more than half-hearted cheers, even from normally demonstrative auds.

A plus is the rousing, synthesizer-based soundtrack by Tony Banks of the pop group Genesis, and songs performed as video clips (this art form will survive into the next century, apparently) by Peter Gabriel and Toyah Willcox.

And there are some nice visuals in the Western Australian desert and in a few studio sequences. Director Christian, who graduated to helming with Paramount's "The Sender" after working in the set designing and art departments on such films as "Star Wars" and "Alien" obviously has talent but it's been squandered on "Lorca And The Outlaws." —*Dogo.*

Niel Lynne
(AUSTRALIAN-COLOR)

Cannes, May 14.
A Niel Lynne production of a David Baker film. Produced by Tom Burstall. Directed by Baker. Exec producers, Baker, Gilda Baracchi. Features entire cast. Screenplay, Baker and Paul Davies; camera (Eastmancolor), Bruce McNaughton; editor, Don Saunders; associate producer, Brian D. Burgess; production designer, Robie Perkins; original music, Chris Neal. Reviewed at the Cannes (Market), May 13, 1985. Running time: **105 MINS.**
Fennimore ....Sigrid Thornton
Niel Lynne ....Paul Williams
Patricia ....Judy Morris
Eric ....Brandon Burke
Reg.....................David Argue
Mather.....................Alan Cinis

A love story which spans 15 years and hops continents from Australia to Vietnam, "Niel Lynne" suffers from one giant credibility gap: it does not make sense.

Whatever problems were encountered in the production or editing, they have not been debugged from the finished product, which is disjointed and in its final reel, unfathomable.

Synopsis from filmmaker David Baker handed out in Cannes refers to the title character's marriage to an 18-year-old girl, an apparently blissful union which ended with her death in an auto accident. In the version caught, the girl does not appear, nor is she mentioned.

That excision won't bother paying audiences, but they will be puzzled, if not entirely mystified, when the narrative jumps eight years with no explanation of what the central characters have done in the interregnum, in particular how Niel manages to segue from a Viet Cong hospital, where he appeared to be on his death bed, to a tranquil and affluent middle-class existence in Melbourne.

All told, it's a muddled effort which reflects no great credit on anyone involved, least of all the cast members who are saddled with overwhelmingly unlovely, unsympathetic characters and slabs of unwieldly, unevenly scripted dialog.

Central quartet are Paul Williams as Niel, a naive country boy who gets caught up in the anti-Vietnam fervor of the late '60s when he edits the university newspaper, volunteers to serve in 'Nam where he cops an unfriendly bullet in the chest, and somehow winds up happily reunited in Melbourne with Judy Morris as an old flame and radical who threw her lot in with the V.C. and did time in an Australian prison as a result; Brandon Burke as Niel's boyhood friend, a firebrand painter whose cynicism and taste for booze and drugs propel him to an early grave via an overdose, and Sigrid Thornton as a screaming harridan, schemer and manipulator who loves, or loved, Burke and who had an affair with Niel.

Of the lot, Williams, a newcomer who graduated from drama school in 1981, fares best. There are some occasional flashes of camaraderie between Williams and Burke, but everyone spends most of the time being unpleasant to everyone else. It leaves a lot of questions unanswered, but at the finale, the question one may well ask is "Who cares?"

Prospects for this botched job are dim indeed. — Dogo.

Future Cop
(U.S.-COLOR)

Cannes, May 12.

An Empire Pictures release. Produced and directed by Charles Band. Features entire cast. Screenplay, Paul De Meo, Danny Bilson; camera (Deluxe color), Mac Ahlberg; special effects makeup design, John Buechler; music, Mark Ryder, Phil Davies. Reviewed at Star 2, Cannes (Market) May 12, 1985. (MPAA Rating: PG-13.) Running time: 85 MINS.
Jack Deth .... Tim Thomerson
Leena .... Helen Hunt
Whistler .... Michael Stefani
McNulty .... Art La Fleur
Hap Ashby .... Biff Manard

———

"Future Cop," originally titled "Trancers," works out of a central idea closely akin to "The Terminator."

That is where resemblances end. This film in no way can match the Arnold Schwarzenegger vehicle — in gritty action, wit and technical knowhow.

Plot centers on Angle City 2247 A.D. The ruins of L.A., as it exists today, lie below the sea following a catastrophic earthquake. A sinister mystic, Martin Whistler (Michael Stefani) threatens the peace with his legion of controlled trancers.

Whistler retreats in time to L.A. 1985 with a plan to murder the ancestors of the rulers of Angel City, thus ensuring that the rulers cease to exist.

Trooper Jack Deth (Tim Thomerson) is sent back to stop him. He is aided by Leena (Helen Hunt) his guide in the "strange world" of today.

Only Hunt in the femme role breaks through a script that rarely rings new.

While a plus might be the low level of violence, that cannot compensate for unlikely leaps in plot and character motivation, and mundane action. —Nic.

The Quiet Earth
(NEW ZEALAND-COLOR)

Cannes, May 11.

A Cinepro/Pillsbury Films production. Produced by Don Reynolds and Sam Pillsbury. Directed by Geoffrey Murphy. Screenplay, Bill Baer, Bruno Lawrence and Pillsbury; camera (color), James Bartle; art director, Rick Kofoed; editor, Michael Horton; music, John Charles sound, Mike Westgate and Hammond Peek; special effects, Ken Durey. Reviewed at Olympia 1, Cannes (Market), May 11, 1985. Running time: 100 MINS.
Zac Hobson .... Bruno Lawrence
Joanne .... Alison Routledge
Api .... Peter Smith

———

Geoff Murphy has taken a man-alone theme and turned it imaginatively to strong and refreshing effect in "The Quiet Earth."

One of the New Zealand's top directors, he helmed "Utu," an historical epic based on the wars between Maori and European, an official selection out of competition at Cannes in 1983. An earlier feature was "Goodbye Pork Pie."

With "The Quiet Earth," Murphy really shows his commercial spurs in a film with a contemporary setting yet containing elements of sci-fi futurism.

A cast of three might spell doom for a less accomplished and innovative hand. Murphy makes it seem an asset.

Plot centers on scientist Zac Hobson (Bruno Lawrence) who wakes one morning to discover he is alone in the world. A global top-secret energy project he has been working on has malfunctioned and altered the fabric of the universe.

While humanity appears to be wiped out, all its materialistic trappings remain. For a time, Zac lives out his fantasies.

Then begins a search for other survivors. He finds two — a woman, Joanne (Alison Routledge), and a man, Api (Peter Smith). The emotions unleashed by this trio in their struggle for survival propels the story, which has an intriguing mystical dimension, to a shattering conclusion.

The film is notable for high production values: photography, special effects, sound mixing and music are among the best-integrated of any Kiwi feature to date.

Acting isn't far behind. Lawrence, a veteran of N.Z. films turns in a performance that is funny and moving, while Maori actor Smith makes a bold debut.

But it is Alison Routledge who is the real find. Possessing a special, delicate, Madonna-like beauty, she invests Joanne with sparky intelligence and strength.

"The Quiet Earth" is a hair's breadth away from being very good indeed. Only hiccups are some untidy narrative stretches and a slight lack of pulsebeat over the final stages. What it achieves without question is the establishment of Murphy as a director of international, commercial caliber. —Nic,

Bombs Away
(U.S.-COLOR)

Cannes, May 12.

A Shapiro Entertainment release of Nexus Group production. Executive producer, Chris Pearce. Features entire cast. Produced, written and directed by Bruce Wilson. Camera (Eastmancolor) Marty Openheimer, music, Skeets McCraw; editor, Jon Newton. Reviewed at the Ambassades-6, Cannes (Market), May 12, 1985. Running time: 82 MINS.
With: Michael Huddleston (Kabale Smith), Pat McCormick, Michael Santo, Ben Tone, Lori Larsen.

———

An advance publicity claim for Bruce Wilson's comedy-farce "Bombs Away" to be Mel Brooksian will rather add to than subtract from critics' and audience claims to have attended a dud if not a total bomb.

Story has Michael Huddleston as cabbie Kabale Smith caught between opposing forces, all running and screaming wildly, when an atom bomb named "M.A.R.Y." from an arsenal in Texas is shipped by mistake to Lillian's Army Surplus Store in Seattle.

Not a single elementary comic device, especially not the topsy turvy maneuvering of the crate containing the nuclear device, works as blueprinted in script. Neither does the intermingling of subplots, while most of the acting consists of facial twists and vocal exhortations.

Having seen the bomb run up and down the Seattle Space Needle, chubby Michael Huddleston utters his only word during the entire proceedings, "oops." Otherwise, his mute, befuddled mien remains film's sole attraction. — Kell.

Kill Zone
(U.S.-COLOR)

Cannes, May 11.

A Shapiro Entertainment release (U.S.) of a Spartan Films production. Produced by Jack Marino. Associate Prodcuer, Thomas Baldwin. Directed by David A. Prior. Features entire cast. Screenplay, Prior and Marino; camera (Eastmancolor) and editor, Victor Alexander; original music, Robert A. Higgins. Reviewed at Cannes (Market), May 11, 1985 (No MPAA Rating.) Running time: 87 MINS.
McKenna .... Fritz Matthews
Mitchell .... Ted Prior
Crawford .... David James Campbell
Ling .... David Kong
Lucas .... Richard Massery
Also with: William Joseph Zipp.

———

A tame action-thriller, "Kill Zone" is notable for one of the longest chase sequences since Sly Stallone played hide-and-seek in the mountains in "First Blood." Unhappily, it is unquestionably the dullest.

Absence of star names, drawnout, derivative plot and B-grade production values likely will relegate this item to a short theatrical life in most territories. It probably will serve as easily digestible fodder for that segment of the homevideo market which has a yen for the run, shoot and slash genre.

Here, object of the pursuit is Fritz Matthews as a Vietnam vet who thinks he is back in 'Nam. His brain snaps when, along with a bunch of other Marines, he is subjected to brutal interrogation by Asian "captors," a bizarre training exercise masterminded by David James Campbell as a sadistic, southern-born, bully of a colonel.

Matthews busts out of the internment camp, killing four Asian guards in the process. That sure as hell annoys Campbell, who orders the platoon to track him down at any cost.

Alone until he is joined by Ted. Prior, his 'Nam buddy, Matthews miraculously manages to keep the hounds at bay. The pursuers are shot, knifed and dispatched by a number of grisly traps while Campbell gets madder and madder, venting his frustrations by wasting a couple of innocent civilians and one of his own men.

It all seems to take an eternity to unfold, and even the introduction of a helicopter into the chase late in the tale fails to enliven proceedings. Finally the protagonists Matthews and Campbell square off with the predictable outcome.

A Stallone without style, Matthews gives a lumbering, bovine performance, Prior is the jut-jawed, teeth-gritted sidekick, and Campbell just rants and cusses a lot. Fight sequences are amateurishly staged, flying hands and feet either clearly missing their mark or landing soft to the echo of patently phony thumps and whacks. Tech credits are okay save for some sloppy editing. —*Dogo.*

Tainted
(U.S.-COLOR)

Cannes, May 12.

A Walter Manley presentation of a Cardinal Pictures production. Executive producers, Orestes Matacena and Phyllis Redden. Written and directed by Matacena. Features entire cast. Camera (Eastmancolor), Ramon Suarez; production design, Randy Barcelo; music, Hayden Wayne, editor, Stephen Sheppard. Reviewed at Cannes (Market). May 12, 1985. (No MPAA Rating.) Running time: 90 MINS.
Cathy . . . . Shari Shattuck
Frank . . . . Gene Tootle
Marion . . . . Park Overall
Also: Magilla Schaus, Blaque Fowler.

Audiences for scare films will have to accept extraordinary slices of outright silliness in plot structure to accept writer-helmer Orestes Matacena's feature thriller, "Tainted." Picture has beautiful blond and well-acting Shari Shattuck as a schoolteacher in an unidentified northern U.S. locale, masturbating in her flimsiest underwear in her remote country house where all doors and windows are left wide open for a prowler to enter and attempt rape. When hubbie accidentally comes home, he takes the rapist's knife and stabs him to death with more than a normal vengeance. After which he himself kneels over, dead of a heart attack.

The teacher, who has been warned by her principal to look out studiously for her reputation, panics, does not call the police, instead buries the rapist in the garden and fixes her husband to look as though he died behind the wheel of his car several miles from the house. Afterwards, she inherits her husband's obviously lucrative crematorium business, but lurking in the shadows are the dead husband's wicked sister and her lover, the crematorium caretaker.

"Tainted" has handsome production values, fine cinematography and some okay menacing acting by the sister and the caretaker. There is some mild softcore sex and

more outright gore, but very little common sense to turn the silliness into true suspense. — *Kell.*

Breaking All The Rules
(CANADIAN-COLOR)

Cannes, May 11.

A New World Pictures release of a Filmline Prods. production. Produced by Pieter Kroonenburg, David Patterson; coproducer, Pierre David; executive producer, Robert Cooper. Directed by James Orr. Features entire cast. Screenplay, Orr, James Cruickshank, based on story by Edith Rey and Rafal Sielinski; camera (color), René Verzier; editor, Nick Rotundo; sound, Claude Hazanavicius; production design, Sandra Kybartas; music, Paul Zaza. Reviewed at Olympia, Cannes (Market), May 11, 1985. (MPAA Rating: R.) Running time: 91 MINS.
Jack . . . . Carl Marotte
David . . . . Thor Bishopria
Debbie . . . . Carolyn Dunn
Angie . . . . Rachel Hayward

"Breaking All The Rules" is a case in point of a promising thriller compromised by a yen to be loose and light and perhaps too many producers' minds at variance.

Possibilities of this one, filmed in Montreal under the title "Fun Park" and set in an amusement park, remain on a roller coaster suspended in mid-air.

A trio of robbers steals a jewel that is to be the park's final summer night prize and tuck it into a stuffed mouse while fleeing police. A park attendant and his pal spend the day at the park, latch onto two girls and make romantic contact after initial skirmishes. One of the males, natch, wins the mouse for his gal. Robbers return to claim their loot and buy up all the mice with no luck.

Police suspect the park attendant and by process of elimination the robbers go after him, too, and get the jewel. They stay in the park just long enough for the attendant's nerd friend to recover it and lead police to the robbers whom he has trapped in a breakdance contest.

Considering the possibilities of thrill rides, the chase sequences are surprisingly tame. Director James Orr displays some gentle touches in the budding romance scenes, but falls flat on the action. Pic is also about wanting to lose virginity and there's some direct language about it. Just talk, though.

René Verzier's camerawork is good as usual. Original songs by Paul Zaza are weak, loud and intrusive. Carl Marotte (the park attendant) and Carolyn Dunn as a middle-class girl who dresses outlandishly punk show some potential — but barely — and acting overall is tepid.

This is a fun park not worth the admission, but tolerable for paycable. —*Adil.*

Evils Of The Night
(U.S.-COLOR)

Cannes, May 12.

A Shapiro Entertainment release of a Mars Production. Executive producer, Mohammed Rustam. Produced and directed by Mardi Rustam. Stars Neville Brand, Aldo Ray. Screenplay, Mardi Rustam, Phillip Dennis Connors; camera (color), Don Stern; music, Robert O. Ragland; editor, Henri Chapro. Reviewed at Les Ambassades, Cannes (Market), May 11, 1985. (MPAA Rating: R.) Running time: 85 MINS.
Kurt . . . . Neville Brand
Fred . . . . Aldo Ray
The Leader . . . . John Carradine
Cora . . . . Tina Louise
Also with Julie Newmar, Karrie Emerson, David Hawk, Tony O'Dell.

A tepid blend of teen sex, sci-fi and low-level horror, this cheap-looking item opens with a group of attractive, sexually active kids camping out by a scenic lake, menaced by Something In The Bushes.

The bushes turns out to be two brainless auto mechanics (Neville Brand, Aldo Ray), in the pay of a team of scientists from outer space, led by John Carradine, that need the blood of kids of a certain age.

Strictly formula stuff, with weak dialog and almost no suspense, this will have to play off fast to undiscriminating audiences to make a buck. Even buffs, lured by the relatively stellar cast, which also includes Tina Louise and Julie Newmar as two of the outer space visitors, will find this a less-than-riveting experience. —*Strat.*

Mr. Love
(BRITISH-COLOR)

Cannes, May 14.

A Warner Bros. and Goldcrest release of an Enigma production. Executive producer, David Puttnam. Produced by Susan Richards, Robin Douet. Directed by Roy Battersby. Stars Barry Jackson. Screenplay, Kenneth Eastaugh; camera (Kay color), Clive Tickner; music, Willy Russell; editor, Alan J. Cumner-Price; art director, Adrienne Atkinson; sound, Tony Jackson; song sung by Rebecca Storm. Reviewed at Cannes (Market), May 13, 1985. (No MPAA Rating.) Running time: 90 MINS.
Donald Lovelace (Mr. Love) Barry Jackson
Theo . . . . Maurice Denham
Also with: Margaret Tyzack, Linda Marlowe, Christina Collier, Helen Cotterill, Donal McCann, Marcia Warren.

This is one of David Puttnam's more modest projects, a slim tale of a legend that grows round an ordinary bloke after his death.

Set in Southport, story involves a municipal gardener whose frigid wife and hostile daughter cause him to stay away from home. He takes part-time job as a cinema projectionist (aren't there unions in Southport?), and another as gardener for a rich widow. Along the way he befriends a number of women, including the movie-mad usherette at the cinema, a young single mother who aspires to be a singer, and another woman with a strange passion for spiders. None of these liai-

sons comes to anything, but when the poor man dies in a freak accident (a statue of Queen Victoria falls on top of his car) just as he thinks he's found love at last, his widow is amazed to see the number of mourning women at his funeral.

The funeral scene comes at the beginning, and is a replica of scenes in both versions of "The Man Who Loved Women." "Mr. Love" is rather less involving than either of those films, thanks to a paper-thin script and Roy Battersby's slow-paced direction. A supposed highlight occurs when the projection equipment fails during a screening of (what else?) "Casablanca," and Mr. Love and the usherette, who know the dialog by heart, play the Bogey-Bergman scenes on stage before the delighted audience; it should be a charming moment, but it comes across as rather embarrassing.

Barry Jackson, as Mr. Love, succeeds in making a very average man rather more insignificant than the role required, though there are some good performances among the supporting cast. This item doesn't look as if it can expect a very bright theatrical career. —*Strat.*

Thunder Alley
(U.S.-COLOR)

Cannes, May 10.

A Cannon Releasing release of a Cannon Group presentation of a Golan-Globus production. Produced by William R. Ewing. Executive producers, Menahem Golan, Yoram Globus. Directed by J.S. Cardone. Stars Roger Wilson. Screenplay by Cardone; camera (color), Karen Grossman; editor, Daniel Wetherbee; music, Ken Topolsky; art direction, Pal Tagliaferro; costumes, Dorothy Baca. Reviewed at the Cannes (Market), May 9, 1985. (MPAA Rating: R.) Running time: 111 Mins.
Richie . . . . Roger Wilson
Beth . . . . Jill Schoelen
Donnie . . . . Scott McGinnis
Lorraine . . . . Cynthia Eilbacher
Weasel . . . . Clancy Brown
Skip . . . . Leif Garrett

"Thunder Alley" seems to compress into a few weeks the classic tale of a rock band's progress from nowhere to the brink of success. Pic has nothing to say about the contempo music scene, but may appeal to mid-teens keen on rock 'n' roll.

Plot is run of the mill. Ace guitar player Richie, who lives on his father's cotton farm near Tucson, is reluctant to join the band assembled by his keyboardist friend Donnie because of the hostility of lead singer Skip. When he is enrolled, the group's fortunes quickly rise.

Concurrently, Richie becomes emotionally attached to Beth, who works in an ice cream parlor with Donnie's girl Lorraine. Rural landscape provides a suggestive setting for the pair's wooing and loving.

Manager Fat Man seems to be giving the band a chance, but he's also feeding drugs to Donnie who dies of an overdose. The band splits up and Richie gets depressed. It's Fat Man's sidekick Weasel who gets the remaining band members together to plot their revenge.

Pic, which could have been trimmed substantially is directed with occasional flair. Among an okay cast Scott McGinnis is standout. Leif Garrett's singing is also a plus. —*Japa.*

Screen Test
(U.S.-COLOR)

Cannes, May 13.

A Farpoint Films production, produced by Sam and Laura Auster. Directed by Sam Auster. Features entire cast. Screenplay, Sam and Laura Auster; camera (Eastmancolor), Jeff Jur, editor, Carol Lastman; music, Don Harrow, Reviewed at Olympic Cannes (Market), May 12, 1985. Running time: **84 MINS.**
With: Michael Allan Bloom, Robert Bundy, Paul Lauken, David Simpetico, Cynthia Kahn, Mari Laskarin, Katharine Sullivan; William Dick, Michelle Bauer, Monique Gabrielle, Dina Delicata, Benjamin Lecompte 3d, Frank Madda.

This west coast youth-oriented sex comedy seems tailored mostly for the drive-in and homevid crowd; some sophomoric laughs and softcore scenes may be a come-on for adolescents seeking fluff.

Tongue-in-cheek yarn concerns four boys who aren't making it with the local chicks. They come up with a scheme of pretending to make a porno videofilm and casting shapely girls in the key roles. The scheme works to perfection, except that one of the girls is the daughter of a Mafioso godfather type, who sweeps down on the unwitting youngsters with a fleet of Cadillacs and rod-toting gangsters to demand a copy of the film which was never made. It all ends happily with a shotgun marriage.

The simulated sex scenes won't embarrass any red-blooded youths in the States, and some of the dialog is amusingly articulate; thesps appropriately ham up some of the scenes, and the four lead actors are fine in their parts of libidinous, bumbling would-be filmmakers. — *Besa.*

Bad Girls Dormitory
(U.S.-COLOR)

Cannes, May 12.

A Films Around The World Inc. release of an Entertainment Concepts production. Written and directed by Tim Kincaid. Features entire cast. Executive producer, Cynthia DePaula. Camera (Eastmancolor) Arthur D. Marks; music, Man Parrish. Reviewed at Cinema Le Star-4, Cannes (Market), May 11, 1985. (No MPAA Rating.) Running time: **95 MINS.**
Lori ....Carey Zuris
Marina ....Teresa Farley

Paige.................Natalie O'Connell
Don Beach ....:....Rick Gianasi
Miss Madison ....Marita
Lisa ....Jennifer DeLora
Rebel ....Donna Eskra
Dr. DeMarco ....Dan Barclay
Nurse Stevens ....Rebecca Rothbaum
Harper ....Rachel Hancock
Valeska ....Charmagne Eckert

Tim Kincaid obviously hopes to reach a wider audience with his feature "Bad Girls Dormitory" than its equally obvious exploitation potential as a female prison sex & violence item, but when he gets maudlin and socially indignant over the cruel fates of his young inmate-protagonists, he loses his otherwise calm grip on dramatic narrative and had — at least at Cannes at a packed midnight showing — audiences laughing.

Most of film, however, is straight action having the 15-20-year-old girls fight each other or with male and female guards when they are not getting raped by a nice, cleancut prison doctor or, of course, by the guards themselves. Kincaid has most of his young actors perform with professional cool, while the head mistress of the New York Female Juvenile Reformatory (an actress named Marita) and a few others are played like characters out of a Charles Addams cartoon.

What is curious about this rape-and-fight-every-other-minute film is the way it pulls its punches so it is never allowed to veer into outright porn or gut-ripping gore. There is an almost antiseptic air about the proceedings, and very little hurt. One girl (Lori, played like a sleepwalker by Carey Zuris), supposedly an innocent victim of circumstance, for a while seems headed for salvation via a young male social worker (Rick Gianasi), but when he, too, turns out to be a baddie, there is really no sympathetic character left. Everybody in "Bad Girls Dormitory" has the look of a scrubbed laboratory rat, and it would take an anti-vivisectionist to really care.
— *Kell.*

Storm
(CANADIAN-COLOR)

Cannes, May 12.

A Groundstar Prods. production. Produced, directed and written by David Winning. Features entire cast. Camera (color), Tim Hollings; editor, Bill Campbell; sound, Per Asplund; music, Amin Bhatia; associate producer-director, Michael Kevis. Reviewed at Salle Jean Cocteau, Cannes (Market), May 12, 1985. Running time: **81 MINS.**
Lowell ....David Palfy
Jim ....Stan Kane
Booker ....Tom Schioler
Burt ....Harry Freedman
Stanley ....Lawrence Elion
Hostage ....James Hutchison

A plodding and often confused thriller, "Storm" is a first feature for all concerned — a learning exer-

cise on an obviously tiny budget that allowed for hardly any production values.

Plot centers on three older men who return to dig up a box of stolen money buried before they were jailed. At the same place in the woods are two young men planning a survival weekend after playing with dart guns on a college campus.

Several shoot-em-ups later, one young man remains alive, digs up the box and finds it empty. Seems it was empty in the first place, a trick played on his pals by one of the older men.

Promising setup is dissipated from the outset and lack of experience by all hands leads to murky scenes of imaginings when tight action is required. The Alberta woods seem so lonely.

Theatrical playoff is doubtful and not much chance for tv use either except where any Canadian content is mandated by law. —*Adil.*

Loose Screws
(CANADIAN-COLOR)

Cannes, May 10.

A Concorde Pictures (New Horizons) release of a Maurice Smith Prods. production. Produced by Smith. Directed by Rafal Zielinski. Features entire cast. Screenplay, Michael Cory; camera (color), Robin Miller; editor, Stephan Fanfara; production design, Judith Lee; sound, Nolan Roberts; sound editor, Al Streeter; music, Fred Mollin. Reviewed at Les Ambassades, Cannes (Market), May 10, 1985. (MPAA Rating: R.) Running time: **92 MINS.**
Brad Lovett ....Brian Genesse
Steve Hardman ......Lance Van Der Kolk
Hugh G. Rection ....Alan Devean
Marvin Eatmore ....Jason Warren

In this sequel to the "Porky's" knockoff "Screwballs," four libidinous males get bounced from Beaver High School to Coxwell Academy for slow learners.

They're not the only ones to bounce. So do too many labored sexual innuendoes, character names included, and the good-sized chests of a cluster of femmes in their late teens.

The boys want one thing, so do the girls. Despite confinement together at the boarding school, there's no action. Pic consists of just a lot of fevered running around, dumb dialog, telegraphed pranks, slow direction and amateurishlooking camerawork.

Reasonable, but not spectacular, bodies must have been the only requirement to get into this low-budgeter. Acting all around is negligible as is the chance of a successful theatrical release. Only hope; homevid. —*Adil.*

American Drive-In
(U.S.-COLOR)

Cannes, May 14.

A Star Media Sales release of a Patel-Shah film. Executive producer, by Shashi Patel. Produced and directed by Krishna Shah. Features entire cast. Screenplay, David Ball, Shah; camera (color), Steve Posey; editor, Amit Bose; music, Paul Sabu. Reviewed at Cannes (Market), May 13, 1985. (No MPAA Rating.) Running time: **89 MINS.**
Bobbie-Ann.....:.....Emily Longstreth
Jack ....Pat Kirton
Also with: Rhonda Snow, Joel Bennett, John Rice, Allison Heath, Mika, Kevin Miller.

A tepid pic in the "Grand Hotel" genre, "American Drive-In" is about an assorted group of characters who assemble at a hicktown drive-in for a double-bill of "Hard Rock Zombies 1 & 2."

Audience includes a fresh-faced young couple recently engaged to be married; a gang of bikers who terrorize them; a nerd-like politician on the lookout for dopepushers; a couple of batty old ladies (who're actually the dope peddlers); a prostie; an intellectual couple intent on analyzing the film; a guy who wants his date to give him sexual favors she's not willing to do; a family of fatties who spend all the time gorging; and a dwarf actor who stars in the picture. There's also the drunken projectionist and beleaguered ticket taker.

Nothing much happens to these uninteresting types, and audiences will become bored quickly at the lack of action. There's some discreet sex, simple humor and a climactic car crackup that's as unmotivated as it is corny.

"Hard Rock Zombies" is also a Patel-Shah production, so the producers of this film didn't have to pay rights for the generous footage seen of the earlier, and apparently equally undistinguished, pic.
—*Strat.*

That's My Baby
(CANADIAN-COLOR)

Cannes, May 13.

A Gemini Film Productions production. Produced by Edie Yolles. Directed, screenplay by John Bradshaw, Yolles. Camera (color), W.W. Reeve; editor, Stephen Withrow; music, Eric N. Robertson. Reviewed at Les Ambassades, Cannes (Market), May 13, 1985. Running time: **98 MINS.**
Louis...................:..Timothy Weber
Suzanne....................Sonja Smits
Sugar ....Joann McIntyre
Sally......................Lenore Zann
Bob Morgan ....Derek McGrath

Honorable in its intentions but bastardized in its execution, this little pic about paternity is destined for video outlets and looks like a pilot for a tv series with its last 30 minutes devoted to highlights of the next six episodes.

The protagonist, would-be-father Louis, is a role that possibly only Robin Williams could deliver with the appropriate zany delight it requires. Timothy Weber delivers a charming but not irrepressible performance as a man who has quit his steady job and become a house-husband for a woman devoted to her apparently meteoric career at a tv station.

Said careerist, Suzanne, is played by Sonja Smits, who can't help but arrange her lovely body in glamorous poses and only briefly sports a pregnant tummy after succumbing to friend Louis' pesky and persistent desire to father her child. Scenes stand or collapse on the strength of the actors, and when the chemistry between the leads is there, it provides an endearing warmth.

The storyline is developed in jerks and starts from Louis' personal crisis to Louis and Suzanne's problem not having a baby, winding up at their role-reversal problems with infant.

Overwritten dialog seems to try much too hard, line for line, to achieve significance, but when the action eclipses it, the strength of the direction and ease of the camera provide cheerful drama, if not quite comedy.

Two directors are credited for the film and they seem to have imposed divergent directions on the pic. A weak or perhaps truncated storyline is compensated by a compassion for the experience of sharing a child in a way that is almost palpable.

Derek McGrath mugs for the camera as Louis' former associate eager to get him back on the fast track. McGrath's acting is suitable for tv commercials and makes Weber look subtle, complex and full of the masculine mystique.

Paternity has spawned so many movies since "Kramer Vs. Kramer" that a sub-genre seems to be developing. "That's My Baby" contributes nothing to it. Perhaps the realm of fatherhood is not really fertile enough ground for all the comedies forced upon it. —*Kaja.*

Déjà Vu
(BRITISH-COLOR)

Cannes, May 9.

A Cannon Releasing release of a London-Cannon Films production. Produced by Menahem Golan and Yoram Globus. Associate producer, Michael Kagan. Directed by Anthony Richmond. Stars Jaclyn Smith. Screenplay, Ezra D. Rappaport, Anthony Richmond, based on an adaptation by Joane A. Gil of a book by Trevor Meldal-Johnsen; camera (color), David Holmes; editor, Richard Trevor; music, Pino Donaggio; production design, Tony Woollard; art direction, John Siddall; costumes, Marit Allen. Reviewed at the Salon Jean Cocteau, Cannes (Market), May 9, 1985. (MPAA Rating: R.) Running time: **90 MINS.**
Maggie Rogers/Brooke
  Ashley . . . . Jaclyn Smith
Gregory Thomas/Michael
  Richardson . . . . Nigel Terry
Eleanor Harvey . . . . Claire Bloom
Olga Nabokov . . . . Shelley Winters

"Déjà Vu" is a lame revenge thriller which involves the seeming

reincarnation of two lovers some 50 years after their death in a mysterious housefire. For an entry in this genre, pic is too short on visual thrills to make any impact theatrically.

Jaclyn Smith and Nigel Terry play the couple in both time periods. Contempo story starts when writer Gregory Thomas observes that his fiancée, Maggie Rogers, is a carbon copy of the late ballerina Brooke Ashley, whom he sees on film.

After learning of the fatal conflagration, Thomas gets to work on a screenplay about the love affair between Ashley and choreographer Michael Richardson. Through dreams and hypnosis administered by Ukrainian spiritualist Olga Nabokov, friend of Ashley whom he happens to visit, Thomas discovers he is Richardson reincarnate.

Script doesn't offer much interaction between the modern lovers (apart from initial carnal activity) nor does it extract any mystery from the indications that Ashley's mother is plotting revenge on her daughter's man. In fact, it's only when Rogers suddenly sets about her bedmate with a knife, about 10 minutes from the film's conclusion, that things really get going.

The performers are unable to breathe conviction into their lines. Smith gives a monotonous performance in both roles. Terry is good as a brooding screenwriter, but cannot cope with his part's other aspects. Shelley Winters is camp as the spiritualist.

Lush scoring contributes atmosphere to the pic, which features lavish art direction. Lensing experience of debutant feature director Tony Richmond (Smith's husband) is only occasionally evident in the film's visuals. — *Japa.*

Shaker Run
(NEW ZEALAND-COLOR)

Cannes, May 10.

A Mirage-Aviscom Production in association with Laurelwood Prods. Executive producer, Henry Fownes. Produced by Larry Parr, Igo Kantor. Directed by Bruce Morrison. Screenplay, James Kouf Jr., Fownes, Morrison; camera (color), Kevin Hayward; production designer, Ron Highfield; editors, Ken Zemke, Bob Richardson; music, Stephen McCurdy; sound, Malcolm Cromle; special effects, Kevin Ohisnall. Reviewed at Olympia I, Cannes (Market), May 10, 1985. Running time: **90 MINS.**
Judd Pierson . . . . Cliff Robertson
Casey Lee . . . . Leif Garrett
Dr. Christine Rubin . . . . Lisa Harrow
Paul Thoreau . . . . Shane Briant
Michael Connolly . . . . Peter Hayden
Barry Gordon . . . . Ian Mune

Billed as "the ultimate chase," Bruce Morrison's second feature, "Shaker Run," gets near earning such an accolade at final fadeout. A clifftop denouement involving pursuers and pursued litarally takes off.

En route, however, the road is

rocky for this action/adventure drama burdened with a story lacking conviction and clear plotline.

High speed motor action, crashes, special effects and meaningful looks cannot work in isolation, nor can New Zealand's superb scenery. There have to be characters audiences can respond to in order to make the formula play.

The story involves two down-on-their-luck American stunt car drivers Judd Pierson (Cliff Robertson) and Casey Lee (Leif Garrett), which research scientist Dr. Christine Rubin (Lisa Harrow).

Rubin, for reasons not made at all clear, has stolen a deadly virus being developed for ulterior political reasons. She is to deliver it to American agent Barry Gordon (Ian Mune) for safe keeping. The CIA seen in a favorable light?

Paul Thoreau (Shane Briant), head of a shadowy military intelligence organization is determined the virus shall not leave New Zealand.

With paucity of script and uneven direction allowing even able performers like Robertson and Harrow little scope, everything depends on the stunts.

Some hit and some miss. Ultimately they are not enough to deliver real excitement and involvement. —*Nic.*

Re-Animator
(U.S.-COLOR)

Cannes, May 14.

An Empire Pictures release of a Re-Animated Prods. film. Produced by Brian Yuzna. Executive producers, Michael Avery, Bruce Curtis. Directed by Stuart Gordon. Features entire cast. Screenplay, Dennis Paoli, William J. Norris, Gordon, from story "Herbert West — The Re-Animator," by H.P. Lovecraft; camera (Deluxe color), Mac Ahlberg; music, Richard Band; special effects makeup, Anthony Doublin, John Naulin; additional makeup effects, John Buechler; stunts, Dan Bradley; art director, Robert A. Burns; editor, Lee Percy. Reviewed at Cannes (Market), May 13, 1985. (No MPAA Rating.) Running time: **86 MINS.**
Herbert West . . . . Jeffrey Combs
Daniel Cain . . . . Bruce Abbott
Megan Halsey . . . . Barbara Crampton
Dr. Alan Halsey . . . . Robert Sampson
Dr. Karl Hill . . . . David Gale
Mace . . . . Gerry Black

Latest entry into the gross-out stakes is "Re-Animator," based on an H.P. Lovecraft tale about a crazy scientist who brings dead bodies back to life with a special serum. Trouble is, they come back violent and ready to kill.

Herbert West (Jeffrey Combs) is the inventor who, like horror film scientists from time immemorial, is too batty to realize the consequences of his actions. Romantic leads are Bruce Abbott and Barbara Crampton, latter a looker who, at the pic's climax, is strapped naked to a lab table as an object of the

lusts of a hateful admirer, who by this time literally has lost his head.

Pic has a grisly sense of humor, and sometimes plays a little like Sam Raimi's "The Evil Dead," in that it's *so* gross and over the top, the film tips over into a kind of bizarre comedy.

Combs signs on as a student at a Massachusetts university where his roommate (Abbott) is having an affair with Crampton, daughter of the puritan dean (Robert Sampson). A senior doctor (David Gale) desires Crampton, and after he's been murdered and beheaded by Combs, all in the course of science, he becomes the time-honored threat to the heroine's chastity.

Pic zips along, making full use of the inventive effects. A music score by Richard Band would be better if it weren't so obviously derivative of Bernard Herrmann's "Psycho" score. Technically pic is tops, with good lensing by Mac Ahlberg. However, the title doesn't really indicate what kind of film patrons for this kind of blood-letting are to expect.—*Strat.*

The Chain
(BRITISH-COLOR)

Cannes, May 9.

A Rank Film Distributors presentation of a Quintet film production. Produced by Victor Glynn. Executive producer, David Deutsch. Directed by Jack Gold. Features entire cast. Screenplay, Jack Rosenthal; camera (color), Wolfgang Suschitzky; editor, Bill Blunden; music, Stanley Myers; production design, Peter Murtori. Reviewed at Ls Ambassades, Cannes (Market) May 9, 1985. (BBFC Certificate, PG.) Running time: **96 MINS.**
Des . . . . Herbert Norville
Keith . . . . Denis Lawson
Carrie . . . . Rita Wolf
Grandpa . . . . Maurice Denham
Mr. Thorn . . . . Nigel Hawthorne
Mrs. Andreos . . . . Billie Whitelaw
Deidre . . . . Judy Parfitt
Thomas . . . . Leo McKern
Paul . . . . Tony Westrope
Nick . . . . Bernard Hill
Bamber . . . . Warren Mitchell
Dudley . . . . David Troughton
Alison . . . . Phyllis Logan
Betty . . . . Anna Massey

"The Chain" is intended as a comic look at the ways in which the emotional upheaval involved in relocating affects people at different levels of British society. Pic, largely cast with actors known to U.K. tv audiences, will have little potential outside Britain.

The chain is started when a black male moves into a recently vacated North London flat after quitting his mother's home. At the end of the film, his former room is taken by a rich old man who comes to lodge in the house so he can end his days in the place where he was born.

Scripter Jack Rosenthal uses a team of moving men, involved in four of the seven moves, to knit together the story. Bamber, their leader, is an amateur philosopher who spouts platitudes about the problems of moving.

The second and third elements in the chain are amusing portraits of two young couples feeling the strain of married life. One pair quarrels about starting a family, the other has to cope with an obstreperous grandfather.

Script identifies each group of people with one of the seven deadly sins. Moving up the social scale, this device results in heavy-handed caricature. Nigel Hawthorne plays a wealthy man whose extreme meanness has disastrous consequences. Judy Parfitt dedicates herself to acquiring more expensive possessions than her neighbors.

Although miscast as a Greek widow, Billie Whitelaw delivers a fine speech describing the moving mania which killed her late husband.

Lensing of the London landscapes is fine and musical score is good. —*Japa.*

Magic Is Alive, My Friends
(SOUTH AFRICAN-COLOR)

Cannes, May 10.

A Film du Scorpion (Paris) release of a Scholtz Films production (Johannesburg). Original story, screenplay, produced and directed by Jan Scholtz. Camera (Eastmancolor) Johan Scheepers; editor, Johan Lategan; music, Terry Dempsey. Reviewed at Cinema Le Star-1 Cannes (Market), May 10, '85. Running time: **105 MINS.**

Thomas Place	Richard Loring
Liz	Ann Powers
Detective Argyrou	Bill Flynn
Jeffrey Fantastic	Bill Curry

Also with: Hall Orlandini, Dennis McLean, Cyril Green.

Jan Scholtz, a journeyman producer-director of feature films and tv shows, in "Magic Is Alive, My Friends" has blond and chubbily handsome Richard Loring play Thomas Place, a con man who, along with his Afro-Indian sidekick Jeffrey Fantastic (Bill Curry), prefers the route of dishonesty whether it is to obtain a free pack of cigarettes or a pouch of stolen diamonds or even the deed to an entire diamond mine.

Along the way, the pair easily and with the use of sight gags galore, outsmarts a clumsy detective, various authorities and The Cat, a bigtime international criminal who has caused a cabinet crisis by stealing top-secret scientific documents. Usually, the two men get away with everything and rather too easily at that, until they come across a stunner of a blond (Ann Powers) geologist in possession of information everybody will pay anything to get.

The semi-farcical fun goes on and on through a multitude of subplots, losing steam here and there, while a good-natured mood is sustained, if

not by cinematic magic then by deft directorial sleight-of-hand. Foreign sales into modest theatrical programming situations are very likely, but film's future would seem to lie mostly with homevideo. — *Kell.*

The Look
(U.S.-COLOR)

Cannes, May 11.

A T.E.M. Programs Intl. release of a Thoremca Productions production. Produced and directed by Robert Guralnick. Features entire cast. Screenplay, Elizabeth Houghton, Laurie Frank, Seth Cagin; camera (color), Ed Lachman; editor, Caroline Ferriol; sound, Dessie Markovsky; original music, Sylvester Levay. Reviewed at Les Arcades, Cannes (Market), May 11, 1985. Running time: **83 MINS.**

With: Julie Wolfe, Carol Alt, Kelly Emberg, Paulina, Carrie Nygren, Patty Owen, Robert Felner, Antonio, Francesco Scavullo, François Lamy, Steven Meisel, Marc Hispard, Patrick Demarchelier, Andy Warhol.

It's difficult to imagine a theatrical playoff for this promotional self-styled drama docu (evidently made for homevideo market) about some of the models and clients of New York model agency chief John Casablancas.

Models portray themselves, talk about pleasures of their work, getting into the business, jetting to Europe and back, pose for name photogs and strut their stuff. Only in one sequence is there a complaint and that's about posing in underwear outdoors in chilly weather. And, oh, hops from Paris to Rome can be so tiring.

Scenes in New York, Paris and Rome are not filmed above travelog-shorts competence. However, the models are quite stunning as are the clothes. Pic's framework is of small town New England girl making it, actually by having her hair cut. Storyline is virtually nonexistent. For the record, Andy Warhol is filmed watching a breakdancing session with models.

Pic is reviewed, also for the record, and doesn't shape up as useful even for educational purposes on homevid. For that purpose more direct info on the modeling world is needed. —*Adil.*

Le Temps Détruit:
Lettres d'une Guerre 1939-40
(Time Destroyed:
Letters From A War, 1939-40)
(FRENCH-DOCU-COLOR/B&W)

Paris, May 9.

An Institut National de l'Audiovisuel production, with the participation of the Ministry of Culture. Conceived and directed by Pierre Beuchot. Camera (color), Jacques Bouquin, Bernadette Marie; editors, Françoise Collin, Anna Csemke; sound, Jean-Pierre Laforce; music, Maurice Jaubert. Reviewed at INA, Paris (In Cannes Film Festival French Perspectives and Intl. Critics Week), May 5, 1985. Running time: **70**

MINS.
With the voices of: Jean-Marc Bory, Frédéric Leidgens, Philippe Nahoun, Anne Terrier.

"Le Temps Detruit" is a pained evocation of France at war in 1939-40 and a moving tribute to three men who died at the front shortly before the nation fell to the German juggernaut in June 1940. Produced by France's enterprising Institut National de l'Audiovisuel, it was presented at Cannes May 8 as part of a special commemoration of VE Day, 40 years ago.

Director Pierre Beuchot dipped into rare West German and French archive and newsreel footage and the daily letters of three soldiers to their wives: novelist and intellectual Paul Nizan, film composer Maurice Jaubert, and Roger Beuchot, the director's father. In a counterpoint montage of voice-over excerpts from the correspondence and the images of yesterday and today, the helmer composes a cinematic dirge about private suffering and waste in an impersonal large-scale landscape of hate and destruction.

The emotion is heightened by the exquisite music of Jaubert, notably themes from Jean Vigo's "Zero For Conduct" and "L'Atalante" and Marcel Carné's "Quai des Brumes," as well as his last composition, written at the front shortly before his death: "Three Psalms For Time Of War." Tears will flow. —*Len.*

Rappin'
(COLOR)

Synthetic trender has its charm.

Hollywood, May 8.

A Cannon production & release. Produced by Menahem Golan, Yoram Globus. Directed by Joel Silberg. Features entire cast. Screenplay, Robert Litz, Adam Friedman; camera (TVC color), David Gurfinkel; editor, Marcus Manton, Andy Horvitch, Bert Glatstein; music supervisor, Larry Smith; music, Michael Linn; production designer, Steve Miller; set decorator, Bruce Miller; choreography, Edmond Kresley; sound, Rolf Pardula; associate producer, Jeffrey Silver; assistant director, Steven Felder; casting, Patricia Ruben. Reviewed at Warner Hollywood Studio, Hollywood, Calif., May 7, 1985. (MPAA Rating: PG.) Running time: **92 MINS.**

John Hood	Mario Van Peebles
Dixie	Tasia Valenza
Duane	Charles Flohe
Allan	Leo O'Brien
Ice	Eriq La Salle
Fats	Melvin Plowden
Cedric	Rony Clanton
Grandma	Edye Byrde

Billed as the craze sweeping the country, "Rappin' " is behind the times. Breakdancing, rappin' and ghetto blasters have long since become common sights at suburban shopping malls and should come as news only to grandmothers, who are obviously not the intended au-

dience. Despite a cliché-ridden script, pic's innocence and simplicity may prove appealing to a younger (and smaller) audience than turned out for Cannon's first two excursions into hip-hop culture, "Breakin' " and "Breakin' 2."

In spite of several good performances and mindlessly pleasant music, "Rappin' " is the kind of Hollywood production that makes street life look like Disneyland. The poor are pure, and the rich are scum with the thugs caught in the middle.

Filmed (just three months ago on a whirlwind schedule) in a Pittsburgh that doesn't live up to its recent designation as the country's most livable city, production designs seems a random sampling of urban decay. The neighborhood people, too, are a diverse collection of every conceivable ethnic group living together in racial harmony in a fantasyland ghetto.

Fantasies, in fact, do come true in "Rappin' " land. Where else could John (Rappin) Hood (Mario Van Peebles) come out of prison, a better man for his experience, rid the neighborhood of evil land developers, land a recording contract and win the girl all in 90 minutes. In the film's finale (shades of "Breakin' 2") the whole community breaks into those funny little singsong poems known as rap music.

On the plus side, "Rappin' " is too sweet and good natured to take seriously, and a packed house in the right mood actually could have some fun with the action. Charles Flohe as Duane, the head of the rival gang of toughs, acts exactly as he should, full of bluff and bluster, but his James Dean good looks seem a bit out of place here.

The girl in question (Tasia Valenza), who has taken up with Duane while John Hood served his time, is also too cute for the gang life. She does hold down a day job with a record company, hence Hood's big break in showbiz.

It's all predictable hokum, but moments when Van Peebles and his brother (Leo O'Brien) and their grandmother (Edye Byrde) do a three-way rap or a group of youngsters rap their way down the street are truly charming.

Editing, however, never really catches the street rhythms and director Joel Silberg has smoothed out too many of the film's rough edges. — *Jagr.*

La Regina del Mate
(The Queen Of Mate)
(SPANISH-COLOR)

Madrid, April 21.

An El Catalejo, Figario Films, Opalo Films production. Directed by Fermín Cabal. Screenplay, Cabal, Paloma Pedrero; executive producers, Carlos Orengo, Ana Huete;

associate producers, Antonio Maria Claret Baquer, José Antonio Pérez Giner; camera (Eastmancolor), José Luis Alcaine; editor, Miguel Angel Santamaria; sets, Félix Murcia; sound, James Willis; music, José Nieto. Reviewed at Cine Gran Via, Madrid, April 19, 1985. Running time: **86 MINS.**

Cristina	Amparo Muñoz
Rafa	Antonio Resines
Carmen	Ana Gracia
Hernan	Héctor Buffa Colome
Emilio	Jorge de Juan
Negro Suarez	Mario Siles
Aurora	Cristina Rota

Neophyte helmer Fermin Cabal has spun a yarn which, if not altogether convincing, is nonetheless sufficiently absorbing to prevent audience interest from flagging.

Antonio Resines, usually cast as a deadpan, muddled funnyman, plays a naive postman used by Amparo Muñoz to help smuggle narcotics into Spain through the post office. Muñoz put on a heavy Argentine accent and intermittently sips *mate,* an herb tea traditionally imbibed by Argentines day and night. The poor postman is hooked on the "queen of mate" and gets drawn into an unsavory circle of Latinos, who use him, threaten him and share some of the profits with him. Pic wraps in a double murder, the only fitting climax for the postman's ill-starred romance.

Cabal throws in some rather silly scenes (lovemaking on a slashed-open mattress stuffed with bills) and there are many plot flaws, as when the impecunious postman can suddenly afford a shiny new motorcycle without arousing suspicion. Also suspect is the stereotyped treatment of knife-toting Latin Americans whose accents are put on a bit too thickly and who are even made to dance a tango. Barring some blemishes, pic moves along deftly enough, though probably only enough for domestic release here.

—*Besa.*

Liberté, Egalité, Choucroute
(Liberty, Equality, Sauerkraut)
(FRENCH-ITALIAN-COLOR)

Paris, May 7.

A UGC release of a Producteurs Associés/Société Investimente Milanese/FR3/Films 21/Ecta Produktion coproduction. Executive producer, André Djaoui. Produced by Manolo Bolognini. Associate producer, Sylvio Tabet. Written and directed by Jean Yanne. Camera (Eastmancolor), Armando Nannuzzi; art directors, Carlo Simi and Jean-Louis Povéda; costumes, Mini Coutelier; editor, Anne-Marie Cottret; sound, Bernard Ortion; music, Yanne; make-up, Phoung Maittret; production managers, Michel Nicolini and Bruno Frasca. Reviewed at the UGC Biarritz theater, Paris, May 6, 1985. Running time: **113 MINS.**

Marat	Jean Yanne
Louis XVI	Michel Serrault
Marie Antoinette	Ursula Andress
Charlotte Corday	Mimi Coutelier
Caliph of Baghdad	Jean Poiret
Grand Vizir	Daniel Prevost
Sheherezade	Catherine Alric
Rouget de Lisle	Darry Cowl
Robespierre	Roland Giraud
Necker	Jacques Francois
Danton	Olivier de Kersauzon
Mirabeau	Gérard Darmon

Jean Yanne is still trying to be France's answer to Mel Brooks. His new film is just as elephantinely unfunny as his last all-star historical spoof, "A Quarter To Two Before Jesus Christ," and cost just as much (reportedly over $4,000,000).

The target this time is the French Revolution. The Bastille is not a prison, but a disco nightclub for aristocrats, where one can nonetheless find Maximilian Robespierre and Danton spinelessly mulling political change, and two-bit composer Rouget de Lisle bemoaning his inability to come up with a hit single.

The chief troublemaker is Marat (played by Yanne), who foments a popular uprising via his incendiary newspaper, and overworks his editorial secretary, Charlotte Corday (Mimi Coutelier), who finally rebels by sticking a knife into him as he prepares for his bath.

Marat survives and pulls off a coup d'état in which he sets himself up as a benign dictator, with the backing of the Caliph of Baghdad (Jean Poiret), who, accompanied by his Grand Vizir and Sheherezade, has come to Paris to check out the guillotine at a Trade Show of Torture and Execution Equipment, and become mired in the turbulence. Meantime, King Louis XVI (Michel Serrault) and Marie Antoinette (Ursula Andress) escape to Baghdad with Robespierre and Corday and create a new regime there.

Thus no heads fall, if not those of filmgoers dropping off to sleep.

Again, the mode of Yanne's high-school skit goofing is anachronistic humor, with numerous political references to the current socialist government. The actors not only don't try to mimic actual state leaders, but bear no physical or temperamental resemblance to their historical models. Roland Giraud's Robespierre for instance is only an innocuous dullard mooning over heartthrob Charlotte Corday, his "Call me Roby" a dull echo of Richard Basehart's growling "Don't call me Max!" in Anthony Mann's 1949 "The Black Book."

Despite the expense, the Franco-Italian coproduction is mostly an eyesore, with elegant real palace interiors showing up the hideousness of the Cinecittà back-lot constructions imagined by Carlo Simi and Jean-Louis Povéda, though Armando Nannuzzi lenses better than Mario Vulpiani in Yanne's previous extravaganza.

Yanne's spiritless direction completes the fiasco. A somewhat different, even longer, version is reportedly aimed for the American market. What this film needs — though it will not improve much —

is heavy cutting, preferably with a guillotine.—*Len.*

Het bittere kruid
(Bitter Sweet)
(DUTCH-COLOR)

Amsterdam, April 26.

A Verenigde Nederlandsche Filmcompagnie presentation of a Rob Houwer production. Release (Netherlands): Concorde Film. Produced by Hans Klap. Executive producer, Houwer. Directed by Kees van Oostrum. Stars Ester Spitz, Gerard Thoolen, Kitty Courbois, Frank Rigter, Mirjam de Rooij, Marion van Wijk. Screenplay, Maurice Noel, based on short novel by Marga Minco; camera (color), Theo van de Sande; editor, Hans Dunnewijk; sound, Lucas Boeke, Wim Hardeman. Reviewed at Cannon Tuschinski Theater, Amsterdam, April 23, 1985. Running time: **92 MINS.**

Sara	Ester Spitz
Father	Gerard Thoolen
Mother	Kitty Courbois
Creet	Mirjam de Rooij
David	Frank Rigter
Lottie	Marion van Wijk

"Bitter Sweet" purports to depict life (especially the life of Jews) in Nazi-occupied Holland, but it doesn't. Dutch helmer Kees van Oostrum, making his feature debut, worked several years in American television, winning an Emmy as director of photography. Born in 1953, he obviously has no affinity with the war years. Script was written, in English, by American Maurice Noel, doubly distant from the subject matter.

Marga Minco on the other hand, the author of the autobiographical novel on which pic is based, was in the middle of it. Her 1957 bestseller "Bitter Herbs" is the story of a 15-year-old Jewish girl who escapes deportation in 1942, while her parents, sister, brother and his fiancée are taken by the Germans. Helped by Resistance friends, she is hidden in different locations until 1945, and survives. The book is moving and effective, and shuns any sensationalism.

The filmmakers changed the English title from "Bitter Herbs" to "Bitter Sweet," which is ludicrous. Their main invention, among many changes, is the addition of a whole family, father, teenage daughter and son. Pop is high up in the Dutch Nazi youth movement. Son is also permanently in uniform. Daughter, very high-strung, slowly dying of T.B., tries to make the most of remaining life.

The two girls had a sickroom friendship while both were in the hospital. They meet again by accident and the Jewish girl, yellow star and all, repeatedly visits the Nazi family, where the kid brother eyes her covetously. This is just as likely as a black girl in 1942 Missouri paying social calls at the home of the local Ku Klux Klan Wizard.

Minco succeeded by lawsuit in getting a text inserted before the ti-

tle, where Minco rejects the relationship between the girl and the Nazi family as "contrary to the spirit of my book and my personal experiences." The picture suffers from a shallow script. The motivation of characters is often unclear. Spitz and de Rooij in their film debuts, although obviously some years too old, battle valiantly and deserve better chances. Only Frank Rigter manages to give life and verisimilitude to his character.

Theo van de Sande's camera work is reliable as always. Other technical credits are adequate. Chances offshore, except some tv airings, seem iffy. —*Wall.*

Brewster's Millions
(COLOR)

Latest remake not funny enough.

Hollywood, May 17.

A Universal Pictures release. Produced by Lawrence Gordon, Joel Silver. Directed by Walter Hill. Executive producer, Gene Levy. Stars Richard Pryor. Screenplay, Herschel Weingrod and Timothy Harris, based on novel by George Barr McCutcheon; camera (Technicolor), Ric Waite; editors, Freeman Davies, Michel Ripps; sound, Jim Webb; production design, John Vallone; assistant director, Beau Marks; associate producer, Mae Woods; art direction, William Hiney, Jr.; music, Ry Cooder; casting, Judith Holstra, Marcia Ross. Reviewed at the Cinerama Dome Theater, Hollywood, May 17, 1985. (MPAA Rating: PG.) Running time: **97 MINS.**

Brewster	Richard Pryor
Spike	John Candy
Angela	Lonette McKee
Warren	Stephen Collins
Charley	Jerry Orbach
Roundfield	Pat Hingle
Marilyn	Tovah Feldshuh
J. B.	Joe Grifasi
Fleming	Peter Jason
Granville	David White
Baxter	Jerome Dempsey
Melvin	Ji-Tu Cumbuka
Vladimir	Yakov Smirnoff
Rupert Horn	Hume Cronyn

"Brewster's Millions" is all about the problems of trying to spend

Original 1914 Version

A Jesse Lasky Co. release (five reels), at Strand theater, N.Y., April 28, 1914.

Monte Brewster/Monte's dad	Edward Abeles
Peggy Gray	Winifred Kingston
Miner/sheik	Richard La Reno

$1,000,000 a day, which pale beside Universal's problem of trying to take in $1,000,000 a day at the boxoffice once an initial flurry is over.

It's hard to believe a comedy starring Richard Pryor and John Candy

1921 Version

A Famous Players-Lasky release (six reels) of a Jesse L. Lasky presentation. Directed by Joseph Henabery. Stars Roscoe Arbuckle (presented by arrangement with Joseph M. Schenck). Screenplay, Frank E. Woods. Reviewed in N.Y., Jan. 28, 1921.

Monte Brewster	Roscoe Arbuckle
Peggy	Betty Ross Clark
Mr. Brewster	Marlon Skinner
Mr. Ingraham	James Corrigan
Barbara Drew	Jean Acker
Col. Drew	Charles Ogle
MacLeod	Neely Edwards
Harrison	William Boyd
Ellis	L. J. McCarthy
Pettingill	Parker McConnell
Blake	John McFarland

is no funnier than this one is, but director Walter Hill has overwhelmed the intricate genius of each with constant background action, crowd confusions and other endless distractions.

All the frenetic motion, unfortunately, never disguises the fact that writers Herschel Weingrod and Timothy Harris haven't done much of distinction with the familiar story that has been produced in

1935 Version
(MUSICAL)
(BRITISH-MADE)

British and Dominion production and United Artists release. Stars Jack Buchanan; features Lili Damita, Nancy O'Neil. Directed by Thornton Freeland. Producer, Herbert Wilcox. From play of same name by Winchell Smith and Byron Ongley; story, Clifford Grey, W. Wilhelm; adaptation and lyrics, Douglas Furber; dialog, Arthur Wimperis, Michael Joseph, D. Pedelty; music, Ray Noble; camera, Bernard MacGill. At Rivoli, N.Y., week April 6, '35. Running time, **80 MINS.**

Jack Brewster	Jack Buchanan
Rosalie	Lili Damita
Cynthia	Nancy O'Neil
Miss Plimsole	Sydney Fairbrother
McLeod	Ian McLean
Freddy	Fred Emney
Rawles, the butler	Allan Aynesworth
Grant, a solicitor	Lawrence Hanray
Mario	Dennis Hoey
Pedro	Henry Wenman
Mrs. Barry	Amy Veness
Frank	Sebastian Shaw
Ferago, the mayor	Antony Holles

many forms, dating back to the 1906 stage version.

In one incarnation or another, the yarn always involves somebody who stands to inherit a huge fortune, but first must squander a small one over a short time. In order to enjoy the fantasy, the audience must be given good reason to root for the hero.

Though Pryor plays it likeably enough, he never seems particularly

1945 Version

United Artists release of Edward Small production. Stars Dennis O'Keefe, Helen Walker, June Havoc, Eddie "Rochester" Anderson; features Gail Patrick, Mischa Auer. Directed by Allan Dwan. Screenplay, Siegfried Herzig, Charles Rogers, Wilkie Mahoney; from novel by George Barr McCutcheon and stage play by Winchell Smith and Byron Ongley; camera, Charles Lawton; editor, Richard Heermance. Previewed at Mayfair, N.Y., March 8, '45. Running time, **79 MINS.**

Monty Brewster	Dennis O'Keefe
Peggy Gray	Helen Walker
Jackson	Eddie "Rochester" Anderson
Trixie Summers	June Havoc
Barbara Drew	Gail Patrick
Michael Michaelovich	Mischa Auer
Hacky Smith	Joe Sawyer
Mrs. Gray	Nana Bryant
Swearengen Jones	John Litel
Nopper-Harrison	Herbert Rudley
Colonel Drew	Thurston Hall
Mr. Grant	Neil Hamilton
Attorney	Byron Foulger
Cab Driver	Barbara Pepper
Notary	Joseph Crehan

deserving of the fun, excitement and brief luxury he falls into in having to spend $30,000,000 in 30 days, much less the $300,000,000 inheritance he stands to receive if he succeeds.

A down-and-out minor league pitcher (with pal Candy behind the

1961 Version:
Three On A Spree
(BRITISH)

United Artists release of a Caralan Prods. production. Executive producer, David E. Rose. Produced by George Fowler. Directed by Sidney J. Furie. Stars Jack Watling. Screenplay, Siegfried Herzig, Charles Rogers, Wilkie Mahoney; adapted by James Kelly, Peter Miller form 1902 novel by George Barr McCutcheon and 1906 play by Winchell Smith, Byron Ongley; camera, Stephen Dade; editor, A.H. Rule; music direction, Philip

Martell. Opened in L.A., June 28, 1961. Running time, **83 MINS.**

Michael Brewster	Jack Watling
Susan	Carole Lesley
Mrs. Gray	Renee Houston
Sid Johnson	John Slater
Mitchell	Colin Gordon
Mr. Monkton	John Salew
Walker	Julian Orchard

plate), Pryor's visions are somewhat limited with or without money. After he learns of the eccentric terms in the will of a distant relative, Pryor's main concerns, in order, are throwing the money away as fast and foolishly as possible, bedding Lonette McKee, hiring the N.Y. Yankees so he can at last play in a major-league game, keeping McKee from thinking he's a self-centered fool so he can bed her, embarrassing New York City politicians, breaking up McKee's engagement so he can bed her, bedding a couple of other floozies on the side, getting all the money and going off into the sunset with McKee so he can bed her and spend the money wisely.

Granted, all of that could still have been funny, but the dialog never snaps and what good lines there are usually are provided by Candy, but not enough. Though McKee tries to function as a conscience, it's a tough role to handle in all the confusion and everyone else, save Pat Hingle in a small role, is strictly one-dimensional.

There are also glaring problems in keeping the highly fanciful storyline from falling through its holes completely, but at least Hill never lingers long enough on one scene for the imperfections to show through completely.

Same cannot be said for the print shown to a sneak-preview audience at the Cinerama Dome, roughly constructed and a mess of washedout colors. Producers and directors often complain that no note should be taken of that at previews since the "professional" release prints will be ready for the general opening. Funny, though, how they never tell that to those paying $5.50 to get into the sneak. —*Har.*

Rambo: First Blood Part II
(COLOR)

Comic book followup.

Hollywood, May 15.

A Tri-Star Pictures release. Produced by Buzz Feitshans. Directed by George Pan Cosmatos. Stars Sylvester Stallone. Exec producers, Mario Kassar, Andrew Vajna. Screenplay, Stallone, James Cameron; story, Kevin Jarre; camera (Technicolor, Panavision), Jack Cardiff; editors, Mark Goldblatt, Mark Helfrich; music, Jerry Goldsmith; sound, Rob Young; production design, Bill Kenney; costumes, Tom Bronson; associate producer, Mel Dellar; assistant director, Fred Rollin; casting, Rhonda Young; helicopter unit director and photography, Peter MacDonald; stunt coordinator, Richard (Diamond) Farnsworth. Reviewed at the Ciner-

ama Dome, Hollywood, Calif., May 15, 1985. (MPAA Rating: R.) Running time: 95 MINS.

Rambo	Sylvester Stallone
Trautman	Richard Crenna
Murdock	Charles Napier
Co Bao	Julia Nickson
Podovsky	Steven Berkoff
Ericson	Martin Kove
Tay	George Kee Cheung
POW Banks	Andy Wood

Propelled by a jumbo blastoff — a record-setting 2,074 opening-day screens — this overwrought sequel to the popular "First Blood" will certainly enjoy a hot week or two. However, production's risible, comic book heroics seriously qualify its boxoffice durability.

Picture is one mounting fireball as Sylvester Stallone's special operations veteran is sprung from a prison labor camp by his former Green Beret commander (Richard Crenna) to find POWs in Vietnam. That the secret mission is a cynical ruse by higher-ups which is meant to fail dramatically heightens Stallone's fury while touching off a provocative political theme: a U.S. government that wants to forget about POWs and accommodate the public at the same time.

Historical timing gives the film's personal sentiment some edge: "I want our country to love us as much as we love it," Stallone's Viet vet declares at picture's end. The picture's conservative stance also curries some favor with diehards: "Do we get to win this time?" Stallone dryly asks his commander in the opening moments. The answer is no; this military adventure is another trick, too.

The charade on the screen, which is not pulled off, is to accept that the underdog Rambo character, albeit with the machine-gun wielding help of an attractive Vietnamese girl, can waste hoardes of Vietcong and Red Army contingents enroute to hauling POWs to a Thai air base in a smoking Russian chopper with only a facial scar (from a branding iron-knifepoint) marring his tough figure. You never even see him eating in this fantasy, as if his body feeds on itself.

The inevitable comparison with "First Blood" (which recorded domestic rentals of $24,000,000) favors the 1982 film because that film's conflict was much more personal. "Part II" is Captain Courageous taking on amorphous forces that no longer even seem like an enemy.

The one real villain is a U.S. government bureaucrat played very well by Charles Napier, the only one who acts. Stallone hardly veers from a Chuck Norris-"Missing In Action"-like determination and seems to have more lines in Vietnamese than English.

Actress Nickson makes a credible film debut, but her makeup, enduring tropical havoc, goes unsmudged. Steven Berkoff is a twisted and nominally chilly Russian advisor, but his performance is essentially the same nasty thing he did in "Octopussy" and "Beverly Hills Cop."

Production, under the direction of George Pan Cosmatos ("Cassandra Crossing," "Massacre In Rome"), is enlivened by the sharp sound mixing of Rob Young (who also mixed "First Blood"). The pic's technical achievement is impressive, particularly in a sampan-river boat encounter and in fiery chopper sequences.

Also reprising services from "First Blood" are Crenna, music composer Jerry Goldsmith, exec producers Mario Kassar and Andrew Vajna, and producer Buzz Feitshans. Stallone cowrote the script with James Cameron, the cowriter and director of "The Terminator." — *Loyn.*

Fletch
(COLOR)

Tour de force for Chevy Chase.

Hollywood, May 15.

A Universal Pictures release of a Douglas/Greisman production. Produced by Alan Greisman and Peter Douglas. Directed by Michael Ritchie. Stars Chevy Chase. Screenplay, Andrew Bergman, based on the novel by Gregory McDonald; camera (Technicolor), Fred Schuler; editor, Richard A. Harris; music, Harold Faltermeyer; production designer, Boris Leven; sound, Jim Alexander; art director, Todd Hallowell; costumes, Gloria Gresham; associate producer, Gordon A. Webb; casting, Patricia Mock; assistant director, Wolfgang Glattes. Reviewed at Universal Studios, May 14, 1985. (MPAA Rating: PG.) Running time: **96 MINS.**

Fletch . . . . .Chevy Chase
Gail Stanwyk . . . . Dana Wheeler-Nicholson
Alan Stanwyk . . . . , ...Tim Matheson
Chief Karlin . . . . .Joe Don Baker
Walker . . . . .Richard Libertini
Larry . . . . .Geena Davis
Dr. Dolan . . . . . , ...M. Emmet Walsh
Fat Sam . . . . .George Wendt
Stanton Boyd . . . . .Kenneth Mars
Gummy . . . . .Larry Flash Jenkins
Creasy . . . . .Ralph Seymour

Arguably Chevy Chase's best work in a feature film, this mystery-comedy, opening nationally at month's end, anticipates some cheery grosses for Universal.

What propels this contempo L.A. yarn about a dissembling newspaper columnist on the trail of a nefarious con man (Tim Matheson) is the obvious and successful byplay between Chase's sly, glib persona and the satiric brushstrokes of director Michael Ritchie. Their teamwork turns an otherwise hair-pinned, anecdotal plot into a breezy, peppy frolic and a long overdue tour de force for Chase.

Working from a popular award-winning novel by Gregory McDonald, screenwriter Andrew Bergman and producers Alan Greisman and Peter Douglas have smartly tilted a story of ordinary corruption to favor Chase at every turn. His patter and one-liners under various identities are consistently funny.

The picture is a fetching launching pad (although she had small roles in "Mrs. Soffel" and "The Little Drummer Girl") for an inviting Hollywood newcomer, Dana Wheeler-Nicholson, as the restless wife of a two-timing Matheson.

In a rather uneventful role, Matheson sets the plot in motion when, under the impression that Chase is a drifter on the Santa Monica beach, he hires our feckless hero to murder him.

Most supporting players have little to do, such as M. Emmet Walsh as an inane M.D. The film is sparked by some hilarious moments, among them Chase as an unwitting surgeon in attendance at an autopsy conducted by a cackling pathologist and, in the script's funniest scene, Chase donning the guise of a legionnaire in a hall full of VFW stalwarts.

Pic is aided by the brisk editing of Richard A. Harris (who cut several previous Ritchie films), a good musical background, and deft glimpses of both the fashion and squalor of L.A. Tone of script is wisecrackingly liberal, and the folks in Utah (which serves as a plot point and takes it lightly on the chin) probably won't be enthralled.
—*Loyn.*

A View To A Kill
(BRITISH-COLOR)

Lackluster 007 epic should earn okay b.o.

Hollywood, May 21.

An MGM/UA Entertainment release of an Eon Productions Ltd. production. Produced by Albert R. Broccoli, Michael G. Wilson. Directed by John Glen. Stars Roger Moore. Screenplay, Richard Maibaum, Wilson from story by Ian Fleming; camera (Panavision, Technicolor; prints by Metrocolor), Alan Hume; editor, Peter Davies; music, John Barry; James Bond theme, Monty Norman; song, Barry, Duran Duran; sound, Derek Ball; production design, Peter Lamont; art direction, John Fenner; set decoration, Crispian Sallis; second unit direction & camera, Arthur Wooster; ski sequence direction & camera, Willy Bogner; special effects supervisor, John Richardson; production supervisor, Anthony Waye; assistant director, Gerry Gavigan; action sequence arranger, Martin Grace; driving stunts arranger, Remy Julienne; costume design, Emma Porteous; associate producer, Thomas Pevsner; casting, Debbie McWilliams. Reviewed at Samuel Goldwyn theater, Hollywood, Calif., May 17, 1985. (MPAA Rating: PG.) Running time: **131 MINS.**

James Bond . . . . .Roger Moore
Max Zorin . . . . .Christopher Walken
Stacey Sutton . . . . .Tanya Roberts
May Day . . . . .Grace Jones
Tibbett . . . . .Patrick Macnee
Scarpine . . . . .Patrick Bauchau
Chuck Lee . . . . .David Yip
Pola Ivanova . . . . .Fiona Fullerton
Bob Conley . . . . .Manning Redwood
Jenny Flex . . . . .Alison Doody
Dr. Carl Mortner . . . . . . .Willoughby Gray
Q . . . . .Desmond Llewelyn
M . . . . .Robert Brown
Miss Moneypenny . . . . .Lois Maxwell
Gen. Gogol . . . . .Walter Gotell
Minister of Defense . . . . . . .Geoffrey Keen

There is hardly a red-blooded American boy whose pulse isn't quicker by the familiar strains of the James Bond theme and the first sight of the hero cocking a gun at any enemy coming his way. Unfortunately, "A View To A Kill," the 16th outing for the Ian Fleming characters, doesn't keep the adrenalin pumping, exposing the inherent weaknesses of the genre. Trading on the Bond name, outlook is good for initial business, but momentum is likely to falter, just as the production does.

The potential for cinematic thrills and chills, what with glamorous locations, beautiful women and exotic locations, is still there, but in "A View To A Kill" it's the execution that's lacking.

A traditionally big Bond opening, this time a daring chase through the Alps, gets the film off to a promising start but proves one of the film's few highlights as it slowly slips into tedium.

Basic problem is on the script level with the intricate plot never offering the mindless menace necessary to propel the plot. First third of the pic is devoted to introduction of characters in a horse-fixing subplot that has no real bearing on the main action.

Bond's adversary this time is the international industrialist Max Zorin (Christopher Walken) and his love-hate interest, May Day (Grace Jones). Bond tangles with them at their regal horse sale and uncovers a profitable scheme in which microchips are surgically implanted in the horse to assure an easy victory.

Horse business is moderately entertaining, particularly when Patrick Macnee is on screen as Bond's chauffeur accomplice. Action, however, jumps abruptly to San Francisco to reveal Zorin's true motives. He's hatching some master plan to pump water from the sea into the San Andreas fault causing a major earthquake, destroying the Silicon Valley and leaving him with the world's microchip monopoly.

Film sags badly in the San Francisco section when it should be soaring, partially due to Bond's joining forces with American geologist Stacey Sutton (Tanya Roberts). Try as you might to believe it, Roberts has little credibility as a woman of science. Her delivery of lines like "I'd sell everything and live in a tent before I'd give," makes the obvious laughable.

While Bond pics have always traded heavily on the camp value of its characters, "A View To A Kill" almost attacks the humor, practically winking at the audience with every move. Director John Glen, who previously directed "For Your Eyes Only," has not found the right balance between action and humor to make the production dangerous fun.

Walken, too, the product of a mad Nazi scientist's genetic experiments, is a bit wimpy by Bond villian standards. With hair colored an unnatural yellow he seems more effete than deadly. As his assistant, Grace Jones is a successful updating of the Jaws-type villain. Jones just oozes '80s style and gets to parade in a number of sensational oufits (designed by Emma Porteous) giving a hard but alluring edge to her character.

As for Roger Moore, making his seventh appearance as Bond, he is right about half the time. He still has the suave and cool for the part, but on occasion he looks a bit old for the part and his coy womanizing seems dated when he does.

Other instances when the film tries to stake its claim to the rock video audience backfire and miscalculate the appeal of the material. Opening credit sequence in MTV style is downright bizarre and title song by Duran Duran will certainly not go down as one of the classic Bond tunes.

With all of its limitations, production still remains a sumptuous feast to look at. Shot in Panavision by Alan Hume, exotic locations such as the Eiffel Tower, San Francisco Bay and Zorin's French chateau are rendered beautifully. Climax hanging over the Golden Gate Bridge is chillingly real thanks to the miniature artists and effects people (supervised by John Richardson). Production design by Peter Lamont is firstrate. —*Jagr.*

The Emerald Forest
(U.S.-COLOR)

Paris, May 10.

An Embassy Pictures release. Produced and directed by John Boorman. Coproducer, Michael Dryhurst. Executive producer, Edgar F. Gross. Features entire cast. Screenplay, Rospo Pallenberg. Camera (Technicolor, Panavision), Philippe Rousselot; editor, Ian Crafford; production design, Simon Holland; art direction, Marcos Flaksman; set decoration, Ian Whittaker; sound (Dolby), Doug Turner; choreography, Jose Possi; assistant director, Barry Langley; co-assistant director, Flavio Tambellini; second unit camera/director, Lucio Kodata; casting, Mary Selway (London), Melissa Skoff (U.S.). Reviewed at the ALMF-Screening Room, Paris, May 7, 1985. Entry at Cannes Film Festival (out of competition). (MPAA Rating: R.) Running time: **113 MINS.**

Bill Markham	Powers Boothe
Jean Markham	Meg Foster
Tomme	Charley Boorman
Kachiri	Dira Pass
Wanadi	Rui Polonah
Jacareh	Claudio Moreno
Caya	Tetchie Agbayani
Mapi	Paulo Vinicius
Werner	Eduardo Conde
Heather Markham	Estee Chandler

Shown as the closing night, out-of-competition attraction at the Cannes Film Festival, "The Emerald Forest" sees John Boorman travelling up a river even wilder than the one he explored in "Deliverance." Ravishingly made and constructed around sociologically popular themes, big-budget release from Embassy packs plenty of adventure and fantasy appeal for young men, in particular, and should prove a good summer b.o. attraction.

Based on an uncredited true story about a Peruvian whose son disappeared in the jungles of Brazil, as well as other similar cases, Rospo Pallenberg's screenplay trades on numerous enduring myths and legends about the return to nature and growing up in the wild.

Tale makes full use of contemporary ecological concerns about the encroachment of the modern world upon the Amazonian rain forests and their inhabitants, and also fits strongly into the Boorman canon, what with its fascination for a magical, mystical world and employment of aspects of the King Arthur story.

Powers Boothe, an American engineer and designer assigned to build an enormous dam in Brazil, loses his young son in the wilderness and, against seemingly hopeless odds, sets out to find him.

Ten years, and about 45 minutes of screen time, later, the two finally meet up under perilous circumstances. By this time, the son, played by the director's own sprig, Charley Boorman, has become well integrated into the ways of a friendly Indian tribe and has little desire to return to the outside world.

Life in the jungle is far from tranquil, however, as the peaceable group is preyed upon by a bloodthirsty tribe of marauding Indians, who in turn trade captured native women to a nearby pleasure camp in exchange for weapons.

To top it off, once he has been exposed to the simple virtues of "uncivilized" life, Boothe begins to have serious doubts about the nature of his work in the area, and dramatic conclusion immediately brings to mind that of "The Bridge On The River Kwai."

Boorman and Pallenberg have a lot of material to work with here and, despite some lumps in the narrative and characterization and some occasionally awkward tension between the documentary realism enforced by the subject and the heavy stylization of the director's approach, film proves engrossing and visually fascinating.

Pic starts out from the father's point of view and gradually shifts to that of the son, who grows into a man and warrior in the course of the telling. By the end, Boothe's character seems rather one-dimensional and almost incidental to the central drama, and his wife, portrayed by Meg Foster, has been forgotten.

Location lensing under doubtlessly difficult circumstances has provided a fabulous setting for the picture, one in which Boorman puts on a terrific display of his virtuosity with the camera. At certain moments, he may have gone too far in elaborating the exotica which is already unusual enough on its own. A few eyebrows might also be raised by the unusually high percentage of sexy, nubile young things among the native women, all of whom naturally appear topless throughout the picture.

Despite these quibbles over emphasis, basic adventure of survival and intertwined study of ethnics and societal mores is boldly told in strong strokes. Buffs will recognize strains of such pic as the Tarzan epics, "The Searchers," "The Wild Child," "The Most Dangerous Game" and "A Man Called Horse," as well as Boorman's earlier efforts, while general viewers, and adolescents in particular, can enjoy the fantasy of imagining themselves in the same unusual situation as Charley Boorman, who has taken on his role with relish and grows with authority as his character matures.

Behind-the-camera contributions are outstanding, especially the lush cinematography by Philippe Rousselot. —*Cart.*

Should I Be Good?
(NEW ZEALAND-COLOR)

Cannes, May 13.
A Grahame McLean and Associates production. Produced, directed and written by McLean. Camera (Eastman color), Warrick Attewell; editor, Jamie Selkirk; sound, Bob Clayton; musical director, Geoff Castle. Reviewed at Olympia 2, Cannes (Market), May 13, 1985. Running time: **90 MINS.**

Nat Goodman	Harry Lyon
Vicki Strassbourg	Joanne Mildenhall
Anne Marie	Spring Rees
Ed	Hammond Gamble
Julie	Beaver

Grahame McLean's "Should I Be Good?," his low-budget feature shot back-to-back with "The Lie Of The Land" (also in the Cannes Market), also is a mixed bag.

The low budget shows in the quality of the print. Great lurches are evident in the plotline, and in character motivation.

When Nat Goodman (Harry Lyon) is released from jail after serving a sentence for drug trafficking, he attempts to free from heroin addiction and prostitution his former Eurasian girl friend, Anne Marie (Spring Rees).

He also returns to a singing spot on the nightclub circuit and meets a crusading television reporter, Vicky Strassbourg (Joanne Mildenhall). The trio works together to expose corruption in high places.

Lyon, a singer in real life, brings a certain shy, rugged charm to Nat Goodman. Among the femmes, Beaver, in a small support role, is the standout. Her account of the fine title song with Ed (Hammond Gamble) is the best scene in the film.

In fact, it is likely to be the song rather than the film that lingers on. —*Nic.*

Le Due Vite Di Mattia Pascal
(The Two Lives Of Mattia Pascal)
(ITALIAN-COLOR)

Cannes, May 15.
A SACIS release of a RAI-TV presentation. Produced by Silvia D'Amico Bendicò and Carlo Cucchi for RAI-TV Channel 1, Cinecittà, Excelsior Cinematografica, with Antenne 2, Telemünchen, TVE, Channel 4, RTSI. Directed by Mario Monicelli. Stars Marcello Mastroianni. Screenplay, Suso Cecchi D'Amico, Ennio De Concini, Amanzio Todini, Monicelli; camera (color), Camillo Bazzoni; art director, Lorenzo Baraldi; costumes, Gianna Gissi; editor, Ruggero Mastroianni; music, Nicola Piovani. Reviewed at the Cannes Film Festival (In competition), May 14, 1985. Running time: **125 MINS.**

Mattia Pascal	Marcello Mastroianni
Terenzio Papiano	Flavio Bucci
Adriana Paleari	Laura Morante
Romilda	Laura Del Sol
Véronique	Caroline Berg
Silvia Caporale	Andrea Ferreol
Paleari	Bernard Blier

This is one of the year's most agreeable and intelligent Italo comedies, shot by veteran Mario Monicelli and based on a Pirandello novel about a man's search for his identity. Tossing out the existential angle, pic plays for ironic, gentle humor, no doubt a minor ambition but at least one that is within its grasp.

Shown in competition at Cannes in its two-hour theatrical release version, "Mattia Pascal" will be seen on the small screen in a much more leisurely format of three 70-minute episodes. Extensive snipping keeps film moving at a brisk pace. Given the cast and six-country production formula, pic looks sure to circulate in the international market and sell even more widely to tv.

Director and scripters have opted to take a new look at Mattia Pascal, a familiar film subject since Marcel L'Herbier's 1925 version starring Mosjoukine and Pierre Chenal's stab in 1936. Here the story has been updated to the present, with a curious framing device of an aged Mattia (Marcello Mastroianni) recounting his story to an old friend in a time that must be the future.

The indolent scion of a wealthy family, Mattia is so disattentive to business he ruins himself. His romantic adventures land him in a loveless marriage with Romilda (Laura Del Sol) and intolerable coexistence with his mother-in-law. He fleetingly contemplates suicide, but decides to jump on a passing train instead.

Mattia ends up in Monte Carlo and wins a fortune. When he returns home, however, he finds an unknown suicide victim being buried in his place. Taking advantage of the ease of mistaken identity, he burns his IDs and starts a new life under the name of Adriano Meis.

Plot takes off on a series of complications, first in Rome, where Mattia attempts to get false documents to legalize his new identity; then in Venice, where he gambles away all his money while on a costly "honeymoon" with a girl he has met; and finally back in his hometown. There he finds his wife has remarried in his absence and had a child. He decides to stay on as "the late Mattia Pascal," a solitary librarian who visits his own grave from time to time.

Most cuts were probably made in the Rome sequence, in which many familiar faces turn up in bit parts. Mattia lives in a spooky boarding house run by Paleari (Bernard Blier) and his daughter Adriana (Laura Morante), who falls for him. Andrea Ferreol and Flavio Bucci are the other inmates.

Top-notch technical talent creates effectively atmospheric locations — the severe, windy Ligurian coast, sunlit Monte Carlo, the gloomy boarding house and Venice as a nightmarish gambling den. Nicola Piovani's score brings the spirit of Pirandello back into pic. Mastroianni, headlining the cast, holds center stage from start to finish as the cad you can't help rooting for. — *Yung.*

Himatsuri
(Fire Festival)
(JAPANESE-COLOR)

Cannes, May 18.
A Shibata Organization release of a Gunro-Seibu Group-Cine Saison Production. Executive producer, Kazuo Shimizu. Directed by Mitsuo Yanagimachi. Features entire cast. Screenplay, Kenji Nakagami; camera (Eastmancolor), Masaki Tamura; art director, Takeo Kimura; sound, Yukio Kubota; mus-

ic, Toru Takemitsu; editor, Sachiko Yamaji. Reviewed at Cannes Film Festival (Un Certain Regard section), May 17, 1985. Running time: **116 MINS.**

Tatsuo .... Kinya Kitaoji
Kimiko .... Kiwako Taichi
Ryota .... Ryota Nakamoto
Yamakawa .... Norihei Miki
Toshio .... Rikiya Yasuoka
Sachiko (Tatsuo's wife) .. Junko Miyashita
Tatsuo's mother .... Kin Sugai
Kimiko's sister .... Aoi Nakajima

Almost a companion piece to his previous film, "A Farewell To The Land," Mitsuo Yanagimachi's "Fire Festival" concerns the erosion of traditional rural life in Japan by encroaching modernity, finally driving a proud man to a desperate act of violence. Pic was inspired by a 1980 newspaper report about a man who killed his entire family and himself.

Setting is a small village by the sea in the south-west of the country. Main industries here are fishing and logging in the wooded mountains which rise steeply from the sea. Tatsuo, whose family has lived for years overlooking this idyllic coastline, works as a logger. Though married and with small children, he has the reputation of being a womanizer, and when a childhood sweetheart, Kimiko, returns to the village from city and sets herself up as a prostitute, he has no hesitation in renewing his association with her.

Meanwhile, the unscrupulous Yamakawa, a land speculator, is pressuring the villagers to sell him their water-frontage land. A new marine park is to be established, and the peaceful area looks like becoming a tourist resort, with hotels to be built on the sites of these old homes. Natsuo refuses to sell.

Yanagimachi reveals a somewhat remote and traditional world of tranquil beauty and order that's threatened by redevelopment. Masaki Tamura's magnificent lensing lingers on images of the sea, the mountains and the graceful forests. Pic is filled with detail about the traditions of the place; the belief in a mountain goddess, the sharp division between those who earn their living from the sea and those who earn it from the land, and the roles of men and women.

A sinister note is struck by the apparent deliberate pollution of the sea, resulting in the death of thousands of fish. Yamakawa throws suspicion on Tatsuo. Matters come to a head at the annual fire festival, when the traditional Tatsuo becomes enraged when some villagers ignore the accepted rituals.

For western audiences, Tatsuo's final tragic act of violence against his family and himself may seem unfathomable. It's certainly not easy, from the information included in the film, to understand his motives. Japanese audiences should have no problems here.

Technically superlative, and with a fine music score by Toru Takemit-su, "Fire Festival" re-confirms Yanagimachi, with his third feature, as one of the brightest of Japan's younger talents.—*Strat.*

Bliss
(AUSTRALIAN-COLOR)

Cannes, May 18.
A Window III-New South Wales Film Corporation production. Produced by Anthony Buckley. Directed by Ray Lawrence. Stars Barry Otto, Lynette Curran, Helen Jones. Screenplay, Lawrence, Peter Carey, from Carey's novel; camera (Eastmancolor), Paul Murphy; editor, Wayne Le Clos; art director, Owen Paterson; costume design, Helen Hooper; music, Peter Best; special effects, Bob McCarron; production manager, Carol Hughes. Reviewed at Cannes Film Festival (In Competition), May 18, 1985. Running time: **135 MINS.**

Harry Joy .... Barry Otto
Bettina Joy .... Lynette Curran
Honey Barbara .... Helen Jones
David Joy .... Miles Buchanan
Lucy Joy .... Gia Carides
Alex Duval .... Tim Robertson
Joel .... Jeff Truman
Rev. Des .... Paul Chubb
Adrian Clunes .... Bryan Marshall
Damian .... Robert Menzies
Ken McLaren .... Nique Needles
Alice Dalton .... Kerry Walker
Aldo .... Jon Ewing
Harry's father .... George Whaley
Dr. Hennessey .... Peter Carmody

A first feature which attempts, with considerable ambition, to translate to the screen a brilliant, wayward novel, "Bliss" is seriously flawed, yet bursting with ideas, originality and invention. It was greeted with considerable controversy in Cannes, with an unusual number of walkouts at all screenings; but, despite being drastically overlong, it nevertheless shapes as a powerful comic statement on many of society's ills.

Pic opens with the death of Harry Joy (Barry Otto), its central character. He runs an ad agency and leads an apparently happy life with wife and two children. A heart attack fells him during a family gathering, and he's dead for four minutes. When he recovers, he believes he has entered Hell.

That's because everything seems to have changed. His loving wife (Lynette Curran) is having an open affair with his sleazy business partner (Jeff Truman); his son (Miles Buchanan) is a drug runner with ambitions to join the mafia; his daughter (Gia Carides) is an addict who gives her brother sexual favors to get free dope; and Harry discovers, too, that his biggest client manufactures products known to cause cancer.

Faced with these unexpected upheavals, Harry goes a little mad. He scurries around noting down everything that's going on, and eventually leaves home to live in a smart suite in a hotel, where he hires a young prostitute, Honey Barbara (Helen Jones) who becomes his constant companion. She's a brown-skinned country girl, who gives him a new meaning in life.

The biggest flaw in "Bliss" is the way the novel has been adapted by its author, Peter Carey, and director Ray Lawrence. The best films of difficult books (and "Bliss" was a difficult book) have pared down the source material while keeping the spirit and intention of the original. Carey and Lawrence have left nothing out; the film teems with characters, some of whom could and should have been dropped altogether or amalgamated.

Lawrence, who has a tv commercial background shared with first-time cameraman Paul Murphy, clearly has talent. Few Australian films have attempted such trenchant satire before, and helmer often takes the breath away with its daring and his ideas. He's good with actors, too, and there are fine performances down the line, with Helen Jones a great new discovery as the earthy little prostitute with whom the beleaguered hero falls in love.

Pic retains, from the book, a narration, delivered by its central character as an old man; voice used is unpleasant and grating — it's a turn-off. On a couple of occasions, characters addressed the camera directly; device doesn't come off. Hospital surgery scenes are graphic.

With trimming, "Bliss" could have a success in up-market houses. Its ecological theme is pertinent, and its sub-text on the marketing of lethally dangerous products without proper testing is devastating. Pic has been invited to Toronto and London film fests.—*Strat.*

Joshua Then And Now
(CANADIAN-COLOR)

Cannes, May 17.
A 20th Century Fox release of a Robert Lantos/Stephen J. Roth-RSL production. Produced by Lantos, Roth. Directed by Ted Kotcheff. Features entire cast. Screenplay, Mordecai Richler, based on his novel; camera (color), François Protât; editor, Ron Wisman; music, Philippe Sarde; production design, Anne Pritchard; art direction, Harold Thrasher; set decoration, Hilton Rosemarin, Rosie-Marie McSherry; costume design, Louise Jobin; sound, Donald Cohen; assistant director, Craig Huston; casting, Ginette D'Amico (Montreal), Dierdre Bowen (Toronto), Lynn Stalmaster (L.A.). Reviewed at the Cannes Film Festival (In Competition), May 16, 1985. (MPAA Rating: R.) Running time: **127 MINS.**

Joshua Shapiro .... James Woods
Pauline Shapiro .... Gabrielle Lazure
Reuben Shapiro .... Alan Arkin
Kevin Hornby .... Michael Sarrazin
Esther Shapiro .... Linda Sorensen
Jack Trimble .... Alan Scarfe
Jane Trimble .... Kate Trotter
Senator Hornby .... Alexander Knox
Seymour Kaplan ...:..... Chuck Shamata
Eli Seligson .... Paul Hecht
Det. Stuart McMaster ... Henry Beckman
Young Joshua .... Eric Kimmel
Dr. Jonathan Cole .... Harvey Atkin
Sydney Murdoch .... Ken Campbell
Colin Fraser .... Robert Joy

"Joshua Then And Now" is a passably entertaining but skin-deep adaptation of Mordecai Richler's semi-autobiographical 1980 novel. Richly performed by a large cast, film gradually loses body and texture after a good start, to the point that it seems thin by the end. Commercial prospects appear moderate.

Director Ted Kotcheff broke into the big time with his screen-version of Richler's "The Apprenticeship Of Duddy Kravitz" more than a decade ago, and once again sets out to tell of a young Jewish Canadian anxious to rise in society.

Initial sections, which nicely depict Montreal life during World War II, contain the best sequences in the film. In flashback from the vantage point of his momentarily ruined adult life, Joshua (James Woods) tells of a childhood dominated by his stripper mother and ex-prize fighter father, who has now turned to illicit activities which land him in the clink.

As papa, Alan Arkin has two priceless scenes in which he tells his son first about sex, then about the lessons of the Bible, all in pragmatic, but quite learned, streetwise fashion.

As a young man in 1950, Joshua heads for London, where he begins establishing a literary reputation and hanging out in radical circles, mainly to court and win the married, WASP daughter of a top politician.

Despite their significant differences, the couple does well for years, until Joshua decides to return to Canada in 1977. At this point, his life crumbles before his eyes — his best friend dies, his wife's beloved brother commits suicide, he is blackmailed by a detective, becomes implicated publicly in a trumped up homosexual scandal and finally has

his wife walk out on him.

Unfortunately, as matters depicted deteriorate, so does the picture. Events go by so quickly they don't register strongly, and the good will built up in the early going is gradually frittered away. Instead of building to a climax, it declines toward one.

This is no fault of the cast, which is uniformly vigorous and engaging. In one of his more conventional roles, James Woods is excellent and entirely believable as he progresses from aggressive youth to troubled middle age. French-Canadian actress Gabrielle Lazure, a pretty blond who looks like a cross between Meryl Streep and Isabelle Adjani, is unusual and fresh as his wife, and the supporting players all make strong impressions.

Philippe Sarde's score adds notable color, and tech credits are good.
—*Cart.*

Kletka Dlia Kanareek
(The Canary Cage)
(SOVIET-COLOR)

Cannes, May 15.

A Mosfilm production, Moscow; world rights, Goskino, Moscow. Directed by Pavel Chukhrai. Features entire cast. Screenplay, Anatoli Sergeyev, Chukhrai, based on a play by Sergeyev; camera (color), Mikhail Bitz; sets, Savet Agaiyan; music, Igor Kantukov. Reviewed at Cannes Film Fest (Critics Week), May 14, 1985. Running time: **85 MINS.**

With: Yevgenia Dobrobloskaya (Alessia), Vyacheslav Baranov (Victor), Alissa Freindlikh, Boris Bachurin.

Pavel Chukhrai, a recent graduate of the Moscow Film School (VGIK), attracted some critical attention with his debut pic, "Men In The Ocean" (1981).

"The Canary Cage," by Anatoli Sergeyev, is about two teenagers on the run from home and friends whose ultimate salvation is in finding each other at the right time in the right place — a railroad station in Moscow. Victor has stolen a canary cage from an apartment on the dare of bad companions, and now decides that enlisting as a sailor in Riga (Latvian Republic on the Baltic Sea) is better than facing the music back home in Moscow. Alessia has had it out with her stepfather, and just wants to run away in mad frustration at the unfairness of it all.

The pair spend the night and part of the next day together at the railroad station, talking over their problems but also trying to bluff their way through as "honest people" in the midst of some rather obvious corruption and passivity going on about them.

It's the girl's hopes that carry the most weight, for she wants badly to see her real father again. As the boy listens to her problems, he tends to forget his own minor ones. Together they come to the conclusion that they can only grow up by facing the music. She telegraphs her mother, he turns himself in to the police.

Despite the talking-heads dramatic context, "The Canary Cage" convinces by the adept use of the trains moving in and out of the station, as well as the variety of corners to hide out from police and railroad officials. The scene keeps changing as the two sort out their troubles in a constant dialog. When the two depart at the end, one has the feeling their encounter only lasted for this one night and day.

Credits are a good cut above the average, particularly thesps Yevgenia Dobrobloskaya and Vyacheslav Baranov as fresh young personalities in the lead roles. — *Holl.*

Latino
(U.S.-COLOR)

Cannes, May 15.

A Lucasfilm/Latino production. Produced by Benjamin Berg. Directed, written by Haskell Wexler. Camera (color), Tom Sigel; editor, Robert Dalva; music, Diane Louie; sound, Pamela Yates; associate producer, James Becket; assistant director, Emilio Rodriguez. Reviewed at the Cannes Film Festival (Un Certain Regard), May 14, 1985. (No MPAA Rating.) Running time: **108 MINS.**

Eddie Guerrero	Robert Beltran
Marlena	Annette Cardona
Ruben	Tony Plana
Attila	Ricardo Lopez
Luis	Luis Torrentes
Malena's son	Juan Carlos Ortiz

Also with: Marta Tenorio, Michael Goodwin, Walter Marin, James Karen.

Although doubtlessly not intended as such, "Latino" comes off distressingly like a left-wing "The Green Berets." A nobly conceived on-the-scene look at the battle between the Sandinistas and the U.S.-backed Contras in Nicaragua, writer-director Haskell Wexler has so woefully simplified a very complex situation that he ill serves the cause for which he feels such sympathy. Commercial chances are dim, more for artistic than political reasons.

Shot quietly in Nicaragua early last year with the knowledge but not the official participation of the government, this is ace cinematographer Wexler's first fictional feature as director since the similarly activist cinema-verité effort, "Medium Cool," 16 years earlier. Over the past few years, he has collaborated on some docus shot in Nicaragua.

Drama centers on Eddie Guerrero, played by Robert Beltran of "Eating Raoul," a Yank Chicano and Vietnam War vet who is assigned to U.S. Special Forces providing assistance to the rebels, or Contras, fighting the leftist Nicaraguan regime.

Beltran and fellow Latino officer Tony Plana join up with a bunch of macho roughnecks, already under the supervision of Americans, who make lightning excursions from Honduras into Nicaraguan territory and blithely kill women and children, capture teenage boys, torture them and force them into service with the Contras.

Beltran enters into a romance with an attractive lady who gradually becomes radicalized through her exposure to the new Nicaraguan society, but Beltran's evolution comes much more slowly and painfully.

Pic spends the bulk of its running time alternating between the lackluster love story and the brutal activities of the Contras, who are misleadingly depicted as consisting of nothing but former Somoza partisans with callous, mercenary-like attitudes toward their jobs.

Weird, unpleasant dynamic of the film derives from the fact that it's largely a war picture in which one is expected to be revolted by all the characters and their actions.

Since virtually the entire drama is played out (negatively) from the Contra side, one never gets to form any opinions about the Sandinistas within the context of the film.

Pic will undoubtedly anger Reaganites for its frontal attack on the Contras, but more opened-minded viewers will be thoroughly frustrated by lack of more balanced information, and those with some knowledge of the situation will be appalled by the hopelessly incomplete and undetailed investigation of the nuances of Latin American politics.

All this is a shame, because Wexler's unique access to Nicaragua itself presented a rare opportunity to clear up some of the confusion stemming from some of the untrustworthy news reporting coming out of the region. Instead, film just adds to it. Director goes no further than exposing the beastliness of war and sentimentalizing the predicament of children. Much more was needed.

Unsurprisingly, indie production, partially backed by Lucasfilm, looks good, but "Under Fire," which was lensed in Mexico, actually conveyed a stronger physical notion of the realities of Nicaraguan combat. Dialog freely mixes English and Spanish in plausible fashion and, among the performers, Tony Plana stands out as a gung-ho U.S. Latin officer. —*Cart.*

La Ciudad y los Perros
(The City And The Dogs)
(PERUVIAN-COLOR)

Cannes, May 12.

An Inca Films production. Directed by Francisco J. Lombardi. Screenplay, José Wantanabe, based on the novel by Mario Vargas Lloso; camera (color), Fili Flores Guerra; editors, Gianfranco Annichini, Augusto Tomayo San Roman; music, Enrique Iturriaga. Reviewed at Cannes Film Festival (Directors Fortnight), May 11, 1985. Running time: **114 MINS.**

The Poet	Pablo Serra
Lieut. Gamboa	Gustavo Bueno
Jaguar	Juan M. Ochoa
Colonel	Luis Alvarez
Slave	Eduardo Adrianzén
Teresa	Liliana Navarro
Arróspide	Miguel Iza
Boa	Aristóteles Picho
Rulos	Antonio Vega
Teresa's Aunt	Isabel Duval
Serrano Cava	David Meléndez

Also with: Alberto Isola, Jorge Rodriguez Paz, Ramón Garcia, Lourdes Mindreau.

When Mario Vargas Lloso's novel was published 22 years ago, copies of the book were burned symbolically at the Peruvian military school in Lima and even now it was by no means easy to film this story of moral corruption among cadets. In fact, according to director Francisco J. Lombardi, several possible locations for the military college became unavailable due to pressures from the army.

Making the film became possible due to the end of military rule in Peru and also thanks to the novelist's very considerable reputation at home and abroad, which should also help "La Ciudad y los Perros" obtain much wider Latin American and foreign sales than normal for a Peruvian film.

Beginning with the hazing of a new class of cadets, the film follows their development over the next three years. A small clique, led by Jaguar, controls the sale of forbidden cigarets and drink. Exam papers are stolen and a cadet is killed. The youngsters are like a cross section of Peruvian society and Lieutenant Gamboa represents the military mentality at its best. The values the army tries to instill in its future officer class are undermined constantly and the system itself is indicted.

This is Francisco Lombardi's fourth film: he tells the story clearly and, although some tightening of the almost two and a half hours running time would not be amiss, sustains interest in his characters and narrative. The film is less complex than the novel and sometimes does not project the issues implied by events in the story in their full breadth, but the acting is on the whole good, with particularly successful performances by José Manuel Ochoa (Jaguar) and Gustavo Bueno (Lieutenant Gamboa). The technical level is quite satisfactory.—*Amig.*

Derborence
(SWISS-FRENCH-COLOR)

Cannes, May 20.

A Sagittaire-Marion's Films-FR3-SSR co-production. Directed by Francis Reusser. Features entire cast. Screenplay, Jacques Beynac, Christiane Grimm, from the novel by C.F. Ramuz; camera (Eastmancolor, Panavision), Emmanuel Machuel; editor, Francis Reusser; sound (Dolby stereo), François Musy, Etienne Metrailler. Reviewed at Cannes Film Festival (In competition), May 19, 1985. Running time: **98 MINS.**

Antoine	Jacques Penot
Thérèse	Isabelle Otéro
Seraphin	Bruno Cremer

Also with: Maria Machado, Jean-Noël Brouté, Jean-Marc Bory.

Dazzling Panavision images shot high up in the Swiss Alps form a sweeping panorama to "Derborence," a mystical tale of death and rebirth.

The newly married Antoine leaves his bride Thérèse behind to climb the high mount over the village of Derborence with his uncle, Seraphin. There is a sudden avalanche, enveloping both men. The villagers assume both have perished. However, nine weeks later, Antoine mysteriously returns. At first the locals think he's a ghost, and one even shoots at him, but, somehow, he has survived, and has a joyful reunion with the now pregnant Thérèse. However, believing that Seraphin may also be alive, Antoine is impelled to return to the mountain top.

Told in the form of a legend, a story handed down from generation to generation, "Derborence" is visually majestic, but emotionally a little thin. Francis Reusser, whose last film was "Seuls" (1981), has created a strange, remote and exceedingly beautiful world in which to set his story, which is no more than an anecdote. The film's usual splendors are its main asset. Acting is fine, and there are some lovely local songs on the soundtrack.
—*Strat.*

Die Nacht
(The Night)
(WEST GERMAN-COLOR/B&W)

Cannes, May 16.
A TMS Film production, Munich. Written and directed by Hans Jürgen Syberberg. Stars Edith Clever. Camera (color, b&w), Xaver Schwarzenberger; music, Johann Sebastian Bach, Richard Wagner; editor, Jutta Brandstätter. Reviewed at Cannes Film Fest (out-of-competition), May 15, 1985. Running time: **360 MINS.**
With: Edith Clever in a monolog.

According to helmer Hans Jürgen Syberberg, "The Night" is to be viewed as the "swan-song of Europe" and "in the tradition of night-meditations." And so, appropriately, pic received its world preem in Berlin on the 40th anniversary of the German capitulation ending World War II in Europe (May 8). In Cannes it was presented in a theater a bit off the beaten path in La Bocca, where the event served as a night meditation for the handful of critics and film buffs who could put aside six hours for this nocturnal pleasure.

All things considered, this appears to be a film-requiem for a series of historically oriented Syberberg films that began over a decade ago, starting with "Ludwig — Requiem For A Virgin King" (1972) through "Parsifal" (1982).

The six-hour monolog was first a theater presentation in Nanterre under the patronage of Patrice Chereau with support of the French Cultural Ministry. The filming of that five-hour performance was done in Berlin, and includes an hour-long overture, so to speak.

Apparently, "The Night" attempts to wed word to music by highlighting Edith Clever's outstanding performance as a "solo voice," while at the same time seeking with black-and-white images to assimilate a dream-poem as far as today's media allow. The key musical composition in the background is Bach's "Well-Tempered Clavier" and, of course, Wagner's "Parsifal" and "Tristan and Isolde."

The text has been put together by Syberberg. He gives the audience no clue as to just when he's using Goethe or Hölderlin, Kleist or Nietzsche — save when the situation calls for it in Clever's dialog. The added treat, coming at the midway point in the film (towards the end of the first half), is a collection of Wagner's youthful letters to his beloved Judith. Here the soft side of Wagner's character is revealed.

The prolog is also of more than passing interest. In this color sequence, Edith Clever sits among the ruins of the Danish Embassy in Berlin and muses on the thoughts and writings of the American Indian chief Seattle (for whom the city is named). Seattle, too, experienced the downfall of his tribe towards the end of the last century, at a time when Wagner was composing his greatest masterpieces. The ruins of the Embassy building provide an appropriate backdrop for the "swan-song" motif.

For music buffs, particularly those who appreciate the art of the fugue, the music in the production is played by Svyatoslav Richter as interpreted by the late Glenn Gould together with Clever (she sings on occasion in the film) and by Pablo Casals.

And that enchanting performance by Clever is enhanced by Xaver Schwarzenberger's lensing: as his work with R.W. Fassbinder indicated at the end of the prolific helmer's career, Schwarzenberger is a lighting genius. The lab work at Geyer-Werke also deserves favorable mention. — *Holl.*

Il Diavolo Sulle Colline
(The Devil On The Hill)
(ITALIAN-COLOR)

Cannes, May 16.
A SACIS release, produced by LP Films. Directed by Vittorio Cottafavi. Features entire cast. Screenplay, Dardano Sacchetti, Elisa Briganti, Cottafavi, with the collaboration of Manuela Cottafavi, based on a short story by Cesare Pavese; camera (Telecolor), Tonino Nardi; art director, Elio Micheli; music, Guido and Maurizio De Angelis. Reviewed at the Cannes Film Festival (Un Certain Regard), May 16, 1985. Running time: **105 MINS.**
Rino .... Alessandro Fontana
Pieretto .... Roberto Accornero
Oreste .... Matteo Corvino
Poli .... Urbano Barberini
Rosalba .... Cristina Van Eyck
Gabriella .... Daniela Silverio

While veteran helmer Vittorio Cottafavi's old films are getting revived in the film clubs, his most recent production, "Devil On The Hill," turned up in the Cannes Un Certain Regard sidebar. Low-budget production, based on a story by Cesare Pavese, and set between the wars, chooses to follow its source as closely as possible. A little like watching a book visualized and read out loud, "Devil" sinks or swims on Pavese's dialog. With its talkiness and unabashed literary feel, it looks destined for the cultural tv market.

Though there is very little action, characters are so sharply sketched they often pull the film along with them. Three idealistic college boys from modest families spend the nights of the fall of 1937 wandering through the hills around Turin, talking about life. One night they cross paths with a handsome youth, Poli (Umberto Barberini), unconscious behind the wheel of his flashy car. Oreste (Matteo Corvino) recognizes him as a childhood companion, and they begin to go out with him.

Through Poli, rich, dissolute, but likable, they meet Rosalba (Cristina Van Eyck), the suicidal mistress he wants to be rid of, and Gabriella (Daniela Silverio), his beautiful wife. On a visit to Poli's country estate the next summer, the three high-minded boys find themselves being drawn into the vacuous irregularity of their rich acquaintances and embroiled in Gabriella's emotional manipulations. At the end of their vacation, they take leave of "the devil on the hill" and his temptations, a little wiser.

In spite of uneven acting from a cast full of non-pros (only Daniela Silverio is a familiar face), film somehow manages to make a potential moralizing thesis convincing. As the boys part ways with the beautiful people, one breathes a sigh of relief at their narrow escape. Technical problems (grainy, blown-up images and imprecise dubbing) somewhat cloud the clarity of the tale. — *Yung.*

Gouloubye Gory
(The Blue Montains)
(SOVIET-COLOR)

Cannes, May 18.
A Gruzia Studios Film Production, Tbilisi, Georgian Republic, Soviet Union; world rights. Goskino, Moscow. Directed by Eldar Shengelaya. Features entire cast: Screenplay, Revaz Cheichvili, Shengelaya; camera (color), Levan Paatachvili; music, Guia Kanchell. Reviewed at Cannes Film Fest (Directors Fortnight), May 18, 1985. Running time: **97 MINS.**
With: Remaz Guiorgobiani, Vassili Kakhnichvili, Telmouraz Chirgadze, Ivan Sakvarelidze.

Eldar Shengelaya, who comes from a Georgian family of filmmakers, first attracted international attention with a feature about "An Extraordinary Exposition" (1968), in which the figure of Stalin (remember: he is Georgian-born) causes a stir at an art show. Now he's scored a hit in the Directors Fortnight with a comedy of manners: "The Blue Mountains."

This time, it's a publishing house in Tbilisi. A young man arrives with a new manuscript under his arm, titled "The Blue Mountains." He goes from office to office, seeking an entré to the right person to read the manuscript, but everybody is interested in his or her own affairs, and the creative piece of work gets pushed aside each time for one ridiculous reason or another.

Meanwhile, the writer notices a crack in the ceiling that hints of a coming disaster if nothing is done about it right away. Nothing is, of course — until the whole building falls into collapse at the end of the film. Shengelaya takes the opportunity, however, to describe in subtle detail each and every one of the various personalities who make up an office.

This makes for a richly entertaining Georgian comedy. "The Blue Mountains" might have been adapted from a successful play (there's no indication of such in the credits), for a musical interlude connects each of three episodes and an appropriate epilog: the whole staff moves to a new building that does look much safer than the one before.

Pic was unspooled in Russian (not Georgian) at Cannes. —*Holl.*

The Innocent
(BRITISH-COLOR)

Cannes, May 17.
A TVS production of a Tempest film. Executive-producer, Dickie Bamber. Produced by Jacky Stoller. Directed by John Mackenzie. Features entire cast. Screenplay, Ray Jenkins, based on the book "The Aura And The Kingfisher" by Tom Hart; camera (color), Roger Deakins; editor, Tony Woollard; production design, Andrew Mollo; music, Francis Monkman. Reviewed at the Cannes Film Festival (Directors Fortnight), May 16, 1985. Running time: **96 MINS.**
Mr. Dobson .... Tom Bell
Carns .... Liam Neeson
Mrs. Dobson .... Kika Markham
Turner .... Clive Wood
The Doctor .... Denis Lill
Win .... Kate Foster
Tim .... Andrew Hawley

"The Innocent" marks a change of direction for its helmer John Mackenzie, whose recent features were the action thriller "The Long Good Friday" and "The Honorary Consul." It's an intimate portrait of a boy's first foray into adult life. Film bears comparison with such British classics of youthful awakening as the Bill Douglas Trilogy and Ken Loach's "Kes," and should win some following on specialized circuits.

Script suffers a little from its attempt to compress the events and revelations of Tom Hart's book "The Aura And The Kingfisher" to feature length. The densely-packed narrative, set in Yorkshire at a time of mass employment in the early 1930s, sometimes suggests that the inhabitants are only just coming to terms with the effects of WWI, which ended 14 years before.

The early sections of the film are deliberately elliptical sketches of the social and human situation in the village seen from the boy's eyeview. What central character Tim has to come to terms with, apart from his own epilepsy, include continuous bickering between his parents, his go-between status in the illicit affair between his friend Carns and a married lady, as well as the brutality of the latter's husband.

Given the violence that simmers beneath the surface, there's something a little sugar-sweet about the warmth that Tim receives from his friends. Against that is set the sometimes cruel attitude of his mother, who does not accept that her child should be different from others, and a doctor who makes no secret of his desire to institutionalize the epileptic boy.

Gradually, the emotional conflicts reach a resolution and a relationship blossoms between Tim and the tomboy Win.

Lensing by Roger Deakins evokes the natural beauty of Yorkshire's hills and rivers. Performances are universally excellent, with Liam Neeson and Miranda Richardson stand out as the adulterous couple whose lovemaking stimulates the first crisis in Tim's life. Newcomer Andrew Hawley is just right as the boy. —*Japa.*

A.K.
(FRENCH-DOCU-COLOR)

Cannes, May 17.
A Greenwich Film (Paris) release of Serge Silberman/Greenwich Film production with Herald Ace Inc. (Tokyo). Written and directed by Chris Marker. Narration (in French), Chris Marker, version with English narration and subtitles available. Camera (color), Frans-Yves Maresco; music, Toru Takemitsu. Reviewed at the Salle Debussy, Cannes Film Festival (Un Certain Regard), May 17, 1985. Running time: **71 MINS.**

"A.K." is a slight, but elegant docu portrait of Akira Kurosawa at work, during a few days of November 1984, on his latest film, "Ran," on two slopes of Mount Fuji locations. The documentarist is France's Chris Marker, and it is evident that he has won the confidence of the Japanese director to be able to work so freely and put in such technically perfect shooting of a major film during its own difficult stages of production with action scenes involving armies of extras and horses.

Of Kurosawa's work with his actors we see little apart from a brief moment with A.K. and his King Lear-styled lead player Tatsuya Nakadai (of "Kagemusha" fame). Many close-ups present the director himself, looking calm and fit at 72, smiling occasionally, unhurriedly smoking a cigaret, always wearing a suede, light blue sailor's cap, bluejeans and sneakers, and rarely raising his voice whether talking to

extras, actors or to his seven (yes, the Samurai coincidence is mentioned) veteran technical collaborators.

Kurosawa is also heard in several little asides on subjects like "Horses" ("Just as important protagonists as human actors, and with horses you must be very calm"), "Fear" ("you look horror in the face, and you will unafraid yourself"), and early morning mist on a day of shooting that needs bright weather ("things you can't use will often haunt you with their uncaptured beauty").

"Fear," "Horses," etc. are words used like captions for various aspects of Kurosawa's thoughts and work processes.

"To create is to remember," is another Kurosawa observation in Marker's film. "Ran" means chaos, and we see how chaos might easily befall so big a production without a genius director-general in charge. Marker has created his own beautifully composed and perfectly lit frames throughout, and when "Ran" has started its theatrical run, "A.K." should do well as a companion piece in smaller rooms almost everywhere.

As to the Shakespearean subject-matter, we are told that "Ran" is Lear, but then again not Lear — rather an echo of him. As a true portrait of a great artist, Marker's work certainly does not go for depth, but the film is perfect in catching the moods and sights of a huge cinematic battlefield workshop. — *Kell.*

Game Of Survival
(U.S.-COLOR)

Cannes, May 15.
A Shapiro Entertainment release of a Laurel Films production. Produced by Walter E. Sear. Directed by Roberta Findlay. Features entire cast. Screenplay, Joel Bender, Rick Marx; camera (color), Roberta Findlay; music, Walter E. Sear, William Fischer; editor, Sear. Reviewed at Cannes (Market), May 15, 1985. (No MPAA Rating.) Running time: **91 MINS.**
Sam Washington . . . . Joe Linn
Hector . . . . Paul Caldron
Carol . . . . Corrine Chateau
Ruth . . . . Mina Bern Bonas

Tale of a rampaging South Bronx gang out for revenge on the inhabitants of a tenement building who called the cops on them, "Game Of Survival" (filmed as "Tenement," which title is still the end-credit song) is a bloody, tacky affair without redeeming features.

It's quite possible to invest style and imagination into this kind of subject, but helmer Roberta Findlay and her team have provided a ragged, silly pic, with copious scenes of stabbing, hacking, shooting and mutilating, none very convincing thanks to poor acting and obvious makeup and effects. It gets to be so

bad that even when a gun is fired it sounds more like a cap pistol than the real thing.

All-pervading sadism of the piece is complemented by the total lack of rudimentary filmmaking skills. There's precious little fun to be had from this dubious "game." —*Strat.*

The Boy Who Had Everything
(AUSTRALIAN-COLOR)

Cannes, May 15.
A Multi Films and Alfred Road Films production. Produced by Richard Mason, Julia Overton. Written and directed by Stephen Wallace. Stars Jason Connery, Diane Cilento. Camera (color), Geoff Burton; editor, Henry Danger; music, Ralph Schneider; art director-costumes, Ross Major; sound, Tim Lloyd. Reviewed at Cannes (Market), May 14, 1985. Running time: **94 MINS.**
Johnny Kirkland . . . . Jason Connery
Mother . . . . Diane Cilento
Robin . . . . Laura Williams
Peter Vandevelt . . . . Lewis FitzGerald
Graham Comerford . . . . Nique Needis
Jock Pollock . . . . Ian Gilmour
Bookkeeper . . . . Tim Burns
Prostitute . . . . Caz Lederman
Actress . . . . Jo Kennedy

An evocation of fraternity life on an Australian college campus in 1965 which couldn't be further from "Porky's" and that ilk, "The Boy Who Had Everything" is a well-directed, but unevenly scripted, drama of rites of passage.

Apparently based in part on some autobiographical reminiscences of its writer-director, Stephen Wallace (who previously helmed two Bryan Brown pics, "Love Letters From Teralba Road" and "Stir"), it's about a youth who comes to college with a reputation from his high school of being popular, intelligent and a superb athlete. Seniors in his frat house, however, decide to bring him down to size, and he undergoes constant humiliations at their hands, all of which he takes more seriously than he should.

At home, meanwhile, he has a troubled relationship with his alcoholic, unstable mother, recently divorced from his (never seen) father who is marrying again. Mother and son, played intriguingly by real-life mother and son Diane Cilento and Jason Connery, live in a superb house by the sea, but the relationship is fraught with traumas and a lack of genuine affection, at least on the mother's side. In addition, the youth's upper-crust girlfriend (Laura Williams) refuses to have sex with him, driving him to cruise the back streets for prosties.

There's the stuff here for some strong drama, but it somehow seems as though vital elements are missing. Johnny tells Robin, his girl, that he feels good with prostitutes, but the film gives no evidence of this, though we're presumably supposed to take it at face

value. Altogether too much screen time is given to the boorish, loutish activities of the seniors in the frat house, and not enough time to develop the relationship between Johnny and his mother. There are continual reminders, via newspaper headlines and tv newscasts, that 1965 was the year Australia entered the Vietnam war; but this, too, isn't developed.

Compounding the script problems is the casting of Jason Connery as Johnny. It must have seemed like a good idea to have a real-life mother and son play a fictitious mother and son on screen, bringing undercurrents into their screen personae. Although Diane Cilento is touching as the rather pathetic middle-aged woman who escaped from a working-class background to marry a successful man and has now been abandoned, Jason Connery not only lacks his father Sean's charisma, but fails to convince in the film's dramatic high points. He's a good-looking, personable young actor, but perhaps lacking experience for this demanding lead part.

Supporting characters are mostly well played, with a special nod to Nique Needis as Johnny's wisecracking best friend. Individual scenes, such as a college race won by Johnny, are well staged, and the film is technically of a high standard. However, it fails to deliver dramatically and its commercial prospects are consequently iffy.

Picture has been selected to be shown at upcoming Moscow Film Festival. —*Strat.*

Io E Il Duce
(Mussolini And I)
(ITALIAN-COLOR)

Cannes, May 14.
A RAI-TV Channel 1, HBO, Antenne-2, Beta Film, TVE coproduction, produced by Mario Gallo. Directed by Alberto Negrin. Stars Susan Sarandon, Anthony Hopkins, Bob Hoskins, Annie Girardot. Screenplay, Nicola Badalucco, Negrin, Ken Taylor; camera (Technicolor), Armando Nannuzzi; editor, Roberto Perpignani; art director, Mario Garbuglia. Reviewed at the Cannes (Market), May 16, 1985. Running time: **120 MINS.**
Galeazzo Ciano . . . . Anthony Hopkins
Edda Ciano . . . . Susan Sarandon
Mussolini . . . . Bob Hoskins
Rachele Mussolini . . . . Annie Girardot
Hitler . . . . Kurt Raab
Claretta . . . . Barbara De Rossi
Felicitas Beetz . . . . Dietlinde Turban

A quality RAI-TV production, "Mussolini And I" is a lush costume drama about the last months of the war as lived by the dictator's family. The story's built-in problem is finding a sympathetic viewpoint from which it can be told; the choice falls on Mussolini's doomed son-in-law, Galeazzo Ciano, without too much success.

Ultimately, pic fails to impart a sense of tragedy to Ciano's being shot by order of his father-in-law.

A second problem is over-hasty pacing that doesn't give characters time to build. Made as four hour-long episodes for television (HBO will cablecast it in two parts in September), it becomes quite a brisk trot through history when pared down to two hours for theatrical release. The tv airing in Italy sparked a national debate on the historical accuracy of the characterizations, particularly the portrait of a weak, domesticated Mussolini padding around the house in slippers, seeming anything but a brutal Fascist. Abroad this shouldn't rankle so much, and pic should sell as above-average entertainment.

Story stretches from the Allied landing in Italy to Mussolini's capture by the Partisans. Against a glamorous backdrop of the Fascist elite at the end of the war, the dictator (Bob Hoskins) tries to separate his loyal followers from those ready to desert him. In the latter category is his daughter Edda's husband, Ciano (Anthony Hopkins), former foreign minister now bent on deserting Mussolini and signing a separate peace.

A handsome, urbane man-of-the-world, Ciano picks up more points from Brit Hopkins' ability to sound natural in the role. Star Susan Sarandon as wife Edda suffers from a clumsy American accent and dialog the likes of: "What happened?" "We've been invaded." "Oh, God." (English screenplay is credited to Ken Taylor, who penned with helmer Alberto Negrin and Nicola Badalucco.)

Story sweeps along, showing the dispersal of Mussolini's family. With Ciano and other Fascist bosses deserting him, Mussolini is arrested by the king. When German commandos free him a few scenes later, he has Ciano arrested in turn. Despite pleading from Edda, the dictator lets Ciano go before the firing squad, fearing Hitler (Kurt Raab) will think him weak if he lets him off. Ciano dies with heroic dignity. Mussolini shows much less when his turn comes.

Popping in for brief appearances are Annie Girardot as Il Duce's wife Rachele, Barbara De Rossi as a pretty, trivial Claretta Petacci, and Dietlinde Turban as a beautiful German spy who falls for Ciano. With all this going on, there is no time left for film to even hint at the greater tragedy sweeping the country outside the palace walls. The family drama is left floating in a timeless aquarium, seeming neither significant nor emblematic.

All praise to Armando Nannuzzi's atmospheric Gotterdammerung camerawork and Mario Garbuglia's posh sets. Most of the film was shot on actual locations. — *Yung.*

Gazl El Banat
(The Adolescent Sugar Of Love)
(LEBANESE-FRENCH-CANADIAN-COLOR)

Cannes, May 14.
An Aleph, Sigmarc, Cine-Video production. Produced by Gabriel Boustani. Directed by Jocelyne Saab. Features entire cast. Screenplay, Gerard Brach; camera (color), Claude La Rue; editor, Philippe Gosselet; art, Rafic Boustani; costumes, Seta Khoubesserian; music, Siegfried Kessler; sound, Pierre Lorrain. Reviewed at the Cannes Film Festival (Directors Fortnight), May 13, 1985. Running time: **100 MINS.**
Karim ....Jacques Weber
Samar ....Hala Bassam
Juliette ....Juliet Berto
Donatien ....Youssef Housni
Mother ....Denise Filiatrault
Father ....Ali Diab
Elie ....Claude Prefontaine
Leila ....Souheir Salhand

For those interested in how the inhabitants of Beirut come to terms with life in war-torn Lebanon, "The Adolescent Sugar Of Love" is a must. This sensitive first feature from Lebanese director Jocelyne Saab, which has French and Arabic dialog, avoids the sensational while transcending a documentary approach. it should have a good run on the fest circuit, with the prospect of sales to public-service tv stations.

Film focuses the city's situation through the eyes of adolescent girl Samar. Having grown up in a war situation, she has a sangfroid and sense of purpose missing from her older acquaintances who remember better times. The sound of bombs and the sight of friends gunned down in the street don't disturb her.

Samar becomes interested in mature artist Karim who rejects the military option espoused by those around him. His abstract paintings are the expression of inner pain, and he finds comfort in Samar's fortitude. She looks in vain for the romance familiar from Egyptian films.

The wrecked Beirut landscape, against which life must continue with some degree of normality, is tellingly filmed. The frequent scenes of Samar wandering through streets and houses are quietly moving.

By contrast, although Gerard Brach's dialog is often sharp, heavily scripted scenes in which characters discourse on subjects such as the changed perception of death or their desire to emigrate, are somewhat stagy.

Acting newcomer Hala Bassam as Samar has considerable screen presence. Jacques Weber conveys the profound grief of Karim. Technical credits are surprisingly good given the conditions under which the film was made. —*Japa.*

Milii, Drorgoi, Lubimil, Edinstvennii
(My Darling, My Beloved)

(SOVIET-COLOR)

Cannes, May 18.
A Lenfilm Production, Leningrad; world rights, Goskino, Moscow. Directed by Dinara Assanova. Features entire cast. Screenplay, Valeri Priemykhov; camera (color), Vladimir Iline; sets. Nathalia Vassilieva; music, Victor Kisine. Reviewed at Cannes Film Fest (Un Certain Regard), May 18, 1985. Running time: **70 MINS.**
With: Valeri Priemykhov (Vadim), Olga Machnaia (Anna).

The Lenfilm Studios in Leningrad enjoy a deserved reputation for a string of realistic feature films reflecting contemporary problems in Soviet life, and one of the most talented directors working there is Dinara Assanova. She made the impressive "Brats," on teenage delinquency problems, which unspooled to critical praise in the Information Section of the 1983 Moscow fest. Now she's at Cannes in Un Certain Regard with the equally eyecatching "My Darling, My Beloved."

The time is the dead of winter in Leningrad, the streets soggy with slush and snow. A taxi driver gets stuck one evening with a young 19 year-old maid with a baby in her arms: she has to get to the airport on time to see her boyfriend, in apparent hopes of winning him back after a trip to Sofia by staging a show with the child in her arms. Meanwhile, she's trying her best to elude contact with the police and other people on her trail — and the taxi driver (played by scripter Valeri Priemykhov) is tricked into helping her, although, at 40, he admits to hardly being able to understand the ways of the younger generation.

In the course of the fastmoving evening together, it comes out that the girl has stolen the baby in order to dupe her boyfriend, while he in turn will have nothing to do with her anymore. Further, she has lied to the taxi driver and doesn't even know how to take care of the baby at feeding and diaper-changing time — it's the driver who takes care of these necessities and thus stumbles on the truth, much to his own chagrin when the police finally catch up with the couple.

Anna, in short, follows her own rules of morality: everything is a matter of getting her own selfish way by going into phases of seemingly uncontrolled hysteria. It's only when she visits the child's true mother in a hospital who, on her deathbed, asks how the child-snatcher has cared for the baby that she finally feels a touch of remorse. By that time it's a bit too late to figure out whether she has learned her lesson, even though she pleads for a new start with the taxi driver (and the audience indirectly).

Pic runs a short 70 minutes, so it's safe to assume that some strong passages have ended up on the cutting room floor. —*Holl.*

Das Mal Des Todes
(The Malady Of Death)
(AUSTRIAN-COLOR)

Cannes, May 18.
A MR-TV Film Production, Vienna. Written and directed by Peter Handke. based on the novel by Marguerite Duras. Camera (color), Xaver Schwarzenberger; music, Sambuca Nigra. Reviewed at Cannes Film Fest (Un Certain Regard), May 18, 1985. Running time: **65 MINS.**
With: Marie Colbin, Peter Handke.

Writer Peter Handke has filmed Marguerite Duras' "Malady Of Death," a self-confessed tale of eroticism and philosophical-theological reflection. Briefly: a woman is paid to pass several days and nights with an apparently rich man in his luxurious apartment — he wishes not only to make love, but also to contemplate her nude body, for he is fascinated by the mysteries of the opposite sex. This very obsession amounts in essence to "the malady of death," as many of the classic Greek and Roman poets and philosophers equally fascinated by art and beauty in human form have confirmed.

The novella concentrates mostly on the morality of erotic and aesthetic obsession. Undoubtably, should this tight piece of narrative writing be transferred to a radioplay, the listener could let his fantasies flow in various directions. Handke's film treatment, however, ties one to the bedpost to gaze at the feminity of Marie Colbin from various angles — often in magnifying-glass closeups. Her eyeball, in particular, forms the filmmaker's prime obsession, rather than those gentle curves of the female figure that usually please a lover.

Handke keeps this up for a full hour, allowing only for a glimpse of the outside world via distant images and noises to assure that it's the 20th century and not in a Victorian drawing-room or the Deer Park of Versailles. The last five minutes introduces a new figure after the woman has gone: filmer Peter Handke himself appropriately dressed in black at the seashore.

Xaver Schwarzenberger's lensing is tops, and the even lilt of the narration allows for easy entry to the sparse, dramatic evenness of the Duras text. However the images don't fit the text in general, and the lack of a firm hand in directing the movements and expressions of thesp Colbin hints that the whole tv-project could have been lensed in a day if need be. — *Holl.*

Novembermond
(November Moon)
(WEST GERMAN-FRENCH-COLOR)

Cannes, May 14.

A coproduction of Ottokar Runze Film, Berlin, and Sun 7 Productions, Paris. Written and directed by Alexandra von Grote. Features entire cast. Camera (color), Bernard Zitzermann; music, Egisto Macchi; editor, Susann Lahayse; sets, Holger Gross, Jean Pierre Bazerolle; costumes, Ingrid Zoré; production manager, Michael Beier, Marie-Annick Jarégan. Reviewed at Cannes (Market), May 13, 1985. Running time: **106 MINS.**

With: Gabriele Osburg (November Messing), Christine Millet (Férial), Danièle Delorme, Bruno Pradal, Stépane Garcin, Louise Martini, Gerhard Olschewski.

"November Moon" is a film whose good intentions form the stumbling-block over which the director, Alexandra von Grote, trips in the making of the project. Everything is stuffed into the story; a Jewish girl fleeing from Germany to Paris in 1933, where she takes refuge with a friendly acquaintance and becomes the object of affection of both the young man and the young woman in the family. Grote, committed to lesbian themes ("Depart To Arrive," 1981), opts for the female-female relationship, and this seems to take first place over all the other historical and catastrophic events around November Messing (the heroine) in the story.

Such an approach might not be bad, but here we have the arrival of the Gestapo, the population flight from Paris, collaborators and resistance fighters among the French, the liberation of Paris, and so on. One has the feeling that a copy of Hollywood-style productions has been attempted on a small scale, with the result that the sets look tacky, the costumes motley and the hairdos out of an album of picture postcards.

Most embarrassing of all are the performances and corny dialog at just those moments when silence might convey a measure of meaning. — *Holl.*

Dediscina
(Heritage)
(YUGOSLAV-COLOR)

Cannes, May 19.
A Viba Film Production, Ljubljana. Written and directed by Matjaz Klopcic. Features entire cast. Camera (color), Tomislav Pinter; sets, Niko Matul; costumes, Alenka Bartl; editor, Darinka Persin; music, Alexander Scriabin, Josip Suk, Billie Holiday. Reviewed at Cannes Film Fest (Un Certain Regard), May 19, 1985. Running time: **116 MINS.**

With: Polde Bibic (Tomaz Vrhunc), Milena Zupancic (Malka, his wife), Bernarda Oman (Mira, their daughter), Miran Bilic (Mitja, their son), Pavle Ravnohrib (Mirko, their son), Matjaz Visnar (Milan, their son), Radko Polic (Dr. Hren), Zvone Petje (the priest), Bine Matóh (Nace, the fool), Judita Zidar (Olga, family servant and later wife of Mirko), Olga Kacjan (Neda, Milan's wife), Tone Gogala (Miha Brus), Iva Zupancic (mother of Miha Brus), Boris Ostan (France Kovic), Bernarda Oman (Veronika, little daughter of Tomaz and Malka Vrhunc).

This is an epic Slovenian story in three parts, presumably cut down from a longer tv version to be en-tered in Un Certain Regard section at Cannes. The events depicted take place in 1914, 1924, and 1944 — these are milestones, so to speak, in the decay and fall of a rich family, the Vrhuncs, in the mining district of Slovenia.

Part One (1914) shows how the rich mine and land owner refuses to bow with the changing times, even though war is imminent with the final breakaway from the Hapsburg Empire. The specter of doom is found in the drunken manners of his wife, who commits suicide rather than go on and live out an existence that's suffocating her.

Part Two (1924) depicts the first rebellions among the population against the new monarchy in Yugoslavia. The Black Guards have taken up the cause of fascism, while the workers are turning to Communism for the answer to their hopes for a better life. In the Vrhunc family the sentiments are split down the middle when the rebellion is put down with blood spilt on both sides of the struggle.

Part Three (1944) sketches the final downfall of the family as the partisans encounter the Nazis and their fascist collaborators in the last bloody struggle. The fortunes of the Vrhunc family are now at an end, the motif for this downfall found in the rape of the youngest member of the new generation by German soldiers and her being shot a short time later by the liberating partisans as a Nazi collaborator.

As it stands in its truncated festival version, "Heritage" is difficult to follow and is often confusing. Neither is the narrative line very clear, nor is it easy to keep track of the various characters. The one major plus is the lensing by Tomislav Pinter, one of Yugoslavia's top cameramen. —*Holl.*

Passage Secret
(Secret Passage)
(FRENCH-COLOR)

Paris, May 6.
A Forum Distribution release of a Scopitone Film/Orca Film coproduction. Directed by Laurent Perrin. Screenplay, Perrin and Olivier Assayas; camera (color), Dominique Le Rigoleur; editor, Denise de Casabianca; sound, Pierre Donnadieu; music, Jean-Claude Nachon. Reviewed at the CNC, Paris, May 5, 1985 (In French Perspectives at Cannes Film Festival). Running time: **87 MINS.**

With: Dominique Laffin, Franci Camus, Francois Siener, Leonard Smith, Julien Dubois, Ged Marlon.

"Secret Passage" is a dull first feature by Laurent Perrin, 30, who coauthored with Olivier Assayas, cowriter of André Téchiné's "Rendezvous." Perrin and Assayas are both scribes of the Cahiers du Cinéma magazine.

Their story revolves around a band of youths who burgle apart-ments during August, when many tenants are away on vacation. Booty is shared with two young women (Dominique Laffin and Franci Camus) who run a bar but remain in deep debt.

Emotional relationships in the group are complicated when a young architect, who has foiled a burglary attempt in his apartment, becomes involved with Laffin and takes advantage of the illicit activity. A final coup designed to end everybody's difficulties results in tragedy.

The rooftops scenes and summer setting offer Perrin the ample opportunity for buff winks to director Jacques Rivette and other Cahiers favorites, but the characters are devoid of credibility or emotion and the direction is slack. Dominique Le Rigoleur's photography is good but doesn't conjure the mystery of Paris abandoned by its citizens. —*Len.*

Bez Konca
(No End)
(POLISH-COLOR)

Cannes, May 18.
A Film Polski Production, Warsaw; world rights, Film Polski, Warsaw. Directed by Krzysztof Kieslowski. Features entire cast. Screenplay, Kieslowski, Krzysztof Piesiewicz; camera (color), Jacek Petrycki; music, Zbigniew Preisner; sets, Allan Starski; sound, Michal Zarnedki; editor, Krystyna Rutkowska; production manager, Ryszard Chutkowski. Reviewed at Cannes (Market), May 18, 1985. Running time: **108 MINS.**

With: Grazyna Szapolowska (Ula), Maria Pakulnis (Joan), Aleksander Bardini (Labrador), Jerzy Radziwilowicz (Antoni Zyro), Artur Barcis, Michal Bajor.

Krzysztof Kieslowski's "No End" scores as the most important film made in Poland since the imposition of martial law in December 1981. As the title indicates, this is an allegorical tale of life in Poland in the crucial year of 1982, a time when heroes were made or broken as the country tried to steer somewhat of an even course into the future after the heady days of the Solidarity movement.

The hero of "No End" is already dead when the film opens: we are attending his funeral. That is not to say that his spirit is gone, for the deceased Antoni Zyro (played by Jerzy Radziwilowicz, the hero of both Andrzej Wajda's "Man Of Marble" and "Man Of Iron" epics on the Gdansk strike) watches silently all that takes place during the weeks to follow as his wife Ula tries to pick up the pieces and start all over again. In the end, she realizes her love for Antoni outweighs everything else — and, in the classical style of a tragedy, draws the proper consequences by joining her husband in death.

The events that take place are viewed through the heroine's (and hero's) eyes, and one immediately has compassion for each character as though they are pawns in a plan of fate.

Ula (a strong performance by Grazyna Szapolowska) comes to the realization that her love for the departed Antoni (killed suddenly in an automobile accident) is too all-consuming to be denied. The only real release is to throw herself into the causes that her husband, a committed lawyer, defended in court with integrity and passion.

The case that presents itself is a worker imprisoned for supposedly organizing an illegal strike. The worker's wife come to Ula to retrieve the files from Antoni's possession, and Ula helps her to find another lawyer, one about to retire. The old lawyer decides to take on the case, together with an assistant who obviously hopes that the imprisoned worker will become a martyr for his cause. The drama in court is heightened by the decision of the worker not to defend himself at all, but stand upon his principles at all costs — even when friends of his opt to "cooperate."

The old lawyer is the most interesting character. He is a decent man trying to find a way out of the labyrinth of conflicting beliefs without compromising the situation any more than is required. The result: the striker is declared guilty, but his sentence is suspended which, in effect, cancels out the cause for the strike in the first place.

It is after the court case is closed that Ula knows what she must do. She delivers her son to the care of Antoni's mother, then returns home to tape the vents in the kitchen — and turn on the gas in the stove. The final shot is of the camera entering the darkness of the oven to blend into an image of Ula reunited with Antoni.

All thesps' performances and credits are tops.— *Holl.*

Dorénavant Tout Sera Comme d'Habitude
(Henceforth Everything Will Be As Usual)
(FRENCH-DOCU-COLOR-16m)

Paris, May 6.
A P.R.O. production. Produced by Hélène Vager. Directed by Roland Allard. Camera (color, 16m) and sound, Roland Allard; editor, Noun Serra, Annie Mendietta. Reviewed at the CNC, Paris, May 5, 1985 (In Perspectives on French Cinema at Cannes fest). Running time: **70 MINS.**

With: Thomas Harlan, Alfred Filbert, Hélène Vager, Henri Alékan, Max Berto, Louis Cochet, Jimmy Glasbert.

This is a confused reportage on a bewildering film-in-the-making. It's two real life characters are Alfred Filbert, former deputy commanding officer of the Nazi SS, and Thomas Harlan, director son of Veit Harlan, the quasi-official filmmaker of the Third Reich.

Harlan Jr., obsessed by his dark double heritage, somehow convinced the aged Filbert to come to Paris and take part in a film about his life (though apparently not about his Nazi career, atrocities of which he has always denied).

Filmmaker's ulterior intention was to confront Filbert with his criminal past and force him to a confession. When some Orthodox Jews, all Holocaust survivors, are brought into the studio for a showdown, the former Nazi denounces Harlan's scheme and tries to leave. Harlan has his technicians block the exit while he bellows a list of charges used at Filbert's war crime trial in 1959 (sentenced to life imprisonment, he was released in 1976 for "failing eyesight," though his view seems quite normal here!)

Harlan's film, "Wundkanal" and a documentary about its making, "Unser Nazi" by Robert Kramer were shown at last year's Venice Film Festival. Now this 16m record, sloppily shot by stills photog Roland Allard, is released by producer by Hélène Vager.

Explanations are denied the viewer, and one doesn't even have the slightest inkling of Harlan's aesthetic intentions for this docu alone. The ironic result is that Filbert comes out a pathetic (perhaps senile) old man, harrassed by the cynical, underhanded Harlan.

—*Len.*

The Protector
(U.S.-COLOR)

Cannes, May 16.

A Warner Bros. release of a Golden Harvest presentation. Produced by David Chan. Executive producer, Raymond Chow. Directed, written by James Glickenhaus. Stars Jackie Chan. Camera (Technicolor), Mark Irwin; editor, Evan Lottman; art, Ken Thorne; art direction, William F. De Seta, Oliver Wong (Hong Kong); set decoration (New York), Christian Kelly; costume design (H.K.), Michele Mao; sound (Dolby), William Daly; stunt coordinator, Alan Gibbs; assistant directors, J. Boyce Harman Jr. (H.K.), Peter Giuliano (N.Y.). Reviewed at Olympia 1, Cannes (Market), May 15, 1985. (No MPAA Rating.) Running time: **95 MINS.**

Billy Wong .... Jackie Chan
Danny Garoni .... Danny Aiello
Mr. Ko .... Roy Chiao
Police Captain .... Victor Arnold
Stan Jones .... Kim Bass
Superintendent Whitehead ... Richard Clarke
Laura Shapiro .... Saun Ellis
Police Commissioner ...... Ronan O'Casey
Benny Garucci .... Bill Wallace

"The Protector" is a crackerjack actioner produced on such a scale that it will give Hong Kong superstar Jackie Chan a legitimate shot as a b.o. attraction in the U.S. Fast-paced item will score heavily in the usual Chan international markets.

Plot is similar to any number of run-of-the-mill chop-socky efforts of the 1970s, as New York cops Chan and Danny Aiello head for Hong Kong to track down a drug kingpin who has kidnaped the daughter of his estranged business partner.

From the beginning, however, director James Glickenhaus makes it clear he's aiming the film for big time status, as a furious barroom shootout at the outset is immediately followed by a speedboat chase in New York harbor that rivals James Bond pictures for elaborate thrills.

What also puts matters on the right track is the tongue-in-cheek humor running throughout. Chan and Aiello both sail through the far-fetched action with insouciance and aplomb as they infuriate their superiors by wreaking havoc wherever they go and knock off enough baddies to momentarily put a dent in Hong Kong's population figures.

Upon arriving in Hong Kong, the pair visits a massage parlor and tries out unusual, double-holed pleasure benches before destroying the place. Chan indulges in almost superhuman acrobatics every 15 minutes or so, running up walls, pole-vaulting and swinging from sampan to sampan in the harbor and generally putting his karate expertise to good use.

The good guys are good, if irreverent, the bad guys are real bad, and audience expectations are consistently met in a predictable but satisfying manner.

Hong Kong and Gotham locales are employed to colorful advantage, nudity is surprisingly copious (including a truly bizarre scene in which the villain's all-girl crew of cocaine packagers work entirely in the raw, presumably so they can't hide anything) and action, stunt and craft contributions are all strong.

—*Cart.*

El Hob Fouk Hadabat Al Haram
(Love Atop The Pyramids)
(EGYPTIAN-COLOR)

Cannes, May 16.

An Abdul Azim el Zogby Films production and release. Directed by Atef el Tayeb. Screenplay, Mostafa Moharem, based on Nagib Mahfouz' novel. Camera (color), Said el Shimy; music, Hani Mehama. Features entire cast. Reviewed at Cannes Film Festival (Directors' Fortnight), May 16, 1985. Running time: **121 MINS.**

Ali .... Ahmed Zaki
Ragaa .... Athar el Hakim

"Love Atop The Pyramids" is an amiable comedy about subjects including young love in the face of stubborn bourgeois traditions, the housing shortage, and the scarcity of jobs for people who took the trouble to achieve an academic education. It all happens in present-day Cairo, and the hustle and bustle of that city plus occasional glimpses of yesterday's world in décor and architecture give a clue that the action is not taking place in some European-Mediterranean country in, say, the 1930s.

The two young protagonists belong to the middle classes, but the girl's family has an edge on the boy's by being civil servants. The first family does not greet with pleasure the news that the young people want to settle down in marriage, especially since he does not yet have the job and money to which his education entitles him. An engagement is, however, celebrated, and apartment hunting begins. The sustained antagonism of the mother-in-law then makes the boy bow out.

True love will, of course, triumph. The couple gets married secretly, and when they, after the ceremony, cannot even find peace in a hotel room, they climb the first step of one of the Giza pyramids, only to be caught in a police spotlight and dragged off on an indecent public conduct charge. En route to the jail, they embrace and swear they will insist on sharing a cell.

Director Atef el Tayeb is rather longwinded in a narrative style that suits Arab-speaking audiences just fine. In other lands, his film will stand limited sales chances. The playing is mutedly charming as far as the two leads go. For the rest of the cast, sly humor as well as frenetic body language is on vigorous display throughout. — *Kell.*

Les destins de Manoel
(Manuel's Destinies)
(FRENCH-PORTUGUESE-COLOR)

Cannes, May 19.

Produced by A. Castro Neves and Paulo Branco for Les Films du Passage, Rita Filmes, Institut National de l'Audiovisuel and Radio Televisao Portuguesa. Written and directed by Raul Ruiz. Camera (color), Acacio de Almeida; music, Jorge Arriagada. Reviewed at Cannes Film Festival. (French Film Perspectives), May 16, 1985. Running time: **130 MINS.**

With: Ruben de Freitas, Marco Paulo de Freitas, Aurelie Chazel, Fernando Heitor.

Reduced from three 52-minute tv episodes to a 130-minute feature, "Manuel's Destinies" contains some vintage Raul Ruiz in its outstanding first section of approximately one hour, but the combination of this with the latter two segments does not quite come off and the three parts do not a feature make.

Ruiz' films are often like Chinese boxes, having stories within stories and full of literary, philosophical and cinematographic allusions. In spite of or perhaps due to the budget limitations of his pics, they are highly imaginative and technically very impressive.

"Manuel's Destinies" starts off very simply and slowly grows more complex. In the first episode, Manuel is a seven-year-old boy tempted by a forbidden garden, where he is confronted by another boy (his older self) and a mysterious fisherman. There are three variations of this basic story which in each case leads to a different outcome. In this manner the little boy finds out about life and the varied shapes destiny can take. The other two episodes are by no means as clear but maintain the basic idea of events seen through the dreams and untrammelled imagination of children (whose acting is very well handled by the director). —*Amig.*

Joey
(U.S.-COLOR)

Cannes, May 20.

A Satori Entertainment release of a Rock 'n' Roll Film production. Executive Producer, Frank Lanziano. Written, produced and directed by Joseph Ellison. Features entire cast. Camera (Precision color). Oliver Wood; editor, Christopher Andrews; original music, Jim Roberge; supervising sound and music editor, Greg Sheldon; associate producer, Jeffrey Silver. Reviewed at Les Ambassades, Cannes (Market), May 19, 1985. (No MPAA Rating). Running time: **95 MINS.**

Joey .... Neill Barry
Joe Sr. .... James Quinn
Janie .... Elisa Heinsohn
Principal O'Neill .... Linda Thorson
Bobbie .... Ellen Hammill
John .... Rickey Ellis
Bonnie .... Dee Hourican
Ted .... Dan Grimaldi
Frankie Lanz .... Frankie Lanz

If the kids who go to see the breakdance musicals and rites of passage comedies can be lured in to see an intelligent, engaging pic about a youngster who's into the rock 'n' roll music of the '50s, then "Joey" could become a minor hit.

Joey (Neill Barry), age 17, likes to play guitar the way his dad, Joe Sr. (James Quinn) used to. In fact, Joe Sr. was lead singer for a rock group, the Delsonics, before falling on hard times and taking to the bottle. Joey and his high school friends have formed a group of their own, and they win a successful audition to play backup to some of the original '50s and '60s groups due to appear in the Royal New York Doo-Wopp Show, to be held at Radio City. Show's creator and producer Frankie Lanz plays himself in the film.

Joey also has a girl, Janie, and when one night she sneaks him into her bedroom and has to keep hiding him when her tipsy mother pays her numerous visits, the stage is set for a charming comedy highlight. The whole film, in fact, is good-natured, quiety amusing, and immensely likeable. Write-producer-director Joseph Ellison, whose previous credit was "Don't Go In The House" (1980), likes his characters and doesn't play down to his audience. There's some cheerful comedy, including a couple of dumb cops, but malice towards nobody.

Leads are excellent, with Barry a very personable hero, Elisa Heinsohn a charming heroine and Quinn managing to give Joey's has-been father genuine dimension. The sock rock concert at Radio City in the final reel will certainly entertain all those 40-year-olds who dug rock 'n' roll. —*Strat.*

Night Magic
(CANADIAN-FRENCH-COLOR)

Cannes, May 17.

A Spectrafilm release of an RSL Entertainment/Fildebroc Production. Produced by Robert Lantos and James T. Kaufman. Executive Producers, Stephen J. Roth and Michelle de Broca. Directed by Lewis Furey. Stars Nick Mancuso, Carole Laure. Screenplay, Lewis Furey, Leonard Cohen; camera (color), Philippe Rousselot; editor, Michel Arcand; art director, François Séguin; sound, Yvon Benoit; music, Lewis Furey; lyrics, Leonard Cohen; choreography, Eddy Toussaint. Reviewed at the Cannes Film Festival (Official noncompeting selection), May 17, 1985. (No MPAA Rating.) Running time: **92 MINS.**

Michael . . . . Nick Mancuso
Judy . . . . Carole Laure
Janice . . . . Stéphane Audran
Sam . . . . Jean Carmet
Frank . . . . Frank Augustyn
Miss Beauty
 (1st Ballerina) . . . . Anik Bissonette
Stardust . . . . Lyne Tremblay
Doubt . . . . Danielle Godin
Pinky . . . . Barbara Harris

For his first effort as a feature film director, Canadian singer-composer Lewis Furey joined forces with poet, songwriter and novelist Leonard Cohen. The combination of these two talents brings forth an ambitious film, "Night Magic" (aka "Angel Eyes"), aspirations will not be easily digested by audiences at large.

The sketchy plot has a music hall star, Michael, preparing a show that would bring new life to a run-down theater named The System. In the course of the one night depicted, he has three guardian angels (female of course) helping him along and one of them falling in love with him at her own peril. This leads to a series of songs and reflections about the clash between art and life, and the dedication of the creative spirit to his creation to the exclusion of everything else.

Furey's past experience on stage and tv is strongly felt here, as the entire film suggests one long, prolongated tv show, very stagy in the conception and limited in its use of the camera. Both the music and the lyrics are reminiscent of the sixties era, and as tuneful as the score is, it lacks the necessary power to grip the listener.

Furey may have attempted to handle too many chores in this first venture, for besides taking credit as co-writer, director and composer, he also supplies the voice for the songs mouthed in front of the cam-

era by Nick Mancuso, who plays the lead. Mancuso, a gifted dramatic actor, is no musical star to begin with and looks uncomfortable in the part: Carole Laure, Furey's partner for several years now, is a musical performer and moves well for the camera. However, the part of the enamoured angel (now we know they are not sexless) has her as befuddled as the audience. Choreography is very much in the spirit of tv extravaganzas, however a team of top Canadian dancers, headed by Frank Augustyn, Anik Bissonette and Louis Robitaille supply strong, professional performances.

Technical credits are way above average, this being a handsome production lavishly shot by Philippe Rousselot with the score being given full symphonic treatment and the soundtrack using the latest technical sophistications. — *Edna.*

Da Capo
(FINNISH-COLOR)

Cannes, May 16.

A P-Kino presentation of P-Kino (Helsinki) production with YLE-TV (Finland), The Finnish Film Foundation, The Swedish Film Institute (handling foreign sales), Filmteknik and Sandrews (Sweden). Directed by Pirjo Honkasalo and Pekka Lehto; screenplay, Honkasalo, dialog, Pirko Saisio; camera (Eastmancolor), Kari Sohlberg, Lars Karlsson; music, Atso Alima, Max Bruch; editors, Dubravka, Antonia, Pirjo Irene, Tuula Mehtonen; executive producers, Lehto, Katinka Farago; production design, Pentti Valkeasuo. Reviewed at Cannes Film Festival (Directors' Fortnight), May 16, 1985. Running time: **120 MINS.**

Arto Arsi . . . . Raimo Karppinen
Arto as a boy . . . . Jan Söderblom
Sergei Rippas . . . . Tarmo Manni
Suvi Ekman . . . . Rea Mauranen
Also with Per Oscarsson, Eeva-Maija Haukinen, Kimmo Otsamo, Jayne Meadows, Marta Becket, Lou Hopson, Virginia Capers.

Mixing facts freely with their own fancy, Finnish writer-helmers Pirjo Honkasalo and Pekka Lehto follow up their flashingly dramatic first effort "Flame Top" (A Cannes competition entry in 1980) with "Da Capo," an account of real-life violin virtuoso Arto Arsi's childhood and early adult career. This time around the team achieves style to the point of suffocation but practically no substance.

"Da Capo" depicts Arto Arsi suffering as a young man from never having had a real childhood, sold as he was (by actual contract) by his mother to leonine teacher-manager Sergei Rippas. During an American concert tour, Arto breaks away regularly from the strict regimen of work and exercise imposed upon him by Rippas and also from the embracing love of Suvi Ekman, his singer-wife. He runs away to gamble and cavort with loose women in Las Vegas or drinks heavily with riffraff in Venice, California. (The real-life Arto Arsi is now in his 60s, still touring and, reportedly

happy with his film portrayal.)

Film comes to an end where Arsi supposedly frees himself by aiming a gun at himself as a child prodigy, clad in white and playing away at Max Bruch's music. All the way through, tortured as well as merely descriptive images are composed to look stunning, which they do but unfortunately leave the narrative floating on air, fragmented, indirect and too dependent on inner dialog. No natural dramatic flow is ever in evidence.

It is no great help that Rea Mauranen is made to overact, while Raimo Karppinen as Arsi most of the time appears to be sleepwalking. All dialog has the hollow ring of girlish young poetry mixed with the philosophy of Chinese fortune cookies.

It is unfortunate that Honkasale and Lehto, who started out rather like prodigies themselves, have not been steered towards cinematic adulthood by a teacher-producer as stern as Sergei Rippas. — *Kell.*

The Rosebud Beach Hotel
(U.S.-COLOR)

Cannes, May 17.

An Almi Pictures release. Produced by Irving Schwartz, Harry Hurwitz. Executive producers, Michael Landes, Stephen Chrystie. Directed by Hurtwitz. Features entire cast. Screenplay, Harry Narunsky, Schwartz, Tom Rudolph; camera (Deluxe color), Raoul Lomas; sound, James Thornton. No other credits available. Reviewed at Les Arcades 2, Cannes (Market), May 16, 1985. (MPAA Rating: R.) Running time: **87 MINS.**

Tracy King . . . . : . . . Colleen Camp
Elliot Gardner . . . . Peter Scolari
Clifford King . . . . Christopher Lee
Linda . . . . Fran Drescher
Liza . . . . Monique Gabrielle
Also with: Eddie Deezen, Hank Garret, Chuck McCann, Hamilton Camp.

Previously known under the title "The Big Lobby," "The Rosebud Beach Hotel" is an inane comedy that falls into no commercially exploitable category. Cheesey look doesn't help either, and it's hard to imagine that Almi will get much mileage out of this one in domestic release, which commenced last November on a regional pattern.

Basic plot contrivance trivializes matters from the outset. An inept Peter Scolari is put in charge of a seaside resort hotel by Christopher Lee, father of his girlfriend, Colleen Camp, so he can prove himself.

Unbeknownst to Scolari, Lee is really plotting to blow up the building in order to collect insurance money, but to everyone's astonishment, Scolari and Camp make a great success of their undertaking, since they hire friendly hookers as bellgirls and generally turn the place into a sex palace.

Pic bounces right along, mainly thanks to the bright presences of Camp, delightful as always, and funny Fran Drescher as the head callgirl. Busty babes and beefy boys

fill out much of the supporting cast, and members of both genders are always ready for action at the drop of a shirt.

Tale is terminally silly, however, and visuals are so crude and grainy as to make even the sexy interludes fairly offputting. —*Cart.*

Herzklopfen
(Heart Beats)
(AUSTRIAN-COLOR)

Cannes, May 16.

A Bannert Film production, in collaboration with the Austrian Film Fund and Austrian Television (ORF). Directed by Walter Bannert. Features Nikolas Vogel and Julia Stemberger. Screenplay, Bannert, Gustav Ernst; camera (color) Hanus Polak; editor, Bannert; music. Roland Baumgartner; sets, Rudolf Czettel, German Pizzinini, Erika Reimer. Reviewed at Cannes (Market), May 15, 1985. Running time: **90 MINS.**

With: Nikolas Vogel (David), Julia Stemberger (Susanne). Adolf Lukan (David's Father), Barbara Focke (David's Mother), Peter Jost (Susanne's Father), Gudrun Velisek (Susanne's Mother), Herta Böhm (Grandmother), Hartmut Brandau (Friedrich Landauer).

Walter Bannert's "Inheritors" (1983) was unspooled at Cannes in the Directors' Fortnight to some critical success; it dealt with the surfacing of neo-fascist groups in Austria. Now he's back in the film mart with "Heart Beats."

"Heart Beats" is a film aimed at the youth audience, leaving out practically nothing — sex, action, sentimentality, romantic music and gorgeous lensing — to assure a box-office gross. Besides the pace, there's little to get excited about.

Nikolas Vogel and Julia Stemberger play two 16-year-olds with sugar-plums in their heads. He's from a working-man's family, she's the rich kid whose dad is in politics. They roll in the hay to their hearts' content until a pregnancy tests their love. Meanwhile, Vogel has to prove his manhood in the boxing ring to get even with a nemesis at work.

Bannert's skills as an editor are more evident here than his prowess in the director's chair.—*Holl.*

A Marvada Carne
(That Damned Meat)
(BRAZILIAN-COLOR)

Cannes, May 16.

An Embrafilme release. Produced by Tatu Filmes Ltda. Executive Producer, Claudio Kahns. Directed by André Klotzel. Features entire cast. Screenplay, Klotzel and C.A. Seffredisi, based on a story by Klotzel; camera (color), Pedro Farkas; art director: Adrian Cooper; decor, Cooper, Beto Mainieri; costumes, marisa Guimaraes; editor, Alain Fresnot; sound, Walter Rogerio; music, Rogerio Duprat; musical theme, Passoca. Reviewed at Cannes Film Festival (Critics Week), May 15, 1985. Running time: **77 MINS.**

Quim . . . . Adilson Barros
Carula . . . . Fernanda Torres
Nho Totó . . . . Dionisio Azevedo

Nhá Policena . . . . .Genny Prado
Nhá Tomaza . . . . .Lucélia Machiaveli
Curupira . . . . .Nelson Triunfo
Devil .Regina Casé
Serafim . . . . .Paco Sanches
Priest . . . . .Henrique Lisboa
Crook . . . . .Chiquinho Brandao
Old Negro . . . . .Tio Celso
Peasants . . . . .Tonico and Tinoco

———

Earlier this year "That Damned
Meat" won the jury, critics and audience prizes at the Gramado Festival in Brazil. It should do well on
its home ground and Latin America, but is by no means clear how
well its humor and local atmosphere
will travel in other countries with a
different cultural background.

Quim is a "caipira" (peasant)
who, although he only lives some
hundred miles from São Paulo,
might just as well be living in
another century, for life out there is
utterly primitive.

This character has two aspirations, almost obsessions: to eat beef
and to find a wife (in that order).
On the other hand Carula, a young
peasant woman, spends a good part
of her time asking Saint Anthony to
help her find a husband; she cheats
Quim into marrying her by promising him the family ox (which does
not exist).

By tricking the devil out of some
money, Quim gets to São Paulo in
search of his beef, but there he is
promptly cheated and, once again,
left with nothing. A supermarket is
looted by the populace and Quim,
without even understanding what's
going on, wanders in, grabs a hunk
of meat and at last fulfills his lifelong ambition. End of pic finds him
and his family settled down in the
big city and the 20th century.

Highly promising as the first feature of 30-year-old André Klotzel,
"That Damned Meat" tells its story with just the right note of naiveté.
The characters are developed within
a framework of the legends and
superstitions they believe in and this
approach makes their underdeveloped environment entertaining
and, at the same time, as true to life
as if a purely realistic approach had
been used. The screenplay could
have done with more detailed development in its last phase (in the
city), but the film's technical level is
good and so is Klotzel's handling of
the actors. Of these, Fernanda
Torres could in due time become
one of the better known names in
Brazilian films. —Amig.

The Toxic Avenger
(U.S.-COLOR)

———

Cannes, May 14.
A Troma Team release of a Lloyd
Kaufman-Michael Herz production. Associ-
ate producer, Stuart Strutin. Directed by
Herz, Samuel Weil. Screenplay, Joe Ritter;
camera (color), James London, Kaufman;
editor, Richard Haines; music consultant,
Marc Katz; sound, John Michaels; special ef-
fects, Jennifer Aspinall; makeup, Tom Lau-
tern. Reviewed at Olimpia Cinema, Cannes
(Market), May 13, 1985. (No MPAA Rating.)
Running time: **100 MINS.**
Sara . . . . .Andree Maranda
Toxic Avenger . . . . .Mitchell Cohen
Wanda . . . . .Jennifer Baptist
Julie . . . . .Cindy Manion
Slug . . . . .Robert Prichard
Melvin . . . . .Mark Torgl
Also, with: Gary Schneider, Pat Ryan Jr.,
Dick Martinsen, Chris Liano, David Weiss.

This madcap spoof on "The
Hulk" has plenty of ingredients that
could make it a winner with youth
audiences in all territories, but especially in the U.S. Pic is an outlandish mix of gory violence and realistic special effects in which sadistic
twists combine with a silly story
about bad guys whose dastardly
deeds range from hit-and-run
drunken driving to tormenting a
blind girl. The sometimes innocuous
fun situations alternate with blood-
steeped gore.

The story concerns Melvin, a 90-
pound weakling who works in a
body-building club pushing around
a mop, and who is hated by the
muscular and healthy types that
flaunt their bodies before him and
the audience. Following some rather
pointless shenanigans in which Melvin is humiliated by the bodybuilders, he jumps out of a window
and lands in a truck carrying toxic
waste. This transforms him into a
hulking monster, but one seeking
only to right wrongs in his town and
persecute the meanies.

As the "Toxic Avenger" he confronts muggers and mauls them,
saves kiddies from being hit by rapacious drivers, rips off the arm of
a holdup hood, fries another's
hands in oil, shoves one into a pizza oven, pokes his fingers through
the eyeballs of an assailant, but then
shows his monster's heart of gold by
befriending and then bedding down
with the poor, pretty blind girl,
whose seeing-eye dog has been
blasted by an assailant's shotgun.

Some good special effects, numerous action sequences, health-
club girls and a script amusing
enough in its mock-heroic overtones
add up to feature-length fluff and
fun, totally silly and forgettable, but
most suitable for the popcorn
crowd. —Besa.

Nomads
(U.S.-COLOR)

———

Cannes, May 14.
A PSO presentation of an Elliott Kastner
production in association with Cinema 7. Ex-
ecutive producer, Jerry Gershwin. Line
producers, George Pappas, Cassian Elwes.
Written and directed by John McTiernan.
Stars Pierce Brosnan, Lesley-Anne Down.
Camera (Easmancolor), Stephen Ramsey;
production design, Marcia Hinds; music, Bill
Conti; editor, Michael John Bateman.
Reviewed at Cannes (Market), May 14, 1985.
(No MPAA Rating.) Running time: **100
MINS.**
Pommier . . . . .Pierce Brosnan
Dr. Flax . . . . .Lesley-Anne Down
Niki . . . . .Anna-Maria Montecelli
"Number One" . . . . .Adam Ant
Ponytail . . . . .Hector Mercado
Silver Ring . . . . .Josie Cotton
Dirty Blonde . . . . .Mary Woronov
Razor . . . . .Frank Doubleday
Cassie . . . . .Jeannie Elias

"Nomads" comes off as the most
stylish supernatural-theme chiller
since Brian DePalma had his breakthrough with "Carrie." Debuting
writer-helmer John McTiernan revives in all departments a genre that
has lately degenerated into mostly
sex & gore.

"Nomads" avoids the more obvious ripped-guts devices in favor of
dramatic visual scares. He even has
some kind of a love interest in his
story without cluttering up the plot
with sticky romance or strained
eroticism. In fact, everything seems
to come naturally in a tale that even
has the supernatural ring true.

Pierce Brosnan plays French anthropologist Pommier who intends
to settle in L.A. with his wife Niki
(Anna-Maria Montecelli), when
flesh-and-blood (seemingly) Evil
Spirits of nomads he once studied in
arctic and desert regions materialize
to haunt him. They now look like
death-pale punkers.

Pommier goes after them, but
they beat him up. He lands in a
hospital, where he attacks and bites
his doctor (Flax, played by Lesley-
Anne Down) before he expires. At
his death, he was possessed by one
of the Evil Spirits and, through his
bit, passes his soul on to Flax.

How Pommier tried to track
down the Big City Nomads is seen in
cross-cuts to Flax fighting her new
soul and what latter drives her to
do. The dénouement is as truly a
surprise as the suspense is sustained
throughout. All technical and production credits are of the most shining order, and the acting of Brosnan
(recruited from tv series "The Man-
ions" and his own show "Remington Steele") and Down is the more
effective for being restrained. Singer
Adam Ant is seen as one of the
Nomads, a mask more of sadness
than of meanness, and Jeannie Elias
is bitingly funny even within the suspense framework as Flax' doctor
colleague.

"Nomads" is a film sure to roam
all worldwide media markets as well
as to establish bright prospects for
the careers of actor Brosnan and
helmer McTiernan. —Kell.

War And Love
(U.S.-COLOR)

———

Cannes, May 18.
A Cannon Group presentation of a Moshe
Mizrahi film. Produced by Jack P. Eisner.
Directed by Moshe Mizrahi. Features entire
cast. Screenplay, Abby Mann, based on Jack
Eisner's book "The Survivor," camera
(color), Adam Greenberg; editor, Peter Zin-
ner, music, Gustav Mahler. Reviewed at
Cannes (Market), May 18, 1985. (No MPAA
Rating.) Running time: **100 MINS.**
Jacek . . . . .Sebastian Keneas
Haling . . . . .Kyra Sedgwick
Aaron . . . . .David Spielberg
Slotka . . . . .Cheryl Giannini

———

There's a fascinating story in
"War And Love," filmed as "The
Children's War," about some Jewish kids from the Warsaw ghetto
who take on the Nazi war machine.
Its impact is squandered within the
film's otherwise mundane account
of Jewish hero Jacek's seemingly
miraculous passage through World
War II Poland. Narrative compres-
sion results in strained plotting.
Jack Eisner's autobiographical
book would have been better realized as a tv miniseries.

Central romance between Jacek
and Jewess Halina is problematic,
because the script has to explain
successive reunions of the two
lovers as well as Jacek's ability to
survive the repeated efforts of German solidery to starve, shoot or gas
him out of existence.

Script seems tailored to chronicle
significant moments in the Nazi
genocide rather than to convey Jacek's courage and endurance.
Perfunctory plot devices make him
a privileged observer of the ghettoi-
zation, deportation and eradication
of the Jews, and later the arrival of
American troops.

The film was expensively made,
with lavish art direction and large
crowd scenes. The action sequences
involving battle on the streets of
Warsaw are finely executed, but too
much of the supposedly affecting
imagery is commonplace.

Lead players Sebastian Keneas
and Kyra Sedgwick fail to deliver
and psychological development for
their characters. Lighting and editing credits are topnotch. The Mahler score is often misjudged.—Japa.

Crimewave
(Broken Hearts And Noses)
(U.S.-COLOR)

———

Cannes, May 12.
An Embassy Pictures release of a Renais-
sance Pictures production. Produced by
Robert Tapert. Coproducer, Bruce Campbell.
Executive producers, Edward R. Pressman,
Irvin Shapiro. Directed by Sam Raimi. Fea-
tures entire cast. Screenplay, Joel Coen,
Ethan Coen, Raimi. Camera (Technicolor),
Claudia Sills; supervising film editor, Michael
Kelly; editor, Kathie Weaver; music, Arlon
Obler; sound, Burr Huntington. Reviewed at
the Olympia 5, Cannes (Market), May 11,
1985. (No MPAA Rating.) Running time: **83
MINS.**
Mrs. Trend . . . . .Louise Lasser
Crush . . . . .Paul L. Smith
Coddish . . . . .Brion James
Nancy . . . . .Sheree J. Wilson
Ernest Trend . . . . . . .Edward R. Pressman
The Heel . . . . .Bruce Campbell
Vic . . . . .Reed Birney
Donald Odegard . . . . .Hamid Dana

"Crimewave" is a boisterous,
goofy, cartoonish comedy in the
"Airplane" mold. Pic is not really
about anything except people's unrelenting aggressiveness toward one

another, and laughs tend to come in bunches rather than being provoked throughout, so final result is more of a mild audience pleaser than a sustained hoot.

Film, previously billed as "The XYZ Murders" (its final U.S. release title will be "Broken Hearts And Noses," while "Crimewave" is used overseas) is framed by the impending execution of nerdy security man Reed Birney and flashes back to the primary setting, which is a particularly dangerous section of downtown Detroit.

Screenwriters Joel and Ethan Coen (of "Blood Simple") and Sam Raimi (of "The Evil Dead"), who also directed, quickly assemble the motley cast of characters, which includes weird security systems operators Hamid Dana and (exec producer) Edward R. Pressman, latter's obnoxious wife Louise Lasser, lounge lizard Bruce Campbell, who pursues cutie-pie Sheree J. Wilson, and Birney, who ineptly attempts to rescue Wilson from Campbell.

Best of all, however, are hulking Paul L. Smith and ratty Brion James as two exterminators who have expanded their field of victims from rodents to human beings.

A great percentage of pic's humor stems from Smith's maniacal pursuit of his prey. Laughing with menacing relish and betraying a gleefully cruel enthusiasm for his work, Smith stalks everyone in sight and turns in a fabulously enjoyable comic performance that singlehandedly keeps the film afloat.

Pic gives the impression of having been storyboarded rather than directed and, despite good execution all around, production looks pretty cheap and its impact evaporates immediately upon final fadeout. However, laughs are abundant enough to make this a passably funny entertainment. —*Cart.*

Delta Pi
(Mugsy's Girls)
(U.S.-COLOR)

Cannes, May 15.

A Pegasus Cinema Releasing release of a Shapiro Entertainment production. Produced by Leonard Shapiro, Kevin Brodie. Written and directed by Brodie. Executive producers, J. Don Harris, Frederick Kunel. Camera (CFI color), Paul Lohmann; editor, Bill Parker; music, Nelson Kole. Reviewed at Les Ambassades 6, Cannes (Market), May 15, 1985. (MPAA Rating R.) Running time: **90 MINS.**
Mugs .... Ruth Gordon
The Girls . . . . Laura Branigan, Joanna Dierek, Estrelita, Rebecca Forstadt, Candace Pandolfo, Kristi Somers
Lane .... Eddie Deezen
Shaun .... James Marcel

The single most remarkable feature "Delti Pi" is that Ruth Gordon, close to 90, is still in there making films.

What is more she shows she can

hoof it with the hunkiest of them in this youth picture of much noise, action and general mayhem. Film was shot as "Mugsy's Girls" and released domestically on a territorial basis beginning with an April launch in Atlanta.

Mugs (Gordon) is a totally off-the-wall sorority mother. She and her six charges (including singer Laura Branigan in her film debut) are about to lose their house on campus. To get the money they need to prevent foreclosure they unsuccessfully try a number of schemes.

Eventually they are persuaded by two young dudes, Shaun (James Marcel) and Lane (Eddie Deezen), to mudwrestle in Las Vegas.

Story is slight and some of the humor gross for a clean-cut bunch of sorority beauties and their hovering beaus. The mud wrestling scenes, in which the femmes pit their skills against the Nevada Nasties, a bunch of leathered ladies with names like Fang, Lungs and Mauling Mama, also may not be to everyone's taste.

The performers are engaging enough, and Gordon, with that famous voice of gravel, bizarre enough to maintain interest.

"Delta Pi" may not make general theatrical release but there should be a place somewhere for it in the video market.—*Nic.*

Hot Resort
(U.S.-COLOR)

Cannes, May 11.

A Cannon Releasing release. Produced by Menahem Golan and Yoram Globus for Cannon Films. Directed by John Robins. Features entire cast. Screenplay, Robins, Boaz Davidson and Norman Hudis; camera (TVC color), Frank Flynn; editors, Brent Schoenfeld, Dory Dubliner; music, Dave Powell, Ken Brown; assistant director-production manager, Roger La Page; associate producer, Christopher Pearce. Reviewed at Cannes (Market), May 10, 1985. (MPAA Rating: R.) Running time: **93 MINS.**
Marty Sullivan .... Tom Parsekian
Liza .... Debra Kelly
Also with: Bronson Pinchot, Mickey Berz, Daniel Schneider, Samm-Art Williams, Marcy Walker, Frank Gorshin.

Quickie sex comedy set in a fancy resort in St. Kitts, "Hot Resort" has enough laughs to go over in teen sexploitation markets and the summer drive-in crowd. The girls and boys show equal enthusiasm for man's favorite sport, as the young resort staff and guests form alliances by the minute. Four-letter-word college humor liberally laces a nominal story line.

Sex is the thing on everybody's mind, especially the boys working for the hotel for the summer. Their access to the bathing beauties around the pool is obstructed mainly by social snobbery in the form of a snooty rich girl and an impossibly stuck up bunch of preppies shooting a commercial at the resort. It's in-

stant war between the preppies and the hotel boys, led by curly haired Marty (Tom Parsekian). Arrows also fly between Marty's boys and the black hotel manager as well as the outfit's paunchy owner.

Only when called on to participate in a crew race for a tv commercial do staff and management band together to beat the snobs.

A lot of fooling around is woven into the tale, though full frontal nudity is kept out. Irreverent humor often rescues pic from tedium. Lensing is unobtrusive and professional throughout, more than can be said for some of the acting. Characters are simple but appealing, like Marty's love interest (Debra Kelly), who doesn't find dating a waiter beneath her dignity.

Even the hotel manager turns out to be an okay guy when he takes over coaching the amateur rowers. —*Yung.*

Leave All Fair
(NEW ZEALAND-COLOR)

Cannes, May 14.

A Pacific Films production, in association with Goldeneye and Challenge Corporate Services. Produced by John O'Shea. Directed by John Reid. Stars John Gielgud, Jane Birkin. Screenplay, Stanley Harper, Maurice Pons, Jean Betts, Reid; camera (color), Bernard Lutic; art director, Joe Bleakley; editor, Ian John; music, Stephen McCurdy; associate producers, Dominique Antoine, Craig Walters. Reviewed at Cannes (Market), May 14, 1985. Runing time: **88 MINS.**
John Middleton Murry .....John Gielgud
Marie Taylor/Katherine Mansfield .... Jane Birkin
André .... Feodor Atkine
Young John M. Murry ......Simon Ward

Lensed entirely in France, this elegiac story about the husband of New Zealand writer Katherine Mansfield, who died in 1922 while returning to places where they'd lived together to oversee the publishing of a book based on her letters to him, is a sober, affecting experience. It marks a complete change of pace for helmer John Reid, who previously made two ebullient comedies ("Middle Age Spread," "Carry Me Back").

John Gielgud, playing another elderly man of letters, returns to France to meet his publisher (Feodor Atkine). The trip brings back memories of his life with Mansfield (Jane Birkin), memories made more painful when he meets Atkine's mistress, Marie (also played by Birkin), who not only resembles his long-dead wife, but is also a New Zealander. Marie is charmed by this courtly old man, especially as he shared, for a while, a life with a writer she greatly admires. As she comes to know him better, and reads some of the letters the dying Mansfield wrote to him, she discovers that in actuality he's a selfish hypocrite, exploiting for personal

gain intimate details of his wife's past, details she never wanted revealed, and, in fact, expressly asked to be destroyed.

Lushly photographed pic is as gentle and nuanced as Mansfield's own writings, and the scenes between Gielgud and Birkin play with subtlety and insight. Less successful are the flashbacks in which Simon Ward appears briefly playing the Gielgud character as a young man, a rather unlikely piece of casting.

On balance, though, this is a refreshing, intelligent film, but one which, by its nature, will have to be handled carefully to find its audience. It's a class act all the way.

Film will be shown at the upcoming Moscow Film Festival. —*Strat.*

Der Bulle Und Das Mädchen
(The Cop And The Girl)
(WEST GERMAN-AUSTRIAN-COLOR)

Cannes, May 17.

A Coproduction of Hanns Eckelkamp Atlas Saskia Film, Dusseldorf, and Neue Studio Film Peter Pochlatko, Vienna, in collaboration with Second German Television (ZDF), Mainz. Directed by Peter Keglevic. Features Jürgen Prochnow, Annette von Klier. Screenplay, Peter Maarthesheimer, Pia Fröhlich; camera (color), Edward Klosinski; music, Brynmor Jones, Alphaville, George Kranz; editing, Susanne Schett. Reviewed at Cannes (Market), May 17, 1985. Running time: **92 MINS.**
With: Jürgen Prochnow (the Cop), Annette von Klier (the Girl), Franz Buchrieser, Stefan Meinke, Krystyna Janda, Daniel Olbrychski, Eduard Erne, Klaus Göschi, Paul Wolff-Plottegg, Ulrike Beimpold, Haymon Maria Buttinger, Rolf Dähne, Pavel Landowski, Rene Henning.

A lot of expectations went into the making of Peter Keglevic's "The Cop And The Girl," and some of them were realized. On the whole, however, the title itself gives away the essence of the theme: an allegory on the nature of force and violence as practiced often within the protection of the law — that grey area between crime and law enforcement found so often in American cinema.

Jürgen Prochnow (the captain in "Das Boot") plays a vice-squad detective in his 40s and on the sour, tough-guy side. His one apparent mistake is losing his gun and ID and car-keys to a youthful girl on the edge of the law, a mistake he decides to make up by taking the law into his own hands by pursuing and capturing the girl — then finding himself pursued in turn by the police for breaking the law in following his illegal methods. On top of that he falls in love with his captive.

Pic's main plus is the nonstop action scenes lensed by the capable Edward Klosinski (he collaborated with Andrzej Wajda on "Man Of Iron"). Both Prochnow and Annette von Klier make an attractive paid when they are handed a meaty piece of dialog. The shootout "Bonnie and Clyde"-style ending is a puzzler in view of what went on before. — *Holl.*

Killing 'em Softly
(CANADIAN-COLOR)

Cannes, May 15.
An Intermarket Pictures Corp. release of a Claude Leger production. Produced by Leger. Directed by Max Fischer. Coproducer, Bruce Mallin. Stars George Segal, Irene Cara. Screenplay, Leila Basen based on a book by Laird Koenig, screen story, Max Fischer; camera (color), François Protât; design, Anne Pritchard; editor, Jean-Guy Montpetit; sound, Michel Bordeleau, Patrick Dodd; music, Art Phillips. Reviewed at Olympia, Cannes (Market), May 14, 1985. (No MPAA Rating.) Running time: **81 MINS.**
Jimmy Skinner . . . . George Segal
Janes Flores . . . . Irene Cara
Michael . . . . Clark Johnson
Clifford . . . . Nicholas Campbell
Poppy Mellinger . . . . Joyce Gordon

Filmed in 1981-1982 in Montreal and New York City under the title "The Neighbor" and "The Man In 5A," and only now offered, this is a loser drama in all respects except François Protât's camerawork and Anne Pritchard's real-feel production design.

George Segal plays a penniless, retired Broadway prop man and Irene Cara a budding rock singer and they have apartments in the same building. Her man is in the band and he attempts to recover $3,000 owed him by the group's manager whom he threatens to kill. Latter's girlfriend, stoned herself, drops cocaine on meat she gives the prop man's dog. The dog dies.

Prop man stabs the manager to death and steals the money. Cara's boyfriend is charged by the police. She suspects Segal, ransacks his apartment, finds nothing and quick as a flash falls in love with him. In the final scene, a tender moment begins between them in the bath and the money flies out of the record player in the living room.

Discrepancies are noted throughout. Segal looks 20 years too young for the role and smiles too much, unrelated to the action. A widow lady character has two different names in separate scene, for no reason. These are just two of many inconsistencies.

Suspicion is that this is meant to be a light comedy, but wandering direction, lackluster acting and uneven sound further undermine a script without much motivation.

Pic is based loosely on the same Laird Koenig novel upon which Louis Malle's "Atlantic City" was based, but that pic made more sense all the way. "Killing 'em Softly," a title which is inexplicable given the subject matter, doesn't. Presence of Segal and Cara adds scant value. She's so-so and he appears to be distracted, but so is the pic itself.

Maybe paycable, only if desperate, for this one. Otherwise, back on the shelf. — *Adil.*

Future-Kill
(U.S.-COLOR)

Cannes, May 15.
An Intl. Film Marketing release of a Magic Shadows presentation. Produced by John H. Best, Gregg Unterberger. Written and directed by Ronald W. Moore. Executive producer, Don Barker. Associate producers, Moore, Edwin Neal, Terri Smith. Camera (color), Jon Lewis; design, Kathleen Hogan; editors, Leon Seith, Charles Simmons; music, Robert Renfrow. Reviewed at Les Arcades, Cannes (Market), May 15, 1985. (MPAA Rating: R.) Running time: **85 MINS.**
Splatter . . . . Edwin Neal
Dorothy Grim . . . . Marilyn Burns

Dandy for markets keen for blood and splatter, "Future-Kill" maintains a quick pace that overrides questions about its thin plot.

Strikingly punk-dressed youths inhabit an abandoned section of a big city to make a peaceful anti-nuclear statement to a world bent on destruction. One of them is a killer, mainly garbed in armor to cover grievous wounds caused by radiation in a laboratory.

Plot centers on playful fraternity boys, punished for a misdemeanor, sent in at night to kidnap one of the residents. They witness the murder of the community's leader by the killer known as Splatter (the film's original shooting title). He and his leather-jacketed hoods hunt them through a maze of streets and buildings. Splatter's hand is a fingered claw that rips bodies apart, men or women, he doesn't care if they get in his way. Blood spurts regularly and with abandon. In some ways, he looks like a nephew of Darth Vader.

The frat boys fend off their pursuers and, helped by two punk women, finally get the baddies as dawn breaks.

Costumes by Kathleen Hogan make the pic a potential draw as does the pic's poster by designer H.R. Giger, who won an Oscar for "Alien." Acting, however, is subpar across the board.

There's even a rest in the action for a scene in a punk music club and a couple of forgettable songs.

Anti-nuclear is claimed to be the pic's major statement. Actually, the message is kill and kill again. Pic accomplishes the latter purpose efficiently. — *Adil.*

City Limits
(U.S.-COLOR)

Cannes, May 15.
A Sho Films/Videoform Pictures presentation. Executive producer, Warren Goldberg. Produced by Rupert Harvey, Barry Opper. Directed by Aaron Lipstadt. Features entire cast. Screenplay, Don Opper, based on a story by James Reigle, Lipstadt; camera (color),

Timothy Suhrstedt; supervising editor, Robert Kizer; art director, Cyd Smilie; music, John Lurie. Reviewed at Cannes (Market), May 14, 1985. (No MPAA Rating.) Running time: **85 MINS.**
Mick . . . . Darrell Larson
Lee . . . . John Stockwell
Helen . . . . Kim Cattrall
Yogi . . . . Rae Dawn Chong
Carver . . . . Robby Benson
Albert . . . . James Earl Jones
Whity . . . . John Diehl
Bolo . . . . Norbert Weisser

Elements of "City Limits," made by the team which earlier did "Android," fit it into the category of the post-holocaust pic, but the historical disaster is a plague which has wiped out an older generation, rather than the bomb. The young survive in a condition of controlled anarchy and resist attempts to impose a centralized government. Pic should have a cultish following.

Most successful aspect of the film is its depiction of a tribal lifestyle regulated according to rules learned from comic strips. Two gangs of bikers, the Clippers and the DAs, have divided up the city and live under a truce. Infractions of their pact are regulated with competitive jousting or acts of reciprocal revenge. The dead are cremated with their vehicles like Vikings in their boats. The two groups may unite against outside threats.

Less convincing is the portrayal, with allusions to Fritz Lang's classic "Metropolis," of the totalitarian-inclined Sunya Corp., which attempts to take over the city with the initial cooperation of the DAs. The nature of the organization and its leader Carver remains shadowy.

The hero, played as a cheerful innocent without fear by John Stockwell, has been brought up in the countryside by surviving veteran Albert. When he comes of age, Lee sets out for the city and, after proving his manhood, is enrolled by the Clippers.

The Clippers are vanquished temporarily by the Sunya outfit. After regrouping at Lee's country ranch and linking up with the DAs, they successfully lay siege to Sunya h.q. and restore disorder.

Film features an ace ensemble cast, although Sunya toppers Carver and Bolo get rather one-dimensional performances from Norbert Weisser and Robby Benson.

Pic's main talking point will be its extraordinary visuals. Lighting, by emphasizing the primary colors in garish costumes, points up the flamboyance of tribal life, while the use of black space in compositions conveys the bleak aspects of life in a rundown city. Action scenes are well-executed and there's a vibrant score. — *Japa.*

Let Ye Inherit
(In Memory Of 450,000 Hungarian Peasant Jews)
(HUNGARIAN-W. GERMAN-COLOR)

Cannes, May 17.
A Television documentary by Imre Gyöngyössy, Barna Kabay, Katalin Petenyi. Camera (color), Gabor Szabo; music, György Pesko. Reviewed at Cannes (Market), May 16, 1985. Running time: **60 MINS.**

Those who have seen Barna Kabay and Imre Gyöngyössy's outstanding "Job's Revolt" (1983 Oscar nomination for Best Foreign Film) will be equally impressed by their docu on the same subject matter: "In Memory Of 450,000 Hungarian Peasant Jews." Among the dozens of films made on survivors of Jewish extermination camps, this is one of the best to surface this year for the 40th anniversary of the German capitulation ending World War II in Europe.

This time, the team of Kabay, Gyöngyössy, and Katalin Petenyi (Gyöngyössy's wife) return to the rich rural farming land where colonies of Hungarians Jews lived and labored before the Holocaust. Some of these villages are ghost towns today, while a few oldtimers have returned to the home of their ancestors simply because there's no other place on earth better suited to them than here. As one old peasant says: "I'm as much Hungarian as Jewish" — a line that weighs heavily in the scales of sociopolitical movements these days.

The beauty of this documentary is the manner in which the lifestyle of these people is sketched: we come to know how they prospered as a farm community before we are made fully aware of the tragedy of their last days. We learn from their non-Jewish neighbors, many of them close friends, how they were one day herded together for a long march to a location center for transport to the death camps. We also hear from the survivors themselves of the dignity and humanity that was maintained in the face of deportation, particularly as the Hungarian Fascists were just the opposite in their conduct.

A highly recommended documentary on the Holocaust. — *Holl.*

French Quarter Undercover
(U.S.-COLOR)

Cannes, May 14.
A Shapiro Entertainment release. Produced by Mark S. Hebert and Thomas M. Hebert for Worldwide Productions. Directed by Patrick C. Poole and Joe Catalanotto. Features entire cast. Screenplay, Bill Holliday; camera (color), Wade Hanks; editor, Steven Van Singel; music, Larry Seyer and Bill Ginn. Reviewed at Cannes (Market), May 14, 1985. (No MPAA Rating.) Running time: **93 MINS.**

With: Michael Parks, Bill Holliday, Layton Martens, Suzanne Regard.

"French Quarter Undercover" is an above-average actioner with a below-average plotline. An international terrorist conspiracy sets out to contaminate the New Orleans water supply with deadly bacteria while the World's Fair is in progress. This is the excuse for a fast-paced series of car chases, shootouts, fist fights and police reports typed across the screen. It should sell well on action markets that aren't fussy about the story making sense.

Two tough undercover FBI agents go after terrorists plotting to spread a horrible disease throughout the world by giving it to tourists at the Fair; they, presumably, will take care of contaminating the rest of humanity. What the goal of this evil scheme may be is never revealed, but its author is a man in a fake-looking Russian uniform talking in sinister fashion on the telephone.

While the cops beat up or shoot everyone in sight, unidentified hands are busy mixing up a bubbling yellow potion which the last surviving terrorist is supposed to dump into the city's water supply. Tragedy is narrowly averted in a climactic gun battle in mid-air, with the villain in a gondola suspended over the Mississippi River and the feds in a helicopter. Except that the thermos of deadly bacteria drops into the river and continues to threaten humanity long after the audience leaves the theater.

Good use is made of fake documentary material to give pic an authentic look. As a break from the action sequences, a reporter is "interviewed;" he claims to have been investigating the astonishing case when the FBI shut the story down.

Cohelmers Patrick C. Poole and Joe Catalanotto channel their energy into shooting non-stop action with a moving camera. Editor Steven Van Singel does a skillful job of machine-gun cutting that leaves few dull moments, with the help of a pulsating music track.

New Orleans is shot in *film noir* night exteriors, where cops make the rounds of the usual grind houses and bars, roughing up hookers, gays and addicts. Achilles' heel of "French Quarter" is its arrogant pair of feds, more brutal, macho and racist than the baddies. Since they're never given distinct personalities or any sympathetic character traits, their final victory is pure filmic convention. —*Yung.*

Die Mitläufer
(Following The Führer)
(WEST GERMAN-B&W)

Cannes, May 18.
A Coproduction of EML-Film, Munich, and Second German Television (ZDF), Mainz, World rights, Futura Film, Munich. Directed by Erwin Leiser and Eberhard Itzenplitz. Screenplay, Oliver Storz; camera (b&w), Gerard Vandenberg, Jochen Rademacher; editors, Elisabeth Imholte, Margo von Oven, Jutta Niehoff; producer, Erwin Leiser; production manager, Christine Carben Stotz. Reviewed at Cannes (Market), May 18, 1985. Running time: **90 MINS.**
With: Karin Baal, Horst Bollmann, Gottfried John, Therese Lohner, Lisi Mangold, Felix von Manteuffel, Armin Mueller-Stahl, Ilsemarie Schnering, Walter Schultheiss, Frank Strecker.

"Following The Führer" is a combination docu and fiction feature, the former assembled by Erwin Leiser and the latter directed by Eberhard Itzenplitz. Leiser, in particular, will be remembered for having made a landmark docu on the Holocaust, "Mein Kampf," a quarter century ago, and this film seems to be a natural sequel in view of both the theme and the treatment. It simply asks: why did so many Germans simply follow a dictator in a world catastrophe?

The answer is more hinted at than given as absolute fact. Some docu footage has been assembled that is indeed rare - for instance, a Christmas celebration by the nation's railroaders that's meant to honor the Führer, but comes across as absurd. As for the fiction scenes, these aren't always convincing, although one in particular rings quite true: a group of tenants from an apartment building assemble in the basement during an air-raid to voice, again in an absurd and tragicomic context, their thoughts and grievances.

Given the 40th anni of the German capitulation and the success of the Edgar Reitz' tv-film series, "Heimat," a film like "Following The Führer" is a welcome addition to German Film Series programming on the fest circuit. — *Holl.*

Dim Sum: A Little Bit Of Heart
(U.S.-COLOR)

Cannes, May 14.
An Orion Classics (U.S.) release of a CIM production. Produced by Tom Sternberg, Wayne Wang, Danny Yung. Executive producer, Vincent Tai. Directed by Wang. Screenplay, Terrel Seltzer, based on a story by Laureen Chew, Seltzer, Wang; Camera (Du Art color), Michael Chin; editor, Ralph Wikke; music, Todd Boekelheide; art direction, Danny Yung; set decoration, Lydia Tanji; sound, Curtis Choy; sound design, Andy Aaron; associate producer, Emily Leung; assistant director, Christopher P. Lee; additional photography, Emitro Omori. Reviewed at the Cannes Film Festival (Directors Fortnight), May 13, 1985. (No MPAA Rating.) Running time: **85 MINS.**

Geraldine Chew	Laureen Chew
Mrs. Tam	Kim Chew
Uncle Tam	Victor Wong
Auntie Mary	Ida F.O. Chung
Julia	Cora Miao
Richard	John Nishio
Amy Tam	Amy Hill
Kevin Tam	Keith Choy

After the offbeat charm and inventiveness of "Chan Is Missing," Wayne Wang's follow-up feature, "Dim Sum: A Little Bit Of Heart," arrives largely as a disappointment. Even more modest in its achievement than in its already limited ambitions, film offers up a few charming observations about cultural differences among assorted generations of Chinese Americans, but the dramatic situations are so underplayed as to be mostly ineffectual. Orion Classics will be hard pressed getting this one past specialized, major city firstrun art houses.

Taking a cue from countless earlier Asian family pictures that have dwelt upon the subject of family traditions and the responsibilities of children for their aging parents, Wang and scripter Terrel Seltzer have focused upon the relationship between a traditional Chinese woman in her 60s and her 30-ish daughter, who unlike her brother and sister, is not yet hitched.

A great deal of the sought-after humor stems from the "So when are you gonna get married?" attitudes of family friends. Other people speak about the daughter's wonderful sense of obligation toward her mother, but her reasons for avoiding matrimony seem to stem just as much from indecisiveness about her potential fiancé as they do from familial traditionalism.

The authenticity of Wang's depiction of San Francisco's Chinese need not be questioned, but the attitudes expressed are predictable in the extreme and are invested with little sense of dramatic urgency. Many of the shots and sequences, while lovely in their own right, are basically inert and filled with dead air.

By the same token, Wang's occasional amusing scenes prove delightful on a momentary basis, but don't connect to fashion anything sustained. When the film is funny it's fine, but when it's not, it just sits there.

Like "Chan Is Missing," pic is an unusual cultural hybrid. Characters alternate between English and Chinese from one sentence to the next, and the subtitler seems to have been utterly arbitrary in selecting what to translate from the Chinese. Use of language in itself provokes smiles at times, but the joke is stretched rather a long way.

Visually, pic represents a major stride from "Chan." Luminously lensed by Michael Chin with fine use of S.F.'s airy, pastel shades, film is a pleasure to look at but, like the Chinese appetizers of its title, is just too insubstantial for a full meal. —*Cart.*

Super
(WEST GERMAN-COLOR)

Cannes, May 17.
A Coproduction of Adolf Winkelmann Film, Dortmund, Westdeutscher Rundfunk (WDR), Cologne, Syndikat "L" and C & H Film, Berlin, and BB-Film, Dortmund. Directed by Adolf Winkelmann. Features entire cast. Screenplay, Jost Krüger, Gerd Weiss, Winkelmann; camera (color), David Slama; editing, Bettina Lewertoff, Claudia Effner; sets, Georg von Kieseritzky; producer, Michael Braun. Reviewed at Cannes (Market), May 17, 1985. Running time: **100 MINS.**
With: Renan Demirkan, Udo Lindenberg, Inga Humpe, Tana Schanzara, Günter Lamprecht, Hannelore Hoger, Ulrich Wildgruber, Gottfried John, Hermann Lause.

Adolf Winkelmann's "Super" is the third feature in a trilogy, following "On the Move" (1978) and "A Lot of Bills to Pay" (1981). All deal with outsiders in an increasingly industrialized and impersonalized society. "Super," however, leans heavily on science fiction for effect and gets lost along the way in the morass of maintaining a line of credibility in a world of practical improbability.

Futuristic setting is a gas-station motel somewhere in an industrial wasteland. Inga, a young lady on the run, has inherited the waystop, whose tenants are the rough-edge Kubella and Fana. They, in order to survive, have taken to trafficking people out of the country to the South Seas. Into their web come an assortment of misfits reminiscent of classic Hollywood and European thrillers, yet this apparent copy is without the charge of the accustomed sharply defined characterizations.

It's something for the German film buffs for the most part, although the closing sequence of the shootout and escape are deftly handled. — *Holl.*

Heated Vengeance
(U.S.-COLOR)

Cannes, May 14.
A Fries Distribution Co. presentation of a Media Home Entertainment production. Executive producer, Joseph Wolf. Written, produced and directed by Edward Murphy. Stars Richard Hatch, Jolina Mitchell-Collins. Camera (Deluxe Color) Frank Johnson; music, Jim Price; editor, Richard Halsey. Reviewed at Cannes (Market), May 14, 1985. (No MPAA Rating.) Running time: **82 MINS.**

Hoffman	Richard Hatch
Michelle	Jolina Mitchell-Collins
Bingo	Ron Max
Pope	Dennis Patrick
Snake	Michael J. Pollard
Cleaver	Robert Walker
Tucker	Mills Watson
Bandit	Cameron Dye

Fast theatrical playoff secured writer-producer-director Edward Murphy a nice profit for his 1982 debut "Raw Force," and his new post-Vietnam military actioner, "Heated Vengeance," may succeed equally well, dealing as it does with gut-basic good guy vs. evil guys fighting for life in the bloodiest of ways in the familiar milieu of jungle warfare. Otherwise, film's future obviously lies with the video trade. It was funded by homevideo outfit MHE, and shot last year under the title "The Jungle."

Plot has Vietnam veteran Hoffman return to the scene to find the girl he left behind (Richard Hatch and Jolina Mitchell-Collins are handsomely personable in these roles), but first he runs into Bingo, a soldier it once was his duty to court-martial for rape of a native teenager. Bingo is now a member of a dope refinery outfit of ex-servicemen somewhere in Laos. Bingo kidnaps Hoffman, Hoffman escapes, but instead of seeking a safe return to his girl he decides to root out the dope gang, while Bingo, of course, played with Rambo-Stallone mien by Ron Max, is happy for his renewed chance to get revenge.

Pic moves swiftly except for a few sequences of vapid romance and sentiment. Michael J. Pollard comes closest to achieving any kind of nuance in his portrayal of a good-at-heart-bad-guy who is also something of a mild-mannered psycho.

Film is a slapped-together effort, but noise and action visuals will probably carry its day. Locations used were the same Francis Coppola had for "Apocalypse Now," but "Heated Vengeance" is a very small bang. — Kell.

Blackout
(U.S.-COLOR)

Cannes, May 15.

A Roger Gimbel production for Peregrine Entertainment in association with Home Box Office. Executive producers, Roger Gimbel, Freyda Rothstein. Produced by Richard Parks, Richard Smith, Les Alexander. Directed by Douglas Hickox. Features entire cast. Screenplay, David Ambrose, based on a story by Ambrose, Smith, Parks, Alexander; camera (color), Tak Fujimoto; editor, Michael Brown; music, Laurence Rosenthal. Reviewed at Cannes (Market), May 14, 1985. Running time: 97 MINS.
Joe Steiner . . . . Richard Widmark
Ed Vinson/Allen Devlin . . Keith Carradine
Chris Graham . . . . Kathleen Quinlan
Mike Patterson . . . . Michael Beck

Pics made for pay-tv rarely convince on the large screen, and "Blackout" is no exception. There are some decent ideas in its thriller plot, but scripting is too loose to provide the sort of payoff that theatrical audiences expect.

Plot centers around a guy horribly mutilated in an auto crash. Since his companion is burned beyond recognition, there's no way of telling whether the amnesiac survivor is Allen Devlin, who hired the car, or someone else. Film becomes too neat for comfort with the inability of the police to trace a background for Devlin.

The accident victim emerges from hospital with a remodeled face and the Devlin name. He promptly tumbles into marriage with his nurse. Six years later, former cop Joe Steiner is tipped off that Devlin could be someone who disappeared after killing his wife and kids. His homelife, it seems, is a carbon copy of the killer's, and the physical details seem to fit.

Anyone remotely familiar with the genre will realize at this stage that the film is going to end with an attempted repeat of the crime. For a start, there's no alternative way to identify Devlin. The script, however, assumes the audience is still guessing.

Richard Widmark is impressive as the failed cop anxious to solve a final crime. For a man who's lost his past, the Devlin role is played too straight by Keith Carradine. He seems to have no problems with a conventional career and marriage.

Some of the film's structural problems might be solved with tighter editing. There's nothing wrong with the direction by Douglas Hickox and scoring is good.
—Japa.

Savage Dawn
(U.S.-COLOR)

Cannes, May 16.

A Mag Enterprises and Gregory Earls presentation. Produced by Earls. Directed by Simon Nuchtern. Stars George Kennedy, Richard Lynch, Karen Black. Executive producer, Pierre Benichou; screenplay, William P. Milling, additional material by Max Bloom; coproducers, Milling, Gerald Feil; camera (Eastmancolor), Feil; editor, Jerry Greenberg; associate producer, Carmen Ventura; production designer, Robb Wilson King. Reviewed at Cannes (Market), May 15, 1985 (No MPAA Rating.) Running time: 102 MINS.
Tick Rand . . . . George Kennedy
Reverend Romano . . . . Richard Lynch
Rachel Wade . . . . Karen Black
Ben Stryker . . . . Lance Henriksen
Kate Rand . . . . Claudia Udy
Pigiron . . . . Bill Forsythe
Zero . . . . Mickey Jones
Sheriff . . . . Leo Gordon

In a variation on the well-worn theme of rampaging bikers terrorizing innocent townsfolk, the denizens under attack in Simon Nuchtern's "Savage Dawn" are the sleaziest bunch of weirdos and wackos you'd never want to meet.

There's an excitable dwarf, a deputy sheriff who displays his physical prowess in bareknuckle fights with all-comers, a preacher (Richard Lynch) who makes a mockery of his faith, and one or two normal people.

Aside from that twist, pic is a fairly routine, predictable depiction of blood-letting and general mayhem. Those with a taste for extreme violence can be expected to roll up at the turnstiles, but as they appear to be a diminishing number at last count, pic seems destined for a short and unrewarding life.

Lance Henriksen limns a war hero, who, tiring of fighting and killing for a living, takes off on his motorbike to meet up with George Kennedy, his old army buddy, and George's blond, attractive daughter Claudia Udy. Having retired, George inexplicably has decided to settle in a rapidly decaying old mining town, peopled with the above misfits.

Not much fun at the best of times, the town turns into a battlefield when the Savages biker gang, led by brutish Bill Forsythe, decide to do the sorts of nasty things which give bikers a bad name.

Confined to a wheelchair, Kennedy exterminates quite a few of the marauders until he cannot get out of the way of an unfriendly bullet, but Henriksen surmounts incredible odds to finish the task.

With this sort of mind-numbing plot, stylish acting is not called for, nor delivered. Henriksen, seen to much better advantage in "The Right Stuff," isn't required to do much more than display a fair bit of agility, and utter such homilies as "You're dead." Kennedy looks relieved when that bullet ends his contribution, and Richard Lynch seems embarrassed in the scene where he is seduced in church by a biker girl, as well he might.

Karen Black, playing a shrewish bar-owner who throws her lot in with the bikies, spends most of her time on screen sitting astride the barrel of a tank, and hissing at Claudia Udy.

Production values are fine, but in other respects it's a substandard effort from director Nuchtern, producer Gregory Earls and coproducer-writer Milling, who last teamed on the 3-D "Silent Madness." —Dogo.

Paradise Motel
(U.S.-COLOR)

Cannes, May 14.

A Saturn International Pictures release of a Frank Rubin-Gary Gibbs presentation. Produced by Gibbs, Rubin. Executive producer, James P. Prichard. Directed by Cary Medoway. Features entire cast. Screenplay, Roger Stone, Medoway; camera (color), James L. Carter; editor, Doug Jackson; music, Rick White, Mark Governor; art direction, Dena Roth; sound, Brian DeMellier; associate producer, Roger Stone; assistant director, second unit camera, Don Jones. Reviewed at the Olympia 8, Cannes (Market), May 14, 1985. (MPAA Rating: R.) Running time: 87 MINS.
Sam Kehoe . . . . Gary Hershberger
Laura Phillips . . . . Jonna Leigh Stack
Mick Thurster . . . . Robert Krantz
Harry Kehoe . . . . Bob Basso
Danny . . . . Rick Gibbs
Strummer . . . . Jeffrey Jay Hea
Debbie . . . . Colleen McDermott
Vicky . . . . Dena Tancata
Coach Martins . . . . Al Hansen
Mrs. Kehoe . . . . Laurie Gould

"Paradise Motel" is a silly little teenage version of Billy Wilder's "The Apartment." Bedroom and poolside locations provide plenty of decisions for teasing nudity and sexplay, but by-the-numbers execution makes for a mostly tedious hour-and-a-half. Film was released domestically in January.

Gary Hershberger is the new boy in town (film's shooting title was "New Kid In Town") whose pa has taken over a seaside motel. Getting wind of the amorous opportunities offered up by the facility's honeymoon suite, local Romeo Robert Krantz instantly decides Gary is his best friend and talks him into making the room available for a non-stop succession of trysts with a parade of nubile high school girls.

Naturally, certain complications ensue, particularly when Gary falls hard for Robert's secret sweetheart, played by winsome Jonna Leigh Stack. School's sports coach becomes convinced that Gary is fooling around with his wife, which creates additional havoc.

Pic's got nothing but inane titillation on its mind, and leering adolescent boys may be satisfied with the scenic diversions. It looks pretty cheap, and collection of soft rock songs layered over the action is awful. What energy the film has stems from the performers, who aren't bad. —Cart.

Les Anges
(The Angels)
(TUNISIAN-KUWAITIAN-COLOR)

Cannes, May 14.

Produced by Ridha Behi for Jugurtha Films, SATPEC, and Dhifaf. Written and directed by Ridha Behi. Stars Madiha Kamel, Kamel Chennaoui. Camera (color), Tonino Nardi; art director, Andrea Crisanti; editor, Kehena Attia. Reviewed at the Cannes Film Festival (Directors' Fortnight), May 14, 1985. Running time: 90 MINS.
Salwa . . . . Madiha Kamel
Youssef . . . . Kamel Chennaoui
Lofti . . . . Fethi Saadallah
Habachi . . . . Lamine Nahdi

The first coproduction between Tunisia and Kuwait, "Les Anges" is pretty to look at, but goes down under the weight of leaden pacing and a non-action script. This unconvincing drama looks like it will have a rough time circulating through the Arab countries for which it was made.

Angels of the title are a theatrical company of young, idealistic actors. Their leader, Lofti (Fethi Saadallah), is the lover of the leading lady, Salwa (Madiha Kamel). The play can't get an okay from the censors and rehearsals are interrupted. At the same time, Salwa's mother dies and she starts having an affair with a wealthy doctor, Youssef (Kamel Chennaoui). Lofti and his rebellious friends tie Youssef up in a villa, where they give him a mild third-degree about his bourgeois life style and dirty money. Youssef has no trouble sending them to jail.

Most motivations have to be inferred, since they're not on the screen. With Lofti out of the way, Youssef's interest in Salwa (now starring in a big production of "Yerma") turns to obsession, though the fascination of the permanently melancholy actress is not readily apparent. Script will have us believe he undergoes a radical change, thanks to the miracle of love. He neglects his career and spends all his wife's money buying Salwa a theater where she can make her dreams come true. Briefly, a smile appears on the girl's face. Moments later, his relatives have him committed to an asylum — end of film.

Chennaoui is convincing as the middle-class doctor, but can't possibly make his conversion credible. Nadiha Kamel is more depressing than irresistible as the g.f. Italo cameraman Tonino Nardi provides the one soothing note with his mysterious lights and shadows, which give an exotic atmosphere to Andrea Crisanti's "1001 Nights" sets. —*Yung.*

Fucha
(The Job)
(POLISH-COLOR)

Cannes, May 13.
A Film Polski Production, Warsaw; world rights, Film Polski. Written and directed by Michal Dudziewicz, based on a work by Jan Himilsbach. Features entire cast. Camera (color), Grzegorz Kedzierski; music, Zygmunt Konieczny; sets and costumes, Andrzej Halinski; sound, Stanislawa Dobak; production manager, Anna Gryczynska, for the Rondo Unit, "Zespoly Filmowe." Reviewed at Cannes Film Fest (Critics Week), May 13, 1985. Running time: 65 MINS.
With: Jerzy Bonczak, Marian Kociniak, Bogdan Baer.

"The Job" is Michal Dudziewicz' debut feature after studying at the Polish Film Academy in Lodz and as part of the film unit under Wojciech Has, as well as working in television. Pic was selected for the Critics' Week due to its stylistic traits. Indeed, this is a quite representative sampling of Polish dry humor with touches of absurdity. Helmer Dudziewicz also admitted having cut some 10 minutes, so one can assume some lines and situations were a trifle too barbed for the officials in the export section of Film Polski.

Two quaint-looking stonecutters (right out of Beckett's "Waiting For Godot" or Roman Polanski's "Two Men And A Wardrobe") are requested by their foreman to deliver, with an aged truckdriver in a dilapidated vehicle, a funeral monument to a cemetery some 60 miles out of

Warsaw. Along the way they experience one absurdity after another: for example, the truck has no brakes and nearly runs over innocent pedestrians at a crossing.

Once at the cemetery to erect the monument for rich widow, they meet a serious gentleman at the gate who requests a moonlighting job: the duo are to aid in the erecting of a long-overdue monument to a hero of the Polish Revolution of 1830, Piotr Wysocki. Wysocki was exiled to Siberia for a time after the failure of the expedition and today is still honored in this backwater provincial town where he's buried.

It turns out that the "Didi and Gogo" stonecutters want to be paid a heavy stipened for their work, to which the apparent chairman of the town council agrees. Later, however, in a local inn to dine over the affair, it turns out the donor for the project is nothing more than a history teacher who also heads a private society interested in preserving the name of Wysocki at all costs. On the next morn, when the job is finished, the stone-cutters decide to take only half their pay while donating the other half to the memory of the Polish hero.

As they are about to depart, an elderly lady happens on the scene: she just might have made the acquaintance of the heroic Wysocki — for he was known in the area as a ladykiller. It's a neat closing touch to this absurd comedy. —*Holl.*

Skyhigh
(U.S.-COLOR)

Cannes, May 14.
An Omega Pictures presentation of a Nico Mastorakis film. Produced and directed by Mastorakis. Executive producer, Isabel Mastorakis. Features entire cast. Screenplay, Robert Gilliam, Fred C. Perry; camera (Eastmancolor), Andrew Bellis; editor, George Rosenberg; music, Denis Haines; art direction, Annie M. Papatolis; costumes, Alice Jonfield; sound, N. Le Lavia. Reviewed at Cannes (Market), May 13, 1985. (No MPAA Rating.) Running time: 100 MINS.
Les . . . . Daniel Hirsch
Bobby . . . . Clayton Norcross
Mick . . . . Frank Schultz
Sally . . . . Lauren Taylor
Joanna . . . . Janet Taylor
Stephanie . . . . Karen Verlaine
Boswell . . . . John Lawrence
Ovidoff . . . . Alan White

Combine a plot about some students on a trip to Greece with an inane tale involving the KGB and the CIA. Throw in some rock videos and shoot the whole thing cheaply under the unvarying Greek sky, and the result would be something like "Skyhigh," a flighty formula pic destined for quick playoff.

Only intriguing plot idea involves an audio tape with both hallucinogenic powers and the capacity to kill at certain frequencies. The phantasmagoric inserts which depict the tape's effect on listeners are well

achieved on video.

The rest is just daft. The invention falls into the hands of three college boys hunting girls on an Aegean cruise. They set out to deliver the tape to a safe place, with a gang of supposedly KGB, but actually CIA, thugs on their tail. Chase is an excuse for much action but, since no one gets hurt, little excitement is generated.

The three male actors give spirited enough performances in their stereotyped roles. The girls, however, were clearly chosen for their looks rather than acting ability. Technical credits are poor. — *Japa.*

Key Exchange
(U.S.-COLOR)

Cannes, May 15.
A 20th Century Fox release (U.S.) of an M-Square Entertainment/Ronald Winston production. Produced by Mitchell Maxwell, Paul Kurta. Exec producers, Michael Pochna, Winston. Co-exec producer, Peer Oppenheimer. Directed by Barnet Kellman. Features entire cast. Screenplay, Kevin Scott, Kurta, from the play by Kevin Wade; camera (Eastmancolor), Fred Murphy; exec in charge of production, Kenin M. Spivak; editor, Jill Savitt; production designer, David Gropman; original music, Mason Daring. Reviewed at Cannes (Market), May 14, 1985. (MPAA Rating: R.) Running time: 90 MINS.
Phillip Bailey . . . . Ben Masters
Lisa Simon . . . . Brooke Adams
Carabello . . . . Danny Aiello
Michael Fine . . . . Daniel Stern
April Fine . . . . Nancy Mette
David Slattery . . . . Tony Roberts
Frank Mars . . . . Seth Allen

Based upon Kevin Wade's off-Broadway play, "Key Exchange" is a charming little romantic comedy about the pitfalls of a mating game which scales no great heights but delivers enough yocks to rate as agreeable entertainment.

This droll item probably can count on moderate returns in the larger urban markets. Younger audiences will readily identify with the dilemma faced by the central characters: deciding when to get serious in a relationship, and they won't mind the salty language, flashes of female flesh, and rock 'n' roll soundtrack by Mason Daring.

In territories outside the U.S. where the theatrical biz is languishing, television and homevideo exploitation should pay reasonable dividends.

Helmer Barnet Kellman and leading players Ben Masters and Brooke Adams obviously know the material well: all toiled in the off-Broadway production.

Masters is a mystery novelist (never seeming to do any writing) who is smugly content with the "open relationship" he has going with Adams, the associate producer of a New York tv talk-show. He researches his detective books by accompanying pro gumshoe Danny Aiello on stakeouts, and when he's

not having the occasional dalliance with other girls, spends his leisure time cycling through Central Park with lawyer buddy Daniel Stern in preparation for a big bike race.

It all goes smoothly for Masters until Adams decides she wants a committed relationship, which means no fooling around, and an exchange of apartment keys. Masters is reluctant since he has seen Stern's marriage bust up after a few weeks. However, he goes along with it, until he lapses back into his old free-wheeling ways and Adams calls it off and demands her keys back.

Stern's wife Nancy Mette returns to the marital fold, nearly catching him out with a girl he picked up at a single bar (one of the pic's funniest scenes). Belatedly, Masters realizes he loves Adams, but she announces she is relocating to Los Angeles with smarmy talkshow host Tony Roberts, and Masters has to move fast (a hair-raising bike ride through Manhattan) to win her back.

Script is peppered with some smart lines and whimsical moments.

Adams, a real looker with tons of charm and style, and Masters turn in classy performances, and the supporting cast do their jobs well, in particular Aiello, whose collapse in an aerobics class is a riot.

Gotham Mayor Ed Koch pops up in a cameo as himself giving a curbside interview in which he gets in a plug for New York and his budget-balancing feat. —*Dogo.*

Richy Guitar
(WEST GERMAN-COLOR)

Cannes, May 17.
A Moviola Dietmar Buchmann/Michael Laux, Berlin. Written and directed by Michael Laux. Features entire cast. Camera (color), Hans-Günther Bucking, Siegmar Brüggenthies; music, Gazi Twist, Die Arzte, Nena, Motorische Reflexe, Plan B.; sets, Edwin Wengoborski, Petra Liebau; editor, Clarissa Ambach, Thomas Brandenburg. Reviewed at Cannes (Market), May 17, 1985. Running time: 90 MINS.
With: Jan Vetter, Dirk Felsenheimer, Hans Runge, Kristina Raschen, Ingrid van Bergen, Horst Pinnow.

On the Berlin Underground side, Michael Laux' "Richy Guitar" does score a few film buff points: the twist on the classic Hollywood title "Johnny Guitar" (the plots, however, are entirely different), the hot Berlin pop scene and the very backdrop of this magical city.

Nevertheless, Laux is aiming for a commercial audience and here is where he could use a scriptwriter and a dash of directorial pace to keep the viewer interested in the fate of the lead character, Richy Guitar, a down-on-his-luck guitarist trying to break into the local pop scene. Gradually, the lad does wed his talents to a band, and the required amplifiers find the group an audience. That group, by the way is to become "Die Arzte" (or "The Doctors"), one of Berlin's best known pop bands with a quite devoted following.

The ripest scenes in the pic have to do with music, the best one featuring the hottest pop singer in all of Germany at the moment: Nena, with her band guesting in Berlin at the time of the shooting.
— *Holl.*

Igor And The Lunatics
(U.S.-COLOR)

Cannes, May 14.
A Troma Team release. Produced by Jocelyn Beard and Billy Parolini. Features entire cast. Directed by Parolini, with additional scenes directed by Tom Doran and Brendan Faulkner. Screenplay, Beard, Parolini; camera (color), John Raugalis; editor, Parolini; special effects and makeup, Simon Deitch; music, Sonia Rutstein. Reviewed at Cannes (Market), May 13, 1985. (No MPAA Rating.) Running time: **84 MINS.**
With: Joseph Eero, Joe Niola, T. J. Michaels, Mary Ann Schacht.

An incompetent slasher film originally titled "Bloodshed,"

"Igor And The Lunatics" has a few entertaining sequences in its first 10 minutes, when it appears to be a madcap genre spoof. Unfortunately, picture loses its audience as soon as it changes register and becomes a simply amateurish rehash of horror clichés. Chances for more than fringe sales look dim, indeed.

Action opens in the late '60s, when a hippie cult living in the woods terrorizes townfolk by murdering girls in grisly ways, such as by tying them to logs and putting them through the sawmill. Bryon is their mad-eyed leader, Igor the leering, cackling butcher.

The police stage a raid on the commune and pack them off to jail. Action then shifts to present-day, when Bryon gets out of prison and assembles his henchmen, perpetrating even more gruesome slaughter on unsuspecting passersby. Gore remains suggested more than seen. Suspense is absent. Characters get cornier. Eventually a pretty redhead, Mary Ann, teams up with Tom and Hawk (Vietnam vet living a hermit's life in the woods) to stop the maniacs and rescue Tom's son. The final confrontation between the forces of good and evil has people jumping clumsily through windows and stabbing each other with anything at hand. Mary Ann drops her gun not once but twice and waits for the boys to save her.

Final twist shows how little audience is made to care who wins.
— *Yung.*

Pray For Death
(U.S.-COLOR)

Cannes, May 18.
A Pray For Death Prods. film. Produced by Don Van Atta. Exec producers, Moshe Diamant, Sunil Shah and Moshe Barkat. Directed by Gordon Hessler. Stars Sho Kosugi. Screenplay, James Booth; camera (color), Roy H. Wagner; editor, Bill Butler; music, Thomas Chase, Steve Rucker; martial arts choreography, Sho Kosugi; special-effects, Wayne Beauchamp; costumes, Ted Sewell. Reviewed at Cannes (Market), May 17, 1985. (No MPAA Rating.) Running time: **123 MINS.**
Akira .... Sho Kosugi
Reiko .... Donna Kei Benz
Limehouse .... James Booth
Dalmain .... Norman Burton
Newman .... Michael Constantine
Also with: Mathew Faison, Alan Amiel, Kane Kosugi, Shane Kosugi, Woody Watson, Charles Gruber, Jude Stephen, Jerry Young, Nik Hagler, Parley Baer, Chris Wycliff, Caroline Williams, Rodney Rincon.

"Pray For Death" is a lively chop-socky actioner that should please martial arts audiences in all territories, as virtuous Japanese emigrants battle with forces of evil and corruption in the States. Though item runs over two hours, interest never flags as there's a nice mix of homespun humor, nasty violence and vigilante heroics .

Sho Kosugi and his half-American wife decide to leave Japan with their two young kids and start a Japanese restaurant in a large American city. Unbeknownst to them, a band of crooks and venal cops have hidden a priceless bracelet under the boards of a deserted storage room. They think honest Kosugi has it, and commence to hound and terrorize him and his family, using a variety of brutal means that range from hit-and-run driving to rape and murder.

The tension builds up nicely, culminating in the former ninja seeking revenge for the outrages perpetrated upon his innocent family. Picture ends with Kosugi deciding not to return to Japan in deference to his murdered wife's wishes.

Pic has good production values, excellent special effects and martial arts sequences. — *Besa.*

Red Heat
(W. GERMAN-U.S.-COLOR)

Cannes, May 16.
A TAT Film production in association with Aida United and Intl. Screen Inc. Produced by Ernst R. von Theumer. Executive producer, Monica Teuber; associate producer, Paul Hellerman; presented by Arnold Kopelson and TAT Filmproductions. Directed by Robert Collector. Stars Linda Blair, Sylvia Kristel. Screenplay, Collector, Gary Drucker; camera (color) Wolfgang Dickmann; editor, Anthony Redman; casting, Annette Benson; art director, Livia Kovats; music, Tangerine Dream; sound, Hans Kunz; special effects, Helmut Graef; makeup, Britta Kraft. Reviewed at Cine Arcades, Cannes (Market), May 15, 1985. (No MPAA Rating.) Running time: **115 MINS.**
Christine Carlson .... Linda Blair
Sophia .... Sylvia Kristel
Hedda .... Sue Kiel
Mike .... William Ostrander
Also with: Albert Fortell, Elisabeth Volkmann, Herb Andress, Barbara Spitz.

"Red Heat," has enough ingredients to make it a big hit with less discriminating mass audiences. Though top-draw stars Linda Blair and Sylvia Kristel downplay the nudity, film is steeped in an erotic atmosphere which should tittillate the libido of male audiences. A spy story, prison brutality, lesbianism and some action sequences are further commercial enhancements.

Yarn concerns a Western femme spy who has just returned from East Germany and is resting in a pretty spa (item was actually shot in Yugoslavia). The spy is kidnaped by East Germans, along with Blair who just happens to be in the wrong place at the wrong time. The two girls are smuggled across the border and thrown into a woman's prison. After interrogation, Blair finally agrees to confess to working for the CIA on the promise of being allowed to return to the West. Instead she gets a three-year sentence.

In prison, a group of inmates, led by Kristel, terrorizes the other girls, humiliates them, brutalizes some and, in cahoots with the warden, obliges them to have sex with the leaders. Meanwhile, intercut with the prison story, is that of Blair's army boyfriend back in West Germany, who, after meeting with total indifference from the U.S. authorities, decides to organize his own rescue operation.

With rather unbelievable ease and simplicity, the boyfriend and his buddy get across the border as tourists and enlist a commando, armed to the teeth, which then runs through some sort of tunnel which leads directly to a trap door right in a basement pantry of the prison, secured only by a padlock. The commandos shoot their way in, rescue the girls, and succeed, somewhat incredibly, in making it back to the West.

Good production values, fast pacing and the aforementioned thesps make pic a natural for the grind circuits, despite the often clumsy dialog. — *Besa.*

Flesh And Bullets
(U.S.-COLOR)

Cannes, May 14.
A Hollywood Intl. Film Corp. release. Produced by Efrain Tobalina for Hollywood Intl. Written and directed by Tobalina. Camera (color), Tobalina; art director, Gloria Nakamura; editor, Tobalina; music, Bullets. Reviewed at Cannes (Market), May 11, 1985. (No MPAA Rating.) Running time: 90 MINS.
Roy Hunter .... Glenn McCay
Gail Hunter .... Susan Silvers
Jeff Borden .... Mic Morrow
Dolores Borden .... Cydney Hill
Also with: Cornel Wilde, Cesar Romero, Yvonne DeCarlo, Aldo Ray.

"Flesh And Bullets" is a quickie thriller in the home movie league. Apart from a catchy title, amateurish effort doesn't have much going for it. Plot, thesping, sets and camerawork have to struggle to come up to adequate level; mostly they hover below the line. Much-flaunted "special performances" by old-timers Cornel Wilde, Cesar Romero, Yvonne De Carlo and Aldo Ray turn out to be disconnected flash cameos that look tacked on as an afterthought.

Roy Hunter (Glenn McKay) and Jeff Borden (Mic Morrow) are two young divorced men suffering from the same malaise: alimony, child support and paying off the mortgage on houses and cars that now belong to their ex-wives. When they meet in Las Vegas and tell each other their troubles, they crib a solution from "Strangers On A Train" — they'll kill each other's wives so the police will find no way to trace the murders.

To convince each other (and viewers) they mean business, frail-looking Jeff describes how he shot a pair of wrestlers who raped him; burly Roy how he brutally murdered women and children in Vietnam. Their manhood established, script moves on to the womenfolk.

Far from finding Roy's ex-mate Dolores (Cydney Hill) a frigid shrew, Jeff falls in love at first bedding. Ditto Roy, for whom Jeff's sportive ex Gail (Susan Silvers) is too sensually fulfilling to bump off right away. Pic meanders while they hesitate awkwardly between plotting mayhem and hopping in the sack. Filmmaker Efrain Tobalina (a.k.a. Carlos Tobalina or Troy Benny when helming porno films) misses chance after chance to build a little suspense. — *Yung.*

The Boys Next Door
(U.S.-COLOR)

Cannes, May 13.
A New World Pictures and Republic Entertainment Intl. presentation. Produced by Keith Rubinstein and Sandy Howard. Executive producers, Mel Pearl and Don Levin. Directed by Penelope Spheeris. Features entire cast. Screenplay, Glen Morgan, James Wong; camera (CFI color), Arthur Albert. Reviewed at Olympia 6, Cannes (Market), May 13, 1985. (MPAA Rating: R.) Running time: 88 MINS.
Roy Alston .... Maxwell Caulfield
Bo Richards .... Charlie Sheen
Detective Mark
Woods .... Christopher McDonald
Detective Ed Hanley .... Hank Garrett
Angie .... Patti D'Arbanville
Chris .... Paul C. Dancer

A before-credits sequence of "The Boys Next Door" helps explain the motives for making the film.

Stills are shown of notorious

figures in the U.S. who, for no apparent reason, have gone on killing sprees. One commentator suggests young criminals today are so brutalized by their own upbringing that they can't see other people as human beings.

Unfortunately the film itself doesn't live up to the expectations. Even if intentions are worthy, it emerges glib and uninvolving.

Two alienated and disturbed 18-year-olds Roy Alston (Maxwell Caulfield) and Bo Richards (Charlie Sheen) graduate from a small high school in California. Before taking up factory jobs, they decide to have a weekend in L.A. in which "anything goes."

An eruption of violence begins with the brutal beating of a gas station attendant. It ends with one boy shooting the other as the police close in on the pair in a shopping mall. In between there are beatings and killings of a homosexual, a young couple and a woman.

One of the problems with "The Boys Next Door" is the casting. With conventional clean-cut good looks, Caulfield and Sheen clearly resemble the title, but they fail to adequately project the "angry stuff" within. This results in one-dimensional characters with whom it is difficult to become dramatically involved. —*Nic.*

On The Edge
(U.S.-COLOR)

Cannes, May 13.

An Alliance Films production. Produced by Jeffrey Hayes and Rob Nilsson. Written and directed by Rob Nilsson. Stars Bruce Dern, Pam Grier. Camera (color), Stefan Czapsky; art director, Steve Burns; editor, Richard Harkness; sound, Bob Shoup; music, Herb Pilhofer. Reviewed at Les Ambassades, Cannes (Market), May 13, 1985. (No MPAA Rating.) Running time: **92 MINS.**

Wes Holman	Bruce Dern
Cora	Pam Grier
Flash Holman	Bill Bailey
Owen Riley	Jim Haynie
Elmo	John Marley

Director Rob Nilsson won the 1979 Camera D'Or at Cannes with a film he codirected with John Hanson, "Northern Lights," about the early 1900s farmers' populist movement in the U.S.

"On The Edge" is his first feature since then. It has taken a long time to get together, and falls on uneasy ground between art film and commercial enterprise.

Story concerns 44-year-old Wes Holman (Bruce Dern) and his bid to win one of the toughest and most demanding foot races, the Cielo Sea run across a northern California Mountain range.

As a young man, Wes had extraordinary talent, but was banned for life from competition after being caught accepting appearance money for racing — a violation of amateur running rules.

His bid to redeem a life he considers one of frustration and failure brings him back into close contact with his former coach Elmo (the late John Marley), his father Flash (Bill Bailey), and one-time lover Cora (Pam Grier).

The race is his catalyst; the result, his catharsis.

Despite some fine, glistening camerawork from Stefan Czapsky, storyline development and performances are too precious.

Dern's interpretation of Wes' personal angst is difficult to respond to, not just because a middle-aged man's concern about wasting his life is tricky territory. The trouble lies in too little motivation being provided for the obsession.

The film also delivers an overdose of lovemaking between Dern and Grier that fails to advance the drama of the piece. Overall, the acting lacks spark.

Ultimately, too, there are too many obvious echoes from a blockbuster like "Chariots Of Fire" — in imagery, music and final feeling — to allow "On The Edge" to achieve its own delicate balance. —*Nic.*

Mystère Alexina
(The Alexina Mystery)
(FRENCH-COLOR)

Paris, May 8.

An F. Distribution Associé release of Cinéastes Associés/TF 1 Films coproduction. Produced and directed by René Feret. Features entire cast. Screenplay, Feret and Jean Gruault, based on the memoirs of Adelaide Herculine Barbin; camera (color), Bernard Zitzermann; editor, Ariane Boeglin; art director, Georges Stoll. Reviewed at CNC, Paris, May 7, 1985. (In Un Certain Regard Section of Cannes Film Festival). Running time: **83 MINS.**

Alexina/Camille	Philippe Vuillemin
Sara	Valérie Stroh
Madam Avril	Véronique Silver
Armand	Bernard Freyd
Marie Avril	Marianne Basler
Priest	Pierre Vial
Dr. Chesnet	Philippe Clevenot

"Mystère Alexina" is a modest but effective dramatization of a bizarre 19th century case history: that of a French hermaphrodite, driven to suicide by bigoted and uncomprehending provincial society. The script by writer-producer-director René Feret, aided by the scenaristic experience of Jean Gruault (who notably collaborated on François Truffaut's "Wild Child"), is based on the extant diary of the protagonist, born Adelaide Herculine Barbin.

Physiologically speaking, Barbin was not a hermaphrodite at all, but a normally developed male, who was the victim of excessive parental prudery and erroneous birth certificate registry ("One doesn't look at such things!", explains the dumbfounded mother over two decades

later at a medical inquiry.

Brought up in a convent and various boarding schools for young girls, Barbin had no inkling of "his" difference from those around him, and was disturbed by nascent sexual desires for another student.

Feret and Gruault choose to begin the film with the arrival of the adult protagonist — familiarly called Alexina — in a provincial boarding school were "she" has found a post as teacher. Alexina's homely flat-chested timidity seems a guarantee of safeguarded morality.

Scandal erupts when Alexina and the pretty young schoolmarm he rooms with (their beds are separated by a thin curtain) become lovers. Chased from the premises, Alexina legally earns recognition as a man, changing his name to Camille (in France, both a male and female Christian name) and returns to claim his sweetheart.

Yet he is too conditioned by his feminine upbringing to impose his will and is condemned by his physical frailty to menial labors (a couple managing a hotel take advantage of the situation by hiring him as a domestic — at women's wages). When his lover is forcibly married off to another, Camille, reduced to desperate loneliness, ends his life.

Feret didn't have the means to reconstruct this tragedy in all its psychological and social ramifications, but he does not betray the essential cruel poignancy of the subject. The intimate scope is well rendered notable by Bernard Zitzermann's excellent lensing.

Pic's trump aesthetic choice was in casting a male actor in the title role: Philippe Vuillemin, a well-known cartoonist, who's somewhat effeminate appearance enforces the character's psycho-sexual ambiguity. Feret had originally thought of Isabelle Huppert for the part, but was happily persuaded to opt for this more logical approach.

— *Len.*

April Fool's Day
(U.S.-COLOR)

Cannes, May 18.

A Vestron Entertainment presentation of a Steve Minasian and Dick Randall Production. Produced by Minasian and Randall. Directed, scripted by George Dugdale, Mark Ezra and Peter Litten. Features entire cast. Camera (uncredited color), Alan Pudney; music, Harry Manfredini; editor, Jim Connock; special effects, Peter Litten. Reviewed at Cannes (Market), May 17, 1985. (No MPAA Rating.) Running time: **89 MINS.**

Carol	Caroline Munro
Marty	Simon Scuddamore
Skip	Carmine Iannoccone
Stella	Donna Yeager
Joe	Gary Martin
Nancy	Sally Cross

Also with: Kelly Baker, Billy Hartman, Michael Saffran, Josephine Scandi, John Segal.

A formula picture in the by now rather tired tradition of "Halloween" and "Friday The 13th," "April Fool's Day" starts slowly, develops predictably, and ends disappointingly. It's for easy-to-please audiences only. This one's a Vestron made-for under its new "Entertainment" banner.

Opening 15 minutes or so plays like a kind of "Porky's," in a protracted locker-room scene in which nered Marty (Simon Scuddamore), who thinks the buxom Carol (Caroline Munro) has the hots for him, gets literally caught with his pants down in front of the entire class; he forgot it was April Fool's Day. A subsequent trick involving Marty in a chemistry lab backfires resulting in a fire and the kid getting a faceful of acid.

A few (unspecified) years pass, and Doddsville County High has long been closed down, when Marty's former classmates gather for an April 1 reunion. They quickly find themselves locked inside the drab building, to be slaughtered one by one, via poison, stabbing, acid bath, electrocution (during the sex act), hanging, drowning and being crushed under a car, until only Carol is left alive to be chased down the endless corridors by the deranged Marty wearing a mask and a jester's cap and bells.

Fadeout has it all a part of Marty's nightmare, not the kind of finale likely to send 'em home happy. It took a trio of writer/directors to concoct this lame affair, which is technically okay, and has a few yukky gore effects, but is generally the mixture we've seen umpteen times before. Acting is poor, and the script is filled with risible lines. In other words, this one's no joke.—*Strat.*

Mission Kill
(U.S.-COLOR)

Cannes, May 16.

A Media Home Entertainment presentation. Produced and directed by David Winters. Screenplay, Maria Dante; camera (Deluxe color), Tom Denove; editor, Ned Humphreys; music, Jesse Frederick, Jeff Koz; executive producers, Howard Goldfarb, Andre Djaoui. Reviewed at New Palais, Cannes (Market), May 16, 1985. (No MPAA Rating.) Running time: **93 MINS.**

Cooper	Robert Ginty
Sidney	Merete Van Kamp
Harry	Cameron Mitchell
Borghini	Harry Darrow
Bingo	Sandy Baron
Revolutionary Girl	Olivia D'Abo

John Wayne gets a lot of mention in "Mission Kill," a film with slight Green Beret connections. If he was still around, the Duke probably would be pleased to be out of it.

The plot, subject to sudden dead ends and equally sudden appearances and disappearances of characters for no good reason, centers on Cooper (Robert Ginty), a demolition expert in an eastern U.S. city.

He visits his Green Beret buddy Harry (Cameron Mitchell) and decides to accompany him on a job smuggling arms to freedom fighters in a mythical Latin American country, Santa Maria.

When Harry gets killed by government troops, Cooper decides to carry through the mission himself.

Technically, the film looks okay. The problems lie in lack of plot coherence and casting. Ginty does not convey the strong macho image the central character demands.

Sidney (Merete Van Camp) is one of the characters lost sight of during the film. After an early appearance as a mysterious blond who hitches a ride with Cooper, she later turns up as a shadowy spy, and, finally, as a kind of Evita.

Sandy Baron, as Bingo, the news agency man in the hot spot, is a caricature of bizarre proportions.

"Mission Kill" probably is solid enough for video material, having been funded by homevideo outfit MHE. There it stops. —*Nic.*

Witchfire
(U.S.-COLOR)

Cannes, May 13.

A Panda Movie Co. presentation. Produced by James R. Orr. Written and directed by Vincent J. Privitera. Associate producer, Shelley Winters; camera (color), Mike Delahonssey; editor, Greg McGee; music, Dave Puchan. Reviewed at Olympia 6, Cannes (Market), May 13, 1985. Running time: **100 MINS.**
Lydia . . . . Shelley Winters
Haddie . . . . Frances De Sapio
Julietta . . . . Corrine Chateau
The Hunter . . . . Gary Swanson

"Witchfire," (which lensed under the title "A Sonnet For The Hunter") presumably is meant to be a horror film in that tradition of grand melodrama perfected in Robert Aldrich's Joan Crawford-/Bette Davis vehicle of 1962, "What Ever Happened To Baby Jane?"

It doesn't make it, although Shelley Winters' florid performance is good for a bellylaugh or two.

The plot centers on three mental hospital escapes, led by Lydia (Winters), who believe they are witches. They trap an unsuspecting hunter (Gary Swanson) while hiding out in a deserted Texas mansion.

Much unintentionally amusing cat-and-mouse action, involving hunter and huntresses, explodes in a flaming finale bereft of credibility and coherence.

Swanson's expression while trapped by the trio is one of pained amazement.

This is not surprising given the ladies around him — Francesca De Sapia's Haddie, pale and panting, and Corrine Chateau's Julietta, languid yet lusty.

However, it is Winters' picture, for what that might be worth, with such memorable lines as: "I may be insane but I'm not stupid ..." and, "I'll get rats to gnaw your face..."
— *Nic.*

When Nature Calls
(U.S.-COLOR)

Cannes, May 16.

A Troma release of a Lloyd Kaufman and Michael Herz presentation. Produced by Frank Vitale and Charles Kaufman. Directed by Charles Kaufman. Features entire cast. Screenplay, Charles Kaufman and Straw Weisman; camera (color), Michael Spera; editor, Michael Jacobi; music, Arthur Custer; production design, Susan Kaufman. Reviewed at Arcade 1, Cannes (Market), May 16, 1985. (MPAA Rating: R.) Running time: **82 MINS.**
With: David Orange, Barbara Marineau, Nicky Beim, Tina Marie Staino, David Strathairn; guest appearances by Willie Mays, G. Gordon Liddy, Myron Cohen and Squirt, the killer poodle.

"When Nature Calls," filmed in 1982 as "The Outdoorsters," is hyped as "the totally out of control comedy." There is wisdom in those words.

Very, very loosely structured, the picture includes its own preview, as well as previews of other coming attractions, like "Baby Bullets" — "the only movie that has to be changed four times a day!"

The feature film, within the film, so to speak, is "The Outdoorsters," featuring the Van Waspishes family, Grey, Barb and their two children, Bambi and Billy.

They decide to escape the hassles of civilization and begin a new life in the great outdoors. They are befriended by a part-time savage, Weejun, a bear and other assorted animals, before it all becomes too, too tough.

It's hardly bellylaugh stuff, but it might just be the kind of material for family night on homevideo. Film was released domestically on a regional basis starting last fall.
—*Nic.*

Scemo Di Guerra
(Madman At War)
(ITALIAN-FRENCH-COLOR)

Cannes, May 19.

Produced by Pio Angeletti, Adriano De Micheli and Claude Berri for Intl. Dean Film (Rome) and Renn Prods. — Films A2 (Paris). Directed by Dino Risi. Stars Coluche, Beppe Grillo. Screenplay, Age, Scarpelli, Risi, based on "The Libyan Desert" by Mario Tobino; camera (Telecolor), Giorgi Di Battista; art director, Giuseppe Mangano; editor, Alberto Callitti, Arlette Langmann; music, Guido and Maurizio De Angelis. Reviewed at the Cannes Film Festival (In Competition), May 18, 1985. Running time: **108 MINS.**
Oscar Pilli . . . . Coluche
Lt. Marcello Lupi . . . . Beppe Grillo
Maj. Bellucci . . . . Bernard Blier
Lt. Boda . . . . Fabio Testi

A bittersweet, surprisingly restrained little comedy, "Madman At War" deserves a special niche in Dino Risi's recent output and in the current Italo comedy season. Unfortunately, in a year of slim pickings, it was the victim of overreaching and in the context of Cannes' competition looked slight and out of place. The gentle brand of humor and actionless plot of this Italo-French coprod could have a rocky time finding an audience.

Pic is based on Mario Tobino's novel "The Libyan Desert" and set during the war in an Italian Medical unit, where the doctors while away the time waiting for the front to draw closer. Young Second Lt. Marcello Lupi (Beppe Grillo), an aspiring psychiatrist, has ample material to study in the camp's resident loony, Capt. Oscar Pilli. Pilli, played by Coluche with likable cunning, is a bull-necked ox with glinting eyes. His bizarre habits are harmless and indulgent, like spreading honey on his body to attract flies, naked sin-worshipping, and stealing sunglasses. His idols are Mussolini and Alida Valli; his sole love, his mother. It's only when Pilli is made camp commander that he becomes dangerous enough to complain about. After he butchers a soldier on the operating table, the other medics start lobbying to get him transferred.

Risi uses a light hand with the tale, which is underpinned by a bitter note. Far from the grotesque war horrors of "Mash" or "Catch 22," "Madman" remains within the limits of the sadly probable. When Pilli's incompetence becomes a menace, he is in due time removed by the army authorities, who are reasonable types, like the rest of the medics. The lovesick Maj. Bellucci (Bernard Blier) may have his idiosyncrasies, but basically Pilli re-

mains an isolated madman in a routine war.

This small-scale drama isn't really dramatic at all, whether out of directorial inertia or because of the way scenes are downplayed. Pilli's first exhibition of tyrannical cruelty, when he makes Lupi run 40 laps in the blazing sun over some imaginary offense, is a tired sequence that conveys nothing. Much more successful is the operating room scene, where the casual horror of a needless death is heightened by film's offhand tone.

Sidestepping metaphor, soft-pedaling the anti-militarist angle and even shying away from sentiment, Risi casts a gently commiserating look at his misfit, whose infantile psychosis is creditably rendered by popular French comedian Coluche. Beppe Grillo, himself a gifted standup comic, plays the straight man Lupi with measured aplomb and subs Risi (once a psychiatry student, too) as on-screen observer.—*Yung.*

Vergesst Mozart
(Forget Mozart)
(WEST GERMAN-COLOR)

Cannes, May 18.

An OKO Film Karel Dirka production, Munich. Directed by Slavo Luther. Features entire cast. Screenplay, Zev Mahler; camera (color), Joseph Simocic; sound, Milan Bor; music, Wolfgang Amadeus Mozart; executive producer, Harald Kügler. Reviewed at Cannes (Market), May 17, 1985. Running time: **93 MINS.**

Mozart . . . . Tidof
Pergen . . . . Armin Mueller-Stahl
Konstanze . . . . Catarina Raacke
Von Swieten . . . . Wolfgang Preiss
Schikaneder . . . . Uwe Ochsenknecht
Salieri . . . . Winfried Glatzeder
Magdalena . . . . Katja Flint
Servant . . . . Jan Biczycki
Physician . . . . Kurt Weinzieri

Far and away the best of the German productions on display at Cannes outside the official selection, Slavo Luther's "Forget Mozart" takes up, as it were, where Milos Forman's "Amadeus" left off. In fact, it was filmed in Prague and apparently made full use of the sets and trappings left over after that Oscar winner left town.

"Forget Mozart" comes across as a detective thriller. It's the day of Mozart's death (Dec. 5, 1791), and the friends of the immortal but capricious composer are gathered around his deathbed. Then the head of the secret police decides to hold a hearing on just who among those present is guilty of Mozart's death.

Once the interrogation begins, each of the witnesses tells his story in flashbacks, so the tale unwinds in bits and pieces. Among those who testify are Konstanze, his wife; von Swieten, the head of the local Masonic Lodge and one of Mozart's benefactors; Schikaneder, the text collaborator on Mozart's operas ("The Marriage Of Figaro"); Salieri, the jealous intriguer at court; Magdalena, one of Mozart's fleeting loves; and an attending servant and doctor.

The police inspector desires to get behind the motives for the death of Mozart on the assumption that the gifted composer might have been murdered, instead of dying a natural death. However, even though everyone in the room reveals reason enough for having done the foul deed, the death itself in the end remains a mystery. But here's the rub: Mozart is shown as an individual with a premonition of his own death as well as possessing an extraordinary lust for life.

This is not only a great idea for a film, but also a fascinating and fast-paced exposé from beginning to end. What's more, most of it is based on fact: the Viennese court and Salzburg under the Catholic archbishop were, indeed, bastions of intrigue, where the young genius made more enemies than friends. Add to this the fears and suspicions generated by the French Revolution (to say nothing of the new sciences), and the sure elements of a thriller are all there.

The central figure, Mozart, is depicted as a contradiction of strength and weakness, courage and fear, with a fidelity to his musical gifts as well as a lust for the pleasures of life. The Mozart of the opera fans and "Amadeus" buffs may feel themselves somewhat betrayed by this unique factual-fantasy approach to a beloved genius, but this is exactly the spark the team of scripter Mahler, helmer Luther, and producer Dirka are out to ignite.
— *Holl.*

Kaminsky
(WEST GERMAN-COLOR)

Cannes, May 15.
A coproduction of Panorama Film, Berlin, and Deininger & Stumpf, Schwäbisch-Gmünd. Written and directed by Michael Lähn. Features entire cast. Camera (color), Jörg Seidl; music, Robert C. Detree; sets, Georg von Kieseritzki; costumes, Maria Schicker; editor, Camilla Bernetti; production manager, Klaus Sungen. Reviewed at Cannes (Market), May 14, 1985. Running time: **90 MINS.**
With: Klaus Löwitsch (Rolf Kaminsky), Hannelore Elsner (his wife), Beate Finckh (Renate), Alexander Radszun (Dieter Stecker).

One of the best of the New Ger-

man films to emerge this season, "Kaminsky" (formerly titled "Kaminsky's Night") is Michael Lähn's debut feature after working for nearly a decade on tv productions. In fact, the pic's only drawback is that the images are wedded to the usual closeup tv format. With a bit more attention to space and camera movement, this might have been a commercial as well as a critical achievement.

The setting is a police station. Two officers, Kaminsky and Stecker, have been shunted to the side, and Kaminsky moves about his job on this hot steaming night like a caged animal. He also suspects his buddy on the beat to be having an affair with his wife, but it emerges during the ongoing encounter that the reasons for it are simply dislike for the brutal Kaminsky himself. This brutality forms the action for the evening — and the film.

A young prostitute is turned over to the policemen. She has a weak heart and dies in the course of a rape committed by Kaminsky in order to get even with both Stecker and his wife. This leads to a showdown between the two men, one a brute, the other a coward, and a tough ending for everyone in the four-person drama.

Klaus Löwitsch (currently on-screen Stateside in "Gotcha!") as the cop passed over in life and now making his last stand gives a strong performance, as do all the principals. "Kaminsky" already has been picked up for fests on the upcoming circuit. —*Holl.*

Dreams Come True
(U.S.-COLOR)

Cannes, May 16.
A Troma Team release. Produced by Carlton J. Albright. Directed by Max Kalmanowicz. Stars Michael Sanville, Stephanie Shuford. Screenplay, Kalmanowicz, Albright, Stephen Kinjerski; camera (color), John Drake; editor, Susan Medaglia, Susana Estellano; music, Spooner. Reviewed at Cannes (Market), May 15, 1985. (MPAA Rating: R.) Running time: **90 MINS.**
Lee . . . . .Michael Sanville
Robin . . . . .Stephanie Shuford

A young couple discovers they have the ability to physically project themselves anywhere in the world while they're asleep. Proclaiming itself the first sensual comedy about astral projection, "Dreams Come True" is an off-beat low-budgeter with a lot of ideas, some better handled than others. Helmer Max Kalmanowicz (whose 1980 horror pic "The Children" is excerpted in one sequence) shines chiefly in the fantasy and special effects departments, faltering on the sensual and the comic. Though material sometimes gets out of control pic is watchable and mostly entertaining, and could find its way onto fringe

teen markets with special handling.

Lee (Michael Sanville) has a rough, dangerous job in a factory where he's under the constant threat of being laid off. He also has a paralyzed mother at home to take care of. Robin (Stephanie Shuford) is a young nurse with an unhappy past who gets away from the world by going on solitary camping expeditions. Together they discover the best escape of all: "soul traveling" while they dream. This hereditary talent allows them to leave their bodies and dine in a Paris bistro, melting into thin air when the bill arrives. They also spend a night in an amusement park, ride a hot-air balloon, and revisit old attics in Salem, Mass. There a dusty tome warns them of the risk soul travelers run if they die while they're on a trip, are suddenly awakened, etc. Oddly, after introducing this caution, pic doesn't do much with the suspense angle; at least we're never convinced Lee and Robin are in serious peril.

The one surprise comes when Lee uses his powers to rob a local bank under the nose of a dumbfounded guard, and his mother suddenly steps in supernaturally to put him back on the straight and narrow.

Pic is interspersed with frank love-making scenes between the leads which are honest, inoffensive and not particularly erotic. Like the characters' down-to-earth backgrounds, the love scenes show Lee and Robin are just a couple of normal kids who have weird powers. Thesps are passable actors, likeable and convincing. Fantasy sequences always kick off with a pretty optical effect of electronic silhouettes dancing through space, the signal that astral hijinks are coming up. Pop score by Spooner is a plus. — *Yung.*

King Of The Streets
(U.S.-COLOR)

Cannes, May 13.
A Shapiro Entertainment release of a Bentsvi-Hunt-Coe production. Produced by Yakov Bentsvi, Edward Coe. Executive producer, Edward Coe. Coproducers, Shaul Yaron, Noam and Rony Schwartz and Barry Pearson. Directed by Edward Hunt. Screenplay, Hunt, Ruben Gordon, Steven Shoenberg and Barry Pearson; editor, Thomas Fucci; music, Contraband. Reviewed at Les Ambassades, Cannes (Market), May 13, 1985. Running time: **100 MINS.**
Buddy .Brett Clark
Laura . . . . .Pamela Saunders
Mr. One . . . . .Reggie DeMorton

Here's yet another example of an evident low budgeter that lacks the wit to spoof the genre of a man from another planet come to rid the world of evil.

Within moments of touching ground in a burst of flames, he encounters a black drug dealer who beats up women and uses them to

corrupt every policeman around. However, production values are so cheap that the drug dealer, who is shown with lots of money, lives in an apartment that from the inside looks like low rent writ large.

The stranger, played woodenly by Brett Clark, and handed such flat lines as, "I must defeat a great evil" and "When I use force, my powers decrease" displays the power to heal the sick but not himself when he is wounded by gunfire.

There's a sweet innocent girl, natch, they fall in love, and when the drug dealer is killed, the stranger leaves for his planet without her. The pic's running time seems twice as long as its 100 minutes.

Some sets, built of models, give off an amateur look. Direction is bland as are the pacing and camerawork. Planetary beings seem to be a specialty of director Ed Hunt who previously did "Starship Invasions."

For the most part, the actors appear to be comatose. No fun in this one, with no snazzy tricks or special powers exhibited. It might play on paycable, and theatrical in non-discriminating sectors. Four script writers and seven producers were involved, obviously a case of too many cooks but no chef. —*Adil.*

A Strange Love Affair
(DUTCH-B&W)

Cannes, May 20.
A CinéTé-All'Arts Ent. BV production. Executive producer, by Cees Kasander. Produced by Willem Thijssen, Linda van Tulden. Written and directed by Eric de Kuyper, Paul Verstraten. Features entire cast. Camera (b&w), Henri Alékan; art director, Ben van Os; editor, Ton de Graaff; sound, Miguel Rejas; costumes, Dien van Stralen. Reviewed at Star Cinema, Cannes (Market), May 19, 1985. Running time: **92 MINS.**
Michael . . . . .Howard Hensel
Jim .Karl Scheydt
Chris . . . . .Sep van Kampen
Ann .Pascale Petit
Linda .Lieke Leo
(English dialog)

"A Strange Love Affair" is a film made for a very specific audience, the gay film-buff set. Outside that audience, there may be admirers for the beautiful grey-toned black and white photography of veteran Henri Alékan, which evokes the films of the '30s, and for the film's knowing inclusion of famous film references. There are fest and cinémathèque possibilities, but commercially pic will have to play in the right theaters in gay centers to pick up any cash.

Story involves a three-sided love affair between Michael, an English teacher living in Holland, Chris, one of his pupils, and Jim, Chris' father and a former love of Michael. There are a couple of women in the film, but they take a back seat. The romance is played out against a myriad of film references. Michael and Chris are first attracted when the former is teaching his class about Nicholas Ray's "Johnny Guitar;" later, after they've kissed, they enjoy a silent dinner listening to the soundtrack of the climax of "Now Voyager."

Pic is stylishly made and has an ethereal quality about it that keeps the viewer reasonably charmed. Co-director Eric de Kuyper previously scored on the fest circuit with "Casta Diva" (1982) and "Naughty Boys" (1983). —*Strat.*

Up Your Anchor
(ISRAELI-COLOR)

Cannes, May 17.
A Cannon Group presentation. Produced by Menahem Golan and Yoram Globus. Directed by Dan Wolman. Features entire cast. Screenplay, Eli Tabor, Wolman; camera (color), Ilan Rosenberg; associate producer, Isaac Kol; editor, Roy Taylor. Reviewed at New Palais, Cannes (Market), May 17, 1985. (No MPAA Rating.) Running time: **82 MINS.**
Benji .... Yetach Katzur
Huey .... Zachi Noy
Donna .... Deborah Keidar
Alberto .... Joseph Shiloah

"Up Your Anchor," subtitled Lemon Popsicle 6 (for those in the know) is a light-weight Israeli youth skin flick dubbed into American.

It has a flavor that could be palatable to some sections of the youth video market — gross though that taste would seem to be.

The story, which is just thin camouflage for periodic bouts of sexual excess, centers on two unlikely young studs, Benji (Yetach Katzur) and Huey (Zachi Noy) with one thing on their minds.

They take jobs on a cruise ship which involves them in mayhem, contraband, sex — and a touch of romance for one of them.

With music out of the 1950s, from the likes of Chubby Checker and Little Richard, "Up Your Anchor" has the bobbysox style of unzippered leather.

It also suggests (not unworthily), with the lard-like Huey, that being overweight is no handicap to scoring. — *Nic.*

Light Blast
(A Colpi Di Luce)
(ITALIAN-COLOR)

Cannes, May 20.
An Overseas Filmgroup rleease. Produced by Galliano Juso and Achille Manzotti. Stars Erik Estrada. Directed by Enzo G. Castellari. Screenplay, Tito Carpi, Enzo G. Castellari; camera (color), Sergio D'Offizi; editor, Jeffrey Bogart; music, Guido and Maurizio De Angelis. Reviewed at Cannes (Market), May 18, 1985. Running time: **85 MINS.**

Ronn Warren .... Erik Estrada
Yuri Soboda .... Michael Pritchard
With: Thomas Moore, Peggy Rowe, Bob Taylor.

Italo action king Enzo G. Castellari here teams up with "Chips" star Erik Estrada in a watchable genre piece shot in San Francisco. With its nonstop car chases, spectacular explosions and a death-a-minute pace, "Light Blast" should be a hot seller on the actioner market.

Mad scientist Yuri Soboda (Michael Pritchard), sacked by the university for performing dangerous experiments in the lab, has created a deadly laser weapon cable of blowing up entire city blocks at a time. The FBI is stymied, the mayor alarmed, the President indifferent. Inspector Ronn Warren, played by Estrada, sets out to save Frisco from total destruction, and naturally succeeds. The final set piece has Warren hopping into a passing racecar and sailing it through the air to land on a river barge, where Soboda meets a grisly end, melted by his own laser beam.

Silly plot is just the glue that holds together a series of extended car chases through the city, which are well-handled if repetitive. Castellari's direction is functional and competent. A pulsating score by Guido and Maurizio De Angelis pumps up the excitement of the action sequences, in which stunt men are run over, burned alive, hurled out of exploding buildings, or disintegrated by the terrible "light blast." By preference, helmer sets his chases and explosions in deserted factories, abandoned train stations and cavernous, empty buildings, which lends pic some stylistic coherence.

With all the mayhem going on, there's not much left for motivation or character development, though Estrada is given a few human traits and a fleeting love interest (Peggy Rowe).

Supporting cast is relaxed and credible, with the exception of the luckless Yuri and city officials who have to get through a lot of stilted dialog about saving the city. Anyway, it's a rare character that makes it through more than one scene, since everybody except Ronn and his burly, big-hearted sidekick Ben gets bumped off almost as soon as they're introduced. — *Yung.*

Rigged
(U.S.-COLOR)

Cannes, May 15.
A CineStar Films presentation. Produced by K.A. Roberson Jr. Executive producer, Gary E. Grote. Directed by C.M. Cutry. Features entire cast. Screenplay, John Goff, Jill Gurr from a story based on James Hadley Chase's novel "Hit And Run;" camera (Eastmancolor), Eddy Van Der Eden; editor, John R. Bowen; associate producers, Eddie Kafafian, Jef Richard; music, Brian Banks, Anthony Marinelli. Reviewed at the Cannes Film Festival (Market), May 15, 1985. (No MPAA Rating.) Running time: **94 MINS.**

Mason Morgan .... Ken Roberson
Monique .... Pamela Bryant
Benjamin Wheeler .... George Kennedy
Cheryl .... Dene Hofteizer Anton
West .... John Goff
Lopez .... Ramon Gonzalez Cuevas

If George Kennedy had squeezed the trigger when he had Ken Roberson in his sights, he would have finished off one of the dullest leading men seen in recent years, and left the audiences puzzling — but without too much vexation — over several mysterious events that occurred in the oil country around Galveston Island, Texas.

Unfortunately, Kennedy, in response to a "Why?" query from Roberson, had to make himself comfortable in a chair, and launch into a fairly lengthy exposition, which gave the cops time to arrive, put a bullet in George and save Roberson.

There's no justice. Indeed, there is very little to get enthused about in director C.M. Cutry's (who replaced Matt Cimber at the helm early in production) pedestrian thriller, "Rigged."

Kennedy, appearing to enjoy his arch-villain role immensely, is a filthy-rich oilman who aims to get richer still by masterminding a cocaine racket in league with a Venezuelan smuggler.

Stumbling unwittingly into the fray is Roberson as a dim-witted rigger, who takes a fancy to Kennedy's girlfriend, Pamela Bryant, quaintly described as an "oil groupie."

Yarn, based on a novel by the late James Hadley Chase, follows a fairly tortuous path and, despite the murders of a crooked cop, a fallen country and western star and her seedy agent, the pace often lags, and with it, the likely audience interest.

Aside from Kennedy, whose tongue-in-cheek approach seems highly appropriate, the rest of the cast plays it straight, and for the most part, badly.

Roberson (who previously starred in "Yellow Hair And The Fortress Of Gold") in this outing registers three expressions: happy, unhappy and blank, with the emphasis on the last. Bryant displays a voluptuous body but little else.

Any dollars generated at the box office will need to come from a fast playoff before word spreads about this dry hole. — *Dogo.*

Ninja Thunderbolt
(HONG KONG-COLOR)

Cannes, May 10.
An IFD Films and Arts Ltd. Production and Presentation. Produced by Joseph Lai. Directed by Godfrey Ho. Stars Richard Harrison, Wang Tao, Randy To, Kulada Yasuaki and Barbara Yuen. Screenplay, Godfrey Ho; camera (color), Raymond Cheung; action sequences designer, Allan Wang; production manager, George Lai; music, Stephen Tsang.

Reviewed at Palais De Festival, Salle H, Cannes (Market), May 10, 1985. Running time: **90 MINS.**
(English soundtrack)

Jackal Chan is the head of a Hong Kong multi-million dollar corporation. He is merciless and corrupt in his business dealings and is assisted by his equally nasty daughter Sara. Father and son later plan to have a valuable antique jade horse stolen for insurance money. Sara employs Shima, a Ninja for the job, but she has no plans of paying him later. She seduces her bodyguard to kill Shima but fails.

The insurance company starts to investigate and they send a girl agent Claudia who happens to be a martial arts specialist. Together with Police Inspector Wong, they plan to solve the mystery and expose the unlawful acts of the Chans. Wong is assistant to foreign cop Superintendent Richard (Harrison) who is also a Ninja. Somehow they get to Japan to finish the Ninja business.

The performers are from the lowest ranks, including an American actor based in Italy, along with unknown local martial artists and leftovers from the kung fu era. However, the Cinemascope photography highlights the touristy sides of Hong Kong, but the other technical aspects of the production are abominable, especially the English-dubbed dialog. —*Mel.*

King Of The City
(U.S.-COLOR)

Cannes, May 18.
An MPR production, with VTC. Executive producer, Charles Aperia, Guy Collins. Produced, directed and written by Norman Thaddeus Vane. Features entire cast. Camera (color), Joel King; editor, David Kern; original score, Jack Conrad; executive music producers, Frank Musker, Evros Stakis; songs by Musker, Michael Sembello, Richard Kerr, Andy Hill, Dominic Bugatti; choreography, Dennon Rawles; art directors, Cynthia Snowden, Phillip Duffin; line producer, Patrick Wright. Reviewed at Cannes (Market), May 17, 1985. (No MPAA Rating.) Running time: **97 MINS.**
Cal McFarlane .... Tom Persekian
Tank .... Michael Parks
Sissy .... Jamie Barrett
Hector .... Tony Curtis
Tillie .... Bleu Mackenzie
Doctor .... Ron Kohlman
Also with: Dee Wallace.

A musical thriller, with a solid soundtrack and some energetic dance scenes, allied to a tale of a young couple from the sticks trying to make it in the depths of Hollywood, "King Of The City" is an uneven affair in which the good and the indifferent vie for audience attention.

Tom Persekian is a personable young lead who arrives in Hollywood as an innocent-at-large and soon is working as a bouncer at The City, a down-market disco run by Tony Curtis. Persekian is taught the tricks of the bouncer trade by old hand Michael Parks, in an all-too-brief, but effective, portrayal of a former actor in the James Dean mold now reduced to this demeaning work.

When Parks is gunned down by a quartet of punks, Persekian is shattered and drops out for a while. Meanwhile his girl (Jamie Barrett) has landed in town looking for him and has been taken in tow by the sinister Ron Kohlman. To make matters worse, Curtis is being squeezed by a new generation of Mafia types who want the lucrative dope deals that take place unofficially at the nightspot.

All this probably sounds stronger than it plays on screen. Writer-director Norman Thaddeus Vane provides some glowing scenes, in which Curtis and Parks, particularly, shine, but the pic is uneven and a bit undeveloped, and the numerous musical numbers seem thrown in rather than properly integrated.

Jamie Barrett makes an appealing heroine, and her waterbed love scene with Persekian is a highlight. Film could attract audiences on its blend of modern music and youthful action, but prospects look somewhat iffy. It's technically tops, with expert lensing by Joel King and a well-produced music soundtrack. —*Strat.*

Hot Water
(CANADIAN-COLOR)

Cannes, May 16.

A Cinema International release in Canada. (No production company credited.) Produced by Don Carmody. Directed by Jim Hanley. Executive producers, Andre Link, John Dunning. Feautres entire cast. Screenplay, John Maxwell and Don Carmody; camera (color). Maurice de Ernsted; editor, Jacques Jean; design, Paola Ridolfi; music, Ken Roberts and Allen Gerber. Reviewed at Olympia, Cannes (Market), May 16, 1985. Running time: **83 MINS.**

K.C.	Suzanne DeLaurentis
Jo	Linda Singer
Luke	Michael McKeever
Bud	Ken Roberts
Junior	Jeremy Ratchford

Nasty minded, bloody and bigoted, "Hot Water" has two hookers released from jail, attacked by their pimp and fleeing to a small waterfront community to reopen a run-down marina.

Townsmen, including the sheriff, have southern U.S. accents and are all slobbering, booze-guzzling rowdies given to random violence, the latter because they resent the ladies' presence. Chief of them is a pathological crazy who rapes and in one sequence destroys the marina's interior with a chainsaw while his demented mother watches gleefully from afar with binoculars.

The curvaceous hookers, who wear a collection of different bikinis throughout the pic, are befriended by the only two men who do not

have southern accents. One of the women saves herself from attack by igniting a Molotov cocktail from a small boat while circled by would-be rapists.

Their two male protectors are killed brutally as is almost everyone else and the hookers decide maybe opening a marina. wasn't such a good idea after all.

Sometime well-paced editing rescues slow direction and brutal plotting. Pic was made on the set of "Meatballs III" in quickie fashion and on a low budget of $C6,000,000 or maybe less.

With little to recommend it beyond repeated acts of violence, pic shows possibilities for homevid and theatrical playoff in grind situations. Acting and other production values are uneven. —*Adil.*

Here Come The Littles
(FRENCH-ANIMATED-COLOR)

Hollywood, May 27.

An Atlantic Releasing Corp. release of a DIC production. Produced by Jean Chalopin, Andy Heyward, Tetsuo Katayama. Executive producers, Chalopin, Hayward. Directed by Bernard Deyries. Screenplay by Woody Kling, from a book by Jon Peterson; camera (CFI color), Hajime Hasegawa, Kenichi Kobayashi; music, Haim Saban, Shuki Levy; editor, Masatoshi Tsurbushi; art director, Mutsuo Koseki; sound, Sound West; animation director, Tsukasa Tannai, Yoshinobu Michihata; tracing and painting, Hiroko Kondo, Mari Nakamura, Tomoko Yamamoto; associate producer, Koji Takeuchi; assistant director, Sunao Katabuchi. Reviewed at the Hollywood Egyptian Theater, Hollywood, Calif., May 24, 1985. (MPAA Rating: G.) Running time: **75 MINS.**

Voice characterizations: Jimmy E. Keegan, Bettina Bush, Donovan Freberg, Hal Smith, Gregg Berger, Patricia Parris, Alvy Moore, Robert David Hall, Mona Marshall.

First feature outing for the Littles, popular Saturday morning kiddie characters, "Here Come The Littles" should prove familiar ground for its target audience. Animated feature lacks the intensity and satisfaction of a true film experience and is closer to an expanded television program. Pic, however, can expect decent returns from the growing kiddie audience in regional playoffs.

Curious creatures something like human mice, the Littles maintain a totally human existence within the walls of a house. Big difference between Littles and humans is that these characters go around with perpetual smiles on their faces, even in the face of numerous calamities.

It seems Henry, the young boy who lives in the Littles' house, is being sent away to live with an evil uncle because his parents have disappeared in the jungle. Little Tom Little and sister Lucy accidently get trapped in Henry's suitcase, setting off a series of misadventures.

Script by Woody Kling explores themes important to kids probably as young as five. Issues raised in-

clude homelessness, loss of parents and the importance of family and friends.

Even when things get darkest for the Littles and young Henry, nothing gets too heavy, and the emotions are basically mild and non-threatening. Consequently, characters come off as agreeable but one-dimensional.

Animation is serviceable without being particularly exciting or imaginative. The Littles and humans have only a limited range of expressions. Like any good stars, the Littles carry the film, but next time they should hold out for better material. —*Jagr.*

Heart Of The Garden
(COLOR)

Washington, D.C., March 18.

A Roland Films presentation. Produced by Raymond Chavez. Written and directed by Lavinia Currier. Camera (color), Ed Lachman, Arthur Ornitz; art direction, Ben Edwards; editor, Denine Rowan; music, J. Aaron Diamond. Reviewed at American Film Institute Theater (Women Make Movies IV), Washington, D.C., March 17, 1985. Running time: **64 MINS.**

Nora	Morgen Leigh
Cully	Freddy Koehler
China, the vagrant	Kaulani Lee
Nimrod	Joe Seneca
Nanny	Madeleine Thornton-Sherwood
Cellist	Yo Yo Ma

The two children, Nora and her little brother of wealthy Virginia landowners are left alone with the servants to get along in a virtual paradise of an old estate in "Heart Of The Garden."

Enter a mad woman. dubbed China after she shatters the china breakfast dishes, who tells the children of the wide world, mesmerizes young Nora, gets her to run away, then confirms what the girl knew in her heart: her parents are dead. Nora drives China away, is fetched back home and has to scale the gate in the last scene as her final attempt to escape her home and childhood. The story is told with care and cunning with little concern for realism.

Structured with flashbacks to show the beauty and love of the past, the pic features elegant locations and dreamy glamor as the child's memory of the not-too-distant past. A Fourth of July fireworks display implies the death of something greater than just the Southern way of life, as the pyrotechnic display lights up as an American flag, then fizzles out.

Ed Lachman has photographed the lush Virginia countryside in a lyrical and languorous sweep, giving the story time, perhaps too much time, to evolve out of the mood of an indulgent Mother Nature. Psychology consumes the dramatic conflict and is appropriately swampy, seen through the eyes of a

pubescent girl.

Thespian credits are tops, with Joe Seneca's entertainment value as an ante-Bellum black named Nimrod leaving us wanting more of him. Actors Studio veteran Madeleine Thornton-Sherwood delivers a small part of the nanny with panache, and Kaulani Lee is histrionically mad.

The powerhouse performance is young Morgen Leigh as Nora. She is never self-conscious before the camera, and director Lavinia Currier modulated the balance so none of the professionals upstage the young protagonist. Her open face gives credibility to the sensitivity of this story of abandoned children and tones down the sometimes excessively poetic dialog.

It's rare that indie debuts assume such a polished and dramatic stance that would earmark them instantly as serious television programming. American Playhouse would be an appropriate goal for "Garden" with its Chekhovian view of the South.—*Kaja.*

Return To Waterloo
(BRITISH-COLOR)

A New Line Cinema release of an RCA Video Prods. presentation. Produced by Dennis Woolf. Written and directed by Ray Davies. Stars Ken Colley; editor, David Mingay; production manager, Paul Sparrow; camera (color), Roger Deakins; sound, Bruce White; art director, Terry Pritchard; choreographer, James Cameron; songs by Davies; music performed by Davies, Mick Avory, Jim Rodford and Ian Gibbons of The Kinks. Reviewed at Magno Preview 9 Theater, N.Y., May 15, 1985. (MPAA Rating: PG-13.) Running time: **60 MINS.**

With: Ken Colley (Traveller); Valerie Holliman (Traveller's Wife); Dominique Barnes (Traveller's Daughter); Hywel Williams Ellis; Aaron Probyn; Gretchen Franklin; Betty Romaine; Michael Cule; Christopher Godwin; Wanda Rokicki; Alan Mitchell; Claire Parker; Timothy Davies; Joan Blackham; Tim Roth; Mike Smart; Sally Anne; Lizzie McKenzie; Sheila Collings; Myrtle Devenish; Nat Jackley; Wally Thomas; Roy Evans; Sue Vanner; Claire Rayner; Michael Fish; Neil Landor, Teresa Pattison.

Conceived by Ray Davies, leader of the veteran English rock group The Kinks, this engagingly bizarre music video sendup of British bourgeois repression was televised originally on England's Channel 4. While "Return To Waterloo" was geared for the homevideo market

here (it will eventually be released on videocassette by RCA), its theatrical distributors could reap a decent turnout in specialty situations if word-of-mouth builds.

With virtually no dialog, "Return To Waterloo" is carried by a melodically strong, lyrically cogent rock 'n' roll soundtrack (including three songs from The Kinks' fine recent LP, "Word Of Mouth") and the visceral, wordless acting of lead Ken Colley as the Traveller, a suburban real estate salesman in mid-life crisis who may or may not be a wanted rapist.

The rollercoaster narrative juxtaposes time/space transpositions representing the buttoned-down Traveller's interior turmoil as he rides to work on the British Rail. The train itself is portrayed as both the lifeline and the regulator of a systemized, ordered society which has rewarded the Traveller with a brick box house, a loveless marriage, a runaway teen daughter and a bubbling emotional cauldron fired by repressed sexual longings.

Along the way the hero meets a trio of clockwork-orange punk rockers, aging war veterans who lament the Empire's nightfall, Monty Pythonesque clucking ladies, and a variety of middle class commuters who seem to be walking the fine line between conformity and flipping out. The vaunted British reserve has a violent underside, Davies is saying, and while his savaging of the middle-class herd instinct is not revelatory, the story is brought off with humorous gusto by the ensemble of skillfully cast character actors populating the pic.

Editing of the overlapping fantasy/reality sequences is first rate, as are the shifting point-of-view camerawork and the sound. Davies makes two brief appearances as a busker in the Underground, but the gripping soundtrack is either laid over the action or-synched to appear as if sung by the various characters. —*Rich.*

Night Train To Terror
(COLOR)

A bumpy ride.

A Visto International release. Executive producer, William F. Messerli. Produced by Jay Schlossberg-Cohen. Directed by John Carr, Schlossberg-Cohen, Philip Marshak, Tom McGowan, Gregg Tallas. Features entire cast. Screenplay, Philip Yordan; camera (United color), Susan Maljan, others; editor, Evan Stoliar, Steve Nielson, others; music supervision, Ralph Ives; visual effects, William Stromberg; stop motion animation, Anthony Doublin, Stromberg. Reviewed at Movieland theater, N.Y., May 18, 1985. (MPAA Rating: R.) Running time: 93 MINS.
Harry Billings . . . . .John Phillip Law
Det. Stern. . . . . .Cameron Mitchell
Weiss/Dieter . . . . .Marc Lawrence
James Hansen/Orderly . . . . . .Charles Moll
Gretta Connors . . . . .Meridith Haze
God .Ferdy Mayne
Devil .Lu Sickler

"Night Train To Terror" is a hodge-podge of at least three separate horror films, crudely edited together as an omnibus picture. Amateurish result is due for one-week stands prior to its entry into the ongoing camp classic slot for bad films.

Wraparound footage has God (Ferdy Mayne sporting an arresting white beard) and the Devil (Lu Sickler) quarreling on a train over which human souls they will get, giving rise to three case histories. (An inept rock group is also on the train with its souls up for grabs, and irritating musical numbers interrupt the action at random.)

First two cases were filmed circa 1982 by director John Carr and play like excerpts from unfinished features, both presented here with the entire story carried by voiceover narration. John Phillip Law toplines in "Harry," sent to a sanitarium after his car crashes, where mad doctors and a crazed orderly (Charles Moll, of tv's "Night Court" series) use him to pickup pretty girls who are then killed, their organs sold to medical schools. Segment includes lots of nudity, gore and many shots filmed out-of-focus. Next, Meridith Haze portrays "Gretta," an aspiring pianist duped into joining The Death Club, where jaded folks play fatal, sadistic games.

Finale, apparently filmed in 1979 as a feature titled "Cataclysm" (which received an R rating in 1981 from the MPAA on its own), is a religious tract in which vet screenwriter Philip Yordan gets on a soapbox. James Hansen (Charles Moll, again) is a Nobel prizewinner who has written a book "God Is Dead" and goes on tv preaching his anti-religion party line. He gets his comeuppance from an ageless Nazi named Olivier who in fact is the devil's emissary. Cameron Mitchell appears as a cop hunting Olivier, while Marc Lawrence has two roles, with beard as a Jewish concentration camp survivor murdered by Olivier and cleanshaven as a fellow cop.

Mishmash features stock footage, including widescreen shots hilariously "squeezed" in an attempt to match the other scenes, plus several stopmotion animation monsters that comically battle tiny puppet versions of the cast members.—*Lor.*

Los Gatos
(The Cats)
(ARGENTINE-COLOR)

Buenos Aires, May 10.
An Argentina Sono Film presentation and production. Associate producer, Salvador D'Antonio. Directed by Carlos F. Borcosque. Screenplay, Jorge Falcón, Pedro Saiz Miramón, Borcosque; camera (Eastmancolor), Aníbal González Paz; music, Jorge Candia; set decoration, Olivo-Marchegiani. Reviewed at the Callao theater; B.A., May 9, 1985. Running time: 91 MINS.
Dolores . . . . .Camila Perissé
Sergio . . . . .Gerardo Romano
Marlene . . . . .Edda Bustamante
Marcela . . . . .Reina Reech
Ethel . . . . .Vicky Olivares
Taxi driver . . . . .Raúl Lavié
Augusto . . . . .Alfonso De Grazia
Paunero . . . . .Enrique Liporace
Cristina . . . . .Gigi Rua
Also with: Ricardo Castro Ríos, Adolfo García Grau, Andrea Bonelli, Daniel Lago, Dorys Perry, Héctor Pellegrini.

"The Cats" is softcore sex for undiscriminating voyeurs. It's impossible to find a plot in this string of rather frenetic sex scenes — rape, lesbianism, incest, besides intercourse between consenting adults — seemingly aimed at getting shock value by utilizing local players. The lack of both stars and taste restrict its b.o. chances to the portfolio trade and the most ardent fans of the genre.

Neither true eroticism nor any degree of subtlety can be found in this pic that starts at a funeral where a character reads an unending eulogy written by the deceased, who apparently ran a clandestine web dealing with drugs and prostitution. Types introduced in the cemetery sequence are later seen in situations kept from believability by blurred storytelling and erratic acting.

Camerawork is okay, but other technical credits are below average. — *Nubi.*

Adiós, Roberto
(Goodbye Robert)
(ARGENTINE-COLOR)

Buenos Aires, April 5.
An Argentina Sono Film presentation of a Jorge and Enrique Dawi production. Executive producer, Jorge Velasco. Directed by Enrique Dawi. Stars Carlos Andrés Calvo, Víctor Laplace. Screenplay, Lito Espinosa; camera (Eastmancolor), Luis Vecchione; editor, Serafín Molina; music, Pocho Lapouble and Pablo Ziegler; sound, José Grammático. Reviewed at the Normandie theater, B.A., April 4, 1985. Running time: 90 MINS.
Roberto . . . . .Carlos Andrés Calvo
Marcelo . . . . .Víctor Laplace
Martha . . . . .Ana María Picchio
Psychiatrist . . . . .Héctor Alterio
Luisito . . . . .Pablo Codevila
Alejandra . . . . . .María Cristina Láurenz
Chabela . . . . .María Vaner
Priest . . . . .Osvaldo Terranova
Roberto's Father . . . . .Onofre Lovero
Friend . . . . .Héctor Pellegrini

"Adiós, Roberto," a witty, very entertaining comedy on the initiation as homosexual of a young man with a macho reputation is doing solid biz here. Director Enrique Dawi and actor-turned-scripter Lito Espinosa have succeeded in making it effective on two levels. For sophisticated viewers it is a spoof on the traditional reactions of straight people when one of their relatives or friends takes such a step. For the mass audience it is a catching probe into a subject long forbidden for native filming and the first approach of the new uncensored Argentine cinema to contemporary themes not related to front-page news.

In the beginning what turns out to be Roberto's imagination confronts him with the reproaches of a friend reminding him of his past as a teenaged lothario and the rage of his dead father who mercilessly beats him. Then unfolds the story of how Roberto, after separating from his unattractive wife, goes to share an apartment with Marcelo, who eventually reveals himself as a homosexual. One night Roberto gets drunk and starts sexual intercourse with Marcelo (there are no explicit sex scenes). After an early feeling of shame and guilt he finds his relationship with Marcelo pleasing, but he has to face the damnation (real or imagined) of his estranged wife, his first fiancée, a priest who punches him after hearing his confession, et al. Puzzled, he resorts to an analyst trying to sort out the contradictions between his macho pride and his other fledgling self. Then past, present and ghosts intertwine in a revealing, often amusing way. Lively dialog is a main asset. —*Nubi.*

The Architecture Of Frank Lloyd Wright
(U.S.-BRITISH-DOCU-COLOR)

Washington, D.C., April 6.
An ABC Video and the Arts Council of Great Britain production. Executive producer, Rodney Wilson. Produced by Barbara and Murray Grigor. Written and directed by Murray Grigor. Camera (color), David Peat, Mick Coulter; lighting, David Moravec: artwork and rostrum photography, Donald Holwill; editor, Russell Fenton; historical advisor, Thomas S. Hines; music, by Frank Spedding, conducted by Marcus Dods. Reviewed at Cine screening room, Washington, D.C., April 5, 1985. Running time: 90 MINS.

Narrator Anne Baxter, the granddaughter of Frank Lloyd Wright, lends an air of authority of this somber, slow docu about some of the buildings designed by one of the world's most famous architects. Wright appears in a brief bit of footage to explain that as a young man he was extremely arrogant, because he always preferred an honest arrogance over a hypocritical humility. His humor is hinted at in similar quotations attributed to him, but in no way affected the filmmakers.

Writer/director Murray Grigor has done three films about architecture prior to this extremely long, overly cautious, pious tribute to Wright. Some of his more magnificent creations are shown as it spans from his Egyptian monumentality in a Southern California socialite's mansion looking as abandoned as a tomb. The camera seems to fear any movement, except for occasional aerial shots revealing Wright's home Taliesin fixed firmly on a hill. Individual shots are too long, as is the entire film. Because the many shots linger on rooms devoid of people where a fireplace inevitably has a fire burning, an absurd sense pervades the pic of Wright's sites having been abandoned or neutron-bombed.

The best achievement of the docu is its summary of Wright's early life and how it affected his ideas about design, which would be just as good in a book. Points being made are seldom supplemented by introducing similar features from other buildings to lend a comprehensive feeling about the value of such a work. The elegaic camera and droning narrative have a somnolent effect, despite an original score, created expressly for pic, that soars rather pointlessly to try to bridge sequences. —*Kaja.*

The Illegal Immigrant
(HONG KONG-COLOR)

Hong Kong, April 24.

A Shaw Bros. presentation and release. Presented by Run Run Shaw; executive producer, Mona Fong; produced by Wong Wa Hee. Directed by Chang Wan Ting. Stars Ching Yung Cho, Wu Fu Sheng, Liao Chun Yu, Li Chu Yuan, Tsen Pao Tsai. Designed by Lo Yi Ling and Alex Law; screenplay, Alex Law; camera (color), Bob Bukowski; music, Kenny Bee, Alan Tsui, Stephen Shing, So Chun Hou. Reviewed at Jade theater; Hong Kong, April 24, 1985. Running time: **98 MINS.**
(Cantonese soundtrack with English subtitles)

Chang Chu-chiu (Ching Yung Cho) is a young man originally from Canton, who enters Hong Kong illegally and then goes to New York's Chinatown, through an illegal syndicate. Chang is eventually caught in a police raid setup by the immigration department and is given one week's appeal, or three months to leave the country automatically or face deportation, never to return.

Bailed out by an uncle, Chang works in a restaurant and studies English at night. To qualify for permanent residency and for that extremely valuable "green card," he accepts an offer from his ex-employer's young son to "marry" on paper that son's sister Hsueh-hung (Wu Fu Sheng) who needs money for plastic surgery to make her nose pointed, like those of Americans.

Chang is accused of deception and is ordered to show his "wife" when immigration officers visit unannounced as he is really living with a male colleague. Chang convinces Hsueh-hung to live in for a few days to cope with future possible checks. Initially turned down, the girl consents late and love blossoms. Just when everything s turning out all right, fate has other things in mind.

Shot entirely in New York City, starring a talented group of unknown, new performers, the film captures the physical ambience and emotional texture of some Chinese living in America.

Lead actor Ching Yung Cho immediately creates audience empathy while the rest of the cast projects engaging exuberance and believability. Director Chang Wan Ting conveys the pain of ordinary people in a foreign environment, with light humor, heart-tugging compassion and deep understanding of the theme.—*Mel.*

Out Of Control
(COLOR)

Self-description for an exploitation misfire.

Hollywood, May 17.

A New World Pictures release of a Fred Weintraub presentation of a Jadran/Incovent production. Produced by Weintraub, Daniel Grodnik. Executive producers, Paul Lichtman, Arnold Fishman. Directed by Allan Holzman. Features entire cast. Screenplay, Sandra Weintraub Roland, Vicangelo Bulluck; camera (CFI color), John Alonzo; editor, Robert Ferretti, Allan Holzman; art director, Veljko Despotovic, Vladmir Spasojevic, Ing. Nemanja Petrovic; sound, John Stein; assistant director, Peter Buntic; casting, Onorato/Franks. Reviewed at Paramount, Theater, Hollywood, Calif., May 17, 1985. (MPAA Rating: R.) Running time: **78 MINS.**

Keith	Martin Hewitt
Chrissie	Betsy Russell
Tina	Claudia Udy
Elliot	Andrew J. Lederer
Robin	Cindi Dietrich
Gary	Richard Kantor
Katie	Sherilyn Fenn
Cowboy	Jim Youngs

"Out Of Control" is an inept exploitation pic which becomes boring before the opening credits are over and goes downhill from there. Attempt to wrap the typical teen sex fare around a stranded-on-a-desert-island plot can hardly be considered ambitious here. Action is totally uninvolving with boxoffice prospects virtually nonexistent.

Shot in Yugoslavia under the title of "Crosswinds," pic was released regionally in January by New World in several markets and is being used now as filler between engagements in other territories.

Pic actually covers three genres in one in an attempt to cram in as much as possible without the least idea how to make the material work. Opening is a standup monolog by Elliot (Andrew Lederer) consisting of some very stale jokes about his paltry sex life. While plot goes off in other directions, Elliot clings to his nerd identity throughout.

Sponsored by the rich kid in the crowd (Martin Hewitt), group of high schoolers dash off in his father's plane to celebrate their graduation. The plane crashes and strands the kids on an island in the middle of nowhere. Fortunately, they find a stash of vodka and get drunk enough to have an orgy. Sequence drags on for 15 minutes as they play strip "spin the bottle," the dramatic highlight of the film.

Later on they get mixed up with some bad guys smuggling drugs off the island. None of it makes much sense and is basically just an excuse to leer at the girls, particularly offensive since the script was written by two women.

Script offers just the barest shadow of character development with the acting not helping much either. At least Sherilyn Fenn as the youngest and most chaste of the girls looks great in her film debut.

Production values are consistent with the rest of the film. Cinematography must rank as some of the worst work ever by John Alonzo. Editing is also surprisingly bad considering director Allan Holzman is an ex-editor and takes a credit here. Numerous scenes are a cloudy tangle of limbs. —*Jagr.*

Ran
(JAPANESE-FRENCH-COLOR)

Tokyo, June 1.

An Orion Classics release of a Herald Ace-Nippon Herald-Greenwich Films co-production. Produced by Masato Hara, Serge Silberman. Directed by Akira Kurosawa. Stars Tatsuya Nakadai. Screenplay, Kurosawa, Hideo Oguni, Masato Ide, based on "King Lear" by William Shakespeare; camera (color), Takao Saito; music, Toru Takemitsu; art directors, Yoshiro Muraki, Shinobu Muraki. No further credits provided. Reviewed at Tokyo Film Festival, May 31, 1985. Running time: **161 MINS.**

Lord Ichimonji Hidetora	Tatsuya Nakadai
Taro	Satoshi Terao
Jiro	Jinpachi Nezu
Saburo	Daisuke Ryu
Lady Kaede	Mieko Harada
The Fool	Peter
Kurogane	Hisashi Igawa
Tango	Masayuke Yui
Lady Sué	Yoshiko Miyazaki

Akira Kurosawa has turned once again to Shakespeare for source material, just as he did nearly 30 years ago when "Macbeth" became the memorable "Throne Of Blood." Now, at age 75, the director has made his most costly epic to date, and it's a dazzlingly successful addition to his distinguished career. Pic should mop up in its home territory, and exceed the business of his previous film, "Kagemusha," in art houses the world over.

The basis of "Ran" (literally, "Chaos") is "King Lear," but with a few minor modifications. Chief of these is that the old king's offspring are now three sons rather than three daughters, though all the basic motivations of the original remain intact. On his 70th birthday, Lord Hidetora announces he's passing authority on to his eldest son, Taro; when his youngest, Saburo, who genuinely cares for his father, violently protests, he's banished. Subsequently, Taro treats his father shamefully, as does the middle son, Jiro, and eventually the two join forces to attack their father's castle. Only the old king, now losing his mind, survives the carnage, and since Jiro has arranged to have his brother murdered, he assumes total power. Pic climaxes with a battle between Jiro's forces and those of Saburo and his allies, with most of the principals expiring.

With great tragic material such as "King Lear" to work with, Kurosawa is in his element. He starts the film in a leisurely way as he sets up the drama and intros the principal characters, but from the very beginning his use of bold color and dynamic camera angles indicates a master at the peak of his powers. The two major battle sequences, the first about an hour into the film, the second providing the climax, are superbly staged and, for sheer spectacle, have not been equaled in the cinema for several years.

Daringly, Kurosawa stages the first part of the attack on the king's castle without any sounds of battle; only sonorous music accompanies the violence and destruction, as lethal arrows zip brutally into bodies; the ladies of the court fall upon each other with daggers when they realize defeat is inevitable, until only the old king sits in the blazing building, miraculously unscathed. Only with the noise of the gunshot that kills Taro does Kurosawa, utilizing a superb stereo soundtrack, introduce the deafening din of the battle.

The second major action sequence is set in spacious fields and hillsides as the colorful armies meet in mortal conflict and riders crash from their galloping horses in countless numbers.

In addition to these genuinely enthralling sequences, Kurosawa provides gripping drama and intrigue in the court scenes. Changing the sexes of the king's heirs provides not only fine roles for three excellent actors, but also gives Mieko Harada, as the evil, scheming Lady Kaede (who goads first one brother than another into war and destruction), the opportunity to play an unforgettable character role, a role similar to that of Lady Macbeth in "Throne Of Blood;" her fate is spectacularly bloody.

Tatsuya Nakadai, in superb makeup, is the king, and it's a tribute to this relatively young actor that he's so convincing in the role; the later scenes of despair and madness are immensely moving. In the part of the fool, the king's loyal jester, Peter, a well-known Japanese transvestite, is startling and touching.

Those who criticized the Westernized music in "Kagemusha" should find no cause for complaint in Toru Takemitsu's excellent score, and visually the film is quite breathtaking. Indeed, all technical departments are firstrate.

At just over two hours and 40 minutes, "Ran" seems not a moment too long; the intensity of the drama easily sustains itself over this running time. Credit must go to French coproducer Serge Silberman (who previously produced films by the late Luis Buñuel) and Kurosawa's Japanese backers for allowing this peerless director to make his long-planned epic. Its success is a credit to all. —*Strat.*

Schakalakadu
(WEST GERMAN-COLOR-16m)

Berlin, May 3.

A Promedia Film production, Munich, in collaboration with the Kuratorium, Junger Deutscher Film. Written and directed by Rigo Manikofski. Features entire cast. Camera (color), Fritz Beckoff; sound, Janos Rosmer; production manager, Achim Tappen. Reviewed at Cinema, Berlin, May 2, 1985. Running time: **83 MINS.**

With: Jochen Schroeder (Rudi), Ulrike Möckel (Petra), Jochen Kolenda (Jürgen), Katharina Gräfe (Claudia), Albert Heins (Bibo), Rigo Manikofski (brother).

"Schakalakadu" is a regional story about young people tucked away in a corner of Germany, helmed by Rigo Manikofski.

Rudi works at the steel mills throughout the week and on the weekend meets his two buddies for a Friday night round of the bars.

Petra is a decent bargirl whose profession is simply to entertain customers over a counter with small talk while a porno flick runs on the wall in the side room. Both are bored with their locked-in routines, but don't quite know how to break out of the lethargy.

Manikofski tells his story from two parallel viewpoints that converge in the second half of the film. As Rudi and his pals prepare for their usual Friday night on the town, Petra and her barmaid friends have a run-in with a local pimp who's out to teach his girlfriend a lesson.

As it happens, Rudi and his buddies hit the bar Petra is tending on their last round of local joints — and it's here that the sleaziness of their existence rises to the surface on both sides. The pair hit it off in a quiet moment, and Rudi decides then and there to break with his pals for good. The arrest of the pimp and the barkeeper for manhandling one of the girls makes it easier for both to go their own way. Rudi wants to prove himself as a man of daring and courage, which forms the twist ending of the tale.

Manikofski is a talented storyteller, relying on visual images and tight acting performances. Some scenes are a bit overdone, and the night backdrop doesn't make it any easier for a lenser working on a restricted production budget. However, these appear to be minor drawbacks. —*Holl.*

Prizzi's Honor
(COLOR)

Offbeat black comedy from John Huston.

Hollywood, May 31.

A 20th Century Fox release of an ABC Motion Pictures presentation. Produced by John Foreman. Directed by John Huston. Stars Jack Nicholson, Kathleen Turner. Screenplay, Richard Condon, Janet Roach, from novel by Condon; camera (DeLuxe color), Andrzej Bartkowiak; editors, Rudi Fehr, Kaja Fehr; music, Alex North; production designer, Dennis Washington; set decorator, Bruce Weintraub; sound, Dennis Maitland, Art Rochester; costume design, Donfeld; casting, Alixe Gordin; assistant director, Benjy Rosenberg. Reviewed at 20th Century Fox studios, May 31, 1985. (MPAA Rating: R.) Running time: **129 MINS.**

Charley Partanna	Jack Nicholson
Irene Walker	Kathleen Turner
Eduardo Prizzi	Robert Loggia
Don Corrado Prizzi	William Hickey
Angelo "Pop" Prizzi	John Randolph
Dominic Prizzi	Lee Richardson
Maerose Prizzi	Anjelica Huston
Filargi "Finlay"	Michael Lombard
Lt. Hanley	Lawrence Tierney
Marxie Heller	Joseph Ruskin
Amalia Prizzi	Ann Selepegno

Certainly one of the most curious and adult films to start off the summer season by a Hollywood major, John Huston's "Prizzi's Honor" packs love, sex, and murder — and dark comedy — into a labyrinthine tale that could draw mature audiences intrigued by a wicked premise and the chemistry of costars Jack Nicholson and Kathleen Turner.

Bizarre nature of the film's tone, however, in which early and slyly funny moments increasingly give way to Godfatheresque drama and a grim uncoupling of the picture's romantic knot, will post a problem for the unsuspecting filmgoer. Pic's length, and even its density, are other drawbacks.

Ad campaign, for initial, national selected run, is keyed to accenting the comedy, but production is considerably more dark than light.

Based on the novel by Richard Condon, and cowritten by Condon and Janet Roach, the Byzantine unfolding of the plot centers on the tragicomedy that results when a hit man for a powerful crime family (Nicholson) falls hard for a svelte blond (Turner) who turns out to be his female counterpart in hired killings.

Pic concludes on a risible note when Turner and Nicholson — after plot convolutions that swing from darkly lit Mafia scenes in Brooklyn to freelance killer Turner's base in sunny L.A. — the loving heroes, are assigned to knock each other off.

Picture is a stretch for Nicholson, who speaks in a street-tough, accented gangsterese that initially takes some getting used to, but shortly becomes totally convincing. His character is not the brightest — once when mob outcast daughter Anjelica Huston tells him about art deco he responds, "Art who?" — but Nicholson is fascinating in catching the amoral rhythms of the syndicate underworld.

Turner manages to use her loveliness to jolting results when she finally turns her gun on a pair of victims in an apartment hallway.

Even more monstrous, in a deceptive way, is the character played by Anjelica Huston, who is the black sheep of the powerful clan, but who maneuvers the plot in insidious ways, all of them tied to the fact that she harbors a lost love for Nicholson.

Production values lend a solid texture. Alex North's music, Donfeld's costumes, and old Huston

colleague Rudi Fehr's editing make strong contributions.

One of film's colorful character turns is by William Hickey as the old don of the family, who is razor sharp beneath his drowsy and frail-speaking figure. John Randolph as Nicholson's affable pop, Robert Loggia as a cool-hard crime chief, and Lee Richardson as the reckless and weak link in the Prizzi tribe etch impressive support as the three sons of the aging head of the family.

Even Lawrence Tierney, B-picture tough guy of yore, shows up as a bald-headed (and tough again) cop on the take.

Dialog deserves high marks for unpredictability. "Do I ice her or marry her?" the flustered Nicholson asks when he discovers his lover's true past and present. Ultimately, it's the question of family honor that turns the screw on Nicholson's character. —*Loyn.*

Nana
(MEXICAN-COLOR)

Mexico City, May 10.

A Películas Mexicanas release of an Irma Serrano Production. Stars Irma Serrano. Directed by Rafael Baledón and José A. Bolaños; assistant directed by Serrano. Screenplay, Serrano; based on the novel by Emile Zola; camera (color), León Sánchez; editor, Carlos Savage; music, Rafael Elizondo. Reviewed at Cine Metropolitan, Mexico City, May 9, 1985. Running time: **97 MINS.**

Nana	Irma Serrano
Companion	Verónica Castro/Isela Vega
Francisco	Roberto Cobo
Count	Manuel Ojeda
Sr. Bonnard	Gregorio Cazals

Also with: Sara Guasch and Jaime Garza.

After five years in production, actress/producer Irma Serrano has finally decided to put her ill-fated "Nana" out of its misery by giving it a commercial release and letting it die a natural death at the boxoffice.

Taking the blame not only for the overacting and assistant directorship, "La Tigresa," as Serrano is known in Mexico, also must bear the brunt of the humorlessly tedious script, which she adapted from her sexy legit musical review which enjoyed a lengthy run in Mexico City.

Based on the novel by Emile Zola about a prostitute who becomes the toast of Paris only to succumb to the deteriorating effects of syphilis, pic reeks of self indulgence, with a half-naked Serrano playing center stage shrieking — never speaking — her vapid dialog while a veritable army of muscular young men declare their undying love for her. Of course, she rejects the advances of any older and more substantial male paramours, even though she accepts their gifts of jewelry, luxury apartments and money. Rather, she beds down with young men whom she can seduce, or with her lesbian lover, alternately played by Isela Vega and Verónica Castro. Due to arguments on the set, Vega walked out on the production and though the trick of using two actresses (replacing a solo actress) to play the same part works in Luis Buñuel's "That Obscure Object Of Desire," the effect here is confusing and sloppy.

Film suffers a poor adaptation from legit to celluloid, where a revue with lots of songs interspliced with nudity can make an agreeable combination. Also, film drags through lack of scene changes.

The use of contemporary Spanish-language romantic ballads is anachronistic to the time period depicted. In fact, the entire musical score by Rafael Elizondo is so uptempo and annoying that it destroys any sense of atmosphere that might have emerged.

As a low-budget soft-porn pic, the film is boring, even though Serrano spends over half the movie with her breasts exposed. Even the graphic lesbian encounter between Serrano and Vega comes across as lifeless.

The confused ending seems like it was intended to be a dream scene shot during Mardi Gras, with Nana's endlessly dramatic death.

— *Lent.*

The Goonies
(COLOR)

Well-crafted fairy tale adventure due for big b.o.

Hollywood, June 3.

A Warner Bros. release of a Steven Spielberg presentation from Amblin Entertainment. Produced by Richard Donner, Harvey Bernhard. Executive producers, Spielberg, Frank Marshall, Kathleen Kennedy. Directed by Donner. Features entire cast. Screenplay by Chris Columbus, from a story by Spielberg; camera (Technicolor, Panavision), Nick McLean; editor, Michael Kahn; music, Dave Grusin; production designer, J. Michael Riva; art director, Rick Carter; set decorator, Linda DeScenna; set design, Virginia L. Randolph, Carrol Johnston, Donald Woodruff; visual effects supervisor, Michael McAlister; special effects coordinator, Matt Sweeney; sound (Dolby stereo), Willie Burton; assistant director, Dan Kolsrud; casting, Mike Fenton, Jane Feinberg, Judy Taylor. Reviewed at Mann's National Theater, Westwood Village, Calif., June 1, 1985. (MPAA Rating: PG.) Running time: **111 MINS.**
Mikey . . . . .Sean Astin
Brand . . . . .Josh Brolin
Chunk . . . . .Jeff Cohen
Mouth .Corey Feldman
Andy . . . . .Kerri Green
Stef . . . . .Martha Plimpton
Data . . . . .Ke Huy Quan
Slouth . . . . .John Matuszak
Jake . . . . .Robert Davi
Francis . . . . .Joe Pantoliano
Mama Fratelli . . . . .Anne Ramsey

"The Goonies" is a dangerous Disneyland sort of a film stamped with the Steven Spielberg style of high fun. Like other Spielberg summer extravaganzas, pic is a roller coaster ride best enjoyed as it's speeding along. Once it stops to consider the sacred state of adole-

scence, it becomes painfully syrupy. Filmmakers, however, have the good sense to keep the action rolling at a high speed with production values sumptuous enough to make it a sizable summer hit, if not as overpowering as previous Spielberg productions.

Though it has much in common with "Indiana Jones And The Temple Of Doom," "The Goonies" is tame in comparison and has toned down the earlier film's much criticized violence. Even the villains here, a mother and her three bumbling sons, are more comical than threatening.

Written by Chris Columbus from a story by Spielberg, script has none of the meanness, either, of his hit from last summer, "Gremlins." Territory is typical small town Spielberg; this time set in a coastal community in Oregon. Story is told from the kids' point of view and takes a rather long time to be set in motion.

Brothers Mikey (Sean Astin) and Brand (Josh Brolin) are being forced to leave their home and friends because land developers are foreclosing on their house to build a new country club. The boys are joined by compulsive eater Chuck (Jeff Cohen) and mumbling Mouth (Corey Feldman) for one final adventure together.

Searching through the attic holding museum pieces under the care of their curator father, the boys uncover a pirate map for the whereabouts of the notorious One Eyed Willie treasure. Sidetracked only temporarily by the nefarious Fratelli family (Robert Davi, Joe Pantoliano, Anne Ramsey), the boys begin their fairy tale treasure hunt.

One Eyed Willie, it seems, was no one's fool, and though he perished in the 17th century, he left a deadly obstacle course to the treasure, reminiscent of the caves in "Indiana Jones." Production designer J. Michael Riva and visual effects supervisor Michael McAlister and their teams have created an eerie array of challenger to match any video game.

Linking the kids together is their identification as "Goonies," residents of the boondocks. Handle apparently imbues them with a mystical bond and idealized state of grace. Mikey is most emphatic in his faith and belief in the possibility of a hidden treasure to save the day. At first trhe girls (Kerri Green and Martha Plimpton) are skeptical, but eventually they too become Goonies united in a mission.

Kids are all given distinct personalities, Ke Huy Quan (Short Round of "Indiana Jones"), for instance, is a James Bond gadget freak, but somehow they are more imagined than real. Separateness of

childhood as a privileged state is a familiar Spielberg theme, but when Mikey declares that "this is our time down here, that's their time up there," the distinction becomes a bit overstated.

Conclusion, too, when the kids are reunited with their parents suggests a love and neatness of emotion that can exist only in film. Good guys and bad guys are recognizable by their hearts and even the hopelessly deformed Slouth (John Matuszak), a third Fratelli brother, wins the love of Chunk.

But the real heart of the film is the search for the gold, and picture uses all the filmmaking skill available to make the adventure seem real. Director Richard Donner has elicited fine performances from his young cast and manages to maintain a balance between danger and humor that carefully modulates the movement of the action. Editing by Michael Kahn also helps keep the audience on its toes.

Widescreen cinematography by Nick McLean simply looks great with the cave shots imbued with a surprisingly wide range of subtle coloring. One shot of the kids through a waterfall can almost make you believe in the magic of the place. Speaking of magic, the climactic view of the great pirate ship, peopled with literally a skeleton crew, has the power of legend about it.

Consummate filmmaking in service of a fairy tale vision of youth is enough to overcome the rocky moments. If only it were true.—*Jagr.*

Perfect
(COLOR)

John Travolta vehicle bites the dust.

Hollywood, June 4.

A Columbia Pictures release from Columbia-Delphi III Prods. Executive producer-production manager, Kim Kurumada. Produced and directed by James Bridges. Stars John Travolta, Jamie Lee Curtis. Screenplay, Aaron Latham, Bridges, based on articles in Rolling Stone by Latham; camera (Panavision, Technicolor), Gordon Willis; editor, Jeff Gourson, music, Ralph Burns; music supervisor, Becky Mancuso; sound, David Ronne; production design, Michael Haller, art direction, Lynda Paradise; set decoration, Tom Roysden; assistant director, Albert Shapiro; costume design, Michael Kaplan; coproducer, Jack Larson; associate producer, Joan Edwards; casting, Howard Feuer, Jeremy Richter; aerobic routines, Kim Connell. Reviewed at Samuel Goldwyn theater, Beverly Hills, Calif., May 31, 1985. (MPAA Rating: R.) Running time: 120 MINS.
Adam . . . . .John Travolta
Jessie . . . . .Jamie Lee Curtis
Frankie . . . . .Anne De Salvo
Sally . . . . .Marilu Henner
Linda . . . . .Laraine Newman
Roger . . . . .Mathew Reed
Mark Roth . . . . .Jann Wenner
Shotsy . . . . .Charlene Jones

"Perfect" pretends to be an old-fashioned love story dressed up in leotards, but more than anything else, it's a film about physical attraction. Set in the world of journalism, pic is guilty of the sins it condemns — superficiality, manipulation and smugness. On any level, "Perfect" is an embarrassment and unlikely to satisfy any audience.

Formula is really quite simple — a man must prove his worth to a reluctant woman — but problems with the plot and profession it's set in keep the affair from flowering.

Jamie Lee Curtis is an ex-Olympic-class swimmer turned aerobics instructor who was burned by a reporter and must be thawed out before she can enter into a relationship with star Travolta.

John Travolta is the heat, but before she can accept him, he must prove himself a decent fellow, something the film never really succeeds in doing. Character, called Adam Lawrence in the film, is a semi-autobiographical version of writer Aaron Latham, who based the script on a searing story he originally wrote for Rolling Stone and now seems to be exorcising here, feeling guilty for his ruthlessness.

Travolta plays a reporter with a preconceived idea of doing a story on health clubs as the singles bars of the '80s. Title of his story is "Looking for Mr. Goodbody," same title as the real piece by Latham.

Unlike Latham, Travolta develops a conscience along the way after seducing, verbally and physically, Curtis, known as "the pied piper of aerobics." He decides not to exploit her but uses other denizens of the L.A. Sports Connection, Laraine Newman and Marilu Henner. Described as the most used piece of equipment in the gym, Newman is hardly a difficult target, and Travolta's reporter laces into her.

When Curtis destroys the story, the hero supposedly has a change of heart and submits a more positive piece only to be sabotaged by Rolling Stone editor Jann Wenner playing himself. There is really little evidence of any change, or any emotion for that matter, in the reporter, and one suspects the character is still capable of anything.

At the same time, Travolta is involved in a convoluted subplot designed to demonstrate his high morals and ethics as a journalist. Story is a drug frame-up by the government against a computer manufacturer, and when the taped evidence is subpoenaed, Travolta sticks to his first amendment guns and is momentarily thrown in jail.

Incident is supposed to demonstrate Travolta's integrity and make him a suitable lover for Curtis, but only bogs down the film with a superfluous and ineffectual long-winded digression. Professionally, Travolta never becomes less than callous, partially because the direction by James Bridges supports that view.

Moments after a character condemns classifying all of the California fitness nuts as airheads, pic cuts to an aerobics class which clearly reinforces the stereotype. Professionally, the film presents a mixed message about journalism as well. On the one hand, an editor classifies obits as the last nice thing a reporter will say about people and, on the other hand, Travolta is considering penning a book defending reporters because they get a lot of bad raps.

Presumably playing a character close to his real-life identity, Wenner is the kind of editor who will do anything for a story and lights up with glee at the thought of lancing another victim, although a New Yorker's attack on California is hardly news anymore.

Given such shaky professional credentials, Travolta cannot rescue his character, and he remains basically an unsympathetic figure. As an actor, Travolta never really gets a hold on the character and is unconvincing as a reporter or a man of feeling.

In Curtis' case, she is more betrayed by lapses in the script by Latham and Bridges than by her own limitations. As an emotionally vulnerable character, it is highly unlikely that she will proposition a hated reporter soon after they meet.

It is also curious that in a film about fitness there is so little physical electricity between the leads. Yes, all the bodies are beautiful, but the attraction is only skin deep with both an aerobics class and a session by a male stripper at Chippendale's offering the same overstated sexual posturing.

Curtis does cut quite a figure in her numerous aerobic outfits, and she does communicate a certain wounded pride and appeal. Newman as the house slut mostly keeps the pathos of her character in check, but she and her sidekick Henner are treated rather like cattle by the script.

Music by Ralph Burns is strident where it should be buoyant and is yet another element threatening to drown the film. Cinematography by Gordon Willis is some of the least impressive work he's done, lacking a distinctive look and sense of time and place. —*Jagr.*

Frankenstein's Great-Aunt Tillie
(MEXICAN-COLOR)

Mexico City, April 1.

A Tillie Prod.-Filmier production, directed and written by Myron J. Gold. Features entire cast. Camera (color), Miguel Garzón; editor, John Horger; sets, Teresa Pecanins; sound, Victor Rojo; music, Ronald Stein. Reviewed on vidcassette, Mexico City, March 30, 1985. (No MPAA Rating.) Running time: **93 MINS.**

Victor Frankenstein/Old
Baron Frankenstein . . . Donald Pleasence
Aunt Matilda (Tillie)
Frankenstein . . . . Yvonne Furneaux
Randy Woonsock . . . . June Wilkinson
Niederhangen . . . : . . . . Rod Colbin
Schnitt . . . . Garnett Smith
Also with guest appearance of Zsa Zsa Gabor.

(English soundtrack)

As its title implies, "Frankenstein's Great-Aunt Tillie" is a spoof, yet with such style that makes it unique in the body of Mexican cinema. Written and directed by Myron J. Gold, the film was shot entirely in English using an all-Mexican crew.

Gold's terse script brims with puns, asides, throwaway lines, anachronisms and verbal jibes, interspersed with slapstick gags on the Keystone Cops level.

Story begins "100 years later," at the beginning of this century. The Frankenstein Castle, lying outside the town of Mugglefugger, has been abandoned. Women in the town are discovering their emancipation as a result of the discovery of bloomers. Besides dealing with such a weighty problem, the crooked town council is plotting to repossess Castle Frankenstein when back taxes become due six days hence.

Of course, as fate and the script would have it, the Frankensteins return: Victor Jr. (Donald Pleasence), his lusty paramour Randy (June Wilkinson) and his 109-year-old Aunt Matilda (Yvonne Furneaux), who has kept herself young using rejuvenating jelly.

The penniless Victor is out to find his father's fortune, believed to be hidden on the estate, while Aunt Tillie is out to win the Trans-Balkan Road Race in her convertible jalopy.

Victor is not so lucky in finding the loot, but he does discover the whereabouts of the Frankenstein monster and with the help of Aunt Tillie, he brings the creature back to life for fun and games with the locals.

Into this confusion, add two bungling policemen and a home for wayward girls, resulting in a comedy that could become a cult film.

Pleasence is hilarious with his underplayed greed and passion, and Furneaux' vitality makes her a talent that warrants more recognition (she appeared in Federico Fellini's "La Dolce Vita" and Roman Polanski's "Repulsion").

Film includes a non-speaking guest appearance by Zsa Zsa Gabor. — *Lent.*

Wild Geese II
(BRITISH-COLOR)

London, May 29.

A Thorn EMI presentation of a Frontier Film production. Executive producer, Chris Chrisafis. Produced by Euan Lloyd. Directed by Peter Hunt. Features entire cast. Screenplay, Reginald Rose, based on the book "The Square Circle" by Daniel Carney; camera (Technicolor), Michael Reed; editor, Keith Palmer; music, Roy Budd; production design, Syd Cain; art direction, Peter Williams; costumes, Diane Holmes; sound, Chris Munro. Reviewed at the Thorn EMI preview theater, London, May 29, 1985. (BBFC Certificate, 15). Running time: **125 MINS.**

John Haddad . . . . Scott Glenn
Kathy Lukas . . . . Barbara Carrera
Alex Faulkner . . . . Edward Fox
Rudolf Hess . . . . Laurence Olivier
Robert McCann . . . . Robert Webber
Heinrich Stroebling . . . . Robert Freitag
Colonel Reed-Henry . . . . . . Kenneth Haigh
Mustapha El Ali . . . . Stratford Johns
Hourigan . . . . Derek Thompson
Murphy . . . . Paul Antrim
Michael Lukas . . . . John Terry
Hooker . . . . Ingrid Pitt

Released seven years after the first entry, "Wild Geese II" opens with a dedication to Richard Burton, who died before he could encore his original role, and a replay of action sequences from the earlier adventure. The new pic fails, however, to deliver the thrills of its predecessor. Marketing will have to be pitched to those who were hooked first time around.

Script has a promising basic premise. An American tv station commissions mercenary John Haddad to kidnap the nonagenarian Nazi leader Rudolf Hess from the impregnable Spandau prison in Berlin, but the follow-through never arrives. A routine car ambush is substituted for the impossible jailbreak. The liberated Hess just doesn't want to play games with history by revealing the Watergate-style story supposedly underlying Hitler's rise to power.

Despite these structural problems, film contains a wealth of incident. Haddad is the object of numerous assassination attempts organized by the German Heinrich Stroebling, who is in league with the Russians and Palestinian terrorists. The British are after Hess too. There's also a supporting role for members of the Irish Republican Army and the kidnap of yank journalist Kathy Lukas occasions a major shootout.

These excuses for violent screen death should, of course, have highlighted the heroic persistence of a mercenary with a mission. In fact, they turn the main story into a subject without putting anything in its place.

Apart from the dramatic shots around the Spandau fortress, there are poorly-motivated but nicely-photographed sequences around a Berlin nightclub, the city's zoo, fairground, the Berlin wall and the Turkish quarter.

Edward Fox plays the Burton character Colonel Faulkner with comic zest. He's one of those absurd Britishers whose favorite pastime is to snipe at passing pedestrians from behind his potted plants. Unintentionally, perhaps, Laurence Olivier also extracts laughs from his Hess cameo. By contrast, Scott Glenn as Haddad and Barbara Carrera in the journalist role take their parts more seriously than the script merits.

Quiet opening scenes show that Peter Hunt can still direct with class, and the action scenes are competently staged. Other technical credits are fine.—*Japa.*

Secret Admirer
(COLOR)

Good acting in another teen comedy.

Hollywood, June 7.

An Orion Pictures release. Produced by Steve Roth. Executive producer, C.O. Erickson. Directed by David Greenwalt. Features entire cast. Screenplay, Jim Kouf, Greenwalt; camera (Technicolor), Victor J. Kemper; editor, Dennis Virkler; music, Jan Hammer, sound, Tom Causey; production design, William J. Cassidy; assistant director, L. Andrew Stone; coproducer, Kouf; casting Mike Fenton, Jane Feinberg. Reviewed at the Academy of Motion Picture Arts & Sciences, June 6, 1985. (MPAA Rating: R.) Running time: **98 MINS.**

Michael Ryan . . . . C. Thomas Howell
Toni . . . . Lori Loughlin
Debora Anne Fimple . . . . Kelly Preston
Connie Ryan . . . . Dee Wallace Stone
George Ryan . . . . Cliff De Young
Elizabeth Fimple . . . . . Leigh Taylor-Young
Lou Fimple . . . . Fred Ward
Roger . . . . Casey Siemaszko
Steve . . . . Scott McGinnis
Ricardo . . . . Geoffrey Blake
Kirkpatrick . . . . Rodney Pearson
Doug . . . . Courtney Gains
Barry . . . . Jeffrey Jay Cohen
Jeff . . . . Cory Haim

Behind the obligatory beer belches, "Secret Admirer" may be hiding an attempt at a reasonably intelligent borderline farce probing for fun in blind passion. That's not too evident, presumably for fear of ruining the usual boxoffice payoff for unencumbered drivel.

Obviously, too much of a reasonably intelligent story would require characters, a risk few major producers are willing to take these days. Fortunately, "Secret" is safe with a group of characters who couldn't keep across and down straight long enough to finish a crossword puzzle.

Cleverly, director David Greenwalt, who processed the script with coproducer Jim Kouf, never lets this be too clear too long. Anytime it beg is to be obvious that some characte could not possibly have made it to age seven, 17 or 37 without detailed instruction on breathing, Greenwalt goes to a closeup of fast food.

The message may be that mankind eventually will be done in by its diet, but the more immediate problem is that some unknown feminine hand has written a passionate love letter to average teenager C. Thomas Howell, who has a best friend and platonic pal in a lovely Lori Loughlin, who may just be the most long-suffering and patient screen friend since Dale Evans.

It may take two or three minutes for the audience to determine that Loughlin is the adoring lovelorn, but as mentioned Howell is no flash and it's going to be at least 90 minutes before he figures it out. And the way he reaches the correct conclusion is simply amazing: He compares her handwriting. The boy should be studied at Harvard.

In the meantime, he has suffered under the delusion that the love letter was penned by the school sexpot, Kelly Preston, and Loughlin with endless charity helps him to pursue this floozy while her own heart breaks.

Enough of this teen twaddle; "Secret" is striving for crossover business here. So one version of this letter reaches Howell's mom, Dee Wallace Stone, who thinks it's been penned to cheating husband Cliff De Young. Preston's pop, Fred Ward, finds another version and thinks it's adulterous evidence against wife Leigh Taylor-Young.

Not having played so much post-office since their own adolescence, De Young and Taylor-Young soon find themselves confusingly tempted to the edge of an affair while Ward and Stone flirt with the idea of a fling of their own for revenge.

Something — it may have been the pizza or the Pepsi — prevents all of this from reaching serious or sensible proportions until Howell finally tires of Preston while their parents sort out their own confusion. Coming out of the spin Howell finally figures out that Loughlin was the one all along.

Actually, though the talented adult players are largely wasted as they usually are in these pictures, once again the teens are really good. For all his denseness, Howell is quite likable and Loughlin is so pretty and appealing she seems miscast as any sort of second choice. Preston seen earlier in Fox' "Mischief" is almost perfect, especially in one self-centered scene as she prattles on about the joys of shopping.

As so often is true, these are bright and interesting young performers hired to portray their generation as absolutely vapid, sex-obsessed, gluttonous, semi-feebleminded hedonists void of all possible mature reflection. It takes more acting than they're getting credit for.
—Har.

Biruma No Tategoto
(The Burmese Harp)
(JAPANESE-COLOR)

Tokyo, June 9.

A Fuji Television Network, Hakuhodo, Kinema Tokyo presentation of a Kon Ichikawa film. Executive producers, Haruo Shikanai, Atsushi Okumoto, Masato Takahashi. Directed by Kon Ichikawa. Produced by Hiroaki Fujii, Masaru Kakutani, Masaya Araki. Planning by Hisashi Hieda, Matsuo Takahashi. Screenplay, Natsuto Wada, based on a story by Micho Takeyama; camera (color), Setsuo Kobayashi; art director, Iwao Akune; editor, Chizuru Osada; music, Naozumi Yamamoto; sound, Tetsuya Ohhashi; lighting, Teiichi Saito. Reviewed at Tokyo Intl. Film Festival, June 9, 1985. Running time: **132 MINS.**

Cmdr. Inoue . . . . Koji Ishizaka
Pvt. Mizushima . . . . Niichi Nakai
Sgt. Ito . . . . Takuzo Kawatani
Pvt. Kobayashi . . . . Atsushi Watanabe
Old man . . . . Fujio Tokita
Old woman . . . . Tanie Kitabayashi
Platoon commander . . . . . Bunta Sugawara

Director Kon Ichikawa has been busy lately, with his "Ohan" screened at the Asia-Pacific Film Festival and his remake of "The Burmese Harp" getting its world premiere as the closing film of the Tokyo Intl. Film Festival. The first

Original Film

A Nikkatsu release and production. Directed by Kon Ichikawa. Screenplay, Michio Takeyama, Natto Wada; camera (b&w), Minoru Yokoyama; editor, Masanori Tsujii; music, Akira Ifukube. At Venice Film Fest, September 1956. Running time: **115 MINS.**
With: Rentaro Mikumi, Shoji Yasui, Tatsuya Mihashi.

"Harp" won the Venice Palme d'Or in 1956, but the new version looks dated and corny. Why Ichikawa chose to remake the same film in essentially the same way, except this time in color, is a puzzle.

A platoon of Japanese soldiers is retreating through Burma to Thailand at the end of World War II. Their brave, kind commander (Koji Ishizaka) was a music graduate, so he's taught his men to sing as a chorus, with Pvt. Mizushima (Kiichi Nakai) accompanying on a Burmese harp. The singing lifts their spirits and helps them survive the hardships of war. It also assures their survival when, in the film's most affecting scene, the platoon members sing as they prepare for battle. Instead of attacking however, the surrounding British troops answer with their own chorus of "Home Sweet Home." It's a moving moment as the enemy forces sing across a nighttime jungle clearing. The Japanese surrender and find out the war had

ended three days before.

Mizushima is later sent by the British to persuade a group of Japanese soldiers to stop fighting. They refuse, and Mizushima is caught in the British bombardment that kills most of the others.

With the help of a Buddhist monk, he recovers from his wounds and sets out walking to rejoin his platoon in a prison camp several hundred miles away. Along the way he passes dead Japanese soldiers and suffers a personal crisis. He decides that no matter how much he wants to return to Japan with his buddies, he has to stay in Burma as a monk, burying the dead and praying for their souls.

The trouble with this pic is it doesn't know where to stop. There are too many scenes of the platoon and its leader in anguish because Mizushima won't join them and of Mizushima agonizing for the same reason. His buddies train a parrot to tell Mizushima to go back to Japan with them, and he trains another parrot to say he can't. At least the birds don't join the soldiers' chorus.

The acting is unrelievedly sincere, and the singing has an artificial quality, with the sound looped in so these battle-scarred veterans sound like they're in a choir loft even in the middle of a jungle. During the first songfest of film, a squirrel comes out and nibbles away while the weary troops sing on a picturesque river embankment. One keeps waiting for Bambi to appear. *—Bask.*

Kayako No Tameni
(For Kayako)
(JAPANESE-COLOR)

Tokyo, June 8.

A Shibata Organization Inc. release of Himawari Theater Group Inc. production. Produced by Fujio Sunaoka. Executive producer, Hiroshi Fujikura. Directed by Kohei Oguri. Features entire cast. Screenplay, Oguri, Shogo Ohta, from the novel by Hwe-Song Lee; camera (color), Shohei Ando; sound, Hideo Nishizake; art director, Akira Naito; music, Durodo Mohri. Reviewed at Towa screening room, Tokyo, June 7, 1985. Running time: **115 MINS.**

Sanjun Im . . . . Sunghil
Kayako Matsumoto . . . . Kaho Minami
Akio Matsumoto . . . . Jun Hamamura
Toshi Matsumoto . . . . Kayako Sono
Kyushi Im . . . . Takeshi Kato
Irujun Im . . . . Takuzo Kawatani
Myoni Chie . . . . Tami Hon
Kayako's Aunt . . . . Toshie Kobayashi

Second feature of Kohei Oguri, whose first was the Oscar-nominated "Muddy River," is an exceptionally beautiful pic dealing with the problem of Koreans living in Japan. Film is visually exquisite, with every image given painterly dimension, and with a meticulous soundtrack of pristine clarity. There is, however, a certain coldness in the personal story told which wasn't evident in the earlier film.

The year is 1957, and Sanjun Im, one of many thousands of Koreans who stayed on in Japan after the war, returns from school in Tokyo to his home in northern Hokkaido. En route, he stops off to visit his father's best friend, who married a Japanese woman and has taken a Japanese name. He has a stepdaughter, Kayako, who's wholly Japanese.

Sanjun keeps in touch with the girl, though his life in Tokyo is a difficult and impoverished one. He tries to stay close to the alienated and disaffected members of the Korean community, who are treated as second-class citizens by the Japanese (although it was Japan's original invasion of Korea which resulted in large numbers of Koreans coming to Japan in the first place).

Eventually Sanjun, the Korean, and Kayako, the Japanese, become lovers, though their happiness is disrupted by the distraught arrival of the girl's parents. Soon afterwards, Kayako disappears. Some 10 years later, Sanjun visits Hokkaido again, searching for his lost love.

Oguri treats this relatively simple story in a rather abstract style. He disrupts the continuity on more than one occasion, so that the viewer has to struggle to pick up the narrative. For instance, towards the end, after Kayako's parents find the lovers together, the young couple go walking in a Tokyo street and have a strange encounter with a water diviner: we see that the girl is crying. Then there's an abrupt cut to icy winter weather, and we find ourselves in Hokkaido 10 years later with Sanjun still searching for Kayako. Abrupt jumps in the narrative like this keep the viewer from getting too emotionally involved with the characters, though the subject of Japan's treatment of Koreans is indeed an emotional one.

This coldness of approach may prevent the film achieving the popular success of "Muddy River," but it's still an important and impressive film from an obviously talented director. It should rep Japan at a major festival later this summer.
— *Strat.*

Ohan
(JAPANESE-COLOR)

Tokyo, June 5.
A Toho Pictures Inc. production. Produced by Tomoyuki Tanaka, Kon Ichikawa. Directed by Kon Ichikawa. Stars Sayuri Yoshinaga, Koji Ishizaka. Screenplay, Ichikawa, Shinya Hidaka; camera (color), Yukio Isohata; sound, Tetsuya Ohashu; editor, Chizuko Osada; art director, Shinobu Muraki; music, Shinnosuke Ohkawa, Tomoyuki Asakawa. Reviewed at Asia-Pacific Film Festival, Tokyo, June 4, 1985. Running time: **112 MINS.**
Ohan . . . . .Sayuri Yoshinaga
Kohkichi. . . . . .Koji Ishizaka
Okayo . . . . .Reiko Ohara
Satoru . . . . .Wataru Hasegawa

"Ohan" is a determinedly old-fashioned pic. Set, apparently, in the '20s, it's about a married couple who separate, against the wishes of Ohan, the wife; her husband, Kohkichi, doesn't know she's pregnant. Seven years later, he's married to Okayo, a former geisha, when he meets Ohan again and falls head over heels for his ex-wife. She doesn't tell him about their son, but they become secret lovers. After a while he meets the lad, and his emotions are further strained, because his new wife apparently can't have children. But, during a fierce thunderstorm, the boy falls into a river and drowns, precipitating a final showdown between Kohkichi and his two women.

Pic is firmly in an earlier tradition of Japanese cinema, and seems a little quaint by today's standards. Director Kon Ichikawa's handling is leisurely and calm, with quietly dramatic scenes interspersed with contemplative images of streets and rooftops.

Sayuri Yoshinaga portrays another of her long-suffering women, at which she's quite superb. Other thesping is all good.

But effortlessly beautiful and gentle as it is, "Ohan" is so out of its time that it already looks like an archive film. Nothing artistically wrong with that, but whether it will attract modern audiences is quite another matter. —*Strat.*

D.A.R.Y.L.
(COLOR)

Farfetched adventure is pleasant at best.

Hollywood, June 7.
A Paramount Pictures release. Produced by John Heyman. Directed by Simon Wincer. Features entire cast. Screenplay by David Ambrose, Allan Scott, Jeffrey Ellis; camera (Panavision, TVC color), Frank Watts; editor, Adrian Carr; music, Marvin Hamlisch; production designer, Alan Cassie; art director, John K. Moore, John Siddall; set decorators, William Aley, Terise Robers, Simon Wakefield; visual effects supervisor, Adrian Carr; sound (Dolby stereo), Simon Kaye; costumes, Shay Cunliffe; coproducers, Burtt Harris, Gabrielle Kelly; assistant directors, Robert E. Warren, Don French; casting, Gretchen Rennell. Reviewed at Paramount Studios screening room, Hollywood, Calif., June 6, 1985. (MPAA Rating: PG.) Running time: **99 MINS.**
Joyce Richardson . . . . .Mary Beth Hurt
Andy Richardson . . . . . . .Michael McKean
Ellen Lamb : . . . . .Kathryn Walker
Elaine Fox . . . . .Colleen Camp
Dr. Stewart . . . . .Josef Sommer
General Graycliffe . . . . .Ron Frazier
Howie Fox . . . . .Steve Ryan
Daryl . . . . .Barret Oliver
Turtle . . . . .Danny Corkill

"D.A.R.Y.L." is the kind of project that must have looked great on paper: a bit of "WarGames" high tech, a bit of "Cloak & Dagger" computer games with a humanizing influence no one could resist. The problem is it doesn't work and result is, at best, a pleasant, if sappy, family adventure. Still, with careful handling pic could garner some modest business as a counterpoint to the summer bombast.

Pic manages to get off to a strong start with a scenic chase through a curving mountain road as a chopper bears down on a racing car. Just before crashing, the driver pushes out a young boy who is rescued and taken into a foster home by the Richardsons (Mary Beth Hurt and Michael McKean).

Fatal mistake of the film is that the audience knows miles ahead of the Richardsons by virtue of the film's tagline, "no one this perfect could be only human," that this strange young man is a robot. Amusing confrontations, such as when the boy learns to play baseball, aren't enhanced enough to justify the advance knowledge.

After establishing a cozy domestic situation the film takes off in a different direction when his "parents" come to take Daryl home. Home is a top security research facility where scientists Josef Sommer and Kathryn Walker have given birth to D.A.R.Y.L. Acronym stands for Data Analyzing Robot Youth Lifeform and Daryl is described as "an experiment in artificial intelligence."

Indeed the idea of a test-tube baby implanted with a highly sophisticated computer brain is hard to believe. Not only is the scientific feasibility of a robot who gains feelings as it comes in contact with humans questionable, the humanizing of a machine is risky business.

With all this said, "D.A.R.Y.L." is still moderately entertaining depending on one's ability to suspend disbelief and go with the action. Director Simon Wincer could have done a better job in keeping the film moving along, especially in the first half..

Second half of the picture is the most farfetched and also the most fun as the young robot gets to show off some of his powers. Production design by Alan Cassie is strongest in the research lab. Other tech credits are adequate with costumes lending an authentic middle America feel to the picture.

As the robot in question, Barret Oliver is suitably stiff and makes as credible as possible a Superman who wants to be Clark Kent.
—*Jagr.*

An Indecent Obsession
(AUSTRALIAN-COLOR)

Sydney, June 7.
A Hoyts Distribution (Australia) release of a Hoyts/Michael Edgley Intl. presentation of a PBL production. Produced by Ian Bradley. Directed by Lex Marinos. Stars Wendy Hughes, Gary Sweet, Richard Moir. Executive producers, Edgley, John Daniell; screenplay, Denise Morgan; camera (color) Ernest Clark; associate producer, Maura Fay; production designer, Michael Ralph; editor, Philip Howe; costume designer, Graham Purcell; original music, Dave Skinner. Reviewed at Hoyts Center, Sydney, June 6, 1985. (Commonwealth Film Censor Rating: M). Running time: **100 MINS.**
Honour Langtry . . . . .Wendy Hughes
Michael Wilson . . . . .Gary Sweet
Luce Daggett . . . . .Richard Moir
Neil Parkinson . . . . .Jonathan Hyde
Matt Sawyer . . . . .Bruno Lawrence
Benedict Maynard . . . . .Mark Little
Nuggett Jones . . . . .Tony Sheldon
Col. Chinstrap . . . . .Bill Hunter
Matron . . . . .Julia Blake
Sally . . . . .Caroline Gillmer

From "The Thorn Birds" authoress Colleen McCullough comes "An Indecent Obsession," a florid tale of thwarted love in the tropics set in the dying days of World War II. McCullough approves of the PBL Productions' rendition of "Obsession" and lent a hand in promoting its theatrical release here, in contrast to the "Thorn Birds"

mini which she reportedly disowned.

Item opened to respectable box-office business in Sydney despite generally unfavorable reviews in the consumer press, which probably proves the drawing power of anything bearing the McCullough name.

The vast audiences which tuned in to the "Thorn Birds" when it aired on ABC in the U.S. are not likely to line up at the pay windows to see this pic which lacks the all-star cast, big production values and wide sweep of its predecessor, but it's strong enough to hold up as moderately entertaining tv fare.

Inviting comparisons with Milos Forman's "One Flew Over The Cuckoo's Nest," action here takes place in Ward X, designated for psychologically disturbed soldiers, in an Australian military hospital on a Pacific island (Lord Howe, north of Sydney). Ward functions normally — or as normal as it can be with the bunch of psychotics — under stern, no-nonsense matron Julia Blake and caring, compassionate sister Wendy Hughes until handsome sergeant Gary Sweet is admitted.

Aside from a nasty temper and a gruff air, Sweet seems relatively sane until sadistic, manipulative inmate Richard Moir discovers his secret: he has homosexual leanings which got him into trouble with a superior officer. After a steamy bath-house encounter between the two, Sweet gets his sexual proclivities back on course by making love to Hughes, who had been a mite frustrated, ministering to all those men in the tropics, and Moir is found dead in the bath-house. It looks like suicide until a clever plot maneuver reveals he was done in by another inmate. Upshot has the chaps closing ranks and heading for home at the end of the war, leaving Hughes alone and no doubt, even more frustrated.

Making his feature film debut, helmer Lex Marinos (a distinguished legit director and actor) does a fair job with the mediocre material, but he often allows the pace to lag, and there are long spells of inactivity when the men sit around sipping tea, and verbally sniping at each other.

Hughes, who has earned international recognition for her roles in two Paul Cox films "Lonely Hearts" and "My First Wife" and in Carl Schultz's "Careful, He Might Hear You," won't do her reputation any harm in this outing, although the character (named, too cutely, Honour) does not give her much scope.

Sweet and Moir register quite well and supporting cast is uniformly good, notably Tony Sheldon as a hypochondriac who injects some much-needed comic relief, Mark

Little as a quivering schizophrenic and from New Zealand, Bruno Lawrence, who tries to stop his wife finding out that he's been blinded by getting other guys to write letters for him (doesn't she know his handwriting?).

Tech credits are fine with one exception: photographing the flashback battle sequences in pale, washed-out colors lessens the realism and impact they should have had.—*Dogo*.

Contrato Con La Muerte
(Contract With Death)
(MEXICAN-COLOR)

Mexico City, May 11.

A Películas Mexicanas release of a Cinematografía Filmex production. Produced by J. Fernando Pérez Galiván. Directed by Alfredo Gurrola. Stars Eduardo Yañez. Screenplay, Tomás Fuentes, based on an idea by Jesús F. Montoya; camera (color), Agustín Lara; editor, Rogelio Zúñiga; music, Raúl Alcantara; special musical appearance, Los Broncos de Reynosa. Reviewed at Cine Variadades, Mexico City, May 10, 1985. Running time: **90 MINS.**

Andrés González . . . . .Eduardo Yañez
José (Pepe) . . . . .Toño Infante
Don Seferino . . . . .Armando Silvestre
Estela . . . . .Julieta Rosen
Luciana . . . . .Maribel Guardia
Gabriel . . . . .Jerry Velaquez
Roberto Gómez . . . . .Jorge Zepeda
Paulino . . . . .Carlos Cardán
  Also with: Narciso Busquets, Bruno Rey, Oscar Fuentes and Prisma.

Actor Eduardo Yañez' first film in a five-picture package with Cinematografía Filmex follows a wellknown formula in Mexican cinema, mixing drug trafficking with the revenge motive. Pic manages to hold its own, perhaps because Yañez comes off as a likeable kid willing to admit his mistakes. When he says he'll be better in the future, we want to believe him.

Story begins with a crooked narcotics deal in which Andrés (Yañez) and his brother Gabriel are doublecrossed. When Gabriel is killed, Andrés shoots one of the villians and is later incarcerated. With time off for good behavior, he returns to his native Durango wanting only to mend his ways and lead a new life. His old buddy Pepe (Toño Infante) gets him a job at a ranch where he falls for the boss' niece Estela (Julieta Rosen).

Everything goes well until the gang discovers Andrés is back in town and decides to reap their own punishment for the murder. So, while on a picnic, Andrés, Pepe and their girlfriends are ambushed. When Pepe and his girl are killed, Andrés is sparked to action and he gets rid of the entire gang singlehandedly.

Rather than build the story around the action, director Alfredo Gurrola has wisely decided to construct well-developed, likeable characters. Thus, the not-so-graphic

violence that follows is a result of self-defense.

Particularly effective is Infante as the sympathetic and flamboyant Pepe, and Rosen as gentle Estela.

Technically, pic is good though there are a few jumps in the narrative due to scenes that ended up on the cutting-room floor.

Also, the ending — where the police chief lets Andrés escape after his umpteenth murder — is unrealistic and more a crowdpleaser than what we have come to expect from the chief's character.

Even so, pic should do well in border areas and the U.S. Hispanic community.—*Lent*.

Ingrid
(DOCU-COLOR/B&W-16m)

Fascinating biopic of Ingrid Bergman.

A Wombat Production, N.Y., produced and written by Suzette Winter and Gene Feldman. Directed by Feldman. Narrator, John Gielgud; camera (color), Lee Kenower, Tony Forsberg, Tery Maher; music supervisor, Diane Ehrlichman; editor, Barbara Glazer. Reviewed at American Film Festival, May 30, 1985. (No MPAA Rating.) Running time: **70 MINS.**

A career-biography of and tribute to the late Swedish actress, Ingrid Bergman, "Ingrid" re-evokes her voice and presence for all. Further, it reveals again the special composure, kindliness and humaneness that put her above mere stardom.

Bergman died of cancer Aug. 29, 1982, on her 67th birthday. Her last performance was "A Woman Called Golda," for television, on the life of the late Israeli premier, Golda Meir. The Venice Festival honored Bergman with a posthumous tribute in August 1983 on the first anniversary of her death.

John Gielgud is appropriate as narrator of "Ingrid." He had costarred with Bergman in "Murder On The Orient Express," directed by Sidney Lumet. Also, he directed her in 1975 for the London stage in "The Constant Wife," by W. Somerset Maugham. He later directed her in Broadway and Los Angeles openings of the play.

"Ingrid" was shot in Stockholm, London, Rome and New York. Among those discussing the late actress is Anthony Quinn, who costarred with Bergman in "The Visit" and in "A Walk In The Spring Rain." Liv Ullmann also appears, having played her daughter in Ingmar Bergman's "Autumn Sonata." Angela Lansbury, who at age 17 appeared with the actress in "Gaslight," is in "Ingrid," as is British actress-director, Ann Todd, a close friend. Richard Goodwin, producer of "Murder On The Orient Express," likewise remembers the actress.

Others appearing in "Ingrid" are Fiorella Mariani, niece of the late Italian director Roberto Rossellini, and Mario Del Papa, his former production manager, who discuss the famous Bergman-Rossellini marriage of seven years, which brought the couple a son, Robertino, and twin daughters, Ingrid and Isabella.

"Ingrid" uses a tv clip from this period, when variety show host Ed Sullivan is seen inviting his viewers to write him their opinions on whether Bergman had done sufficient penance, after the Rossellini scandal, to qualify for invitation to "our" show.

Also interviewed in "Ingrid" are Greta Danielsson, once Bergman's governess; Frank Sundstrom, actordirector and former classmate of Bergman at the Royal Dramatic Theatre School in Stockholm; Kay Brown, former talent scout for David O. Selznick, now a New York agent, who was sent to Stockholm in 1939 to sign up the young Swedish starlet, and who later negotiated her Oscar-winning "Anastasia" performance in 1956; José Ferrer, who costarred with Bergman in "Joan Of Arc;" and Warren Thomas of "The Alvin Gang" of loyal Bergman fans.

In addition to interviews with Bergman colleagues, "Ingrid" uses newsreel clips and excerpts from 25 Bergman films, including both the original Swedish "Intermezzo" and the U.S. remake directed by Gregory Ratoff that launched her American career. "Ingrid" also uses Bergman's screentest for Selznick, wherein her natural beauty was emphasized. In addition, family footage is used, shot by Bergman's doting father, who until his death closely chronicled his daughter's growth to age 13.

"Ingrid" is cowritten and coproduced by wife-husband team Suzette Winter and Gene Feldman for their Wombat Prod., New York. Their previous films about film include "Hollywood's Children," narrated by Roddy McDowall, and "The Horror Of It All," narrated by José Ferrer.—*Hitch*.

Typhoon Club
(JAPANESE-COLOR)

Tokyo, June 7.

An A.T.G. release of a Miyasaka-Sohmai production. Produced by Susumu Miyasaka. Directed by Shinji Somai. Features entire cast. Screenplay, Yuji Katoh; camera (color), Akihiro Itoh; production design, Noriyoshi Ikeya; editor, Isao Tomita. Reviewed at Tokyo Film Festival (Young Cinema '85 Competition), June 5, 1985. Running time: **114 MINS.**

Kyoichi . . . . .Yuichi Mikami
Ken . . . . .Shigeru Benibayashi
Akira . . . . .Toshihiko Matsunaga
Rie . . . . .Yuki Kudoh
Michiko . . . . .Yuka Ohnishi
Yasuko . . . . .Akiko Aizawa

Yumi . . . . .Ryuko Tendoh
Midori . . . . .Yuriko Fuchizaki
Mr. Umemiya . . . . .Tomokazu Miura

Japan's entry in the Tokyo film fest's lucrative Young Cinema '85 contest is a striking pic about alienated youth. Theme itself is a familiar one, but approach in this instance shows originality, even though ultimately there's nothing really very new being said.

Pic intros a clutch of kids in junior high school in the far outer suburbs of Tokyo. Entrance exams are approaching, and there's tension in the air. Youngsters include a loner who acts as a kind of conscience for the rest of the class; a simple-minded type who is still accepted by the others; a couple of girls involved in a lesbian relationship, and others.

Their confidence in authority is eroded when their math teacher is berated in front of his class by the irate mother of his girlfriend. It means loss of face and position for him.

Next day, a Saturday, some kids linger in the school building as a violent storm approaches. The staff closes the school, thinking everyone's gone home, but the principal characters remain locked inside to play out their fantasies as the storm rages around them. They become wildly excited, with the simpleminded one trying to rape one of the girls, the young lesbian lovers indulging themselves, and the loner just looking on. They dance naked in the wind and the wild rain. But, next morning, a strange kind of tragedy awaits them.

Most Japanese films look superb and "Typoon Club" is no exception; Akihiro Itoh's camerawork is marvelous, with memorable image after memorable image on the screen. But, eventually, this boils down to a slight tale of kids without much purpose in life, and their elders who ignore or misunderstand them.

The young actors are all fine, and pic definitely indicates an interesting directorial talent in 35-year-old Shinji Somai, who previously worked as an assistant to the late Shuji Terayama. — *Strat*.

Howling II...Your Sister Is A Werewolf
(U.S.-COLOR)

Tokyo, June 5.

A Thorn EMI release of a Hemdale presentation of a Granite Prods. production. Produced by Steven Lane. Executive producer, Grahame Jennings. Directed by Philippe Mora. Stars Christopher Lee. Screenplay, Robert Sarno, Gary Brandner, from the book by Brandner; camera (color), G. Stephenson; music, Steve Parsons; production design, Karel Vacek; associate producer, Robert Pringle; special effects makeup, Jack Bricker. Reviewed at Tokyo Film Festival (Fantastic section), June 4, 1985. Running time: **90 MINS.**

Stefan Crosscoe	Christopher Lee
Jenny Templeton	Annie McEnroe
Ben White	Reb Brown
Stirba	Sybil Danning
Mariana	Marsha A. Hunt
Vlad	Judd Omen
Erle	Ferdinand Mayne
Punk Group	Babel

Customers led to expect from its title that "Howling II..." will be a werewolf pic in the tradition of Joe Dante's invigorating "The Howling" (1981) are in for a disappointment; this is a generally lackluster horror item. Best bet is to open fast and wide before the word gets out.

Tale opens with the funeral of a femme tv newsperson; in attendance is Christopher Lee as an expert on werewolves. He advises that the dead woman was such a creature, and is joined by her brother (Reb Brown) and colleague (Annie McEnroe) on a trip to Transylvania to destroy the werewolf queen (Sybil Danning), who is actually Lee's sister.

Despite fancy editing tricks and a few touches of grim humor, pic adds up to very little. Suspense is woefully lacking, as Danning is an unformidable villain (she looks as though she's stepped out of a soft-core sex pic) and the plot development is strictly by-the-numbers. Apart from a few moments shot in L.A., pic was lensed in Czechoslovakia, but relatively little is made of the settings, while the production design of Karel Vacek is on the overcrowded side.

Christopher Lee brings a tired authority to his role, but neither Annie McEnroe nor Reb Brown registers very effectively as the (aging) juve leads. A punk rock concert, also shot in Prague with genuine Czech punks, is a redundant sequence. Special makeup effects are okay, but not as shatteringly used as they have been in earlier, better, werewolf sagas. Music score is often inappropriate.

In all, strictly for the undemanding, or the youngsters who haven't seen it all done a million times before, and better. —*Strat.*

Kamata Koshinkyoku
(The Fall Guy)
(JAPANESE-COLOR)

Tokyo, June 6.

A Shochiku release of a Haruki Kadokawa production. Directed by Kinji Fukasaku. Screenplay, Kohei Tsuka, based on his novel; camera (color), Kiyoshi Kitazaka; art direction, Akira Takahashi; music, Masato Kai. No other credits provided. Reviewed at the Tokyo Intl. Film Festival, Shibuya Shochiku Theater, June 5, 1984. Running time: **109 MINS.**
With: Keiko Matsuzaka, Morio Kazama, Mitsuru Hirata.

This contempo melodramatic fable is a welcome change of pace for director Kinji Fukasaku, who's made a considerable splash as a helmer of gangster action pics with beaucoup violence ("Yakuza Papers," 1973) and pics of sharply pointed social statement ("Ohkamito Buta-to Ningen," 1964). Pic was released in 1982, another in producer Haruki Kadokawa's string of slick and commercially appealing ventures.

"Fall Guy" is trickier than it seems at first glance. Essentially, it's a bit of whimsy set in Toei's Kyoto Studios where countless Samurai costumers are lensed. Chief character is a good-natured bit player who turns death-defying stunt man to both establish a personal identity and make enough money to support his new wife, a former actress who's pregnant with another man's child.

That other man is a childish, wildly egocentric leading man whose chief concern is the number of closeups he obtains in any given film. The amiable bumpkin from the southern island of Kyushi idolizes the star for reasons that must be accepted on faith if the pic's comedy is to work.

Laughs come when director Fukasaku and scripter Kohei Tsuka run their characters through the lensing of a Samurai epic complete with off-camera interruptions caused by tantrums from the temperamental topliner and his equally bad-tempered "star" rival. A bit too much melodrama ensues from the humor, however.

This has the effect of forcing the characters to be developed in only the broadest of strokes. The principal figure is a likeable combination of Yoji Yamada's Tora-san and Paddy Chayefsky's Marty. He is kind, faithful as an amiable pooch and courageous beyond measure. In other words, he's not to be taken at face value.

The woman he marries (the leading man's former mistress) is a pretty but overwrought figure in keeping with the Japanese public's apparent preference for femmes as vociferously long-suffering weepers.

Plot comes to a head when the bit player, in a desperate attempt to establish himself as something other than a self-effacing flunkie, agrees to perform a stunt that could well kill him.

The situation is milked both for laughs and suspense in solid fashion. The outcome winds the pic in a breezy style that puts the preceding melodrama somewhat into proportion.

In all, "Fall Guy" is an impressive entry but of limited commercial prospect. —*Sege.*

Deep Blue Night
(SOUTH KOREAN-COLOR)

Tokyo, June 8.

A Dong-Exports Co. Ltd. production. Produced by Lee Woo-Suk. Directed by Bae Chang-Ho. Features entire cast. Screenplay, Choi In-Ho; camera (color), Chung Kwang-Suk; music, Chung Seong-Jo; editor, Kim Hee-Soo; art director, Lee Myung-Soo. Reviewed at Asia-Pacific Film Festival, Tokyo, June 6, 1985. Running time: **110 MINS.**
Ho-Bin Back	Ahn Sung-Ki
Jane	Chang Mi-Hee
Hyung-Sup	Chin You-Young
Mrs. Han	Choi Min-Hee

First-prize winner in the Asia-Pacific film fest, this is a routine drama, lensed entirely in the U.S., about a violent, brutal Korean who'll stop at nothing to get his green card.

Pic opens in Death Valley: he's driving his girlfriend's car but stops to make love to her (it looks uncomfortable) and then beats her up, steals her cash and auto, and abandons her. Nice guy!

In L.A., he meets an alluring Korean girl who works in a bar but specializes in marrying aliens to give them citizenship. They enter into a marriage contract, but she falls in love with him, not knowing he has a pregnant wife back home in Seoul. Once he gets his green card, he abandons her, but she manages to avenge herself on him at fadeout.

Pic may arouse some interest at home, or among the Korean population Stateside, but it's a depressingly ordinary tale of a hideous character and the guillible women he uses and abuses.

Technically slick, it's relentlessly ugly in its theme and its central character. — *Strat.*

La Fuga Del Rojo
(El Rojo's Escape)
(MEXICAN-COLOR)

Mexico City, May 26.

A Peliculas Mexicanas release of a Filmadora Mor Ben, S.A. production. Produced by Carlos Moreno Castilleja. Executive producer, Roberto Moreno Castilleja. Directed by Alfredo Gurrola. Stars Mario Alamada. Screenplay, Jorge Patiño, based on a "corrida" (narrative ballad) by Los Tigres del Norte; camera (color), José Ortiz Ramos; editor, Joaquin Ceballes; music, Los Tigres del Norte and Guadalupe Pineda. Reviewed at Cine Insurgentes 70, Mexico City, May 25, 1985. Running time: **90 MINS.**
Elipido Rojas (El Rojo)	Mario Almada
Adriana	Carmen del Valle
Lieutenant Morán	Noe Murayama
Lieutenant Callahan	Roger Cudney
Carmen	Patricia Rivera

Also with: Mario Cid, Alejandro Parodi, Jorge Reynoso, Carlos González, César Sobrevals, Roberto Rosales, Jorge Patiño, Armado Sumaya and Carlos Vendrell.

"La Fuga Del Rojo" is a routine adventure film that never quite achieves suspense. Pic concerns a group of writers and intellectuals from an unnamed Central American country, which shares a border with Mexico. This group stages a daring escape by famed Mexican safecracker known as EL Rojo (Mario Almada) from a U.S. prison, where he has already done three years time.

The purpose of this escape is to use El Rojo's talents to relieve a U.S. mining company of $3,000,000 in gold to purchase arms for guerrillas fighting for liberation.

Not the idealist, our thief — described as a man of honor — opts for a percentage of the take, which will be given to him on the delivery of said artillery.

On the side of law enforcement, and pursuing El Rojo at every stage, are Lt. Callahan (Roger Cudney), a U.S. police officer, and his Mexican counterpart, Lt. Morán (Noe Murayama). Each one working with his own methods, they join forces to track down the thief.

It is Morán who finally locates him in Central America, surrounded by the guerrilla forces, just after El Rojo has been seduced by the more-than-merely political charms of "Companera" Carmen (Patricia Rivera), a freedom-fighter whose sister was killed in battle and who is destined to share the same fate.

This marks the turning point for El Rojo. Witnessing the valiant death of this sexy revolutionary makes him abandon all thoughts of personal gain and he takes up the cause of the guerrillas — more for the romantic notion of shared brotherhood than any political ideology.

Pic moves along in linear fashion; for an action film, it is not particularly exciting. The characters generate some interest, but not enough to sustain the tale, which can best be described as routine fare.—*Lent.*

Restless Natives
(BRITISH-COLOR)

Tokyo, June 8.

A Thorn EMI Screen Entertainment Ltd-Oxford Film Company production. Produced by Rick Stevenson. Executive producer, Mark Bentley. Directed by Michael Hoffman. Features entire cast. Screenplay, Ninian Dunet; camera (Technicolor), Oliver Stapleton; music, Stuart Adamson, performed by Big Country; editor, Sean Barton; production design, Adrienne Atkinson. Reviewed at Tokyo Film Festival (Young Cinema '85 Competition), June 7, 1985. Running time: **89 MINS.**
Will Bryce	Vincent Friell
Ronnie Wotherspoon	Joe Mullaney
Margot	Teri Lally
Fritz Bender	Ned Beatty
Det. Insp. Baird	Robert Urquhart
Mother	Anne Scott-James
Tourists	Bryan Forbes, Nanette Newman

Ninian Dunet's screenplay for "Restless Natives" won the 1984 National Screenplay Competition sponsored by Britain's Lloyd's Bank; award seems to have been given more for a promising idea than for a fully realized work, for the finished pic is a very uneven affair which starts brightly but soon runs out of ideas and steam.

Set in Edinburgh, it's about two

young men (Vincent Friell, Joe Mullaney) who are bored with life. One is a street cleaner, the other works in a joke shop. They take it into their heads to rob the coaches that take tourists round Scotland's beauty spots, so they don funny masks (one as a clown, the other as a wolfman) and set off on their motorbikes as bizarre latter-day highwaymen.

Premise of the film, an unlikely one, is that the tourists, mostly Yanks, don't mind having their money and valuables stolen by these two eccentrics; in fact, they seem to enjoy it so much that Scottish tourism actually increases. All good comedy is based on reality, albeit heightened reality, and the whole notion of this script is so patently *un*realistic that it quickly becomes dull.

One of the lads falls for a comely tour guide, who reciprocates, while the other becomes involved, for no very good reason, with a criminal type who believes the robberies should involve violence. There's also Ned Beatty as a CIA man who is an early victim of the bandits and becomes obsessed with tracking them down.

Best elements in the film are the engaging performances of the leads, the initial scenes in which the plot is set up, and the fine locations in Edinburgh and the country around Fort William. But, despite its award, the script is a thin one which needed more work before reaching the screen. Michael Hoffman's direction is competent. — *Strat.*

Jacques et Novembre
(Jacques And November)
(CANADIAN-COLOR/B&W)

Tokyo, June 3.

A Les Productions du Lundi Matin production. Produced, written and directed by François Bouvier, Jean Beaudry. Stars Beaudry. Camera (color), Sergae Giguère; sound, Marcel Fraser; music, Michel Rivard; assistant, Marquise LePage; song, Michel Rivard; coproducer, Michel Simard, editor, Beaudry. Reviewed at Tokyo Film Festival (In Competition, Young Cinema '85 section), June 2, 1985. Running time: 72 MINS.
Jacques Landry . . . . Jean Beaudry
Pierette . . . . Carole Fréchetter
Monique . . . . Monique Cantin

Jacques Landry, 31, is dying of cancer. A committed film buff, he decides to make a document about his death, and persuades his friend, Denis, to film his friends at his direction in 16m color, while Jacques films himself with a black and white video camera.

The idea is that, after Jacques' death, Denis will assemble the material together in the form of a visual diary, which covers the last month of Jacques' short life.

Result is a simple, modest, but deeply affecting film, which observes its dying protagonist with quiet humor and sympathy. Jac-

ques, whose favorite film seems to be Alain Tanner's "Jonah Who Will Be 25 In The Year 2000," is seen settling acounts with Monique, the girl he loved and lived with, but who is now pregnant by another man; with his father, in a wonderful scene where the older man, who has double-parked his car outside his son's apartament, tries to tell him he loves him while angry drivers honk their horns outside; and with other friends and lovers.

The directors don't turn this into an unbearably heavy film, though, and there's quiet humor in scenes like one in which Jacques films himself adding up his life's achievements on a calculator (slept 10 years, ate two years, watched tv 472 days, made love 39 days, etc.). At the same time, Jacques' pain, frustration and agony aren't ignored, and his plight is neatly summed up in a scene where he decides to sell off his personal effects to help pay for the film.

Co-director Jean Beaudry is impressive in the title role, and this modest film is made with integrity and skill. Theatrical chances aren't good, because of its subject, length and grainy 16m visuals, but it should have a non-theatrical career and play on enlightened tv networks the world over. —*Strat.*

Matinya Seorang Patriot
(Death Of A Patriot)
(MALAYSIAN-COLOR)

Tokyo, June 6.

A Z.S.A. Film Production. Executive producer, Azmil Mustapha. Directed, screenplay by Rahim Razari. Features entire cast. Camera (Eastmancolor), Zainal Othman; editor, Mior Hashim Manap; music, A. Abu Hassan; sound, Peter Lim. Reviewed at Asia-Pacific Film Fest, Tokyo, June 5, 1985. Running time: 114 MINS.
With: Noor Kumalasari, Saadiah, Zulilifu Zain, Azmil, S. Roomai Noor, Mustaffa Maarof.

Opening reel or so of this contempo political thriller is so muddled and incoherent that half the audience at the screening caught departed. Those who stayed discovered the pic settled down into a revenge saga in which the five sons of a popular local village leader avenge his death.

Seems that Haji Shabhan, the leader, fell afoul of a large business corporation, Melati Holdings, whose board of directors attempted to blackmail him by showing him photos of his wife in the nude, photos taken years earlier by an Englishman for whom she worked. Shock of seeing his wife in the altogether precipitated a fatal heart attack. Now his offspring are out to get the baddies, who are killed off one by one. One brother, however, has infiltrated the family of the head of the company via an affair with his headstrong daughter; he falls in

love, natch, and is torn between his woman and filial duty.

If only writer-director Rahim Razari had opted to tell his tale with a modicum of clarity in the early scenes, the result might have been more gripping. But the pic is all over the place, and the viewer is left completely in the dark. Wretchedly bad English subtitles and a shoddy print that looked as if it had been dragged across the floor of every projection booth in Kuala Lumpur, don't help.

Acting is over the top by Western standards, and motivations are somewhat obscure too. Best to try to enjoy the film on the level of a romantic thriller, though even here it remains resolutely unappealing. —*Strat.*

Zeder
(Revenge Of The Dead)
(ITALIAN-COLOR)

A Motion Picture Marketing (MPM) release of an A.M.A. Film and RAI production in association with Enea Ferrario. Produced by Gianni Minervini, Antonio Avati. Directed by Pupi Avati. Stars Gabriele Lavia, Anne Canovas. Screenplay, Pupi Avati, Maurizio Costanzo, Antonio Avati; camera (Telecolor; prints by Getty), Franco Delli Colli; editor, Amedeo Salfa; music, Riz Ortolani; assistant director, Cesare Bastelli; production manager, Francesco Guerrieri; sets, Giancarlo Basili, Leonardo Scarpa; costumes, Steno Tonelli. Reviewed on Lightning Video cassette, N.Y., April 6, 1985. (MPAA Rating: R.) Running time: 99 MINS.
With: Gabriele Lavia (Stefano), Anne Canovas, Paola Tanziani, Cesare Barbetti, Bob Tonelli, Ferdinando Orlandi, Enea Ferrario, John Stacy, Marcello Tusco, Alessandro Partexano, Aldo Sassi, Maria Teresa Toffano, Adolfo Belletti, Veronica Moriconi.

"Zeder" is a mild excursion into supernatural horror by noted Italian filmmaker Pupi Avati (who had a newer pic screening in the Directors Fortnight at Cannes). Filmed in 1982, it was released Stateside last year as "Revenge Of The Dead."

Legit thesp Gabriele Lavia (previously seen in Dario Argento's horror film "Deep Red") toplines as a budding novelist in Bologna who is gifted by his beautiful wife with a used typewriter on their wedding anniversary. In an interesting variation on the traditional "notebook found in a deserted house" format favored by horror writers, Lavia accidentally discovers on the machine's newfangled carbon ribbon the traces of an essay by the previous owner on experiments breaking through the boundary of death. He laboriously retypes the essay, planning to use it as the plot of his third novel.

Through further research, Lavia discovers the essay was written by Don Luigi Costa, a priest who left the church 10 years ago. He had studied one Paolo Zeder, an experimenter who claimed certain places in antiquity such as Delphi existed in a state of zero-time, with no death or growth occurring there.

With his wife reluctantly in tow, Lavia heads for several of these so-called "K-Zones" and becomes involved in a deadly conspiracy of scientists working to reanimate the dead.

Acceptably English-dubbed and more interesting than most horror films of late, "Zeder" fails to deliver the shocks and thrills that have become *de rigeur* in the genre. There is some gore, but credit Avati with trying to tell a story rather than simply build up a body count. — *Lor.*

The Link
(ITALIAN-COLOR)

Sydney, April 22.

A Zadar Film. Produced by Robert Palaggi. Directed by Alberto de Martino. Stars Michael Moriarty, Penelope Milford. Screenplay, Theodore Apstein, from a story by Max de Rita, de Martino; camera (Technicolor), Romano Albani; editor, Russell Lloyd; music, Ennio Morricone; associate producer, Robert Gordon Edwards; art director, Uberto Bertacca. Reviewed on CBS-Fox video, Sydney, April 19, 1985. Running time: 94 MINS.
Dr. Craig Mannings/Keith
Mannings . . . . Michael Moriarty
Dr. Julie Warren . . . . Penelope Milford
Bud Waldo . . . . Cameron Mitchell
Christine Waldo . . . . Sarah Langenfeld
Hedwig . . . . Martha Smith
Mrs. Thomason . . . . Geraldine Fitzgerald
Ballroom victim . . . . Virginia McKenna
Insp. Hersinger . . . . Reinhold K. Olszewski

This odd little thriller opens in an unnamed U.S. city (filmed in Victoria, B.C., Canada) where Dr. Craig Mannings (Michael Moriarty) and his co-worker/girlfriend Dr. Julie Warren (Penelope Milford) are engaged in some experimentation which leads to Craig discovering he can see through the eyes of his twin brother, Keith. This is something of a shock, because the brothers, born as Siamese twins but successfully separated at birth, were childhood enemies; also because Keith was believed to have perished in a fire at the age of 17; also because it's clear that, as Criag can see, Keith has become a homicidal maniac, busily slaughtering the women of Hamburg and Berlin.

After a quick chat with a hospitalized relative (Geraldine Fitzgerald), who confirms Keith survived the fire, Craig takes off for Germany to seek his murderous sibling. Before long, he's been framed for the murder of his brother's latest victim, and only Julie's intervention, at the risk of her life, can put a stop to Keith's lethal career. Even then, the film has a twist up its sleeve.

Modest pic benefits from the intense dual performance of Michael Moriarty as the twins, and from the suitably sinister music score of Ennio Morricone. Helmer Alberto de Martino and writer Theodore Apstein are somewhat light on credibility but strong on individual scenes,

so that "The Link," made in 1982, generates a certain amount of suspense, not all of it predictable.
— *Strat.*

Yumechiyo Nitsuki
(Yumechiyo's Diary)
(JAPANESE-COLOR)

Tokyo, June 5.

A Toei production. Produced by Yusuke Okada, Masao Satch, Jun Sakagami, Kazuhige Saito. Directed by Kiriro Urayama. Stars Sayuri Yoshinaga. Screenplay, Akira Hayasaka; camera (color), Shohei Ando; art director, Norimichi Igawa. No further credits provided. Reviewed at Tokyo Film Festival (Japanese Films of Today section), June 4, 1985. Running time: **128 MINS.**

With: Sayuri Yoshinaga (Yumechiyo), Kirin Kiki (Munakata), Yuko Natori.

"Yumechiyo's Diary" is a handsomely crafted soap about the last months in the life of a woman who runs a geisha house in a hot springs resort near Kobe. She's dying of cancer, and returning from a trip to the hospital she witnesses a woman falling from the train as it crosses a high bridge over a wild river. She assumes, from the fact that the woman was apparently praying as she fell, that she was a suicide, but the police arrest the dead girl's companion and charge him with murder.

There is one other witness: an actor, Munakata, in a visiting troupe, but he doesn't want to testify. Anxious to help the accused man, Yumechiyo tries to persuade him, and discovers he has a guilty secret; 15 years before he accidentally killed his father. The statute of limitations is about to run out; if he can escape detection for a few more weeks, he's home free. He and Yumechiyo fall in love, and she follows him when he hightails it from the village. They experience a great passion, but when she enters the terminal phase of her illness, he takes her back home and is promptly arrested.

This Japanese love story is filled out with a plethora of subplots involving the geishas in Yumechiyo's house, who have problems of their own, but the central story is quite touchingly told, thanks to the charming performance of Sayuri Yoshinaga as the dying heroine (she does, however look radiantly healthy throughout).

The hot spa setting, during the winter ski season, makes an effective backdrop to these conventional but quite well-handled, goings on. By no means a major film, this is still an appealing one on its central performance, beautiful visuals, and confident direction. —*Strat.*

Rensheng
(Life)
(CHINESE-COLOR)

Tokyo, June 6.

A Xi'an Film Studios production. Directed by Wu Tianming. Screenplay, Lu Yao. Camera (Widescreen, color), Chen Wancai, Yang Baoshi. No further credits supplied. Reviewed at Tokyo Film Festival. June 5, 1985. Running time: **120 MINS.**

With: Zhou Lijing, Wu Yufang.

Billed as a pic about "a youth's frustrations in contemporary China," "Life" is a well made but rather conventional adaptation of a well-known novel. Director Wu Tianming previously came to international attention with his film "River Without Buoys."

Setting is seemingly *not* contemporary, but 20 years ago, the time of the cultural revolution. Action takes place in a picturesque village in the northwestern province of Shaan Xi. Hero is a hardworking youth, politically suspect during this difficult period. Accordingly, the parents of his sweetheart don't approve.

After a good deal of frustration (and screen time) he ankles for the nearest provincial city, where he eventually is able to study as a photo-journalist, and takes up with a new, more sophisticated, femme. When his girl from back home comes to see him, he's churlish towards her.

For those with inside knowledge of the politics of the period. There'll be more to this than meets the eye. However, from the information available, it seems to be little more than a handsomely made, crisply acted romance, with political undertones. The settings are superb and there's a very well staged storm scene, which indicates Chinese technicians are improving all the time. However, post-synching often leaves a lot to be desired.—*Strat.*

Torakku Yaro: Goiken Muyo
(Fireball On Highway)
(JAPANESE-COLOR)

Tokyo, June 5.

A Toei release of a Kenji Takamura production. Directed by Norifumi Suzuki. Screenplay, Suzuki and Shinichiro Sawai; camera (color), Hanjiro Nakazawa; art director, Tadayuki Kuwana; music, Tadashi Kinoshita. No other credits available. Reviewed at the Tokyo Intl. film fest (Japanese Films of Today) at the Shibuya Shochiku theatre, June 5, 1985. Running time: **98 MINS.**

With: Bunta Sugawar, Kinya Aikawa, Yutaka Nakajima.

Produced in 1975, and unaccountably resurrected for the Japanese Films of Today section of the Tokyo festival, "Fireball On Highway," a conventional action comedy drama, is reviewed here for the record. Any commercial prospects it may have had must have been long since exhausted.

The plot focuses on a truck driver, a loner who just lives for his work, who becomes attracted to a waitress at a drive-in. Unhappily for him, she's attracted to someone else, and in a public-spirited gesture reunites the two lovers. That about sums it up, other than to note there's a full quota of action, a daredevil drive to bring the couple together, and a modicum of laughs.

Acting is okay and direction is competent. "Fireball" was first of a series which continued until 1979.
— *Myro.*

Dongdong De Jiaql
(A Summer At Grandpa's)
(TAIWANESE-COLOR)

Tokyo, June 8.

A Marble Road Film Production. Produced by Chang Hwa-kun. Directed by Hou Hsiao-hsien. Features entire cast. Screenplay, Chu Tien-wen; camera (color), Chen Kwen-hou; sound, Shing Johs-son; music, Edward Yang; editor, Liao Ching-song. Reviewed at Asia-Pacific Film Festival, Tokyo, June 7, 1985. Running time: **102 MINS.**

Grandpa	Koo Chuen
Grandma	Mei Fong
Tung-Tung	Wang Chi-kwang
Pi-yun	Lin Hsiao-ling

The best film unspooled in the Asia-Pacific fest was this bright comedy about two kids who spend their summer vacation away from Taipei in the village where their grandfather is the local doctor.

Deliberately light on plot, pic is an observational one in which the oddities of village life are seen through the eyes of two engaging youngsters. Their mother is undergoing a serious operation in the city, so her younger brother escorts them, by train, to the countryside. He's accompanied by his girlfriend, and somehow gets separated from the kids, so that they arrive in grandpa's village before he does. He finds them, however, and the summer holidays begin.

The youngsters find new friends, though the little girl is a bit out of it at first. When her brother and the village boys swim naked in the river, she hides their clothes. Later, she's nearly run down by a train, but is saved in the nick of time by a simple-minded local girl, who becomes her friend.

Their young uncle gets into trouble with his parents because his girl is pregnant; he's forced to leave home, and a painful case of hemorrhoids adds to his woes.

But in the main, this is a peaceful summer in which the city kids observe the placid country ways: the man who places nets across a field to trap birds; the ancestral shrines, adorned with tv aerials; the family photo album. Only real moment of violence is when the kids see a couple of robbers stealing from sleeping truckdrivers.

This is a gentle, enormously likable, film, skillfully directed and acted in a relaxed, human style. It's further evidence that some good things are happening in the Taiwanese film industry right now.
— *Strat.*

Beyond Reason
(Mati)
(COLOR)

Dreary thriller from the vaults.

An Allwyn Pictures and Arthur M. Sarkissian presentation. Produced by Howard W. Koch. Executive producer, Varoujan Assoian; associate producer, Constantine P. Karos. Written and directed by Telly Savalas. Stars Savalas. Camera (CFI color), John A. Alonzo; editor, Frank P. Keller; music, Robert Randles; sound, Larry Jost, Chuck Lewis; postproduction supervisor, William R. Kowalchuk Jr.; production design, Phil Jefferies; set decoration, Reg Allen; production manager, Chuck Murray; assistant director, Jack Aldworth; costumes, Moss Mabry; camera operator, Reynaldo Villalobos; additional photography, Howard Anderson 3d; casting, Remdin. Reviewed on Media Home Entertainment vidcassette, N.Y., May 21, 1985. (MPAA Rating: PG.) Running time: **83 MINS.**

Dr. Nicholas Mati	Telly Savalas
Leslie Valentine	Laura Johnson
Elaine	Diana Muldaur
Vincent	Marvin Laird
Mario	Bob Basso

Also with: Walter Brooke, Barney Phillips, Larry Golden, Tony Burton, John Perak, John Lisbon Wood, Jason Ronard, Walter Mathews, Lilyan Chauvin, Toni Lawrence, Kathy Bendett, Debbie Feuer, Biff Elliot, Lee Terri, Milton Frome, Melissa Prophet, Priscilla Barnes.

"Beyond Reason" represents an unimpressive filmmaking debut by Telly Savalas as writer-director. Shot in 1977 under the title "Mati," theatrically unreleased feature is reviewed for the record as a vidcassette.

Savalas also toplines as Dr. Mati (pronounced mah-tee), an unconventional psychologist who is predictably going crazy (mucho hallucinations) under the pressure of his work. Picture at first resembles a telefilm pilot for a series, loaded with cute characters such as Mati's patients and friendly cabdriver, but detours into its main psychological fear mode with little success. Indecisive ending is unsatisfying.

It's hard to blame Savalas entirely for the film's failure, given that the pic was handed over to film doctor William Kowalchuk. Main evidence of production problems is exposed in the early reels wherein originally announced costar Priscilla Barnes (who had guested on Savalas' "Kojak" tv series before achieving fame in "Three's Company") appears silently, but with camera emphasis, in ensemble shots, while final female lead Laura Johnson is shown in unmatched insert closeups during these scenes in which she is missing from the master shots. Evidently Johnson succeeded Barnes in the role, and acquits herself well in later fully-integrated scenes. Supporting cast is fine, but cannot overcome a repetitious, ho-hum story. — *Lor.*

Die Rückseite des Mondes
(The Other Side Of The Moon)
(WEST GERMAN-B&W-16m)

Berlin, May 31.

An Augenschein Film production, Wolfgang Braden, Münster. Directed by Wolfgang Braden. Features entire cast. Screenplay, Braden, Martina Siefert; camera (b&w), Herbert Baumann; sets, Braden, Siefert, Baumann; editor, Braden, Baumann; music, Harald Budd, Nat & Cannonball Adderley, Miles Davis, Duke Ellington, Tom Archia, Ben Webster, Leo Parker. Reviewed at Filmbühne am Steinplatz, Berlin, May 29, 1985. Running time: **84 MINS.**

With: Axel Schulz (Gregor Urbaniak), Hiltrud Linnemann (Irma), Odilo Weber (Richard), Leonhard Ostendorf (Edgar van Meegeren).

"The Other Side Of The Moon" is the second low-budget feature by Münster-based filmer Wolfgang Braden, one of the more creative talents emerging lately from Northrhine-Westphalia. His "Like A Stranger" (1980) told the story of an outsider coming to grips with both himself and his social surroundings. Now he's expanded the same theme to a group of young sculptors living and working in a provincial town somewhere in northern Germany (possibly Münster, but not exactly indicated).

Four young artists meet regularly in an inn, whose barkeeper (unbeknownst to them) has been eavesdropping on their idle conversation to steal their jointly planned ideas and market them for a profit to commercial and cultural contacts. One day, they see an idea of theirs visualize into a wacky work of art on the town green — the city officials have marketed a screwball idea taken from one of their conversations into a sculptural event. It doesn't take long for the chums to latch on to the barkeeper as the culprit.

We are dealing here with idealists — much like those in the Jules Verne story of travelers to "the other side of the moon" — intent on seeing what the experience will bring. The rest of the story finds the group on a trip to northern Ireland, where they visit another imaginative sculptor who has laid down on the rocky, wave-splashed shore a line of stepping-stones out into the nowhere. —*Holl.*

Warrior Of The Lost World
(ITALIAN-COLOR)

A Visto Intl. release of an A.D.I. production, presented by Eduard Sarlui. Produced by Roberto Bessi, Frank E. Hildebrand. Written and directed by David Worth. Stars Robert Ginty, Persis Khambatta, Donald Pleasence. Camera (Luciano Vittori color), Giancarlo Ferrando; editor-postproduction supervisor, Cesare D'Amico; music, Daniele Patucchi; production manager, Franco Cucco; assistant director, Tony Brandt; production design, Antonello Geleng; special effects, Paolo Ricci; makeup effects, Otello Fava; sound effects, Roberto Arcangeli. Reviewed on Thorn EMI/HBO Videocassette, N.Y., May 24, 1985. (MPAA Rating: R.) Running time: **86 MINS.**
Warrior . . . . .Robert Ginty
Nastasia . . . . .Persis Khambatta
Prosser . . . . .Donald Pleasence
Henchman . . . . .Fred Williamson
McWayne . . . .•. . . .Harrison Muller
Also with: Janna Ryan, Consuelo Marcaccini, Harrison Muller Jr., Russel Case.

"Warrior Of The Lost World" (made in 1983) is a well-directed action fantasy which might have been a winner with a better script. As is, writer-director David Worth (a former cameraman) loads virtually the entire plot into a 170-word opening title crawl.

Robert Ginty toplines as a nameless Warrior, riding in on his supersonic speedcycle to help McWayne (Harrison Muller) and his daughter Nastasia (Persis Khambatta) in their rebellion against evil despot Prosser (Donald Pleasence). The futuristic setting is during a dark age following "radiation wars." Fred Williamson also appears as a henchman whose true loyalties are in doubt.

Picture is firmly in the "Mad Max" groove, though visually Worth aims at a look resembling George Lucas' debut pic "THX 1138." Some excellent fiery explosions highlight the action. Acting is wooden, with Pleasence styled to closely resemble Dr. No in the first James Bond film.

Dialog synchronization in the original English soundtrack varies in quality, and sound effects are on the silly side. —*Lor.*

Otoko Wa Tsurai Yo: Torajiro Yuyake Koyake
(Tora's Sunrise And Sunset)
(JAPANESE-COLOR)

Tokyo, June 5.

A Shochiku production. Produced by Toru Najima, Tokyo. Directed by Yoji Yamada. Screenplay, Yamada, Yoshitaka Asama; camera (color), Tetsuo Takaba; music, Naozumi Yamamoto. Reviewed at Tokyo Intl. Film Festival, June 5, 1985. Running time: **109 MINS.**
Tora . . . . .Atsumi Kiyoshi
Sakura . . . . .Chieko Baisho
Ikenouchi Seikan . . . . .Jukichi Uno

"Tora's Sunrise And Sunset," reviewed here for the record, is a 1976 outing about the good-hearted hapless peddler Tora-san. The Tora-san series, with 34 installments to date, is Shochiku's big money-maker, with two annual releases scheduled in August and at New Year's, the most active seasons for Japanese filmgoing.

Tora-san pictures all fall into a pattern, with Atsumi Kiyoshi playing a sentimental, fast-talking common man who falls in and out of misadventures, always rising above the muddle he creates by the purity of his intentions.

This time around he returns to his parents and sister Sakura's home, connected to a sweets shop in a working-class area of Tokyo, after a long absence peddling trinkets around Japan.

He befriends an old drunk (Jukichi Uno) and impetuously brings him home.

The codger turns out to be a famous artist doing a bit of slumming who, after a comedy of misunderstanding (he thinks Tora's house is a hotel and orders everyone around), repays his debt to Tora. This he does by doodling a little pic that Tora sells for an astounding sum.

Tora later falls for a country geisha who's been swindled out of her life savings. Tora's family and friends rally to help her, but when the swindler proves too wily and incorrigible, Tora turns to the artist and asks him to dash off a painting so they can sell it and replenish the geisha's bank account.

Kiyoshi is a master of comic timing, and the others in the cast, including Chishu Ryu, famous for his roles in Yasujiro Ozu's films, lend strong support. The series' blend of slapstick humor and tear-jerking sentimentality may strike Westerners as unaplatable, but it's a sure-fire formula in Japan, where even now the 35th episode is being prepared for release in August. —*Bask.*

The Passing
(COLOR-16m)

Washington, D.C., May 21.

A Huckert Prods. production; foreign sales, Intl. Cinema Releasing. Produced and written by John Huckert and Mary Maruca. Directed by Huckert. Camera (color, 16m), Jochi Melero, Richard Chisolm; editor, Huckert; music, William-John Tudor; special effects, Mark Chorvinsky, Miguel Munoz; sound, Dennis Towns, Dwayne Dell, David Masser. Reviewed at Biograph theater, Washington, D.C., May 20, 1985. (No MPAA Rating.) Running time: **96 MINS.**
Laviticus Rose . Welton Benjamin Johnson
Ernie Neuman . . . . . .James Carroll Plaster
Wade Carney . . . . .John Huckert
Monica .Lynn Odell

Reviewed for the record after several fest outings, this indie pic opened in its home town for a brief commercial run, self-distributed by the director. Debut feature has been expanded from the effective, tight short "The Water That is Passed" about two old men living out their senile phase together and facing death. This still remains the core of pic's entertainment value, despite attempts to entwine two other threads of plots, one about a young man on his way to jail for a brutally vengeful murder and the other a badly acted piece of science fiction, inspired perhaps by helmer's experience working as an AFI Academy intern on "2010."

Thesp kudos, however, are due the elderly pair whose roles are fleshed out and reflect some promise from young helmer Huckert in directing actors. The production was beset with every tragedy imaginable for some seven years, including the death of lead James Carroll Plaster. Compensatory plot material was woven out of the sci-fi thread, but special effects took over instead of narrative or character development, stranding pic in avant-garde limbo. — *Kaja.*

Kesho
(Make-Up)
(JAPANESE-COLOR)

Tokyo, June 8.

A Shochiku production. Produced by Masatake Wakita. Directed by Kazuo Ikehiro. Features entire cast. Screenplay, Yozo Tanaka, from a novel by Junichi Watanabe; camera (color), Noritaka Sakamoto; music, Sei Akeno; art director, Yoshinobu Nishioka. Reviewed at Tokyo Film Festival, June 7, 1985. Running time: **130 MINS.**
With: Keiko Matsuzaka, Kimiko Ikegami, Machiko Kyo.

A film firmly in the tradition of Japanese family dramas with women in central roles, "Make-Up" is an affecting drama about a family involved in running swank restaurants in Kyoto and Tokyo. These are restaurants served by geishas, and top of the price range.

Matriarch of the family is played by vet actress Machiko Kyo, remembered from many great Japanese films of the '50s. She had four daughters, the eldest two being twins; but one of these, Suzuku, has committed suicide before the film opens for love of the worthless Kumakura. Yoriko, the dead woman's twin, manages a restaurant in Tokyo, and determines to avenge herself against the man who destroyed her sister; she eventually drives Kumakura to suicide when she engineers the failure of his business deals, only to discover too late that the young man she's fallen in love with was his son.

There are subplots in addition to the main story, involving the other two sisters; one is unhappily married and has an affair with a married man, becoming pregnant; and the youngest is arrested for smoking pot, but winds up engaged to marry the son of a rich banker.

All of this is exquisitely mounted, gracefully acted, and delicately handled. Like all films in this genre, "Make-Up" is slowly paced, but it's consistently enjoyable and if it is indeed soap opera, then it's of a most superior kind. — *Strat.*

Prostl Menya, Alyosha
(Forgive Me, Alyosha)
(RUSSIAN-COLOR)

Tokyo, June 5.

A Mosfilm production. Written and directed by Iskra Babych. Features entire cast. Camera (Sovcolor), Alexander Ryabov; art director, Eleanora Nemechek; music, Vladimir Komarov. No further credits supplied. Reviewed at Tokyo Film Festival (Women's section), June 3, 1985. Running time: **91 MINS.**
Alyosha . . . . Igor Marychev
Inka . . . . Olga Kochetkova
Also with: Fyodor Sukhov, Vladimir Andreev.

———

Alyosha is a clean-cut 18-year-old whose parents are working on an engineering site in Siberia. He lives in Moscow with his two sisters. One night, he finds Inka, a genuine damsel in distress, weeping in a city park. She's attempted suicide by slashing her wrists, and is about to give birth. Alyosha, good samaritan that he is, takes her to a hospital, and the authorities assume he's the father. No sooner is Inka up and about than she leaves Alyosha holding the baby, simply ankling her responsibilities. The lad tracks down the mother, and the moustachioed, guitar-playing cad who impregnated her, but they're no help. He decides to look after the sprig himself, though his family is appalled.

This is a decidedly schmaltzy item in which every sentimental moment is underscored both by the saccharine music score and the limpid direction (femme helmer Iskra Babych previously made "Fellows" in 1981). There are occasional moments when the cardboard characters start to become human, but generally speaking this is Russian filmmaking at its most resistable. The continual use of the zoom lens indicates a rather lazy technique, and is far from easy on the eye. Color is okay, though the lab work is shaky at times. — *Strat.*

———

Subessednik Po Zhelanie
(Question Time)
(BULGARIAN-COLOR)

———

Berlin, May 29.

A Bulgarian Film Production, Sofia. Directed by Hristo Hristov. Features entire cast. Screenplay, Vladimir Ganev, Hristov; camera (color), Atanas Tassev; sets, Yordanka Peycheva; music, Victor Chuchkov. Reviewed at ZDF Screening Room, Berlin, May 28, 1985. Running time: **90 MINS.**
With: Vassil Mihailov (Boyan Buchvarov, "Buch"), Lilyana Kavacheva (Miryana), Ivan Kondov (the doctor), Vassil Popiliev (the playwright), Zhana Karayordanova (the nurse), Vulcho Kamarashev (the actor), Kevork Kevorkyan (the tv interviewer), Valentin Ganev (the son).

———

Hristo Hristov's (also spelled Christo Christov) "Question Time" is about a stage actor at the height of his popularity who is told he has leukemia, and comes to the realization that something significant has to be done with his remaining few months.

Protagonist Boyan Buchvarov ("Buch") faces his dilemma while at the peak of his career. In the opening scene he is being interviewed on a live tv broadcast dedicated to personalities in arts and letters, the program titled "Question Time" and featuring impromptu questions from the viewing audience. Shortly thereafter, he goes to a hospital clinic to receive the stern results of recent blood tests. Leukemia is diagnosed, and his option now is either to submit to treatment to prolong his life or burn it out altogether with the few months remaining. He decides on the latter, requesting the doctors don't inform any of his family or friends of the short-term illness.

"Buch" decides it's time to put his own affairs in order. On the stage he is playing a physically demanding role, but he adds to this the onus of directing a new play by a playwright acquaintance that he feels should see the light of day (the play has gone through several versions via self-censorship changes). In his private life he repairs a broken relationship with a woman with whom he once had an affair, she is now a provincial actress on the verge of becoming an alcoholic.

A psychological study, "Question Time" scores remarkably as a portrayal of life with the shadow of death always somewhere in the wings. Credits are a plus, particularly Vassil Mihailov in the title role.
—*Holl.*

———

Kaattathe Kililkkdu
(The Nest Caught In The Wind)
(INDIAN-COLOR)

———

Tokyo, June 7.

A Grihalakrisni production. Directed by Bharathan. Features entire cast. Screenplay, Venun; camera (color), V, Kumar; editor, N. Suresh. No further credits supplied. Reviewed at Asian Pacific Festival, Tokyo June 6. 1985. Running time: **135 MINS.**
With: Gopi Mohanlal, Revathi.

———

Made in Bangalore, in the Malayam language, this Indian entry in the Asian-Pacific festival is an undistinguished affair with zero possibilities for exploitation outside of Indian theaters.

Plot involves a happily married English professor, specializing in Shakespeare, who loves his musically-inclined wife and four kids. But their lives are disrupted by a spoiled young student who comes to stay with her aunt next door. She falls for a somewhat chubby athlete at college, and when they quarrel (over whether to go out for dinner or not) she makes a play for the prof to inflame the athlete's jealousy.

The prof falls for her, and soon moves out of the family home, while the precocious gal gets a bed at the YMCA. Eventually, the chubby athlete can stand it no more and gives the girl what she's evidently been asking for since reel one — a good slapping around. She immediately falls into his arms, he takes a cold shower, and there's a happy ending.

By Western standards, this has no redeeming features; pacing is slack, acting is unrestrained, direction unsubtle, technical qualities modest. There also are several songs, one of which seems almost bad enough to be a parody of this kind of sequence in Indian cinema. It's a shame the fest couldn't have found a better film to rep the world's most prolific film-producing country. — *Strat.*

———

Abortion: Stories From North And South
(CANADIAN-COLOR-DOCU-16m)

———

A Cinema Guild (N.Y.) release of a Studio D group, National Film Board of Canada production, in association with the NFB Ontario Regional Production Studio. Executive producer, Kathleen Shannon. Produced by Signe Johansson, Gail Singer. Directed by Singer. Camera (color, 16m), Susan Trow; sound, Diane Carriere; original music, Maribeth Solomon, Micky Erbe; narrator, Dixie Seatle; editor, Tony Trow. Reviewed at C.W. Post/Long Island U., May 15, 1985. Running time: **60 MINS.**

"Abortion" is a production of Studio D, the Canadian government's all-female film unit, founded in 1974 to make films from the perspective of women. "Abortion" won the grand prize at the 1985 Golden Gate Awards film and video competition of the San Francisco Intl. Film Festival.

"Abortion" takes viewers on an international odyssey that explores different practices of abortion, variously legal and illegal, medically safe and grotesquely primitive.

The picture frankly affirms a woman's right to safe medical care, although it is not stridently agit-prop. It demonstrates that only a small percentage of the world's women have access to safe, legal abortion. In only one episode — that concerning Irish girls who must go to England for their abortions — does the film slip from documentary standards into fictional melodrama, compromising that episode's credibility. Other episodes are better, set in Peru, Colombia, Thailand, Japan and Canada.

"Abortion" conceivably could play theatrically if double-billed with a thematically related companion film in special theaters, e.g., in university towns. For 16m distribution to women's groups, schools, and to public television, its future seems assured. —*Hitch.*

———

Hell Riders
(COLOR)

———

Tepid biker film.

———

A 21st Century Distribution release of a Ciara Prods. production. Executive producers, Art Schweitzer, Lee Frost, Phyllis Frost. Produced by Renee Har . .n. Directed by James Bryan. Features entire cast. Screenplay, Harmon, Bryan; additional material, Dan Bradley, Diane Miller, Ricco Mancini; camera (color), Derek Scott, Juan Valenzuela; editor, Fred Wasser; music, Electra Nova; sound, Tom Sanderson, Margaret Duke; art direction, William A. Luce; assistant director, Frank Millen; production manager, Tom Richer; stunt coordinator, Dan Bradley. Reviewed on Trans World Entertainment vidcassette, N.Y., May 24, 1985. (No MPAA Rating.) Running time: **83 MINS.**
Dr. Dave Stanley . . . . Adam West
Claire Delaney . . . . Tina Louise
Snake . . . . Russ Alexander
Knife . . . . Renee Harmon
Convict . . . . Dan Bradley
Also with: Frank Newhouse, Chris Haramis, Jerry Rattay, Ricco Mancini, Lynn Wiedemayer, Shawn Klugman, Tania Anatole, Debra Morris, Sandra Sterling, Arline Specht.

———

"Hell Riders" is a meek attempt to resuscitate the biker action genre of two decades back. Already released on vidcassette, this 1983 production has little theatrical potential outside the drive-in circuit.

Adam West toplines as Dr. Dave Stanley, physician in the small town of Ransburg beset by the violent Hell Riders biker gang. Besides the local folks, also terrorized is Claire (Tina Louise), a former Las Vegas blackjack dealer on the road.

Archaic cheapie features okay stuntwork but an uninteresting, trite story. Predictably, West saves the day. Film culminates nastily when the townsfolk band together to mercilessly shoot down the bikers like dogs. Pic is more professionally executed than producer Renee Harmon's prior work (such as "Executioner Park II" and "Frozen Scream") but acting by the supporting cast is amateurish (biker extras are credited here to "Rent-a-Gang"). Harmon also casts herself as a sadistic, overage biker — campy at best. — *Lor.*

———

Dances Sacred And Profane
(COLOR-DOCU-16m)

———

Fascinating tour of American sub-cults.

———

A presentation of Valley Filmworks, New York. Producer, Thunder Basin Films. Produced, directed and edited by Mark Jury, Dan Jury. Based on books of photographer-anthropologist Charles Gatewood; narrator, Gatewood; camera (color), Dan Jury; sound, Mark Jury; original music, Larry Gelb. Reviewed at Valley Filmworks, N.Y., May 13, 1985. (No MPAA Rating.) Running time: **80 MINS.**

"Dances Sacred And Profane" is the newest in a series of interesting documentaries, always long and personal, by two Pennsylvania brothers, Mark and Dan Jury, who share all production chores. Film was at the Berlin festival in February and at Antwerp in March.

Inspired by the investigative research of veteran anthropologist Charles Gatewood, whose descents over 20 years into the netherworld of American sub-cults have been documented in his photo-text books, the Jurys take viewers on a bizarre journey rarely seen in American travelogs. In the process, ''Dances'' does not limit itself to dance but examines various rituals, obsessions and practices, often wildly eccentric and painful, that perhaps for some will seem to border on psychopathology.

Picture includes a first-ever filming of the Indian ''Sundance'' ceremony — when a Silicon Valley businessman, a ''Modern Primitive,'' hangs from a Wyoming cottonwood tree by steel hooks through his pectorals. This is grim stuff, but for the businessman, a marketing designer, it is spiritual, ecstasy transcending mere pain, putting him in communion with the Great White Spirit, like Sioux warriors of old. This is ''Mondo Cane'' country, but with class, as the Jury approach is non-sensationalistic and is respectful toward cultists, who can intellectualize and who pursue their beliefs and rituals at great personal sacrifice.

Filming covered four years, following Gatewood's peregrinations, including a visit to ''Naked City'' in Indiana; New York's Belle de Jour Fantasy Theater, a salon of sex cultists; Hindu rites in California; some wild Mardi Gras hijinks in New Orleans, and other scenes. The 1930s b&w anthropological footage shot in India documents the traditions by which physical pain is overcome by spiritual will.

''Dances'' can connect with specialized theatrical situations if properly promoted and perhaps supported with a strong congenial featurette or short. Its 16m distribution to colleges and public television is also indicated. — Hitch.

Cocoon
(COLOR)

Warm fantasy fable is the summer film to beat.

Hollywood, June 12.

A 20th Century Fox release of a Fox-Zanuck/Brown production. Produced by Richard D. Zanuck, David Brown, Lili Fini Zanuck. Directed by Ron Howard. Features entire cast. Screenplay, Tom Benedek, based on a novel by David Saperstein; camera (DeLuxe color), Don Peterman; editors, Daniel Hanley, Michael J. Hill; music, James Horner; sound, Richard Church; production designer, Jack T. Collis; costume designer, Aggie Guerard Rodgers; special visual effects by Industrial Light & Magic; visual effects supervisor, Ken Ralston for ILM; special alien creatures and effects, Greg Cannom; cocoons and dolphin effects, Robert Short Prods.; special creature consultant, Rick Baker; associate producer, Robert Doudell; casting, Penny Perry; stunt coordinator, Ted Grossman; assistant director, Jan R. Lloyd; special music and dance coordinator, Gwen Verdon. Reviewed at Samuel Goldwyn Theater, June 11, 1985. (MPAA Rating: PG-13.) Running time: **117 MINS.**

Art Selwyn	Don Ameche
Ben Luckett	Wilford Brimley
Joe Finley	Hume Cronyn
Walter	Brian Dennehy
Bernie Lefkowitz	Jack Gilford
Jack Bonner	Steve Guttenberg
Mary Luckett	Maureen Stapleton
Alma Finley	Jessica Tandy
Bess McCarthy	Gwen Verdon
Rose Lefkowitz	Herta Ware
Kitty	Tahnee Welch
David	Barret Oliver
Susan	Linda Harrison
Pillsbury	Tyrone Power Jr.
John Dexter	Clint Howard
Pops	Charles Lampkin
Doc	Mike Nomad
Detective	Rance Howard

A fountain of youth fable which imaginatively melds galaxy fantasy with the lives of aging mortals in a Florida retirement home, ''Cocoon'' weaves a mesmerizing tale that's a certified audience pleaser and promising summer bonanza for 20th Century Fox.

Pic is an unquestioned feather in the cap for the key hands — director-with-the-Midas-touch Ron Howard, producers Richard Zanuck, David Brown, and (debuting) Lili Fini Zanuck, and scenarist Tom Benedek, who worked from an unpublished novel by David Saperstein.

''Cocoon'' bows in some 1,000 houses June 21, and if there ever was a classic crossover film, this is it. It not only gilds the career of Howard (following his hit ''Splash'' and who succeeded another director, Bob Zemeckis, before shooting started), but salutes the instincts of heretofore unknown Lili Zanuck (wife of Richard), who nurtured the property through three managements at Fox.

Film inventively taps a wellspring of universal desire: health and youth, a parable set, in this case, among a pallid group of denizens shuffleboarding their twilight days away until a mysterious quartet of normal-looking visitors shows up on their Floridian shores. They are arrivals from another galaxy, led by friendly Brian Dennehy and attractive Tahnee Welch (Raquel's daughter, in her first U.S. film). Another nearly-silent member of the party is a debuting Tyrone Power Jr.

Dennehy hires a young, out-of-pocket charter boat skipper (engagingly played by Steve Guttenberg) for a plan to scuba dive for what appear to be weird, gigantic oyster shells. Dennehy rents an abandoned estate with a big indoor pool and rests the big pods in the pool's bottom.

Effectively intercut with these scenes is the life of the tight circle of nearby retirees, three of whom, played by Don Ameche, Wilford Brimley and Hume Cronyn, pursue a secret, daily recreation: sneaking onto the grounds of the vacated estate and, like a bunch of kids, swimming in the big, unattended pool.

One day they discover the mysterious cocoon-like shells in the pool and after a frolic in the water they are soon diving in like 18-year-olds. They've lucked onto the Bimini that Ponce de Leon couldn't find (if only he had traveled a little farther, from St. Augustine to St. Petersburg, site of the major production location).

The rejuvenation among the trio of aging men also untaps long-dormant sexual activity. The now stalwart old men pour renewed sexual zeal on their dismayed loved ones (Maureen Stapleton, Gwen Verdon, Jessica Tandy). These scenes, which are implied, could have been simply embarrassing but Howard's warm touch makes them humorous and credible.

The effect of rejuvenation on the gray people, the inevitable mania when the whole retirement hospital wants in on the public bath, and the effect of this on the plans of the visitors from outer space propel the feature toward a suspenseful, ironic conclusion.

There are undeniable glimmers of Steven Spielberg's ''E.T.'' and ''Close Encounters Of The Third Kind.'' The endings convey similar tones, hopes and mysteries, but with ''Cocoon'' the filmmakers, having great fun with a boat full of old people heading into a last, awesome exploration, achieve the most touching ending of any fantasy to date.

George Lucas' Industrial Light & Magic contributed solid effects, cinematographer Don Peterman (who also lit Howard's ''Splash'') traps some wonderful moments shot in natural light (a big, '40s-type ballroom scene, for example), and James Horner's score contributes an array of supportive rhythms.

While all the acting is perfectly focused, the performance with a tuning fork of its own is Herta Ware as the wife of codger Jack Gilford. They are the couple that don't dip into the miracle pool until it's too late, and Ware's dying scene is one of the film's finest moments. This is a gentle picture that packs a punch. — Loyn.

Flesh & Blood
(COLOR)

Visceral Medieval adventure.

Hollywood, June 11.

An Orion release of a Riverside Pictures production. Produced by Gys Versluys. Directed by Paul Verhoeven. Stars Rutger Hauer, Jennifer Jason Leigh, Tom Burlinson, Jack Thompson, Susan Tyrrell, Ron Lacey. Screenplay, Gerard Soeteman, Verhoeven, from a story by Soeteman; camera (Deluxe color, Technovision), Jan de Bont; editor, Ine Schenkkan; music, Basil Poledouris; art direction, Felix Murcia; costume design, Yvonne Blake; sound (Dolby), Tom Tholen, Ad Roest; special effects supervisor, Joe Di Gaetano; stunt coordinator, Juan Majan; creative consultant director (Spain), Mischa Muller; associate producer, Jose Vicuna; second unit directors, Steven Charles Jaffe, Jindra Markus; casting, Mike Fenton, Jane Feinberg, Valorie Massalas. Reviewed at Orion screening room, L.A., June 10, 1985. (MPAA Rating: R.) Running time: **126 MINS.**

Martin	Rutger Hauer
Agnes	Jennifer Jason Leigh
Steven	Tom Burlinson
Hawkwood	Jack Thompson
Celine	Susan Tyrrell
Cardinal	Ron Lacey
Arnolfini	Fernando Hillbeck
Karsthans	Brion James
Summer	John Dennis Johnston
Miel	Simon Andreu
Orbec	Bruno Kirby
Anna	Kitty Courbois
Polly	Marian Saura
Father George	Hans Veerman
Little John	Jake Wood
Niccolo	Hector Alterio
Clara	Blanca Marsillach
Kathleen	Nancy Cartwright

''Flesh & Blood'' is a vivid and muscular, if less than fully startling, account of lust, savagery, revenge, betrayal and assorted other dark doings in the Middle Ages. First American-backed, English-language film by Dutch director Paul Verhoeven was world premiered at the Seattle Film Festival and will be released domestically in September. Foreign outlook appears strong, and U.S. take will depend upon current audience appetite for sex and violence rather than fantasy and romance in a period piece.

Buffs know Verhoeven always takes a bold, often shockingly frank approach to his material, so the sight of two young lovers sharing their first intimate moment under the decaying bodies of two lynched men, or the spectacle of a virgin sort of liking getting raped, won't come as a total surprise.

If anything, however, the director may not have gone far enough in portraying a world virtually without morality, ethics or meaningful religious moorings. Verhoeven's original cut is said to have been so explicit it would have garnered an X rating but, be that as it may, director's obvious aim of making a brutally realistic film about barbarism and the meaningless of life in war torn societies has been softened a bit in the execution.

Drama opens with a successful siege on a castle by lord Arnolfini (Fernando Hillbeck), who has recently been ousted from the premises. After promising them loot, Hillbeck goes back on his word and banishes the mercenaries who have helped him in his conquest.

Before long, warrior leader Martin (Rutger Hauer) and his ragtag band get theirs back by nearly killing Hillbeck in an ambush and capturing lovely young Agnes (Jennifer Jason Leigh), the intended bride of Hillbeck's studious son Steven (Tom Burlinson).

Like a medieval Patty Hearst, Leigh quickly adapts to the ways of her kidnapers and, in the wake of her rape, takes up with the rugged Hauer. The troupe wins a castle of its own and captures Burlinson just as the Plague sets in and wipes out virtually the entire supporting cast.

Verhoeven has told his tale in visceral, involving fashion and, for the amount of carnage that piles up, explicit gore is kept to a minimum. On the other hand, there's plenty of nudity, especially from Leigh, who has a rather spicy bath scene with Hauer and has entered with abandon into the raunchy spirit of the director's work.

Dramatic ambiguity of the situation in which Leigh finds herself is played to the hilt. Both the Hauer and Burlinson characters try to force her to choose between them and, since no one in the film is particularly superior morally to anyone else, the choice does become something of a dilemma.

Hauer fills his boots and carries his sword with absolute authority, and Australian actor Burlinson is okay as the student turned military commander. Some of the playing becomes overwrought at times, and one overall problem is the stingy supply of extras; battles appear to be fought between dozens — not hundreds or thousands — of men, with the effect that this is probably the least populated "epic" in memory.

Jan de Bont's cinematography, which frequently employs some great swooping crane shots and striking camera moves, strongly etches the harsh look of the landscape and its treacherous denizens; shooting conditions were clearly horrendous. Fine use is made of Belmonte Castle (on view in "El Cid") and other Spanish locales, while Basil Poledouris' score is on the conventional side. —*Cart.*

Return To Oz
(COLOR)

Somber rendition from Disney with no clear-cut audience.

Hollywood, June 10.

A Buena Vista release of a Walt Disney Pictures presentation produced in association with Silver Screen Partners II. Produced by Paul Maslansky. Executive producer, Gary Kurtz. Directed by Walter Murch. Features entire cast. Screenplay, Murch, Gill Dennis, based on "The Land Of Oz" and "Ozma Of Oz" by L. Frank Baum, camera (Technicolor), David Watkin; editor, Leslie Hodgson; music, David Shire; production design, Norman Reynolds; supervising art director, Charles Bishop; art direction, Fred Hole; set decoration, Michael Ford; costume design, Raymond Hughes; makeup supervision, Robin Grantham; sound (Dolby), Robert Allen; associate producer, Colin Michael Kitchens; assistant directors, Michael Murray, Ray Corbett; second unit director, camera, James Devis; creature design supervision, Lyle Conway; special effects supervision, Ian Wingrove; director of model and process unit-visual effects consultant, Zoran Perisic; optical editorial supervision, Peter Krook; Claymation director, Will Vinton; Claymation producer, David Altschul; casting, Mike Fenton, Jane Feinberg, Susie Figgis, Marci Liroff. Reviewed at Gomillion Sound, L.A., June 7, 1985. (MPAA Rating: PG.) Running time: **110 MINS.**

Dr. Worley/
  The Nome King ...... Nicol Williamson
Nurse Wilson/
  Princess Mombi .... Jean Marsh
Dorothy .... Fairuza Balk
Aunt Em .... Piper Laurie
Uncle Henry .... Matt Clark
Tik Tok .... Michael Sundin, Tim Rose
Voice .... Sean Barrett
Billina .... Mak Wilson
Voice .... Denise Bryer
Jack Pumpkinhead .... Brian Henson,
                    Stewart Larange
Voice .... Brian Henson
Gump .... Lyle Conway,
                 Steve Norrington
Voice .... Lyle Conway
Scarecrow .... Justin Case
Cowardly Lion .... John Alexander
Tin Man .... Deep Roy
Ozma .... Emma Ridley
Mombi II .... Sophie Ward
Mombi III .... Fiona Victory
Lead Wheeler/
  Nome Messenger .... Pons Maar

"Return To Oz" is an astonishingly somber, melancholy and, sadly, unengaging trip back to a favorite land of almost every American's youth. Straight dramatic telling of little Dorothy's second voyage to the Emerald City employs an amusement park-full of imaginative characters and special effects, but a heaviness of tone and absence of narrative drive prevent the flights of fancy from getting off the ground. Built-in interest in the title may provide a little initial draw, but this holdover from the former Disney management will have trouble lasting long even in primetime summer bookings.

The many L. Frank Baum "Oz" books have always held a wealth of marvelous material unused on the screen; perhaps the mere idea of competing with the 1939 MGM classic seemed too intimidating until recently, when remakes of and sequels to even the most venerated of old pictures have become commonplace.

Screenwriters Walter Murch and Gill Dennis have taken elements from the "Oz" books and from the outset, it is clear that the tone of their film will be entirely different from what might have been expected from a Disney view of this material.

Opening finds Dorothy back at home in Kansas but unable to sleep because of her disturbing memories of her recent trip. Reacting harshly, Aunt Em and Uncle Henry decide the girl has become deranged and send her to a clinic to receive electroshock therapy from sinister nurse Jean Marsh and doctor Nicol Williamson.

After nearly a half-hour of these nightmarish goings-on, Dorothy and her talking chicken Billina are delivered to Oz, but not a very inviting section of it. Landed on the edge of the Deadly Desert and hounded by Wheelers, cackling lunatics who have wheels instead of hands and feet and do the bidding of evil Princess Mombi, Dorothy soon discovers the Yellow Brick Road in disrepair, the Emerald City in ruins and her companions from the previous trip turned to stone.

In the eeriest sequence in the picture, Dorothy is captured by Princess Mombi and subjected to her "closet," in which Mombi stores her 30-odd alternate heads.

Along the way, as before, Dorothy accumulates some helpful friends, who in this case are a walking boiler called Tik Tok, the string-bean Jack Pumpkinhead and a moosehead named Gump. All these fellows, particularly Tik Tok, are amiable enough but, not being human, cannot begin to compete with Judy Garland's companions of 46 years ago.

A wonderful touch, however, is the use of Will Vinton's patented Claymation technique to represent the ever-present forces of evil. As soon as Dorothy arrives in Oz, nearby rocks assume different facial shapes as they spy on her, and when she finally makes her way to the lair of the Nome King, ruler of all Oz, he himself is initially animated via the technique until he gradually assumes the form of Nicol Williamson, whose voice in the role sounds uncannily like that of James Earl Jones as Darth Vader.

Ending is perfunctorily happy, and there would be nothing wrong with any of this if it had been told with zest or any unified style. Unfortunately, debuting director Walter Murch, long the celebrated sound wizard for Coppola and Lucas, has been unable to shape the many diverse elements into a coherent entertainment.

Also, in Fairuza Balk, age 10 during the shoot, pic has a Dorothy who is, first and foremost, forlorn and a bit morose, and only then resourceful and adventurous.

Nearly every shot seems to have some sort of special effect, and technical work is both expert and surprisingly sloppy. For every nifty treat, there also is a mismatched shot, obvious matte painting or tacky effect.

It may have been daring to approach Oz as a nightmare that keeps poor Dorothy awake, but it's difficult to pinpoint the audience for which this rendition was made.

David Shire's musical score which runs under the great majority of the action, is unusually turbulent and emotional, underscoring the presumed psychological underpinnings of the film.—*Cart.*

On The Loose
(AUSTRALIAN-COLOR-16m)

Sydney, June 18.

A Health Media Prod., sponsored by the N.S.W. Dept. of Health. Produced by Lyn Norfor. Directed by Jane Oehr. Features entire cast. Screenplay, Ken Cameron (Part 1), Jone Oehr, Mark Stiles (Part 2), Tim Gooding, Tom McPartland (Part 3), from an idea by Oehr; camera (color, 16m), Tom Cowan; sound, John Franks; art director, David Trethewey; music, Todd Hunter. Reviewed at Sydney Film Festival, June 9, 1985. Running time: **83 MINS.**

Part 1: Exit Eddie Leech
Eddie Leech .... Steve Bergan
Russell Leech .... Ray Meagher
Mr. Stenning .... John Smythe
Mr. Cutler .... Ron Hackett
Part 2: Ring of Confidence
Nicole Jones .... Tamsin Hardman
Noel Poulson .... - ...... John Hamblin
Stella .... Maria da Costa
Mrs. Jones .... Carole Skinner
Part 3: Beginner's Luck
Nick Malinowski .... Jim Filipovski
Cane Toad .... Gary Who

An unheralded low-budget feature, which puts some of the more vaunted Australian pics to shame, "On The Loose" is a painfully honest look at three youngsters as they leave school to enter a big-city world of unemployment, corruption and general urban woes. Essayed with grim humor, and wonderfully acted by its mostly unknown cast, pic deserves wide exposure, but 16m format and seemingly restricted scope may limit it.

Three characters are spotlighted in three separate stories, though parts one and three overlap. In the first, scripted by Ken Cameron (who directed "Monkey Grip" and "Fast Talking," a film with a theme similar to this one), Steve Bergan appears as Eddie, a crippled kid who's fed up with school and provokes his teachers into expelling him. The tragedy is that the life he craves *outside* school will be as soul-destroying as it was *inside*.

Part two features Tamsin Hardman as Nicole, an attractive 16-year-old, who gets a job as nursing assistant to a smooth, self-important dentist. Before long, he's making thinly veiled sexual approaches (he is, of course, married) and when she resists, he effectively demotes her to the position of receptionist and hires a presumably more amenable assistant; eventually, she quits, joining the ranks of the unemployed.

Pic ends on a less desolate note with the story of Nick, Steve's best friend from Part One, who gets a job in a security firm, though he lies about being able to drive a car. However, the partner to whom he's assigned covers for him in an emergency, and it seems at fadeout that, of the three, Nick will be the survivor. In the central role, Jim Filipovski is excellent, and there's a generous characterization by Gary Who as his mate who, despite the odds, stands by him.

Oehr (pronounced Air) obviously cares about her three protagonists, and her sympathy for them and anger at the society that's edging them towards lives of unemployment and misery is clearly deeply felt. With a background of docu and short fiction, she's obviously ready to tackle a major feature on the strength of her work here.

Pic was sponsored by a government department, and hopefully will be seen in art-house cinemas before going to the home screen. Abroad it should spark interest among festivals and even find some small distributors who care about it as much as its director obviously does. —*Strat.*

The Return Of The Living Dead
(COLOR)

Some..mes funny zombie sendup should live for a few weeks.

Hollywood, June 14.

An Orion release of a Hemdale Film Corp. presentation of a Fox Films Ltd. production. Produced by Tom Fox. Coproducer, Graham Henderson. Executive producers, John Daly, Derek Gibson. Directed, written by Dan O'Bannon, from story by Rudy Ricci, John Russo, Russell Streiner. Features entire cast. Camera (Deluxe color), Jules Brenner; editor, Robert Gordon; music, Matt Clifford; production design, William Stout; special makeup effects, Bill Munns; sound, Ronald Judkins; assistant directors, Scott Javine, Josh King; casting, Stanzi Stokes. Reviewed at the Orion Screening Room, L.A., June 13, 1985. (MPAA Rating: R.) Running time: **90 MINS.**

Burt	Clu Gulager
Frank	James Karen
Ernie	Don Calfa
Freddy	Thom Mathews
Tina	Beverly Randolph
Chuck	John Philbin
Casey	Jewel Shepard
Spider	Miguel Nunez
Scuz	Brian Peck
Trash	Linnea Quigley
Suicide	Mark Venturini
Colonel Glover	Jonathan Terry
Colonel's Wife	Cathleen Cordell

The "Casino Royale" of the undead genre, "The Return Of The Living Dead" is a sporadically hilarious, frequently draggy takeoff on George A. Romero's celebrated horror entries. Calculatedly hip, sometimes genuinely witty approach of director-writer Dan O'Bannon will win pic a deserved cult following of its own, and there's sufficient mayhem to keep the action fans coming for the first few weeks of wide release. Already playing in France, item will be released by Orion domestically later this summer, when Romero's own entry, "Day Of The Dead," also will be on the screen.

Early on here, one character asks another if he's seen the original "Night Of The Living Dead," then goes on to explain that the 1968 film (cowritten by John Russo, who gets costory credit on this one) altered the facts concerning a real-life zombie attack on the local populace.

Virtually the entire action of the rather threadbare production shuttles among three locations — a medical supply warehouse, where numerous zombies have been sent by the Army; a nearby mortuary, and an adjacent cemetery, where a bunch of punks frolic before being chased out by corpses risen from their graves.

From then on, it's the same old story, as unusually vigorous, athletic zombies besiege the motley bunch of human beings holed up in the vicinity and eat the brains of anyone they get their hands on.

Finally, as in a Godzilla pic or any sci-fi cheapie of the 1950s, the Army is called in and retaliates against the ghouls by nuking Louisville, site of the onslaught. Safe to assume that none of the characters here will be available for a sequel.

O'Bannon deserves considerable credit for creating a terrifically funny first half-hour of exposition, something in which he is greatly aided by the goofball performance of James Karen as a medical supply know-it-all. Initial stretch plays something like "Abbott & Costello Meet The Zombies" might have, and pitting some hardcore punks against the undead was a good idea.

Unfortunately, the inspiration flags in the later-going, despite some bright moments when the zombies call up for more cops to eat, and when the mortician, nicely played by Don Calfa, has a chat with half a female zombie.

Bill Munns has done a good job with the special makeup effects, although pic doesn't begin to approach the gore level of the Romero features. Soundtrack consists of numerous tunes from such punk bands as The Flesheaters, 45 Grave, The Damned and The Cramps.

— *Cart.*

Ikiteru Uchiga Hanananoyo Shindara Soremadeyo to Sengen
(The Nuclear Gypsies)
(JAPANESE-COLOR)

Tokyo, June 1.

A Kinoshita Eiga production. Directed by Azuma Morisaki. Features Yoshio Harada, Mitsuko Baisho, Mitsuru Mirata. Screenplay, Shoji Kondo, Morisaki, Kiyoshide Hara; Camera (color), Tsuyoshi Hamada; sound, Susumu Take; music, Ryudo Uzaki; art direction, Akira Takahashi. Reviewed in Tokyo, February 1985. Running time: **106 MINS.**

Quite a mouthful in any language, the title means "It's great when you're alive and useless when you're dead Party Declaration." Director Azuma Morisaki once read these words in connection with a former Shanghai Red Guard faction, and longed to use it as a film title. The result is this bleak, black comedy, which is shortly to travel abroad under the more succinct title, "The Nuclear Gypsies."

Film is based on a sinister scandal which erupted some years ago in the Japanese press. There have been leaks in Japan's nuclear power stations, and attempts to publicize allegations of poisoned employees reportedly have been stifled brutally. In order to protect power station workers from contamination, it seems local governments hire day laborers to do the dirtiest, most dangerous work — at night. These "nuclear gypsies" spend their lives wandering from one power station to the next. Their services are quite openly recruited by yakuza gangster outfits, while police and local authorities not only look the other way, but actively and ruthlessly strive to maintain a lucrative status quo.

Noro (Mitsuru Hirata), a bumbling, ludicrously diffident Nagoya teacher is kidnaped by a band of high school hooligans and held for ransom.

Loudly proclaiming him to be in league with his kidnapers, the high-school authorities find it more convenient to fire Noro than pay the ransom. Freed anyway, Noro is befriended by an Okinawan stripper Barbara (Mitsuko Baisho) and a nuclear gypsy Miyazato (Yoshio Harada). Their journey takes them through stark tales of nuclear contamination, corruption, vice and violence, taking in every conceivable form of Japanese sociopathy on the way.

There are too many statements about sordid peripheral issues: the more important issue of corruption directly related to the film's evil nuclear core is drowned in a swamp of pessimistic anecdotes.

"Nuclear Gypsies" benefits from performances from an outstanding cast. Yoshio Harada, macho survivor of Japanese hippiedom, seems to generate pent-up rage as a rock-hard monument to indifference. With the loveliest gravelly voice since Marlene Dietrich, the irresistible Mitsuko Baisho excels as usual as the tough, surviving Japanese woman at her most sensual. Mitsuru Hirata is likewise as habitually endearing as the sensitive fool.

The tone is satirical and, along the way, "Nuclear Gypsies" sometimes manages the feat of being a very funny film. The impact of the serious side is relentlessly depressing, however, and overshadows the rest. —*Born.*

St. Elmo's Fire
(COLOR)

The Little Chill.

Hollywood, June 14.

A Columbia Pictures release from Columbia-Delphi IV Prods. of a Channel/Lauren Shuler production. Executive producers, Ned Tanen, Bernard Schwartz. Produced by Shuler. Directed by Joel Schumacher. Features entire cast. Screenplay, Schumacher, Carl Kurlander; camera (Panavision, Metrocolor), Stephen H. Burum; editor, Richard Marks; music, David Foster; sound, Gene Cantamessa; art direction, William Sandell; assistant director, Gary Daigler; casting, Jennifer Shull, Marci Liroff. Reviewed at the Academy of Motion Picture Arts & Sciences, June 13, 1985. (MPAA Rating: R.) Running time: **108 MINS.**

Billy	Rob Lowe
Jules	Demi Moore
Kevin	Andrew McCarthy
Alex	Judd Nelson
Leslie	Ally Sheedy
Kirbo	Emilio Estevez
Wendy	Mare Winningham
Mr. Beamish	Martin Balsam
Howie	Jon Cutler
Mrs. Beamish	Joyce Van Patten
Dale	Andie MacDowell
Felicia	Jenny Wright
Wally	Blake Clark

The audience will have to listen quick to get what the title of "St. Elmo's Fire" has to do with what's happening in the film. On the other hand, the whole picture proceeds with assurance that what's happening is always more important than why.

Judging from events, however, "St. Elmo's Fire" is all about a group of recent college graduates in Washington who were always the best of friends but now are drifting apart as real life approaches, discovering various reasons why they are so individually obnoxious.

Presumably, they would all have been better off to have made the discoveries in their freshman year, but life isn't fair and, when all is said and done, what are you going to do when the only married male and father in the group is the one who wears an earring and lipstick.

That's Rob Lowe and he's a saxophone player who refuses to assume any adult responsibility. The rest of the gang befriends him, especially virginal Mare Winningham, who's a social worker by trade anyway.

The other major problem is beautiful, coked-out Demi Moore who lives in a pink apartment, sleeps with her boss and calls her friends with wee-hour problems like the three sheiks on the sofa who mistook her intentions when she came up to their hotel room. Among other things, "St. Elmo's Fire" would try to convince you that the friends would actually try to rescue this bimbo when she finally attempts suicide.

Moving on to the more admirable products of higher education, there's Yuppie Capitol Hill aide Judd Nelson, a Democrat turned Republican because the pay is better, and his live-in, Ally Sheedy, who won't marry him but has reason to resent his cheating. So Sheedy sleeps with their other good friend Andrew McCarthy, an aspiring writer who loves from afar so long as his pal is watching.

Making them all look good by comparison is Emilio Estevez. Now here's his problem: Accompanying the group to the hospital after an accident, Estevez spots medical student Andie MacDowell, whom he once had one date with several years ago, with no memorable results for her.

Naturally, Estevez decides he must marry MacDowell despite her absolute lack of interest. Living in the shadow of the Post Office Dept., Estevez insists neither rain nor sleet nor fear of gloom will stay him from making a total fool of himself in futile pursuit, up to and including following her soaking wet into a fancy party where he's not invited and to the door of a romantic ski-lodge where she's warming up with another fellow.

Beyond occasional mutterings of words like "love" and "beer," there's never any explanation in the dialog that would hint at motivation. That's okay since nobody's listening, anyway. In the big suicide rescue, for example, Lowe and Moore both mumble away about their own thoughts with no indication at all that either is paying any attention to what the other is saying.

If it doesn't bother them, it probably won't bother those who like the film, either. —*Har.*

Cztery Pory Roku
(The Four Seasons)
(POLISH-COLOR)

Sydney, June 17.
A Polish Corp. for Film Prods.-Polish Television production. Produced, directed by Andrzej Kondratiuk. Screenplay, camera (color), art director, music, sound, Kondratiuk; editor, Maryla Orlowska. Reviewed at Sydney Film Festival, June 12, 1985. Running

time: **73 MINS.**
With: Andrzej Kondratiuk, Iga Cembrzynska-Kondratiuk, Arkadiusz Kondratiuk, Krystyna Kondratiuk, Janusz Kondratiuk.

"The Four Seasons" is that rare thing: a film from a country with a socialized film industry which still manages to be completely personal and even self-financed. Andrzej Kondratiuk raised the budget via a couple of cash prizes for his earlier work (one from West Berlin), plus loans from members of his family. Having done that, he wrote and directed the film himself, and was also in charge of the camera, carpentry, props and lighting. He also composed the music, and played a leading role, together with his parents, his wife and his brother.

The intrepid helmer's lifestyle, as presented in his film, is that of isolation from the rest of the world. He and his family live in a wooden house in beautiful countryside (miles from anywhere, it seems), and pass their days in contemplation as they live off the land. Andrzej himself likes to sit suspended in a kind of swinging cradle, blindfolded, so he can turn on to his own innermost thoughts. His wife produces juices from the herbs and flowers in the area, including nettles. They're interested in determining if plant-life feels pain.

They have dogs, a Siamese cat, and a tame magpie. Andrzej and his brother spy on a neighbor, a fat woman who bathes naked. Nothing really happens, except towards the end when Andrzej's parents visit. His father is very old and obviously unwell (he died a week after filming), but the brothers encourage him to enjoy the sights and sounds of nature (plus the sight of the naked neighbor) and try to make his last days happy.

This, then, is a self-obsessed, inward-looking film, and the viewer will have to have some sympathy for the filmmaker's attitude to life going in, or boredom will quickly follow. It is, in the end, a strangely appealing film about modern dropouts in a country with more than its share of turmoil, and, from a cinematic point of view, an accomplished piece of work form a tenacious and single-minded director. — *Strat.*

Dance Black America
(U.S.-DOCU-COLOR)

Sydney, June 17.
A Pennebaker Associates production. Produced by Frazer Pennebaker. Directed by Chris Hegedus, D.A. Pennebaker. Camera (color), editors, commentary, Hegedus, Pennebaker; sound, Lawrence Hoff, Ellen Haag; narrator, Geoffrey Holder. Reviewed at Sydney Film Festival, June 13, 1985. Running time: **87 MINS.**
With: The Alvin Ailey American Dance Theater (with Donna Wood, Gary DeLoatch), Garth Fagan's Bucket Dance

Theater, Mama Lu Park's Jazz Dancers, The Charles Moore Dance Theater, The Chuck Davis Dance Co., Eleo Pomare, Chuck Green, The Magnificent Force, The Jazzy Jumpers, Al Perryman, Leon Jackson, Halifu Osumare, Dejan's Olympia Brass Band of New Orleans, Rudy Stevenson Band, Ruth Brisbane, Biss Harmonisers.

"Dance Black America" is an excellent, if all-too-brief, record of the four-day April 1983 festival of that name held in Brooklyn by the Brooklyn Academy of Music and the State U. of New York.

Chris Hegedus and D.A. Pennebaker and their team have captured the highlights of what was obviously a dazzling experience, featuring some of the finest black dancers in America. Early sequences feature dancers replicating original African tribal dance routines, such as Charles Moore's extraordinary "Ostrich." Later, archive film footage shows the original turn-of-the-century Cakewalk, while contemporary dancers present new styles.

The two highlights of this exhilarating docu are totally different, yet indicative of the wealth and range to be found in black dance in America today. A quartet of young women, the Jazzy Jumpers, perform a show-stopper with skipping-ropes that had the Sydney fest audience aplauding. Film's climax is an extended ballet, "Fontessa And Friends," composed and choreographed by Louis Johnson (who based it on a Modern Jazz Quartet tune), and brilliantly danced by the Alvin Ailey American Dance Theater. Lead dancer, the talented Donna Wood, proves to be a superb actress and comedienne as well as a fabulous dancer. — *Strat.*

Arhats In Fury
(HONG KONG-CHINA-COLOR)

Cannes, May 10.
A Nan Hai Films Co. (Beijing) and Palace Intl. Film (Hong Kong) coproduction and presentation. Directed by Wong Singloy. Stars Liu Zhenling, Gao Hong Ping, Li Deching, He Fusheng, Wang Xinwu, Wang Zhihua. Distributed by Southern Film Corp. Screenplay, Chen Xi; Music, Wu Dai Jang. (No other credits provided.) Reviewed at Cannes (Market), May 9, 1985. Running time: **98 MINS.**
(Available in Mandarin and Cantonese soundtrack with English subtitles.)

"Arhats In Fury" is the latest Shaolin kung fu film shot entirely in China, in the Szechuan region. It stars well-known and highly respected martial arts champions from the mainland.

"Arhats" centers on a young monk, the orphan Xing Dian, who breaks the peaceful non-involvement code of the Shaolin temple by fighting back to the dismay of the head priest. During a raid, Xing Dian strikes again and the disciplined monks punish him for this noble act. The enemies take the tem-

ple but Dian wins later with the help of volunteer fighter Zhao Xiang, a lady revolutionary. The hero after many fights and much soul searching via the Arhats philosophy finds peace. He saves his religion, his people and his country.

The redeeming asset of this fine production is the exotic novelty of seeing parts of China never seen before on the big screen. The authentic Shaolin kung fu is also exciting to watch. — *Mel.*

The Treasure Of
The Amazon
(El Tesoro Del Amazones)
(MEXICAN-COLOR)

Mexico City, June 1.
A Videocine release of a Star World Prod., Real Intl. and Televicine production. Produced and directed by René Cardona Jr. Screenplay, Cardona; camera (color), Mort Garson; editor, Earl Watson; music, Daniel López. Reviewed at Cine Ermita, Mexico City, May 31, 1985. Running time: **104 MINS.**

Gringo	Stuart Whitman
Paco	Emilio (Indio) Fernández
Klaus	Donald Pleasence
Clark	Bradford Dillman
Priest	John Ireland
Barbara	Ann Sidney
Dick	Clark Jarret
Zapata	Pedro Armendáriz Jr.
Jaime	Jorge Luke
Boat Captain	Hugo Stiglitz
Morimba	Sonia Infante

René Cardona Jr., Mexico's best-known director outside the country, has made a rambling scenic monstrosity with his latest film, "The Treasure Of The Amazon," shot in English with an international cast. He is known for quickie low-budget "docu-dramas" based on bizarre topical events — "Survive," "Guyana, The Cult Of The Damned," "The Devil's Triangle."

This adventure pic supposedly is based on a real incident that took place "deep in the jungles of South America in 1958," yet accompanied by a disclaimer noting all resemblances to anyone depicted in this "unnamed" country is sheer coincidence. Pic attempts to fuse too many diverse elements without achieving a logical coherence. It soon becomes so bogged down in particulars that plot seems unimportant.

Contrived story has Stuart Whitman retrace his journey into the jungle where six years earlier, he and five friends found a wealth in diamonds. He had barely returned to civilization alive, carrying the shrunken heads of his friends. Two unsavory characters, Zapata (Pedro Armendáriz Jr.) and Jaimie (Jorge Luke), have now joined Whitman.

Also on the trail of riches is another trio, made up of Ann Sidney, Bradford Dillman and Clark Jarret, and an unlikely couple composed of a semi-nude Sonia Infante plus Donald Pleasence, who plays a former Nazi (South America is teeming with them, afterall), who wants the wealth to finance renewed experiments in genetics.

Abundance of cut-away shots to the lush flora and fauna seem as if Cardona wants to show us that pic was actually made on location and not in the backlots of Churubusco Studios — the site of most of his films. The local color is given much more attention than the international cast.

Film is absurdly violent: in the first three minutes someone has a finger chopped off, is attacked by alligators and eaten alive by piranhas. This is just a prelude to man-eating crabs, savage headhunters and crooked tax collectors.

Daniel López' predestrian score hinders any attempt for tone.

The film fits well within Cardona's body of work, with emphasis on the grotesque, a convoluted storyline, sketchy character development and a striving for tension that never emerges. It seems destined for limited distribution on the drive-in circuit. —Lent.

Le Déclic
(Turn-On)
(FRENCH-COLOR)

Paris, June 15.
An AMLF release of an Alain Siritzky production. Produced by Siritzky. Written and directed by Jean-Louis Richard, based on the cartoon strip by Milo Manara; storyboard and adviser for sets and costumes, Manara; editor, Martine Baraqué; music, Jacques Lecoeur; production manager, Pierre Cotrell. Reviewed at the Georges V cinema, Paris, June 15, 1985. Running time: **87 MINS.**
With: Jean-Pierre Kalfon, Florence Guérin, Bernard Kuby, Jasmina Maimone, Lisa Marks, Alain Siritzky.

"Le Déclic" doesn't click. This live-action adaptation of Milo Manara's sexy comic strip sort of hums promisingly for a while, but never provides the expected turn-on.

Story, set in Louisiana and shot on location, tells of a certain Dr. Fez, who, to avenge himself on a crooked local tycoon, invents a mysterious black box which, when switched on, sends his antagonist's beautiful but frigid young wife into a libidinous frenzy.

After turning her on in a variety of embarrassing occasions (notably in a department store where she rapes a floorwalker, and at a garden party where a confessional conversation with a priest takes a salacious turn), Fez decides it's time to discard his box and possess her himself. The husband tries to have him eliminated, but fails, allowing Fez and the now sexually thawed out spouse to go off together.

Manara himself visualized the film scene-by-scene with an elaborate storyboard, and director Jean-Louis Richard has apparently executed his treatment faithfully. (It's rumored that Yank helmer Bob Rafelson had a brief hand in the direction.)

The fidelity of film to comic strip only points up the fact that Manara has a tart graphic style that translates the sexual kinkiness of the tale, while Richard has no film style of his own, seeming little more than a smooth technician.

Newcomer Florence Guérin, a nubile 19, is the on-again-off-again bourgeoise, though her acting is monotonously somnambulistic, whether in heat or not. The unsettling Jean-Pierre Kalfon is perfect as the slightly bent Fez, giving the proceedings a quirky flavor that saves it from total blandness.

Producer Alain Siritzky has a mute but effective part as a professional killer hired to get rid of Kalfon. — Len.

Heroic Times
(Dalias Idok)
(HUNGARIAN-WEST GERMAN-ANIMATED-COLOR)

Annecy, June 7.
A Sefel Pictures international release. Coproduced by Pannonia Filmstudio, Budapest, and Infa Film, Munich. Directed, written and designed by Jozsef Gemes from the 19th century epic poem "Tokdi" by Janos Arany; music, Janos Decsenyi. Reviewed at Annecy Festival, June 7, 1985. Running time: **85 MINS.**

A visually stunning medieval epic adventure which should appeal to followers of Arthurian-type tales of chivalry, "Heroic Times" is like stepping into a moving painting about knights and heroes. It is the first feature ever made by fully animating oil paintings.

The workload has led to some repetition of sequences and detailed zooms into every corner of the large canvases, but the action keeps moving and a strong music track helps the lack of narrative, a major flaw.

Set in 14th century Hungary — although armor and costume could indicate anywhere in Europe — the hero is a young man of exceptional strength who wishes to become a knight. As naive as he is good, he is duped by his jealous brother into killing an opponent in a duel and is subsequently exiled. He returns eventually when his country is at war to prove his loyalty, but after some painted battles which rate as among the most exciting scenes ever animated, he is again betrayed and retreats to watch insects climb up blades of grass. He, like the film, can be slow at times.

The storyline is not easy to follow as the film has neither dialog nor narrative. Sequences are frequently repeated at different times in the tale. It's difficult to determine whether a gallop through trees is a similar journey or the memory of a past journey.

Without voices this film can only appeal to a small minority who enjoy visual imagery. A good English script and strong voiceovers could turn it into a successful commercial product appealing to family audiences.

"Heroic Times" is an extraordinary achievement for director Jozsef Gemes who designed, wrote and animated much of the picture. A previous award-winner for shorts such as "Concertissimo," he has already won several awards with this film including the best feature prize at Annecy.—Anmo.

Cannibal Holocaust
(ITALIAN-COLOR)

A Trans Continental Film release of a F.D. Cinematografica production. Presented by Franco Palaggi, Franco Di Nunzio. Directed by Ruggero Deodato. Features entire cast. Screenplay, story, Gianfranco Clerici; camera (Luciano Vittori color), Sergio D'Offizi; editor, Vincenzo Tomassi; music, Riz Ortolani; production design, M.A. Geleng; in charge of production, Giovanni Masini; assistant directors, Salvatore Basile, Lamberto Bava. Reviewed at Embassy 1 theater, N.Y., June 16, 1985. (MPAA Rating: X.) Running time: **95 MINS.**
With: R. Bolla, Francesca Ciardi, Perry Pirkanen, Pio Di Savola, Salvatore Basile.

Filmed in 1979, "Cannibal Holocaust" is an Italian gore picture just now getting its U.S. release. Prospects are poor beyond the gross-me-out market.

Filmmaker Ruggero Deodato, who earlier made the similar "The Last Survivor" (a.k.a. "Carnivorous") in the Far East, travels here to the Amazon to weave a patently phony tale of cannibalism and the white man's mistreatment of native tribes.

New York U. Professor Monroe (played by porno veteran R. Bolla) goes on a mission to the Amazon jungle to locate a missing four-person documentary crew led by director Alan Yates. Monroe finds the quartet's remains and brings back the film footage they've shot.

It seems Yates is an unscrupulous type who in the past paid African troops to stage executions for his camera. On the latest trip, he killed tribesmen and staged massacres for his docu camera, resulting in the cannibals' fatal revenge on him and his crew.

The film's "liberal" message on civilized man's cruelty to primitive peoples is old hat and rendered ludicrous by Deodato's inclusion of much extraneous gore effects and nudity, as well as the genre's usual (and disgusting) killing of animals on camera. Handheld camera film-within-a-film is phony looking, with Yates supposedly lensing (in self-incriminating fashion) loads of evidence that he and his crew are the real killers. End credit laughably pretends that a tv station projectionist illegally smuggled out the "real" footage after it had been ordered destroyed on Prof. Monroe's recommendation. —Lor.

Het Land Van Mijn Ouders
(And Never The Twain Shall Meet)
(DUTCH-DOCU-COLOR)

Sydney, June 17.
A Cinemien production. Produced by Rolf Orthel. Directed by Marion Bloem. Script, Bloem, Ivan Wolffers, Orthel; camera (color), Goert Giltay; editors, Jan Wouter van Reijen, Rimko Haanstra; sound, Bert van den Dungen, Jan Wouter van Reijen; music, Zeth Mustamu. Reviewed at Sydney Film Festival, June 14, 1985. Running time: **88 MINS.**

There are 300,000 Indo Europeans living in Holland, mixed-race people from Dutch-Indonesian parentage. This personal documentary is by one of them; Marion Bloem grew up as a Dutch girl in Holland, but she always knew she was "different." Only when she was at university did she become curious about her background, eventually visiting Indonesia with her husband. As a direct result, she made this film as an exploration of her own background.

That was the intention. In actuality, it has become a film about her parents, and especially her father, an apparently cheerful, good-natured man who, it becomes obvious, misses the country of his birth. Whether demonstrating (with disarming shyness) a traditional dance, or busily preparing some Indonesian food, or explaining that Indonesians peel potatoes differently from the Dutch reveals a more outgoing character, father emerges as a charming and rather sad man.

This focus on the filmmaker's parents makes the original Dutch title, which means "The Land Of My Parents," much more appropriate than the mundane English title.

It's a calm and measured documentary about the attitudes of the Dutch towards their former colony, and Dutch responses to modern-day Indonesia, though the political repression in that country is mentioned only in passing. The pic is too long, but if cut to a little less than an hour could make a fine television docu on a fascinating subject. —Strat.

Back To The Future
(COLOR)

A summertime comedy hit right now.

Hollywood, June 21.

A Universal Pictures release from Amblin Entertainment of a Steven Spielberg presentation. Produced by Bob Gale, Neil Canton. Executive producers, Spielberg, Frank Marshall, Kathleen Kennedy. Directed by Robert Zemeckis. Features entire cast. Screenplay, Zemeckis, Gale; camera (Technicolor), Dean Cundey; editors, Arthur Schmidt, Harry Keramidas; music, Alan Silvestri; sound (Dolby stereo), William B. Kaplan; production design, Lawrence G. Paull; costume designer, Deborah L. Scott; art director, Todd Hallowell; set decorator, Hal Gausman; set designers, Joseph E. Hubbard, Marjorie Stone McShirley, Cameron Birnie; special effects supervisor, Kevin Pike; special effects, Steve Suits, Kimberley Pike, Sam Adams, Richard Chronister. William Klinger; assistant director, Daid McGiffert; makeup, Ken Chase; stunt coordinator, Walter Scott; casting, Mike Fenton, Jane Feinberg, Judy Taylor; second unit director, Frank Marshall; second unit camera, Raymond Stella; visual effects, Industrial Light & Magic. Reviewed at Samuel Goldwyn Theater, June 20, 185. (MPAA Rating: PG.) Running time: **116 MINS.**

Marty McFly . . . . Michael J. Fox
Dr. Emmett Brown . . . . Christopher Lloyd
George McFly . . . . Crispin Glover
Lorraine Baines . . . . Lea Thompson
Jennifer Parker . . . . Claudia Wells
Biff Tannen . . . . Thomas F. Wilson
Mr. Strickland . . . . James Tolkan
Dave McFly . . . . Marc McClure
Linda McFly . . . . Wendie Jo Sperber
Sam Baines . . . . George DiCenzo
Stella Baines . . . . Frances Lee McCain

Once past a shaky opening overloaded with frenetic exposition, the time-travel odyssey "Back To The Future" accelerates with wit, ideas, and infectious, wide-eyed wonder. Following a nationwide, jumbo opening July 3, grosses are sure to brighten the summer of Universal Studios and such key filmmakers as director Robert Zemeckis and co-executive producer Steven Spielberg.

The central winning elements in the scenario by Bob Gale and Zemeckis are twofold; hurtling the audience back to a very accessible year, 1955, which allows for lots of comparative, pop culture humor, and delivering a 1985 teenager (Michael J. Fox) at the doorstep of his future parents when they were 17-year-old kids. That encounter is a delicious premise, especially when the young hero's mother-to-be develops the hots for her future son and his future father is a bumbling wimp.

Film is also sharply anchored by zestful byplay between Fox' Arthurian knight figure and Christopher Lloyd's Merlin-like, crazed scientist. The latter has mounted a nuclear-powered time machine in a spaced-out DeLorean car, which spirits the bedazed Fox 30 years back in time to the same little town in which he grew up.

The film's opening 20 minutes or

so, in present time, are intended to set up almost all you need to know about the characters and the madcap vision of the scientist. Indeed the first image on the screen, of countless timepieces tick-tocking away, is an effective symbolic touch. However, the filmmakers scramble too furiously here and the film doesn't find its control and its feet, and what a relief it is, until the hero is dropped into the same town in 1955 to the becalming background melody of the Four Aces singing "Mr. Sandman." Then the fun begins.

Fox' wonderful goal, it eventually develops, is nothing less than making a man out of his father, who as a teenager is taunted by high school bullies and who is a peeping tom (of his future wife) to boot.

In the film's opening sequences, the father (wonderfully played by Crispin Glover) is an unctuous nitwit, and the mother (Lea Thompson) a plump, boozey, turtle-necked frau. It is the rearranging of time and events by our stalwart heros, the wondrous youth and his magician scientist, that set up the surprise ending when the young lad goes "back to the future" to happily discover his family, including a brother and sister, living a life that would qualify as a trendy Southern California magazine cover.

If the filmmakers' pre-'60s look occasionally suggests the '40s more than the '50s, the screen is constantly full of delightful comparisions: the old village square theater in '55 with a marquee showing Ronald Reagan in "Cattle Queen Of Montana" has become a porno house in '85. The Studebaker lot is now peddling Toyotas. The quaint shops on the square in '55 are now squeezed into the metallic greyness of an outlying shopping mall. The malt shop is now an aeorbics gym.

None of these points is underscored, but merely float in the background as signposts of change. The most rousing, and audience-grabbing scene of culture shock comes when Fox mounts the '55 high school stage, says he's going to play an oldie, and digs into Chuck Berry's "Johnny B. Goode" at the dawn of rock 'n' roll.

You can see the end of doo wop, syrupy ballads and, for that matter, the fade out of strapless prom dresses and baggy cuffed slacks. Yet the mellow motif of the fab '50s is the movie's nice, lingering image.

Performances by the earnest Fox, the lunatic Lloyd, the deceptively passionate Lea Thompson, and, particularly, the bumbling-to-confident Glover, who runs away with the picture, merrily keep the ship sailing. Thomas F. Wilson as the bully (what a change he comes to be) and Claudia Wells as a gorgeous

contemporary girlfriend of Fox contribute good support.

Film's time travel theme is sufficiently imaginative to remind filmgoers of James Stewart's fantasy adventure in Frank Capra's "It's A Wonderful Life." —*Loyn.*

Metropolitan Avenue
(DOCU-COLOR/B&W-16m)

A production of Metropolitan Avenue Film Project, N.Y. Produced, directed, narrated by Christine Noschese; camera (color, 16m), John Bonanno; editor, Stan Salfas; original music, Glen Daum. Reviewed at American Film Festival, N.Y., May 28, 1985. Running time: **60 MINS.**

Winner of the John Grierson Award at the recent American Film Festival for best debut-director of a social-documentary, Christine Noschese's "Metropolitan Avenue" is an affectionate and humorous visit to a typical inner-city community, with small wood-frame family houses, public housing projects, small businesses — a friendly neighborhood where people have their own sports events, school marches, dances and ethnic picnics, but also demonstrations when they get mad at City Hall just across the river. It's set in Central Williamsburg in Brooklyn.

The film emphasizes collective action to preserve the endangered neighborhood from the rapacity of big-business and government, which have ambitious plans for this valuable urban real estate. It affirms the traditional value of small communities with their own vitality and identity.

Because of its warmth and humor, "Metropolitan Avenue" can perhaps connect with general audiences via theatrical exposure in tandem with a compatible film. In addition, "Metropolitan Avenue" is a natural for public TV and also for colleges, urban-planning seminars and the like. —*Hitch.*

Lifeforce
(COLOR)

Vampires terrorize London in unintentional laugh riot.

Hollywood, June 19.

A Tri-Star Pictures release of a Golan-Globus production of a Cannon Group picture. Produced by Menahem Golan, Yoram Globus. Directed by Tobe Hooper. Features entire cast. Screenplay, Dan O'Bannon, Don Jakoby, based on the novel "The Space Vampires" by Colin Wilson; camera (Rank color, J-D-C Widescreen), Alan Hume; editor, John Grover; music, Henry Mancini; additional music, Michael Kamen; production design, John Graysmark; art direction, Alan Tomkins, Bob Cartwright, Tony Reading, Terry Knight; set decoration, Simon Wakefield, Denise Exshaw; costume design, Carin Hooper; prosthetic and makeup effects, Nick Maley; special effects, John Gant; special visual effects, John Dykstra; makeup, Dickie Mills, Michael Morris, Sandra Exelby; special

visual effects produced by Apogee; sound design, Vernon Messenger; sound (Dolby), George Stephenson; associate producer, Michael J. Kagan; assistant director/second unit director, Derek Cracknell; second unit camera, Jack Lowin; casting, Maude Spector, Ann Stanborough. Reviewed at the Picwood, L.A., June 19, 1985. (MPAA Rating: R.) Running time: **101 MINS.**

Carlsen . . . . Steve Railsback
Caine . . . . Peter Firth
Fallada . . . . Frank Finlay
Space Girl . . . . Mathilda May
Dr. Armstrong . . . . Patrick Stewart
Bukovsky . . . . Michael Gothard
Derebridge . . . . Nicholas Ball
Sir Percy . . . . Aubrey Morris
Ellen . . . . Nancy Paul
Lamson . . . . John Hallam

Olde London town hasn't had it this bad since "The Day The Earth Caught Fire." In "Lifeforce," the city is quarantined due to a massive outbreak of zombie-itis, itself caused by a beautiful naked lady vampire recently transported to earth from Halley's Comet. If that sounds ludicrous on paper, it proves even more so in the telling, as "Lifeforce" is the unintentional laugh-fest of the season. By any artistic standards, this is a $22,500,000 bomb, although a big push for last Friday's (21) openings might allow for some quick recoupment.

For about the first 10 minutes, pic indicates it could be a scary sci-fier in the "Alien" mode, as Yank and British space travelers discover seemingly human remains in the vicinity of Halley's Comet and attempt to bring home three perfectly preserved specimens.

The astronauts don't make it back but the humanoids do, and one of them, Space Girl, as she is referred to in the credits, is possessed of such a spectacularly statuesque physique that she could probably have conquered all of mankind even without her special talents, which include a form of electroshock vampirism and the ability to inhabit other bodies.

After the far from uneventful opening reels, which feature space travel, the shocking transformation of normal people into hideous, but undead, cadavers, and minute after minute of Space Girl walking around in the altogether, pic descends into subpar Agatha Christie territory, as fanatical inspector Peter Firth and surviving astronaut Steve Railsback scour the countryside for the deadly Space Girl and make a pit stop at an insane asylum to provide for further hysteria.

Even though she turns millions of Londoners into fruitcakes and threatens the entire world, Railsback just can't get the naked Space Girl out of his mind, and he finally joins her in unholy communion in a cathedral. In the meantime, Firth, in what look like outtakes from one of the "Living Dead" pics, makes his way through scores of zombies in a burning London in hopes of nailing Space Girl.

Film's original title, "Space Vampires," would have been more appropriate than the current moniker on two counts, since it more accurately describes the subject and is more expressive of the generally tacky, exploitative nature of the production. Special effects, particularly the work with moving and transforming human bodies, are elaborate and extensive but can't raise the general tenor of the show.

Director Tobe Hooper and scenartists Dan O'Bannon and Don Jakoby may have intended some of this humorously, but not all of it. Explicitness of the effects and broadness of the performances in the service of preposterous dialog push this toward camp and unendurability.

Railsback and Firth, serious thesps both, are allowed to overact wildly by Hooper, who himself has indulged in plenty of overstated askew camera angles. Although the treatment of women here is unenlightened to say the least, one still can't help but marvel at Mathilda May, who strides through her role as Space Girl with an unembarrassed implacability all the more remarkable for the sordid surroundings. — *Cart.*

Deadly Passion
(SOUTH AFRICAN-COLOR)

Durban, June 10.

A UIP-Warner release of a Deadly Passion Film production. Produced by Anant Singh. Executive producer, Manuel Shaliet. Directed by Larry Larson. Features entire cast. Screenplay, Larson, Curt Allen; camera (color), Vincent Cox; editor, Bill Blunden; music, Jay Ferguson. Reviewed at Oscar Theatre, June 10, 1985. Running time: **98 MINS.**
Sam Black . . . . Brent Huff
Martha Greenwood . . . . Ingrid Boulting
Andy Andrews . . . . Harrison Coburn
Marsha . . . . Lynn Maree
Robert Chandler . . . . Eric Flynn
Abigail Marx . . . . Erica Rogers
Sandra Moore . . . . Gabrielle Lomberg
Harry Marx . . . . John Berks
Also with: Michael McCabe, Jon Maytam, Susan Isaacs, Theresa Iglish, Sunshine, Dennis Folbigge, Rob Smith, Beth Jansen, Louise Saint Claire, Bess Finney, James White, Ron Smerczak.

Anant Singh's first venture into film producing is billed as "South Africa's first adult film." From the outset, however, it becomes obvious this billing is nothing more than a euphemism for a tame softcore sex film built around an appallingly weak script.

Sam Black (Brent Huff) is a slick, smart aleck Los Angeles private investigator who ends up being shot while doing undercover work in the Bahamas.

While recovering at a convalescent home in the island, Black meets Martha (Ingrid Boulting) from Beverly Hills on the beach. He tries his luck rather unsuccessfully as Martha tells him she is recovering from her husband's death.

Undaunted the swashbuckling hero tracks her down on his return to the U.S. and in no time the happy couple are frolicking in the altogether in Martha's swimming pool.

It's the usual love at first sight story. With the odd jealous lover thrown in here and there, the couple go through an endless array of steamy bed scenes.

Martha, a rich widow, is being conned out of her multimillion dollar inheritance by her business manager, Robert Chandler (Eric Flynn). Sam jumps to her rescue with a clever plot to beat both Chandler and the bank at their own game and pulls off an unusual heist. Sam is double-crossed by Martha, who is now shacked-up with his half-brother, Andy Andrews (Harrison Coburn). Chandler is murdered and Sam becomes the suspect. The pic then explodes into violence.

At best, "Deadly Passion" is mildly amusing. A tight budget leaves the pic with a sloppy look. Acting from the topliners is far from good although Coburn does project some enthusiasm. —*Glee.*

Mad Max Beyond Thunderdome
(AUSTRALIAN-COLOR)

Sydney, June 25.

A Warner Bros. release of a Kennedy Miller presentation. Produced by George Miller. Directed by Miller and George Ogilvie. Stars Mel Gibson, Tina Turner. Coproducers, Doug Mitchell, Terry Hayes; screenplay, Hayes, Miller; camera (Panavision, color), Dean Semler; editor, Richard Francis-Bruce; music, Maurice Jarre; casting, Alison Barrett; visual design consultant, Ed Verreaux; costume designer, Norma Moriceau; production designer, Graham Walker; production manager, Antonia Barnard ; exec in charge of production, Su Armstrong; art director, Anni Browning; sound supervisor, Roger Savage. Reviewed at Film Australia theatrette, Sydney, June 25, 1985. (Commonwealth Film Censor Rating: M). (MPAA Rating: PG-13.) Running time: **106 MINS.**
Mad Max . . . . Mel Gibson
Aunty Entity . . . . Tina Turner
The Master . . . . Angelo Rossitto
Savannah Nix . . . . Helen Buday
Scrooloose . . . . Rod Zuanic
The Collector . . . . Frank Thring
Ironbar . . . . Angry Anderson
The Blaster . . . . Paul Larsson
Jedediah . . . . Bruce Spence
Jedediah Jr. . . . . Adam Cockburn

Just as "Mad Max 2" (a.k.a. "The Road Warrior") was a quantum leap above the first of the "Max" adventures, the third in the series represents another significant advance, benefitting from a vastly higher budget (no figure was officially disclosed, but the one mentioned most often is $A13,000,000), the accumulated experience and expanding vision of the Kennedy Miller production team.

Producer Byron Kennedy died in a helicopter crash before "Max Max Beyond Thunderdome" was con-

ceived, but his place seems to have been well filled by director George Miller taking on producer chores in league with coscripter Terry Hayes and Doug Mitchell.

Being released worldwide by Warner Bros., the latest epic looks set to do very good business in the U.S., Australia, Japan and other markets where "Max"/"The Road Warrior" is a proven boxoffice performer.

If "Thunderdome's" takings fall a little short of the second "Max" saga, reason could be that in opting to expand on the characters and strive for more originality in the narrative, the production team has sacrificed some of the pace, tension and rip-roaring action which were at the heart of the genre's appeal.

Mel Gibson needs a hit after the relative disappointments of his last three films, "The Bounty," "The River" and "Mrs. Soffel," and in this outing he is given the chance to take the Max character out of the laconic (monosyllabic?) emotion-deadened strait jacket of the past.

Pic opens strong with Gibson being dislodged from his camel train by low-flying Bruce Spence in an airborne jalopy (providing as much fun here as he did as the Gyro Captain in the earlier "Max" films, this time accompanied by Adam Cockburn as his daredevil son).

To retrieve his possessions, Gibson has to confront Tina Turner, the improbably named Aunty, mistress of Bartertown, a bizarre bazaar where anything — up to and including human lives — is traded as the only form of commerce in the post-apocalyptic world.

Turner throws him a challenge: engage in a fight to the death with a giant known as The Blaster (Paul Larsson) in the Thunderdome, a geometric arena which serves as a kind of futuristic Roman Colosseum for the delectation of the locals. That suits her purpose, since The Blaster functions in unison with The Master (Angelo Rossitto) a clever dwarf who as boss of the Underworld, the town's energy source,

is acting somewhat disrespectful, if not downright mutinous.

The duel — both men flying through the air on elastic ropes, wielding various weapons of destruction — is exciting stuff, laced with bone-crushing violence which seems more explicit than anything in the second "Max" film. Gibson wins, but after being forced to spin a rudimentary wheel-of-fortune is dispatched to the desert, where he is rescued by a tribe of wild children.

Here the pic sags slightly as Savannah (Helen Buday) launches into a lengthy exposition of the children's innocent beliefs in a civilized, sophisticated world which, of course, no longer exists. Touched

by their naiveté, Gibson tells them they're wrong, but Savannah and several of her strong-willed mates won't accept that, and they set off in the direction of Bartertown.

This leads to another bloody encounter with the Bartertown heavies led by Ironbar (Angry Anderson, a diminutive, shaven-headed dynamo who is well known in Australia as the lead singer of a heavy metal band, Rose Tattoo).

Gibson, Rossitto and the kids take off in a massive locomotive, pursued by Turner and henchmen in all manner of strange automobiles. Fast and furious though it is, sequence is not quite as electrifying as the chase in "Mad Max 2" which had Gibson at the wheel of a speeding truck. Neat ending has the children whisked away to safety and Max left to continue his lone odyssey (a cue to "Mad Max 4?")

Miller, sharing the directing with George Ogilvie (with whom he collaborated previously on the Kennedy Miller tv miniseries "The Dismissal") has fashioned a picture which in technical terms is far superior to its predecessors. Dean Semler's camerawork is stunning, making brilliant use of diverse landscapes and settings: a whiter than white desert, red-tinged outback, tranquil bushland of the Blue Mountains (home of the feral children) and the dimly-lit pandemonium of Bartertown and its malevolent circus, Thunderdome. Model work of a Sydney devastated by the holocaust looks chillingly real.

Composer Maurice Jarre's music, played by the Royal Philharmonic Orchestra, is a strong element, beautifully building atmosphere and majestically underscoring the action.

As noted, Gibson impressively fleshes out Max, Tina Turner is striking in her role as Aunty (as well as contributing two topnotch songs, which open and close the picture) and the juves, coached by Ogilvie, a legit director, are uniformly good.

While "Mad Max Beyond Thunderdome" fails by a notch or two to match the velocity and potency of "The Road Warrior," it does take a refreshingly different tack, and it will give cinema patrons full value for their dollars. —*Dogo.*

ˌaux Fuyants
(Hit And Run)
(FRENCH-COLOR)

Tokyo, June 11.

A La Cecilia production. Directed by Alain Bergala, Jean-Pierre Limosin. Features entire cast. Screenplay, Philippe Arnaud, Bergala, Limosin; camera (Telcipro color), Denis Gheerbrant; editor, Claire Simon; music, Kristian Tabuchi; sound, Daniel Ollivier, Jean-Louis Richet. Reviewed at Tokyo Film Festival, June 1985. Running time: **100 MINS.**
Serge . . . . Olivier Perrier

Rachel . . . . .Rachel Rachel
Simon . . . . .Serge de Closets
Patrick . . . . .Nicolas Raynaud
Jacques . . . . .Claude Gaignaire
Also with: Genevieve Brunel, Benedict Christiance, Francoise Guerin, Liliane Mercier, Eddy Zamberlan, Jean-Jacques Henry, Sophie Calle, Christine Pascal.

Non-competitively presented at the 1983 Cannes Film Festival, "Faux Fuyants" was the sole French entry in the competitive Young Cinema '85 section of the first Tokyo Intl. Film Festival.

One night in a quiet Paris street, Serge (Olivier Perrier) accidentally runs over and kills a man who darts out suddenly in front of his car. No one sees, so Serge automatically responds according to the ethics of hit-and-run. From the moment Serge comes to read about the accident in the newspaper, it is the start of a strange obsession and a new life.

It seems the dead man lived in the country town of Yerres and leaves behind an only daughter, aged 16. Renting a room in town, Serge traces the girl and spends his time snooping to find out everything he can about her. Rachel (Rachel Rachel) lives alone and sings with a local rock band, and Serge manages to meet her by pretending to offer them a gig. In one way or another, he will do his utmost to enter her life and stay there.

Although it foregoes the obvious choice of sex to generate a subversive climate, "Faux Fuyants" is defiantly amoral and paints a deceptive sugar coating of charm around a bitterly cynical core.

A clever film, it is nevertheless hampered by its tiny budget, particularly by a rather rudimentary soundtrack. — *Born.*

Gaza Ghetto: Portrait Of A Palestinian Family, 1948-84
(SWEDISH-DOCU-COLOR/-B&W-16m)

A HB PeA Holmquist Film Prod., Orebro, Sweden. Directed by PeA Holmquist, Joan Mandell, Pierre Bjorklund. Written by Holmquist, Mary Khass; camera (color), 16m), Holmwuit, Yoram Millo; sound, Bjorklund, Steve Cameron, Joachim Alling; music, George Totari. (No editing credit.) Reviewed at Film Forum, N.Y., June 6, 1985. Running time: **82 MINS.**

In Arabic, Hebrew and English, with English subtitles.

"Gaza Ghetto" is yet another feature-documentary on the interminable and convoluted Arab-Israeli conflict, this time with a new look, provided by two Swedish film journalists, in association with an American, Joan Mandell, for years a specialist with the Middle East Research and Information Project, Washington, D.C., and writer for El Fahr, English-language Palestinian newspaper in Jerusalem.

Gaza is a long strip of coastline, always Arab, but since 1967 within Israel, wherein dwell a half-million displaced Palestinians in something approaching permanent misery. The film states that these people of Gaza suffer within a ghetto imposed by Israelis, who should know better from their own history.

The film selects and emphasizes the Abu-el-Adel family, spanning three generations, as the microcosm by which we sense the surrounding macrocosm of the Arab-Israeli stalemate. It is a family of intense loyalty to one another, and of nostalgic longing for their ancestral homeland, a fervent hope for a return to their old ways. Also, there is a burning hatred for the Israelis who have dispossessed them of their farmlands and livelihoods. We see the young boys being catechized in patriotism and sacrifice for the P.L.O.

"Gaza Ghetto" makes no pretense of journalistic neutrality. It is not objective. It frankly shows us its bias, its sympathy for the Palestinians, so numerous yet so helpless. But this is not mindless agit-prop. The film skillfully uses the family as continuity for tracing background, inter-cutting old b&w stock footage and interviews. If this film is propaganda on behalf of the Palestinians, its final impression may be negative, that these people are trapped forever in those awful, dreary camps.

Among those talking for the Israelis are Ariel Sharon, minister of trade and industry; Yitzhak Rabin, minister of defense; Reuven Rosenblatt, director of Israeli settlements; and Gen. Ben Eliezar, military coordinator for the West Bank and Gaza.

Within Israel and its occupied territories, "Gaza Ghetto" is banned by the Israeli Board for Censorship of Films and Plays on grounds of its "fabricated and not documented facts" and for its call to viewers "to join the P.L.O., which is an organization hostile to the state." Israeli human rights activist Avigdor Feldman is currently appealing the censor's ruling to the Israeli Supreme Court. —*Hitch.*

Perfect Strangers
(COLOR)

Weak N.Y. thriller.

A New Line Cinema release of a Hemdale Film Corp. presentation of a Larry Cohen production. Executive producer, Carter De-Haven. Produced by Paul Kurta. Written and directed by Cohen. Features entire cast. Camera (color), Paul Glickman; editor, Armond Lebowitz; music, Dwight Dixon; sound, Russel Fager; production manager-assistant director, Kurta; associate producers, Barry Shils, Kato Wittich. Reviewed on Embassy Home Entertainment vidcassette, N.Y., June 19, 1985. (MPAA Rating: R.) Running time:

91 MINS.
Sally .Anne Carlisle
Johnny .Brad Rijn
Fred . . . . .John Woehrle
Matthew . . . . .Matthew Stockley
Lt. Burns . . . . .Stephen Lack
Feminist . . . . .Anne Magnuson
Maletti . . . . .Zachary Hains
Private eye . . . . .Otto Von Wernherr

"Perfect Strangers" is a dull suspense thriller shot in New York under the title "Blind Alley" two years ago by indie filmmaker Larry Cohen, before his recent pics "Special Effects" and "The Stuff." Film was released briefly in Indianapolis last November by distrib New Line and now is entering the homevideo market.

Anne Carlisle (of cult hit "Liquid Sky") toplines as Sally, mother of two-year-old Matthew (Matthew Stockley), who refuses to help the police when her infant witnesses a gangland slaying in an alley near their Greenwich Village apartment. The killer is Johnny (Brad Rijn, male lead in "Smithereens"), a young guy with no criminal record who works for an organized crime syndicate.

Johnny introduces himself to Sally and convinces himself the kid doesn't recognize him, but his crime bosses insist he kill the child to avoid the chance that the police will be able to use psychologists (as happened in a real-life case in the Midwest) to have the kid help create a positive identification.

Johnny refuses, instead becoming romantically involved with Sally and even seemingly protects the child from its father, her estranged husband Fred (John Woehrle). Pic climaxes in Johnny kidnaping the child and having a fatal confrontation with Sally.

Low-budget picture suffers from bland, inexpressive acting and routine development of its premise (there never is any indication that the kid could actually finger the killer). In particular, Carlisle is styled as very plain, with a most unbecoming hairdo, resulting in none of the allure of her dual role debut in "Liquid Sky." —*Lor.*

Traps
(AUSTRALIAN-COLOR)

Sydney, June 19.

A Hughes production. Produced and directed by John Hughes. Stars Carolyn Howard. Screenplay, Hughes, Paul Davies; camera (color), James Grant, Erica Addis, Katrina Bowels; sound, Pat Fiske, Lou Hubbard, John Cruthers, Jack Holt, Laurie Robinson; editor, Zbigniew Friedrich; art directors, Clair Jager, Susan Weis. Reviewed at Sydney Film Festival, June 18, 1985. Running time: **98 MINS.**
Judith Campbell . . . . .Carolyn Howard
Gwenda . . . . .Gwenda Wiseman
Father Coughlan . . . . .John Flaus
Also with: Paul Davies, Lesley Stern, Drew Cottle, Peter Sommerfield, Michael Gill, Anthony McAdam, Marian Wilkinson, Sylvie Le Clezio, John Grenville, Denis Freney,

Gregory Hywood, P.P. McGuinness, Humphrey McQueen, Mark Aarons, Steve Sewell.

"Traps" is a passionate lowbudgeter which, via the device of following the investigations of a dogged femme journalist, explores with deadly accuracy the political atmosphere in Australia today. Over two years in the making, pic will be of great interest to Aussies interested in what's happening in their own country right now, and thus should do well on the local arthouse circuit. Overseas, its references will have to be carefully explained if it's to have an impact.

Pic opens, intriguingly, with actor (and film critic) John Flaus as a Catholic priest hearing confession. Strongly anti-Communist, he advises an unseen parishioner that there's a Communist conspiracy to be faced and fought. Quick inserts from the Phillip Noyce feature "Newsfront" (1978) remind us that Flaus played an anti-Communist priest in that film also.

Film proper begins as Judith (Carolyn Howard), a journalist with a public radio station, becomes involved in politics while preparing a review of the Marian Wilkinson docu feature "Allies" (1983), which was about secret CIA activities in Australia. One theme touched on in that film was that the present prime minister, Bob Hawke, received the support of powerful U.S. interests in 1969 when he was in the running for a key labor union position. Judith begins talking to journalists on both sides of the political spectrum and gradually an intriguing and mysterious political saga begins to unfold.

The film can't be too specific, given Australia's libel laws, and several names are bleeped from the soundtrack, though the points still are made adequately. "Traps" succeeds in following through the investigations of its fictional heroine against a background of actual events, including a Labor Party conference in which an exploding light bulb gave a momentary impression that someone was shooting at the prime minister, and interviews with real people in the know.

John Hughes (no kin to the U.S. director of "Sixteen Candles" and "The Breakfast Club") has probed his subject just about as far as the law will allow, and the result is a sometimes powerful, sometimes frustrating filmic inquiry into the political state of a nation.

Technically, pic — which employed different crew members over a period of time — is a bit ragged, but overall effective. —*Strat.*

Hors-la-loi
(Outlaws)
(FRENCH-COLOR)

Paris, June 10.

An AMLF release of a Sara Films/Cerito Films coproduction. Produced by Alain Sarde. Directed by Robin Davis. Features entire cast. Screenplay, Davis, Patrick Laurent, Dominique Robelet; Camera (color), Jacques Steyn; editor, Marie Castro-Vasquez; music, Philippe Sarde; sound, Michel Laurent; art director, Jean-Claude Sevenet; production manager, Gérard Gaultier. Reviewed at the Studio 28 theater, Paris, May 25, 1985. Running time: **107 MINS.**

With: Clovis, Wadeck Stanczak, Isabelle Pasco, Nathalie Spilmont, Pascal Librizzi, Philippe Chambon, Jean-Claude Tran, Didier Chambragne, Luis Marques, Steven Ronceau, Luc Thuillier, Joel Ferraty, Hatem Boussa, Gilles Stassart, Kamel Meziti, Jean-Paul Roussilon, Madeleine Robinson.

Robin Davis' tale of 15 juvenile delinquents on the run after having escaped from a provincial reform school is a series of adventure setpieces strung out on a barely extant screenplay. Shot on location in the Lozère department in southern France, film is fashioned as a sort of contemporary Western in the way it tries to use natural landscapes into which the group of protagonists is set loose. This intent is underlined — heavily — by Philippe Sarde's score, which strains after unmistakable twanging in strains of American folk music.

Davis, who scored two solid commercial hits previously with the 1979 thriller "The Police Wars" and "I Married A Shadow" in 1982, confirms his technical prowess here and provides a lively number of scenes as the band, doubly outlawed after having provoked a bloody altercation in a dance hall, flees into the wilderness, stalked by police and outraged peasantry.

Obstacles are both human and natural as they are cornered by a vicious hick who humiliates them and they later escape to brave sheer cliffs, dangerous rapids and fragile rope bridges. Perils of on-location shooting helped jack up the initial budget to the point that producer Alain Sarde appealed to Jean-Paul Belmondo, who came in as coproducer to ensure completion of the film.

Apart from some conventional squabbling over a girl by the group's two most authoritative males, individual portraiture is glossed over. This is particularly sad because many of the youths have obvious screen presence (Wadeck Stanczak has since appeared promisingly in André Téchiné's Cannes contending "Rendezvous").

Story logic is also sacrificed from the start as the youths pile into a van and leave the reform insitution unimpeded by any representatives of authority. The writers brazenly try to bluff their way to a conclusion with an unrealistic device — ambushed by police, the youths turn to the camera and defiantly begin to sing a pop song.—*Len.*

Silverado
(COLOR)

Modern approach to the Western should do well.

Hollywood, June 27.

A Columbia Pictures release. Executive producers, Charles Okun, Michael Grillo. Produced and directed by Lawrence Kasdan. Features entire cast. Screenplay, Lawrence Kasdan, Mark Kasdan; camera (Technicolor, Super Techniscope), John Bailey; editor, Carol Littleton; music, Bruce Broughton; production designer, Ida Random; set decorators, Arthur Parker, Anne D. McCulley; assistant art director, William Elliott; set designers, Chas Butcher, Richard McKenzie; sound (Dolby stereo), David Ronne; costumes, Kristi Zea; assistant director, Michael Grillo; associate producer, Mark Kasdan; casting, Wally Nicita. Reviewed at Village Theater, Westwood Village, Calif., June 27, 1985. (MPAA Rating: PG-13.) Running time: **132 MINS.**

Paden	Kevin Kline
Emmett	Scott Glenn
Jake	Kevin Costner
Mal	Danny Glover
Sheriff Langston	John Cleese
Hannah	Rosanna Arquette
Cobb	Brian Dennehy
Stella	Linda Hunt
Slick	Jeff Goldblum

"Silverado" is an entertaining but not totally satisfying attempt to revive the Western genre. While there is much to applaud in Lawrence Kasdan's elaborate production, his modern reworking of mythical themes results in a kind of hybrid form. Whether audiences will find enough in the experience to respond to is one of the more intriguing questions of the summer box-office with bets here on good but not great business.

Rather than relying on legendary heroes of Westerns past, writer Kasdan with his brother Mark have used their special talent to create a slew of human scale characters against a dramatic backdrop borrowing from all the conventions of the genre. "Silverado" strikes an uneasy balance between the intimate and naturalistic with concerns that are classical and universal.

All of Kasdan's characters, introduced in a rather overlong exposition period, are searchers looking for their place in an 1880s world with surprisingly modern rhythms.

Cinematography by John Bailey also emphasizes the intimate over the mythic with a concentration on closeups rather than broad panoramas. When the characters are seen against some striking New Mexico landscape, one wonders how they fit into this tapestry. Even action sequences seem to focus more on the individual effort than the communal experience.

Drifters Paden (Kevin Kline) and Emmett (Scott Glenn) join fates in the desert and follow their destiny to Silverado where they tangle with the McKendrick clan. Along the way they meet up with Glenn's gun happy brother Jake (Kevin Costner) who they break from a jail guarded by Sheriff Langston (John Cleese).

Modern element in the stew is introduction of Danny Glover, an itinerant black returning to Silverado to rejoin what's left of his family. As another outsider looking for some roots, Glover forms an instinctive bond with Glenn and Kline as they travel to a common ground.

On the other side of the fence is arch villian Cobb, sheriff of Silverado and puppet of the McKendricks. As Cobb, Brian Dennehy is an actor born to be in Westerns, so powerful is his sense of destruction. Other performances, especially Kline and Glenn, are equally strong.

Among the classical Western themes explored are loyalty and friendship, with Dennehy and Kline former partners gone their separate ways. Families are the real ties that bind here. Glover has a sister who has become a hooker (Lynn Whitfield) and must be reformed while Glenn and his brother Costner must rescue their young nephew from the gang in the film's finale.

In spite of the abundance of family life, material lacks the emotional payoff it should have. Stella, the proprietress of the local bar in Silverado, Linda Hunt is a crucial character who serves a a barometer of Kline's morality. As a midget who has remade the world to fit her, Stella is a good idea which doesn't really flower as a character.

Kasdan's West is clearly a man's world without an authoritative female to be found. Supposedly supplying an underpinning of love and stability, Rosanna Arquette's Hannah comes off as an underwritten character with little impact though she's on the porch at the film's end begging to be a classical Western presence.

Music, too, by Bruce Broughton, threatens to overshadow the diminutive dimensions of the characters. Score seems to identify more with the landscape than the people.

Real rewards of the film are in the visuals and rarely has the West appeared so alive, yet unlike what one carries in his mind's eye. Ida Random's production design is thoroughly convincing in detail, particularly for the interiors of houses and the Silverado Saloon. Costumes by Kristi Zea give an added texture to the picture as does the lighting by cinematographer Bailey.

Though the landscapes don't always seem attached to the people, they carry a power and authority that has always made the Western irresistible. —*Jagr.*

Genbaku-Shi:
Killed By The Atomic Bomb
(DOCU-COLOR/B&W-16m)

A production of Public Media Arts, Santa Fe, N.M. Produced, directed, written by Gary de Walt. Associate producer, Donna Kuyper; camera (color, 16m), J.K. Parsons; location photography, Joan Myers, Jeff Gates; editor, Rhonda Vlasak; narrator, Connie Goldman; production consultant, Barton Bernstein, Stanford U. Produced in association with NHK, Japan. Partial funding from Southwest Independent Production Fund, National Endowment for The Arts. Reviewed at American Film Prods., N.Y., June 22, 1985. Running time: **60 MINS.**

"Genbaku-Shi" reconstructs the fate of downed American flyers during W.W. II, emphasizing those held as prisoners in Hiroshima and the crews of the B-24s "Taloa" and "Lonesome Lady." Prisoners there died immediately as the atomic bombs hit, except for two who survived to die horribly days later of wounds and radiation sickness. A third American was known to survive the Hiroshima bombing, but his identity is unknown, as both American and Japanese records are incomplete.

Some other American flyers were imprisoned nearby, but escaped death in the bombing. Of those crew-members who survived the war, three appear in this film, filmed in their homes today, 40 years later, remembering their dead buddies.

The film carefully traces a complex series of events, using color and b&w stock footage, stills, military records and interviews with the flyers and their families, and also interviews in English with Japanese officers responsible for the fates of their American prisoners. The film ends with peace memorial ceremonies in Hiroshima today, as Capt. Tom Cartwright, who had piloted "Lonesome Lady," states that a nuclear war today is inconceivable.

"Genbaku-Shi" is a unique document about an unknown corner of World War II, hitherto never explored in film. — *Hitch.*

Parking
(FRENCH-COLOR)

Paris, June 25.

An A.M. Films release of a Garance/FR3 coproduction. Produced by Dominique Vignet. Directed by Jacques Demy. Screenplay, lyrics, Demy; camera (color), Jean-François Robin; editors, Sabine Mamou; Marie-Jo Audiard; music, Michel Legrand; sound, Bernard Ortion; art director, Patrice Mercier; costumes, Rosalie Varda; production manager, Sylia Montalti. Reviewed at the Georges V cinema, Paris, June 22, 1985. Running time: **95 MINS.**

Orpheus	Francis Huster
Eurydice	Keîko Ito
Calaîs	Laurent Malet
Aristée	Gérard Klein
Persephone	Marie-France Pisier
Caron	Hugues Quester
Dominique Daniel	Eva Darlan
Lucienne	Annik Alane
Clément	Jean Amos

Even his die-hard admirers seemed a bit anxious when Jacques Demy announced this pop re-do of the Orpheus myth, with Francis

Huster in the lead role. They were right to worry — "Parking" has none of the wistful charm or ambience of his earlier work, and is even far inferior to his dubious musical tragedy, "Une Chambre en Ville," in which he was at least faithful to his own conventions.

Unfortunately, the Demy touch is absent here, as is his long-time production designer Bernard Evein, whose gifted eye contributed much to the textures of the director's singsong universe. After refusing to take part in "Une Chambre en Ville," Michel Legrand has returned to the Demy fold, but to no avail. The half-dozen or so pop tunes he has composed for Huster — the only warbler in the film — are as insipid as their performer.

It would have needed a personality like Johnny Hallyday to give some essential credibility and magnetism to the script which revives Orpheus as a contemporary pop idol who's giving a series of sold-out concerts at the huge new Bercy sports stadium in Paris. When he's not on stage or busy rehearsing at his splendid country manor, he is strumming and cooing love ditties to his Eurydice, a Japanese sculptor, played by Keiko Ito (probably because Japanese publishing house Kodansha was an important financier of the film). Her struggle with the forces of life and death are not nearly as heroic as her battle with Demy's dialog (which she learned phonetically).

The Underworld, from which Orpheus attempts to recover Eurydice, has now become the lower level of a subterranean parking lot: a vast gloomy concrete bunker where the Dead check in like passengers at an airport.

The premises are presided over by a devil played by Jean Marais, who kicked the bucket for love as the Orpheus of Jean Cocteau (to whom Demy has dedicated this film). Persephone is his fashion-conscious niece, Marie-France Pisier. Both look bored to death.

Demy has tried to stem his commercial misfortunes with a film aimed at a youth audience. In the process he has only compromised his own sensibility and gifts. The saddest thing is that "Parking" is no less a flop than "Une Chambre en Ville."—*Len.*

Red Sonja
(COLOR)

Sword and sorcery intros a new lady warrior for Arnie.

Hollywood, June 28.

An MGM/UA Entertainment release. Produced by Christian Ferry. Executive producer, A. Michael Lieberman. Directed by Richard Fleischer. Stars Brigitte Nielsen, Arnold Schwarzenegger. Screenplay, Clive Exton, George MacDonald Fraser, based on stories by Robert E. Howard; camera (Metrocolor), Giuseppe Rotunno; editor, Frank J. Urioste; music, Ennio Morricone; sound, Amelio Verona; production design/costumes, Danilo Donati; assistant director/associate producer, Jose Lopez Rodero; makeup, Rino Carboni; miniatures, Emilio Ruiz Del Rio; art direction, Gianni Giovagnoni; stunts, Sergio Mioni; mattes, Albert Whitlock; casting, Maude Spector, Johanna Ray, Francesco Cinieri. Reviewed at MGM Studios, June 28, 1985. (MPAA Rating: PG-13.) Running time: **89 MINS.**
Red Sonja . . . . Brigitte Nielsen
Kalidor . . . . Arnold Schwarzenegger
Queen Gedren . . . . Sandahl Bergman
Falkon . . . . Paul Smith
Tarn . . . . Ernie Reyes Jr.
Ikol . . . . Ronald Lacey
Brytag . . . . Pat Roach
Djart . . . . Terry Richards
Varna . . . . Janet Agren

"Red Sonja" returns to those olden days when women were women and the menfolk stood around with funny hats on until called forth to be whacked at.

Except, of course, for Arnold Schwarzenegger, whose Kalidor creation has just enough muscles to make him useful to the ladies, but not enough brains to make him a bother, except that he talks too much. Before he's even on screen 10 minutes, Schwarzenegger blurts out, "Your sister is dying. I'll take you to her." From then on, he speaks up every 15 minutes or so, including one monolog of at least six sentences.

To her credit in the title role, Brigitte Nielsen never listens to a word he has to say, perhaps because he has an unfortunate tendency to address her as "Sony-uh." Nielsen wants to revenge her sister and find the magic talisman all on her own with no help from Kalidor, though she does think it's kind of cute when he wades into 80 guys and wastes them in an effort to impress her.

Some weird old guy with flags strapped to his back has assured Sony-uh that she's the world's best swordsperson, even though she "must learn to like men better — they are not all evil." She knows that; it's just that Kalidor keeps saying things like "Danger is my trade," which she knows is exhausting his vocabulary without noticeably helping the situation.

Shrewd female that she is, Nielsen realizes the real adversary out there is another woman, Sandahl Bergman, whose male companions at least go around bowing and saying, "Oh, great Queens." After many old grudges and knife fights between them, Bergman now has the talisman which can end the world unless Nielsen destroys it.

Along the way they've picked up a spoiled rotten little prince, Ernie Reyes Jr., and his loving mistreated slave, Paul Smith, adding two more males who will prove to be little help except to provide distractions while the two women work out their differences with broadswords.

Eventually, all is saved and Nielsen and Schwarzenegger get their weapons out again and start to kiss, suggesting there may be the start of something big here, maybe even a significant relationship. It might even work if they manage to avoid any attempts at meaningful conversation.—*Har.*

Day Of The Dead
(COLOR)

Lackluster third edition of the zombie series.

A United Film Distribution Corp. release of a Laurel production. Executive producer, Salah M. Hassanein. Produced by Richard P. Rubinstein. Written and directed by George A. Romero. Features entire cast. Camera (color), Michael Gornick; editor, Pasquale Buba; music-assistant director, John Harrison; sound, Rolf Pardula; production design, Cletus Anderson; art direction, Bruce Miller; special makeup effects, Tom Savini; production manager, Zilla Clinton; costume design, Barbara Anderson; second unit camera, Ernest R. Dickerson; stunt coordinator, Taso N. Stavrakis; casting, Christine Forrest Romero, (N.Y.C.) — Bill McNulty, Gaylen Ross; coproducer, David Ball; associate producer, Ed Lammi. Reviewed at Magno Preview 9 screening room, N.Y., June 20, 1985. (No MPAA Rating.) Running time: **102 MINS.**
Sarah . . . . ▪. . . . . . . Lori Cardille
John . . . . Terry Alexander
Capt. Rhodes . . . . Joseph Pilato
McDermott . . . . Jarlath Conroy
Miguel . . . . Antonè DiLeo Jr.
Dr. Logan . . . . Richard Liberty
Bub . . . . Howard Sherman
Steel . . . . Gary Howard Klar
Rickles . . . . Ralph Marrero
Fisher . . . . John Amplas
Also with: Philip G. Kellams, Taso N. Stavrakis, Gregory Nicotero.

"Day Of The Dead" is an unsatisfying part three in George A. Romero's zombie saga. Instead of providing a spectacular climax to the hit series established by "Night Of The Living Dead" (1968) and "Dawn Of The Dead" (1979), "Day" seems to be merely vamping until a payoff in a potential part four. Due to advance interest picture should open well to Romero's hardcore following but has little chance of attracting a much wider audience.

Set in Florida (but filmed mainly in Pennsylvania plus Fort Myers, Fla.), "Day" postulates that the living dead have now taken over the world with only a handful of normal humans still alive, outnumbered by about 400,000 to one. In a claustrophobic format reminiscent of early 1950s science fiction films (such as "The Thing," "Target Earth" and "Invasion, U.S.A."), the human protagonists debate and fight among themselves in an underground missile silo while the common enemy masses topside.

Representing the scientific community are stalwart heroine Sarah (topbilled Lori Cardille), who is working on longrange research to find a way to reverse the process whereby dead humans become unreasoning, cannibalistic zombies, and loony Dr. Logan (Richard Liberty), engaged in conditioning experiments on captured zombies to domesticate them. He has discovered which part of the brain controls the undead and that their craving to devour human flesh is strictly instinctual and not for nourishment.

The military faction is headed by ruthless Capt. Rhodes (Joseph Pilato), who is increasingly impatient with the scientists, preferring the old reliable method of dealing with zombies by shooting them in the head. A divergent point of view is expressed by the group's helicopter pilot, John (Terry Alexander), who puts his faith in God (reminiscent of Charles Lampkin's role in the 1951 sci-fi trailblazer "Five") and opts for escaping to some remote spot where mankind can start anew.

Punctuated by several brief, scary moments, film's opening hour is largely a gabfest, with Romero delivering tough talk and flared tempers in place of the expected action sequences. A final reel of fighting to the death with the zombies is exciting but not enough to save the uneven pic.

The acting here is generally unimpressive and in the case of Sarah's romantic partner, Miguel (Antonè DiLeo Jr.), unintentionally risible. Best performance in fact is Howard Sherman's mime portrayal of Bub, a zombie with a malleable grey face who gives off flickers of remote intelligence much in the manner of popular wrestler George (The Animal) Steele.

The special makeup effects crew headed by Tom Savini has concocted several fanciful model head and torso creations, but the emphasis upon meat-market gore will once again be appreciated only by ironstomached horror fans. Like its predecessors in the series, "Day" has no rating (it wasn't submitted to the Motion Picture Assn. of America), which should also prove limiting at the boxoffice. ("Dawn" eventually got an R rating for 1983 reissue, but surrendered that rating subsequently.)—*Lor.*

Southern Voices, American Dreams
(DOCU-COLOR)

Produced, written and directed by Ken Hey. Camera (color), William Wages, Virginia Brooks, others; editor, Brooks; sound, Jim Hawkins, Sandy Fuller, others. Reviewed at Brooklyn College Screening Room (American Film Festival), May 29, 1985. (No MPAA Rating.) Running time: **78 MINS.**
With (in interviews): Greg Allman, Burt Reynolds, Hal Needham, Andrew Young, Jody Powell, former president Jimmy Carter, Gerry Rafshoon, Ted Turner, Gerry Hogan, Sid Pike, Ed Spivia, Dickie Betts, Paul Hornsby, Phil Walden, Jimmy Hall.

The "good ol' boys" of Georgia, interviewed here by debut helmer Ken Hey, recall the dynamics of the '70s that launched them into the national spotlight and gave rise to the American populism of the Carter era. Tracking that phenomenon from the Civil Rights movement and '60s counter-culture, Hey maps out four areas that Georgia stamped with its good ol' boy style.

Southern rock music got its pace from the Allman Bros., and an interview with Gregg Allman is reinforced with some rare footage of Duane Allman. When the rock singer died in 1971, there was no footage of him performing, but Hey discovered something shot by an amateur at a rock festival and re-edited it to music.

Hey puts Burt Reynolds on screen to define "good ol' boy" as "someone who has a good relationship with the place they're from," while expounding generally on the rise of car-chasin', down-home, drinkin' and stompin', fun-lovin' styles made popular by his pics. Hal Needham talks about the pleasures of making movies in states like Georgia with people such as Ed Spivia, the Georgia film commissioner, all of which begins to sound like a plug.

A nicely edited montage of Jimmy Carter's early campaigns reminds one of the very unlikely nature of his candidacy. Carter compares his own campaigns in 1970 for governor and in 1976 for president. He is the ultimate expression of "making it outside the mainstream," which all these Georgians represent, and Carter is particularly proud of that. He notes, however, that once he had made it, he found himself the mainstream and part of the establishment instead of the attractive alternative.

The most camera-conscious interview material is that with Ted Turner who seems to want to talk about everything but the key to the success of WTBS, although the winner mentality has been paralleled in the previous interviews with Andrew Young, Reynolds, Carter, and the Allman Bros. Their testimony as to the tough stretches in their careers all correspond to having "made it."

Hey's ending shows a rollercoaster collapsing, but pic attests to the survival of good ol' boys, even when they've gone bad. —Kaja.

Marshal Zhukov
Pages From A Biography
(SOVIET-DOCU-B&W/COLOR)

Washington, D.C., June 8.

An Intl. Film Exchange presentation. Produced by the Central Studio of Documentary Films, USSR. Written and directed by Marina Babak. Camera (color), Andrei Kolobrov; military adviser, Lt. Gen. Iaparchev; narrated by Mikail Ulianov. Reviewed at K-B Foun-dry 7, Washington, D.C. (Allied Victory Film Festival), June 4, 1985. Running time: **90 MINS.**

Made to celebrate the end of World War II and circulating as part of the "Allied Victory Film Fest," this documentary's main interest is in its use of archival footage and photos, plus a carefully phrased interview with Marshal Zhukov in the '50s, when he was no longer feared as a potential Napoleon of the Great Patriotic War, as it is called in the pic. Grigori Zhukov was responsible for the heroic defense of Leningrad, the decisive battle for Moscow, the crossing of the Dnieper and the capture of Kiev, and the storming of Berlin, among many other worthy deeds.

While the use of material from the USSR Central Archive may interest historians and the point-of-view on the Marshal offers politically interesting implications, film remains a predictable glorification of a great military hero. His infamous clashes with Stalin are outlined in a way to illustrate his value as a strategist and Stalin's value as a party leader.

The narration is done by actor Mikail Ulianov, introduced here as the "People's Artist." (Ulianov is noted for the dynamic work in "The Chairman," for which he received a Lenin Prize.)

A creative and almost symbolic ending with Zhukov riding in circles on a white horse into a fade-out raises the spectre of a personality cult around his memory.

The Soviet perspective on the enormous role played by Zhukov in ending the war and making the peace, complete with footage of him with Gen. Eisenhower, will come as an instructive surprise to most Western audiences and make for possibly interesting television fare.

The reason for pic being launched here, however, goes beyond a mere introduction of a Starkova-born peasant who joined the Communist Party in 1919 and became the most decorated military leader of World War II. It is couched in the narration's nervous conclusion that "we have been living for 40 years without war, perhaps the highest of military awards." Some audiences may raise eyebrows over a Soviet form of "Pearl Harbor complex" when pic claims they will never again be caught defenseless and unprepared for war. This potential for controversy could be successfully exploited. — Kaja.

Godzilla Meets Mona Lisa
(DOCU-COLOR)

A New Day Films release. Produced by Ralph Arlyck Films. Written and directed by Arlyck. Camera (color), Etienne De Grammont, Jean-Claude Luyat, Bernard Goner, Dominique Le Rigoleur; sound editing, Catherine Temerson. Reviewed at Roosevelt Hotel (American Film Festival), N.Y., June 1, 1985. Running time: **90 MINS.**

The rare documentary that lives up to its title and shows promise of keeping viewers entranced, this trip to the Pompidou Center in Paris is more fun than going there. Guided by indie helmer Ralph Arlyck, architecture meets art, and it's a checkmate. A stolen wallet led Arlyck to a precinct where the cops, too, express unusual views on what art is for: theft.

Through interviews and commentary of his own, Arlyck explores received ideas and traditions about what constitutes an art museum. The constitution of the Pompidou is found to disturb, with its innards hanging on its outer walls, channeling visitors through a maze they accept with a certain perplexed stare that has always been associated with the viewing of "great art," whatever that beast may be. Pic's conclusion is that, in contemporary terms, art is more Godzilla than Mona Lisa. The old "what you can get away with" definition seems to apply, but in an era of outrage, clearly demonstrated by what goes on around the Pompidou's plaza outside, finding that kind of challenge has made the artist turn his focus around 180 degrees on the spectator himself. Arlyck's angles on the Parisian monstrosity are extra-terrestrial.

Interviews with David Hockney try to emphasize the lack of pretension among contemporary artists, but Arlyck catches the paradox in Hockney's own elitist manner and his professed democratizing purposes. The wit of Arlyck's encounters provides the pacing for both versions, the 60 and 90-minute cuts, without losing an ironic distance from a potentially pompous subject. With six awards already to its credit, docu will find its way into many more festivals and programs in quest of humor. —Kaja.

El Judicial (Carne De Cañon)
(Federal Police — Cannon Fodder)
(MEXICAN-COLOR)

Mexico City, June 7.

A Películas Mexicanas release of a Producciones Internacionales de América and Galáctica Films prooduction. Produced by Luis Berkris. Directed by Rafael Villaseñor Kuri. Screenplay, Rafael García Travesi; based on story by Villaseñor and García Travesi; camera (color), Antonio Ruiz; editor, Max Sánchez. Reviewed at Cine Variadades, Mexico City, June 7, 1985. Running time: **85 MINS.**
Rosenda Garza . . . Miguel Angel Rodriguez
Lucio Arrigada . . . . Manuel Capetillo
Capitan José Ramírez . . Armando Silvestre
Elisa López de Garza . . . . Rebeca Silva
Alfonso Bringas . . . . Guillermo Murray
Grandmother . . . . Carmelita González
Alenita . . . . Nicole Urquiza
Also with: Humberto Elizondo, Marta Ortiz, Mario Arévalo.

This quickie low-budget adventure film tries to bring the classroom to the big screen and fails to be either entertainment or a learning device.

Plot centers around a police team (Miguel Angel Rodriguez and Manuel Capetillo) who are cracking down on drug dealing and trafficking in Mexico, with the cargo aimed at the U.S. market.

Comandante Garza wants to quit the force to live a quiet life with his nagging wife and sickeningly sweet daughter. Fellow officers convince him he is needed to curb trafficking and halt drug abuse. So, he and his wife fight for about a third of the film about the fact that policework is his life and danger his daily bread.

Rest of the pic is spent fighting off assassins and raids showing unscrupuplous drug dealers selling joints and cocaine to eight-year-olds, shootouts with machinegun-toting cocaine traffickers and busting a hedonistic party straight out of "Reefer Madness," but without the camp humor.

Film is unduly violent as unarmed dealers are either brutally killed or abused by the police in their efforts to rid the world of evil. This reactionary bent with police officers being both judge and jury is held throughout the pic.

Film also takes advantage of every opportunity to preach the evils of drug abuse with speeches usually accompanied by organ music.

Lowpoint of the film is the sappy graveside epilog — at the death of Comandante Garza's wife and daughter — extolling the bravery of policemen in their ceaseless fight against crime and the sacrifice of their personal life to make this world a better place. Ho-hum!
—Lent.

A Sipolo Macskako
(The Whistling Cobblestone)
(HUNGARIAN-B&W)

Sydney, June 20.

A Studio 1, Mafilm, production. Directed by Gyula Gazdag. Features entire cast. Screenplay, Gazdag, Miklos Gyorffy; camera (b&w), Tamas Andor; music, Lajos Illes; sound, Janos Arato; assistant director, Judit Ember. Reviewed at Sydney Film Festival, June 19, 1985. Running time: **91 MINS.**
Somlo . . . . Zoltan Paulinyi
Professor Dienes . . . . Janos Atkari
Pataki . . . . Andras Mesz
Tokes . . . . Gabor Gergely
Vincze . . . . Janos Bozsogi
Hasznos . . . . Balasz Gyore
Janos . . . . Janos Xantus
The Frenchman . . . . . . Jean-Pierre Falloux

Gyula Gazdag carries the dubious distinction of being the most censored of Hungary's film directors. His woes began with this 1971 feature, which though shown internally at the time, was forbidden to be exported, and was not shown to foreigners. In 1972, his feature docu,

"The Resolution," was canned, not to be released until last year, and the same thing happened to his mock operetta, "Singing On The Treadmill" (1974), which is also finally available now. The Sydney Film Festival has been unspooling all of Gazdag's work, and "The Whistling Cobblestone" is reviewed here for the record.

It's a pic that reflects the youth unrest of the period. A group of city kids are taken on a summer holiday to the countryside where they're to help harvesting corn. Everything in their camp is highly organized, except for the fact that the corn somehow isn't yet ready to be harvested. So the lads mope around with nothing much to do, and get into various kinds of mischief. One even runs away. The irony is that when three youths agree to help a local farmer who seeks their assistance, they're expelled from the camp for going off on their own.

Pic presumably offended authorities of the period because it clearly sides with the kids against the unfair and bloody-minded pedagogs in charge of them. It's a good-natured film, filled with humor and lively, certainly not threatening, young people. The title is derived from a plastic "cobblestone," a memento of the Paris riots of 1968 when students there ripped up the streets, brought to the camp by a Hungarian-speaking Frenchman who becomes an object of envy for the boys because of his freedom (he's driving down to Turkey).

The young Gazdag reveals himself as a creative director, and there's outstanding photography by Tamas Andor. —*Strat.*

Half Life
(AUSTRALIAN-DOCU-COLOR)

Melbourne, July 1.

An O'Rourke & Associates Filmmakers production. Produced, written and directed by Dennis O'Rourke. Camera (color), O'Rourke; editor, Tim Litchfield; sound, Gary Kildea, Martin Cohen; archival research, David Thaxton, Kevin Green. Reviewed at Melbourne Film Festival, June 27, 1985. Running time: **86 MINS.**

Of the dozens of docus made in recent years on the nuclear weapons issue, "Half Life" emerges as one of the most shocking and powerful because it deals with humans who have apparently been subjected to the most unspeakable form of experimentation.

The people concerned are the inhabitants of the Marshall Islands, dots on the map of the Pacific Ocean. The islands were occupied by Japan during World War II and in 1947 were handed by the newly formed Unitd Nations to the U.S. to be held in trusteeship. The UN resolution called upon the U.S. to protect the rights and fundamental freedoms of the islanders. This, the U.S. manifestly did not do. The Marshalls were an ideal spot for testing nuclear weapons, and before long Bikini Atoll was evacuated so tests could take place under the supervision of the Atomic Energy Commission. Sixty-six nuclear bombs were tested on Bikini in the ensuing decade, destroying the environment around the island for generations.

As if this weren't bad enough, in 1954 the first hydrogen bomb was tested, and on that occasion the inhabitants of nearby islands of Rongelap and Utirik were not evacuated as they had been in the past. The explosion rocked the tiny islands and several hours later white powder started to fall on the beaches and on the people.

Officials claimed it was all a mistake; that the wind shifted at the last moment, causing the unintended mishap. However, eyewitnesses, including U.S. weathermen, interviewed in the film strongly suggest weather patterns remained stable throughout the testing period. In any event, the victims of radiation have been examined by doctors every year since, and the results are devastating. A woman testifies that some months after the test, she gave birth "to something that did not look human — like the innards of a beast," and that a subsequent pregnancy also ended in a misshapen, stillborn child. The film shows crippled and deformed children and adults living on the islands today, and notes some who were babies when the tests were held have died young. As late as 1975, a baby was born with its head too big, and no control over its body.

On the evidence presented by Dennis O'Rourke in this memorable film, a terrible crime appears to have been committed against an innocent, trusting people (referred to continually as "savages" by newsreel narrators of the 1940s). The contrast between life on the Marshall Islands today and life before the tests is telling.

O'Rourke is an experienced documentary filmmaker who has hitherto worked mostly among the people of Papua New Guinea. His rapport with the Marshall Islanders most evident.

The combination of footage taken on the islands in recent months, together with newsreel footage of the tests and statements made by past U.S. administrations on the subject, plus the medical and scientific treatment meted out to the victims, provides an agonizing film experience. It ends with the islanders about to celebrate their independence, and a taped message from President Reagan who refers to "our friends in Micronesia" and "the very special relationship" that exists between the U.S. and the islanders: "You'll always be family to us," he says. It gives a bitter new meaning to the term "nuclear family."

"Half Life," blown up to 35m from a 16m original, is technically first-rate and deserves to be screened the world over. —*Strat.*

Joy And Joan
(FRENCH-COLOR)

Paris, June 25.

A GEF release of an ATC 3000 production. Produced by Benjamin Simon. Directed by Jacques Saurel. Screenplay, Jean-Pierre Imbrohoris, Saurel, Emma Geher; camera (color), Dominique Brabant; editor, Eva Zora; art director, Mathilde Merival. Reviewed at the Marignan-Concorde theater, Paris, June 24, 1985. Running time: **94 MINS.**
With: Brigitte Lahaie, Isabelle Solar, Pierre Londiche, Jean-Marc Maurel, Jacques Brylant.

"Joy And Joan" presents the further softcore adventures of Joy Laurey's bestselling top model, hot in the pursuit of love amid glossy exotic settings. In this second installment, the heroine (played by Brigitte Lahaie, succeeding Claudia Udy) is gang-banged in Thailand before meeting Joan, another young French beauty stranded in Bangkok.

Joy and Joan then do it together, lovingly. They're serious about each other, but get separated in Manila when they are kidnaped and dragged to an orgy, where Joy, poor girl, is again gang-banged. She is saved by a weird Thai prince (played by a Westerner in the worst old-time tradition) who has been trailing her because she's the spitting image of a woman he once loved and lost.

Back in Paris, she's reunited with Joan, as well as the cynical journalist who's loved her and left her in the beginning of the story. Naturally a threesome is called for to celebrate. Joy has a baby, and settles down to dull domesticity. The end? Or next episode: Son Of Joy?

Relatively speaking, this is no better or worse than the first film. Director Jacques Saurel has the same advertising spot visual style as Serge Bergon, who helmed the first one. Lahaie and Solar are both well-endowed sex objects, though only latter seems to suggest a personality. There are also the inevitable English-language songs, interspersed throughout. —*Len.*

Living At Risk: The Story Of A Nicaraguan Family
(U.S.-DOCU-COLOR-16m)

Vancouver, June 6.

A Carpenter Center For The Visual Arts production. Produced, directed, edited by Susan Meisalas, Alfred Guzzetti, Richard Rogers. Camera (DuArt Labs), Richard Rog-ers. Assistant editor, Paula Heredia; sound, Steve Izzi. Reviewed at Vancouver Intl. Film Festival (Vancouver East Cinema), June 5, 1985. Running time: **60 MINS.**

Launched at the fourth Vancouver Intl. Film Festival, "Living At Risk: The Story Of A Nicaraguan Family" is a noninflammatory depiction of the private and public lives of a quintet of Christian idealists, all Sandinista members of the privileged Barrios family, in the tumultuous Central American nation five years after the abdication of head of state Anastasio Somoza.

More in sorrow than in anger, the docu presents the adult generation of the Barrios clan: Miguel, a director of land-reform assigned to a volatile zone; his older brother Alberto, another activist and a biochemist in the Ministry of Health; his younger brother Federico, a former medical student; their sister, Martisabel, a sociologist married to Eduardo Holmann, a vice minister in the Agriculture Ministry, and Mauricio, a physician, one of two such serving the remote Wiliwi hospital next to the Honduran border.

Mauricio's predecessor, a West German medico, was killed by counter-revolutionaries.

The irony that these family members are the beneficiaries of college training made possible by their privileged status under the Somoza regime remains latent in the docu's subtext.

Technical credits are seldom more than functional: hand-held camerawork and a reliance upon zoom-lens shots are staples for lenser Richard Rogers' unadorned style.

There is also at times an attempt to revive the 1940s montage "Family of Man" imagery and a casual homage to Walker Evans' style of humanity at bay during the Depression era.

This is a natural for public tv, with the usual festival prospects for any heartfelt political docu that bravely captures the quiet desperation of ideological upheaval.
—*Gran.*

Hungry For Profit
(DOCU-COLOR-16m)

A film by Richter Prods., N.Y. Produced, directed, written and narrated by Robert Richter. Associate producer, Audrey Zimmerman; camera (color, 16m), Burleigh Wartes; sound, Felipe Borrero, Ralph Arlyck; editor, Peter Kinoy; consultant, Joan Gussow, chair, Dept. of Nutrition Education, Teachers College, Columbia U. Reviewed at American Film Festival, N.Y., June 2, 1985. Running time: **85 MINS.**

Hollywood's save-the-farm films — "Places In The Heart," "Country," "The River" — show strong women as madonnas of the plow, fighting courageously to preserve their farms and their families.

Robert Richter's "Hungry For Profit" is a counterpart feature-documentary dealing with the same problem, indeed even using a scene of dispossessed Okies from the feature "Grapes Of Wrath" to dramatize the theme. The film shows small farmers being pushed off their ancestral lands, as trans-national corporations, collaborating with venal Third World governments, seize farmlands and compel peasant families to migrate to sprawling favelas, ugly urban slums in big new cities.

Thus the pun of the title — the hunger for profits causes hunger to millions of dispossessed farmers worldwide who lack a Hollywood happy ending. Abundance in American kitchens connects with famine abroad, states the film, via an intricate international economic cause and effect.

Filmed over two years in 10 countries on five continents, picture is an intelligent and merciless investigation into famine, with global agribusiness as the main culprit, abetted by wars, over-population, drought and pestilence.

Experts pro and con in the film accuse or defend the multi-national "Global Supermarkets" of West Europe and the U.S. for accelerating world hunger and malnourishment, ironically at its most severe today, as the United Nations Food and Agricultural Organization concludes its 1974 pledge to eradicate hunger in a decade.

Near its end, the film demonstrates alternatives to agribusiness, with scenes of model farms, peasant-run cooperatives and other projects aimed to preserve small individual farms. — *Hitch.*

El Hombre De La Mandolina
(The Man With The Mandolin)
(MEXICAN-COLOR)

Mexico City, June 15.
A Películas Mexicanas release of an Estudios América and Conacite Dos production. Executive proder, Guillermo Escobar. Directed by Gonzalo Martínez Ortega. Features entire cast. Screenplay, Rubén Torres, Martínez Ortega, based on an idea by Torres; camera (color), Raúl Domínguez; editor, Angel Camacho; music, Leonardo Valazquez. Reviewed at Cine Madrid, Mexico City, June 14, 1985. Running time: **97 MINS.**
Jardiel Durantes . . . . Omar Moreno
Carlos . . . . Alejandro Camacho
Mother . . . . Alma Defina
Also with: Rosita Qunitana, María Sorte, Héctor Reynoso, Roberto Dumont, Socorro Bonilla, Fernando Balzaretti, Juan Pelaez and Paco Rabell.

"El Hombre De La Mandolina" is an interesting attempt to show the attitudes toward homosexuality in Mexico's conservative provinces, using the Durantes family as a microcosm for society at large.

The story begins in the present day with subjective camera masking the identity of the main character, who is asked about a framed photo of a man with a mandolin. The rest of the film is the answer.

Narration takes the story to 1958 to the town of Querétaro, introducing two friends, Jardiel and Carlos, members of a Renaissance-style Estudiantina group. Mandolin-player Jardiel is beginning to discover adolescent sexual feelings toward Carlos, which are rebuffed though Carlos pledges friendship.

Jardiel's sense of self-awareness is complete during a botched seduction scene set up at a birthday party by a hot-to-trot secretary, who stains his face with lipstick like blood drawn during a battle.

His family must also come to grips with the truth about their son. Under the dictates of a domineering mother, wonderfully played by Alma Defina, Jardiel is stripped of his clothing and locked up at home so he will not disgrace the family. Forced to wear only a sheet, Jardiel is treated as a madman, his homosexuality seen as tantamount to insanity.

Jardiel is not the only one who suffers from this arrangement. His three siblings are also denied their relationships, since their intended spouses can't marry someone with such a skeleton in the family closet.

Except for Jardiel and Carlos, every character in the film is selfish and uses sex as a means of acquiring money, stability and power.

Director Gonzalo Martínez Ortega carefully maintains the pic's tone and use of symbols. As an art film, "El Hombre De La Mandolina" deserves a wider viewing public.
—*Lent.*

Explorers
(COLOR)

Oddball sci-fi fantasy will attract attention but won't reach b.o. stratosphere.

Hollywood, July 8.
A Paramount Pictures release of an Edward S. Feldman production, coproduced by Industrial Light & Magic. Executive producer, Michael Finnell. Produced by Edward S. Feldman, David Bombyk. Directed by Joe Dante. Features entire cast. Screenplay, Eric Luke; camera (Technicolor), John Hora; editor, Tina Hirsch; music, Jerry Goldsmith; sound (Dolby stereo), Ken King; production design, Robert F. Boyle; art direction, Frank Richwood; set decoration, George R. Nelson; set designers, Dan Maltese, Eugene C. Nollman 2d, Les Gobruegge, Donald High; special makeup effects, Rob Bottin; visual effects, ILM; visual effects supervisor, Bruce Nicholson; assistant director, Pat Kehoe; production manager-associate producer, Tom Jacobson; costume design, Rosanna Norton; second unit director/camera, Jack Cooperman; additional photography, Charles Correll; sound effects, Mark Mangini; special effects coordinator, Robert MacDonald Sr.; stunt coordinator, Bill Couch; animal coordinator, Ray Berwick; alien spaceship sequence editor, John Wright; casting, Susan Arnold; computer graphic dream simulations, visual displays, Omnibus Computer Graphics Center; "Starkiller" visual effects, The L.A. Effects Group. Reviewed at National theater, West Los Angeles, Calif., July 8, 1985. (MPAA Rating: PG.) Running time: **109 MINS.**
Ben Crandall . . . . Ethan Hawke
Wolfgang Müller . . . . River Phoenix
Darren Woods . . . . Jason Presson
Lori Swenson . . . . Amanda Peterson
Charlie Drake . . . . Dick Miller
Wak/Starkiller . . . . Robert Picardo
Neek . . . . Leslie Rickert
Mr. Müller . . . . James Cromwell
Mrs. Müller . . . . Dana Ivey
Steve Jackson . . . . Bobby Fite
Mrs. Crandall . . . . Mary Kay Place

After an hour as a perfectly amiable, but rather routine kiddie sci-fi fantasy, "Explorers" become one of the weirdest and most endearingly offbeat alien pictures to have surfaced in recent years. Since it offers virtually no drama or action, film doesn't appear headed for the sort of blockbuster b.o. usually hoped for from a summer entertainment of this sort, but audience expectations stemming from the premise and advertising will undoubtedly generate some solid business.

Appealing hook will be tantalizing to kids of all ages, and to anyone who has ever dreamed of traveling in space. Two young boys, a dreamer (Ethan Hawke) and a nerdy science genius type (River Phoenix), manage, through combining their talents and happening upon an unusual discovery, to fashion a homemade spacecraft.

In league with a lower-class misfit (Jason Presson) who falls in with them, the lads inventively use a leftover Tilt-A-Whirl as their basic chassis and elaborate upon their design with spare parts of all kinds.

Along with their extracurricular Advanced Shop work, opening hour is occupied with passable but far from original stuff devoted to bullies vs. nerds, puppy love, schoolroom antics and domestic *chez* Phoenix which, unfortunately, pales in comparison to similar goings-on in "Back To The Future."

Throughout, director Joe Dante and writer Eric Luke load the proceedings with references to sci-fiers of an earlier day, such as "The War Of The Worlds," "This Island Earth," "Journey To The Center Of The Earth" and many others, but this is nothing compared to what happens when the trio of youngsters finally take off into outer space and make contact with an alien race.

After having their ship swallowed up by a giant whale of a spacecraft and being hurtled down "Lady From Shanghai" — like ramps and chutes, the boys find themselves confronted by a goofy green rubber creature Wak (created by Rob Bottin) who greets them with the universe's most famous cartoon salutation and then proceeds to sing the "Mr. Ed" tv theme song.

The alien's female companion, Neek, who looks like a cousin of Miss Piggy's, comes on to Phoenix while the energetic alien proceeds to deliver an amazing comic monolog comprised of generally well-known snippets of American popular culture, all as a lightning montage of tv clips plays out in the background. Wak winds up by performing Little Richard's "All Around The World" in a sequence that instantly takes its place as unique, an oddball classic.

It turns out, then, that these aliens have learned everything they know about the human race from intercepting American television signals, and they behave accordingly. By the same token, they have been scared off making a trip to Earth, since virtually all the sci-fi films they've seen show humans destroying otherworldly visitors.

To those who have been following Joe Dante's career, it will be clear that this is a very personal film for the director. "Explorers" not only stands as an extension of the central idea of his "It's A Good Life" episode from "Twilight Zone — The Movie," but as a $20,000,-000-plus variation of his first (co-directed) picture, the film-buff-crazed "Hollywood Boulevard."

What mainstream audiences will make of this bizarre contemplation of the effects of pop culture is anybody's guess. Dubbing the monolog into something comprehensible to foreign audiences will rank as one of the toughest such challenges ever undertaken.

Robert Picardo does a sensational job as Wak, and is also briefly seen as the star of a phony 1950s sci-fier. The kids are good, with Jason Presson coming off as intriguingly taciturn and unimpressed with the wild happenings.

Special effects work is highly accomplished, to be sure, and has been pitched in such a way as to conjure up the world of cheap, tacky space epics of 30 years ago without descending to their level.

Jerry Goldsmith's score is excellent, but John Hora's lensing, at least in print caught, frequently appeared fuzzy and lacking sharpness.
—*Cart.*

At Last ... Bullamakanka
The Motion Picture
(AUSTRALIAN-COLOR)

Sydney, July 1.

A Bullamakanka Film prod. Produced by David Joseph. Written and directed by Simon Heath. Features entire cast. Camera (Eastmancolor), David Eggby; editor, John Scott; art director, Terry Stanton; associate producer, Murray Francis; sound, Ross Linton; music, Australian Crawl, Tony Catz Band, The Expression, Jo Jo Zep, Moving Pictures, The Radiators, Rose Tattoo, Skyhooks, Sunnyboys, Wendy and the Rocketts, Uncanny X Men. Reviewed on Thorn EMI vidcassette, Sydney, Australia, July 1, 1985. Running time: **89 MINS.**

Rhino Jackson	Steve Rackman
Waldo Jackson	Gary Kliger
Clare Hampton	Alyson Best
The Senator	Robert Baxter
Senator's Aide	Angry Anderson
Sister Mary	Bassia Carole
Maureen	Debbie Matts
Wally	John Stone
L.D.	Mark Hembrow
T.M.	Iain Gardiner
T.V. Producer	Frank Thring

Presumably inspired by the combination of music and anarchy in "The Blues Brothers," this unreleased 1983 pic emerges as a dispiriting muddle, utterly devoid of entertainment value. It went straight on the shelf before being released on video, and is reviewed for the record.

Plot is incomprehensible, but appears to take place in a small town where a corrupt Mayor (Steve Rackman), running for reelection, invites a senator to attend various functions including a beauty parade and a horse race. Propaganda visit is dogged by noisy demonstrators and disturbances.

Film's gimmick is that cameo roles are taken by a host of well known musicians, television and radio personalities. All that can be said is that the guest spots are as woefully acted as the roles taken by professional actors. This can be laid at the door of director Simon Heath, who shows no feeling for comedy (every single joke is mistimed) or direction.

In all, an amateurish effort, painful to endure, and one which will be quickly and mercifully forgotten.
—*Strat.*

Monique
(Flashing Lights)
(U.S.-FRENCH-COLOR)

An Adolph Viezzi and Henri Lassa presentation of an Alemar Films (N.Y.)/Can't Stop Prod. (N.Y.)/Plan Film (Paris) production. Produced and directed by Jacques Scandelari. Stars Florence Giorgetti, John Ferris. Screenplay, Louisa Rose, from story by Scandelari; camera (uncredited color), François About; editor, Noëlle Balenci; music, Jacques Morali; sound, Michel Brethez; set design, Jed Zuckerman; assistant director, Andre Escargueil; production manager, Jacques Perrier; associate producers, Wallace Potts, Jean Magniez; casting, Potts. Reviewed on VCL-Media Home Entertainment vidcassette, N.Y., June 25, 1985. (No MPAA Rating.) Running time: **93 MINS.**

Monique Raymond	Florence Giorgetti
Richard Lewis	John Ferris
Dr. Mandel	Barry Woloski
Robert	Todd Isaacson
Karl	Rayner Wallwork
Hellen Kahn	Robyn Peterson
Paul Raymond	Pierre Zimmer
Monique's mother	Sonia Petrovna

"Monique" is an extremely odd melodrama, filmed in New York City in 1979 by a mainly French crew under the title "Flashing Lights," subsequently renamed "New York After Dark" and unreleased theatrically. Pic is now available on homevideo as "Monique," not to be confused with the 1970 British sex pic of that name.

Despite opening and end titles insisting this is a true story reported in a 1974 French psychology journal, pic unfolds as an unconvincing exploitation tale with absurd plot hooks. Monique (Florence Giorgetti) is a 35-year-old French art book publisher in Manhattan, who suddenly marries a young artist Richard Lewis (John Ferris), who specializes in oversize drawings of babies. Natch, Monique wants a child but can't seem to have one and is visiting a nasty shrink Dr. Mandel (Barry Woloski) to resolve this and other problems. Her biggest hangup, insecurity, stems from recurring nightmares about a childhood incident involving her mom (since deceased).

Film takes a strange twist when it turns out that husband Richard is cheating on Monique with his prior male lover Robert (Todd Isaacson) and is still a part of Gotham's gay scene, all without informing his wife. Absurd coincidence has the shrink finding out from Monique's dad that the childhood trauma was her witnessing her mom's discovery that daddy was having an affair with another man.

Final reels go way over the top as Monique becomes deranged and hunts for hubbie in Manhattan gay bars, leaving a trail of dead bodies. Filmed around the same time as William Friedkin's "Cruising," pic briefly offers an even stranger glimpse of this N.Y night world, what with Monique dancing on the disco floor with dozens of heavy-leather guys, prior to her stabbing them.

Case history format is very awkward, with frequent inserts of psychoanalysis sessions featuring a most abrasive, obnoxious shrink. Giorgetti, who earlier made a strong impression as Isabelle Huppert's sympathetic roommate in "The Lacemaker," is empathetic in the tortured title role, but is hampered a bit by the requirement of English-language dialog. Supporting cast is weak and underdirected by French helmer Jacques Scandelari. A disco music score by Jacques Morali has become dated. — *Lor.*

Women
(HONG KONG-COLOR)

Hong Kong, June 20.

A Shaw Brothers-Pearl City coproduction. Produced by Mona Fong, Vicky Leung. Directed by Stanley Kwan Kam-pang. Stars Cora Miao, Chow Yun-fat, Chung Chor-hung, Elaine Kam, Yam Hei-Bo, Lee Lam-lam, Cheung Yin-Kwan, Lee Mak, Eric Tsang, Paul Chang. Screenplay, Lai Kit, Chiu Kang-chiang; camera (color), Bill Wong; music, Law Wing-fai. Reviewed at Jade theater, Hong Kong, June 19, 1985. Running time: **98 MINS.**
(Cantonese soundtrack with English subtitles)

Leung Bo-yee (Cora Miao) asks for a divorce from her long-time husband Derek (Chow Yun-fat) and becomes a member of the Happy Spinsters' Club, a group of supposedly well-off divorcees who meet regularly to let off emotional steam.

The center of the story is Leung's on-and-off marriage with Derek who is involved with a liberated woman of today called Ollie (Cherrie Chung).

When not dealing with her eight-year-old son, estranged husband and understanding mother, Leung is seen partying, having tea and trying to be free spirited with her friends Elaine Kam, Yam Hei-bo, Lee Lamlam and Lee Mak.

The women talk about men and sex and other intimate conversations related to being married, getting divorced and the life after.

"Women" has terrific local name stars as marquee attractions in what looks and sounds like a woman's version of "The Boys In The Band."

Picture should do well as a curio piece on the Chinatown circuit as it is a raunchy film about contemporary women trying to survive without men, but subconsciously longing for them all the time. — *Mel.*

Cease Fire
(COLOR)

Timely drama about Vietnam veterans.

A Cineworld Enterprises Corp. release of a Double Helix Films presentation (presented by Stan Wakefield and Jerry Silva) of an E.L.F. Prods. production. Executive producers, George Fernandez, Ed Fernandez. Produced by William Grefé. Directed by David Nutter. Features entire cast. Screenplay, George Fernandez, from his play, "Vietnam Trilogy;" camera (Continental color), Henning Schellerup; editor, Julio Chaves; music, Gary Fry; sound, Henry Lopez; art direction, Alan Avchen; assistant director, Allan Harmon; production manager, Dean Gates; second unit director, Richard Styles; casting, Yonit Hamer. Reviewed at Magno Preview 9 screening room, N.Y., July 3, 1985. (MPAA Rating: R.) Running time: **97 MINS.**

Tim Murphy	Don Johnson
Paula Murphy	Lisa Blount
Luke	Robert F. Lyons
Badman	Richard Chaves
Robbs	Rick Richards
Wendy	Chris Noel
Sanchez	Jorge Gil
Rafer	John Archie

The real-life problems and frustrations of Vietnam vets are dramatically treated in the indie film "Cease Fire." Its theatrical chances will depend on the public's willingness to check out a very serious approach to a subject recently and successfully giving rise to the comic strip heroics of "Rambo." With proper laundering of the R-rated four-letter words, pic will subsequently have solid tv potential.

Don Johnson (currently riding high in tv's "Miami Vice" series) toplines as Tim Murphy, an unemployed Vietnam vet living in Miami with his wife Paula (Lisa Blount), who works as a waitress, and two young children. He is haunted by recurring nightmares of his circa 1970-71 wartime experience, and is becoming increasingly irritable with his wife and other people, interfering with his jobhunting.

Tim meets a fellow Vietnam vet Luke (Robert F. Lyons) on the unemployment line and the two of them become fast friends, sharing their common frustrations and memories of good times as well. Luke is separated from his wife Wendy (Chris Noel), but hopeful of getting back together with her and their son.

Picture climaxes with Luke's tragic suicide when his future plans all fall apart. With the aid of Veterans' Center group therapy sessions for vets and for their wives, Tim finally realizes the nature of his own war guilt and with Paula's help, is ready to rebuild his life.

Adapted by George Fernandez from the third act of his play "Vietnam Trilogy," "Cease Fire" is a hard-hitting problem drama relying mainly on strong performances rather than cinematic devices. Low-budget filming under firsttime director David Nutter adopts an unadorned, flatly-lit visual style which provides a pleasant-looking, neutral Middle American façade for the deep-rooted problems of the characters. Flashback stagings of war battles were also filmed in Florida and lack authenticity, but this is not a major drawback.

Johnson, sporting a moustache to contrast with a cleanshaven, youthful look in his flashbacks, gives a very strong, unglamorized portrayal in the central role, conveying both the anguish and rage of his character. He is ably supported by Blount as his loyal wife and effective source of identification for female viewers. Showiest role of the piece, the impulsive buddy Luke, is expressively handled by well-cast Robert F. Lyons. As his wife, former 1960s starlet Chris Noel ("Soldier In The Rain," "The Glory Stompers") shines in a heartfelt monolog delivered at a group session for veterans' wives.—*Lor.*

A Street To Die
(AUSTRALIAN-COLOR)

Sydney, July 15.

A Mermaid Beach prod. Produced and directed by Bill Bennett. Stars Chris Haywood. Screenplay, Bennett; camera (color), Geoff Burton; production design, Igor Nay; costumes, Magi Beswick; music, Michael Atkinson, Michael Spicer; editor, Denise Hunter; sound, Leo Sullivan. Reviewed at Chauvel theater, Sydney, July 8, 1985. Running time: **91 MINS.**

Col Turner	Chris Haywood
Lorraine Turner	Jennifer Cluff
Peter Townley	Peter Hehir
Dr. Walsea	Arianthe Galani
Craig	Peter Kowitz
Julie	Sussanah Fowle
Sister Sweet	Pat Evison
Dr. Enders	John Smythe
Tom	Robin Ramsay
Dr. Walker	John Hamblin
Deputy President of Commission	Don Crosby

A low-budget feature debut which gets its message across with sympathy and humanity, this is the biography of a Vietnam vet whose death from leukemia was blamed on the after-effects of poisoning by the defoliant Agent Orange.

Col Turner (Chris Haywood), his wife Lorraine (Jennifer Cluff) and their two children move into a home supplied for war veterans; every house on their side of the street is occupied by men who fought in Vietnam and their families. Col and Lorraine quickly notice that there's an unusual amount of sickness and strange behavior among their neighbors. Soon Col discovers rashes on his arms and bruises he can't account for.

Eventually his problem is diagnosed to be leukemia, and he reacts by trying to claim compensation from the authorities for the damage done to him by the defoliation techniques of the Yank forces alongside whom the Aussies fought in Vietnam. After his death, his wife continues the battle for compensation, which she eventually wins.

First-time helmer Bill Bennett, a former tv journalist and docu director, handles this in a straightforward, no-frills style. He's aided immensely by the performance of Chris Haywood as the dying Col, whose laconic humor stays with him almost to the end, but never disguises his pain or his anger. As Lorraine, Jennifer Cluff is also first-rate, especially in the latter sequences.

Chalk this one down as a modest, but highly effective, pic in the realist tradition. With careful handling, it should find an appreciative audience on its no-nonsense approach to a potentially sentimental subject. —*Strat.*

Die Arbeit Und Dann?
..rst The Work—And Then?)
..ST GERMAN-COLOR-16m)

Munich, June 30.

A Cult Film TV Prod., Hamburg. Written and directed by Detlev Buck. Features entire cast. Camera (color), Burkhart Wellmann; editor, Ilona Bruver; sound, Detlev Brozak. Reviewed at Munich Film Fest, June 30, 1985. Running time: **63 MINS.**

With: Detlev Buck, Ela Nitzsche.

"First the Work — And Then?" is a delightful low-budget debut film by director-writer-actor Detlev Buck. It sets out to do no more than depict the daily chores of a young farmer in the Holstein area of northern Germany, using a comic and tongue-in-cheek approach.

The twist is constructed around the old film canard about what a country hick is going to do with an afternoon off in the big city, in this case, Hamburg. Detlev Buck merrily finishes his chores, whereupon he finds himself with time on his hands. He tells Grandma he's decided to go to town.

After siphoning gas from the tractor into the farm Mercedes, he next finds himself in the chic Eppendorf section of Hamburg at an in-bar for long-drinks and musicvideos. This brings the most laughs as he gets into a conversation with a lass with a sports car on how a farmer's lifestyle compares with that of the hip cityfolk. When he finally gets around to the expected midnight kiss, it's time to get back to the homestead for the morning milking. — *Holl.*

The Empty Beach
(AUSTRALIAN-COLOR)

Sydney, July 15.

A Jethro Films production. Executive producer, Bob Weis. Produced by Timothy Read, John Edwards. Directed by Chris Thomson. Stars Bryan Brown. Screenplay, Keith Dewhurst, from the book by Peter Corris; camera (Eastmancolor), John Seale; editor, Lindsay Frazer; music, Martin Armiger, Red Symons; song, Don Walker, performed by Marc Hunter; sound, Max Hensser; production design, Laurence Eastwood; costumes, Miranda Skinner; production manager, Adrienne Read. Reviewed at Chauvel Theater, Paddington, July 13, 1985. Running time: **89 MINS.**

Cliff Hardy	Bryan Brown
Anne Winter	Anna Maria Monticelli
MacLeary	Ray Barrett
Parker	John Wood
Brian Henneberry	Nick Tate
Marion Singer	Belinda Giblin
Fred Ward	Peter Collingwood
Hildegard	Kerry Mack
Sandy Modesta	Sally Cooper
Tal	Joss McWilliam
Manny	Steve J. Spears

Sydney author Peter Corris has been responsible for a successful series of detective novels featuring private eye Cliff Hardy, a character engagingly brought to life by Bryan Brown in "The Empty Beach," first of the books to be filmed. First-time director Chris Thomson, whose trailblazing tv series on police corruption, "Scales Of Justice," was praised widely last year, has moved

effortlessly to the big screen, and the result should do well locally and create some international interest, too.

The plot, as with so many private eye books and movies, is crowded and sometimes a touch confusing. It opens when a rich woman (Belinda Giblin) hires Hardy to find out if her husband, supposedly drowned in a boating accident two years earlier, is alive. The missing man was a business tycoon with powerful friends, and the trail leads Hardy to Henneberry (Nick Tate), an investigative journalist with compromising evidence stashed away somewhere. When Tate is stabbed to death while surfing (a very well-staged scene), his girlfriend, Anne (Anna Maria Monticelli, better known as Anna Jemison by which name she appeared in "Smash Palace" and "Silver City" among others), helps Hardy for a while, until it becomes clear her father is involved in the plot.

Other characters Hardy confronts along the way include John Wood as a cop who lets others do the dirty work for him; Ray Barrett as a wealthy criminal with a taste for very young girls; Peter Collingwood as a more urbane, but equally dangerous, crook; Sally Cooper as the missing man's drug-addict mistress; and Joss McWilliam as her current lover, a hit-man.

Hardy, like his Californian counterparts, is tough, cynical and dogged. Bryan Brown gives the character exactly the right touch, and the flip, sardonic dialog is funny. Cinematographer John Seale (who last toiled on "Witness") makes Sydney a sumptuous backdrop to the mysterious and sometimes violent happenings, and the jazzy music score of Martin Armiger and Red Symons effectively underlines the action, though a title song, performed over both the opening and closing credits, is redundant. —*Strat.*

Idi I Smotri
(Go And See)
(SOVIET-COLOR)

Moscow, July 9.

A production of Belarusfilm and Mosfilm studios. Directed by Elem Klimov. Screenplay, Alexander Adamovich, Klimov; camera (color), Alexei Rodionov; art direction, Viktor Petrov; music, Oleg Yanchenko. Reviewed at Moscow Film Fest, July 9, 1985. Running time: **146 MINS.**

With: Alexei Kravchenko, Olga Mironova, Lubomiras Lauciavicus, Vladas Bagdonas, Viktor Lorents.

"Go And See" is a towering, cathartic experience that left the audience pale and silent after its Moscow fest screening.

Set in Byelorussia in 1943, and based on "The Story Of Khatyn" by Byelorussian writer Ales Adamovich, it starts with a young lad, Flera, joining the partisans, much to his mother's distress. But the boy's family, with the rest of their village, is executed by the Nazis early on. The gruesome experiences mount up, with Flera and his girlfriend Lasha surviving machinegun and mortar attacks interspersed with lyrical interludes.

Finally the lad finds himself in a village which (along with over 620 others in Byelorussia, a credit tells us) the Germans annihilate by herding inhabitants into a barn (taking care not to miss any children) and setting fire to it. They also gang rape any women not incinerated. After the SS men withdraw, there is the question of partisan reprisals against German prisoners. The partisans choose not to emulate the bestial example they have just witnessed.

Technical credits are superlative. Camerawork (the first use of Steadicam in Soviet cinema?) is especially fine, with village interiors and the Byelorussian countryside revealed in soft, warm color. Images such as the hero waking one foggy morning after a mortar attack in the middle of a field, his head resting on a dead cow, stick in the mind. The acting is also remarkable.

It appears a doctor was on hand throughout the grueling shoot to check the health of the young lead player, who is made to age in the film (because of the horrors he encounters) to a middle-aged wreck. The makeup job is astounding, but the trauma in the eyes speaks of real suffering. Music is outstanding as is overall direction. The handling of crowds is extraordinary.

The anti-war message, however, could have come through just as strongly without the near-caricature Nazi villains, falling about in glee at every step of the carnage. There's also some Nazi concentration camp footage included, most inappropriately.

Klimov is known in the West only by the Rasputin film "Agony" now going the rounds, a film whose impact has been lessened by a seven-year delay in its release. If Westerners can overcome their squeamishness to this pic's racist elements and feel up to the ordeal of 146 minutes of raw emotion, this film will be the one to make his name. —*Kits.*

The Killing Hour
(COLOR)

Average thriller

A 20th Century Fox release of a Lansbury/Beruh Prods. presentation of The Hour Co. production, in association with Bert Schneiderman Ltd. Executive producers, Edgar Lansbury, Joseph Beruh. Produced by Robert Di Milia. Directed by Armand Mas-

troianni. Features entire cast. Screenplay, B. Jonathan Ringkamp, from story by Mastroianni, Ringkamp; camera (Movielab color), Larry Pizer; editor, David E. McKenna; music, Alexander Peskanov; sound, Rolf Pardula; assistant director, Costa Mantis; production manager. Kelly Van Horn, art direction, Susan Kaufman; casting, Barbara Quinn, Leonard Finger; associate producer, Nan Pearlman. Reviewed on CBS Fox vidcassette, N.Y., July 7, 1985. (MPAA Rating: R.) Running time: **97 MINS.**

Paul McCormack	Perry King
Virna Nightbourne	Elizabeth Kemp
Larry Weeks	Norman Parker
Lt. Cullum	Kenneth McMillan
Sporaco	Jon Polito
Rich	Joe Morton
Muriel	Barbara Quinn
Willie Gonzales	Antone Pagan

Also with: Thomas DeCarlo, Lou Bedford, David Ramsey, Olivia Negron, Robert Kerman (a.k.a. R. Bolla).

"The Killing Hour" is a well-crafted but mediocre thriller. Lensed in Manhattan in 1981, low-budget indie was picked up by Jensen Farley Pictures and retitled (more appropriately to subject matter) "The Clairvoyant," subsequently acquired by 20th Century Fox after JFP went under, but unreleased theatrically, appearing instead as a cassette via CBS Fox.

Perry King toplines as Paul McCormack, Mack for short, a tv newsman/phone-in talkshow host who successfully exploits on the air a series of handcuffed-victim murders to increase his ratings and secure job advancement. At first he is aided with inside info by policeman Larry Weeks (Norman Parker), who improbably moonlights as an unfunny standup comic/impressionist (he has to identify his carbons, such as Al Pacino or George Burns for the viewer), but his sensationalist reporting soon puts him at odds with the police led by Lt. Cullum (Kenneth McMillan).

Both the police and Mack are aided by Virna Nightbourne (Elizabeth Kemp), a young artist who is clairvoyant and makes drawings of each murder unconsciously.

After a promising beginning, spotlighting the ingenious rather than gory murders, pic becomes sluggish. Because of the script's paucity of suspects, the identity of the killer is quite predictable. Acting is okay and direction by Armand Mastroianni (previously known for "He Knows You're Alone") is effective within the screenplay's limitations. Lensing by British cameraman Larry Pizer is excellent.—*Lor.*

Tango Im Bauch
(Tango In The Belly)
(WEST GERMAN-COLOR-16m)

Munich, June 29.

A coproduction of the Munich Film Academy and Bayerischer Rundfunk Munich. Written and directed by Ute Wieland. Features entire cast. Camera (color), Walter Lindenlaub; sound, Dieter Bayer, Titus Lange; sets, Sherry Hormann; costumes, Esther Walz; music,

Andreas Köbner. Reviewed at Munich Film Fest, June 29, 1985. Running time: **88 MINS.**

With: Karina Fallenstein (Hildi), Peter E. Funck, Dominic Raacke, Dominik Graf, Traute Hoess, Barbara Rudnik.

A low-budget debut feature, Ute Wieland's "Tango In The Belly" comes across as a delightful takeoff on Susan Seidelman's "Smithereens," Bavarian-style. The heroine, Hildi (Karina Fallenstein), lives with two pleasant buffoons in a makeshift flat, borrows money from everybody in sight, and passes herself off as a "composer" (the evidence being a portable music box slung over her shoulder).

Hildi's mark of distinction is a haystack punk hairdo. She's 18, but doesn't know much more about life than the day she's currently living through. Her friends are beginning to duck her.

Yet Hildi is a romantic punk. She dreams of the day when she will be swept off her feet again by Prince Charming. In fact, she's already had the affair and is waiting for him to hit it big in the music field.

One day, she finds herself so broke she tries to earn a few extra bucks by offering herself as a guinea pig for a pharmaceutical drug-testing program, but the results only indicate she's more than likely pregnant. Meantime, she fends off a would-be bed companion by demanding a double-course meal before even making up her mind — the answer is an emphatic no, for Hildi is at heart a good girl.

She finally grows up and accepts the pregnancy, which transforms her into a serious looking lady, but helmer Wieland has a twist to end the pic on yet another upbeat comic note. —*Holl.*

Radikalni Rez
(Radical Cut)
(CZECH-COLOR)

Sydney, July 15.

A Barrandov Film Studios production and Ceskoslovensky Filmexport release. Directed and written by Dusan Klein. Features entire cast. Camera (color), Josef Vanis; editor, Jiri Brozek; music, Zdenek Mart; art director, Jindrich Goetz. Reviewed on SBS tv, July 14, 1985. Running time: **86 MINS.**

With: Lubos Pavlovic, Bronislaw Poloczek, Josef Ropog, Monika Zigova, Ilja Racek, Vera Vlckova.

A whodunit with intriguing social undertones, "Radical Cut," made in 1983, is one of the better recent Czech features.

It's set in a provincial town which has a large gypsy population. The elder son of a local architect, and prominent party member, is found in the gypsy district with his throat cut; his younger brother has disappeared. The father is certain that gypsies are responsible, but the local police, whose senior membership includes a gypsy, aren't so sure. The

investigation turns up various suspects before the not unexpected solution.

What's interesting in the film is not so much the plot but the setting and atmosphere, and especially the depiction of racial tensions between the gypsies and the Czechs. Writer-director Dusan Klein, and a fine cast, make the conflicts seem very authentic, and the suspicions and knee-jerk hostilities on both sides are handled adroitly.

It adds up as a fascinating look at racism in a Central European country today. —*Strat.*

Hälfte Des Lebens
(A Half Of Life)
(EAST GERMAN-COLOR)

Munich, June 26.

A DEFA Studio für Spielfilme production, East Berlin; world rights, DEFA Aussenhandel, East Berlin. Directed by Herrmann Zschoche. Features entire cast. Screenplay, Christa Kozik; camera (color), Günter Jaeuthe; editor, Monika Schindler; sound, Horst Mathuschek; sets, Dieter Adam; costumes, Anne Hoffmann; music, Georg Katzer. Reviewed at Munich Film Fest, June 26, 1985. Running time: **100 MINS.**

With: Ulrich Mühe (Friedrich Hölderlin), Jenny Gröllmann (Susette Gontard), Michael Gwisdek (Gontard), Swetlana Schönfeld, Peter-Mario Grau.

Recent East German film and tv productions have treated the lives of Bach, Beethoven and Martin Luther. Herrmann Zschoche's portrait of poet Friedrich Hölderlin (1770-1843) is titled "A Half Of Life" after one of his works and in view of the fact that the gifted poet went insane at the age of 36, exactly midway through his life. It was one of the prime attractions for the German public at the Munich fest.

Pic focuses on the 12 decisive years in Hölderlin's life, 1796-1806. He had just finished his courses in theology in Tübingen together with two other illustrious friends, Hegel and Schelling. Instead of becoming a minister, he chose the frugal life of a tutor for the rich banking family of Gontard in Frankfurt. There he fell in love with Susette Gontard, wife of his employer and mother of the children he was hired to educate. After a stormy affair on the country estate, the passionate poet is dismissed.

Parallel to this personal conflict — that excruciating experience left a profound mark of isolation and loneliness in his poetry — he saw his friends arrested for espousing the causes of the French Revolution. Suspected himself of being a revolutionary at least in spirit, he could however not be fingered as such due to the enclosed meanings in his verses which tended to become more and more abstract as the years passed. Hölderlin's view of the world was that of a cruel and inhospitable place, even when he left Frankfurt to take refuge in Switzerland and Bordeaux.

Zschoche's approach to Hölderlin is via scripter Christa Kozik's distinctly literary vision. "A Half Of Life" offers some striking insights to the reasons for Hölderlin's apparent growing madness, not all of which can be credited to the poet's forced separation from his beloved "Diotima" (Susette Gontard) as penned in his immortal "Hyperion."

Lensing, costumes, and sets are the major pluses in "A Half Of Life." Ulrich Mühe as Hölderlin gives a strong enough performance, although the affair with Susette Gontard (Jenny Gröllmann) is more smoke signals than a raging passion. — *Holl.*

Infatuation
(HONG KONG-COLOR)

Hong Kong, June 20.
A Centro Films production released in the Golden Harvest theater circuit. Produced and directed by Louis Chan. Stars Lowell Lo, Cecilia Yip and Ricky Hui. Music and songs composed and performed by Lowell Lo. (No other credits provided.) Reviewed at State theater, Hong Kong, June 19, 1985. Running time: **98 MINS.**
(Cantonese soundtrack with English subtitles)

"Infatuation," a serio-comic romantic first feature of commercial director Louis Chan is one of the few fully satisfying productions in a sea of senseless 1985 colloquial comedies. It is glossily presented like a series of carefully staged commercial sequences and subtly acted with civilized sensibilities.

Lowell Lo (a debut for a local recording artist as actor) returns to Hong Kong after seven years traveling abroad to work with friend Ricky Hui in the video lensing business. Lo's first assignment is the wedding of Cecilia Yip to a rich businessman. She apparently doesn't love him and he is involved with another woman who is married. It looks like a marriage of convenience.

How the infatuation of Lo to Yip develops into true love is the film's central theme. Parallel to it is the belief that nothing is absolute and that true happiness is relative. In between some very nicely staged romantic interludes in touristy locales (accompanied by pleasant songs composed by Lo on the soundtrack) are finely honed dramatic moments.

Yip is outstanding as she changes from a girlish, inhibited, well-off housewife to a femme fatale to compete with the husband's trendy mistress.

Classy Cecilia Yip not only photographs well but has a natural flair for serio-comic roles.

Lo in his first film can be praised for his toned down characterization, while Ricky Hui provides comic relief.

Overall, a charming, straightforward picture that is commercial in outlook but good enough to make it to film fests outside the Oriental coast. — *Mel.*

Parad Planet
(Parade Of The Planets)
(SOVIET-COLOR)

Moscow, July 10.
A Mosfilm production. Directed by Vadim Abdrashitov. Screenplay, Alexander Mindadze; camera (color) Vladimir Shevtsik; art direction, Alexander Tolkachev; music, Vyacheslav Ganelin. Reviewed at the Moscow Film Festival, July 10, 1985. Running time: **97 MINS.**
With: Oleg Borisov, Pyotr Zaichenko, Sergei Shakurov, Alexei Zharkov, Sergei Nikonenko, Alexander Pashutin.

"Parade Of The Planets" is an attention-grabber which holds its audience mesmerized right up to the final, enigmatic shot.

In a small town, a group of men of very different backgrounds — an astrophysicist, a fitter, a butcher and a loader — become acquainted through territorial army exercises. They are reunited after two years for more maneuvers (filmed with great panache), during which their group is "killed," and they're told to disappear. Not expected back at home nor at work, they decide to take advantage of the hiatus and take a small trip.

Things, already somewhat surreal, now take on the quality of a waking dream. The men walk into a town full of beautiful women with whom they go skinny dipping in the moonlight to the strains of Beethoven's Seventh. They have an adventure on a deserted island and finally come to a place peopled by somnambulant senior citizens, one of whom is convinced the astrophysicist is her son.

The film is not easy to fathom, but even those viewers who totally gave up on the meaning appeared to respond to its technical excellence and power to fascinate.

Director Vadim Abdrashitov and screenwriter Alexander Mindadze made a big impression in Soviet Film Weeks around the world with "The Train Stopped," a very different kettle of fish, dealing with everyday corruption and inefficiency on the railways. Their next film, like much of the current Soviet product, deals with the problems of youth, another complete change of tack. — *Kits.*

Marie Ward
(WEST GERMAN-COLOR)

Berlin, July 2.

A Hermes Film, Munich, in coproduction with Bayerischer Rundfund, Munich. Written and directed by Angelika Weber. Produced by Padhraic O'Dochartaigh. Features Hannelore Elsner. Camera (color), René Perraudin; editor, Juliane Lorenz; music, Elmer Bernstein; sets, Jürgen Henze; costumes, Egon; production manager, Janusch Kozminski. Reviewed at Hollywood Kino, Berlin, July 2, 1985. Running time: **100 MINS.**
With: Hannelore Elsner (Marie Ward), Irm Hermann (Winn Wigmore), Julia Lindig (Mary Poyntz), Lambert Hamel (Lennard Morriss), Mathieu Carrière (the knight), Wolfgang Reichmann (Father Holtby), Kurt Weinzierl (Father Keynes), Bernhard Wicki (George Abbot), Klaus Guth (Sir Robert Cecil), Anton Diffring (Cardinal Millini), Mario Adorf (Pope Urban VIII), Felix von Manteuffel (Vitelleschi), Hans-Reinhard Müller (Pope Gregory XV), Alexander Kerst (Cardinal Borgia), Hans Quest (English Prelate), Mareike Carrière (Sister Praxedes), Elisabeth Endriss (Sister Allcock), Monika Peitsch (Novice Mistress), Hans Clarin (Maximilian I), Silvia Reize (Elisabeth von Lothringen), Hans Schulze (Mamaduke Ward), Hartmut Becker (Father Roger Lee), Walter Lorenz (Father O'Henry), Jan Biczycki (Decon Golla).

A very costly production, Angelika Weber's "Marie Ward" follows in the now almost forgotten tradition of the good-intentions religious propaganda film. Both France and Italy excelled in the genre with financial assistance from church coffers throughout the 1920s and 1930s, while arguably the best films appeared just when the genre was fading out: Robert Bresson's "Les Anges du Peche" (France, 1943) and Maurice Cloche's "Monsieur Vincent" (France, 1947). "Marie Ward" is a combination of both of these films: a religious woman giving her life and fortune to the poor and the education of young girls in troubled times.

The founder of the Institute of Mary (or Loretto Order), Marie Ward (1585-1645) came from a devout and aristocratic Yorkshire Catholic family. Her wish was to enter the convent from the start of her young adult life, and she finally persuaded her father to let her cross the English channel to St. Omer in Walloon, France to join the austere Order of St. Clare. Returning to England to live and work in lay dress and often in disguise to escape notice by her swarn enemies during the height of religious persecution, she decided to found her own order based on the rules of the Jesuits.

Pic follows Marie Ward through the prisons of London, where her acts of mercy angered the Anglican Archbishop of Canterbury. She's next back in St. Omer, where the Institute of Mary was actually founded in 1606. She goes then to Rome to present her case to, first, Pope Gregory XV and then Pope Urban VIII, the latter making the decision to ban the order on the grounds that nuns should be cloistered instead of out on the streets. Broken from her travels, she finally returns to York just as Cromwell is about to batter

the walls of the city down. She dies.

The Institute of Mary (way ahead of its time) was finally approved by the church in 1703. The film is little more than a picture-book of good lady's travels. In fact, scenes are shot on the actual locations in the manner of a cultural art film just as interested in the places as the persons parading through it. Lensing by René Perraudin is a plus among too many minuses to take this extravaganza seriously. — *Holl.*

Der Fahrrad
(The Bicycle)
(EAST GERMAN-COLOR)

Berlin, June 7.
A DEFA Film production, "Babelsberg" Group, East Berlin; world rights, DEFA Aussenhandel, East Berlin. Directed by Evelyn Schmidt. Screenplay, Ernst Wenig; camera (color), Roland Dressel; music, Peter Rabenalt; editor, Sabine Schmager. Reviewed at ZDF Screening Room, Berlin, June 5, 1985. Running time: **97 MINS.**
With: Heidemarie Schneider (Susanne), Roman Kaminski (Thomas), Anke Friedrich, Hilmar Baumann, Walter Lendrich, Heidrun Bartholmäus, Johanna Clas.

Evelyn Schmidt's second feature, "The Bicycle," scores as one of the best films produced in East Germany this decade. Made in 1982, it's had only limited release abroad due to its rather critical portrait of East Germany. Now that it has made it over the border to West Germany for release, pic deserves to be picked up for fests and femme programs.

"The Bicycle" tells the story of Susanne, an unmarried mother and assembly-line worker nearing the end of her 20s with little else to look forward to other than raising her young daughter. Susanne wastes her free time hanging around discos while an elderly neighbor looks after the child. The mother is always short on funds and can't even pay the modest fees required at the local kindergarten. One day she quits her job out of the usual frustrations.

Her life is about to change. She meets a young engineer, Thomas, who likes her spirit and doesn't waste time or words telling her he'd like to keep company. The difficulty is that Susanne has deceived the social welfare office in order to get the funds she needed to cover immediate bills, and now she has to go to court to face charges. She hides this fact from Thomas even after he's found a job for her at the plant where he works as foreman.

Pic's upbeat note is found in the manner in which the court case is resolved, and the way in which Susanne finds a new lease on life to meet her social responsibilities.

Schmidt is a gifted narrative storyteller. It's her visual comments on the elite establishment in East Germany that are particularly eye-catching. She's also an adept director of actors: Heidemarie Schneider in the lead carries the film with seemingly effortless ease as she adjusts noticeably to the life Fate has dealt her. —*Holl.*

Der Krieg Meines Vaters
(My Father's War)
(WEST GERMAN-B&W-16m)

Munich, June 28.
A Novoskop Film, Mannheim, and Hochschule für Fernsehen und Film (HFF), Munich, coproduction. Written and directed by Nico Hofmann. Features entire cast. Camera (b&w), Ernst Kubitza; sets, Katharina Wöppermann; sound, Winfried Leyh; editor, Roland Suso Richter. Reviewed at Munich Film Fest, June 28, 1985. Running time: **60 MINS.**
With: Hans-Joachim Grau, Gabriele Badura, Heiner Kollhoff, Matthias Kopfmüller.

Nico Hofmann's "My Father's War" is a fiction-documentary by a director completing his diploma studies at the Munich Film Academy (HFF). It is significant in that the theme refers as much to today's military stacking of rockets as it does to the conscientious problems of Germans supporting an entry into World War II under the Third Reich. In fact, the film was prompted by the director's exchange of letters with his father during the autumn of 1983 (the "hot autumn" of the peace demonstrations) about the parent's own experiences during World War II.

The results are gratifying. Hofmann tells the story of a 17-year-old, Hans Witte, drafted into the German army in the winter of 1942. The lad is far from being a hoopla patriot. Instead he's painfully aware of the shortcomings of war when life is about to unfold in all its mysteries. That's one side of the story. The other is the remembrances of a silent departure with choked-back tears and the somber realization that mother and son, husband and wife, may never see each other again after a wave at the train station.

"My Father's War" examines the concept of war and rearmament from a moral standpoint. The fiction scenes are presented in mostly wordless context, the commentary itself setting the mood. Lensing in b&w adds a strong stylistic element. —*Holl.*

Cudo Nevideno
(Unseen Wonder)
(YUGOSLAVIAN-COLOR)

Moscow, July 6.
A Zeta Film release, produced by Centar Film (Belgrade). Directed by Zivko Nikolic. Stars Savina Gersak. Screenplay, Sinisa Pavic; camera (color), Stanislav Somolani; art director, Milenko Jeremic; music, Boro Tamindzic. Reviewed at the Moscow Film Festival, July 6, 1985. Running time: **90 MINS.**

With: Savina Gersak, Dragan Nikolic, Petar Bozovic.

In "Unseen Wonder," an American girl moves to a Yugoslavian fishing village and wreaks havoc among the dazzled male population. Falling somewhere between a plain old sex farce and modern fable with a mini-message of peace and brotherhood between men, this film should have b.o. legs in the East thanks to the unveiled charms of its heroine, a shapely blond very much in the Western centerfold tradition. The look and premise are too dated, however, to travel widely.

In a burg where the standard female attire is a black shift and headscarf and the normal expression a scowl, the sudden appearance of "Yank" Savina Gersak on the scene creates an uproar. Universally detested by the womenfolk, she quickly becomes the obsession of every man. No dumb blond, Savina uses her Frederick's of Hollywood wardrobe to wrap the town around her finger and get back some property once belonging to her family.

Pic's running gag is the surreptitious ogling that goes on when Savina goes skinny-dipping in the lake or prepares for bed. The country bumpkin humor gets monotonous pretty quickly.

Helmer Zivko Nikolic slips a more somber note in with the grotesque story of the mayor's unsuccessful efforts to keep the village from sinking into the lake. His misguided remedies are comic, but at last the townsfolk are forced to wade out of their flooded homes and take to boats. Savina's marriage to a local swain ends in tragedy, too, in a senseless feud between clans.

Pic received one of the Silver Prizes at the Moscow Film Fest.
—*Yung.*

Im Himmel Ist Die Hölle Los
(In Heaven All Hell Is Breaking Loose)
(WEST GERMAN-COLOR)

Munich, June 24.
An Emotion Pictures production, Munich, in coproduction with ZDF, Mainz. Directed by Helmer von Lützelburg. Features entire cast. Screenplay, Andreas Markus Klug, von Lützelburg; camera (color), Klaus Eichhammer, Horst Knechtel; sets, Matthias Hellmer, Erhard Engel; sound, Sylvia Tewes; editor, Illo Endrulat; costumes, Sabine Atzberger; music, Andreas Markus Klug. Reviewed at Munich Film Fest, June 24, 1985. Running time: **88 MINS.**
With: Billie Zöckler (Mimi Schrillmann), Dirk Bach (Willi Wonder), Barbara Valentin, Harry Baer, Ortrud Beginnen, Walter Bockmayer, Cleo Krestschmer, Beate Hasenau, Elma Karlova, Johanna König, Kurt Raab.

Originally titled "Hullygully In Käseburg" at the Hof fest last October, Helmer von Lützelburg's "In Heaven All Hell Is Breaking Loose" tried to improve on its bad luck at that fest by recutting and remounting. The results are pretty much the same: a dull parody of tv entertainment shows.

Willi Wonder (Dirk Bach) is the new superstar from Channel 62, who travels with his tv quiz show from city to city across Germany and arrives at the provincial town of Käseburg. One of his ardent admirers (Billie Zöckler) goes ape once she discovers her idol is in town, and the rest is raw imitation of the underground scenes in Berlin, Cologne (Walter Bockmayer appearing in drag) and Munich. —*Holl.*

Chuchela
(Weirdo)
(SOVIET-COLOR)

Moscow, July 9.
A Mosfilm production. Directed by Rolan Bykov. Screenplay, Vladimir Zheleznikov, Rolan Bykov; camera (color), Anatoly Mukasei; art direction, Yevgeny Markoich; music, Sofia Cabaidulina. Reviewed at Moscow Film Festival, July 9, 1985. Running time: **127 MINS.**
With: Christina Orbakaite, Yury Nikulin.

"Weirdo" is a real chiller, in the guise of a problem picture set in a smalltown school.

It starts slowly, concerning 12-year-old Lena and her grandfather, newcomers to the provincial town. Both are figures of fun because they're different from the rest. Nikolai Nikolaevich is a cranky old man who collects paintings, while Lena is considered a wimp as she tends to simper in a vain effort to please her new schoolmates. For a while her boyfriend, Dima Somov, protects her but it soon becomes apparent that the macho Dima has no guts. He allows Lena to be blamed for something he did, whereupon the rest of the class, having discussed the situation, votes to "boycott" Lena, which means tormenting her constantly, even to the extent of burning an effigy of her, clad in a dress the class has stolen from her. Finally the class discovers the truth and now scampers after Dima like hounds at the scent of blood.

The picture looks great, with its wide-screen images of the dilapidated old town in autumn, wooden houses, brass band and all. It gets a bit bogged down early on with constant discussion between teacher and children, grandpa and children, and children and children on moral issues which would not be of the slightest interest to Western kids.

It becomes riveting as the full extent of the children's cruelty is revealed. From a simple ribbing by some youngsters of others who can't afford Western jeans, it escalates to physical violence and mental cruelty of an extreme kind.

Christine Orbakaite contributes a

wonderful portrait as the girl, gradually growing in stature from a grinning softie to a strong, silent type and, eventually, to a local heroine revered by all. —*Kits.*

Death And Destiny
(AUSTRALIAN-DOCU-COLOR-16m)

Sydney, July 15.
A Look Films production. Produced by Will Davies. Directed by Paul Cox. Screenplay, Cox, Michael Le Moignan, Phillip Adams; camera (color), Yuri Sokol; editor, John Scott, Cox; sound, Max Hensser; narrator, Phillip Adams. Reviewed at Chauvel, Paddington, July 12, 1985. Running time: **76 MINS.**

Paul Cox has throughout his career interleaved documentary projects with his work in fiction features. "Death And Destiny" was made soon after last year's "My First Wife," and centers around excavations at Saqqara in Egypt, just south of the Great Pyramids, where an Egyptian-born Australian archeologist and his team have been making some remarkable discoveries.

Cox and his regular cinematographer, Yuri Sokol, revel in the sights and sounds of Egypt, both ancient and modern. The viewer is shown some of the great archeological treasures already discovered, and the camera is present when impressive new finds are lovingly unveiled after over 4,000 years under the sand. The relative peace and beauty of the archeological site is compared to the noise and confusion of modern-day Cairo with its masses of people and traffic.

As narrator and host of the documentary, Cox uses Phillip Adams, known in Australia as a witty columnist and sometime film producer, as well as being chairman of the Australian Film Commission. Adams' avuncular presence is a bit jarring at first (his opening remarks consist of rather flip comments about treading in the footsteps of Agatha Christie and Hercule Poirot), but he settles into his role, and his obvious fascination for the subject shows.

This is an engaging travelog which is clearly in love with its subject. The camera caresses the ancient carvings, faces and writings with infectious delight and makes Egypt look an immensely attractive place.

It's more for television than theatrical slotting outside the Australian market, but well worth a look.
—*Strat.*

Goethe In D
(WEST GERMAN-DOCU-COLOR-16m)

Munich, June 30.

A Neue Prometheus Film, Düsseldorf, in collaboration with the Northrhine-Westphalian Film Bureau and the Hamburg Film Fund. A documentary with the additional subtitles, ''The Bloody Night On The Schreckenstein'' or ''How Erwin Geschonneck Played A Main Role.'' Directed by Manfred Vosz. Screenplay, Almut Hielscher, Vosz; camera (color), Bernd Bajog, F. Hoffmeister, S. Kempf, R. Neddermann, V. Schwab, M. Vosz; editor, Gerd Pohlmann, Karl Breuer; sound, Rolf Neddermann, Vosz. Reviewed at Munich Film Fest, June 30, 1985. Running time: **85 MINS.**

Manfred Vosz' ''Goethe In D'' is one of those timely documentaries that calls for lengthy discussion after its presentation, just what it got after its debut at the Munich fest. Made in conjunction with the 40th anni of the end of the World War II, the ''D'' in the title referring to the concentration camp at Dachau near Munich.

It tells the story of German inmates in Dachau (a work, not an extermination camp) who found ways to live through the miseries and degradation by turning to art as both a source of courage to live and a means of active resistance under the very noses of the fascist prison guards. The title refers to a particularly extraordinary case. Actor Erwin Geschonneck and his colleagues played Goethe in an improvised production and thus were even able to parody their superiors without the latter being aware.

''Goethe'' symbolically embraces all expressions of art. Vosz recounts how songs and verses were penned, how valuable books could be sneaked into the prison to form a kind of lending library, how theater performances could be organized and presented that had the guards in tears with laughter even though the classics presented satirized individuals like them. One astonishing example after another is presented, and although testimony of this kind is found in pertinent literature, this is the first time a film has chronicled it all.

''Goethe In D'' raises some fundamental questions. How does one make a docu on Dachau that would even permit laughter among the viewing audience? Is the approach a bit too intellectual for the mass audience to grasp all the refined details? Vosz balances the film experience by soberly presenting the despairing side of the coin in the closing scenes. Some inmates could not be cheered even by art into gritting their teeth and continuing the fight for survival. Suicides were commonplace.

Vosz received the help of East German writer-director Günter Rücker in preparing the material. Erwin Geschonneck, too, is a veteran stage-and-screen actor in East Germany. Perhaps a fictional feature film will one day be made from this promising material — indeed, one suspects this is what Vosz would

have liked to accomplish.

Stylistic elements are a standout, particularly the classical music motifs. — *Holl.*

Alle Geister Kreisen
(A Gathering Of Spirits)
(WEST GERMAN-COLOR)

Munich, June 29.

A Juno Film Production, Munich, in collaboration with Westdeutscher Rundfunk (WDR), Cologne. Directed by Peter Przygodda. Features entire cast. Screenplay, Gerd Weiss, Alcides Lopes, Christoph Roth; camera (color), Martin Schäfer, Roth; editor, Przygodda; sound, Martin Müller; music, Irmin Schmidt. Reviewed at Munich Film Fest, July 29, 1985. Running time: **89 MINS.**

With: Gila von Weitershausen, Carlos Alberto Santana, Franz von Stauffenberg, Christopher Roth, Stefan Abendroth.

''A Gathering Of Spirits'' is a film about filmmaking, on how fiction-documentaries about exotic lands tend to get bogged down in the morass of preconceptions. Since filmmaker-editor Peter Przygodda knows Brazil very well, he put many of his own personal experiences into the film. At the same time, he potshots the ineptitude of German filmers who run off to Latin America to make quickie docus and features with preconceived notions on life styles, customs, and traditions. In this case, it's a femme filmer (Gila von Weitershausen), who's to make a film for German tv about the city of Salvador (formerly Bahia) in the Brazilian state of Bahia.

The director, however, doesn't have a script to speak of, can't handle the men in her crew, and ends up shooting most of the footage on the atmospheric pleasures of touristic Bahia. The crew doesn't take her seriously, nor do they seem to care much about the project. When everything seems to be going down the drain, she meets a native seer who tells her a legendary tale from the region and she hits upon an idea to try to finish the film.

The old man dies in the end, but his spirit has been passed on. The femme filmer is no longer as self-centered nor superficial in her thinking as before.

''A Gathering Of Spirits'' commits the same sins as discussed in the film within the film. Helmer Przygodda likes Brazil's captivating images (lensed by the talented Martin Schäfer) more than the narrative line and fails to sew plot and theme together into a filmic whole.

—*Holl.*

Tango Nashevo Detstvo
(Tango Of Our Childhood)
(SOVIET-COLOR)

Moscow, July 11.

An Armenfilm production. Written and directed by Albert Mkrchyan; camera (color)

Rudolf Vatinyan; art direction Rafael Babayan, Gagik Babayan; music, Tigran Mansuryan. Reviewed at Moscow Film Fest, July 11, 1985. Running time: **91 MINS.**

With: Galya Novents, Mger Mkrchyan.

''Tango'' is a curiosity, a family drama where tragedy and comedy jostle for the limelight.

The plot has an Armenian husband, Ruben, return home after the war only to leave his wife and three children and go to live with the wife's friend, a nurse who had saved his life during the war. The wife, Siranush, puts on a brave face and continues her role as Mrs. Fix-it, sorting out the whole town's problems except her own. Finally, she is left entirely alone.

This melancholy tale is interspersed with incidents of high farce — the constant traveling back and forth on a donkey cart of a massive, symbolic sideboard which neither woman will have in her house; the fact that the desperate husband, on one of these sideboard journeys, decides to get rid of it by throwing it under a train, which causes a derailment and lands him in jail for the rest of the film, leaving two ''widows'' to comfort each other.

The lead actors are likeable, especially the lugubrious Mger Mkrchyan, better known for his comedy roles. It's a bit wearing on the eardrums, as all characters find it necessary to shout at all times.

The decor and ambience of the immediate postwar period are impeccably rendered, as are the minor characters, tangoing around their courtyard at the drop of a hat.

— *Kits.*

Banoth
(Girls)
(ISRAELI-COLOR)

Tel Aviv, June 29.

A Nachshon Films presentation of a LA Films production. Produced by Nissim Levy and Harvey Edinoff. Directed by Nadav Levithan. Screenplay, Assi Dayan; camera (color), Marcello Mashyoki; editor, Nissim Mossek; music, Jaroslav Jocobowicz. Reviewed at the Studio Cinema, Tel Aviv, June 29, 1985. Running time: **96 MINS.**

With: Chana Azoulai, Anath Topol, Caroline Langford, Irith Frank, Heli Goldenberg, Orna Rothberg, Sigal Cohen, Rachel Hayimian, Ariela Rabinovitch, Amos Lavie, Doron Zipris, Meir Suissa, Irith Alter.

Seven girls, each representing a different social and ethnic group in Israel, are thrown together for their first training period in the army.

One girl has run away from her parents, who have gone to Canada to make money, and has come on her own to serve in the army. Another is on the verge of becoming a junkie before she is saved by the new life imposed on her. There's also the rich girl who snubs the rest, later learning the meaning of humility and friendship, and so on.

The plot has been concocted by

Assi Dayan, an actor and director in his own right who has limited his contribution here to scripting. There is a bit of nudity, some slapstick and plenty of soul searching, all of it tame. The ending, when the girls take their guns to save one of their own from an attempt on her virtue, is a flight of fancy that has nothing to do with the real army in Israel, but may well prove to be an audience pleaser.

Direction is undistinguished and acting is mostly on the amateurish side. Chana Azoulai is the one actress who seems confident in her part.

Mostly intended for summer audiences here, it has opened to good business and may find a receptive public in Jewish communities abroad. —*Edna.*

The Black Cauldron
(ANIMATED-COLOR-70M)

Painstaking animation aside, Disney effort simply lacks drama.

Hollywood, July 15.

A Buena Vista release from Walt Disney Pictures. A Walt Disney Prods. production, in association with Silver Screen Partners II. Executive producer, Ron Miller. Produced by Joe Hale. Directed by Ted Berman, Richard Rich. Story, David Jonas, Vance Gerry, Ted Berman, Richard Rich, Al Wilson, Roy Morita, Peter Young, Art Stevens, Joe Hale, based on "The Chronicles Of Prydain" series by Lloyd Alexander; additional dialog, Rosemary Anne Sisson, Roy Edward Disney; editor, James Melton, Kim Koford, Armetta Jackson; music, Elmer Bernstein; orchestrations, Peter Bernstein; camera (Technirama 70, Technicolor), various; production manager, Don Hahn; assistant directors, Mark Hester, Terry Noss, Randy Paton; sound effects design, Mike McDonough; sound supervisor (Dolby stereo), Bob Hathaway; special photographic effects, Philip Meador, Ron Osenbaugh, Bill Kilduff; prolog narrated by John Huston. Reviewed at Disney Studios, Burbank, Calif., July 12, 1985. (MPAA Rating: PG.) Running time: 80 MINS.

Animation Credits

Animators: Andreas Deja, Hendel Butoy, Dale Baer, Ron Husband, Jay Jackson, Barry Temple, Phil Nibbelink, Steve Gordon, Doug Krohn, Shawn Keller, Mike Gabriel, Phillip Young, Tom Ferriter, Jesse Cosio, Ruben Procopio, Viki Anderson, David Block, Charlie Downs, Sandra Borgmeyer, Ruben Aquino, Cyndee Whitney, George Scribner, Mark Henn, Terry Harrison, David Pacheco; key coordinating animator, Walt Stanchfield; layout, Don Griffith, Guy Vasilovich, Glenn Vilppu, Dan Hansen, William Frake 3d; layout styling, Mike Hodgson; color styling, James Coleman; background, Donald Towns, Brian Sebern, John Emerson, Tia Kratter, Lisa Keene, Andrew Phillipson; character design, Andreas Deja, Mike Ploog, Phil Nibbelink, Al Wilson, David Jonas; effects animators, Don Paul, Mark Dindal, Jeff Howard, Patricia Peraza, Scott Santoro, Glenn Chaika, Barry Cook, Ted Kierscey, Kelvin Yasuda, Bruce Woodside, Kimberley Knowlton, Allen Gonzales.

Character Voices

Grant Bardsley (Taran), Susan Sheridan (Eilonwy), Freddie Jones (Dallben), Nigel Hawthorne (Fflewddur), Arthur Malet (King Eidilleg), John Byner (Gurgi, Doli), John Hurt (Horned King), Lindsay Rich, Brandon Call, Gregory Levinson (Fairfolk), Eda Reiss Merin (Orddu), Adele Malis-Morey (Orwen), Billie Hayes (Orgoch), Phil Fondacaro (Creeper).

With five years in the imagination, another five at the inkwells and $25,000,000 spent over the decade, nobody can ever say Walt Disney Prods. did not take the time, trouble and expense to do right by "The Black Cauldron." But only the little kids can now say whether they succeeded.

Beyond an appreciation for Disney's unique animation craft, especially in the beautiful pastoral sequences where every little leaf has a movement all its own, elders lacking an innocent influence may never settle with themselves whether "Cauldron" matches their memory of other Disney classics.

And parents may argue too much whether this PG cartoon suffers from an excess of dark and menac-

ing overtones, perhaps forgetting that the old drawings could be pretty scary, too, but enjoyed a less censorious reception from the moral defenders of the day. Fear can be fun, even for the little ones who turn away from the screen to snuggle into mom's bosom.

But by any hard measure, "Cauldron" is not very original. And the characters, though cute and cuddly and sweet and mean and ugly and simply awful, don't really have much to do that would remain of interest to any but the youngest minds. For most of the 80 minutes, things just seem to *happen,* with only the most superficial interplay among the performers, which is fine for the eyeballs but not beyond.

Storyline is fairly stock sword-and-sorcery, with a band of likable youngsters, animals and creatures forced to tackle an evil mob of monsters to keep them from using a magic cauldron to raise an army of the dead. No need to guess who wins.

There is one amusing and original sequence which involves — now how can this be said delicately about a Disney picture — the big breasts of an amorous witch. Interestingly, this, too, would not seem unusual in any other picture, but for Disney it seems daring.

But, busy with the magic swords, bubbling pots and skeletal tyrants, the little kids probably won't get that excited about the witchly flesh at all. That's one of the nice things about being a little kid. —*Har.*

Cementerio Del Terror
(Cemetery Of Terror)
(MEXICAN-COLOR)

A Dynamic Films and Prods. Torrente S.A. presentation. Executive producer, Rodolfo Galindo. Produced by Raul Galindo. Written and directed by Ruben Galindo Jr. Features entire cast. Adaptation, Carlos Valdemar; camera (color), Rosalio Solano, Luis Besina; editor, Carlos Savage; music, Chucho Sarsoza; sound, Daniel Lopez; makeup artist, Ken Diaz; casting, Marta Oliver, Anabel Limon. Reviewed at Cine 1, N.Y., July 17, 1985. (No MPAA Rating.) Running time: 88 MINS.

With: Hugo Stiglitz (Dr. Cardan), Usi Velasco, Erika Buenfil, Edna Bolkan, Maria Rebeca, Eduardo Capetillo, Cesar Velasco, Servando Manzetti, Andres Garcia Jr., Rene Cardona 3d, Jacqueline Castro.

"Cemetery Of Terror" is an okay Mexican horror picture, made last year and currently playing the U.S. Spanish-language theater circuit.

Quite easy to follow without any English translation, Texas-set story concerns a mad Dr. Cardan (Hugo Stiglitz), plagued by nightmares of zombie attacks, who forges (in English) a court order to release a corpse from the morgue to his custody. Unlike the local pragmatic police captain, Cardan is a believer in Satan who is convinced the corpse is

one of the undead about to wreak havoc.

It is Halloween and by a strained coincidence, three teenage couples out on a date at a spooky mansion next to a cemetery find a Black Book of satanic rituals. They need a corpse to carry out a Black Mass (with the book's aid) in the cemetery and, as a prank, head to the morgue and steal the same corpse Dr. Cardan is seeking.

The ritual proves effective, bringing the corpse back to life, whereupon the zombie kills all six teens, accompanied by gore effects. Better makeup work is used on dozens of other varied zombies who subsequently rise from their nearby graves. Several children, including the police captain's kids, visit the cemetery and are barely saved from a horrible fate by the lameduck arrival of Dr. Cardan. Fortunately for them, Cardan is played by Mexican star Hugo Stiglitz (who previously batled atomic zombies in 1980's "City Of The Walking Dead") and he comes up with a new and temporarily effective method of fighting the undead by simply punching them on the nose. Ultimately, the zombies are destroyed by burning when the kids toss the Black Book in a fireplace.

Picture provides good atmosphere and some solid scares, with its oddest element (common to some other Mexican films) being the Texas setting where all signs and visuals are written in English but *everybody* speaks Spanish. Cast is adequate, featuring some new generation talent such as Andres Garcia Jr. (the spitting image of his star father) and Rene Cardona 3d, whose dad and grandfather have directed dozens of action pictures over the years.
—*Lor.*

The Assam Garden
(BRITISH-COLOR)

London, July 15.

A Moving Picture Co. production. Produced by Nigel Stafford-Clark. Directed by Mary McMurray. Screenplay, Elisabeth Bond. Stars Deborah Kerr, Madhur Jaffrey. Camera (color), Bryan Loftus; editor, Rodney Holland; music, Richard Harvey; art direction, Jan Martin; costumes, Cathy Cook; sound, Tony Jackson. Reviewed at the Academy One Cinema, London, July 14, 1985. (BBFC certificate: U.) Running time: 92 MINS.

Helen . . . . Deborah Kerr
Ruxmani . . . . Madhur Jaffrey
Mr. Philpott . . . . Alec McCowen
Mr. Lal . . . . Zia Mohyeddin
Mr. Sutton . . . . Anton Lesser
Arthur . . . . Iain Cuthbertson
Sushi . . . . Tara Shaw
Raju . . . . Dev Sagoo

The British experience in India comes back home in "The Assam Garden," a lowkey entry about an old woman embittered by a loveless marriage passed mostly in the former colony, where her husband worked on a tea plantation.

The film opens with Helen (Deborah Kerr) coming back from her husband's funeral in England. She is preoccupied with the garden surrounding her country home. It's an imitation of those that flourish on the Indian subcontinent and ironically symbolizes her childless marriage. Helen hates the flora and fauna but feels she must realize her husband's ambition to have the place registered in the "Best English Gardens" handbook.

Kerr is fine as the edgy and neurotic old lady, whose bitterness has become a form of madness. She discovers some serenity in an initially difficult friendship with Indian neighbor Ruxmani, played by Madhur Jaffrey. At the film's end Ruxmani leaves for the homeland with her sickly husband and Helen's initial desperation returns.

Elisabeth Bond's scripting is sensitive to the nuances of the evolving relationship between the two women. However, the screenplay should have been pruned of some scenes that do not advance the action or argument.

The film also is spoiled by Mary McMurray's direction in her debut feature. Random camera movements are often poorly motivated and compositions are frequently artless. Apart from the performances by Kerr, Jaffrey and Zia Mohyeddin, acting is poor.

Technical credits are so-so, especially the editing. Although there's a pleasant string score laid over shots of the luxuriant garden, sound is otherwise all clattering teacups and heavy footfalls. — *Japa.*

Skalpel, Prosim
(Scalpel, Please)
(CZECHOSLOVAKIAN-COLOR)

Moscow, July 5.

A Ceskoslovensky Film release. Produced by Barrandov Film Studio. Directed by Jiri Svoboda. Stars Miroslav Machacek. Screenplay, Jiri Svoboda, based on a novel by Valia Styblova; camera (color), Vladimir Smutny; art director, Jaromir Svarc; music, Jozef Revallo. Reviewed at the Moscow Film Festival, July 5, 1985. Running time: 110 MINS.

The professor . . . . Miroslav Machacek
Jitka . . . . Jane Brejchova
Prof. Krtek . . . . Radoslav Brzobohaty
Ruml . . . . Frantisek Rehak

Though its title may lead one to expect a wacky hospital comedy, "Scalpel, Please" is a dead-serious soap opera with a glossy look that could have come out of any studio in the world. It happens to have been made in Czechoslovakia by Jiri Svoboda. This endless succession of tragedies and miracles, life and death in a big-city surgical ward has the compulsive watchability of daytime drama and is equally routine. With nothing in the picture to pin it to a particular time or place, "Scalpel" is a prime candidate for retitling, dubbing and sales on world markets.

The professor (Miroslav Machacek) is an overworked neurosurgeon who sees life in all its variety come trailing through his office. An old friend is brought in suffering from a tumor, reminding the doctor of a rough time in his own past. Tests show an apparently healthy young woman is dying of leukemia. A cute little tyke with a brain tumor has almost no chance of surviving whether he is operated on or not, but his grandfather (a woodcutter) convinces the doctor to go ahead with surgery. A series of dramatic circumstances prevent him from carrying out the operation, but another doctor whose daughter has just died recovers from a nervous breakdown just in time to save the day.

Svoboda has his film technique down pat and "Scalpel" has an anonymous pro look. Story is well paced and thesps are adequate for their roles.— *Yung.*

Robieta W Kopeluszy
(Woman In A Hat)
(POLISH-COLOR)

Moscow, July 5.
A Polish Corp. for Film Prod. "Zespoly Filmowe" film. Written and directed by Stanislaw Rosewicz. Stars Hanna Mikuc. Camera (color), Jerzy Wojcik; art director, Halina Dobrowolska; editor, Urszula Sliwinska; music, Jerzy Satanowski. Reviewed at the Moscow Film Festival, July 2, 1985. Running time: **105 MINS.**
Eve . . . . .Hanna Mikuc
Also with: Henryk Machalica, Wieslawa Mazurkiewicz; Magda Wallejko; Marek Kondrat.

Stanislaw Rosewicz, a helmer with several well-received films, has fashioned a subtly intriguing portrait of a young Polish actress in "Woman In A Hat." Everything that happens in the story is filtered through the consciousness of Eve (Hanna Mikuc), who is seeking her way in life. Well shot, structured and paced, pic is earmarked for further fest play and deserves art house pickups beyond its frontiers.

.The theater stage is presented both concretely as the workplace of Eve and her friends and as a metaphor and reflection on life and its value. As the film opens, Eve is bread-and-buttering it as a mechanical dancer in a play called "Dance Of The Marionette." In a red wig, heavy makeup and 1920s garb, she is the diametric opposite of the rather plain girl who lives on her own, visits a famous old actress to talk about the theater and pays courtesy calls on a poor neighbor.

Much of the film's fascination lies in the believable, multi-sided character Mikuc gradually builds up. She fights with her overly sophisticated, artificial mother, but can't accept the truth about her beloved father, who died an alcoholic. Her obsession with the stage seems genuine, yet she claims she could give it up without regret. At the same time, she'd rather read "King Lear" and dream of playing Cordelia than see her boring boyfriend. She seems to have landed the part she wants in a production by a fashionable young director, but at the last minute he changes his mind and hands the role to a rival. Eve is left as the "real" Cordelia, enacting the play in her imagination.

Besides the oft-repeated dance of the marionettes, showing the actors' complete dehumanization and reduction to store-front dummies, film's central metaphor is the ridiculous hat Eve is told to wear for a brief part in a film. The director angrily refuses to discuss the role with her, because for him she is just "a woman in a hat." — *Yung.*

The Man With One Red Shoe
(COLOR)

Flat adaptation has slim b.o. chances.

Hollywood, July 18.
A 20th Century Fox release. Produced by Victor Drai. Directed by Stan Dragoti. Stars Tom Hanks, Dabney Coleman, Lori Singer, Charles Durning. Screenplay, Robert Klane, based on the film "The Tall Blond Man With One Black Shoe" written by Francis Veber and Yves Robert; camera (Deluxe color), Richard H. Kline; editors, Bud Molin, O. Nicholas Brown; sound, Willis D. Burton; production design, Dean E. Mitzner; associate producers, Jack Sanders, Bill Wilson, Xavier Gelin; assistant director, William Beasley; music, Thomas Newman; casting, Dianne Crittenden. Reviewed at 20th Century Fox Studios, L.A., July 16, 1985. (MPAA Rating: PG.) Running time: **93 MINS.**
Richard . . . . .Tom Hanks
Cooper . . . . .Dabney Coleman
Maddy . . . . .Lori Singer
Ross . . . . .Charles Durning
Paula .Carrie Fisher
Brown . . . . .Edward Herrmann
Morris .Jim Belushi
Virdon . . . . .Irving Metzman
Reese . . . . : . . . . .Tom Noonan
Carson . . . . .Gerrit Graham
Stemple . . . . .David L. Lander
Hulse .Ritch Brinkley
Edgar . . . . .Frank Hamilton

Except for stretches of rather amusing pointlessness, "The Man With One Red Shoe" doesn't look to be much of a summer comedy entry. No matter the color, the shoe has no boxoffice leg to fit.

Pic sports a good cast but Charles Durning and Carrie Fisher have little to do, leaving Tom Hanks, Dabney Coleman and Lori Singer to wrestle with a flat adaptation of the French hit "The Tall Blond Man With One Black Shoe."

Of that trio, Coleman comes off best as a foul plotting CIA chief, but good as he is, Coleman is beginning to be overused as exactly the same type all the time. Hanks is okay at his ill-defined duties, while Singer is certainly pretty enough.

Point of it all is a struggle for control of the spy agency between Coleman and Durning, who has picked Hanks at random as an innocent foil. Singer is a Coleman aide who finds herself, beyond belief, romantically attracted to Hanks, a boring violinist who bicycles.

There is some fun in all the "Get Smart" variations of absurd espionage technology, plus thrown-in confusion from Hanks' adulterous affair with Fisher, married to Jim Belushi, none of it funny enough to overcome the damage to Hanks' likability.

There are also a few good lines and a couple of able action sequences, but director Stan Dragoti never pulls the pic together tightly, leaving a particularly long void in the midsection. Thomas Newman's score is interesting. —*Har.*

Unfinished Business
(AUSTRALIAN-COLOR)

Sydney, July 15.
An Unfinished Business production. Produced by Rebel Penfold-Russell. Executive producer, Andrena Finlay. Associate producer, Patric Juillet. Written and directed by Bob Ellis. Stars John Clayton, Michele Fawdon. Camera (Eastmancolor), Andrew Lesnie; editor, Amanda Robson; production design, Jane Johnston; sound, Gerry Nulifora; production manager, June Henman; assistant director, Jake Atkinson. Reviewed at Chauvel theater, Paddington, N.S.W., July 15, 1985. Running time: **78 MINS.**
Geoff .John Clayton
Maureen . . . . .Michele Fawdon
George . . . . .Norman Kaye
Geoff's flatmate . . . . .Bob Ellis
Telegraph boy . . . . .Andrew Lesnie

For middle-aged audiences, "Unfiished Business" should have an appeal out of all proportion to its modest budget and brief running time. It marks the first job of directing for Bob Ellis, a film critic and co-screenwriter of such distinguished films as "Newsfront," "Goodbye Paradise," "Man Of Flowers" and "My First Wife."

Geoff (John Clayton), a journalist in his mid-40s who's just returned to Australia after 15 years abroad, leaving behind him in the U.S. a failed marriage and three children he misses, accidentally meets Maureen (Michele Fawdon), the girl he was in love with before he went overseas. She's now married to an older man (Norman Kaye) she loves, but they're childless. The meeting reawakens old feelings for both, and Geoff always has wondered why Maureen never joined him in London, as they'd originally arranged. There's obviously still an attraction between them, and it's not long before Maureen is proposing that Geoff try to impregnate her, since she's positive her childlessness is due to her husband's lack of fertility, not her's.

Bulk of the film is set in a beautifully situated house by the sea north of Sydney where the couple go, as Geoff puts it, to "engender a potential taxpayer." At first, Maureen won't allow sex unless her temperature is right, and the increasingly frustrated Geoff begins to find the arrangement less alluring than he'd expected. Later, love blossoms, but the film's ending — an epilog which takes place a year later — is decidedly bittersweet.

"Unfinished Business" is a witty, humane and surprisingly erotic film, confidently directed, beautifully acted and evocatively photographed. It won't appeal to young audiences much, but for older folks its honesty allied to its humor will come as a breath of fresh air. The music, mainly consisting of the old standard "I'll Walk Beside You," as well as Norman Kaye's (offscreen) piano rendition of Sigmund Romberg's "When I Grow Too Old To Dream," is apt. —*Strat.*

Zwischen Den Zeiten
(Between The Times)
(WEST GERMAN-DOCU-COLOR-16m)

Berlin, July 12.
A coproduction of Andreas Oberbach and Hubertus Siegert with the Senator for Urban Planning and Environment, supported by the Audio-Visual Center of the Free University Berlin. Directed by Oberbach and Siegert. Camera (color) and editor, Rainer Meissle; technical advice, Ingo Kowarik; music, Astor Piazzolla, Ludvik Mann; narration, Britta Sommer, Erwin Schastok. Reviewed at the Media Coop, Berlin, July 9, 1985. Running time: **62 MINS.**

Andrea Oberbach and Hubertus Siegert's "Between The Times" is a fascinating educational docu about the railroad tracks leading up to the former Anhalter Bahnhof in Berlin, where in 1939 an average of 111 trains arrived and departed daily. With the end of World War II, the tracks were practically abandoned — and thus a natural landscape of plants, and shrubs and trees sprang into existence over the past 40 years.

"Between The Times" shows how this landscape came about. Oberbach and Siegert went to the socalled "Gleisdreieck" to capture its oasis-like atmosphere and the results are both esthetically pleasing and educationally rewarding.

Pic illustrates from the outset that the Gleisdreieck as it now stands is a circumstance evolving from the political and economic changes at the end of the war. The Anhalter Bahnhof in West Berlin lay in ruins, while the East Berlin officials rerouted traffic to their part of the divided city. Further, the control over the railway sysem in both Berlins fell under East German control — until 1980, when this control was passed over to West

Berlin as the result of an agreement.

Shortly, this area is to be turned into a sprawling traffic museum. The city-jungle as it now stands "between the times," however, will be fortunately left pretty much as it is. —*Holl.*

Jours De Tourmentes
(Days Of Torment)
(BURKINA FASO-COLOR)

Moscow, July 5.

Produced by the Film Direction of Burkina Faso. Written and directed by Paul Zoumbara. Stars Yacine Tall, Sotigui Kouyate. Camera (Color), Sékou Ouédraogo; editor, Andrée Davanture; original music, Sotigui Kouyate. Reviewed at the Moscow Film Festival, July 4, 1985. Running time: **120 MINS.**

Pierre .... Yacine Tall
Boukary .... Sotigui Kouyate
Maria .... Salimata Samake
Seydou .... Lassina Yinace
Jules .... Kassoum Simplice Sama

One of the first features to come out of Burkina Faso (formerly Upper Volta), "Jours De Tourmentes" has the simple, unpretentious appeal of an insider's documentary on life today in rural West Africa. The tale about a modern young man struggling against the prejudices of his native village unfolds without hurry, at the same leisurely pace as village life. While too slow and uneventful for commercial purposes, "Jours" has been making the rounds of African and European festivals.

Picture marks the feature debut of documentarist Paul Zoumbara. Steering clear of complicated narrative, he lets the story glide along through a series of encounters. Pierre (Yacine Tall), a strong-minded boy of 20, is determined to better his social and financial condition by making use of modern farming techniques. This praiseworthy ambition is opposed by the village chief, the local merchant Boukary (Sotigui Kouyate) and his father Seydou (Lassina Yinace), who see in it a challenge to their authority. Things explode when Pierre and his friends form an association to collect money for a new well. In the end, common sense wins out, the villains are justly punished and Pierre plants his field in his own way, with the aid of girl friend Maria (Salimata Samake).

Cast is full of expressive faces and characters are individualized well. Sotigui Kouyate, a well-known actor and musician, is comically villainous as the tall scarecrow Boukary, who spends his days behind a card table lending money, shooing flies off his cigarets and hatching plots. Most expressive of all is the parched, sun-baked land and its typical scenes of village life: women squatting over their cooking, men planting the fields and an assembly where the conduct of members of

---

the village is discussed. A gentle musical theme runs pleasantly through the picture.— *Yung.*

Bao Gio Cho Toi
Thang Muoi
(October Won't Return)
(VIETNAMESE-B&W)

Moscow, July 5.

A Vietnam Feature Film Studios production. Written and directed by Dang What Minh. Features entire cast. Camera (b&w), Nguyen Hanh Lah. (Only credits available). Reviewed at the Moscow Film Festival, July 3, 1985. Running time: **90 MINS.**

With: Nguyen Huu Muoi, Le Van, Minh Vuong, Lai Phu Cuong.

A lyrical black-and-white feature from Vietnam, "October Won't Return" is an appealing mixture of romance, lost love and ghosts with a contemporary setting. Though definitely on the sentimental side, the film can boast astute use of a beautiful heroine, an effective story line and expressive camerawork.

Sven is a young bride whose husband, a soldier sent to the Cambodian frontier a year ago, has been killed in action. The family is never informed of his death, and Sven only finds out when she goes to visit him. On her return, she decides to keep the news a secret out of respect for the boy's father, who is old and sick. It proves a difficult burden to shoulder.

Sven's only confidante is Han, a young teacher she met on the boat trip who rescued her when she fainted and fell in the river. She persuades him to write her letters in her dead husband's handwriting to keep up the pretense he is alive. When it all comes out there is a scandal, but not before the old father can die a peaceful death. Han, who has fallen deeply in love with the inconsolable widow, decides to leave the village.

Thesping is restrained and understated, in contrast to an openly romantic soundtrack that risks overwhelming the film. The most moving sequence involves Sven's encounter with her husband's gentle, melancholy ghost, who urges her to go on living. Always present in the background is the war, an unsettling note that pervades the romantic story and gives pic some much-needed topicality. — *Yung.*

Legenda Suramskoi Kreposti
(The Legend of Suram Fortress)
(SOVIET-COLOR)

Moscow, July 8.

A Gruziafilm production. Directed by Dodo Abashidze, Sergei Paradjanov. Features Levan Uchaneishvili, Zurab Kipshidze, Lela Alibegashvili, Dodo Abashidze, Veriko Andzhaparidze, Sofiko Chiaureli. Screenplay, Vazha Ghigashvili; camera (color), Yuri Klimenko; music, Dzhansug Kakhidze.

Reviewed at the Moscow Film Festival, July 8, 1985. Running time: **76 MINS.**

"The Legend Of Suram Fortress" is the first film in 15 years from persecuted directed Sergei Paradjanov, codirected by Dodo Abashidze. Pic is a magnificent paean to Paradjanov's native Georgia which will consolidate his arthouse reputation gained for Sayat Nova" (The Color Of Pomegranates) and "Memories Of Forgotten Ancestors."

The plot is based on a legend about repeated efforts by the Georgian people to construct a fortress against invaders. The building keeps on collapsing until a fortune teller remembers an old prophecy that the son of her erstwhile lover must be bricked up alive in order for the fortress to stand. The young man sacrifices himself to save his country.

The simple story is told in an allusive, and sometimes baffling, manner. Of no help at the Moscow viewing was a 10-minute deletion early in the film.

However, the painterly images of sailing ships suspended in mid-air over an arid plain or a child changed to a sheep on the sacrificial block are truly breathtaking. Yuri Klimenko's photography is tricky in places but stylish everywhere. The costumes, some of which were borrowed from museums, are especially sumptuous. ,— *Kits.*

The Legend Of Billie Jean
(COLOR)

Tame tale of kids on the run.

Hollywood, July 18.

A Tri-Star Pictures release, from Tri-Star/Delphi III Prods. Produced by Rob Cohen. Executive producers, Jon Peters, Peter Guber. Directed by Matthew Robbins. Stars Helen Slater, Keith Gordon. Screenplay, Mark Rosenthal, Lawrence Konner, camera (Metrocolor), Jeffrey L. Kimball; editor, Cynthia Scheider; music, Craig Safan; production designer, Ted Haworth; set designer, William Durrell; set decorator, Robert Christopher Westlund; sound (Dolby), Charles M. Wilborn; costumes, Donna Linson; coproducer, Lawrence Konner, Mark Rosenthal; assistant director, Tom Mack; second unit director, Rob Cohen; stunt coordinator, Bobby Bass; associate producer, Lori Weintraub; casting, Paula Herold. Reviewed at MGM/UA screening room, Culver City, Calif., July 17, 1985. (MPAA Rating: PG-13). Running time: **96 MINS.**

Billie Jean .... Helen Slater
Lloyd .... Keith Gordon
Binx................. .:.... Christian Slater
Pyatt .... Richard Bradford
Ringwald....... .... Peter Coyote
Ophelia .... Martha Gehman
Putter .... Yeardley Smith
Lloyd's Father .... Dean Stockwell

There is the germ of an idea in "The Legend Of Billie Jean," but hardly a reason for a film. Producers must have envisioned a groundswell of young teens responding to the kid lib theme, but this

---

"Legend" is strictly in their own minds. Despite a good turn by Helen Slater in the title role, pic is really too tame to attract much attention.

Premise is kind of a "Bonnie And Clyde" for kids in which Billie Jean and her gang become outlaws and media heroes by accident. Action, however, is forced, without much personality or dramatic impact.

Part of the problem here is the scale the film was conceived on. For the arch villain, writers Mark Rosenthal and Lawrence Konner have concocted a redneck would-be rapist (Richard Bradford) who is really too petty to take seriously, malevolent though he is.

The inciting incident, too, is a bit of a yawner with Billie Jean's kid brother's motorscooter being trashed by a couple of local rowdies in retaliation for the cold shoulder from Billie Jean. Accidental shooting by the brother (Christian Slater, no relation to Helen) forces them on the lam with friends Yeardley Smith, a pesty whiner given to eating junk food, and the more level-headed Martha Gehman in tow.

Rallying cry for the gang is "fair is fair" (film's original title), plea from Billie Jean for $600 to fix the scooter. Thrown in for good measure is a kidnapping subplot allowing Keith Gordon to become a temporary boyfriend for Billie Jean.

Set up as kind of a martyr and victim at the hands of the mean old adults and inept policeman (Peter Coyote), Billie Jean shaves her hair Joan of Arc style and becomes the new pop savior while the local radio station becomes the oracle. Billie Jean even performs a miracle of sorts by evading the police while kids have no trouble finding her.

Lensed on the Gulf Coast in Corpus Christi, Texas, photography by Jeffrey Kimball manages to suggest the sticky, humid heat of the region. Within the frames, director Matthew Robbins fails to create situations as realistic.—*Jagr.*

The Heavenly Kid
(COLOR)

Weak, derivative supernatural comedy.

Hollywood, July 19.

An Orion Pictures release. Produced by Mort Engelberg. Executive producer, Gabe Sumner, Stephen G. Cheikes. Directed by Cary Medoway. Features entire cast. Screenplay, Medoway, Martin Copeland; Camera (Deluxe color), Steven Poster; editor, Christopher Greenbury; music, Kennard Ramsey; production designer, Ron Hobbs; set decorator, Nicholas Romanac; special visual effects, Louis Schwartzberg; costumer, Mary Lou Byrd; sound, Howard Warren; assistant director, David Whorf; casting, Nancy Foy. Reviewed at UA Coronet Theater, Westwood Village, Calif., July 19, 1985. (MPAA Rating: PG-13.) Running time: **89 MINS.**

Bobby .... Lewis Smith

Lenny	Jason Gedrick
Emily	Jane Kaczmarek
Rafferty	Richard Mulligan
Joe	Mark Metcalf
Bill	Beau Dremann
Fred	Stephen Gregory
Melissa	Nancy Valen
Sharon	Anne Sawyer

Aiming for that special space where filmgoers suspend their disbelief, "The Heavenly Kid" succeeds only in creating a bit of false magic. Borrowing bits and pieces from other films, it seems that only the clichés were kept while the fantasy of a time traveling angel remains leaden and earthbound. With so much supernatural fare to choose from, it is unlikely young filmgoers will find their way to this heaven.

Among the ploys attempted, the idea of an older sensibility set loose in the present day was done more effectively in "Time After Time" and even this summer in "Back To The Future." The idea of an angel coming to help a mortal was more appealing in "Heaven Can Wait" and infinitely more touching in "It's A Wonderful Life."

Director Cary Medoway who wrote the script with Martin Copeland treats the material too literally to let it float.

Action opens with a "Rebel Without A Cause"-like drag race on the edge of a cliff. Bobby Fontana (Lewis Smith) doesn't make it and next stop is the Twilight Zone. Nice touch by production designer Ron Hobbs renders after-life as a sleek silver mass transit system. Bobby, unfortunately, is unable to go uptown until he proves himself worthy.

Sent back to earth to help the fate of a hopeless loser, Bobby approaches the problem with an early '60s style which still makes an impression today. His mission is to endow young Lenny (Jason Gedrick) with some style and confidence so he too can succeed with girls without really trying.

Results are predictable with Lenny becoming a callous cad but later reverting to a nice guy. Even the plot twists that have Bobby turning up at his old girlfriend's house and a surprising discovery about Lenny seem more contrived than felt.

Smith and Gedrick as angel and friend are basically likable with good performances but the crucial points of connection which would make their relationship special are not supplied in the script.

For humor the film relies on some stale marijuana jokes and a visit to a gay leather bar. Visually, sight gags recycle some "Topper"-like effects with a riderless car and bicycle powered by the invisible angel. Other heavenly special effects are equally chintzy.

Production values are borderline with too many static close-ups and editing not speeding things along very well. —*Jagr.*

Pee-wee's Big Adventure
(COLOR)

Charming vehicle for Reubens' creation should please all ages.

Hollywood, July 25.

Warner Bros. release of an Aspen Film Society/Robert Shapiro Prod. Produced by Shapiro, Richard Gilbert Abramson. Directed by Tim Burton. Stars Paul Reubens. Executive producer, William E. McEuen. Screenplay, Phil Hartman, Reubens, Michael Varhol; camera (Technicolor), Victor J. Kemper; production designer, David L. Snyder; editor, Billy Weber; music, Danny Elfman; sound, Peter Hliddal; set designer, James E. Tocci; assistant director, Robert P. Cohen; casting, Wally Nicita. Reviewed at The Burbank Studios, Burbank, Calif., July 24, 1985. (MPAA Rating: PG.) Running time: **90 MINS.**

Pee-wee Herman	Paul Reubens
Dottie	Elizabeth Daily
Francis	Mark Holton
Simone	Diane Salinger
Mickey	Judd Omen
Andy	Jon Harris
Hobo Jack	Carmen Filpi
Terry Hawthorne	Tony Bill
James Brolin	Himself
Morgan Fairchild	Herself

Looney and beguiling opening sequence sets a standard that the rest of "Pee-wee's Big Adventure" can't sustain, but the freshness of comedian Paul Reubens' unique characterization already has disarmed audiences in five regional sites and promises to deliver impressive numbers when Warner Bros. goes wide nationally Aug. 9.

Coproduced by former WB production chief Robert Shapiro and directed by 26-year-old Tim Burton (making the jump to theatricals after a to-date unreleased short, "Frankenweenie," for Walt Disney Prods.), picture is a silly surprise: a performance by an adult who acts like a five-year-old kid.

Children should love the film and adults will be dismayed by the light brushstrokes with which Reubens (one of three credited screenwriters, but star-billed under his stage name, Pee-wee Herman) suggests touches of Buster Keaton and Eddie Cantor.

The lingering question about Reubens' Pee-wee, as this film demonstrates, is the durability of the character over the long haul. Opening 10 minutes of comedy is wonderful introduction to a new film comic. Pee-wee wakes up in a children's bedroom full of incredible toys, slides down a fire station-like brass pole, materializing in his trademark tight suit with white shoes and red bow-tie, proceeds to make a breakfast à la a Rube Goldberg creation, and winds up in a front yard that looks like a children's farm.

It's a delicious bit, with Reubens making noises like a child, walking something like Chaplin, and remarkably drawing for adult viewers the joys and frustrations of being a kid.

Rest of narrative deals with Pee-wee's unstoppable pursuit of his prized lost bicycle, a rambling kidvid-like spoof that includes encounters with a mooney waitress (Diane Salinger), an escaped felon (Judd Omen), a boxcar bum (Carmen Filpi), a fatty rich kid neighbor (Mark Holton), an actual sweetheart (Elizabeth Daily, but, of course, Pee-wee will have none of her), and a wacky ride on his juicy red bike through countless film productions-in-progress on the Warners lot.

There is a nice bicycle-in-the-air homage to "E.T.," and composer Danny Elfman's Felliniesque score contributes the aural illusion of a circus.

Film drags when Pee-wee has to talk too much (a scene in which he harangues a room of listeners to find his bike is jarringly out of sync with character), and the early charm of the material is not sustained. On balance, the achievement is uneven but fetching.

Project initially was at Paramount Pictures, where Reubens, fresh out of a Pee-wee Herman show at the Roxy nitery in Hollywood, signed to make his screen debut in December 1981. He originally came out of L.A. Equity Waiver Theater, with the Groundling Theater group. He's also been seen on tv shows (notably "Late Night With David Letterman"), but majority of film audiences will be caught off guard. —*Loyn.*

National Lampoon's European Vacation
(COLOR)

Uneven sequel not likely to equal predecessor's success.

Hollywood, July 27.

A Warner Bros. release. Produced by Matty Simmons. Directed by Amy Heckerling. Screenplay, John Hughes and Robert Klane; camera (Technicolor) Bob Paynter; editor, Pembroke Herring; music, Charles Fox; production design, Bob Cartwright; coproducer, Stuart Cornfeld; costume design, Graham Williams; sound, Tony Dawe; assistant director, Don French. Reviewed at The Burbank Studios, Burbank, Calif., July 26, 1985. (MPAA Rating: PG-13.) Running time: **94 MINS.**

Clark W. Griswald	Chevy Chase
Ellen Griswald	Beverly D'Angelo
Rusty Griswald	Jason Lively
Audrey Griswald	Dana Hill
Bike rider	Eric Idle
The Thief	Victor Lanoux

Most imaginative stroke is the passport-stamped credit sequence that opens this Warner Bros.' sequel to its popular "National Lampoon's Vacation" (1983 and $30,-300,000 in domestic rentals). Story of a frenetic, chaotic tour of the Old World, with Chevy Chase and Beverly D'Angelo reprising their role as determined vacationers, is graceless and only intermittently lit up by lunacy and satire. Boxoffice outlook is weak.

As the family of characters cartwheel through London, Paris, Italy and Germany — with the French deliciously taking it on the chin for their arrogance and rudeness — director Amy Heckerling gets carried away with physical humor while letting her American tourists grow tiresome and predictable. Structurally, the film unfolds like a series of travel brochures.

Uneven screenplay by John Hughes and Robert Klane never sails, and it's left to Chase to fire up the film. His character is actually rather sympathetic — if boorish — in his insistence on turning every Continental moment into a delight (scanning Paris, he shouts "I want to write, I want to paint, I got a romantic urge!"), and there's an inspired bit of business when Chase does a "Sound Of Music"-Julie Andrews takeoff on a German mountaintop.

As the head of the middle class Yank clan which wins a trip to Europe on a quiz show (including harried wife D'Angelo and kids Jason Lively and Dana Hill), Chase lacks the material of his last two hits ("National Lampoon's Vacation" and the current-running "Fletch").

A scene in a train compartment, in which none of the family can bear the sight of one another, rings with strong identity, and Chase and company quietly register laughs when they spend an evening with a dumbfounded village couple whom they mistake as their German relatives.

Other scenes are crude (quiz show emcee John Astin planting youngster Hill with an endless and lascivious kiss in her piggie costume is particularly tasteless) or even technically rough (the lip-sync for a torrid song by towel-clad D'Angelo).

The whiny and spoiled kids, chiefly daughter Hill in a thankless and highly callow performance, are hard to put up with. Overall, a pretty tacky production, with an ending that is surprisingly banal as the family returns to America. Included in the end-credit sequence of images of life in good ol' America, believe it or not, are pictures of Clint Eastwood from "Pale Rider"and Christopher Reeve as "Superman." Guess which studio made those films?.—*Loyn.*

Harakteristika
(Reference)
(BULGARIAN-COLOR)

Moscow, July 6.
Directed by Hristo Hristov. Screenplay, Alexander Tomov, from his novel; camera (color), Atanas Tassev; music, Victor Chouchkov; art direction, Yordanka Peicheva. Re-

viewed at Moscow Film Festival, July 6, 1985. Running time: **96 MINS.**
With: Ivailo Geraskov (Paliev), Atanas Atanassov (Itseto), Itzhak Fintsi (Penchev), Georgi Kaloyanchev (Bai Louko), Vassil Mihailov (Kroushev), Lilyana Kovacheva (Black Mary), Zhoreta Nikolova (Lilyana), Plamen Sirakov (Petsata).

Hristo Hristov's "Reference" is a low-key but compelling study of the quandary of a man faced with corruption at every turn. Does he continue his one-man struggle or simply give in?

Paliev is a driver who, as party secretary and foreman of his team, is asked to give a reference for a colleague. In all conscience Paliev feels he cannot recommend the corrupt Itseto. Pressure is brought to bear at every point: bribes are offered, housing priority lists tampered with and even, finally, medicine for his sick child withheld. Another colleague joins Paliev's cause, then betrays him, but finally the case is won and all his fellow workers proclaim their solidarity with the decision.

The moral message is by no means as cut and dried as it sounds. In maintaining his principles, Paliev manages to alienate a good friend and he risks his child's life which leads his wife, at the end of her tether, to leave him. The film finishes on a freeze-frame, seemingly *de rigeur* in Eastern Europe these days, indicating the ambivalence of the film's conclusion.—*Kits.*

Shovrim
(Breaking)
(ISRAELI-COLOR)

Tel Aviv, July 8.
A Gelfand Films presentation of an Avi Nesher-Itzhak Tzhayek production. Produced by Nesher, Tzhayek. Written and directed by Nesher. Camera (color), Jorge Gurevitch, Benny Carmeli; editor, Tzhayek; art director, Shlomo Tzafrir; costumes, Bilha Heiman; music; Izhar Ashdoth; "Shafshaf's Song" written and performed by Meir Banai. Reviewed at the Cannon screening room, July 8, 1985. Running time: **95 MINS.**
With: Izhar Ashdoth, Gali Atari, Nathan Datner, Si Heiman, Eyal Geffen, Yair Nitzani, Alona Kimchi, Omra Menkes, Meir Suissa, Moshe Ihs-Kassit, Arik Sinai, Dudu Dotan.

Clumsy is the only way to describe "Breaking," a sad attempt to use the film-within-a-film formula for quick commercial profit. Avi Nesher concocted a story about a production company shooting a Biblical musical about David and Goliath and getting into trouble when the stars fight for control. The whole thing is peppered with pop songs produced by Izhar Ashdoth, a founder of a successful, but defunct pop group, Tislam, which also performs many of them on camera. His Tislam partner, Yair Nitzani, is also in the film, with a non-singing part.

The trouble is that the quickie na-

ture of the whole venture is obvious from the very first moment. Acting is amateurish at best, plot is unbelievable, sets, costumes and choreography are poor, and not even a babe in arms will believe nowadays that films are made in the manner shown here, by people of such total incompetence and lack of professional knowhow.

It is surprising that Nesher, who has directed four full features before this one, would let such a product out of his hands, the only possible explanation being that he was poking fun at local film production.
— *Edna.*

Fright Night
(COLOR)

Vampire thriller is the genuine article.

Hollywood, July 21.
A Columbia Pictures release. Produced by Herb Jaffe. Written and directed by Tom Holland. Camera (Metrocolor), Jan Kiesser; editor, Kent Beyda; sound, Don Rush; production design, John De Cuir Jr.; associate producer, Jerry A. Baerwitz; assistant director, Gerald Sobul; visual effects, Richard Edlund; music, Brad Fiedel; casting, Jackie Burch. Reviewed at the Academy of Motion Picture Arts & Sciences, July 19, 1985. (MPAA Rating: R.) Running time: **105 MINS.**

Jerry Dandridge . . . . Chris Sarandon
Charley Brewster . . . . William Ragsdale
Amy Peterson . . . . Amanda Bearse
Peter Vincent . . . . Roddy McDowall
Evil Ed . . . . Stephen Geoffreys
Billy Cole . . . . Jonathan Stark
Judy Brewster . . . . Dorothy Fielding
Det. Lennox . . . . Art J. Evans

"Fright Night" is a prize, a fundamental, rock-bottom thriller, set up first by charm and humor. With good word-of-mouth to set it apart from the recently worn-out cycle of horror hokum, "Fright" could be a summer sleeper headed for big, big bucks before winter set in.

In his directorial debut on his own script, Tom Holland keeps the picture wonderfully simple and entirely believable (once the existence of vampires is accepted, of course). In a quick 105 minutes, the film simply answers the question of what would probably happen if a charming, but deadly sinister, vampire moved in next door to a likable teenager given to watching horror films on the late show — and the only one the kid can turn to for help is a washed-up actor who hosts the show.

Chris Sarandon is terrific as the vampire, quite affable and debonair until his fingernails start to grow and his eyes get that glow. In contrast to other screen teens of late, William Ragsdale superbly maintains due sympathy as a fairly typical youngster who can't get anybody to believe him about the odd new neighbor next door.

Finally, this is the most fun part

in a long while for Roddy McDowall, hamming it up on the telly as the "fearless vampire killer." Naturally, when Ragsdale comes looking for help, McDowall is more than aware of his humanly limitations, becoming a consistently amusing, unwilling ally in invading Sarandon's lair.

The reason the pair must venture forth is Amanda Bearse, heretofore Ragsdale's sweet, virginal girlfriend who has undergone an amazing personality change since dancing with Sarandon. (Bearse is excellent, too, in handling her split assignment.)

Rounding out the cast in high-spirited style are Jonathan Stark, as Sarandon's equally beguiling sidekick; Stephen Geoffreys, Ragsdale's goofy pal, and Dorothy Fielding, his see-nothing mom.

Make no mistake, as some might ahead of time, this is no send-up of scary films. Thanks to the performances and Richard Edlund's startling effects, once the pair get into Sarandon's house, the horror starts aplenty.

Probably not by accident, Holland slips in a bit of a self-serving plug when McDowall comments at one point: "Nobody wants to see vampires anymore. All they want to see is some demented madman running around in a ski mask hacking up young virgins."

Holland obviously decided to change all that.—*Har.*

Sesame Street Presents:
Follow That Bird
(COLOR)

Amusing, well-made debut feature for Big Bird, et al.

Hollywood, July 19.
A Warner Bros. release of a Children's Television Workshop production in association with World Film Services. Produced by Tony Garnett. Executive producer, Joan Ganz Cooney. Directed by Ken Kwapis. Screenplay, Tony Geiss, Judy Freudberg, camera (Technicolor), Curtis Clark; supervising film editor, Stan Warnow; editor, Evan Landis; music, Van Dyke Parks, Lennie Niehaus; music supervised by Steve Buckingham; art direction, Carol Spier; set decoration, Elinor Rose Galbraith; sound (Dolby), Bryan Day, Michael Lacroix; associate producer, Pat Churchill; assistant director, David Shepherd; special effects director, Colin Chilvers; special effects second unit camera, Thomas Burstyn; second unit assistant director, Jonathan Hackett; casting, Linda Francis, Stuart Aitkins. Reviewed at The Burbank Studios, Burbank, Calif., July 17, 1985. (MPAA Rating: G.) Running time: **88 MINS.**

Big Bird/Oscar . . . . Caroll Spinney
Kermit The Frog/Ernie . . . . . . Jim Henson
Cookie Monster/Bert/Grover . . . Frank Oz
Grouch Cook . . . . Paul Bartel
Grouch Waitress . . . . Sandra Bernhard
State Trooper . . . . John Candy
Newscaster . . . . Chevy Chase
Sid Sleaze . . . . Joe Flaherty
Truck Driver . . . . Waylon Jennings
Sam Sleaze . . . . Dave Thomas
Voices: Laraine Newman (Mommy Dodo), Brian Hohlfeld (Daddy Dodo), Cathy Silvers (Marie Dodo), Eddie Deezen (Donnie Dodo), Sally Kellerman (Miss Finch).

After 16 years of worldwide popularity on television, the Sesame Street characters become film stars in "Sesame Street Presents: Follow That Bird," a breezy, amiable comedy about Big Bird's flight from home and his friends' efforts to bring him back. Since the genuine little kids' market has recently been rediscovered, prospects for solid late summer family trade appear good.

This big screen effort is entirely faithful to the upbeat spirit, integrationist ideals and comic cleverness of the tv series, and is lively and, in spots, wacky enough to keep parents amused while the kiddies delight in the adventures of Jim Henson's muppets.

Simple premise has the slightly goofy yellow, 8' fowl Big Bird taken away from Sesame Street by the officious Miss Finch so he can grow up among his own kind, a bird family named the Dodos, in Oceanview, Ill.

The Dodos are a bunch of loons, however, so B.B. begins the long trek back to New York on foot, while the Sesame Street gang mobilizes in assorted vehicles to find its dear friend.

En route, B.B. has a pleasant encounter with country singing truck driver Waylon Jennings, but a distinctly nasty one with the Sleaze Brothers (SCTV's Joe Flaherty and Dave Thomas), unscrupulous amusement park operators who abduct B.B. for their own nefarious purposes.

All turns out for the best, of course, and spicing things up along the way are Chevy Chase and Kermit The Frog as tv newscasters, Sandra Bernhard and Paul Bartel as the proprietors of a lowdown roadside diner, and John Candy as a motorcycle cop.

Very smoothly directed with an eye to fresh humor by Ken Kwapis, a Northwestern and USC grad who won the 1982 Student Academy Award for "For Heaven's Sake," pic boasts a very crisp and clean visual style, courtesy of Curtis Clark's lensing. Van Dyke Parks and Lennie Niehaus' song is catchy enough, and Carol Spier's art direction contributes a few amusing touches.
— *Cart.*

El Criminal
(The Criminal)
(MEXICAN-COLOR)

Mexico City, July 9.

A Películas Mexicanas release of a Hermanos Tamez Prod. Produced by Orlando Tamez. Executive producer, Leonal Gonzalez. Directed by Fernando Durán. Stars Fernando Almada, Mario Almada. Screenplay, Manuel Cárdenas, based on a corrido (narrative ballad); camera (color), Agustín Lara; editor, Enrique Murillo M.; music, Ernesto Cortazar. Special appearance of musical groups: Los Cadetes de Linares, Carlos y José and Los Rancheritos del Topo Chico. Reviewed at the Mariscala Cinema, Mexico City, July 8, 1985. Running time: **95 MINS.**

Jesús Coronado	Fernando Almada
Demetrio Coronado	Mario Almada
Doña Carmelita Coronado	Maria Eugenia Llamas (La Tucita)
Rosa María	Isaura Espinosa
Don Andrés	Roberto Cañedo
Don Antonio	Tito Junco
Pascual	Eleazar Garcia (Chelelo)

Also with: Leonel González, Wally Barrón, Alfredo Gutiérrez, Tello Mantecón, Ada Carrasco, Raúl Salcedo (Cascarita), "El Fufurufu," Jesús Gómez, Roberto González and Eleazar García Jr.

Mexico's Almada brothers are at it again.

Sometimes they play likeable bad guys with a sense of honor. Other times, they are flawless good guys that are victims of circumstance, or, as in "La Muerte Del Chacal," on opposite sides of the law.

Whichever roles they play, they always wind up in a fair share (about eight a year) of low-budget Mexican films that use the revenge motive and have lots of bodies strewn everywhere. This horse opera is no exception.

"El Criminal" opens with a peg-legged Jesús Coronado (Fernando Almada) on the day of his release following 10 years in prison. He buys a horse and a gun and as he rides along, an extended flashback crosses his mind.

He and his brother Demetrio (Mario Almada) had been happy working their large ranch somewhere in the north of Mexico, which they inherited after the death of their mother. Jesús wanted only to marry Rosa María (Isaura Espinosa) and raise lots of kids. Everything was running smoothly except for some bad-guy neighbors.

Led by Don Antonio (Tito Junco), a gang of dirty desperados wanted to take over the Coronado ranch and dig for valuable minerals that supposedly lay under the property. Don Antonio's son wanted to marry the beautiful Rosa María.

A shootout leaves everyone dead except Jesús, whose leg is shot off. Now, released from prison, he has only one thought on his mind: Revenge!

The pic's contrived plot is so underdeveloped that about a quarter of the screentime is filled with "norteño" (Tex-Mex) music groups, shot with little or no imagination. The groups shown — Los Cadetes de Linares, Carlos y José and Los Rancheritos del Topo Chico — lack screen presence and stare blankly at the camera provoking more than their share of yawns.

All the characters are hastily thrown-together clichés and demand no empathy from either the director or filmgoer. Also, no care has been given to hide such anachronisms in a period Western as a wall telephone in a cantina, light switches or the electric bulbs that glare from a chandelier.
— *Lent.*

Yuganthaya
(The End Of An Era)
(SRI LANKA-COLOR)

Moscow, July 10.

A Tharanga Chithrapata release. Produced by Vijaya Ramanayake. Directed by Lester James Peries. Stars Gamini Fonseka. Screenplay, A.J. Gunawardana, based on the novel by Martin Wickremasinghe; camera (Eastmancolor), Willie Blake; editor, Gladwin Fernando; art director, Hemdaela Oharmasena. Reviewed at the Moscow Film Festival, July 10, 1985. Running time: **102 MINS.**

Saviman Kabalana	Gamini Fonseka
Malin	Richard De Zoysa
Dr. Aravinda	Douglas Ranasinghe

"Yuganthaya" is an epic tracing the organization of trade unions in Sri Lanka. Picture combines the talents of the country's best-known helmer, Lester James Peries, most famous actor, Gamini Fonseka, and novelist Martin Wickremasinghe, who penned the celebrated trilogy about the history of Sri Lanka.

Unfortunately, pic's whole is considerably less than the sum of its parts. Peries, who also brought the first two parts of Wickremasinghe's opus to the screen (New Delhi Grand Prix-winner "Gamperaliya" in 1965 and "Kaliyugaya" in 1982), fails to impart emotion in Part 3 to a horde of filmic and dramatic clichés. Result is a static, heavy-handed message picture.

Epic though the film may be, it is weighted down by all its cardboard characters from interconnected families. Saviman Kabalana (Fonseka) is introduced as the richest and most powerful capitalist in the country. Suave and well-mannered in company, he is more ruthless than "Dallas" ' J.R. when dealing with his cowering employees, who risk being belted one when the boss is in a bad mood.

If father is a Simon Legree of the country club, son Malin (Richard De Zoysa) is painted in terms of a savior of the people. Malin has returned from an upper-crust English education a changed man. Now surrounded by dog-eared tomes of Marx and busts of Lenin, he breaks with his family and school chum Aravinda (Douglas Ranasinghe), a young doctor who has given up his radical convictions all too easily. With revolutionary fervor, young Malin leaves the family mansion for seedy lodgings and gives his inheritance away to the workers.

The climax comes when Malin leads a strike in one of his father's factories. Though wounded, he is hailed as a hero by the grateful masses, while Papa is left disconsolately gazing at his empty riches.

Too heavy-handed and clumsy to make good melodrama, "End Of An Era'" runs its lengthy course with frequent shows of passion but little ability to convince. Thesps simply flow with the tide, being villainous or heroic as the script demands and avoiding fine shades of character. In the spirit of the film, lighting is bright and even throughout. — *Yung.*

The Alien Dead
(COLOR)

Amateur night in the swamp.

A Firebird Pictures production. Executive producer, Henry Kaplan. Produced by Fred Olen Ray, Chuck Sumner. Directed by Ray. Stars Buster Crabbe. Screenplay, Martin Alan Nicholas, Ray; camera (color), Gary Singer, Peter Gamba, Ray; editor, Mark Barrett; music, Franklin Sledge, Sumner; special make-up design, Allen Duckworth; associate producer, Shelley Youngren. Reviewed on Academy Home Entertainment vidcassette, N.Y., July 20, 1985. (No MPAA Rating). Running time: **73 MINS.**

Sheriff Kowalski	Buster Crabbe
Tom Corman	Ray Roberts
Shawn Michaels	Linda Lewis
Emmett Michaels	George Kelsey
Miller Haze	Mike Bonavia
Deputy Campbell	Dennis Underwood

Also with: Martin Alan Nicholas, Norman Riggins, Edi Stroup, John Leirier, Rich Vogan, Shelley Youngren, Fred Olen Ray, Ellena Contello, Nancy Karnz.

"The Alien Dead" (also known under an earlier title, "It Fell From The Sky") is an amateurish monster film made in Florida in 1980 by filmmaker Fred Olen Ray, who has since moved west and graduated to bigger budgets. Unreleased theatrically, pic is a current homevideo entry.

Monsters are on the loose in the Florida swamp, created when a meteorite hit a boat of youngsters and turned them into disfigured, bloodthirsty creatures similar to the zombies of "Night Of The Living Dead." Sheriff Kowalski (topbilled Buster Crabbe, in his final film role) believes gory local killings are the work of a gator and puts out a reward, attracting oddball hunters to the area. Newspaper reporter Tom Corman (Ray Roberts) and game warden Miller Haze (Mike Bonavia) figure out the monsters' cause and do battle with them leading to an unresolved ending.

In-jokes here (especially character name references to Roger Corman's talent troupe) aren't funny and the Halloween makeup worn by the monsters is phony in the extreme. Grossout effects of their ghoulish activities is old hat. Technical credits are poor. — *Lor.*

Terror In The Swamp
(COLOR)

Another genetic mutation runs amuck.

A Martin Folse Prods. presentation. Executive producer, Folse. Directed by Joseph J. Catalanotto. Features entire cast. Screenplay, Billy Holliday, from story by Terry Hebb, Catalanotto; camera (Allied & United color), Wade Hanks; editor, Irina Gregory; music, postproduction supervisor, Jaime Mendoza-

Nava; sound, Kenny Delbert; creature design, Ed Flynn; costume design, David Rau. Reviewed on New World Video cassette, N.Y., July 21, 1985. (No MPAA Rating.) Running time: **85 MINS.**

With: Billy Holliday (Frank), Chuck Long, Chuck Bush, Michael Tedesco (T-Bob), Mike Thomas, Ray Saadie, Gerald Daigal, Mark Peterson, Claudia Wood, Albert Dykes, Keith Barker (nutriaman).

"Terror In The Swamp" is a tame horror picture available as a vidcassette, bypassing domestic theatrical release. Filmed in Houma, La., in 1983, pic is typical of lowbudget, regional horror filmmaking but is rather skimpy in the shocks and violence area.

The late Billy Holliday, who resembles Dabney Coleman onscreen, wrote and toplines as game warden Frank. He finds a mangled body on the Copasaw (local swamp area), but can't figure out whether a gator or perhaps a bear killed the man. It turns out that local scientists, funded by South American backers, have been experimenting on breeding a larger nutria (a brown-furred, webbed-foot water rodent) to be used in making fur coats. Inadvertently, a mutated nutriaman has been created and is killing local folks.

While the police, Frank and military authorities hunt the critter, good ol' boys such as the very fat T-Bob (Michael Tedesco) and his brother also head toward Poacher's Cove to kill it. An unsatisfying ending has the monster burned up on a boat.

Director Joseph Catalanotto (who reteamed with Holliday on latter's final film, "French Quarter Undercover") wisely shows the nutriaman only in longshots or obscured through bushes, avoiding a revelation of a phony guy in a hairy outfit. Main interest here is the local color and interesting regional accents of the folksy cast.—*Lor.*

Los Paraises Perdidos
(The Lost Paradises)
(SPANISH-COLOR)

Madrid, July 26.
A CIC presentation of a Linterna Mágica production. Executive producer, José Luis García Sánchez. Written and directed by Basilio Martín Patino. Camera (Fujicolor) José Luis Alcaine; editor, Pablo G. del Amo; production manager, J.L.P. Tristan; sets, Eduardo Torre de la Fuente; music, Carmelo Bernaola. Reviewed at UIP screening room, Madrid, July 24, '85. Running time: **94 MINS.**

With: Charo López, Miguel Narros, Alfredo Landa, Juan Diego, Ana Torrent, Paco Hernández, Maria Dolores Vila, José Colmenero, Delia Rodríguez de Llera, Francisco Rabal.

Almost a decade after his last memorable film, "Caudillo," Basilio Martín Patino returns to Spanish screens with a bittersweet, poetic film looking back on his own life through the eyes of a returned exile to Spain, majestically played by Charo López.

Patino has opted for a hermetic mood piece without much of a story, a kind of philosophical summing up of his life and its rather downbeat conclusion. The film, presumably, is geared to a minority audience in Spain, who can relate to the problems of those now in their late 40s or early 50s who have never attained the "paradises" dreamt of in their younger years. For others, the film will prove heavy going, since through most of it a voice-over of López reading a Spanish translation of German poet Hölderlin's "Hyperion" will seem pompous.

Patino, who was one of the most outspoken directors opposing the Franco regime, now expounds a philosophy of political and romantic disenchantment throughout the reels. The femme exile looks up old friends and cronies from 20 years ago, none of whom seems to have "made it;" most are intellectually frustrated, and their lives seem wasted.

The advent of democracy has simply been an extension of the former mediocrity. One of the exile's former friends is now in politics, and has become as two-faced as most politicos. López has lived abroad, mothered a child with a German in Frankfurt, but her life is as barren and meaningless as most of the others of her generation presented in the film.

Pic ends rather inconclusively, with her at least finishing the Hölderlin translation, whose sentiments of romantic unfulfillment seem to parallel her own life. Most of the thesping is excellent, especially that by López and Narros, and there's a nice little cameo by Paco Rabal. Patino adds nothing new. His poetic lucubrations will seem heavy handed to most audiences, spelling dim b.o. potential for this pic, even in Spain. —*Besa.*

Wo Andere Schweigen
(Where Others Keep Silent)
(EAST GERMAN-COLOR)

Moscow, July 6.
A DEFA production. Directed by Ralf Kirsten. Stars Gudrun Okras. Screenplay, Michaeil Schatrow; camera (Orwocolor), Günther Haubold; art director, Hans Poppe; editor, Evelyn Carow; music, Peter Gotthardt. Reviewed at the Moscow Film Festival, July 6, 1985. Running time: **114 MINS.**
Clara Zetkin . . . . .Gudrun Okras
Christa .Elke Reuter
Gustav . . . . .Rolf Ludwig
Erich . . . . .Kieter Bellmann
Fritz . . . . .Hans-Uwe Bauer

"Where Others Keep Silent" is an intermittently successful attempt to recreate a critical moment in German history, when the Nazis took over the Reichstag in 1932 and put an end to parliamentary democracy. Traveling back and forth between fact and fiction, helmer Ralf Kirsten and scripter Michaeil Schatrow dramatize the transitional period by showing it through the eyes of a group of leftist intellectuals and Communists.

At the center of the story is Clara Zetkin (Gudrun Okras), a heroic old lady in failing health and Communist member of Parliament. By reason of seniority she has the right to make the inaugural address to Parliament during the fateful session. Half the film details her dangerous journey from Moscow and clandestine life in the home of a Berlin typesetter, where she prepares her historic speech.

Zetkin's impassioned address to the assembly is pic's culminating scene, but the story of her stay in Berlin is interwoven with the life of the typesetter's daughter Christa (Elke Reuter), a nurse. Initially the girl holds herself above politics, but events gradually bring her to an awareness of what is at stake. Her boyfriend decides to emigrate; their best friend Fritz (Hans-Uwe Bauer) is killed by the Nazis, and her own home is burned down. In the end she stays behind to fight with her father.

Pic struggles to tie these two threads together. Mostly it goes out of kilter in the more rhetorical Zetkin passages and comes back on target emotionally where Christa and her family are concerned. Okras brings quiet charisma to the figure of Clara Zetkin, a woman radiating dignity and human values and setting an example for other generations to emulate.

Film is professionally shot, with an accomplished opening sequence of black-and-white stills and newsreels that effortlessly segue into the color fiction film. —*Yung.*

Schatten Der Zukunft
(Shadows Of The Future)
(WEST GERMAN-DOCU-
COLOR-16m)

Berlin, July 12.
A Wolfgang Bergmann coproduction with ZDF and the Kuratorium Kirchlicher Entwicklungsdienst. Directed by Wolfgang Bergmann. Camera (color), Gerd Tönsmann; editor, Vessela Martschewski; sound, Dieter Grönling, Bergmann; music, Wolfgang Hamm. Reviewed at the Audi Max, Technical U., Berlin, July 11, 1985. Running time: **92 MINS.**

There are many reasons for liking and respecting Wolfgang Bergmann's docu on the Israeli-Palestinian conflict, "Shadows Of The Future," but the main one is that he has touched upon the tragedy of this ongoing "war" over the past 40 years.

The tragedy is felt in the interviews. We are introduced to a Israeli woman living in Berlin, whose parents were German Jews who fled Germany and settled in what is today Israel. We are introduced to a Palestinian living in Munich, whose parents were driven from their homeland in Palestine and settled in a refugee camp. Both the woman and the man carry German passports; it's therefore rather doubtful that either will leave the positions they have reached in their private and professional lives to return and settle down in the Middle East.

One feels the tragedy, too, in the discussions with the parents of both parties. The Israeli father admits to a certain miscarriage of justice in regard to the Palestinians, but he defends the Israeli past and is obviously pained by his daughter's statements made in the documentary. The Palestinian mother respects that her son has pulled himself up by the bootstraps to become a Western-oriented computer expert, but she also asks him the numbing question as to when he will return home after 14 years, and why hasn't he even married during this time.

Thus, the two individuals in the docu are people whose own futures are, indeed, shadowed by the past. More than that, the core of the film is found in the contrast of the "Jewish Question" in German history with the "Israeli-Palestinian Problem" of the present. There is a deep-running relationship between the two, which helmer Bergmann deftly underscores at several points in the film. —*Holl.*

The Neglected Miracle
(NEW ZEALAND-DOCU-
COLOR)

Wellington, July 16.
A Pacific Films Prod. presentation. Produced by John O'Shea and Craig Walters. Written and directed by Barry Barclay. Associate director, Peter Hawes; camera (color), Rory O'Shea; sound, Wouter van der Hoevan; editor, Annie Collins; music, Jenny McLeod. Reviewed at Embassy theater, Wellington Film Festival, July 13, 1985. Running time: **120 MINS.**

Preemed at the Wellington Film Festival, "The Neglected Miracle," a riveting examination of the global importance of stewardship of genetic agricultural resources, confirms the position of Barry Barclay as New Zealand's most accomplished and penetrating documentary filmmaker.

What emerges in "The Neglected Miracle," seven years in the making, is a powerful plea for fair play. It is not enough, the film says, for scientists in industrialized countries like the Netherlands and the U.S. to direct and develop the makeup and qualities of basic crops without ensuring benefits flow back to the communities and countries from which the raw materials have come.

In the words of Erna Bennett, Irish-born plant geneticist, and one of the inspirations for the film, it is not enough to produce more. You have to produce more and make sure the poorest man in the world gets his share of it.

Throughout the film, the essential life force connection between human hands, plants and seeds becomes a potent image (fine camerawork by Rory O'Shea), augmenting the director's obvious sensitivities to the priorities of (so-called) "primitive" peoples.

Where the film is less successful is in answering new questions that the material brings to light, particularly in the area of global politics.

Much is made of a U.S. government trade embargo of Nicaragua which, it is claimed, means none of the "ancient" maize material taken out of Nicaragua in the 1960s for use in plant gene banks is being returned in "improved" form.

This is an important ingredient in the film's building of a case suggesting exploitation of Third World countries by the industrialized West in the field of scientific plant breeding.

However, there is no apparent attempt to followup the impact of the embargo with U.S. authorities.

While some audiences might feel some footage could be lopped off this two-hour version without reducing its strength, the cumulative effect of the layering of images and messages ultimately is compelling.
— *Nic.*

The Man Who Knew More
(IRANIAN-COLOR)

Moscow, July 30.
Produced by Hamrah Cooperative. Directed by Yadollah Samadi. Features entire cast. Screenplay by D. Jamal Omid and Hassan Hedayat. Reviewed at the Moscow Film Festival (Competition), July 2, 1985. Running time: 85 MINS.
With: Enayat Shafi-i, Shirin Golkar, Morteza Ahmadi.

A poor man gets rich by laying his hands on tomorrow's newspapers. This bizarre, uncontrolled picture, which announces itself to be about "the destructive power of money," starts out as moralistic sci-fi and ends up as madcap comedy. The idea is a classic (last year saw other remakes of René Clair's "It Happened Tomorrow"), but fails to yield a minute's entertainment.

A young office worker is sitting in the park, bemoaning his lack of money, when a mysterious stranger in black overhears him. The stranger sounds him out on what he'd do if he was rich, and the answers (get married and have kids) are so compelling he hands him a newspaper, dated several months hence.

Recovering from his surprise, the young man uses the advance information to start stockpiling home ap-

pliances, which soon become very scarce. He sells them and makes a killing, but instead of marrying the sweet, chador-veiled coworker who loves him, he gets greedier and more selfish. A miscalculation almost ruins him, but a visit to the stranger in the park saves the day with another post-dated tabloid, accompanied by a stern warning to change his ways or else.

This part of the film is all fake business deals in plush offices lit like train stations. He is set up to get his comeuppance, which arrives with the third paper. It announces his death in a car accident, and from there on pic turns into a wacky comedy, as hero and friends try to keep the preordained from taking place by stopping traffic, locking him up, etc. In the end, the accident takes place but isn't fatal.

Little can be said about the acting and technical side of the film except that they are as amateurish as the direction. — *Yung.*

Avaeté, A Semente Da Vinganca
(The Seeds Of Vengeance)
(BRAZILIAN-COLOR)

Moscow, July 30.
Produced by Embrafilme. Directed by Zelito Viana. Screenplay by José Joffili and Viana. Only credits available. Reviewed at the Moscow Film Festival (Competition), July 11, 1985. Running time: 110 MINS.
With: Hugo Carvana, Renata Sorrah, Milton Rodrigues.

Taking its cue from current headlines, "The Seeds Of Vengeance" is a hard-hitting exposé of the massacre of Amazon Indians and their missionaries by ruthless, stop-at-nothing land speculators. Pic overcomes its lack of technical sophistication through sheer conviction, and frequently succeeds in conveying a raw emotional impact.

Opening sequence is the most horrific. A peaceful village of Indians living in the bush, who have probably never seen a white man, are attacked suddenly by a gleeful crew of murderous roughnecks. Strafed and bombed from an airplane and shot down by a jungle patrol, the Avaetés don't stand a chance. The gruesome slaying of a woman, strung up on a tree and quartered like an animal by a Klaus Kinski lookalike, caps the raid.

The sole survivor is Ava, a five-year-old child saved by the raiders' horrified cook. Cook and boy escape through the jungle and begin a new life together in another part of the forest.

Film follows the boy's quest for revenge but eventually disintegrates into a mass of improbabilities, and the effect of Ava's ritual revenge is more or less lost except at a purely symbolic level. One gets the idea,

but just can't believe all the coincidences involved in bringing Ava and the men behind the massacre, an untouchable politician, together.

Pic's weak spot is introducing a deus-ex-machina woman journalist and her cameraman-lover, a pair of irritating stock characters who are quite unnecessary to the plot, except for buying Ava a plane ticket to the city (why?). Despite its lapses, however, "Seeds Of Vengeance" is a refreshing change from the exploitation jungle pictures that inevitably turn the Indians into the killers.
— *Yung.*

Los Transplantados
(The Transplanted)
(CHILEAN-COLOR-16m)

Santiago, July 7.
Produced by Percy and Juan Matas. Directed by Percy Matas. Screenplay, Waldo Rojas, based on the novel by Blest Gana. Camera (color, 16m), Luis Poirot; editor, Valeria Sarmiento; sound, J.F. Chevalier. Reviewed at French Institute, Santiago, July 5, 1985. Running time: 70 MINS.
With: Nemesio Antúnez, Carla Cristi, Valenzuela Barceló, Sergio Hernandez, Gloria Laso, Guy Mercier, César Moukarzel, Huguette Faget, Sadi Ramirez, and Antonio Espinoza.

Shot in France in 1975 (in two weeks and on a $30,000 budget), "Los Transplantados" has only now surfaced in Chile where the Censorship Board, after thinking it over for six weeks, gave its approval with an "over 18" rating. Surprisingly, the film has not become dated and could do quite well at a local art house. Abroad it is unlikely to go beyond its past exposure at a series of festivals in the 1970s.

Freely adapted by Waldo Rojas from a novel by Alberto Blest Gana published early this century, pic deals with a family of upper class Chilean expatriates who, after Salvador Allende was elected president in 1970, fled the country and settled in Paris out of fear that his leftist regime would lead to communism.

Director Percy Matas was in film studies at the U. of Paris (Vincennes) at the time of the 1973 military coup and later worked as an assistant to Raul Ruiz; he only returned to Chile recently. In "Los Transplantados," although technical credits are unimpressive, he succeeds in recreating the atmosphere of the day-to-day life of the expatriate family and, in the film's last segments, shows their reaction to the military takeover and the arrival in France of a new wave of exiles, this time from the left.

Quite different in its subject matter from the 100-plus films made by Chileans abroad over the last 12 years, Matas' pic is a telling portrait of the bourgeoisie. Except for a few brief scenes in French, the dialog is in Spanish. Actors are mostly Chilean exiles and the leading role is sur-

prisingly well played by Nemesio Antúnez, one of the country's best known painters. — *Amig.*

Terbeschikkinggesteld
(Detention At The Government's Pleasure)
(DUTCH-DOCU-COLOR-16m)

Produced and distributed by Red Dog Prods., Amsterdam, The Netherlands. Directed by Olivier Koning; camera (color), Jules Van De Steenhoven; editor, Teun Pfeil; sound, Erik Langhout. Reviewed at American Museum of Natural History, N.Y., July 19, 1985. Running time: 85 MINS.
(In Dutch with English subtitles)

Set for the Margaret Mead Film Festival in September, this film documents the procedures by which the Dutch government detains for psychiatric observation and treatment the convicted criminals it receives from the courts, but at no time do we learn details of their crimes.

During this evaluation procedure and treatment, the prisoner — perhaps not responsible for his actions, due to temporary or permanent mental aberration — is held utterly in thrall to the government. Committees of experts convene to decide his fate. The images on the screen, and the title of the film, emphasize the government's power versus the helpless prisoner.

Although the filmmakers struggle for journalistic objectivity, their sympathies with the prisoner against the system creep through. While renowned for its tolerance and humaneness, the Dutch government and society that emerge in this film may be sensed by some viewers as coldly functional and bureaucratic.

The film was shot within several high-security mental hospital-prisons, with unprecedented cooperation of the Dutch authorities. Prisoners comment freely to the camera about their feelings. To them, compulsory psychiatric custody and care are unjust. We are also present within the closed chambers of these committees as the destiny of prisoners is debated.

"Detention" differs enormously from Fred Wiseman's 1967 "Titicut Follies," a harrowing exposé of a Massachusetts state hospital for the criminally insane. In contrast, these Dutch prisoners and jailors are civilized and well-mannered, even as they are caught in the same dilemma — to what extent are criminals guilty or innocent if they are deranged and lack free will? —*Hitch.*

Huang Shan Lai De Gu Niang
(The Girl From Mt. Huangshan)
(CHINESE-COLOR)

Moscow, July 30.
Produced by Beijing Film Studio. Direct-

ed by Zhang Yuan and Yu Yan Fu. Screenplay, Peng Ming Yian and Bi Jian Chang. Only credits available. Reviewed at the Moscow Film Festival (Competition), July 4, 1985. Running time: **92 MINS.**

With: Li Ling, Din Yi, Zhang Jun Ying.

A country girl comes to the city to work as a maid and suffers a drama, "Girl From Mt. Huangshan" is naively old-fashioned and artificial. Its main interest is the remarkable glimpse it affords of the changing social configurations of modern-day China.

Filmmakers Zhang Yuan and Yu Yan Fu make a point of insisting that the case they're describing is absolutely typical, one of many common stories. A young girl from the country arrives in Peking and finds a maid's job, thanks to the help of her aunt. The family she works for is straight out of "Cinderella": the father is in the U.S., working and saving for a color tv and cosmetics for his women, the mother is a petty tyrant who won't let the new servant watch tv (an old black & white set), while the spoiled daughter of the house unjustly accuses her of mislaying her best sweater and gets her fired. When the daughter has to undergo an emergency appendectomy, however, she becomes a new person and appreciates the maid's loving care.

Two other episodes flow in the same vein. In one, the maid ends up working without pay for a young mother whose husband has left her; in the other, for the well-to-do family of a politician with another spoiled daughter.

Final scene shows the maid eagerly agreeing to a marriage her parents have arranged, which will permit her to return to the mountains where she was born — a puzzling conclusion that seems aimed at discouraging immigration to the cities. —*Yung.*

Real Genius
(COLOR)

Teen comedy a notch ahead of the usual fare.

Hollywood, Aug. 3.

A Tri-Star Pictures release. Produced by Brian Grazer. Executive producer Robert Daley. Directed by Martha Coolidge. Features entire cast. Screenplay by Neal Israel & Pat Proft, and Peter Torokvei, from a story by Israel & Proft; camera (Metrocolor), Vilmos Zsigmond; editor, Richard Chew; music, Thomas Newman; production designer, Josan F. Russo; set decorator, Philip Abramson; art director, Jack G. Taylor Jr.; set designer, Erin M. Cummins, Steve Wolff; sound (Dolby), Darin Knight; assistant director, Steve McEveety; associate producer, Sam Crespi-Horowitz; casting, Jane Jenkins, Janet Hirshenson. Reviewed at Coronet Theater, Westwood Village, Calif., Aug. 1, 1985. (MPAA Rating: PG.) Running time: **104 MINS.**
Chris Knight . . . . Val Kilmer
Mitch Taylor . . . . Gabe Jarret
Jordan . . . . Michelle Meyrink
Professor Hathaway . . . . William Atherton
Kent . . . . Jonathan Gries
Sherry Nugil . . . . Patti D'Arbanville

"Real Genius" is "Police Academy" with brains. Penned by "Academy" graduates Neal Israel and Pat Proft with Peter Torokvei, pic aims a bit higher than the food fights and crude sex jokes of the common youth fodder, but not much. Result is kind of a hybrid which is by turns clever and juvenile. Consequently, film may have trouble finding its niche at the box-office.

Setting the proceedings at a think tank for young prodigies seems a curious choice as most of the humor of the film comes out of character rather than place. Val Kilmer, punning his way through his senior year at Pacific Tech, is hardly convincing as a world-class intellect.

Plot about creating a portable laser system for the Air Force under the tutelage of campus creep Professor Hathaway (William Atherton) has the authority of an old Abbott and Costello film. Theme about the exploitation of these youthful minds is lost in a sea of sight gags. Laser research probably was chosen for its visual impact.

What lifts the production above the run-of-the-mill is swift direction by Martha Coolidge, who has a firm grasp over the manic material. Aided by production designer Josan F. Russo, Coolidge has literally put skeletons in the dorm closets. Gadgets and gizmos abound with a level of frenetic activity maintained.

In fact, one of the students is the hyperkinetic Jordan (Michelle Meyrink), non-stop talking coed who takes a shine to 15-year-old brain Mitch Taylor (Gabe Jarret). As his mentor, Chris (Val Kilmer) advises Mitch to enjoy life more and study less, a difficult lesson for the young genius.

Point of Chris' instruction is to do as little as possible and film is full of non sequiturs and elaborate digressions such as a mock Hawaiian party complete with water sports and ice skating on a surface of frozen gas in the halls of the dorm.

While the heroes try to do as little as possible, Hathaway and his fawning students race to meet the deadline for creating a secret weapon for the military. But, alas, Hathaway needs the brainpower of the good guys.

While nonsense plot teeters on the brink of bringing down the whole production, Coolidge keeps the appropriate tongue-in-cheek tone, which almost gives the material a sophisticated campy sheen.

Credit must also go to cinematographer Vilmos Zsigmond whose photography contributes a surprisingly stylish look for this kind of fare.

Performances are a plus with Kilmer energetic and enjoyable to watch and Jarret endearingly sincere. Atherton captures well the unctuous quality of a man who will do anything for his creature comforts. —*Jagr.*

Otto — Der Film
(Otto — The Film)
(WEST GERMAN-COLOR)

Berlin, Aug. 1.

A Rialto Film production and Tobis Filmkunst release, Berlin. Produced by Horst Wendlandt. Directed by Xaver Schwarzenberger, Otto Waalkes. Screenplay, Bernd Eilert, Robert Gernhardt, Peter Knorr, Waalkes; camera (color), Schwarzenberger; sets, Hansjürgen Kiebach, Henry Nielebock; editor, Jutta Hering; music, Herb Geller. Reviewed at Royal Palast, Berlin, July 30, '85. Running time: **90 MINS.**
With: Otto Waalkes (Otto), Jessika Cardinahl (Silvia), Elisabeth Wiedemann (Konsulin von Kohlen und Reibach), Sky Dumont (Ernesto), Peter Kuiper (Shark), Karl Lieffen (Floppmann), Gottfried John (Sonnemann), Andreas Mannkopff (Haenlein), Karl Schönböck (Fürst Marckbiss), Eric Vaessen, Tilly Lauenstein, Günther Kaufmann, Erich Bar, Johannes Heesters, Wolfgang Kleff, Lutz Mackensy, Karl Ulrich Meves, Panos Papadopoulos.

Undoubtedly the most successful German film at the boxoffice this season, Otto Waalkes and Xaver Schwarzenberger's "Otto — The Film" is every bit as good on the critical side, despite the imperfections that might very well hinder offshore chances. Waalkes, writer-director-actor-performer, is a well known tv personality whose recent absence from the tube only served to nourish interest in the debut of his screen career.

Further, the media blitz for the film has been nothing short of phenomenal in these parts. Even the evening tv newscast carried a plug for "Otto," to say nothing of the front cover promo in Spiegel and Tip mags. And considering that this is generally the low-count summer season at the German wickets, a risk was obviously taken from start to finish of this polished production.

"Otto — The Film" is little more than a string of stand-up gags, most of them stemming from his well known routines and usually using that famous double entendre: making something nasty out of what seems at first to be a silly straight line. If there's anybody he resembles in antics, however, it's Harpo Marx — in fact, there's a salute to Harpo and Groucho in the mirror-imitation routine right out of "Duck Soup." Waalkes does the scene with a black wig imitating a barber — and when both of the partner's wigs come off, the barber ends up looking like a double of blond-haired Waalkes!

Waalkes plays a number of costume roles in the film. He begins an airplane flight as the stewardess, then becomes the flight engineer, and finally the pilot himself. He's always being pursued by an angry creditor, while he in turn chases a lovely and wealthy aristocrat whose mother wants her to marry a stuffed shift instead of Otto, whom, of course, she really loves after he saved her life one day. Many of the situations seem to be inspired by young Woody Allen or late Peter Sellers routines, while others dip to slapstick à la Jerry Lewis.

"Otto" is good fun, and although much too heavy on the verbal gag and just plain mugging for the sake of Waalkes' faithful tv aud, the humor is quite refreshing. Should a visual gagman be signed on to up the credits even more, Otto Waalkes may one day become an international celebrity. He has all the makings of an anarchic wildman of the screen.

Technical side is a major plus, particularly work by lenser Schwarzenberger. —*Holl.*

Weird Science
(COLOR)

Tame fantasy comedy is not weird enough to make a big dent.

Hollywood, Aug. 1.

A Universal Pictures release. Produced by Joel Silver. Directed by John Hughes. Features entire cast. Screenplay by Hughes; camera (technicolor), Matthew F. Leonetti, editor, Mark Warner, Christopher Lebenzon; Scott Wallace; music, Ira Newborn; production designer, John W. Corso; set decorator, Jennifer Polito; art director, James Allen; sound (Dolby), James Alexander; costumes, Marilyn Vance; assistant director, Deborah Love; associate producer, Jane Vickerilla; casting, Jackie Burch. Reviewed at Plaza Theater, Westwood Village, Calif., July 29, 1985. (MPAA Rating: PG-13). Running time: **94 MINS.**
Gary . . . . Anthony Michael Hall
Lisa . . . . Kelly LeBrock
Wyatt . . . . Ilan Mitchell-Smith
Chet . . . . Bill Paxton
Deb . . . . Suzanne Snyder

Hilly . . . . Judie Aronson
Ian . . . . Robert Downey
Max . . . . Robert Rusler

"Weird Science" is not nearly as weird as it should have been and, in fact, is a rather conventional kids-in-heat film, and a chaste one at that. Director-writer John Hughes squanders the opportunity to comment on the power struggle between the sexes for a few easy laughs. Tameness of the film targets it solely for a young teen crowd who should turn out in fair numbers, but without the possibility of much of a crossover audience.

Starting with the delectable premise of two high school nerds who create a woman through some inexplicable computer hocus-pocus, "Weird Science" veers off into a typical coming-of-age saga without exploring any of the psychological territory it lightly sails over in the early going.

Helplessly horny chums Gary (Anthony Michael Hall) and Wyatt (Ilan Mitchell-Smith), in an act of creative frustration, put their brains together and create the answer to their fantasies — the beautiful and very available Lisa (Kelly LeBrock). The trouble is the boys hardly use her.

Although clearly not grounded in reality, the film really goes nowhere with its central conceit, opting instead for a more ordinary approach. Hughes never capitalizes on the idea that Lisa is a creation of 15-year-old psyches or examines the intriguing question of who controls whom in this relationship. Instead, Lisa becomes sort of a big sister with magical powers, guiding the boys to girls who are infinitely less interesting than herself.

Road to maturity is bumpy and LeBrock turns out to be the ideal guide. Her no-nonsense sexuality is the perfect counterpoint to the uptight boys who can't even take a shower with her with their clothes off. First and funniest stop is a black nightclub where the 15-year-olds get down and Hall takes on the manner and accent of an aging black bluesman.

Other stops are less imaginative and though Hughes has become more sophisticated visually, all of his films seem to be set in shopping malls, school and a climactic party, where, in this case, the boys get the girls of their dreams.

Special effects are plentiful but disconcerting since Hughes never really establishes the boundaries of Lisa's powers or what rules apply here.

Hughes' true gift is at capturing the naturalistic rhythms and interaction between the boys wth a great ear for dialog. Unfortunately he gives Hall too much rein and the young actor is seen bugging his eyes in amazement a few too many times. LeBrock is just right as the film's calm but commanding center.

Tech credits are fine but overall production has the feel of a good idea that wasn't thought through enough to make it work. — *Jagr.*

Es Liegt An Uns, Diesen Geist Lebendig Zu Erhalten
(It's Up To Us To Keep This Spirit Alive)
(WEST GERMAN-COLOR-DOCU-16m)

Berlin, July 29.
A Chronos Film production, Berlin, produced by Bengt von zur Mühlen. Written and directed by Irmgard von zur Mühlen. Camera (color), Peter Tamm; editor, Gisela Bienert; optical effects, Studio Bartoschek. Reviewed at the Memorial for German Resistance Auditorium, Berlin, July 20, '85. Running time: **75 MINS.**
With: Barbara von Haeften, Freya Graäfin Moltke, Rosemarie Reichwein, Charlotte Gräfin von der Schulenburg, Marianne Gräfin Schwerin von Schwanenfeld, Clarita von Trott zu Solz, Hedwig Wirmer, Marion Gräfin Yorck von Wartenburg, Johanna von Bennigsen-Foerder, Maria Hermes, Marianne Meyer-Krahmer.

Little doubt, Berlin-based Irmgard von zur Mühlen deserves a great deal of praise and credit for making "It's Up To Us To Keep This Spirit Alive," a docu on the German Resistance leading to, and following, the attempted assassination of Hitler on July 20, 1944. Pic preemed at the Berlin Memorial to the German Resistance 41 years after the fact, while the impulse for making the film began there a year ago when the widows of the executed resistance leaders gathered for the anniversary service and memorial tribute.

One wonders, in fact, why this theme was never attempted sooner. Here are eyewitnesses — widows, by the way, who never married again and kept the flame of their husband's memories burning in their hearts over the decades — telling the story of the July 20 conspiracy as though it had happened yesterday. Von zur Mühlen, a talented compilation documentarist, simply lets them tell their stories on camera at a leisurely pace, intercutting the footage with contemporary newsreels to maintain both a historical perspective and a chronological storyline.

Documentary follows the route of the Christian-Socialist reformers, those conspirators molded in the traditions of the Old Prussian nobility. These included a mixture of the military, the nobility and the well-to-do middle class. The fate of the conservative Lord Mayor of Leipzig, Carl-Friedrich Goerdeler, also is followed.

Von zur Mühlen touches upon an important element of the German Resistance: although hardly organized within the context of an overbearing totalitarian state, it was the spirit of the conspirators that was shared to the core by the wives who were willing to risk everything together with their husbands (who, in turn, did everything possible to protect them from the truth). Once the assassination failed and the horrific "people's trial" under the infamous Roland Freissler took place (ending in slow deaths by hanging in Berlin-Plötzensee Prison), it was the wives and the next-of-kin who were to suffer under Hitler's demands that "their kind" be wiped out.

Many were arrested, even though they often were the mothers of small children. Others were separated from families and children, sons and daughters sent to state schools where they were given other names in order to further dishonor their parents. Their land and property was confiscated.

The irony of the whole situation is that the families of the oppositionists were not exonerated right after the war — indeed, for a long time after the war — while some criminal judges belonging to the infamous "people's courts" continued on in their legal positions by a stretching of the "can't-condemn-all-Germans" principle for the reconstruction of the country.

To this reviewer's taste, the women in "It's Up To Us To Keep This Spirit Alive" are to be admired. Some of them — Barbara von Haeften, Freya Gräfin Moltke, Rosemarie Reichwein — are such dignified personalities in their own right that added films on this or that "profile in courage" should be made. —*Holl.*

Summer Rental
(COLOR)

Funny in spots, Candy vehicle looks to do modest biz.

Hollywood, Aug. 6.
A Paramount Pictures release. Produced by George Shapiro. Executive producer Bernie Brillstein. Directed by Carl Reiner. Stars John Candy. Screenplay by Jeremy Stevens, Mark Reisman; camera (Continental Film Labs color), Ric Waite; editor, Bud Molin; music, Alan Silvestri; production design, Peter Wooley; set decorator, Gary Moreno; costumes, Larry K. Johnson; sound, Al Overton Jr.; assistant director, Albert Shapiro; associate producer, Stevens, Reisman; casting, Penny Perry. Reviewed at Director's Guild Of America, Hollywood, Aug. 5, 1985. (MPAA Rating: PG.) Running time: **88 MINS.**
Jack Chester . . . . John Candy
Sandy Chester . . . . Karen Austin
Jennifer Chester . . . . Kerri Green
Bobby Chester . . . . Joey Lawrence
Laurie Chester . . . . Aubrey Jene
Al Pellet . . . . Richard Crenna
Scully . . . . Rip Torn

Amusing in spots, "Summer Rental" is another light summer confection that threatens to float away before it's over. More a collection of bits about taking the family to the shore for the summer than a coherent story, John Candy manages to elevate some of those bits to the hilarious and therein lies the film's appeal, but only enough for modest b.o. prospects.

As an airport flight controller, Candy starts hallucinating planes on his screen when his boss strongly suggests a vacation. With three kids, dog and a U-Haul, family sets off for r&r at the Florida shore. It comes as little surprise when things don't go as planned and Candy finds himself sunburned with an injured leg.

Script by Jeremy Stevens and Mark Reisman also is lame and dreams up only the most pedestrian domestic castastrophes from a young daughter's (Kerri Green) budding interest in boys and a gay divorcee's interest in Candy's wife (Karen Austin).

After an hour of meandering around the beach and environs, Candy locks horns with local denizen and resident sailing champ Richard Crenna. Climax is the local regatta with Candy racing with a pirate crew of misfits to maintain his summer rental from owner Crenna.

Best bits in the film are supplied by Candy's wardrobe; he turns up in everything from a hockey jersey to Hawaiian shirts and various beach and sailor outfits, all designed to show off his ample bulk. Highlight may be Candy in a Japanese robe with his face covered in Noxzema for sunburn making him look like an actor in a Noh drama.

Despite supplying a few good laughs, it is unclear if Candy can sustain a whole film as an actor rather than the punchline in isolated skits. Other performances are merely adequate with the exception of Rip Torn who, as a modern day pirate with a heart of gold, demonstrates once again that he can make any role believable regardless of how silly it is.

Tech credits seem better suited to the small screen with much voice-over dialog and limited use of the seaside locations. Film was edited in a hurry for summer release with direction by Carl Reiner lacking the polish of his previous film, "All Of Me." —*Jagr.*

Egungun
(BRAZILIAN-COLOR-DOCU)

A production of SECNEB, Desenbanco, distributed by Embrafilme, Brazil. Director, Carlos Brajsblat. Camera (color), Edson Santos; editor, Juana Elbein, Brajsblat; sound editor, Walter Goulart. Narrated in Portuguese, with English subtitles. Reviewed at American Museum of Natural History, N.Y., as part of Margaret Mead Film Festival, July 26, 1985. Running time: **60 MINS.**

If you are of Nago Afro-Indian

ancestry and live on the islands off northeast Brazil, you may worship "Eguns," your ancestors who materialize wearing elaborate colorful costumes during the great festival of "Baba Olukorun." This pagan cult is 200 years old and is found only in these islands and in Nigeria and Dahomey, West Africa.

The "Egun" sect embodies the values and customs of the Nago people, who are fishermen, hunters and fruit-harvesters. "Egun" is a faith that gives unity and meaning to the Nago. On camera, young men who have been newly initiated speak of the peace they now feel, their new sense of continuity and purpose: "I feel joy. I feel reverence. I honor my ancestors. They guide us. We obey their rules."

Although the "Egun" rituals seem primitive and crude — composed of animal sacrifice, fireworks, mock-violence, incantations, dancing, chanting, clapping, torchlit walks by night in the surf, with children scampering to join the fun — the basic stuff of sophisticated religion appears to be there, satisfying man's need for transcendence, a kinship with nature, a sense of life's mystery.

But there's trouble in paradise. The simple island tranquility is menaced by vulgar tourism. Developers converge like locusts, buying up and despoiling the topography. A form of oppressive share-cropping is imposed. In addition, factionalism breaks out among the "Egun" elders. As the sect's 108-year-old patriarch dies, his succession is disputed. Finally, a triumvirate restores a shaky peace.

"Egungun" is relevant to anthropologists, theologians, scholars of Third World culture, college communities, and perhaps also is suitable for public television. — *Hitch*.

Hamara Shahar
(Bombay, Our City)
(INDIAN-COLOR-DOCU-16m)

An Icarus Films, New York, release Produced, directed and edited by Anand Patwardhan. Camera (color), Ranjan Palit; sound, Inderajit Neogy. Reviewed at American Museum of Natural History, N.Y., as part of Margaret Mead Film Festival, July 26, 1985. Running time: **82 MINS.**

"Instead of removing poverty, they remove the poor" is the line of

complaint in this docu against the Bombay city government from the thousands of dispossessed squatters living miserably in clusters on the city's edges. In the distance, mocking their shacks, are high-rise luxury and middle-class housing.

Like many other mushrooming cities within the developing Third World, Bombay has a huge underclass of unemployed and marginally employed day-laborers who live

cramped together in boxes and tents, barely subsisting. Periodically, city bulldozers push them out, like garbage heaps, crushing their few belongings. But the squatters resurface in colonies elsewhere, often whole families living precariously on sidewalks and on the shoulders of highways, posing safety problems.

In these ghetto communities, which must float about to survive, street-theaters act out grievances for audiences of appreciative squatters, dramatizing the lack of toilets, and satirizing the pompous and cruel authorities, whose plans for urban beauty are being sullied. Civil liberties attorneys argue with the police, who are readying a baton charge against the squatters. As babies suckle, their mothers rave at the camera — Here, take my picture, this is what it's like to be poor! Grotesque cripples bare their souls — is there a job for me somewhere?

Meanwhile, government officials are interviewed in their splendid homes and gardens, speaking neatly in English, coldly justifying the harsh measures being taken by the police against the poor. As they talk, the camera ironically peers about at the luxurious settings.

Frankly agit-prop, intended to enflame, this documentary has commendable energy and drama, but offers no solutions. These people, it appears, simply must suffer and endure, barely. Distribution to schools and to public television seems likely. — *Hitch*.

Shennu
(The Goddess)
(CHINESE-B&W-SILENT)

Sydney, Aug. 5.
A Lian Hua Film Co. production. Directed, screenplay by Wu Yonggang. No further credits supplied. Reviewed at Chauvel, Paddington, Aug. 1, 1985. Running time: **82 MINS.**
With: Ruan Lingyu, Li Keng, Zhong Zhizhi, Li Jupan.

Reviewed for the record, this 1934 silent production is evidence of an extremely vital and innovative film production in China 50 years ago.

It seems Chinese film producers, like some Japanese producers, were still making silent features well into the '30s; this one looks like a late-'20s production, in that it's fabulously well photographed (cameraman's credit was not available) and luminously acted by Ruan Lingyu, who was obviously a firstrate actress.

She plays a prostitute (the film's title is a euphemism for the oldest profession) who's on the game to feed and house herself and her son. She's taken under the wing of a plump, vicious pimp, who robs and beats her. Her son suffers at school

where his fellow pupils call him names because of his mother's profession, and parents petition the school to expel him. Eventually, the prostie kills her pimp and is sentenced to die; the boy's kindly teacher comes to the death cell to tell her he'll be well cared for.

Pic treats its subject without flinching, and probably wouldn't have passed the Production Code back in 1934. Ruan Lingyu gives a genuinely warm and moving performance as the protective mother who suffers nobly throughout. Supporting roles are subtly essayed. Cinematography, as noted, is firstrate, with interesting compositions and lighting. Script and direction by Wu Yonggang are likewise up to the best international standards of the period.

Print caught had suffered nitrate stock decomposition, but was restored in 1981. For buffs, the prospect of more discoveries from the vaults of Chinese cinema archives will be tantalizing. — *Strat.*

Xiangyin
(A Country Couple)
(CHINESE-COLOR)

Sydney, Aug. 5.
A Pearl River Studio production. Directed by Hu Bingliu. Features entire cast. Screenplay, Wang Yimin; camera (color), Liang Xiongwei; art director, Li Gan. No further credits supplied. Reviewed at Chauvel, Paddington, July 24, 1985. Running time: **85 MINS.**
With: Zhang Wixin, Liu Yen, Zhao Yue.

This recent offering from China's Pearl River Studio is a straightforward piece in which the messages contained are glazed with a reasonably entertaining sugar coating.

The setting is a small village set in spectacular mountain scenery (the film's alternative title is "Song Of A Mountain Village"), where Musheng, who runs a hand-operated ferry across the river, lives with his hard-working wife Taochun and their two children. Message No. 1 is that Musheng treats his wife in the old-fashioned way; although he works hard, she works harder, looking after the kids, the pig, the chicken and the house, while he takes her for granted.

Message No. 2 is that you should have regular medical checkups; Taochung ignores a pain in her stomach until terminal cancer is diagnosed.

Musheng doesn't tell his wife how ill she is, but suddenly starts treating her less like a slave and more like a woman. This upsets her outspoken cousin, Xingshi (presumably speaking for the modern Chinese woman), who berates Musheng for the past treatment of his wife. The pic eschews a final lingering death scene and ends rather abruptly as Mush-

eng takes his wife, by wheelbarrow, across the mountains to see the nearby city for the first time in her life; he knows if they wait a few months until a new road is opened, it will be too late.

Though the film is a bit pedantic it's helped by fine color photography and attractive performances from the principal players. It's an academic exercise, more intent on getting a message across than in telling a wholly satisfactory narrative, but though its commercial chances in the West are nil, it adds to the viewer's sum of information about the rapidly maturing Chinese film industry. — *Strat.*

Kölner Erinnerungen Aus 40 Jahren
(40 Years Of Cologne Recollections)
(WEST GERMAN-COLOR-DOCU-16m)

Berlin, July 29.
A WDR-3 (Cologne) production, for the "Germany, Germany..." tv series. Produced by Christhart Burgmann. Written and directed by Viktor Böll and Herbert Hoven. Camera (color), Paul Ellmerer. Reviewed at SFB Screening Room, Berlin, July 24, '85. Running time: **65 MINS.**
With: Heinrich Böll, Wolfgang Niedecker.

The last film of more than two dozen featuring the stories or the personality of Nobel Prize-winner for literature Heinrich Böll and rock music composer-singer Wolfgang Niedecker, "40 Years Of Cologne Recollections" was made by the writer's nephew Viktor Böll together with Herbert Hoven. It's part of a WDR-3 series of docus called "Germany, Germany..." told from various political and humanistic viewpoints.

In this case, the older writer Böll engages himself in conversation with the young composer Niedecker about the southern part of the city of Cologne in which they both grew up. Böll (who died recently at 67) views Cologne as a museum today, particularly after the devastating bombing of World War II. Nothing is much the same as he remembered it in his youth. As for Niedecker (born 1951), he remembers playing in the ruins and how the restored city grew up about him; for him it's the social, political and environmental problems of the day that characterize his music. Obviously the two like each other and have a lot in common.

The conversation takes place in Böll's home in the Eifel (near Cologne). The one-day shoot is then matched with docu newsreel footage of the past and with a well-attended rock concert featuring Niedecker and his band. Both men were associated with the peace movement demonstrations of 1983-84, and this is where a lot of the conversation between the two leads on different occasions. Böll also has some pointed remarks on the postwar political situation in West Germany.

At the end of the docu, Böll receives an award of merit from the French Cultural Ministry. This was in November of last year, when the writer was in fairly good health despite a vascular problem. He comments on how the French Assn. of Writers was the first to welcome the new postwar generation of German authors in 1947, almost immediately after the catastrophe of the Third Reich and the end of World War II.

A warm and engaging docu for scribe fans as well as film buffs.

—*Holl.*

Un Hombre, Cuando Es Un Hombre

(A Man, When He Is A Man) (COSTA RICAN-WEST GERMAN-COLOR-DOCU-16m)

Produced by ZDF, West Germany. Distributed in the U.S. by Women Make Movies, New York. Directed and written by Valeria Sarmiento. Camera (color), Leo de la Barra; editor, Claudio Martinez; sound editor, Joaquim Pinto; special effects, Claude Porcher. Reviewed at American Museum of Natural History, N.Y., as part of Margaret Mead Film Festival, July 26, 1985. Running time: **60 MINS.**

(In Spanish, with English subtitles.)

Manliness is more than macho virility, the morality of the muscle. As this film's title implies, a man, when he is a true man, is respectful of woman and is worthy of her love. But the film states that such true manliness is uncommon, at least in Costa Rica, where this film was produced by West German television.

Distributed in the U.S. by Women Make Movies, a feminist media center in New York founded in 1972, "Un Hombre" is deceptively simple, without narration, letting its images reveal its messages about the corrosive psycho-social conditioning of Costa Rican youth. Boys are seen insisting on virgin brides even as they seek relief with prostitutes. Boys practice and memorize the vanity and assertiveness of being male, as defined by macho convention.

In "Un Hombre," men and women, both old and young, talk about masculinity. The film's theme — the rareness of sensitive democratic reciprocal love between man and woman — occurs naturally, like a realization, as we watch Catholic school segregation of the sexes, debut parties, courting rituals, guitar serenades under the balcony, male pride of possession after the elaborate church wedding. Scenes with the popular Mexican film star, the late Jorge Negrete, romantic machismo personified, are intercut as ironic commentary.

A darker note intrudes, as two male prisoners describe for the camera their own infidelities, and those of their wives, whom they jealously murdered.

"Un Hombre" can circulate well among schools and community groups, with special value to the youth culture, especially if the right programming context can stimulate discussion. Public television also seems a possibility. —*Hitch.*

Year Of The Dragon
(COLOR)

Solid action in Chinatown thriller.

Hollywood, Aug. 5.
An MGM/UA Entertainment release. Produced by Dino De Laurentiis. Directed by Michael Cimino. Screenplay, Oliver Stone, Cimino, based on novel by Robert Daley; camera (Technicolor, Widescreen), Alex Thomson; editor, Françoise Bonnot; music, David Mansfield; sound, David Stephenson; production design, Wolf Kroeger; assistant director, Brian Cook; art direction, Vicki Paul; casting, Joanna Merlin. Reviewed at MGM Studios, Culver City, Aug. 2, 1985. (MPAA Rating: R.) Running time: 136 **MINS.**

Stanley	Mickey Rourke
Joey	John Lone
Tracy	Ariane
Angelo	Leonard Termo
Louis	Ray Barry
Connie	Caroline Kava
McKenna	Eddie Jones
Chang	Joey Chin
Yung	Victor Wong
Bin	K. Dock Yip
Hung	Pao Han Lin
Sullivan	Mark Hammer
Herbert	Dennis Dun

"Year Of The Dragon" is never as important as director Michael Cimino thinks it is, but there's a fair amount of solid action and gunplay, all set securely in the intricate, mysterious enigma of New York's Chinatown and its ties to worldwide drug-dealing. Beyond the action crowd, film will certainly attract the curious about Cimino's first effort since "Heaven's Gate," leaving them doubtlessly with mixed reactions.

Unquestionably, Cimino's eye for detail and insistence thereon has paid off in his impressive recreation of Chinatown at producer Dino De Laurentiis' studios in North Carolina. Crammed with an array of interesting characters, including the extras in the background, "Dragon" brims with authenticity.

That helps a lot in bringing a sense of veracity to a world (or underworld) that neither Cimino, cowriter Oliver Stone, novelist Robert Daley or any other Caucasian really knows very well, no matter how much time they spend on research.

Chinatowns from coast to coast and beyond are impenetrable to outsiders, but "Dragon" proceeds as best it can with a plot structured around just how difficult it is for a Polish-American police captain to apply his rigid ideals to a closed community.

Assigned to Chinatown to clear up a probelm of murderous youth gangs, Mickey Rourke quickly proves to be one of those lone renegade cops that fiction favors more than real-life. Beyond the teen toughs, Rourke wants to undo a criminal system rooted in a culture for thousands of years. Needless to say, this is a bit upsetting for both the Chinatown elders and his superiors at City Hall, who only want the streets safe for tourists.

Rourke is particularly annoying to John Lone, the urbane young crimelord who has his own problems in modernizing an ancient drug racket. Rourke is also a vexation for Chinese-American newscaster Ariane (are all heroines newscasters these days?) who veers between intense anger at Rourke's antics and wanting to jump his bones in her bathtub. That, along with everything else, is more than enough for Rourke's long-patient wife, Caroline Kava.

Beyond the color and the corpses, though, Cimino fails to focus on an idea and stick with it. He ends up playing with significant thoughts in between awkward lessons in Chinese history, losing most of them as they filter through half-baked resentments Rourke has left over from the Vietnam war.

Consequently, Rourke starts out as a sympathetic hero and proceeds to wear out everyone around him in lonely pursuit of ill-defined goals, not helped by his highly improbable fling with the newscaster. Nothing is clearly resolved beyond the last dead body.

Performances, though, are generally excellent and "Dragon" certainly never drags. —*Har.*

Volunteers
(COLOR)

Tedious, grating comedy.

Hollywood, Aug. 6.
A Tri-Star release of an HBO presentation in association with Silver Screen Partners. Produced by Richard Shepherd, Walter F. Parkes. Directed by Nicholas Meyer. Stars Tom Hanks. Screenplay, Ken Levine, David Isaacs from story by Keith Critchlow, camera (Metrocolor), Ric Waite; editors, Ronald Roose, Steven Polivka; music, James Horner; production design, James Schoppe; art direction, Jose Rodriguez Granada; set design, Arturo Brito; sound (Dolby), Claude Hitchcock; special effects coordinator, Raul Esquivel; associate producer, Theodore R. Parvin; assistant directors, Elie Cohn, Jesus Marin (Mexico); additional photography, Jack Green; casting, Joyce Robinson, Penny Ellers. Reviewed at the Picwood, Los Angeles, Aug. 5, '85. (MPAA Rating: R.) Running time: **106 MINS.**

Lawrence Bourne 3d	Tom Hanks
Tom Tuttle from Tacoma	John Candy
Beth Wexler	Rita Wilson
John Reynolds	Tim Thomerson
At Toon	Gedde Watanabe
Lawrence Bourne Jr	George Plimpton
Chung Mee	Ernest Harada

"Volunteers" is a very broad and mostly flat comedy about hijinx in the Peace Corps, circa 1962. Toplined Tom Hanks gets in a few good zingers as an upperclass snob doing time in Thailand, but promising premise and opening shortly descend into unduly protracted tedium. Pic probably will be an immediate candidate for foreign aid to the b.o.

Hanks plays Lawrence Bourne 3d, an arrogant, snide rich boy from Yale who trades places with an earnest Peace Corps designate when his enormous gambling debts land him in danger at home.

The sight of this snooty fellow, who arrives in Asia wearing a white dinner jacket, amidst a planeload of hootenannying naive liberals is good for a few yocks, as are some of his insolent, nasty cracks made in the direction of cohort Rita Wilson and anyone else he finds underfoot.

Once ensconced in a remote village, the contentious couple and ultra do-gooder John Candy set out to build a bridge across a river. Kidnaped and brainwashed by the commies, the gung-ho Candy disappears from the scene for a long stretch and, by the time he returns, the guerrillas and some fierce black marketeers have plans of their own for the bridge.

With Candy absent most of the time, Hanks' one-note, if sometimes clever, attitudinizing wears out its welcome after awhile. He also is deprived of anyone effective to play off, since newcomer Wilson fails to register and everyone else is frozen within the most exaggerated of caricatures.

Lensed in Mexico, pic features a muddy, truly ugly look that puts a damper on the proceedings from the outset. Also present is undoubtedly the most offensively blatant plug for Coca-Cola yet seen in the new era of Coke-owned entertainment companies. Sequence in which Hanks gets Wilson to stay with him by offering her that rarest of jungle commodities — a Coke — could play unaltered as a tv commercial.
— *Cart.*

The Bride
(COLOR)

Romantic remake lacks punch.

Hollywood, Aug. 9.
A Columbia Pictures presentation from Columbia-Delphi III Prods. of a Victor Drai production. Produced by Drai. Directed by Franc Roddam. Features entire cast. Screenplay by Lloyd Fonvielle, based on characters by Mary Shelley. Executive producer, Keith Addis; coproducer, Christ Kenny; camera (Rank color), Stephen H. Burum; editor, Michael Ellis; production designer, Michael Seymour; music, Maurice Jarre; costume designer, Shirley Russell; sound, David John; special makeup, Sarah Monzani; set decorator, Tessa Davies; Frankenstein laboratory designer, Jim Whiting; associate producer, Lloyd Fonvielle; casting, Ellen Chenoweth; assistant director, Patrick Clayton. Reviewed at the Samuel Goldwyn Theater, Beverly Hills, Calif., Aug. 8, 1985. (MPAA Rating: PG-13.) Running time: **118 MINS.**
Frankenstein .... Sting
Eva .... Jennifer Beals
Viktor .... Clancy Brown
Rinaldo .... David Rappaport
Mrs. Baumann .... Geraldine Page
Clerval .... Anthony Higgins
Magar .... Alexei Sayle
Bela .... Phil Daniels
Countess .... Veruschka
Dr. Zalhus .... Quentin Crisp
Josef .... Cary Elwes

Despite attractive cast and imaginative premise — two "Pygmalion" characters who create their own "Beauty And The Beast" fable — this "Frankenstein" tale is too randomly paced and, ultimately, too flat to spark any lasting marriage at the boxoffice.

Production departs for the host of other "Frankensteins" (including its most immediate predecessor, the 50-year-old "Bride Of Frankenstein") in its bright visual look, its lush Maurice Jarre score, its modern-day view of women, its younger characters, and its romantic scope. Pic also opens with a jolting laboratory sequence, when Sting as Baron Frankenstein brings to life the gauze-wrapped Jennifer Beals as the doctor's original monster creation looks on with frothing agitation.

The ensuing fairy tale aura of the story, directed by Franc Roddam and written by Lloyd Fonvielle (who also collaborated on "Lords Of Discipline"), is merely leisurely rather than enthralling. In opting to tone down the horror aspect of the genre, producer Victor Drai and his team have created another kind of monster: a "Frankenstein" movie that's not scary. The result culminates in silliness when the bride and her hulking mate-to-be (wonderfully played by Clancy Brown) collapse in each other's arms at the top of the baron's castle.

While there is deliberate humor at times, most of it successfully produced by a lilting dwarf character who steals the movie (David Rappaport), the intention of the filmmakers is not camp. That's both the pic's virtue and, at the conclusion, its downfall.

Screenwriter Fonvielle weaves, in concept, a nice balancing act between the Sting-Beals relationship and the similar "Pygmalion" act simultaneously occuring between Dr. Frankenstein's male monster and a vagabond friend, the dwarf. Latter pair is a truly engaging friendship as they head for Budapest to join a ragtag circus. Increasingly, this odd couple attracts interest while momentum flags in the Sting-Beals relationship.

Stephen Burum's lensing, largely in southern France, is a strong production value, and Michael Seymour's period production design ripely conveys old Europe.

One scene at an aristocratic social gathering, featuring Veruschka as a countess, crackles when a chic parlor discussion about Shakespeare is interrupted when a cat crosses Beals' path and the girl snarls like a lion. It's an electrifying moment and emblematic of the kind of punch the film otherwise lacks.

The modern thesis of a young, beautiful Frankenstein creation declaring her independence and her freedom to have an affair with a man if she wants (in this case, in opposition to Frankenstein's own long-suppressed sexual designs), is moderately ironic in the context of another century. If the film does draw supporters, they are more likely to be women, abetted by Sting's stylish blond arrogance. —*Loyn.*

My Science Project
(COLOR)

Funniest of the current crop of science pics, but slight.

Hollywood, Aug. 10.
A Buena Vista release of a Touchstone Films presentation. Produced by Jonathan Taplin. Directed by Jonathan Betuel. Features entire cast. Screenplay, Betuel; camera (Technicolor), David M. Walsh; editor, C. Timothy O'Meara; music, Peter Bernstein; production design, David L. Snyder; set decorator, Jerry Wunderlich; art director, John B. Mansbridge; visual effects supervisor, John Scheele; assistant director, Jerry Sobul; sound, Jim Webb; associate producer, E. Darrell Hallenbeck; casting, Bill Shepard. Reviewed at Egyptian Theater, Hollywood, Calif., Aug. 9, '85. (MPAA Rating: PG.) Running time: **94 MINS.**
Michael Harlan .... John Stockwell
Ellie Sawyer .... Danielle Von Zerneck
Vince Latello .... Fisher Stevens
Sherman .... Raphael Sbarge
Bob Roberts .... Dennis Hopper
Lew Harlan .... Barry Corbin
Dolores .... Ann Wedgeworth
Detective Nulty .... Richard Masur

Dennis Hopper has been seen in a lot of weird situations, but who would have expected to see him passing through a time warp riding to "the headwaters of creation." Such is the business of "My Science Project" and though it may not have much of a story it is probably the funniest of the three neo-science summer films thanks to comic turns by Hopper and Fisher Stevens as a Brooklyn-born grease monkey. If audiences can distinguish it from the other test tube babies, it could have a decent run at the boxoffice.

"My Science Project," along with "Weird Science" and "Real Genius," would have done well to use their intelligence to cure the summer disease plaguing Hollywood — lack of story. Though the films are not really similar they share a reliance on a manufactured high-tech plot as a pretext to the usual hijinx of the three. "My Science Project" is most dependent on its premise with little else on its mind.

Picture plays a bit like "Lifeforce" as a comedy with young Michael Harlan (John Stockwell) pillaging a military junkyard to come up with his high school science project, a super power contraption able to break the space and time barriers. It all plays like an excuse for some not-so-fancy special effects and the film's finale in the high school features a cast made up of Cleopatra, a Neanderthal man, Nazi soldiers, Godzilla and gladiators all collecting in battle.

Although there is little that is compelling about the action, luckily there is Harlan's sidekick Vince Latello (Fisher Stevens) to keep the proceedings lively with a steady stream of one-liners. Vince's car is lit up like a Christmas tree and he's the kind of guy who refers to school as a brain press, sits in class with sunglasses and a cigar and has a wisecrack for every occasion.

Director Jonathan Betuel, who also wrote the screenplay, seems to lavish most of his attention and best lines on Vince. Elsewhere script falls flat and romance between Harlan and fox-in-nerd's clothing Danielle Von Zerneck generates nary a spark despite all the pyrotechnics going off around them.

There is something irresistible about Hopper as the hippie science teacher, complete with VW van and Country Joe tapes, who tries to crack the mystery of the machine and winds up taking a cosmic ride. His return is equally spectacular, arriving in fringe jacket and cowboy hat looking like he just stepped out of "Easy Rider," announcing that "the future is a groove."

Despite the thinness of the idea, Betuel manages to keep up a brisk pace and delivers a helter-skelter climax with Vince, Harlan and Sherman (Raphael Sbarge), high school nerd tuned hero, literally taking on all the world to rescue the lovely Ellie (Von Zerneck).

Tech credits are adequate with effects often having a homemade quality which somehow links the film more to "Son Of Flubber" than "Close Encounters." Although film is a Disney production through its Touchstone label, the Disney moniker is nowhere to be found.— *Jagr.*

American Flyers
(COLOR)

Bicycle drama goes off in too many directions at once.

Hollywood, Aug. 8.
A Warner Bros. release. Produced by Gareth Wigan, Paula Weinstein. Directed by John Badham. Features entire cast. Screenplay by Steve Tesich; camera (Technicolor, Panavision), Don Peterman; editor, Frank Morriss; music, Lee Ritenour, Greg Mathieson; production designer, Lawrence G. Paull; set decorator, Garrett Lewis; set designer, Joseph Nemec 3d; sound (Dolby), Willie Burton; costumes, Marianna Elliott; assistant director, Jerry Ziesmer; associate producer, Gregg Champion. Reviewed at Samuel Goldwyn Theater, Beverly Hills, Calif., July 25, 1985. (MPAA Rating: PG-13.) Running time: **114 MINS.**

Marcus ......•.......... Kevin Costner

David	David Grant
Sarah	Rae Dawn Chong
Becky	Alexandra Paul
Mrs. Sommers	Janice Rule
Muzzin	Luca Bercovici
Jerome	Robert Townsend
Dr. Conrad	John Amos

Story of two brothers who untangle their mixed emotions as they compete in a grueling bicycle race, "American Flyers" is most entertaining when it rolls along unencumbered by big statements. Unfortunately, overblown production just pumps hot air in too many directions and comes up limp. Boxoffice appeal is limited with even biking aficionados likely to find the action inauthentic.

Everything from whirling aerial cameras tracking the race to overheated family strife and Panavision lensing attempt to give more import to events than the film can hold. Although scripter Steve Tesich hit the bull's eye with the bicycling-set "Breaking Away," "American Flyers" is off-center and poorly structured, displaying only an occasional deft touch.

Basic conflict between underachiever David (David Grant) and older brother Marcus (Kevin Costner), a fierce competitor and no-nonsense sports doctor, is crammed into a hotbed of family problems including a career-woman mother (Janice Rule) who emotionally abandoned her dying husband.

If this isn't enough, one of the boys is destined for the same fate as the father. So, with the shadow of death hanging over them, the brothers set off for Colorado for "the toughest bicycle race in America."

Troupe is joined by Marcus' girlfriend Sarah (Rae Dawn Chong) and a hitchhiker (Alexandra Paul) who becomes David's girl and immediately fast friends with the group.

Combativeness between brothers yields to comaraderie, but true nature of their conflict is difficult to get a handle on. David's reactions are often inexplicably hostile. He's not just a quirky character, he's a crank. Characters emote freely with no underpinnings for their feelings.

Women's roles are hopelessly underwritten as well, with little more to do than stand around and cheer their men. Mother also is a mystery and one more cog in a not very well oiled machine.

Bicycles, however, run smoothly and race sequences are the strongest part of the film as cyclists climb scenic Rocky Mountain slopes. But even here production resorts to clichés by portraying the Russian champion as a stereotypical thick-waisted and thick witted Soviet. Also contributing to the contrived atmosphere are a series of glaring

commercial product tie-ins.

Performances are adequate considering that over-production makes the characters seem larger than life without being lifelike. — *Jagr.*

De Veras Me Atrapaste
(You Really Got Me)
(MEXICAN-COLOR)

Mexico City, July 15.
A Películas Mexicanas release of a Producciones Manchuria and Clasa Films Mundiales production. Produced by Manuel Barbachano Ponce and Gerardo Pardo Neria. Executive producers, Sonia Valenzuela, Maggie Rincón Gallardo. Directed by Pardo Neria. Features entire cast. Screenplay, Pardo Neria, Tony Pardo, based on an idea by René Avila Fabila; camera (color), Oscar Palacios; original music, Grupo Manchuria; editor, Gerardo Pardo Neria, Oscar Palacios; sound, Emilio Cantón. Reviewed at Cine Insurgentes 70, Mexico City, July 13, 1985. Running time: **90 MINS.**

Aída Villanueva	Lucy Reyna
El Humo	Gerardo de la Peña
Tenoch	Tenoch Ramos
Laura	Annette Fradera
Pecas	Armando Martín
Aída's father	Claudio Brook
El Tira	Eduardo López Rojas

With the title coming from The Kinks 1965 hit, "De Veras Me Atrapaste" (You Really Got Me), debut pic by Gerardo Pardo Neria, allows us to see a young Mexican filmmaker who knows how to use camera and sound to turn a basically weak storyline into a disturbing film looking at today's youth.

Plot concerns Aída (Lucy Reyna), the adolescent daughter of a provincial politician who comes to the capital, where friends introduce her to the world of sex, drugs and rock 'n' roll, such as it exists in Mexico.

She has almost mystical premonitions about young ghost rocker El Humo (Gerardo de la Peña), who she later meets at a party and the two fall in love.

When he confesses that he can't possibly marry her, she decides to return to Tamaulipas, although at the last minute she changes her mind.

The ending of the film has Aída, after not hearing from El Humo (his name means "Smoke" in Spanish) for five days, decide to try smoking marijuana and taking hallucinogenic mushrooms. Alone in the darkness of her room, she "sees" El Humo's death in a motorcycle accident and realizes she is truly alone.

This skimpy plotline is not the film. Rather, what there is is a sympathetic look at disillusioned Mexican youth in their quest to live. Through stark images and deft use of sound, Pardo Neria maintains an enigmatic tension.

The acting is strong, especially Reyna, her best friend Laura (played by Annette Fradera) and the drugged-out guitar player/singer Tenoch, also a member of the Mexican heavy metal group Newspaper.

The music alternates with the ac-

tion, though it does not take center stage as with most rock films. The sound is spare and raw, and does not lend itself to a soundtrack album.

With a low budget, the director has had to cut some corners, but usually he manages to clean up after himself. Much of the language is made up of Mexico City street slang, wich may limit the audience to adolescents. —*Lent.*

Diesel
(FRENCH-COLOR)

Paris, Aug. 6.
A UGC release of a Stephan Films/Filmedis/Farena Films/TF-1 Films coproduction. Produced by Vera Belmont. Directed by Robert Kramer. Screenplay, Serge Leroy, Richard Morgiéve, Kramer, camera (color), Ramon Suarez; sound, Alain Curvelier; art director, Max Borto; costumes, Edith Vesperini; music, uncredited. Reviewed at the UGC screening room, Neuilly, August 5, 1985. Running time: **92 MINS.**
With: Gérard Klein, Agnès Soral, Richard Bohringer, Niels Arestrup, Magali Noël, Xavier Deluc, Roland Blanche, Laurent Terzieff, Souad Amidou, Jacques Penot, Caroline Lang.

Mad Max has a poor cousin in France. He's called Diesel, lives in the desolate near future, drives about in a souped-up pickup truck and sometimes acts as savior and avenger when the occasion calls for it. Here the occasion comes in the form of a young prostitute (Agnès Soral) who has escaped from a subterannean city where she has witnessed the murder of a colleague and is being pursued by a trio of goons unleashed by the town's vengeful pimp.

No parody is intended. "Diesel" takes its clichés with a straight face and feeds them back to the audience without a glint of humor — worse, without imagination or energy. Though the tale takes the form of a series of pursuits and confrontations, there is no suspense or sense of movement (an early car chase has all the dash of a turtle race).

In the title role, Gérard Klein generates no masculine authority and often looks like a nebbishy Mel Gibson. There are unintentional laughs to be had at the expense of most of the other players, notably Magali Noël as a tender-tough truckstop mamma and Laurent Terzieff as the megalomaniac mastermind of the totalitarian metropolis.

The ultimate unpleasant shock is that the director is Robert Kramer, the estimable Yank indie filmmaker who has been working in France since 1980. Nothing in this glum mainstream product reflects the talent and personality of his previous work. —*Len.*

Elsa, Elsa!
(FRENCH-COLOR)

Paris, Aug. 4.
A Bloody Mary/Films A2 coproduction, with the participation of the Ministry of Culture. Produced by Didier Haudepin and S. Alvarez de Toledo. Directed by Haudepin. Screenplay, Haudepin, Alain LeHenry, S. Alvarez de Toledo; Camera (color), Gilberto Azevedo; editor, Yves Deschamps; art director, Jacques Rouxel; sound, Antoine Ouvrier and Jean-Paul Loublier; music, Eric Lelann. Reviewed at Unifrance Films, Paris, Aug. 3, 1985. Running time: **77 MINS.**

Ferdinand	François Couzet
Ferdinand (child)	Maxime Manson
Elsa 1	Lio
Elsa 2	Christine Pascal
Felix	Tom Novembre
Juliette	Catherine Frot
Yvonne	Anne Letourneau
Nenesse	Romain Bouteille
Albert	Jean-Paul Roussillon

A slight but pleasant comedy in a familiar film-within-in-a-film vein, "Elsa, Elsa!" concerns a young scripter-director (François Cluzet) who is commissioned to write a feature based on his own experience as a child actor. Distracted by the departure of his girl-friend, Elsa, Cluzet starts to write in a sub-plot about his romantic problems, which drives his producer to distraction and menaces the production. After wrestling with both professional and personal obstacles, Cluzet gets his film in front of the cameras.

Writer-director Didier Haudepin offers some amusing anecdotes on the difficulties of being a child thesp — something he knows well since at age eight he was launched prematurely into cinema as Jeanne Moreau's son in Peter Brook's "Moderato Cantabile" — and manages some spry variations in an overworked autobiographical mode. Yves Deschamps' editing of the flip-flop between Cluzet's real present and his cinematically re-fashioned past is deft.

Mostly young cast is fresh and engaging, with Cluzet back in an effective wistful register. Tom Novembre, a pop singer, and Lio, another singer in debut here, has sweetness as Elsa, as re-imagined by Cluzet. In one of the pic's nicest touches, Christine Pascal makes a cameo appearance late in the film as the more mature-looking, real-life Elsa.—*Len.*

Return
(U.S.-COLOR)

Indie return-of-the-dead chiller just making the rounds.

Berlin, Aug. 7.
A Silver Prod., Boston. Executive producers, Andrew Silver, Yong-Hee Silver. Produced by Philip Spinelli. Features entire cast. Written and directed by Andrew Silver, based on Donald Harrington's novel "Some Other Place, The Right Place." Camera (color), Janos Zsombolyai; sets, Charles Tomlinson; editor, Gabrielle Gilbert; music, Ragnar Grippe, Michael Shrieve. Reviewed at Ber-

liner Screening Room, Berlin, Aug. 6, '85. Running time: **82 MINS.**

With: Karlene Crockett (Diana Stoving), John Walcutt (Day Whittaker), Lisa Richards (Ann Stoving), Frederic Forrest (Brian Stoving), Anne Lloyd Francis (Eileen Sedgely), Lenore Zann (Susan), Thomas Rolopp (Lucky), Harry Murphy (MDC Officer), Lee Stetson (Daniel Montross), Ariel Aberg-Riger (Diana, three years old).

"Return," debut pic directed by Boston-based Andrew Silver, carries the subtitle "A Case Of Passion" and thereby gives away the twist on which both the film and the theme is structured. This is one of those "restless souls beyond" tales about a murdered man whose presence is felt by both strangers and relatives on Earth as he apparently tries to "return" and make contact with a young woman for some mysterious reason. That reason forms the nucleus of the story.

For those who enjoy the presence of poltergeists in the house and a few friendly ghosts in the closet, "Return" should prove fascinating. The heroine (Karlene Crockett) has a premonition that her mother never has fully told her the story of her childhood in Massachusetts, so she leaves home in Arkansas and sets out to find out some things for herself. By chance, she stumbles across a woman adept at "age-regression" hypnosis — in fact, she happens to be experimenting with a strange case related to Crockett's own background.

After checking out the details, it turns out Crockett can truly make contact with her murdered grandfather via the person of a young man the grandfather now appears to be "possessing" from time to time in efforts to make contact with the real world. The theory here is that when people die, their spirits or souls enter into the bodies of people in the next generation, sometimes even staying rather close to home in making the transfer.

Possession being the initial thematic crux of "Return," an attempt is made to shift gears to a psychological thriller. It works to the exent that the story itself provides material to digest. Here the film, after a promising start, just runs out of gas, and the punch line is given away too soon.

Unspooled at fests in Houston, the Virgin Islands and Munich, "Return" thrusts helmer Andrew Silver in the forefront of Boston independents. Lensing is a plus, by Hungary's Janos Zsombolyai who has collaborated on all of Peter Bacso's films. —*Holl.*

Ah-Fei
(TAIWAN-COLOR)

Santiago, July 28.
An MBR Film Co. production. Produced by Liu Shan Chung. Directed by Wan Jen. Screenplay, Hou Hsiao Hsien, Liao Hui In. Reviewed at the Taiwanese Film Week, Espaciocal, Santiago, Chile, July 26, '85. Running time: **115 MINS.**

With: Cheng Chuo Yen, Ke I-Cheng, Su Ming Ming, Yen Cheng Kuo, Pai Pai, Chang Ei Tzi.

This story of a young girl's rise from rags to riches, from the boondocks to the big city and from subordination to her family to independence is a rather simplistic soap opera unlikely to make it in Western markets, although it may be of interest on a more limited scale in its depiction of women's lib, Taiwanese-style.

Hsiu Chin and her daughter, Ah-Fei, represent two generations of Chinese women. Hsiu was married off by her family and is frequently beaten by her husband, who also squanders her dowry and has an affair with another woman. When Hsiu tries to return to her father, she is sent back; the traditional view has it that women must accept their fate, whatever it be. Strong and determined, she somehow manages to keep her family afloat and educate her children, but, understandably, she becomes frustrated and bitter in the process.

Meanwhile, Ah-Fei grows up. A bright young girl, she finishes high school and college, becoming a junior executive in an advertising agency. This enables her to move mother and family out of their slum dwellings and maintain them in middle-class comfort. Ah-Fei then reencounters her high-school sweetheart, leading to a conflict with her mother. Ah-Fei ultimately succeeds in breaking away and living her own life.

The interesting contrast between the two women is marred by poor transitions and superficial handling of the characters. Technical credits are okay, but the makeup of the aging parents could have been better. —*Amig.*

Escalier C
(Staircase C)
(FRENCH-COLOR)

Paris, Aug. 2.
An AMLF release of a Films 7/FR3 coproduction. Produced by Marie-Dominique Girodet. Directed by Jean-Charles Tacchella. Screenplay, Tacchella and Elvire Murail, based on the latter's novel; camera (Fujicolor), Jacques Assuerus; art director, Georges Levy; editor, Agnès Guillemot; sound, Pierre Lenoir; music, Raymond Allessandrini; production manager, Patrick Delauneux. Reviewed at the Gaumont Colisée theater, Paris, Aug. 1, 1985. Running time: **102 MINS.**

Forster Lafont	Robin Renucci
Bruno	Jean-Pierre Bacri
Florence	Catherine Leprince
Claude	Jacques Bonnafé
Conrad	Jacques Weber
Mr. Lafont	Claude Rich
Joss	Michel Aumont
Beatrice	Catherine Frot
Al	Hugues Quester
Mrs. Bernhardt	Mony-Rey
Charlotte	Florence Giorgetti

Jean-Charles Tacchella, who has never managed to repeat the Stateside success of his "Cousin, Cousine," confronts his first adapted script in "Escalier C," based on a prizewinning first novel by Elvire Murail, a 27-year-old French graduate of Cambridge U., who aided the filmmaker in his screenplay. The book's action, set in Manhattan, has been transposed to Paris and its personages Gallicized. The geographic shuttle presents no real problems, though Tacchella's treatment of the material does.

Protagonist (Robin Renucci) is a cynical, misogynistic young art critic who gets his comeuppance in a series of personal entanglements and dramas. A wary friendship with a homosexual neighbor (Jacques Bonnafé), an ambivalant relationship with a pretty young press agent (Catherine Leprince), the discovery of an unknown artist of brilliance (Jacques Weber) and the suicide of a lonely Jewish woman in his building, are the major interacting elements in his emotional thaw-out.

Tacchella does not seem at ease with the novelist's world and personages, and his generally benign attitudes tend to sentimentalize people and events to excess. Murail must no doubt share the blame for the self-consciously "in" dialog that rings false in many of the film's crucial scenes. She has allowed Tacchella to change her tale's piquant twist: the protagonist's newfound equilibrium is associated with his move towards homosexuality. Tacchella chickens out by pairing off Renucci and Leprince and keeping latter's rapport with Bonnafé strictly platonic.

Many scenes are set in the stairwell of the apartment building where Renucci lives, in which a gallery of minor characters comes and goes, in a series of vignettes that are meant perhaps to recall the populist French films of the 1930s. Here too Tacchella is not at his best, and is technically sloppy with these studio-shot sequences.

Renucci, one of the promising new crowd of young screen talent, is only fair as the hard-nosed snot who finally ends up an over-sensitive humanist, at first professing a visceral hatred for Auguste Renoir paintings, only to later melt into tears before one of his canvases. Most of the secondary performances suffer from sketchy scripting. Claude Rich, as Renucci's bemused businessman father, and Michel Aumont, as a tipsy neighbor, come out a little better than the others.

Tacchella's indulgent musings on the endearing foibles of the French middle-class have provided some genuine charm and feeling in past films, but "Escalier C" lacks his usual address. — *Len.*

Legend
(U.S.-COLOR)

Lavishly produced but thin-scripted fantasy.

London, Aug. 19.
A 20th Century Fox (Universal Pictures in U.S.) release of a Legend Production. Produced by Arnon Milchan. Directed by Ridley Scott. Features entire cast. Screenplay, William Hjortsberg; camera (Panavision, Fujicolor), Alex Thomson; editor, Terry Rawlings; music, Jerry Goldsmith; special makeup, Rob Bottin; production design, Assheton Gorton; costumes, Charles Knode; special effects supervisor, Nick Allder; production supervisor, Hugh Harlow; choreography, Arlene Phillips; 1st assistant directors, Garth Thomas, Bill Westley; additional photography, Max Mowdray, Harry Oakes; supervising art directors, Norman Dorme, Les Dilley; set decorator, Ann Mollo; coproducer, Tim Hampton; The Rob Bottin Crew: Production manager, Richard White; sculptural design, Henry Alvarez; lead special make-up artist, Vince Prentice; lab technician supervisor, John Goodwin; cosmetic print supervisor, Margaret Beserra; Visual Optical Effects: Matte photography consultant, Stanley Sayer, Fotherly Ltd., Peerless Camera Co. Reviewed at National Film Theater, London, Aug. 18, 1985. Running time: **94 MINS.**

Jack	Tom Cruise
Princess Lili	Mia Sara
Darkness	Tim Curry
Gump	David Bennent
Blix	Alice Playten
Screwball	Billy Barty
Brown Tom	Cork Hubbert
Pox	Peter O'Farrell
Blunder	Kiran Shah
Oona	Annabelle Lanyon
Meg Mucklebones	Robert Picardo
Nell	Tina Martin

"Legend" contains all the exhilarating visual elements audiences have come to expect from Ridley Scott. It is a fairy-tale produced on a grand scale, a classic tale of the struggle between darkness and light, good and evil, set in some timeless world and peopled with fairies, elves and goblins, plus a spectacularly satisfying Satan.

At the same time, the basic premise is alarmingly thin, a compendium of any number of ancient fairytales including "Jack And The Beanstalk" and "The Sleeping Beauty," with borrowings from dramatic works such as "A Midsummer Night's Dream" and "Peter Pan." Plot concerns a heroic young peasant, Jack, who takes his sweetheart, Princess Lili, to see the most powerful creatures on earth, the last surviving unicorns. Unknown to the young lovers, Darkness (i.e., The Devil) is using the innocence of Lili as a bait to trap and emasculate the unicorns, and succeeds in removing the horn of the male beast, triggering an instant ice-age. Soon after, Darkness kidnaps the princess, intending to have her as his bride. It's up to intrepid Jack, and a friendly band of elves, to come to the rescue.

Perhaps realizing that the plot mechanics aren't very interesting, Scott has kept them to a minimum and concentrated on the action and the bizarre, magical characters. All too often, though, William Hjortsberg's script contains such deliberately anachronistic lines as "Time goes fast when you're having fun" or "I get the point, Lord," which may be intended humorously, but which fall pretty flat. Another minus is the rather insipid hero, as played by Tom Cruise.

Kids of all ages should be entranced by the magnificent make-up effects of Rob Bottin and his crew, from the smallest elves to the giant Darkness. The latter is unquestionably the most impressive depiction of Satan ever brought to the screen. Tim Curry plays him majestically with huge horns, cloved feet, red, leathery flesh and yellow eyes, plus a resonantly booming voice. Pic's best scene comes when he threatens the lovely Lili and she tells him he's an animal: "We're all animals, my dear," he replies.

Also registering strongly is David Bennent (the lead in "The Tin Drum" a few years back) as a knowing pixie with large, pointed ears. Annabelle Lanyon is also very effective as a jealous fairy, apparently based on J. M. Barrie's Tinkerbell. As clumsy elves, Billy Barty and Cork Hubbert provide plenty of fun.

Ironically, for a film that celebrates nature, "Legend" was almost entirely lensed on the large Bond set at Pinewood (production was interrupted by a fire which destroyed the set). It is technically wondrous to behold, but the very slender basis on which so much imagination and expertise is resting makes it a rather fragile production. Terry Rawlings' editing has resulted in a very tight 94-minute running time, leaving audiences no time to ponder the script's inadequacies. Jerry Goldsmith's score is one of his best.

"Legend" is set to open the Venice Film Fest Aug. 26, but theatrical openings have been put back until year's end. With its legendary elements, it does seem more of a Christmas film than a summer one, but it will have to be handled carefully if results commensurate with the big budget are to be achieved. —*Strat.*

Paradise View
(JAPANESE-COLOR)

Edinburgh, Aug. 14.

A Hitoban production. Produced by Mitsuzo Anan. Written and directed by Tsuyoshi Takamine. Features entire cast. Camera (color), Takao Toshioka; music, Haruomi Hosono; sound, Mitsuo Azuma; assistant director, Tsuyoshi Yamada. Reviewed at Edinburgh Film Festival, Aug. 13, 1985. Running time: **111 MINS.**
Reishu . . . . Kaoru Kobayashi
Chiru . . . . Jun Togawa
Ito . . . . Haruomi Hosono
Papa . . . . Shizuko Osemi

Kamado . . . . Tomi Heira
Bindare . . . . Hiroko Taniyama
Micha . . . . Kat-chan
Machu . . . . Eddie

This genuine oddity is supposedly the first indigenous Okinawan feature, and is largely spoken in the Okinawan language, with Japanese subtitles. The strange story is set in the early 1970s, just before the island, which had been occupied by the U.S. since World War II, was returned to Japan.

There are a dozen or more odd characters living in this subtropical paradise, chief among them Reishu, who used to work for the Americans and now spends his time idly gluing numbers on ants and catching poisonous snakes. At a traditional *moashibi* ceremony (a gathering of young people where sexual partners are exchanged) he impregnates a girl who's engaged to a mainland Japanese, considered by her mother to be a good catch. The pregnancy complicates everything, of course, and the girl's burly brothers seek vengeance on Reishu.

Pic is filled with reference to strange customs and rituals (Japanese audiences have been supplied with a glossary of Okinawan terms), including "Inton Grass," a kind of tropical foliage which, when eaten by pigs, can drive them mad so they become "rainbow pigs" and can attack humans. This, indeed, is the fate of the unfortunate Reishu at the film's end.

Item's bizarre sense of humor and unfamiliar rituals make it something of a puzzle for uninitiated audiences, so "Paradise View" is unlikely to get any commercial attention outside the Japanese market. Its very originality of setting and lingo could, however, appeal to fest programmers, though program notes will have to be carefully prepared if viewers are to appreciate this most unusual effort. —*Strat.*

Agnes Of God
(COLOR)

Well-made drama suffers from brittle Jane Fonda performance.

Hollywood, Aug. 13.

A Columbia release of a Columbia-Delphi IV production. Produced by Patrick Palmer, Norman Jewison. Directed by Jewison. Stars Jane Fonda, Anne Bancroft, Meg Tilly. Screenplay, John Pielmeier, based on his play; camera (Metrocolor), Sven Nykvist; editor, Antony Gibbs; music, Georges Delerue; production design, Ken Adam; art direction, Carol Spier; set decoration, Jaro Dick; costume design, Renee April; sound (Dolby), Richard Lightstone; associate producers, Charles Milhaupt, Bonnie Palef-Woolf; assistant director, John Board; casting, Gretchen Rennell. Reviewed at the Burbank Studios, Burbank, Aug. 13, 1985. (MPAA Rating: PG-13.) Running time: **98 MINS.**
Dr. Martha Livingston . . . . Jane Fonda
Mother Miriam Ruth . . . . . . Anne Bancroft

Sister Agnes . . . . Meg Tilly
Dr. Livingston's mother . . . Anne Pitoniak
Detective Langevin . . . . . . Winston Rekert
Father Martineau . . . . Gratien Gelinas
Justice Joseph Leveau . . . . . Guy Hoffman
Monsignor . . . . Gabriel Arcand
Eve LeClaire . . . . Françoise Faucher
Eugene Lyon . . . . Jacques Tourangeau

"Agnes Of God" is solidly crafted, middlebrow, issue-oriented drama that pits opposite each other the forces of logic and religion. The property's past history as a hit play, its cast and theological orientation will insure a serious reception among many critics and audience groups, and pic appears headed for the same level of success achieved by Jewison's previous dramatic adaptation, "A Soldier's Story."

John Pielmeier penned the screenplay from his own 1982 play about a young nun who is found to have given birth and then strangled the baby at an isolated convent. A psychiatrist, played by Jane Fonda, is appointed by the court to determine whether or not the young woman is fit to stand trial, and is assured that the seemingly innocent, naive girl has no recollection of the child or conception.

In her aggressive quest for the facts in the case, Fonda goes head to head with Mother Superior Anne Bancroft, a cagey, very hip woman of God whose past as a wife and mother gives her a strong knowledge of the real world values represented by Fonda.

At first, Meg Tilly's Sister Agnes seems like a devout hysteric who in all probability is merely covering up for deeds of her own she'd rather not face. Under hypnosis, stranger, more mysterious aspects of her personality come to light, although Fonda finally finds that her traditional sleuthing can lead her only so far.

Three-character theater piece has been expanded extensively for the screen, and one of the film's strongest assets is the on-location lensing in Ontario and Quebec. French Canadian characters lend some unusual color to the tale, and Sven Nykvist's crystal-clear lensing superbly catches the cold winter light, the warmth of fresh milk and people's breath, and the impeccable values of Ken Adam's production design.

On the downside, about 80% of Fonda's dialog must consist of questions, and her relentless interrogating, mannered chain-smoking and enforced two dimensionality cause her to become tiresome very early on. Half-hearted attempts are made to flesh out the character by giving her a senile mother and a barren personal life, but she remains a brittle cliché of a modern professional woman.

At a couple of moments, Bancroft comes across as almost too wise for her own good, but actress

gives a generally highly engaging performance as a religious woman too knowledgeable to be one-upped by even the craftiest layman.

Meg Tilly is angelically beautiful as the troubled youngster and more than holds her own with the two veteran Oscar winners. Her eyes do become increasingly moist with emotion as the picture progresses, but she brings a convincing innocence and sincerity to the role that would be hard to match.

Predictably, religion and reason play to something like a draw, and the world can move on even if the major questions — both specific and general — remain unanswered.

Georges Delerue's score is discreetly lovely. — *Cart.*

My Beautiful Laundrette
(BRITISH-COLOR)

Edinburgh, Aug. 19.

A Working Title-SAF production, with Channel 4. Produced by Sarah Radclyffe, Tim Bevan. Directed by Stephen Frears. Features entire cast. Screenplay, Hanif Kureishi; camera (Technicolor), Oliver Stapleton; editor, Mick Audsley; music, Stanley Myers, Hans Zimmer; art director, Hugo Wyhowski; costumes, Lindy Hemming. Reviewed at Edinburgh Film Festival, Aug. 17, 1985. Running time: **97 MINS.**
Johnny . . . . Daniel Day Lewis
Omar . . . . Gordon Warnecke
Nasser . . . . Saeed Jaffrey
Omar's papa . . . . Roshan Seth
Rachel . . . . Shirley Anne Field
Tanya . . . . Rita Wolf

The script for this intelligent, up-to-the-minute film is by Hanif Kureishi, a respected Pakistani playwright resident in Britain. Which is just as well, because if this tale of profiteering middle-class Pakistani capitalists making a fortune out of unscrupulous wheeling and dealing in an impoverished London had been written by an English writer it would probably be labeled racist.

Focus is on two youths, friends from schooldays. Johnny is a working-class white whose punkish mates are members of the National Front, a fascist group of thugs. Omar lives with his left-leaning widower father in a rundown house by the railway line. When the film begins, Omar is given a menial job by his wealthy uncle, Nasser, a flagrant go-getter who's on the way to earning his second million. He likes young Omar and eventually gives him a rundown laundrette which he and Johnny quickly convert into a veritable palace of a place, complete with video screens and other amenities. Meanwhile, a repressed love blossoms between Omar and Johnny, adding a further degree of tension to the already volatile racial situation.

As always, director Stephen Frears does a superb job of work when given a good script, and this is a very good script. It's peopled with interesting characters, allowing for a gallery of fine performances and situations, intelligently marshalled to make a strong statement about race relations in Britain today (and sexual stereotyping, too). In an excellent cast, standout performances come from Saeed Jaffrey as the avuncular Nasser and Shirley Anne Field as the white mistress, holding her head high despite an increasingly embarrassing situation.

Technically, pic is first rate in all departments. —*Strat.*

Warning Sign
(COLOR)

Failed thriller about germ warfare contamination.

Hollywood, Aug. 16.
A 20th Century Fox release of a Barwood/Robbins production. Produced by Jim Bloom. Executive producer, Matthew Robbins. Directed by Hal Barwood. Features entire cast. Screenplay, Barwood, Robbins; camera (Deluxe color), Dean Cundey; editor, Robert Lawrence; music, Craig Safan; production design, Henry Bumstead; set decoration, Mickey S. Michaels; costume design, Aggie Guerard Rodgers; sound (Dolby), Michael Evje; associate producer, Robert Latham Brown; assistant director, Nick Marck; casting, Susan Arnold. Reviewed at 20th Century Fox Studios, L.A., Aug. 16, 1985. (MPAA Rating: R.) Running time: **100 MINS.**

Cal Morse	Sam Waterston
Joanie Morse	Kathleen Quinlan
Major Connolly	Yaphet Kotto
Dan Fairchild	Jeffrey De Munn
Dr. Nielsen	Richard Dysart
Tom Schmidt	G.W. Bailey
Vic Flint	Jerry Hardin
Bob	Rick Rossovich
Dana	Cynthia Carle

"Warning Sign" is a woefully bad paranoid thriller for 20th Century Fox limning how germ warfare research could make the United States into the land of the living dead. Lensed under the title "Biohazard" (a moniker previously claimed by an indie horror film made coincidentally by 21st Century Distribution), first-time director Hal Barwood attempts to establish wall-to-wall, high-pitched tension, but result is deadly dull and pretty ridiculous to boot. Count on this one to make a quick transition from the big screen to the homevid market.

Film stands as an ideal companion piece to the 1982 MGM/UA effort "Endangered Species," in that both pit a solitary cop against both some difficult Far West citizens and a deadly plague that's threatening to spread and contaminate more than a limited number of victims. Pic also falls in the same genre as Fox' 1984 flop "Impulse."

Central setting here is a lab ostensibly devoted to agricultural research but secretly involved in illegal development of biological weapons. An accidental spill causes the building to seal itself off. Some

of those trapped inside seem to die, but then bounce back as homicidal maniacs bent on destroying the rest of the survivors.

Cop Sam Waterston has his hands full with concerned citizens and high-handed military rep Yaphet Kotto, but has a personal stake in trying to save the day since wife Kathleen Quinlan, a security guard, is among the sequestered.

Everyone here acts so feverishly that it's impossible to identify the sick ones without a scorecard, and the electrifying pace Barwood tries to set merely seems punishing and exhausting. Each scene has people desperately trying to get in or out of some room or building, and the characters all exhibit such abusive attitudes toward one another that the germ, which is supposed to make people angry and mean as well as ill, hardly seems to make a difference in the personalities.

Toward the end, a scientist makes a medical discovery worthy of the Nobel Prize in two minutes' time, and climactic action is so poorly staged that one begins longing for the clarity of Republic serials by comparison.

This is not the film that Sam Waterson needed to follow up "The Killing Fields," and remainder of the cast has seen nothing but brighter times. —*Cart.*

Special Police
(FRENCH-COLOR)

Paris, Aug. 9.
A UGC release of a Cathala Prods./TF 1 Films coproduction. Executive producer, Norbert Saada. Produced by Norbert Chalon. Directed by Michel Vianey. Screenplay, Vianey, Simon Mickael; camera (color), Claude Agostini; editor, Geneviève Winding; sound, Jean-Bernard Thomasson; production manager, Annia-Maria Otta. Reviewed at the UGC Normandie theater. Aug. 7, 1985. Running time: **92 MINS.**
With: Richard Berry, Carole Bouquet, Fanny Cottençon, Jean Pierre Malo, Jean Jacques Moreau, Georges Lavaudant, Jean-Claude Dauphin.

"Special Police" is nothing special, just another ineptly contrived thriller off the unstoppable assembly line of local genre pictures. Richard Berry is a wisecracking police functionary and Carole Bouquet a damsel-in-distress, both on the run from killers dispatched to recover tapes implicating people in high places of lowly deeds. Berry, a computer whiz kid, finally prevails by dispatching the compromising material across every electronic billboard in the French capital.

Director Michel Vianey wrote the script with Simon Mickael, the pseudonymous ex-police inspector who brought his experience to the script of Claude Zidi's smash "Les Ripoux" (My New Partner). That sense of authentic detail is totally missing here, where everybody talks

and acts as only tritely conceived movieland cops and criminals can.

Typical of the script's sloth is the Berry's talents with computers have little place in the action until quite late in the film, by which time the hero has dispatched his antagonists in the usual blood-and-guts fashion. Maybe this film was written with a computer. —*Len.*

The Flying Devils
(DANISH-COLOR)

Copenhagen, Aug. 9.
A Metronome release of an Erik Crone Film Sales and Continental Pictures production with the Danish and Swedish Film Institutes. Produced by Erik Crone. Executive producer, Benni Korzen. Directed by Anders Refn. Stars Mario David, Senta Berger, Pete Lee Wilson. Screenplay, Sigvard Olsson, Anders Refn; camera (Eastmancolor), Mikael Salomon; production managers, Michael Christensen, Florian von Hofen (Germany), Bertrand Gauthier (France), Roberto Bessi (Italy); music, Kasper Vinding; title song lyrics written and sung by Murray Head; production design, Sören Krag Sörensen; editor, Kasper Schyberg; casting directors, Lynn Stalmaster, Marlene Thomasie, Linda Chabert, Simone Reynolds, Francesco Cinieri. Reviewed at the Grand, Copenhagen, Aug. 9, '85. Running time: **110 MINS.**

Lazlo Hart	Mario David
Miranda Hart	Karmen Atias
Max Hart	Jean-Marc Montel
Mory	Pete Lee Wilson
Nina Rosta	Senta Berger
Oscar Seidenbaum	Erland Josephson
Arno	Warren Clarke

With: Ole Michelsen, Margaretha Krook, Nadeem Razag Janjau, Guy Godefroy, Johnny Wade, Erik Clausen.

Originally conceived as a strictly Danish, funny-melancholy film retelling of a turn-of-the-century short story by Herman Bang, "The Flying Devils" soon got into international hands with a cast of near-marquee names and international financing plus an English dialog track.

Helmer Anders Refn combines the outward excitement of aerial circus acts with a fine feeling for the dramas beyond the ring and a good ear for the essentially phony, but obviously heartfelt dialog of his showbiz protagonists.

Titular characters are father Lazlo (Mario David, a graduate of many Claude Chabrol features and cast in the Lino Ventura mold), son Max (Jean-Marc Montel), daughter Miranda (Karmen Atias) and adopted son and son-in-law Mory (Pete Lee Wilson, who has a very modern punk, but friendly air about him). The quartet lives on the dream of one day accomplishing The Quad, a quadruple somersault, for the performance of which (if ever recorded by a camera) Hollywood's Burt Lancaster is said to have set a $250,-000 award aside. But the quartet's manager (Erland Josephson) washes his hands of them, leaving them to work their way through the hassle of at first higher, soon the lower ranks of the European circus circuit.

The dream of doing the Quad gets sidetracked when young Mory, the troupe's flyer hope, strays from the fold with a woman journalist twice his age (Senta Berger), and when father Lazlo gets into bad gambling debts to mean-spirited fellow circus artist Arno (Warren Clarke).

Although the Quad is finally achieved, it happens in a run-down circus in Italy, with nobody there to record it or even to care. Apart from shying from a happy ending, film has every plot twist, turn and cliché of the classic circus meller, and most of the acting, except for Pete Lee Wilson's, is done accordingly. Nevertheless, production values are of a high order; sharp cinematography by Mikael Salomon, and, especially, helmer Refn's sweet-tempered compassion for all the adult children who people his circus world, along with a few salty dashes of irony, add up to a high-class piece of cinematic entertainment. Though rather short of achieving artistic heights, and occasionally lagging in tempo, pic is full of the fun and inevitable sadness of the circus game in a world that has turned to sharper experiences for its kicks. —*Kell.*

Happy Ghost II
(HONG KONG-COLOR)

Hong Kong, Aug. 2.
A Cinema City production, released by Golden Princess. Directed by Clifton Ko Chisum. Produced by Karl Maka, Dean Shek, Raymond Wong. Stars Raymond Wong, May Law, Melvin Wong, Charine Chan, Fennie Yuen and Jean M. Kanai. Production designer, Raymond Fung; camera (color), Bob Thompson; editor, Tony Chow; music, Mahood Rumjahn; costumes, Shirley Chan. Reviewed at President theater, Hong Kong, Aug. 1, 1985. Running time: **98 MINS.**
(Cantonese soundtrack with English subtitles)

Hoi Sum-Kwai (Raymond Wong) is the reincarnation of Happy Ghost Chu Kam-chun. He is a dedicated teacher who recently got a job in a girl's school. Fennie Yuen, May Law and Charine Chan form a clique who's motto is to do mean things in school with Hoi as their primary target.

Hoi's use of his supernatural power to discourage the boys from the next school to date the young girl students backfires and he is forced to apologize to the headmistress who happens to be an attractive woman. It was love at first sight for him despite the clumsy meeting which did not amuse Jean M. Kanai.

After a few more embarrassing incidents, Hoi gets dismissed from the girl's school. Later, he is reinstated when the student culprits petition to make amends for all the awful things they have done in the past. Hoi resumes work, helps the girl to win a volleyball match and wins their affection and trust.

Cinema City has a summer blockbuster in "Happy Ghost II" (the sequel). Not bad, considering the erratic quality of the cinematography, extremely noisy dubbed soundtrack and the inexperience of the three newcomers (teenagers). Here's mass Cantonese low-budget entertainment for the school holiday period that is slated to gross over $HK15,000,000 just on the domestic market. —*Mel.*

Malibu Express
(COLOR)

Oldfashioned skin show for drive-ins and homevid/pay-cable.

A Malibu Bay Films release of a Sidaris Co. production. Executive producers, Robert L. Perkis, Anatoly Arutunoff. Produced, written and directed by Andy Sidaris. Features entire cast. Camera (Foto Kem color), Howard Wexler; editor, Wexler, Craig Stewart; music, Henry Strzelecki; sound, Neil Wolfson; production manager, Mike Freeman; production design, Sal Grasso; costume design, Phillip Dennis; casting, Deborah Kurtz; coproducer, Bill Pryor. Reviewed on MCA Home Video cassette, N.Y., Aug. 16, 1985. (MPAA Rating: R.) Running time: 101 MINS.
Cody Abilene . . . . Darby Hinton
Contessa Luciana . . . . Sybil Danning
Matthew . . . . Art Metrano
Anita Chamberlain . Shelley Taylor Morgan
Shane . . . . Brett Clark
Lady Lillian Chamberlain . . . Niki Dantine
Beverly McAfee . . . . Lori Sutton
Stuart Chamberlain . . . . . Michael Andrews
    Also with: Lorraine Michaels (Liza Chamberlain), Barbara Edwards (May), Kimberly McArthur (Faye), Lynda Wiesmeier (June Khnockers), John Alderman (Lt. Arledge), Robyn Hilton (Maid Marian), Richard Brose (Mark), John Brown (Luke), Suzanne Regard (Sexy Sally), Les Steinmetz (Jonathan Harper), Robert Darnell (Douglas Wilton), Jeanine Vargas (Rodney, photographer), Peggy Ann Filsinger (Peggy), Abb Dickson (P.L. Buffington), Busty O'Shea (Doreen Buffington), Randy Rudy (Bobo Buffington).

"Malibu Express" is a pleasant though underachieving throwback to the naughty but nice, lightweight entertainment that used to flourish on the drive-in circuit. Made by ABC Sports director-cum-filmmaker Andy Sidaris, pic is similar to but less fun than Sidaris' 1979 William Smith-starrer "Seven," made for Melvin Simon Prods. and American Intl. Pictures. "Malibu" was backed by The Playboy Channel (and features a song plugging Playboy as well as four former Playmates in the cast), but was self-distributed regionally last May ahead of its current homevideo release.

Darby Hinton toplines as country boy private eye Cody Abilene who, along with glamorous Contessa Luciana (Sybil Danning), is hired by the government to investigate a Bel Air household suspected of selling U.S. computer secrets to the Russi-

ans. Mansion is presided over by Lady Lillian Chamberlain (Niki Dantine), an old friend of the Contessa's. Her chauffeur Shane (Brett Clark) is sexually involved with her nephew Stuart (Michael Andrews), her niece Liza (Lorraine Michaels) and Stuart's wife Anita (Shelley Taylor Morgan), and is blackmailing them in order to pay his gambling debts.

Aided by a sexy policewoman Beverly McAfee (Lori Sutton), Abilene uncovers the skullduggery while working along parallel lines, the Contessa exposes the heavy who is selling computer secrets, Jonathan Harper (Les Steinmetz).

Storyline and minimal action sequences play second fiddle here to an awesome display of undraped chests, with the male cast including Hinton, Clark and a Mr. Arizona (Richard Brose) and Mr. Universe (John Brown) providing not quite equal time in the beefcake department to the dozen or so female pinups. No full-frontal nudity is included, however.

Other than car-racing scenes, director Sidaris is niggardly in the action department, a major detraction. Comic relief is weak, particularly the pointless interludes of the oddball Buffington family challenging Abilene to drag race in his red De Lorean and other vehicles.

Hinton is personable as a blond Sam Elliott-type in the lead and Danning is at her most beautiful in a variety of revealing costumes. No one should mind that the supporting cast is mainly there for posing rather than acting. —*Lor.*

Teen Wolf
(COLOR)

One-joke teen comedy starring Michael J. Fox.

Hollywood, Aug. 1.
An Atlantic Releasing release of a Thomas Coleman and Michael Rosenblatt presentation of a Wolfkill production. Produced by Mark Levinson, Scott Rosenfelt. Executive producers, Coleman, Rosenblatt. Directed by Rod Daniel. Stars Michael J. Fox. Screenplay (associate producers), Joseph Loeb 3d, Matthew Weisman; camera (United color), Tim Suhrstedt; editor, Lois Freeman-Fox; music, Miles Goodman; set decorator, Rosemary Brandenberg; special makeup effects, The Burman Studios: Tom Burman, Jefferson Dawn, Kyle Tucy; costume design, Nancy Fox; sound, Douglas Arnold; assistant director, Jim Nasella; casting, Paul Ventura. Reviewed at the MGM Studios, Culver City, Calif., July 31, 1985. (MPAA Rating: PG.) Running time: 91 MINS.

Scott Howard . . . . Michael J. Fox
Harold Howard . . . . James Hampton
Kirk Lolley . . . . Scott Paulin
Boof . . . . Susan Ursitti
Stiles . . . . Jerry Levine
Mr. Thorne . . . . Jim Mackrell
Pamela . . . . Lorie Griffin
Mick . . . . Mark Arnold
Lewis . . . . Matt Adler
Chubby . . . . Mark Holton
Coach Finstock . . . . Jay Tarses

Also with: Elizabeth Gorcey, Melanie Manos, Doug Savant, Charles Zucker, Harvey Vernon, Clare Peck, Gregory Itzin, Doris Hess, Troy Evans, Lynda Wiesmeier, Rod Kageyama.

If summer audiences have already tired of the majors' teenpix of the season, they will have little use for the low-budget "Teen Wolf." Atlantic Releasing will open this one in about 1,000 theaters nationally on Aug. 23, and its major commercial hope lies in playing up the participation of "Back To The Future" star Michael J. Fox to the utmost, a factor which should make for good initial results.

Lightweight item is innocuous and well-intentioned but terribly feeble, another example of a decent idea yielding the least imaginative results conceivable.

The Beacontown Beavers have the most pathetic basketball team in high school history, and pint-sized Michael J. Fox is on the verge of quitting when he notices certain biological changes taking place. Heavy hair is growing on the backs of his hands, his ears and teeth are elongating — lots of strange things that go way beyond the usual punishment for self-abuse.

Instead of turning into a horrific teen werewolf, however, Fox takes to trucking around school halls in full furry regalia, becoming more successful with the ladies (since he can alternate between his normal self and hirsute version virtually at will, girls request which guise they want as their partner) and, most importantly, winning basketball games. The wolfy Fox so freaks out the opposition with his red eyes and new physical prowess that the Beavers become champs.

There's little more to it than that, which is why the pic is so thin. If becoming a better basketball player is the only thing a kid can think of making out of such unique circumstances, someone is lacking some creative juices — the writers.

Fox is likeable enough in the lead, something that cannot be said for the remainder of the lackluster cast. Cheapness of the undertaking has not been disguised in any way, and the rock song score is awful.—*Cart.*

Hoehenfeuer
(Alpine Fire)
(SWISS-COLOR)

Locarno, Aug. 15.
A Rex Films presentation of a Bernard Lang production. Written and directed by Fredi M. Murer. Camera (color), Pio Corradi; editor, Helena Gerber; art director, Bernhard Sauter; costumes; Greta Roderer; sound, Florian Eidenbenz; music, Mario Beretta. Reviewed at Morettina Film Center, Locarno Film Festival, Aug. 14, 1985. Running time: 120 MINS.
Boy . . . . Thomas Nock
Belli . . . . Johanna Lier
Mother . . . . Dorothea Moritz

Father . . . . Rolf Illig
Grandmother . . . . Tilli Breidenbach
Grandfather . . . . Jörg Odermatt
(Dubbed in Swiss dialect, with German and French subtitles.)

"Alpine Fire" is a slow and deliberate, moody story of life on top of a mountain, away from the rest of the human race. It depicts the solitary life of silent, industrious, introverted people who are closer to nature surrounding them than to their fellow men. There are only six characters in this film, two of them separated from the others by a whole mountain, and one of the other four departing at a certain point for self-imposed exile on another mountain top.

The plot is simple enough. We watch one closely-knit family as they go through their daily routines. Their home is completely isolated, the closest available communication being through binoculars to the house of the wife's parents, living on the other side of the valley. It is a hard life, determined by the lay of the land and its nature, by the changing seasons of the year, by ancient traditions and customs.

The drama is introduced gradually by the sexual awakening of the son, a deaf-mute who has never been sent down the valley to get proper education. His deformity is explained by the fact that his parents have married too late, after being engaged for 15 years but being prevented from creating their own home by the tyrranical mother-in-law who refused to part with her son.

Sexual impulses are nothing new and the mountain people have always treated them by having their progenies work off their steam by building stone hedges and undertaking other heavy labors. For the boy, however, who suffers from the additional frustration of being unable to express himself, this is soon translated into bouts of violent rage. After one such bout, fearing the wrath of his father, he escapes to a mountaintop hut, there to be visited only by his sister, a couple of years older than him and the closest to him, of all the family. The sister, the only character with a name in the film, is given to daydreams of a different kind of life and responsible for the boy's rudimentary education. She spends the night with her brother, after bringing food for him up the hill, and the inevitable happens: incest, which is unacceptable to the concepts of this family, as much as it is shown to be unavoidable under these specific conditions.

Director Fredi M. Murer builds a sound background by detailing peasant routines in an almost documentary fashion at times, and by piling up indications of the suspicious attitude the father has towards anything even slightly alien to him, such as the "valley people," the rejection of contact with the rest of the world unless absolutely necessary, and the obvious decision to consider solitude imposed by objective conditions as a feature to be cultivated.

Given the fact that only one of these characters is identified by name, and since the entire situation is so clearly stylized, dramatically, there is a strong temptation to approach it all on an allegorical level, as Murer's own very critical vision of his country and his people.

Dialog is sparse, nature is formidable and quite often adverse, people tend to be dour, but to Murer's credit he manages to get under the armor and allows human nature to emerge. In the quiet, more relaxed scenes, he handles his cast efficiently, and merges the natural background into the picture very effectively. Visually, the film is indeed very impressive.

However, at 120 minutes, Murer tends to be too slow and repetitive, even for a story which requires this kind of tempo. Also, some of the climactic scenes are handled in a rather clumsy way, indicating that Murer may be more at home when implying instead of portraying feelings. This is also true of his cast, particularly the boy who has to compensate for his deformity by facial expressions. Nice performances by Dorothea Moritz, Johanna Lier and Rolf Illig are slightly marred at times by the dubbing process, but luckily, dialog is of secondary importance here.

German-speaking Swiss see Murer's film as their own answer to another mountain item, shown earlier in Cannes, "Derborence," made by the Francophone Swiss. Therefore it is expected to have as warm a reception in Zurich and Bern as the previous one had in Geneva and Lausanne. The film is already skedded for the Montreal fest and is bound, by its nature, for a fruitful festival career, after winning first prize in Locarno. — *Edna.*

Tajvanska kanasta
(Taiwan Canasta)
(YUGOSLAVIAN-COLOR)

Pula, July 24.

A Centar Film production, Belgrade. Directed by Goran Markovic. Screenplay, Markovic, Milan Nikolic; camera (color), Milos Spasojevic; art director, Miljen Kljakovic; music, Zoran Simjanovic. Reviewed at Pula Film Fest, July 24, 1985. Running time: **93 MINS.**
With: Boris Komnenic, Neda Arneric, Gordana Gadzic, Radko Polic, Predrag Monojlovic.

Goran Markovic ("Special Education," "National Class," "Variola Vera") emerges as a leading critic and spokesman among his own film generation of Yugoslavian life with this subtly ironic comedy about an aging hippie — a "man of '68" — who now faces personal crisis at turning 40 and sentenced to live in a society he feels has betrayed his once-youthful idealism.

Ironic, because what is for most of its length an amusing portrait of generational conflict in socialist Yugoslavia, on reflection turns out to be the small tragedy of a sincere but naive and ridiculous man who can't find a position in life and is literally left hanging in mid-air. It could be suicide but audience must decide.

Hero Sasa is an out-of-work architect-cum-artist whose funky, life-size mobiles catch the eye of modish gallery patrons, who eventually offer him work in a shady scheme to build high-rises. Between proving himself a great heartbreaker (his family life is consequently a mess) as well as still fancying himself to his nonconformist art student girlfriend (half his age) a revolutionary role model from the 1968 student protest days, he is constantly caught in the sack with the wrong woman, including the wife of his new boss, who has introduced him to influence and money.

The times are out of joint, however, even for nostalgia about changing the world, the filmmakers are saying, and the young don't want to participate, nor do they want to soil their hands in Sosa's social engagements.

His prankish, porno mobiles satirizing the police get him arrested; his new bosses set him up with a phony hand of "Taiwan Canasta" at a house party, where he is enticed into doing faulty blueprints for their housing scheme. Too late he realizes the collapse of his house of cards.

Music adapts nicely to '60s and '80s themes and characters. Screenplay by Markovic and Nikolic, student of Markovic at the Belgrade Faculty of Dramatic Arts (where Markovic teaches), is ably realized by leads Boris Kemnenic and Gordana Gadzic as the young art student (she won Pula's "Golden Arena" for best supporting actress). Film is well worth fest outings and art houses interested in current state of "the Yugoslavian soul," as director phrased it at his Pula press conference. Critics there saw its fresh approach as a "breakthrough" in the now thematic "open door" for Yugoslavian filmmaking.—*Milg.*

Girl With The Diamond Slipper
(HONG KONG-COLOR)

Hong Kong, Aug. 1.

A Shaw Brothers production and release. Produced by Run Run Shaw. Executive Producer, Mona Fong. Directed by Wang Tsing. Stars Maggie Cheung, Chen Pai Chiang, Wang Tsing, Wang Yu, Wang Lung Wei, Brenda Lo, Wei Yi Ching and Pan Chun Wei. Reviewed at Jade Theater, Hong Kong, Aug. 1, 1985. Running time: **98 MINS.** *(Cantonese soundtrack with English subtitles)*

Maggie Cheung (a real beauty-title holder) is a tv starlet who shares an apartment with two other girls. She auditions for a lead role and gets the job and a chance to meet once again a rich man's son and sponsor, Tom Poon. Meanwhile, Wang Tsing and Chen Pai Chiang are petty thiefs who accidentally gets hold of a precious diamond from a dying millionaire. During a chase, Chen slips the diamond into a shoe eventually bought by Maggie for a supposedly high-society ball à là Cinderella. She borrows a gown that she must return before midnight. Have we heard this story before?

Thus, Maggie becomes the innocent victim and while she dashes to the escalator before midnight, she leaves behind one shoe (with the diamond) that the supposedly Prince Charming gets hold of without knowing the valuable content. There are more chases and fights but the story ends happily (what else) when the baddies are stopped and the heroine finds her true love and hero while bicycling by Clearwater Bay.

Extremely idiotic, "Girl With The Diamond Slipper" clearly shows why the Shaw Brothers' box-office ratings have been going downwards. The film looks and sounds like it was made for young children (age five) and the style is old-fashioned, untrendy and totally unreal even for an escapist romantic comedy. Most of the jokes are unfunny and the saving graces are the pleasant visual presence of lovely Maggie Cheung and a host of well-known character performers doing cameo bits. — *Mel.*

Qingmei Zhuma
(Taipei Story)
(TAIWANESE-COLOR)

Edinburgh, Aug. 13.

A Huang-Liu production. Produced by Huang Young, Liu Shenzhong. Directed by Edward Yang. Features entire cast. Screenplay, Edward Yang, Hou Xiaoxian, Zhu Tianwen; camera (color), Yang Weihan; editors, Wang Jiyang, Song Fanzhen; sound, Du Duzhi; music, Edward Yang; executive producer, Lin Rongfeng; production planner, Hou Xiaoxian. Reviewed at Edinburgh Film Festival, Aug. 10, 1985. Running time: **117 MINS.**

Chin	Cai Qin
Lon	Hou Xiaoxian
Kim	Wu Nianzhen
Ling	Lin Xiuling
Gwan	Ke Suyuan
Miss Mei	Chen Xufang
The young man	Sun Peng
Chin's father	Wu Binnan
Chin's mother	Mei Fang

Here's another feather in the cap for Chinese cinema, this time from Edward Yang, a relatively new director (his second feature) who was born on the mainland, studied for a while in the U.S., and now lives and works in Taiwan. "Taipei Story" is a refreshing, intelligent study of a disintegrating relationship involving a young couple who, on the surface, have everything going for them.

Chin (Cai Qin) is a successful career woman, personal assistant to a woman executive in a computer company. Lon (Hou Xiaoxian) works for a fabric company, but is a bit restless, clinging to memories of his past success as a baseball player and to a former girlfriend, Gwan, who married a Japanese and lives in Tokyo. Chin and Lon have been engaged a long time, but somehow never got married. Chin is moving into a smart new apartment, and expects Lon to live there with her, but everything goes wrong.

Chin loses her job when her company is taken over; her father starts borrowing large sums of money from her; Ling, her younger sister, leads a wild life and needs an abortion; and she suspects that Lon, on a trip to L.A. to see relatives, stopped over in Tokyo to see Gwan.

Lon has his problems too. He gambles away his money, can't decide to take the final step and marry Chin, and is worried for his old friend, Kim, who's fallen on hard times. The relationship starts to fall apart, and ends in an unexpected, futile tragedy.

All this is deftly presented in crisp, telling sequences. Yang shows the breakdown of traditional family life and subtly indicates the uncertainties of life in Taipei itself, with its mighty neighbor becoming more assertive and nothing as permanent as it used to be.

Technically the film is very good, with fine lensing by Yang Weihan and notable performances by the leads and large supporting cast of interesting characters. Hou Xiaoxian, who plays Lon, is an important Taiwan-based director in his own right, having made "The Boys From Fengkuei" (1983) and the impressive "A Summer At Grandpa's" (1984). — *Strat.*

Tsui Tai-Chi
(Drunken Tai-Chi)
(TAIWANESE-COLOR)

Santiago, July 28.

A Dragons Group Film Co. production. Directed by Yuang Ho-Ping. Screenplay, Yu- and Ho-Ping. Reviewed at the Taiwanese Film Week, Espaciocal, Santiago, Chile, July 25, '85. Running time: **90 MINS.**
With: Donnie Yen, Shen Tan-Shen Tan-Sheay, Wang Tad, Yuang Family.

Although more imaginative in its staging of martial arts scenes than other films of this genre, plotlines in

"Tsu Tai-Chi" do not quite converge and often fail to create the required suspense and climax. In spite of this, pic should find access to what is left of the international Kung Fu market.

After Tao Swee's offer to buy Chen Nu Tsai's salt business is rejected, he hires Tieh Wu-Ching, the Ironheart, to do away with the merchant and his two sons. The youngest son escapes the massacre and, in the end, gives both the hired fighter and Tao Swee their comeuppance. In between, Chen falls in with an old puppet master and his portly but agile wife and is trained by the former in the martial arts specialties that lead him to victory.

The use of the puppets, a fireworks boobytrap and other ingenious ingredients, plus a sense of humor, bring the film to life. Technical credits and special effects are good, and acting is satisfactory.

— *Amig.*

Honor, Profit And Pleasure
(BRITISH-COLOR)

Edinburgh, Aug. 14.

A Spectra production. Produced by Ann Skinner. Written and directed by Anna Ambrose. Features entire cast. Camera (color), Peter MacDonald; editor, George Akers; music, Nicholas Kraemer; production design, Miranda Melville; costumes, Doreen Watkinson; production manager, Donna Grey; executive producer, Michael Whyte. Reviewed at Edinburgh Film Festival, Aug. 13, 1985. Running time: **73 MINS.**

Handel	Simon Callow
Quin	Alan Devlin
Elizabeth	Jean Rigby
Swift	T.P. McKenna
Addison	James Villiers

A micro-budget biopic of Handel which may or may not have been inspired by the success of "Amadeus," "Honor, Profit And Pleasure" is a modestly engaging effort on the period spent in Britain by the German-born composer.

Simon Callow is effective as Handel, while Alan Devlin gives an amusingly rich performance as his friend and confidant, Quin, and also narrates the film. Rather campy staging of 18th century operas is fun.

Writer-director Anna Ambrose, who tragically died soon after completing the film, has managed to achieve a great deal out of what was undoubtedly a minimal budget, though the film will play better on tv than in theaters. For music buffs, it will be a great treat. — *Strat.*

Tarang
(Vibrations)
(INDIAN-COLOR)

Edinburgh, Aug. 19.

A National Film Development Corp. of India production. Directed by Kumar Shahani.
Features entire cast. Screenplay, Roshan, Kumar Shahani, Vinay Shukla; camera (Scope, color), K.K. Mahajan; sound, Narendra Singh; music, Vanraj Bhatia; editor, Ashok Tyaoi; art director, Bansi Chaterji; costumes, B. Athaya; executive producer, Ravi Malik. Reviewed at Edinburgh Film Festival, Aug. 16, 1985. Running time: **169 MINS.**

Janaki	Smita Patil
Rahul	Amol Palekar
Hansa	Kawal Gandhiok
Namdev	Om Puri
Dinseh	Girish Karnad
Sethji	Dr. Shriram Lagoo
Patel	Jayanti Patel
Abdul	Miki Raiha

"Tarang" is an ambitious saga about a widowed working class woman who is hired by a seedy, calculating industrialist as nurse to his son. Rahul, the industrialist, a man whose morals are as dubious as his taste in neckties, has married the highly strung daughter of the head of the company, an old man near death. As Rahul fights for control with the equally corrupt London-based cousin of his wife (played by actor-director Girish Karnad), he is having a secret affair with the nurse. She, in turn, is using her privileged position to help the more radical workers with their claims for better pay and conditions.

There are plenty of interesting characters in the plot, but director Kumar Shahani, making only his second feature in 12 years, somehow lacks the flair and elan to bring it all together. Nor does it work as a study of two classes locked in a lethal battle; pacing is too slow and too much is over-stated.

On the plus side there's some lush widescreen lensing, and a handful of fine performances, notably Smita Patil as the widowed worker and Om Puri as a radical union leader. As Rahul, Amol Palekar is rather too much the stock villain to be very convincing.

Songs are kept to a minimum (only two) in the film. — *Strat.*

Compromising Positions
(COLOR)

Silly comedy-thriller doesn't make it.

Hollywood, Aug. 15.

A Paramount Pictures release. Produced, directed by Frank Perry. Executive producer, Salah M. Hassanein. Stars Susan Sarandon, Raul Julia, Edward Herrmann, Judith Ivey, Mary Beth Hurt, Anne De Salvo. Screenplay, Susan Isaacs, based on her novel; camera (uncredited color), Barry Sonnenfeld; editor, Peter Frank; music, Brad Fiedel; production design, Peter Larkin; set decoration, Victor Kempster; costumes, Joe Aulisi; sound, Danny Michael; associate producer, Patrick McCormick; assistant director, Ron Bozman; casting, Howard Feuer. Reviewed at the Paramount Studios, L.A., Aug. 14, 1985. (MPAA Rating: R.) Running time: **98 MINS.**

Judith Singer	Susan Sarandon
David Suarez	Raul Julia
Bob Singer	Edward Herrmann
Nancy Miller	Judith Ivey
Peg Tuccio	Mary Beth Hurt
Bruce Fleckstein	Joe Mantegna
Phyllis Fleckstein	Anne De Salvo
Dicky Dunck	Josh Mostel
Brenda Dunck	Deborah Rush
Mary Alice Mahoney	Joan Allen

Falling midway between a campy send-up of suburban wives soap operas and a legitimate thriller, "Compromising Positions" emerges as a silly little whodunnit that's a mild embarrassment to all involved. Since a stylistic groove is never established, none of the many talented thesps here is able to perform with any confidence or conviction. Pic has nowhere to go commercially.

As in Frank Perry's last two films, "Mommie Dearest" and "Monsignor," there's a barrel-full of hilarity here that seems bursting to escape but never quite manages to hit the brim.

Unlikely material, about the murder of a philandering Long Island dentist, the reactions of his many mistresses, and the official and unofficial investigations into it, has hardly been approached with a straight face. The victim is a loathesome gold chain type, and most of his conquests are ladies who lunch with little redeeming social or intellectual value.

Intrigued and naively amazed that nearly everyone she knows has been involved with the late Dr. Fleckstein, upper-middle-class housewife Susan Sarandon undertakes some amateur sleuthing with an eye toward reviving her old profession of newspaper reporter with startling revelations about the case.

With her husband growing increasingly angry about her obsession with the matter, Sarandon begins taking a fancy to detective Raul Julia, and their tentative romance is accompanied by increasing jeopardy.

Action moves along snappily enough, supporting players such as Judith Ivey and Josh Mostel contribute some tolerably amusing comedy turns, and Sarandon is, as always, highly watchable, even if her reactions to the goofy goings-on here are too consistently wide-eyed.

Julia, on the other hand, seems to be smirking while trying to play it straight, and Edward Herrmann is stuck with the utterly thankless role of Sarandon's super-straight hubbie who wants his wife to be a doormat.

Warner Bros. acquired Susan Isaacs' novel when it was published in 1978, and Nora Ephron was the first to be assigned to the adaption. Isaacs ended up doing the job herself, and the one thing that can be said of the pic is that it evokes a strong sense of setting.

Tech credits are routine. — *Cart.*

Beni Ecen Vete
(Beni Walks By Himself)
(ALBANIAN-BLACK & WHITE)

Giffoni Valle Piana, Aug. 1.

Produced by the New Albanian Film Studio. Written and directed by Xhanfise Keko, P. Herion Spiro, Pandi Raidhi, Yilka Mujo, Dhorka Orgocka. Camera (b&w), Saim Kokona; music, Limos Dizdari. Reviewed at the Giffoni (Italy) Film Festival, July 29, '85. Running time: **90 MINS.**

An Albanian version of the "wholesome rural life vs. evil city decadence" film, "Beni Walks By Himself" is the story of a spoiled, neurotic city kid who straightens out in the country.

When Beni's country uncle Thoma comes to visit the family in the city, he finds Beni a lazy, spoiled child without friends. Thoma invites the boy to his village fo the summer, and Beni reluctantly leaves for the rigors of country life. At first, wimpy Beni is scared of the strong, independent farm children, but soon he gets with the commune and learns to be a lively, hardworking Socialist.

Keko's film is very primitive technically but intriguing culturally. Pic is just as schematic as the recent spate of American country films but with better reason — the city Beni inhabits is so grim looking he might be better off in the South Bronx.

— *Brom.*

Doña Herlinda Y Su Hijo
(Doña Herlinda And Her Son)
(MEXICAN-COLOR)

Mexico City, July 21.

A Peliculas Mexicanas release of a Clasa Films Mundiales production. Produced by Barbachano Ponce. Written and directed by Jaime Humberto Hermosillo, based on a story by Jorge López Páez. Features entire cast. Camera (color), Miguel Ehrenberg; editor, Luis Kelly; sound, Fernando Cámara; special appearance of Lucha Villa and group Madres y Comadres. Reviewed at Sala 1 of Cineteca Nacional, Mexico City, July 19, 1985. Running time: **90 MINS.**

Rodolfo	Marco A. Treviño
Ramón (Moncho)	Gustavo Meza
Doña Herlinda	Guadalupe del Toro
Olga	Leticia Lupercio
Billy	Billy Alva
Ramón's mother	Angélica Guerrero
Ramón's father	Donato Castañeda

Jaime Humberto Hermosillo, one of Mexico's most daring directors, makes no compromise about the theme of his 12th feature film, "Doña Herlinda Y Su Hijo." He has produced a gay domestic comedy that, despite some horrendous technical flaws, offers an entertaining story.

Tale concerns the relationship between young surgeon Rodolfo (Marco A. Treviño) and musician Ramón (Gustavo Meza), studying french horn at Guadalajara's Conservatory of Music.

Rodolfo laments the fact that Ramón lives in a noisy boarding house where their amorous attempts are constantly interrupted. He lives with his mother Doña Herlinda (Guadalupe del Toro) who, although she knows about her son's sexual habits, chooses to accept it. In fact, she inviests Ramón to live with them.

She also knows Rodolfo is planning to marry Olga (Leticia Lupercio), a fact that torments Ramón when he finds out. He gets drunk, cries over corny melodramatic ranchero songs and mopes about confiding in his friend and fellow classmate Billy (Billy Alva).

Rodolfo wants his cake and eats it too. After his marriage, he continues his relationship with Ramón both in his new apartment and at his mother's house where Ramón still stays.

Later, when Olga has a baby, Ramón is chosen as godfather. Doña Herlinda is also capable of a few surprises: she has an addition built onto her house and the five of them live happily ever after.

"Doña Herlinda And Her Son" is certainly not your typical Mexican film, but then Hermosillo has never been Mexico's typical director. Technically, the film suffers through bad sound, grainy blowup of the film from 16 to 35m and some embarrassingly poor acting. Also, the graphic male sex scenes may put some viewers off.

Overall, pic is interesting within the body of Hermosillo's work and also within the context of Mexican cinema, but is not for everyone's tastes. —*Lent*.

Don Ratón Y Don Ratero
(Don Mouse And Don Thief)
(MEXICAN-COLOR)

Mexico City, July 26.

A Películas Mexicanas release of a Televicine production. Produced, written and directed by Roberto Gómez Bolaños (Chespirito). Features Chespirito. Camera (color), Luis Medina; editor, Carlos Savage; music, Nacho Méndez. Reviewed at Cine Insurgentes 70, Mexico City, July 25, 1985. Running time: **92 MINS.**
Pérez Pérez (Don
  Ratón) . . . . Roberto Gómez Bolaños
  (Chespirito)
Rufino Rufián (Don
  Ratero) . . . . Rubén Aguirre
Astadolfa . . . . Florinda Meza
Rufián's mother . . . . . . María Antonieta de
  las Nieves
Kilos . . . . Edgar Vivar
Vinagre . . . . Alfredo Alegría
Boxer . . . . Raúl Chato Padilla

Cashing in once again on his popular tv show, Mexican comedian Roberto Gómez Bolaños (Chespirito) offers an extended sketch that has somehow grown into a feature-length collection of worn-out tired jokes aimed at the whole family. Other regulars from the tv show fill the rest of the cast.

This time pic's action centers round the activities of gang warfare during the 1920s. A famed Chicago hitman accidentally dies as a result of eating bad seafood. A rival gang erroneously takes bumbling exter-minator Pérez Pérez (Gómez Bolaños) — called in to rid the place of mice — for the new hired gun and the comedy revolves around this case of mistaken identity.

Astadolfa (Florinda Meza), the hitman's young widow, supplies both romantic interest and a tap dance partner for Bolaños.

There are a few funny moments such as a running gag concerning hysterical widows of newly deceased gang members, but overall, we have seen this all before and we'll probably see it again. —*Lent*.

Huang Tudi
(Yellow Earth)
(CHINESE-COLOR)

Edinburgh, Aug. 14.

A Guangxi Film Studio production. Directed by Chen Kaige. Features entire cast. Screenplay, Zhang Ziliang; camera (color), Zhang Yimou; art director, He Qun; music, Zhao Jiping. Reviewed at Edinburgh Film Festival, Aug. 14, 1985. Running time: **89 MINS.**
Cui Qiao, the girl . . . . Xue Bai
Gu Qing, the soldier . . . . Wang Xueqi
The father . . . . Tan Tuo
Hanhan, the boy . . . . Liu Qiang

"Yellow Earth" is the most impressive film from mainland China unveiled so far in the West. Its simple story is told with considerable depth of feeling, allied to classical direction and impeccably composed images.

The year is 1939, and China is at war with Japan. However, in the remote north of Shaanxi Province, where peasant farmers live and work in grinding poverty, the war is unknown and far away. There is a punishing drought, and at the wedding with which the film opens the customary fish consumed by the guests has had to be replaced by wooden fake "fish" in order to keep the tradition alive. Though bordering the swiftly flowing Yellow River, the terrain is rocky, dusty and arid.

Gu Qing, a Communist soldier, is sent from the Army h.q. at Ya-n'an (depicted as a place of cheerful celebration) to Shaanbei, partly to collect folk songs of the region, partly to influence the locals in favor of Communism. He stays with a poor family; a widower, his 12-year-old daughter, Cui Qiao, and 10-year-old son, Hanhan. At first they're suspicious of the stranger, but gradually he wins them over, telling them about the new future, including the possibility for girls to choose their own husbands instead of being forced into arranged marriages.

When it's time for him to leave, Cui Qiao, who herself is being forced to marry an older man, asks to go with him; he refuses, but promises to return for her. By the time he does, she has gone, presumably drowned attempting to cross the river and join the Army.

For 32-year-old director Chen Kaige, working out of the small Guangxi Film Studio, this is a quite remarkable achievement. He tells the story with great subtlety and delicacy, allowing silences, looks and gestures to convey the feelings of his characters. The compositions of cinematographer Zhang Yimou are outstanding, and the film's images are consistently rich and evocative. Only in the somewhat shaky postsynchronization of the songs does the film falter technically.

Pic will compete in the upcoming Montreal Film Fest. — *Strat*.

Gros Dégueulásse
(Superslob)
(FRENCH-COLOR)

Paris, Aug. 5.

An SFDI release of a A.S. Prod. Sara Films coproduction. Produced by Alain Siritzky. Written and directed by Bruno Zincone, from the comic strip by Jean-Marc Reiser; camera (color), Max Monteillet; sound, Alain Contrault; supervising editor, Bruno Zincone; music, Yasuaki Shimizu; theme song, Michel Munz; lyrics, Felix Landau; performed by Helen Wendel. Reviewed at the UGC Ermitage theater, Paris, Aug. 5, 1985. Running time: **85 MINS.**
With: Maurice Risch, Valérie Mairesse, Martin Lamotte, Jackie Sardou, France Dougnac, Dora Doll, Françoise Dorner, Florence Guérin, Maria Laborit.

"Gros Dégueulasse" is a live-action adaptation of the late Jean-Marc Reiser's caustic comic strip about a slob whose chief occupation in life is to gross others out with his repulsive physique and toilet philosophy. Clad only in a soiled, oversized pair of underwear, through which can be glimpsed one horrendous testicle, he is the embodiment of human crassness and indecency who holds up an unseemly mirror to his more decorous peers.

In Maurice Risch, who has portrayed the character on the stage (and briefly in a previous Reiser screen transposition, "Vive les Femmes"), Gros Dégueulasse has the best possible flesh-and-blood correspondent. But this film by Bruno Zincone, debuting in theatrical features after work in commercials, fails like so many previous efforts to find the tone and style of its cartoon source, and degenerates quickly into a monotonous series of sketches in which Reiser's aggressive ribaldry is betrayed by the commonplace vulgarity of the direction. — *Len*.

The Dark Room
(AUSTRALIAN-COLOR)

Devizes, England, Aug. 8.

A Filmco presentation of a Nadira-Artis Films production. Produced by Tom Haydon. Directed by Paul Harmon. Stars Alan Cassell, Anna Jemison. Screenplay, Michael Brindley, Harmon, from a story by Harmon; camera (Eastmancolor), Paul Onorato; editor, Rod Adamson; music, Cameron Allan; art director, Richard Kent; associate producer, Michael Brindley; assistant director, David Bracknell; production manager, Michael McKeag; sound, Ken Hammond; costumes, Liz Keogh. Reviewed on Medusa Videocassette. Devizes, England, Aug. 7, '85. Running time: **92 MINS.**
Dr. Ray Sangster . . . . Alan Cassell
Nicky . . . . Anna Jemison
Michael Sangster . . . . Svet Kovich
Martha Sangster . . . . Diana Davidson
Liz Llewellyn . . . . Rowena Wallace
Susan Bitel . . . . Oriana Panozzo
Sam Bitel . . . . Ric Hutton
Himself . . . . Hayes Gordon

Three singularly unappealing characters form the triangle at the center of this turgid melodrama which was made in 1982, but which has never seen the light of day in Australia. It's out on vidcassette in the U.S. and Britain, and is reviewed for the record.

Pic marked the feature debut of cowriter/director Paul Harmon, whose inexperience shows, especially in his handling of the film's young lead actor, Svet Kovich, who gives a hopelessly inadequate performance. He plays the disturbed teenage son of a successful doctor (Alan Cassell) who's secretly having an affair with a young dress designer (Anna Jemison). Kovich, whose hobby is photography, has realized the liaison before the film begins, and spends his time following his father and the girl and sneaking snapshots of them. From a rooftop, he gets pics of them in the sack, too.

However, blackmail isn't on his mind. He manages to meet the girl, under an alias, and eventually gets to bed her, but proves to be not up to the task. This sends him off his rocker completely; he kidnaps the girl and brings about his own death in a fiery climax.

Since Kovich doesn't for one moment convince as the deranged youth, it falls upon Cassell and Jemison, professionals both, to give some semblance of reality to the proceedings. They both perform creditably under the circumstances. Diana Davidson is fine in the small role of Kovich's wronged mother.

Even bad Australian films are usually good to look at, and this one's no exception, its main, indeed only, strength being Paul Onorato's photography, making excellent use of various Sydney landmarks. The film is dedicated to Peter Fox, topper of Filmco at the time it went into production.—*Strat*.

Zai Na Hepan Qing Cao Qing
(Green, Green Grass Of Home)
(TAIWANESE-COLOR)

Edinburgh, Aug. 12.

A Dong-Da Film Xing-Jiao Film coproduction. Produced by Zhang Huakun. Written and directed by Hou Xiaoxian. Features entire cast. Camera (Scope, color), Chen Kun-hou; editor, Liao Qingsong; art director, Ji Kaiqin; music, Zuo Hongyuan; sound, Qi Jiangsheng; assistant director, Xu Shuzhen. Reviewed at Edinburgh Film Festival, Aug. 11, 1985. Running time: **89 MINS.**

Lu Ta-Nien .... Kenny Bee
Chen Su-Yun .... Jiang Ling
Lu's ex-girlfriend .... Chen Meifeng
Lu's father .... Gu Jun
Mr. Chou .... Shi Ying
Su-Yun's father .... Li Po

This 1982 production was the third feature of Hou Xiaoxian, who subsequently made two more impressive films, ''The Boys Of Fengkuei'' (1983) and ''A Summer At Grandpa's'' (1984), as well as playing the leading role in Edward Yang's ''Taipei Story'' (1985). It seems Hou and Yang make up the core of a vital new school of cinema in Taiwan.

''Green, Green Grass Of Home,'' however, plays like a film in which the director is still feeling his way. Characteristic of his later films is the country setting and the handling of child actors, but on this occasion the hand is a little heavy and the incidents a bit mundane.

Theme involves a country school where a new teacher arrives with new methods. He throws over a former girl in favor of an attractive fellow teacher, and encourages the school to lead the way in a conservation plan for the district.

The kids are natural and engaging, but the adults rather too flatly drawn. The use of widescreen is a little awkward at times, too. Still, Hou has shown subsequently that he's a sympathetic director of youth films, and if he's working within rather limited commercial constraints this time, it's an apprentice work which obviously paid off.

— *Strat.*

Taulanti Kerkon Nje Moter
(Taulant Wants A Sister)
(ALBANIAN-COLOR)

Giffoni Valle Piana, Aug. 2.
Produced by the New Albanian Film Studio. Written and directed by Xanfise Keko. Camera (color), Saim Kokona; Music, Hajg Zaharian. Reviewed at the Giffoni (Italy) Film Festival, Aug. 1, '85. Running time: **90 MINS.**
With: Yilka Mujo, Viktor Zhusti, Donald Kokona, Roza Anagnosti.

This picture takes the prize for Most Babies and Pregnant Women per Shot. Purpose is to convince Albanian women that staying home and having kids is more important than devoting themselves to fulltime careers, interesting topic considering pic was made by Albania's most prominent woman director.

Little Taulant is the only child of an intellectual family. He begs his parents for a little sister, but all his pianist mother wants to do is practice and play concerts and dad is always at work. Mom's in the family way, but feels unable to take care of another child, so she applies to a committee of doctors to get an abortion. They chew her out for being a selfish intellectual and order her to have the kid.

Ever helpful and responsible Dad just says, ''I don't want to become a criminal.'' Western viewers may sympathize with Mom, but she clearly is the villain. Finally she sees the light and Taulant gets his sister in the end.

Film is very crude technically and interesting only for its treatment of feminist issues inside the self-proclaimed one, true, Marxist-Leninist society. — *Brom.*

Hurlevent
(Wuthering Heights)
(FRENCH-COLOR)

Locarno, Aug. 13.
A La Cecilia, Renn production, French Ministry of Culture production. Produced by Martine Marignac. Directed by Jacques Rivette. Screenplay, Pascal Bonitzer, Suzanne Schiffman, Rivette based on the first chapters of ''Wuthering Heights'' by Emily Brontë; dialog, Pascal Bonitzer; camera (color), Renato Berta; editor, Nicole Lubtchansky; sets, Manu Chauvigny; sound, Alix Comte; music, Pilentze Pee, Strati na Angelika, Polegnala e Pschenitza. Reviewed at the Locarno Film Festival, Aug. 12, 1985. Running time: **130 MINS.**

Catherine .... Fabienne Babe
Roch .... Lucas Belvaux
Guillaume .... Olivier Cruveiller
Isabelle .... Alice de Poncheville
Helene .... Sandra Montaigu
Olivier .... Olivier Torres
Joseph .... Philippe Monier-Genoud

Here again is that classic warhorse of English literature, already adapted several times before both for the big and the small screen, getting the personal attention and treatment of Jacques Rivette.

For the Brontë fans, Rivette's decision to move the story, with the help of his two faithful script partners, Pascal Bonitzer and Suzanne Schiffman, from 19th century England to the French countryside of the early 1930s, couldn't be that felicitous. Also the fact that he is content to use only certain parts of the early chapters hints at Rivette's intention to use Brontë as only a departure point.

All names have been transferred into French, when possible (Heathcliff is now Roch) but otherwise the plot is easily identifiable: the revenge of a spurned lover against all those who betrayed him. The powerful, romantic spirit that once blew through the novel, the impetuous emotions that elevated characters, even when unsympathetic, to a noble level, is all gone. Rivette treats the story in a straightforward manner, and keeps it at such distance from the audience that no real involvement, other than purely intellectual, is elicited here. He also eliminates parts of the plot that are not immediately relevant to his observations on human nature, which means that for anyone who is not familiar with the book, some of the elliptical plot jumps may be rather enigmatic, and the disappearance of certain characters unexplained.

Rivette directs Renato Berta's camera in a most fluid cinematic way, both in the choice of camera set-ups and movements, and in the powerful atmosphere he extracts from an old farm in the region of Beaune. Yet there is a prevalent feeling that the actors were given stage directions, and indeed entrances and exits seem to be ordained only by dramatic needs, and are orchestrated accordingly, logically or not.

The young, inexperienced actors strike poses as if they were training for live portraits on stage, all their expressions and movements stylized and exaggerated beyond the call of a movie camera.

Since Rivette refrains from analyzing the characters, one is tempted to go for easy labels, moving between brutes and decadents, all devoid of a degree of personal charm that would have made them plausible, if not acceptable. This is particularly painful in the case of Fabienne Babe, playing Catherine as a monster of selfishness; one is almost happy to see, at the end, getting her just retribution. — *Edna.*

Ni Chana Ni Juana
(Neither Chana Nor Juana)
(MEXICAN-COLOR)

Mexico City, Aug. 11.
A Películas Mexicanas release of a Producciones Matour, S.A. de C.V. production. Produced by Antonio Matour. Directed, written by and starring María Elena Velasco (La India María). Screenplay based on an idea by Ivette Lipkies; camera (color), Fernando Alvarez Colin; editor, Angel Camacho; music, J. Antonio Zavala; technical coordinator for script and direction, Tito Novaro. Reviewed at Cine Chapultepec, Mexico City, Aug. 9, 1985. Running time: **97 MINS.**

Juana Cruz/Adrà (Chana) ... María Elena Velasco (La India María)
Pilar del Río(Pico de Oro) .... Carmen Montejo
Sweet Potato vender .... Rubén Olivares (El Púas)
Armando .... Armando Calvo
Also with: Polo Salazar, Atony Fonti, Pedro de Urdimalas, Alfredo Bustamante, Los Kaluris, Regina Herrera, Bernabe Palma, Jorge Saldana, Rolando de Castro and magician Cristian Cri-Shan.

''Ni Chana Ni Juana,'' the latest comedy by María Elena Velasco (La India María), is surely one of Mexico's most dismal films this year.

Velasco, who has written the scripts to almost all of her popular ''India María)'' films concerning the bumbling misadventures of an ignorant Indian woman (usually when confronted with sophisticated urban life), has decided to add a few new feathers to her headdress. She not only took the helm as film's director, assisted by Tito Novaro, but she also plays two disparate roles.

Story concerns twins from the countryside separated at birth. While Juana, the typical India María character, stayed in her village with her father, her sister Chana went off to Mexico City with their mother, who found employment as servant for Spanish singer-actress Pilar del Río (Carmen Montejo), better known in the trade as ''Pico de Oro,'' or ''chatterbox.''

When her mother dies, Chana is adopted by Pilar, who brings the infant to Spain and raises her as her own child. She grows up to become a refined popular singer-actress, and speaks with a Castilian accent.

After years in Spain, Pilar decides to take her world-famous troupe on a tour of Latin America and thus they return to Mexico and our story begins.

Juana has been on the lookout for her sister and hears about the visit of El Pico de Oro and her troupe. Her search involves shenanigans at a tv studio and in a theater, where she wreaks havok at every step. Sideplot has Juana kidnapped by Chana's ex-husband. The comedy is forced and filled with tired old gags that resist any attempt to bring them out of retirement.

Pic resolves with a confrontation: Chana learns that the pitiful "Indian" woman is indeed her sister, but they both understand that they can no longer bridge the cultural gap that now separates them.

Possibly the only merit in this depressing comedy is to see Velasco sing and dance during the Chana routines, which is a side seldom shown, especially in the series of films featuring the India María character. —Lent.

The Stuff
(COLOR)

Fun sci-fi pic about a deadly dessert.

Hollywood, Aug. 14.

A New World Pictures release of a Larco Production. Written and directed by Larry Cohen. Executive producer, Cohen. Produced by Paul Kurta. Features entire cast. Camera (color), Paul Glickman; editor, Armond Lebowitz; sound, Rolf Pardula; special effects makeup, Steve Neill, Rick Stratton, Ed French; associate producer, Barry Shils; art director, Marleen Marta, George Stoll; assistant director, Harvey Waldman. Reviewed at New World Pictures, L.A., Aug. 14, 1985. (MPAA Rating: R.) Running time: 93 MINS.

David . . . . .Michael Moriarty
Nicole . . . . .Andrea Marcovicci
Col. Spears . . . . .Paul Sorvino
Jason .Scott Bloom
Chocolate Charlie . . . . .Garrett Morris
Vickers . . . . .Danny Aiello
Evans . . . . .Alexander Scourby
Richards . . . . .Russell Nype

The bottom line on "The Stuff" is that, at a reported $2,800,000 production cost, New World Pictures should turn a tidy bundle on this untidy diversion about a monstrous yogurt-like dessert that eats people from the inside out.

It's sci-fi with no hardware but lots of white goo. It's a certified Larry Cohen film ("Black Caesar," "It's Alive") that seems to fly right out of the '50s horror genre. It also has an underlying humor about it, plays around with satirizing fast foods, and cloaks a sly little subtext about people who ingest stuff they know is not good for them.

What's not to like? The film enjoys a larky sense of innocence, some hideous gaping mouths full of

a curdling, parasitic menace, and a fey performance by Michael Moriarty as an industrial saboteur who, along with Andrea Marcovicci and little Scott Bloom, track down the scourge of the countryside and the heavies.

Film should play well with teens, particularly those who like to stuff themselves. It also benefits from a hilarious performance played straight by Paul Sorvino as a self-styled paramilitary nut. The 11-year-old Bloom is appealing, and Garrett Morris as a chocolate cookie mogul and Danny Aiello as Vickers lend flavor in support.

Tech credits are sufficient to shore up the taste craze of America. —Loyn.

La Sonata A Kreutzer
(The Kreuzer Sonata)
(ITALIAN-COLOR)

Locarno, Aug. 15.

An RAI Piemonte Production. Directed by Gabriela Rosaleva. Written by Paola di Monreale based on story by Leo Tolstoy; camera (color), Maurizio Donadoni; editor, Fernando Muraro; music, Ludwig van Beethoven (the Kreuzer Sonata is played by Mario Lo Guercio and Tamas Vasary). Reviewed at the Morettina Film Center, Locarno Film Fest, Aug. 15, 1985. Running time: 100 MINS.
Husband . . . . .Maurizio Donadoni
Wife . . . . .Daniela Morelli
Violinist . . . . .Maurizio Lo Guercio

Leo Tolstoy's short novel about a husband's tragic obsession that his wife is unfaithful to him, considered in the past as a misogynist piece of literature, has become here almost a women's lib tract.

The strong autobiographical nature of the original, in which Tolstoy accused women of being incapable of reaching the highest levels of human sensitivity, has been turned around here, to show woman as the eternal victim of man's irrascible possessiveness, of his insecurity and perverse sense of honor. The husband who suspects that his wife is having an affair with an old friend, a violinist with whom she plays the famous Beethoven sonata, is definitely the tormentor here, making life miserable for everyone, first of all himself. His wife desperately tries to maintain some sort of equilibrium in a marriage which has become a prison. Her spouse's suspicions are certainly confirmed, for indeed it is only through music that she manages to escape, temporarily, from the gilded but infernal cage in which she has been confined.

The film stays close, dramatically, to the structure of the original novel, the plot being unfolded in flashback in a train station.

The recording of the voices, an immensely important part in a film based mostly on dialog, sounds to-

tally inauthentic, like it had been made in a sterile recording studio. On the other hand, the decision to use a real violinist as the third party works very well. Maurizio Lo Guercio lacks dramatic experience, but compensates with a strong screen personality. He certainly knows what he is doing with his violin, something one could never accuse actress Daniela Morelli of in her handling of the piano. She retreats too easily in the image of the pale victim who won't ever lift a finger to improve her fate. Maurizio Donadoni offers some heavy theatrical acting as the husband. Some of the camera work done by Maurizio Donadoni is impressively moody. —Edna.

Kazetachi No Gogo
(Afternoon Breezes)
(JAPANESE-B&W)

Edinburgh, Aug. 16.

An Oiwake-Nagasaki production. Produced by Shiro Oiwake, Shunichi Nagasaki. Directed by Hitoshi Yazaki. Features entire cast. Screenplay, Yazaki, Nagasaki; camera (b&w), Isamu Ishii, Atsushi Komatsubara; editors, Goro Nakajimma, Kiyomi Ishizawa; music, Kazuo Shinoda, Masashi Abe, Tatsuo Uchida, Hiroshi Yano, Boozy; sound, Akihiko Suzuki; assistant, Goro Nakajima. Reviewed at Edinburgh Film Festival, Aug. 14, 1985. Running time: 106 MINS.
Natsuko . . . . .Setsuko Aya
Mitsu .Naomi Ito
Hideo . . . . .Hiroshi Sugita
Etsuko . . . . .Mari Atake

This low-budget, privately funded pic, made in 1980 but only now surfacing abroad, is an intriguing study of obsession and lust, though handled sans any sensationalism.

Natsuko and Mitsu are two attractive young women who share an apartment. Natsuko, however, is jealous of her friend's relationship with Hideo, who sleeps over from time to time. Seeming to be barely aware at first of the causes of her jealousy, Natsuko proposes to Hideo that if she sleeps with him he will agree not to see Mitsu again. He agrees, discovering in the process that Natsuko was a virgin.

With Hideo temporarily out of the way, the two girls seem innocently happy together, until Natsuko discovers she is pregnant and Hideo returns to spill the beans. Mitsu throws Natsuko out of the apartment.

Natsuko's unrequited lesbian passion for her friend is so understated as to become quite frustrating at times. Yet the film, awkward and amateurish as it sometimes is, does exert a strange fascination. Performances are good, and the limpid, over-exposed black and white photography quite effective. Director Hitoshi Yazaki, whose first and so far only feature this was, bears watching. —Strat.

Oragens fange/I na kamnjakh rastut derévja
(Captive Of The Dragon/Even On Rocks, Trees Grow)
(NORWEGIAN/SOVIET-COLOR)

Haugesund, Aug. 20.

A Kommunernes Filmcentral release of Norsk Film (Norway) coproduction with Gorky Film (USSR). Sales (Western hemisphere), Norsk Film (Frieda Ohrvik) and Wagner-Hallig Film (Bad Soden-Ts. 2, West Germany). Executive producers, Erik Borge, Harald Ohrvik, Vjatsjeslav Sjumskij. Directed by Stanislav Rostotsky. Co-director, Knut Andersen. Screenplay, Alexandr Alexandrov, Stanislav Rostotsky, Gennedij Sjumski, based on story by J. Vronski; camera (Eastmancolor), Vjatsjeslav Sjumski; production design, Sergei Serebrenikov; costumes, Elsa Rapoport; music, Egil Monn-Iversen; editor uncredited. Reviewed at Norwegian Film Festival (official entry), at the Edda Cinema, Haugesund, Norway, Aug. 20, 1985. Running time: 110 MINS.
Kuksja/Ejnar . . . . .Alexandr Timoskin
Signy . . . . .Petronella Baker
Torir .Tor Stokke
Sigurd . . . . .Torgeir Fonnlid
Harald . . . . .John Andresen
Tyra . . . . .Lise Fjeldstad
Guttorm . . . . .Per Sunderland
Levius . . . . .Mikhail Gluzskij
Olav . . . . .Victor Sjulgin

"Captive Of The Dragon," a Norwegian-Russian coproduction (to be released later this year in Russia by Sovexportfilm in a 145-minute version under the title "Even On Rocks, Trees Grow") tries to probe a little deeper than earlier pictures into the souls of the sea-faring Vikings, but fails to bring them into any kind of social perspective.

Veteran helmer Stanislav Rostotsky (a Sergei Eisenstein pupil and collaborator who has had two of his own features, "The Dawns Are So Quiet Here" and "White Bim Of The Black Ear" nominated for Oscars in the Best Foreign-language film category) and his Norwegian co-director Knut Andersen have delivered a clean, but rather stodgily told classical adventure-thriller story about love, honor, skullduggery and swordplay among the Norwegian vikings.

Chieftain Torir raids an Eastern Baltic village and abducts its best young defender. Kuksja in his name, but the vikings call him Ejnar The Peaceful after he has bashed a few of their heads, convincing Torir that the boy is worthy of adoption as his son.

Back in Norway, Torir fights off some evil (by this time his own bunch are the good guys) Danish vikings, then is allowed to settle for the winter on the estate of another chieftain and latter's strong and handsome wife Tyra. Kuksja/Ejnar strikes up a friendship with Harald and Signy, the chieftain's near-adult children. Signy, a bit of a wildcat, soon makes it clear that she prefers the new arrival to her old suitor Sigurd The Berserk (this means The

One Blessed By The Gods) who, his name notwithstanding, has a scraggly beard and narrow-set eyes. Kuksja/Ejnar (by now speaking a little Norse: 80% of film's dialog is in Norwegian, the rest is in Russian) is drawn to Signy, but he also considers it his duty to somehow manage to return to his real home.

After much intrigue, some amourous cavorting, lots of heavy fighting and some bloodshed, none of it overdone, film has a part-tragic, party-happy ending.

"Captive Of The Dragon" has a splendid production dress, and the cinematography makes the most of mountains rising steeply above fjords and of the sun seeping through leaves of birch trees. The elegant viking ships are also seen in smooth operation, making it rather hard to believe that they were built by the same simpletons who man them. —*Kell.*

Desert Hearts
(U.S.-COLOR)

Locarno, Aug. 13.

A Samuel Goldwyn Co. release of a Desert Hearts production. Produced and directed by Donna Deitch. Screenplay, Natalie Cooper, based on novel "Desert Of The Heart" by Jane Rule; camera (color), Robert Elswit; editor-musical supervisor, Robert Estrin; music, original recordings of Fifties hits; sound, Austin McKinney; production design, Jeannine Oppewall; art direction, David Brisbin; set decoration, Rosemary Brandenburg; costume design, Linda Bass; assistant director, George Perkins. Reviewed at the Morettina Film Center, Locarno Film Festival, Aug. 12, 1985. Running time: 93 MINS.

Vivian Bell . . . . Helen Shaver
Cay Rivers . . . . Patricia Charbonneau
Frances . . . . Audra Lindley
Silver . . . . Andra Akers
Darrell . . . . Dean Butler
Lucille . . . . Katie La Bourdette
Jerry . . . . Jeffrey Tambor
Gwen . . . . Gwen Welles

For the first few minutes, one is almost tempted to believe helmer Donna Deitch is taking off where Clare Boothe Luce's "The Women" left off, in a Nevada ranch, amid society women waiting for their divorce to come through and passing the time of day, bitchily taking each other apart.

This impression is soon dispelled, however, once the plot focuses on one of the guests at the ranch, Vivian Bell, an English Literature lecturer from New York, frozen stiff by middle class morality and inbred prejudices, and totally confused by the drastic step she is about to take at the age of 35, after an exemplary and uneventful life.

To make matters much worse for her, once on the ranch, she catches the fancy of the owner's adoptive daughter, who starts making advances, first timidly and then in a pressing fashion, until the prim, respectable East Coast intellectual has

to drop her armor and face her own latent homosexuality.

Since the story is placed in the fifties, it is clear that what, by today's standards, would have been an unconventional but by no means an exceptional case, becomes an act of defiance against the accepted rules of society. This, as a matter of fact, is the best aspect of the movie, since Deitch does not go for extremes. She does not present a repressive environment nor drag in excessive dramatics. She prefers to dwell on the incapacity of many people to condone something which is beyond their own experience and comprehension, and on the fear of being alienated from people one loves by an emotion that is considered against nature.

However, once this is established, Deitch lacks both the inventiveness necessary to keep audience attention with the plot and the characters that would fascinate it. Everything proceeds smoothly, according to all the traditions of film melodrama, including the obligatory love scene between the two women, all wrapped up in filters and soft focus. Some of the dialog preceding this climax, is a bit awkward.

Helen Shaver, playing the lead, does a most commendable job as a character who starts by being all tied up inside, and ends up by melting and opening up to emotions she couldn't even conceive before. Audra Lindley, as the older woman who will go along with any kind of heterosexual irregularity but balks at the thought of homosexuality, is both humorous and touching. Patricia Charbonneau, as the avowed lesbian desperate for true affection in female companionship, tends to look too much like the spoiled brat who will have her own way.

Considering the evidently low budget of the production, Deitch offers some sound film making, even if she could tighten up her narrative style for better results.

Technical credits are above par and soundtrack, featuring some of the more notable hits of the fifties (mostly the country and western variety), helps to establish a credible mood and at the same time offer comments on the plot itself.
— *Edna.*

Liebe Und Tod
(Love And Death)
(WEST GERMAN-COLOR)

Locarno, Aug. 16.

A Nanna Rélia Film, Bonn. Written and directed by Nanna Rélia. Features entire cast. Camera (color), Dieter Fitzke; editor, Robert Süd; music, Guy Boulanger, Jean Yves Rigaud; sets, Gi Brenig. Reviewed at Locarno Film Fest (competition), Aug. 16, 1985. Running time: 110 MINS.
With: Maria Laborit, Billi Rubien.

Nanna Rélia's "Love And Death" is one of those audience chasers moving at an extremely slow pace. All the same, it's a film with some style and obvious commitment, even though it leans too heavily on arty experimental aesthetics to cover its many imperfections.

The setting is some fictitious time in the future. A war without end is going on, the soldiers are at the front, and the wives are left behind in an isolated highrise in a desolate land-area to carry on some ritual of "love and death" that's never fully explained.

A woman teacher of history kills a child one day with a gun. Then she is sentenced to death herself before a council of women. Years pass: another woman teacher happens on the scene to visit an old friend, stays for a while, and then sets off on a long trip to see her brother at the front. She has to kill a man, too, out of this apparent ongoing conflict between love and death. Then we find her back at the desolate highrise again, the Council of Women sitting at a kind of da Vinci "Last Supper" table.

It's the music and camera that make "Love And Death" worth sitting through. Lenser Dieter Fitzke's statically composed shots are also a delight to the eye over the long viewing haul. — *Holl.*

Black Hills
(W. GERMAN-DOCU-COLOR)

Edinburgh, Aug. 13.

A Michael Kuball Filmproduktion, in collaboration with SWF. Produced, directed and written by Michael Kuball. Camera (color), Jörg Jeschel; editor, Conny Galle; music, John Surman, Buddy Red Bow. Reviewed at Edinburgh Film Festival, Aug. 12, 1985. Running time: 92 MINS.

A German film crew examines the lives of Sioux Indians in the Black Hills of Dakota in this interesting but overlong documentary.

Wizened old-timers, sometimes speaking in their own language (which is not translated) relate their experiences at the hands of the government. Ironically, the focal point of these survivors of the Sioux nation, Bear Butte Mountain, is also a radar checkpoint for a USAF base controlling Minutemen missiles. The contrast between the Indians, some of whom are still trying to live a traditional life, and the frightening modern weapons, is telling.

The film takes much too long to get its message across, and quite a bit of it looks like routine travelog, with trips to Mt. Rushmore and other tourist sites of marginal interest. When director Michael Kuball concentrates on the Indians themselves, among them Grover

Horned Antelope and Frank Kills Enemy, he's on much surer ground.
—*Strat.*

Parole de Flic
(Cop's Honor)
(FRENCH-COLOR)

Paris, Aug. 21.

A UGC release of an Adel Productions picture. Produced by and starring Alain Delon. Directed by José Pinheiro. Screenplay, Delon, Pinheiro and Frédéric Fajardi, from an original story by Philippe Setbon; camera (Eastmancolor), Jean-Jacques Tarbes; art director, Théo Meurisse; editor, Claire Pinheiro-L'Heveder; sound, Louis Gimel, Jean-Paul Loublier; music, Pino Marchese; theme song lyrics, "I Don't Know," Charles McLoughlin; theme song performed by Phyllis Nelson and Alain Delon; production manager, Michel Crosnier. Reviewed at the Gaumont Ambassade theater, Paris, Aug. 21, 1985. Running time: 99 MINS.
With: Alain Delon, Jacques Perrin, Fiona Gélin, Jean-Francois Stévenin, Stéphane Ferrara, Vincent Lindon, Eva Darlan, Aurelle Doazan.

Alain Delon's new film may be the most auteur-oriented local production out on French screens currently. Not because he is producer, co-scripter and star (he also performed the English theme song, with Phyllis Nelson) of this otherwise routine revenge thriller.

But the film tellingly seems to channel into genre conventions all the anger and disappointment the star has poured out in the local press over the past year, not only over the fickleness of the public (his previous film, "Notre Histoire," was a resounding b.o. dud), but also over what he considers the rotten sociopolitical scene in France. Latter prospect recently prompted Delon to request a residence permit from Swiss authorities to settle in Geneva (though his film production house remains based in Paris).

So it's interesting to find the protagonist of "Parole de Flic" is also a bitterly disillusioned hero who has abandoned the native sod to live abroad. Here the character is a former cop who has quit job and country after French justice allowed the apparent murderer(s) of his wife go free on a legal loophole.

When the film opens he is living the life of Reilly in a coastal village in the Congo, where he spends his days playing cards, treating himself to the local women, beating up a black collosus for fun, or playing in the surf with the native kids.

The idyll is destroyed by a telegram announcing the murder of his teen daughter at the hands of a band of vigilantes, who are determined to clean up the Lyons suburbs of undesirable elements: North Africans, gays, dealers, delinquents and other menaces to wholesome France. Delon jumps on the plane for France where, ignoring official police warnings, he begins tracking down the killers and exterminating them with sadistic glee (maiming them first before delivering the final coup de grace). He then returns to his palm trees in the company of the pretty young police inspector who was on the case (a surrogate daughter and bed-mate?).

Delon, who caused some shock waves by publicly expressing his sympathy for France's increasingly popular extreme-Right political leader Jean-Marie Le Pen, doesn't make much of an effort to disguise the tale's odious ideology, and the character's cold blooded egoism. If the personage wipes out the vigilante band it's exclusively to avenge his daughter (whom the prolog reveals, was coaxed into a delinquent act against her will), not to pay lipservice to justice or defend society's outsiders. It is significant that the story's principal "villain," a police inspector who has created the vigilante group because he believes that the moral rot will otherwise smother the nation in a few years, does not die at Delon's hand. Film doesn't overtly condone or condemn vigilantism, but cleverly loads the dice, notably in assigning the role of the warped cop to the clean-cut and sympathetic Jacques Perrin.

America has Dirty Harry and Rambo; France now has Delon to knock out some bloody home-truths to film audiences.

José Pinheiro, the promising helmer of "Family Rock" and "Les Mots Pour le Dire" is the director of "Parole de Flic." Technically it's no better or worse than most other local genre product, only more insidious. — Len.

┌─────────────────────────────────┐
│   Pics At Montreal Fest   │
└─────────────────────────────────┘

The Assisi Underground
(U.S.-COLOR)

Montreal, Aug. 21.

A Golan-Globus Production for The Cannon Group. Produced by Menahem Golan and Yoram Globus. Directed by Alexander Ramati. Features entire cast. Screenplay, Ramati, based on his own "documentary novel." Camera (color), Giuseppe Rotunno; editor, Michael Duthie; music, Dov Seltzer; production designer, Luciano Spadoni; costumes, Adriana Spadaro; associate producer, John Thompson; production supervisor, Mario Cotone; production manager, Attilio Viti; assistant director, Albino Cocco; technical advisor, Father Mario Bigaroni; historical advisor, Don Aldo Brunacci; advisor on Jewish refugees, Daniel Dropf; 2d unit camera, Silvano Ippoliti; special effects, Giovanni Corridori. Reviewed at Montreal World Film Festival (Parisien 1), Aug. 21, 1985. (MPAA Rating: PG.) Running time: **178 MINS.**
Padre Rufino . . . . Ben Cross
Bishop Nicolini . . . . James Mason
Mother Giuseppina . . . . Irene Papas
Colonel Mueller . . . . Maximilian Schell
Captain von Velden . . . . . Karl-Heinz Hackl
Luigi Brizzi . . . . Riccardo Cucciola
Giorgio Kropf . . . . Angelo Infanti
Paolo Josza . . . . Paolo Malco
General Bremer . . . . Tom Felleghy
Countess Cristina . . . . Delia Boccardo
Professor Rieti . . . . Roberto Bisacco
Mrs. Eva Rieti . . . . Didi Ramati

At a three-hour running time, this otherwise interesting piece of history falls between a frustrated miniseries and an attempt at a grand splash of a two-part epic vision of the role the city of Assisi played in saving Jewish targets of the holocaust by lending them refuge in the convents and monasteries of that august and glorious holy city. Beyond all that, it also features one of James Mason's last performances.

Beginning with Mason as a bishop, who with drawn expression opines, "It couldn't happen here," it proceeds with the inevitable. Just as the rabbi entrusts a religious treasure to the bishop's care, soon a group of 15 Jews will be put under the stewardship of the Church. Emerging from his simple wine drinking, witty ways, one Padre Rufino is appointed shepherd of these black sheep from all over Europe. Among them is a nuclear physicist wanted by the Germans to help them beat the Americans to the bomb, but this Professor Rieti is more concerned about his diabetic wife, who dies in the course of the film. Irene Papas appears in some briefly dramatic scenes trying to keep folks out of her convent, which has not been penetrated by men in some 700 years.

Soon there are kosher kitchens in the convent, followed by Nazi raids. What in the beginning is a command compared to Saint Francis' guidance to "kiss the leper," becomes an act — even a movement — of Christian charity, all of which might never have occurred without Padre Rufino's ebullient habits.

Ben Cross lends a great deal of charm to the role of a callow young monk who will grow into a saint-like stature after he is arrested and given 24 hours to betray Assisi or be executed. The salvation of the pic is Cross, who bears his own quite well, with a face that fits right in with the magnificent frescos of Assisi.

Some of the best acting is found in scenes between Padre Rufino and a local printer Luigi Brizzi, played by Riccardo Cucciolla with credible ambivalence about churning out identity cards for the Jews not only in Assisi but the surrounding Umbrian monasteries.

A subplot of a local countess carrying on with the German commandant promises her damnation, in the post-war world if not in the hereafter, but she manages to redeem herself by seducing the general one last time in order to convince him to grant a stay of execution for Padre Rufino. She's so convincing he hires the other three Jews to work as translators, and from within the Nazi headquarters, they can be even more subversive. They forge a letter declaring Assisi an open city and deliver it to Colonel Mueller, who is the good German running a hospital as opposed to the bad German Captain von Velden, who is neither Catholic nor educated. These examples of the polarized German army are well-acted by the all-purpose German Max Schell and Karl-Heinz Hackl in a constant snit.

There is simply not enough story to fill three hours, so the filmmakers let the scenery upstage the actors. Breathtaking panoramas of the golden tones of Umbria reflect the talent of Giuseppe Rotunno, who also focuses the camera on the art and architecture of Assisi in such a way as to make it far more interesting than its underground. A ponderously melodramatic score weighs down the mood, which is not tragic as most holocaust pics are, but rather chipper in a Franciscan sort of benevolence.

Certainly the potential for cultural clash in the convent was not explored in this version, but various versions of pic seem to be possible. This three-hour, two-part dyptich has some jump cuts that reflect the conflict over its editing. Music can't compensate for choppy vignettes bridged by landscapes. Ramati's journalistic account of this little-known episode in the last two years of World War II has not been served well by his film. —Kaja.

Tristesse et Beauté
(Sadness And Beauty)
(FRENCH-COLOR)

Paris, Aug. 26.

A Parafrance release of a Pacific/-GPFI/FR3 Films coproduction. Produced by Pierre Novat. Directed by Joy Fleury. Screenplay, Fleury, Pierre Grillet, inspired by the novel by Yasunara Kawabata; camera (color), Bernard Lutic; editor, Nelly Meunier; music, Jean-Claude Petit; art director, Dan Weil; sound, François de Morant; production manger, Hugues Nonn. Reviewed at The Publicis screening room, Paris, Aug. 22, 1985 (In Montreal Film Festival.) Running time: **97 MINS.**
Hugo Pierjoyre . . . . Andrzej Zulawski
Lea Ueno . . . . Charlotte Rampling
Prudence . . . . Myriem Roussel
Martin . . . . Jean-Claude Adelin
Mathilde . . . . Isabelle Sadoyan
Agathe . . . . Béatrice Agenin

To adapt a Japanese literary masterpiece to the screen, transposing it in a European context, would be quite a challenge for even the most skilled Western filmmaker. So it seems doubly ambitious (and maybe foolhardy) for a newcomer to attempt the operation. For her first film, Joy Fleury (wife of film's coproducer, Jean-Claude Fleury) has taken the plunge, and comes up with neither glory nor disgrace, in her adaptation of Yasunara Kawabata's "Sadness And Beauty."

Fleury and her coscripter, Pierre Grillet, claim to have retained the "skeleton" of the novel's plot, though admit to having kept in certain specifically oriental symbols and cultural notions. Fleury's attempt to find a style for the film, notably in her use of facial closeups and body poses, is more mannered than mystical, and in the absence of conventional psychological dramatization, the characters seem artificial and inscrutable.

Tale begins with Hugo, a middle-aged novelist, who finds a pretext to renew contact with Lea, a sculptor of some repute, whom Hugo had loved when she was 16. That affair, which ended with his desertion, gave him the material for a novel that has made his literary reputation. His inspiration since then has been tepid and so he now comes back to Lea, asking for a "sequel."

Lea, who has never recovered from this unique passion, rejects him, but not before presenting him to her beautiful young disciple, Prudence. The young firl is profoundly attached to Lea and feels immediate hatred for the writer. Bent on vague notions of revenge, she makes several trips to Paris where she visits Hugo, who lives with his adoring wife, and their son. Latter immediately falls in love with Prudence, while she seduces the father. In their single night of lovemaking, she perversely stages the act as Hugo had described it in his emotionally vampiric literary work.

Prudence has nonetheless allowed her relationship with Hugo's son, Martin, to develop along more apparently healthier lines. He eventually decides to visit her and the young couple go off together for an idyll in the mountains. One day they take a speedboat out on the lake and meet with an accident. The boy drowns, but Prudence survives. Hugo and Lea, who have rushed to the scene of the accident, have one final, silent encounter. She plants a mysterious kiss on his lips and they separate.

Despite the film's remoteness and lack of palpable emotion, Fleury was at least done some smart casting, first with Andrzej Zulawski, the expatriate Polish filmmaker, and Charlotte Rampling, as Hugo and Lea. The trump part as Prudence is Myriem Roussel, the lovely newcomer who was Jean-Luc Godard's virgin in "Hail, Mary." She alone succeeds in dredging up some of the mystery lacking in the direction and gives meaning to the film's title.

—Len.

Illustres Inconnus
(Notorious Nobodies)
(FRENCH-COLOR)

Montreal, Aug. 26.

A Soleil Fertile production. Produced, directed and written by Stanislav Stanojevic. Camera (color), Georges Barsky; editor, Anne-France Lebrun; music, Benito Merlino. Reviewed at World Film Festival, Montreal, Aug. 24, 1985. Running time: **87 MINS.**
(Cast members not identified in press material supplied)

The denial of human rights in many countries around the world has been the concern of Amnesty Intl. and other like-minded organizations for some time now. "Notorious Nobodies" is a fictionalized documentary on the subject which is a bit schematic and awkward, but which gets across a feeling of anger and frustration very well.

An opening title tells us that the situations here are "inspired by real life." The countries mentioned, we're told, could be replaced by others where things could be better, but are probably worse. A day at random is chosen: Nov. 10, 1983. On this day, around the world, violations of human rights are taking place. In Prague, a dissident just released after serving three years in prison, finds himself boycotted by former friends and takes dramatic steps to draw attention to his plight. In Montevideo, plain-clothed cops arrest a man in his home, murder him, and make it appear he swam out to sea. Ironically, the victim is found guilty of the crime of leaving the country without permission. In Zaire, a man is wrongly arrested, then murdered to conceal the mistake. In Ho Chi Minh City, two women make a bet that one can't stand in a public place and cry "Long Live Freedom," with grim results.

Director Stanislav Stanojevic also shows people trying to help the situation. In Geneva, an Englishman tries to shame the representatives of a Third World country into not executing four peasants. A West German woman travels to Prague with a present, which is smashed to pieces by Czech customs officers. In Paris, two victims of the terror in Argentina try to live normal lives. In a small French village, a farmer decides it's time he protested the abuse of civil rights.

In covering so much ground, the film sacrifices cohesion and depth, but at the same time provides a panorama of human rights abuses that's cumulatively impressive. The film is unduly naive at times, with the Vietnamese scenes extremely unconvincing, and some misguided comedy in the Montevideo sequence, showing that the fascist cops are also buffoons. "Notorious Nobodies," for all its flaws, has impact, and could certainly be used by Amnesty Intl. and other like-minded bodies to promote their cause. Tv and video, rather than theatrical, distribution is indicated. Tech credits are good. —*Strat.*

Frida: Naturaleza Vita
(Frida)
(MEXICAN-COLOR)

Montreal, Aug. 26.

A Clasa Films Mundiales production. Produced by Manuel Barbachano. Directed by Paul Leduc. Stars Ofelia Medina. Screenplay, Alejandro Luna; dialog, Jose Joaquin Blanco, Paul Leduc; camera (color), Angel Goded; editor, Rafael Castanedo; sound, Ernesto Estrada, Penelope Simpson; costumes, Luz Maria Rodriguez. Reviewed at World Film Festival, Montreal, Aug. 24, 1985. Running time: **107 MINS.**
Frida Kahlo . . . . Ofelia Medina
Rivera . . . . Juan Jose Gurrola
Leon Trotsky . . . . Salvador Sanchez
Frida's Father . . . . Claudio Brook
With: Max Kerlow, Cecilia Toussaint, Valentina Leduc, Juan Angel Martinez, Gina Morett, François Lartique.

Responses to this bio of Frida Kahlo (1907-54) will vary according to individual taste, for, as a long opening title explains, this isn't a conventional bio but a series of loosely collated scenes from the life of the famous Mexican painter and leftist, supposedly as they flashed across her mind as she was dying. This enables the filmmakers to ignore such bothersome things as story, structure and dialog, and instead present a kind of filmic collage.

No doubt Frida was an exceptional woman, fiercely independent though troubled with various infirmities, including eventually the amputation of a leg, and passionate about her art, her friends and her lovers. Her involvement in politics results in giving shelter to the exiled Leon Trotsky, who's as attracted to her as everyone else. Trotsky's murder is depicted in this film as committed not by a young man with an ice-pick but via some Stalinist members of the Mexican military with machine guns, a curious distortion of history.

Ofelia Medina is perfectly cast as Frida and gives a vibrant performance. Pic is perhaps overly academic, but audiences may well respond to its visual richness and somewhat simplistic presentation of its heroine and those around her. A great music score certainly helps.
—*Strat.*

Le Pouvoir du Mal
(Power Of Evil)
(FRENCH-ITALIAN-COLOR)

Paris, Aug. 26.

A Films Molière release of a Pierson production/TF1 Films/Maki Films - Enzo Peri (Rome) coproduction. Producers, Claude Pierson, Jean-Pierre Voronowsky, Enzo Peri. Written and directed by Krzysztof Zanussi. Camera (color), Slavomir Idziak; music, Wojciech Kilar; sound, Eric Vaucher, A. Magara. No other credits provided. Reviewed at the CELTEC screening room, Paris, Aug. 23, 1985. (In both Venice and Montreal Film Festivals.) Running time: **110 MINS.**
Sylvie . . . . Marie-Christine Barrault
Gotfried . . . . Vittorio Gassman
Hubert . . . . Benjamin Voelz
Lab director . . . . Raf Vallone

Polish intellectual director Krzysztof Zannusi made this film under Franco-Italian auspices, and shot most of it on location in eastern France (near Nancy). Zanussi has worked away from home before, but "Le Pouvoir du Mal" shows him floundering between a preposterous script and a mixed cast unable to reconcile the highfalutin' talk and ill-contrived action.

Zanussi attempts here a sort of philosophical melodrama about the influence of evil on the individual and society. Script's protagonist is a penniless theological student who gets into something more than a metaphysical jam when he finds himself the lover of the wife of a rich arms manufacturer who has agreed to finance his university studies.

The student (Benjamin Voelz) seems at first rigid in his moral beliefs, but gradually begins to compromise those values as he is confronted with each new assault on his supposed integrity. Dissuading the wife (Marie-Christine Barrault) from suicide in a church, he becomes her lover. When Barrault gets pregnant, he implores her on moral grounds not to abort. She then maneuvers him into confronting her husband (Vittorio Gassman) with the truth after latter suffers a heart attack, in the hope that the revelation will bring about a fatal relapse.

Voelz and Gassman have a heated showdown, and latter does indeed expire. The widow's perverse relief turns to dismay when the will reveals that the student is principal beneficiary. Barrault, who is actually in cahoots with a revolutionary group plotting to gain control of Gassman's arms factory, offers Voelz a swap of her baby against his inheritance. He accepts and is last seen some years after, a bible-quoting tramp, trundling his son around in a poor working-class village.

Even Douglas Sirk might have recoiled from some of the oddball scenes Zanussi has imagined. When several characters gather around the body of the deceased arms magnate, Voelz proposes that all kneel and pray. Suddenly a revolver, which had been thrown aside in the student's final argument with his benefactor, goes off by itself, and somebody remarks that if they hadn't gone down on their knees, the shot would have killed one of them.

Given these unlikely situations, and the philosophy-larded artifices of dialog, it's not their fault that the chief players are dreadful (Voelz is the only actor in the French-track version who is dubbed). Gassman's sheer professionalism saves him from ridicule though he is hardly convincing. In a cameo appearance, Raf Vallone also injects some moral gab as the head of the medical school morgue.

The tale is set in some unspecified country in the 1920s. Zanussi and his compatriot lenser Slavomir Idziak try to create a morbid Eastern European atmosphere, with its somber industrial landscapes and contrasting bourgeois swankness. Some of the photography is effective, though Idziak makes excessive use of light filters.

Film is unspooling at both the Montreal and Venice festivals. Helmer is jury president at the former, where film is being shown out-of-competition. —*Len.*

Amargo Mar
(Bitter Sea)
(BOLIVIAN-CUBAN-COLOR)

Montreal, Aug. 23.

A Productora Ukamau-I.C.A.I.C. coproduction. Directed by Antonio Eguino. Features entire cast. Screenplay, Oscar Soria, Paolo Agazzi, Raquel Romero, Antonio Eguino; camera (color), Armando Urioste, Eguino; editor, Justo Vega. No further credits supplied. Reviewed at World Film Festival, Montreal, Aug. 22, 1985. Running time: **96 MINS.**
General Campero . . . . Edgar Vargas
Daza . . . . Eddy Bravo
Arco . . . . Alfredo Ribera
Manuel Davalas . . . . Edwin Morales

In 1879, Chile invaded neighboring Bolivia which, as a result, lost possession of its coastline. That's an important and exciting theme for a film, but not the way it's mishandled in "Bitter Sea."

The blame for this inept pic can be laid at several doors. There's a dreary script in which characters make speeches rather than speak dialog; plotting is choppy and confused; a plethora of characters are used, none involving. Then there's the indifferent acting, the flat, fuzzily processed photography and the sparse but over-emphatic music. Finally, though, the blame rests with Bolivian helmer Antonio Eguina ("Chuquiago," 1978), whose handling is completely uninspired.

The machinations of Chilean sympathizers within Bolivia, especially evil industrialists, and the duplicity of a senior army officer with political ambitions, plus various battles and confrontations with the enemy amid spectacular South American settings — all this is the stuff of a drama which is quite spectacularly mishandled. — *Strat.*

Ni Avec Toi, Ni Sans Toi
(Not With You, Not Without You)
(FRENCH-COLOR)

Montreal, Aug. 23.

A Mikado Films-FR3-Lyric International coproduction. Directed by Alain Maline. Stars Evelyne Bouix, Philippe Léotard. Screenplay, Joelle Pilven, Yves Josso, Maline, from the novel "L'Ecureuil dans la Roue" by Hortense Dufour; camera (Panavision, Fujicolor), Joel David; editor, Hughes Darmos; music, Kolinka; sound, Harald Maury. Reviewed at World Film Festival, Montreal, Aug. 22, 1985. Running time: 83 MINS.
Mathilde . . . . Evelyne Bouix
Pierre . . . . Philippe Léotard
Also with: Tanya Lopert, Charles Gerard.

At a family party to celebrate the New Year, Pierre (Philippe Léotard) disappears. Mathilde (Evelyne Bouix), his wife, remembers their life together in extended flashback.

Pierre's problem is that he's a drunk, and a rather charmless drunk at that. Pic is thus full of scenes in which Léotard, good actor that he is, gets violent and irrational and generally a pain in the butt. Evelyne Bouix suffers nobly throughout.

Firsttime director Alain Maline was a former assistant to Claude Lelouch among others, and the Lelouch influence is there in midscreen shots of lovers driving by the sea or mulling over their plight. As movies about drunks go, this is somewhat below average, though lushly shot by Joel David. — *Strat.*

Jenny Kissed Me
(AUSTRALIAN-COLOR)

Montreal, Aug. 26.

A production of Nelson Premiere Ltd. Produced by Tom Broadbridge. Directed by Brian Trenchard-Smith. Screenplay, Warwick Hind and Judith Colquhoun with dialog by Alan Lake; camera (color) Bob Kohler; set design, Jon Dowding; music, Trevor Incas, Ian Mason; choreography, Aphrodite Kondos. Reviewed at Montreal World Film Festival (Parisien 2), Aug. 25, 1985. Running time: 98 MINS.
Jenny West . . . . Tamsin West
Lindsay Fenton . . . . Ivar Kants
Carol Grey . . . . Deborah-Lee Furness
Gaynor . . . . :Paula Duncan
Grace . . . . . : . . . . Mary Ward
Neighbor . . . . Steven Grimes

Proceeding from a very sentimental 18th Century poem by Leigh Hunt that denounces all earthly accomplishments in comparison to the incomparable kiss of one Jenny, an ambitious script for "Jenny Kissed Me" of nonparental care and parental non-caring remains sufficiently shallow and graced only by fastidious attention to decor and hairdos that it could easily replace a whole week of soap opera.

In the hills near Melbourne live Carol, her daughter Jenny, and Lindsay, whom Jenny calls and treats like her daddy. His response is to return the affection and dote on the child in a way that lovable kids inspire. We see little of Jenny's lovable qualities, nor even her point-of-view except for ephemeral eruptions followed by running away. The girl is given no character development whatsoever, which makes the story of Lindsay's devotion to her possibly "an unnatural" obsession, as Carol once accuses him.

When Jenny gets a glimpse of her mother's flirtation with a neighbor Mal, she warns Lindsay that "some women are tarts," with implications for her mother, who actually is. After Carol leaves Lindsay in outrage, she moves into a mauve apartment with her bimbo friend Gaynor and is easily talked into working in the same bordello where she earns $500 in her first night. A cocaine bust in the apartment is quickly dropped from the storyline, in favor of following Lindsay's kidnapping of Jenny in order to spend his last loving days camping with her, because he's dying of brain damage.

The child languishes in an orphanage, giving her mother a chance to clean up her act, change her mind and marry Lindsay in a death-bed ceremony that sends the dialog lunging into the embarrassing "till death us do part," accompanied by titters from the audience. Those are not the only titterable titillations in pic. An up-against-the-wall seduction of Carol by her neighbor makes it problematic as youth fare, where some sympathy for the kid might be expected.

Jenny's love of Lindsay turns into a leap of faith after his death when she decides he has been reincarnated into some koala-like creature in the trees around the house, and pic' ends on a cute little pink nose, while the score sends in the violins to saw away at the ham-strung heartstrings of mother-love.

Lensing is solidly commercial, paying attention to actresses' good sides but ignoring a few continuity problems. Acting is mannered as can be expected from the trendiness built into the sets and social message of a life worth living for the kiss of a kid. If it were only clichéd, the television markets might kiss Jenny back, but the dialog leaves a saccharine aftertaste, even for tv.
— *Kaja.*

Private Practices:
The Story Of A Sex
Surrogate
(U.S.-DOCU-COLOR-16m)

Montreal, Aug. 23.

A Kirby Dick production. Produced and directed by Kirby Dick. Camera (video, color), Christine Burrill, Catherine Coulson; editors, Lois Freeman, Dick; music, Tom Recchion; sound, Alan Barker. Reviewed at World Film Festival, Montreal, Aug. 22, 1985. Running time: 78 MINS.
With: Maureen Sullivan, Christopher Walker, John Christ.

Los Angeles men with sexual problems can, on referral, pay for the help of sex surrogates. This quite fascinating docu, shot on video and transferred to film, studies one such sex surrogate, attractive Maureen Sullivan, and two of her clients, a painfully shy 25-year-old and a divorced 45-year-old.

Sullivan, who has a lively personality, treats her clients with delicacy and seemingly unforced affection. Both are nervous and reticent at first (no surprise considering they were being filmed), but blossom under her treatment, which includes touching, frank talk and eventually, intercourse. Latter stage of the therapy isn't shown in the film, which though dealing with an explicit theme remains tactful; genitals are not seen.

It's an interesting and somewhat bizarre profession, and "Private Practices" is an interesting and somewhat bizarre film. Sullivan's father and brother are shown talking with her, as are her neighbors, plus her analyst, with whom she has a tearful session. Also, the ex-wife of one of the clients is seen in a rather uneasy reunion with her former partner.

Despite the theme, this isn't for voyeurs. Adults seriously interested in sexual problems will be interested, possibly even helped, by it, if they get a chance to see it. —*Strat.*

Strawberry Fields
(WEST GERMAN-COLOR)

Montreal, Aug. 24.

A Cine-International presentation of a Marten Taege Filmproduktion and Channel 4 production. Produced by Martin Taege. Directed by Kristian Kuhn. Screenplay, Kuhn, Stephen Poliakoff; camera (color), Martin Schäfer; editor, Alexander Meisel; music, Eberhard Weber. Reviewed at Montreal World Film festival (Parisien), Aug. 24, 1985. Running time: 82 MINS.
Charlotte . . . . Beate Jensen
Karl . . . . Rolf Zacher
Nicki . . . . Thomas Schmucke
Frau Ruprecht . . . . Lisa Kreuzer

Skimpy production values and a desperate concern with anxieties that seem specific to Germany make this otherwise well-scripted pic an unlikely proposition beyond the borders of German-speaking Europe. A road movie through the landscapes of visually polluted West Germany, it comments on the psychology that is pushing young people into neofascist thinking.

Thesp kudos go to Beate Jensen whose pixie face and intelligent manner make her fascinating to watch, as she seems to represent the last thing worth looking at among the Teutons. Her traveling companion, Karl, is an individualistic, alienated radical-turned-reactionary, or he is a demented slob. The script keeps him on seesaw for sympathy. Another young kid who is studying education hitches a ride with them, against their wishes, and sticks with them, fascinated by the kind of dime-store political movement they think they are launching with something called "The National People's Front."

Plot is less political than it is a psychodrama of this trio who shoot two policemen, an act which welds them together. Two stolen cars later, they reach their destination at a combination cocktail/neo-Nazi party. This nostalgic elegy to preindustrial Germany is empty of any real dynamism over the experience of Germany as a contaminated culture full of imported kitsch and bumbling political notions. Imbedded in the dialog is a beautiful sense of German at its dramatic best, which unfortunately does not penetrate the subtitles. — *Kaja.*

Breaking Silence
(U.S.-DOCU-COLOR)

Montreal, Aug. 24.

Produced by Future Educational Films. Produced and directed by Theresa Tollini. Written by Michelle Morris; camera (color), Francis Reid; editor, Jennifer Chinlund; music, Paul de Benedictis. Reviewed at Montreal World Film Festival (Conservatoire d'art cinematographique), Aug. 24, 1985. Running time: 62 MINS.

"Breaking Silence" is primarily intended as an educational film, but its sensitivity and scope in dealing with one of today's major social problems, child abuse, has put it on the festival circuit, where it successfully competes among its socially concerned ilk. In a recent study cited in the film, one out of three people had been molested as a child, and one out of six is an incest victim within the U.S. An estimated 96% of the offenders are male, and pic has the courage to interview convicted offenders.

Keeping the focus primarily, however, on victims, interviews dealing forthrightly with the actual assault and the delayed reaction are mixed with children's naive drawings that reveal the incidents and the perpetrators implicated in obviously symbolic ways. Precisely because the finger-pointing in the fingerpainting reveals shocking relationships within the family, traditional responses have hesitated to believe the children and gone with Freud's own fear of his findings. (He retreated from his theory of incest and abuse, and got on the safer ground of "projection.")

Director Theresa Tollini has put all this together in a palatable if not totally savory fashion, and the elegance of pace and use of color alleviates the fairly dreadful dealing out of unpleasant information. Television prospects are very good, and classroom use inevitable.—*Kaja.*

Tupac Amaru
(PERUVIAN-CUBAN-COLOR)

Montreal, Aug. 23.

A Cine Kuntur-ICAIC coproduction. Produced by Pilar Raco, Santiago Llapur. Directed by Federico Garcia. Features entire cast. Screenplay, Yolanda Rodriguez; dialog, Federico Garcia; camera (color), Rodolfo Lopez; sets, Pilar Roca Palacio; editor, Roberto Bravo; music, Juan Marquez; sound, Leonardo Sorrell; costumes, Isabel Salazar. Reviewed at World Film Festival, Montreal, Aug. 23, 1985. Running time: **92 MINS.**
Tupac Amaru . . . . Reynaldo Arenas
Bastades . . . . Zully Azurin
Moscoso . . . . Enrique Almirante

There seems to be a trend for Latin American coproductions recreating political events of the past from an historical perspective. The Bolivian-Cuban coproduction "Bitter Sea" is one example, and now here's a Peruvian-Cuban coproduction about an ill-fated revolution against Spanish rule in 1780 by the Incan leader, Tupac Amaru.

The setting is the old Incan capital of Cusco where unrest against Spanish colonialism grew into a full-scale revolt combining workers, slaves and Indians under Tupac's inspired leadership. His main opponent is the corrupt Bishop of Cusco (seen at one point in bed with a nun just to indicate how really evil he is), and after Tupac's inevitible defeat he has the leader horribly executed in the city square (torn apart by four horses) while all members of his family are also killed.

The film ends on a polemical note with black and white newsreel footage from 1975 of the birth of an agrarian revolutionary movement in Peru that carries the name of Tupac Amaru. The pic is handsomely mounted, a bit stolid early on, but improves as it continues, with a powerful climax. Acting is quite impressive, especially Reynaldo Arenas as the eponymous hero.—*Strat.*

I Jizn, I Slezy, I Liubov
(Life, Love, Tears)
(SOVIET-COLOR)

Montreal, Aug. 23.

A Mosfilm Production. Written and directed by Nikolai Gubenko. Features entire cast. Camera (Sovcolor), Leonid Kalachinkov; art director, Yuri Kladienko; music, Igor Nazarouk. Reviewed at World Film Festival, Montreal, Aug. 22, 1985. Running time: **101 MINS.**
With: Janna Bolotova (Varvara Voloshina), Elena Fadeeva, Fedor Nikitine, Piotr Scherbakov, Sergei Martinson, Eugeny Evstignev.

"Life, Love, Tears" is a sentimental tale of a run-down old people's home transformed by the arrival of an enthusiastic woman doctor.

The home, set in a magnificent old house, has leaky ceilings and a shabby look until Dr. Voloshina (Janna Bolotova) arrives and starts putting things right. She also brings a new lease of life to the inmates, her greatest success being a bedridden old man who starts taking an interest in life again and even falls for an 80-year-old former singer.

"Cocoon" minus the sci-fi trappings, "Life, Love, Tears" is modestly engaging, and told with a keen sense of humor. The oldsters reminisce about the old revolutionary days, while a tv set plays loud modern rock music. In a slightly sinister touch, the proximity of the home to a helicopter base means that choppers are constantly flying overhead, bringing discomfort to the senior citizens.

Former actor turned director Nikolai Gubenko ("The Orphans") has turned out a charming, typically Russian, pic. — *Strat.*

Rate It X
(DOCU-COLOR-16m)

A film by OTM Prods., N.Y., in association with Channel Four, London. Produced by Lucy Winer, Paula de Koenigsberg, Lynn Campbell, Claudette Charbonneau. Directed by Winer and De Koenigsberg; based on a concept by Charbonneau; camera (color); De Koenigsberg; production manager, Robin de Crespigny; sound and creative consultant, Jan Oxenberg; editor/interviewer, Winer; music and lyrics, Elizabeth Swados; singer, William Parry; associate producer, Karen Eaton. Dedicated to the late Lynn Campbell (coproducer). Reviewed at TVC Labs, N.Y., Aug. 15, 1985. (No MPAA Rating.) Running time: **95 MINS.**

Already set for the Berlin festival, "Rate It X" is a docu selection of perhaps 20 scenes showing American males exercizing their machismo. Alternately funny and outrageous, these men collectively personify male-dominated American society from the cradle to the grave, literally — as men in the film talk about inculcating masculine values into the man-child (no dolls!), to shopping for caskets (for men, heavy oak; for women, silk ruffles and floral designs). Even side by side in the cemetery, wife and husband maintain their differences.

"Rate It X" is financed in part by British tv, with additional funding from the Money for Women Fund; the Women's Project of The Film Fund; The Film Fund; New York State Council for The Humanities; New York State Council on The Arts; Beva and Lucius Eastman Foundation; George Gund Foundation; Skaggs Foundation; and the Astraea Foundation. Total production cost is $250,000.

Men only appear in "Rate It X," men talking about men and the nature of manhood and the limitations of womanhood. These are males proudly propagandizing for men, in a film produced by females that, in effect, reverses their sexist pride and instead searches for a common humanity with women. Are the men being set up? — well, yes, but they ask for it. A few of them sheepishly realize they are victims of their own sexist prejudices, doing themselves as well as women an injustice.

The men in the film explain their vocations, which invariably are rationalized by their sexism. For example, a young Fundamentalist minister intones from his pulpit the holy law of the division of the sexes, with Eve subordinate to Adam. Business executives explain the prosperity of their "Lily of France" bras, disguising the imperfections of the female body. A fancy baker makes cakes as headless torsos of curvaceous women, for display and sale. A toy salesman demonstrates machine-guns, tanks and helicopters for the little boys and across the aisle the cuddly dolls and play-cosmetics for the little girls. The chief humor editor of the Larry Flynt periodicals justifies his "Chester The Molester" cartoon series about a "goofy," but laughable psychopathic rapist.

The producer of a splatter film, "Bloodsucking Freaks," reveals audiences harmlessly enjoy the gory thrills he contrives for them. A black editor of "Players," monthly aimed at yuppie black males, justifies nude centerfolds of black women as fostering black pride. Self-described as a millionaire, cable-cameraman Ugly George equates his show's success with the fulfillment of every immigrant's American dream. A half-dozen elderly war veterans in uniform clearly know what little boys do and must not do, but are baffled by the idea of "tomboy" girls who enjoy playing football.

These and other scenes in "Rate It X" make a composite montage on the theme of male chauvinist pigheadedness, produced with humor, insight and irony, especially as men trap themselves in their own clichés. The film is a natural for public tv and can prosper in specialized theatrical situations and in 16m distribution. —*Hitch.*

Havlandet
(Northern Lights)
(NORWEGIAN-COLOR)

Haugesund, Aug. 19.

A UIP release of Marcusfilm production. Foreign sales, Norsk Film (Frieda Ohrvik). Directed by Lasse Glomm. Stars Stein Björn, Sven Wollter, Björn Sundquist, Arja Saijonmaa; executive producer, Bente Erichsen. Screenplay, Glomm and Andrew Szepesy based on novels by Idar Kristiansen; camera (Eastmancolor), Erling Thurmann-Andersen; music, Klaus Schultze; editors, Lars Hagström, Peter Ekvall, Mats Krüger; production design, Frode Krogh; costumes, Anne Siri Bryhni, Erna Störkson. Reviewed at Norwegian Film Festival (official entry) at the Edda, Haugesund, Aug. 19, 1985. Running time: **91 MINS.**
Heikki . . . . Stein Björn
Taavi . . . . Björn Sundquist
Hilma . . . . Arja Saijonmaa
Matti . . . . Sven Wollter
Anne-Kreeta . . . . Anitta Suikkari
Blind old man . . . . Jens Bolling
Inkeri . . . . Benedicte O. Marthinsen
Marja . . . . Hege Sandvik
Hillka . . . . , ... Kaja Glomm
Child Hillka . . . Camilla Eriksrud Nordwall
Mauri . . . . Harald Woll

Shot on a lavish budget, Lasse Glomm's "Northern Lights" (original title "Havlandet" means the Country By The Sea), has production values to match. As an epic of poor people, whose fates are molded by the austere and often vicious Nature of Northern Norwegian regions in the 1860s, film has the Grand Design written all over it. Where it comes to describing Nature and her whims, sounds and visuals are stunning even to the fastidious ear and eye, and even if Glomm has a tougher time coming to grips with narrative dramatics, "Northern Lights" will surely travel the major film festival circuit and also reach at least selected commercial situations worldwide.

Story, based on two out of a quartet of novels about life among farmers, woodsmen and other poor folks, has Heikki, in his earliest teens, see the Northern Lights as tradition among his people always saw them: as celestial designs, spelling out the hope of one day reaching the coast and a sea expected to abound with fish. One day, Heikki really ups and leaves on a horse-drawn sledge. He braves a snowstorm and finds temporary refuge in a cabin amidst a snowswept wasteland, where a blind old man is taken care of by a young woman driven to madness after her husband's death at sea. Heikki sees her set fire to the house and fails to save anybody but the girl's baby. Boy and baby finally reach the sea.

Glomm rarely succeeds in making the components of his story jell. The narration comes in jerks and bumps and too often has to be helped along by sudden downpours and thunderclaps. Most protagonists are left to speak their lines stiffly (Sweden's Sven Wollter as the boy's real father is a notable exception) while looking stoic and austere even if oozing pink-cheeked health throughout. Only with Finland's Arja Saijonmaa has make-up care been taken to add grimness to her otherwise beautiful face. — *Kell.*

Brennende blomster
(Burning Flowers)
(NORWEGIAN-COLOR)

Haugesund, Aug. 18.

A KF release of Norsk Film (artistic director, Lasse Glomm) production. Foreign sales, Norsk Film (Frieda Ohrvik). Executive producer, Harald Ohrvik. Directed by Eva Dahr and Eva Isaksen. Original story and screenplay, Lars Saabye Christensen; camera (Eastman color), Rolv Haan; editor; Pal Gengenbach; production design, Anne Siri Bryhni; costumes, Kari Elfstedt; music, Geir Böhren, Bent Aserud; additional music, Pussycats, Rina Ketty. Reviewed at Norwegian Film Festival (official entry), at Haugesund, Aug. 18, 1985 in the Edda Cinema. Running time: **85 MINS.**

Herman .... Torstein Hölmebakk
Rose Stern .... Lise Fjeldstad
Unni .... Karoline Waal
Willy .... Jan Petter Berglund
Britt .... Nina Myhrvold
Herman's mother ... Anne Marit Jacobsen
Herman's father .... Björn Sothberg
Also with: Per Christensen Sr., Elisabeth Riseng, Anne Stray, Ingolf Karinen, Anitta Sukkari, Aamund Johannesen, Lasse Lindtner and The Two Angelos.

Scriptwriter Lars Saabye Christensen and cohelmers Eva Dahr and Eva Isaksen were all born in the late '50s. They nevertheless manage in their feature comedy-meller "Burning Flowers" to evoke the mid-'60s with much truth and atmosphere. With old guard Norsk Film production professionals to help them, trio has also come out with a teenage sexual initiation story that has total credibility and that is helped along by young nonprofessional as well as veteran actors made to shine with ease and natural airs about them.

Schoolboy-teenager Herman (Torstein Hölmebakk has all the necessary handsome charm and casual shyness for the role) studies his sex magazines, buys Beatles records and, on the sly, booze, and keeps his classmate date Unni at a distance because he, as a parttime delivery boy in a florist's shop, has struck up an acquaintance with a woman, who, it would seem, orders flowers sent to herself. She is a fading beauty, living alone in a perennially semi-dark apartment full of inexpensive art deco.

She does not exactly throw herself upon young Herman, and neither does he force himself upon her, but they are obviously attracted to each other, while she seems to subsist on wine, and while she tells him the sad story of her life as a flyer with a trapeze act. Her catcher-friend disappeared into the German army while she found herself pregnant. Obviously, hers is a tragic fate, but Lise Fjeldsted plays the role with discretion. Discretion also reigns in the inevitable sexual encounter between the two.

Some of the rougher aspects of private lives and feelings of everybody around Herman are observed with rather sharp wit and robust boldness, dispensing with the otherwise predominant discretion.

A film like "Burning Flowers" may, as a sales item, attract mostly tv buyers offshore. Carefully nur-sed, film could also gather a rose or two for itself on the minor fest circuit and even see some sales into limited arthouse situations. — *Kell.*

Fetish & Dreams
(SWISS-COLOR)

Locarno, Aug. 16.

An Alive Film & Video production. Produced, written and directed by Steff Gruber. Camera (video, color), Rainer Klausmann; editor, Beni Müller; video editing, Phil Haines; music, William Stephen. Reviewed at the Morettina Film Center, Locarno Film Festival, Aug. 16, 1985. Running time: **90 MINS.**
With: Steff Gruber, Michele Rusconi, Marcy Boucher, Lea Lerman, Rip Wilson, Peter Schilling.

As in a previous film, "Moon In Taurus," director Steff Gruber shot "Fetish & Dreams" in America, using the English language, except for some short incursions in the Swiss-German dialect.

The point of the exercise, this time, is to explore some of the means and ways of the 7,000,000 singles in New York, to break through the barrier of solitude. It shows Gruber, whose exotic appearance includes a mane of straight red hair coming down to his hips, as he is taking his theme to a course on "Fifty ways to meet your lover." He follows up, again with his crew beside him, on other suggestions to reach one's neighbors.

The decision to deal both with a theme and with your own approach to it results in some fascinating and also amusing observations, but also some tedious stretches. Shot entirely on ¾-inch videotape and then transferred to film, this item may be well attuned to special outlets interested in film experiments. However, neither the treatment of the theme, nor the quality of the image, which suffers mostly in the darker passages, could encourage a commercial release. —*Edna.*

Mienai
(Blind Alley)
(JAPANESE-COLOR)

Edinburgh, Aug. 19.

An Ozawa production. Produced by Tsuyoshi Ozawa. Written and directed by Go Riju. Camera (video,color), Go Abe; editor, Koji Tanaka; music, Gulliver Otsuka. Reviewed at Edinburgh Film Festival, Aug. 16, 1986. Running time: **60 MINS.**
With: Koji Sano, Asao Kobayashi, Go Riju.

Go Riju, who recently played the teenage Mishima in Paul Schrader's film, has made a distinctly off-beat and diverting featurette on the very nature of "cinema verité" documentary filming.

Shooting on video, later transferred to film with mixed results, he latches on to a young man, a truck-driver who works nights, and simply follows him around, filming him. At first the trucker is bemused and tolerant; but when Riju spends more and more time in the poor man's apartment, quizzing him constantly, and even urging him to pick a fight with a noisy neighbor, matters come to an amusing climax.

A twist at the end turns the whole film around, and calls into question everything seen before. It's a clever notion, nothing commercial, but useful for fests who want to show something of the best of young Japanese cinema. —*Strat.*

La Baston
(The Rumble)
(FRENCH-COLOR)

Paris, Aug. 21.

An AAA release of a Productions du Dau-nou/Sherwood Productions/FR3/Artistique Caumartin coproduction. Produced by Denise Petitdiddier. Directed by Jean-Claude Missiaen. Screenplay, Missiaen, Jacques Labib. Camera (Fujicolor), Jean-Claude Vicquery; art director, Dominique André; editor, Armand Psenny; sound, Michel Desrois; music, Hubert Rostaing and Ivan Jullien. Reviewed at the Marignan-Concorde theater, Paris, Aug. 19, 1985. Running time: **95 MINS.**
With: Robin Renucci, Véronique Genest, Gérard Desarthe, Michel Constantin, Patrick Depeyrat, Dominique Pinon, Natacha Finlay, Elizabeth Margoni.

"La Baston," the third film by ex-press agent Jean-Claude Missiaen, is yet another thriller that makes no concessions to originality or imagination. A trio of stereotypically cynical hoods lure some young and stereotypically basically-good-at-heart delinquents into a decoy burglary while they pull a bigger job elsewhere. When latter learn they've been had, they go after the thugs and exact revenge, though at a high price.

Protagonist, played by Robin Renucci, is that familiar antihero: the former convict who wants to go straight, but is forced by necessity back to crime. Seems he and his wife, Véronique Genest, have a young son with a rare ailment, which, of course, can only be treated in far-away America and naturally, at astronomical expense. Renucci manages to salvage some loot amid the bloodshed and pursuits but is nonetheless carted away by police. Pathos. The end.

"La Baston" is what is euphemistically called in France "an exercise in style." It's not the meaning but the method. However, Missiaen's method is pure mimicry. There's hardly a gesture, a pose, an exchange, a pursuit or a gun battle that is not cribbed from some old French or Hollywood thriller. More clever and technically expert directors have been able to make a name on their ability to recycle movie clichés. Missiaen doesn't have the pyrotechnical skills necessary for a career in cinematic ersatz.—*Len.*

Ljubavna pisma s predumis-lajem
(Love Letters With Intent)
(YUGOSLAVIAN-COLOR)

Pula, July 30.

A Marjan Film, Split and Croatia Film, Zagreb production. Direction and screenplay by Zvonimir Berkovic. Camera (color), Goran Trbuljak; art director, Zeljko Senecic; music, W.A. Mozart. Features entire cast. Reviewed at Pula Fest, July 29, 1985. Running time: 93 MINS.
With: Irina Alferova, Zlatko Vitez, Kunoslav Saric, Relja Basic, Mustafa Nadarević, Sinisa Popovic.

Veteran director Zvonimir Berkovic ("Rondo"), in his first feature in eight years, manages to pull off an elegantly told romantic tale of a music professor lecturing on Mozart who wakes up one morning in the hospital following a traffic accident and becomes fixated on the face of a woman hovering above the neighboring bed.

Triggered by conversations he overhears between the wife and husband, with whom he shares the ward, he coldly begins an experiment of sending anonymous love letters and then observing her behavior during hospital visits. (The haunting face belongs to Soviet star Irina Alferova.)

The history of his growing obsession intersperses with work on "The Magic Flute" and its theme of marital harmony as well as the rocky time he is having with his own marriage and convalescence. All this is shrewdly noticed by attending interns.

But he is carried away by both his increasing confessional fantasies and imagined trysts, and sensing a response from his neighbor's wife, the stage is set for the moment of revealing himself the author of the love letters. The onetime distant and breathtakingly blondish beauty of Alferova meantime also has become carnal.

How the wife delicately succumbs, but to neither her husband or the professor, is a sly play on the Mozart theme.

This rather intellectual love story has universal arthouse appeal.
— *Milg.*

Tagediebe
(Hanging Around)
(WEST GERMAN-B&W-16m)

Locarno, Aug. 15.

A Coproduction of Marcel Gisler Filmproduktion and Renz-Film, Berlin, in collaboration with Second German Television (ZDF), Mainz. Written and directed by Marcel Gisler. Features entire cast. Camera (b&w), Rüdiger Weiss; editor, Catharine Steghens. Reviewed at Locarno Film Fest (Competition), Aug. 15, 1985. Running time: **90 MINS.**
With: Dina Leipzig (Lola), Rudolf Nadler (Max), Lutz Deisinger (Laurids), Matthieu Hornung.

Swiss-born Marcel Gisler's debut feature "Tagediebe" (rough translation: "Hanging Around") is right out of the Berlin Underground and is yet another example of how vital this movement is.

The charm of "Hanging Around" is that it's so typically Berlin. Here we have three outsiders who mutually form a commune in an apartment of one of the occupants' friend, Karl, who happens to be away on a trip for the time being. Theoretically the three should be out looking for an apartment of their own and some kind of paying job as well, but all of them are of the same vague opinion that opportunity will come knocking on the door one day — and daily cares will simply vanish.

Lola comes from Paris. She wants to break into the music and (Underground?) film scene in Berlin. Her outlandish hairdo requires cash for the spray can alone, so on the side she gives French lessons to a shy student in Marlene Dietrich-like undress. On one occasion, her 10-year-old son visits her, the father dropping him off at the apartment (he fears the hairdo more than the meeting with Lola itself).

Max is a would-be writer. He regularly receives money from his parents for his makebelieve studies in Berlin, and he has a loose relationship with Lola. His main problem, apparently, is literary inspiration, so until that comes along, he gives in to distractions.

Laurids, Karl's friend, is the least complicated of the lot. He likes his flute and appreciates Bach, while his homosexuality is satisfied with casual affairs here and there. He earns his day-to-day living by playing his flute before Schloss Charlottenberg, or reading to needy elderly matrons.

The setting is in West Berlin (apparently Kreuzberg) in the winter of '84-'85, inclusive of cafes and sidewalks and the come-and-go ease of-life on this Vegas-isle of a city.

Major pluses are the thesp performances as they improvise lines and situations to keep the story moving along. —*Holl.*

Ironmaster
(ITALIAN-FRENCH-COLOR)

An American National Enterprises presentation of a Nuovo Dania Cinematografica/Medusa Distribuzione/Imp. Ex. Cl./Les Filmes Jacques Leitienne Production. Executive producer, Carlo Maietto. Produced by Luciano Martino. Directed by Umberto Lenzi. Features entire cast. Screenplay, Alberto Cavallone, Dardano Sacchetti, Lea Martino, Gabriel Rossini; camera (Telecolor), Giancarlo Ferrando; editor, Eugenio Alabiso; music, Guido & Maurizio de Angelis; art direction, Antonello Geleng; stunt coordinator, Nazareno Cardinali. Reviewed on Prism Entertainment vidcassette, N.Y., Aug. 20, 1985. (No MPAA Rating.) Running time: **99 MINS.**
With: Sam Pasco (Aela), Elvire Audray,

George Eastman (Vude), Pamela Field, Jacques Herlin, William Berger (Mogo), Brian Redford, Benito Stefanelli, Arena D'adderio, Giovanni Cianfriglia, Nello Pazzafino, Walter Lucchini.

———

Made in 1982, "Ironmaster" is an Italian adventure fantasy right off the assembly line that has copied recent trends in Yank and Aussie action pics. In this case, it's mainly "Quest For Fire" time, though the primitive men here are far more advanced.

George Eastman is in the title role, portraying a power-hungry Iron Age man who discovers the art of iron smelting and uses it to make swords. He has been passed over by his tribe elders who want a woman to succeed them, but Eastman as Vude plans to conquer his and other neighboring tribes.

In opposition is young muscleman Aela (Sam Pasco), who not only steals Vude's swords but invents a bow & arrow to easily subdue the baddies. Corny finish has him destroying all these weapons of war after they've done the job.

Picture is strictly routine, with no nudity, discreet (mainly) violence and little period atmosphere. Lensing is competent, including unusual (for this genre) locations shot in South Dakota with a small buffalo herd grazing nearby.—*Lor.*

Stranger Than Fiction
(BRITISH-COLOR/B&W)

Edinburgh, Aug. 19.
A British Film Institute production. Produced by Jill Pack. Executive producer, Peter Sainsbury. Directed by Ian Potts. Screenplay, Potts, Angus Calder; editors, Don Fairservice, Amanda Smith; music, Benedict Mason; camera (color), Patrick Duval; sound, Simon Hayter. Reviewed at Edinburgh Film Festival, Aug. 17, 1985. Running time: **91 MINS.**
With: Will Knightley (Tom Harrison), Muriel Lawford, Howard Crossley, Sheila Vaudrey, Anthony Benson, Tom Brierley.

———

There's probably an interesting film to be made about Mass-Observation, a pioneering public opinion poll organization, but this isn't it.

Mass-Observation was founded in 1936 by a group of intellectuals who felt it important to discover how the British public *really* felt about such issues of the day as the abdication of the King. They set themselves up in Bolton, Lancashire, and started polling people, and their work continued on into the war years.

Director Ian Potts and his crew haven't been able to come up with a very interesting approach to the subject. It starts out fascinatingly enough with the initial establishment of Mass-Observation as told by members who are still with us. Brief interspersed re-enacted scenes, with Will Knightley as the group's leading light, add little but running time.

Ironically, today Mass-Observa-

tion is still working as a public opinion research company, with a turnover of £1,500,000; very different from its original concept, but the film makes nothing of this.

In all, an uninvolving, disappointingly bland effort, and saddled with a singularly inappropriate music score into the bargain.—*Strat.*

Sest dana juna
(Six Days In June)
(YUGOSLAVIAN-COLOR)

Pula, July 30.
A TRZ SFR Art Film 80 production, Belgrade. Directed by Dinko Tucakovic. Features entire cast. Screenplay, Nebojsa Pajkic; camera (color) Goran Trbuljak; art director, Marina Milin; music, Vladimir Divljan. Reviewed at Pula Film Festival, July 30, 1985. Running time: **88 MINS.**
With: Nebojsa Krstic, Cintija Asperger, Mladen Nelevic, Sinisa Copic, Peda Belac, Mladen Andrejevic.

———

This picture of Yugoslav smalltown life in the '60s played against the backdrop of the June 1968 student riots in Belgrade (echoing dimly over the lives of five young buddies laying about town during the balmy summer) recalls the youthful "vitelloni" of Fellini's classic film of smalltown life as well as "American Graffiti." It has enough Balkan variations, however, to make this debut effort by 24-year-old Belgrade Film Academy grad Dinko Tucakovic (student of director Goran Markovic) a very different and engaging work.

Story centers on a young metal worker, Rajko lounging around with friends while waiting to go back to the Army, listening to Beatles records, bike-riding through town, chasing girls and hardly perceiving what might be happening in the big city as his returning grad student friend brings home news of unrest and change. They all flirt with Vesna, also home for the summer from university, whom Rajko approaches, finally summoning up the courage. But their "social distance" is too great. In his crude perception of a relationship, she rejects him as a "peasant." On the eve of his departure, and an attempted rape, he boards the train in flight, with police in pursuit. What began as a somewhat jaunty summer idyll, unexpectedly turns into tragedy as Rajko's life heads for a crash.

Shot by one of Yugoslavia's best cinematographers (Goran Trbuljak) in 16m and successfully blown up to 35m film has the casual humor and neo-realistic look of Czech '60s films and an interesting Yugo political and social theme ('68 student events were taboo subject until only recently) to make it a candidate for fest outings, university and arthouse circuits. — *Milg.*

Zivot je lep
(Life Is Beautiful)
(YUGOSLAVIAN-COLOR)

Pula, July 30.
A Neoplant Film. Novi Sad, and Slavija, Union production, Belgrade. Direction and screenplay by Bora Draskovic. Features entire cast. Camera (color). Bozidar Nikolic; art director, Milenko Jeremic; music, Vojislav Voki Kostic. Reviewed at Pula Fest, July 30, 1985. Running time: **100 MINS.**
With Rade Serbedzija, Sonja Savic, Dragan Nikolic, Ljubisa Samardzic, Pavle Vujisic, Predrag Lakovic, Milan Erak, Snezana Savic.

———

In an isolated country tavern somewhere in the northern Yugoslavian plain (Vojvodina province), a trainful of unruly passengers show up early one morning for food and lodging because the overworked engineer stalls and refuses to go further. Thus begins 24 hours in this separate little Noah's Ark housing a range of boisterous national types, from seasonal workers in the hop fields, to local manipulators and party hacks to musicians and transients who wait either for a new engineer or the local party committee to decide on how to get the train going.

As a leitmotif, everybody in the tavern is forced by a strong-arm functionary to sing the song "Life Is Beautiful," struck up by a ragtag bunch of musicians.

Amid this richly metaphoric and fast-moving kaleidescope of a place, a truckful of chickens arrives to provide sustenance after the local peacock is dispatched to the kitchen.

The nasty energy and high spirits, aided by the fluid camerawork and the shifting spotlighting of characters, tone down when the local committee arrives along with the police.

Most sympathetic character is a wired-up accordion player, who chivalrously tries to protect the band's chanteuse from maulers. He finally can't take the whole scene, and opens up on the crowd with his pistol before drawing a bullet himself and walking off into the new dawn with his accordion.

Multi-talented Bora Draskovic, who did postgrad film work at Lodz, Poland, in the '60s, before '70s work in documentaries and three books on film directing, adapted "Life Is Beautiful" from the short stories of contemporary author Aleksander Tisma.

Film is a candid illustration of current freedom by Yugo directors to tackle probing political and social themes and has been invited to the Venice film fest.—*Milg.*

Kaiser Und Eine Nacht
(Kaiser And One Night)
(SWISS-COLOR)

Locarno, Aug. 13.
An Aspekt Telefilm Production, Hamburg, BOA Filmproduktion Zürich coproduction

with MOMENT AG, ZOF and SRG. Produced by Markus Trebitsch. Directed by Markus Fischer. Stars Emil Steinberger. Written by Alex Gfeller and Markus Fischer; camera (color), Jörg Schmidt-Reitwein; editor, Gerhard Ertlmaier; art director, Hans Gloor; sound, Hanspeter Fischer; music, Markus Fischer. Reviewed at the Locarno Film Festival, Aug. 13, 1985. Running time: **95 MINS.**

Robert Kaiser . . . . Emil Steinberger
Sandra . . . . Brigitte Karner
Eddie . . . . Rolf Hoppe
Chérie . . . . Rosemarie Fendel
Rosa . . . . Vera Schweiger

A businessman gets off a train in Lugano to make a phone call, the train leaves before he is through, and he finds himself stranded in the middle of his trip, soon to embark on a strange adventure when a strange girl offers to take him to the next station on her scooter.

This is the starting point of what should be a situation comedy but turns out to be a heavy-handed attempt at humor and satire, out of breath long before it is on its way.

The point should be that the businessman, named Kaiser, a typical specimen of the humorless, square bourgeois, is dragged to a delapidated hotel, the perfect symbol of every un-Swiss quality in its disorder, both physical and mental. It is inhabited only by the girl's parents, a couple of has-beens, a boxer and nightclub singer, and a maid with a tendency to get passionate at times, but whose reason to stick with the rest of the unseemly, and obviously quite deranged family, is not quite clear.

This is as far as the script goes into creating a backbone for all the episodes stringed together here in a haphazard way.

Acting, on the whole, is rather better than parts warrant, with Emil Steinberger, major star locally after his tremendous success in ''The Swissmaker,'' embracing again the image of the perfect Swiss, and Rolf Hoppe, the East German actor who played the Nazi general in ''Mephisto,'' trying for measure the part of the dazed ex-prizefighter who is still going the rounds against the same one adversary who had felled him in the ring. —*Edna*.

Bimini Code
(COLOR)

Low-interest adventure opus.

An American National Enterprises presentation. Executive producer, Rip Coalson. Produced by George Gale. Directed by Barry Clark. Features entire cast. Screenplay, Gabrielle Rivera; camera (Getty color), Ralph White; editors, Beth Conwell, Lawrence Ross; music, Marc Ellis; second unit director, White; production manager, Jennifer Carter; stunt coordinator, Jeff Habberstad; associate producer, Richard W. Long; additional photography, Long, Milas Hinshaw, Brian Burton. Reviewed on Prism Entertainment vidcassette, N.Y., Aug. 21, 1985. (No MPAA Rating.) Running time: **95 MINS.**

With: Vickie Benson, Kristal Richardson, Rosanna Simanaitis, Frank Alexander, Dolores Penn, Wayne Thomsen, Darrin Horowitz, Richard Sonoda, Anthony P. Brooklier, Tom Crosser.

''Bimini Code'' is an amateurish adventure film shot two years ago on the West Coast and in the Caribbean, now making its debut in videocassette form.

Episodic storyline has two pretty girls, blond Stacy and brunette Sheryl, running a skin diving shop in Catalina. When a local boy is kidnapped while playing near the ocean, the good samaritan gals decide to investigate and rescue him.

They discover that the boy found some containers that were part of a drug shipment. The evil Countess Magda von Cress (a hissable blond with an eyepatch) is using the drug trafficking to finance her quest to find the lost Mayan Power Stone, which supposedly contains the secret of nuclear fusion and offers the holder unlimited power.

After numerous escapes and recaptures, the girls free the kid and then trek all the way to Aruba, Bimini and other Caribbean sites in a race for the stone. Ultimately they find it in a jar, but when exposed to water the stone dissolves, leaving them empty-handed.

Vickie Benson and Kristal Richardson are good-looking leading ladies, but director Barry Clark and scripter Gabrielle Rivera unfold their adventures in flat, uninteresting fashion, emphasizing boring underwater footage and corny dialog. —*Lor*.

Police
(FRENCH-COLOR)

Paris, Sept. 2.

A Gaumont release of a Gaumont/TF1 Films coproduction. Produced by Emmanuel Schlumberger. Directed by Maurice Pialat. Stars Gérard Depardieu, Sophie Marceau. Screenplay, Catherine Breillat, Sylvie Danton, Jacques Fieschi, Maurice Pialat, from an original story by Breillat; camera (Eastmancolor), Luciano Tovoli; art director, Constantin Méjinsky; sound, Bernard Aubouy; editor, Yann Dedet; makeup, Thi Loan N'Guyen; costumes, Malika Brahim; music, Henryk Mikolaj Gorecki; production manager, Jean-Claude Bourlat. Reviewed at the Gaumont Champs-Elysées, Paris, Sept. 2, 1985. Running time: **113 MINS.**

Mangin . . . . Gérard Depardieu
Noria . . . . Sophie Marceau
Lambert . . . . Richard Anconina
Marie Vedret . . . . Pascale Rocard
Lydie . . . . Sandrine Bonnaire
René . . . . Franck Karoui
Simon . . . . Jonathan Leina

In ''Police,'' director Maurice Pialat subverts the mainstream thriller genre for a personal film that deliberately works against conventional expectations. Gaumont must have had supreme confidence in its helmer (who enjoyed both critical and commercial success with his previous film, ''A Nos Amours,'' also produced by the French major) and its topbilled players, Gérard Depardieu, Sophie Marceau and Richard Anconina, to have sunk a reported 25,000,000 francs (nearly $3,000,000) into ''Police,'' which will need strong local playoffs and important foreign sales to recoup its investment.

As with previous Pialat pics, ''Police'' underwent long, tortuous and frequently stormy gestation and production phases. Film was first announced as an adaptation of a Yank detective novel, ''Bodies Are Dust'' by P. J. Wolfson. Pialat suddenly dropped the idea and asked writer-scripter Catherine Breillat for an original screenplay, but then discarded most of what she came up with (which nearly occasioned a law suit by Breillat against Pialat and Gaumont). Shooting finally began with only the embryo of a script available for cast and technicians. Backed by a small battery of writers, the filmmaker improvised story development as production rolled.

Not surprising then that the film hasn't much of a plot, and what plot there is is treated offhandedly by Pialat, who is more interested in character and ambience than gunplay and sharp plot turns. Formally, the film is daring, though finally unsuccessful, in the way it introduces a number of characters and interlocking situations, and then ruthlessly strips everything down to a deliberately anti-climactic study of an ill-fated romance between a cop and a drug dealer's girlfriend.

Gérard Depardieu gives a superb, buttressing performance as the flic, transcending the usual tender-tough clichés in his composition of an apparently committed law-enforcer, whose boisterous, macho manner hides an abyss of mediocrity and desperate loneliness. When off duty, he often knocks around with a shady young lawyer (Richard Anconina, in a perfect depiction of vulnerability and sleazy ethics) and doesn't shun the company of hookers (one of them played by Sandrine Bonnaire, who was launched into the spotlight in ''A Nos Amours'').

It is also through Anconina that Depardieu gets closer to a young girl (Sophie Marceau), who has been arrested along with her Arab boyfriend during a drug raid. She stands up to Depardieu's grilling, and is soon let off thanks to Anconina. Depardieu begins to see her socially, and soon falls in love with her. When he learns she has in fact stolen the booty of a drug deal, he saves her from imminent underworld vengeance by recovering the goods and delivering them to the hoods he had been hunting previously. Yet Marceau abandons him.

The first half of ''Police'' is vivid and vigorous, as the director situates his protagonist in his professional milieu. There's an anecdotal richness, a sly sense of observation, and considerable humor, in Pialat's personal revision of the police procedural. Also, his penchant for improvisation here enriches more than it diminishes.

When the perspectives narrow, however, and the Depardieu-Marceau relationship comes to the fore (and story and secondary characters all but disappear) the film begins to unravel badly. The piecemeal approach to the script proves inadequate for these intimate stretches, which often slide into banality and tedium. It is difficult to whip up much concern for Depardieu's unexpected (and not all that convincing) passion for Marceau. She is perfectly credible as the sullen, chronically mendacious misfit who drifts into and out of the cop's life as she has done with every man before him, yet she is eclipsed by Depardieu's massive, vital screen presence.

On the technical level, ''Police'' is one of Pialat's most assured and polished performances, with Italian lenser Luciano Tovoli imparting a haunting aquarium-like feel to the blue-dominated police station settings.

Film, which unspooled at the Venice festival and opens commercially in France this week, was the last production initiated at Gaumont by its former general manager, Daniel Toscan du Plantier.

—*Len*.

American Ninja
(COLOR)

Minor No.4 entry in the series.

A Cannon Releasing release of a Golan-Globus production from Cannon Films. Produced by Menahem Golan and Yoram Globus. Directed by Sam Firstenberg. Features entire cast. Screenplay, Paul de Mielche, from story by Avi Kleinberger, Gideon Amir; camera (TVC color), Hanania Baer; supervising editor, Michael J. Duthie; music, Michael Linn; sound, Jacob Goldstein, Donald Santos; assistant director, Ron Tal; production manager, Michael Kansky; production design, Adrian Gorton; stunt coordinator, Steve Lambert, Renato Morado; martial arts choreography, Mike Stone; special and visual effects, Danilo Dominguez; postproduction supervisor, Michael R. Sloan; costumes, Audrey Bansmer; casting, Robert MacDonald, Perry Bullington, Maria Metcalfe; associate producers, Kleinberger, Amir, Ken Metcalfe. Reviewed at UA Twin 1 theater, N.Y., Sept. 3, 1985. (MPAA Rating: R.) Running time: **95 MINS.**

Joe	Michael Dudikoff
Jackson	Steve James
Patricia Hickock	Judie Aronson
Col. Hickock	Guich Koock
Shinyuki	John Fujioka
Ortega	Don Stewart
Rinaldo	John LaMotta
Black Star Ninja	Tadashi Yamashita
Charlie	Phil Brock

"American Ninja" is a bland fourth entry in Cannon's successful martial arts series. Minus Sho Kosugi this time and (despite the title) set in the Philippines rather than the U.S., pic is okay as a B-picture, but unlikely to hold its own as a solo title.

Michael Dudikoff is the titular hero, a sullen G.I. named Joe who arrives at U.S. Army base Fort Sonora with a chip on his shoulder. He quickly alienates everyone except the pretty daughter of the commanding officer, Patricia Hickock (Judie Aronson) by singlehandedly saving her from the deadly ninjas working for corrupt arms dealer Ortega (Don Stewart).

This storyline has Joe ultimately defeating Ortega, with the aid of Shinyuki (John Fujioka), Ortega's Japanese gardener who predictably turns out to be Joe's original martial arts tutor before Joe got amnesia six years ago. One plot thread, in which Hickock's dad (Guich Koock) is in league with Ortega, is clumsily handled.

Director Sam Firstenberg (who did Cannon's last two ninja pics) stages the numerous action scenes well, but engenders little interest in the nonstory. Dudikoff, in a lead role originally announced for Chuck Norris before Cannon and Norris decided to change his martial arts image, comes off awkwardly as a new James Dean clone who's been pumping iron. Most winning performance is turned in by Steve James, Joe's sole pal on the base who turns into a gung-ho, black Rambo in the final reel. —*Lor.*

No Man's Land
(FRENCH-SWISS-COLOR)

Paris, Aug. 27.

An MK2 release of an MK2, Paris/Filmograph, Geneva coproduction, in association with Westdeutscher Rundfunk/Channel 4, London/Film on Four Intl./SSR/Films A2. Produced by Marin Karmitz and Alain Tanner. Written and directed by Alain Tanner. Camera (color), Bernard Zitzerman; editor, Laurent Uhler; music, Terry Riley, performed by Riley and Krishna Bhatt; art director, Alain Nicolet; sound, Jean-Paul Mugel; production manager, Gérard Ruey. Reviewed at Studio 407, Paris, Aug. 21, 1985. Running time: **108 MINS.**

Paul	Hugues Quester
Madeleine	Myriam Mézières
Jean	Jean-Philippe Ecoffey
Mali	Berry Berr
Lucie	Marie-Luce Felber
Hitchhiker	Maria Cabral
The banker	Jean-Pierre Malo
Informer	Teco Celio
French policemen	André Steiger, Jacques Michel

After several films of itinerant filmmaking abroad, Swiss director Alain Tanner has come home, or just about. The title of his new film is both geographical and figurative, referring to the Franco-Swiss frontier, across which the story moves unceasingly, and the gray psychological and social zone through which the four young protagonists grope, as they engage in smuggling

Paul (Hugues Quester) is French and works in his father's garage, but runs people and things illicitly across the border to make the money he hopes will allow him to go to Canada with an aviation license he is soon to get. His girlfriend Madeleine (Myriam Mézières) runs a local discotheque and dreams of a pop music career in Paris. Despite their conflicting dreams, they enjoy a strong sexual compatibility.

Mali, a young Algerian (Berry Berr), lives on the French side as well, but works in a factory across the border. She too is part of the smuggling activities, hiding pouches of dope in her underwear during the daily frontier crossings.

Only Jean (Jean-Philippe Ecoffey), a young Swiss who works on his uncle's farm, is not afflicted with the frustration and wanderlust of the others. His accidental involvement in the illicit activity and especially his meeting with Mali, with whom he falls in love, pulls him into the tragic web of events.

Despite the knowledge of a tightening police web, Quester agrees to a final smuggling venture — taking into Switzerland bars of gold for a French banker. Border police are waiting for him and Ecoffey. Quester is shot and dies in the hospital, while Ecoffey gets away with a leg wound, and escapes the subsequent police investigation, thanks to Berr, who refuses to reveal his identity.

Tanner's seductively furtive camera manner, his sense of nature and

his talent for implicating his characters in their respective environments have not diminished. However, the script, in good part improvised with the collaboration of the actors, presents us with characters who neither grow nor deepen as the predictable action develops and who finally inspire more irritation than pathos or empathy. Only Ecoffey and Berr suggest some depth, and it's regrettable that Tanner didn't favor their guarded rapport in story development. The dialog smacks of straight-from-the-heart platitudes.

Technically, film is first-rate, with subdued lensing by Bernard Zitzerman and a marvelous musical score by Terry Riley. — *Len.*

Mamma Ebe
(ITALIAN-COLOR)

Venice, Aug. 29.

Produced by Giovanni Di Clemente for Clemi Cinematografica. Directed by Carlo Lizzani. Stars Stefania Sandrelli, Barbara De Rossi, Ida Di Benedetto, Berta Dominguez. Screenplay, Iaia Fiastri, Gino Capone, Lizzani; camera (color), Romano Albani; editor, Franco Fraticelli; art director, Massimo Razzi; music, Franco Piersanti. Reviewed at the Venice Film Festival (competition), Aug. 28, 1985. Running time: **98 MINS.**

Mamma Ebe	Berta Dominguez
Sandra Agostini	Stefania Sandrelli
Laura Bonetti	Barbara De Rossi
Mario Bonetti	Alessandro Haber
Maria Pia Sturla	Ida De Benedetto
Lidia Corradi	Laura Betti

Choosing to forego the more sensationalistic side of a story that has been stealing the Italo headlines — a fake religious order put on trial for making millions out of the weak and gullible — "Mamma Ebe" is a serious-minded, balanced and fairly engrossing version of the facts, mostly taken from public record. This feature-length docu-drama was in production before the outcome of the trial against charismatic Ebe Giorgini, called a miracle-worker by some and a skilled extortionist by others, was known. Luckily for filmer Carlo Lizzani and associates, pic's point of view against Mamma Ebe was upheld by the court, which sentenced her to a light prison term later reduced to house arrest. Pic should benefit at the b.o. from its timeliness and interest generated in the case nation-wide, though parallel phenomena in other countries are not hard to find.

Lizzani has often been attracted to the possibility of filming real-life events, and he stolidly sets about getting his reportage down without fireworks or undue speculation. Scripters Iaia Fiastri and Gino Capone tell the story through the eyes of the father of one of the young "noviates," Laura (Barbara De Rossi), a frail girl who falls under Ebe's spell. Père Bonetti, warmly played by Alessandro Haber with a well-applied sense of humor, is a

concert violinist who realizes only when it's too late that an absent father is worse than one who occasionally makes mistakes. Laura's obsessive attachments to Mamma Ebe is explained in terms of her absent parents' need for affection, and search for a mother figure. To underline the point, Laura Betti cameos as the dippy parent of another boy whose possessiveness masks her lack of feeling for him.

There is ample material for an exciting film in the factual story, but at times pic seems too restrained to make full use of it. Lizzani steadfastly avoids the ever-present temptation to excess suggested by the anguish of the relatives, fanatical devotion of Ebe's followers, and horrors perpetrated within the sect. The convent girls are worked 18 hours a day and sadistically punished for imaginary crimes, but much more is suggested than actually shown. A psychologically frail ex-prostitute who has lost her son, Sandra (Stefania Sandrelli), is seen kneeling on a bed of nuts and licking up broken glass; and Ebe's rebellious vicar Maria Pia (Ida Di Benedetto) appears bruised, beaten and brainwashed after trying to write to the bishop.

When it comes to treating the self-appointed holy-woman herself, pic is cautious and careful to bring out conflicting testimony (as attested by the fact the real Mamma Ebe approved the script before shooting). While on the one hand she really does seem to perform miracles, film casts serious doubt on her claim to be chaste and virginal after two husbands and a rumored lover among the seminarians who accompanied her on champagne cruises aboard her yacht. In a chic wardrobe and long raven tresses, Berta Dominguez's Mamma Ebe is an intriguing figure that the picture only begins to explore. — *Yung.*

Sans Toit Ni Loi
(Vagabond)
(FRENCH-COLOR)

Venice, Aug. 30.

A Cine-Tamaris and Films A 2 coproduction, Paris, in collaboration with the French Ministry of Culture and Channel Four, London. Written and directed by Agnès Varda. Features Sandrine Bonnaire. Camera (color), Patrick Blossier; sound, Jean-Paul Mugel; editor, Varda, Patricia Mazuy; music, Joanna Druzdowicz. Reviewed at Venice Film Fest (competition), Aug. 29, 1985. Running time: **105 MINS.**

With: Sandrine Bonnaire (Mona, the vagabond), Macha Meril (Madame Landier, the plantologist), Stephane Freiss (Jean-Pierre, the agronomist), Laurence Cortadellas (Eliane, his wife), Marthe Jarnias (Aunt Lydie, the old woman), Yolande Moreau (Yolande, the maid), Joel Fosse (Paulo, the conman), Patrick Lepczynski (David, the Jew), Yahiaoui Assouna (Assoun, the vineyard worker).

The first highlight in the competition at Venice and an inside favorite to win one of fest's top prizes, Agnès Varda's "Vagabond" (title translates: "Without A Roof And Beyond The Law") should easily do well on the arthouse circuit with proper handling and a boost from other key fests on the circuit. It numbers among Varda's best films.

"Vagabond" begins with a worker in the southern vineyards discovering the body of a young girl frozen to death in a ditch. When the police arrive, they inspect the corpse under suspicion of possible foul play. Then the entire story is told in a kind of seamless flashback, the case-history bridges offered when a succession of characters "testify" before the camera on what they know about the girl. It is gradually revealed that the girl has no one to blame but herself for dying as she did.

Mona is one of those all-too-common contemporary teenagers who aimlessly drifts. She carries her tent on her back, swims (in the opening shot) in the Mediterranean in the warmer weather to bathe herself from time to time, sleeps during the particularly cold spells in railroad stations or abandoned villas, and makes acquaintances or has relations with whomever she wishes as she goes along. She never stays in any one place very long, yet an impression of her visit is always left behind due to her rather amoral attitude to sex, stealing-to-eat, and her practice of sleeping where she pleases.

In fact, it's the people she meets that provide the moral and narrative context to the story. She is equally at home with Arab workers (a Moroccan, a Tunisian), garage attendants (when broke, she sleeps with one or other of them arbitrarily), and middle-class inhabitants of the district (a woman who pursues the medicinal value of plants and herbs, a rich old woman in a villa).

Mona covets her freedom most of all. So, too, do a couple raising goats and making cheese to sell for a living. The girl lives with them for a while, then one day steals a few bars of cheese for her knapsack to be on her way — which she then exchanges for a few francs with a prostitute on a highway soliciting customers among passing cars. From time to time, she teams with other vagabonds of her own age, sleeping together in villas they've broken into.

Varda's style is reminiscent of Robert Bresson's in exposing the evil in the world without judging the motives of the protagonist herself. There's also a scene toward the end that hints of the impending doom, as though Mona is a victim of fate or a moral code more alien and cold-hearted than her own. Now ill

from a lung infection and without tent or blankets (burned in her last abode, an unheated shack for the Arab workers and riff-raff), she ventures into a village — only to be surprised and mishandled by youths in a season vineyard ritual, an annual Halloween-style celebration during which passers-by are rather maliciously sprayed with the purple of the grape.

Sick, drenched and humiliated, she flees into the countryside, falls into a ditch — and freezes to death.

Credits are all top-grade. Outstanding are the performance by Bonnaire, the sparse musical soundtrack, and Varda's risky refusal to dramatize the story any more than necessary. — *Holl.*

Svindlande affärer
(Business Is Booming)
(SWEDISH-COLOR)

Stockholm, Aug. 29.

A Svensk Filmindustri (SF) release of a Christer Abrahamsen for Cinema Art/SF/Attlaxeras/Filmteknik/TV-Cuba/Smart Egg Pictures (London) production. Directed by Peter Schildt, Janne Carlsson. Screenplay, Theodore Folke, Janne Carlsson, Gösta Wälivaara; camera (Eastmancolor), Dan Myhrman, Bertil Rosengren, Noclas Jensen; production design, Eric Lison Johnson; editor, Sylvia Ingemarsson; music, Bengt Palmers; title song performed by Pernilla Wahlgren. Reviewed at the Spegeln cinema, Stockholm, Aug. 29, 1985. Running time: **103 MINS.**

Rolle	Janne Carlsson
Gösta	Gösta Wälivaara
Rita	Sanne Salomonsen
Bertil	Thomas Hellberg
Pekka	Johan Holm
Otto	Lars Amble
Arvidsson	Ingvar Kjellson
Alessandra	Marika Lindström
The Rev. Moloch	Michael Segerström
La Lagarte	Alba Marina
Chiquita	Elisabeth Morales
Cuba Police Chief	Reinaldo Miravalles

"Business Is Booming" — or seems to be — when a crooked used-car dealer sells a wreck to a naive hairdresser whose vampish hairdresser wife invents a punk perfume that sells exactly because it stinks. Most of the business booms when the naive man's petty criminal of a brother is released from jail and decides to take the used-car dealer for a ride in the financial balloon.

So it goes from boom to bust and back again, endlessly and, occasionally pretty aimlessly, in this Swedish feature farce that winds up in Cuba.

This would clearly be the stuff of classical crook-cheats-crook farce, and sometimes it works that way, especially since the two main actors, Janne Carlsson (a walrus of friendly-cunning mien) and Gösta Wälivaara (moist-eyed and bearded to the navel), team up with expert comedy timing. One is brash, the other timid, and both of them know how to pull their punches sufficiently to cause the delayed laughter. For

a good part of film, these two characters look like true human beings, worth rooting for, amidst the production noise surrounding them.

Then things fail to jell. Director Peter Schildt is obviously not working harmoniously with co-director and actor Janne Carlsson. Latter, a beloved comedian on home turf, has even pitched in as a scriptwriter. The natural flow of narrative is clogged, the inner logic of all good comedy gets lost and too much wreckage farce is introduced merely to keep things going, not springing from sources of true dramatic continuity.

In female semi-leads, Denmark's mock-vamp Sanne Salomonsen and Cuba's sweetly bubbling Elisabeth Morales perform with youthful sensuality, charm and gusto. Considering the two male leads' huge popularity with Swedish audiences, "Business" may boom on its home turf, and since Cuban TV is involved with a minor production share, Cubans will probably also be let in on the rather strenuous fun. With a Spanish-dubbed version and smart sales handling, film might even reach the Latin American homevideo trade. — *Kell.*

Los Naufragos Del Liguria
(The Shipwreck Of Liguria)
(MEXICAN-COLOR)

Mexico City, Aug. 17.

A Peliculas Mexicanas release of a Cooperative Rio Mixcoac-Conacine (Imcine) production. Executive producer, Jorge Santoyo; associate producer, Héctor López. Directed by Gabriel Retes. Features entire cast. Screenplay, Pilar Campesino, Sergio Molina, Antonio Orellana, Retes, based on book of same name by Emilio Salgari; camera (color), Guadalupe García; music, Juan José Calatayud; editor, Carlos Savage; sets, Zeth Santacruz. Reviewed at Cine Insurgentes 70, Mexico City, Aug. 17, 1985. Running time: **98 MINS.**

Constanza	Tina Romero
Emilio Albani	Ignacio Retes
Teresa	María José Garrido
Héctor	Juan Claudio Retes
Sofia	Frida Maceira
Piccolo Seri	Ernesto Rivas
Harry Thompson	Gonzalo Lora
Marino Albizetti	Abel Woolrich
Capt. Talcone	Jaime Casillas
Scott	Enrique Ontiveros
Midshipman	Raul Ruiz
Passenger	Leonor Llausas
Groom	Rigoberto Carmona
Bride	Laura Ximena

Also with: Cecilia Romo, Sergio Morante, Jorge Beckris, Raúl Sierra, Héctor Avilia and Santiago Adan.

This adventure film is sort of a Mexican "Swiss Family Robinson," set in the 19th century and based on the children's adventure classic "The Shipwreck of the Liguria," by Italian writer Emilio Salgari.

Story begins when a bag-guy sailor (Gonzalo Lora) attempts to steal a cache of gold and jewels aboard the Italian passenger vessel Liguria and is caught in the act by

the captain (Jaime Casillas). His struggle and frenzied escape inadvertently set off a blaze causing the ship to explode.

Seven survivors (three adults and four children) make their way to a deserted tropical island and live as castaways as best they can.

There are long, loving scenes of their search for fresh water, the construction of a not-so-rustic dwelling and attempt to escape by using a crude raft that later falls apart.

These scenes are intercut with shots of the villain and his captive sailor companion, who have also landed on another part of the island. Besides bullying his captive, he buries and reburies the stolen loot. Eventually he discovers the children and they have a confrontation with the result that he falls from a cliff.

Pic ends with our group celebrating its first anniversary on the island and the whereabouts of the treasure remain unknown. Spliced onto the end of the film is a trailer for part II, "Naufragos II: Los Piratas" (The Pirates). Sequel was shot at the same time as part I and from the looks of it, our gang is not destined for an easy life.

The film holds up as family entertainment and is exciting despite occasional technical flaws and obvious low-budget problems. The score, by Juan José Calatayud, adds to the tone as does the apt camera work by Guadalupe García. — *Lent.*

Amor Estranho Amor
(Love Strange Love)
(BRAZILIAN-COLOR)

Santiago, Aug. 23.

A Sharp Features release (U.S.) of a Cinearte production. Produced by Anibal Massaini Neto. Directed by Walter Hugo Khouri. Screenplay, Khouri; camera (color), Antonio Meliande; editor, Eder Mazini; musical coordination, Rogerio Duprat. Reviewed at Cine Lido, Santiago, Chile, Aug. 21, 1985. Running time: **96 MINS.**

With: Vera Fischer, Tarcisio Meira, Xuxa Meneghel, Mauro Mendonça, Iris Bruzzi, Otavio Augusto, Walter Forster, Marcelo Ribeiro, Matilde Mastrangi.

Basically fluffy, but with the trappings of artsiness and significance, "Love Strange Love" displays actors who strike meaningful poses and glare at each other or the infinite, as if expressing deep emotion or innuendo. In the right context this could be called style; in this case it is only window-dressing.

The film begins with an elderly man exploring a now abandoned but still splendid mansion. The action then slides back to 1937: what could once have been the stately home of a coffee baron had become Sao Paulo's most luxurious brothel, leased by Osmar Passos, a local politician, to Doña Laura, the Madam. The aloofly beautiful Ana — as his present favorite — is the establishment's leading lady.

Preparations are afoot for a grand party Osmar is throwing to welcome a leading politician from another state, with whom he is negotiating a bid for power on a national scale. At this rather inopportune moment Ana's son, an approximately 12-year-old boy, is delivered there by his grandmother. He is packed off to an attic where he will be out of the way, but curiosity gets the better of him; he catches glimpses of the establishment's local color and proceedings. Unwittingly, he also becomes a participant in same.

This boy obviously becomes the elderly man exploring the mansion and remembering his experience there, in a series of flashbacks. The ambience, suggestive of sex and political intrigue, has the disadvantage that non-Brazilians are liable to be left out in the cold, lacking knowledge of the historical context of events. For example, they won't know that the coup that puts an end to the frolics was Getulio Vargas' dissolution of Congress. This does not imply that familiarity with the background would make the film politically significant. — *Amig.*

Luces de Bohemia
(Bohemian Lights)
(SPANISH-COLOR)

Madrid, Aug. 23.

A Laberinto production, in collaboration with TVE S.A. Directed by Miguel Angel Diez. Screenplay, Mario Camus, based on play by Ramón del Valle-Inclán; camera (Eastmancolor), Miguel Angel Trujillo; sets, Félix Murcia; editor, José Salcedo Palomeque; sound, Carlos Faruolo; production manager, José Jacoste. Reviewed at Cine Palafox, Madrid, Aug. 22, 1985. Running time: 95 MINS.
Max Estrella . . . . Francisco Rabal
Don Latino . . . . Agustín González
Minister . . . . Fernando Fernán Gómez
Catalan Prisoner . . . . Imanol Arias
M. Collet . . . . Berta Riaza
La Lunares . . . . Paula Molina
Zaratustra . . . . José Vivó
Also with: Azucena de la Fuente, Viki Lagos, Manuel Galiana, Mario Pardo, Manolo Zarzo, Jaoquín Hinojosa, Manuel Sánchez, Saturno Cerra, Alfredo Mayo, Angel de Andrés López.

The filmic adaptation of Ramon Valle-Inclán's most famous play, "Luces de Bohemia," brimming with iconoclastic comment and set in the impecunious literary circles of turn-of-the-century Madrid, is a daunting task, since local audiences will inevitably compare it to the original. Neophyte helmer Miguel Angel Diez seems to have stepped into every pitfall, despite a script written by Mario ("La Colmena") Camus, whose most recent credit was the excellent "The Holy Innocents."

Diez had a topnotch cast to draw upon plus a handsome budget forwarded by the Culture Ministry and

Spanish Television, but the result is a murky, confusing and ultimately boring film that never makes its point and which fails to do justice to the poetry and wit of the original play. Even Spaniards will have a hard time disentangling the story of the last day on earth of the bohemian poet Max Estrella and his cohort Don Latino, as they wander about the low-life scenes of Madrid, mostly in a drunken stupor.

Estrella (meaning "star"), a blind poet who seems to have few compunctions about letting his wife and daughter starve in their miserable tenement, proclaims himself "the greatest poet of his day." He indefatigably declaims and pontificates in the gutters, sympathizes with a violent anarchist whom he meets in a prison cell, barges into the office of a government minister who was his childhood friend only to revile him for his success, and sputters forth abstractions about the Spanish character. Much of the dialog used is from the early part of the century, which today sounds rather strained.

Despite the coin spent, sets are rather modest and direction is uninspired. Paco Rabal as Estrella is fine, but the heavily made-up Agustín González is barely recognizable. Few spectacles are as quickly tiresome as that of an actor doing the "drunk" bit for the full length of a film. Item is bound to be soon shelved and its budget written off as a loss to the Spanish taxpayer.

— *Besa.*

Creator
(U.S.-COLOR)

Montreal, Sept. 2.

A Universal Pictures release of a Kings Road production. Produced by Stephen Friedman. Directed by Ivan Passer. Stars Peter O'Toole, Mariel Hemingway, Vincent Spano. Screenplay, Jeremy Leven, based on his novel; camera (color), Robbie Greenberg; art director, Josan F. Russo; associate producer, Charles Mulvehill; music, Sylvester Levay; editor, Richard Chew; assistant director/executive in charge of production, Wolfgang Glattes; "Zeno" built by Michael & Richard Prather; costumes, Julie Weiss. Reviewed at World Film Festival, Montreal, Sept. 1, 1985. (MPAA Rating: R.) Running time: 107 MINS.
Dr. Harry Wolper . . . . Peter O'Toole
Meli . . . . Mariel Hemingway
Boris . . . . Vincent Spano
Barbara Spencer . . . . Virginia Madsen
Sid Kuhlenbeck . . . . David Ogden Stiers
Paul . . . . John Dehner
Lucy Wolper . . . . Karen Kopins
Pavlo . . . . Kenneth Tigar
Mrs. Mallory . . . . Elsa Raven
Mrs. Pruitt . . . . Lee Kessler
Mr. Spencer . . . . Rance Howard
Mrs. Spencer . . . . Ellen Geer
Dean Harrington . . . . Jeff Corey

If ever there was a pic suffering from a lack of focus, it's "Creator," which preemed as the closing night attraction at the Montreal festival. The Ivan Passer film, adapt-

ed by Jeremy Leven from his own novel, starts out as an amusing tale of an amiably nutty scientist (Peter O'Toole) attempting to re-create his beloved wife, dead for thirty years, from her living cells which he's preserved. Film then shifts into a two-tiered love story, and finally into an intense tear-jerker revolving around a young woman in an apparently permanent coma. The various elements don't mix well, and Universal will probably find audience resistance as a result.

Early scenes are quite fun, with O'Toole giving a delightful, if familiar, performance as a shambling, fey Nobel Laureate genius, forever chomping a huge cigar and coming out with pithy quips as he goes about "negotiating with God" to restore his long-dead wife and at the same time battle with rivals within the laboratory outfit where he works.

Romance comes when his young, eager assistant (Vincent Spano) falls head over heels for a lab technician (Virginia Madsen) and they shack up together after coy hesitations on her part. This relationship is amusing, touching and convincing, which is more than can be said for the parallel love story between Mariel Hemingway, as a self-styled 19-year-old nymphomanic who agrees to give O'Toole an ovum to help in his experiments, and the aging scientist.

Intense drama takes over when Madsen unexpectedly goes into a coma and is pronounced dead. The distraught Spano begs that her life support system be left on, and gets a 48-hour reprieve, at the end of which an apparent miracle occurs.

Individually, these differing segments of the film work well enough, but Passer has trouble melding them together into one coherent picture. Audiences lulled by the light comedy of the early scenes may be surprised by the eroticism of the Madsen-Spano love affair, and turned off by the pain and grief of the scenes in which it appears Madsen is dead. "Terms Of Endearment" managed to shift gears in a somewhat similar vein without losing its audience; "Creator" may not be so lucky.

Apart from O'Toole, there are several good performances in the pic. Vincent Spano is effective as the passionate Boris, while Virginia Madsen is quite memorable as Barbara in a role which should bring her plenty of attention. Mariel Hemingway has a rather thankless part, not appearing for the first 30 minutes, and disappearing for long stretches thereafter. She's charming as far as it goes, but she really doesn't have the key femme role, despite being second billed. Supporting actors are solid, though David Ogden Stiers is another vic-

tim of the changing mood of the film, expected to be accepted as a figure of derision for most of the running time, then as a serious man of science at the climax.

Despite its many enjoyable bits, including a great moment when Hemingway, playing football for O'Toole's team against Stiers, demonstrates a unique new way to score a touchdown, "Creator" is frustrating. A rough ride at the box-office is to be expected. — *Strat.*

Satyajit Ray
(INDIAN-DOCU-COLOR/B&W)

Montreal, Aug. 30.

Produced by the films division of the government of India. Directed by Shyam Benegal. Camera (color), Govind Nihalani; editor, Bhanudas Divkar; sound, Hitendra Ghosh; technical advisor, Gamal Khanekar; assistant director, Dev Benegal. Reviewed at Montreal World Film Festival (Conservatoire d'art cinematographique), Aug. 29, 1985. Running time: 140 MINS.

The man who brought dignity to Indian films and made Bengali cinema the voice of reason and realism relative to other entertainment on the subcontinent does not appear ready to pass on his sceptre. Even in this respectful but rather elegaic review of Satyajit Ray's life and work by another very talented Bengali helmer, Shyam Benegal, it is Ray who is in control of the situation as master and mentor. His precepts are handed down with illustrations from his extensive oeuvre. Yet, the word "auteur" never slips from his tongue.

Ray's own account of his life extends to a commentary on the autobiographical elements in his pictures, such as his father's death when he was an infant, his closeness to his mother and her strong belief in the salvation of education. His business studies at university fortunately came to naught, and further studies in design turned him toward commercial art. The outlines of Ray's life are fairly well known, and the version here is consistent with the details and his image known abroad. Particularly interesting, however, are his confessions of the difficulty of finding a way to appreciate Indian art, his assessments of his own contributions, and a confession that he never intended the "Apu Trilogy" to be constituted as such until asked at the Venice Film Festival, where he found himself telling the journalists what they wanted to hear.

His shift away from the cosmetic and manufactured style of Indian cinema was inspired by the photographs of Cartier-Bresson, and he recounts how he began operating his own camera with "Charulata," in order to gain more control over the kind of zooms and camera movements that punctuate his work. Watching the clips included here, which lack subtitles and force the non-Bengali-speaker to observe only the visuals, reveals how Ray's signature acquired certain flourishes generally forgotten in the overall impression of his simple approach.

Because Ray's health has been bad recently, it is reassuring to see him puffing his pipe and commanding the set of "The Home And The World" in some location footage. The length of the docu seems to wear on its subject as much as on the audience, however, as he slowly begins to appear weary of Benegal's inquisition and questions about his "splendid isolation." Ray's comment that "one makes a film for an ideal audience" extends to this pic. The ideal audience will know Bengali, filmmaking techniques, Ray's stature, and the poignance of the meaningful final shot, as the camera pulls back to reveal him in profile in his library window with the sun setting on Calcutta in the background. — *Kaja.*

Tangos - L'Exil De Gardel
(Tangos - Gardel's Exile)
(FRENCH-ARGENTINE-COLOR)

Venice, Aug. 28.

A Gaumont Presentation of a Tercine-Cinesur production. Produced by Vincente Diaz Amo. Executive Producer, Sabina Sigler. Written and directed by Fernando Solanas. Camera (color), Felix Monti; editor, Cesare d'Angiolillo, Jacques Gaillard; sets, Luis diego Pedreira, Jimmy Vansteenskiste; backdrops, Hermenegildo Sabat; music, Astor Piazzola; songs, Jose Luis Castineira de Rios, Fernando Solanas, performed by Roberto Goyeneche, Susana Lago, Osvaldo Pugliese Orchestra, also original recordings by Carlos Gardel; choreography, Susana Tambutti, Margarita Balli, Robert Thomas, Adolfo Andrade. Reviewed at the Excelsior Screening Room, Venice Film Festival, Aug. 27, 1985. Running time: **130 MINS.**

Mariana . . . : . . . . .Marie Laforêt
Pierre . . . . .Philippe Léotard
Juan Dos . . . . .Miguel Angel Sola
Florence . . . . .Marina Vlady
Jean-Marie . . . . .Georges Wilson
Gerardo . . . . .Lautaro Murua
Ana . . . . .Ana Maria Picchio
Maria . . . . .Gabriela Toscano
San Martin . . . . .Michel Etcheverry
Carlos Gadel . . . . .Gregorio Manzur
Miseria . . . . .Jurge Six
Dancers: Roberto Thomas and Manon Hullu, Gloria and Eduardo, Nora Codina and German Altamiramo, Ines Banguinetti.

Anyone expecting Argentine director Fernando Solanas to return, after 15 years of silence (except for one documentary made on order), to the angry, militant and revolutionary cinema which made him famous at the time on the Latin American continent is bound to be disappointed by his latest picture.

He is concerned exclusively, as indicated by the title, with the exiles, those Argentines living abroad, more precisely in Paris. The movie is clearly about them, about the cultural gap they are confronted with away from home.

Solanas, who had to leave Argentina himself in 1976 because his radical political opinions were endangering his life, uses many personal experiences in shaping the incidents within the film. To establish his point of view beyond doubt, story is narrated by Maria, a 20-year-old girl, whose memories of Argentina stem more from hearsay than from personal experience, and who concedes she is not sure just what are her national identity and preferences.

Film is supposed to follow the creative process of a troupe consisting of Argentine exiles in Paris, about to produce a show about themselves, titled "Gardel's Exile," Carlos Gardel being the living personification of the Argentine spirit, the top tango star who spent the last years of his career as a movie idol in France and America, before he was killed in a 1935 auto accident. The show is being prepared by Juan Uno, who lives in Argentina, and writes it there surreptitiously and Juan Dos, who composes the texts, sent to him in the strangest fashion, in Paris.

Instead of proceeding with a traditional tale, Solanas goes for a complex fresco, in which many themes intermingle, and everything is bound together by the music of the tango and the spectacular ballets it generates.

Thus, it is not only the story of young Maria, who is supposed to take part in the show, it is also the story of her mother, Mariana, who is its star, of the composer Juan Dos, who is Mariana's lover, and of Philippe, the Frenchman who helps them produce the play, soliciting the support of reknowned local artists for it. In addition, there is Gerardo, the older intellectual visited by nightmares, who hopes to find the little Marita, born in prison to his daughter, one of countless political victims who simply disappeared, and Miseria, whose specialty is to rip off the Paris phone company and allow his friends to call Buenos Aires free of charge.

All these stories advance side by side while Solanas proceeds at the same time to dwell on the creative process leading to the final show.

Visually, the film is most gratifying, with Solanas' old team, headed by cameraman Felix Monti doing a great job as the plot moves from musical scenes to dramatic ones, from tense and nervous moods to humorous and light ones. Surprisingly, Solanas uses much humor in this description of despair and longing, a kind of humor which drifts easily into the absurd.

With most interiors shot in Buenos Aires, including the musical scenes, and Paris exteriors, the film is remarkably homogenous. The tangos themselves are brilliantly choreographed, and acting, both by the French and the Argentine cast, is on a high level, with Miguel Angel Sola and Marie Laforêt distinguishing themselves, in particular.

Another tremendous advantage for the film is the pulsating, energetic Astor Piazzola score, driving the film forward, its jagged rhythms and syncopations fitting in perfectly with Solanas' purposes.

A first coproduction between Argentina and France, supported by the Film Institute in Buenos Aires and also the Ministry of Culture in Paris, the film was indeed made possible only after the change of regime in Buenos Aires. An ideal item for festivals, careful nursing may help if find a market, even beyond the art circuit, given its visual impact, if the problem of overlength is solved. —*Edna.*

The Song For Europe
(BRITISH-COLOR)

Venice, Aug. 29.

A Channel Four, London, coproduction with Stern TV, Hamburg, and Second German Television, Mainz. Produced by Renée Goddard, Johann Hinrich Gerhard. Directed by John Goldschmidt. Features entire cast. Screenplay, Peter Prince; camera (color), Wolfgang Treu; sets, Ingo Tögel, Mathias Matthies; costumes, Regina Bätz; sound, Terry Hardy; editor, Richard Key; music, Carl Davis. Reviewed at Venice Film Fest (TV Section). August 28, 1985. Running time: **95 MINS.**

With: David Suchet (Steven Dyer), Maria Schneider (Madeleine), Anne-Marie Blanc (Maman), Reinhard Glemnitz (Weigel), George Claisse (Dutourd), Dietmar Schönherr (Junger), Robert Freitag (Moser), Michael Gempart (Ehrli).

John Goldschmidt, a veteran award-winning helmer of British tv-films, scored at Venice with his latest, "The Song For Europe," selected for the "Venezia TV" section. Pic deserves more fest exposure on thematic content alone, but with proper handling might also find its way into selected art houses.

This is the true story of a British citizen (born in Malta) caught in the middle of a complicated legal court case that has still to reach its complete end. Here is an executive of a giant drug consortium based in Basle who is aware of the company's malpractices, so he takes the evidence to the Common Market commission for prosecution and fining. However, by doing so, he has engaged in industrial espionage, and for this offense he is held guilty by Swiss law — and thus is arrested upon returning to Switzerland from his early retirement to a pig-farm in Italy. The next move is up to the Common Market commission in Brussels.

This is where the drama really begins. It turns out that our naive hero is left stranded in the middle. Since Switzerland is not a member of the Common Market, but merely has signed an agreement with same, the Brussels commission can only impose the fine in the end without being able to take any real action on helping the informer who acted in the interest of justice and his own sense of fair play. So, as all too often happens in cases of truth-and justice, an innocent is caught in a spider-web of deception that leads to tragic personal consequences.

First, his wife, a Swiss citizen, commits suicide under the pressure. Then, after languishing in a cell for three months of interrogation (not allowed even to attend his wife's funeral), he is freed on bail only because he managed finally to contact a lawyer on the outside. Finally, having been advised to jump bail by his Brussels advisers, he discovers that he will lose his farm in Italy for the simple reason that Italian officials don't wish to offend their Swiss neighbors (not to mention that Italy is also a member of the Basle drug consortium).

Put all of this together, and you have an intriguing tale of legal entanglements hindering the human cause of justice. If helmer Goldschmidt's premise is accurate, then the Swiss drug consortium in question is powerful enough to manipulate the world market in terms of global crises by say, withholding vitamins and medical aid at crucial moments to jack up the price and register enormous profits. Thus the fact that this film was produced and aired on various European tv-stations last spring is as astonishing as the fact that Goldschmidt was indeed able to film "The Song For Europe" partially in Switzerland.

Pic suffers from the usual drawbacks of a docu-drama. One knows pretty much how the story is going to turn out at the very beginning, and the lines often appear to have been passed through a legal wringer to imply as much as possible without saying everything. Acting and direction are also according to conventional tv formulas.

An epilog at the end in the context of a press conference indicates that the protagonist's appeals to clear his name are still going on.
—*Holl.*

Karnabal
(Carnival)
(SPANISH-COLOR/B&W)

Venice, Aug. 27.

Produced by Aura Films, Figaro Films and Imatco Productions. Directed by Carles Mira. Features entire cast. Screenplay, Joan Mallarach and the Comedians; camera (color, b&w), Tomas Pladevall; editor, Teresa Alcocer; art direction, the Comedians, Jordi and Josep Castells; music, the Comedians. Reviewed at the Venice Film Festival, Aug. 26, 1985. Running time: **80 MINS.**

"Karnabal" is the self-celebrating compendium of the mime talents of a well-known Spanish troupe called "Les Comedians," who have participated in virtually every aspect of the film's production, from direction and scripting to sets, costumes and, of course, performance. Unhappily, most of the picture remains in the realm of recorded theater, which in this case is particularly cold and distant. The hilarity on the screen brings no answering echo from the audience.

Without a story, film is an 80-minute anthology of loosely-connected antics performed in traditional carnival mask. Though the children's market may find much of the material appealing, main audience will probably be limited to fellow thesps and stage-watchers interested in the work of this group. As far as general audiences go, there is little here to captivate or even instruct historically, for though the group makes use of traditional mask — and many of the costumes are fantastic — they are updated into a very modern and personal idiom.

Pic skips merrily from one setting to another, in dream-like fashion. It opens with a man driving through the country who is stopped by a balloonist and induced to step into a hot-air balloon, which sails him into a magical kingdom peopled by carousing merry-makers who name him King of Fools. He follows a beautiful, mysterious woman, only to discover an old hag lurks under her mask. The hag takes him to a sumptuous, empty theater where a performance is given. In it, God and his angels humorously re-enact the creation of the world.

Only in a last, long sequence in black and white does picture get a laugh. While technically "Karnabal" is first-rate filming, with skillful use of camera, lighting, costumes and sets, it is only at the end that helmer Carles Mira synthesizes his know-how into an original and successful piece of film comedy. The hero is drawn into a parable about the progress of man from primitive, naked cave-dweller to clothed, brain-washed consumer who is convinced by a traveling salesman to adopt everything from tvs to toilets in one day. In b&w, with speeded-up motion and jump-cut editing, the sequence goes beyond the distant conventions of mask (which pic unwittingly makes seem like dead relics) to a contemporary exploration of the conventions of modern life. — *Yung.*

Yesterday
(POLISH-COLOR)

Venice, Aug. 31.

A Film Polski production, "Rondo" Unit, Warsaw; world rights, Film Polski, Warsaw. Written and directed by Radoslav Piwowarski. Features entire cast. Camera (color), Witold Adamek; sets, Tadeusz Kosarewicz; costumes, Iwona Szymanska; editor, Irena Chorynska; music, John Lennon, Paul McCartney; sound, Alexander Golebiowski. Reviewed at Venice Film Fest (Critics' Section), Aug. 30, 1985. Running time: **87 MINS.**
With: Piotr Siwikiewicz (Ringo), Andrzej Zielinski (John), Robert Piechota (Paul), Waldemar Ignaczak (George), Anna Kazimierczakk (Anna), Krystyna Feldman (Aunt), Henryk Bista (Director), Stanislaw Brudny (Priest).

For a while, there appeared a slew of pics in Europe referring back to the Elvis Presley craze of the 1950s. Now it's the Beatles' turn. One of these is the Polish entry in the Critics' Section of the Venice fest, Radoslav Piwowarski's "Yesterday," the English-lingo title stemming directly from one of the group's 1965 hit songs.

We're in a small provincial town in Poland at the time when the Beatles are making it big in Liverpool and on tour. Four lads are facing graduation, but all they can think of is how to wow the home crowd and their school chums with a band concert chock-full of Beatles hits. They don't have the amplifying equipment necessary to do their show, so they put together some makeshift equipment which goes haywire during a rehearsal and puts one of the group in a hospital with an electrical shock!

The lads, who use all the Beatles' names in addressing each other, have another problem. A girlfriend of the one in-shock (John) has been compromised by being caught in a clinch one day by the school authorities. So while our erstwhile lothario is still in shock, his friend (Ringo) goodheartedly steps in and saves her from ultimate shame before parents and friends. Years later, with the mantle of adulthood placed upon the group, we find the romantic couple of yesterday divorced.

Piwowarski, a tv-director leaning on autobiographical data, follows the conventional formula with little extra to offer. — *Holl.*

Signé Renart
(Signed Renart)
(SWISS-FRENCH-COLOR)

Venice, Aug. 31.

A coproduction of MS Productions Geneve, MK2 Productions, Television Suisse Romande, and CAB Production. Executive producer, Jean-Louis Porchet. Directed by Michel Soutter. Features entire cast. Screenplay, Soutter, Bernard Meister; camera (color), Jean-Bernard Menaoud; editor, Hélène Viard; music, Tom Novembre; sound, Luc Yersin, Peter Begert. Reviewed at Venice Film Fest (Special Program I), Aug. 30, 1985. Running time: **89 MINS.**
With Gerald Battiaz (Renart, Françoise Dupertuis (Hermeline), Nader Farman, Rita Gay, Marka Lehmann, François Margot, Christophe Merian, Michel Rossy, Lou Scarol Marcos Tsacopoulos.

Unspooled in the Special Program section, and one of three Swiss pics on display at Venice, Michel Soutter's "Signed Renart" comes across as a slight-of-hand feature on little people in show-business. Renart is a club entertainer who can charm an audience with suitcase full of objects he can manipulate into a sound-effects sketch. One day, his wife, Hermeline, is fired for the offense of being pregnant — so Renart up and quits.

Next we find the couple in an industrial town in the mountains, where they've opened a club of their own. But now that he's the boss himself, Renart changes in character and temperament. His friends in the show tolerate his indispositions for a while, but it's soon clear that only Hermeline will take his side as things go from bad to worse.

Soutter, who helped to establish French-Swiss cinema two decades ago via scripts (often for Claude Goretta) and self-directed features (among them, "Les Arpenteurs" in 1972 and "Repérages" in 1977), has made better films than "Signed Renart." Here he seems to have slowed that narrative pace too much, as though stretching an hour-long tv-production into a full-length feature. Acting, too, is one-dimensional without nuance or esprit as befits a showbiz theme.
—*Holl.*

Nicht Nichts Ohne Dich
(Not Nothing Without You)
(WEST GERMAN-B&W)

Venice, Aug. 27.

A Pia Frankenberg Film production, Hamburg. Produced, written, directed and acted in by Pia Frankenberg. Features entire cast. Camera (b&w), Thomas Mauch; editor, Ursula West; sets, Brigitte Abel; sound, Sven Funke; music, Horst Mühlbradt. Reviewed at Venice Film Fest (Critics' Section), Aug. 27, 1985. Running time: **88 MINS.**
With: Pia Frankenberg (Martha), Ilona Ribowski-Bruwer (Ilona), Klaus Bueb (Alfred), Emma Israel (Old Woman In U-Bahn), Fats G. Pachsteffl (Man in U-Bahn), Jörn Hüsing (shares apartment with Alfred), Gabriela, Felipe, Adelina, Guilherme, Almeida-Sedas (share apartment with Martha), Thomas Struck (Frau Strach), José Aparicio (the Portuguese), Adelina Almeida (Teresa).

The nonsense title used in Pia Frankenberg's "Not Nothing Without You" pretty well sums up this low-budget debut pic unspooled in the Critics' Section at Venice. Pic is without a conventional narrative form and wanders through the wintery Hamburg landscape picking up impressions as the femme helmer goes along. Two characters continu-ally interchange life experiences, Martha (Pia Frankenberg) and Alfred (Klaus Bueb), and their observations have to do with people on the marginal side of life: communes, foreigners, a family of Turks and a family from East Germany, people on the street and in offices (one of them a transvestite), and so on.

Since pic has no thematic direction to speak of, a lot depends on whether or not Frankenberg and Bueb are clever enough to improvise before the camera. They're not, nor is their self-indulgence of much interest.

Only plus is Thomas Mauch's b&w lensing — that, and the brief recitation of an Erich Fried poem that offers the excuse for the title.
Budget was just over $100,000.
— *Holl.*

Running Out Of Luck
(BRITISH-COLOR)

Venice, Aug. 27.

Produced by Nitrate Film Ltd. and the Julien Temple Production Co. Directed by Julien Temple. Stars Mick Jagger, Jerry Hall, Dennis Hopper and Rae Dawn Chong. Screenplay, Temple; camera (color), Oliver Stapleton; sound, Chris Monroe; editing, Richard Bedford; music, Jagger. Reviewed at Venice Film Festival, Aug. 26, 1985. Running time: **90 MINS.**

After bringing dozens of rock songs to life on screen in his pacesetting videos, Julien Temple has done the same for an entire album, Mick Jagger's "She's The Boss," in this cheerfully sardonic, exotic and totally predictable star vehicle, essentially a long-playing vidclip. A must-see for Jagger fans, it will keep most other audiences amused. Authentic Brazilian backdrops are entertaining just to look at. Main obstacle — and a big one — to b.o. success is previous exposure of much of the material on tv in vidclips of various album cuts.

Playing your average drunken slob who just happens to be an international superstar, irresistible to every woman who sets eyes on him, Jagger is not surprisingly at his best in the musical sequences. Real-life girlfriend Jerry Hall as his wife and Dennis Hopper, playing a crazed video director, are fine in limited caricatures.

In what there is of a plot to supply the bridges from song to song, Jagger has a marital spat in Rio, gets mugged and winds up in the interior on a chain gang-style plantation run by a boss lady who can't spend a night without his English love. With the help of a local beauty (Rae Dawn Chong), he escapes back to civilization, only to find that his place has been taken by a lookalike.

One scene sure to have audiences howling involves Jagger's energetic attempts to convince the proprietors of a general store in the bush that he's really a big deal. Finding a copy of an old Rolling Stones album among the Julio Iglesias LPs in the bin, he gyrates and lip-synchs to "Brown Sugar" while they look on blankly.

"Running Out" is helmer Temple's second feature after "The Great Roack And Roll Swindle" docu in 1979 and amply demonstrates that his talent for composition and flair for the surreal are worthy of big-screen fiction. There have been many worse full-scale movie musicals than this vidclip of his, which could be the harbinger of an LP-based feature trend. —*Jay.*

Jagode U Grlu
(Caught In The Throat)
(YUGOSLAVIAN-COLOR)

Venice, Aug. 29.
An Avala-Pro Film, Belgrade; world rights, Yugoslavia Film, Belgrade. Written and directed by Srdjan Karanovic. Features entire cast. Camera (color), Zivko Zalar; sets, Miljen Kljakovic; costumes, Mirjana Markovic; editor, Branka Ceperak; music, Zoran Simjanovic. Reviewed at Venice Film Fest ("Young Venice" Section), Aug. 28, 1985. Running time: **90 MINS.**
With: Branko Cvejic (Bane Bumbar), Alexander Bercek (Uske), Pedrag Miki Manojlovic (Mike Rubiroza), Bogdan Diklic (Boca), Dobrila Stojnic (Biljka), Gordana Maric (Goca), Mira Banjac (servant), Gala Videnovic (young girl), Lepi Jovica (band leader).

Pic is a nostalgic glance over the shoulder at a popular 13-part tv-serial made by Karanovic in 1974 with young actors who were later to make it in film and theater: Bane Bumbar, Alexander Bercek, and Pedrag Miki Manojlovic in particular. The idea was to construct a loose tale about what happened to the characters in that original serial, providing at the same time an opportunity to analyze what the passage of time does to old friendships.

The reunion takes place on a raft-restaurant on the river. A local band is hired for the occasion, and off the characters go in a game of one-upsmanship — until it's all too evident that none of them has been very successful since departing to go their separate ways a decade ago. When the raft breaks away to move off with the current at the end, and a fire breaks out on board as well, a note of absurdity is added to the happening. A minor film, but all-around fun for the Yugo film buff.
—*Holl.*

La Donna Delle Meraviglie
(Woman Of Wonders)
(ITALIAN-COLOR)

Venice, Aug. 30.
An Italnoleggio Cinematografica release. Produced by Gianni Federici for RAI-TV Channel 1, Arnoldo Mondadori Publishers.

VE. GA. Produzioni. Written and directed by Alberto Bevilacqua, based on his novel. Stars Ben Gazzara, Lina Sastri, Claudia Cardinale. Camera (color), Giuseppe Ruzzolini; art director, Mario Garbuglia; editor, Sergio Montanari; music, Carlo & Paolo Rustichelli, Rinaldo Muratori. Reviewed at the Venice Film Festival (Competition), Aug. 29, 1985. Running time: **106 MINS.**
Alberto . . . . Ben Gazzara
Luisa . . . . Lina Sastri
Maura . . . . Claudia Cardinale
Ulisse . . . . Orazio Orlando
Astolfo . . . . Flavio Bucci
Gianni . . . . Fabrizio Bentivoglio

Novelist, poet and filmer Alberto Bevilacqua, best known for his book-turned-film "La Calipha" (starring Romy Schneider), brings another part of his literary output to the screen in "Woman Of Wonders." There is obviously a lot of autobiographical material in this story of a successful writer/director going through a mid-life crisis. The less-than-original premise is developed in two directions: an exploratory tour through the hero's childhood memories and an acting-out of his current obsession with locating the perfect woman. Both trails hit a dead end early on, but picture limps on to a patently incredible conclusion, long after it's lost most of the audience.

Alberto (Ben Gazzara) lives alone in a comfortable old Roman villa where he is editing a film he has just made. The only thorn in his side is a noisy neighbor, Luisa (Lina Sastri), who is one of Alberto's old lovers and cause of the breakup of his marriage to Claudia Cardinale. Though Alberto doesn't know it yet, both women secretly nurture an undying love for him, and pic evolves through a series of encounters with adoring females (including his mother) in a way reminiscent of a Fellini film like "8½," minus the fantasy and irony.

Alberto is obsessed with finding the woman of his dreams, who has been making anonymous phone calls for some time which intrigue him profoundly. Audience is a little less breathless, since the voice over the phone is immediately recognizable as Luisa's (yes, there are difficulties in transposing novels to film.)

With a Mona Lisa smile, Luisa sets about ensnaring Alberto's heart again through teasing and flattery. Alberto consults everyone from his best friend to worst enemy over the "mystery," but no one has a clue.

The tiresome search is intercut with scenes on a moviola, where Alberto is working (but when?) on a film about his boyhood in the Po Valley. Little of it bears any but a tenuous relation to the rest of the film. In one bizarre episode a riverboat full of prostitutes captures a strong, shy young peasant and subjects him to psycho-sexual torture

while the boy Alberto looks on. Striking but unreal, the incident fails to connect emotionally with the grown-up's problems.

Gazzara is personable and at ease in a difficult role, and works well with bright new actress Sastri and a super-chic Cardinale. Technically picture falls short in special effects, which are, sorely lacking in what is supposed to be a climactic flood scene when Alberto finds inner peace once more. A calm river, a little rain, and a few praying villagers does not a tempest make — though given the teapot dimensions of the drama, it hardly makes much difference. —*Yung*

Biohazard
(COLOR)

Imitative monster pic.

A 21st Century Distribution presentation of a Viking Films Intl. production. Executive producers, Art Schweitzer, T.L. Lankford. Produced and directed by Fred Olen Ray. Features entire cast. Screenplay, Ray; additional dialog, Lankford, Miriam L. Preissel; camera (color), Paul Elliott, John McCoy; editor, Preissel, Jack Tucker; music, Eric Rasmussen, Drew Neumann; sound, Rex Baille, Craig Tomlin; assistant director, Donald E. Jackson; special effects makeup, Jon McCallum; Bio-Monster suit created by Kenneth J. Hall; special effects animation, Bret Mixon; coproducer, Ray Guttman; associate producers, Richard Hench, Preissel. Reviewed on Continental Video cassette, N.Y., Aug. 26, 1985. (No MPAA Rating.) Running time: **79 MINS.**
General Randolph . . . . Aldo Ray
Lisa Martyn . . . . Angelique Pettyjohn
Mitchell Carter . . . . William Fair
Mike . . . . Frank McDonald
Reiger . . . . David Pearson
Bio-Monster . . . . Christopher Ray
Jack Murphy . . . . Charles Roth
Rula Murphy . . . . Carroll Borland
Dr. Williams . . . . Arthur Payton
Roger . . . . Richard Hench
Jenny . . . . Loren Crabtree

Made in 1983 and just released on vidcassette, "Biohazard" is a silly horror film that slavishly imitates (as have many other low-budgeters) the monster effects in the 1979 hit "Alien." Ironically, pic made for 21st Century release retained its monicker though 20th Century Fox reportedly tried to buy the name to affix to its recent "Warning Sign" film. Postscript is that 20th Fox is itself back in production with the Sigourney Weaver-starred sequel "Aliens.

Thin story has Dr. Williams (Arthur Payton) experimenting in his remote desert research lab on matter transfer, not the process used in the Fox classic "The Fly" but rather bringing objects here from another, unknown dimension. One such foot-long object has been materialized and is being shown to military observers led by Gen. Randolph (Aldo Ray). The object is stolen by a journalist who wishes to write about it, and it opens, releasing a se-

ries of monsters that go on the rampage.

Mitchell Carter (William Fair) of the Army tries to track down the monsters, using a geiger counter (they are radioactive). He is aided by Lisa (Angelique Pettyjohn), an ESP-sensitive who has been instrumental in Dr. Williams', experiments. Climax has a leading character revealed to be one of the monsters.

Spectacle of seeing the "Alien" monster imitated in each of its guises is a sad excuse for a film, loaded with gore and in-jokes (at one point a monster angrily tears up a poster displaying "E.T."). This short feature ends ludicrously with the director audibly yelling "Cut!" from off-screen, followed by nearly 10 minutes of outtakes as padding. Funniest bit is when mature bombshell Angelique Pettyjohn's platinum blond wig slips off during a sex scene, duly recorded in the outtake section. — *Lor.*

The Seven Magnificent Gladiators
(COLOR)

The Magnificent Seven ride again, in ancient Rome.

A Cannon Releasing release of a Cannon Group presentation. A Cannon Films production. Produced by Alexander Hacohen. Directed by Bruno Mattei. Stars Lou Ferrigno, Sybil Danning, Brad Harris, Dan Vadis. Screenplay, Claude Fragass (Claudio Fragasso); camera (Luciano Vittorio color), Silvano Ippoliti; editor, "A. Swyftte;" music, Dov Seltzer; assistant director, Gerard Olivier; production manager, Ned Linke; art direction, Armand Mellon; stunt coordinator, Hank O'Leary; costumes, Belle Crandall; post-synchronization supervisor, Lewis Lester. Reviewed on HBO, N.Y., Aug. 25, 1985. (MPAA Rating: PG.) Running time: **86 MINS.**
Han . . . . Lou Ferrigno
Julia . . . . Sybil Danning
Scipio . . . . Brad Harris
Nicerote . . . . Dan Vadis
Also with: Carla Ferrigno (Pandora), Barbara Pesante (Anakora), Yehuda Efroni (Emperor), Mandy Rice-Davies (Lucilla), Robert Mura (Vendrix), Ivan Beshears (Goliath), Jody Wanger (Festo), Michael Franz (Glafiro).

"The Seven Magnificent Gladiators" is an uncredited (and subpar) remake of John Sturges' "The Magnificent Seven," itself a remake of "Seven Samurai." Action has been transplanted to ancient Rome in this quickie, made in 1982 as a warmup for Lou Ferrigno just prior to his starring in Cannon's "Hercules." Like "Hercules," the film set no boxoffice fires when released regionally in August 1984. A third pic, "Hercules II," remains on the shelf.

Ferrigno toplines as Han, a barbarian who, after proving his prowess as a chariot racer, is asked by the women of the beleaguered village of Clusium to defend their town against the supposedly immortal demigod Nicerote (Dan Vadis), who annually descends upon them to exact a tribute and kill off any able-bodied men. Han passes their test as the only man able to wield the magical Sword of Achilles.

Accepting the assignment, Han teams up with a gladiator Scipio (Brad Harris), whom he bested in the chariot race, Scipio's pal Julia (Sybil Danning) and four other out-of-work warriors.

Plot twists and individual scenes are right out of the Yul Brynner-Steve McQueen classic, with Goliath (Ivan Beshears) introed chopping wood in a vignette identical to Charles Bronson's entrance in the original film and Glafiro (Michael Franz) going through a truncated version of Horst Buchholz' role. Main changes are the introduction of campy scenes in Rome of the emperor (Yehuda Efroni), including the anachronism of oiled-up women in bikinis wrestling for his entertainment. Also, instead of the strategy of defense in the original films, director Bruno Mattei stages two ho-hum swordplay battles. Only point of interest is Sybil Danning's femme warrior, convincingly integrating the previously all-male, he-man format.

Cast, though articulating in English, is sabotaged by poor dubbing and film develops very little period atmosphere.—*Lor.*

Pics At Montreal Fest

Le Matou
(The Alley Cat)
(CANADIAN-FRENCH-COLOR)

Montreal, Sept. 2.

A Cinevideo Inc.-Antenne 2 coproduction. In association with Telefilm Canada, Societe-Radio Canada, La Societe de Radio-Television du Quebec. Produced by Justine Héroux. Directed by Jean Beaudin. Features entire cast. Screenplay, Lise Lemay-Rousseau, from the novel by Yves Beauchemin; camera (color), Claude Agostini; set design, François Lamontagne; editor, Jean-Pierre Cereghetti; music François Dompierre; sound, Claude Hazanavicius. Reviewed at World Film Festival, Montreal (In Competition), Aug. 28, 1985. Running time: **140 MINS.**

Florent . . . . .Serge Dupire
Elise . . . . .Monique Spaziani
Ratablavasky . . . . .Jean Carmet
M. Emile . . . . .Guillaume Lemay-Thivierge
Picquot . . . . .Julien Guiomar
Mme. Jeunehomme . .Madeleine Robinson
Slipskin . . . . .Miguel Fernandes
Gladu . . . . .Julien Poulin
Mlle. Lydie . . . . .Alexandra Stewart
M. Boissonneault . . . . .Yvan Canuel
Mme. Boissonneault . . . . . .Rita Lafontaine

The simultaneous production of a feature film and a tv mini-series may make economic sense, but it rarely works artistically, as such recent failures as "Louisiana," "The Blood Of Others" and the Australian "Robbery Under Arms" can testify. "The Alley-Cat," a lavish adaptation of a popular Quebec novel, is rather better than any of the above, but it's still comprised by its inelegant format. Had the novel been adapted solely for the screen, it would surely have been produced to play at less than its present 2 hour 20 minute running time.

Tale involves a struggling Montreal clerk (Serge Dupire) whose good deed in helping an injured man on the street brings him to the attention of the mysterious and satanic Ratablavasky (Jean Carmet). Dupire's road to eventual success is a rocky one indeed. He's cheated out of a restaurant where he's made a success, and has to start all over again. A cute little street kid, Monsieur Emile (Guillaume Lemay-Thivierge), who latches on to Dupire and his wife (Monique Spaziani), is eventually killed in a rooftop fall. Every time Dupire thinks he has it made, he gets put down, but he keeps on struggling.

Pic teems with characters, of which the most engaging is the devious Slipskin, wonderfully played by Miguel Fernandes. Slipskin, who turns out to be Ratablavasky's agent in the campaign against Dupire, is an Anglophone who mostly speaks English, while everyone else speaks to him in French. His confrontation with cockroaches and rats in his restaurant, placed there by young M. Emile, is a highlight.

In the end, though, the story simply isn't strong enough to sustain a pic of this length. That shouldn't matter in French-speaking Canada, where the book is well known and there's an eager and ready-made audience (film opened in Montreal the day after the World Film Festival preem). In other territories it may not be such clear sailing.

Director Jean Beaudin, who competed last year in the Montreal fest with "Mario," has surrendered his usually crisp style to the more flaccid demands of the production. Pic is technically good, with fine production dress, and a sprightly music score by François Lamontagne.
—*Strat.*

Alem Da Paixao
(Happily Ever After)
(BRAZILIAN-COLOR)

Montreal, Sept. 2.

A Producoes Cinematograficas production. Produced by Lucy Barreto, Antonio Calmon. Directed by Bruno Barreto. Features entire cast. Screenplay, Bruno Barreto, Antonio Calmon; camera (color), Affonso Beato; editor, Vera Freire; sets Oscar Ramos; sound, Romeu Quintas, Helio Ramos. Reviewed at World Film Festival, Montreal, Aug. 30, 1985. Running time: **106 MINS.**
Fernanda Sampaio . . . . .Regina Duarte
Miguel . . . . .Paulo Castelli
Bom Bom . . . . .Patricio Bisso
Roberto . . . . .Flavio Galvao
Also with: Flavio Sao Thiago, Ivan Setta.

Fernanda is a seemingly happy wife, mother and career woman living in a comfortable home in Sao Paulo. Since her father's death she's been depressed, and the film begins with a dream: in a nightclub she's dancing intimately with a blond woman who turns out to be a transvestite.

Next day, she literally runs into the self-same transvestite (she hits him with her car), and when her husband goes off to the U.S. on a business trip (despite the fact that it's Christmas week) she's soon seeking out the man, Miguel, and is attracted to him despite the fact that he's living with Bom Bom, another transvestite. When Bom Bom conveniently leaves by sea for France, Fernanda and Miguel take off into the hinterlands for a steamy affair, even thought everyone she meets warns her he's dangerous, proving to be a drug dealer.

Many viewers will have trouble accepting the fact that this particular woman would be sufficiently attracted to this particular man to abandon her children and go off after him. In addition, the AIDS scare suggests that a sexual relationship with a known bisexual is less likely than heretofore, as is Fernanda's impetuous act in getting herself tattooed, another dangerous practice.

Despite, these drawbacks, Bruno Barreto, who had a hit with "Dona Flor And Her Two Husbands," is a good enough director to make the film reasonably gripping. It moves along swiftly, hardly pausing along enough to let the viewer question the irrational acts of its heroine, and is shot against a backdrop of colorful and interesting locations. Most performances are good, too, though Patricio Bisso overdoes his caricature of a blowsy middle-aged transvestite.

All technical credits are very good, but the pic is unlikely to garner much international interest, either at fests or on the arthouse circuit. As a softcore sex item, it's too tame, apart from one reasonably explicit sequence at around mid-point.
— *Strat.*

Le 4eme Pouvoir
(The 4th Power)
(FRANCE-COLOR)

Montreal, Sept. 2.

A Consortium Financier de Production de Films-Compagnie Française Cinematographie production. Produced by Jean Kerchner. Directed by Serge Leroy. Stars Philippe Noiret, Nicole Garcia. Screenplay, Yonnick Flot, Serge Leroy; camera (color), André Domage; music, Alain Bashung; editor, François Ceppi; sound, Bernard Aubouy. Reviewed at World Film Festival, Montreal (In Competition), Aug. 28, 1985. Running time: **99 MINS.**
Yves Dorget . . . . .Philippe Noiret
Catherine Carré . . . . .Nicole Garcia
Network President . . . .Jean-Claude Brialy
Also with: Roland Blanche, Michel Subor.

An extremely topical thriller about attempts by the French government to muzzle the media, "The 4th Power" is a satisfying pic on just about every count. Sock lead performances from Philippe Noiret, as a tough newspaper reporter, and Nicole Garcia as a courageous tv news anchorwoman, enhance a taut script and slick direction.

Plot hinges on the assassination of an Arab diplomat in Paris. He was opposed to the sale to his country of two French nuclear reactors, and Noiret and Garcia, ex-lovers who come together in the course of the drama, are convinced he was killed by, or with the knowledge of, the French Secret Service. The suave Minister of the Interior is outraged by Garcia's probing on-air questions, and orders her boss, head of the state-owned tv network (Jean-Claude Brialy) to muzzle her. Meanwhile, Noiret writes a story in which a known gangster claims to have witnessed the Arab's murder, and as a result is thrown in the cooler, despite an outcry in the media.

With the recently successful attempt of the British government to prevent the BBC from putting on the air a program on an IRA leader, plus the suspicions that have fallen on French involvement in the sinking of a Greenpeace ship in a New Zealand harbor, the up-to-the-minute aspects of the screenplay by Yonnick Flot and helmer Serge Leroy are plain to see. It's to the pic's credit that it doesn't play like a contrived series of government-baiting incidents, but as a well-rounded and suspenseful thriller. The low-key climax seems apt.

Handsomely packaged item should do okay at home on its controversial theme and popular stars, and should also get some attention offshore. —*Strat.*

L'Orchestre Noir
(The Black Orchestra)
(BELGIAN-DOCU-COLOR)

Montreal, Aug. 24.

Produced by Essel Films/Contrechamp and La Communaute Française de Belgique.

Produced, written, and directed by Stephan Lejeune. Camera (color), Philippe Defosse; sound, Charles Bernard, Thierry Ferret, Dominique Warnier; music, Jean-Francois Maljean; editor, Lejeune. Reviewed at the Montreal World Film Festival (Parisien), Aug. 23, 1985. Running time: **97 MINS.**
With: Walter De Bock, Rene Haquin, George-Henri Beauthier, Jean-Paul Collette, Jean-Claude Garot, Jose Happart, Serge Moureaux.

The increased activity of neo-fascist groups that attract membership among young people has occupied European journalists' attention and become the subject of several European art films. This investigative docu of Stephan Lejeune focuses on the well-organized perpetuation of violence.

Beginning with two groups in Belgium, the VMO and the Front de la Jeunesse, Lejeune interviews members, exposing their ideology of racism, anti-Marxism, and anti-semitism. Although they claim to be sports clubs, Lejeune traced their weekend outings to training sessions for close combat and guerrilla warfare. He takes a look at a bombing of a magazine editorial office, after a negative article about neo-fascist youth and interviews a baron at Chateau Bonvoisin, where an international conference of rightist leaders launched a Christians for Peace convention.

Interviews with members reveal almost ridiculously absurd attitudes, but Lejeune warns against dismissing them as harmless. The wildest speeches are delivered at a forum for "The Courage of Your Convictions," where fascists opine that the only error of national socialism was the loss of the war. Lejeune illustrates the spread of these clubs and attitudes into Portugal, Spain, England, and Germany, in a three-pronged strategy emanating from Belgium. Fascinating viewing and in-depth inquiry makes it ideal for the television market, but French language and lack of subtitles may be the major obstacle. —*Kaja.*

Agonia
(Agony)
(VENEZUELAN-COLOR)

Montreal, Aug. 31.
A Joel Films Production. Produced by Elia Schneider. Directed by Jose Novoa. Written by Novoa and Aminta de Lara; dialog by Novoa; camera (color), Novoa, Hernan Toro; editor, Novoa; set design, Silvia I. Vallejo; sound, Robert Katz; music, Gilberto Harquez; costumes, Silvia I. Vallejo. Reviewed at Montreal World Film Festival (Parisien), Aug. 31, 1985. Running time: **85 MINS.**
Jorge .... Juan Manuel Montesinos
Aida .... Aminta de Lara
Galindo .... Roberto Fontana
Arturo .... Jorge Diaz
Crescencio .... Rodney Rochester
Isabel .... Maria Eugenia Carrasco
Maneto .... Mario Pena
Tatiana .... Carlota Sosa
Jorge's father .... Nelson Serge
Jorge as boy .... Danniel Garmendia

Grandmother .... Marianella Rojas

"Agonia," the debut feature of New York-based helmer Jose Novoa, moves too slowly and carefully, a major mistake of an otherwise well-crafted, moody psychological study. Cut to an hour, it would make a quality tv pic.

Jorge, the central character, is about to turn his family's plantation into real estate in order to leave the country and the jungle for the sake of his lonely wife, Aida. Story stretches across two days and a night of the visit and negotiations with two visiting men. They have brought along a sex-bomb named Isabel whom Aida instantly dislikes. Flirtations and signals of interest lead to various forms of seduction.

The hacienda's sale will include the two servants, a lovely young Indian girl and a dwarf Crescencio, who is the manager. The Buyer's son Arturo arrives to collect his allowance, and when his father proves unwilling to fork over the money, Arturo enters a liaison with the servant girl who is eager to have a baby.

The women are portrayed as universally frustrated, and even the proper Aida winds up in the arms of the dwarf and is discovered by her husband. Generation gaps and class conflicts are drawn with decadent overtones. The wife sinks ever deeper into the lush nature of the jungle of the plantation as well as the corrupt relationships around her. When it becomes clear that Jorge will continue drinking and cling to his roots, she puts a bullet through her temple.

A score put together of soulful opera arias makes for lovely listening, but the story is stretched too thin and the characters left undeveloped, while the camera explores the exotic Venezuelan landscapes. —*Kaja.*

Mode In France
(FRENCH-COLOR)

Montreal, Aug. 31.
A Kuiv production. Produced by Michael Rotman. Written and directed by William Klein. Camera (color), Gérard DeBattista; editor, Nelly Quettier; music, Serge Gainsbourg. Reviewed at Montreal World Film Festival, Aug. 31, 1985. Running time: **90 MINS.**
With: Claudi Huidobro, Bambou, Sapho, Anne Rohard, Chantal Thomass, Grace Jones.

As the title implies, this docudrama showcases high fashion in France. Just as most of the creators and their creations are avant-garde, so too is the tone of this free-form film fashion show.

Essentially a dramatization by models of the works of such designers as Kenzo, Agnes B., Castel-

bajac, Gaultier, Montana and more, film is frequently as jumbled as the fashion statements being made. However, to the credit of director William Klein, the New York-born, Paris-based painter, photographer and filmmaker, the film is never static.

Pic is primarily geared for high fashion afficionados as both commercial and avant-garde film buffs will likely find docudramatic sequences by models painfully theatrical and narcissistic. At least in the fashion mags, the models don't engage in pretentious, superficial chit-chat on the meaning of life and haute couture.

A segment devoted to a mini-history lesson of French fashion is the most comprehensible. In a couple of entertaining minutes, Klein makes the quick transition from corset to Coco Chanel to Christian Dior to Courreges. Also to the point is a Kenzo fashion display set to a romantic movie motif.

Unfortunately, the balance of the pic is given to much incoherent, mumbo-jumbo on alleged style where absolutely anything goes, including the wearing of foot galoshes as trendy head gear.

Apart from name designers and celebrated French mannequins and cover girls, the biggest headliner is disco starlet/movie actress Grace Jones, who looks smashing in a potpourri of revealing leather-ware but who unfortunately can't carry a film singlehandedly.

Photography and Serge Gainsbourg music are perfectly in keeping with pic's tempo, which is very frantic. — *Bro.*

Le Choix D'un Peuple
(The Choice Of A People)
(CANADIAN-DOCU-COLOR)

Montreal, Aug. 31.
A Les Films De La Rive production. Directed by Hugues Mignault, Camera (color), various; editor, Jean Saulnier; music, Pierre Langevin and Marc O'Farrell. Reviewed at Montreal World Film Festival, Aug. 30, 1985. Running time: **100 MINS.**

In the past, the Montreal World Film fest has been accused of not addressing sensitive, socially significant local Quebec concerns.

Hugues Mignault's docu touches on the granddaddy of sensitive, socially significant local Quebec concerns — the Quebec Sovereignty Association Referendum of May 20, 1980.

Forests of timber have been felled and countless miles of celluloid and cassette tape exposed in dealing with one of the most passionate, divisive issues to have ever confronted Quebecers, not to mention all Canadians. That is, the poignant question of Quebec independence from Canada.

Montreal filmmaker Hugues Mignault has sifted through all the pulp, celluloid and videotape, added his own footage and emerged with an evocative, moving and balanced view of events that led to the victory of then Canadian P.M. Pierre Trudeau's "No" (to independence) forces over Quebec Premier René Levesque's "Yes" faction.

From first tabling of the Referendum question in Quebec's provincial National Assembly to final tabulation of results, Mignault and his minions of cameramen catch virtually all the nuances of this colossal media extravaganza. All the principal combatants are there: Trudeau, his former cabinet minister Jean Chrétien, the unheralded, then Quebec Liberal Party leader Claude Ryan and their opposite numbers, Quebec Premier Levesque and noted, articulate separatist Pierre Bourgault.

Beyond their impassioned pleas and varied reactions of "the little people," Mignault closely chronicles the events that really solidified the final outcome. Most noteworthy are the Quebec labor movement's fallout with the provincial Levesque government and the staggering, roller-coaster effect of the non-separatist women of Quebec, who upon being slurred by a provincial cabinet minister rallied to the Canadian cause with unabated enthusiasm.

Voices of eloquence and reason, fear and paranoia come blaring through. So too does the voice of absurdity, and never more ludicrously than in a boxing match contested by two beefy, over-aged representatives of the "Yes" and "No" options.

That Mignault dramatically sustains the tension throughout and has done a yeoman's job in culling footage is amply evident, but the question really is whether or not Quebecers will want to relive this painful period. The raging political fires of five years ago barely flicker today. On a global level, it remains to be seen if audiences will be at all aroused by this ongoing Quebec-Canada fracas. — *Bro.*

---

90 Days
(CANADIAN-COLOR)

Montreal, Aug. 25.
Produced by the National Film Board of Canada. Executive producer, Andy Thomson. Directed by Giles Walker. Written and co-produced by Giles Walker and David Wilson. Features entire cast. Camera (color), Andrew Kitzanuk; editor, David Wilson; sound editor, Bill Graziadei; music editor, Diane Le Floc'h; original music, Richard Gresko; music recording, Louis Hone. Reviewed at Montreal World Film Festival (Parisien), Aug. 24, 1985. Running time: **99 MINS.**
Blue .... Stefan Wodoslawsky
Hyang-Sook .... Christine Pak
Alex .... Sam Grana
Laura .... Fernanda Tavares

The firing line of the men's liberation movement seems to be in Canada, where two young Quebec filmmakers have struck their second blow for their sex with this year's feature follow-up to last year's "The Masculine Mystique."

Cashing in on "Masculine Mystique's" clever idea of a men's therapy group, pic has abandoned group grope for a focused story of two men, one an irretrievable Don Juan and the other a sensitive male needing to give with no prospects of someone taking all of him. Stefan Wodoslawsky as Blue leads an alarmingly well-ordered life, but is so tender that he resorts to shopping for a mate in a Korean catalog. His buddy Alex, whose wife has thrown him and his golf clubs out, is intrigued at Blue's mating list, but contrary to the principles of sharing, men's libber Blue tries to shoo him away.

Alex' persistence in pursuing relationships reflects the triumph of optimism over experience, or he's simply too arrogant to know he's not wanted. Approached by a woman who has selected him for a mysterious client in need of healthy sperm, Alex is shocked she is more interested in his sperm count than his human potential, wherever that is.

Christina Pak plays Blue's mail-order bride with such candid charm that she takes the character beyond the confines of the catalog. She is oriental and even does windows, but she shows that she has seen the world and wants her share of it. Blue has 90 days to decide to marry her, and she perceives his "to flee or not to flee" tactics early enough to decide to leave him. There ensues a happy ending with Blue and Hyang-Sook marrying and Alex proving to have an astounding sperm count. So much for liberation.

Director Giles Walker has kept the performances toned down to quiet comedy, so that the actors deliver their one-liners with the naturalness of well-trained actors, although they are, for the most part, amateurs. Ensemble's nerd-like qualities make them seem quite normal in the fairly outrageous situations they have created for themselves. Their lethargy is convincing within a tightly paced, zippy comedy. The lensing and technical credits are workmanlike, but the soundtrack features some brilliantly matted musical numbers for the individual sequences. A big hit at the Montreal festival, pic could be a boxoffice bonanza on the art-house circuit, if handled as a discovery. —Kaja.

Timing
(CANADIAN-COLOR)

Montreal, Sept. 2.
A Hania production. Produced by Eric Weinthal, Miles Dale. Written, directed and edited by Weinthal. Features entire cast. Camera (color), Keith Hlady; sets, Andrew Stearn; music, James Dale; sound, David Taylor. Reviewed at World Film Festival, Montreal, Aug. 31, 1985. Running time: 73 MINS.
Diane . . . . Heather-Lynne Meacock
Jeff . . . . Eric Weinthal
The Blonde . . . . Alice Lafleche
Friend . . . . Tom Melissis
Also with: Nancy Merritt Bell, Michael Kopsa.

———

A first feature for Eric Weinthal, who co-produced, directed, plays the leading role, scripted, edited, wrote the song and probably made the coffee, "Timing" is as predictable and familiar as it is charmless.

Weinthal plays a student actor who falls for a divorced actress. They live together for nine months, then split when she gets offered work in L.A. Sometime later they're reunited when they're cast in the leads in a production of "Romeo And Juliet."

Despite all the footage given over to students practising the art of acting, the performances on display here are uniformly weak. So is the by-the-numbers scripting and the tentative, plodding direction. If a film like this is going to work, the audience must care about and feel for the characters. This couple is simply too dull to bother about.

Only plus is the brief running time. This case of bad "Timing" is the kind of pic that has, in the past, given Canadian cinema a bad name. Commercial possibilities are zero. —Strat.

L'Araignée de Satin
(The Satin Spider)
(FRENCH-COLOR)

Montreal, Sept. 2.
A Baraka production. Produced by Louis Duchesne. Written and directed by Jacques Baratier, from "Les Detraquées" by P.L. Palau, P. Tjiery. Features entire cast. Camera (color), Roger Fellous; editor, Marie-Ange Baratier, Danielle Fillios; music, Bruno Gillet; sound, Jean-Philippe Le Roux; sets, Guenole Azerthiope; costumes, Eve-Marie Arnaud. Reviewed at World Film Festival, Montreal, Aug. 31, 1985. Running time: 86 MINS.
Solange . . . . Catherine Jourdan
Marthe . . . . Ingrid Caven
Lucienne . . . . Alexandra Sycluna
Also with: Michel Albertini, Daniel Mesguich, Roland Topor, Diane Deriaz, Fanny Bastien, Michèle Guigon, Alexandra Masbou, Jacques Baratier.

———

Jacques Baratier, who once upon a time directed some excellent films ("Goha" in 1958, "La Poupée" in 1962) enters Walerian Borowczyk territory with "The Satin Spider," a turgid, fatuous entry about lesbians in a girls' boarding school in the twenties.

The headmistress (Ingrid Caven) of a school populated entirely by beautiful, voluptuous and scantily-clad young women is impatiently awaiting the return from a psychiatric hospital of her lover, Solange (Catherine Jourdan), a drug addict with strange phobias. Meanwhile, the school's most beautiful pupil, Lucienne (Alexandra Sycluna), who has mysteriously disappeared, returns accompanied by a policeman. The cop sticks around, expecting trouble, and sure enough Lucienne is eventually strangled.

None of this is very interesting, despite an intrinsically intriguing premise, a clutch of beautiful young actresses, some nudity and a general air of decadence. The dialog is so filled with pretentious clichés it had the Montreal fest audience rolling in the aisles, and the deadly serious actors, faced with impossible material, can do nothing but emote. Visually the film, blown up from 16m, is very grainy but oddly beautiful.

Baratier himself plays the small role of an elderly servant in the strange establishment. —Strat.

Visage de chien
(Dogface)
(FRENCH-COLOR)

Montreal, Aug. 28.
Produced by JPC & Co. Directed by Jacek Gasiorowski. Screenplay, Gasiorowski. Dialog by Jacques Labas. Camera (color), Gerard Grenier; editor, Tamara Pappe; sound, Piotr Zawadski; music, Didier Vasseur; artistic advisor, Andrzej Wajda. Reviewed at Montreal World Film Festival (Parisien 5), Aug. 27, 1985. Running time: 82 MINS.
Denis . . . . Hugues Quester
Monqiue . . . . Anne Alvaro
Pierrot . . . . Pierre Champenois
Also with: Roland Blanche, Jacques Dumur, Serge Lemkin, Gerard Lorin, Martin Trevieres, Jacques Vincey.

———

Distinguished by the prize in the "Perspectives du cinema francais" at Cannes and the artistic advice or virtual guarantee of status by Andrzej Wajda, "Dogface" reflects good directorial talent, but remains too artistic for easy marketing.

Full of Parisian locations and breathless movement, it has an urgency that makes sense of the protagonist's frenetic attempt to collect on debts and the perspective of a young boy to link together the vignettes.

Denis is an unemployed designer and part-time drug drealer forced into a one-day suicide mission while concurrently spending time with his eight-year-old son, Pierrot. His suppliers have put the heat on and given him until sundown to pay them off. His odyssey through the underground to collect from his own clients delivers confrontations with well-played and curiously universal types. Another dealer/musician, a Vietnamese girl on heroin, a trip to a morgue, fast-talking his way into a fast-food joint, a strange encounter with a man who seems intent on buying his drawings, if not his son, all make for a quick-paced, desperate search.

Hugues Quester is extremely good as the dealer-by-default with a soul to lose along with his life, if he doesn't succeed. Pierrot, given a delicate turn as an unwilling accomplice by young Pierre Champenois, watches his father fail, and through his eyes comes compassion. The secondary roles are well-cast with regulars from French cinema.

Polish-born Jacek Gasiorowski was an assistant on Wajda's "Danton," has worked with the other major Polish directors, and became a member of unit "X" before it was disbanded. His first feature shows the marks of recent Polish cinema's love affair with the low-budget thriller. Despite the budget, lensing is sharp and sensitive to the hide-and-seek situations of the story, and the editing tight enough to make Pierrot's observations of his father come through as an awakening to a brutal and truly seedy world. —Kaja.

Baryton
(The Baritone)
(POLISH-COLOR)

Montreal, Aug. 27.
A Perspektywa Film Unit of Polish Corporation for Film production. Directed by Janusz Zaorski. Stars Zbigniew Zapasiewicz. Screenplay, Feliks Falk; camera (color), Witold Adamek; music, Jerzy Satanowski; production design, Allan Starski; sound, Danuta Zankowska; editor, Halina Prugar-Ketling; production manager, Barbara Pec-Slesicka. Reviewed at World Film Festival, Montreal (In Competition), Aug. 26, 1985. Running time: 95 MINS.
Antonio Taviatini . . . Zbigniew Zapasiewicz
Artur Netz . . . . Piotr Fronczewski
Sophie . . . . Malgorzata Pieczynska
Stella Stern . . . . Zofia Saretok
Leon Stern . . . . Aleksander Bardini
Froelich . . . . Jan Englert
Steinkeller . . . . Janusz Bylczynski
Leonardo . . . . Marcin Tronski

———

Feliks Falk, one of Poland's best writer-directors, scripted but did not helm "Baritone," Poland's entry in the Montreal Fest competition. Under Janusz Zaorski's rather surface direction, pic emerges as a busy soap-opera set in Poland in 1933, just as Hitler was coming to power in Germany.

Zbigniew Zapasiewicz plays a famous Polish singer who's been abroad for 25 years. He returns to his home town, accompanied by his faithless third wife, scheming, ambitious private secretary, and a hefty entourage. They all check into a plush hotel, where almost all the film's action unfolds, and the stage is set for plenty of plotting against the maestro by his employees and his family.

The baritone is using his own funds to build an opera house in Strasburg; the private secretary (Piotr Fronczewski) will stop at nothing to get the job of opera house director, even stooping to blackmail. Meanwhile the singer's wife is having an affair with Fronczewski, his business manager is absconding with the funds, and to top it all the poor man loses his voice just prior to his home town performance.

Background to all this is encroaching fascism and fascist methods (the singer's hotel room is being bugged) and it's no surprise that at the end the control of the baritone's destiny falls into the hands of the most devious character in the film, a German. Solid acting, fine production design and quality lensing make for an agreeable, if ultimately none too significant, picture. Maybe the handling needed a touch more irony.—*Strat.*

Racetrack
(U.S.-DOCU-B&W)

Montreal, Aug. 31.

A Zipporah Films production. Produced, directed and edited by Frederick Wiseman; Camera (b&w), John Davey; sound, Wiseman. Reviewed at Montreal World Film Festival, Aug. 26, 1985. Running time: **111 MINS.**

Documentary filmmakers are invariably drawn to the spectacular for film fodder and occasionally emerge with the pedestrian. Frederick Wiseman, arguably North America's greatest documentarist, is, by contrast, drawn to the seemingly pedestrian and invariable emerges with the spectacular.

Wiseman has set his sharp focus on all facets and foibles of the thoroughbred racing world in "Racetrack."

Utilizing the same modus operandi, no narrative voice-over, unobtrusive placement of his cameras (to the extent they appear hidden) and shooting in stark black-and-white, Wiseman doesn't miss much in this quasi-probe. From conception to creation to a first-place finish at the coveted Belmont Stakes, he makes the viewer acutely aware that these steeds are definitely not destined for the inside of an Alpo can.

To complete the picture, Wiseman also trains his cameras on the folks who make their daily bread with these prized beasts, everyone from the grooms and jockeys to the eccentric owners and legions of starry-eyed bettors camped in the always littered bleachers.

It's the little whimsical touches that put everything in perspective: the minister of the local racing chapel who admonishes his flock to seek the sort of spiritual pleasure which is not a 50-to-1 longshot coming home in the stretch, and to put God first, and presumably not in Place or Show.

The bottom line is, of course,

winning and those wondrous clichés: the joy of winning and the agony of defeat (and for the horses, them aching hooves). And Wiseman is again in the proverbial money.

Minor technical lapses are evident and understandable considering Wiseman's budgetary constraints, but occasional graininess of image shouldn't detract. Perhaps this could be the Wiseman pic to open previously locked distribution doors. — *Bro.*

On Ne Meurt Que 2 Fois
(You Only Die Twice)
(FRENCH-COLOR)

Montreal, Aug. 28.

A Swanie Production. Produced by Norbert Saada. Directed by Jacques Deray. Stars Michel Serrault, Charlotte Rampling. Script, Michel Audiard, from the novel by Robin Cook; camera (Eastmancolor), J. Penzer; music, Claude Bolling; sound, Pierre Lanoir; editor, Henri Lanoe; art director, François de Lamothe. Reviewed at World Film Festival, Montreal (In Competition), Aug. 27, 1985. Running time: **105 MINS.**

Inspector Staniland .... Michel Serrault
Barbara Spark .... Charlotte Rampling
Margo Berliner ...... Elisabeth Depardieu
With: Xavier Deluc, Riton Liebman, Julie Jezequel, Gerard Darmon, Jean-Pierre Bacri.

Jacques Deray has made a number of thrillers over the years, none with the same commercial clout as "Borsalino" (1969). His latest won't set boxoffice records either, but it's one of his best films, a cool, cunning policier, adapted by the late Michel Audiard from a book by Robin Cook.

The body of a pianist is found savagely beaten and dumped on a railroad track. The unconventional Inspector Staniland discovers in the dead man's apartment a stack of audio tapes in which the victim poured out his love for certain Barbara, for whom he left his wife. Barbara arrives at the apartment and almost immediately confesses to the murder; the intrigued and attracted Staniland doesn't believe her.

The investigation continues with suspicion pointed at various characters, including an unstable young tough, a devious photographer, and Barbara's estranged husband. But, inexorably, Staniland finds himself drawn to the enigmatic Barbara, and before long they're having a passionate affair, and the cop begins to realize he's stepped into the shoes of the victim.

Core of the film is another beautifully-timed performance by Michel Serrault as the questing, lusting, unconventional cop. This fine actor, the mainstay of many a French film since he soared in popularity with his "female" role in "La Cage Aux Folles," is perfect as Staniland. Charlotte Rampling's brand of off-hand sexuality is becoming a little familiar by now, but

she has a certain presence in her femme fatale role.

Crisply directed, well shot, and with a fine jazzy score by Claude Bolling, this engaging thriller (whose alternative English title is "He Died With His Eyes Open") is, basically, a formula whodunit; but thanks to the wit of its dialog and its central performance it improves on the formula and comes up shining.
—*Strat.*

Vaudeville
(FRENCH-B&W)

Montreal, Sept. 2.

A Films du Chantier Production, assisted by the Ministry of Culture. Produced, written and directed by Jean Marboeuf. Features entire cast. Camera, (b&w), G. Simon; sets, J. Clement; editor, A.F. Lebrun; music, Sylvain Kassap; sound, C. Coiffier. Reviewed at World Film Festival, Montreal, Aug. 30, 1985. Running time: **89 MINS.**

Madeleine .... Marie-Christine Barrault
Gaston .... Guy Marchand
Victor .... Roland Giraud
Pierre .... Jean-Marc Thibault
Yvette .... Annie Jouzier

It's the discovery of an unheralded little gem like "Vaudeville" that makes festival-going worthwhile. Overlooked for all sections at Cannes, and passed by other fests held since, "Vaudeville" is a modest, cool, amusing item, along classical lines, which affords plenty of pleasure. All credit to Montreal fest for giving it some attention.

Gaston (Guy Marchand) and Victor (Roland Giraud) work at the same department store, and are firm friends. Gaston has been married for twenty years to the lovely, caring Madeleine (Marie-Christine Barrault), while Victor is a bachelor ceaselessly seeking new sexual partners, bringing his pal stories of one exciting conquest after another. Needless to say, the domesticated Gaston is painfully jealous of Victor while Victor himself yearns for domesticity and stability. In contrast there's Pierre (Jean-Marc Thibault), Gaston's older brother. He has a sexy younger wife, Yvette (Annie Jouzier), but is wracked with jealously as he suspects she's cheating on him. She is, with Victor among others, and when she's hit by a bus while hurrying home from an assignation, Pierre is as affected by the fact that she wasn't wearing panties at the time as he is by her death.

Eventually, Madeleine — who needs a little romance in her life too — ankles, leaving Gaston the opportunities to play the field and follow his dictum that "Man is a hunter." Needless to say, it's no more successful for him than it was when he was married. Victor tries to change his ways, too, but to no avail.

"Vaudeville" is quietly amusing

throughout, with sharp dialog, wry situations and a bitter-sweet mood that doesn't cloy but which reveals a lot about the sexual hang-ups of its quintet of characters. Acting is perfection, starting with Marie-Christine Barrault as the loyal, but frustrated, wife, Guy Marchand as the absurdly twitchy husband, and Roland Giraud as the rather gross womaniser, whose perfect woman, he says, would have "the boobs of Liz Taylor, the legs of Cyd Charisse, the wiggle of Monroe — and the smile of Michel Simon," a line sure to amuse those who remember the last named, the late actor not known for his good looks.

In all, an old-style film in the best sense, one that has plenty to recommend it. It should be checked out by upcoming fests, and art house distribs should also take a look.
— *Strat.*

Permeke
(BELGIAN-COLOR)

Montreal, Aug. 27.

Produced by Iblis Films. Produced by Pierre Drouot. Directed by Henri Storck and Patrick Conrad. Screenplay, Conrad, Drouot, Storck; camera (color), Marc Koninckx, Gilberto Azevedo; editor, Ton De Graaff; music, John Surman, David Darling; set design, Alain Negre, Yvan Bruyere; sound, Dominique Warnier. Reviewed at Montreal World Film Festival (Parisien), Aug. 26, 1985. Running time: **92 MINS.**

With: Ilse Uitterlinden and Paul Steenbergen.

An art film about the painter Constant Permeke, pic attempts to straddle the art docu and the avant-garde and loses its footing. A 28-year-old photographer Anna plays herself on a quest for the real Permeke, making a pilgrimage to every location he himself had ever set foot on in France, Belgium and England as he layed the foundations for Flemish expressionism in the first decades of this century.

Framed by Anna in a sequined dress recalling her own aesthetic struggles in conversation with a man in a tux, the pic is burdened by its own self-consciousness. It does, however, bring to light a rather obscure painter and reveals his work with precision while reliving his life through dramatic recreations, such as his grand gesture of casting his canvases into the sea when they dissatisfied him — "a sacrifice worthy of the ancients," as it is called.

Good archival footage of James Ensor accompanies the account of Permeke's friendship with that English artist. In another sequence, the canvases burst into flame, a symbol of the spontaneous combustion of that artistic movement, and the image of an elusive coach being pushed into the darkness finally turns out to be a painting Permeke produced.

The dreams of the art historian tend to eclipse the importance of the work under discussion, as the docu has the irritating habit of foregrounding its obsession with itself as an art film instead of a film about art. An intriguing score gently sets the moods, and it should make its mark in museums where informed audiences will appreciate it. Technical credits are tops and stunning images speak for the craftsmanship invested here. —*Kaja.*

Babel Opera, ou La Repetition De Don Juan
(Babel Opera, or The Rehearsal Of Don Juan)
(BELGIAN-COLOR)

Montreal, Aug. 30.
A Nouvelle-Imagerie s.a. production. Produced by Jean-Claude Batz. Directed by André Delvaux. Features entire cast. Screenplay, Denise Debbaut, Jacques Sojcher, Delvaux; camera (Fujicolor), Michel Baudour; sound (Dolby stereo), Henri Morelle, André Defossez; editor, Albert Jurgenson, assistant director, Susi Rossberg; production manager, Jacqueline Louis. Reviewed at World Film Festival, Montreal (In Competition), Aug. 29, 1985. Running time: 94 MINS.
François . . . . .François Beukelaers
Stéphane . . . . .Stéphane Escoffier
Sandra . . . . .Alexandra Vandernoot
Ben .Ben Van Ostade
Jacques . . . . .Jacques Sojcher
The Singers
Don Giovanni . . . . .José van Dam
Il Commendatore . . . . .Pierre Thau
Donna Anna . . . . .Ashley Putnam
Don Ottavio . . . . .Stuart Burrows
Donna Elvira . . . . . . .Christiane Eda-Pierre

The latest film from Belgium's best known director is, as the title suggests, built around preparations for a performance of Mozart's Don Giovanni at the splendid old Theatre Royal de la Monnaie in Brussels. As the rehearsals get underway, characters involved on the periphery of the production act out roles similar to those in the opera itself.

François, who is planning an ambitious open-air production of the opera, is married to the charming Sandra, but his womanizing ways are driving a wedge between them. When he starts an attempted conquest of Stéphane, Sandra is enraged, as is François' assistant, Ben, who is in love with Stéphane himself.

The interaction between the (rather slight) real-life drama and the opera is not an especially original idea, but Delvaux through his immaculate imagery brings an extra dimension to the piece. The misty, slightly sinister countryside north of Antwerp, where François goes to seek locations for his production, becomes a major element in the film itself. Perhaps this is a film that could only be made in Belgium, where the spreading of urban communities threatens what's left of some of Europe's loveliest and most mysterious countryside.

Visually and aurally (with an excellent Dolby stereo mix), the film is impeccable. It's a mood piece which may move too slowly for many, but those who surrender to its style will be well rewarded.

This may be the first feature ever financed by a lottery. Pic was funded by the Loterie Nationale de Belgique to celebrate its 50th anniversary, a charming idea and one rewarded by a scene in which one character buys a lottery ticket. He doesn't win. — *Strat.*

La Moitié de l'amour
(Half Of Love)
(BELGIAN-COLOR)

Montreal, Aug. 30.
Produced by Les Productions de la Phalene and La Communaute Française de Belgique. Produced by Carole Courtoy. Directed by Mary Jimenez. Screenplay, Jimenez; camera (color), Michel Houssiau, Raymond Fromond; editor, Jacqueline Lecompte, France Duez; music, Ramon de Herrera; sound, Henri Morelle; set design, Michette Noterman; costumes, Suzanne Van Well; special effects, Manfred Frank. Reviewed at Montreal World Film Festival (Conservatoire d'art cinematographique), Aug. 29, 1985. Running time: 95 MINS.
Yvi . . . . .Margit Carstensen
Adrian . . . . .Christopher Donnay
Alain . . . . .Patrick Bauchau
Maurice . . . . .Alexandre Von Sivers
Henriette . . . . .Carole Courtoy
Sandra . . . . .Luce Bonfanti
Emma . . . . .Nadine Castagne
Dreyer . . . . .Christian Maillet

Elegant production design and a morbidly erotic atmosphere make this psychological thriller an intriguing but marginal pic reflecting the surrealistic influence of South American literature on Peruvian helmer Jimenez, now living and working in Belgium. Margit Carstensen's fragile sneer makes her riveting in the lead, eclipsing the more melodramatic thesp tendencies of the rest of the cast.

Carstensen plays Yvi, a doctor who has developed amnesia after being wounded by a bullet in the brow. She has been confined to the Dekay Institute where she previously had a position of authority and her own following among the patients. Persisting in certain mannerisms and concerns as a doctor, she functions well enough to respond to a young man named Adrian (Christopher Donnay), who comes to find her and take her to his family's villa to recuperate. The atmosphere in his home proves to be no less bizarre than the one she has abandoned. Adrian has a sado-masochistic relationship with his domineering butler Maurice, and Yvi's presence threatens that.

A continual persecution of Yvi, Adrian and several secondary characters by criminal elements at the Institute features eruptions of bloody violence alternating with extremely stylized gangster clichés.

The prostitutes are blowsy broads, the killers lithe sadists, the victims refined while the power over all these people is wielded by a toad-like physician totally devoid of medical ethics.

The production design has the artistic flair to make for interesting images, inspired apparently by Magritte, but the melodrama of the relationships often lunges into the absurd, and one explicit shot in a bordello could lead to awkward or censorious reactions. The highly literary story is solved by Adrian two-thirds through the pic. The rest is an ethereal inquiry into selective amnesia that is quite forgettable. — *Kaja.*

Le Caviar Rouge
(Red Caviar)
(SWISS-FRENCH-COLOR)

Montreal, Aug. 28.
A Slotint SSR-Philippe Dussart production. Directed by Robert Hossein. Stars Robert Hossein, Candice Patou, Ivan Desny. Script, Hossein, Frederic Dard, from their novel; camera (color), Edmond Richard; music, Jean-Claude Petti, Claude-Michel Schonberg, with pan-pipes by Gheorghe Zamfir; editor, Sophie Bhaud; art director, Jacques D'Ovidio; sound, Jean Labussiere; production manager, George Casati. Reviewed at World Film Festival, Montreal (In Competition), Aug. 27. 1985. Running time: 91 MINS.
Alex . . . . .Robert Hossein
Nora . . . . .Candice Patou
Yuri . . . . .Ivan Desny

Robert Hossein, actor and director for both cinema and theater has come up with a clinker this time, based on a book he co-authored with Frederic Dard. It's a predictable, lethargic tale of Soviet spies setting traps for each other, and is set almost entirely in a big old house near Lake Geneva.

Alex (Hossein) and Nora (Candice Patou, making her film debut) play a former spy team who used to be lovers, but split up seven years earlier when Patou was ordered to seduce a pro-American Egyptian and get him to join the Soviet team. Now the couple is brought together again by Yuri (Ivan Desny), the Soviets' Swiss spy chief, because the Egyptian has been found murdered in Geneva. Someone evidently betrayed him, and Desny, suspecting one of the two, shuts them in a room for a night so that they can come up with the guilty party.

What follows is as predictable as it is silly, with intense acting, feeble dialog and obvious plotting leading to a ludicrous climax as the reunited lovers are gunned down on the empty streets of Geneva by the very Egyptian they thought was dead. With its almost one-set drama, pic seems like a transposed theater piece, and would certainly play better on tv than on the cinema screen, although the top quality of Edmond Richard's

cinematography, with its images of rainy, bleak Geneva, is the film's chief asset.

Hossein and Patou are merely adequate. Ivan Desny brings a tired charm to his role as the devious spy chief. — *Strat.*

Sheng Gang Qi Bing
(Red Guards In Hong Kong)
(HONG KONG-COLOR)

Montreal, Sept. 2.
A Golden Harvest release of a Johnny Mak-Bo Ho Film coproduction. Produced by Chan Pui Wah. Directed by Johnny Mak Don Hung. Features entire cast. Screenplay, Philip Chan; camera (color), Koo Kwok Wah; sets, Ho Kam Kai; editor, Cheung Yiu Chung; music, Mahmood Rumjahn; sound, Chow Kwok Hung. Reviewed at World Film Festival, Montreal, Sept. 1, 1985. Running time: 106 MINS.
With: Lam Wai, Wong Kin, Yeung Ming, Angel Lau.

"Red Guards In Hong Kong" is a violent actioner in which a group of thugs from the mainland infiltrates Hong Kong to perpetrate the robbery of a jewelry store. Not really fest fare, this is a fast-paced item which should go over well with Chinese audiences.

One member of the gang is shot and then savaged by guard dogs while trying to cross the border. The others make it, but can't go ahead with the robbery (the store is closed, having been robbed once already). So the guys hang around, enjoying sex with prosties, and become inexorably involved in a violent local gang war. Finally they rob the store, but they're all gunned down by the police before they can get back home.

The plot and characters beggar belief, but helmer Johnny Mak Don Hung stages his action scenes with some flair, especially the killing of a gangster at a skating rink and the final-reel chase through the dank back-alleys of the city. The blood-letting is overdone.

Lengthy opening explanatory titles went untranslated in the print caught. —*Strat.*

After Hours
(COLOR)

Successfully dark comedy of urban paranoia.

Hollywood, Aug. 30.

A Geffen Co. release through Warner Bros. of a Double Play production. Produced by Amy Robinson, Griffin Dunne, Robert F. Colesberry. Directed by Martin Scorsese. Screenplay, Joseph Minion. Camera (Duart color), Michael Ballhaus; editor, Thelma Schoonmaker; music, Howard Shore; production design, Jeffrey Townsend; art direction, Stephen J. Lineweaver; set decoration, Leslie Pope; costume design, Rita Ryack; sound, Chat Gunter; associate producer, Deborah Schindler; assistant director, Stephen J. Lim; casting, Mary Colquhoun. Reviewed at The Burbank Studios, Burbank, Calif., Aug. 29, 1985. (MPAA Rating: R.) Running time: **97 MINS.**

Paul Hackett	Griffin Dunne
Marcy	Rosanna Arquette
June	Verna Bloom
Pepe	Thomas Chong
Kiki	Linda Fiorentino
Julie	Teri Garr
Tom The Bartender	John Heard
Neil	Cheech Marin
Gail	Catherine O'Hara
Waiter	Dick Miller
Horst	Will Patton
Mark	Robert Plunket
Lloyd	Bronson Pinchot

The cinema of paranoia and persecution reaches an apogee in "After Hours," a nightmarish black comedy from Martin Scorsese. Something like a combination of "The Trial" and "Mean Streets," anxiety-ridden picture would have been pretty funny if it didn't play like a confirmation of everyone's worst fears about contemporary urban life. Morbid spiritual malaise on display won't be everyone's cup of tea, to be sure, but pic will be a must for serious-minded filmgoers and stands as one of the quality entries of the fall season.

A description of one rough night in the life of a mild-mannered New York computer programmer, film is structured like a "Pilgrim's Progress" through the anarchic, ever-treachous streets of SoHo. Every corner represents a turn for the worse, and by the end of the night, he's got to wonder, like Kafka's K, if he might not actually be guilty of something.

It all starts innocently enough, as Griffin Dunne gets a come-on from Rosanna Arquette and ends up visiting her in the loft of avant-garde sculptress Linda Fiorentino. Both girls turn out to be too weird for Dunne, but he can't get home for lack of cash, so he veers from one stranger to another in search of the most mundane salvation and finds nothing but trouble.

All because he thought Arquette seemed like a nice girl, Dunne ends up witnessing a murder, suspecting he's been the cause of a woman's suicide, is chased as a burglar and nearly lynched by a local vigilante squad, assaulted in a heavy-duty punk club and, in a tip of the hat from Scorsese to Roger Corman's "A Bucket Of Blood," made into a piece of living sculpture. Dick Miller, the star of that Corman film, appears here in a cameo role.

Given Dunne's uncanny resemblance to Dudley Moore and his similar mannerisms in the face of adversity, it is easy to imagine all of this being played for laughs. But it's apparent that Scorsese felt that comedy would have represented the simpler approach to the wild material in Joseph Minion's screenplay, and has rigorously denied himself plenty of easy laughs and any occasion to comfort the audience.

Strangely, for the extreme nature of the goings-on, this is undoubtedly Scorsese's quietest, least frenzied film to date. The characters rarely shout, Mozart and Bach play on the soundtrack, and many of the scenes are stylized in a way that make them seem as though they are being played in a vacuum. This creates a certain distancing odd for a Scorsese picture, but the silence also contributes to the feeling of dread, that something awful lies in wait. And it does.

This is Scorsese's first fictional film in a decade without Robert De Niro in the leading part, and Griffin Dunne, who doubled as co-producer, plays a mostly reactive role, permitting easy identification of oneself in his place.

Supporting roles have been filled by uniformly vibrant and interesting thesps, all of whom have limited screen time but make strong impressions.

With the exception of one shot in which camera tracks are visible, film is technically superb, notably Michael Ballhaus' luminous lensing, Thelma Schoonmaker's tight editing and Jeffrey Townsend's imaginative production design.
— *Cart.*

Sudden Death
(COLOR)

Weak female vigilante entry.

A Marvin Films release of a Lodestar production. Executive producer, Marvin Friedlander. Produced by Steven Shore and David Greene. Written and directed by Sig Shore. Features entire cast. Camera (Technicolor), Benjamin Davis; editor, John Tintori; music, Arthur Baker; sound, Steve Rogers, Dorielle Rogers; art direction, Charles Weaver; assistant director, Ron Gorton Jr.; unit production manager, Michael Shore; special effects-stunt coordinator, Wilfred Kaban; costume design, Rosemary Ponzo; makeup, Harvey Livingston Jr.; casting, Mary Jo Slater. Reviewed at Lorimar screening room, N.Y., Sept. 5, 1985. (MPAA Rating: R.) Running time: **90 MINS.**

Valarie Wells	Denise Coward
Det. Marty Lowery	Frank Runyeon
Willie	Jamie Tirelli
Herbert	Robert Trumbull
Peggy	Rebecca Hollen
Kosakowski	J. Kenneth Campbell
Raphael	Joe Maruzzo
Sailor	Arnold Mazer

"Sudden Death" is an unimpressive thriller likely to get okay playoff on the action circuit by virtue of its femme vigilante theme. Filmmaker Sig Shore (best-known as producer of the WB hit "Superfly") has put together commercial elements, but directed them flatly.

Denise Coward (a former Miss Australia beauty contest winner) toplines as Valarie Wells, a New York City rape victim who buys a gun and, not unlike the Charles Bronson in "Death Wish" archetype, starts hanging around in sleazy locations. Sure enough, other men try to assault her with fatal results.

Her businessman boyfriend Herbert (Robert Trumbull) is patronizing, thereby alienating her affections which are transferred to the cop on the case, Det. Lowery (Frank Runyeon). Quite improbably, when Lowery discovers she is what the press has dubbed The Dum-Dum Killer (after the lethal bullets she uses), he jumps in bed with her and later successfully covers up her guilt when closing both cases.

Low-budgeter suffers from a paucity of action, with a lengthy final reel footchase by Lowery after the rapist that is thoroughly unexciting. Coward is a looker, but her impassive, expressionless acting wins little audience sympathy. Runyeon, a tv soap opera star, looks uncomfortable in action scenes.

Though advertised as "the first female vigilante," pic actually suffers by comparison to its more stylish forerunners, "Ms. 45" and "Alley Cat." Tech credits are okay, with an emphasis on exploding bloodpacks in the various victims.
— *Lor.*

Jagged Edge
(COLOR)

Solid courtroom thriller.

Hollywood, Sept. 6.

A Columbia Pictures release of a Martin Ransohoff Prod. Produced by Martin Ransohoff. Directed by Richard Marquand. Stars Jeff Bridges, Glenn Close. Screenplay, Joe Eszterhas; camera (Metrocolor), Matthew F. Leonetti; editor, Sean Barton, Conrad Buff; music, John Barry; production design, Gene Callahan; art direction, Peter J. Smith; set design, John Warnke, Christopher Burian-Mohr, Beverli Eagan; costume design, Ann Roth; sound, Gene Cantamessa; associate producer, Michele Conners-Raley; assistant director, Michael Daves; casting, Lynn Stalmaster. Reviewed at Columbia Pictures, Sept. 6, 1985. (MPAA Rating: R.) Running time: **108 MINS.**

Jack Forrester	Jeff Bridges
Teddy Barnes	Glenn Close
Thomas Krasny	Peter Coyote
Sam Ransom	Robert Loggia
Virginia Howell	Leigh Taylor-Young
Judge Carrigan	John Dehner
Bobby Slade	Marshall Colt
Eileen Avery	Diane Erickson
Fabrizi	Louis Giambalvo
Greg Arnold	William Allen Young
David Barnes	Brandon Call

A well-crafted, hardboiled mystery by Joe Eszterhas, with sharp performances by murder suspect Jeff Bridges and tough-but-smitten defense attorney Glenn Close, "Jagged Edge" should find fans in the public jury if Columbia Pictures smartly promotes for a scheduled early October release.

Developed from a concept by producer Martin Ransohoff and helmed by Richard Marquand with some of the same illusionary surfaces he captured in "Eye Of The Needle," pic manages to really have it both ways. The intrigue is fun whether one surmises the identity of the killer midway or whether one rides out the see-saw to the bloody conclusion. Primary credit for that must go to writer Eszterhas.

In either case, the filmmakers fashion a suspenseful variation on what used to be called neighborhood programmers or, in contemporary terms, what conjures up the appearance of a nifty telefilm. The difference is the stars and the colorful support of foul-talking gumshoe Robert Loggia, corrupt, smooth district attorney Peter Coyote, and, in smaller but telling characterizations, a subtly sensual turn on the witness stand by bulbous-eyed Leigh Taylor-Young and a judge one comes to like in the robes of actor John Dehner.

The opening reel is a certified, chilly grabber, no matter how many variations of it have been seen before. In a storm-slashed, luxurious beach house, a masked man in black walks up a flight of stairs, jumps on a woman asleep on her silky sheets, whips out a serrated, jagged hunting knife — and the unspeakable (off-screen) happens.

The victim was a socialite and heiress. Her husband (Bridges), a very upwardly mobile San Francisco newspaper publisher, now owns his wife's fortune. He's boyish and rides horses and he's a charmer. He's also indicted for murder by wily and sardonic prosecutor Coyote.

Embittered by past experiences in criminal law, Close is pressed to defend Bridges, once he convinces her of his innocence. Then she falls in love with him. Triple-Oscar nominees Bridges and Close play a balancing act that is both glossy and psychologically interesting.

Courtroom drama, which is becoming increasingly hard to make work for gobs of time on the big screen, consumes perhaps 30% of this film and, for the most part, the benchmarks are compelling.

John Barry's score is unobtrusive, which is testament to the proceedings. Editors Sean Barton and Conrad Buff stitch the Bay Area lensing of Matthew Leonetti. Pace is measured, not jumpy.

Pic, in quick strokes, raises jagged questions about an imperfect justice system. Although the conflicting parameters of mother-lover-professional woman are becoming naggingly repetitive, the Close persona (unlike the Bridges character) is a fully realized and dimensional one. —Loyn.

Plenty
(COLOR)

Cold drama boasts strong Meryl Streep performance.

Hollywood, Aug. 13.

A 20th Century Fox release of an RKO Pictures presentation of an Edward R. Pressman production. Produced by Pressman, Joseph Papp. Executive producer, Mark Seiler. Directed by Fred Schepisi. Stars Meryl Streep. Screenplay, David Hare, based on his play; camera (Technicolor, Panavision), Ian Baker; editor, Peter Honess; music, Bruce Smeaton; production design, Richard Macdonald; art direction, Tony Reading, Adrian Smith (France); set decoration, Peter James; costume design, Ruth Myers; sound (Dolby), John Mitchell; associate producer, Roy Stevens; assistant director, David Tringham; casting, Mary Selway. Reviewed at the 20th Century Fox Studios, L.A., Aug. 12, 1985. (MPAA Rating: R.) Running time: **124 MINS.**

Susan Traherne	Meryl Streep
Raymond Brock	Charles Dance
Alice Park	Tracey Ullman
Sir Leonard Darwin	John Gielgud
Mick	Sting
Sir Andrew Charleson	Ian McKellen
Lazar	Sam Neill

A picture possessing a host of first-class pedigrees, "Plenty" emerges as an absorbing and fastidiously made adaptation of David Hare's acclaimed play, but also comes off as cold and ultimately unaffecting. Material holds more than enough dramatic, historical and symbolic weight for educated, upscale audiences to chew on, and prestige elements, led by star Meryl Streep, will assure considerable attention and good biz in urban openings.

Hare's ambitious drama, first staged in London in 1978 and then in New York in 1982-83, with Kate Nelligan in the lead (Blair Brown toplined a 1980 edition in Washington), charts the growing social malaise of Western Europe and, specifically, Great Britain, over the years following World War II. He does this through the character of Susan Traherne, a difficult, unsettled, neurotic young woman who moves from idealism to frustration and madness in her passage through a succession of bleak political and personal events.

Pic opens with Susan, played by Streep, involved in derring-do with the Resistance in France during the war. In the midst of all the excitement, intrigue and danger, she has a brief affair with commando Sam Neill, an event that becomes so wrapped up with her sense of optimism and hope for the future that no man can ever displace Neill from her mind.

Personally and historically, it's all downhill from there. Action is set principally in the British diplomatic world, and moves across a stage backdropped by post-war economic difficulties, Coronation Year, the Suez crisis and further developments in the Middle East.

After working in middle range business and functionary posts, and trying to conceive a child with a specially selected working class member portrayed by Sting, Streep marries career diplomat Charles Dance, creating a relationship that freezes over and finally cracks, with dire results.

Hare, who wrote the screenplay himself, has fashioned any number of sharply etched scenes, most of which reflect the deception, hypocrisy and wrongheaded moves he sees as having comprised the general mode of Western behavior after the Allied victory. Particularly memorable is a dinner party scene in which senior official John Gielgud, who has just resigned from the Foreign Office, can ill conceal his scorn for both his duplicitous superiors and the uncomprehending younger generation. This marks yet another first-rate late career supporting characterization by the octogenarian actor.

Thematically and structurally, "Plenty" bears striking parallels to one of the late Rainer Werner Fassbinder's greatest films, "The Marriage Of Maria Braun," which looks at the phenomenon of the German postwar economic miracle through the figure of an opportunistic young woman. The characters are very different, as Susan Traherne is a deeply troubled and sternly moralistic person, but many of the conceits are similar, and Fassbinder's is much the superior work.

Fred Schepisi has staged the events in a sober, stately but overly brittle manner. Given their importance, the opening action in France plays a bit awkwardly and lacks sufficient excitement, and Streep in this section appears too frosty for an idealistic 18-year-old, although she later takes command and strongly carries the picture.

Casting overall is highly disparate, with the American Streep mixing it up with distinguished stage performers Gielgud and Ian McKellen, rockers Sting and Tracey Ullman and screen newcomer Charles Dance, who made such a strong impression as Guy Peron in "The Jewel In The Crown."

As Streep's husband and a decent man of limited horizons, Dance scores with quiet authority, much in the manner of Michael Caine. Ullman is odd and lively as Streep's friend through the years. Sting shows both street smarts and a welcome vulnerability. McKellen embodies aristocratic power with icy brilliance, and Neill is fine as the heroic lover of a young girl's dreams.

Film has been most handsomely produced on locations in the U.K., Belgium, France and Tunisia, and technical contributions, notably those of lenser Ian Baker, production designer Richard Macdonald and costume designer Ruth Myers, are superior. —Cart.

Elise
(DANISH-COLOR)

Copenhagen, Sept. 3.

A Metronome release of Palle Fogtdal production (with the Danish Film Institute/Jörgen Melgard). Directed by Claus Ploug, with postproduction assistance from Henning Carlsen. Features Frits Helmuth, Ole Ernst, Ann-Mari Max Hansen. Screenplay, Mogens Rukow, based on short story by Steen Steensen Blicher; camera (Eastmancolor), Dan Lausten; production design, Sven Wickman; costumes, Jette Termann; editor, Grete Möldrup; production management, Per Arman; music, quotes from Chopin, Strauss, others. Reviewed at the Dagmar, Copenhagen, Sept. 3, 1985. Running time: **107 MINS.**

Elise	Ann-Mari Max Hansen
Her husband	Ole Ernst
The vicar	Frits Helmuth
Captain of Dragoons	Henning Jensen
Rachel, his wife	Kirsten Olesen
Vicar's wife	Anne Birch
Elise's sister	Anne-Lise Gabold
Bandleader	Peter Schröder
Housekeeper	Lene Vasegard
Anne	Lene Bröndum

"Elise" is an austere piece of cinematic chamber music scored for six characters who are seen as three married couples. It is based, by writer Mogens Rukow, on a 19th century Danish short-story classic, "Belated Awakening" by Steen Steensen Blicher, himself a vicar like the man who tells this story about the burden of one person's adultery as hurting, possibly, everybody else more than the sinner herself.

She is Elise, vivacious, talented wife of Henry, a small-town doctor. She loves Henry and she loves to sing and act in amateur theatricals (Ibsen's "A Doll's House" of course) and to play games with people. She does so with Henry, too, when they relieve provincial boredom by going off secretly to a bigger town where they set up clandestine meetings between themselves.

Accident throws her into the arms of William, a captain of dragoons. She bears William's children (he cannot have any with his wife Rachel) along with those of Henry's, she keeps up her regular secret trysts with both men without ever batting a revealing or guilty eyelash to disturb the small-town round of picnics, dinners and dances. Only Carl, the vicar, and his wife Henriette suspect what is going on, but Henriette keeps her thoughts to herself, and Carl closes out all suspicion from his mind. Until one day the bubble bursts.

Much finesse and inverted narrative technique is at display in the telling of the story as experienced mostly via the vicar's eyes, ears and mind, but occasionally also through direct or indirect exposure of his wife's and of the doctor's sensibilities.

What will make Claus Ploug's "Elise" a candidate for the festival circuit and for art-oriented international sales is that audiences will be kept guessing, deliciously, about what really makes the main protagonists tick. Is this Elise of the glossy surface and the tempestuous lovemaking actually a hardheaded innocent, or is she, unconsciously, a crusader for some kinds of Women's Lib? And is this vicar, so abject in the face of so much Sin, the biggest sinner of them all and, secretly even to himself, the spreader of the gossip that ultimately makes tragedy's cup run over? At the end, we see Elise and the vicar as the only survivors, she seemingly untouched by it all, he forever tantalized by the shadows of events.

Ole Ernst as the happy-go-lucky doctor riding for a fall and Frits Helmuth as the maybe not so innocent bystander both deliver acting of depth and discretion, while Ann-Mari Max Hansen's big-boned facial beauty radiates just the mystery of smile and gleam of eye the Elise role calls for. —Kell.

****

Venice Fest Reviews

****

The Lightship
(U.S.-COLOR)

Venice, Sept. 1.

A Warner Bros. release of a CBS Productions film. Produced by Bill Benenson and Moritz Borman. Executive producer, Rainer Söhnlein. Directed by Jerzy Skolimowski. Stars Robert Duvall and Klaus Maria Brandauer. Screenplay, William Mai, David Taylor, based on Siegfried Lenz's novel; camera (color), Charly Steinberger; sets, Holger Gross; editor, Barry Vince; music, Stanley Myers. Reviewed at Venice Film Fest (Competition), Sept. 1, 1985. Running time: **89 MINS.**

Caspary	Robert Duvall
Captain Miller	Klaus Maria Brandauer

Coop . . . . Tom Bower
Stump . . . . Robert Costanzo
Nate . . . . Badja Djola
Gene . . . . William Forsythe
Eddie . . . . Arliss Howard
Alex . . . . Michael Lyndon
Thorne . . . . Tim Phillips

Jerzy Skolimowski's "The Lightship" is based on a well-known novella by the highly regarded German writer Siegfried Lenz. It was filmed in West Germany on the island of Sylt with an all English-speaking cast, the story transferred from its North Sea setting to the coastal waters off Norfolk. The setting is the only seaworthy lightship left, and it's on this precarious wreck that everything takes place. That thematic element alone makes the film well worth the viewing time.

The other major plus is the acting duel between Robert Duvall and Klaus Maria Brandauer, both with thespian styles of their own and in direct contrast to each other. Since the roles of the hijacker Caspary and the Coast Guard captain Miller had to be switched before shooting began, one senses a battle of wits all the way down the line. Further, Skolimowski is notorious for improvisation himself, so the script reportedly went through three changes — in addition to adding a saving narrative commentary on the editing table.

Captain Miller (Brandauer) suffers from severe pangs of conscience. A German-born American, he served in the U.S. Navy during World War II as the commander of a destroyer. During a submarine attack, he went after the U-Boat to sink it at the cost of picking up American survivors in the open sea, who later drowned.

Although he made a correct military decision and was exonerated in an investigation, the assignment on the lightship now seems to be the end of his career. Further, he breaks naval traditions by bringing his high-school son on board one evening just to save the latter from being thrown into jail for a minor offense. The son comments on the events as they happen.

The lightship picks up a boat on the open sea just as a storm is approaching and is promptly hijacked by a trio of psychopathic crooks led by a New Orleans wag named Caspary (Duvall). Duvall was to rendezvous with a contact ship in the vicinity (a drug shipment?), and now decides to wait it out on the lightship until the storm passes. The rest is the showdown between the crew and the hoods.

As a psychological thriller, "The Lightship" has its tense entertainment moments, but the narrative line takes so many detours that the problem is trying to figure out the non sequiturs as they surface out of nowhere. Those film buffs who appreciate Skolimowski's finesse in patching on a cutting table should appreciate the results more than the average arthouse clientele. The rest will enjoy the acting of Duvall and Brandauer in a game of mutually enjoyable oneupsmanship.

A lightship offers some room for metaphorical interpretation of both the story and the characters. Seen from novelist Lenz's viewpoint, one can sense a threat to the social fabric. Viewed from the psycho-thriller aspect, however, this has about as much sociopolitical reference as John Huston's 1948 "Key Largo," with which "The Lighthouse" bears a remarkable thematic resemblance.

Pic might get arthouse legs with proper handling. Duvall's savvy thespian nuances are a delight.
—*Holl.*

Pervola
(Tracks In The Snow)
(DUTCH-COLOR)

Venice, Sept. 4.
A Maya Film production, Amsterdam. Produced by Jan Kaandorp. Executive producers, Jan Musch, Orlow Seunke, Tys Tinbergen. Directed by Orlow Seunke. Features entire cast. Screenplay, Seunke, Dirk Avelt Kooiman, in collaboration with Maarten Koopman and Gerard Thoolen; camera (color), Theo Bierkens; special effects, Peter Borgli; sets, Misjel Vermeire; costumes, An Verhoeven; editor, Seujke; music, Koopman; sound, George Bossaers. Reviewed at Venice Film Fest (Competition), Sept. 4, 1985. Running time: **95 MINS.**
With: Gerard Thoolen (Simon von Oyen), Hein van der Vlugt (Hein van Oyen), Melle van Essen (Aapo), Jan Willem Hees (Van Oyen, Sr.), Thom Hoffman (Ron), Jaap Hoogstra (Olga), Brigitte Kaandorp (Truusje), Phons Leussink (Adelaar).

After scoring at Venice three years ago with "A Taste Of Water," Dutch helmer Orlow Seunke is back with an equally impressive entry in the Lido sweepstakes: "Pervola" (Tracks In The Snow).

This is the story of two brothers at odds with each other. A successful stockbroker goes into early retirement, intending to turn over his company and fortune to his two sons on an equal-share basis. However, Hein dupes his brother Simon into believing that his father has disinherited him, so Simon lives an impoverished existence as a variety entertainer. Then comes the news from the "far north" (Norway was the location setting) that the father is about to die. Simon hastens there to seek reconciliation with his father, Hein to prevent his brother from ever learning the truth about the fraud.

In the arctic north, the father dies as expected in the arms of the clever Hein before Simon can reach him to beg forgiveness. However, the father requests in his dying breath to be buried even farther north in the isolated village of Pervola, a place associated with his late wife. So Simon is determined to honor this last wish, while Hein goes along just to be sure that his brother never finds out the deception by some accident.

Along the way, Simon does stumble on the truth due to his brother's own clumsiness in seeking to hide the matter. As a result a quarrel takes place, and Simon begins to discover his inner strength while Hein his inherent weakness. Since the journey is also extremely difficult in the dead of winter, "Pervola" becomes a thriller of sorts as the two brothers are not only pitted against each other, but also struggle to survive against the harsh elements.

The twist at the end not only offers reconciliation between the two brothers, but also comments on how life can be changed via such a confrontation with the real self.

Credits are tops, and with proper handling pic has solid offshore chances. —*Holl.*

Echo Park
(AUSTRIAN-COLOR)

Venice, Sept. 4.
A Sasha-Wien Film, Vienna. Produced by Walter Shenson. Directed by Robert Dornhelm. Features entire cast. Screenplay, Michael Ventura; camera (color), Karl Kofler; editor, Ingrid Koller; music, David Rickets; musical consultant, Bill Wyman. Reviewed at Venice Film Fest ("Venice Youth" section), Sept. 3, 1985. Running time: **92 MINS.**
May . . . . Susan Dey
Jonathan . . . . Thomas Hulce
August . . . . Michael Bowen
Henry . . . . Christopher Walker
Gloria . . . . Shirley Jo Finney
August's father . . . . Heinrich Schweiger
Hugo . . . . John Paragon
Sid . . . . Richard Marin
Sheri . . . . Cassandra Peterson

Although lensed on location in Echo Park section of Los Angeles, both the greater part (three-quarters) of its financing and the director come from Austria — so "Echo Park" (like Wim Wenders' "Paris, Texas") is another of those quite successful views of the States made by talented European directors. Helmer Robert Dornhelm received an Oscar nomation for his "The Children Of Theater Street" (1977), which first brought him Stateside. Then he made "She Dances Alone" in and around San Francisco, a prizewinner that bowed at Cannes in 1981.

Now, with "Echo Park," he's hit pay dirt, as pic should do well on the independent feature circuit with proper handling. On the Lido it scored in the "Venice Youth" section, and is reportedly headed for Deauville and the London fest.

Wittily scripted and full of oddball twists from start to finish, "Echo Park" features three hapless people looking for the big break as they share an old-style duplex-apartment house in the rundown area of East Los Angeles. May works as a waitress while dreaming of an acting career, but she also has to take care of her eight-year-old son Henry (who's growing up fast and can't be fooled anymore about the facts of life and his own mother's sexual promiscuity).

Next door to her lives August, a body-builder from Austria who wants to become the second Arnold Schwarzenegger. He's always thinking up ways to revolutionize the body-building business with home-made, questionable scientific techniques relating muscle and adrenalin to sexual orgasm. One night, he and May enjoy a mutual wrestling match, then she decides it's too risky to roll in the hay with a neighboring border.

May needs a tenant in her own flat to meet the payments, and this turns out to be the friendly pizza delivery boy, Jonathan, who reads books and writes poetry. Jonathan falls in love with May while trying to help her out on the side and playing the surrogate father to Henry. May wants to respond, but doesn't want to give up her dreams.

If all of this sounds vaguely like Nathaniel West's "Day Of The Locust," well, no matter. Helmer Dornhelm has a vision of his own. May takes to delivering birthday-party stripteases in order to improve her status in L.A. and give up the waitress job. August gets a job doing a viking strongman act for a tv spray can ad, but he goes crazy on the job one day when he realizes that his employer has been stringing him along all the while as he goes from one goofy body-building gimmick to another.

The best gag of all has Jonathan — played by Tom Hulce of "Amadeus" fame-playing around with a ditty for a recording company, then telling his more than interested listeners that "it's not ready yet." Jonathan prefers rolling with life's punches, rather than struggling upstream like his two friends.

In the end, May gets an offer to do a tv commercial as well, so she feels she's on her way up. Played by Susan Dey, it's a firstclass performance in a role cut snugly to her talent. Ditto for Hulce as Jonathan and Michael Bowen as August.
— *Holl.*

Turtle Diary
(BRITISH-COLOR)

Hollywood, Sept. 10.
A Samuel Goldwyn Co. (U.S.) release of a CBS Theatrical Films presentation of a United British Artists/Britannic production. Produced by Richard Johnson. Executive producer, Peter Snell. Directed by John Irvin. Stars Glenda Jackson, Ben Kingsley. Screenplay, Harold Pinter, based on the novel by Russell Hoban; camera (Technicolor), Peter Hannan; editor, Peter Tanner; music, Geoffrey Burgon; productin design, Leo Austin;

art direction, Diane Danklefsen, Judith Ariadne Lang; costume design, Elizabeth Waller; sound (Dolby), David Hildyard; assistant director, Michael Zimbrich; casting, Susie Figgis. Reviewed at the Samuel Goldwyn screening room, L.A., Sept. 9, 1985. (No MPAA Rating). Running time: **97 MINS.**

Neaera Duncan	Glenda Jackson
William Snow	Ben Kingsley
Mr. Johnson	Richard Johnson
George Fairbairn	Michael Gambon
Mrs. Incheliff	Rosemary Leach
Miss Neap	Eleanor Bron
Harriet	Harriet Walter
Sandor	Jeroen Krabbe
Publisher	Nigel Hawthorne
Mr. Meager	Michael Aldridge

Audiences hungry for a witty, well-spoken, ultra-civilized entertainment will be amply provided for by "Turtle Diary," a wonderfully eccentric British picture starring Oscar winners Glenda Jackson and Ben Kingsley as two misfits bent upon rescuing sea turtles from their imprisonment at the London Zoo. Gentle, unassuming and always slyly observant, film obviously wasn't made for the mass public, but will appeal strongly to the art house crowd and viewers interested in Harold Pinter, who penned the delicious screenplay. Domestic distrib The Samuel Goldwyn Co. should know how to zero in on the appropriate target audience for good results upon release early next year. Pic preemed Tuesday (10) at the Toronto Film Festival.

Principal subject of the comic drama fits in neatly with current concern about captive animals (something especially pervasive in the U.K.), but this is far from a "cause" problem picture. Love of turtles is merely the one odd obsession that draws strangers Jackson and Kingsley together. Throughout, Pinter sketches wonderful quick portraits of a number of offbeat, lonely individuals who are connected by the most fragile of lines, and in the process creates a subtle but telling picture of frugal, middle-class London life.

Kingsley, who works in a bookshop, and Jackson, the author of animal-oriented children's books, are presented as being among the world's meeker, more reticent citizens, and one of Pinter's impressive coups is his demonstration of how even these painfully repressed, unassertive folks become terrorists of a sort.

With the collusion of the zoo's aquarium keeper, the two self-described "turtle freaks," who have virtually nothing else in common and never pursue anything resembling a romance, ever-so-quietly scheme to spirit three large turtles out of their confinement and off to the seashore, from where they can return to their natural environment.

That this simple, subversive act may be the most satisfying thing either of them has ever done is clear but never spoken, and Pinter at all times avoids the sentimental clichés of virtually all animal-lover stories.

On one level, the film represents a splendidly amusing treatise on the vagaries of apartment living. Jackson's sole pet is a water beetle, and her across-the-hall neighbor, portrayed by vet actor and the film's producer Richard Johnson, is a man of many secrets, while Kingsley shares a small apartment building with an assortment of real misfits, including the pathetically lonely Eleanor Bron and a hulking slob, Jeroen Krabbe.

Kingsley allows himself to be casually seduced by fellow bookstore employee Harriet Walter, and it falls to her to take the outsider's view of incomprehension that anyone could be interested in turtles, much less devoting oneself to their cause.

In adapting Russell Hoban's novel to the screen, Pinter proves himself as alert as ever to the comedy and subtext of banal conversation; author also puts in a cameo as a bookshop customer.

Director John Irvin has served the unusual material well by concentrating on performances and the background touches that help it all come alive.

As he did in "Betrayal," Ben Kingsley asserts himself as the peerless Pinter actor. His razor-sharp delivery, meaning-laden vocal nuances and frequently funny glances make him a thoroughgoing delight, and his performance is the centerpiece of the picture. Glenda Jackson has rather less to do and fewer people to interact with, but creates an unusual, for her, characterization of an unnecessarily withdrawn woman who comes out of her shell only with difficulty.

The whole story, indeed, is about how these two unlikely creatures emerge, however briefly, from their protective coverings to accomplish something they consider worth doing. Handsomely produced in all regards, film is a special treat for specialized audiences. —*Cart.*

Naked Spaces
(WEST AFRICAN-U.S.-DOCU-COLOR)

Toronto, Sept. 7.
Produced by Jean-Paul Bourdier. Directed and written by Trinh T. Minh-ha. Camera (color), editor, Minh-ha; assistance, Bourdier. Reviewed at the Toronto Festival of Festivals (Varsity), Sept. 6, 1985. Running time: **134 MINS.**

Avant-garde director Trinh T. Minh-ha is known for the clarity and elegance of her camerawork, which serves her tour of West Africa quite well. At a prohibitive length, she enters into the intimate domestic lives within the tribes of six African countries, documenting their architecture, rituals and peaceable village life. A narrative full of poetic pronouncements mourns the loss of traditions and argues that the word primitive is misapplied to tribal life.

The importance of the music to village life is translated to the film, where the hypnotic steady beat unifies the transitions from country to country, but also runs the risk of lulling the viewer into a complacent viewing of elegantly composed shots, which is not what the effort is all about. Minh-ha's desire to mobilize opinion so as to preserve the civilization she is documenting runs into her own romanticism with the primitive. Oblique and almost pretentious commentary such as, "Space has always reduced me to silence," must be granted a literary suspension of disbelief.

"Naked Spaces" will make the festival circuit, and beyond that, with the appropriate length imposed on pic, good television product for upscale art/travelog programming.—*Kaja.*

Shokutaku No Nai Ie
(Fate Of A Family)
(JAPANESE-COLOR)

Venice, Sept. 3.
A Marugen Building production in association with Herald Ace, Tokyo. Produced by Genjjiro Kawamoto, in association with Haiyuza Movie Broadcasting. Executive producers, Masayuki Satoh, Masato Hara. Written and directed by Masaki Kobayashi (from an idea by Fumiko Enchi). Features entire cast. Camera (color), Kazuo Okazaki; sets, Shigemasa Toda; sound, Hideo Nishizaki; editor, Nobuo Okazaki; music, Toru Takemitsu. Reviewed at Venice Film Fest (Competition), Sept. 2, 1985. Running time: **143 MINS.**
With: Tatsuya Nakadai (Nobuyuki Kidoji), Mayumi Ogawa (Yukimo Kidoji), Kie Nakai (Tamae Kidoji), Kiichi Nakai (Otohiko Kidoji) Takayuki Takemoto (Osamu Kidoji), Shima Twashita (Kiwa Nakahara), Mikijiro Hira (Kawabe's Lawyer), Azusa Mano (Kanae Sawaki).

Masaki Kobayashi's "Fate Of A Family" is nourished by the family-tragedy tradition of the fruitful 1950s in Japan, when directors like Ozu and Naruse honed the feelings and emotions of modest people to a fine art of cinematic expression.

The story is set in the early 1970s, when Japanese terrorists held the tv spotlight during a shootout with the police at a mountain hideout in central Japan. Taking its cue from this national event, Kobayashi examines what might have happened to the family of a terrorist, one university student known as Otohiko Kidoji. In fact, the family nearly falls apart in the face of the shame heaped upon it by the oldest son's anti-social and inhuman act. The central motif Kobayashi uses for his theme is the dining-room table, the place when the family was at last together before the son leaves for a trip to the mountains — and his rendezvous with fate.

Television coverage shows that the young terrorists killed their own members for deserting the cause and the shootout with the police produced more deaths on both sides. When the terrorists went to prison to await trial, the parents of most of them publicly apologized to society for the crimes of their children. Not so the father of Otohiko Kidoji. This stoic corporate executive felt that his son was solely responsible for his actions (a Western moral position, fundamentally alien to Japanese tradition). Throughout the film he maintains this stance in the face of almost unbearable family suffering.

First, the engaged daughter marries secretly (with the compassionate help of the aunt, the distraught mother's sister), and departs for a new life in America (albeit with tears of embarrassment and shame). Then the mother loses control of her senses, is committed to a psychoward, and eventually commits suicide. Left alone now with only the younger son, the latter at first rebels. Then, upon meeting with his older brother in prison, both sons grudgingly come to admire the position of the stoically suffering father. The sister-in-law to the father, always on hand to see things through, also confesses her unfulfilled love for him, a position that naturally is in vain under the circumstances.

The twist at the end has the son freed from prison (another historical fact) by the hijacking of a plane by fellow terrorists, but he acts to join the rest only after long deliberation. He is much like his father in the long run although despising Japanese society in general. The father and young son watch the plane fly off in the closing shot.

The story might easily be classified as melodrama, save that this is just too authentic to be taken as a soaper. Each shot is perfectly composed, while each image is interwoven with the last and the next in a pattern of seamless editing. Further, the acting is consistent throughout — particularly that of the father and sister-in-law in the key scenes of what to do in regard to crucial family matters.

A fine film, it is another outstanding example of the current revival in Japanese cinema. — *Holl.*

Mi Hijo El 'Chei': Un Retrato De Familia De Don Ernesto Guevara
(My Son Che: A Family Portrait By Don Ernesto Guevara)
(ITALIAN-SPANISH-CUBAN-DOCU-COLOR)

Venice, Sept. 3.
Produced by Laboratorio de poeticas Cinematograficas de Fernando Birri, Televi- sion Espanola, and ICAIC (Cuba). Written and directed by Fernando Birri. Camera (col- or), Adriano Moreno; editor, Birri, Alfredo Muschietti; music, Tata Cedron. Reviewed at the Venice Film Festival, Aug. 28, 1985. Run- ning time: 60 MINS.

As intimate as the home movies it contains and as simple as the single interview at its core, "My Son Che" will be a valuable historical docu- ment for future biographers of Ar- gentine revolutionary Che Guevara, the smiling young doctor who earned fame as a guerrilla leader during the Cuban revolution and who was canonized as an interna- tional myth in the '60s.

Docu is designed not only to pre- sent unseen photos and films from the family's private collection, but to point up the contrast between the poster-hero legend and the current eclipse of interest in the man and his deeds. At the same time, fil- mer Fernando Birri captures a sharp picture of another surprising figure, Che's 84-year-old father, Don Er- nesto Guevara Lynch, a lively, re- fined upper-class gentleman whose political sympathies clearly in- fluenced his offspring.

Made for Spanish television and for theatrical release in Cuba in an 80-minute version, "My Son Che" is a free-flowing chronicle that pours out of Guevara Père, a gifted narrator whose anecdotes accompa- ny 8m films of baby Che at the beach with his mother and siblings or riding the family dog around the back yard.

In one story he tells how the jun- ior guerrilla once surprised the fa- mily by marching alongside a train, uttering the mysterious phrase "I am a soldier of America!" over and over.

In addition to family material, there is rare footage from 1957 of Cuban guerrillas marching through the Sierra Maestra jungles. An ap- pealing score of Argentine tangos by avant-garde composer Tata Cedron underlines all. — Yung.

Tex And The Lord Of The Deep
(ITALIAN-COLOR)

Venice, Sept. 4.
A Titanus release, produced by RAI-TV Channel 3 and Cinecitta. Directed by Duccio Tessari. Stars Giuliano Gemma. Screenplay, Gianfranco Clerici, Marcello Coscia, Tessari, Giorgio Bonelli; camera (color), Pietro Morbidelli; art director, Antonello Geleng, Walter Patriarca; editor, Mirella Mencio; mu- sic, Gianni Ferrio. Reviewed at the Venice Film Festival, Sept. 4, 1985. Running time: 103 MINS.
Tex Willer . . . . Giuliano Gemma
Tiger Jack . . . . Carlo Mucari
Kit Carson. . . . . William Berger
Tulac . . . . Isabel Russinova
Kanas . . . . Flavio Bucci
Witch doctor . . . . . . Giovanni Luigi Bonelli
El Morisco . . . . Peter Berling

The rage for transposing the two-dimensional pen-and-ink he- roes of young readers to big and lit- tle screens has reached the heart of Italo production, RAI-TV, where "Tex And The Lord Of The Deep" was conceived.

Based on three issues of the popu- lar Italo comic book that recounts the adventures of a Texas ranger and his partners, Kit Carson and Ti- ger Jack the Indian, "Tex" marks what Italian tv clearly hopes will be- come the first in a series of formu- la Westerns capable of cashing in on the comic's 500,000 readers scattered from Yugoslavia to Brazil, Greece, Finland, Turkey and most Spanish-speaking lands.

Tex Willer was created in 1948 (only 10 years after "Superman" first appeared), and his loyal fans will recognize the finicky fidelity with which helmer Duccio Tessari and associates have handled him. Recognize, but not appreciate, be- cause somewhere in the process the excitement has slipped away, and Tex the movie proves a rousing dis- appointment, unable to make even the simplest suspense mechanisms function.

Pic has something of a corporate look to it, as though once the per- fect Old West sets designed by An- tonello Geleng and Walter Patriar- ca were in place and the three main characters physically replicated in Giuliano Gemma (Tex), William Berger (Carson) and Carlo Mucari (Tiger), there was nothing left to do but sit back and let the complicated tale perform its magic on the screen. Unfortunately, it does nothing of the sort.

Story is a melange of adventure plots any kid will recognize. Tex and his pals are investigating a robbery of guns from an army convoy. The trail leads them to a tribe of Yaqui Indians who dream of avenging the slaughter of their ancestors, the Az- tecs, by joining forces with other tribes and launching an Indian War. Their secret weapon, manufactured by a hooded alchemist in the belly of a volcano, is a glowing green rock capable of turning their enemies into instant mummies.

The violence is fast and furious, but as make-believe and bloodless as a comic strip. On the screen, the effect is curiously uninvolving, as in dynamite explosions that toss the wrong extras into the air a few se- conds too late, making for anything but a realistic impression. Each mini-adventure ends in the miracu- lous escape of the heroes, who pull each other out of swamps and up from ravines before the least sense of danger can be communicated.

Predictable on the level of action, "Tex" makes another mistake in taking it for granted that everyone has a clear idea of who the charac- ters are and why we should root for them. Gemma makes an archetypal Ranger in a white hat, but is too re- strained and anonymous to arouse gut-level sympathy.

Berger gives Carson the right dose of aging awareness, but the role is too slender to develop, while Carlo Mucari's Indian of few words seems barely on the screen at all. Every- body looks dated circa the 1960s, particularly Isabel Russinova in the one female role of Tulac, Yaqui queen, who gives new meaning to the words impassive acting.

Introducing the story, and con- cluding it with hopeful hints of a se- quel, is an old witch doctor played by Giovanni Luigi Bonelli, creator of the comic book. — Yung.

Montreal Fest Reviews

Le Voyage à Paimpol
(Journey To Paimpol)
(FRENCH-COLOR)

Montreal, Aug. 30.
Produced by Jomy Productions. Produced by Dominique Laurent. Directed by John Berry. Screenplay, Berry and Josiane Le- veque; dialog by Leveque; camera (color), Bernard Zitzerman; editor, Jean Bernard Bo- nis; set design, Olivier Paultre; music, Serge Franklin; sound, Henri Roux; costumes, Anne Schotte. Reviewed at the Montreal World Film Festival (Conservatoire d'art cin- ematographique), Aug. 29, 1985. Running time: 92 MINS.
With: Myriam Boyer, Michel Boujenah, J.F. Garreaud, Dora Doll, Andre Rouyer.

American director John Berry has turned up on the other side of the Atlantic again with a likeable and lively comedy in the mad- housewife vein. Mining working class frustrations, he takes his her- oine through the realities and fanta- sies of her life leading up to a trip to Paimpol, during which her flash- backs construct the story.

Myriam Boyer plays Maryvonne, a cheeky, bouncy, appealingly plump worker on an assembly line in a well-defined factory situation. She meets an Arab co-worker, Joel, who's cute enough to sweep her out of the factory and off her feet long enough to produce a son. Although Maryvonne initially refuses to mar- ry him, they get together, renovate a house and share a life affected by variously humorous trends and gad- gets.

A search for her G-spot renders some silly sex, and a strike at the plant inspires wild-eyed fantasies in Maryvonne, seeing herself as Joan of Arc, as the writer of a red book for the Chinese masses, and as a fur-collared Russian revolutionary.

A journalist visiting the strike in search of a story uses Maryvonne's irreverent humor to focus his report and seductively encourages her to write her own story for him. Her in- fatuation spurs her to pen several notebooks on her life and take them to Paimpol, where the disingenuous journalist wants to take her on his next assignment but refuses to take her seriously. Disappointed, she re- turns home to a furious husband, and pic glides to a satisfactory end.

Lensing seems effortless and lets the characters do the moving, par- ticularly in Maryvonne's fantasy se- quences which might have tempted a less sure hand than Berry's to hype them with special effects. Berry's confidence in his actors to carry their roles and guarantee the nor- malcy of the lives he is portraying is reflected in casting of less than glamorous types. Myriam Boyer's smile is as earthy and charming as her flights of fancy are soaringly ri- diculous.

Pic keeps its eye focused on Maryvonne and achieves its modest ambitions as a solid French comedy with reasonable market expecta- tions within that realm. — Kaja.

Bian Cheng
(Border Town)
(CHINESE-COLOR)

Montreal, Sept. 2.
A Beijing Film Studios production. Direc- tied by Ling Zifeng. Features entire cast. Screenplay, Yao Yun, Li Juanpei, from the book by Shen Congwen; camera (Scope, col- or), Liang Ziyong; music, Liu Zhuang. Reviewed at World Film Festival, Montreal (In Competition), Aug. 31, 1985. Running time: 98 MINS.
Grandfather . . . . Feng Hanyuan
Cui-cui . . . . Dai Na
Da-lao . . . . Liu Hui
Er-lao . . . . Shi Lei

Another quality item from main- land China. "Border Town" is a film based on a 1934 novel and set in the mountainous country on the border between Hunan and Szechu- an. Tale is a bitter-sweet yarn of un- requited love, and the unfortunate meddlings of a well-meaning but muddled old man.

He's an elderly ferryman (in- teresting how many characters in Chinese films are ferrymen or boat- men of some sort) whose orphaned granddaughter Cui-cui, is 14 going on 15. Her mother died unmarried, and the old fellow is afraid the na- ive, impressionable girl will meet the same fate. She's loved by two brothers, sons of an important local man, and in trying to mediate be- tween them the grandfather only succeeds in messing everything up, leaving the girl, at fadeout, alone and still unwed.

Helmed by 76-year-old vet Ling Zifeng, pic is slow-moving but quite disarming in its naive charm and depiction of village life fifty years ago. The little town where grandad does his shopping is a marvelous setting for the love story, with its annual festivities including a Dragon Boat race and a Duck Hunt.

Feng Hanyuan is very good as the foolish old ferryman, while young Dai Na, herself only 14 when the film was made, is exquisite as the shy young girl not certain how to cope with the confusing situation in which she finds herself. Overall, "Border Town" is not as impressive as "Yellow Earth," the Locarno prize-winner, but it reconfirms the qualities of Chinese cinema.

— *Strat.*

No Sad Songs
(CANADIAN-DOCU-COLOR)

Montreal, Aug. 29.

Produced by Cell Prods. Produced and directed by Nick Sheehan. Executive producer, Kevin Orr. Camera (color), Paul Mitchnick; location sound, Clarke McCarron; set design, Monte Douglas; production consultant, Ron Mann; editor, Miume Jan; production manager, Sheryl Wright; music, Allen Booth, David Woodhead. Reviewed at Montreal World Film Festival (Cinema Desjardins), Aug. 28, 1985. Running time: 62 MINS.
Narrator ....Kate Reid
Fireman ....David Roche
Monolog artist ....David Maclean
Preacher.................Henry Van Rijk
Organist ....David Sereda
Jim ....Joe Norman Shaw
Martha..........:.......Martha Cronen

The first docu about the crisis of AIDS, "No Sad Songs" offers testimony from victims and loved ones about the problems of dealing with the epidemic and its side effects, such as ostracism. The interviews range through the entire homosexual landscape from leather bars to mourning families. The most interesting opinions and information come from Kevin Orr, who is the film's executive producer as well as

the representative of the AIDS Committee of Toronto. He speaks with refreshing bluntness and candid charm.

Pic is burdened with the sob-sister confessions of several of the affected people, which seem aimed at the gay community rather than the public at large, where they might serve a better purpose. The featured victim and his "emotional lover," as they term their necessarily limited relationship, don't seem to have any other means to their lives since this disease has struck. One hears the litany of medical problems that has led to a politics of caution, but what recommends the pic is its lack of caution, actually. It is obviously no time to be coy.

Nevertheless, debut director Nick Sheehan has studded the pic with enacted monologs and dramatic theatrical pieces that are simply weird and affected in contrast to the honesty of the interviews. Apparently, he has edited a version for television sales clocked to 49 minutes that omits these attempts at gay art forms. Their humor is strained and angry and leaves the feeling of being even more puritanical than the attitudes the pic openly condemns when it attacks the moral majority for thinking AIDS is God's signal of condemnation.

Although tech credits are workmanlike and efficient, the structure is confused and could have benefited from a logical development that moves from outsiders and mourners to victims, since the punch is delivered by a victim who explains that for his family he "no longer exists." That in the face of imminent death demands the kind of concern that is, in fact, being galvanized and led by many courageous people in the entertainment industry. Pic's market will lay in that concerned community and probably not extend beyond it, unfortunately. —*Kaja.*

Venice Festival
Continued

Les Lendemains Qui Chantent
(Song-Filled Tomorrows)
(FRENCH-COLOR)

Venice, Sept. 10.

An Antenne 2, RTBF Production. Directed by Jacques Fansten. Stars Wojtek Psoniak. Screenplay, Jean-Claude Grumberg; camera (Kodak color), Bernard Zanni; editor, Andre Chaudagne; art director, S.F.P.; music, Jean Marie Senia. Reviewed at the Venice Film Festival, Sept. 2, 1985. Running time: 95 MINS.
Marcel ....Wojtek Psoniak
Dora ....Anne Marev
Claire ....Marilyne Canto
Thomas ....Thomas Gromb
Yaneck..............Teodor Komaniecki

At the center of "Tomorrows" is Marcel Slivovitz, a warm-hearted artisan furrier naive to the point of neurosis. The Slivovitz household, which includes wife Dora and kids Claire and Thomas, spends Sundays with the local cell, singing songs about Peace, Justice, and Friendship between men. Marcel, who was born in Lithuania (once Polish territory now Soviet), still has a sister in the fabled USSR, and one day he learns his nephew Yaneck, whom he has never seen, is coming to Paris with a ballet company.

Trembling with excitement, pride and nervousness, the Slivovitzes meet their relative and even manage to bring him to a neighborhood party, where they are the heroes of the day. Just when everyone is happily glowing from the dancing, drinking and toasts to socialism, Yaneck steals out a bathroom window and vanishes forever.

The family is stunned, unable to understand why anyone would want to defect from the glorious fatherland into such a grim, unjust world as theirs. The Soviets accuse them of complicity in Yaneck's defection and put their apartment under surveillance, the Party abandons them, and Marcel develops a series of psychosomatic illnesses. Meanwhile, Claire, a law student, and Thomas, a schoolboy, begin asking themselves some hard questions about the world, beginning with a mysterious message Yaneck leaves behind for them in Yiddish that seems to hint at the fate of Jewish intellectuals under Stalin.

This small jewel of craftsmanship, characterization and situation owes much to a team of fine thesps, lead by Polish actor Wojtek Psoniak as Marcel, Belgian Anne Marev as his wife, and Marilyne Canto as the daughter. Young Thomas Gromb stands out in the role of the son, through whose eyes the story passes. — *Yung.*

A delightful glimpse into a corner of the world rarely approached by filmmakers, Jacques Fansten's "Song-Filled Tomorrows" is the story of a happy Parisian family in the early '50s who find their identity as Communists and Jews suddenly challenged by circumstance. Intriguing and believable, pic has a roguish humor that never abandons its sensitivity to its characters' plight or sinks into facile moralizing. Though made for television by Antenne 2 and RTBF (it won a prize in the Venice Fest's tv section), pic could easily find its way to appreciative art house audiences.

Petrina Chronia
(Stone Years)
(GREEK-COLOR)

Venice, Sept. 2.

A Coproduction of the Greek Film Center, ERT 1, Panelis Voulgaris, and Greek television, Athens. Written and directed by Pantelis Voulgaris. Features entire cast. Camera (color), Giorgos Arvantis; sets & costumes, Julia Stavridi; sound, Andreas Achladis; editor, Andreas Andreadakis; music, Stamatis Spanoudakis. Reviewed at Venice Film Fest (Competition), Sept. 1, 1985. Running time: 142 MINS.
With: Themis Bazaka (Eleni), Dimitris Katalifos (Babis), Maria Martika (Mother), Irene Iglesi (Cleo), Nikos Birbilis (Prison warden), Illias Katevas (Michalis), Thanos Grammenos (Detainee).

A strong entry in the Venice Festival, Pantelis Voulgaris' "Stone Years" is based on probable fact in that surely some innocent people

suffered a similar fate during the two troubled decades depicted between 1954 and 1974. The film was conceived as a tribute to simple Greek people caught in the political vice of those "stone years," when illegal membership in the Communist Party was punished with de facto prison sentences under successive intolerant governments practicing an ongoing censorship policy.

Pic begins in Thessaly in 1954. A couple, ages 22 and 18, meet and fall in love — then Babis is arrested for disseminating pamphlets on the Communist Party. Eleni, also hunted, escapes arrest and goes into hiding in Athens. With the help of friends she goes on as before, always maintaining her love for Babis from afar, until his release 12 years later, in February 1966, when a leniency measure was introduced.

Now comes the ironic twist of fate. Just as Babis and Eleni are reunited and they spend a brief respite with each other (she becomes pregnant), Eleni is arrested on the old charge via an informer. Now it's her turn to go to prison for a 10-year sentence.

While serving her sentence in an Athens prison, the lenient officials and inmates there care for her during her child's birth. She is allowed to raise her child in the prison under the mitigating circumstances. Then comes the military coup of April 21, 1967. Once again, her relatives and political acquaintances are arrested, Babis escaping and going into hiding. When he is caught by chance in 1970, he is again tried and sentenced this time to a more severe 17-year term.

Struggling to maintain contact with each other in prison, Babis and and Eleni are in fact married behind bars — with their own son allowed to serve as best man to the wedding. It's not until 1974, when the dictatorship falls, that the two are finally released and given the chance to live their lives in peace, 20 years after their initial engagement.

Told at a lesiurely pace, "Stone Years" impresses with the frank honesty of the tale and the attention to detail. Words are not really needed to express the love and commitment between the couple, and Voulgaris leaves the actors (Themis Bazaka is particularly fine as Eleni) plenty of room to deliver the moral and human message with glances and gestures. However, at two hours plus, the going can be tough even for the sympathetic viewer.

—*Holl.*

---

44 Ou Les Recits De La Nuit
(44 Or Tales Of The Night)
(MOROCCAN-COLOR)

Venice, Sept. 3.

Produced by Ody Roos. Written and

directed by Moumen Smihi. Stars Pierre Clémenti, Marie-France Pisier. Camera (color), Pierre Lhomme, Abdelkrim Darkaoui; art director, Farid Belkahia, Patrice de Mazieres; music, Benjamin Yarmolinsky, Guido Baggiani. Reviewed at the Venice Film Festival, Sept. 2, 1985. Running time: **115 MINS.**

Moussa . . . .•. . . . . . . .Pierre Clémenti
   Also with: Marie-France Pisier, Abdelsam Farawi, Christine Pascal, Naima Elmcharki, Habachi.

A visually beautiful, ambitious film, "44 Or Tales Of The Night" recounts in elliptical sketches the almost half-century that Morocco was under the European protectorate from 1912-1956. Half Scheherazade's "1001 Nights" and half James Joyce (to whom pic is dedicated), film has an original look that borders the avant-garde in its unsequential editing and narrative technique. A handful of characters fade in and out of the film, and their stories, which are not easy to follow, provide the tenuous thread that takes the viewer through a maze of historical scenes.

The most identifiable character is Moussa, credibly limned by Pierre Clémenti, a young student at the beginning of the picture and later a scholar, an actor and a tormented intellectual who watches his country pass to the hands of foreigners. Other characters that come and go are El Haj, a patriarch incarnating the past and traditions; Ba Driss, an old story-teller who was once almost blinded to serve in a harem; Iakout, a beautiful black slave; and two young women of the new generation, played by French thesps Marie-France Pisier and Christine Pascal, neither of whom looks remotely Moroccan.

Pic spans the declaration of the Spanish-French protectorate in 1912, the nationalist revolts led by Abd el-Krim in the 1920s, the official attempt to recruit locals in the Spanish Civil War, more nationalist uprisings after the Second World War guided by the United Independence Party, and finally the withdrawal of France and Spain leading to Morocco's independence in 1956.

Captivating imagery is a constant, with characters framed around colorful fountains, courtyards and mosques. In spite of the evident stylization, however, there is a ring of authenticity to "Tales" and a real intensity about the country's troubled history. — *Yung.*

Frau Holle
(CZECHOSLOVAK-WEST GERMAN-COLOR)

Venice, Sept. 4.

A coproduction of Omnia Film (Munich), Slovensky Film (Bratislava), MR-Film (Vienna), in collaboration with Second German Television (ZDF), Mainz, Austrian Television (ORF), Vienna, RAI-1, SACIS, and RTVE (Italy). A Beta Film release, Munich. Directed

by Juraj Jakubisko. Features entire cast. Screenplay, Lubomir Feldek, Jakubisko, based on a fairy tale by the Brothers Grimm; camera (color), Dodo Simoncic; sets, Viliam Gruska; costumes, Sarka Hejnova; editor, Patrik Pass; music, Petr Hapka; sound, Csaba Török. Reviewed at Venice Film Fest (competition), Sept. 3, 1985. Running time: **95 MINS.**

With: Giulietta Masina (Frau Holle), Valerie Kaplanova (Death), Sona Valentova (Stepmother), Pavol Mikulik (Father), Tobias Hoesl (Jakob), Petra Vancikova (Elisabeth), Milada Ondrasikova-Krsikova (Dora), Karel Effa (Ringmaster), Eva Horka (Death as a young woman).

The Czechoslovak cinema is noted for its expertise in making live-action fairy tales. This one, Juraj Jakubisko's "Frau Holle" deals with a kind old granny type who governs the passing of the seasons from her perch on high. During one natural catastrophe — an avalanche of snow buries a circus caravan — Frau Holle takes pity on a youngster named Jakob and brings him into her enchanted world as a kind of assistant.

One day, Jakob sights below on Earth a young girl named Elisabeth, who must suffer under a cruel stepmother and two evil and jealous sisters. So the daring youngster decides to leave the world of immortality for the time being to become a mortal once again in order to right the wrongs on Elisabeth. Death — in the form of an old hag — now sees the chance to recapture her lost prey. Frau Holle, however, keeps a casual eye on her errant ward and steps in to save Jakob and Elisabeth from any unnecessary evil.

Giulietta Masina as Frau Holle makes for a charming fairy godmother. Production credits in general are also topgrade.

Pic was made for tv, where it will find its proper audience. — *Holl.*

Orfeo
(Orpheus)
(FRENCH-ITALIAN-COLOR)

Venice, Sept. 6.

A Pierre Vozlinsky presentation of an Antenne-2 (Paris), Radio France (Paris), Total Foundation for Music (Paris), SSR (Geneva) Istituto Luce (Rome) and SRC (Canada) coproduction. Executive producers, Manolo Bolognini, Geroges Dybman. Written and directed by Claude Goretta, based on "Orfeo" by Antonio Striggio and Claudio Monteverdi; camera (color), Giuseppe Rottuno; editor, Marie-Sophie Dubus; art director, Jacques Bufnoir; costumes, Gabriella Pescucci; sound, Guy Level; music recording, Pierre Lavoix; music performed by the Lyon Opera Orchestra, conducted by Michel Corboz. Reviewed at the Excelsior Screening Room, Venice Film Festival, Sept. 5, 1985. Running time: **92 MINS.**

Orpheus . . . . .Gino Quilico
Eurydice . . . . .Audrey Michael
Messenger . . . . .Carolyn Watkinson
Apollo . . . . .Eric Tappy
Prosperine . . . . .Danielle Borst

Unlike its companion piece for the last day of Venice, Istvan Gaal's "Orpheus And Eurydice," there is no attempt in "Orfeo" to transport

opera into natural surroundings. Swiss director Claude Goretta follows in the tracks of Ingmar Bergman's "Magic Flute," by keeping close to the stage origins, his sets never even trying to suggest realism.

"Orfeo," written by Monteverdi in the early 17th century as "La Favola d'Orfeo," is a masterpiece of the baroque repertoire. In the last few years it has been revived often which may be one reason behind the many joint forces of this production, officially presented here as Franco-Italian, but using Swiss and Canadian funds as well.

Goretta does his best to draw little attention away from the score. His direction is simple and unadorned, leaving the main impact to the soundtrack. Some of the sets are highly effective, for instance, the dark recesses of the underworld, and the singers themselves play on camera (except in one case), adding much to the general verisimilitude.

More of a spectacle than the Gluck opus, Monteverdi's opera gives a fuller version of the Greek myth, starting with the wedding of the semi-god and the nymph. An inspired musical performance by the Lyon Opera under Michel Corboz is another important asset.

As Goretta does not have the felicitous visual inventions that made Bergman's interpretation of Mozart so attractive, this entry may finally be restricted mainly to an audience of opera buffs, but it is sure to find a niche on tv, as the list of coproducers indicates. —*Edna.*

Orfeus es Eurydike
(Orpheus And Eurydice)
(HUNGARIAN-COLOR)

Venice, Sept. 6.

A Hungarofilm Presentation of a Mafilm Budapest/RAI Rome coproduction. Directed by Istvan Gaal. Written and edited by Gaal, based on opera by Ranieri de Calzabigi (libretto) and Christoph Willibald Gluck (music); camera (color), Sandor Sara, Sandor Kurucz; sets; Tamas Zanko; costumes, Judit Gombar; sound, Gyorgy Pinter; music performed by the Franz Liszt Chamber Orchestra, conducted by Tamas Vasari. Reviewed at the Excelsior Screening Room, Venice Film Festival, Sept. 5, 1985. Running time: **95 MINS.**

Actors
Orpheus . . . . .Sandor Teri
Eurydice . . . . .Eniko Eszenyi
Amor . . . . .Akos Sebastyen
Singers
Orpheus . . . . .Lajos Miller (baritone)
Eurydice .Maddalena Bonifaccio (soprano)
Amor . . . . .Veronika Kincses

Hungarian helmer Istvan Gaal is a leading director in his country but he is working against impossible odds here, attempting to transfer Gluck's poetic chamber opera into a film spectacle. The original material offers neither the drama nor the color which made for successful similar ventures in the past, for example "La Traviata" and

"Carmen."

The picture proceeds in what appears to be perpetual slow motion, from beginning to end, that is from the death of the nymph Eurydice through Orpheus' trip to the underworld to bring her back and until the final separation between lovers. Here Gaal has departed from the original score and libretto which allowed the couple to benefit from celestial clemency, and he wraps up the story with Orpheus wandering across a frozen landscape, his hair white, singing the lament which is the best known music in this opera.

Throughout there are desperate efforts to create a dreamy, mystical atmosphere out of the natural landscape used as scenery, but no amount of filters and smoke machines helps in this instance. The three scenes intended as spectacular — the burial rites, the encounter with Furies and then with the Blessed Spirits — are heavy-handed and repetitious. The dramatic climax, the lovers' hike through caverns of the underground back to the world of the living, will register its full impact only with those who are familiar with the original text and follow Eurydice's pleas to Orpheus to look at her, in spite of his pledge, before they are out of Hades.

The casting doesn't help too much either, since both the actor playing Orpheus and the singer performing the music on the soundtrack are too stodgy and inflexible, suggesting the character to be a warrior rather than a poet.

Technical credits are of a high order, with the camera moving through miles of tracking shots and keeping its distance from the characters whenever possible.—*Edna.*

Kasic Ousmani
(The Wedding Chamber)
(TURKISH-COLOR)

Venice, Sept. 4.

Produced by Mustafa Ozbey. Written and directed by Bilge Olgac. Camera (color), Umit Gulsay; editor, Bilge Olgac. (Only credits available). Reviewed at the Venice Film Festival, Sept. 4, 1985. Running time: **104 MINS.**

Ousman .Halil Ergün
   Also with: Perihan Savas, Mesdot Engin, Ismet Ay, Aloye Rona, Aysegul Unsal.

Beginning with a tragic gas explosion and ending with an absurd wedding that fails to come off, "Wedding Chamber" is an eclectic film that veers from beautifully handled tragedy to gentle comedy and outright farce, and back again

to a touching, melancholy finale. Helmer Bilge Olgac doesn't manage to keep absolutely everything under control, but even those parts of the film that falter are imbued with such vitality and pointed meaning the rough edges are forgiven. Neither polished nor academic (it appeared in the Venice Fest's People section rather than in competition), pic has an originality that keeps it watchable throughout.

Taking its cue from real-life events that occurred in a small Turkish village in 1978, pic opens in mysterious slow motion. Preparations for a wedding are in progress, and every woman in the village except one, the mad girl Elif, has gathered in a house. Suddenly the joyful festivities are interrupted as a gas tank — a wedding present — explodes. Those who aren't killed on the spot are trapped in the house and burnt to death, while their frantic menfolk struggle in vain to free them.

A mass grave is dug for the 97 women and children who have been killed. A tv unit comes to film the aftermath and interviews Ousman (Halil Ergün). Elif, laughing happily because Ousman, whom she loves has no wife now, is roughly pushed aside by the mourners. Even though she is the last marriageable woman left in the village, they won't have anything to do with her.

Before long, daily life resumes and the men realize the impossibility of living without women. Deftly swinging into gentle comedy, the film sketches their woes and Elif's taunts. A wife-hunt begins, but no one has the money to pay another dowry.

Least successful part of the film starts when a tubby German woman sees Ousman on tv and writes, offering to marry him. Flattered and excited, he agrees to the marriage, but an abominable German tv director decides to film "the meeting of two cultures" and sends a spacey actress down to play the bride. The cruel joke goes all the way, and the unfeeling (and very unbelievably portrayed) German crew makes a mockery of Ousman and the whole village, before revealing their deception. They are avenged by Elif, who has the perspicacity to steal the film as the crew is departing.

Excellent in depicting the villagers and their lives, with many comic bits, film goes off-target when it tries to make the leap to German culture and mentality — ironically illustrating its own point about inter-cultural misunderstanding. In passing, it strikes a few well-aimed blows at traditional Turkish marriages as money-oriented and male-dominated. — Yung.

Montreal Festival
Continued

O-Bi, O-Ba — Koniec Cywilizacji
(O-Bi, O-Ba — The End Of Civilization)
(POLISH-COLOR)

Montreal, Aug. 30.
Produced by Polish Film Corp., Perspektywa Unit. Written and directed by Piotr Szulkin. Camera (color), Witold Sobocinski; editor, Elzbieta Kurkowska; music, Jerzy Satanowski; set design, Andrzej Kowalczyk; sound, Nikodem Wolklaniewski. Reviewed at Montreal World Film Festival (Parisien), Aug. 29, 1985. Running time: 88 MINS.
With: Jerzy Stuhr, Krystyna Janda, Kalina Jedrusik, Mariusz Dmochowski, Marek Walozewski, Jan Nowicki, Henryk Bista, Leon Niemczyk.

A grand metaphor movie that thrives in intellectual circles and festival situations, this Polish pic comes dangerously close to being boring with its anti-nuclear message about some mythical Boers who shut down civilization with a bomb. Feeling inspired by Luc Besson's "Le Dernier Combat," its austerity is muddied by its riddles and symbols.

Set in an underground labyrinth peopled by bundled, ragged leftover human beings, the story follows the wanderings of the hero through situations that represent an archaeology of civilized values. The platform where people wait for the Ark that will mean their salvation is relentlessly smoky, and a loudspeaker system repeats incessantly; "There is no Ark. It will not be coming." Despite this the people wait, and the hero searches for what is behind the myth of the Ark. The only remnant of color in this vision is carried by the women who can be found in a neon-laced bordello, where the hero falls in love with Krystyna Janda, who confesses, "I sell my body. You sell your mind. Who's worse?"

Some comic relief is supplied by one of the repairmen, who claims to realize that the dome will crack before the Ark comes, because he was there when it was designed, and it was only a one-year plan. He has rigged himself a refrigerated room to which he will retreat, and he has frozen two women in ice in order to thaw them out later in order to continue the human race, when the time comes. He tells the hero, "Come the big freeze, make for the icebox."

Studded with unmistakably meaningful quips, the script seems to derive from a theatrical sense that allows one scene for each problem. The characters are brutal, no-neck, heavy-jowled abstractions, and the future in this dystopia is pointedly bleak.

But the ending reveals the truth of hope, as the Ark arrives and the masses on the platform rush toward the disembodied light that represents the Ark as a Mother-ship. It's like the old joke about the operation, here Operation Ark, succeeding but the patient dies. There may not be lift, but there is love after the end of civilization, such as it is portrayed here. —Kaja.

Tosha 1/250 Byo
(Indecent Exposure)
(JAPANESE-COLOR)

Montreal, Sept. 2.
A Nippon Television production. Produced by Akira Okubo, Yoshinori Moniwa. Written and directed by Masato Harada. Features entire cast. Camera (color), Motoyoshi Hasegawa; editor, Riichi Fuke; music, Takayuki Inoue; sets, Yuji Maruyama; sound, Makio Ika. Reviewed at World Film Festival, Montreal, Aug. 31, 1985. Running time: 93 MINS.
Nobi Namekawa . . . . Keiko Saito
Gozen . . . . Mari Natsuki
Kashiba . . . . Ryudo Ozaki
Also with: Chin Naito, Yoshio Harada.

A rare instance of a pic made for Japanese television but planned for cinema release, "Indecent Exposure" is a finely crafted, gripping behind-the-scenes tale of people working for a sensational news-magazine, appropriately called "Out of Focus." Story centers on Nobi, a girl from the sticks, who rises from the bottom to become the paper's best camerawoman, but at a high price.

First part of the film is rather funny, as the intrepid sensation-seekers flirt around Tokyo trying to get scoop pictures (a politician who's shacked up with a bimbo, a visiting singer hiding out to practice zen) or to shoot pictures (illegally) at a criminal trial. The dogged and ingenious ways Nobi and her friends deliver the goods is convincingly depicted, and their camaraderie is fun to watch.

The last third of the film provides an unexpected change in mood. Nobi, who has started an affair with Gozen, the most experienced scribe on the paper, is present when he, together with two children, is kidnapped by a crazed gunman, and, from a safe distance, she is clicking away at the very moment her lover is shot in the head at point-blank range. At fadeout, she has to decide whether to allow her pictures to be used, thus guaranteeing her status as a journalist, or, in deference to Gozen, refuse permission.

Director Masato Harada (who aroused interest in 1979 on the fest circuit with his first feature, "Goodbye, Flickmania") presents a persuasively realistic look at the way such a magazine operates and the team that gets it all together. The documentary look of the film is impressive, and the humor of the early scenes lures the viewer into a cosy state of mind which is abruptly shattered in the tense and tragic finale.

There's also the pointed aside that when President Reagan inadvertently mispronounces the name of the Japanese Prime Minister Nakasone, he makes it sound like "cry baby."

"Indecent Exposure" has already been shown on the tube in Japan, with a theatrical release in the works (usually a TV-produced feature opens in cinemas before being transmitted), and could garner some art house interest abroad on its insightful look into the world of journalism. — Strat.

Adela
(RUMANIAN-COLOR)

Montreal, Sept. 2.
A Group 4, Romaniafilm, production. Written and directed by Mircea Veroiu, from the novel by G. Ibraileanu. Features entire cast. Camera (color), Doru Mitran; art director, Calin Papura; costumes, Hortensia Georgescu; music, Adrian Enescu. Reviewed at World Film Festival, Montreal, Sept. 1, 1985. Running time: 85 MINS.
Adela . . . . Marina Procopie
Dr. Emil Codrescu . . . . George Motoi
Raluca . . . . Valeria Seciu
Tuliu Dragan . . . . Stefan Sileanu
Also with: Florina Luican, Jeana Gorea.

Reminiscent of the best of Soviet or Polish turn-of-the-century literary adaptations, "Adela" is a subtle, attractive tale of youth vs. middle-age during a hot, lazy summer more than 80 years ago.

It's 1899, and Dr. Emil Codrescu returns to a place he once knew some years earlier. There he meets Adela, a child last time he saw her, but now a beautiful, grown woman, already briefly married and divorced. Codrescu is evidently attracted to the girl, but he procrastinates. It's quite obvious that, at over 40, he's too old for her, or so he tells himself. Meanwhile he resumes an acquaintance with an old army buddy, Dragan, living a reclusive life on a houseboat.

During the course of the film there are several moments when Codrescu could have swept Adela off her feet, but he always hesitates. Finally he leaves as he came, alone, not willing to make a commitment. Dragan, meanwhile, has eloped with Adela's beautiful mother.

This is a film of quiet beauty, limpidly shot in hazy color, with sumptuous art direction and costumes, evoking a long-lost era. Eventually, Codrescu's inertia is to be seen not as shyness or laziness, but simply as an acceptance of his own middle-age.

Probably not strong enough to garner art house attention, pic still deserves to be seen at festivals and on tv where possible. It won the Grand Prix at the recent San Remo Festival for 'author's films.'
—Strat.

The Last Hunt
(U.S.-FRENCH-COLOR)

Montreal, Sept. 2.

A Films du Soleil production, in association with the French Ministry of Culture. Produced, written, directed and edited by Maryse Leon. Features entire cast. Camera (color), Afshin Chamasmany, Amy Halpern; music, Gray Castle; sound, Neetzchka Keene. Reviewed at World Film Festival, Montreal, Aug. 31, 1985. Running time: **86 MINS.**

Pia.......................Joyce Hyser
Mother......................Sally Kemp
Also with: Bernie White.

A misguided attempt at an Ingmar Bergman-like chamber-piece, along "Autumn Sonata" lines, "The Last Hunt" is a failure in almost every respect.

Pia lives in a lovely house in the Hollywood Hills and yearns for the black lover who rejected her. The unexpected arrival from the east of her mother, with whom she doesn't get along, makes her irritable. Mother and daughter spend about 80 minutes arguing with each other. Mother reveals she has cancer. Pia is shocked, but checks it out by phone with her brother, who says it can't be true. More fights, until mum leaves; only then does Pia check with her doctor and find out she *did* have cancer after all.

To get away with something like this one has to have a top-flight script, fine actors and delicate direction. "The Last Hunt" has none of the above, and furthermore is poorly photographed and saddled with an irritatingly pretentious music score. Participation of the French Ministry of Culture is a total mystery. — *Strat.*

Venice Festival
Continued

Ablakon
(IVORY COAST-COLOR)

Venice, Sept. 10.

Produced by Henri Dupare for Radio-Télévision Ivoirenne. Written and directed by M'Bala Roger Gnoan. Features entire cast. Camera (color), N'Gouan Kacou; editor, Aboussy Diangoye; music, Les Mystics. Reviewed at the Venice Film Festival, Aug. 31, 1985. Running time: **90 MINS.**

With: Kodio Eboucié, Issa Sanogo, Matvieu Attawa; Joel Okou, Bitty More, Ladii Sidibé.

Independent filmer M'Bala Gnoan, who has produced several shorter works with Ivory Coast television (the last was "Le Chapeau" in 1976), filled the void of sub-Saharan cinema in the Venice Film Festival's People section with a social comedy. "Ablakon." Between spoofing the pretentious capitalist-crook Charlemagne Ablakon and lamenting the desolate life of a gang of child runaways living out of garbage cans, pic struggles to achieve a tone and to get its message across without being heavy-handed. Results are mixed, but there are some memorable moments along the way on both sides of tragicomedy.

Abandoned by their parents, hunted day and night by the police, a drove of street urchins scrounges around the city, surviving by their wiles, imagination and group solidarity. In one episode, a one-legged boy distracts the adults with an incredible break-dance performance while his cohorts swipe food from a grocery store. In another, the older boys walk the streets at night as transvestites, narrowly escaping a police roundup.

In the same city live a foolish pair of *nouveau riche* folk. Ablakon and his wife, who lord it over a swarm of servants and a French butler. When the master of the house literally loses his pants during a nocturnal visit to his mistress, he is pulled into the police station and treated like a common delinquent, until the chief recognizes him as a respected businessman and lets him off with profuse apologies.

Fleeing to his native village in the bush, Ablakon reveals his true colors as a swindler who makes his money robbing the gullible. Among his victims is an innocent girl he sends to the city, who gets murdered. His crooked schemes are exposed by Yapi, a young villager who also left for the city, and came home more wretched than ever.

Music by Les Mystics has extraordinary vitality when dealing with the gang of kids. Technically pic suffers from uncertain lensing overrun with zooms and a lack of timing. Thesping is uneven. — *Yung.*

Die Förstenbuben
(The Forester's Sons)
(AUSTRIAN-WEST GERMAN-COLOR)

Venice, Sept. 1.

A Coproduction of MR-Film, Vienna, Austrian Television (ORF), Vienna, and Second German Television (ZDF), Mainz. Directed by Peter Patzak. Features entire cast. based on Peter Rosegger's novel; camera (color), Dietrich Lohmann; sets, Herta Hareiter-Pischinger; costumes, Edith Almoslino; music, Ennio Morricone. Reviewed at Venice Film Fest ("Venezia TV" section), Aug. 31, 1985. Running time: **88 MINS.**

With: Franco Nero (Böhme), Heinz Moog (Michel), Thilo Prückner (Krauthas), Anja Jaenicke (Gunda), Georg Friedrich (Elias), Thomas Siegwald (Friedel), Horst Klaus (Rufmann), Hanna Lussing (Sali), Mirjam Ploteny (Helene), Brigitte Antonius (Mariedel), William Berger (Pastor Gerhalt).

Peter Patzak shot "The Forester's Sons" against the striking backdrop of the Steiermark Alps. It's this stylistic element that makes the film worth seeing. This is also a "Heimatfilm," a genre now experiencing a revival of sorts on the German-language film scene.

A mysterious stranger (Franco Nero), arrives in an isolated village one cold wintry day. His presence causes suspicion among the mountain folk, particularly as he appears to be investigating something other than just the neighborhood's fauna. The two sons of the forester become attracted to him for different reasons as well, one a sensitive student and the other a gruff youngster longing to emigrate to America.

The stranger finally reveals to the villagers that he's here to investigate the murder of an old woman in a nearby town, who was in fact his mother. The murderer, an unseemly lout, kills Nero in the end when he finds himself trapped with the evidence piling up against him. The village can now go back to its passive slumber.

Credits are a good cut above the norm for tv dramas, particularly the lensing by Dietrich Lohmann.

—*Holl.*

Ce Fou De Peuple Russe
(This Folly Of The Russian People)
(FRENCH-COLOR-DOCU-16m)

Venice, Sept. 1.

A Dess Production, Pais. A documentary by Galya Milovskaya. Camera (color, 16m), John Cressey; editor, Agnes Molinard; music, Glinka, Shostakovich, Tchaikovsky, Vedel. Reviewed at Venice Film Fest ("Venice People" section), Aug. 31, 1985. Running time: **60 MINS.**

For those docu buffs and political historians interested in following the fortunes of Russian émigré artists living in Paris, Galya Milovskaya's "This Folly Of The Russian People" is highly recommended. The femme helmer is a Russian living in Paris; thus having an open-door access to the studios of the eight painters and one sculptor introduced in the docu.

What is particularly interesting is the link between these artists with the vibrant experimental era of the 1920s. It's obvious that the tenets of Socialist Realism were alien to this group, wich sprang up in the so-called "Unerground" movement in and around Moscow in the 1960s during the thaw briefly inaugurated in all the arts under Nikita Khrushchev. The artists could not sell their experimental works to the state, so they invited friends and colleagues to their studio-apartments for unauthorized exhibitions of their own — until granted permission to emigrate abroad.

Paris is not the only center for Russian émigrés, to be sure. Similar artistic movements can be found in New York, London, and West Berlin. The Paris group, however, appears to be more cohesive as an avant-garde movement. Helmer Milovskaya effectively matches interviews with examples of the artists' best works. This is the kind of docu that would be most effective when shown in conjunction with traveling art shows by ex-Soviet, Russian artists. —*Holl.*

A Tanitvanyok
(The Disciples)
(HUNGARIAN-COLOR/B&W)

Venice, Aug. 27.

A Hungarofilm presentation of a Hungarofilm production. Written and directed by Geza Bereményi. Camera (Eastmancolor), Sandor Kardos; editor, Terez Losonci; art direction and costumes, Byula Pauer; sound; Peter Laczkovich; music, Ferenc Darvas. Reviewed at the Venice Film Festival Palazzo del Cinema (International Critics Week), Aug. 26, 1985. Running time: **103 MINS.**

Josef Feher...............Károly Eperjes
Joltan Magyary...........Kornél Gelley
Count Alex...........György Cserhalmi
Countess.....................Juli Básti
Imra Török..............Beza Balkay
Peter Engel...............Byörgy Kézdi

"The Disciples" is a typical first film, overbrimming with good intentions and visual gimmicks, but not quite sure of its style.

The plot based on historical facts taken out of the Hungarian chronicles of the late thirties deals with a subject highly relevant to today's modern technocratic society of today.

Józef Feher, a peasant's son, wants to get an education at any price, manages to get into the graces of a radical professor, Magyary, who accepts him, nurses him along and drafts him into his fascinating new program of analyzing what is wrong with the basically agrarian Hungarian society of that time. The research most accurately points out that too many lands are concentrated into too few hands, that reforms to rectify the situation are urgent. Everything is to be exposed in an exhibition to be inaugurated by the minister in charge.

What the professor does not realize is that his work will never be accepted as long as it is presented in a purely scientific manner, without taking into consideration the human and political aspects. Which means, as Magyary puts it towards the end of the film, that whoever will come into power, right, left or center, will need superlative administrators.

With some sections in black and white, others using color saturation to indicate an historical perspective, and with reality slipping from time to time into pretty transparent symbolism, Bereményi simply tries too hard to drive his message home. His use of characters stays mostly on the allegorical level.

The importance of his theme, the dangers of technocracy, is probably the main reason for pic's inclusion in the Critics' Week. Technically, the film has a glossy look, with careful art direction and costumes. There is a dedicated performance by György Cserhalmi, as the dissipated symbol of decay.
—*Edna*.

Requiem Por Un Campesino Espanol
(Requiem For A Spanish Peasant)
(SPANISH-COLOR)

Venice, Sept. 10.
Produced by Angel Huete for Nemo Films and Venus Producción. Directed by Francesc Betriu. Stars Antonio Ferrandis, Antonio Banderas. Screenplay, Raul Artigot, Gustav Hernandez, Betriu; camera (Eastmancolor), Raul Artigot; editor, Guillermo S. Maldonado; art director, Julio Esteban, Josep Rossell; music, Anton Varcia Abrie. Reviewed at the Venice Film Festival (Competition), Aug. 29, 1985. Running time: **95 MINS.**
Mosén Millán . . . . Antonio Ferrandis
Paco . . . . Antonio Banderas
Don Valeriano . . . Fernando Fernán Gómez
Jeronima . . . . Terele Pavez

Moving, sincere and simple, "Requiem For A Spanish Peasant" uses the story of the life and death of a farm boy and his friendship with a priest who betrays him to denounce the collaboration of the Catholic Church with Franco's Fascists during the Spanish Civil War. Though there is evident dramatic potential in the tale, helmer Franceso Betriu deliberately downplays the suspense in favor of a quieter, but no less effective, moral condemnation. Well-acted and lensed, pic seems made for art house audiences.

As the film opens, Paco (Antonio Banderas), a young farm-worker who had promoted land reforms in his town during the Republic, has been dead for a year. The old priest who had been like a father to him tiredly waits to start a requiem mass in Paco's memory, but mysteriously no one appears except three rich men who had been Paco's political enemies and are as responsible as the priest for his death. The congregation of believers has abandoned the church. The three men — along with Paco's riderless white horse, which gallops through the church like a ghost come back to haunt them — will be the only ones to attend the requiem mass.

Paco's life is told entirely in flashbacks, as the priest recalls administering all the Church's sacraments to him, from baptism to first communion, confession and confirmation, through his marriage to a village girl. Little Paco, once his altar boy, grew into a leader respected by the townsfolk, who strove to reform the feudal land-leasing system that had the farm-workers in a stranglehold. He encounters opposi-

tion from the priest, who is on the side of the landowners. When the Civil War breaks out, black-shirts appear and summarily execute the populace. Paco goes into hiding in the hills. The priest, however, bends under pressure and reveals his hiding-place. The final sacrament he gives Paco is the last rites just moments before his is shot by a Fascist firing squad.

The story is depressingly believable, aided by the honest directness of Antonio Banderas as Paco and the unconfessed hypocrisy of Antonio Ferrandis as the priest, whose punishment for placing his rich parishioners above the poor hardly seems adequate to his sin. Picture closes on a disturbing note that leave one's sense of justice unsatisfied, as the three rich men offer to pay for Paco's mass. —*Yung*.

I Ragazzi Della Periferia Sud
(The Kids From The South Side)
(ITALIAN-COLOR)

Venice, Sept. 2.
Produced by Società Coop. TV Cine 2000. Directed by Gianni Minello. Features entire cast. Screenplay, Gianni Minello, Piergiovanni Anchisi; camera (color), Silvio Fraschetti; editor, Emanuele Foglietti; music, Alessandro Sbordoni. Reviewed at the Venice Film Festival, Sept. 2, 1985. Running time: **90 MINS.**
Angela . . . . Alessandra Mida
Andrea . . . . Stefano Sabelli
Rosa . . . . Marta Bifano
Gianni . . . . Walter Toschi
Mother . . . . Gisella Burinato

"The Kids From The South Side" originated with the respectable idea of giving an update on the sub-prole denizens written about by Pier Paolo Pasolini and filmed in "Mamma Roma" and "Accattone." Unfortunately it is no simple matter to capture the tragic grandeur and humiliated dignity of the Roman slums, particularly in the wake of a master of dialect and screen poetry. Though the intention is unquestionably sincere, "Kids" disappoints on all levels.

Story begins on the outskirts of the city, where a gang of unemployed kids on mopeds gathers under the ancient Roman acqueducts of "Mamma Roma." Among the petty thieves who steal to pay for their heroin are Cesare, boyfriend of Rosa (Marta Bifano), and Pino, her little brother. During a hold-up Cesare is shot to death and Pino arrested. Rosa, a juvenile streetwalker, commits suicide on a trash heap after being brutally gang-raped. Pino's other sister Angela (Alessandra Mida) leaves the factory for a life of prostitution and resists being "saved" by a middle-class architect (Walter Toschi). Mother Gisella Burinato disowns the whole family.

Bleak tale is too predictable to be

more than intermittently interesting, and helmer Gianni Minello (whose "A Boy Like All The Others" tackled a similar social theme) has little knack for dramatizing. Dismaying events follow each other like clockwork, but the impact just isn't there.

Cast of newcomers has been selected for their resemblance to what Roman proles are supposed to look like and not for thesping talents, though some, like actresses Mida and Bifano, occasionally rise above their inexperience. They get no help from the amateur-looking shooting, and attempts at a couple of nude lovemaking scenes are memorably disastrous. —*Yung*.

Letter To Brezhnev
(BRITISH-COLOR)

Venice, Sept. 2.
A Circle Releasing release (U.S.) of a production of Yeardream Ltd., Film Four International, and Palace Productions, London. Produced by Janet Goddard. Associate producers, Paul Lister and Caroline Spack. Directed by Chris Bernard. Features entire cast. Screenplay, Frank Clark; camera (color), Bruce McGowan; sets, Lez Brotherstone, Nick Englefield, Jonathan Swain; costumes, Mark Reynolds; sound, Ray Beckett; editor, Lesley Walker; music, Alan Gill. Reviewed at Venice Film Fest ("Venice Youth" section), Sept. 1, 1985. Running time: **95 MINS.**
Elaine . . . . Alexandra Pigg
Sergej . . . . Alfred Molina
Peter . . . . Peter Firth
Teresa . . . . Margi Clarke
Tracy . . . . Tracy Lea
Mick . . . . Ted Wood
Girl at bar . . . . Susan Dempsey

Unspooled in the "Venice Youth" section, Chris Bernard's "Letter To Brezhnev" was one of the discoveries of the fest. It should score easily at the home wickets, and with proper handling has solid offshore chances — provided viewers can relate to an ear-denting Liverpool dialect.

This is a farce, penned with wit and acted with appropriate deadpan honesty by all the principals. Picture a Russian ship docking in Liverpool. Two sailors go ashore for a night on the town, both primed with Beatles folkore and one speaking enough English to get them both by with the lasses in a dancehall.

As for the girls, one works in a chicken-factory and does little else than look forward to the weekend conquests. The other is on the dole, but has a romantic view in regard to her bed partners. Both are low on ready cash and the free-and-easy Teresa manages to pick the wallet of a chump pawing her at a bar after a brief acquaintance. Off they go to the dancehall for the precipitous meeting with the Russians.

Elaine, the Liverpool innocent, meets Peter, the Russian romantic from the Black Sea. They fall in love at first sight. So with Teresa's

pickpocket money and her hankering for the robust Sergei, off they go to a sleazy hotel to spend the night. Elaine and Peter spend it talking, however, and the next day they experience Liverpool together as they wander arm-in-arm and talk about life and Peter's lucky star in the heavens (to remind them forever of their meeting).

When they part, the naive Elaine finds it unfair that the world's political stage should prove a hindrance to their ever seeing each other again. So — on an impulse given by her friend Teresa, she writes a letter to Brezhnev — and gets an answer. To wit: if you really love your Russian sailor, come to the Soviet Union to marry him and settle down as an adopted citizen.

Elaine likes the idea, but her parents and government officials are distraught. Not even the bogus news that Peter is really happily married is enough to qualm her passion, to say nothing of the lucky star in the heavens encouraging her on. In the end, off she flies to see Peter, while Teresa waves goodbye with a "give my love to Igor" kiss!

"Letter To Brezhnev" doesn't make fun of the thematic situation by exploiting it for unneeded laughs or strained political satire.

Alexander Pigg (Elaine) and Margi Clarke (Teresa) are a tickling pair of working girl types right out of that British tradition going back to "free cinema" days. Helming by Chris Bernard is also a plus, although geared too much to the visual dictates of the tv screen. —*Holl*.

Maxie
(COLOR)

Old-fashioned romantic fantasy.

Hollywood, Sept. 10.

An Orion Pictures release of an Aurora presentation of a Carter De Haven production in association with Elsboy Entertainment. Produced by Carter De Haven. Executive producers, Rich Irvine, James L. Stewart. Directed by Paul Aaron. Stars Glenn Close, Mandy Patankin. Screenplay, Patricia Resnick, based on the novel "Marion's Wall" by Jack Finney; camera (Deluxe color), Fred Schuler; editor, Lynzee Klingman; production design, John Lloyd; set decoration, George Gaines; music, Georges Delerue; costume design, Ann Roth; sound (Dolby), David MacMillan; assistant director, David Sosna; casting, Judith Holstra, Marcia Ross. Reviewed at the Directors Guild Theater, L.A., Sept. 9, 1985. (MPAA Rating: PG.) Running time: **90 MINS.**

Jan/Maxie . . . . Glenn Close
Nick . . . . Mandy Patinkin
Mrs. Lavin . . . . Ruth Gordon
Bishop Campbell . . . . Barnard Hughes
Miss Sheffer . . . . Valerie Curtin
Father Jerome . . . . Googy Gress
Cleopatra director . . . . Michael Ensign
Commercial director . . . . . Michael Laskin
Harry Hamlin . . . . Himself

As forgettable as it is well-meaning, "Maxie" represents a stab at an old-fashioned sort of romantic fantasy, as well as a chance at a full-blown starring role (two of them, in fact) for perennial supporting actress Glenn Close. A concoction like this needs lots of fizz, but the bubbly here has gone mostly flat, and what's left evaporates quickly. In the old days to which the picture so fondly harks back, female viewers would have comprised the main audience for a project like this, but the modern public is not likely to get too worked up over this featherweight conceit. Film was first unveiled at festivals in Toronto and Deauville.

Pic does start off with a bit of charm and promise, squanders most of it during a sagging mid-section, then does a fair job of recapturing a fanciful spirit in the final reel. Much of the credit for keeping it alive at all must go to Mandy Patinkin, who, after launching his film career behind a bushy beard in ethnic roles, here shows himself to be a good-looking leading man with a rare light touch for romantic comedy in fairly dubious circumstances.

Based on a novel by Jack Finney, tale will divert the easily entertained, but proves trying to those who have more than once before been exposed to a story in which a dead person returns to inhabit the body of a living soul.

Such is what happens to Close, the normal, cheerful wife of book specialist Patinkin. When he uncovers a message on the wall from a certain "Maxie" who lived in their San Francisco apartment back in the 1920s, Patinkin becomes quite taken with the jazz age flapper who bore a striking resemblance to his wife and appeared in just one motion picture before meeting an untimely end.

In short, Maxie returns to wreak no end of tiresome havoc in Patinkin's life. Finally, to get rid of her, he agrees to take her to Hollywood to audition for the lead in, of all things, a remake of "Cleopatra," so that the actress whose career was nipped in the bud can know if she had what it took to become a star.

Screen test scene, in which an unbilled Harry Hamlin plays himself portraying Marc Antony, provides some of the picture's more amusing moments.

Getting there, however, is an ordeal at times, since the simple idea that has limited possibilities to begin with seems done to death by midway point. Maxie's misadventures don't prove amusing enough to warrant extended elaboration and seem, as often as not, to merely provide excuses for Close to try on a new period outfit and act goofy again.

She has some very good comic moments, but Close may be too down-to-earth an actress for foolishness of this kind. Like her character, she often seems to be doing too much and coming on too strong.

The late Ruth Gordon, in her last film role, contributes another of her patented nutty neighbor turns, this time with a little extra feeling as the former vaudeville partner of Maxie.

Production was clearly on the economical side. Tech credits are strictly average, and a few camera moves and cuts are decidedly awkward. —*Cart.*

A Matter Of Struggle
(DOCU-COLOR-16m)

A Parallel Films, N.Y., production and release. Produced by Ralph Klein and Saul Newton. Associate producer, Albee Gordon. Directed by Joan Harvey. Camera (color), Peter Schnall, Jeff Wayman, Mark Peterson; sound, Gordon, Chat Gunter, Samantha Heilwel; editor, Harvey. Previewed at Movielab, N.Y. Sept. 5, 1985. (No MPAA Rating.) Running time: **90 MINS.**

The two previous feature documentaries by Parallel Films have used a fixed format that persists in "A Matter Of Struggle," a style of non-stop verbal information and persuasion. The avalanche of discourse is close to overwhelming. One is grateful to Parallel for facts and interpretation on urgent socio-political issues, but one wishes they were more graciously imparted, and with some impartiality.

This third and most recent Parallel film, like the others directed by film/tv stage actress Joan Harvey, traces an odyssey of enlightenment by singer-composer Richie Havens, progressive troubador, who sings as he learns, full of affirmation.

Havens is accompanied by two charming waifs, ages eight and 10, who pose precocious questions on Reaganomics and foreign policy to those they meet on this journey for peace — Congressmen Ron Dellums, Theodore Weiss, George Crocket; Kremlinologist Genrikh Borovik; civil liberties attorney William Kunstler; a Catholic sister who risks jail to shelter Central American refugees; Vietnam veterans; El Salvador guerrillas; Black Panthers; Brown Berets; Green Party of West Germany; labor unionists, church activists; spokespersons for the American Indian Movement, Urban League, Communist Party, Republic of New Afrika — a sampling of American opinion, all discontented with Reagan.

These interviews are usually very brief, almost fragmentary, and are intercut with comments and songs by Havens and his two young friends. Stock footage from world archives and excerpts from other documentaries are also used, including rare scenes from our National Archives of U.S. troops invading the USSR at Murmansk in 1918.

"A Matter Of Struggle" has cumulative impact even though its style is stridently one-note.

The film was seen this summer at Edinburgh, Moscow and Munich, will have a Carnegie Hall benefit in November, and will circulate within Parallel's loyal and impressively large network of churches, colleges, peace groups and community centers. — *Hitch.*

Buddies
(COLOR)

Modest AIDS meller.

San Francisco, Sept. 12.

A New Line Cinema release of a Film and Video Workshop production. Executive producer, Frederick Schminke. Produced, directed, edited and written by Arthur J. Bressan Jr. Features entire cast. Camera (color), Carl Teitelbaum; music, Jeffery Olmsted; sound, Steve Hirsch; associate producer, John Hartis; casting, Jeff Hochhauser. Reviewed at Castro Theater, San Francisco, Calif., Sept. 12, 1985. (No MPAA Rating.) Running time: **81 MINS.**

Robert Willow . . . . Geoff Edholm
David Bennett . . . . David Schachter
Edward . . . . Billy Lux
Steve . . . . David Rose

What is billed as the "first dramatic movie" about AIDS (acquired immune deficiency syndrome) was written in five days and shot in nine (on 16m) by New Yorker Arthur J. Bressan Jr., known previously for his 1983 feature "Abuse" and a PBS compendium of JFK presidential press conferences.

"Buddies" world-preemed at a benefit showing at the Castro Theater and then next night opened first commercial run at Frisco's Roxie. The timing of the release, from a promotional point of view, couldn't be more propitious considering daily breaking news stories. With well-publicized accounts of AIDS incursion into heterosexual community, there is clearly universal interest in this mysterious ailment.

Although "Buddies" is clearly well-meaning and intelligently wrought, yarn lacks universality that can draw straights in sufficient numbers to guarantee decent b.o. Further, technical quality of this pic might offput commercial audiences — because there are occasional sound deficiencies, excessive close-up shots and minimal production values.

Yarn plays more like a legit two-hander with two sets: the hospital room of an AIDS victim and the apartment of victim's volunteer "buddy." The performing pair are, respectively, Geoff Edholm and David Schachter, who make up virtually the entire cast. Schacter's roommate is seen briefly in a shower, Edholm's former lover in home movies. Other characters are only heard.

Screenplay does brush on the politics of AIDS — the sanctimonious homophobia — but could have spent more time on exposition of the disease. Focus mainly is on the buddy's feelings about himself and the victim and is laden with persistent sexual connotations. It's straightforward, never mawkish but never particularly interesting either.

Opening and closing credits roll over a printout of AIDS victims — moments more compelling than much of what occurs in the film.
—*Herb.*

Visage Pale
(Pale Face)
(CANADIAN-COLOR)

Montreal, Aug. 31.

A Yoshimura-Gagnon production. Produced by Yuri Yoshimura-Gagnon and Claude Gagnon. Written and directed by Claude Gagnon. Stars Luc Matte, Allison Odjig and Denis Lacroix. Camera (color), Serge Ladouceur; editor, Gagnon; music, Jerome Langlois, sound, Daniel Masse, Robert Girard. Reviewed at Montreal World Film Festival, Aug. 29, 1985. Running time: **102 MINS.**

Derivative, implausible and occasionally patronizing, the Quebec-made "Visage Pale" may have its heart in the right place, but is ultimately sabotaged by director Claude Gagnon's generally jumbled script. Gagnon would have done well to stick to just one topic, and not cram the quintessential Quebec hockey saga, the remaking of "Deliverance," survival in the bush and native-white race relations all in one film.

Principal protagonist of pic is C.H. (Luc Matte), an esthete, a Don Juan, a chess master and a former Montreal Canadiens hockey star. On the other hand, C.H. is not a millionaire athlete. He actually toils as a waiter, and as a result, is in dire need of some R&R in the quaint Quebec bush.

It's there C.H. encounters unexpected trouble from three rowdy locals. Former hockey playing esthetes-cum-chess masters don't mean much to these guys.

Hard as this may be to fathom, the situation suddenly metamorphoses into "Deliverance." Things get downright grisly as the boys proceed to brutalize C.H. Fortunately, a sympathetic Indian guide (Denis Lacroix) comes to his rescue.

Unfortunately, one of the rowdy locals gets accidentally murdered in an ensuing scuffle, and the duo are forced to flee, seeking refuge in an outlying Indian reservation.

Acting is on the amateur side, while sharp photography and occasional hard action are film's only redeemable facets. —Bro.

Toronto Fest Reviews

Twice In A Lifetime
(U.S.-COLOR)

Toronto, Sept. 10.
A Yorkin Co. presentation. Produced and directed by Bud Yorkin. Executive producer-production manager, David Salven. Stars Gene Hackman, Ann-Margret, Ellen Burstyn, Amy Madigan, Ally Sheedy, Darrell Larson, Brian Dennehy. Screenplay, Colin Welland, based on his tv play "Kisses At 50;" camera (Alpha Cine color), Nick McLean; editor, Robert Jones; music, Pat Metheny; title song, Paul McCartney; sound, Darin Knight; production design, William Creber; set design, Kenneth Creber; set decoration, Antony Mondello; assistant director, Tommy Thompson; costume design, Bernie Pollack; casting, Deborah Lucchesi. Reviewed at Toronto Festival of Festivals, Sept. 9, 1985. (MPAA Rating: R.) Running time: 117 MINS.

Harry . . . . Gene Hackman
Audrey . . . . Ann-Margret
Kate . . . . Ellen Burstyn
Sunny . . . . Amy Madigan
Helen . . . . Ally Sheedy
Keith . . . . Stephen Lang
Jerry . . . . Darrell Larson
Nick . . . . Brian Dennehy
Tim . . . . Chris Parker
Joanne . . . . Rachel Street
Also with: Kevin Bleyer, Micole Mercurio, Doris Hugo Drewien, Lee Corrigan, Ralph Steadman, Rod Pilloud, Art Cahn, Anne Ludlum.

An edgy, shifty-eyed 50th birthday tribute for hero Harry Mackenzie gets this midlife-crisis film off to a risky, sentimental start, and from there on out it's Ellen Burstyn, the abandoned wife, versus Gene Hackman, the not-unsympathetic-but-risk-taking husband, vying for audience affections in the friendliest competition ever in marital-dissolution pictures.

Burstyn claims the film as Kate, who has to cope with her own life and family, and some rather mediocre lines, alone. Whether the marquee value will bring the over-30 audience into the theaters will depend on the pic filling a gap in the marketplace, much as "The Four Seasons" did.

Hackman is stalwart and determined in his resolve to make a new life with Ann-Margaret, but she is far too sexy and he far too underdeveloped for anybody to understand what she sees in him. Their scenes are very abbreviated, and his entire motivation attenuated.

Nevertheless, the day of Harry Mackenzie's birthday has great ambience and establishes the working class ethics and frustrations upon which the plot plays with a modicum of success.

Sometimes his family is unemployed and scared; sometimes they are off defining honesty on the job versus honesty to one's spouse.

Everybody's point-of-view is given equal time, which means the members of the Mackenzie family are treated with egalitarian interest, even if Amy Madigan as the infuriated daughter presents the most original perspective of intolerance and infantile tyranny over changes in the family.

Ann-Margret as Audrey throws off the balance in Harry's life when she goes to work at his neighborhood bar.

It is obvious, even to Harry, that Ann-Margret looks too classy for a wench tapping beer in the suburbs. Behind that major objection lays the reasoning that it would take someone that exhilarating and sexy to revive Harry and give him a second chance of a lifetime.

Brian Dennehy as his best friend has the burly bravado to make the pic feel down home.

Burstyn is such a hang-in-there housewife, with a life devoted to making bridesmaid dresses, pies and babies, that the contrast with Ann-Margret makes it desperately clear why Harry doesn't live here anymore.

The pic is loaded with jock humor and incidental comments that allow the characters' frustrations to seep out.

Audiences will love Burstyn's warm wrinkles and visit with her daughters to a male strip joint, as well as Hackman's workmanlike heroism. After all his son tries to explain it all, when he wings in from California to say, "Dad's no older than Clint Eastwood."

What the script tries to prove is that Harry's departure is just what Kate needed to make a new woman of herself, and the wedding plans of their younger daughter provide a wealth of clichés to reflect the hopes and naive convictions of every new marriage.

These scenes are done with the shorthand of television sitcoms, but it allows filmmaker Bud Yorkin to weave in scenes of new beginnings in everybody's life and draw the pic to a happy ending, with Harry taking a handful of flowers from the church home to Audrey, and Kate carrying on nobly even if, as she claims in the scene central to pic's conflict, she didn't deserve to be treated like this.

Colin Welland's screenplay tries to be tender and tough about everybody's elected role in life and succeeds well enough to make smashing stuff for pay and cable.

True to its working class milieu, pic avoids being artsy and proceeds from its premise that Hackman can and must leave so abruptly with a similar straight-ahead, unreflective pace. — Kaja.

The Journey Of Natty Gann
(U.S.-COLOR)

Toronto, Sept. 9.
A Buena Vista release of a Walt Disney Pictures presentation and production. Produced by Michael Lobell. Directed by Jeremy Paul Kagan. Features entire cast. Screenplay-associate producer, Jeanne Rosenberg; camera (color), Dick Bush; editor, David Holden; music, James Horner; production design, Paul Sylbert; art direction, Michael S. Bolton; sound design, Leslie Schatz; sound, Ralph Parker; assistant director, Michael Steele; production manager, Les Kimber; costumes, Albert Wolsky; casting, Janet Hirshenson, Jane Jenkins. Reviewed at Toronto Festival of Festivals, Sept. 8, 1985. (MPAA Rating: PG.) Running time: 105 MINS.

Natty Gann . . . . Meredith Salenger
Harry . . . . John Cusack
Saul Gann . . . . Ray Wise
Sherman . . . . Scatman Crothers
Parker . . . . Barry Miller
Connie . . . . Lainie Kazan

More a period piece of Americana than a rousing adventure, "The Journey Of Natty Gann" is a generally diverting variation on a boy and his dog: this time it's a girl and her wolf. If the kids respond to the emotional hook of this sentimental yarn, Disney can count on snappy commercial prospects.

Set in the Depression in Chicago, story has widower Saul Gann desperate to find employment to support himself and daughter Natty. He's offered a job at the lumber camp out in Washington State and reluctantly takes it, promising to send for Natty as soon as he can. He leaves her under the auspices of a floozie hotel manager, who has zero interest in taking Natty into her custody.

The girl runs away and remainder of pic is her sojourn across America in search of her dad. Natty, who is by nature feisty and enterprising, instantly learns how to ride the rails, eat beans from a can, forage through the forest for berries, and hitchhike. Along the way she rescues a wolf from its captors, and he becomes her endearing traveling partner, forewarning her of danger and supporting her in her plight.

Ultimately, after the requisite glitches and hitching near-misses, and a lot of growing up, Natty is reunited with her father while she tearfully sets the wolf free in the forest.

Chicago is not even set by an establishing shot, and Natty's journey cross country isn't exactly so — entire pic was lensed in Canada, so the Canadian Rockies sub for Colorado and points west.

But Dick Bush's photography is lovely and the art direction evokes the gray-brown mood of the Depression. Natty gets a sociological crash course on the national desperation in the 1930s.

Director Jeremy Paul Kagan extracts an engaging performance from Meredith Salenger as the heroine, who is convincing in her vitality, industriousness, and vulnerability. Rest of the cast is fine, with John Cusack as her begrudging but good buddy and Barry Miller as the witty entrepreneurial leader of a hobo brat pack.

The film rambles on with too many cuts to Natty and the wolf sauntering dejectedly down the country roads. Cut to an hour, it would make a fine Disney telepic.
—Devo.

Ruthless Romance
(SOVIET-COLOR)

Toronto, Sept. 8.
An Intl. Film Exchange release. Produced by Mosfilm Studios. Directed by Eldar Ryazanov. Features entire cast. Screenplay, Ryazanov, based on "The Dowerless Bride" by Alexander Ostrovsky; camera (color), Vadim Alisov; set design, Alexander Borisov; music, Andrei Petrov. Reviewed at the Toronto Festival of Festivals (Varsity), Sept. 7, 1985. Running time: 140 MINS.

Sergei Paratov . . . . Nikita Mikhalkov
Larisa . . . . Larisa Guseeva
Madame Ogudalova . . . . . . Alisa Friendlikh
Yuli Karandyshev . . . . Andrei Myagkov
Knurov . . . . Alexei Petrenko
Vasya Vozhevatov . . . . . . Victor Proskurin

Only handsome Russian actor/director Nikita Mikhalkov could get away with entering on a white horse in a white suit at the opening of a film set on the Volga, where Olga has just married. Looking more like Omar Sharif than ever, Mikhalkov opens pic with panache as he casts flowers to the bride and turns to woo her sister. He owns the fastest boat on the Volga, and life picks up for the flirtatious Larisa, who is courted with assiduity by a motley crowd of types recognizable from Russian drama and literature.

While the story revolves around the seduction, abandonment and betrayal of the lovely Larisa, it also attempts to address the larger question posed by the dissatisfied suitor, who will shoot Larisa at the end, "Why do women usually prefer immoral men to decent ones?" Because they sing instead of whine, if this pic can be believed, and indeed, Mikhalkov as the dashing Volga boatman Sergei shows off his singing, dancing, and lust for life that keeps the movie afloat through the first half. The second half gets swamped by the turn of the screw when Sergei returns home after a year's absence to settle the family estate and finds Larisa is about to marry Yuli, the Georgian equivalent of a nerd. Sergei and his cronies humiliate Yuli and steal Larisa.

The final scenes on the boat, The Swallow, which Sergei is selling to a rising businessman, drag on much too long, while the message condemning materialistic decadence is spelled out all too carefully. The lighter moments with the gypsies singing and dancing and Larisa's love songs that have substituted for dialog to track her emotional development fail to make the reversal of her fate seem tragic. There is a frustration that turns to utter boredom in the *longeur* of Larisa's fall into the arms of Sergei, which promised more excitement in a single night than an entire life with the priggish Yuli.

Enough splendid panoramas of the Volga and carousing sequences stretch the film out, so if 30 minutes were cut it would still be effective, particularly with the ironic portrayal of collapsing aristocrats and burgeoning bourgeoisie. It need only be as pithy as the play upon which it is based, and it would make quite respectable art-house viewing. Because the material is basically the stuff of melodrama, it does not lend itself to helmer Eldar Ryazanov's epic vision. Ryazanov's forte is in the Russian romance of a less ruthless tradition than this, such as his recent "Station For Two," a much tighter, more focused story.
—Kaja.

Relasyon
(The Affair)
(FILIPINO-COLOR)

Toronto, Sept. 13.

A Regal Films production. Directed by Ishmael Bernal. Screenplay, Ricardo Lee, Raquel Villavicencio; camera (color), Sergio Lobo; editor, Augusto Salvador; sound, Vic Macamay; music, Winston Ravel. Reviewed at Toronto Festival of Festivals, Sept. 13, 1985. Running time: **97 MINS.**

With: Christopher de Leon, Vilma Santos, Jimi Melemdrez, Bing Caballero, Olive Madrilejos, Beth Monodragon.

In a country that doesn't allow divorce, the Filipino pic "The Affair" will prove a risky but entertaining effort. Prolific director Ishmael Bernal, whose "Himala" was shown at the Berlin Festival in 1982, weaves a story about an adulterous affair and its implications for the families involved.

Marilou (Vilma Santos) is a pretty guide at the Planetarium who is having an affair with handsome Emil (Christopher de Leon), who is married and has a son. Marilou can't give him up, despite the urging of her father and friends. When Emil's wife leaves him he moves into a house with Marilou, only to discover gradually the compromises and personal quirks that have to be tolerated when living together.

Emil's a boorish chauvinist in many ways, and Marilou is too eager to please. She becomes more and more frustrated with her inability to change society. She checks out the possibility of Emil getting an annulment, but it would be too mired in bureaucratic red tape. After a contrived finale to the relationship, Marilou is left with nothing.

There's a vital dynamism between Santos and de Leon which relays the passion and sexual urgency in their affair, and Bernal gets fine performances from them. The script is trite and hokey in parts and dilutes some of the more cutting insights into the false morality ascribed to marriage.

Tech aspects are efficient, but lighting is too flat and stark throughout and print shown at fest was grainy. Pic can cruise the festival circuit to showcase what other Filipino directors are up to, but its natural market is Southeast Asia.
— Devo.

La Dame En Couleurs
(Our Lady Of The Paints)
(CANADIAN-COLOR)

Toronto, Sept. 11.

Production of the National Film Board of Canada and Les Prods. Pierre Lamy Ltee. Produced by Lamy. Executive producers, Lamy and Jean Dansereau. Directed by Claude Jutra. Screenplay by Jutra, Louise Rinfret, based on an original idea of Rinfret; camera (Eastmancolor), Thomas Vamos; editing, Clair Boyer; sound, Richard Basse; first assistant director, Mireille Goulet; second assistant, Pierre Plante; continuity, Marie Theberge. Reviewed at the Festival of Festivals (Cumberland), Toronto, Sept. 10, 1985. Running time: **119 MINS.**

Ti-Cul . . . . Guillaume Lemay-Thivierge
Gisele . . . . Ariane Frederique
Sebastien . . . . François Methe
Regis . . . . Mario Spenard
Ti-Loup . . . . Jean-François Lesage
Denis . . . . Gregory Lussier
Francoise . . . . Lisette Dufour
Agnes . . . . Charlotte Laurier
Barbouilleux . . . . Gilles Renaud
Sister Gertrude . . . . Paule Baillargeon

Mother Superior . . . . . . Monique Mercure
Mario . . . . Martin Guay
L'abbe Menard . . . . Rolland D'Amour
Serge . . . . Eric Dubois
Simon . . . . Zachary de Rioux-Perra
Madame Gregoire . . . . Gisele Schmidt

Claude Jutra has made a sensitive and fascinating picture about children and childhood that resounds on many levels and bears its air of intrigue lightly, with a rare agility in films that treat children and psychopaths, not to mention nuns, seriously. Small films that succeed against so many odds — a huge cast, an unruly amount of children, an obscure historical period that yields an unlikely plot, and religious intonations — invite words like serendipity to be attached to them, for better or worse.

It is common knowledge in Quebec, apparently, that the province's psychiatric institutions were opened up during the '40s to take in homeless children, since the orphanages were bursting. Fortunately, an excess of anything deprives it of its romance, and Jutra has stripped his orphans who dominate the story of qualities too endearing. They are as rebellious and bratty as children are supposed to be, but their drive to create a family for themselves in the literal underground of an institution dominated by maniacs and neurotic clergy is the driving force of the many stories of the cloister braided into a single story of hiding behind insanity.

A bus unloads a group of kids to a distressed convent in the first scene, establishing that the children are not wanted anywhere and, indirectly, justifying their retreat from all authority. Charlotte Laurier plays Agnes, a young girl reaching adolescence in this awkward environment where the best she can hope for is to become as frustrated as the one sister who is intermittently kind and receptive to her needs, or to lead the younger children into establishing a secret society in the cellars.

Little Ti-Cul has explored a labyrinth of passageways from the convent to the garden, and the children begin to spend more and more time there, where only a mad painter discovers them and, in delight, joins them. He teaches them to paint the walls, and all this self-expression is what yields the title, "Our Lady Of The Paints," a rainbow virgin of the underground.

The children are finally discovered when one of them falls ill and dies in the infirmary, only to have his body disappear. The nuns carry out a search that evacuates the cellars and leads to a rather dark and surprising conclusion. A flash-forward of two of the children still in the convent years later, only as insane parodies of their childlike selves, jerks the gentle pace and wis-

dom of the entire story into bitter despair. Its necessity is questionable, particularly in view of the marketplace's limited tolerance of sudden mood shifts in that direction.

Lensing has a lyrical quality that suits Jutra's temperament, and since his film "Mon Oncle Antoine" was recently voted the best Canadian film ever, he has worked to live up to the reputation. An even-handed direction of a very large cast and willingness to let the children become fairly outrageous, as when they mime shock-therapy while carrying out their duties among the mental patients, makes the pic more than just another homage to innocence.

Pic should find good reception in French-speaking territories.
— Kaja.

Smooth Talk
(U.S.-COLOR)

Toronto, Sept. 11.

A Spectrafilm release of a Goldcrest presentation of a Nepenthe/American Playhouse production. Produced by Martin Rosen. Executive producer, Lindsay Law. Directed by Joyce Chopra. Features entire cast. Screenplay, Tom Cole, based on a short story by Joyce Carol Oates; camera (color) James Glennon; production designer, David Wasco; editor, Patrick Dodd; music director, James Taylor; score, Bill Payne, Russell Kunkel, George Masenburg. Reviewed at Toronto Festival of Festivals, Sept. 11, 1985. Running time: **92 MINS.**

Arnold Friend . . . . Treat Williams
Connie . . . . Laura Dern
Katherine . . . . Mary Kay Place
Harry . . . . Levon Helm
Jill . . . . Sara Inglis
Laura . . . . Margaret Welch
June . . . . Elizabeth Berridge

Much of Joyce Carol Oates' fiction is populated with ordinary, working-class heroines to whom unfamiliar and extraordinary things happen. Joyce Chopra uses Oates' short story, "Where Are You Going, Where Have You Been?" as the framework for an elliptical, haunting and finely crafted debut.

"Smooth Talk" starts out as a teens-at-the-shopping mall foray and is transformed into something totally different — a sultry exploration of a girl's tentative plunge into sexuality and the dark lures of adulthood.

Story concerns 15-year-old Connie (Laura Dern) languishing in the hot California summer between her freshman and sophomore years in high school. She's basically an unsympathetic, selfish character. She's insolent to her mother (Mary Kay Place), deceitful to her father (Levon Helm), and jealous of her sister (Elizabeth Berridge). Connie and her two best friends spend their days putting on makeup and jewelry, teasing boys in the malls and at the local burger stand and dallying in first flirtations and teases with macho boys .

On a Sunday afternoon, Arnold Friend (Treat Williams), a tattooed psycho who's been following Connie, comes by to pick her up, informing her that he will be her lover. She's scared to death but he assures her he's as safe as his license plate: A FRIEND.

Connie's experience with Arnold is ambiguous and dangerous and she's transformed in a delicately eerie way.

Cast is first rate. Dern is magnetic as the teen, and Place imbues her character with zest and love. Helm is fine as the lunky father, and Williams is creepy, threatening and tops as the mysterious stranger.

Chopra, who has worked in docus for 20 years, directed this with an assured hand, telegraphing Connie's vulnerability in treading the dangerous line to adulthood and making Williams' entrance darkly foreboding.

While it's a classy "American Playhouse" tv entry, pic could also score at the boxoffice with the right marketing moves.—*Devo*.

Chain Letters
(U.S.-COLOR-16m)

Toronto, Sept. 9.

A Chain Letters production. Produced by Mark Rappaport and Harvey Wildman. Written and directed by Rappaport. Camera (color), Martin Schäfer; editors, Rappaport and Anthony Szuk; art director, John Arnone; sound, Barbara Zahm; music, Robert Previte. Reviewed at Toronto Festival of Festivals, Sept. 9, 1985. Running time: **96 MINS.**

With: Mark Arnott, Reed Birney, David Brisbin, Randy Danson, Daniel Davis, Marilyn Jones, Ellen McElduff, Joan MacIntosh.

A convoluted script with absurd but uneven comic touches peppers New York director Mark Rappaport's sixth feature, "Chain Letters." It's a mystery whether this effort is self-consciously smug, tongue-in-cheek or earnest, so it'll be snug on the arthouse circuit but rather tough going commercially.

The choppy story finds nine people receiving chain letters. The characters are murkily interrelated. A college prof is having an affair with a woman who is involved with the prof's brother, an acutely paranoid Vietnam vet furiously working on a plan to decode the letter. He's sure there's a plot that will find everyone who received the letter being inoculated with a cancer-causing virus.

A dark-haired woman also involved with the vet is the sister of an alcoholic soap opera star, who lives with a macho man she accuses of not being able to satisfy her, so she has a secret affair with a businessman in the surveillance biz. A blond bisexual hunk who is getting it on with a woman who does research for nerve gas (and was married to the surveillance man) and

used to date the professor, comes on to the macho guy for a gay fling. Two Frederick's of Hollywood-clad teen' hookers deliver bunches of chain letters as they're en route to serve the vet. Two deaths occur.

The cast delivers its lines with deader-than-deadpan irony with no affect in their voices, but without the intentional shocks.

Rappaport made the film for about $125,000 and it shows in the minimal and confining sets. He did have some fun with secret lensing in a New York City post office letter sorting department, but the rest of the photography is in the studio.

Rappaport touches on themes of political paranoia, sexual dilemmas and general ennui, but it's all very confusing and not consistently engaging to sustain the labyrinth of interconnected characters.—*Devo*.

My American Cousin
(CANADIAN-COLOR)

Toronto, Sept. 5.

A Spectrafilm release of a Peter O'Brian Independent Pictures production in association with Borderline Prods. Produced by O'Brian. Coproducer, Sandy Wilson. Written and directed by Wilson. Features entire cast. Camera (color), Richard Leiterman; art director, Phillip Schmidt; editor, Haida Paul; set decoration, Joey Morgan; sound, Bruce Nyznik; assistant director, Edward Folger. Reviewed at Toronto Festival of Festivals, Sept. 5, 1985. Running time: **95 MINS.**

Sandy Wilson	Margret Langrick
Butch Walker	John Wildman
Major Wilcox	Richard Donat
Kitty Wilcox	Jane Mortifee
Lenny McPhee	T.J. Scott
Shirley Darling	Camille Henderson

First-time feature director Sandy Wilson delivers an affectionate and charming entry with "My American Cousin," and Spectrafilm can look forward to some b.o. sparks with proper handling. Word of mouth is already buoyant about this tale of an adolescent girl's golden summer in British Columbia.

It's 1959 and just as 12-year-old Sandy (Margret Langrick) scribes furiously in her diary, "Nothing ever happens," her world is transformed when her handsome, bad boy American cousin Butch (John Wildman) descends on the Wilcox household.

Sandy lives on a sprawling ranch on Lake Okanagan in B.C. with her five siblings and ultraconservative parents. Eighteen-year-old Butch's arrival from California in a snazzy red Cadillac sparks titillation and fear in Sandy. Butch has run away from home, which makes his visit all the more enigmatic.

Butch meets the local kids and has a mini-fling of heavy petting with pert Shirl, girlfriend of the town's ladies man, Lenny. Sandy is quietly going ga-ga over Butch, and convinces him to take her and three girlfriends out for a spin in the Caddy, all to their giggling glee. He

turns them on to chewing gum, candy, and his American wisdom.

Butch ultimately gets in a tiff with Lenny and the local boys over Shirl, and gets Sandy in hot water by keeping her out all night at a verboten teen dance. When Butch's obnoxious parents come up to Canada to whisk him home, Sandy plots her own escape from oppressive small-town B.C., but relents and winds up staying on.

The cast is solid, especially young Langrick, who captures just the right sensibility of a 12-year-old praying she were 17. She's alternately smug, sweet, insecure, and confused. John Wildman's Butch is a hunk and has the insouciant manner of a rebel, but is often not sufficiently troubled. Richard Donat and Jane Mortifee have fun as the pristine parents.

Script is deft, with nice touches about quirky things femme teens do: e.g., rehearsing lines to potential boyfriends in a hand mirror and then kissing "his" image on it.

A musical soundtrack with '50s hits such as "Summertime Blues" and "Sea Cruise" sets the period, and Richard Leiterman has shot the pic handsomely.

Wilson, who helmed this autobiographical feature with great care, has also turned the tables on this summer's glut of pubescent boy hacker pics by posing the girl's p.o.v. Despite stretches of little action, the pic moves along a lazy summer where nothing and everything happens at once. —*Devo*.

Beer
(COLOR)

Unsuccessful satire attacking the hucksters.

Hollywood, Sept. 11.

An Orion Pictures release of a Robert Chartoff production. Produced by Chartoff. Executive producer, James D. Brubaker. Directed by Patrick Kelly. Stars Loretta Swit, Rip Torn. Screenplay, Allan Weisbecker; camera (Deluxe color), Bill Butler; editor, Alan Heim; music, Bill Conti; production design, Bill Bordie; art direction, Tony Hall, Bill McAllister (Nevada); set decoration, Steve Shewchuk, Michele Guiol (Nevada); sound, Bruce Cawardine, Gary Cunningham (Nevada); associate producer, Maryanne Ziegler; assistant director, Martin Walters; casting, Lynn Kressel, Canadian Casting Associates. Reviewed at the Orion Screening Room, L.A., Sept. 10, 1985. (MPAA Rating: R.) Running time: **82 MINS.**

B.D. Tucker	Loretta Swit
Buzz Beckerman	Rip Torn
A.J. Norbecker	Kenneth Mars
Elliot Morrison	David Alan Grier
Merle Draggett	William Russ
Frankie Falcone	Saul Stein
Harley Feemer	Peter Michael Goetz
Stanley Dickler	David Wohl
Talkshow host	Dick Shawn
Mary Morrison	Ren Woods
Thief	Alar Aedma

"Beer" selects as its satiric target the holy shrine of Madison Avenue

and comes up with the shocking revelations that the American advertising industry manufactures phony images, lies to the public and promotes dubious values. Prospective viewers are certainly not going to lay down their $5.50 to learn that when they can figure it out by staying home and watching tv. Pic recently opened in test engagements in Colorado, and further playoff remains questionable.

Originally announced under the title "The Selling Of America," film began lensing with Sandra Bernhard in the leading role, but she was replaced after a week or so by Loretta Swit. Part is that of a high-powered ad exec who hypos sales for Norbecker Beer by developing a campaign featuring three regular Joes off the street who become macho media figures.

Allan Weisbecker's script manages a few easy laughs from the easy prey, but film has trouble passing as satire since the commercials, directed by tough-guy old pro Rip Torn in something of a John Huston turn, are so close to the real thing. Remove the lewd "Whip Out Your Norbecker" tagline and the spots are little different than those that turn up on every football game.

The ads created by Swit are unrelentingly sexist, and gays will have little reason to be pleased by the thrust of the final reel or two. What they don't know won't hurt them, and few will end up seeing this.

Director Patrick Kelly keeps things moving along at a tv commercial pace. Set in New York, pic was lensed mostly in Toronto with adequate visual results. With the exception of the three men recruited for the campaign, the characters are uniformly obnoxious, and the thesps play them accordingly.

— *Cart*.

Il Risveglio di Paul
(Paul's Awakening)
(ITALIAN-COLOR)

Venice, Sept. 7.

Produced by Michele Saponaro for Sigla Emme. Written and directed by Saponaro. Camera (Color), Riccardo Pizzocchere; art director, Ninni Migliotta; music, Marco Canepa, Kalib Khallab. Reviewed at the Venice Film Festival, Sept. 6, 1985. Running time: **85 MINS.**

Paul Mendàs	Michele Saponaro
Alice	Bianca O'Feeney
Tao Ling	Thomas Wu Tao Ling

The most fun of the new Italian films unspooled in Venice's De Sica section, "Paul's Awakening" overcame some technical shortcomings with pure imagination. Sci-fi plot involves a time machine that whisks athletes and other gifted souls into the future to participate in "The Great Game." Though not strictly original, pic proved able to hold audience attention from start to finish and helmer Michele Saponaro, whose background is in tv commercials, showed a lively hand with his material.

Saponaro (45), who also scripted, plays the title role of Paul Mendàs, a French decathlon champ who is pulled off his deathbed in 1946 (his corpse is replaced by a double to avoid arousing suspicion among the relatives) and projected into the year 2262. Machines rule the world and mankind lives under their yoke. Rebellious impulses are detected instantaneously and quelled with a quick hit of drugs. In addition to the regular robot-citizens, there live a number of exceptional men and women pulled out of the past, like Paul, who form a kind of zoological garden, each living in his own re-created natural habitat. They are kept in hibernation 11 months out of the year, and only are awake for one.

Paul wakes up to find he has been chosen a participant in the Great Game of Spring. Prize: a shot at possible freedom in the mysterious Northwest Zone. As he trains for the encounter, at which he must be capable of killing his opponent, he meets Alice Meyers (Bianca O'Feeney), a young teacher from the 21st century, and an attachment develops. Thomas Wu Tao Ling plays Paul's secret kung fu master, whose Chinese pagoda garden is the high point of set designer Ninni Migliotta's imaginative work.

There are a lot of holes in the story that wouldn't pass muster in a comic book, but film has a dream-like quality that absorbs the incongruities and lets the fantasy shine through. In a climactic game scene that doesn't come off very well, Paul discovers his opponent is none other than Alice, who has somehow grown a monstrous red claw-arm with homicidal intentions of its own. He cuts off the nauseating protuberance and the couple (again with four normal arms between them) heads for the great Northwest.

Amateurish thesping contributes to the aura of enjoyable B-sci-fi pulp. —*Yung.*

Frog Dreaming
(AUSTRALIAN-COLOR)

Sydney, Sept. 10.
A Greater Union (Australia) release of a U.A.A. presentation of a Middle Reef production. Produced by Barbi Taylor, Everett de Roche. Executive producers, David Thomas, John Picton-Warlow. Directed by Brian Trenchard-Smith. Stars Henry Thomas. Screenplay, Everett de Roche; camera (color), John McLean; editor, Brian Kavanagh; music, Brian May; production design, Jon Dowding; costumes, Aphrodite Kondos; special lab consultant, Bill Gooley; production manager, Jan Tyrell; assistant director, Terry Needham; underwater camera, Ron Taylor. Reviewed at Chauvel, Paddington,

July 23, 1985. Running time: **93 MINS.**
Cody Walpole . . . . Henry Thomas
Gaza . . . . Tony Barry
Wendy Cannon . . . . Rachel Friend
Jane Cannon . . . . Tamsin West
Sgt. Ricketts . . . . John Ewart
Mr. Cannon . . . . Dennis Miller
Mrs. Cannon . . . . Katy Manning
Charlie Pride . . . . : . . . . . . Dempsey Knight
Neville . . . . Peter Cummins

An ingenious, handsomely produced fantasy-adventure for youngsters, "Frog Dreaming" should score with the young set Down Under and has definite offshore possibilities.

Original screenplay by coproducer Everett de Roche, an old hand at this sort of thing by now, is about an adventurous 14-year-old, played by E.T.'s friend, Henry Thomas, who becomes obsessed with the idea that some kind of marine monster, perhaps a cousin to the Loch Ness monster, is lurking under the murky waters of a small lake in the picturesque hills of southern Australia. Gripping opening sequence shows a lone fisherman at first intrigued, then petrified by something he sees bubbling up from the depths of the lake, and it's the later discovery of his skeletal remains that sparks the youngster's interest. Resolution of the drama is clever, but may be overly down-to-earth for youngsters who expect pretty heavy fantasy in their movies these days.

John McLean's superlative photography takes full advantage of the beauty of the area, and de Roche's script gives helmer Brian Trenchard-Smith ample opportunity to jangle the nerves of the audience. There's a strong subtext of aboriginal legend and mystery in the film, much as there was in Peter Weir's "The Last Wave," and the aboriginal scenes are evocatively presented. Brian Kavanagh's editing is very tight, and Brian May's music always effective. Insert shots of frogs, carnivorous lizards and snakes add to the atmosphere of it all.

Thesping is fine, with Rachel Friend a pert newcomer as Thomas' young girlfriend and Tamsin West (the eponymous heroine of Trenchard-Smith's previous pic, "Jenny Kissed Me") often funny as Friend's smartass younger sister. The adults, led by Tony Barry as Thomas' easy-going foster-father, John Ewart as the local cop, and Dempsey Knight as a mysterious aboriginal, are all fine. Henry Thomas was obviously cast with an eye to the U.S. boxoffice. He's okay, but despite the obligatory line in the script about his American antecedents, seems misplaced. It's odd that, after apparently some time in this rural backwater, he hasn't picked up a hint of an Aussie accent.

Overall, though, "Frog Dreaming" is a modest winner, and should repay local distrib Greater Union

with healthy returns. U.S. distribution remains up for grabs, after an early potential Stateside backer (20th Fox' since-defunct TLC Films) dropped out. — *Strat.*

No Surrender
(BRITISH-COLOR)

Toronto, Sept. 13.
A production of Dumbarton Films, National Film Finance Corp., Film Four International, William Johnston, Ronald Lillie, and Lauron International Inc. Produced by Mamoun Hassan. Directed by Peter Smith. Written by Alan Bleasdale; executive producer, Michael Peacock; camera (color), Mick Coulton; editor, Rodney Holland; art director, Andrew Mollo; sound, Sandy Macrae, Brian Holland; music, Darryl Runswick. Reviewed at the Toronto Festival of Festivals, Varsity Theater, Sept. 12, 1985. Running time: **101 MINS.**
Mike . . . . Michael Angelis
Martha Gorman . . . . Avis Bunnage
George Gorman . . . . J.G. Devlin
Paddy . . . . James Ellis
Ross . . . . Tom Georgeson
Bernard . . . . Bernard Hill
Billy . . . . Ray McAnally
Norman . . . . . . : . . . . Mark Mulholland
Cheryl . . . . Joanne Whalley

The first British film to be linked under the Canadian/British "twinning" agreement, pic is surprisingly uncommercial. A fair amount of talent has been invested in Alan Bleasdale's darkly comic script, but look is just as dark and the dialog so thickly Liverpudlian that a great deal of concentration is required to **catch the jokes. A lot of promising debuts here, from the director and several leads, but they don't link up in a unified and consistent delivery.**

Confined for the better part of pic to a seedy nightclub on the outskirts of town, the threads of various stories are finally woven together at the Charleston Club on New Year's Eve.

A new manager (Michael Angelis) is about to assume the responsibility for keeping the club's chaos under control, after his sabotaging predecessor has booked two warring factions of old folks as an aud. Angelis' reaction shots have a non-plussed desperation, as he tries to figure out how to provide entertainment for the oldsters using a young punk band, an hysterical magician and a comedian he simply sends home. His discomfort is palpable in this joint where old Christmas decorations come to die.

Adding to the outrageousness, three or four octogenarians hobble or roll in wheelchairs, laughing insanely to punk group lyrics like "Die, die, die!" Good taste never gets in the way of the hard-bitten humor, and the shift of moods can be startling. Numerous plot contrivances are never spelled out, and difficult to follow.

Hints at political alliances riddle the situations, such as with the **murder of an Ulster terrorist by a**

former gunman called, somewhat incredibly, "Billy The Beast." Ray McAnaly does a smarmy Billy, giving some comic wrinkles to the edges of the character. But Bernard Hill upstages everyone as the bouncer delivering wildly funny lines about his old days in the foreign legion.

Pic's ending gives it a bittersweet aftertaste, feeling ultimately slightly high concept, along the lines "Long Good Friday" meets "Secret Policeman's Other Ball."

Club's rundown ambience is quite *noir,* and the sleight-of-hand dialog that turns disaster into parody saves pic from depression, concluding with a shrug over the deaths, violence, police, and odd prize for the best costume in a pensioners' masquerade.

Peter Smith puts it all together as a series of deliberately mismanaged moments, confrontations over half-forgotten issues, and reunions of enemies who lives have no meaning without each other, and regularly returns to Michael's point of view, seeing it as all in a night's work. — *Kaja.*

Antonio Gaudi
(JAPANESE/SPANISH-DOCU-COLOR)

Toronto, Sept. 8.
Produced by Teshigahara Prods. Produced by Hiroshi Teshigahara, Noriko Nomura. Directed by Teshigahara. Camera (color), Hunichi Segawa, Yoshikazu Yanagida, Ryu Segawa; edited by Teshigahara; sound, Koji Asari; music, Toru Takemitsu, Kurodo Mori, Shinji Hori. Reviewed at Toronto Festival of Festivals (Varsity), Sept. 7, 1985. Running time: **82 MINS.**

Known in the film world for the use Antonioni made of the organic and illusionary quality of his architecture in "The Passenger," Antonio Gaudi is the Catalan architect who was part of the late 19th-century revival of Catalan culture from the Middle Ages. This surprising tribute to him by the man whose photography and equally organic vision in "Woman Of The Dunes" shows off Gaudi's brilliance and audaciousness without burdening it with any narration full of caveats and pre-digested interpretations.

Beginning with a brief outline of other Catalan creators, such as Picasso, Antoni Tapies, Joan Miro, as well as a wall bearing bullet marks from the Spanish Civil War, Teshigahara traces Catalan art from the Romanesque period of 1000 to 1300 A.D. and shows how the extraordinary architecture of Gaudi draws on that more ancient and pious tradition.

Teshigahara appreciates with the camera alone the fantasy, the molding of shapes and the eruption of mosaic-like surfaces in Gaudi's work, revealing their curvaceous, even erotic forms through the simplicity of his camera. He does not attempt to compete with Gaudi's sometimes erratic imagination, and includes the context with shots of the streets and the Sunday morning dance of the Sardana on the main square of Barcelona.

The undular walls and designs that remind one of marine life and little else in the history of architecture are accompanied by a score compiled of baroque harpsichord, organ pieces, and even a glass orchestra. The protean perfection of Gaudi's work on the houses for Guell, his faithful patron, is painstakingly illustrated, building up to show his wild dreams of a temple, as he called it, in Barcelona, that looks more like a Disney structure than a religious edifice.

But Teshigahara makes the overwrought designs and bejeweled fairy world quite accessible. — *Kaja.*

Desert Warrior
(COLOR)

Weak imitation of Mad Max.

Hollywood, Sept. 13.
A Concorde Pictures release of a Rodeo Prods. production. Produced and directed by Cirio H. Santiago. Features entire cast. Screenplay, Fredrick Bailey; editor, George Saint; music, Chris Young; associate producer, John Carlos; casting, Dick Raye. Reviewed at the Hollywood Pacific Theater, Hollywood, Calif., Sept. 13, 1985. (MPAA Rating: R.) Running time: **85 MINS.**
Trace .... Gary Watkins
Stinger .... Laura Banks
Harley .... Lynda Wiesmeier
Spike .... Linda Grovenor

"Desert Warrior" is a bargain basement rip-off of the "Road Warrior" series obviously designed for the foreign action market. Pic is so poorly played and ridiculous it is difficult to imagine anyone with a low enough I.Q. to qualify as the target audience. B.O. prospects are nonexistent.

"Desert Warrior" has copied only the bare bones of the Mad Max pictures without the imagination to create a memorable hero or even threatening villains for that matter. Form is merely an excuse for crudely executed shootups and extended nude scenes.

Hero is Trace (Gary Watkins), who squares off against the Scourge and his men in an attempt to rescue his sister (Lynda Wiesmeier) who spends most of the film being raped by the bad guys. In his quest Trace is joined by a female bounty hunter (Laura Banks) and a psychic child (Linda Grovenor).

Action is staged clumsily with effects unconvincing and set design more World War II surplus than futuristic. Acting is commensurate with the rest of the production.

Pic was shot in the Philippines in 1984, first known as "Vindicator" and then "Wheels Of Fire." —*Jagr.*

Fratelli
(Brothers)
(ITALIAN-COLOR)

Venice, Sept. 1.
Produced by RAI-3. Directed by Loredana Dordi. Stars Rüdiger Vogler, Enzo Cosimi. Screenplay, L. Dordi, Franca Ongaro Basaglia, based on a novel by Carmelo Samonà; camera (Color), Angelo Sciarra; editor Mirella Mencio; art director, Nicola Rubartelli; music, Egisto Macchi. Reviewed at the Venice Film Festival, Aug. 31, 1985. Running time: **100 MINS.**
The brother .... Rüdiger Vogler
Pietro .... Enzo Cosimi
Anna .... Mimsy Farmer

"Brothers" is Loredana Dordi's first feature film; helmer has been a tv director and documaker. Both experience and sensitivity show through in the pic, which shared first prize in its Venice De Sica debut. Tale of two brothers is a rigorous exploration of mental illness as an unsolvable enigma that makes few concessions to viewer comfort. Though headliner Rüdiger Vogler, an international art house name, could get pic into a few theatrical sites, its main audience will be the fans of cultural tv stations, like producer RAI-3.

Vogler plays the enlightened, intellectual frère of Pietro (Enzo Cosimi), a handsome schizophrenic youth. Viewer's first hurdle is to accept the screen convention that would make the blond German and dark Italian flesh and blood, as they're about as far apart as two thesps can get.

Most of pic has Vogler shut up in a big, empty, labyrinthine apartment with the boy, trying every means he can think of to penetrate the wall of irrationality and illness that separates them. Visually this translates as long, slow sequences of Pietro moving his hand over a pane of glass, spinning around the room in circles, and hiding behind curtains. With the patience of a saint, Vogler helps him remember the names of common objects, eat and dress.

It is hard to depict obsessive behavior without making it seem unbearably repetitive. Dordi takes such pains to faithfully describe the psychological mechanisms and their subtle variations, she sometimes misses the emotional key that would have given a scene resonance and meaning.

Mimsy Farmer cameos as a sensitive friend who partially suceeds in getting through to Pietro via emotional communication.

Brother Vogler's linguistic attempts are doomed to failure, as Pietro evades all his efforts to talk

and reason. Both thesps show great tenacity in difficult roles, and both win our grudging sympathy. We share some of their frustration at story's end when, after an apparent breakthrough, Pietro retreats into isolation once more, and both men are left stranded before his painful suffering. — *Yung.*

Dark Lullabies
(CANADIAN-DOCU-COLOR/B&W)

Montreal, Sept. 2.
A National Film Board of Canada production. Produced by Irene Lilienheim Angelico, Abbey Jack Neidik, Edward Le Lorrain, Bonnie Sherr Klein. Directed by Irene Lilienheim Angelico, Neidik. Written by Lilienheim Angelico, Gloria Demers; camera (color), Susan Trow; music, Lauri Conger, Michael Beinhorn; sound, Jean-Guy Normandin. Reviewed at World Film Festival, Montreal, Aug. 29, 1985. Running time: **80 MINS.**

To the increasing number of films and documentaries on the subject of the Holocaust, add this Canadian item which covers the responses of the children of the survivors of Nazi atrocities, as well as the offspring of their oppressors.

The parents of codirector Irene Lilienheim Angelico spent the war in separate concentration camps, but survived. As the title of this film suggests, filmmaker's childhood was haunted by the painful, but unspoken, memories of her mother and father, and only much later did she come to realize what they'd suffered before she was born.

Seeking to discover more about this agonizing past, Lilienheim Angelico travels to Israel and then to Germany to ask the question nobody is really able to answer: Why did it happen? She also talks to the children of the Nazis in an effort to discover how they were affected by the guilt of their parents.

A sober, sometimes painful, documentary. —*Strat.*

Blu Cobalto
(Cobalt Blue)
(ITALIAN-COLOR)

Venice, Aug. 30.
Produced by Marco Bianchi for Alias-Babele Cinematografica in cooperation with RAI-TV Channel 3. Directed by Gianfranco Fiore Donati. Stars Anna Bonaiuto, Enrico Ghezzi. Screenplay, Donati, Aldo Braibanti; camera (color), Vittorio Bagnasco; editor, Enzo Meniconi; art director, Leonardo Scarpa, Giancarlo Basil; music, Daniele Bacalov. Reviewed at the Venice Film Festival, Aug. 28, 1985. Running time: 77 MINS.
Anna .... Anna Bonaiuto
Doctor .... Enrico Ghezzi
Enea .... Enea Cesari
Actress .... Susanna Javicoli
Actor .... Flavio Bonacci

A promising first feature by Gianfranco Fiore Donati (whose background was in advertising),

"Cobalt Blue" is a film about neurotics, set in a hospital cancer ward. In spite of the somber setting and up-in-the-air ending, it is not a gloomy film. The name of the disease everybody has is hidden under a cloak of silence, and attention is focused on character relations and reactions. Nobody looks sick. The only one who dies is an old man (Enea Cesari) who has made peace with the world, and among the younger patients total recovery seems to be the rule.

Anna (Anna Bonaiuto), a pretty young actress, finds little satisfaction in her personal life. She runs between stage, dressing room, and hospital with a restlessness that is underlined by flashbacks and flashforwards, eventually developing an attachment to the wise old peasant Enea and her neurotic young medic, Enrico Ghezzi. The doctor himself is an ex-cancer patient and obviously has a tormented relationship to his professional specialization. Will their affection survive after Anna leaves the hospital?

Watchable enough but inconclusive, "Cobalt" channels most of its energy into playing with film technique — fancy editing, discontinuous storyline, division into sections with titles like "Presages," "Night," "Malus;" plus overhead camera angles. Lensing by cameraman Vittorio Bagnasco is sharp and crisp. Actors are interesting and out of the ordinary, though slick dubbing takes a lot away from both the old man and the doctor. Their faces cry out for real voices, not flawless studio sound.— *Yung.*

L'Amara Scienza
(The Sadness Of Knowing)
(ITALIAN-COLOR)

Venice, Aug. 28.
Produced by RAI-3. Directed by Nicola de Rinaldo. Stars Lina Polito, Remo Girone. Screenplay, De Rinaldo, Giorgio Vitale, freely based on the novel by Luigi Compagnone; camera (color), Antonio Baldoni; editor, Orlando Marini; art director, Nicola Rubertelli; music, Fiorenzo Rizzone. Reviewed at the Venice Film Festival, Aug. 25, 1985. Running time: **86 MINS.**
Nino .... Remo Girone
Lucia .... Lina Polito
Isidro .... Massimo Abbate
Salvatore .... Mario Scarpetta
Father .... Luigi Compagnone

Nicely lensed and solidly acted, "L'Amara Scienza" is a quiet little Neapolitan tragedy made by RAI-3. No fireworks, but honest craftsmanship from helmer Nicola de Rinaldo, who likes thesps Remo Girone, Lina Polito and Massimo Abbate comes from a serious stage background. Script, touching without being sentimental, revolves around the sacrifice asked of three siblings in the name of their family. Pic shared first prize in Venice's De Sica section, where it was preemed.

It is the director's first feature.

Action takes place in a single day in Naples. Unknown to the elderly Capt. Alinei (Luigi Campagnone, author of the novel on which the story is based), the family house in a coastal fishing village, full of memories and traditions, will have to be sold unless his three grown children can come up with a large sum of money to pay back taxes. In defense of their family's identity and continuity, the trio of young people go to the city to look for the money.

Nino (Girone), a promising actor, lowers himself to begging for an advance from a rich producer. Isidro (Abbate), the youngest, casually makes friends with a transvestite his own age, but ultimately refuses to prostitute himself. Lucia (Polito), an average-looking woman of 30 without husband or fiancé, swallows her pride and feelings and asks her old betrothed Mario Scarpetta for the sum. After seducing her in a sordid trailer and letting her glimpse his blond wife, he takes her to a rich man who suggests she have a baby in his wife's place and sell it to them. She flees in disgust.

In the end it is Nino who bitterly ruins his career to get the money.

Various moods alternate throughout pic, from the shame, fear and anger of having to search for money, to brief moments of joy and release, as when Isidro runs down the street with the whole city appearing to be at his feet. The somber realism of the story is softened by a gentle, understanding musical comment by Fiorenzo Rizzone which acts as a plaintive counterpoint. — *Yung.*

Damul
(Bonded Until Death)
(INDIAN-COLOR)

Montreal, Aug. 27.
A Prakash Jha-National Film Development Corporation production. Produced, directed, written by Prakash Jha. Features entire cast. Story, dialog, Shalwal; camera (color), production design, Rajen Kothari; editor, Apurwa Yagnik; sound, A.M. Padmanabhan, S.M. Basu; music, Raghunath Sheth; production manager, P.K. Vasu; associate director, Subhankar Ghosh. Reviewed at World Film Festival, Montreal (In Competition), Aug. 26, 1985. Funning time: 106 MINS.
With: Manohar Singh, Annu Kapoor, Sreela Mazumdar, Deepti Naval, Pyare Mohan Sahay, Braj Kishore, Vani Singh, Shyamall.

An angry, passionate film about the feudal system known as Panha still operating today in Bihar state, "Damul" presents a grim picture of the shameless and ruthless exploitation of the lowest caste, the Harijan (Untouchables) by the ruling Brahmin class.

Setting is a Bihar village in 1984. The place is run by the Brahmin Madho, and elections are rigged against anybody from another caste standing a chance. This creates even more dissatisfaction among the poverty-stricken Harijan, who stage a walk-out, refusing to work on Madho's land. The Brahmin's men react by massacring most of the Hairjan men and burning their homes. When the police and a government minister arrive to investigate, it goes without saying that the testimony of the surviving Harijan is ignored and the situation will go on as before.

We've seen films about the ruthless caste system in the Indian hinterlands before, but few as pessimistic and devastating as this one. It's a pity, then, that Prakash Jha's direction is a bit precious, with his camera continually on the move, tracking and circling his characters in a manner that becomes thoroughly irritating after a while. Apart from this annoying directorial trait, film is handsomely mounted with excellent color, solid acting and a confident sense of narrative. Jha has dedicated it to his parents. — *Strat.*

Beethoven's Nephew
(FRENCH-WEST GERMAN-COLOR)

Venice, Sept. 5.
An Orfilm Internazional production. Produced by Marita Coustet. Directed by Paul Morrissey. Features entire cast. Screenplay, Mathieu Carrière, Morrissey; camera (color), Hans Polak; sets, Mario Garbuglia; costumes, Claudia Bobsin; editor, Albert Jurgenson, Michèle Lauliac; musical direction, Elena Rostropovitch; sound, Philippe Lemanuel, Claude Gazean. Reviewed at Venice Film Fest (Special Programs I), Sept. 4, 1985. Running time: 100 MINS.
With: Wolfgang Reichmann (Ludwig van Beethoven), Dietmar Prinz (Karl van Beethoven), Jane Birkin (Johanna van Beethoven), Nathalie Baye (Léonore), Mathieu Carrière (Archbishop Rodolfo), Ulrich Beer (Shindler), Erna Korhel (Holz).

Not much in the way of critical praise can be showered on Paul Morrissey's "Beethoven's Nephew," a French-German coproduction shot in English and unspooled in a special program on the Lido. It's one of the several films on music and musicians presented towards the end of the fest as an informational series.

This is an attempt to diagnose the great composer's obsession with the company of his nephew in Vienna during the last years of his life. Morrissey, together with scripter-thesp Mathieu Carrière, apparently feel that this odd relationship between uncle and nephew was about all that counted.

Beethoven is plagued with paranoia as he fights to keep the nephew away from his own mother with costly court cases. All that is well and good supposing it's all true as here presented by Morrissey & Co. — but to keep hitting the audience over the head with banal dialog on the matter for the full course of a film is enough already. The waste of good actors is equally painful. — *Holl.*

Prima del Futuro
(Before The Future)
(ITALIAN-COLOR)

Venice, Sept. 3.
Produced by Renato Ostuni for RAI-2, Cinecittà, U.P.C., A.D.C. Written and directed by Fabrizio Caleffi, Ettore Pasculli, Gabriella Rosaleva. Features entire cast. Camera (color), Armando Bolzoni, Ildo Chiappin, Benedetto Spampinato; editor, G. Neri, Antonella Galassi; art director, Mauro Radaelli and Anna Mari; music, Riccardo Senigallia. Reviewed at the Venice Film Festival, Sept. 1, 1985. Running time: 100 MINS.
Seneca . . . . David Brandon
Teacher . . . . Laura Marconi
Janitor . . . . Elda Olivieri
Spartacus . . . . Maurizio Donadoni
Woman . . . . Olimpia Carlisi
Inspector . . . . Peter Chatel
Actress . . . . Valeria Cavalli

A three-director effort produced by RAI-2 and Cinecittà, "Before The Future" aims to be a spoof with a message, but succeeds only in stringing together a collection of vaguely futuristic images without wit, humor or emotional charge. It radiates a strong aura of first-year film school project.

The trio of episodes is set in an indefinite future world, where tv has made predictably greater inroads into daily life and where homo sapiens has become predictably more dehumanized. All three start with the premise that the winner of a great telematic contest is being sought among subscribers to the tv. In the first sketch, "Seneca," David Brandon is a young professor of mythology who conducts his classes in pajama bottoms from his apartment via closed-circuit tv. Feeling he is losing popularity with his students and won't get his contract renewed, Seneca goes for comfort to a sexy colleague, Laura Marconi, who counsels him to upgrade his image. After a high-tech lecture on centaurs, he goes horseback riding and is killed in a fall, before he can collect his prize money.

Second winner to be picked is "Spartacus." As might be imagined, hero Maurizio Donadoni is an exploited prole of the future. He rebels against his machine masters after falling in love with a romantic woman (Olimpia Carlisi) on a "therapy cassette." More controlled than the other episodes, "Spartacus" (helmed by Gabriella Rosaleva) contains a touching note of loneliness and isolation.

Last lucky winner is "Caligola." Here actors and extras anxiously strain to be chosen in a completely automated tv studio, where aspiring actress Valeria Cavalli is made over, only to be rejected. Telematics inspector Peter Chatel finally realizes Caligola is a sheepdog.

Dialog and dubbing compete with each other for last place in the technical department.

Part of the pic's strange look can be accounted for by the fact that all filming took place in Milan's Intl. Exhibition of Architecture for the Electronic Civilization, judged the most suitable locale to probe the possibilities of film production based on new technological images. The makers promise future products in the same "Cinema And Paradox" series which will mine other untried talents. — *Yung.*

Le Dernier Glacier
(The Last Glacier)
(CANADIAN-COLOR)

Toronto, Sept. 9.
National Film Board of Canada production. Produced by Jean Dansereau. Written and directed by Roger Frappier, Jacques Leduc. Camera (color), Leduc, Pierre Letarte; editor, Monique Fortier; sound, Claude Beaugrand; music, Rene Lussier, Jean Derome; optical effects, Jimmy Chin, Susan Gourley. Reviewed at the Toronto Festival of Festivals, Cumberland Theater, Sept. 8, 1985. Running Time: 83 MINS.
Raoul . . . . Robert Gravel
Carmen . . . . Louise Laprade
Leonard . . . . Michel Rivard
Benoit . . . . Martin Dumont
Montagnais Indian . . . . Marie St-Onge

When Prime Minister Brian Mulroney was still president of an iron ore company, he closed down a company town called Schefferville, effectively displacing 5,000 inhabitants and returning the land to the 800 Native Americans still there. The filmmakers have used this raw material "torn from the headlines" in such a slipshod style that the outsider might well wonder who Mulroney is and why the NFB thought this was a story worth documenting, much less dramatizing. The actual events during the death of Schefferville have been drowned in the melodrama of a marital breakup that itself lacks motivation.

In this last outpost of civilization, a generation has been born which is about to be uprooted. To prove this, interviews with school kids are meant to provide the barometer of the success of this town as a home, but the kids come off as merely manipulative extensions of writers/directors Roger Frappier and Jacques Leduc. Whenever the lack of activity threatens to bring pic to an utter standstill, they use split-screen images, thus doubling the boredom.

Title derives from the perspective of a local scientist, brought in as one of many detours, offering some archeological and geological data plus a bit of sophistic reasoning. In the long haul, he explains, the closing down of one mining town is not a major historical event, and certainly the pic's not impressed with its historical importance, to judge from its failure to show anything but the most emotional reaction by abandoned adolescents.

Pic's obsession with fancy film techniques has muddled the interest in its subject matter and betrayed its own purpose. It would be hard for an outsider to know if the footage of Mulroney was real or also a dramatization, or who this man actually is. Minimal marketing possibilities beyond Canada result.

—*Kaja.*

Crime Wave
(CANADIAN-COLOR)

Toronto, Sept. 12.

Produced, directed and written by John Paizs. Director of photography, Paizs; camera (Total color), Tom Fijal; editor, Paizs, Gerry Klym, Jon Coutts; sound, Klym; graphics and miniatures, Paizs; special effects, Shawn Wilson, Dave Peter. Reviewed at Toronto Festival of Festivals, Cumberland Theater, Sept. 11, 1985. Running time: **80 MINS.**

Cast: John Paizs, Eva Kovacs, Darrel Baran, Jeffery Owen Madden, Tea Andrea Tanner, Mark Yuill, Neil Laurie, Mitch Funk, Barbara MacDonald.

The debut feature of one of Canada's funniest and, by virtue of his budgets, most inventive directors, John Paizs makes a splendid splash that fulfills the promise of his previous 10 shorts. Winnipeg-based and movie-obsessed, Paizs has fashioned a meditation on the frustrations of a would-be scriptwriter with ambitions of producing the world's best color crime films.

As narrator Doug Syms tells us, in confessional comic tones, hero Steven Penny can wrote only beginnings and endings, but can't cope with middles. Paisz shows several of Penny's scripting attempts, each taking only a few moments and presumably seen through the eyes of the little girl who is his neighbor and reads his trashed manuscripts. She learns about persistence of vision and of frustrations, along with the hows and whys of movie-making. Her pronouncements on Steven's self-doubt have a childlike tone of over-simplification while mocking entire pose of amateurs.

Regularly comes a warning in title cards, "From the North would come ...". Further visual jokes include extraordinary gadgetry, such as a gadget called the "jaws of life" which hoists a wrecked car in a rescue attempt. Paizs' wizardry is the achievement of a hyperkinetic humor and pungent vignettes.

Penny's adventurous search for a solution to his crime-script problem leads to Dr. Jolly, an alleged scriptdoctor in Kansas. Heading south,

he encounters in the woods an old woman and she gives Penny the impetus to overcome his writing block — a kick in the pants. The only problem with the final trip south is that Paizs' wit slackens, an illustration or parable if not a caveat for Canadians who look to the U.S. for solutions.

This is guaranteed to regale festival crowds and has a quirky potential, if developed as a cult or midnight movie. — *Kaja.*

Strictement Personnel
(Strictly Personal)
(FRENCH-COLOR)

Toronto, Sept. 14.

A Michelle de Broca and Yvan Valensi production for YF. Produced by Simona Benzakein, Pierre Jolivet. Directed by Jolivet. Script, Jolivet, Luc Beraud, Bernard Balavoine, Christiane Kruger; camera (color), Christian Lamarque; editor, Gerard Lamps; music, Serge Perathoner; set design, Christian Grosrichard; sound engineer, Yves Osmu; first assistant director, Ginette Mejinsky; second assistant director, Fabrice Roche; continuity, Sylvie Koechlin; costumes, Magali Bassenne. Reviewed at Toronto Festival of Festivals (Varsity), Sept. 14, 1985. Running time: **90 MINS.**

Jean	Pierre Arditi
Benoit	Jacques Penot
Helene	Caroline Chaniolleau
Villechaize	Jean Reno
The father	Robert Rimbaud
Julia	Christiane Kruger
Judith	Simona Benzakein
The concierge	Maurice Baquet
Isabelle	Voice of Berangere Bonvoisin

Following the notable critical success of "Le Dernier Combat," the writer-producer and lead actor of that virtually silent, post-apocalyptic vision has returned with a clever (and talking) psychological police thriller about a man who is as bad a writer as he is a cop.

Pierre Arditi plays Jean with a wry longing to do great things without having to exert himself, and his pinched resignation when his novel is rejected by both his publisher and girlfriend, because he has only managed to recreate "Madame Bovary," is writer-director Pierre Jolivet's own cynicism at work in this highly intellectual but entertaining genre pic.

Behind the policier lies a story about a policeman investigating his own family and his own psychological trauma over the loss of his mother at an early age, after which his father, brother and sister abandoned him in Lyons and moved to Paris.

Jean goes to Paris for a rare family reunion and finds his father has married a very young woman whose parttime work in an art gallery is bringing in suspicious amounts of money. Jean's investigation of her implies she is moonlighting as a prostitute, and the father, himself a frustrated painter, commits suicide.

Jean discovers that his sister, who

runs a jazzercise joint, is keeping a whole string of hookers fit, and his brother is a junkie. Willing to use his police connections, Jean is prepared to get his brother a desperately needed fix, but it turns out the boy has killed their step-mother.

The camera work is clear, to-thepoint and serves the pace, which is determined by the psychological development of Jean rather than the storyline.

A haunting piano score and some built-in ironies are managed as subsidiary to the story, which Jolivet keeps in the foreground. As the mystery of the murdered stepmother unravels, the entire family is implicated in a plot of producing forgeries and replacing them in the dead clients' homes after stealing the originals, which get put on the market in the father's gallery.

Jean's showdown with brother Benoit, who had been hired by their brother-in-law as a killer, brings him face-to-face with his feelings of betrayal and his own little brother's accusations of Jean's having abandoned the family. As they all begin to pull guns on each other, the disintegration of the family as a theme quickly replaces the whodunnit drive of the plot.

This pic marks debut helmer Jolivet's emergence as an uncompromising and marketable talent, and deserves the special handling required for genre pics on the arthouse circuit. — *Kaja.*

Yeh Kahani Nahin
(An Event)
(INDIAN-COLOR)

Montreal, Sept. 2.

An S.N. Production. Produced by Subhash, Shreyasi and Prabodh Godbole. Written and directed by Biplab Ray Chaudhuri. Features entire cast. Camera (Eastmancolor), Rajan Kinagi; sets, Nikhil Sen Gupta; editor, B.R. Chaudhuri; music, Bhubaneswar Misra. Reviewed at World Film Festival, Montreal, Sept. 1, 1985. Running time: **134 MINS.**

With: Subhash Godbole, Simantini Das, Charushila Sable, Anil Ranade, Ramesh Bhatkar, Satish Alekar.

"An Event" is a rather overwrought and overemphatic drama about a racist industrialist, a firm believer in India's caste system, and member of a sinister secret society founded on bigotry, who undergoes a heart transplant and winds up with the heart of an Untouchable.

The familiar tale of the bigot hoisted with his own petard is given a slow, solemn treatment by helmer Biplab Ray Chaudhuri, with every point carefully emphasized and underlined. Fantasy and dream sequences are rather awkwardly integrated.

Acting is variable, though coproducer Subhash Godbole is effective as the ruthless businessman who

finds it hard to come to terms with the marvels of modern medicine. Pic is technically okay except for some tinny sound recording.

—*Strat.*

Pisingana
(Hopscotch)
(COLOMBIAN-COLOR)

Monteal, Sept. 2.

A Focine production. Directed by Leopoldo Pinzon. Features entire cast. Screenplay, German Pinzon; camera (color), Jorge Ruiz; editor, Leopoldo Pinzon; music, Paul Dominguez. Reviewed at World Film Festival, Montreal, Aug. 31, 1985. Running time: **98 MINS.**

Graciela	July Pedraza
Jorgito	Carlos Barbosa
Consuelo	Consuelo Luzardo

Graciela is an attractive young peasant woman whose life in the beautiful hinterlands of Colombia is rudely shattered when she comes across the decapitated body of her father. Leaving her roots, she goes to Bogota where she gets a job as maid in a household headed by a groveling businessman with a neurotic wife and fascist mother. One night, the businessman comes to her room and seduces her. They're caught in the act by the wife, and Graciela is forced to leave. Her fate is inevitable.

Director Leopoldo Pinzon's idea in "Hopscotch" is to depict, via the tragic story of this one woman, how the poor in Colombian society are oppressed and violated. It's a calm, slowly evolving case history, charmingly acted by July Pedraza as the victim, and well shot by Jorge Ruiz. In all, one of the better and more accessible Colombian films to appear on the festival circuit in recent years. — *Strat.*

Glissandro
(RUMANIAN-COLOR)

Venice, Aug. 28.

A Romaniafilm production, "Three" Unit, Bucharest; world rights, Romaniafilm, Bucharest. Features entire cast. Written and directed by Mircea Daneliuc, based on Cezar Petrescu's short story "The Man In The Dream." Camera (color), Calin Ghibu; sets, Magdalena Marasescu; costumes, Catalina Iakob; music, Vasile Sirli; editor, Maria Neagu. Reviewed at Venice Film Fest (Competition), Aug. 27, 1985. Running time: **165 MINS.**

With: Stefan Iordache (Ion Theodorescu), Tora Vasilescu (Nina), Petre Simionescu (Elderly Gentleman), Ion Fiscuteanu (Alexandru Algiu), Rada Istrata (Maria Algiu), Rodica Maianu (Doctor Steriu), Victor Ionescu (Doctor Stircu).

One of Rumania's leading film artists, Mircea Daneliuc is deservedly in the main event at Venice with "Glissandro" (the title referring to a musical expression dealing with the violin). As in most of his films, Daneliuc attempts a metaphorical statement on Rumania.

This time, however, he waits two hours before getting down to the point during the last important phase of the film. It's well worth waiting for, nonetheless.

In this tale set in the 1930s, the central character is a middle-class intellectual who is dissipating his life away at the gambling table. One day, he meets an elderly gentleman, who in turn brings him a bit of unexpected good luck. He quickly betrays this trust by giving into his weaknesses. He rapes a woman in his friend's house, then defeats the elderly gentleman at a game of cards — thus driving his opponent to suicide.

Meanwhile, he sinks deeper into depression and madness. One of his obsessions is a portrait of a woman who looks like his mother. The realization that the mansion of his friend is full of these same portraits is enough to unbalance him permanently, and he commits suicide.

In the last half-hour of "Glissandro" the gambler's fantasies take possession of reality in his mind. The visual metaphor is a group of inmates from a mental asylum roaming the streets and once even invading the premises of the neighboring casino.

Pic could find its way to other fests on the circuit, but its overlength and heavy theatricality in general eliminate most chances of arthouse distribution. All the same, this one is a standout at Venice.

—Holl.

Marie
(COLOR)

Impressive though familiar political drama.

Hollywood, Sept. 14.
An MGM/UA Entertainment release of a Dino De Laurentiis presentation. Produced by Frank Capra Jr. Executive producer, Elliot Schick. Directed by Roger Donaldson. Stars Sissy Spacek. Screenplay, John Briley, based on the book "Marie: A True Story," by Peter Maas; camera (Technicolor, J-D-C widescreen), Chris Menges; editor, Neil Travis; music, Francis Lai; art direction, Ron Foreman; set decoration, Tantar Leviseur; costume design, Joe Tompkins; sound, David Hildyard; assistant director, Bob Howard; casting, Lynn Stalmaster and Associates. Reviewed at the MGM Studios, Culver City, Sept. 13, 1985. (MPAA Rating: PG-13.) Running time: 112 MINS.

Marie Ragghianti	Sissy Spacek
Eddie Sisk	Jeff Daniels
Kevin McCormack	Keith Szarabajka
Charles Traughber	Morgan Freeman
Fred Thompson	Himself
Toni Greer	Lisa Banes
FBI Agent	Trey Wilson
Deputy Attorney General	John Cullum
Governor Blanton	Don Hood
Charlie Benson	Graham Beckel
Murray Henderson	Macon McCalman
Virginia	Collin Wilcox Paxton
Dante Ragghianti	Robert Green Benson 3d
Therese Ragghianti	Dawn Carmen
Ricky Ragghianti	Shane Wexel
Dave Ragghianti	Vincent Irizarry
Bill Thompson	Michael P. Moran

"Marie" is a powerfully made political melodrama, the many strengths of which are vitiated only by the relative familiarity of the exposé, little person-vs.-the establishment framework. Sissy Spacek adds another excellent characterization to her credits, and Roger Donaldson reestablishes himself as one of the most exciting young directors on the scene with his first U.S.-lensed picture. Film will involve audiences without inflaming them, which indicates a moderate-to-good b.o. life.

Based upon a true-life book by Peter ("Serpico") Maas, tale opens in 1968 with a rough scene in which Spacek and her small kids leave home after she is brutalized by her husband.

Five years later, after educating herself further, she gets a job as extradition director and, before long, is appointed chairman of the parole board for the State of Tennessee. Helping guide her up the twisting stairway of the political system is ostensible friend Jeff Daniels, a close aide of Governor Blanton who frequently comes to Spacek with overt suggestions that she speed through the parole of certain individuals.

It doesn't take her long to figure out that the governor is in cahoots with some scummy, criminal types, and once the officals realize that Spacek is working against their interests, they railroad her out of her job.

Instead of taking this lying down, like a good little southern girl, Spacek takes the administration to court over wrongful dismissal, with the specter of widespread government corruption looming large in the background.

John Briley, who won an Oscar for "Gandhi," has set the story down in cogent fashion, and Donaldson has brought tremendous freshness to its telling, but there is just no avoiding that most of this ground has been trod many times before, and recently at that. The Watergate era produced any number of corruption-in-high-places sagas, and Spacek, for all her individuality, comes off rather like a Norma Rae Silkwood, an average woman with a brood of kids who all of a sudden finds herself playing hardball in the big leagues.

What makes the film noteworthy, then, is Donaldson's virtuoso style. Frankly displaying his documentary roots, he and ace cameraman Chris Menges move the camera urgently, restlessly, constantly reframing the elements within the widescreen image to accommodate the quick pace with which the events unfold.

Spacek is right at home with her role, coming off as spunky but not offensively cute, determined but hardly holier-than-thou, a victim who can still be painted with warts and all. Jeff Daniels is outstanding as her duplicitous associate, and Keith Szarabajka is highly sympathetic as Spacek's best friend.

Remainder of the cast has been astutely selected for absolute believability, and entire collection of characters represents an interesting view of the underside of the Southern coalition that got Jimmy Carter into the White House.

Along with Menges' superior lensing, other technical contributions are firstrate. —Cart.

La Gabbia
(The Cage)
(ITALIAN-SPANISH-COLOR)

Rome, Sept. 24.
An ACTA release, produced by Ettore Spagnuolo for Visione Cinematografica (Rome) and Bridas Productions (Madrid). Directed by Giuseppe Patroni Griffi. Stars Tony Musante, Laura Antonelli and Florinda Bolkan. Screenplay, Alberto Silvestri, Francesco Barilli, Lucio Fulci; camera (color), Juan Amoras, Hans Burmann; editor, Sergio Montanari; art director, Esio Altieri; music, Ennio Morricone. Reviewed at Quirinale Cinema, Rome, Sept. 22, 1985. Running time: 98 MINS.

Michael	Tony Musante
Marie	Laura Antonelli
Helene	Florinda Bolkan
Jacqueline	Blanca Marsillach
Young Marie	Christine Marsillach

Returning to pictures after a 10-year stint of stage work, helmer Giuseppe Patroni Griffi comes up with an elegantly lensed pic of muddy origins, somewhere between a thriller and very softcore eroticism.

Marketed on the strength of its many heroines in and out of lace undies, "The Cage" will probably garner its biggest audiences in the old-fashioned hinterlands. Laura Antonelli fans will find the vehicle pretty creaky.

Michael (Tony Musante) and Helene (Florinda Bolkan), an unmarried Parisian couple, split up for a few days at Christmas while Helene takes her son to grandma's house. In a mysterious apartment across from Helene's, Michael recognizes Marie (Antonelli) a woman he had a brief fling with when she was a brooding teenager (Christine Marsillach). Sexy flashbacks flit through both their minds and one thing leads to another on the dining room table, culminating in a mutual striptease artily lensed in slow motion.

The plot thickens slowly. Michael wakes up after a wild night to find himself tied to the bedstead, and sweet-faced Marie refuses to let him leave her a second time. With teen daughter Jacqueline (Blanca Marsillach), she holds him prisoner with nylon stockings, guns and razor blades. While the women vie for his attention and favors, Helene tries to figure out where her boyfriend has disappeared to. In the end, thanks to an incredible coincidence, she succeeds.

Story has the underpinnings of a decent thriller, but the tension is continually defused by sex scenes tacked on for obviously calculated reasons. Musante is too much of a tough playboy to attract much sympathy in the victim's role. Like the picture, he can't seem to decide whether to concentrate on getting out of the apartment or dallying with the occupants. Beautiful, gentle, and composed, Antonelli looks the opposite of mentally deranged. Sets and costumes are exceptionally gorgeous, and technical work (including an Ennio Morricone score) is generally of high quality.

—Yung.

Troupers
(DOCU-COLOR)

San Francisco, Sept. 17.
An Icarus Films release of a Catalyst Media production. Produced and directed by Glenn Silber and Claudia Vianello. Associate producer-camera (color), Michael Anderson; editor, Mary Bauer; sound, Andy Wiskes. Reviewed at Jack Wodell Screening Room, San Francisco, Calif., Sept. 17, 1985. (No MPAA Rating.) Running time: 85 MINS.

"Troupers" traces the 26-year history of the San Francisco Mime Troupe and includes archival footage of and current interviews with early Troupers Peter Coyote and Bill Graham, who went on to theatrical feature stardom and rock promotion, respectively.

Troupe began as a sort of "guerrilla theater," working Frisco parks and passing the hat, and in recent years has toured nationally and internationally with series of fresh, political musicomedies. The staging of one of those, "Steeltown," in East Chicago, Ind., takes up a long segment of the pic and is most compelling because of the reaction of trade unionists to the Troupers and the show, itself full of fun.

Portions of the pic concentrate on politics within the Troupe — how it was transformed from one-man rule of founder R.G. Davis into a "collective." Pros might be interested in company's kvetching about pay and working conditions, but the lay spectator will likely respond with a "get on with the show" attitude.

Pic has been booked into the York in Frisco for one week and will likely stir b.o. interest in the Bay area. Otherwise, commercial prospects are modest. Technical credits are sure-footed all the way.
—*Herb.*

Gesher Tzar Me'od
(On A Narrow Bridge)
(ISRAELI-COLOR)

Tel Aviv, Sept. 16.
A Nachshon Films presentation of a Tom production. Produced by Micha Sharfstein. Directed by Nissim Dayan. Screenplay, Haim Heffer, Nissim Dayan, based on an original idea by Haim Heffer; camera (color), Amnon Salomon; editor, Danny Shick; art director, Yoram Bdrzilai; music, Poldi Shatzman. Reviewed at Berkey-Pathe-Humphries Studios, Sept. 15, 1985. Running time: **100 MINS.**

Benny Tagar	Aharon Ipale
Layla Mansour	Salwa Hadad
Anwar Mansour	Tuncel Curtiz
Abadi	Makhram Khouri
Azoulai	Uri Gauriel
Menashe	Jacques Cohen
Tony Hilu	Youssouf Abou-Warda
Ilana Tagar	Rachel Dayan

This is Nissim Dayan's best effort to date, a strong, impressive and topical film, far more relevant and outspoken in its approach to the Middle East conflict than either Costa-Gavras' "Hanna K." or George Roy Hill's "The Little Drummer Girl," with which the subject bears some resemblance.

The story concerns an Israeli lawyer, Benny Tagar, called for his annual reserve service and sent to the West Bank to act, for one month, as a military prosecutor there.

Chasing kids who have stoned his car on the street, he meets a local widow, working as a librarian in a school, and once initial antagonism between them is over, a strong attraction pulls them towards each other, stronger than all the ethnic and national differences separating them.

Naturally, everybody around them is against this awkward relationship. For the Israelis, the affair is one more headache nobody needs, a complication in an already thorny and explosive situation. For the Arabs, it is an affront, since the widow is the daughter-in-law of the town dignitary, and as such has a certain position to respect.

Shooting almost the entire film in the West Bank, Dayan has managed to capture the hate-filled atmosphere to perfection, never taking sides. Effective camerawork by Amnon Salomon, close enough to a documentary style to add to the credibility, is a great help throughout.

These are incisive performances from a trio of actors, Salwa Hadad, as the Arab widow, is endowed with a personality that comes through easily, her steely eyes capable of expressing both gentleness and astounding ferocity.

Makhram Khouri, an Arab actor playing the Military Governor of the area, displays a considerable degree of sensitivity, by allowing what could have been a one-dimensional part to grow in depth and give a glimpse into the moral conflicts of a honest man doing a job he feels has to be done, even if he is not all that happy about it. Turkish actor Tuncel Curtiz, as the Arab dignitary, draws another one of the strong-headed, silent and determined types he did so well for Yilmaz Güney.

It is a wonder the film was finished, given the countless obstacles in its way during production. The film, to bow first in the San Sebastian competition, hasn't as yet been scheduled for home release.
— *Edna.*

Va Banque II
(POLISH-COLOR)

Gdansk, Sept. 10.
A Film Polski production, "Kadr" Film Unit, Warsaw; world rights, Film Polski, Warsaw. Written and directed by Juliusz Machulski. Features entire cast. Camera (color), Jerzy Lukaszewicz; music, Henryk Kuzniak; sets, Andrzej Przedworski; production manager, Andrzej Soltysik. Reviewed at Gdansk Film Fest, Sept. 10, 1985. Running time: **101 MINS.**
With: Jan Machulski (Kwinto), Leonard Peetraszak (Kramer), Bronislav Wroclawski (Sztyc), Witold Pyrkosz (Duncayk), Jacek Chmielnik (Moks and the Jazzband Singer, two roles), Krzystof Kier-sznowski (Nuta), Marek Walczewski (Inspector Twardyjewicz), Ewa Szykulska (Marta).

The 1984 sequel to Juliusz Machulski's popular home hit, "Va Banque" (1981), "Va Banque II" features the same thesps in a duel of wits between a former safecracker and a crooked bank manager (imprisoned for fraud at the end of the first episode).

Machulski seems to have hurried the production through without paying much attention to tight cutting, oft-needed dialog wit and scene continuity. Plot has imprisoned ex-banker Kramer breaking out with the help of a recently released accomplice, and now he's out to get even with his nemesis Kwinto by hiring a killer first and deciding on a trap to imprison him second. Kwinto has to call up the old gang to meet the threat.

Some of the situations are quite amusing, but they are few and far between. The best has Kramer, seemingly victorious, on his way to Switzerland with the loot via a prearranged plan to cross the German border and then take off by hired plane to Zurich. Since the story is set in the 1930s (when capitalism was in vogue in Poland), the crooks sweat it out with Nazi border guards as they try to bribe their way into the country. They eventually succeed, make their contract with the pilot, and fly off to what the crooks believe is Switzerland — only to discover a film-team has duped them with sets, props and actors, so they end up back in the arms of the police inspector.

Pic's strength is the cast of colorful characters, led by the helmer's own father in the Kwinto role — Jan Machulski, one of Poland's most popular screen personalities.
— *Holl.*

Invasion U.S.A.
(COLOR)

Nasty Chuck Norris actioner aimed at the 'Rambo' market.

Hollywood, Sept. 20.
A Cannon Group presentation of a Golan-Globus production. Produced by Menahem Golan, Yoram Globus. Directed by Joseph Zito. Stars Chuck Norris. Screenplay, James Bruner, Chuck Norris, from a story by Aaron Norris and James Bruner; camera (TVC color), Joao Fernandes; editors, Daniel Loewenthal, Scott Vickrey; music, Jay Chattaway; production designer, Ladislav Wilheim; sound, Gary Rich; set design, Monica Paige; assistant director, David Anderson; casting, Louis DiGiaimo. Reviewed at Celluloid Services screening room, Sept. 19, 1985. (MPAA Rating: R.) Running time: **107 MINS.**

Matt Hunter	Chuck Norris
Rostov	Richard Lynch
McGuire	Melissa Prophet
Nikko	Alexander Zale
John Eagle	Dehl Berti
Kurt	Shane McCamey
Tomas	Alex Colon
Mickey	Billy Drago

A brainless plot would be almost forgiveable were it not for the perverse depiction of innocents butchered in "Invasion U.S.A." Star Chuck Norris, who cowrote the script and has recently chiseled a popular niche with his "Missing In Action" and "Code Of Silence" pictures, hits his nadir with this vicious-minded commodity from the Cannon Group. The "Rambo" audience will blink at this one. Yes, it will make some money.

An international hoard of ruthless mercenaries, led by foreign agents with Russian-sounding names like Rostov and Nikko, invade the southeast U.S., turn neighbor against neighbor in selective slaughters, and are ultimately throttled by Norris' loner of a hero.

Film has a message: Americans are sitting ducks because they are soft and ignorant of the nature of their own freedom. That fanatic moral is voiced by arch heavy Richard Lynch, whose performance is so richly pernicious that he, and not Norris, is the linchpin of the film. A picture like this needs a terrific crazie and Lynch, with solid classical training, is the only excuse to see the film.

Melissa Prophet plays a callow, strident photojournalist in what might generously be termed the year's least credible supporting performance in an exploitation film. The multi-faceted Prophet (she was associate producer on "The Cotton Club") will make out-of-work actresses scream. Where was director Joseph Zito when the cameras rolled?

As for innocents slain, a boatload of dying Cuban refugees are methodically gunned down just at the point when they think rescue has arrived. A teenage couple necking on a Miami beach is dispatched in a particularly blood-curdling fashion. In addition, a collection of cheerful homes, with frolicking children at Christmas time, are randomly blown up by a bazooka-brandishing Lynch.

These specific episodes, in the manner of their writing and execution, give the film its vile stamp. Lynch also blows away a couple of weasels with a low-ball technique dramatized as sticking a fat revolver down a guy's crotch and pulling the trigger not once but two or three times.

There's one thing about this movie — there's no blood, or as the filmmakers would say, no gore.
—*Loyn.*

Sweet Dreams
(COLOR)

Jessica Lange is impressive as Patsy Cline.

Hollywood, Sept. 26.

A Tri-Star Pictures release of an HBO/Silver Screen picture. Produced by Bernard Schwartz. Directed by Karel Reisz. Stars Jessica Lange, Ed Harris. Screenplay, Robert Getchell; camera (Technicolor), Robbie Greenberg; editor, Malcolm Cooke; music, Charles Gross; sound, Jeff Wexler, Don Coufal, James Stuebe; coproducer, Charles Mulvehill; production design, Albert Brenner; costumes, Ann Roth; assistant director, Patrick Crowley; art direction, David M. Haber; casting, Ellen Chenoweth. Reviewed at the Directors Guild of America, Hollywood, Sept. 25, 1985. (MPAA Rating: PG-13.) Running time: **115 MINS.**

Patsy Cline . . . . Jessica Lange
Charlie Dick. . . . . Ed Harris
Hilda Hensley . . . . Ann Wedgeworth
Randy Hughes . . . . David Clennon
Gerald Cline . . . . James Staley
Woodhouse . . . . Gary Basabara
Otis . . . . John Goodman
Wanda . . . . P.J. Soles
Sylvia. Caitlin Kelch
Singer . . . . Terri Gardner

Clearly the coal miner's daughter's cousin by both birthright and ambition, "Sweet Dreams" upholds the family honor quite well, with Jessica Lange's portrayal of country singer Patsy Cline certainly equal to Sissy Spacek's Oscar-winning recreation of Loretta Lynn.

If the resemblance holds at the boxoffice, "Dreams" might well match the more than $40,000,000 taken by "Coal Miner's Daughter" since its release in 1980. There are serious problems, however.

For one thing, Lynn is a superstar still at the top of her career, Cline was far more obscure, not handily remembered today and still only a rising country & western star when she died in a plane crash more than 20 years ago.

Secondly, Lange's last biopic, "Frances," flopped in telling its own tale of a tragic star, Frances Farmer, despite excellent notices for the actress. That brings up the third thorn: Lange usually gets lavish reviews (and one Oscar), but has a string of losers except for "Tootsie," whose success usually is credited to Dustin Hoffman.

So it remains to be seen whether "Coal Miner" producer Bernard Schwartz will succeed commercially with a full-length followup on Cline, portrayed much differently in the earlier picture by Beverly D'Angelo. Artistically, however, there's no question Schwartz, director Karel Reisz and writer Robert Getchell have combined with Lange and costars Ed Harris and Ann Wedgeworth to come up with a touching and entertaining marital love story, stricken by tragedy within and without.

Seemingly to stress the personal angles and avoid more "A Star Is Born" clichés, the film slants Cline's biography toward romance as likeable redneck Harris meets Lange at a roadside inn and their initially blissful marriage tackles the rough, upward climb to stardom, with many a shabby waystop.

Apart from the deftly interwoven singing sequences, most of Cline's career takes place off-camera. There are unavoidable references and inferences to the pressures the success of one spouse has on the other, but they never really intrude dramatically.

Instead, "Dreams" deals with what could have been any marriage of its time and place: an ambitious, independent wife — a bit too sassy and sharp-tongued at times — versus an essentially loving working stiff, whose macho insecurities inspire him to too much booze, a little infidelity and boorish brutality.

In some hands, either or both of these characters could have been personally unsympathetic, but they emerge here as genuinely worth caring about, neither all-bad nor all-good.

"Dreams" is a film of small scenes, often with only two people present. Usually, it's Lange and Harris excellently or Lange and Wedgeworth quite worthily or Lange and manager David Clennon, very capably. Beyond those four, the credits slip into bit parts quickly.

A fifth essential element, however, is the dubbed singing voice of Cline herself, who possessed a special, emotional grip on heartfelt lyrics that works perfectly within this story.

Period work is first-rate throughout, particularly the vintage cars, which are splendid (maybe overly so in scenes where it seems everybody in a poor town owns a new car). As the day-to-day surroundings show, life was still a bit sparse in the '50s and '60s, even for Grand Ol' Opry stars. That's where the sweet dreams were born. —*Har.*

Code Name: Emerald
(COLOR)

Old-fashioned espionage programmer.

Hollywood, Sept. 27.

An MGM/UA Entertainment release of an NBC Prods. presentation of a Martin Starger production. Produced by Starger. Coproducers, Jonathan Sanger, Howard Alston. Directed by Jonathan Sanger. Features entire cast. Screenplay, Ronald Bass, based on his novel "The Emerald Illusion," camera (Metrocolor), Freddie Francis; editor, Stewart Linder; music, John Addison; production design, Gerard Viard; set decoration, Albert Rajau; costume design, Jean Zay; sound, Daniel Brisseau; assistant director, Paolo Barzman; casting, Maggie Cartier. Reviewed at the MGM Studios, Culver City, Sept. 27, 1985. (MPAA Rating: PG.) Running time: **93 MINS.**

Gus Lang . . . . Ed Harris
Jurgen Brausch . . . . Max Von Sydow
Walter Hoffman . . . . Horst Buchholz
Ernst Ritter . . . . Helmut Berger
Claire Jouvet . . . . Cyrielle Claire
Andy Wheeler . . . . Eric Stoltz
Colonel Peters . . . . Patrick Stewart
Sir Geoffrey Macklin . . . Graham Crowden

"Code Name: Emerald" is just what the world is breathlessly waiting for, a 1960s-style World War II espionage thriller in which the fate of the free world hinges upon a successful undercover mission. Little could be further from current audience tastes or concerns than this thoroughly routine programmer. NBC Prods. will make hardly a dent with its debut theatrical feature, which opened via MGM/UA in test engagements in Texas Friday (27).

As old-fashioned and unimaginative as its title (it was shot simply as "Emerald"), pic features Ed Harris as a very Aryan-looking American double agent who has both the British and the Nazis trusting him.

After the Germans capture a young Yank officer who knows details of the upcoming Normandy invasion, Harris is dispatched to Paris to make sure the imprisoned kid, played by Eric Stoltz, doesn't divulge the all-important secrets.

Harris has the inevitable dalliance with possible Resistance fighter Cyrielle Claire, and hobnobs with Nazi bigwigs Horst Buchholz, Max Von Sydow and Helmut Berger to make sure they still believe he's loyal to the Führer.

Although handsomely dressed and lensed in a depopulated-looking Paris by Freddie Francis, pic has virtually no action at all and insists upon underlining its plot points in heavy crayon. Jonathan Sanger, in his directorial debut, sets a plodding pace, and only Von Sydow among the thesps is able at all to crack through the one-note script to invest his character with any humanity.

— *Cart.*

Huey Long
(DOCU-COLOR/B&W-16m)

An RKB/Florentine Films production. Produced by Ken Burns and Richard Kilberg. Directed by Burns. Screenplay, Geoffrey C. Ward; camera (color, 16m), Burns, Buddy Squires; editor, Amy Stechler Burns; sound, Greg Moring; music, John Colby with additional music by Randy Newman; narration, David McCullough; consultants, William Leuchtenburg, Alan Brinkley, Arthur M. Schlesinger Jr., William Snyder, Jerome Liebling. Reviewed at Alice Tully Hall, N.Y. (23d New York Film Festival), Sept. 26, 1985. (No MPAA Rating.) Running time: **88 MINS.**

The career of Huey P. Long — the charismatic demagog whose populist politics first changed the face of his native Louisiana, then shook the ruling establishment of the United States — remains unique in the annals of American history 50 years after his assassination. Although likely to surface only for limited runs in specialty exhibition situations, this solid, absorbing documentary about the life and times of the self-styled "Kingfish," who ruled Louisiana like a benevolent fiefdom from 1928 to 1935 as governor and U.S. senator, deserves a broad showing on cable and public television and should be required viewing on college campuses.

Director Ken Burns succeeds admirably in presenting complex perspectives on a man who was seen variously as a heroic savior of the poor, a tyranically evil enemy of democracy and a tragically flawed political genius. Through skillful intercutting of talking head reminiscences by Long's common and exalted contemporaries, remarkaby well-preserved archival footage and a narrative balancing anecdotal humor and historical overview, the docu captures the mercurial momentum of Long's rise and fall while evoking a sense of once fiery political emotions recollected from the tranquil vantage point of a vanished era's survivors.

The first half of the documentary is sympathetic to its subject as it traces Long's rise from a middle class farm family (his sister Lucille debunks the myth Long cultivated that he grew up dirt poor in a log cabin) to a brilliant career in law and politics. Long's Louisiana, the docu notes, was wracked by poverty, disease and illiteracy and lacked all but the most primitive roads, utilities and public services. Determined to achieve radical reform and aggrandize himself in the process, the wily Long was elected state railroad commissioner, then governor (after one failed attempt) and never looked back as he rallied the state's previously neglected poor with the promise to make "every man a king."

Recollections by Louisianans testify to Long's dramatic impact on the common folk. They praise him as a champion who provided free textbooks, night schools, hospitals and massive employment in one of the largest road and bridge-building programs every undertaken. If pervasive corruption was part of the process and Long became rich as a matter of course, that was all right with people who previously had been scorned by the state's political power-brokers. Unlike that latter-day southern populist, George Wallace, Long never resorted to race-baiting, the docu says, and credits him with uniting Louisiana's French Acadian, Baptist and New Orleans population groups as he modernized the state.

Long's spellbinding personality survives in extensive archival footage that captures his magnetic affability, gopher-like smile and oratorical genius. As he gained more power and prominence, Long increasingly indulged in Machiavellian expedients, and the documentary's tone becomes more critical as it traces Long's rough and tumble tactics in consolidating his position as an American Caesar. His bouts with the bottle and flamboyant lifestyle are not overlooked.

In interviews, critics like historian Arthur M. Schlesinger Jr. and newspaper publisher Mrs. Hodding Carter say Long was dangerous and unprincipled. Defenders, like his son, U.S. Sen. Russell Long, say he took extraordinary measures in the extraordinary times of the Great Depression. Detached observers like author Robert Penn Warren (whose 1946 novel "All The King's Men" was based on Long's life and made into a 1949 pic starring Broderick Crawford) revel in the Falstaffian dimensions of the man.

With a bitterly divided Louisiana on the brink of civil insurrection, Long was gunned down by the son-in-law of a political rival, as his "Share The Wealth" party was mounting a serious national challenge to F.D.R. The documentary imparts a sense of how his success might have transformed the United States into something far different than the society envisioned by the framers of the constitution, but leaves the impression that Huey Long could have happened only in America. —*Rich.*

Kim Jest Ten Czlowiek?
(Who Is That Man?)
(POLISH-COLOR)

Gdansk, Sept. 10.

A Film Polski production, "Iluzjion" Film Unit, Warsaw; world rights, Film Polski, Warsaw. Directed by Ewa and Czeslaw Petelski. Screenplay, M.H. Gromar, based on his novel; camera (color), Jerzy Jaruga; music Jerzy Maksymiuk; sets, Jerzy Skrzepinski; sound, Krzysztof Grabowski; editor, Elicja Torbus-Wosinska; production manager, Wieslaw Grzelczak. Reviewed at Gdansk Film Fest, Sept. 10, '85. Running time: **100 MINS.**
With: Henryk Talar (Adam Iwinski), Ewa Szykulska (Maria), Wienczyslaw Glinski (Colonel Kuziemski), Krzysztof Chamiec (Major Stanislaw), Witold Prykosz (Examining Officer), Miroslawa Nyckowska (Neighbor), Wlodzimierz Adamski (Stefan).

It's 1939 and a military officer is stripped of his rank by superior officers without explanation other than that he apparently collaborated with a counter-espionage agent while on a mission to Paris. Next we find him suddenly being enlisted in his own country's counter-espionage activities, a job he's qualified for in view of his knowledge of languages. His assignment is Danzig (Gdansk), where he sets about trying to uncover and trap the mysterious "Wotan" in the German Secret Service.

A twist here has to do with Danzig/Gdansk as the next pawn to be moved on the chessboard (after the occupation of Czechoslovakia by the Germans) toward the onset of World War, II some six months into the future as this tale of adventure goes. Our erstwhile hero kills his femme associate by error (after con-

veniently rolling in the hay with her on more than one occasion), then finally tracks down "Wotan" to the door of his own superior officers. He kills the agent, but by doing so cancels out the possibility of proving his own innocence before a tribunal.

Just as the sentence of death is about to be carried out, war breaks out on Sept. 1, 1939 and a stray bomb landing on the prison frees him to go on fighting for his country among the Partisans.

It adds up to a cornball spy caper.—*Holl.*

Yasha
(JAPANESE-COLOR)

Tokyo, Aug. 30.

A Toho release of Group Encounter and Toho Co. production. Produced by Yoshishige Shimatani and Kiyotomo Ichiko. Directed by Yasuo Furuhata. Features Ken Takakura. Screenplay, Tsutomu Nakamura, based on his original story; camera (color), Daisaku Kimura; score, Mitsuhiko Saito, Jean "Toots" Thielemans ("Winter Green, Summer Blue" sung by Nancy Wilson); art direction, Senichi Benitani; editor, Akira Suzuki; assistant directors, Haruo Ichikura, Junichi Shino, Tomoo Ito; production assistant, Yuki Sato. Reviewed at Toho screening room, Tokyo, Japan, Aug. 28, 1985. Running time: **118 MINS.**
Shuji . . . . Ken Takakura
Fuyuko . . . . Ayumi Ishida
Ume . . . . Nobuko Otowa
Hotaruko . . . . Yuko Tanaka
Yajima . . . . Beat Takeshi
Keita . . . . Kunie Tanaka
Tora . . . . Aki Takejo

With a stellar cast headed by Japan's number one boxoffice star returning to form as a Yakuza-with-heart, "Yasha" bodes boffo at the national wickets. The pic is an uneven rural melodrama sparked by powerful performances, notably that of topliner Ken Takakura.

"Yasha's" director is Yasuo Furuhata, a close associate of Takakura's who worked with the actor on at least three pics: "Fuya No Hana" seven years ago, "Station" in 1981 and "Izakaya Choji" in 1983. Scripted by Tsutomu Nakamura from his original story, "Yasha" has Takakura as a burned-out hit man (who wields a lethal sword) trying to live out his life quietly in a fishing village near Osaka.

The character keeps secret his unsavory Yakuza past. He blends in as a working fisherman, takes a wife (played by singer-actress Ayumi Ishida) and makes close local friendships, notably with a financially pressed fisherman with a heart problem (nicely played by character actor Kunie Tanaka).

The closer Takakura becomes to the villagers, however, the more tangled his personal involvements get. A friendship with a barmaid (superbly played by Yuko Tanaka) winds up in a scuffle with the young woman's husband (Beat Takeshi). Takakura's jacket is cut in half by a

knife revealing an elaborate tattoo on his character's back (the tattoo is a colorful replication of the mythical Japanese goddess Yasha; thus the pic's title). Since only Yakuza gangsters are so marked, Takakura's character is exposed, and shunned by the townspeople.

To complicate matters, the barmaid's husband is addicted to hard drugs supplied by a visiting pusher from the same gang that Takakura's character departed. A large chunk of "Yasha" is spent sorting out ensuing complications with Takakura returning to the mob's Osaka base to take matters into his own hands.

The plot's unwieldiness underscores the melodrama and detracts from the action. As usual, Takakura is admirably restrained. His action scenes are handled adroitly although a love scene with the barmaid is conducted in curiously listless fashion.

Yuko Tanaka as the barmaid is a revelation. She combines tart sexiness with a powerful emotional punch, and is always most convincing. Beat Takeshi, a tv personality in Japan, is an exuberant presence who requires stronger directorial control that Furuhata apparently was willing to provide. His drug-crazed, violent husband seems out of control, in marked contrast to the kind of potent reserve Takeshi showed in his role as a tough Japanese sergeant in Nagisa Oshima's "Merry Christmas, Mr. Lawrence."

Director Furuhata and cinematographer Daisaku Kimura excel at showing the pleasures of life in a picturesque Japanese fishing village. Jean (Toots) Thielemans' harmonica work on the soundtrack proves surprisingly effective. Production values, in all, are topnotch.

"Yasha" is a film of strong emotional content that required what it most lacks, a controlling hand to rigorously shape the story material. Export potential outside of key Far East territories appears limited at least partially because key plot twists hinge upon cultural factors not fully understood in the West.—*Sege.*

Janyo-nok
(The Noblewoman)
(SOUTH KOREAN-COLOR)

Venice, Aug. 30.

Produced by Chung Jin-Woo for Jin Woo Film Co. Directed by Chung Jin-Woo. Stars Kim Yong-Sun, Won Mi-Kyung. Screenplay, Ji Sang-Hak; camera (color), Lee Sung-Chonn; editor, Hyun Dong-Chun; music, Han Sang-Key. Reviewed at the Venice Film Festival, Aug. 28, 1985. Running time: **120 MINS.**
Young noblewoman . . . . Kim Yong-Sun
Old noblewoman . . . . Park Jung-Ja
Sa-Wol . . . . Won Mi-Kyung
Chun-dang . . . . Choi Byung-Kun
Sung-Sam . . . , ... Kim Hi-Ra
The doctor . . . . Chun Mu-Song

Veteran Korean filmer Chung Jin-Woo, who has directed some 70 features in the last 25 years, brings

all his technical knowhow and sensitivity to bear in "The Noblewoman," a finely shot family costume drama that turns to melodrama by the end.

The ingredients are classic: to solve the problem of an aristocratic couple's childlessness, concubines and lovers are brought in to wreak havoc with everybody's feelings. The story is updated to include a good deal of eroticism and barely off-camera sex, which got past the national censors on the basis of its good taste. Classy and watchable, if a little too protracted, pic could have arthouse and paycable pickups with the right handling.

Husband Chun-dang (Choi Byung-Kun) and wife Kim Yong-Sun have been childless too long and tough matriarch Park Jung-Ja is worried. Film starts with the arrival of a second concubine, beauteous Sa-Wol (Won Mi-Kyung), who is paid to procreate in the wife's place. In a titillating character introduction, the old lady has the girl strip and knowingly fingers her naked body, looking for "good omens." Best omen of all is the fact Sa-Wol has already had a child, taken away from her by her traveling circus father.

The noble family's supposed virtue is symbolized by twin red gates in front of the house, earned by virtuous widows whose resistance to temptations officially exempted them from paying taxes. With this kind of reputation to keep up, it's no wonder sex is the family obsession. When the matriarch discovered another daughter-in-law indulged in a brief affair after her husband's death, she demanded the girl commit suicide to preserve the family honor. She obeyed, but hanged herself on the "janyo-nok," the adulterer's tree, creating a scandal that had to be hushed up.

The ghostly tree keeps creeping into the story, as the current daughter-in-law, obedient to tradition, meets her former suitor there and kills him when he tries to rock the boat and take her away.

The soap really starts foaming when Sa-Wol the concubine realizes the husband is impotent and has a friendly, oafish servant (Kim Hi-Ra) get her pregnant. The baby is a boy and matriarch and son rejoice at the birth of their "heir." At this point the unassailable rights of maternity raise their head and Sa-Wol refuses to give up the child.

Pic has a satisfying number of twists and turns, though by the end they grow a little thin. Luckily helmer is skilled at guiding audience sympathy, even for stereotyped and shallow characters. As in his previous "Does The Cuckoo Sing At Night?" a strong pro-woman message comes out through a refusal of enforced female chastity and arranged marriages. — *Yung.*

Kobieta Z Prowincji
(The Woman From The Provinces)
(POLISH-COLOR)

Gdansk, Sept. 17.

A Coproduction of Polish Television (PRF "Zespoly Filmowe") and Film Polski, "Oko" Film Unit, Warsaw. Written and directed by Andrzej Baranski, based on the novel by Waldemar Sieminski. Features entire cast. Camera (color), Ryszard Lenczewski; music, Henryk Kuzniak; sets, Pawel Mirowksi, Adam Kopczynski; production manager, Marek Depczynski. Reviewed at Gdansk Film Fest, Sept. 14, 1985. Running time: **104 MINS.**

With: Ewa Dalkowska (Andzia), Katarzyna Rubacha (Andzia as 12-year-old), Ryszarda Hanin (the mother), Aleksander Fogiel (the father), Bozena Dykiel (the sister), Jan Jankowski (Henryk), Magdalena Michalak (Celinka), Maciej Goraj (Szczepan)

One of the discoveries at Gdansk, Andrzej Baranski's "The Woman From The Provinces" well deserved its runnerup recognition at the festival. It's the type of portrait of the Polish provinces that speaks for the dignity of man, thus pic should easily find further support and recognition on the fest circuit. Offshore chances are possible.

And aging woman of 60 recalls in patchy, disconnected fashion the high points of her life. As a child from a poor background, she showed the utmost respect for her parents and the social community about her. When she went to school barefoot, the priest in the religion class offered to buy the necessary shoes, but the father could not accept the offer as an upright and honest man with a sense of his own responsibility. The girl, Andzia, is to carry this simple code of living life frugally but honestly to the present.

Andzia meets the equally unpretentious Szczepan, and they marry. Their wedding night proves an evening of comic embarrassment, but two children eventually come of the union. Szczepan drowns suddenly and Andzia is left a widow with the chore of raising a son and daughter on the meager wages she earns as a dishwasher in a plant restaurant. The daughter grows up and marries and Andzia is there to help when she can during brief marital problems. The son enters the army and again Andzia is on hand when the lad has to make a decision one Sunday morning to go to church or not. Andzia offers a practical argument about "believing in something," and wins him over.

This is a poetic, realistic film about the everyday. Ewa Dalkowska as Andzia gives an extraordinary performance, depending for the most part on simple facial expressions and gestures to get the essentials across without embellishment or reliance upon superfluous words. Sets and costumes, lensing and lighting, thesps in supporting roles — all contribute to this human comedy. —*Holl.*

Flanagan
(COLOR)

Solid acting in story of a N.Y. cabbie/Shakespearean actor.

Mill Valley, Sept. 23.

A United Film Distribution release of a Tenth Muse production. Produced and directed by Scott Goldstein. Stars Philip Bosco. Screenplay, Edmond Collins and Goldstein; camera (color), Ivan Strasburg; editor, Scott Vikery; art director, Ruth Ammon; associate producer, Mark Slater. Reviewed at Sequoia Theater, Mill Valley Film Festival, Sept. 22, 1985. (No MPAA Rating.) Running time: **97 MINS.**

James Flanagan	Philip Bosco
Mama	Geraldine Page
Andrea	Linda Thorson
Papa	William Hickey
Mary	Olympia Dukakis
Danny	Brian Bloom
Sean	Steven Weber

Highlighted by the affecting, title role performance of Philip Bosco as a 50ish cabbie-Shakespearean thesp, "Flanagan' is the first theatrical feature of New York legit-tv producer-director Scott Goldstein and has been picked up by UFDC for gradual, major market bookings starting in early November.

Goldstein produced, directed, cowrote and scored pic and, with Bosco's boost, makes a decent, promising big-screen debut. Picture suffers from sluggish pacing, too many scenes which appear to be climactic and an aura which smacks more of legit than feature.

Yarn is labeled as "a success story of self-realization" as cabbie Bosco tries to reconcile his past — a rummy of a long-dead daddy (William Hickey) who instilled him with love of the Bard — with his present, which includes an estranged, pony-playing wife (Olympia Dukakis), a pair of teen-aged sons and a supportive artist-girl friend (Linda Thorson).

Sugestions that Flanagan has "trapped" his "creative spirit in a cab" are clear to him, but he struggles to be true to thine ownself. In flashbacks, often spun off conversations with his mama (Geraldine Page), the child Flanagan is seen with his father, a figure who needs more exposition in screenplay.

There's a particularly cathartic scene at Central Park's Delacorte Theater as the hero, just after being tossed out of an audition and left by his ankling g.f., starts shredding his much-loved book of the bard in his belief that "I have nothing to look forward to." By daylight he is picking up the pages, and his life, as pic heads toward an upbeat ending.

The performances are universally nifty, but commercial prospects appear minimal. —*Herb.*

Zhong Shen Da Shi
(The Rejuvenator)
(TAIWANESE-COLOR)

Sydney, Sept. 23.

A King Hu production. Produced, directed, and written by King Hu. Executive producer, Ling Ching. Camera (color), Chou Yeh-hsing; editor, Hu. No further credits available. Reviewed on SBS TV, Sydney, Sept. 15, 1985. Running time: **99 MINS.**

With: Tao Wei (Tao Limin), Tai Ho-shih (Ji), Sylvia Chang, Hu Hui-chung, Sun Yueh, Kuan Kuan, Tai to-to.

"The Rejuvenator" is a comedy King Hu ("A Touch Of Zen") made in Taiwan in 1981, reviewed here for the record.

Comedy is clearly not Hu's forte, as this embarrassingly bad pic can attest. Apparently attempting to cash in on a type of film popular in the Taiwanese-Hong Kong market in the early 1980s, Hu merely came up with a shambling, humorless farce with a creaking plot that makes even "Brewster's Millions" seem fresh.

The accident-prone hero (Tao Wei), an ad designer for a company trying to do business with a powerful Japanese concern, is told he can handle a highly profitable account — marketing a new rejuvenating elixir — only if he is married before a certain date. Apparent idea is that, if married, he'll achieve greater stability, thus be more reliable. Story involves his predictable efforts to snare a wife by the due date, involving liaisons with call girls, a free-living artist, and an immensely tall, and hearty, nutritionist.

Lackluster proceedings, which are adequately acted, are accompanied by a bizarre music score (uncredited) which contains themes from "Camptown Races" and "12 Days Of Christmas." Pic, whose original title can be roughly translated as "A Lot Of Fuss About A Wedding," had a disastrously short two-day run in Taipei in 1981 before being yanked, and has only been screened in Hong Kong as part of a retrospective of King Hu films.

—*Strat.*

Sam Posrod Swoich
(Alone Among His Own)
(POLISH-COLOR)

Gdansk, Sept. 10.

A Film Polski production. "Zodiak" Film Unit, Warsaw; world rights, Film Polski, Warsaw. Written and directed by Wojciech Wojcik. Features entire cast. Camera (color), Krzysztof Ptak; music, Zbigniew Gorny; sets, Marek Morawski; editor, Jaroslaw Ostanowko; sound, Marek Wronko; production manager, Joanna Kopczynska. Reviewed at Gdansk Film Fest, Sept. 9, 1985. Running time: **116 MINS.**

With: Jan Jankowski (Lt. Andrzej Kmita), Jerzy Trela (Capt. Feliksik), Marek Frackowiak (Capt. Lenczak), Jolanta Mielech (Danka), Piotr Dejmek (Garbowski), Artur Barcis (Pielarz), Janusz Bukowski (Head Master).

Wojciech Wojcik's "Alone Among His Own" is one of those Polish pictures set in the immediate postwar years, made for patriotic reasons by government film officials primarily for the home public. It's set in a small town in Pomerania in 1946, a time when Poland's borders were being pushed westward at the expense of a defeated Germany and when Poles themselves quarreled over the course of their national political heritage.

As the title hints, helmer Wojcik describes the fate of a young lieutenant in the newly established Polish army trying to come to grips with a restless Polish band of underground bandits and terrorists. Since Lt. Kmita (played engagingly by Jan Jankowski) belonged to the partisan fighters as a teenager, he hopes to complete his secondary education. Instead, he finds his former partisan comrade, Capt. Feliksik, on the other side among the reactionaries hiding out in the forests. It's the Polish People's Army vs. the Home Army, in other words.

Kmita has been appointed the local "propaganda officer," which assumes he now adheres to the Polish Provisional Government of National Unity before national elections are held in January 1947. His job apparently is to get the population to vote in the elections, but people are afraid to leave their homes for fear of getting killed while terrorist actions are carried out arbitrarily.

Besides the brother-against-brother theme, a romantic interest is played upon. Kmita falls in love with a rebel lass and it becomes a personal tragedy when the girl is killed in a raid. After a moral showdown with the renegade captain, the latter commits suicide and Kmita is killed by the forest bandits.

"Alone Among His Own" might prove a curiosity for the informed Polish history fan, but the film buff is referred to Andrzej Wajda's classic "Ashes And Diamonds" (1958) for a more accurate portrait of this troublesome era. — *Holl.*

Hard Traveling
(COLOR)

Nicely-made rural drama.

Mill Valley, Sept. 26.

A Shire Films production. Produced by Helen Garvy. Written and directed by Dan Bessie, based on novel "Bread And A Stone" by Alvah Bessie. Features J.E. Freeman, Ellen Geer. Camera (color), David Myers; editor, Susan Heick; music, Ernie Sheldon; costumes, Karen Mitchell; sound, Anne Evans; assistant director, Garvy. Reviewed at Sequoia Theater, Mill Valley, Sept. 25, 1985. (No MPAA Rating.) Running time: **107 MINS.**

Ed Sloan	J.E. Freeman
Norah Sloan	Ellen Geer
Frank Burton	Barry Corbin
Sgt. Slattery	James Gammon
Lt. Fisher	Jim Haynie
Bill Gilbert	W. Scott DeVenney
Judge	Joe Miksak
Sheriff	William Paterson
Jim Baldwin	Al Blair
Joey Gilbert	Anthony Danna
Tim Gilbert	T.J. Thompson
Capt. Patrick	John Allen Vick
Mike	Jack Tate
D.A. Cobb	Charles Martinet

Winnie Hoskins..........Kathryn Trask
Ella Horton..............Marcia Taylor
Earl Horton...........William Ackridge

Discerning distribs will find "Hard Traveling" an appealing pick-up. It's not about to yield boffo b.o. bucks for either the Santa Cruz, Calif.-based Shire Films or the distrib, but it's the sort of well-crafted pic that should recover everybody's investment and garner word-of-mouth prestige for all concerned.

This period (1939-40) love story of an illiterate ne'e'r-do-well and the woman who finds the good within him is adapted by Dan Bessie, 53, (in his feature directing debut) from a 1951 novel by his late father Alvah Bessie, one of the blacklisted "Hollywood Ten." The novel was about Dan's mother and stepfather, with theme generally, but without contrivances, in the ilk of "Places In The Heart" and "Tender Mercies."

Most of the performers have a legit background and appear to have stepped right out of Steinbeck. That's the kind of feel pic has: an old-fashioned, uncomplicated yarn about affection clearly made with affection.

Ellen Geer is just right as a pilot's widow who is taken with her landlady's handyman, a gangly, boastful loser who has spent all his life seeking to be part of a family. The affair and marriage of the aptly cast J.E. Freeman and Geer is intercut in uncomplicated flashback form with the handyman's arrest and trial for murder.

The death sentence is inevitable, but the storytelling maintains interest throughout via the characterizations of the couple. Fine in support are Barry Corbin, as Freeman's lawyer, and Marcia Taylor, the landlady.

Pic is marred slightly by police caricatures early on, and pace could improve with minute tightening of any number of scenes. — *Herb.*

Leila And The Wolves
(BRITISH-LEBANESE-COLOR)

Mill Valley, Sept. 24.

A British Film Institute, Leila Films, Belgian Ministry of Culture, NCO and NOVIB (Holland) production. Written and directed by Heiny Srour. Features Nabila Zeitouni, Rafiq Ali Ahmed. Camera (color), Charlet Recors, Curtis Clark; editor, Eva Houdova; postproduction supervisor, Christopher Sutton. Reviewed at Sequoia Theater, Mill Valley Film Festival, Sept. 23, 1985. Running time: **90 MINS.**

This 1984, multi-national docudrama won the Mannheim fest grand prix a year ago and was one of the few subtitled offerings at the Mill Valleyfest this year. (Print source is London's Playpont Films.)

Director-writer Heiny Srour has a fine premise — the ennoblement of the Arab woman in a framework of a half century of Palestinian and Lebanese history. Trouble is, he packs in too much information, and symbolism, and nearly winds up dissipating the theme that women, and children, are the real victims of "guns and endless politics."

The "wolves" who confront pic's Everywoman are multiple: British, Nazis, Israelis, Arab men and, ultimately, the activist, militant Arab woman herself.

Technical credits are decent enough in this Brechtian-like discourse. Several of the thesps have multiple roles, and the rubble of Beirut itself plays a compelling role. Forecast for feature is brief play in selective urban art venues. —*Herb.*

Hodja fra Pjort
(Hodja From Pjort)
(DANISH-COLOR)

Copenhagen, Sept. 27.

A Metronome Film release of a Metronome Prods. production. Executive producer, Tiwi Magnusson. Directed by Brita Wielopolska. Features entire cast. Screenplay, Brita Wielopolska, based on novel by Ole Lund Kirkegard; camera (Eastmancolor), Peter Klitgaard; production design and special effects, Peter Höimark; editor, Ghita Beckendorff; music, Sebastian; costumes, Evelyn Olsson, Jette Termann; production managers, Jacob Eriksen, Karsten Grönborg (Denmark), Zafer Dogan, Ayse Kulin, Filiz Bala (Turkish locations); production consultant, Ida Zeruneith (The Danish Film Institute); postproduction director, Astrid Henning Jensen. Reviewed at the Dagmar, Copenhagen, Sept. 27, 1985. Running time: **82 MINS.**
Hodja..................David Bertelsen
Emerald................Zuhal Özdemir
The Rat................Lars Junggreen
El Faza.................Holger Boland
Old Woman.......Astrid Henning Jensen
Also with: Stig Hoffmeyer, Leif Sylvester Petersen, Debbie Cameron, Michele Björn Andersen, Bent Börgesen, Jörn Fauerschou, Zihni Kücümen, Cevat Kultulus, Macit Koper, Kadir Savun, Yadigir Ejder.

"Hodja From Pjort" is producer Bent Fabricius-Bjerre's fourth Metronome feature based on the writings of the late, beloved absurdist children's novelist Ole Lund Kirkegaard. Each film has had a new director to benefit from Lund Kirkegaard's rich comic invention in plots and characters and have appealed to worldwide audiences and been rewarded with a number of fest and other awards.

"Hodja" was Lund Kirkegaard's last book and the first to take place outside an urban Danish environment. It was not a successful departure, but aided by rich production values and many loans from the 1001 Nights' treasure chest, scripter-helmer Brita Wielopolska has brought in an opulent kiddie entertainment of mild humor and moderate suspense. She has, however, probably lost the adult audiences the books and their earlier film versions had by constantly pulling her suspense as well as her absurdist comic punches. Also, her handling of narrative is choppy and, sometimes insecure. A further drawback is an abundance of night sequences too badly lit to make it clear what is happening.

Still, little Turkish boy Hodja and his wanton girlfriend Emerald ooze charm as they come aloft on a flying carpet given them by the village elder. They fall into traps and get out of scrapes as they are being chased by The Rat, a villain who hopes to be appointed by the Sultan's general by bringing latter the carpet as the only gift that would, literally, lift the fat fellow out of his enormous, luxury-imposed boredom. Flying — on the carpet or otherwise — belongs only to those with true belief in wonders in their hearts. So runs the moral of the tale, when the Sultan and The Rat have been up in air for a brief spell only to be dropped into the sea (and oblivion) at the children's command.

Kiddie programmers everywhere will probably take "Hodja From Pjort" to their hearts and secure item's sales into many specialized (children's) theatrical situations plus, of course, late afternoon television slots for tots. Most of film was shot on romantic-looking Turkish locations, and Peter Höimark's special effects work with the flying carpet are impressive. —*Kell.*

Dot And The Koala
(AUSTRALIAN-ANIMATED-COLOR)

Sydney, Sept. 25.

A Yoram Gross presentation. Produced and directed by Gross. Screenplay, Greg Flynn, Gross; camera (color), Graham Sharpe; associate producer, Sandra Gross; animation director, Gairden Cooke; editor, Neil Thompson, Ted Otton, Ian Spruce; music, Bob Young, John Sangster; production manager, Narelle Hopley. Reviewed at Yoram Gross Film Studio, Sydney, Sept. 24, 1985. (Commonwealth Film Censor Rating: G.) Running time: **70 MINS.**
Featuring the character voices of Robyn Moore and Keith Scott.

Fourth in the series of the "Dot" films from prolific producer-director Yoram Gross, "Dot And The Koala" is arguably the most accomplished, displaying a more sophisticated and imaginative animation style than its forerunners.

Debuting scripter Greg Flynn and new animation director Gairden Cooke have brought a fresh, more adventurous and humorous approach to the successful "Dot" formula.

The characters are drawn with more detail and intricacy, the colors are softer and subtler and the overall effect will likely beguile the targeted 10 years and under audience.

Earlier "Dot" vehicles have reaped handsome dividends internationally on television and home-video, and "Koala" seems destined for the same route.

There's a moral slyly tucked away in every Gross film, and here it is the need to ensure that the march of progress does not trample all over the environment.

Dilemma is dramatized neatly in a battle between small town residents led by Mayor Percy Pig (shades of George Orwell's "Animal Farm") and bush creatures over plans to build a hydro-electric plant which involves damming a river.

Mayor Percy and his followers are determined that work should proceed, no matter that trees will be uprooted and soil and air polluted. The natives led by Bruce the Koala try to foil them, but their puny resistance is pushed aside easily and Dot, a super smart little girl, is summoned to help the greenies.

Despite the hamfisted efforts of detectives Sherlock Bones — a real rat — and a feline Watson, the bush animals' cunning, with Dot as the mastermind, prevails over the town progressives.

The Gross trademark — matching animation over live footage — is particularly effective in this pic, using the background setting of the Tasmanian wilderness (a region that recently had its own conservation controversy over a proposal, since rescinded, to dam the Franklin River).

It's a simple story, well-told and attractively sketched, and the lilting score by Bob Young and John Sangster is a plus. —*Dogo.*

Savage Island
(COLOR)

Patched-together sexploitation pic.

Hollywood, Sept. 27.

An Empire Pictures release. Producers, Robert Amante, Mark Alabiso. Directed by Edward Muller (L.A. sequences directed by Nicholas Beardsly). Stars Linda Blair. Screenplay, Michelle Tomski, Nicholas Beardsly, camera (color), uncredited; editor, Michelle Tomski; music, Mark Ryder, Phil Devies. (Only credits available.) Reviewed at Hollywood Pacific, Sept. 27, 1985. (MPAA Rating: R.) Running time: **74 MINS.**
Daly......................Linda Blair
Laredo.................Anthony Steffen
Marie.....................Ajita Wilson
Muriel...................Christina Lai
Luker.....................Leon Askin

This patchwork slave women's picture, picked up by Empire Pictures, is actually a combination of an Italian/Spanish coproduction ("Orinoco — Prison Of Sex") and a few minutes of wraparound footage shot later in L.A. and featuring the top-billed Linda Blair.

Empire bought the film for video distribution but threw it into its theatrical pipeline at the last second. Pic is sexploitation on the level of mud wrestling, with a laughable, English-dubbed soundtrack.

Core of the film is formula women's prison sleaze, with considerable nudity, unraveling on a steamy tropical island. Some of the bodies are great (Ajita Wilson and the towering Christina Lai), but the enterprise is so gimcrack that box-office will be lifeless.

Blair, in what must certainly qualify as a theatrical embarrassment, is on camera perhaps 10 minutes, an appendage to the real movie. Appearing as a vengeful former island slave, she sets up the "savage island" portion of the story in flashback and then reappears at the end pulling an automatic from under a fur coat and blowing away the villain (who was also an afterthought).

The director of the island portion of the film, which runs a little more than an hour, is Edward Muller. The helmsman of the Blair-Century City wraparound stuff is Nicholas Beardsly.

Snake lovers will gape at a couple of scenes. In one, a boa constrictor curls itself around the neck and face of a girl buried in sand. In another — the movie's riotous highpoint — actress Lai bites off the head of a snake and spits it back at her tormentors. —*Loyn.*

Gregorio
(PERUVIAN-COLOR)

Montreal, Aug. 30.

Produced by Grupo Chaski. Directed by Fernando Espinoza, Stefan Kaspar, Alejandro Legaspi, Maria Barea, Susana Pastor of the Grupo Chaski. Written by Grupo Chaski; camera (color), Alejandro Legaspi; music, Arturo Ruiz del Pozo; sound, Francisco Adrianzen and Fernando Espinoza. Reviewed at Montreal World Film Festival (Parisien 5), Aug. 29, 1985. Running time: **85 MINS.**

With: Marino Leon de la Torre, Vetzy Perez-Palma, Agusto Varillas, Manuel Acosta Ojeda, Rafael Hernandez, Julio Pacora, Oscar Huayta, Marco Jaime, Jose Saavedra.

First fiction feature of a Peruvian collective, "Gregorio" portrays the inevitable disintegration of a family of peasants in the Andes who are forced from the land and into the city, where the father is more likely to find work. Sketched in a lyrical and impressionistic fashion, the story benefits from a score that provides continuity with its hypnotic indigenous instruments and rhythms.

A wonderful long take of Gregorio playing in the surf naked sets the tone of pic, as the child pursues some kind of freedom and sense of independence in the anarchy of Lima's barrios. Filmmakers have carefully avoided graphic violence or shocking brutality, and what penetrates is the inevitability and hopelessness of the family's situation in busy streets with nothing to do. Gregorio's father works night and day until there is no more work, then dies. His widowed mother, played with delicate vulnerability and grace by Vetzy Perez-Palma, tries to come to terms with the bare existence Gregorio can provide with his shoe-shine operation and eventually takes up a relationship with a

man, which inspires Gregorio's jealousy. He stays away from home more and more, until his mother confronts him. But the city has drained the love from the family and they are unable to communicate any longer. Their dialog is cautious, and their emotions reflected in simple scenes of isolation.

Gregorio's life on the streets develops from clumsy attempts to earn some respect from other boys to his joining up with a gang who live in an abandoned equipment yard.

Pic focuses primarily on the faces rather than the fates of its subjects, and this seems to lend a documentary tone to the kids' confessions of why they have run away from home.

The Grupo Chaski was formed in 1982 and has produced two documentaries, which may explain why they let the characters tell their stories rather than attempting to stage them. Although this is not as heartwrenching as "Pixote," it draws from the same material and is blessed with able child actors. In markets specializing in Spanish-language product, pic ought to do well, and the festival circuit will snap it up to do justice to a rarely represented country like Peru and this special brand of filmmaking. — *Kaja.*

Drei Gegen Drei
(Three Against Three)
(WEST GERMAN-COLOR)

Berlin, Sept. 24.

A Neue Constantin Film Prod., Munich, produced by Bernd Eichinger and Thomas Schühly. Directed by Dominik Graf. Features the Trio pop group. Screenplay, Martin Gies, Bernd Schwamm, from an idea by Peter Berecz; camera (color), Klaus Eichhammer; sets, Rainer Schaper; costumes, Esther Walz; production managers, Klaus Keil, Michael Wiedemann. Reviewed at Gloria Palast, Berlin, Sept. 23, 1985. Running time: **100 MINS.**,

With: Stephan Remmler (General Weingarten/Stephan), Gert "Kralle" Krawinkel (General Ludovico/Kralle), Peter Behrens (General Klotz/Peter), Sunnyi Melles (Ms. Pelikan), Ralf Wolter (Kaminski), Günter Meisner (Professor Holl), Peer Augustinski (Brunnmeier), Peter E. Funck (Eric), Michael Wittenborn (Gernot), Uwe Büschken (Walter), Ute Lemper (Marianne).

Dominik Graf's "Three Against Three" stars the pop group Trio in a vehicle designed to put them over as comedians as well as a quite talented band. They don't perform one number in the pic as a pop attraction, while their debuts as madcap double-identity comedians are pale imitations of the Three Stooges.

Storyline has three Latin American dictators hitting on the plan of having themselves rubbed out via three lookalike doubles — the trio of Stephan Remmler, Kralle Krawinkel and Peter Behrens. Once the three generals reach Germany, they hope to use the triple assassination to

dupe the revolutionaries back home into thinking they're completely out of the picture. Then it's off to Switzerland, where they've stashed away the people's wealth in illegal bank accounts.

Cornball comedy routines over the mistaken identities make Graf a dull helmer and "Three Against Three" a miscalculation. —*Holl.*

Trzy Stopy Nad Ziemia
(Three Feet Above The Ground)
(POLISH-COLOR)

Gdansk, Sept. 15.

A Coproduction of Polish Television (PRF "Zespoly Filmowe") and Film Polski, "Oko" Film Unit. Written and directed by Jan Kidawa-Blonski. Features entire cast. Camera (color), Andrzej Wolf; music, Zbigniew Raj; sets, Wojciech Majda; production manager, Zbigniew Tolloczko. Reviewed at Gdansk Film Fest, Sept. 14, 1985. Running time: **87 MINS.**

With: Jaroslaw Dunaj (Nowaczek), Tadeusz Chudecki (Gienio), Zdzislaw Kozien (Ewald), Magdalena Wollejko (Mariola), Zdzislaw Wardejn (Kapusta), Zdzislaw Kuzniar (Zybel), Ferdynand Matysik (Kuciara), Emilian Kaminski (Henio).

Jan Kidawa-Blonski's "Three Feet Above The Ground" describes life in the coalmining districts. It's the 1970s, and a young man decides that being an army recruit is not for him. Having dropped out of school, he becomes a voluntary miner instead. He lives with his buddies in a barracks where the only recreation is a ping-pong table — and dreams about the opposite sex.

He has a friend he hangs around with on nearly every occasion, and it's their adventures together that supply the few-and-far-between laughs. When they go to a nightclub in town, their fake identities get them to a front table for the striptease show, but they make little headway with the girls at the bar.

There's an accident on the job that kills a careless buddy, and a quarrel with a stubborn foreman on the job, and the rendezvous with a girlfriend that has all the other barracks chums gaping, and the nearly tragic accident to the close buddy at the end to round it out. These turns in the narrative resemble a rerun of your favorite soap opera.—*Holl.*

Godnosc
(Dignity)
(POLISH-COLOR)

Gdansk, Sept. 15.

A Coproduction of Polish Television (PRF "Zespoly Filmowe") and Film Polski, "Profil" Unit. Directed by Roman Wioncek. Features entire cast. Screenplay, Jerzy Grzymkowski; camera (color), Wladyslaw Nagy; sets, Jerzy Zielinski; production manager, Ryszard Jasionowski. Reviewed at Gdansk Film Fest, Sept. 14, 1985. Running time: **95 MINS.**

With: Jerzy Aleksander Braszka (Karol Szostak), Halina Kossobudzka (Szostakowa, Karol's wife), Magda Celowna (Bozena Rzepinska, Szostak's daughter), Edward Sosna (Waldemar Rzepinski, Szostak's son-in-law),

Boguslaw Sar (Jedrak Szostak), Piotr Krasicki (Marcin Rzepinski, the grandson).

The most embarrassing film on view at Gdansk, Roman Wioncek's "Dignity" is an anti-Solidarity feature seeking to present the government's side in giving its blessing to members of the official state union vs. reforms pushed through by Lech Walesa and his 10,000,000 backers in the laboring ranks. Since Solidarity was founded just around the corner from the festival center in Gdansk, it was not surprising that no one showed up from the production to present Wioneck's case at a press conference. Further, the film has met with practically no audience success in Poland, per reliable reports. It's an all-around dud.

Depicted are the last days of December, just when events in Poland were leading up to the declaration of martial law. According to this fictitious tale by Wioneck, a worker at a steel plant is elected to head the old official branch union that's trying to hold its own against the heavy inroads made by Solidarity. When he refuses to join a strike, he's run out of the plant in a wheelbarrow — to all intents and purposes, by Solidarity.

Pic is so clumsily made that it achieves the opposite of what's intended.—*Holl.*

Medium
(POLISH-COLOR)

Gdansk, Sept. 10.

A Film Polski production, "Tor" Film Unit, Warsaw; world rights, Film Polski, Warsaw. Written and directed by Jacek Koprowicz. Features entire cast. Camera (color), Wit Dabal, Jerzy Zielinski; music, Krzesimir Debski; sets, Rafal Waltenberger; production manager, Michael Szczerbic. Reviewed at Gdansk Film Fest, Sept. 10, '85. Running time: **98 MINS.**

With: Wladyslaw Kowalski (Commissioner Selin), Michal Bajor (Assistant Krank), Grazyna Szapolowska (Luiza Skubijewska), Jerzy Zelnik (Andrzej Gaszewski), Jerzy Stuhr (George Netz), Jerzy Nowak (occultist), Ewa Dalkowska (occultist's sister).

Jacek Koprowicz' "Medium," also titled "Deja Vu" in the program, is the first feature film made in Poland on the theme of parapsychology. It deals with four people in Sopot (Baltic Sea resort) in 1933 mysteriously brought together to an old villa to reenact a murder ritual that took place there 50 years ago by people who look exactly like the people in question.

One of the hapless individuals is a 1930s police commissioner; another is a school teacher; the third is a visitor on a train from Berlin, the fourth is a hunchback. At first, none of the afflicted knows why he keeps being drawn to the site of the previous murder, but an occultist and his psychic sister know what's going on without being able to interfere in the course of events. Gradually the police commissioner gets an inkling of the bloody deed ahead. It's his attempt to ward off the inevitable that forms the nucleus of this tale of woe.

Pic has some tense and entertaining moments as a suspense thriller, but the ending is pedestrian and uninspired.—*Holl.*

Bekci
(The Guard)
(TURKISH-COLOR)

Venice, Sept. 6.

Produced by Asya Film Productions. Directed by Ali Ozgentürk. Stars Müjdat Gezen. Screenplay, Isil Ozgentürk; camera (Kodachrome color), Ertune Senkay; editor, Katicha Berina; music, Sarper Ozsan. Reviewed at the Venice Film Festival (Competition), Sept. 6, 1985. Running time: **115 MINS.**
Murtaza ....Müjdat Gezen
Murtaza's wife ....Güler Okten
The boss ....Halil Ergün

"The Guard" is the third feature of Ali Ozgentürk, former assistant and scriptwriter to Yilmaz Güney. Film is a tragicomedy focused on an incredible character named Murtaza, a naive, deluded oaf who takes his job as a factory guard so seriously he makes himself the town laughingstock.

Though lensed with aplomb and snatches of fantasy, pic has something heavy and repetitive about it and an unmistakably literary quality that suggests the story would make a better book than a film. In the last scene, in fact, Murtaza comes back after this death and oddly turns up in a bank, where someone is reading "the book about him."

With the simple motto "duty is sacred" engraved in his mind like stone, dense, pompous Murtaza Bey (played by stage and screen veteran Müjdat Gezen) dons his plain green uniform with all the obtuse pride of Emil Jannings' hotel doorman in "The Last Laugh." Here it's not the uniform that makes the man, but rigid adherence to the ideas of "discipline and education" and the like, all confused with vague notions of patriotism. A comic figure with no real authority or power, except that mockingly conferred by the factory's suave director (Halil Ergün), Murtaza is the butt of jokes and the despair of his family. His wife, who seems much too intelligent for him, lovingly puts up with the humiliation when the boss invites them to his son's circumcision, only to have his guests laugh at Murtaza's excited stories of his heroic grandfather who died in the war (but who is remembered in history books chiefly for his stupidity).

His two daughters, however, are his victims. One finally chooses to live out of wedlock with her beloved rather than be given in marriage to a rich stranger. The pretty younger girl is forced to go to the factory because Murtaza won't ask for a raise.

One day he catches her sleeping on the night shift and strikes her so hard she later dies, but he seems less upset by the tragic accident than by her "desertion of duty." After the funeral he is knifed to death by the girl's boyfriend.

Ending has a potential for dramatic power which would richly cap the melange of comedy and melancholy that goes before, but editing is so poorly worked out, skipping to other incidents in the midst of the daughter's tragedy, that all emotion is undercut. Ozgentürk is best at gentle spoof and characterization, like the tiny fellow in the factory who earnestly salutes Murtaza whenever he sees him, throwing the officious guard into confusion.
—*Yung.*

To Kill A Stranger
(COLOR)

Weak thriller.

A VCL release of an Angel Films and Radio Video Prods. presentation, in association with Star World Prods. Produced by Raul Vale. Directed by Juan López-Moctezuma. Features entire cast. Screenplay, Emerich Oross, with revisions by Rafael Buñuel, Michael Elliot, López-Moctezuma, Morrie Ruvinsky; camera (color), Alex Phillips; editor, Carlos Savage; music, Mort Garson; sound, Roberto Camacho; production manager, Jaime Alfaro; second unit camera, David Golia; postproduction supervisor, Paul Leder. Reviewed on Media Home Entertainment vidcassette, N.Y., Sept. 18, 1985. (No MPAA Rating.) Running time: **88 MINS.**
Cristina Carver ....Angelica Maria
John Carver ....Dean Stockwell
Col. Kostik ....Donald Pleasence
Inspector Benedict ....Aldo Ray
Major Keller ....Sergio Aragones
Tom ....Ken Grant
Susan ....Jill Franklyn

Shot in Mexico in 1982, "To Kill A Stranger" is a low-voltage, theatrically unreleased thriller currently available in homevideo stores. Merely competent direction by horror vet Juan López-Moctezuma and okay thesping add up to an overfamiliar entry unlikely to find a niche in the market place.

Latin actress-singer Angelica Maria toplines as Cristina Carver, naturalized American wife of tv reporter Dean Stockwell, who flies in after a night club gig to be with him in an unnamed country run by the military. After a traffic accident, she foolishly goes home with a Good Samaritan played by Donald Pleasence, who predictably attacks her with sex and murder on his mind. Killing Pleasence in self-defense, she hides the corpse and covers up the crime when a not-so-helpful truck driver tells her Pleasence is a local war hero whose death will set off the wrath of the government (and military).

Hubbie Stockwell tries to protect his wife, but ultimately a wily police detective (Aldo Ray) uncovers the crime and ties matters up a bit too

neatly, while holding off the blood-thirsty military elements led by Major Keller (Sergio Aragones).

English-language sound recording is adequate, but film is unengrossing. General plot structure and twists are very reminiscent of René Clément's 1970 international hit "Rider On The Rain," but executed without style. —*Lor.*

The Man Who Envied Women
(U.S.-COLOR-16m)

Toronto, Sept. 11.

A Rio Grande Union production. Written and directed by Yvonne Rainer. Camera (color), Mark Daniels; editors, Rainer and Christine Le Goff; art consultant, Aimee Rankin; sound, Helene Kaplan. Reviewed at Toronto Festival of Festivals, Sept. 10, 1985. Running time: **125 MINS.**

"The Man Who Envied Women" is a tough-going exercise in feminist theory and intellectual mind games that will tax even the most ardent fans of Yvonne Rainer and the New York avant-garde movement. There are some clever comic asides, but mostly it's a tedious pic with limited appeal.

The voiceover narration of a 50-year-old woman who just split up with her husband provides the context for a mix of the fictional break-up, docu footage of public hearings on artist housing in lower Manhattan and responses to a collage of political and sexual newspaper editorial spreads.

Rainer delves into a mix of themes ranging from menstruation to political involvement in Central America, all through loose connecting threads. She links victims of biology (women) with victims of the state. Pic was shot on a few minimal sets with a switch to New York City streets as a backdrop for conversational snippets.

Film does have its moments: Rainer uses some effective juxtapositions of a background of b&w movies (from "Dark Victory" to "Un Chien Andalou" to "Double Indemnity") running simultaneously while Jack relates his urgent confessionals about the confused state of his sexuality to the shrink/camera.

Mostly the pic rambles on in a dense barrage of sexual and philosophical polemics and it becomes boring. —*Devo.*

Der Unbesiegbare
(The Invincible)
(WEST GERMAN-COLOR)

Montreal, Sept. 1.

A production of Salinas-Film in cooperation with ZDF, Austrian television ORF, Swiss television DRS, Belgian television RTBF, the Wallonie Image Prod. and the German Film and Television Academy in Berlin. Produced by Bernhardt Stampfer. Directed by Gusztav

Hamos. Screenplay, Hamos, Ed Cantu, Astrid Heibach, Juri Kozma; camera (color), Wolfgang Knigge; set decoration, Tomas Bergfelder; costumes, Kristen Johannsen; makeup, Ulrike Madej. Reviewed at the Montreal World Film Festival (Parisien 2), Aug. 29, 1985. Running time: **85 MINS.**
Argon.......................Udo Kier
Hurry Cane ....Piero von Arnim
Daisy Bit ....Linda Himbert
Dr. Rath ....Kurt von Ruffin
Samurai ....Makato Ozaki
Dr. Popov........Hans-Peter Hallwachs

The daring use of electronic images and video makes "The Invincible" work as a comic book, but the action does not have the zany quality one might expect of such a comic, perhaps done better in the past via animation. Actors such as Udo Kier are quite willing to ham it up, and the casting of the blond *Ubermensch* Piero von Arnim as hero Hurry Cane shows filmmakers are moving in the right direction, but editing is not tight enough to keep the pace funny, or even as inventive as a music video to which this is related.

Daisy Bit (Linda Himbert) tires to do a Marilyn Monroe imitation accompanying Hurry Cane and mad scientist Dr. Popov in a voyage to Mars, in order to protect the Earth from a space bandit Argon. Self-parody of contemporary styles does credit to designer Tomas Bergfelder, with his campy Third Reich inspirations, but the acting does not achieve the same stylization.

Debuting helmer Gusztav Hamos is a Hungarian just graduated from the Berlin academy with a vision that promises much more, once the technical marriage of video and film in consummated. When the posing stops and the action takes over, this is original and delightfully silly entertainment. —*Kaja.*

For Your Heart Only
(HONG KONG-COLOR)

Hong Kong, Sept. 10.

A Cinema City production. Released by Golden Princess. Produced by Dean Shek, Raymond Wong, Carl Maka. Directed by Raymond Fung. Stars Leslie Chung, Loletta Lee, Mang Hoi, Ann Bridgewater, Jimmy Wong. Screenplay, Edward Li, Raymond Fung; production design, Clifton Ko chi-sun; art direction, Benjamin Lau Man Hung; music, Danny Chung. Reviewed at President Theater, Hong Kong, Sept. 9, 1985. Running time: **98 MINS.**
(Cantonese soundtrack with English subtitles)

Disk jockey Piggy Chan (Leslie Chung), a plump mechanic called Sapi (Mang Hoi) and cousin Hayden (Jimmy Wong), a student with an apartment, are close friends.

They form a trio called "Lovebusters." Piggy falls in love at first sight with Jane (Loletta Lee, the young girl in "Shanghai Blues," grownup now and looking good), while on a bus.

Piggy still looks like a teenager and tries everything to win Jane's heart and unspoiled body. With the victory, she loses her virginity at 18 (her mother confesses to her that she lost hers at 17).

Piggy then resumes his flirting and cruising around with other wild girls in the usual disco background.

The Cinema City production is busy, but totally disorganized and without any specific direction. It was made for the simplest of teenage tastes.

As can be expected, it is bawdily funny most of the time in its own predictable, schoolboyish fashion. For the most part it is slanted to amuse the young regulars looking for easy rude situations. —*Mel.*

Osnisty Aniol
(Angel Of Fire)
(POLISH-COLOR)

Gdansk, Sept. 13.

A Coproduction of Polish Television (PRF "Zespoly Filmowe") and Film Polski, "Tor" Film Unit, Warsaw. Directed by Maciej Wojtyszko. Features entire cast. Screenplay, Maciej Siatkiewicz, Wojtyszko, based on the novel by Valery Bryusov; camera (color), Ryszard Lenczewski; music, Romuald Twardowski; sets, Jerzy Sniezawski; production manager, Michal Zablocki. Reviewed at Gdansk Film Fest, Sept. 12, 1985. Running time: **100 MINS.**
With: Jerzy Radziwilowicz (Ruprecht), Bozena Krzyzanowska (Renata), Jerzy Gralek (Henryk), Wiktor Grotowicz (Archbishop), Zygmunt Hübner (Faust), Janusz Michalowski (Hans).

The interesting aspect regarding Maciej Wojtyszko's tv-film production, "Angel Of Fire," is not that it's set in the Grand Inquisition period of the late 16th century, but that the literary source is from the same Russian author whose work inspired Prokofiev to compose his opera of the same title.

"Angel Of Fire" comes across as a film for youth and the young at heart, rather than as an esthetic experiment drawing upon the poetic, symbolist imagery found in the original. Ruprecht (Jerzy Radziwilowicz), stops overnight at an inn, only to meet and fall in love with the lovely Renata. She, however, has fallen under the spell of Count Henryk, whom she believes (from a childhood dream) to be an "angel of fire." The girl eventually brings him before the Inquisition.

Pic has some eyecatching costume scenes, but otherwise not much else. —*Holl.*

Objection
(POLISH-COLOR)

Gdansk, Sept. 11.

A Film Polski production, "Kadr" Film Unit, Warsaw; world rights, Film Polski, Warsaw. Written and directed by Andrzej Trzos-Rastawiecki. Features entire cast. Camera (color), Przemyslaw Skwirczynski; music, "Siekiera;" sets, Zenon Rozewicz; production manager, Tadeusz Lampka. Reviewed at Gdansk Film Fest, Sept. 11, '85. Running time: **77 MINS.**
With: Rafal Wieczynski (Jacek), Anna Gornostaj (Jola Pietrzyk), Jolanta Pietek (Kasia), Daniel Olbrychski (Grzegorz), Ewa Dalkowska (Krystyna), Mieczyslaw Hryniewicz (Iskierka), Zbigniew Zapasiewicz (Jacek's father).

Andrzej Trzos-Rastawiecki's "Objection" is a docudrama dealing with drug abuse among young people in Poland. Trzos-Rastawiecki hints that trading in marijuana, cocaine and the socalled "hard stuff" is seldom, but it is possible to get ready substitutes (even for injections) from local pharmacies, clinics, and medical centers and hospitals. By taking massive doses kids get hooked.

Storyline has a teenager from a well-to-do family learning the ropes through a girlfriend who's already hooked. The girl dies in the emergency room of a hospital, the death caused because Jacek, her boyfriend and pic's protagonist, has given in to her requests for a second drug injection.

"Objection" begins with this death in the hospital, whereupon Jacek seeks help voluntarily at a rehabilitation center. This is Jacek's second time at the center, which means that the others are required to vote on whether or not he can be admitted at all. The lad goes before his peers to plead his case by telling his story in flashbacks. In the end the experience is so painful that he decides to leave the center of his own free will. He is told by the center's director that if he stays clean for six months, he will be welcomed back.

The final shot shows Jacek giving in to his addiction and breaking the window of a pharmacy in the middle of the night.

Picture's major plus is the documentary approach on real locations, while a big minus is helmer's ineptitude with thesps on a professional scale.—*Holl.*

Remembrance
(BRITISH-COLOR)

Toronto, Sept. 8.

A production of Channel 4. Produced and directed by Colin Gregg. Screenplay, Hugh Stoddart; camera (color), John Metcalfe; editor, Peter Delfgou; art director, Jamie Leonard; sound, David Stephenson; assistant director-associate producer, Selwyn Roberts. Reviewed at the Festival of Festivals, Toronto (Varsity), Sept. 7, 1985. Running time: **106 MINS.**
Steve .... John Altman
John .... Al Ashton
Malcolm .... Martin Barrass
Chris .... Nick Dunning
Sue .... Sally Jane Jackson
Mark .... David John
Vincent .... Pete Lee-Wilson
Daniel .... Gary Oldman
Sean .... Ewan Stewart
Douglas .... Timothy Spall
Christine .... Kim Taylforth
Gail .... Michele Winstanley
Joe .... Kenneth Griffith

After winning first prize at the Taormina Film Festival in 1983, "Remembrance" (shot in 1981 for Channel Four) slipped into relative obscurity and has been flushed out again, apparently by the declaration of the year of the British film. It remains art house fare and is hampered by dialog so thickly accented it defies understanding. On the other hand, that failing does not seem that important, because the events are self-explanatory.

Long at over 100 minutes, the story revolves around the day spent before a group of very young sailors embark on NATO maneuvers. While in Plymouth enjoying their last shore leave, their experience embraces the totality of English existence, and helmer Colin Gregg demonstrates an impressive ability to range across a society, illustrating with vignettes its worst and finest moments.

These sailors of the Royal Navy prove a motley lot. Mark is determined to play sleuth and discover the identity of a badly beaten kid. Steve is on the point of developing a new love affair, adding some lighter but still anxious moments. Vincent is a victim of the generation gap, and Douglas will become a fathe at sea after bidding his sadly pregnant wife farewell. Malcolm drinks it up en route on the train from the Midlands, oblivious to responsibility and the future.

All these characters are given strongly delineated characteristics, and thesp kudos are well deserved. However, the slice of society Gregg so analytically surveys is a tad too depressing to make for marketable entertainment. —*Kaja.*

Saltimancii
(The Clowns)
(RUMANIAN-COLOR)

Montreal, Aug. 29.

Presented by Romaniafilm. Produced by Bucuresti Film Production Center, Group 5, in cooperation with Mosfilm Studios. Directed by Elisabeta Bostan. Written by Vasilica Istrate, based on the novel "Fram The Polar Bear," by Cezar Petrescu; camera (color), Ion Marinescu and Nicolae Girardi; art direction, Dumitru Georgescu; costume design, Nelly Merola; editor, Iolanda Mintulescu; music, Tomistocle Popa; sound, A. Salamanian. Reviewed at World Film Festival, Montreal, Aug. 28, 1985. Running time: **104 MINS.**
Lisette .... Gina Patrichi
Cezar Marcelloni .... Octavian Cotescu
Fanny .... Carmen Galin
Geo .... Adrian Vilcu
The Polar bear Fram .... Fram

Aiming for a big pic in the constrained circumstances of Rumanian production, "The Clowns" takes advantage of the Bucharest circus, one of the best in the world. The circus performances are featured prominently, providing the most entertaining moments plus the kind of material that could lead to marketing beyond its own region, particularly in the realm of kidpics, especially with the terrific shots of the bear.

Promising beginning scenes among the eskimos in polar climes, sweeping panoramas of ice and a polar bear initiate the story, representing the dream of young Geo to explore the North Pole. After this, the story is reduced to a mostly predictable and theatrically staged drama of a circus family. At the turn of the century in the provincial Rumanian city of Jassy, itinerant circus artistes enjoy the slap-dash of their shows and their own tinsel egos. Minor melodramas are sketched in brushstrokes to indicate Madame Lisette's glamor, Cezar's sad clowning and Fanny's romantic running away from the circus to elope into respectability.

A fire wipes them out and causes Lisette's death, putting them back on the road where they join up with the Sidoli Circus.

The subsequent story involves the training of a polar bear cub as well as young Geo, who must rise above disdain for circus life and realize that the life of a clown is the very essence of humanity.

Circus sequences seem to incorporate performers and locations of the Bucharest big top, which means dancing girls, elephants, and even a dramatic fall from the trapeze by Fanny. Attempts at humor are sometimes childlike

Thesping is primitive with the exception of young Adrian Vilcu, who restrains himself in the role of the young dreamer. Carmen Galin is pretty enough as an ingenue, but on the highwire acts, she really swings. Pic could benefit from more circus displays, since the story leaps through momentous changes without providing much motivation for psychological changes in the characters. —*Kaja.*

Dawandeh
(The Race)
(IRANIAN-COLOR)

Venice, Sept. 7.

Produced by the Institute for the Intellectual Development of Children and Youth. Written and directed by Amir Naderi. Stars Madjid Niroumand. Camera (color), Firouz Malekzadeh; editor, Bahram Beyzai; art director, Amir Naderi, Mohammad Hassanzadeh. Reviewed at the Venice Film Festival, Sept. 6, 1985. Running time: **94 MINS.**
Amiro .... Madjid Niroumand
Also with: Mousa Torkiradeh, A. Gholamzadeh, C. Bechkal, A. Pasdarzadeh, M. Kabiri.

Produced by Iran's Institute for the Intellectual Development of Children and Youth, "The Race" has nothing of an institutional air about it. This tale of a street urchin intent not just on surviving but on "winning the race" harks back to neorealist works like De Sica's "Shoeshine" and Buñuel's "Los Olvidados," but with weight of the film all resting on the frail shoulders of its remarkable pint-sized hero, Madjid Niroumand. Filmed on the shores of the Persian Gulf, pic is of great pictorial beauty, and a sure bet for future fest outings.

Amiro lives by himself in a rusty old hulk, but all day long he's out and about hustling a living and playing with his friends, abandoned urchins like himself. To whatever he does Amiro brings fierce intensity, driven by a mysterious, undefined rage. Scavenging in a junkyard, collecting bottles in shark-infested waters, shining shoes for sailors on leave or selling water, all of his activities are tinged with desperation.

Even more chilling, however, are Amiro's favorite pastimes. On the one hand he is obsessed with trains, ships and planes, anything that moves fast. He shouts senselessly at ships off the shore, at small aircraft coming in for a landing on a field, and with his friends plays a dangerous game of chasing after trains.

Helmer and writer Amir Naderi tells his tale without sentimentality or condescension, which lends pic a disturbing realism. At times the barren, vast panoramas of a developing landscape — new roads, docks, trucks and little else — appear monotonously tedious. At other moments pic captures something of its hero's breathlessness and achieves scenes of burning intensity. Most successful sequence is the heart-breaking, climactic race, where the kids run across the desert, tripping each other up, to reach a melting block of ice, outlined against the inferno of a blazing oil field. Cutting, lensing, thesping and pace converge in a powerful emotion all the stronger for being not quite definable. In the context of the film, winning the race — which might mean learning to read and write and bettering one's condition in life — remains ambiguous and problematic. — *Yung*.

Prague
(ITALO/CZECH-
DOCU-COLOR)

Toronto, Sept. 8.

A Trans World Film presentation. Produced by Karel Kvitak. Directed by Jiri Menzel and Vera Chytilova. Written by Chytilova; camera (color), Jan Malir; editor, Alois Fisarek; music, Michael Kocab. Reviewed at the Toronto Festival of Festivals, Varsity theater, Sept. 7, 1985. Running time: **60 MINS.**

An exhausting display of virtuoso camera work and a pretentious commentary traces the history of the city of Prague from pagan times to modern, with the architecture and cultural monuments — even a local production of "Amadeus" — serving as a photographic fodder.

Taking up the intellectual tones of Vera Chytilova's tribute to Milos Forman, produced in Belgium in 1981 and orginally titled "Continuity Of Consciousness," the narration

relentlessly repeats its exhortation to be conscious of continuity with a religious fervor. It turns into an exasperating self-consciousness, reinforced by the appearance of stylish fashion models posing against the stones of history every time the camera slows to a simple pan.

Quite likely to be snapped up by festivals because of the marquee value of Menzel and Chytilova, it is likely to experience difficulties in its natural habitat, television, where the vertiginous camera work and pedantic tone may appear too artsy.
—*Kaja.*

Cien Juz Niedaleko
(A Looming Shadow)
(POLISH-B&W)

Gdansk, Sept. 10.

A Film Polski production, "Rondo" Film Unit, Warsaw; world rights, Film Polski, Warsaw. Written and directed by Kazimierz Karabasz. Features entire cast. Camera (b&w), Czeslaw Swirta; music, Zbigniew Rudzinski; sets, Anna Bondziewicz, Andrzej Plocki; production manager, Stefan Lojec. Reviewed at Gdansk Film Fest, Sept. 10, 1985. Running time: **87 MINS.**

With: Mariusz Dmochowski (Jozef), Jaroslaw Kopaczewski (Henryk), Wlodzimierz Kwaskorski (Leon), Michal Bajor (manager's assistant), Jerzy Kryszak (clerk).

Kazimierz Karabasz' "A Looming Shadow" comes across as a docu drama, told very simply while relying heavily on scenes shot on actual locations for overall realistic detail and dramatic effect. There's a docu newsreel shown midway through the story dating from the mid-1950s, when Karabasz was just cutting his filmmaking teeth in the same genre.

This is the story of an ex-steelworker at the Nowa Huta plant near Cracow, now living in retirement as a 60-year-old cripple in the distant city of Szczecin, returning to his former place of employment for the purpose of receiving an award together with colleagues on the occasion of the plant's 30th anniversary. It turns out, however, that the deserving old veteran of the Nowa Huta origins is not on the list of recipients for some undisclosed reason, and a cursory investigation is made into his, and another exworker's, case to find out the reason for the oversight.

At the same time, the man's son is facing an eviction problem from the apartment belonging to the father and family over the years. This comes while his wife is delivering their second child. An investigative look into this matter reveals the oddity that the son hasn't any right to the apartment anymore since he left the steelworks to seek employment elsewhere, the irony being that the father was made a cripple while working a difficult job at the mill over a number of years.

The retired worker and frustrat-

ed father finds his hands tied. He can neither right the injustice of his own case, nor help his son to retain the apartment for which both have labored long and hard throughout their working lives. Such a pessimistic though dignified portrait of contemporary labor conditions in Poland has seldom been sketched so clearly.

In the end, the father departs without having cleared up anything. He is left with the thought that perhaps he should have conducted his private affairs with as much care and devotion as he gave to his job. His pride obviously hindered him as well at a crucial moment in the past: he refused to take a desk job after his injury at the mills, then lost desire and interest upon his wife's death.

"A Looming Shadow" epitomizes the aura of futility sensed in Poland these days. —*Holl.*

The Vals
(U.S.-COLOR)

Sydney, Sept. 23.

An Entertainment Artists production. Produced and directed by James Polakof. Executive producer Shirley Rothman. Features entire cast. Screenplay, Polakof, Deborah Amelon, from a story by Polakof; camera (color), G.W. (Dink) Read; editor, Millie Paul; art director, Charles Tomlinson; music, Daphna Edwards, Unicorn Records; assistant director/production manager, Pamela Hauser; associate producers, John Cannon, Fred Ziems, Edward T. Stein. Reviewed on Sundowner videocassette, Sydney, Sept. 19, 1985. (MPAA Rating: R.) Running time: **100 MINS.**

Samantha	Jill Carroll
Trish	Elena Stratheros
Beth	Michelle Laurita
Annie	Gina Calabrase
Trish's father	Chuck Connors
Samantha's mother	Tiffany Bolling
TV star	Sue Anne Langdon
Spaced-out guest	Sonny Bono
Mr. Stanton	John Carradine
Keith	Matthew Conlon
Julie	Sharon Lea
Mike	Tony Longo
Lance	Michael Leon
Stone	Robert Dryer

Made in 1982, thus pre-dating Martha Coolidge's definitive film on the subject of valley girls, "The Vals" is a drab low-budgeter, routinely plotted and executed. Pic was orignally set for release in 1983 by since-defunct Jensen Farley Pictures.

Central characters are four high-school students who hang around together. Trish (Elena Stratheros) is upset because her handsome boyfriend (Matthew Conlon) respects her too much to have sex with her. Samantha (Jill Carroll) is the conscience of the group, who persuades the others to help her in a Capra-esque scheme to save an orphanage facing foreclosure. Beth (Michelle Laurita) is a cheerful, plump highliver, while Annie (Gina Calabrase) is the sexually active member of the group (and involved in an R-level

sex scene).

Odd combination of teen comedy, with lotsa valley slang (we get "Grody to the max" no less than four times), sex, social concern and drama (when the girls try to raise money for the orphans by ripping off two cocaine dealers), makes for a muddle of a film. Given the poor material provided, the four young actresses are surprisingly effective, but as the coke-snorting, partner-swapping older generation, Chuck Connors, Sonny Buno, Tiffany Bolling and Sue Anne Langdon are merely cyphers. John Carradine is in for a benign cameo as the kindly manager of the orphanage. —*Strat.*

The Women's Olamal — The Origins Of A Maasai Fertility Ceremony
(DOCU-COLOR-16m)

A presentation of Films Inc. (Wilmette, Ill.). A production of BBC-TV, Bristol; coproduced by Chris Curling and Melissa Llewelyn-Davies. Directed by Llewelyn-Davies. Camera (color), Dick Pope, Barry Ackroyd; sound, Bruce White; translations, Moses Ole Simel; spoken in Maasai, with subtitles in English, and with English voiceover. Reviewed at Margaret Mead Film Festival, N.Y., Sept. 12, 1985. Running time: **120 MINS.**

The Maasai — variously hunters and nomadic shepherds and farmers — live on the high plains of Kenya and Tanzania, East Africa. This film emphasizes Maasai women and their duty to reproduce. The women do not question this duty and indeed are eager to obey.

A barren woman, or a woman whose children have died, is unfulfilled and suffers loss of social face. The husband loves only the wife who gives him children.

It is a Maasai custom for women of neighboring villages to come together periodically under the leadership of women-elders to plan and perform ritual Olamal fertility ceremonies. The climax of this ceremony is a kind of parade or dance, with an incantation evoking God's blessing for pregnancy.

A remarkable aspect of this film is the intimacy of the Maasai women who speak to the director, a British woman, through an interpreter. Their comments are very detailed, personal and emotional, showing a strong sense of woman's subordinate place in nature's grand design and their sacred function to give birth.

Although overlong at two hours, perhaps because of scrupulous fidelity to ethnographic authenticity, the film could be vastly improved for popular audiences, e.g., public tv and 16m to colleges, by sharpening its points through cutting and condensing. The film's portrayal of Maasai tribal life, perhaps a miniature of our own prehistory, has resonances that reach out to our own culture. —*Hitch.*

Quel Numero?
(What Number?)
(CANADIAN-DOCU-COLOR)

Toronto, Sept. 13.

A DEC Films release of a production of Les Prods. du Regard and Les Prods. Contrejour. Produced by Jean-Roch Marcotte, Sophie Bissonnette. Directed by Bissonnette. Researched by Bissonnette, Diane Poitras, Suzanne Belanger; camera (color), Serge Giguere; sound, Diane Carriere, Claude Beaugrand, Marcel Fraser, Michel Charron, Pierre Blain; editor, Liette Aubin; an animation, Herve Bedard; character design for animation, Andree Brochu; original music, Jean Sauvageau. Reviewed at Toronto Festival of Festivals (Cumberland), Sept. 11, 1985. Running time: **81 MINS.**

A clever and accessible look into the changes wrought by computers and word processors, "What Number?" is handicapped only by its many speeches in French creating a need for elaborate subtitles, but it is entertaining and informative as tv viewing.

What has happened since the introduction of microchip technology into the workplace is behind the testimonies of the secretaries, checkout clerks, telephone operators and postal employees here.

Problems such as loss of control over the information, shifts in authority within the office and new types of strain and stress don't come as a surprise, but the expression of all that from the mouths of these lively women has a human interest that suggests even more could be made of this material that would be appropriate to fiction features about the workplace. — *Kaja.*

Otryad
(The Unit)
(SOVIET-COLOR/B&W)

Montreal, Aug. 30.

A Mosfilms Studio production. Directed by Alexei Simonov. Screenplay, Evgeny Grigoriev; camera (color, b&w), Jonas Gritsus; music, Vladimir Kamolikov. Reviewed at Montreal World Film Festival, Aug. 27, 1985. Running time: **96 MINS.**

With: Alexander Feklistov, Sergei Garmash, Dmitri Brusnikin, Mikhail Morozov, Yakov Stepanov, Alexander Peskov, Viktor Nesterov.

In what shouldn't come as much of a shock, the Germans don't come across at all well in the USSR-made "The Unit," a dry, grim account of life on the run behind enemy Nazi lines in Lithuania.

No sooner does World War II break out in Russia than a ragtag unit of young Soviet soldiers finds itself facing all sorts of adversity and humiliation from hordes of advancing Germans. Though outmanned, the unit is undaunted in seeking to reach the front-line and to valiantly save the motherland.

In lieu of much derring-do, the movie is mostly given to rhapsodizing about the Red Army and to adhering to the rigid Stalin Party-line. Perhaps to ensure audience interest,

director Alexei Simonov resorts to continually cross-cutting color and black-and-white footage for effect, an exceedingly annoying effect at that. Otherwise, pic's production values are impressive. — *Bro.*

Nadzor
(Custody)
(POLISH-COLOR)

Gdansk, Sept. 13.

A Film Polski production, Karol Irzykowski Film Studio; world rights, Film Polski, Warsaw. Written and directed by Wieslaw Saniewski. Features entire cast. Camera (color), Przemyslaw Gintrowski; sets, Andrzej Kowalczyk; production manager, Krzysztof Was. Reviewed at Gdansk Film Fest, Sept. 13, 1985. Running time: **112 MINS.**

With: Ewa Blaszczyk (Klara Molosz), Grazyna Szapolowska (Klinga), Teresa Sawicka (Beata), Ewa Szykulska (Stacha), Gabriela Kownacka (Danusia "Wabik"), Justyna Kulczycka (Justyna), Elzbieta Zajacowna (Ala), Ewa Dalkowska (Gabyrsiakowa).

Completed in 1981 and shown in film clubs around Poland, Wieslaw Saniewski's "Custody" ran at a reported two-and-a-half-hours and received a "Solidarity Award" for its frank exposition of prison life. With the advent of martial law (December 1981), Saniewski found his film on the shelf for the duration — until its current release

"Custody" is about the trials and tribulations of a young woman picked up by the police on her wedding day for embezzlement, promptly sentenced to life imprisonment. If the punishment seems exaggerated for the crime, well, Saniewski stretches the point all the way down the line to the limits of prison-life credibility. One has the feeling helmer Saniewski doesn't want to leave anything out in describing the severe knocks handed out to the relatively innocent Klara: she enters the prison pregnant, has the baby under trying conditions, then suffers an almost immediate separation from her child — only to discover later it's been confined to an orphanage for a time and has suffered a severe spinal injury there.

Further, the guards and many of her cellmates are pretty ornery types. One guard, in particular, demonstrates a cruel streak every chance she gets — not only to Klara, but also to a student (why she's jailed is not exactly explained) who exercises her option for passive resistance every chance she gets.

The year of entering the prison is 1967, and later it's stated that the Polish authorities in a declaration of amnesty have commuted her sentence from life to 25 years. Thus, 12 years later, we find her leaving prison on parole. She hopes to find her daughter waiting for her, but the departure keeps to the overall tone of the story by having her leaving the prison gate alone on as equally a depressing day on the outside as

they were on the inside.

Despite reservations, however, "Custody" is an important film and one that stands out in the annals of contemporary Polish cinema for its forthrightness. The performance by Ewa Blaszczyk as Klara is quite extraordinary, and she's supported by several other fine performances. Blaszczyk won the Best Actress kudo at Gdansk, while helmer Saniewski copped a belated debut prize. — *Holl,*

Dluznicy Smierci
(Indebted To Death)
(POLISH-COLOR)

Gdansk, Sept. 14.

A Coproduction of Polish Television (PRF "Zespoly Filmowe") and Film Polski, "Profil" Film Unit, Warsaw. Directed by Wlodzimierz Golaszewski. Features entire cast. Screenplay, Maciej Zenon Bordowicz, based on his own story; camera (color), Henryk Janas; music, Wlodzimierz Nahorny; sets, Roman Wolyniec; production manager, Roman Kowalski. Reviewed at Gdansk Film Fest, Sept. 13, 1985. Running time: **94 MINS.**

With: Krzysztof Kolbasiuk (commander), Tomasz Zaliwski (Jezewski), Wieslaw Golas (Listwa), Henryk Talar (Koldak), Andrzej Precigs (Wertep), Karol Stasburger (prosecutor), Wlodzimierz Golaszewski (poet).

Wlodzimierz Golaszewski's "Indebted To Death" is an "Eastern" set in the still troublesome days of 1946, when the Bialystok province witnessed regular showdowns between the state militia and underground bandits. Pic opens with the bridegroom at a wedding reception being spirited away by the militia into the night in order to get him to identify Grom, a feared leader of the bandits. Grom, hardly the man's real name, is believed to be among a group of prisoners held by the state police at the county seat.

The trick is to get the bridegroom safe and sound to a trial in order to finger Grom. Meanwhile, attempts are made on the potential betrayer's life as the militia passes through dangerous country. Just as there have been boring B-Westerns, this is an equivalently weary B-Eastern.

— *Holl.*

Cronica dos bons Malandros
(A Chronicle Of Good Hoodlums)
(PORTUGUESE-COLOR)

Montreal, Aug. 29.

Produced, written and directed by Fernando Lopes. Camera (color) Manuel Costa e Silva; music, Rui Veloso. Reviewed at the Montreal World Film Festival (Parisien), Aug. 28, 1985. Running time: **90 MINS.**

With: Joao Perry, Lia Gama, Maria do ceu Guerra, Nicolau Breyner, Paulo de Carvalho, Pedro Bandeira Freire, Duarte Nuno, Antonio Assuncao, Virgilio Castelo, Zita Duarte.

This zany story has much appeal, but it has a gang of Lisbon bandits aiming at a jewel heist who seem a bit long in the tooth for the agility required by the singing and dancing.

There is the usual range of per-

sonalities — the gang's intellectual, the Judas, the hooker, the nice girl, and a car chase.

An overlay of computerized video effects makes this seem like a very long rock video without the rock, although there are some parodic musical numbers on it. Fernando Lopes demonstrates some provincial attempts at sophisticated, trendy fashion photography, especially in the closeups of the jewels from the Lalique collection at the Portuguese Gulbenkian Foundation Museum. For the most part, there are little prospects of travel beyond the festival circuit. — *Kaja.*

Pobojowisko
(Battlefield)
(POLISH-COLOR)

Gdansk, Sept. 14.

A Coproduction of Polish Televison (PRF "Zespoty Filmowe") and Film Polski, "Iluzjon" Film Unit. Written and directed by Jan Budkiewicz, based on the novel by Waclaw Bilinski. Features entire cast. Camera (color), Waclaw Dybowski; music, Andrzej Zarycki; sets, Szeski; production manager, Dariusz Bielawski. Reviewed at Gdansk Film Fest, Sept. 13, 1985. Running time: **104 MINS.**

With Janusz Rafal Nowicki (Bogdan Ianowiecki), Halina Bednarz (Lucja), Jacek Strama (Wrobel), Karin Gregorek (Mathilde von Paulitzky), Zygmunt Malanowicz (Los), Jacek Kalucki (Piotrowski), Wieslaw Wojcik (Gradkowski).

Set in the Baltic port of Pobojowisko (formerly known as Schlachtenfeld, or "Battlefield") in the autumn of 1945, Jan Budkiewicsz' "Battlefield" is another one of those postwar good guys vs. bad guys action films made for both Polish tv and theater audiences. People are trying to get resettled. The native Germans want to move west, while Polish families from other districts (mostly what was formerly eastern Poland) are arriving in the area.

The hero in charge of maintaining a semblance of law and order is a former partisan now in the militia and suffering from intermittent bouts of typhus. He has to receive regular injections from a friendly nurse (at the local overworked hospital) whom he gradually pursues for other convenient reasons.

In order to legitimize its "Eastern" status, the commander comes across as the lonely town marshal having to combat the prejudices of even his own people at times — while at the same time clearing the port of booby-trap mines. — *Holl.*

Memoirs
(CANADIAN-COLOR)

Toronto, Sept. 15.

A production and release of Les Productions Chbib. Produced and directed by Bachar Chbib. Screenplay, John Beckett Wimbs, Chbib, based on the play "Memoirs Of Johnny Daze" by Wimbs; camera (color 16m), Christian Duguay, Bill Kerrigan; editor, Chbib, Amy Webb; music, Julia Gilmore, Edward Straviak, Philip Vezina; sound, Gabor Vadney. Reviewed at the Festival of Festivals, Toronto (Cumberland), Sept. 14, 1985. Running time: **91 MINS.**

Johnny Daze . . . . Philip Baylaucq
Ida Rage . . . . Norma Jean Sanders
Lotta Lov . . . . Julia Gilmore
Rotwang. Rotwang

The inspiration of "Liquid Sky" and Susan Seidelman is all too evident in this pilgrimage through "a big city" which is clearly Canadian. Debut helmer Bachar Chbib has a good sense of perverted punk style yawning over the emptiness of young lives, but his approach is simply too derivative. Film opened theatrically in New York last November as a midnight attraction.

Pic centers around the misadventures of Johnny Daze, played with a catatonic expression by Philip Baylaucq, who hooks up with Ida Rage, a young woman who steals art or facsimiles thereof under the guise of collecting. She will also collect Johnny, to help her in her search for increasingly rarified trash, the kind of *objets d'art* she leaves in front of her door overnight and nobody steals.

On one of their explorations, they hear a woman singing (or doing performance art or something approximating entertainment) and Ida is thoroughly captivated by the wildly Teutonic Lotta Lov. What at first looks like a sendup of German performance art turns out to be the ultimate junk sought after by Ida Rage. The two women throw in their lot together, which means Lotta moves in with Ida and Johnny, who is elbowed out. He comes to reconsider the glamor and artistic life he craved in the city as a writer. The two women's consuming desire drives Lotta Lov to a theatrical self-mutilation, carried off surprisingly well by Norma Jean Sanders. Sanders has some acting ability hiding beneath the nonplussed airs she adopts in most of her scenes.

Given more original material than rhinestones in the rubble and a stud in the rough coping with a *menage à trois,* these not untalented people could afford to appear more human and thereby appeal to a wider audience. —*Kaja.*

Pismak
(Write And Fight)
(POLISH-COLOR)

Gdansk, Sept. 12.
A Film Polski production, Rondo Film Unit, Warsaw; world rights, Film Polski, Warsaw. Directed by Wojciech Jerzy Has. Features entire cast. Screenplay, Wladyslaw Terlecki, based on his novel; camera (color), Grzegorz Kedzierski; music, Jerzy Maksymiuk; sets, Andrzej Halinski; production manager, Konstanty Lewkowicz. Reivewed at Gdansk Film Fest. Sept. 11, 1985. Running time: **120 MINS.**
With: Wojciech Wysocki (Rafal), Gustaw Holoubek (Inspector), Zdzislaw Wardejn (Safecracker), Jan Peszek (Sykstus), Janusz Michalowski (Prison Doctor), Gabriela

Kownacka (Maria), Hanna Mikuc (Sykstus' Lover).

Wojciech Jerzy Has' "Write And Fight" takes place during World War I, and the setting is a prison cell. Here a newspaper satirist, a safecracker, and a clerical murderer have been cooped up together until the investigation into each of their supposed crimes has been completed. The newspaperman, Rafal, decides to take copious notes on the situation in view of writing a social novel based on his experiences.

Since all the characters — including the prison officials — prove to be quite colorful personalities, the film moves along nicely at the beginning. Then the writer catches typhus, and in his delirium fantasy mixes with reality until he is no longer able to differentiate between the characters in his manuscript and those in real life.

Static camera angles offer many possibilities for the distant observation of lifestyles, but when the cell brothers don't have much of interest to say and don't even seem worth writing about in a novelist's farfetched fantasy, the result is dullsville. —*Holl.*

Darse Cuenta
(Becoming Aware)
(ARGENTINE-COLOR)

Santiago, Sept. 13.
A Rosales y Asociados S.R.L. production. Executive producer, Diana Frey. Directed by Alejandro Doria. Screenplay, Jacobo Langsner, Doria; camera (color), credit not reported; music, Silvio Rodriquez. Reviewed at Cine Ducal, Week of New Argentine Cinema, Santiago, Chile, Sept. 11, 1985. Running time: **105 MINS.**
With: Luis Brandoni, Dora Baret, Luisina Brando, Lito Cruz, Oscar Ferrigno, María Vaner, China Zorrillà, Darlo Grandinetti, Matlas Puelles.

At first it seems that "Becoming Aware" is heading towards an indictment of the bureaucratic hangups of the Argentine Health Service and the medical profession in general, including doctors' cynical attitude towards malpractice and their callousness towards patients.

The action then concentrates on Doctor Carlos Ventura and one patient, a young man who was run over by a car and so seriously hurt that, upon admission to the hospital, doctors consider it a waste of time to try and patch him up. Ventura, in his mid 40s, is a character not normally given to grand gestures, but he senses this human wreck's will to live, takes over the case and, over many months, brings about his recovery and rehabilitation.

Long before this outcome, Ventura's marriage, already in the doldrums, breaks up and his son leaves the country, accusing dad of never communicating with him. Because of all this, taking care of the young patient becomes a way of making up

for the shortcomings and frustrations of the doctor's personal life.

Whatever platitudes the film may be aiming at, the one-note characters like Ventura's wife, the patient's relatives and other doctors, are stilted stereotypes, more befitting of a soap opera. There is, however, an outstanding performance by China Zorilla, a veteran Uruguayan actress, in a small supporting role as a nurse.

Technical credits are professional, but otherwise unimpressive. Pic is unlikely to obtain commercial exposure beyond its home ground. — *Amig.*

Zabicie Ciotki
(Killing Auntie)
(POLISH-COLOR)

Gdansk, Sept. 12.
A Film Polski production, "Rondo" Film Unit, Warsaw; world rights, Film Polski, Warsaw. Directed by Grzegorz Krolikiewicz. Features entire cast. Screenplay, Krzysztof Skudzinski, Krolikiewicz, based on novel by Andrzej Bursa; camera (color), Krzysztof Ptak; music, Janusz Hajdun; sets, Wojciech Szpotakowski; production manager, Anna Gryczynska. Reviewed at Gdansk Film Fest, Sept. 11, 1985. Running time: **105 MINS.**
With: F. Robert Herubin (Jurek), Maria Kleydysz (Jurek's aunt), Wanda Luczycka (grandmother), Krystyna Feldman (Aunt Emily), Gustaw Holoubek (sacrilegious man), Jozef Pieracki (priest), Wladyslaw Dewoyno (professor).

Grzegorz Krolikiewicz' "Killing Auntie" comes across as a grotesque fairy tale of what goes on in 21-year-old Jurek's apparently twisted mind and rampant imagination. We first find the lad in a confessional telling the priest about killing his aunt. Then we see him mailing off parcels at the post office as though deliveries from the butcher shop are properly sent through the mail. Has he hacked his aunt to pieces, as he claims?

The rest is a trail through the labyrinth of Jurek's wildest fantasies. Just when it appears that an arrest is about to be made, along comes Auntie alive and well, back from a trip to begin doting on her weird nephew once again. This time, though, Jurek braces himself to really do the naughty deed.

Krolikiewicz draws upon poet-novelist Andrzej Bursa's autobiographical experiences and includes a strong scene in the confessional that matches Irish writer Frank O'Connor's anti-clerical sentiments and would probably have amused Luis Buñuel in its forthrightness. —*Holl.*

Carry On Doctors
And Nurses
(HONG KONG-COLOR)

Hong Kong, Sept. 9.
A Shaw Bros. production and release. Produced by Run Run Shaw. Executive producer, Mona Fong. Directed by Chen Yu. Stars

Chen Yu, Lin Chien-ming, Chang Chien-ting, Chung Pao-lo, Kuan Chao-chung, Chen Hsui-wen. Planning by Chang Chien-ting; screenplay, Hung Hung-chi, Wen Chuan, Chang Chien-ting. (No other credits provided by producers.) Reviewed at King's Theater, Hong Kong, Sept. 9, 1985. Running time: **98 MINS.**
(Cantonese soundtrack with English subtitles)

The Medical and Health Dept. sends a special investigative team to check the alleged bad management at St. Moren hospital. (The name of the hospital when translated from Cantonese to English means "sexually impotent.")

Lin Chien-ming is the nursing officer who is also in charge of the reorganization. A number of young student nurses have been recruited to improve the service (Lin Shanshan, Chen Hsui-wen and others).

The men in the hospital are naturally overzealous in their schemes to make advances to the supposedly innocent nurses. Luckily, the nursing officer is always around to save the day and their virginity.

There are scenes that depict the training of the student nurses, but more are devoted to the games that young boys and girls play.

Fast-moving, "Carry On Doctors And Nurses," has lots of energy but there's really no serious story, merely a string of brisk, little jokes loosely strung together. Some are good, others sick and the rest imitative.

The cast includes a mixture of old-timers, non-professionals trying to be celebrities and disk jockeys moonlighting on the big screen. — *Mel.*

Remo Williams: The Adventure Begins
(COLOR)

Pale shadow of James Bond antics, minus the fun.

Hollywood, Oct. 1.

An Orion Pictures release of a Dick Clark, Larry Spiegel, Mel Bergman production. Produced by Spiegel. Executive producers, Clark, Bergman. Directed by Guy Hamilton. Stars Fred Ward, Joel Grey, Wilford Brimley. Screenplay, Christopher Wood, based on "The Destroyer" series by Richard Sapir, Warren Murphy; coproducer, Judy Goldstein; camera (DeLuxe color), Andrew Laszlo; editor, Mark Melnick; production designer, Jackson De Govia; music, Craig Safan; set decorator, Frederick C. Weiler; costumes, Ellen Mirojnick; art director, N.Y., Woods Mackintosh; art director/-Mexico, Brandy Alexander, John R. Jensen, Michael Minor; stunt coordinator, Glenn H. Randall Jr.; sound, James J. Sabat; assistant director, U.S., Alex Hapsas; assistant director, Mexico, Richard L. Espinoza; casting, Amanda MacKey, Jane Jenkins, Janet Hirshenson. Reviewed at Samuel Goldwyn Theater, Beverly Hills, Calif. Sept. 30, 1985. (MPAA Rating: PG-13.) Running time: **121 MINS.**

Remo Williams	Fred Ward
Chiun	Joel Grey
Harold Smith	Wilford Brimley
Conn MacCleary	J.A. Preston
General Scott Watson	George Coe
George Grove	Charles Cioffi
Major Rayner Fleming	Kate Mulgrew

"Remo Williams: The Adventure Begins" is a poor man's James Bond with a dash of two or three other popular genres thrown in for good measure. It is not surprising, then, that the film never seems to know where it's going and, when the smoke has cleared, doesn't seem to have got there either. Although it tries hard, pic mostly just spins its wheels. Its b.o. outlook is modest.

With Guy Hamilton, veteran of four Bond films, directing and Christopher Wood, writer of two Bond adventures, one might safely expect some of the flash and wit of the Ian Fleming character. Not so.

Although "Remo Williams" is adapted from the popular "Destroyer" series, the filmmakers have chosen to play the characters seriously without any of the camp charm that has endeared James Bond to audiences for years. Bond was always so suave and tongue-in-cheek that he could get away with almost any outlandish plot and often did.

Williams, on the other hand, is sort of a proletarian Bond — a new York City cop recruited for some secret government agency supposedly working undercover for the President himself. Although he acquits himself as well as he can, Fred Ward as Remo, looking surprisingly like Charles Bronson, is too distant and mysterious to root for.

There is also something disturbing about Remo's kidnaping and unwilling enlistment in the service of his country. Any chance that this could all be a big joke goes out the window when Ward is escorted to meet Wilford Brimley as head of the secret group (his assistant, J.A. Preston is the only other member). Brimley, so appealing in other roles, delivers his lines here with a world-weary solemnity usually reserved for heads of state.

What levity occurs in the film is mostly reserved for the long middle section in which Remo is placed under the tutelage of the last living master of the Korean martial art Sinanju. It comes as a bit of a shock to realize this ancient Korean soul is really Joel Grey transformed, but the disguise and the performance are probably the most enjoyable ingredients in the film.

The relationship between Remo and Chiun (Grey) is an adult version of "The Karate Kid" with the master unveiling a host of secrets for his gradually more receptive pupil. Small feats such as walking on water and dodging bullets are simply routine for the great man.

Unfortunately all the nifty tricks Remo is storing up are to be used against villains that generate no sense of menace. Charles Cioffi as an arms manufacturer in cahoots with the military is a cardboard heavy surrounded by a supply of bumbling bad guys. Politically there is also something about the setup that robs it of any possible credibility.

Thrown in for a slight romantic interest is Kate Mulgrew as an honest officer stumbling on the nefarious plot. Several scenes of Remo on the run with Mulgrew in tow are reminiscent of the pairing in "Romancing The Stone," but nothing much comes of it here.

Since Remo is too thinly drawn and the villains too comic-book-like to take seriously, the procession of stunts are rendered basically flat, although there is some impressive dangling from the Statue of Liberty and hanging logs. The conclusion of all this stunting is rather sudden and anticlimactic considering what has come before it.

The musical score by Craig Safan tends to be overwhelming and although individually the production values are solid they never contribute to a unified tone for the film. "Remo Williams" is simply not that much fun. —*Jagr.*

O Viasmos Tis Aphrodites
(The Rape Of Aphrodite)
(GREEK-CYPRIOT-COLOR)

Thessaloniki, Oct. 4.

A Cyprus Film Center, Greek Film Center, ERT-1 production. Written and directed by Andreas Pantzis. Camera (color), Andreas Bellis; editor, Panos Papakyriakopoulos; sets, Antis Partzilis, costumes, Stefanos Athienitis; sound, Nikos Achladis; music, Michalis Christodoulidis. Reviewed at the Thessaloniki Film Festival Oct. 4, 1985. Running time: **150 MINS.**

Evagoras	Costas Timvios
Aphrodite	Thalia Argiriou
Taxi Driver	Ilias Aletras

For anyone unfamiliar with recent Cypriot history, this film is bound to be particularly heavygoing: attempting to retrace the tragedy of this island in the last 30 years in a highly symbolic fashion, throwing dates and information at the audience, and using long soliloquies to fill in the details.

The plot itself is a pretext. A former member of the anti-British resistance movement, EOKA, who has lived in London since the island had been granted independence from Great Britain in 1960, returns 14 years later, to look for his wife and son who had gone there to visit his mother just when the Turkish military invasion had thrown the whole place into havoc. The picture is fashioned as a long search.

Evagoras, the protagonist, establishes his base in a Nicosia hotel, overlooking the mountains behind which his native village, the original destination of his family, lies under Turkish occupation. Every day he sets out in another direction, with a taxi driver who serves as his companion, and each trip serves as an excuse for another flashback, sometimes visually, sometimes only narrated, into the history of the Greek Cypriot community.

Director Andreas Pantzis is trying to fashion a kind of cinema which blends Greek tragedy, mythology, symbolism and politics together. By presenting his people (Pantzis is a Cypriot) as victims, blaming the British, the Greek and the Turks, equally for what has happened to his homeland, and leads towards a militant conclusion, suggesting that violence may be the only issue out of the impossible impasse Cyprus finds itself now.

—*Edna.*

Dreamchild
(BRITISH-COLOR)

A Universal Pictures release of a PFH Ltd. production, in association with Thorn EMI Screen Entertainment. Executive producers, Dennis Potter, Verity Lambert. Produced by Rick McCallum and Kenith Trodd. Directed by Gavin Millar. Stars Coral Browne, Peter Gallagher, Ian Holm. Screenplay, Potter; camera (Technicolor), Billy Williams; editor, Angus Newton; music, Stanley Myers; additional music, Max Harris; sound, Godfrey Kirby; production design, Roger Hall; art director, Len Huntingford (locations), Marianne Ford (sets); assistant director, Guy Travers; costume design, Jane Robinson; Alice In Wonderland characters' design and performance, Jim Henson's Creature Shop; design supervisor, Lyle Conway; workshop supervisor, Constance Peterson; creature producer, Duncan Kenworthy. Reviewed at Cinema II, N.Y., Oct. 5, 1985. (MPAA Rating: PG.) Running time: **93 MINS.**

Alice Hargreaves	Coral Browne
Rev. Charles L. Dodgson	Ian Holm
Jack Dolan	Peter Gallagher
Lucy	Nicola Cowper
Sally	Caris Corfman
Mrs. Liddell	Jane Asher
Little Alice	Amelia Shankley

Also with: Imogen Boorman, Emma King, Shane Rimmer, William Hootkins.

Creature Performers

Gryphon	Ron Mueck
Mock Turtle	Steve Whitmire
Dormouse	Karen Prell
March Hare	Michael Sundin
Mad Hatter	Big Mick
Caterpillar	Steve Whitmire

Creature Voiceovers

Gryphon	Fulton Mackay
Mock Turtle	Alan Bennett
Dormouse	Julie Walters
March Hare	Ken Campbell
Mad Hatter	Tony Haygarth
Caterpillar	Frank Middlemass

"Dreamchild" is an ambitious but unsatisfying and gimmicky film about Rev. Charles L. Dodgson, a/k/a Lewis Carroll, the creator of "Alice's Adventures In Wonderland." A gem of a performance by Coral Browne is wasted in the picture's rickety setting.

Browne toplines as the widow Alice Hargreaves, who as a child inspired Dodgson to write his famous work, published in 1865. In 1932, Hargreaves, nearly 80 and dying, travels to New York to receive an honorary degree from Columbia University in conjunction with the celebration of Lewis Carroll's birth centenary.

Screenwriter-executive producer Dennis Potter relies upon several conceits for his story, notably Dodgson/Carroll's attraction to underage girls, as well as 1930s nostalgia (seeming to be a companion piece to his "Pennies From Heaven" opus), comedy about U.S./-British cultural differences and other themes. Utilizing flashbacks, dreams, hallucinations and "illustrative" footage, director Gavin Miller comes up with an awkward and frequently distracting structure to the picture.

While Browne has a grand time commenting on the incivilities of Americans, the flashback material starring Ian Holm as Dodgson and an expressive debuting child actress, Amelia Shankley, as Alice is sketchy and merely interrupts the main story. In brief doses, elaborate creatures from Jim Henson's company are a further narrative disruption, calling attention to themselves and away from Browne.

Peter Gallagher scores points as a surprisingly sympathetic mercenary — an ex-newspaper reporter who attaches himself to Mrs. Hargreaves and romances her young traveling companion Lucy (Nicola Cowper giving a rather flat reading of the role). Rest of the cast has small parts, including the ubiquitous group of Americans in British-made films, including Shane Rimmer and William Hootkins.

Thinness of the material and a lack of subtlety is evident right from the opening reel, as Holm is directed to gaze so longingly and lustily at young Alice that there is no ambiguity as to his (repressed, fortunately) sexual attraction. Though Browne's character ultimately sorts out her memories and feeling toward the kindly man by film's conclusion, the picture has already been set in the wrong direction.

While the craftwork on display, particularly Billy Williams' lovely photography, is laudable, a lack of verisimilitude is offputting. Grey tarpaulins (à la Federico Fellini's "Casanova") substitute phonily for ocean waves in a studio-bound scene at film's outset and conclusion, destroying the grounding in verity that fantasy requires. In the New York opening, a Gotham reporter exclaims "Columbia *are* going to give her an honorary degree," using the British plural construction which rings quite false here.

Commercial future for this addendum to "Alice'"'s screen history (though Potter takes potshots here at the 1933 all-star Paramount "Alice" feature, yet another all-star edition, for tv, has just been made by Irwin Allen) is weak, as the project would have worked better in a less elaborate tv-play version.

—*Lor.*

Kalt In Kolumbien
(Cold in Colombia)
(W. GERMAN-COLOR)

Toronto, Sept. 14.

A production of Planet-Film, Munich, and Miramar Films, Cartagena. Executive producers, Anja S. Zaeringer, Victor Nieto. Directed and written by Dieter Schidor. Camera (color), Rainer Klausmann; assistant director, Jane Seitz; editor, Petra Mantoudis; music, Peter Maloney, Michael McLernon; sound, Christian Moldt; production designer and costumes, Karen Lamassonne; artistical collaboration, Marcel Odenbach. Reviewed at Festival of Festivals, Toronto, Sept. 13, 1985. Running time: **79 MINS.**

With: Ulrike S., Burkhard Driest, Richard Ulacia, Gary Indiana, Gerald Uhlig, Dieter Schidor, Karen Lamassonne, Marcel Odenbach, Michael McLernon, Victor Nieto.

Part of the Fassbinder legacy, "Kalt In Kolumbien" features the conceptual intrigue of cocaine, Colombia and sundry literary citations, but the camera never moves and the visual images remain so flat and distanced that pic gets stranded between minimal chic and self-parody.

The German colony living in Colombia read lines to each other such as, "Ah, back from the Reich?" or "I am a murderer but not a thief." Try as it might, the highly stylized dialog never achieves the implied comic bent.

Norbert Haims arrives in Colombia and is spotted at the airport by Ulrike, the girlfriend of the man who betrayed Norbert years before

after a bank heist. She is an aging, sagging cabaret singer, who shows Norbert and Gary Indiana around, bringing them to the fortified villa of one Philip Grosvenor who is a German parody of Pee-wee Herman, uttering exasperated, breathless babble, while surrounded by a bevy of beautiful boys. Finally, Norbert is thrust together with his target, with whom he plays cards, then murders, returning to the airport, where Ulrike sees him off and returns for a sex scene with Norbert over the final credits.

Pic resists its own story throughout, preferring a display of over-rehearsed, but underacted petulance. The long speeches create theories of government, justice and suppression, sexuality and torture, studded with snippets that will betray the shallow decadence of these exploiters of the Third World. It's hard to see the film as anything other than an exploitation of existing myths about the Third World and an excuse for filming in Cartagena a pic about chilling alienation. —*Kaja.*

Private Conversations
(DOCU-COLOR-16m)

A Punch Prods. production. Produced and directed by Christian Blackwood. Camera (color, 16m), Blackwood; editor, Donna Marino; sound editor, Mona Davis; sound/camera assistant, Pam Katz; assistant editors, Cornelia Kiss, Amy Black rerecording, Rick Dior; production supervisor, Lisa Tesone; music, Alex North; title design, Hillsberg-Meyer Inc. Reviewed at Alice Tully Hall, N.Y. (23d New York Film Festival), Oct. 4, 1985. (No MPAA Rating). Running time: **88 MINS.**

With: Arthur Miller, Dustin Hoffman, John Malkovich, Volker Schlöndorff, Stephen Lang, Michael Ballhaus, Charles Durning.

The CBS-TV broadcast Sept. 15 of Arthur Miller's "Death Of A Salesman" was a magnificent achievement for all concerned, but the same cannot be said for this fawning, self-congratulatory documentary about the making of the telemovie production. In order to film the star Dustin Hoffman, director Volker Schlöndorff, Miller and other principals at work, docu helmer Christian Blackwood obviously made an implicit bargain to take none but the most reverential view of the behind-the-scenes proceedings. In spite of shapeless pacing and the total absence of probing narrative analysis, however, the popularity of the televised play (reviewed n *Variety,* Sept. 18) and the presence of the charismatic Hoffman should guarantee this docu a run in art house locations and eventual tv exposure.

The docu might have been titled private monologs by Hoffman, whose approach to the legendary American Everyman role of the washed-up salesman and failed fa-

ther, Willy Loman, dominates the goings-on. Retaining the scratchy whine he developed for his Willy, Hoffman goes on at length about his own youth as a salesman's son and his idolization of Miller and the play as a struggling young actor in New York. So deep is his passion for the play that Hoffman is not shy about stepping on the professional Schlöndorff's directorial toes when he thinks a scene is not working in the right way.

Miller comes across as a sage *eminence grise,* joining in skull sessions with Hoffman, Schlöndorff and, occasionally, supporting actor John Malkovich as they plumb the play's nuances as if it were the Rosetta Stone. Blackwood never ventures to ask Miller hardball questions about the play's relevance in 1985 — particularly the datedness of son Biff's trauma over Willy's infidelity. The docu director also accepts without response Miller's ungenerous denigration of the original Willy, Lee J. Cobb, and Hoffman's callow sniping at producer Robert F. Colesberry, as if Cobb were not an important element in the play's initial success and as if Colesberry shouldn't be concerned about skyrocketing expenses. What about Hoffman's and other stars' huge salaries? What about unenthusiastic critical reception for Miller's recent plays? Blackwood never dares to ask. Instead, the docu offers lots of camera's-eye eavesdropping on endless retakes, backstage politics and horsing around.

As for the impressive final product that was shown on America's tv screens, those interested in more would be wise to follow the familiar injunction of a Gotham sportscaster and go back to the videotape. — *Rich.*

The Holcroft Covenant
(BRITISH-COLOR)

London, Sept. 31.

A Thorn EMI Screen Entertainment production (Universal release in U.S.). Produced by Edie and Ely Landau. Directed by John Frankenheimer. Stars Michael Caine, Anthony Andrews, Victoria Tennant. Screenplay, George Axelrod, Edward Anhalt, John Hopkins, from the book by Robert Ludlum; camera (color), Gerry Fisher, editor, Ralph Sheldon; music, Stanislas; production designer, Peter Mullins; assistant director, Don French. Reviewed at the ABC Fulham Road, London, Sept. 29, 1985 (BBFC Rating: 15.) (MPAA Rating: R.) Running time: **112 MINS.**

Noel Holcroft	Michael Caine
Johann von Tiebolt	Anthony Andrews
Helden von Tiebolt	Victoria Tennant
Althene Holcroft	Lilli Palmer
Erich Kessler	Mario Adorf
Ernst Manfredi	Michaël Lonsdale
Leighton	Bernard Hepton
Oberst	Richard Munch
Anthony Beaumont	Carl Rigg
Frederick Leger	Andre Penvern
Hartman	Andrew Bradford
Lieutenant Miles	Shane Rimmer
General Clausen	Alexander Kerst
General Kessler	Michael Wolf
General von Tiebolt	Hugo Bower

This muddled thriller is seemingly aimed at cinemagoers fearful of a fourth Reich. Since the prospect of a new Nazi regime is of little concern to today's audiences, b.o. prospects for "The Holcroft Covenant" would be poor even if the film had been convincingly executed, which it isn't.

Various scripters credited on "The Holcroft Covenant" have not created a clear narrative line out of Robert Ludlum's complex potboiler novel. Result is a muddled narrative deficient in thrills or plausibility.

Film starts with the revelation to Noel Holcroft (Michael Caine) that his father, the financial wizard who kept Hitler's plans afloat, together with two partners, left a bequest valued at over $4-billion with which the son is to make amends for the evils of Hitler's Germany.

Although Holcroft is enthusiastic about the assignment, his mother (Lilli Palmer) suspects that the money is designated for the building of a new Nazi empire. Argument is supported by various deaths that happen around Holcroft.

Knowing that his life is in danger, Holcroft is led on a scenic tour from New York to Geneva and on to London's Trafalgar Square and the lowlife quarter of Berlin. The character doesn't attempt to discover what is going on and his attractive escort Helden von Tiebolt (Victoria Tennant) has to keep on reminding him that their lives are in danger.

It's when Holcroft is taken to meet his mother in rural England that he learns that his supposed partner, Helden's brother Johann von Tiebolt, is actually in league with nazi sympathizers and plans to use the money for that purpose.

Character plausibility is not helped by misguided casting. Michael Caine, whose reputation was built acting wily Britishers in local thrillers, just doesn't convince as a naive New Yorker. (James Cann wsa originally to play the role.) Putting young-faced Anthony Andrews in the role of Caine's contemporary is just silly. And Victoria Tennant plays her part of *femme fatale* as if she doesn't know which side she's on.

Mario Adorf has a cameo as the other son and Nazi plotter who just happens to be a great orchestra conductor. The role's only significance is to indicate that conductors, and Nazis, sweat a lot.

Film's final twist is that Helden von Tiebolt is working with her brother, who's also her incestuous lover. Following the killing of the other partners in the lobby of a Geneva bank, Holcroft reveals that he has fallen in love with her. She obligingly gets him out of the fix by shooting herself.

John Frankenheimer's direction is about as convincing as the film's plotting. Gerry Fisher's photography is okay, but sound quality on print caught for viewing was frequently patchy. —*Japa.*

Commando
(COLOR)

Impressive Schwarzenegger action fantasy, ably supported by Rae Dawn Chong.

Hollywood, Oct. 2.

A 20th Century Fox release of a Silver Pictures production. Produced by Joel Silver. Directed by Mark L. Lester. Stars Arnold Schwarzenegger. Screenplay, Steven de Souza, based on a story by Joseph Loeb 3d & Matthew Weisman and de Souza; camera (DeLuxe color), Matthew F. Leonetti; editor, Mark Goldblatt, John F. Link, Glenn Farr; music, James Horner; production designer, John Vallone; set designer, Dan Maltese; sound, Don Johnson; assistant director, Beau E.L. Marks; casting, Jackie Burch. Reviewed at 20th Century Fox studios, Oct. 1, 1985. (MPAA Rating: R.) Running time: **88 MINS.**

Matrix	Arnold Schwarzenegger
Cindy	Rae Dawn Chong
Arius	Dan Hedaya
Bennett	Vernon Wells
Sully	David Patrick Kelly
Jenny	Alyssa Milano
General Kirby	James Olson
Cooke	Bill Duke

In "Commando," the fetching surprise is the glancing humor between the quixotic and larky Rae Dawn Chong and the straight-faced killing machine of Arnold Schwarzenegger. Chong lights up the film like a firefly, Schwarzenegger delivers a certain light touch of his own, the result is palatable action comics guaranteed to draw solid business via 20th Century Fox' release on 1,400 screens.

Pic was the first project greenlighted by production chief Lawrence Gordon after his arrival at Fox. While it's not in the class of Schwarzenegger's last hit ("The Terminator"), "Commando" is actually superior to "Rambo: First Blood Part II" because of its deft mixture of humor and action (with most of the action also brushed with humor) and its deliberate evasion of any political message. It won't do "Rambo" business, but it could attract patrons who normally eschew weapons-crazy movies.

Director Mark L. Lester, compelled to deal with an absurd plot, is blessed by the decision to cast Chong, who enjoys an offbeat sexuality and an insouciance that is irrestible. Credit Lester with chiseling the quick, subtly romantic byplay between the two stars — unlikely mates thrown together in pursuit of a deadly Latin neo-dictator — and pulling off a terrific series of tracking shots during a riotous chase in a crowded galleria complex.

Heavies are vividly drawn in the cases of the obsessed Vernon Wells, the punk David Patrick Kelly, and sullen, ice-cold Bill Duke. Editor Mark Goldblatt ("The Terminator," "Rambo: First Blood Part II"), cuts to a crisp 88 minutes. Scenarist Steven de Souza and producer Joel Silver bring to this fantasy the mixture of action and light ballast that juiced up their "48 HRS."

Production, which used the famed Harold Lloyd estate as a backdrop to the concluding slaughter by Schwarzenegger's one-man assault, features some sharp martial arts stuff choreographed by Mike Vendrell and introduces to the big screen 12-year-old Alyssa Milano (who plays Samantha on ABC's tv series "Who's The Boss") as the hero's abducted daughter. — *Loyn.*

The Doctor And The Devils
(COLOR)

Uncompelling period morality tale.

Hollywood, Sept. 24.

A 20th Century Fox release of a Brooksfilms Ltd. presentation. Produced by Jonathan Sanger. Executive producer, Mel Brooks. Directed by Freddie Francis. Features entire cast. Screenplay, Ronald Harwood, based on an original screenplay by Dylan Thomas; camera (J-D-C Widescreen Rank color), Gerry Turpin, Norman Warwick; editor, Laurence Mery-Clark; music, John Morris; production designer, Robert Laing; art director, Brian Ackland-Snow; set decorator, Peter James; sound, Ken Weston; costumes, Imogen Richardson; assistant director, Peter Bennett; associate producer, Jo Lustig; casting, Maggie Cartier. Reviewed at 20th Century Fox Little Theater, Sept. 23, 1985. (MPAA Rating: R.) Running time: **93 MINS.**

Dr. Thomas Rock	Timothy Dalton
Robert Fallon	Jonathan Pryce
Jenny Bailey	Twiggy
Dr. Murray	Julian Sands
Timothy Broom	Stephen Rea
Elizabeth Rock	Phyllis Logan
Dr. Thornton	Lewis Fiander

Based on an original screenplay by Welsh poet Dylan Thomas, "The Doctor And The Devils" is destined to become an odd footnote to film history. Thomas' credit seems to be the only reason for having made this grisly morality tale of 18th century grave robbers and their anatomy professor patron. Unrelentingly serious treament of the gruesome subject matter is unlikely to attract many warm bodies at the boxoffice.

Original script penned for pay by Thomas in the late '40s has been revised, but not updated by Ronald Harwood. Although there are glimpses of Thomas' poetic vision, particularly in his rendering of the squalor and poverty of the lower class, production never manages to make its issues of conscience timely or compelling.

(Project from Thomas' script originally was set to be directed in 1965 by Nicholas Ray, but went unrealized. —*Ed.)*

What Thomas was playing with was whether a good man involved in bad deeds for good ends is responsible for his actions. General ethical issues, however, tend to get lost in the muddle of the story.

Given only a small supply of bodies to dissect by the state, Dr. Thomas Rock (Timothy Dalton) takes matters into his own hands. He starts paying a price for his flesh, never questioning where it comes from. Vagabonds Robert Fallon (Jonathan Pryce) and Timothy Broom (Stephen Rea) soon are making a living delivering freshly butchered corpses to the good doctor, only they are doing the butchering themselves.

Moving back and forth between the peasants in "Pig Town" and the respectable citizens at the medical academy, director Freddie Francis never achieves a consistent tone for the morality play. Human activities are quite literally reduced to the basics with little shading to humanize the characterizations.

As Dr. Rock, Dalton strikes a single note in his insistence on the supremacy of science. He also renders too much of a matinee idol pose further stilting the virtues of the doctor.

While Pryce and Rea clearly are more fascinating as the low-lifes, they are hardly likable characters. Only sympathetic character is prostitute Jenny Bailey, nicely played by Twiggy.

Basically it's an ugly world we see where life is cheap and people are worth more dead than alive. Owing to his background as a cinematographer, Francis has created a distinctive style for the film, but even that starts to look too much like a film set, so pervasive is the filth and debauchery.

Although costumer Imogen Richardson and production designer Robert Laing have done their jobs in creating a period atmosphere, there are too many plot threads to give the film the feel of real life. Other tech credits are above average. —*Jagr.*

San Sebastian Festival

La Corte de Faraon
(Pharaoh's Court)
(SPANISH-COLOR)

San Sebastian, Sept. 24.

A Line Films production. Executive producer, Luis Sanz. Directed by José Luis Sánchez. Screenplay, Rafael Azcona, García Sánchez; camera (Eastmancolor), José Luis Alcaine; editor, Pablo G. del Amo; production coordinators, Mónica Delbosco, Ignacio Soriano; sets, Andrea d'Odorico; costumes, Miguel Narros; choreography, José Granero; sound, Enrique Bañuls; music, Luis Cobos. Reviewed at Cine Victoria Eugenia, San Sebastian Film Festival, Sept. 23, 1985. Running time: **101 MINS.**

Lota/Mari Pili	Ana Belén
Roque	Fernando Fernán Gómez
Friar José	Antonio Banderas
Putifar/Tarsicio	Josema Yuste
Father Calleja	Agustín González
Police commissioner	José Luis López Vázquez

Also with: Quique Camoiras, Mary Carmen Ramirez, Juan Diego, Guillermo Montesinos, Maria Luisa Ponte, Millan Salcedo, Antonio Gamero, Guillermo Marin, Luis Ciges.

Handsomely produced, "Pharoah's Court" is a real crowd-pleaser and is sure to rack up tidy grosses in theatrical and homevideo for its producer and distrib (latter is Incine) in Spain.

Beautifully costumed and crisply lensed by Spain's top cameraman, José Luis Alcaine, pic flashes back and forth from the performance of a zarzuela loaded with sexual double meanings, "Pharoah's Court," written in the 1910s, but prohibited under the Franco regime; scenes in a police precinct to where the whole troupe has been hauled off for creating a public scandal; and interspersed episodes illustrating the depositions given by the thesps.

The outraged censor-priest, the complacent, libidinous commissioner, and the bumptious actors and actresses still clad in their "Egyptian" costumes, are all elements of the comedy as the often outrageous goings-on behind stage are counterpointed with the pandemonium and histrionics in the police station.

In addition, several numbers from the old zarzuela are staged, some of the best-known songs performed, and no end of on-stage clowning represented, with a dazzlingly beautiful Ana Belén flirting with "chaste Joseph" on stage and a handsome, young, self-mortifying friar offstage. The censors, police, political oppression, ecclesiastical strait-jacketing and misery of the times are all passed over with levity.

Even the photos of Franco and José Antonio on the wall of the police station seem to wink in collusion at the bizarre antics, part of a sinister past now turned into farce. However, due to its local slant, interest in pic will be limited to the Spanish domestic market. —*Besa.*

Una Novia Para David
(A Girlfriend For David)
(CUBAN-COLOR)

San Sebastian, Sept. 23.

An Instituto Cubano de Arte e Industria Cinematográfica production. Executive producer, Sergio San Pedro. Directed by Orlando Rojas. Screenplay, Senel Paz, Rojas; camera (color), Livio Delgado; editor, Nelson Rodriguez; sound, Carlos Fernandez, Raul Garcia; music, Pablo Milanes. Reviewed at Cine Miramar, San Sebastian Film Festival. Sept. 22, 1985. Running time: **100 MINS.**
David..................José Luis Alvarez
Ofelia................Maria Isabel Diaz
Miguel..............Francisco Gattorno
Olga....................Edith Massola
Marisela...................Thais Valdés

"A Girlfriend For David" is a somewhat simplistic but nonetheless sincere yarn set in a Havana high school in 1967, revolving around a provincial boy's first love affair. Using mostly amateur thesps, director Orlando Rojas delves into the social pressures that prevent the protagonist, David, from carrying on a romance with a homely, plump girl whom none of the other boys wants to date.

More than just a cute yarn about school life, Rojas is standing up for the boy's personal freedom of choice, as his companions egg him on to make it with other girls and mercilessly rib his romance with the overweight girl.

José Luis Alvarez is rather *too* flat in the role of David, never generating the dramatic tension needed to get audiences involved. The other kids put in better performances, but the story is far too slim and the girl far too physically unattractive to make the film effective. —*Besa.*

Ete und Ali
(Ete And Ali)
(EAST GERMAN-COLOR)

San Sebastian, Sept. 24.
A DEFA/Filmlustspiel production. Produced by Wolfgang Rennebarth. Directed by Peter Kahane. Screenplay, Waltraud Meinreis, Henry Schneider; camera (color), Andreas Köfer; editor, Sabine Schmager; music, Rainer Böhm. Reviewed at Cine Miramar, San Sebastian Film Festival, Sept. 23, 1985. Running time: **97 MINS.**
Ete.....................Jorg Schüttauf
Ali....................Thomas Putensen
Also with: Daniela Hoffman, Johannis Thal, Hilma Eichhorn, Otto Heidemann.

"Ete And Ali" is a droll youth pic about a couple of 22-year-olds, just finished with their military service, who return to the village whence one of them comes, and whence he has family and an estranged wife.

The antics of the two boys as they indulge in practical jokes, court the wife and place obstacles in the path of a new suitor are occasionally funny, as is some of the dialog. Unfortunately given the rambling, directionless non-plot, pic at times tends to become tedious.

Despite its lack of direction, pic has a winning, youthful quality, a spontaneous devil-may-care flair which is gratifying and which hel-

mer Peter Kahane may turn to better effect in future films. —*Besa.*

Zina
(BRITISH-B&W/COLOR)

San Sebastian, Sept. 27.
A TSI/Looseyard production. Executive producers, Andrew Lee, Penny Corke, Adrian Munsey, Paul Levinson. Produced and directed by Ken McMullen. Screenplay, McMullen, Terry James; camera (color, b&w), Bryan Loftus; editor, Robert Hargreaves; production designer, Paul Cheetham; line producer, Kim Nygaard; music, David Cunningham, Barry Guard, Simon Heyworth. Reviewed at Cine Victoria Eugenia, San Sebastian Film Festival, Sept. 27, 1985. Running time: **92 MINS.**
With: Domiziana Giordano, Ian McKellen, Philip Madoc, Rom Anderson, Micha Bergese, Gabrielle Dellal, Paul Geoffreys, William Hootkins, Leonie Mellinger, Maureen O'Brien, Dominique Pinon, Tusse Silberg, George Yiasoumi.

Despite certain ambiguities and poetic license in "Zina," helmer Ken McMullen has made a film that could captivate arthouse audiences in all countries. He skillfully probes into the unhappy life of Zina, the daughter of Leon Trotsky, believed to have committed suicide in Berlin in 1931, shortly before the advent of National Socialism.

Much of the story unfolds during Zina's bouts with a psychoanalyst cum political historian, in which she remembers some of the incidents of her own life and that of her father when in exile. The director intersperses dream sequences, reenactments of some of the historical events of the times and suggestive, metaphorical episodes intended to give a clearer insight into Zina's life, at times comparing it to the Greek classics in theme, particularly "Antigone."

For the most part the fairly complex texture and structure of the film works, maintaining interest through the psychoanalysis, the political discussions and theorizings, all of which are subservient to the study of Zina as a person.

Thesping all around is topnotch, especially Ian McKellen as the silently intense analyst and Domiziana Giordano as the disoriented Zina, alternately diffident and outspoken. In all, an intelligent, sensitively made film that skillfully and imaginatively handles a difficult subject. —*Besa.*

Macho y Hembra
(Male And Female)
(VENEZUELAN-COLOR)

San Sebastian, Sept. 26.
Produced and directed by Mauricio Walerstein. Screenplay, Walerstein, Irene Tapias; camera (color), Mario Robles; editor, José Alcalde; music, Alejandro Blanco Uribe. Features Orlando Urdaneta, Elba Escobar, Irene Arcila. Reviewed at Cine Victoria Eugenia, San Sebastian Film Festival, Sept. 25, 1985. Running time: **90 MINS.**

"Male And Female" is a tiresome, talky and seemingly pointless pic involving the amorous relations between two women and a man seen over the course of 10 years. The relationships shift and vary, as the threesome progresses from combative university days in 1973 to the sober realities of a compromised present.

Director Mauricio Walerstein is constantly sidetracked by irrelevancies, and fails to provide any kind of continuity to the plot, which is so vague as to be virtually nonexistent. Most of pic is shot in interiors, and the evolution of Venezuela outside is surmised rather than seen.
—*Besa.*

La Vieja Música
(The Old Music)
(SPANISH-COLOR)

San Sebastian, Sept. 25.
A Brezal, Estela Films and Anem Films production. Executive producers, José Luis Olaizola, Félix Tusell. Directed by Mario Camus. Screenplay, Camus, Joaquín Jordá; camera (Eastmancolor), Hans Burman; editor, José María Biurrun; sets, Rafael Palmero. Reviewed at Cine Victoria Eugenia, San Sebastian Film Festival, Sept. 24, 1985. Running time: **108 MINS.**
Martín Lobo.............Federico Luppi
Paloma....................Charo López
Paloma (child)..............Eva Cooper
Ramón.................Antonio Resines
Luz....................Assumpta Serna
Also with : Agustín González, Francisco Rabal, Jim Wright, Miguel A. Rellán.

Mario Camus, who in the past has scored with pics such as "La Colmena" and "The Holy Innocents," here wades into a disappointing, downbeat and frustrating film about an Uruguayan exile who comes to Spain with his daughter seeking a former flame.

"The Old Music" is set in the rainy, northwestern city of Lugo, where Martín, the exile, well thesped by Federico Luppi, has managed to get a job as basketball coach under false pretenses, since in fact he knows little about the game.

During most of pic, Martín is seen moping about the city and trying to track down his former girlfriend in Madrid. A subplot, which never really is developed, concerns a Spanish coach from whom Martín is taking over and his marital woes. Meanwhile, Martín's American daughter is being urged to return to the States by her mother's lawyer.

Boredom of the feeble plot is compounded by considerable footage of basketball practice and games. At the end, Martín finds the lady of his heart, but, though sympathetic, she is loath to take up again with a loser who seems to have no future.

The daughter flies back to the States and Martín is left playing old tangos on his accordion and trying to learn how to be a basketball

coach.

Pic delves into the loneliness of exiledom and the vanity of trying to resuscitate past loves, but the mood is so unrelievedly bleak, the end so mournful and some of the thesping so unconvincing that item seems destined to fast oblivion. —*Besa.*

Golfo de Vizcaya
(Gulf Of Biscay)
(SPANISH-COLOR)

San Sebastian, Sept. 22.
A Lan Zinema production. Produced by Juan Ortuoste. Directed by Javier Rebollo. Screenplay, Joaquin Jordá, Santiago Gonzales, Ortuoste, Rebollo; camera (Eastmancolor), Javier Aguirresarobe; editor, José María Biurrun; sets, José María Lago; music, Angel Muñoz. Reviewed at Cine Victoria Eugenia, San Sebastian Film Festival, Sept. 21, 1985. Running time: **90 MINS.**
Lucas.................Omero Antonutti
Olatz...................Silvia Munt
Itxaso.................Amaia Lasa
Ander..................Patxi Bisquert
Mateo...................Mario Pardo
Police Commissioner........Juan Diego
Also with: Juan M. Segues, Miguel Angel Albisu, Luis Iturri, Julio Maruri, Cristina Collado.

"Gulf Of Biscay" is a murky film set in the Basque city of Bilbao with so many twists and veiled allusions, most of them involving local politics and the Basque terrorist group ETA, that even Spanish audiences were hard put to understand what the story was all about.

Neophyte helmer Javier Rebollo pussyfoots with the subject of Basque terrorism and never lets the audience know where his sympathies lie. He touches upon the protagonist's brushes with the police, the ETA, exiled Republicans and (presumably) rightwing activists, but never clearly. Pic does capture the mood of political confusion and uncertainty in the Basque community, but the story is anemic and dramatic tension aborted.

Story revolves around a somewhat mysterious journalist (Omero Antonutti) who after years of exile in Argentina returns to Bilbao to make a new start. Before he can say "Euskadi," he becomes embroiled in the local tensions, is beaten up by thugs (who they are is never explained), has a half-hearted romance with a local girl, gets a job with a newspaper and is finally saved from assassination by one of the groups when his girlfriend warns him and we're served a freeze-frame ending.

Italo thesp Antonutti, who gave a memorable performance a few years back in Victor Erice's "El Sur," puts in a fine job of thesping, but seems miscast as a Basque journalist. Support by Silvia Munt and Juan Diego is good, but not enought to buoy up the onerous weight of this rambling story.
—*Besa.*

Otra Vuelta De Tuerca
(The Turn Of The Screw)
(SPANISH-COLOR)

San Sebastian, Sept. 27.

A Gonzalo Goikoetxea production for Gaurko Filmeak. Directed by Eloy de la Iglesia. Production manager, Francisco Ariza; screenplay, Goikoetxea, Eloy de la Iglesia, Angel Sastre, based on the novel by Henry James; camera (Eastmancolor), Andrés Berenguer, Joan Gelpi; editor, Julio Peña; sets, Simón Suárez; music, Luis Iriondo; sound, Enrique Molinero. Reviewed at Cine Victoria Eugenia, San Sebastian Film Festival, Sept. 27, 1985. Running time: **119 MINS.**

Roberto ....Pedro María Sánchez
Antonia....................Queta Claver
Mikel ....Asier Hernández Landa
Flora ....Cristina Reparaz Goyanes

Eloy de la Iglesia's films are usually known for their sensationalist commerciality, but in this case the results are unmitigated boredom rather than scandal. The scriptwriters have transferred the action of Henry James' "The Turn Of The Screw" to the Basque area and changed the governess into a young man straight out of a seminary, enabling the director to throw in at least one scene suggesting a homosexual interest of the tutor in the young boy.

More than just a travesty upon James' work, which the film otherwise follows fairly closely, pic is a stultifying exercise in wooden acting by Pedro María Sánchez. He sees all the right ghosts and is properly shocked at his little charges' misdeeds, but pic has such a flat quality, lack of mood, and such clumsy dialog, that is is a veritable relief when Mikel, the Basquified boy, succumbs all on his own to a heart attack!—*Besa.*

Les Trottoirs de Saturne
(The Sidewalks Of Saturne)
(FRENCH-B&W)

San Sebastian, Sept. 28.

A Caliban Audiovisuel production, in collaboration with Euro America Films, the Culture Ministry, the Ministry of Foreign Affairs and Teleprogramas Argentinos. Executive producer, Hubert Niogret. Produced by Pierre Henri Deleau. Directed by Hugo Santiago. Screenplay, Santiago, Juan José Saer, Jorge Semprun; camera (b&w), Ricardo Aronovich; editor, Francoise Belleville; sets, Marcial Berro; music, Rodolfo Mederos, Eduardo Arolas; arrangements, Rodolfo Mederos; musicians, Mederos, Tomás Gubitsch, Osvaldo Calo, Jean Paul Celea, Hugh McKensie, Jon Toth, Eric Shumsky, Vincent Limousin, François Craemer. Reviewed at Cine Victoria Eugenia, San Sebastian Film Festival, Sept. 28, 1985. Running time: **168 MINS.**

Fabián Cortés ....Rodolfo Mederos
Danielle Mallet ......Berangere Bonvoisin
Mario ....Edgardo Lusi
Marta ....Andrea Aronovich
Also with: Philippe Clevenot, Emmanuelle Dechartre, Catherine Jarrett, Sophie Loucachevsky, Diego Mas Trelles, Mónica Mortola, Juan Quirno, Stanislas Stanojevic, Maurice Vallier, Louis René des Forets.

A nearly three-hour film made by Hugo Santiago, an Argentine exile living in Paris, about his own political and personal hangups, "The Sidewalks Of Saturn" contains large doses of modern tango music but amazingly succeeds in avoiding hermeticism. Santiago unfolds a riveting, sometimes larger-than-life story which to an extent is that of exiles anywhere in the world.

Pic works on many levels. As a drama, Santiago and cowriters Juan José Saer and Jorge Semprun, latter noted for scripting many famous political thrillers, skillfully develop the plot so audiences are kept guessing throughout the film what each new development will bring. Camerawork is nimble and restless, preventing boredom. Thesping all around is so convincing as to be virtually cinema-verité, and the music, a key part of the film, is brilliant, impeccably performed by Rodolfo Mederos and his group, considered to be one of the modern tango greats.

Anyone with a taste for modern tango will be mesmerized by this tour de force, superbly thesped by Maderos himself as the tormented celeb who has made it in exile but nonetheless longs to return to his homeland despite fascist repression.

This is a very special film, for a select audience. Its length, subject matter, black and white photography and heavy dose of modern tango music will make it a hard sell, but over the years it may carve a niche for itself as a landmark in the lore of exiledom and modern tango.
— *Besa.*

Ana
(PORTUGUESE-COLOR-16m)

Rimini, Sept. 24.

An Antonio Reis/Margarida Cordeiro production; world rights, Instituto Portugues de Cinema, Lisbon. Directed by Antonio Reis and Margarida Martins Cordeiro. Screenplay, Reis, Cordeiro; camera (color, 16m), Acacio de Almeida, Elmo Roque; sound, Carlos Pinto, Joaquim Pinto, Pedro Caldas. Reviewed at European Film Fest, Rimini, Italy, Sept. 24, 1985. Running time: **120 MINS.**

With: Ana Maria Martins Guerra, Octavio Lixa Filgueiras, Manuel Ramalho Eanes, Aurora Alfonso, Mariana Margarido.

Written and directed by a psychiatrist and a poet, "Ana" is a portrait of a simple, selfless grandmother, filtered through the memory of her now grown granddaughter. The extremely slow, static, almost liturgical film is often breathtakingly beautiful, yet its rejection of conventional acting, plot, and character is cold and distancing.

Everyone is waiting for a young girl to come home in the midst of a storm. She returns, soaked to the skin. Her silent grandmother dries and tends her. The girl is wrapped in a blue cloak and an infant is put into her arms. All kneel and gaze at her in a Madonna and Child tableau.

In a series of memories from childhood, we feel the eternity of nature and the senses in a timeless, peasant present. An historian gives a long, technical explanation of some prehistoric rafts used in the area, and the impossibility of knowing the truth about the past.

In an especially beautiful, strange scene, the grandmother walks through a snowless winter landscape — the valley of death — to a sparkling lake, where she sees blood on her hands. She walks home and lies down. The children she has tended now tend her. She dies.

"Ana" is performed stiffly and the filmmakers reject conventional editing for extended master shots. The 16m photography is full of the pleasures of thick, richly colored fabrics.—*Brom.*

O Lugar Do Morto
(Place Of The Dead)
(PORTUGUESE-COLOR)

Rimini, Sept. 24.

An Antonio-Pedro Vasconcelos/Jose Luis Vasconcelos production. Directed by Antonio-Pedro Vasconcelos. Screenplay, Vasconcelos, Carlos Saboga; camera (color), Joao Rocha; editor, Manuela Viegas; music, Alain Jommy; set design, Manuel Graca Dias; sound, Paola Porru, Vasco Pimentel, Joaquim Pinto. Reviewed at European Film Fest, Rimini, Italy, Sept. 24, 1985. Running time: **118 MINS.**

With: Ana Zanatti (Ana), Pedro Oliveira (Alvaro Serpa).

A chump journalist falls for a mysterious temptress, has family troubles, and is bumped off in Antonio-Pedro Vasconcelos' plodding, self-conscious imitation of a '40's detective yarn "Place Of The Dead."

Alvaro (Pedro Oliveira) leaves his girlfriend's house when her daughter discovers them in bed together. He drives to the beach to think and sees a couple quarreling. The woman, Ana (Ana Zanetti), jumps into Alvaro's car and orders him to drive away, then, just as capriciously, to return to the beach, where they discover her companion dead in his car, an apparent suicide. Ana disappears.

Alvaro tracks down a long series of clues, meeting a lot of stereotypical characters out of half-remembered, dubbed B-movies. He is apparently propelled by passionate desire for Ana, though they didn't even look at each other in their brief moments in the car together. Finally, he happens upon her in a train, and she seduces him.

Meanwhile, Alvaro has been neglecting his two sons by previous marriages. One boy runs away from home because his mother wants to remarry. Alvaro's current girlfriend discovers she's pregnant, and the film suddenly turns into a soap opera, with Ana making periodic, irritating reappearances. Worried about family problems, Alvaro parks by the sea, falls asleep, and is pushed off the cliff to his death, by an unseen hand. Ana looks out to sea, but what she feels behind her sunglasses is a mystery.

It takes a lot of work to drain every bit of pleasure out of a thriller, but the filmmakers manage it here. The plot is incoherent and based entirely on coincidence, the characters are flat, and a lot of pointless smoking substitutes for acting. There is never any sense of sexual tension or danger. Uniformly bad technical credits, an overwrought chamber music score and snail's-pace cutting add up to an endless two hours.

The only line that rings true is when Alvaro's gruff boss-with-a-heart-of-gold tells him, "You're not Philip Marlowe." —*Brom.*

Calamari Union
(FINNISH-B&W)

Rimini, Sept. 23.

A Villealfa Film Productions Oy/Aki Kaurismaki production; world rights, Jörn Donner Productions Oy, Helsinki. Directed by Aki Kaurismaki, Screenplay, Kaurismaki; camera (b&w), Timo Salminen; editor, Kaurismaki, Raija Talvio; music, Casablanca Vox; sound, Jouko Lumme; production manager, Jaakko Talaskivi. Reviewed at European Film Fest, Rimini, Italy. Sept. 23, 1985. Running time: **80 MINS.**

With: Markku Toikka, Kari Vaananen, Osmo Hurula, Matti Pellonpaa, Mato Valtonen, Saku Kuosmanen.

"Calamari Union" features young men joining together on a quest to cross the dirty, dangerous city and reach a beautiful suburb by the sea. "The Warriors" did it as an actioner with liberal doses of fantasy, but substitute antispetic Helsinki for the subways of New York, and a bunch of hammy buddies for gang warfare, and you're left with an amateurish, unfunny comedy.

Seventeen young Finns, all wearing dark glasses and all named "Frank," gather to plan their escape from the slums to the mythic suburban peace of Eira. They commandeer an empty subway train. When they get off, one of them is shot for no reason. His companions don't react; they just give him a last smoke and watch him die, then keep going.

Splitting into smaller groups, they go their separate ways through the city. All the Franks appear onstage as a rock band and sing to an adoring crowd about how "bad" they are. Two Franks finally make it to the shore, which turns out to be covered with dead fish. They end up fighting over a rotten rowboat.

The dialog consists of arch, pretentious non sequiturs. Derivative use of film noir visual style and low-down blues and R&B is supposed to be funny in wholesome Helsinki, but only serves to remind the audience of all the feeling missing from the film. Mediocre technical credits and really shocking misogyny played for laughs round out a dismal vanity production.
—Brom.

Den kroniske uskyld
(Chronic Innocence)
(DANISH-COLOR)

Copenhagen, Oct. 1.
An Obel Film release of Gunnar Obel/Edward Fleming/Nordisk Film production. Written and directed by Edward Fleming, based on novel by Klaus Rifbjerg. Executive producer, Bo Christensen. Camera (Eastmancolor) Dirk Brüel; production consultant, Claes Kastholm Hansen (The Danish Film Institute); music, Anne Linnet; editor, Lars Brydesen; production design, Henning Bahs. Reviewed at the Palads, Copenhagen, Oct. 1, 1985. Runing time: 100 MINS.
Janus .... Allan Olsen
Tore .... Thomas Algren
Helle .... Simone Bendix
Mrs. Junkersen, Helle's
    mother .... Susse Wold
Inger .... Helle Fastrup
Headmaster .... Axel Ströbye
Mrs. Reimer, Janus'
    mother .... Anne-Lise Gabold
Also with: Ole Ernst, Lisbet Dahl, Per Pallesen, Lars Simonsen, Ernie Arneson, Lars Svenning Jensen, Jonas Elmer.

Klaus Rifbjerg's 1958 novel "Chronic Innocence" remains a high school favorite in Denmark because of its crisp dialog and fresh insights in late teenagers' world of sweat and fear and striving for cool appearances. It is, however, as sloppily constructed and loose in its drawing of characters as is most of Rifbjerg's work thus serves scripter-helmer Edward Fleming poorly in his turning of the subject matter into a feature film. Fleming, otherwise known for his smart, witty, folksy and dramatically cleancut films based on literary works by others, this time has had to pad and add to an extent that cuts suspense from a narrative that simultaneously remains far too vague about three of its four central characters.

The three are dead-faced pawns moved around in a plot that has the fourth (and much livelier and better explained) character merely tag along to get hurt. We see him as Janus, who is at his happiest when in the company of class-mate Tore (Thomas Algren, seen as vacuously attractive), the school's leading light in all respects. When Tore finds a girl to go steady with (Helle, played by beautiful Simone Bendix with more vacuity), Tore settles for just being along as the faithful friend to both of them. He is convinced they are very happy together and take their having sex for granted while he himself is reduced to finding disgusted solace with a nice little semi-whore. Actually, Helle refused all Tore's physical advances, leaving the field wide open for her own Mrs. Robinson caricature of a vampire mother. Susse Wold, one of Denmark's most accomplished actresses, plays this mother with a too-feeble attempt at making her appear human, which defuses the intended drama even further. Title's "Chronic Innocence" covers both the poor young Helle, who takes her own life when she sees her mother seduce her boyfriend, and the utter lack of perspective evident with all players, young and old, of this parlor game of bourgeois manners & morals.

"Chronic Innocence" will probably make its way with local audiences, but off-shore, item's thematic innocence is liable to spell boredom. —Kell.

Better Off Dead
(COLOR)

Nasty teen comedy aims low.

Hollywood, Oct. 6.
A Warner Bros. release of a CBS Prods. presentation of an A&M Films production. Produced by Michael Jaffe. Executive producers, Gil Friesen, Andrew Meyer. Directed by Savage Steve Holland. Features entire cast. Screenplay, Holland. Camera (Technicolor), Isidore Mankofsky; editor, Alan Balsam; music, Rupert Hine; production designer, Herman Zimmerman; art decorator, Gary Moreno; sound, Bud Alper; costumes, Brad Loman; assistant director, Uydi Bennett; associate producer, William Strom; casting, Caro Jones. Reviewed at Regent Theater, Westwood Village, Calif. Oct. 6, 1985. (MPAA Rating: PG.) Running time: 98 MINS.
Lane Myer .... John Cusack
Al Myer .... David Ogden Stiers
Jenny Myer .... Kim Darby
Johnny Gasparini .... Demian Slade
Badger Myer .... Scooter Stevens
Monique Junot .... Diane Franklin
Mrs. Smith .... Laura Waterbury
Charles .... Curtis Armstrong
Beth .... Amanda Wyss
Ricky .... David Schneider
Roy .... Aaron Dozier

Yet another lonely-teenager-in-love film, "Better Off Dead" would have been better off unmade. It's a case of grownups with the imagination of 12-year-olds trying to give the kids what they want and under-shooting the mark. Kids deserve better than this.

"Better Off Dead" pokes fun at virtually anything but not with wit, with malice. People, especially adults, are not characters but caricatures of people. It's an ugly view of human nature and only the hero (John Cusack) and his friends are excused from the savage treatment of writer/director Savage Steve Holland.

Film has not so much a plot as a series of mishaps directed at Cusack after his fickle girlfriend (Amanda Wyss) leaves him for a more popular guy. Cusack even tries a few mock suicides before he is saved by the love of a good schoolgirl, the French foreign exchange student Monique (Diane Franklin).

All this nonsense is supposed to build up to a climactic ski race between Cusack and his rival in love, Pretty Boy Roy (Aaron Dozier). Along the way there are, of course, the mandatory loutish parents, with the mother and nextdoor neighbors being treated especially cruelly here.

Cusack, who was so promising in "The Sure Thing," is occasionally able to lift the material off the ground with his manic energy and puppy dog face, but it would be nice to see him try something other than a bumbling nerd with heart. David Ogden Stiers is likable as the father despite the character and is Diane Franklin charming as the exchange student trying to win Cusack's heart.

Good production values are wasted on this material. Kids should be smart enough to stay away. —Jagr.

Final Justice
(COLOR)

Fun but overly familiar action film.

An Arista Films release of an Arista Films and Mediterranean Film Prod. presentation of an L&G production. Executive producer, Louis George. Produced and directed by Greydon Clark. Stars Joe Don Baker. Screenplay, Clark; camera (color), Nicholas von Sternberg; editor, Larry Bock; music, David Bell; sound, Joe Debono; assistant director-production manager-associate producer, Daryl Kass; special effects, Mario Cassar; stunt coordinator, Roberto Messina. Reviewed on Vestron Video vidcassette, N.Y., Sept. 27, 1985. (MPAA Rating: R.) Running time: 90 MINS.
T.J. Geronimo .... Joe Don Baker
Palermo .... Venantino Venantini
Don Lamanna .... Rossano Brazzi
Wilson .... Bill McKinney
Gina .... Patrizia Pellegrino
Maria .... Helena Abella
Sheriff .... Greydon Clark

"Final Justice" is an enjoyable action picture, well directed by Greydon Clark who, unfortunately, falters in the screenplay department in terms of originality. With fresher material, it could have been a useful entry on the action circuit, but instead emerges as a homevideo title. Picture was filmed last year under the shooting title "The Maltese Connection."

Joe Don Baker is cast perfectly as T.J. Geronimo, a gung-ho Texas deputy sheriff working on the Mexican border after having been booted off the Dallas force for being trigger happy. When a criminal Palermo (Venantino Venantini) blows away his sheriff (played by director Clark), Geronimo is assigned by federal agent Wilson (Bill McKinney) to take the prisoner to Europe and turn him over to Italian authorities.

The plane is sabotaged, forced to land in Malta and the rest of the pic has Geronimo repetitiously tracking down Palermo there with the aid of local cop Maria (Helena Abella). Rossano Brazzi guests as a local crimelord who protects Palermo.

The film's basic premise is derived heavily from the Don Siegel-Clint Eastwood thriller "Coogan's Bluff" (plus their subsequent "Dirty Harry"), with emphasis on cultural clash as the Texan brings cowboy justice to the European island. Baker is excellent, bringing a tongue-in-cheek approach to the role, but the supporting cast is weak. Maltese locations are attractive and Clark stages some vigorous chases and explosions.—Lor.

Caffé Italia
(CANDIAN-COLOR/B&W)

Montreal, Sept. 21.
A Cinema Libre release of an ACPAV production. Produced by Marc Daigle. Directed by Paul Tana. Screenplay, Tana, Bruno Ramirez; camera (color), Michel Caron; sound, Serge Beauchemin; editor, Louise Suprenant; music, Pierre Flynn, Andrea Piazza. Features Pierre Curzi and Tony Nardi. Reviewed at L'Autre Cinema, Montreal, Sept. 20, 1985. Running time: 82 MINS.

Like most immigrants, members of Montreal's sizable Italian community find themselves torn between allegiances toward the old country and the new. The resultant attempts at bridging this gap and adapting to another culture are the scope of Italian-born Montrealer Paul Tana's highly personal docudrama "Caffé Italia."

In his pursuit of roots, Tana specifically focuses on the wave of Italian immigration into Montreal from the onset of the century to the present. Through frequent cross-cutting of sepia-toned archival footage, dramatic vignettes, excerpts from a musical stage production and interviews — conducted mainly at Caffé Italia, a Little Italy culture hotspot on St. Lawrence — Tana is able to cleverly weave seemingly disparate sources of material into a unique and revealing look at the Italo-Montreal experience.

Between bouts of levity highlighting an out-of-shape, out-of-tune street band and chaos at the border as Canadian Customs officials bust immigrants bearing homemade pepperoni and pasta, Tana delves into some still-tender and sensitive issues. In particular, he zooms in on the formation of the Facist Movement of Ville Emard (a Montreal suburb) in conjunction with the rise of Mussolini, its divisive effect on the community, and subsequent crackdown on it by Canadian authorities.

Within the fictionalized confines of the film, noted Montreal actors Pierre Curzi and Tony Nardi, both of Italian origin, assume a variety of well-executed roles. Toward the conclusion, both remove their performing masks and makeup and, echoing the sentiment of many of the young Italians interviewed, passionately regale in their roots and traditions despite the increasing blurring of cultural lines.

So much for the Thomas Wolfe contention that you can never go home again. —*Bro.*

San Sebastian Festival

Continued

Figlio Mio Infinitamente Caro
(My Dearest Son)
(ITALIAN-COLOR)

San Sebastian, Sept. 27.

An Istituto Luce and Ager Cinematografica production. Produced by Giuliani G. de Negri. Directed by Valentino Orsini. Screenply, Orsini and Vincenzo Cerami and Giuliani based on idea by Orsini and Furio Scarpelli; camera (color), Luigi Kuveiller; editor, Roberto Perpignani; music, Guido E. Maurizio de Angelis. Reviewed at Cine Victoria Eugenia, San Sebastian Film Festival, Sept. 27, 1985. Running time: **100 MINS.**

With: Ben Gazzara, Sergio Rubini, Valeria Golino, Fabrizio Temperini, Wanda Pasquini, Mariangela Melato.

"My Dearest Son" is a sincere, well-paced pic that tackles the drug problem in Italy, giving it a few new twists as a father voluntarily goes on hard drugs in a frantic, last-ditch effort to free his son from the habit. Pic flows along well enough; but seems more geared to the tv market than theatrical release, since the story is a bit thin at times. Ben Gazzara puts in a fine performance, but the supporting cast is weak.

Antonio Morelli is a respected lawyer who lives with his son, who's in high school. When the father finds out the boy is on heroin, he struggles to rehabilitate him, neglecting his own law practice. After the father also goes on drugs, the son manages to shake off his addiction in a rehabilitation camp. Pic ends, after the father has gone "cold turkey" in his apartment, with the son waiting for days in the hallway outside. Final scene has father and son walking in conciliatory peace across the town square. Item is a nice drama, but fails to get the adrenalin flowing. — *Besa.*

Los Dias de Junio
(Days In June)
(ARGENTINE-COLOR)

San Sebastian, Sept. 25.

A Producciones Fischerman-Santos film. Executive producer, Natalio Koziner. Produced by Quique Santos. Directed by Alberto Fischerman. Screenplay, Fischerman, Marina Gaillard, Gustavo Wagner; camera (Eastmancolor), Jorge Behnisch; editor, Juan C. Macias, Carlos Marquez; sets, Jorge Sarudiansky; costumes, Mirta Tesolin, Beatriz Trento; music, Luis María Serra. Reviewed at Cine Victoria Eugenia, San Sebastian Film Festival, Sept. 24, '85. Running time: **95 MINS.**

With: Norman Briski, Victor Laplace, Arturo Maly, Lorenzo Quinteros, Ana María Picchio, Julia von Grolman, Inda Ledesma, Guillermo Battaglia, Aldo Braga, Monica Galán, Gustavo Garzón.

"Days In June" is another Argentine film set in the years of the recent military dictatorship chronicling the lives of four friends who have shared a common liberal political philosophy and who, each in his own way, are victimized by the repressive forces in the country. Despite touching performances by Norman Briski and his cohorts, script is rather too ponderous and talky, the plot slim and interest only sporadically aroused.

Pic starts and ends with the four friends hoisting a burning flag, more as a joke than a political gesture. They are surprised by a group of fascist thugs who beat up Briski and put hoods over the other three. The scene shifts to Briski's return from exile at the time of the Falklands war, his reunion with his friends and their reminiscing over the past. Flashbacks tell us of each member of the group's traumas and difficulties during the years of repression. The talking is incessant and what starts out as a good political thriller turns into a mood piece reflecting upon man's loss of ideals. To an extent, pic is the story of Briski's own life in exile for many years in Madrid and New York.

Pic may click in its home market, but is rather too hermetic for any kind of offshore sales. —*Besa.*

Extramuros
(Extramurals)
(SPANISH-COLOR)

San Sebastian, Sept. 26.

A Blau Films, Miguel Picazo production. Produced by Antonio Martin; head of production, Jesus García Gargoles. Written and directed by Picazo, based on novel by Jesús Fernández Santos; camera (Eastmancolor), Teo Escamilla; editor, José Luis Matesanz; sets, Rafael Palmero; costumes, Javier Artiñano; music, José Nieto. Reviewed at Cine Victoria Eugenia, San Sebastian Film Festival, Sept. 25, 1985. Running time: **120 MINS.**

Sor Ana	Carmen Maura
Sor Angela	Mercedes Sampietro
Prioress	Aurora Bautista
The Guest	Assumpta Serna
The Doctor	Antonio Ferrandis

Also with: Manuel Alexandre, Conrado San Martín, Marta Fernández Muro, Valentín Paredes, Nacho Martinez, Beatriz Elorrieta.

Miguel Picazo's "Extramurals," a tale of self-induced stigmata and lesbian love between two nuns in a 16th century Spanish convent, makes an alternately compelling and ponderous film which is certain to stir up plenty of controversy wherever it plays.

In Spain, pic's commercial release in Madrid was preceded by a certain amount of scandal when two exhibs refused to book the item into their theaters. Problems in other Catholic countries may ensue. Nonetheless, within its sensationalist premises, story is handled with good taste and sensitivity, never catering to gratuitous exploitation.

Superbly acted by Mercedes Sampietro and Carmen Maura, tale unfolds in a convent which has come on hard times and is threatened with closure if strong sponsorship is not found. One nun, Sor Angela, hits upon the idea of faking stigmata on her hands, with the connivance of another nun, Sor Ana, who is carrying on a lesbian relationship with her, and agrees to inflict the wounds on Sor Angela's palms.

Word spreads fast of the "miracle," causing the old prioress to be ousted from her job, which the young "miracle-worker" usurps. Ultimately, the Inquisition calls for a court hearing of the case. Both Sor Angela and Sor Ana are put on trial and sentenced to banishment. Before the punishment can be carried out, Sor Angela dies in the arms of her lover.

Pic has its slow moments, but on the whole holds audience interest, largely due to topnotch thesping by Sampietro and Maura, with good supports by Aurora Bautista, Assumpta Serna and Antonio Ferrandis. Director Picazo, who hasn't had a hit since his 1960s pic, "La Tia Tula," should attract good-sized audiences in this offbeat and outspoken film, which might even be of interest to art circuits offshore. — *Besa.*

Silver Bullet

Ludicrous Stephen King horror film.

Hollywood, Oct. 7.

A Paramount Pictures release of a Dino De Laurentiis presentation. Produced by Martha Schumacher. Directed by Daniel Attias. Features entire cast. Screenplay, Stephen King, based on his novelette, "Cycle Of The Werewolf;" camera (J-D-C Widescreen, Technicolor), Armando Nannuzzi; editor, Daniel Loewenthal; music, Jay Chattaway; sound, Richard Goodman; production design, Giorgio Postiglione; associate producer — production manager, John M. Eckert; assistant director, John Kretchmer; creatures, Carlo Rambaldi; casting, Jeremy Ritzer. Reviewed at the Academy of Motion Picture Arts & Sciences, Beverly Hills, Calif., Oct. 7, 1985. (MPA Rating: R.) Running time: **95 MINS.**

Uncle Red	Gary Busey
Marty Coslaw	Corey Haim
Jane Coslaw	Megan Follows
Rev. Lowe	Everett McGill
Sheriff Haller	Terry O'Quinn
Nan Coslaw	Robin Groves
Bob Coslaw	Leon Russom
Andy	Bill Smitrovich
Brady	Joe Wright
Herb	Kent Broadhurst
Tammy	Heather Simmons
Milt	James A. Baffico

"Silver Bullet" is a Stephen King filmette from his scriptette from his novelette which may sell some tickettes but not without regrettes.

Since this is the time of year for both Halloween horror pictures and those with intense "adult" themes, first-time director Daniel Attias has covered both bases well: he puts a pumpkin on the front porch in one scene and fills the remainder with a remarkably regressive group of grownups.

Full moon or not, the little town of Tarker's Mill is not the kind of place where people catch on real quick. First, something mysterious knocks the head off a railroad worker and they think he was run over by a train. Then this woman hears all this growling and grunting upstairs and rushes up to find a slashed body and they start to get suspicious.

At sunset, consequently, people begin to stay indoors, except for the kid who would rather fly his kite. When he ends up torn to pieces, the menfolk form a posse and head into the fog-filled woods to find a maniac. First they have to get past director Attias and a couple of goofy, gruesome sight gags.

Persisting, the posse finally comes upon some noisy thing in the fog which has a hairy arm and throws people through the air and crushes their skills and stuff like that.

Since this sort of thing only goes on once a month in Tarker's Mill, however, nobody seems to get too upset or call for reinforcements. In between the bloodshed, life drones on in the summer, allowing time to get better acquainted with the Coslaw family.

There's little Marty (Corey Haim), unfortunately confined to a wheelchair, his sometimes impatient sister (Megan Follows), protective parents (Robin Groves and Leon Russom) and alcoholic uncle Gary Busey.

The Coslaws are a lot like the other folks in town, meaning that when the fair and fireworks show are closed down for fear of the monster, they go ahead and plan an outdoor barbeque after dark. Better still, little Marty motors off into the night to shoot fireworks down by the bridge by himself.

Well, wouldn't you know, the whatever shows up and gets a rocket through the eyeball, creating a grudge against the little boy that's sure to last for months.

By the way, one of the problems in the Coslaw household is that mom is overprotective of her son. With a crazed killer on the loose, she and dad decide to take a holiday in the city, leaving the kid and the sister with uncle boozer. Yes, they do.

Across town, the sheriff has wound up dead, too, and a prominent citizen has suddenly started wearing an eyepatch, but nobody's called the army yet.

Fortunately, the kids have a silver bullet, the only known power that will stop a werewolf. Unfortunately, there's no known power that will stop films like this. —Har.

Treffpunkt Leipzig
(Rendezvous Leipzig)
(WEST GERMAN-COLOR)

Berlin, Oct. 9.

A Fritz Wagner Film, Berlin, in coproduction with Second German Television (ZDF), Mainz. Directed by Jürgen Klauss. Features entire cast. Screenplay, Claus Legal; camera (color), Michael Steinke; editor, Clarissa Ambach; sets, Anita Möller; music, Peter Schirmann, Franz Bartzsch; production manager, Fritz Fühlert; tv-producer, Franz Neubauer. Reviewed at ZDF Screening Room, Berlin, Oct. 8, 1985. Running time: **89 MINS.**
With: Hansjoachim Krietsch (Berthold Kohlgrub), Dorothea Carrera (Gertrud Kohlgrub), Heike Schrötter (Rosi), Robert Naegele (Adalbert Pfiffling), Bernd Hoffmann (Konrad Trenkelfuss), Knut Reschke (Hans Berner), Günther Stocklöv (GDR Customs Officer).

Jürgen Klauss' "Rendezvous Leipzig" is set at the Leipzig Fair, skedded twice a year in the spring and fall. It's here that several West German manufacturers and small-time businessmen convene to maintain contracts for continued East/West trade (made beneficial for East Germany due to the fact that Western countries do not recognize a permanently divided Germany, particularly West Germany). What Klauss is underscoring is another kind of East/West relationship at the Leipzig rendezvous — namely, businessman/mistress ties.

The story opens with Berthold, born in Leipzig but now a drainpipe manufacturer in the West, getting ready to depart for Leipzig. A bourgeois type at home with family and house (replete with overgrown dog), he fairly itches to get underway with his bundle of provisions (and wife's discarded clothes) for the rendezvous with Rosi, a divorcee who always takes her vacation when the Leipzig Fair rolls around in order to profit in West German marks for "services rendered." At the border, in one of the film's best scenes, the East German customs agent inspects just about everything in the car — even the lingerie, which Berthold manages to explain away due to his wife's intentions to visit him in Leipzig this time.

Berthold has to work fast to mix pleasure with business in the few days of respite left him. He and Rosi hit it off as usual, but things take on a new tint when Bertold discovers for the first time that the East Germans want to make a deal with him for drainpipes, even though the offer carries with it round-about trades that would involve selling pigs to Berthold's brother-in-law, a butcher in the West. The hero prevails upon his wife, Gertrude, who is then to prevail upon her brother to clinch the deal. Meanwhile, Berthold lives it up with his West cronies and their mutual friends in the bars and restaurants, the "business as usual" rendezvous points in Leipzig.

The twists at the end as Berthold, Gertrude and Rosi glide toward a collision are worth waiting for.
—Holl.

Mangiati Vivi
(Doomed To Die)
(ITALIAN-COLOR)

A Continental Inc. release of a Dania/National/Medusa production. Produced by Luciano Martino, Mino Loy. Written and directed by Umberto Lenzi. Stars Robert Kerman (a.k.a. R. Bolla), Janet Agren. Camera (Luciano Vittori color), Federico Zanni; editor, Eugenio Alabiso; music, Budy & Maglione; production design-costumes, Massimo Antonello Geleng; assistant director, Francesco Fantasia; special effects, Paolo Ricci. Reviewed at 42d St. Liberty theater, N.Y., Oct. 12, 1985. (No MPAA Rating.) Running time: **93 MINS.**
Mark Butler .... R. Bolla
Sheila Morris .... Janet Agren
Prof. Carter .... Mel Ferrer
Rev. Jonas................. Ivan Rassimov
Diana Morris .... Paola Senatore
Widow .... Me Me Lai

"Mangiati Vivi" (translated: "Eaten Alive") is an above-average Italian cannibalism feature, originally titled "Defy To The Last Paradise" and finally released Stateside as "Doomed To Die." Pic is the third cannibal film made by prolific helmer Umberto Lenzi in 1980 to be released here, following "City Of The Walking Dead" and "Make Them Die Slowly." Its revolting gore and brutality content target the film for fringe audiences only.

Porno star R. Bolla (using his alternate monicker Robert Kerman) toplines as soldier of fortune Mark Butler, hired for $100,000 by Shelia Morris (Scandinavian star in Italian pics, Janet Agren) to help her find her missing sister Diana (Paola Senatore). In New York City, Prof. Carter (guest star Mel Ferrer) matches a super 8m film belonging to Diana with his research to indicate she is in New Guinea.

Sheila and Butler travel to New Guinea (actually filmed in Sri Lanka) where they battle with local cannibals and become trapped in a religious cult headed by Reverend Jonas (Ivan Rassimov), who opposes civilization and is attempting to reunite man with nature by various ancient purification rituals. Ultimately Sheila and Butler esscape, aided by a sympathetic native girl (Me Me Lai), and Jonas flees after having his followers commit mass suicide, in the manner of the Guyana Jonestown massacre.

For those who can stomach the explicit butchering of animals on screen and fake-looking people-mutilation footage, pic boasts atmospheric location photography, a fine musical score and effective cast.
— Lor.

Le Mariage de Siècle
(The Marriage Of The Century)
(FRENCH-COLOR)

Paris, Oct. 10.

A Fechner/Gaumont release of a Trinacra Films/Films Christian Fechner/Films A2/Machinassou coproduction. Produced by Yves Rousset-Rouard. Directed by Philippe Galland. Stars Anémone, Thierry Lhermitte. Screenplay, Galland, Jean-Luc Voulfow, Anémone; camera (color), Eduardo Serra; editor, Martin Barraque-Curie; sound, Michel Laurent; art director, Noelle Galland; music, Jean Morlier; producer, Denis Mermet; production manager, Philippe Schwartz. Reviewed at the Gaumont Colisée theater, Paris, Oct. 10, 1985. Running time: **104 MINS.**
Princess Charlotte .... Anémone
Paul...... .... Thierry Lhermitte
Kaffenberg .... Jean-Claude Brialy
The king .... Michel Aumont
Adrienne .... Dominique Lavanant
Grand Duke Guillaume ... Martin Lamotte
Alexandra .... Michèle Moretti

"Le Mariage du Siècle" asks audiences to accept Anémone, the homely French legit and screen comedienne, as a royal princess of a fictional European kingdom, who naively dreams of slumming among the less privileged classes. It also asks them to believe that Thierry Lhermitte is an unethical young

Paris playboy who seduces her on a bet, further stains her honor by publishing photos of his deed, but then falls genuinely in love with her and finally steals her away in the midst of a pompous church ceremony in which she is to wed a stuffy young duke from a neighboring land.

The film asks too much. All the more so because it offers in return so little as either a send-up of Royal Family domesticity and public image crises, or as a romantic comedy. Evidently in part inspired by "Roman Holiday" and even "The Graduate," for its final scenes, script (in which Anémone had a part) and direction, by Philippe Galland, fall back on the hoariest variety of low comedy gags and cheap class-difference ribs to generate gaiety.

Apart from the howling miscasting of Anémone as a patrician booby (the noun only is credible), other players suffer too from implausibility of characterization and gaucherie of execution. Only Michel Aumont as the king, Jean-Claude Brialy as the chamberlain and Dominique Lavanant as the palace press agent maintain some comic hauteur amid the droopy-drawers tomfoolery.

With its exteriors shot in Hungary, "Marriage Of The Century" registers as another overblown local comedy in which extravagant production and name topbilling fail to hide the poverty of elements essential for a marketable international commercial item. —Len.

Hercules II
(Adventures Of Hercules)
(COLOR)

Cheapo Lou Ferrigno vehicle.

Chicago, Oct. 9.

A Cannon Releasing release of a Cannon Group production. Produced by Alfred Pecoriello. Executive producer, John Thompson. Directed by Luigi Cozzi (a.k.a. Lewis Coates). Stars Lou Ferrigno. Screenplay, Cozzi; camera (color), Alberto Spagnoli; editor, Sergio Montanari; music, Pino Donaggio; production designer, Massimo Antonello Geleng; costumes, Adriana Spadaro. Reviewed at the United Artists Theater, Chicago, Oct. 9, 1985. (MPAA Rating: PG.) Running time: **90 MINS.**
Hercules .... Lou Ferrigno
Urania .... Milly Carlucci
Glaucia .... Sonia Viviani
King Minos .... William Berger
Athena .... Carlotta Green
Zeus .... Claudio Cassinelli
Poseidon .... Nando Poggi
Hera .... Maria Rosaria Omaggio
High Priest .... Venantino Venantini
Flora .... Laura Lenzi
Aphrodite .... Margi Newton
Ilia .... Cindy Leadbetter
Atreus .... Raf Baldassarri
Also with: Serena Grandi, Era Robbins, Sandra Venturini, Andrea Nicole, Allessandra Canale, Pamela Prati, Cristina Basili.

Thanks, apparently, to a clause in a subsidiary rights deal — mandating theatrical playoff in one of the country's top three markets — Chicago is "blessed" with the firstrun bow of Cannon's "Hercules II" with Lou Ferrigno. Theatrical b.o. potential as demonstrated here is virtually nil immediately thrusting this feature to the netherworlds of video and tv playoff.

Lensed in Rome about two years

along with predecessor "Hercules," pic has Ferrigno as the invincible son of Zeus sent to earth to retrieve seven thunderbolts stolen by rebellious gods. Curiously, Ferrigno is given little to do except flex his muscles combating objects created by the special effects department.

Cast is largely Italo, and hams up the weak material furnished by scripter-director Luigi Cozzi (a.k.a. Lewis Coates). Pic might have been interesting had it explored a sexual subtext promised by the original which featured the likes of Sybil Danning and Rossana Podestà. No such luck here; rating is an innocuous PG.

Special effects of a routine nature unsuccessfully attempt to make up for cast deficiencies. Pino Donaggio's score is ersatz John Williams. Production designer Massimo Antonello Geleng's sets and Adriana Spadaro's costumes show humorous and imaginative touches.—*Sege*.

Trois Homme et Un Couffin
(Three Men And A Basket)
(FRENCH-COLOR)

Paris, Oct. 2.
An AAA release of a Flach Films/Soprofilms/TFI FIlms coproduction. Produced by Jean-François Lepetit. Written and directed by Coline Serreau. Camera (color), Jean-Yves Escoffier; art director, Yvan Maussion; editor, Catherine Renault; sound, Daniel Ollivier; music, Schubert; production manager, Henri Vart. Reviewed at the Gaumont Ambassade theater, Oct. 1, 1985. Running time: **100 MINS.**
Pierre ....Roland Giraud
Michel ....Michel Boujenah
Jacques ....André Dussollier
Sylvia ....Philippine Leroy Beaulieu
Mme. Rapons ......Dominique Lavanant
Antoinette ....Marthe Villalonga
Pharmacist ....Annik Alane

Coline Serreau's comedy about three hardened bachelors saddled with a newborn baby has turned into the sleeper hit of the new local season, and it's success is well-merited. Produced on a modest budget and without bankable talent, "Three Men And A Basket" is warm, hilarious and well-made, a happy alternative to the continuing trend of costly, over-produced star comedy vehicles that usually clutter French screens.

Serreau's direction is bright and confident, avoiding the saccharine pitfalls of the material, and her three actors Roland Giraud, Michel Boujenah and André Dussollier incarnate beleaguered male egos with delightful verve.

Most of the story is set in the sprawling Paris apartment that serves as the macho sanctuary of the three liberty-loving bucks (a house rule restricts female presence to one-night stands). The baby is the unannounced deposit of a girl whom Dussollier has already bedded and forgotten (he is the alleged father), and who has taken off for the States for several months.

With Dussollier, an airline pilot, away for the time being, Giraud and Boujenah react with the expected panic and their calamitous first attempts to take care of their new ward are chronicled with a sure sense of farce pacing by Serreau. Added complications arise in the form of a small package of heroin, which the trio has been unwittingly harboring, and which is sought by both its dealers and the police drug squad. The boys foil the cops by hiding the dope in the baby's disposable diapers until they can get rid of it.

Eventually Dussollier returns and assumes his share of the nursing chores. By this time the initial terror has changed to guarded affection as the now three experienced babysitters start eyeing one another with paternalistic jealousy.

The mother eventually returns home and claims her baby. The boys think they're relieved, but soon find that all the flavor has gone out of their erstwhile bachelor activities. The girl, unable to cope as a working single mother, finally asks them to look after the baby just a little while longer, a request which the men accept with undisguised joy.

Film marks the full-fledged screen debut of Boujenah, an exuberant young Tunisian Jewish stand-up comic who has enjoyed success with his one-man shows. Giraud, who has already shown deft comic abilities in previous films, hits his full stride under Serreau's direction. The scene in which he sends packing a pushy professional nurse (played by the always funny Dominique Lavanant), is one of the best in the film. Dussollier comes across with skillful aplomb.

Jean-Yves Escoffier's lensing is smart and Catherine Renault's editing provides much of the snap and crackle. Other credits are fine.
—*Len*.

Ville des Pirates
(City Of Pirates)
(PORTUGUESE-FRENCH-COLOR)

A production of Metro Films (Lisbon) and Les Films du Passage (Paris). Executive producer, Paolo Branco. Written and directed by Raul Ruiz. Camera (color), Acacio de Almeida; editor, Valeria Sarmiento; sound, Joaquim Pinto and Vasco Pimental; production manager, Anne-Marie La Toison; music, Jorge Arriagada. Reviewed at the New York Film Festival, Oct. 8, 1985. Running time: **111 MINS.**
Tobi ....Hugues Quester
Isidore ....Anne Alvaro
Malo...................Melvil Poupaud
The fisherman ....Andre Engel
The father............Duarte de Almeida
The mother............Clarisse Dole
The rifleman ....Andre Gomes

Appearing at the New York Film Festival for the second time — last year his "Three Crowns Of The Sailor" was shown — Raul Ruiz is a prolific Chilean playwright and

film/video director with a considerable following within Europe. Ruiz has lived in France, in exile, since the military coup that deposed President Allende. His "City Of Pirates" has screened at other festivals — Venice in 1983, London 1984, Berlin 1985.

"City Of Pirates" is a strange film that alternates outrageous scenes and gross ugly business with comic and dramatic episodes, unmotivated non sequiturs, capricious asides, borrowings from this or that cinema classic, in all a strange and provocative murder-mystery with special photographic effects at times that are oddly beautiful.

Within the first 20 minutes of "City Of Pirates," a goodly exodus from the Alice Tully Hall began, and many who remained groaned and snickered during the rest of the film. It is impossible to synopsize the film's plot, as none exists.

Although the commercial prospects for "City Of Pirates" within the U.S. seem dubious, Ruiz remains a phenomenon to keep under surveillance: he has produced 30 works, from shorts to two-hour features, since 1974. —*Hitch*.

A Hora Da Estrela
(The Time Of The Star)
(BRAZILIAN-COLOR)

Brasilia, Sept. 30.
An Embrafilme release of a Raiz Produções Cinematográficas production. Directed by Suzana Amaral. Features entire cast. Screenplay, Suzana Amaral, based on the novel "A Hora da Estrela" by Clarice Lispector; camera (Eastmancolor), Edgar Moura; art direction, Clovis Bueno; editor, Idê Lacreta; music, Marcus Vinicius; assistant director, Silvia Bahiense. Reviewed at Cine Brasilia, XVIII Brasilia Festival of the Brazilian Film, Sept. 30, 1985. Running time: **96 MINS.**
Macabéa ....Marcélia Cartaxo
Olimpico...................José Dumont
Gloria ....Tamara Taxman
Carlota ....Fernanda Montenegro
Seu Raimundo ....Umberto Magnani
Pereira ....Denoy de Oliveira
Maria da Penha........Claudia Rezende
Maria ....Lizete Negreiros
Maria do Carmo ..Maria do Carmo Soares
Hostal owner ....Sonia Guedes

"The Time Of The Star" is the first feature directed by Suzana Amaral, a former cinema student at New York U. It is based on the last novel by the late Brazilian writer Clarice Lispector, about the urban drama of a lonely northeastern young lady living in São Paulo.

The woman, Macabéa, is portrayed by newcomer Marcélia Cartaxo, who got a fair ovation after the screening. Amaral demonstrates a fine sensibility in directing, also getting strong performances from José Dumont and Fernanda Montenegro as special guest star. It is the touching story not only of Macabéa, an almost Chaplinesque character, but also of thousands of lonely and hopeless people living in a big city and moved primarily by a dis-

tant fantasy.

The story of Macabéa can be compared to Federico Fellini's "Nights Of Cabiria," for her ingenuity drives her to a second class role in life. She is oppressed permanently by her roommates and office colleagues, but especially by boyfriend Olimpico (Dumont), for whom São Paulo can be the ultimate instance of a search for success by any means, fantasy included.

Amaral treats her characters with a fine sense of humor, plenty of local references in great part made clear by the outstanding acting of Cartaxo, Dumont and Tamara Taxman. — *Hoin*.

Aqueles Dois
(That Couple)
(BRAZILIAN-COLOR)

Brasilia, Sept. 30.
A Roda Filmes release of a Roda Filmes production. Directed by Sergio Amon. Features entire cast. Screenplay, Sergio Amon, Pablo Viersi, based on the short story "Aqueles Dois" by Caio Fernando Abreu; camera (Eastmancolor), Cesar Charlone; editor, Roberto Henkin, Sergio Amon, Alex Sernambi; art direction, Marta Biavaschi, Jose Artur Camacho, Marlise Storchi, Sayonara Ludwig; music, Augusto Licks; assistant director, Giba Assis Brasil; executive producers, Rudi Lagemann and Marlise Storchi. Reviewed at Cine Brasilia, XVIII Brasilia Film Festival, Sept. 29, 1985. Running time: **85 MINS.**
Saul.....................Pedro Wayne
Raul ....Beto Ruas
Clara Christina ....Syzana Saldanha
Jussara ....Maria Ines Falcao
Gordo Carlos ....Oscar Simch
Juarez ....Carlos Cunha Filho
Seu Ferreirinha ....Edu Madruga
Dr. Andre ....Birata Vieira
Also with: Isabel Ibias, Araci Esteves, Simone Castiel, Marco Antonio Sorio, Zeca Kiechaloski, Java Bonamigo, Angel Rojas, Marley Danckwardt, Rusa Cali.

"Aqueles Dois" deals with a story of between two men working at a depressive office in downtown Porto Alegre. Both are lonely and coping with problems. Their deep friendship drives office colleagues to conclusions about their intimacy. Saul and Raul are taken as homosexuals and snubbed by their lower middle-class colleagues until they are fired.

Description of the environment is undertaken by director Sergio Amon, 25, as is the relation between the men. Raul and Saul's friendship reveals a mutual necessity and love, though sexual relations are never implied. Amon reveals the absurd world in which two sensible people are forced to live and the hell of human relations surrounding them.

Unsolved, however, are probelms with dialog and acting. Both lack the necessary sophistication to make the film convincing.

"Aqueles Dois" is a fine effort by the group which is giving life to a cinema industry at Rio Grande do Sul. —*Hoin*.

That Was Then...This Is Now
(COLOR)

Weak outlook for troubled teens.

Hollywood, Oct. 18.

A Paramount Pictures release of a Media Ventures and Alan Belkin production. Produced by Gary R. Lindberg, John M. Ondov. Executive producers, Alan Belkin, Brandon K. Phillips. Directed by Christopher Cain. Stars Emilio Estevez, Craig Sheffer, Kim Delaney, Jill Schoelen, based on the novel by S.E. Hinton; camera (TVC color), Juan Ruiz-Anchia; editor, Ken Johnson; music, Keith Olsen, Bill Cuomo; art director, Chester Kaczenski; set decorator, Victoria L. Hinton; costumes, Ann Wallace; sound, Mark Berger; assistant director, Robert Koster; associate producers, Jim Geib, Martin M. Weiss; casting, Penny Perry. Reviewed at the Paramount Studios, Hollywood, Calif., Oct. 17, 1985. (MPAA Rating: R.) Running time: **102 MINS.**

Mark Jennings	Emilio Estevez
Bryon Douglas	Craig Sheffer
Cathy Carlson	Kim Delaney
Angela Shepard	Jill Schoelen
Mrs. Douglas	Barbara Babcock
M&M Carlson	Frank Howard
Mr. Carlson	Frank McCarthy
Terry Jones	Larry B. Scott
Charlie Woods	Morgan Freeman

God save the kids who live in an S.E. Hinton novel. They're firecrackers waiting to go off. "That Was Then...This is Now" is the fourth film to venture into the gloomy world of adolescents with few friends and lots of enemies. Despite its fascination for filmmakers, it's not a place many filmgoers have been anxious to visit and this time should be no exception.

While the direction of Francis Coppola ("The Outsiders" and "Rumblefish"), Tim Hunter ("Tex") and now Christopher Cain has brought different filmmaking styles to the material, it is Hinton's vision that prevails. A very peculiar vision it is, where adults are basically in the background and kids are left on their own to battle their way into an adulthood that promises them even less.

Filmmakers and kids are probably attracted to Hinton's novels because they see her troubled characters as "real," but on the screen, their worlds seems artificial, almost surreal. Around every corner is a fight and the worst that could happen invariably does.

Also appealing to readers is the rage percolating in all the characters. But in "That Was Then...This Is Now," it becomes not a way into the people but a one-dimensional portrait of teenage angst.

Most trouble of the kids here is Emilio Estevez as Mark Jennings, a lonely, brooding child anxious to be through with his adolescence. Title refers to his youthful bond with Bryon Douglas (Craig Sheffer) with whom he has grown up after his own father shot his mother and went to prison. To Mark's dismay, their friendship is falling apart as Bryon taks on a girlfriend and starts to accept some adult responsibility.

Mark is too locked into his own suffering to grow up, and Estevez is best at suggesting a youth who is always uncomfortable with himself. Estevez also wrote the screenplay and as a writer he fails to raise the pronouncements and revelations of youth ("help people out and you just get screwed") beyond the mundane to the universal.

Dark tone is also reinforced by cinematographer Juan Ruiz-Anchia who captures well the look of the street, but that's all one sees. It's an oppressive world without being particularly insightful.

What is important here is friendship, and the central relationship between Estevez and Sheffer does have some touching moments. Kim Delaney is perfectly likable as Sheffer's girlfriend, but their tie is no more understandable than the instant antagonism between other characters.

Barbara Babcock is sympathetic as the caring but ineffectual den mother to the boys although her role is only sketched by the script.

Also likable is Morgan Freeman as a friendly barkeeper who gets blown away by one of the many acts of gratuitous violence in the film.

"That Was Then...This Is Now" is an admirable attempt to make something other than teen comedies for kids, but it is probably too sour for their tastes and too simple for an older audience, although parents may find it cuts closer to the bone. —*Jagr.*

De Dream
(The Dream)
(DUTCH-COLOR)

Amsterdam, Oct. 6.

A Cannon Tuschinski release of a Roeland Kerbosch Filmproduktie production. Produced by Roeland Kerbosch. Directed by Pieter Verhoeff. Screenplay, Dirk Ayelt Kooiman, Verhoeff; camera (color), Paul van den Bos; editor, Edgar Burcksen; art direction, Hendrik Jan Visser; costumes, Jany Hubar; music, Cees Bijlstra. Reviewed at Cinecenter, Amsterdam, Oct. 3, 1985. Running time: **95 MINS.**

Wiebren Hogerhuis	Peter Tuinman
Police inspector	Huub Stapel
Ymkje Jansma	Joke Tjalsma
Pieter Jelsma	Freark Smink
Police commissioner	Hans Veerman
Public prosecutor	Adrian Brine
Marten Hogerhuis	Geert Lageveen
Keimpe Hogerhuis	Fokke de Vries
Mother Hogerhuis	Catrien Wolthuyzen
Tjeerd Stienstra	Rients Gratama
Sieds Jansma	Eelco Vellema
Farmer Haitsma	Wytze Hoekstra
Judge	Arend Jan Heerma van Vos

"The Dream" is a piece of regional filmmaking, shot in the northern province of Friesland, which prides itself on its independent spirit and its own language.

The screenplay is based on a notorious judicial scandal 90 years ago, at a time of severe economic crisis and social unrest. Hunger and desperation gripped the Frisian countryside in the harsh winter of 1895. The new doctrines of socialism and anarchism attracted starving farm workers, who burned well-stocked farms and stole what they could lay their hands on to feed their families.

One winter night, three masked men broke into the house of a well-to-do farmer, shots were fired and two men were wounded. Wiebren Hogerhuis (Peter Tuinman) and his two brothers, though never near the crime, eventually were arrested, tried, convicted and given long prison sentences. Their appeals failed. Even after new evidence had proved three other men guilty, the judiciary refused to reopen the case.

The scriptwriters have skillfully fashioned this true story into a moving drama of love and revenge, solidarity and betrayal, social history and private passions.

Peter Tuinman as Wiebren electrifies the screen in an extraordinarily discreet — but very physical — performance of a proud and taciturn man. Two Frisian newcomers to the screen should also be singled out: Joke Tjalsma as the young woman who, ditched by her lover Wiebren, falsely testifies against him and thus seals the brothers' fate; and Freark Smink as the schoolmaster who runs from pillar to post to prove the scapegoats' innocence. Well-known Dutch actor Huub Stapel (from "The Lift") puts in an effective performance as the solitary police inspector .

Director Pieter Verhoeff and producer Roeland Kerbosch have worked wonders with their budget of $500,000: a beautiful and original picture, consistently sober and terse.. —*Ewa.*

Burke & Wills
(AUSTRALIAN-COLOR)

Sydney, Oct. 7.

A Hoyts Edgley production. Produced by Graeme Clifford, John Sexton. Executive producers, Terry Jackman, Michael Edgley. Directed by Graeme Clifford. Stars Jack Thompson, Nigel Havers, Greta Scacchi. Screenplay, Michael Thomas; camera (Panavision, Eastmancolor), Russell Boyd; music, Peter Sculthorpe; production design, Ross Major; costumes, George Liddle; editor, Tim Wellburn; sound, Syd Butterworth; associate producer, Greg Ricketson; production manager, Carolynne Cunningham; assistant director, Mark Turnbull; camera (U.K. sequences), Egil Wozholt. Reviewed at Hoyts Center, Sydney, Oct. 1, 1985. Running time: **140 MINS.**

Robert O'Hara Burke	Jack Thompson
William John Wills	Nigel Havers
Julia Matthews	Greta Scacchi
John King	Matthew Fargher
Charley Gray	Ralph Cotterill
William Brahe	Drew Forsythe
Tom McDonagh	Chris Haywood
Dost Mahomet	Monroe Reimers
George Landells	Barry Hill
Bill Wright	Roderick Williams
Ambrose Kyte	Hugh Keays-Byrne
Sir William Stawell	Arthur Dignam
Dr. John Masadam	Ken Goodlet
Ludwig Becker	Edward Hepple
Dr. William Wills	Peter Collingwood
Bessie Wills	Susanna Harker
Mayor of Melbourne	Martin Redpath
Mrs. Kyte	Julia Hamilton

Big in scope, and emotionally stimulating, this eagerly awaited new Australian pic about the doomed 1860 expedition of explorers Burke and Wills to cross the continent and back, is satisfying entertainment despite its length and seemingly downbeat subject. Prestige item should attract audiences worldwide on its lavish production values and gripping recounting of a real-life tragedy.

On paper, the project sounded rather dull. Every Aussie school kid knows Robert Burke and William Wills led an expedition to cross the island continent from Melbourne in the south of the Gulf of Carpenteria in the north, and that the explorers died on the return journey. With the outcome a foregone conclusion, there loomed the possibility of a dreary trek of little popular appeal. That the story emerges quite differently on film is very much to the credit of director Graeme Clifford and screenwriter Michael Thomas, two expatriate Australians (Clifford, based in L.A., previously directed "Frances" and worked as a film editor; Thomas, who lives in London, has contributed to the screenplays of several pics).

The expedition began as a race with another explorer, who turned back before achieving his goal. Burke and Wills set out with a large party consisting of 19 men, 28 horses, 27 specially imported camels, six wagons and 21 tons of equipment. Two base camps were established along the way, and a final group of four men with camels and a horse made the final dangerous trek to the northern coast, crossing rocky desert and crocodile-infested swamp before reaching the sea. On the trip back, a series of unexpected delays and incredibly frustrating setbacks prevented the four from keeping their scheduled rendezvous — though they missed their crucial appointment by only a few hours.

Russell Boyd's superior cinematography, on the locations originally traversed by the explorers, is quite ravishing. The authenticity of the picture is a tribute to the grueling location work of the film crew. Clifford shrewdly inserts flashbacks into the desert material evoking scenes of Wills at home in England and Burke's dalliance with a comely opera singer with whom he had a long-standing affair. Footage also is devoted to the machinations of the businessmen and politicians who originally financed and supported the expedition, but whose failure to follow through with needed money and supplies contributed to the deaths of three of the explorers. The motivation for their behavior and this lack of support, remain somewhat ambiguous.

Ultimately, with all its handsome production values and precise period detail, pic would fail if audiences did not care for the characters. Jack Thompson, with full beard, is an imposing Burke, a fiery-tempered Irishman whose determination to succeed clouds his judgment. This is one of Thompson's best performances. British actor Nigel Havers also is excellent as the scientist, Wills, stubbornly following his friend into the unknown while barely concealing his fears for the outcome. In support, Matthew Fargher impresses as the youngest member of the expedition and its only survivor; scene of his return to Melbourne and impassioned speech before the stuffy members of the Geographic Society is a knockout. Ralph Cotterill, Drew Forsythe, Chris Haywood and Hugh Keays-Byrne, among a large cast, are standouts, with Greta Scacchi giving a charming portrayal of the singer adored by Burke.

"Burke & Wills" has similarities with the 1948 British Ealing Studios pic "Scott Of The Antarctic" which also dealt in very human terms with the courageous heroes of a doomed expedition. The climax of the Australian film will have many reaching for their handkerchiefs.

At 140 minutes, pic is undeniably long, but thanks to its visual splendors, the exotic locations, and the strong performances, doesn't seem so. It should perform very well when it opens in Australia next month after a Royal premiere (before Prince Charles and Lady Diana), although the release one week earlier of a parody on the same subject, "Wills And Burke," may have an effect on the boxoffice. Internationally this will be seen as another major, and most prestigious, Australian production. —Strat.

Wills And Burke
(AUSTRALIAN-COLOR)

———

Sydney, Oct. 9.
A Greater Union Distributors release of a Stony Desert production. Produced by Bob Weis, Margot McDonald. Directed by Weis. Starts Garry McDonald, Kim Gyngell. Screenplay, Philip Dalkin; camera (Panavision, Eastmancolor), Gaetano Nino Martinetti; editor, Edward McQueen Mason; production design, Tracy Watt; music, Red Symonds, Paul Grabowsky; costumes, Rose Chong, Karen Markel; sound, Ian Ryan; assistant director, John Wild; choreography, Jo-Anne Robinson. Reviewed at Greater Union screening room, Sydney, Oct. 8, 1985.

Running time: 101 MINS.
Robert O'Hara Burke ... Garry McDonald
William John Wills .... Kim Gyngell
John Macadam .... Jonathan Hardy
Sir William Stawell .... Peter Collingwood
John King .... Mark Little
Charley Gray .... Roy Baldwin
Julia Matthews .... Nicole Kidman
George Landells .... Roderick Williams
Charles .... Henry Maas
William Brahe .... Alex Menglet
Constable .... Chris Haywood
Publican .... Colin Hay

———

Rushed into release to cash in on Graeme Clifford's "Burke & Wills," this humorless, pointless parody is as dismal a failure as its rival is a success. It's scheduled to open a week before the other film, but it won't last long.

It's possible to make a good comedy out of death or disaster, "Dr. Strangelove," for instance, but the "Wills And Burke" makers have merely come up with a tasteless mocking of two brave, but misguided, explorers who crossed the Australian continent in 1860 and died on the way back. Philip Dalkin's screenplay is so poor that it never even makes clear exactly where the expedition is heading, leaving the uninitiated viewer in the dark. There are almost no laughs, and what jokes there are (the aristocratic Wills wearing full formal attire right through his desert trek) are mercilessly overworked.

As Burke, Garry McDonald, a popular and talented tv comedian, does his best to get laughs from the sophomoric dialog, but fails. Kim Gyngell, as Wills, fails to register. Nicole Kidman, a bright young actress in other films, is cruelly wasted as a Melbourne singer who winds up incongruously playing for Burke in a ghastly musical sequence that climaxes the picture. Of the entire cast, only Peter Collingwood, as a British administrator who takes unusual steps to ensure the love of the people, and Chris Haywood, as a trigger-happy country cop, make any impression; coincidentally, both are in the Clifford film, Collingwood as Wills' father, Haywood as a member of the expedition.

Debuting director Bob Weis, who as a producer was responsible for some good pictures including, in the U.S., Bobby Roth's "Heartbreakers," brings nothing but a heavy hand to the proceedings. Technically the film is okay, though the music score is weak.

Down Under there may be initial interest on Garry McDonald's reputation and an advertising campaign ("They double-cross the continent") that's funnier than the picture. Word of mouth, however, and critical drubbing, will ensure that this misguided affair will fade fast. Offshore chances are zero. —Strat.

Rocking The Foundations
(AUSTRALIAN-DOCU-B&W)

———

Sydney, Oct. 14.
A Pat Fiske production. Produced and directed by Fiske. Narration, Graham Pitts, Fiske, spoken by Fiske; camera (b&w), Martha Ansara, Fabio Cavadini; sound, Lawrie Fitzgerald; editor, Stewart Young, Fiske; music, Davood Tabrizi; associate director, Jim Stevens; research, Fiske. Reviewed at Academy Twin theater, Sydney, October 14, 1985. Running time: 90 MINS.

———

"Rocking The Foundation" is a lucid, passionate documentary about the activities of what must have been one of the world's most innovative and progressive unions, the New South Wales branch of the Building Laborers' Federation, which, in the early '70s, used socalled Green Bans to prevent the demolition and redevelopment of some of Sydney's most beautiful and historic streets and buildings, at the same time infuriating redevelopers and their backers.

Director Pat Fiske, herself a member of the B.L.F. (among other policies, the union encouraged the employment of women in the building industry), tells the story of this most unusual union via interviews with former members and officials, plus generous amounts of newsreel and tv coverage of the sometimes bitter events.

Prior to 1961, according to Fiske, the union was run by corrupt officials who were ousted finally by the rank-and-file who joined political forces to form a coalition of communists, Labor Party supporters and independents, a rare enough achievement. One important decision was to restrict the terms of senior office holders to six years so long-term power bases could not be established. The union also took a stand on the social and political issues of the day — the Vietnam War,

the aboriginal land rights question, etc.

The unquestioned hero of "Rocking The Foundations" is Jack Mundey, secretary of the N.S.W. branch of the B.L.F. from 1968-1973, when the union's most radical decisions were made. The wholesale redevelopment of the inner-suburbs of Sydney, destined for highrise apartments and office blocks, was halted effectively by the B.L.F., with the assistance and enthusiastic support of residents' groups, but at the same time facing hostility from the developers and the conservative state government of the day. Scenes of police violently evicting residents from their homes and bulldozers moving in are still powerful 12 years later. Fiske also touches on the mysterious disappearance of Juanita Nielsen, editor of a small newspaper which supported the residents and the B.L.F. against the developers. Nielsen, whose body was never found, was the subject of two 1981 feature films, Phillip Noyce's "Heatwave" and Donald Crombie's "The Killing Of Angel Street."

"Rocking The Foundations" will be of considerable interest to all those who remember the turbulent days when the ordinary people of Sydney found a union willing to support them against powerful business and political interests. The theme of the docu is the stuff of a Frank Capra movie. Whether Fiske's lament for things past (the union was decertified and taken over by more conservative elements) will attract paying customers is open to question. Docu is booked into a Sydney cinema for a two-week run and undoubtedly will have a long life on the nontheatrical circuit and, probably, television. It should also be caught at festivals specializing in documentaries. —Strat.

Thessaloniki Festival

I Skiachtra
(The Enchantress)
(GREEK-COLOR)

———

Thessaloniki, Oct. 2.
A Cooperation EPE production. Written and directed by Manoussos Manoussaukis. Features Akis Kourkoulos, Lilly Koukodi, Antigoni Amanitou, Vicky Koulianou, Nicos Papaconstantinou, Stratos Pahis, Sophia Aliberti, Costas Balademas. Camera (color), Aris Stavrou; music, Demetris Papademetriou; sets, Tasos Zografos; costumes, Costa Valinopoulos, sound, Marinos Athanasopoulos, Thanasis Arvanitis. Reviewed at the Thessaloniki Film Festival, Oct. 1, 1985. Running time: 98 MINS.

———

Manoussos Manoussaukis makes a departure with a charming fairy tale, "The Enchantress," a fantasy adventure for youngsters as well as adults. It is the first Greek picture of this type and got an enthusiastic reception from the fest audience.

The hero is a young boy who works with his father and two brothers. He is a fearless lad, ignorant of joy, sorrow or love, in contrast with his brothers who are afraid of the fairies and especially of an enchantress who supposedly appears at night at a nearby spring.

After seeing the Enchantress, the hero begs his father to let him go and sets out to travel. He visits villages and haunted castles and becomes the favored human being of the fairies who help him find hidden treasures. He returns back home very rich still longing for the Enchantress.

He marries a local girl, but soon wants to leave to search for the Enchantress.

Lensing by Aris Stavrou has a lyrical quality and takes full advantage of its picturesque background. Akis Kourkoulos, son of actor Nicos Kourkoulos, turns in a good performance as the hero. All other credits, especially the music, are of a high standard. —Rena.

Topos
(GREEK-COLOR)

Thessaloniki, Oct. 2.
Produced by the Greek Film Center. Directed by Antoinetta Angelidi. Features entire cast. Screenplay, Angelidi, Clery Mitsotaki; camera (color), Stavros Hassapis; editor, Antonis Tembos; art director, Costas Angelidakis; music, Giorgos Apergis. Reviewed at the Thessaloniki Film Festival, Oct. 1, 1985. Running time: 85 MINS.
Maria .... Jany Gastaldi
Eleni .... Maya Liberopoulou
Anna .... Anita Santorineou
Little girl................. Clery Mirtseki

"Topos" is a second feature by helmer Antoinetta Angelidi and one of the very few experimental films produced in Greece. Its bow at the Thessaloniki Film Festival earned it a special jury prize and kudos for its remarkable soundtrack by Giorgos Apergis. Meticulously crafted around visuals that hark back to Renaissance painting and Dutch masters, among others, film has only the thinnest of narrative threads to hold it together, and by the end pretty much collapses into repetitiveness. Along the way, however, there is evidence of a fine pictorial sensibility at work, making it of fest and film archive interest.

More than the fragments of situations which relate to female life — maternity, childhood/maturity/old age, prostitution, etc. — pic has a unity of tone and imagery, which remain in the realm of pure nightmare. Dramatically-lit paintings spring to life, but with a monstrous feeling. Contributing to the atmosphere of an art critic's horror film is Apergis' abstract soundtrack that rhythmically scans the sequences, echoing the actors' ritual gestures. Dialog is seant and is used more for sound than meaning.

The fact that virtually all the actors are women offers a clue to where pic is headed. From the ethereal Medieval maidens and bloodless virgins of Cranach to the unsettling abstractions of De Chirico (some paintings actually appear in the film), Angelidi traces the artist's vision of woman as isolating, alienating, and dehumanizing, where maternity and sexuality appear as chillingly unnatural.

Camerawork by Stavros Hassapis and sets by Costas Angelidakis are standouts, in which a few bright colors like red and purple are set against an abstract gray background. —Yung.

Ta Paidia Tou Kronou
(Children Of Chronos)
(GREEK-COLOR)

Thessaloniki, Oct. 4.
Produced by the Greek Film Center. Written and directed by George Korras. Stars Takis Moschos. Camera (color), Philippos Koutsaftis; editor, Christos Voupouras; music, Manolis Logiadis; art director, Damianos Zarifis. Reviewed at the Thessaloniki Film Festival, Oct. 3, 1985. Running time: 107 MINS.
Aris .... Takis Moschos
Stella.................... Anna Makraki
Thanos .... Minas Hadjisavvas
Petros .... Thanassis Mylonas

As voluble as a radio drama, "Children Of Chronos" is a talky but contemporary peek into the private lives of some young Athenians in their 30s who live in a rented apartment. Since pic's main merit is the way it succeeds in capturing its characters in the modern idiom, it isn't likely to travel well, though younger viewers could go for it on home territory.

Title is a double entendre, both to time (helmer George Korras demonstrates a sure feel for his own day and age) and to Chronos, the primitive god who devoured his offspring. The old moldings in the apartment (miraculously saved from the demolition of most of modern Athens) and curious posters and cutouts of ancient art the residents have put up are obsessive visuals in the film. Almost all the story takes place within its four walls, shot from only a few angles.

In this enclave live Aris (Takis Moschos) and his friends. Dubbing himself a perennial medical student, Aris dabbles in journalism for a living, but spends most of his time talking and debating with Thanos (Minas Hadjisavvas) and the actress Stella (Anna Makraki), who moves in with them. A *menage à trois* develops very casually, but is not sensationalized in the film. Petros, Aris' journalism teacher and ex-lover, and a girl his mother would like him to marry, are other well-drawn characters who come in and out of talks around the kitchen table and livingroom tv.

Top-flight performances from Takis Moschos, a rising young thesp appreciated in several quality films this year, and Anna Makraki charge the gabby script with real screen presence. Editing is paced briskly. The pair of brief nude scenes are determinedly desexualized, but fail to achieve the naturalness they were after. Pic is much more successful in

proposing its offbeat romantic liaisons without fuss or prudery.
—Yung.

Mia Toso Makrini Apousia
(Such A Long Absence)
(GREEK-COLOR)

Thessaloniki, Oct. 3.
A Greek Film Center and Stavros Tsiolis production. Written and directed by Stavros Tsiolis. Features Pemi Zouni, Demetris Hatoupis, Betty Valassi, Costas Tzoumas, Manos Hatzisavvas, Zaharias Rohas, Nicos Lytras. Camera (color), George Arvanitis; music, Stamatis Spanoudakis; sets and costumes, Mikes Karapiperis; editor, Costas Jordanides; sound, Nicos Achladis, George Michaloudis, Nicos Varouxis. Reviewed at the Thessalonniki Film Festival, Oct. 3, 1985. Running time: 75 MINS.

"Such A Long Absence," the third picture made by filmmaker Stavros Tsiolis, is a compelling modern drama skillfully handled.

The central character is Agueliki, a young girl desperately concerned about her psychopath sister, while all other members of the family don't care. Realizing the case is hopeless, the family decides to commit the girl to a state mental hospital. Angueliki suffers seeing her sister in such a helpless plight and tries to keep her in a private clinic.

Finally, the family succeeds in transfering the sick girl to the hospital. Angueliki, unable to persuade them to care for her sister, gets her out of the hospital, deciding to keep her in her house. She prefers to live in isolation like her sister since all refuse to understand and accept her decision.

Tsiolis directed with a sure hand avoiding pitfalls that would make it a cheap melodrama. Ending gives a bitter aftertaste, however, the director trying to point out, perhaps, that there is no communication and compassion between people in our days.

Pemi Zouni as the heroine turns in a sensitive performance. Other assets are the sharp camerawork by George Arvanitis and the editing by Costas Jordanides. All other technical credits are above average.
— Rena.

Scenario
(GREEK-COLOR)

Thessaloniki, Oct. 4.
A Greek Film Center and Dinos Mavroidis production. Written and directed by Mavroidis. Camera (color), Dimitris Papaconstantis; editor, Takis Yannopoulos; sets and costumes, Damianos Zarifis; choreography, Yannis Flery; music, George Hadzinassios; lyrics, Dimitris Iatopoulos, Yannis Kanthoulis, Dinos Mavroidis; orchestration, Mike Rozakis. Reviewed at the Thessaloniki Film Festival, Oct. 3, 1985. Running time: 98 MINS.
With: Martha Vourtsi, Maro Kontou, Timos Perlengas, Katy Grigoratou, Michalis Mitrousis, Melina Botelli, Straits Tsopanellis, Christos Kallow, Lakis Lazopoulos, guest ap-

pearances: Christiana, Nikos Dimitratos.

A satirical sendup of the traditional melodrama, for years the trademark of Greek cinema, "Scenario" doesn't miss much in the way of typical characters and situations, delivering it all tied in a pink ribbon.

From the golden-hearted tart, victim of society, to the rich bitch representing society, from the innocent young lovers who dream of escaping into a world of their own, to the tough old nuts who talk only about money and profits, all the protagonists of the staple tearjerker are here. That some of the actors indeed have made a career of such characters is by no means accidental.

Situations are equally parodical. A poor flower girl falls for a rich playboy, who immediately stops playing and falls in love. His parents and the girl's mother are opposed to the union.

To make the whole thing even more absurd, director Dinos Mavroidis adds music, has his protagonists break into song, and sometimes even dance, to display their sentiments. The bitch naturally is dressed in black, the repentant sinner is in black, the innocent lover has long tresses and a Mary Pickford smile, and whenever one's feelings are purified, he is immediately clad in white, even if it is after death.

The story drifts into obvious repetitions of itself and of the genre it makes fun of, until it becomes just like the object satirized.

If the whole thing promised to be hilarious at the beginning, it ends up by being quite tedious. Neither a professional, but not very inspiring, score combining average tunes of the Western musical type with local folklore, nor the overdone sets and camerawork can do much to salvage the project by its second half. The performances fit in with the requirements of the commercial melodrama.

The numerous stars in this film, some highly prized by the Greek public (Christiana is a well known singer, Lakis Lazopoulos, a popular standup comic), may carry their own weight at the home boxoffice.
—Edna.

Meteoro kai Skia
(Meteor And Shadow)
(GREEK-COLOR)

Thessaloniki, Oct. 3.
Produced by the Greek Film Center. Written and directed by Takis Spetsiotis. Stars Takis Moschos. Camera (color), Philippos Koutsaftis; editor, Despina-Danae Maroulakou; music, Marinos Athanassopoulous. Reviewed at the Thessaloniki Film Festival, Oct. 2, 1985. Running time: 101 MINS.
Napoleon Lapathiotis ..... Takis Moschos
Also with: N. Alexiou, A. Aposkitis, G. Zavradinos, M. Marmarinos, G. Kentros.

"Meteor And Shadow" is a costume biopic no less eccentric in style than the life of its hero, Greek poet Napoleon Lapathiotis. A homosexual aesthete reminiscent of Oscar Wilde, an opium eater and communist by persuasion (not by party), Lapathiotis makes a natural subject for film. Helmer Takis Spetsiotis has pared his life down to its bare bones with mixed results. The look is much too effete for most markets, but pic could make other fest passes.

The poet's life (1888-1984) is told as a rise-and-fall story. Born into a wealthy, doting family, indulged by his adoring mother, the young poet is shown in a series of theatrically-staged situations as he strolls through public gardens or converses in drawing rooms on political, social, and literary matters. As played by Takis Moschos, one of Greece's top new talents who won the best actor laurels for this role at the Thessaloniki Film Fest, Lapathiotis is an attractive, sympathetic figure, but the stagy technique puts a deliberate distance between him and the audience. In the end, the main impression that comes across is a pretty conventional Athenian society with his outré behavior and leftist leanings. The latter are visualized mainly in late-night opium sessions with working men.

Pic is clearly meant to be a sympathetic portrait, but has some trouble penetrating the mysteries of its subject. It comes back in focus by the end, when a prematurely aged Lapathiotis dies with dignified pathos, practically a suicide, during a war he claims no part in.

Visually pic is often striking, thanks to award-winning sets and costumes by Dora Lelouda.

— *Yung.*

Mania
(GREEK-COLOR)

Thessaloniki, Oct. 8.
A George Panoussopoulos Ltd. Greek Film Center — Spentzos Film and Synergasia production. Written and directed by Panoussopoulos. Features Alessandra Vanzi, Aris Retsos, Antonis Theodoracopoulos, Stavros Xenides. Camera (color), Panoussopoulos; music, Nicos Xidakis, sound, Marinos Athanassopoulos; art direction, Nicos Perakis; executive producer, Yorgos Tsemberopoulos. Reviewed at the Thessaloniki Film Festival, Oct. 7, 1985. Running time: **92 MINS.**

In "Mania," one-man filmmaker George Panoussopoulos, who wrote, directed, photographed and edited, manages to tell an unbelievable story with symbolic aspects in a convincing way.

Based on an original and imaginative script, the film narrates the story of Zoe, a married woman with two children who is employed by a foreign computer company as a program analyst. She is the only person from Greece to be chosen for a special program of advanced training in the United States due to her intelligence and knowledge. She is, however, totally unaware of all that will happen to her in the National Gardens of Athens where she goes for a walk with her daughter.

Zoe does not suspect that within herself memories and instincts of primitive ages affect her subconscious and work. Through a series of events in the park she is captivated by these internal powers, losing all sense of identity. Her actions arouse the sensitive children in the park and all the animals in the zoo. She creates such a panic that the police cannot control it and finally hunt her like a wild beast. She is the last to remain in the park, with her daughter, while her husband makes a desperate effort to save them.

The film is somewhat uneventful at first, but picks up speed and suspense in its second half sustains the unbelievable plot.

Alessandra Vanzi manages to appear creedible as Zoe and the rest of the cast is efficient in support.

— *Rena.*

En Plo
(On Course)
(GREEK-COLOR)

Thessaloniki, Oct. 4.
A Greek Film Center and Stavros Konstantaracos production. Directed by Konstantaracos. Screenplay, Konstantaracos, in collaboration with Stratis Karas and Yannis Negrepontis. Features George Kimoulis, Stratis Tsopanellis, Lila Kafantari, Nicos Kalogueropoulos, Mimis Fotopoulos (guest star). Camera (color), Stavros Hasapis, music, Heleni Karaendrou, sets, Agnes Doutsi, costumes, George Patsas, editor, Antonis Tempos. Reviewed at the Thessaloniki Film Festival, Oct. 3, 1985. Running time: **95 MINS.**

Stavros Konstantaracos' debut film, "On Course," is an amateurish attempt to present the social and political problems in Greece today.

Based on a naive screenplay, the film narrates the adventures of a young man who sets sail with two friends for an island in the Aegean Sea. Their object is to search for something which the deceased father of the hero had hidden in a cave. This information was passed to him by a cellmate of his father before his execution for underground action during the German occupation.

Since the exact spot of the hidden "thing" is unknown, the hero has to overcome many obstacles and difficulties to carry out his mission. Konstantaracos clumsily directed this tale with political hints in flashback scenes. The picture's two assets are excellent photography by Stavros Hasapis and the music by Heleni Karaendrou. —*Rena.*

Osa
(COLOR)

Weak gender switch on Mad Max.

Washington, D.C., Oct. 20.
Produced by Constantin Alexandrov. Written and directed by Oleg Egorov. Camera (color), John Drake; editor, Suzanne Fenn; music, Mason Daring; sound, Tom Fleishman. Reviewed at the Cine Screening Room, Washington, D.C., Oct. 19, 1985. Running time: **94 MINS.**

Osa	Kelly Lynch
Mr. Big	Daniel Grimm
Speedway	Phillip Vincent
Allan	Etienne Chicot
Crooner	John Forristal
Trooper	Peter Walker
Preacher	Clayton Day
Weasel	David Hausman
Quilt Face	Bill Moseley
Mr. Hammond	Len Stanger
Mrs. Hammond	Brenda King

Glossy lensing and unintentionally funny dialog strand "Osa" somewhere between being a sendup of the "Mad Max" style it intended to rework (with a female road warrior) and a stylish Cormanesque dystopia. In a landscape littered with corpses, imbecile thugs are on the rampage, annihilating what little remains of western civilization.

Three statements offering data on water contamination preface this U.S.-made exploitation pic about post-apocalyptic conditions. The water resources of the entire globe have been contaminated, but for a mysterious place where one Mr. Hammond has cornered the market on unpolluted water and driven up the price to $200 a gallon. Several instances of despair detour the plot, before turning to a family in the desert about to be wiped out by Mr. Hammond's new head of security, a black-leather homosexual called Mr. Big.

The title character Osa is a sexy blond introduced by pivoting her in a cut from her target practice as an orphaned child to the stunning dead-eye avenger she has become under the tutelage of an old state trooper. Still, we see too little of Osa and too much of the demented killers, whose violence is actually fairly clean, except for one shot directly in someone's eye, delivered in a graphic closeup. Essentially sadistic in storyline, pic is so loosely limned that the various encounters stand alone and succeed or fail according to the complexity leading up to the inevitable termination of the good guys by the bad guys.

By the time Osa gets to her showdown with Mr. Big, an elaborate game called Bird Hunt must be invented, the ground rules of which are spouted forth somewhat pedantically. This final game is choreographed for one contestant in a blindfold to shoot the other who must dodge the bullet with a bell in one hand, all of this in an enclosed circle. They cheat. Mr. Big gets blown away in slow-mo.

Pic is like a catalog of old Corman devices, and characters enter and exit, usually at the end of a muzzle, without concern for such classical concerns as motivation. Thesps range from cool to dead-pan deliveries with an honorable mention for John Forristal as a hunk of a villain. Drive-in circuit action is guaranteed. —*Kaja.*

Partisans Of Vilna
(DOCU-COLOR/B&W-16m)

Washington, D.C., Oct. 12.
A Ciesla Foundation production. Produced by Aviva Kempner. Directed by Josh Waltezky. Camera (color, 16m), Danny Schneuer; editor, Josh Waltezky; sound recording, Danny Natovich; sound editor, Ela Troyano; photo animation, Edward Gray, Danny Schneuer. Narrated by Roberta Wallach. Reviewed at the Cine Screening Room, Washington, D.C., Oct. 12, 1985. Running time: **133 MINS.**

A fascinating chapter from the horrific documentaries on the Holocaust makes this account of fighting back a moving and necessary pic, even at its prohibitive length. The underground Jewish resistance based in the Vilna ghetto is pieced together out of interviews with over forty survivors in several languages. Archival footage supplements their stories, by now familiar but aching to be told by these particular witnesses.

Toward the end of a gruelling tale of how the resistance provided a commando group to sabotage the fascist forces comes a devastating account by Abba Kovner, who tells of his mother coming to their hideout and asking what she should do. The principles of secrecy and discipline were such that he could not take her in, and he had no answer to her question. His admission that the heroics of such a resistance are punctured by the failure to deal with the problem on a personal level leave the audience stunned, particularly after two hours of painful discourse.

Drawing its historical background from "Ghetto In Flames" by Yitzhak Arad and using the vast research available in archives from the Abraham F. Rad Contemporary Film Archives to the Library of Congress, pic is an impeccable contribution to history and should find strong non-theatrical life. A draconian editing job will be necessary for theatrical and vid venues. —*Kaja.*

L'Alcova
(The Alcove)
(ITALIAN-COLOR)

Rome, Oct. 21.
A C.R.C. release, produced by MAD Film productions. Directed by Joe D'Amato (Aristide Massaccesi). Stars Laura Gemser, Lilli Carati. Screenplay, Ugo Moretti, based

on a novel by Judith Wexley; camera (Color), Federico Slonisko; editor, Frank Martin; music, Manuel De Sica. Reviewed at Rouge et Noir Cinema, Rome, July 20, 1985. Running time: **85 MINS.**

Zelba	Laura Gemser
De Silverstrim	Al Cliver
His wife	Lilli Carati
Secretary	Annie-Belle

———

"The Alcove" is one of the softest-core erotica pieces to be helmed by Joe D'Amato (Aristide Massaccesi), Italy's premiere red-light director, on the wave of recent softcore hits led by the Giovanni Tinto Brass films. Though targeted for wider audiences, pic carries with it such ugly vices as a dull, meaningless story, no credible psychology for any of the characters, and undirected thesps left to follow their instincts. Genre fans will have to be satisfied with plentiful views of the female cast, lead by Laura Gemser as an Abyssinian slave, Lilli Carati in the depraved housewife role, and Annie-Belle as her jealous lesbian secretary.

The excuse for getting these characters together is *paterfamilias* Al Cliver, an unscrupulous Fascist officer just back from the war in Africa with the beauteous Zelba (Gemser) in tow. Though at first willing to obey only Cliver, she is soon passed on in ownership to his bemused wife Carati, who has other uses for her, while her old lover Annie-Belle smoulders in the next room.

In an hommage to his profession, helmer stages a film-within-the-film during which Annie-Belle, who thinks she's merely acting in a good old porn film, is actually raped by the gardner. This dastardly deed plants the seed of revenge in her heart, and with the help of Carati's son, a priggish military cadet, she turns the tables on the accomplices. In practice, this means getting rid of her rival, Zelba, by burning her alive in an unconvincing backyard bonfire.

Gemser looks best without clothes, while Carati has a malicious gleam of irony in her eyes that puts her out front in the thesping dept. The entire film is shot in a period villa with a nice green garden around it. As Cliver sums up when he shoots his own movie: "The setting can be approximate. What counts is the story, nice and crude." — *Yung.*

———

Twisted Passion
(HONG KONG-COLOR)

———

Hollywood, Oct. 1.
A Shaw Brothers production and release. Produced by Wong Ka Hee. Directed by Yang Chuan. Stars Hsu Shu Yuan, Chang Kuo Chu, Tang Chen Tsung, Hung Hsin Nan, Charlie Tsao, Li Chia Li, Wu Shu Yi. Designed and written by Chen Shu Kuang; camera (color), Ma Chin Chiang; editor, Chiang Hsing Lung; music, Stephen Shing,

So Chun Hou. Reviewed at King's Theater. Hong Kong, Sept. 30, 1985. Running time: **98 MINS.**
(Cantonese soundtrack with English subtitles)

In "Twisted Passion," an ambitious businessman, Chang Kuo Chu, who wants to be a local politician, marries model Tina (Hsu Shu Yuan) and his social fantasies come true.

The worldly and restless Tina is not happy as a rich Tai Tai (local version of a socialite) and her dissatisfaction is further fueled by her husband's neglect, especially in the bedroom.

To keep his sex-starved wife busy, Chang has her run a modelling agency, which becomes a success. Chang even arranges that his male secretary Hung Hsin Nan should help her organize a fashion extravaganza.

Tina is introduced to a young designer, Sam (Tang Chen Tsung), who falls in love with her. Unable to control her sexual drive, Tina starts a love affair with him. When news of their relationship reaches Chang, he sends someone to threaten Sam.

Later, Tina finds her husband is really a homosexual (still a controversial subject here). To top it all, there's a murder to contend with. Then Tina finishes the whole affair by exposing all to the local press.

Twisted indeed in its portrayal of what's happening in modern Hong Kong society, film is fictionalized in typical, showy Shaw Bros. style. There's lots of feminine skin exposure, simulated but daring sex scenes and even male nudity.

Pic is doing well at the boxoffice because of its sensationalistic appoach and side promotion of Hsu Shu Yuan, a bold, sexy actress recruited from Taiwan, to portray Tina. — *Mel.*

———

Dormire
(WEST GERMAN-COLOR)

———

A Visual Film, Munich, in coproduction with Maran-Film, Munich, and Süddeutscher Rundfunk (SDR), Stuttgart. Produced by Elke Haltaufderheide. Directed by Niklaus Schilling. Features entire cast. Screenplay, Schilling, in collaboration with Sunnyi Melles and Sabina Trooger; camera (color), Schilling, Thomas Meyer; sound, Stefan Meisel; sets, Gretel Zeppel; music, Andreas Hofner. Reviewed at Arsenal Kino, Berlin, Sept. 28, 1985. Running time: **91 MINS.**
With: Sunnyi Melles (Claudia), Sabina Trooger (Inge), Markus Helis, Antony Paul, Gert Burkhard, Hans-Rudolf Stein, Gerhard Acktun.

———

Niklaus Schilling's "Dormire" (the Italian verb for "sleep") deserves attention because of the unique way in which the film was made. Everything was shot originally on one-inch videotape, and then transferred to film stock with care. Indeed, this does look like a film on screen.

Two women share a sleeping compartment on a deluxe train traveling

from Hamburg to Munich Inge is a professional journalist, an independent hardened type who is not above tricks and deception to root out a story for the yellow press. Claudia is a well-known pianist whose specialty is Mozart. As the train pulls out of Hamburg, Claudia arrives just in time but without money.

Inge helps her traveling companion out by paying for the ticket. The two settle down for the night journey with cognac and conversation. It's here that the plot heats up for a while as a game of hide-and-seek and oneupmanship develops, so much so that the truth becomes clouded in lies and exaggerations. A Hitchcockian element is introduced as well: Claudia attempts to tear out and destroy a page in the evening paper that indicates a foul deed has been perpetrated, for which a famous pianist is being sought.

Once Inge finds that she's been doped with a sedative in a slug of cognac (she drinks only half and the effect wears off quickly), she decides to get behind the story with a tape recorder running and her camera poised and ready. Claudia admits to running away, but she feels she's innocent and still a bit confused as to just what happened in regard to poisoning her husband. Inge apparently wants to help Claudia to get a head-start at least in evading her pursuers, all of which leads to a twist at the end.

Pic's main drawback is that it's neither fish nor fowl, neither a movie thriller nor an eyecatching video experiment. Thesp performances are also uneven. — *Holl.*

———

The Fix
(COLOR)

———

Subpar action programmer.

———

A Reverie Prods. production. Executive producer, George Harriss. Produced by Ervin T. Melton. Directed by Will Zens. Stars Vince Edwards, Richard Jaeckel. Screenplay, Esty F. Davis Jr., Lance Smith Jr., Zens; camera (TVC color), William VanDerKloot; editor, Frank Johnson; songs, Zens, Tony Dale, Billy Schaefer, others; sound, Richard E. Pitstick; assistant director, Don Dubbins; production manager, Robert (Sy) Vance Jr.; stunt coordinator, Jerry Rushing; set decoration, Lynn Wolverton. Reviewed on World Video Pictures vidcassette, N.Y., Sept. 29, 1985. (No MPAA Rating.) Running time: **95 MINS.**

Frank Lane	Vince Edwards
Charles Dale	Richard Jaeckel
Doug Davis	Tony Dale
Kelly	Julie Hill
Esty	Byron Cherry
Hawkeye	Charles Dierkop
Spook	Robert Tessier
Sheriff Bower	Don Dubbins
Deputy George	Lou Walker
Cherry	Leslie Leah
Bobby	Bob Hannah
Redneck	Jerry Rushing

"The Fix," alternately titled "The Agitators," is a dull action film lensed about two years ago in North Carolina.

Vince Edwards heads an okay cast as a drug kingpin, whose front is a business as a building contractor. With henchmen Charles Dierkop (the familiar sidekick of the "Police Woman" tv series) and Robert Tessier (bald action film villain) he decides to use a traveling country music band as dupes in his drug shipments through the South.

Federal Drug Enforcement agent Richard Jaeckel is hot on Edwards' trail, using his agent Julie Hill to infiltrate the operation. Several country music songs later, Jaeckel literally talks Edwards out of his upper hand in the climactic confrontation.

Vet B-picture director Will Zens ("The Starfighters," "Road To Nashville") stages okay chase scenes but fails to develop this material beyond its opening premise. As a result, film is unengrossing (with the country music padding showing through) and went to homevideo directly without a domestic theatrical release. Oddly, the vidcassette displays no distributor logo on tape or even the usual FBI warning crawl. — *Lor.*

———

Casas Viejas
(SPANISH-B&W/COLOR)

———

San Sebastian, Sept. 25.
An Andalusi-Cline production. Written and directed by José L. López del Río. Camera (b&w, Easmancolor), Jusuf L. Ibn Lubb An Nahari, José E. Izquierdo, Antonio Pérez Olea; editor, José A. Rojo, David Raposo; sets, José L. López del Río; music, Victor Monge "Serranito." Features villagers of Casas Viejas and thesps of Andalusian theater. Reviewed at Cine Miramar, San Sebastian Film Festival, Sept. 24, 1985. Running time: **142 MINS.**

"Casas Viejas" is an overlong semi-documentary reconstruction of the event surrounding a minor footnote to modern Spanish history. In 1933, in the Andalusian village of Casas Viejas, an anarchist uprising was put down brutally by the Republican government.

Most of pic is in black and white, though occasional color footage is inserted for no obvious reason. Long sections are dedicated to political speeches in congress by lookalikes of Spanish politicians of the time, condemning or defending the repression in which a dozen villagers were killed. Helmer José L. López del Río also reenacts the fighting and carnage that followed.

Pic loses some of its dramatic potential by skipping back and forth in time. Commercial outlook is limited to tv sales, though even there the events portrayed are probably too oscbure to arouse any interest. — *Besa.*

To Live And Die In L.A.
(COLOR)

Overdone thriller is a turnoff.

Hollywood, Oct. 25.

An MGM/UA Ent. release from UA of a New Century Prods. Ltd. and SLM Inc. presentation of an Irving H. Levin production. Produced by Levin. Executive producer, Samuel Schulman. Directed by William Friedkin. Stars William L. Petersen, Willem Dafoe, John Pankow. Screenplay, Friedkin, Gerald Petievich, based on the novel by Petievich. Coproducer, supervising film editor, second unit director, Bud Smith. Camera (Technicolor), Robby Müller; editor, Scott Smith; music, Wang Chung; production design, Lilly Kilvert; art direction, Buddy Cone; set decoration, Cricket Rowland; costume design, Linda Bass; sound (Dolby), Jean-Louis DuCarme, Rodger Pardee; production manager, John J. Smith; assistant director, Charles Myers; second unit camera, Robert Yeoman; stunt coordinators, Pat E. Johnson, Buddy Joe Hooker; casting, Bob Weiner. Reviewed at the MGM Studios, Culver City, Calif., Oct. 24, 1985. (MPAA Rating: R.) Running time: 116 MINS.

Richard Chance	William L. Petersen
Eric Masters	Willem Dafoe
John Vukovich	John Pankow
Bianca Torres	Debra Feuer
Carl Cody	John Turturro
Ruth Lanier	Darlanne Fluegel
Bob Grimes	Dean Stockwell
Jeff Rice	Steve James
Thomas Bateman	Robert Downey
Jim Hart	Michael Greene
Max Waxman	Christopher Allport
Jack	Jack Hoar
Judge Filo Cedillo	Val DeVargas
Doctor	Dwier Brown
Thomas Ling	Michael Chong
Claudia Leith	Jackelyn Giroux

"To Live And Die In L.A." looks like a rich man's "Miami Vice." As hip as can be and as cynical as all getout, William Friedkin's evident attempt to fashion a West Coast equivalent of his "The French Connection" is engrossing and diverting enough on a moment-to-moment basis but is so overtooled as to invite scorn for the fetishistic care lavished on this otherwise straightforward *policier*. Film is very commercially intended, but the intense vulgarity of the characters and stylistic overkill will, like that of MGM-UA's just-previous release, "Year Of The Dragon," turn off mainstream audiences.

Friedkin leaves no doubt about his technical abilities, as he has created another memorable car chase and, with the considerable assistance of cinematographer Robby Müller, has offered up any number of startling and original shots of the characters inhabiting weirdly ugly-beautiful L.A. cityscapes.

As usual, the people in a Friedkin film are living intensely under high pressure situations that rarely let up. William L. Petersen plays a highly capable Secret Service agent who decides to nail a notorious counterfeiter responsible for the murder of his partner.

Petersen's search leads him into the kinky, high-tech world of Willem Dafoe, a supremely talented and self-confident artist whose

phony $20 bills look magnificent and whose tentacles reach into surprising areas of the criminal underworld, both high and low-class.

Like any self-respecting special agent these days, Petersen is a freewheeling sort who doesn't like to play by the rules, and in persuit of his objective he goes so far as to rob and kill at least one innocent person. He's also a heartless user where the opposite sex is concerned, but at one point his mistaken sense of compassion gets him into one heap of trouble.

As is the fashion, Friedkin keeps dialog to a minimum, but what conversation there is proves wildly overloaded with streetwise obscenities, so much so that it becomes something of a joke. Someone's always threatening to stick something up somebody else's something-or-other, and while they occasionally succeed in doing so, the taunts grow wearing and hollow before long.

Petersen, a powerful Chicago stage actor, is initially appealing mainly because he's clearly good at his job as an agent. As structured, however, the film gradually pulls away from him. Like Al Pacino's undercover cop in Friedkin's "Cruising," the character goes too far, and Friedkin's rigorous denial of psychological insight prevents any comprehension of why. With his intense villainy, Dafoe makes a strong bid to establish himself as the Lee Marvin of the 1980s.

But the surfaces are brilliant, from Lilly Kilvert's L.A. new wave production design to Bud and Scott Smith's editing to Wang Chung's relentless music.

Pic is also extremely well cast. Everyone here seems capable of deception and moral duplicity, and then proceeds to live up to those expectations. —*Cart.*

Tears Are Not Enough
(CANADIAN-DOCU-COLOR)

Toronto, Oct. 18.

A Pan-Canadian release of a Canadian Broadcasting Corp. tv production in association with Northern Lights for Africa Society. Executive producer, Sandra Faire. Produced and directed by John Zaritsky. Associate producers, Gordon McClellan and Virginia Storring. Camera (color), Chris Elias, Tony Mountford, Bob Asgersson, Brian Tyson, Al McPherson, Dennis Beauchamp, Hans Vanderzande, Patrick Bell; editor, Gordon McClellan; audio, Bruce Graham, Mark Parkham, Brian Radford. Reviewed at Carlton Cinema, Toronto, Oct. 18, 1985. (No MPAA Rating). Running time: 90 MINS.

"Tears Are Not Enough" is a celebratory documentary on the making of the Canadian video for Ethiopian famine relief. Rather than enlarging the scope to tackle the political and social problems of starvation in Africa, producer-di-

rector John Zaritsky (Academy Award-winning director of "Just Another Missing Kid") focuses on the process and preparation of recording the video and the result is a vital landmark assembly of 50 Canadian music greats.

David Foster, who wrote the tune and produced the video, is the troop leader whose voiceover narrative sets the warm tone in recalling the feelings and drama of the event. Zaritsky reenacts some key scenes: Foster getting zapped by inspiration crossing a bridge in Victoria, B.C., and humming "Tears" into a handheld tape recorder, and rock organizer Bruce Allen pacing and screaming into the telephone as he keeps convincing artists to commit to the project.

Behind the scenes antics and good humor abound, but the real joy comes from the meeting of the musicians in rehearsals and endless takes. High points include oldtimer Ronnie Hawkins kidding newcomer Corey Hart about being pretty good for a punker; Neil Young in sunglasses and headband, responding to Foster's assessment that the take was flat with "that's my sound, man;" Joni Mitchell, Jane Siberry and Lorraine Segato discussing the I Ching; Burton Cummings doing a mean Rodney Dangerfield; Anne Murray graciously getting her line right on the first take; Bryan Adams playing Boy Scout by assisting everyone in getting the right notes; John Candy hamming it up with Paul Shaffer.

The sign on the recording studio said, "Please Check Your Egos At The Door," and all the Canadian musicians did just that. Zaritsky and Gordon McClellan edited down 50 hours of the session (including videos and performance footage of many of the artists) to a crisp insightful, and euphoric tribute to the Northern Lights effort. — *Devo.*

Bring On The Night
(DOCU-COLOR)

Rewarding portrait of Sting's new band.

A Samuel Goldwyn Co. release of an A&M Films production. Produced by David Manson. Executive producers, Gil Friesen, Andrew Meyer. Directed by Michael Apted. Stars Sting. Camera (color), Ralf D. Bode; editors, Robert K. Lambert, Melvin Shapiro; music by Sting, produced by Sting and Pete Smith; art director, Ferdinando Scarfiotti; costumes, Colleen Atwood; associate producer, Lambert; technical adviser, Vic Garbarini. Reviewed at Magno screening room, N.Y., Oct. 24, 1985. (MPAA Rating: PG-13.) Running time: 97 MINS.

With: Sting, Omar Hakim, Darryl Jones, Kenny Kirkland, Branford Marsalis, Dolette McDonald, Janice Pendarvis, Trudie Styler, Miles Copeland.

Lensed in nine days last spring, Michael Apted's documusical

"Bring On The Night" is a more than worthy addition to the genre. Pic details the formation of Police leader Sting's current jazz-rock ensemble, following them through an introductory press conference, numerous rehearsals at the lavish Chateau du Courson in France, and, finally, a triumphant concert unveiling (actually filmed during several performances).

Apted, as experienced with docus as with features, effectively lets the performers speak for themselves, keeping himself and his crew out of the picture. While Sting's premise — that his idea for a blending of rock and jazz is unique and original — is a bit presumptuous, the soft-spoken songwriter and his outspoken sidemen come across as affable, thoughtful, generous sorts. Their comments about the nature of their music, their backgrounds and their opinions of each other are both pointed and humorous.

The interviews are intercut with scenes of jovial rehearsals marked by extraordinary good will on all sides. Bassist Darryl Jones and saxophonist Branford Marsalis break into an impromptu vocal rendition of the theme from tv's "The Flintstones," which reaches hilarious proportions when the normally aloof Briton Sting joins in ... and knows every word. Marsalis is especially wonderful as, when he's asked if he's nervous about playing this new music to an audience for the first time, he quickly responds, "I'm a jazz musician, I'm used to playing stuff that no one wants to hear."

One sour note in the pic is struck by Police manager Miles Copeland (brother of Police drummer Stewart), who aggressively points out why Sting deserves more money for the concerts than the other band members. He also gets in a dither over the clothes the musicians are to wear onstage, which doesn't exactly endear him to costume designer Colleen Atwood or to the viewer.

The filmmakers had the added boost of being able to film the birth of Sting's son Jake by his longtime companion Trudie Styler, who is seen in interviews during rehearsals leading up to the birth (which actually took place on the second night of concert filming). Fairly explicit hospital scene documenting the birth, with Sting on hand to cut the cord, is movingly backed on the soundtrack by a new song, "Russians," which posits love of children as a nuclear war preventative.

Musically and aurally, pic is on the money, offering a satisfying mixture of old Police songs and the new ones that would eventually make up the current "Dream Of The Blue Turtles" album. Sting's gratification upon seeing this new conglomeration (which also includes drummer Omar Hakim, keyboardist Kenny Kirkland and vocalists Dolette McDonald and Janice Pendarvis) being rousingly accepted by its first live audience is evident.

Ralf D. Bode's photography is luminous, especially the romantically lit concert footage. The effectiveness, however, of one of Sting's most potent compositions, "Message In A Bottle," about universal despair, is undercut by the end credits crawl.

There's enough, though, to please Sting/Police fans and then some. He's in his element here.
—*Gerz.*

Appointment With Fear
(COLOR)

Unconvincing thriller.

Hollywood, Oct. 22.

A Galaxy International Releasing release. Produced by Tom Boutross. Executive producer, Moustapha Akkad. Directed by Ramzi Thomas. Features entire cast. Screenplay, Thomas, Bruce Meade; camera (United color), Nicholas Von Sternberg; editor, Paul Jasiukonis; music, Andrea Saparoff; art director, David Gladstone; associate producer, M. Sanousi; sound, Paul F. Shremp, Mark Linden; casting, Dan Guerroero. Reviewed at De Mille Screening room, Laird Studios, Culver City, Calif., Oct. 21, 1985. (MPAA Rating: R.) Running time: **98 MINS.**
Carol . . . . Michele Little
Bobby . . . . Michael Wyle
Heather . . . . Kerry Remsen
Detective Kowalski . . . . Douglas Rowe
The Man . . . . Garrick Dowhen
Ruth . . . . Deborah Sue Voorhees
Samantha . . . . Pamela Bach
Cowboy . . . . Vincent Barbour

"Appointment With Fear" is a stylish looking but nearly incomprehensible low-budget thriller which can only leave the audience wondering what it all means. Plot is so ludicrous that suspense unintentionally turns to laughter. Crowd looking for a good scare will likely be disappointed.

Film strikes a portentous tone as it opens with the recitation of an ancient Egyptian myth about the god Attis who must sacrifice his child at harvest time. Among the god's magical powers is the ability to raise himself out of a dream state for a series of bloody murders.

All this silliness is transposed to modern day L.A. (where else?) where a mental patient (Garrick Dowhen) becomes the latter day Attis. After he murders his wife, his child, it seems, is in the hands of Heather (Kerry Remsen) and a group of her high school friends. The girls take off for a party at some mysterious desert house and wait for Attis to appear.

Film is dotted with bizarre non sequiturs such as a philosophical bum (Danny Dayton) who live in the back of a pickup truck. Perhaps

even stranger than the killer/god is the cop chasing him. As Detective Kowalski, Douglas Rowe introduces some "Repo Man"-like humor and even looks a bit like Harry Dean Stanton.

Somehow, ritual dances, shotgun microphones, glowing bushes and a boyfriend who comes to save the day all play a part in sorting out this nonsense. When all is said and done, it doesn't make much sense.

Despite its denseness, "Appointment With Fear" is never dull to look at, thanks to the glossy sheen produced by Nicholas Von Sternberg's photography. Cast of young actors is also attractive, particularly Michèle Little as the herione. Although she has a charming smile, it often seems to be directed at the material rather than part of the action.

Ramzi Thomas' direction is flashy, but he is his own worst enemy as a writer. —*Jagr.*

Eleni
(COLOR)

Flat drama is headed nowhere.

Hollywood, Oct. 22.

A Warner Bros. release of a CBS Productions presentation of a Vanoff/Pick/Gage production. Produced by Nick Vanoff, Mark Pick, Nicholas Gage. Directed by Peter Yates. Stars Kate Nelligan, John Malkovich, Linda Hunt. Screenplay, Steve Tesich, based on the book by Gage; camera (color), Billy Williams; editor, Ray Lovejoy; music, Bruce Smeaton; production design, Roy Walker; art direction, Steve Spence, Fernando Gonzalez (Spain); set decoration, Martin Atkinson, Jacques Bradette (Canada); costume design, Tom Rand; sound (Dolby), Ivan Sharrock; associate producer, Nigel Wooll; assistant directors, Chris Newman, Derek Cracknell, Carlos Scola; casting, Noel Davis. Reviewed at The Burbank Studios, Burbank, Calif. Oct. 22, 1985). (MPAA Rating: PG.) Running time: **117 MINS.**
Eleni . . . . Kate Nelligan
Nick . . . . John Malkovich
Katina . . . . Linda Hunt
Katis . . . . Oliver Cotton
Spiro . . . . Ronald Pickup
Grandmother . . . . Rosalie Crutchley
Joan . . . . Glenne Headly
Ana . . . . Dimitra Arliss
Christos . . . . Steve Plytas

"Eleni" is as lofty in ambition as it is deficient in accomplishment. Adapted from Nicholas Gage's best-selling book about his search for the truth about his mother, who was executed by the communists in Greece in the late 1940s, pic has the most noble of intentions, but comes off as flat, tedious and crudely biased. Without strong reviews, there's not much b.o. future in store for this sort of serious-minded undertaking.

Steve Tesich's screenplay cuts back and forth between events separated by 30 years. The Gage figure, portrayed by John Malkovich, is assigned to the New York Times' Athens bureau, a base from which he can strategically investigate the

events surrounding his mother's death during the civil war. Having been a child at the time, Nick can remember incidents and places but feels compelled to research matters fully from an adult perspective and, most important, hopes to exact revenge upon the man who acted as judge and executioner.

Eleni, Nick's mother, played by Kate Nelligan, was a peasant woman in the tiny village of Lia. Portrayed as entirely apolitical, she was forced from her home when the communists occupied the area in the fractions period following World War II, then courageously suffered countless other indignities until being convicted as a traitor in a mock trial for having arranged for her children to escape.

The communist guerrilla fighters depicted here are guilty of everything from rudeness and snideness to treachery and betrayal. While there is no doubt that they committed all the barbarisms displayed here and more, the film plays virtually as a catalog of leftist crimes against their fellow citizens. The opposing side is alternately referred to as monarchist or fascist, but never is it characterized in any way, nor is there the slightest reason offered why some of the resistance members might have the motivation to oppose the ruling government in the first place.

Pic's cheap political analysis might go over with smugly conservative viewers, who can point to what's up on the screen as evidence of how awful the commies are, but the approach here is more insidiously slanted than something like "Rambo," which at least is upfront with its attitudes.

Just as bad is the dramatization of the historical incidents, which, despite the highly charged emotions involved, come off as drab and lacking in tension. Peter Yates has filmed it all in a plain, head-on manner, and paced the action so that the picture seems much longer than its two hours.

The scenes involving Malkovich's extended search for the evil judge prove more successful than the period stuff, and the climactic scene of their confrontation is undeniably tense, by far the best in the film. It comes as much too little, too late.

Nelligan, Malkovich and Linda Hunt, superior performers all, have strong grips on their characters, but the women, in particular, are victimized by the sorry artistic circumstances surrounding what they are required to do. Oliver Cotton, as the chief villain, looks like Satan himself.

Tech credits are fine, with the impoverished Greek village having been suitably recreated in Spain by production designer Roy Walker.—*Cart.*

Death Wish 3
(U.S.-COLOR)

Monotonous shootout.

London, Oct. 23.

A Cannon Group presentation of a Golan-Globus production. Produced by Menahem Golan and Yoram Globus. Coproduced and directed by Michael Winner. Stars Charles Bronson. Screenplay, Michael Edmonds, based on characters created by Brian Garfield; camera, (color) John Stanier; editor, Arnold Crust (Michael Winner); music, Jimmy Page; production designer, Peter Mullins; associate producer, Michael Kagan; production supervisors, Malcolm Christopher, Ron Purdie; production manager (U.S.) George Manasse. Reviewed at the Cannon Classic preview theater, London, Oct. 22, 1985. (MPAA Rating: R.) Running time: **90 MINS.**
Paul Kersey . . . . Charles Bronson
Kathryn Davis . . . . Deborah Raffin
Richard S. Shriker . . . . Ed Lauter
Bennett . . . . Martin Balsam
Fraker . . . . Gavan O'Herlihy
Giggler . . . . Kirk Taylor
Hermosa . . . . Alex Winter
Angel . . . . Tony Spiridakis
The Cuban . . . . Ricco Ross
Tulio . . . . Tony Britts
Rodriguez . . . . Joseph Gonzalez
Charley . . . . Francis Drake
Maria . . . . Marina Sirtis

"Death Wish 3" adds significantly to the body count scored to date in this street-rampant series. Thrills, however, are way down due to script's failure to build motivation for Paul Kersey's latest killing spree.

Set in N.Y., but lensed mostly in London, pic's release is timed to capitalize on the controversy around subway vigilante Bernhard Goetz. Latter's single killing seems timid in comparison with what goes on in "Death Wish 3."

It's been a miserable few years for Kersey. In the original "Death Wish" he lost his wife. Maid and daughter expired in the first sequel. The problem with "Death Wish 3" starts from the fact that there's no-one else for the killing-machine to lose.

Attempts to justify the ensuing mass-murder are perfunctory. Film opens with the butchering of an old man who turns out to be an old mate of Kersey, but there's no suggestion that the relationship was intimate. Kersey sees an attractive Latino lady being terrorized by a local punk. A few moments in a local jail make a deadly enemy out of gang-leader Fraker (Gavan O'Herlihy). Finally, a lady lawyer (Deborah Raffin) sufficiently entranced by Kersey to lure him to bed is promptly incinerated.

Kersey's response, like Bronson's acting, is automaton-like. Mystery is why he came to New York in the first place without the tools of his brutal trade and has to make regular visits to the post office to accumulate firepower. Quality of guns acquired is sufficient to ensure that the pic's hero is never in serious jeopardy.

The oldies living in the flats which Kersey uses as a base endure regular muggings as they wander the streets with overflowing shopping bags. The police, it seems, are prevented by law from intervening. Although various crimes are seen on film, no attempt is made to focus on particular groups of miscreant youths. Kersey uses various forms of bait to lure the young to their deaths.

Michael Winner directs with customary tongue-in-cheek panache. There are occasional moments of wit as when apartment resident Bennett (Martin Balsam) wields his rusty machine gun, or gang-boss Fraker ends up on a flicker of flame on the street. The musical score by Jimmy Page is pleasing and technical credits are fine. —*Japa.*

The Island (Life And Death)
(HONG KONG-COLOR)

Hong Kong, Oct. 15.

A D&B Films Co. Ltd. production, released by the Golden Princess theater circuit. Presented by Dickson Poon and Samo Hung. Directed by Leong Po-chih. Production suprvisor, Deanie Ip. Stars John Sham, Tse Ching Yuen, Ronald Wong, Timothy Zau, Amy Kwok, Kitty Ngau, Helen Au. Production manager, Ip Wing-cho; art direction, Yee Chung-man; camera (color), Poon Hang-sang. Reviewed at President theater, Hong Kong, Oct. 14, 1985. Running time: **98 MINS.**
(Cantonese soundtrack with English subtitles)

"The Island's" format (Life And Death) is unoriginal, but it remains a remarkable and competent rehash of the "survival against all odds" theme. Fortunately, this latest D&B production, loaded with assorted bloodbaths is suspense-filled and visually stunning.

On a deserted island lives a Chinese family. There's a paralyzed mother who rules her three mentally unbalanced grown-up sons who run a grocery store. The first is fat and sullen, the second vulgar and cruel and the third is mentally retarded. The mother's final wish before her demise is to have number three son married. They luckily find a girl refugee from China who is forced into marriage until the mother discovers that she is no longer a virgin. She's made a prisoner instead. The opening build-up is actually to frame the arrival six months later of nature loving teacher "Coffin Cheung" (John Sham) and his six young students for camping. A boat is expected to pick them up two days later to return to Hong Kong.

The initial reaction of the city folks to the rural environment is that of fascination. That is soon changed when the three strange island men start meddling with the group's activities. This leads to a lot of hide and seek, scare and run, see and be shocked sequences. The once passive human nature of the teach-er and the students is put to the test as they face a primitively violent world and how they eventually solve their problems is what the rest of the picture is all about.

Comedian John Sham changes into a serious actor, but retaining his special Chui Chau accent which has become his trademark to local popularity. Sham proves his versatility, along with the young cast.

The clever craftsmanship, especially the cinematography of Poon Hang-sang is more than commendable. —*Mel.*

Sällskapsresan II — Snow Roller
(The Package Tour II - (Snowroller) (SWEDISH-COLOR)

Malmö, Oct. 24.

An SF (Svensk Film) release of Viking Film (Bo Jonsson) production for SF, The Swedish Film Institute, Sonet Film/Balkdakinen, Smart Egg Pictures. Executive producer, Bo Jonsson. Original story and directed by Lasse Aberg. Camera (Eastmancolor), Hanno Fuchs; production management, Rune Hjelm, Bamse Ulfung; editor, Sylvia Ingemarsson; music, Bengt Palmers; costumes, Ingabritt Adriansson; Inger Martin; technical director, Peter Hald; Bo Jonsson's personal production aide, Britt Ohlsson. Reviewed at the Palladium, Malmö, Sweden, Oct. 24, 1985. Running time: **90 MINS.**

Stig Helmer Ohlsson ....Lasse Aberg
Ole of Norway ....Jon Skolmen
Kärran ....Eva Millberg
Lotta ....Cecilia Walton
Mr. Jönsson ....Björn Granath
Mrs. Jönsson ....Ingrid Wallin
Their son ....Oscar Franzén
Their daughter ....Erica Larsson
Brännström ....Bengt Andersson
Hedlund...................Staffan Ling
Nalle....................Jan Waldecranz
Mackan ....Klasse Möllberg
Algernon of England........David Kehoe

Also with: Barbro Hjort af Ornš, Lars-Olaf Lihwall, Carl-Henry Cagarp, Dieter Augustin, Elianne Gagneaux, Felix St. Clair, Franz Hanfstingel.

Any feature film by Lasse Aberg bears the stamp of the happy amateur at work as a writer and director of the human comedy farce in which he stars himself as a latter-day cross between Buster Keaton and Joe E. Brown. This stamp made Aberg's "The Call-Up" a runaway hit in 1978, while his first "Package Tour" since its release in 1988 has had more admissions (and enjoyed larger homevideo sales) than any other film in the history of Swedish cinema. It has been sold well and done nicely in several offshore territories as well, and a similar good fortune can be predicted for Aberg's "Package Tour II - Snow Roller."

Any feature film by Aberg also gives every member of the cast a chance to develop as a full-fledged character, villainous or in-spite-of-himself heroic but all of them always winding up with audience sympathy secured. As a writer-director, Aberg is a true humanist, and as a one-role comedy actor he has made his shy, 40-ish, mother-dominated bachelor Lasse Helmer a Scandinavian institution, instantly recognizable whether he fumbles the ball with bureaucracy, smart-aleck youngsters, women or whoever. This Lasse Helmer is a loser-winner and so are, in various ways, all other specimens, absurd but never grotesque, of humanity surrounding them.

This time around, Aberg has taken his little human zoo on a winter holiday to Verbier, Switzerland. Only Aberg as Helmer and jolly, warm-hearted, irrepressible Jon Skolmen as his Norwegian pal Ole are veterans of the first "Package Tour," which took the Swedish innocents-abroad to the sun, fun & liquor games of the Canary Islands. The fun behind the sequel remains more or less the same with Spanish swimming-pools, cantinas and package tour mechanics replaced by ski slopes, *bierstuben* in Alpine heights and more package tour guide manipulation of their defenseless herd.

Not much happen in terms of a plot, but hapless Helmer really gets the girl this time, thus indicating that Aberg does not plan further sequels. Apart from Helmer, we meet a youthful gang of slalom samurais, a tyrannical head of family who winds up in a cast while his wife wife blossoms during an innocent enough flirt with a local inn-keeper, and we meet the two smart young girls who are not to be bowled over by professional Romeos, and sundry other guys and dolls we might have met before during Vermont winters or Carribean peak seasons.

Although aided by Bo Jonson's production-knowhow and Hamme Fuchs' expert cinematography, Aberg does seem a little bogged-down by the sheer challenge of having to maneuver with helicopters, ski-lifts, etc. on Swiss locations where before he and his team just seemed to take a stroll while recording what happened in and around the Las Palmas swimming pools. Still, his new film is already breaking house-records at home, and its special low-key, almost soft-spoken farcial style should make him many friends on foreign slopes, too.

— *Kell.*

School Spirit
(COLOR)

Low-grade teen comedy.

A Concorde Pictures/Cinema Group release from New Horizons Film Corp. of an Amritraj/Chroma III production. Executive producers, Sidney Balkin, Ken Dalton. Produced by Jeff Begun and Ashok Amritraj. Directed by Alan Holleb. Features entire cast. Screenplay, Geoffrey Baere; camera (Deluxe color), Robert Ebinger; editor, Sonya Sones; music, Tom Bruner; sound, Steve Nelson; production design, Peter Knowlton; production manager, Bill Tasgal; assistant director, Stephen Buck; special effects-second unit director, Ken Soloman; optical effects supervisor, Jim Stewart; casting, Gino Evans; associate producers, Vijay Amritraj, Chandru Manchnani. Reviewed at RKO National I theater, N.Y., Oct. 25, 1985. (MPAA Rating: R.) Running time: **90 MINS.**

Billy Batson.................Tom Nolan
Judy Hightower ....Elizabeth Foxx
Mrs. Grimshaw ....Roberta Collins
Pinky Batson.............John Finnegan
Pres. Grimshaw ....Larry Linville
Madeleine ....Daniele Arnaud
Ursula Grimshaw ....Marta Kober
Also with: Nick Segal, Toni Hudson, Julie Gray, David Byrd, Johnny Lee, Michael Miller, Liz Sheridan, The Gleaming Spikes.

"School Spirit" is a weak, low-budget comedy that arrives way too late in the overdone teen fantasy cycle. Announced as an Almi Pictures release last year, film debuted instead through Roger Corman's new distribution company in April 1985 in Atlanta.

Tom Nolan (imagine Michael J. Fox as a 6-foot-tall football player) toplines the overage-looking cast as Billy Batson (no relation to Captain Marvel), a college student who is killed in a car crash while rushing heedlessly home from a drugstore with an all-important condom to bed down with campus beauty Judy (Elizabeth Foxx). His late uncle Pinky appears in the hospital as a transparent ghost to take Billy to heaven, but our hero, discovering that a hand motion (reminiscent of Curly's schtick for the Three Stooges) can materialize him as flesh-and-blood, escapes to stay on Earth one more day. Object: get laid.

With chintzy special effects, the pic's ghost gimmick is extraneous, mainly used for an obligatory scene of eavesdropping (invisibly) in the girls' shower room to ogle various siliconed cuties. Grainy photography, muffled sound recording and dinky production values all indicate that picture was ground out carelessly as just another title for market.

Cast is sunk by the material, but executes the pratfalls acceptably. Only surprise is the presence of a Corman mainstay of 15 years ago (in all those Filipino women's prison pictures) Roberta Collins as the perenially drunken wife of the college president. —*Lor.*

A Nightmare On Elm Street, Part 2: Freddy's Revenge
(COLOR)

Solid followup to horror hit should please the same audience.

A New Line Cinema release of a New Line

Cinema, Heron Communications and Smart Egg Pictures presentation of a Robert Shaye production. Produced by Shaye. Executive producers, Stephen Diener, Stanley Dudelson; line producers, Michael Murphey, Joel Soisson; coproducer, Sara Risher. Directed by Jack Sholder. Features entire cast. Screenplay, David Chaskin; camera (Deluxe color; prints by Technicolor), Jacques Haitkin; supervising editor, Arline Garson; editor, Bob Brady; music, Christopher Young; sound, Ed White; assistant director, Matia Karrell; special effects, A&A Special Effects/Dick Albain; Freddy makeup, Kevin Yagher; transformation effects, Mark Shostrom; puppet effects, Rick Lazzarini; special visual effects supervisor, Paul Boyington; stunt coordinator, Dan Bradley; costumes, Gail Viola; casting, Annette Benson. Reviewed at Magno Preview 9 screening room, N.Y., Oct. 17, 1985. (MPAA Rating: R). Running time: **84 MINS.**

Jessee Walsh	Mark Patton
Lisa Poletti	Kim Myers
Grady	Robert Rusler
Mr. Walsh	Clu Gulager
Mrs. Walsh	Hope Lange
Coach Schneider	Marshall Bell
Freddy Krueger	Robert Englund

Beneath its verbose, marquee-busting title, Jack Sholder's followup to Wes Craven's year-old hit is a well-made though familiar reworking of demonic horror material (in the vein of "The Amityville Horror" series). Prospects are very fine for the New Line release, thanks to effective special effects work that will please the target audience.

David Chaskin's screenplay for Part 2 basically makes a sex change on Craven's original: a teenage boy Jesse Walsh (Mark Patton) is experiencing the traumatic nightmares previously suffered by a young girl, Nancy Thompson.

Walsh's family has moved into Thompson's house, five years after the events outlined in the first film. The slouch-hatted, long, steel fingernails-affixed, disfigured monster Freddy (Robert Englund) is attempting to possess Walsh's body in order to kill the local kids once more, and judging from the film's body count, is quite successful. While Walsh's parents (Clu Gulager and Hope Lange) look on in disbelief to the supernatural going-on, the boy enlists the iad of his girl friend Lisa (Kim Myers) and buddy Grady (Robert Rusler) to protect him (and the neighbors) from himself.

Episodic treatment is punched up by an imaginative series of special effects. The standout is a grisly chest-burster setpiece which makes explicit the story's stress on Freddy taking over the heros body and will in order to carry out his nefarious deeds.

Mark Patton carries the show in the central role as not quite a nerd, but strange enough to consistute an outsider presence. Kim Myers scores as his sympathetic girl friend, surmounting her obvious teen lookalike for Meryl Streep image. Reprising his monster role, Robert Englund is a frightening addition to the horror pantheon (and even gets a brief scene as a bus driver, sans his heavy makeup).

Pic could have done without the disappointing (and now almost obligatory) final twist scene, but works overall. Director Sholder is ably supported by Jacques Haitkin's colorful lensing and Christopher Young's dramatic musical score. —*Lor.*

Odd Birds
(COLOR-16m)

Okay Chinese-American success story.

Washington, Oct. 22.

A Pomeranian Pictures presentation. Produced by Jeanne Collachia and Charles A. Domokos. Written and directed by Collachia. Camera (color, 16m), John Morrill; editor, Collachia, Domokos; music, Dick Hamilton. Reviewed at Cine Screening Room, Washington, D.C., Oct. 21, 1985. (No MPAA Rating.) Running time: **90 MINS.**

Brother T.S. Murphy	Michael Moriarty
Joy Chan	Donna Lai Ming Lew
Mrs. Chan	Nancy Yee
Gower Champion	Bruce Gray
Eric	Scott Crawford

Debut helmer Jeanne Collachia enters the territory carved out by Wayne Wang about Chinese-Americans trying to enter mainstream U.S. "How many Chinese movie stars are there in America?" asks Joy Chan's mom in this star-is-hatched youth pic, "Odd Birds."

The misfits hit their pace when Michael Moriarty enters in a likable, contained performance as a high school math teacher in a collar at a parochial school, Brother T.S. Murphy, whose status as an old duck in the religious life encourages young Joy Chan to persist in her dreams. Moriarty is careful not to eclipse Donna Lai Ming Lew's performance as a vulnerable, round-faced wallflower, which the debut thesp carries off with dignity, but sometimes Moriarty's patient modulation is visible.

His concern of Joy sometimes seems to extend beyond the appropriate bounds of "Brother" Murphy, but the script tries to leave the romantic illusions all on Joy's side. She remains dreadfully innocent, considering the number of taboos facing her, not the least of which will be thwarting her family's plan of a nursing career for her.

The final scene reveals Joy's true singing talent in an audition for the late Gower Champion (portrayed by Bruce Gray) who actually is looking for dancers. The number she belts out leaves us believing in her talent, something that had not been established by an opening song in her own attic that, in fact, puts her entire effort into the realm of the improbable. To sympathize with her character, the audience needs to believe in her potential. If the first 20 minutes were pared away to allow Moriarty an earlier entrance, pic would gain momentum and lose little in ambience, and probably discourage dial-flopping at pic's final destination, the discreet side of television. —*Kaja.*

South Bronx Heroes
(COLOR)

Well-meaning but soft approach to a tough topic.

A Continental Inc. release of a Zebra Prods. Ltd, and Walter Manley presentation. Executive producer, Phil Mercogliano. Produced and directed by William Szarka. Features entire cast. Screenplay, Szarka, Don Schiffrin; additional dialog, Marc Shmuger, Mario van Peebles; camera (color), Eric Schmitz; supervising editor, Jim Rivera; editor, Eli Haviv, Szarka; music, Al Zima; additional music, Mitch Herzog; sound, Michael Trujillo; assistant director, Sean Ward; production manager, George Szarka Sr.; associate producers, Jon Kurtis, Schiffrin. Reviewed at RKO National 2 theater, N.Y., Oct. 26, 1985 (No MPAA Rating.) Running time: **85 MINS.**

Paul	Brendan Ward
Tony	Mario van Peebles
Chrissie	Megan van Peebles
Michelle	Melissa Esposito
Bennett	Martin Zurla
Scott	Jordan Abeles

Also with: Barry Lynch, Dan Lauria, Bo Rucker, Sean Ward.

William Szarka's "South Bronx Heroes" is the sort of earnest U.S. indie feature which might play on public tv but lacks the oomph and tough approach to make waves on the action film circuit. Filmed two years ago as "Runaways" (with another alternate title, "Revenge Of The Innocents"), pic is the second theatrical release in the last month from Continental Video.

Unusual story structure presents parallel tales of two sets of brother-sister combos, one white and one black. Paul (Brendan Ward) and Michelle (Melissa Esposito) are, respectively, 14 and 11-year old runaways from their evil foster father Bennett (Martin Zurla), who hole up in the basement of a derelict South Bronx apartment building, scrounging food out of trash cans. Tony (Mario van Peebles), is just out of a Mexican jail and moves in with his sister Chrissie (Megan van Peebles), who earns their keep working as a teacher while Tony loafs.

The two couples meet halfway through the pic when Paul & Michelle (it sounds like a Lewis Gilbert pic) break into the van Peebles' apartment in order to take much-needed showers. Fleeing, Paul accidentally drops his cache of incriminating kiddie porn photos taken by Bennett, who used another foster child, six-year-old Scott (Jordan Abeles) in his porn pictures before killing the kid. When Paul returns to fetch the stills, Tony grabs him and they decide to blackmail Bennett together. A highly artificial happy ending has the young heroes trapping Bennett and turning him over to the FBI.

With child abuse and perils of existence on the South Bronx turf (filmed on location) as topics, Szarka takes an unfortunately wimpy approach, even substituting the artificially squeaky-clean pairs of siblings format for any romantic or sexual content. Hoary use of fadeouts between scenes and generally sluggish pacing hurt as well.

Brendan Ward is impressive as the young hero, particularly in a lengthy monolog recalling how Bennett abused his foster brother Scott. Mario van Peebles is overly theatrical at times, but has some entertaining scenes, especially when he dresses up, referring to himself as "Dark Gable," and serves his sister some "brown champagne" (a bottle of Pepsi). Effective casting has his real-life, beautiful sibling Megan van Pebbles as sister Chrissie. These central performances deserved a more realistic, hardhitting story treatment. —*Lor.*

Nous Etions Les Rois du Monde
(We Were Once The Kings Of The World)
(SWISS-COLOR-DOCU-16m)

Nyon, Oct. 2.

A production of Films Henry Brandt, Geneva, with the Institut du Film, Berne. Director and editor, Brandt; camera (color, 16m), Willy Rohrbach; sound, Jacqueline Brandt. Reviewed at Nyon Film Festival Oct. 19, 1985. Running time: **72 MINS.**

The purpose of this film seems to be encouragement of efforts to salvage and preserve the sweet lifestyle and charm of the picturesque Swiss villages. The film argues that the Old Switzerland must homogenize new incoming technologies, to survive and thus win a new lease on life. If "we were once the kings of the world," then perhaps we can become so again.

Doubtlessly a topic of intense interest to the Swiss, the film and its problems are relevant as well to other nations undergoing threatening social changes. Although overlong, and over-sweet, this is a nice film about nice people having troubles that they now seem determined to solve. —*Hitch.*

Hong-Kong Graffiti
(HONG KONG-COLOR)

Hong Kong, Oct. 2.

A Lo Wai production, released by Golden Princess. Produced by Lo Wai and Hsu Li Hwa. Directed by Terry Tong. Stars Olivia Cheng, Ni Shu Chun, Billie Tan, Polly Chan,

Yeung Kwan, Chan Chun Kwok. Screenplay, Lee Mak; music, Alvin Kwok; lyrics, James Wong; singer, Elisa Chan, production designer, Chiao Chiao.(No other credits provided by producer.) Reviewed at President theater, Hong Kong, Oct. 1, 1985. Running time: **98 MINS.**
(Cantonese soundtrack with English subtitles)

Lovely Olivia Cheng is a successful career woman in Hong Kong in a promotions-ad agency, whose entire family has immigrated to Canada. She is having an affair with a divorced middle-aged man (Yeung Kwan) who has a teen-age daughter (Ni Shu Chun).

The problems begin when Olivia's sister-in-law Polly Chan from China, who's about to be divorced, decides to live in Hong Kong. From a country bumpkin we see the transformation of the provincial woman to a typical Hong Kong lass of ambition with greed who would stop at nothing to get what she wants.

Olivia's parents die in a car crash and she is suddenly all alone. She now values a more lasting relationship (not the weekend type), or one night stands, but something more permanent.

"Hong Kong Graffiti" is a Cantonese film with serious substance and a potent message about life and living in a busy transitory environment that inhibits closeness and possible deep emotional ties. Screenwriter Lee Mak has fashioned and sensitively molded characters that jell realistically and intelligently from fragments to a solid scenario uncommon in Hong Kong-made films.

Olivia Cheng is perfect as the citified girl as is Polly Chan who does not lose her provincialism despite the trappings of material wealth. The supporting cast provides the right emotional convolutions.—*Mel.*

Festa di Laurea
(Graduation Party)
(ITALIAN-COLOR)

Rome, Oct. 28.
A D.M.V. release. Produced by Antonio Avati for DUE-A Films, Dania Cinematografica, Filmes Intl. and National Cinematografica. Directed by Pupi Avati. Stars Aurore Clément, Carlo Delle Piane. Screenplay, Pupi Avati, Antonio Avati; camera (Telecolor), Pasquale Rachini; editor, Amadeo Salfa; music, Riz Ortolani. Reviewed at Quirinale, Rome, Oct. 27, 1985. Running time: **96 MINS.**

Vanni . . . . Carlo Delle Piane
Gaia . . . . Aurore Clément
Daughter Sandra . . . . Lidia Broccolino
Nicola . . . . Nik Novecento

After that somewhat anomalous "Employees," set in a modern bank, Pupi Avati is back with one of his better Bolognese country comedies, a period pic in the vein of "A School Outing." Penned with Pupi's brother-producer Antonio Avati, script makes the gentle heart of eccentric character actor Carlo Delle Piane beat for the unattainable bourgeoise Aurore Clément. Pic has a sharper aftertaste than previous works by this helmer and more acute social vision. It has done well onshore and can be expected to receive offshore play in specialized houses.

Rimini of 1950 is a small town where ordinary people live, like Vanni (Delle Piane) the baker, his gawky teenage son Nicola (Nik Novecento) and his divorced wife, who works on the beach burying customers in the sand for dubious health reasons. In another category altogether are the "chic," monied crowd from Bologna, who come to spend a few days now and then in their beach houses. To this group belong Gaia (Clément), her philandering husband, her lying daughter, and snooty friends.

Vanni has worshiped Gaia ever since the day, 10 years before, she impulsively gave him a kiss on the cheek on hearing the news Italy had declared war. When she asks him to remodel her country house and organize a graduation party for her daughter Sandra (Lidia Broccolino), he goes into debt to advance the money for the work.

Pic builds slowly as it follows the stages of rebuilding and several innocent love intrigues. Besides Vanni's dreams about his employer, Nicola has more concrete designs on Sandra, while one of the local boys working for Vanni sneaks off to see a pretty vacationer from the city. She belongs to yet a third group of characters who run in and out of the film, a comical bunch of working folk from Bologna who, in 1950, want to go back and brag to their friends they've been "on vacation."

Characters are drawn sharply throughout, and Avati gets just the right tone and nuance from his principals. Stock player Delle Piane gives a standout performance as the humble little baker, the embodiment of common sense and integrity even when he knows he's the victim of an illusion. In the end the party is a dismal failure, Sandra doesn't even graduate (she doctored up her report cards), and Gaia and her husband let Vanni foot the bill. The baker is left to chalk it up bitterly as a "present" to the woman he loves.
— *Yung.*

Krush Groove
(COLOR)

Minor rap musical.

Hollywood, Oct. 22.
A Warner Bros. release. Produced by Michael Schultz and Doug McHenry. Exec producers, George A. Jackson, Robert O. Kaplan. Directed by Michael Schultz. Features entire cast. Screenplay, Ralph Farquhar; camera (Technicolor), Ernest Dickerson; editor, Alan J. Koslowski, Jerry Bixman, Conrad M. Gonzalez; sound, Lawrence Loe-winger; production design, Mischa Petrow; costumes, Dianne Finn-Chapman; coproducer, Russell Simmons; assistant director, Dwight Williams; choreography, Lori Eastside; music, various artists; casting, Pat Golden. Reviewed at The Burbank Studios, Brubank, Calif., Oct. 21, 1985. (MPAA Rating: R.) Running time: **97 MINS.**

Russell . . . . Blair Underwood
Run . . . . Joseph Simmons
Sheila E. Sheila E.
Fat Boys . . . . Mark Morales, Damon
Wimbley, Darren
(Buffy) Robinson
DMC . . . . Daryll McDaniels
Jam Master Jay . . . . Jason Mizell
Kurtis Blow . . . . Kurtis Blow
Jay B . . . . Richard E. Gant
Aisha . . . . Lisa Gay Hamilton
Rev. Walker . . . . Daniel Simmons
Rick . . . . Rick Rubin
Sal . . . . Sal Abbatiello
Terri . . . . Charles Stettler

Beyond a bare pretense at plot, "Krush Groove" is really no more than 97 minutes of the current rock and rappin' fad, meaning it may front for those who want to get down and get chilled or whatever else the younger set does these days. For anybody else, subtitles would have helped.

Given the outcry over porn and pop music, though, the picture does offer an interesting footnote, introducing the underage audience to the basic dramatic structure — if not content — of the average X-rated film.

In those, of course, the hero says, "Hi, I'm here to do the windows" and the action starts until somebody says "let's go to Mary's house" and there's 10 seconds of exteriors before the action starts again, etc.

As directed by Michael Schultz and written by Ralph Farquhar, "Krush" is a bit more ambitious than that, but not much. Quickly introducing its rapertoire company — Run-DMC, Sheila E., The Fat Boys and Kurtis Blow — as unknown street kids in New York City, "Krush" consumes several musical numbers before young manager Blair Underwood needs financing to press the records to meet demands for Run-DMC's first hit.

After a few more raps, Underwood borrows a bundle from sinister Richard E. Gant. More rap and he's had a falling out with brother Joseph Simmons ("Run") over Sheila E. and a recording contract.

More rap and more rock and Underwood is left behind while the performers move on to stardom and he's got the problem of paying off Gant. More rap and the old gang comes back to help him out and they all rap happily ever after.

Oh yes, there's a subplot of the Fat Boys who rap and walk up and down the street and eat gluttonously until they get to be big stars, too.

Story aside, however, there's no question that the performers exhibit infectious energy and more than passing ability with high-speed, tongue-twisting rhymes, all pounded out to a booming beat and flashy choreography. Perhaps more praise is even due beyond what's evident, but subcultures do enjoy their secrets, and are entitled to them.
—*Har.*

Macaroni
(Maccheroni)
(ITALIAN-COLOR)

A Paramount Pictures release of a Filmauro-Massfilm production. Produced by Luigi & Aurelio De Laurentiis and Franco Committeri. Directed by Ettore Scola. Stars Jack Lemmon, Marcello Mastroianni. Sceenplay, Ruggero Maccari, Furio Scarpelli, Scola; camera (Eastmancolor), Claudio Ragona; editor, Carla Simoncelli; music, Armando Trovajoli; sound, Carlo Palmieri; production design, Luciano Ricceri; set decorator, Ezio Di Monte; costumes, Nanà Cecchi. Reviewed at Paramount screening room, N.Y., Oct. 10, 1985. (MPAA Rating: PG.) Running time: **104 MINS.**

Bob Traven . . . . Jack Lemmon
Antonio Jasiello . . . . Marcello Mastroianni
Laura De Falco . . . . Daria Nicolodi
Carmelina Jasiello . . . . Isa Danieli
Also with: Maria Luisa Saniella, Patrizzia Sacchi, Bruno Esposito, Marc Berman, Jean-François Pérriere, Fabio Tenore.

"Macaroni" is a mild comedy-drama teaming the formidable talents of Jack Lemmon and Marcello Mastroianni. Stronger in expression of honest sentiment than in its humorous component, the picture faces weak theatrical prospects via Paramount release as a pickup. It was originally scheduled to be an HBO Premiere Films presentation domestically (a slot it would fill comfortably) until the pay-cable outfit dropped out of the project.

Jack Lemmon toplines as Bob Traven (the joke on the mysterious novelist B. Traven's name is never made explicit here), a v.p. at McDonnell Douglas visiting Naples as a consultant to Aeritalia. It's his first time back there since 1946 when, as a G.I., he was stationed there.

An acquaintance from that period whom he has completely forgotten, Antonio Jasiello (Marcello Mastroianni) looks Traven up and takes the at-first unwilling (too busy) American around town to meet the family and friends.

It seems that everybody knows Traven, because Jasiello has been surreptitiously writing letters using Traven's name over the years to his own sister Maria, who had a brief romance in 1946 with the American. She's long-since been married and now has adult grandchildren.

Relying too heavily on its two stars, at first abrasive adversaries but later best of friends as Lemmon unbends to Mastroianni's exuberant *joie de vivre,* "Macaroni" rarely achieves the comedic heights of director Ettore Scola's previous work. There simply isn't an abundance of funny situations or witty dialog here.

Best sequence has amateur playwright Mastroianni filling in as the villain in one of his monthly poverty productions. Heavily made-up (and looking oddly like the late Ernie Kovacs), Mastroianni is genuinely funny in the brief skit acted with Italian dialog.

Elsewhere, this English-language film is hampered by the dialog, with merely okay readings by Mastroianni, artificial dubbing of Isa Danieli as his empathetic wife and rote, direct-sound speeches by Daria Nicolodi as Aeritalia's p.r. officer. Thesps' acting is okay but diluted by the language distraction.

Lemmon throws himself into his role with customary passion, pumping life into some routine scenes. Pic would have benefited from some period flashback material set in 1946 (especially given Scola's memorably nostalgic work in his 1974 "We All Loved Each Other So Much") but is rooted in the present. A contrived, melancholy ending doesn't come off.

Tech credits are merely adequate, with Naples' natural beauty shining through Claudio Ragona's strictly functional photography. —*Lor.*

Het Kortste Eind
(The Wrong End Of The Rope)
(DUTCH-DOCU-COLOR-16m)

Amsterdam, Oct. 17.

A D.D. Filmproductions production. Produced by Phil van der Linden. Directed by Corla Risseeuw. Camera (color, 16m) Cees Samson; script and research, Risseeuw, Kamala Peiris; sound, Otto Horsch; editor, Teresa Caldas. Reviewed at Filmmuseum, Amsterdam, Oct. 4, 1985. Running time: 82 MINS.

There are some 25,000 female coir workers in Sri Lanka. (Coir is a fiber derived from coconut husk.) Officially they supplement the family income in their spare time. In reality, most of them work fulltime, in addition to their tasks as mothers and homemakers.

They work for the local or regional middleman who is also owner of the only local store. Wages are low, prices high. The middleman will make personal loans at fabulous interest rates.

The coir industry is in decline. Man-made fibers are cheaper, uniform, easier to process than the natural coir. It lasts longer, but that consideration has a low priority nowadays.

Carla Risseeuw is a Dutch sociologist who has studied the coir workers' problems since 1977. She has made an eminently viewable docu, beautifully photographed by Cees Samson. The main plot is about some of the women who form a co-operative to grade the coir themselves and sell it directly to exporters. They were opposed by the middlemen and some of the husbands who saw their status endangered. The women succeeded, but it remains to be seen if their co-op can survive in view of international market conditions.

Risseeuw did not make a sociological docu about downtrodden paragons or near-saints. The women in the film bicker and gossip (passionately), cheat and giggle, pray, look after their families, and are wonderfully alive.

The scenario was cleared and the players chosen by the women themselves. Pic preemed at the U.N. Women's Conference in Nairobi last July. It was funded by the Ministry of Foreign Affairs in the Hague, and deserves to be seen at universities, and fests. There are Dutch and English versions.

— *Wall.*

To Kollie
(The Necklace)
(GREEK-COLOR)

Salonica, Oct. 5.

A Greek Film Center, Nikos Kanakis Prod. Written and directed by Nikos Kanakis. Dialog, Yannis Negrapontis; camera (color), Alexis Grivas; editor, Nikos Kanakis; sound, Dinos Kittou; sound mixing, Thanassis Arvanitis. Reviewed at the Thessaloniki Film Festival, Oct. 5, 1985. Running time: 90 MINS.

With: Antonis Antoniou, Sofia Mirmingou, Minas Hatzisavvas, Jenny Kaliva, Maria Marmarinou, Chritos Simandaris, Fotis Polychronopoulos.

Whatever merits this comedy might have on its own home ground, it is hard to imagine it transferring to any other market. Excessively talky, very static, devoid of any character development and extremely loud, "The Necklace" offers a series of sitcom situations that are hardly original and beats them to death.

The plot follows the efforts of several people to lay hands on an inheritance left by a despicable general. They play up to his widow, who makes the most of it as long as she is around. It is supposed to be a satire on middle class rapacity, in all its ugliness. Indeed, none of the characters elicits the least sympathy, but that is hardly sufficient to flesh out an entire feature.

Acting is very loud and overdone. Dialog, according to some Greek critics, has puns that are untranslatable. —*Edna.*

The Unwritten Law
(HONG KONG-COLOR)

Hong Kong, Oct. 5.

A Seasonal Film (H.K.) Corp. production, released by the Golden Harvest theater circuit. Produced by Ng See Yuen. Directed by Ng See Yuen. Stars Lau Tak Wah, Yip Tak Han (Deanie Ip), Nam Kit Ying, Tang Lai Ying, Lai Siu Ming, Chun Pin. Art direction, Poon Hung; camera (color), Ma Kwun Wah; assistant director, Poon Hung. (No other credits provided by producer.) Reviewed at Ocean Theater, Hong Kong, Oct. 3, 1985. Running time: 98 MINS.
(Cantonese soundtrack with English subtitles)

In "The Unwritten Law," Lau Che Pang is an intellgient boy, raised in an orphanage managed by a Catholic mission. He grows up to be handsome Lau Tak Wah, who is admitted to a British law school in London on a scholarship.

Many years later, Lau returns with his girlfriend Annie Lam who is from a rich family. Through Annie's influential father, Lau finds work in a top Hong Kong law firm.

Lau soon gets tied up in a murder case involving the bizarre killing of a rich businessman. The accused is an aging prostitute from the poor Western District.

It is a difficult case that nobody wants to handle, but the idealistic Lau takes a keen professional interest. After meeting the defendant (in a melodramatic situation staged by singer-turned-actress Deanie Ip), Lau is convinced she is innocent and agrees to be her attorney.

The story, general mood and presentation are extremely old-fashioned, but the film is doing well at the domestic boxoffice.

The success of this feature will surely give birth to more of the same to join the bandwagon in the four-hankie tearjerker genre. —*Mel.*

Los Motivos de Luz
(Luz' Reasons)
(MEXICAN-COLOR)

San Sebastian, Sept. 26.

A Chimalistac Postproduccion presentation. Production Manager, Carlos Resendi. Executive producer, Enrique Cuanda. Produced by Hugo Scherer. Directed by Felipe Cazals. Screenplay, Xavier Robles; camera (color), Angel Goded; editor, Sigfrido Garcia. Reviewed at Cine Victoria Eugenia, San Sebastian Film Festival, Sept. 26, 1985. Running time: 117 MINS.

With: Martha Aura, Ana Ofelia Murguia, Alsono Echanove, Carlota Villagran, Dunia Saldivar, Adriana Rojo, Georgina Chavira, Maria Prado, José Angel Garcia, Carlos Cardan.

"Luz' Reasons" is a quasi-documentary filmic investigation of a case in which a mother of four children living in a Mexican slum strangled her offspring. Director Felipe Cazals presents the yarn from the perspective of two social workers cum lawyers who question the accused in multiple sessions, trying to find out what motivated her.

These scenes are intercut with flashbacks of the woman's life of despair in the slum, scenes in a woman's prison as she awaits trial and interviews with some of her neighbors. No answer is ever found. Cazals reflects effectively upon the sordid social conditions of a large sector of Mexicans which on occasion gives rise to such desperate and tragic outbursts of violence.

Pic is by its very nature slow and talky. An excellent performance by Martha Aura as the murderess adds a dimension of realism. —*Besa.*

Irith, Irith
(ISRAELI-COLOR)

Tel Aviv, Sept. 29.

A Noah Films Presentation of a G&G production. Produced by Itzhak Kol. Written and directed by Naftali Alter, based on an original idea by Irith Alter and Irith Razili. Camera (color), Gad Danzig; editor, David Tur; art director, Michal Yeffet; music, Naftali Alter. Reviewed at Tevath Noah screening room; Tel Aviv, Sept. 28, 1985. Running time: 90 MINS.

Irith Shor . . . . Irith Alter
Irith Katz . . . . Liora Grossman
Benny Shor . . . . Hanan Goldblatt
Ronnie Shor . . . . Ronnie Pinkovitch
Irith Katz' Suitor . . . . Oded Be'eri

After years of producing films for his former partner, Assi Dayan, and writing music for them, Naftali Alter is trying his hand, for the first time, at directing in "Irith, Irith" with mixed results. His inexperience is evident in the direction of actors and dramatic situations. His gentle, sympathetic approach to the characters, however, atones for many of his sins.

The script is based on an idea originating with Alter's wife, Irith, and a friend of hers, also named Irith. In its final form it reads as a romantic comedy with feminist undertones. It is the age-old story of two women each of whom discovers she is unhappy with her identity and would gladly exchange it for the other one's.

The first Irith is a successful lawyer, a single woman navigating from one lover to another with easy insouciance. The second Irith is married to a surgeon, has a son and a daughter and feels trapped by her home, her family and her routine. She doesn't know anything about it, until Irith the lawyer moves next to her, bringing a whiff of sweet liberty. Thanks to a pretty transparent and not very original plot, the two grow closer until the change of identity is effected, without any protest from the husband who doesn't mind as long as food is on the table and there is a neighbor next door, to peep at when she takes a shower.

Whatever semblance of realism or social significance the story carries initially, is soon dispelled as its style slips into farce, fortunately devoid of the usual vulgarities marring many local comedies.

The leading actresses, Irith Alter (the one whose idea started the film) and Liora Grossman, are both beginners in film, their acting shaky and not always in control. Hanan Goldblatt, as the insensitive, mixed-up surgeon, is much more experienced, but soon falls into his usual grotesque pattern. — *Edna.*

Thermokipio
(Greenhouse)
(GREEK-COLOR)

Salonica, Oct. 1.

A Greek Film Center and Vaguelis Serdaris production. Written and directed by Serdaris. Features Tassos Halkias, Christina Theodoropoulos, Chritos Daktylides, Yannis Kyriakidis. Camera (color), Theordore Marguas, sets and costumes, Despina Athanassiadou; music, Michalis Christodoulides; editor, Panos Kyriacopoulos; sound, Th. Georgiades. Reviewed at the Thessaloniki Film Fest, Oct. 1, 1985. Running time: **112 MINS.**

Vaguelis Serdaris' "Greenhouse" is a mediocre effort describing the inner fight between a man's principles and his ambition.

The story is set in 1975 when Stelios, a man in his 30s returns to Athens from Germany where he studied law. He pays a brief visit to his mother in their native village and comes back to Athens to work as an assistant at a prominent lawyer's office. He is opposed to his boss' methods and soon resigns to open his own office accepting, however, the financial support and sexual favors of his ex-boss' wife.

His girl, Mariana, does not want him. She copes with her own life, cultivating a greenhouse inherited from an uncle. Compromising his feelings to succeed professionally, he sets more and more involved in the demands of his career.

Thesp credit goes to Christina Theodoropoulos very convincing in her determination and vulnerability. Tassos Halkias is good in the central role.

Camerawork and other technical aspects are up to standard. — *Rena.*

Working Class
(HONG KONG-COLOR)

Hong Kong, Sept. 1.

A Cinema City production, release by Golden Princess. Directed by Tsui Hark. Stars Sam Hui, Teddy Robin, Tsui Hark, Angie-Leon Leung, Wong Joe Yin. Executive producer, Catherine Hun; associate producer, Andy Ma; screenplay, Chan Kam-kuen; art direction, Yiu Yau Hung; music Teddy Robin; camera (color), Henry Chan; production design, Lo Yuk Ying; editor, David Wu. Reviewed at President theater, Hong Kong, Sept. 1, 1985. Running time: **98 MINS.**
(Cantonese soundtrack with English subtitles)

In "Working Class," Yam (Sam Hui), Sunny (Tsui Hark) and Ah Hing (Teddy Robin) portray good friends, all dismissed for creating havoc in their jobs.

The trio later are employed by a noodle factory which has very poor labor relations. The manager, supervisor and foreman always pick on their subordinates. The workers decide to take a united front to oppose their superiors. Caught in this situation between romantic and financial problems is the trio.

Yam meets a beautiful girl, Amy (Wong Joe Yin) who is the daughter of the proprietor of the noodle factory. A series of lighthearted events happen as Yam tries to court her.

The plant's electricity is cut as a result of overdue payment and brings on a crisis. Realizing Amy's father is in deep financial trouble, the workers decide to use manual labor to carry on production. The stricken factory survives to the credit of its workers.

"Working Class" is a standard comedy lined with a bit of satire.
— *Mel.*

Pink Nights
(COLOR-16m)

Nice, squeaky clean teen sex comedy.

Chicago, Oct. 10.

A Koch/Marschall production. Produced by Phillip Koch and Sally Marschall. Written and directed by Koch. Camera (color, 16m), Charlie Lieberman; editor, Koch, Marschall; set design, Gail Specht; costumes, Rachel Herbener; music, Jim Tullio, Jeffery Vanston; sound, Hans Roland; choreography, Shaun Allen, Don Franklin. Reviewed at Facets Multimedia, Chicago, Oct. 9, 1985. (No MPAA Rating.) Running time: **84 MINS.**

Terry	Shaun Allen
Danny	Kevin Anderson
Esme	Peri Kaczmarek
Jeff	Larry King
Zero	Jonathan Jancovic Michaels
Marcy	Jessica Vitkus
Bruno	Mike Bacarella
Pop	Ron Dean
Ralph the Lounge Lizard	Tom Towles
Danny's Mother	Denyse Leahy

Debut helmer Phillip Koch has blazed a new detour with this competent teen sex comedy *sans* sex. With a soundtrack by rockers Bohemia, it could find audiences among preteens and make safe vid-viewing with its teasing, alluring limning of teen fun without baring a single supple thigh. Per Koch, younger girls are intimidated by older girls' state of undress, and his credibility is reinforced by previous credits, revolving around teenage sexuality, for which he has won a string of prizes.

Kevin Anderson delivers a likeable performance as Danny, a diffident kid who is too nice and not too hip. His friend Jeff takes the opposite approach and hits on girls constantly, but their scores total zero. Both actors have the gangly rubber-legged movements of insecure teenagers, making for credible adolescence.

Shaun Allen plays Terry, daughter of two punked-out motorcycle mavens who find her too straight. After first picking up Danny on a bet, she finds herself dropping in on him looking for a place to sleep, only to crash a romantic scene he is attempting in his mother's absence with the utterly gorgeous Esme. The fragility of Peri Kaczmarek as Esme makes for a nice contrast with yet another girl mad for Danny's company, the pseudo-sophisticated deb Marcy, played tough by Jessica Vitkus. In short, thesp credits are tops, and even the marginal roles are expanded with a charming humor. Tom Towles deserves a hand for his sleazy lounge lizard.

Plot takes its twists and turns around Danny's stability being destabilized by three girls moving in with him looking for family, not for love. They redecorate Danny's room as an Arabian tent, giving the set designer some imaginative opportunities. Danny's mother comes home to find an apartment full of kids, but what looks to her like an orgy turns out to be more like an orphanage, and she becomes a den mother. A happy ending finds the kids affectionately pairing off as well as being reunited with their families, all in a spare and gently paced pic.

Cute dialog and straightforward lensing are interrupted only once by a rather implausible pause as Danny waxes a bit too clever in a punk club by giving a speech that stalls the action and the ensuing chase, which also fails to distinguish Koch as an action director. With his feet firmly on midwestern ground, Koch can create light fare for average kids. —*Kaja.*

Bordello
(GREEK-COLOR)

Rimini, Sept. 26.

A Profilm/Greek Film Center production. Directed by Nikos Koundouros. Screenplay, Vangelis Goufas, Angel Wagestein; camera (color), Nikos Kavoukidis; editor, Alexis Pezas; music, Nikos Mamangakis; sound, Thanasis Georgiadis; set design, Michel Karapiperis; costumes, George Pastas. Reviewed at European Film Fest, Rimini, Italy, Sept. 26, 1985. Running time: **130 MINS.**

With: Marina Vlady (Rosa Bonaparte), Eleonora Stathopoulou (Sarah), Vassilis Lagos (Vassilis), Aris Retsos (Homer), Agapi Manoura (Emma), Vladimir Smirnof (The Russian Captain), Antigone Amanitou (Antigone), Fanis Hinas (Captain Mason).
(English-language soundtrack)

Based on real events associated with a 19th century rebellion on the island of Crete, "Bordello" seems inspired by genuine passions, but they are buried beneath an incoherent script and ludicrous dialog.

Thirteen whores arrive on the island of Crete in 1897, just after a local rebellion against the Turks has been put down by an Allied flotilla of British, French, Italian, and Russian warships. The first thing they see as they step ashore is an execution by firing squad. We meet a lot of characters in brief vignettes; the Madame, Rosa Bonaparte (Marina Vlady), the whores, soldiers, a disappointed revolutionary artist named Vassilis (Vassilis Lagos), and various Cretan collaborators with the Allies.

Vassilis' sister is married in a funereal wedding ceremony. When the newlyweds are murdered, Vassilis finds out who did it and kills the murderer and his entire family. A crazy woman burns down the whorehouse, and the prostitutes move on to the next port, leaving behind their washed-up Madame.

Despite a creditable performance by Marina Vlady and well-controlled, if extreme, art direction, the pleasures of sustained ranting aren't enough to carry this "Caligula"-like trip into the lower depths.

Obsessively filthy dialog is delivered in whispers. National stereotypes of the most primitive kind stand in for plot, but are hard to follow because they are played by Greeks in thickly accented English, speaking lines that bear no relationship to English syntax as we know it. A slow pace, disembodied sound, and hand-held camerawork don't help.—*Brom.*

Tacos Altos
(High Heels)
(ARGENTINE-COLOR)

Buenos Aires, Oct. 22.

An Argentina Sono Film presentation of a Chango production. Executive producer, Jorge Velasco. Directed by Sergio Renán. Stars Susú Pecoraro. Screenplay, Máximo Soto, Renán, based upon Bernardo Kordon's short stories; camera (Eastmancolor), Daniel Karp; editor, Carlos Márquez; music, Pocho Lapouble, Pablo, Ziegler; assistant director, Horacio Guisado; costumes, Nora Renán. Reviewed at the Ambassador theatre, B.A., Sept. 5, 1985. Running time: **90 MINS.**

Luisa	Susú Pecoraro
Rubén	Miguel Angel Solá
Herminda	Ana Maria Picchio
Tula	Arturo Maly
Nato	Willie Lemos
Antonio	Julio De Grazia
Don Domingo	Franklin Caicedo
Fabián	Alejandro Copley
Amalia	Chany Mallo
Julián	Cacho Espíndola
Cholo	Juan Leyrado

Loosely based on two short stories by Bernardo Kordon, "High Heels" has an uneven script that compensates its lack of a solid structure with the keen observations of characters and situations (within a given psychosociological context) that were the late writer's main gifts.

Director Sergio Renán — who got an Oscar nomination in 1975 with "La Tregua" (The Truce) — has attained an overall satisfying entertainment, as good b.o. results indicate.

Susú Pecoraro, winner of the best actress award at Karlovy Vary for her performance in "Camila," plays here a sort of young Gelsomina from the pampas "working" as a streetwalker in Buenos Aires with her elder sister Ana María Picchio. Latter urges Susú to go back to their rural hometown to convince their family to move to B.A. because she needs someone to take care of her illegitimate baby.

Susú, after being savagely raped by her resentful former boyfriend and his cronies, returns to the big city with her mother Chany Mallo and her 10-year-old brother Alejandro Copley, since her humble but honest father chose to remain at home.

Sur'. starts an affair with a mediocre painter, Miguel Angel Solá, then upgrades as prostitute by joining the staff of a massage parlor. When for reasons of taste, she refuses to go to bed with a client, she is fired and returns to the freedom of the streets.

Her sister scorns her for her lack of professional ethics while her lover turns against her the rage of frustration, but she finds solace in a true friendship with Willie Lemos, a cheerful, streetwise transvestite who teaches her some secrets of the trade. Willie is eventually killed in a fight with a potential client, Solá abandons Susú after a wild picnic with her uninhibited friends and she resumes her streetwalker's routine seemingly unscathed despite all that happened to her.

Susú Pecoraro clicks as the ignorant, free-spirited, wishful-thinking prostitute used to accept happiness and sadness, love and hate, as short-lived experiences, but instinctively faithful to her self-esteem. Ana María Picchio also shines with the funny matter-of-fact outbursts of an archetypically amoral whore. Ditto Willie Lemos as the screwball gay, especially when wearing female garb. The other members of the generally able cast have less chance to excel.

Photography is good; other technical credits okay. — *Nubi.*

Destroyer Of Illusion/Lord Of The Dance
(FRENCH-U.S.-DOCU-COLOR-16m)

Nyon, Oct. 15.

A Skywalker production, Paris. Executive Producer, Franz-Christoph Giercke. Directed by Richard Kohn. Camera (color), Jorg Jeschel; editor, Noun Serra; sound, Barbara/Becker; narration script, Amanda-Beth Uhry; translations from the Tibetan, Kohn; narrator, Peter Hudson. Reviewed at Nyon Film Festival, Oct. 14, 1985. Running time: **105 MINS.**

The American Tibetologist Richard Kohn, 37, spent seven years studying the Mani-Rimdu Festival and translating its obscure texts. This film signals his debut as a film director.

Theme of this film on Tibetan religious life: everything is impermanent, and to achieve absolute freedom, one must overcome desire, hate and ignorance, the three destructive no-no's preventing the full

life. The film was shot in Nepal, adjacent to Mount Everest, in monasteries dependent on contributions from poor communities. These Sherpas and Tibetans preserve a unique way of life and a special vision of the world. The film chronicles closely the daily routine of these Buddhist monks and nuns.

"Destroyer Of Illusion" deserves a salute for its having penetrated a secret world, although it is doubtful that the film can have general distribution. —*Hitch.*

Fiebre de Amor
(Love Fever)
(MEXICAN-COLOR)

Santiago, Sept. 22.

A Televicine production. Written and directed by René Cardona Jr. Camera (color), Raúl Domínguez; musical arrangements, León Rey; choreography, Milton Ghio. Reviewed at Cine Santa Lucia, Santiago, Chile, Sept. 21, 1985. Running time: **99 MINS.**

With: Luis Miguel, Lucerito, Guillermo Murray, Lorena Velázquez, Mónica Sandoz Navarro, Carlos Monden and Maribel Fernández (La Pelangocha).

Whatever the quality of his films, 16-year-old singer Luis Miguel provides Mexican cinema with the sort of hit it has lacked for a long time in Spanish America. His audiences are mostly in their early teens, but there are also younger kids (plus their parents).

In "Fiebre de Amor," Miguel plays himself on a visit to Acapulco, where a concert is scheduled. Lucerito is a fan who, while listening to his songs (of which there are plenty) constantly daydreams about him. On occasion, in an amusing role reversal, she imagines herself a star, followed by Miguel as a fervent fan.

Once they actually meet, about two-thirds through the film, it's downhill all the way. The screenplay clumsily introduces mayhem as Lucerito becomes an unwitting witness to a murder, is pursued by the villains and, on the way picks up Miguel as a protector. In the end, safe again and with the baddies put away, they walk hand in hand into a colorful sunset.

The principals and their songs are pleasant enough, but René Cardona Jr.'s direction is poor and almost primitive. Particularly poor are the chase scenes around a condominium and later in cars. The acting in some 10 supporting roles is mostly unsatisfactory. As Miguel grows up and faces audiences in a less naive age range, he certainly will need better crafted films. —*Amig.*

Tigipió
(Tigipió)
(BRAZILIAN-COLOR)

Brasilia, Sept. 29.

An Embrafilme release of an Animatographo/Embrafilme production. Directed by Pedro Jorge de Castro. Features entire cast. Screenplay, Pedro Jorge de Castro and Carlos Alberto Ratton, based on the novel "Tigipió," by Herman Lima; camera (Eastman color), Miguel Freire; editor, José Tavares de Barros; music, Ednardo; sound, Chiquinho de Souza. Reviewed at Cine Brasilia, XVIII Brasilia Festival of Brazilian Film, Sept. 28, 1985. Running time: **100 MINS.**

With: José Dumont, B. de Paiva, Regina Dourado, João Falcão, Ricardo Guilherme, Lilian Mendel.

The novel which inspired "Tigipió" takes place in the Brazilian northeastern state of Ceará during the first decade of this century. The region is suffering from the habitual lack of rain. Colonel Cesario, once a wealthy man, now a poor widower, lives there with his only daughter, Matilde. An engineer, Heitor, comes from the big city to work on a government project. He gives work to Cesario in order to be free to romance his daughter. Questions of honor and misery generate a conflict that leads to tragedy.

Working with scenery international audiences know very well from "Barren Lives" by Nelson Pereira dos Santos, Pedro Jorge resumes the theme which almost became a trademark of the Brazilian cinema of the '60s, and develops an emotional plot full of elegance and dignity. His images are almost always strong and beautiful, fully integrating the scenery into the dramatic necessities.

Helping out is effective camera-work by Miguel Freire, music by Ceará-born composer Ednardo and solid acting by José Dumont (doubtless one of the best Brazilian actors today), Regina Dourado and B. de Paiva. —*Hoin.*

To Aroma Tis Violetas
(The Scent Of Violets)
(GREEK-COLOR)

Salonica, Oct. 4.

A Greek Film Center-Maria Gavala production. Written and directed by Maria Gavala. Features Yota Festa, Maritina Passari, Nicos Kamtsis, Akis Davis, Yannis Hatziyannis. Camera (color), Philippos Koutsaftis; sets and costumes, Amalia Michaelidou; sound, Marinos Athanassopoulos; editor, Despo Maroulakou. Reviewed at the Thessaloniki Film Festival, Oct. 4, 1985. Running time: **91 MINS.**

Maria Gavala's "The Scent Of Violets" is a disappointing, naive story about the painful shattering of a girl's romantic dreams.

Dina is a cynical modern girl who wants to succeed by any means. Her cousin Ismene is a sensitive girl who reads romantic novels, dreaming of someday meeting an ideal man to marry. Dina persuads her to rob their grandmother with the help of a gay cousin. Dina spends her share of the stolen money in a couple of days and succeeds in becoming an actress. Ismene does not touch the

cursed money and later gives more of it to the gay cousin who wishes desperately to leave the country.

Ismene's dreams are shattered when she realizes the man she hoped would love her is her cousin's lover. Coming face to face with the bitter reality of life, she agrees to marry an old friend who truly loves her.

Yota Festa tries hard to be convincing in a role charged with monologs and Maritina Passari is efficient in support. —*Rena.*

Caso Cerrado
(Closed Case)
(SPANISH-COLOR)

Valencia, Oct. 8.

A Tango Producciones S.A. film. Produced by Concha Infante. Directed by Juan Caño Arecha. Screenplay, J.C. Arecha, Gonzalo Goicoechea; camera (Eastmancolor), Alfredo Mayo; editor, Jolio Peã; sound, Carlos Faruolo; sets, Tony Cortés; music, Luis Mendo and Bernardo Feverrigel. Reviewed at Cine Marti, Valencia, Spain, Oct. 8, 1985. Running Time: **90 MINS.**
Isabel . . . . Pepa Flores
César . . . . Patxi Bisquert
Mother . . . . Encarna Paso
Teresa . . . . Isabel Mestres
Also with: Santiago Ramos, José Viv, Lola Gaos, Nacho Martinez, Fernando Delgado, Antonio Banderas.

Neophyte helmer Juan Caño Arecha goes off on so many tacks in "Closed Case" he never hits the bull's eye, though he does at least keep things lively. Pic lurches between prison scenes, a mysterious cover-up of a bank scandal, and rather vague criticism of Spain's court system, none of it effectively handled.

For no obvious reason, scripters decided to make the central character a rabbi's son (Patxi Bisquert), married to a Jewish girl (Pepa Flores, a.k.a. Marisol). This paragon of liberalism is a conscientious objector, and activist in all liberal causes and, rather incongruously, a supposedly brilliant banker.

Before long he's gotten himself into multiple dilemmas. He neglects his new wife, tries to reveal bank irregularities, and finally is thrown into prison to await trial for forging a check. After a hunger strike (never shown) and for no immediately obvious reason, he commits suicide.

Motivations throughout pic are tissue thin. Worse, the whole negative yarn is told in flashback, thereby diminishing any potential element of suspense. The Jewish element is barely alluded to after the opening scenes, nor is the battler for lost causes theme adequately followed up.—*Besa.*

I Played It For You
(DOCU-COLOR-16m)

Vanity production.

Hollywood, Oct. 23.

A Ronee Blakley production. Produced, directed, written by Blakley. Camera (Du Art color), Ed Lachman; additional photography, Wim Wenders; additional camera, Tony St. Jacques, Pat Darrin; editor, Elton Soltes; music composed by Blakley; music produced by Rob Fraboni; sound, Maryte Kavaliauskas; executive producer of Shangri La segments, Chris Sievernich; associate producers, Kimball Chen, Alexandra Roosevelt. Reviewed at the Aidikoff Screening Room, L.A., Oct. 23, 1985. (No MPAA Rating.) Running time: 70 MINS.
With: Ronee Blakley, Wim Wenders, Scarlet Rivera, Harley Stumbaugh, Eulogy, The Old Dog Band.

"It Played It For You" would stand as Ronee Blakley's psychodrama about her marriage to Wim Wenders, except that it has no psychological insight or drama to offer. A most curious amalgam of musical numbers, Super 8m travel footage, cinema verité doodlings and ruminations about life and love, this one-of-a-kind home movie opened Oct. 24 at the Fox International in Venice for a week's Oscar qualifying run in the feature documentary category. Commercial prospects will be limited to offbeat venues and double bills with Wenders features.

To the accompaniment of some 14 Blakley tunes, a semblance of a story is played out involving the actress-singer and German director Wenders, with what amounts to self-generated found footage. In a barroom, the couple enacts a version of their meeting for the first time, at which Wenders is mysteriously called "Howard," and over which he seems to have exercised dominant artistic control. Later, one sees the two cavorting on Santa Monica pier, on vacation in the Caribbean, and on trips to Idaho and Germany.

Along the way are mentions of how they worked together, notably on "Lightning Over Water," how they married, separated and divorced, and of Wenders' advisory role in the completion of this film. Nowhere to be found, however, is evidence of what drew the two together, of an emotional dynamic between them, or of reasons for their split.

Those are conventional, biographical questions, and this is a patently unconventional film. But, for lack of being offered any real substance, one quickly begins speculating upon why Blakley made it. For reasons that the picture does not express, it must have been very important for her to preserve something of this relationship, to fashion something vaguely artistic.

Although the film begins in 1979, it quite uncannily evokes an earlier era, one of sweetly half-baked hippie philosophizing, slightly spacey long-haired musicians and self-styled artists hanging out, one which conjures up the period embracing BBS, Robert Altman and "The Rolling Thunder Revue," of which Blakley was a part.

Given the private, flat nature of the footage shot, it is impossible to imagine a professional context in which Wenders might have imagined this stuff ending up. As for Blakley, she seems unquenchably determined to be expressive in both her songs and her attempt at a confessional, but it's hard to say what she is trying to express.

The film will also pose a problem to audiences on a technical level. All manner of material has been transferred to 16m, resulting in a visual hodgepodge, and the sound mix, such as it is, renders some of the dialog and most of her lyrics incomprehensible. —Cart.

Denver Film Festival

Sotto ... Sotto
(Softly ... Softly)
(ITALIAN-COLOR)

Denver, Oct. 22.
A Triumph Films release of an Intercapital production. Executive producers, Mario & Vittorio Cecchi Gori. Directed by Lina Wertmüller. Stars Enrico Montesano. Screenplay, Wertmüller, Enrico Oldoini; camera; (color) Dante Spinotti; editor, Luigi Zita; music, Paolo Conte. Reviewed at Denver Film Festival, Oct. 21, 1985 (MPAA Rating: R.) Running time: 98 MINS.
With: Enrico Montesano (Oscar), Veronica Lario (Ester), Luisa de Santis (Adele), Massimo Wertmüller (Ginetto).

Lina Wertmüller's "Softly ... Softly" bowed at the 1984 Munich fest as part of an all-embracing retro, then popped up here and there on the fest circuit. Last stop was the Denver fest, where it scored with film buffs and the general audience.

This is a one-joke film with rambunctious macho Oscar (Enrico Montesano) interpreting his wife's dream of a lesbian embrace with a mutual girlfriend as an attack on his own masculinity. First Oscar thinks he's been cuckolded (which is bad enough) and then he's sure that he has to defend the very course of nature against inroads of a feminist conspiracy against the male animal. He goes berserk, charging like a bull into private home and chasing his wife down public streets like a mercenary on a one-man kill mission.

It's all good fun at the outset, but the joke wears thin when it's clear that only caveman tactics are at the core of this Adam and Eve conflict. Title is a sardonic twist on the action as it unfolds.

Wertmüller, with such fine art pics as "Seven Beauties" to her credit, has shelved the subtlety of prior visual imagery to give her actors full play without embellishment. Enrico Montesano makes for an appropriate ape-like Oscar in grimaces and contortions, but when he flays away at the gentle sex in raging fits, the macho is compared with a lunatic in end effect. Thus, taking Wertmüller as a femme filmer, this is her most direct statement on the war of the sexes. The rest is ho-hum. —Holl.

Choosing Victory
(DOCU-COLOR)

Upbeat story of the disabled.

Denver, Oct. 20.
An MKD production. Produced and directed by Muffett Kaufman. Camera (color), Philip Hurn. Only credits available. Reviewed at Denver Film Festival, Oct. 19, 1985. (No. MPAA Rating.) Running time: 95 MINS.

Femme documentarist Muffett Kaufman went to the 1984 Summer Olympics in Los Angeles to zero in on a sidebar event set up for wheelchair athletes. The results are to be found in "Choosing Victory," a humanistic viewing of how five different individuals came to grips with their disabilities and used competitive events as a way to overcome despair and frustration on a personal level.

One gets to know each of these individuals rather intimately before the Olympics are presented as a key moment in their lives. They discuss what their lives were before the critical accident, then describe the emotional conflicts the disabled face in today's society. Sport offered for these individuals an outlet for a "return to normalcy" — just as artistic expression might be the ultimate cure for others in the same boat.

Several such films have been made on the subject ever since a "year" was set aside for the disabled at the beginning of this decade in order to call the world's attention to the plight of the unfortunate. This is one of the best.
—Holl.

The Old Forest
(COLOR-16m)

Charming piece of Americana.

Denver, Oct. 29.
A Memphis State University (Dept. of Theater & Communication Arts) production, in collaboration with the Tennessee Committee for the Humanities. Produced and directed by Steven J. Ross. Features entire cast. Screenplay, Ross, David Appleby, Susan Howe, Joseph Mulherin, based on a short story by Peter Taylor; camera (color 16m), Larry McConkey; music, Mark Blumberg; narrated by Taylor. Reviewed at Denver Film Fest, Oct. 19, 1985. (No MPAA Rating.) Running time: 60 MINS.
With: Peter White, Jane Wallace, Beverly Moore, Shannon Cochran, Cynthia Moore, Amy Shouse, Kathryn Murry, Bennett Wood, Betty May Collins, Jeffrey Posson, Keith Kennedy.

Steven J. Ross' "The Old Forest" is based on a short story by Tennessee writer Peter Taylor, who fortunately narrates the tale off-screen to give the whole a ring of authenticity. This is one of those state funded projects that works particularly well.

Set in Memphis in 1937, author Taylor reviews class distinctions between aristocratic Southern families and working people struggling with the Depression. Story first appeared in New Yorker in 1979, where it was recognized as part of the tradition of Southern scribes John Crowe Ransom and Robert Penn Warren. Ross set out to recapture the atmosphere of those times: it succeeds in this regard due to Memphis' own desire to preserve its landmark traditions. Every shot manages to capture the aura of the 1930s.

Nat Ramsey (Peter White) is the heir apparent to a wealthy Memphis cotton brokerage, but like any Southern Gentleman he wants to get in his playboy kicks before settling down to marriage and family. The tables are turned on him when he has a car accident with an easygoing girlfriend just a week before his wedding: the girl disappeared into the forest while he's knocked out by a conk on the head. The incident brings the police into the affair to investigate possible foul play, so the girl has to be found before the wedding can take place at all.

The young gentleman with his bride-to-be then decide to carry on an investigation of their own. It's here that the rub between the classes surfaces with all the nasty class hangups proper to the old southern traditions. In the end, several key individuals learn what it means to be human first and self-righteous second, the lessons experienced on both sides of the fence.

Pic has a low-key tone throughout. Well acted and directed, it's a fine debut effort that shows just what can be done in regional filmmaking in America far off the beaten path of Hollywood and stereotyped tv values, albeit with forgivable flaws and minor credit imperfections —Holl.

American Rebel
(DOCU-COLOR)

Country boy goes East.

Denver, Oct. 21.

An Ohio River Films release. Produced and directed by Will Roberts, in collaboration with Dean Reed. Reviewed at Denver Film Festival, Oct. 18, 1985. (No MPAA Rating.) Running time: **93 MINS.**

"American Rebel" focuses on the life and times of Yank pop singer Deen Reed, who presently lives in East Germany and is often referred to as "the Johnny Cash of Communism " (N.Y. Times). One finds him entertaining huge auditorium or stadium crowds in Moscow or Cuba or East Berlin or Baghdad (where this reviewer has seen him in action over the past decade or more), and he well deserves to have a docu made on the phenomenon if not the personality behind it. This one took filmer Will Roberts some three years to complete.

Reed grew up in Denver (thus the world preem of pic at the Denver Film Fest), attending the U. of Colorado for a brief spell before slinging his guitar over his shoulder and setting off to Hollywood to seek his fortune. There he recorded a couple songs for Capitol Records, one of which hit the top of the charts in South America.

Reed then hit the trail for Latin America on a promo tour, deciding to stay there for a while when he discovered he could entertain huge crowds while lending his allegiance to Allende's cause in Marxist/Socialist Chile. He learned to converse and sing in Spanish, and departed reluctantly when the military governments took charge in Chile and Argentina.

Next Reed is seen doing Italo Westerns with the late Yul Brynner — until he received an invitation to sing his politico folk songs at fests and concerts in Socialist countries in East Europe. The Soviet Union and the German Democratic Republic in particular adopted him wholeheartedly, and Dean Reed suddenly found himself doing concerts, making films (directing and starring), and finally marrying an East German thesp to settle down in East Berlin with a family.

All along, Reed has kept his passport. Occasionally, he returns to the States — only, in 1978, to find himself in the middle of controversy when he was jailed in Minnesota with demonstrators marching to halt power lines going through a farming district. All these headline events and extracurricular activities have been duly recorded for posterity in "American Rebel."

Docu is both informative and eyecatching as something a bit out of the ordinary. It's when Reed has to sit down before a camera to explain his political views that he limps like a lame duck across the pages of contemporary history. He believes in peace and goodwill among men as though every day is Christmas, or as if all one has to do is to collectively wish for the same to attain it. Roberts would have done well to nail him down on his views in a repartee on camera, instead of allowing his subject to repeat his notions over and over again. In the end effect, the best that can be said about Dean Reed is that he has often shown personal courage to put his own life on the line in some rather dangerous Latin American demonstrations.

Those interested in Reed's movie career are recommended to see his "Sing, Cowboy, Sing" comedy produced in East Germany at the end of the 1970s. It set b.o. records in the home market — and it's not bad. As for his singing talent, the chairsma is more attached to his tall athletic build (replete with cowboy boots) than to a voice that's slightly fading at 45.

Reed showed up at Denver for the world preem of "American Rebel." Again, controversy flared up when he made an appearance on a talk-show. All the same, as the docu shows in interviews with Reed's mother and father and friends, Denver welcomed back the local home-town boy in typical homespun manner and with a warm embrace as liberal, democratic America is wont to do.—*Holl.*

The Return Of Ruben Blades
(BRITISH-U.S.-DOCU-COLOR)

Denver, Oct. 21.

A Film Four International (London) and Mug-Shot coproduction. A Documentary by Robert Mugge features Ruben Blades and his band, Linda Ronstadt, Peter Hamill, Anoland Blades, Ruben Blades Sr., Dean Frederick Snyder. Camera (color), Lawrence McConkey. Reviewed at Denver Film Festival, Oct. 19, 1985. (No MPAA Rating.) Running time: **82 MINS.**

Robert Mugge, a producer-director-editor based in Philadelphia, has made a string of fascinating docus for Channel Four in London together with tv producer Andy Park: "Black Wax," "The Gospel According To Al Green," "Cool Runnings: The Reggae Movie," and now "The Return Of Ruben Blades." Each focuses on a personality and/or movement on the contemporary musical scene, and all are unforgettable portraits of living-and-working artists as they piece together on camera the reasons that make them tick and perform.

Ruben Blades, a Panamanian who resides in New York and recently graduated from Harvard Law School, has carved out an enviable reputation as a salsa music star and latterly film actor ("The Last Fight," "Crossover Dreams"). A handful of his hit tunes are performed on camera live with his band — particularly "Buscando America" and "Silencios" — and one can sense the passion and originality of his music right at the outset. He is, indeed, a gifted musician, composer, and band leader.

Just as fascinating, however, is his witty and intelligent way of handling the on-camera interviews. He defends the Latin American political sensibility to the point of admitting that he may one day even run for public office in Panama (where his popularity seems to assure election), but he is also his own man down to business manager (at least none other appears in the film) and aspiring graduate of the Harvard Law School. Docu opens with the commencement exercises in the Harvard yard, where he's surrounded by family and friends.

Mugge then accompanies Blades back to Panama City. His parents are presented as the core of a sound family tradition, and one notes that Ruben's songs do indeed spring from the feelings of the people. With the "Americanization" of Latin America (Europe, too, for that matter), it's the traditional values and way-of-life that count the most. Helmer Mugge lets Blades speak pretty much for himself, using the musical interludes as poetic illustrations of his opinion.

All well and good, but one has to be pretty well acquainted with the personality himself to grasp the full message of the docu. There's only one instance in which Mugge exposes the man's burning pride in his career and reputation: that's when Blades lets it be known that he does have political aspirations strictly on the grounds that he's more or less the hottest number in town. It's at this point that the filmer should have laid it on the line with a give-and-take firing-line approach, for the whole film theme is about commitment in the first place.

"The Return Of Ruben Blades" should score anywhere that music docus are favored by a built-in audience. Performances are lensed quite professionally, so much so that these segs tend to be the most revealing about the Blades personality.
— *Holl.*

Stripper
(DOCU-COLOR)

Insightful look behind the G-strings.

Denver, Oct. 20.

A 20th Century Fox release of an Arnon Milchan presentation of a Visionaire production. Executive producer, Milchan. Produced by Jerome Gary, Geof Bartz, Melvyn Estrin. Directed by Gary. Camera (color), Ed Lachman; editor, Bartz, Bob Eisenhardt, Lawrence Silk; music, Jack Nitzsche, Buffy Sainte-Marie; additional music, Joe Lynn Turner; coproducers, Thom Tyson, Michael Nolin. Reviewed at Denver Film Festival, Oct. 19, 1985. (MPAA Rating: R.) Running time: **90 MINS.**

With: Janette Boyd, Sara Costa, Danyel (Kimberly Holcomb), Mouse (Loree Menton), Gio (Lisa Suarez).

"Stripper" delivers everything it sets out to do. In fact, it comes across more like a fiction film than a documentary in the accepted sense. Because the subject matter is an attraction in itself, it's probably better off in the docu class where the camera can serve as a voyeur tactic to get "behind the scenes" of one of the world's more exotic professions on stage.

Helmer Jerome Gary, ably assisted by ace lenser Ed Lachman, uses the First Annual Strippers' Convention in Las Vegas in 1983 as the focal point of his treatise. Here the finalists of the strippers' contest will determine the beginnings or the ends of the careers of several contestants — for some of the girls are pushing 30, and have to push hard to compete with the sleek finesse of the 18-year-olds just starting out. The girls who score — particularly the winner — can look forward to bookings across the country, while those who don't are doomed to the provinces, so to speak.

Gary picks out Lisa, a 30-year-old, to crystalize the human side of the affair. She's got a young daughter to care for, has the predictable marriage and round of love interests behind her, and knows that she's good when the situation demands it. But she's vulnerable; time is running out.

Contrasted with Lisa are girls who have heavy hangups. One girl is such an emotional bag of nerves that she feels she's got to win or else. Another hopes to win in order to be able to face up to the truth of having to tell her mother what she has been doing all these years. Still another doesn't take anything at the convention very seriously, save that this is a job and an opportunity.

The angle is stripping is more or less an escape for most girls on the Las Vegas stage. They need it either to save face or maintain a front or simply to immerse themselves in the gaping admiration of the customers. However, like everything else in the flesh business, the profession has become warped and neutralized by competing male-strip shows, porno-houses, and live-sex acts. In fact, the Las Vegas audience doesn't even appear to work up a sweat during the numbers: this is business, not burlesque.

Docu's pluses are the flowing narrative line and tight cross-cutting during the Strippers' Convention. The one drawback is the slickness of the whole affair. When Lisa comes home to her daughter to let her know that she didn't win, the followup to that is a birthday party on the lawn the next day. We've been accompanying a hometown girl on the salesman routes all along, as the kid pictures from family albums testify over the closing credits.

"Stripper" should do well in art houses and other docu venues, with solid chances to cross over to commercial stages given proper handling as offbeat "family" fare for grownups. University auds are a natural.—*Holl.*

Target
(COLOR)

Involving thriller marred by several botched scenes.

Hollywood, Nov. 1.

A Warner Bros. release of a CBS Pros. film. Produced by Richard D. Zanuck and David Brown. Directed by Arthur Penn. Stars Gene Hackman, Matt Dillon. Screenplay, Howard Berk, Don Petersen; camera (Technicolor), Jean Tournier; editor, Stephen A. Rotter, Richard P. Cirincione; music, Michael Small; sound, Bernard Bats; art direction, Willy Holt; assistant director, Alain Tasma; casting, Gene Lasko. Reviewed at The Burbank Studios, Burbank, Calif., Oct. 29, 1985. (MPAA Rating: R.) Running time: 117 MINS.

Walter Lloyd . . . . Gene Hackman
Chris Lloyd . . . . Matt Dillon
Donna Lloyd . . . . Gayle Hunnicutt
Lise . . . . Victoria Fyodorova
Taber . . . . Josef Sommer
Clay . . . . Guy Boyd
Schroeder . . . . Herbert Berghof
Carla . . . . Ilona Grubel
Colonel . . . . Richard Munch
Mason . . . . Ray Fry
Glasses . . . . Jean-Pol Dubois

"Target" is a spy thriller that's not only completely understandable and involving throughout, but also continually surprising along the way. These might seem like simple virtues, but they have been so rare of late in this kind of picture that it's most commendable.

Presumably, this must say a lot for the writing of Howard Berk and Don Petersen and the direction of Arthur Penn. The praise must be balanced by the fact that "Target," for all its pluses, also strangely contains a few scenes of dreadful writing, acting and direction.

Other than to set the audience laughing at times in the wrong spots, these errant efforts fortunately do not harm the overall results much. They are more than offset by Gene Hackman's generally superb performance and fine supporting efforts by Matt Dillon, Josef Sommer and Victoria Fyodorova.

Initially, Hackman is a seemingly dull lumberyard owner in Dallas and Dillon is his sporty roughneck son, affectionately contemptuous of his stodgy father. Loving but a bit bored, too, mother Gayle Hunnicutt finally has decided to vacation in Paris alone because Hackman has an odd aversion to visiting Europe.

While away, she hopes the two boys will make an effort to get to like each other better and there are some good scenes as Hackman and Dillon make an awkward attempt to pal around. Then comes news that mom has been kidnaped abroad.

The plot proceeds logically and the suspense holds with each new character taking a minimum of dramatic license to contribute to the unfolding drama.

Although there are the obligatory preposterous auto chases, the action overall is supportive of the plot

rather than a substitute. Ditto bloodshed and pyromania. All in all, "Target" might have been an exemplary film of its type — if it just wasn't for those few dumb scenes. — *Har.*

Nieuwe Golf
(New Waves)
(DUTCH-DOCU-COLOR-16m)

Amsterdam, Oct. 17.

A Pan Film production. Directed by Digna Sinke. Produced by P. Hans Frankfurther. Camera (color, 16m), Albert van der Willdt; sound, Erik Langhout; editor, Jan Wouter van Reijen. Reviewed at Kriterion, Amsterdam, Oct. 7, 1985. Running time: 87 MINS.

In Europe, 1985 — the 300th anni of the births of Bach, Handel and Scarlatti — has been proclaimed the Year of Music. In Holland, the World Music Days of the International Society for Contemporary Music, organized by the Gaudeamus Foundation, closed recently.

Gaudeamus commissioned Digna Sinke to make a docu exploring and explaining the differences and affinities between composed and improvised modern music. Commission Impossible, one might think, but Sinke, helped by excellent photography and by well-nigh flawless sound recording and mixing, came up with an informative, intelligent and very entertaining pic.

A number of the foremost modern Dutch composers, some singers, and two small avant-garde orchestras (joined into one for the occasion) collaborated. The composers' work is very heterogeneous, minimal, serial, anything. One works with a computer, another with blueprints; for another, music is "all emotion."

They all like to play improvisations. Why? "When you're improvising you don't have time to clear away the muck like you do when you're composing." "When you improvise, audacity gives you ideas." "To play written music is always striving towards perfection, whereas in improvisation communication comes first."

"New Waves" listens in at rehearsals and concerts, talks to musicians, but does not confine itself only to registering its subject matter. Basically strictly composed, the pic also improvises, for instance by inserting shots of the sea, of trees, of freeways with their own specific sounds, surprisingly used. Quite different from most docus about art, full of highfalutin' vapor and mush, it's a civilized and robust bit of culture. — *Wall.*

Hay Unos Tipos Abajo
(There Are Some Guys Downstairs)
(ARGENTINE-COLOR)

Buenos Aires, Oct. 22.

An R.F. Producciones presentation and production. Produced and directed by Emilio Alfaro and Rafael Filipelli. Story, Antonio Dal Masseto; screenplay, Dal Masseto, Alfaro and Filipelli; camera (Eastmancolor), Yito Blanc; art director, Jorge Sarudiansky; music, Jorge López Ruiz. Reviewed at the Alfa theatre, B.A., Sept. 26, 1985. Running time: 90 MINS.

With: Luis Brandoni, Luisina Brando, Marta Bianchi, Emilio Alfaro, Soledad Silveyra, Elsa Berenguer.

This is one of those films which leaves you wondering what did they try to tell. One day in mid-1978, while most Argentines are hypnotized by the victories of their national soccer team in the World Cup being played in Buenos Aires, others still fear being abducted by secret agents of the military regime.

On that day Luis Brandoni, a journalist living alone, starts to worry when his neighbor Elsa Berenguer calls his attention to some men in a car in the street, who are seemingly watching the building they live in.

Brandoni, with the help of his lover Luisina Brando, tries to find out whether they are after him, and although it isn't so, he becomes increasingly scared. He eventually runs away, doesn't find the refuge he seeks at the home of a couple too cowardly to hide him, spends some hours with a former lover who accidentally crosses his path and finally, he boards a train, imagines a passenger watches him and steps down in a rural station leaving his bag aboard. That's all.

It is hard to find any trace of dramatic development, less so psychological insight, in this almost plotless film revolving around the same situation all the time. Corny dialog helps to excite some laughs at the wrong times.

Static camera, shadowy images, obtrusive music and elementary editing add to the boring results. — *Nubi.*

Hold-Up
(FRANCO-CANADIAN-COLOR)

Paris, Nov. 4.

An AMLF-Cerito release of a Cerito Films/Films Ariane/Ciné-Vidéo (Montreal) coproduction. Executive producers, Alexandre Mnouchkine, Georges Dancigers, Denis Héroux. Producer, Alain Belmondo. Directed by Alexandre Arcady. Stars Jean-Paul Belmondo. Screenplay, Francis Veber, Daniel Saint-Hamont, Arcady, based on the novel "Quick Change" by Jay Cronley; camera (Eastmancolor), Richard Ciupka; art director, Jean-Louis Poveda; editor, Joëlle Van Effenterre; makeup, Charly Koubesserian; sound, Alain Sempé; music, Serge Franklin; stunt director, Rémy Julienne; reviewed at the Gaumont Ambassade theater, Paris, Nov. 3, 1985. Running time: 112 MINS.

Grimm . . . . Jean-Paul Belmondo
Georges . . . . Guy Marchand
Lise . . . . Kim Cattrall
Labrosse . . . . Jean-Pierre Marielle
Lasky . . . . Tex Konig
Cab driver . . . . Jacques Villeret

"Hold-Up" is the most watchable Jean-Paul Belmondo film in years. The 60,000,000 franc ($7,-000,000) Franco-Canadian coproduction doesn't quite come off as a fully satisfying entertainment, but it gives the impression that Belmondo is trying a little harder.

More important, his current collaborators have made an effort as well to surround the actor with a story, cast and direction that will occupy the viewer (a common denominator to many earlier Belmondo vehicles is that scripters and helmers seemed to have executed their chores lying down) rather than serve as an indifferent backdrop and foil to the star's easygoing charm and athletic skills.

"Hold-Up" is a combination caper-chase comedy, inspired by a novel by Jay Cronley, "Quick Change," of which apparently only the caper angle has been preserved. A bank job occupies the first half of the film, while the rest of the action concerns the protagonists' potholed attempts to get themselves and the loot out of the country.

Belmondo is the mastermind of course, and the heist involves his apparently single-handed stickup, dressed as a clown, of a major Montreal bank, where his two cohorts (Guy Marchand and Kim Cattrall) mingle with the hostages. Belmondo deliberately sets off the alarm and in no time hordes of police surround the building. Playing cat and mouse with a humiliated police captain (Jean-Pierre Marielle), the "trapped" thief passes his partners and himself through the police barricade as hostages. Cattrall is hugely "pregnant" with over $2,000,000 in cash, while Belmondo mimicks an exasperated elder.

Their subsequent race to get out of town is complicated by a number of obstacles, most notably a burly ex-cellmate of Belmondo and Marchand who has cottoned on to the job and pursues them, by pickup, then trailer truck, all the way to the airport. The outlaw trio, who finally batter their way across the highways in a hijacked school bus, also have to put up with police blockades, a blackmailing cabbie (Jacques Villeret), and the always illtimed "human element" when, in the midst of it all, Cattrall jilts pathetic boyfriend Marchand and tries to seduce Belmondo into splitting with her alone.

In its construction, comic hijinks and sometimes clever dialog, one recognizes the welcome hand of Francis Veber, France's leading architect of screen situation comedy, who was brought into help director Alexandre Arcady and his cowriter Daniel Saint-Hamont lick thorny scripting problems.

Arcady, who carved his commercial niche with a trio of increasingly expensive films inspired by his French Algerian heritage, graduates to the international coproduction scene with "Hold-Up," and, if he lacks any genuinely creative comic sense, at least confirms sound craftsmanlike ability in the execution of a complex, technically slick production. (Veteran stunt coordinator Rémy Julienne deserves mention for his "second unit" direction of the dangerous highway pursuits.)

Still, despite its real qualities (and the spirited performances are on the plus side) "Hold-Up" leaves an impression of déja vu, with its overworked theme of the "heist of the century ' and its umpteenth motorized pursuit.

Belmondo obviously is making more of an acting effort than usual, but he never creates a character capable of doubts and temptations, which would add a genuine element of suspense to the threatening romantic subplot. —Len.

Wizards Of The Lost Kingdom
(U.S./ARGENTINE-COLOR)

Hollywood, Oct. 28.

A Concorde/Cinema Group release. Produced by Frank Isaac, Alex Sessa. Directed by Hector Olivera. Stars Bo Svenson. Screenplay, Tom Edwards; camera (color), Leonard Solis; editor, Silvia Roberts; music, James Horner, Chris Young; production design, Mary Bertram; special effects makeup, Mike Jones; special effects, Richard Lennox; stunt coordinators, Arthur Neal, Guy Reed; assistant director, Andrew Sargent. Reviewed at the Hollywood Pacific, L.A., Oct. 28, 1985. (MPAA Rating: PG.) Running time: 75 MINS.
Kor .... Bo Svenson
Simon .... Vidal Peterson
Shurka .... Thom Christopher
Udea .... Barbara Stock
Acrasia .... Maria Socas
Aura .... Dolores Michaels

Lensed two years ago under the title "Wizard Wars" and test marketed regionally in May, "Wizards Of The Lost Kingdom" is about as marginal an item as can make it into theatrical release these days. Incredibly cheap and infinitely derivative, pic will be lucky to last more than a week even in the least demanding situations.

This tacky looking Roger Corman Argentine-produced fantasy possesses limited appeal to adults due to the very soft PG rating, but at least has the saving grace of selfmocking humor, most of it contributed by leading man Bo Svenson.

Big Bo plays an easy going, rather past-his-prime masterless warrior who decides to help out a little prince whose wizardly father has been murdered and kingdom overrun by mean magician Thom Christopher.

These two, along with the prince's pet, a lumbering oaf that looks like the result of a mating between a sheepdog and the abominable snowman, roam the countryside attempting to return to the castle. They meet with occasional obstacles in the form of gruesome halfhumans, monsters and even regular soldiers, all of whom are dispatched with so little as a shove from Svenson. Despite some scenes that pass for action, there's no violence or even much contact here.

Every prominent storybook myth receives a tip of the hat here, and Svenson, knowing exactly what kind of project he was involved with down Argentine way, makes it passably tolerable thanks to his surprising cheerfulness under the circumstances.

Some of the monster masks are okay, and the special effects primarily consist of red and blue light rays and frequent superimpositions. —Cart.

White Nights
(COLOR)

Okay outlook for muddled romantic thriller.

Hollywood, Oct. 31.

A Columbia Pictures release of a New Visions production from Columbia-Delphi V Prods. Produced by Taylor Hackford, William S. Gilmore. Directed by Hackford. Stars Mikhail Baryshnikov, Gregory Hines. Screenplay, James Goldman, Eric Hughes, from a story by Goldman; camera (Metrocolor), David Watkin; editors, Fredric Steinkamp, William Steinkamp; music score, Michel Colombier; music supervisor, Phil Ramone; production design, Philip Harrison; art direction, Richard Dawking, Malcolm Middleton, Austen Spriggs; set decoration, Joan Wollard; costume design, Evangeline Harrison; sound (Dolby), Clive Winter; choreography, Twyla Tharp; "Le Jeune Homme et la Mort" choreographed by Roland Petit; tap improvography, Gregory Hines; additional choreography, Mikhail Baryshnikov; associate producer, Bill Borden; assistant directors, Ray Corbett, Matti Ollila (Finland), Jose Sa Caetano (Portugal); additional photography, John Harris, Ken Withers; casting, Nancy Klopper. Aerial unit: director, Jim Gavin; coordinator, Jeff Hawke; camera, Frank Holgate; special effects, Martin Gutteridge, Ian Wingrove, Garth Inns. Reviewed at The Burbank Studios, Burbank, Calif., Oct. 31, 1985. (MPAA Rating: PG-13.) Running time: 135 MINS.
Nikolai (Kolya) Rodchenko ...... Mikhail Baryshnikov
Raymond Greenwood ..... Gregory Hines
Colonel Chaiko .... Jerzy Skolimowski
Galina Ivanova .... Helen Mirren
Anne Wyatt .... Geraldine Page
Darya Greenwood ...... Isabella Rossellini
Wynn Scott .... John Glover
Captain Kirigin .... Stefan Gryff
Chuck Malarek .... William Hootkins
Ambassador Smith .... Shane Rimmer
Ballerina (Death) .... Florence Faure

In their determined effort to make mainstream commercial entertainment out of material that, in several ways, borders on the specialized, the makers of "White Nights" have tried to have it both ways on too many counts. The result is a vaguely uncomfortable compromise which is neither fish nor fowl, good nor bad, b.o. gold nor poison. The Columbia release possesses the stellar cultural components to establish it as a major, serious year-end entry, but business prospects appear just okay.

At its core a political thriller about the dilemma of a famous Russian defector who, after a plane crash, finds himself trapped back in his mother country, pic shies away from the world of classical dance, personified by leading man Mikhail Baryshnikov, in favor of Gregory Hines' "improvography" and assorted modern stuff in blatant music video contexts.

Mix all this in with KGB intrigue, racial tensions, numerous emotional breakdowns and several suspense sequences, all played at the broadest levels of melodrama, and one has quite a mish-mash indeed.

A film creates serious difficulties for itself when the first two major scenes are far and away the two best in the entire picture, and that is the case here. The extended title sequence, in which Baryshnikov and Florence Faure dance Roland Petit's "Le Jeune Homme et la Mort," is strikingly performed and photographed, and creates high hopes for further displays of same that remain unmet.

This is followed directly by an astonishing sequence depicting the crash landing of a 747 at a Soviet military airstrip in Siberia. The close shots of the plane quickly descending are thrilling, and the moments in which the plane cracks up while hurtling off the runway and through a fence are as realistic as could possibly be. Full honors are due the aerial unit for their accomplishments here.

With the plane down, the Soviets find themselves with a celebrated defector on their hands, and intend to use the opportunity to get him to "return" officially to Russia. Without so much as an interrogation by the KGB, Baryshnikov is moved to the dingy Siberian residence of Gregory Hines, a black American tap dancer who jumped to the other side when his disgust with the U.S. during the Vietnam era reached the breaking point, and his Russian wife Isabella Rossellini.

The trio shortly is installed in Baryshnikov's luxurious old apartment in Leningrad, and the dancer is expected to begin preparations for a triumphant homecoming at the Kirov. Inevitably, an escape attempt climaxes the picture, with results that seem as unlikely as most of what has come before.

Despite the pressured situations in which the characters find themselves, surprisingly little sympathy or emotion is generated for them. Baryshnikov, while naturally appealing, never goes much past his attitude of arrogant defiance. What's more, he seems to spend more time limbering up than actually dancing.

Hines plays a bitter, ornery man with a quick trigger, and the deed performed by the character many years before makes him difficult to warm up to. His tap dancing, of which there is a great deal, is accomplished, but rather incongruous in context.

Isabella Rossellini, in her Hollywood film debut, has disappointingly little to do. Her utterly convincing peasant looks here are at odds with her recently acquired glamorous image, and many of her mannerisms are startlingly reminiscent of those of her mother (Ingrid Bergman).

Emigré Polish director Jerzy Skolimowski exudes intelligent villainy in the stock role of the foxy KGB agent who tries to manipulate the leads, and Helen Mirren has some intense, tearful scenes as the lover Baryshnikov left behind when he defected.

Director Taylor Hackford has made a film with good looks but no style. Lenser David Watkin and production designer Philip Harrison have done superior work in making it all attractive and convincing. —*Cart.*

There Were Times, Dear
(COLOR-16m)

Fictional story on Alzheimer's Disease.

A presentation of the Northeastern Gerontological Society, the N.Y. Commission on Aging and Sardoz (Dorsey Pharmaceuticals and Sardoz Pharmaceuticals). Produced by Lilac Prods., Hollywood. Executive producer and coproducer, Linda Hope. Directed by/coproducer, Nancy Malone; unit production manager and coproducer, Flora Lang; screenplay, Harry Cauley; camera (color), Brianne Murphy; music, Jay Gruska; editor, Kenneth Miller; medical consultant, Jack Rowe, M.D. Reviewed at N.Y. Cultural Center, Oct. 31, 1985. (No MPAA Rating.) Running time: **60 MINS.**
Susanne Millard . . . . Shirley Jones
Bob Millard . . . . Len Cariou
Jenny, their daughter . . . Cynthia Eilbacher
Don Mason . . . . Dana Elcar
Dr. Rosen . . . . Alan Haufrect
Marsha . . . . Ina Balin

A labor of love and social commitment for busy director Nancy Malone ("Dynasty," "Hotel," "St. Elsewhere," etc.), "There Were Times, Dear" is a moving fictional drama based on documentary authenticity that traces the devastating impact of Alzheimer's Disease on an American family.

Well-known professional performers worked for guild minimums as their contribution to the project. Funding comes from various sources, including Norman Lear, Bob and Dolores Hope, and the Lawrence Welk Foundation. Additional funding came from Women in Film Project, a national organization, and from the American Film Institute, in association with the National Endowment for The Arts ($20,000).

Purpose of the film is to educate the public about early symptoms of Alzheimer's Disease that may be overlooked or minimized by a protective family as the patient's deterioration continues. Film spans eight years as Bob Millard (Len Cariou) slips inexorably toward doom. His wife (Shirley Jones) and family can only look on in horror. Because Alzheimer's Disease has no cure, and because science at present can barely slow its destructive course, the dramatic suspense of the film does not center on the husband-father — for him there is no hope — but instead centers on the frictions between Jones as the mother and their daughter, well played by Cynthia Eilbacher. They must face the daily death of a man who still lives before them, until finally he is taken away to a nursing home. Meanwhile, their friends, or rather ex-friends, cease to visit, and their doctor can merely offer perfunctory platitudes of consolation.

Len Cariou is especially effective in creating the transition from ardent loving husband, a vigorous outdoorsman in the sporting-goods business, to the helpless state of emotionless vegetation. He's so far gone he could not even organize his own suicide.

"There Were Times, Dear" — its title suggests an earlier, better time — is available free of charge to all organizations that pledge to use it for non-profit educational screenings. The film's value to television, and to non-theatrical distribution, can hardly be overestimated, as Alzheimer's Disease is so widespread (5,000,000 Americans) that it must be confronted in the media.
—*Hitch.*

Mother Teresa
(DOCU-COLOR-16m)

Inspiring biopic on Nobel Laureate.

A film by Petrie Productions, N.Y. Coproduced by Ann and Jeanette Petrie. Directed by Ann Petrie. Camera (color, 16m), Ed Lachman, Sandi Sissel; sound, Barbara Becker; music, Suzanne Ciani; editor, Tom Haneke; consultant and narrator, Richard Attenborough; additional consultants, William Petrie, SS. CC., Philip Kravitz, Scott Morris, Jerald F. Wagner. Reviewed in General Assembly, United Nations, N.Y. Oct. 26, 1985. (No MPAA Rating.) Running time: **81 MINS.**

Shot over five years in 10 nations on four continents, "Mother Teresa" traces the career of the famed Nobel Peace Prize winner (1979) and founder of the Missionaries of Charity. Catholic order presently has 230 centers in 60 nations, with 1,650 missionaries and 750 novices.

Mother Teresa shuttles restlessly among these centers providing leadership, inspiration and an example of hard work. The film, much of it shot with *verité* immediacy, shows Mother Teresa constantly on the move, always optimistic, yet seemingly always one step ahead of overwhelming adversity. We see her tending the sick, changing diapers in India and rescuing spastic children in Beirut who are caught in the crossfire. Stock news footage shows her with many world leaders. Her voice-over in English alternates with that of Richard Attenborough.

Some information in "Mother Teresa" deals with her 1910 birth in Yugoslavia to a wealthy family, the decline in the family's fortune, her taking vows as a nun, which required total separation from her family, and her transfer to India as a teacher. Finally, at age 38, while riding a train to a retreat in Darjeeling, Mother Teresa suddenly underwent a miraculous realization that she was being called upon or singled out for special missionary work. Starting among the poor of Calcutta, she enlarged her Charity order into a worldwide movement.

Now 75, small and bent but relentlessly pressing on, Mother Teresa is warned in the film by doctors to moderate her breathless pace, but does not heed their advice.

Overall impression of "Mother Teresa" is a documentary tribute to a dynamic, dedicated workaholic-idealist who combines practical realism and the spirit, who preaches and practices love and duty as the path to personal and global salvation. In the film, and in her speech in the United Nations on the film's world premiere, Mother Teresa placed strong emphasis on the search for peace.

"Mother Teresa" was conceived by director Ann Petrie as an outgrowth of her 1981 PBS documentary "The World Of Mother Teresa." Her new "Mother Teresa" is privately financed and has no commitments yet in regard to festivals, television, theatrical or non-theatrical. As the definitive portrait of a unique soul who is having continuing impact on world consciousness, "Mother Teresa" is an important documentary for our time. —*Hitch.*

Interno Berlinese
(The Berlin Affair)
(ITALIAN-WEST GERMAN-COLOR)

Rome, Nov. 5.
An Italian Intl. Film release (Italy), Cannon Releasing release (U.S.). Produced by Menahem Golan and Yoram Globus for Italian Intl. Film, Cannon Films and KF-Kinofilm Prods. (Munich). Directed by Liliana Cavani. Stars Gudrun Landgrebe. Screenplay, Cavani, Roberta Mazzoni, based on the novel "The Buddhist Cross" by Junichiro Tanizaki; camera (color), Dante Spinotti; editor, Ruggero Mastroianni; art director, Luciano Riccieri; music, Pino Donaggio. Reviewed at Fiamma Cinema, Rome, Nov. 3, 1985. (No MPAA Rating.) Running time: **115 MINS.**
Louise . . . . Gudrun Landgrebe
Mitsuko . . . . Mio Takaki
Heinz . . . . Kevin McNally
Also with: Massimo Girotti, Philippe Leroy, William Berger.

Suggestively billed as another elegant brew of torrid eroticism and Nazis by the maker of "The Night Porter," "Berlin Affair" is likely to attract initial interest but fade fast. Liliana Cavani's adaptation of "The Buddhist Cross" by Japanese scribe Junichiro Tanizaki is pretty to look at, but so uninvolving it's baffling. Somewhere in the process of scripting a four-cornered tale of passion-unto-death, the story has vanished. The Cannon release might have looked good on paper, but that paper was obviously not the screenplay.

Everything is told as a flashback which Louise (Gudrun Landgrebe) is telling her literature prof, just before the Gestapo hauls him off on a charge of writing immoral novels. The Nazi morality campaign (actually just an excuse to bump off political rivals, we're told) supplies the backdrop to the characters' multiple relationships, which cross sexual, marital and racial lines in a dizzying succession of alliances. First Louise, the beautiful upper-class wife of a party diplomat (Kevin McNally), falls for a Japanese girl in her art class, Mitsuko (Mio Takaki). Mitsuko initiates the inexperienced Louise into the pleasures of lesbian love, hiding her secret relations with their (male) art teacher.

Heinz, Louise's husband, has the teacher arrested when he tries to blackmail him with homemade Japanese erotica depicting the two ladies and himself, but once he's out of the picture — literally — Heinz discovers he's as obsessed with the oriental girl as his wife is. He abruptly loses all interest in his career and ends up on the losing end of a death pact *à trois*. So does Mitsuko. Louise, who knows why, lives to tell the tale to her lit prof, who may end up writing "The Berlin Affair" from his prison cell.

To cover all this in under two hours, pic speeds along from encounter to encounter without even a token attempt to make the ruinous obsessions of its principals psychologically credible. Though Landgrebe, McNally and Takaki make a valiant effort, none is given a chance to convince us of the fatal charm of Mitsuko, who is embarrassingly slighted by the camera in favor of Landgrebe, to the detriment of the film as a whole. In the end, the only fascination imputable to the inscrutable Japanese girl with a kimono full of sleeping potions is being oriental, which really isn't enough.

On the erotic plane, pic is positively subdued, almost demure in minimizing on-screen flesh (there is no full nudity in the picture), and never voyeuristic, whatever the couplings. Probably the most interesting thing in the film is the way Cavani handles the lesbian relationship between Louise and Mitsuko, whose uninhibited passion is clearly expressed, but not used as an easy come-on for the audience.

Dante Spinotti's camera and Luciano Riccieri's '30s sets give pic a classy look of soothing elegance, even in the cheapest hotel rooms.
—*Yung.*

La Tentation d'Isabelle
(The Temptation Of Isabelle)
(FRENCH-SWISS-COLOR)

Paris, Nov. 4.

An MK2 release of an MK2 (Paris)/Strada Films (Geneva)/Films A2/Télévision Suisse Romando coproduction, with the participation of the Centre National de la Cinématographic (CNC). Executive producer, Marin Karmitz. Produced by Jean-Louis Porchet. Directed by Jacques Doillon. Screenplay, Doillon, Jean-François Goyet; camera (color), William Lubtchansky; editor, Noëlle Boison; music, Philippe Sarde; sound, Jean-Claude Laureux; art director, Alexandre Ghassem; production manager, Catherine Lapoujade. Reviewed at the Elysées Lincoln theater, Paris, Nov. 1, 1985. Running time: **90 MINS.**

With: Jacques Bonnafé, Ann Gisel Glass, Fanny Bastien, Xavier Deluc, Françoise Brion, Henri Virlogeux, Anne-Marie Maillé, Charlotte Gainsbourgh, Marie-Luce Felber.

Jacques Doillon, one of the more talented young French filmmakers to have emerged in the 1970s, seems of late to be working in two distinct modes of dramaturgy: the first, best characterized by such pictures as "La Drolesse" and the recent "La Vie de Famille," functions in a subdued, often understated style.

His other manner, in which his new film is cast, is based on shrill, head-on collisions between usually hysterical, neurotic individuals. "La Tentation d'Isabelle," set for no discernible dramatic reason in the Swiss Jura region (film is a coproduction), matches in sheer obnoxiousness the sadomasochistic antics of Doillon's "La Pirate," the obligatory seat-emptier at the 1984 Cannes Film Festival.

The master of excessive ceremonies here is a young man (Jacques Bonnafé) who loves a young woman (newcomer Ann Gisel Glass), who used to love a young man (Xavier Deluc), who now loves another young woman (Fanny Bastien). Since Bonnafé loves not wisely but only too well, he arranges, as a birthday surprise for Glass, a reunion with former flame Deluc in a hotel. Since latter is a no-more wiser ex-lover, he is accompanied by current mate Bastien, who is miffed by Deluc's birthday gift to Glass.

Not surprisingly, the festivities quickly degenerate into a long, loud night of mutual recriminations, jealousies and breast-beatings. The morning after brings little relief, and pretty soon the foursome resume their game of amorous musical chairs, with both males vacillating between Glass and Bastien. Finally Bonnafé prevails over his wishy-washy rival and is reunited with Glass in a desperate sexual embrace.

It becomes clear early on in this sub-Cassavetes exercise in self-indulgence that Bonnafé is an uncertified nutcase who is setting out to put his girl friend's love to the acid test in the most perverse, roundabout of ways. Doillon and his coscripter Jean-François Goyet (who worked on the vastly superior "La Vie de Famille") tip us off heavily on Bonnafé's weirdness in a pre-credits sequence in which the young man is seen napping in a dell among grazing cows and entering the chalet of Glass' family by climbing in the first-story balcony.

Doillon has directed without regard for dramatic contrast and rhythm, or for how much self-punishment an average audience can take in the course of 90 minutes. William Lubtchansky's superb photography helps alleviate viewer distress and boredom. —*Len.*

Once Bitten
(COLOR)

Weak combo of teen sex comedy and vampire genre.

Hollywood, Nov. 4.

A Samuel Goldwyn Co. release. Produced by Dimitri Villard, Robby Wald, Frank E. Hilderbrand. Executive producer, Samuel Goldwyn Jr. Directed by Howard Storm. Features entire cast. Screenplay, David Hines, Jeffrey Hause, Jonathan Roberts, from a story by Villard; camera (Metrocolor), Adam Greenberg, editor, Marc Grossman; music, John Du Prez; production designer, Gene Rudolf; art director, Robert Howland; set decorator, Jerie Kelter; sound, Mark Ulano; assistant director, Gene Sultan; associate producer, Russell Thacher; casting, Vivian McRae. Reviewed at Coronet Theater, Westwood Village, Calif., Nov. 2, 1985. (MPAA Rating: PG-13). Running time: **93 MINS.**
Countess .... Lauren Hutton
Mark Kendall .... Jim Carrey
Robin Pierce .... Karen Kopins
Sebastian .... Cleavon Little
Jamie .... Thomas Ballatore
Russ .... Skip Lackey

"Once Bitten" is one more silly variation of the teen sex comedy, but it is too timid to make its premise interesting. Intrusion of Lauren Hutton as a vampire into the lives of a young couple grappling with their own sexual identities comes as nothing more than a flat gimmick, offering few laughs and certainly no new insights into this overworked territory. Any initial curiosity from filmgoers about the supernatural subject matter should quickly fade.

For all their supposed daring in combining a modern female vampire story with a teen romantic comedy, the filmmakers have taken the easy way out. Rather than injecting new life into the tired teen genre, the vampire material merely sinks to the commonplace.

Neither the screenplay by David Hines, Jeffrey Hause and Jonathan Roberts nor the direction by Howard Storm manages to enliven the characters or the setting. Perhaps zombies would have been more appropriate than vampires.

Mark Kendeall (Jim Carrey) and Robin Pierce (Karen Kopins) are your typical high school couple. He wants it while she is holding out for the right time and place.

If she's unsure, the Countess (Lauren Hutton) is not. She needs the blood of a virgin three times before Halloween or she will lose her illusion of youth and beauty. Unfortunatley, the chase lacks danger, suspense or imagination. She just turns up from time to time.

While Hutton is an interesting casting choice as the vampire, neither she nor the script manages to give her character the least bit of personality. In fact, she's upstaged by the stylized elegance of her modern mansion (designed by Gene Rudolf).

As her vampire valet, Cleavon Little is the only thing worth watching as he glides through the house. Even here the filmmakers were too meek to explore the amusing possibilities of a gay vampire.

Carrey as the all-American boy has a few good moments and shows some talent for physical comedy, but again the character is basically one-dimensional, especially when he teams up with his pals Thomas Ballatore and Skip Lackey in their futile hunt for girls.

As the girlfriend, Kopins is attractive but her character has about as much depth as a wading pool.

"Once Bitten" isn't executed well enough to escape the limitations of its conception. The kids never have anything on their minds except sex, and neither do the vampires. No wonder eternal life is a bore.
—*Jagr.*

Bad Medicine
(COLOR)

Obvious, unfunny medschool comedy.

Hollywood, Nov. 9.

A 20th Century Fox release of a Lantana production. Produced by Alex Winitsky, Arlene Sellers. Executive producer, Sam Manners. Coexecutive producers, Michael Jaffe, Myles Osterneck. Directed by Harvey Miller. Stars Steve Guttenberg, Alan Arkin. Screenplay, Miller; story, Miller based on the novel "Dr. Horowitz" by Steven Horowitz, Neil Offen; coproducer, Jeffrey Ganz; camera (DeLuxe Color), Kelvin Pike; editor, O. Nicholas Brown, John Jympson; music, Lalo Schifrin; production designer, Les Dilley; set decorator, Ian Whittaker; costumes, Rita Riggs; sound, Bud Alper; assistant director, Jose Maria Ochoa; casting, Howard Feuer (N.Y.), Joan Sittenfield (L.A.), Alan Foenander, Leslie DePettitt (London). Reviewed at 20th Century Fox screening room. Century City, Calif., Nov. 8, 1985. (MPAA Rating: PG-13.) Running time: **96 MINS.**
Jeff Marx .... Steve Guttenberg
Dr. Madera .... Alan Arkin
Liz Parker .... Julie Parker
Dr. Gerald Marx .... Bill Macy
Dennis Gladstone ...... Curtis Armstrong
Cookie Katz .... Julie Kavner
Gomez .... Joe Grafasi

There's probably a good comic film in the adventures of American medical students who because of the law of supply and demand are forced into going to medical school in Mexico or other more exotic parts of the world.

Unfortunately, not much of it is in "Bad Medicine." Despite some amusing situations and a few good yocks, pic tries too hard to embellish the material and comes out a bit thin. Boxoffice prospects are not healthy.

Coming from a long line of doctors, Jeff Marx (Steve Guttenberg) is in a bind. No medical school will have him. His father (Bill Macy), a hotshot plastic surgeon, arranges for him to attend Madera Medical School somewhere in Central America.

With great trepidation, Guttenberg sets off to become a doctor. Much of the humor comes out of his encounter with a Third World country that is examined with American eyes. In showing the worst and most predictable part of another culture, where most of the characters are made to look foolish, writer/director Harvey Miller has relied too much on cheap shots.

Rather than let the inherent cultural differences carry the comedy, Miller (who cowrote "Private Benjamin" and here directs his first film) widens the gap to milk laughs. Plot is not advanced by school doings, but sidetracked by a subplot involving an illegal clinic set up by the would-be doctors in a remote village to help the peasants. Film then becomes an overextended sitcom.

Consistent with the condescending tone of the film, the American students, in the best tradition of knowing what's best for another country, possess more social conscience than the natives. Not only does this episode trivialize the medical profession it endows these wunderkinder with superior skills — Guttenberg delivers what appears to be a three-month-old infant.

Nemesis of the students is the school founder and resident dictator Dr. Madera (Alan Arkin) who runs the institution like a Boy Scout camp, complete with dress code and morning flag raising. Although Arkin supplies some deft comic touches, his character shifts from the realistic to the ludicrous, sometimes in the same scene, making him a cardboard creation.

There's romance too. Guttenberg falls for fellow student Julie Hagerty who seems totally miscast as an earnest but dipsy nurse who wants to be a doctor.

As for Guttenberg, he relies on his boy-next-door charm with Miller doing little to control his "gosh-gee whiz" acting style. Supporting cast, however, is fine and the best moments are in the lowkey camaraderie between the American friends when the film isn't trying to whip up another funny situation.

Shot in Spain, film looks consistently drab, more from the photography than the country. To emphasize the poverty some of the least appealing scenery is selected.—*Jagr.*

Hustruer, 2 — Ti ar etter
(Wives, 2 — Ten Years Later)
(NORWEGIAN-COLOR)

Lübeck, Nov. 3.

A Norsk Film release of Norsk Film production. Foreign sales, Norsk Film (Frieda Ohrvik). Executive producer, Bente Erichsen. Directed by Anja Breien. Features entire cast. Original story and screenplay, Breien, Knut Faldbakken; camera (Eastmancolor), Erling Thurmann-Andersen; editor, Lars Hagström. Reviewed as official entry in the 27th Nordic Film Days at the Kammerspiele, Lübeck, West Germany, Nov. 3, 1985. Running time: **90 MINS.**
Heidrun . . . . Fröydis Armand
Kaja . . . . Katja Medboe
Mie . . . . Anne-Marie Ottesen
Heidrun's lover . . . . Per Frisch
Kaja's husband . . . . : Henrik Scheele
Mie's senior lover . . . . Jon Eikemo
Hotel porter . . . . Brasse Brännström

Although already a boxoffice hit on home turf, helmer Anja Breien's comedy feature "Wives, 2 — Ten Years Later" may prove an embarrassment to the otherwise meticulous filmmaker who is noted abroad mostly for serious fare, but whose first "Wives" outing had flash and wit plus a topicality the sequel has substituted with staleness, repetition and erratic technique in all departments.

Item is already on the international fest circuit with London and Chicago coming up after Lübeck, however, and a pre-preem showing at Rimini and may enthuse some offshore die-hard anything-goes feminists because of the cause it either espouses or — so it would seem to others — mocks cruelly.

In the first "Wives," Breien had the same three actresses plan a weekend away from their Oslovite men and homes, but they got caught up and frustrated in various ways, both melancholy and hilarious, that had the snap of deep-cutting satire as well as plenty of warm feeling for the female victims of male manners & morals. The second time around, the three women seemed to have learned nothing while they stumble, mostly drunkenly, around Oslo on the night before Christmas, bemoaning their fates with the very same men who remain the targets of their desires. The trio seems exhibitionist and prone to locker-room dialog. If the men in their lives remain slightly ridiculous, the women appear stuck at a very tedious, near-pubescent level. They do succeed in running away this time — to a southern Sweden luxury hotel where they get to quarrel with each other before they return, nothing learned, nothing achieved, to their Oslo status quo. At the hotel, they — and audiences — are treated to a first-rate comedy performance by Sweden's Brasse Brännström.

His bit part as a hotel porter seems, however, to be completely of his own making, while it serves to make all the other comedy conceits of "Wives, 2 — Ten Years Later" sound and look tinny. The three actresses, Fröydis Armand, Katja Medboe and Anne-Marie Ottesen, are said to have collaborated on film's script but in this, they have not furthered the cause of scripting by committee any more than the cause of women's lib. —*Kell.*

P.R.O.F.S.
(FRENCH-COLOR)

Paris, Nov. 11.

An AMLF release of a Madeleine Films production. Produced by Gilbert de Goldschmidt. Directed by Patrick Schulmann. Features entire cast. Screenplay, Schulmann, Didier Dolna; camera (Fujicolor), Jacques Assuerus; art director, Jean-Claude Gallouin; editor, Aline Asséo; sound, Gérard Lamps; music, Schulmann. Reviewed at the UGC Biarritz theater, Paris, Nov. 10, 1985. Running time: **95 MINS.**
With: Patrick Bruel, Fabrice Luchini, Laurent Gamelon, Christophe Bourseiller, Martine Sarcey, Etienne Draber, Camile de Casabianca, Yolande Gilot, Charlotte Julian, Isabelle Mergault, Chantal Neuwirth.

"P.R.O.F.S.," one of the rare domestic films to score at the boxoffice this season, features four young subversive teachers in a typical French lycée, where they upset the establishment with their unconventional notions and sense of vengeful outrage.

Despite its open reference to "Mash," pic is too timid and familiar in its hijinks to claim any sort of parentage by the corrosive Robert Altman satire, and in its weaker moments has the assembly line-gag feeling of a Claude Zidi classroom farce.

Yet this is the most agreeable feature of director Patrick Schulmann, who debuted with the sex comedy "Et la Tendresse? Bordel!" the sleeper smash of 1979, but thereafter failed to repeat that success (though he directed last year the commercially profitable Aldo Maccione vehicle, "Aldo And Junior").

Schulmann here at least seems to have made a happy union with Didier Dolna, a professional teacher who wrote the original story and worked on the script. Between Schulmann's obsessive interest with sex games people play and Dolna's iconoclastic ideas on education, the film gains in its episodic ironies and more realistic humor.

The four young musketeers of academia are played with quirky warmth by Patrick Bruel, the most progressive of the lot, Christophe Bourseiller, the ever-goofy Fabrice Luchini and Laurent Gamelon, as the cool gym instructor who flips out after a disastrous romance.
—*Len.*

Miranda
(ITALIAN-COLOR)

Rome, Nov. 6.

A C.I.D.I.F. release. Produced by Giovanni Bertolucci for San Francisco Film. Written and directed by Giovanni Tinto Brass. Stars Serena Grandi. Camera (Color), Silvano Ippoliti; editor, Brass and Muller; art director, Paolo Biagetti; music, Riz Ortolani. Reviewed at Quirinale Cinema, Rome, Nov. 5, 1985. Running time: **99 MINS.**
Miranda . . . . Serena Grandi
Norman . . . . Andy J. Forest
Berto . . . . Andrea Occhipinti
Toni . . . . Franco Branciaroli
The consul . . . . Franco Interlenghi

In "Miranda," a silly, plotless pic whose lone virtues of freshness and irreverency pale long before the end, Giovanni Tinto Brass ("Caligula") seems to be slumming it, thumbing his nose at his own audience. This very Mediterranean fantasy is designed for worshippers of big-boned Earth Mother figures and unsophisticated couplings.

If in "The Key" Brass discovered that the ample flesh of mature actresses could exert an irresistible attraction on audiences, in "Miranda" he takes the concept a step further and builds an entire film around the over-indulged, under-exercised charms of newcomer Serena Grandi. Grandi's role, luckily, calls not so much for acting as merely exhibiting the body of a monumental nude with maternal attributes straight out of Fellini. With her sweet child's face, irrepressible grin and all-consuming lust for men, Grandi hogs the screen, clumsy but not unappealing.

This early-'50's version of Mirandolina, heroine of Carlo Goldoni's celebrated 18th century play "La Locandiera," runs a roadside tavern-inn in the marshy countryside around Venice. Her beloved young spouse has been missing since the end of the war, but Miranda still hopes he'll turn up. In the meantime, the maybe-widow consoles herself with a handsome local trucker named Berto (Andrea Occhipinti) and a rich Consul, played by the badly aged Franco Interlenghi.

Pic adopts the classic A-B-A-B structure of sex scene-story-sex scene-story. This uncomplicated approach works as long as Grandi and the situations she finds herself in remain startling, which is about the first half of the picture. After that Brass' imagination flags and pic sinks into a positively anti-climactic ending — Miranda marries the one man she never gave herself to, her waiter at the inn (Franco Branciaroli), who demurely beds her in full legality.

The cutest setpiece, underscored by Riz Ortolani's playful score, has Miranda and a girlfriend lasciviously eyeing boys on the beach and imagining what they look like without their drawers, in what must qualify as the most sustained male back nudity sequence in Italian cinema. There is also a fleeting orgy scene in a hotel with Norman (Andy J. Forest), a left-over American G.I.; a romp in the back of a truck; a rained-out picnic in the woods that turns into a roll in the mud by 10 people; and a coupling against the scenic background of an outdoor urinal. All in a spirit of good, clean fun, for Miranda is not one to be hypocritical and moralistic about sex, although one gets a strong feeling Brass is.

Despite a few lovingly shot landscapes of the Veneto region, Silvano Ippoliti's camerawork is prone to unsteady zooms in the bedroom and obsessive anatomical views of Grandi front and back, especially lower front and lower back.
—*Yung.*

Hot Target
(NEW ZEALAND-COLOR)

Hollywood, Nov. 7.

A Crown International Pictures release of an Endeavour Prods. Ltd. film. Produced by John Barnett, Brian Cook. Directed by Denis Lewiston. Features entire cast. Screenplay, Lewiston, based on a story by Gerry O'Hara; camera (Colorfilm (N.Z.) color), Alec Mills; editor, Michael Horton; music, Gil Mellé; production designer, Jo Ford; art director, Kirsten Shoulder; set designer, Paul Radford; costumes, Patrick Steel; assistant director, Terry Needham; sound, Colorfilm Pty Ltd.; casting, Onorato/Franks-U.S., M&L Casting-Australia. Reviewed at Nossack Screening Room, Los Angeles, Calif., Nov. 7, 1985.

(MPAA Rating: R.) Running time: **93 MINS.**
Christine Webber . . . . Simone Griffeth
Greg Sandford . . . . Steve Marchuk
Clive Webber . . . . Brian Marshall
Detective Nolan . . . . Peter McCauley
Suanne Maxwell . . . . Elizabeth Hawthorne
Douglas Maxwell . . . . Ray Henwood
Benjamin . . . . John Watson

An unlikely pickup for teen-oriented Crown International, "Hot Target" starts out as a soft-core romance, complete with appropriately tacky music, but eventually hardens into a Claude Chabrolesque exploration of obsessive passion among the rich and restless. Unusual hybrid leaves the film floating in a commercial nether world with no help from its non sequitur title. Crown will have its work cut out for it to find an appreciative audience for this New Zealand oddity.

Part of the problem is that pic is neither good enough to win over more discerning filmgoers nor bad enough for the exploitation crowd. "Hot Target," is in fact, a good deal above average with writer/director Denis Lewiston displaying considerable talent as well as lapses from his inexperience.

Rather than getting inside the lives of his rich heroine (Simone Griffeth) and her burglar boyfriend (Steve Marchuk) who kills the husband (Brian Marshall) in an act of passion, Lewiston plots their progress too methodically, too coldly. One never gets caught up in the heat of their relationship and even their lovemaking scenes seem more forced than essential.

Griffeth, an American, is married to a wealthy and heartless New Zealand businessman when she gets entagled with Marchuk who masterminds a casual meeting in order to arrange a heist from her house. Lust turns to love and the plot thickens with some fairly interesting turns along the way.

"Hot Target" picks up considerably in its second half after the crime has entrapped the lovers in an inextricable web. Climactic chase scene at a racetrack has the nailbitting suspense necessary to make the genre satisfying but which is largely missing elsewhere.

Lewiston takes too long in getting around to the deadly business at hand with the editing never really hitting the mark. Griffeth gets close to the cool blond exterior and burning core that Hitchcock was so fond of but Marchuk plays it with too much cool and not enough charm.

Marshall is a pushover as the despicable tycoon and Peter McCauley as a hardnosed cop almost tips over into a caricature. Trick to pulling off this kind of fare is a delicate sense of balance which Lewiston is able to sustain only part of the time.

Production values are passable without really achieving the required sheen and high gloss for the material. —*Jagr.*

Transylvania 6-5000
(COLOR)

Frantic, unfunny spoof.

A New World Pictures release of Mace Neufeld production, in association with Jadran Film. A New World Pictures/Dow Chemical Co. picture. Executive producers, Paul Lichtman, Arnie Fishman. Produced by Neufeld, Thomas H. Brodek. Written and directed by Rudy DeLuca. Stars Jeff Goldblum, Joseph Bologna, Ed Begley Jr. Camera (color), Tomislav Pinter; editor, Harry Keller; music, Lee Holdridge; sound, Pat Mitchell; sound design, David Lewis Yewdall; production design, Zeljko Senecic; set decoration, Trpcic Ivica; visual consultant, Steve Haberman; production manager, Milan Stanislic; production manager, Milan Stanislic production representative, Robert F. Lyons; production supervisor, Donko Buljan; postproduction supervisor, Trevor Jolly; costume design, Christine Glazier, Latica Ivanisevic; special effects, Marijan Kuroglan; special effects makeup, Cosmekinetics' Bob Williams & Ellis Burman; casting, Joseph D'Agosta, Monica Swann; associate producer, Glenn Neufeld. Reviewed at Magno Penthouse screening room, N.Y., Nov. 6, 1985. (MPAA Rating: PG.) Running time: **94 MINS.**
Jack Harrison . . . . Jeff Goldblum
Dr. Malavaqua . . . . Joseph Bologna
Gil Turner . . . . Ed Begley Jr.
Lupi . . . . Carol Kane
Lepescu . . . . Jeffrey Jones
Radu . . . . John Byner
Odette . . . . Geena Davis
Also with: Michael Richards (Fejos), Donald Gibb (Wolfman), Norman Fell (Mac Turner), Teresa Ganzel (Elizabeth), Bozidar Smiljanic (Inspector Percek), Inge Apelt (Madame Morovia), Petar Buntic (Hunyadi — Frankenstein's monster), Rudy DeLuca (Lawrence Malbot), Dusko Valentic (Twisted man), Ksenija Prohaska (Mummy), Sara Grdjan (Laura), Robert F. Lyons (Victim).

"Transylvania 6-5000" is a terminally unfunny spoof of horror films, aimed at the kindergarten audience. Debuting filmmaker Rudy DeLuca (who has contributed to the scripts of Mel Brooks comedies) encourages frantic overplaying with embarrassing results.

Tabloid editor Mac Turner (Norman Fell) sends his son Gil (Ed Begley Jr.) and fellow reporter/buddy Jack (Jeff Goldblum) to Transylvania to come back with a "Frankenstein Lives!" banner story, based on a home movie he shows them (in which the film's production rep, actor Robert F. Lyons, plays, uncredited, a victim of the monster).

In Transylvania, film closely resembles a squeaky clean version of the 1979 West German sex comedy "Dracula Blows His Cool." The town mayor (Jeffrey Jones) doubles as hotel manager, planning to open a castle as theme hotel. There the two intrepid reporters find all manner of monsters, traceable to the mad experiments of Dr. Malavaqua (Joseph Bologna doing a Sid Caeser-like turn). It's basically 90 minutes of filler until a happy ending reveals, to the chagrin of fantasy fans, that the monsters aren't monsters after all.

Though they make an engaging screen team, Goldblum and Begley aren't given any funny lines to work with. With several scenes lapsing into improvisation, Goldblum has trouble keeping a straight face, while Begley doesn't get any real laughs until the finale.

Bologna and his two aides, Carol Kane and John Byner, seem to be trapped in old-fashioned burlesque (or tv sketch) routines that drone on endlessly. For the kids, Michael Richards executes goofy slapstick moves and Geena Davis provides the PG-rated skin as a Vampirella comic creation. The monsters are disappointing, with a wolfman whose makeup seems lifted from George Lucas' Chewbacca.

As evidence to the real reason such poor films are produced, Yugoslavian-lensed pic bears a "New World Pictures/Dow Chemical Co." copyright, presumably turning the alchemist's trick of converting blocked funds into exportable celluloid. —*Lor.*

Falsk som vatten
(False As Water)
(SWEDISH-COLOR)

Malmö, Nov. 7.

A Svensk Film release of Svenska Ord/Svensk Film production. Executive producers, Waldemar Bergendahl, Hans Alfredson. Original story, screenplay and directed by Alfredson. Camera (Eastmancolor), Jörgen Persson, Rolf Lindström; editor, Jan Persson; music, Stefan Nilsson; production management, Anita Tesler, Eva Ivarsson; production design, Stig Boquist; costumes, Lenamarie Wahlström; assistant director, Hakan Bjerking. Reviewed at the Camera, Malmö, Nov. 7, 1985. Running time: **102 MINS.**
Clara . . . . Malin Ek
John . . . . Sverre Anker Ousdal
Stig . . . . Stellan Skarsgard
Anna, John's wife . . . . Marie Göranzon
Carl . . . . Orjan Ramberg
Fia . . . . Lotta Ramel
Jens . . . . Philip Zandén
Tina . . . . Catharina Alinder
Lill-John . . . . Martin Lindström
Mr. Schült . . . . Magnus Uggla
Weirdo . . . . Folke Lind

Having veered between satrical comedy and realistic symbolism in his first three features, author-actor-producer Hans (Hasse) Alfredson graduates as a European filmmaker of major status with "False As Water," a Hitchcockian suspenser that probes deeply into the soul of jealousy and into the excesses that this Black Sickness, as it is known in Swedish, may lead to among people otherwise considered to be in control of themselves. "False As Water" (title is a quote from Shakespeare's "Othello") will, aided by superior acting and the shiniest production gloss, travel far and wide both as art and as immediate-impact entertainment.

Plot has book publisher John (Norway's Sverre Anker Ousdal) as the husband who is prone to philandering, but who is ready to play for keeps when he meets young poetess Clara (Malin Ek). This leaves John's taciturn wife Anna (Marie Göranzon) and Clara's novelist-lover Stig (Stellan Skarsgard) high and dry and, seemingly, not ready to do very much about it. Somebody does object, since the new couple soon finds their love-nest apartment in a slum area house turned into a virtual death trap with menace spelled out in the misplacing of objects, gas leaks, mysterious grafitti, etc.

Frail Clara soon seeks refuge in drinking wine before noon and eventually has a nervous breakdown. There is to be, however, no escape for John and Clara, but the whodunit aspect of Alfredson's film comes as a complete shock although the denouement is psychologically sound and even seems inevitable when finally absorbed during a whirlwind ending of chase and bloodletting.

The subject of jealousy is explored via sharp vignettes of film's secondary characters, too. These people of the intellectual elite (which Alfredson greets wryly by having such Scandinavian leading lights of literature and television as Suzanne Brögger and Nils-Petter Sundgren appear in cameos) are made to seem truly human. Alfredson may take a dim, if not downright bleak, view of humanity but he shows sympathy with its individual members. —*Kell.*

Le Phenix Et Le Dragon Ou Une Messe Pour La Chine
(SWISS-DOCU-COLOR-16m)

Nyon, Oct. 17.

A production of City-Films Geneve, Television Romande and Choeur Universitaire, Geneva. Produced, directed and edited by Bertrand Theubet; camera (color, 16m), Simon Edelstein; sound. Alain Klarer. Reviewed at Nyon Intl. Film Festival, Oct. 17, 1985. Running time: **62 MINS.**

This conventional but pleasant documentary chronicles a trip to China by the University Choir of Geneva. Film shows charming young Swiss singers enjoying themselves, making friends among the Chinese, swapping how-to's about interpreting Mozart, touring about and personifying strong argument for cultural exchange and building international amity through the arts.

Chen Lianv-Seng, for 20 years the group's choirmaster in Geneva, returns with them to his native China. For him, it is a wrenching but rewarding homecoming. He and his 70 Swiss singers are impressed by Chinese respect for Western music and by their multiple sylistic approaches to Mozart. Film's finale is a joint performance of Mozart's "Mass In C Minor," epitomizing triumph of culture over ideological differences.

This is a sweet film with an uncomplicated message that can fit into U.S. school distribution and into some tv usage. —*Hitch.*

Männer
(Men)
(WEST GERMAN-COLOR)

Hof, W. Germany, Oct. 28.
An Olga Film, Munich, in coproduction with Second German Television (ZDF), Mainz. Written and directed by Doris Dörrie. Features entire cast. Camera (color), Helge Weindler; editor, Jörg Neumann; music, Claus Bantzer; sets, Neumann. Reviewed at Hof Film Fest, Oct. 27, 1985. Running time: **98 MINS.**
With: Heiner Lauterbach (Julius), Uwe Ochsenknecht (Stefan), Ulrike Kriener (Paula), Janna Marangosoff (Angelika), Marie-Charlott Schüler (Marita Strass), Dietmar Bär (Lothar), Edith Volkmann (Frau Lennert).

A leading femme helmer and a very gifted storyteller, Doris Dörrie scored one of the biggest audience hits of the Hof film fest with her third feature, "Men."

The protagonist is a successful ad man who discovers he's being cuckolded at home. Being the macho type, it galls him to find he's suddenly playing second fiddle in the boudoir, and on his 12th wedding anniversary at that. Immediately, Julius takes a leave-of-absence from the firm, walks out of the matrimonial nest and takes up spying on his wife for a hobby.

It turns out that Julius' rival for Paula's affections is a down-and-out, would-be artist who leads a bohemian life in the commune lifestyle section of Munich. Julius hits upon an idea: why not join the group as the roommate of Stefan, Paula's lover? It works — and that's the twist that gives "Men" a thematic lift to place it a bit above the ordinary.

Pic is constructed tightly. The only lesson Dörrie has yet to learn is to dare delving into gag-writing and witty dialog, for things tend to bog down in the middle of all her films once she has established character and motivation. —*Holl.*

Zahn um Zahn
(On The Tracks Of The Killers)
(WEST GERMAN-COLOR)

Berlin, Nov. 2.
A Bavaria Atelier production in coproduction with Neue Constantin Film-produktion, Munich, and Westdeutscher Rundfunk (WDR), Cologne. Directed by Hajo Gies. Stars Götz George. Screenplay, Horst Vocks, Thomas Wittenburg; camera (color), Jürgen Jürges; editor, Margot von Schliefen; music, Klaus Lage Band; sound, Karsten Ullrich; sets, Winfried Henning. Reviewed at Zoo Palast, Berlin, Nov. 1, 1985. Running time: **95 MINS.**
With: Götz George (Schimanski), Renan Demirkan (Ulli), Rufus (Hacker), Eberhard Feik (Thanner), Charles Brauer (Grassmann), Herbert Steinmetz (Krüger), Louis-Marie Taillefer (Bonano), Julien Maurel (Jean Pierre), Ulrich Matschoss (Königsberg), Martin Lüttge (Wilkens), David Gabison (Corti), Claude Carliez (Jules), Erich Bar (Manni), Bilal Inci (Barkeeper).

Hajo Gies' "On The Tracks Of The Killers" (German title translates as "A Tooth For A Tooth") is another worthy attempt to win back part of the fading home audience with an action-thriller. It's inspired by the tv-detective series that came into their own over the past decade.

In fact, the lines between tv and film production are wiped out completely in "On The Tracks Of The Killers," for the hero, Schimanski, comes right out of the popular "Kommissar" (police inspector) series bearing his name, while helmer Gies was one of those creatively responsible for the success formula of an offbeat cop with a Polish moniker fighting for law-and-order in the rough-and-tumble industrial Ruhr area of western Germany. The only difference is that the cop gets suspended from duty in the film version.

This suspension allows Schimanski to go his own way as a lone powerhouse to solve the convoluted crime that includes the murder of a schoolboy friend and his family in their home, the foul deed happening during a police raid on a housing settlement in Duisburg where the police inspector grew up. Götz George (Schimanski) gets particularly riled when he finds the eviction and the murder can be traced to a rich speculator, Grassmann, who in turn has connections with crime bosses in Marseilles.

To keep him off the trail, Grassmann pulls strings to get Schimanski into trouble for his unorthodox investigative ways, and then suspended. A liberated woman reporter steps in whenever needed to detour her bullheaded boyfriend as together they try to outwit each other in getting to the incriminating evidence. Just like in the Saturday serials, the pair gets in over their heads every quarter hour — only to walk away from each knock-off attempt in the nick of time. In the end, the bad guys are pegged as ex-French Foreign Legion pals.

All action without storyline or dialog, however, doesn't add up to much of a thriller in the long run. One hardly feels the presence of danger at any particular time, while the camera tricks and superhuman antics have more in common with slapstick routines rather than derring-do realism.

Götz George is tops as Schimanski. —*Holl.*

Paul Chevrolet en de ultieme hallucinatie
(Paul Chevrolet And The Ultimate Hallucination)
(DUTCH-B&W)

Amsterdam, Oct. 28.
A Cupido Films release of an Altamira Films Prod. Produced by Lea Wongsoredjo, Ruud den Drijver. Directed by Pim de Parra. Features entire cast. Screenplay, de la Parra, Dorna van Rouveroy, Karin Loomans; camera (b&w), Fans Bromet; editor, Hans van Dongen; music, Lodewijk de Boer; sound, Jac Vleeshouwers. Reviewed at Cinepress, Amsterdam, Oct. 26, 1985. Running time: **110 MINS.**
Leopold (Paul Chevrolet) . . . . . Peter Faber
Willie, his wife . . . . Jenny Arean
Suzanne (his lover) . . . . Liz Snoyink
Elizabeth, the editor . . . . Ellen Vogel
Herman du Bois, Leopold's
friend . . . . Cas Enklaar
Charlotte, Herman's
wife . . . . Moniek Toebosch
Boy Pappa, a gangster . . Eddie Constantine

Helmer Pim de la Parra hopes "Paul Chevrolet" will be the start of a continuous flow of mini-budget features, able to recoup costs in the small and depressed Dutch film market. Shooting took 14 days, main editing 10. Pic preemed 10 weeks after lensing started, with total costs of $100,000.

Result is an entertaining film, which misses becoming wholly satisfactory because the scenario remains inferior to directing, thesping and technical credits.

Story is about Leopold (Peter Faber), 40, divorced, with one teenage daughter, who writes rather successful detective stories under the pseudonym Paul Chevrolet. He wants to become a serious author, but his novel "The Ultimate Hallucination" is rejected by the publisher as being too juvenile. Small wonder, because Leopold himself is not a really grownup person.

The editor's daughter has an affair with Leopold, and our hero also has an affair with a girl who is the mistress of Leopold's best friend. The friend dies, Leopold is drawn back to wife and child. But he always is drawn easily to attractive women. The annoying thing is that most sequences remain separate, entertaining bits and never become a whole. —*Wall.*

Betrogen
(Betrayed)
(WEST GERMAN-COLOR)

Hof, W. Germany, Oct. 26.
A Common Film production, Berlin, in coproduction with Cinegrafik/Helmut Herbst, Adolf Winkelmann Filmproduktion, and Bayerischer Rundfunk, Munich. Written and directed by Harun Farocki. Features entire cast. Camera (color), Axel Block; lighting, Holger Greiss, Joachim Scholz, Peter Arendt; sets, Ursula Lefkes, Hermann Pitz, Raimund Kummer; music, Andreas Köbner; editor, Renate Merck; tv producer, Silvia Koller. Reviewed at Hof Film Fest, Oct. 26, 1985. Running time: **90 MINS.**
With Roland Schäfter (Jens Baumann), Katja Rupé (Anna Mewis), Nina Hoger (Edith Mewis), Timo and Denis Menzel, Swenja and Ilka Höwe (Micha and Laura).

Harun Farocki specializes in avant-garde features soaked in social or political meaning, but generally running at a snail's pace — "Between Two Wars" (1978), "Something Becomes Visible" (1982), and now "Betrayed." For the film buff captivated by images and mannerisms, his unique approach to cinematic art deserves to be better known.

"Betrayed" follows the classic double-identity formula. Story (based on a newspaper account) offers a study of a man who has murdered his wife accidentally, then confesses the crime to his sister-in-law, with whom he has been having an affair while the wife was in a hospital (apparently a psychological clinic). The sister-in-law is pretty much a lookalike, so she simply changes roles with the dead partner, going so far in her new identity as to adopt her own children via a complicated but credible legal route.

What happens then is a round of role-playing until the cat is out of the bag some years later. —*Holl.*

Harom Nover — Filmregeny
(Three Sisters — A Film Novel)
(HUNGARIAN-DOCU-B&W)

Minneapolis, Oct. 25.
A Hungarian Film production, Studio Budapest. A documentary with fiction elements by Istvan Darday. Screenplay, Darday, Györgyi Szalai; camera, Lajos Koltai. Reviewed at Minnesota Film Center, Minneapolis, Oct. 24, 1985. Running time: **270 MINS.**
With: Szuzsa Szakacs (Mari), Maria Himmer (Agi), Eszter Bognar (Zsuzsa), Imre Dezsi (Father), Mrs. Dezsi (Mother).

Istvan Darday's "Three Sisters — A Film Novel" (1977) was made at a time when the lines between fact and fiction in the so-called "fiction-documentary" and "docu-drama" were being blurred beyond viewing visibility. A corresponding technique, known as the "film-novel," was formulated at the Bela Balazs Studio in Budapest, a kind of sociographic documentary film that's ultimately designed to make important statements about both society and the conditions that mold it.

"Three Sisters" is as appealing in its film structure as it is in its sociological theme. Darday and writer Györgyi Szalai have set out to make an authentic portrait of life and times in Budapest today. The way they do it is to seek out non-professionals to fit their given roles like a glove, then to flesh out given personalities along a tightly constructed narrative line.

Zsuzsa, Agi and Mari are all at the critical age of life-decisions between 20 and 30. They live with their parents in a very crowded apartment in Budapest, the parents ordinary working people (who came to the city from the country) looking forward to retirement and the day when the girls will marry and move out.

Zsuzsa already has been married and divorced. She works in a textile factory and hopes one day to become a clothes designer of some rank and recognition, but meantime contends herself with a love affair with a married man. When she attempts to force her lover to make a decision, he can't do it, so she quits both job and the liaison.

Agi, the second oldest, attends the university and studies economics. She hangs out with a cynical indifferent son of well-to-do parents, but the casual affair leads to a pregnancy. Agi hopes to marry her rich lover, but he is adamant about an abortion. It's done, but only after long deliberation and with resignation.

Mari, the youngest, works as a clerk. She, too, hopes to move up the ladder of success by enjoying a new boyfriend to find her a job on the factory newspaper he works for as a reporter. Guts and hard work result in writing articles for the paper on her own, but she eventually drops her macho boyfriend to marry a friendly type quickly, on the rebound, and have a child to delight the family.

The film-novel method prompts improvising before a running camera as though it's not there at all.

Even more important: life under the Socialist system is held up to a magnifying glass. There is one scene of the family getting up in the morning to follow a ritual in the tiny apartment that takes it all in from an intimate distance in one long take. Visits to a factory contrast ironically with the milieu of a state artist. Problems of housing and employment and management are treated squarely without ducking the issue, for even the use of a slogan or cliché can be detected under this filming method. —*Holl.*

Ofelia kommer til byen
(Ophelia Hits Town)
(DANISH-COLOR)

Copenhagen, Nov. 5.

A Kärne Film release of Palle Fogtdal/Per Holst Film production with the Danish Film Institute (Christian Clausen, Peter Poulsen) and DR/TV. Original story, screenplay and directed by Jon Bang Carlsen. Camera (Eastmancolor), Alexander Gruszynski; editor, Anders Refn; music, Hans-Erik Philip, Henrik Langkilde, Carl Nielsen; production management, Jens Arnoldus, Jane Graun; stunts, Svenska Stuntgruppen (Johan Thoren); costumes, Pia Myrdal. Reviewed at the Grand, Copenhagen, Nov. 5, 1985. Running time: **96 MINS.**
John . . . . Reine Brynolfsson
Molly . . . . Stine Bierlich
Vagn . . . . Flemming (Bamse) Jörgensen
Rita, John's mother . . . . Anna Lise Hirsch Bjerrum
Arne . . . . Ingolf David
School teacher . . . . . . Hans Chr. Aegidius
Theodora . . . . Else Petersen
Also with: Axel Larsen, Gustav Bentsen, Kristen Poulsgard, Niels Nygard, Peter Ruby, Anders Pedersen, Margrethe Madsen, Viggo Madsen, Bent Ove Jacobsen.

Jon Bang Carlsen's "Ophelia Hits Town" has the minuscule population of a fishing village on the remotest, poorest stretch of the Jutland peninsula's North Sea coast coached by a school teacher from a bigger city into doing an amateur production of "Hamlet." The verbiage of the play's monologs are then put to the test against the fumblings and stumblings of the nonactors.

John, a near-half-wit gravedigger and church handiman, gets the Hamlet role and struggles mightily. The King is played by a bus driver of pagan instincts and of holierthan-thou parentage. Ophelia has an elderly lady plunging into the mad scene until Molly hits town to take over. Molly is a young Copenhagen prostitute who has sought refuge out west from a client with demands so bizarre that she has been tempted to kill him. The Queen is played by John's real-life mother who has slept around so much he does not know who fathered him.

Along with evocative cinematography, Bang Carlsen tells the ensuing story in a rather abrupt vignette style that keeps audiences guessing too often about who is doing what to whom and about where dreams begin and reality ends. The general idea seems to be that the gravedigger is helped out of his various traumas by the visiting prostitute, and that his love for her gives her the strength to go ahead and kill the client who one day turns up to claim her body.

"Ophelia Hits Town" has a style uniquely its own and a cool mix of beauty and brutal frankness in the depicting of its characters. Last are played convincingly by a few professionals and by more amateurs from the chosen North Sea coast locations.

In the Hamlet and Ophelia leads, Reine Brynolfsson, a Swede, and Stine Bierlich perform with muted and aggressive charm respectively, while pop singer Flemming (Bamse) Jörgensen in an acting debut as the bus driver & Danish King often seems to walk away with the show. Film is a small-scale art item that should be attractive on the minor fest circuit. It will take canny effort to get it into many commercial situations (apart from television) outside its native territory. —*Kell.*

City Hero
(HONG KONG-COLOR)

Hong Kong, Oct. 28.

A Cinema City Co. Ltd. production and presentation. Released by Golden Princess. Directed by Dennis Yu. Produced by Dennis Yu Film Production Co. Ltd. Stars Mark Cheng, Anthony Tang, Dean Shek, Pang Kin Sang, Michael Wong, Billy Lau, Patricia Ha. Executive Producer, Yu Chung Hung. Screenplay, Lam Koon Kiu; camera (color), Gary Ho; art direction, Robert Luk; music, Danny Chung; editor, Tony Chow; special effects, Kevin Chisnall. Reviewed at President theater, Hong Kong,, Oct. 27, 1985. Running time: **98 MINS.**
(Cantonese soundtrack with English subtitles)

Five young and idealistic policemen, Mark Cheng, Anthony Tang, Pang Kin Sang, Michael Wong and Billy Lau join the special cop squad in "City Hero."

It is the elite unit of the local police force, and to be accepted they must undergo a rigorous training and elimination process headed by meanie Dean Shek.

Meanwhile, Mark Cheng falls in love with the neighborhood grocery girl (Pat Ha) and that gets him into a series of troubles with Shek and the girl's family.

Despite the hostilities and hard work, the healthy-looking men work out well and at the same time begin to understand the total devotion of their well-meaning instructor. This gives them inspiration and respect for the man.

During an emergency assignment on Christmas day, Mark Cheng is killed. At the burial service, his buddies mourn his death, but his demise serves as guiding light in their future careers with the force.

The corny direction of Dennis Yu (once an innovative director now trapped in the "system" he once avoided), is flat and one-dimensional. All the clichés from "Police Academy" and low-grade American B-features are in this lowbudget, slapstick comedy.

Judging from the audience response, Dennis Yu and Cinema City will be laughing all the way to the bank. — *Mel.*

Heart Of The Dragon
(HONG KONG-COLOR)

Hong Kong, Oct. 28.

A Bo Ho production for Golden Harvest presentation and release. Directed by Samo Hung. Stars Jackie Chan, Samo Hung, Emily Chu, Melvin Wong, Chung Fat, Chan Friend, Lam Ching-Ying. Screenplay, Barry Wong; song sung by Julie Sue (WEA Records), composed by Lam Man-Yee. (No other credits provided by producer). Reviewed at Queen's theater, Hong Kong, Oct. 27, 1985. Running time: **98 MINS.**
(Cantonese soundtrack with English subtitles)

Samo Hung and Jackie Chan play brothers in "Heart Of The Dragon." But Samo portrays the mentally retarded one while Jackie is a cop with a bright future, except that he is in constant disagreement with his superior, Melvin Wong.

Jackie wants to travel, but he knows his family responsibility is to take care of his brother. Samo, while playing with his toy gun, scares a gangster who is carrying stolen jewelry. He is held hostage by the gangster to force Jackie to do something about the situation.

Our kung-fu comedy hero is around to save the day, but first he must kill some of the baddies to save his beloved brother.

This bread and butter Cantonese action drama has already grossed nearly $HK20,000,000 and is still running. —*Mel.*

Edvige Scimitt
(WEST GERMAN-COLOR-16m)

Hof, W. Germany, Oct. 27.

A Von Vietinghoff Film, Berlin in coproduction with Xanadu Film, Zurich, and Second German Television, Mainz. Written and directed by Matthias Zschokke. Features entire cast. Camera (color, 16m), Adrian Zschokke; sound, Christian Moldt; sets, Jan Schlubach; costumes, Marlis von Soden; editor, Barbara von Weitershausen; production manager, Udo Heiland; producers, Jochen von Vietinghoff, Georg Radanowicz. Reviewed at Hof Film Fest, Oct. 26, 1985. Running time: **89 MINS.**
With: Ingrid Kaiser (Edvige Scimitt), Fritz Schediwy (mesmerist), Wolfgang Michael (the candid one), Klaus Völker (the indirect one), Verena Buss (Mrs. Smallwood), Pia Waibel (Anna Robel), Bruno Ferrari (clergyman).

Better known as a writer than a filmmaker, Matthias Zschokke joined German avant-garde ranks after penning a handful of novels and working in theater in Stuttgart and Bochum. Swiss-born, he has a peculiar approach to language and a bent for using the film image as a psychological exploration of the self. His "Edvige Scimitt" was the farthest out of many experimental features unspooled at Hof, but also the easiest to digest.

Hedwig Schmitt, known as Edvige Scimitt to the mispronouncing authorities in Italy during her stay there (names are often "nationalized" for easier pronunciation in Europe), led a quite contradictory life in the early 1920s as she described it in her biography. She worked in London as a maid, in Milan as a waitress, in Zandvoort (Holland) as a servant, and in New York as a bathroom attendant. Without much trouble, Zschokke reconstructed these stages in her Swiss life in the Esplanade, a former deluxe hotel in Berlin that's about to be turned into a film house for cultural film activities.

The question arises at the outset as to whether everyone in the film is a bit off his rocker. The rather innocent miss regularly is bumping into people who leer and stare at her. Her schizophrenia mounts till she is pushing herself to the borderline between dream and reality. As a servant throughout her life, she finds herself put upon by employers and colleagues. She becomes pregnant in Zandvoort, migrates to America and bears a son in New York.

Upon the death of her three-year-old child, she breaks down completely and is admitted to a psychological clinic. Her brother in Switzerland eventually sees to it that she is transferred to Switzerland for care and treatment.

Zschokke views Hedwig Schmitt's journey as though nearly all of the scenes take place in her fantasies. Color, costumes and sets thus form a fundamental stylistic component to the whole. Pic was made on a low budget for the "Little Television Show" on ZDF in a late-night slot. —*Holl.*

Der Angriff der Gengenwart au die übrige Zeit
(The Assault Of The Present Upon The Rest Of Time)
(WEST GERMAN-COLOR/B&W)

Berlin, Nov. 5.

A Kairos-Film production, in coproduction with the Second German Television (ZDF), Mainz, and the Städtische Bühnen Frankfurt/Main - Oper. A Film Essay with fictional and documentary elements written and directed by Alexander Kluge. Camera (color, b&w), Thomas Mauch, Werner Lüring, Hermann Fahr, Judith Kaufmann; editor, Jane Seitz; sets, Jürgen Schnell; tv-producer, Willi Segler. Reviewed at Lupe 1, Berlin, Nov. 3, 1985. Running time: **113 MINS.**
With: Jutta Hoffman (Gertrud Meinecke), Armin Müller-Stahl (Blind movie director), Michael Rehberg (Herr von Gerlach), Peter Roggisch (Big boss), Rosel Zech (Superfluous employee), Maria Slatinaru ("Tosca" in Verdi Opera), Günther Reich ("Scarpia" in Verdi Opera), Piero Visconti ("Cavaradossi" in Verdi Opera), Edgar M. Böhlke (Scrap iron dealer), Heinning Burk (Computer worker at home), Gunna Wardena and her children (Computer worker's family).

Alexander Kluge's "The Assault Of The Present Upon The Rest Of Time" is the third in his series of film essays employing both documentary and fictional elements to form a literary whole.

Jutta Hoffman plays a court-appointed foster-parent, who has been assigned to care for a little girl still in psychological shock after the death of her parents in an automobile accident she herself witnessed. The time comes when the girl is to be turned over to her aunt's family, particularly to a cold and calculating mistress of a newly purchased mansion. The aunt and her servants couldn't care less about the young girl's mental state. So the foster-parent up and leaves with the child in the middle of the night.

The "blind director" sequence is a real howler. In the middle of a subsidized (or safely financed) film production, the director goes blind — and the responsible producer is obliged to keep him on the job simply because contractually he apparently has no other alternative. A newspaper interviewer asks why the blind man is still in charge of the whole affair — and the producer does his very best to explain the situation.

The core of Kluge's thesis has to do with our perception of art in the revolutionary 20th century. He opens with a passage from a Frankfurt Opera production of Verdi's "Tosca," thus defining how moral and aesthetic issues were viewed by leading artistic figures of yesterday. Kluge then seeks to redefine these same issues through the lens of a movie camera, citing the seventh art as today's dominating moral and aesthetic force. Such being the case, the filmmaker contends, the classical concepts of tragedy and dramatic resolution (as exemplified in Verdi's opera) have now been negated by the cinematic art's "assault of the present upon the rest of time."
—*Holl.*

Die Wolfsbraut
(The Wolf's Bride)
(WEST GERMAN-COLOR-16m)

Hof, W. Germany, Oct. 27.

A Dagmar Beiersdorf Film in coproduction with Norddeutscher Rundfunk, Hamburg. Produced, written and directed by Beiersdorf. Features entire cast. Camera (color, 16m), Christoph Gies; sound, Christian Siewers; editor, Lothar Lambert; music, Pete, Wyoming-Bender; tv producer, Eberhard Scharfenberg. Reviewed at Hof Film Fest, Oct. 26, 1985. Running time: **85 MINS.**
With: Imke Barnstedt (Mascha), Martine Felton (Dennis), Lothar Lambert (Kurtchen, alias "Marilyn"), Albert Heins (Frank), Mustafa Iskandarani (Rajab), Roswitha Tischler (Cleo), Erika Rabau (Hannchen).

Some of the best of the Berlin no-budget pics were made by Lothar Lambert with Dagmar Beiersdorf assisting. Occasionally Beiersdorf branches out on her own with Lambert assisting as house editor and supporting actor. Of Beiersdorf's three features "Dolly Kaput" (1977), "Dirty Daughters" (1981) and now "The Wolf's Bride" — the last is the most polished and the least inventive.

Tale has a successful tv producer and femme filmmaker deciding to become a dropout for a while due to approaching middle age and a corresponding creative crisis. Along comes a mulatto whom she meets in a moviehouse cleaning up butts, and it's fascination at first sight. Shortly thereafter, she parts from her longstanding boyfriend to enter upon a precarious lesbian relationship. To make things merrier, along comes a happy-go-lucky transvestive (Lambert) who joins the duo on a vacation spree, where nature steps in to resolve the conflicts — if there ever were any there to begin with.

Lambert's scenes are ribticklers.
—*Holl.*

De Deur Van Het Huis
(The Door Of The House)
(DUTCH-B&W-16m)

Amsterdam, Oct. 17.

A The Movies/Classics release of a Rolf Orthel production. Produced by Orthel. Written and directed by Heddy Honigmann, Angiola Janigro; camera (b&w, 16m), Mat van Hensbergen; sound, Piotr van Dijk, Marcus Nijssen; editor, Jan Wouter van Reijen. Reviewed at The Movies, Amsterdam, Oct. 14, 1985. Running time: **98 MINS.**
Karel . . . . Johan Leysen
Johan . . . . Titus Muizelaar
Iris . . . . Catherine ten Bruggencate
A pollster . . . . Anke van't Hof

"The Door Of The House" is an art film, but not artsy, about two young men. They share a small apartment, have indifferent jobs and indifferent lives. They're used to each other, and good friends, though very different. If they have expectations, these are not great, but vague. They would like things to happen, but don't make them happen. They just hover.

Though they surreptitiously rebel against it and each other, they are afraid of anything that may disrupt the routine of their relationship, the only peg they have to hang their petty lives on.

Heddy Honigmann calls the film "a little tragedy in 20 scenes." She says that it is "probably about the difficulty of growing up." The two characters are about 30, but still more adolescent than adult. Johan Leysen (excellent) and Titus Muizelaar were directed so as to express themselves largely with their bodies, by gestures and movements.

The third protagonist, the camera, does the same. It stands still, then moves, then crawls. It noses close to things and people when it gets interested, and takes the viewer along.

"The Door Of The House" is an avant-garde film without gimmicks. It is simply cinema: pictures plus good, sometimes witty dialog, and made with the severe self-discipline which the characters completely lack. Considering pic was made on a tiny bit of shoestring (total budget was $21,000), one stands amazed at the talent, assiduity and perseverance which created an exceptional film which never loses its grip on the viewer's interest. It's fest fare for gourmets. — *Wall.*

Mein Lieber Schatz
(My Sweet Darling)
(WEST GERMAN-COLOR-16m)

Hof, W. Germany, Oct. 28.

A Beate Klöckner Film Prod., Munich. Written and directed by Klöckner. Features entire cast. Camera (color, 16m), Peter Gauhe; sound, Michael Sombetzki; sets and costumes, Gabriele Friedel; music, Verdi, Cassiber; editor, Suso Berthel Ying, Gisela Castronari, Birgit Klingl. Reviewed at Hof Film Fest, Oct. 27, 1985. Running time: **85 MINS.**
With: Renate Muhri (Tusnelda), Karlheinz Maslo (Nabucco), Rita Bastardo (Don Giovanni), Carlos Pavlidis (Napoleon), Thomas Scholz (Goethe), Doris Michel (Brischitt), Horst Schweimler and Andreas Köhler (the Twins).

Beate Klöckner divides her time between publishing and avant-garde features: "Head Shot" (or "Nightfall") (1981) and now "My Sweet Darling." As a femme helmer there's something ideologically safe about her experiments, though nothing here commercially to get excited about.

"My Sweet Darling" is a one-joke film. In some nether-netherland where people never leave their highrise apartments and the only visible job is serving a battery of computers, it's the women who rule the roost and the men who are robots aching for something to break the monotony on the home front (even tv offers little more than a dull repeat of the same show daily: somebody apparently drowning in a lake). All the principal roles are based on literary and musical and historical figures. Tusnelda, married to Nabucco, decides to skirt the indignities of married life by ordering her children from mail-order catalogs — she gets a dwarf Goethe and dwarf Napoleon to sweeten her life. They are about as crazy as the movie is.—*Holl.*

L'Amour Propre Ne Le Reste Très Longtemps
(Clean Loving Never Stays That Way For Long)
(FRENCH-COLOR)

Paris, Oct. 30.

An AMLF release of a Films 7 production. Produced by Claude Zidi and Marie-Dominique Girodet. Written and directed by Martin Veyron, based on his comic strip. Camera (color), Denis Lenoir; editor, Claudine Bouché; music, Jean-Claude Vannier; art director, Jean-Louis Poveda; sound, René Levert; production manager, Pierre Gauchet. Reviewed at the George V theater, Paris, Oct. 8, 1985. Running time: **90 MINS.**
Gautier . . . . Jean-Claude Dauphin
Rose . . . . Nathalie Nell
Blanche . . . . Marianne Basler
Roussel . . . . Jean-Luc Bideau
Violette . . . . Béatrice Houplain
Olivier . . . . Yves Beneyton
Anne Sophie . . . . Corinne Touzet

A routine sex comedy about a young white-collar lecher in search of the ultimate female erogenous zone, "L'Amour Propre..." is the film debut of cartoonist Martin Veyron, who scripted and directed from his own bestselling comic strip album.

Though he is adapting his own work, Veyron meets the same difficulties other filmmakers have encountered trying to render in live-action, cinematic terms a starkly caricatural cartoon universe. His aggressively sarcastic strip of self-deluding hedonism peters out on the screen into a series of timid vignettes on Making It and the quest for the true female orgasm.

Probably due to his unfamiliarity with film, Veyron directs timidly, even if he has faithfully transposed much of the crudely blunt dialog.

The comedy at least has the support of a good cast, which provides a certain human dimension that makes some scenes work modestly. Jean-Claude Dauphin is the priapic hero, striking a nice balance between lust and vulnerability, and Nathalie Nell is the principal object of his desire, who shows him the whereabouts of the mysterious "G Zone," only in order to manipulate the desperate male into wedlock later.

Jean-Luc Bideau offers reliable support as Dauphin's even more libidinous pal (a role he's already done in Patrick Schulmann's smash 1979 sex comedy, "Et la Tendresse? Bordel!").—*Len.*

China — Die Kunste, Der Alltag
(WEST GERMAN-DOCU-COLOR-16m)

Nyon, Oct. 18.

A film from Ulrike Ottinger Filmproduktion, West Berlin, in collaboration with West Deutscher Rundfunk, produced in cooperation with China Film Co-Production Corp. Director, and camera (color, 16m), Ulrike Ottinger. Production supervisor, Hanna Rogge; sound, Margit Eschenbach; editor, Dorte Volz; translator, Ting-I Li; English subtitles, Susanne Hoppmann-Lowenthal. Reviewed at Nyon Intl. Film Festival, Oct. 17, 1985. Running time: **270 MINS.**

Respected in West Germany since 1972 as scenarist, director and cinematographer of a half-dozen fiction features, Ulrike Ottinger has delivered a mammoth four-and-a-half-hour tableau of modern China, emphasizing the arts of dance and drama, cinema, cuisine, architecture and design.

Film also details the routine daily life of ordinary Chinese in commonplace activity like shopping, cycling and working. Total impact is overlong but stunning and saturating, a prolonged immersion in a China rarely seen, a film that seems itself Chinese, not West German, because shots often are held interminably on unstructured spontaneous events. The editing is simple and functional, without an omniscient narrator providing data and statistics and intoning Westernized interpretations.

This everyday "China" was commissioned by WDR TV as a 90-minute ocumentary but grew instead to three times that length. Anything shorter, the director apparently thought, would be merely an *hors-d'oeuvres* or sampling of China, a huge country needing a huge film.

"China" was shot in January and February of this year, travelling from the urban east to the remote western undeveloped provinces. Almost entirely visual, and self-explanatory, we read only occasional subtitles as translations from the Chinese, e.g., the meaning of street signs, Mao slogans on banners, the dialog of opera performers, the comments of makeup artists and directors, etc.

Not informational, this "China" is instead an impressionistic tour of an exotic culture.

"China" seems a natural for public tv and perhaps also for colleges if edited into shorter, manageable units for classroom purposes.
— *Hitch.*

2020 Texas Gladiators
(ITALIAN-COLOR)

A Continental Motion Pictures presentation of a Eureka Cinematografica s.r.l. production. Directed by Kevin Mancuso. Features entire cast. Screenplay and story, Alex Carver; camera (Luciano Vittori color), John Larson; editor, Caesar White; music, Francis Taylor; production design, Robert Jenkins; production supervisor, Helen Handris; costume design, Linda Connors; production manager, Charles Kellin. Reviewed on Media Home Entertainment vidcassette, N.Y., Nov. 1, 1985. (No MPAA Rating.) Running time: **91 MINS.**

Jab	Harrison Muller
Nisus	Al Cliver
Maida	Sabrina Siani
Catch Dog	Daniel Stephen
Halakron	Peter Hooten
Red Wolfe	Al Yamanouchi
Black One	Donal O'Brien

"2020 Texas Gladiators" is an incomprehensible action pic, made during the 1982-83 boom in Italian takeoffs on "Mad Max" and similar films. New Line Cinema mulled a theatrical release last year (under new title "Sudden Death") for this item from Helen Sarlui's Continental Motion Pictures banner, but instead it is going direct to homevideo by MHE release.

Absent any Texas location establishing footage, this made-in-Rome property opens with a telltale scene of post-nuclear war marauders attacking a priest and nuns. A group of "rangers" (our heroes) defeat the baddies, but one ranger, Catch Dog (Daniel Stephen) tries to rape heroine Maida (Sabrina Siani) and is banished from their group by nominal leader Nisus (Al Cliver).

Without any exposition, next sequence is apparently several years later, with Nisus working at a petroleum refinery and Maida taking care of a cute little girl (revealed to be her daughter several reels later). Catch Dog shows up leading a bunch of marauders on 250-cc. motorcycles, riot police arrive in a battletruck and are protected by bullet-repelling thermal shields, and a Nazi-styled leader named Black One (Donal O'Brien) tries to set up a new order.

Though action sequences are directed adequately, film totally lacks connective tissue and makes no sense whatsoever. Only laughs are provided by guys dressed up like cowboys, wielding whips presumably left over from the 1960s pasta oaters craze, and very fake Indians riding to the rescue. In a shaggy dog joke, Catch Dog carries around a weird-looking, multi-barreled prop gun, which he finally tries to shoot in the final reel — it doesn't work, so he tosses it away in disgust unfired.

Multinational cast is okay, with ubiquitous leading lady Sabrina Siani styled to resemble Daryl Hannah this time out. —*Lor.*

Piccoli Fuochi
(Little Fires)
(ITALIAN-COLOR)

Rome, Oct. 20.

A 20th Century Fox release (Italy). Produced by Claudio Argento for Intersound Prods. Directed by Peter Del Monte. Features entire cast. Screenplay, Del Monte, Giovanni Pascutto; camera (color), Tonino Nardi; editor, Anna Napoli, Simona Paggi; art director, music, Riccardo Zampa. Reviewed at Holiday Cinema, Rome, Oct. 18, 1985. Runnng time: **95 MINS.**

Tomasso	Dino Jakosic
Mara	Valeria Golino

Also with: Carlotta Wittig, Mario Garriba, Ulisse Minervini.

Not a film for children, "Little Fires" presents a schizophrenic look at the sexual life of a five-year-old boy, from a viewpoint that ambiguously fuses the child's and the adult's. Result is an original work that sometimes interests, sometimes irritates. Peter Del Monte has slowly and laboriously built up a solid reputation among younger Italo helmers, without ever having made a big hit. His films, like the French coproduction "Invitation au Voyage," are too far out for most audiences, but have a pleasing idiosyncracy and carefully de-Italianized, pan-European look that has earned them an arthouse following. "Little Fires" is headed for the same market.

Like "Sweet Pea" (one of helmer's most successful films in Italy), "Fires" adopts the p.o.v. of a cute tyke whose mental preoccupations would make Freud's hair stand on end. The offspring of modern, liberated parents who don't know how to treat him and so don't do anything at all, Tom (Dino Jakosic) fills his day with imaginary companions. These are visualized as a sinister trio of creatures, a little king, an alien-robot and a dragon, who are not the nicest playmates mommy could wish her baby to have. They specialize in playing nasty tricks on baby-sitters, until one day Mara (Valeria Golino) arrives.

It's love at first sight for little Tom, whose passion is nursed by seeing his beloved naked very frequently in the bathroom and while she makes love to her boyfriend. At first his attachment to the new baby-sitter alienates him from his imaginary companions, but in the end they band together to help him rid himself of Mara's boyfriend. In this version, childhood cruelty triumphs. They tie him to the bed and burn him alive, and Tom gets the girl. The premature end of his childhood is coyly underlined by the landing of a spaceship straight out of "Close Encounters" that whisks away his three murderous pals.

The whole thesis is a little too pat to be shocking, and most viewers will take the happy ending in stride. Still there is something unsavory in "Fires," possibly the way a wooden child thesp is supposed to represent untrammeled imagination, or how the explicit nudity of Golino (a promising newcomer) is suspiciously titillating. Del Monte, a master at using the camera, can't be accused of not knowing the weight of his shots. —*Yung.*

Bras de Fer
(Operation Judas)
(FRENCH-COLOR)

Paris, Oct. 30.

A Fechner/Gaumont release of a Carthago Films/TF1 Films coproduction. Executive producer, Tarak Ben Ammar. Produced by André Pergament and Carlo Lastricati. written and directed by Gérard Vergez. Stars Christophe Malavoy, Bernard Giraudeau, Angela Molina. Camera (color), André Diot; editor, Jacques Witta; art director, Jean-Jacques Caziot; sound, Alain Sempé; costumes, Elisabeth Tavernier; music, Michel Portal; song lyrics, Georges Moustaki, Claude Lemesle; production manager, Dominique Rigaux. Reviewed at the Publicis Matignon Theater, Paris, Oct. 29, 1985. Running time: **107 MINS.**

With: Bernard Giraudeau, Christophe Malavoy, Angela Molina, Mathieu Carrière, Pierre-Loup Rajot, François Lalande, Thierry Ravel, Agnés Garreau.

Tunisian producer Tarak Ben Ammar turned a neat profit last year locally with Gérard Vergez' Great War actioner, "The Horsemen Of The Storm." He now has tried to repeat his success with a new film by Vergez, "Bras de Fer," a World War II cloak-and-dagger item, but the public hasn't bitten this time.

"Horsemen," a Franco-Yugoslav coproduction, ladled on lots of old-fashioned bravado and action against vast Balkan vistas, but "Bras de Fer" is just another cramped studio thriller, with over-familiar figures plodding through a series of typically convoluted plots and counterplots. This routine melodrama has more exposition than dramatic payoff, and the final multiple revelations bring neither illumination nor retrospective pleasure.

Topbilled male leads Christophe Malavoy and Bernard Giraudeau are two former friends who, in pre-war days, were competitive fencing opponents and romantic rivals for a cabaret singer (Angela Molina), whom Giraudeau finally married.

Film begins with Malavoy, as an exiled Resistance fighter, being sent back into Occupied France on an undercover mission to divert German Intelligence from the true timetable of the planned Normandy invasion. His contact turns out to be Giraudeau, who now runs a gymnasium in a swank Paris hotel, where he hobknobs with a German secret service chief (Mathieu Carrière).

Most of what follows hinges on the question of Giraudeau's allegiances as double or triple or quadruple agent. Though in charge of a top secret assignment he himself is manipulated by the Nazis, who have isolated Molina and continue her drug habit in order to extort services from Giraudeau. Malavoy, still in love with the girl, comes to doubt his colleagues when he is ordered to sacrifice a fellow resistance man and suspected traitor.

Not that any of this matters, because long before the final duel between the protagonists, the viewer is anesthesized by the stolid performances and humdrum direction. Plot is no more or less credible than most other espionage tales, but has none of the well-oiled logistics of a good old-fashioned thriller. — *Len.*

Nickel Mountain
(COLOR)

Routine piece of Americana.

A Ziv Intl. presentation of a Nickel Mountain Prods. production. Executive producer, David S. Shanks. Produced by Jakob Magnusson; line producer, Steve Golin. Directed by Drew Denbaum. Features entire cast. Screenplay, Denbaum, based on novel by John Gardner; camera (Deluxe color), David Bridges; editor, Robert Jenkis; music, Lincoln Mayorga; sound, Steve Nelson; art direction, Nancy Mickelberry; set decoration, Cynthia Sowder; assistant director, Tom Phelps; additional photography, George Posedel; casting, Jeff Gerrard, Don Pemrick. Reviewed on HBO, N.Y., Oct. 28, 1985. (No MPAA Rating.) Running time: **88 MINS.**

Henry Soames	Michael Cole
Callie Wells	Heather Langenkamp
Willard Freund	Patrick Cassidy
George	Brian Kerwin
Ellie Wells	Grace Zabriskie
Doc Cathey	Don Beddoe
W.D. Freund	Ed Lauter
Frank	Harry Northrup
Trucker	Cotter Smith
Kuzitski	E.J. Andre
Dr. Costard	Peter Hobbs
Reception nurse	Liz Sheridan

Adapted from the late John Gardner's massive novel, "Nickel Mountain" is a well-acted bit of Americana, lacking the freshness and dramatic bite to make it as a

theatrical entry. Filmed in 1983, title went unreleased until its current exposure on paycable and as a vidcassette.

The romantic story is set in rural, upstate New York (though exact locale is not mentioned in the film), where 16-year-old Callie (Heather Langenkamp) becomes pregnant after dallying with Willard (Patrick Cassidy). After Willard goes away to work for the summer and then on to agricultural college, his dad (Ed Lauter) oppposes any marriage, offering Callie $300 to get an abortion. He has become a bigtime farmer and doesn't want his son to marry a relatively poor girl.

Coming to Callie's rescue is Henry Soames (Michael Cole), a friendly, overweight neighbor who dated Callie's mom (Grace Zabriskie) when they were teens. Callie works as a waitress at Henry's diner and takes care of him when he's ill. Henry marries Callie and the baby is born, but a violent confrontation ensues when a jealous Willard comes home to ask Callie to run off with him. An unconvincing finale contrives a happy ending for everybody.

Ranging from "Where The Lilies Bloom" to "Coal Miner's Daughter," the rural drama is an enduring genre, but as "The River Rat" and "Sylvester" have shown recently, its b.o. impact is lessening. Writer-director Drew Denbaum fails to bring the necessary contemporary relevance to "Nickel Mountain" to attract an audience.

Michael Cole (well-remembered as star of "The Mod Squad" series) has an effective change-of-pace, fitted here with a bloated body suit and handling heartfelt monologs as the selfless hero.

Pic "introduces" (per screen credit) Heather Langenkamp, a lovely young actress from Tulsa who previously had small roles in Francis Coppola's "The Outsiders" and "Rumble Fish" and received her main exposure as the leading player in "A Nightmare On Elm Street" in 1984. Her winning smile and sympathetic thesping are "Mountain's" chief assets. Supporting cast is okay. —*Lor.*

One Magic Christmas
(U.S./CANADIAN-COLOR)

Winning family film bowing for Thanksgiving.

Hollywood, Nov. 13.

A Buena Vista release of a Walt Disney Pictures presentation of a Peter O'Brian production in association with Fred Roos, Silver Screen Partners II and Telefilm Canada. Produced by O'Brian. Executive producer, Phillip Borsos. Directed by Borsos. Stars Mary Steenburgen. Screenplay, Thomas Meehan; story by Meehan, Borsos, Barry Healey; camera (Deluxe color), Frank Tidy; editor, Sidney Wolinsky; music, Michael Conway Baker; production design, Bill Brodie; art direction, Tony Hall; set decoration, Rondi Johnson; costume design, Olga Dimitrov; sound (Dolby), Bruce Carwardine, Glen Gauthier; sound design, Bruce Nyznik; makeup design, Ann Brodie; special effects coordinator, John Thomas; associate producer, Michael Macdonald; assistant director, Tony Lucibello; casting, Gail Carr, Janet Hirschenson and Jane Jenkins (L.A.), Bonnie Timmerman (N.Y.). Reviewed at The Burbank Studios, Burbank, Nov. 13, 1985. (MPAA Rating: G.) Running time: **88 MINS.**

Ginny Grainger	Mary Steenburgen
Jack Grainger	Gary Basaraba
Gideon	Harry Dean Stanton
Caleb Grainger	Arthur Hill
Abbie Grainger	Elizabeth Harnois
Cal Grainger	Robbie Magwood
Betty	Michelle Meyrink
Eddie	Elias Koteas
Harry Dickens	Wayne Robson
Santa Claus	Jan Rubes

"One Magic Christmas" represents an emotionally rewarding and artistically successful attempt to pull off the sort of uplifting family fare Hollywood used to do so well but lately has forgotten how to make. Pic proves dramatically involving for adults due to the legitimacy of real-life dilemmas faced by the family here, yet there is plenty of fantasy in which the kids can revel. B.O. prospects for this Thanksgiving release look good.

Drawing for inspiration both upon "A Christmas Carol" and "It's A Wonderful Life" (certainly two of the best models extant), director Phillip Borsos keeps sentimentality nicely in check as he presents the sad Christmas season being faced by the Grainger family.

Dad has been laid off, Mom is hardly managing to pay the bills with her checkout girl's salary, and they and the two kids are being evicted from their small suburban home just in time for the holidays. Not only is there insufficient money to buy Christmas presents, but Mom has lost the Christmas spirit so entirely that she mopes around in bitter despair and snaps disapprovingly at the kids when they dare voice their belief in Santa Claus.

Just when it appears things can't get any worse, they get very much worse indeed. Although not in any way violent, the drama does become quite intensely grim at midpoint, as Mom, rather like Jimmy Stewart in "Wonderful Life," hits the absolute bottom-of-the-barrel.

As has been seen periodically up to now, however, Mom has had an angel appointed to restore the proper spirit to her, and he quickly takes over to remedy matters. What the picture is really trying to say with its flight into fantasy remains somewhat unclear, but a trip to the North Pole makes for a delightful ride, and it may be said the picture effectively wins the heart even if it leaves the mind behind.

Film succeeds, first, because Borsos and scenarist Thomas Meehan have approached the material seriously and utterly without cyncism.

Second reason for the pic's winning qualities is the casting. Mary Steenburgen is very mom-like in the pivotal role, is very realistically depressed for a long while, and is then very wonderfully won over to optimism and warmth by the satisfying turn of events.

The real find is Elizabeth Harnois for the role of the little daughter who, while pathetically deprived of what any kid wants, doesn't give up on Mom and gets to visit the real Santa Claus on her way to reawakening her mother's belief. An astonishingly beautiful six-year-old blond, Harnois has the necessary innocence and sense of wonder and adventure to carry the picture, which she does enchantingly.

In his long, dark coat and wide-brimmed hat, Harry Dean Stanton looks more like a Sergio Leone Western villain than an emissary from heaven, and his way of approaching people is so abrupt and blunt that he often seems sinister. His roughness is offset by a purity and sweetness of manner, and the unusual strategy of his casting finally pays off.

Other performances are fine, and behind-the-scenes contributions on the Canadian-lensed effort are good, with the exception of Michael Conway Baker's music, which is exemplary.—*Cart.*

Rainbow Brite
And The Star Stealer
(ANIMATED-COLOR)

Old-fashioned, flat kiddie fare.

Hollywood, Nov. 13.

A Warner Bros. release of a DIC Enterprises production. Produced by Jean Chalopin, Andy Heyward, Tetsuo Katayama. Executive producers, Chalopin, Heyward. Directed by Bernard Deyries, Kimio Yabuki. Screenplay, Howard R. Cohen, from a story by Chalopin, Cohen; based on characters devloped by Hallmark Properties; editor, Yutaka Chikura; music, Haim Saban, Shuki Levy; art director, Rich Rudish; associate producer, Victor Villegas, Alan Lee; voice casting, Marsha Goodman, Ginny McSwain. Reviewed at Warner Bros. Screening Room, Burbank, Calif., Nov. 13, 1985 (MPAA Rating: G.) Running time: **97 MINS.**
Character Voices

Rainbow Brite	Bettina
Lurky	Patrick Fraley

Murky	Peter Cullen
Twink	Robbie Lee
Starlite	Andre Stojka
The Princess	Rhonda Aldrich
Orin	Les Tremayne
Krys	David Mendenhall

"Rainbow Brite And The Star Stealer" is the first recent venture into the burgeoning pre-youth market by one of the majors apart from Disney. Produced by DIC Enterprises and based on characters developed by Hallmark, pic is old-fashioned (in the bad sense of the word) and stifflingly sweet. It's hard to tell what the b.o. potential is for a film like this with parents rather than the target audience making the choice, but word around nursery schools could be to stay away from this one.

Animated flatly by a Japanese team, "Rainbow Brite" has few of the ups and downs and textures of a theatrical film for tots. Hero, a perky little girl who spreads color throughout the universe, must face the challenge of a wicked princess set on capturing the planet Spectra and thereby darkening the world.

Assisted by the young warrior Krys and a pair of magical horses, Rainbow Brite battles the bad guys who are rendered without much flair.

Emotional range of the Rainbow dwellers is limited by facial expression that makes them look as much like cookies as kids. Furthermore, Krys is disparaging about waging his fight assisted by a "girl." While she does ultimately prove her worth, it's a point that could have been bypassed by now.

Despite that popularity of these characters from Hallmark's merchandising and five television specials in this form, they are too short on character and invention to stir a child's imagination at any age.
— *Jagr.*

Fever Pitch
(COLOR)

So bad it's almost good.

Hollywood, Nov. 14.

An MGM/UA Entertainment release from MGM Film Co. Produced by Freddie Fields. Directed by Richard Brooks. Stars Ryan O'Neal. Screenplay, Brooks; camera (Metrocolor), William A. Fraker; editor, Jeff Jones; music, Thomas Dolby; production design, Raymond G. Storey; set designer, Jim Teegarden; set decorator, John M. Dwyer; sound, Al Overton Jr.; assistant director, Jerry Ballew; casting, Joseph D'Agosta. Reviewed at MGM/UA screening room, Culver City, Calif., Nov. 13, 1985. (MPAA Rating: R.) Running time: **96 MINS.**

Taggart	Ryan O'Neal
Flo	Catherine Hicks
Charley	Giancarlo Giannini
Amy	Bridgette Andersen
Dutchman	Chad Everett
Sports editor	John Saxon
Sun publisher	Hank Greenspun
Panama Hat	William Smith
Casino boss	Keith Hefner

"Fever Pitch" may be the best bad film of the year. Weak script, poor acting and miscasting aside, it's the power of the subject that makes this an enjoyable ride. Writer/director Richard Brooks thoroughly researched the territory of the compulsive gambler and captures the obsession with almost a documentary eye. Popularity of the subject could generate some interest if distrib MGM/UA doesn't dump it.

As the film labors to make clear in its opening minutes, everyone gambles. Some $200-billion is bet each year. The possibility of turning your life around with one roll of the dice or one swing of the bat is something no one can resist. It's the American religion. Even the film director is a gambler betting on a hit.

"Fever Pitch" is not a good film, but Brooks does manages to get inside the material with an old-fashioned, hard-hitting, exposé style. Unfortunately, it backfires for several reasons. Plot is a totally unconvincing jumble and Ryan O'Neal as a sports reporter hooked on the gambling game is wooden and unsympathetic.

Up to his ears in gambling debts, Taggart (O'Neal) just gets in deeper with loansharks and operators. He's already lost his wife due to gambling (she was killed in a car accident bringing him money for a payoff). His excuse for his downfall is that he's doing a story about the gambling world and he becomes a guide through the rings of gambling hell.

Most of the action takes place in Las Vegas where Taggart wins and loses huge sums and gets involved with big-timer Giancarlo Giannini. Brooks tries to spice up the action with some contempo music (by Thomas Dolby), nudity and gratuitous violence, but basically this is old line filmmaking.

Brooks does better with action sequences at the crap tables and the roll of the dice or the turn of the roulette wheel becomes infectious. Even though one doesn't believe for a moment O'Neal as a reporter or gambler, so devoid of passion is his performance, there is still a certain pleasure in watching him go down.

Rest of the cast is as stiff as the script. Catherine Hicks as a Vegas cocktail waitress and sometime call-girl goes through a few turns that don't quite fit. Keith Hefner is equally baffling as the casino boss and John Saxon as O'Neal's editor at the L.A. Herald Examiner seems to be playing a different game.

Even gambling can't save the last 20 minutes of the film as O'Neal becomes repentant and joins Gambler's Anonymous. Of course, he has one last fling left in him. The pieces simply don't make any sense here and the only thing that matters is the bet. The story is really an excuse to watch the action.

William Fraker's photography is suitably dark and occasionally penetrates the surface of the fever. Other tech credits are adequate but can't save the film. The cards are stacked against it.—*Jagr.*

Démoni
(Demons)
(ITALIAN-COLOR)

Rome, Nov. 15.

A Titanus release. Produced by Dario Argento for DACFilm Prods. Directed by Lamberto Bava. Stars Urbano Barberini and Natasha Hovey. Screenplay, Bava, Argento, Dardano Sacchetti, Franco Ferrini; camera (Eastmancolor), Gianlorenzo Battaglia; editor, Pietro Bozza; music, Claudio Simonetti, art director, Davide Bassian. Reviewed at Madison Cinema, Rome, Nov. 14, 1985. Running time: **85 MINS.**

Cheryl	Natasha Hovey
George	Urbano Barberini

Also with: Paolo Cozzo, Fiore Argento, Nicoletta Elmi, Carl Zinni, Fabiola Toledo.

"Demons" is a medium-quality blood and gore horror pic produced by Dario Argento and shot by protégé Lamberto Bava. Story has kids trapped in a film theater who progressively "zombie-fy" each other till only the two leads are left. The picture has done brisk business at the national b.o. and has been placed in major markets. An audience for bloodletting is out there.

One day in the Berlin metro, Cheryl (Natasha Hovey) and her girlfriend are handed free tickets to a mysterious sneak preview in a creepy old theater nobody knew existed. There they meet George (Urbano Barberini) and his friend. The film they see is about a demonic mask that scratches whoever puts it on and turns them into a yellow-eyed, pustulent, foaming-at-the-mouth special effect.

Lo and behold, there is an identical mask out in the lobby, just waiting to be tried on. First to get scratched is a black streetwalker, who undergoes a nasty transformation in the ladies' room. After infecting her horrified girlfriend, she/it takes off for the balcony to wreak more havoc. In pic's most effective sequence, the girlfriend stumbles behind the screen and bursts through it, her screams mingling with those of the victims on-screen.

Pic loses impetus after this, as contamination swiftly spreads through the audience. They run for the exits in panic, only to find they have been walled in (how and by whom we never know). The slaughter is intercut awkwardly with four coked-up punks cruising the streets of Berlin, looking for trouble. They are sucked into the no-exit theater and quickly zombie-fied.

If all this seems like something that's made the rounds before, helmer also has tipped his hat slyly to the directorial debut of his late father Mario Bava in "Maschera del Demonio" ("Black Sunday"). The special effects are a gory cross between George Romero and "Alien," with weird things popping out of people's skins at the least provocation. The Dario Argento touch is recognizable in a loud rock score (songs by Billy Idol and Rick Springfield, among others), a couple of action sequences, including hero and heroine zooming around the theater on a motorcycle with the creepie-crawlers after them, and a consistent disregard for logic and psychology.

The large teen cast looks wholly non-pro, with the exception of leads Hovey and Barberini, who don't do much besides survive. At pic's end, when one is lost in an obligatory surprise twist, it comes as no great loss.—*Yung.*

Tornado
(ITALIAN-COLOR)

A Gico Cinematografica production, presented by Gianfranco Couyoumdjian. Directed by Anthony M. Dawson (Antonio Margheriti). Features entire cast. Screenplay, Tito Carpi, from story by Couyoumdjian; camera (Luciano Vittori color), Sandro Mancori; editor, Marcello Malvestito; music, Aldo Tamborrelli, performed by Sound of Eden; production design, Antonio Visone; assistant director, Edoardo Margheriti. Reviewed on Lightning Video cassette, N.Y., Nov. 10, 1985. (No MPAA Rating.) Running time: **90 MINS.**

Sgt. Sal Maggio	Timothy Brent
Capt. Harlow	Tony Marsina
Lee Freeman	Alan Collins

"Tornado" is a well-made little war picture, currently available in the homevideo market. Filmed in the Philippines in 1983 by an Italian production company, nicely dubbed item comes off credibly as an American-style film.

Set in Vietnam during the closing stages of the U.S. war there, pic's title refers to the code name of helicopters for a unit of Green Berets, headed by Captain Harlow (Tony Marsina). Newspaper reporter Lee Freeman (Alan Collins) is tagging along with the unit, trying to write an exposé about Harlow.

It seems Harlow is trying to achieve personal advancement at the expense of his troops, recently suffering a 60% casualty rate. He leaves Sergeant Maggio (Timothy Brent) behind when latter is trying to save a wounded comrade and later orders Maggio court martialed after the Sarge punches Harlow.

Maggio escapes en route to jail and film climaxes at the Cambodian border as Maggio nearly escapes permanently.

Filmmaker Antonio Margheriti, who has made over 50 action pictures of various types since 1960, keeps the action cooking, highlighted by effective battle sequences and location photography. Film has only a minimum of clichés, understandably taken from hits "The Deer Hunter" and "First Blood." Except for a hokey ending, "Tornado" is a refreshingly simple B-picture with appropriate underplaying by an Italian cast headed by Timothy Brent. —Lor.

L'Eveillé du Pont d' Alma
(The Insomniac On The Bridge)
(FRENCH-COLOR/B&W)

Paris, Nov. 7.
A Citevox release of a Films du Passage production, with the participation of the Ministry of Culture and the Maison de la Culture of Grenoble. Produced by Paolo Branco. Written and directed by Raul Ruiz. Camera (color, b&w), François Ede; editor, Rodolfo Wedeles; sound, Antoine Bonfanti; music, Gérard Maimone. Reviewed at the Republique Cinema, Paris, Nov. 5, 1985. Running time: 73 MINS.
With: Michaël Lonsdale, Jean Badin, Olimpia Carlisi, Jean-Bernard Guillard, Melvil Poupaud, Kim Massée, Frank Oger.

Raul Ruiz, the prolific expatriate Chilean director who shoots (film) faster than his shadow — he made six last year! — knocked this one off on a shoestring budget, prior to embarking on his more ambitious modern-day redo of "Treasure Island," already in postproduction.

Pic seems like the kind of avant-garde prank the helmer has done before, and more entertainingly. "L'Eveillé" has Michaël Lonsdale at his most bleary-eyed as an insomniac voyeur who, in the company of another criminal loon (Jean-Bernard Guillard), rapes a pregnant woman on the banks of the Seine. There are numerous consequences and surprises in this metaphysical farce, but little enjoyable sense or nonsense to be had by the viewer.

Ruiz has directed as if he himself were in a comatose state. Technical credits are indolent. —Len.

Une Femme ou Deux
(One Woman Or Two)
(FRENCH-COLOR)

Paris, Nov. 13.
An AAA-Hachette Première release (Orion Classics in U.S.) of an Hachette Première/Philippe Dussart production. Directed by Daniel Vigne. Stars Gérard Depardieu, Sigourney Weaver. Screenplay, Vigne, Elisabeth Rappeneau, based on an original idea by Vigne; camera (color), Carlo Varini; art director, Jean-Pierre Kohut-Svelko; editor, Marie-Joseph Yoyotte; sound, Guillaume Sciama; music, Kevin Mulligan, Evert Verhees, Toots Thielmans; theme song "Tracks Of Love" performed by Talkback; production manager, Michel Choquet. Reviewed at the Gaumont Colisée theater,

Paris, Nov. 12, 1985. Running time: 97 MINS.
Julien Chayssac . . . . Gérard Depardieu
Jessica Fitzgerald . . . . . . Sigourney Weaver
Pierre Carrière . . . . Michel Aumont
Mrs. Heffner . . . . Dr. Ruth Westheimer
Constance . . . . Zabou
Gino . . . . Jean-Pierre Bisson
Alex . . . . Yann Babilée
Patrick . . . . Robert Blumenfeld

"The Return Of Martin Guerre," Daniel Vigne's medieval drama of imposture, no doubt owed part of its Stateside success to its exoticism: it was the kind of picture the Yanks couldn't make. So it will be curious to see U.S. reaction to Vigne's new effort in a genre in which Hollywood has always excelled.

"One Woman Or Two" is a contemporary comedy, and though this may seem light years away from "Martin Guerre," there is again the theme of impersonation, and the notion of reconstructing the past. Its hero is a young French paleontologist (Gérard Depardieu) who discovers the fossilized remains of the first French woman, age 2,000,-000 years, and applies to an American research foundation for a much-needed grant to continue his explorations.

The foundation director he picks up at the airport is in fact a shrewd, attractive advertising woman (Sigourney Weaver) who at first uses Depardieu to evade a former boy friend waiting in the terminal, then continues the charade when she realizes the archeological revelation would make an ideal ad gimmick for a new perfume line she's promoting.

The basic ingredients of the screenplay by Vigne and Elisabeth Rappeneau are potentially appealing, but what develops from them lacks the bone structure and marrow of good, meaty film comedy.

Too often the plot seems to move to the wrong climaxes, while subsidiary situations and characters, which promise daft complications, are left unexploited or abandoned. Vigne sometimes short-circuits his own good ideas by not taking them far enough (like the parallels between the romantic plight of the prehistoric woman and the modern-day imbroglio of Weaver and her jealous ex-flame) and generally tends to vacillate indecisively between the madcap and the romantic.

Uncertainty of the script and direction are reflected in the lead performances. Depardieu, who displayed a breezy sense of comedy in Francis Veber's films, seems less confident as the scientist torn between his three women (Weaver, his wife and his fossil lady), and Weaver appears handicapped by her French dialog. The sparks of conflict and affection one awaits between the two never really fly.

On the credit side is a droll film debut by Dr. Ruth Westheimer, who plays the real American foundation director. Ironically, her role is superfluous to the central story and hovers peripherally, until she merely disappears. Michel Aumont is fine as Depardieu's envious colleague and Westheimer's principal foil, while Zabou is perky as Depardieu's wife.

There is also fine lensing by Carlo Varini as well as a humorously alert music track by Kevin Mulligan, Evert Verhees and Toots Thielmans (the bongo motif for Westheimer's huffy entrances is particularly successful).

Film was presold for Canada and the U.S. to René Malo Films and Orion Classics, respectively. —Len.

Lamb
(BRITISH-COLOR)

Chicago, Nov. 12.
A Films Four Intl./Flickers-Limehouse release. Produced by Neil Zeiger. Directed by Colin Gregg. Features entire cast. Screenplay, Bernard MacLaverty, based on his novel with same title; camera (color), Mike Garfath; sets, Austen Spriggs; editor, Peter Delfgou; music, Van Morrison. Reviewed at Chicago Film Fest (Competition), Nov. 11, 1985. Running time: 109 MINS.
With Liam Neeson (Michael Lamb), Ian Bannen (Owen Kane), Frances Tomelty, Dudley Sutton, Hugh O'Connor.

Colin Gregg's "Lamb" scored as a worthy British entry preeming at the Chicago film fest during "British Film Year" celebrations. Based on a novel written by proven scriptwriter Bernard MacLaverty ("Cal"), it's a religioso theme handled with care to the humanistic side and attention to psychological detail.

The setting is a correctional school located on the forbidding coast of Antrim County in Ireland. One of the boys sent to the "borstal" conducted by the Christian Brothers is a lonely lad, Owen, who suffers from epileptic fits and bed wetting. His mother, a floozy, doesn't want to take responsibility anymore, as Owen often runs away.

Contrasted with the boy's fate is that of Michael Lamb, a young and rather immature religious brother who dotes on his aged and dying father in his permitted time away from the school. When the old man dies, Lamb (his name carrying symbolic meaning) faces a crisis. Naturally, the gap in his life is filled by turning his attention to Owen, particularly as the lad is mistreated badly by the home's superior, the dour and just-plain-mean Brother Benedict.

A decision is made when Brother Benedict tries to get his religious order's hands on the inheritance left to Brother Lamb by the deceased father. Lamb pockets the inheritance and takes off from the home illegally with Owen. Since this amounts to a breach of the law, Lamb leaves the country for London to throw pursuers off the trail.

Once in London, the two develop a missing father/son relationship desired by both. However, a religious brother on the loose experiencing a new-found freedom leads to complications. Further, the radio reports indicate the "kidnaping" is being taken seriously by the authorities. So it's back to Ireland to a seacoast refuge of Brother Lamb's childhood.

It's here that Owen has a fatal epileptic fit. At the same time, Lamb makes an agonizing decision to "free" the lad completely at the one and only time the boy is truly happy.

A solid performance by Liam Neeson as Brother Lamb makes the film convincing enough as far as the storyline is concerned. Unfortunately, helmer Gregg wants to get in his licks at religion at the same time, much in the literary manner of a Frank O'Connor or J.F. Powers (Catholic satirists par excellence). This approach just doesn't pay dividends in the end. —Holl.

La Messa E' Finita
(The Mass Is Over)
(ITALIAN-COLOR)

Rome, Nov. 16.
A Titanus release, produced by Achille Manzotti for Faso Film. Starring and directed by Nanni Moretti. Screenplay, Moretti, Sandro Petraglia; camera (color), Franco Di Giacomo; editor, Mirco Garrone; music, Nicola Piovani; art director, Amedeo Fago, Giorgio Bertolini. Reviewed at Capranica Cinema, Rome, Nov. 16, 1985. Running time: 96 MINS.
Don Giulio . . . . Nanni Moretti
Mother . . . . Margarita Losanno
Father . . . . Ferrucio De Ceresa
Valentina . . . . Enrica Maria Modugno

One of the highlights of the season, "Mass Is Over" is an idiosyncratic little comedy about the contemporary generation of 30-year-olds. Its hero is a childish, neurotic priest. Nanni Moretti led a new wave of successful young actor-director comics to fame several years ago ("Ecce Bombo," "Golden Dreams," "Bianca"). His fifth feature confirms him at the head of the class, with undiminished powers of invention and renewal.

"Mass" is off to a fast start onshore. Though too closely tied to Italo situations and nuances to travel widely, it deserves to be seen in special outings for quality product.

Moretti plays Don Giulio, a late convert to the priesthood who was once part of the radical '60s. Now his long hair has been cut in a preppie trim, his moustache shaved off, his old friends gladly forgotten. They come back one by one in the course of the film, often bearers of uncomfortable memories, or equally uncomfortable examples of deluded conformism.

One has lost the woman he loved and turned into a recluse in his run-down, terraced apartment; another, a jazz pianist, suddenly decides to become Catholic and joins the first-graders' catechism class. A book-store owner is disposing of tomes on Mao and Albania by the boxload, while a fourth is in jail, awaiting trial for terrorism.

Moretti's is a painfully self-conscious brand of comedy, bent on avoiding easy gags, punchlines, and clichés at all costs. When a monolog veers into the realm of the conventional, it is deliberately drowned out by music. The secret of pic's success is its total impatience with all the bunk and baloney of everyday life, which turns out to be almost everything. Over and over, Moretti cuts scenes perilously short, as though unable to continue them without falling into a trap of convention. Result is a jerky overall rhythm.

Center of laughs is always Don Giulio in his outmoded soutane, trying to follow a set of values it would be so comfortable to believe in, except that they simply don't work anymore. To start with, the former priest of his parish lives next door with his wife and kid. The young couples who flock to his pre-marital class all want to see films and hear him talk about sex. The church is deserted unless there's a wedding or a funeral. To show the regard wearers of the cassock are held in these days, Don Giulio is practically drowned in a public fountain by four men out to steal his parking spot.

Many tragi-comic episodes concern another of helmer's familiar themes, loneliness and the possibility of banishing it through family life. Don Giulio himself is a mama's boy unable to live alone in the rectory, who sees his family primarily as a haven of security and sure values. In reality, his unwed sister is pregnant and plans to have an abortion, and his aged father leaves his mother for a younger woman. None of Don Giulio's efforts can piece the family together again, and eventually his mother commits suicide.

Instead of offering easy answers, "Mass" ends with Don Giulio throwing in the towel and heading for a mythical windy parish in the mountains.

Pic achieves a rare ring of sincerity. Moretti is able to inject large portions of autobiographical confession without turning pic into a diary. The mainly non-pro cast works splendidly. —*Yung*.

La Hora Bruja
(The Witching Hour)
(SPANISH-COLOR)

Madrid, Nov. 8.

A Serva Films production, directed by Jaime de Armiñán; screenplay, Armiñán and Ramón de Diego; camera (Eastmancolor), Teo Escamilla; production manager, Enrique Bellot; editor, José Luis Matesanz; sets, Tony Cortés; sound, Antonio Bloch; music, Alejandro Masso, partly performed by Gulams de Pontevedra. Reviewed at Cine Roxy B, Madrid, Nov. 7, 1985. Running time: **108 MINS.**

César	Francisco Rabal
Pilar	Concha Velasco
Saga	Victoria Abril
Rubén	Sancho Gracia
Nun	Asunción Balaguer

Helmer-scripter Jaime de Armiñán, best known for his Oscar nominees "The Nest" and "My Dear Miss," has turned his talents to "The Witching Hour," a whimsical story about an itinerant couple of entertainers who, as they travel about the northwest province of Galicia, tangle with a pixie-like witch.

Though the young girl (Victoria Abril) who helps their touring house-bus out of a ditch on a lonely road is never identified positively as such, the strange goings-on soon tip off the viewer to her special powers, as she ingratiates herself first with the phony, drum-thumping "wizard," César and then to his alternately bossy and tender sidekick, Pilar.

With three of Spain's top thesps in the vehicle, Armiñán cuts a droll caper as the pixie patches up marital differences between the couple and ultimately enables each to realize the full worth of his and her partner. Pic blends elements of fantasy with a steady flow of wry humor, as the pixie's ambiguous relationship to the couple shifts from highminded friendship to sexual teasing.

The subject of witchcraft (indigenous to Galicia province) is dealt with lightheartedly, as the wizard and his companion put on live shows in the little villages, supplementing their income by screening films as well. To their astonishment, the wizard's hokum actually starts to work, as the pixie and her warlock friend, who are the real thing, intervene to make the couple's efforts turn out well.

In a charming climax, after the pixie has slipped away into the forest, César treats Pilar to a sumptuous meal in a country villa. To their amazement, the prices are what they were 100 years ago. After downing a dozen oysters each, César stands up and publicly declares his love for Pilar before the astonished diners at the other tables. The following day when they return to the villa, they find only an old, abandoned building. The pixie, however, is watching complacently from a distance in the forest,

mounted on a white stallion.

Though a trifle slow and directionless at times, pic's topnotch thesping and a mellow and often amusing story should especially please those audiences who have reached the age of discernment. Film has been submitted as Spain's official entry in the Best Foreign-language Film category for the upcoming Academy Awards. —*Besa*.

Basic Training
(COLOR)

Basically insulting.

Hollywood, Nov. 16.

A The Movie Store release. Produced by Otto Salamon and Gil Adler. Executive producers, Paul Klein, Lawrence Vanger; assistant producer, Allison Rosenfeld. Directed by Andrew Sugerman. Features entire cast. Screenplay, Bernard M. Kahn; camera, (Deluxe color), Steven W. Gray; editor, Larry Bock; music, Michael Cruz; art director, John Carter; set design, Susan Emshwiller; sound, Jonathan Stein; costume design, Warden Neil; casting, Barbara Claman, Victoria Burrows. Reviewed at Pacific's Eagle Rock theater, L.A., Nov. 15, 1985. (MPAA Rating: R.) Running time: **88 MINS.**

Melinda	Ann Dusenberry
Debbie	Rhonda Shear
Cheryl	Angela Aames
Lt. Cranston	Will Nye
Ambassador Gotell	Walter Gotell

What is outrageous about "Basic Training," a low-budget film that is being billed as an "outrageous comedy," is how it manages to insult nearly every group of people represented — in a very unfunny way. While the picture might do well as a drive-in entry, its boxoffice prospects in urban hardtops appear meager. Pic was filmed in 1983 as "Up the Pentagon," backed by The Playboy Channel.

The film ostensibly is about how an unsophisticated new employee in the Pentagon's Public Information office, Melinda (Ann Dusenberry), rises through the ranks to become the first female Secretary of State by outfoxing her stupid and lecherous military bosses who see her only for her body and not her brains.

Unlike her female counterparts who revel in their sexual conquests over their superiors, Melinda refuses to engage in playing games such as "Prisoner Of War" with her boss and gets fired for insubordination.

Being the altruistic woman she is, Melinda is determined to be rehired at the Pentagon so she can make the country safe for democracy by ridding the U.S. Armed Services of these boobs.

Not only does she get rehired, she manages to bring every man at the Pentagon to his knees as she flaunts her lithe and buxom self without ever losing her virtue.

Rather than use clever dialog to carry this film, which tries desperately to be "Stripes" and "Private Benjamin," screenwriter Bernard M. Kahn relies heavily on the bad use of double entendres to provide what is really a vehicle for showing the naked upper torso of women's bodies at every possible occasion.

Besides reducing women to vacuous playthings for men's pleasure and the military to a bunch of incompetent sex maniacs, the film also manages to insult blacks — portraying them as jive-talking people in servile positions such as shoe shine boys and delivery men.

— *Jaga*.

The Loser, The Hero
(TAIWANESE-COLOR)

Chicago, Nov. 16.

A Kwang Ha Mass Communications release. Produced by Ho In-Li. Directed by Peter Mak. Features entire cast. Screenplay, Wu Nen-Gan; camera (color), Lin Chi-Zon. Reviewed at Chicago Film Fest (out of-competition), Nov. 16, 1985. Running time: **97 MINS.**

An entry from Taiwan, Peter Mak's "The Loser, The Hero" deals with the social issue in Taipei of mistreatment of teenagers in a so-called "cram school," a place where kids have to go in order to bone up to pass college entry exams. As a feature film document on the difficulties of getting into choice schools, it has its merits. The lack of a strong narrative line, however, leads to the doldrums and a wasted effort in the long run.

The protagonist is a lad who just barely missed on the point system, ending up in the authoritarian-style cram school. The menace here is a hulky disciplinarian who wields a mighty ruler, with which he slaps palms of hands and occasionally the tender backs of knees.

One young student decides he won't stand for the mistreatment any longer. Since the system is obviously corrupt in the first place, or so it's presented, the rest of the film describes how he gets even with the tough by not showing up at the school one day. This puts the teacher on the spot, for he's "paid by the head," so to speak.

Pic has subpar credits and a ho-hum storyline. —*Holl*.

Santa Claus
(COLOR)

Overlong hokum muffs a good beginning.

Hollywood, Nov. 21.

A Tri-Star Pictures release of an Alexander Salkind presentation of an Alexander & Ilya Salkind production, made by Santa Claus Prods. Ltd. Produced by Ilya Salkind and Pierre Spengler. Directed by Jeannot Szwarc. Features entire cast. Screenplay, David Newman, from story by David & Leslie Newman; camera (Rank color, J-D-C Widescreen), Arthur Ibbetson; editor, Peter Hollywood; music, Henry Mancini; songs, Mancini & Leslie Bricusse, Bill House & John Hobbs, Nick Beggs, Stuart Croxford, Neal & Steve Askew; sound (Dolby), David Crozier; production design, Anthony Pratt; supervising art director, Tim Hutchinson; art directors, Don Dossett, John Hoesli, Malcolm Stone; set decorator, Stephanie McMillan; flying and second unit director, David Lane; visual and miniature effects director, Derek Meddings; optical effects supervisor, Roy Field; costume design, Bob Ringwood; assistant director, Derek Cracknell; production supervisor, Vincent Winter; additional photography, Paul Beeson; visual effects photography, Paul Wilson; choreography, Pat Garrett; supervising animatronic designer, John Coppinger; casting, Lynn Stalmaster & Associates; associate producer, Robert Simmonds. Reviewed at Coronet theater, L.A., Nov. 21, 1985. (MPAA Rating: PG.) Running time: 112 MINS.

Santa Claus	David Huddleston
Patch	Dudley Moore
B.Z.	John Lithgow
Anya Claus	Judy Cornwell
Joe	Christian Fitzpatrick
Cornelia	Carrie Kei Heim
Towzer	Jeffrey Kramer
Dooley	John Barrard
Puffy	Anthony O'Donnell
Ancient Elf	Burgess Meredith
Goober	Melvyn Hayes
Groot	Don Estelle

"Santa Claus" is a film for children of all ages, but will probably skew best toward infancy or senility. In any case, a baffling PG rating and a running time beyond the attention span of most young children will surely confound its touted test as a family film.

Oddly enough, even Scrooge himself might adore the first 20 minutes when "Santa" develops a charming attitude, lovely special effects and a magical feeling that the audience may indeed be settling down for a warm winter's eve.

After that, however, the picture becomes Santa Meets Son of Flubber or something in a mad rush to throw in whatever might appeal to anybody. Bah, humbug.

David Huddleston is a perfect Claus, first introduced several centuries ago as a real-life woodcutter who delights in distributing Christmas gifts to village children. Determined to disappoint none, he and his pleasant wife, Judy Cornwell, drive their reindeer sled on through a blizzard, losing their way until team and couple can go no further.

Wondrously, Mr. and Mrs. Claus awake to discover they are at the North Pole, where their arrival is excitedly hailed by elves led by Dudley Moore. It seems they have fulfilled a prophecy and Claus will not serve eternity delivering toys made in an enchanting workshop.

To be sure, the workshop is something to witness, and, for this part of the film, it's easy to see where the production money went (as contrasted later with cheap sets that seemed left over from old B-pictures.) For awhile the wonder continues as Huddleston is outfitted with his red suit and introduced to his team of flying antlers.

Then Moore manufactures a batch of bad toys and, sorry to have disappointed Santa, flees to 20th Century New York City, where he ends up working in a crooked toy factory run by John Lithgow, saddled with an absolutely horrible, child-theater, cigar-sucking performance as a greedy corporate monster.

After that, Moore invents a car that soars and candy that makes people fly and Santa gets depressed and the reindeer get sick and the street urchin, Christian Fitzpatrick, doesn't believe in Santa until he does and the little rich girl, Carrie Kei Heim, overhears Lithgow's plot to take the money and run to Brazil and there's going to be Christmas II in March and ... oh, bah, humbug again.

At the end, the two little kids get permission to spend a year with Santa at the North Pole. After 112 minutes, the rest of the little kids will probably think they already have. —Har.

The Gig
(COLOR)

Warm tale of buddies who want to be jazzmen.

A release and production of The Gig Co., presented by McLaughlin, Piven, Vogel Inc. Produced by Norman I. Cohen. Directed by Frank D. Gilroy. Features entire cast. Screenplay, Gilroy; camera (Duart Color), Jeri Sopanen; editor, Rick Shaine; music director, Warren Vaché; sound, Eric Taylor; production manager, Cohen; assistant director, Ken Ornstein; casting, Abigail McGrath; associate producer, Scott Hancock. Reviewed at Magno Preview 4 screening room, N.Y., Nov. 13, 1985. (No MPAA Rating.) Running time: 92 MINS.

Marty Flynn	Wayne Rogers
Marshall Wilson	Cleavon Little
Jack Larmon	Andrew Duncan
Aaron Wohl	Jerry Matz
Arthur Winslow	Daniel Nalbach
Gil Macrae	Warren Vaché
Abe Mitgang	Joe Silver
Rick Valentine	Jay Thomas

Also with: Stan Lachow (George), Celia Bressack (Lucy), Georgia Harrell (the blond), Michael Fischetti (Vincent Amati), Susan Egbert (Laura Macrae), Karen Ashley (Janet Larmon), Virginia Downing (Mrs. Winslow), Chuck Wepner (the driver).

"The Gig" is a winning little film about a group of guys who try to fulfill their dream of being jazz players. Self-distributed by filmmaker Frank D. Gilroy, this comedy-drama should win favor with older audiences who can identify easily with the ingenious premise and situations.

Wayne Rogers toplines as a New York businessman who has played Dixieland Jazz with his five pals for their own amusement once a week since 1970. He arranges a two-week pro engagement at Paradise Manor hotel in the Catskills and ultimately talks the group into taking the step, the convincing argument being when their bass player George (Stan Lachow) drops out due to a major illness, promoting solidarity among the other five.

The replacement bassist, veteran player Marshall Wilson (Cleavon Little), causes friction in the group, not so much because he's black and they're white but because of his unfriendly personality and condescending attitude towards the budding amateurs. Filmmaker Gilroy gets maximum comic mileage out of this contrast, while making good points concerning the snobbism and purist stance that pervades many jazz circles.

At Paradise Manor, the group's dream of self-realization is almost snuffed out when hotel owner Abe Mitgang (Joe Silver, perfectly cast), immediately objects to their loud "biff, bang, bam" playing, and requires the band to play quiet, schmaltzy music. They ultimately succeed in winning over the resort audience to swinging Dixieland music. Disillusion comes when crooner Rick Valentine (played by actor-dj Jay Thomas) makes a comeback engagement and nastily insults the band's abilities when they can't play his Vegas-style arrangements, forcing Mitgang to fire them.

Aided by a very entertaining portrait of life at a Catskills resort, Wayne Rogers and Cleavon Little make a solid team. They're supported ably by reallife jazz artist Warren Vaché (who plays his own cornet here and doubled as film's musical director) portraying, natch, the most talented musician in the group, Jerry Matz as the clarinetist with an inflated view of his abilities, Andrew Duncan as the henpecked pianist and Daniel Nalbach as the morose drummer/dentist.

"The Gig" stands as an effective peek at the wish-fulfillment fringes of show business, previously treated from a jazz vantagepoint in the 1976 Swedish pic "Sven Klang's Combo." — Lor.

King Solomon's Mines
(COLOR)

Overactive remake is too imitative of Indiana Jones.

Hollywood, Nov. 22.

A Cannon Releasing release of a Cannon Prods. production. Produced by Menahem Golan, Yoram Globus. Directed by J. Lee-Thompson. Stars Richard Chamberlain, Sharon Stone, Herbert Lom, John Rhys-Davies. Screenplay, Gene Quintano, James R. Silke, based on the novel by H. Rider Haggard; camera (Rank color, J-D-C Widescreen), Alex Phillips; editor, John Shirley; music, Jerry Goldsmith; production designer, Luciano Spadoni; art director, Leonardo Coen Cagli; set decorator, Nelle Giorgetti; stunt coordinator, Peter Diamond; second unit director, Carlos Gil; costume designer, Tony Pueo; sound (Dolby), Eli Yarkoni; assistant director, Miguel Gil; associate producer, Rony Yacov; casting, Cianna Pissanello. Reviewed at the Hollywood Pacific Theater, Hollywood, Calif., Nov. 22, 1985. (MPAA Rating: PG-13). Running time: 100 MINS.

Allan Quatermain	Richard Chamberlain
Jessie	Sharon Stone
Colonel Bockner	Herbert Lom
Dogati	John Rhys-Davies
Umbopo	Ken Gampu
Gagoola	June Buthelezi

Cannon's remake of "King Solomon's Mines" treads heavily in the footsteps of that other great modern hero, Indiana Jones — too heavily. It's a three-aspirin film that many filmgoers will no doubt find stirring entertainment, and at times it does prove good fun. Too much of a good thing is numbing and "King Solomon's Mines" is that if anything.

From the Indiana Jones-type logo to the derivative Wagnerian musical score by Jerry Goldsmith, Cannon has tried to update the hero of the H. Rider Haggard novel for today's impatient audience. Surprisingly the production has not turned out as schlocky as it might have thanks to generally good production values and snappy effects and direction by J. Lee-Thompson.

Action sequences are edited almost too rapidly and come at a fevered pitch so that at times it is impossible to distinguish the blur of movement passing across the screen. Pacing is, perhaps, more than any other ingredient what made Indiana Jones in "Raiders Of The Lost Ark" and its sequel so entertaining and leaves "King Solomon's Mines" as a second-rate imitation.

Where Jones was deft and graceful in moving from crisis to crisis, "King Solomon's Mines" is often clumsy with logic and probability totally out the window, making the action hopelessly cartoonish. Once painted into the corner, scenes don't resolve so much as end before they spill into the next cliff-hanger.

It's an unrelenting pace with no variation that ultimately becomes tedious. Neither the camp humor nor the romance between Richard Chamberlain as the African adventurer Allan Quatermain and heroine-in-distress Sharon Stone (aptly named) breaks the monotony of the action.

Script by Gene Quintano and James R. Silke plays something like a child's maze with numerous dead-ends and detours on the way to the buried treasure, in this case the booty of King Solomon's Mines.

Things start out on the run with Jessie Huston (Stone) hiring Quatermain to help her find her archeologist father who has been kidnaped because of his knowledge of the location of the treasures. Once he is rescued from the clutches of the German Colonel Bockner (Herbert Lom) and the Turkish mercenary Dogati (John Rhys-Davies), joined in an unholy alliance, it's a race to the gold through alligators, lions, cannibals, tribes of savages and the German army.

Many of the effects are shamelessly "borrowed" from the Indiana Jones pictures, especially the finalé inside the mines. One scene in particular featuring a wall closing in on the heroes is lifted almost verbatim.

"King Solomon's Mines," however, never captures the charm of its model. Part of the problem is the lack of chemistry between the leads. (Chamberlain and Stone have already reteamed in a recently-shot sequel, "Quatermain.") Nothing is at stake if they don't make it and at the end they prove as mercenary in their own way as the bad guys. It's not surprising, given contemporary values, that the heroes are given their fair share of the gold. Glory is not enough anymore.

Elsewhere, characterization of the Germans and Turks as ugly colonialists and the natives as heathens has the ring of another era. Several scenes of savage rituals look more like a rock concert than ceremonial rites.

In other words there is scarcely a believable person in this mix. Chamberlain tries hard but doesn't have the *sang froid* to give Quatermain credibility. Rest of the cast generally overacts making even more of a cartoon of the proceedings than it need be. A little lighter touch could have made the film easier to digest.

Lensed on location in Zimbabwe, Alex Phillips' widescreen photography makes ample use of the scenery but it is also hard to swallow.
— *Jagr.*

Rocky IV

Big b.o. outlook for sappy Cold War installment.

Hollywood, Nov. 25.

An MGM/UA Entertainment release from United Artists of a Robert Chartoff-Irwin Winkler production. Executive producers, James D. Brubaker, Arthur Chobanian. Produced by Chartoff, Winkler. Directed by Sylvester Stallone. Features entire cast. Screenplay, Stallone; camera (Metrocolor), Bill Butler; editor, Don Zimmerman, John W. Wheeler; music, Vince DiCola, with themes from "Rocky" by Bill Conti; sound (Dolby), Chuck Wilborn; production design, Bill Kenney; set decoration, Rick T. Gentz,

Marti Wright (Vancouver); assistant director, Duncan Henderson; production manager, Jo Ann May-Pavey, Mary Eilts (Vancouver); montage editor, James Symons; casting, Amanda Mackey. Reviewed at Village Theater, L.A., Nov. 24, 1985. (MPAA Rating: PG.) Running time: **91 MINS.**

Rocky Balboa ....Sylvester Stallone
Adrian.....................Talia Shire
Paulie ....Burt Young
Apollo Creed ....Carl Weathers
Ludmilla ....Brigitte Nielsen
Duke ....Tony Burton
Nicoli Koloff ....Michael Pataki
Drago ....Dolph Lundgren

Sylvester Stallone is really sloughing it off shamelessly in "Rocky IV," but it's still impossible not to root for old Rocky Balboa to get up off the canvas and whup that bully one more time. Familiarity breeds boxoffice.

Beyond its visceral appeal, "Rocky IV" is truly the worst of the lot, though Stallone himself is more personable in this one and that helps. Dolph Lundgren is the most contrived opponent yet and that hurts.

Obviously, it's almost pointless to note that this is really the fourth version of the same story. The care and intensity of the first three — especially in the choreography of the fights — is missing this time.

Lundgren, an almost inhuman giant fighting machine created in Russian physical-fitness labs, comes to the U.S. to challenge the champ, but is first taken on by Apollo Creed (Carl Weathers), anxious to prove himself one last time. Weathers fails to take the amateur seriously and will not be back for "Rocky V."

So it's on to Moscow where, surprise, surprise, it's going to take a lot of training to get Stallone in shape for the Soviet. Though it really makes no difference, the story gets truly dumb at this point.

Arriving for a world-televised summit match, Rocky and his trainers are dispatched to a cabin in Siberia or somewhere, void of amenities and equipment. (Had Stallone been scripting the recent Geneva conference, he doubtlessly would have isolated President Reagan in a motel on the outskirts of town.)

Anyway, while the Soviets are prepping Lundgren with the latest and best boxing technology, poor old Rocky is out there in the snow, chopping wood and hauling sleds. Eventually, though, the training is over and, lacking any stairs on the steppes, Rocky runs to the top of Mount Everest or whatever the Russian equivalent is to spread his arms.

Lundgren, according to the digital readout, has developed a punch of 2,000 p.s.i., which should be enough to send Rocky back to Philadelphia without a plane. Once the fight starts, however, there's no way Rocky fans can resist getting caught up in it, predictable and preposterous though it be.

Through it all, Talia Shire stands around and worries as usual and brother-in-law Burt Young returns to hold the robe. Looking back at the mortality rate among the originals from first episode, however, they should be getting nervous.

Coming soon, no doubt, will be Rocky vs. Rambo, taking whatever money is left in the world. — *Har.*

Fool For Love
(COLOR)

Unsuccessful widescreen adaptation of Sam Shepard play.

A Cannon Releasing release of a Golan-Globus production. Produced by Menahem Golan, Yoram Globus. Directed by Robert Altman. Stars Sam Shepard, Kim Basinger, Randy Quaid, Harry Dean Stanton. Screenplay, Shepard, based on his play; camera (Rank color, J-D-C Widescreen), Pierre Mignot; editor, Luce Grunenwaldt, Steve Dunn; music, George Burt; songs, Sandy Rogers; production design, Stephen Altman; set decoration, John Hay; sound, Daniel Brisseau; associate producers, Scott Bushnell, Mati Raz; assistant director, Ned Dowd. Reviewed at Magno Penthouse screening room, N.Y., Nov. 18, 1985. (MPAA Rating: R.) Running time: **106 MINS.**

Eddie.....................Sam Shepard
May.......................Kim Basinger
Old Man............Harry Dean Stanton
Martin....................Randy Quaid
May's Mother ....Martha Crawford
Eddie's Mother.............Louise Egolf
Teenage May ....Sura Cox
Teenage Eddie ....Jonathan Skinner
Young May................April Russell
The Countess ......Deborah McNaughton
Mr. Valdez ....Lon Hill

Robert Altman has directed a fine cast in "Fool For Love" with all the authority and finesse a good play deserves, so it's too bad the play fooled them all. Sam Shepard's drama of intense, forbidden love in the modern West has proved a solid attraction in small legit houses over the past two years, and some individual strong scenes manage to arrest the attention, but this closeup rendition, at least, makes it seem like specious stuff filled with dramatic ideas left over from the 1950s. Some highbrow critics here and abroad likely will proclaim this a masterpiece, but general audiences will react as they did to the last Shepard-scripted pic, "Paris, Texas" — with a yawn.

Altman is a great admirer of John Huston's "The Misfits," and "Fool For Love" certainly qualifies as its equivalent in his career. Both build up potent emotional connections among a bunch of losers in the once wild West, and the talent involved proves more than enough to provide some absorbing moments.

Ultimately, however, the two films suffer from a similar, overweening literariness, from trying to fill the wide open spaces with too much jabber.

Shepard's work also leans, to a

surprising degree, on many of the dramaturgical conventions of the Miller-Williams-Inge-Albee era — the twisted, brutal sexuality, the warped family connections, the deep, dark secrets and the public revelation of same in the third act are here in all their clichéd, inescapable ingloriousness.

In Altman's best films during the 1970s, he rarely held to the text of his scripts and, in any event, was always undercutting his material. Whether successful or not, his more recent legit adaptations have seen him serving the plays in more expected ways. Working with Shepard, there was probably no way Altman could have subverted or transcended the material, but it sure could have used it.

Opening up the play, which was set entirely in a dingy motel room, Shepard and Altman have spread out the action all around a rundown motel complex on the edge of the desert. Eddie, a rangy, handsome cowboy, returns after a long absence to try to get back with the sexy May, with whom he has a can't-live-with-or-without-her relationship.

The two shout, argue, make up, make out, split up, pout, dance around each other and start up all over again, while an old drunk observer takes it all in.

Finally, the arrival of another fellow to take May out prompts a nocturnal spilling of the beans about Eddie and May's taboo love affair. Altman illustrates this lengthy explanation with snippets of flashbacks, some of which, intriguingly, somewhat contradict the accompanying narration. Wrapup is unsatisfyingly inconclusive.

Altman has worked overtime trying to make it all convincing and, technically, the film is superior. Other than seeming a bit over-edited, pic displays a total command of the medium, and many of Altman's effects could be labelled virtuoso. Aiding him notably are Pierre Mignot's very mobile camera and Stephen Altman's seedily evocative production design.

Beginning with the impressive Shepard, cast was hand-picked with care. As the saucy May, Kim Basinger alternately conjures up Marilyn Monroe in "The Misfits" and "Bus Stop" and Brigitte Bardot in "And God Created Woman."

Harry Dean Stanton is excellent as the washed-up cause of all the problems here, while Randy Quaid is perfect as the gullible, likeable audience standin to whom the sordid story can be explained.

Emphasizing the 1950s feel of the production is George Burt's very Leonard Rosenman-like score. Sandy Rogers (Shepard's sister) wrote and sang several effective c&w tunes. — *Cart.*

Contrary Warriors
(DOCU-COLOR)

San Francisco, Nov. 15.

A Rattlesnake Prods. (Missoula, Mont.) release. Produced by Connie Poten, Pamela Roberts, Beth Ferris. Camera (color), Stephen Lighthill; editor, Jennifer Chinlund; music, Todd Boekelheide; sound, Ann Evans. Narrator, Peter Coyote. Reviewed at the Palace of Fine Arts Theater, San Francisco, Nov. 14, 1985. (No MPAA Rating.) Running time: **60 MINS.**

This well-crafted, straightforward docu, unspooled at 10th annual American Indian filmfest, is an examination, through family and background of nonogenerian Robert Yellowtail, of the troubled history of Montana's Crow nation. Bureaucrats have deprived these Indians of buffalo, land and water, yet Yellowtail's legacy of "contrariness" and advocacy has not been dispelled. The spirit lives on and this pic, clearly tv docu fodder, manages to express that ardor handily.

The no-nonsense, informative narration by thesp Peter Coyote tells us all we need to know about the attempted U.S. government subjugation of the Crow. It's a valuable history lesson, an example of how scholarship and technicals can be blended. Todd Boekelheide's score is impressive and elevating.

— *Herb.*

Harem
(FRENCH-COLOR)

Paris, Nov. 21.

A UGC release of a Sara Films production. Produced by Alain Sarde. Directed by Arthur Joffé. Stars Nastassja Kinski, Ben Kingsley. Screenplay, Joffé, Tom Rayfiel, with the collaboration of Richard Prieur; camera (color), Pasqualino de Santis; production design, Alexandre Trauner; sound, Pierre Gamet; costumes, Olga Berlutti; editor, Dominique Martin (editing consultant, Ruggero Mastroianni); makeup, Charles Koubesserian, Stefano Fava; hairdo, Sergio Gennari; art director (N.Y.), George Goodridge; music, Philippe Sarde, Beethoven and Mozart; production managers, Christine Gozlan, Bernard Bouix, Pierre Cottrell (N.Y.), Lilo Capoano (Italy). Reviewed at UGC, Neuilly, Nov. 5, 1985. Running time: **113 MINS.**

Diane	Nastassja Kinski
Selim	Ben Kingsley
Massoud	Dennis Goldson
Affaf	Zohra Segal
Monsieur Raoul	Michel Robin
Zelide	Julette Simpson

"Harem" is an album of gorgeous images, aligned to tell a story, but it's a poor excuse for a dramatic motion picture packaged for the international marketplace. France's Alain Sarde, who last year had done a test run in English-language production with Paul Morrissey's offbeat, Gotham-set low-budgeter, "Mixed Blood," splurged for this feature debut by director Arthur Joffé, whose 1982 short, "Merlin ou le Cours de l'Or," won the Gold Palm at the Cannes Film Festival that year.

Despite an investment of $10,-000,000, which afforded stars Ben Kingsley and Nastassja Kinski, lenser Pasqualino de Santis and designer Alexandre Trauner, Sarde has skimped on the essential — a screenwriter. Instead he has disastrously allowed Joffé, obviously not yet at ease with an elaborate full-length narrative, to develop his own original story idea, with the help of another neophyte feature screenwriter, Tom Rayfiel (nephew of veteran scripter David Rayfiel). To cite just one elementary plotting problem: how do you create dramatic action around two protagonists of indecisive and essentially passive natures?

Tale concerns a fabulously wealthy Arab prince who kidnaps a beautiful young New York girl and has her brought to his desert palace, where she joins his harem. The idea is fraught with possibilities of kitsch extravagance and romantic delirium, but Joffé is into contemporary de-mystification and an oddly restrained view of *l'amour fou.*

As played by Kingsley, the unscrupulous potentate turns out to be a hypersentive esthete, trapped by tradition to maintain, for appearances' sake at least, a way of life he doesn't believe in. Though he keeps his harem and goes through the motions of exercising his sexual authority, he never has consummated the act with any of the ladies, who are content to idle away the hours watching porno vidcassettes.

As it turns out, he has kidnapped Kinski as a desperately romantic gesture. She, a blasé stock exchange trainee who drifts shallowly through sexual relationships, might have treated Kingsley as just another passing bedfellow had he courted her in a more banal fashion.

Up to this anti-climactic revelation, Joffé manages his unlikely tale with some skill and visual flair, but once he pulls away the final veil of mystery, the last vestiges of exoticism and dramatic interest also vanish. Poor exploitation of subsidiary characters also reflects Joffé's inability to master his material, as do the injection of some bogus melodramatic incidents.

Yet the film is visually ravishing, with the consummate artistry of de Santis and Trauner often happily distracting the viewer from the emptiness of the script and the exasperating indigence of the main characters. Some of the interiors were shot in the Palais Baya in Marrakesh, while others were conceived in a warehouse-cum-studio, and at a crumbling Moroccan desert fortress, superbly reconstructed to serve as Kingsley's palace.—*Len.*

The Supergrass
(BRITISH-COLOR)

London, Nov. 16.

A Recorded Releasing Co. presentation of a Comic Strip film. Executive producer, Michael White. Produced by Elaine Taylor. Directed by Peter Richardson. Features entire cast. Screenplay, Pete Richens, Richardson; camera (color), John Metcalfe; editor, Geoff Hogg; music, Keith Tippet, Working Week Big Band; art director, Niki Wateridge; costume design, Frances Haggett; sound, John Hayes. Reviewed at the ABC Cinema, Shaftesbury Avenue, London, Nov. 4, 1985. (BBFC Certificate, 15.) Running time: **105 MINS.**

Dennis	Adrian Edmondson
Lesley	Jennifer Saunders
Harvey Duncan	Peter Richardson
Andrea	Dawn French
Wong	Keith Allen
Gunter	Nigel Planer
Troy	Robbie Coltrane
Jim Jarvis	Daniel Peacock
Robertson	Ronald Allen
Perryman	Alexei Sayle
Collins	Michael Elphick
Franks	Patrick Durkin
Landlady	Marika Rivera

"The Supergrass" marks the feature debut of the Comic Strip group, who have a tv show with a cult following. Despite a somewhat rickety plot, pic has scored in broad playoff at the U.K. boxoffice and should merit some offshore exposure.

Story is sparked by a boorish innocent who tries to impress a would-be girlfriend with talk of his involvement in a drugs ring. Since his yarn tallies with information otherwise available to the police, Dennis is sent off to the South Coast to wait for the white powder-shipment, in the company of two undercover police.

Film's best moments involves the evolving relationship between the three. They put up in a comfortable hotel and have plenty of time on their hands. Policewoman Lesley, posing as the lover of the boorish Dennis, is in fact policeman Harvey's former girlfriend. That creates plenty of well-exploited comic scope for lust, jealousy and anger. This strand of the plot culminates in a tense scene of mutual drunken confession.

Pic makes up for the absence of any substantial external plot by multiplying characters with some abandon. Fine performances just about pull the film through. Ronald Allen as Inspector Robertson, the policeman who fell for Dennis' story, is depicted as an aspirant priest who prays for a breakthrough in the case before he takes the cloth. Robbie Coltrane, whose ominous arrival is never quite explained, plays a fat policeman with a belief in torture rather than romantic parlor games. Alexei Sayle almost steals the show with his set-piece as a uniformed cop patrolling the roads of Devon who longs to get into plain clothes. There's an amusing pair of real male drug smugglers posing as a married couple, with resulting sex-

ual tensions.

The film has some *longeurs* where it seems editing has been done to a preordained musical score. Peter Richardson, who also plays Sergeant Duncan, directs with a keen eye for the scenic, however. Noteworthy moments involve a drive through southern England and a splendid sequence when policeman Troy walks along an esplanade surrounded by splashing waves, with his chainsaw at the ready.

Lensing of this seaside laffer is uneven, but technical credits are generally fine.—*Japa.*

Young Sherlock Holmes
(COLOR)

Too much emphasis on special effects wizardry.

Hollywood, Nov. 19.

A Paramount Pictures release of a Steven Spielberg presentation of an Amblin Entertainment production, in association with Henry Winkler/Roger Birnbaum, coproduced by Industrial Light & Magic. Executive producers, Spielberg, Frank Marshall, Kathleen Kennedy. Produced by Mark Johnson. Directed by Barry Levinson. Features entire cast. Screenplay, Chris Columbus, suggested by characters created by Sir Arthur Conan Doyle; camera (Technicolor), Stephen Goldblatt; editor, Stu Linder; music, Bruce Broughton; sound (Dolby), Tony Dawe; production design, Norman Reynolds; art direction, Fred Hole, Charles Bishop; set decoration, Michael Ford; special effects supervisor, Kit West; visual effects produced by Industrial Light & Magic — supervisor, Dennis Muren; animatronics supervisor, Stephen Norrington; second unit director, Andrew Grieve; second unit camera, Steven Smith; costume design, Raymond Hughes; stunt arranger, Marc Boyle; production manager, Donald Toms; assistant director, Michael Murray; casting, Irene Lamb, Joselyn Morton, Mike Fenton/Jane Feinberg, Judy Taylor. Reviewed at Paramount Studios, Nov. 18, 1985. (MPAA Rating: PG-13.) Running time: **109 MINS.**

Sherlock Holmes	Nicholas Rowe
John Watson	Alan Cox
Elizabeth	Sophie Ward
Rathe	Anthony Higgins
Mrs. Dribb	Susan Fleetwood
Cragwitch	Freddie Jones
Waxflatter	Nigel Stock
Lestrade	Roger Ashton-Griffiths
Dudley	Earl Rhodes
Master Snelgrove	Brian Oulton
Bobster	Patrick Newell
Reverend Nesbitt	Donald Eccles

"Young Sherlock Holmes" is another Steven Spielberg film corresponding to those lamps made from driftwood and coffee tables from redwood burl and hatchcovers. It's not art but they all serve their purpose and sell by the millions.

The formula this time is applied to the question of what might have happened had Sherlock Holmes and John Watson first met as teenage students. As usual, Speilberg's team — this time led by director Barry Levinson — isn't really as interested in the answer as it is in fooling around with the visual effects possibilities conjured by George Lucas'

Industrial Light & Magic shop.

Did you know, for example, that as a teenager Sherlock Holmes perfected the first flying machine? Well, according to this picture he did because that's what he and Watson needed to chase the villain across town to the hidden temple. Exactly why Holmes did not go on to a lucrative career in aviation is never considered.

Similarly, though the adult Holmes mysteries are brilliant with deduction and logic, there's little time for that stuff here beyond an early sequence that's supposed to show how smart young Holmes is at picking up clues. Mostly, though, the young boys just rush from one scene of the adventure to the next.

The adventure itself, true to the Spielberg touch, comes straight from the Saturday matinees, complete with a murderous costumed cult sacrificing virginal maidens in elaborate ceremony.

Nicholas Rowe as Holmes and Alan Cox as Watson maturely carry off their roles, assisted by Sophie Ward as the necessary female accomplice. The adults are just there to fill in the spaces.

As expected, the effects are splendid, ranging from terrifying to cloying. Again, there's always the feeling they came first and the story idea was structured around them.

The boxoffice testifies that none of this is very negative at all. Taken for what it is, "Sherlock" is certainly well crafted, satisfying entertainment. Fans of Baker Street probably don't really care what Holmes was like as a teenager anyway.
—*Har.*

London Fest Reviews

Defence Of The Realm
(BRITISH-COLOR)

London, Nov. 22.
A Rank Film Distributors presentation (Warner Bros. release in U.S.) of an Enigma film, in association with the National Film Finance Corp. Executive producer, David Puttnam; producers, Robin Douet, Lynda Myles. Directed by David Drury. Stars Gabriel Byrne, Greta Scacchi, Denholm Elliott. Screenplay, Martin Stellman; camera (color), Roger Deakins; editor, Michael Bradsell; music, Richard Hartley; production design, Roger Murray-Leach; art director, Diana Charnley; costumes, Louise Frogley; sound, Tony Jackson, Howard Lanning. Reviewed at the London Film Festival, Nov. 21, 1985. (No MPAA Rating.) Running time: **96 MINS.**

Nick Mullen . . . . Gabriel Byrne
Nina Beckman . . . . Greta Scacchi
Vernon Bayliss . . . . Denholm Elliott
Dennis Markham . . . . Ian Bannen
Victor Kingsbrook . . . . Fulton Mackay
Jack Macleod . . . . Bill Paterson
Harry Champion . . . . David Calder
Arnold Reece . . . . Frederick Treves
Leo McAskey . . . . Robbie Coltrane

The state of the nation's press and the evil antics of its secret services in the nuclear age have recently become a key topic for local filmmakers and legit writers. This fast-paced thriller combines both themes in a package with sufficient controversy value to assure good local b.o. performance. The film may not register quite as strongly with offshore audiences.

Script unravels a relatively uncomplicated story of events following the near crash of a nuclear bomber on an American airforce base in the English countryside. A leftwing MP who gets wind of the event is framed as a Russian spy and forced to resign. His journalist friend is bumped off secretly shortly before publishing details of the incident.

The story centers, however, on a younger hack who enjoys the triumph of cracking the link between parliamentarian Markham and a Russian agent, only to discover after the death of his friend that he has been set up by the secret services. Like many another cinema scribe, he searches for the truth.

Onward propulsion of the narrative eclipses other characters. The journalists around Nick Mullen are seen as sturdy professionals little affected by the events around them. The secret services are kept at a distance. Ditto the journalistic establishment which initially prevents Mullen's story getting out.

A female character, Nina Beckman, played by Greta Scacchi, is strangely marginal. By the time she enters center stage as Mullen's journalistic accomplice, her only function is to tie up a few loose ends. There's a jokey allusion to an ongoing relationship at the film's ending, shortly before Mullen's apartment is incinerated by a bomb.

Pic fights a little shy of its messages about the rotten state of Britain. The final sequence seems embarrassed and confused.

Gabriel Byrne is somewhat one-dimensional as Mullen and attempts to depict his moral turnaround from cynical journalist to sincere seeker after the truth are minimal. He's a perfect foil, however, to the older journalist between friendship, the truth and his career. Denholm Elliott gives an extraordinary performance in that role.

What really marks the film out amongst recent British medium budgeters is the vigor and wit of David Drury's direction. Some credit must also go to debutante producer Lynda Myles, formerly a film writer and festival organizer. Production design, centered on the scruffy newsroom, is firstrate.

Film is also interesting for its evocative use of London street locations, which here have an atmosphere not previously caught on film. Cinematographer Roger Deakins, whose other recent credits include Michael Radford's "1984" and Philip Saville's "Shadey," does a remarkable job. —*Japa.*

The McGuffin
(BRITISH-COLOR-16m)

London, Nov. 22.
A BBC-TV Prod. Produced by Kenith Trodd. Directed by Colin Bucksey. Features entire cast. Screenplay, Michael Thomas, based upon the book by John Bowen; camera (color), John Walker; editor, Clare Douglas; music, Richard Hartley; production design, Jim Clay; costumes, Anushia Nieradzik; sound, Peter Edwards. Reviewed at the London Film Festival, Nov. 21, 1985. Running time: **95 MINS.**

Paul Hatcher . . . . .Charles Dance
Man in brown . . . . .Brian Glover
Celestia . . . . .Ritza Brown
Silver-haired man . . . . . .Francis Matthews
Anne .Phyllis Logan
Mrs. Forbes-Dutchie . . . . .Ann Todd
Gavin .Mark Rylance
Nina . . . . Anna Massey
Marty de Rezke . . . . .Jerry Stiller
Archie . . . . .Calaban

An homage to Alfred Hitchcock risks being judged by the highest standards. "The McGuffin," however, gets egg all over its face and then some. It's a botched job that doesn't merit the spotlight of a film festival screening.

Film was considered for 35m production as the first theatrically released pic to be made by BBC Television. Even when considered as just a jolly romp, "The McGuffin" confirms the impression given by other BBC films screened during the London Film Festival that the corporation needs a shakeout in its script department.

Film starts promisingly with an allusion to "Rear Window" to establish that something interesting is going on opposite the flat where the tired but agile film critic Paul Hatcher (Charles Dance) lives. Several red herrings then suggest pic's intended theme is a film devourer's inability to distinguish between fantasy and reality.

There is a splendidly inconsequential scene where the critic returns from the screening of a Japanese film to imagine the lady living opposite appearing in the window dressed as Madame Butterfly and being strangled.

What is going on over the way is that a transvestite is not getting on very well with an old woman. The former is being pursued by hoods interested in the whereabouts of a set of pictures of a senior politician performing lewd sex acts.

There is little attempt at mystery. The pair living opposite are killed, in one case with the cameras running. The hunt then is focused on Hatcher who quickly discovers a hyperactive dog has the vital negative around its neck.

With the "Rear Window" theme gone, the script has to introduce some new characters to keep things moving. They include a mysterious policeman and a girlfriend. Hatcher promptly goes off to Italy where he's been invited to sit on the jury of a festival of "cinema puro," which turns out to be a beanfeast of porno films. Welcome distraction is found in a black-haired lady who happens to be in league with the tough guys.

It all looks as if someone decided to shoot a promising first-draft script. Several narrative jumps in the resulting film suggest a few nightmares ensued in the editing room. —*Japa.*

Past Caring
(BRITISH-COLOR)

London, Nov. 18.
A BBC-TV production. Produced by Kenith Trodd. Directed by Richard Eyre. Features entire cast. Screenplay, Tom Clarke; camera (color), Kenneth McMillan; editor, Ken Pearce; music, George Fenton; production design, Geoff Powell; costumes, Hazel Pethig; sound, Ron Brown. Reviewed at the London Film Festival, Nov. 15, 1985. Running time: **77 MINS.**

Victor . . . . .Denholm Elliott
Edward . . . . .Emlyn Williams
Linda . . . . .Connie Booth
Stella . . . . .Joan Greenwood
Warden . . . . .Dave Atkins
Warden's wife . . . . .Barbara Keogh
Margaret . . . . .Matyelock Gibbs
Minibus driver . . . . .James Duggen
Em . . . . .Madeline Thomas

"Past Caring" is a portrait of a callous, seemingly virile man on the edge of old age. Victor finds himself in the unlikely position of being accommodated in a home for senile oldies where the only object of sexual-romantic interest is the youngish hostel keeper.

The piece's most dramatic moment is an opening scene where an act of lechery between Victor and his married neighbor leads to the incineration of the protected apartments in which each intended, until that moment, to end their days.

It's downhill from then on as Victor willfully ignores the petty regulations by which the institution is run and causes havoc among his fellow inmates. Eventually he finds himself in the bed of the hostel's chief officer. The mismatched couple's attempts to form some life together abort when Victor falls asleep during lovemaking.

Denholm Elliott's distempered rendition of old age is most effective in the first half of the film.

Most touching performance is from Emlyn Williams as an aging queen who hopes, through his relationship with Victor, to find a way of reliving for a while his days of glory.

Ken McMillan's lighting of the hostel's corridors is heavily dependent on back light seemingly designed to illustrate the oppressive horrors of institutional living. Effect is ultimately a drag. —*Japa.*

Letters To An Unknown Lover
(Les Louves)
(BRITISH-FRENCH-COLOR)

London, Nov. 16.
A Portman production, made in association with Channel Four and Antenne-2. Executive producer, Tom Donald. Produced by Ian Warren. Directed by Peter Duffell. Features entire cast. Screenplay, based on their novel "Les Louves," by Pierre Boileau and Thomas Narcejac, camera (color), Claude Robin; editor, Teddy Darvas; music, Raymond Alessandrini; production design, Michael Janiaud; costumes, Liselle Roos, Jean-Philippe Abril. Reviewed at the London Film Festival, Nov. 16, 1985. Running time: **101 MINS.**
Helene . . . . Cherie Lunghi
Agnes . . . . Mathilda May
Gervais . . . . Yves Beneyton
Bernard . . . . Ralph Bates
Julia . . . . Andrea Ferréol
Elderly Man . . . . Gabriel Gobin
Elderly Woman . . . . Cadine Constant
Lawyer . . . . Les Clack

"Letters To An Unknown Lover," is a collaboration between French and British tv stations shot concurrently in two language versions with the French title of "Les Louves." Film was made on locations in Lyons, France and at Joinville Studios earlier this year.

It's an intriguing piece of *film noir* which, at least in the English-track version caught for review, fails to provide persuasive characterization. Problem may have been the two-track shooting arrangement. Dialog placed in the mouths of Mathilda May and Yves Beneyton just doesn't sound right.

Story originates in a pen-pal love affair between Bernard, a Frenchman imprisoned by the Germans during World War II, and a faded aristocrat with a sordid family history. When the prisoner escapes with his friend they're destined for the Lyons apartment where Helene (Cherie Lunghi) lives with her much younger sister Agnes (Mathilda May). Since Bernard is killed under a train, his companion Gervais stands in as the POW romantic.

Caught between the charms of the two sisters, Gervais is forced to marry Helene. Beneyton plays the role of Gervais as an innocent who doesn't have a clue what's happening to him. It's only when trapped in the nuptial knot that he discovers it's all a plot to win a large inheritance left to Bernard. The eventual outcome is, needless to say, a

surprise.

Film is moderately interesting as a portrait of French bourgeois life which has adapted to a German occupation, whose effects are conveyed in shots from an apartment window.

The plot has too many flaws to justify theatrical playoff. There is, however, some stylish direction from Peter Duffell. Also, Mathilda May gives an entrancing performance as the psychic sister caught up in a web of her sister's devising.—*Japa.*

The End Of The World Man
(IRISH-COLOR)

London, Nov. 23.
An Aisling Films production in association with the Irish Film Board. Executive producer, Tiernan MacBride. Produced by Marie Jackson. Directed by Bill Miskelly. Features entire cast. Screenplay, Jackson, Miskelly; camera (color), Seamus Deasy; editor, Maurice Healey; music, John Anderson; production designer, Diane Menaul; costumes, Jacqueline Young; sound, Brendan Deasy. Reviewed at the London Film Festival, Nov. 23, 1985. Running time: 85 MINS.
Johnson . . . . John Hewitt
Mrs D'Arcy . . . . Maureen Dow
Sir George . . . . Michael Knowles
Paula . . . . Leanne O'Malley
Noel . . . . Ian Morrison
Joe . . . . Rowan Moore
Colm . . . . Anthony McClelland
Pete . . . . Eoin O'Callaghan
Mr D'Arcy . . . . Kevin Flood
Architect . . . . Ian McElhinney

One of six films aimed at a kid audience to be screened during this year's London Film Festival, "The End Of The World Man" is a comedy with an ecological theme. Without any standout production values, it's destined largely for tv playoff.

Pic starts unevenly with a series of loosely associated visual gags, and the narrative generally wanders down one fruitless byway too many. Overall, however, the story is entertaining.

Leanne O'Malley has a sparkling naturalness as Paula, a spirited tomboy who leads a campaign to protect the wooded area in which the kids play. This is linked to a touching concern that the death of the last tree will mean the end of the world.

Paula works in association with an unassertive girl friend. They raise a petition against the transformation of their play area into a concrete leisure center, lobby the "government" and finally take direct action. The main obstacle initially comes from two bullying little boys.

There's rather a superfluity of characters, with the adults being generally dull. There is, however, a charming portrait of an utterly cynical politician who gets his comeuppance in the film's final frame.

Incidentally interesting aspect of the film is its depiction of life in Bel-

fast, Northern Ireland, where kids walk the streets without noticing the alert machine guns, and every incident provokes a seeming overreaction from the security forces. —*Japa.*

Honest, Decent and True
(BRITISH-COLOR)

London, Nov. 16.
A BBC-TV production. Produced by Graham Benson. Written and directed by Les Blair. Features entire cast. Camera (color), John McGlashan; editor, Sue Wyatt; music, Simon Brint; production designer, Jim Clay; costumes, Andrew Rose; sound, Richard Manton, Ken Hains. Reviewed at the London Film Festival, Nov. 14, 1985. Running time: **97 MINS.**
Mike . . . . Derrick O'Connor
Alun . . . . Adrian Edmondson
Davina . . . . Juliette Mole
Derek . . . . Gary Oldman
Moonee . . . . Richard E. Grant
Prish . . . . Arabella Weir
Patsy . . . . Yvonne French
James Fletcher . . . . Thomas Wheatley
Graham . . . . Tony Portacio
Lucinda . . . . Lyndsay Russell
Scott . . . . Rupert Baker

"Honest, Decent and True" is an amusing but flawed account of the advertising scene in London. Improvised nature of the script shows in the wayward narrative.

Pic centers on the evolution of a tv campaign for a lager from an old-fashioned brewing enterprise. There are some dramatic scenes in which the old-fashioned client attempts to restrain the unrestrained creativity of an art department. The resulting compromise commercial is an absurdity.

The only other thing the story has to say about those working in the advertising business is that they are involved in an endless quest to get into or out of each other's beds. Even as a metaphor for the superficiality of their lives, such an assumption has scant interest.

A subplot which suggests more meanings than it provides has boorish art director Alun living in a flat with a real artist. Adrian Edmondson brings comic zest to his role as Alun.

Derrick O'Connor is a standout as the raffish advertising executive who has sold out his principles in the pursuit of an exciting life which has lost its appeal.

Les Blair's direction is fairly artless, but technical credits are fine.—*Japa.*

Agada
(Agatha)
(SOUTH KOREAN-COLOR)

London, Nov. 18.
Produced by Pak Jong-ch'an for Hwa Jon Film. Directed by Kim Hyeon-myeong. Screenplay, Ji Sang-hak, from a story by Yu Hong-jong; camera (color), I Seog-gi; editor, Hyeon Dong-chun; music, I Pil-weon; sets

Kim Byeong-su. Reviewed at the London Film Festival, Nov. 17, 1985. Running time: **97 MINS.**
With: I Bo-heui (Agada), Yu In-chon (Father Da-du), Kim Weon-seob (Hyeon-uk, Agada's boyfriend), I Gyeong-heui (Jeong Yeo-sin, Father Da-du's mother)

A painterly eye on the part of the film's director, a subtle shifting of narrative time sequences and strong performances from the principals save "Agatha," which might have degenerated into an irritatingly melodramatic oriental "nun's story."

Although the conflict between commitment to a religious calling and the desire for sexual fulfillment is not the most trendy of subjects these days, seeing Roman Catholicism taken seriously as a personal code of conduct and — in of all place, strongly Buddhist South Korea — is striking.

The film's action revolves around the young woman of the title who, about to take the veil, hesitates long enough to return home to nurse her dying father. His death sets off a series of crisis which eventually unhinge Agatha. The young priest of the village church struggles against his passion for Agatha, finally deciding to enter a Carmelite monastary to free himself from her.

Fighting against her own passion, Agatha lets herself succumb to another admirer, a highly Westernized businessman, by whom she has a child. He too abandons her, for his previous fiancée, and Agatha is talked into turning her child over to them.

This final blow deadens Agatha, leaving her mute and without memory. Eventually she is taken back to her hometown where memories of happier times reawaken her religious calling. We last see her fallen prostrate in front of the church altar.

Despite the sometimes excessive melodrama, director Kim Hyeon-myeong has largely dignified the plot by an intelligent use of visual imagery and poetic conceits. The natural landscape, beautifully photographed, shifts tellingly as the characters' anguish grows.

Whether one reads the film as a criticism of repressive values which menace human health and happiness or as an acceptance of those strict values as the only sure refuge from human suffering, the treatment is moving, the images haunting.

What is lacking is more sustained reference to Korean society or of the Buddhist approach to life with which to contrast the effects of Roman Catholicism on the heroine. A real clash of cultures might have made the film less dependent on melodrama and denser thematically. As it is, it is one woman's descent into hell and her redemption by being reunited with the only force which hasn't actively abandoned her, God. —*Guid.*

Silas Marner
(BRITISH-COLOR)

London, Nov. 16.

A BBC-TV production. Produced by Louis Marks. Directed by Giles Foster. Stars Ben Kingsley. Screenplay, Marks, Foster; camera (color), Nat Crosby; editor, Robin Sales; music, Carl Davis; production design, Gerry Scott; costumes, Anushia Nieradzik; sound, John Pritchard. Reviewed at the London Film Festival, Nov. 16, 1985. Running Time: 92 MINS.
Silas Marner . . . . Ben Kingsley
Nancy Lammeter . . . . Jenny Agutter
Godfrey Cass . . . . Patrick Ryecart
Dunstan Cass . . . . Jonathan Coy
Squire Cass . . . . Freddie Jones
Mr. Lammeter . . . . Frederick Treves
Molly . . . . Angela Pleasence
Eppie . . . . Patsy Kensit
Dolly Winthrop . . . . Rosemary Martin
William Dane . . . . Paul Copley
Sarah . . . . Natalie Ogle

"Silas Marner" is a moving account of George Elliot's novel characterized by none of the stylistic stodginess often associated with British television's treatment of classic tomes.

Ben Kingsley gives a passionate performance as the weaver who, after being exiled from a religious community on the false charge of theft, becomes a recluse in the village of Faveloe. His only solace is a stack of gold put by for an unspecified purpose. Kingsley's eyes and gestures perfectly convey the character's quiet suffering and ultimate goodness.

Script moves somewhat slowly at first as the complex details of village life are sketched in. Giles Foster directs, however, with precision and a fine eye for the telling moment.

When Silas is robbed by the younger son of the local squire, his life seems wrecked. Then, one winter night a little blond girl, the secret daughter of the squire's son, finds a way to Silas' humble hearth while her mother, an opium addict, dies outside.

The woman's death frees the squire to marry a local lass, but he is unable to declare the true parentage of the girl. That lays the seeds for his tragedy. His wife becomes barren and the squire tries unsuccessfully to claim the 16-year-old Eppie from her adoptive father. The aristocratic couple played by Patrick Ryecart and Jenny Agutter are doomed to hollow-eyed unhappiness, while Silas basks in human love.

Film is saved from excessive schematism by its detailed depiction of Silas' daily chores and activities at the manor house, which are just the cover for degenerate goings-on.

Lensing by the BBC's top cameraman Nat Crosby is topnotch. Carl Davis' score, which attempts to match the richness of the image, is sometimes rather overblown.
—*Japa.*

The Insurance Man
(BRITISH-COLOR-16m)

London, Nov. 16.

A BBC-TV production. Produced by Innes Lloyd. Directed by Richard Eyre. Features entire cast. Screenplay, Alan Bennett; camera (color), Nat Crosby; editor, Ken Pearce; music, Dominic Muldowney; production design, Geoff Powell; costumes, Janet Tharby. Reviewed at the London Film Festival, Nov. 15, 1985. Running time: 77 MINS.
Young Franz . . . . Robert Hines
Mr. Kafka . . . . Daniel Day-Lewis
Gutling . . . . Jim Broadbent
Culick . . . . Hugh Fraser
Pohlmann . . . . Tony Haygarth
Collecting Girl . . . . Oona Kirsch
Miss Weber . . . . Geoffrey Palmer
Trapp . . . . Ralph Hammond
Reisz . . . . Roger Hammond
Doctor . . . . Alan McNaughtan
Old Franz . . . . Trevor Peacock
Landlady . . . . Diana Rayworth
Christina . . . . Tessa Wojtczak

Writer Alan Bennett plunges into despair in this telefilm homage to Franz Kafka. It combines allusions to various of Kafka's novels, including "Metamorphosis" and "The Trial," with information about his working life. It's an imaginative and ambitious piece.

Whereas the intensity of Kafka's novels comes from the first person narrative of characters metamorphosed into a monstrous cockroach or lost in a bureaucratic nightmare world, Bennett's script covers a diffuse range of characters. Bookending scenes involve the sick lead character 35 years after the main incident.

Robert Hines plays an innocent whose body is covered in a rash. He blames the malaise on his toils in a dyeworks, and seeks an explanation from the state insurance office where various officials dedicate themselves to repelling the importunate. It is shortly after finally meeting with the kind Mr. Kafka that the true cause of his malaise becomes clear. He is afraid of his fiancée's sexual advances. The explanation of the disease from which he is suffering in 1945 is subsequent labor in an asbestos works.

Construction of the narrative around disassociated scenes in the state bureaucracy weakens the dramatic impulse and throws the audience onto a quest for some underlying philosophy. It lies in a vision of a world where everyone busies himself with attempting to conceal that he knows nothing.

Among a distinguished group of performers, Raymond Day-Lewis is standout as the kindly Mr. Kafka. The film is shot in an impressive expressionist style by Richard Eyre, with Nat Crosby's blue-tinged lensing giving a consistently oppressive hue throughout. —*Japa.*

The Silent Twins
(BRITISH-COLOR)

London, Nov. 17.

A BBC-TV production. Executive producer, Graham Massey. Produced by Martin Thompson. Directed by Jon Amiel. Features entire cast. Screenplay, Marjorie Wallace; camera (color), Ken Westbury; editor, Bill Wright; music, Nicholas Carr; production design, Tony Snoaden; costumes, Odile Dicks-Mireaux, Lynda Woodfield; sound, Malcolm Webberly. Reviewed at the London Film Festival, Nov. 17, 1985. Running time: 85 MINS.
June Gibbons . . . . Sharon Parker
Jennifer Gibbons . . . . Shirley Parker
Gloria Gibbons . . . . Ena Cabatyo
Audrey Gibbons . . . . Ruddy L. Davis
Greta Gibbons . . . . Beverley Martin
Rosie Gibbons . . . . Natasha Dixon
Young June . . . . Juliette Tony
Young Jennifer . . . . Jillian Tony
Wayne Kennedy . . . . Marcus D'Amico
Carl Kennedy . . . . David Blackburn
Tim Thomas . . . . Ifan Huw Dafydd
Cathy Arthur . . . . Madeline Adams
Helen . . . . Sandra Voe

"The Silent Twins" tells the intriguing true story of identical twins who form a pact when young to remain silent in dealings with the outside world. The story came to public notice when the two 18-year-olds were imprisoned for arson.

That vow of silence presents the filmmakers with their dramatic problem. It is not resolved by frequent voiceovers. The rare scenes showing the two relating to each other generally are characterized by extreme physical violence. The world conjured in their creative writing, which might have provided some clue to the enigma, is not depicted.

The psychological facts established about the two girls are that, within their shared life, each was striving to defeat the other, creating constant tension between their inseparability and occasional murderous aggression. Also, they sought as a pair to distinguish themselves in some remarkable way, leading to the conflagrations and their imprisonment in a high-security prison for the insane.

The film rather overplays the comic aspects of the two peculiarly dressed girls who refuse to respond to outside interventions. The most telling moments are when they set out to lose their virginity to two visiting American kids. Significantly, those encounters do involve some words.

Film, destined for tv playoff, is a fascinating commentary on the ultimate limitations of our knowledge about the workings of the human mind. —*Japa.*

Hitchcock, Il Brivido Del Genio
(The Thrill Of Genius)
(ITALIAN-DOCU-COLOR-16m)

London, Nov. 16.

An RAI-1 production. Produced and directed by Francesco Bortolino and Claudio Masenza. Camera (color), Michael Bernard, Philippe Blaess, Jim McCalmont, Digby Elliott; editor, Lidia Bordi. Reviewed at the London Film Festival, Nov. 14, 1985. Running time: 129 MINS.
With: Patricia Hitchcock, Sylvia Sidney, Anne Baxter, Joan Fontaine, Judith Anderson, Hume Cronyn, Joseph Cotten, Ann Todd, Alida Valli, Farley Granger, Richard Todd, Ray Milland, John Michael Hayes, Donald Spoto, Mildred Natwick, Daniel Gélin, Anthony Perkins, Janet Leigh, Tippi Hedren, Jessica Tandy, Lila Kedrova, Philippe Noiret, Barry Foster, Jon Finch.

Some of the legwork involved in putting together this documentary could have been usefully replaced with a little more attention to the questions posed to the people interviewed about their work with Hitchcock.

The three-part docu made for Italian tv might have been entitled "Hitchcock And The Performers" were it not for the occasional intrusion of another commentator like the nauseating (in this context) Donald Spoto, and the space given to the generally ill-informed views of actresses on Hitchcock's working methods and philosophy.

The comments about Hitchcock's dealings with actors too often are restricted to simple refutations of the view that the master of suspense regarded actors as mere "cattle." Another oft-reiterated platitude is that Hitchcock was a sad man who would have liked to have been a star. This is Hitchcock for the innocents.

There are, however, some amusingly told stories and moments of fresh insight, particularly from Philippe Noiret, Joan Fontaine and Ann Todd. General effect is diminished by the appalling reproduction of the film clips.—*Japa.*

Gospodin Za Edin Den
(King For A Day)
(BULGARIAN-COLOR)

London, Nov. 18.

A Bojana Studio production for Bulgariafilm. Directed by Nikolai Volev. Stars Todor Kolev. Screenplay, Nikola Stratkov; production design, Konstantin Rusakov; music, Ivan Staikov. Reviewed at the London Film Festival, Nov. 18, 1985. Running time: 100 MINS.
With: Todor Kolev, Yordanka Stefanova, Stoyen Gudev, Veliko Stoyanov, Ivan Grigorov, Itzhak Fintsi.

It may surprise audiences outside the Balkans to find the talents of early silent comedians so delightfully revived in a drama set on the Turkish-Bulgarian border at the turn of the century. "King For A Day" is sufficiently dependent on its visual gags to be universally comprehensible.

Todor Kolev gives a splendid deadpan performance as Purko, a down-on-his luck peasant whose simple-minded attempts to find the werewithall to pay off his taxes only serve to further complicate his life. The eggs he buys with stolen church silver are promptly crushed by a bird A visiting motorcyclist sells him a useless clothes shredder.

Purko's true nemesis, and also a rival for top billing, is a pig whose never-ending hunger is not satiated even by the legs of a municipal statue or the foundations of the local tavern. The film's best slapstick humor revolves around this hyperactive beast.

It's to the credit of London Film School-trained director Nikolai Volev that he uses silent-film devices like speeded-up motion to make ribald comedy, but also tells a touching story about a father who never gives up hope of providing for a senuous wife and consequently expanding brood of children. Purko's emotional resilience is symbolized in skilled clarinet-playing.

Film loses its way somewhat when Purko makes a journey into town to raise a loan to finance a trip to America. He hands over his final hope of redemption to a local prostitute who's in league with a conman. However, the hiatus is justified in a climactic penultimate sequence when Purko's return to the village in a suit reminiscent of that worn by Chaplin secures credit from the local innkeeper for a final revel. The next morning, Purko is led off to prison by the local tax-collector.

"King For A Day" is a sensitive account of life in a newly-independent Bulgaria when the dream of escape from an impoverished country to the U.S. offered the only hope of rising out of the penury trap.

—*Japa.*

Jangnam
(First Son)
(SOUTH KOREAN-COLOR)

London, Nov. 26.

A Dae Heung film release. Produced by I. Tae-weon. Directed by Lee Doo-yong. Features entire cast. Screenplay, Doo-yong, An Jin-weon, based on a story by Jin-weon; camera (color), Jeong Il-seong; editor, I. Gyeong-ja; sets, Do Yong-u; music, I Jeol-hyeok. Reviewed at London Film Fest, Nov. 25, 1985. Running time: **115 MINS.**

With: Shin Seong-il (First Son), Hwang Jeong-sun (Mother), Kim Il-hae (Father), Tae Hyeon-sil (First Son's Wife), Kim Hui-ra (Second Son), Seong Hui-yeon (Second Son's Wife), Kim Seong-su (Third Son), Min Boggi (Third Son's Wife), Mun Jong-sug (First Daughter), Nam Gung-weon (First Daughter's Husband), O Yeong-hwa Il Dae (Second Daughter's Husband).

Lee Doo-yong's "First Son" focuses on the problems many South Koreans have in adapting to a new Westernized culture that automatically requires the jettison of traditional customs — like the obligations of children to care for their aging parents, who are usually without

pensions and thus totally dependent on their children for support in their last years. With more and more Koreans moving from the country to urban housing developments, there is simply no place there for the parents, nor do old people care to be confined to homes for the aged.

An elderly couple who have raised three sons and two daughters left their country residence to move to Seoul, to settle in with the "first son" — now a computer exec — but the quarters are too small. The parents also find it difficult to adjust to the lifestyles of the new generation, while the Old Peoples Home is a cold block of concrete. A decision is made to build a house to accommodate everyone, but father has cancer and mother dies suddenly.

Theme is marred by overacting and conventional direction. —*Holl.*

Um Adeus Português
(A Portuguese Goodbye)
(PORTUGUESE-COLOR/B&W)

London, Nov. 24.

A Portuguese film production, Lisbon. Produced and directed by João Botelho. Features entire cast. Screenplay, Botelho, Leonor Pinhão; camera (color, b&w), Acácio de Almeida; music, Olivier Messiaen, African songs; sound, Joaquin Pinto, Vasco Pimental. Reviewed at London Film Fest, Nov. 23, 1985. Running time: **85 MINS.**

With: Rui Furtado (Raul), Isabel de Castro (Pledade), Maria Cabral (Laura), Fernando Heitor (Alexandre), Cristina Hauser (Rosa).

Returning to the London fest after his initial success here in 1981 with "The Other One," Portuguese helmer João Botelho scored again with "A Portuguese Goodbye," a natural for the fest circuit. So far as subject matter is concerned, it's also one of the most forthright features to emerge from Portugal this decade.

Botelho tells two stories parallel to each other, the b&w sequences following a patrol through the jungles of Portuguese Africa (more like Mozambique than Angola) in 1972, while the color segments are a depiction of the present. The link between the two is in the memory and compassion of parents who have lost a dearly loved son in the colonial war that now no one officially or unofficially wants to talk about anymore. The experience after a decade is still too painful.

The parents come from their country home to visit the younger son in Lisbon, who is having a difficult time making ends meet while penning trite erotic tales for a pulp publisher. During the visit, rendered in warm colors and static camera placements — the fragile and still mourning mother simply "takes leave of this world" one evening.

— *Holl.*

A Chorus Line
(COLOR)

Attenborough gets the job done, with good results.

Hollywood, Dec. 3.

A Columbia Pictures release of a film from Embassy Films and Polygram Pictures, produced by Cy Feuer and Ernest Martin. Directed by Richard Attenborough. Features entire cast. Executive producer, Gordon Stulberg. Screenplay, Arnold Schulman, based on stage play directed by Michael Bennett with book by James Kirkwood and Nicholas Dante; camera (color), Ronnie Taylor; editor, John Bloom; sound, Chris Newman; music, Marvin Hamlisch; lyrics, Edward Kleban; arrangements, Ralph Burns; costumes, Faye Poliakin; production design, Patrizia Von Brandenstein; choreography, Jeffrey Hornaday; associate producer, Joseph M. Caracciolo; assistant director, Robert Girolami; art direction, John Dapper; casting, Julie Hughes, Barry Moss. Reviewed at Century Theater, L.A., Dec. 2, 1985. (MPAA Rating: PG-13). Running time: **113 MINS.**

Zach	Michael Douglas
Larry	Terrence Mann
Cassie	Alyson Reed
Paul	Cameron English
Sheila	Vicki Frederick
Val	Audrey Landers
Mark	Michael Blevins
Morales	Yamil Borges
Kim	Sharon Brown
Richie	Gregg Burge
Al	Tony Fields
Kristine	Nicole Fosse
Connie	Jan Gan Boyd
Bebe	Michelle Johnston
Judy	Janet Jones
Maggie	Pam Klinger
Mike	Charles McGowan
Greg	Justin Ross
Don	Blane Savage
Bobby	Matt West

Director Richard Attenborough has not solved the problem of bringing "A Chorus Line" to the screen, but he at least got it there after nearly a decade of diddling around by others, and the result should be to-

'Chorus Line' On B'way

The original stage production of "A Chorus Line" is the longest-running show in Broadway history with 4,290 performances at the Shubert Theater as of Saturday (30). Show opened July 25, 1975 after transferring from Joseph Papp's Public Theater, where it preemed several months earlier.

"Chorus Line" bypassed "Grease" as the Broadway long-run champ Sept. 29, 1983 when it played its 3,389th performance. It's also the most dollar-profitable show in U.S. legit history, with total net profit of roughly $40,000,000. Its worldwide gross is also a record, somewhere above $300,000,000. The legit show is a coproduction of Papp's N.Y. Shakespeare Festival and Michael Bennett, the conceiver-director-choreographer.

The legit production stands to earn considerable extra income from the film if it clicks

since the authors, who share on a 60-40 basis with the show, are due to receive a percentage of the distributor's gross above $30,000,000.

tally enjoyable for sophisticated audiences, if not in theaters, then in a long life of homevideo.

There's a common wisdom, of course, that a stage show must be "opened up" for the camera, but Universal Pictures had no idea of how to do that when it paid $5,500,-000 for the film rights in 1976. Since then, "Chorus" passed through the hands of additional talent such as Sidney Beckerman, Mike Nichols, Sidney Lumet, Allan Carr, John Travolta and whomever else in Hollywood and Broadway who might have had an idea.

Finally locked into place by Polygram and Embassy, Attenborough clearly chose to ignore the problem and film the stage show as best he could. To a large extent, the common wisdom prevails and "Chorus" often seems static and confined, rarely venturing beyond the immediate.

Nonetheless, the director and lenser Ronnie Taylor have done an excellent job working within the limitations, using every trick they could think of to keep the picture moving. More importantly, they have a fine cast, good music and a great, popular show to work with. So if all they did was get it on film, that's not so bad.

The only boxoffice name on the bill, Michael Douglas, is solid as the tough choreographer and Terrence Mann is good as his assistant. Aly-

Original Broadway Cast

N.Y. Shakespeare Festival Public Theatre presentation of a musical without intermission (13 numbers), conceived, choreographed and staged by Michael Bennett, with book by James Kirkwood and Nicholas Dante, music by Marvin Hamlisch and lyrics by Edward Kleban. Co-choreographer, Bob Avian; setting, Robin Wagner; costumes, Theoni V. Aldredge; lighting, Tharon Musser, orchestrations; Bill Byers, Hershy Kay, Jonathan Tunick; music coordinator, Robert Tunick; music coordinator, Robert Thomas; musical direction and vocal arrangements, Don Pippin; associate producer, Bernard Gersten. General manager, David Black; production manager, Andrew Mihok; publicity, Merle Debuskey, Bob Ullman; stage managers Jeff Hamlin, Frank Hartenstein; advertising, Blain Thompson Co. (Don Josephson). Opened May 21, '75, at the Public-Newman Theatre; $9 top weeknights; $10 weekend nights.

Cast: Scott Allen, Renee Baughman, Carole Bishop, Pamela Blair, Wayne Cilento, Chuck Cissel, Clive Clerk, Kay Cole, Ronald Dennis, Donna-Drake, Brandt Edwards, Patricia Garland, Carolyn Kirsch, Ron Kuhlman, Nancy Lane, Baayork Lee, Priscilla Lopez, Robert Lupone, Cameron Mason, Donna McKechnie, Don Percassi, Michael Serrecchia, Michel Stuart, Thomas J. Walsh, Sammy Williams, Crissy Wilzuk.
Musical numbers: "I Hope I Get It,"

"I Can Do That," "And...," "At The Ballet," "Sing," "Hello Twelve, Hello Thirteen, Hello Love," "Nothing," "Dance: Ten, Looks, Three," "The Music and the Mirror," "One," "The Tap Combination," "What I Did For Love," "One" (reprise).

son Reed also is sympathetic as Douglas' dancing ex-girlfriend.

Worth special note, too, are Cameron English as the troubled young gay, Vicki Frederick as the older hoofer and Audrey Landers, who romps delightfully through the "T&A" number. Beyond the special mention, each member of the cast is totally pro. —*Har.*

La Hora Texaco
(The Texaco Hour)
(VENEZUELAN-COLOR)

Rio de Janeiro, Nov. 27.

A Latinoamericana de Cine and Studio Heller presentation of a Bohemia Films production. Produced by Pancho Toro. Directed by Eduardo Barberena. Screenplay, Ibsen Martinez; camera (color), Ricardo Younis; art director, Haydee Ascanio; editor José Alcalde; associate producer, Jaime Pinto Cohen. Reviewed at Rio Film Festival (competition) Nov. 25, 1985. Running time: **88 MINS.**

"The Texaco Hour" has a little bit of everything, but little of it makes sense. Montoya, a foreman on one of Texaco's Venezuelan oilfields, is having career troubles, apparently because a man who reads books during his lunch hour really can't be trusted. Guerrillas blow up pipelines, while Montoya's son doesn't quite know what to do with his life and his wife ends up cheating on him.

The screenplay spreads out in many different directions, without establishing or developing either characters or the situations with enough clarity or depth. To this, one must add wooden acting and somewhat unsatisfactory camera work. —*Amig.*

Runaway Train
(COLOR)

Outstanding action picture.

Hollywood, Nov. 6.

A Cannon Releasing release of a Golan-Globus production for Northbrook Films. Produced by Menahem Golan, Yoram Globus. Executive producers, Robert Whitmore, Henry Weinstein, Robert A. Goldston. Directed by Andrei Konchalovsky. Stars Jon Voight, Eric Roberts, Rebecca DeMornay. Screenplay, Djordje Milicevic, Paul Zindel, Edward Bunker, based on a screenplay by Akira Kurosawa; camera (Rank color), Alan Hume; editor, Henry Richardson; music, Trevor Jones; production design, Stephen Marsh; art direction, Joseph T. Garrity; set decoration, Anne Kuljian; costume design, Kathy Dover; sound, Susuma Tokunow; special effects, Keith Richins, Rick Josephson; associate producer, Mati Raz; assistant director, Jack Cummins; second unit director, Max Kleben; second unit camera, Don Burgess; second unit sound, Neal Thomas; casting, Robert MacDonald. Reviewed at the Directors Guild of America Theater, L.A., Nov. 6, 1985. (MPAA Rating: R.) Running time: **111 MINS.**

Manny	Jon Voight
Buck	Eric Roberts
Sara	Rebecca DeMornay
Frank Barstow	Kyle T. Heffner
Ranken	John P. Ryan
Dave Prince	T.K. Carter
Eddie MacDonald	Kenneth McMillan
Ruby	Stacey Pickren
Conlan	Walter Wyatt
Jonah	Edward Bunker
Al Turner	Reid Cruickshanks

"Runaway Train" is a sensational picture. Wrenchingly intense and brutally powerful, Andrei Konchalovsky's second American film rates as the most exciting action epic since "The Road Warrior" and, like that film, is fundamentally serious enough to work strongly on numerous levels. Cannon's distribution arm will be tested to the limit by the challenge of attracting both the college-buff crowd and the mainline audience. Pic unquestionably delivers, but the word must be got out to both groups.

An exercise in relentless, severe tension, tale begins with a half-hour of excruciatingly violent prison drama, then never lets up as it follows two escaped cons as they become inadvertent passengers on some diesel units that run out of control through the Alaskan wilderness after the engineer dies.

The two desperate men who, after an hour's running time, are surprised to find themselves joined by a young lady, are tracked throughout their headlong journey by railroad officials bent on avoiding a crash, and eventually are stalked by the law.

In the meantime, however, Konchalovsky and company paint a startling portrait of the most vehement sort of antisocial behavior, a vivid but shrewdly unemphatic picture of how the dispossessed can take over society's inventions and, at least momentarily, turn them against their creators.

Jon Voight portrays a two-time loser determined never to return to prison after his third breakout, no matter what. After a series of memorably rough and bloody incidents, which may turn off some viewers, Voight and younger con Eric Roberts effect their escape into the frigid wasteland, from which a hitched ride on a train represents the only possible way out.

Complication is piled upon complication as the men first discover that the powerful locomotives have no driver, then go barreling through the countryside, manage to slow it down somewhat and finally, after many punishing attempts, make their way toward the lead engine.

Pic is based upon a screenplay by Akira Kurosawa, and it is taking nothing away from Konchalovsky and his team of writers to assert that the imprint of the renowned Japanese director can be felt throughout. To the contrary, the challenge posed by Kurosawa's artistic and physical demands has forced them to rise to the occasion and dare to be great in ways perhaps new to all of them. This is also, incidentally, the most palpably "cold" picture since Kurosawa's own "Dersu Uzala."

Although the grainy and gray location lensing by Alan Hume is no way pretty, the images are invariably strong, bold and muscular; as linked by Henry Richardson's unforgivingly assaultive editing, they forge a supremely visceral moving picture which never stops surprising the viewer despite the cramped quarters in which most of the yarn is played out.

Working in a style and genre that could not be more different from those of his first film for Cannon, "Maria's Lovers," Konchalovsky has pitched the action boldly at maximum intensity throughout and has managed to sustain it for close to two hours in a tour de force display of virtuoso filmmaking.

Entirely in concert with the director's approach are the feverish performances, especially that of Jon Voight as the total misfit who is able to achieve a certain nobility through his recognition that the animal has won out over the civilized creature in him, and to experience flashes of spirituality when he fails to kill Roberts in the frenzy of an argument.

Watching Voight, one can easily see how brilliant Toshire Mifune might have been in the role had he played it for Kurosawa, but no more brilliant than Voight in fact is. Somewhat deformed (via makeup effects) around the face, the actor goes way out on the edge with his nonstop risk-taking, and it pays off in a characterization that ranks with his other career highlights.

Roberts impressively manages to hold his own under the demanding circumstances, and DeMornay works herself well into the essentially all-male surroundings despite the curveball her entrance represents.

Standout supporting turn comes from John P. Ryan, whose relentlessly tracking prison warden proves a delicious sadistic heavy. Coscenarist and "Straight Time" author Edward Bunker puts in a brief appearance as a longtime prison inmate. Pic ends with the "No Beast So Fierce," quotation from Shakespeare's "Richard III," previously used by Bunker as the title for his novel which was filmed as "Straight Time."

Some stupendous shots, stunts, crashes and effects were captured under what had to be bitterly cold and difficult working conditions. Images of the train literally plowing through the virgin snow remain haunting well after the film is over, and the entire technical crew deserves kudos for the top results here.

Film is dedicated to the memory of Rick Holley, pilot who was killed on a flight during production.

—*Cart.*

Dubbelbeeld
(Double Image)
(DUTCH-DOCU-COLOR-16m)

Amsterdam, Sept. 10.

An Olga Madsen production. Directed and edited by Hans van Dongen. Camera (color, 16m), Marc Felperlaan; sound, Kees Linthorst; music, Dick Maas. Reviewed at Dutch Filmmuseum, Amsterdam, Sept. 9, 1985. Running time: **60 MINS.**

"Double Image" explores the influence, integrity and ingenuity of film editors while also drawing a fascinating picture of a legendary "giant of the cutting room," Helen van Dongen, 76, petite, opinionated and full of spunk.

Amsterdam-born van Dongen edited Joris Ivens' "Zuiderzee" and "Borinage" in 1932-33, before going to Berlin and Paris to learn how to register and edit sound. From there she went to Moscow as a student and lecturer at the film academy. The Rockefeller Foundation called her from Moscow to N.Y. in 1936 to develop a project about film in higher education.

A year later, she edited "Spanish Earth," about the contemporary civil war; in 1938, Ivens' "400 Million" (about China); in 1939, she collaborated with Joseph Losey on an animated pic for the oil industry, "Pete Roleum And His Cousins," and in 1941, Robert Flaherty's "The Land."

Between 1942-45 she directed and edited compilation films about the Allied war effort, including "News Review No. 2," which established her at the top of her profession.

After the war, Helen worked for about 18 months as coproducer and editor on Flaherty's "Louisiana Story." She then produced and directed "Of Human Rights," commissioned by the United Nations.

She was at the height of her career in 1950 when she met historian Kenneth Durand, whom she married a year later. Shortly afterwards she decided to give up film and work with her husband in Vermont. They collaborated for 22 years until his death, after which she continued his work.

Director Hans van Dongen (no relation) expresses here Helen's simple credo: look for the truth; don't manipulate the facts or the public; let the shots tell their own story and, at all times, resist the ever-present temptation to cheat.

This dedication to her trade and

her personality, plus the well-chosen excerpts from her work (particularly "Spanish Earth," "News Review No. 2" and "Louisiana Story") make the docu most attractive for universities, film schools and fests. — *Wall.*

The Peanut Butter Solution
(CANADIAN-COLOR)

Toronto, Nov. 22.

A Cineplex Odeon release of a Les Productions La Fête production. Executive producer, Rock Demers. Produced by Demers, Nicole Robert. Written and directed by Michael Rubbo. Features entire cast. Camera (color), Thomas Vamos; editor, Jean-Guy Montpetit; music, Lewis Furey; sound, Claude Langlois; art director, Vianney Gauthier; production manager, Lyse Lafontaine; costumes, Huguette Gagne; casting, Helene Robitaille. Reviewed at Cineplex Odeon screening room, Toronto, Nov. 22, 1985. Running time: **90 MINS.**
Michael ....Mathew Mackay
Connie ....Siluck Saysanasy
Suzie ....Alison Podbrey
Billy ....Michael Hogan
The Signor ....Michel Maillot
Mary ....Helen Hughes
Tom....................Griffith Brewer

Rock Demers, producer of the highly likable and lyrical "The Dog Who Stopped The War," now launches the second feature of his "Tales For All" package, deliciously titled "The Peanut Butter Solution." Despite a fanciful premise that taps into the spooky fantasies of both kids and adults, pic slows down and lands with a thud as its plot stretches and characters become more obtuse.

An amusing storyline gets things going. Eleven-year-old Michael (Mathew Mackay) has a wild imagination and sense of daring. When his buddy Connie pops in to tell him that an old deserted "haunted" mansion burned down, Michael is compelled to go to the scene and check out if any of the winos who lived there survived.

Michael climbs the rickety planks and peeks in, screaming with fright at what he sees. In fact, he's so petrified his hair literally falls out and he's as bald as Kojak.

Rest of pic deals with Michael's ploys to grow back his hair. Two ghosts of bag people who survived the fire visit him and dictate a concoction of dead flies, kitty litter, and peanut butter to apply to his scalp.

Within a few hours Michael's hair is as long as Rapunzel's and he must suffer the indignations of his school chums' taunts. The plot congeals when Signor (Michel Maillot) kidnaps Michael along with 20 other kids and sets up a magic paintbrush factory in an abandoned part of town, using the boy's tresses as a constant source of supply.

The factory is a Dickensian dream, with kids on an assembly line and hairballs everywhere. Spe-

cial effects are delightful as Signor paints a magic canvas that is so realistic he walks right into it.

This film is docu director Michael Rubbo's first feature, and he gets bogged down in a plodding pace of a story that should be zippy and melodic.

He's served well by Mathew Mackay as a distraught Michael and Alison Podbrey as the bossy, superefficient big sister. Michael Hogan is perhaps a bit too grounded as the artistic father, while Michel Maillot is a fine overblown villain.

There's a real everyday neighborhood feel to the photography, which transmits the core twist of extraordinary things happening to an ordinary boy. The hair special effects are okay, given that this is not an effects pic but a shaggy boy story.

"Peanut Butter" will open wide in Canada in early December with a hefty promo campaign that includes two single records of Québeçois Celine Dion's songs, a novel, and a coloring book. Pic should score big at the b.o. initially on the strength of the producer's previous hit, and will be a lowkey welcome to the Christmas season big-budget fluff. Word of mouth may not be so spirited. — *Devo.*

Spies Like Us
(COLOR)

Strained comedy points to ratings shortcoming.

Hollywood, Nov. 27.

A Warner Bros. release, produced by Brian Grazer and George Folsey Jr. Directed by John Landis. Features entire cast. Executive producer, Bernie Brillstein. Screenplay, Dan Aykroyd, Lowell Ganz, Babaloo Mandel; camera (Technicolor), Robert Paynter; editor, Malcolm Campbell; sound, Ivan Sharrock; production design, Peter Murton; assistant director, Dusty Symonds; costumes, Deborah Nadoolman; associate producers, Sam Williams, Leslie Belzberg; music, Elmer Bernstein; casting, Debbie McWilliams, Marion Dougherty. Reviewed at The Burbank Studios, Nov. 26, 1985. (MPAA Rating: PG.) Running time: **109 MINS.**
Emmett Fitz-Hume ....Chevy Chase
Austin Millbarge...........Dan Aykroyd
Gen. Sline ....Steve Forrest
Karen ....Donna Dixon
Ruby ....Bruce Davison
Keyes ....William Prince
Col. Rhumbus ....Bernie Casey
Gen. Miegs................Tom Hatten

Teamed together for the first time in "Spies Like Us," Chevy Chase and Dan Aykroyd will need a sub-teen audience for their juvenile humor. But theaterowners better watch out for parents thinking the PG pic is innocent holiday fare; they may be a bit upset.

Getting on the soapbox again, it's now obvious the Ratings Administration is as addled as ever, even with the PG-13 as an additional choice. It's absolutely absurd that

squeaky-clean "Santa Claus," whose PG defies rational analysis, will be out in the same marketplace with "Spies" and its bathroom jokes, flatulence and four-letter references to anatomical parts. Pity the family that opts for the latter if it can't get into the former.

Pity them doubly if they expect to find "Spies" very amusing. Though Chase and Aykroyd provide moments, the overall script thinly takes on eccentric espionage and nuclear madness, with nothing new to add.

Chase and Aykroyd are a couple of bumbling bureaucrats with aspirations for spy work, but no talent for the job. They unknowingly are chosen for a mission, however, because they will make expendable decoys for a real spy team headed by pretty Donna Dixon.

What's up is really never very clear, which wouldn't matter if the picture were funny. When it's not, it would help to care what's going on just to make the time pass faster.

Much of the time, Aykroyd is fooling with gadgets, Chase is fooling with Dixon and director John Landis is fooling with half-baked comedy ideas, trying to get something going before the American and Soviet plotters blow up the world.

Out of sheer willpower, "Spies" starts to gather steam toward the end, but by then it's too late. But Dixon really is pretty. —*Har.*

Johannes' Hemmelighed
(John's Secret)
(DANISH-COLOR)

Copenhagen, Nov. 14.

A Nordisk Film release of Nordisk Film production with the Danish Film Institute (Ida Zeruneith). Original story, screenplay and directed by Ake Sandgren. Camera (Eastmancolor), Dan Lausten; editor, Leif Axel Kjeldsen; music, Anders Koppel, Tiakovsky; production design, special effects, Henning Bahs; costumes, Annelise Hauberg, production management, Sanne Gläsel, Lene Nielsen. Reviewed at the Palads, Copenhagen, Nov. 14, 1985. Running time: **60 MINS.**
Johannes ....Jacob Katz
Dream Jesus .....Ina-Miriam Rosenbaum
Johannes' mother ....Kirsten Olesen
His father ....Claus Strandberg
Grandfather ....Poul Thomsen
Mrs. Jensen ....Bodil Lindorff
Little girl ....Liv Lövetand Hansen
Girl's mother ....Karen-Lise Mynster
Her father ....Nis Bank-Mikkelsen
Also with: Ole Möllegard, Sammy B. Samuelsen, Johannes Rebel.

In Swede Ake Sandberg's Danish feature film bow, five-year-old John is a child whose parents are divorced and he misses his father, a nice enough man but kept from seeing his son by his ex (played by perenially weepy-eyed Kirsten Olesen).

When the child wakes up from a dream to find family and friends re-

united, he has been given a guided tour by Jesus himself through at least the outlying districts of the powers of good and evil. He has found out that there is no absolute good nor any absolute evil and that ambiguity lies at the root of most men's actions and decisions.

The Dream Jesus has taken on the shape and costume of a latter-day street urchin of obvious Middle East origin. She — because — a she it turns out to be — also carries an apparently empty rucksack and has chosen to make her entries and exits via toilet bowls, a bit of whimsy that otherwise contains no symbolism.

It is highly doubtful that moppets will be anything but confused by film's spouting of shallow wisdoms, but they will like, and identify with, John as he is played with wide-eyed candor by Jacob Katz. —*Kell.*

The Trip To Bountiful
(COLOR)

Oscar-caliber Geraldine Page performance in dramatic winner.

An Island Pictures release of a FilmDallas and Bountiful Film Partners Prod. Produced by Sterling VanWagenen and Horton Foote. Executive producers, Sam Grogg, George Yaneff. Directed by Peter Masterson. Stars Geraldine Page. Screenplay, Foote, from his play; camera (color), Fred Murphy; editor, Jay Freund; music, J.A.C. Redford; production design, Neil Spisak; art direction, Philip Lamb; set decorator, Derek R. Hill; costume design, Gary Jones; sound, John Pritchett; makeup, Jimi White; line producer, Dennis Bishop; assistant director, Stephen McEveety; casting, Ed Johnston. Reviewed at the Broadway Screening Room, N.Y., Nov. 19, 1985. (No MPAA Rating.) Running time: **106 MINS.**
Mrs. Watts ....Geraldine Page
Ludie ....John Heard
Jessie Mae..................Carlin Glynn
Sheriff ....Richard Bradford
Thelma ....Rebecca DeMornay

"The Trip To Bountiful" is a superbly crafted drama featuring the performance of a lifetime by Geraldine Page in the leading role of Mrs. Watts, a woman whose determination to escape the confines of life in a small Houston apartment with her selfless son Ludie (John Heard) and his domineering wife Jessie Mae (Glynn) leads her on a moving and memorable journey across the Gulf Coast to return to Bountiful, the town where she was born and raised. Adapted by Horton Foote from his 1953 teleplay that enjoyed

Original Play

A Theatre Guild & Fred Coe production of drama in three acts, by Horton Foote. Stars Lillian Gish; features Jo Van Fleet, Gene Lyons, Eva Marie Saint. Staged by Vincent J. Donehue; settings, Otis Riggs; costumes, Rose Bogdanoff; lighting, Peggy Clark. At Henry Miller's, N.Y., Nov. 3, '53; $4.80 top ($6 opening).
Mrs. Carrie Watts ....Lillian Gish
Ludie Watts ....Gene Lyons

Jessie Mae Watts	Jo Van Fleet
Thelma	Eva Marie Saint
Houston Ticket Man	Will Hare
Traveler	Salem Ludwig
2d Ticket Man	David Clive
Harrison Ticket Man	Frederic Downs
Sheriff	Frank Overton
Travelers	Patricia MacDonald, Neil Laurence, Helen Cordes

theatrical success on Broadway, the 1947-set film recalls the days of scripts with real plots and dialog and should be a strong attraction to holiday filmgoers dazed by a blizzard of teen-themed releases.

Life for Mrs. Watts with Ludie and Jessie Mae is a claustrophobic and harsh existence of forced politeness, petty battles and demanded apologies. Heard is excellent as the downtrodden Ludie burdened with keeping the peace while contending with money problems and self doubts. Glynn likewise puts in a strong performance, giving a human edge and depth to what could have been an otherwise nagging wife stereotype.

Mrs. Watts stashes away a pension check, waits for Ludie to go to work and Jessie Mae to the hairdresser, and embarks on her odyssey. She befriends Thelma (Rebecca DeMornay) while waiting for the bus. DeMornay is delightful in an ensuing scene when Mrs. Watts hides from the searching Ludie and Jessie Mae, leaving her new friend in the quandry of turning Mrs. Watts in or letting her continue her quest.

Mrs. Watts and Thelma, traveling to her in-laws while her husband's away in the army, share the long bus ride. Page's work is excellent throughout, but no more so than here as she half laughs and half cries remembering the harsh paradoxes of her life.

Brief scenes at a rural gas station at night and other moments in her trip are as breathtaking as Hopper still-lifes and a testament to the understated direction of Peter Masterson, making a strong feature film debut.

Seemingly defeated when confronted by a small-town sheriff (admirably limned by Richard Bradford) instructed to hold the woman until Ludie and Jessie Mae can pick her up, Mrs. Watts' passionate despair wins him over and he opts to drive her the last 12 miles to the now abandoned town of Bountiful.

A rewarding climax is the result of Mrs. Watts' journey as Ludie and Jessie Mae catch up to her on the porch of her delapidated, overgrown home.

Tech credits are firstrate, especially Murphy's photography, Spisak's production design and costumes by Gary Jones. —Roy.

Il Pentito
(The Repenter)
(ITALIAN-COLOR)

Rome, Nov. 23.

A Columbia release (Italy), produced by Mario and Vittorio Cecchi Gori for C.G. Silver Films. Directed by Pasquale Squitieri. Stars Franco Nero and Tony Musante. Screenplay, Orazio Barrese, Lino Jannuzzi, Squitieri; camera (color), Silvano Ippoliti; editor, Mauro Bonanni; art director, Umberto Turco; music, Ennio Morricone. Reviewed at Supercinema, Rome, Nov. 22, 1985. Running time: **93 MINS.**

Judge Falco	Franco Nero
Vanni Ragusa	Tony Musante
Spinola	Max von Sydow
Corleone gangster	Erik Estrada
Lidia	Rita Rusic

Pasquale Squitieri tackles the Sicilian Mafia in "The Repenter," a fairly routine policier with a dash of "The Godfather" thrown in. Virtually everything that happens in the film has a real-life reference, which makes it more interesting for Italo auds who can plug in the headlines. Undoubtedly there are a lot of explosive issues in this compendium of killers, gang wars and creaky judiciary cases, but pic stays in the safer waters of the conventional actioner. Genre fans won't be disappointed.

Investigating magistrate Falco (Franco Nero) is sent to Palermo on the hot Mob beat. As might be imagined, he is under tremendous pressure — keenly visualized — living in a kind of super-security cell to conduct the investigaton. A bloody gang war is in progress, with all the honorable old Dons and their venerable families getting mowed down by the young hot-bloods, led by Erik Estrada. So much for the good old days.

Meanwhile, in New York, a banker named Spinola (Max von Sydow) is in trouble at the Hotel Pierre. The feds are onto him over a bank crack and won't let him out of the States, so he engineers a fake kidnaping to get to Sicily and have it out with his financiers, the Dons. His righthand man, Vanni Ragusa (Tony Musante), is tied to the old families, and when they begin to be eliminated he agrees to testify as a star witness for Judge Falco.

Pic makes the point that his testimony, while valuable, also is biased and aimed at his own ends — revenge — and that the real baddies (Estrada, et al.) always get away in the end, and that honest judges are risking their necks without support from the government. Nero and Musante throw themselves into their parts with a passion, but dialog remains flat and wooden.

Pic works best as a shoot-em-up actioner, with lots of blood spattered on carpets, snappy cutting, and clearcut roles for the good guys in police uniforms and judges' mantles (one exception), and bad guys with machineguns and sluttish blonds on their arms. Technically pic can boast a pro look and a soundtrack by Ennio Morricone. —Yung.

A Zed And Two Noughts
(BRITISH-DUTCH-COLOR)

London, Nov. 30.

An Artificial Eye production in association with the British Film Institute and Channel Four (U.K.), and Allarts Enterprises and VPRO (Netherlands). Produced by Kees Kasander and Peter Sainsbury. Written and directed by Peter Greenaway. Features entire cast. Camera (color), Sacha Vierny; editor, John Wilson; music, Michael Nyman; production design, Ben van Os; sound, Garth Marshall; costumes, Patricia Lim. Reviewed at the London Film Festival, Nov. 30, 1985. Running time: **115 MINS.**

Alba Bewick	Andrea Ferreol
Oswald Deuce	Brian Deacon
Oliver Deuce	Eric Deacon
Venus de Milo	Frances Barber
Van Hoyten	Joss Ackland
Van Meeregen	Gerard Thoolen
Caterina Bolnes	Guusje van Tilborgh

Despite its visual pyrotechnics and an impressively woven texture of intellectual allusions, Peter Greenaway's second full-length feature fails to go beyond its predecessor, "The Draughtsman's Contract," in engaging the audience's sympathies. While it will no doubt have pull on the arthouse circuit, both in Europe and in the U.S., it's unlikely to speak to a larger public.

In the end, it remains the work of a highly talented British eccentric who hasn't yet managed to thresh out his private fantasies and obscurantist intellectual preoccupations to connect with major concerns or touch the emotions. "A Zed And Two Noughts" invites praise for its stylishness, but its own lack of feeling ultimately leaves one cold.

This said, it has to be admitted that the film moves on ground which few have dared — or even thought of — traveling. The action centers on a zoo (its letters making up the zed and two noughts of the title). In this lurid arena there are no balloon-holding kids feeding peanuts to the elephants; Greenaway, rather, is intent on upturning the seamier, humiliating side of animal existence in captivity (including that of homo sapiens).

He approaches this material neither rationally nor self-righteously, but elliptically and obliquely, with farcical fictions, sophisticated references to Vermeer's paintings, witty musical citations, mythological motifs, snippets of wildlife, timelapse photography of decaying animals, full-frontal male nudity, doppelgangers, mirror-images, three-legged apes, verbal puzzles and visual puns.

Beyond the unusual setting and provocative approach, the film takes up (again obliquely and not always successfully) large themes like death, decay and man's relationship to other animal species. It even deigns to develop a storyline of sorts, though any reconstruction of the events of the plot would give a misleading impression of causality and plausibility.

Suffice to say the film opens with a witty, preposterous coup de théâtre and closes with a whimsically horrific sequence. Both are beautiful to look at, suggestive in their implications, and the best effects of the film. In the opening, a pregnant swan crashes into the windshield of a car, killing two women and maiming a third. In the finale, twin brothers, animal behaviorists of a kind, manage to satisfy their obsession with physical decay by filming their own demise and decomposition. Their efforts are undermined ironically by the snails which jam the workings of the camera.

In between, the plot works to bring the Junoesque, though legless, accident victim (Andrea Ferreol) into fruitful relationship with the two scientist-zookeeper brothers, whose wives, it turns out, died in the crash with the swan. It succeeds when Ferreol copulates with each of them and gives birth to twins. A secondary strand involves the brothers in increasingly bold acts of liberating the caged animals — at first butterflies, eventually a rhino — and in procuring carcasses for their scientific experiments. Jocular comic relief is provided by the zoo prostitute Venus de Milo, who sells her favors in return for getting her obscene animal stories published — and who just may be getting it on with a zebra.

Meanwhile, lots of pseudo-philosophical conundrums are tossed at the audience like peanuts to hungry caged animals: Is a zebra a white horse with black stripes or a black one with white? etc. Needless to say, the resulting stilted dialog does not make the acting much of a treat.

Although the initial effect of the film is tonic (photography, sets and music are superb), all but diehard enthusiasts will eventually find it either too obscure, too inane or just plain tedious. —Guid.

Doin' Time
(COLOR)

Lame prison comedy.

Sydney, Nov. 28.

A Ladd/Warner Bros. release of a Filmcorp production. Produced by Bruce Mallen, George Mendeluk. Executive producers, Ken Sheppard, Carol Mallen. Directed by Mendeluk. Stars Jeff Altman, Dey Young. Screenplay, Franelle Silver, Ron Zwang, Dee Caruso; camera (DeLuxe color), Ronald V. Garcia; music, Charles Fox; production design, Jack McAdam; editor, Stanford J. Allen; production manager, Michael Bennett; 1st assistant director, David M. Robertson. Reviewed at Village Cinema City, Sydney, Nov. 27, 1985. Running time: **77 MINS.**

Duke Jarrett	Jeff Altman
Vicki Norris	Dey Young
Mongo Mitchell	Richard Mulligan
Big Mac	John Vernon
Nancy C. Catlett	Colleen Camp
Linda Libel	Melanie Chartoff
Prescott	Graham Jarvis
Fallis	Pat McCormick
Wetback	Eddie Velez
Shaker	Jimmie Walker
The Bride	Judy Landers
Animal	Nicholas Worth
Bruno	Mike Mazurki
Himself	Muhammad Ali

According to the credits, it took five people, including director George Mendeluk, to concoct the inane story for this feeble comedy. They came up with something Abbott & Costello would have discarded as hopeless 40 years ago, for this dismal attempt to do for prisoners what "Police Academy" did for the police force has few laughs and little entertainment value. Ladd Co./WB pickup, which opened in Australia in October but has yet to open Stateside, will open and close fast and for the undiscriminating.

Hero Jeff Altman is imprisoned on the most specious grounds (a traveling salesman, he is seduced by the wife of a government official). In the John Dillinger Memorial Penitentiary he finds chaos reigning under the lax control of Gov. Pat McCormick, until the latter is replaced by disciplinarian Richard Mulligan. Mulligan, never the subtlest of actors, mugs his way shamelessly through the pic in a vain search for laughs.

Jokes, such as they are, are sexist, vulgar and derivative, even to the "Mash"-style p.a. announcements frequently heard above the din. John Vernon appears as a senior convict, Colleen Camp is the governor's eager secretary, Melanie Chartoff a crusading tv newshen called Linda Libel, and Dey Young is Altman's love interest.

Mendeluk and his team lurch from one misfired gag to the next with little sense of structure or pacing. Climax is a boxing bout in which Muhammad Ali makes the briefest of guest appearances. Pic is technically sloppy, too, with shadows of mike booms clearly evident in more than one shot. Abnormally brief running time for a feature film these days suggests possibly even less funny material than that included here may have been junked. —*Strat.*

Static
(COLOR)

Witty spoof of American culture.

Chicago, Nov. 19.

A Necessity Film production and release. Produced by Amy Ness. Directed by Mark Romanek. Stars Keith Gordon, Amanda Plummer. Screenplay, Romanek, Gordon; camera (color), Jeff Jur; sets, Cynthia Sowder; editor, Emily Paine; music, pop tunes; casting, Judy Courtney. Reviewed at Chicago Film Fest, Nov. 18, 1985. (No MPAA Rating.) Running time: **93 MINS.**

With: Keith Gordon (Ernie), Amanda Plummer (Julie), Bob Gunton (Frank), Barton Heyman (Sheriff William Orling), Lily Knight (Patty), Jane Hoffman (Emitly), Reathel Bean (Fred Savins), Kitty Mei Mei Chen (Li).

One of the pleasant surprises of the Chicago fest, Mark Romanek's "Static" also scores as one of the best indie productions of the season. This is a witty, tongue-in-cheek spoof of American culture, each of the key individuals drawn from typical clichéd situations.

Ernie (Keith Gordon) hasn't quite been the same since the loss of his parents in an automobile accident some years ago. The insurance allows him to live a quiet, unobtrusive life in the Prairie Guest House in northern Arizona, where in a back room he's been working on the construction of a tv-set that can tune in on heaven. This will enable people "to be happy, and not sad" if and when he ever completes the invention. He does — just in time for Christmas.

Ernie's friends are an oddball preacher into Green Beret militarism on the side, a lunch-counter waitress with a crush on him, and a childhood sweetheart who recently dropped out of a tour with a pop band. As Christmas approaches, Ernie has been fired from his job in a religious artifacts factory for pocketing defective crucifixes on the assembly line. He has a collection of these on his wall in the motel, where they form a kind of private gallery.

Ernie hopes to be able to market his invention, and the townspeople take sides betting on his fortune. The moment of truth takes place Christmas Eve; the unveiling of the tv set before friends and the local attorney. It's here they discover our young Edison is convinced he can tune into a live broadcast from heaven. All anybody sees is static — save for Ernie, of course, who's still waiting for a glimpse of his parents (they're still a no-show on the screen).

Switch to Christmas Day on a bus to Albuquerque, loaded with senior citizens of the Fleetwood Township Charity Council on an outing. Ernie plans to hijack the bus in order to get media coverage on his new invention. The senior citizens, of course, are thrilled by the idea of the kidnaping, so they go all out to help Ernie by convincing the local sheriff they just may be in danger of their lives after all. Pic's surprise ending is its weakest element.

Romanek is a promising talent with a finesse for visual flair and low-key acting. "Static," with proper handling, could score on the arthouse circuit, as well as at fests abroad. —*Holl.*

Rebel
(AUSTRALIAN-COLOR)

Sydney, Oct. 21.

A Phillip Emanuel-Village Roadshow Corp. production. Executive producers, Robyn Campbell-Jones, Bonnie Harris. Produced by Phillip Emanuel. Directed by Michael Jenkins. Stars Matt Dillon, Debbie Byrne, Bryan Brown. Screenplay, Jenkins, Bob Herbert, adapted from Herbert's play, "No Names ... No Packdrill;" camera (Panavision, Eastmancolor), Peter James; editor, Michael Honey; production design, Brian Thomson; costumes, Roger Kirk; music, Chris Neal; musical director, Ray Cook; original songs, Peter Best; choreography, Ross Coleman; sound, Mark Lewis; 1st assistant director, David Evans; production manager, Susan Wild. Reviewed at Village Cinema City, Sydney, Oct. 14, 1985. Running time: **91 MINS.**

Rebel	Matt Dillon
Kathy McLeod	Debbie Byrne
Tiger Kelly	Bryan Brown
Browning	Bill Hunter
Bubbles	Ray Barrett
Joycie	Julie Nihill
Bernie	John O'May
Hazel	Kim Deacon
Barbara	Sheree da Costa
Mrs. Palmer	Isabelle Anderson
Mary	Joy Smithers
Lambert	Chris Hession
Madam	Annie Semler
Ringman	Ray Marshall
Bea Miles	Beth Child

Also with: Cassandra Delaney, Antoinette Byron, Nicky Crayson, Nikki Coghill, Sally Phillips, Betti Summerson, Lissa Ross (All Girl Band).

Brash, noisy and defiantly anachronistic, "Rebel" is a basically unappealing tale of the love affair between a U.S. marine sergeant (Matt Dillon) who is on the run in wartime Sydney having deserted his outfit, and a lonesome nightclub singer (Debbie Byrne) whose hubby is away fighting. Compared with these two, the lovers in "Swing Shift" were models of good behavior.

Pic is crammed with songs, some of them excellent, to an extent that it sometimes seems as though the plot, such as it is, is only an excuse on which to hang the musical numbers. Yet the project started life as a stage play ("No Names ... No Packdrill," starring Mel Gibson as the Yank and Noni Hazlehurst as the girl) sans musical numbers. Film version originally was to star Olivia Newton-John, but when she dropped out Debbie Byrne stepped in to play Kathy, her first film role. Byrne, who currently is a hit in the Australian production of "Cats," is great in a rather unlikable role, and whatever business "Rebel" does Down Under will be largely thanks to her. Her final song, "Heroes," is especially effective and ends the film on a high note. She also acquits herself well as an actress, and is rather moving in a scene where she learns that her husband has been killed in action.

Matt Dillon, as the Yank on the run, gives an irritatingly mannered performance and elicits little sympathy not only because he's a deserter, but also because of the single-minded way he pursues a vulnerable woman he knows is married to a soldier fighting for his country.

As a local con-man, Bryan Brown brings much-needed humor to the proceedings. Bill Hunter is solid as a sympathetic cop, but Ray Barrett, as the nightclub emcee, has almost nothing to do, his role having been largely excised from the picture (the release version of "Rebel" is 15 minutes shorter than the version shown to judges at the Australian Film Awards earlier this year). As members of the all-girl band and back-up singers, Kim Deacon, Julie Nihill and Joy Smithers stand out.

"Rebel" definitely is not a film for audiences with lingering nostalgia about the early '40s. Byrne and her friends are no Andrews Sisters, and all the songs are defiantly of the '80s. This is a film aimed at young audiences, who may or may not respond.

Director Michael Jenkins, who scripted Carl Schultz' successful "Careful He Might Hear You" two years ago, goes along with the garish visual style of the film, and handles the dramatic scenes in a busy, cluttered style. As a director, he gives the film some energy, but little genuine feeling.

Local business will very much depend on some of the songs getting into the charts, but interest in Debbie Byrne should get things off to a good start.

However, sustained business over the Christmas period, with stiff competition, looks doubtful. Despite presence of Matt Dillon, offshore business doesn't look promising. —*Strat.*

Stitches
(COLOR)

Outdated sex comedy.

Hollywood, Nov. 29.

An Intl. Film Marketing release of a Marcucci/Kerr production. Produced by William B. Kerr, Robert P. Marcucci. Directed by Alan Smithee. Screenplay, Michel Choquette, Michael Paseornek; camera (Deluxe color), Hector R. Figueroa; editor, John Duffy; music, Bob Floke; art direction, Diane Campbell; costume design, Richard E. La Motte; sound, Ed Somers; assistant director, Ron L. Wright; second unit camera, Daryn Okada. Reviewed at the Paramount Theater, L.A., Nov. 27, 1985. (MPAA Rating: R.) Running time: **89 MINS.**

Bobby Stevens	Parker Stevenson
Ralph Rizzo	Geoffrey Lewis
Sam Boon Tong	Brian Tochi
Nancy McNaughton	Robin Dearden
Al Rosenberg	Bob Dubac
'Barfer' Bogan	Tommy Koenig

Sheldon Mendlebaum . . . . .Sydney Lassick
Dean Bradley . . . . .Eddie Albert
Howard Pierce . . . . .Ken Stovitz
Dr. Sidney Berman . . . . .Russ Marin
Osgood Hamilton Sr. . . . . . .Ed McNamara
Bambi Bilenka . . . . .Rebecca Perle

"Stitches" will have people on the floor and rolling in the aisles — backwards, out the doors and into the streets. This imbecilic comedy about med school was made more than two years ago, and the wait was in no way worth it. The whole class flunked on this one.

One of the many inane gross-out comedies so bad as to make "Porky's" look like a masterpiece, "Stitches" features such bursts of inspiration as having the three lead wiseacres posing as corpses in order to scare members of an autopsy class; instructing all the girls to undrape and give each other examinations while the guys watch from behind a one-way mirror; disrupting a reception at the dean's house with punk rock music, and having the nice femme lead catch her boyfriend playing doctor with a naked busty blond.

Socalled protagonists are all smarmy and obnoxious, and members of the establishment are invariably uptight and flustered. Pic's racial and sexual stereotypes date back at least 20 years.

Only intriguing aspect of the film is the directorial credit to "Alan Smithee." The differently spelled "Allen Smithee" is Hollywood's most famous nonexistent producer-director of the past 15 years. Rod Holcomb was listed as director during production, but, for whatever reason, the fictitious name was applied to the credits. Maybe even Allen Smithee didn't want his name on this one. — *Cart.*

Is That It?
(BRITISH-COLOR-DOCU-16m)

London, Nov. 30.
A Four Corner production for Channel Four, London. An Experimental Film Workshop picture written and directed by Wilf Thust. Camera (color), Patrick Duval; editor Anthea Kennedy; music, Schaun Tozer. Reviewed at London Film Festival, Nov. 29, 1985. Running time: **83 MINS.**

Wilf Thust's "Is That It?" represents a long period of involvement with young people on creative experimental film projects. The teenagers in the Four Corners Film Workshop have the benefit of professionals trained at the London Film School, particularly helmer Wilf Thust (co-founder of the workshop). Channel Four stepped in to spotlight the improvised projects made in a working-class district on London's East Side, and the NFT2 venue was filled the day of showing with a young crowd to present their wares and discuss what the ex-

perience meant to them.

The filmmakers are around 15 years old. They are straightforward in conducting interviews with each other and "staging" scenes on the steps on a subway station (Bethnal Green in the program booklet). The film is a compilation of three years of activity at Four Corners. To Thust's credit he doesn't pull punches when the young people decide to put directly on film their deepest frustrations and blighted hopes.

Pic suffers from one blatant technical flaw: printed-word poster bridges that could have been rendered on the narrative soundtrack.
— *Holl.*

Out Of Africa
(COLOR)

Intriguing period romance, engagingly acted by Redford and Streep but the pace is at times languid. Broad appeal iffy.

Hollywood, Dec. 7.
A Universal Pictures release. Produced and directed by Sydney Pollack. Stars Meryl Streep, Robert Redford. Executive producer, Kim Jorgensen. Screenplay, Kurt Luedtke, based on writings by Isak Dinesen, Judith Thurman and Errol Trzebinski; camera (Rank color), David Watkin; editors, Fredric Steinkamp, William Steinkamp, Pembroke Herring, Sheldon Kahn; sound, Peter Handford; coproducer, Terence Clegg; production design, Stephen Grimes; costumes, Milena Canonero; assistant director, David Tomblin; associate producers, Judith Thurman, Anna Cataldi; music, John Barry; casting, Mary Selway. Reviewed at Universal Studios, L.A., Dec. 6, 1985. (MPAA Rating: PG.) Running time: **150 MINS.**
Karen . . . . .Meryl Streep
Denys . . . . .Robert Redford
Bror . . . . .Klaus Maria Brandauer
Berkeley . . . . .Michael Kitchen
Farah . . . . .Malick Bowens
Kamante . . . . .Joseph Thiaka
Kinanjui . . . . .Stephen Kinyanjui
Delamere . . . . .Michael Gough
Felicity . . . . .Suzanna Hamilton
Lady Belfield . . . . .Rachel Kempson
Lord Belfield . . . . .Graham Crowden

At two-and-a-half hours, "Out Of Africa" certainly makes a leisurely start into its story. Just short of boredom, however, the picture picks up pace and becomes a sensitive, enveloping romantic tragedy. Nonetheless it's a long way to go for a downbeat ending, which may hurt broad appeal.

Getting top billing over Robert Redford, Meryl Streep surely earns it with another engaging performance. Still, the film rarely really comes to life except when Redford is around, which unfortunately is not often in the first hour.

Ably produced and directed by Sydney Pollack, "Africa" is the story of Isak Dinesen, who wrote of her experiences in Kenya. Though Dinesen (real name: Karen Blixen) remembered it lovingly, hers was not a happy experience.

She arrives in 1914 for a marriage of convenience with Baron Bror Blixen (well played by Klaus Maria Brandauer) who offers his title and friendship in exchange for her money. But he doesn't provide love, fidelity or even much company, leaving her alone with the natives for the gritty work of getting a coffee plantation going.

Often, her only amusements are the occasional visits of white hunters Redford and Michael Kitchen (also good), attracted by her strong will and love of the land. With one landscape after another, Pollack and lenser David Watkin prove repeatedly why she should love the land so, but at almost travelog drag.

The mannered speech and customs of the times do not hurry matters along, either.

Eventually, Streep and Brandauer split, leaving an opening for Redford to move in. True love follows, but not happiness because he's too independent to be tied down by a marriage certificate. And the coffee plantation isn't perking along too well, either.

Within the doomed dimensions, however, it's a wonderful romance, probably Redford's best since "The Way We Were." He plays his initially casual counterpoint to her seriousness perfectly, followed by his gradual coming to grips with the concessions that will be needed to keep her.

Maybe the problem of the pacing is simply the nature of the beast these days with expensive period pieces. Once the difficult details are all in place, it may be too much to expect a director to resist milking every scene for more than it's worth. And that's probably equally true for every strong scene with a solid cast. But too long remains too long.—*Har.*

The Jewel Of The Nile
(COLOR)

Thin script but solid action and appealing thesping in "Stone" sequel.

Hollywood, Dec. 7.
A 20th Century Fox release. Produced by Michael Douglas. Directed by Lewis Teague. Stars Michael Douglas, Kathleen Turner. Screenplay, Mark Rosenthal, Lawrence Konner; camera (Technicolor), Jan DeBont; editor, Michael Ellis, Beter Boita; music, Jack Nitzsche; sound, Sandy MacRae; production design, Richard Dawking, Gerry Knight; assistant director, Kuki Lopez; coproducers, Joel Douglas, Jack Brodsky; costumes, Emma Porteous; art direction, Leslie Tomkins, Damien Lanfranchi; casting, Rose Tobias-Shaw, Caroline Mazauric. Reviewed at the Egyptian Theater, L.A., Dec. 6, 1985. (MPAA Rating: PG.) Running time: **104 MINS.**

Jack . . . . .Michael Douglas
Joan . . . . .Kathleen Turner
Ralph . . . . .Danny DeVito
Omar . . . . .Spiros Focas
Holy Man . . . . .Avner Eisenberg
Tarak . . . . .Paul David Magid
Barak . . . . .Howard Jay Patterson
Karak . . . . .Randall Edwin Nelson
Arak . . . . .Samuel Ross Williams
Sarak . . . . .Timothy Daniel Furst
Rachid . . . . .Hamid Fillali
Gloria . . . . .Holland Taylor

As a sequel to "Romancing The Stone,'" the script of "The Jewel Of The Nile" is missing the deft touch of the late Diane Thomas but Lewis Teague's direction matches the energy of the original and the only boxoffice question is whether the film comes late in the cycle for Saturday matinee revivals.

Though action fans will have

plenty to keep them interested, others may grow restless, depending on how many of these pics they've seen by now. With their characters already firmly established, Michael Douglas and Kathleen Turner again play off each other very well, but the story is much thinner.

The main problem is the dialog, which retains some of the old spirit with lines like "Jack's favorite author is the guy who wrote 'pull tab to open,' " but too often relies on the trite ("When we get out of this alive, I'm going to kill you").

Even some of the stunts are old, though presumably may seem fresh to the younger end of the audience. But with a train heading for a tunnel, it does launder some of the fun to know what's sure to happen next.

Story picks up six months after "Stone's" happy ending and Douglas and Turner have begun to get on each other's nerves after being confined to his boat most of the time. She accepts an invitation from a sinister potentate (Spiros Focas) to accompany him and write a story about his pending ascendency as desert ruler.

Left behind, Douglas runs into the excitable Danny DeVito and they become unwilling allies, again in pursuit of a jewel. Naturally, their quest will take them into Focas' kingdom, where Turner has already run into trouble.

There's a twist in the identity of the jewel, but it's given away early and turns out to be an unsatisfactory substitute, though Avner Eisenberg has what fun he can with it. As usual, all of this takes place amidst mass destruction, endless gunfire and a fiery finish.

Film is dedicated to Diane Thomas, who died earlier this year in a car accident, and to Richard Dawking, Bryan Coates and Richard Kotch, who perished in a plane crash while scouting locations.
—*Har.*

Time After Time
(BRITISH-COLOR-16m)

London, Nov. 29.

A BBC-TV production in association with the Arts & Entertainment Network and the Australian Broadcasting Corp. Produced by Terry Coles. Directed by Bill Hays. Features entire cast. Screenplay, Andrew Davies, from the novel by Molly Keane; camera (color), John McGlashan; editor, Dave King; music, Jim Parker; production design, Don Taylor; costumes, Michael Burdle; sound, Dick Boulter, Geoff Cutting, Antonia Sherman. Reviewed at the London Film Festival, Nov. 26, 1985. Running time: **103 MINS.**

Jasper Swift . . . . John Gielgud
Leda Klein . . . . Googie Withers
April Grange-Gorman . . . . . . Helen Cherry
May Swift . . . . Ursula Howells
June Swift . . . . Brenda Bruce
Christy Lucy . . . . Mark Lambert
Brigadier Croshawe . . . . . . Trevor Howard
Ulick Uniake . . . . Freddie Jones

Lady Alys Crowshawe . . . . . . Mavis Walker

This adaptation of Molly Keane's book features three sisters and a brother trapped in lives of mutual scorn and resentment within their rotting Irish mansion. It's a wordy effort occasionally leavened by some witty performances and evocative flashbacks.

The bickering brood is comprised of a body-conscious but deaf widow, an embittered spinster with a taste for flower arranging and shoplifting and a jovial rustic. The John Gielgud character not only does the cooking and gardening but tries vainly to restrain the sniping.

Script's flashbacks unravel the traumatic history of this group. The main revelation concerns a German cousin called Leda who was expelled from the family nest because of her sexual allure.

Leda, a Jewess whom everyone thought had perished in World War II, materializes and sets about uncovering family secrets. Plan is to further disrupt the family in revenge for her expulsion. It later emerges she had spent the war in Paris where she survived only by collaborating with the Nazi occupiers.

The film ends in sweetness and light for all but Leda. Her visit, it seems, has washed away the family pain, freeing its members to plan for a happier future.

Director Bill Hays doesn't attempt to bring out the symbolic aspects of the original story and films the piece in an unimaginative style. Technical credits are nothing to write home about. —*Japa.*

Sotto Il Vestito Niente
(Nothing Underneath)
(ITALIAN-COLOR)

Rome, Dec. 3.

A Titanus release, produced by Achille Manzotti for FASO Film. Directed by Carlo Vanzina. Screenplay, Carlo Vanzina, Enrico Vanzina, Franco Ferrini based on a novel by Marco Parma; camera (color), Beppe Macari; editor, Raimondo Crociani; music, Pino Donaggio. Reviewed at Ariston 2 Cinema, Rome, Nov. 29, 1985. Running time: 97 MINS.

Bob . . . . Tom Schanley
Barbara . . . . Renée Simonsen
Inspector . . . . Donald Pleasence
Also with: Nicola Perring, Maria McDonald, Catherine Noyes, Paolo Tomei, Cyrus Elias.

"Nothing Underneath" is a flyweight Italo thriller about high-fashion models, with precious few chills, surprises or suspense. Its youthful helmer, Carlo Vanzina, is best known for (and much better at) teen comedies. Of interest is a production footnote: producer Achille Manzotti originally had planned to make pic with Michelangelo Antonioni but changed his mind mid-project, opting for a domestic quickie over heavier au-

teurist fare. Pic takes its cue not from "Blow-Up" as much as "Blow Out," making DePalma and even Kubrick the victims of passing homages. It looks promising on the local market and macabre screens elsewhere despite the fact hero and his sister are Yanks.

Pic opens with some dazzling footage of Yellowstone Park, where clean-cut blond Bob (Tom Schanley) is a forest ranger. One day in a fit of telepathy he realizes his twin sister, a punkish fashion model working in Milan, is in mortal danger, and he hops on the next jet to Italy. He checks into her hotel, peopled exclusively by tall, willowy beauties, and tries to convince kind Police Inspector Donald Pleasence the girl has been murdered.

The sister's corpse doesn't turn up till the last reel, but in the meantime there is no shortage of bodies, dead and alive, to look at. Undoubtedly the best thing in "Nothing Underdeath" is the girls. Though rather uncharitably described by a solemn Japanese photographer as "empty under their clothes," they beat the rest of the lackluster cast hands down on screen presence. A black-gloved, scissor-wielding killer whose face we never see bumps off several more before the finale, to a mellifluous score by Pino Donaggio.

Besides its generous amounts of gratuitous nudity, pic attempts to play up the decadence of the high-fashion world via a smarmy atmosphere of playboys, orgies, drugs, lesbianism, discos, bribery, even a fatal round of Russian roulette. All contrasted to the unspoiled purity of the great Wyoming landscape. (If only sis had taken that job in the supermarket ...)

For comic relief there is a dirty-minded hotel clerk, who seems to be on duty night and day. When a murder victim is covered with a sheet before being wheeled off to the morgue, he remarks, "Her last dress." —*Yung.*

Out Of The Darkness
(BRITISH-COLOR-16m)

London, Dec. 2.

A Children's Film and TV Foundation production for Rank Film Distributors. Produced by Gordon L.T. Scott. Directed by John Krish. Features entire cast. Screenplay, Krish, from the novel "The Ivy Garland" by John Hoyland; camera (color), Ray Orton; music, Ed Welch; production design, Keith Wilson; sound, Robert Allen, Rupert Scrivener; costumes, Lynette Cummin, Imogen Magnus. Reviewed at the London Film Festival, Dec. 1, 1985. Running time, **75 MINS.**

Tom . . . . Garry Halliday
Mike . . . . Michael Flowers
Penny . . . . Emma Ingham
Ghost boy . . . . Anthony Winder
Mrs. Nell . . . . Jenny Tarren
Julian Reid . . . . Michael Carter
Blacksmith . . . . Roy Holder

Jenny . . . . Vivienne Moore

This atmospheric kid's film is based on the story of an English village afflicted by the Plague during the 17th century. Story imagines a boy who escaped from the guards around the village, only to be murdered by the neighboring population.

Script focuses on the contempo story of three boys staying in the latter village who see the ghost of the boy victim as well as scenes of lynching. They enlist the support of the local museum keeper to discover what really happened and, in the process, free the village from its guilt for the killing.

With a spirited cast of children, writer-director John Krish creates a convincing narrative of a group alternately intrigued and frightened by what they see, but also inclined to bicker about the proper course of action.

Thanks also to skillful lensing and scoring credits, pic is a powerful story of ghosts and guilt. There's a thrilling dénouement.—*Japa.*

La Cage aux Folles 3
(FRENCH-ITALIAN-COLOR)

Paris, Dec. 4.

A WB/Col release (France)/Tri-Star elsewhere of a Da. Ma., Produzione (Rome)/Columbia (Paris) coproduction. Produced by Marcello Danon. Directed by Georges Lautner. Stars Michel Serrault and Ugo Tognazzi. Screenplay, Philippe Nicaud, Christine Carere, Marcello Danon, Jacques Audiard, Michel Audiard, Georges Lautner, Gérard Lamballe, inspired by characters in Jean Poiret's play, "La Cage aux Folles," camera (Eastmancolor), Luciano Tovoli; art director, Mario Garbuglia; costumes, Piero Tosi; editor, Michelle David; music, Ennio Morricone; production manager, Mario D'Alessio. Reviewed at the Gaumont Ambassade theater, Paris, Dec. 3, 1985. Running time: 87 MINS.

Albin . . . . Michel Serrault
Renato . . . . Ugo Tognazzi
Charrier . . . . Michel Galabru
Jacob . . . . Benny Luke
Matrimonia . . . . Stéphane Audran
Cindy . . . . Antonella Interlenghi
Moritmer . . . . Saverio Vallone
Dulac . . . . Gianluca Favilla
Kennedy . . . . Umberto Ramo

There are lots of cooks but not much broth for the third screen concoction featuring the gay odd couple profitably imagined for the Paris stage by Jean Poiret, prior to its international success in film and in a Broadway musical version. With five years gone by since the "La Cage aux Folles 2," there should be enough fans out there anxious enough to know what's become of Albin (Zaza) Napoli and his long-suffering mate Renato, to make this return visit a profitable one for producer Marcello Danon and Tri-Star, which is handling the film worldwide. It has opened in France via WB/Col to mainly boxoffice results.

It took no fewer than seven — count 'em seven — credited writers to dream up the weak premise and poorly sustained consequences in which our limpwristed hereos are embroiled. Among them one can spot producer Danon and the late Michel Audiard, specifically credited with the dialog, for which he certainly will not be remembered.

Albin and Renato are alive and well and still living in Saint-Tropez, but their gay nightclub, where Zaza is preparing his high-flying new revue as the Queen of Bees, is in financial straits. Fortunately, Albin stands to inherit a magnificent castle and vast property in Scotland that will have the couple sitting pretty for the rest of their days. Unfortunately, the will stipulates Zaza must marry and provide an heir within 18 months, or the inheritance will go to his virile, greedy young cousin.

Naturally, Zaza, furiously faithful and every inch a queen, shuns the idea of such an abnormal alliance, even for appearances' sake. Renato, more pragmatic and wily, hits on a number of schemes to goad his obstinate mate into wedlock, including a pretense that an accident has restored him to heterosexuality; and a matchmaking arrangement with a lonely young beauty who has been jilted and left pregnant by her ex-lover. A solution finally is found, if only because the small army of scripters seems to call a sudden truce of imagination.

The poor screenplay and indifferent direction by Georges Lautner probably won't matter to those who find a full evening's entertainment in Michel Serrault, who is always a scream, literally and figuratively, as the daintily shrill and sentimental drag artist. Serrault does his number with all his usual technical facility, and even if it's all thoroughly familiar by now, he keeps the film from slipping into droning insignificance.

Ugo Tognazzi resumes his role as Renato, but still looks bored playing the, ahem, straight man to Serrault. Benny Luke is back as Jacob, the dainty domestic, and Michel Galabru repeats his performance as a hapless conservative politician, here accused of having the "Cage aux Folles" club. Stéphane Audran does a forgettable guest turn as the head of a matrimonial agency. Other players, mostly Italian, and mostly badly dubbed, leave no impression.

Technically, production is more handsome than the previous 1981 installment, with pleasing, if unexceptional, lighting by lenser Luciano Tovoli; discreet set design by Mario Garbuglia, and aptly bright costumes for the leads by Piero Tosi. —Len.

Tiempo de Morir
(A Time To Die)
(COLOMBIAN-CUBAN-COLOR)

Rio de Janeiro, Nov. 28.
A Focine (Colombia) production in association with Icaic (Cuba). Executive Producer, Gloria Zea. Directed by Jorge Ali Triana. Screenplay, Gabriel García Márquez; camera (color) Mario García Joya; music, Leo Brower, Nafer Durán; editor, Nelson Rodriquez. Reviewed at Rio Film Festival (competition), Nov. 25, 1985. Running time: **98 MINS.**
With: Gustavo Angarita, Sebastian Ospina, Jorge Emilio Salazar, Maria Eugenia Dávila, Lina Botero, Enrique Almirante, Carlos Barbosa, Mónica Silva, Héctor Rivas, Luis Chiape, Rodolfo Miravalles, Lucy Martinez, Edgardo Román, Nelly Moreno and Patricia Bonilla.

In a very impressive first film, director Jorge Ali Triana, working from an original screenplay by Gabriel García Márquez, has turned out what may well be the best film to date based on the Nobel Prize novelist's work. Written at the beginning of the '70s, the screenplay's themes are in many ways similar to those of "Chronicle Of A Death Foretold," García Márquez most recent novel, soon to be filmed by Francesco Rosi.

Juan Sayago once killed a man and spent 18 years in jail for it, and the film begins with his release from prison and return to his native village. It soon becomes obvious he is not welcome. Julián and Pedro Moscote are now grown men and, following unwritten laws of machismo and revenge, are waiting to do away with the man who killed their father. The whole town is aware of what is about to happen; Sayago also knows, but refuses all advice to leave and settle elsewhere. Neither the villagers nor he try to prevent the inevitable and in the behavior of Julián, the older brother, the film develops another of its main themes: that the fear of killing is even worse than the fear of dying.

On the one hand, "Tiempo de Morir" has some of the ingredients of a traditional Western, final shootout and all; on the other, with an inexorable fate moving on to its inevitable conclusion, this is the stuff of which tragedies are made. There is a great deal more to it than the obsession of revenge. All sorts of social mores are involved and even the younger characters who try to rebel against them end up equally involved and victimized by events.

The pace is perhaps slow, but the film's tension and atmosphere are handled well by director Triana and most of his actors. The local background is firmly etched in by Cuban cinematographer Mario García Joya, and Gustavo Angarita (as Juan Sayago) turns in a performance that, with a minimum of dialog, gives his character considerable depth. A large part of the film was shot in Armero, a small town

recently destroyed by the eruption of the Nevado del Ruiz volcano.

Both on its own merits as a film and also thanks to García Márquez' involvement, "Tiempo de Morir" well could obtain wider international arthouse exposure than any other Colombian film to date. — Amig.

Shadey
(BRITISH-COLOR)

London, Nov. 17.
A Larkspur Films production for Film Four Intl. Produced by Otto Plashkes. Directed by Philip Saville. Features entire cast. Screenplay, Snoo Wilson; camera (color) Roger Deakins; editor, Chris Kelly; music, Colin Towns; production design, Norman Garwood; costumes, Tudor George; sound, Sandy Macrae, Anthony Sloman. Reviewed at the London Film Festival, Nov. 17, 1985. Running time: **106 MINS.**

Oliver Shadey	Antony Sher
Dr. Cloud	Billie Whitelaw
Sir Cyril Landau	Patrick Macnee
Carol Landau	Leslie Ash
Captain Amies	Bernard Hepton
Dick Darnley	Larry Lamb
Lady Landau	Katherine Helmond
Shulman	Jon Cartwright
Carl	Jesse Birdsall
Manson	Olivier Pierre
Winston	Stephen Persaud

"Shadey" is the sort of film you either love or hate. Its rich store of surpises, enigmas and mysteries defies an audience to be bored. Pic is the most imaginative comedy to come out of Britain in some time.

Quality of the script derives from its combination of surrealism with strict contemporaneity. Scattered references to terrorism, espionage and the weird world of pop promo makers give an edge to the humor.

Antony Sher, a distinguished legit actor making his screen debut, gives a standout performance as a bankrupt car mechanic who uses his power to project images onto film in order to secure the funds he needs for a sex change operation. Only condition is that he shouldn't be involved in anything involving defense or violence.

Discovered in his garage by a wealthy banker, played by Patrick Macnee, he is lured into his weird family situation comprising a delightful aspirant model, Carol (Leslie Ash) and an agoraphobic wife whose pastimes include eating coal. Katherine Helmond plays the latter role of Lady Landau as an extension of her performances in the "Soap" tv show and "Brazil."

Concurrently, Oliver Shadey is traded by the banker to the defense establishment, which uses drugs to force him to reveal details of Soviet submarine bases. Representation of Shadey's mental images is enhanced by witty scoring.

Although the film rollicks along in early scenes, leadup to the film's dénouement is rather clumsy. A protracted engagement party crowded out by South Africans

hungry for access to the new espionage tool is a dull backdrop to an emotionally charged confrontation between Shadey and a knife-wielding Lady Landau. A subsequent chase in an elevator shaft also seems rather conventional within the film's zany framework.

Director Philip Saville does a splendid job of orchestrating the various human confrontations throughout the film from an imagined scene of incest between father and daughter to a hilarious beach scene where Carol is pursued by an aggressive group of Mongols to the dismay of her watching mother. All technical credits are firstrate.—Japa.

Grunt! The Wrestling Movie
(COLOR)

Loser by disqualification.

Coral Springs, Fla., Nov. 30.
A New World Pictures release of a New World Pictures and James G. Robinson presentation. Executive producer, Robinson. Produced by Don Normann, Anthony Randel. Directed by Allan Holzman. Features entire cast. Screenplay, Roger D. Manning, from story by Holzman, Randel, Lisa Tomei, Barry Zetlin; camera (Foto-kem & Du Art color; prints by Technicolor), Eddie van der Enden; editor, Holzman, Zetlin; music, Susan Justin; sound, Walter Martin; assistant director, Kristine Peterson; exec production manager, William C. Edwards; second unit camera, Donald C. Jackson; casting, Mary Ann Barton, Michael Greer. Reviewed at Loews Coral Springs 6 theater, Nov. 30, 1985. (MPAA Rating: R.) Running time: **90 MINS.**

Lesley Uggams	Jeff Dial
Tweed	Robert Glaudini
Sweet Lola	Marilyn Dodds Farr

Also with: Greg Magic Schwartz, Bill Grant, Steve Cepello, Dick Murdoch, Exotic Adrian Street, John Tolos, Wally George, Victor Rivera, Count Billy Varga, members of Duck's Breath Mystery Theater.

"Grunt! The Wrestling Movie" is an unfunny, amateurish feature, notable only as the first to be released of three recent productions tied to wrestling's new-found popularity.

Format slavishly imitates that of Rob Reiner's "This Is Spinal Tap." A documentary filmmaker, Lesley Uggams (Jeff Dial), is making a verité film about wrestler Mad Dog Joe Di Curso, who in 1979 accidentally decapitated opponent Skull Crusher Johnson in a match, after which he supposedly committed suicide. Six years later, a new "good guy" wrestler, The Mask, is thought to be Mad Dog Joe and Uggams boringly inteviews anybody on the subject while incorporating old footage of Mad Dog in action and lensing The Mask's matches.

Screenwriter Roger D. Manning and director Allan Holzman err in merely presenting a series of clichés about wrestling, featuring unknown or relatively obscure wrestlers. The viewer may nod in recognition or perhaps nod off into slumberland, but for laughs the televised real matches are far more exaggerated and laugh-producing. Photography is alternately pretentious or incompetent, but mainly designed to lamely hide the fact (through low-angles and smoke sets) that even at a massive 10-man elmination tournament there are only about 20 extras in the audience for this low-budget opus, not the 20,000 who show up for the real thing. Artsy editing and other tech credits are way below par. —Lor.

Scandalosa Gilda
(Scandalous Gilda)
(ITALIAN-COLOR)

Rome, Dec. 3.
A D.M.V. release, produced by Pietro Innocenzi for Globe Films, Dania Film, Filmes International, National Cinematografica. Directed by Gabriele Lavia. Screenplay, Lavia and Riccardo Ghione; camera (color), Mario Vulpiani; animated cartoon, Gibba; art director, Giovanni Agostinucci; editor, Daniele Alabiso; music, Giorgio Carnini. Reviewed at the Quirinale Cinema, Rome, Nov. 26, 1985. Running time: **94 MINS.**
He . . . . Gabriele Lavia
She . . . . Monica Guerritore

"Scandalous Gilda" is an eclectic film which veers recklessly between softcore sex, a few good laughs, and a doomed love affair between strangers.

Gabriele Lavia had made a name as a stage helmer and thesp of the classics. In "Gilda" he takes a brief vacation to cash in on the fad for disreputable pictures by reputable directors, where half of the fun from the filmgoer's point of view is seeing how low the famous man (inevitably accompanied by a famous lady) will sink. This picture goes just so far before Lavia balks and tries to inject a dose of serious sentiment into the nitty-gritty raunch the public paid for.

Nowhere close to an unblushing crowd-pleaser like Tinto Brass' "Miranda," "Gilda" basically has three things to recommend it over staying home and leafing through a men's magazine: a lovely leading lady (Monica Guerritore), an intermittently appealing leading man (Lavia), and a very funny cartoon lasting approximately five minutes.

Story is a dismal cross between "Brief Encounter," film noir and a New German road movie. A rich, loving wife (Guerritore) catches her husband having an affair, seen in panting close-up in the opening scene. She tearfully jumps in her sportscar and takes off down the highway, where she meets a wacky cartoon animator (Lavia) weaving down the road in a jeep, singing "Carmen." It takes quite a while before the two can make it into a motel room for the next coupling. By then the best part of the picture is over, a short cartoon called "Scandalous Gilda" in which little men shaped like private parts meet a long pair of female legs.

Attempting to eat its cake and have it, too, pic plays its sex scenes for psychology as well as titillation. Unlike the French, Italians have little talent for this. Results are disappointing in both camps and pic drags toward the end. Back at the motel, Guerritore sheds her middle-class look for a wilder appearance and begins to systematically humiliate the nice cartoonist. First she has a roll in a tractor-trailer with a truck driver, then goads Lavia into raping a strange woman; finally she drives them both off the road. Diabolically, only she survives.

Lensing and sets create a lurid mortuary atmosphere that complements the story. —Yung.

Scout Toujours
(A Scout Forever)
(FRENCH-COLOR)

Paris, Dec. 3.
An AMLF release of a Films 7/Arturo Prod./Films A2 coproduction. Produced by Pierre Gauchet. Starring and directed by Gérard Jugnot. Screenplay, Jugnot, Pierre Geller, Christian Biegalski; camera (color), Gérard de Battista; editor, Catherine Kelber, sound, Bernard Auboy; music, Gabriel Yared. Reviewed at the Gaumont Colisée theater, Paris, Dec. 3, 1985. Running time: **97 MINS.**
With: Gérard Jugnot, Jean-Claude Leguay, Jean Rougerie, Jean-Paul Comart, Agnès Blanchot, Maurice Barrier.

Gérard Jugnot, one of the several Paris cafe-theater comics to make a successful switch to films, last year directed himself to more or less happy results in "Pinot, Simple Flic," in which he played a soft-hearted cop. He fails to keep the promise of his debut in his second vehicle.

Working again with the scripting team of "Pinot," Pierre Geller and Christian Biegalski, Jugnot casts himself as a French boy scout master assigned to head a summer camp in the mountains. Lacking a genuine sense of authority, he runs into a series of disasters as he tackles some unmanageable scouts, a band of gypsies, a homosexual associate who's secretly keen on him, and the precocious teen daughter of the wealthy farmer who's leased a plot of land to the scout camp.

This is formula stuff, with the bumbling Jugnot of course coming through in the end when he leads a lost scout troop out of the wilds, and earns their esteem. The gags are lame, the direction ill-timed and Jugnot lacks the credible human base that made "Pinot" a heart-warming bumbler with a secret reserve of spunk. Better luck next time.—Len.

AIDS — Gefahr
für die Liebe
(AIDS — A Danger For Love)
(WEST GERMAN-FRENCH-COLOR)

Berlin, Dec. 6.
A Coproduction of CCC-Filmkunst (Arthur Brauner), Berlin, and S.N. Lira Films, Paris; released by Cinevox, Munich. Directed by Hans Noever. Screenplay, Paul Hengge, Alex Kersten; camera (color), Hans-Günther Bücking; music, Francis Lai, Roman Romanelli; sets, Holger Scholz; sound, Gunter Kortwich; editor, Sybille Windt. Reviewed at Atelier am Zoo, Berlin, Dec. 3, 1985. Running time: **95 MINS.**
With: Fritz Cat, a.k.a. Friedrich Graner (Frank), Geraldine Danon (Jessica), Piero von Armin (Georg), Oliver Rohrbeck (Ritchie), Claudia Arnold (Tamara), Aliver Pascalin (Max).

The first of a series of such pics now in production in Germany, Hans Noever's "AIDS — A Danger For Love" leans too heavily on the current press and media coverage of the disease to be taken very seriously as a film. Nevertheless, there is enough here to warrant the attempt, and one wonders what might have been accomplished given a clear shot at the theme with a more weighted screenplay.

Tale is of a young taxi driver, Frank (nicknamed Prince, after a name imprinted on his Yank-style car, plus his penchant for working whenever he cares to), who is suffering from the immunity deficiency disease due to have been on the needle: one assumes that he contracted it via a none too hygenic drug fix. He picks up a young mannequin type in his cab one day, and it's love at first sight. Prince also has a younger brother still on the needle, who has debts to pay off to a local mafia boss. While trying to straighten out these affairs, while pursuing a seemingly normal love relationship, the lad is stricken by frequent fevers.

Oops, there's also an odd twist thrown in for good measure involving a brief encounter (minus intimacy) with a gay admirier of Prince. Why this should enter the picture is not clear at all — in fact, since one tends to associate the disease with gay relationships, the red herring only confuses the issue in the long run.

Main weakness is in the dialog, however, along with an irritating musical score on the soundtrack resembling that employed for typical tv thrillers. The pity is that everyone associated with the project appears to be talented enough to handle just such a contemporary treatment, particularly as Berlin (where pic was lensed) offers more AIDS true-life experiences than elsewhere.—Holl.

In Her Own Time
(DOCU-COLOR)

Hollywood, Dec. 6.
A Direct Cinema Limited release. Produced by Vikram Jayanti, Lynne Littman. Directed by Littman, based on the field work of Dr. Barbara Myerhoff. Camera (color), William Moffitt; editor, Suzanne Pettit; music, James Horner; sound, Tom Koester; consulting producer, Jonathan Bernstein. Reviewed at the Royal Theater, Santa Monica, Calif., Nov. 27, 1985. (No MPAA Rating.) Running time: **60 MINS.**

"In Her Own Time" is a unique blend of anthropology and personal history based on the exploration of the diverse Fairfax district Jewish community in Los Angeles by Dr. Barbara Myerhoff. After starting her investigation, Myerhoff learned she had cancer and it is that knowledge that gives the film a compelling edge. Although the film probably will only reach a limited audience, anyone encountering it is bound to be moved by the story.

Using the tools of the social scientist, Myerhoff investigates the orthodox Hasidic community in Fairfax and finds people with a strong spiritual commitment in their lives. As a Jew and a woman with a terminal illness, Myerhoff is attracted to the community, both personally and professionally.

The Hasidim may appear simply an oddity in today's world but Myerhoff discovers there is a deep universal humanity to these unusual people. Filmmaker Lynne Littman ("Testament") follows Myerhoff around as she investigates the meaning of rituals of orthodox Jewish life.

As conventional medical treatment for her illness fails, Myerhoff turns more to the spiritual and healing powers of her religion, albeit in a more extreme form than she has ever practiced it. Ultimately "In Her Own Time" becomes a moving document of an insulated community that has maintained its own values and its meaning in a spirtually bankrupt society.

Myerhoff was a respected anthropologist at the U. of Southern California at the time of her death. Her quest is treated in a matter-of-fact fashion that elevates it above just another fatal disease soap opera. The material is sentimental without being cloying.

Production values are adequate without being overly polished, enough to let the feeling and affection of the filmmaker for her subject to come through. Littman, in fact, had made an earlier film with Myerhoff, "Number Our Days," about a senior citizens center in Venice, Calif., which is a suitable bookend for "In Her Own Time."
—Jagr.

Underworld
(BRITISH-COLOR)

London, Nov. 30.

A Limehouse Pictures-Green Man Prods. film. Produced by Kevin Attew and Don Hawkins. Coproducer, Graham Ford. Executive producer, Al Burgess. Directed by George Pavlou. Features entire cast. Screenplay, Clive Barker, James Caplin; camera (color), Sydney Macartney; editor, Chris Ridsdale; sets, Len Huntingford; music, Freur; special effects, Richard Perkis. Reviewed at London Film Festival, Nov. 29, 1985. Running time: **100 MINS.**

With: Denholm Elliott (Dr. Savary), Steven Berkoff (Hugo Motherskille), Larry Lamb (Roy Bain), Miranda Richardson (Oriel), Art Malik (Fluke), Nicola Cowper (Nicole), Ingrid Pitt (Pepperdine), Irina Brook (Bianca), Paul Brown (Nygaard), Philip Davies (Lazarus), Gary Olsen (Red Dog), Brian Croucher (Darling), Trevor Thomas (Ricardo), Paul Mari (Dudu).

Without doubt, George Pavlou's "Underworld" will do well by the audience for which it's intended. This is a pop horror thriller beefed up by a synthesizer on the soundtrack, jellied Halloween masks, and a thin narrative thread based on a book by writer Clive Barker, word-processed onto the familiar thriller terrain outlined in Dashiell Hammett's "The Glass Key." The formula works — all that's missing to score on the video mart is a soundtrack featuring a current hot pop band. Pic also moves too slowly just when the tension is supposed to climb to the climax.

It's about mutants living underground as a result of tests made by a crazy medicine man, who's into the gangland drug trade, to produce a chemical formula that allows his young patients to live out their fantasies in real life. When their fantasies are allowed to run free, deformities take place in the body (primarily facial), and only a fair maiden named Nicole escapes the ill effects of the dreamdrug. The mutants kidnap her one evening from a house of ill repute, holding her hostage in order to get the daily doses from the doctor they need to survive — even eventually be cured of their lumping sores and facial miseries.

The gangland boss intends to rub out everybody concerned, so he prompts a retired gunman, now reformed, to come to the rescue of the fair damsel whom he once loved. As the hardboiled detective sets out on the tracks of the underworld goons, he's shadowed by the Big Boss' own henchmen. Nicole, meanwhile, helps her former friends as best she can, which means antihero Bain gradually is prompted to turn the tables on his old gang, one at a time like an avenging angel.

Okay thriller marred by cornball dialog. — Holl.

Hechos Consumados
(An Accomplished Fact)
(CHILEAN-B&W/COLOR-16m)

Santiago, Nov. 19.

Produced by Luis R. Vera. Executive Producer, Myriam Braniff. Directed by Vera. Features entire cast. Screenplay, Vera, based on a play by Juan Radrigán; camera (b&w, color), Andrés Martorell Jr.; sound, Eugenio Gutierrez; music, Patricio Solovera; costumes, Maya Mora. Reviewed at Conate screening room, Santiago, Nov. 18, 1985. Running time: **100 MINS.**

With: Nelson Brodt, Loreto Valenzuela, José Soza, Mónica Carrasco, Myriam Palacios, Jorge Gajardo.

Juan Radrigán's plays usually deal with the have-nots, the dropouts from society who struggle to maintain their dignity as human beings. This is also one of the themes of "An Accomplished Fact," Luis R. Vera's first feature, running the festival gauntlet (Biarritz, Cartagena, Bogotá, Huelva, Havana). Vera left Chile 12 years ago, studied at the Rumanian film school and now lives in Stockholm where his $60,000-budgeted film was produced with the assistance of Swedish television.

Shot in Santiago a year ago, most of the pic takes place on a barren piece of land somewhere outside Santiago. There Emilio, a former textile worker and now a ragged vagabond, finds Martha dumped into the dirty waters of a nearby rivulet by unidentified individuals.

He revives her and slowly, subtly, without their even touching each other, a bond is formed between them. Miguel (José Soza), caretaker of the private property the other two are on, is torn between feelings of solidarity with the couple and fear of losing his job if he does not obey orders and throw them out.

Somewhere in the background, there is a procession of the poor leaving the city. To stress their symbolic value, these sequences are portrayed in unfocused yellow-orange, an effect which does not accomplish its objective. André Martorell Jr.'s black and white photography in the rest of the film is adequate, but perhaps too flat and conventional, given pic's many ambiguities, which leave ample scope for readings on different levels.

Director Vera is most successful in establishing the personal relationships between the three main characters, thanks to good performances, especially by Soza and his projection of the caretaker's thoughts and feelings. It is an interesting, albeit partly flawed film, particularly striking in its poetic moments. It could do quite well in Chile and is likely to obtain tv exposure abroad. —Amig.

Broken Rainbow
(DOCU-COLOR)

Powerful indictment of government's callous treatment of Navajos.

San Francisco, Nov. 22.

An Earthworks presentation of a documentary produced, written and edited by Maria Florio and Victoria Mudd. Directed by Mudd. Narrated by Martin Sheen; historical voice, Burgess Meredith. Camera (color), Michael Anderson, Fred Elmes, Joan Weidman, Tony St. John, Baird Bryant, Mudd; original music, Laura Nyro; associate director, Thom Tyson; associate producers, Roslyn Dauber, Tommie Smith; sound, Sesumu Tukunow, Jim Rossolini, Trevor Black, Clyde Smith, Haline Paul, Johanna Demetrakas. Reviewed at the York Theater, San Francisco, Nov. 21, 1985. (No MPAA Rating.) Running time: **69 MINS.**

This deeply compelling, anger-inducing docu was unspooled first at 10th annual Indian film fest in San Francisco, then played commercially for two nights at nabe York.

Pic concerns the federal government's relocation of some 10,000 Navajos in northeastern Arizona to clear land for energy (mostly coal) development projects. The story is complicated by a century of what amounts to bureaucratic racism. That the feds have discriminated historically against Native Americans is not news; that this commercially inspired insensitivity and seeming inhumanity persists in 1985 is. Yet national media have been unable to cover the story adequately.

A docu such as this — told with clarity, technically clean — merits wide exposure; it's a natural "60 Minutes" seg. Frisco pubcaster KQED already is trying a docu for eventual PBS airing, so the spinoff success of "Broken Rainbow" beyond its Indian Filmfest honors is questionable, unless some earnest booker in an urban or college town situation perceives the innate humanism of the story.

Even the most bottom line-oriented Yuppie can't see this yarn without being moved. In some ways, pic leaves one with the perverse feeling that all of this — the movement of thousands of people who don't wish to be moved or transplanted from their culture — is happening in another time in a far-off land.

"Broken Rainbow" speaks eloquently for a silent minority and could, if seen by popular media mavens, lead to reason. —Herb.

Amateur Hour
(COLOR)

Amateurish parody of a tv station.

Washington, Nov. 1.

Produced by Susan Kaufman. Directed by Stanford Singer. Screenplay, Singer, Kevin McDonough; camera (color, 16m), Lisa Rinzler; art director, Ann Williams; editor, Richard King; music, Cengiz Yaltkaya. Reviewed at the Cine screening room, Washington, D.C., Nov. 1, 1985. Running time: **85 MINS.**

Paul Pierce . . . . Adam Nathan
Donna Rose . . . . Julie Hanlon
John Reid . . . . John MacKay
Bill Johnson . . . . Walt Willey
Frank Romance . . . . Saul Alpiner
Miss Murphy . . . . Mikhail Druhan
Marcel Pederewsky . . . . . . Michael Griffith
Rico . . . . Guillermo Gonzalez

Debut pic about a very young couple corrupted by the vicious and untalented folks in a third rate New York tv station lives up to its title. An ambitious plot full of characters meant to parody the evils of broadcasting fails to deliver because thesps are not up to comic delivery and the central characters lack warmth to sustain interest in their moral perils.

Donna and Paul run away from Gus Grissom High School after stealing a camera, a harbinger of the thefts that will keep them alive in the Big Apple, as they plunder the storeroom of the tv station where Paul's sleazy father gives them jobs worthy of criminal talent. Their supervisor is the venal Miss Murphy, played for every penny she is worth by Mikhail Druhan, as she slinks and slurps after their young blood and bodies. Paul's tough father has arranged living quarters for the couple in an abandoned building, where the supervisor is a hip young Cuban named Rico, played with the most conviction of anybody in the cast by Guillermo Gonzalez. They, of course, keep thinking he is Puerto Rican, allowing for some ethnic minority jokes, but he is the only character who has not had his courage and integrity done in by New York City.

The thrust of pic is a sendup of the television biz, but it falls into many of the same traps as its object of ridicule, most obviously, bad acting. Director Stanford Singer has pushed the performances beyond realism but not quite into parody, so the line deliveries are full of bravado much like the sitcom style but without the heartwarming centers and laugh machine.

By the time Donna and Paul have established a terrorist front of two called the "Collective for a Clear Channel" to eliminate vid pollution, the story should be racing along, but the various plots have trouble untangling. The last sequence, in which a talk-show suddenly becomes a "Network"-like confrontation with the meaning of the media, needs to be clipped to half the time taken to tie up all the characters. The happy ending has Paul losing Donna to a Stanislavsky theorist named Pederewsky who looks like what he sounds like, while Paul and his father resolve their Oedipal conflicts on the way to jail. —Kaja.

Silip
(FILIPINO-COLOR)

Chicago, Nov. 17.

A Viking Films Intl. release. Produced by Wilson Tieng. Directed by Elwood Perez. Features entire cast. Screenplay, Ricardo Lee; camera (color), Johnny Araojo; editor, Edgardo Vinarao; music, Lutgardo Labad; sets, Alfred Santos. Reviewed at Chicago Film Fest (out-of-competition). Nov. 16, 1985. Running time: **130 MINS.**

With: Maria Isabel Lopez (Tonya), Sarsi Emmanuelle (Selda), Myra Mannibog (Mona), Mark Joseph (Simon).

One might question the selection of Elwood Perez' "Silip" in a respectable international film festival, save that Chicago is celebrating Filipino Culture Week and helmer Perez does happen to be the country's leading b.o. filmmaker. Pic is scripted by Ricardo (Ricky) Lee, who's also responsible for the inanities found in the other Filipino pic on the Chifest schedule, Sixto Kayko's "Private Show," a softcore sex film. Ditto for "Silip."

Picture village life with an idyllic sun-bathed beach, where fair maidens can romp in the buff and be pursued over the dunes by the furies and a roving camera. Plot has to do with a village stud hankering for a virgin teacher, who in turn decides one day that her emancipation is there for the asking. There are also a jealous widow and a schoolgirl, the latter a victim of circumstances that lead to an accidental death, followed by vengeance on the stud by her classmates (they behead him).

The innocent schoolteacher now has but one friend, an attractive femme arrival, and together they are the victims of a gang rape and burning-at-the-stake execution. It's blood and sex, Filipino style.

—Holl.

Walter & Carlo: Op pa Fars hat
(Walter & Carlo: Up At Dad's Hat)
(DANISH-COLOR)

Copenhagen, Nov. 28.

A Regnar Grasten release (Denmark), Kaerne Film (foreign sales) of Per Holst Produktion production. Executive producer and directed by Per Holst. Stars Jarl Friis-Mikkelsen, Ole Stephensen. Screenplay, Jarl Friis-Mikkelsen, Stephensen, Jane Amund, Holst, John Hilbard; camera (Eastmancolor) Peter Roos; production manager, Ib Tardini; assistant director, John Hilbard; editor, Sven Methling; production designer, Palle Arestrup; music, Jan Gläsel; costumes, Pia Myrdal; special effects, Sören Skjär; stunts, Svenska Stuntgruppen, Pank's Parateam; produced with the support of the Danish Film Institute (consultant Peter Poulsen). Reviewed at the Palads, Copenhagen, Nov. 28, 1985. Running time: **87 MINS.**

Walter	Ole Stephensen
Carlo	Jarl Friis-Mikkelsen
Inge	Benedikte Hansen
Viola	Kirsten Rolffes
Osvald	Kai Lövring
Manfred	Paul Hagen
Vera	Lisbeth Dahl
Ateza	Poul Bundgaard

Also with: Tommy Kenter, Ulf Piilgard, Claus Ryskjär, Jesper Holst, Kirsten Norholt, Niels Skousen, Tom McEwan, Peter Ronild, Poul Glargaard, Jess Ingerslev, Sös Egelind,

Kerry Riebel, Max Hansen.

Busy film producer and sometime helmer Per Holst wears both hats for "Walter & Carlo: Up At Dad's Hat," and feature-length farce proves not to be his stronger suit. Actually, the man behind such original Danish mellers as "Zappa," "Twist & Shout" and "The Element Of Crime," which all bore his producer's imprint of quality and knowhow, has this time around fallen into the old trap of thinking good television fun fodder equally serviceable for the big screen.

Film's two title characters were invented for more or less intermission fooling-around by television entertainer-host Jarl Friis-Mikkelsen and Ole Stephensen, former as a loud mouth, quick-service cobbler Carlo, latter as Walter, his handsome hulk of an airline steward straight man. Blown up into characters supposed to carry the plot of a feature-length farce, Carlo comes off as an intolerable bore of one pitch only, Walter as a romantically inclined dimwit who couldn't hold a candle, let alone a highball, to Dean Martin even when given a good ballad to sing and a bathing beauty to sit in his lap.

Plot is intended to be updated Brothers Marxian and does have some of the ingredients with clownish-tough Carlo and sweetly daffy Walter getting involved with pretty dames and diamonds-and-weapons smuggling thugs while on a package tour to sunny Spain. There, they and assorted other stock characters of crime thrillers and family sitcoms are crammed into an endless succession of spots so tight neither sight-gags nor quick-repartee dialog ever gets a chance to breathe or in any other way function within the suspense-cum-surprise mechanics essential to all farce.

Stephensen, appearing somnolent most of the time, does get an idea or a word across now and then, while Friis-Mikkelsen maintains a sustained level of shrill, hectoring and mostly unintelligible punster's yakkety-yakking all the way through a one-note performance. Veteran film comedians like Paul Hagen, Lisbeth Dahl, Poul Bundgaard, Kristen Rolffes and Kai Lövring are close to scene-stealing wherever they appear but their punch is soon snatched away from them by Holst's hurry to hurtle everything from his Farce For Beginners Guide onto the screen, again ignoring the all-important dictum of the pause that refreshes.

If "Walter & Carlo: Up At Dad's Hat" is to make back its costs, it will have to happen via its saturation booking on local turf where the title characters are still riding the crest of television popularity. If an offshore viewer should ever get

stuck in Holst's too tightly packed fun parlor of a film, he won't have to worry about the meaning of its title. It has none, but carries the slangy notion of somebody being out of their skull. *— Kell.*

Rouge Baiser
(Red Kiss)
(FRENCH-WEST GERMAN-COLOR)

Paris, Dec. 8.

A U.G.C. release of a Stephane Films-Farena Films-Films A2 (Paris)-C&H Films (Berlin) coproduction. Produced, directed, and written by Vera Belmont. Stars Charlotte Valandrey, Lambert Wilson. Script collaborators, Guy Konopnicki, David Milhaud; camera (Fuji color), Ramon Suarez; editor, Martine Giordano; music, Jean-Marie Senia; sound, Alain Curvelier. Reviewed at the UGC Biarriz theater, Paris, Dec. 8, 1985. Running time: **111 MINS.**

Nadia	Charlotte Valandrey
Stéphane	Lambert Wilson
Bronka	Marthe Keller
Moishe Maldelman	Laurent Terzieff
Hershel	Günter Lamprecht
Roland	Laurent Arnal
Henriette	Audrey Lazzini

Producer Vera Belmont made her directing debut in 1979 with the ambitious "Prisoners Of Mac," a quasi-documentary denunciation of totalitarianism in Red China in the 1950s, shot on location in Taiwan and Hong Kong with a cast of nonprofessionals. Six years later she is back with a second film as writer-director, again criticizing Communist dogmatism. This time she is working more intimately in a semi-autobiographical vein, with apparent borrowings from her own family background and youth.

Belmont's script follows the gradual political disenchantment and romantic warming-up of 15-year-old Nadia, born in Paris to Polish Jewish immigrant parents who have brought her up as an unquestioning Stalinist (for whom she has knitted a pair of slippers, complete with hammer and sickle, and to whom she has written a letter, as yet unanswered). As a member of a local Communist youth cell, she acts the committed, dispassionate young activist, who has a soft spot for Guillaume Apollinaire, but seems out of touch with the swinging social life of 1952.

During a demonstration that turns violent, she is saved from police clubbing by a young photographer (Lambert Wilson) for Paris-Match, whose intervention is inspired partially by a cynical quest for a scoop reportage. Despite their political, emotional and age differences, a guarded, on-again-off-again relationship begins.

Nadia's pained emotional thawing is quickened by events among her comrades and family, notably with the return of Moishe (Laurent Terzieff), her mother's first lover

before the war, and in fact her real father. At a homecoming party Terzieff, who has spent years atoning for his faith in Stalin in a Siberian labor camp, shocks everyone with a bitter outburst against the Soviet system. Later Nadia eavesdrops on a scene between Terzieff and her mother (Marthe Keller). Her eventual rupture with her Communist cell, and her move towards Lambert coincide with the announcement of Stalin's death.

Belmont has tried to cram too much into her film, which lacks an overall dramatic unity and rhythm and tends to dilute the emotional buildup of scenes. Her reconstitution of the period is adept, though there is occasional technical awkwardness and trite direction (the opening sequence recounting the separation of Terzieff and Keller in 1938, is shot in predictable b&w).

Pic gains, however, from its generally solid cast. Newcomer Charlotte Valandrey is striking as the temperamental but vulnerable Nadia, one of a number of fine performances by youngsters in recent French films. Wilson is seductively crass as the apolitical lover-photog, obliged to enlist for service in Indo-China to escape charges of having abducted a minor when Nadia disappears with him on a photo assignment. Terzieff and Keller are both fine in the limited screen time they have together. *—Len.*

Lune de Miel
(Honeymoon)
(CANADIAN-FRENCH-COLOR)

Paris, Nov. 27.

An AAA/Revcom Films release of a Hugo Films/La Gueville/René Malo Films/-C.A.P.A.C./TF 1 Films coproduction. Produced by Xavier Gelin. Directed by Patrick Jamain. Stars Nathalie Baye, John Shea, Richard Berry. Screenplay, Philippe Setbon, Patrick Jamain; camera (color), Daniel Diot; editor, Robert Rongier; music, Robert Charlebois, Boris Bergman; art director, Aimé Deudé; production manager, Bernard Grenet. Reviewed at the Marignan-Concorde theater, Paris, Nov. 26, 1985. Running time: **100 MINS.**

Cécile Carline	Nathalie Baye
Zack Freestamp	John Shea
Michel	Richard Berry
Garnier	Michel Beaune
Sally	Marla Lukovsky
Novak	Peter Donat

"Honeymoon," a Gotham-set Franco-Canadian thriller, brings Nathalie Baye to New York to be near her jailed boyfriend, Richard Berry, who has been caught smuggling drugs into the country. When her tourist visa expires, Baye desperately contracts a marriage of convenience through an agency and lands a job in a delicatessen. Her problems are only beginning when "husband" John Shea comes knocking at the door, with every intention of moving in.

For his theatrical feature debut,

tv helmer Patrick Jamain opts for the clichés of the psycho killer tradition, with lurid, unfriendly New York as the obvious backdrop to a familiar progression of events in which Shea, of course, turns out to be a razor-wielding lunatic who already has shredded a previous spouse and is ready to do the same to Baye if she doesn't give him the attention and affection he requires.

Jamain and coscripter Philippe Setbon base their situation on the platitudinous premise that the vulnerable heroine is too naive to realize she's dealing with a psychotic, though this is clear almost immediately to the audience. Viewers may respond more with irritation than concern to Baye's naive attempts to befriend the unpleasantly tenacious Shea, who lacks the twisted charm of memorable screen madmen.

The film does not so much create suspense as mark time, until Shea blows his last fuse and goes after Baye in a deserted amusement park.

Most of the exteriors were lensed on location in New York, with interiors and more anonymous street scenes apparently shot in Montreal. In version playing in France, everybody communicates in French, which notably robs the Baye-Shea scenes of dramatic possibilities.
—*Len.*

You Got To Move — Stories Of Change In The South
(U.S.-DOCU-COLOR-16m)

Nyon, Oct. 15.
A presentation of the Cumberland Mountain Educational Cooperative, New Market, Tenn. Produced by Lucy Massie Phenix. Directed by Phenix, Veronica Selver. Camera (color, 16m), Alan Dater, Gary Steele, Peter O'Neill, Roger Phenix; editor, Lucy M. Phenix, Selver; archival and photo research, Catherine Coates, Mary Lance. Funded in part by National Endowment for The Arts; the Tennessee, Kentucky and South Carolina humanities and arts councils; the Film Fund; others. Reviewed at Nyon Intl. Film Festival (Switzerland), Oct. 14, 1985. Running time: **87 MINS.**

Winner of two prizes at the recent Nyon all-docu festival, only U.S. film of 10 in the program to be so honored, "You Got To Move" is a delightful, hard-nosed retrospective retelling of the Southern civil rights struggle, told by Southerners, black and white, but updated to deal with contemporary social problems. Title expresses film's theme — you got to keep moving and keep confronting ongoing injustices, as part of the democratic process, and to affirm your self-worth. Belief in preceding leads logically to activism.

Social problems in the film include industrial abuse of the land, poverty, lack of decent rural education, struggle for women's equality, strengthening of unionism and con-

tinuing efforts to combat racism. New issues in the Old South include gay rights, help to Vietnam vets and keeping out of Central America.

Not a grim didactic documentary or political tract, "You Got To Move" is often funny and dramatic, with plenty of foot-stompin' mountain music, as colorful Southern characters in homespun anecdotes describe their metamorphoses from passivity to activism. "There's nothing fixed that you can't unfix," muses one veteran of the famous Highlander Folk School, 53-year-old center in the Tennessee mountains, where courage and social change are the curriculum.

Film uses stock footage, old recordings, still photos and newspaper headlines to chronicle attacks on Highlander by state authorities fearful of alleged "subversion."
—*Hitch.*

Christmas Present
(BRITISH-COLOR-16m)

London, Dec. 2.
A Telekation Intl. production for Film Four Intl. Produced by Barry Hanson. Written and directed by Tony Bicât. Features entire cast. Camera (color) Gabriel Beristain; editor, Bill Shapter; music, Nick Bicât; production design, Nigel Phelps; costumes, Andrea Galer; sound, Terry Hardy. Reviewed at the London Film Festival, Nov. 30, 1985. Running time: **75 MINS.**
Nigel Playfayre . . . . Peter Chelsom
Sir Percy . . . . Bill Fraser
Judy Tall . . . . , ... Lesley Manville
Anne . . . . Karen Meagher
Pamela . . . . Hetty Baynes
Ned . . . . Richard Ireson
Mr. Mehrban . . . . Baddy Uzaman
Mrs. Mehrban . . . . Jamila Massey
Viv . . . . Danny Wooder
Gos . . . . Clive Parker
Sticky . . . . Mark Harvey

Although conceived only for tv playoff, this imaginative interpretation of Charles Dickens' "A Christmas Carol" could be a hit as a homevideo release for family viewing.

The "Scrooge" character in this story is an arrogant investment manager entrusted to deliver a Christmas turkey to a poor family. If he doesn't fulfill the company custom he'll lose his job, but what's really on his mind is bedding his fiancée.

When Nigel Playfayre loses the address of the chosen household, he's set on a journey through the world of the social services, street types and the poor of a housing estate, all resulting in his moral transformation.

The witty script skillfully weaves in the lowly background of a boy who finds the letter. Also contributing to the comedy is the reappearance of Christ's parents on a donkey to see if they can find a place to stay on the streets of London.

Writer-director Tony Bicât handles the more incredible aspects of

this story with subtle flair, as well as bringing humanity to his depiction of the meek and humble. Lensing and editing credits are good.—*Japa.*

Roman Behemshechim
(Again Forever)
(ISRAELI-COLOR)

Tel Aviv, Oct. 21.
A Berkey-Pathé-Humphries presentation. Produced by Nurith Shani. Directed by Oded Kotler. Stars Chaim Topol. Screenplay, Itzhak Ben-Ner, based on his short story "Dime Novel;" camera (color), Hanania Baer; editor, Anath Lubarsky; art director, Avi Avivi; music, Shem-Tov Levi. Reviewed at the Lev Cinema, Tel Aviv, Oct. 20, 1985. Running time: **91 MINS.**
Effi Avidar . . . . Chaim Topol
Ariela . . . . Galia Topol
Hadara . . . . Efrat Lavie
Amos Rudnik . . . . Ori Levi
Orna . . . . Anath Topol
Jonathan . . . . Nathan Dattner
Levia . . . . Saria Tzuriel

The combination of the top Israeli international film star, in a story by one of the country's best known writers, under the direction of a highly rated stage personality, seems a sound boxoffice bet, but the result falls short of expectations.

Itzhak Ben-Ner adapted one of his short stories, "Dime Novel," also using elements from another of his stories, to fashion a plot that mixes middle-age personal angst (and nostalgia for the past) with highly relevant political aspects which drastically changed the nature of the Israeli regime in 1977.

Stage director and actor Oded Kotler tries his hand here for the first time at film direction, while Chaim Topol has brought both his wife, Galia, and his daughter, Anath, to stand by him in a picture which he has to carry himself most of the way.

Topol plays a highly successful lawyer who, after a cardiac warning, realizes he may have squandered his life in the wrong direction when he left his first wife and all the ideals of youth, which she stood for, in order to marry a neurotic poet and join the rat race for success, money and power. He desperately tries to revive his first love, while at the same time facing the internal moral corruption eating away at his fellow leaders in the Labor movement and facing uncomprehendingly the generation gap separating him from his daughter and her friends.

Trying to convey what is obviously a complex and multifaceted dilemma, Kotler doesn't manage to do much more than mention the problems, without ever getting down to analyzing them.

Topol has no trouble handling the lead. He is a confident actor with strong screen presence, and for the local audience he certainly represents the upright, commendable

moral values once identified with the Labor movement here. However, he is a bit self-assured for someone doubting himself and the sense of his entire life.

His wife, Galia, lacks the subtle qualities that would justify the rekindling of an old fire in her former husband, and his daughter, Anath, is too shaky and aggressive as his on-screen daughter. Miscast is Efrat Lavie as a pale caricature of a poet in pain.

All technical credits are okay but the musical score tends to be repetitive.—*Edna.*

Rosso
(FINNISH-COLOR)

Lübeck, Nov. 2.
A Finnkino release of a Villealfa production with Jörn Donner Prods. and Arthouse. Executive producer, Jaakko Talaskivi. Directed by Mika Kaurismäki. Stars Kari Väänänen, Marti Syrjä. Original story and screenplay, Kaurismäki, Väänänen; camera (Eastmancolor), Timo Salminen; music, Marco Cucinatta; editor, Raija Talvio; Sicilian location management, Angelo Strana; Finnish production management, Heikko Ukkonen; narrator, Walter Benigni. Reviewed as official entry in the 27th Nordic Film Days at the Kammerspiele, Lübeck, West Germany, Nov. 2, 1985. Running time: **80 MINS.**
Rosso . . . . Kari Väänänen
Maria . . . . Leena Harjupatana
Maria's brother . . . . Martti Syrjä
Dumb blond . . . . Mirja Oksanen

"Rosso" is a small-scale feature takeoff on French intellectual thrillers and on Michelangelo Antonioni-type colorful-empty-space-and-enigmatic rhethoric. Helmer and coscripter Mika Kaurismäki is tongue-in-cheek all the way through this brief story about a young Sicilian hitman who is falling down on his job and in a true fix when he is sent to Finland to bump off his former Finnish summer love, Maria. Rosso (Finland's Alain Delon-like Kari Väänänen who speaks credible Italian along with film's narrator, Walter Benigni) arrives in Helsinki only to find Maria gone off to some remote rural area which Rosso now sets out to explore in an old American car along with the girl's halfwit, but enthusiastic, brother.

Film also has the road movie genre within kidding range, while pursuers are killed and banks and stores are robbed to the accompanying soundtrack spouting of quotations from Dante's "Divine Comedy" and blaring of typical Italian village brass band music. The brother, played with fine comedy timing by Martti Syrjä, gets a bullet through his head rather too early on. Maria is seen only in Sicilian flashbacks that contrast nicely with the dullish winter landscapes of Finland's vast Osterbotten district. She is blond as can be although she later gets competition from a girl even blonder and, possibly, dumber, too. As Rosso, Kari Väänänen, who co-scripted, puts in a performance of stoicism tinged with the slightest irony.

"Rosso" looks good and most likely will find a modest niche for itself on the international fest circuit. At home, film has made it to second place on the boxoffice lists. Item has sparkle, speed and high production gloss to reach at least limited theatrical sales abroad. Its English-language subtitling works in fine rhythm with the spoken dialog.

—Kell.

Private Show
(FILIPINO-COLOR)

Chicago, Nov. 16.
A Clock Work Films Intl. release. Produced by William Pascual. Directed by Sixto Kayko. Features entire cast. Screenplay, Ricky Lee; camera (color), Joe Tutanes; sets, Dante Mendoza; sound, Ramon Reyes; editor, Joe Solo; music, Jaime Fabregas. Reviewed at Chicago Film Fest (out-of-competition), Nov. 16, 1985. Running time: 135 MINS.
With: Jaclyn Jose (Myrna), Gino Antonio (Jimmy), Leopoldo Salcedo (Ador).

One of the Filipino features brought in to complement the weeklong celebration of Filipino arts and culture during the Chicago film fest, Sixto Kayko's debut pic "Private Show" exploits to the fullest the country's recent lifting of censorship in regard to sexual mores. Title refers to the live sex acts in major cities, and helmer Kayko plays peekaboo for two hours plus, thereby practically canceling out any good intentions he might have had at the beginning with a rather promising theme.

Myrna takes up the life of a "torera" (the "stud" here is called a "torero") after quitting the nightclubs elsewhere. She's had a child who died tragically in an accident, so she wants to forget by delving into private shows. Her partner, Jimmy, also has been a victim of hard knocks. They gradually warm to each other as human contact is sought in a pit of decadence. The attempt to break out, however, fails due to lack of employment elsewhere, so the finale finds them back where they started, with Myrna in particular now showing definite signs of physical wear-and-tear as a result of getting heavily into drugs.

Thesp performances by Jaclyn Jose and Gino Antonio as torera & torero hold up rather well throughout, even in the more graphic scenes. The same topic, however, was handled better in another recent Filipino pic, "Boatman." —Holl.

Enemy Mine
(COLOR)

Familiar story of friendship between the best of enemies is well-executed in visually arresting space saga.

Hollywood, Dec. 12.
A 20th Century Fox release of a Kings Road Entertainment production. Produced by Stephen Friedman. Executive producer, Stanley O'Toole. Directed by Wolfgang Petersen. Stars Dennis Quaid, Louis Gossett Jr. Screenplay, Edward Khmara, based on a story by Barry Longyear; camera (DeLuxe color, Arriflex Widescreen), Tony Imi; editor & 2d unit director, Hannes Nikel; music, Maurice Jarre; production design, set decoration & matte paintings design, Rolf Zehetbauer; scenic artist, Frieder Thaler; art director, Werner Achmann, Herbert Strabel; Aliens design-special creature makeup, Chris Walas; space dog fights sequences and matte paintings, Industrial Light & Magic; sound, Milan Bor, Christian Schubert; visual effects pervisor, Don Dow; special effects supervisor, Bob MacDonald Jr.; costumes, Monika Bauert; assistant director, Bert Batt; model effects supervisor, Guy Hudson; stunt coordinator, Martin Grace; casting, Mike Fenton, Jane Feinberg, Troy Neighbors. Reviewed at 20th Century Fox, L.A., Dec. 11, 1985. (MPAA Rating: PG-13.) Running time: 108 MINS.
Davidge .... Dennis Quaid
Jeriba, the Drac .... Louis Gossett Jr.
Stubbs .... Brion James
Arnold .... Richard Marcus
Morse .... Carolyn McCormick
Zammis .... Bumper Robinson
Old Drac .... Jim Mapp

"Enemy Mine" is proof once again that there are but a few basic models for films. Regardless of how it's dressed up, most pictures revert to models that have been used over and over again. In the case of "Enemy Mine" it's a friendship story between two disparate personalities carried to extreme lengths. It may be a long way to go to a distant sun system to get to a familiar place, but "Enemy Mine" is largely successful in establishing a satisfying bond. Whether an audience will also go that distance is uncertain.

As a kind of hybrid film, "Enemy Mine" is neither nonstop action for the teen audience nor thoughtful relationship fare for the older crowd. It's a bit of both. Obviously 20th Century Fox, which has stayed with the project through two directors (Richard Loncraine was replaced by Wolfgang Petersen after two weeks of lensing) and some $33,000,000, is hoping to lure both groups. It's a neat trick when it works, but it's always iffy to try to make a film all things for all people.

Difficulty for an older audience is to overcome the antipathy that may exist towards a relationship between an alien Drac and a human. To its credit the screenplay by Edward Khmara manages to find the core of real feelings that makes the story come alive. Sworn enemies, the Drac and the human discover, not their common humanity, but their common universality.

Story is set up by a kind of videogame battle between the Earth forces and the warring Dracs from the distant planet of Dracon. Space pilot Willis Davidge (Dennis Quaid) goes down with a Drac ship and is the only survivor on a desolate planet. His initial response to the half-human, half-reptilian is inbred hatred, distrust and combativeness, all recognizable human triggers.

Hostility soon gives way to a common goal-survival. Davidge and the Drac (Louis Gossett Jr.) peel away their outer layers and reveal two similar beings. It's an anthropomorphic view of life but touching nonetheless.

Appearances form a key part of this emerging friendship. Gossett is unrecognizable, covered with scales, an oval head and a tail. Davidge, too, goes through a metamorphosis in the harsh winter conditions, his long hair and beard giving him the look of a savage.

Gossett has also devised an unusual tone and speech pattern for the Drac and both parties must overcome the language barrier before they can be friends.

Once the strength of the bond is established it must be tested and here the story lags a bit. The ramifications of their friendship are not quite as interesting as it was in the making. This is the part of the film that satisfies the action/adventure requirement and again looks like so many other pictures. Even in space, bad guys sit around and drink, cuss and play cards.

Visually, director Wolfgang Petersen and production designer Rolf Zehetbauer have gone to great lengths to create new images and have at least, partially succeeded. Look of the harsh Fryine IV landscape is actually modeled after the volcanic island of Lanzarote off the west coast of Africa.

Special effects including a space dogfight by Industrial Light & Magic are routine but photography by Tony Imi manages to capture vast panoramas while maintaining the human scale of the story. It is Petersen's accomplishment that he had the restraint to keep this a film more about people than hardware.

—Jagr.

Barbarian Queen
(COLOR)

Adventure cheapie aimed at voyeurs.

A Concorde/Cinema Group release of a Rodeo Prods. production. Produced by Frank Isaac, Alex Sessa. Directed by Hector Olivera. Features entire cast. Screenplay, Howard R. Cohen; camera (Metrocolor; prints by The Film House Group), Rudy Donovan; editor, Sylvia Roberts, Leslie Rosenthal; music, Chris Young, James Horner; sound, Daniel Castle; art director, Julia Bertram; assistant director, Andrew Sargent; stunt coordinators, Arthur Neal, Guy Reed; postproduction supervisor, Deborah Brock. Reviewed at 42d St. Liberty theater, N.Y., Dec. 14, 1985. (MPAA Rating: R.) Running time: 71 MINS.
Amethea .... Lana Clarkson
Estrild .... Katt Shea
Taramis .... Dawn Dunlap
Tinara .... Susana Traverso
Also with: Frank Zagarino, Victor Bo.

From Roger Corman's production and distribution stable comes the Argentine-lensed "Barbarian Queen," a throwback to the cheap skin flicks of the mid-1960s that preceded (and were usurped by) the porno glut. Very minor pic has been in regional release since April.

The extremely well-built Lana Clarkson toplines as Amethea, a blond whose wedding day is disrupted by black-clad bad guys raping her younger sister Taramis (Dawn Dunlap), abducting the groom and either killing or abducting the rest of her village's townsfolk. Amethea teams up with surviving pals Estrild (Katt Shea) and Tinara (Susana Traverso) to trek to the evil tyrant's village and rescue everyone.

Episodic tale of rebels attacking the villain and his henchmen is just an excuse for routine broadsword fights and frequent scenes of female nudity. Sets are crummy and fake-looking, while the special visual effects of previous Corman entries in this genre (fantasies such as "Sorceress" and "The Warrior And The Sorceress") have been discarded.

Concept of female warriors besting male opponents on the battlefield is unconvincing as presented, with the gals more effective as sex objects. They're definitely a good-looking group, particularly Latin beauty Traverso. Emphasis on rape and torture is overdone.—Lor.

The Color Purple
(COLOR)

Overproduced, overly manipulative Steven Spielberg drama is saved by outstanding performances.

Hollywood, Dec. 11.
A Warner Bros. release of an Amblin Entertainment presentation, in association with Quincy Jones. A Guber-Peters Co. production. Produced by Steven Spielberg, Kathleen Kennedy, Frank Marshall, Quincy Jones. Executive producers, Jon Peters, Peter Guber. Directed by Spielberg. Features entire cast. Screenplay by Menno Meyjes, based on the novel by Alice Walker; camera (DeLuxe color), Allen Daviau; editor, Michael Kahn; music, Quincy Jones; production design, J. Michael Riva; set decorator, Linda DeScenna; art director, Robert W. Welch; sound, Willie Burton; costume design, Aggie Guerard Rodgers; assistant director, Pat Kehoe, Richard Alexander Wells; second unit director, Frank Marshall; stunt coordinator, Greg W. Elam; associate producer, Carol Isenberg; casting, Reuben Cannon and Associates. Reviewed at Samuel Goldwyn Theater, Beverly Hills, Calif., Dec. 10, 1985. (MPAA Rating: PG-13.) Running time: 152 MINS.

Albert . . . . .Danny Glover
Celie . . . . .Whoopi Goldberg
Shug Avery . . . . .Margaret Avery
Sofia . . . . .Oprah Winfrey
Harpo . . . . .Willard Pugh
Nettie . . . . .Akosua Busia
Young Celie . . . . .Desreta Jackson
Old Mr. . . . . .Adolph Caesar
Squeak . . . . .Rae Dawn Chong
Miss Millie . . . . .Dana Ivey

There are some great scenes and great performances in "The Color Purple," but it is not a great film. Steven Spielberg's turn at "serious" filmmaking is marred in more than one place by overblown production that threatens to drown in its own emotions. But the characters created in Alice's Walker's novel are so vivid that even this doesn't kill them off and there is still much to applaud (and cry about) here. Box-office outlook is promising without approaching other Spielberg super-hits.

Comparisons to Walker's novel are inevitable and it seems safe to say that those who haven't read the book will be more favorably disposed to the film. It is not that the film need slavishly recreate the book — no film does. It is more a question of whether the film preserves and translates what made the book special and the answer here is yes, and no.

Much of what is successful in the film is from the book. Walker has created truly memorable characters and some very touching scenes. Some of them have made it onto film while other are missing. Overall, the film lacks the depth, variety and richness of the book.

Walker's tale is the story of a black family's growth and flowering over a 40-year period in the south starting around 1909. At the center of everything is Celie, who as a young girl gives birth to two children and is then married into a life of virtual servitude to a man she can refer to only as "Mr." (Danny Glover).

Above all "The Color Purple" is a love story between Celie and her sister, Nettie, from whom she is separated at childhood, and, later in life, the blues singer Shug Avery. It is this love which holds together the extended family and the loosely structured narrative. Unfortunately the script by Menno Meyjes doesn't bind the lives together well enough and the film often feels cluttered with too much going on in too small a space.

Relationship between Celie and Shug as written by Walker is a complex and deeply felt friendship fueled, in part, by a strong sexual attraction. While Spielberg touches on this it remains pretty much in the background.

Shug is a wonderful Bessie Smith-type character who Celie is attracted to because of her pure joy for living. For Celie, her love for Shug is her lifeblood but the film never dares to get under her skin to feel its heat. As a result one of the central relationships of the story is weakened.

As for the other crucial relationship between the sisters, Nettie is basically not heard from for the first half of the film because Mr. is not giving her letters to Celie. The film finally comes alive when Celie stands up for herself at a family dinner and claims the letters and her freedom.

Things also pick up with the reentry of Nettie (Akosua Busia) into the picture. She has spent years as a missionary in Africa where, through a strange twist of 'fate, she has been raising Celie's children. Cross-cutting between Africa and Georgia draws some interesting visual and cultural parallels between the two lives.

Other isolated scenes are striking but they don't pack much emotional wallop until the last half hour when the scales of justice are balanced. Subplot involving Mr.'s son Harpo (Willard Pugh) and his bossy wife Sofia (Oprah Winfrey) are good examples of the struggle for family power playing itself out a generation later.

There are few surprises in the story and Spielberg leans heavily on all the key emotional scenes so that the audience knows what to feel and what's coming. Music by coproducer Quincy Jones reenforces the cues set up by Spielberg, although the score is much more subtle and affecting in the African segments.

Spielberg has smoothed out most of the rough edges giving the film a rather limited emotional range. There are numerous shots of the Georgia landscape dusted with snow and portentous shots of the mailbox waiting for news from Nettie. The emotional notes are familiar, sometimes they ring true, more often they seem manipulated and overstated.

Texture of Southern black life is well drawn, if a bit too perfect and homogenized. J. Michael Riva's period production design looks authentic and Aggie Guerard Rodgers' costumes are lovely but perhaps too numerous. These people seem to be doing a lot better than simply eking out a living.

Saving grace of the film are the performances. As the adult Celie debuting Whoopi Goldberg uses her expressive face and joyous smile to register the character's growth. Equally good is Glover who is a powerful screen presence. He is, however, too likeable to suggest the evilness of his character, but here, even more than in Walker's novel, no one is truly evil.

Other standouts include Oprah Winfrey's burly Sofia and Margaret Avery's spicy Shug Avery. Rae Dawn Chong as Harpo's girlfriend Squeak is one of the casualties of the film with little remaining of her part. She is one of several fringe characters who seem to come and go without much holding them to the story.

Tech credits are outstanding. The film looks great. Allen Daviau's photography is bright and colorful aided by Michael Kahn's snappy editing which is exceptional at melding images together.

Ultimately, "The Color Purple" is not that different from other Spielberg pictures despite the setting. It comes out as a fairy tale of black life in the South where family and friends can live in peace and harmony happily ever after. It is an appealing fantasy, if it were only true. — *Jagr.*

Trouble In Mind
(COLOR)

Stylish, off the wall drama from Alan Rudolph works in fits and starts.

Hollywood, Nov. 20.

An Alive Films release of an Island Alive and Terry Glinwood presentation. Produced by Carolyn Pfeiffer, David Blocker. Executive producer, Cary Brokaw. Directed by Alan Rudolph. Features entire cast. Screenplay, Rudolph; camera (CFI color), Toyomichi Kurita; editor, Tom Walls; music, Mark Isham; songs performed by Marianne Faithfull; production design, Steven Legler; set decoration, K.C. Fox; set design, Don Ferguson; costumes, Tracy Tynan; sound, Richard Portman; assistant director, Bruce Chevillat; casting, Victoria Lee Pearman. Reviewed at MGM/UA screening room, Nov. 15, 1985, Culver City, Calif. (MPAA Rating: R.) Running time: **111 MINS.**
Hawk . . . . .Kris Kristofferson
Coop . . . . .Keith Carradine
Georgia . . . . .Lori Singer
Wanda . . . . .Genevieve Bujold
Solo . . . . .Joe Morton
Hilly Blue . . . . .Divine
Lt. Gunther . . . . .George Kirby
Nate Nathonson . . . . .John Considine

The first release for Alive Films (formerly partnered in Island Alive), "Trouble In Mind" is a stylish urban melodrama instantly recognizable as an Alan Rudolph picture. It is peopled by a strange collection of off-center characters living in a stylish, almost-real location. Consistent with his previous indie efforts, "Trouble In Mind" will find its champions, but it is unlikely to bring in new fans.

"Trouble In Mind" expands the emotional landscape Rudolph established in "Choose Me," taking it outside into a territory that's hard to pin down. One never really knows what's going on in a Rudolph film. It suggests more than it explains. Sometimes it's intriguing and other times it falls flat.

Set in a town known as RainCity, action could be taking place in the 50s, 80s or 90s, so stylized is the production design by Steven Legler and script by Rudolph. What flourishes in the RainCity hothouse are the disconnected emotions of the characters looking for something to attach themselves to.

The good people of RainCity are like a microcosm of the larger world seen through the lens of 40s gangster pictures with several other influences thrown in for good measure. At the core of the film is a not-so-classic romantic triangle involving Hawk (Kris Kristofferson), Georgia (Lori Singer) and her boyfriend, Coop (Keith Carradine).

Hawk blows into town fresh from the slammer. He's an ex-cop who did time for what seems to have been a just murder to avenge a friend. Hawk is kind of a guardian angel for lost souls who somehow always get left out in the cold. Kristofferson is fine at suggesting a hardened exterior with a vulnerable heart.

As he returns to society, such as it is, Hawk's job is to rescue Coop from a life of petty crime and to salvage his relationship with Georgia, although he would rather have her for himself. In RainCity, as in earlier film versions of the same territory, sacrifice is the code of the road.

Center of this emotional landscape is Wanda's cafe, owned and operated by Wanda (Genevieve Bujold), a former lover of Hawk's and the woman for whom he committed the murder. Also on the scene is Solo (Joe Morton) as Coop's eccentric partner in crime and the kingpin of the underworld Hilly Blue, played by Divine in his first male role after winning recognition in drag in a series of John Waters' cult pictures.

Rudolph stirs all the ingredients around — love, crime, friendship, responsibility — and ties them together with a charged score by Mark Isham highlighted by a searing but disorienting version of the title tune by Marianne Faithfull as the film opens.

Even when all the elements don't add up to a cohesive whole, there are few directors who can fill a frame with as much interesting business as Rudolph and here, assisted by cinematographer Toyomichi Kurita, he creates at least a visually tantalizing terrain if somewhat emotionally arid. Shot on location in Seattle, "Trouble In Mind" captures well the look of a paranoid nether world.

Performances on the fringes are often more rewarding then the leads, although Singer looks great as the hippy heroine. Comedian George Kirby as Hawk's ex-boss Lt. Gunther is a real find as is Morton. It is hard to know what to make of Divine in man's clothes, but it is that kind of hit-or-miss mystery on which "Trouble In Mind" is built.—*Jagr.*

Boggy Creek II
(COLOR)

Mild followup to the 1972 regional hit.

A Howco Intl. Pictures release of a Charles B. Pierce Pictures production. Produced and directed by Pierce. Features entire cast. Screenplay, Pierce; camera (Movielab color) & editor, Shirah Kojayan; music, Frank McKelvey; sound, Greg Perdue; narration, Pierce; associate producer, Joy N. Houck Jr. Reviewed at Criterion 6 theater, N.Y., Dec. 14, 1985. (MPAA Rating: PG.) Running time: **91 MINS**.

Prof. Lockhart . . . . Charles B. Pierce
Leslie Ann Walker . . . . Cindy Butler
Tanya . . . . Serene Hedin
Tim Thorn . . . . Chuck Pierce
Crenshaw . . . . Jimmy Clem
Deputy Williams . . . . Rick (Rock) Hildreth
Adult creature . . . . Fabus Griffin
Young creature . . . . Victor Williams

Charles B. Pierce's "Boggy Creek II," made in 1983, finally arrived in New York with the misleading retitle "The Barbaric Beast Of Boggy Creek Part II." Pic is actually a very mild and folksy piece of regional filmmaking in which it is clear that the filmmaker (who doubles as his own leading man) really likes the creatures. Though labeled number 2, pic is actually the third trip to Boggy Creek, since Pierce's 1972 hit "The Legend Of Boggy Creek" was followed in 1977 by a film aimed at the kiddies (and made not by Pierce but by Tom Moore) called "Return To Boggy Creek."

Pierce stars as Bryant Lockhart, a U. of Arkansas professor of anthropology who is pulled away from a football game (where the Razorbacks are beating Tulsa) to investigate reports that the Boggy Creek creature is on the loose again. He quickly rounds up an expedition peopled by student Tim (Chuck Pierce, the director's son) and two pretty girls (Cindy Butler, Serene Hedin).

Quartet travels south to Texarkana to interview folks who've sighted the beast. Camping out, they set up a computerized system of sensors to track the nearly 400-pound creature's movements. Pierce includes fuzzy-focus flashbacks illustrating previous tales of the creature's contacts with humanity. Pic doesn't really pick up steam until the final reel when Jimmy Clem appears in a fine acting turn as a hermit who has captured the creature's offspring which he is holding as bait to attract the parent. Prof. Lockhart lets both creatures go, intoning the film's message that they're part of nature living in harmony and ought to be left alone to roam free.

The creature looks like a man in a gorilla suit and film is painfully short on thrills. This type of filmmaking went out with the wilderness adventures, whose heyday was a decade ago. — *Lor*.

Blastfighter
(ITALIAN-COLOR)

A National Cinematografica/Nuova Dania Cinematografica/Medusa Distribuzione production. Directed by "John Old Jr." (Lamberto Bava). Features entire cast. Screenplay, Max von Ryt, Luca von Ryt; camera (Luciano Vittori color), Lawrence Bannon; editor, Bob Wheeler; music, Andrew Barrymore; song, "Evening Star," composed by Barry, Robin & Maurice Gibb, sung by Tommie Baby; sound, Ralph Luca; art direction, Ray Cliver; assistant director, Michael Saroyan; stunt coordinator, Patrick O'Neil; special effects-weapons, Paul Callard. Reviewed on Vestron Video vidcassette, N.Y., Dec. 10, 1985. (No MPAA Rating.) Running time: **87 MINS**.

Tiger . . . . Michael Sopkiw
Connie . . . . Valerie Blake
Tom . . . . George Eastman
Also with: Mike Miller, Richard Raymond, Patrick O'Neil Jr., Elizabeth Forbes, Carl Savage, Michael Saroyan, George Williams.

"Blastfighter" is a routine action picture, filmed in Georgia in 1983 by Italian filmmakers. Unreleased theatrically, it is now available Stateside in homevideo format.

Yank actor Michael Sopkiw (of "After The Fall Of New York") toplines as Tiger, a cop on the Atlanta police force just released from a lengthy prison term for killing the thug who murdered his wife and partner (but couldn't be proved guilty in court).

Returning to his small hometown in Georgia, Tiger soon runs afoul of the young Good Ole Boys there, who are mistreating animals — they hunt deer and other forest denizens but do not kill them, delivering them seriously wounded to a local Hong Kong-derived merchant who requires live animals to fabricate medicine and aphrodisiacs from their innards. Tiger tries to run the H.K. dude out of town and stop the cruelty to animals, but as a result the heavies kill his pet deer and terrorize him.

Matters deteriorate further when Tiger is hiking in the woods with his grownup daughter and two friends — the locals kill the friends and later shoot down his daughter, precipitating a fight-to-the-death climax. Film's title derives from a high-tech rifle Tiger uses in the final reel, which blasts out fireballs rather than conventional ammunition.

Cast is personable, especially Sopkiw and Valerie Blake as his attractive, feisty daughter, but the crude postsynched dialog stamps this effort as an Italian import rather than an All-American picture. Dumb, inconclusive ending involving a shootout between Sopkiw and Italian thesp George Eastman (duo previously teamed in "After The Fall Of New York") is very disappointing.

Oddest touch here, perhaps a first, is pseudonym used for the director's credit. Lamberto Bava helmed the picture, but is credited as "John Old Jr.;" his late father Mario Bava occasionally used the Anglicized name John Old with the fake moniker apparently handed down.—*Lor*.

Clue
(COLOR)

Funny, camp version of the game, with gimmick of three endings to lure repeat business.

Hollywood, Dec. 11.

A Paramount Pictures release. Executive producers, Jon Peters, Peter Guber, John Landis, George Folsey Jr. Produced by Debra Hill for Guber-Peters Prods. Directed and written by Jonathan Lynn. Story by Landis, Lynn, based on the Parker Brothers board game. Features entire cast. Camera (Metrocolor), Victor J. Kemper; editor, David Bretherton, Richard Haines; music, John Morris; sound, Thomas D. Causey; production design, John Lloyd; costumes, Michael Kaplan; set decorator, Thomas L. Roysden; casting, Jane Jenkins, Janet Hirshenson. Reviewed at Paramount Studios, Dec. 10, 1985. (MPAA Rating: PG.) Running Time: **87, 87 and 86 MINS**. depending upon the version seen.

Mrs. Peacock . . . . Eileen Brennan
Wadsworth . . . . Tim Curry
Mrs. White . . . . Madeline Kahn
Professor Plum . . . . Christopher Lloyd
Mr. Green . . . . Michael McKean
Colonel Mustard . . . . Martin Mull
Miss Scarlet . . . . Lesley Ann Warren
Yvette . . . . Colleen Camp
Mr. Boddy . . . . Lee Ving

"Clue" is campy, high-styled escapism and should prove for adult audiences what the board game has for years been for children — pure fun! In a short 87 minutes that just zip by, the game's one-dimensional card figures like Professor Plum and others become multidimensional personalities with enough wit, neuroses and motives to intrigue even the most adept whodunnit solver. That's what Paramount is counting on. By releasing the film with three endings, they can almost be assured that some "Clue" fans will be back in the audience to see a different solution.

(This reviewer saw all three endings in succession and still hasn't figured out which works best.)

Tim Curry plays the loquacious organizer of the evening's murder game, which takes place in a Gothic hilltop mansion in New England in 1954 during a storm (of course).

He sends six individuals a letter providing the incentive to attend dinner at the mansion and when each arrives, assigns them a pseudonym — Professor Plum, Mr. Green, Mrs. White and so on.

The unlikely assemblage of characters is mostly portrayed by well-known actors and comedians of which Lesley Ann Warren's Miss Scarlett, Martin Mull's Colonel Mustard and Eileen Brennan's Mrs. Peacock performances stand out.

As expected, they all turn out to have something in common — something that gives each of them enough motive to commit murder. It's when the lights go out and the first victim meets his untimely end that the intrigue begins.

Screenwriter Jonathan Lynn has written a clever script utilizing all kinds of rhetorical tricks that haven't been spoken since the early works of Woody Allen. (Most notably "Bananas" and "Love And Death.")

Other than Curry's wordiness, which gets a bit tiresome during the expository parts of the picture, the dialog is almost always funny and at times hilarious. Curry's confusing conversations with Mull should send semanticists reeling.

Terrific performances also are given by relative unknowns: Michael McKean as Mr. Green and Colleen Camp as the French maid, Yvette.

According to Clue aficionados the film is true to the game. That is, the cast of characters live up to their names; the secret passageways are the same and so are the weapons.

It's too bad the picture got a PG rating since children play the Parker Brothers game probably starting as early as eight years old. But then, murder is treated rather lightly here.
—*Brit*.

Murphy's Romance
(COLOR)

Pleasant but uncompelling May/December love story.

Hollywood, Dec. 10.

A Columbia Pictures release. Produced by Laura Ziskin for Martin Ritt/Fogwood Films Ltd. Directed by Martin Ritt. Stars Sally Field, James Garner. Screenplay, Harriet Frank Jr., Irving Ravetch; camera (Panavision, color), William A. Fraker; editor, Sidney Levin; music, Carole King; sound, Jack Finlay; production design, Joel Schiller; assistant director, Jim Van Wyck; costumes, Joe I. Tompkins; art direction, Rick Gentz; casting, Dianne Crittenden, Ilene Starger. Reviewed at Columbia Pictures, Burbank Studios, Dec. 9, 1985. (MPAA rating: R). Running time: **107 MINS**.

Emma Moriarty . . . . Sally Field
Murphy Jones . . . . James Garner
Bobby Jack Moriarty . . . . Brian Kerwin
Jake Moriarty . . . . Corey Haim
Freeman Coverly . . . . Dennis Burkley
Margaret . . . . Georgann Johnson

Director Martin Ritt has just the right touch to keep "Murphy's Romance," a fairly predictable May/December love story, from lapsing into gushy sentimentality of clichés. Unfortunately, this sweet and homey picture which casts two very decent actors (Sally Field and James Garner) in two very decent roles, falls far short of compelling filmmaking. It's nice, family fare that is undeserving of an R rating for one brief scene where two profane words are spoken.

. "Murphy's Romance" reunites Field, Ritt and screenwriters Harriet Frank Jr. and Irving Ravetch, who previously collaborated on the Oscar-winning (for Field) "Norma Rae."

The cumulative quality of their experience shows here with a fine, light-hearted script delivered by solid and believable performances all around. The problem is a lack of either a new or an interesting story.

Field plays a divorced mother who is determined to make a living as a horse trainer on a desolate piece of property on the outskirts of a one-street town in rural Arizona.

On practically her first day in the area, she meets Murphy, a widower who is the town's pharmacist and local good guy.

He takes a liking to her almost immediately, but it isn't much later until her n'er-do-well former husband, Brian Kerwin, rides back into her life expecting instant acceptance from her and their son, 13-year-old Corey Haim.

What unfolds is how the Field, Garner and Kerwin triangle is resolved with Field leaning toward Garner the whole time.

Field does a convincing job of playing a good and caring mother who is also, perhaps, too good to her charming and irresponsible ex-husband.

Garner also is sincere as the love interest who's close to twice Field's age — playing the part without trying to act or look any younger than his 57 years.

Brian Kerwin is the surprise find following tv, legit and minor film experience.

Here, he plays a terrific, affable rake in a performance that is enhanced by his blond, All-American good looks.

"Murphy's Romance" represents the first film scoring effort of master songwriter, Carole King, who also wrote the title song. The music is fitting, but not memorable.

Production design by Joel Schiller deserves a special note. The picture has an authentic bucolic feel throughout.—Brit.

Mitt liv som hund
(My Life As A Dog)
(SWEDISH-COLOR)

Malmö, Dec. 12.
An SF (Svensk Filmindustri) release of SF with AB Filmteknik production. Executive producer, Waldemar Bergendahl. Directed by Lasse Hallström. Screenplay, Hallström, Brasse Brännström, Pelle Berglund and Reidar Jönsson, loosely based on Jönsson's novel; camera (Fujicolor), Jörgen Persson, Rolf Lindström; sound, Eddie Axberg; costumes, Inger Pehrsson, Susanne Falck; production design, Lasse Westfelt; editor, Susanne Linnman, Christer Furubrand; music, Björn Isfält; production management, Ann Collenberg, Erik Spangenberg. Reviewed at the Metropol, Malmö, Sweden, Dec. 12, 1985. Running time: **100 MINS.**
Ingemar Johansson . . . . .Anton Glanzelius
His mother . . . . .Anki Liden
His uncle . . . . .Tomas von Brömssen
His brother . . . . .Manfred Serner
Saga, the boy-girl . . . . .Melinda Kinnaman
Berit, the artist's
    model . . . . .Ing-Marie Carlsson
Ulla .Kicki Rundgren
The artist . . . . .Lennart Hjulström
Old man Sandberg . . . . .Leif Ericsson
Mrs. Sandberg . . . . .Christina Carlwind
    Also with: Ralph Carlsson, Didrik Gustavsson, Vivi Johansson, Jan-Philip Hollström, Arnold Alfredsson, Fritz Elofsson, Per Ottosson, Johanna Udehn, Susanna Wetterholm.

The skill and artistry of recent Swedish cinema is evident in helmer Lasse Hallström's fifth feature effort in 10 years, "My Life As A Dog," an exquisite look at childhood.

Based loosely on Reidar Jönsson's 1983 novel about a rural-provincial 12-year-old equivalent of J.D. Salinger's Holden Caulfield, Hallström, a script collaborator, obviously put a lot of personal recollections into his telling of Ingemar Johansson, who has a hard time adjusting to the atmosphere of his beloved mother's house. She is bedridden with a terminal illness, but also given to temper tantrums alternating with a refuge behind heavy literary tomes. Ingemar tries his level best to control his mischievous pranks and high spirits.

To secure the mother her peace and quiet, the boy is sent away to some relatives in a rural community near the famous Boda glass-works. When his mother eventually dies, Ingemar finds elbow-room for his mischief when settling permanently with his soccer-playing, glassblower uncle, an amiable prankster himself, in a cozily tolerant household of no-nonsense love and happiness. The year of the action is 1959, when the boy's countryman-namesake won over Floyd Patterson in the world boxing champion fight, and little Ingemar, literally and in other ways, has some fighting of his own to do before he comes out the winner over his haunting memories of a dead mother and a dog left behind.

Actually, getting down on his knees to bark and to feign barking turns out to be the boy's best means of getting around various moments of crisis. Otherwise, he is endowed with a charm so obvious that nobody can quite help loving him. As played by amateur Anton Glanzelius, dark-haired, slant-eyed and with a mouth of a multitude of expressions, there is nothing slick or cute about this Ingemar as there is nothing maudlin nor prearranged about the whole film. Tomas von Brömssen as the curly-haired, blond uncle is a marvel of subdued humor and strength, and all supporting players seem caught in mid-action of real life.

Even though "My Life As A Dog" is obviously anecdotal, it has a smoothly moving narrative flow. Executive producer Waldemar Bergendahl, a veteran of his trade, has filled the big screen with every value of sight and sound a fair-sized budget would allow. The only value not on display on this film's sleeve is its nostalgia. —Kell.

Revolution
(BRITISH-NORWEGIAN-COLOR)

A Warner Bros. release of a Goldcrest (U.K.) and Viking (Norway) coproduction. Produced by Irwin Winkler. Executive producer, Chris Burt. Directed by Hugh Hudson. Stars Al Pacino. Screenplay, Robert Dillon; camera (System 35 Widescreen, Rank color, Technicolor), Bernard Lutic; editor, Stuart Baird; music, John Corigliano; sound (Dolby), David Crozier; production design, Assheton Gorton; art director, Malcolm Middleton, John Bunker; set decorator, Ann Mollo; stunt coordinator, Eddie Stacey; costumes, John Mollo; production manager, David Barron; assistant director, Derek Cracknell; special effects supervisor, Alan Whibley; casting, Noel Davis. Reviewed at Warner Bros. screening room, Burbank, Calif., Dec. 12, 1985. (MPAA Rating: PG.) Running time: **125 MINS.**
Tom Dobb .Al Pacino
Sergeant Major Peasy . .Donald Sutherland
Daisy McConnahay . . . . . .Nastassja Kinski
Mrs. McConnahay . . . . . . .Joan Plowright
Mr. McConnahay . . . . .Dave King
Sergeant Jones . . . . .Steven Berkoff
Corty . . . . .John Wells
Liberty Women . . . . .Annie Lennox
Ned Dobb . . . . .Dexter Fletcher
Young Ned . . . . .Sid Owen
Lord Hampton . . . . .Richard O'Brien
Betsy . . . . .Felicity Dean

Watching "Revolution" is a little like visiting a museum — it looks good without really being alive. The film doesn't tell a story so much as it uses characters to illustrate what the American Revolution has come to mean. Despite attempting to reduce big events to personal details, "Revolution" rarely works on a human scale. Victory at the boxoffice seems unlikely.

The American Revolution has been a subject basically ignored by Hollywood, even in the bicentennial year, and apparently with good reason. Neither D.W. Griffith's "America" in 1924, Disney's "Johnny Tremaine" 30 years later nor the film version of the stage play "1776" in 1972 have made a dent at the boxoffice. The new patriotism notwithstanding, there is little reason to think filmgoers will welcome this "Revolution."

Major miscalculation by all concerned was the contemporary reading given to characters in order to interest an audience. Decision to tell the story through the lives of ordinary people rather than major historical figures could have worked but backfires. In Robert Dillon's script, people become walking symbols mouthing positions and ideals that only could have been taken years later.

Also with an eye towards a contemporary view of the revolution, director Hugh Hudson and Dillon have made sure to include representation from all minority groups. Blacks, Jews and women all have their democratic place in this revolution. Maybe they did, but it's all too neat here.

Street action, too, has echoes of the 1960s and costumes and heady atmosphere in the streets of old New York seem vaguely reminiscent of the youth revolution.

While intimate story of Tom Dobb (Al Pacino) and his son Ned (Dexter Fletcher, Sid Owen as young Ned) and Tom's love for renegade aristocrat Daisy McConnahay (Nastassja Kinski) is full of holes, the larger canvas is staged beautifully and realized, due in good part to Assheton Gorton's production design.

Battle scenes especially are stirring as rows of British troops line up in their red coats and march in unison against an outmanned Colonial makeshift army. Soldiers drop like flies along the way as little drummer boys keep time.

Unfortunately, against this well-drawn background the small story that is meant to serve as a way into the drama for viewers looks too much like an historical reenactment. As the spirited and independent trapper Dobb, Al Pacino seems to be battling his role. His speech pattern, something of a coarse mumble, sounds like a pre-Brooklyn Brooklyn accent.

As a character, Dobb is more of a device than a person. He is a comment on the revolution rather than a person who is inside of it. Result is a kind of two-dimensionality which gives a false core to even the most authentically staged material.

Case in point is a scene where Ned is having his feet cauterized by the good Indians. What should have been a key dramatic moment is lessened by Pacino's speech about how they will find the freedom they seek. Even so, the relationship between father and son is considerably more effective than the love between Kinski and Pacino.

For starters the audience is asked to accept Kinski as an exemplary revolutionary when she bolts out of the family carriage to join the people on the street. What the origins or underpinnings of her convictions are remain a mystery. She just seems to be caught up in the emotion of it all and breaks down crying at least three times.

In World War II films, a soldier often would go into battle with the vague image of a woman becoming his ideal. This, however, is not the connection the filmmakers are seeking here, although there is little more substance to it.

Performances fail to elevate the material with only Pacino and Fletcher and Owen as Ned giving their characters a personal touch. Donald Sutherland is wasted and distant as an English officer, partially because it is nearly impossible to understand what he's saying through his thick brogue. When the dialog is clear, script is full of clinkers.

Music by John Corigliano is flavorful, but not enough to validate what is going on in front of it. For one brief moment at the end of the film, as Catherine Kenny sings a mournful period-flavored folk song, "Revolution" finally captures the turbulent emotions of a nation being born and film becomes what it should have been all along. —Jagr.

O Tempo dos Leopardos
(The Time Of Leopards)
(MOZAMBICAN-YUGOSLAV-COLOR)

Rio de Janeiro, Nov. 25.
Produced by Instituto Nacional de Cinema Mozambique and Avala Films Yugoslavia. Directed by Zdravko Velimirovic. Screenplay, Luis Patriquim, Branimir Scepanovic, Velimirovic; camera (color), Dusko Ninkov; music, Kornelije Kovac. Reviewed at Rio Film Festival (competition), Nov. 23, 1985. Running time: 95 MINS.
With: Santos Mulungo, Ana Mazuse, Marcelino Alves, Simiao Mazuse, Armando Loja.

This coproduction handles Mozambique's struggle for independence in a manner far too reminiscent of the partisan films Yugoslavia at one time churned out by the dozen. The action takes place in 1971 and deals with Pedro's (Santos Mulungo) band of guerrillas and Portuguese efforts to capture him, at which they finally succeed. When his men take the barracks of the commando troops that hold him, it is too late, for Pedro has been killed.

Cast of Mozambican actors is rather uneven, but Mulungo gives credibility to Pedro, in spite of a screenplay that at times makes him look too good to be true. There is a tendency toward oversimplification and the dialog tends to become stilted at times. Direction, cinematography and music, plus two of the screenwriters, are Yugoslav and, at best, routine. —Amig.

She
(ITALIAN-COLOR)

An American National Enterprises presentation, presented by Eduard Sarlui, of a Royal Film production. Executive producers, Eduard Sarlui, Helen Sarlui. Produced by Renato Dandi. Directed by Avi Nesher. Stars Sandahl Bergman. Screenplay, Nesher, inspired by the novel by H. Rider Haggard; camera (Telecolor), Sandro Mancori; editor-sound design (Dolby stereo), Nicholas Wentworth; music, Rick Wakeman; additional music, Justin Hayward, Bastard, Motorhead; sound, Gaetano Testa; art direction, Umberto Turco, Ennio Michettoni; production manager, Annabella Andreoli; stunt coordinator, Sergio Mioni; costume design, Ivana Massetti; special effects, Armando Grilli; associate producers, Michael-John Biber, Sue Cameron. Reviewed on Cinemax, N.Y., Dec. 11, 1985. (No MPAA Rating.) Running time: 106 MINS.
She	Sandahl Bergman
Tom	David Goss
Shanda	Quin Kessler
Dick	Harrison Muller

Also with: Elena Wiedermann (Hari), Gordon Mitchell (Hector), Laurie Sherman (Taphir), Andrew McLeay (Tark), Cyrus Elias (Kram), David Brandon (Pretty Boy), Susan Adler (Pretty Girl), Gregory Snegoff (Godan), Mary D'Antin (Eva), Mario Pedone (Rudolph), Donald Hodson (Rabel), Maria Quasimodo (Moona), David Traxlor (Xenon).

Israeli filmmaker Avi Nesher must have been in a strange mood when he made the latest, very loose remake of "She," lensed in Italy in 1982 and theatrically unreleased. Pic surfaced recently on paycable service Cinemax, only mildly embarrassing those involved.

Incoherent, episodic narrative has athletic Sandahl Bergman as She,

1917 Version
(B&W)

A William Fox Film Corp. release. Directed by Kenean Buel. Screenplay, Mary Murillo, adapted from Sir H. Rider Haggard's novel; camera (b&w), Frank Kugler. Reviewed in N.Y., week of April 27, 1917.
Ayesha (She)	Valeska Suratt
Leo	Ben L. Taggart
Ustane	Miriam Fouche
Billall	Wigney Percyval
Holly	Tom Burrough
Job	Martin Reagan

1926 Version
(BRITISH-B&W)

Lee-Bradford productions, featuring Betty Blythe. Directed by Leander Cordovo. Adapted from novel of same title by Sir Rider Haggard with captions written by author. At Tivoli, N.Y. as half double bill. One day, July 7, 1926. Running time: 64 MINS.

1935 Version
(B&W)

RKO Radio production and release. Features Helen Cahagan, Randolph Scott, Helen Mack, Nigel Bruce. Directed by Irving Pichel and Lansing Holden. From Rider Haggard's novel; adapted by Ruth Rose; additional dialog, Dudley Nichols; camera, J. Roy Hunt; effects, Vernon Walker; music, Max Steiner; dance director, Benjamin Zemach. Merian C. Cooper production. At Radio City Music Hall week July 25, 1935. Running time: 90 MINS.
She	Helen Gahagan
Leo Vincey	Randolph Scott
Tanya Dugmore	Helen Mack
Holly	Nigel Bruce
Prime Minister	Gustav von Seyffertitz

1965 Version
(BRITISH-COLOR)

Metro-Goldwyn-Mayer release of Seven Arts Hammer (Michael Carreras) production. Stars Ursula Andress; features rest of cast. Directed by Robert Day. Screenplay, David T. Chantler, based on novel by H. Rider Haggard; camera (C'Scope-Metrocolor), Harry Waxman; supervising editor, James Needs; editor, Eric Boyd-Perkins; art direction, Robert Jones; music, James Bernard; sound, Claude Hitchcock; special effects, Bowie Films Ltd.; asst. director, Bruce Sharman. Reviewed at Metro studio, Hollywood, April 7, 1965. Running time: 104 MINS.
Ayesha	Ursula Andress
Major Holly	Peter Cushing
Job	Bernard Cribbins
Leo Vincey	John Richardson
Ustane	Rosenda Monteros
Billall	Christopher Lee
Haurneid	Andre Morell

queen of an adoring cult, the Urech, 23 years after an unspecified holocaust. Various other competing gods and leaders coexist, notably, Godan (Gregory Snegoff), who can make people he disagrees with levitate by staring at them with green-glowing eyes; Hector (Gordon Mitchell), ruler of the Norks, a gladiatorial bunch; and disfigured mutants led by Kram (Cyrus Elias), whose arms fall off if you tug on them.

With her trusty Amazonian aide Shanda (Quin Kessler), She has random adventurers wandering around with two ne'er-do-wells, Tom (David Goss) and Dick (Harrison Muller). The guys are trying to find Tom's pretty sister Hari (Elena Wiedermann), who was kidnapped in the opening reel by Hector.

With an unworkable, pointless script, Nesher stresses instead funny-looking costumes and cheap sets, generally failed black humor, outbursts of violence and dumb jokes (e.g., Tom, Dick & Hari arrive at film's start at a little town labeled "Heaven's Gate"). Resemblance to H. Rider Haggard's novel "She" is quite remote, with Bergman skinny-dipping in a hot springs bathtub to be rejuvenated, rather than passing through the memorable Eternal Fire of previous screen versions.

Special effects are minimized and acting is generally poor. Bergman and Kessler are physically well-cast but done in by the script. Best scene has David Traxlor as a nutty comedian who does Groucho Marx, Jimmy Cagney and Popeye impressions while guarding a bridge — soon there are 10 of him on screen since he clones himself every time a violent passerby hacks off one of his limbs.

Rick Wakeman contributes a very energetic, successfully distracting heavy metal music score, which includes songs sung by Justin Hayward and Maggie Bell. Ironically, Hayward's romantic ballad "Eternal Woman" has more plot material relevant to Haggard's saga in its lyrics than does Nesher's script. The filmmaker even leaves out the tagline "She who must be obeyed."

For the record, the last outing of the oft-filmed (at least nine times) character was in a 1968 Hammer sequel "The Vengeance Of She," toplining Czech actress Olinka Berova. —Lor.

Se Infiel y no Mires con Quien
(Be Unfaithful And Don't Be Concerned With Whom)
(SPANISH-COLOR)

Rio de Janeiro, Nov. 29.
A Cia. Iberoamericana de TV production. Executive producer, Andrés Vincente Gómez. Written and directed by Fernando Trueba, based on novel "Move Over Mrs. Markham" by Ray Cooney and John Chapman. Camera (Eastmancolor), Juan Amorós; editor, Carmen Frias; production designer, Gerarde

Vera; sets, Josep Rossell; music, Angel Muñoz-Alonso; sound, Bernard Orthion. Reviewed at Rio Film Festival (competition), Nov. 27, 1985. Running time: **90 MINS.**
Rosa ....Ana Belén
Carmen ....Carmen Maura
Fernando ....Antonio Resines
Also with: Santiago Ramos, Verónica Forqué, Guillermo Montesinos, Bibi Andersen, Chus Lampreave, Pirri.

A comedy of manners, this pic provides an occasional droll moment, but is more suited to the legit stage than film. Thesps try hard to bring the proper histrionic tone to the silly goings-on (about a jealous husband and multiple misunderstandings and martial mixups), but the bubbly original here tastes like stale champagne.

The silly, talky bedroom scenes mostly are fatiguing instead of funny as the two partners of a publishing house on the skids and their wives get entangled with a conservative authoress of children's books, a hysterical secretary, an undersized friend, a prostitute and several other characters who trip in and out of the scenes, only rarely providing a laugh. —Besa.

Baton Rouge
(FRENCH-COLOR)

Paris, Dec. 5.

A Films du Sémaphore release of a Lyric International/TF 1 Films coproduction. Produced by Hubert Balsan and Jean-Pierre Mahot. Directed by Rachid Bouchareb. Screenplay, Bouchareb, Jean-Pierre Ronssin; camera (color), Jimmy Glasberg (France) and Pierre Dupouey (U.S.); art director, Jean-Pascal Chalard; editor, Guy Lecorne; sound, Thierry Sabatier; original music, John Faure. Reviewed at the Publicis screening room, Paris, Dec. 4, 1985. Running time: **85 MINS.**
Abadenour Colbert .... Pierre-Loup Rajot
Karim Brahimi .... Hammou Graia
Alain Lefebvre "Mozart" .. Jacques Penot
Bruno .... Frédéric Wizmane
Victoria Paine .... Elaine Foster
Becky .... Alexandra Steinbaum
Mr. Temporary .... Romain Bouteille
Karim's father .... Larbi Zekal
Social worker .... Katia Tchenko

A breezy, genial first feature by Rachid Bouchareb, who has made some shorts and has worked in television, "Baton Rouge" describes the ironic adventures of three young unemployed Parisians who set out to find their American Dream. A sort of contemporary fairy tale, Bouchareb's tale is not so fanciful as it might seem: its characters are based on real-life models who returned from a sojourn in the U.S. to start up a successful hamburger restaurant in the suburbs of Paris.

Jacques Penot, Pierre-Loup Rajot and Hammou Graia are three buddies with little to dream about other than escaping to America where, naturally, they will certainly fulfill their destinies.

After a failed attempt to stow away on a New York-bound plane while working at the Paris airport, the trio hit the jackpot during sani-

tation chores at an international organization, where they intercept a call from a travel agency and book themselves onto a plane for the U.S. (first-class).

They do a flash tour of Gotham, pay a visit to the grass roots family whose daughter Rajot has met in Paris, and at last hit the road for their set destination: Baton Rouge.

Only Penot, a lover of jazz and blues who has brought his tenor saxophone along, finds his lot when he falls for a beautiful young black singer in a Louisiana nightclub, and later returns to New York with her.

Rajot and Graia are nabbed on a job by immigration officers, jailed, and deported.

Back home, and dejected to be there, the two come to realize their experiences stateside were not as futile as they seem. While sitting in front of the tv watching an old Fernandel comedy, "Ali Baba And The 40 Thieves," they hit upon the scheme that with 40 partners, each scraping together an equal investment, they can start and run a hamburger joint, profiting from the knowledge they've picked up working in Southern fast food chains.

Bouchareb's script (coauthored by Jean-Pierre Ronssin) and brisk direction manage a nice mixture of naiveté and wisdom that carries the tale over the potholes of the road movie cliché. Though this is his first feature, the helmer (like one of his personages, he is of Algerian emigré origins) also displays a keen sense of ellipse and storytelling economy.

Rajot, Penot and Graia are perfect as the footloose trio, bringing winning personality, humor and warmth along on their travels. Elaine Foster, a lovely blues singer who has an act with her two sisters, has sweetness and talent in the sketchy role of the warbler with whom Penot links up.

Bouchareb had the good idea of using two different lensers for the French and Stateside scenes (Jimmy Glasberg and Pierre Dupouey), and both do fine work. Other credits are smart. —Len.

L'Effrontée
(The Hussy)
(FRENCH-COLOR)

Paris, Dec. 9.

A UGC release of an Oliane Prods./Films A2/Téléma/Monthyon coproduction, with the participation of the C.N.C. Produced by Marie-Laure Reyre. Directed by Claude Miller. Screenplay, Miller, Luc Béraud, Bernard Stora, Annie Miller; camera (color), Dominique Chapuis; art director, Jean-Pierre Kohut-Svelko; editor, Albert Jurgenson; sound, Gérard Lamps; original music, Alain Jomy; plus Mendelssohn, Mozart, Beethoven and the song "Sara' Perche'ti Amo" by D. Farina, E. Ghinazzi and D. Pace, perrformed by Ricchi & Poveri; production manager, Armand Barbault. Reviewed at the UGC screening room, Neuilly,

Dec. 6, 1985. Running time: **96 MINS.**
Charlotte .... Charlotte Gainsbourg
Léone .... Bernadette Lafont
Sam (Fruit of the Loom)Jean-Claude Brialy
Antonie .... Raoul Billery
Clara Bauman .... Clothilde Baudon
Jean .... Jean-Philippe Ecoffey
Luly .... Julie Glenn

Director Claude Miller, who has shown skillful eclecticism and growing technical prowess in the four films he has made in the past 10 years, returns in his new venture to the quietly observant manner of his debut feature "La Meilleur Façon de Marcher" (The Best Way).

"L'Effrontée," which the helmer scripted with his wife Annie, writer-director Luc Béraud, and Bernard Stora, is a psychologically acute study of adolescent growing pains and juvenile admiration and jealousy. In addition to the understanding script and fluent direction, film has one of the best child performances to be seen anywhere in years.

Charlotte Gainsbourg is the memorable lead, a plain gangly 13-year-old, blindly revolting against her drab environment in a lakeside provincial French town during a summer vacation. Daughter of actress Jane Birkin and singer Serge Gainsbourg, (from whom she has inherited her mom's gawkiness and her dad's homely looks), she is vividly on screen for every major sequence, translating her character's naiveté, lack of confidence and rebellion with fierce, poignant immediacy.

Gainsbourg, who lives with her vulgar brother, preoccupied father (delicately etched by Raoul Billery) and adoptive mother (Bernadette Lafont, in one of her best recent performances) sees escape from her surroundings when she strikes up an awed friendship with a visiting child prodigy pianist her own age (Clothilde Baudon), who is to give a classical recital in town.

Latter casually flatters the diffident Gainsbourg by telling her she'd love to take her on as her impressario, even though she has Jean-Claude Brialy, a former pop manager, who now lives the easy life as Bauman's agent. Gainsbourg naively takes the offer to heart, to the point of preparing her bag to leave the pianist right after her concert.

At the same time, she experiences her first vague sexual attraction to a young merchant seaman (Jean-Philippe Ecoffey), who is holding down a temporary job in a local metal shop. Gainsbourg makes herself out to be older than she is, and Ecoffey clumsily and unsuccessfuly tries to seduce her.

Gainsbourg herself is idolized by her sickly, clinging seven-year-old neighbor (Julie Glenn, daughter of lenser Pierre-William Glenn, who almost steals some scenes from Gainsbourg), who cannot accept the

idea of her friend leaving and nearly wrecks Baudon's concert when she wails her protest in the middle of the show.

Miller again proves his ability as a sensitive director of actors, both adult and adolescent, and his technical fluency in recreating a lethargic, sensuous seasonal ambience in a town divided into the chic residential lakeside quarter (where Baudon lodges) and the working class sector from which Gainsbourg wants to flee. Use of music — juxtaposing the classical pieces associated with the child pianist, and the summertime pop hit — also adds texture to this pained depiction of juvenile crisis.

Tech credits are firstrate down the line. —Len.

Sword Of Heaven
(COLOR)

Stupid martial arts actioner, aimed at the homevideo trade.

A Trans World Entertainment release of a Sword of Heaven Prods. production. Produced by Joseph J. Randazzo; coproducer, Britt Lomond. Directed by Byron Meyers. Features entire cast. Screenplay, James Bruner, Lomond, William P. O'Hagan, Randazzo; camera (Deluxe color), Gil Hubbs; editor, Warren Chadwick; music, Christopher L. Stone; sound, Charles King 3d; production manager, Terry Spazek; stunt coordinator, Jeff Halberstad; fight director, Lomond, martial arts coordinator, Tadashi Yamashita; associate producer, Don Wilkerson; casting, Crystal Nadine Shaw. Reviewed at UA Twin 2 theater, N.Y., Dec. 21, 1985. (MPAA Rating: R.) Running time: **85 MINS.**
Tadashi .... Tadashi Yamashita
Dirk .... Mel Novak
Patrick .... Gerry Gibson
Cain .... Joe Randazzo
Satoko .... Mika
Cal .... Wynston A. Jones
Also with: Bill (Superfoot) Wallace, Karen Lee Shepherd, Venus Jones.

"Sword Of Heaven" is an idiotic action picture that attempts to mix the martial arts ingredients with a touch of fantasy and a lot of B-movie clichés. California-lensed offering is being self-distributed theatrically by homevideo indie TWE, with its obvious best market being in homevideo stores.

Tadashi Yamashita toplines as Tadashi, a Japanese cop on vacation in California, where he lends his martial arts expertise to Irish pal Patrick (Gerry Gibson) of the L.A.P.D. Patrick is investigating the murders of millionaires who have been subjected to extortion threats, masterminded by fellow cop Cal (Wynston A. Jones). Cal is using the money to equip a paramilitary force to fight crime, led by martial arts whiz Dirk (Mel Novak).

An extraneous fantasy element is injected into this crime format, as Tadashi helps a pretty prostitute Satoko (played by Mika) retrieve a magical glowing sword, forged 400 years ago by Zen priests from a meteorite to fight the forces of evil. The sword has been in her family's care, but is now possessed by Cal and Dirk. Other major protagonist is Satoko's pimp Cain (hammily overplayed by Joe Randazzo).

This nonsensical storyline, which relies heavily on coincidences, is an excuse for okay chase sequences, dull dialog and rather flat martial arts fights (including a minor final reel appearance by champ Bill (Superfoot) Wallace). The only saving humor occurs when Tadashi goes undercover made up most unconvincingly as a woman, and then has to spend 10 minutes of kicking bad guys while wearing a red dress. An extremely tasteless joke attempt designed to offend Catholics should have been edited out.

Yamashita is okay physically, but is far more convincing when cast as a villain than as a tough good guy. The glowing sword special effect is inconsistently applied, appearing in only some shots. —*Lor.*

Private Resort
(COLOR)

Sex comedy formula is worn out.

A Tri-Star Pictures release from Tri-Star/Delphi III Prods. A Unity Pictures production. Produced by R. Ben Efraim, Don Enright. Directed by George Bowers. Features entire cast. Screenplay, Gordon Mitchell, from story by Ken Segall & Alan Wenkus, Mitchell; camera (Metrocolor), Adam Greenberg; editor, Sam Pollard; songs, Bill Wray, others; sound, John Stein, James Thornton; production manager, Russell Vreeland; assistant director, Ernest Johnson; production design, Michael Corenblith; set decoration, Gayle Simon; stunt coordinator, Gary Jensen; casting, Elizabeth Leustig. Reviewed on RCA/Columbia Pictures Home Video vidcassette, N.Y., Dec. 20, 1985. (MPAA Rating: R.) Running time: **82 MINS.**
Ben . . . . Rob Morrow
Jack Marshall . . . . Johnny Depp
Patti . . . . Emily Longstreth
Dana . . . . Karyn O'Bryan
The maestro . . . . Hector Elizondo
Amanda Rawlings . . . . Dody Goodman
Bobby Sue . . . . Leslie Easterbrook
   Also with: Tony Azito, Andrew Clay, Hilary Shapiro, Michael Bowen, Greg Wynne, Ron House, Susan Mechsner, Lisa London, Nora Gaye.

The third in a loose series of sex comedies from producer R. Ben Efraim (preceded by "Private Lessons" and "Private School"), "Private Resort" is an example of going to the well once too often. Formula of nubile women on display, teen antics and rock music is worn out, and Tri-Star elected to give the picture only a token theatrical release last May, ahead of its current homevideo release.

Episodic nonstory concerns two young guys (Rob Morrow, Johnny Depp) on the prowl at an expensive resort (filmed partly in Miami) peopled almost exclusively with beauti-

ful young women. Exceptions, for mainly embarrassing comic relief, include Hector Elizondo, fitted with a wig (and running gags which involve his hairdo) and playing a jewel thief, and Dody Goodman, miscast as an aristocratic type whose diamond necklace is Elizondo's target.

Depp is doing his thinking with another part of his anatomy than his brain, trying to hop in the sack with every girl in sight, including the genre's inevitable older woman, statuesque Leslie Easterbrook. He gets his buddy Morrow into constant trouble, including giving Elizondo a drastic haircut and, also inevitably, dressing in drag to escape from the understandably angry Elizondo.

The slapstick here is old hat and overdone. What's left is an old-fashioned display of female flesh (mainly in bikinis but with some nudity) that in these porno-glutted times is no longer enough to attract an audience. Cast tries hard in a losing cause. — *Lor.*

Pelle Svanslös i Amerikatt
(Peter No-Tail In Americat)
(SWEDISH-ANIMATED-COLOR)

Malmö, Dec. 18.
A Sandrews release (Sweden) of Farago Film & Team Film for the Swedish Film Institute, Sandrews, Semic International, Thorn EMI Video and Filmhuset. Executive producers, Katinka Farago, Bengt Forslund. Designed and directed by Stig Lasseby and Jan Gissberg. Based on Gösta Knutsson's novelettes. Screenplay, Leif Krantz; camera (color), Eberhard Fehmers, others; paintings, Ruth Lasseby, Orvar Ottosson; animation, Jonny Eriksson and Swedish staff, Vaclav Polak and staff of Art Centrum, Prague, Czechoslovakia; music, Berndt Egerblahd; voices: Erik Lindgren (Peter), Ewa Fröhling (Maya Creamnose), Ernst-Hugo Järegard (Hobo Mans), Carl Billquist (Bill), Björn Gustafsson (Bull), Stellan Skarsgard (Peter Swanson). Reviewed at Sandrews 1-2-3, Malmö, Sweden, Dec. 18, 1985. Running time: **83 MINS.**

Stig Lasseby and Jan Gissberg's second animated cartoon feature based on Gösta Knutsson's tiny tots novelettes has, per its title, "Peter No-Tail In Americat," that friendly little petit-burgeois cat dreaming himself away from the cruel onslaughts and merciless kidding (Peter really is without that proudest of feline's extremities, a tail) of villainous Hobo Mans. While asleep at home in Uppsala, where he is a recent university graduate wearing a freshman hat and a green bow tie, he sees himself getting the better of his bully during little set pieces of American West dramatic lore. When he wakes up again, he has to prove to himself, and to his girlfriend Maya Creamnose, that he really can outwit Hobo Mans. During a forest trip, where he is trapped again and again by Mans and latter's young comedian-twin sidekicks (cats also, everybody is a cat in this

film), Peter finally triumphs and even adds a halo to his head by rescuing Mans from the fate of being boiled alive for a bearcat's supper.

Chance more than brains gets Peter out of his scrapes. In film's string of episodes, nary any dramatic suspense is built. The animation technique is rather simplistic. No subsidiary character is developed as more than a vague sketch. The villain and his small henchmen are strictly out of Disney. So are the little bits of theater of cruelty, but again the sketching is too vague to be likely to make much of a scare impression on anyone regardless of age group.

Overall feel of "Peter No-Tail In Americat" is sweetness with little dashes of Disneyesque grit and gumption added with the most extreme care. Film's predecessor sold well in many territories, and so may this one even if only an audience of 3 to 7 year olds with patient parents is likely to enjoy the mild-to-bland fun. A running time of 83 minutes seems overlong for tots to stay put for one program in a cinema seat, but items is obviously fashioned for eventual serialization into television kiddie programming. Dialog, in the original version spoken by a cast of top-notch Swedish actors, is kept simple, facilitating dubbing into other languages — or tuning down for voice-over narration. — *Kell.*

Astérix et la Surprise de César
(Asterix vs. Caesar)
(FRENCH-ANIMATED-COLOR)

Paris, Dec. 13.
A Gaumont release of a Gaumont/Dargaud/Prods. René Goscinny/Gutenberghus coproduction. Produced by Yannick Piel. Directed by Paul and Gaëtan Brizzi. Screenplay, Pierre Tchernia, adapted from the cartoon albums, "Astérix Legionnaire" and "Astérix Gladiateur," by René Goscinny and Alberto Uderzo (Dargaud Press); music, Vladimir Cosma; storyboard and layouts, Jack Stokes; art director, Michel Guérin; special effects, Keith Ingham; camera, Philippe Lainé; editor, Robert and Monique Isnardon; production manager, Philippe Grimond; Astérix theme song performed by Plastic Bertrand. Reviewed at the Gaumont Ambassade theater, Paris, Dec. 12, 1985. Running time: **76 MINS.**
   Voices: Roger Carel (Astérix), Pierre Tornade (Obélix), Serge Sauvion (Caesar), Pierre Mondy (Caius Obtus), Pierre Tchernia (Terminus), Henri Labussière (Panoramix), Séverine Morisot (Falbala), Patrick Préjean (Superbus), Jean-Pierre Darras (Abraracourcix), Roger Lumont (Briseradius).

Gaumont's animation feature, "Asterix vs. Caesar," first of two megabuck adaptations of the beloved comic strip created by René Goscinny and Albert Uderzo, is a pleasing kidpic that should do nicely on home grounds as a year-end holiday attraction, and fare well in other markets where the adventures of the resourceful little Gaul, Asterix, have carved out a faithful audience (160,000,000 copies of the print al-

bums have been sold to date in 33 languages).

Adapted from two separate albums by Pierre Tchernia, pic following Asterix and big dimwitted but strong-armed sidekick, Obelix, as they venture abroad to save the handsome young Tragicomix and his gorgeous fiancée Falbala, who have been kidnapped from their Gallic village (the only one to have resisted colonization by the Roman Empire), and sold into slavery.

The trail leads Asterix and Obelix (and their mutt, Idéfix) to North Africa, where they enlist in the Foreign Legion, and then on to Rome, where they find themselves on the bill of Imperial Games at the Coliseum, where the young couple are on the lions' menu.

The numerous incidents offer occasions for good-humored ribbing of picaresque desert sagas and a sendup of costume genres pic characterized by "Spartacus" and "Ben-Hur."

This is not champion stuff, but reflects nonetheless quality craftmanship in all production departments. Directors Paul and Gaëtan Brizzi, who have previously made a number of highly regarded animation shorts, come out with good marks in their first major commercial cartoon assignment (they also supplied a complete storyboard for Roman Polanski's "Pirates" feature) as does the large crew of skilled animators and artists recruited from all over Europe and North America. —*Len.*

Carné: l'Homme à la Caméra
(Carné: The Man Behind The Camera)
(FRENCH-DOCU-COLOR/B&W)

Paris, Dec. 15.
A Discop release of a Télébulle/Antenne-2 coproduction. Produced by Paule Sengissen. Directed by Christian-Jaque. Commentary, Jacques Robert, Henri-François Rey, Didier Decoin, Roland Lasaffre, spoken by Jean-Louis Barrault and Arletty; camera (color), Pierre Petit; editor, Yvonne Martin; music, Georges Delerue. Reviewed at the Studio 28, Paris, Nov. 13, 1985. Running time: **80 MINS.**
   With: Roland Lasaffre, Marcel Carné, Yves Montand.

"Carné: l'homme à la Caméra" is a re-edited theatrical version of a two-part 1980 tv docu portrait of the veteran French director Marcel Carné. It had a brief commercial run in Paris recently in company of revivals of several Carné classics, and may be of interest in homevid and education tv and non-theatrical situations, provided further editing and a new commentary are undertaken.

Tone of the film is effusively celebratory rather than objectively informative, with an often unctuous commentary by journalist Jacques

Robert, novelist Henri-François Rey, author-scripter Didier Decoin and actor Roland Lasaffre, all good friends of the filmmaker. Decoin and Lasaffre (who has appeared in most of Carné's later, poorer films) in particular have had an annoyingly proprietarial hand in Carné's affairs and public image in recent years, and their pushy press agent manner shows negatively in this portrait. (What's more, clips from Carné's more recent work are all selected to showcase Lasaffre's acting talent, which is forgettable.)

Though this is essentially a film about Carné, it's a regrettable example of the writers' table-turning intentions to give only belated and brief recognition to Jacques Prévert, the poet-screenwriter who wrote Carné's greatest films. Detractors of Carné, notably in light of his disappointing post-war, post-Prévert career, have tended to re-evaluate him as a polished hack who owed everything to Prévert.

Instead of merely reducing Prévert to a gifted backup man in Carné's cinematic universe, this film would have been more honest in stressing the artistic interaction between the two men. If it is true that Carné made little of worth without Prévert, it is also true that Prévert's films with other directors rarely attained the heights of work like "Le Jour Se Lève" and "Les Enfants du Paradis." Their creative osmosis has never been seriously studied.

Essential value of this docu then remains in the nostalgia of clips from Carné's most famous pictures, though ironically the selection tends to favor dialog scenes (like the memorable Louis Jouvet-Arletty exchanges, written by Henri Jeanson, in "Hotel du Nord") over predominantly visual scenes that illustrate Carné's directorial mastery (like the magnificent finale of "Le Jour Se Lève").

Some of the most exhilarating moments come from several minutes extracted from Carné's debut short in 1929, "Nogent, Eldorado du Dimanche," a silent docu two-reeler that marvelously captures the populist pleasures of Sunday outings in the Paris suburb of Nogent.

Carné himself makes a few appearances before the camera, if only to tell us that he has nothing much to say. Yves Montand, who debuted under Carné's aegis in 1946, is also on hand in a scene that would have been charming if it had been staged less self-consciously.

—Len.

Joey
(WEST GERMAN-COLOR)

Berlin, Dec. 9.
A coproduction of Centropolismus Film with Pro-ject im Filmverlag der Autoren and Bioskop Film, Munich. Produced by Klaus Dittrich. Directed by Roland Emmerich. Features entire cast. Screenplay, Emmerich, Hans J. Haller, Thomas Lechner; camera (color), Egon Werdin; editor, Tomy Wigand; music, Hubert Bartholomae; sets, Holger Schmidt. Reviewed at Gloria Palast, Berlin, Dec. 8, 1985. Running time: 94 MINS.
With: Joshua Morrell (Joey), Eva Kryll, Jan Zierold, Tamy Shields, Barbara Klein, Matthias Kraus.
(English-language soundtrack)

Since he scored with an entry in the Berlinale two seasons ago with "The Noah's Ark Principle," helmer Roland Emmerich has been fairly aching to be adopted into the Hollywood colony of sci-fiers. So what better way to crash the party than making an imitation special effects production on home grounds with an English-speaking cast that combines elements dearly remembered in Steven Spielberg's "Close Encounters" and Wolfgang Petersen's "Neverending Story."

"Joey" never really gets off the ground, however, as anything more than second-rate imitation. It's about a precocious 11-year-old who misses his recently deceased dad. He and his mother live in a smalltown American community, where the neighboring youngsters are the heckling sort for the most part. Joey compensates by communicating with his father in the nether world on his toy red telephone — what's more, he can telekinetically activate his toys via a special transcendental power mysteriously bestowed upon him.

These magic powers are not exactly controllable. A wicked ventriloquist's dummy tends to take over at times when Joey's imagination runs too wild, so much so that strange poltergeists are threatening to demolish the household, Joey's mother included. The weird chain of events in this Middle American setting leads to a showdown in the end: Joey has to sacrifice his life for others, and only true love can bring him back to Mother Earth.

Emmerich demonstrates a rather sure hand for visual fantasy on the screen, but quality science-fiction lies in the narrative skills of making the incredible credible. "Joey" suffers from a crooked narrative line and lame dialog, most of all, while the imitation factor can prove for him to be downright embarrassing to those familiar with the sources. —Holl.

Kücken für Kairo
(A Chick For Cairo)
(WEST GERMAN-COLOR)

Berlin, Dec. 16.
A Topas Film, in coproduction with West Deutscher Rundfunk (WDR), Cologne. Directed by Arend Aghte. Features entire cast. Screenplay, Aghte, Monika Seck-Aghte; camera (color), Karl F. Koschnick; editor, Yvonne Kölsch; music, Matthias Raue; sound, Uwe Thalmann; costumes, Corinna Dreyer; production manager, Michael Alexander; tv-producer, Enrico Platter. Reviewed at Akademie der Künste, Berlin, Dec. 15 1985. Running time: 72 MINS.
With: Friedrich Karl Praetorius (Piet Osswald), Hans Beerhanke (Michael Alexander), Timmo Niesner (Lester McCormick), Cornelia Köndgen (Lilly McCormick), Leo Seck-Aghte (Max Oswald), Peter Schiff (Hartmut Henke), Gottfried Breitfuss (Customs Agent).

After scoring a solid b.o. and critical success with his debut children's film, "River Trip With Hen" (1984), helmer Arend Aghte has done nearly as well with his second, "A Chick For Cairo," which preemed at the kidpic fest in Berlin just before the holidays. Only a couple lapses in the storyline marred its reception here to a SRO crowd at the Academy of Fine Arts.

Aghte believes in making the narrative as realistic as possible — in other words, everything in the story could really have happened, the twist being that one absurd situation is more likely the spark to ignite another, and so on. Here we have a Lufthansa Air Freight delivery to begin with: crates of newly hatched chicks are being transported to Cairo. One chick escapes the crate, and is discovered in turn by a warm-hearted copilot stuck peeping away in the matting of the fusilage.

Since the plane is about to take off for Nairobi on the next assignment, there's nothing left to do but take the abandoned chick along with them. The pilot is the gruff type, however, but he also slowly demonstrates that he has a heart beneath his rhino-hide when it comes down to a crisis. This happens when the copilot takes sick with a stomach virus, thus incapacitating him for a spell and thereby ruining the pilot's plans to spend Christmas in sunny Sydney on the golf links. It's the pilot who has to care for the chick, as well as his flight companion.

The chick disappears one day from the hotel room. In comes a nosy master detective, a 9-year-old Agatha Christie fan who deduces that the crime was the result of a rational chain of coincidences. Once well and able to travel, the pilots are off with the chick for the return flight to Frankfurt - where a final twist with the customs agents there makes for a closing round of absurdities.

Credits are tops and acting fresh and credible for the young crowd, particularly thesps Friedrich Karl Praetorius and Hans Beerhanke as the pilot-pair who come across as distant cousins to Laurel & Hardy in their dialog routines. "A Chick for Cairo" should do well on the kidpic fest circuit. —Holl.

Guardian Of Hell
(ITALIAN-COLOR)

A Film Concept Group release, presented by John L. Chambliss and Michael Franzese, of a Cinemec Produzione S.r.l. production. Directed by Stefan Oblowsky. Camera (color; prints by CFI), uncredited. No credits on release print. Reviewed at UA Twin 2 theater, N.Y., Dec. 13, 1985. (MPAA Rating: R.) Running Time: 85 MINS.
With: Sandy Samuel, Frank Garfeeld.

"Guardian Of Hell" is a poorly-made Italian horror film, bearing a 1980 copyright but no other credits or identification on its U.S. release prints. Pic has been in regional release since September.

Story would make this a candidate for a double feature with "Agnes Of God." A series of priests are sent to a convent to investigate the mysterious killings of several nuns there. The convent's mother superior committed suicide many years ago and the current mother superior, Sister Vincenza, obstructs the investigations.

It turns out that one of the nuns has borne a child supposedly fathered by the devil who becomes one of the Evil One's instruments on Earth. The kid, named Louisa, also has the power to bring the dead back to life, starting with the convent's inevitable creepy gardener, named Boris.

Very poor dubbing fails to disguise the wide-eyed, over-the-top performances of the film's unknown Italian cast. Filming technique is crude, with overuse of handheld camera and painfully underlit interiors. Matters aren't helped by the slapdash U.S release print caught, which looked like a dupe of a dupe.

Pic's rock music score has one effective scene merging with the convent's choir singing. —Lor

L'Homme aux Yeux d'Argent
(The Man With The Silver Eyes)
(FRENCH-COLOR)

Paris, Nov. 28.
An AAA/Revcom Films release of a T. Films/Films A2 coproduction. Directed by Pierre Granier-Deferre. Stars Alain Souchon and Jean-Louis Trintignant. Screenplay, Granier-Deferre, Guy-Patrick Sainderichin, based on the novel "The End Of Someone Else's Rainbow," by Robert Rossner; camera (color), Renato Berta; art director, Dominique André; editor, Marie Castro Vasquez; music, Philippe Sarde, performed by Wayne Shorter, Herbie Hancock, Clark Terry, Larry Coryell, Ron Carter, Tony Williams and Toots Thielemanns, production manager, Philippe Lièvre. Reviewed at the Marignan-Concorde Pathé cinema, Paris, Nov. 28, 1985. Running time: 93 MINS.
Thierry . . . . Alain Souchon
Inspector Mayène . . Jean-Louis Trintignant
Francine . . . . Tanya Lopert
Villain . . . . Lambert Wilson

Yet another French melodrama

based on an Anglo-Saxon print source, "L'Homme aux Yeux d'Argent" compounds the weakness of its script with some miscasting and dull direction. Helmer Pierre Granier-Deferre, a conscientious professional who has never been able to transcend a mediocre screenplay, is also the uninspired coauthor of the adaptation, which mixes the unlikely and the obvious.

Alain Souchon, the sympathetically nonchalant pop singer who has acted in four films previously (notably in Jean Becker's "One Deadly Summer"), never musters the requisite credibility as a man who has spent 15 years in prison on a bank robbery and manslaughter charge and now returns to his hometown to recover the loot he had buried at the foot of a tree before his capture.

Souchon discovers the entire area has been transformed and modernized, though the tree is still there, now grown so tall that its thick roots prevent inconspicuous access to the money from above ground. Souchon befriends a lonely municipal librarian (Tanya Lopert) who works just a few feet away and gains her complicity in a plan to dig a tunnel from the library basement to the foot of the tree.

Souchon's chief worry is the vindictive police inspector (Jean-Louis Trintignant) who has been trailing him. The cop wants to recover the money and then avenge the murder of a fellow policeman, shot down during Souchon's bank job with an accomplice. Trintignant is soon joined by a younger, vaguely perverse detective (Lambert Wilson)

Granier-Deferre's bland direction reflects the bloodless characterizations, unconvincing performances and uncompelling plotting, which comes to a head without stirring up any genuine suspense. A sturdier leading man may have helped; Souchon's laid-back manner is far from embodying world-weary experience. —*Len.*

Zivile Knete
(Fun Raising)
(WEST GERMAN-COLOR-16m)

Berlin, Dec. 17.
A Kängaruh Film production, Berlin, in collaboration with Westdeutscher Rundfunk (WDR), Cologne. Written and directed by Detlef Gumm and Hans-Georg Ullrich. Features entire cast. Camera (color), Ullrich; editor, Ute Wenzel-Spoo; music, original music by "Zivil" band; assistant, Hanna Blösser; tv-producer, Dieter Saldecki. Reviewed at Akademie der Künste, Berlin, Dec. 15, 1985. Running time: **80 MINS.**

With: Stefan Hülsemann, Oliver Jahn, Andreas Kobelt, Thorsten Küster, Robert Raguse, each playing himself.

The magic that flows from Detlef Gumm and Hans-Georg Ullrich's "Fun Raising" is the same that can be found on the back streets of Berlin nearly every day of the week. There are an estimated 1,000 pop bands scattered around the city trying to make their marks with the teenage pop crowd in dozens of concert halls and at various band competitions organized and occasionally financed by the city of Berlin.

The story of "Fun Raising" — title is a free translation for collecting money (Knete) to buy proper musical instruments for a new band called Zivil (meaning civic or public) — is about a real group of youngsters just into their teens who want to make it one day to a Waldbühne concert (the arena holds 20,000 and is SRO for pop concerts), just like other name Berlin bands have made it before them.

Pic opens with the five-piece band making just such an entry into the Waldbühne, albeit on an empty stage before an empty arena. It's a warmup for the big moment when the group has earned enough pocket money doing odd jobs to buy their own instruments. The rest is how they go about doing it.

It's fun from start to finish. Lensed spontaneously with nonprofessionals throughout and at various on-the-spot settings, one gets an inside glimpse into how original pop bands in Berlin get their acts together in the first place. The lads have a couple of beaten-up instruments to begin with, and they can practice in the padded basement of one of the city's numerous old-style tenements. The question is how can kids between 12 and 14 earn extra pocket money in the first place to buy even secondhand guitars and drums.

They do it by adroitly informing car drivers of hidden radar speedtraps, by raking the leaves in backyards, and by landing a job in a kid-pic production in Berlin (a film-within-a-film gambit).

Sprinkled with wit and gags throughout, "Fun Raising" is a light, free-wheeling affair. —*Holl.*

Naar Engle Elsker
(Angels In Love)
(DANISH-COLOR)

Copenhagen, Nov. 20.
A Warner & Metronome Films release of a Metronome Film (Bent Fabricius-Bjerre) production with the Danish Film Institute (Claes Kastholm Hansen). Directed by Peter Eszterhas. Stars Jesper Langberg, Lone Hertz. Screenplay, Nils Schou; camera (Agfa Gevaert color), Claus Loof; editor, Maj Soya; music, Anne Dorte Michelsen; production design, Sven Wickman; costumes, Günther Rossen, Marcella Kjeldtoft; executive producer, Tiwi Magnusson; production management, Michael Christensen, Jane Garun. Reviewed at the Danish Film Studio at Kongens Lyngby, Nov. 20, 1985. Running time: **94 MINS.**

Arne Mortensen	Jesper Langberg
Bente, his wife	Lone Hertz
Their son	Lars Simonsen
Their daughter	Josephine Sascha Olsen
Dagwood	Henrik Kofoed
Blondie	Tammi Oest
Gabriel	Ove Sprogöe
Kurt, the chauffeur	Paul Hüttel
Lis	Birthe Neumann Hüttel
Frits Guldborg	Flemming Enevold
Meta Nielsen	Ann Hjorth
Ms. Nikolaisen	Puk Schaufuss
Bent Petersen	Poul Thomsen
Carsten Nielsen	Jens Arentzen

Writer Nils Schou and helmer Peter Eszterhas in their feature "Angels In Love" pick up a time-honored theme of romantic film comedy to give it several new twists and turns of dialog and plot while they tell the story of a mean guy being transformed into a finer specimen of humanity through a truly celestial touch or two.

The meanie, shoe-factory owner and corporate struggler Mr. Mortensen, is a tyrant at home and at work. One day, at the dinner table with two near-adult children, he calls his wife a junkie because she swallows vitamin pills. She responds by calling him an alcoholic. The children flee the table and seek refuge with Kurt, the family chauffeur, who reads Pascal's "Thoughts" in his spare time. Mortensen gets behind the wheel, puts the chauffeur in the back seat and smashes them both into the nearest wall.

In Heaven, a boy-girl couple of angels named Dagwood and Blondie have had 200 years to rid themselves of earthly lusts. Not having succeeded, they are now sentenced by the Archangel Gabriel to a tour of duty on Earth where they may save their standing as angels only by turning some true-blue bad guy into a good guy. Mortensen is the meanie chosen for them to work on, but Mortensen ups and dies on them, while the chauffeur miraculously survives and has the Mortensen inner characteristics transferred to his body. Re-entering the scheme of things, Mortensen looks to audiences like his former self while to film's protagonists he is clearly the surviving chauffeur.

All possibilities of such a plot are now explored when Mortensen comes back to live in a different corner of his former household. With him, he has insights into the factory's more shady financial dealings and thus holds a strong hand when the new manager tries to edge into ownership as well as into possession of Mrs. Mortensen.

Film has dexterous casting, fine production credits, glossy but inventive cinematography plus performances of warmth and vigor by such Danish stalwarts of stage and screen as Jesper Langberg and Lone Hertz, Paul Hüttel and Ove Sprogöe, and younger talent like Tammi Oest and Henrik Kofoed (the angels), Josephine Sascha Olsen and Lars Simonsen (the youngsters) along with Flemming Enevold and Ann Hjorth. As a technically and dramatically brilliant piece of giddy fluff, "Angels In Love" is bound to be a hit at home, while offshore sales for such fare would seem obtainable as well. —*Kell.*

1986

Lejanía
(Distance)
(CUBAN-COLOR)

An ICAIC production. Produced by Humberto Hernandez. Written and directed by Jesús Díaz. Camera (ICAIC color), Mario Garcío Joya; editor, Justo Vega; sound, Jerónimo Labrada. Reviewed at the Cine 23 y 12 (Havana Film Festival), Dec. 9, 1985. Running time: **83 MINS.**
Susana .... Verónica Lynn
Reinaldo .... Jorge Trinchet
Ana .... Isabel Santos
Aleida .... Beatriz Valdés
Also with: Mónica Guffanti.

Havana — The most ambitious and controversial new Cuban film unspooled at the Havana Film Festival was "Lejanía" ("Distance"), the first local feature to deal with the issue of Cuban exiles returning to the island for visits with relatives. Although pic would be restricted by its nature to select art and specialized houses, its creative virtues and U.S.-related subject matter are such that it deserves some limited commercial playoff in addition to international fest slottings.

Second fictional effort by Jesús Díaz, whose powerful first feature "Polvo Rojo" ("Red Dust") made the fest rounds in 1981, centers upon the first reunion in 10 years between a son and the mother who abandoned him for the easy life in Miami. Also along for the trip is the young man's sexy cousin who loves living in New York.

In the interim, the son, Reinaldo, has grown from a juvenile delinquent into a responsible husband and stepfather, while his own father has died in Florida without seeing Reinaldo one last time.

Opening reel offers up some broad comedy, as Susana, a middle-aged woman of deep-rooted bourgeois tastes, arrives in Havana loaded with tantalizing gifts made in the U.S.A. that Cubans would supposedly kill for.

However, the tensions arising from political, emotional and generational differences can't remain submerged for long, and Díaz ends up painting a devastating and exceedingly bleak picture of the possibilities of any reconciliation between mother and son, and, by extension, between the two countries.

Ironically, Díaz has been attacked by certain quarters in his native country for trading as extensively as he does in ambiguities, for admitting that some contemporary Cubans can be seduced by the supposedly superficial attractions of "decadent" American society.

By contrast, Western viewers will be amazed by the diffidence with which Reinaldo is able to treat his mother, and perhaps a bit appalled at the manner in which American values are exclusively tied to material possessions.

Film could have used a more dynamic center than the relatively passive and reactive Reinaldo, whose age, 26, is, not coincidentally, made to be precisely that of the revolution. By default, most of the dramatic fireworks are set off by the women. It takes Reinaldo's spirited wife to tell mama that she can just pack up her things and take them all back to Miami, while Isabel Santos, whose raspy voice and provocative ordinariness qualify her as the Cuban Debra Winger, is especially effective as the New York cousin.

Pic both benefits and suffers from the simplifications implicit in the symbolic weight of the characters, but Díaz is to be commended for tackling such a politically sensitive and tricky subject in such a forthright manner. He has also pulled off an impressive formal exercise, as the entire picture, up until the final shot, is played out in a single apartment building. Mario García Joya's very mobile lensing in the tight quarters is superior.
—*Cart.*

En Tres Y Dos
(Full Count)
(CUBAN-COLOR)

An ICAIC production. Produced by Humberto Hernandez. Directed by Rolando Díaz. Screenplay, Eliseo Alberto Diego, with the collaboration of Díaz; camera (ICAIC color), Guillermo Centeno; editor, Jorge Abello; assistant director, Roberto Viña. Reviewed at the Cine 23 y 12 (Havana Film Festival), Dec. 14, 1985. Running time: **95 MINS.**
With: Samuel Claxton (Mario Lopez Garcia), Mario Balmaseda, Alejandro Lugo, Irela Bravo, Luis Alberto García.

Havana — "Full Count" is an intelligent, sympathetic but poorly structured look at a top Cuban baseball star who is forced to confront his retirement from the sport. Jarring transitions and insufficient explanations of what's going on make this somewhat confusing even for baseball fans, and anyone who doesn't understand or like the sport will probably tune out early due to frustration. A popular favorite in Cuba and one of the nation's better productions of the year, its subject matter and very mainstream nature make it problematic for most offshore audiences.

Pic opens at a pitch of high excitement at Havana Stadium, as the Industriales and Villa Clara meet in the championship series. Mario Lopez García, the veteran centerfielder for the Industriales, will be retiring when the series is decided, and is honored before the game.

Here beings a progression of flashbacks depicting Lopez' private and professional life, his problems with wife and son, his hesitations about retiring, his horsing around with fellow athletes and his feelings about his career.

Rolando Díaz attracted favorable attention with his first feature, "Los Pajaros Tirandole A La Escopeta" in 1984, and here he has avoided the sentimentality latent in this sort of tale by giving Lopez a relatively tough, fatalistic attitude about what's happening to him.

Instead, the problem is that he keeps jumping around so much in time that you never quite know if one event is supposed to have happened before or after something else you've just seen. The championship series games are all identified as taking place on the same date, and it takes the entire film to figure out that this is, indeed, the way it's done in Cuba, with multiple games being played at the same stadium on the same night. And how can the same pitcher start two games on the same evening, as seems to be the case here? These are just samples of the confusion confronting even a student of the game.

On the other hand, sports buffs will get their fill of local color and detail from the film. The sight of fans wildly dancing in the stands to the accompaniment of hot salsa music is something to behold, and it is fascinating to listen to veterans reminisce about how they beat the Yankees back in 1959.

Díaz also provides some unique digressions by way of vintage newsreel footage of, and contemporary interviews with, such Cuban sporting legends as boxers Kid Chocolate and Teofilo Stevenson, and Olympic gold medalist runner Albert Juantorena. Use of music, which ranges from Vivaldi's Violin Concerto No. Six to the latest from the hot group Los Van Van, is also interesting. —*Cart.*

El Corazón Sobre La Tierra
(The Heart On The Land)
(CUBAN-COLOR)

An ICAIC production. Produced by Miguel Mendoza. Directed by Constante Diego. Screenplay, Eliseo Alberto Diego, Constante Diego; camera (ICAIC color), Livio Delgado; editor, Roberto Bravo; music, Jose Marie Vitier; sound, Germinal Hernandez. Reviewed at the Cine 23 y 12 (Havana Film Festival), Dec. 9, 1985. Running time: **95 MINS.**
With: Reinaldo Miravalles, Nelson Villagra, Annia Linares, Tito Junco, Argelio Sosa.

Havana — "The Heart On The Land" is a predictable and quickly tiresome tract designed to demonstrate how even independent-minded roughnecks in the Cuban mountains can rally 'round the spirit of the revolution. The inexplicable winner of numerous local prizes, tedious effort is of no interest to international audiences.

This first feature film by Constante Diego wears its "correct" political credentials proudly. A father and son in Havana dream of starting a cooperative in the far-off Sierra Maestra mountains, but when the son is killed in action in Ethiopia, the father throws himself into the cause of the cooperative with maniacal devotion.

Along the way, the tough old-timer, who resembles a heavier Lee Van Cleef and whose body posture is utterly convincing as a veteran cowpoke, meets nominal resistance from some of the locals who haven't yet been converted to principles of the revolution. His relentlessness finally wins the day, and the coop, as well as the pic, is dedicated to a Cuban youth who lost his life in Africa.

Filmmakers' intentions are all too obvious from the outset, and pic feels heavily padded even at 95 minutes. —*Cart.*

Igreja De Libertaçao
(Church Of Liberation)
(BRAZILIAN-DOCU-COLOR-16m)

An Embrafilme release of a Lumiar Producoes Audiovisuais production. Written and directed by Silvio Da-Rin. Camera (color), Walter Carvalho; editor, Aida Marques. Reviewed at the Cine Charles Chaplin (Havana Film Festival), Dec. 8, 1985. Running time: **80 MINS.**

Havana — "Church Of Liberation" makes up in timeliness what it lacks in dramatic urgency. Exhausting in its attempt to be an exhaustive examination of the Roman Catholic Church's social and political engagement in Brazil, sincere docu is valuable as an utterly up-to-date report on a newsworthy and ongoing activity. Catholic orgs worldwide represent a large audience for mostly nontheatrical playoff.

Endorsing church activism all the way, methodical pic begins in the more sparsely populated areas of the Amazon, the Northeast and the South, where priests have worked on behalf of efforts to improve land use, agricultural conditions and the Indian heritage.

Moving to the urbans centers of São Paulo and Rio, film documents the struggle to establish a Christian presence in the workers' movement, and climatically focuses upon the case of Brother Leonardo Boff, an activist condemned to silence by the Vatican for his outspokenness.

Docu promotes the church's involvement in liberation politics as its natural role and argues that, despite opposition from conservative elements in Rome, the church will have to prove even more flexible and responsive in the future if it is to keep pace with social developments.

All of this is laid out in too plodding a manner, but limiting the analysis to one country, South

America's largest, helps keep this informative pic in good focus.
— Cart.

Rei Do Rio
(King Of Rio)
(BRAZILIAN-COLOR)

An Embrafilme release of a Producoes Cinematograficas L.C. Barreto LTDA. production. Directed by Fabio Barreto. Screenplay, Jorge Durán, José Joffily, Barreto; editor; Raimundo Higino. No other credits available. Reviewed at the Cine Charles Chaplin (Havana Film Festival), Dec. 6, 1985. Running time: **90 MINS.**
With: Nuno Leal, Maia, Nelson Xavier, Milton Concalves, Amparo Grisales, Andrea Beltran, Marcia Barreto.

Havana — A crazy, unpredictable picture, "King Of Rio" keeps the viewer guessing as it starts off like a road company version of "Scarface," borrows bits and pieces from such gangster sagas as "The Public Enemy," "Manhattan Melodrama" and "The Godfather," then careens into a sort of "Romeo And Juliet" where the old folks die instead of the youngsters. This may go over big with antive audiences, but somehow doesn't connect squarely with a foreign sensibility despite the familiar references.

Tragic but farcical tale charts nearly two decades in the lives of two close friends who get their bread when they hit it big in a lottery. Tucan, the top dog, forms a gang of his own, moves in and finally rubs out the leading mobster in the area. With the assistance of helpful newspapermen and government officials, Tucan is soon sitting pretty.

Fifteen years later, he's more comfy than ever, what with his wife, mistress and lavish home all in place. But after unscrupulous modern drug dealers threaten him and an arrest lands him in jail, he decides to go straight, even though he knows his lurid past will always be nipping at his heels.

Tucan's daughter and his old buddy's untrustworthy son get involved in a torrid romance, the two friends shoot it out on a beach, with goofy results, and it all ends up at a carnival parade, where the past finally arrives to snatch up Tucan.

Director Fabio Barreto, 28, has plenty of tricks up his sleeve, and this, his second feature, is sexy, lively, very commerically minded and anything but dull. Effects are quite scattershot, however, indicating that Barreto must refine his storytelling ideas before he'll come up with a truly first-rate piece of work. But this makes it clear that he's got a knack for punchy, often outrageous moments. —Cart.

Vampiros En La Habana
(Vampires In Havana)
(CUBAN-ANIMATED-COLOR)

An ICAIC production. Written and directed by Juan Padrón. Camera (color), Adalberto Hernández, Julio Simoneau; editor. Rosa María Carreras; design, Padrón; animation, Mario García-Montes; Josés Reyes, Noel Lima. Reviewed at the Cine 23 y 12 (Havana Film Festival), Dec. 11, 1985. Running time: **75 MINS.**

Havana — Recalling something of the raunchy irreverent spirit, if not the style, of "Fritz The Cat," "Vampires In Havana" is a mostly amusing animated send-up of gangster and vampire pictures. Very knowing in its hip allusions and a fount of gags and one-liners, farce spins exhaustingly out of the control toward the end, but proves diverting overall. A natural for animation fests and programs internationally, pic could also warrant unspooling where offbeat curiousities are sought out.

Bubbling brew of a plot has leading vampire members of the international mafia converging on Havana, circa 1933, to try to lay their hands on a new invention called Vampisol, a potion that allows vampires to survive in sunlight.

Leading character is a happy-go-lucky trumpet player named Joseph, son of Vampisol's inventor. Joseph is actually walking proof that the formula works, since he has been raised on it and leads a perfectly normal life. In fact, he doesn't even know he's a vampire, but that soon changes, much to the distress of his girlfriend.

Everything is played in delightfully broad caricature. Animation style is crude but witty, and director-writer-designer Juan Padrón has slipped in lots of sly pokes at gangster and vampire mythology, the Machado dictatorship, tourists and morally slack musicians.

Unfortunately, the action gets out of hand in the final reels, as the various factions of bad guys, police, musicians, et. al., are all chasing after one another trying to snatch the formula.

A lively, bawdy effort on the whole, this is certainly not the sort of film one expects to be produced by a state-controlled film industry.
—Cart.

Come La Vida Misma
(Like Life Itself)
(CUBAN-COLOR)

An ICAIC production. Produced by José R. Perez, with the collaboration of José Rodriguez. Directed by Victor Casaus. Screenplay, Casaus, Luís Rogelio Nogueras, based on works by Rafael Gonzalez; camera (ICAIC color), Raúl Rodríguez; editor, Roberto Bravo; music, Silvio Rodríguez; sound, Ricardo Istueta; assistant director, Lourdes Prieto. Reviewed at the Cine 23 y 12 (Havana Film Festival), Dec. 13, 1985. Running time: **100 MINS.**
With: Fernando Echevarría (Fernando), Beatríz Valdéz (Madelene), Pedro Rentería, Sergio Corrieri, Flora Lauten and the Theater Group of Escambray.

Havana — An amiable comic drama designed to demonstrate how the theater can be important and relevant to real life, "Like Life Itself" suffers from its own divided attention between two plot strands. Pic succeeds as a domestic audience pleaser, but is too deeply flawed to stand as a promising item for export.

Debut feature by Victor Casaus starts well enough, as a likable young man leaves Havana to join a thriving theater company in the mountain community of Escambray. He quickly gets into the swing of the group's life, which includes agricultural work and domestic chores as well as rehearsals and performances, and he shortly embarks upon a romance with a local beauty.

As if he felt some troubling drama were needed to stir up these relatively placid waters, Casaus has devoted altogether too much time to an uninvolving subplot concerning a student who has cheated on an exam. All the exposition is devoted to generating sympathy for and interest in the newcomer to the group, so one resents the sudden intrusion of the ne'er-do-well and his problems.

Finally, the group decides that the cheater's difficulties can be resolved by dramatizing them, which, in the event, makes for better drama than psychology. At least the company can thereby justify its activities with respect to the revolutionary process which, of course, wants to wipe out cheating.

Film is punctuated by sizeable helpings of lowbrow, but frequently funny, comedy, which helps offset the dull seriousness with which the subplot is presented. —Cart.

Jíbaro
(Wild Dog)
(CUBAN-COLOR)

An ICAIC production. Produced by Santiago Llapu. Directed by Daniel Díaz Torres. Screenplay, Torres, Norberto Fuentes; camera (ICAIC color), Pablo Martínez; editor, Justo Vega; sound, Jerónimo Labrada. Reviewed at ICAIC screening room (Havana Film Festival), Dec. 12, 1985. Running time: **84 MINS.**
With: Salvador Wood, René de la Cruz, Adolfo Llauradó, Flora Lauten, Ana Viña.

Havana — "Wild Dog" is a didactic modern-day Western that probably only a doctrinaire Marxist could swallow whole. Tale of Cuban cowboys dedicated to flushing counterrevolutionaries out of the hills in 1960 is filled with obvious action and sentiment and proves of little interest except as a grafting of genre elements onto a political body.

Felo is a tough old bird who specializes in hunting down wild dogs that kill livestock. He, like most of the other rugged, older men living in the country, has always lived quite independently and has some initial trouble adapting to the cooperative spirit implicit in the revolution.

A rag-tag peasant militia is formed, which allows first-time director Daniel Díaz Torres to indulge in some of the oldest boot camp comedy in the book, and finally Felo becomes a real cowboy bureaucrat, organizing his comrades just as a sheriff would gather a posse and leading them off to shoot it out with the counterrevolutionary holdouts up in the hills.

Obvious eponymous metaphor relates the wild dogs to the reactionary elements that finally need killing off, and Torres and co-screenwriter Norberto Fuentes (author of "Hemingway In Cuba") haven't probed deeply enough to create an interesting character study of a man forced to change his priorities and way of life at a relatively late age. —Cart.

Chico Rei
(King Chico)
(BRAZILIAN-COLOR)

An Embrafilme release. Written and directed by Walter Lima Jr. Camera (color), José Antonio Ventura, Mario Carneiro; editor, Carneiro, Lima. No other credits available. Reviewed at the Cine Charles Chaplin (Havana Film Festival), Dec. 8, 1985. Running time: **112 MINS.**
With: Severo D'Acelino, Othon Bastos, Cosme dos Santos, Carlos Kroeber, Antonio Pitanga, Alexander Allerson, Rainer Rudolf, Mario Gusmao.

Havana — "Chico Rei" is like a Brazilian version of "Mandingo" topped off with thick layers of political and mystical significance. Main point is to show how liberation movements sprang up from the enslavement of the blacks, but pic spends much of its time richly detailing the horrors of slavery and the period in which it thrived. Chances outside of its native country are slim.

Lensed in 1979-1980 but tied up in court until recently, this historical epic from former Glauber Rocha collaborator Walter Lima Jr. was produced handsomely, even opulently, but is without style. Dramatically, it lurches from one momentous event to the next without modulation, with the result that it feels even longer than its nearly two-hour running time.

After a prolog depicting three black men in chains fleeing from an unseen enemy, film proper begins in the 18th century, as some nasty traders capture Galanga, the King of the Congo, and his clan and pack them off for sale in Brazil.

First couple of reels vividly display the evil deeds visited upon the captured slaves to almost comically caricatured effect, since film acts as though the audience never before heard of how awful some of those white boys could be.

Long after one has begun wondering if "Chico Rei" might have been made only to fully catalog every known atrocity meted out to the blacks, one of the white characters, a suddenly enlightened slave owner, begins getting it, since the local authorities have decided that he is being too lenient with his workers.

Slipped in here sideways somewhere is the story of Galanga, who is promised his freedom, and then receives it, for finding a major gold lode in his master's mine. In short order, he becomes the nation's first black mine owner, the emancipator of others of his race and, finally, the subject of wild Brazilian songs and carnivals.

Although it looks and sounds good, film tries to hit a home run when a double would have done nicely, and ends up fouling out.
— Cart.

Pequeña Revancha
(Little Revenge)
(VENEZUELAN-COLOR)

An Alfredo J. Anzola production. Produced by Anzola. Directed by Olegario Barrera. Screenplay, Barrera, Laura Antillano; camera (color), Alfredo J. Anzola, Carlos Bricaño, Jorge Naranjo; editors, Barrera, Marisa Bafile. Reviewed at the Cine Charles Chaplin (Havana Film Festival), Dec. 4, 1985. Running time: 95 MINS.

With: Eduardo Emiro García, Elisa Escámez, Carlos Sánchez, Pedro Durán, Carmencita Padrón, Yoleigret Falcon, Cecilia Todd.

Havana — Simple in its aims and straightforward in its storytelling, "Little Revenge" represents a satisfying little parable about how the wisdom of children can triumph over the insidiousness of facism. Too direct and unadorned to be taken to heart by the art house crowd, pic could nevertheless merit showcasing at foreign fests with room for modestly talented, if unspectacular, Third World fare.

In a quiet, desolate village, the ruling military government initiates a series of untoward events designed to stamp out any opposition among the relatively placid citizenry but which, in fact, slowly but surely foments a united resistance movement.

Debut feature by Olegario Barrera begins somewhat awkwardly, as he opens with a mawkish scene of a boy's dog being run over by a military jeep and has some difficulty establishing the p.o.v. of the 12-year-old.

Pic gathers force, however, as the father of his playmate is suddenly taken away as a subversive. Having heard that big word for the first time, little Pedro runs home and innocently asks his father, "Are you subversive?"

It turns out papa does have possibilities in that direction, which makes for a tense scene when a pompous military officer struts into the local schoolroom to ask the unsuspecting kids to write a paper revealing everything their parents do and say in the evening.

With time out for a kiddie romance and some mild adventure along the way, pic demonstrates how an oppressive regime prompts an early political awakening among its youth, how facism is fundamentally anti-human and how it must protect itself from the very people it governs.

Barrera seems to develop greater directorial confidence reel by reel, and his sympathetic intentions and unpretentious approach carry the viewer over the occasional crude spots. —Cart.

Amigos
(COLOR)

Humorous, upbeat tale of Cuban refugee.

A Manicato Films presentation. Produced by Camilo Vila. Executive producer, Marcelino Miyares. Directed by Ivan Acosta. Features Ruben Rabasa, Reynaldo Medina, Lucy Pereda. Screenplay, Acosta; camera (color), Henry Vargas; editor, Gloria Pineyro; music, Sergio Garcia-Marruz; sound, Phil Pear; art direction, Siro Del Castillo; assistant director, Oscar Costo; assistant camera, Orson Ochoa; production manager, Edy Chea. Reviewed at Cine 1, Dec. 19, 1985, N.Y. (No MPAA Rating). Running time: 108 MINS.
Ramon .... Ruben Rabasa
Pablo .... Reynaldo Medina
Magaly .... Lucy Pereda
Olmedo .... Juan Granda
Gavilan .... Armando Naser
Cecilia .... Blanca de Abril
Mirta .... Lilian Hurst
Consuelo .... Luisa Gil
Pellon .... Juan Troya
Also with: Dania Victor, Uva Clavijo, George Prince, Mercedes Enriquez, Celia De Munio, Manuel Estanillo, Ellen Cody, Carlos Bermudez and Tony Calbino.

(In Spanish with English subtitles)

This is the first film feature by Cuban-American Ivan Acosta, whose Off-Off Broadway play "El Super" was adapted in a droll, captivating 1979 film by Leon Ichaso ("Crossover Dreams") and Orlando Jimenez-Leal ("Improper Conduct"). Although "Amigos" is slated for initial release at an Hispanic speciality house, the first-rate subtitles indicate the filmmaker hopes for crossover distribution to the mainstream market. While this film about the adjustment of a Cuban refugee from the 1980 Mariel boat flotilla has its share of humor and thematic sharpness, it's less ironic

and more loosely structured than "El Super," and seasoned with the type of sentimentality and broad comedy likely to have its greatest appeal in the specialty sector.

After spending 18 years in one of Fidel Castro's prisons simply for being in the wrong place at the wrong time, born loser Ramon (Ruben Rabasa) is allowed to leave in the Mariel boat exodus for Miami, where he's taken in by childhood pal Pablo (Reynaldo Medina), a suave and successful truck salesman whose family left Cuba in 1958. The world of Miami's well-to-do, hard working Cuban middle class is depicted in microcosm here, and the conflict between the comfortable Cuban-American establishment and the Mariel newcomers, stigmatized by the convicts and social outcasts in their midst, is a thematic backbone of "Amigos."

Ruben's life changes overnight as he's accepted immediately into Pablo and his girlfriend Magaly's (Lucy Pereda) cozy circle of friends in bountiful Miami, U.S.A., where, as Pablo says, "there's lot's of bread and the freedom to enjoy it." Balding, self-effacing Ramon is easygoing on the surface, but he's still haunted by his long and terrible prison ordeal. Although he shares a common language and homeland with engaging characters like construction boss Gavilan, undertaker Olmedo and aerobics instructor Magaly (who sets him up on a phenomenally successful blind date) the culture-shocked Ramon feels isolated by his uncommon experiences from their prosperity and hustling American lifestyle.

No one in Miami, it seems, wants to hire *Marielitos*, and gradually Ramon sinks into a depression over his inability to find even the most mundane work. After a short, hilarious stint with Olmedo in the hearse and a boatyard job that ends when his boss discovers his origins, the guileless Ramon is duped by unsavory criminal Pellon into a scheme to drive stolen goods to Union City, N.J. This puts him in a big jam in the Big Apple from which only his new amigos can hope to rescue him.

There's a funny subplot involving Ramon and his obese ex-wife Consuelo (Luisa Gil) who deserted him in Cuba when he was imprisoned but longs to win him back with witchcraft and womanly wiles. Although Acosta is clearly anti-Castro he neatly satirizes the military fantasies of Cubans who still dream of reconquering the island, and also casts some deft barbs at machismo, materialism and the paradox of cultural assimilation.

Ensemble performances are appealing and location shooting in Miami is keenly evocative of the Cuban-American milieu there.
— Rich.

Blauvogel
(Bluebird)
(EAST GERMAN-COLOR)

A DEFA Film production, "Johannisthal Gruppe," East Berlin; world rights, DEFA Aussenhandel, East Berlin. Directed by Ulrich Weiss. Screenplay based on novel with the same title by Anna Jürgen. Only credits available. Reviewed at Hollywood Kino, Berlin, Dec. 15, 1985. Running time: 96 MINS.

Berlin — One of the curiosities of the Children's Film Fest in Berlin skedded just before the holiday season, Ulrich Weiss' "Bluebird" (1979) was one of four East German entries included in the program. Helmer is known for his offbeat features — and this one is no exception: he offers a personal study of American Indian life in frontier colonial times of the mid-18th century.

The setting is the western Ohio country during the bloody French and Indian War (1754-63). Weiss in his and novelist Anna Jürgen's version of historical events places the Iroquois on the side of French against the British, although these federated Indian tribes were mostly neutral throughout the campaign.

This is the tale of a 9-year-old lad among the British colonials captured one day by a roving Indian band, who is then adopted into the tribe to take the place of a recently deseased son of an Iroquois chief.

The boy ultimately finds himself siding, and fighting, with the Indians during an attack (including the attempted massacre of women).

Seven years later, in a time jump, the war is over and George is returned back to his family as part of the peace treaty. He now finds that his family has taken on slaves, George's father (formerly a serf) now taking on illusions of grandeur as a landowner. George decides he's more Indian than White Man, so back he goes to the reservation.

Lensed in Rumania (where an Indian/Western backlot has been constructed), pic is neither historically nor anthropologically correct in factual details. It does illustrate how fascinated East German (other Socialist lands as well, for that matter) are with American Indian culture. Minus the legacy of Karl May adaptations (West Germany has dibs on Winnetou and Shatterhand tales), other approaches to the subject have been sought in order to praise the nobility of the savage against the imperialism of the European powers in settling America. "Bluebird" is a prime example of exploiting legends from a different point-of-view.
— Holt.

The Violent Breed
(ITALIAN-COLOR)

A Cannon Films release of a Visione Cinematografica production. Produced by Ettore Spagnuolo. Directed by Fernando Di Leo. Stars Henry Silva, Harrison Muller, Woody Strode, Carole Andrè. Screenplay, Di Leo, Nino Marino; camera (Technicolor), Roberto Gerardi; editor, Arnold Jury; music, Paolo Rustichelli; stunt coordinator, Gil Galimberti; special effects, Paolo Ricci; associate producer, Fabio Diotallevi. Reviewed on MGM/UA Home Video vidcassette; N.Y., Dec. 21, 1985. (No MPAA Rating). Running time: **91 MINS.**
Kirk Cooper . . . . Henry Silva
Mike Martin . . . . Harrison Muller
Paolo . . . . Woody Stode
Also with: Carole Andrè, Debora Keith, Danika.

Italian filmmaker Fernando Di Leo seems to have made the actioner "The Violent Breed" without a finished script. Story and characters' behavior makes no sense at all and action is perfunctory. Domestic distributor Cannon Films elected to send this 1983-lensed junker direct to homevideo without theatrical exposure.

Henry Silva toplines (in a very small role) alongside the ubiquitous Harrison Muller and vet Woody Strode as three commandos whose mission to rescue kids in Southeast Asia leads to an unexplained falling out when Strode turns against his buddies.

Without transition, next scene is back in the States, with Silva now a CIA honcho sending Muller back to the Cambodia/Thailand/Laos border area in search of Strode. It seems that Strode, in league with the KGB and the Mafia, is running drugs and arms and generally acting like a nogoodnik. Muller teams up with a beautiful, underage prostitute there to find Strode's camp and ludicrously offer him a deal whereby the U.S. government would best the Russians and the Mafia's price for drugs. This leads to pointless shootouts.

Finale, making no sense from what has gone before, has Silva, Muller and Strode suddenly teamed up for another mission, the slate magically wiped clean.

If you can believe this nonsense, you'll probably believe in Strode, dubbed with another person's voice, as a character named Paolo.
—*Lor.*

Solidarnosc - The Hope From Gdansk
(DANISH-WEST GERMAN-DOCU-COLOR-16m)

Berlin, Dec. 17.
A Riverside Pix Tv Journalism production, Copenhagen, in collaboration with Westdeutscher Rundfunk (WDR), Cologne. A Documentary by Henrik Byrn. Only credits available. Reviewed at Landesbildstelle Berlin, Dec. 16, 1985. Running time: **80 MINS.**

Berlin — Henrik Byrn's docu

"Solidarnosc - The Hope From Gdansk" is much more than the typical tv news coverage of regular events going on in Poland these days. This one attempts to dig below the surface to take the pulse of the people who remember well and still stubbornly continue to support the days filled with hope when Lech Walesa and "Solidarity" practically revolutionized Socialism at the beginning of the present decade.

Docu opens with an interview (face concealed) with underground Solidarity leader, Jan Dzwonek. That such an interview could be filmed demonstrates how effective the organization is, as well as the constant difficulties Polish authorities face in keeping track of what foreign media journalists can and cannot do these days. From there it goes to covering events that led up to the Polish Election on Oct. 13, 1985, one that reporter Byrn feels was hardly as heavily observed by the masses as the government ultimately claimed.

On camera are contrasting life styles in Poland today. There's a silversmith who's obviously pleased with the way situations are right now, for he stands to make a small fortune for himself as a private businessman with all the material comforts of life and a government-approved passport that allows him to travel at will.

Compare this accommodating type, however, with the priest Henryk Jankowski, who is the friend and confessor of Lech Walesa and in charge of the administration of St. Brigit's Church in Gdansk (the current "haven" of the spirit of Solidarity) — and you have the full range of believers and nonbelievers in the once freely independent trade union. Byrn talks to the Party manager of the Lenin Shipyard, who pegs Walesa as a common electrical worker, but little more. He finds a schoolteacher who still stubbornly belongs to the Party — but when his back is turned, up goes a child's two fingers in a "v for victory" sign. When he interviews the election judges at a voting place, an extra judge — from Solidarity — lets it be known that a secret count is being made by Solidarnosc at the same time.

Finally, there's footage of the masses gathered at St. Brigit's Church for a public demonstration on the part of the Solidarity Movement. During a kind of medieval religious play, a child performer poignantly presents the case for Solidarity by exorting the crowd to pray for its leaders and its future success. It's on this note that the docu ends.

"The Hope From Gdansk" has been made available in several lengths and language versions for export abroad. Riverside Pix is a private tv enterprize in Denmark set up to secure the flow of information from Poland, particularly to present the case of the Radio Solidarnosc resistance against General Jaruzelski. —*Holl.*

Terry On The Fence
(BRITISH-COLOR)

A Rank Films presentation of an Eyeline Film and Video production of a Children's Film and Television Foundation film. Produced by Frank Godwin. Coproduced by Harold Orton. Written and directed by Godwin. Features entire cast. Camera (color), Ronald Maasz; editor, Gordon Grimward; music, Harry Robertson; production design, Maurice Fowler; sound, Stanley Phillips, Daryl Jordan, Colin Martin; stunts, Alan Stuart. Reviewed at the London Film Festival, Nov. 23, 1985. Running time: **70 MINS.**
Terry . . . . Jack McNicholl
Les . . . . Neville Watson
Tracey . . . . Tracey Ann-Morris
Mick . . . . Jeff Ward
Denis . . . . Matthew Barker
Plastic-head . . . . Brian Coyle
Mum . . . . Susan Jameson
Dad . . . . Martin Fisk
Gran . . . . Margery Mason

London — This uneven drama supposedly represents a move to more ambitious storylines for the sponsoring Children's Film and TV Foundation. Although pic touches on contempo themes of youth criminality, domestic cruelty and gang violence, it remains somewhat old-fashioned kid's film.

Story concerns Terry, a youth who runs away from home after a family squabble, only to find himself caught up in the frightening world of a youth gang.

Credible characterization generally is sacrificed to moral message. Gangleader Les goes through abrupt psychological transformations, from the personification of mindless violence to canny crook and then misunderstood youth with a heart of gold. His antisocial behavior is credited to a mother's cruelty.

Terry also behaves a little strangely, joining in a raid on his school with some bravado. The following day, he confesses his involvement in the crime and then hunts down Les so they can return the stolen goods together. Drawn up before a court, he has to explain why he did not surrender Les to the police.

Film has some moments of stirring comedy and pathos, but effect is diminished by uneven lighting.
— *Japa.*

Moi Vouloir Toi
(Me Want You)
(FRENCH-COLOR)

A Fechner/Gaumont release of a Christian Fechner/Films Optimistes/Films A2 coproduction. Produced by Fechner. Directed by Patrick Dewolf. Stars Gérard Lanvin, Jennifer. Screenplay, Dewolf, Patrice Leconte, Lanvin; camera (Fujicolor); Eduardo Serra; editor, Joëlle Hache; art director, Ivan Maussion; sound, Alain Lachassagne; music, Eric Demarsan, the groups Jerrycan and Blessed Virgins; production manager, Henri Brichetti. Reviewed at the Gaumont Colisée theater, Paris, Dec. 11, 1985. Running time: **86 MINS.**
With: Gérard Lanvin (Patrick Montanet), Jennifer (Alice Wexler), Patrick Russo, Corine Marienneau, Bernard Giraudeau, Clémentine Célarié.

Paris — Back to the basics in "Moi Vouloir Toi," tediously familiar corn in which Boy Meets Girl, nearly loses her, but wins her back because True Love Triumphs in the End. Despite a screenplay and direction that seem computer-programmed, this latest production by the green-thumbed Christian Fechner is off to a good start at local wickets.

Picture toplines actor Gérard Lanvin (costar of Fechner's recent b.o. smash, "The Specialists") and pop singer Jennifer. Fact that they are also off-screen husband and wife was no doubt seen as extra commercial spice, as was the idea of Lanvin himself writing the hip, contemporary dialog.

Lanvin is an early morning disk jockey for a private radio station and Jennifer the artistic director of an important recording house. Though they don't keep the same hours, they meet, fall in love, and move in together before the film is halfway through.

A perfect match made in screenwriters' heaven apparently, but, Lanvin has these bizarre notions about getting married and hearing the pitter-patter of little feet, while Jennifer, who's just been through a disappointing relationship (with walkon guest star Bernard Giraudeau, the other costar of "The Specialists"), is unwilling to tie herself down and compromise her career opportunities.

A real dilemma, but it's nothing a picturesque beachside cottage, an overload of dewy-eyed closeups and the sun setting into the sea behind the final slow-motion/freeze frame embrace can't resolve.

Pic was directed by newcomer Patrick Dewolf, who wrote the script with Lanvin and Patrice Leconte (who directed "The Specialists"). Production credits are handsome. —*Len.*

Inganni
(Deceptions)
(ITALIAN-COLOR)

An Off Limits release, produced by Marina Piperno for M.P. productions. Directed by Luigi Faccini. Stars Bruno Zanin. Screenplay, Faccini, Sergio Vecchio; camers (color), Marcello Gatti; editor, Gino Bartolini; music, Luis Bacalov. Reviewed at Rialto Cinema, Rome, Dec. 14, 1985. Running time: **90 MINS.**
Dino Campana . . . . Bruno Zanin
Sibilla Aleramo . . . . Olga Karlatos
Dr. Pariani . . . . Mattia Sbragia
Nun . . . . Daniela Morelli

Rome — "Deceptions" belongs to the category — becoming rarer all the time on the Italo scene — of the small, serious-minded indie, aimed at whatever audience chances its way in limited art house engagements. Based on the troubled life of poet Dino Campana and set mostly in a psychiatric institution of the 1920's, pic has had no easy commercial life since it won a prize at Locarno this summer. Sensitive and slow-moving with bursts of intensity, it seems a natural pickup for fests in search of quality Italo product in a lean year.

Helmer Luigi Faccini is appreciated for two previous features, "The Red Carnation," based on a Vittorini novel, and "In The Lost City Of Sarzana." The literary origins of "Deceptions" are present throughout the film, even though Campana (Bruno Zanin) has stopped writing by the time he is institutionalized at the age of 30. Visits from a patient psychiatrist, Dr. Pariani (Mattia Sbragia) are aimed at reawakening some lust for life and literature in the embittered, disillusioned poet, who isn't mad but merely lonely, indigent, and disgusted with society beyond the high walls that enclose him. In the meantime his work has been reevaluated and his poetry republished, and it's hard not to read the good doctor's interest in his famous patient as that of a licensed literary parasite. When at pic's end he opens the "secret diary" Campana has given him as reward for his perseverance and discovers it's all blank pages, we feel Campana has had the last laugh. At the cost of living out his days in the gruesome, melancholy asylum, he has remained true to himself.

All hands turn in excellent performances, particularly Bruno Zanin (who many years ago played the young hero in Federico Fellini's "Amarcord") as the hypersensitive, angry poet. Olga Karlatos is very credible as the well-known writer Sibilla Aleramo, who haunts Campana as he remembers their tempestuous love affair. Atmospheric lensing of natural landscapes is by Marcello Gatti. Many of the gentle, quiet inmates are non-actors, actually institutionalized. —Yung.

A Me Mi Piace
(I Like Her)
(ITALIAN-COLOR)

A CEIAD release, produced by Made In Italy 81 productions. Directed by Enrico Montesano. Stars Montesano. Screenplay, Laura Toscano, Franco Marotta. Montesano; camera (color), Danilo Desideri; editor, Antonio Siciliano; music, Vincent Tempera. Reviewed at Etoile Cinema, Rome, Dec. 14, 1985. Running time: 93 MINS.
Arturo . . . . Enrico Montesano
Marion . . . . Rochelle Redfield
Mike . . . . Dan Doby
Michela . . . . Lara Wendel

Rome — Roman comic Enrico Montesano makes his helming debut in a modest but likable tale in which he falls for his best friend's girl. Pic is professionally packaged and can boast one of the most attractive new discoveries of the year, Yank model Rochelle Redfield in her screen debut. Despite these virtues pic bottomed out quickly at the local boxoffice.

A timid, bespectacled program director for a great Milanese private tv network, Arturo (Montesano) leads a quiet, womanless existence (thanks to romantic heartbreak in his past) until his old schoolchum Mike (Dan Doby) walks back into his life, having been absent since '68 when they built barricades together. Since Mike is revealed to be an American millionaire, it is hard to accept this oft-repeated bit of background info, but it gives a clue to the kind of closet idealism lurking in Arturo's heart. Moving force of the story is Marion (Redfield), a tall, gorgeous, redheaded singer who has just left Mike for her manager. In the course of trying to get her back together with the heartbroken Mike, Arturo falls for her — of course — and she for him (why?).

Up to this point Mike has done nothing but drink, run up bills, and tear Arturo's Casa Vogue apartment to pieces. Like most of pic's gags, the joke is drawn paper thin, and carried to grotesque lengths (like Mike gambling away every stick of furniture, and all Arturo's money, while he sleeps). None of the comedy is hilarious, but it gently entertains with cultural crashes as the two Yanks, Mike and Marion, breeze through Arturo's carefully constructed world like fresh air, ingenuously trampling on the material values that have crept up on him with age while they liberate him from same.

As a director Montesano is unobtrusive, backed up by a top-flight technical crew. Sets and costumes are particularly fun. —Yung.

Yu Qing Sao
(Jade Love)
(TAIWANESE-COLOR)

A Cosmos film production. Executive producers Zhang Yutian, Xiao Jing. Produced by Li Xing. Directed by Zhang Yi. from a short story by Bai Xianyong; camera (color), Lin Zirong; editor, Lin Shanliang; music, Zhang Hongyi; production design, Zou Zhiliang; costumes, Song Shu Lanying; sound, Wang Rongfang, Chedna Jianhua. Reviewed at the London Film Festival, Nov. 15, 1985. Running time: 104 MINS.
Yu Ch'ing . . . . Yang Hulshan
Ch'ing-sheng . . . . Ruan Shengtian
Li Jung-jung . . . . Ling Dingfeng
Chin Yen-fei . . . . Fu Juan

London — Like the short story on which it is based, "Jade Love" takes a boy's eye view on the adult world, gradually focusing in on the ill-fated relationship between his nanny, a maturing beauty, and a sickly stripling. It's the first serious feature directed by Chang Yi, who emerges as a director to watch.

The boy Jung-jung is the energetic and mischievous son of the ruling family in a town in China during World War II. His wickedness is restrained with the arrival of his beautiful nanny Yu Ch'ing whom he guards jealously from wagging tongues and importunate suitors.

Dramatic thrust of narrative comes from the boy's unwitting role in creating tragedy. Discovering the nanny has a secret lover whom she supports and cares for, Jung-jung befriends Ch'ing-sheng. He takes him to the theater and introduces him to a young actress. Ch'ing-sheng finds liberation and health in his relationship with the actress. Yu Ch'ing, unable to reestablish the former relationship, kills him and herself.

The qualities of Chang Yi's direction rest in his evocation of the atmosphere of an aristocratic household, the subtle performances extracted from all performers and constant fixing of the camera onto illuminating psychological moments. Film is shot in muted colors which occasionally burst into magical brightness. —Japa.

The Final Executioner
(ITALIAN-COLOR)

A Cannon Films release of an Immagine production. Produced by Luciano Appignani. Directed by Romolo Guerrieri. Stars William Mang, Marina Costa, Harrison Muller, Woody Strode. Screenplay, Roberto Leoni; camera (Luciano Vittori color), Guglielmo Mancori; editor, Alessandro Lucidi; music, Carlo De Nonno; production manager, Umberto Innocenzi; assistant director, Filiberto Fiaschi; set design, Eugenio Liverani; special effects, Roberto Ricci; associate producer, Pino Buricchi. Reviewed on MGM/UA Home Video vidcassette, N.Y., Dec. 21, 1985. (No MPAA Rating.) Running time: 94 MINS.
Alan . . . . William Mang
Edra . . . . Marina Costa
Erasmus . . . . Harrison Muller
Sam . . . . Woody Strode
Also with: Margi Newton, Stefano Davanzati, Renato Miracco, Maria Romano, Luca Giordana, Karl Zinny.

"The Final Executioner," also known as "The Last Warrior," is a subpar 1983 Italian science fiction film set after a nuclear holocaust (represented by lowercase stock footage of volcanic eruptions and bombed out neighborhoods). Cannon pickup wisely bypassed U.S. theaters in favor of homevideo release.

Story vaguely borrows from classics such as "The Most Dangerous Game" and "The Tenth Victim," postulating humanity divided into two groups, the rich, privileged few and the radiation contaminated masses. The rich folk hunt down the contaminated population for sport.

Cybernetics expert Alan (top-billed William Mang) discovers that after 80,000,000 people have been killed in hunts there are no more contaminated folks to shoot down. To keep their privileges, however, the rich class continues to designate people as "target material" and kill off healthy folks, perpetuating the system.

Alan teams up with a tough, ex-cop Sam (Woody Strode) to launch an assault on a hunters' headquarters. It takes many reels of filler, punctuated by extraneous sex scenes, until the good guys make some headway.

With no special effects, little atmosphere and a one-joke script, pic is science fiction in name only. Poor dubbing negates the cast's efforts, though Strode is an impressive screen presence convincingly beating up multiple young guys in hand-to-hand combat. —Lor.

Billy Ze Kick
(FRENCH-COLOR)

An AAA/Hachette Première release of a Hachette Première/Hamster/FR3 Films coproduction. Produced by Pierre Grimblat and René Cleitman. Stars Francis Perrin. Directed by Gérard Mordillat. Screenplay, Gérard Guérin, Mordillat, from the novel by Jean Vautrin (a.k.a. Jean Herman); camera (Eastmancolor), Jean Monsigny; editor, Michèle Masnier-Catonné; art director, Théo Meurisse; sound, Guillaume Sciama; costumes, Caroline de Vivaise; make-up, Maud Baron; music, Jean-Claude Petit; song lyrics, Mordillat; songs performed by Zabou and Marie-France; production manager, Eric Lambert; producers, Nicolas Traube, Michel Faure. Reviewed at the UGC Biarritz theater, Paris, Dec. 21, 1985. Running time: 87 MINS.
Roger Chapeau . . . . Franics Perrin
Juliette Chapeau . . . . Zabou
Madam Achère . . . . . Dominique Lavanant
Zulie-Berthe Chapeau . . . . Cerise Bloc
Commissioner Bellanger . Michaël Lonsdale
Alcide . . . . Yves Robert
Miss Peggy Spring . . . . Marie-France
Inspector Cordier . . . . Jacques Pater
Hippo . . . . Pascal Pistacio
Little Ed . . . . Benjamin Azenstarck
Eugène . . . . Patrice Valota

Paris — "Billy Ze Kick" is an absurdist comedy-mystery based on a novel by noted thriller author Jean Vautrin, who has moonlighted less successfully as a screenwriter-film director under the name Jean Herman. Screen rights for the book passed through the hands of several producers, writers and directors, who could not lick the story's essential adaptation problems, until it reached producer Pierre Grimblat, of Hamster Films, and helmer Gérard Mordillat. They initially planned it as an episode in Hamster's popular tv thriller skein, "Série Noire," then decided to revamp the project as a theatrical feature.

Vautrin's novel is about a third-rate cop who discovers that the tall-tales he has been spinning to his daughter about a mysterious killer called Billy Ze Kick have been coming true and that the murderer is in fact knocking off women in his own neighborhood. Story is written in a style immersed in slang, fractured narrative and neologistic wordplay that is in good part inspired by writers like Raymond Queneau and his ''Zazie dans le Metro.''

Mordillat, who displayed imaginative handling of non-realistic narrative in his debut feature in 1983, ''Vive la Sociale,'' applies himself with verve to finding a cinematic equivalent to Vautrin's literary conceits. The results, though full of visual exuberance and energetic performances, fail to convince.

He is adroit in creating a bizarre, often cartoon universe with offbeat characters and surreal incidents, but he and his co-scripter Gérard Guerin offer no key to reading the puzzle, which concludes without one being any the wiser about what has gone on.

Cast is headed by Francis Perrin, as the mediocre *flic* who becomes the victim of his own imagination, and the vivacious Zabou, as his frustrated wife, who winningly performs two musical numbers. Michaël Lonsdale is a Shakespeare-quoting police inspector who is kidnaped by Yves Robert, an anarchist who has turned his suburban house into a stronghold against urban renewal, and Dominique Lavanant is the stuck-up, lovelorn concierge of the apartment complex in which the murders take place. Adolescent newcomer Cerise Bloc is fine as Perrin's strange daughter, who seems to be the catalyst of all the story's catastrophes.

Production credits, and Jean-Claude Petit's peppy music, are smart. —*Len.*

Le Transfuge
(The Turncoat)
(FRENCH-WEST GERMAN-COLOR)

An I.D. Films release of a Plaisance Presentations/TF 1/Telemunchen/RTBF coproducton. Produced by Daniel Vaissaire. Directed by Philippe Lefebvre. Screenplay, Simon Michael and Philippe Lefebvre; camera (color), Jacques Guérin; editor, Elisabeth Fernandez; sound, Michel Picardat; music, Luis Bacalov. Reviewed at the Monte Carlo theater, Paris, Nov. 26, 1985. Running time: **85 MINS.**
Bernard Corain ....Bruno Cremer
Heinz Steger .... Heinz Bennent
Captain Clement .... Jean-François Balmer
Mrs. Steger ....Lisa Kreuzer

Paris — ''Le Transfuge'' is a conventional espionage tale about an unassuming French provincial industrialist (Bruno Cremer) recruited by the Secret Service to make contact with and sound out a potential top-level defector during his periodic business trips to East Germany.

When he confirms that the subject, a former executive intelligence man now in official disgrace, would consider coming over to the West, Cremer is sent back to set up the operation, gets entangled in escape plans and must accompany the defector in his flight.

Philippe Lefebvre, a tv helmer who made his theatrical debut last year with ''Le Juge,'' a trite but well-executed drama about a crusading French magistrate, confirms his technical skill in John Le Carré country, moving the story along with detached efficiency. Script, by Lefebvre and Simon Michael (author of Claude Zidi's ''Les Ripoux''), is nonetheless familiar in its twists and turns and final surprise revelation, which any self-respecting filmgoer will guess before long.

Acting by Bruno Cremer as the reluctant industrialist, Heinz Bennent as the defector and Lisa Kreuzer as latter's wife is adequate for story's purposes. Tech credits are good.

But Lefebvre needs a first-class script to land him firmly in the camp of active feature directors. —*Len.*

Arunata Pera
(Before The Dawn)
(SRI LANKAN-B&W)

A New Wave Films production. Produced by Ananda Gunasekara. Directed by Amarnath Jayatilaka. Features entire cast. Screenplay, Jayatilaka, Kumara Karunaratna, from a story by Karunaratna; camera (b&w), Suminda Weerasingha; editor, Elmo Halliday; production design, Joe Dambulugala; music, W.B. Makuloluwa. Reviewed at the London Film Festival, Nov. 17, 1985. Running time: **80 MINS.**
Banda ....Wijeratna Warakagoda
Menika ....Chandi Rasika
Banda's mother .D.M. Denawaka Hamine
Landlord ....Joe Dambulugala
Eldest child .Ranjeewa Amarajit Jayatilaka
Youngest child Sundeep Sanjaya Jayatilaka
Daughter .....Madhuri Anjana Jayatilaka

London — Conceived as part of a trilogy about the Sri Lankan peasantry, ''Before The Dawn'' tells of the oft-narrated story fo a peasant forced into penury by the exploitative practices of a local landholder. Film's style is simple but emotionally devastating.

Film's impact comes from its double flashback structure. The imprisoned peasant Banda initially recounts the tale of happy days reaping a good harvest. When that crop is confiscated by his creditors, he has to seek work elsewhere and is arrested.

Returning to his village in high spirits, Banda asks after his absent wife. He is told how domestic service and wagging tongues had resulted in her death during childbirth.

Director Amarnath Jayatilaka, who nurtured this project over 15 years, uses the camera tellingly to chronicle the joys and hardships of peasant life. When tragedies befall the family, the responses of its members are emphasized through precise editing and skillfully orchestrated shots. The film reaches a chilling climax as the older son runs around the village with a blazing torch to seek help for his suffering mother, only to return and find her dead.

The black and white lensing is skillful, and the film is scored sensitively. —*Japa.*

La Nuit Porte Jarretelles
(The Night Wears Suspenders)
(FRENCH-COLOR)

A Forum Distribution release of an Avidia production. Written and directed by Virginie Thevenet. Features entire cast. Camera (color), Alain Lasfargues; editor, Jacqueline Mariani; sound, Pierre Donnadieu; music, André Demay and Mikado. Reviewed at the Republique theater, Paris, Dec. 15, 1985. Running time: **85 MINS.**
With: Jezabel Carpi, Ariel Genet, Caroline Loeb, Jacques de Gunsbourg, Eva Ionesco, Arielle Dombasle.

Paris — ''La Nuit Porte Jarretelles' is a low-budget sleeper that opened early this year in a specialized situation and has worked its way tenaciously to over 100,000 admissions in Paris, a score more expensive arthouse items usually fail to attain.

It's hard, however, to find much in this first feature by 28-year-old actress Virginie Thevenet that warrants its unusual success. Thevenet, who also scripted, shows an intermittent sense of provocative fun and irreverence, but her debut suffers from her filmmaking inexperience and technical inadequacies.

Story, which might have had more effect as a short, relates the adventures of a hip young girl who tries to pervert a timid young man by dragging him through the erotic nightlife of Paris. There are visits to a sex shop, and the Bois de Boulogne with its transvestite hookers.

All of this has the feeling of a series of sketches tied loosely together, and this overlong guided tour through seedy, nocturnal Paris finally is wearing because its two protagonists remain insignificant and because its shock value seems outdated.

Thevenet is preparing a second film shortly and has received state coin support on the basis of her script. —*Len.*

Brás Cubas
(BRAZILIAN-COLOR)

An Embrafilme release of a Julio Bressane/Embrafilme production. Directed by Julio Bressane. Features entire cast. Screenplay, Bressane, Antonio Medina, based on the novel ''Brás Cubas,'' by Machado de Assis; camera (Eastmancolor), José Tadeu; editor, Dominique Paris; art direction, Luciano Figueiredo; costumes, Vera Barreto Leite, Kika Lopes; sound, Didi Gupper, Guaracy Rodriges; production direction, Sonia Dias, Romulo Marinho. Reviewed at Sala Glauber Rocha, II Intl. Festival of Cinema, TV and Video of Rio de Janeiro, Nov. 24, 1985. Running time: **100 MINS.**
Brás Cubas.....Luiz Fernando Guimarães
Virgilia ....Bia Nunes
Bento Cubas ....Ankito
Marcela ....Regina Casé
Quincas Borba............Renato Borghi
Tio João ....Colé
Lobo Neves ....Paschoal Vilaboim
Cotrim ....Guará
Sabina...................Cristina Pereira
Also with: Helio Ari, Maria Gladys, Wilson Grey, Telma Reston, Breno Moroni, Marcia Rodrigues, Ariel Coelho, Dedé Veloso, Sonia Dias, Jorge Cherques, Sandro Siqueira, Marise Farias, Martim Francisco.

Rio de Janeiro — Julio Bressane is the main architect of the Brazilian underground movement of the late sixties which generated a set of experimental features, from 1968 to the mid seventies, that can be compared in importance to the *cinema novo.*

The experimental Brazilian cinema, however, did not manage to find a market, even through University circuits, that would allow it continuity. Some local experimentalists, therefore, turned to the conventional cinema; others simply gave up. Bressane, together with his fellow filmmaker from the early times Rogerio Sganzerla, are among the very few that kept following his way.

''Brás Cubas'' has its starting point in a novel by Machado de Assis, a celebrated Brazilian writer of the late nineteenth century. Bressane follows Assis' ironic view of Rio's social structure of that time. The plot is not much more than an excuse for the inclusion of many other Machadian characters, including the writer himself. Bressane harmonically blends two universes, his and Machado de Assis' to build a third one, rich, unpredictable and frequently very funny.

This is the same strategy used by the author on his previous film, ''Tabu,'' when three actual characters of Rio's cultural life, who lived in three different epochs, are seen together interacting their philosophy. As in ''Tabu,'' Bressane develops a high technical standard, especially through cinematography (then by Murilo Salles, now by José Tadeu). The apparently chaotic narrative is in fact highly sophisticated.) ''Brás Cubas'' is a statement on the medium to be consumed by sophisticated filmgoers who have the disposition to get into this kind of discussion. Those who are willing to do that will get into a fantastic and beautiful universe.—*Hoin.*

Wurlitzer
(WEST GERMAN-DOCU-B&W)

An Antje Starost Film Production, Berlin. A Documentary written and directed by Antje Starost and Hans-Helmut Grotjahn. Camera (b&w), Axel Brandt, editor, Christiane Fazlagic; Starost; sound, Ulrike Isenberg, Wolfgang Schukrafft; text, Manfred Flügge; narrator, Maren Kroymann; music, Büdi Siebert, Wolfgang Stryi; production manager, Klaus Volkenborn. Reviewed at German Film & TV Academy, Berlin, Dec. 20, 1985. Running time: **103 MINS.**
With: Christine Vogt, Bianka Vogt, Liane Vogt, Helmut Vogt, and Gustav Vogt.

Berlin — More in the style of a film-essay than in the genre of documentary, Antje Starost and Hans-Helmut Grotjahn's "Wurlitzer" — its subtitle is "The Discovery of the Present" — will fascinate film historians for the peek it offers into the development of the sound movie. As hinted in the title, the same corner of Bavaria that helped to initiate the sound film is also the birth-area of the pioneer who put his name on the Wurlitzer organ and jukebox.

In the village of Wurlitzer in the Franken hills (near Hof) still live the family and brother of inventor Hans Vogt, who, together with fellow inventors Engel and Massolle, developed the Tri-Ergon system in 1918-19 that led to sound being recorded photographically on film. Hans Vogt's brother, Gustav (b. 1900), is still alive — and recollects in the film on the personality and fledgling exploits of the older Hans (b. 1890) as the son of a farmer-blacksmith.

Starost and Grotjahn appear to have simply fallen in love with the roll of the seasons on the rolling and rather idyllic landscape. More footage is spent lensing the daily labors of a farming community than probing into the personality of the inventor himself. The docu reverently captures the rhythms of life in Bavarian Vogtland, or Upper Franconia, and as such it is a pleasure to watch.

When the helmers dip into the font of film history throughout the treatise, however, the well is dry. It appears that the legacy of Hans Vogt — old film footage, professional and private photographs, and other cinemabilia — is still in the hands of a family squabbling over an inheritance. Film archives have made bids on the legacy, all to no avail up to the present. ♦

What's known is that the Tri-Ergon inventors — Vogt, Engel, Massolle — presented their first "talkie" in 1922, but the industry was not yet ready to give up silent movies supported by the strains of a Wurlitzer organ (invented by another Bavarian, who made his fortune later in America). So eventually the patent was sold to a firm in Switzerland, which in turn resold it to Fox in Hollywood in 1926. As for Vogt, he entered upon a prosperous engineering career after giving up the ghost on revolutionizing the motion picture industry.

"Wurlitzer" preemed at the recent Hof fest, and will next be on view at the Rotterdam fest. Stunning lensing and a feeling for rural landscape make the docu side of the project something special. Promo shorts (one by Lotte Reiniger) are also a delight to watch, and whet the appetite for more.—*Holl.*

Scream
(COLOR)

Tedious in the extreme.

A Cal-Com Releasing release of a Calendar International Pictures/Cougar Films Ltd. production. Executive producer, Byron Quisenberry. Produced by Clara Huff, Hal Buchanan, Larry Quisenberry. Written and directed by Bryon Quisenberry. Features entire cast. Camera (Cinereel color), Rick Pepin; editor, B.W. Kestenberg; music, Joseph Conlan; sound, Harold Belbin; assistant director-production manager, Fred Allison; stunt coordinator, John Nowak. Reviewed at UA Twin 2 theater, N.Y., Dec. 27, 1985. (MPAA Rating: R.) Running time: **81 MINS.**

Bob	Pepper Martin
John	Hank Worden
Al	Alvy Moore
Stan	(John) Ethan Wayne
Laura	Julie Marine
Ross	Gregg Palmer
Charlie	Woody Strode

Also with: Bobby Diamond, Joseph Alvarado, Anna Bronston, Nancy St. Marie.

"Scream" is one of the crummiest horror films made during the late, unlamented boom of five years ago. Shot in 1981 under the title "The Outing," pic was briefly released in Florida in 1983 and has just bowed in New York.

Filmmaker Byron Quisenberry uses the hoary formula of several folks out hiking for the weekend at a remote western ghost town, where they are killed off one by one. Most of the killings occur offscreen (with sound effects) and the killer is never shown. What makes the film so bad is that Quisenberry does not include any interesting incidents between killings. All there is consists of people wandering around foolishly in the dark or sitting around moping (they're 30 miles from the nearest town and unable to get help).

Tedious exercise in minimalist horror is not helped by poor acting and sluggish editing. The only interesting moment comes when after an hour Woody Strode rides into town on horseback out of a mist, styled like his Western persona from John Ford and Sergio Leone films. He cryptically regales the confused cast with a tale of his exploits 40 years ago as a sailor, rides out of town, and then comes back to save the day with a well-timed rifle shot.

Final explanation scene is completely bungled, with unintelligible voiceover narration and panning camera over to a 1891 sea captain's portrait which attempts to connect the murders with Strode's seafaring story.—*Lor.*

A Pushkin Trilogy
(SOVIET-ANIMATED-COLOR)

A Soyuzmuitfilm release. A feature animation film in three parts written and directed by Andrei Khrzhanovsky, based on illustrations by Alexander Pushkin. Design, V. Yankinevsky, Yu, Batanin, G. Arkadyev; camera (color), I. Skidin-Bosin, V. Strukov; music, Alfred Shnitke; editors, L. Georgiyeva, N. Trescheva. Reviewed at London Film Fest, Nov. 23, 1985. Running time: **98 MINS.**

London — Soviet animation master Andrei Khrzhanosky, known particularly for his adaptation of fables and fairy tales, spent five years researching a legacy of some 2,000 pen drawings by poet Alexander Pushkin on the pages of his manuscripts over a century ago. Although one can find these drawings in publications on the work of Pushkin, this is the first time attention has been given totally to assessing the sharp satirical value of what some might simply classify as doodling.

The project was undertaken in three parts: "I Fly To You In Memory," "I Am With You Again" and "Autumn" each remarkable for amusing portraits of both the characters in the poem and self-portraits. When these figures are set in motion via the animation technique, we find Pushkin wandering among his contemporaries commenting quite sarcastically on the life and times about him. He is on the side of tried-and-convicted revolutionaries, is in constant quarrels with the censors on his publications, and has to explain his position on more than one occasion with the czar.

Pushkin's turbulent life (ending in a tragic death by duel) is covered to good effect in the choice of the passages, while the spoken texts come across like an enlightening "Readers' Theater" exercise. Music by Alfred Shnitke is a standout.
— *Holl.*

Samuel Lount
(CANADIAN-COLOR)

A Moonshine Prods. presentation. Produced by Elvira Lount. Executive producers, Keane, Don Haig. Directed by Laurence Keane. Screenplay, Phil Savath, Keane; camera (color), Marc Champion; editor, Richard Martin; sound, Clark McCarron; art director, Kim Steer; costumes, Olga Dimitrov; music, Kitaro. Reviewed at Ridge Theater, Vancouver, Dec. 15, 1985. Running time: **95 MINS.**

Samuel Lount	R.H. Thomson
Elizabeth Lount	Linda Griffiths
William Lyon Mackenzie	Cedric Smith
Bishop Strachan	Donald Davis
David Wilson	David Fox
Sir Francis Bond Head	Andrew Gillies

Vancouver — The factual basis for this modest period pic will prove a real eye-opener for many North American viewers. Seldom in its brief history has the new Canadian film industry taken a long, hard look at the historical roots of its social system. Unhappily the Canadian Broadcasting Corp., in alliance with Telefilm Canada, chose to proceed with a dynamic yarn without adequate funding ($C1,800,000) or a practical shooting schedule (33 days).

In 1837 firebrand orator and journalist William Lyon Mackenzie provoked a rebellion among dispossessed settlers in Upper Canada, resulting in an abortive march upon Toronto. Blacksmith Samuel Lount, a devout pacifist, against his better judgment became a leader in this revolt and was hanged for treason. Mackenzie and Lount sought to overthrow The Family Pact that denied the colonists a fair chance at becoming property owners in the New World.

Tyro helmer Laurence Keane, working against considerable odds, has fashioned a respectable action-drama, with an emphasis upon religious conviction, that is distinguished by a trio of fine performances. R.H. Thomson strives manfully to overcome the saintliness that seemingly characterized the real-life Samuel Lount. Cedric Smith lends his extensive legit savvy to the wild-eyed, wayward Mackenzie, who survived the fiasco and was the recipient of an unofficial pardon. David Fox is never less than riveting as Lount's mentor, leader of the Children of Peace sect, and a public figure as elusive as any master politico.

The lesser roles in Keane's ambitious socio-political canvas regrettably are played on a single note that lends a facetious aspect to the villainy on display. Keane has a sharp eye for the telling image and an acute ear for the impassioned belief of the era. The music of Japanese composer Kitaro lacks the full-bloodedness needed by the genre.

All other credits are above par. The pic's future lies primarily in the art house and college circuits, on paycable and possibly on vidcassette in Canada. —*Gran.*

Big Shots
(ISRAELI-COLOR)

A TOMLI Prods. Ltd. film. Produced by Ron Ackerman. Directed by Yankul Goldwasser. Screenplay, Haim Merin, Goldwasser; camera (United Studios Color), Ilan Rosenberg; editor, Anat Lubarski; music, Shlomo Gronich; art direction, Yoram Barzilai; costumes, Zmira Hershkovitz. Reviewed at the Royal Theater, L.A., Nov. 22, 1985. (No MPAA Rating.) Running time: **100 MINS.**

Sammy	Uri Gavriel
Herzl	Moshe Ivgi

Jhanna . . . . Zadok Zarum
Yacov . . . . Juky Arkin
Miriam . . . . Judith Millo
Ben-Shoshan . . . . Makram Churi

Hollywood — One of the joys of watching foreign films is to get some insight into another country's culture. Unfortunately, that's not the case with the Israeli film "Big Shots," which follows the same storyline as any low-budget American cops-and-robbers caper, but leaves out any of the humor. Students of Hebrew might come away with a couple of new off-color colloquial sayings, but it's doubtful that it will appeal to the usual high-brow foreign film audience.

Central characters are a couple of bumbling petty criminals, Sammy and Herzl, who fantasize about scoring big so that one day they can read about themselves on the crime page of the newspaper.

Sammy (Uri Gavriel) likes to play the stud, while Herzl (Moshe Ivgi) is constantly preoccupied with securing his next cocaine fix.

They read about the largest local police bust in history where the cops recover $500,000 and decide to break into police headquarters to get it.

Instead of trying to pull off the job alone, they convince two retired burglars — Jhanna and Yacov — to join in their scheme.

After the first few minutes of the film, it's pretty easy to figure out what happens to these inept and greedy low-lifes whose lives become increasingly sordid with each successive frame.

However, the actors do a fine job playing criminals devoid of charm or a sense of humor, working with a script that is essentially pretty pat stuff.

"Big Shots" is the first feature film directed by Yankul Goldwasser, who also coscripted.

It is obvious that he had very little money because the picture never looks or sounds anything less than a crude production.

It doesn't explain how he could do so little with so many reasonably good actors to show something of Israeli life other than the seedy world of unsympathetic criminals. —*Brit.*

Martin Niemöller
(WEST GERMAN-COLOR/ B&W-DOCU-16m)

A Karnick & Richter, Darmstadt coproduction with Sender Freies Berlin (SFB). Written and directed by Hannes Karnick and Wolfgang Richter, in collaboration with Dietmar Schmidt. Camera (color, b&w), Richter; sound Karnick; editor, Richter; music, Frank Wolff. Reviewed at Bali Kino, Berlin, Dec. 2, 1985. Running time: **95 MINS.**
With: Martin Niemöller.

Berlin — Historians will recognize the name of Martin Niemöller as one of those on Adolf Hitler's hate list and Eleanor Roosevelt's save list during seven years of imprisonment in concentration camps at Sachsenhausen and Dachau. Docufilmers Hannes Karnick and Wolfgang Richter's "Martin Niemöller" approached the Protestant pastor just after he passed his 90th birthday in 1982 through a mutual friend, Dietmar Schmidt. A lengthy interview was conducted on positions held by the "fighting pastor" over the decades from U-Boat commander to spiritual leader of today's peace movement. Two years later, before the docu was completed, both Niemöller and Schmidt died.

Thus, as a statement on the times, Karnick and Richter's "Martin Niemöller" scores as one of the more interesting portrait documentaries released hereabouts recently. The Grand Old Man talks about his past experiences as a U-Boat commander in World War I ("where real democracy was practiced, as everybody's life depended on everybody else's opinion on how to come through it all"), his confrontation with Hitler and imprisonment as the Führer's "personal captive" in the camps, his narrow escape from the SS hit list at the end of the war and then further internment under the Americans for various political reasons (he was released upon going on a hunger strike), his warm contacts with Gandhi, Albert Schweitzer and Karl Barth, his publicized trips to Washington, Moscow and Hanoi in the cause of world peace, and his controversial role as church leader in postwar Germany — particularly as a spokesman from a position of authority for the World Council of Churches — that was to infuriate Chancellor Adenauer and on several occasions nearly cost him his job.

If ever a Lutheran pastor since the inception of Protestantism stamped his personality on the pages of history, then it was Niemöller. Much like Martin Luther, he was stubbornly tenacious when he made up his mind. But he also had a simplicity in expressing himself and a way of absorbing criticism like a lightning rod in the middle of a storm. His disarming argument was always that he spoke out in the name of humanity — "What would Jesus have said?"

Karnick and Richter intersperse their and Schmidt's questions with illustrative film and tv clips, excerpts from newspapers and published statements by Niemöller on all his lifelong stances in the name of peace and pacifism. A chronological approach gives the docu a certain logical order, as well as engendering a feeling of expectancy for those familiar with the history of the world peace movement and the personality in question.

Perhaps it's well that little in the way of contradictory material surfaces throughout the interview, for the positions themselves are clear enough in the long run. After all, one agrees with Niemöller, or he doesn't. This particular pastor wouldn't have had it any other way. More than a docu, this is a legacy.

Pic was winner of a Silver Dove at the recent Leipzig fest. —*Holl.*

Ginger e Fred
(Ginger And Fred)
(ITALIAN/FRENCH/W. GERMAN-COLOR)

An Istituto Luce/Italnoleggio Cinematografico release, produced by Alberto Grimaldi for P.E.A. Produzioni (Rome), Revcom Films (Paris), Stella Films (Munich) in cooperation with RAI-1. Directed by Federico Fellini. Stars Giulietta Masina and Marcello Mastroianni. Screenplay, Fellini, Tonino Guerra, Tullio Pinelli; camera (color) Tonino Delli Colli, Ennio Guarnieri; editor, Nino Baragli, Ugo De Rossi, Ruggero Mastroianni; music, Nicola Piovani; art director, Dante Ferretti; costumes, Danilo Donati. Reviewed at International Recording, Rome, Jan. 9, 1986. Running time: **126 MINS.**
Amelia Bonetti (Ginger) . . Giulietta Masina
Pippo Botticella
(Fred) . . . . Marcello Mastroianni
Show host . . . . Franco Fabrizi
Admiral . . . . Frederick Von Ledenburg
Asst. Director . . . . Martin Blau
Toto . . . . Toto Mignone
Transvestite . . . . Augusto Poderosi
Mafioso . . . . Francesco Casale
Also with: Frederick Von Thun, Henri Lartigue, Jean Michel Antoine, Antonio Iurio, Nando Pucci Negri, Laurentina Guidotti, Elena Cantarone.

Rome — For those who identified the sinking vessel of "And The Ship Sails On" with the cinema, Federico Fellini's "Ginger And Fred" can be read as a kind of Part II, showing the apotheosis of its rival, tv. This utterly Fellini entertainment, set in a tv studio before and during the live broadcast of a variety-talk show, brings together the director's pet themes with his two sterling thesps, wife Giulietta Masina and Marcello Mastroianni.

With the first dating back to Fellini's co-directorial debut "Variety Lights" ('50) and the second to "La Dolce Vita" ('60), and a little bit of almost every other picture thrown in, watching "Ginger And Fred" is like seeing a fast-forward recap of a long and fruitful career. Though the action is fast and fun, a dark hand of melancholy overshadows all. Easy viewing for nostalgia fans, pic is headed for the same prestige art house runs as its recent predecessors. Pic is being released 10 days earlier in France than Italy; MGM/UA will handle U.S. and Canadian distribution this spring.

Visually and structurally pic hales back to "City Of Women." Center of gravity rests with Amelia Bonetti (Masina) and Pippo Botticella (Mastroianni), a long-broken-up ballroom and tap dance team who were famous 30 years ago as "Ginger And Fred," homegrown imitations of Astaire and Rogers. The aging pair has been brought out of oblivion and called to Rome to appear on a tv show peopled with an unholy mixture of lookalikes, cheap imitations of Clark Gable and Marcel Proust, Ronald Reagan and Kojak.

At a time when most filmgoers are under 30, the pic chooses to view the world of the '80s from an oldster's point of view as all trashy advertising and apocalyptic horror, a universe of omnipresent boob tubes broadcasting non-stop nonsense and vulgarity.

Ginger, a widow who now runs a large family and small industry in the north, arrives like a babe in the woods at the chaotic, uncivilized train station. By the time she has been herded into the Manager Palace Hotel with all the other tv guests, she bitterly regrets having let her dignity in for a beating. The real reason she came was to see Fred again. She finds him that night, drunk and snoring in the next room. Badly aged and down-at-the-heels, he's spent some of the intervening years in an asylum and has agreed to come out of retirement for the meager recompense.

While pic casts shuddering glances at a seemingly endless universe of grotesque characters (as usual, virtually all thesps are non-pros), soulless tv personnel, menacing motorcyclists, punks, transvestites, etc., it also achieves a few moments of real magic. These involve Fred and Ginger, who are perfect counterpoint, alone.

Masina wavers between the big-eyed innocent of "Cabiria" and a more realistic bourgeoise granny, who probably spends the regulation number of hours in front of the tv set herself. Mastroianni outdoes himself in adding another classic to his growing gallery of last-legs oldsters who still have a spark of feisty rebellion in them and intend to go down swinging. He is embarrassing when he starts in with his dirty jokes, exhilarating as the unrepentant anarchist who wants to use his moment of televised fame to call the viewers "pe-co-ro-ni!" a more contemptuous word than sheep. Wearing long white hair that is thinning fast, Fellini's topcoat, hat and scarf, his resemblance to helmer is even physical.

Hard as it is to parody a tv show, the Fellini touch at least makes it lavishly visual, a treat of incredible costumes (Danilo Donati) and sets (Dante Ferretti). Franco Fabrizi plays the toothful host who presents a succession of levitating monks and hysterical housewives.

Gorgeously lensed by Ennio Guarnieri and Tonino Delli Colli, the tv studio is transformed into a circus ring, with a dwarf orchestra and long-legged showgirls. When Fred and Ginger's turn comes, there is a power failure; in a dreamlike moment of frozen time, they talk about running off in the dark. The lights come on and, despite the fact Fred falls down and has a hard time remembering the steps, they dance through "The Continental" and Irving Berlin with real style.
— *Yung.*

Titan Serambut Dibelah Tujuh
(The Narrow Bridge)
(INDONESIAN-COLOR)

A Bustal Nawawi production for Kofina Film, released by Prasidi Teta Film, Jakarta. Directed by Chaerul Uman. Features entire cast. Screenplay, Asrul Sani, Uman, based on Sani's 1959 film of same title; camera (color), M. Soleh Ruslani; editor, Cassim Abas; sets, Rajul Kahfi; music, Franki Raen. Reviewed at London Film Festival, Nov. 25, 1985. Running time: **99 MINS.**

With: Dewi Irawan (Ibrahim), Rachmat Hidaya (Pak Sulaiam), Soekarno M. Noor (Pak Harun), Soultan Saladin (Arsad), Darussalam (the Traveler), Menzano (Syamsu), Sum Hutabarat (Syamsu's wife), Youtine Rais (Suleha, Harun's wife), Firman D.A. (Ukan, Harun's friend), Marlia Hardi (Maimunah).

London — Something can be said about inviting Asian entries to participate in lazy afternoon slots for London ethnic cultures, and certainly on this score Chaerul Uman's "The Narrow Bridge" deserved its invite on the ground of impressing visitors to the recent Hong Kong Film Festival.

Pic is set in an Indonesian village far off the beaten path of technological civilization. A young idealistic teacher arrives there to bring a more liberal stance on traditional mores, but by trying to do so he runs headlong into opposition from all sides — and is accused, along with an innocent girl, of corrupting public morals. The woman, however, is the victim of an attempted rape by the self-righteous keeper of the local mosque, for which she gets thrown into irons for public condemnation according to ancient custom.

The teacher, too, is accused of attempted rape by the jealous wife of the local despot. Good triumphs over evil, however, thanks in good part to a passing wandering Moslem preacher. — *Holl.*

The Clan Of The Cave Bear
(COLOR)

Prehistoric Daryl Hannah needs a new club.

A Warner Bros. release of a Producers Sales Organization, in association with the Guber-Peters Company, presentation of a Jozak/Decade production from Jonesfilm. Produced by Gerald I. Isenberg. Coproducer, Stan Rogow. Executive producers, Jon Peters, Peter Guber, Mark Damon, John Hyde. Co-executive producer, Sidney Kimmel. Directed by Michael Chapman. Stars Daryl Hannah. Screenplay, John Sayles, based on the novel "The Clan Of The Cave Bear" by Jean M. Auel; camera (Technicolor, Technovision), Jan De Bont; editor, Wendy Greene Bricmont; music, Alan Silvestri; production design, Kelly Kimball; sound (Dolby), Larry Sutton; co-head of makeup department/special makeups created and designed by Michael G. Westmore; head of makeup department, Michele Burke; clan body movement, Peter Elliot; stunt coordinator, John Wardlow; narrator, Salome Jens; associate producer, Richard Briggs; assistant director, Jerry Grandey; second unit director, Max Kleven; casting, Curtis Burch, Amanda

Mackey. Reviewed at The Burbank Studios, Burbank, Calif., Jan. 13, 1986. (MPAA Rating: R.) Running time: **98 MINS.**

Ayla	Daryl Hannah
Iza	Pamela Reed
Creb	James Remar
Broud	Thomas G. Waites
Brun	John Doolittle

Hollywood — "The Clan Of The Cave Bear" is a dull, overly genteel rendition of Jean M. Auel's novel. Handsomely produced on rugged Canadian exteriors, story of pre-history's first feminist may well appeal to teenage girls, who, despite the R rating, represent the main market for this uninspired effort.

Although set 35,000 years ago in a period of transition from the Neanderthal age to the Cro-Magnon era, pic could more or less have been set in any time, as it displays little of the anthropological ambition of "Quest For Fire" and is pitched to appeal to the same sensibilities that responded to "The Blue Lagoon."

Blond orphan girl Ayla is adopted reluctantly by the small Cave Bear Clan, most of whose members constantly remind her she's an outcast even though she pitches in when it matters. Because she is considered grotesquely ugly by the dark, hairy clansters, Ayla is told she'll never have a mate or a baby.

After more than a half-hour, Ayla grows up to be Daryl Hannah, which proves to be too much of a provocation for arrogant leader-apparent Broud, who makes her submit to him and gives her a baby.

Ayla is temporarily banished for having learned to use "male" weapons, but ultimately returns to prevail over Broud and emerge as, presumably, the first warrior heroine to walk the earth.

Setting would seem to allow for plenty of room to exercise the imagination, but little is in evidence here. A primitive language has been invented for these early humans to speak (subtitles run throughout), but nothing in the customs, habits or attitudes of the people proves very interesting.

Similarly, virtually all the possibilities for harsh, raw power in the many confrontation scenes have been softened for palatability by the faintest souls. R rating must certainly have stemmed from the two or three occasions when Broud savagely, and briefly, takes Ayla, for the rest of the action barely merits a PG.

Due to lack of drama developed by Michael Chapman's rendering of John Sayles' script, one is left only with the pleasures provided by Jan De Bont's splendidly colorful location lensing. After a while, however, even this isn't enough, and result is finally a bore.

Hannah, at least, is a fetching and sympathetic center of attention, but emoting of the entire cast is limited to expressive grunting. Thanks to the limited amount of di-

alog, Alan Silvestri's score is ever-present; it isn't bad, but strains of Vangelis' "Chariots Of Fire" threaten to intrude at many moments. —*Cart.*

My Name Ain't Suzie
(HONG KONG-COLOR)

A Shaw Bros. presentation and release. Presented by Sir Run Run Shaw. Produced by Mona Fong, Wong Ha Hee. Directed by Angie Chan. Stars Pat Ha, Angela Yu, Anthony Perry, Kuan Yi Nan, Li Shih Ping, Ku Chia Ling, Wang Hei, Deanie Yip and Betty Ting. Designed and written by Chang Koon Chung; camera (color), Bob Huke; art directors, Chen Ching Shen, Teng Kuang Hsien; original music, Anders Nelsson, Stephen Shing, So Chun Hou. Reviewed at Jade Cinema, Hong Kong, Nov. 15, 1985. Running time: **98 MINS.**
(Cantonese soundtrack with English subtitles.)

Hong Kong — "My Name Ain't Suzie" is a detailed recollection of the old Wanchai area of Hong Kong in the late '50s, when the bar were centralized and the exotic oriental bar girls were mysteriously legendary in an exotic fashion. One can almost say this is the other side of Suzie Wong. It's a rehash, all right, but more of a contemporary Cantonese version of a Suzie Wong story, set in the girlie bars with American soldiers from Vietnam.

Sui Mei (Pat Ha) and Leung are close friends living on a sampan in Lantau Island like most of the sampan people of that time. They live in extreme poverty and the only way to improve their conditions is to go to Wanchai and be "money honey" girls. They are recruited by Auntie Monroe (played by onetime sex symbol Betty Ting who reached international fame with her involvement with the late Bruce Lee).

Sui Mei falls in love with Jimmy, illegitimate son of an American sailor. He does not know the identity of his father and still is desperately looking for some leads about his "Dad from America." His intimate relationship with Sui Mei leads to a confrontation between Sui Mei and the aging owner of Lucky Bar, Sui Ling Yuk, who keeps Jimmy in her bedroom purse. Sui Mei is forced to leave the bar to become a common streetwalker.

When Jimmy finally finds his father, he simply leaves for the States. As time passes, the deserted Sui Mei becomes a typical Ma Ma-San or Madam. She tries to set up her own business, but is beaten up by hoods in the area because of her lack of a powerful sponsor and protection money, and pic limns her efforts to start a new business.

Though the film itself has flaws in pacing, confusion and some prolonged sequences that need drastic editing, it manages to show a cross section of an era when thousands of women made their living by selling their bodies. Director Angie Chan, once an erratic, undisciplined filmmaker ("Let's Make Love"), is ambitious enough to cinematically show how it was in the era, through an individual story.

The sincerity of making an awardwinning picture with controlled histrionics is evident with the creditable performance of Pat Ha. Deanie Yip, as a lesbian friend, is stunning.

Production is commendable, with the costumes and songs of the '50s and '60s utilized to great advantage to provide instant nostalgia for Suzie and sisters in the oldest profession whose simple battle cry is "No Money, No Honey."

The film failed at the local box-office, but the director made some good marks with critics. It should do well in international filmfests as a Hong Kong entry.—*Mel.*

Youngblood

(COLOR)

The brat pack on ice.

An MGM/UA Entertainment release from United Artists of a Guber-Peters Co. production. Executive producers, Jon Peters, Peter Guber. Produced by Peter Bart, Patrick Wells. Directed by Peter Markle. Stars Rob Lowe, Cynthia Gibb, Patrick Swayze; screenplay, Markle, from story by Markle, John Whitman; camera (color), Mark Irwin; editor, Stephen E. Rivkin, Jack Hofstra; music, William Orbit/Torchsong; art director, Alicia Keywan; set decorator, Angelo Stea; casting, Penny Perry. Reviewed at the Village Theater, L.A., Jan. 10, 1986. (MPAA Rating: R.) Running time: **109 MINS.**

Dean Youngblood	Rob Lowe
Jessie Chadwick	Cynthia Gibb
Derek Sutton	Patrick Swayze
Murray Chadwick	Ed Lauter
Kelly Youngblood	Jim Youngs
Blane Youngblood	Eric Nesterenko
Racki	George Finn
Miss McGill	Fionnula Flanagan

Hollywood — "Youngblood" will interest the crossover audience of girls infatuated with handsome Rob Lowe and hockey lovers, which couldn't add up to much at the box-office.

The picture has a simple premise: Lowe desperately wants to leave the hard life on his father's farm to join a minor league Canadian hockey team where he believes he will be the star player. His half-blind brother (Jim Youngs), who once played for the same team before he was injured, tells their Dad (Eric Nesterenko) he'll do double-duty so Lowe can be free to try and fulfill his dreams.

Dad agrees and Lowe takes off. He is an innocent who, after less than a week in this small rural Canadian town, is seduced by his landlady (a strange role for Irish actress Fionnula Flanagan) ridiculed by his teammates and enamored of the first girl he meets (Cynthia Gibb) — the coach's daughter who becomes his girlfriend.

Scenes on the ice look great and Lowe truly looks like the fast and accurate son-of-a-gun hockey player he's supposed to be. Credit here

goes to the editors, Stephen E. Rivkin and Jack Hofstra, who've spliced Lowe's doubles in beautifully.

While Lowe often looks too pretty and unscarred to be a hockey star (and too tan), his teammates — including best friend Derek (Patrick Swayze) — look like they grew up hitting pucks at each other. Best casting here is for Lowe and Swayze's arch rival, Racki (George Finn) who has a crazed look of intimidation equal to his athletic prowess.

Women count for little in this superficial story. The biggest role goes to Cynthia Gibb, who plays Lowe's girlfriend Jessie. She doesn't seem to have any sexual hangups at the age of 17 at the same time she's glib on the absence of morality in competitive hockey players.

There are no mothers around in this picture for some reason. Lowe's mom split the farm scene and Jessie's dad is divorced.

Flanagan plays the other major female role as a nymphomaniac woman who runs a boarding house for hockey players and calls on them for sex with a hot cup of tea. What is intended to be funny is instead pandering. —*Brit.*

Marcel Carné's "Les Enfants du Paradis" will be shown as part of the "Cinema Montparnasse" series Feb. 2 at Manhattan's The Jewish Museum.

Corinth Films has acquired American rights to "Huey Long," Richard Kilberg & Ken Burns-produced docu which preemed at last year's New York Film Festival.

Down And Out In Beverly Hills

(COLOR)

Very enjoyable Mazursky comedy of west coast manners.

A Buena Vista release of a Touchstone Films presentation. Produced by Paul Mazursky. Coproducer, Pato Guzman. Directed by Mazursky. Stars Nick Nolte, Richard Dreyfuss, Bette Midler. Screenplay, Mazursky, Leon Capetanos, based on the play "Boudu Sauvé des Eaux" by René Fauchois; camera (Technicolor), Donald McAlpine; editor, Richard Halsey; music, Andy Summers; production design, Pato Guzman; art director, Todd Hallowell; set decorator, Jane Bogart; sound (Dolby), Dave Dockendorf, Paul Wells, Kevin Cleary; costumes, Albert Wolsky; associate producer, Geoffrey Taylor; assistant director, Peter Bogart; casting, Ellen Chenoweth. Reviewed at Plitt Century Plaza, L.A., Calif., Dec. 31, 1985. (MPAA Rating: R.) Running time: **97 MINS.**

Jerry Baskin	Nick Nolte
Dave Whiteman	Richard Dreyfuss
Barbara Whiteman	Bette Midler
Orvis Goodnight	Little Richard
Jenny Whiteman	Tracy Nelson
Carmen	Elizabeth Peña
Max Whiteman	Evan Richards
Matisse	Mike
Dr. Von Zimmer	Donald F. Muhich
Sidney Waxman	Paul Mazursky
Pearl Waxman	Valerie Curtin

Hollywood — "Down And Out In Beverly Hills" continues Paul Mazursky's love-hate relationship with the bourgeoisie and its institutions, especially marriage. It's a loving caricature of the *nouveau riche* (Beverly Hills variety) and although it is more of a comedy of manners than a well-developed story, there are enough yocks and bright moments to make it a thoroughly en-

---

Original Film
Boudu Sauvé des Eaux (1932)
(FRENCH-B&W)

A Pathe Contemporary Films release of a Michel Simon-Jean Gehret production. Written and directed by Jean Renoir, from play by René Fauchois. Stars Michel Simon. Camera (b&w), Marcel Lucien Asselin; editor, Suzanne de Troyes; music, Rapheael; assistant director, Jacques Becker. Reviewed in N.Y., Feb. 17, 1967. Running time: **84 MINS.**

Boudu	Michel Simon
Monsieur Lastingois	Charles Grandval
Madame Lastingois	Marcelle Hainia
Anne-Marie	Severine Lerczynska
Student	Jean Daste
Godin	Max Dalban
Vigour	Jean Gehret
Poet on bench	Jacques Becker

joyable outing. With a crafty blending of youth and adult elements, pic has a good chance for crossover audience and should not go begging at the boxoffice.

The first R-rated film produced by Disney (under its Touchstone banner), "Down And Out" is an updating and considerable reworking of Jean Renoir's 1932 classic "Boudu Saved From Drowning" about a bum who jumps into the Seine and is saved by a bookseller only to turn his domestic life upside down.

Mazursky and cowriter Leon Capetanos have cleverly taken the basic premise and used it as a looking glass for the foibles of the rich and bored. Mazursky obviously feels at home in this land of conspicuous consumption and has seamlessly created a world where even the gardener has a condo in Hawaii.

Assisted by Pato Guzman's detailed production design, Mazursky's direction has never been more on the mark offering numerous keenly observed and revealing touches. Mazursky also strikes a style rich in visual humor to complement his cast of caricatures.

Head of the household is the aptly named David Whiteman (Richard Dreyfuss in a toned down, grown-up and successful variation of his hustling Duddy Kravitz) who has made his fortune in the hanger manufacturing business. Bette Midler is the lady of the house with Tracy Nelson their near anorexic daughter and Evan Richards the son who's not sure he wouldn't rather be a daughter. Also on the scene is Elizabeth Peña as the maid and Dreyfuss' sexual outlet.

In short it's a household of unhappy people whose collective psyche represents a virtual catalog of pop culture fads, trends and affectations of the last 20 years. And the fly (perhaps flea is more accurate) in the ointment is Nick Nolte as the bum Jerry Baskin.

A disheveled and dirty street person, Jerry is an artist of sorts, a con artist. But there is an element of creativity to his personality as he good-naturedly becomes what people want him to be. For the Whitemans he becomes their idealized bum, the family pet.

Jerry's role is to give each of the Whitemans what they need and to revive their hold on life, even if it means having sex with most of the family.

The problem with the Jerry character is that he doesn't have an identity of his own and is not allowed to be himself. He is most affecting in the one scene where he does expose his vulnerability.

Mazursky has painted himself into a bit of a corner by using Jerry only as a catalyst. After he has served as a family aphrodisiac what's to become of him? Even though these people have come to need each other it is hard to believe that they have a continuing place in each other's lives.

The climax for the story devised by Mazursky and Capetanos revolving around some of Dreyfuss' business dealings with the Chinese is unsatisfying and beside the point. There's still the problem of what to do with Jerry and the film takes the easy way out.

Jerry hasn't changed so much as the people around him and though Mazursky ridicules them, the audience comes to like them as much as he does. Much of the credit must go to the actors who are able to find the humor in basically obnoxious traits.

Midler has mastered a Beverly Hills walk while Dreyfuss is pompous while still being likable. Nolte too has managed to turn himself into a mirror for bourgeois aspirations and to reflect their inherent humor and humanity.

As usual in a Mazursky film the supporting cast is accomplished, supplying odd bits of business and diversions along the edges. Elizabeth Peña is winning as the lusty maid as is Tracy Nelson as the starving daughter. Evan Richards gets under the skin of the troubled son and, in his film acting debut (after many musical roles), rock 'n roller Little Richard is not your average next door neighbor.

Music is also a plus with a surprisingly tasty collection of pop tunes ranging from The Talking Heads to Little Richard, who performs one song with a trace of his old fire. Midler warbles a delightful postcoital "You Belong To Me" to Nolte.

Production values are fine all

around with Donald McAlpine's photography supplying a sunny sheen but also capturing the less savory shadows of life in Beverly Hills. —*Jagr.*

Warner Bros. in Gotham confirmed that "Greetings From Nantucket" is the new title for **Savage Steve Holland's** "My Summer Vacation," bowing next summer.

Alan Silvestri is composing the music for **Menaham Golan's** "The Delta Force," starring **Chuck Norris** and **Lee Marvin.**

Black Moon Rising
(COLOR)

Action film suffers from continuity and credibility problems.

A New World Pictures release. Produced by Joel B. Michaels, Douglas Curtis. Directed by Harley Cokliss. Stars Tommy Lee Jones. Screenplay, John Carpenter, Desmond Nakano, William Gray; camera (CFI color), Misha Suslov; editor, Todd Ramsay; music, Lalo Schifrin; sound, Jonathan Stein, Steve Nelson; production design, Bryan Ryman; assistant director, Betsy Magruder; special visual effects, Max W. Anderson; stunts, Bud Davis; casting, Linda Francis. Reviewed at 20th Century Fox, L.A., Jan. 6, 1986. (MPAA Rating: R.) Running time: 100 MINS.
Quint .... Tommy Lee Jones
Nina .... Linda Hamilton
Ryland .... Robert Vaughn
Earl .... Richard Jaeckel
Ringer .... Lee Ving
Johnson .... Bubba Smith
Billy .... Dan Shor
Tyke .... William Sanderson
Iron John .... Keenan Wynn

Hollywood — "Black Moon Rising" is all about a very fast car and a lot of very slow people in pursuit of it. The car almost flies, but the running time doesn't.

The Black Moon is one of those jet-powered machines that races across the salt flats and has to be stopped by a parachute. While hauling it back from a test, inventor Richard Jaeckel pulls into a Nevada service station where Tommy Lee Jones is hanging around for no apparent reason.

Jones is some sort of unofficial thief for the U.S. government who the night before has ripped off some evidence from a casino company and has a small army of killers after him, which makes it odd that he's frittering away time at the filling station instead of high-tailing it back to L.A.

Jones is not going to be a genius anywhere throughout this picture and, again for no real clear reason, he decides to hide the evidence in the back of the Black Moon. Already there's a continuity problem building up which is bound to get worse.

For a moment, though, the lack of continuity is a blessing: When the killers show up at the station, Jones jumps in his car and roars off into the desert, presumably to set up the film's first endless car chase.

The killers rush off after him, but the film then cuts instantly to Jones sitting in a bar in Hollywood, where he's going to meet up with the unpleasant feds led by Bubba Smith.

In a few four-letter words, Smith tells Jones he better get that evidence back because it's needed in court in 72 hours.

Jones catches up with the car, but Linda Hamilton steals it before he can retrieve the tape. He chases after her through crowded L.A. streets, but she turns on the jet power, not even needing a parachute to make all those squealing turns.

Anyway, Hamilton and the Moon wind up hidden in a skyscraper run by Robert Vaughn and his gang of car thieves.

Naturally, Jones catches up with Hamilton again, in bed and out, but that's not the good part. The wonder begins when the Vegas boys, led by vicious Lee Ving, catch up with Jones again and beat him up.

Jones then finds it no problem at all to climb to the top of a skyscraper neighboring Vaughn's, crossing over on a wire and sneaking back down through the second building to rescue Hamilton and the car.

With his usual planning, Jones manages to drive Hamilton and the Moon from the basement of the skyscraper to a floor near the top. Now he has a problem of getting the Moon from Skyscraper number 1 to Skyscraper number 2.

Emerging from the car unscathed in the second building, Jones still has to have a fight with Ving and make love one more time with Hamilton. By now, the wear is starting to show because he is beginning to moan a bit, or maybe that was the audience.—*Har.*

Head Office
(COLOR)

Unfunny comedy about the executive suite.

A Tri-Star Pictures release, presented by HBO Pictures in association with Silver Screen Partners. Produced by Debra Hill. Executive producers, Jon Peters, Peter Guber. Written and directed by Ken Finkleman. Features entire cast. Camera (color); Gerald Hirschfeld; editor, Danford B. Greene, Bob Lederman; music, James Newton Howard; sound, Norval D. Cruther; production design, Elayne Barbara Ceder; casting, Judith Holstra, Marcia Ross; art director, Gavin Mitchell; assistant director, Michael Zenon. Reviewed at Hollywood Pacific Theater, L.A., Calif. Jan. 3, 1986. (MPAA Rating: PG-13). Running time: 90 MINS.
Helmes .... Eddie Albert
Stedman .... Danny DeVito
Rachael .... Lori-Nan Engler
Don King .... Don King
Sal .... Don Novello
Jack Issel .... Judge Reinhold
Jane .... Jane Seymour
Hoover .... Wallace Shawn
Gross .... Rick Moranis

Hollywood — The advertisements for "Head Office" promote the well-deserved credits for past comedic performances of several of the film's actors, including those by Judge Reinhold ("Beverly Hills Cop"), Danny DeVito ("Romancing The Stone") and Rick Moranis ("Ghostbusters"). Unfortunately, they aren't given anything even faintly humorous to work with in this script, another story of an impersonal autocratic multinational corporation run by a bunch of racist and blindly ambitious individuals. Boxoffice potential should prove to be as dull as the humor.

Cast is led by Reinhold, the son of a U.S. senator, who is handed a job at INC Intl. due to his father's involvement with the company.

Reinhold doesn't care that the corporation manufactures everything from depilatory cream to nuclear warheads, but he's assigned to the public relations department where he's forced to deal with those who do care.

Along comes cute, blond Rachael (Lori-Nan Engler), who is leading the protest against INC's callous decision to close a plant in a one-company town in favor of moving the operation to South America where labor is cheaper.

Reinhold predictably falls for Engler, who even more predictably turns out to be the disenfranchised daughter of INC's chairman (Eddie Albert).

Danny DeVito makes an all too brief appearance as a frenzied INC executive exposed for illegal stock trading and comes to an untimely end.

Same is true for Rick Moranis and Wallace Shawn — each of whom is given about five lines of dialog before their characters are whisked offscreen in favor of Reinhold's unfunny failure up the corporate ladder.

Playing a minor role of a bitchy, ambitious woman (again) is Jane Seymour, who is involved in a subplot that has virtually nothing to do with anything. She is beautiful but that's about it.

Also wasted is Don King (as himself), whose wild hair and nonsensical speech should have been a natural bright spot.

Actors would have saved face if they could have parodied Ken Finkleman's script, rather than appearing to just endure it. — *Brit.*

Joan Lui: Ma un Giorno nel Paese Arrivo io di Lunedi
(Joan Lui: But One Day In The Country I Come On Monday)
(ITALIAN-COLOR)

A C.D.E release, produced by Mario and Vittorio Cecchi Gori for C.G. Silver Film Prods. Written, directed, edited by and starring Adriano Celentano. Camera (Color), Alfio Contini; art director, Lorenzo Baraldi; choreography, Franco Miseria; music, Celentano, Ronny Jackson, Pinuccio Pirazzoli and Gino Santercole. Reviewed at Adriano Cinema, Rome, Jan. 1, 1986. Running time: 140 MINS.
Joan Lui .... Adriano Celentano
Newswoman .... Claudia Mori
Judy .... Marthe Keller
Jarek .... Al Yamanouchi
Emanuela .... Federica Moro

Rome — Adriano Celentano's $10,000,000 rock musical-religious fable "Joan Lui" is something more than a disappointment. It's so far-out it's bizarre, nonsensical without a smile, and the least religious viewer is likely to be put off by the filmmaker's swaggering presentation of himself as Jesus Christ in the Second Coming. By the time this two hour-plus epic reaches its all song-all dance conclusion amidst scale models of Manhattan burning and sets toppling on actors' severed limbs, audience puzzlement has long since turned to definite dislike. Pic has had predictably poor returns at the Christmas b.o.

Name of the main character, Joan Lui, and pic's full title (But One Day In The Country I Come On Monday) introduce the kind of liberties Celentano, who wrote, helmed, edited and stars, is willing to take with such a trivial thing as language. When he gets around to scripting the Second Coming his imagination is positively turned loose. Joan Lui arrives in Italy on a beautiful 19th century train rolling across a landscape that looks like the Old West. Wearing rimless specs and a flowing headband, he looks like an updated hippie. The train's passengers are equally hard to place: all are young, black, and hostile to the presence of the lone white.

Soon the train breaks down, he walks to a dusty station, and emerges on the other side in a murderous Future world that seems to be a cross between Beirut and "Escape From New York." While stuntmen plow cars into each other, Army helicopters circle menacingly, and gunmen kidnap an industrialist's daughter (Federica Moro, who returns at the end of the film), Joan Lui stands around and raps with the locals in demented dialog (his specialty: rapid-fire tongue-twisters). This lengthy scene ends in a song and dance number on a cloverleaf.

When we next catch Joan Lui, he has already become famous as a type of singer-prophet, managed by greedy career woman Marthe Keller. At the opening of a new disco called The Temple inside a church, with half-dressed nuns as the waitresses and gold crucifixes and tabernacles as the decor Joan Lui surprises everyone by getting mad and wrecking the joint, but not before we have been treated to abundant cross-cutting between gyrating female thighs and Christ's suffering face from the cross. Like a sacrilegious tv variety show, Celentano stages number after number of rock preening, while supposedly condemning the decadence and impiety of the modern world. Few filmgoers will identify with this wild mixture of hedonism, egotism and garbled fundamentalism.

Of note is the performance of Al Yamanouchi as a handsome Japanese devil, so much more likeable than his antagonist, and Franco Miseria's choreography. A large percentage of the cast and extras are either blond or black. Claudia Mori plays a hardbitten newswoman for "The Easter Herald," a fantasy version of Pravda perhaps. Though Communism is one of the pic's favorite targets, Mori is perversely Joan Lui's choice as love interest — the one woman who can't stand him. At least in the film. — *Yung.*

The Alchemist
(COLOR)

Sluggish supernatural horror pic.

An Empire Pictures release of an Ideal Films production. Produced by Lawrence Appelbaum. Executive producers, Billy Fine, Jay Schultz. Directed by James Amante (Charles Band). Stars Robert Ginty. Screenplay, Alan J. Adler; camera (Deluxe color), Andrew W. Friend; editor, Ted Nicolaou; music, Richard H. Band; sound, Eric Appelbaum; assistant director, Mark Allen; production manager, J. Larry Carroll; stunt coordinator, Harry Wowchuck; production design, Dale A. Pelton; art direction, Pam Warner; special photographic and optical effects, John Lambert, Paul Gentry, Guy Marsden; second unit camera, Lambert; special effects makeup, Steve Neill, Rick Stratton, Martine Vogel, Sheri Short, Gillian Hathaway; casting, Lorinne Vosoff. Reviewed at UA Twin 2 theater, N.Y., Jan. 4, 1985. (MPAA Rating: R.) Running time: **84 MINS.**
Aaron McCallum . . . . Robert Ginty
Lenore/Anna . . . . Lucinda Dooling
Cam . . . . John Sanderford
Hester McCallum . . . . Viola Kate Stimpson
Delgatto . . . . Robert Glaudini

"The Alchemist" is a dull, old-fashioned (with gore added) supernatural horror film. Onscreen credits are garbled: direction is attributed to James Amante, probably a pseudonym, since Craig Mitchell was listed as director when film went into production in February 1981 and Charles Band received the credit when pic was released overseas in 1983. Band opened the pic domestically beginning last May through his Empire Pictures banner.

Robert Ginty stars (though his role is abbreviated) as a Virginia maker of beautiful glass figurines who, in 1871, is cursed to live and kill forever as a beast when he accidentally kills his wife Anna (Lucinda Dooling) in a struggle with alchemist Delgatto (Robert Glaudini), who is using a spell to seduce her.

Ginty doesn't age and is cared for by his daughter (Viola Kate Stimpson) until 1955, when she casts a spell trying to free him by substituting another soul for his. Anna's lookalike (and presumably her rein-

carnation) Lenore is driving to Charlotte, North Carolina and becomes involved as the substitute soul until a contrived climax in the woods at a portal to the nether world sorts out winners and losers.

Whoever really directed this junker, the screenplay by Alan J. Adler is extremely weak in failing to develop any of the alchemist's lore or to make credible the plot coincidences. As a hitchhiker who tags along with Leonore, John Sanderford acts as the audience's surrogate, continually striking poses of bewilderment as he witnesses each phony plot turn unfolding. Ginty is unconvincing in a period role, while Stimpson as his 90-year-old daughter engenders the most sympathy. Dooling, who was most impressive in her next film, starring as the karate expert of "Lovely But Deadly," is wasted here as a stock gothic heroine.

California lensing generates no atmosphere for the story's Southern setting and the 1955 dateline (with no period music) is presumably chosen to avoid the extreme silliness of such a hoary plotline in a contemporary setting. — *Lor.*

Sharma And Beyond
(BRITISH-COLOR)

A Cinecom Intl. Films release of an Enigma Prods. production. Executive producer, David Puttnam. Produced by Chris Griffin. Directed by Brian Gilbert. Features entire cast. Screenplay, Gilbert; camera (color), Ernest Vincze; editor, Max Lemon; music, Rachel Portman; sound, David Crozier; art director, Maurice Cain. Reviewed at Preview 9 screening room, Jan. 9, 1986. (No MPAA Rating). Running time: **83 MINS.**
Natasha Gorley-Peters . . . . Suzanne Burden
Evan Gorley-Peters . . . . . . Robert Urquhart
Stephen Archer . . . . Michael Maloney
Myrna . . . . Antonia Pemberton
Anton Heron . . . . Benjamin Whitrow
Vivian . . . . Tom Wilkinson

A romantic comedy at heart, "Sharma And Beyond" spins a winning and witty tale with a minimum of cardboard clichés and a maximum of genuine characters, humor and emotion. Pic is one of several films in producer David Puttnam's "First Love Series" and shows his quality touch throughout, a necessary ingredient in generating the word-of-mouth that could draw more than an arthouse crowd to this warm and memorable import.

Stephen, sharply portrayed by Michael Maloney, is a young man supporting himself in London as an English teacher to a humorous mix of enthusiastic foreigners. Aspiring to be a science fiction writer and lionizing the prodigious works of one Evan Gorley-Peters in that field, Stephen takes his class on an unscheduled field trip to see the celebrated novelist's country home.

Riding in a field on their arrival is the writer's daughter, Natasha, finely acted by Suzanne Burden,

who, through a number of previous intercuts, we know is rebounding from a recent breakup of a relationship and seems to be adrift in the currents of life. Upon learning her identity and close connection with his literary hero, Stephen returns alone the next day, takes the emotionally fragile Natasha to tea and soon is invited to the house for lunch with her and her father.

The tension building up to and carrying through the budding science fiction writer's lunch with the renowned Gorley-Peters, excellently limned by veteran Scottish character actor Robert Urquhart, leads to a funny sequence as Stephen eagerly chirps high-sounding quotes from the master's past works which Gorley-Peters, slowly getting drunk, doesn't recall writing and doesn't really seem to care about.

Natasha's nagging fear as to whether her new boyfriend is in love or just using her to get to her father runs throughout, and Brian Gilbert's taut script and crisp direction rightly leave the question hanging till the end.

Film features a number of enjoyable minor characters, among them Benjamin Whitrow as Anton, Stephen's world-weary colleague at the language school, in addition to the eager classroom of foreigners who consistently provide strong comic relief.

Ernest Vincze's camerawork nicely captures the beautiful rolling English countryside and Rachel Portman's music helps establish the quirky moods of "Sharma And Beyond." — *Roy.*

Fernando Rey toplines in **Jana Bokova's** "Hotel du Paradis."

The Annihilators
(COLOR)

Cornball Vietnam on the home front picture.

A New World Pictures release. Produced by Allan C. Pedersen, Tom Chapman. Directed by Charles E. Sellier Jr. Features entire cast. Screenplay, Brian Russell; camera (color), Henning Schellerup; editor, Dan Gross; music, Bob Summers; art direction, Simon Gittins; set decoration, Annette Serena; sound, Alan Silk; visual consultant & stunt coordinator, Don Shanks; assistant director, Leon Dudevoir; associate producer & second unit director, Perry Husman. Reviewed at the World Theater, L.A., Jan. 3, 1986. (MPAA Rating: R.) Running time: **84 MINS.**
Bill . . . . Christopher Stone
Woody . . . . Andy Wood
Garrett . . . . Lawrence Hilton-Jacobs
Ray . . . . Gerrit Graham
Joe . . . . Dennis Redfield
Roy Boy . . . . Paul Koslo
Leon . . . . Cavanaugh Yelling
Jesse . . . . Bruce Evers
Doc . . . . Tom Harper
Virgil . . . . Lonnie Smith
C.C. . . . . Josh Patton
Lt. Hawkins . . . . Jim Antonio
Capt. Lombard . . . . Bruce Taylor

Hollywood — "The Annihilators" is the latest, and quite possi-

bly the least, in the cycle of pics featuring Vietnam vets reverting to their old tricks. Booking it on a double-bill with "Rambo" will be the only way to get good grosses out of this one.

Twist here is that, instead of heading back to Nam to rescue somebody or other, former unit regroups to battle punks on the streets of Atlanta. The nasties here are so baaaad that they even assault cripples and bag ladies, so the audience feels no hesitation in cheering the good guys on every time they blow someone away.

Pic has been directed with sometimes surprising good cheer by former Sunn Classics topper Charles E. Sellier Jr. It is remotely possible, but highly unlikely, that Brian Russell's script is a gem of wit and brilliant dialog; it's impossible to know for sure, however, since the soundtrack is hopelessly garbled and frequently unintelligible.
— *Cart.*

Tutta Colpa del Paradiso
(Blame It On Paradise)
(ITALIAN-COLOR)

A C.E.I.A.D. release, produced by Gianfranco Piccioli for Union P.N. productions and C.G. Silver Film. Directed by Francesco Nuti. Stars Ornella Muti, Francesco Nuti. Screenplay, Vincenzo Cerami, Giovanni Veronesi, Nuti; camera (Eastmancolor), Giuseppe Ruzzolini; editor, Sergio Montanari; music, Giovanni Nuti. Reviewed at Fiamma Cinema, Rome, Jan. 4, 1986. Running time: **109 MINS.**
Romeo . . . . Francesco Nuti
Celeste . . . . Ornella Muti
Husband . . . . Roberto Alpi
Social worker . . . . Laura Betti

Rome — A pleasant, well-constructed bit of family entertainment, "Blame It On Paradise" brings Francesco Nuti ("Me, Chiara and Darkness," "Casablanca, Casablanca") back to the screen for his second try at directing.

A young father just out of jail looks for his son. Given the sentimentalism inherent in the tale, Nuti does a good job of deflating it and rides out the film on the gentle, wistful comedy that has become his trademark. Local boxoffice has favored the film in the Christmas grab-bag.

Romeo Casamonica (Nuti) gets out of prison after serving five years for armed robbery. Far from being a hardened criminal, Romeo is the same soft-spoken, clownish regular guy we've met in other films. His old neighborhood has been turned into a haven for S&M punks, his wife is missing, but he follows a trail through the office of a comically malevolent social worker (the fantastic Laura Betti, an expert at harpies, ably sketches this one in a few killing strokes) that leads to his six-year-old son Lorenzo.

The boy has been adopted by a beauteous mountain woman (Ornella Muti) and her ethnologist husband (Roberto Alpi). Determined to get the child back at all costs, Romeo spends a month in their Alpine retreat, pretending to be a vacationer. In the end he falls for Muti, realizes Lorenzo is growing up in the world's greatest surroundings, and nobly packs off with a wry grin.

The story is slight, but thesps fill it out skillfully. Co-star Muti works splendidly as a modern pioneer woman whose sensuality is accentuated in boots and blue jeans. The romance between her and the visitor is handled with maximum discretion, though their attraction to each other is always present. Alpi makes a convincing mate who spends his time looking for a rare albino ram, which of course Romeo is the only one to see.

Scenery of the Aosta Valley is absolutely stunning and is wisely kept in the frame as much as possible.
— *Yung.*

Revenge For Justice
(FILIPINO-COLOR)

A Saga Film International (Denmark and international sales), Sittis Film Exchange (Manila) production. Produced by Hadja Sitti Aiza Ummar. Directed by Manuel "Fyke" Cinco. Stars Rudy Fernandez, Donna Villa. Original story and script, Dave Brodett; camera (Eastmancolor), Edmund Cupcupin; music, Jimmy Fabregas; editor, Augusto Salvador. Reviewed at Ankerstjerne screening room, Copenhagen, Denmark, Dec. 10, 1985. Running time: **95 MINS.**

Bobby . . . . .Rudy Fernandez
Malou . . . . .Donna Villa
Police lieutenant . . . . .George Estregan
Police sergeant . . . . .Yusuf Salim
Sergeant's younger brother .Ronnie Lazaro
Crime syndicate boss . . . . . .Johnny Wilson
Also with: Paquito Diaz, Max Alvarado, Rodolfo "Boy" Garcia, Dick Israel, Philip Gamboa, Dave Brodett.

Copenhagen — "Revenge For Justice" is an English-dubbed version of Manuel "Fyke" Cinco's Tagalog-language vigilante-vs.-cops-and-mafiosos actioner that has already wowed them in Manila where Rudy Fernandez is a current heart-throb. Film is now up for international grabs via Danish distributor Arne Hübertz, whose Saga International setup will start marketing it at the American Film Market in February.

Rudy Fernandez looks and moves like a very young and curiously baby-faced Charles Bronson and does so in a story to match his vigilante role as Bobby who works in a gunsmith's repairshop. Here he has fashioned his own bazooka-like supergun to use it with quiet expertise against just about every hoodlum, bigtime or small-scale, that crosses his path. It seems that gangsters killed his policeman father when Bobby himself was only a small kid. Today, he believes in no justice meted out by anybody but himself and soon finds himself chased with equal ardor by the police and by a

crime syndicate boss whose henchmen he has started killing off like flies. When the girl he carries a torch for is killed by the gangsters, he out-Rambos Rambo in a final assault on their rural headquarters.

The dialog is crude, the characterizations of all protagonists mostly ludicrous, but the narrative and the action sequences, latter making up to 80% of the proceedings, move swiftly and with vitality. There will probably be few big screens left for this kind of item, but homevideo business, especially in territories where rentals are dominant, will probably be lively.
— *Kell.*

Love Circles
(BRITISH-COLOR)

A Playboy Programs presentation of a Jerawood Ltd. production. Executive producer, Harry Alan Towers. Produced by Wilfred Dodd. Directed by Gérard Kikoïne. Features entire cast. Screenplay, uncredited, based (uncredited) on the play "Reigen" by Arthur Schnitzler; camera (Kay color), Gerard Loubeau; editor, Allan Morrison; music, Bunny Anton; art direction, Giorgio Fenu; assistant director, Dominique Combe; Hong Kong photography, Bob Huke; production managers: Philippe Pinceloup (Paris), Lynn Rayner (L.A.), Debborah Lee (N.Y.), Tony Leung (H.K.). Reviewed on vidcassette, N.Y., Jan. 1, 1986. (No MPAA Rating.) Running time: **97 MINS.**

Suzy . . . . .Marie France
Brigid . . . . .Josephine Jacqueline Jones
Jill . . . . .Lisa Allison
Dagmar . . . . .Sophie Berger
Yo Yo/Ko Ko . . . . .Michele Siu
Jack .John Sibbit
Count Crespi . . . . .Pierre Burton
Gino . . . . .Philippe Baronnet
Blake .John Allen
Michael . . . . .Timothy Wood

"Love Circles" is the latest remake of "Reigen," oft-filmed Arthur Schnitzler play which gave rise to Max Ophüls' classic 1950 version, "La Ronde." New one is a feature made for cable, shown by The Playboy Channel last fall.

In common with other recent updates such as "N.Y. Nights" and "Ring Of Desire," "Love Circles" emphasizes the sexual aspect of the format. With very attractive women and impressive globehopping locations, it is okay adult programming for Playboy, but a rather weak entry for theatrical use abroad.

Marie France sets the circle of love in motion when she beds down an American deejay in Paris, John Sibbit. A cryptic warning about her

1950 Version
La Ronde
(FRENCH-B&W)

A Sacha Gordine release and production. Directed by Max Ophüls. Stars Anton Walbrook, Simone Simon, Daniel Gélin, Danièlle Darrieux. From a play by Arthur Schnitzler. Camera (b&w), Christian Matras; editor, Axar. At Palais De Chaillot, Paris, June 24, 1950. Running time: **109 MINS.**

Raconteur . . . . .Anton Walbrook
Streetwalker . . . . .Simone Signoret
Soldier . . . . .Serge Reggiani
Chambermaid . . . . .Simone Simon

Student .Daniel Gélin
Wife . . . . .Danièlle Darrieux
Husband . . . . .Fernand Gravey
Seamstress . . . . .Odette Joyeux
Playwright . . . . .Jean-Louis Barrault
Actress . . . . .Isa Miranda
Count . . . . .Gérard Philipe

fails to reach him in time, as in this modernized (and poor taste) version, the woman apparently is carrying a social disease.

The chain continues through a variety of liaisons, including black actress Josephine Jacqueline Jones (who has appeared in several made-for-Playboy features including "Black Venus") as a jewelry clerk in the Carlton Hotel in Cannes; Lisa Allison as a film and legit actress auditioning for play director Timothy Wood; and Michele Siu portraying twins who can be told apart by butterfly tattoos positioned on different sides of their posteriors.

Credit filmmaker Harry Alan Towers with rounding up an attractive cast, particularly Lisa Allison, who easily could qualify for Playboy Playmate status. Poor dubbing and a weak script detract from some stylish direction by Gérard Kikoïne (better known for his many hardcore porn features). Besides the veiled reference to venereal disease, the chain concept is demonstrated here (with attempted irony) by a pack of clove-scented cigarets which is passed along in each segment until it is returned to a puzzled Marie France at film's end.—*Lor.*

Denis Quilley, Amanda Donohoe and Eve Ferret into "Foreign Body," rolling in London under **Ronald Neame.**

Hannah And Her Sisters
(COLOR)

Smashing comedy-drama by Woody Allen.

An Orion Pictures release of a Jack Rollins and Charles H. Joffe production. Produced by Robert Greenhut. Executive producers, Rollins, Joffe. Written and directed by Woody Allen. Features entire cast. Camera (Technicolor processing, Deluxe prints), Carlo Di Palma; editor, Susan E. Morse; production design, Stuart Wurtzel; set decoration, Carol Joffe; costume design, Jeffrey Kurland; sound, Les Lazarowitz; associate producer, Gail Sicilia; assistant director, Thomas Reilly; casting, Juliet Taylor; additional photography, Jamie Jacobsen. Reviewed at the Orion Screening Room, L.A., Jan. 13, 1986. (MPAA Rating: PG-13.) Running time: **106 MINS.**

Mickey . . . . .Woody Allen
Elliot . . . . .Michael Caine
Hannah . . . . .Mia Farrow
April . . . . .Carrie Fisher
Lee . . . . .Barbara Hershey
Hannah's Father . . . . .Lloyd Nolan
Hannah's Mother . . . .Maureen O'Sullivan
Dusty . . . . .Daniel Stern
Frederick . . . . .Max Von Sydow
Holly . . . . .Dianne Wiest

Hollywood — "Hannah And Her Sisters" is one of Woody Allen's great films, the answer to the prayers of Allen fans who have found his work since "Annie Hall" and "Manhattan" a bit slight. In fashioning this picture about the many different stages of romantic love, the writer-director has set his sights high and realized all his aims. This should settle in for long runs in traditional Allen territory and score more decisively at the b.o. over the long haul than his last several pictures.

One gets the feeling in the early going, as Allen swiftly introduces his large cast of characters, that this is going to be a major achievement. Indeed, he makes nary a misstep from beginning to end in charting the amorous affiliations of three sisters and their men over a two-year period.

In its structure and successful mixture of outright comedy, rueful meditation and sexual complications, "Hannah" most closely resembles "Manhattan" among the director's previous films. As before, most of the characters are relatively successful and creative New Yorkers with more than their share of angst and neuroses. Where "Manhattan" focused on single people or childless couples, however, the new film is loaded with family ties, children and parents, and has an essentially positive, rather than melancholy, thrust.

All of this makes for an exceedingly rich set of relationships and plot possibilities. Pic begins at a Thanksgiving dinner, and ends at one two years later, with most of the characters going through mate changes in the interim.

Hannah, played by Mia Farrow, was formerly married to tv producer Woody Allen but is now happily wed to agent Michael Caine, who, in turn, secretly lusts for his wife's sexy sister, Barbara Hershey, the live-in mate of tormented painter Max Von Sydow.

The third sister, Dianne Wiest, is by far the most neurotic of the bunch and, while waiting for her acting, singing or writing career to take off, runs a catering business with Carrie Fisher. She is no more successful with men than she is in her professions, and her disastrous date with Allen, her former brother-in-law, is one of the comic high points of the picture.

Everyone here endures some romantic anguish and trying times during the course of the two years. Allen suffers a mid-life crisis that is both uproarious and painful. A hypochondriac, he puts himself through endless medical tests for fear that he has a brain tumor and, after much soul-searching, considers converting from Judaism to Catholicism, only to find, as Joel McCrea did in "Sullivan's Travels," salvation in comedy.

Structure and ever-changing relationships allow Allen to present the many different colors in the romantic rainbow: Caine's intense infatuation with Hershey, Von Sydow's fury at her breakup with him, Wiest's depression when Fisher beats her out for the attentions of an eligible man, Farrow's confusion and fear at Caine's growing remoteness, Maureen O'Sullivan and the late Lloyd Nolan's fondness for each other in old age.

Unsurprisingly, all the actors are seen in top form under Allen's astute direction, but it must be said that, under impossible odds, Dianne Wiest steals the show. She exhibits brashness and vulnerability in equal measure, and beautifully captures that sort of contemporary woman who is always busy but has nothing to show for it.

Hershey has just as much screen time and is also a revelation; never before has she seemed so natural and humanly appealing in a film. Farrow is depicted as an absolute angel, the only blameless individual in the picture, and looks even younger here than she did last year and the year before that. An emotional scene among the three sisters in a restaurant is an all-time classic of writing, acting and direction.

For the first time in a decade, Allen has not had Gordon Willis behind the camera, but Italian lenser Carlo Di Palma has done an exemplary job in his stead. Like all of the director's films, it looks and, with a soundtrack loaded with old show tunes, sounds great.

Putting in uncredited appearances here are Tony Roberts, in the usual best-friend role, and Sam Waterston, as Wiest and Fisher's dreamboat. —*Cart.*

Gipgo Pureun Bam
(Deep Blue Night)
(SOUTH KOREAN-COLOR)

A Motion Picture Promotion Corp. release. Produced by Lee Woo Suk. Directed by Bae Chang-Ho. Features entire cast. Screenplay, Choi In-Ho; camera (color), Jung Kwang-Suk. Only credits available. Reviewed at Chicago Film Fest (out-of-competition), Nov. 9, 1985. Running time: **110 MINS.**
With: Ahn Sung Kec (Ho Bin Back), Chang Mee Ho (Jane), Choi Min-Hee, Jin Yoo-Young.

Chicago — Bae Chang-Ho's "Deep Blue Night" has strong curiosity value, for this South Korean entry at the Chicago fest was produced in the States and deals with the familiar "Green Card" dilemma facing aliens living and surviving illegally in the U.S.

A Korean sailor hopes to fulfill his dream of permanent residence in the U.S. by marrying an Asian-American citizen, thereby allowing him to work and live here with permission of the Immigration Bureau. Being the handsome type, he's left a girlfriend pregnant at home and now feeds on the hopes of gullible native Asiatics on the west coast to get what he wants.

The twist has the protagonist meeting his match with a lady bartender who came the same route by marrying a black GI when the latter was stationed in South Korea. Now she marries alien Koreans under a contract that permits her to divorce as soon as the bogus husband gets his Green Card. This time, however, she falls in love with her prey, and it's a game of cat-and-mouse until she discovers what a heel he really is, upon which she kills both him and herself.

Shot almost entirely in English, pic suffers from sloppy production values. Exaggerated acting is the primary drawback. —*Holl.*

Lady Jane
(BRITISH-COLOR)

A Paramount Pictures release of a Peter Snell production. Produced by Snell. Directed by Trevor Nunn. Features entire cast. Screenplay, David Edgar, from story by Chris Bryant; camera (Technicolor), Douglas Slocombe; editor, Anne V. Coates; music, Stephen Oliver; production design, Allan Cameron; art direction, Fred Carter, Martyn Hebert; set decoration, Harry Cordwell; costume design, Sue Blane with David Perry; sound (Dolby), Roy Charman; associate producer, Ted Lloyd; assistant director, Barry Langley; casting, Rebecca Howard, Joyce Nettles. Reviewed at Paramount Studios, L.A., Jan. 9, 1986. (MPAA Rating: PG-13.) Running time: **142 MINS.**

Lady Jane Grey	Helena Bonham Carter
Guilford Dudley	Cary Elwes
John Dudley	John Wood
Dr. Feckenham	Michael Hordern
Mrs. Ellen	Jill Bennett
Princess Mary	Jane Lapotaire
Frances Grey	Sara Kestelman
Henry Grey	Patrick Stewart
King Edward VI	Warren Saire
Sir John Bridges	Joss Ackland
Sir John Gates	Ian Hogg
Renard	Lee Montague
The Marquess of Winchester	Richard Vernon
Archbishop Cranmer	David Waller
The Earl of Arundel	Richard Johnson
Thomas	Pip Torrens
Dr. Owen	Matthew Guiness
Robert Dudley	Guy Henry
John Dudley	Andrew Bicknell

Hollywood — With its emphasis on youthful idealism despoiled by treacherous, manipulative adults, "Lady Jane" emerges as a tragic historical romance tinged with a strong 1960s feeling. As such, impressively mounted and acted piece may strike youthful contemporary viewers as rather anachronistic and out of synch with current attitudes. Another marketing negative facing

---

1936 Version
Lady Jane Grey
(Tudor Rose)
(BRITISH-B&W)

A Gaumont-British release of a Gainsborough production. Directed and adapted by Robert Stevenson. Stars Cedric Hardwicke, Nova Pilbeam, features John Mills. Cameraman, Mutz Greenbaum. At Tivoli, London, April 28, 1936. Running time: **78 MINS.**

Earl of Warwick	Cedric Hardwicke
Lord Guilford Dudley	John Mills
Edward Seymour	Felix Aylmer
Thomas Seymour	Leslie Perrine
Henry VIII	Frank Cellier
Edward VI	Desmond Tester
Mary Tudor	Gwen ffrangcon Davies
Jane's parents	Martita Hunt, Miles Malleson
Ellen	Sybil Thorndike
Lady Jane Grey	Nova Pilbeam

Paramount is the unfortunate lack of interest modern audiences have generally shown for pre-20th century period pieces. Nevertheless, unique story told here has its fascinations, and a small, but devoted, following could develop for this quite traditional British production.

Tale seized upon by producer Peter Snell and directed by theatrical wizard Trevor Nunn is one little-known to Americans. In 1553, six years after the death of King Henry VIII and upon the death of his 16-year-old son, Edward VI, some extraordinary maneuverings brought to the British throne Henry's 15-year-old great-niece, the scholarly but unprepared Lady Jane Grey.

She ruled for only nine days, after which she was toppled, imprisoned and finally executed by the Catholic Mary.

Every chapter of the story is loaded with sinister intrigue on the part of the hierarchy of the Royal Court. Particularly active are Lady Jane's parents, the Duke and Duchess of Suffolk, and the Duke of Northumberland, who scheme to force a marriage between Jane and the latter's dissolute 17-year-old son, Guilford Dudley, in order to position Jane on the throne, enhance their own power and keep Britain free of the Pope's influence.

Very much centerstage, however, is the unlikely love story of Jane and Guilford. A grimly serious, exceedingly virginal girl at the outset, Jane is literally beaten into submission by her mother and unwillingly marries Guilford with the condition that he not touch her.

A drunk and a whoremonger, Guilford shortly shapes up and seduces his wife, who in turn is very quickly liberated in body and mind. Outraged by the poverty and injustice they observe around them, the pair fantasizes about how they would make the world a better place and rhapsodize about a socialist-type utopia where all citizens would have equal rights, no noblemen could tell other men what to do.

Before they know it, these dreamers are actually installed in power, and the first commands Queen Jane issues involve the restoration of land rights to farmers who lost them during the Reformation. This is all too much for the members of the Royal Council, who had imagined that Jane and Guilford would be as puppets on a string, and Jane a moment later seals her fate by ordering her father-in-law to lead an army to defeat Mary and her forces.

Without a constituency of her own, Jane is doomed. She is given the chance by Mary to save herself by converting to Catholicism, but Jane doesn't have it in her to become a hypocrite, so she and Guilford, like Romeo and Juliet, go to their deaths with the hope that the next world will be more hospitable to them than this one was.

Indeed, film's attitudes and approach remind of nothing so much as Franco Zeffirelli's 1968 "Romeo And Juliet," also a Paramount release. The idealization of youthful hope, purity and love is similar in both, as is the disapproving view of the way adults run the world.

Disappointingly, Trevor Nunn, whose only previous film was a 1975 rendering of his stage production of "Hedda Gabler" with Glenda Jackson, has brought little of his tremendous theatrical flair to the screen here. Direction is perfectly decent — excellent, in fact, when it comes to the actors — but pacing is slow and visual presentation is entirely conventional. Pic belongs squarely within the traditions of good taste and literate dialog one associates with the British cinema from the 1930s onward.

Given the dearth of these commodities these days, however, there are plenty of old-fashioned pleasures to be had here. Script by David Edgar, who penned the adaptation of "Nicholas Nickleby" for Nunn, does trade in numerous clichéd notions, but is intelligent, well-structured and full of interesting historical details and ironies.

Performances are all top-drawer, beginning with newcomer Helena Bonham Carter in the title role. Bearing a slight resemblance to both

Isabelle Adjani and Genevieve Bujold, she grows most believably from studious introvert to sexually delighted progressive, and is refreshingly different enough from other actresses on view today to keep attention riveted upon her.

Cary Elwes also impresses as he matures rapidly from lout to royal consort, and entire supporting cast of British stage stalwarts, notably including John Wood, Michael Hordern, Jane Lapotaire, Patrick Stewart and Lee Montague, performs admirably.

Pic is too long and leisurely at nearly two-and-a-half hours. Douglas Slocombe's lensing, Sue Blane and David Perry's costumes, and Allan Cameron's production design, mainly centered around existing castles, are excellent, but best of all is Stephen Oliver's beautiful, traditional, always supportive orchestral score. —Cart.

House
(COLOR)

___

Silly, unconvincing horror pic due for fast playoff.

___

A New World Pictures release of a Sean S. Cunningham production. Produced by Cunningham. Directed by Steve Miner. Screenplay, Ethan Wiley, from story by Fred Dekker; camera (Metrocolor, prints by Technicolor), Mac Ahlberg; editor, Michael N. Knue; music, Harry Manfredini; sound, Richard Lightstone; production design, Gregg Fonseca; art direction, John Reinhart; set decoration, Anne Huntley; production manager-associate producer, Patrick Markey; assistant director, H. Gordon Boos; creatures design, Kirk Thatcher, James Cummins; special visual effects, Dream Quest Images; costumes, Bernadette O'Brien; stunt coordinator, Kane Hodder; casting, Melissa Skoff. Reviewed at Manhattan 2 theater, N.Y., Jan. 18, 1986. (MPAA Rating: R.) Running time: **92 MINS.**
Roger Cobb .... William Katt
Harold .... George Wendt
Ben .... Richard Moll
Susan .... Kay Lenz
Tanya .... Mary Stavin
Chet .... Michael Ensign
Aunt Elizabeth .... Susan French
Jimmy .... Eric Silver, Mark Silver

___

"House" is an unconvincing, derivative horror picture which takes a time-tested premise and proceeds to muck it up. New World has a workable title and trailer but no film to back up the campaign, indicating a couple weeks of business before the word gets out.

Filmmakers Sean S. Cunningham and Steve Miner scored hits with several simple "Friday The 13th" films but tackle a more complex story here with embarrassing results. Cornball script by Ethan Wiley posits Roger Cobb (William Katt) as a successful horror novelist who moves into the spooky house where he was raised following the suicide of his aunt, aiming for solitude as he writes a personal book based on his war experience in Vietnam.

Cobb immediately experiences odd happenings which play as hallucinations, but which the audience is supposed to believe are real. A wall-mounted fish comes to life, household implements (as in "Carrie") levitate and fly dangerously at him and goofy-looking monsters appear. His estranged tv actress wife Susan (Kay Lenz), shows up, apparently changes into a puffy monster and is killed by Cobb.

Though much of this nonsense is played tongue-in-cheek, an audience can hardly be expected to swallow the screenplay's inconsistent and arbitrary approach to Cobb's character. At one moment Cobb is desperately trying to hide any evidence of the monsters, burying parts of them all over the yard or feverishly hiding his wife's (back to her normal state) corpse from inquisitive police. A minute later he is just as desperately trying to get kindly neighbor Harold (George Wendt of "Cheers," providing much-needed comic relief) to witness the monsters' materializations. Then in the next scene he's back to a hiding mode.

Compounding such credibility problems is a ludicrous subplot in which his other neighbor is a wolf-whistle beauty Tanya (Mary Stavin, a Miss World contest winner imported from James Bond films), who after coming on seductively to Cobb at their first meeting suddenly pops up with her two-year-old son and literally forces the kid on Cobb, needing latter (who the audience knows to be dangerously nutty) as a babysitter.

Cobb's own young son Jimmy (played by twins Eric and Mark Silver) has been missing for some time, a key plot element. It turns out that the cause of his manifold problems is a supernatural vengeance quest by Ben (Richard Moll), a Vietnam sidekick who requested euthanasia from Cobb after being severely wounded but whom Cobb left bleeding to be captured by the torture-prone enemy. Many Vietnam flashbacks are included here as filler.

Cast cannot be faulted, especially lead Katt who apparently never balked to question the director about his motivation. The monsters are fake and rubbery, better suited to a comedy than a film in search of scares. Other tech credits are acceptable but can't save an idiotic script. Sneak preview audience roundly booed the film at its conclusion. —Lor.

Troll
(COLOR)

___

'Gremlins' clone for the younger set.

___

An Empire Pictures release. Produced by Albert Band. Executive producer, Charles Band. Directed by John Buechler. Features entire cast. Screenplay, Ed Naha; camera (Technicolor), Romano Albani; editor, Lee Percy; music, Richard Band; set decorator, Gayle Simon; set dresser, Mariangela Capuano; sound (Dolby stereo), Amelio Verona; costumes, Jill Ohanneson; assistant director, Mauro Sacripanti; Troll creatures and special effects makeup; Buechler and Mechanical and Makeup Imageries Inc.; associate producer, Debra Dion. Reviewed at Empire Pictures screening room, Hollywood, Calif., Jan. 15, 1986. (MPAA Rating: PG-13.) Running time: **86 MINS.**
Harry Potter Jr. .... Noah Hathaway
Harry Potter Sr. .... Michael Moriarty
Anne Potter .... Shelley Hack
Wendy Potter .... Jenny Beck
Peter Dickinson .... Sonny Bono
Malcolm Malory/
Troll .... Phil Fondacaro
William Daniels .... Brad Hall
Young Eunice St. Clair .... Anne Lockhart
Jeannette Cooper ..... Julia Louis-Dreyfus
Barry Tabor .... Gary Sandy
Eunice St. Clair .... June Lockhart

Hollywood — "Troll" is a predictable, dim-witted premise from Empire Pictures executed for the most part with surprising style. Horror fantasy of a universe of trolls taking over a San Francisco apartment house is far-fetched even for this genre, but above-average cast and production values make it almost bearable. Pic could catch the imagination of a young audience.

Creatures designed by John Buechler, who also directed, are a repulsive assortment of hairy, fanged evil-looking elves inspired more than a little by "Gremlins." Lightning-like special effects are also reminiscent of "Ghostbusters." But the plot is pure shlock.

No sooner does the Potter family move into an ordinary looking building than the young daughter (Jenny Beck) is possessed by the troll. While the troll in Jenny's body becomes totally irascible at home he also starts swallowing up the other inhabitants and setting up beachheads for the new order of trolldom in the other apartments.

Explanation has something to do with a resident witch (June Lockhart) who, in a previous life, had battled the terrible trolls. Here she joins forces with the young Potter boy (Noah Hathaway) to keep them from spreading.

The business with the trolls is, surprisingly, the least interesting part of the film. Characters are truly revolting and forest fantasyland they create inside each apartment is more odd than fascinating.

Where the film rises above the ordinary is in the domestic scenes when, thanks to her acquired personality, young Beck can flaunt all the conventions of how a good girl should act. She's mean to her brother, who is the first to catch on to what's happened to her, and disobeys her parents.

Performances by the kids are convincing and, as the mother, Shelley Hack is attractive and sympathetic. As the head of this crumbling household, Michael Moriarty has at least one great scene in which he gyrates around the living room to strains of rock group Blue Cheer performing "Summertime Blues." It perfectly fits his slightly dazed personality.

Script by Ed Naha is also better with the commonplace than the fantastic. Despite the ridiculousness of the action, Buechler manages to move the film along at a reasonably brisk pace and create a modicum of suspense.

Cinematography by Romano Albani and other tech credits for the Italian-shot production are fine although choral music composed by Richard Band to accompany the troll invasion is laughable. —Jagr.

Kuei-Mei, A Woman
(TAIWANESE-COLOR)

___

A Central Motion Picture Corp. release. Produced by Lin Dun-Fei. Directed by Chang Yi. Features Loretta Yang. Screenplay, Sho Sa, Chang Yi, based on the novel "The Chavannes House," by Sho Sa; camera (color), Yang Wei-Han; art direction, Wang Shai-Chun; music, Chang Hung-Yi. Reviewed at the Chinatown Theater, N.Y., Jan. 13, 1986. (No MPAA Rating). Running Time: **116 MINS.**
Kuei-Mei .... Loretta Yang
Ho .... Lap Kwan Li
(In Mandarin with English and Chinese subtitles)

In its grim portrayal of working-class life, this official Taiwanese submission for consideration in the best foreign-language film Oscar race reportedly defied the customary censorship of socially critical films in the Chinese island nation. This well-acted but slowly paced family epic aims to present some 25 years of recent Taiwanese history in the story of one woman's heroic struggles in an ultimately redeemed lifetime of unending hardships.

While "Kuei-Mei, A Woman" is valuable for its insights into Taiwanese culture, its realism is framed by gloomy lensing. Lacking the grand sweep and impressive production values of such international-class regional efforts as the 1983 Chinese/Japanese coproduction "The Go Masters," it will not easily find playdates on the art house circuit in spite of potential interest to aficionados of Asian film.

When the film opens in 1959, young Kuei-Mei has been exiled to Taiwan, presumably because of her family's sympathy for the defeated Chiang Kai-Chek. Leaving behind a lover on the mainland she lives with her cousin's family who are anxious to marry her off to Ho. He's a widower with three truculent kids, a penchant for gambling and a waiter's job in a ritzy American-owned hotel. Using her characteristic blend of strength and sensitivity, Kuei-

Mei wins the love and respect of her new family.

Coscripter and source novelist Sho Sa's feminist outlook is evident throughout the story, as the indomitable heroine suffers the consequences of her husband's irresponsible conduct with the implicit obedience demanded by an ancient, male-dominated culture. Although he's basically a decent fellow, Ho's a self-pitying weakling and, when he's fired by the hotel for gambling and left saddled with debt, it's up to Kuei-Mei to figure out a way to feed their new twins and the three other kids.

Reluctantly, they split up the kids and set off for Japan, where Kuei-Mei has landed a job for the couple as servants to a wealthy Taiwanese family. The work is not too hard and, blessing of blessings, the pay is in American dollars. Their mean mistress is constantly fighting with her philandering husband (money, we are meant to understand, does not buy happiness) and her cruelty eventually proves too much for the proud Kuei-Mei. She and Ho move on to a backbreaking job as illegal workers in a Chinese-owned restaurant, dreaming of the day they'll have enough money to return to Taiwan and open their own eatery. This finally comes to pass, and leaving behind their oldest son to study cooking in Japan they go home and open the Chavannes restaurant, named after a fancy street in old Shanghai.

The final third of the film deals with Kuei-Mei's continuing struggles to raise the family. As Taiwan prospers so does the restaurant, but troubles still find Kuei-Mei. The oldest daughter, whose fondness for dating, miniskirts and Western ways is indulged by Kuei-Mei, needs an abortion. Her husband has an affair and a typhoon wrecks the restaurant. Kuei-Mei perserveres and a lifetime of selfless struggle results in a family of educated, successful children and middleclass affluence for the reconciled parents.

Life, however, is not replete with happy endings, and as Kuei-Mei says in voiceover, "we grow old, we are subject to illness." It seems everyone has realized too late the extent of her sacrifices, but the Buddhist ideal of an exemplary life is her legacy and the film's bittersweet resolution undoubtedly had a powerful affect on Taiwanese audiences accustomed to celluloid pablum. —Rich.

Iron Eagle
(COLOR)

I was a teenage Rambo.

A Tri-Star Pictures release. Executive producer, Kevin Elders. Produced by Ron Samuels and Joe Wizan. Directed by Sidney J. Furie. Stars Louis Gossett Jr. Screenplay, Elders, Furie; camera (Metrocolor). Adam Greenberg, editor, George Grenville; music, Basil Poledouris; sound, Alan Holly; production design, Robb Wilson King; assistant directors, Alan C. Blomquist, Elie Cohn; associate producer, Lou Lenart; second unit director, James W. Gavin; aerial camera, Frank Holgate; casting, Barbara Claman. Reviewed at Pacific Theater, Hollywood, Jan. 15, 1986. (MPAA Rating: PG-13). Running time: **119 MINS.**

Chappy	Louis Gossett Jr.
Doug	Jason Gedrick
Defense minister	David Suchet
Ted	Tim Thomerson
Reggie	Larry B. Scott
Elizabeth	Caroline Lagerfelt
Tony	Jerry Levine
Milo	Robbie Rist
Knotcher	Michael Bowen
Matthew	Bobby Jacoby
Katie	Melora Hardin
Kingsley	David Greenlee

Hollywood — Normally, it's best to beware of any film that begins with a digital display, but "Iron Eagle" quickly becomes a crackerjack fighter-pilot picture with decades of heritage heading straight into today's outbreak of Ramboism. Theaters may have to stay open from high noon to red dawn to handle the crowd.

"Eagle" is going to give the commentators plenty to chew on, especially those worried about a right-wing renaissance among young people. It won't be welcomed, either, by those concerned that the Arabs are being used as stereotyped villains by Hollywood.

The film's focus on a daring rescue of a hostage in a small Middle East country has lucked into the most real-life headlines since "China Syndrome" and Three Mile Island.

"Eagle" could have starred John Wayne in one or more roles and that says a lot about shifting sentiments in the young audience (at least for the moment). Beyond that, it's certainly a change to see a kid determined to rescue his captive father instead of sitting around with the gang and moaning about how the old man mistreated him.

Young Jason Gedrick swings into action when word comes that pilot pop Tim Thomerson has been shot down for venturing too near the borders of the little nation defended by swarthy David Suchet, who almost twirls his moustache in anticipation of hanging the Yankee intruder.

At first Gedrick is hopeful that the U.S. will respond officially, despite precedent to the contrary. Reminded of Iran, a pal assures, "That was different. Mr. Peanut was in charge. But this guy in there now don't take no ---- from no gimpy country," a line that seemed much appreciated by the young preview audience.

But the government waffles and, fortunately, dad has often taken Gedrick up in an F-16 and that, along with a lot of simulator time, has made the lad into quite a fighter pilot himself. Equally fortunate, all his high-school friends are Air Force kids, too, trusted by their elders to move about the base freely.

With the gang ferreting out all the necessary information about the target and faking the military computers into assigning two jets for their use, Gedrick persuades veteran combat pilot Louis Gossett Jr. to lead the mission and off the pair goes into the wild blue yonder.

Director Sidney J. Furie fills in the rest with breakneck action and some dandy dogfights staged with the assist of aerial director James W. Gavin. Even if the odds against success are a bit overwhelming, there's never much doubt about the ultimate outcome, complete with a surprise happy ending.

Furie has not aimed for art here and Gossett, though good, hardly needs his multiple talents for this one. Much of the dialog is simply laughable, which seemed to please the young audience that much more.

Young Gedrick can't quite hit a target unless he's got rock-and-roll playing in the cockpit. That's how you get a music video out of a fighter-pilot picture. —Har.

The Longshot
(COLOR)

Unfunny and unsympathetic racetrack comedy.

An Orion Pictures release of a Longshot Prods. production. Executive producer, Mike Nichols. Produced by Lang Elliott. Directed by Paul Bartel. Screenplay, Tim Conway; camera (DeLuxe color), Robby Müller; editor, Alan Toomayan; music, Charles Fox; sound, Jon Earl Stein; production design, Joseph M. Altadonna; set decoration, Bob Schulenberg; costumes, Sandra Culotta; assistant director, Michael Schroeder; associate producer, Tom Egan; casting, Longshot Prods. Inc. Reviewed at Orion screening room, Century City, Calif., Jan. 14, 1986. (MPAA Rating: PG-13.) Running time: **89 MINS.**

Dooley	Tim Conway
Elton	Jack Weston
Lou	Harvey Korman
Stump	Ted Wass
Madge	Anne Meara
Santiago	Jorge Cervera
Nicki Dixon	Stella Stevens
DeFranco	George DiCenzo
Fusco	Joseph Ruskin
Tyler	Jonathan Winters

Hollywood — Is there anything worse than teenage food, sex and toilet jokes? Yes, when middle age men do them. Such is the lot of "The Longshot" and there is nary a laugh to be found in this dismal racetrack comedy. Odds against a boxoffice win provide the real longshot.

Despite an impressive collection of comic talent "The Longshot" is surprisingly lacking in humor. Large part of the responsibility must fall on the script by Tim Con-way about a group of aging losers who are suckered into a race fixing scheme that even a child could see through. They may be grown men but they are too pathetic to even inspire sympathy or concern.

Group includes Conway, Jack Weston, Harvey Korman and the youngster of the crowd, Ted Wass. These inseparable losers spend most of their time on petty gambling — cards, football and, their favorite, the ponies. Needless to say they are a sorry lot with nagging wives and broken-down cars.

Apparently Conway's idea of comedy is a man talking to a goldfish, castration and sexual prowess bits, overflowing toilets and frozen food. Santiago (Jorge Cervera), the gentleman who entices them with visions of the big score, is an offensively stereotypical Mexican who can't wait to escape with their money to Tijuana.

Plot complicates, but only slightly, when the boys go to comic book mafioso (George DiCenzo) for a loan. Other pratfalls along the way to easy money are equally boring.

Probably the only funny bit in the picture is supplied by Anne Meara as Conway's nagging wife par excellence. She could give lessons in the fine art of shrieking. Rest of the cast is fine but given such flimsy material to work with can't buy a laugh.

Pic is directed by Paul Bartel, obviously for cash, without his usually offbeat wit. All he does is film the script and that's enough to destroy the film. One saving grace is photography by Robby Müller.
—Jagr.

Der Schwarze Tanner
(Black Tanner)
(SWISS-W. GERMAN-
AUSTRIAN-COLOR)

A Columbus Film AG Zürich release of a Catpics AG Zürich (Alfi Sinniger & Alex Grob)-SRG (Swiss Television)-ZDF (Second German TV net)-ORG (Austrian TV)-Egli Film & Video AG-Glass Family Trust coproduction. Directed by Xavier Koller. Screenplay, Koller, Walter Deuber, based on a story by Meinrad Inglin; camera (color), Elemér Ragalyi; editor, Fee Liechti; sound, Hans Künzi; music, Hardy Hepp; executive producer, Alfi Sinniger; production manager, Peter Spoerri; makeup, Anna Wyrsch, Anne-Rose Schwab; costumes, Sylvia de Stoutz; art direction, Rolf Engler, Karl-Heinz. Previewed at the Alba, Zürich, Jan. 10, 1986. Running time: **106 MINS.**

With: Otto Mächtlinger, Renate Steiger, Dietmar Schönherr, Liliana Heimberg, Susanne Betschart, Elisabeth Seiler, Ernst Sigrist, Albert Freuler, Dieter Moor, Ingold Wildenauer, Heinz Bühlmann, Giovanni Früh, Nikola Weisse, Johannes Peyer, Volker Prechtel, Herbert Leiser, Wolf Kaiser, Eva Rieck, Ilja Smudla, Martin Steiner, Jürgen Cziesla, Othmar Betschart, Michael Gempart, Vera Schweiger, Beat Fäh.

Zurich — Following Francis Reusser's "Derborence" and Fredi M. Murer's "Höhenfeuer" (Alpine Fire), last year's Locarno Grand

Prize winner, Xavier Koller's "Der Schwarze Tanner" (Black Tanner) is the third in a recent string of Swiss films set in rural regions, away from big-city life with its hangups and dominant materialism.

While "Höhenfeuer" may emerge as the top of the three, artistically and commercially, "Der Schwarze Tanner" has definite merits. Koller's previous entry, "Das Gefrorene Herz" (The Frozen Heart), was the most successful local film of 1980. "Tanner," too, stands a good chance on the Swiss market.

Loosely based on a story by the late Swiss author Meinrad Inglin, it is set in 1941. According to a government decree, every available piece of soil had to be cultivated as farmland in order to ensure the country's self-provision with food after being cut off from imports. A farmer in a mountain region in Central Switzerland stubbornly refuses to follow government orders, arguing that their grazing land is unfit for other plantings and that nature should not be violated. The other villagers stand by him at first, but not for long. Tanner and his family are left on their own.

They start making their own butter and cheese, bypassing wartime food rationing measures. This, in addition to his obstinate refusal to observe the law, lands Tanner in jail where he goes on a hunger strike. After his release, he returns home, unbroken in spirit.

Koller has succeeded in making plausible Tanner's authority-defying stand as an early predecessor to today's young protestors. There's no nostalgia involved when he evokes the past. The general style is straightforward, unsentimental and authentic. Apart from a leisurely-paced first half, the pace is just right. Elemér Ragalyi's excellent lensing, in mostly subdued colors, is an important asset.

The title refers to Tanner being accused of black market practices with his self-supplying. Otto Mächtlinger in the title role, his last — he recently died in Zürich and was already fatally ill last summer when he made the picture — is most impressive by sheer presence and facial expression, as he has relatively little dialog. Remainder of the large cast is just right, with special mention due to Renate Steiger's strong characterization at Tanner's wife and Dietmar Schönherr as a village official charged to supervise the government's farming measures. Hardy Hepp's music score helps to underline the mood, but sounds a bit self-conscious at times. —*Mezo*.

Power
(COLOR)

Trite tale of politics and the media.

A 20th Century Fox release of a Lorimar Motion Pictures presentation of a Polar Film production. Produced by Reene Schisgal and Mark Tarlov. Directed by Sidney Lumet. Features Richard Gere, Julie Christie, Gene Hackman, Kate Capshaw, Denzel Washington, E.G. Marshall, Beatrice Straight. Screenplay, David Himmelstein; camera (Technicolor, prints by Deluxe), Andrzej Bartkowiak; production design, Peter Larkin; costume design, Anna Hill Johnstone; film editor, Andrew Mondshein; music, Cy Coleman; production manager, Kenneth Utt; assistant director, Wolfgang Glattes; sound, Chris Newman; associate producers, Glattes, Utt; art direction, William Barclay. Reviewed at Broadway screening room, N.Y. Jan. 22, 1986. (MPAA Rating: R.) Running time: **111 MINS.**

Pete St. John . . . . Richard Gere
Ellen Freeman . . . . Julie Christie
Wilfred Buckley . . . . Gene Hackman
Sydney Betterman . . . . Kate Capshaw
Arnold Billings . . . . Denzel Washington
Senator Sam Hastings . . . . . . E.G. Marshall
Claire Hastings . . . . Beatrice Straight
Wallace Furman . . . . Fritz Weaver
Gov. Andrea Sandard . . . Michael Learned
Jerome Cade . . . . J.T. Walsh
Irene Furman . . . . E. Katherine Kerr
Lucille DeWitt . . . . Polly Rowles
Phillip Aarons . . . . Matt Salinger
Sheikh . . . . Tom Mardirosian
Roberto Cepeda . . . . Omar Torres

Not so much about power as about p.r., this facile treatment of big-time politics and media, featuring Richard Gere as an amoral imagemaker, revolves around the unstartling premise that modern politicians and their campaigns are calculatedly packaged for tv. In spite of relentless jet-propelled location hopping that helps to stave off bordedom, "Power" never gets airborne as contemporary drama or corrosive satire. Boxoffice outlook is mediocre for a pic with little appeal to teens and questionable prospects among adults at a time when polls show overwhelming popular satisfaction with the most tube-savvy President ever.

Pete St. John (Richard Gere) is a peripatetic public relations wiz whose services practically guarantee political success. He's not just good, he's "the best there is," and he's got the offices, wardrobe and fee schedule ($25,000 per month, plus expenses) to match. He also needs a private jet to wing between his far-flung clients. At the outset, these are a populist South American prexy prospect, a recently divorced and remarried female governor of Washington who's up for reelection, and a multimillionaire cipher from the East who's carpetbagging for governor of New Mexico. To relax, St. John knocks out jazz licks on a drum pad.

Busy as he is, Pete decides to make time for one more client, Jerome Cade (J.T. Walsh) a humorless superyuppie industrialist from the Midwest who's eyeing the Ohio U.S. Senate seat being mysteriously

vacated by Sam Hastings (E.G. Marshall), Pete's friend and political idol from the long-gone time when political issues and ideals still "mattered" to the cynical media maven. Something about Cade bothers Pete, but the ambitious businessman agrees to submit to St. John's inviolate mandate of "total control," so he takes him on anyway. Besides, there are only so many clients out there who can afford Pete's tab.

With his "Cotton Club" moustache Gere bears an uncanny resemblance to Robert DeNiro's Rupert Pupkin character in "The King Of Comedy," and something about the whole business of media manipulation must strike St. John as funny since he's usually smirking. His exwife, British journalist Ellen Freeman (Julie Christie), and alcoholic former mentor and partner Wilfred Buckley (Gene Hackman) both remember Pete when the kid had ideals. He's dumped them both but they still care for him. Nothing succeeds like success.

Ellen's lost out to Pete's right-hand gal Sydney Betterman (Kate Capshaw) who takes quick shower meetings with the boss on his pit-stops back in Gotham. Ellen's only solace is her work (seems that she's also "the best") even though she's another one of those movie journalists who rarely take notes, never go to the office and are always too busy "investigating" things to actually write.

Ellen wants to know why Sen. Hastings is really giving up his seat. Gere wants to know who's bugging his office, messing with his jet, and running him off the highway with a Mack truck (what, no chauffeur?). Could it all be linked to be Cade's hard-as-nails advisor Arnold Billings (Denzell Washington) who's tied to insidious Arab oil sheikhs whom oppose Hastings and Gere's banana republic populist? Scripter David Himmelstein's transparent scenario telegraphs all the answers.

All that remains to be seen is if Pete will find some sort of redemption by helping out on-the-skids Wilfred (in a phoned-in turn by Hackman) boost the candidacy of an idealistic professor (Matt Salinger) in the race against his own client Cade. Director Sidney Lumet wraps it all up with a coda of "The Stars And Stripes Forever" and a pan of sophisticated tv studio hardware. In the world of power, anything goes. —*Rich*.

The Imagemaker
(COLOR)

Hard to swallow black comedy about media manipulation.

A Castle Hill Prods. release of a Melvyn J. Estrin production. Produced by Marilyn and Hal Weiner. Executive producer, Estrin. Directed by Weiner. Screenplay, Dick Goldberg, Weiner; camera (Fuji color), Jacques Haitkin; editor, Terry Halle; production designer, Edward Pisoni; music, Fred Karns; art director, Russell Metheny; costumes, Catherine Adair; assistant director, Jim Reynolds; associate producers, Charles P. Abod, James P. Hristakos; special effects, Frank Rogers; casting, Lois Planco. Reviewed at AFI screening room, Washington, D.C., Jan. 16, 1986. (No MPAA Rating.) Running time: **93 MINS.**

Roger Blackwell . . . . Michael Nouri
Molly Grainger . . . . Anne Twomey
Byron Caine . . . . Jerry Orbach
Cynthia . . . . Jessica Harper
The ambassador . . . . Farley Granger
Morris Brodkin . . . . Richard Bauer
Victor Griffin . . . . Roger Frazier
Talk show host . . . . Maury Povich
Gossip columnist . . . . Diana McLellan

Washington — The first feature to be produced locally in Washington by local production company Screenscope, this political thriller tells the age-old tale of the incestuous relationship between the press and politicos in the nation's capitol. The media manipulates the public, but the powerbrokers manipulate the media-brokers. The use and abuse of the press is presented as brutal, cynical and ruthless in what should confirm, in case anyone ever doubted it, that the Washington beat is sexy and violent.

The imagemaker of the title is Roger Blackwell, a media adviser to some 50 politicians in his brief career, which stretches the credibility of the young character played with equally dubious credibility by Michael Nouri. Nouri's approach to playing this hotshot as a hollow man correspond to the poses struck by many press spokesmen whose self-confidence seems to surpass their integrity and will be a type recognized by insiders. The story requires, however, that Nouri be a neurotic, haunted by a nightmare of his wife's suicide, which he failed to inhibit.

Blackwell has discovered a thoroughly ingenius use of video that allows him to supplant his dead wife with tapes of her. The woman in these tapes that run on monitors throughout the house is an actress, who is his own ex-lover and made up to be his wife's double. In this role, Jessica Harper offers an unnerving portrayal of what it means to lack ambition.

The plot begins around a Nixonesque tape that ought to reveal the President's link to an undetermined organized crime honcho. Blackwell intends to make it public, and to observe this triumph, he appropriates the attentions of an ambitious woman journalist named Molly Grainger, who has toppled him from his White House position some three years earlier.

What Blackwell really wants is to make a movie about the manipulation of the media. To realize the funding for this, he appears on a talkshow, where he plays the disputed tape, then denies its authenticity, after which he pulls out a pistol and shoots himself, a la "Network." This ruse for funding a film would all be unnecessary, if his partner, played defiantly by Jerry Orbach, would simply accept a proposal from an unnamed "ambassador."

Several threads remain untied in the surprise ending, or rather, endings, since pic comes to several conclusions. The point of departure for the plot was an on-camera suicide in 1974 by Channel 40's anchorwoman Christine Chubbuck.

Lack of marquee value for the cast will make theatrical distribution difficult beyond its politically obsessed Washington base. For its low budget and high tech credits, however, it is an extremely successful indie product. —*Kaja.*

A Room With A View
(BRITISH-COLOR)

A Cinecom Intl. Films release of a Merchant Ivory production in association with Goldcrest. Produced by Ismail Merchant. Directed by James Ivory. Screenplay, Ruth Prawer Jhabvala, based on a novel by E.M. Forster; camera (Technicolor), Tony Pierce-Roberts; editor, Humphrey Dixon; music, Richard Robbins; costume design, Jenny Beavan, John Bright; production design, Gianni Quaranta (Italy), Brian Ackland-Snow (U.K.); assistant director, Kevin Barker; production managers, Ann Wingate, Lanfranco Diotallevi; associate producers, Paul Bradley, Peter Marangoni (Italy); casting, Celestia Fox; assistant camera, Graham Hazard; sound, Ray Beckett. Reviewed at the Magno Penthouse screening room, N.Y., Jan. 15, 1986. (No MPAA Rating). Running time: 115 MINS.

Charlotte Bartlett . . . . .Maggie Smith
Lucy Honeychurch .Helena Bonham Carter
Mr. Emerson . . . . .Denholm Elliott
George Emerson . . . . .Julian Sands
Cecil Vyse . . . . .Daniel Day Lewis
Reverend Beebe . . . . .Simon Callow
Miss Lavish . . . . .Judi Dench
Mrs. Honeychurch . . . . . .Rosemary Leach
Freddy Honeychurch . . . . . .Rupert Graves
Mr. Eager . . . . .Patrick Godfrey
Catherine Alan . . . . .Fabia Drake
Teresa Alan . . . . .Joan Henley
Mrs. Vyse . . . . :. . . . . .Maria Britneva
Also with: Amanda Walker, Peter Cellier, Mia Fothergill, Patricia Lawrence, Mirio Guidelli, Matyelock Gibbs, Kitty Alridge, Freddy Korner, Elizabeth Marangoni, Lucca Rossi, Isabella Celani, Luigi Di Fiori.

Quality-starved filmgoers will welcome this thoroughly entertaining Merchant Ivory screen adaptation of novelist E.M. Forster's comedy of manners about the Edwardian English upper class at home and abroad. Distinguished by the same type of superb ensemble acting, intelligent writing and stunning design that marked the team's production of "The Bostonians," this film has excellent prospects for selective theatrical release in all major markets.

Set in 1907, when Victorian innocence was slowly giving way to the animated forces of a new age, "A Room With A View" opens in a pensione in Florence, Italy where a well-to-do young English lady,

Lucy Honeychurch (Helena Bonham Carter) is traveling on the type of compulsory horizon-broadening tour that was the prerogative of her class, chaperoned by her fussy, punctilious aunt Charlotte (Maggie Smith). At the hotel they encounter a number of garrulous, slightly eccentric fellow Britishers including rough-edged but delightful self-made businessman Mr. Emerson (Denholm Elliott) and his handsome railway executive son George (Julian Sands), a gentlemanly but strong-willed young man who takes an immediate shine to the appropriately aloof Lucy.

Ruth Prawer Jhabvala's sparkling screenplay is replete with razor-sharp observations of class behavior. The travelers demonstrate an inbred sense of superiority to the Italians — "they're all peasants, you know," hack novelist Miss Lavish remarks to aunt Charlotte on a walking tour of the city — even as they're held spellbound by Florence's historicity and profusion of artistic riches.

When Lucy, off on her own, witnesses a murder in the town square, she's rescued by George, who later boldly presses his affections during a brief torrid interlude in an idyllic pasture. Chancing to observe their embrace and horrified at the thought of scandal, Charlotte cuts the trip short and hastens Lucy back home to the insular Surrey countryside where she lives with her mother and irrepressible younger brother.

Soon Lucy's engaged to wealthy, foppish dilettante Cecil Vyse (played with comic spiritedness by Daniel Day Lewis), and the relationship between the beautiful, self-confident and musically talented girl and the callow, insufferably snobbish esthete becomes the central concern of all who know them. When Mr. Emerson and George, by the oddest of coincidences, happen to move into their village, the course of true love begins to take a tortuous new turn.

Ivory's direction makes what might have been a talky period piece in lesser hands a consistently engaging study of the mores and morality of a bygone time. Tony Pierce-Roberts' cinematography splendidly complements outstanding performances by the major character actors and skillful supporting turns by Simon Callow, Fabia Drake, Joan Henley, Rosemary Leach and Rupert Graves. —*Rich.*

The Adventures Of The American Rabbit
(ANIMATED-COLOR)

An Atlantic Releasing/Clubhouse Pictures release of a Toei Animation Co. production. Produced by Masaharu Etoh, Masahisa Saeki and John G. Marshall. Coproduced by Robert Kaplan. Executive producers, Thomas

Coleman and Michael Rosenblatt. Directed by Fred Wolf and Nobutaka Nishizawa. Screenplay, Norm Lenzer, based on characters by Stewart Moskowitz; music and lyrics written and performed by Mark Volman, Howard Kaylan and John Hoier. Reviewed at Lorimar Screening Room, N.Y., Jan. 23, 1986. (MPAA Rating: G.) Running time: 85 MINS.

Voices by: Bob Arbogast (Theo); Pat Freley (Tini Meeny); Barry Gordon (Rob/American Rabbit); Bob Holt (Rodney); Lew Horn (Dip/various characters); Norm Lenzer (Bruno); Ken Mars (Vultor/Buzzard); John Mayer (Too Loose); Maitzi Morgan (Lady Pig); Lorenzo Music (Ping Pong); Lauri O'Brien (Bunny O'Hare); Hal Smith (Mentor); Russi Taylor (Mother); Fred Wolf (Fred/Red).

Take a long-eared bunny, paint him red, white and blue and put him on roller skates and you'll have the American Rabbit — the upright, offbeat and mildly humorous hero around which this well-intentioned and harmless animated film is based. Simple plot and dialog might prove slow going for accompanying adults as "The Adventures Of The American Rabbit" is definite kiddie fare, but to this group pic should be a nice little diversion.

Loosely based along the lines of Superman, the mild-mannered and bespectacled Rob Rabbit grows up in a sleepy little town displaying an innate knack, or power, to master everything he tries. This early section is sprinkled with lessons in morality upon which our hero will be forged.

When a boulder comes crashing down on a peaceful family outing Rob makes his first transformation into the American Rabbit to save the day. A wizened old rabbit appears to explain Rob has been chosen to battle evil in the world, and after a tearful farewell Rob sets out to do just that.

A motorcycle-riding pack of jackals terrorize Rob before and after he gets to a city (supposedly San Francisco) and lands a job playing piano at a bar called Panda-Monium, run by an overly polite Panda named Teddy. When Teddy's bar is burned down by the Jackals, various "good" animal citizens of the city stage a rally to protest the lawless bikers.

Teddy announces he's launching a crosscountry tour of "The White Brothers Band," five white rabbits, to earn money to rebuild. Rest of the film follows Rob and his new found friends as they're thwarted by the jackals at every stop and only saved by the last-minute appearances of the American Rabbit. Even preschoolers may find the final plot sequences flat as the ill-conceived climax abruptly clunks to an end.

Animation is fair, sound particularly good and extensive music sections above-average. —*Roy.*

My Chauffeur
(COLOR)

Fine screwball comedy aimed at young women.

A Crown Intl. Pictures release. Produced by Marilyn J. Tenser. Written and directed by David Beaird. Camera (Deluxe color), Harry Mathias; editor, Richard E. Westover; sound, Don Summer; production design, C.J. Strawn; assistant director, David M. Robertson; coproducer, Michael Bennett; costumes, Camile Schroeder; makeup, Christa Reusch; music, Paul Hertzog; casting, Paul Bengston, David Cohn. Reviewed at the Bruin Theater, L.A., Jan. 23, 1986. (MPAA Rating: R.) Running time: 97 MINS.

Casey Meadows . . . . . . .Deborah Foreman
Battle Witherspoon . . . . .Sam J. Jones
O'Brien . . . . .Sean McClory
McBride . . . . .Howard Hesseman
Witherspoon . . . . .E.G. Marshall
Bone . . . . .Penn Jillette
Abdul . . . . .Teller
Catfight . . . . .Leland Crooke
Giles . . . . .John O'Leary
Johnson . . . . .Julius B. Harris
Jenkins . . . . .Laurie Main
Downs . . . . .Stanley Brock
Moses . . . . .Jack Stryker
Doolittle . . . . .Vance Colvig
Dupont . . . . .Ben Slack

Hollywood — Of all things, Crown Intl. — normally the home of hokum — has come up with a picture that is sweeter, nicer, kinder and generally just more entertaining than 90% of the films released in the past five years. "My Chauffeur" could be a big draw among teens and preteen girls.

Writer-director David Beaird avowedly set out to imitate the screwball comedies of the 1930s and 1940s and has succeeded admirably, thanks to adorably spunky Deborah Foreman and her stuffy foil, Sam J. Jones. They make quite a pair.

Foreman is a real find who may go far after this one, fitting into the mold of Goldie Hawn, Carole Lombard and Claudette Colbert. She not only can say a lot when saying nothing, she's a real pro when it comes to the difficult task of combining high-tuned dialog with physical action.

Summoned mysteriously by millionaire limo company owner E.G. Marshall, Foreman takes a job as a driver, much to the objections of ramrod Howard Hesseman and a wonderful assortment of chauvinistic chauffeurs who want to maintain their male-dominated domain.

She gets the impossible assignments, starting with a crazed rock group led by Leland Crooke, whom she gets to the concert on time despite their worst efforts. Among her other clients are a sheik and a con man out to get his cash (an amusing film debut by the stage comedy team of Penn & Teller).

Her toughest assignment is Jones, a spoiled, domineering industrialist who is, unknown to her, Marshall's son. Dumped by his girlfriend, Jones sets off on a wonderous drunk, beginning in the back seat of her limo and proceeding ultimately to a naked romp through a public park. (Per screen footage, there is far more male nudity in this pic than female, setting a Crown record and establishing the softly feminist attitude of the film.)

Romance gradually blossoms between Foreman and Jones, once she has him well under control. The other drivers even grow fond of her and the mysterious relationship to Marshall is revealed and life works out just fine.

This is not a big-budget picture, but Beaird and lenser Harry Mathias have done a lot with what they have. Sometime, though, the errors of scale are glaring and one rock "concert" looks like it's taking place in somebody's living room with a crowd of 20.

The cars, to be sure, are lovely. Best of all, they rarely go over 30 m.p.h. and never chase each other.
— *Har.*

Where Are The Children?
(COLOR)

Unsuccessful tear-jerker about missing kids.

A Columbia Pictures release. Produced by Zev Braun. Directed by Bruce Malmuth. Screenplay, Jack Sholder, based on the novel by Mary Higgins Clark; camera (Metrocolor), Larry Pizer; editors, Roy Watts; music, Sylvester Levay; sound, Carey Lindley; production design, Robb Wilson King; set decorator, Jane Cavedon; costumes, Mary Ellen Winston; assistant director, Donald J. Newman; associate producer, Bryant Christ; casting, Bonnie Timmermann. Reviewed at Columbia Pictures screening room, Burbank, Calif., Jan. 24, 1986. (MPAA Rating: R.) Running time: 92 MINS.

Nancy Eldridge	Jill Clayburgh
Clay Eldridge	Max Gail
Michael Eldridge	Harley Cross
Missy Eldridge	Elisabeth Harnois
Dorothy Prentiss	Elizabeth Wilson
Jonathan Knowles	Barnard Hughes
Courtney Parrish	Frederic Forrest
Robin Legler	James Purcell
Chief Coffin	Clifton James

Hollywood — "Where Are The Children?" is too much of a tear-jerker to be successful as a suspense picture, but this doesn't stop the filmmakers from trying. Pic moves in too many directions at once without ever really getting anywhere. Good intentions of the project notwithstanding, this is another example of a film that didn't need to be made and audiences should agree.

Based on a novel by Mary Higgins Clark about a child abduction, the project has been kicking around Hollywood since 1979 and arrives at a time when disappearing kids are a staple of the nightly news. Columbia reportedly has been sheepish about releasing the film and all mention of Rastar's involvement has been dropped from the credits.

At one time announced as a Brian DePalma project, that version presumably would have relied more on the suspense of the situation in-stead of the melodrama.

This is not to minimize the serious issues raised by the film but they are so complicated and convoluted here as to dissipate much of the emotional charge. Story opens with an idyllic family scene in autumnal New England, soon complicated when the Eldridge children (Harley Cross and Elisabeth Harnois) are methodically kidnaped.

If this weren't enough, lurking in the closet is the mysterious death of two children by the same mother (Jill Clayburgh), several years earlier. What surfaces is an old rap charging her with the murder of her kids by a former husband. Though she was found innocent, the scars remain.

Plot is so thick with detail and implication that director Bruce Malmuth has difficulty balancing the exposition with the action. On hand is a former husband (Frederic Forrest), an accomplice (James Purcell) and a retired shrink (Barnard Hughes) to help sort it all out. At the crux is a very sick man and a child molestation tragedy. The film uses the material without really having anything to say about it.

Dealing with this kind of charged material is always dangerous and here the real life concerns do not fuel the action but detract from it. Malmuth resorts to clichéd slamming doors and other obvious portents of evil acts to come. Clues are telegraphed throughout.

Forrest as the kidnapper and former husband gives a riveting and unexpected performance. Almost unrecognizable with a paunch and a grey beard, Forrest is by turns loving and deadly with the children. Youngsters are also credible if a bit too sweet at times.

Clayburgh, called upon to look ashen throughout most of the film, is effective at communicating a mother's love and desperation, but has little to do until the rather overblown ending. Also appealing is Max Gail as her loving husband.

Outside of a few suspenseful turns biggest plus for the film is the lush Cape Cod scenery photographed mostly in the rain by Larry Pizer. Other tech credits are better than average. — *Jagr.*

Born American
(FINNISH-U.S.-COLOR)

A Concorde/Cinema Group (U.S.) release of a Cinema Group in association with Larmark production. Executive producers, Venetia Stevenson, Markus Selin. Directed by Renny Harlin. Features Mike Norris, Steve Durham, David Coburn. Screenplay, Renny Harlin, Markus Selin; camera (Fujicolor), Henrik Paerchs; editor, Paul Martin Smith; music, Richard Mitchell. Reviewed at the Palads Teatret, Copenhagen, Jan. 16, 1986. Running time: 95 MINS.

Savoy	Mike Norris
Mitch	Steve Durham
K.C.	David Coburn
The Admiral	Thalmus Rasulala
U.S. emissary	Albert Salmi
Nadja	Piita Vuosalmi

Copenhagen — Totally banned by the Finnish censors before its imminent U.S. release in 800 prints, "Born American" is a joint Finnish-American effort that has been nearly three years in the making. It is a slam-bang actioner, fast-paced and handsomely produced, that is likely to ride the crest of give-the-Commies-hell pictures currently in demand. It hardly merits the publicity garnered via its local ban, since latter was decided upon as a political consideration in Finno-Soviet relations. But the bad guy Russians of "Born American" are no worse than the caricatures of Germans in SS roles we have lived with peacefully for the last forty years.

Film makes no pretense about being anything but fictional. It has three young Amerians on a Lapland hunting trip straying, on a dare, across the border into the USSR. Here they make friends with a local girl who hides them until the Army's soldier-hunters move in to fight it out with the boys. Together, they succeed in burning a whole village to the ground. Major part of the film has the original innocents learning about life in a Gulag-prison which has, in its center, a permanent chess game going with the inmates as do-or-die pawns.

A rascally U.S. emissary (for a change, the CIA is not mentioned) makes a deal with the Russians that the three Americans aren't worth any diplomatic trouble. A caviar-and-champagne toast plus some nibbling at suddenly available female flesh serve to celebrate the boys' sentence to be considered nonexistent. The rest is a series of prison escape set pieces sprinkled with a few surrealistic or Kafkaesque overtones as a black American fellow prisoner with strange privileges turns up to help at least one of the youngsters (along with a rather glamorous little Russian girl) gain the way back to freedom.

"Born American" lags whenever women appear on the scene, but that happens only at very long intervals. Film's plotting is often contrived to the point of obscurity. Still, energy and flash of action staging is displayed throughout, and Mike Norris (son of Chuck), Steve Durham and David Coburn (no relation to James) put in convincing, natural performances that ought to soon make them familiar names and faces for casting directors to consider. There is plenty of violence spouting from the Rambo vein, but where it occurs, it makes sense. Henrik Paerchs' cinematography has a no-nonsense steadiness that works hand-in-glove with director Renny Harlin's smooth handling of a large cast through the plot's minefields. —*Kell.*

I Soliti Ignoti ... Vent'Anni Dopo
(Big Deal On Madonna Street ... 20 Years Later)
(ITALIAN-COLOR/B&W)

A Medusa Distribuzione release. Produced by Excelsior Film Tv-Medusa Distribuzione. Directed by Amanzio Todini. Stars Marcello Mastroianni, Vittorio Gassman. Screenplay, Age, Suso Cecchi D'Amico, Todini; camera (Kodacolor), Pasqualino De Santis; editor Ruggero Mastroianni; art director, Emilio Baldelli; music, Nino Rota, chosen and directed by Bruno Moretti. Reviewed at Royal Cinema, Rome, Jan. 22, 1986. Running time: 109 MINS.

Tiberio Brashi	Marcello Mastroianni
Peppe	Vittorio Gassman
Ferribotte	Tiberio Murgia
Orderly	Francesco De Rosa

Also with: Giorgio Gobbi, Clelia Rondinella, Concetta Barra, Gina Rovere, Natale Tulli, Ennio Fantastichini, Federica Pacifici.

Rome — One of the season's most curious ideas is bringing back an Italian comedy classic, "Big Deal On Madonna Street," by using the same cast and updating their saga. The original gem was helmed by Mario Monicelli in 1958 (strictly speaking, thesps have aged 27 years in the interim) and was penned by the towering quartet of Age, Scarpelli, Suso Cecchi D'Amico and the director. Amanzio Todini, a longtime assistant director making his helming debut, has replaced Monicelli, and Scarpelli (who has professionally separated from partner Age) has dropped out, but pic has rounded up Marcello Mastroianni, Vittorio Gassman and Tiberio Murgia from the original and Toto-lookalike Francesco De Rosa in the nostalgic role of Toto's son.

And yet, despite its promise, "20 Years Later" is more like a melancholy visit to the cemetery of Italian comedy than a worthy followup. In part, the lingering air of sadness is intended. Intercut scenes in black and white from the original film underline the effect of the years on our heroes, and also how the urban landscape of Rome has changed for the worse in the unzoned high-rises beside junk yards where petty thieves live these days.

That the quality of life has deteriorated substantially is the first thing Tiberio (Mastroianni) notices when he gets out of jail for the second time, after serving time for robbery. In spite of his efforts to avoid the gang's "mastermind," Peppe (Gassman), he soon is forced to look him up when other attempts to earn a living fail.

Peppe is about to take a van to Yugoslavia to export some hot money when he has a stroke and has to be hospitalized. Tiberio carries out the job with a carload of decoys, who include the wizened old Ferribotte (Tiberio Murgia), an old lady, his son and a girl with a baby. The happy vacationers get past the border police, but on their way back are tricked by their Mafia-type bosses. The bosses in turn think they've been betrayed by Peppe, and have him killed just when they're celebrating their "big deal."

Direction is attentive but lacks verve. Though the perfect ensemble acting of the earlier film is missing, individual performances are high quality. All the original characters remain sharply drawn; it is the new bits — the romance between Tiberio's son and the girl, his wife's relationship with their lodger — that have the empty-as-air feeling of current comedy. With a haunting score selected from old Nino Rota pieces, pic remains a ghostly curiosity item that draws a harsh line between yesterday's gold and today's tin.

—*Yung.*

U.S. Fest Reviews

Seven Minutes In Heaven
(COLOR)

Charming teen comedy, arrives late in cycle.

A Warner Bros. release of an FR production from Zoetrope Studios. Produced by Fred Roos. Directed by Linda Feferman. Screenplay, Jane Bernstein, Feferman; camera (Technicolor), Steven Fierberg; editor, Marc Laub; production design, Vaughan Edwards; art direction, Thomas A. Walsh; set decoration, Deborah Schutt; costume design, Dianne Finn Chapman; sound, Mike Rowland; associate producer, Mark Silverman; assistant director, Kelly Van Horn; casting Aleta Wood-Chappelle. Reviewed at the Holiday Village Cinema I (U.S. Film Festival), Park City, Utah, Jan. 20, 1986. (No MPAA Rating). Running time: 90 MINS.
Natalie Becker ....Jennifer Connelly
Polly Franklin..........Maddie Corman
Jeff Moran...............Byron Thames
Casey ....Alan Boyce
Aileen Jones ...'.........Polly Draper
Gerry Jones ....Marshall Bell
Bob Becker ....Michael Zaslow
Aunt Gail ....Denny Dillon
Lenore Franklin..........Margo Skinner
Stew Franklin ....Mathew Lewis
Richie Franklin...........Tim Waldrip
Zoo Knudsen..............Billy Wirth
Tim Williams ....Paul Martel
Bill the photographer ....Terry Kinney

Park City, Utah — A modestly charming entry in the teenpic field, "Seven Minutes In Heaven" features some of the outrageous farcical elements mandatory in the genrè but distinguishes itself in its more serious and realistic moments.

There's little here that hasn't been seen before, in both better and worse pictures, and fact of its coming late in the cycle can't help. Careful nurturing through gradual playoff, with special attention to the teen-age female audience, would seem to be the way to go.

The first feature effort by Linda Feferman, director of several well-received shorts, film shares with "Fast Times At Ridgemont High," another femme-directed teenpic, an unusual frankness concerning youthful sexuality.

Kids here have been caught at their most sex-on-the-brain stage, but, as usual, the ones who talk the most are the ones with the least action.

Story charts the burgeoning love lives of two 15-year-old girls, the serious, reserved, already beautiful Jennifer Connelly, whose ambition is to become President of the United States, and the aggressive, inadequacy-plagued Maddie Corman, whose fantasies run more toward becoming a groupie for major league baseball players.

Pic's most amusing and telling moments stem from the numerous tentative brushes with romance experienced by both girls.

Connelly becomes involved, but resists going all the way, with the local high school Lothario, then has a sweet but unphysical tryst with a young Presidential aide in Washington, D.C., where she has gone as a Future Leader.

For her part, Corman, who just can't wait to leave her girlhood behind, flies from Ohio to New York to meet a baseball jock with whom she's made out in a car one afternoon and subsequently bluntly propositions a hip photographer who saves her from the stadium's security police.

Dragging the proceedings down a bit is some protracted farce involving a local buddy, Byron Thames, who decides he's had enough of his mother and stepfather and camps out at Connelly's while her papa is away.

Too much is made of how neighbors and classmates imagine the worst about the pair's "living together." Connelly seems to have nothing in common with him, and the gag appears artificial compared to the rest of the events in Feferman and Jane Bernstein's screenplay.

Feferman exhibits a good feel for her young characters, and one can say that the casting of the male sex objects here seems different and more believable than in most pictures directed by men.

Some of the direction is as awkward as the characters are at times, but the good moments outweigh the weak ones.

Connelly, so striking as the young dancer in "Once Upon A Time In America," is equally gorgeous here and quite believable to boot as the determined achiever. Corman gets her character's brashness across but doesn't have the depth to evoke all the vulnerability that is implicit in the dialog.

Developed in the heyday of Zoetrope Studios, pic has been handsomely produced on a low budget by longtime Francis Coppola associate Fred Roos on location in New Jersey suburbs. —*Cart.*

F/X
(COLOR)

Implausible but entertaining action pic.

An Orion Pictures release. Produced by Dodi Fayed, Jack Wiener. Executive producer, Michael Peyser. Directed by Robert Mandel. Screenplay, Robert T. Megginson, Gregory Fleeman; camera (Technicolor), Miroslav Ondricek; editor, Terry Rawlings; music, Bill Conti; production design, Mel Bourne; art director, Speed Hopkins; set decorator, Steven Jordan; set dresser, David Weinman; sound, Les Lazarowitz; special effects consultant, John Stears; special makeup, Carl Fullerton; costumes, Julie Weiss; assistant director, Thomas Lofaro; casting, Alixe Gordin. Reviewed at the U.S. Film Festival, Egyptian Theater, Park City, Utah, Jan. 23, 1986. (MPAA Rating: R.) Running time: 106 MINS.
Rollie Tyler ....Bryan Brown
Leo McCarthy ....Brian Dennehy
Ellen ....Diane Venora
Lipton ....Cliff DeYoung
Colonel Mason ....Mason Adams
Nicholas ....Jerry Orbach
Mickey ....Joe Grifasi
Andy ....Martha Gehman
Captain Wallenger ....Roscoe Orman
Lt. Murdoch ....Trey Wilson
Varrick ....Tom Noonan

Park City, Utah — As contrived and plot-hole ridden as it is, "F/X" still works quite effectively as a crowd-pleasing popcorn picture. Despite inside reference of the title, and lack of star names, Orion should be able to pull good winter biz with the fast-paced actioner.

Basic premise here is so strong that it proves well-nigh indestructible, even in the face of numerous implausibilities, some silly dialog and less-than-great casting in secondary roles. Done properly, this could have been a first-rate film; as is, pic plays as a serviceable entertainment, the cinematic equivalent of a paperback thriller that's hard to put down.

Crackerjack film special-effects man Bryan Brown is recruited by the Justice Dept. to stage a phony assassination of big-time mobster Jerry Orbach, who is ready to squeal. The authorities want the Mafia to think Orbach is dead so they won't try to rub him out before he takes the stand.

Brown is convinced to act the role of the hitman himself, but once he pulls off the convincing stunt, he finds himself a marked man, the target of both government goons and New York police.

Last 80 minutes of the film constitute a relentless, multi-faceted chase, as Brown must rely on his wits and resourceful talents as an F/X wizard to elude and, ultimately, hunt down the baddies who set him up. At the same time, old-style Irish cop Brian Dennehy so flagrantly disobeys the rule book in his pursuit of justice that he gets tossed off the force. But even this doesn't stop him.

Both of the lead characters, then, are victims of a corrupt and anti-human system. Roles are one-dimensional, but Brown and Dennehy possess sufficient personality and physical presence to fill them well.

It would be an understatement to say that Robert Mandel directed with a lack of attention to strong characterization in the remaining parts. In a genre piece such as this in which characters are important for what they represent, not who they are, supporting actors, especially villains, must be chosen for their immediate recognizability and unusual traits. Blandness of most of the cast, with the exception of Orbach, reduces the force of evil and general sense of melodrama.

Contrivances in Robert T. Megginson and Gregory Fleeman's screenplay are preposterous at times, but Mandel just keeps the thing barreling along to most diverting effects. Much of the amusement stems from Brown's diverse disguises and use of special effects, with which he variously fools, distracts, misleads and does in his adversaries.

Special effects, stunts and special makeup are all they needed to be — top drawer — while regular technical contributions are straightforwardly pro. —*Cart.*

The Boy In Blue
(CANADIAN-COLOR)

A 20th Century Fox release of an ICC-Denis Héroux-John Kemeny production. Produced by John Kemeny. Directed by Charles Jarrott. Executive producer, Steve North. Screenplay, Douglas Bowie; camera (color), Pierre Mignot; editor, Rit Wallis; music, Roger Webb; production designer, William Beeton; production manager, Stephane Reichel; costumes, John Hay; assistant director, Jacques Methe. Reviewed at Towne Cinema, Toronto, Jan. 18, 1986. (MPAA Rating: R.) Running time: 93 MINS.
Ned ....Nicolas Cage
Margaret..................Cynthia Dale
Knox.............Christopher Plummer
Bill....................David Naughton
Walter....................Sean Sullivan
Dulcie ....Melody Anderson
Collins ....James B. Douglas
Mayor....................Walter Massey
Bainbridge ....Austin Willis
Kinnear...................Philip Craig
Trickett ....Robert McCormick

Toronto — "The Boy In Blue" is a largely uninspired and lackluster affair about one of Canada's grand sports heroes, Ned Hanlan, a world-class rower. Subject matter and star attraction of Nicolas Cage may spark initial interest, but a host of weak reviews and poor word of mouth make b.o. future look dim. And for its quick brush with nudity, pic doesn't merit an R rating.

Ned (Nicolas Cage) is a young backwoods Ontario bootlegger, whose skills at sculling bring him to the attention of sneaky Bill (David Naughton), who sees a good investment in Ned and becomes his manager. He grooms him for the Philadelphia Centennial Regatta on the Schuylkill.

Pic covers the rowing period of 1874-1884, in which time Hanlan wins in Philly, gets disqualified from the Boston race for unsportsmanlike behavior, and regains his coveted title after the world championship Thames River competition.

There's a love interest, of course — Margaret, the snooty niece of the venal Col. Knox (Christopher Plummer). Knox uses Ned as a gambling tool for his own purposes, and Margaret, while engaged to a rich Harvard man, is won over by Ned's downhome manner and his Rocky-esque physique.

Cage is too lunky and too much of a Yankee for the victorious oarsman's role here, although he looks great throughout the pic. His personality is all brawn. Kudos to Cage, though, for doing his own rowing and giving some credence to the action scenes.

David Naughton is also a peculiar choice for Bill, the shifty manager who gives up Ned to Knox. Cynthia Dale (''Heavenly Bodies'') is all poutish coquetry here, and Christopher Plummer delivers his character in one note, twirling his moustache with evil glee.

Charles Jarrott (''Anne Of The Thousand Days,'' ''The Amateur'') directs ''Boy'' at a sluggish pace. Even the grand racing finale is stripped of its excitement by the predictable camerawork and upbeat music. And none of the backstabbing gambling intrigue ever takes off either. Script by tv writer Douglas Bowie pales with unconvincing characterizations. Location shooting by Pierre Mignot, however, is sometimes glimmering.

There's still a film to be made about this engaging Canadian rower, the glory of sculling, and the energy associated with a sport that in the late 1800s inspired the same public fervor that football and baseball do today. — *Devo.*

Windschaduw
(Windshade)
(DUTCH-COLOR-16m)

A Film Intl. release of a Frans van de Staak production. Produced and edited by van de Staak. Screenplay, van de Staak, in collaboration with Gerrit Kouwenaar; camera (color, 16m), Mat van Hensbergen; music, Berend Hunnekink; sound, Pjotr van Dijk. Reviewed at Desmet Theater, Amsterdam, Jan. 21, 1986. Running time: 71 MINS.
Man ....Gerrart Klieverik

Woman ....Isabelle Guillaume

Amsterdam — Producer and avant-garde filmmaker Frans van de Staak constructed ''Windshade'' around two poems by Gerrit Kouwenaar, one of the best Dutch poets, who reads his own verse off-screen. The decisive part which poetry has in the film makes distribution in non-Dutchspeaking countries unlikely, except for some fests.

Vacations are mentioned in Kouwenaar's verses, and pic is built around shots of a man and a woman packing, going away, arriving at their destination, packing again, going back to square one. These shots are intercut with beautifully photographed views of fields, forests, trees.

The people in the film (which will preem at the Rotterdam Film Fest) never say more than occasional half-sentences. They don't really communicate. ''Windshade'' tells of people who lead indefinite lives and can't find definitive solutions to their problems.

As in van de Staak's recent pics people are used as near abstractions. This makes for an interesting structure, though hardly for human interest. The poems provided some of the needed counterweight. —*Wall.*

Devil In The Flesh
(AUSTRALIAN-COLOR)

A J.C. Williamson Film Management Ltd.-World Film Alliance presentation of a Collins Murray production. Produced by John B. Murray. Executive producer, Peter Collins. Written and directed by Scott Murray. Stars Katia Caballeo, Keith Smith. Adapted from the novel ''Le Diable au Corps'' by Raymond Radiguet; camera (Eastmancolor), Andrew de Groot; editor, Tim Lewis; music, Philippe Sarde; art director, Paddy Reardon; sound, Laurie Robinson; production manager, John Hipwell; line producer and assistant director, Tom Burstall; costumes, Frankie Hogan. Reviewed at Colorfilm screening room, Sydney, Nov. 26, 1985. Running time: 103 MINS.
Marthe ....Katia Caballero
Paul Hansen ....Keith Smith
John Hansen ....John Morris
Jill Hansen ....Jill Forster
Pierre Fouriner ....Colin Duckworth
Madeleine Fournier ....Reine Lavoie
Ermanno ....Luciano Martucci
Blond model ....Louise Elvin
Simon Greene ....Jeremy Johnson
Simone ....Odile Le Clezio
Brother Murphy ....John Murphy
Disciplinarian Brother ....Peter Cummins

Sydney — Raymond Radiguet's novel ''Le Diable au Corps'' was memorably filmed by Claude Autant-Lara in 1947. Now the book has become the inspiration for the first feature of Scott Murray, for many years editor of Australia's leading film magazine Cinema Papers, and it's an impressive debut.

Murray has taken a few liberties with the book. He has set the story, not in France during World War I but in rural Australia in 1943. Fur-

Original Film
Le Diable au Corps
(FRENCH-B&W)

A Universal Intl. release of a Paul Graetz production (Transcontinental Films). Directed by Claude Autant-Lara. Stars Gérard Philipe, Micheline Presle; features Denise Grey, Debucourt. Screen adaptation, Jean Aurenche and Pierre Bost, from the novel by Raymond Radiguet; camera (b&w), Voinquel; music, Rene LeCloarec. At Normandie, Olympia and Moulin Rouge, Paris, Sept. 16, 1947. Running time: 122 MINS.
François ....Gérard Philipe
Marthe.................Micheline Presle
François' father ....Debucourt
Marthe's mother ....Denise Grey
François' pal ....Emile François
Schoolmaster ....Maxudian
Headwaiter ....Francoeur

thermore, he has drastically altered the book's ending, in which the adulterous heroine died in childbirth. However, despite these changes, Murray has faithfully retained the spirit and feel of the original, both book and film, and his handling of the narrative displays a firm confidence.

Marthe, a young Frenchwoman married to an Italian who has been interned by Australian authorities for the duration of the war, is attractively played by newcomer Katia Caballero. Another newcomer, Keith Smith, is properly awkward at first as the shy schoolboy, Paul, who becomes infatuated with Marthe and eventually becomes her lover. First part of the film, prior to the couple's first sexual encounter, is the best; the erotic tension is palpable and craftily maintained by Murray.

The once-sensational theme of a schoolboy sleeping with a married woman is no longer as shocking as it was thanks to films like ''Summer Of '42,'' although the fact that this couple long for the war to continue so that Marthe's husband will stay imprisoned does add a dark note to their affair. Second half of the pic is filled with secret meetings, small-town gossip and the horrified reaction of Paul's troubled parents, though the lowkey approach makes for rather understated drama.

Though strongly influenced by French cinema, the film is undeniably Australian. Beautifully shot by Andrew de Groot, in complete contrast to his only other feature, ''Strikebound,'' the handsome visuals emphasize the landscape: the dusty dirt roads, the gum trees, the quaint railway stations, the sleepy town. There's male and female nudity on display, but strictly softcore. In one striking scene, Paul picks up the artists' model (Louise Elvin) and makes love to her, but they have nothing to say to each other.

Pic has arthouse possibilities on its superb look and feeling for period and place, its eroticism, and its sensitive lead performances.

Coincidentally, Italian director Marco Bellocchio is now complet-

ing another version of Radiguet's book which is expected to be unveiled at Cannes. Murray's version has already secured distribution in France, via Georges Alain-Vuille, and it's set to open in Paris shortly. —*Strat.*

Nachruf auf eine Bestie
(Obituary For A Beast)
(WEST GERMAN-B&W)

An Oase Film, Essen, in coproduction with Second German Television (ZDF), Mainz. A documentary written and directed by Rolf Schübel. Camera (b&w), Niels Bolbinker; sound and editor, Harald Reetz; research, Michael Föster; tv-producer; Ingeborg Janiczek. Reviewed at ZDF Screening Room, Berlin, Dec. 9, 1985. Running time: 107 MINS.

Berlin — Programmed last year in the Forum of Young Cinema at the Berlinale, Rolf Schübel's ''Obituary For A Beast'' then won immediate broad critical acclaim as one of the most fascinating German docus on a criminal case. It tells the story of child sex murderer Jürgen Bartsch, who in his teens killed four boys in a hideous manner and aroused the wrath of the entire population. His case was referred to in the press as ''the crime of the century,'' while a survey ranked him second only to Hitler as a cold-blooded murderer.

Schübel picks up the traces nearly a decade after Bartsch died in 1976 on an operating table during voluntary castration surgery, aged 30. He interviews everyone of note in the case, save for Bartsch' foster-parents and the operating surgeon. The killer is presented via a lengthy taperecorded interview. The research into the case is so thorough one gathers voluminous information on both the criminal and the crime, enough to analyze the whys and wherefores down to rather minute detail. A parallel example in portrait criminology might be Truman Capote's ''In Cold Blood,'' although the points of departure are fundamentally different.

''Obituary For A Beast'' is less interested in the crimes committed than the criminal who perpetrated them, and the viewer often is nudged into reflecting upon whether or not society might not have given Jürgen Bartsch a bum deal from the start. He never knew his real parents, was raised in a clinic before being adopted by a butcher's family, and apparently never received love and understanding enough to look at life squarely in the face. By 15, he was ''driven'' to become a child killer.

Particularly praiseworthy is the manner in which helmer Schübel tells his story without extra commentary or even notifying subtitles under those interviewed. One bit of testimony simply dovetails with another — it's like piecing together a puzzle or constructing a mosaic. Pic's lensing also adequately captures an atmosphere.

What's missing are interviews with friends and relatives of the victims. Then again, that might mean another kind of documentary altogether — extra testimonials instead of a single obituary. —*Holl.*

On Valentine's Day
(COLOR)

Modest prequel to Horton Foote's '1918.'

An Angelika Films release of an American Playhouse presentation of a Guadalupe/Hudson production in association with Lumiere Prods. Produced by Lillian V. Foote, Calvin Skaggs. Executive producers, Lewis Allen, Lindsay Law, Ross Milloy, Peter Newman. Directed by Ken Harrison. Screenplay, Horton Foote, from his play, "Valentine's Day"; camera (DuArt color), George Tirl; editor, Nancy Baker; music, Jonathan Sheffer; art direction, Howard Cummings; set decoration, Donnasu Schiller; costume design, Van Broughton Ramsey; sound, Skip Frazee; associate producers, Carl Clifford, James Crosby. Reviewed at the Egyptian Theater (U.S. Film Festival), Park City, Utah, Jan. 22, 1986. (No MPAA Rating.) Running time: **105 MINS.**
Elizabeth Robedaux .... Hallie Foote
Horace
Robedaux .... William Converse-Roberts
Mr. Vaughn .... Michael Higgins
George Tyler .... Steven Hill
Mrs. Vaughn .... Rochelle Oliver
Bobby Pate .... Richard Jenkins
Miss Ruth .... Carol Goodheart
Bessie .... Jeanne McCarthy
Steve Tyler .... Horton Foote Jr.
Brother Vaughn ...... Matthew Broderick

Park City, Utah — "On Valentine's Day" represents a prequel to, and something of an improvement upon, the first filmed installment in Horton Foote's trilogy of Texas plays, "1918." With a better critical response, new film should improve upon the meager b.o. performance of the original, but theatrical audience is still extremely limited.

To anyone who found "1918" exceptionally dull and lifeless, the first half-hour or so of "On Valentine's Day" offers up more of the same.

Adapting his own play, Horton Foote at considerable length delivers all the necessary exposition about how Elizabeth Vaughn, daughter of the most prominent citizen of a small Texas town, and Horace Robedaux, a hard-working self-made man, eloped on Valentine's Day, 1917.

Primary action is set at Christmastime of that year. Elizabeth's parents have not spoken to her since she ran off, but the holidays afford the opportunity for a reconciliation and, slowly but surely, one sets in.

Drama embraces different layers of family, from the nucleus to such secondary relatives as the strange and mysterious cousin George and the unrelated family of happen-stance represented by the eccentric boarders in the Robedaux household.

As before, Ken Harrison's direction emphasizes the stagy nature of the proceedings. He gives the piece over to the actors and presents the script without illuminating it.

And yet, after the boredom of the first third, a certain integrity makes itself felt. This, in turn, is followed by some very quiet but palpable dramatic explosions which create some genuinely earned emotional effects. Nothing major is achieved, but there are some real feelings conjured up here.

Foote's dialog consists of nothing but small-town small talk, and sponding favorably to the film depends almost entirely upon one's ability to find charm in the ways of these middle-class Texans.

This is also emphatically the cinema of the screenwriter. Pic is wall-to-wall words, all enunciated clearly and cleanly by a well-chosen cast, most of who also appeared in "1918." Most prominent here are Hallie Foote as the sweet, ever-thoughtful Elizabeth, William Converse-Roberts as her husband, Michael Higgins as her father and Steven Hill as cousin George.

Lensed in Waxahachie and Venus, Tex., modest production is solid in all technical departments.
—*Cart.*

The More Things Change
(AUSTRALIAN-COLOR)

A Hoyts release of a Syme Intl. production, in association with the New South Wales Film Corp. Produced by Jill C. Robb. Directed by Robyn Nevin. Stars Judy Morris, Barry Otto. Screenplay, Moya Wood; camera (Panavision, Eastmancolor), Dan Burstall; editor, Jill Bilcock; music, Peter Best; sound (Dolby), John Phillips; production design, Josephine Ford; associate producer, Greg Ricketson; production manager, Trish Hepworth; assistant director, Adrian Pickersgill. Reviewed at Film Australia screening room, Sydney, Dec. 4, 1985. Running time: **95 MINS.**
Connie .... Judy Morris
Lex .... Barry Otto
Geraldine .... Victoria Longley
Barry .... Lewis Fitz-Gerald
Roley .... Peter Carroll
Lydia .... Louise Le Nay
Nicholas .... Owen Johnson
Angela .... Brenda Addie
Bridesmaid .... Joanne Barker
Karen .... Adrienne Barrett
Eric .... Bill Bennett
Mim .... Paddy Burnet
Vince .... John Egan

Sydney — Robyn Nevin, a distinguished stage and film actress, has moved behind the camera with distinction. "The More Things Change" is a universally topical film about a modern marriage, told with humor and insight. It's also splendidly acted.

Connie (Judy Morris) and Lex (Barry Otto, from "Bliss") are happily married with a small son, Nicholas (Owen Johnson). They've decided to opt out of the rat race, and have purchased a small but spectacularly beautiful farm two hours' drive from the city. This is to be their future, but until the farm is self-sufficient one of them has to keep working. The onus falls on Connie, who has an excellent job with a publishing company. The laid-back Lex settles down to work, single-handed, on the farm, but finds the child to be very much in his way. A live-in baby-sitter is the answer, and Connie engages Geraldine (newcomer Victoria Longley), young, engaged to be married, and pregnant — though not by her fiance.

The viewer's expectations are, naturally, that Lex and Geraldine will have an affair, but Moya Wood's sharp screenplay is much more subtle than that. The two do, indeed, strike up a warm and intimate friendship, but there's no sex involved, and somehow that's even more worrying for the increasingly busy and frustrated Connie. Instead of charting the obvious course, the film, with great affection, explores the way Connie and Lex slowly grow apart just as Geraldine and her understanding fiance (Lewis Fitz-Gerald) grow closer together.

This is a film where all the characters are a pleasure to spend time with. Lex, as played to perfection by Barry Otto, is constantly cheerful, irresponsible, lazy, infuriating and yet loving. Connie is far more serious, dedicated to her work, determined to make her marriage succeed, and yet not willing to be pushed around too much. Geraldine is painfully immature, naive and open, but in a strange way old-fashioned and genuinely sweet. They're all flesh and blood people.

Pic is most handsomely shot by Dan Burstall, who makes the farm and its environs look like paradise on earth. The Panavision format seems a bit unnecessary for this intimate subject, and the Dolby stereo sound is sometimes irritatingly over-loud and over-emphatic, but these are minor quibbles in a generally delightful film. Peter Best's music score is well integrated, and the production design of Josephine Ford is first-rate. Editor Jill Bilcock deserves special praise for seamlessly turning out a tightly-structured pic that doesn't overstay its welcome. Producer Jill Robb also deserves a nod for putting it all together.

This is a film which, if properly handled, should find an appreciative audience for its genuinely funny comedy, its understated pathos, and its forthright honesty.—*Strat.*

Konzert für Alice
(Concert For Alice)
(SWISS-WEST GERMAN-AUSTRIAN-COLOR)

A Columbus Film Zurich release of a Condor Features Zurich-SRG-ZDF-ORG coproduction. Written and directed by Thomas Koerfer, from story by Alexander & Lev Schargorodsky. Executive producer, Edi Hubschmid. Camera (color), Martin Fuhrer; lighting, Benjamin Lehmann, Salvatore Piazzitta; sound, Hans Künzi; art direction, Kathrin Brunner; costumes, Monika Schmid; production manager, Marcel Just; editor, Fee Liechti; music, Louis Crelier. Reviewed at the Alba, Zurich, Nov. 19, 1985. Running time: **87 MINS.**
Alice/Margot .... Beate Jensen
Ljova .... Towje Kleiner
Frau Keller .... Anne-Marie Blanc
Conductor .... Erwin Parker
Also with: Angelica Arndts, Grete Heger, Heinz Bühlmann, Peter Holliger, Johannes Silberschneider, Yvonne Kupper, Michael Gempart, Patrick Frey, Hermann Guggenheim, Matthias Günther.

Zurich — Swiss helmer Thomas Koerfer attempts a complete change of pace with his latest film, "Concert For Alice." His previous entries, notably "Der Gehüfld," "Alzire oder der neue Kontinent" and "Glut," were either intellectual exercises or politically motivated stories. "Alice" is neither. Instead, Koerfer has tried his hand at a lightweight, contempo romantic comedy with music. The result seems to indicate the director lacks the light touch, paired with poetic substance, to create a sort of 1985 Zurich version of René Clair's "Sous les Toits de Paris," as might have been his goal.

The story has charm, but little else. A famous Russian flutist who has defected to Switzerland falls in love with a young Zurich street musician, also a flutist. He decides to finance a concert for her without revealing his identity. She, in turn, sees through his plan and assumes a false identity as a rich sponsor determined to further his career in the West.

The concert finally takes place, but instead of Alice as the star soloist, it is the Russian who, thanks to her manipulations, takes her place on the concert stage. Naturally, all ends well, with the couple last seen floating "into happiness" in an illuminated boat along the Limmat River.

Koerfer adapted this modern fairytale from a story by the Schargorodsky brothers, Alexander and Lev, Russian writers and scripters who defected from Leningrad in 1979 and live in Geneva. Apart from too many "accidents" straining credibility, the film does have a nice romantic touch, but it seems settled in a never-never land too far beyond reality.

Obviously, music plays an important part. Besides an excerpt from a flute concerto by Antonio Vivaldi, Swiss composer Louis Crelier has written an original score, notably a leitmotif entitled "Close To Me." It is pleasantly melodic, but sounds too much like a love theme heard before. Lensing by Martin Fuhrer succeeds in turning Zurich, the banking and business metropolis, into a kind of enchanted dream city.

Koerfer showed a good hand in casting his leads. Towje Kleiner, a Munich-based tv actor originally from Israel, as the sad-faced Jewish artist, and young German actress Beate Jensen, at times almost a young Leslie Caron lookalike, as the dual-identity flutist, are among the picture's definite assets.

— *Mezo.*

Isle Of Fantasy
(HONG KONG-COLOR)

A Cinema City production, released by Golden Princess. Executive producers, Karl Maka, Dean Shek, Raymond Wong. Directed by Michael Mak. Stars Wong, Teresa Carpio, Ann Bridgewater, Fennie Yuen, Loletta Lee, Charine Chan, May Lo, Bonnie Law and Tang Kee Chun. Screenplay, Wong; camera (color), Johnny Koo; editor, Wong Ming; music, Mahood Rumjahn. Reviewed at President theater, Hong Kong, Jan. 5, 1986. Running time: 95 MINS.
(Cantonese soundtrack with English subtitles)

Hong Kong — Fantasy all right in "Isle Of Fantasy" ... with all the giggly young girls from Cinema City that the producers packaged as juvenile "actresses (?)" for the mass Cantonese moviegoers.

Singer turned actress Teresa Carpio looks bright and sprightly, but overacts outrageously, in a bloated performing style as predictable as the gorilla jokes and her feline screams.

A plane with six Girl Scouts on board ditches into the sea and the six are washed up on a supposedly deserted island with salesman Raymond Wong. The apparent make-believe paradise emerges only to submerge readily.

The girls, along with Teresa, do a lot of running around and shouting in shrill voices. Bizarre characters later enter the picture, with Mark Cheng tagging along as the undercover hero they nurse back to health.

Ridiculous, corny and plastic, but the domestic public seems to like this kind of cartoon celluloid monstrosity. A delighted romp into the world of cliché-crammed low-budget quickies.—*Mel.*

Heathcliff: The Movie
(ANIMATED-COLOR)

An Atlantic Releasing/Clubhouse Pictures release of a DIC Audiovisuel-LBS Communications-McNaught Syndicate production. Produced by Jean Chalopin. Executive producers, Chalopin, Andy Heyward, Tetsuo Katayama. Supervising director, Bruno Bian-

chi. Head screenwriter, Alan Swayze; Heathcliff voice characterization, Mel Blanc. Reviewed at Lorimar screening room, N.Y., Jan. 23, 1986. (MPAA Rating: G.) Running time: 73 MINS.

"Heathcliff: The Movie" is a colorful animated feature culled from several episodes of the syndicated tv series and with a good portion of new material added to tie everything together. While supplying little animation sophistication or wit that might enthrall older kids and adults, preschoolers nevertheless should enjoy it for its slapstick humor.

New material introduces Heathcliff, an orange wise-acre cat, as he's trying to entertain his three silent cat nephews. Pulling them next to him with a vacuum cleaner, he regales them with several of his past experiences as a means of whiling away a quiet afternoon. His various tales — greatly exaggerated, one assumes — recount his exploits with a bullying bulldog, whom Heathcliff cagily outwits time and again; a Heathcliff lookalike who lacks the star's braggadocio; his escaped con of a father (whose coat is orange with black horizontal stripes); and two Siamese cat twins who are martial arts masters.

Humor throughout is on the broad side, despite the efforts of master cartoon voice Mel Blanc to enliven Heathcliff. While animation technique is nothing that can't be seen on a Saturday tv cartoon, there are moments when it appears something ambitious in the way of foreground/background juxtaposition is being attempted.—*Gerz.*

Parting Glances
(COLOR)

Impressive drama about gay yuppies.

A Cinecom International Films release of a Rondo production. Produced by Yoram Mandel, Arthur Silverman. Executive producer, Paul A. Kaplan. Directed, written, edited by Bill Sherwood. Camera (DuArt color), Jacek Laskus; production design, John Loggia; sound, Scott Breindel; associate directors, Yoram Mandel, Tony Jacobs; associate producers, Nancy Greenstein; Victoria Westhead; casting, Daniel Haughey. Reviewed at the Holiday Village Cinema 2 (U.S. Film Festival), Park City, Utah, Jan. 20, 1986. (No MPAA Rating.) Running time: 90 MINS.
Michael . . . . Richard Ganoung
Robert . . . . John Bolger
Nick . . . . Steve Buscemi

Park City, Utah — "Parting Glances" is an up-to-the-minute gay yuppie picture, and an excellent one at that. Bracingly forthright and believable in its presentation of an all-gay world within contempo New York City, indie production looks sensational and is well-acted down to the smallest bits.

Commercial possibilities are inherently limited by subject matter

and lack of selling points, but film deserves the strongest push possible by Cinecom to try to break down conventional b.o. boundaries.

Most recently gay-themed pics, from militant political tracts to campy underground fare and even studio-financed projects, seemed to be trying to make some kind of point about homosexuality; in any event, "it" was the subject matter.

In "Parting Glances," "it" is taken for granted and instantly becomes the fabric of an exceedingly vibrant evocation of a multifaceted social scene, which in turn assumes background status for a tale of strong emotions among some quite recognizable characters.

Set within a 24-hour period, Bill Sherwood's highly sophisticated pic centers around a series of farewell events for Robert, good-looking boyfriend of ultra-yuppie Michael.

Robert, for reasons finally discovered by his lover, is leaving for a stint in Kenya, which will bring about the interruption, if not the end, of a six-year relationship.

Tale sees them through some bickering, an intimate dinner party at the home of Robert's wealthy, effete British boss, their final lovemaking session and — the film's centerpiece — an intense, all-night SoHo party populated almost entirely by the arty gay crowd.

Intertwined with all this is Michael's very responsible dealing with his former lover Nick, a caustic, cynical rock musician who has recently learned that he has AIDS.

Fortunately, film indulges in no special pleading with regard to the disease, merely regarding it as another fact, however tragic, of gay life.

The one substantial criticism that could be made of the film is that all of the secondary characters are so much more colorful than either Michael or Robert; indeed, the latter remains an emotional cipher, but their relationship is entirely plausible.

White putting the two characters through the motions of finding out what's going on between them, Sherwood avoids any awkwardness in dialog or acting, and Richard Ganoung and John Bolger are to be commended for pulling off scene after difficult scene. Steve Buscemi is superb as the acerbic, doomed artist.

Production is terrifically classy in every respect. Particularly outstanding is Jacek Laskus' lensing, which unerringly and gorgeously captures several different Gotham milieus rendered by production designer John Loggia. Mix of rock and classical music is also extremely effective.

An absorbing entertainment, film always seems authentic, never calculated. It's an impressive achievement. — *Cart.*

U.S. Fest Reviews

Raw Tunes
(COLOR-16m)

Amateurish musical.

A Changing Horses production. Produced, directed, written, edited by Gary Levy, Dan Lewk. Camera (Cine Craft color), Randy Sellars; music, Lewk, Julie Christensen, Levy; sound, John Fero, Jeanine Moret; assistant director, Mark Cornett. Reviewed at the Holiday Village Cinema 2 (U.S. Film Festival), Park City, Utah, Jan. 21, 1986 (No MPAA Rating.) Running time: 72 MINS.
With: Gary Levy (Johnny Columbus), Dan Lewk (Laird Bonnet), Malcolm Hurd, Steve Peterman, Mitchell Laurence, Jim Purcell.

Park City, Utah — Watching "Raw Tunes" is like catching a Ramada Inn lounge act on a bad night. As it happens, that is also more or less what this ear and eyesore is about, but that's no excuse for the appalling amateurishness of the effort here. Commercial possibilities are zilch.

The outgrowth of a graduate-film project at Los Angeles City College, pic doesn't quite look its $24,000 production budget.

This is the sort of film that has a green line running through the middle of the frame, not just on one reel, as sometimes happens, but through the entire picture. Somebody should have called the lab.

Story has something to do with a road tour by the eponymous group, a band which the press materials state has cumulative I.Q. of 48.

Unfortunately, band members quickly drop out along the way, and the remaining member and the manager, portrayed by filmmakers Dan Lewk and Gary Levy, would be lucky to reach double digits together.

The best that can be said is that a few moments of off-the-wall humor manage to get through the imbecilic shenanigans. But this is a long, long 72 minutes. —*Cart.*

Desert Bloom
(COLOR)

Intelligent family drama needs special handling.

A Columbia Pictures release of a Carson Prods. Group production in association with The Sundance Institute, from Columbia-Delphi IV Prods. Produced by Michael Hausman. Executive producer, Richard Fischoff. Written and directed by Eugene Corr, based on a story by Linda Remy, Corr, camera (Metrocolor), Reynaldo Villalobos; editor, David Garfield, John Currin, Cari Coughlin; music, Brad Fiedel; art direction, Lawrence Miller; set decoration, Bob Zilliox; costume design, Hilary Rosenfeld; sound, Michael Evje; associate producer, Remy; assistant director, Hausman; casting, Deborah Lucchesi. Reviewed at the Egyptian Theater (U.S. Film Festival), Park City, Utah, Jan. 24, 1986. (MPAA Rating: PG.) Running time: **104 MINS.**

Jack	Jon Voight
Lily	JoBeth Williams
Starr	Ellen Barkin
Mr. Mosol	Allen Garfield
Rose	Annabeth Gish
Robin	Jay D. Underwood
Dee Ann	Desirée Joseph
Barbara Jo	Dusty Balcerzak

Park City, Utah — After more than a year on the shelf, "Desert Bloom" emerges as a muted, intelligently observed story of a girl's growing pains in an emotionally deprived and politically warped environment. Inherently a small picture, the greatest assets of which are mood and performance, Columbia release presents clear-cut marketing challenges. Good reviews will be necessary to attract discerning domestic audiences, and prestige fests could help further its reputation internationally.

Although artfully made, this is not really an art film per se, as it trades very directly in the emotional problems and situations of a lower-class family in ways that would be entirely recognizable to any audience.

Nevertheless, writer-director Eugene Corr develops his drama in an understated, measured manner that requires some patience, at least in the opening reels. Arid setting in question is Las Vegas, 1950, where World War II vet Jon Voight runs a gas station and is stepfather to JoBeth Williams' three daughters, the oldest of whom is the 13-year-old Rose, played by Annabeth Gish.

Big events in the household are the arrival of the girls' Aunt Starr (Ellen Barkin), a glamorous showgirl type who will live with the family for the 42 days necessary to obtain a quickie divorce, and the impending atmospheric A-bomb test, for which the entire community is preparing as if it were the second coming.

Devoted to his shortwave radio and military rumors more than he is to his family, Voight stupidly compensates for feelings of inadequacy and impotence by mistreating his stepdaughters, particularly Rose,

and taking to the bottle. He also precipitates a huge blowup by making a play for his wife's sister, the sexually provocative Starr.

Except for isolated moments, the drama is handled in a subdued, low-key manner, and viewers looking for sensitive, discreetly handled fare will be amply rewarded. Gish, whose character narrates as an older woman, is the centerpiece of the tale, rebelling against the man she refuses to accept as her father but, as a scholarly girl, finding the exciting Starr a tempting but incomplete role model.

The promised atomic blast is fraught with meaning and significance, of course, but fortunately, it is not inflated with phony symbolic weight vis-à-vis Gish's emotional traumas. It is just there as a foreboding but strangely fascinating backdrop, and when the explosion finally does come, the screen moments are unexpectedly haunting.

As he did in "Lookin' To Get Out" and "Runaway Train," among other films, Voight again plays a dumb, limited man capable of tremendous insensitivity and loathesome behavior. As much as one might feel sorry for the oaf, one feels even sorrier for those around him, resulting in growing dislike for the character. It must be a very effective performance.

Due to her good housewife role, Williams can do little but be overshadowed by Barkin, who delivers a wonderfully splashy turn as the unlucky but resilient sexpot. She's probably never looked better onscreen, and by the way she sinks her teeth into this role, enlivens the picture whenever she shows up.

Gish is a find as Rose. Obviously bright and physically reminiscent of another actress of about the same age, Jennifer Connelly, she almost singlehandedly lends the film its intelligent air and makes one root for Rose to survive her squalid upbringing.

Project was developed at the 1983 Sundance lab, and Corr makes a promising fictional feature debut here. Dramatic structure and pacing could be surer, and some of his points are ultimately obscure, but the portrait of infertile, stultifying conditions for personal growth is powerful.

Postwar setting has been well evoked on Tucson-area locations, and Reynaldo Villalobos' outstanding lensing paces the good technical contributions. —*Cart.*

Un Complicato Intrigo di Donne, Vicoli e Delitti
(Camorra)
(ITALIAN-COLOR)

An Italian Intl. Film release (Cannon Releasing in U.S.), produced by Menahem

Golan and Yoram Globus for Italian International Film in association with Cannon Tuschinski. Directed by Lina Wertmüller. Stars Angela Molina, Harvey Keitel. Screenplay, Wertmüller, Elvio Porta; camera (color), Giuseppe Lanci; editor, Luigi Zita; music, Tony Esposito; art director, Enrico Job; choreography, Daniel Ezralow. Reviewed at Barberini Cinema, Rome, Jan. 30, 1986. (MPAA Rating: R.) Running time: **115 MINS.**

Annunziata	Angela Molina
Frankie Acquasanta	Harvey Keitel
Antonio	Daniel Ezralow
Guaglione	Francisco Rabal
Tango	Paolo Bonacelli
Carmela	Isa Danieli

Rome — "Camorra," competing for Italy at Berlin, marks a step away from the grotesque comedy Lina Wertmüller is most often associated with and a natural segue into a genre mixing drama, melodrama and fantasy. Wertmüller is surefooted in this Neapolitan Camorra element, and guides an able cast through a winding and truly complicated tale that unexpectedly blossoms into a stirring group finale. Pic could be one to win the helmer new fans.

Social concerns, usually found lurking under the surface of Wertmüller pictures, are here woven into a mystery. Annunziata (Angela Molina), a former child prostitute, has set up a small pensione with Antonio (Daniel Ezralow), who runs a dance school in the adjacent church. When a Camorra boss comes by for the rent one day, he is murdered trying to rape Annunziata. The girl is interrogated by cops and the underworld alike, but she didn't catch a glimpse of the killer.

A series of murders, which like the first are signed by a needle stuck through the victims' testicles, make it look like a gang war over the drug traffic. Annunziata's ex, an Italo-american charmer named Frankie (Harvey Keitel), is waiting for a shipment from the Orient while trying to win his girl back. The decadent boss Tango (Paolo Bonacelli) isn't safe even in an armored vault guarded by a vast harem of women.

Pic is carried largely on the strong shoulders of Molina, an uninhibited, uncowed heroine in the best tradition. Her small son is being used as a juvenile (and thus unpunishable) dope runner. In pic's most sustained sequence, Antonio, the gay dancer who loves Annunziata, races desperately through the city after two fiendish motorcyclists, who are leading the little boy to his doom. Miraculously, he catches up to them in time, but is stabbed to death in the ensuing scuffle.

The truth behind the murders gives the story a powerful final twist. All the mothers of the neighborhood, whose kids have been drawn into the drug trade and killed at ages 9, 12, 13, have organized themselves into a secret vigilante

squad. Final sequence, somewhere between a fantasy and a call to arms, shows dozens of defiant women in black being tried collectively for murder, supported by a courtroom full of mothers and kids.

Pic is punctuated by several top-notch modern dance numbers by Daniel Ezralow, who also choreographed, and whose freckled, muscular Antonio lends the story a dose of tragic humanity. Francisco Rabal cameos as an old-time boss opposed to drugs. Tony Esposito's lyrical score is also of note.— *Yung.*

The Great Wall Is A Great Wall
(U.S.-CHINESE-COLOR)

An Orion Classics release of a W&S production. Produced by Shirley Sun. Executive producers, Wu Yangchian, Zhu Youjun, E.N. Wen. Directed by Peter Wang. Screenplay, Wang, Sun; camera (color), Peter Stein, Robert Primes; editor, Graham Weinbren; music, David Liang, Ge Ganru; assistant director, Lishin Yu. Reviewed at the Egyptian Theater (U.S. Film Festival), Park City, Utah, Jan. 21, 1986. (MPAA Rating: PG.) Running time: **97 MINS.**

Leo Fang	Peter Wang
Grace Fang	Sharon Iwai
Paul Fang	Kelvin Han Yee
Lili Chao	Li Qinqin
Mr. Chao	Hu Xiaoguang
Mrs. Chao	Shen Guanglan
Liu Yida	Wang Xiao
Yu	Xio Jisn
Jan	Ran Zhijuan
Old Liu	Han Tan

Park City, Utah — A charming but unduly lightweight film, "The Great Wall Is A Great Wall" has carved a place for itself in the history books as the first fictional, feature-length Chinese-American coproduction to have been realized since the revolution. Lensed on location in the environs of Peking in 1984 by actor and former documentary filmmaker Peter Wang, pic humorously accentuates the many cultural differences between the two giant nations, but goes out of its way to avoid dealing with politics or any other issues of substance. Upbeat tone and unique nature of the film make it a decent bet for art house runs domestically.

Wang, who appeared in "Chan Is Missing," himself portrays a San Francisco computer executive who takes advantage of the opening up of China to visit relatives there as well as to introduce his American-born wife and son to his native land.

Film begins with tremendous promise and good cheer, as Wang quickly sketches in his key players on both sides of the Pacific and deftly characterizes their differing lifestyles.

Most of the Chinese kids, especially Lili, Fang's niece, are shown to be very achievement-oriented, intent upon succeeding in their studies so they can join the elite of modern Chinese society.

By contrast, Wang's teenage son Paul is a gung-ho jock who thinks studying Chinese is a waste of time and considers his father a racist for disapproving of his white girlfriend.

After failing to be promoted (due to racism, he believes), Wang quits his company and carts the family to China, where they are met with an awkward but friendly reception. Although uncomprehending of certain Yank customs, the Chinese soon are seduced by the surfaces of many things American, and Wang makes it look as though China willingly will become another American cultural colony if given half a chance.

After an hour or so of amusing little insights into Chinese ways and genuinely fascinating footage of unfamiliar locations, one begins to hunger for some drama or thematic concerns to surface, but none ever do. Disappointingly superficial climax has young Paul battling it out with a local hotshot for a ping pong championship in a "Rocky"-like sequence unlike anything else in the picture.

Wang simply glosses over too many important issues for the film to be considered a true artistic success. One never learns what Wang's somewhat batty brother-in-law does or did in life, how he obtained such a relatively spacious home, or what Chinese think of their country and what is happening to it today. The Communist Party and its leaders, old and new, are never mentioned, and Wang avoids complexity and dealing with issues on all levels.

Nevertheless, film announces itself primarily as a comic view of human attitudes and behavior, and has enough to offer audience a good time. Performances, in English and Chinese, are broad but personable, and technical quality is fine.

Title is derived from Richard Nixon's comment when asked what he thought of the Great Wall. "The Great Wall is a great wall," he remarked.—*Cart.*

Hamburger ... The Motion Picture
(COLOR)

Poor grossout comedy.

An F/M Entertainment release, produced by Edward S. Feldman, Charles R. Meeker. Directed by Mike Marvin. Screenplay, Donald Ross; camera (CFI Color), Karen Grossman; editor, Steven Schoenberg, Ann E. Mills; music, Peter Bernstein; sound, James Thornton; art direction, Maria Rebman Caso; production design, George Costello; assistant director, Mary Ellen Woods; coproducers, Robert Lloyd Lewis, Donald Ross; associate producer, Jeffrey Sudzin; costumes, Shari Feldman; casting, Melissa Skoff. Reviewed at the 4-Star Theater, L.A., Jan. 27, 1986. (MPAA Rating: R.) Running time: **90 MINS.**

Russell	Leigh McCloskey
Drootin	Dick Butkus
Mrs. Vunk	Randi Brooks
Dr. Mole	Chuck McCann
Nacio Herb Zipser	Jack Blessing
Lyman Vunk	Charles Tyner
Mia Vunk	Debra Blee
Fred	Sandy Hackett
Prestopopnick	John Young
Magneto	Chip McAllister
Sister Sara	Barbara Whinnery
Conchita	Maria Richwine
Dr. Gotbottom	Karen May-Chandler

Hollywood — By titular history, "Hamburger ... The Motion Picture" is something of a followup, though not a sequel, to "Hot Dog The Movie," which has returned more than $8,000,000 in domestic film rentals since its 1984 release, despite critical disdain. Edward S. Feldman, who produced the dog, has now produced the ham with Charles Meeker. Mike Marvin, who wrote and coproduced the first, directed the second.

"Hot Dog" was a metaphorical title alluding to skiing while "Hamburger" is more metazoan, its interests aimed mainly at the waist and directly below. When the credits list "Man On Toilet" as one of the characters, there's a hint that an uplifting lesson in the humanities does not lie ahead. That's before the gang of gaseous, gluttonous fat people crowd into the stall with him and the whole building explodes.

For various reasons, none remotely interesting, the ususal gang of teenagers involved here are trying to graduate from a 12-week course at Busterburger U., an apparent center of higher learning in the fast-fold biz.

Per formula, the bad adult male is Dick Butkus and the addled adult males are Chuck McCann and Charles Tyner. The bad adult girls are Randi Brooks and Karen May-Chandler and the bad young girl is Maria Richwine (that takes care of all of those who remove their tops). The good young girls (those who don't) are Debra Blee and Barbara Whinnery. Who the boys are doesn't make much difference.

As their final test, the students must run a food outlet for the public and among the first customers are the aforementioned horde of fatties. After they eat the joint out of food, the motorcycle gang shows up to wreck the place, followed by a troupe of angry black motorcycle cops and two Mexican farmers in a chicken truck.

All is saved when one of the chickens flies through the air and lands in a hot fat vat introducing a new product to the franchise, marking the kids as proud fast-food servants of tomorrow. —*Har.*

The Best Of Times
(COLOR)

Contrived football comedy.

A Universal Pictures release of a Kings Road Entertainment presentation of a Gordon Carroll production, in association with Cinema Group Venture. Produced by Carroll. Directed by Roger Spottiswoode. Stars Robin Williams, Kurt Russell. Screenplay, Ron Shelton; camera (Monaco color; prints by Technicolor), Charles F. Wheeler; editor, Garth Craven; music, Arthur B. Rubinstein; art director, Anthony Brockliss; set decorator, Marc E. Meyer, Jr.; costumes, Patricia Norris; sound, James Dehr; assistant director, James Robert Dyer; associate producer, Fredda Weiss; casting, Lynn Stalmaster and Associates, David Rubin. Reviewed at Universal Studios screening room, Universal City, Calif., Jan. 23, 1986. (MPAA Rating: PG-13.) Running time: **104 MINS.**

Jack Dundee	Robin Williams
Reno Hightower	Kurt Russell
Gigi Hightower	Pamela Reed
Elly Dundee	Holly Palance
The Colonel	Donald Moffat
Darla	Margaret Whitton
Charlie	M. Emmet Walsh
Eddie	Donovan Scott
Schutte	R.G. Armstrong

Hollywood — "The Best Of Times" is a poorly executed, shamelessly manipulative redemption fable that, despite its shortcomings, manages a reasonably satisfying ending. It's the familiar formula of losers transformed into winners more through the trickery of cinema than anything resembling real life. Required magic is in too short supply here and boxoffice returns should be also.

Although the ending of this fairy tale is never in doubt it's rather static along the way. Screenwriter Ron Shelton has failed to people his small California desert town with full-blooded characters. Instead, the script delivers a predictable collection of would-be eccentrics and ne'er-do-wells who could live only within a motion picture.

Ever since he dropped the winning touchdown pass in his big high school game against arch rival Bakersfield, Jack Dundee (Robin Williams) has been trying to live down the disgrace. His life became infected with failure. Also on the skids is one-time star quarterback Reno Hightower (Kurt Russell) who, despite his glory days, has lost the spark that once made him a hero.

It's a dreary existence out there in the city of Taft and getting worse all the time. First Reno's wife Gigi (Pamela Reed) leaves her grease-monkey husband, telling him her life's out of tune, not her VW. Next Jack's wife (Holly Palance) throws him out of the house when he becomes obsessed with the idea of playing the big game over again.

Film's tone is too preachy when Jack tries to convince the town it should pull itself up by the bootstraps. Lessons of self-reliance and the possibility to turn one's life around are delivered without much punch or conviction.

Fortunately, the film is a good deal more lively when Williams does his physical bits. As a character, he's a bit of a whiney nerd, but when he performs he's a winning clown. Director Roger Spottiswoode stacks the deck methodically for the film's finale, hopelessly hokey but somehow still moving.

Performances, too, have a few highpoints and some effective scenes but are handicapped by the pedestrian characters. Reed and especially Palance are appealing as the objects of desire, but Donald Moffat as a kind of cross between Colonel Sanders and General Patton is a cartoon character and seems to be encouraged to overact. It's touches like this that make the film a yawner until it gets to the promised endzone.

Production values are competent.

—*Jagr.*

Eliminators
(COLOR)

Minor fantasy trend pic.

An Empire Pictures release of a Charles Band production. Produced by Band. Directed by Peter Manoogian. Screenplay, Paul De Meo, Danny Bilson; camera (Fotofilm color), Mac Ahlberg; editor, Andy Horvitch; music, Bob Summers; production design; Phillip Foreman; art direction, Gumersindo Andres Lopez; line producer, Alicia Alon; special effects makeup, John Buechler; stunt coordinator, Jose Luis Chinchilla; special effects chief, Juan Ramon Molina; costume design, Jill Ohanneson; sound, Antonio Bloch Rodriquez; associate producer, Debra Dion; assistant director, Betsy Magruder; casting, Anthony Barnac. Reviewed at Empire Pictures screening room, L.A., Jan. 28, 1986. (MPAA Rating: PG.) Running time: **96 MINS.**

Harry Fontana	Andrew Prine
Nora Hunter	Denise Crosby
Mandroid	Patrick Reynolds
Kuji	Conan Lee
Abbott Reeves	Roy Dotrice
Ray	Peter Schrum
Bayou Betty	Peggy Mannix
Luis	Fausto Bara
Takada	Tad Horino
Maurice	Luis Lorenzo

Hollywood — "Eliminators" is a good-natured but undisguisedly cheap entry in the ever-expanding half-man, half-robot genre. Ample amount of action will probably keep undiscriminating fans happy through the tiresomely predictable revenge plot, so Empire should be able to pull decent b.o. with the exploitable item.

The rugged Patrick Reynolds stolidly portrays the Mandroid, a being of human birth who might have died in an air crash had it not been for the sinister Dr. Abbott Reeves (Roy Dotrice), who equipped him with a toy store-full of mechanical parts, colored lights and nifty weapons.

Far from being thankful to Reeves for keeping him alive, Mandroid considers himself the genius' victim and sets out to seek revenge. He's joined, for various reasons, by intense blond Denise Crosby, aging hippie and jungle boat captain Andrew Prine, a martial arts he-man with the great film name of Conan Lee, and a tiny flying robot named

S.P.O.T., which is like a combination of Tinkerbell and R2-D2.

Gang travels up river in pursuit of Reeves and along the way encounters plenty of obstacles, including a lesbian river queen and her mangy entourage, some prehistoric tribesman that time forgot and some Reeves goons who look like Klu Klux Klan rejects.

Ultimate confrontation is pretty unconvincing, but there are at least moments of amusing kung fu by Lee and a prevailing awareness that some humor is needed every few minutes to distract the viewer from the threadbare circumstances surrounding the enterprise.

Prine rather overdoes the goofiness of his oddball river rat, while the remainder of the thesps take things far too seriously considering the material.

Pic was produced in Spain, with the exception of a few L.A. location shots, although set in Mexico. Pic leans more toward action than special effects, although latter are okay. Empire exec Peter Manoogian made his full-length feature directorial bow on the film. —*Cart.*

Dot And Keeto
(AUSTRALIAN-ANIMATED-(COLOR)

A Yoram Gross Film Studio presentation. Produced and directed by Yoram Gross. Screenplay, John Palmer; camera (color), Graham Sharpe; director of animation, Ray Nowland; editor, Rod Hay, Andrew Plain; original songs, Guy Gross, John Levine, John Zulaikha, John Palmer; associate producer, Sandra Gross. Reviewed at the Yoram Gross Studios, Sydney, Jan. 1, 1986. (Commonwealth Film Censor rating: G.). Running time: **70 MINS.**
Featuring the character voices of Keith Scott and Robyn Moore.

Sydney — Fifth in the series of the seemingly never-ending "Dot And ...." kidpics, "Dot And Keeto" is another pleasant outing which should find favor with the targeted under-10 audience, chiefly via television and homevideo.

The Gross trademark — skillfully matching animation and live footage — works a treat here, as the producer/director weaves his characters through the insect kingdom.

After eating something unpleasant, Dot literally is reduced to knee-high to a grasshopper size.

Her home becomes a potential minefield as she is nearly knocked over by a cookie, swept away by her mom's broom, and sucked perilously close to the vacuum cleaner.

Outside, life suddenly takes on new and scary proportions. Ants and beetles loom as giants in her vision, a wasp decides Dot would be ideal fodder for her young, and she nearly comes to a sticky end in a spider's web.

Aided by Butterwalk, a slow-talking, lugubrious caterpillar, and Keeto, a camp mosquito who is fond of talking in rhyming couplets, Dot survives these scrapes and eventually reverts to her normal size.

It's a charming fantasy, attractively presented and enlivened by a sprinkling of appealing, original songs ranging from jazz to blues and pure pop.

Pic is gently instructive in its depiction of the insect world (e.g., caterpillars transforming themselves into butterflies) and as such serves as a painless nature lesson.
—*Dogo.*

Tuntematon Sotilas
(The Unknown Soldier)
(FINNISH-COLOR)

A Kinosto release (foreign sales: Carlton/-Raoul Katz, Paris) of Arctic Film with Kinosto and Finnish Film Foundation production. Produced and directed by Rauni Mollberg. Screenplay Mollberg, Väino Linna, Veikko Aaltonen, based on Linna's novel; camera (Eastmancolor), Esa Vuorinen; editor, Olli Soinio; production management, Eila Werning; sound (Dolby Stereo), Tuomo Kattilakoski; production design, Ensio Suominen. Reviewed at the Royal, Malmö, Sweden, Jan. 30, 1986. Running time: **193 MINS.**
Rahikainen . . . . Mika Mäkelä
Lahtinen . . . . Pertti Koivula
Heitanen . . . . Pirkka-Pekka Petelius
Vanhala . . . . Tero Niva
Lehto . . . . Pauli Poranen
Riitaoja . . . . Hannu Kiviola
Lt. Kariluoto . . . . Pekka Ketonen
Rokka . . . . Paavo Liiski
Koskela . . . . Risto Tuorila

Copenhagen — "The Unknown Soldier," already in preproduction assured of a modicum of worldwide sales and brought in after two years of shooting at a local record budget of $3,000,000, is the "Big One" from Finland, looming to be a Cannes entry after having enthused critics and audiences at home and in test foreign territory Sweden.

The more than three hours war epic is based on Väino Linna's 1954 novel, a national Finnish treasure and an international bestseller. An earlier film version (1955) by Edvin Laine achieved classic status, but Rauni Mollberg's version competes favorably with both book and Laine's work by bringing viewpoints and technical credits handsomely, but never abrasively, up to date.

"The Unknown Soldier" tells of a single machinegun platoon's bloody way through Finland's so-

Original Film
(FINNISH-B&W)

A Suomen Filmiteollisuus (SF) release of a T.J. Sarkka production. Directed by Edvin Laine. Screenplay, Juha Nevalainen, based on novel by Väino Linna; camera (b&w), Pentti Unho, Osmo Harkimo, Olavi Tuomi, Antero Ruuhonen; music, Jean Sibelius, Ahti Sonninen; sets, Aarre Koivisto; editor, Armas Vallasvuo. At Berlin Film Festival, July 10, 1956. Running time: **133 MINS.**

Lt. Koskela . . . . Kosti Klemela
First Lt. Lammlo . . . . Jussi Jurkka
Lt. Kariluoto . . . . Matti Ranin
Corp. Heitanen . . . . Heikki Savolainen
Corp. Lahtinen . . . . Veikko Sinisalo
Corp. Rokka . . . . Reino Tolvanen
Major Sarastie . . . . Tauno Palo
Soldier Rahikainen . . . . . Kaarlo Haittunen
Soldier Maatta . . . . Pentti Simes
Soldier Riitaoja . . . . Olavi Ahonen
Corp. Lehto . . . . Ake Lindman

called Continuation War (1941-44) with Russia over the Karelia province, which the Finns had already once, in the winter of 1939-40, fought for valiantly. They lost both rounds, but while the Winter War made the Finns heroes in the eyes of the world, they fought the followup war in the shadows of not only World War II, but burdened with the ignominy of suddenly finding themselves allied with Hitler's Germany.

Did Finland do right in entering, albeit forcedly, such an alliance? Was the war they fought really just, or did they get swelled heads when, after early victories, they pushed too deeply into the USSR, at the final cost of both Karelia and 80,000 men? Where the novel is ambivalent, the first film version often verges on hero worship. There are heroes in Rauni Mollberg's film as well, but they are mostly heroes in spite of themselves. Mollberg, who had author Linna as co-scripter, puts his platoon under the microscope and rarely lets his vision widen too far outside his chosen microcosm of war.

In classic war movie style, we follow a little flock through induction and training into ferocious action in terrain that appears barren and impersonal to most of the soldiers. Moments of relief and temporary victory such as the retaking of the burned-out city of Petroskoi are precious few. The gunning down of advancing enemy or the being gunned down by the same enemy when retreat is inevitable constitute the bulk of a film that is rich in closeups, ferocious and swift in depicting individual forays or other action.

Mollberg does not have the narrative build dramatically, and relying mostly on his subject matter's raw appeal to every audience's natural soul and gut sensitivity, his long sequences at times turn leaden, especially so since he has chosen to dispense totally with soundtrack music.

Even at its bloodiest, the film has no excess or reveling in gore. Mollberg is very good with his actors, keeping the performances muted. His soldiers are mostly heroes in spite of themselves, and they are more than a little villainous, too — not above shooting captured Russians and robbing the dead of rubles and insignia.

Members of the Finnish officer

corps are rather less benevolently observed, but Mollberg has abstained, in big things and small, from the hectoring role of political analyst/commentator. "The Unknown Soldier" is not a pacifist tract. It is staunchly anti-war in its impact, but it is also a soberly honest, straight goods piece of entertainment. — *Kell.*

Belizaire The Cajun
(COLOR)

Rewarding period drama.

A Cote Blanche Feature Films production. Produced by Allan L. Durand, Glen Pitre. Executive producer, James B. Levert Jr. Line producer, Sandra Schulberg. Written and directed by Pitre. Stars Armand Assante, Gail Youngs, Michael Schoeffling. Camera (DuArt color), Richard Bowen; editor, Paul Trejo; music, Michael Doucet; production design, Randall LaBry; art direction, Deborah Schild; costume design, Sara Fox; sound, David Gisclair; creative consultant, Robert Duvall; associate producers, Paul Hardy, George Graham, Jacob Landry; assistant director, David Ross McCarty; local casting, choreography, Miriam Lafleur Fontenot; N.Y. casting, Cyrena Hausman. Reviewed at the Egyptian Theater (U.S. Film Festival). Park City, Utah, Jan. 21, 1986. (No MPAA Rating.) Running time: **101 MINS.**
Belizaire Breaux . . . . Armand Assante
Alida Thibodaux . . . . Gail Youngs
Hypolite Leger . . . . Michael Schoeffling
James Willoughby . . . . . Stephen McHattie
Matthew Perry . . . . Will Patton
Rebecca . . . . Nancy Barrett
Sheriff . . . . Loulan Pitre
Dolsin . . . . Andre Delaunay
Amandee Meaux . . . . Jim Levert
Old Perry . . . . Ernie Vincent
Sosthene . . . . Paul Landry
Priest . . . . Allan Durand
Preacher . . . . Robert Duvall

Park City, Utah — An unusual ethnic period piece about the persecution of Cajuns by Louisiana landowners in the last 1850s, "Belizaire The Cajun" is a well-made, entertaining indie effort. Easily accessible to all audiences due to a plot framework drawn straight from many Westerns, pic is nevertheless limited by dialog that is frequently difficult to understand. Worthy of distribution (producers have opened it themselves in their native area), film arrives at a time when things Cajun are fashionable, so some good promo inroads are possible.

Portrayed by Armand Assante, title character is an affable, charismatic herbal doctor who still carries a torch for his former sweetheart, Gail Youngs. She, in turn, lives with farmer Will Patton in a sort of common-law arrangement and tries to keep her ardent medicine man at a safe distance.

Even though the local Cajuns seem to be peaceable types, the white powers-that-be, portrayed clearly as Ku Klux Klan forerunners, decide the French-speaking settlers are undesirables and have to go.

Some, such as Belizaire, are exempted from exile, but shortly things escalate into violence. The doctor's buddy, the unreliable Michael Schoeffling, is hunted down for murder, and Belizaire ends up confessing to having committed it just to put an end to the violence. All this culminates in one of the looniest hanging scenes ever committed to film.

Dramatically, film is engaging but is perhaps painted in overly black-and-white terms. The vigilantes who attempt to chase the Cajuns out have no reason to want them out, so one just has to assume they are just old-fashioned, racist good-ol'-boys. Writer-director Glen Pitre tends toward simplification when a little complexity and irony would be welcome.

Nevertheless, film plays quite winningly, and individual scenes sparkle with color, warmth and robust humor. Outfitted with long hair, beard and nifty period garb, Assante is magnetic and enjoyably expansive as the resourceful medic who becomes involved unexpectedly in social issues.

Gail Youngs is very good as the object of his attentions, and others in the cast — many recruited locally — acquit themselves nicely.

It takes awhile to conect with the dialog as delivered. Most of it is in an accented English, but characters sometimes slip into dialect as well as French, and one has to listen very hard to keep up with what is being said.

Lenser Richard Bowen has come up with many fresh and fine images, but too much latitude has been given to the hand-held camera with which the majority of scenes has been shot, resulting in some irritation.

Film's screenplay was developed in part at the Sundance lab, gives prominent thanks to both Robert Duvall (credited here for a bit as a preacher at a funeral) and Robert Redford, and was lensed last year under the title "Acadian Waltz." —Cart.

Arthur's Hallowed Ground
(BRITISH-COLOR)

A Cinecom Intl. Films release of an Enigma Prod. for Goldcrest in association with Techno Sunley Leisure. Produced by Chris Griffin. Executive producer, David Puttnam. Directed by Freddie Young. Screenplay, Peter Gibbs; camera (Kay color), Chic Anstiss; editor, Chris Ridsdale; associate producer, David Bull; production manager, Dominic Fulford; location manager, Scott Wodehouse; sound, David Crozier; costume design, Tudor George; series script editor, Jack Rosenthal. Reviewed at Magno Preview 9 screening room, N.Y., Jan. 27, 1986. (No MPAA Rating). Running time: **84 MINS.**
Athur ....Jimmy Jewel
Betty ....Jean Boht
Lionel ....David Swift
Len ....Michael Elphick
Eric....................Derek Benfield
Henry ....Va Blackwood
Norman ....John Flanagan
George ....Bernard Gallagher
Sales Representative ....Sam Kelly
Billy ....Al Ashton
Kev ....Mark Drewry

"Arthur's Hallowed Ground" concerns itself with craft vs. commerce, traditional values vs. modern expediency and the problems of growing old in a leisurely little fable about a crusty old groundsman's proprietary hold on the cricket pitch he's tended for nearly half a century. Although there are a few nice performances in this entry in exec producer David Puttnam's "First Love" series of British indie pics, its narrative plods along to an unsurprising resolution.

Part of the trouble with "Arthur's Hallowed Ground" is that groundskeeper Arthur (Jimmy Jewel) is an unlikable old curmudgeon whose opposition to compromise is rooted as much in fossilized stubborness as in idealism. Seems some directors of the perennially losing cricket team want Arthur to shape the pitch to give thier sad-sack side the same home field advantage their opponents enjoy.

Arthur's chief antagonist on the board is Len Draycott (Michael Elphick"), a no-nonsense builder who wants to apply to cricket the pragmatic principles that have made his business flourish. He'd like Arthur to retire so the club can spend less on things like automatic seeders and more on amenities for the players and "the paying public."

Arthur doesn't give a fig for the players and the public, but "that ground is out there seven days a week," and he's not about to tamper with it just to please some second-rate cricketeers and the stuffed shirts who pay his salary.

Of course there's nothing wrong with this kind of thinking, but Arthur makes things difficult for himself and the audience with a petulant irascibility that brooks no contradiction. There's little of the customary wisdom of old age in his world view, just the conviction that everything, like the jumbled inventory in his toolshed, has its "proper place" and shouldn't be tampered with. When he's saddled with Henry (Vas Blackwood), a young black helper hired by the club from a government subsidized youth employment program, Arthur does his best to make the lad's life miserable.

In spite of solicitous treatment by long-suffering souls like his wife, Betty (Jean Boht) and club official Lionel (David Swift) Arthur seems concerned with nothing but the lay of his greensward, which is bordered by the most symbolically English landmarks: a factory, rowhouses, trees and a white picket fence. Eventually, however, a crisis triggers something of a self-examination in the old codger's attitude towards others.

Because this is all presented rather dryly and the scenario only passingly links Arthur's story to the world at large, the ending is less uplifting than simply a relief. — Rich.

Wildcats
(COLOR)

Formula football pic masks Goldie Hawn's talent.

A Warner Bros. release of a Hawn/Sylbert production. Produced by Anthea Sylbert. Directed by Michael Ritchie. Stars Goldie Hawn. Screenplay, Ezra Sacks; camera (Technicolor), Donald E. Thorin; editor, Richard A. Harris; music, Hawk Wolinski, James Newton Howard; production design, Boris Leven; set decorator, Phil Abrahmson; art director, Steve Berger; sound (Dolby stereo), Jim Alexander; costumes, Eddie Marks; assistant director, Tom Mack; associate producer, Gordon A. Webb; casting, Marion Dougherty. Reviewed at Warner Bros. screening room, The Burbank Studios, Burbank, Calif., Jan. 29, 1986. (MPAA Rating: R.) Running time: **107 MINS.**
Molly ....Goldie Hawn
Verna ....Swoosie Kurtz
Alice ....Robyn Lively
Marian....................Brandy Gold
Frank ....James Keach
Stephanie ....Jan Hooks
Darwell ....Bruce McGill
Edwards ....Nipsey Russell
Bird ....Mykel T. Williamson
Finch ....Tab Thacker
Trumaine ....Wesley Snipes
Cerulo ....Nick Corri
Krushinski ....Woody Harrelson
Coes.................M. Emmet Walsh

Hollywood — Not without its charm and a few good laughs, "Wildcats" is a prime example of taking a star and a premise and attaching it to a story. The result, unfortunately, is an artificial hybrid without a life of its own.

In her fourth film for Warner Bros. since "Private Benjamin" in 1980, Hawn again has been pushed into the mold of the adorable but goofy independent woman. It's true few actors do it better, but by "Wildcats" she has become reduced to a type and is looking a bit old for the part. Why not give her the opportunity to do more challenging dramatic roles?

Hawn, however, is the least of the problems amid cardboard characters with cardboard conflicts. When Hawn, the daughter of a legendary football coach, tangles with high school varsity coach Bruce McGill, anyone can foresee the final confrontation.

Sure enough, when McGill has her appointed football coach at the unspeakable ghetto school, Central High, it's an inevitable collision course. Along the way crises pop up at carefully placed intervals, the first being winning the confidence of the rag-tag collection of players.

This is a team well stocked with overgrown kids and the average age seems well over high school vintage, but age is not the real problem there, it's more of a behavioral thing. These would-be ghetto heavies are more pussycats than wildcats.

Also short on credibility is James Keach as Hawn's ex-husband. He's a man with a perpetual scowl designed to elicit hatred for him and sympathy for Hawn as he tries to win custody of the couple's two too-adorable girls (Robyn Lively and Brandy Gold). To make matters worse, Keach's girlfriend is a super straight-laced caricature (Jan Hooks) who threatens to turn the girls into conservative clones.

Even when the case comes to court, not surprisingly before a black woman judge (Royce Wallace), the sides are too sharply drawn to pose a real threat.

Hawn's spunkiness and bucking of convention to take "her best shot" is the film's meager message which must have seemed perfect on paper. When she tells her daughters they can be whatever they want to be, it's an empty promise because the film is too safe in proving its point.

Micheal Ritchie's direction lacks his usual bite and eye for detail. There is nothing spontaneous about the action and, when a train passes in the background, it looks like a prop. Football footage is also surprisingly dull, filmed mostly at close range making it look more like bodies bouncing off each other than a sport.

Script by Ezra Sacks is a write-by-numbers affair — now some humor, now some pathos. Supporting characters such as Hawn's sister (Swoosie Kurtz) have little to do but smile and frown and conform to the model.

As for the football team, it has the mandatory ethnic mix, with Mykel T. Williamson as the tamed renegade quarterback. One nice touch is the presence of the enormous Tab Thacker as a William Perry-like mass of humanity. (The action takes place in Chicago, too.)

Hawn, seemingly on screen for the entire film, is fun to watch as she runs her team through aerobics and mugs for the camera, but even better is Nipsey Russell as the roughhewn high school principal with a word for all occasions.

Tech credits are adquate, although Donald E. Thorin's photography is grainy without being gritty. Score by Hawk Wolinski and James Newton Howard is appropriately urban, complemented by a slew of rhythm and blues numbers.

Ironically, the best moment of the film is saved for the end-credits as Hawn and her teammates perform the funky and funny "Football Rap," each of them isolated in turn for a verse returning to Hawn for the one-word chorus — "football." It's the kind of inventive, original touch sorely lacking in the rest of the film. —Jagr.

February 12, 1986

De l'Argentine
(About Argentina)
(FRENCH/BRITISH-COLOR-16m)

A FR3/Out One production. Written, produced and directed by Werner Schroeter. Camera (color, 16m), Schroeter, Carlos Bernardo Wajsman; editor, Cathérine Brasier, Claudio Martinez; sound, Albelardo Kuschnir. Reviewed at Rotterdam Film Festival, Jan. 28, 1986. Running time: **90 MINS.**

Rotterdam — "About Argentina" is another film about a regime of terror, but different from all others and more impressive than most because of the restraint which director Werner Schroeter exercised over his feelings.

There are no scenes of violence, but the film shows instruments of torture, clean, well-lit, as if they were exhibits in a gallery. Only the politicians shout grandiose phrases. The children, parents, grandmothers of the victims repeat routinely their tales of abduction, rape, mutilation and murder.

Schroeter adds poignancy to the narrative by a few bars from Mahler's "Kindertotenlieder" (songs for the dead children). Pic starts with an actress playing Galileo forced by the Inquisition to abjure the truth of his theories. He underlines the grotesque absurdity of historic events by staging scenes in which a film star (who played Eva Peron in successful movies) is shown with Evita's real life dress designer.

He adds vitality and wide-eyed innocence through the sequences with Gabriel, an orphan left over for profitable adoption when his parents were killed right after his birth. Schroeter quotes the governor of Buenos Aires: "First we kill the subversive elements, then the sympathizers, then their henchmen, and last of all the weak." Gabriel survived because he was strong. So is the film.

Schroeter gives an artist's vision of a diabolical regime, but pic is never arty. It's sincere, emotional and never melodramatic.—*Wall.*

Nine ½ Weeks
(COLOR)

Unsexy depiction of an obsessive love affair is headed nowhere.

An MGM/UA Entertainment release of a Producers Sales Organization and Sidney Kimmel presentation of a Keith Barish production from Jonesfilm, in association with Galactic Films and Triple Ajaxxx. Produced by Antony Rufus Isaacs, Zalman King. Executive producers, Barish, Frank Konigsberg. Co-executive producer, Richard Northcott. Directed by Adrian Lyne. Stars Mickey Rourke, Kim Basinger. Screenplay, Patricia Knop, Zalman King, Sarah Kernochan, based on the novel by Elizabeth McNeill; camera (Technicolor processing, Metrocolor prints), Peter Biziou; editor, Tom

Rolf, Caroline Biggerstaff; co-editor, Mark Winitsky; additional editing, Kim Secrist; music, Jack Nitzsche; additional music, Michael Hoenig; production design, Ken Davis; art direction, Linda Conaway-Parsloe; set decoration, Christian Kelly; costume design, Bobbie Read; sound (Dolby), Bill Daly; associate producers, Steven D. Reuther, Stephen J. Ross; assistant director, Benjy Rosenberg; casting, Lynn Stalmaster & Associates, Nan Dutton. Reviewed at the MGM Studios, Culver City, Calif., Feb. 4, 1986. (MPAA Rating: R.) Running time: **113 MINS.**

John	Mickey Rourke
Elizabeth	Kim Basinger
Molly	Margaret Whitton
Harvey	David Margulies
Thea	Christine Baranski
Sue	Karen Young
Ted	William De Acutis
Farnsworth	Dwight Weist
Sinclair, The Critic	Roderick Cook

Hollywood — "Nine ½ Weeks" is a steer, not the bull it surely wanted to be when it grew up, although there's plenty of the latter in it anyway. Bland, conventional and entirely untitillating, this soft stab at a "Last Tango In Manhattan" has pretty clearly been disemboweled, defanged and desexed since it began production as a Tri-Star project nearly two years ago. Ultimate distributor MGM/UA will have to locate some folks in real desperate need of some cheap thrills to dig up an audience.

Only and entire *raison d'etre* for this screen adaptation of Elizabeth McNeill's novel would be to vividly present the obsessive, all-consuming passion between the two main characters, a successful Wall Street type and a beautiful art gallery employee, who embark upon an intense love affair that lasts as long as the title indicates.

The film is about the crazy, overwhelming attachment they have with one another, and nothing else. What happens in the scenes when they're apart is of no relevance. Therefore, the virtual absence of anything interesting happening between them — like plausible attraction, exotic, amazing sex, or, God forbid, good dialog — leaves one great big hole on the screen for two hours.

There are hints that Mickey Rourke's trendy, self-satisfied stockbroker is into some mildly kinky scenes — he insists upon blindfolding Kim Basinger during an early encounter, and a later sequence sees him buying a riding crop, which he never uses.

Despite some unusual, almost public locations for their lovemaking sessions — a clock tower, Bloomingdale's, a filthy alley — what they actually do together is utterly normal and, far from explicity presented. Anyone looking for a hot time will be sorely disappointed, victims of the irresistible pressure filmmakers and distributors feel to win an R rating. A spicier version is said to be headed for release overseas.

In retrospect, filmmakers probably shouldn't have gone ahead with such a picture if they weren't prepared to go all the way and have the guts to really make a film about sexual obsession, ratings be damned. Otherwise, there is no point, a fact this malarky bears out.

Not that signs indicate it would have been much good anyway. Adrian Lyne persists in his flashy, commercials/music video style, although Peter Biziou's lensing often has trouble finding or holding focus. Collection of pop tunes is mediocre in the extreme.

Rourke is less than totally convincing as a big businessman, but Basinger is the film's one saving grace, as she manages to retain a certain dignity despite incessant attempts by Rourke and Lyne to despoil her. —*Cart.*

TerrorVision
(COLOR)

Tedious sci-fi comedy.

An Empire Pictures release of an Altar Prods. production. Produced by Albert Band. Executive producer, Charles Band. Written and directed by Ted Nicolaou. Camera (Technicolor), Romano Albani; editor, Tom Meshelski; music, Richard Band; production designer, Giovanni Natalucci; assistant director, Mauro Sacrapanti; associate producer, Debra Dion; special effects makeup, John Buechler and Mechanical and Makeup Imageries Inc.; optical effects, Motion Opticals Inc.; casting, Anthony Bay Barnao. Reviewed at Preview 4 screening room, N.Y., Feb. 7, 1986. (MPAA Rating: R.) Running time: **83 MINS.**

Suzy	Diane Franklin
Stanley Putterman	Gerrit Graham
Raquel Putterman	Mary Woronov
Sherman	Chad Allen
O.D.	Jonathan Gries
Medusa	Jennifer Richards
Spiro	Alejandro Rey
Grampa	Bert Remsen
Cherry	Randi Brooks

Also with: Ian Patrick Williams, Sonny Carl Davis.

"TerrorVision," filmed in Italy, is an uninvolving sci-fi thriller comedy that relies heavily for its shock value on gooey monster effects rather than cinematic finesse. With performances that are almost uniformly overwrought, pic will have a hard time attracting any but the most kitsch-loving viewers.

With the apparent intent of making some comments about our unnatural reliance on television, and technology in general, filmmakers have perhaps bit off too much. Film opens with swinging husband and father Stanley Putterman installing a do-it-yourself satellite dish on his patio. At the same time, on a distant planet, a heavily made up alien is feeding refuse into some sort of grotesque living garbage disposal that eats anything within its powerful tongue's reach. Through a freak combination of lightning and the dish's positioning, the beast is transported to Earth and eventually appears on all the television sets in the Putterman house.

It pops out of the sets on occasion to attack various folk unlucky enough to be around it. Besides Putterman and his pleasure-seeking wife, there are their two children, the daughter a pink-haired heavy metal follower, the young son (most normal character in the pic) a gun-toting adventurer. Also on hand, and among the first to be consumed and "reborn" à la "Invasion Of The Body Snatchers," is a horny grandfather.

While Giovanni Natalucci's production design is colorful and clever, featuring a house with all the amenities including a large hot tub in the bedroom, it also is crowded and garish and never gives the impression that the film was shot anywhere but inside a studio. Most unsettling of all, however, are the performances, textbook examples of pregnant pauses going beyond the call of duty. Characters deliver such lines as "Will you look at those hooters!" then gawk for two or three seconds before another sound is heard. Of course, the director and writer, Ted Nicolaou, is as much to blame.

Pic hints strongly at the aforementioned "Body Snatchers," and makes direct references to "E.T." (the young blond boy who befriends the monster might as well be Henry Thomas) and "Poltergeist," but in its overall appearance more closely resembles a mediocre '50s sci-fier.

The ever-increasing practice of aiding production financing through product placement rears its head here in the form of commercials for a certain imported beer. There's a lingering swig and a loving closeup of a bottle, and there's Stanley expending an undue amount of breath pushing his "heinies" on a houseguest. —*Gerz.*

Hyinch Ha'gdi
(The Smile Of The Lamb)
(ISRAELI-COLOR)

A Dotan-Aroch production. Produced by Jonathan Aroch. Directed by Shimon Dotan. Screenplay, Dotan, Shimon Riklin, Anath Levi-Bar, based on a novel by David Grossman; camera (color), Danny Schneuer; editor, Netaya Anbar; sets, Charles Leon; costumes by Rona Doron; music by Ilan Virtzberg. Reviewed in Tel Aviv, Jan. 23, 1986. (In competition at Berlin Film Festival). Running time: **93 MINS.**

Hilmi	Tuncel Curtiz
Laniado	Rami Danon
Katzman	Makhram Khouri
Sheffer	Dan Muggia
Shosh	Iris Hoffman

Tel Aviv — Halfway between legend and realistic documentation of political facts, Shimon Dotan's second feature film uses parts of a highly rated local novel, which attempts to deal with the Israeli-Arab crisis not just on the immediate, front page news level, but as a more profound and complicated clash between different traditions and cultures.

In the main, it is the confrontation between three different characters, each representing a world of his own. Hilmi is an old Arab, living in a cave in the mountains, near a village on the West Bank. His whole existence is conditioned by old traditions and customs. He stays close to nature and accepts it as a wondrous presence as he stubbornly preserves his primitive solitude. Katzman is the Israeli military governor of the region, a Jew of Polish origins and hawkish politics, somehow reminiscent of old time European colonialists. In between, there is Laniado, a military doctor, who desperately tries to find a way to establish a basis of communication between his friend Katzman and the old Arab whose presence fascinates him.

An abortive terrorist attack on an Israeli patrol creates the tension which leads each character to act in an extremist way. Katzman is bent on breaking down the resistance of the villagers and forcing them to hand over the culprits. Hilmi is drawn into the conflict unwittingly when it turns out that his son is directly implicated, and Laniado is prepared to go to any lengths to force a dialog, even at his own peril.

Using a narrator and a text that suggests the style of a folk story, slipping time and again into Hilmi's past, director Dotan tries to point at the basic differences that separate these three characters, with present, and very real events, lending the story its urgency.

Turkish actor Tuncel Curtiz, a familiar face from Yilmaz Güney's films, carries the film as Hilmi, a man perplexed by the centuries he has to cover in one existence. An effective casting idea has Israeli-Arab actor Makhram Khouri as Katzman, the second time he has played a Jewish military governor in a local production. Rami Denon does a creditable job as the soulful, well-intentioned Laniado.

Ilan Virtzberg's score, using mostly traditional Arab rhythms and percussion instruments, is an important contribution to the overall atmosphere. Pic was produced by old-time friends and associates Dotan and Jo ..than Aroch on their own. No distribution deal has been secured for the film as yet, allowing them to work in complete freedom. The decision of the Berlin Fest to include the pic in competition certainly will aid in securing distribution.
— *Edna.*

Georges Lautner directed "La Cage aux Folles 3," Tri-Star Pictures film which preemed in France

and Belgium Nov. 20 and bows in the U.S. this month.

Pretty In Pink
(COLOR)

Well-made but predictable saga of growing up.

A Paramount Pictures release. Produced by Lauren Shuler. Directed by Howard Deutch. Exec producers, John Hughes, Michael Chinich. Screenplay, John Hughes; camera (Technicolor), Tak Fujimoto; editor, Richard Marks; music, Michael Gore; sound, C. Darin Knight; production design, John W. Corso; assistant director, Stephen Lim; associate producer, Jane Vickerilla; casting, Paula Herold, Marci Liroff. Reviewed at the Chinese Theater, Hollywood, Jan. 29, 1986. (MPAA Rating: PG-13.) Running time: **96 MINS.**
Andie .... Molly Ringwald
Jack .... Harry Dean Stanton
Duckie .... Jon Cryer
Blane .... Andrew McCarthy
Iona .... Annie Potts
Steff .... James Spader
Donnelly .... Jim Haynie
Jena .... Alexa Kenin
Benny .... Kate Vernon

Hollywood — In his mid-30s, John Hughes' much-vaunted teen thinking now seems to be maturing a bit in "Pretty In Pink," a rather intelligent (if not terribly original) look at adolescent insecurities. Question will be whether Hughes' teen following will want to mature with him.

With "Pink," it's possible the difference is that Hughes is not both writing and directing, leaving latter chores to the first-timer Howard Deutch. Whatever the cause there is a definite improvement.

Teamed with Hughes for the third time, Molly Ringwald is herself growing as an actress, lending "Pink" a solid emotional center that largely boils down to making the audience care about her.

Like scores of leading ladies before her, Ringwald is the proverbial pretty girl from the wrong side of the tracks, called to a motherless life with down-on-his-luck dad (Harry Dean Stanton) and the misfortune to have to attend high school where the rich kids lord it over the poor.

That's enough to make any young lady insecure, even before the wealthy nice guy (Andrew McCarthy) asks her to the senior prom. Teased by his rich pals for slumming, McCarthy is also a bundle of uncertainties. So are Ringwald's pals, Annie Potts and Jon Cryer, both contributing a lot. And, as a couple of nicely played scenes ultimately reveal, elder Stanton is no statue of confidence either after having been dumped by Ringwald's mother.

Moving predictably, none of this is unique drama, but "Pink's" points may seem fresh to a younger audience and the pic puts them forth sincerely, with no excess. In the end, the wrong guy still gets the girl,

which is a lesson youngsters might as well learn early. —*Har.*

The Hitcher
(COLOR)

Cornball slasher film.

A Tri-Star Pictures release of an HBO Picture in association with Silver Screen Partners. An Edward S. Feldman and Charles R. Meeker production. Directed by Robert Harmon. Produced by David Bombyk and Kip Ohman; coproducer, Paul Lewis. Screenplay, Eric Red; camera (Metrocolor), John Seale; editor, Frank J. Urioste; music, Mark Isham, production design, Dennis Gassner; casting, Penny Perry. Reviewed at MGM Screening room 23, Culver City, Calif., Feb. 5, 1986. (MPAA Rating: R.) Running time: **97 MINS.**
John Ryder .... Rutger Hauer
Jim Halsey .... C. Thomas Howell
Nash .... Jennifer Jason Leigh
Captain Esteridge .... Jeffrey DeMunn

Hollywood — "The Hitcher" is a highly unimaginative slasher that keeps the tension going with a massacre about every 15 minutes and a series of car chases (and car crashes) in-between. Scenes provide enough gore to keep fans of the genre happy through to its bloody conclusion, when pic falls flat with an essentially downbeat ending. Absence of a powerful dramatic payoff will limit its breakout potential.

Film proves mom's admonition not to pick up hitchhikers, especially if they're anything like John Ryder, a psychotic and diabolical killer played with a serene coldness by Rutger Hauer.

Along comes an innocent young man (C. Thomas Howell), who is falling asleep at the wheel of his drive-away Seville on a trip through a desolate part of Texas and stops to pick Hauer up in the hopes that having a companion will keep him awake.

It's only a couple of miles into the ride when Howell figures out the hitchhiker is a psychopath and pushes him out the door.

What ensues for the rest of the film is a cat and mouse game where Hauer eliminates just about everyone Howell comes in contact with, but always stops short of killing the kid because, he tells him, "I want you to stop me."

In the meantime, the Texas sheriffs confuse Howell with the killer until miraculously near the end, and with no explanation they gets things straight.

Playing Howell's only friend is the winsome Jennifer Jason Leigh, the waitress who has a gut feeling that Howell is an okay guy even if he looks, acts and smells strange.

It seems her character was inserted to create something of a love interest for Howell and a diversion for the audience, but she's history before anything can be made of their relationship.

In addition to working with a script that has many holes, film-

makers didn't allow for one laugh in the entire 97 minutes.

Their effort, however, is redeemed somewhat by John Seale's stunning cinematography and Mark Isham's haunting music, which sets the pic's ominous tone from the start of the opening credits.

While the scenes are unrealistically empty of people, they have a surrealistically beautiful quality. Credit here goes to production designer Dennis Gassner. —*Brit.*

Eva Gabor, Lu Leonard and **Richard Paul** head the cast of **Weintraub Prods.'** "Princess Academy."

Quicksilver
(COLOR)

Pointless attempt to followup 'Footloose' on bikes.

A Columbia Pictures release from Columbia-Delphi IV of IndieProd. production. Produced by Michael Rachmil, Daniel Melnick. Written and directed by Tom Donnelly. Stars Kevin Bacon. Camera (Metrocolor), Thomas Del Ruth; editor, Tom Rolf; music, Tony Banks; production designer, Charles Rosen; art director, James Shanahan; set decorator, Marvin March; sound (Dolby), John V. Speak; costumes, Betsy Cox; assistant director, Duncan Henderson; associate producer, Christopher Meledandri; casting, Pennie du Pont. Reviewed at Plitt's Century Plaza theater, Century City, Calif., Feb. 6, 1986. (MPAA Rating: PG.) Running time: **106 MINS.**
Jack Casey .... Kevin Bacon
Terri .... Jami Gertz
Hector Rodriguez .... Paul Rodriguez
Gypsy .... Rudy Ramos
Gabe Kaplan .... Andrew Smith
Mr. Casey .... Gerald S. O'Loughlin
Voodoo .... Larry Fishburne
Tiny .... Louis Anderson
Rand .... Whitney Kershaw
Airborne .... Charles McCaughan

Hollywood — "Quicksilver" is six films in one — all of them bad. Core story of a hotshot financial wiz who drops out to become a bicycle messenger is lame enough on its own without being complicated needlessly with street crime, car chases, romance and ethnic drama. Pic is stuffed with as much action as possible to disguise the fact that it's not really about anything.

More than anything pic seems designed to cash in on the success of "Footloose" (by the same producers) with an infusion of blaring and often superfluous rock 'n' roll and the presence of star Kevin Bacon. Lacking a center or a character to believe in, b.o. prospects are dim.

Events get underway when Bacon blows his fortune playing the stock market. He is supposed to be a brilliant broker, but somehow the touch has deserted him. With a three-piece suit and a hideous moustache, Bacon is, for starters, a ridiculous creation.

Bacon winds up as a bicycle messenger in San Francisco which, he explains to his baffled parents, who only want to get him on his feet and back making money again, allows him the freedom to be responsible only for himself.

Once on the street Bacon is an unlikely addition to a crew of messengers diverse enough to be a World War II platoon. Main plot device centers around a cartoon street tough (Rudy Ramos) who uses some of the messengers to make drug deliveries for him. Into this web falls the young and vulnerable Terri (Jami Gertz), who ultimately must be saved by Bacon.

While all this nonsense is going on there is time along the way for breakdancing on bicycles, a bike race through the streets of San Francisco and a hit-and-run murder. Writer-director Tom Donnelly has thrown in everything but the kitchen sink and does little to unify a string of not very interesting or related set pieces.

As the sidewalk heavy, Ramos is about as menacing as a bee sting and no more believable than Bacon. The good performance of the film is turned in by Paul Rodriguez as Bacon's Mexican messenger friend whose dream is to own a hot dog cart.

Gertz as the would-be girlfriend down on her luck is appealing but left stranded by a script that gives the character little texture. Bacon, too, can do little to salvage his part.

Score by Tony Banks with a handful of strategically placed tunes supervised by Becky Mancuso is a prime example of a film threatening to drown in a sea of music. Songs attempting to explain the action of characters that even the script can't is at best a risky business.

Production values are slick but even Thomas Del Ruth's stylish lensing of San Francisco doesn't make it an interesting place to visit.
—*Jagr.*

Foxtrap
(ITALIAN-U.S.-COLOR)

A Snizzlefritz Distribution release of a Realtà Cinematografica presentation of a Po' Boy production. Produced and directed by Fred Williamson. Executive producers, Linda Radovan, Marcello & Pier Luigi Ciriaci. Stars Williamson, Chris Connelly. Screenplay, Aubrey K. Rattan, from story by Williamson; camera (Luciano Vittori color), John Stephens, Steve Shaw; editor, Giorgio Venturoli; music, Patrizio Fariselli; sound, Clark Will, Olivier Schwos, Giuseppe Testa. Reviewed at UA Twin 2 theater, N.Y., Feb. 7, 1986. (MPAA Rating: R.) Running time: **88 MINS.**

Thomas Fox	Fred Williamson
John Thomas	Chris Connelly
Emily	Arlene Golonka
Susan	Donna Owen
Mariana	Beatrice Palme
Josie	Cleo Sebastian
Lindy	Lela Rochon

"Foxtrap" is an uneventful, so-called action picture, marking ac-

tor/athlete Fred Williamson's ninth feature as director. B.o. prospects are weak.

Overreaching in its attempt to masquerade as a globehopping adventure in the James Bond vein, pic has Williamson as Thomas Fox, a bodyguard who reluctantly agrees to a private eye-type job for John Thomas (Chris Connelly). J.T. says his brother's daughter Susan (Donna Owen) is missing in Europe and sends Fox to find her.

After several dull reels and pointless killings, Fox finds Susan, unconvincingly bamboozles her into coming back to Los Angeles with him and then exposes J.T.'s secret, which has to do with those old genre standbys: blackmail, drug addiction, pimps and whores. At fadeout, a threatening title alerts the viewer to "Watch for 'The Fox And The Cobra' next summer."

Pic has almost no action, with Williamson padding the proceedings with sluggishly edited wandering around shots and scenic transition footage. Locations in Cannes, Rome and L.A. are naturally photogenic but spoiled by the constant distraction of dozens of people in each exterior shot ogling the camera — apparently no extras were used for this cheapie.

In place of action, Williamson applies his budget to frequent costume changes for himself. Another personal touch is the presence of an array of international beauties who, naturally, can't keep their hands off the star.—*Lor.*

Rise And Fall Of The Borscht Belt
(DOCU-COLOR/B&W)

Excellent docu bridges entertainment and cultural history.

Produced by Villon Films, Hurleyville, N.Y. Produced, written, directed, camera (color) and edited by Peter Davis. Sound, David Langton, Joy Davis, Danny Aranowitz, David Messenbring; narrator, Joseph Wiseman. Historical footage from private sources, and from Jewish Film Archives (Brandeis U.), National Archives and Library of Congress. Reviewed at C.W. Post (Long Island U.), Jan. 25, 1986. (No MPAA Rating). Running time: **80 MINS.**

Highbrow terms for a film about lowbrow entertainment come to mind, but such terms invite that mockery of pretense for which the Borscht Belt was once famous. The Borscht Belt, that cradle of iconoclastic humor, eschews or sneezes at pomposity.

By 1910, 1,200 Jewish families had settled in Sullivan County, 110 miles northwest of New York City, in the Catskill Mountains. The settlers began renting barns and spare rooms to city tourists, refugees like themselves from the sweltering slums. Bungalow colonies and boarding-houses and resort hotels

developed. Emphasis was on keeping the guests happy. "Goldberg's Spanish Villa" expressed an attempt to fit in. Comics and musicians and children's vaudeville and amateur-hour theatrics — every family had a would-be star. Social mobility — upward, of course — was the obsession and also the butt of satire.

These Catskill live-in summer communities were run by women, mothers, while the fathers slaved in New York, visiting only weekends. One million New Yorkers, mostly Jews, called the Catskills their summer home. Borscht, beet/cabbage soup, was a nourishing staple, as was home-grown family-style entertainment. Orchards were cut down to make swimming pools, sports fields, dance pavilions, space for religious services, as the Borscht Belt thrived.

The Catskills were once tremendously popular, and many talents trained there, a who's who of Hollywood, Broadway, television, nightclubs — Eddie Fisher, Sid Caesar, Jerry Lewis, Robert Merrill, Jack Carter, Dick Shawn, many others.

Today, omnipresent television and its spinoff technologies have much reduced the informal live entertainment once so popular in the Catskills. Only a comparatively few big glossy hotels survive. The rise and fall are shown in this film — a happy film, but with a sad ending.

"Borscht Belt" uses old newsreels, promotional travelogs, home movies, scraps and fragments of sound and picture, new interviews with ancient survivors, and other materials, both b&w and color, bridged by a humane and ironic narration, spoken by Joseph Wiseman.—*Hitch.*

De aanslag
(The Assault)
(DUTCH-COLOR)

A Cannon Films release of a Fons Rademakers production. Produced and directed by Rademakers. Screenplay, Gerard Soeteman, based on the novel by Harry Mulisch. Stars Derek de Lint, Monique van de Ven, John Kraaykamp Sr., Huub van der Lubbe. Camera (color), Theo van de Sande; music, Jurriaan Andriessen; assistant director, Lili Rademakers; sound & editing, Kees Linthorst; art direction, Dorus van der Linden; costumes, Anne Marie van Beverwijk. Reviewed at Cannon showroom, Amsterdam, Jan. 20, 1986. Running time: **140 MINS.**

Anton Steenwijk	Derek de Lint
Truus Coster/	
Saskia de Graaff	Monique van de Ven
Cor Takes	John Kraaykamp Sr.
Fake Ploeg	Huub van der Lubbe
Anton Steenwijk	
(12 years old)	Marc van Uchelen
Mrs. Beumer	Elly Weller
Karin Korteweg	Ina van der Molen
Liesbeth	Mies de Heer

Amsterdam — Collaboration of author Harry Mulisch, scripter Gerard Soeteman and helmer Fons Rademakers results in a gripping film, "The Assault," which, not-

withstanding the specifically Dutch story, has universal themes and should have appeal in many countries.

The story starts in 1945. Part of Holland is already liberated, but the Germans are still in command in Haarlem, 20 miles from Amsterdam. A sadistic Dutch Nazi-policeman is liquidated by the resistance and his body is found in front of the Steenwijk home. As a reprisal the house is burned down and 19 people are shot, including the Steenwijk family, except for Anton, 12 years old.

He is adopted by an uncle in Amsterdam, becomes a successful anesthetist, marries (twice) and has two children. He should be a contented man, but his whole life is marked by the night of the assault, and by encounters, partly by chance, with people who were connected with that night.

"The Assault" treats important issues, but the pic is never highbrow or morbid. It stays primarily a whodunnit. Pic has lots of intriguing twists, focusing on many individuals, unraveling over a period of nearly 40 years what happened during that night in 1945.

The most difficult part is that of the grown-up Anton Steenwijk. The part of 12-year-old Anton is mastered with astonishing ease by 14-year-old Marc van Uchelen. Derek de Lint then takes over. Anton is a man who does not make things happen. They happen to him. He's the center of the story, but a soft center. De Lint successfully evades the perils of this part, and delivers a convincing performance.

Monique van de Ven plays two characters: a member of the resistance and Anton's first wife. She is moving in a taxing scene as the extraordinary resistance woman, and credibly ordinary as young wife and mother. John Kraaykamp as one resistance fighter whose war will not end as long as he lives, impressively creates a tormented character.

Historical newsreel shots are used sparingly, as is voiceover narration. Through these devices the narrative is kept taut and pic never sags during nearly two-and-a-half-hours of running time. This is due partly to subtle changes of pace in the acting and editing of sequences, but much of the credit should go to Soeteman's remarkable scenario which translates Mulisch's writing into cinematic storytelling.

Technical credits are outstanding.
—*Wall.*

Billy Drago joins cast of New World's "Vamp," which **Richard Wenk** is directing from his own script. **Donald Borchers** produces.

Saarbrücken Film Festival

Schwarz und Ohne Zucker
(Black And Without Sugar)
(WEST GERMAN-B&W)

An Optische Werke, Lutz Konermann, film production, Munich. Written and directed by Konermann. Camera (b&w), Tom Fährmann; music, Adrian Vonwiller. Reviewed at Saarbrücken Film Fest (Max Ophüls Prize competition), Jan. 26, 1986. Running time: **94 MINS.**

With: Edda Backman, Lutz Konermann, Kolbrun Halldorsdottir, Gudjon Petersen, Hanna Maria Kardottir, Thröstur Gudjartson, Gudjon Ketilsson, Herbert Linkesch, Thorgeir Gunnarsson, Franca Mannetti, Niki Lauda, Ayrton Senna.

Saarbrücken — One of the high-lights of the Saarbrücken fest and a prizewinner there, Lutz Konermann's "Black And Without Sugar" impressed for its widescreen, black-and-white images.

It's a road movie, a loose tale of a couple coming together, parting, and coming together again on a narrative journey following the routes of one or the other from Iceland to Sicily.

Konermann himself plays a filmmaker taking photographs of sites in Italy. The encounter that forms the core of the story is with Edda, member of an Icelandic street-theater group called S.O.S. — it stands for, in translation, Black Without Sugar. She has a spat with the leader of the group one day, decides to go off on her own for a while as a hitchhiker, and then meets Herrmann. They like each other's company, but when a declaration of love is made, Edda opts to return to the group.

It's only a matter of time before their paths cross again, in a seaside resort town where the street-theater group is doing another show. Herrmann now has to make a decision as to whether to return to Germany or join the group on the ferry from Italy to Sicily. Both thesps, Lutz Konermann and Kolbrun Halldorsdottir, make for an ideally amusing couple from the start.

"Black And Without Sugar" is full of observations and tongue-in-cheek twists. It also scores on camera and direction. —*Holl.*

Westler
(WEST GERMAN-COLOR-16m)

A Searcher Filmproduktion Sunger & Grüttgen, Berlin, in collaboration with Second German Television (ZDF), Mainz. Directed by Wieland Speck. Screenplay, Speck, Egbert Hörmann; camera (color), Klemens Becker; music, Engelbert Rehm; sets, Herbert Weinand; tv-producer, Andreas Schreitmüller. Reviewed at Saarbrücken Film Fest (Max Ophüls Prize competition), Jan. 23, 1986. Running time: **94 MINS.**

With: Sigurd Rachman (Felix), Rainer Strecker (Thomas), Andi Lucas (Bruce), Sascha Hammer (Elke), Frank Redies (Bernie), Andreas Bernhardt (Jürgen), Hans-Jürgen Punte (Lutze), George Stamokski (Pavel), Zazie de Paris (Zazie), Harry Baer (Customs Agent).

Saarbrücken — Wieland Speck's "Westler" concerns a gay relationship between a West Berliner and East Berliner. Speck shot some scenes with a Super-8 camera in East Berlin, film then blown up to 16m insert footage for good effect.

"Westler" begins in L.A., about as far west in Continental America as a German tourist can go. The trip from Berlin to Los Angeles is infinitely easier to make for a West Berliner than it is for an East Berliner to cross over or through the Wall to West Berlin. Speck gets this point across at the outset by underscoring a contact between two gays from West Berlin and the west coast on the streets of L.A., then having the American travel to Berlin to visit his friend — and ask for a day in East Berlin as one-day-visa tourists.

They meet a young man and it's love at first sight for Felix-West and Thomas-East.

Felix often visits his friend in East Berlin. They are mutually fascinated by each other's perception of contrasting realities and social patterns of life. When a "Westler" crosses too often over the border, suspicion is aroused — so, one day, a border guard asks Felix to step into an examination room for closer inspection to see if any undue smuggling is going on.

It's the border scenes that ring true to life. Some dialog is also witty and to the point. The love story is nothing in particular as far as the gay genre is concerned. The one twist is when Thomas decides to attempt an illegal crossing via a trip to Prague. Whether he makes it is another story, as is whether Felix is ready for a continuing relationship now that circumstances have changed.—*Holl.*

Walkman Blues
(WEST GERMAN-COLOR-16m)

A Basis-Film Verleih production, Berlin, in collaboration with Second German Television, Mainz, and Channel Four Television, London. Written and directed by Alfred Behrens. Camera (color), Claus Deubel, Martin-Theo Krieger; editor, Gabriele Herms, Heidi Heisuck; music, "Blurt," Peter Radszuhn/Marius des Mestre, Heikko Deutschmann, "Ludus;" sets, Klaus-Jürgen Pfeiffer, Irene Kraft. Reviewed at Saarbrücken Film Fest (Max Ophüls Prize competition), Jan. 22, 1986. Running time: **91 MINS.**

With: Heikko Deutschmann, Jennifer Capraru, Madeleine Daevers, Jörg Döring, Sema Engin, Werner Koller.

Saarbrücken — Writer-director and experimentalist filmmaker Alfred Behrens won a German Film Prize for his docu "S-Bahn Pictures" (1982), which in turn appears to have supplied the inspirational basis for "Walkman Blues." Both films are about Berlin, render their states in visual images rather than the spoken word, and deal with life on the edge of society and usually in transit from one place to another.

Just as in "S-Bahn Pictures," it's a ride on a public transportation vehicle, a bus through Berlin-Moabit, that sets the tone at the beginning of the pic. The protagonist (Heikko Deutschmann) is a withdrawn lad wearing his walkman, who simply walks into the frame of the filmmaker's camera — and from there is followed without comment from place to place. Due to this voyeuristic and dispassionate technique, we learn very little about the young man.

Since the lad likes his music and can play an organ with a pop group, he appears to be quite gifted. He also lives poorly in a factory loft, works a night shift in a slaughterhouse, and has few contacts on a social level other than letters to a former girlfriend in Hamburg. The real subject of "Walkman Blues" is the city itself, in the dead of winter and most at night.

Pic won the Saarbrücken University Jury Prize at the Max Ophüls competition. —*Holl.*

Va Banque
(WEST GERMAN-COLOR)

A Fuzzi Film, Berlin, and Roxy Film, Munich, coproduction. Written and directed by Diethard Küster. Camera (color), Wolfgang Pilgrim; editor, Karl Brandenburg; music, Achim Reichel, Toni Nissl; sets, Albrecht Konrad; producer, Manuela Stehr. Reviewed at Saarbrücken Film Fest (Max Ophüls Prize competition), Jan. 24, 1986. Running time: **105 MINS.**

With: Grazyna Dylong (Helen), Winfried Glatzeder (Stefan), Achim Reichel (Paul), Claus-Dieter Reents (Alfred S.), Joschka Fischer (Puhdy), Mink DeVille, Joy Rider, Rolf Zacher, Maximilian Ruethlein, Aurelio Malfa, Vera Müller, Helmut Stauss, Dorothea Moritz, Rio Reiser, Kevin Coyne.

Saarbrücken — Diethard Küster's "Va Banque" draws heavily on the genre of tried-and-true bankrobbery thrillers for its inspiration, but there is more than enough original material here to guarantee a good run at home and possibly legs for offshore chances on the arthouse circuit as well.

Three down-and-out types figure they have nothing to lose by attempting an armored-car hold-up. Stefan is a lawyer turned taxi-driver who plans the job; Helen can't makes ends meet at a boutique nor suffer along anymore with a macho Italian hubby; and Paul has debts that have risen astronomically at his auto-repair shop. They decide to pull off a job together that seems to be pretty much of a snap, considering that Stefan has made the acquaintance of a bank pick-up driver on a tennis court and now knows the operation from the inside out.

The heist works — in fact, it's the best segment in the film — and the trio feel they're home free with a cool million apiece.

The final twist has "crime pays" instead of the opposite. Each of the gang end up being bourgeois citizens putting their loot to tax-paying use.

Pic's only drawbacks are the slow pace at the beginning as characters are being respectively introduced and the lack of flair among the lead thesps. Indeed, it's the bit-players who walk away with the bacon at the end: Claus-Dieter Reents as a conman, Rolf Zacher as a cynical gangster boss, and Joschka Fischer (presently a Greens Party Minister for Environment in the State of Hessia) as a taxi driver writing a book in his spare time.

Note: Diethard Küster's "Va Banque" should not be confused with Juliusz Machulski's same-title Polish production of 1980.—*Holl.*

Ab Heute Erwachsen
(Grown Up Today)
(EAST GERMAN-COLOR)

A DEFA Film, Group "Berlin," production, East Berlin. World rights, DEFA Aussenhandel, East Berlin. Directed by Gunther Scholz. Screenplay, Helga Schubert, Scholz; camera (color), Micheal Göthe; music, Jürgen Balitzki. Reviewed at Saarbrücken Film Fest (Max Ophüls Prize competition), Jan. 25, 1986. Running time: **86 MINS.**

With: David C. Bunners (Stefan), Jutta Wachowiak (His Mother), Kurt Böwe (Herr Grünbaum), Katrin Sass (Christel).

Sarrbrücken — Gunther Scholz' "Grown Up Today" doesn't aim any higher than the home youth aud in East Germany. Because it succeeds very well on this level, pic can cross the border easily to find its way to the general teen public.

Stefan is an 18-year-old who lives alone with his mother. He choses his coming-of-age birthday to strike out on his own: he decides to rent his own apartment and, follow his own life style. The only real trouble is that he doesn't have the backbone to tell his mother of the decision to move out.

She is a progressive type (working in a bookshop) and wants to meet her son's wishes on the human level — as long as he stays home for a while.

As a young construction worker ranked "one of our best" in the brigade, he's liked by his fellow workers and strikes up a warm relationship with a maid from the local post office. He's too blind at first to notice his landlord in the rented apartment uses every opportunity to have him do all the house chores, as well as hiring him out for friends and colleagues at a restaurant where he is employed as house manager. When his mother sees how her son is being exploited, she hits the roof.

Another twist occurs when Stefan's mother attempts a reconciliation by leaving him in charge of her apartment while she takes a short trip. Stefan and his new girlfriend fumble their way through a botched overnight affair (the funniest scene in the film), then wake up to find this little innocent escapade has damaged family relations even more upon the mother's return home. The lad has to spend a night walking the streets of East Berlin before coming to the realization that being grownup means taking full responsibility for one's actions and mistakes.

Well acted and with a strong performance by Jutta Wachowiak as the beleagured mother, "Grown Up Today" should do well on the Youth Film Fest circuit. —*Holl.*

Der Polenweiher
(The Polish War Worker)
(WEST GERMAN-COLOR-16m)

A Nico Hoffmann Film, in collaboration with Südwestfunk Baden-Baden, Susan ·Schulte, tv-producer. Directed by Hoffmann and Thomas Strittmatter. Screenplay, Strittmatter; camera (color, 16m), Ernst Kubitza; music, Thomas Timmler, Dieter Gutfried. Reviewed at Saarbrücken Film Fest (Max Ophüls Prize competition), Jan. 24, 1986. Running time: 104 MINS.
With: Ursula Cantieni, Gerhard Olschewski, Wolf-Dietrich Sprenger, Eberhard Feik, Britta Pohland, Manfred Epting.

Saarbrücken — "The Polish War Worker" is based on a play by young dramatist Thomas Strittmatter. Its success earlier this decade on the stage led to a collaboration with another talented young artist, filmer Nico Hoffmann, who graduated from the Munich Film Academy and impressed with his debut feature, "My Father's War" (1984).

Tale is set in the Black Forest during the last of World War II. A Polish POW, Anna, is sent to work on a farm. Young and by nature timid, she does her job well and is given a place at the family table during meals, although this is strictly forbidden by Nazi regulations.

The war is drawing to a close. For the local police commissioner it means finding a place to go into hiding when the allied Forces take over the area, which, according to BBC newscasts (listening to these forbidden broadcasts was then punishable by death), is fairly imminent. He choses the family of the farmer for his coverup, the situation made easier in light of the fact that a criminal investigation has to be

undertaken there when the Polish girl is mysteriously murdered and thrown into a nearby lake.

One of the suspects is a hired hand and village idiot, but it soon surfaces that the girl was pregnant when drowned and that the real culprit is the farmer. The first to discover the crime is the farmer's wife, upon which the guilt-ridden husband promptly joins the German Wehrmacht to seek his death on the approaching war front.

The police chief oils his way into the good graces of the neglected wife and succeeds in his aim to take the husband's place at the table. The war now over, he and a country doctor look into the future of a new Germany filled with the promise of continued opportunism.

Pic has its quiet, somber moments, but its main drawback is a slow-paced narrative and theatrical, rather than filmic, approach to the material. Thesp performances are a major plus. —*Holl.*

Zelda Rubinstein will star in **Bigas Luna's** thriller "Anguish," now rolling in Barcelona.

German Dreams
(WEST GERMAN-COLOR-16m)

A Regina Ziegler Film, production, Berlin. Written and directed by Lienhard Wawrzyn. Camera (color), Claus Deubel; music, Jügen Buchner, "Haindling." Reviewed at Saarbrücken Film Fest (Max Ophüls Prize competition), Jan. 25, 1986. Running time: 90 MINS.
With: Angela Leiberg (Margot Schulze), Ilona Lewanowski (Jeannette Schulze), Ulf Steihann, Claus Eberhard Schultze, Diana Berndt, Ilja Schellschmidt.

Saarbrücken — A grad of the Berlin Film Academy, Lienhard Wawrzyn scored as a kidpic helmer until he got the chance to make his first feature "German Dreams," one of the important films unspooled at Saarbrücken.

This is the story of a mother and her 16-year-old daughter leaving East Germany to settle in West Berlin. Margot Schulze has spent a year and a half in prison for attempting to make the illegal crossing to the West, and now the GDR is ready and willing to part with her company. In fact, she can take her daughter Jeanette with her. Jeanette, however, has a boyfriend back East, and is unhappy to leave him despite her general curiosity about lving in West Berlin. She communicates with her friend Philipp by mail (censored and controlled on the other side), with the hope he will one day be able to join her via a border-crossing from Hungary to Yugoslavia.

The dream of settling in the "Golden West" is shattered almost from the beginning. The pair take over a city-subsidized apartment previously occupied by a despondent Turkish couple as underprivileged foreign workers. Margot's first job is at a fast food hamburger joint in West Berlin, then in a slaughterhouse on the sausage-making counter. Both jobs are degrading and a blow to the pride of a woman from the provinces whose only previous experiences were rooted in the smalltown ethic.

Mother and daughter eventually recognize the values of East German life — in fact, Margot is always listening to GDR radio, while Jeanette leaves home when her mother suddenly takes up with the old good-for-nothing boyfriend. Their mutual saviors turn out to be host-type acquaintances "just around the corner," so to speak.

The way out is via a painful suicide attempt that reunites mother and daughter — whereupon they're both off on a trip to Paris as advertised in a travel-saver plan common to West Berlin citizens. By this time, Jeanette has just about forgotten Philipp who, in turn, has announced in a letter his success in crossing the Hungarian border into Yugoslavia.

Wawrzyn researched his story well, living for a couple of months

in East Berlin under a permit. As for his two leads, both are nonprofessionals who lived until recently in East Germany: Angela Leiberg (Margot) in Dresden as a teacher, and Ilona Lewanowski (Jeanette) in East Berlin as a streetcar driver. They provide the glue to hold the docu-fiction together. The title gag takes place in a disco-bar where a "German Dream" can be ordered: half vodka, half whiskey. —*Holl.*

Vistar Films has completed its sale of 3,000,000 common shares and warrants, a $3,000,000 private placement which will be used to purchase 3,000,000 shares. Company is headed by Seymour Malamed, Gabriel Katzka and Herb Jaffe.

Robert Hughes will direct his first feature, "Hunter's Blood," for producer **Myrl Schreibman.** Pic rolls Feb. 18 in Newhall, Calif.

The Delta Force
(COLOR)

Solid actioner for wishful thinkers looks to hijack quick b.o.

A Cannon release of a Golan-Globus production. Produced by Menahem Golan, Yoram Globus. Directed by Golan. Stars Chuck Norris, Lee Marvin. Screenplay, James Bruner, Golan. Camera (color), David Gurfinkel; editor, Alain Jakubowicz; music, Alan Silvestri; production design, Lucisano Spadoni; set design, Leonardo Coen Cagli; set decoration, Ladi Wilheim; costumes, Tami Mor; sound (Dolby), Eli Yarkoni; special effects, John Gant; stunt coordinator, Don Pike; associate producer, Rony Yacov; assistant director, Tony Brandt; second unit director, Carlos Gil; second unit camera, Hans Khules Jr.; second unit a.d., Avner Orshalimi; second unit sound, Danny Natovitz; casting, Robert MacDonald, Perry Bullington (L.A.), Tova Cypin (Israel). Reviewed at the Warner Hollywood Studios, L.A., Feb. 12, 1986. (MPAA Rating: R.) Running time: 129 MINS.

Major Scott McCoy	Chuck Norris
Colonel Nick Alexander	Lee Marvin
Ben Kaplan	Martin Balsam
Harry Goldman	Joey Bishop
Abdul	Robert Forster
Sylvia Goldman	Lainie Kazan
Father O'Malley	George Kennedy
Ingrid	Hanna Schygulla
Debra Levine	Susan Strasberg
Captain Campbell	Bo Svenson
General Woodbridge	Robert Vaughn
Edie Kaplan	Shelley Winters
Pete Peterson	William Wallace
Sister Mary	Kim Delaney
Mustafa	David Menahem
Raffi Amir	Assaf Dayan

Hollywood — "The Delta Force" represents a rather astounding mix of fact and fantasy, documentary-like recreation and macho fairy tale. Constantly entertaining both of its own accord and in spite of itself, comic book actioner delivers the expected heavy duty adventure and political goods, and should rack up some hefty numbers for Cannon in quick, wide release.

Directed with the throttle wide open by Cannon cotopper Menahem Golan, pic roots itself firmly in very fresh history, then proceeds to brashly rewrite it, thereby turning itself into an exercise in wish fulfilment for those who favor using force instead of diplomacy.

First hour is mostly devoted to what seems to be a quite accurate rendition of last summer's TWA Athens hijacking. It's all there — the one Arab nabbed at the gate, the weapons hidden in the washroom, the forced landing at Beirut and subsequent departure, the German-born stewardess who balks at separating the Jewish passports, the three Navy divers mistaken for Marines, and so on.

All this seems more or less true to life except for the passenger list, which resembles a weekend's entertainment card at a Catskills resort. Here we have Joey Bishop and wife Lainie Kazan, heading back to the States with tans you couldn't beat in Miami. Sitting nearby are Martin Balsam and — have you met the wife? — the inevitable Shelley Winters, who one might have thought could easily have taken care of a couple of measly hijackers singlehandedly.

Lending a sense of historical continuity to the flight is "Airport" veteran George Kennedy as Father O'Malley, no less. Hanna Schygulla is present for the edification of the highbrows, while Robert Vaughn struts pensively as chairman of the Joint Chiefs.

While the tension in the Mediterranean keeps crackling, Delta Force topper Lee Marvin gets packing. Frustrated by defeats in Vietnam and in the desert of Iran during the aborted hostage rescue attempt (latter opens the picture), lone wolf Chuck Norris joins his former team for the long flight, first to Algiers, then on to Israel, from where the good guys launch their attack upon Arab safehouses in Beirut holding the hostages.

From here, film is purest fantasy pitting the noble Yankees against the dirty, low-down Palestinians. In an attempt at "make my day" immortality, Norris growls at one of them, "Sleep tight, sucker," before blowing him away, and gets a chance to make ample use of his martial arts skills, as well as a James Bond-style motorcycle, before spectacularly catching the flight back to safety.

Seeing as how all the hostages except the murdered sailor were eventually released in real life, film's argument seems to be that a show of force is preferable to negotiations because, one, it's impressive, and, two, the criminals are punished. As the later Maltese episode proved, that doesn't always work, but this isn't a pic that encourages much thought or meditation.

Lensed entirely in Israel, film features excellent stunt and special effects work down the line, and Golan's direction proves crudely efficient. Composer Alan Silvestri has

set it all to a throbbing disco action beat difficult to get out of one's system for hours afterward.—*Cart.*

The Hills Have Eyes Part II
(BRITISH-U.S.-COLOR)

A Castle Hill Prods. release of an Adrienne Fancey presentation of a New Realm Entertainment production in association with VTC. Produced by Barry Cahn, Peter Locke. Written and directed by Wes Craven. Camera (color), David Lewis; editor, Richard Bracken; music, Harry Manfredini; sound, Art Names; production manager-assistant director, John Callas; associate producer, Jonathan Debin. Reviewed at 42d St. Liberty theater, N.Y., Feb. 15, 1986. (MPAA Rating: R.) Running time: **88 MINS.**
With: Michael Berryman (Pluto), Tamara Stafford (Cass), Kevin Blair, John Bloom, Janus Blythe (Ruby), Peter Frechette, Robert Houston (Bobby), Penny Johnson, John Laughlin, Willard Pugh, Colleen Riley, David Nichols, Edith Fellows, James Whitworth (Reaper).

"The Hills Have Eyes Part II" is a lower case followup by Wes Craven to his 1977 cult horror pic. With funding from British homevideo companies, pic was lensed in fall of 1983 in California and has been in territorial release since last summer.

Following a hokey, narrated opening crawl that recounts the "true story" of Part I (a family from Cleveland attacked on a trip out west by a family of primitive cannibals), film proper concerns two grownup survivors of the earlier pic. Young Bobby Carter (Robert Houston) is plagued by nightmares of the desert massacre that he survived. He has invented a super formula of gasoline which his local moto-cross club (featuring lots of product plugs for a particular brand of motorcycle) is testing in an upcoming race. Ruby (Janus Blythe), a nice-gal survivor of the cannibal family, is taking the bikers in a red school bus to the race, when they foolishly try a shortcut across the desert to make up lost time.

From then on, it's dull, formula terror pic clichés, with one attractive teenager after another picked off by the surviving cannibals, Michael Berryman and James Whitworth. Craven, who has gone on to bigger and better films, shows his contempt for the project in one very funny scene: after numerous flashbacks by characters recalling the first film's events (and padding the running time with old footage), Craven runs out of survivors so suddenly the dog (named Beast) has a flashback of its own!

Acting is on the level of a formula shocker, with a winsome Candice Bergen-lookalike, Tamara Stafford, introduced in the unbelievable role of a blind girl who does most of the film's wandering around.—*Lor.*

Knights Of The City
(COLOR)

Dated picture mixes gang rumbles, rap music and breakdancing to little purpose.

A New World Pictures release of a Grace production, presented by Michael Franzese and Jerry Zimmerman. Executive producers, Franzese, Robert E. Schultz. Produced by Leon Isaac Kennedy, John C. Strong 3d. Directed by Dominic Orlando. Stars Kennedy. Screenplay, Kennedy, from story by David Wilder, Kennedy; camera (CFI color), Rolf Kesterman; editor, John O'Connor, Nicholas Smith; music, Misha Segal; additional music, Paul Gilreath; additional editing, Paul LaMori; sound, Joe Foglia; production manager-assistant director, Allan Harmon; stunt coordinators, Jeff Moldovan, Steve Boyun. Reviewed at 42d St. Harris theater, N.Y., Feb. 15, 1986. (MPAA Rating: R.) Running time: **88 MINS.**
Troy . . . . .Leon Isaac Kennedy
Mookie . . . . .John Mengati
Joey . . . . .Nicholas Campbell
Carlos . . . . .Jeff Moldovan
Eddie . . . . .Stoney Jackson
Brooke . . . . .Janine Turner
John . . . . .Michael Ansara
Also with: Wendy Barry, Karin Smith, Smokey Robinson, Fat Boys, K.C., Jeff Kutash, Deney Terrio, Cammy Garcia, T.K. & Jessie, Kurtis Blow.

"Knights Of The City" is a silly mishmash filmed in South Florida two years ago under the title "Cry Of The City" (retained as a theme song). Filmmaker-star Leon Isaac Kennedy attempts to mix elements form the youth gang pics of the late 1970s with the recently demised ("Beat Street," "Flash Forward") genre of dance/rap music contests. Hokey result, picked up by New World, is yet another dud ready to line the shelves of homevideo stores.

Pic gained some notoriety when its production company, Miami Gold (not credited on screen in release print) left Florida after much local ballyhoo and exec producer Michael Franzese was later charged by the feds with racketeering and allegedly using his film companies to launder funds.

With new producers, music and postproduction changes, pic emerges as a diffuse tale of three urban gang members (setting is indeterminate despite Florida lensing) played by Kennedy, John Mengati and Nicholas Campbell, at war with a rival gang, The Mechanix, led by Jeff Moldovan, that is invading their turf. Kennedy and Mengati also head up a musical group, which looks like their ticket out of the ghetto when they are briefly befriended in jail by drunk record company owner Michael Ansara.

Kennedy crosses both the color line and social classes by romancing Ansara's daughter, statuesque Janine Turner (named Brooke here and styled after Brooke Shields), who, á la "Flash Forward," organizes a street talent contest. After being coached in the latest dance steps by (fellow ex-Clevelander) Jeff Kutash, Kennedy & crew win the $10,000 prize and a recording con-

tract, even though their much-applauded performance is pretty bad.

Campbell is a hardliner who wants to keep the gang together, and there is some chummy solidarity in the final reel when the good guys unite to wipe the floor with The Mechanix.

Filmed by director Dominic Orlando with too much back lighting and smoke machine effects, pic is padded with quickie turns by numerous guest stars from the music world, including Smokey Robinson as the contest emcee. Sammy Davis Jr.'s stint ended up on the cutting room floor, however.

Kutash's choreography is unimpressive and pic's musical sequences never generate the excitement of such models as "Breakin'" or even NW's own "Body Rock." The hope to modernize a "West Side Story" format is stillborn because this is not a musical but rather an action pic with interpolated musical performances.

Campbell wins the overacting honors with a strident, screaming act, while his future teammate on tv's "The Insiders" series, Stoney Jackson, has little to do as the group/gang's drummer. Kennedy's script is extremely self-serving, unbelievably adding to his screen persona as "a lover and a fighter" the status of rap singer. —*Lor.*

Troppo Forte
(He's Too Much)
(ITALIAN-COLOR)

A Titanus release. Produced by Augusto Caminito for Scena Film Prods. Directed by Carlo Verdone. Stars Verdone. Screenplay, Verdone, Rodolfo Sonego, Alberto Sordi; camera (Eastmancolor), Danilo Desideri; editor, Nino Baragli; music, Antonello Venditti; art director, Franco Velchi. Reviewed at Adriano Cinema, Rome, Feb. 12, 1986. Running time: **101 MINS.**
Oscar . . . . .Carlo Verdone
Nancy . . . . .Stella Hall
Lawyer . . . . .Alberto Sordi
With: John Steiner, Mario Brega, Sal Da Vinci.

Rome — Versatile young comic Carlo Verdone — one of the b.o. toppers in his generation of clowns who successfully shifted from cabaret to film — comes up with a minor act in his latest pic, "Troppo Forte." Characters and story are reprised from Verdone hits of the past with little variation, and pic as a whole has a tired, rerun look. Helmer-star knows his local audience, however, and pic has quickly climbed the charts thanks to younger viewers, especially.

Verdone plays Oscar, a pudgy motorcycle punk who likes to style himself the Rambo of the outlying Roman slum he lives in. When he tries out for the part of a tough guy in a film, he's rejected because he's not tough enough, and to avenge himself Oscar stages an accident to milk the producer of insurance money.

Instead pretty American actress Nancy (Stella Hall) is driving the car, and the accident costs her her job. She moves into Oscar's apartment and runs up his phone bill, till her husband (a turkey farmer) comes to take her back to Texas.

The pathos and humanity Verdone habitually injects into his characters fall flat here. Even Oscar, the most likable of the lot, is unfocused and shallow. His dream-girl Nancy may inflame the imagination of local viewers, but bears little resemblance to a living woman, despite a melancholy finale. Ditto the portrait of Yank filmmakers, who end up offering Oscar a suitcase full of money if he'd just sign on the dotted line.

Pic's single highlight is Alberto Sordi in the role of a crazy shyster out to defend Oscar's interests at all costs, even to the point of gratuitously removing his spleen. In bowtie and curled looks, Sordi looks like he's thoroughly enjoying hamming it up, and gets the few genuine laughs in the film.

An extended cycle race sequence against unearthly landscapes, lensed like a commercial with driving background sound from Antonello Venditti, is inserted for a change of pace.—Yung.

'Crossroads' R Sustained

Motion Picture Assn. of America's Classification and Rating Appeals Board on Feb. 13 sustained the R rating tagged to Columbia Pictures' "Crossroads."

"Crossroads" helmer Walter Hill and Columbia worldwide production v.p. Robert Bookman made appeal statements to CARA.

Visszaszamlalas
(Countdown)
(HUNGARIAN-B&W)

A Tarsulas Studio, Mafilm, production. Directed by Pal Erdöss. Screenplay, Istvan Kardos; camera (b&w), Ferenc Papp, Gabor Szabo; editor, Klara Majoras; music, Jozsef Czencz; sets; Andras Gyürki; sound, György Fek. Reviewed at Hungarian Film Week, Budapest, Feb. 12, 1986. Running time: **103 MINS.**
Jutka Meszaros . . . . Erika Ozsda
Sandor Meszaros . . . . Karoly Eperjes
Peter . . . . Denes Ujlaky
Fireman . . . . Zoltan Bezeredi
Selmeczi (The Shark) . . . . Jenö Dekleva

Budapest — A somber, finely crafted film about the pitfalls of the system of private enterprise now taking hold in Hungary, "Countdown" is a very pessimistic film but an emotionally involving one. It's already invited to the Cannes Directors' Fortnight in May, and should get plenty of attention from noncompeting festivals, as did its director, Pal Erdöss, with his first feature, "The Princess."

Sandor Meszaros (Karoly Eperjes) is a truck driver who decides to go into business for himself. He puts all his savings into a truck he buys at an auction. At first things go well ("Just Like America!" says the jubilant Sandor as he counts the first day's takings), but before long jobs are hard to find and Sandor has to pay bribes to get work as well as doing ever more back-breaking hauling. Meanwhile, to pay their debts (they're building a new house), Sandor's pretty, supportive wife, Jutka (beautifully played by Erika Ozsda), starts working at home as a seamstress.

Then disaster strikes. Sandor's back gives way, he can't work and can't keep up the payments. In an agony of despair, he and Jutka quarrel furiously. Eventually he adapts himself and learns how to work a sewing machine.

Erdöss is obviously making a cautionary tale about too enthusiastic an embrace of the private enterprise system. The good goes along with the bad, with a vengeance in this case. "Countdown" is very well made in the documentary tradition, with gritty black and white photography and fine, realistic performances. It's not a cheerful night's entertainment by any means.

Pic was the easy winner of the Gene Moskowitz award, given as best film of the Hungarian Film Week by foreign journalists.—Strat.

Az Eluarázsolt Dollar
(The Enchanted Dollars)
(HUNGARIAN-COLOR)

A Hungarofilm Presentation of a Mafilm — Moviecoop production. Written and directed by István Bujtor. Camera (color), György Illés, László Baranyai; editor, Mária Szécsényi; sets, Tomás Hornyánszky; sound, István Sipos; music, Károly Frenreisz. Reviewed at the Budapest Congress Center (Hungarian Film Week), Feb. 12, 1986. Running time: **94 MINS.**
With: István Bujtor, András Kern, István Avar, László Kozák, Barbara Kristály, László Horesnyi, Edit Frajt.

Budapest — István Bujtor, a beefy Hungarian actor, has made a career for himself playing heavyweight bruisers who enforce the law by beating it on the heads of criminals. He has written and directed the new installment in the adventures of Lieutenant Tiny of the Balathon Police Force.

This comical actioner shows Tiny chasing a gang of counterfeiters. The action scenes, car races and fist fights are clumsily handled.

There is much over-acting and under-direction, but the scenery of the Balathan district, Hungary's top tourist attraction, is enjoyable to watch.

Technical credits are acceptable.
—Edna.

L'Unique
(The One And Only)
(FRENCH-COLOR)

An AAA Revcom Films release of a Les Prods. Belles Rives production. Produced by Jérôme Diamant-Berger. Stars Julia Migenes Johnson. Screenplay, Jérôme Diamant-Berger, Olivier Assayas, Jean-Claude Carrière; camera (Fujicolor, Panavision), Jean-François Robin; music, Guy Boulanger; choregráphy, Rick Odums; art director, Nikos Meletopoulos; special effects director, Christian Guillon; graphic conception, Jean-François Henri; computer images production, Xavier Nicolas; computer images animation, Christian Foucher; sound, Philippe Lioret, Michel Vilain; editor, Luc Barnier; makeup, Sophie Landry, Alain Moize; costumes, Dona Turnier; production manager, Jean Lefèvre. Reviewed at the Georges V cinema, Paris, Feb. 11,1986. Official entry (out of competition) at Berlin Film Festival. Running time: **81 MINS.**
The Singer . . . . Julia Migenes Johnson
Michel . . . . Tcheký Karyo
Colewsky . . . . Sami Frey
Vox . . . . Charles Denner
Aline . . . . Jézabel Carpi
Sarah . . . . Fabienne Babe
Rey . . . . Thierry Rode
Tom . . . .̇. . . Benjamin de Borda

Paris — "L'Unique" is both a science fantasy and a monster hi-tech music video for its star, Julia Migenes Johnson, who, after an impressive debut in Francesco Rósi's "Carmen" is now a no less fiery hologram genius. If Migenes Johnson can be packaged as a pop star for young audiences, "L'Unique" may have fair chances in the marketplace. But as a sci-fi fable it is unfocused in theme, shaky in development and anticlimactic in conclusion.

This reportedly is the first European film to use computer-generated images and effects, necessary for the sequences of the creation of the star's hologram double. Created by Sogitec, a French computer technology company with an audiovisual sector, these scenes are first-rate, if only moderately exciting in a dramatic context. Kudos to all those who worked on the scenes integrating computer effects into conventional live-action footage.

The script lacks definition and drama. Migenes Johnson is to be replaced on stage by a double by her producer, who is fed up with her capricious behavior (she has stopped in mid-concert, and sometimes doesn't even show up). The producer subsidizes a research scientist, who promises to duplicate the star with a hologram that can perform in her stead, without the public being any wiser.

One expects piquant melodramatic complications from this intriguing premise, but what the writers — debuting director Jérôme Diamant-Berger, Olivier Assayas and Jean-Claude Carrière — finally lead us to is an unexpectedly low-keyed denouement, which doesn't work because they have not limned flesh-and-blood characters of any dramatic weight. If Migenes Johnson pulsates with energy and talent in her rock and blues numbers, she hardly exists offstage, though it's not the actress' fault.

Migenes Johnson gets some needed and superb support from her male partners, notably Tcheky Karyo, as an electronics video pirate who is thrown out of her concert when he tries to film it with a hidden microcamera. Karyo is in fact her former lover, who lives with the son she gave him (and whom she at last recognizes in the final scene, thanks ironically to the hologram double). Karyo has to deal with another underwritten role and some pot holes — he seems to have no trouble entering obviously off-limits precincts, like the scientist's lab — but his mere presence proclaims an actor of extraordinary intensity and force.

Charles Denner and Sami Frey offer a stylishly entertaining duo of voices as the ruthless record tycoon and the scientist. Their opposing dictions, and the extraordinary way in which Denner can break up and modulate a line of dialog, are a subsidiary treat.

As director, Diamant-Berger sacrifices a personal style to the special effects and the very special Migenes Johnson, but does at times affirm technical assurance and a sense of rhythm. He has been aided invaluably by Jean-François Robin's sleek lensing and Luc Barnier's editing.

François Valery and the rock group Heaven 17 provided the good rock and blues numbers. —Len.

Der Rosenkönig
(King Of The Roses)
(WEST GERMAN-COLOR)

A Film Intl. release of a Werner Schroeter production. Produced and directed by Schroeter. Screenplay, Schroeter, Magdalena Montezuma; camera (color), Elfi Mikesch; art direction, Caritas de Witt; editor, Juliane Lorenz; sound, Joacquim Pinto. Reviewed at Rotterdam Film Festival, Feb. 1, 1986. (In Forum Of Young Cinema at Berlin Film Fest.) Running time: **115 MINS.**
Anna . . . . Magdalena Montezuma
Arnold . . . . Antonio Orlando
Albert . . . . Mostea Djayam

Rotterdam — Seventeen years ago Werner Schroeter made his first film, with Magdalena Montezuma in the lead. She went on to star in a number of other Schroeter films and remained one of his closest friends and collaborators. The idea of "Der Rosenkönig" originated with her, she wrote all the dialog and worked on scenario together with the helmer. Camerawoman Elfi Mikesch came in at an early stage. Shooting (in Portugal) took place with everyone in the crew aware Montezuma was dying of cancer but determined to finish the film. She died two weeks after shooting ended, and pic is dedicated to her.

It's about love, beauty, death, religion and ritual sacrifice. Schroeter evokes his themes through beautiful pictures, imaginative cutting,

Feature Films At Berlin Film Festival

fantastic shots of animals; through music, opera, lieder, a waltz, chamber music; through poetry, American, German, Portuguese, English; through voices and the movements of camera and actors.

Schroeter records the bleating of sheep, the croaking of a toad, the serenity of statues of saints hanging on a church wall, breaking waves, playing children, rose petals, a white mouse, a burning barn. Miraculously, this does not become a pretentious hodgepodge of phony art. Pic is very disciplined, the structure meticulously planned, the acting subdued. Montezuma is touching through a gentle approach to her part.

There's no sense in describing the story, slender as it is. This is a film to see, to listen, to experience emotionally. One will love it or hate it. It will be unforgettable for some, a waste of time for others. The audience at the Rotterdam world preem loved it. When the lights went on, spectators remained silent for quite a while before they got up and spontaneous applause broke out. It is a pic for arthouses and fests, currently unspooling at Berlin.— Wall.

Stammheim
(WEST GERMAN-COLOR)

A coproduction of Bioskop Film, Munich, and Thalia Theater, Hamburg. World rights, Futura Film, Munich. Produced by Eberhard Junkersdorf and Jürgen Flimm. Directed by Reinhard Hauff. Screenplay, Stefan Aust; camera (color), Frank Brühne, Günter Wulff; sets, Dieter Flimm; editor, Heidi Handorf; music, Marcel Wengler; sound, Jan van der Eerden. Reviewed at Lankwitz Screening Room, Berlin, Jan. 27, 1986. (In competition at Berlin Film Festival.) Running time: 107 MINS.

With: Ulrich Pleitgen (Presiding judge), Ulrich Tukur (Andreas Baader), Therese Affolter (Ulrike Meinhof), Sabine Wagner (Gudrun Ensslin), Hans Kremer (Jan-Carl Raspe), Peter Danzeisen (Defense attorney), Hans Christian Rudolph (Defense attorney), Holger Mahlich (Defense attorney), Marina Wandruszka (Defense attorney), Horst Mendroch (First states attorney), Günther Flesch (Second states attorney), Fred Hospowsky (New presiding judge), Fred Maertens (Public defender), Matthias Bramberger (Public defender), Hans Michael Rehberg (Federal attorney), Dominique Horwitz (Witness), Günther Heising (Witness), Rainer Philippi (Witness), Angela Buddecke (Witness), Circe (Witness), Michael Schönborn (Witness), Eric Schildkraut (Witness), Klaus Schreiber (Witness), Silvia Fenz (Witness), Lothar Rehfeldt (Witness), Alexander Duda (Reporter).

Berlin — Reinhard Hauff's "Stammheim," an official German entry in the Berlinale, is an extraordinary film. Performed by the Thalia Theater ensemble in Hamburg and lensed on a tight schedule in a Hamburg factory, it scores first and foremost as an historical event — that is, one of those rare films that well needs a festival like the Berlinale to launch it into international orbit.

"Stammheim" is about the Baader-Meinhof trial in the Stuttgart-Stammheim prison. On trail were Andreas Baader, Ulrike Meinhof, Jan-Carl Raspe, and Gudrun Ensslin. A fifth member of this politically active group modeled after the "Tupamaros" (guerrillas in underground) movement in Latin America, Holger Meins, died at the trial's opening as a result of a hunger strike. Ulrike Meinhof died next, during the trial, of apparent suicide, followed by the other three shortly after receiving life sentences.

The trial took two years, 1975-77, but the roots of the national hysteria surrounding it date back to the student revolt of 1968 — and long before that to National Socialism and the subsequent postwar break between fathers and sons, parents and students, past Nazis and contemporary revolutionaries.

"Stammheim" is also a film belonging not only to helmer Hauff but equally to its scriptwriter, Stefan Aust, for his newly published book "The Baader-Meinhof Complex" is a compendium of research and a distillation of the trial protocol in order to present facts without passion or prejudice and thus leave the whole matter open to the viewing public to decide for themselves. "Stammheim" is thus one big question mark.

Thesp performances are a plus, particularly Ulrich Pleitgen as the hair-splitting presiding judge and Ulrich Tukur as the rambunctious Andreas Baader. One would have liked, however, that an older truer-to-reality actress had played the key role of Ulrike Meinhof, yet the fact that an entire theater ensemble has taken on the task in the first place is remarkable.

"Stammheim" is not a pioneer work. British theater director Pip Simmons produced "The First Baader-Meinhof Play" on a Bochum stage in Germany a decade ago, which suffered a canceled preem and a short run due to bomb threats. Upcoming at Cannes is Markus Imhoof's Swiss-German coproduction, "The Trip," based on Bernward Vesper's (Gundrun Ensslin's husband and father of her child) autobiographical book. There was also Margarethe von Trotta's "German Sisters" (a.k.a. "Marianne And Juliane") (1981), winner of the Golden Lion at Venice, which dealt with the Ensslin sisters.

When one considers that "Stammheim" had to be made without subsidy coin from either of the German tv funds, and that only the liberal Hamburg film-aid plan and the generosity of the Thalia Theater there made this modestly budgeted project possible in the first place, then many of the film's shortcomings can be accepted for what they are under the circumstances. And praise should be handed out to lenser Frank Brühne for the capturing of the flourescent-lighting prison-courtroom atmosphere. One feels the tension of the highly explosive trial and that's something one can't say about scores of other fictionally reconstructed movies on the same theme. — Holl.

Elsö Ketszaz Evem
(My First 200 Years)
(HUNGARIAN-COLOR)

An Objektiv Studio, Mafilm, production. Written and directed by Gyula Maar, from the novel by Pal Kiralyhegyi. Camera (Eastmancolor), Ivan Mark; editor, Julia Sivo; sets, Tamas Banovich; costumes, Judit Schaffer; sound, Karoly Peller. Reviewed at Hungarian Film Week, Feb. 9, 1986. (In competition at Berlin Film Festival.) Running time: 103 MINS.

Pali	Zoltan Bezeredi
Maud	Anna Kubik
Ernö	Endre Harkanyi
The Movie Mogul	Jiri Adamira
His wife	Mari Töröcsik
Krausz Jr.	Laszlo Markus
Krausz Sr.	Bela Both

Budapest — Uneven in tone and ultimately rather uninvolving, "My First 200 Years" follows the fortunes of a rather listless Hungarian Jew (Zoltan Bezeredi) during the 1930s. Pic opens as he returns from America, and early scenes promise some quiet satire at the expense of Budapest's famous cafe society.

The gentle humor continues for awhile as Pali, the protagonist, heads off for England where he has an odd meeting with a movie mogul obviously based on Alexander Korda (this expatriate Hungarian claims the main theme of all his films is: "Long Live England!"). In London, Pali has an affair with an unsuccessful and cheerfully promiscuous actress (Anna Kubik) before returning to a Budapest already in the grip of facism.

At this point, the film loses its way. The quiet satire of the early scenes gives way to a glum yet emotionally undemanding approach to the subject of Jewish persecution. Admittedly, this subject hasn't been covered all that often before in Magyar films, but director Gyula Maar seems unable to find the right way to tackle it here. As the film gets bleaker and more violent it only becomes an audience turnoff since we don't really care about the characters in the way we certainly should.

Acting is rote, and though the film is quite elegantly made on a technical level, it remains an ultimately unsatisfactory experience. The climax, a sort of dream of death, is a cop-out.

Pic is representing Hungary in competition at the Berlin Film Fest.
—Strat.

Heiderlöcher
(Hideouts)
(AUSTRIAN-WEST GERMAN-B&W)

A coproduction of Voissfilm, Munich, Marwo-Film, Vienna, and Bayerischer Rundfunk (BR), Munich. Written, directed and edited by Wolfram Paulus. Camera (b&w), Wolfgang Simon; sets, Christoph Kanter; sound, Michael Etz. Reviewed at Berlin Film Fest (Competition). Feb. 15, 1986. Running time: 102 MINS.

With: Florian Pircher (Santner), Albert Paulus (Ruap), Helmut Vogel (Jacek), Matthias Aichhorn (Dürlinger), Rolf Zacher (Guard), Claus-Dieter Reents (Gestapo man), Maria Aichhorn (Frau Dürlinger), Gerta Rettenwender (Frau Santner), Joanna Hadej (Agnes), Franz Hafner (Forester), Doris Kreer (Lisabeth), Hubsi Aichhorn (Festl), Darius Polanski (Staschek), Piotr Firackiewicz (Kowal), Hans-Jörg Unterkrainer (Weissbauer), Jürgen Bretzinger (2d gestapo man), Günther Mixdorf (2d guard), Walter Oczlon (Soldier on furlough), Milena Oczion, Barbara Reitter, Marzena Krupinski (Three Polish girls).

Berlin — This year's Berlinale nod to a newcomer goes to Wolfram Paulus' "Hideouts" (actual title is an expression for a mountain cave).

Pic comes across as an exercise in b&w esthetics, so much so that the story gets buried somewhere along the way, and never really surfaces thereafter.

In an isolated Austrian village in the winter of 1942 a deserter has been hiding away for a year. His wife has been feeding him while villagers help out any way they can in addition to keeping a tight lip before the gestapo and military authorities. The village has also received POWs of various nationalities (French, Polish, Russian), who are there to make up for the manpower gone to war.

One Austrian lad is embittered because his brother was allowed to go to the front, which only means that his lot at home amounts to harder chores in the company of the POWs. His father even shells out more praise to a decent hard-working Polish POW, and one day clouts his own son on the ear for his continued nagging arrogance. Then comes the news that the brother was killed on the front: It leads to a betrayal of the hidden deserter to the Gestapo and a tragic ending for both the informed and the informer.

The story itself is rather thin, so Paulus stretches the tale by describing the daily routine of POW life (one prisoner dies of typhus because the guard refuses to consign him to a hospital) and hard physical labor in the dead of winter in the high Alps. One senses the tension in the village, for these independent farmers tolerate the POWs more than they do the alien military forces in their presence.

Pic's chief drawback is the helmer's confusing storyline, plus patches of dialog in foreign tongues that could be picked up on fest earphones but not via needed subtitles. Okay for a debut effort, but little hope for an offshore launch even with proper handling. —*Holl.*

Director **Andrei Konchalovsky** has rolled "Duet For One," starring **Julie Andrews**, for Cannon Films in London.

Sky Pirates
(AUSTRALIAN-COLOR)

A Roadshow (Australia) release of a John Lamond Motion Pictures production. Produced by Lamond, Michael Hirsh. Directed by Colin Eggleston. Stars John Hargreaves, Meredith Phillips. Screenplay, Lamond; camera (Panavision, color), Garry Wapshott; music, Brian May; editors, Lamond, Hirsh; production design, Kristian Fredrickson; sound, Gary Wilkins; 2d unit director, Ross Hamilton; 2d unit camera, John Wheeler; stunts, Max Aspin; special visual effects, Dennis Nicholson; assistant director, John Powditch; production manager, Kevin Powell. Reviewed at Village-Roadshow screening room, Sydney, Jan. 15, 1986. Commonwealth Film Censor Rating: M.) Running time: **86 MINS.**

Harris ....John Hargreaves
Melanie Mitchell ....Meredith Phillips
Savage ....Max Phipps
O'Reilly ....Bill Hunter
Reverend Mitchell ....Simon Chilvers
General Hackett ....Alex Scott
Hayes ....David Parker
Valentine ....Adrian Wright
Colonel Brien ....Peter Cummins
Barman ....Tommy Dysart
Logan ....Wayne Cull
Sullivan ....Alex Menglett
Spencer ....Nigel Bradshaw

Sydney — Eighteen months after the completion of shooting, "Sky Pirates" limps into release as the first Australian pic of the new year, sans advance hype. Apparent lack of interest on the part of Roadshow, the distrib, is understandable, since the film is a woefully conceived ripoff of the Indiana Jones epics, which aims for large-scale entertainment but falls flat via a puerile script (by coproducer John Lamond), flabby direction and second-rate effects.

Set in 1945, plot starts out along the lines of "The Philadelphia Experiment" as an aircraft piloted by the supposedly intrepid Harris (John Hargreaves) en route from

Sydney to Washington via the Pacific island of Bora Bora, enters some kind of time warp, crashes in the sea and ends up near Easter Island. Story then leaps forward to take in the court martial of Harris, by which time audiences probably will be confused completely. Presumably Lamond knew what his story was about, but few others will, nor will they care.

Subsequent footage deals with the attempts of the villain, blond and jackbooted and badly acted by Max Phipps, to locate a magical stone, supposedly left behind by prehistoric spacemen, which contains the power to build such edifices as Stonehenge or the Easter Island statues, but which can also destroy. Harris is there to frustrate his desperate efforts, of course. There's also a heroine, a feisty young woman (Meredith Phillips) who manages to look elegant during all the mayhem. Not a demanding role for this newcomer.

As the hero, John Hargreaves acquits himself better than might have been expected given the quality of his material. The actor, one of Australia's best, brings just enough charm and grit to the role to avoid embarrassment.

Script borrows not only from Indiana Jones, as noted, but also knowingly introduces scenes and even lines of dialog lifted from such varied pics as "The Road Warrior," "The Deer Hunter," "Dirty Harry" and the risqué scene in the train from "North By Northwest;" but it all plays as silly and second-rate here.

"Sky Pirates" fails to take off because the direction of Colin Eggleston lacks the pace and zip sorely needed, the stunts look phony (even if they aren't) and the special effects seem tatty. Brian May's music goes along with the hand-me-down spirit of the enterprise, and is re-cycled John Williams.

Entire sorry affair seems to indicate this kind of madcap adventure is just not the kind of thing Australian filmmakers can get away with. It's all too half-hearted, self-conscious and muddled to enthrall audiences the way it should. —*Strat.*

In de schaduw van de overwinning
(In The Shadow Of Victory)
(DUTCH-COLOR)

A Concorde Film release of Sigmafilm production. Produced by Matthijs van Heijningen. Directed by Ate De Jong. Stars Jeroen Krabbé, Edwin de Vries, Linda vna Dyck, Marieke van der Pol. Screenplay, De Jong, de Vries; camera (color), Eddy van der Enden; editor, Ton Ruys; music, Henny Vrienten; art direction, Ben van Os, Jan Roelfs; sound, Victor Dekker. Reviewed at Cinema International, Amsterdam, Jan. 14, 1986. Running time: **109 MINS.**

Peter van Dijk ....Jeroen Krabbé
David Blumberg ....Edwin de Vries
Sanne ....Linda van Dyck
Hansje ....Marieke van der Pol

Vos ....Rijk de Gooyer
Doctor ....Ton Lutz
Kohler ....Tom Jansen
Schwarz ....Hein Boele

Amsterdam — A thriller in which what happens inside the characters is as important as what happens to them, pic is situated in Nazi-occupied Amsterdam in 1943. The two main characters are based very loosely on historical figures. Few incidents in the film correspond to actions of the resistance movement as they really happened.

Peter van Dijk (Jeroen Krabbé), a talented painter, with a wife and two kids (also a womanizer) becomes through traumatic circumstances the brave leader of the resistance group. He organizes some brilliant raids against the Germans. He's very much a wanted man.

David Blumberg (Edwin de Vries) wants to save himself, his family and other Jews from deportation. A German general, von Spiegel, himself in Berlin, appoints Blumberg his agent to select Jews who will be sent to Switzerland, provided they buy their tickets with plenty of money, jewels or gold. Blumberg shows the general's letter to the Gestapo and secures their cooperation. Soon there are some 600 Jews on the "Blumberg list." There's one snag: von Spiegel exists only in Blumberg's imagination.

This part of the story might strike non-Dutch viewers as ludicrous and unbelievable, but it is one of the things which are historically true. Such a list saved hundreds from deportation for nearly a year, before the Gestapo stumbled onto the fact that no such general existed.

Writer-director Ate De Jong very cleverly intertwines the stories of Blumberg and van Dikj; their families; van Dijk's women friends; other members of the resistance group; the moneygrabbing black marketeer (Rijk de Gooyer) who is an invaluable source of weapons, papers, safe houses etc. to the resistance; even one or two of the Gestapo.

De Jong got remarkable acting performances from his entire cast. Helped by excellent production design, imaginative music, and purposeful cutting pic moves vigorously along at a great pace, with plenty of action.

"In The Shadow Of Victory" should easily find theatrical distribution outside the Netherlands. —*Wall.*

Endgame
(ITALIAN-COLOR)

An American National Enterprises release of a Cinema 80 presentation of a Filmirage production. Directed by Steven Benson. Features entire cast. Screenplay, Alex Carver, from story by Carver, Benson; camera (Telecolor), Federico Slonisco; editor, Tony Larson; music, Carlo Maria Cordio; production manager, Charles Kellin; production supervisor, Helen Handris; production design, Robert Connors; costume design, Linda Jenkins. Reviewed on Cinemax, N.Y., Jan.

10, 1986. (No MPAA Rating.) Running time: **99 MINS.**

Ron Shannon ....Al Cliver
Lilith ....Laura Gemser
Kurt Karnak ....George Eastman
Prof. Levin.................Jack Davis
Ninja ....Al Yamanouchi
Bull ....Gabriele Tinti
Kovack ....Mario Pedone
Col. Morgan ....Gordon Mitchell
Tommy ....Christopher Walsh

"Endgame" is a rather weak entry in the crowded post-WWIII series of Italian action films made circa 1983. Emanating from the Helen Sarlui pic stable (though she does not take a screen credit), item was mulled for a while as a New Line theatrical release but went instead to pay-tv and homevideo.

Misleading opening reel establishes a tv game in the year 2012 called "Endgame," quite similar to Robert Sheckley's concept used in the classic "The Tenth Victim" (and recently updated in another Italian pic, "The Final Executioner"). Al Cliver toplines as a successful warrior in the killing game who is recruited by a telepathic mutant Lilith (Laura Gemser) to help her band of mutants leave the city (where they are subject to extermination by storm trooper-styled soldiers) to set up a new community.

The tv game is over in 20 minutes, with remainder of the film given over to fights en route to delivering the mutants. Action scenes are perfunctory, with none of the thrills in the model for this genre, "The Road Warrior."

Given the poor dubbing of these pictures, "Endgame" benefits from its telepathy gimmick, which allows many dialog scenes to have staring faces with no lips moving as the thoughts are voiced-over on the soundtrack. Acting is stilted, with the ubiquitous husband-wife team of Laura Gemser and Gabriele Tinti both credited with different "real" names, Moira Chen and Gus Stone, respectively. Freeze-frame nonending is poor. —*Lor.*

Red Desert Penitentiary
(DUTCH/U.S.-COLOR)

A Cupido Films release of an MGS Film Amsterdam and The Sweetwater Little Theater production. Produced, directed and written by George Sluizer, based on a short story by Tim Krabbé. Stars James Michael Taylor, Cathryn Bissell. Camera (color) Toni Kuhn; editor, Julie Sloane, Sluizer; music, James Michael Taylor; sound, Bernardine Ligthart. Reviewed at Cine Press Club, Amsterdam, Jan. 9, 1986. Running time: **94 MINS.**

Dan McMan ....James Michael Taylor
Myrna Grenbaum ....Cathryn Bissell
James Gagan ....Bill Rose
Chet Kofman ....Jim Wortham
Mickey Slavasky .....Giovanni Korporaal
Rosalie................Trudy Wortham

Amsterdam — George Sluizer is a Dutchman, but born and partly educated in France, who since 1961 has directed, written and mostly produced some 30 films all over the world, all but three documentaries.

His latest, "Red Desert Penitentiary" was shot in West Texas in 1984.

It's an elegant little romp, spoofing B-films. A producer (played by Sluizer) assembles cast and crew for a routine western with a new angle: leading man Dan McMan has to be seduced by his daughter to commit incest in a swimming pool. McMan, a veteran B-hero, objects, protecting his image. The girl, a newcomer, is dumb, overweight, a virgin, can't act, but has what may turn out to be star qualities.

Film-within-the-film (also called "Red Desert Penitentiary") is based on the autobiography of one Gagan, who states that two very rich and kinky students have managed to keep him in a fake one-room prison in the desert for 20 years.

Gagan's autobiography itself turns out to be a colossal fake. He's a convicted criminal lately let out of prison. McMan, through a nice twist in the story, gets 20 years for the murder he did not commit, and this time the trial is completely honest, the judge above reproach, and the witnesses are absolutely truthful.

Nearly all actors are amateurs. James Michael Taylor, a country and western singer (he also wrote the music), is very good in an Eastwoodish way, Cathryn Bissell very acceptable as the dumb blond. The lack of production money never becomes obtrusive.

Helmer keeps a light touch nearly all of the time. The exception is Gagan's story, told in flashback, two-thirds through the film. Pic then sags, and there is not time enough before the ending to regain the aloof stance of an amused storyteller. Camerawork and other credits are very good.

Theatrical chances except for fests and special situations are slim, but pic should fare well on tv and cassettes.—*Wall.*

Les Loups Entre Eux
(The Wolves Among Themselves)
(FRENCH-COLOR)

An AAA CCFC/Revcom Films release of a C.O.F.C.I./TF 1 Films coproduction. Produced by William Oury, Dany Cohen. Directed by José Giovanni. Screenplay, Giovanni, Jean Schmitt, based on their novel; camera (color) Jean-François Gondre; editor, Jacqueline Thiédot; music, Pino Marchese; art director, Jacques Dugied; sound, Jean-Louis Ughetto; production manager, Guy Azzi. Reviewed at the Marignan-Concorde theater, Paris, Jan. 13, 1986. Running time: **114 MINS.**
> With: Claude Brasseur (Larcier), Bernard-Pierre Donnadieu (De Saintes), Gérard Darmon ("La Cavale"), Niels Arestrup (Mike), Edward Meeks (Straub), Jean-Hugues Anglade (Richard Avakian), Patrick Edlinger (Patrick), Daniel Duval (The Gypsy), Jean-Roger Milo (Bastien), Gabriel Brian (Spartacus), Lisa Kreuzer (Carla), Isabelle Lorca (Jennifer), Robert Arden (General).

Paris — Picaresque male-bonding action in the vein of "The Guns Of Navarone" and "The Dirty Dozen," "Les Loups Entre Eux" is curiously unenthralling adventure fare, despite its gallery of virile but flawed antiheroes and an adequate quota of bullets, bombs and man-to-man confrontations.

Director José Giovanni and co-scripter Jean Schmitt adapted the story from their own print thriller. It is trite stuff about an assorted band of mercenaries and rogues who are recruited by a NATO intelligence service for a top-secret commando mission.

An American general with highly confidential European defense info has been kidnapped by terrorists and is being held in a cliff-top fortress in the Mediterranean.

The Dirty Dozen Minus Two must scale the cliffs, lay siege to the fort and recover the general unharmed before he can be induced to spill the beans.

They accomplish their mission with some losses. When they are paid off, the remainder of the unit find themselves the targets of NATO assassins who are bent on insuring total silence on the mission. The chief of the band and a professional alpinist escape the massacre and manage to find refuge from their treacherous employers.

Giovanni has rounded up a sound male cast though none of the performances rise above the dull scripting, which recycles the clichés of the genre without brio.

Claude Brasseur is the chief, a professional mercenary; Bernard-Pierre Donnadieu, a former French military officer and champion sharpshooter; Gérard Darmon, a light-fingered safe-cracker; Niels Arestrup, a cancer-stricken explosives expert; Daniel Duval, a gypsy who can tame watch-dogs, etc. Professional mountain climber Patrick Edlinger plays the alpinist who leads the men up the steep rock-face. Edward Meeks is the double-faced NATO attaché who supervises the unit's formation and training and later their elimination. Lisa Kreuzer has a superfluous cameo as a double agent who infiltrates the terrorist lair.

Giovanni is a veteran novelist and filmmaker whose own experiences on the wrong side of the law and prison during his youth provided fascinating matter for a number of books on criminal mentality and the carceral universe (his 1957 novel, "Le Trou," was brilliantly adapted to the screen, with Giovanni's help, by Jacques Becker).

As helmer however Giovanni has increasingly tended to trade on movieland sentimentality about tender-tough adventurers and outsiders. "Les Loups Entre Eux" is one more flabby ode to virile masculinity.—*Len.*

Love Scenes
(COLOR)

Adult soap opera look at filmmaking.

A Playboy Programs presentation of a Starways Pictures production. Produced by Vernon P. Becker. Directed by Bud Townsend. Features entire cast. Screenplay, C. Panning Master; camera (color), Tony Forsberg; editor, Bruce Stubblefield; music, Ted Scotti; sound, Rob Newell; assistant director, Bill Tasgal; production manager, John O'Connor; production design, George Costello; art direction, Jay Burkhart; set decoration, Maria Caso, Renee Johnston; casting, Bob Morones, Dee Dee Bradley. Reviewed on vidcassette, N.Y., Jan. 11, 1986. (MPAA Rating: R.) Running time: **90 MINS.**

Val	Tiffany Bolling
Peter Binnes	Franc Luz
Melinda	Julie Newmar
Sydney	Jack Carter
Rick	Daniel Pilon
Don	John Warner Williams
Annie	Britt Ekland

Also with: Susann Benn, Carol Ann Susi, Dante D'Andre, Laura Sorrenson, Monique Gabrielle, Michael Collins, Lisa Zebro, Dee Dee Bradley, John Eby, David Ursin.

"Love Scenes" is a behind-the-scenes look at filmmaking, styled as a soap opera with nudity and simulated sex scenes included (since the feature was made for The Playboy Channel). Shot in 1983, pic was cablecast by Playboy last fall and has recently been programmed by another cable service, Cinemax.

Tiffany Bolling, a promising starlet over a decade ago and now a handsome, mature woman, toplines in a story which plays like Blake Edwards' "S.O.B.," but without the intended humor and acid satire. Val (Bolling) is a bankable Hollywood star eventually won over by her director husband Peter (Franc Luz) and his agent-producer Sydney (Jack Carter) to star in a frankly erotic feature penned by former actress Melinda (Julie Newmar).

Though the film project, entitled "Lovescene," is aimed for a hard-R rating, Val becomes aroused in her first love scene with costar Rick (Daniel Pilon), resulting in tastefully filmed footage of an actual sex act, complete with her having an orgasm. Complicating matters is the fact, which Val confides to her photographer pal Annie (Britt Ekland), that she has been faking the big O with hubbie Peter throughout their five-year marriage.

Film suffers from overly predictable story development, with Melinda quitting as rewrites alter her original screenplay conception, Val having an affair off-camera with Rick and ultimately making up with her husband. Also, as often happens in backstage stories, the film-within-a-film is uninteresting and often merely an excuse to get in some more sex scenes. At times it seems that the issues raised would have relevance only to Bo and John Derek, though they would likely be amused at the old-fashioned hang-ups presented here. Ironically, "Love Scenes" had "Ecstasy" as its alternate title, the same alternate title (spelled differently) used by the Dereks briefly for their "Bolero" film.

Bolling gives an uninhibited performance featuring frequent nudity but hampered by the gauche soap opera acting style which permeates the project. Costar Luz is miscast, coming off as way too laidback for the dramatic scenes. Director Bud Townsend, best known for helming several horror pics, "Coach" and the 1976 porno version of "Alice In Wonderland," does a competent job but despite the subject matter errs on the side of blandness.—*Lor.*

The Unheard Music
(DOCU-COLOR)

A Skouras Pictures release of an Angel City production. Produced by Christopher Blakeley. Coproducer, Everett Greaton. Directed, written by W.T. Morgan. Stars X. Camera (CFI color), Karen John Monsour; editor, Charlie Mullin, Kent Beyda, Curtiss Clayton, Morgan; music, X: original songs, John Doe, Exene Cervenka; production design, Alizabeth Foley; sound, (Dolby), John Huck, Greaton; associate producers, Foley, Morgan; additional photography, Marino Colmano. Reviewed at the Egyptian Theater (U.S. Film Festival), Park City, Utah, Jan. 24, 1986. (MPAA Rating: R.) Running time: **83 MINS.**
> With: John Doe, Exene Cervenka, Billy Zoom, D.J. Bonebrake, Ray Manzarek, Rodney Bingenheimer, Brendan Mullen, Frank Gargani, Alizabeth Foley, Denis Zoom, Dinkey Bonebrake, Bob Biggs, Al Bergamo, Joe Smith, Robert Hilburn, Jello Biafra, Tom Hadges.

Park City, Utah — This long-in-the-works documentary look at the Los Angeles-based rock group X is a frequently imaginative, even striking, piece of work. In some ways, however, it is also curiously evasive and incomplete, which might leave some of the band's hardcore fans somewhat dissatisfied. Technical quality and first-rate sound represent strong points, and lively pic has some decent theatrical potential in carefully selected venues before hitting possibly more lucrative ancillary markets.

Since sprouting as part of the L.A. punk scene in 1978, the four-member group has been a perennial critics' favorite that, despite intense loyalty among its fans, has never really crossed over to gain mass acceptance.

Using a disciplined shotgun approach embracing concert footage, interviews, home movies, photographic montages, dramatic docu recreations, tv show clips and many 1950s cultural artifacts, writer-director W.T. Morgan has put together an evocative pastiche which nevertheless fails to illuminate what made X speical among countless punk bands.

After briefly introducing the band members and establishing lead singer Exene Cervenka's credentials as a natural-born poetess, Morgan deftly charts X's rise out of the bowels of the hardcore The Masque club via vastly amusing interviews with former club manager Brendan Mullen and member of the Doors turned-producer Ray Manzarek.

Once X has been launched in a chronological sense, however, pic's fabric begins to become undone. Interesting and provocative at first, Morgan's use of superficially unrelated newsreel and television footage as visual counterpoints to the songs becomes over-elaborated, and eventually threatens to take over the picture.

Increasingly, one hungers to see more concert footage. Further, music scenesters will expect some insight into the evolution of the relationship between Exene and her husband-collaborator John Doe. Famous and perhaps unique within the punk world for extolling the virtues of marriage, the pair saw their personal union fall apart, but came through it well enough to keep the band together.

Perhaps certain constraints were put upon Morgan by the couple, but it remains amazing that an uninitiated viewer could watch the film and never learn the two were ever married, or even together.

Similarly, one gets little sense of how the other band members, Billy Zoom and D.J. Bonebrake, relate to one another and the others, why they play the music they do, or where they may be headed artistically. The hardcore punk scene depicted here is already history, but the internal evidence offered by the film gives little indication of how the group is handling this.

Still, for anyone who likes X's music or who might enjoy a retrospective look back at the club scene of the late 1970s, film proves sufficiently diverting. Despite the shortcomings, Morgan displays a sympathetic affinity for the band and an often dazzling imagination and technique.

A title card at the beginning reads, "Play This Movie Loud." Certainly, no one coming to see it would want it any other way, and the parade of X's greatest hits is heard to maximum advantage under the circumstances. —Cart.

Forest Of Bliss
(DOCU-COLOR-16m)

A production of Film Study Center, Harvard U. Produced by Robert Gardner and Akos Ostor. Directed, photographed (color, 16m) and edited by Gardner. Sound, Ned Johnston. Reviewed at C.W. Post (L.I. U.), N.Y., Jan. 25, 1986. (No MPAA Rating.) Running time: 90 MINS.

"Forest Of Bliss" was a winner in December of the Golden Marzocco at the 26th annual ethnographic Festival Dei Popoli, second win there by Prof. Robert Gardner, anthropologist at Harvard.

Gardner's newest film took him to Benares, India's holy city on the Ganges, for 10 weeks of filming, af-

ter many earlier visits.

Benares seems to have only one industry and preoccupation — death. Death is everywhere. Cremation is a lifestyle, it's big business, it helps support the living. This theme is expressed in the film's opening titles, quoting Yeats — "Everything in the world is eater or eaten, the seed is food and the fire is eater."

Both savage and spiritual, Benares is a strange city of wild dogs attacking and eating one another, of endless parades of mourners bearing shrouded bodies down steep roads to the burning ghats at the river.

Connecting these images are three men — a genial healer, who tends the sick and dying; a priest who performs sacred rites; and the boss of the cremation grounds, who sells sacred fire and grass to grieving families.

"Forest Of Bliss" is a natural for public tv and can do well abroad, presenting no language problems and wisely avoiding didactic narration. — Hitch.

La Galette du Roi
(A Piece Of The Royal Pie)
(FRENCH-COLOR)

An AMLF-Hachette Première release of a Hachette Première/Partner's Prod./MG Prod. coproduction. Produced by Ariel Zeitoun. Directed by Jean-Michel Ribes. Screenplay, Ribes, Roland Topor; camera (Fujicolor), François Catonné; editor, Geneviève Winding; music, Vladimir Cosma; art director, Pierre Gompertz; sound, Christian Vallée; production manager, Bernard Bouix. Reviewed at the Havas screening room, Neuilly-sur-Seine, Jan. 24, 1986. Running time: 90 MINS.
Arnold III . . . . Jean Rochefort
Victor Harris . . . . Roger Hanin
Maria-Héléna . . . . Pauline Lafont
Utte of Denmark . . . . Jacques Villeret
Jo Longo . . . . Eddy Mitchell
L'Elégant . . . . Jean-Pierre Bacri
Leo . . . . Pierre-Loup Rajot
Clermont . . . . Philippe Khorsand
Costerman . . . . Claude Pieplu
Jeremie . . . . Christophe Bourseiller
Morrisson . . . . Jess Hahn

Paris — Only months after the witless "Marriage Of The Century," here is another send up of royal weddings. "La Galette du Roi," scripted by director Jean-Michel Ribes and caricaturist Roland Topor. It's better cast and considerably more spirited than "Marriage," but there's not enough bite and cinematic imagination to keep it going for a full feature's entertainment.

Ribes and Topor come up with a mythical Mediterranean island kingdom, Corsalina, whose suave but spineless monarch (Jean Rochefort) is preparing the marriage of his beautiful daughter (Pauline Lafont) with the nudnik son of a self-made millionaire businessman (Roger Hanin).

Neither knows the other is deep in debt, however and both are counting on this marriage of convenience to pull them out of the red. Roche-

fort, an inveterate gambler, has lost millions to a Mafioso-crooner (Eddy Mitchell) and has desperately sold exclusive tv coverage rights on the wedding to the Americans. Hanin, whose affairs are on the verge of bankruptcy, plans to refloat his deep-freeze business with the royal dowry — half the island of Corsaline — which he already has presold to a powerful Arab magnate.

Script is more disposed to broad comedy than satire and the gags more often than not fall flat. Ribes, whose debut feature in 1979, "Rien Ne Va Plus," was a sketch film derivative of his café-theater background, is more assured technically here, but has not really sharpened his sense of visual humor.

Most amusing sequences revolve around the hapless trio of second-rate security men who are hired to escort the paranoid Hanin to the wedding. As played with brio and sure comic timing by Philippe Khrosand, Jean-Pierre Bacri and Pierre-Loup Rajot, they provide the punch missing from the rest of the story. Another standout performance comes from Eddy Mitchell, the rock singer, whose comedic abilities are just waiting for the right leading part, script and director.

Tech credits are fine, with handsome locations lensed around Lake Como. —Len.

Diggers
(DOCU-COLOR/B&W-16m)

A film by Diggers Prods., N.Y. Produced and directed by Roman J. Foster. Camera (color), Richard Adams, Vincent Galindez, Karma Stanley; editor, Joseph Burton; sound, Clive Davidson, Jonathan Weld; music, Ken McIntyre; narration written by Mel Williamson; narrator, Brock Peters; historical consultants, Dr. George Priestley, Dr. George Westerman. Reviewed at C.W. Post (L.I.U.), N.Y. Jan. 28, 1986. (No MPAA Rating.) Running time: 90 MINS.

They were called "diggers," 100,-000 black laborers from Jamaica and Barbados, some of them teenagers, who came to Panama to dig the big ditch connecting the two oceans. Some 30,000 died of disease and construction accidents.

Roman Foster's "Diggers" reconstructs the work of these black laborers through old photographs, drawings, stock footage, fragments of newsreels and travelogs, and most important from the testimony on-camera of 12 diggers, age 86-96, three of whom died during the filming. These old men recall their youth in Panama, years of hardship in jungle heat, beset by voracious insects, decimated by cholera, malaria, smallpox, dysentery and the dreaded yellow fever, discriminated against by their racist white masters, who overworked and underpaid them.

The diggers in the film describe how they were paid 10¢ an hour, 10 hours a day, six days a week —

some earning more for working closely with dynamite. After 500 working days, a digger earned his passage home. Many stayed and became, in effect, Panamanians, some working 35 or 45 years maintaining the completed canal, then retired on tiny pensions. There were no disability payments to "aliens" injured on the job. Some Chinese, Europeans, Hispanics and Louisiana blacks also worked on the canal, but most diggers were West Indian blacks, bossed by the engineers of the U.S. Army.

"Diggers" ends with recent news footage of labor organizing in the Canal Zone. Also seen are treaty ceremonies between Panama and the U.S., negotiated under ex-President Jimmy Carter, formalizing the end of U.S. control of the big ditch by the year 2000.

"Diggers" is the first film of Roman Foster, whose grandfathers were diggers and who was born in Panama. It is more than an impressive debut film and greatly contributes to the documentation of our own history, produced not a minute too soon, as the last of these diggers are dying. Finally, "Diggers" is a moral lesson about uncomplaining hard work, survival, pride in accomplishment — satisfactions not diminished by the injustices they endured. — Hitch.

Morrhar & ärtor
(Cat's Whiskers & Green Peas)
(SWEDISH-COLOR)

An SF release of Cinema Art (Christer Abrahamsen), SF, Filmteknik and Deadline production. Executive producer, Christer Abrahamsen. Directed by Gösta Ekman with Rolf Börlind. Screenplay, Ekman, Börlind; camera (Eastmancolor), Lars Björne; editor, Jan Persson; music, Stefan Nilsson; production design, Gert Wibe. Stars Gösta Ekman, Margaretha Krook, Lena Nyman. Reviewed at the Grand, Copenhagen, Feb. 3, 1986. Running time: 101 MINS.
Claes-Henrik (Double H) Ahlhagen
. . . . Gösta Ekman
Mamma . . . . Margaretha Krook
Boel . . . . Lena Nyman
Crille . . . . Kent Andersson
The Principal . . . . Sten Ljunggren
Tompa . . . . Claes Jansson
Lina . . . . Sanna Ekman
Also with; Robert Sjöblom, Margareta Pettersson, Iwa Boman, Peter Huttner, Wallis Grahn, Börje Nyberg, Carl-Axel Elfving.

Copenhagen — In his helmer debut, the farcical comedy "Cat's Whiskers & Green Peas," popular actor Gösta Ekman has cast himself as Double H, timid layabout son of a domineering mother. He's a would-be flim-flam man but mostly out of luck, and perennial hopeful for a quick sexual conquest without strings. His impressive monicker has only to do with the odd occurrence of two h's in his real surname, otherwise he is thoroughly mild mannered and devoted to practical jokes to distract from the harsh realities of his life.

Film relates a few days in the non-career of luckless Double H who cannot pay his rent, but who sees a chance at making a fast buck when a team of porno filmmakers wants to borrow his mother's big apartment in Stockholm for three days of shooting.

Double H tries to get his mom out of the way by offering her a country holiday with some relatives. Mother and son reach the railroad station where everything starts going amiss, and a long sequence in a sleeping compartment has some of the happy insanity about it of the famous ocean steamer stateroom sequence in the Marx Bros.' "A Night At The Opera" although considerably fewer people are involved.

Mom gets left on the platform in her nightie when the train pulls out, and Double H finds himself in the lower berth without a ticket and with a jolly little near-middle-age woman in the upper. Together, they become involved in a bottle of Irish whiskey and later some screwball romance.

Toward the end, Double H finally tears himself out of mommy's clutches and jumps into the new woman's arms. His life will hardly be less complicated, but the whole story has been told without cloying sentimentality, sustaining a note of the farcical and the bizarre.

Film's title has to do with a daydreaming scheme to do away with mommy by using an old Spanish murder recipe: you cut the tips of a cat's whiskers and insert them in green peas which you later serve with the victim's meal. When the peas have been digested, the cat's whiskers will enter the blood stream and cause an untraceable heart failure. No such death actually occurs. Film remains lighthearted all the way and never sacrifices the credibility of its characters.

Dialog is sparse and the story well told visually. If "Cat's Whiskers" gains limited access to offshore theaters in its Swedish version, dubbed editions could work wonders.—*Kell.*

The Global Assembly Line
(DOCU-COLOR)

Produced by Lorraine Gray, Anne Bohlen, Maria Patricia Fernandez Kelly. Directed by Lorraine Gray. Associate producers, Beatriz Vera, Rachael Grossman, Judy Davis; camera (color), Sandi Sissel, Baird Bryant, Lorraine Gray; editor, Mary Lampson, Sara Fishko; sound, Michael Boyle, Kathleen King; music, Steven Gray. Reviewed at the AFI Screening Room (Kennedy Center), Washington, D.C., Jan. 9, 1986. (No MPAA Rating.) Running time: **62 MINS.**

Washington — From the makers of the well received "With Babies And Banners" comes this indictment of the exploitation of the primarily female labor force in the developing world.

Lorraine Gray toured the factories to interview assembly line workers throughout the world as well as the American businessmen who are lowering their labor costs by moving their manufacturing to off-shore facilities in places such as Manila, Mexico, Taiwan, and Korea. In interviews, the industrialists from Zenith, Interlek, and several Silicon Valley companies state the economic arguments as clearly as possible, but these people are such stereotypes of capitalist exploiters that they elicited hoots and derision at the premiere screening. The international consortium reps may seem set up by the filmmakers.

The profit motive means that workers in the Philippines earn about 5% of what American laborers would make. Yet cheap labor keeps prices down in the highly competitive American marketplace, whose sympathies are not explored in the film.

The helmer explores the sad consequences for the jobless in a Tennessee town that the Philips Corp. is abandoning. She takes Filipino discontent seriously in lengthy interviews contrasting conditions and wages. She had the luck or what could only be called serendipity to cull a quote from Imelda Marcos, who announces that she has been in the U.S. and discovered that Americans love Filipino workers, because "only beautiful products can come from happy people."

The plight of Gray's oppressed workers is made to seem all the more miserable next to the disingenuous management and the "let them eat cake" approach of their oppressors. It is a sobering survey, intelligently conducted, but it doesn't make us want to pay more for beautiful products from happy people. —*Kaja.*

El Caballero del Dragon
(The Knight Of The Dragon)
(SPANISH-COLOR)

A Cinetel release (U.S.) of a Salamandra production. Produced and directed by Fernando Colomo. Executive producer, Carlos Orengo. Associate producer, Ana Huete. Screenplay, Andreu Martín, Miguel Angel Nieto, Colomo; camera (Eastmancolor), José Luis Alcaine; editor, M.A. Santamaría; music, José Nieto; production design, Enric Ventura; art director, Félix Murcia; special effects, Reyes Abades; optical effects, Oscar Núñez and Chuck Comisky; costumes; sound, James Willis; Javier Artiñano. Reviewed at Cine Avenida, Madrid, Jan. 5, 1986. Running time: **90 MINS.**

Boetius	Klaus Kinski
Clever	Harvey Keitel
Fray Lupo	Fernando Rey
Alba	Maria Lamor
Count of Ruc	José Vivó
Ix	Miguel Bosé

Also with: Julieta Serrano, José María Pou, Carlos Tristancho, Santiago Alvarez.
(Spanish soundtrack; also available with English soundtrack)

Madrid — Director Fernando Colomo, known in the past for such wry comedies as "La mano negra" and "Skyline," here turns his whimsical talent to a yarn about a medieval village visited by an extraterrestrial. Although by internation-

al standards the special effects, sets and occasional swordplay are far from spectacular, Colomo fills in the shortcomings by winning humor and amusing performances by his cast.

Klaus Kinski is aptly cast as a necromancer and alchemist, whose arch-enemy is a bigoted priest (Fernando Rey); both try to curry the favors of a doddering count (José Vivó), while a bumbling knight (Harvey Keitel) seeks the hand of the count's pretty daughter. The local intrigues are upstaged by the supposed appearance of a dragon in the region, which in truth is an ET arriving in a flying saucer. The being from outer space (Miguel Bosé) is clad in a space suit with a bubble around the head, which enables us to see his face, but Bosé never gets to utter a single word throughout the film.

The spaceman and the count's daughter fall in love, and after various misadventures, the former gets to meet the local power clique. At the end, the priest and the knight are whisked off into space in the flying saucer, while the ET, after being slain, is revived by the necromancer, knighted and given the hand of the pretty countess. All of the scenes are done tongue-in-cheek, as a kind of fable, with the priest cast as the heavy. Unlike what the Monty Python group did with the subject, there is never any violence nor melodrama.

This is the film's weakness. It is amusingly blah, an innocuous, occasionally droll fable, but one that never packs a punch. Some offshore sales might be racked up on basis of the international cast, but mellowness of story will limit any wider appeal. —*Besa.*

Fracchia Contro Dracula
(Fracchia Vs. Dracula)
(ITALIAN-COLOR)

A Titanus release. Produced by Bruno Altissimi and Claudio Saraceni for Maura Intl. Film and Faso Film. Directed by Neri Parenti. Stars Paolo Villaggio. Screenplay, Laura Toscano, Franco Marotta, Villaggio, Parenti; camera (color), Luciano Tovoli; editor, Sergio Montanari; art director, Giovanni Licheri; music, Bruno Zambrini. Reviewed at Cola di Rienzo Cinema, Rome, Jan. 1, 1986. Running time: **91 MINS.**

Fracchia	Paolo Villaggio
Filini	Gigi Reder
Dracula	Edmond Purdom
Countess Oniria	Ania Pieroni

Also with: Isabella Ferrari, Giuseppe Cederna, Filippo Degare, Romano Puppo, Federica Brion.

Rome — "Fracchia Vs. Dracula" is one of those embarrassing misfires that looks like a hard sell even to insomniacs on late-night tv. On its maiden voyage around the first-run circuit it has fared poorly. Fans of Paolo Villaggio's wonderful characters (Fracchia is an alter-ego incarnation of the better-known Fantozzi) would do well to sail around it.

Little thought has gone into working out new twists to this creaky Dracula spoof done so much better elsewhere. Villaggio, the short, funny-faced veteran comic who has often shown a propensity for tackling old movies as comic vehicles, gets almost nothing out of Transylvanian lore. The best gag comes in the first five minutes, when watching a chiller at the movies with his girlfriend, back turned and eyes shut, Fracchia overturns a row of seats that knocks down the next dozen rows like dominoes. Simple and original, the joke gets a much bigger laugh than what follows.

Fracchia is a bumbling real estate agent whose boss is going to fire him if he doesn't make a sale within three days. The only prospective client is Filini (Gigi Reder), old-fashioned, blind as a bat, and convinced he can buy a five-bedroom vacation house for $3,000. The only piece of property going for that price is a castle in Transylvania, and the two take off to examine it.

The rest is not hard to guess. Helmer Neri Parenti rallies his resources and makes a decent stab at atmosphere on a limited budget, aided by a great castle and the decision to make some special effects deliberately tacky, like puppet bats squeaking through the skies. After Edmund Purdom's classic Dracula sneers through a few scenes at our ignorant heroes, and his sister Countess Oniria (Ania Pieroni) makes lascivious eyes at the still-virginal Fracchia, Frankenstein turns up, then a pretty blond ghostbuster (Isabella Ferrara), then a horde of zombies. Villaggio's absurdist humor makes no headway in this make-believe world. As an indestructible character who can fall off castle walls without getting scratched, he needs a real environment to come off funny. In "Dracula" he's just another monster.— *Yung.*

Disconnected
(COLOR)

♪ Okay regional horror film.

A Reel Movies Intl. release of a Generic Films production. Executive producer, Bob Stewart. Produced and directed by Gorman Bechard. Features entire cast. Screenplay, Virginia Gilroy, Bechard, from story by Gilroy; camera (Du Art color, 16m), Bechard; editor, Bechard; music, Steve Asetta; sound, Bill LaCapra; assistant director-associate producer, Carmine Capobianco. Reviewed on Active Home Video vidcassette, N.Y., Jan. 1, 1986. (No MPAA Rating.) Running time: **81 MINS.**

Alicia/Barbara Ann	Frances Raines
Franklin	Mark Walker
Mike	Carl Koch
Lt. O'Donovan	Ben Page
Trimaglio	Carmine Capobianco

"Disconnected" is a low-budget horror film made by locals in Waterbury, Conn., which tries to surmount the clichés of the genre, but emerges as a routine picture. One-man filmmaker Gorman

Bechard shows some style, especially in flashy insert shots, but needs to come up with more original material.

Frances Raines toplines as Alicia Michaels, a young woman who works as a sales clerk at Valley Video, a homevideo store. She's had a fight with her deejay boyfriend Mike (Carl Koch), accusing him of having slept with her twin sister Barbara Ann (also played by Raines), and now a young guy Franklin (Mark Walker) keeps hanging around Valley Video trying to get a date with Alicia.

Meanwhile, the cops are investigating a series of slasher murders, with evidence (shown to viewer but not known to the cops) implicating Franklin. Alicia is plagued by annoying phone calls that feature harsh noises. She also becomes involved romantically with Franklin.

Although Bechard plants some interesting clues in the opening reel, plotline goes haywire when Franklin is seduced by twin Barbara Ann, murders her and then, in a poorly designed scene (it's largely omitted, referred to verbally later) is killed by the cops. The killings continue after Franklin's death with an open-ended finale pointing at the real killer.

Bechard's exposition scenes, particularly with the lackadaisical cops, continually mock the rigid format of slasher films, but ultimately his picture lapses into these clichés, such as the overuse of the phone call gimmick. Leading lady Raines, who has been featured in many B-films of late, is impressive in her dual role, combining vulnerability with the ambiguity of possible madness necessary in a ''Repulsion''-type heroine. —*Lor.*

La Jeune Fille et l'Enfer
(The Young Girl And Hell)
(FRENCH-SPANISH-COLOR)

An Orphée release of an Orphée Arts-Accord Prods.-Producciones Balcazar coproduction. Produced by Lucien Duval. Directed by François Mimet. Screenplay, Jean-Claude Carrière; camera (Eastmancolor), Juan Gelpi; editor, Michel Lewin; music, Michel Stelio, Fernand Boudou; sound, Juan Quilis; art director, Yves Brover; production manager, Antonio Liza. Reviewed at the Paramount City Triomphe theater, Paris, Jan. 27, 1986. Running time: 85 MINS.
With: Philippe Etesse, Florence Guérin, Assumpta Serna, Manuel Serra.

Paris — Made in 1984, this soporific tale of eroticism is only now emerging in a confidential release by its producing firm, which has been involved in the ''Emmanuelle'' and ''Madame Claude'' series. It's only noteworthy aspect is that it was written by Jean-Claude Carrière, the talented (and often overactive) screenwriter. This looks like something from the bottom of a crowded drawer of unproduced scripts.

Tale is set in Spain where a youngish university prof has come to spend some time with an old school chum, now living with his ripe teenage daughter from a first marriage, and his second wife, whom he neglects for extramarital sexual pursuits.

The two friends stir up old memories when they pore over rare editions of classic libertine literature that are still locked away in the library's locked cache (the ''hell'' of the title).

When the nubile daughter (Florence Guérin, seen in last year's erotic item, ''Turn-On'') learns of the books, she coaxes the timid prof into giving her late night readings. Pretty soon (though not soon enough to forestall viewer boredom) they are in the sack for the girl's unsentimental education. The teacher also gets to service his friend's lonely and frustrated wife before his own mate departs with baby to put an end to his hedonistic interlude.

Maybe Jean-Luc Godard would have made sometime really piquant from on-screen readings of truly bawdy literature, but director François Mimet is content to film tritely. —*Len.*

Movie House Massacre
(COLOR)

Amateurish horror spoof.

A Movie House Prods. production. Produced and directed by Alice Raley. Features entire cast. Screenplay, Raley; camera (color), Bill Fishman; editor, uncredited; music, uncredited; sound, Steve Williams. Reviewed on Active Home Video vidcassette, N.Y., Jan. 8, 1986. (No MPAA Rating.) Running time: 75 MINS.
With: Mary Woronov, Jonathan Blakely, Lynne Darcy, Cynthia Hartline, Lisa Lindsley, Pam McCormack, Joni Barnes, Laurie Tidemanson, Barrie Metz, Terry Taylor, Joe Howard, Alice Raley, Bruce Nangle, Kim Clayton, Sam Bowe, Dee-Dee Hoffman.

''Movie House Massacre,'' made in 1984, is an unimpressive spoof of horror films which went directly to the homevideo market, bypassing theatrical release. Despite the presence of accomplished actress Mary Woronov, it plays like amateur night at the bijou.

Gimmick is a presumably haunted movie theater (originally a legit theater house), where many years ago the manager went nuts, started a fire (creating a panic) and stabbed the ticket booth girl to death. Now the owner of the 11-screen Spotlite Theaters chain attempts to reopen the accursed place, sending three hapless employees to clean up the site for a big opening night. Supposedly he will get a $25,000 reward from parties unknown for daring to reopen the joint.

Hokey subplot has one of the employees being a school cheerleader, so her fellow cheerleaders can visit her at the theater and become standard victims of the ghostly killer.

Body count mounts until a botched nonending.

Filmmaker Alice Raley demonstrates an ignorance of rudimentary technique, with poorly matched shots, minimal sound mix and incompetent editing. Woronov keeps busy with irrelevant bits of business as the theater owner's assistant, but the rest of the cast is blah. Location filming at the Beverly Theater in Beverly Hills and Fairfax Theater in Los Angeles delivers some atmosphere.

If ''Massacre'' had been released theatrically, exhibitors would not have been pleased by its silly injokes, emphasizing a corrupt theater owner who is more interested in videotaping bootleg versions of films off his screen than in satisfying his (less lucrative) filmgoing clientele. — *Lor.*

The Riverbed
(U.S./DUTCH-COLOR-16m)

A Film Intl. release of a Rachel Reichman/VPRO production. Produced, directed, written and edited by Reichman. Camera (color, 16m), Steven Giuliano; music, Josh Colow. Reviewed at Desmet Theater, Amsterdam, Jan. 21, 1986. Running time: 95 MINS.
The Man . . . . John Beuscher
Mother . . . . Elaine Grove
Daughter . . . . Sharon Bellanoff-Smith

Amsterdam — St. Louis-born Rachel Reichman's ''The Riverbed'' is a fable, a folk story, situated in the American South during the Depression.

A young man travels around, seeking work. He's not above swiping money from a cash register, but he's not really bad, rather a kind of half-honest con man.

He gets a job with a widow who has a teenage daughter. The girl is mentally disturbed; she never speaks. She's retarded and has fantasies about water: rivers, ponds, lakes.

Mother, in a polite way, offers the man money to marry the daughter and take her away. The man respectfully accepts. The marriage is never consummated. It's more of a father-daughter relationship. Times are bad, no work to be found, no money left.

The girl does not mind. She has her fantasies: soft, clear water surrounding her. In the end the man takes her in his arms, wades into a pond, lets her sink onto the riverbed. It's not clear if she is still alive while he does it. It is clear that he means her no harm. There's no question of murder. He performs a ritual. He restores quiet and order by putting her where she belongs.

Rotterdam Fest director Huub Bals saw Rachel's work on this film lensed in 1983 and brought it to the attention of tv-station VPRO in Holland. They furnished the money needed to finish the picture.

Reichman has the gift to convey people, their motives and feelings through images. Helped by the camerawork of Steven Giuliano, pic focuses on bearings, postures, but mainly on people's expressive and insinuating movements.

John Beuscher (pious forehead, brutal chin) is the only one with any acting training. He's very good, as are Sharon Bellanoff-Smith in the difficult part of the daughter and Elaine Grove as the mother. Dialog is used sparingly. ''Natural'' sounds are put to good effect. The music, partly folk songs, partly composed, is an important component.

''The Riverbed'' has faults. Some shots, put in for their visual beauty, detract from the story. Some sequences would benefit from tightening. All in all Reichman's fairy tale is an extremely auspicious helming debut.—*Wall.*

Le Médecin de Gafiré
(The Doctor Of Gafiré)
(NIGERIAN-MALIAN-COLOR)

A Lasa Films release of a Dipka-Film (Nigeria)/ORTN (Nigeria)/CNPC (Mali) coproduction. Written and directed by Mustapha Diop. Camera (color), Yousouf Djibo; editor, Hubert Martin; sound, Abdoulaye Dia, Harouna Diarra; music, Mali instrumental ensemble. Reviewed at the UGC Marbeuf, Paris, Jan. 19, 1986. Running time: 92 MINS.
With: Sidiki Bakaba, Marlin N'Diagne, Fifi Dalla Kouyate, Hima Adamou, Djingarey Miaga, Sotigui Kouyate, Djeneba Dao, Harouna Diarra, Mustapha Diop.

Paris — A fable about tradition vs. modernity, this Nigerian-Malian coproduction, made in 1984, is getting a theatrical release in Paris via new art film distrib Lasa Films. Despite the laudable intentions to impose Third World filmmaking on the art circuit, it seems too slight an effort to make commercial headway outside of home markets and festival screenings.

Script by director, Mustapha Diop, who also plays a supporting part, tells of a young African doctor, trained in France, who is sent to an isolated village to practice. He is accompanied by his wife, who teaches the local youngsters French.

His practice is menaced immediately by the presence of a renowned local witch doctor, who shows up the at first incredulous newcomer with some magical healings. The physician decides that if you can't beat 'em, join 'em, and becomes the sorcerer's disciple. Latter surpasses his master in black magic when, after being poisoned by the witch doctor for having made notes of the tribal teachings in view of making them available to others, he comes up with a last minute antidote.

Diop's direction has the leisurely pace of a folk tale, but the scripting is sketchy and the acting, with the exception of Sidiki Bakaba's single-mindedly convincing sorcerer, inadequate. At average feature running time, it seems like an appealing

idea for a medium-length picture that got unnecessarily distended.
—*Len.*

Señor Turista
(WEST GERMAN-DOCU-COLOR-16m)

A Gerlinde Böhm Film production, Berlin. A documentary written and directed by Böhm, assisted by Liz Gutte. Camera (color), Clemens Frohmann; sound & editor, Michael J. Küspert; collaborators, Rolf Wittwer, Vera-Lynn Sorrentino; Samuel Elray Wooten; musical accompaniment, "Grupo Mitimaes." Reviewed at Filmbühne am Steinplatz, Berlin, Jan. 19, 1986. Running time: 86 MINS.

Berlin — Every now and then, a young, inexperienced filmmaker in Germany will pack a camera in a suitcase and journey to a far corner of the world to shoot an original documentary of an ethnographic nature.

Gerlinde Böhm began her film career as an editor and assistant director, but her studies in ethnology and Latin American affairs whetted her appetite to make a film on the Indios living on the shores and islands of Lake Titicaca in Peru. Three years ago, January-May 1983, she prepared her project, then spent six months living among the natives later that year. The actual shoot for "Señor Turista" took only two months — upon its completion last January, it made the rounds of several fests.

The docu's first cut proved too long and ambling, but after its initial test with a well-informed audience at the Intl. Forum of Young Cinema last year, Böhm has come up with a tightly edited and quite informative thematic treatment of just over 80 minutes. The strength of the film is that it doesn't preach, but simply tells a story with pictures for the most part.

Lake Titicaca is the largest and highest lake in South America, situated between Peru and Bolivia. Small steamboats cross from La Paz Bolivia, to reach a railway system in Peru for a connection with ports on the Pacific. The traffic brings its fair share of tourists, and it's the arrival of these tourists that is hinted at ironically in the title.

Böhm shows two different worlds clash when tourists invade the floating islands of the Uros Indios to take pictures and buy woven baskets and other trinkets. The tourists, indeed, are the life-blood of these people, so they comply with their role — while at the same time maintaining their independence and freeing themselves of various forms of slavery and subservience to the white man.

She and her crew move on to the larger island of Taquile farther out in the lake, where a form of communal sharing has been introduced to keep the natives from being ex-

ploited by playing prices off against one another. Tourists come here to go native overnight by living in huts on a rather primitive scale.

"Señor Truista" impresses for its docu footage and is highly recommended for ethnological film outings like the Margaret Mead festival. —*Holl.*

Phei Hamered
(Flames In The Ashes)
(ISRAELI-DOCU-B&W)

A Teudah Films production for the Ghetto Fighters House. Produced by Monia Avrahami. Directed by Haim Guri and Jacquot Erlich. Historical advisers: Prof. Yehuda Baver, Mulka Baranchuk; editor Jacquot Erlich. Still photographer, Marco Yaakobi; sound, Yaacov Shem-Tov; Music, Yossi MarHaim. Reviewed at the Diaspora House, Tel Aviv, Jan. 8, 1986. Running time: 96 MINS.

Tel Aviv — A valuable addition to the documentation of the Holocaust, this is the second in a three-part cycle produced by the "Lohamey Haghettaot" Museum (in English: The Ghetto Fighters House). The earlier released "The 81st Blow" dealt mostly with the raise of antisemitism in Europe which led almost inevitably to the Holocaust and its horror, while "The Last Sea," concluding the cycle but finished previously, focused on the aftermath of the Holocaust and the survivors' effort to come back to terms with life in a land of their own.

Poet Haim Guri and editor Jacquot Erlich concentrated their efforts here in the period of the Holocaust itself, covering Europe with a thin brush to find filmed documents of which there aren't many as the Nazis themselves didn't allow movie cameras in the extermination camps. Still, the footage assembled is terrible enough to leave little to the imagination, and at least some of it is unveiled here for the first time, such as the images of Ukrainian peasants torturing Jewish deportees.

The thrust of Guri and Erlich is to prove that the generally approved concept maintaining that Holocaust victims let themselves be butchered without lifting a finger is historically inaccurate, and that wherever there was the slightest chance of putting on some sort of resistance, the victims did fight to the bitter end.

The soundtrack consists once again, as it did in the previously released parts of this trilogy, only of testimonies from survivors, taken separately and sometimes converging in an eerie fashion with the images on the screen. This has been the basic idea behind the entire project ("The 81st Blow" soundtrack was only excerpts from the recording of the Eichmann trial) and quite often, when the visual documents presented are familiar to the eye, the impact

of the living witnesses heard behind them lends a totally new dimension.

Museums, archives, cinematheques and TV programmers are bound to find this most useful.
—*Edna.*

Il Mistero di Bellavista
(The Mystery Of Bellavista)
(ITALIAN-COLOR)

A Columbia release. Produced by Mario Orfini and Emilio Bolles for Eidoscope Intl. productions. Directed by Luciano De Crescenzo. Screenplay, De Crescenzo, Riccardo Pazzaglia, based on a novel by De Crescenzo; camera (color), Nino Celeste; editor, Anna Napoli; art director, Carlo Leva; music, Renzo Arbore, Claudio Mattone. Reviewed at Etoile Cinema, Rome, Jan. 19, 1986. Running time: 103 MINS.
Prof. Bellavista .... Luciano De Crescenzo
Cazzaniga................Renato Scarpa
The old ladies...........the Fumo sisters
Housemaid ....Marina Confalone

Rome — "The Mystery Of Bellavista" is a followup to last year's successful "Thus Spake Bellavista," based on author-helmer Luciano De Crescenzo's whimsical book of modern-day Naples lore. This second round lacks the originality and charm of its predecessor.

In "Mystery," the homey guided tour of Neapolitan philosophy for the practical man gives way to a series of sitcom dialogs that cry out for a laugh track. Patrons at onshore locations haven't reacted with much spontaneous mirth.

De Crescenzo again appears in the role of Prof. Bellavista, a dignified, white-bearded sage who is spiritual leader to a crew of neighborhood disciples — a garbage man, the housemaid, etc. While peering through a telescope in the prof's apartment, looking for Halley's Comet, they happen to spy what they think is foul play in the next building. The prof and his laid-back gang of Keystone Cops plot how to discover the murderer of the missing woman next door, and launch a series of unconvincing investigations.

The point seems to be that in Naples not even a murder mystery unwinds the way it would elsewhere. In fact, it doesn't unwind at all. When our gang notices a big chest being carried out of the suspect building, they jump in a taxi to race after it, but the usual traffic jam brings pursuers and pursued to an instant standstill. So?

Locations include a museum, where the value of modern art is tiresomely debated, and an underground monks' cemetery full of bones and skulls, used far better in other films. In a subplot, the professor's son-in-law tries to sell prefabricated fallout shelters to Naples. His only taker is a crooked Italo-American merchant who speaks in a confused cross of English and Italian. Though the comedy falls flat more often than not, there is a faint echo from the Renzo Arbore "alter-

native" tv talk shows that raises a smile. A number of the offbeat thesps are graduates of Arbore's shows and Arbore himself gets a music credit. —*Yung.*

L'Executrice
(The Executor)
(FRENCH-COLOR)

A Films Jacques Leitienne release of a Tiphany Films/Fil à Film/Zoom 24 coproduction. Produced; written and directed by Michel Caputo. Stars Brigitte Lahaie. Camera (Fujicolor), Gérard Simon; editor, Annie Lemesles, sound, Francis Baldos; reviewed at the Paramount City-Triomphe theater, Paris, Jan. 19, 1986. Running time: 87 MINS.
With: Brigitte Lahaie, Pierre Oudry, Michel Godin, Michel Modo, Dominique Erlanger, Jean-Hugues Lime.

Paris — "L'Executrice" is a cheap personal justice thriller with its protagonist a female police inspector who turns her back on law enforcement regulations when she goes gunning for the well-protected procuress who has murdered her kid sister in a kidnap plot.

Writer-director Michel Caputo is a sharpshooter for genre clichés, but is no worse on the draw than many other local helmers who boast bigger budgets and more bankable cast names.

The femme-flic is played by Brigitte Lahaie, who displayed her assets in last year's softcore slush item, "Joy And Joan." Here she displays them less.

Gérard Simon's color lensing is so dark, one wonders if Caputo takes the term *film noir* a bit too seriously, or if he wants to save his cast the embarrassment of being recognized.
—*Len.*

Killing Machine
(SPANISH-MEXICAN-COLOR)

An Embassy Home Entertainment release of a Golden Sun (Spain), Esme Intl. (Mexico) production. Produced by Carlos Vasallo. Written and directed by J. Anthony Loma (Jose Antonio de la Loma). Stars George (Jorge) Rivero, Margaux Hemingway. Camera (color), Alexander (Alejandro) Ulloa; music, Guido and Maurizio de Angelis; editor, Nicholas Wentworth; script supervisor, Robert A. Miller; stunts, Remy Julienne; international distribution, Overseas Filmgroup. Reviewed on Embassy Videodisc, Jan. 24, 1986. Running time: 95 MINS.
Chema ....George (Jorge) Rivero
Jacqueline ....Margaux Hemingway
Maitre Julot ....Lee Van Cleef
Tony ....Willie Aames
Martin ....Richard Jaeckel
Liza ....Ana Obregon
Picot ....Hugo Stiglitz

Sydney — A thoroughly routine revenge pic, "Killing Machine" was shot in Spain and France in November 1983. George (Jorge) Rivero emulates Charles Bronson as a Spanish trucker whose wife (Ana Obregon) is burned alive when his truck is set afire by French farmers at the frontier. He swears vengeance on two of the farmers, plus the lawyer who defended them. Latter is played with a malevolent sneer by Lee Van Cleef.

Pic is merely an excuse for various acts of violence. The hero is beaten to a pulp on two occasions, but emerges unscarred. Needless to say, he succeeds in eliminating his three enemies.

Viewers without some knowledge of the friction between farmers in parts of Europe over the dumping of farm produce will doubtless be baffled by the plot and, since everyone speaks English, it's sometimes hard to work out if the characters are supposed to be Spanish or French. It doesn't matter much.

An unflatteringly photographed Margaux Hemingway has little to do, and looks uncomfortable. The rest is strictly macho nonsense, as unpleasant as it is fatuous. Typical of the shoddy, careless approach of the filmmakers is that, in a scene where the hero confronts an enemy in a supposedly deserted forest, the legs of someone, presumably a crew member, are clearly to be seen dodging out of the way as the protagonists fight. Surely the production could have afforded a retake?—*Strat.*

Ballet Black
(ENGLISH-COLOR-16m)

A Stephen Dwoskin, Urbane production. Written, produced, directed, photographed (color, 16m) and edited by Dwoskin. Sound, Roger Ollerhead; music, Schaun Tozer. Features Patricia Clover, Ben Johnson, Pearl Johnson, Johnny Lagey. Reviewed at Rotterdam Film Festival, Jan. 27, 1986. Running time: **87 MINS.**

Rotterdam — Stephen Dwoskin's "Ballet Black" is about the "Ballets Nègres," the first dance group in Europe consisting entirely of (mainly Caribbean) blacks. Founded in 1946, the company created, under leader Berto Pasuka, a unique style of dance, mime and music, and had considerable influence on the development of ballet all over the world.

Although it was very successful it suddenly was dissolved in 1952. Pic explores its history and the attitudes towards and within the group.

Dwoskin arranged a meeting of original members after 35 years, and used their memories plus some reenacting of their dancing and old photographs. The veterans advised him while he reconstructed rehearsals of Ballets Nègres work with young dancers.

Dwoskin managed to blend these various parts into a well-structured whole. Film conveys the impression that something intriguing and special had been wrought by Pasuka's company. — *Wall.*

Schleuse 17
(Lock 17)
(WEST GERMAN-B&W)

A Munich Film Academy (HFF) film production. Written and directed by Sebastian Lentz. Camera (b&w), Jo Heim; music, Paul Hornyak. Reviewed at Saarbrücken Film Fest (Max Ophüls Prize competition), Jan. 22, 1986. Running time: **68 MINS.**
With: Roxane, John Cooper, George Lentz, Oliver Strietzel.

Saarbrücken — A debut feature by a grad of the Munich Film Academy, Sebastian Lentz' "Lock 17" was lensed in a village called Gien in the middle of France. It's the story of three Yanks involved in a bank robbery that bags $1,000,000 but results in the death of one of the trio during the getaway. The two remaining gunmen, John and Roy, quarrel over leaving Harry behind — so Roy momentarily gets the upper hand to escape with his share of the loot to Paris. John stays behind with his dying buddy until there's nothing more to do, save to meet Niki, a tourist guide, and promptly fall in love.

Niki is not aware that John is being hunted by the police for the bank robbery until, on a trip to Paris, he avenges himself on the hapless Roy in a shoddy hotel room. Then it's back to Gien and a police blockade along the way, which adds more spice to the soup by having a wounded John fall on the doorstep of the loving Niki. The young lady, it turns out, has a close platonic friend in the writer Kleefuss, who has the best lines in the picture as a pulp writer holed up in his villa.

Kleefus comes reluctantly to the couple's help by finding a doctor friend to help the wounded bandit back to enough health to leave the area by way of a boat through a canal lock (thus the title).

Lentz is particularly adept at directing thesps in English, German, and French. —*Holl.*

Afzien
(Abandon)
(DUTCH-COLOR-16m)

A Film Intl. release of an R. Orthel Filmproductie production. Produced by Orthel. Directed by Gerrard Verhage. Screenplay, Verhage, Gerrit van Elst, Jose Alders; camera (color, 16m), Goert Giltay; sound, Lukas Boeke; music, Bernard Hunnekink; editor, Jan Wouter van Reijen; art direction, Hadassah Kann; costumes, Inger Kolff. Reviewed at Rotterdam Film Festival, Jan. 28, 1986. Running time: **77 MINS.**

Rotterdam — "Abandon" is an astonishingly mature feature debut of Gerrard Verhage who made some excellent documentaries, especially about political and social subjects.

Pic takes place during a day and half a night in a roomy house with spacious grounds about 20-30 miles from Amsterdam. It belongs to a well-known architect (at the moment in America with a girl friend)

and his wife, who is very active in the international peace movement. The marriage is breaking up.

They're paying their son, a struggling painter, to redecorate the house before it is put on the market. Some friends of the son arrive, all in their 30s, and a thunderstorm forces them to stay longer than planned.

They are a tightly knit group who have known each other for years. Personal problems are poured out, discussed, dissected. Solid relationships show cracks, egos are dented, love is threatened by sex.

An excellent script makes it easy to follow all entanglements. Verhage creates credible parts helped by imaginative camerawork and editing. The players, all from the top echelon of young Dutch actors, give flesh and blood to their characters. The film has style and is elegant entertainment.—*Wall.*

I Love Dollars
(DUTCH/FRENCH/SWISS-DOCU-COLOR-16m)

A Film Intl. release of a VPRO Televisie, TF-I Paris, Télévision Suisse Romande, Film Intl. Rotterdam production. Produced, written, directed and photographed (color, 16m) by Johan van der Keuken. Sound, Noshka van der Lely; editor, Jan Dop, Van der Keuken; music, Willem Breuker. Reviewed at Rotterdam Film Festival, Jan. 27, 1986. Running time: **147 MINS.**

Rotterdam — Johan van der Keuken has an international reputation as an outstanding documentarist and original cinematographer. He wanted to make a film about money; the people who trade in it; the specialists who create it; and ordinary guys who need it and have to scramble for it. Pic was shot in Amsterdam, New York, Hong Kong and Geneva.

He interviewed brokers, jobbers, investment counselors, electronics manufacturers, slumdwellers etc. He let his handheld camera nose around in cities, streets and in betting shops in Hong Kong with long rows of cheerless punters in front of computer terminals.

Pic took two years to make with a low budget of $90,000. Pic is musical; it is emotional, sometimes a shade too much; pictorially, it contains some stunning shots. The helmer shows his mastery of creating tension and expectation through cunningly inserting quiet pictures of inanimate objects. Yet the handheld camera at times becomes too excited. To be fair, several cameras would be necessary to convey in a more fluent way the mad goings-on at a stock exchange in full action.—*Wall.*

Hijos de la Guerra Fria
(Children Of The Cold War)
(CHILEAN-FRENCH-COLOR)

A Conate release of an Arca (Chile) and Out One (France) production. Executive pro-

ducer, Jorge Benitez. Directed by Gonzalo Justiniano. Screenplay, Justiniano; camera (color, 16m), Jorge Arriagada; editor, Rodolfo Wedeles, Claudio Martinez; sound, Eugenio Gutierrez. Reviewed at Cine Ducal, Santiago, Jan. 4, 1986. Running time: **75 MINS.**
With: Eugenio Morales, Pachi Torreblanca, Javier Maldonado, Néstor Corona, Sonia Mena, Nené Larrain, Juan Enrique Forch, J.L. Gutty, Ernesto Muñoz, Sigfrid Polhammer.

Santiago — Winner of the opera prima award at last year's Biarritz fest, "Children Of The Cold War" was blown up to 35m for commercial release in Chile. Shot on a shoestring in 16m, the film has visual flair, but fails to overcome the handicap of an uneven screenplay that does not blend its openly symbolic material with the more realistic scenes that make up the bulk of the pic.

Action begins as the Chilean boom of the late 1970s (based on abundant foreign loans, largely squandered on consumer goods) brusquely starts to fade. Rebeca and Gaspar are lonely and frustrated. None of the characters is much to look at and there is a despondent feeling about the city (Santiago) and its rundown bars.

Gaspar works at a liquor import firm whose owner goes abroad, leaving him in charge. His shy romance with Rebeca leads to marriage but he soon discovers, with a helping hand from the police, that the business he is supposed to handle consists of nothing but debts.

From here on it's downhill all the way. Neither the couple nor their friends manage to find work until Gaspar can take it no more, explodes and sets out, first with Rebeca and others, then by himself, on what seems to be a pilgrimage. Where to and what for is by no means clear. In fact, this vague 10-minute final sequence, besides being stylistically inconsistent with the rest of the film, is likely to alienate most of the audience.

Technical credits, particularly Jorge Roth's camerawork, are satisfactory, as is the acting. Gonzalo Justiniano is a promising filmmaker, particularly in the way he visually establishes his environment and the characters' relationship with it. His film should do reasonably well on its home ground and further festival exposure is also likely.
—*Amig.*

Les Interdits du Monde
(The Forbidden Of The World)
(FRENCH-DOCU-COLOR)

A LMD release of an ATC 3000 production. Produced by Benjamin Simon. Directed by Chantal Lasbats. Commentary, Monique Pantel; camera (color), François About; music, Big Bucks; no other credits available. Reviewed at the Paramount City-Triomphe theater, Paris, Jan. 19, 1986. Running time: **82 MINS.**

Paris — "Les Interdits du Monde" is another "Mondo

Cane''-styled reportage that suggests the bottom of the barrel has been scraped. Director Chantal Lasbats apparently took her camera abroad to places like Togo and the Philippines, though she comes back to home turf (France) so often, one begins to wonder if the planet has exhausted its shock value.

In any case, what she has to spread out before our blasé eyes is insignificant: voodoo rites, Black Magic initiations are paraded across the screen with pseudo-sociological casualness, as are more banal scenes of middle-class prostitution and orgies. All this, accompanied by a gaseous commentary by Monique Pantel, is interlarded with arty shots of predatory beasts, to whom we (humans) are compared with nauseating insistence. It's not nice for the beasts.

What finally irks one most is the phoniness of its objective posturing. Though several sequences are quite openly staged, other episodes pretend to be real, but the frequent cutting and changes of camera angle tip one off otherwise.

Perhaps the most dishonest section of all is a "scoop" reportage on necrophilia in what is announced as a New York morgue, where a chic couple begin groping one another before a fresh cadaver. Maybe the corpse is real, but the couple and their petting are quite obviously not. And if the morgue attendant is genuine, would he have allowed himself to be filmed so overtly? The only thing shocking about this film is the apparent cynicism of those who made it.—*Len.*

Transittraüme
(Transit Dreams)
(WEST GERMAN-COLOR-16m)

A Pentafilm production, Berlin, Hartmut Jahn, in collaboration with Second German Television (ZDF). Written and directed by Hartmut Jahn and Peter Wensierski. Camera (color), Carlos Bustamente; music, Bernhard Voss. Reviewed at Saarbrücken Film Fest (Max Ophüls Prize competition), Jan. 25, 1986. Running time: **95 MINS.**

With: Marita Marschall, Pascal Lavy, Gerald Uhlig, Edith Neitzel, Kurt Raab, Peter Heusch.

Saarbrücken — Hartmut Jahn and Peter Wensierski's "Transit Dreams" is as much documentary as it is fiction. The situations described here are known to any Berliner accustomed to cross the border at regular intervals.

The basic idea is a charmer. What would happen if lookalike girlfriends from East and West Berlin exchanged roles and idenities so that Anne from the East and Marie from the West could experience firsthand the fundamental differences in the two cultures? At the same time, wouldn't it be additionally interesting to review the historical film footage that chronicled the

gap between the two Germanys over the decades? By a fortunate coincidence codirector Peter Wensierski just made the transfer himself from East to West but a couple of years ago, so everything in "Transit Dreams" has been researched in detail to provide a certain authenticity.

The joke is that the friends and acquaintances of both Anne-East and Marie-West don't grasp that an identity switch has been made, thereby treating insiders to patches of merriment over the contrasting cultures and realities, both social and political.

Marie-West goes to Anne's small apartment with its leaky pipes in the plumbing, and takes her place in a garment factory. Anne-East is now happy to have the opportunity to play her tuba somewhere else then in her bathroom. Marie-West comes from the theater, and is more than amused by the chance to take Anne-East's place in a rehearsal exam that involves playing in Goethe's "Urfaust" before professionals; in fact, she brings a new slant into the staid production.

Docu footage and interludes with a pair of identical girls of around 10 years of age provide additional spice in this absorbing document. Minus factors are the overblown and often silly scenes with neighbors and officials in East Berlin. —*Holl.*

Mukhamukham
(Face To Face)
(INDIAN-COLOR)

A General Pictures production.Executive producer, Rajasekharan Nair. Produced by Ravi. Written and directed by Addor Gopalakrishnan. Features entire cast. Camera (Eastmancolor), Ravi Varma; editor, M. Mani; music, M.B. Srinivasan; production design, Sivan; art director, Meera; sound, Devades. Reviewed at the London Film Festival, Nov. 20, 1985. Running time: **107 MINS.**
Sreedharan . . . . .P. Ganga
Old Farmer . . . . .B.K. Nair
Savitri .Ponnamma
Sreedharan's son . . . . .Krishna Kumar
Trade union leader . . . . .Karamana
Trade union leader . . . . .Thilakan
Child Sudhakaran . . . . .Vishwanathan
Sudhakaran . . . . .Ashokan
Party worker . . . . .Lalitha
Teashop owner . . . . .Vembayan

London — Despite its subject matter — the history of the Communist Party in director Gopalakrishnan's home state of Kerala between the 1940s and today — "Face To Face" is more "Citizen Kane" than agit-prop. Script follows a fictional leader's development from political action to despair. Approach adopted shifts from lowkey drama to enigmatic and tantalizing allegory.

Early part of the film draws together the testimonies of, among others, the teashop keeper who first welcomes Sreedharan to the village, a young boy who idolizes the new arrival and a farmer who adopts him into his family. Throughout,

Sreedharan's activities are seen from a distance.

When Sreedharan returns to the village 10 years later, it's hoped he will resolve differences between the state's bickering politicians, but the hero desires only sleep. Dragged into wakefulness by the various members of a divided Communist Party, he soaks himself in drink. The great Sreedharan has become, in short, a total wreck.

In contrast to the film's rather dull first section, the scenes that follow are amusing as well as painful. The metaphorical significance of Sreedharan's despair however, that of a visionary looking on the outcome of his former work, never acquires real resonance.

P. Ganga, a non-professional, conveys an extraordinary sense of physical pain in his depiction of Sreedharan's later life. Other roles are persuasive.—*Japa.*

Noah und der Cowboy
(Noah And The Cowboy)
(SWISS-B&W-16m)

A Felix Tissi film production, Bern. Written and directed by Tissi. Camera, Hansueli Schenkel; music, Andreas Litmanowitsch. Reviewed at Saarbrücken Film Fest (Max Ophüls Prize competition), Jan. 24, 1986. Running time: **82 MINS.**

With: Frank Demenga (Noah), Yves Progrin (Cowboy), Claude-Inga Barbey, Felix Rellstab, Marion Widmer, Philipp Engelmann.

Saarbrücken — Winner of the Saarbrücken Zeitung's "Readers' Prize," Felix Tissi's debut feature "Noah And The Cowboy" is packed with comic situations and witty, spontaneous dialog from start to finish.

Two buddy types living in the same building have trouble with girlfriends: Bede has just quarreled with his and she's moved out for good, while Luki has had four or five passing relationships over the past year. They decide to wander off in a battered car after an accident.

Along the way to French Switzerland they pick up an elderly gentleman, who thanks them by inviting the pair to a dinner of natural food at the local ecological commune — the car ends up being stuffed with cauliflower when they set out on their way again. As in vintage road movie style, they quarrel and part over some silly difference of opinion.

Bede meets the old gentleman again, who hands him a bag of "cauliflower seed" to deliver to a customer in Lausanne: the "coke" transaction needs a naive type, of which our hero fits the bill. The transfer is made in an underground garage, and Bede now finds himself with a bag full of Swiss Francs. Little does anyone know, however, that at the bottom of the cache is really cauliflower seeds — and the

one who later gets it in the neck is Luki, when he finds his friend's car by chance while hitchhiking and decides to spend the night in it to await Bede's return.

Bede and Luki eventually separate for good. Bede wants to return by foot to play "Noah" on his new girlfriend's ark, while Luki opts to be a "Cowboy" on the open Alpine range with his cattle.—*Holl.*

Thomas en Senior op het spoor van brute Barend
(Thomas And Senior On The Track Of Barend The Brute)
(DUTCH-COLOR)

A Gofilex Film release of a Castor Film production. Produced by Frank van Balen, Simon Jansen, Arthur Hornstra. Directed by Karst van der Meulen. Screenplay, van der Meulen, Piet Geelhoud; camera (color), Fred Tammes; music,Tonny Eyk; sound, Bert Flantua. Reviewed at Cineac, Amsterdam, Nov. 25, 1985. Running time: **110 MINS.**
Thomas . . . . .Bart Steenbeek
Senior . . . . .Lex Goudsmit
Sandra . . . . .Karin van Ee
Hageman . . . . .Cor van Rijn
Drenth . . . . .Henk van Ulsen
Chief of Police . . . . . .Carol van Herwijnen

Amsterdam — Karst van der Meulen has been making kidpics regularly since 1972. They are meant for children from about eight years on and their familes — nice, clean, no violence. Characters are good (but no goody-goodies), bad (with gusto), or rather dumb (always grownups). The sustained success of van der Meulen's films is due to his excellent direction of children, all amateurs, and to outstanding generally thrillerish, scripts.

Thomas, a schoolboy, and especially Senior, a nice old gentleman with lots of imagination and gumption, who also is the father of the local chief of police, are finding things dull compared to some more adventurous times. Senior plans new excitement for Thomas, and fakes clues about a (nonexistent) treasure buried by ancient pirates. But the supposed secret leaks out. The media get the message; the underworld goes a-hijacking and a-kidnaping; advertising moguls scent big money in merchandising; a venal scientist and a blackmailed teacher become tools of evil.

Finally, of course, right triumphs, all loose ends are neatly tied, the baddies are behind bars and Thomas and Senior (and Karst van der Meulen) can wonder what the next adventure will be. Helming, thesping and all credits contribute to this enjoyable family pic. Van der Meulen has won international prizes before, and Thomas and Senior might very well travel outside their native Holland. —*Wall.*

Police Story
(HONG KONG-COLOR)

A Golden Harvest-Golden Way production and release. Executive producers, Raymond Chow, Leonard Ho, Jackie Chan, Willy Chan. Directed by Jackie Chan. Stars Jackie Chan, Priggy Lim, Maggie Cheung, Li Hsing Hsia, Ken Tong. Screenplay and production by Edward Tang; music, Michael Lai. (No other credits provided by producers.) Reviewed at Queen's theater, Hong Kong. Jan. 1, 1986. Running time: **98 MINS.**
(Cantonese soundtrack with English subtitles)

Hong Kong — Jackie Chan capped the Hong Kong holiday season with this fast-moving widescreen cops and robbers feature. It is pure entertainment, highlighted with superb chase scenes. "Police Story" should do well in Hong Kong (expected to gross over $HK25,000,-000).

Chan, this time around is once again a police officer trained for special assignments and the hero in a police crackdown on drug king Chee. Mob king Chee's special secretary Salina has turned witness for the prosecution. Jackie is assigned to protect her, gathering more evidence on the side.

On the day of trial, Salina mysteriously disappears. Chee is set free on lack of evidence. Jackie is demoted for the major mistake and socalled inefficiency. Chee, however, wants Jackie dead and dishonored. Jackie is lured to a house where he is disarmed and his gun is used to kill another police officer. In the confusion, Salina escapes.

The cops order Jackie's arrest. Jackie sees his superior to present his case, only to be charged with murder. Jackie escapes by holding his superior hostage. A long chase ensues and you know the rest.

Athletic Chan as director has improved to present a totally engrossing, convincing production. How can he outdo his stunts after "Police Story?" As actor, he has even given himself sufficient time to do gags, plus a dramatic encounter from Ken Tong, and love interest from Li Hsing Chia, a lovely Taiwanese actress. —*Mel.*

Daheim Sterben die Leut
(To Live And Die In Westallgäu)
(WEST GERMAN-COLOR)

A Klaus Gietinger, Westallgäuer Filmproduktion, Lindenberg. Written and directed by Gietinger, Leo Hiemer. Camera (color), Marian Gzura; editor, Clara Frykowsky; music, Klaus Roggers; sets, Peter Krammer, Johannes Frick; production manager, George Veit. Reviewed at Saarbrücken Film Fest (out-of-competition), Jan. 23, 1986. Running time: **98 MINS.**
With: Walter Nuber (Hans Allgeier), Norbert Hauber (Werner Allgeier), Luise Zodel (Fini Allgeier), Josef Lau (Grandpa Allgeier), Constanze Maier (Hanni Allgeier), Heribert Weber (Dr. Franz Strobel), Jockel Tschiersch (Franz Branntwein), Sepp Preiss (Sebastian Guggemoos), Anni Rapps Silke), Stefan Huth (Devil).

Saarbrücken — One of the best regional films of the season is Klaus Gietinger and Leo Hiemer's "To Live And Die In Westallgäu" (original title is a colloquialism meaning something like "People Are Bored To Death At Home"), set in the western section of Bavaria near Lake Constance and within the shadow of the Alps. However, this is not a "Heimatfilm" — more a satire of such.

It's little more than a series of vignettes spurred by an old-fashioned local showdown on a public issue — in this case, a community waterline is to be laid. The nub of the question is whether the local gentry really need a water system, for the wells are sufficient and have been for ages. It's the case of politicians coupling their interests with construction firms angling to earn a pot of subsidized gold.

In the end, the water line laid and tapped, the gentry gather for the first glass of water to be celebrated as nectar from a wine harvest. Unfortunately the piped-in water looks like mud. The final pun has the town politico having to down his own medicine to defend his position on the matter. Great fun!—*Holl.*

Merken Sie Sich Dieses Gesicht
(Make A Note Of This Face)
(AUSTRIAN-COLOR)

A Polypol film production, Vienna. Written and directed by Gerhard Meseck. Camera (color), Gerhard Hierzer; music, Pas Paravant. Reviewed at Saarbrücken Film Fest (Max Ophüls Prize competition), Jan. 23, 1986. Running time: **80 MINS.**
With: Ursula Siller, Roselinde Renn, Sibylle Courvoisier, Gertrud Roll, Jessica Fruh, Otto David, Rudolf Buczolich, Günter Einbrodt.

Saarbrücken — One of the most polished and professionaly done films at Saarbrücken, Gerhard Meseck's "Make A Note Of This Face" deals with murder and corruption in higher aristocratic places of contemporary Viennese society.

The owner of a glass factory fears assassination by some unknown assailant, which happens in the dead of night in his plush villa when he goes to the door to welcome an acquaintance. His sister suspects the brother-in-law, for under an intricate blood-related clan system he stands to benefit the most by taking over the factory as the next heir in line.

While the sister at the graveside ceremonies plots revenge, a female reporter is also on the trail of a tax shelter fraud involving the beneficiary of all these shading dealings. She stumbles on proof of same, although the exposé in the media requires permission from the tv editorial board. This is, of course, a bit out-of-bounds, for a case built on circumstantial evidence can blow up in anybody's face when it comes to Austrian aristocracy. In the middle of her investigation, the reporter receives news of the death of a good friend in Latin America while pursuing an "honest beat," in tv parlance.

It's a crime story done in good taste and with a penchant for esthetic filmmaking values. Gerhard Hierzer's lensing is a standout.
—*Holl.*

Orissia
(Destiny)
(BULGARIAN-COLOR)

A Bulgarian Film release, produced by Studio for Feature Films. Stars Lyuban Chatalov and Maria Hristova. Written and directed by Nikola Korabov, based on a short story by Nikolai Haitov. Camera (color), Plamen Somov; art directors, Tsvetana Yankova and Eliana Stoyanova. Reviewed at the Cairo Film Festival, Dec. 3, 1985. Running time: **81 MINS.**
Boy .... Lyuben Chatalov
Girl .... Marika Hristova
Also with: Elefteri Elefterov, Leda Tasseva, Yordan Spirov.

Cairo — Veteran helmer Nikola Korabov bases this lyrical, almost ironic film on a folk tale about Nikolai Haitov's poetic Rhodope Mountain called "The Dervish Seed." Beautifully lensed, with sensitive performances from its two young principals Lyuben Chatalov and Marika Hristova, film combines human poignancy with disturbing regions of myth and superstition.

The unnamed hero is a young goatherd who one day finds himself married off to a bride he has never laid eyes on. When she takes off her veil after the wedding ceremony, he falls in love with her. Grandfather locks them in the bedroom and demands "blood" to prove the marriage has been consummated and the girl is a virgin, but for one reason or another, mostly out of mutual embarrassment, the young couple makes the girl's nose bleed instead.

As weeks go by, they find it increasingly difficult to perform their marital obligations and plant what Grandfather calls "the dervish seed." Getting wind the bride is still a virgin, the lustful next-door neighbor has her abducted by her crude brothers and buys her for two goats. The boy imagines all the ways he'll kill his neighbor, but is actually incapable of murder or cruelty. He ends his days as an old man, breaking his back to bring firewood to the home of his hated rival, because if he didn't cut the wood, the woman he still loves would have to.

Pic has a great moral force in its natural imagery and innovative lensing, with gorgeous travelling shots through the snow. The musical soundtrack, used only in dramatic moments, superbly reinforces the folk tale. — *Yung.*

Am Nächsten Morgen Kehrte der Minister Nicht an Seinen Arbeitsplatz Zurück
(On The Next Morning The Minister Didn't Return To His Post)
(WEST GERMAN-COLOR-16m)

A Monika Funke-Stern film production, Berlin. Produced, written and directed by Monika Funke-Stern. Camera (color, 16m), Nicolas Joray; music, Frieder Butzmann. Reviewed at Saarbrücken Film Fest (Max Ophüls Prize competition), Jan. 24, 1986. Running time: **70 MINS.**
With: Udo Kier (the Minister), Magitta Haberland, Ciliane Dahlen, Ric Schachtebeck, Frieder Butzmann, Peter Althoff, Walter Sprungalla, Christian Golusda, Günther Nolden.

Saarbrücken — Before making her first experimental feature film, Berlin-based helmer Monika Funke-Stern made a handful of shorts and videofilms while working at the Academy of Art there in the department of visual communication. It's the visual aspects of this part film/part video exercise that captivates.

As the title "On The Next Morning The Minister Didn't Return To His Post" hints, this is a trip into the subconscious of a "Minister For LUST" in some sci-fi world of computers, new forms of energy, and other visionary expressions of a technological utopia.

Udo Kier as the minister has a manner of acting that conveys a certain plausibility in dealing with psycho-physical phenomena. The erotic scenes and splashes of nudity can be defended as more than just futuristic wet dreams, although the general public probably will look upon the pic as little more than that.

The fact that Funke-Stern seems to be very much at home in the world of visual communication is a point in her favor, but this is still not much of a movie when images give way to dialog scenes. — *Holl.*

Retouche
(WEST GERMAN-B&W-16m)

A Berlin Film Academy (DFFB) film production. Written and directed by Dieter Funk and Beat Lottaz. Camera (b&w, 16m), Peter van den Reek; music, Konrad Haas. Reviewed at Saarbrücken Film Fest (Max Ophüls Prize competition), Jan. 22, 1986. Running time: **74 MINS.**
With: Bernd Tauber (Rotter), Gaby Pochert (Rita), Martina Gedeck, Marc Cevio, Barbara Boschan.

Saarbrücken — Dieter Funk and Beat Lottaz' "Retouche" refers in the title to a camera expression for retouching photographs. This is a diploma film made by two students at the Berlin Film Academy about small-town life in Baden-Württemberg (southwest Germany) — in fact, it's set in Funk's hometown of Rottweil.

Rotter, played with perceptive sensitivity by thesp Bernd Tauber, returns to Rottweil after a long absence to settle his father's business after the latter's recent death. The father ran a photo-shop, where the son first learned the trade of photography firsthand.

He decides to dump the place on a speculator. It's at this moment that the shop's hired girl Rita throws up her hands in disgust and applies for a job on an assembly line at a film developing plant. Then comes the twist: a nearly blind man with a bit of vision comes into the shop to pick up his developed pictures. It turns out that the man uses his camera, with the use of a magnifying glass, in appreciating what he can't really see (save for shapes) with the naked eye. The pictures turn out to be gems of photography due to the man's careful attention to detail.

Rotter suddenly realizes that he's been spiritually blind all these years. So instead of selling the shop, he goes out of his way to win back the faithful Rita to help him to manage the store. The ending alone makes "Retouche" a winner. —*Holl.*

Zwischenzeit
(Time Interval)
(WEST GERMAN-DOCU-
COLOR-16m)

A Wendländische Filmkooperative production, Marleben. A documentary by Roswitha Ziegler, Niels Bolbrinker, Jochen Fölster and Gerhard Ziegler. Camera (color), Bolbrinker; music, "Einstürzende Neubauten;" text and commentary, Roswitha Ziegler, Gerhard Ziegler. Reviewed at Saarbrücken Film Fest (out-of-competition), Jan. 24, 1986. Running time: **125 MINS.**
With: Jochen Fölster.

Saarbrücken — The subtitle for "Time Interval," docu made by an on-the-spot film collective, is "Gorleben 1982-1985," meaning the film was shot over three years in chronicling the resistance in a town of the Wendland district of Lower Saxony (near the East German border) to the construction there of an atomic energy plant. "Gorleben," in fact, was a clarion call for the Green Party in West Germany's political make-up. And as its filmmakers — Roswitha Ziegler, Niels Bolbrinker, Jochen Fölster, Gerhard Ziegler — take pains to underscore, the squatters' resistance and ecological demonstrations will continue on into the foreseeable future despite setbacks.

Via a commentator (Jochen Fölster) a flashback of the events is provided, the commentary often ironic and cynical as well as analytical and full of self-criticism. The high moments deal with the masses that turned out for human-chain demonstrations, plus examples of government reactions to the challenge.

In general, the film collective (particularly Roswitha Ziegler) is turned on by sociopolitical questions. Yet a documentary also needs a visual strength of its own, or a

poetic style in presenting a thematic argument. "Time Interval" is more of a film seminar than a stimulating docu in its own right.—*Holl.*

Mexicano, Tú Puedes
(Mexican, You Can Do It)
(MEXICAN-COLOR)

A Peliculas Mexicanas-Peliculas Nacionales release of a Conacite Dos production. Directed by José Estrada. Screenplay, Olivia Michel; camera (color), Miguel Garzón; editor, Maximo Sánchez Molina; art direction, Francisco Magallón; music, Pedro Plascencia Salinas and Pancho Saenz. Reviewed at Cine Viaducto, Mexico City, Nov. 5, 1985. Running time: **110 MINS.**
Carmen . . . . Carmen Salinas
Vicente . . . . Sergio Jiménez
Héctor . . . . Arturo Alegro
Lucha . . . . Lupita Sandoval
Ismael . . . . Ernesto Yañez
Benito . . . . Juan Angel Martínez
Georgina . . . . Roxana Frias
Irma . . . . Alma Delfina

Mexico City — The comedy "Mexicano, Tú Puedes" is one of the most genuinely funny Mexican pics to emerge in some time. Based on Olivia Michel's awardwinning script (it won the 1981 writers society Sogem screenplay competition), the pic concerns the havoc caused when a lower-income Mexican family decides to change its lifestyle.

Enticed by all the glittering ads on tv announcing a new real estate development, Carmen (admirably played by Carmen Salinas) decides her tenement surroundings are no longer sufficient.

What is seen on tv as a virgin forest setting is actually a barren plot of wasteland. Yet, she is convinced — at the cost of everyone's happiness — that a beautiful new home can be built there, which will mark the beginning of a new life for her and her family. Trouble plagues this group at every step, including a hilarious view of Mexico's bureaucracy and government corruption, and problems with the "compadre" extended-family system. Their whole former life falls apart.

Although there are some holes in the plot, the film manages to penetrate the particularly Mexican idiosyncrasies and milk them of their comedic value. It also shows a very Mexican cynical view of life — as every hope for a better future is dashed, Mexicans shrug and continue.

Acting honors go to Salinas and Sergio Jiménez for creating believable everyday characters in a film that should say something to most Mexicans or those of Mexican blood.—*Lent.*

Berlin Festival

At Close Range
(U.S.-COLOR)

Impressive but downbeat father/son drama.

An Orion Pictures release of a Hemdale production. Produced by Elliott Lewitt, Don Guest. Executive producers, John Daly, Derek Gibson. Directed by James Foley. Stars Sean Penn, Christopher Walken. Screenplay, Nicholas Kazan; camera (Panavision, CFI color), Juan Ruiz-Anchia; editor, Howard Smith; music, Patrick Leonard; sound, David Brownlow; production design, Peter Jamison. Reviewed at Berlin Film Festival, Zoo Palast (in competition), Feb. 19, 1986. (MPAA Rating: R). Running time: **111 MINS.**
Brad Whitewood Jr. . . . . Sean Penn
Brad Whitewood Sr. . . . Christopher Walken
Terry . . . . Mary Stuart Masterson
Tommy Whitewood . . . . . Christopher Penn
Julie Whitewood . . . . Millie Perkins
Grandmother . . . . Eileen Ryan
Ernie . . . . Alan Autry
Mary Sue . . . . Candy Clark
Dickie Whitewood . . . . R.D. Call
Patch . . . . Tracey Walter
Boyd . . . . J.C. Quinn
Tony Pine . . . . David Strathairn
Lester . . . . Jake Dengel
Lucas . . . . Crispin Glover
Tim . . . . Kiefer Sutherland
Jill . . . . Noelle Parker

Berlin — A downbeat tale of brutal family relations, James Foley's "At Close Range" is a very tough picture. Violent without being vicarious, this true story runs the risk of being an audience turnoff, though the presence of Sean Penn will give it a needed lift at the boxoffice.

Pic really achieves its full impact only in the last third, though early scenes are vitally important in setting up characters and theme. Set in a small Pennsylvania town (though shot in Tennessee) in 1978, story introduces young Brad (Penn) as just another rather tough kid with an eye for a new girl (the charming Mary Stuart Masterson) and fiercely protective of his brother (Christopher Penn).

Along comes Brad's father (Christopher Walken), who's stayed away for years. Brad Sr. has a reputation as a criminal, and in fact heads a gang of tough safecrackers. Intrigued by his seemingly exciting parent, Brad Jr. is encouraged to form his own gang to carry out more modest heists, and on one foray is slightly wounded.

First two-thirds of the pic concentrate on the growing relationship between father and son, and between Brad Jr. and his sweet 16-year-old girl (his mother, played by Millie Perkins, gets hardly a look-in). Then federal investigators start to close in on Brad Sr., and he realizes that the junior gang knows far too much about his activities. One by one, the youngsters are mur-

dered, including Brad's kid brother. Brad Jr. and his girl decide to flee, but as they sit in their car they're repeatedly fired on (like Bonnie and Clyde) by unseen gunmen, and the girl is killed. Brad Jr. survives, however, and sets off to avenge himself on his father.

Following on the relatively light, amoral mood of the early part of the film, climax comes as unexpectedly brutal. It says much for Masterson that her character of Terry has won the audience over to the extent that her savage murder comes across as an exceptionally shocking and brutal act.

General audiences will respond to the very strong performances of the two leads, especially Walken whose smiling, dangerous killer is one of his best roles — and the agonizing developments of the plot. As he did in "Reckless," Foley moves his camera around a lot, with plenty of tracking shots and cranes. Cynics may accuse him of a rock video mentality, but his style is more solid and traditional than that. Editing by Howard Smith is often brutally abrupt, but even so the film is a bit lengthy at 111 minutes.—*Strat.*

Caravaggio
(BRITISH-COLOR)

A British Film Institute production, in association with Channel 4 and Nicholas Ward-Jackson. Produced by Sarah Radclyffe. Executive producer, Colin MacCabe. Written and directed by Derek Jarman. Camera (Technicolor), Gabriel Beristain; editor, George Akers; music, Simon Fisher Turner, assisted by Mary Phillips; production design, Christopher Hobbs; costumes, Sandy Powell; assistant director, Glynn Purcell; production manager, Sarah Wilson; sound, Billy McCarthy. Reviewed at Berlin Film Festival, Zoo Palast (in competition), Feb. 17, 1986. Running time: **89 MINS.**
Caravaggio . . . . Nigel Terry
Ranuccio Thomasoni . . . . Sean Bean
Davide . . . . Garry Cooper
Jerusaleme . . . . Spencer Leigh
Lena . . . . Tilda Swinton
Cardinal Del Monte . . . . . Michael Gough
Marchese Giustiniani . . . . Nigel Davenport
Cardinal Borghese . . . . Robbie Coltrane
Baglione . . . . Jonathon Hyde
Young Caravaggio . . . . Dexter Fletcher
Boy Caravaggio . . . . Noam Almaz
The Pope . . . . Jack Birkett

Berlin — Derek Jarman's "Caravaggio" triumphantly rises above its financial restrictions and proves, once again, that less can be a lot more.

Pic is an imagined biopic of one of the last Renaissance painters. Michelangelo Merisi da Caravaggio (1571-1610), but the inspiration seems to be Italian film director Pier Paolo Pasolini, since both artists came from poor backgrounds and used beautiful young men from the slums in their work. Both also became involved in scandal and violence.

Jarman's film, in classical tradition, is told in flashback as the artist lies dying in poverty. Story fragmentarily traces his life from childhood, his early struggles, the patronage he receives from an art-loving Cardinal (a wonderful performance from Michael Gough) and his obsesssion with Ranuccio Thomasoni (Sean Bean), a low-life gambler with whom he falls in love and who he eventually murders.

Story takes a backseat, however, since much of the joy of the film is to be found in the way Jarman and his team, including cinematographer Gabriel Beristain, production designer Christopher Hobbs and costume designer Sandy Powell, recreate the look and color of the original paintings. Caravaggio is said to have invented chiaroscuro (theatrical lighting employing artfully placed shadows), a style embraced hundreds of years later by the cinema.

Film is not flawless, however, despite the extraordinary achievements of Jarman given the limited funds at his disposal. It lacks a certain warmth and emotional depth, and the fact that location shooting was not possible makes for a claustrophobic feeling.

If "Caravaggio" is lacking in heart, it's not lacking in humor. Jarman includes many jokes and deliberate anachronisms. These renaissance characters used pocket calculators, motor-bikes and typewriters. The jokey asides aren't over-stressed.

Pic will have obious cult appeal for the gay crowd, and should also be wholeheartedly embraced by artlovers, as long as they don't object to Jarman's engaging irreverence. — Strat.

Pas in Doi
(Paso Doble)
(RUMANIAN-COLOR)

An Artexim Bucharest presentation of a Romaniafilm production. Directed by Dan Pita. Screenplay, George Busecan, Pita; camera (color), Marin Stanciu; editor, Cristina Ionescu; art director, Calin Papura; costumes, Maria Malita, music, excerpts from Haydn's ''Creation.'' Reviewed at Berlin Film Festival (in competition) at Zoo Palast, Feb. 22, 1986. Running time: **110 MINS.**
With: Claudia Bleant, Ecaterina Nazare, Petre Nicolae, Anda Onesa, Mircea Constantinescu, Valentin Popescu, Aurora Leonte.

Berlin — "Paso Doble" is a highly stylized film carrying some incisive social criticisms that aren't all that familiar in Rumanian production.

On the face of it, this is a love story, using classical characters in a classical situation. Two friends sharing the same room in a hostel are diametrically opposed characters and get devoted to each other. One is a charmer, handsome and agile, the other is the silent, introverted type. The first is practically engaged to a pretty, nice girl, from a nice family, the second is desperately in love with, but spurned by an unwed mother. The conflict erupts when the charmer meets this second girl and she falls for him. He has to juggle the two women with whom he feels equally in love, and on top of it, to deal with his moody friend who now feels betrayed. Being sincere in his feelings towards all of them, the lucky winner turns finally to be the loser, for wanting too much from too many people.

If the story isn't all that new, its background permits a fascinating glimpse into present-day Rumanian society, a glimpse that isn't all flattering. The hostel which the two male protagonists, and all the workers employed by the same factory, occupy, looks very much like a college dormitory. Their ideas about life and their future seem to be limited strictly to catching a woman and marrying her, for that is their only chance to get a flat of their own and move out of collective lodgings.

The relations between men and women are old-fashioned, at best, and marriage, as desirable as it may be, is far from paradise, as it is indicated by one of the boys, who manages to find a spouse in the course of the film.

Claudia Bleant, as the man who is too well loved, and Petre Nicolae as the unloved one, offer a nice contrast physically and emotionally, while both Ecaterina Nazare, as the unwed mother, and Anda Onesa, as the other woman, are equally well matched. — *Edna.*

Yari No Gonza
(Gonza The Spearman)
(JAPANESE-COLOR)

A Shochiko Hyogensha production. Produced by Kiyoshi Iwashita, Tomiyuki Motomochi, Masatake Wakita. Directed by Masahiro Shinoda. Screenplay, Taeko Tomioka, from a play by Monzaemon Chikamatsu; camera (Eastmancolor), Kazuo Miyagawa; editor, Sachiko Yamachi; sound, Shotaro Yoshida; music, Toru Takemitsu; sets, Kiyoshi Awazu. Reviewed at Berlin Film Festival. Zoo-Palast (in competition), Feb. 20, 1986. Running time: **121 MINS.**
Gonza Sasano .... Hiromi Goh
Osai .... Shima Iwashita
Bannojo Kawazura .... Shohej Hino
Oyuki .... Misako Tanaka
Oyaki's governess .... Haruko Kalo
Ichinoshin Asaka .... Takashi Tsumura
Okiku .... Kaori Mizushima

Berlin — A resolutely classical adaptation of an early 18th century play by Monzaemon Chikamatsu, "Gonza The Spearman" is a richly-textured piece of traditional film-making. Wonderfully shot by the veteran Kazuo Miyagawa and delicately directed by Masahiro Shinoda, this is a stately tale of honor and disgrace, steady in pace and sometimes convoluted in the telling.

The original play, in the *bunraku* tradition, was penned by Chikamatsu in 1717. Set in the Edo period, when provincial lords were required to spend long periods of time serving in the capital city, it concerns the Matsue clan of Izumo whose leader, Asaka, is away on shogunate business. In his absence, his wife, Osai, requests that Gonza, her husband's most handsome and popular retainer, marry her daughter, Okiku, who is in love with him.

Although already engaged to Oyuki, sister of one of his fellow retainers, the ambitious Gonza agrees. His main reason is that, as a member of the Asaka family, he will be privy to the closely guarded secrets of the tea ceremony, which will add to his prestige. When Osai discovers Gonza's prior commitment to Oyuki, she rashly agrees to bind him to her daughter by illegally revealing to him the tea ceremony secrets before the wedding. She's discovered, and word is put out that she and Gonza have committed adultery. Although it's not true, they're forced to flee, pursued by the vengeful Asaka and his retainers.

There are a few moments of outdoor pageantry, but almost all the film unfolds in interiors and consists of exploring the rigid code of honor by which those people must live. At the climax of this tempest in a teacup, Gonza and Osai finally make love before their inevitable capture. They're trapped on a bridge crowded with people, and Gonza, who has sold his samurai sword, makes only a token effort at defense; his death, and that of Osai, is bloody.

Hiromi Goh and Shima Iwashita are fine as the fugitives, but the film's most memorable performance comes from Takashi Tsumura as the vengeful husband who rigidly adheres to his code of honor. There's another fine music score from Toru Takemitsu. — *Strat.*

Sininen Imettäjä
(The Blue Mammy)
(FINNISH-B&W)

A Finnkino (Helsinki) release of Gironfilmi Oy with Swedish Television (Lulea) and Finnish Film Foundation production. Directed by Markku Lehmuskallio. Story and screenplay, Lehmuskallio, Helmi Paula Pulkkinen, Niilo Hyttinen; camera (b&w), Pekka Martevo; editor, Juhu Gartz; music, Pekka Jalkanen; production design, Seiia Kiisi; paintings, Niilo Hyttinen. Reviewed at Berlin Film Festival (market), the CineCenter Studio 6 screening room on Feb. 16, 1986. Running time: **95 MINS.**
Joel Ström .... Niilo Hyttinen
Kerttu .... Aino-Maija Tikkanen
The Muse .... Kaija Kiiski
Ström's mother .... Aino Lähdenpera
Also with: Jaako Raulamo, Esko Hukkanen.

Berlin — ''The Blue Mammy'' is about an introvert artist (born a deafmute) living in a remote area of Lapland where he works quietly and stubbornly.

The story, if there really is one, seems to be about the salvation of the longsuffering talent in the face of mundane everyday demands. Director and co-scripter Markku Lehmuskallio, has chosen real-life painter Niilo Hyttinen, (balding, bespectacled and scraggly-bearded) to play the lead and used Hyttinen's own work to illustrate (in occasionally inserted color frames) the art in question. Hyttinen performs with properly mute persuasion, and all actors around him, professional or non-professional, also keep their expressions subdued.

Film's title refers to Nature and the Universe as Mammy, actually wet-nurse, to the painter's dreams and ambitions. —Kell.

Achalgazrda Kompozitoris Mogzauroba
(The Journey Of A Young Composer)
(SOVIET-COLOR)

A Gruzia Film production, Tbilisi, Georgian Republic, USSR. World rights, Goskino, Moscow. Directed by Georgi Shengelaya. Screenplay, Erlom Achwlediani, Shengelaya, based on Otar Chcheidze's novel "The Nameless Wind;" camera (color), Levan Paatashvili; editor, S. Machaidze; sets, Boris Chakaya, Nikolai Shengelaya; music, Gustav Mahler. Reviewed at Berlin Film Fest (in competition), Feb. 18, 1986. Running time: **105 MINS.**
With: Giya Peradze (Leko Tatasheli), Levan Abashidze (Nikusha Chachanidze), Zubar Kipishidze (Elisabar Chetereli), Rusudan Kvilvidze (Thekla Chetereli), Ruslan Mikaberidze (Shalva Chetereli), Lili Yoseliani (Elfimiya Chetareli), Teimuraz Dshaparidze (Georgi Ozcheli), Ketevan Orachelashvili (Guranducht), Zinaida Kverenchchiladze (Gulkan), Chabua Amiredshibi (David Itrieli), Teimuraz Bichinashvili (Rostom).

Berlin — Georgian director Georgi Shengelaya made one of the memorable films of Soviet cinema, "Pirosmani" (1969), the story of a national folk painter. His entry at this year's Berlinale, "The Journey Of A Young Composer," won best director honors.

This is an atmospheric, slowly paced film based on a literary work with deep roots in Georgian history and tradition. The period is 1907 in an eastern Georgian community during the last bitter phase of repression following the 1905 rebellion against the tsarist government. A young and rather naive composer is commissioned by his tutor to go through the land to certain marked areas on a map to collect folk songs.

The tsar's brutal soldiers are everywhere, and the people live in hope of some kind of redeemer. The young composer's journey is viewed by many as a secret mission, while his map and letters of introduction beg to be decoded for a possible insurrection to come.

A friendly physician decides to entrust the composer Nikusha to the braggart Leko, and the two are to journey by secretive routes to Tbilisi. The situation is only worsened by having Leko along, for he is convinced destiny has chosen him to become the needed martyr to rally the people to victory over tyranny.

As for the populace, they look upon the presence of the two as "redeemers" of some kind, although it's not known exactly what. Finally, at a religious festival, a fire breaks out that spurs the soldiers to act and make arrests. Leko is recognized for the charlatan he is, but Nikusha's mysterious map arouses suspicion. Further, it contains the addresses of all the places the composer has visited, and thus ignites a mass arrest, torture and killings, and a whole new wave of terror.

In a final confrontation, the military officer discusses the matter of the map with the composer's tutor. They understand each other completely: the wave of terror is a mistake, for folk songs were in truth the only reason for the journey. However, and here's the core of the matter, the people are simply too passive in their silent resistance to be trusted. The reign of terror must go on.

"The Journey Of A Young Composer" is conceived as a profoundly moral and refinely philosophical film. All well and good, but for average audiences pic simply moves too slowly. Another minus is the inferior print sent to the Berlinale with its pale, washed-out colors. —Holl.

Tong nien Wang shi
(A Time To Live And A Time To Die)
(TAIWANESE-COLOR)

A Central Motion Picture Co. production. Produced by Lin Tong-fei. Directed by Hou Hsiao-hsien (Hou Xiaoxian). Screenplay, Chou Tien-wen, Hou Hsiao-hsien; camera (color), Li Ping-Pin; editor, by Wang Ch'i-yang; sets, Lin Tsong Wen; costumes, Chou Ching-wen; sound, Hsi Chiang-Sheng; music, Wu Ch'u-ch'u. Reviewed at the Berlin Film Festival (forum), Feb. 17, 1986. Running time: **145 MINS.**
With (as adults): T'ien Feng, Nei Fang, T'ang Ju-yün, Hsiao Ai, Yu An-shun, Wu Su-ying, Ch'en Shu-Fang; (as children): Chang Ning, Luo Tse-chung, Luo Ch'eng-ye, Chiang Chia-Pao, Luo Hsün-Lin, Liu Kuo-Pin.

Berlin — After the success reaped by his "Summer At Grandpa's" last year, Hou Hsiao-hsien is back with another beautifully controlled and highly nostalgic picture of child-

hood, based on his own boyhood, a period coinciding with the last years of the Chinese revolution and establishment of an independent Taiwanese identity.

Not that politics have anything to do directly with this film. What the script is mostly concerned with is growing up in a lower middleclass family, culturally bridging between the ancient superstitions and the new modern ways of education. It is also about the economic struggle to keep afloat in those difficult years.

Mostly episodic in nature, the film impresses by its exquisite camerawork which suggests perfectly framed paintings.

Time is one of the essential elements of the story, the changing seasons contributing to establish moods and the passing years indicating a change in mentality.

Time, however, may also be one of the film's drawbacks, overlong at 145 minutes. —Edna.

L'Aube
(The Dawn)
(FRENCH-ISRAELI-COLOR)

A World Marketing Film presentation of a Swan Prod. (Paris), VNYL (Tel Aviv), Odessa Films production. Produced by Evelyne July. Directed by Miklos Jancso. Screenplay, Jancso, based on novel by Elie Wiesel; camera (color), Armand Marco; editor, Jean-Paul Vauban; music, Zoltan Simon; sets, Yves Brocer; costumes, Pierre Albert; sound, François Groult. Reviewed at the Zoo Palast. Berlin Film Fest (in competition), Feb. 21, 1986. Running time: **92 MINS.**

God	Philippe Léotard
Elisha	Redjep Mitrovitsa
Dawson	Michael York
Ilana	Christine Boisson
Yoav	Serge Avedekion
Dan	David Burstein
David	Paul Blain

Berlin — Distinguished Hungarian director Miklos Jancso, who has been out of the limelight lately, tries to depart in "L'Aube" (Dawn) from some of the typical trademarks of his work, and yet remain faithful to them, a feat which leaves him somewhere in the middle.

While his camera remains constantly on the move, Jancso has foregone the the wide open spaces of a Hungarian locale in preference for the intimate landscape of the actors' faces, and instead of spectacular crowds and beautifully disrobed women, he goes for a claustrophobic atmosphere.

The script is based on an episode from an early Elie Wiesel novel, which suits perfectly a theme dear to Jancso: how far is a freedom movement entitled to infringe the basic rights of man in order to bring a change for the better?

In the period before the State of Israel declared its independence, a resistance movement catches a British officer as hostage after one of their own had been sentenced to

death by the English. The plot takes place during one night, evolving around a young member of the resistance who is told he is to execute the hostage at dawn. In this one night, he has to come to terms with the moral issue of killing in cold blood, the memories of the Diaspora and the Holocaust which led him to where he is now, and with his own conscience and responsibility to the other members of his group.

The conclusion is absolutely clear. Nothing justifies killing, not even the loftier ideals, and whoever takes the life of his kin, murders his own identity as a human being.

Jancso keeps the story mostly on an abstract level, as he switches from reality to fiction, from present to past and indulges long discussions.

Very well shot, picture uses a cast which may not be all that accustomed to Jancso's declamatory style. —Edna.

Gilsodom
(S. KOREAN-COLOR)

A Hwa Chun Trading Co. Ltd. production. Produced by Lee Woan-Ho. Directed by Im Kwon-Taek. Screenplay, Song Kil-Han; camera (color), Jong Il Song; sound, Kim Yong Soo; music, Kim Jong-Kil; sets, Kim Yoo Joon; assistant director, Yoo Yong Jin. Reviewed at Berlin Film Festival, Zoo-Palast (in competition), Feb. 19, 1986. Running time: **97 MINS.**

Hwayong	Kim Ji Mi
Tongjin	Sin Song-Il
Soktschol	Han Ji-Il
Tuknam	Kim Ji-Yong
Hwayong as a girl	Lee Sang-A
Tongjin as a young man	Kim Jong Sok
Tongjin's father	Kim Ki Ju
Tongjin's mother	Kim Bok Hi
Hwayong's husband	Jon Moo-Song

Berlin — An up-to-the-minute pic of extreme topicality in Korea, "Gilsodom" tackles the theme of the reuniting of families separated as a result of the Korean War more than 30 years ago. It opens with scenes from Korean tv in which people with missing relatives try to find their lost family, and in many cases were reunited over the airwaves. The programs, broadcast in 1983, were watched by an estimated 88% of the population.

One of them is Hwayong, happily married and living a comfortable life. Years before she's had a young sweetheart and a child, both lost. She sets out to locate them, and soon finds her former lover, Tongjin. In long flashbacks they tell each other their experiences during and after the war. Unlike Hwayong, Tongjin is unhappily married and not well off. There's a strained relationship between the former lovers, but they decide to try to locate their missing son. When they eventually find him (or at least a young man who could be him) there are more disappointments as he's oafish, a drunk and a wife-beater.

Last part of the film, in which it becomes clear that Hwayong doesn't really want her son, are powerfully handled, though the central section involving flashbacks to the past contains more familiar material.

Director Im Kwon-Taek has approached a burning subject with perhaps a bit too much reverence. Nonetheless, this is a strong entry, telling an emotional story of separation and loss and disappointment with a steadily building momentum, and with excellent performances from the principals. The sub-text is the reunification of the country itself. After years of hoping, if the day comes when the two halves of Korea finally get together, will they still be compatible?

The title of the film refers to the town where Hwayong and Tongjin grew up, which is now in North Korea.—Strat.

Dokument: Fanny och Alexander
(Document: Fanny And Alexander)
(SWEDISH-DOCU-COLOR)

A Cinematograph with Swedish Film Institute production. World Sales, Swedish Film Institute (Lena Enquist). Arranged by Ingmar Bergman; camera (Eastmancolor) Arne Carlsson; editor, Sylvia Ingemarsson. Reviewed at CineCenter Studio 2, Berlin Film Fest (forum), Feb. 21, 1986. Running time: **110 MINS.**

Berlin — Cameraman Arne Carlsson recorded for posterity with Ingmar Bergman's blessing and guidance (on 16m film) much of the helmer's work with his actors and crew, especially cinematographer Sven Nykvist, during the seven months it took to shoot "Fanny And Alexander." The resulting "Document: Fanny And Alexander" is now on display as an "arrangement" by Bergman himself.

Bergman at work helming is seen as an endlessly patient, but relentless meticulous and demanding artist who maintains an atmosphere of easy camaraderie with everybody around him. He acts out movements and nuances in dialog for his actors but rarely engages in discussions with them as he does, gladly, with cinematographer Nykvist. It is obvious that everybody is in loving awe of him and ready to do their damnedest to heed his advice and admonitions.

This has the look of a professional's home movie, and the sound is terrible. It gives a good idea of Bergman's work processes and will belong in any film school's library. To the layman, docu is tediously overlong. An abbreviated version probably could enjoy wide television sales. — Kell.

Anne Trister
(CANADIAN-COLOR)

A Ciné 360 Inc. released. Produced by Roger Frappier and Claude Bonin for the Natinal Canadian Film Office and Les Films Vision 4. Directed by Léa Pool. Stars Albane Guilhe. Screenplay, Marcel Beaulieu, Pool; camera (color), Pierre Mignot; editor, Michel Arcand; music, René Dupéré; art director, Vianney Gauthier. Reviewed at the Berlin Film Festival (in competition), Feb. 20, 1986. Running time: 115 MINS.
Anne Trister . . . . Albane Guilhe
Alix . . . . Louise Marleau
Sarah . . . . Lucie Laurier
Thomas . . . . Guy Thauvette
Pierre . . . . Hugues Quester
Simon . . . . Nuvit Ozdogru

Berlin — As in her first feature, "La Femme de l'Hotel," Swiss-Canadian director Léa Pool tackles deeply felt, intense female portraiture in "Anne Trister." A visually sumptuous, slow-moving and deliberate work, "Trister" teeters on the brink of dramatic stasis and psychological cliché. In the moments it finds its feet, film is lovely.

Heroine Anne (Albane Guilhe) is a young Swiss painter who had just lost her father. From the stunning opening sequence when he's buried in the Israeli desert, it is clear his death will be the mental event at the heart of the film. Bidding farewell to her mother and boyfriend Pierre (Hugues Quester), Anne goes to Quebec for an indeterminate period. Things proceed as smoothly as they only can in the movies: an old friend of her father's who runs a Jewish bistro rents her a mammoth studio out of his own pocket. her friend Alix (Louise Marleau), a child psychologist, insists she moves into her comfortable apartment, despite the friction this occasions with Alix' lover Thomas (Guy Thauvette).

Moody, melancholy and fragile, Anne throws herself into a mad project, which is to paint a vast mural on the walls of the decrepit atelier. The moments depicting Anne at work are the most exciting in the picture. Rarely has the artistic process been rendered so strikingly, as the mural gradually progresses and absorbs all of her energy and creativity.

Outside the studio, Anne suffers from the realization she's no longer in love with Pierre, who is patiently waiting for her back home, but instead has fallen for Alix. The Alix-Anne relationship is handled with maximum delicacy and sensitivity, yet never seems truly convincing or even very interesting.

At times Pool's magnificently refined, unhurried style bogs down in banal plotting, like the recurring parallel made between Anne's mental suffering and that of a little girl (Lucie Laurier) Alix is treating in her clinic. When the child feels hurt and aggressive and paints her teddy bear's face a wound-like red, pic cuts to Anne destroying part of her mural in blind despair. Only the intense performance of young thesp Guilhe keeps this portrait of the suffering artist from sinking into cliché.

In Anne's eventual return to the desert sands, she finally loses her mask of moody impenetrability and blossoms into a smile, as though she had at last found identity and roots at her father's grave.

Cinematography by Pierre Mignot is uniformly excellent, as is art direction and music. —*Yung.*

Toby McTeague
(CANADIAN-COLOR)

A Spectrafilm release of a Filmline Intl. production. Produced by Nicolas Clermont. Directed by Jean-Claude Lord. Executive producers, David Patterson, Pieter Kroonenburg. Screenplay, Jamie Brown, based on an original screenplay by Jeff Maguire and Djordje Milicevic; camera (color), Rene Verzier; editor, Yves Langlois; music, Claude Demers; production designer, Jocelyn Joly; stunt coordinator, Jerome Tiberghien; special effects, Bill Orr; sled-dog advisers. Judy Pearce and Bryan Pearce. Reviewed at the Carmichael, Smithsonian Institution, Washington, D.C., Feb. 6, 1986. (MPAA Rating: PG.) Running time: 95 MINS.
Toby McTeague . . . . Yannick Bisson
Tom McTeague . . . . Winston Rekert
Edison Crowe . . . . Timothy Webber
Sara . . . . Stephanie Morgenstern
Sam McTeague . . . . Andrew Bednarski
Jenny Lessard . . . . Liliane Clune
Chief George Wild Dog . . . . George Clutesi
Jacob . . . . Evan Adams

Washington — Reinforcing its Canadian identity, Spectrafilm makes an unexpected turn into family fare with this story of parenting and dog sled racing in the snows of northern Quebec.

A tiny community called Silver Creek is obsessed with mushing, a sport that can mean economic survival for the McTeagues, if they win the $6,000 Provincial Championship prize. Yannick Bisson is rather good as the 15-year-old Toby who is alternately awkward and recklessly self-confident. He is on the way to replacing his dad as the champion, which provides the thrust of the plot, and every subplot is a deflection from that potential Oedipal conflict.

The life of the kids in Silver Creek is affected by the arrival of a new teacher, played by the vapidly lovely Liliane Clune. She is idealized as a caring, probing, computer-savvy teacher, who would make a good mom for the two McTeagues, of course, a plot device signalled with her first appearance out of the plane.

Missing from the story of widower Tom McTeague struggling to raise huskies and boys is a psychological depth that would sustain the tension in the family that is posited but never felt. Toby's pattern of rebellion, running away, and remorse has the formulaic assurance of television. Andrew Bednarski as Toby's little brother Sam is called in like a laugh track to lighten up the mood when Toby is in a conflict. Toby's awakening sexuality is delicately developed in some of the best moments opposite Stephanie Morgenstern, who never seems self-conscious of how she is expressing her concern about Toby. She stands out, because she is convincing in her simple little role.

Pic tries very hard to be warm and reassuring about the teenage problems it addresses, as well as about the benefits of living life in the snows of Alaska. Pointed comments about city life declare it an inferior life style. The dogs are fun and unruly, but with all the concern for domestic details, pic never opens out into a vision of nature as grandiose and absorbing the way such pics as "Never Cry Wolf" and "Natty Gann" so successfully did. When Toby runs away into the mountains he has an encounter with an old Indian Chief, who later shows up like a *deus ex machina* before Toby's final race to lend an unpracticed lead dog that will hurl him literally over the finish line.

The script has spread out the action across too many individual incidents that don't achieve a accumulative effective creting the portrait of a young musher. An otherwise workmanlike production has put too much emphasis on keeping the dogs instead of the plot racing. —*Kaja.*

Dream Lover
(COLOR)

Dull picture on an interesting topic.

An MGM/UA Entertainment release from MGM. Produced by Alan J. Pakula and Jon Boorstin. Executive producer, William C. Gerrity. Directed by Alan J. Pakula. Stars Kristy McNichol. Screenplay, Jon Boorstin; camera (Technicolor, prints by Metrocolor), Sven Nykvist; editor, Trudy Ship; music, Michael Small; sound, Chris Newman; art direction, John J. Moore; production design, George Jenkins; assistant director, David Tringham; production manager, Gerrity; associate producer, Susan Solt; casting, Alixe Gordin. Reviewed at MGM Studios, Culver City, Feb. 5, 1986. (MPAA Rating: R.) Running time: 104 MINS.
Kathy Gardner . . . . Kristy McNichol
Michael Hansen . . . . Ben Masters
Ben Gardner . . . . Paul Shenar
Kevin McCann . . . . Justin Deas
Martin . . . . John McMartin
Claire . . . . Gayle Hunnicutt
Danny . . . . Joseph Culp
Billy . . . . Matthew Penn
Shep . . . . Paul West
Vaughn Capisi . . . . Matthew Long

Hollywood — Directed by Alan J. Pakula, "Dream Lover" certainly can not be dismissed as another mindless thriller, as it might have been in other hands. Pakula's problem is that the picture often has more mind when it needs more thrills.

To his credit, Pakula dares to play around in the wayout areas of brain behavior, particularly dream research. With the advice of a Yale University Sleep Laboratory consultant, "Dream" firmly sets itself among some rather fascinating scientific notions.

Specifically, some dream doctors believe that, while "asleep," part of the brain reacts to dreams as if they were really happening and sends signals to the muscles to take appropriate action. Another part of the brain nullifies the signals with a chemical that paralyzes the muscles during the dream.

What would happen if another chemical were injected to uncheck the paralysis and allow the dreamer to act out his reactions to the nocturnal imaginations?

Pakula and writer Jon Boorstin get started in the right direction, setting up Kristy McNichol as an average young lady living alone in a N.Y. apartment. As sometimes happens to young ladies living alone, McNichol becomes victim to an intruder (Joseph Culp) whom she stabs in the back.

Was the stabbing really necessary for self-defense or did it leap out of some subconscious fury connected to her domineering father (Paul Shenar) or unfaithful lover (Justin Deas)?

Only her brain knows for sure (or does it?) and when she tries to sleep, the events of that night torment her severely. Coming to her aide, dream researcher Ben Masters unwittingly makes matters worse with a treatment designed to free her dreaming thoughts into controlled action.

Unfortunately, for cinematic purposes, all of this just goes on and on, with a lot of (almost padding) replays of her dreams of the stabbing incident. The ultimate attempt to channel the unwelcome results of her dream treatments limps to a conclusion with no real excitement. —*Har.*

Flucht in den Norden
(Escape Into The North)
(FINNISH-W. GERMAN-COLOR)

An NEF (Munich) release of a Theuring-Engström (Munich and Versailles) with Jörn Donner (Helsinki) production. World sales, Cine-International Filmvertrieb (Munich). Written and directed by Ingemo Engström, based on Klaus Mann's 1934 novel "Entkommen zum Leben/Escape To Life." Stars Katharina Thalbach, Jukka-Pekka Palo. Executive producers, Ulrich Möller, Carl von Willebrand, Helmi-Paula Pulkkinen, Tuula Söderberg. Camera (Eastmancolor), Axel Block; editor, Thomas Balkenhol; production design, Kristiina Tuura, Jukka Vikberg, Ben Gyllenberg; costumes, Heidi Wujek, Marja-Liisa Tielinen, Leila Oksanen; music, quotes from Bach, Sibelius. Reviewed (in competition) at Zoo Palast, Berlin Film Festival, Feb. 17, 1986. Running time: 130 MINS.
Johanna . . . . Katharina Thalbach
Ragnar . . . . Jukka-Pekka Palo
Karin . . . . Lena Olin
Jens . . . . Tom Pöysti

The Mother . . . . Käbi Laretei
The Maid . . . . Britta Pohland

Berlin — Ingemo Engström has based her big-production feature "Escape Into The North" on Klaus Mann's written-in-exile novel "Escape To Life," an elegantly sad work, and blown it into a sprawling, repetitive and deadly boring feature film. What evoked sadness in the book has been turned into hectoring expressions of opinion and sullen solemnity. Only fine production credits save this Finnish-German Berlin Fest competition entry from being dismissed as wholly ridiculous.

It is Johanna, a young Berlin woman, who in 1934 flees the Nazis, whom she is actively engaged in fighting. Having visited a Finnish girl friend (a lesbian affair is more than hinted but abruptly dropped again without having had any bearing on the drama that follows), Johanna goes to the girl's family's country estate. There she has verbal fights with one brother of strongly fascist leanings, and soon enters into a blazing love affair with another brother, Ragnar, who shares her own political views and who is by far the handsomer of the two.

A road movie theme follows when the lovers ride slowly North. This film's lovers are busy with their impersonal lovemaking which takes place in and out of beds and windowsills and in the grass and on the beach.

This film's lovers are busy with their impersonal lovemaking which takes place in and out of beds and windowsills and in the grass and on the beach.

At long last, the lovers reach an Arctic port. Ragnar advises Johanna to live the new life offered here and to forget Germany, but news of a friend's death in Nazi hands has her insist on joining other exiled Germans in Paris where they are planning ways and means of resistance to Hitler. The dialog here sounds like tract quotations and is unconvincing, coming from two characters who have proved so self-obsessed that the world will most likely pass them by anyway.—*Kell.*

Skupa Moya, Skupi Moy
(My Darling, My Darling)
(BULGARIAN-COLOR)

A Bulgarian Film Production, "Boyana" film studio, Sofia. World rights, Bulgariafilm. Directed by Eduard Zahariev. Screenplay, Zahariev, Plamen Maslarov, based on motifs in Alexander Tomov's novel "The Saintly Anna;" camera (color), Stefan Trifonov; editor, Magda Krusteva; sets, Georgi Gutsev; music, Mitko Schtorev. Reviewed at Berlin Film Fest (in competition), Feb. 16, 1986. Running time: **107 MINS.**
With: Marianna Dimitrova (Anna), Plamen Sirakov (Ivan), Ivan Donev (Glado), Raya Buchvarova (Raya), Andrei Todorov (Andro), Anton Radichev (Mitko), Stoyan Stoev (Grigor), Anna Cuncheva (Minka), Bozhidar Iskrenov (Bozho), Katya Todorova (Neighbor), Blagovest Argirov (Blago), Svetoslav Argirov (Svet), Penka Armanakova (Pepa).

Berlin — Edward Zahariev has a well-earned reputation for film satires. Now he's on a romantic melodrama kick with "My Darling, My Darling."

Anna and Ivan with their two kids are from the provinces. Ivan has got a new job in an industrial plant, while Anna can work the night shift in a textile factory to earn a bit more money and allow both of them the chance to look after the children in their free time. They are opposites in nature, the husband a merry country type and the wife a shy, attractive individual.

A young poet on the same factory night shift falls in love with Anna and begins to pester her on the streets and on her doorstep. Naturally, Ivan gets jealous, and so one misunderstanding follows another until Anna is at the end of her nerves as the innocent one caught in the middle.

To make matters worse, Ivan still hasn't found an apartment for them, while the friend who runs the villa wants to use the place again for his weekend parties. A telegram arrives announcing the death of Anna's mother. The couple return briefly to the provinces for the burial returning now to Sofia a bit wiser and more than a little resigned to the future.

Well acted by the lead players, "My Darling, My Darling" may not be Zahariev at his challenging best, but it does offer rare insights into working-class mores in a country still making the change-over from a rural to an industrial society. One feels the pain of being uprooted and the despair that goes with it.—*Holl.*

Mon Beau-Frère a Tué Ma Soeur
(My Brother-in-law Has Killed My Sister)
(FRENCH-COLOR)

A World Marketing Film presentation of a Cineproduction film. Produced by Giorgio Silvagni. Directed by Jacques Rouffio. Screenplay, Rouffio, Georges Conchon; camera (color), Jacques Loiselleux; editor, Anne Ruiz; muic, Philippe Sarde; sets, Jean-Jacques Caziot; costumes; Michèle Oerf; sound, Patrice Guisolet. Reviewed at the Zoo Palast, Berlin Film Fest (in competition), Feb. 18, 1986. Running time: **100 MINS.**
Octave . . . . Michel Serrault
Etienne . . . . Michel Piccoli
Esther . . . . Juliette Binoche
Jocelyn . . . . Jean Carmet
Renata . . . . Milva Biolcati

Berlin — It is difficult to understand what is a film like "My Brother-in-law Has Killed My Sister" is doing in the competition of a prestigious film festival. That it might do quite nicely, on home basis, as a boulevard farce, is one thing, but putting it up for awards is rather too much to expect of it.

A very broad spoof of a Raymond Chandler-like plot, with plenty of French sauce, heavy on dialog, it veers away from the main thrust of the story at the slightest excuse, to indulge in pure inconsequential vaudeville.

Two respectable members of the illustrious Académie Française, smitten for rather unclear reasons with a pretty, young and zany veterinarian, are prepared to take at face value her accusation that her brother-in-law has murdered her sister. They start investigating and soon blunder their incompetent way into an incomprehensible maze, with bodies galore. Altogether, there are at least 16 victims around, but keeping with the spirit of the spoof, no dead body is actually shown.

Nothing much comes of this bantering, in the same way that the first verbal duel of the two academicians is nothing more than fireworks for fans of the French language.

Given the obvious talents of Michel Piccoli and Michel Serrault, there are some amusing moments strewn through the movie, but both are worthy of much more challenging material. Juliette Binoche, a rising new star, does pretty well for herself. Technical credits are of a high order.—*Edna.*

Alska mig
(Love Me)
(SWEDISH-COLOR)

An SF (Stockholm) release of the Swedish Film Institute, Swedish TV-2, Svensk Filmindustri, Esselte Video, FilmStallet production. Produced by Staffan Hedquist with Anders Birkeland, Göran Lindström. Executive producer, Klaes Olafsson. Directed by Kay Pollak. Stars Anna Lindén. Original story and screenplay, Pollak with Binnie Kristal-Andersson, Johanna Hald, Ola Olsson; camera (Fujicolor), Roland Sterner; editor, Thomas Holewa; production design, Pelle Johansson, Lotia Melanton. Reviewed at Zoo Palast, Berlin Film Festival (in competition), Feb. 23, 1986. Running time: **126 MINS.**
Sussie . . . . Anna Lindén
Martha . . . . Lena Granhagen
Gunnar . . . . Tomas Laustiola
Son Thomas . . . . Tomas Fryk
Daughter Ann . . . . Jenny Kai-Larsen
The social worker . . . . Ernest Cünther
The ox . . . . Örjan Ramberg

Berlin — For production values and general artistic handling, Sweden's official entry, Kay Pollak's "Love Me" may well remain unsurpassed in this year's Berlin competition. Pollak tells his story with visual flash and burning passion. The trouble is he has no new insights to offer a story that has been told so often in recent years that by now audiences will be justified in branding it tedious.

Sussie, 15, is taken away from her widowed, alcoholic mother by authorities willing to give her a final lease on non-institutional life in a foster home. She fights her foster parents and their own children with cunning as well as tooth & claw (plus spray can). The man and wife have taken Sussie in only as a last-ditch attempt to save their marriage.

The 18-year-old son falls in love with Sussie. The father, abject and insecure, makes clumsy overtures to her. The mother puts up a savage fight to ensure Sussie's love.

Inside and outside their idyllic rural retreat, Sussie wreaks havoc on furniture and real estate in endless temper tantrums. She uses a razor blade to hurt herself and others. During numerous escapes, she repeatedly is a near-victim of rape. Almost everyone in "Love Me" seem to cry the words of the title mutely while they are just as mentally damaged as Sussie.

Pollak unashamedly uses the family unit as a microcosm of society. The film ends, however, amidst the debris of her foster home, with Sussie sitting down at a piano to play softly to the awed people around her. Has she perhaps run the gamut of her tormented feelings? Probably not, but things and people seem to be given one more chance by Pollak.

While the film is overlong and repetitious (it was cut by 25 minutes against the wishes of the helmer), it offers strong and subtle performances by professional actors as well as newcomer Anna Lindén, who is at turns burningly vicious, sweetly demure and just plain touching. Some foreign sales were obtained by its fest showing in Berlin. —*Kell.*

Rosa-La-Rose, Fille Publique
(Rosa-The-Rose, Public Woman)
(FRENCH-COLOR)

A Diagonale/Stephan Films coproduction, with the Ministry of Culture. Produced by Pierre Bellot. Written and directed by Paul Vecchiali. Camera (Eastmancolor), George Strouve, Renato Berta; editor, Vecchiali, Franck Mathieu; sound, Jean-François Chevalier; music, Roland Vincent; costumes, Nathalie Cercuel; sets, Michel Roques; assistant director, Didier Albert; production managers, Yves Dutheil, Eric Dangremont. Reviewed at Berlin Film Festival, Atelier (out of competition), Feb. 17, 1986. Running time: **87 MINS.**
Rosa . . . . Marianne Basler
Gilbert . . . . : . . . . Jean Sorel
Julien . . . . Pierre Cosso
Laurent . . . . Laurent Levy
40 . . . . Catherine Lachens
35 . . . . Evelyne Buyle

Berlin — Paul Vecchiali continues to make odd, idiosyncratic films ("Women, Women," "Body To Heart") which have a small but loyal following. His latest is arguably more accessible than some of his others, but overall still a dangerously thin effort about a spectacularly beautiful prostitute and her fate.

Set in the Les Halles district of Paris, pic focuses attention on a group of hookers working for pimp Jean Sorel of which Rosa (Marianne Basler) is the star attraction. All goes well until Rosa falls for a working class character, which results in agony and tragedy.

Pic's chief asset is Basler, a looker with a fresh-faced charm which indicates she has a future with the right roles. Free-wheeling nudity will appeal to some sections of the audience.

The plot is pretty familiar, and though Vecchiali intros some oddball characters, such as a stunted youth who follows Rosa around and eventually gets to bed her before the tragic finale, he really adds little of interest to an old theme, despite buff allusions.

Pic is dedicated to several great names of French cinema, including Jean Renoir, Max Ophüls and Danielle Darrieux. —*Strat.*

Das Haus am Fluss
(The House On The River)
(EAST GERMAN-COLOR)

A DEFA Film production, "Roter Kreis" unit, East Berlin. World rights, DEFA Aussenhandel, East Berlin. Written and directed by Roland Gräf, based on Friedrich Wolf's story "The Russian Pelt;" camera (color), Roland Dressel; editor, Monika Schindler; music, Günther Fischer; sets, Alfred Hirschmeier. Reviewed at Berlin Film Fest (in competition), Feb. 21, 1986. Running time: **88 MINS.**

With: Katrin Sass (Agnes Eckert), Manfred Gorr (Jupp Eckert), Jutta Wachowiak (Mother Voss), Rolf Hoppe (Director Hüsgen), Corinna Harfouch (Emmi Voss), Johanna Schall (Lena Brinken), Sylvester Groth (Heinz Hüsgen), Peter Zimmermann (W. Tiedemann), Werner Codemann (Schimmelpfennig), Mathis Schrader (Ferdinand Belz), Arianne Borbach (Lisbeth Voss), Hermann Beyer (Piter Dressen), Eckhard Becker (Gestapo man).

Berlin — Roland Gräf's "The House On The River" is based on a story by one of East Germany's respected authors, Friedrich Wolf (1888-1953), the father of the equally renowned filmmaker Konrad Wolf. Friedrich Wolf's story "The Russian Pelt" (1942), the source for "The House On The River," served back then a double purpose as literature and propaganda. Today it stands up well on its merits alone.

Mother Voss and her daughters, Agnes (married) and Emmi (engaged), live in a house on the river near Berlin in 1941. The German army is victorious on the Russian front, and one day Emmi's boyfriend sends home a Ukrainian blouse for her. She puts it down and dances like a carefree sprit on the water's edge. The Voss family is poor but hardworking, employed as fishermen and in a nearby factory, and this gesture of accepting a wargoods present from the front strikes the note of doom for them all.

The married sister, Agnes, is desired by the factory boss where she works. Since he's in cahoots with the local Gestapo chief, who in turn desires his own wife, an effective deal is made to have Agnes' husband Jupp conscripted for service. This done, and with the distraut Agnes now in need of affection of any kind, she acquiesces after loneliness sets in and she can resist no longer.

The summer turns to winter, and the bitter news of the death of Emmi's love on the front hits hard. Emmi loses control, falls into depression and hangs herself. Jupp returns home from the front a cripple, but he carries with him a Russian pelt taken from a dead civilian, something as dear to him as his own life. Agnes, who has been courted by the factory boss with a similar fur piece, feels the irony of the situation, but she is now more desperate than ever to keep Jupp at her side, whatever the cost.

The final scene in the house on the river has a showdown between the arrogant factory boss and the repentive Jupp concerning the crimes being committed by the Germans on the Eastern front. The evildoer in the show wants to report Jupp for treason against the state, while at the same time decrying a possible sabotage by communist underground workers at the plant. It's the frail and weak Agnes who rises in protest at the precise moment to strike the death blow against her seducer and manipulator. Justice is done, but the SS man and the Gestapo are at the door like wolves in the final shot.

"The House On The River" is a metaphorical statement on German guilt and blind compliance. It's presented on an appropriately low-key note and is well acted by all the principals. —*Holl.*

Just Between Friends
(COLOR)

Maudlin treatment of a mid-life crisis.

An Orion Pictures release of an MTM Enterprises production. Produced by Edward Teets, Allan Burns. Written and directed by Burns. Stars Mary Tyler Moore. Camera (Deluxe color), Jordan Cronenweth; editor, Ann Goursaud; music, Patrick Williams; production design, Sydney Z. Litwack; set decorator, Bruce Weintraub, Chris Butler; set designer, Joseph Lucky; sound, Kirk Francis; costumes, Cynthia Bales; assistant director, Patrick Crowley; associate producer, James H. Rascoe; casting, Geri Windsor, Eugene Blythe. Reviewed at MGM/UA screening room, Culver City, Calif., Feb. 27, 1986. (MPAA Rating: PG-13.) Running time: **120 MINS.**

Holly Davis	Mary Tyler Moore
Chip Davis	Ted Danson
Sandy Dunlap	Christine Lahti
Harry Crandall	Sam Waterston
Helga	Salome Jens
Kim Davis	Susan Rinell
Jeff Davis	Timothy Gibbs
Carla	Diane Stilwell
Bill	James MacKrell

Hollywood — The main difference between "Just Between Friends" and a tv film is that "Just Between Friends" doesn't have commercials. It is also slower even than tv and more packed with improbable life crises than any telefilm. Despite numerous melodramatic developments, nothing much seems to be happening and even with Mary Tyler Moore, audiences should stay away in droves.

It is nice to see a film dealing with adult issues for a change, but "Just Between Friends" chronicles a middle age few people will experience. In an attempt to be "real" and "relevant," Allan Burns screenplay has included far too many maudlin turns to allow any real feeling to survive.

Mary Tyler Moore is the envoy into this middle-class wasteland and it's hard to believe anyone will want to spend much time there. As Holly Davis, Moore is a timid homebody who has sacrificed her independence for a well-oiled domestic life. Her husband Chip (Ted Danson), however, misses the excitement and takes up with tv newscaster Sandy Dunlap (Christine Lahti) for a little adventure.

Burns, who also directed and coproduced the film, throws a few wild curveballs to get at some very predictable emotions. First, the women become friends in Moore's aeorobics class. The real surprise of the film comes about halfway through when Burns kills off Danson in an off-camera car wreck while he's away at an anti-nuke rally.

If this isn't enough, Lahti discovers Danson has left her a souvenir from beyond the grave, as it were. She's pregnant with his baby. This puts a crimp in the girls' friendship and it takes the rest of the film's excessive 120 minutes for them to accept how much they need and like each other.

Moore plays an odd kind of character who seems unsure about even the most fundamental decisions in life. It probably comes from having her husband around to make most of her decisions and her growth in the film is to become more confident and self-reliant.

Lahti is once again the best friend and is every bit as good, if not better, than she was in a similar role in "Swing Shift." Here she is by far the more interesting character partially because Burns has given her most of the film's good lines. It's no small wonder that she's a breath of fresh air for Danson after spending years with the oh-so-perfect Moore.

As Danson's best friend with an eye for Moore, Sam Waterston moves out of type to play a timid, insecure man. It's a good performance but not a terribly appealing character. Overall there is little chemistry between these friends and lovers with Danson and Moore basically an unconvincing couple. On her own Moore is master of the mannerism with not enough substance to back up the action. Again partial blame must go to Burns.

Most of the action takes place in the Davis' suburban household with Burns creating little momentum. Camerawork by Jordan Cronenweth is surprisingly static and given to dark tones. In his first directorial outing, after developing many of the MTM tv hits, Burns frames too many silhouetted lovers and other equally clichéd shots.

Other tech credits are adequate with Patrick Williams' music supplying the proper syrup at key moments.—*Jagr.*

Hell Squad
(COLOR)

Amateurish action film.

A Cannon Films release of a Cinevid production, in association with Cannon Group. Written, produced and directed by Ken Hartford. Camera (color), John McCoy; editor, Robert Ernst; music, Charles P. Barnett; sound, Robert Bourne, Dave Fisher, Jim Watt; assistant director, Steve Wallace; production manager, Mangann Zvoleff; special effects, Harry Woolman. Reviewed on MGM/UA Home Video vidcassette, N.Y., March 1, 1986. (MPAA Rating: R.) Running time: **87 MINS.**

Jan	Bainbridge Scott
Jack	Glen Hartford
Tina	Tina Lederman

Also with: Maureen Kelly, Penny Prior, Kimberly Baucum, Delynn Gardner, Lisa Nottingham, Kathy Jinnett, Loren Chamberlain (members of squad); Jace Damon (Mark), Walter Cox (Jim), Frank Romano (Drill Sgt.), Marvin Miller (Sheik), Sally Swift (Ann), William Bryant (Nightclub owner), Lee Coy (Col. Balin).

"Hell Squad" is a laughable action picture about Las Vegas showgirls who become instant commandos. Made circa 1983, pic was released theatrically overseas last year but domestic distrib Cannon sent the film directly to homevideo stores (via its MGM/UA deal) domestically.

Bainbridge Scott is a pretty blond who toplines as Jan, a manager of Vegas showgirls enlisted by her former boyfriend Jim (Walter Cox) to help him rescue a diplomat's son (Glen Hartford) who's been kidnaped by Arabs demanding the secret of a neutron bomb weapon.

Nearly 20 statuesque girls go through a week's crash training course, after which nine are chosen (including Jan, the only one with previous fighting skills) to mount a commando raid in the Middle East. Typical of the film's carelessness, only eight girls are identified in the poolside selection scene, yet a squad of nine carries on for the rest of the picture.

Poor action scenes ensue, revolving around the running gag of the girls repeatedly returning to their hotel suite and together hopping into a big, communal bathtub, due to a local water shortage. Reversing the usual pecking order of exploitation films, only leading player Jan has nude scenes while the other girls manage to remain covered up.

Filmmaker Ken Hartford is known for buying and selling features "by the pound" for international distribution, but he seems to have short-changed the viewer here. Filmed out west, picture includes unconvincing stock footage to represent the Middle East, plus cheap sets and a library music-type score. Level of humor is evidenced by an end credit that thanks "42 members of PLO who played themselves as terrorists." —*Lor.*

Salvador
(COLOR)

Controversial, semi-docu drama of a photojournalist in Central America.

A Hemdale release and presentation. Produced by Gerald Green, Oliver Stone. Executive producers, John Daly, Derek Gibson. Directed by Stone. Stars James Woods. Screenplay, Stone, Richard Boyle; camera (color), Robert Richardson; editor, Claire Simpson; music, Georges Delerue; production design, Bruno Rubeo; art direction, (Mexico), Melo Hinojosa; costume design, Kathryn Greko Morrison; special effects supervision, Yves De Bono; associate producers, Bob Morones, Brad H. Aronson; assistant directors, Ramon Menendez, Jose Luis Ortega (Mexico). Reviewed at the Avco Cinema, W. Los Angeles, Feb. 23, 1986. (MPAA Rating: R.) Running time; **123 MINS.**
Richard Boyle .... James Woods
Dr. Rock .... James Belushi
Amb. Thomas Kelly ..... Michael Murphy
John Cassady .... John Savage
Maria .... Elpedia Carrillo
Major Max .... Tony Plana
Jack Morgan .... Colby Chester
Cathy Moore .... Cynthia Gibb
Col. Hyde .... Will MacMillian
Pauline Axelrod .... Valerie Wildman
Archbishop Romero .... Jose Carlos Ruiz
Col. Julio Figueroa .... Jorge Luke
Army Lieutenant .... Juan Fernandez

Hollywood — The tale of American photojournalist Richard Boyle's adventures in strife-torn Central America five years ago, "Salvador" is as raw, difficult, compelling, unreasonable, reckless and vivid as its protagonist. Oliver Stone's picture, which had its world premiere at the Santa Barbara Intl. Film Festival on Feb. 28, will serve as the first release of Hemdale's distribution arm, and the b.o. road will not be easy. Contemporary political pictures in general, and those on Central America in particular, such as "Under Fire" and "Latino," have not appealed to the public. There's plenty here to provoke discussion, enough to spark sufficient controversy to give the film a foot in the door of the specialized and art market.

Designed to expose as many outrages, injustices and human tragedies as possible, pic naturally comes down savagely upon the Salvodoran military, the Death Squads and U.S. government backing or tolerance for at least some of their excesses. Nevertheless, it would be far from accurate to label this a left-wing tract.

Despite a brief sequence which embarrassingly idealizes the peasant insurgents, Stone seems anxious to straddle the political fence. He makes sure to point out that the left can be just as brutal as the right, and seems to conclude by saying that Central America is such a chaotic mess that no coherent attitude or policy is possible until a return to some basic human values is effected. Indeed, nothing in Stone's previous filmography ("Midnight Express," "Scarface," "Year Of The Dragon") would lead one to believe that he stands in the forefront of Hollywood's liberal-left humanists.

James Woods portrays the real-life Boyle, who at the outset is shown to be at his lowest ebb as a virtual bum and professional outcast in San Francisco.

With no particular prospects, he shanghais fun-loving buddy James Belushi for the long drive down to (El) Salvador, where Woods has left behind a native girlfriend and where he thinks he might be able to pick up some freelance work.

Hard to warm up to because of his extreme irresponsiblity, crudeness and irrepressible need to take advantage of everyone in sight for selfish reasons, Woods/Boyle nevertheless cuts an amusing figure as he bumps up against glowering Death Squad officers, double-talking U.S. Embassy types, self-righteous military officers and priggish, clean-cut establishment reporters.

A man of such manic energy and mighty enthusiasm that even vast quantities of alcohol can't douse the flames, Woods finally sobers up when he discovers the true magnitude of suffering going on in the country he formerly visited for its great surfing and pretty women.

The film's major problem as a story is that its course feels determined by historical events, rather than by the imperatives of good dramatic structure. Stone makes sure his hero is present at every conceivable moment of significance — a 1980 U.S. Embassy party where Ronald Reagan's election is celebrated, the assination of Archbishop Romero, the immediate aftermath of the rape and murder of the American nuns, a decisive battle between the government and rebels — but hasn't adequately shaped matters to artistic ends.

Woods' transition comes too abruptly, Belushi virtually disappears from the story, and Stone unfortunately allows his spokesman to figuratively mount a platform and, for many sanctimonious minutes, tell off American government personnel and chastise them for their lack of "human decency," when he himself is a walking illustration of incivility.

Nevertheless, the film has an immediacy, energy and vividness that is often quite exciting, and the essential truth of much of what Stone has put on display will prove bracing for many viewers. Except for his occasional missteps, the director rivets the attention in scene after scene.

Working in a documentary-like style, Stone, lenser Robert Richardson and production designer Bruno Rubeo have very effectively caught the teeming confusion, appalling poverty, natural beauty and festering danger of this Third World region.

Woods and Boyle seem to go together like hand and glove. It's unimaginable that any actor could be more convincing as such a crazed, impassioned correspondent. John Savage pops in from time to time as a combat photographer who wants to be Robert Capa and finally gets his wish. Michael Murphy feels right as the outgoing U.S. ambassador, and remainder of the cast is uniformly good.

Despite the dramatic problems, Stone has gotten a great deal of visual and political material up on the screen, and it's all worth grappling with. A fine point: Woods' repeated use of the term "yuppies," a category of people he naturally can't stand, is decidedly premature in 1980. —*Cart.*

Bokuchan No Senjou
(Bokuchan's Battlefield)
(JAPANESE-B&W)

A Kobushi production, Shinjuku. Produced by Seijiro Kohyama, Yutaka Osawa, Toshio Gotoh. Directed by Osawa. Screenplay, Yoko Yamamoto, Osawa, based on Tsuguo Okuda's story "Bokuchan's War;" camera (b&w) Shun Yamamoto; editor, Jun Nabeshima; music, Masao Hario; sound, Shimpei Kikuchi; sets, Aira Haruki. Reviewed at Berlin Film Fest (Children's Festival), Feb. 25, 1986. Running time: **106 MINS.**
With: Takanori Kurumagi (Minamoto), Yoshiyuki Ohmori (Asahina), Daijiro Nakamura (Makino), Gin Maeda (Teacher), Yukari Yamamoto (Matrone), Yumiko Fujita (Minamoto's mother).

Berlin — Yutaka Osawa's "Bokuchan's Battlefield" is more of a film for adults that deals with children than it is a kidpic per se, although the thin line between a film for children and youth does qualify it in the fest competition for audiences 12 years of age and older. It's a very fine film on wartime Japan, third in a trilogy of "War Orphans In Hiroshima" (1980), "Sensei - Teacher" (1982), on events in Nagasaki, and now "Bokuchan's Battlefield" (1985) set partially in Osaka.

Since the cities of Hiroshima, Nagasaki and Osaka were all heavily hit by fire and/or atomic bombings during the spring and summer of 1945, helmer Osawa has molded an overall impressive and apparently autobiographical (he was born in 1935) statement on horrors of war experienced and seen through the eyes of children.

Bokuchan, a lad of about 10, lives with his family in the industrial city of Osaka (Japan's second largest). It is early 1944 and Japan is losing the war, so the children have to be evacuated to a youth camp and training center as future soldiers once the bombings start. Since Bokuchan's father is a soldier on the front, he is intensely loyal to his family and country, but he is also a frail athletic specimen and has trouble being the class leader the teacher expects of him.

As the title indicates, Bokuchan has to fight his own battles before becoming a respected leader and a strong personality. He finds very quickly that the bullies in the camp can terrorize the children as they please, and if he doesn't stand up to them soon, all self-respect will be lost. The camp bully leader gradually has his way, and the situation is further complicated by Bokuchan's being lonely and not receiving a weekend visit from his mother. Moreover, regulations by a nationalist-type teacher require blind obedience above all — particularly when the war is being lost and disconcerting news of the imminent defeat reaches school authorities.

The first shadows of the war reach the children via the increasing shortage of food, a situation that plays into the hands of the bullies: food has to be turned over by the weaker to the stronger. Bokuchan's best friend protects him as a stronger and tougher individual, but tragedy strikes when the friend loses his family in a bombing raid.

Next comes news of the death of Bokuchan's father, and the boy is convinced his mother needs him more at home than the teacher does at the school. The 1945 air raids wipe out Bokuchan's home in Osaka, kill his grandmother, and disperse the family to some unknown refuge. The boy rises to the moment by deciding to fight his own battles: he confronts his school enemy and, despite being the weaker, fights him to a draw — and wins his respect as a friend for his courage and determination.

The final scene has Bokuchan leaving the school illegally to catch a train to Osaka, where we find him caught in the midst of a catastrophic fire bombing. The death and destruction around him is horrendous.

Directed with an able hand and well acted by kid thesps and adult professionals, "Bokuchan's Battlefield" stands out in particular for its b&w lensing. On the minus side, pic is a mite too long and could be tightened without losing on theme or message. —*Holl.*

Treťi Sarkan
(The Third Dragon)
(CZECHOSLOVAK-COLOR)

A Czechoslovak Film production, Prague. World rights, Czechoslovak Film Export, Prague. Directed by Peter Hledik. Screenplay, Igor Rusnak, based on an idea by Jozef Zarnay; camera (color), Vincent Rosinec; editor, Eduard Klenovsky; music, Petr Hapka; sets, Anton Krajčovič. Reviewed at Berlin Film Fest (Children's Festival), Feb. 24, 1986. Running time: **83 MINS.**
With: Patrik Šima (Pato), Ján Križik (Jano), Boris Trsťan (Boris), Marjo Malatinsky (Mogam), Radovan Lukavsky (Ravadar) František Husák (Museum director), Marian Sotnik (Tubar), Margita Lopatová (First scientist), Jeno Siposs (Second scientist).

Berlin — The Czechoslovaks have a respected tradition of making original kidpics, and Peter Hledik's "The Third Dragon" is no exception. It scores as one of the best of the many quite outstanding entries in the increasingly important children's section of the Berlinale.

Three boys are prone to adventure, and one of their favorite Mark-Twain-like hideaways is at the Dragon's Rock. While on an expedition to the rock, their dog falls into a crevice. While trying to rescue him, they discover a cave.

The cavern turns out instead to be the inside of a space-ship, sent from the planet Lurida during the Middle Ages (originally three space ships were sent) to find out how Earthlings were handling the problem of acid rain, industrial waste, and other technological scourges destroying life on Lurida. The twist here is that Lurida is some eight centuries ahead of Earth, so the one space-ship is left behind to wait until the Earthlings catch up to ecological scare — and perhaps stumble on a scientific solution helpful to all in the meantime.

The boys are confronted with rather frightening images of a dying planet once they wake out of a deep sleep and find they are on Lurida. At the same time, their parents back home are concerned over their whereabouts, and a search around the Dragon's Rock takes place parallel to the lads' experiences on Lurida. By chance, the boys brought along corn kernels, and these are planted on the wasted planet. It turns out to be the saving grace motif: a fortunate rainfall nourishes the seeds, and up sprouts corn shoots — the planet is saved!

The grateful Luridans get the boys back home, carrying with them in their consciousness the bitter lessons of environmental pollution. Once back home, they do take everything to heart too: they look around only to discover that trees are dying and the waters are polluted and a dark haze hangs over their town. Considering that Czechoslovakia has a high acid rain count, this kidpic is stating the case in pretty strong terms in regard to industrial misery in a socialist society.

Indeed, up until only a few years ago, sociocritical themes of this sort were rarities in E. European cinema. Now that a children's film in Czechoslovakia has taken such a progressive stand on a common ecological problem is a sure sign of better things to come in Czech and Slovak film circles.

Credits in general are a solid plus, particularly kid thesps and musical score. —*Holl.*

Untermehmen Geigenkasten
(Operation Violin Case)
(EAST GERMAN-COLOR)

A DEFA Film production, "Johannisthal" group, East Berlin; world rights, DEFA Aussenhandel, East Berlin. Directed by Gunter Friedrich. Screenplay, Anne Gossens; camera (color), Günter Heimann; editor, Vera Nowark; sets, Marlene Willmann; music, Bernd Menzel; production manager, Siegfried Kabitzke. Reviewed at Berlin Film Fest (Children's Fest), Feb. 15, 1986. Running time: **85 MINS.**
With: Alexander Heidenreich (Ole), Dirk Bartsch (Andreas), Peggy Steiner (Marie), Matthias Krohse (Jens), Swetlana Schönfeld (Ole's mother), Gerd Grasse (Ole's father), Peter Bause (Lt. Vogel), Fred Delmare (Grandpa Tönnchen), Andreas Schumann (Herr Neumann), Gerd Hartmut Schreier (Herr Franke).

Berlin — One of the delightfully amusing kidpics at the Berlinale, Gunter Friedrich's "Operation Violin Case" has a pair of fun-raising youngsters playing Sherlock Holmes in a small provincial town. Ole is always scheming up something. His attempt to fly with a Leonardo da Vinci contraption gets him into the air on a windy day off a steep hill — but the resulting crash puts him in a hospital for a spell. There he watches an older Holmes film on tv and hits upon the idea to become a detective.

The summer vacation now over, the kids in school make fun of the inventive youngster. Only his friend Andreas goes along with the new scheme, taking on the role of Dr. Watson. The rest is finding the right costumes: they pretend to be interested in taking violin lessons to get their hands on an empty violin case, as shown in the film. While out scouting for a case to solve, they stumble on a real burglary.

Helmer Friedrich has packed his kidpic with witty jokes, both visual and verbal. The added note that crooks are running around in socialist society, just as in the capitalist countries, is worth reflecting on as well. —*Holl.*

El Rigor Del Destino
(Hardships Of Destiny)
(ARGENTINE-COLOR)

A Gerardo Vallejo production. Produced, written and directed by Vallejo. Camera (color), Yito Blanc; editor, Luis Mutti; sound, Miguel Babuini; sets, Abel Facello; costumes, Beatriz di Benedetto. Reviewed at Berlin Film Festival (forum), Feb. 24, 1986. Running time: **100 MINS.**
With: Carlos Carella, Alejandro Copley, Lenor Manso, Ana Maria Picchio, Victor Laplace, Alberto Benegas.

Berlin — Set in Tucuman, a province in northern Argentina, "Hardships Of Destiny" is a film about three generations of a family who live through the tumultuous period of the last 10 years. It opens in 1976 as an old farmer, living in an isolated country house, is brought the news that his son is dead and his daughter-in-law and beloved grandson have left for Spain.

Seven years later, with the country returning to normal, they return home and the old man is reunited with the little boy, who worships him. Pic's main concerns are the relationship between these two, the oldster conveying to the lad his homespun philosophies about life and also explaining what happened to his father. The father, we discover, is not the paragon we might have expected, but a rather unsavory drunk and womanizer.

From its title, viewers might expect a more rugged film than this actually is. It's more of a hymn to the Tucuman people who survived the bad years and are now looking forward, with the rest of the country, to a brighter future. Technically pic is fine in every department. —*Strat.*

Erzi De Da Wanou
(The Sandwich Man)
(TAIWANESE-COLOR)

A Sunny Overseas Corp. production. Produced by Ming Chi. Directed by Hou Shao-Shen, Jen Wan, Jong Cheung-Tsang. Screenplay, Wu Nien-Chun, from stories by Hwan Tzen-Ming; production supervisor, Wu Chung Ling. No further credits supplied. Reviewed at Berlin Film Festival (market), Feb. 22, 1986. Running time: **102 MINS.**
With: Chen Bo Jeng, Yang Li-Ying, Jo Shen-Li, Chiang Sha, King Ding, Chan Chi.

Berlin — Now that international interest in Taiwanese cinema has been aroused by such films as Edward Yang's "Taipei Story" and Hou Shao-Shen's "Time To Live And Time To Die" (unspooled in the Berlin Forum), some of the earlier films of this new wave are being unveiled including the 1983 three-part pic "The Sandwich Man." Hou Shao-Shen directed the first part only, but this apprentice work already shows a confident talent.

His episode is "Son's Big Doll" and is set in 1962. Long out of work, a man manages to get a job dressed as a clown promoting the films at the local cinema. His peculiar get-up makes him a laughing stock and shames some of his relatives. Worse, his baby son only recognizes his father when he's in clown makeup. To the child, he's a "big doll." It's a touching, beautifully handled featurette.

Part 2, "Vicky's Hat," directed by Jen Wan, takes place in 1964 and deals with two friends selling Japanese-made pressure cookers in small towns. One is strangely attracted to a schoolgirl who always wears a hat to hide a disfiguring scar, while the other, married with a pregnant wife, dies when a pressure cooker explodes during an outdoor demonstration. It's a grim, but effective, centerpiece.

"A Taste Of Apples," directed by Jong Cheung-Tsang, and set in 1969, has a cyclist on his way to work hit by a car driven by an American officer. Ironically his misfortune brings to his family more money and food than they ever had before including, for the first time, apples.

All three stories deal with the plight of poor people trying to get by and, to a degree, with foreign influences on Taiwanese society. In the first story, the hero gets the idea for the clown makeup from a Japanese magazine, and the outside influences on stories two and three are obvious.

Mandarin-track pic would be an integral part of any future programming by archives or fests on

Taiwanese cinema, but tv exposure is also indicated in certain countries.
—*Strat.*

Paris Minuit
(Paris Midnight)
(FRENCH-COLOR)

A Mai production. Produced by Jean-Pierre Malignon. Associate producer, Olivier Donnet. Directed by Frédéric Andrei. Screenplay, Philippe Malignon, Andrei; camera (Fujicolor), Bertrand Chatry; editor, Dominique Roy; music, Christophe Donnet; sound, Eric Vaucher; production manager, Jacques Perrier; assistant director, Jean-Marie David; sets, François Carton. Reviewed at Berlin Film Festival (market), Feb. 23, 1986. Running time: **94 MINS.**
Serge Cartan ....Frédéric Andrei
Marie ....Isabelle Texier
Lt. Belland ....Gabriel Cattand
Rougier ....Philippe Malignon
Leproux ....Michel Creton
Carmona ....Jean-Pierre Malignon
Martin ....Alain Sachs
Alexis ....Jean-Paul Comart
Roubaud ....Jerome Nobecourt
The Tramp................Ginette Garcin
Frederique ....Isabelle Willer

Berlin — Frédéric Andrei, the young actor who scored in the lead role in "Diva" and since has made a trio of short films, turns feature director with this offbeat crime pic. "Paris Midnight" starts out like any other French cop film (armed bandits rob a fashionable jewelery story in mid-August; three are killed; two, slightly wounded, escape) but then goes off in some intriguingly odd directions. Result is quite a lot of fun. It opens in France mid-April.

The couple who get away, played by the director himself and newcomer Isabelle Texier, are lovers. They decide to split up, but keep in touch via a series of coded messages broadcast by radio stations. Using picture postcards which they leave in strategic positions, they move around the famous monuments of Paris by night, always a step or two ahead of the police.

The cop in charge of the case (Gabriel Cattand) latches on to the postcards — all of which carry a line from a poem by Appolinaire — and the broadcast messages, but can never work out where the young outlaws will rendezvous next.

Matters are complicated by the fact that Andrei's sister is a member of a large bike gang roaming the streets, and that his mother, on hearing of her son's trouble, is rushed to a hospital.

Credit Andrei for injecting a few new ideas into a tired genre. He and Texier are properly tough yet vulnerable, while the cops are generally seen as being a bit thick. Sharp lensing by Bertrand Chatry on famed locations all over the city almost all shot at night, is an added plus.
—*Strat.*

Los Insomnes
(The Insomniacs)
(ARGENTINE-COLOR)

A Ferlain S.A. production, Buenos Aires. Directed by Carlos Orgambide. Screenplay, Beatriz Guido, Bernardo Raitman, Orgambide based on story by Guido; camera (color); Eduardo Legabia, Silvart; editor, Eduardo López; music: Luis Maria Serra; sets, Leandro Rogucci; sound: Sergio Stavropulos. Reviewed at the Delphi Palace, Berlin Film Fest (forum), Feb. 21, 1986. Runing time: **80 MINS.**
With: Elsa Berenguer, Betiana Blum, Carlos Leyrado, Selva Aleman, Mirta Busnelli, Roberto Carnaghi, Alberto Fernández de Roso, Marta Gam, Marcos Zucker, Antonio Grimau, Hugo Midon, Boy Olmi.

Berlin — Obviously intended as an allegory of pre-Alfonsin Argentina, "The Insomniacs" is so excessively concerned with the meaning behind the lines, that it doesn't care whether the lines themselves make any sense at all.

The entire story takes place in one building, populated by a crowd which is supposed to reflect everything that is wrong with Argentine society. They range from the janitor, on the ground floor, who pretends to have been once a successful cabaret star and still lives on the past glories of the old continent, in memories of Gardel and stories about holidays in Cannes, to the top floor, in which a handsome youth is tied to a bed and is tortured by a businessman type and his henchman — a transvestite, a tough lady with sexual hangups and a moron.

Everyone is busily hustling for himself, and all are delighted to ignore anything that might disturb their miserable existence. Only the children of the house, running up and down the stairs day and night (the insomniacs of the title) are conscious of what is going on and try to warn the grownups of the horrors under their own noses, but to no avail.

Carlos Orgambide doesn't even try to tell a real story here. He goes on repeating his statements and his warnings from different angles, often resorting to quick montage of short excerpts from sequences already seen. Heavy makeup and overdress suggest the utter decadence of the country, in a cabaret style calling to mind Germany in the '20s. References are made to Argentina's dependence on American money, on the machismo that rules the social conventions, on the perversity of murderers who like cats but kill people, and to top it all, some characters have significant names such as Pandora.

The style itself is rather old-fashioned and the dramatic material insufficient. Technical credits are satisfactory. —*Edna.*

Mala Noche
(Bad Night)
(U.S.-B&W)

A Northern Film Co. production. Produced, written and directed by Gus Van Sant, from the novella by Walt Curtis. Camera (b&w), John Campbell; editor, Gus Van Sant; music, Creighton Lindsay; sound, Pat Baum. Reviewed at Berlin Film Festival, Atelier (panorama), Feb. 24, 1986. Running time: **75 MINS.**
Walt Curtis ....Tim Strecter
Johnny ....Doug Cooeyate
Roberto Pepper ....Ray Monge

Berlin — A low-budget adaptation of an autobiographical novella, "Mala Noche" seems to be aiming for the same audience as "Stranger Than Paradise" via its offhand humor, studied yet vaguely realistic dialog and throwaway acting. The Jim Jarmusch film was much more successful, but this debut by Gus Van Sant shows lots of promise and is basically a likeable effort.

Central character is Walt, who works in a small store in Portland, Ore., and lives with his understanding sister. Walt is gay, and develops an almost uncontrollable lust for a young Mexican drifter, one of many illegal immigrants. Johnny, the Mexican, agrees to come to Walt's home for dinner, but insists on bringing his friend Roberto along. Johnny prefers Walt's sister to Walt, and Walt has to settle for Roberto as a lover instead of the object of his desires.

Later Roberto is killed in a fracas with the police, and Johnny disappears. Film ends abruptly as the sister decides to go to Anchorage to work in a strip club and Walt finally sees Johnny again on a street corner.

Shot in very high contrast black and white, with lots of oppressive shadows, pic looks good on the big screen, but will probably suffer when transferred to video. Dialog is peppered with four-letter words and an almost Henry Miller-ish use of rough language. It all rings true, and the yearning is there, plus the plight of these oppressed young men from south of the border who try to stay alive while on the run in the inhospitable northwest. —*Strat.*

Vladimir Horowitz, The Last Romantic
(U.S.-DOCU-COLOR)

A Peter Gelb production. Directed by David Maysles and Albert Maysles. Features Vladimir Horowitz, Wanda Toscanini Horowitz. Camera (color), Albert and David Maysles, Don Lenzer; editor, Deborah Pickson, Patricia Jaffe; music, Jack Pfeiffer; sound, Michael Shoskes. Reviewed at Berlin Film Festival (forum), Feb. 24, 1986. Running time: **87 MINS.**

Berlin — "Vladimir Horowitz, The Last Romantic" is a touching portrait of one of the greatest pianists of this century in his old age.

The Russian-born master's New York apartment on the Upper East Side was converted into a sound studio and lensed live with no prearranged script. Between sessions at the keyboard, beginning with a Busoni transcription of a Bach choral, Horowitz and wife Wanda, daughter of the last conductor Arturo Toscanini, keep up a relaxed and often humorous conversation. Despite his advanced age, Horowitz shows a lively wit, mugging and clowning at the Steinway before and after serious playing.

Much of the 87 minutes is taken up in performances of Mozart, Schubert, Chopin, Liszt, Rachmaninoff and Scriabin, for whom Horowitz played when he was 10. Between times, the master stretches out on the sofa and reminisces about the greats he has known in a career extending well over 60 years.

He describes Rachmaninoff as "My best friend, composer, conductor and pianist, first class all." As Horowitz plays, the camera gives closeups of his hands and top shots in virtuoso passages.

Wanda Horowitz recounts their courtship and brings out a family album with a picture of Vladimir when he was 24 with the remark, "Doesn't he look like Chopin?"

To his wife's feigned annoyance, Horowitz strums a few bars of his famed arrangement of "Stars And Stripes Forever," a bravura piece reserved for encores. After a transcendental performance of Chopin's B-minor scherzo, in a real understatement Horowitz quips, "Good for an old man."

The docu gives an intimate glimpse of piano playing in the grand manner, and is very spontaneous. It's a natural for the art circuits, public television, and video, with offshore prospects bullish.—*Kind.*

Tras El Cristal
(In A Glass Cage)
(SPANISH-COLOR)

A TEM Productores Asociados production. Produced by Teresa Enrich. Written and directed by Agustin Villaronga. Camera (color), Jaume Peracaula; music, Javier Navaretto; editor, Raul Roman; art director, Case Candini. Reviewed at Berlin Film Festival, Atelier (panorama), Feb. 23, 1986. Running time: **112 MINS.**
Klaus..................Gunter Meisner
Angelo ....David Sust
Griselda.................Marisa Paredes
Rena ....Gisela Echevarria
Maid ....Imma Colomer
Also with: Josue Gausch, Alberto Manzano, Ricart Carcelero, David Cuspinet.

Berlin — A horrifying film about a sexual deviant who gets his kicks torturing and killing young boys, "In A Glass Cage" is, perversely, a well-made and probably seriously intentioned pic. Its very evident qualities only add to its power to disturb and shock.

Presumably set in the '50s, pic opens with a scene in which a middled-aged man is beating a naked boy who's hanging from the ceiling by a rope attached to his wrists. The man (Gunter Meisner) kisses the child on the lips before delivering the death blow. It's a harrowing opener.

It seems the man, Klaus, was formerly a doctor at a German concentration camp who discovered sexual pleasure when torturing and killing little boys. An offscreen accident has put him in an iron lung, where he live in a house somewhere in the Spanish countryside with a wife (Marisa Paredes) who despises him and an innocent pre-teen daughter, Rena (Gisela Echevarria). Enter a mysterious, scarred young man, Angelo (David Sust) who offers to care for the invalid. It soon becomes clear that Angelo was one of Klaus' camp victims who survived, but he's not after revenge. Indeed, the film suggests, he has inherited the sexual desires and obsessions of his tormentor, and delights in reading passages from Klaus' wartime diary in which his gruesome acts are lovingly described.

Before long, Angelo has murdered the wife (in a classical suspense sequence, beautifully shot and edited) and is bringing young boys from the village home to kill them in front of his helpless mentor, using methods described in the diaries. He also sleeps (offscreen) with the daughter.

It's a nightmarish theme, but valid one for a probing insight into the mind of a madman and his victims. It seems certain that few people will see it. Where there is film and video censorship, it will certainly be banned on the grounds of child pornography, and even where it can be freely shown it's hard to imagine an arthouse audience willing to sit through such a catalog of horrors. Fests could give it screening time, but even there it may be risky.

For the record, the audience at the screening caught appeared to be about 50% appalled and the rest respectful. There were many walkouts, but strong applause from some sections of the crowd at the end, especially when the young helmer made an appearance. —*Strat.*

Hungarian Film Week

Embriok
(Embryos)
(HUNGARIAN-B&W)

A Tarsulas Studio, Mafilm, production. Directed by Pal Zolnay. Screenplay, Zolnay, Orsolya Szekely; camera (b&w), Elemer Ragalyi, Tamas Sas, Gabor Halasz; music, Zdenko Tamassy; editor, Marianna Miklos; sound, Ferenc Csonka. Reviewed at Hungarian Film Week, Budapest, Feb. 10, 1986. Running time: **90 MINS.**
Terez .... Erzsebet Gaal
Kati .... Kati Lazar
Tamas .... Tamas Jordan

Budapest — Although he's only made three features in the last 15 years, Pal Zolnay has a deserved reputation for sensitivity in his chosen field, the dramatized documentary. "Embryos" presents an interesting dilemma: a 33-year-old obstetrician/gynecologist, Terez, divorced for 11 years, is pregnant by her lover, a married man. She is indecisive about how to handle the situation. She's 11 weeks pregnant — one more week and an abortion will be impossible.

In her daily work she performs abortions, and also assists at births. While she accepts the necessity for some abortions (which are legal in Hungary), the actual act of abortion (heard but not seen once in the film) is something of a horror to her. She instinctively wants to keep her baby, and doesn't seem to balk at pushing her selfish, vacillating lover into leaving his wife and children. When the crunch comes, he won't leave, and he's violently against the proposal that she has the child — an abortion is his only solution.

In this tense and difficult situation, all three characters — the pregnant woman, the lover, the wife — behave in ways that will often be inexplicable for western audiences. Terez, for example, though an intelligent and sensitive woman, accompanies her lover to his home for a brutal confrontation with his distraught wife. She behaves in a thoroughly despicable fashion in this scene. Nor is the wife's motivation clear at times, while the lover is predictably swinish throughout, and thus hardly worth bothering with.

Shot in 16m, and blown up to 35m with a good deal of grain, "Embryos" is a pic that could spark pros and cons, especially among feminists and on both sides of the abortion issue. The film itself takes no stand either way. It ends with a question mark, which in the circumstances is something like a cop-out. It boasts good performances, however, from the nonprofessional actors.—*Strat.*

Bábolna
(HUNGARIAN-DOCU-B&W/COLOR)

A Hungarofilm presentation of a Mafilm. Hunnia Studio, Hungarian Television production. Written and directed by Sándor Sára. Camera (color). Sándor Kuruez; editor, Mihály Morelli; sound, György Fék. Reviewed at the Budapest Congress Center (Hungarian Film Week, in competition), Feb. 10, 1986. Running time: Part 2 - **102 MINS.**; Part 3 - **82 MINS.**, Part 4 - **80 MINS.**

Budapest — This major undertaking by leading cameraman and director Sándor Sára attempts to trace the history of Hungary from 1945 until today through a series of six feature length documentaries on the fate of the cooperative farm of Bábolna. In the heyday of the Austro-Hungarian Empire, this was an important center for breeding the finest studs in that part of the world. After the war, as the profile of the society and its needs changed, so did the farm, and Sára sees it in development a faithful reflection of the political, economical and moral struggles of his country today.

Judging by the three episodes shown by the Hungarian Film Week, Sára is trying to combine the history of the place with incisive social comment, using as much archive footage as was available on the subject and adding interviews with witnesses who were involved in shaping the profile of the place. The second episode contains some scorching commentaries about well-intentioned incompetents who were allowed to bungle their jobs only because they held the right party cards, and some not-so-well intentioned political troublemakers who exploited every bit of unrest to further their interests and settle accounts with opponents. All this, while the farm itself was falling to pieces, for lack of adequate know-how on the managerial level.

The third episode, unfolding the transformation of the stud stables into chicken coops by the early 1960s, consisting mostly of talking heads interviews dealing with the intricacies of the Hungarian economy, starting to look for support outside the limited horizon of the Socialist countries. The fourth episode goes on to elaborate on that same theme, and the frictions resulting therefrom.

Evidently prepared for tv, it seems now that the importance of the document is such, it will be preserved for theatrical purposes as well, even if outlook is definitely limited. A non-Hungarian audience would have to be very dedicated to

sit through it all, but as an unusual attempt to establish audio-visual history, this may well turn into a work of reference that many archives and film schools could use. —*Edna.*

Agitatorok
(Agitators)
(HUNGARIAN-B&W)

A Bela Balazs Studio production. Directed by Deszö Magyar. Screenplay, Gabor Body, Magyar, Jozsef Lengyel, György Lukacs, Ervin Sinko, Szilagyi Szamuelyne; camera (b&w), Lajos Koltai. No further credits supplied. Reviewed at Film Museum, Budapest, (Hungarian Film Week), Feb. 9, 1986. Running time: **71 MINS.**
With: Gabor Body, György Cserhalmi. Laszlo Bertalan, Tamas Szentjobi, Peter Dobay, Sandor Oszter, Mark Zala, Andras Kozak, Sandor Simenfalvy, György Kezdy, György Pinter, Iren Süto, Laszlo Földes.

Budapest — Produced by a group of young people at the experimental Bela Balazs Studio in 1969, the year after student unrest in Europe and the Soviet intervention in Czechoslovakia, "Agitators" seems to have been a deliberately provocative pic which was unsurprisingly banned by the Magyar authorities.

It's set in 1919, during the 133-day Communist revolution led by Bela Kun. The film team uses old newsreels from that turbulent year, some of them shockingly savage, and reenacts scenes of debate about Party principles. During these debates, the forbidden name of Trotsky crops up more than once, and with dialog to the effect that, despite the advent of Communism, there's still a class system and the poor still worry about the price of bread, it's no wonder the axe fell on the picture. It is, in truth, a rather academic and dry affair, not without interest, of course, but of limited appeal. —*Strat.*

Idö Van
(Time)
(HUNGARIAN-COLOR)

A Hunnia Studio, Mafilm, production. Directed by Peter Gothar. Screenplay, Peter Esterházy, Gothar; camera (Eastmancolor), Zoltan David; editor, Maria Nagy; music, György Selmeczi; sound, Janos Reti. Reviewed at Hungarian Film Week, Budapest, Feb. 12, 1986. Running time: **105 MINS.**
Mihaly Halasi .... Mark Zala
Ilona Halasi .... Kati Lazar
Mihaly's brother .... Tamas Cseh
Mihaly's mother .... Eva Ruttkai
Hotel caretaker .... Gyula Bodrogi
Professor Edelhorn ...... Laszlo Csakanyi
Jutka .... Zita Toth
Marci .... Barna Gara

Budapest — In "Time," Peter ("Time Stands Still") Gothar is working with a new writer (Geza Beremenyi wrote both his earlier films) and has come up with a weird, surreal tale that suffers from having no really coherent plotline.

It starts naturalistically enough as the Halasi family set off on their summer holiday. On to Lake Balaton, where the hotel at which they've reserved rooms is deserted and partly under water. The caretaker insists the family, including two children, share a single room, and furthermore has them fill out forms in which they comment on the hotel service and facilities before they've even checked in.

The film consists of one bizarre situation after another, some of them superbly realized, some of them a bit precious. Gothar also has fun with Hungarian tv commercials.

"Time" is just a collection of clever bits and pieces without much substance. A stronger narrative was needed as a peg on which to hang all these dazzling doodles. — *Strat.*

Elysium
(HUNGARIAN-COLOR)

A Daniel Films presentation of a Hungarian Television, Daniel Films, Mafilm production. Produced by Akos Ravasz. Directed by Erika Szanto. Screenplay, Eva Schulze, Szanto, based on the novel by Imre Keszi; camera (color), Ferenc Zádori; editor, Vera Hertzka; art director, Tamás Vayer; costumes, Fanny Kemenes; sound, Marianne Takáos; music, W.A. Mozart, compiled by László Herczeg. Reviewed at the Hungarian TV Studios, Budapest (Hungarian Film Week), Feb. 10, 1986. Running time: **118 MINS.**

Zsámboki	Ferenc Bács
Gyuri	Zoltan Nágy
Doctor Helmer	Klaus Abramowsky
Father	Tibor Szilágyi
Mother	Anna Ráckevei
Aunt	Erzsébet Kutuälgyi
Grandmother	Risarda Hanin

Budapest — "Elysium" is one of the rare instances of a movie dealing with the Holocaust which manages to suggest horror and despair without the use of any traditional concentration camp shots.

Based on a real incident and on a highly rated novel by the same title, the script focuses on one of the lucky Jewish families, not deported during the war, but allowed to remain in their own flat and lead a more or less normal life inside, even if they did have to wear a yellow star once they stepped outside.

One day, their 10-year-old son visits a family friend living nearby, is picked up on the way by a patrol arresting Jews, and is sent with a group of total strangers to a deportation camp. In Budapest, the parents are struggling, with the help of a faithful Christian friend, to discover what has happened to their little son and bring him back home, while the boy finds himself in a kind of a beatific summer colony for deported children, named Elysium. It's almost a paradise, except that the cultured Germans tending it are

using the internees for medical experiments.

Helmer Erika Szanto keeps the film subdued. The matter of fact behavior of what could be taken as average people creates a horrific image of the world. Everybody seems very civilized and well-behaved while helping the world sink to its lowest point. Using Mozart music, highly polished photography which dresses the scenery in warm, romantic hues, and memories of the good pre-war life which somehow persists to keep appearances in the middle of the tragedy taking place just around the corner, only helps stress the absurdity of the situation.

The tempo of the film is uneven, some intercuts are annoying and the prettiness sometimes goes too far, but Szanto makes her point nevertheless: art, music, culture — everything we believe represents the best in mankind, are meaningless, faced with the ruthless immorality our race is capable of. Lofty research on the origins of Hungarian music do not prepare the father to defend his family, the staunch belief that he is a Hungarian like all the others, is an illusion he can't get rid of, and practically none of the respectable people surrounding him all his life have the moral fiber to put themselves in danger, when required by circumstances.

Well played and shot, the project was originally intended as two one-hour tv episodes, but Szanto is now planning to recut it for a theatrical version, to give it more of a punch. —*Edna.*

Kovbojok
(Cowboys)
(HUNGARIAN-DOCU-COLOR)

A Hungarofilm presentation of a Mafilm-Hunnia Studio production. Directed by Pal Schiffer. Screenplay, Gábor Havas; camera (color), Tamás Andor, Gabor Balogh; editor, Mária Rigó; sound, Gyula Traub; music, János Novák. Reviewed at Hungarian Film Week (competing), Budapest Congress Center, Feb. 10, 1986. Running time: **224 MINS.**

Budapest — This very long documentary takes a critical view of the conditions of the independent peasants trying to make a decent living as big business is crowding them out of their existence and the state does nothing to help them.

Instead of the banks and the big companies playing the villains, as they did in similar American pictures, here it is the state cooperatives that are undermining the efforts of private initiatives. Except for the very few who manage to catch the right wave, the loners and the independents are doomed to fail.

The dramatic aspects of the Hungarian situation are further stressed by the fact that recent openings for individual enterprises could have

made such initiatives tempting, but those who embark upon them are bound to discover they face practically unsurmountable obstacles in a state-controlled economy.

Schiffer tells the story of five young persons, four men and a woman, who take over cattle from a six-village cooperative which does not have the manpower to tend to it. Once they are handed the animals, they discover that they lack both the knowhow and what's worse, the elementary conditions to do their job. They don't have enough fodder, they are not given pastures or proper stables, and a milking machine is a mystery for them.

Trimmed to normal length and tightened up around the climactic scene which pack a wallop thanks to the utter credibility of the characters, this could turn out to be a fascinating document on the development of social conditions and relations in Hungary. — *Edna.*

A Nagy Generacio
(The Great Generation)
(HUNGARIAN-COLOR/B&W)

A Dialog Studio, Mafilm, production. Directed by Ferenc Andras. Screenplay, Geza Beremenyi, Andras; camera (Eastmancolor), Elemer Ragalyi. No further credits available. Reviewed at Mafilm Studios, Budapest, Feb. 12, 1986. Running time: **114 MINS.**

With: György Cserhalmi, Karoly Eperjes, Mari Kiss, Dorottya Udvardos, Robert Koltai, Tamas Major, Peter Andorai.

Budapest — This is a stylish pic which contains all the pessimism and bleakness found in other current Hungarian films, but has been fashioned by top scripter Geza Beremenyi and helmer Ferenc Andras into an accessible and emotionally affecting drama. A major fest outing this summer is indicated.

The "great" generation of the title is the generation of the 1960s, and the film actually opens with a black and white prolog set in 1968 which introduces the three main characters, friends and drinking partners. One of the trio (György Cserhalmi) steals a passport from another (Karoly Eperjes) and leaves the country with his girlfriend, heading for success in America.

Some 17 years later he returns to Budapest with a teenage daughter in tow. His wife (Mari Kiss) long since left him and returned home. At first, Eperjes is delighted to see his old friend. They go off drinking together and talking about old times. It quickly becomes clear that Cserhalmi hasn't been successful in the States. He's still the shallow cheat and drifter he was, and his homecoming simply muddies the waters for his erstwhile friends, opening up old wounds and causing fresh pain.

Pic also explores two other gener-

ations. Today's teenagers are repped by the Americanized daughter and by Eperjes' son, who's been called up to do military service. In a frantic effort to help the youth avoid the draft, Eperjes has him apply for admission to a mental home, with devastating results. Then there's the older generation, the ones who suffered the war and the social changes that followed it. Strangely enough, these old men seem to have adjusted and accept their lives. They're resigned and content, where the other generations are not.

"The Great Generation" is a probing look at Hungarian society today, but handled in a relaxed and quite entertaining fashion. It's probably the most accessible of this year's crop. Solid thesping and sharp cinematography are added pluses for this intelligent item which, while quite pessimistic about the way Hungary may be heading, is sufficiently cinematic to give considerable artistic pleasure. —*Strat.*

Falfuro
(The Wall Driller)
(HUNGARIAN-COLOR)

A Hunnia Studio, Mafilm, production. Directed by György Szomjas. Screenplay, Szomjas, Ibolya Fekete, Ferenc Grunwalsky; camera (Eastmancolor), Grunwalsky; editor, Anna Korniss; music, Janos Karacsony; sets, Attila Kovacs; sound, György Kovacs. Reviewed at Hungarian Film Week (Congress center), Budapest, Feb. 8, 1986. Running time: **92 MINS.**

Geza	Janos Ban
Eva	Renata Szatler
Geza's wife	Agi Szirtes
Caretaker	Peter Andorai
Gyula	Denes Ujlaky

Budapest — A free-wheeling, iconoclastic comedy about some of the stranger forms of private enterprise to be found in Hungary today, "The Wall Driller" is a solid followup to director György Szomjas' last hit, "Light Physical Injuries."

Geza (Janos Ban), the film's lugubrious hero, lives in an ugly apartment block with his wife and children. He works in a factory and lives a routine life until one day two things happen: as he leaves his apartment he catches a glimpse of a new neighbor, the comely Eva (Renata Szatler) and it's lust at first sight. Later, at work, the machine he operates refuses to start and, after an argument with his boss, he quits. It's time, he feels, to start life anew.

Of all the possibilities open to him, he chooses wall drilling. He buys an electric drill (which he carries by a sling round his neck like a machine gun) and offers to drill holes to hang pictures or fixtures in apartment walls. Before long his neighbor has invited him in for another kind of drilling, and his life is even more confused.

Another kind of private enterprise is flourishing in the area; amateur prostitution. Bored wives, many of them on maternity leave, see this as a way to earn extra money.

Some of the jokes are strictly local, but the film is fun and will benefit from first-class subtitles which catch the humor in the dialog, including the occasional use of alliteration to create a stylized effect. Less successful as an alienating device is the somewhat arbitrary use of color filters.

Its raunchy humor and the nude scenes involving the spectacular Renata Szatler could spark international interest.

Janos Ban is very good as the sad sack hero, but the pic is stolen by Peter Andorai giving a wonderfully over-the-top performance as the apartment building's hateful caretaker, who terrorizes all and sundry.—*Strat*.

Paulette
(FRENCH-COLOR)

An AMLF release of a GPFI-AMLF-CAPAC coproduction. Produced by Jean-Claude Fleury. Written and directed by Claude Confortes, based on the comic strip by Wolinski and Pichard. Camera (Fujicolor), Claude Agostini; editor, Ghislaine Desjonquères; music, Nicolas Errera; theme song performed by Jeanne Marine; art director, Françoise de Leu; sound, Dominique Levert; costumes, Edith Vesperini; makeup, Maryse Felix; special effects makeup, Reiko Kruk, Dominique Colladant; production manager, Patrick Delauneux. Reviewed at the Gaumont Colisées theater, Paris, Feb. 26, 1986. Running time: **91 MINS.**

With: Jeanne Marine (Paulette), Luis Rego (Georges), Catherine Leprince (Joseph, female), Charles Schmitt (Joseph, male), Gérard Desarthe (Guillaume), Roland Blanche (Albert-Henri), Christian Sinniger (Gilbert), Eric Metayer (Prosper), Georges Beller (Alphonse), Roland Dubillard, Mylène Demongeot, Jean-Marie Rivière, Guy Montagné, Michèle Bernier, Philippe Avron, Maurice Risch, Jean-François Perrier, Dominique Besnehard, Jean-Paul Farre, Marie-Chrisine Descouard, Roland Giraud, Cerise, Maurice Baquet, Clause Evrard, Gérard Caillaud, François Cavanna, Professor Chron.

Paris — "Paulette" is another failed attempt to bring comic strip characters to a live-action feature film. Writer-director Claude Confortes, who's become a specialist in the matter, adapted several cartoon albums by Georges Wolinski and Pichard about Paulette, a "poor little rich girl," a sort of Little Orphan Annie with developed breasts, whose naive sense of social concern leads here into troubled waters.

Luscious newcomer Jeanne Marine plays the heroine like an inflated, full-scale doll, who has as much trouble keeping her clothes on as fellow cartoon sex symbol Gwendolyne. Good-natured Paulette, who has inherited a huge fortune from her prematurely deceased parents (Roland Dubillard and Mylène Demongeot), wants to spread happiness among the less privileged.

She makes an unsuccessful attempt to slum as a worker in her factory, then decides to distribute her wealth to all those who come to her with an appropriate sob story. The good deed goes down badly with the crooked estate administrator (Roland Blanche) who has her certified as a nut and carted off to a funny farm, where she eventually escapes with an inmate (Gérard Desarthe).

In the course of her adventures, the poor undraped thing is knocked unconscious into a river and saved from drowning by a friendly colony of bargemen, who help her foil the machinations against her.

The large cast is composed mostly of guests and cameos (including cartoonist Wolinski himself and many other personalities of Parisian satiric magazine society), which makes this look like a home movie with a big budget and an in-joke script. There are a number of good supporting players and comics, though most have little time to overcome the bad dialog and self-consciously theatrical direction.

Confortes did somewhat better with his two earlier features, "Le Roi des Cons" and "Vive les Femmes," respectively based on cartoons by Wolinski and the late Jean-Marc Reiser (to whom "Paulette" is dedicated), which both had funny moments. "Paulette" is naked in more senses than one. Technical credits, however, are good.
—*Len*.

Whatever It Takes
(COLOR)

Well-intentioned post-Vietnam adjustment drama.

An Aquarius Films release. Produced by Bob Demchuk, Walter J. Scherr. Executive producer, Scherr. Directed by Demchuk. Stars Tom Mason, Martin Balsam, Chris Weatherhead, James Rebhorn. Screenplay, Weatherhead, Demchuk; camera (color), John Drake; editor, Demchuk; music, Garry Sherman; sound, Felipe Borrero; production design, Maher Ahmad; assistant director, Joseph Winogradoff. Reviewed at Lorimar screening room, N.Y., Feb. 24, 1986. (No MPAA Rating.) Running time: **93 MINS.**
Jeff Perchick . . . . Tom Mason
Hap Perchicksky . . . . Martin Balsam
Lee Bickford . . . . Chris Weatherhead
Michael Manion . . . . James Rebhorn
Eren Haberfield . . . . Maura Shea
Timmy Shaughnessy . . . . Bill Bogert
Millie . . . . Rosetta Lenoire
Curley . . . . Joey Ginza
Mr. Bunyon . . . . Fred Morsell
Mr. Kingsley . . . . Edward Binns
Hilbourne . . . . Thomas Barbour

The lead characters in this warm, well-intentioned but occasionally rocky film represent a kind of post-Vietnam "lost generation," struggling to come to grips with their lives, relationships and careers against the backdrop of New York City. At its best, "Whatever It Takes" succeeds in capturing the gritty realism and quiet desperation that comes when dreams collide with reality. As its ebbs, the film lacks pacing and crispness, relying on a number of ill-conceived scenes for comic relief and a sugar-coated ending that contrasts sharply with the bulk of the picture.

Jeff Perchick (finely acted by Tom Mason) is a Vietnam vet supporting himself, and his father's failing diner, by driving a New York City cab and working a number of offbeat and demeaning jobs. His ambition of becoming a syndicated cartoonist has been buffeted by years of rejections, dad's diner has been delivered the death knell of an outrageous rent increase and his personal life is a shambles.

Jeff's ex-girlfriend, a photojournalist from the Vietnam days, seems to miss the excitement and simplicity of the war and now lives with a public defender, a man who has clung to the ideals of the '60s and now is jumping ship to a cushy law firm.

A series of Vietnam paintings Jeff made upon coming back, now stored in a warehouse, provides a nice subplot and offers an immediacy of the war's impact across a void of time. In one of the more moving and cryptic scenes in the film, Jeff recounts holding a dying soldier in his arms and asking if he wants morphine. "No thanks," replies the soldier, "as long as I can feel the pain I know I'm still alive."

Martin Balsam, Chris Weatherhead and James Rebhorn all register good performances, and newcomer Maura Shea provides a nice diversion as Jeff's young girlfriend.
— *Roy*.

Unfinished Business
(DOCU-COLOR/B&W)

A Mouchette Films presentation. Produced, directed, camera (color) and edited by Steven Okazaki. Written by Okazaki, Jane Kaihatsu, Kei Yokomizo and Laura Ide; associate producer, Kaihatsu; narrated by Amy Hill. Reviewed at Castro Theater, San Francisco, Jan. 15, 1986. (No MPAA Rating.) Running time: **60 MINS.**

San Francisco — This current nominee in the Academy's best documentary feature category originally was broadcast on PBS. It was funded by the Corp. for Public Broadcasting and the Gerbode Foundation and is notable mostly for archival footage illustrating internment of American citizens of Japanese descent within the first six months of our entry into World War II.

Pic is a mix of this b&w footage, contemporary interviews with three men who challenged the legality of the internment and news conference shots related to these lawsuits. One additional element of the project captures scenes from a play, "Point Of Order," based on the case of one of the three litigants. These scenes prove more discursive than illuminating. Often, too, the exposition of the legal issues lack clarity.

Yet despite these flaws, the implicit civil rights-deprivation issue is told so compellingly that the docu serves to provide dramatic and historical impact. —*Herb*.

Les Longs Manteaux
(The Long Coats)
(FRENCH-ARGENTINE-COLOR)

A Fechner-Gaumont release of a Les Films de la Tour-T.F. 1 Films-A.K.F. (Buenos Aires) coproduction. Produced by Adolphe Viezzi, Henri Lassa. Directed by Gilles Behat. Stars Bernard Giraudeau. Screenplay, Jean-Louis Leconte, Behat, from the novel by G.J. Arnaud; camera (Fujicolor), Ricardo Aronovich; editor, Geneviéve Vaury; sound, Paul Lainé; music, Jean-François Léon; end theme written and performed by Daniel Lavoie; associate producer, Hugo Kusnet; production manager, Alain Queffelean. Reviewed at the Publicis screening room, Paris, Feb. 13, 1986. Running time: **106 MINS.**
Loïc Murat . . . . Bernard Giraudeau
Julia . . . . Claudia Ohana
Laville . . . . Robert Charlebois
Garcia . . . . Federico Luppi
Lama . . . . Ricardo Darin
Miguel . . . . Lito Cruz
Vinchina . . . . Franklin Caicedo
Cesario . . . . Victor Laplace
Figueras . . . . Oscar Martinez
Zarate . . . . Raul Rizzo
Ruiz . . . . Vincente Buono
Juy . . . . Juan Palomino
Gayata . . . . Dario Grandinetti

Paris — One of the coproductions made under the recent Franco-Argentine accords, "Les Longs Manteaux" is an adventure yarn that brings Gallic leading man Bernard Giraudeau to the wide open spaces of Latin America where he is embroiled in a political plot.

Director Gilles Behat, who made his commercial reputation with his David Goodis transposition, "Street Of The Lost," extracted the plot from a print thriller by G.J. Arnaud (no relation to Georges Arnaud, author of the classic suspense novel, "The Wages Of Fear") and has given it a certain flavor of the Western. Call it "High Noon In The Andes" maybe, since the lonesome and reluctant hero spends much screen time running around a near-abandoned frontier town (the Argentine-Bolivian frontier, that is) seeking help to stave off the threatened tragedy that arrives with a passenger train at midday.

It's not his life that is directly endangered, but that of a beloved Argentine novelist and symbol of anti-totalitarian struggle, who is to be freed from a Bolivian prison by the nation's new democratic regime, and escorted by train to the border, where he is to regain his homeland.

The deadly obstacle to the author's repatriation is a fascist general who has sworn that he will never return home alive. With a faithful group of parliamentary officers (the "long coats" of the title), he takes over the town and its station, to await the train. Some of his men have already infiltrated the special escort occupying an armored coach in the coming choo-choo.

Behat's direction is sound, but the conventional scripting and characterizations — Giraudeau is that stock anti-hero, the world-weary fellow who wants to mind his own business, but gets involved up to his neck — take up a lot of time before hell breaks loose in the last half-hour or so.

Giraudeau, a solitary geologist who comes down from this mountain camp to buy spare tool parts, has a pretty face to fight for in the person of Claudia Ohana ("Erendira") as the exiled writer's daughter, who has come to meet him at the border. Though Ohana has no qualms about changing her dress in front of the embarrassed Frenchman, no romance blooms between them.

Secondary parts are skillfully filled by a host of name Latin American talent, who know how to make the most out of their sketchy personages. Casting should help commercial performance in Latin and Spanish-speaking markets.

French Canadian pop singer Robert Charlebois is also on hand as a European photojournalist who hops the train in search of a scoop and provides the tale's ironic coda.

Pic was handsomely lensed on location in northern Argentina by a native son, Ricardo Aronovich, today one of France's ace cinematographers. — *Len.*

Malcolm
(AUSTRALIAN-COLOR)

A Cascade Films presentation of a Nadia Tass/David Parker film. Produced by Tass, Parker. Directed by Tass. Stars Colin Friels, John Hargreaves, Lindy Davies, Camera (color), screenplay, mechanical effects, Parker; executive producer, Bryce Menzies; associate producer, Timothy White, production designer, Rob Perkins, editor, Ken Sallows; music, The Penguin Cafe Orchestra. Reviewed at Hoyts Cinema Center, Melbourne, Feb. 15, 1986. Running time: **90 MINS.**
Malcolm . . . . Colin Friels
Frank . . . . John Hargreaves
Judith . . . . Lindy Davies
Willy . . . . Chris Haywood

Melbourne — "Malcolm" is 90 minutes of sheer joy. What could have been a trite story is transformed into great entertainment by the devoted professionalism of first-time filmmaker Nadia Tass and David Parker.

Parker made his name as a stills photographer working on such Australian pictures as "The Man From Snowy River," "Phar Lap" and "The Coolangatta Gold."

Collaborating here with his wife, director Nadia Tass, Parker serves as cameraman and scripter, and the couple shares producer chores.

The result is a handsomely directed, lensed and acted, original comedy that should click with local audiences.

Narrative starts when Malcolm is aged 30. His mechanical aptitude is exceptionally high but his social and emotional development stopped long ago. He works for the tramways as a maintenance man and, instead of going home after a night-shift, Malcolm makes his own tram which he eventually takes on a hair-raising run through Melbourne's streets. He's deservedly fired.

Malcolm quickly runs out of the funds necessary to keep alive his primary objective — a house full of very clever, but mainly useless, mechanical devices — and there are no funds and quite a few overdue bills for his secondary objective, food.

He is forced to take in borders and, despite an elaborate questionnaire, settles on Frank who is just out of jail and Judith who is Frank's ever-loving moll. Frank and Judith are as fascinated with Malcolm's incredible inventions as Malcolm is with Frank and Judith's lovemaking.

Frank is a quicker learner than Malcolm and he sees more potential in mechanical gimmicks than Malcolm sees in learning about women. Soon, this unlikely trio is embarking on a bank heist laden with surprising and inventive twists.

It is a very funny film. It moves quickly and has some unforgettable lines which Tass has ensured are delivered with perfect timing.

Colin Friels is cast superbly as Malcolm. He shows the humor and pathos called for in the script. His performance is equalled by John Hargreaves and Lindy Davies as Frank and Judith.

The mechanical props are highly original but the real-life cockatoo, Arnold, makes three appearances which is two too many.

Parker has lensed mostly at night, catching the drabness of a Melbourne winter. The darkness gradually disappears as Malcolm's fortunes improve. One of the most pleasing features of "Malcolm" is its music. Some of it is obscure, some well-known, some specially written. Like the film, it all works. — *Pher.*

Dreptate In Lanturi
(Chained Justice)
(RUMANIAN-B&W)

An Artexim, Bucharest, presentation of a Bucharest Film Studios, Group 1 production. Directed by Dan Pita. Screenplay, Pita, Mihai Stoian; camera (b&w), Vlad Păunescu; editor, Cristina Enescu; sets, Călin Papură; costumes, Daniela Codareco; music, Adrian Enescu. Reviewed at Berlin Atelier, (in Berlin Film Festival's Black Sea Panorama) Feb. 16, 1986. Running time: **116 MINS.**
With: Ovidiu Iuliu Moldovan, Victor Rebengiuc, Claudiu Bleont, Nicolae Petrică, Sebastian Comanici, Ana-Maria Călinescu, Maia Istodor, Patricia Grigoriu.

Berlin — This 1983 production shows director Dan Pita at his creative best, as he unfolds the tale of a real-life, peasant Robin Hood, stealing from the rich and giving to the poor, who lived in Rumaina at the turn of the century.

Fearful of condemning him in a court of law, because of his widespread popularity, he is allowed by the police to escape from prison and then his pursuers are instructed specifically not to capture but to kill him. At the same time, these bounty killers also moonlight as highway robbers, pretending to be his acolytes, and steal from the poor, in order to ruin his reputation.

While the subject suggests an action film, Pita goes for stylization, using the camera to create moody images of the grim popular hero, confronted by a totally corrupt and decadent society.

The film's main strength is its black and white photography, with strong backlighting, candle-lit interiors, dark backgrounds and fog machines lending the early morning scenes a mysterious, ominous feeling.

At 116 minutes, the script tends to be repetitive and the inevitable action scenes lack the necessary tension and drive.

Acting is on the theatrical side, but Ovidiu Iuliu Moldovan cuts a fine figure as the rebel with a cause.
—*Edna.*

Lejania
(The Parting Of The Ways)
(CUBAN-COLOR)

A MECLA presentation of an ICAIC production. Produced by Humberto Hernandez. Written and directed by Jesús Diaz. Camera (color), Mario Garcia Jowa; editor, Justo Vega; sets and costumes, José M. Villa; sound, Jerónimo Labrado. Reviewed at Studio 7 Berlin Film Fest (market), Feb. 22, 1986. Running time: **90 MINS.**
Susana . . . . Veronica Lynn
Reinaldo . . . . Jorge Trinchet
Ana . . . . Isabel Santos
Aleida . . . . Beatriz Valdés
Also with: Monica Guffanti, Mauricio Renterio, Roselia Blain, Polcma Abraham.

Berlin — This otherwise nicely shot and acted little film suffers from a surfeit of ideology at the expense of human interest.

A woman who left Havana for Florida 10 years earlier comes back for the first time, to visit the son she left behind when he was only 16. She is accompanied by her niece and carries with her all the typical presents an American tourist would take to poor relatives in an underde-veloped country. While some of her relatives jump with joy when given blue jeans and transistor radios, her son balks, resenting the parent who had abandoned him in the most difficult moment of his life.

The division is clearcut: on the one hand, the dropout who had opted for comfort and ease and left her people and her family to fend for themselves, is trying to buy her way back into their hearts in a clumsy way. On the other hand, those who stayed behind are the worthy pioneers who fought valiantly and are justifiably proud of their achievements, sufficiently so to reject the demeaning offers coming from across the sea. Not that there aren't some bad apples here, too, such as the dignitary accused of exploiting his position to extract material advantages that are immoral in the eyes of a young idealist, or his son who is envious of a stereo set more sophisticated than the one he owns.

No effort is made to explain why people were so powerfully compelled to leave the country in the past, to the point of leaving their offspring behind. Without clarification of this point, the relations between mother, son and daughter-in-law she had never met are superficial at best. More interesting is the encounter between the protagonist and his visiting cousin, offering a glimpse at the plight of those who left a home to live elsewhere, and now are strangers both where they were born and in their country of choice.

The three actresses — Veronica Lynn as the mother, Isabel Santos as the cousin and Beatriz Valdés as the daughter-in-law — do a creditable job and carry the film. They have to struggle with a script which crams almost everything it has to say into the dialog and leaves little for the visuals to express.—*Edna.*

Novemberkatzen
(November Cats)
(WEST GERMAN-COLOR)

A Quadriga Film production, Sigrun Koeppe and Volker Tittel, in collaboration with Südwestfunk, Susan Schulte, Baden-Baden. Directed by Koeppe. Screenplay, Vera von Wilcken, based on a novel by Mirjam Prossler; camera (color), Tittel; sets, Dieter Reineke; music, Günter Ress; editor, Sabine Schönecker. Reviewed at Berlin Film Fest (panorama), Feb. 22, 1986. Running time: **100 MINS.**
With: Angela Hunger (Ilse), Ursela Monn (Mother), Katharina Brauren (Grandma), Robert Zimmerling (Grandpa), Jürgen Vogel (Dieter), Andreas Kastning (Horst), Katja Engelhard (Marga), Dorothea Carrera (Frau Schuster), Christian Woyda (Bruno Schuster), Jens Schuldt (Philipp Schuster), Claudia Schuldt (Katrin Schuster).

Berlin — Sigrun Koeppe's "November Cats" introduces a new woman helmer to the German film scene, one who worked on several earlier projects as a camerawoman as well as all-around hand on tv-productions. This is a rather typical "woman's film" from script to camera angle, the story stemming from a novel by a coming kidpic author, Mirjam Prossler.

Setting is a provincial village in the postwar years before the economic boom was anything more than a rumor. Life is hard for 11-year-old Ilse, who has to do all the house chores after school for her abandoned mother and two older brothers. She lives a pretty lonely existence, and this makes her rather aggressive at times as she tries to get even with the unjust world about her.

One day she finds a discarded kitten still alive in a trash heap, and takes the "November Cat" home as her sole friend. Her mother, now pregnant via her latest weekend beau, understands her daughter's desperation to a point — so she eventually gives in to letting Ilse go to live next door with the kindly grandma. The girl begins to mature.

"November Cats" is full of good intentions, and there are moments when the story seems to come to life, particularly with the grandma on camera or upon the return of Ilse's long lost father with a new wife and kid and shiny new car. In general the dialog is too stiff, the script too predictable, and the acting too restrained in a straight-jacket. —*Holl.*

We Were So Beloved
(U.S.-DOCU-COLOR/B&W)

A Manfred Kirchheimer production. Written, directed and edited by Kirchheimer. Camera (color), James Callonan, Steven Giuliano; additional camera, Walter Hess. Kirchheimer; sound, James Steele. Reviewed at Berlin Film Festival (Forum), Minilux, Feb. 21, 1986. Running time: **145 MINS.**

Berlin — Documentary filmmaker Manfred Kirchheimer didn't have to go very far to prepare this portrait of a German-Jewish community living in Washington Heights, in New York City, since he is one of them. Born in Germany and brought by his parents to America when he was only five, Kirchheimer had only to interview family, friends and acquaintances he has known since childhood, to put together this film. That by doing so he manages to expose some unexpected and sometimes unsettling aspects of this community, is to his credit.

This is a first-person narrated film. Kirchheimer uses archive footage to establish the milestones of the Nazi takeover, and copious interviews, taken at length with survivors who are trying to give an idea of what they had gone through at the time.

Obvious is the amazement of all, that such a thing could happen in Germany, where Jews were completely assimilated and felt full and equal citizens. One elderly person, for instance, still is convinced her immediate entourage of gentiles couldn't possibly be to blame, it was strangers who came from elsewhere who were really responsible for it all. She is prepared even today to find excuses for the behavior of those she knew personally.

Intercuts of quotes from Hitler's "Mein Kampf" stress even further the single-minded purposefulness of the Holocaust, as witnesses attest to the horrors, but at the same time let slip numerous remarks that won't be cherished by a Jewish audience. The filmmaker's father recounts how he rejected an offer to help the FBI in the war and supply information on Bremerhaven, a strategic German port, because he knew the intention was to bomb the place and he was not prepared to be a traitor to the place he was born. Somewhere else he also says that had he been a Gentile, he would have been afraid to help Jews, as he is a natural coward. Other remarks, suggesting there wasn't much love lost among German Jews for their Polish brethren and explaining the annihilation of those Jews who stayed in Germany by pointing out they had been brought up in the strict German spirit of obedience, also are bound to reopen some old, uncomfortable wounds.

As this is a very personal document, Kirchheimer indulges himself too often, his narrative interfering and commenting excessively. A tightening of the material would make this sprawling picture more effective, for it has plenty of intriguing material to attract attention.
— *Edna.*

Kak Molody My Byli
(How Young We Were Then)
(SOVIET-COLOR)

An Alexander Dovzhenko Studio (Kiev) production. Written and directed by Mikhail Belikov. Camera (Sovcolor), Vassili Truschkovski; music, Yuri Vinnik; art director, Alexi Levtschenko; sound, Anatoli Tschernotschenko. Reviewed at Berlin Film Fest (out of competition), Atelier, Feb. 18, 1986. Running time: **92 MINS.**
Sascha . . . . Taras Denisenko
Julka . . . . Jelena Sehkurpelo
Maria . . . . Nina Sarolapova
Uncle Petja . . . . Alexander Paschutin
Uncle Valja . . . . Alexander Sviridovski
Viktor . . . . Anatoli Lukjaneko
Tosja . . . . Tatiana Kravtshenko
Gavril Michalovich . . Mikhail Kokshenkov

Berlin — A plot synopsis of this film from the Ukraine will inevitably sound very over-familiar; set in the late 50s, it's about a romance between two young people, interrupted when they have to go away to study. Their love is under the shadow of the fact that, as a child during the war, the girl was subjected to some kind of chemical poisoning.

The delightful thing about this third feature of Mikhail Belikov is that he has made a thoroughly sweet, funny film from such tried and true material. His eye for comedy is notable, and he treats his characters with affection and admiration. This is evident from the start in a delightfully handled scene of a family reunion at which everything stops so that they can watch a popular tv comedian. Later, the youngsters go to an outdoor dance where the emcee enthusiastically introduces a sports hero and then forgets his name.

Later in the film, when the subject of Julka's illness is raised, Belikov never allows the material to become maudlin.

It's an unexpected charmer of a film, beautifully acted by its two young leads, and imbued with a nostalgic innocence for the 50s, a time when that shooting star the lovers gaze at in the sky is almost certainly a sputnik. — *Strat.*

En Penumbra
(Among The Shadows)
(SPANISH-COLOR)

A José Miguel Juárez Producciones Cinematograficos production. Produced by Juárez. Directed by José Luis Lozano. Stars Antonio Canto, Amparo Muñoz. Screenplay, Luis Ariño Torre, Lozano; camera (Eastmancolor), Tote Trenas; editor, Luis Manuel de Valle; music, Fernando Civil, Mariano Diaz; sound, Antonio Bloch; sets, Victor Alarcon; costumes, José Maria Garcia; special effects, Reyes Abades; assistant director, José Luis Garcia Berlanga. Reviewed at Atelier, Berlin Film Festival (out of competition), Feb. 21, 1986. Running time: **89 MINS.**
Daniel . . . . Antonio Canto
Helena . . . . Amparo Muñoz
Maniqui . . . . Miguel Bosé
Mother . . . . Lola Herrera
Father . . . . Antonio Garisa
Rosario . . . . Miguel Molina
Reyes . . . . Emilio Lain
Braulio . . . . Miguel Ortiz

Berlin — After a couple of interesting short films, director José Luis Lozano has come up with a rather old-fashioned first feature "Among The Shadows" about a young man from a good family who enters into a world of vice and depravity through love for a seemingly unattainable woman.

Daniel, well played by Antonio Canto, breaks his jaw in a foolish accident, and is hardly able to speak thereafter. Alienated from family and friends, he becomes obsessed with a beautiful older woman, Helena (Amparo Muñoz), and abandons his usual life to pursue her at a never-ending string of vacuous parties and orgies during which he meets a variety of bizarre characters.

The endless party scenes are flashy and basically old-hat. The suggestion that Daniel is a victim of modern vampires is a throwaway, that doesn't add up to anything in the end. We're supposed to feel for this man as he descends into a hell of his own making, but pic remains stubbornly uninvolving, and the visions of hell are often simply laughable. Pic takes itself with deadly seriousness, though, which adds to audience discomfort.

Technically, it's a fine production with quite an inventive soundtrack. Final resolution ("It's all a lie anyway!") is an apt summing up of an ambitious but misconceived effort. —*Strat.*

Den' Gneva
(Day Of Wrath)
(SOVIET-COLOR)

A Studio Yalta Central Gorki Studios production. Directed by Sulambek Mamilov. Screenplay, Alexander Lapshin, from a story by Sever Gonsovski; camera (Widescreen, Sovcolor), Alexander Rybin; art director, Boris Dulenkov; sound, Stanislav Gurin; music, Gija Kantscheli. Reviewed at Atelier, Berlin Film Festival (panorama), Feb. 25, 1986. Running time: **85 MINS.**
Donald Batley . . . . Juosas Budrajtis
Meller . . . . Alexei Petrenko
Fiedler . . . . Anatoli Ivanov
Batley's wife . . . . Grazyna Bajkschtite

Berlin — Presumably set in the U.S., "Day Of Wrath" is a rather half-hearted and bloodless Soviet adventure film about an intrepid tv newsman on the track of a story involving an evil professor and strange laboratory experiments.

The hero, aided by a local guide, treks deep into mountain country in search of his goal. The guide is played by an actor who looks so unnervingly like Paul Bartel that the viewer may half expect some comedy, but this is all in deadly seriousness. Indeed, pic takes itself so seriously that it entirely lacks the entertainment values U.S. films of this type generally supply.

Explorers come across a community of farmers where everyone looks mysterious and depressed, but where even children can perform extraordinary feats of mathematics without the aid of a calculator. Something's fishy.

Nearby, the heroes stumble on the underground lab, and the journalist is savaged by a barely glimpsed creature. That's about as much action as the film provides. It's all a tract about the dangers of science when allied to capitalism.

We don't get to see many Soviet films in this style, but this one is certainly no rival for its Hollywood counterparts. —*Strat.*

Hollywood Vice Squad
(COLOR)

Silly spoof of action/exploitation pictures.

A Concorde/Cinema Group release of a Cinema Group presentation of a Sandy Howard production. Produced by Arnold Orgolini, Howard. Executive producers, Mel Pearl, William Fay. Directed by Penelope Spheeris. Screenplay, James J. Docherty; camera (Foto-kem color; prints by Film House Group), Joao Fernandes; editor, John Bowey; music, Keith Levine, Michael Convertino; additional music & songs, Chris Spedding; sound, Jan Brodin; assistant director, Elliott Rosenblatt; production manager, Scott White; production design, Michael Corenblith; set decoration, Donna Stamps; costumes, Jill Ohanneson; stunt coordinator-second unit director, Dan Bradley; second unit camera, James Tynes; associate producers, Jeff Gary, David Witz; executive in charge of production, Venetia Stevenson; casting, Paul Bengston, David Cohn. Reviewed at UA Eastside theater, N.Y., March 1, 1986. (MPAA Rating: R.) Running time: **100 MINS.**

Capt. Jensen	Ronny Cox
Walsh	Frank Gorshin
Hawkins	Leon Isaac Kennedy
Pauline Stanton	Trish Van DeVere
Betty Melton	Carrie Fisher
Daley	Ben Frank
Chang	Evan Kim
Lori Stanton	Robin Wright
Romero	H.B. Haggerty
Stevens	Joey Travolta
Judy	Cec Verrell
Jesse	Julius W. Harris
Luchessi	Robert Miano
Man with doll	Marvin Kaplan

"Hollywood Vice Squad" is producer Sandy Howard's silly, unfunny spoof followup to his 1982 action hit "Vice Squad." Earlier film worked well as a thriller but the new one is an episodic mishmash that is strictly dullsville.

Main storyline is an elaborate injoke taking off on Paul Schrader's "Hardcore:" Pauline Stanton (Trish Van DeVere) asks the Hollywood police, led by kindly Capt. Jensen (Ronny Cox reprising his "Beverly Hills Cop" role) to help find her runaway daughter Lori (Robin Wright). (Van DeVere's real-life spouse George C. Scott became mired in a similar cesspool of vice in "Hardcore.")

Lori has become a hooker working for nasty James Walsh (Frank Gorshin hamming it up) and Jensen assigns several cops, led by Hawk (Leon Isaac Kennedy) to entrap Walsh as a white slaver.

Two dumb subplots also compete for attention. In one, gung-ho cop Betty Melton (Carrie Fisher enacting a "Saturday Night Live" tv skit) heads up a team trying to bust a filmmaker shooting S&M pornography with underage actors. The other has Det. Romero (H.B. Haggerty) trying to use a bookie (Julius W. Harris) to get the goods on N.Y. mob figure Luchessi (Robert Miano).

Not helped by James Docherty's vulgar, unfunny dialog, director Penelope Spheeris muffs the timing of the comedy scenes and fails to integrate exposition & dramatics with the requisite action footage. Slapdash production was filmed last summer, but an extraneous car-stunt sequence jarringly features theater marquees (displaying "Clue" and other pics) filmed much later, around Christmastime.

Tech credits are acceptable, but the musical score, mainly percussion, is a drag. — *Lor.*

La Gitane
(The Gypsy)
(FRENCH-COLOR)

An AMLF release of a T. Films-Films A2 coproduction. Produced by Alain Terzian. Written and directed by Philippe De Broca, from an original scenario by Jean-Loup Hubert. Stars Claude Brasseur, Valérie Kaprisky, Camera (Eastmancolor), Robert Fraisse; editor, Françoise Javet; music, Claude Bolling; art director, Dominique André; sound, Jean-Charles Ruault, Jean-Paul Loublier; makeup, Muriel Baurens; production managers, Françoise Galfre, Philippe Lievre. Reviewed at the Marignan-Concorde theater, Paris, Feb. 17, 1986. Running time: **92 MINS.**

Hubert Durieux	Claude Brasseur
Mona	Valérie Kaprisky
Elsa	Clémentine Célasié
Brigitte	Stéphane Audran
Florence	Valérie Rojan
Miss Chaprot	Marie-Anne Chazel
Mme. Chomard	Rosine Cadoret
Commissioner	Martin Lamotte
Pilu	Jacques Legras
The old gypsy	Henri Virlojeux

Paris — "La Gitane" is another disappointing comedy from Philippe De Broca. Claude Brasseur stars as a bored, overworked provincial banker who is beleaguered by females.

De Broca has adapted an original script by Jean-Lou Hubert, but it's the same old story of an apparently complacent, if somewhat harried, middle-aged bourgeois who gets the *coup de grace* from a spirited younger woman. That the lady in question is a beautiful young footloose gypsy (played by a tanned Valérie Kaprisky), who taunts and victimizes Brasseur with a band of juvenile thieves, adds little to the formula. De Broca sides predictably with the amoral, anarchic Kaprisky and tritely sends up the hypocritical life style of Brasseur, who must deal daily with an importuning ex-wife (Stéphane Audran), a nympho mistress (Clementine Célarié), a problematically married daughter (Valérie Rojan) and a homely, quietly adoring secretary (Marie-Anne Chazel).

It doesn't take long for Brasseur's head to turn when Kaprisky enters his life by stealing his cherished car, embarrassing him in front of genteel society, and finally robbing his bank in order to finance their future outlaw life together when Brasseur passes the series of acid tests she puts him through.

As always, there are still sporadic moments of style that made De Broca an internationally admired practitioner of light romantic comedy, but "La Gitane" is often frantically in search of a tone and resorts to labored farce to give its stock characters some freshness and energy.—*Len.*

Peau d'Ange
(Angel Skin)
(FRENCH-COLOR)

A Films de l'Atalante release of a Zora Prods. film. Produced by Danièle Molko. Directed by Jean-Louis Daniel. Screenplay, Jean-Louis Daniel, Philippe Setbon; camera (Fujicolor), Richard Andry; editor, Isabelle Rathery; music, Philippe Servain; art director, Denise Cohen; sound, Jean-Marcel Milan; makeup, Tania Martin. Reviewed at the UGC Marbeuf theater, Paris, Feb. 16, 1986. Running time: **69 MINS.**

Milo	Robin Renucci
Héléna Werner	Alexandra Stewart
Angélina	Véronique Delbourg
Alexandre	Jean-Paul Muel
The gigolo	Jeffrey Kime
Héléna (young)	Agnès Cassandre
The lover	Patrice Melennec

Paris — Shot in 1983, the technically polished but pretentious "Angel Skin" has surfaced commercially only now, probably because its male lead, Robin Renucci, has finally come into the spotlight, notably as the lead of Jean-Charles Tacchella's "Staircase C."

Story by director Jean-Louis Daniel and Philippe Setbon has echos of Joseph Losey and Harold Pinter's "The Servant." Renucci is an obnoxious, self-assured young man who pushes his way into a job as private secretary to a well-heeled but reclusive woman (Alexandra Stewart). She seems to accept him because he resembles her dead husband, who hung himself in the building's stairwell after witnessing her infidelity.

The still-traumatized Stewart passively allows Renucci to reorganize and dictate her life, which is essentially limited to weekly visits from her gigolo and her nurse, and periodic nightmares about her husband's suicide. Renucci tries to cut Stewart off completely from the outside world, and even has to murder the well-meaning friend who invites Stewart for a trip abroad.

The act of violence takes on a supernatural tone because Renucci crushes the man's skull between his bare hands and stuffs him in a garbage bin. Later, after he has asserted his complete control over Stewart by raping her, he is apparently clubbed to death by the neurotic nurse, who returns to the apartment, herself succombs to him and reacts with violence when he announces his departure.

The mystery peaks when Renucci's body suddenly disappears from the landing. A jack-in-the-box shock climax confirms the suggestion that Renucci is Stewart's dead husband, who has returned to take his revenge.

Daniel's direction is full of underlined symbolism and emphatic effects, though Renucci and Stewart came out fairly well from this unconvincing cross between Grand Guignol and "The Twilight Zone." Richard Andry's lensing is slick.
— *Len.*

Filme Demência
(The Last Faust)
(BRAZILIAN-COLOR)

Produced by E.M. Cinematográfica/Cinearte Produções Cinematográficas/Beethoven Street Films/Embrafilme. Written and directed by Carlos Reichenbach. Camera (color), José Roberto Eliezer; editor, Eder Mazini; music, Manoel Paiva, Luiz Chagas; sound, Antonio Cesar S. Santos. Reviewed at Rotterdam Film Festival, Jan. 29, 1986. Running time: **90 MINS.**

With: Enio Goncalves, Emilio di Biasi, Imara Reis, Fernando Benini, Rosa Maria Pestana, Benjamin Cattan, Orlando Parolin.

Rotterdam — The Faust of this film is in his 30s. The cigaret factory he has inherited just went bust, and so has his marriage. So Faust cracks up, grabs a gun from the janitor and goes on a rampage. Pic shows what happens to Faust, what he thinks is happening and what he would like to happen. However, the pic never makes clear which of these is represented by which sequence. Helmer Carlos Reichenbach seems to consider many things in Faust's reality, nightmares and sweet dreams equally absurd.

The viewer can to some extent identify with Faust. He's mad, of course, but quite nice. He shoots people, but only awful baddies. He runs risks to procure for a chance acquaintance the brand of cigarets he craves. That the acquaintance is really Mephisto in disguise is unfortunate.

Pic is rich in funny sequences, as well as in lightly clad ladies. There is a hilarious scene of a "symbolical symposium" with two pixilated members of the forum called E.V. Stroheim and C.Th. Dreyer. Faust's encounters with the dregs of humanity are never tragic; Mephisto in drag and ravenously hungry, is a new experience. Faust has many visions of a young girl, generally clad in white, obviously representing Innocence, with an angelic smile. But it's as sexy as it is childlike. Innocence might very likely be a little devil.

This irreverent pic is the first Reichenbach film coproduced by Embrafilme of the Ministry of Culture. Tech credits all are above average.—*Wall.*

Lulu de Noche
(Lulu By Night)
(SPANISH-COLOR)

A Kaplan, Fernando Trueba P.C. production. Executive producers, Fernando Trueba, Emilio Martinez-Lazaro. Written and directed by Emilio Martinez-Lazaro. Camera (color), Juan Amoros; editor, Nieves Martin; Music, Angel Munoz-Alonso; art direction, Carlos Ruiz Castillo. Reviewed at Coconut Grove Playhouse (Miami Film Festival), Feb. 10, 1986. Running time: **95 MINS.**

Rufo	Imanol Arias
Nena	Amparo Munoz
Germain	Antonio Resines

Amelia . . . . Assumpta Serna
Lola . . . . Patricia Adriani
Josefina . . . . Asuncion Balaguer
Cesar . . . . Fernando Vivanco
Paco . . . . El Gran Wyoming

Miami — "Lulu By Night" is an inventive and amusing installment of Spain's New Wave movement which cleverly combines screwball comedy with *film noir* in a likable mix of styles and elements.

Directed by Emilio Martinez-Lazaro ("Everything's Going Wrong"), "Lulu" is about an amiably muddled theater director Germain (Antonio Resines) struggling to produce a play about a mother-obsessed psychotic and a free-spirited seductress. The title of his comically ultra-serious production-to-be is "The Wolfman's Politics."

Before Germain can proceed, he must first cast the play and find backers. Germain's actress ex-wife Amelia (Assumpta Serna) would like the role, but Germain would rather have former girlfriend Nena (Amparo Munoz) — whom he still secretly loves — play the seductress Lulu. Nena, alas, has no aspirations to the stage. For the part of Lulu, Germain also considers Lola (Patricia Adriani), a sexy, flaky woman he encounters in a taxicab.

The director hopes to persuade Rufo (Imanol Arias), a dark-eyed and mysterious petty thief, to fill the male lead. To further complicate matters he hopes to receive financial backing from his beloved Nena's rich new husband Cesar (Fernando Vivanco), who does not know about Nena and Germain's affair.

Lazaro deftly juggles his comic characters and oddball situations against a dangerously intriguing background. As it turns out, Germain can't put aside his clumsy longings for Nena. Nena falls for Rufo, Cesar for Lola, and Amelia for a virile, but none too intellectual soccer player (El Gran Wyoming). Rufo cares only for his nagging, drug addicted mother Josefina (Asuncion Balaguer) and also is plagued by psychedelic images of the Pope blessing the masses.

Lazaro's life-imitates-art theme culminates in the grisly murder of a prostitute and the crime's blithe resolution.

Arias and Resines pair off as devastatingly funny opposites. Resines is especially appealing as a kind of intellectual buffoon whom nobody takes too seriously, yet everyone can't help but like.

The results are a hilarious, unpredictable mix of laughs and thrills. Cinematographer Juan Amoros cleverly lends polish to the look of "Lulu" with a lethally amusing mix of dark interiors and psychedelic imagery. — *Bux.*

Martial Arts Of Shaolin
(HONG KONG-CHINESE-COLOR)

A Pearl River Film production, released by Sil-Metropole Organization Ltd. Directed by Lau Kar-Leung. Stars Jet Lee, Hu Jiang-Qiang, Huang Qui-Yan, Yu Cheng-Hui, Yu Hai, Sun Jian-Kiu, Liu Huai-Liang, Ji Chun-Hua. Produced by Ann Tse Kai, Liu Yet Yuen. Executive Producer, Fu Chi; planner, Chan Man. Producers, Lam Ping Kwan, Lu Yin Pei, Wong Ying Cheong. Screenplay, Sze Yeung Ping; theme song, James J.S. Wong, performed by Lu Fang. Reviewed at King's Theater, Hong Kong, Feb. 11, 1986. Running time: **97 MINS.**
(Mandarin soundtrack with English and Chinese subtitles)

Hong Kong — Publicized as a production that was two years in the making with a budget of $HK15,-000,000, "Martial Arts Of Shaolin" was scheduled for the 1986 Chinese Lunar New Year. It has the reigning star of China, Jet Lee (the country's answer to Jackie Chan and Bruce Lee) and has Hong Kong's leading exponent of kung fu movies, Lau Kar-Leung.

The story begins at the Imperial Palace, as an official hurries to rescue his friend who has been framed by Lord He Suo. However, he is too late: his friend is executed before he can intervene. He confronts Lord He Suo, and is killed as well.

Many years later the children of both victims have grown up. One is Zhi Ming who was taken to North Shaolin by his mother. The other is Sima Yan who took refuge with her uncle Fa Ren at South Shaolin.

One day news spreads that officials from all over the country are going to congratulate Lord He Suo on his coming birthday. Simultaneously, Zhi Ming & Sima Yan make plans to take their revenge.

The thin story acts as framework to many stunning fights. Besides the leading martial artists in top roles, more 300 other experts in the field were recruited from all over China as extras for the film. Lacking in plot, the film offers unlimited energy, spectacular mob scenes and fresh, unseen exotic locations. There is a duel on the highest point of the Great Wall of China, an ambush in the Forbidden City in Beijing, marvelous shots of the South Shaolin Temple in Fujian and the Imperial Palace. — *Mel.*

Las Madres: The Mothers Of Plaza De Mayo
(DOCU-COLOR)

A First Run Features release. Produced, written and directed by Susana Muñoz and Lourdes Portillo. Camera (color), Michael Anderson; music, Inti-Illimani and Astor Piazzola; narrated by Carmen Zapata. Reviewed at the Castro theater, San Francisco, Jan. 15, 1986. (No MPAA Rating.) Running time: **64 MINS.**

San Francisco — This is an emotionally moving, technically solid exposition of the disappearances in military-ruled Argentina in the 1970s of thousands. By featuring the politically organized mothers of the missing, the filmmakers have deftly told the entire grisly story and earned a nomination in the Academy's feature documentary category.

Sans Franciscans Susana Muñoz and Lourdes Portillo offer a first-rate piece of reportage. Interviews with survivors are subtitled, but narration in print reviewed — a crisp job of writing — is in English.

Score is highly complementary and mood-inducing without being overbearing. There is a universality to the comments of the interviewees. As one of the mothers notes: "we were all the same person."

Pic concludes by analogizing Argentine tragedy with repression in other politically reactionary nations but ducks similar acts of terror in leftist lands. — *Herb.*

Heilt Hitler!
(Heal Hitler!)
(WEST GERMAN-COLOR)

A Herbert Achternbusch Film production, Munich. Written and directed by Achternbusch. Camera (color), Achternbusch, Gunter Freyse, Adam Olech; sound, Hartmut Geerken; makeup and costumes, Ann Poppel. Reviewed at Berlin Film Fest (Special Screening), Feb. 23, 1986. Running time: **145 MINS.**
With: Gunter Freyse (Gunter and Traudylein), Herbert Achternbusch (Herbert the cripple), Gabi Geist (Gaby and Gabylein), Waltraud Galler (Traudy), Annamirl Bierbichler (Annamirl and Annamirl), Anita Geerken (Annytta and Anita), Judit Achternbusch (the girl), Luisa Francia (Luise), Josef Bierbichler (farmer), Franz Baumgartner (the man), Hias Schaschko (Hi), Helmut Neuayer (He), Hartmut Geerken (Penisdiener), Ruth Drexel, Hans Brenner.

Berlin — The Berlinale has been featuring a Herbert Achternbusch evening regularly for a couple of years. It means his latest homemade movie, like "Heal Hitler!" (blown up to 35m from super-8), gets shown in the Zoo Palast in a late-night slot. Afterwards, Herbert leads his entourage to a local Kneipe for an all-night "press conference" and victory celebration.

Achternbusch is a showman par excellence. As a filmmaker, however, he would be better off specializing in Robert Benchley and W.C. Fields type shorts than persecuting his public under a two-hour-plus shower of lusty words and static images on the Hitler syndrome still pestilently infecting the rural mores of Bavaria. Super-8 tracts are arguably better off shown on super-8 screens. — *Holl.*

Zabravote tozi slochai
(Forget That Case)
(BULGARIAN-COLOR)

A Bulgaria Film release of Bojana Studio (Sofia) production. Directed by Krassimir Spassov. Stars Filip Trifonov. Screenplay, Spassov, Georgi Danailov, based on Danailov's stage play "The Autumn Of An Investigating Magistrate," camera (color), Radoslav Spassov; production design, Georgi Todorov; music, Kiril Donchev. Reviewed at Berlin Film Fest (Panorama section), Feb. 17, 1986. Running time: **100 MINS.**
Magistrate Andreev . . . . Filip Trifonov
Petrov . . . . Boris Loukanov
Sarafov . . . . Lyubomir Kabakchiev
Maria . . . . Tsvetana Maneva
Petrov's wife . . . . Ruth Spassova
Elena . . . . Tanya Shahova

Berlin — Veteran stage director Krassimir Spassov took one of his stage hits, Georgi Danailov's "The Autumn Of An Investigating Magistrate," as the basis of his feature film bow "Forget That Case." He has opened up the play nicely by having the protagonists move with natural ease in and out of cityscapes, landscapes and houses in a provincial town.

Young Andreev (Filip Trifonov), bewildered and stubborn, wants to pursue a legal career as a barrister, but at first he has to prove himself able of handling a small-town magistrate's job. This turns out more difficult than expected when he runs smack into the stone-walling and elusive double-talking of nearly everybody in town in connection with his initially innocent search for the reasons for his predecessor being in jail.

The imprisoned man himself does not want himself cleared even when Andreev finds out that the real culprit in local municipality shenanigans is the mayor of the town. Andreev repeatedly finds his questions evaded, while he also suffers physical abuse when getting close to the heart of the matter.

It turns out that the solving of the crime hurts practically everybody, and Andreev's victory is a Pyrrhic one. (Plot closely resembles David Friedkin's fine 1958 U.S. film "Handle With Care," starring Dean Jones — *Ed.*)

Spassov has his actors handle their evasive miens and flagrant doubletalk with quiet conviction and a certain kind of sad wisdom to help them uphold the fiction that everything should be left alone. Filip Trifonov manages to appear a sympathetic victim throughout.
— *Kell.*

Die Nachtmeerfahrt
(The Nocturnal Voyage)
(AUSTRIAN-COLOR)

A Thalia Film production, Vienna, in collaboration with Austrian Television (ORF). Written and directed by Kitty Kino. Camera (color), Hanus Polak, Frédéric G. Kacek; editor, Charlotte Müllner, Brigitte Frischler; sets Elisabeth Klobassa; music, Polio Brezina;

costumes, Cera Graf; sound, Herbert Koller, Dieter Laske. Reviewed at Berlin Film Fest (info show - special screenings), Feb. 21, 1986. Running time: **80 MINS.**

With: Anita Kolbert (Lilly), Wilfried Scheutz (Richard), Christine Jirku (Margret), Beatrix Wipperlich (Sue), Anne Mertin (Lady Caretaker), Lotte Loebenstein (Lady caretaker's daughter), Joesi Prokopetz (Pepo).

Berlin — Kitty Kino's "The Nocturnal Voyage" is an impressive Austrian feature which has a lot in common with another talented femme helmer's ironic statement on the ad world, Doris Dörrie's "Men."

Lilly, a photographer's model, is bored both by the routine of her empty-headed work and the whims of her married boyfriend, but she's also not the type to go out and change things. One day, however, she's surprised to find she's sprouting whiskers on her chin, a situation that becomes increasingly more desperate to control. Finally she decides to let it grow and get used to the idea of passing herself off as her brother.

The twist is to see everything around her through a man's eyes, which leads her to seek a new role in life and take her affairs into her own hands for the first time. Also, as a male personality that can go unnoticed even by her close friends, she begins to have a bit more fun than usual and even gets into trouble on occasion (the nightclub scene ends with her being thrown out on her ear during a striptease show).

The way back to reality after this "nocturnal voyage" through the spiritual self finds Lilly in demand again as a photographer's model, a job she takes by deciding to shave off the beard and posing in an outlandish victory goddess costume wearing only the mustache. The ad customer, of course, is delighted, and Lilly wins the day. She has the gumption to split with her macho boyfriend. At just this moment, what should happen but her beard vanishes.

Nice, witty situations, but Kino doesn't get enough out of the overall story to sustain the joke. Dialog and thesp performances are pluses.

Suuri illusioni
(The Grand Illusion)
(FINNISH-COLOR)

A Finnkino release of Elokuvatuottajat Oy (Matti Penttilä) with the Finnish Film Institute production. Directed by Tuija-Maija Niskanen. Screenplay, Anja Kauranen, based on Mika Waltari's 1928 novel; executive producers, Claes Olsson, Matti Pentilä; camera (Eastmancolor), Kari Sohlberg; sound, Paul Jyrälä; lighting, Kari Kekkonen; production design, Erkki Saarainen; costumes, Sari Salmela; editor, Irma Salmela; music, Kaija Saariaho. Reviewed at Berlin Film Festival (market), Feb. 17, 1986. Running time: **92 MINS.**
Hart . . . . Pekka Valkeejärvi
Caritas . . . . Stina Ekblad

Hellas . . . . Markku Toikka
Madama Spindel . . . . Rea Mauranen

Berlin — In Tuija-Maija Niskanen's feature melodrama "The Grand Illusion," the trio of lead characters and everybody around them drink menthe liqueur, read Baudelaire's "Les fleurs du Mal" and Hemingway and are pretty desperate in their search of outré fun and games, sexual and otherwise. The characters are taken from Mika Waltari's youthful 1928 novel of which the author is said to have been ashamed (over its superficiality) in later years when he had achieved world fame for such works as "Sinuhu, The Egyptian" and "The Unknown Soldier."

Niskanen's film has stunning looks, sounds, lighting and décor plus demure acting. Story does, however, appear ludicrous after a short while as clean-cut blond Hart drops his divinity studies for nocturnal observations at Madame Spindel's opulent cabaret-brothel-fortune-telling establishment in Helsinki of the 1920s. Hart watches and falls in love with similarly blond and cleancut Caritas (Stina Ekblad in another exquisite performance) who herself is hopelessly in love with leather-clad, bald-headed and loud-mouthed Hellas, a poet aiming for the big score with the novel about his own generation.

The trio repairs to Paris, where they suffer and booze and, finally, come to grips with some various tragic facts of life. Caritas is then off on the Oriental Express alone, and divinity may yet gather Hart to its bosom.—*Kell.*

Teo El Pelirrojo
(Teo The Redhead)
(SPANISH-COLOR)

A Pena Amaya Films production. Produced by Pedro Roman. Executive producer, Francisco Merayo. Written and directed by Paco Lucio. Camera (Eastmancolor), Federico Ribes; editor, Luis Manuel del Valle; music, Jan Garbarek, Rosita Perrer; sound, Antonio Bloch; production design, Luis Valles; assistant director, Gabriel Villanueva. Reviewed at Berlin Film Festival, Zoo-Palast (in competition), Feb. 24, 1986. Running time: **94 MINS.**
Teo . . . . Alvaro de Luna
Santiago . . . . Juan Diego Botto
Viviana . . . . Maria Luisa San José
Luis . . . . Ovidi Montillor
Grandfather . . . . Luis Escobar
Aunt Maria . . . . Concha Leza
Valeriana . . . . Sarai Hermosa
Matias . . . . Daniel Barros

Berlin — Spain's competitive entry into the Berlin fest is a first feature of considerable charm and promise. Helmer Paco Lucio, who also scripted, formerly worked as an assistant to both Carlos Saura and Victor Erice, and it's hard not to see their influence in his handling of a story involving children who act older than their years.

Pic is set in 1960. Young Santiago travels from Madrid with his parents to the countryside to see his dying grandfather. The old man is delighted to see his favorite grandson, and makes a big show of confiding to him a special secret. Soon after, he dies. It seems he left his property to young Santiago, so his parents stay on, sharing the old farmhouse with his father's brother's family, which includes two children Santiago's age.

The boy quickly befriends Teo, for many years his grandfather's foreman. Teo is an exotic character, big and strong and with a variety of strange animals in tow. Santiago hero-worships the rugged countryman, especially after the boy gets lost exploring the rocky crags of the district and is found by Teo.

Things turn dark when Teo is imprisoned for drunkenness and takes a savage revenge on the men who put him there. Teo is now a murderer, but that doesn't affect the frightened boy's love for his friend.

For Spanish-speaking audiences, the clue to the close relationship between Teo and the boy (and to the secret the dying grandfather confided in Santiago) is probably obvious from the start: "tío" is Spanish for uncle.

It's not the plot that counts so much as the feel for the brown-tinged, rugged setting, the small town with its petty officials, and the everyday discoveries of the growing children. Acting is solid, with two notable performances: Luis Escobar, remembered for playing the cantankerous old Marquis in "The National Shotgun" and its sequels, makes a wonderful but brief cameo out of the old grandfather, and Juan Diego Botto is another of those alert Spanish kids with huge black eyes and a questioning nature.

What the film lacks is a somewhat harder edge. It does entertain, especially via such charming scenes as a visit to a rundown circus in which a woman miming to an old record is discomfited when the needle gets stuck in a groove. Could that be a metaphor for Spain in 1960, also stuck in some kind of groove under the long reign of Franco? —*Strat.*

Müllers Büro
(Müller's Bureau)
(AUSTRIAN-COLOR)

A Wega Film production, Vienna. World rights, Wega Film, Vienna. Written and directed by Niki List. Camera (color), Hans Selikovsky; editor, Ingrid Koller; music, Ernie Seubert; sets, Rudolf Czettel; costumes, Martina List; sound, Moshar Nasiri. Reviewed at Berlin Film Fest (info show), Feb. 18, 1986. Running time: **95 MINS.**
With: Christian Schmidt (Max Müller), Andreas Vitasek (Andy), Barbara Rudnik (Bettina Kant), Sue Tauber (Frau Schick), Gaby Hift (Frau Copain),

---

Berlin — Austrian helmer Niki List's "Müller's Bureau," unspooled in the Special Screenings of the Info Show at the Berlinale, is also a rare treat for film buffs, Bogie-and-Bacall fans, and incurable night-table readers of the hard-boiled detective story.

"Müller's Bureau" is also a musical. The thesps frequently break into pop songs to comment mostly on the confusion already visible within the plot.

Max Müller is a private eye who's commissioned by the lovely Bettina Kant to find her missing fiance. Down on his luck, Müller takes the case, only to discover in the morning paper that his client was supposed to have been killed the day before. Together with his sidekick Andy, Müller is off to investigate in the Underworld — only to discover that the top Mafia leaders are out to stop him from poking his nose around. One corpse piles up on top of another, until the missing boyfriend is found with a couple of intimidating bordello photos taped to his back.

There's a final shootout, plus a series of twists and sight-gags. Pic does hang in parts and thus loses its drive, a matter that could easily be corrected on the editing table.
—*Holl.*

Nem Tudo e Verdade
(Not Everything Is True)
(BRAZILIAN-COLOR/B&W)

A Rogério Sganzerla Cinematográficas production. Written and directed by Sganzerla. Camera (color), José Madeiros, Edson Santos, Edson Batista, Carlos Alberto Ebert, Afonso Viana, Vitor Diniz; editor, Severino Dadá, Denise Fontoura; sound, Sganzerla; music, João Gilberto. Reviewed at the Mini-lux Berlin Film Fest (forum), Feb. 23, 1986. Running time: **95 MINS.**
With: Arrigo Barnabe (Orson Welles), Grande Otelo, Helena Ignez, Nina de Pádua, Mariana de Maraes, Vania Magalhães, Abrão Farc, Otavio Terceiro, Gudrá, José Marinho, Geraldo Francisco, Mario Cravo, Nonato Freire.

Berlin — This peculiar Brazilian docu-drama ostensibly attempts to pay tribute to the late Orson Welles and to his visit to Brazil in 1942, when he tried to shoot a film known as "It's All True," which he never finished.

In order to do so, a complicated hodge-podge of different elements are stuck together, from newsreel footage of Brazil at the time, to excerpts from "Citizen Kane" and "Touch Of Evil," interviews with people who met Welles, recordings from Welles' radio shows and on top of it all, dramatized episodes describing his visit. It's all very impressionistically fashioned with a local actor playing the part of Welles.

Narration tries to tie it all together, with one voice aiming to ape the unique timber of Welles' voice. There are many references to the political situation in Brazil at the time, which, the film suggests, had much to do with Welles' failing to finish the picture.

The trouble is that as considerate as the intentions may have been toward Welles, the film becomes an uneasy caricature of the man, particularly in the dramatized sequences showing his relations with local women journalists or referring to later wine commercials, in what comes out as a derogatory manner.

A final title indicates that after this film was completed, it turned out that contrary to what is stated in it, Paramount did find more than 300 reels Welles shot in Brazil lying in its vaults. Which shows, just as the title of the film states, paraphrasing Welles' own title, that "not everything is true," not even the things you have just seen.

— *Edna.*

Morena
(FINNISH-COLOR)

A Reppufilmi Oy (Helsinki) production. Foreign sales, the Finnish Film Foundation. Executive producers, Mika Kaurismäki, Günther Stocklöv. Original story, screenplay and directed by Anssi Mänttäri; camera (Agfa color), Heikki Katajisto; editor, Raija Talvio; music, Jukka Hakoköngäs, Costas Papanastasiou, Asko Mänttäri, Claes Andersen. Features Anssi Mänttäri. Reviewed at Berlin Film Festival (market), Feb. 20, 1986. Running time: **78 MINS.**
Redbeard . . . . .Anssi Mänttäri
Morena . . . . .Caroline Krüger
Pianoplayer . . . . .Claes Andersson
Painter . . . . .Dan van Husen
The layabout . . . . .Klaus Tonke

Berlin — Anssi Mänttäri's pic was shot in Berlin a year ago over just 10 days, but looks like more than its budget's modest $140,000.

In the leading role Mänttäri leaves Finland to spend days and nights in Berlin wandering in and out of bars. He says that he is looking for a countryman who knows a tune he has lost. The countryman turns out to be a jazz pianist who has lost his own tune in life. He is incredibly lucky in charming his way into the heart of a radiantly beautiful Italian waitress, the Morena of the title. She comes to spend one night with him, but is then cooly dismissed.

It is never indicated whether this man is running away from anything, but if he is, it could be from his childhood, since interpolated scenes show a little German boy, who has tried to make friends with him, being exposed to coldness and adult fighting in his home. Having spouted a good deal of dimestore philosophy, Redbeard, as he calls himself, gives up on Berlin. Not yet ready to return to Finland, we find him blowing a bluesy bit on a clarinet on a Copenhagen, Denmark, streetcorner.

Lacking any exploration of the character of Morena (given mute but stunning presence by Germany's Caroline Krüger, a non-professional like most everybody else in the small cast), film simply does not have enough of an anchor for sustained attention in Mänttäri's own mild-mannered persona. His work then comes across at best as an academic exercise. —*Kell.*

El Hombre que gano la razon
(The Man Who Gained Reason) (ARGENTINE/DUTCH-B&W)

A Film Intl. release of a Movimiento Falso/Haags Filmhuis production. Written, produced and directed by Alejandro Agresti. Camera (b&w), Agresti, Nestor Sanz; editor, Rene Wiegmans; sound, Jorg Ventura; music, Agresti, Stravinski. Reviewed at Rotterdam Film Festival (also in Forum of Young Cinema at Berlin Film Fest), Jan. 30, 1986. Running time: **68 MINS.**
Ricardo . . . . .Elio Marchi
Leticia . . . . .Marina Skell
Sergio . . . . .Sergio Poves Campos

Rotterdam — Alejandro Agresti has, at 24, worked nine years in tv and films, published a novel and reinvented for himself a goodly part of modern filmmaking. He began at 15 as assistant to lenser Anibol di Salvo, became cameraman at 18 and worked mainly on commercials.

He started "El Hombre" four years ago, under the Argentine military dictatorship, with film stock "found" at tv stations and with no script, in order to delude secret police who continuously followed the film crew. Came the Alfonsin government and authorities doled out very little money. (Total budget is under $20,000.)

Funds were depleted before shooting was finished, so helmer went to Europe to try his luck. He ended up in the Netherlands, "because life was cheap there;" learned English and found the Hague Film House, which provided editing facilities and paid for lab work.

Pic is about Ricardo, a writer who also wants to make films. Suffering from writer's block, he meets Letitia, and later Sergio, who offer to help him. He also meets a motley crew of curious characters, including a woman who wants to sell Argentina to the Japanese who could then go on expanding. The Argentines could then use the money to fulfill their dearest wish: get themselves an island. He also meets his ex-wife's new husband, a crippled officer, who warns him of the danger to artists in Argentina, namely disappearing. In the end Ricardo, until then a softboiled weakling, decides to become his own man, and to face all perils.

"El Hombre," however, is no pessimistic dirge, but a lively, ironic, witty, provocative escapade. It has style, and its form is the success-

ful result of choice and necessity. Agresti preferred black and white as a contrast to tv culture. Lack of money forced him to use sparse lighting, existing locations, practically no sets. He managed to get positive effects from these disadvantages.

Pic, which had critical and popular success in Rotterdam, went on to the Berlinale. —*Wall.*

Ganz Unten
(Right At The Bottom) (W. GERMAN-DOCU-COLOR/B&W)

A Kaos Film and Video Team (Cologne) and Pirat Film production, in coproduction with Radio Bremen. A documentary by Jörg Gfrörer, in collaboration with Günter Wallraff. Camera (color, b&w), Gfrörer, Dieter Oeckl; editor, Peter Kleinert, Tom Meffert; music, Heinrich Huber, Nehmet Ipek; sound Jochen Schemm. Reviewed at Berlin Film Fest (Info Show), Feb. 20, 1986. Running time: **100 MINS.**

Berlin — The run on tickets for Jörg Gfrörer and Günter Wallraff's documentary "Right At The Bottom" is due to the notoriety of the bestseller upon which it is based and which shares its overall concept.

A research reporter disguises himself as a Turkish worker to apply for odd jobs available to the unemployed in the industrial Ruhrgebiet area of West Germany. Everything he does is then filmed by hidden video cameras, with the intention of releasing the footage later to the film and public tv.

Once Wallraff's book became a nonfiction bestseller the interest in the film/video footage rose accordingly, so much so that word-of-mouth on this Berlinale entry in the "Documents" section of the Info Show was nothing short of phenomenal before anyone had officially even seen the docu. This is a deadly way to market such a film. For, upon viewing the results, "Right At The Bottom" is fine as a contemporary document, but only so-so as a documentary film.

Little else than that could really be expected in the first place. The video footage was made under the most restrictive conditions possible. While Wallraff was appearing as Turkish worker Ali Levant each morning at a local job-placement agency in Cologne, helmer Gfrörer was a few steps behind him as his Italian foreign-worker assistant. The two had worked out a system of communication signs to determine how and when to film a scene. Lighting could be extremely poor, while tape recordings were equally a question mark or far as clarity is concerned.

Wallraff's aim was to show how badly Turkish foreign-workers are treated in Germany's work force. In this he has succeeded admirably. Ali

Levant was given jobs dangerous to his health and safety at the Thyssen Steel Mills in Duisburg. His housing was in a dilapidated, condemned section of an industrial complex and he and others were being exploited constantly by the job agency whose penny-pinching boss is one of the most undesirable creatures in the entire film. Wallraff and Gfrörer get their sweet revenge when they set the agency crook up with a ruse of their own. "People from Bonn" arrive on the scene to commission the job agent with a false contract to hire Turkish labor for a health-damaging job at an atomic-energy plant — how this one turns out forms the dramatic core of the film.

New media technology being what it is, one is satisfied with the blowup results for "Right At The Bottom." On the other hand it all seems so lacking in luster and without that sense of immediacy docus must possess to stand out at all. —*Holl.*

El Suizo - Un Amour En Espagne
(El Suizo, A Love In Spain) (SWISS-COLOR)

A Richard Dindo, Robert Boner, SAGA production. Directed by Dindo. Screenplay, Dindo with Georg Janett; camera (color), Ranier Trinkler, Jürg Hassler; editor, Trinkler, supervised by Georg Janett; sound, Laurent Barbey. Reviewed at the Minilux, Berlin Film Fest (forum), Feb. 21, 1986. Running time: **90 MINS.**
Hans . . . . .Jürg Löw
Anne . . . . .Aurore Clément
Margareta . . . . .Silvia Munt
Also with: Alfredo Mayo, Luis Barbero, Juan Folguera, Carmen Liano, Jesus Munt, Walter Ruch, José Solans, Maria Soley Marti.

Berlin — Almost the entire length of "El Suizo" is a very long flashback. A Swiss journalist remembers a trip he had taken seven years earlier to Spain, ostensibly in order to cover the events that would ensue after Franco's death. Actually, he's to follow in the footsteps of his recently deceased father, a veteran of the Spanish Civil War.

The script tries to follow the father-fixation of a man who obviously feels his generation has been doomed to a life of insignificance compared to the previous one. At the same time it deals with the failed relations he has with two women, to neither of which he succeeds in relating. They are vastly different, one a liberated, independent Frenchwoman whose father probably also fought in Spain, the other a traditional Spanish girl, who fascinates him because she is the daughter of the woman his father used to love before the war.

Richard Dindo adopts a cool, detached approach to the story. There are no great affecting moments. The pace is slow, the mood introspective, and the audience is asked to make an effort to get close to what is defined in the script itself as "timid Swiss."

Jürg Löw plays the lead role accordingly, doing his best to suggest emotions without showing them. Aurore Clément offers solid presence as the Frenchwoman who will not allow herself to be crowded. Silvia Munt is given the liveliest part, as a high-society girl whose dependence on traditions and the roles imposed on men and women is so strong, she is bound by them even though she knows they don't work.
— *Edna.*

La Republica Perdida II
(The Lost Republic II)
(ARGENTINE-DOCU-COLOR)

A Noran and Enrique Vanoli production. Directed by Miguel Pérez. Text, Maria Elena Walsh, Pérez; editor, Pérez, Luis Mutti; music, Luis Maria Serra. Reviewed at the Berlin Film Festival (forum), Feb. 23, 1986. Running time: **140 MINS.**

Berlin — This is the second part of a sweeping historical documentary ("The Lost Republic I" appeared in 1983) detailing events in Argentina from 1976-83. Filmmaker Miguel Pérez has assembled a wide range of materials into an informative trip through recent history that speeds by on winged feet. A strong point-of-view lends a sense of urgency to the torrent of facts and figures that pour out of the commentary, and generally keeps the plethora of images from becoming simply overwhelming.

By way of introduction, the brief presidency of the Perons is shown in terms of a chaotic, conservative democracy, the end of an epoch that was to precede a reign of state terror. Founding their rule on ideas like, "democracy is the sign of a healthy nation, our country is too sick for it" and "our society is insane, so orders must be followed without question," leaders of the military coup banned the Congress and Supreme Courts. The film documents the kidnapings, torture and summary executions that followed in a lightning round of images — famous faces that joined the ever-lengthening missing lists, interviews with survivors and relatives. While none of this is new, Pérez is skillful in interweaving it with such material as government propaganda films and reactions from various U.S. presidents. Occasional diplomatic nuggets are to be found, like how war with Chile was avoided in 1979 thanks to the Pope's mediation.

Pérez is particularly good in using plain quotes from the historical record to ridicule personages like Gen. Videla and Co. A section on the economic recession, skyrocketing unemployment, inflation, and for-eign debt is less interesting on film. When the road of Argentine history winds through the Falklands, Pérez interprets it as the government's clever and highly successful move to get the people on its side, and shows the population firmly united, for those fleeting weeks, behind a deeply felt national cause. As soon as the venture is over, Plaza de Mayo again fills with the outraged voices of mothers and grandmothers of the desparecidos (missing persons).

The return of democracy and election of Raul Alfonsin provide an upbeat finalé for a film that is essentially the tragic record of a country's suffering. Though it is based on no brilliantly original thesis and chooses to avoid easy emotion and impassioned prose (a linear chronological text is alternately read by male and female narrators), "Lost Republic" succeeds in presenting these unhappy years of recent history cogently and compactly. — *Yung.*

Mati Manas
(The Mind Of Clay)
(INDIAN-DOCU-COLOR)

Produced by Infrakino Film Prod. Directed by Mani Kaul. Text, Kamal Swaroop, Kaul; camera (color), Venu; editor, Renna Mohan; music, T.R. Mahalingam. Reviewed at the Berlin Film Festival (forum), Feb. 23, 1986. Running time: **91 MINS.**

Berlin — Indian documentarist and feature filmmaker Mani Kaul crafts a marvelously visual film poem on the art of simple pottery in "The Mind Of Clay." As in some of his other experimental films, Kaul manages to impart a spell of ancient myth and legend to his subject, where visuals blend with mesmerizing music and commentary in an expressive whole.

Film opens with a shot of dozens of plain clay pots, one of which has some cats playing inside. A soft-spoken commentary begins to weave together several threads — animals, language, mothers and fathers. Rural potters unself-consciously carry on their "primordial craft" in front of the camera. A girl in a museum examines ancient pottery shards. Gradually the images of the clay take over: horses seem to come to life, becoming mythical figures to send messages to the viewer.

Approaching pottery as an anonymous popular art form, Kaul uses form and texture, color, light and framing to create a magical atmosphere. His skilful camera knows when to move and when to be still, harmonically accompanied by a lovely Indian score. The subject of the film is pots, but they resonate to include myth, fable, dream, and a child's relationship to his ancestors. — *Yung.*

Poteryalsya Slon
(An Elephant Got Lost)
(SOVIET-COLOR)

A Soviet Film production, Central Studio for Popular Science, Moscow. World rights, Goskino, Moscow. Directed by Yevgeni Ostashenko. Screenplay, Arkadi Krassilscho-hikov, Otashenko; camera (color), Pavel Filimonovi; music, Sandor Kallosh; sets, Alexander Petrov; sound, L. Shutova. Reviewed at Berlin Film Fest (Children's Festival), Feb. 19, 1986. Running time: **74 MINS.**
With: Sasha Komarov (Yegorska), Maxim Sidorov, Slava Galiullin, Vera Panassenkova (the other children), Raissa Ryassanova (Yegorska's mother).

Berlin — Yevgeni Ostashenko's "An Elephant Got Lost" is set in the wilds of the Taiga region of northern Siberia, where children grow up in the lap of nature with all its mysteries.

A touring circus suffers a near catastrophic fire, the result of which leaves an elephant (Chandru) wandering around on the loose. Since the Taiga is partially natural forest reserve, the elephant should have nothing to fear from the human species, but illegal poachers are on the prowl for wild game and fire upon the movement in the brush, only to wound the pachyderm and anger him.

Right about this time, our young hero Yegorska happens upon the scene. He befriends the elephant, nurses his wound, and takes him home to be put up in the family shed. The lad lives with his mother on a farm on the edge of the forest, and she in turn is not too surprised at the boy's action so long as he takes care of the huge beast until the summer is over.

Yegorska's mother also happens to be the local gamekeeper. The mother and son intuitively understand each other, more so than Yegorska with his own school chums who simply don't believe he's got an elephant at home until they see it with their own eyes.

The authorities finally arrive on the scene and take Chandru into custody. Not for long: the animal breaks loose, and heads back to his newly found chum. The final twist in the story has Chandru catching bronchial pneumonia, which necessitates a shift to warmer climate for the winter. The two bid farewell in the closing scene.

It's a nice youth film for lads crazy for the circus. — *Holl.*

Noe heit annet
(Something Entirely Different)
(NORWEGIAN-COLOR)

A KF/Kommunernes Filmcentral (Oslo) release of Norsk Film A/S with Media Vision A/S production. Executive producer, Odd Wenn. Written and directed by Morten Kolstad. Based on story by Trond Kirkvaag, Knut Lystad, Lars Mjöen; camera (color) Halvor Näss; production design, Jon Arvesen, Dagfinn Kleppan; editor, Tore Tomter; music, Hissa Nyberget; costumes, Wenche Petersen. Reviewed in CineCenter Screening Room Studio 6, Berlin Film Fetival (Market section), Feb. 15, 1986. Running time: **77 MINS.**
Buff .Trond Kirkvaag
Judge, others . . . . .Knut Lystad
Vulvatt, others . . . . .Lars Mjöen
Svalbard . . . . .Linn Stokke
Mrs. Bull . . . . .Minken Fosbeim
Valentino . . . . .Geir Börresen
Also with: Dag Vagsas, Sigve Böe, Lars Andreas Larsen, Henrik Scheele, Kine Allebust, Per Christonsen Sen., Anne Stray, Mari Björgan, Ingolf Karinen.

Berlin — "Something Entirely Different" is a title on loan from early Monty Python tv fun. The borrowers are a trio of Norwegian tv fun & punsters who, in their feature film bow, also pay homage to old Dracula movies and to Swedish stage & film funnymen Povel Ramel and Yngve Gamlin plus, of course, to the Pythons themselves. While latter made the transition to feature films look like a piece of cake, the Norwegians, aided and abetted by writer-director Morten Kolstad, seem burdened by the strain of throwing their satirical pies towards too many targets at once.

Story has mild-mannered, blond Trond Kirkvaag growing up mobbed and generally burdened by his Dracula-type teeth and corresponding thirst on nights of a full moon. Garlic also spurs him on. It turns out that he really is a descendant of Dracula but his heart isn't really in it, and he is seen most of the time as the victim of various social and class superiority attitudes given wildly exaggerated life by everybody around him except one sweet girl whose blood he is loath to taste.

Some sequences should evoke mild guffaws even with non-Norwegian audienes, but the strictly visual fun and the satirical digs are too scattered and diffuse to endear the trio of lead players (in several roles each) to many beyond their home fans. Punster translation of characters' names and dialog works nicely in English subtitles.
—*Kell.*

Die Zeit die Bleibt
(The Time That Remains)
(EAST GERMAN-DOCU-B&W/COLOR)

A DEFA-Studio für Dokumentarfilm production, East Berlin. World rights, DEFA Aussenhandel, East Berlin. A documentary by Lew Hohmann. Artistic director and scriptwriter, Wolfgang Kohlhaase; coauthors, Hohmann, Christiane Mückenberger, Regino Sylvester; camera (b&w, color), Christian Lehmann; editor, Karin Wudtke; music, Günther Fischer; sound, Eberhard Pfaff; production managers, Harry Funk, Klaus Dörrer; narrators, Alexander Lang, Klaus Piontek. Reviewed at Berlin Film Fest (Forum), Feb. 22, 1986. Running time: **107 MINS.**

Berlin — "The Time That Remains" is a memorial tribute to East German filmmaker and president of the GDR Academy of Fine Arts, the late Konrad Wolf (1925-1982), directed by Lew Hohmann but conceptualized and supervised by its scriptwriter Wolfgang Kohlhaase. It offers a rare opportunity to view the postwar period in East Germany through the experiences of a man who helped to mold social and artistic commitment to the German Democratic Republic. The docu achieves more than that: it stands up as a fascinating and quite balanced study of a crucial period in postwar East European history.

Konrad Wolf, son of writer-dramatist Friedrich Wolf, was a rather unique socialist filmmaker in that he pointed the way for others to follow in East German cinema, particularly at times when the going was rough diplomatically.

Excerpts from his films are selected by Kohlhaase for comment and discussion, and it's here that one notes how progressively liberal the filmmaker was in his dual role as director and prez of the Academy of Fine Arts.

Docu begins with fragmented childhood recollections when the family left Germany in 1933 (Konrad was eight years old) to emigrate to Moscow: rare docu footage seems to have been employed here to register his impressions. Next come clips from Alexander Ptushko's animated feature "The New Gulliver" (1935) and Sergei and Georgi Vasilev's "Chapayev" (1934), from which motifs in Wolf's own "Sun Searchers" appear to have originated. Konrad's brother Markus Wolf recalls these days in the Soviet Union, as well as two close childhood friends, the Americans George and Victor Fischer (interviewed in New York and Alaska).

Wolf enlisted in the Red Army at 17, and as a young lieutenant witnessed firsthand the closing days of the war on the eastern front: these impressions paved the way for the autobiographical "I Was Nineteen" and "Mama, I'm Alive." Then comes his return to Moscow to enroll at VGIK for film courses, after which he quickly established himself as a natural filmmaking talent. Appropriate clips are selected from his ouvre to match comments by cameraman Werner Bergmann, scripters Wolfgang Kohlhaase and Angel Wagenstein, actor Kurt Böwe, and others.—*Holl.*

Bir Avuç Cennet
(A Handful Of Paradise)
(TURKISH-COLOR)

A Mine Film (Istanbul) production. Produced and directed by Muammer Özer. Screenplay, editor, Özer; camera (color), Hüseyin Özsahin; sound, Frkan Aktas; music, Tarik Öcal; sets, Yurdaer Hrsan. Reviewed at Berlin Film Festival, Atelier (out of competition), Feb. 19, 1986. Running time: **99 MINS.**
With: Tarik Akan, Hale Soygazi.

Berlin — "A Handful Of Paradise" is a somewhat familiar tale of a Turkish family who leaves its village for greater prosperity in Istanbul. Needless to say, it doesn't work out. They plan to stay with a friend from home, but when they arrive they find he's been killed in an industrial accident. With nowhere to stay, they squat in an abandoned bus left near a garbage dump.

The husband gets a job working on the railroad, while the wife makes the bus more comfortable, even planting a garden in the wasteland. The authorities, spurred on by venemous apartment dwellers who resent the squatters, eventually force them to leave and remove the bus. They carry on, living in a tent.

Tale is a bit too glossy to be convincing, with the actors looking too much like actors and not enough like desperately poor slum-dwellers. Apart from that, there are a few interesting points that set this ahead of the average Turkish film. The wife, for instance, stands up to her husband and is less of a weakling than is usually the case.

Overall, pic lacks the anger present in the best and most memorable Turkish films.—*Strat.*

Romantichna-Istorija
(Romantic Story)
(BULGARIAN-COLOR)

A Bulgariafilm production. Directed by Miaden Nikolov. Screenplay, Aleksander Tomov, from his short story, "Condor," camera (color), Georgi Georgiov; editor, Catherine Stanley; music, Aleksander Burzitsov; art director, Vladimir Lokarski. Reviewed at Berlin Film Festival, Atelier (panorama), Feb. 24, 1986. Running time: **98 MINS.**
Zhana .... Irene Krivoshieva
Ivan Chunov ("Condor") .... Ivan Ivanov
Zhoro .... Vladimir Kolev

Berlin — "Romantic Story" is a routine Bulgarian romance, featuring two singularly unappealing characters. It starts in the '70s as male chauvinist Ivan bosses pretty Zhana around, but postpones marrying her. Later, he's willing to marry but she wants independence (i.e., she wants to play the field). He goes off and 10 years later comes back with some smart clothes and a case full of (illegal) money. They marry, but the dismal drama continues.

Neither the oafish hero nor the infuriating heroine are pleasant characters to spend much time with, although they model themselves after Romeo and Juliet (and there's a generous excerpt from Zeffirelli's film). Acting is rote, and the film is slackly and uninventively directed. — *Strat.*

Inughuit — folket vid jordens navel
(Inughuit — The People At Earth's Navel)
(SWEDISH-DOCU-COLOR)

An Eden Film (Stockholm) production with The Swedish Film Institute, Swedish Television, Channel-2, Greenland's Homerule Cultural Affairs Fund, The Nordic Cultural Affairs Fund. World Sales, The Swedish Film Institute (Lena Enquist). Written, directed and edited by Staffan Ylva Julén. Camera (Fujicolor), Michael Rosengren, Staffan Julén; music, Juakka, Chrichan Larsson; performed by Chrichan Larsson, Staffan Larsson, Juakka, Anna Lindal; executive producer, Staffan Julén; sound, Julén & Julén. Reviewed at Atelier am Zoo, Berlin Film Fest (panorama), Feb. 22, 1986. Running time: **85 MINS.**

Berlin — The "Inughuit — The People At Earth's Navel" of Staffan Julén's and his sister Ylva Julén's feature-length docu are a tribe of Arctic Eskimos numbering only a few thousand and belonging to the larger tribe Inuit, the name for all Greenland/Danish, Canadian, Alaskan and Siberian Eskimos. They were forced to move one of their major homesteads in 1953 when the Danes allowed the U.S. to build a major military base in the Thule (Qaanaaq) area.

In the Juléns' film, the Inughuit, 100% dependent for their livelihood on hunting seals (babies and fully grown), whales and other ocean fauna, express themselves stoically about all that threatens their existence. They are worried that oil tankers will soon be allowed to pass through their waters, destroying Inughuit hunting with hand-thrown harpoons, since the animals are strongly susceptible to sound and may flee to farther reaches of the ocean.

The bloodiness of killing is not hidden by the Juléns, but it isn't wallowed in, either. The hunters smile with pained tolerance at Brigitte Bardot's insistence, from a safe distance, that they ought to become vegetarians. They have no natural access to vegetables, and their region's low temperatures and their hard work make them physically dependent on the fatty meat of seals and whales and on animal furs for clothing.

The Inughuit are gradually adapting to rock 'n' roll and tv, but they have rejected being turned into a tribe of storekeepers. They are proud and happy to be hunters, and the younger generation is eager to stay in touch with the traditions, music and fantastic tales of their ancestors. With the six months of summer being eternal day, the other six uninterrupted pitch darkness, the beautiful locale and the movements of men and animals in and out of water have been caught by cameramen Michael Rosengren and Staffan Julén with loving care, fine compository flair and technical adeptness.

"Inughuit" is obviously in favor of these Eskimos being allowed to thrive and develop in an unforced way, but there are no hectoring overtones or the least trace of tractmaking. Film is occasionally long-winded and could be cut by a near half-hour to fit the traditional 58-minute tv programming slot. Made for modest coin, "Inughuit" looks rich. — *Kell.*

Egeszseges Erotika
(Sound Eroticism)
(HUNGARIAN-B&W)

A Dialog Studio, Mafilm, production. Written, directed and edited by Peter Timar. Camera (b&w), Sandor Kardos; sets, Laszlo Gardonyi; sound, Tamas Markus. Reviewed at Hungarian Film Week (Congress Center), Budapest, Feb. 11, 1986. Running time: **88 MINS.**
Manager .... Adam Rajhona
Fire officer .... Robert Koltai
Chairman .... Peter Haumann
Ibi .... Kata Kristof
Mrs. Hajdu .... Judit Nemeth
Veterinary .... Jozsef Sotonyi

Budapest — A good idea for a funny comedy is to be found at the center of this depressingly bad film. The trouble is that any chances for real humor are destroyed by first-time director Peter Timar's hideous handling of the subject.

Setting is a small factory with exclusively women workers who make wooden crates. Inspired by an official survey into the sexual habits of his workers, the venal factory manager, aided by his fire officer, sets up a hidden video camera in the women's changing room. Every morning and evening they sit back to watch the strip-tease show on their monitor. Word spreads, and soon the local Party Chairman is coming along for a look. As more and more important people come to see the show, the factory's orders increase greatly. Then the women discover the hidden camera.

Given this promising idea, Timar unaccountably manages to wreck it via his self-indulgent and frenetic style. The actors are encouraged to overact so that, instead of real people in an absurd situation, we get absurd caricatures and the humor is entirely lost. Timar has his cameraman, fish-eye lens in place, scurry about in search of the oddest angle. It only adds to the mess. Timar's own editing is as incompetent as the rest. He uses stop-motion effects for no good reason, further diminishing the potential comedy in the basic material.

The actors can only go along with the director's ideas, but it's sad to see Kata Kristof, as a screeching secretary, giving such an awful performance. — *Strat.*

Szerelem Elso Verig
(Love Till First Blood)
(HUNGARIAN-COLOR)

A Dialog Studio, Mafilm, production, written and directed by György Dobray, Peter Horvath. Camera (Fujicolor), Tamas Andor; editor, Marianna Miklos; music, Laszlo Des; sets & costumes, György Csik; sound, Janos Reti. Reviewed at Hungarian Film Week, Budapest, Feb. 10, 1986. Running time: **96 MINS.**

Füge	Ari Bery
Agota	Mariann Szilagyi
Füge's mother	Erzsi Galambos
Füge's father	Denes Ujlaki
Agota's mother	Ilona Kallai
Agota's aunt	Jolan Jaszai
Mili	Christine Harbourt
Gyula	Attila Epres

Budapest — "Love Till First Blood" (no, it's not about Sly & Brigitte's courtship), is a routine tale of teenage troubles, but lacking the kind of insights and sensitivity to be found in Danish films on a similar theme. The young hero, Füge, lives in a school hostel and has formed a jazz band with some friends. He's in love with the chubby Agota, and jealous of her former boyfriend. During the course of the film, Füge gets Agota pregnant (a rather coy little love scene) and his mother succumbs to cancer. He also dallies with one of his father's ex-mistresses, an opera singer.

For a film about youth, this one's sorely lacking in verve. It's mildly pleasant but quite forgettable. It appears to be the first Magyar feature shot in Fujicolor, and contains a blatant plug for the company as, in the opening scene, a light plane scatters leaflets advertising Fuji film all over the town. Hollywood, it seems, isn't alone in product pushing.—*Strat.*

Varosbujocska
(Tandem)
(HUNGARIAN-COLOR)

A Budapest Studio, Mafilm, production. Directed by Maria Sos. Screenplay, Adam Rozgonyi, Sos; camera (Eastmancolor) Gabor Szabo; music, Janos Masik, Jiri Stivin. The Europa Kiado Group; sets, Andras Györky; costumes, Nora Kovats; editor, Julia Sivo; sound, Istvan Sipos. Reviewed at Hungarian Film Week (Congress Hall), Budapest, Feb. 11, 1986. Running time: **97 MINS.**

Janos	Janos Masik
Tamas	György Dörner
Tamas' wife	Annamaria Prepeliczay
Sara	Margit Földessy
Henrik	Simon Gevai
Lauri	Lauri Törhönnen

Budapest — A gentle, slow moving tale of a group of jazz musicians and their relationships. "Tandem" is beautifully shot, has good music, but is too diffuse to attract art house audiences. It's a mood piece, but the numerous characters are introduced awkwardly making the viewer confused for too long as to who's who.

Janos and Tamas are former friends, both musicians, who've drifted apart. One day, Janos returns to be reunited with his former pal and to re-enter his life. There are "Big Chill" aspects to the pic, but it lacks precision and depth, though it's always worth watching.
—*Strat.*

Kepvadaszok
(The Picture Hunters)
(HUNGARIAN-COLOR)

A Dialog Studio, Mafilm, production. Directed by Andras and Miklos Szurdi. Screenplay, Istvan Farkas, Andras Szeker, Andras Szurdi, Miklos Szurdi; camera (Eastmancolor), Andras Saimi; music, Zsolt Döme; sets, Tamas Vayer; costumes, Judit Szekulesz; editor, Hajnal Spellö; sound, Istvan Sipos. Reviewed at Hungarian Film Week (Congress Hall), Budapest, Feb. 10, 1986. Running time: **85 MINS.**

Richter	Andras Kern
Gal	Peter Andorai
Bakos	Tamas Vegvari
Lengyel	Frigyes Hollosy
Varga	Sandor Gaspar
Annamaria	Maria Gor Nagy
Mystery woman	Adriana Riedryzska

Budapest — "The Picture Hunters" is a comedy-thriller based on the old joke in which identical suitcases get mixed up with tumultuous results.

Three petty crooks rob the National Gallery of some valuable paintings, placing the canvases in a suitcase. Later, on the street, they bump into a drunken musician, also carrying a suitcase and an inadvertent swap is made. Things get more complicated when one of the three robbers is killed and his body stuffed in yet another identical suitcase.

This stage is set for plenty of comical coming and going, and for a mildly enjoyable pic which would have been better with a bit more discipline in the timing of the jokes. It's visually very handsome, thanks to Andras Szalai's sharp lensing, and there are some engaging players in the cast. But the joke tends to outstay its welcome before the end, despite the presence of a beautiful mystery woman to muddy the waters still further.

Pic is directed by brothers, and is something of a letdown from the younger brother, Miklos, who made an impression with "Midnight Rehearsal" a few years ago. This new film is far more routine.—*Strat.*

A Rejtözködö
(The Absentee)
(HUNGARIAN-COLOR)

An Objektiv Studio, Mafilm, production. Written and directed by Zsolt Kezdi-Kovacs. Camera (Eastmancolor), Janos Kende; music, Laszlo Sary; sets, Tamas Banovich; costumes, Fanni Kemenes; editor, Eva Karmento; sound, Peter Kardos. Reviewed at Hungarian Film Week (Congress Hall), Budapest, Feb. 10, 1986. Running time: **87 MINS.**

Janos	Peter Breznyik Berg
Marti	Lili Monori
Mother	Mari Töröcsik
Agi	Vera Pap
Odette	Camille de Casabianca
Jozsef	Andor Lukats
Mari	Enikö Eszenyi
Jano	Kalman Nemes

Budapest — A story of a rather foolish young man's problems with women, "The Absentee" takes itself rather too seriously to succeed. Janos (Peter Breznyik Berg) loves flying and works for a crop-dusting company. He's in love with a pretty but vacuous French girl (Camille de Casabianca) who's visiting the country. When she suddenly heads home for France, he takes his company's plane to pursue her car along the highway. This romantic gesture ends in an accident and the loss of his pilot's license, not to mention heavy fines.

Disillusioned, Janos returns to his mother's house where there are plenty of other women to keep him occupied. The mother herself (Mari Töröcsik), heavily involved with a much younger lover; his sister (Vera Pap, who played title role in "Angi Vera") who belongs to a sect preaching love and understanding; and Marti (Lili Monori), his ex-wife, an unstable, neurotic alcoholic and seemingly a failed actress, who quickly brings her new lover into the house.

Zsolt Kezdi-Kovacs is one of the better Magyar directors, but it's hard to see what interested him in this particular subject. None of the characters is very appealing and after a crisp opening scene sans dialog, there's altogether too much talk for the rest of the picture. It's technically fine, but just a rather mundane tale of a none too-interesting young man and his self-made problems. Best performance comes from Vera Pap as the loving, understanding sister. — *Strat.*

Keserü Igazsag
(The Bitter Truth)
(HUNGARIAN-B&W)

A Hunnia Studio, Mafilm production. Directed by Zoltan Varkonyi. Screenplay, Endre Kövesi, Laszlo Nadasy, Varkonyi; camera (b&w), Barnabas Hegyi; editor, Zoltan Kerenyi; music, Ferenc Farkas; songs, Peter Bacso, Szabolcs Fenyes; sets, Melinda Vasary; production managers, Jozsef Bajusz, Jozsef Teuchert. Reviewed at Film Museum, Budapest (Hungarian Film Week), Feb. 9, 1986. Running time: **88 MINS.**

Sztanko	Ferenc Bessenyej
Palocz	Miklos Gabor
Klari	Eva Ruttkai
Mrs. Sztanko	Vera Szemere
Bonis	Tibor Molnar
Buvesz	Imre Sinkovits
Barczen	Bela Barsj
Old Bela	Oszkar Ascher
Bönczöl	György Kalman
Ornagy	Gabor Madj Szabo

Budapest — On the shelf for 30 years, and reviewed here for the record, "The Bitter Truth" is a hardhitting drama about corruption within the lower ranks of the Communist Party. Made in the summer of 1956, it was understandably 'frozen' after the upheavals in the country that November, culminating in the invasion of Soviet forces. Despite its age, it comes up fresh and exciting.

Central characters are old friends who have gone their separate ways. Sztanko (Ferenc Bessenyé) is a Party Member with plenty of ambition; he's a building engineer who's been promised a fat promotion if the current project on which he's working, a housing development, is completed on schedule. At the site, he comes across his old buddy Palocz (Miklos Gabor) who's fallen on hard times. He's gone abroad and on his return to Hungary had been imprisoned. Now he's out of the cooler and starting afresh. Sztanko instantly befriends him, knowing that Palocz is tops in his field. But the friendship quickly turns sour when Palocz points out that the new building may be unsafe due to cost-cutting methods of Sztanko. Matters are further complicated because Sztanko, a married man, is having a secret affair which is occupying a lot of his time.

Climax of the drama is suitably dramatic. A wall of the building collapses, a worker is killed. But needless to say the wily and well connected Sztanko is able to shift the blame onto his friend.

It says a lot for the climate in Hungary in the first half of 1956 that a film in which a Party Member is revealed as dishonest, adulterous and cowardly while an ex-convict (presumably jailed for his political beliefs) represents morality and goodness, could be made at all. Small wonder it was put on the shelf. Pic is extremely well made, shot in the kind of lyrical black and white photography common at the time, tightly structured and persuasively acted. Belated kudos to all concerned. —*Strat.*

De Mislukking
(The Failure)
(DUTCH-COLOR-16m)

A Hans de Ridder Filmproduktie production. No distributor. Written, produced, directed, camera (color, 16m) and edited by Hans de Ridder. Music, Lelijke Mannen; sound, T-Track-Gewande. Reviewed at Rotterdam Film Festival (market), Jan. 31, 1986. Running time: **78 MINS.**

Erik	Peter Kolpa
Paul	Pie Slot
Leo	Theun Huisman
Martin	Ruud Mes
Old Man	Jan Cudde
Mother	Puck van Loon

Rotterdam — Hans de Ridder has worked in television for many years, producing-directing three documentaries. "The Failure," his feature debut, is a short story, told soberly and with style. The soberness is partly due to a mini-budget of $18,000, but the use of lifelike people and situations reflects his documentary past.

Erik, about 30, has a decent office job and lives alone in a low-rent apartment, a most melancholy gay whose lover has left.

He falls in love again, and — after a while — is left again. His roommate at the office gets promoted but Erik doesn't.

His experiences are most disheartening. However, (helmer quoting Aldous Huxley) "experience is not what happens to a man. It is what a man does with what happens to him." Pic ends with Erik buying a very small puppy and getting acquainted with a nice old neighbor with hope looming in the distance.

De Ridder, who took more than a year to assemble his non-pro cast, gets astonishingly credible performances out of them. He conveys much about Erik through small details, without dwelling on them. The love scenes are tender, fragile and caring. Erik, when utterly desolate, shows no sign of rebellion, but the behavior of one tamed by unhappiness. — *Wall.*

Crossroads
(COLOR/B&W)

Superficial tale of hero worship and blues music.

A Columbia Pictures release of a Mark Carliner production from Columbia-Delphi IV Prods. Produced by Carliner. Executive producer, Tim Zinnemann. Directed by Walter Hill. Stars Ralph Macchio, Joe Seneca. Screenplay, John Fusco; camera (Technicolor), John Bailey; editor, Freeman Davies; music & blues guitar, Ry Cooder; blues harmonica, Sonny Terry, John 'Juke' Logan; production design, Jack T. Collis; art direction, Albert Heschong; set design, James Tocci, Nancy Patton; set decoration, Marvin March; sound (Dolby), Richard Goodman; associate producer, Mae Woods; assistant director, Chris Soldo; casting, Judith Holstra, Marcia Ross. Reviewed at the Regent Theater, W. L.A., Feb. 27, 1986. (MPAA Rating: R.) Running time: **96 MINS.**

Eugene Martone	Ralph Macchio
Willie Brown	Joe Seneca
Frances	Jami Gertz
Scratch's assistant	Joe Morton
Scratch	Robert Judd
Jack Butler	Steve Vai
Lloyd	Dennis Lipscomb
Bartender	Harry Carey Jr.
Sheriff Tilford	John Hancock
Dr. Santis	Allan Arbus
Beautiful girl/dancer	Gretchen Palmer
Robert Johnson	Tim Russ
Woman at boardinghouse	Akosua Busia

Hollywood — As appealing as its premise may be and as good-natured as many of its interludes are, "Crossroads" just doesn't make the strong impression it should have. For a tale which argues for the irreplaceability of real life experience, this emerges as just a bit too slick, contrived and faintly ridiculous by the end to be swallowed completely. Although the blues territory of the deep South is rather off the beaten track for modern teens, and the R rating seems excessive, pic has enough going for it to result in good off-season grosses for Columbia.

Penned partly on the basis of actual experiences he had as a teenager touring the South as a musician, John Fusco's screenplay makes ample use of the legend of the late bluesman Robert Johnson, who left behind a tiny but potent legacy.

Ralph Macchio, a classical guitar student at Juilliard, discovers an old travelling and playing companion of Johnson's in a New York hospital. Hoping to make his reputation by finding and recording Johnson's alleged "unknown 30th song," Macchio springs old Joe Seneca from the facility, and the unlikely pair hits the road for Mississippi Delta country.

Constantly chiding his young idolator for his illustrious Long Island roots, the crusty Seneca goads Macchio and pushes him into mildly tough situations which, if experienced over a period of many years, might lead one to be able to feel the blues and maybe even play them.

Along the way, they also pick up sultry little road urchin Jami Gertz, who gives Macchio a tumble and is willing to commit some petty crime on her way to L.A. to become a dancer.

Finally, invoking mythic and religious elements, Fusco and director Walter Hill pit the now experienced Macchio against The Devil, whose henchman is impersonated by a heavy metal guitar freak who matches his opponent riff for riff until Macchio pulls an ace from his sleeve which has absolutely nothing to do with the blues.

It's not being overly sensitive to feel that there is something vaguely insulting about climaxing a picture fundamentally about blues and black culture with a music contest populated by two white boys. What one is supposed to take away from this off-putting sequence is anybody's guess.

Nevertheless, it remains entirely possible that kids might get off on it, just as it is conceivable that Macchio's appeal to his contemporaries is lost on somewhat older viewers. Not bad in the opening sequences when he insinuates himself into Seneca's life, he quickly loses his charm on the road. His guitar playing simulations are quite convincing, however.

Seneca, a veteran singer and actor, acquits himself very nicely, while Gertz is appealing despite the artificial nature of her character.

Hill pulls off the expected professional job, but he pushes so hard for pace that he skates right over the opportunities for emotion, thought and meditation that the subject and the music call for. Director allows nothing to sink in, and glosses over the felt experience necessary for the story to mean anything.

Aside from Ry Cooder's strong music, soundtrack is loaded with a dozen tunes of assorted varieties. Tech credits are all good. — *Cart.*

The Statue Of Liberty
(DOCU-COLOR)

A Direct Cinema release of a Florentine Films production. Produced by Ken Burns and Buddy Squires. Directed by Burns. Written by Bernard Weisberger, Geoffrey Ward; camera (color), Burns, Terry Hopkins, Squires; editor, Paul Barnes; narrator, David McCullough; voice-overs, Jeremy Irons, Arthur Miller, Derek Jacobi. Reviewed at The Museum of Modern Art, N.Y. March 4, 1986. (No MPAA Rating.) Running time: **60 MINS.**

Constructed in a quiet Paris suburb, almost lost in a storm during its crossing of the Atlantic, unceremoniously left in crates for over a year while America wrangled over whether this was a French political ploy, distasteful or just plain eyesore, the Statue of Liberty is a lady with a past and the subject of Ken Burns' lively and informative documentary.

It's said the statue's creator, Auguste Bartholdi, took the face of his mother and the body of his mistress for his massive work. Scores of old photographs detail its painstaking construction in the early third of the picture, and Burns wisely varies the pacing with interviews of prominent first-generation immigrants such as Milos Forman and Jerzy Kosinski and others such as New York Gov. Mario Cuomo and historian David McCullough discussing the statue's importance on personal and national levels.

When it finally stood in New York harbor, the statue was the tallest structure in the U.S., a point in American history nicely captured in old footage and newspaper stories from the time. England took a dim view of its construction, one journalist noting it came from a country with too little liberty and went to a country with too much. Art critics loathed it, and yet, the Statue of Liberty had a life of its own, becoming America's best-known symbol as a steady stream of immigrants steamed past to Ellis Island.

Burns' examination is thorough. One of the more memorable moments coming when James Baldwin concludes "to black Americans, the State of Liberty is a bitter joke." It's use in films (Charlie Chaplin's short "The Arrival' and the 1968 "Planet Of The Apes" among them) and in advertising is well chronicled, as is its place in American music. "The Statue Of Liberty" is worthy of its subject. — *Roy.*

Gung Ho
(COLOR)

Funny treatment of cultural clash.

A Paramount Pictures release of a Ron Howard production. Executive producer, Howard. Produced by Tony Ganz, Deborah Blum. Directed by Ron Howard. Stars Michael Keaton. Screenplay, Lowell Ganz, Babaloo Mandel, from story by Edwin Blum, Ganz, Mandel; camera (Panavision, Continental color; prints by Technicolor), Don Peterman; editor, Daniel Hanley, Michael Hill; music, Thomas Newman; songs performed by Stevie Ray Vaughan, others; sound, Richard S. Church; production design, James Schoppe; art direction, Jack G. Taylor Jr.; set decoration, John Anderson; assistant director-associate producer, Jan R. Lloyd; production manager; Neil A. Machlis (U.S.), Carlos Olveira (Argentina), Yuji Yoshida (Japan); second unit director, Tony Ganz; second unit camera, Nick McLean; casting, Karen Rea. Reviewed at Paramount Studios, Hollywood, March 5, 1986. (MPAA Rating: PG-13.) Running time: **111 MINS.**

Hunt Stevenson	Michael Keaton
Kazihiro	Gedde Watanabe
Buster	George Wendt
Audrey	Mimi Rogers
Willie	John Turturro
Sakamoto	Soh Yamamura
Saito	Sab Shimono
Googie	Rich Overton

Paul ....Clint Howard
Junior ....Jihmi Kennedy
Heather ....Michelle Johnson
Ito ....Rodney Kageyama
Mayor Zwart.............Rance Howard

Hollywood — With "Gung Ho," director Ron Howard comes close to a Norman Rockwell magazine cover, nicely drawn, good for a chuckle and chock full of old-fashioned virtues. Even though there's not much on the other side of the page, it's still popular entertainment whose only problem may be how much teenagers relate to the notion of work as its own reward.

As for the virtues of labor, Howard and writers Lowell Ganz and Babaloo Mandell initially have a nice time with the fact the Puritan Ethic of the American worker has been exported to Japan, leaving sloth and inefficiency behind.

Trying to save his town, auto worker Michael Keaton journeys abroad to plead with Japanese industrialists to reopen the plant in Hanleyville, Pa. that's been closed by foreign competition. Soon after, the Japanese invasion begins.

From the first morning of calisthenics, it's clear the American workers will not adapt well to Japanese management, which relies absolutely on an employee's selfless devotion to the company, including shame at shoddy products and willingness to work endless hours to make sure their output is high.

In contrast, the Americans are used to union featherbedding, a lot of time off and a general acceptance of the idea that, thanks to a shortcut here and there, not all the cars coming off the assembly line will be driveable for long.

Drawn from real life (coproducer Deborah Blum's screenwriter father Edwin Blum suggested the idea after watching a similar situation on "CBS Reports"), the conflict between cultures is good for both a laugh and a sober thought along the way. Howard has problems straddling the two, sometimes getting bogged down in the social significance.

Keaton can be funny as he puzzles the Japanese with his wacky mannerisms. However, his character is often just a plain selfserving liar, which distracts. A big problem is with all the Americans. In fact, they ofter are no more than a bunch of lazy whiners.

Gedde Watanabe is excellent is the young Japanese exec whose career is threatened by the lack of output by the Americans and the fact that his superiors back home (led by the superbly stone-faced Soh Yamamura) can't understand why Watanabe's work force is so disloyal.

Keaton gradually comes to realize there is some merit in the oriental's discipline just as Watanabe begins to believe there is something to say

in favor of the occidental's individual pursuit of life and happiness beyond the assembly line.

Circumstances will eventually demand that East meet West to reach a happy ending, but there's no real feeling that the fundamental differences have been solved permanently. This shouldn't matter much in a comedy and wouldn't here if Howard hadn't made such a big deal of trying to tackle real issues.

The performances are all good, with Rodney Kageyama deserving additional mention as Watanabe's assistant, and the production values are first-rate. Overall, "Gung Ho" is a lot like the average American car: good for the short distance, but don't look too closely under the hood. — *Har.*

Bad Guys
(COLOR)

Unfunny wrestling comedy.

An InterPictures Releasing release of a Tomorrow Entertainment production. Produced by John D. Backe, Myron A. Hyman. Coproducers, Brady Westwater, John Pashdag. Directed by Joel Silberg. Screenplay, Brady W. Setwater, Joe Gillis; camera (Cinema color), Hanania Baer; editor, Peter Parasheles, Christopher Holmes; music, William Goldstein; music supervision, Russ Regan; sound, Ron Judkins; art direction, Ivo Cristante; assistant director, Jerram Swartz; production manager, Paul Lewis; stunt coordinator, Eddy Donno; wrestling consultant, Verne Gagne; associate producer, Shirley J. Eaton; casting, Caro Jones. Reviewed at Magno Preview 9 screening room, N.Y., March 5, 1986. (MPAA Rating: PG.) Running time: **86 MINS.**
Skip Jackson ....Adam Baldwin
Dave Atkins ....Mike Jolly
Janice Edwards ....Michelle Nicastro
Petal McGurk ....Ruth Buzzi
Lord Percy ....James Booth
Turk McGurk ....Gene LeBell
Capt. Watkins...........Norman Burton
Kremlin Krushers ....Alexia Smirnoff, Jay York
Murphy Green ....Dutch Mann
Also with: Sgt. Slaughter, Allan Rich, Prof. Toru Tanaka, Chief Jay Strongbow, Jack Armstrong, Buddha Kahn, Curt Henning, Count Billy Varga, Pepper Martin.

"Bad Guys" is a poorly-scripted, would-be comedy attempting to cash in on the current popularity of wrestling. Theatrical prospects are weak for this inauspicious debut film from distrib InterPictures Releasing and production company Tomorrow Entertainment.

Merest pretext of a story has young cops Adam Baldwin and Mike Jolly suspended from the L.A. police after a brawl with bikers in a bar owned by Dutch Mann (who pointlessly keeps popping up in the film as their nemesis). After tasteless footage detailing their odd jobs (including a leering stint as male strippers), they turn their wrestling avocation into a fulltime job under the tutelage of pretty reporter-turned manager Michelle Nicastro.

Quickly discovering that the dirty

practitioners are the stars in wrestling's firmament, the heroes don masks and become the Boston Bad Guys, tutored in illegal moves by Gene LeBell and his wife, played by Ruth Buzzi. Pic's anti-climax is their big match against the Kremlin Krushers (played by pro wrestlers Alexia Smirnoff and Jay York). Though still called the Bad Guys, heroes have changed costumes and unconvincingly become flagwavers in the interim.

Burdened with hoary, unfunny dialog, director Joel Silberg directs in frantic, comic strip fashion, having the lines exclaimed as if they were displayed in balloons above the actors' heads. The gags aren't funny and there's very little wrestling action amidst extraneous car chases and horseplay. Patriotic U.S. vs. Russia finale has already been done to death in "Rocky IV" and on tv broadcasts of all the competing wrestling leagues. As in the other disappointing current release, New World's "Grunt! The Wrestling Movie," only a handful of extras appear in the audience during big matches that attract many thousands in real life.

Topliner Baldwin (title roler from "My Bodyguard") is unrecognizable here with blond-dyed hair. He doesn't have the body weight to be convincing as a wrestler, with his ring action adequately doubled by pro Jeff Dashnaw. Costar Jolly (stunt-doubled by champ Curt Henning) is bland while Nicastro looks out of place in a role better suited to a comedienne in the Cyndi Lauper style. As in "Breakin'," Silberg builds up the promise of romance among the three young leads and then pretends that sex doesn't exist in their world.

Pic was made with the assist of Verne Gagne and his American Wrestling Assn., but fans will be disappointed in AWA's Sgt. Slaughter only showing up for a brief cameo in the final reel. Young kids might believe that the fights and feuds presented are real, but pic's in-joke of a ringside commentator named Vince (a jab at Vince McMahon, who runs the rival World Wrestling Federation, where Slaughter used to work) indicates a more interesting, truthful scenario could be built around the wars between leagues.

Film is overlaid with a relentless rock music score but fails to integrate the music with the wrestling the way Michael Hayes, Junkyard Dog and other popular wrestlers do in their live and tv performances.
—*Lor.*

Speriamo Che Sia Femmina
(Let's Hope It's A Girl)
(ITALIAN-FRENCH-COLOR)

A C.D.E. release. Produced by Giovanni Di Clemente for Clemi Intl. Prods. and Producteurs Associes. Directed by Mario Monicelli. Stars Liv Ullmann, Catherine Deneuve, Giuliana De Sio, Philippe Noiret, Bernard Blier. Screenplay, Leo Benvenuti, Piero De Bernardi, Suso Cecchi d'Amico, Tullio Pinelli, Jacqueline Lefevre, Monicelli; camera (color), Camillo Bazzoni; editor, Ruggero Mastroianni; music, Nicola Piovani; art director, Enrico Fiorentini. Reviewed at Capranica Cinema, Rome, March 1, 1986. Running time: **121 MINS.**
Elena ....Liv Ullmann
Count Leonardo ....Philippe Noiret
Uncle Gughi...............Bernard Blier
Aunt Claudia ....Catherine Deneuve
Francesca ....Giuliana De Sio
Fosca ....Athina Cenci
Bambina.....Lucrezia Lante Della Rovere
Guido Nardoni ....Giuliano Gemma
Gym owner ....Stefania Sandrelli

Rome — Mario Monicelli has made one of his most appealing films in years, "Let's Hope It's A Girl," with an all-star cast of femme thesps that whets the appetite. In its gentle, refreshing, off-beat way, the picture delivers.

Neither comedy nor tragedy but more of a single-sex family saga, "Let's Hope" cleverly mixes its broad cast of characters in interweaving stories, whose point is that women can find alternative ways of living happily sans male companionship.

To film's credit, this simple thesis is demonstrated entertainingly with the help of a little black humor and a little forcing. It opened strong in Italy, thanks to its what-next script as much as the b.o. draw of its cast, led by an amusingly displaced Liv Ullmann as a strong-shouldered Countess-farmer.

As film begins, Philippe Noiret's Count Leonardo actually seems to be the main character. He drives up to a sprawling old Tuscan farmhouse, intent on persuading separated wife Elena (Ullmann) to finance his latest hare-brained scheme. A maid (fine comic thesp Athina Cenci) keeps the household running while mothering her daughter and that of Elena's sister, a famous movie star played by Catherine Deneuve at her most glamorous.

Elena's other girl, Bambina (Lucrezia Lante Della Rovere), is a grownup teen who wants to raise horses. Her eldest, Francesca (Giuliana De Sio) is paired off comically with a nerdish ethno-musicologist who records songs from the lips of dying peasants. In the midst of these introductions, which amiably take up the first half of the picture, Leonardo drives his car off a cliff and disappears.

Monicelli realistically depicts the family breaking up in the wake of the accident. Later, though, the eldest daughters accuse Elena of being hard-hearted and uncaring about Papa, and Francesca abruptly leaves the house to get married. The film star takes her daughter to Rome to live with her, where a nasty lover provokes plate-smashing fights that terrify the chid.

Elena decides to sell the farm, partly to repay Leonardo's lover Stefania Sandrelli, owner of a gym, the money she unwisely has lent him. Giuliano Gemma, overseer of the property, hesitates between marrying Elena (she refuses) and buying the farm (which he does). Forgetful Uncle Gughi (a show-stealing Bernard Blier) is packed off reluctantly to the old folks' home, and so on, until a turnaround conclusion shows the only logical thing for everybody to do is move in together at the farm. — *Yung*.

Highlander
(COLOR)

Mishmash mixes genres to ill effect.

A 20th Century Fox release. Produced by Peter S. Davis, William N. Panzer. Executive producer, William N. Panzer. Directed by Russell Mulcahy. Stars Christophe Lambert. Screenplay, Gregory Widen, Peter Bellwood, Larry Ferguson from story by Widen; camera (Technicolor), Gerry Fisher; editor, Peter Honess; music, Michael Kamen; songs and additional music, Queen; production design, Allan Cameron; sound, Peter Pennell; art direction, Tim Hutchinson, Martin Atkinson; associate producers, Harold Moskovitz, John Starke, Eva Monley; casting, Michael McLean and Diane Dimeo & Assoc. Reviewed at 20th Century Fox, L.A., March 6, 1986, (MPAA Rating: R.) Running time: **111 MINS.**
Connor MacLeod .... Christophe Lambert
Brenda Wyatt .... Roxanne Hart
Kurgan .... Clancy Brown
Ramirez .... Sean Connery
Heather .... Beatie Edney
Lt. Frank Moran .... Alan North
Rachel Ellenstein .... Sheila Gish
Det. Walter Bedsoe .... Jon Polito

Hollywood — It takes a while to figure out what "Highlander" is about. Film starts out with a fantastic sword-fighting scene in the garage of Madison Square Garden and then jumps to a medieval battle between the clans set in 16th century Scotland.

While there are entertaining moments, total work is a mess and should generate disappointing b.o.

Adding to the confusion in time, director Russell Mulcahy can't seem to decide from one scene to the next whether he's making a sci-fi, thriller, horror, music video or romance — end result is a mishmash.

Film opens to the music of rock group Queen as Christophe Lambert, playing an adept sword-brandishing antiques dealer in modern day New York, encounters an equally skillful swordsman in the bowels of the Garden's parking structure following a wrestling match and beheads him in one clean slice.

While the soundtrack continues to pulsate, the action moves to the lowlands of Scotland where Lambert is transformed back in time as a wimpy clansman named Connor MacLeod whom no other warrior will fight except the evil Kurgan (Clancy Brown).

Following the battle, MacLeod survives what would normally have been fatal stab wounds which Kurgan inflicts but is banished from his village by the other town folk who are convinced he has the devil in him.

He comes to understand why he returned from near death after a visit by Sean Connery, playing a campy Obe Wan Kenobi-type character named Ramirez. Connery teaches MacLeod how to wield a sword like a warrior and understand his fate is to be immortal man who cannot have children, facing instead a life fending off other immortals like Kurgan.

Lambert looks and acts a lot better in a tartan and long, scraggly hair than as a nearly non-verbal antiques dealer in SoHo.

Brown never seems to frighten, whether as the supposedly-terrifying Kurgan or as the shaven-headed punker menacing the back alleys with his awesome blade.

His character seems right out of "The Rocky Horror Picture Show," best illustrated in a hilarious sketch inside a Catholic church where he flicks his tongue in and out to a couple of nuns.

Even though Ramirez admonishes Lambert for keeping close female company since the women will grow old and die and he never will, he ignores the advice and takes a couple of loves anyway.

The first is the blond maiden Heather, played by the innocent-looking Beatie Edney as a wonderfully romantic young Bonny, but a very unconvincing old woman. Make-up artists could have done a more thorough job.

Five centuries later, Lambert takes up with a New York police forensics expert investigating the first beheading that occurred.

Wouldn't you know, she just happens to be an expert on medieval weapons and has written an authoritative book on the subject.

Roxanne Hart does the best that she can with this character, considering that for most of the film she is in some terrifying situation where other mortals would go mad.

Overall, the picture is beautifully photographed by Gerry Fisher, especially in the Steadicam scenes shot in the Scottish woods where Ramirez instructs MacLeod on the craftiest ways to duel.

Production values range from outstanding special effects by Optical Film Effects Ltd. to some very fake-looking sets, most notably the castle where Kurgan battles Ramirez.

The Queen soundtrack is fitting in Manhattan sequences, but ridiculous as a backup for the foppishly-dressed Connery as he runs along the beach in his medieval red velvet outfit alongside the tattered-looking Lambert. —*Brit*.

The Naked Cage
(COLOR)

Dumb exploitation film.

A Cannon Releasing release presented by Cannon Group of a Cannon Films production. Executive producers, Menahem Golan, Yoram Globus. Produced by Chris D. Nebe. Written and directed by Paul Nicholas. Camera (TVC color), Hal Trussell; editor, Warren Chadwick, Nino DeMarco; music, Christopher Stone; sound, Morteza Rezvani; art direction, Alex Hajdu; set decoration, Marlene McCormick; assistant director, Bradley Gross; production manager, Dan Schneider; stunt coordinator, Al Jones; post-production supervisor, Michael R. Sloan; casting, Perry Bullington. Reviewed at Pacific theater, Hollywood, March 7, 1986. (MPAA Rating: R.) Running time: **97 MINS.**
Michelle .... Shari Shattuck
Warden Wallace .... Angel Tompkins
Rhonda .... Lucinda Crosby
Rita .... Christina Whitaker
Sheila .... Faith Minton
Amy .... Stacey Shaffer
Smiley .... Nick Benedict
Abbey .... Lisa London
Willy .... John Terlesky
Brenda .... Aude Charles
Vonna .... Angela Gibbs
Peaches .... Leslie Huntly
Trouble .... Carole Ita White
Randy .... Seth Kaufman
Doc .... Larry Gelman

Hollywood — Though they call it "The Naked Cage," a woman's prison is actually kind of a nice place, with lots of showers and beds and they don't make the ladies wear brassieres or very long dresses or much of anything if they don't want to. If the menfolk don't believe that, they'll just have to go see for themselves.

At first, pretty little Michelle (Shari Shattuck) doesn't know any of that because she's an innocent farm girl with a mom and a pop and a horse named Misty, plus a good job at a small-town bank. The bank gets robbed and Michelle winds up in the joint.

There she meets the other girls, like Amy the drug addict and Sheila, a rather large woman with a tattoo. They are full of good advice, "You look like a nice kid. Don't mess with the Warden. Whatever she wants, just give it to her."

The warden in question is Angel Tompkins who lives on the premises in an art deco apartment with an aquarium. A friendly sort when she wants to be, Tompkins likes to invite a favorite inmate over from time to time to take their clothes off and watch the fish and stuff like that.

Tompkins takes a liking to Michelle right away, but Michelle

isn't into aquariums, preferring to lie around dreaming she's back home riding Misty. She can't do that as much as she'd like because there are various fights she has to take part in, a prison ritual apparently designed to let the girls show off their clean underwear.

Then there's Rita (Christina Whitaker): what a pill she is. It was Rita who framed Michelle for the bank robbery and it seems the two are just never going to get along, especially after Rita stabs Michelle through the hand with a screwdriver.

What with Rita and the rejection of the warden and Smiley the male guard who likes to rape girls and hang them from the ceiling, even good-natured Michelle starts to use dirty words and wonder if she'll ever ride Misty again.

Lucky for her, though, good-guard Rhonda shows up on some sort of undercover mission to right all wrongs at the prison, starting with Rita, the warden and Smiley. Best of all, she suspects Michelle never robbed the bank in the first place.

Before Rhonda can reach a conclusion, there's a riot and right there in a fog of pink teargas the warden and Smiley get killed and Michelle and Rita face off in the basement.

When Michelle gets the drop on her, Rita says she's sorry and promises to tell everybody the truth about the bank robbery. Still a farm girl at heart, Michelle actually says at that point, "Okay, let's contact the authorities."

Rita was lying, but Rhonda was listening and before long Michelle is back on the farm riding Misty into a freeze frame, hoping to forget that upon arriving at the naked cage she said, "God, it's strange here." Sometimes it feels the same way in a theater.—*Har*.

16 Days Of Glory
(DOCU-COLOR)

A Paramount Pictures release of a Cappy Prods. production in association with Milton Okun. Produced and directed by Bud Greenspan. Screenplay, Greenspan; executive producer, Nancy Beffa; senior producer, Okun; camera (Panavision, color), Robert E. Collins, Gil Hubbs, Michael D. Margulies, Robert Primes; editor, Andrew Squicciarini; music Lee Holdridge; soloist, Placido Domingo; narration, David Perry; second unit director, Beffa. Reviewed at the Guild 50th St. Theater, N.Y., March 7, 1986. (MPAA Rating: G). Running time: **145 MINS.**
With: Joan Benoit, Rowdy Gaines, Michael Gross, Juergen Hingsen, John Moffett, Dave Moorcroft, Edwin Moses, Mary Lou Retton, Ecaterina Szabo, Daley Thompson, Yasuhiro Yamashita and Grete Waitz.

A lavish documentary tribute to the 1984 Los Angeles Olympics, "16 Days Of Glory" splendidly captures the pageantry and noble competitive spirit of that event in an unabashedly devotional overview. While slated primarily for the homevideo market, this "official film record" of the XXIII Olympiad has outsized docu production values uniquely suited to big-screen viewing. Its theatrical prospects will depend largely on the extent of nostalgia for the Olympics and the eagerness of people to relive the uplifting experience of that widely shared media event.

The millions who were not at the Los Angeles Memorial Coliseum witnessed the Olympics on television through coverage that was both a ratings and artistic triumph for ABC-TV, and audiences are bound to compare the docu with their memories of the events as experienced on live tv. Director Bud Greenspan, a veteran of tv sports, has fully utilized the magnifying properties of film to differentiate the documentary recollection from tv's microscopic coverage of the unfolding events.

Technically, "16 Days Of Glory" is a marvel of contemporary editing and camera techniques, particularly in its subtle use of slow motion and exploitation of privileged camera angles that yielded unusual and evocative closeups of athletes in the white heat of competition.

Journalistically, the docu is somewhat lacking. Just as the absence of the boycotting Soviet Union and 13 other Eastern bloc nations was virtually forgotten by the media once th Olympics began, the docu mentions this once specifically, together with passing references to the dashed hopes of individual athletes who did not compete at the 1980 Moscow games due to the U.S.-led boycott over the Russian invasion of Afganistan. How the various winners might have fared against the absent competition is never speculated upon. Topics such as amateurism and under-the-table payments to athletes by equipment makers, or the use of performance-enhancing drugs are studiously avoided.

Although there's a relatively brief montage of events and athletes not covered in depth, the docu focuses on a selective sampling of athletes and their sports: marathoners Joan Benoit and Grete Waitz; swimmers Rowdy Gaines, Michael Gross and John Moffett; distance runner Dave Moorcroft; decathaletes Daley Thompson and Juergen Hingsen; judo player Yasuhiro Yamashita; gymnasts Mary Lou Retton and Ecaterina Szabo and hurdler Edwin Moses.

The selection process must have been difficult for Greenspan and his colleagues and, inevitably, memorable Olympic highlights are glossed over and omitted. These included the victory of New York messenger Nelson Vails in the bicycle sprint, the fateful duel between runners

Mary Decker and Zola Budd and the triumphs of the American men gymnasts.

Although the narrative script has stretches of blandness and the fanfare music score tends to be overbearing, "16 Days Of Glory" succeeds fully in capturing the exhilaration of the elaborately staged games and surrounding ceremonies. Most of all it's an effective tribute to the superhuman talents of athletes meeting the ultimate test of their careers. —*Rich.*

Clockwise
(BRITISH-COLOR)

A Thorn EMI Screen Entertainment presentation of a Moment Films production. Executive producers, Verity Lambert, Nat Cohen. Produced by Michael Codron. Directed by Christopher Morahan. Screenplay, Michael Frayn; camera (Technicolor), John Coquillon; editor, Peter Boyle; music, George Fenton; sound, Don Sharpe; production design, Roger Murray-Leach; art direction, Diana Charnley; assistant director, Tony Hopkins; associate producer, Gregory Dark. Reviewed at the Warner West End, London, March 10, 1986. (BBFC Rating: PG.) Running time: **97 MINS.**
Brian Stimpson . . . . John Cleese
Gwenda Stimpson . . . . Alison Steadman
Pat Garden . . . . Penelope Wilton
Mr. Jolly . . . . Stephen Moore
Mrs. Trellis . . . . Joan Hickson
Laura . . . . Sharon Maiden

London — "Clockwise" is a somewhat uneven comic road film. It should, however, garner a strong following among audiences sensitive to the talents of Monty Python member John Cleese, who turns in a characteristic performance as a beleaguered common man.

Cleese plays the headmaster of a secondary school, whose main trait, obsessive timewatching, turns out to be a strategy to dam up the natural disarray of his personality.

Film's plot is triggered when Stimpson (Cleese) misses the train for a headmaster's conference over which he has been invited to preside. Immediately panic-struck, he seeks some other way to get to the meeting on time.

The best moments in "Clockwise" depict his gradually going to pieces as he struggles to complete his journey in the company of an abducted schoolgirl (Sharon Maiden) and former girlfriend (Penelope Wilton).

Pic gets off to a slow start, however, as it chronicles the gathering of relations of the journeying duo and assorted old ladies, who give chase across the countryside. These comic cameos provide no light on Stimpson's character or depth to the plot.

Contrast drawn between the regiment in Stimpson's school and the attitudes of the headmasters gathered from noted private schools (Eton, Harrow, etc.) to hear Stimp-

son's speech, is not likely to interest many viewers.

"Clockwise" would be a bore were it not for Cleese's comic ability, which derives from broad expressive gesticulations and expressions which mark the simple man still trying to control his world long after he has gone over the edge.

Cleese's two female companions are also well played. Maiden, in her debut, is the knowing and plucky young girl who gradually takes control as her affection for Stimpson grows. Wilton plays the older woman driven to distraction by male idiocy.

Cleese's final speech, in which, dressed in the stolen and torn clothes of a passing driver, he reverts to his headmasterly persona, is a brilliant piece of comic embarrassment, reminiscent of the best Monty Python television sketches.

Christopher Morahan's direction, in his first feature since the late 1960s, is adequate, while George Fenton's music is witty and lensing by John Coquillon is pristine.

—*Japa.*

The Money Pit
(COLOR)

Terminally unfunny comedy.

A Universal Pictures release of a Steven Spielberg presentation from Amblin Entertainment. Produced by Frank Marshall, Kathleen Kennedy, Art Levinson. Executive producers, Spielberg, David Giler. Directed by Richard Benjamin. Stars Tom Hanks, Shelley Long. Screenplay, Giler; camera (Du Art color; Deluxe prints), Gordon Willis; editor, Jacqueline Cambas; music, Michel Colombier; sound (Dolby), Nat Boxer; production design, Patrizia Von Brandenstein; art direction, Steve Graham; set decoration, George De Titta Sr.; costume design, Ruth Morley; special effects supervisor, Michael Wood; assistant director, Michael Haley; casting, Howard Feuer. Reviewed at Universal Studios, Universal City, March 13, 1986. (MPAA Rating: PG.) Running time: **91 MINS.**
Walter Fielding . . . . Tom Hanks
Anna Crowley . . . . Shelley Long
Max Beissart . . . . Alexander Godunov
Estelle . . . . Maureen Stapleton
Art Shirk . . . . Joe Mantegna
Curly . . . . Philip Bosco
Jack Schnittman . . . . Josh Mostel
Shatov . . . . Yakov Smirnoff
Brad Shirk . . . . Carmine Caridi
Ethan . . . . Brian Backer
Benny . . . . Billy Lombardo
Marika . . . . Mia Dillon
Carlos . . . . John van Dreelen
Walter Fielding Sr. . . . . . Douglass Watson

Hollywood — "The Money Pit" is simply the pits. Shortly after the starring couple has bought a beautiful old house which quickly shows itself to be at the point of total disrepair, Tom Hanks says to Shelley Long, "It's a lemon, honey, let's face it." There is really very little else to be said about this gruesomely unfunny comedy, except that the presence of Steven Spielberg's name on it may actually enable the film to make a few bucks it otherwise would have no hope of earning.

Unofficial remake of the 1948 Cary Grant-Myrna Loy starrer "Mr. Blandings Builds His Dream House" begins unpromisingly and slides irrevocably downward from there. Unmarrieds Hanks and Long take on the suburban New York mansion for a bargain basement price, only to discover in the course of an excruciating 91 minutes that the stairs, plumbing, floors, walls, chimney, stove — indeed, the entire abode — are about as solid as a house of cards.

Most of the scenes in this demolition derby begin with something or other caving in or falling apart, an event which is invariably followed by the two leads yelling and screaming at each other for minutes on end. Members of the vast construction crew engaged to rebuild the house not only look but act like mercenaries, and it is typical of the inanities of the screenplay that, after Hanks grovels to come up with the relatively modest purchase price, not a single mention is made of the undoubtedly far higher repair bills.

All involved will want to move along from this mutual career low as quickly as possible. —*Cart.*

Pouvoir Intime
(CANADIAN-COLOR)

A Vivafilm release of a Les Films Vision 4 production. Produced by Claude Bonin. Directed by Yves Simoneau. Screenplay, Simoneau, Pierre Curzi; camera (color), Guy Dufaux; editor, André Corriveau; music, Richard Gregoire; art director, Michel Proulx. Reviewed at the Berri Cinema, Montreal, March 3, 1986. Running time: **87 MINS.**
With: Marie Tifo, Pierre Curzi, Jacques Godin, Eric Brisebois, Robert Gravel, Jacques Lussier, Jean-Louis Millette, Yvan Ponton.

(French-language soundtrack)

Montreal — Be it a Coke commercial with Quebecois chanteuse Diane Dufresne or the award-winning doc "Pourquoi Monsieur Zolock s'interesse-t-il tant a la bande dessinée?," a partly animated history of the comic book, innovation has been the hallmark of 25-year-old Quebecois filmmaker Yves Simoneau.

Simoneau outdoes himself once again in "Pouvoir Intime," a jolting, shoot-em-up affair that has the slickness of a film many times its budget of $C1,700,000 and a sophistication that belies the youth and experience of its director. A non-stop explosion of enticing colors and sounds, the psychodrama is as stylish — albeit in a steely, cold fashion — as it is involving.

Simoneau takes viewers for a plunge inside Montreal's sordid underbelly on a botched-up heist of an armored, cash-laden van. A crusty con Théo (Jacques Godin) appears to have the operation under perfect control with a crackerjack gang comprised of an ex-cellmate (Pierre Curzi), the latter's tough-as-nails girlfriend (Marie Tifo) and Théo's trigger-happy teenage son (Eric Brisebois).

However, an unscheduled changing of the van's guard inadvertently touches off a bizarre and bloody chain reaction. Two of the guards are killed in the ensuing melee, while the third lies wounded inside the van. The catch is that the bad guys can't get in to the loot, and the good guy can't get out.

What transpires is a nail-biting battle of wits as emotions become frayed. Simoneau tosses in enough intriguing plot twists to keep everyone off-track until the end — although the murky political connection and corruption implied is never satisfactorily explained.

The husband/wife tandem of Curzi and Tifo, along with veteran character actor Godin, are once again rock-solid, but it's Robert Gravel, as the trapped and tormented guard, who steals the show with an overwhelming, power-packed performance.

In addition to Guy Dufaux for his precision and stylized camera-work, plaudits also go to art director Michel Proulx, editor André Corriveau and Richard Gregoire, for a pulsating score that perfectly punctuates the proceedings.—*Bro.*

The Millionaire's Express
(HONG KONG-COLOR)

A Bo Ho Films and Golden Harvest coproduction. Executive Producers, Samo Hung, Raymond Chow. Directed and story by Hung. Stars Hung, Olivia Cheng, Yuen Biao, Kenny Bee, Wang Yu, Lydia Sum, Kwan Pak Hing. Title and end music performed by Julie Sue. (No other credits provided by producers.) Reviewed at State theater, Hong Kong, Feb. 18, 1986. Running time: **98 MINS.**
(Cantonese soundtrack with English subtitles)

Hong Kong — There is an incongruous, eclectic variety in favor of "The Millionaire's Express" so it achieves enjoyable awfulness. Properly edited it could be repackaged for foreign action markets.

"Millionaire's Express" is a Cantonese version of the American Western that has just about everything. There are established domestic stars, familiar faces, starlets and bit parts for local celebrities. There are excellent stunts, ladies in distress, high comedy and Marx Bros./Keystone Cops style slapstick sequences. It's also a mixed bag that includes samurai, karate, kung fu and lots of horses in a "Magnificent Seven" format.

Samo Hung, Olivia Cheng, Yuen Biao and Kenny Bee are some of the marquee names that ramble from the snowy mountains of Canada to a fictitious town near Shanghai in what looks like the '20s. Locals can sitback and let their favorite stars jump, run, fight and ride horses in this corn-bred picture geared for the Chinese New Year crowds. —*Mel.*

Car Trouble
(BRITISH/U.S.-COLOR)

A Thorn EMI Screen Entertainment presentation of a GTO/Goldfarb production. Executive producers, Howard Goldfarb, Laurence Myers, Maxwell Meltzer, Judith Goldfarb. Produced by Howard Malin, Gregory J. De Santis. Directed by David Green. Screenplay, James Whaley, A.J. Tipping; camera (color), Michael Garfath; editor, Barry Reynolds, costume design, Vanegga Clarke. Reviewed at the ABC Bayswater, London, March 12, 1986. (BBFC certificate: 18.) Running time: **93 MINS.**
Jacqueline Spong .... Julie Walters
Gerald Spong .... Ian Charleson
Reg Sampson .... Stratford Johns
Kevin O'Connor .... Vincenzo Ricotta

London — "Car Trouble" plays with some promising comic material but ultimately doesn't know whether to aim for an indictment of male attitudes to their cars, a satire of contempo marriage or something quite else. Film's offshore prospects are dim.

Initial premise for this British-lensed comedy has a woman trapped with a lover in her husband's racing car. When the police arrive to cut them out, she's more concerned about the vehicle than its male occupant.

Screenwriters evidently had problems in building a feature film around this little joke. Since they hold their punches anyway for the climax, it's difficult to know why they bothered.

First part of the pic shows Mr. Spong (Ian Charleson) gradually alienating his wife with excessive concern for the newly acquired E-type Jaguar. The bickering couple, just about the most unpleasant wedded duo ever to grace a film, are a real turnoff.

Things don't get much more light-hearted when Mrs. Spong (Julie Walters) meets up with a hunky car salesman for their cramped encounter. Following the car's demise, the humor gets even more strained as Mr. Spong attempts to kill his wife by burning down their home and then arranging a collision between two airplanes.

"Car Trouble" may attract some attention due to double-billing of Walters and Charleson, who both try rather too hard to extract some humor out of their scenes. Technical credits are okay.—*Japa.*

American Commandos
(Hitman)
(COLOR)

Clumsy, made-in-the Philippines action film.

A Panorama Film Intl. release. A Just Betzer presentation of an Ader/Spiegelman release. Executive producers, Benni Korzen, Bobby A. Suarez. Produced by Betzer. Directed by Bobby A Suarez. Screenplay, Ken Metcalfe, Suarez, from story by Suarez; camera (Technicolor), Jun Pereira; editor, Suarez, Sing Yim & Associates; music, Ole Hoyer; sound, Jack Cooley; production design, Butch Santos; assistant director, Asset Bernabe; action coordinator, Lauro Flores & Associates. Reviewed at RKO National 1 theater, N.Y., March 14, 1985. (MPAA Rating: R.) Running time: **88 MINS.**
Dean Mitchell ...... Christopher Mitchum
Kelly .... John Phillip Law
Somsak .... Franco Guerrero
Creeper .... Willie Williams
Brutus .... Robert Marius
Brady .... Ken Metcalfe
Lisa .... Kristine Berlandson
Mitchell's wife .... Karen Lopez

"American Commando" is a subpar action picture made in the Philippines for undemanding international audiences. It opened domestically last November in Miami under the title "Hitman," a moniker retained in its theme song. (Shooting title was "Mr. Salvage.")

Christopher Mitchum toplines as Dean Mitchell, the owner of an L.A. gas station who thwarts a robbery of his business by young punks. The youths later descend on his home, kill his young son and rape his wife (Karen Lopez), who subsequently commits suicide.

Bent on revenge, Mitchell accepts a mission assigned by vaguely CIA operative Brady (Ken Metcalfe, film's cowriter who frequently pops up in Far East pics) to go to the Gold Triangle and wipe out drug operations there. Mitchell recruits members of his old Vietnam War platoon for the job and, despite treachery within his unit, wipes out numerous Filipino bit players pretending to be Thais. In flashbacks the Filipinos pretend to be Vietnamese.

Mitchum's stone-faced nonacting here sets new low standards for the second-generation thesp, while the Filipino victims are quite funny in their exaggerated, choreographed death scenes. Opening reel in which the Philippines awkwardly doubles for L.A. is a hoot, with Mitchum sent to Siesta Inn (Filipinos doubling for Chicanos) for a rendezvous at what is described in the silly dialog as an "AC/DC joint."

Much of the action footage involves the outnumbered heroes working out of an armored van, which looks like a cheap version of tv's "The A-Team," perhaps an homage to that show's coproducer John Ashley, who pioneered in making U.S. action films in the Philippines in the 1960s. —*Lor.*

Care Bears Movie II:
A New Generation
(CANADIAN-ANIMATED-COLOR)

Disappointing sequel loaded with plugola.

A Columbia Pictures release of a Nelvana Ltd. production. Produced by Michael Hirsh, Patrick Loubert, Clive A. Smith. Executive producers, John Bohach, Jack Chojnacki, Harvey Levin, Carole MacGillvray, Paul Pressler. Directed by Dale Schott. Screenplay, Peter Sauder; director of animation, Charles Bonifacio; editor, Evan Landis; music, Patricia Cullen, songs, Dean & Carol Parks; production supervisor, Dale Cox; voice casting, Arlene Berman. Reviewed at Columbia Pictures, Burbank, March 10, 1986. (MPAA Rating: G.) Running time: **77 MINS.**

Voice of:
True Heart Bear .... Maxine Miller
Noble Heart Horse .... Pam Hyatt
Dark Heart/the boy .... Hadley Kay
Christy .... Cree Summer Francks
Dawn .... Alyson Court
John .... Michael Fantini

Hollywood — While "The Care Bears II: A New Generation" has a likable cast of cuddly characters espousing morals we should all ascribe to, the work is little more than a thinly veiled commercial for Care Bears and has more of the qualities of a Saturday morning cartoon than a feature film. Its story is neither interesting enough nor songs clever enough to capture an audience other than eight-year-olds or younger, thereby limiting boxoffice.

Missing from the original "Care Bears Movie" are the voices of Mickey Rooney, Georgia Engel and Harry Dean Stanton and the music by John Sebastian and Carole King.

This film features several saccharine songs by Dean & Carol Parks, performed by Stephen Bishop and Debbie Allen, that revolve monotonously around the word care.

In this production from the Toronto-based animation house of Nelvana, scripters manage to mention in the first 20 minutes nearly every Care Bear, Care Bear Cub and Care Cousin product (mostly stuffed animals) for sale at the local toy store.

Once that obligation has been met, action picks up as the main characters True Heart Bear and Noble Heart Horse venture from their home base at The Great Wishing Star on a mission to a summer camp to teach a couple of self-centered youngsters the virtue of sharing and caring.

It turns out that behind the plot of turning the campers against each other and into insufferable brats is the scheming Dark Heart, who also gets most of the good scenes.

In one of the film's more surprisingly funny moments, the evil Dark Heart invades The Great Wishing Star Compound and becomes entangled in the antics by the playful Care Bear and Care Cousin cubs.

Animation is very colorful, sometimes spectacularly so. Too bad the story isn't commensurate with the quality of the production. —Brit.

Zone Rouge
(Red Zone)
(FRENCH-COLOR)

An AAA/Revcom Films release of a Revcom Films-TF 1 Films coproduction. Executive producer, Jean Nachbaur. Produced by Jean Bolvary. Directed by Robert Enrico. Stars Sabine Azéma, Richard Anconina. Screenplay, Enrico, Alain Scoff, based on the novel "Brulez-les tous" by G. J. Arnaud; camera (Fujicolor), Didier Tarot; editor, Patricia Neny; music, Gabriel Yared; sound, Guillaume Sciama; art direction, Jean-Claude Gallouin; assistant director, Jérôme Enrico; production manager, Jean-Claude Bourlat; special effects, Georges Demetrau. Reviewed at the Publicis screening room, Paris, March 13, 1986. Running time: 114 MINS.
Claire Rousset . . . . Sabine Azéma
Jeff Montellier . . . . Richard Anconina
Claire's mother . . . . Hélène Surgère
Pierre Rousset . . . . Jacques Nolot
Nathalie Cheylard . . . Dominique Reymond
Also with: Pierre Frejek, Thierry Rode, Jean Reno, Bernard Freyd, Jean-Pierre Bagot, Philippe Vacher, Christin Pereira, Jean-Pierre Bisson, Henri Villon, Daniel Langlet, Jean Bouise.

Paris — "Zone Rouge," first initiating majority production of Revcom Films, motion picture affiliate of the Editions Mondiales publish-

ing and media giant, is a formula thriller, but smartly turned out by veteran director Robert Enrico and a fine cast. It's another in the line of paranoid suspense dramas in which innocent portagonists stumble onto dark, apocalyptic dealings and are at a loss as to informing the authorities, since the authorities seem to be in cahoots with the chief villains.

Sabine Azéma is a Lyons schoolteacher who survives the sudden and mysterious destruction by fire of a small village, where she has gone to pay a sick call to her ex-husband, who (like the other neighbors apparently) has been poisoned by something in the drinking water.

Official explanation of the catastrophe is the explosion of a gas truck passing through the hamlet, but Azéma heatedly denies this, claiming that the houses were doused with gasoline and ignited, but that there never was an explosion of any kind before the conflagration.

No one seems willing to listen to the distraught Azéma until she meets Richard Anconina, who is an employee for the giant insurance, transportation and security company that seems directly involved in an illegal traffic of dangerous chemical product. His own investigating reveals a transport accident of the material that has poisoned the water supply of the town, which was deliberately destroyed as a cover-up.

The parallel (later united) snooping of Azéma and Anconina opens the familiar Pandora's Box of top-level hanky-panky, harrassment and final mortal pursuit in which the stalked protoganists seem to run into a dead-end before a providential (and ironic) last-minute intervention.

None of this earns much for novelty but the script by Enrico and Alain Scoff, based on a novel by G. J. Arnaud (also the author of the print source for Gilles Béhat's current Latin American actioner, "Les Longs Manteaux") is well-constructed and executed with streamlined efficiency by Enrico.

Of course the acting helps audience adhesion: Azéma's emotive, high-strung manner is perfect for her role. Anconina adds his own notes of casualness and vulnerability to the role of her unwitting savior. Other performances are okay.

All tech credits are excellent.
—Len.

Cool Change
(AUSTRALIAN-COLOR)

A Hoyts release of a Delatite (Melbourne) production. Executive producer, Geoff Burrowes. Produced by Dennis Wright. Directed by George Miller. Stars Jon Blake, Lisa Armytage. Screenplay, Patrick Edgeworth; camera (Eastmancolor), John Haddy; editor,

Philip Reid; music, Bruce Rowland; sound, Terry Rodman; production design, Leslie Binns; art director, Barry Kennedy; assistant director, John Powditch; production manager, Bill Regan; stunt coordinators, Bill Stacey, Chris Peters; casting, Suzie Mazells and Associates. Reviewed at Hoyts 7 theater, Sydney, March 10, 1986. Running time: 90 MINS.
Steve . . . . Jon Blake
Joanna . . . . Lisa Armytage
Lee . . . . Deborra-Lee Furness
Also with: David Bradshaw (James Hardwicke), Alec Wilson (Bull Raddick), James Wright (Snr. Ranger), Mark Albiston (Frank Mitchell), Marie Redshaw (Rob Mitchell), Clive Hearne (Ray Regan), Christopher Stevenson (Jim Regan), Jennifer Hearne (Jennifer Regan), Robert Bruning (Minister), Wilbur Wilde (Wally West), Alistair Neely (Joanna's child), Chris Waters (Agent), Ray Pattison (Curly).

Sydney — In the continuing worldwide argument between those who want to conserve the beauties of nature and those who want to make money from them, "Cool Change" comes firmly down on the side of the latter. Set in the spectacular high country of Victoria, setting for the previous Geoff Burrowes-George Miller hit, "The Man From Snowy River" (still the No. 1 Australian film of all time at the local boxoffice), pic tells a trite and cliché-ridden story of a handsome young forest ranger (Jon Blake) caught up in two feuds: between the cattlemen and the greenies and between his family and the family of the woman he loves. It's Romeo and Juliet in the mountains.

The conservationists are portrayed as grubby troublemakers in league with the devious socialist government. It's a point of view that will infuriate as many as it will appeal to, but the conservationist cause will not be seriously harmed by this basically silly effort.

Leads Blake and Lisa Armytage are wooden, while Deborra-Lee Furness is ludicrous as a femme fatale employed by the government's minister in charge of conservation. Patrick Edgeworth's script is composed of such tried and true material that it's almost possible to predict the lines of dialog before the actors (laboriously) utter them.

John Haddy's scenic cinematography often looks like outtakes from "Snowy River," and Bruce Rowland's music score is syrupy. Anyone who's still confused with the two Australian directors named George Miller may rest assured: there's no possibility that the flat, TV-style direction of "Cool Change" could be credited to the man who made the "Mad Max" films. The title is meaningless.
—Strat.

Bleu Comme l'Enfer
(Blue Like Hell)
(FRENCH-COLOR)

A UGC release of a Garance-Transcontinentale-FR3 Films coproduction. Produced by Dominique Vignet. Directed by Yves Boisset. Screenplay, Boisset, Jean Herman, Sandra Majerowicz, based on the novel by Philippe Djian; camera (color), Dominique Brenguier; editor, Jacques Witta; music, Pierre Porte; sound, Jean-Pierre Ruh; art director, Patrice Mercier; costumes, Rosalie Varda; production manager, Sylvia Montalti. Reviewed at Havas screening room, Neuilly, Feb. 27, 1986. Running time: 100 MINS.
Ned . . . . Lambert Wilson
Lilly . . . . Myriem Roussel
Franck . . . . Tcheky Karyo
Carol . . . . Agnès Soral
Sara . . . . Sandra Montaigu
Henri . . . . Benoit Regent

Paris — "Bleu Comme l'Enfer" is an absurd but fast-paced thriller about a mad-dog cop on the trail of the outlaw who not only has slipped out of his clutches, but has taken the cop's wife with him. Director Yves Boisset, adapting a novel by Philippe Djian (with Jean Herman and Sandra Majerowicz, latter featured in cast under the name Montaigu), seems to have recovered the directorial punch and sense of movement that first earned him some note as an action director à l'américaine.

Tcheky Karyo is again riveting as a weird, rabid lawman who nabs Lambert Wilson for robbing a roadside cafe, but, instead of taking him down to the station, brings him home and handcuffs him to a bathroom pipe. Karyo's attentions are distracted when he finds his long-suffering wife, Myriem Roussel (Jean-Luc Godard's titular "Hail, Mary") packing her bag and about to leave with her sister, Agnès Soral. In an ensuing domestic fight, the women bean Karyo and hit the road with Wilson.

Eventually, Wilson and Roussel are alone and bent on putting the border between them and the increasingly frenzied cop. On the way, they take refuge with friends of Wilson, a couple (Sandra Montaigu and Benoit Regent) who live with their daughter in the mountains. Wilson steps into a deadly jam Regent has gotten into with some dangerous hoods, but the resulting clash draws Karyo back on their trail, for the eventual and satisfying showdown.

Boisset is in his element when he trains his abilities on motion and suspense, which he handles with flamboyant style. But — Karyo's ambiguous performance aside — he doesn't break through to the *film noir* lyricism the script reaches for. Part of the problem is the Wilson-Roussel tandem, who don't quite convey hell-bent desperation. At it's weakest, film seems a pale reflection of Godard's "Pierrot le Fou" and its joyriding outlaw couple.

Dominique Brenguier has lensed vividly, and other technical credits are fine.—Len.

Take It Easy
(DANISH-COLOR)

A Metronome release of a Crone Film Produktion A/S with the Danish Film Institute production. Executive producer, Nine Crone. Consulting producer, Peter Poulsen. Directed and written by Jesper Höm; camera (Agfacolor), Peter Klitgaard; editor, Anders Refn; music, Leo Mathisen; music arranged and directed by Kenny Drew, Kasper Winding; sound, Leif Jensen; production design, Sören Krag Sörensen; costumes, Evelyn Olsson; production management, Jörgen (Nico) Nicolaisen. Reviewed at the Dagmar Teatret, Copenhagen, March 13, 1986. Running time: **103 MINS.**

Herbert . . . . Nikolaj Egelund
Allan . . . . Martin Elley
U.S. Army captain . . Maurice Weddington
Leo Mathisen . . . . Eddie Skoller
Erik Parker . . . . Mek Pek Falk
Erik "Spjät" Kragh . . . . . . Kasper Winding
Henry Hagemann . . . . Jesper Thilo
Carlo Jensen . . . . Gert Rostock
Herbert's mother . . . . Helle Hertz
Victor . . . . Tommy Kentner
Anita . . . . Nadia Klövedal Reich
  Also with: Jeanne Boel (blonde), Louise Frevert (Bitten), Masja Dessau (Miss Andersson), Stig Hoffmeyer (greengrocer), Ole Ernst (Vedel).

Copenhagen — Jesper Höm, celebrated photographer, occasional cinematographer and sometime writer-helmer, was 14 when World War II ended and he rushed to Copenhagen's München Inn where he and his friends went jitterbug-wild to the Fats Waller-ish music of pianist-singer-composer Leo (The Lion) Mathisen's easygoing jazz band. Now, Höm has fashioned a bit of nostalgia fluff comedy about young kids trying their hands at clumsy black marketeering in order to get closer to cigar-chomping Mathisen and his merry men. He has named his picture "Take It Easy" after one of Mathisen's most popular tunes.

Flocking to the München were also British and U.S. servicemen and their Danish girlfriends. Youngsters Herbert and Allan sell the family silver to be able to buy cigars, cigarets and nylon stockings from the Americans. They also, especially Herbert, get into deep water with authorities and hoodlums. They are befriended by a black U.S. Army captain who might have steered them into a healthier course if he had not been so busy black-marketeering, boozing and wallowing in blonds. All comes out reasonably well, however, and the end of an era of innocence is suggested when the night spot's radio announces the atomic bullseye on Hiroshima.

What does not come out in good shape is Höm's film. Nina Crone, as producer and exec producer, has seen to it that 1945 looks and styles are reproduced with fair accuracy. Höm, on the other hand, has let the sounds go adrift, and using amateur actors almost throughout has been a fatal mistake. Everyone speaks their lines with awkward stiffness, and the sound recording is shrill to boot.

The music fares even worse. Instead of using the original Leo Mathisen recordings (which still sell well here), a bunch of rock and post-bop jazz musicians plus one entertainer with imitation as his specialty (Eddie Skoller) comes nowhere near the swing phrasing and the animal gusto of Mathisen's original outfit. On the soundtrack, America's Kenny Drew (who co-arranged the music with rock drummer Kasper Winding) emulates Mathisen's often ham-fisted style of playing with too much gentlemanly finesse.

Onscreen, Eddie Skoller just cannot make his honeyed voice hit a swing groove. In spite of a rascally moustache and the big cigar, he also looks baby-faced, kind and dressed up like an adult, where the original Mathisen radiated a near-vicious charm.

Ultimately, "Take It Easy" lacks ease and rhythm in its story-telling. Some thrown-in sex scenes only serve to clutter up proceedings further. It winds up looking like a youth comedy suffering from a bad case of arthritis.—*Kell.*

Inspector Lavardin
(FRENCH-COLOR)

An MK2 production and release, coproduced by Films A2, la Télévision Suisse Romande, and Cab Prods. Produced by Marin Karmitz. Directed by Claude Chabrol. Screenplay, Chabrol, Dominique Roulet; camera (Eastmancolor), Jean Rabier; editor, Monique Fardoulis; music, Mathieu Chabrol; art director, Françoise Benoit-Fresco; production manager, Catherine Lapoujade. Reviewed at Publicis screening room, Paris, Feb. 28, 1986. Running time: **99 MINS.**
Jean Lavardin . . . . Jean Poiret
Hélène Mons . . . . Bernadette Lafont
Claude Alvarez . . . . Jean-Claude Brialy
Raoul Mons . . . . Jacques Dacqmine
Véronique Manguin . . . . . . Hermine Claire
Max Charnet . . . . Jean-Luc Bideau
Marcel Vigouroux . . . . Pierre-François
                                           Dumeniaud
Francis . . . . Florent Gibassier
Buci . . . . Guy Louret
Volga . . . . Jean Depussé

Paris — The law of sequels applies to Claude Chabrol's new film: it is not as good as last year's "Poulet au Vinaigre," which brought the old New Wave master back into the critical and commercial spotlight after a series of undistinguished commercial assignments unsuited to his talent and temperament.

Unfortunately, "Poulet au Vinaigre," in which Chabrol returned to his old stamping grounds of provincial bourgeois crime, itself wasn't much of a film — merely a wafer-thin entertainment saved from insignificance by Jean Poiret's performance as an unorthodox police inspector. "Inspector Lavardin" is just as slight, but rarely entertaining or suspenseful, even though Poiret (who made a late entrance in "Poulet") is on screen for most of the film.

Problem begins with a poorly constructed and dramatically arbitrary screenplay by the director and Dominique Roulet (who co-scripted "Poulet," based on his print whodunit). It brings Poiret's Inspector Lavardin to a picturesque coastal town to investigate the murder of a well-known but obnoxious Catholic author, whose nude body is found on the beach one day.

There is the usual round of interrogations and confrontations, virtually none of it interesting, because everybody puts on a show of nonchalance and indifference, which the spectator soon feels obliged to join. Poiret pulls some skeletons out of various closets, but the bone rattling reflects a story starved of novelty or tension. The plot doesn't thicken, it just peters out into a somewhat cynical climax in which Poiret frames an innocent but unsympathetic nightclub owner to save the honor of the real guilty party, who acted in self-defense.

Bernadette Lafont and Jean-Claude Brialy, veterans from Chabrol's early days, have been recruited for service in this pastiche of the director's better work, but neither brings flavor to this insipid tale. Poiret himself seems already weary of a role that is designed to operate on a small repertory of dramatic responses and personality ticks. It worked in "Poulet" because some of the dialog was genuinely tart and funny. None of that here.

Chabrol's humdrum, academic direction provides the coup de grace. Tech credits are adequate. —*Len.*

Ninja Turf
(L.A. Streetfighters)
(COLOR)

Poorly-dubbed west coast action pic.

An Ascot Entertainment Group release of an Action Brothers Prods. production. Produced by Phillip Rhee. Executive producer, Jun Chong. Directed by Richard Park. Screenplay and story, Simon Blake Hong; camera (DeLuxe color), David D. Kim, Maximo Munzi; editor, Alex Chang; music, Charles Pavlosky, Gary Falcone, Chris Stone; sound, John Dunne, Hilliary Wong; production design, David Moon Park; associate producer, Richard Park. Reviewed at Hollywood Pacific Theater, Hollywood, Calif., March 14, 1986. (MPAA Rating: R.) Running time: **86 MINS.**
Young . . . . Jun Chong
Tony . . . . Phillip Rhee
Chan . . . . James Lew
Lily . . . . Rosanna King
Kruger . . . . Bill (Superfoot) Wallace
Dorin . . . . Dorin Mukama
Chan's girlfriend . . . . Arlene Montano

Hollywood — "Ninja Turf" must be the first martial arts film to include a toga party and a scene in a Mexican dance hall. Filmed in Los Angeles, pic introduces some unexpected locations but it's still the same old turf. Theatrical life is just a brief stop on the way to homevideo and the foreign market where the film is being released as "L.A. Streetfighters."

A poorly lit, poorly staged and crudely made film, "Ninja Turf" features the dubious distinction of dubbing even the caucasian members of the cast. Luckily, or unluckily (depending on one's viewpoint) much of the conversation goes on in dark backgrounds making most of the dialog seem like it's off camera.

As for the story, it's really a little bit of this and a little bit of that. First there's the group of enemy gangs squaring off, then there's the broken family riff and, finally, there's the crucial confrontation with drug dealers.

Young (Jun Chong) is the kung fu ace with a wounded soul who longs to return to his native land. Unfortunately, he gets mixed up with the wrong crowd and reaches a bloody end.

Although there are some decent action scenes, pic is lacking in the necessary sense of humor to make the comic book material fun. For some reason director Richard Park seems to be taking all this nonsense seriously.

Since voices are poorly dubbed it's nearly impossible to judge the performances, but Chong does give off a certain animal magnetism as the gang leader. As the killer imported from New York, Bill (Superfoot) Wallace has the baddest sneer this side of Hong Kong.—*Jagr.*

Absolute Beginners
(BRITISH-COLOR)

An Orion Pictures release of a Virgin and Goldcrest presentation of a Palace production. Produced by Stephen Woolley, Chris Brown. Executive producers, Nik Powell, Al Clark, Robert Devereux. Directed by Julien Temple. Screenplay, Richard Burridge, Christopher Wicking, Don MacPherson, based on the novel by Colin MacInnes; camera (Super Techniscope, Rank color), Oliver Stapleton; editors, Michael Bradsell, Gerry Hambling, Richard Bedford, Russell Lloyd; music, David Bowie, Ray Davies, Gil Evans, Paul Weller, Patsy Kensit, Sade, Tenpole Tudor, Jerry Dammers, Nick Lowe, Ekow Abban, Working Week; music arranged & conducted by Gil Evans; sound (Dolby), David John; production design, John Beard; art direction, Ken Wheatley, Stuart Rose; choreographer, David Toguri; costume design, Sue Blane, with David Perry; additional dialog, Terry Johnson; associate producer, David Wimbury; assistant director, Ray Corbett; casting, Susie Figgis, Mary Selway, Leonora Davis. Reviewed at the Orion screening room, L.A., March 14, 1986. (No MPAA Rating.) Running time: **107 MINS.**

Colin	Eddie O'Connell
Suzette	Patsy Kensit
Vendice Partners	David Bowie
Henley	James Fox
Arthur	Ray Davies
Big Jill	Ege Ferret
Dido Lament	Anita Morris
Harry Charms	Lionel Blair
The Fanatic	Steven Berkoff
Athene Duncannon	Sade Adu
The Wizard	Graham Fletcher Cook
Ma	Mandy Rice-Davies
Flikker	Bruce Payne
Ed Ted	Tenpole Tudor
Cool	Tony Hippolyte
Call Me Cobber	Alan Freeman
Baby Boom	Chris Pitt
Dean Swift	Paul Rhys
Misery Kid	Julian Firth
Hoplite	Joe McKenna
Amberley Drove	Ronald Fraser
Mrs. Larkin	Irene Handl
Cynthia Eve	Sylvia Syms
Salt Beef Man	Eric Sykes
Vern	Peter Hugo Daly
Saltzman	Johnny Shannon
Dorita	Amanda Jane Powell
Mario	Robbie Coltrane

Hollywood — "Absolute Beginners" is a terrifically inventive original musical for the screen, the likes of which hasn't been seen in quite some time. Daring attempt to portray the birth of teenagedom in London, 1958, almost exclusively through song has some probably inevitable ups and downs, but comes out well ahead overall in the plus column.

A strong bet in its native Britain, elaborate pic faces an uncertain commercial future domestically, as its thoroughgoing Englishness may prove too much of a barrier for Yank youths. Soundtrack is spectacular, and full cross-plugging promo efforts will need to be made via videos and music outlets to stir up interest. World premier takes place March 30 at the San Francisco Intl. Film Festival.

Based upon the late Colin MacInnes' cult novel about teen life and pop fashion in the percolating moments just before the youth cultural explosion in the early 1960s, first major film from Julien Temple since "The Great Rock 'N' Roll Swindle" in 1980 cleverly spans nearly 30 years of musical tastes, neatly bridging the gap between jazz maestro Gil Evans and rock star David Bowie, who sings three tunes and costars as well.

In addition to interpreting the genesis of teen culture, Temple is interested in the political and radical backdrop in Britian at the time, including the Notting Hill race riots. Temple has thrown an untold number of musical, sociological and stylistic ingredients into the pot and stirred vigorously, so it's amazing the result has turned out as palatably as it has.

Tenuous storyline is a typical one of teen love achieved, lost and regained, and is used as a mere string to which a constant parade of musical numbers and flights of fancy are attached. Aspiring photographer Colin and tyro fashion designer Suzette seem a perfect match, but when the latter begins getting ahead and becomes engaged to a snooty couturier played by James Fox, Colin decides to sell out and make the most of his connections in a last-ditch effort to win back his lady love.

In the mad swirl of events which constitute the picture, Colin meets up with such colorful characters as a musical mogul who specializes in pre-pubescent boy singers, a mid-Atlantic ad exec played by Bowie who tempts him into the material world, sinister real estate promoters, a fanatic racial separatist and assorted pimps, hustlers, hipsters, jazzers and scenesters in the happening world of Soho.

In creating a stylized view of 1950s culture, Temple and lenser Oliver Stapleton have made great use of fabulous sets fashioned by production designer John Beard. An astonishing moving camera take throughout the Soho set in the early going represents a fully worthy homage to the opening shot of Orson Welles' "Touch Of Evil." More to the point, however, the film is constantly conjuring up impressions of two of the key directors of the era, Vincente Minnelli and Frank Tashlin, Minnelli for the lush surfaces, color schemes and camera style, Tashlin for the fun vulgarity. Visually, pic represents a constant barrage of pleasures.

Unfortunately, such stylized, studio-enclosed works usually have difficulty finding favor with modern audiences. For Americans, there will be the additional problems of the occasionally thick accents and obscure references. The jazz connection, however rewarding, and the involvement of arranger Gil Evans, will be for aficionados.

Given the diversity of sources, soundtrack coheres very impressively. Bowie scores strongly with both the title tune and a fancy production number, Ray Davies contributes an amusing setpiece as a hip old fogey, and Sade's delivery of her song "Killer Blow" is stunning.

Overall, music is used to advance the storyline and flesh out the concerns of the tellers; but not necessarily in the conventional manner of Broadway or opera. There's a little of everything here, which keeps it almost constantly stimulating. When the invention sags, which it does at times, film seems heavy and pointlessly brassy, but Temple manages to recover quickly.

The expensive Palace production, its first since "The Company Of Wolves," financed in conjunction with Virgin, Goldcrest and U.S. distrib Orion, is tops in every technical department. Young leads Eddie O'Connell and Patsy Kensit are attractive and natural, all they are really called upon to be, and the racial turbulence which jumps from the background to centerstage at the end provides a rawer social context than one finds in most musicals.
—*Cart.*

April Fool's Day
(COLOR)

Unappetizing mixture of horror and put-on comedy.

A Paramount Pictures release of a Hometown Film production. Produced by Frank Mancuso Jr. Directed by Fred Walton. Screenplay, Danilo Bach; camera (Panavision, Metrocolor), Charles Minsky; editor, Bruce Green; music, Charles Bernstein; sound (Dolby), Peter Shewchuk; sound design, David Lewis Yewdall; art direction, Stewart Campbell; set decoration, Della Johnston; assistant director, Lee Knippelberg; production manager, Randolph F. Cheveldave; special effects coordinator, Martin Becker; stunt coordinator, John Wardlow; special effects & makeup effects, Reel EFX, Martin Becker, Christopher Swift, Jim Gill, Bettie Kauffman; casting, Fern Champion, Pamela Basker. Reviewed at Guild 50th St. theater, N.Y., March 21, 1986. (MPAA Rating: R.) Running time: **88 MINS.**

Harvey	Jay Baker
Clara	Pat Barlow
Ferryman	Lloyd Berry
Muffy/Buffy	Deborah Foreman
Nikki	Deborah Goodrich
Potter/Uncle Frank	Tom Heaton
Buck	Mike Nomad
Rob	Ken Olandt
Skip	Griffin O'Neal
Nan	Leah King Pinsent
Chaz	Clayton Rohner
Kit	Amy Steel
Arch	Thomas F. Wilson

While continuing the profitable "Friday The 13th" film series (the sixth one has just started lensing in Georgia), producer Frank Mancuso Jr. unsuccessfully attempts to send up the terror genre with another calendar title, "April Fool's Day." This uneasy mixture of terror and laughs is likely to confuse and/or alienate fans of both genres, indicating brief strength at the boxoffice.

Ironically, since a catchy title is often more important than the contents of a horror pic, another film titled "April Fool's Day" was filmed in Britain in 1984 for Vestron by the original "Friday The 13th" makers, Georgetown Prods., starring Caroline Munro. That pic remains unreleased while Paramount's newer film goes into distribution with the title. Coincidentally, Sean Cunningham's original "Friday" for Georgetown and Paramount in 1980 superceded an earlier, unlucky film titled "Friday The 13th ... The Orphan."

Danilo Bach's underdeveloped screenplay has young heiress Muffy St. John (Deborah Foreman) inviting eight college chums for a premature "Big Chill" (the kids are only about 20 years old) get-together at her family's mansion on an island. Beginning with a gory accident involving the ferryman on the way over, the April 1 weekend is punctuated by the kids being killed or disappearing sequentially in "10 Little Indians" fashion.

Except for their hostess played by Foreman, the youngsters are an undifferentiated lot, unappealing in their whining about "what am I gonna do after college?" and tiresome in the corny practical jokes essayed (collapsing chairs, spraying water). Prevalence of jokes is the main clue to the film's twist outcome, while other gimmicks such as Foreman's dual role are highly predictable. Far from being the novelty it pretends to be, picture's "it never happened" switcheroo is a hoary device dating back to silent films in which supernatural goings-on were explained away as a ruse in the final reel.

Cast struggles with the intractable material. Foreman overdoes her smile in the opening reels before becoming unconvincingly spooky later on. Deborah Goodrich tries to be the sexiest of the group, but, to be charitable, she'd never make the physical for a Russ Meyer feature. In the briefest of the lead roles, Griffin O'Neal is looking more and more like his pop Ryan.

Director Fred Walton, who had a most influential hit in the recent horror cycle with "When A Stranger Calls" in 1979, emphasizes effects over substance here. As part of a hokey, overdone Dolby stereo soundtrack, one of the silliest gaffes has a guy unzipping his zipper in what sounds like Sensurround.

Apart from sound, other technical credits are okay including effective widescreen lensing of British Columbia locations by Charles Minsky. —*Lor.*

Tuttobenigni
(All Benigni)
(ITALIAN-DOCU-COLOR)

A Mario and Vittorio Cecchi Gori presentation of a C.E.I.A.D. release, produced by Ettore Rosbach for Best Films Intl. Directed by Giuseppe Bertolucci. Stars Roberto Benigni. Camera (color), Renato Tafuri; editor, Jannis Christopulos. Reviewed at Ariston Cinema, Rome, March 7, 1986. Running time: 88 MINS.

Rome — The funniest stand-up comic in Italy is Roberto Benigni, a dimunitive Tuscan mumbler in ill-fitting clothes and uncombed hair, whose stage appearances play to packed houses all over the country. "All Benigni" was shot by Giuseppe Bertolucci as a tv special, but blown up to grainy 35m after a belated decision was made to release it theatrically.

Though the material is irreverent and addresses figures ranging from Prime Minister Craxi to God, it is handled with such a gentle touch that the theatrical run may be assumed to pave the way for eventual small screen airing. It is breaking b.o. records in Florence, and doing well in other situations where it is in release.

Basically, film is a record of the comic on stage in some of his best moments and routines. Editing by Jannis Christopulos is lightning fast (like its subject), rarely cuts away to audience reaction, but intercuts a few hilarious interviews by journalists and some footage shot in a car. As a docu it is a model of concise, no-frills filmmaking. From a pre-credits opener with Benigni running down village streets in some kind of blindfolded race, to his final bravura improvisation on stage, there is a rarely a dull moment in which audiences are not laughing.

Unfortunately, the only public able to appreciate this mile-a-minute talker whose words pour out on top of each other in garbled Tuscan dialect will be Italian speaking. Benigni's comedy, though also gestural, is so rooted in lightning-fast puns and word play it defies translation of any sort. This is particularly a shame because those who have seen him in feature films, like Giuseppe Bertolucci's "Berlinguer I Love You," Marco Ferreri's "Chiedo Asilo," his own "You Bother Me," or "Nothing Left To Do But Cry," which he co-directed with Massimo Troisi, have only glimpsed the lesser part of this dynamic wordsmith. Less an actor able to perform prewritten dialog than a masterful improviser, Benigni is at his best when he asks the audience to call out a few nonsense phrases, which he then instantaneously works into side-splitting routines.

Freely leaping from one thought to another, he somehow gets from the Pope ("the greatest living Pope in Italy") to Poland, and thence to the Mideast and Khomeini, until he explains how Italy could solve its economic problems with the conquest of Switzerland. When an interviewer calls him the Italian Woody Allen, Benigni very seriously suggests he'd rather be thought of as "the Swiss Anna Magnani."
— *Yung.*

Police Academy 3: Back In Training
(COLOR)

Watered-down formula still works.

A Warner Bros. release. Produced by Paul Maslansky. Directed by Jerry Paris. Screenplay, Gene Quintano, based on characters created by Neal Israel and Pat Proft; camera (Technicolor), Robert Saad; editor, Bud Molin; music, Robert Folk; sound, David Lee; production design, Trevor Williams; art director, Rhiley Fuller; set decorator, Sean Kirby; assistant director, Michael Zenon; associate producer, Donald West; casting, Fern Champion, Pamela Basker. Reviewed at Mann's Chinese Theater, Hollywood, Calif., March 21, 1986. (MPAA Rating: PG.) Running time: 82 MINS.

Sgt. Mahoney	Steve Guttenberg
Sgt. Hightower	Bubba Smith
Sgt. Tackleberry	David Graf
Sgt. Jones	Michael Winslow
Sgt. Hooks	Marion Ramsey
Lt. Callahan	Leslie Easterbrook
Commandant Mauser	Art Metrano
Cadet Sweetchuck	Tim Kazurinsky
Cadet Zed	Bobcat Goldhwait
Commandant Lassard	George Gaynes
Cadet Adams	Shawn Weatherly
Sgt. Copeland	Scott Thomson
Sgt. Fackler	Bruce Mahler
Lt. Proctor	Lance Kinsey
Cadet Nogata	Brian Tochi
Cadet Fackler	Debralee Scott
Governor Neilson	Ed Nelson

Hollywood — It comes as no surprise, but "Police Academy 3: Back In Training" is no finishing school. There is no class in wit or humor, in fact, there's no class at all. This hasn't seemed to discourage business and "3" should follow in the great tradition of the first two.

Most noticeable about "Police Academy 3" is a continued trend to softer material which should also be reflected at the boxoffice. The first "Police Academy" was a raunchy R and delivered $38,500,000 in domestic rentals. "Police Academy 2" was PG-13 and made $27,200,-000. "Police Academy 3" is PG and should fall off some more.

Cast of cartoon misfits is still basically intact and if "Police Academy 3" has any charm it's in the good-natured dopeyness of these people. No bones about it, these people are there to laugh at.

Leading the charge for the third time is Steve Guttenberg turning in another likable boy-next-door performance. His role, however, as the cute straight man seems a bit abbreviated, with the comic burden spread out among the cast.

New additions Tim Kazurinsky and Bobcat Goldhwait as cadets are only intermittently amusing. Kazurinsky, from tv's "Saturday Night Live," generates a few yocks as the timid, would-be cop but Goldhwait adds an element of animalistic humor that is boorish.

Plot has something to do with one of the two rival police academies being shut down by the penny-pinching governor (Ed Nelson). Bad guys led by Commandant Mauser (Art Metrano) try to sabotage the forces of virtue led by Commandant Lassard (George Gaynes).

What has made the police academy formula work for audiences is that it's really just a formula for a running string of mostly sight gags and noisy accidents. Director Jerry Paris manages a few well-executed bits without varying his attack here. Gene Quintano's screenplay is almost beside the point.

Along for the ride without a whole lot to do are returnees Bubba Smith as the baddest cop in town, David Graf as the most dangerous and Leslie Easterbrook as the best endowed. Michael Winslow turns in some off-beat vocal tricks but like most of the running jokes in the film, they go on too long.

Tech credits are fine and pic looks polished. Who would have imagined cuddly cops 10 or 15 years ago? — *Jagr.*

Amarosa
(SWEDISH-COLOR)

A Sandrews release of a Sandrews with the Swedish Film Institute and SR/TV-2 production. Executive producer, Brita Werkmäster. Artistic supervising producer, Bengt Forslund. Original story, screenplay and directed by Mai Zetterling. Stars Stina Ekblad, Erland Josephson. Camera (Agfacolor), Rune Erickson, Mischa Gavrjusjov; editor, Darek Hodor, Zetterling; production design, Jan Oquist; costumes, Gertie Lindgren, Kerstin Lokrantz; production management, Marianne Persson, Eva Ivarsson. Reviewed at the Sandrews 1-2-3, Malmö, Sweden, March 20, 1986. Running time: 113 MINS.

Agnes von Krusenstjärna	Stina Ekblad
David Sprengel	Erland Josephson
Adolf von Krusenstjärna	Philip Zandén
Gerhard Odencrantz	Peter Schildt
Ernst von Krusenstjärna	Olof Thunberg
Eva von Krusenstjärna	Catharina de Seeynes
Ava de Geer	Lena T. Hansson
Edward von Krusenstjärna	Rico Rönnbäck
Hugo Hamilton	Lauritz Falk
Evelina Hamilton	Gunnel Broström

Also with: Helen Friberg, Efva Lilja, Heinz Hopf, Eva von Hanno, Anita Björk, Annelie Martini, Inga langré, Aina Landgré, Inga Gill, Börje Ahlstedt, Mimi Pollak.

Malmö — Mai Zetterling, who converted an international career as a comedy actress into a career as a director of often controversial feature films ("Loving Couples," 1964, "The Girls," 1968, "Scrubbers," 1982) has over the years expressed a very special empathy with the figure and fate of her Swedish countrywoman Agnes von Krusenstjärna (1894-1940), a writer of girlish romances, later of a novel brimming with explicit (for the day) sex and spiteful portraitures of her own family of landed but poor gentry. From the latter, she had broken away to share life with David Sprengel, a literary charlatan, collector of erotica, bisexual vagrant and 14 years her senior.

In "Amarosa," Zetterling's first Swedish picture in 18 years, von Krusenstjärna is seen as a phsyically frail, mentally schizophrenic victim of both hereditary madness and of the narrow-minded and snobbish values of her family. She is also described as the strong-willed woman and artist, thriving on whatever sexuality she could find to explore and certainly aided and abetted in both sexual exploits and literary output by Sprengel.

Descriptions of insanity generally afford filmmakers too free a rein, with audiences left without any anchor of common denominator recognition. Likewise, descriptions in films of the creative processes of a literary person are usually confined to hand-wringing, brow-mopping and floor-pacing in the neighborhood of idle writing utensils. Zetterling, fortunately, has the essential toughness of her heroine's writing instincts in evidence as the natural link to the reality of work as a healing process. Her bouts of utter madness come as equally natural expressions of generated inner heat and turmoil.

Stina Ekblad's gaunt, rawboned face has a wistful, but also somehow willful beauty that is far from conventional. Her sinewy acting talent is just right for Zetterling's intense dramatic style and obsession with sexuality versus Establishment mores. Ekblad's Krusenstjärna is first seen behind a mask in Venice at carnival time where she has a nervous breakdown and has to be taken to a hospital in a strait jacket. Sprengel is with her, and he tries desperately to keep her from tearing to pieces a manuscript she has just completed.

At film's end, we return to Venice after having been shown, in one long flashback, how Krusenstjärna's life and career evolved through inner and outer pressures into her seesaw life with Springel. He doctored her writings, administered her morphine shots and kept her writing along with having her joyfully join him in sundry games of sexual excess.

Sprengel is played with sly cunning by Erland Josephson, who also turns the neat trick of parading sexual abrasiveness, sensual submissiveness along with a quivering lower lip, lecherous jelly-fish eyes and slicked down curls plus greyish makeup while nevertheless emerging as an essentially sympathetic character and good guy. It soon seems a pretty sensible move for Krusenstjärna to have left the sun-bathed and idyllic rural idyll of her family's life in favor of a desk and a bed in the stuffy, shadowy world of art deco drawing-rooms belonging to a man whose ideas of comforting her in moments of stress would run along the lines of having a servant girl in nun's habit baring herself in readiness for triangular fun & games.

In clumsier hands, all this would have come out silly and suffocating. Zetterling and her two cinematographers, however, make summer outings on boats, the goings-on in dens of vice, the tentative sexual approaches between two young girls shivering with cold in their swimsuits, and even screaming madness look stunningly real and strangely haunting as natural extensions of the involved characters' acts and emotions. All production values are sumptuous, and the Venice of bizarre costumes, masks and gondolas on placid lagoons, worked to death in numerous films, has a new magic, albeit somewhat morbid, added to it here.

Venice, or some other major fest site, would also seem just right for the international launching of this feast-for-the-eyes meller of inner and outer worlds on a strange collision course. —Kell.

He Stands In A Desert Counting The Seconds Of His Life
(U.S.-COLOR-16m)

A Film-makers' Co-op release of a film by Jonas Mekas. Reviewed at International Forum of Young Cinema, Berlin Intl. Film Festival, Feb. 16, 1986. (No MPAA Rating.) Running time: 150 MINS.

Berlin — Jonas Mekas' "He Stands In A Desert" was a popular item at the recent Berlin festival, which always has friendly audiences for U.S. independents. "He" is also being shown abroad soon at the Amsterdam and Malaga festivals, also at the Walker Art Center, Minneapolis, and currently in New York. "He" is an auto-biographical film, a continuation of Mekas' diary series, using his recurrent format of staccato color fragments, provocative but incomplete morsels, cut very fast.

"He" was shot by Mekas between 1969-84, edited in 1984-85. It consists of 124 brief sketches, ranging from 30 seconds to two minutes, with quick informal mini-portraits of Mekas' artist-friends, including Hans Richter, Roberto Rossellini, Nam June Paik, Elia Kazan, Shirley Clarke, John Lennon and Yoko Ono, Jackie Onassis, Allen Ginsberg, Henri Langlois, Kenneth An-

ger, Ken Jacobs, Hollis Frampton and Willard Van Dyke. Inter-titles identify personages, locales and dates.

The abrupt transitions of "He," the non-sequiturs, the unlikely juxtapositions, the arbitrary and unpredictable montage, make for a style difficult for the layman, even alienating. Mekas' bursts of imagery, his jagged and irregular rhythms, may tire and puzzle the uninitiated. —Hitch.

Cry From The Mountain
(COLOR)

Religious-themed effort is achieving some crossover recognition.

A World Wide Pictures release of a film produced by the Billy Graham Film Ministry. Produced by William F. Brown. Directed by James F. Collier. Screenplay, David L. Quick; camera (color), Gary D. Baker; editor, J. Michael Hooser; music, J.A.C. Redford; sound, Michael Strong, Les Kisling; production design, Hooser; costumes, M. Butler; production coordinator, Twila Knaack; set design, James Sewell. Reviewed at Metcalf Theater, Kansas City, March 6, 1986. (MPAA Rating: PG.) Running time: 90 MINS.
Larry Sanders . . . . Wes Parker
Carolyn Sanders . . . . Rita Walter
Cal Sanders . . . . Chris Kidd
Jonathan . . . . James Cavan
Marian Rissman . . . . Coleen Gray
Dr. Carney . . . . Jerry Ballew
Laurie Matthews . . . . Allison Argo
The pilot . . . . Glen Alsworth
Dr. Blake . . . . Myrna Kidd

Kansas City — This current release from the Billy Graham organization has a young family-religious theme set in the Alaskan wilderness with a sufficient story to earn it some crossover recognition in its market-by-market distribution which began last November in Seattle.

Wes Parker, the one-time L.A. Dodger first baseman, plays the young husband-father, who has dallied with his office secretary, Allison Argo, and has his wife, Rita Walter, pregnant and looking toward the divorce court possibly even to the extent also of an abortion. As promised to their 10-year-old son, Chris Kidd, the father takes the boy on a camping trip to the Alaskan mountain wilderness before the parents, unknown to the boy, will break up.

While attempting to shoot some treacherous rapids in a roaring mountain stream, their twin-seater kayak is overturned and the father survives a nasty head wound, but is beached unconscious. Young Kidd enlists the help of mining camp recluse James Cavan, and they save the father's life. Eventually they have to fly him by helicopter from the rickety old cabin to a hospital in Anchorage, where surgery relieves the concussion and the father recovers.

The mother is persuaded by Cavan, who is struggling with his own lifelong grudge against an obstreperous son, to attend the Billy Graham Revival in Sullivan Auditorium. She joins those who "come down front" to commit to Christ, and later at the hospital tells the husband she is forgiving him, with a resultant family re-huddling.

The story line proceeds directly, but the treatment is episodic and the pace somewhat languid. It could have gotten there better with more pungent dialog to focus the dramatic highlights and tighter scripting and editing. What the picture has going for it more than anything else is the wilderness setting, and the producers have been sharp about including generous footage of the Alaskan mountains-forest-streams, indeed eye-filling and compelling. Much of the filming was on location in the historic Willow Creek mining district, including the once-famous Independence Mine.

Parker looks every bit the rugged outdoorsman and is adequate as the father. Walter, a soap-opera veteran, is first-rate as the wife, and young Kidd is 100% the outdoors boy. Cavan does the most with what he has to work as the old miner who comes out of his shell.

The PG rating is explained by the inclusion of the divorce threat and the discussion about abortion, no bad language or suggestive scenes.

Some lengthy footage is devoted to the Graham revival crusade, as would be expected, but nowhere as on the big screen is his effectiveness brought home so graphically, while being an integral part of the story. —Quin.

RAD
(COLOR)

Conventional bike-riding pic.

A Tri-Star Pictures release of a Jack Schwartzman presentation of a Taliafilm II Ltd./Robert L. Levy production. Produced by Levy. Coproducer, Sam Bernard. Executive producer, Schwartzman. Directed by Hal Needham. Screenplay, Bernard, Geoffrey Edwards; camera (Technicolor), Richard Leiterman; editor, Carl Kress; music, James Di Pasquale; art direction, sound (Dolby), Frank H. Griffiths; Shirley Inget; set decoration, Cindy Gordon, Clay Weiler, Grant S. Goodman; costume design, Jerry Allen; associate producer, Mary Eilts; assistant director, Gordon Robinson; casting, Annette Benson. Reviewed at the Hollywood Pacific, L.A., March 21, 1986. (MPAA Rating: PG.) Running time: 91 MINS.
Cru . . . . Bill Allen
Christian . . . . Lori Loughlin
Mrs. Jones . . . . Talia Shire
Burton Timmer . . . . Ray Walston
Eliott Dole . . . . Alfie Wise
Duke Best . . . . Jack Weston
Bart Taylor . . . . Bart Conner
Becky . . . . Marta Kober
Luke . . . . Jamie Clarke
Wesley Jones . . . . Laura Jacoby
Sgt. Smith . . . . H.B. Haggerty
Rod Reynolds . . . . Carey Hayes

Foxy . . . . Kellie McQuiggin
Tiger . . . . Beverly Hendry

Hollywood — BMX bikes are this month's fad, a fact the world can apprise itself of in "RAD," a simple but action-filled meller about and for middle-class teens. Except for the sharp bike riding, pic is minor-league in all departments, and b.o. performance should follow suit.

Credit sequence, which displays all the wild contortions of which the little BMX bikes are capable, was designed by John Schwartzman and provides for the most arresting moments in the entire picture.

As for the remainder, scripters Sam Bernard and Geoffrey Edwards have strung about a dozen bike action sequences together with a Capra-esque fable which pits nice local kid Bill Allen against the corrupt, conniving racing establishment personified by Jack Weston.

Weston comes to town to stage a nationally televised race on the aptly named Helltrack. A $100,000 prize is held out to the winner, but the competition is rigged so that locals are effectively prevented from taking on Weston's hand-picked champ.

Most of the running time is devoted to Allen circumventing Weston's ever-changing regulations, a process which does not entail much suspense since his participation in the final is a foregone conclusion. Despite the pressures on him, Allen still finds time for a dalliance with pretty girl rider Lori Loughlin.

Conventional in almost every conceivable way, "RAD" actually seems "rad" in the context of many post-"Risky Business" youth films in that it rejects financial gain as the ultimate goal of life and actually dares to suggest that there may be some higher values, such as honesty, integrity, loyalty and the like. Who knows what they'll think of next.

Director Hal Needham covers the action competently, but then, bikes move a lot more slowly than the speed vehicles he's used to. Richard Leiterman's lensing, on Calgary locations, is on the dark side, and James Di Pasquale's music keeps things hopping with the help of numerous pop songs. —Cart.

Conseil de Famille
(Family Council)
(FRENCH-COLOR)

A Gaumont release of a K.G. Prods.-Gaumont-Films A2 coproduction. Produced by Michèle Ray. Written and directed by Constantin Costa-Gavras, from the novel by Francis Ryck. Stars Johnny Hallyday, Fanny Ardant and Guy Marchand. Camera (Eastmancolor), Robert Alazraki; editor, Marie-Sophie Dubus; music, Georges Delerue; sound, Jean-Paul Mugel; art direction,

Eric Simon; assistant director, Frédéric Blum; production manager, Gérard Crosnier, casting, Dominique Besnehard, Margot Capelier, Marie-Christine Lafosse. Reviewed at Gaumont screening room, Paris, March 14, 1986. Running time: 123 MINS.

The father . . . . Johnny Hallyday
The mother . . . . Fanny Ardant
Faucon . . . . Guy Marchand
François (teen) . . . . Laurent Romor
François (adult) . . . . Remi Martin
Martine (child) . . . . Juliette Rennes
Martine (teen) . . . . Caroline Pochon

Also with: Ann Gisel Glass, Fabrice Luchini, Patrick Bauchau, François Bette, François Michaud, Laurent Peters, Rosine Cadoret, Vincent Martin, Julien Bertheau, Philippe de Brugada, Robert Deslandes, Michel Cremades, Anne Macina, Gérard Dubois, Charly Chemouny, Mouss, Alexandra Vidal, Stéphanie Vidal, Emmanuelle Collomb, Florence Collomb, Anne Loisel, Emmanuelle Loisel.

———

Paris — Humor has never been an element in the socio-political film world of Constantin Costa-Gavras, so it's a surprise to see the director now taking a stab at this ironic comedy about a family of burglars done in by its own double standard of morality. Costa-Gavras himself adapted a novel by well-known thriller author Francis Ryck, and has directed with his usual conscientious professionalism. Despite some sporadic moments of mirth, "Conseil de Famille" is stolidly lacking in visual imagination and narrative brio.

Johnny Hallyday, the top rock singer who made a much-remarked starring debut in Jean-Luc Godard's "Détective" (he has had small roles in films before) confirms his screen presence if not yet much range as a professional safecracker who returns to the bosom of his family after a jail term. Reunited with his patient wife (Fanny Ardant) and his two children, Hallyday intends to pursue a conventional family life (with the kids getting a classical Catholic education), and take up his old métier of burglary with his long-time sidekick, Guy Marchand.

Unfortunately, the kids have long since learned the true reasons for daddy's long absence, and François, the son, wants to be a chip off the old block. Using some of dad's less commendable traits, he "blackmails" Hallyday and Marchand into taking him along on their next job. The initiation, though not quite glorious, leads to a new team spirit, to which François brings his own abilities.

The years pass and the family moves up the social ladder. Soon their exploits impress organized crime circles in America, and during a visit Stateside the family is offered a contract as a Riviera affiliate. François, now a young man with a sweetheart and dreams of another profession (cabinet-making) announces he wants out. His dad, enraged by his son's attitude, calls for a family council and imprisons his son in his room until he decides to change his mind. François, again following the example established by dad, delivers Hallyday and Marchand to the police so that he, his sister and his mother can lead a normal life.

This odd family chronicle runs for a full two hours, but exhausts much of its interest before it is half over. In its best moments the straight-faced, sober direction gives the action an offbeat tone, but too often the filmmaker seems uncertain about how to approach his material and the action drags.

Hallyday is brightly complemented by Marchand, who embodies the comic spirit the director cannot provide, but Ardant's personage has little relief. Laurent Romor and Remi Martin, as François at different ages, are good, as are the girls who play his slangy kid sister. Supporting cast and tech credits are okay. —*Len.*

———

Hame'ahev
(The Lover)
(ISRAELI-COLOR)

A Cannon Releasing release of a Cannon Films Presentation of a G.G. Studios Production. Produced by Menahem Golan, Yoram Globus. Executive producer, Itzhak Kol. Directed by Michal Bat-Adam. Stars Michal Bat-Adam, Yehoram Gaon. Screenplay, Bat-Adam, Zwika Kertzner, based on novel by A.B. Yehoshua; camera (color), David Gurfinkel; editor, Tova Asher; music, Dov Seltzer; art director, Eytan Levy. Reviewed at the Shahaf Cinema, Tel Aviv, March 2, 1986. (No MPAA Rating.) Running time: **90 MINS.**

Assia . . . . Michal Bat-Adam
Adam . . . . Yehoram Gaon
Daffi . . . . Avigail Arieli
Gavriel . . . . Roberto Pollak
Naim . . . . Awas Khatib
Grandmother . . . . Fanny Lubitsch

———

Tel Aviv — The original A.B. Yehoshua novel on which "The Lover" is based is one of the most successful literary works of the new generation of Israeli writers. As such, it has been discussed for years as a possible subject for a film adaptation, until Menahem Golan, who had acquired the rights from the American publisher, Doubleday, settled on Michal Bat-Adam as director and star.

The results falls short of the expectations, as it reduces both the scope and the depth of the original. The story concerns a middle-aged couple. The husband owns a profitable car-repair business, the wife teaches in high-school, their only daughter a teenager. Shortly before the 1973 Yom Kippur War, a stranger penetrates this staid and conventional family cell. The wife falls desperately in love with him, the husband tries his best to cope with the situation without bringing it into the open, until the war breaks in, the man disappears and the family is thrown into a profound state of crisis.

For Yehoshua, this was much more than a torrid love story. Through the different participants in the story, each presenting his separate point-of-view, which gave the novel a kind of "Rashomon" construction, it offered a social, economical and psychological image of Israel at a critical point in its history. The introduction of a young Arab boy working for the husband and being used, at a certain stage, as an active factor in the relations between the characters, brings into the picture the additional aspect of the Jewish-Arab relations and their particular nature at that time.

Bat-Adam, however, chose to simplify the approach by offering only one point-of-view, and by stressing the sexual connotations of the plot, at the expense of all other aspects. Her adaptation is about the last fling of a woman facing menopause, and the response of her family, her husband being awakened from his middleage sexual lethargy by his wife's affair, and the daughter going through the first confused pangs of lust and jealousy.

The problem is that neither Bat-Adam nor Gaon look anything like the age of their characters. Avigail Arieli as their daughter is far too inexperienced to handle her part, and all the rest of the cast doesn't really get a chance to develop real characters. The one who does, Roberto Pollak, as the stranger, doesn't even begin to suggest a reason for anybody's infatuation with him.

A rift with the censors concerning a love scene between Gaon and a 15-year-old-girl, widely publicized shortly before the film was released, helped promote it on the local market and results, up to now, have been satisfactory if not remarkable. —*Edna.*

———

GoBots: Battle Of
The Rock Lords
(ANIMATED-COLOR)

Well-produced action feature holds attention.

A Clubhouse Pictures/Atlantic Releasing release of a Hanna-Barbera/Tonka Corp. production. Produced by Kay Wright. Executive producers, William Hanna, Joseph Barbera, Joe Taritero. Directed by Ray Patterson. Screenplay, Jeff Segal; story consultant, Kelly Ward; supervising animation director, Paul Sabella; production supervisor, Bob Marples; supervising editor, Larry C. Cowan; musical director, Hoyt Curtin; sound direction, Alvy Dorman, Phil Flad. Reviewed at Amboy Mutliplex, Sayreville, N.J., March 22, 1986. (MPAA Rating: G.) Running time: **75 MINS.**

Voice of:
Solitaire . . . . Margot Kidder
Nuggit . . . . Roddy McDowall
Boulder . . . . Michael Nouri
Magmar . . . . Telly Savalas

Also with voices by: Arthur Bughardt, Ike Eisenmann, Bernard Erhard, Marilyn Lightstone, Morgan Paul, Lou Richards, Leslie Speights, Frank Welker, Dick Gautier, Foster Brooks.

———

Based on the cartoon tv series, "GoBots: Battle Of The Rock Lords" is an all-new feature-length actioner keyed to youngsters familiar with the robot characters who can transform into spaceships, land rovers and other assorted vehicles. A new group of characters, not part of the tv series, is the Rock People, humanoid types who can ball up into rocks for protection, or bound down a cliffside to escape attackers.

Film is solidly scripted and fast-moving, with the good guys (the GoBots) coming to the aid of the oppressed Rock People, who are under seige by the evil Rock Lords. A fourth faction, the Renegades, are GoBots gone bad who team up with the Rock Lords to wreak havoc. The Great amount of characters, each with a name and individual characteristics, adds both depth to the genre but also may cause confusion to those not familiar with them from television.

Vet animators Hanna-Barbera and the Tonka toy firm, who together produce the "Challenge Of The GoBots" tv series, haven't settled for simply stringing together a bunch of episodes, but rather have put together a complete work with a beginning, middle and end. Animation is colorful, with nicely conceived battle sequences and terrain layouts.

Curiously, voice characterizations by such name actors as Margot Kidder, Roddy McDowall and Telly Savalas (as the head bad guy) are electronically altered so as to make them almost unrecognizable; less-expensive talent could have probably achieved the same results.

Business for this effort will likely be confined to young boys and attendant parents, but it should also do well on vidcassette shelves. Pic ends on a "The battle's over but the war continues" note, indicating a second feature may be in the offing.—*Gerz.*

———

Eat The Peach
(IRISH-COLOR)

———

A Film Four Intl. and Strongbow Marketing presentation of a Strongbow production. Produced by John Kelleher. Executive producer, David Collins. Directed by Peter Ormrod. Screenplay, Ormrod, Kelleher; camera (color), Arthur Wooster; editor, J. Patrick Duffner; music, Donal Lunny; production designer, David Wilson. Reviewed at the Savoy I Cinema, Dublin, Ireland, March 12, 1986. (Irish Film Censorship Certificate: All ages.) Running time: **95 MINS.**

Arthur . . . . Eamon Morrissey
Vinnie . . . . Stephen Brennan
Nora . . . . Catherine Byrne
Boots . . . . Niall Toibin
Boss Murtagh . . . . Joe Lynch
Sean Murtagh . . . . Tony Doyle
Bunzo . . . . Takashi Kawahara

———

Dublin — Strongbow's first theatrical feature film "Eat The Peach" was produced on a budget of $2,300,000, mainly raised last year in Ireland, supplemented by the Irish Film Board and the British Channel 4 and lensed in Ireland.

The story is simple and tells of two ordinary men who try to do something extraordinary. Living on a peat bog in frustration they see a video of "Roustabout" in which Elvis Presley rides a Wall Of Death at a fairground. They decide to build their own Wall Of Death and become performers.

Seeking to finance their project they become aides in a smuggling racket which creates a lively comedy element, although it may not be entirely clear to audiences outside Ireland that smuggling gasoline and booze from Northern Ireland to the Irish Republic is a profitable enterprise. The Wall Of Death gets built and arouses excitement locally, which terminates in fear and the destruction of the Wall by one of the partners, ending a dream.

Family loyalty is a background to the endeavors of the major participants, and the woman in the piece is still backing them when their dream is demolished and they start on something fresh and maybe simpler.

This is a gentle piece, perhaps a little confusing in its local Irish jokes but beautifully photographed and well edited. Stephen Brennan, who is tops among the younger generation of actors in Ireland, is a strong lead with Eamon Morrissey, a good comic actor providing an excellent back-up. Catherine Byrne, wife to the lead, projects a gentle character supportive of a husband's endeavors and has a quiet beauty to go with it. Direction is unobtrusive.

Good character playing by Niall Toibin as the pseudo-American who would be a racketeer and general fixer provides a comedy element, and there's a firm performance from Joe Lynch as the racketeer who knows his business.

There's a puzzling (for people outside Ireland) sequence at the start involving Japanese industrialists ending an involvement in Ireland. Otherwise this story of simple but imaginative and hopeful characters holds up. It's due for screening at Cannes. —Max.

Die Liebeswüste
(The Desert Of Love)
(WEST GERMAN-B&W-16m)

A Lothar Lambert film production. Produced, written, directed, camera (color), edited, and sound by Lothar Lambert. Assistant camera, Eberhard Geick; assistant soundman, Michael Eiler. Reviewed at Berlin Film Mart screening room, March 6, 1986. Running time: 85 MINS.
With: Ulrike S., Dieter Schidor, Dorothea Moritz, Jessica Lanée, Doreen Heins, Abbas Kepekli, Semra Uysallar, Stefan Menche, Friederike Menche, Hans Marquardt, Michael Hülsmann, Lothar Lambert, Dagmar Beiersdorf, Albert Heins, Erika Rabau.

Berlin — The film lab erred grievously in developing Lothar Lambert's last pic and inadvertently destroyed meters of film.

He solved the problem by making a film about the catastrophe: Lambert sits with a desperate expression on his face at the editing table trying to put some semblance of continuity to separate patches of a loosely fitting and improvised story. The project was titled "The Desert Of Love."

Into the cutting-room walks Berlin Underground colleague Dagmar Beiersdorf, who asks embarrassing questions on what all this mess was supposed to mean in the first place. They discuss their differences on the social and psychological aspects of outsiders in sex and society (Lambert's bread-and-butter theme). Along comes producer Albert Heins, who would like to help Lambert out of his financial difficulties by finding a potential tv backer, but what is there to do when the entire project can only be pasted together with rejects from the cutting-room floor.

As for the failed film project itself, it has Lambert's Underground star Ulrike S. escaping from a mental institution with nothing covering her bare body but a raincoat — which she opens to expose herself whenever insulted by a bourgeois passerby. For the most part, too, everyone she bumps into wants to exploit her presence for one erotic aberration or another — and she has to flee time and time again to save her own self-respect.

Back in the cutting-room, Ulrike S. visits to echo Beiersdorf's running commentary on the oddities in Lambert's burgeoning film career.

"The Desert Of Love" also stars Dieter Schidor as a gay searching for a sexual fix, plus Dorothea Moritz as a voyeur in a wheelchair at a window getting in her say on all the strange characters congregating at the corner public relief station. —Holl.

Aces Go Places IV
(Mad Mission IV)
(HONG KONG-COLOR)

A Cinema City production and released by Golden Princess. Produced by Raymond Wong, Dean Shek. Directed by Ringo Lam. Stars Sam Hui, Karl Maka, Sally Yeh, Sylvia Cheng, Ronald Lacey, Peter Macauly, Onno Boulee, Sin Lam Yuk, Sandi Dexter, Gayle Anne Jones. Coproduced by Karl Maka. Overseas executive producer, Murray Newey; screenplay, Karl Maka, Ringo Lam; special effects consultant, Kevin Chisnall; stunts by Joe Chi, Peter Bell; camera (color), Sander Lee; editor, Tony Chow; art direction, Vicent Wai. Reviewed at State theater, Hong Kong, March 1, 1986. Running time: 98 MINS.
(Cantonese soundtrack with English subtitles)

Hong Kong — In "Aces Go Places IV," a special rain stimulant has been developed somewhere in New Zealand that gets Sam Hui, Karl Maka, Sylvia Chang, Baldy Junior and Sally Yeh into trouble.

The first 10 minutes of the picture are visually exciting but that's about it. The project lacks cohesion and is no better or worse than a "Cannonball Run" concept.

There is screen movement, but it is sorely lacking in a credible storyline. The producers could have invested more in the screenplay instead of having Karl Maka do the acting, producing and writing.

Sam Hui looks tired of it all. Sylvia Chang is a tough cop who's suddenly reduced to a sobbing, defeated housewife in trouble while plump Sally Yeh is wasted as yet another typecast dumb girl in love with the hero.

Partly shot in New Zealand, this production is in keeping with the '80s trend in Cantonese films to shoot abroad for armchair travelers. Despite the huge budget allocated, Cinema City should recoup with the domestic run and international sales. —Mel

Bröderna Mozart
(The Mozart Brothers)
(SWEDISH-COLOR)

A Sandrews release (international sales via Swedish Film Institute/Lena Enquist) of Crescendo and Swedish Film Institute with SR/TV-2 production. Produced by Bengt Forslund (for Swedish Film Institute). Executive producer, Göran Lindström. Directed by Suzanne Osten. Stars Etienne Glaser, Philip Zander. Original story and screenplay, Etienne Glaser, Suzanne Osten, Niklas Radström; camera (Fujicolor), Hans Welin; editor, Lasse Hagström; music, Mozart, Björn J:son Lindh; sound, Claes Engström; production design, Roland Söderberg; costumes, Eva Fenger. Reviewed at the Cinema 1-2-3, Lund, Sweden, March 20, 1986. Running time: 98 MINS.
Stage director .... Etienne Glaser
Rehearsal conductor/
  Mozart's ghost .... Philip Zander
Production designer .... Henry Bronell
Don Giovanni .... Loa Falkman
Donna Elvira .... Agneta Ekmanner
Donna Anna .... Lena T. Hansson
Don Ottavio .... Helge Skoog
The Stone Guest .... Niklas Ek
Mazetto .... Krister S:t Hill
Leporello .... Rune Zetterström
Zerlina .... Grith Fjelmose
Switchboard operator .... Malin Ek
  Also with: Okko Kamu, Anders Claeson, Ana Yrsa Falenius, Henrik Holmberg, Björn Gedda, Amanda Ooms.

Lund — In the footsteps of Milos Forman's "Amadeus" followed "Forget Mozart" from West Germany and "Babel Opera: A Don Juan Rehearsal" from Belgium. Now add Suzanne Osten's feature comedy satire "The Mozart Brothers" to the current Mozartian sweepstakes and watch a winner sure to make it into specialized situations across most borders.

Suzanne Olsen's chosen title refers both to the Marx Brothers' "A Night At The Opera" and to Mozart's ghost appearing, to nod approval, to his brother in the spirit. That's the balding, intense, warmly human, errant-eyed director who has decided, in "The Mozart Brothers," to stand "Don Giovanni" on this revered opera's head, to strip it of its libretto and to strip also the singers of both hair and clothing in favor of colorful rags.

The director (played by film's cowriter Etienne Glaser with gentle strength and cool wit) runs, of course, into trouble with traditional-minded singers as well as with the musicians who are asked to dress up in gaudy costumes, too. Inflated egos have to be soothed. Union regulations have to be flaunted without interference from shop stewards. Old and more recent lovers among the cast have to be flattered and cajoled into going on with rehearsals at all. All along, the Marx Brothers as well as Fellini's "Orchestra Rehearsal" come to mind, but Osten and her players, many of them recruited from the Stockholm Opera, not only appear to have glorious fun themselves, but also succeed in getting the fun "across the boards" in a gently human way.

Two-thirds through the fun, which is visual enough to cover certain verbal obscurities, picture is obviously in need of some kind of an "11 o'clock song" to break what threatens to become repetitions of the same jokes. We are given some brief, but straight renditions of Mozart's music and the opera's main aria instead and are thus maneuvered past the narrative lag. A finale has the entire cast taking curtain calls after a first-night performance that proved successful enough for the cast to take credit for it, ignoring their director completely. It would appear, however, that it was Mozart's music and the opera's essential drama mechanics that once again prevailed over any director's oddball inventions. —Kell.

Douce France
(Gentle France)
(FRENCH-W. GERMAN-COLOR)

A Les Films 2001 production and release. Coproducers, TF1 Films and Anthea Film (Munich). Produced and directed by François Chardeaux. Screenplay, Chardeaux, Serge Schoukine, Michel del Castillo, from a story by Del Castillo; camera (Fujicolor), Jean-Claude Larrieu; editor, Anna Ruiz; original music, Nicolas Skorsky; song lyrics, Vera Baudey; songs performed by Barbara Rudnik; sound, Louis Gimel; production manager, Nicole Flipo. Reviewed at the Empire theater, Paris, March 7, 1985. Running time: 90 MINS.
Lise .... Barbara Rudnik
Mme Maurin .... Andréa Ferreol
Frédéric .... Hito Jaulmes
Karl .... Hanns Zischler
Roland .... Patrick Bouchitey
Jeannot .... Jacques Nolot
Frédéric's mother .... Bernadette Le Sache
Frédéric's grandfather .... Paul Le Person

Paris — "Douce France" tritely chronicles passions in a small town in the south of France, where a beautiful German exile seeks refuge during the German Occupation. Producer-director François Chardeaux adapted a story, inspired by a true incident, by novelist Michel del Castillo and enlisted the author's aid for the script. The results lack psychological and social insight, falling back on the platitudes and facile pathos that plague too many productions about the war years.

German thesp Barbara Rudnik is unconvincing in the principal role of a one-time German Jewish cabaret star who left her homeland for France when Hitler came to power, and must once again flee when the German army invades France's southern "Free Zone" in 1942. Her impresario (Hanns Zischler) finds her room and board in a mountain town where, posing as an Alsacian to hide her true identity, she settles down to wait out the war.

Her beauty, fancy clothes and accent provoke varying responses among the townspeople who begin to nurture suspicions about her as a German spy. Antipathy deepens when it is revealed she is sleeping with a teen-age boy she has befriended. When the region finally is liberated in 1944, Rudnik is cold-bloodedly executed by a local resistance fighter whose sexual advances the German had once rejected.

Rudnik grapples weakly with a role that is poorly limned (why is she careless about leaving her personal belongings around if she is concerned about hiding her true identity?), while her partners fare only a little better in more conventionally motivated parts. Chardeaux' direction keeps the film intimate, but never really renders a specific sense of time, place and circumstance. Lenser Jean-Claude Larrieu's exteriors are often striking, though he seems less at ease with lighting the indoor scenes. Other credits are good.—*Len.*

Killing Cars
(WEST GERMAN-COLOR)

A Sentana Film Production, Munich. Produced, written and directed by Michael Verhoeven. Camera (color), Jacques Steyn; editor, Fred Srp; music, Michael Landau. Reviewed at Berlin Film Market Screening Room, March 6, 1986. Running time: **115 MINS.**

With: Jürgen Prochnow (Ralph Korda), Senta Berger (Marie), Agnes Soral (Violet, Daniel Gélin (Kellermann), Stefan Meinke (Niki), Bernhard Wicki (von der Mühle), Peter Matić (Dr. Hein), Marina Larsen (Dina), William Conrad (Mahoney).

Berlin — Lensed in English with a potpourri of international stage and screen stars, Michael Verhoeven's "Killing Cars" is apparently aiming at some specific market, al-

though it's not quite clear which one. If the Yank commercial mart is in mind, then the confusing narrative line and inept dialog dooms it from the start. If it's the current concept of a Eurofilm that takes priority, then the typical stereotyped tv thriller on view each weekend on German tv is by far a better model for imitation than this one.

"Killing Cars" is a film without any point-of-view. The idea evolves around a new type of worldcar motor that dispenses with gasoline — and thus the oil cartel — in favor of a lightweight accumulator of cellular energy. Chief engineer and playboy is Ralph Korda, whose patent on the worldcar has been provisionally handed over to a Berlin-based motor company in view of mass production as soon as the invention has been properly test-driven and proven commercially viable.

Korda, however, finds himself being tailed by mysterious characters bent on buying his patent. Natch, it's the Arab oil cartel and some unknown big-money bosses that want to wipe the worldcar out before it ever hits the highways. Even the board members of the Berlin motor company have been afflicted by the power play.

Meanwhile, our macho engineer (Jürgen Prochnow) wrestles with his psyche, spends more time rolling in the hay than on the car's development, and finally joins forces with a femme tv-reporter after it's clear that even his chummy office assistant (a rejected flame) and co-workers are part of the plot to do him in. The twist in the end has punk hoodlums stealing the car for a spin of their own around town, which means that Korda has to track down his own car while dodging hitmen sent to rub him out.

At the close our hero is in Gotham and more in the spider's web than ever before. —*Holl.*

Silent Love
(HONG KONG-COLOR)

A D&B production and release. Executive producer, Dickson Poon. Directed by David Chiang. Stars Season Ma, Lau Ching Wan; music, Lam. (No other credits provided by the producers.) Reviewed at Jade Theater, Hong Kong, March 8, 1986. Running time: **98 MINS.**
(Cantonese soundtrack with English subtitles)

Hong Kong — Sadly, the desire to create a sensitive film about physical disability in a modern society did not succeed in "Silent Love."

Ah Yeung (Season Ma) who is plain dumb but not deaf is the leader of a gang of deaf and dumb pickpockets operating in the Causeway Bay area. They live on a houseboat located at the Typhoon Shelter, next to the Royal Hong Kong Yacht Club with four of her comrades.

Yeung and her gangmates encounter Kee, an angry young man just released from prison after eight years. Their friendship and his platonic involvement with Ah Yeung create complications with another gang of young gangsters. Violence, revenge, bloodshed, physical attacks, and deaths occur as the competing groups try to dominate each other.

In the process, the possibilities of serious high drama are waylaid by director David Chiang. Petite lead star Season Ma (superb in "Boat People") has learned sign language. She is effective in silence and her brooding final sequence shows her ability to portray vulnerability and inner strength.

The touching final sequence and Season Ma's non-verbal interpretation of singer Lam's pop song "Needing You Every Moment" are the only high points in this self-defeating endeavor.

"Silent Love" is the type of ambitious low-budget production that should be tried again. Maybe they will get it right next time. —*Mel.*

Very Close Quarters
(COLOR)

Unfunny sex comedy.

A Cable Star Ltd. production. Executive producers-produced by Harold Sobel, Jack Bean. Directed by Vladimir Rif. Stars Shelley Winters, Paul Sorvino, Theodore Bikel, Farley Granger. Screenplay, Rif; additional material, Dennis Pearlstein; camera (Guffanti color), Mikhail Suslov; editor, Lorenzo Marinelli, Rudolph Marinelli; music, Jay Chattaway; sound, Michael Lonsdale; production design, Mikhail Fishgoit; art direction, Hilda Stark; assistant director, Kato Wittich; casting, Leonard Peters. Reviewed on Vestron Video vidcassette, N.Y., March 9, 1986. (MPAA Rating: R.) Running time: **101 MINS.**

Galina	Shelley Winters
Kiril	Paul Sorvino
Victor	Theodore Bikel
Pavel	Farley Granger
Vera	Lee Taylor Allen
Luda	Ellen Barber
Vadik	Frederick Allen
Alex	Dennis Boutsikaris
Irina	Kathleen Doyle

"Very Close Quarters" is a hopelessly unfunny sex comedy filmed in 1983 under the title "The Communal Flat." With no conceivable audience in mind, picture has ended up as a direct to homevideo release by default.

Resembling an off-Broadway play on film rather than a feature, episodic pic is unconvincingly set in a communal flat in Moscow, with 31 inhabitants sharing one kitchen and one toilet. This hoary format gives rise to various slapstick gags and lack of privacy mishaps that seem better suited to a youthful "Porky's" comedy than an ethnic piece.

In place of a developing storyline, writer-director Vladimir Rif

substitutes vignettes which are barely knitted together. Main thrust has unwed mother Galina (Shelley Winters) trying to get her pretty daughter Vera (Lee Taylor Allen) married to Vera's prosperous boss Kiril (Paul Sorvino in a tiresome drunk routine). Young hero Vadik (Frederick Allen) has a crush on Vera, while Vera pretends to be having a lesbian relationship with artist neighbor Luda (Ellen Barber), just to bug the nosy neighbors.

Corny dialog is mainly vulgar, American vernacular and film never develops any Russian atmosphere (except for Theodore Bikel, the cast relies on neutral American accents). The wafer-thin characters are generally overacted, with declamatory, theatrical thesping. Unlike Jean-Charles Tacchella's successful recent apartment house comedy-drama "Staircase C," Rif has not solved the problem of the claustrophobic premise — all scenes except a final tracking shot take place inside the crowded place.—*Lor.*

Lien de Parenté
(Next Of Kin)
(FRENCH-COLOR)

A Les Film de la Rochelle release of a Plaisance Presentations/Plaisance Prods. production. Produced by Daniel Vaissaire. Directed by Willy Rameau. Stars Jean Marais. Screenplay, Rameau, Jean-Pierre Rumeau, Didier Kaminka, based on the novel, "Next Of Kin" by Oliver Lang; camera (Panavision, Fujicolor), Jimmy Glasberg; editor, Delphine Desfons; music, Bruno Coulais; sound, Michel Brethez; art direction, Benedict Beaugé; production manager, Daniel Vaissaire; assistant director, Sonia Cauvin. Reviewed at the Ponthieu screening room, Paris, March 13, 1986. Running time: **97 MINS.**

Victor Blaise	Jean Marais
Clem	Serge Ubrette
Patricia Guérin	Anouk Ferjac
Philippe Guérin	Roland Dubillard
Cécile	Diane Nierderman

Also with: Charles Millot, Michel Amphoux, Bernard Farcy, Ivan Romeuf, Marie Palmieri, Giselle Touret, Jane Watts.

Paris — Jean Marais, the French screen's most popular romantic leading man back in the 1940s and 1950s, tries for a full-fledged comeback in this hokey first feature by Willy Rameau, a 38-year-old West Indian-born assistant director and production manager, who has adapted an English-language novel by Oliver Lang.

Story bears a superficial resemblance to Claude Berri's 1966 film "Le Vieil Homme et l'Enfant" (The Two Of Us) in which Michel Simon had one of his best-remembered late career roles as a bigoted peasant who is given the care of a young Jewish boy during the German Occupation of France. Here Marais, now 72, and long absent from films (except for a cameo in Jacques Demy's "Parking," meant as a tribute to the star's mentor, Jean Cocteau) is a similarly crotchety and insufferable hick who agrees to take charge of the offspring of his long estranged and recently-deceased ne'er-do-well son. His grandson, whom he must fetch in London, is a delinquent — and mulatto.

One can imagine the problems that arise from this meeting of dissimilar mentalities and cultures. Rameau and his coscripters, see it all much too caricaturally, with the arrogant brash young black (played with stereotypical fervor by Serge Ubrette) not only worming his way noisily into his granddad's heart but also seducing the town's sexpot and standing up to the intolerant rage of the latter's boyfriend and his roughneck pals, who mysteriously cool down into alcoholic stupor later on.

Marais does a pretty hammy job himself as the irascible but goodhearted rube who finally realizes he needs his weird grandson to fill the loneliness of his old age and replace the son with whom he never got along.

Rameau allows just about everybody else in the cast to overact, which is suited to the emphatic direction. Best "performance" however is that of lenser Jimmy Glasberg, whose photography here is superb.—*Len.*

Il Bi e il Ba
(The Bi And The Ba)
(ITALIAN-COLOR)

A Medusa release of a San Francisco Film — New Team production. Produced by Giovanni Bertolucci and Nicola Carraro, with the collaboration of RAI-TV Channel 1. Directed by Maurizio Nichetti. Stars Nino Frassica. Screenplay, Nichetti, Frassica, Daniela Conti, Silvia Napolitano; camera (Telecolor), Cristiano Pogany; editor, Fiorenza Muller; music, Detto Mariano. Reviewed at Ariston theater, Rome, Italy, March 14, 1986. Running time: **89 MINS.**
Antonino . . . . Nino Frassica
Also with: Maria Giovanna Elmi (herself).

Rome — "The Bi And The Ba" is a surprisingly lightweight entry by director Maurizio Nichetti, whose "Ratataplan" was a memorable event at the 1979 Venice film festival. It is the first feature in which the helmer-mime doesn't appear before the cameras. Instead pic celebrates the art of tv comic Nino Frassica, a far less sophisticated funnyman.

Were it not for a few faint echoes of silent film comedy (Nichetti's trademark), this would appear to be a wholly Frassica film. The Afro-haired actor's schtick is malapropisms, mangling the Italian language until a word comes out as something close to, but not quite, what it should be. Thus we hear that an expensive item costs "a gastronomic sum," and learn of a cousin who bought a refrigerator in "18 episodes." There is also a lot of mistaken endings to words, calling men

"Signora," and so forth. Most gleeful laughter comes from younger kids, for whom this kind of linguistic contortion is new and hilarious. Needless to say, the film has little chance of surviving subtitles or dubbing. As a purely local product, it has opened strongly.

Storyline follows Frassica's hallowed tv (and now book) tradition: a supremely self-confident hick from a Sicilian town convinces his amazingly gullible pals to finance a trip to Rome, to look for a cure for dandruff from a mystic seer. In the capital, he passes through every type of misadventure unharmed, never noticing he was even in danger. This sort of cartoon fantasy also helps film center in on kiddie market. It is lensed haphazardly, but usually with a bright-colored, busy background. Italy's favorite tv announcer, Maria Giovanna Elmi, appears in a cameo as herself, which may represent the involvement of RAI-TV in the film. — *Yung.*

Sonnensucher
(Sun Searchers)
(EAST GERMAN-B&W)

A DEFA Film Production, East Berlin; world rights, DEFA Aussenhandel, East Berlin. Directed by Konrad Wolf. Screenplay, Karl Georg Egel, Paul Wiens; camera (b&w), Werner Bergmann; music, Joachim Werzlau; sets, Karl Schneider. Reviewed at DEFA Screening Room, East Berlin, March 6, 1986. Running time: **115 MINS.**
With: Ulrike Germer (Lutz), Günther Simon (Franz Beier), Erwin Geschonneck (Jupp König), Victor Avdyushko, Vladimir Yemelyanov, Willi Schrade, Manja Behrens, Norbert Christian, Erich Franz, Brigitte Krause.

Berlin — Konrad Wolf's "Sun Searchers" (1958) waited 14 years for general release in both East and West German cinemas and tv airings. Following Wolf's death in 1982 at the age of 57, the pic has been revived in both Germanys as a tribute to one of the major postwar directorial figures.

The film was originally banned by the East German authorities for the apparent reason that too much emphasis was placed on the Soviet drive for the mining of uranium in the midst of the Cold War. Since uranium equals atom bombs in most chemistry primers, it was then felt that such a film theme need not be duly exploited in such a way that propagandists in the West could make hay while the sun shined.

To be sure, "Sun Searchers" (as the title suggests) does deal with Soviets' frantic priority to catch up with the West in the atom bomb race (or at least the processing of uranium). But the young director Konrad Wolf had other things well in mind in telling this story of outsiders in East Germany struggling to find their places in a new socialist

society. Nearly all of the central figures are losers: a young girl pawed by too-friendly males on work shifts, a one-armed brigade leader sour over his wartime misfortune, a circus figure who contantly gets into quarrels in local pubs, a sadder-but-wiser barmaid whose whole life has been catering to the weaknesses of the stronger sex, and so on.

Seldom has a feature film produced in Eastern Europe presented so many interesting full-dimensional characters, even though the general framework of the project has the schematic rules of Socialist Realism written all over it. Konrad Wolf apparently hoped to make a feature much in the line of Soviet "realist" films produced in the early 1930s — indeed, his Russian commissar officer appears to be modeled after the similar figure in Sergei and Georgy Vasiliev's Soviet classic "Chapayev" (1934), a human being first and a bloodless military leader second.

More important, the description of working in mines in the reconstruction period of the 1950s presents a hard case against the East German economy amid forecasts of better times to come in the future. Everywhere the protagonists turn in "Sun Searchers," their ways seem to be lined with thorns and other evident obstacles. The Germans don't really trust the Russian commandants, and there's not a common bond of unity felt until the tragedy strikes in the mine towards the end. The figures all try to understand each other as they go along from one deterring barrier to another. Wolf, in other words, appears to be throwing his theme open for pro and con dialog.

Pic may be too dated to find its way into art houses, but it does deserve festival and archive exposure as one of the more forthright and challenging films made in both East Germany and Eastern Europe in the late 1950s. —*Holl.*

Rosa Luxemburg
(WEST GERMAN-COLOR)

A Bioskop Film production, Munich, in coproduction with Pro-ject Film im Filmverlag der Autoren, Munich, Regina Ziegler Film, Berlin, Bären Film, and Westdeutscher Rundfunk (WDR), Cologne. Produced by Eberhard Junkersdorf; WDR-TV producer, Martin Wiebel. Written and directed by Margarethe von Trotta. Camera (color), Franz Rath; editor, Dagmar Hirtz; music, Nicolas Economou; sets, Bernd Lepel, Karel Vacek; sound, Christian Moldt, Hellmut Röttgen. Reviewed at Cinema Paris, Berlin, March 24, 1986. Running time: **122 MINS.**
Rosa Luxemburg . . . . Barbara Sukowa
Leo Jogiches . . . . Daniel Olbrychski
Karl Liebknecht . . . . Otto Sander
Luise Kautsky . . . . Adelheid Arndt
Karl Kautsky . . . . Jürgen Holtz
Clara Zetkin . . . . Doris Schade
Kostja Zetkin . . . . Hannes Jaenicke
August Bebel . . . . Jan-Paul Biczycki
Mathilde Jacob . . . . Karin Baal
Paul Levi . . . . Winfried Glatzeder
Gertrud . . . . Regina Lemnitz
Rosa's Mother . . . . Barbara Lass
Rosa, Age 6 . . . . Dagna Drozdek

Berlin — Headed for Cannes as a likely West German entry in the competition, Margarethe von Trotta's "Rosa Luxemburg" measures up as a frontrunner in the Riviera sweepstakes and scores as von Trotta's most balanced film to date. One might expect that after she took over the project upon the untimely death of Rainer Werner Fassbinder, the costly production might turn out to be another of her ardent pleas for women's lib today. Far from being so, this is essentially a fiction documentary based on several key letters of the roughly 2,500 written by the prolific propagandist and intellectual leader of the left wing of the German Socialists known as "Spartacus" (forerunner, too, of the German Communist Party).

Films about revolutionary figures and other historical personalities have been on the increase: John Reed was the subject of Warren Beatty's "Reds" and Sergei Bondarchuk's two-part epic, while "Colonel Redl" by Istvan Szabo was in the running at last year's Cannes fest.

All the same, the raw difficulty of approaching an almost legendary revolutionary figure should not be underestimated. No matter how von Trotta made "Rosa Luxemburg," critical voices would be raised to discount either the factual side or the fictional narrative line. She appears to have taken the middle course: the letters bring a chronological sweep to the film, while at the same time introducing a maze of characters that belonged not only to her political circle but also numbered among her intimate friends.

The key historical figures number: Karl Liebknecht, with whom she was brutally murdered on the night of Jan. 15, 1919 and her body dumped in the Landwehrkanal in Berlin; Leo Jogiches, a Polish Jewish compatriot with whom she had an on-again, off-again affair since her student days in Zurich exile; Karl and Luise Kautsky, the former a former private secretary of Friedrich Engels and chief ideologist of the Marxist movement in the German Socialist Party and the latter a close friend and biographer of Rosa Luxemburg; Clara Zetkin, an older acquaintance and leader in the women's lib movement who co-founded the ''Spartakus'' group; and Kostya Zetkin, Clara's son who had an affair with Rosa and whose figure in the film is joined to that of another young lover (Hans Diefenbach, who died on the front in World War I).

Other historical figures — August Bebel, Mathilde Jacob, Paul Levi — pass through the crowd scenes on the edges of the main action. They are important to support the underpinnings of the documentary frame.

Rosa Luxemburg spent months of her life in prison, and it's in the Warsaw Citadel that the film opens. She left her job as editor of the Socialist newspaper ''Vorwärts'' in Berlin to help pave the way in 1905 for the first failed Russian Revolution. Back in Germany (1906), she spends more time in jail and then tours Europe tirelessly to support Socialist and Marxist movements in London, Basel, Copenhagen, and throughout Germany. It's the opening scene in the Polish prison, during which she is treated to a mock execution while other Polish revolutionaries are murdered about her, that sets the tone for the film — and underscores von Trotta's directorial finesse as narrative storyteller. This sequence, plus the final murder episode at the end, are the major highlights of ''Rosa Luxemburg.''

What comes in between, however, is difficult to sort out. A clear portrait of Rosa Luxemburg is lacking: we see her mostly as a fragile and peace-loving woman, a standpoint that may be appropriately filmic in a fiction story but oddly out-of-place in a fiction documentary and contrary to most historical opinion. Further, without a definitive stand on Luxemburg's role in history, it's hard to understand just what motivates her actions among friends and colleagues on multiple occasions. Yet von Trotta's intentions may have been only to whet the audience's appetite to go to the letters and books via a film sketch of one of the most dynamic women in modern European history.

Barbara Sukowa as Rosa Luxemburg is outstanding among many fine performances in impersonating the character of a frail and worn-out revolutionary. Indeed, during the three long years of political imprisonment during World War I (she took a pacifist position), she appropriately ages and grows in dignity and self-assurance through her theoretical writings and by calling on her last reserves of inner strength.

Without her performance, the entire project might have caved in like a house of cards.

Another major plus is Franz Rath's lensing, particularly in its application of the innovative color-bleaching lab process whereby the historical turn-of-the-century atmosphere is conveyed in muted colors hinting of the impending catastrophic war and its bloody street-fighting aftermath. By contrast, the musical score is rather silly and redundant in an apparent losing attempt to spice up the mass scenes.

''Rosa Luxemburg'' will be liked by film buffs and history fans, but the public will grow more than a bit weary through the two-hour talk marathon. Fest laurels would help considerably. —*Holl.*

The Check Is In The Mail
(COLOR)

Potential contemporary fun film can't get it all together.

An Ascot Entertainment Group release of a Joseph Wolf presentation of a Robert Kaufman-Ted Kotcheff production. Executive producers, Wolf, Simon Tse. Produced by Kaufman, Robert Krause. Directed by Joan Darling. Screenplay, Kaufman; camera (color), Jan Kiesser; music, by David Frank; associate producer, David Wolf. Reviewed at Ranch Mart theater, Kansas City, March 13, 1986. (MPAA Rating: R.) Running time: **91 MINS.**
With: Brian Dennehy, Anne Archer, Hallie Todd, Chris Hebert, Michael Bowen, Nita Talbot, Dick Shawn.

Kansas City — What may have looked on paper as though it had the potential for a film of generous laugh content never gets transferred to the screen in ''The Check Is In The Mail.'' It is somewhat deceiving in that a few sparks of humor and a couple of endearing moments pierce the otherwise draggy, disjointed pace, but on the whole it has to be labeled a lame entry. Boxoffice prospects are slim.

Surprisingly, the film has established actors, Brian Dennehy and Anne Archer in the lead roles. It is probably the first major lead for Dennehy, who has been one of the most sought after actors for major supporting roles and chalked up numerous successes recently. He even manages to sustain some semblance of stature as the besieged California pharmacist in this one. Archer is called upon for little more than being a supporting spouse.

Dennehy and Archer are the parents of three rapidly maturing youngsters, a family which Dennehy is unable to support as troubles rain upon him. A new car is a bucket of bolts, a Hawaiian vacation turns into a ripoff, utility bills cascade upon him. If that isn't enough, a Mafia hit-man is on his trail for (unexplained) huge gambling debts, for which always the check is in the mail. Amidst these assorted pres-

sures, he reasons the system is cheating him and lying to him, and he resolves to fight back by living outside the system. Out come the light bulbs, the telephone line is cut, and gas, water and electric service are discontinued. He digs a well in the back yard, grows vegetables on the front lawn, stocks up on lanterns and other basic supplies. It comes to naught, as the family members are oblivious to the social pressures felt by the father and are stand-offish about opposing the system.

The R rating is on the soft side, likely stemming from a blatant sex scene involving the teenage son with a hospital nurse and a generous supply of bad language. By contrast a brief scene of Dennehy and Archer togther in bed achieves an almost endearing level, possibly traceable to director Joan Darling's background in sitcom tv. Of the several episodes comprising the story, the Hawaiian vacation interlude and the making over of the house into a bastion against the system are vastly overdone, while others are treated so sparingly as to wonder why they are included. Dick Shawn as a friendly neighbor muffs his part in grand style and Nita Talbot as his wife is lost in a bit role.

What might have been a light-hearted, flippant, current comedy turns out to be largely pointless as screen entertainment. —*Quin.*

Lucas
(COLOR)

Winning teen pic.

A 20th Century Fox release of a Lawrence Gordon production. Produced by David Nicksay. Written and directed by David Seltzer. Stars Corey Haim, Kerri Green, Charlie Sheen. Camera (Deluxe color), Reynaldo Villalobos; editor, Priscilla Nedd; additional editing, Scott Conrad; music, Dave Grusin; sound (Dolby), Ray Cymoszinski; art direction, James Murakami; set decoration, Linda Sutton; costume design, Molly Maginnis; associate producer, Kristi Zea; assistant director, David Sosna; casting, Mary Gail Artz; Jane Alderman, Shelley Andreas (Chicago). Reviewed at the 20th Century Fox Studios, L.A., March 21, 1986. (MPAA Rating: PG-13.) Running time: **100 MINS.**
Lucas .... Corey Haim
Maggie..................... Kerri Green
Cappie .... Charlie Sheen
Alise ....Courtney Thorne-Smith
Rina .... Winona Ryder
Bruno ....Thomas E. Hodges
Ben ....Ciro Poppiti
Coach ....Guy Boyd
Spike .... Jeremy Piven
Tonto ....Kevin Gerard Wixted

Hollywood — If Hollywood tried often enough, and God knows it has, it was bound to make a first-class, authentic-feeling teen pic one of these days. So now, at what is said to be the tail end of the comedy trend, we have ''Lucas,'' a soft, ''small'' picture, to be sure, but one of the few films of its ilk of genuine merit. This warm, appealing direc-

torial debut by David Seltzer will certainly generate strong word-of-mouth, but lack of upfront b.o. allure poses a formidable marketing challenge for Fox.

Many of the stock high school ingredients are present here — the jocks who bully the wimps, a girl's first love, the unphysical, four-eyed, nerdy science types, the football players and cheerleaders lording it over the other students — but Seltzer has reinvented these clichés with their original meanings. More impressively, he has systematically refused to indulge in conventional, comforting conclusions, or to ignore the pain that goes along with growing up. ''Lucas'' is charming, but it is also sufficiently realistic to ring true to life.

Simple tale centers upon the title character, a pre-pubescent 14-year-old who has skipped a grade or two and is thus physically way behind most of the other kids in school. During the summer, Lucas meets a cute girl, Maggie, new to the neighborhood, and by September the two are best friends, although ''involved'' only in Lucas' mind.

Once the school year begins, Lucas doesn't have Maggie all to himself anymore, and the bullying and humiliation he routinely receives from some of the muscle men take on new meaning for him when Maggie witnesses it. Good-looking footballer and in-crowd member Cappie protects Lucas from his cohorts' worst assaults, and also begins taking an interest in Maggie, who considers herself entirely available.

The jealousies and hard feelings extend far beyond the threesome to include a cute, shy little girl, who genuinely likes Lucas, and Cappie's golden cheerleader girlfriend, who will brook no competition. Realizing his shortcomings lie in the physical department, the cerebral Lucas resorts to desperately absurd measures to prove his worth, and it is here that Seltzer so refreshingly denies himself the easy way out of conventional heroics and wishful sentimentalizing.

Seltzer's central concern is the essential unfairness of life, especially at that critical moment when the whole world seems to turn on whether certain people, especially members of the opposite sex, like you or not. Despite the enormous sympathy generated for the pint-sized Lucas, who at this stage can't begin to compete with his more mature classmates, Seltzer also manages to expose the character's undue selfishness and self-absorption.

Casting and performances are all ideal, with Corey Haim proving very engaging in the title role, Kerri Green coming across in appealing, offbeat fashion as the girl in the middle, and Charlie Sheen cutting an impressive profile as the sensitive jock. Winona Ryder quietly steals all her scenes as the sweet, studious type who bravely tries to cultivate a relationship with the distracted Lucas.

Attractively lensed by Reynaldo Villalobos in northern Chicago suburbs, pic offers up many points of identification to virtually anyone who went to high school in the U.S. within the last 25 years, and is done in a pleasantly naturalistic style. While hardly earthshaking, pic impressively accomplishes everything it sets out to do, and Seltzer the director here makes Seltzer the writer look better than any other director ever has. —Cart.

Tiempo de Silencio
(Time Of Silence)
(SPANISH-COLOR)

A Lolafilms-Morgana Films production. Executive producer, Carlos Durán. Directed by Vicente Aranda. Screenplay, Aranda and Antonio Rabinat, based on novel by Luis Martin Santos; camera (Eastmancolor), Juan Amorós; editor, Teresa Font; sets, Josep Rosell; costumes, Gumersindo Andres; production manager, Francisco Lara; assistant producer, Oriol Regas. Reviewed at Cine Lope de Vega, Madrid, Spain, March 16, 1986. Running time: 95 MINS.
Pedro . . . . Imanol Arias
Dorita . . . . Victoria Abril
Charo/Mother . . . . Charo López
Muecas . . . . Francisco Rabal
Matías . . . . Juan Echanove
Also with: Francisco Algora, Joaquin Hinojosa, Diana Peñalver, Enriqueta Claver.

Madrid — Three or four topnotch films are produced each year in Spain that can hold their own with the best in other countries. "Tiempo de Silencio" is one of them. Superbly adapting Martin Santos' post-war classic, director Vicente Aranda limns an intriguing tale of love and passion with philosophical overtones that should appeal to discriminating audiences anywhere.

Set in the Franco Madrid of the late 1940s, tale concerns a young man engaged in cancer research who is involuntarily drawn into a sordid affair concerning a girl who dies of an abortion in a shanty-town outside the capital. Pedro tries to do what he can to save the girl's life, but is then wrongly accused by the jealous girl's lover of having aborted the child and killed the mother.

Subplots concern the scientist's friendship with an upper-class friend, with whom he goes carousing, relations with his mother, and his budding romance with a neighbor in the boardinghouse where he lives. Story wonderfully brings out the oppressive feel of those postwar years in Madrid under the shadow of Franco's regime and the yearning for freedom and enlightenment.

Superb thesping from an all-star Spanish cast makes this a truly memorable film, probably the best thing Aranda has ever done, which is saying a lot. Sets effectively capture the mood of those days, and Juan Amorós' crisp lensing plus a script which is literate without being obtrusive all contribute to this topnotch effort.—Besa.

El Amor Brujo
(Bewitched Love)
(SPANISH-COLOR)

An Orion Classics release (U.S.) of an Emiliano Piedra presentation. Produced by Piedra. Directed by Carlos Saura. Screenplay and choreography, Saura, Antonio Gades, based on ballet by Manuel de Falla; camera (Eastmancolor), Teo Escamilla; editor, Pedro del Rey; music, de Falla, with Jesús López Cobos conducting the National Orchestra of Spain; songs sung by Rocio Jurado; sound (Dolby), Daniel Goldstein; sets and costumes, Gerardo Vera; production manager, Emiliano Otegui. Reviewed at Cine Cid Campeador, Madrid, March 21, 1986. (No MPAA Rating.) Running time: 100 MINS.
Carmelo . . . . Antonio Gades
Candela . . . . Cristina Hoyos
Lucia . . . . Laura del Sol
José . . . . Juan Antonio Jiménez
   Cataores: Gómez de Jerez and Manolo Sevilla; guitarists, Antonio Solera, Manuel Rodriguez and Juan Manuel Roldán; also, Emma Penella, La Polaca, Enrique Ortega, Diego Pantoja, Giovana, Candy Román and the Antonio Gades ballet troupe.

Madrid — "El Amor Brujo" is the third of the Carlos Saura-Antonio Gades Spanish dance trilogy, begun with "Blood Wedding" and "Carmen," and is doubtless the most difficult and austere. From the superb, long opening shot, in which the camera takes us from the outside of the Bronston Studios into the elaborate set inside, a reconstruction of a gypsy shantytown on the outskirts of Madrid, to the end of the film, Saura first tells the audience this is a contrived set, scene, and then successfully makes us forget the fact due to topnotch dancing and a superb track sung by Rocio Jurado.

Technically, the dancing is probably better than in "Carmen," and the music is performed impeccably, but neither is the original de Falla score as familiar and stirring as that of Bizet, nor is the choreography in this film as spectacular as its predecessor. Cristina Hoyos who plays the main part is a far better dancer than Laura del Sol, but audiences abroad may find her less attractive than her younger counterpart, who has a far smaller part in the new film.

Saura put in one telling scene, in which Gades is showing Laura del Sol how to do a certain dance step. It is as though he's saying, "Laura is prettier, but less accomplished as a dancer." Gades has choreographed three dances which stand out in this longish film. One is an opening scene of a gypsy marriage ceremony; the second is of a knife fight between two gangs; and the third is the famous "Fire Dance;" but none is as memorable as, say, the tobacco factory number in "Carmen."

Story concerns a couple, Candela and José, who have been bethrothed since childhood. Upon reaching maturity, they are wed, but another gypsy, Carmelo (Gades), has always loved Candela, while José has carried on an affair with a pretty young gypsy, Lucia. A while after the wedding, during a dance, a fight breaks out with some other toughs (the best dance number of the film) and José is killed. Carmelo is accused wrongly of the deed committed by a member of the other gang and is arrested.

When Carmelo returns after four years in jail, he finds Candela is still pining for her late husband. Each night she goes out and meets his ghost and dances with him. Carmelo is told by an old crone that the only way to exorcise José is to confront him with his ex-lover, Lucia. This is done, and Candela finally is freed to marry Carmelo.

Pic can be expected to do good biz in art circuits and with discriminating audiences who can appreciate the artistry of the production and especially the superb music on the soundtrack. — Besa.

Komba Dieu Des Pygmées
(Komba, God Of The Pygmies)
(FRENCH-CENTRAL AFRICAN REPUBLIC-COLOR)

A Ya Films production. Directed by Raymond Adam. Screenplay, Christine Miller; camera (Eastman color), Pierre Dupouey; editor, Nguyen Long, Michel Lavigne; music, Hector Zazou, Angelo Zursolo; sound, Patrick Bordes. Reviewed at Roy and Niuta Titus Theater 2, Museum of Modern Art, N.Y. (in New Directors/New Films series), March 27, 1986. Running time: 90 MINS.
Forester . . . . Didier Sauvegrain
Ekoma . . . . Ekoma
   With: Jacques Besnier, residents of the area around the Sangha River in the Central African Republic.
(In French and indigenous languages with English subtitles)

Filmed in the Central African Republic (part of French Africa during the colonial era), "Komba, God Of The Pygmies" deals with a forest-dwelling pygmy's passage to manhood and his conflict with a feudal social system controlled by French businessmen and African Bantu villagers. In spite of an engaging scenario ostensibly based on "true stories," this pic will appeal mainly to anthropological film buffs, and is best suited for limited runs in those venues that specialize in offbeat and experimental fare.

To put "Komba" into perspective it's important to remember that only a few years ago the location country was named the Central African Empire and ruled by a self-crowned neo-Napoleonic emperor,

Jean Bedel Boukassa, a madman whose bloody reign was notorious for horrifying brutalities that made the Duvaliers look like progressives by comparison.

Although Boukassa was overthrown and exiled, "Komba" suggests that a cruel feudalism, which binds the hunter pygmies to French-speaking African villagers, still survives in the CAR. Director Raymond Adam and scripter Christine Miller take an unabashed "noble savage" view of the pygmies' way of life, captured with fascinating effectiveness by the filmmakers. Organized in communal tribes, the pygmies are spirit-worshiping hunter-gatherers, tracking down game with spears and crossbows and supplementing their diets with fried caterpillars. In return for pathetic payments of pots, pans, grain and cheap liquor they also hunt for the villagers who "own" them but never really control the comings and goings of the nomadic pygmies.

When Ekoma's father is killed by a poison snake after dreaming of serpents, the youth sets off to marry Zaba, a girl from another pygmy tribe who's chattel to a mean-spirited bantu village boss who pitilessly exploits the pygmies under his control. This African is also the link between the pygmies and a forester for the French-owned lumber mill (Didier Sauvegrain) who retains a group of the little guys as guides for a deep forest expedition in search of fellable trees.

Though they're treated with contempt and condescension by their black and white masters, the pygmies are masters of the forest, a lesson learned by the Frenchman when he's suddenly abandoned deep in the jungle. In return for saving the white man's life, Ekoma gets a beatbox portable radio, a big cash reward and a job at the lumber mill. Things start looking up for the plucky pygmy and his pregnant wife.

However, his success is bitterly resented by the villagers who accuse him of sorcery and precipitate a bloody denouement that's in keeping with the pic's theme of pygmy life as a fight for survival against stacked odds.

The pygmies in "Komba" are remarkably natural on camera and the filmmakers obviously achieved a trusting rapport with this childlike but extremely resourceful people whose oral literature and indigenous religion based on a creator deity reflect an ancient culture untouched by the outside world. Their very survival into the nuclear-digital-space age is a minor miracle that the film documents with intimate clarity.
—Rich.

37°2 Le Matin
(Betty Blue)
(FRENCH-COLOR)

A Gaumont release of a Constellation-Cargo Films coproduction. Produced by Claudie Ossard. Written and directed by Jean-Jacques Beineix, from the novel by Philippe Djian. Camera (Fujicolor), Jean-François Robin; editor, Monique Prim; music, Gabriel Yared; sound, Pierre Befve; art direction, Carlos Conti; costumes, Elisabeth Tavernier; makeup, Judith Gayo; assistant director, Jean-François Chaintron; production manager, Volker Lemke; casting, Dominique Besnehard. Reviewed at the Gaumont screening room, Neuilly, March 27, 1986. Running time: **120 MINS.**
Betty . . . . Béatrice Dalle
Zorg . . . . Jean-Hugues Anglade
Lisa . . . . Consuela de Haviland
Eddy . . . . Gérard Darmon
Annie . . . . Clémentine Celarié
Bob . . . . Jacques Mathou
Bungalow owner . . . . Claude Confortes
Publisher . . . . Philippe Laudenbach
Also with: Vincent Lindon, Raoul Billeray, Claude Aufaure, André Julien, Nathalie Dalyan, Louis Bellanti, Bernard Robin, Nicolas Jalowyz, Dominique Besnehard.

Paris — Though the artiness is not quite gone, there's a sense of dramatic purpose and intensity in "Betty Blue" that was missing in Jean-Jacques Beineix' first two films, in which the decorative and photographic aspects were predominant. Most of all there is the heat generated by its lead performers, Jean-Hugues Anglade and newcomer Béatrice Dalle, that gives Beineix' film a human conviction one searched for in vain ami the studio artifices of "The Moon In The Gutter" and the playfulness of "Diva."

Beineix has adapted a novel by Philippe Djian, considered here as an *enfant terrible* of the new literary generation. It's another feverish tale of *amour fou* and Beineix has used some of the writer's own first-person text as the male protagonist's voice-over commentary in the film.

Film begins with the animal attraction between Zorg, a young man living off odd jobs in a coastal bungalow colony, and Betty, a waitress who quits her job to move in with her new lover. The carnal links soon deepen into stronger bonds, particularly for Betty, who comes across a stashed-away manuscript that reveals Zorg's long-suppressed literary ambitions. She declares Zorg an undiscovered genius who is wasting away in demeaning labors and burns down their bungalow to precipitate their departure for Paris.

They move into a suburban house shared by a girl friend of Betty's (Consuela de Haviland) and her mate (Gérard Darmon), who gives them work as waiters in his pizzeria. Betty types up Zorg's manuscript and sends it off to numerous publishers, but what little response there is is negative.

The disappointment incites them to accept an offer from Darmon, who needs someone to take over the provincial apartment and piano store of his just-deceased mother. They try to settle down, but Betty's failed pregnancy and her unrealized hopes of stability push her into madness. She tears out her eye, is committed to a hospital and declared incurable by the doctors. Zorg slips into her room one night to save her, and (in a scene reminiscent of "One Flew Over The Cuckoo's Nest") smothers her with a pillow.

Though Beineix hasn't abandoned his esthetic preoccupations (notable here in the preponderant use of primary colors in clothing and decors, with the blues finally taking priority), he has concentrated on his two actors, who are extraordinarily genuine. Béatrice Dalle, a model, makes a moving debut as the desperate baby-doll who fails to mold reality to her own conceptions of happiness. Jean-Hugues Anglade, who played the rollerskating thief in Luc Besson's "Subway," is more introvertedly affecting as the lucidly casual, but devoted Zorg. (Anglade also merits the Gérard Depardieu Male Nudity Prize since he pads around entirely naked for many scenes, as Depardieu first started doing in Marco Ferreri's "The Last Woman.")

Secondary parts, like Darmon's risible restaurateur, who wears a pornographic tie to his mother's funeral, or Clementine Celarié's sexually frustrated village grocer's wife, who vainly propositions Anglade, are more conventionally conceived to set off the main characters by their comic mediocrity, but Beineix' hand with humor is often heavy.

Jean-François Robin's lensing, Carlos Conti's art direction and Gabriel Yared's music all contribute vividly to Beineix' dramatic design.

Gaumont is distributing in France, while 20th Century Fox Intl. will release in all markets except U.S., Canada and French-speaking territories. It could bring Beineix back the audience he alienated with "Moon In The Gutter." —*Len.*

Comic Magazine
(Komikku Zasshi Nanka Irani)
(JAPANESE-COLOR)

A New Century Producers production. Produced by Yutaka Okada. Directed by Yojiro Takita. Stars Yuya Uchida. Screenplay, Uchida, Isao Takagi; camera (color), Yoichi Shiga; editor, Masatsugi Kanazawa; music, Katsuo Ono. Reviewed at Lorimar screening room (in New Director/New Films series) N.Y., March 24, 1986. Running time: **120 MINS.**
Kinameri . . . . Yuya Uchida
Also with: Yumi Asou, Beat Takeshi, Hiromi Go, Yoshio Harada, Taiji Tonoyama, Masahiro Kuwana, Rikiya Yasuoka, Tsurutaro Kataoka, Daisuke Shima and Kazuyoshi Miura.

The vitality and excesses of the current Japanese "new wave" cinema are on display in this mordant satirical drama about a tv gossip reporter's quest for self-respect in a society obsessed with scandal. Using the most sensational Japanese news stories of 1985 as its backdrop, "Comic Magazine" is a wicked sendup of contemporary Japanese junk-culture, electronic pack-journalism and the success-at-all-costs ethos that drives its professional classes. It should be one of the most provocative pics to emerge from the 15th New Directors/New Films series where it's making its U.S. debut.

Kinameri (Yuya Uchida) makes his living tailing celebrities through Narita airport or camping on their doorsteps in the hope of gathering crumbs of gossip for his nightly report on a tv news show. He endures insult, humiliation and an occasional roughing-up in order to hold his own in the frantic, competitive world of Japanese showbiz reporting. "Go after scandals and keep pushing hard," Kinameri's editor commands, and the stone-faced reporter obeys with a compulsive persistence that spoofs the Japanese fear of failure.

He barges into the businessplace of a man suspected of a sensational wife murder (Kazuyoshi Miura, now under arrest, plays himself in a typically bizarre touch), noses around into the affairs of warring Japanese mafiosos, the Yakuza (real gangsters are used), tries to crash the (real) wedding of girl pop idol Seiko Matsuda and is punched-out for his trouble and brazenly intrudes with tactless questions into the funeral of a murdered teenage prostitute. When he's arrested for trespassing at a singer's home, Kinameri is moved to "eyewitness" reporter, investigating sex clubs, porn films and illegal immigrants.

These goings-on give director Yojiro Takita and Uchida ample opportunity to lampoon contemporary Japanese society and the double standard which both worships and disdains showbiz idols. Through pacing and camera perspectives that evoke a jittery comic-surreal feeling, the filmmakers effectively present events from the reporter's steadily disintegrating viewpoint. Played by Uchida with laconic stoicism, Kinameri's life fragments under the pressures of his directionless but all-consuming ambition. Scorned by his friends, abandoned by his wife, Kinameri's one refuge is his hotly depicted affair with a popular model (Yumi Asou), and even that is ironically turned against him when a photo spread of one of their dates appears in a pulp magazine.

His self-redemption comes at the biggest story of the year: the internationally reported "tv murder" of a fraudulent gold dealer who was stabbed to death in Tokyo as crowds of newspeople stood by and recorded the event. The film's dramatic revision of the bloody killing is followed by Kinamera's ultimate transgression — the rejection of all things Japanese.

Camerawork by Yoichi Shiga presents an imaginative, disjointed view of the oft-photographed Tokyo cityscape, and helps carry the film through stretches that might have been compressed. Although the presence of some of Japan's rock 'n' roll elite (Uchida, Beat Takeshi and Hiromi Go) will mean little to Western audiences, the film's dark humor and "real events" hook could make "Comic Magazine" a sleeper with the young, hip art house crowd here if properly handled by the right distributor. Gotham-based Kuzui Enterprises is repping the pic.—*Rich.*

Maine-Ocean
(Maine-Ocean Express)
(FRENCH-COLOR)

An AAA Classic release of a Films du Passage-French Line-FR3 coproduction, with the participation of the Ministry of Culture (CNC). Produced by Paolo Branco. Directed and edited by Jacques Rozier. Screenplay, Lydia Feld, Rozier; camera (Eastmancolor), Acacio de Almeida; music, Chico Buarque, Hubert Dege, Anne Frédéric; sound, Nicolas Lefebvre, production manager, Danièle Behara. Reviewed at the Club de l'Etoile, Paris, March 20, 1986. Running time: **132 MINS.**
Le Garrec . . . . Bernard Menez
Pontoiseau . . . . Luis Rego
Lawyer . . . . Lydia Feld
Dejanina . . . . Rosa-Maria Gomez
The judge . . . . Bernard Dumaine
Impresario . . . . Pedro Armendariz Jr.
A lawyer . . . . Mike Marshall
The sailor . . . . Yves Afonso

Paris — "Maine-Océan" is a self-indulgent, ludicrously overlong comeback by Jacques Rozier, a fringe New Wave figure whose debut feature "Adieu Philippine" (1962) was highly praised for its free-wheeling style, charm and naturalness. Rozier has made only two other films since, the last one a decade ago, and has finally been able to make this film thanks to producer Paolo Branco. It could have been a delightful medium-length film, but "Maine-Océan" goes nowhere, and takes well over two hours to get there. Significantly Rozier is credited as co-author, director and editor, which typifies *auteur* filmmaking at its most wastefully undisciplined.

There is no plot or theme, just a number of characters from differing backgrounds who happen to fall in together in a series of loosely constructed sequences. Rozier is apparently interested in dissimilar personages and the way fate brings them together and separates them, but these folks, caricatures for the most part, overstay their welcome. Their adventures eventually try the viewer's patience.

Pic starts on a Britanny-bound train from Paris (the "Maine-Océan" express) where a pair of ticket-inspectors come across a Brazilian samba dancer and a young woman lawyer. Latter is on her way to defend a sailor on an assault and battery charge, but she bungles the defense. Circumstances soon bring everybody together on a Brittany island, where a showbiz impresario shows up. There is an improvised samba rehearsal in a dance hall. One of the ticket inspectors is offered a contract for a show, then just as suddenly dropped as the others pile into a plane for the States.

The first part of the film entertains in a zany sketch-like manner, notably in the frustrated attempts of the ticket inspectors (Bernard Menez and Luis Rego) to communicate with the Brazilian girl (Rosa-Maria Gomez), and especially in the courtroom scene in which the lawyer (Lydia Feld, who co-scripted) and her client (Yves Afonso) both make hilarious incoherent pleas. Unfortunately after that the action plods on vacuously to an obsessively protracted finale, in which for no apparent reason we follow the hapless Menez' attempts to get back to the mainland after the others abandon him.

Pic was handsomely lensed by the Portuguese Acacio de Almeida; and Chico Buarque, the popular Latin composer, is on the music credits.

"Maine-Océan" just won the 1986 Jean Vigo prize. —Len.

Secvente
(Sequences)
(RUMANIAN-COLOR)

A Romaniafilm (Bucharest) production. Written and directed by Alexandru Tatos. Camera (color), Florin Mihăilescu; editor, Iulia Vincenz; art direction, Nicolae Schiopu, Andrei Both; costumes, Svetlana Mihăilescu, Andreea Haznas. Reviewed at Museum of Modern Art, N.Y. (in New Directors/New Films series), March 26, 1986. Running time: 98 MINS.

With: Geo Barton, Ion Vîlcu, Emilia Dobrin- Besoiu, Mircea Diaconu, Dragos Pîslaru, Alexandru Tatos, Florin Mihailescu.

"Sequences" is a film whose parts are greater than their sum: a film with three sequences that substitute for a beginning, a middle and an end. Western audiences accustomed to plot continuity will be put off by its lack of structure. However, the film's final section focuses on a fascinating situation that in itself could have been expanded into another, far more interesting, film.

We are presented with a situation similar to François Truffaut's "Day For Night," as a Rumanian film crew is shown dividing its time between making films for the State on the benefits of Communism and shooting scenes for their own narrative film.

This promising opening is quickly sidetracked when the family-like troupe of filmmakers, which include a producer, director, actress, actor, script girl and other related jobs, stop at a roadside restaurant while scouting locations. A long sequence follows with the only result being the filmmakers' joke of passing the producer off as a prosecutor (to get good food from the dimwitted proprietor) backfires when he gets chummy with the crew and spills out the depressing details of his life.

Action abruptly shifts to a studio where one gathers the crew is now working on their 'real' film entitled "Happiness." Focus here is on two elderly male extras paired at a table in a restaurant shot as background for a climactic scene. One extra gradually recognizes the other as his torturer from a World War II concentration camp. The sequence, which runs the last third of the picture, is riveting, memorable and bears little connection to the action preceding it.

Writer-director Alexandru Tatos makes liberal use of shooting point-of-views through other cameras as a rather heavyhanded device to underline the art-versus-reality theme of "Sequences." Tech credits are average, while pic's subtitling is spotty and at times confusing.
—Roy.

Por Un Vestido De Novia
(All Because Of A Wedding Dress)
(MEXICAN-COLOR)

A Peliculas Mexicanas release of a Producciones Potosl production. Directed by Arturo Martínez. Based on song and original story by Vicente Fernández. Camera (color), Augustin Lara; music, Luis Arcaráz. Reviewed at Cine Sonora, Mexico City, Feb. 10, 1986. Running time: 86 MINS.

Reynaldo . . . . .Pedro Infante Jr.
Lauro . . . . .Arturo Martínez Jr.
Marsela . . . . .Mónica Prado
Don Rafael Garza . . . . .Víctor Alcocer
Bertha . . . . .Socorro Bonilla
Mother . . . . .Ana Luisa Petuffo
    Also with: Rodolfo de Anda, Juan Gallardo, Humberto Elizondo, Bruno Rey and Paty Maldonado.

Mexico City — The cheapo Mexican production "All Because Of A Wedding Dress" is a grab-bag of diverse scenes that never come together.

Tale, told in retrospect, concerns a duel fought by best buddies Reynado (Pedro Infante Jr.) and Lauro (Arturo Martínez Jr.) over the disagreeable, money-grubbing, social-climber Marsela (Mónica Prado).

Inserted in an overlong secondary story about a gang of bad guys who must be hunted down and killed one by one.

The gang's appearance does not distract from some of the more obvious holes in the script, such as the fact that Marsela refused to marry her beloved Lauro because she wanted a large wedding held in Mexico City's Basilica of Guadalupe, whereas her wedding to Reynaldo is set to take place at the local town church.

The proposed wedding ceremony is interrupted by the gunfight in which the heroes mortally wound each other, while the pending bride can only watch in horror.

Hokey emphasis is placed on the two friends managing to crawl towards each other and their hands meeting mid-screen as they utter their final gasps, making it seem they would have been much happier married to each other than the ungrateful Marsela.

This horse opera's only real interest stems from the sympathetic characterizations of pic's leads, Infante and Martínez, and in the naive exploitation of a Mexican folk theme. —Lent.

Mama is boos!
(Mama Is Mad!)
(DUTCH-COLOR)

A Meteor Film/The Movies release of a Movies Film Prods. production. Produced by Chris Brouwer, Haig Balian. Directed by Ruud van Hemert. Screenplay, van Hemert; camera (Eastman), Theo van de Sande; editor, Wim Louwriter; music, van Hemert; sound, Georges Bossaers, Paul Veld; art direction, Jan Blokker, Dirk Debou, Dorus van der Linden; assistant director, Pieter Walther Boer; production manager, Arnold Heslenfeld; special effects, Harry Wiessenhaan, Leo Cahn. Reviewed at Bellevue Theater, Amsterdam, Holland, March 19, 1986. Running time: 110 MINS.

John Gisberts . . . . .Peter Faber
Danny Gisberts . . . . .Geert de Jong
Jan-Julius Gisberts . . .Sanne van der Noort
Valentijn Gisberts . . . .Alexander Mouissie
Pete Stewart . . . . .Rijk de Gooyer
Jane Fongler . . . . .Adelheid Roosen

Amsterdam — A sequel to helmer Ruud van Hemert's feature debut "Schatjes" (Darlings) (a cash bonanza which saw 10% of the total Dutch population buying tickets, and Warner Bros. picking up world rights), "Mama Is Mad!" should amass plenty of coin, though perhaps somewhat less than the first pic.

"Schatjes" told of guerilla warfare between flying officer John Gisberts (Peter Faber), his wife Danny (Geert de Jong), and their two eldest children. Now the kids have left home, and "Mama" is the story of a battle royal between the parents, with the two younger boys as spectators and pawns.

Papa has a girlfriend, while mama has a temper. Smashed furniture, assault and battery, divorce proceedings, kidnaping — it's all there. Helmer keeps up a furious pace so spectators have no time to wonder about logic. Mama's mayhem ends during the great finale to a sumptuous entertainment put on at papa's airbase (with him as the star), to mark the NATO jubilee of 1989, the capping absurdity of the film.

The charm of "Darlings" was the ingenuity with which the teenagers perpetrated their diabolical pranks. The fun in "Mama" comes from the exaggerated reactions of the characters to more or less normal problems, and also from van Hemert's satirical investigation if a crowd of yuppies.

Geert de Jong in the "impossible" part of frenentic avenger, and Peter Faber (very impressive through movements and gestures) are excellent. All others are also good in a film which combines farce, comedy, gags, an occasional tear and razzmatazz aplenty.

The big show number put on by amateurs and not-too-hot professionals at the NATO fest is wittily executed. Credits, especially art direction and camerawork, are above average. "Mama" seems set for traveling abroad. —Wall.

Almacita di Desolata
(DUTCH-COLOR)

A Hungry Eye Pictures release of a Cosmic Illusion production. Written and produced by Norman Ph. de Palm. Directed by Felix de Rooy. Stars Marian Rolle. Camera (color), Ernest Dickerson; editor, Ton de Graaff; music, Grupo Issoco; sound, René van den Berg. Reviewed at Rotterdam Film Festival, Jan. 30, 1986. Running time: 100 MINS.

Solem . . . . .Marian Rolle
Lucio . . . . .Gwendomar Roosje
Mama Grandi . . . . .Nydia Ecury
Alma Sola Yon . . . . .Yubi Kirindongo
Papia Un Papia Dos . . . .Imelda Valerianus
Palomba . . . . .Ana Muskus
Marga . . . . .Irene van Grieken

Rotterdam — Curaçao in the West Indies is part of the Dutch Commonwealth. Norman de Palm and Felix de Rooy, having worked in the U.S. and in Holland, went back to their native island to make a picture that would convey the culture, nature, language, history and heritage of Curaçao and its people. Except for the star of their previous pic, "Désirée," Miami-born actress/singer Marian Rolle, the cast comes from the island.

De Palm's excellent script is based on old folktales. Desolato is an isolated small village where old customs still prevail. The time is around 1900.

Solem is a young mute woman, a priestess whose task is to conciliate the mighty spirits so they send rain for the parched soil, and keep away the Alma Sola of the empire of evil who can appear as men or beasts. Accompanied by a boy named Lucio, she leaves the village to gather medicinal and other herbs.

A priestess must stay virgin, but Solem is seduced by an evil spirit, Alma Sola Yon, masquerading as a wounded young man. When she gives birth to a daughter, she and Lucio are chased away from Desolato. The Alma Solo follows them on their way to Matriz di Piedat, a distant place where the spirits of former generations of villagers happily are gathered together. Alma Sola Yon repeatedly tries to take the baby away from Solem. Pic winds up with death and eventual rebirth.

Pic was shown in work copy, with colors and sound still uneven, but the music is stunning, the native language, Papiamento, in itself musical. The landscapes are intriguing. Some of the actors, mostly amateurs, have fascinating faces, but performances are weak, and one can see in crowd scenes and dances when and how players execute helmer's directions. The camera catches impressive natural beauty, but can add little to the storytelling.

The magic of the West Indies conquered the audience at the Rotterdam Fest, where pic was one of the popular favorites. Well marketed, film should have a chance in special situations and with Latin auds. —*Wall.*

She's Gotta Have It
(B&W)

Flawed rites-of-passage feature.

A Forty Acres and a Mule Filmworks production. Produced by Shelton J. Lee. Written and directed by Spike Lee. Camera (b&w), Ernest Dickerson; editor, Spike Lee; music, Bill Lee; sound, Barry Alexander Brown; prodction design, Wynn Thomas; art direction, Ron Paley. Reviewed at SRO screening room, San Francisco, Calif., March 26, 1986. (No MPAA Rating.) Running time: **100 MINS.**
Nola Darling . . . . Tracy Camilla Johns
Jamie Overstreet . . . . Redmond Hicks
Greer Childs . . . . John Terrell
Mars Blackmon . . . . Spike Lee
Opal Gilstrap . . . . Raye Dowell
Clorinda Bradford . . . . Joie Lee
Dr. Jamison . . . . Epatha Merkinson
Sonny Darling . . . . Bill Lee

San Francisco — This worthy, but flawed attempt to examine an independent young woman of the '80s is the work of Spike Lee, whose New York U. grad school thesis pic, "Joe's Bed-Stuy Barbershop: We Cut Heads," earned him fest appearances and various awards. To say Lee shows promise is to understate the exemplary depth and talent he displays in "She's Gotta Have It," a Frisco filmfest world premiere.

Pic was lensed, in Super 16m, in 15 days but doesn't appear jerrybuilt; the camerawork of Ernest

Dickerson is most impressive and stylish.

All the elements of an interesting yarn are implicit here — save one: a compelling central figure. The young woman who's the locus of the pic is, clearly, trying to find herself. She juggles three beaus, fends off a lesbian's overtures and consults a shrink to determine if she's promiscuous or merely a lady with normal sexual appetites.

There's a good deal of bedding down in "Gotta," but Dickerson's lensing keeps it subtle and in context. While Lee offers plenty of flesh in his screenplay, he has failed to flesh out the character of Nola Darling (Negro Ensemble Company thesp Tracy Camilla Johns in her first screen chore).

Aside from her bod, viewer can't be certain why the three guys are so drawn to her — and what makes her so impulsive, so uncertain about how she wishes to conduct her life. Amplification of the brief scene with the shrink could have accomplished that and manifested some insight into the young woman.

The three beaus, an upscale male model, a sensitive sort and a funny street flake, all essayed nicely by, respectively, John Terrell, Lee and Redmond Hicks, serve to keep the scenario moving with interest. In the end, Nola ankles all three as she decides life is "all about control ... My body, my mind. Who's gonna have it — them or me?''

In a decade of rites-of-passage pictures, this one does have some thoughtfulness about it. But "She's Gotta Have It" has got to have more mind than body if it wishes to control an audience. —*Herb.*

3:15
(COLOR)

Gangs rumble & audience snoozes.

A Dakota Entertainment release of a Wescom Prods. in association with Romax Prods. presentation, produced in association with Jones-Kenner Picture Co. and Brody Films. Executive producers, Charles C. Thieriot, Sandy Climan, Jean Bullians, Andrew Bullians. Produced by Dennis Brody, Robert Kenner. Directed by Larry Gross. Screenplay, Sam Bernard, Michael Jacobs; camera (CFI color), Misha Suslov; editor, Steven Kemper; music, Gary Chang; sound, Steve Nelson; production design, Paul Ahrens; set decoration, Anne Huntley; assistant director, Gordon Boos; production manager-associate producer, Nancy Israel; costume design, Nina Padovano; stunt coordinator, Dan Bradley; casting, Valorie Massalas. Reviewed at Magno Penthouse screening room, N.Y., March 24, 1986. (MPAA Rating: R.) Running time: **95 MINS.**
Jeff Hanna . . . . Adam Baldwin
Sherry Havilland . . . . . . Deborah Foreman
Principal Horner . . . . Rene Auberjonois
Moran . . . . Ed Lauter
Chris . . . . Scott McGinnis
Cinco . . . . Danny De La Paz
Jim . . . . John Scott Clough
Whisperer . . . . Mario Van Peebles

Smiley . . . . Jesse Aragon
Lora . . . . Wendy Barry
Whitey . . . . Bradford Bancroft
Norman . . . . Joseph Brutsman
Draper . . . . Wayne Crawford
Patch . . . . Lori Eastside
Ponch . . . . Jeb Ellis-Brown
Chooch . . . . Panchito Gomez
Mrs. Havilland . . . . . . Nancy Locke Hauser
Mr. Havilland . . . . Wings Hauser

"3:15" is a weak entry in the trickle of gang rumble films which made some b.o. noise back when Walter Hill's "The Warriors" was released. Debuting helmer Larry Gross, formerly a scriptwriter for Hill, minimizes the action and comes up with a fortgettable pic ill-suited to theatrical release. Filmed two years ago, it has been in regional distribution since January.

Adam Baldwin (title roler in "My Bodyguard") is too old to be the high school student here, a former member of the Cobras gang who is now at odds with the Cobras' leader, Danny De La Paz. Crisis comes when a drug bust, organized by cop Ed Lauter, nabs De La Paz and Baldwin refuses to help his former leader. Branded a traitor by most kids at school, Baldwin is also being pressured by principal Rene Auberjonois to fink on his former crony.

On a half-day of school (morning only), Baldwin sets up a final confrontation with De La Paz' gang at, surprise, 3:15 p.m. Showdown is an anticlimax, with only Baldwin's girl friend Deborah Foreman and a nerd played by Joseph Brutsman coming to his aid against five armed toughs. Pledges of support to Baldwin from a black gang and an Oriental one amount to nought.

Pic suffers from the absence of action, with fights mainly consisting of kids running down school hallways and stabbing each other. Low budget and weak production values are inferior to a typical telefilm.

Acting is also weak, with Baldwin generating little sympathy in the lead underdog role (he physically towers over the rest of the cast) and Foreman stuck with an inconsistent part. De La Paz is the most impressive performer, upsetting the script's balance since he wins sympathy by virtue of forceful thesping yet is supposed to be the hissable villain. Screenplay skirts over racial conflicts, though the good guys are all white and the bad guys are mainly Chicanos.—*Lor.*

Violets Are Blue
(COLOR)

Superficial romance fails to blossom.

A Columbia Pictures release of a Rastar production, from Columbia-Delphi IV Prods. Produced by Marykay Powell. Executive producer, Roger M. Rothstein. Directed by Jack Fisk. Stars Sissy Spacek, Kevin Kline. Screenplay, Naomi Foner; camera (DeLuxe color, Metrocolor prints), Ralf Bode; editor, Edward Warschilke; music, Patrick Williams; production design, Peter Jamison; art director, Bo Welch; set decorator, Jane Bogart; costumes, Joe I. Tompkins; sound, Jim Alexander; assistant director, Jim Van Wyck; casting, Pat McCorkle. Reviewed at Samuel Goldwyn theater, Beverly Hills, Calif., April 2, 1986. (MPAA Rating: PG-13.) Running time: **88 MINS.**
Gussie Sawyer . . . . Sissy Spacek
Henry Squires . . . . Kevin Kline
Ruth Squires . . . . Bonnie Bedelia
Ralph Sawyer . . . . John Kellogg
Addy Squires . . . . Jim Standiford
Ethel Sawyer . . . . Augusta Dabney
Sara Mae . . . . Kate McGregor-Stewart
George . . . . Adrian Sparks

Hollywood — Baby boomers looking for a return to their glory days are the target audience for "Violets Are Blue," but even they are likely to find that this tale of the road not taken promises more than it delivers. As an antidote to the epidemic of kiddie films, "Violets Are Blue" is a commendable effort, but unfortunately, not the cure. B.o. prospects are limited.

Premise of high school sweethearts, now settled into separate and vastly different lives, meeting again 15 years later seems like a rich vein to tap. After all, who has not wondered about the one that got away. But the whole business is orchestrated in a rather baroque fashion without ever getting to the emotional core of the characters.

Film opens with Gussie Sawyer (Sissy Spacek) and Henry Squires (Kevin Kline) plotting their escape form the small resort town of Ocean City, Md., where their imaginations have ripened for bigger places. Gussie does manage to get away and, in one of the film's more artificial developments, returns as a world-class photo-journalist.

Kline is not so lucky and after his father's death he takes over the local newspaper and settles in with his wife (Bonnie Bedelia) and raises a son (Jim Standiford). Spacek's return to this idyllic little setting threatens to destroy all their lives.

Although there is clearly an attraction between Spacek and Kline there is no urgency to their love. Director Jack Fisk takes his time developing Naomi Foner's script at the expense of any intensity or necessity. For the first half hour the film is a rudderless ship with no motor to propel it.

When the star-crossed couple does get together their choices are perhaps too personal to justify. In true yuppie fashion all they seem to think about are themselves. In an uncharacteristic role as the other woman, Spacek rather callously moves in on Bedelia's turf.

As they demonstrated even as kids, they are reluctant to accept the consequences of their actions. In short, these are not terribly sympathetic people although Foner's script does have flashes of insight and wit. The long spaces in between are the problem. Somehow this relationship never becomes the major love it needs to be to carry the story and make everything forgivable.

Opportunity to supply some necessary depth and texture with a subplot involving would-be land development on the pristine Assateague Island is mishandled and abruptly dropped.

Performances are competent but don't do enough to flesh out the inner workings of these people. One never cares very much one way or the other what happens. At the center of the triangle, Kline's ambivalence is weak. More understandable and convincing is Bedelia's vulnerable yet solid housewife.

Production values are strong as one might expect from Fisk, a former art director. Locales along the Maryland coast are scenic and not overexposed from other films. However, accompanied by Patrick Williams' sappy score, vistas occasionally have a postcard sheen. —*Jagr.*

Aufforderung zum Tanz
(Invitation To Dance)
(WEST GERMAN-COLOR-16m)

A Westdeutscher Rundfunk Film production, Cologne. Directed by Peter F. Bringmann. Screenplay, Matthias Seelig; camera (color, 16m), Axel Block; editor, Diana Kischkel; music, Ingfried Hoffmann; tv-producer, Alexander Wesemann; sets, Manfred Lütz; production manager, Eberhard Forck. Reviewed at Landesbildstelle. Screening Room, Berlin, March 25, 1986. Running time: **105 MINS.**

With: Marius Müller-Westernhagen (Theo Gromberg), Guido Gagliardi (Enno Goldini), Riad Gholmié (Jussuf), Elga Sorbas (Maria), Dan van Husen (Zaplata), Alexander Malachowsky (Siggi Leicht), Gudrun Landgrebe (Ulla), Karl-Heinz Walter (Schneider), Johannes Buzalski (Zwickel-Pit), Eberhard Steib (Jupp), Werner Eichhorn (Hermann), Kurt Zips (Ludwig), Sabine Eichner (Karin).

Berlin — Occasionally a pure tv-film production that hit the top of the ratings upon its initial airing finds its way via film clubs and public institutions to the mass film public. A fortunate example is Peter F. Bringmann's "Invitation To Dance" (1976), the forerunner of his "Theo Against The Rest Of The World" (1979), b.o. winner and companion to yet another tv-film hit, "Paul Is Back" (1977).

Put all three together, and the trilogy forms a unique and witty social commentary on the underworld of conmen and petty thieves in-

habiting the industrial Ruhrgebiet area of western Germany where the Rhine and Ruhr rivers join amid coal mines and steel mills.

The reason the two "Theo" pics have become audience favorites is primarily because of scripter Matthias Seelig. He knows the world of the smalltime hoodlum groups inside out, but he has also carved out the figure of the perpetual lovable loser who just never learns a lesson — on the contrary, when he gets a pocketful of change, he'll splurge it almost immediately on the next card game or horserace or whatever pie-in-the-sky that next comes along.

Theo is a truckdriver longing to buy his own rig. He needs a spare couple of thousand marks to make the down payment with a partner on a truck of his own, and he needs it within the next few days or lose everything. On top of that, Theo has temporarily lost his driver's license, while a friend of his has got into a fight with gypsies — the result of which was an accidental death — and the dead gypsy's chums are constantly after him.

Theo keeps pumping his Italian pal Enno for money to play the horses (he loses), join in a backroom card game (he wins and loses), and chase after the girls in his spare time (he wins). After agreeing to join in an illegal insurance job by changing papers at a freight yard, he suddenly finds himself up to his neck in Mafia tricks — and tries to bluff his way through to a pot of blackmailing gold. He ends up with saving his hide amid beatings from every side only because of his agility and instinct for running like hell whenever things get too hot.

Marius Müller-Westernhagen, built like a stove-pipe and with a Cheshire cat grin, obviously has the charm and talent for playing a lamebrain loser.—*Holl.*

P.O.W. The Escape
(COLOR)

Effective he-man action pic.

A Cannon Releasing release of a Cannon Group presentation of a Golan-Globus production. Produced by Menahem Golan, Yoram Globus. Directed by Gideon Amir. Stars David Carradine. Screenplay, Jeremy Lipp, James Bruner, Malcolm Barbour, John Langley, from story by Avi Kleinberger, Amir; camera (TVC color), Yechiel Ne'eman; supervising editor, Marcus Manton; editor, Roy Watts; theme music, David Storrs; music supervision, Michael Linn; sound, Jacob Goldstein; production design, Marcia Hinds; art direction, Bo Johnson, Ramon Nigado (Philippines); production manager, Michael Kansky, Antonio Ezpeleta (Philippines); assistant director, Adi Shoval, Ricardo De Guzman (Philippines); second unit director, Ron Tal; stunt coordinators, John Barrett, Steve Lambert; costume design, Audrey Bansmer; additional photography (L.A.), Gideon Porath; postproduction supervisor, Michael R. Sloan; associate producer, Kleinberger; casting, Robert MacDonald, Perry Bulling-

ton. Reviewed at Hollywood Pacific, L.A., Calif., April 4, 1986. (MPAA Rating: R.) Running time: **90 MINS.**
Col. Cooper ....David Carradine
Sparks ....Charles R. Floyd
Capt. Vinh ....Mako
Jonston ....Steve James
Adams ....Phil Brock

Hollywood — "P.O.W. The Escape" is yet another Cannon picture about our heroic fighting boys mowing down the commies in Vietnam, this time as a band of determined prisoners desperate to reach freedom in the last days before the fall of Saigon. Although script contains about 10 minutes of plot spread out over 90 minutes, winning combination of likeable G.I.s and chockablock action sequences should enlist a winning boxoffice.

Macho leading man in this Philippines-shot actioner (formerly titiled "Behind Enemy Lines") is David Carradine as the infamous Colonel Cooper, who when taken as a prisoner by the Veitcong, becomes the enemy's highest-ranking American in captivity.

He immediately becomes a major concern of the North Vietnamese Army's hierarchy in Hanoi, who want him executed before the cease fire, and of his captor, Captain Vinh (Mako) who instead offers Cooper a way out if the prisoner will take him and his booty to the U.S.

Cooper stands fast as a leader of *men,* meaning he'll only cooperate with Vinh if all the P.O.W.s are promised freedom — holding out through a couple of hairy scenes until Vinh finally relents.

Carradine's characterization, not unlike his "Kung Fu" personality, is of supreme coolness and verve as he gets his boys (most of 'em) through the jungle and the crossfire.

Getting the role of Mr. Warmth, such as exists in this hard pic, is the colonel's loyal sidekick, Jonston (Steve James), who is as good maneuvering around gunfire, grenades and white water rapids as he is keeping this cheerless band of escapees from giving up hope.

Compounding the usual hurdles of surviving guerrilla warfare is the perverbial thorn-in-the-side character, in this case a rebellious soldier named Sparks (Charles R. Floyd) who breaks ranks with Cooper to save his own neck.

Floyd, a former soap star, manages to give his renegade character much more complexity and depth than is usually afforded comic book bad boys.

While entire cast looks scruffy and unattractive from one explosive scene to another, Floyd always manages to look appealing — his vulnerablity showing through his translucent blue eyes.

How unfortunate that this kind of pic attracts a mostly male crowd. (There are no female roles.) Floyd

will be missed by what could be his most appreciative audience.

Physical scope of the film is ambitious, including a lot of fancy pyrotechnic work that makes combat scenes actually look pretty.

Except for Mako, who is nondescript as the fickle Captain Vinh, Asians are nonentities whose only function in this picture is to get wasted.

Maybe if they were given anything more — like human qualities — picture wouldn't work nearly as well. —*Brit.*

La Machine à découdre
(The Unsewing Machine)
(FRENCH-COLOR)

A Films Jacques Leitienne release of an M. Films production. Produced, written and directed by Jean-Pierre Mocky, based on the novel, "A Killer Is Loose" by Gil Brewer. Camera (Eastmancolor), Edmond Richard; editor, Bénédicte Teiger; music, Jacky Giordano; sound, Jack Jullian; art direction, Etienne Mery; makeup, José De Luca; production manager, Sophie Moyse. Reviewed at the Ponthieu screening room, Paris, March 26, 1986. Running time: **82 MINS.**
Ralph Enger ....Jean-Pierre Mocky
Steff Muller................Peter Semler
Liliane ....Patricia Barzyk
Betty ....Françoise Michaud
Rubis ....Sophie Moyse
Sam ....Hervé Pauchon
The mayor ....Jean Paul Massoni
Thomas Bourne.....François Toumarkine
Yoyo ....Isabelle Strawa
Henri....................Patrick Granier
Jack Mironi ....Alan Dan

Paris — The main attraction of writer-director Jean-Pierre Mocky's new film "The Unsewing Machine," based on a Yank print thriller by Gil Brewer, is the helmer's performance as a madman on a killing spree in the monied neighborhoods of the French Riviera.

The lunatic is a one-time doctor who has become unhinged and been locked up in an asylum. He escapes and begins a quest for funds to build a hospital for infant war victims. He comes into possession of a Mauser pistol and a pair of hostages who are forced to accompany him on his grotesque charity rounds, in which he responds to contrariness with the weapon. When the police finally close in on him, his hostages, who have come to see some sympathetic method in this madness, help him to escape.

Mocky, who began his career as an actor (notably in Georges Franju's asylum-set drama, "La Tête contre les murs," which he also co-scripted) is a black comedy treat as the killer, an unlikely mixture of psychotic altruism, lucid brutality and likable, sleezy desperation. Though Mocky, as writer-director, loads the dice conventionally by making victims and pursuers caricatural egotists, it's understandable that his captives side with him in the end.

Unfortunately, direction and other performances are not on the same level as Mocky's offbeat playing, and the picture suffers from the same sense of hurried casualness as the filmmaker's previous productions.

Peter Semler and Patricia Barzyk are Mocky's hostages: an unemployed immigrant carpenter who is trying to sell his collector's item Mauser to pay for his pregnant wife's hospital expenses; and a luscious dancer whom Mocky keeps locked naked in his posh hotel room. Barzyk, last seen delivering Paul Claudel's classic verse dialog in Manoel de Oliveira's "The Satin Slipper," here looks like a vixen escaped from a Russ Meyer picture. Both serve as litte more than foils for mocking Mocky. —*Len.*

Critters
(COLOR)

Inane creature feature.

A New Line Cinema release of a Sho Films production, in association with Smart Egg Pictures. Executive producer, Robert Shaye. Produced by Rupert Harvey. Directed by Stephen Herek. Screenplay, Herek, Domonic Muir; camera (DeLuxe color), Tom Suhrstedt; editor, Larry Bock; music, David Newman; sound, Donald Summer; production design, Gregg Fonseca; assistant director, Leon Dudevoir; art director, Philip Foreman; set decoration, Anne Huntley; special effects (Critters), Chiodo Brothers Prods.; Critters design, Charlie Chiodo, Steve Chiodo; Zanti transformations makeup, Chris Biggs; special visual effects, Quicksilver FX/Studio; stunt coordinator, Mike Cassidy; Critter voices, Corey Burton; additional photography, Russ Carpenter; casting, Elisabeth Leustig. Reviewed at Magno screening room, N.Y., March 7, 1986. (MPAA Rating: PG-13.) Running time: **86 MINS.**

Helen Brown	Dee Wallace Stone
Harv	M. Emmet Walsh
Jay Brown	Billy Green Bush
Brad Brown	Scott Grimes
April Brown	Nadine Van Der Velde
Bounty hunter/Johnny Steele	Terrence Mann
Charlie McFadden	Don Opper
Steve Elliot	Billy Zane
Jeff Barnes	Ethan Phillips
Preacher	Jeremy Lawrence
Sally	Lin Shaye
Warden Zanti	Michael Lee Gogin
Ed	Art Frankel

Critters resemble oversize hairballs and roll like tumbleweeds when prodded into action, the perfect menace for this irritatingly insipid and lightweight film which unfolds with plodding predictability and leaves few clichés unturned.

From necessity "Critters" doesn't dwell on its threadbare beginnings. Within minutes of film's start, a small band of voracious Krites (a.k.a. Critters) easily escape from a "maximum security asteroid" and are whizzing toward Kansas with two crack bounty hunters in pursuit.

Establish the sleepy life of farmer (yes) Brown and wife Helen, as credibly performed by Billy Green Bush and Dee Wallace Stone as can be expected with such material, rambunctious son Brad and sexually budding daughter April. There's also M. Emmet Walsh as the familiar smalltown sheriff and several other stock characters stripmined from science fiction films of the past.

The Critters land, eat a cow and soon have the Brown family cowering and cut off from the rest of the world. The action mercifully shifts to the bounty hunters, one portrayed by Terrence Mann who has taken the likeness of a rock star from an intercepted musicvid, and the other an indecisive sort who goes through the film changing into the likenesses of various people.

The bounty hunters destroy the town in search of the escapees, angrily demanding "Where are the Krites?" to all the confused earthlings they encounter, not that anyone would shield these furry garbage disposals from recapture. Young Brad Brown finally slips away from the house on his bike, Mom, Dad and Sis too weak from Critter encounters, and manages to drag the aliens back to the farm.

Payoff is getting to watch a systematic destruction of the Browns' once peaceful home as the Critters are picked off one-by-one, to the stock denouement.

Cowriters Domonic Muir and Stephen Herek, latter doubling as film's director, manage to deflate what little suspense is created by subtitling the Critters' chatter among themselves with inane snippets of dialog. The final result is neither scary nor humorous and the only real feeling a viewer leaves with is the hope that the sequel intimated in the final frames never gets made.—*Roy.*

Matador
(SPANISH-COLOR)

An Andrés Vicente Gómez production. Executive producer, Andrés Vicente Gómez. Directed by Pedro Almodóvar. Screenplay, Almodóvar, Jesús Ferrero; camera (Eastmancolor), Angel Luis Fernández; editor, José Salcedo; music, Bernardo Bonezzi; sound, Bernard Orthión; production designer, Fernando Sánchez. Reviewed at Cine Rex, Madrid, March 27, 1986. Running time: **115 MINS.**

Maria	Assumpta Serna
Angel	Antonio Banderas
Diego	Nacho Martinez
Eva	Eva Cobo

Also with: Julieta Serrano, Chus Lampreave, Carmen Maura, Eusebio Poncela, Bibi Andersen, Luis Ciges, Eva Siva, Verónica Forqué, Jaime Chávarri.

Madrid — Pedro Almodóvar's iconoclastic and often zany new pic "Matador" follows the tongue-in-cheek style of his previous works (last one, "What Have I Done To Deserve This!" got Stateside release), but is more polished. The Spanish helmer's wry humor and acute eye for the outrageous make this an amusing mixture of the bullfight and detective genres.

The word matador is used in double sense of one who kills a bull and a murderer. Helmer uses a very large cast for the convluted but droll story, including even director Jaime Chávarri as a priest. Story concerns a young man, who comes from a very pious family (members of the Catholic lay organization Opus Dei which is poked fun at) and is training to be a torero. After unsuccessfully trying to rape the girlfriend of his bullfight teacher, he gives himself up in repentance to the police. While in the precinct he confesses to the murder of two men.

It turns out the kid is psychic and eventually leads police to the bodies buried in the garden of his instructor. His femme defense attorney turns out to be the murderess. She in turn falls for the instructor and they consume their passion for murder by killing each other with deadly passion. The police arrive too late, having stopped to look at a solar eclipse.

Pic has a number of kinky scenes involving nudity and lovemaking, allusions to drugs, homosexuals and a mocking anti-Catholic vein running through it. Without those it wouldn't be an Almodóvar film. Item should do well with audiences who have already latched on to the films of this Spanish original, even if some of the local jokes are lost on them. —*Besa.*

Suivez mon regard
(Follow My Gaze)
(FRENCH-COLOR)

A UGC release of a Protecrea production. Produced by Dagmar Meyniel. Written and directed by Jean Curtelin. Camera (color), Michel Cenet; editor, Martine Barraqué; music, Tom Novembre, Charlélie Couture; sound (Dolby), Henri Roux, Paul Bertault; assistant director, Elisabeth Parnière. Reviewed at UGC, Neuilly, March 26, 1986. Running time: **80 MINS.**

With: Pierre Arditi, Feodor Atkine, Stéphane Audran, Jean-Pierre Bacri, Christian Barbier, Macha Beranger, Richard Berry, Jean-Pierre Bisson, Jean-Claude Brialy, Patrick Bruel, Jean Carmet, Claude Chabrol, Farid Chopel, Charlélie Couture, Darry Cowl, Gérard Darmon, Michel Duchaussoy, Roger Dumas, Andréa Ferreol, Michel Galabru, Véronique Genest, Hippolyte Girardot, Julie Jezequel, Riton Liebman, Vincent Lindon, Léo Malet, Macha Meril, Roger Mirmont, Tom Novembre, Dominique Pinon, Annette Poivre, Robin Renucci, Mort Shuman, Beth Todd, Patrice Valota, Jacques Weber, Zabou, Jean Curtelin, Joel Santoni, Brigitte Lahaie, Caroline Lang, Charly Chemouni, Jezabel Capri.

Paris — A huge cast, mixing veteran names and new generation talent, parades before the camera in this witless sketch film written and directed by Jean Curtelin in his helming debut. Curtelin, who has fashioned a reputation as a caustic screenwriter crusading against human stupidity and intolerance in such films as Denis Amar's "L'Addition" and Roger Hanin's "Train d'enfer" comes a cropper with his grabbag of half-baked satiric bits and sketches, assembled with no particular purpose, structure or rhythm.

A few amusing ideas pop up on occasion but are bludgeoned quickly by Curtelin's inexpert direction. Among those players who manage to survive through sheer professionalism are Jean Carmet, as an unintelligible hick being filmed for a dog food commercial, Michel Galabru, as a callous schoolmaster who fails a pupil for his composition on his mother's death and Farid Chopel, in a mute bit as an airport cleaning man at odds with an automatic door. —*Len.*

Wohin mit Willfried?
(What To Do With Willfried?)
(WEST GERMAN-COLOR)

A Coproduction of Dieter Köster Film, Berlin, and Sender Freies Berlin. Directed by Dieter Köster. Screenplay, Hannelore Conradsen, Köster; camera (color), Wolfhard Osswold; editor, Dagmar Bleasing; sets, Mandus Köhler; assistant director, Jürgen Volkevy; tv-producers, Frauke Klinkers, Pierre Le Page; production manager, Horst Jonas. Reviewed at Berliner Screening Room, Berlin, March 25, 1986. Running time: **81 MINS.**

With: Geseke Piper (Valerie), Gisela Probst (Susanne), Dagmer Biener (Doris), Rainer Hunold (Paul), Dorothea Moritz (Frau Frisch), Christoph M. Ohrt (Walker), Beate Tober (Rose), Alexander Hauft (Freddy), Dorothee Kremps-Ehrlich (Gundula), Peter Schlesinger (Stallkeeper), Horst Pinnow (Cowboy).

Berlin — As kidpic helmers go, Dieter Köster has one of the best records among directors spending equal time between tv productions and theatrical films. His formula is simple: find a believable but outlandish story set in familiar surroundings, then start the narrative in the middle and end it in the middle, so that the young viewer has the feeling that life is one big adventure after another.

Working together with scripter Hannelore Conradsen on all his projects, Dieter Köster latest, "What To Do With Willfried?" has an average family (father is a postman) winning a horse in a raffle. When they arrive at an ad agency to pick up the lottery surprise they discover it's a white stallion named Willfried. Since they live in the back courtyard apartment of an old-style Berlin tenement house, this is great for adman photos with all the curious and somewhat envious neighbors, particularly as Valerie's girlfriend Susanne has recently dropped her for a beau, so this is a way to settle the score in a game of oneupmanship.

Then the family is stuck with the stallion for the weekend and a deluge of rain comes pouring down on the unprotected horse. What to do with Willfried, but take him into the house, where he relieves himself on the stairs. Next comes the real surprise: the ad agency has had its fun and doesn't want to take the horse back, while renting a stall at a riding academy would wreak havoc on the family budget. So back to a summer cottage of a family acquaintance for the duration of the autumn, which means transporting Willfried illegally on an S-Bahn train out to the suburbs.

One witty joke follows another until finally a solution is found. The idea of having Pappa and Momma Postman joining the local Wild West Club in Berlin (it really does exist) so that Willfried receives free boarding there, is the ribtickler that makes "What To Do With Willfried?" one of the most memorable kidpics of the season.—*Holl.*

Sita in de noordzee
(Sita In The North Sea)
(DUTCH-DOCU-COLOR-16m)

A Cinemien release of a De Maatschap BV Filmproduktie production. Produced by Jonne Severijn. Directed by Alma Popeyus. Stars Sita A. Kallasingh. Screenplay, Popeyus; camera (Kodak Highspeed color, 16m), Alex Boon, Paul van den Bos, Mat van Hensbergen; editor, Erik Disselhoff; music, Gerard Stokkink & Tommy Bachmann, Gurudath Kallasingh; sound, Mark Glynne, Bert Koops; production manager, Eric Hafkamp, Marion Hilhorst. Reviewed at Desmet Theater, Amsterdam, Holland, March 19, 1986. Running time: **80 MINS.**
With: Sita A. Kallasingh, Gurudath Kallasingh, Gaytree Kalpoe, Koeldiep Kalpoe, Nellie van Os, Cynthia Kasi, Barryl Biekman.

Amsterdam — This is an interesting, lighthearted, but not lightweight docu about Sita, a Hindu girl from Surinam, now living with her family in Holland. She is integrated, but not assimilated. She tries to give their due to the different cultures, traditions, religions which all helped to form her. She recognizes that "If you get to live in the North Sea, you've got to make friends with the fish."

Pic, meant as a lesson in discovering Sita, does it with lots of humor and an intelligent screenplay which seems haphazard, but is very tightly structured.

We see Sita looking for a job, from salesgirl to police woman, learning classical Hindu dances, helping with a Hindu wedding and discussing her religion — the normal life of a Hindu girl in Holland. Truthful docu is also informative through what we do not see: no boy friend, no contact with Surinam Creoles. As in the Caribbean the two communities (black Creoles, Indian Hindus), while slowly integrating with the Dutch, remain completely segregated from each other.

A companion pic about a Creole girl in Holland would be a good subject for writer/helmer Alma Popeyus who, with "Sita," makes instruction entertaining, with imaginative use of music, the help of clever editing and good, but unobtrusive camerawork. — *Wall.*

Manden i maanen
(The Man In The Moon)
(DANISH-COLOR)

A Metronome release of Film-Cooperativet Denmark 1983 with the Danish Film Institute, Metronome Prods. (Bent Fabricius-Bjerre) and C.C. Cosmos production. Executive producer, Tiwi Magnusson. Film Institute consultant producer, Peter Poulsen. Original story, screenplay and directed by Erik Clausen. Camera (Eastmancolor), Morten Bruus; editor, Ghita Beckendorff; production design, Leif Sylvester Petersen; sound, Henrik Langkilde; costumes, Gitte Kolvig; music, Robert Broberg; songs performed by Broberg with Lotte Römer, Oyvind Ougard, Maria Bramsen, Thomas Grue, Henning Pold. Reviewed at the Dagmar, Copenhagen, March 6, 1986. Running time: **90 MINS.**
Johannes . . . . Peter Thiel
Maria Bianca . . . . . . Catherine Poul Jupont
Christina . . . . Christina Bengtsson
Her husband . . . . Kim Jansson
Turkish guest worker . . Yavuzer Cetinkaya
African guest worker . . . . Roy Richards
Johannes' mother . . . . . . Berthe Quistgaard
Police lieutenant . . . . Erik Truxa
First hooker . . . . Anne Nöjgard
Second hooker . . . . . . Marianne Mortensen
Waiter . . . . Stig Hoffmeyer

Copenhagen — Erik Clausen, whose previous feature comedies ("Circus Casablanca," etc.) grew out of variety shows and political satire with the social underdog emerging triumphant, is off in an entirely different and more ambitious direction with "The Man In The Moon," although the underdog remains the protagonist. The little guy, slim, hollow-cheeked and played with quiet strength by screen newcomer Peter Thiel, is released from the prison where he has spent 16 years for the passion-inspired murder of his wife. Middle-aged, he enters life in freedom to find himself closed in between narrow walls where he listens to sounds that echo the slamming doors and footsteps along the corridors of the penal institution he has just left.

Clausen, originally a painter, and his cinematographer Morten Bruus elaborate on the shabby, threatening new world of Johannes in shots that are small marvels of neo-expressionism couched in soft focus and camera angles suggesting the little guy's awe of everything that meets his tender consciousness.

Johannes does not have many words to express his longing to tell first his dying mother and later his now fully grown daughter about the misguided love that made him commit his fatal crime. Nobody, except for some "cheap labor" guest workers from Turkey and Africa, seems inclined to waste any sympathy on

his plight. Still, film does have a happy ending of a kind. Otherwise, it meanders almost wistfully through its non-plot with writer-helmer Clausen pulling every melodramatic punch. —*Kell.*

Gritta vom Rattenschloss
(Gritta Of The Rat Castle)
(EAST GERMAN-COLOR)

A DEFA Film production. "Johannisthal" group, East Berlin. Directed and photographed (color) by Jürgen Brauer. Screenplay, Christa Kozik; editor, Evelyn Carow; sets, Alfred Hirschmeier; music, Stefan Carow; production manager, Hans-Erich Busch. Reviewed at Berlin Film Fest (Children's Fest), Feb. 14, 1986. Running time: **91 MINS.**
With: Kadja Klier (Gritta), Hermann Beyer (Count Julius Ortel), Fred Delmare (His servant Müffert), Suheer Saleb (Countess Nesselkrautia), Mark Lubosch (Peter), Wolf-Dieter Lingk (Pekavus), Peter Sodann (King), Ilja Kriwoluzky (Prince Bonus), Peter Dommisch (First guardian), Horst Papke (Second guardian), Heide Kipp (Abbess).

Berlin — Based on motifs in a fairytale novel by Bettina and Gisela von Arnim, Jürgen Brauer's "Gritta Of The Rat Castle" is a somewhat silly kidpic for the youth auds with a yen for romantic stories filled with castle and knights and the ancient rules of battle between the forces of good and evil. In this case a 13-year-old lass saves the day with help from her mice friends in a castle owned by her neglectful, eccentric father that is about to fall completely into ruins.

Gritta's father spends more time on trying to invent useful machinery, and he's rather sure that a throne-saver is what's required these days. He figures that when an armored foe charges through the doors, then an ejection switch can be pushed to catapult the king to safety in the eaves of the throneroom. When he tries it out on his faithful servant and Gritta, however, the two get stuck hanging from the ceiling with no way to get down.

The father, an eccentric count, has other goofy ideas as well. One day he meets a countess passing by in entourage, falls in love, and then up and marries her — only to discover to his dismay that the new lady of the house wants to change everything, including declaring war on the rats and sending Gritta off to an evil abbess to be locked up in a cloister. Gritta finds out that the abbess and her scheming friends plan to lock up plenty of girls in order to get their hands on the inheritances. All seems lost until her rat-friends come to the rescue by chewing her way to freedom. She and her friends then set make-believe. —*Holl.*

Maria
(DUTCH-COLOR)

A Cannon Tuschinski Film Distribution release of a Kaktus-CNR Film Produktie production. Executive producer, Jules Bruessing. Written and directed by Peter Jan Rens. Camera (color), Frans Bromet; editor, Victorine Habets; sound, Peter Flamman; music, Tony Eyk. Reviewed at Cinema International, Amsterdam, Feb. 17, 1986. Running time: **90 MINS.**
Maria . . . . Jeanne Marleau
Maria (young) . . . . Liesbeth Sjollema
Erik . . . . Peter Jan Rens
Paolo Pietrosanti . . . . Huub Stapel
Sister Elisabeth . . . Annemieke Hoogendijk
Anneke . . . . Kika Keus
Daniëlle . . . . Rosita Steenbeek
Luca . . . . Tony Maples

Amsterdam — "Maria's" most original feature is the way it got financed. Debuting director Peter Jan Ren asked the public in press advertisements to buy certificates of 10 guilders ($3.50) each of which would be accepted at boxoffices in payment for tickets when the film reached theaters. This brought him about 20% of a total budget of $270,000.

"Maria" is based on the experiences of a lady in her 80s whom Rens nursed and befriended while in his 20s. It concerns a young Dutch woman in pre-Mussolini Italy, around 1920. She falls in love with Paolo, a member of a fascist elite. They marry, but Paolo is doomed, mainly because of the jealousy of his immediate superior, a homosexual.

Maria, old and lame, tells the (in flashback) story to nurse Erik, played by Rens, during a summer vacation of some patients of a nursing home.

Unfortunately, helmer's complete ignorance of filming prevents "Maria" from coming to life. His script and dialog are wooden. So are the actors, even Huub Stapel (excellent in "The Lift") and Rens himself. Camera and editing fight hard, but in a losing cause. Chances abroad seem less than slim. — *Wall.*

Der Ruf
(The Summons)
(WEST GERMAN-B&W)

An Objectiv-Film production, Munich. Directed by Josef von Baky. Stars Fritz Kortner. Screenplay, Kortner; camera (b&w), Werner Krien; sets, Fritz Maurischat, Hans Sohnle, Fritz Lück; production manager, Richard König. Reviewed at Berliner Screening Room, Berlin, March 12, 1986. Running time: **104 MINS.**
With: Fritz Kortner, Johanna Hofer, Rosemary Murphy, Lina Carstens, William Sinnigen, Michael Murphy, Ernst Schröder, Paul Hoffman, Arno Assmann, Charles Regnier.

Berlin — As German cinema begins to reexamine its postwar past, neglected treasures like Josef von Baky and Fritz Kortner's "The Summons" (1949) suddenly loom large out of a period in which they were rather unjustly neglected. Shot half in English and half in German, this story of a German émigré professor in Los Angeles deciding to return to Germany to accept a teaching post at the same university he departed a decade before parallels the career of Fritz Kortner (1892-1970) himself. It's reviewed here for the record.

Kortner wrote and acted in the film, while Josef von Baky (the director of the classic "Münchhausen" in 1943) directed. Credits are all top grade, and "The Summons" well deserved its invitation to participate at the third Cannes fest in 1949 as the German entry.

This is the story of two expulsions from Germany, the first being the emigration from Germany under the Nazis and the second being the returning professor's rejection by colleagues and some of the students at the university when he resumes a lecture on history and morality that marked the interruption in his career at this very place 10 years before. The title refers to a summons to take up a vacant post at a prestige institution of higher learning.

Pic opens with Kortner in Los Angeles during a house party filled with German emigrants. He contemplates returning "home" and astounds the others by making this decision in 1948, when respect for the German nation was at its lowest ebb and his own career and professional esteem was at its height. Next we find him in Paris with an entourage of American friends and students, one of them a young personal secretary whose admiration remains platonic but could be easily more upon request. Kortner wants to find his long lost wife and discover what has happened to his son in Germany, particularly as the latter would have had to live under a different name and guise in Nazi Germany. He visits the ruins of Berlin, alone.

He does find his ex-wife and true love (played by Kortner's own wife, Johanna Hofer), but she hesitates over telling him what has happened to his son — other than that he was last heard of under internment in a POW camp. Intrigue mounts thereafter at the university (apparently in Munich) due to the jealousy of a former professor who had, like so many others, compromised his career under the Nazis. Kortner takes ill when he notes that his position becomes untenable, but before dying he is reconciled with his wife and greets his son again on his deathbed.

"The Summons" sparkles in dialog and true-to-life situations, at its wittiest in the ping-pong-like English/German exchanges.—Holl.

Chto u Senjki Bylo
(The Unjust Stork)
(SOVIET-COLOR)

A Filmstudio Odessa production, Ukraine. World rights, Goskino, Moscow. Directed by Radomir Vassilevsky. Screenplay, Radi Pogodin; camera (color), Vadim Yefrimov. Reviewed at Berlin Film Fest (Children's Festival), Feb. 18, 1986. Running time: 79 MINS.
With: Alyshoa Vesselov (Senka); Yulia Kosmacheva (Matruska), Vladimir Nossik, yekaterina Vassilyeva, Nadeshda Butyrzewa.

Berlin — Radomir Vassilevsky's "The Unjust Stork" is a charming kidpic, one of the best of those on view at the Berlinale. The preschool youngsters in this idyllic Ukrainian country tale steal the show from the first moment on the screen.

The story is hardly new. Little Senka learns from his mother that he's going to have a baby brother soon to play with. That's fine, but where do babies come from? Some say the stork is to blame, others that they're simply found inside of cabbages out in the fields. Senka shares all this thoughts on the matter with Matruska, the little girlfriend next door. Because mother's off to the hospital for some mysterious reason, this gives the two of them much more of an opportunity to cook up a bit of mischief on the side.

One day, the two of them are playing near a stream, and fall in — only to be rescued by an elderly widow (the kids think she's a witch because she's a recluse dressed in black). As for the grown-ups, they tend to take everything in stride. This is, after all, a rural community where everyone keeps an eye on youngsters on the loose.

When the baby brother finally arrives, it turns out to be a baby sister — and this after all the scolding Senka has been going through up to now. Here comes the twist: Senka decides the nurse in the community (who's going to marry soon) deserves to have the baby sister instead, so he and Matruska lug the bundle of joy out to the fields and dump it right in the middle of the cabbage patch. The parents and neighbors are distraught when this happens, but the day is saved by the old widow in black, who carries the child back to the mother. —Holl.

Djamila
(SOVIET-COLOR/B&W)

A Coproduction of Mosfilm and Kirghizfilm; world rights, Goskino, Moscow. Directed by Irina Poplavskaya. Screenplay, Chengiz Aitmatov. Only credits available. Reviewed at Sovexport Film Office, West Berlin, March 12, 1986. Running time: 95 MINS.
With Natalia Arinbassarova, Sulmenkul Chokmovrov, Nasreddin Dibashev.

Berlin — With the swing back to a more liberal position in the Soviet film ministry, a certain progressive attitude is currently being taken in key locales like West Berlin that seems to bode well for Soviet cinema in the future. On view in a Soviet-German friendship meet was Irina Poplavskaya's "Djamila" (1968), produced in Kirghizia and based on Chengiz Aitmatov's classic love story (published in 1958) with the same title. It's reviewed here for the record.

"Djamila" was the third of three important features made by Moscow-based filmmakers in the progressive 1960s, when it was more advantageous for grads from the Moscow Film School (VGIK) to seek work in a Soviet republic like Kirghizia where a cinematic culture was just beginning to develop. First Larissa Shepitko adapted Aitmatov's "Heat" (1963); then Andrei Mikhalkov-Konchalovsky collaborated with the author on "The First Teacher" (1965); and then Aitmatov worked closely with Irina Poplavskaya on the story "Djamila" (1968) that was acclaimed by Louis Aragon in its time of publication as "the world's loveliest love story."

The story has an autobiographical bent, for it takes place in traditional Kirghizia at the time of the Second World War when Chengiz Aitmatov (born 1928) was growing into manhood but still too young to go to the front. In his village where a commune labors under the summer heat to provide grain for the cause there lives a young girl, a vital and spirited being.

According to ancient traditions, however, she is betrothed to a young man who must shortly thereafter leave for the army.

The girl's best friend and youthful companion (though younger than her) is the teenaged storyteller, who also happens to be the younger brother of her betrothed. While working in the fields, she's once mishandled by a greedy sort and is rescued by the nagging combative boy who arrives in the nick of time to save her honor. Next arrives a young worker on the scene, a silent lad whose afflicted health leaves him a lonely outsider among the rest. The lad and Djamila take to teasing him until, one day, he proves his courage and stamina by toting an extra loaded bag of grain up a ramp to spite the teasing pair for their spiteful trick. Thereafter, the love story grows, as Djamila comes to realize that she has fallen in love with the man she has previously tormented. In the end, just when the betrothed returns home from the war, she decides to break ancient customs and go off to live with the one she truly loves.

Pic's major pluses are its tight narrative style, colorful lensing (in a blend of b&w, color, and sepia tones), and a strong performance by Natalia Arinbassarova in the title role. —Holl.

Der Sexte Sinn
(The Sexth Sense)
(WEST GERMAN-COLOR)

A Horizont Film Production, Berlin. Written and directed by Dagmar Beiersdorf, Lothar Lambert. Camera (color), Hans Günter Bücking; editor, Verena Neumann; music, Albert Kittler; sound, Slavco Hitrov; Reviewed at Berlin Film Market screening room, March 15, 1986. Running time: 85 MINS.
With: Albert Heinz (Alfred), Ingolf Gorges (Hans), Ulrike Schirm, Ela Behrends, Barbara Morawiecz, Jutta Klöppel, Susanne Stahl.

Berlin — Lothar Lambert and Dagmar Beiersdorf's combined effort "The Sixth Sense," represents a parody of all they've stood for in the no-budget asphalt vineyard of West Berlin. What's apparently happened is that the success of Lambert's two coproductions with NDR-Hamburg television ("Paso Doble" and "Drama In Blond") spurred a producer to strike while the iron was hot.

Following a formula can be deadly, particularly when inspiration and spontaneity are hammered into stereotyped idiocy. The story has a mama's boy stripped of his dominating mother, which means in turn that he now has the chance to emancipate himself sexually. His brother is a ladies' man with plenty of experience to pass on, all of which leads to blunted situations aimed at spoofing the world of bourgeois manners. They meet Angelika, who's trying to cure her sexual frustrations as well — again, a dud.

"The Sexth Sense" hopefully will not put a damper on that otherwise quite original movement known as the Berlin Underground. —Holl.

Carré Blanc
(White Squares)
(CANADIAN-FRENCH-DOCU-COLOR)

A Les Films Molière release of Pierson Prods. (Paris) — Citel Inc. (Montreal) coproduction. Produced by Isabelle Pierson and Jacques Jean. Directed by Gilles Delannoy and Michel Campioli (for the fiction scenes); conceived by Pierson, Delannoy. Camera (color), Dominique Bouilleret, Laurent Dailland (fiction scenes); editor, Huguette Boisvert; music, Flavien Pierson, Dan Belhassen, performed by Miss Thing (CBS Records); sound, Raymond Marcoux and Michel Brethez (fiction scenes); production managers, Carole Aurousseau (Paris) and Gisèle Sornin (Montreal). Reviewed at the Paramount City Triomphe theater, Paris, March 1, 1986. Running time: 82 MINS.
With: Jacques Paoli, Alain Hamon, Alain Stanke, Marc Menant, Estelle Ghouzi, Jean-Marie Bioteau.

Paris — "Carré Blanc," which opened here just weeks after the cheapo "Mondo Cane"-styled "Les Interdits du Monde," is another peek-a-boo potpourri of the shocking and the bizarre. However, it bears a certain seal of official approval since it was made with the collaboration of several noted media and print journalists.

Each provides a filmed reportage in his field, which range from the trivial (a look at a motorized couple-swapping on Paris' swank Avenue Foch) to the gruesome (an interview with a corpse "restorer" in a Gotham morgue). The only scoop of any genuine interest is a disturbing interview with Donald Lavoie, a one-time hit man for the Montreal underworld who turned stool pigeon and lives under constant police protection.

Episodes are linked by a fictional editorial conference in which the reporters play themselves. Though it is meant to put their work in a context and authenticate the whole it has the reverse effect, at times bordering on parody.

A pop music track has been tacked on to make the enterprise more marketable. Gilles Delannoy, the director, was involved with "La France Interdite," a 1984 exercise in docu sensationalism.—*Len.*

Matanza En Matamoros
(Slaughter In Matamoros)
(MEXICAN-COLOR)

A Películas Mexicanas release of a Cinematográfica Rodríguez production. Produced by Roberto Rodríguez; assistant producer, Roberto Lozano. Directed by José Luis Urquieta. Stars Jorge Luke, Sergio Goyri. Screenplay (based on real events), Jorge Patiño; camera (color), Alberto Areltanos; editor, Francisco Chiu; music, Susan Rodriguez, with groups Chola y Yeni, Carlos y José, Carmen Cardenal and Rojo Gran. Reviewed at Ermita Cinema, Mexico City, Feb. 8, 1986. Running time: **86 MINS.**
Maximino Castro . . . . Jorge Luke
Silverio Bernal . . . . Sergio Goyri
Estela . . . . Patricia Rivera
Elena . . . . Marcela Camacho
Also with: Jorge Fegan, Aaman Méndez, Antonio Zubiaga, Servando Manzetti, Alfredo Mutiérrez, Jorge Victoria, Carlos Terán.

Mexico City — Not only does the low-budget Mexican film "Slaughter In Matamoros" fail to deliver the bloodbath promised in the title, but the feature also fails to give the viewer one full minute of entertainment.

Pic's poster notes that "the Italian mafia is the most well known while the Mexican mafia is the most efficient." Too bad the filmmakers didn't borrow any of this efficiency for the script, photography or acting.

Confused storyline concerns a gang war among drug traffickers along the Mexican-U.S. border. Although pic is touted as being based on true events, it seems "borrowed" in part from "The God-

father," with such elements as a gun hidden in a restaurant lavatory, a murdered thug falling face-first in a plate of spaghetti and a joyful wedding ceremony intercut with scenes of violence.

Add to this two disagreeable heroes (Jorge Luke and Sergio Goyri), lots of badly choreographed shootouts, inane dialog and cheap cutaways to bored ranchero and norteño musicians.

The heroes manage to kill everyone they can before killing each other. The film's tediousness is possibly much more effective in killing any real audience potential. —*Lent.*

Abel
(DUTCH-COLOR)

A Concorde Film release of a First Floor Features production. Produced by Laurens Geels, Dick Maas, Robert Swaab. Written and directed by Alex van Warmerdam. Camera (color), Marc Felperlaan; editor, Hans van Donegen; sound, Georges Bossaers; art direction, Harry Ammerlaan; music, Vincent van Warmerdam. Reviewed at Cinema Intl., Amsterdam, Feb. 21, 1986. Running time: **100 MINS.**
Abel . . . . Alex van Warmerdam
Victor . . . . Henri Garcin
Duif . . . . Olga Zuiderhoek
Zus . . . . Annet Malherbe
Christine . . . . Lous Luca

Amsterdam — Alex van Warmerdam's comic debut feature about Abel, who refuses to go outdoors, is an enjoyable but overlong entry in which the helmer still shows traces of his legit background.

Story follows theatrical farce tradition, piling coincidence upon absurdity, in telling Abel's story via a series of separate, well-constructed sequences, all of which contain imaginative lensing, exceptional art direction and excellent acting.

Unfortunately, writer van Warmerdam runs out of steam while helmer and lead actor van Warmerdam are still amusing themselves, and the pic becomes a drag. Lacking a final super gag, the film would benefit from losing 10 or so minutes.

Van Warmerdam has a sense of humor at times reminiscent of Blake Edwards, and should be given another chance soon.—*Wall.*

Charley
(DUTCH-B&W-16m)

A Kriterion Filmverhuur release of a Wanker Bros. production. Written and directed by Theo van Gogh. Camera (b&w), editor and sound, Willem Hoogenboom. Reviewed at Kriterion Theater, Amsterdam, Holland, Feb. 17, 1986. Running time: **80 MINS.**
Charley . . . . Marie Kooiman
Berte . . . . Rosita Steenbeek

Amsterdam — "Charley" sets out to tease and shock, break rules and taboos, and ends up being very

annoying on two counts. In the first place, it irritates by relentlessly using dirty words, being ornery, doing avidly what's forbidden. It's not witty, it's boring. Secondly, Theo van Gogh's enormous cinematic talent sometimes breaks through the slithery mixture of murder, necrophilia, cannibalism, the culinary use of private parts and excrement, incest and so on.

One regrets that he slid back from the level of his second film ("A Day At The Beach," very successful in many respects) to that of his debut, "Luger." Helmer flashes wicked iniquity with the giggling glee of a precocious adolescent.

Van Gogh is now 28 and in danger of developing into that sad phenomenon, a permanently promising director. On the other hand, newcomer Marie Kooiman in the title role is a delight. —*Wall.*

The Family
(HONG KONG-COLOR)

A D&B production and release. Produced by Dickson Poon. Directed by Raymond Fung. Supervisor, Linda Kuk. Stars Richard Ng, Fung Bo Bo, Lui Fong, May Law, Pauline Kwan, Danny Chan, Lee Lai Chun. Screenplay, Ko Chi Sum; organizers, Ronny Yu, Ko Chi Sum; camera (color), Chan Hou Ming; Art Direction, Li Yiu Kwong; editor, Chan Fung; music, Lam Mun Yee. Reviewed at Jade theater, Hong Kong, March 1, 1986. Running time: **95 MINS.**
(Cantonese soundtrack with English subtitles)

Hong Kong — "The Family" has a built-in light comedy appeal and should be attractive to those who enjoy simple stories with happy endings. Richard Ng is enjoyable to watch, his comic timing still intact. His screen family is composed of lovely child star Fung Bo Bo (in her comeback to film) and the children. Singer-turned actor Lui Fong plays a most convincing teenager.

"The Family" has a happy, charming outlook with the right sentiment, corny jokes, warmth, humor, and a likeable cast. The McDonna (reference to singer Madonna) is portrayed by starlet Lee Lai Chun.

Made on a shoestring budget, the boxoffice gross exceeded $HK6,-000,000 locally. — *Mel.*

Sera Posible El Sur — Mercedes Sosa
(Mercedes Sosa Sings)
(W. GERMAN-DOCU-COLOR)

An Arsenal-Film production, Tübingen. Produced by Gerd Unger and Chris Sievernich. A documentary written and directed by Stefan Paul. Features Mercedes Sosa. Camera (color), Hans Schalk, Hans Warth, Jorge Casal; editor, Hildegard Schroder. Reviewed at Berlin Film Mart Screening Room, March 7, 1986. Running time: **86 MINS.**

Berlin — Known to her faithful Argentine public as "Mother Courage" and "The Voice Of The Andes," Mercedes Sosa had to leave her native country under the military dictatorship and go into exile. Upon her return from a stay in Europe (where she toured Spain, France, the Nethelands and Germany), she took to the road again with two German camera teams to travel the length and breadth of Argentina on a welcome back mission. The footage shot on this occasion forms the substance of Stefan Paul's docu "Sera Posible El Sur — Mercedes Sosa," or "Mercedes Sosa Sings."

Mercedes Sosa comes from the foothills of the Andes. She was born in the Tucumán province of northwestern Argentina. The interview segments are particularly revealing about her past. She roamed the country as a young singer to play every hamlet reachable by public transportation, while her presence at national folk festivals provided the necessary media springboard to fame.

Then, when the dictatorship loomed, she sang for "peace" and supported in her original songs the plight of mothers searching in vain and demonstrating on the Plaza de Mayo for their missing sons and husbands. Her voice and her presence proved to be too much for the authorities. She left for over two years, and then returned rather triumphantly when the censorship ban on her lyrics was lifted.

Helmer Stefan Paul shows her singing at several touring concerts, talking with people in her free time in the squares and on the streets, and only interrupts with moments of dialog that seem to pour forth without the need of prompting questions. To his credit, he and his camera teams stay entirely in the background while making the docu. When Sosa is drifting off with heart and soul into the lyrical rendering of one of her popular numbers, the camera lingers on some of the country's lovely background scenery for visual effect.

Docu deserves continued exposure on the festival circuit, particularly those accenting folk music and concert singers. — *Holl.*

El Día De Los Albañiles II
(Bricklayers Day, Part II)
(MEXICAN-COLOR)

A Películas Mexicanas release of a Frontera Films production. Produced by Gilberto & Adolfo Martínez Solares and Alejandro & Santos Seberon. Directed by Gilberto Martínez Solares. Screenplay, Gilberto & Adolfo Martínez Solares; camera (color), Fernando Colín; editor, José J. Munguía; music, Ernesto Cortázo. Reviewed at Cine Insurgentes 70, Mexico City, Feb. 9, 1986. Running time: **89 MINS.**
Roberto . . . . Alfonso Zayas

Beatriz/Julieta . . . . .Angélica Chain
Fernando . . . . .Hugo Stiglitz
Juan . . . . .Luis de Alba
Compadre (El Enano) . . . . .René Ruiz
(Tun Tun)
Lupita . . . . .Lupita Sandoval
Letitia . . . . .Arlette Pacheco
Reynardo (Chiquilln) . . . .Gerardo Zepeda
(Chiquilln)
Also with: "Pelon Solares" and Yhira
Aparicio.

Mexico City — The sequel to the 1984 Mexican boxoffice hit "Día De Los Albañiles" (Bricklayers Day) is about as unfunny as its predecessor and, like the first film, is not so much about laying bricks as other things.

Low-budget sex comedy pic centers on the marital problems of Beatriz (Angélica Chain) and her husband-with-a-roving eye Roberto (Alfonso Zayas).

The two appear together in so many Mexican comedies with more or less the same situations and accompanied by the same motley band of misfits (René Ruiz "Tun Tun," Luis de Alba, Lupita Sandoval, etc.) that it is difficult to differentiate this pic from so many others ("Los Verduleros," "Rateros De La Vecindad," etc.).

The Chain-Zayas comedy is unhappily wed to a shock horror pic about a psychotic murderer who has a deadly attraction for prostitutes.

To complicate the already-confused plot, Chain plays two roles: blond Beatriz and her identical redhead sister Julieta, who takes her clothes off all the time. Unfortunately, no one seems to notice the resemblance, least of all her husband.

There are several other plot leads that only confuse the story further and very little is resolved by the time the final credits roll. —*Lent.*

Nipagesh Ba'Sivuv
(No Milk Today)
(ISRAELI-DOCU-COLOR-16m)

A Rejuan & Daniel release of a Roy Films production. Produced by Yehuda Barkan, Ezra Shem-tov. Directed by Barkan and Igal Shilon. Camera (color, 16m), Yehiel Neeman, Beni Carmeli, Dror Simchoni; editor, Jonathan Masson: music, compiled by Shilon; sound, Danny Natovich; production manager, Udi Soffer. Reviewed at the Berkey-Pathe-Humphries Studios, Givatayim, Israel, March 17, 1986. Running time: **85 MINS.**
With: Yehuda Barkan, Carolyn Langford, Moshon Albocher, Moshik Timor, Danuta, Igor Borisov.

Givatayim, Israel — After an unhappy experiment with fiction film direction, Yehuda Barkan is back, for the third time around, with a candid camera feature, bound to score as heavily on the local market as the previous two did.

Barkan, who enjoys the reputation of a local Allen Funt, uses his gang to pull fast ones on unsuspecting victims and comes out with some funny gags, some obvious ones, and some sketches that look suspiciously rehearsed before being shot. He uses the considerable physical dimensions of Igor Borisov and the ample bosom of Danuta to put unsuspecting targets in embarassing situations, for instance when Big Igor asks to taste every fruit at a greengrocer's before buying it, to the utter despair of the shopkeeper.

The best gag, however, does not involve people at all. One of the crew hides inside a tree trunk, and every time a dog approaches, intending to relieve itself, the trunk moves away, to the animal's complete discomfiture. The spontaneous reaction on camera is better than anything obtained from humans.

Israelis have already shown their predilection for this genre, and given the sprightly tempo of the gags, the upbeat music and the many familiar faces they will encounter on the screen, this has to be a winner locally, in spite of too many commercials inserted all through the film. Abroad, it looks more like tv fare. Technical credits are satisfactory.—*Edna.*

Xiao Cheng Zhi Chun
(Spring In A Small Town)
(CHINESE-B&W)

A Wen-Hua-Film production, Shanghai Studios. Directed by Fei Mu. Screenplay, Li Tian Ji; camera (b&w), Li Sheng Wei; sound, Miao Zhen Yu; sets, Zhu De Xiung; editor, Xu Ming, Wei Shun Bao; music, Huang Yi Jun; costumes, Qi Qiu Ming. Reviewed at Arsenal-Kino, Berlin, March 14, 1986. Running time: **85 MINS.**
With: Wei Wei (Zhou Yu Wen), Shi Yu (Dai Li Yan), Li Wei (Zhang Zhi Chen), Zhang Hong Mei (Dai Xiu), Cui Zhao Ming (Lao Wang).

Berlin — A rediscovered classic of Chinese cinema, Fei Mu's "Spring In A Small Town" (1948) surfaced at the Berlinale in the Forum of Young Cinema section, won immediate critical acclaim, and is reviewed her for the record. Little doubt, since its bow at both the Hong Kong and Berlin fests, pic will be making the rounds of other fests and archives specializing in the neglected and forgotten high points of cinematic art.

The oddity here is that it appears to be the Peking Film Archive that made the key decision to take the film off the shelf after nearly four decades simply because of the desire to give belated recognition where it was due. Director Fei Mu (1906-1951) left Shanghai shortly after making "Spring In A Small Town" to settle in Hong Kong permanently in 1949 until his death. Apparently, upon Fei Mu's departure, his film was buried.

The story is simple, indeed almost Western in its style and conception. It's a love story, involving a married woman who has to make a decision between her ailing husband and her first and true love who has suddenly reappeared on the scene in this small town near Shanghai shortly after the destructive Second World War. Each day the wife takes long walks along the ruins of the town's wall, while the husband — formerly a wealthy and respected landowner — idles his time away in a garden under a seemingly incurable fit of constant depression.

Enter the long-gone friend, now a physician, who renews acquaintances with the husband but is really there because of an aching heart for the wife, whom he deserted in the midst of the war for unexplained reasons. The husband's younger sister has a crush on the visiting doctor to boot, and now the relationships in the household become more complex. The question of love and morality surfaces. The wife has to make a decision between her heart and the traditional sense of marital duty. It's when the husband, apparently suspecting the worse, falls ill and has to be attended by his friend that the either/or situation reaches a head. She decides for the moral side.

The original script called for a propaganda message to end the film. The doctor was to awaken to the cause of Chinese Communism and seek his destiny in the arms of the people. Fei Mu, however, used his influence as one of Shanghai's most respected directors to mold the story instead into a exposition of traditional Chinese morality in regard to family and marriage. Pic's entire tone is one of resigned pessimism in which the emotions are the guiding force of the characters' actions from beginning to end. Wei Wei as the wife gives a top performance in particular. —*Holl.*

Il Etait une Fois la Télé
(Once Upon A Time There Was Television)
(FRENCH-DOCU-COLOR-16m)

A Dopa release of a Périphérie Prod.- Bibliothèque Pulique d'Information du Centre Pompidou-Centre Regional de Création Cinématographique en Ile de France-Antenne-2 coproduction. Produced by Claudine Bories. Written and directed by Marie-Claude Treilhou. Camera (color, 16m), Lionel Legros, Michel Souriouy; editor, Khadicha Bariha. Reviewed at the 14 Juillet Parnasse theater, Paris, March 1, 1986. Running time: **60 MINS.**

Paris — "Once Upon A Time There Was Television" is a modest but interesting medium-length docu on the influence and role of tv as seen by the inhabitants of a small French village. Director Marie-Claude Treilhou, who has directed two quirky theatrical features and a funny prize-winning short set in Lourdes, went back to her home town in southern France to query the residents on what they think of the boobtube.

Film culls a variety of reactions that deflate the usual clichés of comic hick ignorance one tends to expect when well-meaning Paris tv and film people go out into the sticks with a camera and mike. While some opinions provoke laughter it is never at the expense of the interviewees, who come across as simple, sincere folk nonetheless aware of how the media affect their lives. Treilhou's respectful distance allows a certain melancholy to color her portrait of an isolated burg abandoned by its young people and linked to the larger world by tv.

Film, coproduced by the Antenne-2 network, is getting a one-screen theatrical chance by new art film distrib Dopa Films. It's a worthwhile item for specialized fests and media-themed manifestations. —*Len.*

Gardien de la Nuit
(Night Guardian)
(FRENCH-COLOR)

A Forum Distribution release of a Films du Passage-Forum Prods. Intl. coproduction, with the participation of the Ministry of Culture (CNC). Executive producer, Paolo Branco. Produced by Renaud Victor. Directed by Jean Pierre Limosin. Screenplay, Limosin, Pascale Ferran; camera (Eastmancolor), Thierry Arbogast; editor, Claire Simon; music, Tabuchi; sound, Vasco Pimentel; art direction, Laurence Brenguier; assistant director, Marie-Line Chesnot. Reviewed at the Ponthieu screening room, Paris, March 18, 1986. Running time: **104 MINS.**
Yves . . . . .Jean-Philippe Ecoffey
Aurore . . . . .Aurelle Doazan
Vaillant . . . . .Nicolas Silberg
Armand . . . . .Vincent Perez
Lecoeur . . . . .Olivier Perrier
Post office clerk . . . . .Mireille Perrier
Achard . . . . .Philippe de Brugada
Also with: Jean-Claude Frissung, Serge Giamberardino, Jean-Paul Bonnaire, Guy Pannequin, Anne Gautier, François Bourcier.

Paris — Eccentric humor and imaginative direction characterize "Night Guardian," a beguiling solo debut feature by Jean Pierre Limosin, who codirected (with Alain Bergala) the offbeat 1983 feature, "Faux Fuyants," which suffered from inadequate technical conditions. Now directing alone, from an original script he penned with Pascale Ferran, Limosin offers a technically polished comedy-drama that is at once personal and entertaining, though its most receptive audience will be found in the art houses.

Film follows the erratic adventures of a young man in a provincial city, who does night rounds for the municipal police force, but steals cars during the day, and occasionally ventures into other criminal activities, like the robbery of the local post office and even attempted murder.

His acts seem for the most part

gratuitous, though there's no doubt the reason for his behavior is the fact that he's in love with a childhood friend. He has trouble seeing her because she works as a nurse during the day and he hangs around too often with the spoiled sons of the town notables who have hired him for the police force (his father, whom we never see, has used his influence to find him the job). His double life is made knottier because he doesn't want her to know about his police work — he wants to impress her with his picaresque boasts.

He constantly puts himself into perilous situations, robbing the post office where he has previously sent his heart throb a romantic telegram. Trailing the girl, who is horseback riding with a current wooer, he tries to run the latter down (in yet another stolen car) and finds himself being hunted by a police dragnet (in which he normally should have served). His superior eventually stumbles onto the truth, but uses a no less roundabout method to expose him.

Limosin's brisk, allusive style, underscored by Claire Simon's editing, slyly keeps the viewer off-balance in any attempts to pin down his protagonist's circuitous behavior. Jean-Philippe Ecoffey, who attracted attention in Alain Tanner's "No Man's Land" and Claude Miller's "L'Effrontée," is fine as the rebel without a cause, or perhaps too many. Aurelle Doazan is charming as the immature light of his life. Nicolas Silberg, as Ecoffey's boss, leads a good supporting cast. —*Len*.

'Round Midnight
(FRENCH-U.S.-COLOR)

A WB/Col release (WB in U.S.) of a Little Bear-P.E.C.F. coproduction. Produced by Irwin Winkler. Directed by Bertrand Tavernier. Stars Dexter Gordon, François Cluzet. Screenplay, Tavernier, David Rayfiel, inspired by incidents in the lives of Francis Paudras and Bud Powell; camera (Panavision, Eastmancolor), Bruno de Keyzer; editor, Armand Psenny; music composed, arranged and conducted by Herbie Hancock; sound, Michel Desrois, William Flageollet; production design, Alexandre Trauner; costumes, Jacqueline Moreau; production managers, Pierre Saint-Blancat, Monty Diamond (N.Y.). Reviewed at Billancourt studios, Paris, March 7, 1986. Running time: **133 MINS.**
Dale Turner . . . . Dexter Gordon
Francis Borier . . . . François Cluzet
Bérangère . . . . Gabrielle Haker
Buttercup . . . . Sandra Reaves-Phillips
Darcey Leigh . . . . Lonette McKee
Sylvie . . . . Christine Pascal
Eddie Wayne . . . . Herbie Hancock
Ace . . . . Bobby Hutcherson
Mr. Borier . . . . Pierre Trabaud
Mrs. Borier . . . . Frédérique Meininger
Ben . . . . John Berry
Goodley . . . . Martin Scorsese
Also with: Ron Carter, Billy Higgins, Freddie Hubbard, John McLaughlin, Eric Le Lann, Pierre Michelot, Palle Mikkelborg, Mads Vinding, Wayne Shorter, Cedar Walton, Tony Williams, Liliane Rovère, Ged Marlon, Hart Leroy Bibbs, Benoit Regent, Victoria Gabrielle Platt, Arthur French, Alain Sarde, Philippe Noiret, Eddy Mitchell.

Paris — " 'Round Midnight" is a superbly crafted music world drama in which Gallic director Bertrand Tavernier, whose passion for American jazz is second only to his mania for films, pays a moving dramatic tribute to the great black musicians who lived and performed in Paris in the late 1950s. Film is dedicated to jazz giants Bud Powell and Lester Young, the composite inspiration for the story's central personage.

Produced by Irwin Winkler for Warner Bros., which financed the $3,000,000 picture for world distribution rights, the largely English-lingoed " 'Round Midnight" is a rare example of Franco-American filmmaking in the truest sense of the term: where transatlantic coproduction and collaboration are dictated by subject matter, treatment and technique. Tavernier, who already explored the roots of jazz more casually in his docu (with Robert Parrish) on the American South, "Mississippi Blues," seems to have made the film he set out to make. He has done so in a style that reflects his reality as a European looking at a culture he loves, but which remains nonetheless not his own.

With his American coscripter, David Rayfiel, he has placed deftly the themes of cultural roots, affinities and distances at the heart of the screenplay, which dramatizes the friendship between an aging jazz saxophonist, who has accepted an engagement at the legendary Blue Note club in Saint-Germain-des-Près, and a passionate young French admirer who is ready to make personal sacrifices to help his idol. Story is in fact inspired by the real-life rapport between Bud Powell and French illustrator Francis Paudras.

Like Paudras, the film's Gallic protagonist tries to save his hero by moving him out of his milieu and into his own home, where he can control his excesses and goad him into working (and also provide a motivation for his own desperate life). When the jazz man apparently recovers some of his erstwhile form and creativity, his young friend thinks he has won. But, as subtly and poignantly limned by Rayfiel and Tavernier, the rehabilitation is illusory despite the profound affection that links the two men, nevertheless divided by culture and experience.

Again playing on a hunch (as he did with 73-year-old Louis Ducreux in "A Sunday In The Country") Tavernier has cast a non-professional in the central role: Dexter Gordon, the 63-year-old jazz veteran whom Tavernier has long admired. With his hoarse, hesitant diction and his lanky shuffle, Gordon fills the part of the world-weary artist with his own personality and jagged warmth. François Cluzet, one of France's most promising young actors, is excellent as the ardently helpful but finally uncomprehending French friend.

Large supporting cast boasts a fine mix of Franco-American actors, singers and musicians, notably Sandra Reaves-Phillips, Lonette McKee, Christine Pascal (as Cluzet's estranged wife), and John Berry, the Paris-based Yank director, who plays the boss of the Blue Note. As his Gotham counterpart, director Martin Scorsese offers a vivid, hilarious cameo as the owner of the Birdland jazz club.

The many musical sequences, well-integrated into the narrative, were arranged and conducted by Herbie Hancock, who added some new compositions to the selected standards, and also plays one of the members of Gordon's band (along with other noted jazzmen). All the music was performed live during the lensing, which posed problems galore for sound engineers who come out of the ordeal with their heads held high.

Film is no less a treat for the eye as for the ear. Shot almost entirely in the Epinay studios north of Paris (with some exteriors in New York and Lyon), production has been vividly designed by veteran Alexandre Trauner. Eyes may pop at his reconstruction of a Saint-Germain-des-Près street on Epinay's sound stages, though he is at his most imaginative best with less spectacular interiors, like the jazz club sets and the Louisiane Hotel, the Bohemian Left Bank abode for many artists and intellectuals in the 1950s.

(Trauner once said nothing is harder to design than a hotel room, because of its general lack of distinction.)

Bruno de Keyzer, who lovingly lensed the natural locations of "A Sunday In The Country," shows masterly versatility with the artificial lighting of "Midnight." Other tech credits are all firstrate.

Planned for a fall release, pic reportedly will be trimmed slightly from its current 133-minute running time. —*Len*.

Off Beat
(COLOR)

Unfunny police comedy wastes a lot of talent.

A Buena Vista Distribution release of a Touchstone Films presentation of a Ufland/Roth/Ladd production, in association with Silver Screen Partners II. Produced by Joe Roth, Harry Ufland. Directed by Michael Dinner. Screenplay, Mark Medoff, from story by Dezso Magyar; camera (Technicolor, prints by DeLuxe), Carlo di Palma; editor, Dede Allen, Angelo Corrao; music, James Horner; sound, Frank Warner; production design, Woods MacKintosh; casting, Howard Feuer. Reviewed at Disney Studios, Burbank, Calif., April 7, 1986. (MPAA Rating: PG.) Running time: **92 MINS.**
Joe Gower . . . . Judge Reinhold
Rachel Wareham . . . . Meg Tilly
Abe Washington . . . . Cleavant Derricks
Pete Peterson . . . . Joe Mantegna
August . . . . Jacques D'Amboise
The Commissioner . . . . Fred Gwynne
Mickey . . . . Harvey Keitel

Hollywood — The worst thing one can say about a comedy is that it isn't funny, which is the case for Touchstone Films' latest offering, "Off Beat," a tedious film that suffers visibly from the involvement of several artists known for good work on more serious fare. Effort here is not embarrassingly bad, it's just boring and bets are that no path will be beaten to the boxoffice.

Credits include three Tony winners: scripter Mike Medoff ("Children Of A Lesser God") and actors Joe Mantegna ("Glengarry Glen Ross") and Cleavant Derricks ("Dreamgirls"); National Dance Institute founder Jacques D'Amboise, who plays a choreographer here, noted cinematographer Carlo di Palma ("Blow Up" and "Hannah And Her Sisters"), and Academy Award-nominated Meg Tilly ("Agnes Of God"), as well as actor Harvey Keitel ("Mean Streets," and "Taxi Driver").

Except for Derricks, who shows a natural comedic talent playing a New York City cop in over his head in a mixup involving a friend (Judge Reinhold) subbing for him at the annual police benefit dance auditions, cast led by Reinhold seem so conscientious about trying to be funny, they forget to lighten up.

Reinhold, a library clerk who zips through the stacks on roller skates to retrieve books, returns a favor and agrees to replace friend Abe Washington (Derricks) in the chorus line where he falls instantly for a cute little policewoman (Tilly).

He's supposed to fail the audition, but instead woos the choreographer (D'Amboise) so he can stick around and get to known Tilly better.

To keep up the charade for Tilly, he ends up in uniform more often than he should and unwittingly gets himself involved in a few incidents that wouldn't cause the ordinary urbanite to bother crossing the street — a purse snatching, a car chase, a hapless car theft and an amiable bank robbery.

Romance between Reinhold and Tilly is lackluster, attributable partially to some dreary dialog where they try to redefine how to be in love and be cops at the same time. They can't dance, either.

End result is a film with zero tension and a predictible ending.
—*Brit.*

Band Of The Hand
(COLOR)

Okay actioner with a tv pedigree.

A Tri-Star Pictures release of a Michael Mann production from Tri-Star-Delphi IV and V Prods. Produced by Michael Rauch. Executive producer, Mann. Directed by Paul Michael Glaser. Screenplay, Leo Garen, Jack Baran; camera (Metrocolor), Reynaldo Villalobos; editor, Jack Hofstra; music, Michael Rubini; sound (Dolby), Howard Warren; production design, Gregory Bolton; art direction, Mark Harrington; set decoration, Don K. Ivey; costume design, Robert De-Mora; associate producer, Don Kurt; assistant director, Patrick Kehoe; casting, Pat McCorkle. Reviewed at the Hollywood Pacific, L.A., April 11, 1986. (MPAA Rating: R.) Running time: **109 MINS.**

Joe .... Stephen Lang
Ruben .... Michael Carmine
Nikki .... Lauren Holly
J.L. .... John Cameron Mitchell
Carlos .... Daniele Quinn
Moss .... Leon Robinson
Dorcey .... Al Shannon
Aldo .... Danton Stone
Tito .... Paul Calderon
Cream .... Larry Fishburne
Nestor .... James Remar

Hollywood — "Band Of The Hand" is like a socially conscious "Miami Vice," in which a bunch of society's misfits pull together to try to rid the streets of some of the drug kingpins Crockett and Tubbs missed. Exec produced by "Vice" mastermind Michael Mann and directed, in his feature debut, by three-time "Vice" helmer Paul Michael Glaser, pic has very much the look and sound of the hit series, and its concerns are roughly the same. B.o. for this unpreviewed item could be okay in short runs.

With a dramatic trajectory along the lines of a "Lord Of The Flies" in reverse, script by Leo Garen and

Jack Baran has five of Miami's scummiest lowlifes jailed and quickly dumped in the middle of the Everglades, where they encounter a super tough survivalist named Joe who lets them know they'll either learn to work with each other and survive or die.

The boys, who represent a perfect ethnic melting pot consisting of a hot-blooded Latin, a self-styled Romeo, one bad black dude, an illiterate poor white trash specimen and a punkish father killer, learn to clean fish, hunt wild boar and eat worms and like it. Pic's main source of comedy stems from watching how wimpy these street toughs instantly become when confronted with the rigors of the wild, although there are more than enough shots of the boys taking to the trees when bears and other beasts head their way.

For his part, Joe turns out to be a local Indian and Vietnam War vet with not a little of Billy Jack in him. A probation officer by trade and a do-gooder by instinct, Joe finally leads his shaped-up crew back to Miami, where they occupy a house in the seediest part of town and begin cleaning up the neighborhood.

This doesn't go down too well with the local druglords, particularly the arrogant Larry Fishburne and his boss and top dog, the ever-evil James Remar, who has stolen Romeo's girlfriend while the latter has been slogging through the swamp.

Two climactic shootouts are spectacular enough, and film seems to be saying that, with the military draft gone, some other way has to be found to discipline young punks into such positive pursuits as duking it out, *mano a mano*, with the big bad boys.

Nifty use of slow dissolves and fade-outs is identical to style seen on "Miami Vice," as is the lengthy use of rock songs. Bob Dylan's excellent title tune, on which he is backed by Tom Petty & The Heartbreakers, harks back to his protest song groove, and pops up three times during the running time.

A few of the film's simplifications are laughable, but Glaser keeps matters moving at a resonable pace and cast, headed by the very capable Stephen Lang as Joe, proves engaging. For what this is, it's not so bad. —*Cart.*

What Happened To Kerouac?
(DOCU-COLOR/B&W)

A New Yorker Films release. Produced by Richard Lerner. Directed by Lerner and Lewis MacAdams. Coproduced by MacAdams, Nathaniel Dorsky, Malcolm Hart. Editor, Dorsky, Robert Estrin; interviews photographed by Lerner; poetry sequences photographed by Dorsky; associate producer, Eve Levy.

Reviewed at Roy & Niuta Titus Theater 2, Museum of Modern Art, N.Y. (in New Directors/New Films series), March 27, 1986. (No MPAA Rating.) Running time: **96 MINS.**

With: Steve Allen, William Burroughs, Carolyn Cassady, Neil Cassady, Ann Charters, Gregory Corso, Robert Creeley, Diane DiPrima, Lawrence Ferlinghetti, Allen Ginsberg, John Clellon Holmes, Herbert Huncke, Joyce Johnson, Jack Kerouac, Jan Kerouac, Fran Landesman, Michael McClure, Father "Spike" Morissette, Edie Kerouac Parker, Gary Snyder, Edward White.

Originally a 55-minute videotape, "What Happened To Kerouac?" was transferred to 35m after well-attended showings at a Los Angeles video theater demonstrated greater theatrical potential than the producers originally had thought. In the specialized market, docu does have a lot going for it given the apparent unwaning interest in the Beatnik writer, although it faces a healthier commercial life in non-theatrical.

Presenting footage from various sources (fascinating old tv talk shows and home movies, new on-location footage and recent interviews), the makers of this creditable documentary on American cult hero Jack Kerouac come up with many answers to the title question: Why, in other words, did the gifted, influential author of "On The Road" drink himself into an early grave?

Given several pieces of the author's troubled and puzzling personality, viewers will have a field day making their own judgments. They get input, for example, from Kerouac cónfidante Gregory Corso, who says his late friend didn't know how to handle success. William Burroughs, a little less superficial in his assessments, says the essentially apolitical man was deeply disturbed when the Beat Movement took on political dimensions.

Filmmaker Richard Lerner and poet Lewis MacAdams also incorporate pastoral scenes shot in one-time Kerouac stomping grounds (hometown Lowell, Mass., and San Francisco). Their choice of soundtrack music, the jazz of the late Thelonious Monk, works well throughout.

Very nearly losing control over their voluminous source material, filmmakers allow viewers' attention to rise and fall, depending on the appeal and intelligence of the Kerouac friends and relatives who are interviewed. Not all of them are as interesting as Kerouac.

Technically, the tape-to-film transfer yielded good results. The route from 3/4-inch to 1-inch tape then to a 16m transform and finally to a 35m negative made the extreme closeups of the "cast" larger and sharper.

More routinely competent than trail-blazing as a docu, "What Happened To Kerouac?" might have trouble escaping the commerical confines of the genre, but it's

still an honest and thorough bio of a cultural figure who has rarely lacked attention in the media.
—*Binn.*

Zone Troopers
(COLOR)

Good war actioner marred by aliens' intervention.

An Empire Pictures production and release. Produced by Paul De Meo. Executive producer, Charles Band. Directed by Danny Bilson. Screenplay, Bilson, De Meo; camera, (Technicolor Rome), Mac Ahlberg; editor, Ted Nicolaou; music, Richard Band; sound, Mario Bramonti; special effects, John Buechler; costumes, Jill Ohanneson; assistant director, David Boyd; associate producer, Debra Dion; casting (Italy), Rita Forzano. Reviewed at Pacific World Theater, April 11, 1986, Hollywood. (MPAA Rating: PG.) Running time: **88 MINS.**

Sarge .... Tim Thomerson
Joey .... Timothy Van Patten
Mittens .... Art La Fleur
Dolan .... Biff Manard
Alien .... William Paulson

Hollywood — Imagine outerspace aliens in Italy helping our boys win World War II. Somebody did and therein lies the plot of Empire Pictures latest offering, "Zone Troopers." In reality this premise is neither as ridiculous nor terrible as it sounds. Surprisingly "Zone Troopers" is a competent, moderately amusing war saga with the aliens just along for the ride.

Obviously shooting for the sci-fi effects crowd, pic is likely to be more pleasing to World War II buffs since it is basically the same old story with many of the pleasing clichés and characters intact. Arrival of aliens is actually the least entertaining part of the pic and, with little for them to do, the film comes to a virtual standstill.

On the plus side, director Danny Bilson, who wrote the script with Paul De Meo, has a good film sense and understanding of the elements that make a decent war story — and a sense of humor to boot.

Story starts out with the typical cast of characters and starts to unravel as a good war-themed B-picture. Surrounded by evil "Krauts" in the middle of occupied Italy, Sarge (Tim Thomerson) and his men try to find a way back behind the American lines. Instead they run into an inexplicable spaceship.

The platoon in question includes the mandatory buck private still wet behind the ears (Timothy Van Patten), the dumb but lovable corporal (Art La Fleur) and the pain-in-the-neck journalist (Biff Manard) just out for a story. Sarge himself is quite a character, seemingly defying death so many times he's been nicknamed "Iron Sarge" by his men.

Bilson has fun with the rituals, even allowing Mittens (La Fleur) to take a swipe at the Führer himself Unfortunately, the aliens are mostly dead weight and the mission to find out what they're about and to keep them out of the hands of the Germans leads nowhere. Someone should have had the sense to look at the picture they were making instead of the boxoffice potential.

Too bad because performances are mostly right on the money. Cast seems to be having a good time playing out these pat characters. Thomerson as Sarge is suitably gruff while La Fleur is the kind of soldier who really would walk a mile for a camel.

Van Patten also does a good job as the only one in the group young and innocent enough to believe in the existence of aliens. It's a bit much for 1944, but who's counting.

Effects by John Buechler are passable, but unlikely to raise too many oohs and aahs from the crowd. Otherwise Mac Ahlberg's lensing on Italian locations looks fine and actually manages to capture the wartime dankness. Other tech credits including Richard Band's score are a step up for Empire. —Jagr.

Esther
(FRENCH-ISRAELI-COLOR)

An Agav Films Intl. Distribution of an Agav Films production in association with Channel 4 Television (U.K.), ORF, IKON and United Studios, Israel. Executive producer, Reuven Kornfeld. Produced and directed by Amos Gitai. Screenplay, Gitai, Stephen Levine based on the Biblical story; camera (Fujicolor, prints by LTC France, United Studios, Israel), Henri Alékan; editor, Sheherezade Saadi; music, Sikumar Tumar (santouri), Ishi Yashi (flute), traditional Yemenite and Armenian songs performed and arranged by Sarah Cohen, traditional Arab songs by Rin Banah; sound, Claude Bertrand; production designer, Richard Ingersoll; costume design, Thierry Fortan; production manager, Edgar Tenenbaum; casting, Levia Hon, Ziad Fahoum. Reviewed at the Tel Aviv Museum, Tel Aviv, Israel, March 25, 1986. Running time: 93 MINS.
With: Mouhammad Bakri (Mordechai), Simona Binyamini (Esther), Shmuel Wolf (narrator), Giuliano Mer (Haman), Zare Vartenian (Ahashverosh), David Cohen (Hatak).

Tel Aviv — This picture, selected by the Critics' Week for the next Cannes Film Festival, in all probability will delight film theoreticians and left-wing politicians alike, but will be received less enthusiastically by a general audience which may find it a cold intellectual exercise. Shots that seem to go on forever, a camera that is either motionless or gliding very slowly and deliberately, actors delivering their lines in a declamatory fashion and most of the action taking place off-screen, pedantic framing of each setup, deep focus exploited to enhance dramatic intentions and sound harnessed to imply modern aspects in an otherwise historical pageant, these are only some of the aspects in

Amos Gitai's first foray into fiction, which will invite frequent discussions and admiration from professionals.

Plot is based on the Bible's Book of Esther, which tells the story of a Jewish girl in ancient Persia, chosen by the Emperor as his spouse, who shrewdly manages to save her own people from extermination.

Gitai's treatment allows the Biblical story to proceed in an almost straightforward fashion, using actors mostly as moving pawns reciting the old texts, into which some quotes from other Books, like Song of Songs and Ecclesiastics as well as additional modern narration, are inserted.

The political context, which obviously lured Gitai to this subject, emerges only in the last 10 minutes, when we are offered a first moral, that in the Bible, the Jews saved from extermination are allowed to massacre their foes, and a second moral, when the leading actors walk in the last shot, in modern dress, through the streets of the city of Acre, and introduce themselves, their biographies implying that ancient history is repeating itself now, in Israel, in the relations between Jews and Arabs (the cast is a mixed one, on purpose).

All along the way, however, Gitai slips in hints of present-day reality, whether in the sound of modern traffic in the background, or the sight of burning tires which have become a typical expression of political protest.

Shot among the dilapidated half-ruins of a Haifa slum where Gitai shot an earlier documentary, and on the walls of the old city of Acre, the film, except for the end, looks much like a traditional Purim play, usually put on in Jewish schools for the special religious festival celebrating the ancient victory of Esther the Queen over the enemies of her people. It is impossible to refer to acting in this case, since no such thing is required here, but both the lighting by veteran Henri Alékan and the camerawork by Nurith Aviv, a director of photography in her own right who gladly accepted to work under Alékan's supervision, are admirable, using modest resources of maximum effect.

Gitai, better known for a string of radical leftist documentaries, often criticizing Israeli official politics, already has established a sound reputation for himself, and his film, while obviously restricted to art house circuits, will probably get a lot of attention.—Edna.

Was geschah wirklich zwischen den Bildern?
(What Really Happened Between The Images?)
(W. GERMAN-DOCU-COLOR)

A Werner Nekes Film production, Mühlheim/Ruhr. Produced, written, and directed by Werner Nekes. Camera (color), Bernd Upnmoor; editor, Astrid Nicklaus; music, Anthony Moore; sound, Andreas Wölki; sets, Dore O. Reviewed at Berliner Screening Room, Berlin, April 1, 1985. Running time: 83 MINS.

Berlin — "What Really Happened Between The Images?" by experimental filmmaker Werner Nekes is a film lexicon on the pre-history of the cinema. Viewers will be fascinated by Nekes' own collection of cinemabilia, as well as his knowledge of which museums should be visited and which authorities should be read on the topic.

Recently, a number of books have appeared on the "archaeology of the cinema," but an authoritative research has yet to be made. Nekes' docu is a step in the right direction. His "kinematographic" findings include quaint 17th-century peep shows, 19th-century magic lantern shows, flicks, books and the kinetoscope parlors, zoetropes and phenakistoscopes, thaumatropes and mutoscopes, lithophanes and traxinoscopes, and whatever else in terminology borrowed mostly from the Greeks.

This is a simple, straightforward documentary designed entirely to deliver information in as pleasant a manner as possible via the use of film images to present other film images. When one has seen the film at one sitting, the urge comes to sit through it again to sort out the puzzles and note the subtleties in the development of cinematic art — for the pioneers themselves were mostly interested in toying with visual tricks and an increasingly accessible mechanical and electrical invention.
—Holl.

I Love You
(FRENCH-ITALIAN-COLOR)

A UGC release of an Alliance Film et Communications-Films A2-UGC-23 Guigno (Rome) corproduction. Produced by Maurice Bernart. Directed by Marco Ferreri. Stars Christophe Lambert. Screenplay, Ferreri, Didier Kaminka, Enrico Oldoini; camera (Panavision, Eastmancolor), William Lubtchansky; editor, Ruggero Mastroianni; music, Les Jivaros, Zéme Prix de Beauté, and Les Illuminés du 8 Décembre; art direction, Jean-Pierre Kohut-Svelko; makeup, Maud Baron; production manager, Daniel Deschamps; assistant director, Laurent Laubier. Reviewed at UGC, Neuilly, April 7, 1986. Running time: 100 MINS.
Michel . . . . .Christophe Lambert
Yves .Eddy Mitchell
Hélène . . . . .Agnès Soral
Barbara . . . . .Anémone
Maria . . . . .Flora Barillaro
Pierre . . . . .Marc Berman
Camelia . . . . .Laura Manszky
Prostitute . . . . .Jeanne Marine

Dentist . . . . .Jean Reno

Paris — In Marco Ferreri's new film, "I Love You," Christophe Lambert plays an emotionally shriveled young man who develops a fetish for a doll-like talking key holder, which declares "I Love You" when its owner whistles. It's a typically bizarre romantic situation from Ferreri — still putting contemporary decadent civilization under a distorted magnifying glass — but it's one of his feeblest, and, cinematically, pedestrian efforts, to date. Franco-Italian coproduction may ride briefly on its star's popularity in local playoffs, but it's unlikely general audiences elsewhere will warm up to it.

We meet Lambert, a travel agency clerk who lives in a suburban warehouse-turned-apartment building, breaking up with Anémone, who has reproached him for not giving her a child. He seems subsequently pretty turned off on the fair sex and their unfair demands, so it's understandable that he gets perversely obsessed with the key gizmo, which he finds one evening in a lot. It has luscious red lips, blue eyes and only responds with its welcome one-liner when you call it. Lambert seems to have found, true, uncomplicated love. He can just stick it on his tv screen, and sit back happily, whistling and masturbating.

Unfortunately, even key rings can be promiscuous: one day it responds not to his call, but to a whistle from Lambert's lonely, unemployed neighbor (Eddy Mitchell). In a fit of jealousy, Lambert runs his motorcycle into a brick wall, and loses some teeth. Tragedy: he can no longer whistle.

The story doesn't end there, but it might just as well for all the dramatic mileage Ferreri and co-scripters Didier Kaminka and Enrico Oldoini get out of it. They have mistaken an amusing sketch idea for another of the filmmaker's protracted fables of modern society, and Ferreri dutifully has unloaded his familiar bag of bloated symbolism and grotesque props. His indictment of loveless mankind and soulless urban landscapes is becoming as tediously mechanical as his talking key doll.

Though William Lubtchansky's lensing is fine, Ferreri seems to have lost all of his filmmaking sense, and the editing is clumsy. The actors fare the worst: Lambert flounders in what must be one of his emptiest roles to date; Mitchell, the rock singer, moons about insipidly with monologs on loneliness; and a supporting cast of lovelorn ladies and eccentrics performs heavily italicized roles. —Len.

Happy Din Don
(HONG KONG-COLOR)

A Golden Harvest-Paragon Films production and release. Executive producers, Raymond Chow, Michael Hui. Directed by Hui. Stars Hui, Cherie Chung, Tung Pui, Michael Lai, Wong Ching, Wong Waan Sze, Ricky Hui, Anita Mui, Winnie Chin, Tin Ching, Shen Wai. Camera (color), Ardy Lam; editor, Chueng Yiu Chung; production supervised by Louis Sit; production design, David Chan; art direction, Carman Wan; music, Michael Lai. Reviewed at State theater, Hong Kong, April 1, 1986. Running time: **98 MINS.**
(Cantonese Soundtrack with English subtitles)

Hong Kong — Michael Hui, after a long shaping-up phase, is happily in top comedic form for his Easter presentation. Picture is a simple but ingeniously diversified bit of Cantonese slapstick.

Hui is an ordinary musician, a nightclub guitarist. His indulgence in gambling costs him his job and unpaid apartment. Wandering in a dark alley, he accidentally overhears a gang of drug dealers on a murder assignment. Seen by the baddies, Hui tries to fool them by acting as a blind man, in an hilarious sequence.

Eventually he escapes with the help of friend and roommate Michael Lai as a female performer in an all-girl band bound for Thailand. While in Bangkok, Hui falls for lead singer Cherie Chung. Tung Pui tries to court Hui in a "Some Like It Hot" predicament. Cherie Chung makes a glamorous decorative attraction as romantic interest.

"Happy Din Don" is a jovial, unpretentious Cantonese comedy that is very agreeable for the cinemagoing families of Hong Kong. Properly edited, its humor could be universal. Hui is still Hong Kong's number one film clown.
—*Mel.*

The Ladies Club
(COLOR)

Rapists beware: castrating women are on patrol.

A New Line Cinema release of a Media Home Ent./Heron Intl. production. Produced by Nick J. Mileti, Paul Mason. Directed by A.K. Allen. Screenplay, Mason, Fran Lewis Ebeling, from novel "Sisterhood" by Betty Black, Casey Bishop; camera (color), Adam Greenberg; editor, Marion Segal, Randall Torno; music, Lalo Schifrin; production design, Stephen Myles Berger; assistant director-production manager, H. Gordon Boos; associate producers, John Broderick, Richard Kahn, Rosemary Dennis; casting, Ellen Meyer. Reviewed at Regency 2 theater, Philadelphia, April 11, 1986. (MPAA Rating: R.) Running time: **90 MINS.**

Joan Taylor	Karen Austin
Lucy Bricker	Diana Scarwid
Dr. Constance Lewis	Christine Belford
Richard Harrison	Bruce Davison
Eva	Shera Danese
Georgiane	Beverly Todd
Rosalie	Marilyn Kagan
Carol	Kit McDonough
Ed Bricker	Arliss Howard
Harriet	Randee Heller
Eddie	Paul Carafotes
Jack Dwyer	Nicholas Worth
Pete Campanella	Scott Lincoln

Philadelphia — A formula vigilantes' revenge film about rapists' victims, direct or indirect, who band together to give justice-evading criminals their comeuppance or, more precisely, their comeoffance, "The Ladies Club" reflects its distaff helming by omitting even a tittle of titillation.

Its graphic rape scenes avoid any voyeuristic peek at exposed female flesh, depicting only perpetrators' violence and ravishees' suffering.

Director A.K. Allen (a pseudonymn for a woman director from television), also detours from standard substandard exploitation film practice by eliciting commendably lowkey performances from several of her principals, notably Karen Austin as the policewoman whose vicious brutalization triggers the plot, Diana Scarwid as the sister of a permanently traumatized rape victim, and Christine Belford as a grieving mother who is also, conveniently, a skilled surgeon.

This particular "magnificent seven," with token integration balancing a black baddie, conspires to track down recidivist rapists via the policewoman's access to official files, immobilize them with doctored liquor and deprived them of their crime-causing testes. (Ads for the film get right to the point: "Men who attack women have two big problems. 'The Ladies Club' is about to remove them both.")

There are several suspenseful sequences and one mildly amusing one, in which a policeman ponders whether to list castration as assault or robbery. However, the quick release of some of the offenders defies credibility. Would the testimony of three hoodlums, for instance, outweigh that of a viciously battered policewoman?

Awkwardly inserted statistics about the frequency of rape (every seven minutes) and low conviction rate (2%) fail to justify such lapses in logic.—*Hari.*

Home Of The Brave
(COLOR)

Arty rocker Laurie Anderson caught in eye-popping ear-blasting performance.

A Cinecom Intl. Films release of a Talk Normal and Warner Bros. Records production. Produced by Paula Mazur. Executive producer, Elliott Abbott. Written, directed and visuals by Laurie Anderson. Camera, John Lindley; editor, Lisa Day; artistic director, Perry Hoberman ; soundtrack coproducers, Roma Baran, Laurie Anderson; sound engineer, Leanne Ungar; production designer, David Gropman; electronics designer, Bob Bielecki; costumes, Susan Hilferty. Reviewed at Mark Goodson auditorium, N.Y., March 19, 1986. (No MPAA Rating.) Running time: **90 MINS.**
With: Laurie Anderson, Joy Askew (keyboards, vocals), Adrian Belew (guitar, vocals), Richard Landry (horns, winds), Dollette McDonald (vocals), Janice Pendarvis (vocals), Sand Won Park (kayageum and voice), David Van Tiegham (persussion), Jane Ira Bloom (horns), Bill Obrecht (horns), and William S. Burroughs.

Not long ago, pics like "Home Of The Brave," an unpredictable musical art film showcasing the talents of "performance artist" Laurie Anderson, had few, if any, chances to score at the boxoffice. But in this era of realistic commercial expectations and specialized audiences, the right courting of the entertainer's cultish but rabid following will mean big bucks — on a modest level. Down the line, home-video prospects look even better.

Pulling in converts with this pic won't be impossible for the Illinois-born performer and Gotham-bred bandleader. Sporting an infectious grin and mod duds straight out of clubland, topped off by a spiky but mainstream punk haircut, Anderson sings or merely speaks her witty lyrics. The colorful verse is backed by a compelling fusion of conventional rock instruments (electric guitar and saxophone dominate) and loopy electronic sonics.

The heretofore unseen or unheard result is general embraceable and only rarely offputting, at least in the visually sensational context of Anderson's debut film. Lensed in the New York area, largely in a studio and in part before a live audience, "Home Of The Brave" is an eye-popping tapestry stitched with video, chaotic choreography, subtitles, and wild props such as dancing shirts and a so-called drum suit that turns the singer's entire body into a percussive instrument.

The proceedings have to be seen to be believed, although there will be some who won't want to believe. Her experimental efforts are at times too distancing. The wearing of masks turning her and the musicians into Gumby-like wraiths, for example, achieved mixed results.

Still, whatever she does is done with tongue firmly implanted in cheek. Anderson loves the odd turn of the phrase, and to demonstrate her literary influence, she dances a tango with novelist William S. Burroughs, the coiner of one Anderson title, "Language Is A Virus."

In all, the nine-piece band delivers 18 Anderson compositions, some very brief. Others are lengthy, such as "Gravity's Rainbow," an edgy, atmospheric piece (an apt description of all her material). Every tune demonstrates the expertise of the backing musicians, although guitarist Adrian Belew often upstages his colleagues.

Belew, as well as background vocalists Dolette McDonald and Janice Pendarvis, once performed with the Talking Heads. Comparisons between "Home Of The Brave" and TTH's "Stop Making Sense" are inevitable. Both Anderson and David Bryne are unlikely but likeable rock stars who are pros on film. Pushing the boundaries of mainstream accessibility, both artists peddle funk-influenced rock, recorded for the screen via state-of-the-art digital processes.

Farther than Bryne, however, Anderson presses into artistic ground that some may find trying. Indeed, the artist is aware of this, at one point assuming a d.j. role for a "difficult listening hour."

Still, she and her film may be a downright breeze to market, given the backing of her record label (Warner Bros.), promo tie-ins with MTV, her support from critics, as well as the distributor's experience with the kind of audience to attract (Cinecom also handled "Stop Making Sense" domestically).—*Binn.*

Follia Amore Mio
(Madness My Love)
(ITALIAN-COLOR)

Produced by Film 73 Prods. and RAI-TV Channel 2. Directed by Gianni Bongioanni. Stars Carlotta Wittig. Screenplay, Bongioanni and Carlotta Wittig; camera (Kodakcolor, 16m), Gianni Bongioanni; editor, Luciana Bartolini, Gino Bartolini; music, Francesco De Masi; art director, Vittoria Guaita. Reviewed at Cinecittá Lab, Rome, Apr. 17, 1986. Running time: **158 MINS.**

Carlotta	Carlotta Wittig
Stefano	Piero Di Jorio
Professor	Gabriele Ferzetti

Also with: Felice Andreasi (engineer), Mirella Falco (old lady), Amy Werba (Lucia), Margarita Baffico (Mirella), Umberto Craco (redhead), Francesco Scali (Tonino), Massimo Bonetti (psychologist).

Rome — Gianni Bongioanni's "Madness My Love" is a whimsical, very personal view of mental illness, as seen through the eyes of a woman volunteer who works with former patients in a type of halfway-house apartment. Not a clinical picture, film prefers to focus on the woman (played by co-scripter Carlotta Wittig) and dramatize her reactions, problems and satisfactions.

Though it is over 2½ hours long, "Madness" has a gallery of human and often humorous characters that makes it as easy to watch as a soap. If anything, story could have gone on to tie up some loose ends, or round out a few of the characters.

Film's strong point is its firm grip on the psychology of Carlotta (Wittig), a film dubber married to a college prof (Piero Di Jorio). Her life is an empty round of problems on the job, boring evenings with the husband's colleagues (he's ambitious), and misunderstandings at home. Though a little stilted and caricatured, the portrait of Carlotta's life is easily recognizable. When she stumbles onto an opportunity to supervise a new coop apartment for a group of mental patients, we get a euphoric feeling of her life opening up.

If the parts dealing with Carlotta's home life are unevenly scripted, pic comes into its own when dealing with the apartment dwellers. A happy balance is struck between their laughable quirks and funny ideas, and touching moments of tenderness or sadness. Thesps are well-chosen and absolutely convincing, particularly Felice Andreasi as a paranoid gentleman who tries unsuccessfully to rescue a mistreated girl (finely limned by Amy Werba) kept strapped to a bed and drugged by her relatives.

No easy solutions are offered to the many problems the film brings up, such as Italy's closing its mental institutions without adequate provisions for home care. Wittig's performance is humble and right on key.

Film was made for tv and blown up to 35m, which shows. Despite technical limits, it is an example of the much greater range of subjects now coming from Italo tv than the narrowing sphere of theatrical film producers.—*Yung.*

Willy/Milly
(COLOR)

Effective fantasy comedy about sex roles.

A Concorde Cinema Group release from Cinema Group. Produced by M. David Chilewich. Directed by Paul Schneider. Coproducer, Fred Berner. Executive producers, Dal la Magna, David Helpern. Associate producers, Eva Fyer, Griffon Productions, Walter Carbone, Carla Reuben. Screenplay, Walter Carbone and Carla Reuben from the story by Alan Friedman; camera (color), Dominique Chapuis; production designer, Nora Chavooshian; editor, Michael Miller; music, David McHugh; special effects, Lenna Kaleva. Reviewed at the MPAA Screening Room, Washington, D.C., April 11, 1986. (MPAA Rating: PG-13.) Running time: **90 MINS.**

Milly/Willy . . . . Pamela Segall
Alfie . . . . Eric Gurry
Stephanie . . . . Mary Tanner
Mrs. Niceman . . . . Patty Duke
Mr. Niceman . . . . John Glover
Malcolm . . . . Seth Green
Tom . . . . John David Cullum
Harry . . . . Jeb Ellis-Brown

Washington, D.C. — The rather

silly title "Willy/Milly" caps this charming and substantial kidpic about sex roles. Rather than face the trauma of crossing the threshold of womanhood, 14-year-old Milly turns into a boy under the effect of a magic spell she tries out during an eclipse. As a girl, the would-be astronomer is constantly under pressure to be more feminine, and her exasperation is very nicely portrayed by Pamela Segall, last seen as the tomboy in "Grease II." Having become a hermaphrodite, Milly is forced by her horrified parents to choose one sex or the other. The matter-of-fact reaction of Milly is captured when she spins the first letter of her name upside-down and decides to try out Willy, effectively turning her entire world upside down.

The effects of the kid's crossover are explored on all fronts, going beyond locker room humor and capturing the kinds of expectations that spark the war between the sexes at all ages. The strategies of boys include learning to box, be confrontational and eat like an animal, and Willy struggles to be macho enough to take on the toughs in his new school. It's hard to forget that Willy is actually Milly as a boy, although Segall's androgyny has more appeal than will be expected from a kid's pic dealing with this subject.

Film's biggest asset is in the performances of the unknown adolescent actors. Helmer Paul Schneider may be remembered from the festival circuit where his short "Sweetwater" circulated. Here he reveals a sure hand at getting normal behavior out of the kids, more than can be said for what he gets out of Patty Duke and John Glover as the overreacting parents of Milly/Willy.

Schneider shows real finesse in handling a subplot romance that develops between Willy and his new but handicapped buddy Alfie, whose fear that he is homosexual has to be gently dispelled and replaced by heterosexual health on all sides. Schneider's fearless poking around into kids' subliminal urges has a bittersweet honesty.

Since the lack of marquee value and dicey subject matter will make this a tough theatrical release, its eventual favorable exposure will be on the small screen. The challenge there, however, will be getting the rough language Willy must learn as a boy past the censors.

When Willy finds the courage to go back to being a Milly, the plot finds an appropriately marketable resolution to all the nuances of behavior it exposes in both sexes when they are most nervous about the opposite one. There is a clarity in the lensing and production design that mark this as a thoroughly professional production and not just beginner's luck. —*Kaja.*

8 Millions Ways To Die
(COLOR)

Seamy crime thriller with an improbable scenario.

A Tri-Star Pictures release of a Producers Sales Organization picture. Produced by Steve Roth. Coproduced by Charles Mulvehill. Directed by Hal Ashby. Stars Jeff Bridges, Rosanna Arquette. Screenplay, Oliver Stone, David Lee Henry, based on book by Lawrence Block; camera (color), Stephen H. Burum; editor, Robert Lawrence, Stuart Pappe; music, James Newton Howard; production design, Michael Haller; sound, Jeff Wexler, Don Coufal, Jim Stuebe; assistant director, Andy Stone; casting, Lynn Stalmaster & Associates. Reviewed at MGM Studios, L.A., April 16, 1986. (MPAA Rating: R.) Running time: **115 MINS.**
Scudder . . . . Jeff Bridges
Sarah . . . . Rosanna Arquette
Sunny . . . . Alexandra Paul
Chance . . . . Randy Brooks
Angel . . . . Andy Garcia

Hollywood — In its favor, "8 Million Ways To Die" falls somewhere short of being a "Miami Vice" clone since neither the settings or main characters are made to look anything less than seamy. What could have been a better film delving into complexities of one tough-but-vulnerable alcoholic sheriff out to bust a cocaine ring, instead ends up an oddly-paced work that is sometimes a thriller and a sometimes love story, succeeding at neither. Boxoffice expectations are modest.

A former L.A. Sheriff named Scudder (Jeff Bridges) comes close to death less than a handful of times while trying to dismantle a scummy Latino drug smuggler's empire and at the same time winning his girl (Rosanna Arquette).

Respected director Hal Ashby was reportedly fired from this picture before it was finished, which could explain its unevenness as he wasn't privvy to what happened in the editing room. Producer Steve Roth was also relieved of his duties and both filmmakers sued production company PSO.

Plot is contrived and built upon an improbable scenario wherein Scudder agrees to a high-priced call girl's pleas to buy off her pimp and win her freedom, quickly finding himself entangled with her and her unsavory associates.

Lackluster story line gets no help from the scripters, who relie too much on profane shouting matches that escalate towards the end of the picture to the point that lines become unintelligible — signaling desperate measures to try and create drama where none exists.

In isolated scenes, the actors manage to rise above it all to bring some nuances to their fairly stereotypical roles. Arquette is best as the hooker with a heart, coyly playing off main squeeze Angel (Andy Garcia), the ultra-chic cocaine dealer,

until she goes over to Scudder's side.

A few one-liners do little to lighten this girm slice of tawdry life and filmmakers overestimate an audience's willingness to sit through all 115 minutes to wait for the violent payoff.

Stephen Burum's lensing sometimes lightens the load, especially aerial shots above L.A. freeways.

Scoring is overdone and frequently gives the opposite tone to a scene than it should, notably those with Bridges and Arquette *tête à tête.*

Film has no sex scenes, surprising considering the story content. Filmmakers compensated by use of coarse language and a couple of bloody confrontations. —*Brit.*

Crocodile Dundee
(AUSTRALIAN-COLOR)

A Hoyts Distribution (Australia) release of a Rimfire Prods. film. Produced by John Cornell. Directed by Peter Faiman. Stars Paul Hogan. Screenplay, Hogan, Ken Shadie, camera (Kodakcolor), Russell Boyd; editor, David Stiven; music, Peter Best; sound, Gary Wilkins; production design, Graham Walker; assistant director, Mark Turnbull; production manager, Peter Sjoquist; line producer, Jane Scott; assoc. producer, Wayne Young; Reviewed at Film Australia, Sydney, Australia, April 16, 1986. (Commonwealth Censor rating: M.) Running time: **102 MINS.**
Michael J. "Crocodile Dundee" Paul Hogan
Sue Charlton . . . . Linda Kozlowski
Wally Reily . . . . John Meillon
Richard Mason . . . . Mark Blum
Same Charlton . . . . Michael Lombard
Neville Bell . . . . David Gulpilil
Also with: Irving Metzman (doorman), Graham Walker (bellhop), Maggie Blinco (Ida), Steve Rackman (Donk).

Sydney — Paul Hogan, Australia's most popular televison comedian for a decade, makes a reasonably effective leap to the wide screen in "Crocodile Dundee." Though rarely scaling great heights of comedy, item will probably deliver enough mirthful moments to click with Australian audiences who venerate Hogan as something akin to a folk hero.

Compared with run-of-the-mill Aussie pics, "Dundee" will have a head start in cracking the U.S. market since Hogan's weatherbeaten face — if not his name — is familiar through those "slip another shrimp on the barbie" tv blurbs. His brand of humor — extremely broad — plus the film's partial New York locationing (by far its most entertaining passages) and presence of Yank actors, will give it some chance of success Stateside.

As the title character, Hogan limns a laconic if rather dim crocodile hunter who achieves some notoriety after surviving an attack by a giant croc. New York reporter Linda Kozlowski (young actress who appeared with Dustin Hoffman in both stage and tv versions of "Death of a Salesman") journeys to the Northern Territory to cover the story.

Plot bogs down somewhat as Hogan and Kozlowski trudge through the outback, lingeringly and lovingly photographed at dusk, sunset and in between. That, plus such scenes as an Aboriginal corroboree, will be stock travelog footage for most Aussies, but may offer more novelty and interest to offshore audiences. However, proceedings are intermittently enlivened by John Meillon who is slyly humorous as Dundee's manager and partner in a safari tour business.

Rather implausibly, Kozlowski persuades Hogan to return to Gotham with her to finish the assignment (and, one suspects, for more personal liaison). Here at last the tempo quickens as he is initiated into the delights of the Big Apple. If he can survive muggers, prosties, waiters, the drug culture, Kozlowski's ostentatiously wealthy newspaper magnate father (Michael Lombard) and her smarmy fiance (Mark Blum) he probably deserves a good time with her.

Director Peter Faiman, essaying his first theatrical venture after an impressive career in Australian tv, directing Hogan's shows among others, has problems with the pacing and a script (by Hogan and longtime tv colleague Ken Shadie) that has its flat, dull spots.

Hogan is comfortable enough playing the wry, irreverent, amiable Aussie that seem close to his own persona, and teams well with Kozlowski, who radiates lots of charm, style and spunk.

Tech credits are good without quite attaining the level suggested by pic's $A8,900,000 budget.—Dogo.

Torment
(COLOR)

Well-lensed but unconvincing thriller.

A New World Pictures release. Produced by Samson Aslanian, John Hopkins. Coproduced by Stacey Giachino. Written and directed by Aslanian, Hopkins; camera (Mŏnaco color), Stephen Carpenter; editor, John Penney, Earl Ghaffari, Bret Shelton; music, Christopher Young; art director, Chris Hopkins; sound, Walter Gorey, Larry Hoki, Paul Fischer; associate producers, John Penney, Deane Weaver; assistant director, Jay Vincent, Ghaffari. Reviewed at Lion's Gate Studios screening room. L.A., April 15, 1986. (MPAA Rating: R.) Running time: **85 MINS.**
Jennifer .... Taylor Gilbert
Father .... William Witt
Mrs. Courtland .... Eve Brenner
Michael .... Warren Lincoln
Helen .... Najean Cherry
Bogartis .... Stan Weston
Officer Tilman .... Doug Leach

Hollywood — "Torment" is a psychological thriller without the psychology. What's left is a slick-looking, competently made low-budget feature without the inner workings to grab hold of an audience and take it for a ride. Even so, New World should be able to coax some warm bodies in to see it.

Obviously shot on a shoestring in San Francisco, newcomers Samson Aslanian and John Hopkins, who produced, wrote and directed, have concentrated on the form at the expense of content. Often imaginatively lit and shot by cinematographer Stephen Carpenter, style frequently overshadows what is going on inside the frame.

Story is constructed around a psychopathic killer who stalks young couples and then turns up on the doorstep of the most unlikely couple — the detective who's chasing him. Film starts to unravel when the detective's fiancee (Taylor Gilbert) moves in with her boy friend's invalid mother (Eve Brenner) in an uppercrust suburb.

Premise that a homicide detective (Warren Lincoln) could come from this environment doesn't wash and completely throws the picture out of balance. Other dramatic twist also falls like a lead balloon and strains the bounds of credibility. For this kind of fare to work the filmmakers must set up a universe with its own logic and probability. With that lacking, the audience just watches from a safe distance.

Luckily what they see is not all bad and there are some nicely executed turns of the screw. Gilbert, a Meg Tilly type, is likable in an undeveloped role. Also effective and truly creepy is William Witt as the slasher. Brenner has a few good scenes as the hysterical mother, but script never gives the characters the connections they need to work on the imagination.

Tech credits are fine; in fact, they're the best part of the film.
—Jagr.

The Fantasy Film World Of George Pal
(DOCU-COLOR)

Produced, written and directed by Arnold Leibovit. Technical supervisor, Anthony Magliocco; camera (color), George Gerba; editor, Leibovit; sound, Tom Scherman; art direction, Mike Minor; production animation, Walt Disney Prods.; advisor and consultant, Mrs. George Pal. Reviewed at Library of Congress, Washington, D.C., April 10, 1986. (No MPAA Rating.) Running time: **96 MINS.**

Washington, D.C. — Basically fanzine stuff, this docu is sure to make the festival rounds just for its pleasant compilation of producer George Pal's better works. This father of modern sci-fi began as an animation man, and the footage from his "puppetoons" shows the imaginative talents to which a horde of friends and colleagues testify. Talking heads ranging from Ray Harryhausen, Roy Disney, Gene Warren, Tony Curtis to Barbara Eden, Ray Bradbury and Walter Lantz are primarily interesting for the before-and-after effect of their

appearances in '50s footage, then today.

At Paramount George Pal made some of the finest sci-fi of the time. In an interview with Pal, we hear him claim to have been projecting "the near future" into his films rather than fantasy. Despite the seriousness of his own approach, the style today strikes one as campy. At a desperate attempt at an all-embracing critical statement, narrator Paul Frees (doing his Walt Disney impersonation) argues that "When Worlds Collide" illustrates Pal's basic message — the Noah's Ark principle of taking it all with you, if it looks like civilization is threatened.

Pal's principles are attested to by Tony Curtis who complains that Pal refused to use special photography, so that the long takes of "Houdini" strained Curtis' ligaments. The real strain, ultimately is trying to figure out who cast George Pal's pictures. The collection of clips used here comprises a veritable hommage to bad acting, especially in the absurd reduction of dialog and situation that such snippets impose on the material. But nostalgia will win out with film buffs, and the fantasy of George Pal will make the festival rounds.—Kaja.

Carnage
(COLOR)

Trite horror opus.

A Jaylo Intl. Films production. Executive producer, Lew Mishkin. Written and directed by Andy Milligan. Camera (color), Milligan; editor, Gerald Bronson; sound, Dennis Malvasi. Reviewed on Media Home Ent. vidcassette, N.Y., April 13, 1986. (No MPAA Rating.) Running time: **91 MINS.**
Carol .... Leslie Den Dooven
Jonathan .... Michael Chiodo
Walter .... John Garritt
Susan .... Deeann Veeder
Ann .... Chris Baker
Minister .... Jack Poggi
Tony .... Albert Alfano
Mother-in-law .... Ché Moody
Margaret .... Rosemary Egan
Judy .... Ellen Orchid
Also with: Chris Georges, Bill Grant, Judith Mayes, Lola Ross.

"Carnage" is an old-hat, poorly made horror picture, shot in New York in 1983 under the title "Hell House." Filmmaker Andy Milligan, whose heyday was about 15 years earlier with pics like "The Ghastly Ones," delivers pure corn here and the feature went directly to homevideo without a domestic theatrical release.

Leslie Den Dooven and Michael Chiodo portray newlyweds Carol and Jonathan who move into a bargain house (a la "The Money Pit") where three years earlier a groom killed his bride and then committed suicide. Of course the site is haunted by that couple and many a visitor is killed in gory fashion while inanimate objects move around amid other supernatural happenings.

For unexplained reasons, Carol and Jonathan love the house and won't leave no matter what mayhem occurs. Not surprisingly, they also become eternal residents. Picture is padded with inconsequential footage and a boring subplot involving a pregnant friend of theirs, Ann (Chris Baker) whose marriage is on the rocks.

Gore is exaggerated and phony, while special effects shots are amateurish. Milligan's use of a background score made up of library music makes the film seem at least 20 years older than its copyright date.—Lor.

Yuppies, I Giovani di Successo
(Yuppies, Youngsters Who Succeed)
(ITALIAN-COLOR)

A Filmauro release. Produced by Luigi and Aurelio De Laurentiis for Filmauro Prods. Directed by Carlo Vanzina. Screenplay, Enrico and Carlo Vanzina; camera (Technicolor), Luigi Kuveiller; editor, Raimondo Crociani; music, Detto Mariano. Reviewed at Ariston Cinema, Rome, April 10, 1986. Running time: **96 MINS.**
Gianluca .... Jerry Calá
Sandro .... Christian De Sica
Lorenzo .... Massimo Boldi
Car salesman .... Enzo Greggio
Françoise .... Corinne Cléry
Magazine editor .... Federica Moro
Amanda .... Sharon Gusberti
Virginia .... Valeria D'Obici

Rome — Carlo Vanzina's latest formula comedy, "Yuppies, Youngsters Who Succeed," has nothing to do with the rising culture of young urban professionals. Title (which rhymes with groupies in Italian) is a gimmick to market a tired story about bed-hopping husbands, reluctant virgins and promiscuous moms. This local product pulled through the Easter holiday b.o. with good grosses.

Cast is a collection of teen favorites of the moment, some with faces familiar from tv. Little ensemble acting is called for, though, since the various stories intertwine only casually.

Funniest in the lot is Massimo Boldi, who plays a staid young notary public. When the wives and kids of Boldi and dentist Christian De Sica pack off for a ski week in the mountains, the mice decide to play. De Sica finds them a slew of easy dates, but Boldi prefers to have an affair with his neurotic secretary, Valeria D'Obici, which ends in disaster when his wife comes back.

Milanese comic Jerry Calá walks through the role of a brown-nosing young ad excec on the move. His love affair with magazine editor Federica Moro is fraught with misunderstandings, but ends happily. Enzo Greggio, an unnerving car salesman who chatters a mile a minute, chases every female in sight, from virginal Sharon Gusberti (who turns out otherwise) to freewheeling

French mom Corinne Cléry.

So, nothing new under the sun, least of all these "youppies." On the plus side, film is lacking in vulgarity (a Vanzina trademark) and the girls are pretty to look at. Soundtrack is a medley of recent pop hits.—*Yung.*

Vor der Flut
(Before The Flood)
(WEST GERMAN-DOCU-COLOR-16m)

A De Campo-Film and Tag/Traum Film and Video production, Cologne. A Documentary by Hinnerick Bröskamp and Thomas Schmitt. Music, P. Oliveros, Saxophon Mafia, Jochen Vetter, Jana Heimsohn, Dario Domigues, Christian Bollmann & Christoph Müller, the Tanzforum der Oper Köln. Reviewed at Berliner Screening Room, Berlin, April 1, 1985. Running time: **70 MINS.**

Berlin — Hennerick Bröskamp and Thomas Schmitt's "Before The Flood" has a lot in common with Handel's classical "Water Music" (composed 1715-17), for this is a genuine and original concert dealing with water in its most elementary sense. By chance, it was discovered that an emptied reservoir serving the city of Cologne built in 1899 had the architectural capacity to hold an echo for an incredibly long 45 seconds — that is, longer than anything known before in existence (the Taj Mahal, it's said, has the next longest echo resonance capacity).

Since the city reservoir (it holds 20,000,000 liters of drinking water when filled) was under repair, it was decided to hold a spontaneous concert within its extraordinary echo chambers. The results are indeed amazing: various musical instruments (saxophones, in particular), the human voice, modern ballet and music numbers, and literally all kinds of innovative happenings are staged to be filmed and recorded for posterity. One regrets in the end that the water faucet had to be turned on to get back to the business of quenching a city's thirst.—*Holl.*

Murphy's Law
(COLOR)

Nasty meller for Charles Bronson fans

A Cannon Releasing release of a Cannon Group presentation of a Golan-Globus production. Produced by Pancho Kohner. Coproducer, Jill Ireland. Executive producers, Menahem Golan, Yoram Globus. Directed by J. Lee-Thompson. Stars Charles Bronson. Screenplay, Gail Morgan Hickman; camera (TVC color), Alex Phillips; editor, Peter Lee-Thompson, Charles Simmons; music, Marc Donahue, Valentine McCallum; sound, Craig Felburg; production design, William Cruise; set decoration, W. Brooke Wheeler; associate producer, Hickman; assistant director, Steven Lazarus; casting, Robert MacDonald, Perry Bullington. Reviewed at the Cannon screening room, L.A., Apr. 14, 1986. (MPAA Rating: R.) Running time: **100 mins.**

Jack Murphy	Charles Bronson
Arabella McGee	Kathleen Wilhoite
Joan Freeman	Carrie Snodgress
Art Penny	Robert F. Lyons
Frank Vincenzo	Richard Romanus
Jan	Angel Tompkins
Ben Wilcove	Bill Henderson
Ed Reineke	James Luisi
Lt. Nachman	Clifford A. Pellow

Hollywood — Cannon Films, star Charles Bronson and director J. Lee-Thompson all stalk exceedingly familiar territory in "Murphy's Law," a very violent urban crime meller. Tiresome but too filled with extreme incident to be boring, seamy vehicle recycles innumerable conceits from earlier Bronson revenge epics as well as Clint Eastwood's "Dirty Harry" entries. Cut from such a commercial pattern, pic should score well in quick, wide release, but fall off quickly.

Title refers not only to the w.k. axiom that, "Whatever can go wrong will go wrong," but to Bronson's personal version of it: "Don't ---- with Jack Murphy." Title character is an L.A. cop who's down but not quite out, a tough loner whose main companion in life is his flask now that his wife has left him.

Murphy's life is shaken up even more when the ex-wife, her new boyfriend and, before long, numerous others around him are mowed down. Booked for the crimes, he escapes handcuffed to a foul-mouthed female street urchin, and after many more bodies hit the deck, he clears his name by tracking down killer Carrie Snodgress, a looney bent on offing everyone who had a hand in sending her to the nuthouse.

Preposterousness and frequency of the action hold the attention, but Gail Morgan Hickman's script panders to the lowest common denominator in viewers. Virtually every character relationship here is a hostile one, everyone is heavily armed and anxious to use their hardware, and the little punk delivers a torrent of vile one-liners that should have been funny but aren't.

Snodgress' character is repellent, but at least having the killer played by a woman reps a bit of change from the usual hung-up, psychopathic madman. Nasty little touch has Snodgress sprayed in the face with blood when she blasts people to smithereens.

Alex Phillips' lensing is awfully dingy, and remainder of tech credits are utterly routine.   — *Cart.*

Wise Guys
(COLOR)

Low-brow Mafia comedy misfires.

A UA/MGM Distribution release from MGM Entertainment. Produced by Aaron Russo. Executive producer, Irwin Russo. Directed by Brian DePalma. Stars Danny DeVito, Joe Piscopo. Screenplay, George Gallo; camera (Technicolor, prints by Metrocolor), Fred Schuler; editor, Jerry Greenberg; music, Ira Newborn; production design, Edward Pisoni; art director, Paul Bryan Eads; set decorator, Leslie Bloom; sound, Les Lazarowitz; assistant director, Joe Napolitano; associate producer, Patrick McCormick; casting, Dianne Crittenden. Reviewed at UA/MGM screening room, Culver City, Calif., April 11, 1986. (MPAA Rating: R.) Running time: **91 MINS.**

Harry Valentini	Danny DeVito
Moe Dickstein	Joe Piscopo
Bobby Dilea	Harvey Keitel
Marco	Ray Sharkey
Anthony Castelo	Dan Hedaya
Frank The Fixer	Captain Lou Albano
Lil Dickstein	Julie Bovasso
Wanda Valentini	Patti LuPone
Aunt Sadie	Antonia Rey
Grandma Valentini	Mimi Cecchini

Hollywood — "Wise Guys" misfires on all cylinders and the end result is even more disheartening given the previous solid achievements of director Brian DePalma. His early indie ventures, "Greetings" and "Hi, Mom!" notwithstanding, this attempted small-time Mafia comedy does not seem to be his genre. B.o. results also are likely to be minimal.

Gone are the flamboyant excesses that made a DePalma film instantly recognizable. What's left is a limp, visually dull look at limp, mentally dull people.

Equally guilty is the cast of unfunny comics led by Joe Piscopo and Danny DeVito. DeVito is so grating as Mafia messenger boy Harry Valentini, that this character makes his Louie DePalma of tv's "Taxi" seem charming.

As his Jewish sidekick, Piscopo seems to be mimicking Jerry Lewis throughout with not very funny results. There is little chemistry between the two to suggest their supposed great friendship and more often than not they appear to be acting separately, each in a different film.

On the script level, George Gallo has provided a feeble plot involving a heist by DeVito and Piscopo of funds belonging to Mafia kingpin Anthony Castelo (Dan Hedaya). The pair of bumblers invest the mob money at the racetrack and must avoid getting killed at the same time they try to come up with the dough to pay back Castelo.

Level of humor along the way is strictly low-brow led by the massive Frank The Fixer (former wrestler Captain Lou Albano) who eats up the screen and almost everything else in his path. Low point comes with Albano lying naked in his hotel room getting a pedicure from one of his henchman.

Only performance rising above the material is Harvey Keitel as an old neighborhood pal made good in the hotel business. Just sleazy enough to make his motives questionable, Keitel gives the production a touch of class, but, alas, not nearly enough.

Tech credits are fine although cinematography looks a bit grainy at times. Production design by Edward Pisoni and choice of urban locations in Newark and Atlantic City have an appropriately rundown look.—*Jagr.*

Hong Kong Festival

Ping Pong
(BRITISH-COLOR)

A Film Four Intl. presentation of a Picture Palace Film production. Produced by Malcolm Craddock, Michael Guest. Directed by Po-chih Leong. Screenplay, Jerry Liu; camera (color), Nic Knowland; editor, David Spiers; music, Richard Harvey; production design, Colin Pigott; assistant director, Sean Fleming; production manager, Annie Rees; casting, J&R Hubbard. Reviewed at Hong Kong Film Fest (City Hall), April 4, 1986. Running time: **103 MINS.**

Mike Wong	David Yip
Elaine Choy	Lucy Sheen
Mr. Chen	Robert Lee
Ah Ying	Lam Fung

Hong Kong — Spurred on, no doubt, by the success of Wayne Wang's "Dim Sum," set in San Francisco's Chinatown, the latest Film Four presentation, "Ping Pong," takes place in the Chinese section of London. It's a slight, but engaging, comedy-drama about a young femme lawyer trying to sort out the complicated last will and testament of a prominent member of the Chinese community, Sam Wong.

Wong's will places heavy restrictions on his family, and the tyro lawyer, Elaine, has to bring the bickering factions together before the will can be finalized. They include the dead man's eldest son, the charming, Cambridge-educated Mike, with whom Elaine has a love affair.

Matters are further complicated by the fact that the dead man wanted to be buried in the village where he was born in Mainland China, and someone has to go there to accompany the body. Nobody is very willing.

The plot is a bit slight, and the film overstays its welcome by the end, but thanks to the charming playing of Lucy Sheen, a beautiful Chinese woman with a splendidly incongruous London accent, it's always worth watching.

There is pleasure to be found in the various jokey asides, such as a

Chinese waiter accurately predicting in advance what food a group of American tourists is going to order, or Elaine, emerging from a friendly interview at the Chinese Embassy with some unwanted pamphlets about modern China, trying to stuff them into the nearest wastepaper bin which is already overflowing with identical brochures.

Director Po-chih Leong was born in London, but has made his previous eight films in Hong Kong, including "Hong Kong 1941," about the Japanese invasion of Hong Kong, which played at some festivals a couple of years ago. He's handled his chores adequately here, working especially well with a large group of actors, but his basic material is a bit thin.

"Ping Pong" lacks the appeal that made "Dim Sum" a modest success in art houses, but is a perfectly pleasant entertainment which may find its eventual home on video or tv. Most of the dialog is in English, while some Cantonese dialog is subtitled expertly. —Strat.

Amansiz Yol
(The Desperate Road)
(TURKISH-COLOR)

A Sineray Film, in association with T.C. Kultur ve Turizm. Directed by Omer Kavur. Screenplay, Kavur, Baris Pirhasan; camera (color), Orhan Oguz; music, Ugur Dikmen. (No further credits supplied.) Reviewed at Hong Kong Film Fest (Ko Shan theater), April 8, 1986. Running time: **94 MINS.**
With: Kadir Inanir (Hasan), Zuhal Olcay (Sabahat), Yavurer Cetinkaya (Yavuz).

Hong Kong — "The Desperate Road" is an under-charged road movie which generates little excitement or involvement from its sluggishly handled chase theme.

A truck driver returns home to Turkey after spending time in a German prison. He discovers his former best friend is now an embittered cripple (after an accident) and is involved in some unspecified criminal activities. When a couple of thugs come after the friend, he disappears, leaving the hero with a wad of money and responsibility for the missing man's wife (the hero's ex-girl) and daughter. They set out on a drive across country, half-heartedly pursued by the two villains.

Pic is in low gear from the start, and though the scenic trip across Turkey has some marginal interest, the main subject of the film (the chase) is a bore. Characters are conventional and their actions predictable. It's a trucking pic that's going nowhere. —Strat.

Ye Shan
(Wild Mountains)
(CHINESE-COLOR)

A China Films release of a Xi'an Film Studio production. Directed by Yan Xueshu. Screenplay, Zhu Zi, Yan, from the novel "The People of Jiwowa" by Jia Ping'ao; camera (color), Mi Anqing; music, Xu Youfu; art director, Li Xingzhen. Reviewed at Hong Kong Film Fest (Kings theater), April 2, 1986. Running time: **99 MINS.**
With: Du Yuan, Yue Hong, Xin Ming, Xu Shaoli, Tan Xihe, Qiu Yuzhen.

Hong Kong — A film on the subject of wife swapping might sound like a pretty wild item to come from Mainland China, but that's the theme of "Wild Mountains." "Bob & Carol & Ted & Alice" it isn't, but like Paul Mazursky's film this one does attempt to show the logical grass-roots conclusions to the bewildering social changes sweeping the country.

Pic is set in a village in the province of Shanbei. Huihui is a pig farmer happily married except for the fact that his wife, Guilan, has never had a child. He's a hard worker, unlike his rather shiftless brother, Hehe, who has a pretty young wife, Qiurong, and a baby.

At the outset, the brothers appear a bit bewildered by what's happening in the country. Even in this isolated spot, the changes are obvious. As Huihui says, "There are no team leaders anymore; we have to lead ourselves." Going into business for themselves, after years of regimented communal life, means big upheavals.

Before long, the couples fall out of love with their original partners. Hehe takes his sister-in-law for a (strictly platonic) trip to the nearest town, where she's amazed by the unusual sights and sounds. The out-ragged Huihui divorces his wife, and decides to marry Qiurong instead. Pic ends with the couples completely reversed.

This is eyebrow-raising stuff in the Chinese context, a study of sexual roles in the hinterlands that goes further than one would have dreamed only a year or so ago. Unsensational in tone, the film is visually splendid as the isolated village forms a picturesque backdrop to the unusual goings-on.

Another top quality pic to emerge from China, "Wild Mountains" is technically fine and has a superior music score by Xu Youfu. Its unusual theme and the placid beauty of its images should get it attention in the West. —Strat.

Peesua lae Dokmai
(Butterflies And Flowers)
(THAI-COLOR)

A Five Stars production. Produced by Chareon Iamphungporn. Directed by Euthana Mukdasnit. Screenplay, Mukdasnit; camera (Widescreen, color), Panya Nimchareonpong; music, M.L. Varapa Kasaemsri; music, Butterfly; sound, Nivat Sumneangsanor; production manager, Yuvanee Thaihirun. Reviewed at Hong Kong Film Fest (Columbia Classics theater), April 7, 1986. Running time: **125 MINS.**
With: Suriya Yaovasang (Huyan), Vasana Pholyiem (Mimpi), Suchow Phongvilai (Father), Rome Isra (Naka).

Hong Kong — Sympathetic tale of a village youth trying to scrape together a living after his father is injured in a railway accident, "Butterflies And Flowers," despite a rather sugary music score, is not as sentimental as it title suggests. In fact, it's one of the best Thai films to emerge in recent times.

Huyan, his widower father and his young brother and sister are Muslims (Thailand is basically a Buddhist country, with a small Muslim minority). He's a good student, but making ends meet is desperately difficult. He decides to take the risk of joining some acquaintances in smuggling rice by train across the border into Malaysia.

The train sequences are expertly handled. When the youths are forced to hide from customs officials on top of the fast-moving carriages, scenes handled without any obvious faking, the film becomes genuinely gripping. Acting is very good, too, with every character well-delineated in the screenplay and by the individual performers. The colorful bordertown setting of most of the latter part of the film is quite fascinating.

Early scenes are a bit slow, and the pic could be speeded up overall with tighter editing. This is a pic that fests interested in showing top quality Asian fare should try to grab. English subtitles in the version caught were adequate, though print itself was in poor shape.

The film copped seven prizes in the 1985 Thai Film Awards, including Best Film and Best Director. —Strat.

Jue Xiang
(Swan Song)
(CHINESE-COLOR)

A China Film presentation of a Pearl River Film Studio (Youth Division) production. Directed by Zhang Zeming. Screenplay, Zhang, from a novel by Kung Jiesheng; camera (color), Zheng Kangzhen, from a novel by Kung Jiesheng; camera (color), Zheng Kangzhen, Zhao Xiaoshi; music, Zhao Xiaoyuan; artistic adviser, Wang Jin. Reviewed at Hong Kong Film Fest (Kings theater), April 3, 1986. Running time: **99 MINS.**
With: Kung Zianzhu, Chen Rui, Feng Diqing, Mo Shaoying.

Hong Kong — This first feature by a 34-year-old director is another major breakthrough for the new Chinese cinema. It's very different in every way from last year's discovery, "Yellow Earth," but equally impressive. It is, on the other hand, a deeply pessimistic saga of the betrayal and destruction of a gifted artist.

The artist in question is a musician, a composer of classical Cantonese music who learned his craft from one of the master musicians. The story spans some 30 years, beginning when the musician already is being attacked for his old-fashioned compositions, attacks that intensify during the Cultural Revolution when even his *zheng* (a Cantonese musical instrument) is prohibited.

His ambitious wife has left him. His son, imprisoned in a labor camp on Hainan, becomes alienated from him and, when released, sells the priceless *zheng* to pay for an illegal passage to Hong Kong, only to be ripped off and left behind. Even after his death, the betrayals continue. His music is discovered and adapted to be performed at an excruciating Western-style concert by the daughter of his ex-wife.

Zhang Zeming spares nothing in his disenchanted depiction of life in Canton over the last three decades. The slogan-spouting reps of the Mao Tse-Tung government are satirized as sharply as is the rush to Western consumerism in the present day (the final scenes take place amid a barrage of well-known brand-name products and Taiwanese music). An old friend from Hong Kong is a crook, so there's no hope there. The old traditions and customs are dead or dying.

This forthright pic is top-notch in all departments, with good performances, fine camerawork and tight editing. Only drawback for Chinese-speaking audiences is the fact that, though set in Canton, the dialog is in Mandarin, which won't ring true. Westerners won't be bothered by this.

It's to be hoped that "Swan Song" will feature strongly at international festivals this summer. Art house distribution in major cities is not out of the question. —Strat.

Subarnarekha
(INDIAN-B&W)

A J.J. Films production. Produced by Uday Row Kavi. Directed by Ritwik Ghatak. Screenplay, Ghatak; camera (b&w), Dilip Ranjan Mukhopadhyay; editor, Ramesh Joshi; music, Ustad Bahadur Khan; art direction, Ravi Chattopadhyay. Reviewed at Hong Kong Film Fest (Space Museum theater), April 11, 1986. Running time: **126 MINS.**
With: Abhi Bhattacharya, Madhavi Mukhopadhyay.

Hong Kong — Since he died in poverty in 1976, Bengali director Ritwik Ghatak's work has been recognized as being of importance and distinction; some think he's the equal of Satyajit Ray. Last year, the Hong Kong Film Festival presented a Ghatak retrospective from which "Subarnarekha," made in 1965, was omitted. The film was presented instead this year and is reviewed for the record.

Spanning a number of years, it's a grim tale of refugees from the countryside who flocked to Calcutta in 1948, the year of Gandhi's assassination. One, Isvar, is accompanied by his young sister, Sita, and a boy, Abirham, who has been left alone after his mother was kidnapped. An old friend offers Isvar a job at a steel foundry by the Subarnarekha River east of Calcutta, and he goes there with the two children.

Years pass, the children grow up, fall in love and marry. They move to the overcrowded city, but Abirham, a bus driver, is killed in an accident and Sita, left with a small baby, is forced to turn to prostitution. One night a drunken Isvar, who has lost his spectacles and can hardly see, becomes his sister's customer.

It's strong stuff, extremely pessimistic in tone, although the final message is of the innate goodness in man. Classically photographed, it's certainly an impressive work, though the numerous songs rendered by the actress playing Sita, though acceptable to Bengali audiences, simply add to the running time. Acting is fine right down the line.

If Ghatak's other films are of this quality, he certainly deserved the recognition he apparently never had in life.—*Strat.*

Doea Tanda Mata
(Mementos)
(INDONESIAN-COLOR)

An Indonesian Film Council presentation of a Citra Jaya Film. Produced by Haryoko Punarwan. Directed by Teguh Karya. Screenplay, Karya, Alex Komang; camera (color), George Kamarullah; editor, Rizal Asmar; music, Idris Sardi. Reviewed at Hong Kong Film Fest (Ko Shan theater), April 3, 1986. Running time: 93 MINS.
With: Alex Komang, Hermin Chentini, Sylvia Wdiantono, Corbi, Eka Gandara, Bambang.

Hong Kong — Teguh Karya is Indonesia's best known director ("November 1828," "Behind The Mosquito Net") and the 1984 production "Mementos" must rank as one of the best Indonesian films unveiled at fests to date. It's still dramatically a bit thin, however, and by no means a breakthrough.

Set in Bandang in the early 1930s in what was then the Dutch East Indies, story concerns a young man who joins the anti-Dutch freedom movement. When his best friend is shot dead during a confrontation with the authorities, Goenadi vows vengeance against the police commissioner who gave the order to fire.

He spends most of the rest of the film trying to make up his mind how, where and when to carry out the assassination, while dallying with the sister of the dead man and (understandably) infuriating his comrades who want more action.

The film could do with a little more action, too, mainly because Alex Komang, who plays the indecisive hero and who coscripted with the director, is a rather bland young actor. Some of the extras and supporting players seem slackly directed, too, and the post-synching is wayward at times. On the plus side, the film looks very good, with handsome art direction and first-class lab work, producing a crisp, clear color print.

On the basis of this effort, Indonesian film production is making strides but not yet quite in the same quality class as the best productions from other Asian countries.
—*Strat.*

Qingchun Ji
(Sacrifice Of Youth)
(CHINESE-COLOR)

A China Film release of a Peking Youth Studio production. Directed by Zhang Luanxin. Screenplay, Zhang Luanxin, from the novel "There Was That Beautiful Place" by Zhang Manling; camera (color), Mu Deyuan, Deng Wei; editor, Zhao Qihua; music, Liu Suola, Qu Xiasong. Reviewed at Hong Kong Film Fest (Kings theater), April 2, 1986. Running time: 95 MINS.
With: Li Fengxu, Feng Yuanzheng, Song Tao, Guo Jianguo.

Hong Kong — A beautiful, serene pic calling for harmony between the different ethnic groups within China, "Sacrifice Of Youth" is an accomplished second feature by a woman director, Zhang Luanxin.

Story takes place during the upheavals of the Cultural Revolution. Li Chun (Li Fengxu), a city girl whose family has fallen foul of the authorities, is exiled to the remote province of Yunnan, close to the border with Burma. She has been told to live with a farmer and work on the land as penance for the alleged misdeeds of her parents, though she was studying medicine. She takes a liking to the truculent old man, and even more to his aged mother, and enters into the hard farm work with a will, though finding herself at first shunned by the other farmworkers because of her strange city ways.

Main theme of the film is to contrast the uptight, regimented city girl with the uninhibited, fun-loving local girls, who wear colorful sarongs and unselfconsciously bathe naked in the river (discreetly shot sequence is probably a first in Chinese cinema). Gradually, Li comes to love the country life, though her idyll has to end eventually. There's a sad little post-script in which the world in which she was so happy literally has disappeared.

This is possibly the first time the somewhat paternalistic approach of the Han people towards the ethnic minorities of China has been dissected so acutely. Director Zhang seduces the viewer with the richness of the lives of the Dai people. Alongside these happy folk, the inhibited northerner sticks out like a sore thumb.

There's the hint of romance between Li and the son of the farmer, but it's kept to a few looks and the frustrated reaction of the man when Li spends time with a youth from Peking with the same refugee status as herself.

Technically the film is tops, with the sub-tropical climate of the region lushly photographed (a sequence devoted to the monsoon season is strikingly handled). Li Fengxu is charming as the heroine, and though ultimately the film may appear a bit lightweight to foreign audiences, for whom the underlying implications may not be obvious, it's another feather in the cap for the new Chinese cinema.—*Strat.*

Bei Aiqing Yiwang Di Jiaoluo
(The Corner Forsaken By Love)
(CHINESE-COLOR)

A China Film presentation of a E Mei Film Studio (Sichuan) production. Directed by Zhang Qi, Li Yalin. Screenplay, Zhang Xian (based on his novel); camera (color), Mai Shuhuan; editor, Li Ling; art direction, Chen Desheng, Wu Zujing; music, Wang Ming. Reviewed at Hong Kong Film Fest (Ko Shan theater), April 8, 1986. Running time: 95 MINS.
With: Shen Danping, He Xiaoshu, Yang Hailian, Zhang Shihui.

Hong Kong — Made in 1981, and banned until now, "The Corner Forsaken By Love" is an outspoken film about the effects of the upheavals in China in recent years on a farming community. If it had been shown five years ago, it certainly would have been considered daring and impressive. Today it has been superceded somewhat by the high quality productions of the last couple of years.

Told in a series of complex flashbacks akin to an early Alain Resnais film, the pic explores the lives of three peasant women. In the mid-1940s, the people eagerly await the coming of communism, and when the revolution comes, a woman breaks off a marriage arranged by her parents ("Am I just a commodity?") to marry a young tree farmer she loves. Some years later she's living in dire poverty with her children. Her husband has been expelled from the party for objecting to the destruction of the orange trees on which the wealth of the village was based (to make way for corn). "To hell with the party!" she cries. "What did communism ever do for us?"

Her eldest daughter grows up in an atmosphere of fear and sexual ignorance, is seduced by her boyfriend, becomes pregnant and commits suicide. The youngest daughter hates all men as a result, but lives to see the downfall of the Gang of Four, the rehabilitation of her father, the return of the orange trees, and a new prosperity.

All this is handled (despite the flashbacks) in a rather old-fashioned, melodramatic style. Acting is uneven, with the young hero of the final sequences seemingly incapable of any expression save for a vacuous grin.

"The Corner Forsaken By Love" will have its place in the history of the Chinese cinema as an important trailblazer, but it already looks like a museum piece, an indication of how fast things are moving in film production on the mainland.
—*Strat.*

Amerasia
(W. GERMAN-DOCU-COLOR)

A Red Harvest Film production. Produced and directed by Wolf-Eckart Bühler. Screenplay, Bühler; camera (color), Bernd Fiedler; editor, Thomas Balkenhol; music, Terry Allen, Surachai Jantimatorn; sound, Martin Müller. Reviewed at Hong Kong Film Fest (City Hall), April 4, 1986. Running time: 96 MINS.
With: John Anderson.

Hong Kong — A German team made this feature docu in Thailand about leftovers from the Vietnam War — the children of mixed American and Thai blood and the G.I.s who never went home — and how these people are affecting the country.

Beginning with an I.F. Stone quote about "the evil of banality" of the Nixon years, film probes the reasons many Americans decided not to go home. Most speak of the friendliness of the Thai people, though some are still bitter about the war and the way the media handled it. In Bangkok, the film observes that Thailand, the one Southeast Asian country that was never colonized, has been transformed since the American invasion and now has become Americanized. Out in the countryside, Americans are living like Thais, often happily married to Thai women and growing rice.

The real tragedy is the half-caste children, kids who're teased or bullied by other children and who hate the fathers they never saw and sometimes their mothers, too. Often the girls wind up as prostitutes or strippers.

There are thousands of such unwanted children in Thailand today, and Wolf-Eckart Bühler's film usefully draws attention to their plight. They're innocent victims of the Vietnam War, and their tragedy continues.—*Strat.*

Rokkasho Ningenki
(People Of Rokkasho)
(JAPANESE-DOCU-B&W)

A Kuraoka Prod. Produced by Akiko Kuraoka. Directed by Kuraoka, Nobuki Yamamura. Camera (b&w), Hiroshi Oda; editor, Yamamura; interviews, Kuraoka. Reviewed at Hong Kong Film Fest (City Hall), April 5, 1986. Running time: **171 MINS.**

Hong Kong — "People Of Rokkasho" is an overlong and indulgent study, by a husband-and-wife team of documentary filmmakers, of the people displaced by the establishment of a vast chemical plant on the Shimokita Peninsula.

The project, in the works for 15 years but slowed due to the recent recession, has disrupted the lives of some 3,000 farmers and fishermen in the hitherto peaceful area. Akiko Kuraoka and Nobuki Yamamura set out to interview many of them, but for undisclosed reasons the filmmakers take their small child along, who continually gets in the way, even grabbing the mike on occasion. There seems no point to this indulgence.

Otherwise, this is yet another, painfully long, plea for a return to nature and a slowdown of industrialization. Its length and the rough-hewn, amateurish way it's made will limit it to a minimal audience.
—*Strat.*

Zuodian Yuanyang
(Love With The Perfect Stranger)
(HONG KONG-COLOR)

A Shaw Bros. release and production. Presented by Run Run Shaw. Directed by Lu Chien-ming (Jamie Loke). Screenplay, Lu, Teng Yung-kung; camera (color), Li Hsin-yeh; editor, Shao Feng, Ma Chung-yao, Chao Cho-wen; music, Stephen Shing, So Chun-hou; art direction, Hao Yung-tsai; set decoration, Chen Ching-shen, Ho Chien-sheng. Reviewed at Hong Kong Film Fest (City Hall), April 7, 1986. Running time: **94 MINS.**
With: Erh Tung-sheng (Ah Pao), Wang Hsiao-feng (Chin Chin), Pan Chen-wei, Tso Yen-ling.

Hong Kong — A comedy in the tradition of the Rock Hudson-Doris Day outings of the early 1960s, "Love With The Perfect Stranger" is about a man who finally plucks up the courage to ditch his bossy fiancee and almost immediately marries a pretty girl he meets the same day. Trouble is, after a deliriously happy honeymoon, he discovers she's two months pregnant by a former lover.

The screenplay, which was prized in the 1985 Hong Kong Film Awards, is pleasantly old-fashioned, though in siding with the pregnant wife against her shocked new husband and possessive ex-lover it does, arguably, make a pitch for feminism, Chinese style.

Director Lu Chien-ming, an ex-stuntman making his first feature, handles the material in a slick, superficial way which is characteristic of Hong Kong comedy. The actors tend to overplay, again a local tradition. It's strictly for home consumption, or one of the many small cinemas in major city Chinatowns.
— *Strat.*

Sand
(HONG KONG-COLOR-16m)

A Modern Films production. Produced by Roger Garcia. Directed by Jim Shum. Screenplay, Hwang Chenfan; camera (color, 16m), Kirk Ng; editor, Fong Ling-ching; music, Jam Machine. Reviewed at Hong Kong Film Fest (City Hall), April 5, 1986. Running time: **74 MINS.**
With: Antonio Mak, Wendy Mok, Fiona Hawthorne, Susan Fung, Boriana Varbanov-Song.

Hong Kong — An experimental, abstract feature by a young director who has hitherto dabbled in 8m production, "Sand" is an oddity for a very limited inside audience. Dialog is in Cantonese, Mandarin, English and French, which is confusing to begin with.

Jim Shum seems to be psychoanalyzing himself and the pull of Mainland China is a major factor. His central character journeys to Peking and stands in its famous central square. There's also an English girl droning on about death on a video, and a girl who talks in Mandarin to the Cantonese-speaking protagonist. There are deserted beaches, train journeys, streets, a clay figurine, telephones that never answer, and a very handsome tiger in the zoo.

Dreams and memory are jumbled up in a way that will make sense to few. There are some striking images at times, but "Sand" is a curiosity that would need repeated viewings and analysis for its meanings, if any, to be fully revealed. It appears to have no commercial audience whatsoever.—*Strat.*

Rose
(HONG KONG-COLOR)

A Manshi Yonfan production, released by Golden Harvest. Directed by Manshi Yonfan. Adapted from the novel by Yik Shue; soundtrack theme performed by Jenny. (No other credits provided by the producers.) Reviewed at Queen's theater, Hong Kong, March 1, 1986. Running time: **99 MINS.**
With: Chow Yan-fat, Maggie Cheung.
(Cantonese soundtrack with English subtitles)

Hong Kong — "Rose" is a ridiculous film. Rose, as played by Maggie Cheung, is an undercover soap opera variation of a courtesan, with very subtle hints of incest hidden deep in her subconscious. Now that local filmmakers have discovered Paris as an opulent location and a place to show they have been influenced by arty Continental films, the City of Light will never be the same.

Everyone is posing and talking slowly, moving with studied civility. They light cigarets, puff the smoke and recite their lines followed by a soul-searching gaze into space. These are sure signs that they are suffering from the pains of trying hard to be trendy and sophisticated, brought about by the new breed of social Hong Kong upstarts who would like to have a European image.

The story is said to have been adapted from a popular love story (read by adolescent girls) written by Yik Shue. Maggie Cheung (swathed often in black, socalled French costumes), shows some dramatic possibilities as the confused sister of Chow Yan-fat who plays a dual role (older brother and then lover and about to be husband). Cheung was dubbed by a local d.j. which made her voice deeper.

The film was a boxoffice winner due to the popularity of the book, the presence of matinee idol Chow Yan-fat, the glamour of Maggie Cheung and the touristy sights of Paris with the help of arty director-cinematographer-artist Manshi Yonfan. —*Mel.*

Separati in Casa
(Separated At Home)
(ITALIAN-COLOR)

A Columbia release. Produced by Mario Orfini, Emilio Bolles for Eidoscope Prods. Written and directed by Riccardo Pazzaglia. Stars Riccardo Pazzaglia, Simona Marchini. Camera (Telecolor), Nino Celeste; editor, Anna Napoli; music, R. Pazzaglia and others; art director, Giovanni Agostinucci. Reviewed at Eden Cinema, Rome, April 3, 1986. Running time: **100 MINS.**
Husband . . . . Riccardo Pazzaglia
Carolina . . . . Simona Marchini
Luciano . . . . Massimiliano Pazzaglia
Lawyer . . . . Marina Confalone
Lawyer . . . . Lucio Allocca

Rome — In a lean year for Italo comedy, "Separated At Home" stands out for its gentle humor, original characters and unstressed pungency. Director Riccardo Pazzaglia up to now has been known best as a radio announcer (a role he plays in the film) and for his tv appearances on a madcap summer program run by Renzo Arbore. He is competent if not specially gifted behind the camera, but in front of it comes across as whimsical and appealing. Film failed to bring in local audiences, perhaps because it has no stars and follows no familiar genre.

The basic idea is simple enough: a husband (Pazzaglia) and wife (Simona Marchini), married long enough to have a teenage son (Massimiliano Pazzaglia), are fed up with living together but can't afford separate residences. After a series of small episodes (he accuses her of snoring, and brings in a panel of "witnesses" to prove it, etc.), their lawyers (Maria Confalone and Lucio Allocca), who are in the same situation in their private lives, draw up a set of rules for cohabitation without contact. The headboard on the bed is sawed in half, a wall unit built between the beds, food rigorously divided in the kitchen. They throw separate parties, to which the same friends are invited.

Thesps carry the show with consistently good banter. Playing two eccentrics, Pazzaglia and Marchini work together splendidly. More than an integrated film, "Separated At Home" has the feel of sketches from a variety show, and its eventual airing on the small screen should earn it the audiences it deserves.

In spite of a little awkwardness towards the end when an attempt is made to introduce drama briefly (son tells mom dad is dying), the final sequence of gluing the headboard back together neatly rounds off the tale. —*Yung.*

Last Song In Paris
(HONG KONG-COLOR)

A Chor Yuen production, released by Golden Harvest-Gala theater circuits. Directed by Chor Yuen. Stars Leslie Chung, Anita Miu, Wong Joe Ying, Cecilia Yip, Chu Kwong and Lam Hung. Executive producer, Doris Tse; assistant director, Tony Kwan. (No other credits provided by producers and distributor.) Reviewed at Golden Harvest theater, Hong Kong, April 6, 1986. Running time: **98 MINS.**
(Cantonese soundtrack with English subtitles)

Hong Kong — "Last Song In Paris" is a ridiculously monotonous, commercially measured and leisurely promenade in the dated romanticism that seems to be sweeping Hong Kong cinema.

Leslie Chung, supposedly a singing idol, holds his concert in Hong Kong's biggest stadium. Leslie later holds a celebration party in a disco where he meets Anita Mui, a dancer in his concert who really is a frustrated singer. They have an accidental, casual one-night stand. Leslie doesn't care for Anita as he is really in love with himself.

The next day, Leslie meets his pleasant businessman father at the airport. He is a widower with a young mistress, Wong Joe Ying, a lovely girl Leslie once encountered and fell in love with. Before the confrontation, Leslie surprises Anita on the final day of the concert by allowing her to do a solo number which catapults her to fame.

Heartbroken, angry and disturbed, poor rich boy Leslie leaves for Paris to escape the beach girl, father, fans, everything. High living, drinking and gambling get him broke fast and there's no financial support from home. One cold evening, the soiled, spoiled kid meets Cecilia Yip, a sweet Vietnamese girl who takes him home and nurses him back to health. They fall in love after endless footage of romantic, touristy interludes. Leslie and Cecilia get married and they work hard in a restaurant. She eventually dies, but Anita comes in just in time to rescue her real love.

The saving grace is Cecilia Yip, a competent actress who bravely acts out the role of a dying woman in love. —*Mel.*

Jo Jo Dancer, Your Life Is Calling
(COLOR)

Unsatisfying Richard Pryor opus.

A Columbia Pictures release. Produced and directed by Richard Pryor. Stars Pryor. Screenplay, Rocco Urbisci, Paul Mooney, Pryor; camera (Deluxe color), John Alonzo; editor Donn Cambern; music, Herbie Hancock; production design, John De Cuir; set decorator, Cloudia; sound, Willie D. Burton; assistant director, Jerry Ziesmer; costumes, Marilyn Vance; associate producer, John Wilson; casting, Reuben Cannon and Associates. Reviewed at the Samuel Goldwyn Theater, April 17, 1986, Beverly Hills, Calif. (MPAA Rating: R.) Running time: **97 MINS.**
Jo Jo Dancer/Alter Ego .... Richard Pryor
Michelle .... Debbie Allen
Arturo .... Art Evans
Grace .... Fay Hauser
Dawn .... Barbara Williams
Grandmother .... Carmen McRae
Satin Doll .... Paula Kelly
Mother .... Diahnne Abbott
Father .... Scoey Mitchlll
Johnny Barnett .... Billy Eckstine
Little Jo Jo .... E'lon Cox

Hollywood — Anyone looking for a soul-searching glimpse at the rise and fall and rise of Richard Pryor is bound to be disappointed by "Jo Jo Dancer, Your Life Is Calling." As autobiography, pic delivers few insights and mostly skates on the surface of events. As a performance piece, it is slightly better with enough of Pryor and his irreverent humor on display to satisfy his multitude of fans and create reasonably good boxoffice results.

Sorting out how much of the story is true will probably become the hot topic at cocktail parties with Pryor seemingly willing to fan the flames.

Obviously the story of a performer who goes into a drug-induced decline and ultimately has a life-threatening accident is based on Pryor's much publicized burn-out of several years back. At the same time Pryor denies the film is autobiographical while allowing it to be publicized as "the role of his life."

Probably what Pryor was shooting for was an emotional landscape approximating his own up and down career and it is here that the film is most deficient. Pryor and his coscreenwriters Rocco Urbisci and Paul Mooney have crammed the script full with four wives, and numerous benchmarks in Jo Jo's life, from his childhood in Peoria to stardom in Hollywood, without really fleshing out characters or getting beyond clichéd explanations.

On a structural level film is, at best, clumsy. Borrowing techniques from "All That Jazz," pic starts with the wounded comic being taken to the hospital where his alter ego steps from his body and reassesses his life from its beginnings. Gimmick misfires as much as it works with Pryor's spirit turning up seemingly arbitrarily to fill the screen with a fuzzy double vision.

Device is most effective as Pryor looks in on himself as a child. Here he is able to create a textured world with a depth of feeling lacking elsewhere in his travels. For starters, as the young Pryor, E'lon Cox is a lovable little kid surrounded by interesting people.

Best here is Carmen McRae as Jo Jo's grandmother and owner of the local whorehouse where the boy's mother (Diahnne Abbott) is employed. In the few scenes in which she appears, McRae virtually lights up the screen. Equally enjoyable a bit later in the journey is Billy Eckstine as a nightclub veteran who gives Jo Jo some tools of the trade which also include an introduction to drugs. Paula Kelly as the stripper Satin Doll is also appealing as one of Jo Jo's early mentors.

From here things go downhill as Jo Jo meets and marries Barbara Williams, Debbie Allen and Tanya Boyd and apparently develops a growing dependency on alcohol and cocaine, although the need and attraction remain pretty much a mystery.

Much of the responsibility for the failure of the film must go to Pryor for failing to draw out a truly involving character who is willing to go beneath the performer's facade. While Pryor relies too much on his wit and charm to get by, he is undeniably entertaining.

As a director Pryor still has some lessons to learn to keep a film on its feet. Pacing and editing are often choppy and staging gives the action an artificial feeling. Production design by John De Cuir is best in the early going while John Alonzo's photography is fine except in the overly grainy special effects section.

Herbie Hancock's score is generally a plus, peppered with an intelligent use of tunes such as Muddy Waters' "Mannish Boy" as Jo Jo leaves home to become a man. At other times, however, songs are applied like wallpaper with Marvin Gaye's "What's Going On" covering the action. —*Jagr.*

The Big Hurt
(AUSTRALIAN-COLOR)

An Ultimate Show-Big Hurt Ltd. production. Executive producer, Phillip Dwyer. Produced by Chris Kiely. Directed by Barry Peak. Stars David Bardshaw, Lian Lunson. Screenplay, Peak, Sylvia Bradshaw; camera (Eastmancolor), Malcolm Richards; editor, Ralph Strasser; music, Allan Zavod; sound, John Rowley; art director, Paddy Reardon; assistant director, Ross Hamilton; production manager, Ray Pond. Reviewed at Ultimate Show screening room, Melbourne, March 24, 1986. Running time: **93 MINS.**
Price .... David Bradshaw
Lisa .... Lian Lunson
Algerson .... Simon Chilvers
Harry .... John Ewart
Brake .... Alan Cassell

Also with: Nick Waters (McBride), Abbe Holmes (Jenny), Alethea McGrath (Mrs. Trent), Robin Cuming (Monk), Tommy Dysart (Schwartz), Syd Conabere (O'Neal), Joanne Canning (Ballerina), Dorothy Cutts (Rachel), Gary Adams (Fletch).

Sydney — A relaxed and disarmingly old-style crime thriller, "The Big Hurt" is a low-budget genre item about an investigative journalist involved in a case embracing murders, an apparent suicide, secret government departments, and dangerous scientific experiments. This kind of pic has not scored at the Aussie boxoffice (e.g., "The Empty Beach"), but this one could have cult appeal.

Director Barry Peak, whose previous pic was the cultish "Future Schlock," has aimed at a wider audience this time around. His screenplay, written with Sylvia Bradshaw, is cleverly plotted and the inevitable twists and turns of the story are adroitly handled. In the lead, David Bradshaw gives a solid performance in the Bryan Brown mold, but lacks humor, while Lian Lunson seems inexperienced as the inevitable femme fatale.

An essential requisite of this kind of film is a strong line-up of supporting characters, and these "The Big Hurt" has in abundance: John Ewart as a panicky newspaper editor, Simon Chilvers as a high-level secret service man and Alan Cassell as a scientist suspect are all good.

The moody musical score by Allan Zavod helps things along, but pic is lacking in action until quite near the end, depending on an intriguing plot to keep the audience happy. Small-scale production will probably make more of a mark on tv or on videocassette than in cinemas, but it might get bookings if promoted with the same level of grassroots enthusiasm that's gone into its production. Film noir addicts, certainly, should have an enjoyable time. —*Strat.*

Il Diavolo in Corpo
(Devil In The Flesh)
(ITALIAN-FRENCH-COLOR)

An Istituto Luce/Italnoleggio release of a L.P. Film (Rome), Istituto Luce/Italnoleggio Cinematografico (Rome), Film Sextile (Paris) coproduction. Produced by Leo Pescarolo. Directed by Marco Bellocchio. Stars Maruschka Detmers. Screenplay, Bellocchio, with the collaboration of Ennio De Concini; camera (color), Giuseppe Lanci, editor, Mirco Garrone; music, Carlo Crivelli; art director, Andrea Crisanti; production managers, Angelo Barbagallo, Stefano Bolzoni; costume design, Lina Nerli Taviani. Reviewed at C.D.S., screening room, Rome, April 21, 1986. Running time: **110 MINS.**
Giulia .... Maruschka Detmers
Andrea .... Federico Pitzalis
Mrs. Pulcini .... Anita Laurenzi
Giacomo Pulcini . Riccardo De Torrebruna
Mrs. Dozza .... Anna Orso
Prof. Raimondi .... Alberto Di Stasio
Also with: Catherine Diamant (Mrs. Raimondi), Claudio Botosso (Don Pisacane),

Lidia Broccolino and Stefano Abbati (terrorists).

Rome — The much-publicized tiffs between director Marco Bellocchio and producer Leo Pescarolo over the final cut of ''Devil In The Flesh,'' and a notoriously explicit oral sex scene between stars Maruschka Detmers and Federico Pitzalis, have this gracious film off to a fast start at the national b.o. Scandal-seekers looking for torrid auteurist eroticism will have to readjust their sights, however, as ''Devil'' is paradoxically one of the sunniest, lightest works Bellocchio has come up with in some time. Yes, eroticism is a key theme and, thanks to an electrifying performance by Detmers, sparks fly in all directions. However, sex between the attractive late-teen hero and heroine tends to be playful, joyous, and basically tasteful.

Though title recalls the famous novel by Raymond Radiguet ''Le Diable au Corps'' and Claude Autant-Lara's film, also something of a scandal in its time, present film retains only a few echoes of the original story. Andrea (Pitzalis) is quietly and studiously finishing his last year of high school when Giulia (Detmers) comes into his life. He's the son of a precariously balanced shrink (Alberto Di Stasio); she's a rich girl whose father was killed by terrorists and who is engaged to be married to a middle-class terrorist (Riccardo De Torrebruna) on his way out of prison for recanting and naming names. Though opposed by everyone for various reasons, Giulia and Andrea's love story triumphs in the end.

One of the most appealing things about the film is its paradoxes, turnabouts, and unexpected characters (one of the best is certainly Anita Laurenzi in the role of the young terrorist's mother, shocked by nothing and hell-bent on getting her son out of jail and embarked on a ''normal'' life). Bellocchio is in top form as far as lensing is concerned, and cameraman Giuseppe Lanci bathes scenes in the superb, glowing color of bright clear sunlight.

However, the many finely staged scenes fail to come together to make the emotional impact story demands. Ultimately, ''Diavolo'' reads like an intelligent, studied, interesting miss.

Center of the tale is Giulia, gorgeous but neurotic (viewed as mad by the psychiatrist, but viewer will have to decide autonomously). Living in a world of expensive objects and vast but empty apartments (especially the one she's gradually furnishing for her married life), Giulia, like her two lovers, is in search of normality and stability, but has a lot harder time finding it.

Next to Detmers' dynamic, high-strung character who is always laughing a little desperately, Pitzalis (a debuting thesp) can't do much but pale, though he imparts calm clarity to the unexciting Andrea. In baring her body (both male and female frontal nudity is shown) or lewdly gesturing to her jailed boyfriend, she is disturbingly expressive. In scenes focused on other characters, film's eros-related symbolism goes embarrassingly off the mark (e.g., a courtroom scene where two terrorists make love publicly).

Particularly noteworthy is Carlo Crivelli's melodious score, imaginatively used throughout. A curious footnote to the film is the contribution of Bellocchio's own analyst, anti-psychiatrist Massimo Faggioli, to the picture's making. He receives a large ''personally dedicated to'' credit right under the director's name. — *Yung.*

The Still Point
(AUSTRALIAN-COLOR)

A Colosimo Film Prod. Produced by Rosa Colosimo. Directed by Barbara Boyd-Anderson. Screenplay, Colosimo, Anderson; camera (Cinevex color), Kevin Anderson; editor, Zbigniew Friederich; music, Pierre Pierre; sound, Geoffrey White; production supervisor, Reg McLean; production manager, Robert Kewley; art director, Paddy Reardon. Reviewed at Walker Street theater, North Sydney, April 16, 1986. Running time: **82 MINS.**
Sarah . . . . Nadine Garner
Barbara . . . . Lyn Semmler
Grandfather . . . . Robin Cuming
Paul . . . . Alex Menglet
David . . . . Steve Bastoni
Simone . . . . Kirsty Grant

Sydney — A very low-budget feature about a deaf 14-year-old girl, ''The Still Point'' is well-meaning but too awkward and uninvolving to be of much interest.

The slight screenplay, by the producer and director, revolves around Sarah (Nadine Garner) who has had a hearing impairment from birth, but whose ability to lip-read is perfect, and who speaks with no suggestion of a disability. Her problems seem not to be so much that she's deaf, but that, in the middle of puberty and troubled by the fact that her parents have divorced and her mother has a new lover, she's become surly and unpleasant, unendearing traits referred to throughout as her shyness.

On a holiday visit to her grandfather she falls afoul of some older, drug-taking, girls, but corrals the ex-boyfriend of one of them.

Nadine Garner has something of the looks of a young Hayley Mills, and it will be interesting to see how she performs in a more flattering role in the future. Her temper tantrums and continual pouting here make for an unendearing character. Lyn Semmler is lively as her youthful mother. Other thesping is merely average.

Technically, the pic is just about adequate, but since it was obviously made on a miniscule budget, it's doubtless a small achievement that it was completed at all. A pity the screenplay wasn't stronger, or more interesting. It really doesn't have enough content for a feature-length film, and might better have been made into a short subject. —*Strat.*

Kangaroo
(AUSTRALIAN-COLOR)

A Filmways (Australia) release of a Naked Country production. Produced by Ross Dimsey. Executive producer, Mark Josem, William Marshall, Peter Sherman, Robert Ward. Directed by Tim Burstall. Stars Colin Friels, Judy Davis. Screenplay, Evan Jones, from the novel by D.H. Lawrence; camera (Panavision, Eastmancolor), Dan Burstall; editor, Edward McQueen-Mason; music, Nathan Waks; production design, Tracy Watt; costumes, Terry Ryan; sound, Paul Clark; production manager, Darryl Sheen; assistant director, Stuart Freeman; casting, Liz Mullinar Casting; made in association with Film Victoria. Reviewed at Hoyts screening room, Sydney, April 24, 1986. Running time: **108 MINS.**
Richard Lovat Somers . . . . Colin Friels
Harriet Somers . . . . Judy Davis
Jack Calcott . . . . John Walton
Vicky Calcott . . . . Julie Nihill
''Kangaroo'' . . . . Hugh Keays-Byrne
 Also with: Peter Hehir (Jaz), Peter Cummins (Willy Struthers), Tim Robertson (O'Neill).

Sydney — There have been several aborted attempts over the years to film ''Kangaroo,'' written in 1922 by D.H. Lawrence after a brief visit to Australia, and it's much to the credit of screenwriter Evans Jones and director Tim Burstall that the difficulties inherent in the project have finally been overcome. The resulting film is a serious, literary pic, handsomely produced and boasting a very strong cast of accomplished players. It's a solid bet for quality exhibition in most territories.

Pic opens with a 10-minute prologue set in Cornwall, England, in 1916 and establishing the problems that Lawrence, called Somers in the book and film, and his German-born wife Harriet, experienced during the war; his books were being attacked as pornography, and since he refused to enlist on conscientious grounds, his patriotism was questioned.

Setting then shifts to Sydney in 1922 as the couple arrive and settle into a suburban house next to Jack and Vicky Calcott. Jack is a war hero, holder of the Victoria Cross, while Vicky is an innocent for whom the Somers are exotic, fascinating people. Jack is secretly involved with a society of returned soldiers, known as The Diggers; under the leadership of the wealthy and charming ''Kangaroo,'' they're training to fight an expected socialist revolution. Somers, whose literary reputation has preceded him, is courted both by the socialist leader, Struthers, who offers him a newspaper to edit, and by the dangerously charming 'Kangaroo,' a sexually ambivalent fascist, who seeks not only the loyalty of his followers but also their love.

Of necessity, given the source material, the film is full of dialog, but it's interesting, well-written dialog (Harriet describes the brown Australian landscape, saying ''It feels as though men had never loved it'').

Judy Davis gives another outstanding performance as a very modern woman, abrasive and a bit cynical and world-weary, yet passionate. As Somers, Colin Friels gives a tense, brooding performance, filled with charm. He has one intimate scene with Julie Nihill, perfectly cast as the winsome Vicky, which has a strong sexual charge, even though nothing actually happens.

John Walton is fine as the easygoing, yet fanatical, Jack, while Hugh Keays-Byrne gives his best screen performance to date as the frightening fascist leader, who puts across his terrible ideas with sincerity and force.

Audiences expecting something steamy from the D.H. Lawrence reputation will be disappointed: this is a film of ideas, not sex or, until the violent scenes of the last reel, action. Indeed, the only major miscalculation of Burstall is a Friels-Davis love scene on a pounding surf beach which is so like the much-parodied scene in ''From Here To Eternity'' that it seems bound to be greeted with unwanted guffaws at many screenings.

Dan Burstall's Panavision cinematography coupled with Tracy Watt's production design make for a very handsome picture, which will appeal to the growing world-wide audience for class pictures. Some may find that the pic skirts the edges of the very strong drama at the center, but this elliptical approach is faithful to the Lawrence original and is inherent in the success of the film. —*Strat.*

Ryder, P.I.
(COLOR)

Lowbrow comedy has its moments.

A YGB Distribution release of a Long Island Entertainment Group production. Produced by Karl Hosch. Executive producers, Taimi Kivikko, Tony DeMartino, Angelo DeMartino. Directed by Hosch, Chuck Walker. Screenplay, Hosch, Walker, Dave Hawthorne, Bob Nelson, from story by Hosch, Walker; camera (color, video), Phil Arfman; editor, Keith Brooke; music, Kevin Kelly; sound, David Greenbaum; art direction, Kenneth Hosch; production manager, George Steinholz; associate producer, Walker.

Reviewed at UA 85th St. East theater, N.Y., April 26, 1986. (MPAA Rating: PG-13.) Running time: **92 MINS.**
Sky Ryder . . . . Dave Hawthorne
Eppie . . . . Bob Nelson
Valerie . . . . Frances Raines
Gang leader . . . . John Mulrooney
Prof. Throckmorton . . . . Bob Woods
Ben Wah . . . . Howard Stern
Maria . . . . Kim Lurie
Det. Hoolihan . . . . Chuck Rader

Though closely resembling a backyard, homemade film in structure and technique, ''Ryder, P.I.'' is an amusing little feature made in Port Washington, N.Y. Fans willing to take a goof on a low-budget pic will enjoy it.

Dave Hawthorne (who cowrote the screenplay) toplines as a pudgy private eye named Sky Ryder, who is given to halting the story in order to essay his okay impressions of Jack Nicholson and other celebrities. He is teamed, in Bowery Boys fashion, with nerd assistant Eppie (Bob Nelson), whose idea of getting a license plate number is to unscrew the plate and bring it to Ryder.

The duo is on a case trailing a woman for her husband (actually watching the wrong lady for a whole year) when they save a lovely young woman Valerie (Frances Raines) who is being assaulted by three bikers. Ryder takes her under his wing, romance blossoms and he succeeds in saving her from a group of South American drug smugglers out to get her inherited land holdings south of the border. The bikers turn out to be undercover federal drug enforcement agents.

Loaded with silly shtick and a sense of humor drawing upon tv culture, ''Ryder'' has its share of funny gags. Best sequence is a throwback to the 1960s, a lyrical interlude of the three leads romping at the beach and a miniature golf course.

Hawthorne holds the film together in a warm performance while sidekick Nelson overdoes his scatterbrained routine, using a voice similar to Frank Fontaine's Crazy Guggenham impression. Raines is a fresh new face as the vulnerable heroine in one of her best showcases yet (after roles in ''Model Behavior,'' ''Disconnected'' and other east coast B-pictures).

Among numerous comedians in small roles, radio personality Howard Stern is unimpessive as a goofy tv anchorman named Ben Wah and Chuck Rader's carbon of Dirty Harry is subpar.

Picture was lensed on videotape with a Betacam system. Its transfer to 35m film for theatrical release is adequate, though blurring (especially of street signs and other written material) is evident in longshots and some panning shots. —*Lor.*

Twelfth Night
(AUSTRALIAN-COLOR)

A Twelfth Night production. Produced by Don Catchlove. Directed by Neil Armfield. Screenplay, Armfield, from the play by William Shakespeare; camera (Agfacolor), Louis Irving; editor, Nicholas Beauman; music, Allen John; production designer, Stephen Curtis; sound, Rob Stalder; production manager, Steven Salgo; assistant director, Corri Soeterboek. Reviewed at Dendy theater, Sydney, April 13, 1986. Running time: **120 MINS.**
Viola/Sebastian . . . . Gillian Jones
Orsino . . . . Ivar Kants
Olivia . . . . Jacqy Phillips
Malvolio . . . . Peter Cummins
The Fool . . . . Kerry Walker
Sir Toby Belch . . . .: . . . John Wood
Sir Andrew Aguecheek . . . . Geoffrey Rush
Also with: Tracy Harvey (Sarah), Stuart McCreery (Antonio), Odile Le Clezio (Olivia's maid), Igor Sas, Russel Kiefel.

Sydney — An exhilirating modern-dress version of Shakespeare's comedy play, this Aussie film version of a successful local stage production attempts no more than to be a film record of a legit hit, but does so with élan. It's fun.

Right from the start, when Orsino bursts into a frenzied party with his ''If music be the food of love'' speech, adaptor/director Neil Armfield presents an engagingly irreverent version of the play. Purists won't be happy, but this is Shakespeare for the widest audience. Subsidiary characters, such as John Wood's Sir Toby Belch, are presented as defiantly 'ocker' Australian types, complete with beer gut and strong accent.

Stephen Curtis provides a set design that's deliberately artificial and extremely simple. Music is modern, too, with Allen John setting Shakespeare's lyrics to his own compositions, to good effect.

All the players are excellent. Gillian Jones is intriguingly androgynous in the Viola/Sebastian role (this version brings out the sexual ambiguities of the original very strongly); Ivar Kants a forceful Orsino; Jacqy Phillips a suitably vulnerable Olivia; and Peter Cummins an hilarious Malvolio, especially when tricked into courting Olivia in hideous yellow shorts and socks, yellow being a color she loathes.

Kerry Walker gives another topnotch performance as The Fool, a male character to which this fine actress brings a mysterious, knowing edge. Wood and Geoffrey Rush, as his hapless buddy, Sir Andrew Aguecheek, steal all their scenes.

With its broad humor, asides to camera and contagious irreverence, this version of ''Twelfth Night'' could become a cult item with youthful audiences. Made on a tiny budget, it provides excellent entertainment value once the concept of hearing the medieval poetry of The Bard spoken by these defiantly modern characters is accepted.

Careful handling is essential, and could pay off. It's technically passable. —*Strat.*

For Love Alone
(AUSTRALIAN-COLOR)

A Greater Union (Australia) release of a Waranta production, in association with U.A.A. Produced by Margaret Fink. Executive producer, David Thomas. Directed by Stephen Wallace. Stars Helen Buday, Sam Neill, Hugo Weaving. Screenplay, Wallace, from the novel by Christina Stead; camera (Eastmancolor), Alun Bollinger; editor, Henry Dangar; music, Nathan Wax; production designer, John Stoddart; art director, John Wingrove; sound, Syd Butterworth; costumes, Jennie Tate; casting, Hilary Linstead (M & L Casting); production manager, Susan Wild; assistant director, Mark Turnbull. Reviewed at Greater Union screening room, Sydney, March 18, 1986. Running time: **104 MINS.**
Teresa Hawkins . . . . Helen Buday
James Quick . . . . Sam Neill
Jonathan Crow . . . . Hugo Weaving
Harry Girton . . . . Huw Williams
Andrew Hawkins . . . . . . Hugh Keays-Byrne
Kitty Hawkins . . . . Odile Le Clezio
Also with: Linden Wilkinson (Miss Havilland), Judi Farr (Aunt Bea), Anna Phillips (Ann), Regina Gaigalas (Jean), John Polson (Leo Hawkins), Nicholas Opolski (Lance Hawkins), Naomi Watts (Marion), Jill Clayton (Aunt Di), Renee Wray (Landlady), Jennifer Hagan (Manette), Fiona Stewart (Martha), Anna North (Lucy), Mercia Dean-Jones (Clara), Tracey Higginson (Malfi).

Sydney — It's been seven years since ''My Brilliant Career,'' but Margaret Fink's handsome new production, ''For Love Alone'' will, for many, be worth the wait. Stephen Wallace, rather than Gillian Armstrong, directs this time around, but the similarities between the two films strongly indicate the personality of the producer behind the scenes.

Like the earlier film, ''For Love Alone'' is a period romance centering around a plain-jane heroine with career ambitions. Set in the 1930s, pic opens in a snow-covered Britain but quickly flashes back to sunny Australia where the central character, Tess (Helen Buday) lives with her bullying father (Hugh Keays-Byrne), her sister and brothers. Times are hard (the depression), but the intelligent, lively Tess is in love with Jonathan Crow (Hugo Weaving), a university lecturer, and though he treats her badly more often than not, she decides to follow him to England when he departs for a job in London.

It takes her years of saving to raise the fare (though, unaccountably, she seems to travel first-class by ocean liner) and on the voyage she meets James Quick (Sam Neill), a banker, who falls in love with her. He gives her a job in London, but she spends most of her time trying to break through to the increasingly distant Jonathan, whose time in England seems to have made him even more difficult than he was back home.

''For Love Alone'' is, as might be expected, a visually magnificent production. Cinematography by New Zealand's Alun Bollinger (''Vigil'') and production design by John Stoddart are impeccable. About half the story takes place in Britain, but there was only a few days shooting there (with stand-ins). Thanks to the sets and camerawork, it doesn't show.

Just as ''My Brilliant Career'' launched Judy Davis, so this new film should draw attention to Helen Buday, another excellent young actress whose unconventional looks exactly fit the requirements of her role; when necessary, she's radiant. Sam Neill is in fine form as the sympathetic banker, while Hugo Weaving, as the caddish Jonathan, is suitably and properly unpleasant. Hugh Keays-Byrne gives a Charles Laughton-ish portrayal as Buday's bombastic father, and there's a charming cameo from Odile Le Clezio as her sister.

Pic is what used to be known as a woman's picture, but it is a little cold and passionless. So was the Christina Stead novel on which director Wallace based his screenplay, but a little more emotion, and thus audience identification, would have helped the boxoffice.

It's a prestige item, technically up to the highest standards of Australian cinema, and, with the right handling, should make its mark internationally. —*Strat.*

Low Blow
(COLOR)

Hamfisted, dull action flick.

A Crown Intl. Pictures release of an Action Communications production. Produced by Leo Fong. Executive producers, Bertrand Ungar, Mark Moldenhauer. Directed by Frank Harris. Screenplay, Fong; camera (color), Harris; editor, Harris; music, Steve Amundsen; additional music, Samuel S. Cardon; sound, John Torrijos; assistant director-second unit director, Gene Lehfeldt; art direction/costume design, Diane Stevenett; production manager, David Cox; stunt coordinator, George Chung; associate producer, Hope Holiday. Reviewed at UA Twin 2 theater, N.Y., April 25, 1986. (MPAA Rating: R.) Running time: **85 MINS.**
Joe Wong . . . . Leo Fong
Karma . . . . Akosua Busia
Yurakunda . . . . Cameron Mitchell
Templeton . . . . Troy Donahue
Diane . . . . Diane Stevenett
Duke . . . . Stack Pierce
Daughter . . . . Patti Bowling

In ''Low Blow,'' filmmakers Leo Fong and Frank Harris (who previously teamed on ''Killpoint'') reduce an action picture to its basic elements: fights, shootouts and simple delivery of expository dialog, with tedious results. This test of an audience's patience was filmed in Stockton, Calif., under the title ''Savage Sunday.''

Fong, who also produced and

scripted for his Action Communications banner, toplines as private eye Joe Wong, an ex-cop who is hired by rich guy Templeton (Troy Donahue, looking like he's been to a nearsighted barber) to bring his daughter Karen (Patti Bowling) out of a religious cult. Karen has been renamed Purity by the cult, which is led by blind guru Yurakunda (Cameron Mitchell), with the real power vested in his gorgeous black assistant Karma (Akosua Busia).

Fong spends most of the film killing time by staging tough man contests and otherwise recruiting a team to go in and rescue the girl. Script fails to establish the evilness of the cult (other than their hypnotizing and seemingly drugging kids to keep them), but Fong & Co. go in and kill the cult's guards anyway in ruthless fashion. Karma shoots Yurakunda, but her fate is just another loose end.

Sole point of interest in this clunker is the presence of Akosua Busia, actress whose next role after this in "The Color Purple" earned her an Oscar nomination. She is funny, vivacious and ultimately a bit touching in the stock, evil dragon lady role. This film won't appear on her resumé, but it's a wild performance nonetheless. Busia's thesping contrasts with that of Fong and the rest of the players, who are strictly monotone. In fact, many of the smaller roles look like they're being filled with pals who work out with Fong at the local gym.—*Lor.*

Sweet Liberty
(COLOR)

Behind the scenes comedy fails to realize its potential.

A Universal Pictures release of a Martin Bregman production. Executive producer, Louis A. Stroller. Directed and written by Alan Alda. Camera (Kay color), Frank Tidy; editor, Michael Economou; music, Bruce Broughton; production design, Ben Edwards; sound, Al Mian; art direction, Christopher Nowak; set decoration, John Alan Hicks; costume design, Jane Greenwood, associate producers, Judith Stevens, Michael Economou; assistant director, Yudi Bennett; casting, Mary Colquhoun. Reviewed at MCA/Universal screening room 1, Universal City, Calif., April 22, 1986. (MPAA Rating: PG.) Running time: **107 MINS.**
Michel Burgess . . . . Alan Alda
Elliot James . . . . Michael Caine
Faith Healy . . . . Michelle Pfeiffer
Stanley Gould . . . . Bob Hoskins
Gretchen Carlsen . . . . Lise Hilboldt
Cecelia Burgess . . . . Lillian Gish
Bo Hodges . . . . Saul Rubinek
Leslie . . . . Lois Chiles

Hollywood — There was a terrific concept behind writer-director-star Alan Alda's "Sweet Liberty," with the emphasis on *was*. Comedic potential is too rarely realized in this story of a college professor who watches filming of his historical tome become bastardized by Hollywood into a lusty romp. Alda in-

stead favors focusing on characters' sappy relationships, which is sure to please certain filmgoers who are amused watching middle-aged men pant after younger women.

Playing their true ages are Alda as college professor Michael Burgess who teaches history of the American Revolution at a small North Carolina college, and Michael Caine as boxoffice draw Elliot James, set to play an English Greencoat in the filmed version of Burgess' book.

When the film company arrives on location in buccolic Sayeville, Alda falls for leading lady Faith Healy (Michelle Pfeiffer), at the same time stringing along girlfriend Gretchen Carlsen (Lise Hilboldt).

Caine at first lunges after the college president's wife (Lois Chiles) before luring Faith away, all the while managing to keep the slightly wounded Miss Carlsen enticed.

Film starts slowly focusing around Burgess and Carlsen's insipid conversations about her wanting to get married and his wanting to live together.

Effort picks up when action moves to film location sequences, especially encounters between Alda and film's slick director, Bo Hodges (Saul Rubinek), who is determined to make a youth-oriented picture at the expense of historical accuracy.

Working to change the script any way can, Burgess pulls all-nighters with the film's scripter rewriting dialog and seduces Faith with his knowledge of history and how to make a salad, scenes that were more bemusing than amusing.

Hilarity comes when he attempts to be a swashbuckler like Caine, always the better swordsman as well as being much more adept at playing the Cavalier with the ladies.

Alda gets bogged down with too much dialog explaining every little nuance that would have been better shown and not explained, including those attempted by his mother (the very lucid Lillian Gish) pining away for a love who hasn't called here in 25 years.

Less believable is Hilboldt as the almost too goody-two-shoes girlfriend determined to make it down the altar with Burgess, smiling through nearly every scene, even ones that are quasi-dramatic.

Pfeiffer and Chiles are good, though neither of their roles demands too much.

Production has a nice, true feel to it. The Hollywood cast and crew look and act the part, notably the macho stuntmen out to strut their stuff, as do the townsfolk who appear eager to do something other than endure another stifling Southern summer.—*Brit.*

Fire With Fire
(COLOR)

Tame and predictable romantic drama.

A Paramount Pictures release of a Gary Nardino production. Produced by Nardino. Executive producer, Tova Laiter. Directed by Duncan Gibbins. Screenplay, Bill Phillips, Warren Skaaren, Paul Boorstin, Sharon Boorstin; camera (Alpha Cine Service color; Metrocolor prints), Hiro Narita; editor, Peter Berger; music, Howard Shore; production design, Norman Newberry; art direction, Michael Bolton; set decoration, Rondi Johnson; costume design, Enid Harris; sound, Larry Sutton; assistant director, Jules Lichtman; casting, Jackie Burch. Reviewed at the Paramount Studios, L.A., April 25, 1986. (MPAA Rating: PG-13.) Running time: **103 MINS.**
Joe Fisk . . . . Craig Sheffer
Lisa Taylor . . . . Virginia Madsen
Boss . . . . Jon Polito
Mapmaker . . . . Jeffrey Jay Cohen
Sister Victoria . . . . Kate Reid
Sister Marie . . . . Jean Smart
Jerry . . . . Tim Russ
Ben . . . . David Harris
Baxter . . . . D.B. Sweeney
Sandy . . . . Dorrie Joiner
Manuel . . . . Evan Mirand
Sister Harriet . . . . Ann Savage

Hollywood — "Fire With Fire" throws off very few sparks. Even though it is based on a true story, pic, lensed under the title "Captive Hearts," plays as a thoroughly unconvincing rich girl-poor boy romance. Innocuous and tame in treatment, Paramount release is lackluster in every department and doubtlessly will disappear from screens quickly as the summer product moves in.

Script, worked over by several hands, unfolds in so predictable and unimaginative a fashion that only young girls who have never been exposed to "Romeo And Juliet" and its countless offspring could conceivably become enthralled with the story.

Up in the remote woods somewhere (production was lensed in British Columbia), a parole camp for ne'er-do-wells and a Catholic girls school coexist in relatively close proximity. After blond beauty Virginia Madsen and independent-minded inmate Craig Sheffer spy one another one day, Madsen arranges for her school to host a dance for the socially deprived fellows, which allows for the fated couple to get together.

Before long, Sheffer is sneaking past the nuns in the middle of the night to steal into Madsen's room, and they finally scurry off to the local cemetery and consummate their love on the cold cement floor of a crypt.

Naturally, the powers-that-be don't cotton to any of this. After much earnest chasing around, the outcasts make their way to an abandoned cabin, where they would be happy ever after if only society would leave them alone.

But no, the cars and helicopters and guns are nipping at their heels, and a conflagration as well as a few

action stunts must take place before matters can be resolved.

This being the mid-1980s, and a Paramount film to boot, story can't be told without any number of rock songs accompanying the characters to their destinies, although it must be said that debuting feature director Duncan Gibbins displays little evidence of his background in music videos in his work here. In fact, he displays little of anything resembling style.

In fairness, however, the script is equally sorry, as none of the characters, not even the two leads, are provided with dimensional personalities or histories. Jon Polito's heavy is embarrassingly caricatured, and the boys in the camp come off like insipid versions of the Bowery Boys, nice lads who'd be fine if given half a chance. The small talk at the long dance sequence is staggering in its banality.

Gone very bright blond here, Madsen is stuck with a character who makes too many unbelievable choices for a young lady of her intelligence, while Sheffer lacks the emotional urgency needed in a fellow willing to take such risks for his sweetheart.

Chaste, seemingly abbreviated love scenes prove disappointing, and PG-13 rating doesn't allow pic to approach living up to its title. Tech contributions are adequate.
— *Cart.*

Cannes Fest Reviews

Tenue de soirée
(Evening Dress)
(FRENCH-COLOR)

An Hachette Première-AAA release of a Hachette Première/Philippe Dussart Prods./Ciné Valse/D.D. Prods. coproduction. Executive producer, Dussart. Produced by René Cleitman. Written and directed by Bertrand Blier. Stars Gérard Depardieu, Michel Blanc, Miou-Miou. Camera (Panavision, Eastmancolor), Jean Penzer; editor, Claudine Merlin; art direction, Théo Meurisse; sound, Bernard Bats, Dominique Hennequin; music, Serge Gainsbourg; makeup, Michel Deruelle and Joel Lavau; costumes, Michèle Cerf; production manager, Michel Choquet; assistant director, Bertrand Arthuys; casting, Margot Capelier. Reviewed at the Gaumont Ambassade theater, Paris, April 29, 1986. (In competition at Cannes Film Festival). Running time: **81 MINS.**
Bob . . . . Gérard Depardieu
Antoine . . . . Michel Blanc
Monique . . . . Miou-Miou
Art collector . . . . Bruno Cremer
Depressed husband . . . Jean-Pierre Marielle
Depressed wife . . . . Caroline Sihol
Burgled couple . . . . Jean-François Stevenin,
Mylène Demongeot
Pedro . . . . Michel Creton
Man in night club . . . . Jean-Yves Berteloot

Paris — There's nothing like a good shot of insolence for getting one's flagging career out of a rut. After the failure of his two previous films ("My Best Friend's Girl" and "Our Story"), writer-director Bertrand Blier finally has recovered the abrasive imagination and tonic bad taste that fired some of his early films, notably "Les Valseuses" ("Going Places").

"Tenue de soirée" is a tart black comedy of sexuality in which, among others things, Blier energetically turns the French star system on its head. Despite his impressive range, one did not quite expect to see robust Gérard Depardieu falling for another man, especially somebody so nebbishy as Michel Blanc, the bald, wispy funnyman who had tremendous success with his 1984 film, "Marche à l'ombre," which he wrote, directed and starred in.

Happily, "Tenue" has much more than its purported shock value, which no doubt will fade even more quickly than that of "Going Places" in the 1970s. Blier charges what could have been little more than a clever gay variation on the romantic triangle with a bulldozing wit and cynicism, and his talent for writing raw, bristling, strangely lyrical dialog is exhilarating. After the sluggishness of his recent pictures, it is good to see Blier's direction again so assured in its bite and forward-leaning pace. The film runs a breathless 81 minutes.

Depardieu, a burglar whose sexual tastes have undergone a change in prison, meets a down-and-out couple, Blanc and Miou-Miou, and drags them into a series of housebreakings with promises of lucre and a new life. Blanc is hopelessly in love with his now-contemptuous mate, and naturally is disturbed when their new friend begins making advances — at him.

He's even more unsettled when he finds himself slowly giving in to Depardieu's husky wooing. They become lovers, and shack up together, with Depardieu secretly paying off a pimp to take the now intrusive wife off their hands. They meet up again in a disco where the desperately enamored Blanc, now in drag, kills Miou-Miou's pimp and wounds a young man the fickle Depardieu has picked up in the toilets. In the final scene, Blanc and Depardieu, decked out in their feminine best, are walking the streets with fellow hooker Miou-Miou.

Blier's script is shot through with dark, ferocious humor. It is not devoid of an ambiguous poignancy, best expressed in Blanc's astonishing performance of a straight milquetoast whose sexual calvary leads to a new identity and sense of self — the film's last, unforgettable, image is of the totally feminized Blanc applying lipstick with a hand mirror, casting quick smiles and inviting glances at the camera.

Depardieu has a field day as Blanc's exuberant dark angel, at first bizarrely sincere in his fervent pursuit of love (his seduction scenes with Blanc are among the film's best) and his later mercenary

wantonness. As the odd-woman-out, Miou-Miou too has several outstanding scenes, notably the film's opening in a seedy dance hall, where she unleashes a torrent of abuse on her meek mate.

Far from the ironic pastoral tone of "Going Places" (which launched Depardieu, Miou-Miou and the late Patrick Dewaere, for whom Blier first wrote the Blanc role years ago), "Tenue" is closer visually to the cold, nocturnal textures of the director's underrated 1980 black comedy, "Buffet Froid," which he reprised in "Our Story." Blier again is working with the same lenser and art director, Jean Penzer and Théo Meurisse, and their contributions are stylishly evocative. Claudine Merlin's editing provides snap to the fast-moving events, and Serge Gainsbourg's music is discreetly effective. —Len.

In The Shadow Of Kilimanjaro
(COLOR)

Hungry Baboons attack.

A Scotti Bros. Pictures release of a Sharad Patel presentation of an Intermedia production. Executive producer, Sharad Patel. Produced by Gautam Das, Jeffrey M. Sneller. Directed by Raju Patel. Stars John Rhys-Davies, Timothy Bottoms. Screenplay, Sneller, T. Michael Harry; camera (Technicolor), Jesus Elizondo; supervising editor, Paul Rubell; editor, Pradip Roy Shah; music, Arlon Ober; sound, Russell Williams; art direction, Ron Foreman; production manager, Joyce Warren; assistant director, Mila Rocho; animal trainer, Clint Rowe; baboon voices created by Percy Edwards; casting, Laurie Ronson. Reviewed at Magno Penthouse screening room, N.Y., April 30, 1986. (MPA Rating: R.) Running time: **97 MINS.**
Chris Tucker . . . . John Rhys-Davies
Jack Ringtree . . . . Timothy Bottoms
Lee Ringtree . . . . Irene Miracle
Ginny . . . . Michele Carey
Maitland . . . . Leonard Trolley
Lucille Gagnon . . . . Patty Foley
Mitushi Uto . . . . Calvin Jung
Julius Odom . . . . Don Blakely
Eugene Cruz . . . . Patrick Gorman
Gagnon . . . . Jim Boeke

Filmed over two years ago in Kenya, "In The Shadow Of Kilimanjaro" is an old-fashioned adventure thriller in the borderline horror genre of a last-stand-at-the-house against predators, previously essayed in such films as "Kingdom Of The Spiders," "Savage Harvest" and "Roar." Boxoffice outlook is weak.

A famine has caused the 90,000 baboons on a Kenya wildlife reservation to begin banding together and preying on humans (film claims on-screen to be based on a true story, but the 1984 date given is impossible). Wildlife ranger John (Jack to his friends) Ringtree wants to evacuate the area of about 200 people but the government and manager of the local mine Chris Tucker (John Rhys-Davies) view him as an alarmist and oppose his efforts. As usual

in corny horror films like this one, the cast (especially female) is given to wandering alone in the bush long after word of animal attacks has been announced, making them easy prey.

Eventually the danger comes close to home and all survivors huddle together in a hotel run by Michele Carey. The last stand against the marauding animals is successful and a convenient rainstorm spells the end of the drought and the problem.

Hokey film benefits from atmospheric location photography, but suffers from sometimes inaudible dialog recorded in direct sound. Rhys-Davies uses a prop cigar and a new accent in a fun job as a villain, but by the final reels he has become a true-blue good guy, with only the baboons as hissable targets. Bottoms is merely okay as the bland hero, Irene Miracle is extremely glamorous as his "please come home with me to America" nagging wife (in a role reserved decades ago in these films for Elsa Martinelli) and it's fun to see 1960s starlet Michele Carey again as the friendly neighborhood hotelier. Leonard Trolley is so hammy as an old British colonial type recalling the good old days that one wishes he had been fed to the baboons early on.

Director Raju Patel substitutes gore effects for suspense in an episodic presentation that fails to knit individuals scenes together. Unconvincing matte shots are used to show hundreds of baboons storming down from the hills, while more manageable stagings of a dozen or so animals are used to enact the attacks on humans. Situation inevitably conjures up memories of Cy Endfield's minor 1965 classic "Sands Of The Kalahari," but instead of that film's genuinely chilling climax of the baboons descending in longshot on the surviving protagonist (which left the horror to one's imagination), we now get severed limbs, half-eaten faces and torsos and other ineffective gimmicks. — Lor.

Agent On Ice
(COLOR)

Chintzy nonaction film.

A Shapiro Entertainment release of a Louis And Clark Expedition production. Executive producer, Robert J. Dupere. Produced by Louis Pastore. Directed by Clark Worswick. Screenplay, Worswick, Pastore; camera (Du Art color), Erich Kollmar; editor, Bill Freda; music, Ian Carpenter; sound, Don Paradise; production manager, Jeff Switzer; casting, Donna De Seta. Reviewed at UA Twin 2 theater, N.Y., May 3, 1986. (MPAA Rating: R.) Running time: **97 MINS.**
John Pope . . . . Tom Ormeny
Kirkpatrick . . . . Clifford David
Frank Matera . . . . Louis Pastore
Joey . . . . Matt Craven
Secretary . . . . Debra Mooney
Jane . . . . Donna Forbes

Helen Pope . . . . Jennifer Leak

Take an uninteresting story, executed on the cheap in perfunctory fashion and you have the nonthriller "Agent On Ice," shot in New York and New Jersey with such alternate titles as "And Then You Die" and "Silent Partners." With a no-name cast, pic will have trouble getting attention in international markets.

Tom Ormeny (who looks like an uncle to actor John Ericson) toplines as John Pope, an ex-CIA agent now on the skids as a slovenly insurance adjustor. A Mafioso he supposedly killed, Frank Matera (Louis Pastore), is back in New York after hiding out in Sicily, and orders Pope and other CIA agents to be killed.

Pope's ex-bosses at the CIA are corruptly in cahoots with the Mafia, so everyone wants him dead. It takes six boring reels and a bulletproof vest for Pope to wipe out everybody and have the obligatory final scene letting the government know what it can do with its jobs and perks.

Acting is lousy in a film which cries out for an international cast of character actors. Shot in winter (with New Jersey unconvincingly filling in for a prolog supposedly set in Hungary), film has consistently ugly locations and dreary colors. With producer Louis Pastore doubling as the Mafia villain, film is closer to a vanity production than the tough guy, B-picture it strives to be. —Lor.

Blue City
(COLOR)

Embarrassing attempt at brat film noir.

A Paramount Pictures release of a Hayward/Hill and Jones/Kenner production. Produced by William Hayward and Walter Hill. Executive producers, Robert Kenner, Anthony Jones. Directed by Michelle Manning. Screenplay, Lukas Heller, Walter Hill, based on novel by Ross Macdonald; camera (Technicolor), Steven Poster; editor, Ross Albert; sound, C. Darin Knight; art direction, Richard Lawrence; assistant director, Doug Claybourne; additional photography, Ric Waite; second unit camera, Donald M. Morgan; camera (Florida), Egon Stephan; associate producer, Katherine Morris; music, Ry Cooder; casting, Jackie Burch. Reviewed at Paramount Studios, Hollywood, April 28, 1986. (MPAA Rating: R.) Running time: **83 MINS.**
Billy Turner . . . . Judd Nelson
Annie Rayford . . . . Ally Sheedy
Joey Rayford . . . . David Caruso
Luther Reynolds . . . . Paul Winfield
Perry Kerch . . . . Scott Wilson
Malvina Kerch . . . . Anita Morris
Lt. Ortiz . . . . Luis Contreras
Debbie . . . . Julie Carmen

"Blue City" is fictionally set in Florida, but was lensed principally in California, thus managing to shame the citizenry on one coast and the filmmaking industry on the other, all at the same time. Judd

Nelson and Ally Sheedy have attracted young fans to bad films before, so who knows.

It's doubtful that any small town in Florida could have contained so many dopey people and not have been overgrown with swamp grass and alligators. The townfolk are reasonably content until Nelson returns to his hometown, carrying a basketball.

Within a couple of minutes, Nelson has started a bar-room brawl for no clear-cut reason, then seemingly wisecracks to his jail guard that they should call his dad the mayor to get him out and a couple of minutes later it turns out his dad really was the mayor, but he's dead now.

By then it's impossible to care at all and it never gets better as Nelson rampages back and forth between Blue City's dopey police chief (Paul Winfield), dopey local crimelord (Scott Wilson) and his dopey stepmother (Anita Morris) to find his father's killer.

Nelson's going to need a couple of hometown dimwits to help him through all this and he finds two beauties in Sheedy and David Caruso, her brother and his old pal from high school.

Caruso isn't anxious to help because Wilson's boys have already busted up his kneecaps and the film's action sequences are going to require a lot of running and jumping. Suddenly, though, Caruso says he can do it because "I've been soaking my leg," something he apparently never thought of before.

Sheedy isn't anxious to help, either, but Nelson gives her a ride on his motorcycle and they start kissing and taking their shirts off and talking about sleeping on the couch but end up in bed where she apparently decides Nelson's cause is just.

It's the hero himself who must take credit for the ultimate triumph. Thoroughly unlikable, Nelson is equally unstoppable. After three of Wilson's huge thugs beat on him at length, he emerges with a slightly smudged cheek, just like Claudette Colbert used to look after enduring several hours of Japanese dive-bombing.

Sheedy does tell him, "You don't look too good all beat up," but this girl is not given to acute observations about anything going on. Typically she does make a big discovery that Wilson married Morris before his dad died, but that adds nothing to the plot one way or the other.

Nothing else does either, but Nelson will eventually work his way through the plot turns before the audience stops laughing. When he doesn't know what else to do, he gets on his motorcycle and goes for long rides.

When director Michelle Manning doesn't know what else to do, she photographs him.—*Har.*

Getting Even
(Hostage: Dallas)
(COLOR)

Topical thriller lacks energy until a rousing final reel.

An American Distribution Group release of an AGH Prods. production. Executive producer, Alan Belkin. Produced by J. Michael Liddle; line producer, Jean Higgins. Directed by Dwight H. Little. Stars Edward Albert, Audrey Landers, Don Baker. Screenplay, M. Phil Senini, Eddie Desmond, from story by Liddle; camera (CFI color), Peter Lyons Collister; editor, Charles Bornstein; music, Christopher Young; sound design, David Lewis Yewdall; sound, John Pritchett; production design, Richard James; set decorator, Derek Hill; assistant director-production manager, Joe O'Har; special effects, Jack Bennett, Jack Bennett Jr.; special effects makeup, Larry Aeschlimann; second unit camera, Allen Facemire; casting, Linda Francis, Pat Orseth. Reviewed at RKO Warner 2 theater, N.Y., May 3, 1986. (MPAA Rating: R.) Running time: **90 MINS.**
Taggar .... Edward Albert
Paige Starsen .... Audrey Landers
King Kenderson .... Joe Don Baker
Doc .... Rod Pilloud
Ryder .... Billy Streater
Kurt .... Blue Deckert
Roone .... Dan Shackelford
Molly .... Caroline Williams

"Getting Even," filmed in Texas as "Hostage: Dallas" (a title retained for international distribution), is an uninteresting thriller that finally picks up steam in its last reel due to some exciting aerial and building-top stunts. Pic has been in regional release since February.

Edward Albert toplines as Taggar, a successful Dallas industrialist who steals a deadly new poison gas from the Russkies in Afghanistan (an unconvincing, chintzy opening, also shot in Texas) on orders of our government. His chemical company is under government contract to develop an antidote, and federal agent Paige Starsen (Audrey Landers), who trained and romanced years ago with Taggar, is sent to Dallas to see what's taking him so long in the lab.

Rival chemical magnate King Kenderson (Joe Don Baker, king of the good ole boys) is in sorry financial condition, and hits upon the dumb idea of stealing the poison gas from Taggar. After the theft, his scientific whiz Molly (Caroline Williams) immediately self-destructs via some sloppy lab technique that contaminates her, whereupon Kenderson sends Taggar a ransom note asking for $50,000,000 or he will kill off the denizens of Dallas with the gas.

Taggar gets the money out of petty cash and several double crosses later he and Starsen retrieve the gas, vow to get out of the weapons business and live happily ever after. As stated, final reel of helicopter chases, stunt climbs & falls almost counteracts the four preceding reels

of relentless dullness. Until that finale, director Dwight Little lets the pace lag and gives no evidence that there is anything to worry about, hardly the approach necessary for a doomsday thriller.

Edward Albert smirks his way through the main role, Landers is merely decorative and Joe Don Baker hard to hate as a villain for a change. Remainder of the cast is weak. —*Lor.*

Short Circuit
(COLOR)

Cute robot comedy.

A Tri-Star Pictures release, from Tri-Star and PSO. Produced by David Foster, Lawrence Turman. Executive producers, Mark Damon, John Hyde. Coproducer, Dennis Jones. Directed by John Badham. Screenplay, S.S. Wilson, Brent Maddock; camera (Panavision, Metrocolor), Nick McLean; editor, Frank Morriss; music, David Shire; sound, Willie D. Burton; art direction, Dianne Wager; set design, Garrett Lewis; robotics, Syd Mead, Eric Allard; assistant director, Jerry Ziesmer; casting, Mike Fenton, Jane Feinberg, Judy Taylor. Reviewed at Coronet theater, L.A., May 1, 1986. (MPAA Rating: PG.) Running time: **98 MINS.**
Stephanie Speck .... Ally Sheedy
Newton Crosby .... Steve Guttenberg
Ben Jabituya .... Fisher Stevens
Howard Marner .... Austin Pendleton
Skroeder .... G.W. Bailey
Frank .... Brian McNamara
Voice of No. 5 .... Tim Blaney

Hollywood — Summer is here, signaled by the release of "Short Circuit," a hip, sexless sci-fi sendup featuring a Defense Dept. robot who comes "alive" to become a pop-talking peacenik. Pic is the kind to draw teens in out of the sun at the folks' expense, adding up to a long circuit at the b.o.

Robot is the one-dimensional No. 5 at film's opener, the ultimate weapon designed by playful computer whiz Dr. Newton Crosby (Steve Guttenberg) who treats the Nova classified military complex where he works like his personal playground without ever contemplating the real consequences of his creations.

By a fluke, No. 5 gets short-circuited by a bolt of lightning on the day the DOD debuts it and Nos. 1-4 during a demonstration before the Washington rubber stampers.

No. 5 begins to malfunction and finds itself outside the high-security Nova compound in a chase that lands it on top of a natural foods catering truck and under the influence of its sweet but tough animal-loving owner, Stephanie (Ally Sheedy).

In contrast to unoriginal and overwrought scenes involving military as either zealous warmongers or mindless bureaucrats, those with the altruistic and charming Sheedy make an otherwise predictable story seem clever, funny and fresh.

Scripters S.S. Wilson and Brent

Maddock get credit for some terrific dialog that would have been a lot less disarming if not for the winsome robot and Sheedy's affection for it.

Basically, No. 5 is cute, especially when it becomes a sponge of information, whipping through encyclopedia volumes in milliseconds and absorbing and regurgitating nuances it takes in from watching commercial tv.

Guttenberg plays his best goofy self — the wide-eyed scientist with a naive innocence who offends no one.

Playing off him is a malapropism-prone sidekick named Howard (Austin Pendleton) with the awsome load of memorizing skewed one-liners that are often a bit too convoluted.

Credit goes to robotics engineer Eric Allard who has created a warm, but not lovable, character in No. 5.

While Sheedy doesn't seem to have any trouble hugging the mechanical beast, or even kissing it, facsimilies aren't likely to end up cherished toys like E.T.—*Brit.*

Death Of A Soldier
(AUSTRALIAN-COLOR)

A Scotti Bros. Pictures presentation of a Suatu Film Management production. Produced by David Hannay, William Nagle. Executive producers, Oscar Scherl, Richard Tanner. Directed by Philippe Mora. Screenplay, Nagle; camera (Panavision, color), Louis Irving; editor, John Scott; music, Alan Zavod; coproducer, Lance Reynolds; associate producers, Honnan Page, Richard Jabara; art direction, Geoff Richardson; costumes, Alexandra Tynan; production supervisor, Geoff Pollock; postproduction supervisor, Charles Hannah. Reviewed at Magno Preview 9 theater, N.Y., April 28, 1986. (MPAA Rating: R.) Running time: **93 MINS.**
Maj. Patrick Dannenberg ..James Coburn
Edward J. Leonski .... Reb Brown
Det. Sgt. Adams .... Bill Hunter
Det. Sgt. Martin .... Maurie Fields
Margot Saunders .... Belinda Davey
Maj. William Fricks .... Max Fairchild
Gen. MacArthur .... Jon Sidney
Maj. Gen. Sutherland ...... Michael Pate
Gallo .... Randall Berger
Also with: John Cottone, Nell Johnson, Mary Charleston, Jeanette Leigh, Rowena Mohr, Duke Bannister, John Murphy, Brian Adams, Arthur Sherman, Terry Donovan, Ken Wayne and Ron Pinnell.

Based on a true story of Edward J. Leonski, a psychopathic G.I. who was hanged by the U.S. Army for the 1942 murders of three women in Melbourne, Australia, "Death Of A Soldier" is a psychological murder mystery that's short on mystery and pathology, and an anti-capital punishment tract that fails to opened new ground. In spite of decent performances, first-rate period re-creation and provocative insights into U.S.-Australian wartime relations, "Death Of A Soldier" is marked by an inexorable predictability and glumness that will likely limit its theatrical prospects to a brief run prior to paycable playoff.

The film is at its most interesting in its revisionist view of the uneasy alliance between the Americans and the Australians, who had engaged the Japanese in bitter fighting for years before the Yanks arrived. The film suggests that the rosy romanticism of the Andrews Sisters' soundtrack tune, "Boogie Woogie Bugle Boy Of Company B" was belied by tensions seething just beneath the surface of relations between the embattled Aussies and their swaggering U.S. allies. When an American G.I. was spotted fleeing the scene of the first of three brutal murders of young local women, the tensions erupted into openly bitter enmity capped by a bloody, surreal train station shootout between U.S. and Aussie troops.

The shootout is hushed up by Maj. Patrick Dannenberg (James Coburn), an M.P. with a legal background (character is based on American attorney Ira C. Rothberger who headed the case) who's trying to capture the killer before he strikes again. His mission is particularly urgent because, according to "Death Of A Soldier," American brass up to and including Gen. Douglas MacArthur considered the apprehension and execution of the perpetrator essential to preserving allied unity.

Coburn and his gruff sidekick Maj. William Fricks (Max Fairchild) are in a sort of race with two Aussie gumshoes, Det. Sgts. Adams and Martin (splendidly essayed by Bill Hunter and Maurie Fields), to capture Leonski in a competition that mirrors the larger Aussie-Yank rivalry. The local cops are interested only in getting the madman off the streets and bringing him to Australian justice, but the Army wants his blood to set an example no one will forget. Coburn is caught in the middle.

Played by Reb Brown as a passingly charming scatterbrained New York redneck with a penchant for hard drinking and rambunctious womanizing, Edward Leonski does not emerge as a sympathetic character. His psychopathic nature is evident from the start, but never satisfactorily delineated, aside from casual references to family alcoholism and a brother in the slammer during the compressed trial sequences.

Two-thirds of the film is given over to Leonski's carousing in the Gommorah-like fleshpots of wartime Melbourne, his murderous rampage, and the flabbergasting indecision of his tentmate, Gallo (Randall Berger), to whom he confesses early on but who waits through three murders before reporting his suspicions.

When Leonski's military defender is struck down by hepatitis, a reluctant Coburn takes on the case, convinced Leonski's confession (he killed the women because he "wanted their voices") demonstates his insanity and unfitness for execution. A postwar investigation of the Leonski case was said to have produced permanent changes in the military justice system. However, the film's court martial sequences are familiar formula stuff and the arguments over insanity and criminal culpability don't challenge the viewer with an original presentation of their moral urgency. —*Rich.*

Cut And Run
(ITALIAN-COLOR)

A New World Pictures release of a Racing Pictures production. Produced by Alessandro Fracassi. Directed by Ruggero Deodato. Stars Lisa Blount, Leonard Mann, Willie Aames. Screenplay, Cesare Frugoni, Dardano Sacchetti; camera (Telecolor), Alberto Spagnoli; editor, Mario Morra; music, Claudio Simonetti; sound, Piero Fondi; art direction, Claudio Cinini; production manager, Maurizio Anticoli. Reviewed at RKO National 2 theater, N.Y., May 2, 1986. (MPAA Rating: R.) Running time: **87 MINS.**
Fran Hudson . . . . Lisa Blount
Mark . . . . Leonard Mann
Tommy . . . . Willie Aames
Col. Brian Horne . . . . Richard Lynch
Bob . . . . Richard Bright
Karin . . . . Karen Black
Ana . . . . Valentina Forte
Quecho . . . . Michael Berryman
Vlado . . . . John Steiner
Manuel . . . . Gabriele Tinti

"Cut And Run" is an incoherent, relatively tame action film from Italian director (of "Zenabel" and "Cannibal Holocaust") Ruggero Deodato. Pic was lensed in the summer of 1984 in Venezuela and Miami.

Unconvincing plotline posits that a Green Beret colonel who served in Vietnam, Brian Horne (Richard Lynch), was the real force behind Jim Jones' Jonestown massacre in Guyana. He's still on the loose in South America running a drug operation, and cable newshen Fran Hudson (Lisa Blount) and her trusty cameraman Mark (Leonard Mann) trek from Miami to get the story.

In the jungle, they encounter a war between Indians and drug smugglers, and also find the son (Willie Aames) of their news boss (Richard Bright). Many characters are injected into the story arbitrarily, such as Cable Video News owner Karen Black (embarrassingly overreacting to every event in a small role) and Italian starlet Valentina Forte (taking care of the requisite nudity and suddenly killed off midway through the picture). In a nebulous role as the bald leader of the Indians, Michael Berryman has no dialog and is photographed as a monstrosity, tastelessly heading him towards the status of a new Rondo Hatton (the acromegalic 1940s actor exploited in horror films back then).

Most of the inane dialog is in direct sound English, with Aames coming off as the silliest of the lead players. Forte is also laughable with her heavily accented, post-synched dialog. The best that can be said for star Blount's role is that, against all odds, she gets to keep her clothes on throughout.

Picture give evidence of having been edited heavily, with numerous opportunities for Deodato's trademark gore going unfulfilled. Claudio Simonetti's musical score has its moments but is a far cry from his best work (such as "Suspiria") with the rock group Goblin.—*Lor.*

The Last Emperor
(Pu Yi's Latter Life)
(HONG KONG-CHINESE-COLOR)

A New Kwun Lun Film Production Co. (Li Han Hsiang) and China Intl. Television Corp. coproduction. Released by Southern Films in the Nanyang theater chain. Directed by Li Han Hsiang. Stars Tony Leung (Liang Jia Huei), Pan Hung, Li Dien Lang (Margaret), Li Dien Xing (Mary). Screenplay cowritten by Li Han Hsiang, based on Li Shu Xian's "Pu Yi And I," "Pu Yi's Latter Life" and "Pu Yi's My Former Life." (No other credits provided by the producers.) Reviewed at Nanyang theater, Hong Kong, April 19, 1986. Running time: **100 MINS.**
(Mandarin soundtrack with Chinese and English subtitles)

Hong Kong — Li Han Hsiang is one of the most important directors in the history of Chinese films, known for his period costume and historical epics for Shaw Brothers.

"The Last Emperor" was filmed in Beijing and Inner Mongolia. Though laden with touristy shots of the Palace Museum, Beijing Zoo and Zhen Xie where the People's National Congress was held, along with valuable sepia-tinted authentic footage of the Cultural Revolution, the center of the production is more on the human side of the last emperor.

While Bernardo Bertolucci is set to direct a film about the early days of Emperor Pu Yi, director Li has successfully done the final chapter on the man's life, with Tony Leung (Liang Jia Huei) in the emperor's role. The scenario focuses on the man who was made an emperor as a young boy and grew up to be the puppet ruler during the Japanese occupation. After the war, he is brought to life as a simple, reformed ordinary citizen who is faced with modernism, lost wealth, the emerging Cultural Revolution, the recriminations of his past wives/concubines and a forthcoming new marriage to a hospital nurse. There are some epic scenes with thousands of people but Li Han Hsiang zooms in on humanistic emotions instead of the detailed visual splendor of Chinese arts, crafts and traditions as seen in his past historical-dramatic epics.

"The Last Emperor," when properly edited, has great potential in art theaters, college circuits, film festivals abroad and retrospective programs of Li's prolific and controversial career.

It is the first joint production between New Kwun Lun Film Prod. and China Intl. Television Corp.

The acting of Tony Leung is superior and is ably supported by Pan Hung as Li Shu Xian (award-winning actress from China), Li Dien Lang (Margaret) as the Empress Wan Rung and Li Dien Xing (Mary) as Li Yu Qin. The production qualities are good but cannot be compared to Li's big-budget extravaganzas in the 1960s and 1970s.

"The Last Emperor" is a serious but entertaining film, and should be of great interest to those interested in Asian history. The authentic footage on the Cultural Revolution is rarely seen and is stunning to behold.—*Mel.*

The Fringe Dwellers
(AUSTRALIAN-COLOR)

A Fringe Dwellers Prod., in association with Ozfilm. Executive producer, Hilary Heath. Produced by Sue Milliken. Directed by Bruce Beresford. Screenplay, Bruce Beresford, Roishin Beresford, from the novel by Nene Gare; camera (Eastmancolor), Don McAlpine; editor, Tim Wellburn; music, George Dreyfus; production designer, Herbert Pinter; sound, Max Bowring; costumes, Kerri Barnett; production manager, Helen Watts; assistant director, Mark Egerton; casting, Alison Barret. Reviewed at Film Australia screening room, Sydney, April 14, 1986. (In competition at Cannes Film Festival.) Running time: **98 MINS.**
Trilby Comeaway . . . . Kristina Nehm
Mollie Comeaway . . . . Justine Saunders
Joe Comeaway . . . . Bob Maza
Noonah Comeaway . . . . Kylie Belling
Also with: Denis Walker (Bartie), Ernie Dingo (Phil), Malcolm Silva (Charlie), Marlene Bell (Hannah), Michelle Torres (Audrena), Michele Miles (Blanchie), Kath Walker (Eva), Bill Sandy (Skippy), Maureen Watson (Rene), Robert Ugle (Tom), Alan Dargin (Bruce), Terry Thompson (Horrie), Annie Saward (May), Wilkie Collins (Dr. Symons).

Sydney — "The Fringe Dwellers," an accomplished adaptation of Nene Gare's early 1960s novel about an Australian aboriginal family, will probably be dubbed Bruce Beresford's "The Color Purple." After the disappointing results of his Biblical epic "King David," Beresford returned to Australia to make this long-cherished project, and has succeeded admirably. Pic has been invited to compete in Cannes.

Set in a small outback town in Queensland, it's the story of the Comeaway family, who live in appalling conditions in makeshift shacks on the edge of town. Despite their poverty, the Comeaways make the best of things. Mollie (Justine Saunders), a Jane Darwell type, is forever nagging her lazy spouse, Joe (Bob Maza) to do some work and earn some money. Elder daughter Noonah (Kylie Belling) is a trainee nurse at the town hospital, while the sensitive Trilby (Kristina Nehm), focus of the story, is a high school student who dreams of leaving to live in the city, but who is made pregnant by her boyfriend, Phil (Ernie Dingo).

Pic is made up of lots of incidents, with editor Tim Wellburn frequently cross-cutting between the various members of the family. Screenplay, by Beresford and his wife, Roishin, is a seamless adaptation of the novel, while Don McAlpine's camerawork is up to his usual high standard in capturing the tones of the little town and the landscape around it, as well as some eye-catching sunsets.

But the film will be remembered for its ensemble acting. A large cast of mainly aboriginal players, for which casting director Alison Barret deserves credit, are faultless under Beresford's sympathetic direction. Always good with actors, he elicits memorable performances from all concerned, with Justine Saunders a stand-out as the woman who has to cope with a lazy husband, fractious daughters and various unwanted in-laws and who barely remembers the few aboriginal words taught to her by her beloved mother. Kath Walker, a well-known poetess, also gives a forceful performance as a mystic who frightens the children with strange stories of aboriginal legends.

Despite the film's humor, tenderness and drama, there will doubtless be those who will criticize it for its essentially white Anglo-Saxon approach to the aboriginal people. It is, in some ways, old-fashioned. The political issues and land rights problems that have become such a factor in white-aboriginal relations in recent years simply aren't mentioned. The racism of some whites towards blacks is indicated, but at times the film gets close to the old stereotypes of lazy, drunken black man who never does anything positive.

Critical pros and cons may be anticipated, but the film should appeal to audiences around the world for its humanity and beauty.

—*Strat.*

Cactus
(AUSTRALIAN-COLOR)

A Roadshow (Australia) release of a Dofine production. Produced by Jane Ballantyne, Paul Cox. Directed by Paul Cox. Stars Isabelle Huppert, Robert Menzies. Screenplay, Cox, with the collaboration of Norman Kaye, Bob Ellis; camera (Fujicolor), Yuri Sokol; editor, Tim Lewis; sound, Ken Hammond; production designer, Asher Bilu; executive producer, Jeannine Seawell; associate producer, Tony Llewellyn-Jones; production manager, Milanka Comfort; assistant director, Virginia Rouse. Reviewed at Roadshow screening room, Sydney, March 26, 1986. (In Directors Fortnight at Cannes Film Festival.) Running time: **93 MINS.**

Colo . . . . Isabelle Huppert
Robert . . . . Robert Menzies
Tom . . . . Norman Kaye
Bea . . . . Monica Maughan
Bunduk . . . . Bunduk Marika
  Also with: Peter Aanesen (George), Sheila Florance (Martha), Jean-Pierre Mignon

(Jean-François), Julia Blake (Cactus lecturer), Erwin Rado, Ann Rado.

Sydney — With "Cactus," Paul Cox, Australia's most innovative director, has made his most challenging and intriguing film to date. Visually extraordinary and dramatically satisfying, pic is a unique blend of emotional drama, documentary and visual experimentation.

Isabelle Huppert is ravishing as a French woman visiting friends in Australia to escape a crumbling marriage back home. Early in the film she's involved in a car accident. A sliver of glass pierces one eye, blinding it. Doctors tell her the eye must be removed or the blindness will spread to her other, uninjured, eye; she vacillates.

Her contrite friends (Norman Kaye, Monica Maughan) introduce her to a neighbor, a shy, rather uptight young man (Robert Menzies), blind from birth, whose symbolic hobby is growing cacti. The two become friends, then lovers.

Around this simple plotline, Cox brilliantly embroiders in his usual quirky style. His long-standing interest in both experimental film and documentary explain the integration of both in all his major films. In "Cactus" there are sequences where the fictional characters step into real-life situations, such as a rather quaint meeting of a cactus society. There's also a riveting moment, grainily captured on blown-up 8m, where Menzies recalls from his childhood the one split-second in his life when he actually *did* manage to see.

Visually and aurally the film is masterly. Yuri Sokol's complex camerawork, beginning with an imposing 500° pan, is his best work to date, while the soundtrack, recorded by Ken Hammond, adds the weird noises of the Australian bush, including the unearthly cry of the whip bird, to the visuals making this the most tactile film about the Australian countryside since "Picnic At Hanging Rock."

Huppert gives a very strong performance as the visitor to Australia to whom tragedy strikes. Robert Menzies (grandson of a former Prime Minister of the same name), in his first major screen role (he had a small part in "Bliss"), proves a major discovery.

"Cactus" is an unusual, fascinating, deceptively complex film, filled with odd little asides and off-beat peripheral characters. With proper handling, it should enhance Cox's reputation in art houses and at festivals the world over. —*Strat.*

Top Gun
(COLOR)

Flashy but empty military pic, with good b.o. outlook.

A Paramount Pictures release. Produced by Don Simpson, Jerry Bruckheimer. Executive producer, Bill Badalato. Directed by Tony Scott. Screenplay by Jim Cash, Jack Epps Jr.; camera (Metrocolor), Jeffrey Kimball; music, Harold Faltermeyer; editor, Billy Weber, Chris Lebenzon; production design, John F. DeCuir Jr.; set decorator, Robert B. Benton; supervisor of special photographic effects, Gary Gutierrez; sound (Dolby), William B. Kaplan; assistant director, Daniel P. Kolsrud, Sharon Mann; associate producer, Warren Skaaren; casting, Margery Simkin. Reviewed at Paramount Studio's Little Theater, Hollywood, Calif., April 29, 1986. (MPAA Rating: PG.) Running time: **110 MINS.**

Maverick . . . . Tom Cruise
Charlie . . . . Kelly McGillis
Ice . . . . Val Kilmer
Goose . . . . Anthony Edwards
Viper . . . . Tom Skerritt
Jester . . . . Michael Ironside
Cougar . . . . John Stockwell
Wolfman . . . . Barry Tubb
Slider . . . . Rick Rossovich
Merlin . . . . Tim Robbins
Sundown . . . . Clarence Gilyard Jr.
Hollywood . . . . Whip Hubley
Stinger . . . . James Tolkan
Carole . . . . Meg Ryan

Hollywood — "Top Gun" is revved-up but empty entertainment from producers Don Simpson and Jerry Bruckheimer. Watching the film is like wearing a stereo Walkman, so pervasive and insistent is the music. It has the aggressive good looks of a television commercial and a formula that has worked for Simpson/Bruckheimer before. "Top Gun" should be a sizable summer hit.

Set in the world of Naval fighter pilots, pic has strong visuals and pretty young people in stylish clothes and a non-stop soundtrack. Result is a film that tries hard to please — too hard.

This is not to say the film is not entertaining in spots. Audiences prepared to go with it will be taken for a thrilling ride in the wild blue yonder. Cinematographer Jeffrey Kimball and his team have assembled some exciting flight footage, an updated version of the classic war pictures. But too much of any good thing becomes a bit tedious, especially if there isn't a story to tie it all together or vary the intensity.

Tom Cruise is Maverick, a hotshot fighter pilot with a mind of his own and something to prove. Assigned to the prestigious Top Gun training school at the Miramar Naval Station in San Diego with his sidekick Goose (Anthony Edwards), Maverick has a skeleton in his closet and a rocket in his pocket.

Along for the ride as a romantic interest is Kelly McGillis as Charlotte (Charlie) Blackwood, a civilian astrophysicist brought in to teach the boys about negative G's and inverted flight tanks. Cruise, however, has his sights set on other targets.

Maverick gets broken by a few mishaps and one tragedy, but Charlie is there to pick him up and all the while the music is blaring. It seems there is no experience, from lovemaking to jets taking off, that isn't accompanied by Harold Faltermeyer's soundtrack. Life is given the emotional texture of a three-minute pop song.

Sometimes, the sheer power of the imagery is enough to keep the film going, but more often than not the action is forced. Script by Jack Epps Jr. and Jim Cash fails to make the necessary emotional connections. Also, buried in the background are some very disturbing political notions for anyone who wants to bother to consider them.

Tony Scott's direction pushes the film with numerous closeups designed to certify the importance of events. Pic works best in the few instances where Scott allows it to take off on its own power.

Perfomances don't help to put across the romantic and dramatic imperatives either. McGillis is blessed with an intelligent and mature face that doesn't blend that well with Cruise's one-note grinning. There is nothing menacing or complex about his character. Edwards, on the other hand, gives some rough edges to his ill-fated Goose and almost makes his friendship with Cruise believable.

Tom Skerritt turns in his usual nice job as the hardened but not hard flight instructor. Rest of the cast is stocked with plenty of beefcakes for the teenage girls.

But perhaps more than anything it is the production values that star here. Production design by John F. DeCuir Jr. and costumes by James W. Tyson and Bobbie Read look great, almost as if the film were posing for a picture. —*Jagr.*

Thunder Run
(COLOR)

Silly 'Mad Max' imitation.

A Lynn-Davis production in association with Panache Prods. Produced by Carol Lynn. Executive producer, Peter Strauss. Coproducer, Lawrence Applebaum. Directed by Gary Hudson. Stars Forrest Tucker, John Ireland, John Sheperd. Screenplay, Charles Davis, Carol Heyer, from a story by Clifford Wenger Sr., Carol Lynn; camera (DeLuxe color), Harvey Genkins; editor, Burton Lee Harry; music, Matthew McCauley, Jay Levy; stunt coordinator, Rod Amateau; special action unit, Alan Gibbs; special effects, Clifford Wenger Sr., Charles Davis; associate producers, Clifford Wenger Sr., Charles Davis; production manager, Steve Traxler; assistant director, Rob Roda; art director, Carol Heyer. Reviewed on Delta vidcassette, Sydney, April 29, 1986. (No MPAA Rating.) Running time: **91 MINS.**

Charlie Morrison . . . . Forrest Tucker
George Adams . . . . John Ireland
Chris . . . . John Sheperd
  Also with: Jill Whitlow (Kim), Wally Ward (Paul), Cheryl M. Lynn (Jilly), Marilyn O'-

Connor (Maggie Morrison), Graham Ludlow (Mike), Alan Rachins (Carlos), Tom Dugan (Wolf).

———

Sydney — After a slow start, and some preposterous plot development, "Thunder Run" develops into a stunt-filled chase film obviously patterned after the "Mad Max" pictures. Vet action icon Forrest Tucker plays a grizzled granddad and retired ex-trucker hired by a former comrade-in-arms from the Korean War (John Ireland) to drive a truckload of radioactive plutonium across Nevada and Arizona, knowing that evil terrorists (with unlimited resources) will be out to stop him.

For the teen audience, there's plucky, resourceful Chris (John Shepherd), the old man's loving grandson, who insists on going along on the mission despite Tucker's objections.

Story is even sillier than usual for this kind of effort, but once-the truck is on the road and the terrorists, equipped with heat-seeking rockets, set out after it, things get more exciting. The large stunt team, headed by Rod Amateau, does sterling work, with some spectacular smash-ups captured by the camera.

This 1985 pic, which has gone straight to video in Australia, is acceptable action fare for undemanding audiences. It's dedicated to Clifford Wenger Jr. —*Strat.*

Around The World In Eighty Ways
(AUSTRALIAN-COLOR)

———

A Palm Beach Entertainment production in association with Australian European Finance and Commonwealth Bank of Australia. Produced by David Elfick, Steve Knapman. Directed by Stephen Maclean. Screenplay, Maclean, Paul Leadon; camera (Colorfilm), Louis Irving; editor, Marc von Buuren; music, Chris Neal; production design, Lissa Coote; costume design, Clarrissa Patterson; sound, Paul Brincat; production manager, Catherine Phillips Knapman; assistant director, Ian Page. Reviewed at Colorfilm screening room, Sydney, April 23, 1986. Running time: **91 MINS.**
Wally Davis . . . . Philip Quast
Roly Davis . . . . Allan Penney
Nurse Ophelia Cox . . . Gosia Dobrowolska
Mavis Davis . . . . Diana Davidson
Eddie Davis . . . . Kelly Dingwall
Alec Moffatt . . . . Rob Steele
Also with: Judith Fisher (Lotte Boyle), Jane Markey (Miserable Midge), John Howard (Dr. Proctor), Frank Lloyd (Mr. Tinkle), Cathren Michalak (Mrs. Tinkle), Ric Carter (Financier), Jack Allan (Mailman), Nell Schofield (Scottish Scrooge), Kaarin Fairfax (Checkout chick), Micki Gardner, Helen Simon, Elizabeth Burton (Geisha girls).

Sydney — At a time when traveling overseas on vacation seems more than ever fraught with danger, "Around The World In Eighty Ways" should strike a few chords: It's about a world trip experienced entirely at home. Wayout comedy has a most original premise, which has, in the main, been realized by director and coscripter Stephen Maclean, helming his first pic.

Old Roly (a top performance from Allan Penney) is much older than his wife, Mavis: as she puts it, "He didn't age gracefully," and, indeed, he's senile, virtually blind and unable to walk. Mavis decides to go off on a package tour around the world, leaving Roly in an old folk's home, but when the old man discovers his hated neighbor and erstwhile business rival, the nouveau riche and loathesome Alec (Rob Steele) is going on the same tour, evidently with lustful intent, he is determined, despite his infirmities, to go, too.

Enter his two sons: the elder, Wally, a gay, smalltime tour guide, wants the old man's money; the younger, Eddie, a sound effects wiz, goes along with the scam. The idea is to take the cash Roly would have spent on his trip, but simulate a trip for him; after all, he can hardly see, so won't know the difference. With Wally impersonating everything from an airline pilot to a geisha girl to Elvis Presley, and Eddie providing convincing sound effects, and with the absent Alec's luxury home providing an all-purpose international hotel setting, Roly is convinced he's overseas. They go first to Honolulu, then on to Las Vegas, Rome and Tokyo. Aided by a pretty nurse (Gosia Dobrowolska), Roly has so much fun that gradually he regains his faculties; before long he's able to walk, then dance, even see. Meanwhile, on the real tour,

Mavis and Alec are having a dreadful time: rushed schedules, bad food, bad weather, forced landings, etc.

It says a lot for Maclean's direction that the audience is always well aware of what's going on in this rather complicated, but clever, plot. Principal actors work hard, especially Quast with his various impersonations, and have lots of fun. Subsidiary characters are less interesting, and the film does have a few flat patches, especially in the scenes of the real tour. Also, the budget seems to have limited the quality of the special effects required, especially in the last reel when a fully recovered Roly destroys the luxury home of his rival.

Lissa Coote's production design is on the garish side, but it's in keeping with the unusual situations: there's nothing very subtle here, but the film's not aiming for subtlety. Chris Neal's score is tops, and Louis Irving's camerawork is pro. Marc von Buuren edited to a tight 91 minutes.

Cheerful ending to the pic contains a nod to "Cocoon," and audiences will come away similarly pleased to see an old man rejuvenated. Mark this down as a genuinely original comedy which, with proper handling and promotion, could do good business on its intriguing premise and ingenious development. —*Strat.*

```
***********************************
*                                 *
*       Competing At Cannes        *
*                                 *
***********************************
```

Offret
(The Sacrifice)
(FRENCH-SWEDISH-COLOR)

———

A Sandrews release (international sales, Swedish Film Institute) of a Swedish Film Institute/Argos Films (Paris) production in association with Josephson & Nykvist, SR/TV-2, Sandrews (Stockholm), Film Four Intl. (London), with participation of the French Ministry of Culture. Executive producer, Anna-Lena Wibom. Produced by Katinka Farago. Written and directed by Andrei Tarkovsky. Stars Erland Josephson. Allan Edwall. Camera (Eastmancolor), Sven Nykvist; editor, Tarkovsky, Michael Leszczylowski; music; Watazumido Shuso; sound, Owe Svensson, Bo Persson; art direction, Anna Asp; costumes, Inger Pehrsson; assistant director, Kerstin Eriksdotter; casting, Priscilla John, Claire Denis. Françoise Menidrey; production manager, Göran Lindberg; stunts, special effects, Richard Roberts, Johan Torén, Lars Höglund, Lars Palmquist. Reviewed at the Cannes Film Festival (in competition), May 12, 1986. Running time: **150 MINS.**
Alexander . . . . Erland Josephson
Adelaide, his wife . . . . Susan Fleetwood
Otto, the mailman . . . . Allan Edwall
Victor, the physician . . . . Sven Wolter
Maria, the witch . . . . . . Gudrun Gisladottir
Julia . . . . Valerie Mairesse
Marta . . . . Filippa Franzén

Cannes — "The Sacrifice," which writer-director Andrei Tarkovsky calls "as Russian a film as any other made by me" is primarily a Swedish production with Swedish dialog. It takes place in and around a house on the desolate and marshy coastal plains of a Swedish island in the Baltic Sea adjacent to the Soviet Union.

Although decidedly overlong, "The Sacrifice" is a continuously brilliant exercise in Tarkovsky's finely honed *clair obscure* of cinematic techniques, as well as of larger meanings not given any explanation by way of what's accepted commonly as plot or character developer. Still, the doomsday film is Tarkovsky's most generally accessible work ever, indulging as it does in the current atomic scare while dealing with a small group of people facing the Earth's ultimate disaster.

Parts of "The Sacrifice" will

main open for very diverse interpretation, but what appeals directly to the hearts and minds of intellectuals and the common man alike is not only the scare appeal, but also the relief offered by an ending that turns out to be rather upbeat.

Forgetting about poetic digressions and themes developed in asides, Tarkovsky's film concerns a middle-aged intellectual (Erland Josephson) whose birthday dinner is interrupted by what is obviously the nuclear Big Bang, although it is seen (an icy light followed by near darkness) rather than heard. The man's wife has an understandable fit of hysterics, and is sedated by a doctor friend who is largely preoccupied with his now-dashed hope of emigrating to Australia. Another friend, a mailman (Allan Edwall) of philosophical bent and knowledge, advises the host to go sleep with a local witch, reportedly a good one, and use her innocence to seek atonement, for the sins of mankind.

Alexander the intellectual, played with nervous intensity under a façade by Josephson, follows the mailman's advice. But first he sinks to his knees and promises God to leave behind all his worldly possessions, including his young and cherished son, if the world may be allowed, so to speak, another lease on life. His wish is granted, but to underscore his personal responsibility for the eventual outcome, Alexander burns down his own house. He is considered looney by the survivors and is taken away, destined for the nuthouse.

His small son, however, a deafmute, pre-Armageddon regains his voice and repeats a Biblical quote told him by his father: "In the Beginning was the Word." In a wealth of Tarkovsky symbolism, the boy carries water to a withered tree his father had planted on the beach with the admonition that any repeated act by a human may one day change the world. The tree doesn't spring into bloom again, but a message of hope lies in the final frame's dedication of the film to Tarkovsky's own son, and to hope for the world in general.

For Tarkovsky followers — and there are enough to ensure art house playoff of this film worldwide — "The Sacrifice" has enough assets to propel it over its self-imposed hurdles of near-somnambulistic tempos and sometimes ritualistic acting. All Tarkovsky's pet imges and sounds — e.g., water dripping into stale pools, black & white flashbacks of decay and disaster, Japanese art and lifestyles — are emulated to heighten film's aesthetic values. And there is Sven Nykvist's camera wizardry with ultralong takes, and lighting that provides a sheen to even the most somber frames.

With all these elements, anybody not expecting an outright actioner should be able to enjoy being taken into Tarkovsky's wonderland of emotionally charged deepthink.

—*Kell.*

Mona Lisa
(BRITISH-COLOR)

An Island Pictures release (U.S.) of a HandMade Films presentation of a Palace production. Produced by Stephen Woolley, Patrick Cassavetti, coproduced by Chris Brown, Ray Cooper. Executive producers, George Harrison, Denis O'Brien. Directed by Neil Jordan. Stars Bob Hoskins. Screenplay, Jordan, David Leland; camera (Technicolor), Roger Pratt; music, Michael Kamen; editor, Lesley Walker; production design, Jamie Leonard; sound, David John; production manager, Linda Bruce; assistant director, Ray Corbett; casting, Susie Figgis; special production consultant, Richard Starkey MBE. Reviewed at Gaumont Screening room, Neuilly (Paris), May 6, 1986. (In competition at Cannes Film Festival.) (No MPAA Rating.) Running time: **104 MINS.**

George .... Bob Hoskins
Simone .... Cathy Tyson
Mortwell .... Michael Caine
Thomas .... Robbie Coltrane
With: Clarke Peters (Anderson), Kate Hardie (Cathy), Zoe Nathenson (Jeannie), Sammi Davies (May), Rod Bedall (Terry), Joe Brown (Dudley), Pauline Melville (Dawn), David Hallwell (Devlin).

Cannes — The couple at the center of this wide and wayward romantic thriller are about as odd as you could find anywhere. George (Bob Hoskins), short in stature as well as intellect, is just out of prison and trying to pick up the pieces of his life. Simone (Cathy Tyson) is a tall, slender black whore who plies the poshest London hotels for her up-market trade. George gets a job driving Simone to her various assignations and, though he's not very good at it, and feels awkward and ill at ease, he finds himself falling in love with her.

What follows is a pic that skillfully combines comedy and thriller, romance and sleaze. Simone takes advantage of George's feelings for her and assigns him to search for her missing girlfriend, a teenage blonde hooked on heroin and involved in the kinkier areas of the vice trade. Dutifully, George starts his search and in doing so enters dangerous and unpredictable terrain.

Bob Hoskins gives another memorable performance as the earnest ex-con who's so dumb that he chatters to his beautiful friend disparagingly about "darkies," forgetting she's one herself. There probably isn't another actor around right now who could play the role to such perfection, and it's his film, though Cathy Tyson brings charm and sensuality to the role of Simone and Robbie Coltrane, the rotund actor who seems almost a mascot to the new British directors, is very funny as George's loyal friend. Michael Caine is around, too, in a generously self effacing supporting role as a sinister, dangerous cockney vice king.

In his third feature, (after "Angel" and "The Company Of Wolves"), Irish-born Neil Jordan confirms his talent as one of the most inventive and daring helmers working in Britain. "Mona Lisa" (named after the Nat (King) Cole standard first featured in Mitchell Leisen's "Captain Carey U.S.A." in 1950) is a stylish and genuinely original pic which injects unexpected humor even at the most suspenseful moments and which builds inexorably to a violent and chilling climax.

Not a predictable selection to rep Britain for Cannes, but a most satisfying one. —*Strat.*

★★★★★★★★★★★★★★★★★★★★★★
Cannes: Non-Competing
★★★★★★★★★★★★★★★★★★★★★★

Pirates
(FRENCH-TUNISIAN-COLOR)

An AMLF release (France), Cannon Releasing release (U.S.) of a Carthago Films Paris/Accent-Cominco production. Produced by Tarak Ben Ammar. Executive producer, Thom Mount; co-executive producers, Marc Lombardo, Umberto Sambucco. Directed by Roman Polanski. Stars Walter Matthau. Screenplay, Gerard Brach, Polanski, with the collaboration of John Brownjohn; camera (Panavision. Satpec & Eclair Color; Folair prints), Witold Sobocinski; editor, Herve de Luze, William Reynolds; music, Philippe Sarde; sound (Dolby), Jean-Pierre Ruh; art direction, Pierre Guffroy; costume design, Anthony Powell; assistant director, Thierry Chabert; casting, Maude Spector, Mary Selway, Dominique Besnehard. Reviewed at Cannes Film Festival (official selection, non-competing), May 8, 1986. (No MPAA Rating.) Running time: **124 MINS.**

Captain Red .... Walter Matthau
Don Alfonso .... Damien Thomas
Padre .... Richard Pearson
The Frog .... Cris Campion
Dolores .... Charlotte Lewis
Boumako .... Olu Jacobs
Also with: David Kelly, Roy Kinnear, Bill Fraser, Jose Santamaria, Ferdy Mayne, Anthony Peck, Georges Trillat.

Cannes — Roman Polanski's "Pirates" is a decidedly underwhelming comedy adventure adding up to a major disappointment, given the director's decade-plus quest to get this pet project off the ground. Commercial prospects loom okay in foreign markets where slapstick action pictures thrive, but U.S. release through Cannon shapes up as a loser.

"Pirates" first was announced as a 1976 Polanski feature to star Jack Nicholson and Isabelle Adjani, and the project bounced from United Artists to Paramount, Filmways, Universal and MGM as well as being bandied about by several European production banners before finally being produced (commencing in 1984) by Tarak Ben Ammar in Tunisia, Malta and the Seychelles.

Walter Matthau, sporting a difficult-to-classify and thick brogue, gainfully essays the central role of Capt. Thomas Bartholomew Red, a peg-legged British pirate captain with plenty of Robert Newton's Long John Silver in his manner. Teamed with a handsome young French sailor he derisively calls the Frog (Cris Campion), Red is captured by Don Alfonso, captain of the Spanish galleon Neptune. In a series of turnabout adventures, Red causes the Neptune's crew to mutiny, takes the niece (Charlotte Lewis) of the governor of Maracaibo hostage, and steals a golden Aztec throne from the Spaniards.

Bookended by scenes of Red and the Frog adrift on a raft that recall Polanski's short film "The Fat And The Lean," "Pirates" is surprisingly short on large-scale action and scope for a feature that cost in excess of $30,000,000. A goodly chunk of the budget went to fabricating the full-size galleon, but like Dino De Laurentiis' costly boat for "The Bounty" remake, it's not the vessel that counts with audiences. Ultimately, "Pirates" suffers from a blah script leading to an unexciting nonending.

Casting is unimpressive, with Matthau unable to carry the picture singlehandedly. He has his moments, however, particularly in handling physical business such as in an extended scene where his captors force him to eat a rat for dinner. Newcomer Campion projects a pleasant personality, more than can be said for Polanski's discovery Charlotte Lewis, thoroughly inexpressive here, though she since has landed the costarring role in Eddie Murphy's latest feature, "The Golden Child." Absence of a truly hissable villain doesn't help.

Technical credits are all pro, but hardly on a par with previous Polanski films. Oddly, the fight sequences, supervised by William Hobbs, are dull, yet he handled the rollicking swordfights in Richard Lester's "The Three/Four Musketeers" films. Throughout 'Pirates' one is aware of Polanski painstakingly setting up and delivering each gag almost as an end in itself. The closest modern model is Sergio Leone's irreverent reworking of the Western. Leone ended up adding to Western lore but "Pirates" is merely a lampoon.—*Lor.*

Blackout
(NORWEGIAN-COLOR)

A KF release of a Norsk Film production in association with Esselte Video and Kodak Film (Oslo). Produced by Anders Enger. Screenplay, Erik Gustavson, Eirik Ildahl. Directed by Gustavson. Stars Henrik Scheele, Juni Dahr, Elizabeth Sand. Camera (Eastmancolor), Kjell Vassdal; sound, Niels Bokkenheuser; editor, Torleif Hauge; music, Oistein Boassen; costumes, Inger Derlick; art direction/set decoration, Frode Krohg. Reviewed at the Cannes Film Festival (Market), May 10, 1986. Running time: **88 MINS.**

Werner .... Henrik Scheele
Stella Hvidtsteen .... Juni Dahr
Lill .... Elizabeth Sand
Max .... Tommy Körberg
Police chief .... Per Bronken
Also with: Peter Lindbeck, Ella Hval, Hans-Jacob Sand, Kalle Oeby, Terje Strömdal, Espen Dekko, Pal Skjönberg, Ramon Gimenz, others.

Cannes — "Blackout," by first time helmer Erik Gustavson, balances neatly as a *film noir* tribute, toeing the line between John Huston's "Maltese Falcon" and Wim Wenders' Francis Coppola production of "Hammett." Shot entirely on studio sets and following original story-boarding meticulously, film was brought in on a modest budget. But every cent and then some shows up on screen. Pic may achieve some international sales on its curio value as well as on its innocent charm.

Walking down the mean 1937 streets of some unidentified city, big enough to have its own Chinatown, private eye Werner (Henrik Scheele) fishes corpses out of rivers, has beautiful women dumping tough assignments (and themselves) on him, is beaten up by corrupt police and sundry thugs, and very nearly is fooled by Establishment and Mafia bigwigs. He has a beautiful secretary who forgives his errant ways and finally saves him in the bloodbath climax.

Faithfulness to classic Warner Bros. gangster film style and to the set of behavior patterns associated with Sam Spade and Philip Marlowe keeps "Blackout" going at a brisk pace. All production values contribute to state of the art pop design. Acting throughout is tongue-in-cheek with the irony hardly showing. In fact, film's only drawback would seem to be its inability to work beyond its own curiosity value.

While "Blackout" is a collection of upbeat genre clichés, it has no real moral indignation and no true belief in the need for Sam Spades, Philip Marlowes or even Werners to make the world a cleaner place to live in. Film takes you down those mean streets all right, but it also leaves you feeling you have seen it all through bullet-proof glass. Filmgoers don't run the risk of taking any of it personally.—*Kell.*

El Rio de Oro
(The Golden River)
(SPANISH-SWISS-COLOR)

A Tesauro (Spain) and Marea Film Prod. (Zurkh) coproduction in collaboration with INCINE Industrial Cinematografica and Federal Films presentation. Executive producers, Tadeo Villalba and Küde Meier. Produced by Hervé Haohuol. Written and directed by Jaime Chávarri. Associate producers, Miguel Angel Rivas and Adi Lipp; camera (Eastmancolor) Carlos Suáres; editor, Pablo del Amo; sound, Jürg von Ailmen; artistic director, Adi Gisler; costumes, Yolanda Alimbau. Reviewed at Cannes Film Festival (Market), May 11, 1986.

Laura . . . . Angela Molina
Peter . . . . Bruno Ganz
Dubarry . . . . Francesca Annis
Juan . . . . Stefan Gubser
Also with: Nacho Rodriguez, Juan Diego Botto and Carolina Norris.
(English soundtrack available)

Cannes — The trauma of growing old and the quest for recovering the unattainable past are the themes of this ponderous, rambling film, where make-believe and reality are often inseparable. Some have interpreted the story as being a kind of updated Peter Pan yarn, but the analogy is questionable.

Though there are some winning moments in the film, on the whole script is closer to an exercise in sleight-of-hand than a live drama; the personages remain sketchy, the air of mystery is often too thin to hold audience interest.

An eccentric and palpably unhappy middle-aged man, Peter (Bruno Ganz) returns to a country house, near a pretty stream, where he had long before spent a happy summer. He comes with his dissipated wife to visit a writer friend whose wife he always has coveted. The houseowners have three children and "Uncle Peter" fascinates them with his antics, builds a pirate's raft, plays children's games and seeks to retrieve the times gone by, and his own youth.

Each of the characters' shifting relationships with the enigmatic Peter is probed, until one night he disappears down the river on the raft. Despite excellent thesping by Ganz, Angela Molina and Francesca Annis, plot is too thin to maintain interest. Commercial outlook is iffy. In Spain, pic failed to click during its recent release. —*Besa.*

A State Of Emergency
(U.S.-COLOR)

A NorKat Co. release of an Esstar Prod. Produced and directed by Richard Bennett. Stars Martin Sheen. Screenplay, Ray Cunneff, Tom Guggino; camera (Fujicolor), Willy Kurant; music, George Garvarentz; editor, Catherine Kelber; associate producer Kurant; production manager, Richard Hahn. Reviewed at the Cannes Film Festival (Market), May 10, 1986. Running time 97 MINS.
Dr. Alex Carmody . . . . Martin Sheen
Dr. Kenneth Parrish . . . . Peter Firth
Father Joe Ryan . . . . Tim Pigott-Smith
Diane Carmody . . . . Fionnula Flanagan
Also with: Frances Tomelty (Jackie Hampton), Ramon Sheen (Brian Carmody), Dudley Sutton (Soviet professor), Daniel Wozniak (Uri), Francois Guetary, Kenneth Haigh, Bob Sherman.

Cannes — An earnest, preachy film on a topical and important theme, "A State Of Emergency" is just too talky and slow to appeal to audiences other than those already committed to the anti-nuclear cause. Even they may be turned off by this film's strong religious theme.

Martin Sheen and Peter Firth are physicists working on American nuclear warfare programs (there's a great deal of incomprehensible scientific talk about "electro magnetic pulses" and the like). They become convinced that continued testing of nuclear devices will set off an atomic chain reaction that will destroy the world. Further, Sheen is certain this destruction was prophesied at the miracle of Fatima, a 1917 event in Portugal when the Virgin Mary appeared to three young girls and, among other things, supposedly prophesied the start of World War II.

Sheen journeys to the Fatima shrine, and tries (unsuccessfully) to see the surviving member of the three girls; but, even more certain that a pending Soviet test in the Arctic must be stopped, he goes to the Soviet Embassy in Paris to try to convince the Russians not to go ahead with it. Needless to say, the C.I.A. guys aren't amused.

But this is no thriller in the normal sense. Sheen is allowed to address a joint U.S. Soviet disarmament conference and to tell them "The hand of God" is on them. The Soviets seem as unconvinced as their U.S. counterparts.

Shot last year in French studios, pic is technically okay but the slow pacing of the early scenes and the combination of anti-nuclear message with religious preaching makes for an uneasy mix, at least as presented here. Pic is unquestionably well intentioned, but finding an audience will be tough. — *Strat.*

Two Friends
(AUSTRALIAN-COLOR)

An ABC production. Produced by Jan Chapman. Directed by Jane Campion. Screenplay, Helen Garner; camera (Eastmancolor), Julian Penney; editor, Bill Russo; designer, Janet Patterson; sound, Chris Alderton; production manager, Carol Chirlian; assistant director, Kate Woods. Reviewed at A.F.C. screening room, North Sydney, April 18, 1986. (In the Un Certain Regard section at Cannes Film Festival.) Running time: 76 MINS.
Louise . . . . Emma Coles
Kelly . . . . Kris Bidenko
Janet (Louise's mother) . . . . Kris McQuade
Chris (Kelly's mother) . . . . Debra May
Malcolm (Stepfather) . . . . Peter Hehir
Also with: Tony Barry (Charlie, Kelly's father), Steve Bisley (Kevin), Sean Travers (Matthew), Kerry Dwyer (Alison), Giovanni Marangoni (Renato), Stephen Leeder (Jim), Paul Mason (Father at funeral), Martin Armiger (Philip), Lisa Rogers (Little Helen), Amanda Frederickson (Kate), Rory Delaney (Wally), Emily Stocker (Soula).

Sydney — A recent recruit from the Australian Film and Television School, Jane Campion has started her career with a bang: three of her Film School shorts have been tagged for screening in official sections at Cannes this year (one in competition, two in Un Certain Regard) and her first feature, made as a telefilm for the Australian Broadcasting Corporation, has also made it to Un Certain Regard, practically guaranteeing it wider distribution than could ever have been predicted.

Deservedly, too, for "Two Friends" is a painfully honest, cannily structured and genuinely moving drama about two 15-year-old girls. It takes place in Sydney, but could happen anywhere in the Western world.

As with the Harold Pinter play and film, "Betrayal," "Two Friends" tells its story backwards. The screenplay, by Helen Garner (on whose novel the 1981 film "Monkey Grip" was based), introduces the two girls, Louise (Emma Coles) and Kelly (Kris Bidenko) after they've gone their separate ways. Louise goes with her divorced mother (Kris McQuade) to the funeral of another girl who's dead from a drug overdose. Meanwhile Kelly, in bleached mohawk hair and punk gear, is living in a communal house on the beachfront and, presumably, involved in sex and drugs herself.

As the story moves backwards over the preceding months (the film begins in winter and ends in the previous spring) we discover that Louise and Kelly were best friends at high school who did everything together until separated when Kelly's stepfather refused to allow her to attend a smart private school, believing it to be too elitist.

Throughout, "Two Friends" is brutally honest in laying the blame, not on the deliberate acts of the parents, or step-parents, of these girls from broken homes. The adults mean well, are caring and try to understand. The generation gap is just too wide, and they have their own problems, their own day-to-day dramas and relationships. The girls have to fend for themselves. Louise manages it, but Kelly doesn't.

With its pin-point accuracy down to the smallest detail of everyday behavior of kids and adults alike, this is a film which is far more important than its modest format would suggest.

It is, ultimately, a heartbreaking experience as we see how these intelligent, lively youngsters have changed over a period of just a few short months. The final image of them, happily toasting each other in their school uniforms for having just passed some exams, makes for a devastating ending to an immensely accomplished production.

Technical credits are modest, but perfectly acceptable, and the acting, right down to the smallest bit part, is painfully realistic. —*Strat.*

The Manhattan Project
(U.S.-COLOR)

A 20th Century Fox release (U.S.) of a Gladden Entertainment presentation. Produced by Jennifer Ogden, Marshall Brickman. Directed by Brickman. Screenplay, Brickman, Thomas Baum; camera (Technicolor; Deluxe prints), Billy Williams; editor, Nina Feinborg; music, Philippe Sarde; sound, Les Lazarowitz; production design, Philip Rosenberg; special visual effects, Bran Ferren; assistant director, Ron Bozman; production manager, Ogden; costumes, Shay Cunliffe; associate producer, Roger Paradiso; second unit camera, Dick Kratina; casting, Juliet Taylor. Reviewed at the Cannes Film Festival (Market), May 10, 1986. (MPAA Rating: PG-13.) Running time: 117 MINS.
John Mathewson . . . . John Lithgow
Paul Stevens . . . . Christopher Collet
Jenny . . . . Cynthia Nixon
Elizabeth Stevens . . . . Jill Eikenberry
Lt. Col. Conroy . . . . John Mahoney
Night guard . . . . Sully Boyar

Cannes — Marshall Brickman's "The Manhattan Project" is a warm, comedy-laced doomsday story which packs plenty of entertainment for summer audiences, but falls short of its potential as a thriller.

Topical premise has 16-year-old student Paul Stevens (Christopher Collet) tumbling to the fact that the new scientist in town, Dr. Mathewson (John Lithgow) is working with plutonium in what fronts as a pharmaceutical research installation. While Mathewson is romancing Stevens' mom (Jill Eikenberry) — the husband having split years ago — the genius kid is plotting with his helpful girlfriend Jenny (Cynthia Nixon) to steal a cannister of plutonium and build an atomic bomb. Their goal: to expose the danger of the secret nuclear plant placed in their community in the strongest possible terms.

Using clever one-liners and many humorous situations (particularly when Lithgow is clumsily coming on to Eikenberry early in the film), Brickman manages successfully to sugarcoat the story's serious message concerning the ongoing folly of arms buildup and reliance upon nuclear deterrence for security. What keeps the film from being a thriller is his matter-of-fact direction, extremely sluggish in many scenes early on. Only a very interesting "Rififi"-style silent (background sound only) reel in which the hero steals the plutonium from the well-secured lab is strong enough to keep interest from wandering. Fortunately, later situations regain the story's momentum and lead to a rousing climax.

Collet is very appealing as the brilliant hero, almost convincing in situations that require him to be more resourceful than is truly possible. Lithgow adds quirky personality and charm to what might have become a standard "bad guy sees the light" assignment. As their respective sounding boards, Nixon and Eikenberry both contribute to the film's emphasis upon human values over mere hardware in a genre which has increasingly been upstaged by its special effects work.

Those special effects here are entirely realistic rather than showy, another feather in the cap of wiz Bran Ferren, who also appears in an opening reel cameo as a lab assistant. Philip Rosenberg's production design and Billy Williams' camerawork are exemplary.

Feature was financed by Thorn EMI Screen Entertainment, but print caught already had the Cannon logo at introduction, reflecting Cannon's recent buyout of what was once TESE.—*Lor.*

Rebel Love
(U.S.-COLOR)

A Troma release of a Raven Cliff Prods. film. Produced by John Quenelle. Written and directed by Milton Bagby Jr. Camera (Panavision) Joseph A. Whigham; editor, Mellena Bridges; music, Bobby Horton; casting, Debra Neathery; associate producer, Shirley Fulton Crumley. Reviewed at the Cannes Film Festival (market), May 9, 1986. Running time: **80 MINS.**
Columbine Cromwell........Jamie Rose
Hightower................Terence Knox
Granny....................Fran Ryan
Captain...................Charles Hill
Yankee sergeant..........Carl Spurlock
Corporal....................Rick Waln
Also with: Larry Larson, Thom Gossom Jr., Harry Howell.

Cannes — Set in the American Civil War, "Rebel Love" is a turgid melodrama lacking in almost every department. Theatrical prospects are zilch; lackluster item won't light any fires in the homevideo market, but might serve as acceptable filler material on television.

Threadbare script, dopey dialog, by-the-numbers acting and uninspired direction are lead weights in this donkey's saddlebags.

Jamie Rose limns a Yankee widow living alone on a farm, tormented by memories of her late husband, who ill-treated her.

On her doorstep one stormy night she finds the unconscious figure of Terence Knox, a Southern spy who's on the run from the Yankees while posing as a traveling salesman.

Initially straight-laced and demure, she falls into his arms with very few preliminaries. After a brush with two Northern soldiers, he declares his true identity, but she, by now deeply in love, forgives him. Duty calls, however, and he returns to his undercover mission.

In between these labored passages, Rose fills in time nattering with merchant and local gossip Fran Ryan, who tells her about the many men she's loved, or at least bedded. From both Ryan and Knox, Rose gets a lot of simple-minded claptrap about breaking free from the past, being herself and striking out for a new life, and that gives her the strength to cope with another tragedy that lies ahead.

Thesps struggle to rise above the sappy material, from writer-director Milton Bagby Jr. Tech credits are generally okay, although some scenes, both interiors and exteriors (lensed in Alabama), are dimly lit. About as dim as the picture itself.
—*Dogo.*

Lost!
(CANADIAN-COLOR)

A Norstar release in Canada of a Peter Rowe production. Produced by Rosebud Films in association with Victor Solnicki Prods. and the Canadian Broadcasting Corp., with the participation of Telefilm Canada. Written and directed by Peter Rowe, based on the novel "Lost!" by Thomas Thompson. Camera (color), Don Wilder; editor, Christopher Hutton; music, Micky Erbe, Maribeth Solomon; line producer, Sean Ryerson; art direction, Bill Fleming; set decoration, Lizette St. Germaine; sound, David Joliat; assistant director, Ty Haller; production coordinator, Nan Skiba. Reviewed at the Cannes Film Festival (market), May 13, 1986. Running time: **93 MINS.**
Jim....................Kenneth Welsh
Linda....................Helen Shaver
Bob....................Michael Hogan
Wilma.................Linda Goranson
Nick..................Charles Joliffe

Cannes — Much of a potentially riveting awash-at-sea storyline gets diluted in "Lost!" based on a true story by Thomas Thompson. Writer-director Peter Rowe sets up the tension early on with some fine character delineations, but the suspense — and the special effects — waxes and wanes with the waves in this actioner. Since it's largely a saga of family relationships under duress, it will be a spitfire tv movie, but only a so-so proposition at the boxoffice.

Story centers on Jim (Kenneth Welsh), an earnest man of the cloth, who annouces to his brother Bob (Michael Hogan) and wife Linda (Helen Shaver) that he's going down to Costa Rica to be a missionary. He wants Bob and Linda to sail the 2,000 miles from Vancouver with him on his boat, since he needs a crew and sees the trip as a good way to reconcile the brothers' shaky relationship.

As soon as they're esconced in the Pacific and Bob beams that the ship is sailing itself, a fierce storm blows up. It turns into a gale, capsizing the boat. Rest of pic deals with survival at sea. The group rigs up a way to use the upside-down craft as a makeshift bunker. They ration food, try to impart a daily routine, and keep up their spirits.

Linda cracks first, hallucinating rescue planes. She also uses the trip to spring the news to hubby that she's pregnant, so it's not only the accident that's been making her violently queasy. But the dark side of the dilemma exacerbates the division between the two brothers.

Rowe directs the capsize scenes with vigor, with quick cuts into the water, camera angles under the boat, and a style that captures the terror. But the day-to-day desperation (they were lost at sea for 72 days) isn't built up sufficiently. When Linda dies midway on, we should be overwrought, but somehow it's not wrenching.

Michael Hogan is tops as Bob, who manages to keep his bearings and humor amid Shaver's histronics and Welsh's "PTL Club" zeal. There are one too many near-misses of planes flying overhead

Welsh's religious desperation is overbearing, as he tries to use the accident as a mystical experience; even his t-shirt reads "God is my skipper." At least Hogan lightens things up a bit with his "Damn Seagulls" baseball cap.—*Devo.*

Hellfire
(U.S.-COLOR)

A Manley Prods. presentation of a Howard Foulkrod production. Produced by Foulkrod. Directed by William Murray. Screenplay, Murray; camera (Du-Art color), Dennis Peters; editor, Keith L. Reamer; music, Mark Knox; art director, Robert Zeier; special effects, David DiPietro; assistant director, David Swift; sound, Aaron Smith. Reviewed at the Cannes Film Festival (market), May 11, 1986. Running time: **88 MINS.**
Corby McHale.......Kenneth McGregor
Samantha Kelly..........Sharon Mason
Caitland Foster..............Julie Miller
Also with: Jon Maurice (Frank Gitto), Joseph White (Nicky Fingers), Stephen Caldwell (Colan Foster), Edward Fallon (Kesselman), Mickey Shaughnessy (Waxman).

Cannes — Set in 1997, when a new kind of energy known as "hellfire" is in hotly contested use, this is a confusing thriller which awkwardly combines private eye and sci-fi genres.

The private eye takes on an assignment from a beautiful blond whose brother is one of the bosses of the private corporation handling the powerful but ultra-dangerous fuel. One slip-up and victims quickly are burned to a crisp, and emit blue sparks.

Unfortunately, a promising idea gets nowhere thanks to the incoherent scripting and direction of William Murray; most private eye pics are a challenge to follow, but this one is mostly incomprehensible. Nor are any of the characters very interesting, least of all the sullen hero as played by Kenneth McGregor.

Special effects are strictly cheap and won't pass muster with most audiences.

Item lensed in south New Jersey and Pennsylvania is dedicated to the late Mickey Shaughnessy, who plays a tiny role. It's technically merely adequate. —*Strat.*

Backlash
(AUSTRALIAN-COLOR)

A Mermaid Beach-Multifilms production. Produced and directed by Bill Bennett. Screenplay, Bennett, with dialog by David Argue, Gia Carides, Lydia Miller, Brian Syron; camera (Atlab color), Tony Wilson; editor, Denise Hunter; music, Michael Atkinson, Michael Spicer; sound, Leo Sullivan; production manager, Sue Seeary. Reviewed at A.F.C. screening room, Sydney, April 14, 1986. (In the Un Certain Regard section at Cannes Film Festival.) Running time: **89 MINS.**
Trevor Darling.............David Argue
Nikki Iceton................Gia Carides
Kath.....................Lydia Miller
The Executioner...........Brian Syron
Mrs. Smith.................Anne Smith
Mr. Smith..................Don Smith
Waitress.................Jennifer Cluff

Sydney — An intriguing, often powerful, drama set in rugged outback country, "Backlash" is an unusual attempt, for an Australian feature, to have its actors improvise dialog around a carefully plotted storyline. Best point of reference is probably Jerzy Skolimowski's 1970 "Deep End," with which the current pic has many similarities save for newie's wide open spaces setting.

Two young police constables, Darling (David Argue) and Iceton (Gia Carides), are assigned to transport a young aboriginal woman (Lydia Miller), accused of murdering a bar-owner, from Sydney back to the outback township where the crime occurred. Darling is a foul-mouthed bigot, whereas his partner is the well-educated daughter of a barrister, herself studying law. Iceton is shocked at Darling's racist and sexist attitudes towards the prisoner, but the characters undergo some subtle changes after two flat tires strand the trio miles from nowhere on an abandoned sheep station.

As is the case with most improvised pics, this one is marvelous when it works and awkward when it doesn't. Fortunately, it does work, most of the time, and, given lots of leeway, the three principal actors acquit themselves very well.

David Argue, always a volatile actor, convincingly undergoes his character modification, while Gia Carides (last seen as the daughter in "Bliss") is a knockout as the sensual policewoman. In a less showy role, Lydia Miller also scores as the prisoner.

Unfortunately, scenes involving actors other than the principals are less successful, with one crucial sequence (the extortion of a confession from the murdered man's widow) failing because of the inexperience of the actress involved.

There are also a few improbabilities and one serious technical gaffe (the camera crew clearly reflected in a car window). But, despite the flaws, "Backlash" is dynamic and original filmmaking, and another plus for producer-director Bill Bennett (whose last was the award-winning Agent Orange drama, "A Street To Die"). Camerawork by Tony Wilson is very fine, and the editing of Denise Hunter is pro.

Bennett is certainly a director of talent; almost every moment in the film is charged with suspense and undefined menace and, despite the flaws as noted, it's a most creditable low-budgeter which could well find wide acceptance. It has one most unusual credit: you'll have to ask an Australian what a "yabbie handler" is.—*Strat.*

The Second Victory
(BRITISH-COLOR)

A J&M Film Sales release of a Melaleuka production of a Gerald Thomas film. Executive producer, John Murray. Produced and directed by Gerald Thomas. Stars Anthony Andrews, Helmut Griem, Mario Adorf, Renee Soutendijk, Birgit Doll and Max Von Sydow. Screenplay, Morris West; camera (Rank color), Alan Hume; music, Stanley Myers; associate producer, Peter Manley. Reviewed at the Cannes Film Festival (market), May 11, 1986. Running time: **112 MINS.**
Major Hanlon . . . . Anthony Andrews
Dr. Huber . . . . Max Von Sydow
Karl Fischer . . . . Helmut Griem
Dr. Sepp Kunzli . . . . Mario Adorf
Anna Kunzli . . . . Birgit Doll
Max Holzinger . . . . . Wolfgang Reichmann
Traudi Holzinger . . . . Renee Soutendijk
Liesl Holzinger . . . . Immy Schell
Rudi Winkler . . . . . Gunther Maria Halmer
Father Albertus . . . . Wolfgang Preiss
Johann Wikivill . . . . Jacques Breuer

Cannes — Produced at Pinewood Studios and filmed largely on location in Austria, "The Second Victory," financed out of Australia to the tune of $5,000,000, represents a remarkable change of pace for producer-director Gerald Thomas. For years he has devoted himself almost exclusively to the direction of the highly successful "Carry On" features, and has some 30 to his credit, plus a tv series based on the same formula.

Under Thomas' thoughtful and painstaking direction, there are consistently reliable performances from the entire cast. Andrews fills his role as the British major with a deft mix of authority and charm. For most of the film he's a man obsessed with a mission to capture the wanted man, but it turns out to be some-

thing of an anti-climax for him when the mission is accomplished. Max Von Sydow as the surgeon in charge of the hospital who has to plead for drugs to save human lives is typically sympathetic, in striking contrast to the interpretation of Helmut Griem as the police chief who just fails to bluff his way out of trouble. Mario Adorf portrays the lawyer with calm conviction, Birgit Doll as his niece is appealing and attractive, and Renee Soutendijk is appropriately seductive as the major's secretary who would happily take the place of the other girl. Jacques Breuer as the fugitive, Gunther Maria Halmer on the ex-Dachau surgeon, and other members of the big cast acquit themselves admirably.

The opening sequences on the mountain slopes as Breuer skis his way to the sanctuary of his home village, are extremely effective and handsomely lensed, while in the latter part of the film there is a sustained degree of menace as the Nazi doctor is driven to his death by a horde of ex-concentration camp victims. Music background is unobstrusive, editing is compact, and other credits are up to standard.
—*Myro.*

Playing Beatie Bow
(AUSTRALIAN-COLOR)

A CEL (Australia) release of a South Australian Film Corp. production. Produced by Jock Blair. Executive producer, John Morris. Associate producer, Bruce Moir. Directed by Donald Crombie. Screenplay; Peter Gawler, from the novel by Ruth Park; camera (Eastmancolor), Geoffrey Simpson; production design, George Liddle; music, Garry McDonald, Laurie Stone; editor, A.J. Prowse; sound, Robert Cutcher; production manager, Pamela Vanneck; assistant director, Philip Hearnshaw; casting, Audine Leith. Reviewed at Cannes Film Festival (market), May 9, 1986. Running time: **89 MINS.**
Abigail . . . . Imogen Annesley
Judah/Robert . . . . Peter Phelps
Beatie Bow . . . . Mouche Phillips
Dovey . . . . Nikki Coghill
Granny . . . . Moya O'Sullivan
Also with: Don Barker (Samuel), Lyndel Rowe (Kathy), Barbara Stephens (Justine), Damian Janko (Gibbie), Phoebe Salter (Natalie), Su Cruickshank (Madam), Henry Salter (Swanton), Jo England (Doll), Edward Caddick (Legless), Edwin Hodgeman (Sir).

Cannes — A distaff variation on "Back To The Future," "Playing Beatie Bow" is a time-travel fantasy which looks extremely handsome but which suffers from an uncertainty of tone and direction.

Pic opens in present-day Sydney where 16-year-old Abigail (played by an appealing newcomer, Imogen Annesley) is suffering from the usual teen problems (broken home, no boyfriend, etc). Watching some younger kids play a game they call "Beatie Bow," she sees a strange, lost child and, when she tries to help her, is suddenly whisked back to

1873, whence the child, whose name is Beatie Bow (Mouche Phillips), has come.

Since Beatie has a handsome brother (Peter Phelps) and a wise, mystical old grandmother (Moya O'Sullivan), Abigail doesn't seem overly anxious to get back to 1986, though she makes some token efforts to escape, one of which results in her being kidnapped and delivered to a brothel. Phelps and his friends rescue her. Eventually, of course, she gets back to the present, is able to trace the family tree of the Bow family, and finds that a descendant of her 19th century beau is alive and well and just as attracted to her as his ancestor had been.

Aided immeasurably by topnotch production design by George Liddle, with some spectacular sets built at the SAFC Adelaide film studio, "Playing Beatie Bow" is another visually splendid Australian pic, but it never seems to decide if it's aiming at 10-year-olds or 15-year-olds. There are scenes which would surely be too naive and childish for the mid-teens and others a bit too adult for the little ones. Above all, it never has the dash and the assurance of its American counterparts.

Indeed, when helmer Donald Crombie tries hardest to make a U.S. style entertainment, as in the slapstick fight in the brothel, he's more unsure of himself than usual, resulting in the same kind of strained jocularity that marred the SAFC's "Robbery Under Arms," which Crombie co-directed.

When the magic works, which it does from time to time, it works beautifully; but, more often than not, the strain shows. There are, apparently, plans to re-dub two of the actors, though the voices seemed perfectly adequate. The film's problems lay elsewhere, and will prevent it becoming the smash success it might have been if handled with more assurance and elan. As it is, it will have to be content with modest returns. —*Strat.*

Le Déclin de l'empire Américain
(The Decline Of The American Empire)
(CANADIAN-COLOR)

A Corporation Image M&M Ltée/Office National du Film du Canada coproduction. Executive producer, Pierre Gendron. Produced by René Malo & Roger Frappier. Written and directed by Denys Arcand. Camera (color), Guy Dufaux; sound, Richard Besse; editor, Monique Fortier; art direction, Gaudeline Sauriol; music, François Dompierre, from themes by Handel; assistant director, Jacques Benoit; production manager, Lyse Lafontaine. Reviewed at Club 70, Paris, May 2, 1986. (In the Directors Fortnight section at Cannes Film Festival.) Running time: **101 MINS.**
Pierre . . . . Pierre Curzi
Rémy . . . . Rémy Girard

Claude . . . . Yves Jacques
Alain . . . . Daniel Brière
Dominique . . . . Dominique Michel
Diane . . . . Louise Portal
Louise . . . . Dorothée Berryman
Danièlle . . . . Geneviève Roux
Mario . . . . Gabriel Arcand

Paris — Behind the ironically sweeping title of Denys Arcand's film is a mordant small-scale study of private lives and sexual mores among a group of contemporary Canadian academics. From the long opening dolly shot through a vast modern interior university mall to the final fixed images of a lakeside chalet cloaked in snow and deathly silence, writer-director Arcand deploys a smart script, fluent technique and a first-rate cast for this deviously sardonic comedy of carnal manners.

Arcand gives his story a theatrical cast, with a distinct two-act structure, two principal settings (a modern gym complex and the above-mentioned chalet) and its eight principal characters — four men and four women, all teaching or studying at the same university — at first presented like two separate sexual choruses.

They are to gather that evening at the chalet for a casual, friendly dinner. However, it is the menfolk who are in the kitchen while the ladies work out in the gym, with each group engaging in supposedly frank and liberated exchanges of jocular sex talk and reminiscences.

But the day's mood of levity and well-being disintegrates around the dinner table, notably when Dominique (Dominique Michel), a history professor whose just published tome, "The Decline Of The American Empire," expounds on the disintegration of marital values during eras of socio-political decadence, reveals suddenly her affairs with two of the men present, Pierre and Rémy (Pierre Curzi and Rémy Girard), both profs in the same department.

The disclosure throws a pall over the evening, hitting hardest Rémy's wife, Louise (Dorothée Berryman), who despite her self-professed emotional equilibrium, is crushed by the revelation of her mate's obsessive promiscuity.

The smooth ensemble acting throws into trenchant relief the differing comportments in the group, and the shallowness and hypocrisy of their attitudes. Pierre, a divorcé who clings to his freedom despite his relationship with the much younger Danièlle (Geneviève Roux), who pays for her studies with a job in a sexual massage parlor, where the two met; Diane (Louise Portal), a faculty member who is engaged in a kinky affair with a sinister hippie lover (Gabriel Arcand) who disrupts the dinner to unceremoniously drag her off to bed; Claude (Yves Jacques), homosexual prof who sets himself apart from the group as ironic observer, though he keeps secret the venereal malady he has contracted; and Alan (Daniel Brière), a young faculty assistant who also keeps his distance, until he finds himself seduced by Dominique.

Arcand, aided by Guy Dufaux' limpid photography and Monique Fortier's fluid editing of the numerous subjective flashbacks, strikes a balance between satire and realism, which makes this a superior literate entertainment that forgoes the usual graphic vulgarity of most sex comedy-dramas.—*Len.*

Rezhou
(Sunrise)
(CHINESE-COLOR)

A China Film release of a Shanghai Film Studio production. Directed by Yu Benzheng. Screenplay, Cao Yu; camera (Scope, color), Zhu Yongde; music, Xu Jingxin; production manager, Yang Gongming. Reviewed at the Cannes Film Festival (Un Certain Regard section), May 10, 1986. Running time: 131 MINS.
Also with: Pang Shu (Lulu Chen), Wang Shihuai, Yan Xiang, Wang Futang, Wan Fuli.

Cannes — A new version of a perennially popular stage play, filmed at least once before, 30 years ago. "Sunrise" is a stylish drama which often has the feel of a Douglas Sirk/Ross Hunter production of the 1950s. Use of Scope system and rather gaudy color enhances the impression.

Set presumably in the '30s, tale revolves around a beautiful young woman who's left her devoted husband and child to become a popular nightclub warbler and generally to live life in the fast lane. She lives in a lavishly furnished apartment with servants, a cute little dog, and lots of male admirers on the side. When her husband comes to beg for a reconciliation, she rebuffs him; but she's not all bad. She takes care of a very young girl who has narrowly escaped rape at the hands of an evil capitalist. In the end, though the only way out for the heroine after her sinful life is suicide.

Followers of Asian cinema who have only seen more "serious" Chinese films, dealing with contemporary or historical social problems, may at first be bemused with this long, glossy picture which looks like a Joan Crawford or Bette Davis vehicle relocated. But it's all handled with consummate skill by director Yu Benzheng who, if he hasn't seen a Sirk movie, may at least have seen a Fassbinder pic or two.

As the libidinous heroine, Fang Shu gives an all-stops-out performance that's fun to watch. Technical credits are good, with excellent use made of the widescreen.
—*Strat.*

Mille et une marguerites
(A Thousand And One Daisies)
(FRENCH-DOCU-B&W/COLOR)

A Gaumont production and release. Executive producer, Martine Offroy. Written and directed by Pierre Philippe. Narrated by Aurelle Doazan and Jean-Hugues Anglade. Editor, Marie-Jeanne de Susini; sound, Alain Carnier; music, Philippe Eidel; production managers, Monique Pautas, Benedicte Aulois. Reviewed at the Cinémathèque Gaumont, Joinville-le-Pont, France, May 5, 1986. (Special screening at Cannes Film Festival.) Running time: 88 MINS.

Paris — For its 90th anniversary French major Gaumont, whose emblem is the "Marguerite" (daisy), has produced a feature-length documentary about its checkered history, compiled entirely from footage in the company's extraordinary cinémathèque. Writer-director Pierre Philippe, who probably knows the Gaumont archives better than anyone else (he made a series based on the firm's early silent films for Gaumont's now-shuttered tv subsidiary back in the late 1970s), put the film together in a record two months, though the haste is not evident in the pleasantly polished results.

Philippe forgoes the historian's approach for a more freewheeling presentation of the house built by Léon Gaumont back in 1895 (at first a photographic equipment firm, before moving into motion picture materials the following year). Using clips from about 140 fiction titles and numerous Gaumont Actualité newsreels about films and filmmaking, Philippe and his editor Marie-Jeanne de Susini adroitly time-trip the viewer back and forth, from striking early images of Mr. Gaumont showing foreign dignitaries around his studios (today housing SPP French tv facilities on the Buttes-Chaumont) and primitive biopics about Jesus and Molière, to the latest Gaumont productions, like the Gérard Krawczyk's adaptation of Ben Hecht's Hollywood-set novel, "I Hate Actors," which now is in post-production.

Film buffs and casual viewers alike will no doubt be most captivated by the imagination and visual exuberance of pioneering Gaumont silent films in various genres; early French Westerns starring the daredevil Gallic cowboy Joë Hamman (prefiguring the stunting antics of a later Gaumont star, Jean-Paul Belmondo), the surreal pre-Mack Sennett lunacies of the "Onésime" series directed by Jan Durand; the elegant comedies and melodramas of Léonce Perret; and, of course, the crime serials made by Gaumont's longtime production chief and star director, Louis Feuillade: "Fantomas," "Judex" and "Les Vampires" (the last recently restored by the Cinémathèque Française under the supervision of Feuillade's filmmaker grandson, Jacques Champreux).

Film also takes us, less satisfactorily, through Gaumont's more highbrow pictures of the 1920s by Marcel Lherbier and Léon Poirier; and on into the sound period: the company's collapse in the mid-1930s, rebirth during the war, and its subsequent return to moneymaking popular comedies and thrillers of the '50s and '60s, and Daniel Toscan du Plantier's culture reign of the past decade.

Philippe's casual commentary is voiced by two young actors, Aurelle Doazan and Jean-Hugues Anglade (seen in clips from Jean-Jacques Beineix' "Betty Blue"), and debuting fim composer Philippe Eidel has scored effectively, if not always discreetly.

Only serious caveat to be made is about the many silent film scenes that have been stretch printed (printing every second or third frame twice in order to approximate the original projection speeds). It's an abominable technique that tends to impose an irritatingly slow and jerky rhythm, and should be outlawed by archives and laboratories. —*Len.*

Salomé
(FRENCH-ITALIAN-COLOR)

A Cannon Group release of a Cannon Prods., TF-1 and Dedalus coproduction. Produced by Henry Lange. Executive producers, Menahem Golan and Yoram Globus. Director, Claude d'Anna. Screenplay, d'Anna adapted from Oscar Wilde's play, "Salomé," camera (Panavision, Fotocinema color), Pasqualino DeSantis; editor, Robert Perpignani; production design, Giantito Burchiellaro; costumes, Adriana Spadaro; score, Egisto Macchi; choreographer, Christopher Bruce; production supervisor, Mario Cotone; associate producer, John Thompson. Reviewed at the Cannes Film Festival (Un Certain Regard), May 8, 1986. Running time: 97 MINS.
Herod .... Tomas Milian
Herodias .... Pamela Salem
Nerva .... Tim Woodward
Salome .... Jo Champa
Yokanaan .... Fabrizio Bentivoglio
Nerva's aide ...... Jean-Francois Stevenin
Narraboth .... Fabio Carfora
Nelim .... Richard Paul Majewski
Messenger .... Feodor Chaliapin
Doctor .... Paul Muller
Philip .... Lorenzo Piani
Salomé as a child .... Fabiana Torrente

Cannes — This pretentious howler certifiably ranks as the 1986 Cannes fest's first hands-down clunker. Designed, apparently, to spruce up the Cannon Group's "prestige" film portfolio, "Salomé" should find modest use as filler on the European specialty circuit.

The cultural credentials of the pic, aside from a reference to its free — very free — derivation from the Oscar Wilde play, are hard to come by. Lensed on a shoestring in Rome by director-scripter Claude d'Anna, the pic is deficient in every respect with the possible exception of cameraman Pasqualino DeSantis' darkly atmospheric photography and Gaetano Testa's sound mix that delivers more dramatic punch than anything the cast is up to.

"Salomé" deliberately obscures the source material by shifting settings from Judea in 30 A.D. to what appears to be contemporary times. Adriana Spàdaro's costumes are equally as schizophrenic.

In a set that slightly resembles a New York subway express stop, King Herod (Tomas Milian) anguishes about ominous symbolism — blackbirds flying noisily about — and his uneasy hold on a slipping term in office. He also worries about the garrulous Caesar.

To complicate matters, Herod's prior misdeeds — he and wife Herodias (Pamela Salem) murdered his brother, Salomé's father — have left his subjects permanently shrouded in darkness and incapable of experiencing sexual pleasure.

Several confusing plot turns into the pic, Salomé (Jo Champa) appears to right prior wrongs and shmooze with the John-the-Baptist figure, here called Yokanaan (Frabrizio Bentivoglio). He's stuck in a stony basement in chains.

The inevitable seduction occurs in such listless fashion that Salomé's climactic dance of the seven veils looks like an arty aerobic exercise. There's a fair amount of nudity in the pic spiced by simulated sex with a decided whiff of kinkiness. Despite this, "Salomé's" erotic quotient is slightly to the left of that of "Song Of Bernadette."

Director d'Anna force-fed his cast with dialog of striking pomposity and allows the performers to founder. As for Salomé's climactic dance, Rita Hayworth did it better.

"Salomé" was the opening film in the fest's Un Certain Regard section.—*Sege.*

Hollywood Zap
(U.S.-COLOR)

A Troma Team release of a Protovision Prods. and Ben/Bar Prods. production. Executive producer, Dror Soref. Produced by Bobbi Frank, Ben Frank. Written and directed by David Cohen. Stars Ben Frank, Ivan E. Roth, De Waldron. Camera, Tom Frisby Fraser; editor, Rick Westover; music, Jaap. Reviewed at the Cannes Film Festival (market), May 10, 1986. (MPAA rating: R.) Running time: 93 MINS.
With: Ben Frank, Ivan E. Roth, De Waldron, Neil Flanagan, Annie Gaybis, Claude Earl Jones, Chuck Mitchell, Stan Ross, Helen Verbit.

Cannes — A self-described action comedy but weak on both counts, "Hollywood Zap" would be lucky to go straight to homevid where only its title might keep it from gathering dust.

Plot concerns a Southern nerd who quits his job at a women's clothing store and drives to Los Angeles in search of his father who abandoned him 24 years before. A videogame shark attaches himself to the nerd, and in well-populated L.A. runs into him everywhere.

Nerd finally locates pa, now a female nun, and drives back home with the video shark's all-but silent girlfriend. Writer-director David Cohen, in his first feature, has problems keeping the action going, but seems fascinated with videogame stores and little else.

Comedy is non-existent, action is restricted to getting in and out of cars and working the videogames; the music is loud and nothing else. R rating comes in both language and a flash of bare breasts, which the nerd doesn't touch.

Even the bouncy title is wasted.
—Adil.

The Supernaturals
(U.S.-COLOR)

A Republic Entertainment Intl. presentation of a Sandy Howard production. Executive producers, Mel Pearl, Don Levin. Produced and written by Michael S. Murphey and Joel Soisson. Directed by Armand Mastroianni. Camera (color), Peter Collister; music, Robert O. Ragland; production manager, Angela Heald; art director, Jo-ann Chorney; special effects coordinator, Gregory Landerer; associate producers, Victoria Plummer, William Fay. Reviewed at the Cannes Film Festival (market) May 9, 1986 (MPAA rating: R.) Running time: **80 MINS.**
Pvt. Ray Ellis . . . . Maxwell Caulfield
Sgt. Leona Hawkins . . . . . Nichelle Nichols
Pte. Angela Lejune . . . . Talia Balsam
Pte. Tom Weir . . . . Bradford Bancroft
Pte. Michael Osgood . . . . Levar Burton
Pte. Tim Cort . . . . Bobby Di Cicco
Also with: Margaret Shendal (Melanie), Patrick (Grampy) Davis (old man), James Kirkwood (Captain).

If audiences can swallow the inherently silly premise of "The Supernaturals" — and that's a big IF — this sci-fi thriller could make a modest impression at the wickets, despite the absence of a big-name cast. For the small-screen market (homevideo, tv) it's a moderately enjoyable piece of hokum.

Saga by cowriters and producers Joel Soisson and Michael S. Murphey opens in Alabama in 1865 during the Civil War. A group of captured Confederate soldiers is ordered to walk across a minefield while their horrified wives and children look on helplessly. All but one — a boy in a Rebel uniform — is blown to smithereens.

Cut to the same terrain in the present, where a motley assortment of Army recruits are out on bivouac, driven hard by tough-talking female sergeant Nichelle Nichols. Suspense builds nicely through a series of puzzling incidents; one rookie collects a bullet between the eyes; discovery of an underground bunker inhabited by an ancient, unspeaking man, and

of barricades from the Confederate era; appearance out of nowhere of a beautiful girl who says little more than her name; and finally an all-out attack on the troops by skeletal figures.

Link between the two events spaced a century apart ultimately is explained, but it stretches credibility a long, long way.

Maxwell Caulfield as the soldier who uncovers the secret is a fairly lightweight leading man, with a limited range of expressions (scared/befuddled), but just about all the other thesps put in strong performances.

Director Armand Mastroianni keeps the plot moving along at a snappy pace, and Peter Collister's photography is stylish, most notably the sequences in the fog-shrouded forest.

Robert O. Ragland's rousing score heightens the tension very effectively.—Dogo.

La Venexiana
(The Venetian Woman)
(ITALIAN-COLOR)

A Titanus release of a Lux Intl. production. World sales, Intra Films. Executive producer, Ciro Ippolito. Directed by Mauro Bolognini. Screenplay, Bolognini, Massimo Franciosa, from an anonymous 16th century play; camera (Luciano Vittori color), Beppe Lanci; editor, Alessandro Lucidi; music, Ennio Morricone; assistant director, Francesco Papa; costumes, Aldo Buti. Reviewed at the Cannes Film Festival (market), May 9, 1986. Running time: **84 MINS.**
Angela . . . . Laura Antonelli
Valeria . . . . Monica Guerritore
Foreigner . . . . Jason Connery
Also with: Claudio Amendola, Clelia Rondinella, Cristina Noci, Annie-Belle, Stefano Davanzati.

Cannes — In "La Venexiana," director Mauro Bolognini rides the crest of the wave of Italian audiences' fondness for older woman-accented erotic cinema, while adding an element of class to the commercial equation. Result is a disarmingly simple, technically proficient period romance, which has a strong home market future on the basis of casting two top actresses in the genre.

Based on an anonymously penned 16th-century play (recently revived on stage internationally), feature is set in Venice at a time following the devastation of The Black Plague. Laura Antonelli toplines as Angela, a widow with unfulfilled sexual yearnings who spots a handsome, blond foreigner (Jason Connery) from her window one day and immediately is infatuated with him. The foreigner, in turn, catches sight of Angela's married neighbor Valeria (Monica Guerritore), and is just as smitten with her.

With each of the ladies' maids Nena and Oria acting as a go-between, there ensues a sexual round-

robin in which the foreigner ends up satisfying (separately) both ladies' appetites before exiting just in time as Valeria's husband returns home. During the well-timed shenanigans, Angela's maid Nena also gets to do some comforting of her mistress as well as dally with Bernardo, a bearded young man who earlier had used some fast talking to divert the foreigner from a rendezvous with Valeria in order to visit Angela first.

Erotic content of "La Venexiana" is high, while Bolognini opts for lush settings and tasteful photography which avoid pornographic detail. Beppe Lanci's warm visuals and Aldo Buti's period costumes conform to Bolognini's usual high standard of technical quality. Ennio Morricone's music has fun with the kitschy material, segueing smoothly from liturgical music to highly romantic scoring and even throwing in some trademark breathy vocalese.

Laura Antonelli is a delight, playing her scenes of romantic longing straight (leaving the intrinsic humor underplayed) and throwing herself into sex scenes with her usual fervor. Pic might garner her the first U.S. theatrical pickup in several years for Italy's top cinematic export of the late 1970s.

Monica Guerritore is overshadowed by Antonelli, but still is effective in a smaller role. Jason Connery projects the kind of raw masculinity of his dad Sean and his acting fits smoothly into the Italian ensemble (with convincing dubbing in Italian by Tonino Accolla). Supporting cast works hard, with a priceless scene in which the maid hands Connery his belongings as he rushes out of Guerritore's apartment (just as the husband approaches) in the manner of passing a baton in a relay race. —Lor.

Arriving Tuesday
(NEW ZEALAND-COLOR)

A Cinepro production in association with the New Zealand Film Commission and Walker Films Ltd. Executive producer, Campbell Stevenson. Produced by Don Reynolds and Chris Hampson. Directed by Richard Riddiford. Screenplay, Riddiford, David Copeland; camera (color) Murray Milne; editor, John McWilliams; music, Scott Calhoun; sound, David Madigan; production design, Roger Guise; assistant director, Chris Graves; associate producer, Hammond Peek. Reviewed at the Cannes Film Festival (Market) May 12, 1986. Running time: **90 MINS.**
Monica . . . . Judy McIntosh
Nick . . . . Peter Hayden
Riki . . . . Rawiri Paratene
Also with: Heather Bolton, Lee Grant, Te Paki Cherrington, Sarah Peirse.

Cannes — First film from New Zealand director Richard Riddiford, "Arriving Tuesday" is a triangular love story that takes a long time to reach its predictable conclusion.

Often-explored subject, its gentle,

understated treatment and parochial elements will restrict the pic's chances of theatrical playoff outside Kiwiland, but it should be accessible enough for homevid and tv exploitation in some territories.

Fairly simple plot has Judy McIntosh returning to her lover, Peter Hayden, after spending 10 months in Europe. The reunion proves a bit awkward after the long separation, and to try to patch up their differences, she suggests they take a vacation on the beaches on the north of the North Island.

At a hotel they meet up with Rawiri Paratene, an itinerant Maori with a poetic turn of phrase, and they agree to give him a lift.

Hayden senses a growing attraction between Judy and Rawiri, and he cannot stomach the Maori's sentiments about how the white settlers damaged his homeland. Tension mounts until Hayden ditches Rawiri and decides to go back home, presenting his girlfriend with a sticky dilemma.

Performances by the three leading thesps are equally strong and convincing. Script by Riddiford and David Copeland has its absorbing moments despite the slow pacing, and Murray Milne's photography ranges over some impressive locations.

Concentration on Maori customs and beliefs, and the white man's problems in coming to terms with them, is a common preoccupation in Kiwi films. That may play well for the locals, but it does not necessarily translate or relate to audiences elsewhere. —Dogo.

Doorman
(U.S.-COLOR)

A Just Spokes production. (World sales, Manley Prods.) Produced by Stratton Leopold. Directed by Gary Youngman. Screenplay, Barbara Brenner, Youngman, from story by Youngman; camera (TVC color), William Wages; editor, Tod Lending; music, Claude Gaudette; sound, Jim Hawkins; assistant director, Greg Torre; art direction, Bea Swanson; set decoration, Hilary Henkin; stunt coordinator, Don Schisler; casting, Jerry Saviola. Reviewed at the Cannes Film Festival (market), May 10, 1986. (No MPAA Rating.) Running time: **80 MINS.**
Linda Regan . . . . Sharon Schlarth
Terry Reilly . . . . Bradley Whitford
Lu . . . . Haru Aki
Also with: Dan Biggers, Bruce Taylor, Dan Devendorf, Robin Cahall, Johnny Pophell, Ted Henning, Mike Smith, Susan Wolf, Lou Walker, Stuart Culpepper, Allison Biggers.

Cannes — "Doorman" is an uneventful, lowbudget mystery thriller shot and set in Atlanta. Pic has the earnest, simple approach of a B-picture, but lacks any attention-grabbing elements to make it competitive in international markets.

Bradley Whitford plays Terry Reilly, an apartment building doorman, who is a budding mystery writer on the side. When three doormen (including the worker on the other shift at his building) are killed and Riley's name is in the newspaper as an eyewitness, he is marked as a murder target. Teaming up with Linda Regan (Sharon Schlarth), whose uncle was one of the murdered doorman, he tries to unravel the mystery of who broke their necks and why.

Following up on a clue of missing packages being delivered to new residents in each of the three buildings, Riley pieces together evidence of a conspiracy. With Regan's help, he corners the baddies in a contrived climax at a local roller skating rink.

Cast, particularly Whitford, performs capably but not only is this story uninteresting, it is enacted too cheaply. Verbal mentions of gunrunning and other elements of international intrigue are no substitute for exotic locations and large-scale action set pieces. Filmmaker Gary Youngman delivers a dull car chase and squeaky-clean content that would probably garner a G rating. Pic's best chances would be in a tv syndication package.—Lor.

Sleepwalk
(U.S. WEST GERMAN-COLOR)

A Driver Films Inc. Ottoskop Filmproduktion (Munich) coproduction. Executive producer, Otto Grokenberger. Produced and directed by Sara Driver. Screenplay, Driver, Lorenzo Mans; camera (color), Franz Prinzi, Jim Jarmusch; editor, Li Shin Yu; art director, Robert Cooney, Andrea Degette; sound, Drew Kenin; music, Phil Kline; production manager, Rachel Reichman. Reviewed at the Cannes Film Festival (Critics Week), May 9, 1986. Running time: 75 MINS.
Nicole .... Suzanne Fletcher
Isabelle .... Ann Magnuson
Jimmy .... Dexter Lee
Dr. Gou .... Steven Chen
Barrington .... Tony Todd
Also with: Richard Boes (The Thief), Ako (Ecco Ecco), Harvey Perr (Matt), Jim Stark (Detective), Roberta Wright (Fence), Simon Daillie (Cross Me Kid).

Cannes — Because Sara Driver produced "Stranger Than Paradise," the international cult hit by Jim Jarmusch, comparisons certainly will be made between that film and Driver's feature debut, "Sleepwalk." Pics have the urban setting and loosely constructed plot in common, but "Sleepwalk" has less humor and less immediate appeal. Nonetheless, a most interesting debut.

Nicole (Suzanne Feltcher) works in a small print shop where she operates a word processor that's getting her down. Because she understands Chinese, she accepts an assignment to translate an ancient Chinese manuscript in her own time; the text is a series of poems. But there's something mysterious about it: the first page has been stolen by a Japanese girl who, we hear, is murdered later; and after a while the manuscript simply crumbles to dust.

Meanwhile Nicole's friend and roommate, Isabelle (Ann Magnuson) loses all her hair and Nicole's small, Asian looking, son, Jimmy (Dexter Lee) is kidnaped accidentally when he's sleeping in the back of Isabelle's car and it's stolen. Nicole goes searching for her missing son.

Driver has created some memorable moments during the course of the film, most notably a mysterious scene in an old-fashioned elevator which keeps stopping at the wrong floors whereupon the doors open to reveal strange scenes and characters. Final scenes, as Nicole searches near the docks for the kidnaped Jimmy, not realizing he's very close at hand, also carry a charge.

There are some amusing peripheral characters, too, such as a cop with such a sore throat that he can hardly be understood, and a very pregnant fence who refused to accept the stolen car with a kid sleeping in the back of it.

Technically, pic is excellent (Jarmusch assisted on the camera), and Li Shin Yu has edited to a very tight 75 minutes. It looks to find a cult following, and may be expected to turn up at several fests later this year, though commercially it seems less of a bet than the Jarmusch effort. —Strat.

Laputa
(WEST GERMAN-COLOR)

A Von Viettinghoff Films production. Produced by Johakim Von Viettinghoff. Written and directed by Helma Sanders-Brahms. Camera (Color), Eberhard Geick; editor, Eva Schlensag; music, Matthis Meyer; sound, Lothar Mankewitz. Reviewed at the CNC, Paris, May 1, 1986. (In the Un Certain Regard section at Cannes Film Festival). Running time: 90 MINS.
Paul .... Sami Frey
Malgortzata .... Krystyna Janda

Paris — A familiar romantic recipe for lovers separated by space, condition and experience, re-served with a sauce of socio-political topicality, "Laputa" is a minor effort from German director Helma Sanders-Brahms. The two-person drama enacted mostly in French, has Gallic architect Sam Frey and Polish photographer Krystyna Janda during one of their all-too-brief trysts in West Berlin, perhaps their last, trying to come to terms with their situation .

Most of the film is set in a large apartment-atelier where Janda wants to develop the photos she has shot during a professional jaunt in Africa. Enervated by her desire to remain in Poland, where her ex-lover is a political prisoner, Frey, who himself has a wife and daughter to return to in Paris, tries to

force open a new horizon on their narrow relationship, offering to leave everything and come to her in Warsaw. They argue, make up, argue again. Finally she decides to return home as planned, and he promises to settle his affairs in France and come shortly to join her in Poland.

Frey and Janda provide the story's requisite poignancy, but do not fulfill the filmmaker's parable design of embodying West and East attitudes, because the script reduces most of the essentially trite story to talk rather than action. Film's title refers to a voice-over device in which Frey cites passages from Jonathan Swift's "Gulliver's Travels" about the flying city of Laputa, which is meant to reflect the character's perceptions of West Berlin as a backdrop to his feelings of absurd futility. —Len.

Captive
(BRITISH/FRENCH-COLOR)

A Virgin Films release of a Don Boyd production. Executive producers, Al Clark and Stanley Sopel. Produced by Don Boyd. Written directed by Paul Mayersberg. Stars Irina Brook, Oliver Reed, Xavier Deluc, Corinne Dacla, Hiro Arai. Camera, (Fuji-color), Mike Southon; editor, Marie-Therese Boiché; music, The Edge and Michael Berkeley; art director, George Djurkovic. Reviewed at the Cannes Film Festival (market), May 12, 1986. Running Time: 95 MINS.
Rowena Le Vay .... Irina Brook
Greogry Le Vay .... Oliver Reed
'D' .... Xavier Deluc
Bryony .... Corinne Decla
Hiro .... Hiro Arai
Leo .... Nic Reding
Pine .... Annie Leon

Cannes — The kidnaping of a beautiful rich young girl, not for money, nor for sex, but just for the joy of doing it is the theme intricately developed by Paul Mayersberg in "Captive." The intriguing situation, with its obvious suspense potential, as well as generous helpings of nudity, suggest encouraging boxoffice possibilities.

In the opening sequence, the rich girl is enjoying a romp in the hay to the musical accompaniment of "Tosca" with a boyfriend who is never seen again. Thereafter, it's the trio of kidnapers who take over: A French boy, a Japanese boy and an English girl. She's drugged, handcuffed, blindfolded and gagged before being locked up in a chest for the night. At that point what's happening on screen is never really clarified, but as the action proceeds it becomes evident the object of the mission is a brainwashing exercise, to mold the girl to their mode of life. Gradually, they succeed. Eventually, she's free to go, but quickly returns to her captors when she discovers her father is sharing his bed with a girl.

Subsequent action, including a

shootout at an airport and the destruction of works of art is somewhat preposterous, as is the heroine's calm acceptance of a couple of years in prison, during which time she miscarries the French boy's child. At the end, the Japanese slices his throat when his love is not reciprocated.

It would appear that the premise of the Mayersberg screenplay is to suggest that environment plays a significant role in shaping character, and that's realized by her cordial behavior after her return. She's become one of them, sharing their anarchic way of life with enthusiasm and abandon. It's a bit tough to swallow all along the line, but vigorous direction and crisp editing more than compensate for any inconsistencies. Every now and then, there is a little directorial "cheating," as when the captive is placed fully clothed in a bath, and the Japanese holds a dagger above her. But it's only used to rip her clothes apart.

Irina Brook (daughter of Peter Brook) is a handsome girl with a firm young body, and willing to show it off. Fortunately, she's also a competent actress, and adds substance to the difficult role of the captive. Oliver Reed gives a commanding performance as the girl's father, the rich tycoon who is hated by his daughter. He's particularly impressive in the scene in which he sets fire to his luxury yacht to meet one of the demands of the kidnapers. Xavier Deluc, Corinne Dacla and Hiro Arai as the three kidnapers are an unlikely trio, though they work together well enough. Annie Leon is the clairvoyant detective who "smells the lilies" and knows the kidnapers have moved from London to the country!

Background music by The Edge and Michael Berkeley is a distinct plus. George Djurkovic has designed some highly imaginative sets, and Mike Southern's lensing is first rate.

"Captive" was financed by Virgin, World Audio Visual Entertainment, Les Productions Belles Rives, and Bill Colegrave, who is Don Boyd's partner. —Myro.

What Comes Around
(U.S.-COLOR)

A W.O. Associates release of a Jerry Reed Prod. production. Executive producer, Jerry Reed. Produced by Ted Evanson. Directed by Jerry Reed. Screenplay, Peter Herrecks, based on an original story by Gary Smith and Dave Franklin; camera (color), James Pergola; editor, William Carruth; production designer, Don K. Ivey; music, Al Delory; associate producer, Gary Neill. Reviewed at Cannes Film Festival (Market), May 11, 1986. Running time: 86 MINS.
Joe Hawkins .... Jerry Reed
Leon .... Barry Corbin
Tom Hawkins .... Bo Hopkins
Malone .... Arte Johnson

Esther Houston . . . . Nancy
Big Jay . . . . Ernest Dixon
Ralph . . . . Hugh Jarrett
Chester . . . . Buck Ford

Cannes — Country singer Jerry Reed will have trouble finding audiences for "What Comes Around" as he already has in spotty playoffs in Texas and other regional U.S. centers.

He portrays a boozy, drugged-out country singer celebrating his 25th anniversary in showbusiness whose brother kidnaps him from the ravages of the toll of the road.

Sure enough, Reed's manager has been pocketing his money to the tune of about $8,000,000 hived off in a Swiss bank. And sure enough that discovery leads to a settling of accounts as Reed and his brother wreck a shopping center the manager has put in his name.

Acting and technical credits are as lame as the plot. But underneath, way underneath, there lurks what might have been a snappy story about the hard time coping with success on the stage.

For Reed, the producer, director and actor, the stage never leaves the hitching post. Outlook: dim at best.—*Adil.*

The Return Of Josey Wales
(U.S.-COLOR)

A Reel Movies Intl. release of a Multi/Tacar Prods. presentation of a Ron Taylor film. Executive producer, Taylor. Produced by Mickey Grant. Directed by Michael Parks. Stars Parks. Screenplay, Forrest Carter; camera (color), Brant A. Hughes; editor, Ivan L. Bigley; music, Rusty Thornhill. Reviewed at Cannes Film Festival (market), May 9, 1986. Running time: **90 MINS.**
Josey Wales . . . . Michael Parks
Chato . . . . Raphael Campos
Ten Spot . . . . Bob Magruder
Paco . . . . Paco Vela
Escobedo . . . . Everett Sifuentes
Charlie . . . . Charlie McCoy

Cannes — The good news, for anyone who may be interested is that notwithstanding what seemingly happened in an earlier film, Josey Wales is still alive, still an outlaw, and still committing mayhem with indiscriminate abandon. The dubious news is that not too many people will be sufficiently concerned. Thus prospects for this Western must be rated slim, though the title may attract some of the audience of the original pic.

The action is set in rural Mexico and a fair slice of the dialog is in Spanish, which may add a degree of authenticity, but is a handicap for those who do not understand the lingo. That apart, it's a fairly stereotyped yarn in which a determined and callous chief of police is outwitted constantly by the outlaw.

In one scene a young Apache girl, due for the hangman's rope the following morning, successfully resists a rape attempt by the police captain, and she and two others in the condemned cell are freed by the outlaw. One of them, Ten Spot (Bob Magruder) later falls to a police bullet, while the police chief is left buried up to his neck, with the vultures already flying overhead.

Michael Parks, who directs as well as stars, appears to have given more thought to the gunfights than the clear delineation of the other characters, resulting in a minor degree of confusion. The title character is clear enough, and confidently portrayed, although spoken lines are not easy to follow. More than likely it's due to the quality of the print shown at Cannes, as the presentation was preceded by an on-screen statement that it was a working print.—*Myro.*

40 m² Deutschland
(40 Square Meters Of Germany)
(GERMAN-COLOR)

A Tevfik Baser Film Prod. Studio Hamburg Film Prod. co-production. Executive producer, Frank Winterstein. Written and directed by Tevfik Baser. Camera (Color), Izet Akay; editor, enate Merck; sound, Bernhard Ebler; music, Claus Bantzer; costumes, Marina Heinrich. Reviewed at the Cannes Film Festival (Critics' Week), May 10, 1986. Running time: **80 MINS.**
Cast: Osay Fecht, Yaman Okay, Deir Gokgol, Mustapha Gupinar.

Cannes — "40 Square Meters Of Germany," a first feature by Turkish-born filmer Tevfik Baser, is a harrowing account of claustrobia and imprisonment in the apartment of a couple of Turkish immigrants living in Hamburg. Victim of the story is Turna, the young and inexperienced bride of a factory worker whose bright hopes for leading a new life in Germany are dashed when her husband locks the door behind him on his way to work. The tale is chilling, but unfortunately develops with few surprises.

From the moment Turna discovers Dursun has locked her in "like an animal," the smile fades from her face and the tedium begins. She spends her days scrubbing floors, wringing out the laundry, and gazing wistfully at life outside in a dark back courtyard. Director Baser works skillfully within the narrow limits of realism he sets for himself, and keeps sympathy high for the plight of his meek and increasingly depressed heroine.

But potentially touching moments, such as her brief visual contact with a little neighbor girl through the window, or her excitement at being taken to a fair (which doesn't come off because hubby goes to play cards and forgets the time), are too pat and predictable to have much impact. Dursun is such an ogre, and Turna such a martyr, that picture gets stuck on a very elementary emotional level — despair.

Interest suddenly picks up in the final sequence when Dursun dies and Turna is liberated unexpectedly. But to do what, being pregnant, speaking no German, and knowing literally nothing about the real world outside her four walls? This is where the picture should have begun in the first place?

Performances are excellent, however, and Baser's talent for storytelling promises more —*Yung.*

Dr. Otto And The Riddle Of The Gloom Beam
(U.S.-COLOR)

A Sweat Equities production. Executive producers, Coke Sams and John Cherry. Produced by Coke Sams. Directed by John Cherry. Associate producers, Gunnar Gelotte and Sharon Weil; screenplay, Cherry, Sams; camera, Jim May; editor, Scott Arnold; music, Shane Keister; special visual effects, Frank Cappello; costumes, Kathy Cherry. Reviewed at the Cannes Film Festival (market), May 11, 1986. (MPEA rating, PG.) Running time: **88 MINS.**
Dr. Otto, Rudd Hardtact,
Laughin' Jack, Guy Dandy,
Auntie Nelda . . . . Jim Varney
Lance . . . . Myke Mueller
Doris . . . . Jackie Welch
Slave Willis . . . . Daniel Butler
Tina . . . . Esther Huston
· Also with: Tina Goetze, Jennifer Wood, David Landon, Mac Bennett, Winslow Stillman, Mary Jane Harvill, Ivy Kane, Leslie Potter, et al.

Cannes — This pop fantasy is replete with sophomoric humor about an "evil genius, mad scientist" who's trying to dominate the world and destroy the world economy, and a bumbling non-hero who's assigned the job of stopping him. The all-too-apparent low-budgeter is an ordeal to watch as campy shenanigans and ham acting punctuate silly situations and comicbook type gibberish. Item is so amateurish it is a penance to sit through it.

Idea supposedly is to generate some sales on basis of idiosyncratic Yank pitchman Jim Varney in the cast, who plays five different parts. Whatever mileage he may get in local U.S. tv markets, it is hard to conceive audiences anywhere else would latch on to the farcical humor that runs through the film.
—*Besa.*

Thrashin'
(U.S.-COLOR)

A Fries Entertainment release of a David Winters film. Executive producers, Charles Fries, Mike Rosenfeld. Produced by Alan Sacks. Directed by David Winters. Screenplay, Paul Brown, Sacks; camera (color) Chuck Colwell; editor, Nicholas Smith; production designer, Katheryn Hardwick; music, Barry Goldberg; casting, Gino Havens. Reviewed at the Cannes Film Festival (market), May 11, 1986 (No MPAA rating.) Running time: **90 MINS.**
Cory Webster . . . . Josh Brolin
Tommy Hook . . . . Robert Rusler
Chrissy . . . . Pamela Gidlay
Tyler . . . . Brooke McCarter
Bozo . . . . Brett Marx
Radley . . . . Josh Richman
Little Stevie . . . . David Wagner
Velvet . . . . Sherilyn Fenn

Cannes — For those who enjoy endangering life and limb by hurtling along roads and up and down ramps on flimsy bits of wood known as skateboards, "Thrashin' " might be a fun way to spend 90 minutes. Since that lets out the vast majority of the world's cinemagoing audience, write down this one as very much of a special-interest film.

Theatrical prospects likely will be limited to the youth market, but even that age group probably is going to groan at the cliché-ridden saga of gang wars fought on skate wheels, and a tepid on/off romance between leading players Josh Brolin and Pamela Gidley.

Contrary to those who thought the title referred to brawling or a form of sado-masochism, pic explains that "thrashin' " is teenage argot for an aggressive style of skateboard riding.

And there is an interminable amount of "thrashin' " as rival gangs the Ramp Locals and the Daggers (who hate the other bunch for no reason other than they have the fortune, or misfortune, to live in the San Fernando Valley) prepare for a 20-mile downhill race billed as "The Massacre."

In between these less than gripping encounters, Ramp Local Josh Brolin takes a shine to Pamela Gidley, sister of Dagger Robert Rusler. Natch, Rusler does not welcome such attention from one of the enemy, and he shows his displeasure by severely beating Brolin in a duel.

Miraculously, Brolin recovers in time to compete in the "Massacre," although by this time he's sore at Pamela, who threatens to go home to Indiana, where life is no doubt more peaceful.

There are no prizes for guessing who wins the race and the girl.

The skateboarding sequences are photographed imaginatively by Chuck Colwell, but director David Winters can't extract much drama or genuine excitement out of what is basically a very filmsy, dull plot.

Heavy use of rock tracks from such acts as Devo, Meatloaf, Bangles, Animotion and Fine Young Cannibals will go down well with the youth brigade, and for the rest, may relieve some of the boredom of all that whizzing downhill.—*Dogo.*

Bridge To Nowhere
(NEW ZEALAND-COLOR)

A Challenge Film Corp. presentation of an Mune film. Executive producer, Henry Fownce. Produced by Larry Parr. Directed by Ian Mune. Screenplay, Bill Baier, Mune, based upon the story by Parr; camera (Kodacolor), Kevin Hayward; editor, Finola Dwyer; music, Stephen McCurdy; sound Hammond Peek; art direction, Mike Becroft; assistant director, Lee Tamahori; stunt coordinator, Peter Bell; special effects coordinator, Selwyn Anderson; associate producer, William Grieve. Reviewed at the Cannes Film Festival (market) May 10, 1986. (No MPAA rating.) Running time: **90 MINS.**

Carl	Matthew Hunter
Tanya	Margaret Umbers
Julie	Shelly Luxford
Gray	Stephen Judd
Leon	Philip Gordon
Mac	Bruno Lawrence
Lise	Alison Routledge

Cannes — Take five fairly typical teenagers, strand them in a spectacularly rugged countryside, then have them stalked by a rifle-toting foe. Not a terribly original premise, but director and cowriter Ian Mune gives the theme some intriguing twists in "Bridge To Nowhere."

It's an engaging, if occasionally gory and slightly drawn-out thriller probably will do healthy business in its native New Zealand, particularly with youth audiences who will identify with the imperiled characters, and enjoy the sprinkling of rock tunes, some by Kiwi bands.

Another big plus is the presence of Bruno Lawrence, arguably New Zealand's top actor, whose growing international reputation ("The Quiet Earth," "Utu," "Heart Of The Stag," "Smash Palace") could help open doors to some territories for this pic.

Lawrence specializes in playing taciturn, brooding guys with a violent streak, and his latest role is tailor-made. Living in a remote mountain shack with enigmatic Alison Routledge (his "Quiet Earth" costar) Lawrence gets testy when the teenagers, out on a weekend hike, destroy the area's peace and quiet.

In a confrontation with Lawrence and Routledge, one of the group is killed, the rest flee in terror. Lawrence's motives, while hardly justified, at least go some way. towards explaining his ruthless pursuit of the kids. Routledge's character remains a puzzle.

After a slow start, Mune deftly maintains the tension right up to the climax, and the payoff likely will satisfy most customers.

Lawrence brings the right kind of menace to his role, Routledge will keep the audiences guessing, and the young thesps are uniformly good, although one or two are prone to go over the top with a surfeit of shouting and facial contortions.

Kevin Hayward's camerawork is handsome, his wide shots making maximum capital out of the wilderness of New Zealand's North Island (the bridge of the title is a remarkable structure, a relic of the 1920s' interspersed with plenty of closeups of the thesps as they go through their traumatic experiences.)

Music, a blend of vocal tracks and synthesizer-based score by Stephen McCurdy, neatly reinforces the onscreen action. — *Dogo.*

Shtay Etzba'ot m'Tzidon
(Ricochets)
(ISRAELI-COLOR)

A Marathon Films Presentation of an Israeli Defense Forces Unit production. Produced by Eli Dori. Directed by Eli Cohen. Screenplay, Cohen, Tzvika Kertzner, Baruch Nevo; camera (Eastmancolor, 16m), Yehiel Ne'eman; editor, Avigdor Weill; music, Benny Nagari; title song, Nagari,, Eli Madorski, performed by Boaz Ofri; sound, Danny Yeger. Reviewed at the IDF Film Unit screening room, April 30, 1986 in (Un Certain Regard section, Cannes Film Festival). Running time: **91 MINS.**
With: Ronnie Pinkovitz (Gadi), Shaul Mizrahi (Tuvia), Alon Aboutboul (Georgie), Ossi Hillel (Micky).

Tel Aviv — Eli Cohen's first feature film, "Ricochets," is bound to raise plenty of controversy both in Israel and when it unspools May 15 in Cannes. Much of the home audience will balk at the idea of the Army producing an anti-war picture about Lebanon, in which its own soldiers are shown to be fed up with their jobs. Abroad, the film's narrow focus on a handful of soldiers on patrol in South Lebanon, probably will be interpreted by some critics as an attempt to draw a curtain over the larger problems and refer only to its fringe effects.

Cohen lensed the entire pic in Lebanon, utilizing real-life settings and incidents. Unfortunately, real time and the film's plot got entangled while moving on parallel paths, making it difficult to discern fact from fiction.

Plot revolves around a young officer, fresh out of training camp, who replaces a more experienced one killed at a checkpoint. Energetic and cocksure, he soon realizes there are no answers at all in war, only questions. The screenplay's basic episodic construction follows several subplots involving the men serving under the officer. One of them nurses a mute affection for a pretty Lebanese girl seen at a distance whenever the patrol goes through her village. Another tries to win the confidence of a young boy playing in the streets, a third's allegiance to his uniform cannot wipe out his strong link with his own people, the Druse, who live on the other side of the border as well.

All these paths lead uniformly to tragedy, however, and whatever political opinions each of the soldiers holds, conclusion is the same: war kills guilty and innocent alike, military and civilian, and there is no such thing as enlightened occupation.

The authentic locations and the actors' youth help create a thick, palpable atmosphere of anguish, anger and frustration. The young and spontaneous cast do a fine job, with Ronnie Pinkovitz as the greenhorn officer and Alon Aboutboul, as his most troublesome soldier, standing out.

Repetitious script is indictive of the stifling routine in military life, but the film holds up nicely. And Yehiel Ne'eman's sensitive camera really has caught events in the raw. The action scenes lack the sleek professional touch of a Hollywood production, which is all for the best, as it contributes to the almost documentary qualities of the pic. Some dialog could have been more carefully fashioned. Benny Nagari's mechanical score is the least imaginative contribution to this picture.

Originally produced for military instructional purposes, film has been put on the local market and handed to an indie distrib. Distribution abroad probably will depend on the political inclination of the different markets. —*Edna.*

Valkoinen kääpiö
(The White Dwarf)
FINNISH-COLOR

A Finkino release (foreign sales: Finnish Film Foundation) of a Panfilm Humaloja & Innanen production. Executive producer, Heikki Innanen. Written (based on a story by Bo Carpelan) and directed by Timo Humaloja. Stars Kari Heiskanen. Camera (Eastmancolor), Pertti Mutanen; sound, Mikael Sievers; music, Johnny Lee Michaels; editor, Tapio Suominen; art director, Mattheus Marttila. Reviewed at the Cannes Film Festival (market), May 10, 1986. Running time, **104 MINS.**
Cast: Kari Heiskanen, Lilga Kovanko, Jaana Raski, Jaakko Pakkasvirta, Esko Salminen, Riitta Selin, Kimm Gunnel.

Cannes — There is no dwarf in Timo Humaloja's atomic scare feature "The White Dwarf." There is no scare, either, only a stilted solemnity and a few flashes of morose anger in the story of a young mining engineer's escape through a mine shaft after a nuclear explosion in the Finnish Arctic region, and in his subsequent despair at fitting into a normal life when he finds himself inflicted with leukemia. Mostly he acts like a thoroughly spoiled kid on a continuous sulk.

The stricken man has visions of a young blond woman, but these do not relieve the steady dreariness of Humaloja's narrative style either. He uses the widest of screens and carefully composed frames but fills them mostly with mute boredom, set to music of dull austerity. Acting in all roles is correspondingly devoid of life.

Flashed for a split second on the screen in the final crawl is an explanation of the title's dwarf being the tag applied by scientists to a small dose of deadly radiation. Program notes supplied by the director describe all kinds of inner meanings never actually in evidence in the film.—*Kell.*

Krysar
(The Pied Piper of Hamelin)
(CZECHOSLOVAKIAN-COLOR)
(ANIMATED)

A Filmexport (Prague) release of a Studio J. Trnka production, in cooperation with TV-2,000 and Gunther Herbertz for Südwestfunk Baden-Baden. Directed by Jiri Barta. Screenplay, Kamil Pixa; čamera (color), Vladimir Malik, Ivan Vit; editor, Helena Lebduskova; music, Michael Kocab. Reviewed at the Cannes Film Festival (Un Certain Regard), May 10, 1986. Running time: **62 MINS.**

Cannes — The art of animating puppets for the screen reaches deep into the heart of fairy tales in this extraordinary Czech version of "The Pied Piper Of Hamelin," Filmmaker Jiri Barta and his team start from a variation of the story, set in northern Germany in the Middle Ages, in which a town is overrun by rats. A mysterious piper, who saves the town by piping the rodents into the sea, is mocked when he comes to claim payment for his services. He justly turns the townspeople into the rats they really are, and vanishes into thin air.

Kamil Pixa's story eliminates the unsettling presence of children who, in one version of the tale, are led into a mountainside by the piper. Instead, it makes his vengeance easier to swallow by having him punish the villagers directly. As the prolog states, this is a story about greedy men and greedy rats, and the film underlines their similarities.

The amazing puppets are creations of pure fantasy, somewhere between futuristic, expressionist and Medieval. They move in a no-less-fantastic space of metalized miniatures, and talk an imaginary language, miming the action. Animation techniques are integrated with footage of real rats and special process shots, like the puppets bickering over prices in the market with coins coming out of their mouths. Overall, top quality children's entertainment. — *Yung.*

Dead Time Stories
(U.S.-COLOR)

A Bedford Entertainment release of a Scary Stuff Prods. production. Produced by Bill Paul. Executive producers, William Links, Steven Mackler. Directed by Jeffrey Delman. Screenplay, Delman, Charles Shelton, J. Edward Kiernan; camera (color), Daniel Canton; supervising editor, Jim Rivera; editor, William Szarka; music, Taj; sound, Rick Waddel; assistant director, Bill Paul; makeup effects, Bryant Tansern, Edward French.

Reviewed at the Cannes Film Festival (Market), May 11, 1986. (No MPAA Rating.) Running time: 81 MINS.
With: Scott Valentine (Peter), Nicole Picard (Rachel), Cathryn De Prume (Goldi Locks), Melissa Leo (Ma Ma Baer), Michael Mesmer (Mike), Matt Mitler, Kathy Fleig, Brian De Persia, Kevin Hannon, Tim Rule, Casper Roos.

Cannes — "Dead Time Stories," originally titled "Freaky Fairy Tales," is an unsatisfactory horror comedy in three segments. Only audience is diehard fans for special makeup effects.

Structure closely resembles that of "Creepshow," with a little boy demanding that his uncle recite scary bedtime stories to help him go to sleep.

Only the first tale is effective: a low-budget but interesting to look at medieval story of Peter (Scott Valentine), a fisherman's son sold into slavery to two witches. He saves a girl they intend to sacrifice in order to conjure back to life their warlock brother (using remains of his heart fetched from his grave). Makeup effects are very impressive here as the heart gradually recreates the whole body by spouting blood vessels, sinews and red creeping flesh in an amazing setpiece. Half-hour story also features a funny trickending.

The following two segments of "Dead Time Stories" are truly terrible and a test of any audience's endurance. Part Two has the story of Red Riding Hood updated to the present with Rachel (Nicole Picard) as a sexy girl in red jogging togs who goes to the drugstore to fetch Maalox for her granny. The Maalox is accidentally mixed up with a drug fix for wolf Willie, who is a sleaze-bag as well as a werewolf. He bites and kills granny when he goes to her house to exchange the drugstore parcels and is in turn done in by resourceful Rachel. Guess what Granny turns into?

Idiotic finale revamps the "Goldilocks And The Three Bears" tale into sophomoric slapstick. Goldi (Cathryn De Prume) is a blond with a big chest who killed her parents at age eight, followed by other killing sprees. She's just escaped from an insane asylum as have Mr. Baer and his lame-brained son, sprung from stir by Ma Ma Baer (Melissa Leo). The four of them team up and fight it out with the local cops. Oddest element of this amateurish segment is casting of Melissa Leo, a talented young actress, with black wig and some makeup as the matriarch with an adult son.

Technical credits and acting are weak throughout. —Lor.

Eins og skepnan deyr
(The Beast)
(ICELANDIC-COLOR)

A Bio release of a Bio/Finnish Film Foundation production. Produced by Jon Olafsson. Written and directed by Hilmar Oddsson. Camera (Agfacolor), Sigudur Sverrir Palsson; editor, Oddsson, Kristin Palsdottir, Valdis Oskarsdottir; music, Hrodmar Sigurdbjörnsson, Oddsson W.A. Mozart; sound, Gunnar Helgason; art director, Togeir Gunnarsson; costumes, Hulda Magnusdottir; production manager, Marin Magnusdottir. Reviewed at the Cannes Film Festival (market) May 9, 1986. Running time: 97 MINS.
Helgi . . . . Tröstur Gennarsson
Lara . . . . Edda Heidrun Backmann
Baldur . . . . Johann Sigurdarson
Also with: Torgeir Gunnarsson, Sigurdur Palsson, Hallgrimur Helgasson, Torarinn Gudnason, Fridgeir Olgeirsson, Hilmar Oddsson, others.

Cannes — Original title of Hilmar Oddsson's psycho-meller feature "The Beast" is first part of a Biblical quote stating that "as the beast dies, so does man." The beast in Oddsson's story is an imaginary one although it is symbolized by a reindeer.

Helgi, an aspiring young novelist, goes with girlfriend Lara to a lonely house near a fjord to exorcise, through writing, the torment in his soul stemming from the fact that his mother left him when he was a small boy. She went to Germany with a reindeer researcher named Wolfgang.

When writing fails him, Helgi has dreams of herds of reindeer. After have been given lots of red herrings to create suspense, audiences are, at the finale, left with Helgi nearly killing himself with a gun that was supposed to have hit a reindeer standin for seductor Wolfgang.

Tröstur Gunnarsson and Edda Heidrun Backmann seem insecure about what to do with their muddily written roles. Plot development is jerky and all technical credits are executed modestly at best. Psychology as well as suspense suffer accordingly. — Kell.

Bullies
(CANADIAN-COLOR)

A Universal release (U.S.) and Norstar Releasing release (Canada) of a Simcom Prods. production. Executive producers, Peter Simpson and Peter Haley. Produced by Peter Simpson. Directed by Paul Lynch. Screenplay, John Sheppard and Brian McCann; camera (color), Rene Verzier; editor, Nick Rotundo; art direction, Jack McAdam; music, Paul Zaza; associate producer, Ilana Frank; casting director, Lucinda Sill. Reviewed at Cannes Film Festival (market), May 12, 1986. (MPAA Rating: R.) Running time: 90 MINS.
Jenny Morris . . . . Janet Laine-Green
Clay Morris . . . . Stephen Hunter
Matt Morris . . . . Jonathan Crombie
William Crow . . . . Dehl Berti
Becky . . . . Olivia D'Abo

Cannes — Non-discriminating exhibs and homevid retailers will be happy with "Bullies," a bloody violence effort which has no pretense of socially redeeming values.

The plot in a nutshell: A family of three, pretty blond wife, wimpy husband and her teenage son by another marriage, move to a small town ruled by a family of brutal men.

The lords of violence, a father and three sons, force an elderly couple off the road to their death over some slight offense, rape the pretty blonde, terrorize everyone else (even the town's sheriff) and get their comeuppance when the teenage son successfully frees the wimp they have tied up and plan to kill.

A wise and friendly Indian is kind to the teenage son but gets his home burned when he thwarts a first rape attempt.

It's a nasty pic from start to finish, well photographed in picturesque British Columbia by Rene Verzier and competently directed by Paul Lynch.

The cast performs well, notably Jonathan Crombie (the teenager) in his first feature. A $2,000,000 pickup by Universal puts this low-budgeter in profit. And as steady as the violence is the certainty pic will find fast boxoffice and returns in homevid. Blood money for sure. —Adil.

Huomenna
(Tomorrow)
(FINNISH-COLOR)

A Kinosto release of a Skandia Filmi/Finnish Film Foundation production. Produced and executive produced by Kaj Holmberg. Written and directed by Juha Rosma. Stars Juka Puotila, Katja Kiuru, Bibi Andersson. Camera (Fujicolor), Esa Vuorinen; editor, Kristina Schulgin; sound, Johan Hake; music, Edward Vesala; art director, Janusz Sosnowksi; costumes, Kaija. Reviewed at the Cannes Film Festival (market section), May 9, 1986. Running time: 90 MINS.
Lieutenant Leimu . . . . Jukka Puotila
Irene . . . . Katja Kiuru
Kott . . . . Aake Kalliala
Luke . . . . Heikki Luukas
The singer . . . . Bibi Andersson
Also with: Pertti Sveholm, Mikko Majanlahti, Jukka-Pekka Palo, Markku Maalismaa, Jussi Parviainen.

Debuting writer-helmer Juha Rosma's "Tomorrow" has superior production credits in all departments except the screenplay. The feature has the look of a master filmmaker's work, but had the storyline been clearer and Rosma indulged less in asides of an experimental character, wider international sales might have been predicted. As it stands, however, "Tomorrow" is a promising bow that brings to mind early Ridley Scott.

Action spans the last two days of a civil war in an unidentified country. The writer-director, who has worked closely with his art director, Poland's Janusz Sosnowski (a graduate of several Andrzej Wajda and Krzystof Zanussi films), claims events in Poland inspired his vision of a world in which nobody can trust anybody but himself.

In a barracks prison camp, Lieutenant Leimu (Jukka Puotila) has to interrogate, and most of the time, subsequently order the execution of prisoners coming from the Other Side. Gradually he becomes involved more personally with a few of them. On the day peace is declared, he succeeds in rising above partisan stands, and defies execution orders so he can bring at least one prisoner to safety.

The camp has a Kafkaesque look of a walled and corridored no-man's land. Acting in all roles is muted even when cruelty is indicated. No character is defined beyond a few basic traits, but neither are any to be dismissed as one dimensional. Each is a victim of the war, and this includes the children who beg for a knife rather than for a piece of bread.

This also goes for Sweden's Bibi Andersson who brings grim sadness to a cameo role as a singer who may double as a spy, but who shelters a small boy refugee named — as is the film — Huomenna (Tomorrow). The boy is hardly seen in the film, but there is no doubt about his part in making the adults around him come to terms with themselves.
—Kell.

Hulyeseg nem Akadaly
(Idiots May Apply)
(HUNGARIAN-COLOR)

A Hungarofilm release of a Dialog Studio/Mafilm production. Directed by Janos Xantus. Screenplay, Xantus, Ildiko Korody; camera (Eastmancolor), Andras Matkocsik; music, Janos Masik; art director, Gabor Bachmann; production manager, Andras Elek. Reviewed at the Cannes Film Festival (market), May 9, 1986. Running time: 86 MINS.
Robi . . . . Andor Lukats
Iren . . . . Jadwiga Jankowska
"Einstein" . . . . Gabor Mate
Dr. Korosi . . . . Jan Nowicki
Prof. Nopcsa . . . . Robert Koltai
Also with: Eszter Csakanyi (Sara), Ferenc Sebestyen (Uncle Joska), Barnabas Torh, Sandor Szers (Sons).

Cannes — Janos Xantus' first feature, "Eskimo Woman Feels Cold," was a promising, uneven, anarchic affair, but "Idiots May Apply," his second, is a flat, conventional situation comedy. It represents a step back for this young director.

Central character is a supposedly wacky, but irritating, character who keeps embarrassing his wife with his oddball behavior, such as getting on the table during a smart dinner party or paddling in a fish tank. Doctors can't help, but the tutor of their eldest son, nicknamed "Einstein" has a theory as to how the husband can be "cured."

Main trouble is that the film simply isn't funny, though it tries to be.

Even such a surefire sequence as one where the hero is locked in a flooding toilet and can't get out goes for virtually nothing. Acting throughout is as strained as the direction.
—*Strat.*

Loyalties
(CANADIAN-COLOR)

A Norstar Releasing release (in Canada) of a William Johnson/Ronald Lillie Lauron Intl. production in association with Wheeler-Hendren Enterprises and Dumbarton Films and Telefilm Canada. Produced by Ronald Lillie and William Johnson. Coproduced and directed by Anne Wheeler. Stars Susan Wooldridge, Kenneth Welsh, Tantoo Cardinal. Screenplay, Sharon Riis based on a story by Wheeler and Riis; camera (color), Vic Sarin; editor, Judy Krupanszky; art direction, Richard Hudolin. Reviewed at the Cannes Film Festival (market), May 12, 1986. Running time: 100 MINS.
David Sutton . . . . Kenneth Welsh
Lily Sutton . . . . Susan Wooldridge
Rosanne Ladouceur . . . . . Tantoo Cardinal
Beatrice . . . . Vera Martin
Leona . . . . Diane Debassige
Eddy . . . . Tom Jackson
Nicholas Sutton . . . . Jeffrey Smith

Cannes — "Loyalties" marks a classy feature debut for Canadian director Anne Wheeler and scripter Sharon Riis.

It's a tight, neatly executed drama about a British doctor's family that moves to a remote northern community where their secret is not known.

Wheeler and Riis unfold details slowly and with depth of characterization. The wife and mother (Susan Wooldridge) is upper-class and banks her emotions skilfully. The husband (Kenneth Welsh) is sexually cool toward her because, as it is hinted by fleeting shots that don't signal too much of what is to come, he lusts after young adolescent girls.

Against this foreground is a backdrop of a halfbreed Métis population where life is played out in the raw: The Métis woman, who becomes their housekeeper, orders her man out of their home because he has been violent to her. The woman (Tantoo Cardinal) has a barely teenaged daughter who the doctor rapes in a powerful rainy night scene.

Wooldridge, who learns about life from the Métis, finally calls the cops near fadeout.

Sounds trite, but not in Wheeler's accomplished hands. Wooldridge, Welsh and Cardinal are outstanding and the pic, which offers divergent depictions of women trapped by their emotions, or lack of them, has strong possibilities for theatrical playoff and also for festivals.

Wheeler and Riis leave some key questions: No explanation is offered why Wooldridge let her husband's problem go on so long, especially after a violent session between them back in England (depicted without actors). And while Wooldridge

makes contact with the resident white women of the town, there is no scene of them calling on her to follow up.

The problem is reflected by their 11-year-old son, well played by Nicholas Sutton, who has witnessed the first fight, though unseen by them.

Production values are terrific, especially camerawork by Vic Sarin on location in Lac La Biche, Alberta.

This is not just a women's pic and requires special handling. But for a low-budget effort ($C1,800,000), the rewards are evident. Though set in Canada, the story is universal.
—*Adil.*

Abducted
(CANADIAN-COLOR)

An Interpictures release in association with Modern Cinema Marketing of an Erin Films production. Produced by Harold J. Cole. Executive producer, Alex Massis. Directed by Boon Collins. Screenplay, Collins, from story by Lindsay Bourne, Collins; camera (Medallion color), Robert McLachlan; editor, Bruce Lange; music, Michel Rubini; sound, Peter Clements; art direction, Kim Steer; set design, Alan Wilson; assistant director, Judy Kemeny; wildlife footage, Tommy Tompkins. Reviewed at the Cannes Film Festival (market), May 12, 1986 (No MPAA Rating.) Running time: 87 MINS.
Joe . . . . Dan Haggerty
Renee . . . . Roberta Weiss
Vern . . . . Lawrence King-Phillips

Cannes — "Abducted" is a modest little picture, which achieves its goal of presenting a simple story of survival in the mountainous wilds of British Columbia. Tameness of treatment indicates its best market will be for tv audiences.

Shot on handsome, treacherous locations, story ironically recalls the strictly claustrophobic tale "The Collector." Renee (Roberta Weiss) is a beautiful, young student out jogging in the woods who is kidnapped by primitive backwoodsman Vern (Lawrence King-Phillips). He forces her to climb steep rock faces and trek for several days with him to his remote mountain cabin, where he plans to live with her.

Though Renee gradually comes to understand Vern and even pity him, she resists his frequent attempts to assault her and is finally saved from a fate worse than death by the appearance of Vern's dad, Joe (Dan Haggerty) on the scene. Joe warns his son not to hurt the lady and agrees to return her safely to civilization.

After an altercation with some hunters (out to kill the mountain sheep Joe loves and protects), Vern runs off. An Oedipal conflict occurs when he returns, savagely bashes his father with a rifle butt and leaves Joe for dead. Ever the rugged survivor, Joe manages to recover and track Vern down in a predictable

conclusion that spells freedom for Renee.

Director Boon Collins smoothly handles this basic material, pulling his punches in the frequent scenes that promise some sex or nudity but never deliver. Roberta Weiss is easy on the eyes even under such a tasteful approach while Lawrence King-Phillips chews the woodsy scenery as a young villain reminiscent of John Drew Barrymore. Haggerty is perfectly cast as a kindly mountain man not too distantly related to his Grizzly Adams persona.

Tech credits are modest but effective, with an assist provided by nice wildlife photography by Tommy Tompkins. —*Lor.*

Der Sommer des Samurai
(Summer Of The Samurai)
(WEST GERMAN-COLOR)

A Cine Intl. release of a Radiant Films production, in association with Cinenova-ZDF. Produced by Michael Bittins. Directed by Hans Christof Blumenberg. Screenplay, Blumenberg, with the collaboration of Carol H. Stern, Frederick Spindale; camera (color), Wolfgang Dickmann; music, K. Bartholome; editor, M. Barius; sound, G. Kortwitch; sound, Gunther Korwich; assistant director, Wilhelm Engelhardt. Reviewed at the Cannes Film Festival (market), May 10, 1986. Running time 105 MINS.
Christiane Land . . . . Cornelia Froboess
Wilcke . . . . Hans Peter Hallwachs
Gerhard Krall . . . . Wojciech Pzoniak
Dr. Feuillade . . . . Nadja Tiller
Schirmer . . . . Peter Krauss
Doris . . . . Hannelore Hoger
Weinrich . . . . Anton Diffring
Also with: Matthias Fuchs (Dr. Herbst), Karl-Heinz von Hassel (Heideman), Miko (Marianne).

Cannes — Critic turned director Hans Christof Blumenberg seems to be opting to make his mark with disarming thrillers based on a style of cinema harking back to the silent days, when directors such as Fritz Lang and, even earlier, Louis Feuillade, made dashing mysteries involving criminal masterminds. For his second feature (after "Thousand Eyes"), Blumenberg even has a character called Dr. Feuillade, and jokingly has the character played by Nadja Tiller.

Far fetched but engaging, pic is about a mysterious samurai terrorizing Hamburg businessmen one summer. A femme journalist, recovering from a broken relationship and a bout with alcoholism, is assigned to write the story, and discovers the samurai is a German Zorro type, raised in Japan, out to seek vengeance for the theft of an antique samurai sword, a theft which occurred when some German businessmen visited Japan several years earlier.

The actual thief is a Howard Hughes type, amusingly played by Polish actor Wojciech Pzoniak, who cowers in a heavily guarded

castle surrounded by a moat and modern surveillance systems: he even has ninja to protect him, but to no avail, of course.

There might have been a bit more Zorro-type derring-do to keep things bubbling a little faster, but Blumenberg's affection for an older genre of cinema is appealing, and he brings off one superb moment: when the journalist on a rooftop on one side of Hamburg is linked to the samurai on the other side of the city via a breathtaking helicopter shot.

Cast is solid, with Cornelia Froboess fine as the dogged newshen and vet actor Anton Diffring doing a good bit as a businessman who's had "trouble" with dioxin.

All tech credits are tops, with fine lensing by Wolfgang Dickmann giving a good gloss to the adventurous goings-on. — *Strat.*

America 3000
(U.S.-COLOR)

A Cannon release of a Cannon Group presentation of a Golan-Globus production. Produced by Menahem Golan, Yoram Globus. Written and directed by David Engelbach. Camera (Rank color), David Gurfinkel; editor, Alain Jakubowicz; music, Tony Berg; sound, Danny Natovich; art direction, Kuli Sander, Stephen Dane; stunt coordinator, Mario de Barros; fight arranger, Ernie Reyes; special effects, Carlo de Marchis; postproduction supervisor, Michael Sloan; costume design, Debbie Leon; designer of Aargh the Awful, Laine Liska; associate producer, Itzhak Kol. Reviewed at the Cannes Film Festival (market), May 10, 1986. (MPAA Rating: PG-13). Running time: 92 MINS.
Korvis . . . . Chuck Wagner
Vena . . . . Laurene Landon
Rhea . . . . Camilla Sparv
Lakella . . . . Victoria Barrett
Gruss . . . . William Wallace
Morha . . . . Sue Giosa
Lynka . . . . Galyn Görg
Lelz . . . . Shai K. Ophir

Cannes — "America 3000" is a silly sci-fi pic from Cannon, scheduled for domestic release in August, but better suited to homevideo use.

Following the killing of her mother Rhea (Camilla Sparv in a campy performance), blond female warrior Vena (Laurene Landon) succeeds to leadership of her fighting clan in an America (actually filmed in Israel) 900 years after a devastating nuclear war. She has a sibling rivalry with her sister Lakella (Victoria Barrett), who was passed over for the leadership post and Morha (Sue Giosa), the aggressive leader of another ruling clan.

In this environment, men are enslaved in various categories (workers, procreators, etc.), but Korvis finds a bunker designed to protect the U.S. President in time of nuclear war. He returns with advanced weaponry (including laser guns and hand grenades) to lead a successful rebellion against the women and create a happy, coexistence ending.

Film is relentlessly silly, with the

madeup language, based on English, producing infantile jokes. Writer-director David Engelbach thinks he's funny, with Korvis bringing back a big ghetto blaster to impress everyone typical of the failed humor. Though the bleak Israeli landscapes (which look like limestone quarries) are atmospheric, film never becomes more than an imitation of numerous pics like "Conan" and "Quest For Fire."

Barbarian women of the future apparently wear too much eye makeup from the evidence here, just one of many camp elements likely to elicit audience groans. A hairy monster mascot named Aargh the Awful has some cute bits, but film plods along listlessly until an energetic final reel battle featuring some martial arts skills. Aimed at kids, film omits nudity. The actors do the best they can, but are made to appear ridiculous in most scenes. —Lor.

Combat Shock
(U.S.-COLOR)

A 2000 AD production from Troma. Executive producers, Lloyd Kaufman and Michael Herz. Written, produced and directed by Buddy Giovinazzo. Camera (color), Stella Varveris; lighting design, Jim Grib; music, Ricky Giovinazzo; special makeup effects, Ralph Cordero 2d, Ed Varuolo, Jeff Matthes; special effects, Brian Powell. Reviewed at the Cannes Film Festival (market), (MPAA rating: R.) Running time: **96 MINS.**
With: Mitch Maglio, Asaph Livni, Nick Nasta, Michael Tierno.

Cannes — "Combat Shock" is a raw, violent, downbeat film that endeavors to lay open the underbelly of America, as experienced by a former Vietnam POW, but which degenerates into an almost ludicrous elaboration of the antihero's woes. Nonetheless Buddy Giovinazzo's vision of the lower depths occasionally may touch a responsive nerve with under-30 audiences who are currently attuned to the present stresses of unemployment, drugs and crime in urban peripheries like Staten Island, where pic was lensed.

Via occasional flashbacks and opening sequences, we learn of a loser's former war experiences in Vietnam in which he was involved in the slaughter of a village and later held prisoner for two years and tortured. These sequences add nothing to the standard footage on the subject in former films.

The downer's experiences in a dilapidated neighborhood progress from bad to worse. He and his family are literally starving. He lives in a kind of human pig sty for which he has already received an eviction notice; the drug pushers are after him to pay for dope he owes them for; his wife is a bedraggled, nagging, slovenly, overweight harridan; their one-year-old offspring is a distorted monster (the poor make-up

on this E.T. is one of the weakest elements of the film, and provoke laughter in the audience here), and the local unemployment officer (inexplicably with a poster of "Day Of The Dead" on the wall) can't find work for the unskilled drifter.

Helmer takes us through a series of shock scenes. Explicit ugliness and revolting realism are the order of the day, and we know that nothing will be left to the viewer's imagination. The dreary debacle comes when the ex-POW gets hold of a handgun and polishes off the drug ring, and then follows up with wife, child and finally himself. We practically see the bullet entering the cranium and the blood gushing out, all most graphically, after he has placed the body of the baby in a lit oven.

Pic might rack up some bucks in the blood and gore circuits, but its schlumpy protagonist and often exaggerated situations, which provoke mirth rather than involvement, will limit its acceptance even in sectors seeking blood curdling explicitness. —Besa.

Pobre Mariposa
(Poor Butterfly)
(ARGENTINE-COLOR)

An Instituto Nacional de Cinematografía presentation. Executive producer, Kiko Tenembaum. Produced by Ben Silberstein. Directed by Raúl de la Torre. Screenplay, Aida Bortnik and De la Torre. Camera (color), Marcelo Camorino; art director, Jorge Sarudiansky; editor, Carlos Macías; costumes, Tita Tamanes, Rosa Zamborain. Reviewed at the Cannes Film Festival (Official Competition), May 9, 1986. Running time: **118 MINS.**
Clara . . . . Graciela Borges
Julio . . . . Lautaro Murúa
Shloime . . . . Pepe Soriano
José . . . . Victor Laplace
Juana . . . . Cipe Lincovsky
Irma . . . . Ana María Piccio
Luis . . . . Cacho Fentana
Armando . . . . Augusto Bonardo
Gertrud . . . . Bibi Andersson
Pereyra . . . . F. Fernán Gomez
Bruno . . . . Duilio Marzio
Tía Amelia . . . . China Zorrilla

Cannes — "The Official Story" may prove to have been only a taste-whetter for new Argentine cinema. Raul de la Torre's new tour-de-force "Pobre Mariposa" is a memorable and distinguished film which should have art-houses audiences waiting on line.

Item has all the elements to make it a winner, especially in areas with sizable Jewish populations, dealing as it does with the survival of Nazis in Argentina in 1945, and the difficulties of a half-Jewess who is now a famous radio broadcaster. On one level, pic is effective as an actioner set against the turmoil and intrigues marking the immediate post-war period in Argentina, when Communists, Anarchists and Fascists all were vying for power.

On another level, pic scores bril-

liantly in portraying the struggles and doubts of a woman who must come to grips with her partly Jewish heritage and ancestry as well as that of the Communist background of her late father, a journalist who had been actively combatting the Fascists and has obtained a list giving the names and contacts of the top Nazi exiles.

Buoying the film are memorable performances, especially by Graciela Borges, who tops even that of Norma Aleandro, and a topnotch supporting cast, among them Argentina's most talented thesps. Despite its two-hour running time, item has only a few sagging interludes in the second half.

Even before the credits come on, film sets the mood and pace by chronicling the tumult in Buenos Aires on the day Berlin falls to the Allies at the end of World War II. De la Torre intercuts the plottings of the Nazis — who vow continued allegiance to the Third Reich and land war criminals and agitators in U-boats on the beach — with the personal story of Clara, the wife of an aging surgeon and daughter of a Communist agitator.

Clara's introduction to the Jewish community and her brushes with left-wing radicals, especially via a former lover, jettison her out of her smug bourgeois world into the conflictive uncertainties of what eventually is to become Peronist Argentina. The only ideologically questionable point here might be the equating of Jewish and leftist causes. Occasionally, pic will belabor a point, as when Clara is shown a reel on Nazi atrocities, but the objections are minor.

Productionwise, pic has a handsome look, nicely recreating the historical period in which it is set. With top thesping, a lively story and the ever-topical subject of Nazis hunting Jews, pic is likely to be an aesthetic and commercial winner when it is released internationally. —Besa.

Eu Sei Que Vou Te Amar
(Love Me For Ever Or Never)
(BRAZILIAN-COLOR)

A Sagitário Filmes production. Produced by Arnaldo Jabor and Helio Paula Ferraz with Embrafilme. Executive producer, Angelo Gastal. Written and directed by Jabor. Camera, Lauro Escorel; editor, Mair Taveres; sets, Oscar Niemeyer, Sergio Silveira; wardrobe, Gloria Kalil; props, Maria Helena Salles. Reviewed at the Cannes Film Festival (Official Competition) May 9, 1986. Running time: **104 MINS.**
Cast: Fernanda Torres and Thales Pan Chacon.

Cannes — As in "I Love You" (1981) Arnaldo Jabor deals with two characters in an enclosed environment in "Eu Sei Que Vou Te Amar," but this time around he is

unlikely to find a broad audience in foreign markets.

Pics depicts a young couple that has split up after two years of marriage and one child. Three months after their separation they meet again. Emotionally scarred, still loving and hating each other, they talk about their past relationship. At first realistically but soon alternating with interior dialog, they try to make sense of their experience together and to exorcise the past.

Throughout all these psychological probings and confrontations there are moments of truth and others where they try to evade reality. As they delve deeper and deeper, verbalizing feelings that had up to then been locked in the subconcious, the scene might well be described as psychological sado-masochism. All the while, although not even admitting it to themselves, they still are attracted to each other.

The stylized decor and acting, with an outstanding performance from Fernanda Torres, plus Lauro Escorel's good camera work, are on the plus side. The film's extreme talkiness is liable to alienate most audiences, but its main flaw could well be that, in its analysis of love and a deteriorated relationship it has moments of insight but in the long haul, it does not have very much to say. — Amig.

Kurbagalar
(The Frogs)
(TURKISH-COLOR)

A Gulsah Film production, Istanbul. Directed by Serif Gören. Screenplay, Osman Sahin; camera (color), Erdogan Engin; music, Atilla Özdemiroglu. Reviewed at Istanbul Film Fest (Turkish series), April 19, 1986. Running time: **98 MINS.**
With: Hülya Kocyigit, Talat Buluk, Yavuser Cetinkaya, Yaman Okay, Hikmet Celik, Metin Cekmez, Cengiy Ekinci, Nesrin Cetinel.

Istanbul — The best of the Turkish films on display at the Istanbul fest, "The Frogs" has director Serif Gören, who codirected with the late Yilmaz Güney the Golden Palm winner at Cannes 1982, "Yol," busy again on sociocritical themes.

"The Frogs" is set in the swamp country along the Turkish-Greek border, where rice is planted for sustenance and frogs are captured at night for an export delicacy. A widow with a young son has lost her husband at the work camp — he was mysteriously murdered, and the true killer is never found — so she steps into his shoes in a desperate effort to earn a living during the height of the working season in this quarter of the country.

Meanwhile, a beau she first refused years ago has returned from a stretch in prison, but he is too shy to make advances to the still mourning widow. Since this is a work camp, other men have eyes for the young widow in the fields. In fact, this is one of those places where muslim traditions have given way to Western customs, so the women are rather emancipated. Pic recalls the Italian neorealist film set in the Po Valley, "Bitter Rice," also dealing with love and lust in the fields.

The only trouble with "The Frogs" is that Gören (by training, a cameraman) has jettisoned his script for images alone, even though the local censors are known to have a sharp eye out for subversive material of a political or sociopolitical nature. Perhaps he had no script at all to begin with, but preferred to shoot between the lines.

Whatever, there are some striking village scenes in the labor compound, but the docu footage appears too slick to be taken seriously. So, too, the lead personalities: one can't believe Hülya Kocyigit, as wonderful an actress as she is, taking on a man's role as required in the story.

"The Frogs" is a cameraman's pallet of images for the most part. For some reason, Gören loves shooting silhouettes against the rays of a setting sun. Quite impressive, but not what the story needs.

—*Holl.*

Killer Party
(COLOR)

Mad-killer pic is tamer than the norm.

A UA/MGM release of a Marquis Prods. presentation. Produced by Michael Lepiner. Executive producer, Kenneth Kaufman. Directed by William Fruet. Screenplay, Barney Cohen, camera (Technicolor), John Lindley. Editor, Eric Albertson; music, John Beal; production designer, Reuben Freed; assistant art director, Alicia Keywan; set decorator, Enrico Campana; costumes, Gina Keillerman; sound, Bryan Day, Michael Lecroix; coordinating producer, Majorie Kalins; associate producer, Grace Gilroy; assistant director, Gordon Robinson; casting, Peg Halligan (L.A.), Armstrong/Clydsdale (Toronto). Reviewed at MGM/UA screening room, Culver City, Calif., May 8, 1986. (MPAA Rating: R) Running time: **91 MINS.**
Blake . . . . Martin Hewitt
Martin . . . . Ralph Seymour
Phoebe . . . . Elaine Wilkes
Professor Zito . . . . Paul Bartel
Vivia . . . . Sherry Willis-Burch
Veronica . . . . Alicia Fleer
Harrison . . . . Woody Brown
Jennifer . . . . Joanna Johnson
Melanie . . . . Terri Hawkes

Hollywood — "Killer Party" is a cut above standard splatter fare in production values and casting, but sinks to the lower depths in script and execution. A pickup for UA/-MGM, pic us unlikely to generate much heat in regional playoff.

April Fool's Day seems to be becoming as much of an excuse for nefarious doings among teenagers as Halloween these days. "Killer Party" uses the holiday as a setting for springtime bloodletting, although much of the gore is thankfully implied rather than witnessed.

Action revolves around the initiation of three pledges into the fun-loving Sigma Alpha Pi sorority at an unindentified eastern college. The sadistic sisters, known fittingly as goats, put the three lovelies through trial by fire, but then some weird things start happening for real at the old campus haunted house where else?

What exactly is going on is anybody's guess; something to do with a murdered student whose spirit has come back for revenge and possessed young Jennifer's body.

Script by Barney Cohen is full of strange characters even without the supernatural happenings. There are also a number of non sequiturs such as two bizarre opening sequences, one a funeral, the other a mock rock video, that serve as prologs except they don't have anything to do with the rest of the film.

Direction by William Fruet is strongest when he goes for the camp humor, but fails to generate very much suspense of involvement, even for the film's overlong finale at the scene of the crime.

On the camp side, bit part by Paul Bartel as a literature professor who is gruesomely murdered (not by his students), is the tongue-in-cheek highlight of the pic.

Rest of the cast is attractive but with hardly a character among them, Joanna Johnson, a young Cybill Shepherd look alike, is appealing as the most reticent of the girlfriends. Elaine Wilkes and Sherry Willis-Burch also are likable as the sidekicks, and together the three almost hold the film together.

As for the men, Martin Hewitt receives top billing for a smallish part, probably due to his previous work in "Endless Love" and others. He suffers through like the others. As the resident crazy, Ralph Seymour has a few good moments when he isn't bludgeoning his part to death.

Tech credits are fine . — *Jagr.*

Poltergeist II
(COLOR)

They're back and scary enough for success.

A UA/MGM Distribution release from MGM Entertainment. A Freddie Fields presentation of a Victor-Grais production. Written, produced by Mark Victor, Michael Grais. Executive producer, Fields. Directed by Brian Gibson. Camera (Panavision, Metrocolor), Andrew Laszlo; editor, Thom Noble; music, Jerry Goldsmith; production design, Ted Haworth; set design, Roy Barnes, Greg Papalia; sound, Al Overton; visual effects supervisor, Richard Edlund; conceptual art, H.R. Giger; associate producer, Lynn Arost; first assistant director, William S. Beasley; casting, Joseph D'Agosta. Reviewed at Samuel Goldwyn theater, Beverly Hills, Calif., May 16, 1986. (MPAA Rating: PG-13.) Running time: **90 MINS.**
Diane Freeling . . . . JoBeth Williams
Steve Freeling . . . . Craig T. Nelson
Carol Anne Freeling . . . Heather O'Rourke
Robbie Freeling . . . . Oliver Robins
Tangina Barrons . . . . Zelda Rubinstein
Taylor . . . . Will Sampson
Kane . . . . Julian Beck
Gramma Jess . . . . Geraldine Fitzgerald
Old Indian . . . . John P. Whitecloud

Hollywood — It's another horrifying house party at the Freelings' in "Poltergeist II" and that's all that counts for fans of the first pic to want a second invitation. MGM accountants can expect to smile at boxoffice receipts.

Sequel finds the poor Freeling family a year later mooching off Gramma Jess (Geraldine Fitzgerald) as they now are penniless and slightly crazed after their Cuesta Verde tract house was obliterated by poltergeists and the insurance company is having a hard time swallowing the claim.

When Gramma dies, little Carol Anne's play telephone spontaneously rings with a call from "the other side," and that's all the warning there is before the thumping, shaking and hysteria begin all over again.

This time around, coscripters Mark Victor and Michael Grais (who wrote the first "Poltergeist" with Steven Spielberg) have the focus of evil in human form, in the perfectly cast, since deceased, Julian Beck.

Story gets a little bogged down explaining Kane as a charlatan frontier parson who was buried in the graveyard under the Freelings' Cuesta Verde house, but never really died and instead remains in hell's limbo.

Representing the good side, sent as spiritual leader at the advice of "Poltergeist" psychic Tangina Barrons (the squeaky-voiced Zelda Rubinstein with only a minor role) is a stoic, towering Native American called Taylor (Will Sampson).

Taylor arrives on the Freelings' doorstep unannounced and engages in hilariously cryptic conversations with Steve Freeling (Craig T. Nelson) on how to deal with the family curse.

Unlike the first film that focused all the action around the innocent blond and persecuted Carol Anne (Heather O'Rourke), juiciest moments in "II" revolve around Nelson playing a soppy drunk, a lustful husband (again to the warm JoBeth Williams), a loving father and a ghoulie-spewing monster. Ultimately, the macho man learns the hard way that only the power of love is strong enough to send Beck into the underworld forever.

Script has enough humorous breaks and high-wire moments to make up for some of the overly expository sections in the dialog.

While the payoff is a bit weak and less tension-filled than would be expected considering what the Freeling family has just endured, tech credits from beginning to end look like they cost a mint and filmmakers probably figured they had to stop somewhere.

Four-time Academy Award-winner Richard Edlund and his team of special effects magicians at Boss Film Co. are to be commended as well as are other Academy winners Ted Haworth for production design and H.R. Giger for conceptual art.

Jerry Goldsmith is also back for another haunting score to warn when things are about to get scary, and they always do.—*Brit.*

No Retreat No Surrender
(COLOR)

Amateur-night action film.

A New World Pictures release of a Seasonal Films/Balcor Film Investors/New World presentation of a Ng See Yuen production. Produced by Ng See Yuen. Directed by Corey Yuen. Screenplay, Keith W. Strandberg, based on an original story by Yuen; camera (Technicolor), John Huneck, David Golia; editor, Alan Poon, Mark Pierce, James Melkonian, Dane Davis; music, Paul Gilreath; sound, Jim Murphy; martial arts choreographer, Harrison Mang; assistant director, Tony Lee; casting, Paul Maslak, Jean Ferguson, Thaddeus Hejker. Reviewed at the Hollywood Pacific, L.A., May 2, 1986. (MPAA Rating: PG.) Running time: **83 MINS.**
Jason Stillwell . . . . Kurt McKinney
Ivan, Russian . . . Jean-Claude Van Damme
R.J. Madison . . . . J.W. Fails
Kelly Reilly . . . . Kathie Sileno
Sensei Lee . . . . Kim Tai Chong
Scott . . . . Kent Lipham
Ian Reilly . . . . Ron Pohnel
Dean . . . . Dale Jacoby
Frank . . . . Pete Cunningham
Tom Stillwell . . . . Tim Baker
Mrs. Stillwell . . . . Gloria Marziano
New York Agent . . . . Joe Vance

Hollywood — It's easy to imagine the producer's pitch for "No Retreat No Surrender": "It's a cross between 'The Karate Kid' and 'Rocky IV,' and we'll make it so cheap that you can't possibly lose any money." Result is marginally entertaining for the least discriminating audiences on a crude good guys vs. bad guys level, but this is basically an amateur night production. Okay quick biz should be found in target action markets.

"The Karate Kid" angle figures here first. Karate student Kurt McKinney is treated like a wimp by local toughs upon moving to Seattle, so he decides to toughen himself up and receives some help from a martial arts expert who is a spiritual standin for Bruce Lee.

Much frustration is accumulated during the initial hour, since McKinney's dad doesn't believe in fighting, and both he and his son suffer repeated humiliation at the hands of an assortment of goons, most of whom are grossly fat.

"Rocky IV" enters in at the climax, where three of Seattle's best are pitted against an impossibly handsome, muscular karate star from guess where. Ivan the terrible dispatches his opponents like cupcakes, but he hasn't figured on the newly acquired skills of McKinney, who furiously jumps into the ring to teach the Russkie a lesson, even though the fighter is twice his size.

Pic, made by the U.S. subsidiary of Hong Kong's Seasonal Films banner, is set in Seattle for the presumed reason that it allows for a pilgrimage to Bruce Lee's grave. Tech credits are skimpy — no art director is credited, and it shows — and it would appear nonactors have been employed throughout. Jean-Claude Van Damme is undeniably impressive as the villain. —*Cart.*

Dangerously Close
(COLOR)

Well-intentioned suspenser degenerates, sadly.

A Cannon release of a Golan-Globus production. Produced by Harold Sobel. Executive producers, Menahem Golan, Yoram Globus. Directed by Albert Pyun. Screenplay, Scott Fields, John Stockwell, Marty Ross, based on a story by Ross; camera (TVC color), Walt Lloyd; editor, Dennis O'Connor; music, Michael McCarty; production design, Marcia Hinds; art direction, Bo Johnson; set decoration, Piers Plowden; sound (Dolby), Ed Novick; associate producers, Susan Hoffman, Karen Koch; assistant director, Bradley Gross; second unit camera, Charles Minsky; casting, Robert McDonald, Perry Bullington. Reviewed at the Cannon screening room, L.A., May 5, 1986. (MPAA Rating: R.) Running time: **95 MINS.**
Randy McDevitt . . . . John Stockwell
Donny Lennox . . . . J. Eddie Peck
Julie . . . . Carey Lowell
Krooger Raines . . . . Bradford Bancroft
Ripper . . . . Don Michael Paul
Brian Rigletti . . . . Thom Mathews
Lang Bridges . . . . Jerry Dinome
Corrigan . . . . Madison Mason
Smith Raddock . . . . Anthony DeLongis
Matty . . . . Carmen Argenziano
Leon Biggs . . . . Miguel Nunez
Nikki . . . . Dedee Pfeiffer
Betsy . . . . Karen Witter
Morelli . . . . Greg Finley
Ms. Hoffman . . . . Debra Berger
Ms. Waters . . . . Angel Tompkins

Hollywood — "Dangerously Close" comes surprisingly close to being quite a good film. For its first two-thirds an engrossingly tense suspenser about teen vigilantes run amok, pic becomes distressingly conventional in its final act, its unusual qualities virtually dissolving before one's eyes. But even as it stands, third directorial effort by Albert Pyun shows plenty of talent and is distinguished by its lively style and notable serious-mindedness. Cannon release falls somewhat between b.o. stools, but can be pitched to mainstream urban audiences while still developing a certain cult reputation.

Drama does not announce its intentions at the outset, but gradually reveals itself as a devastating attack on the fascistic potential among Reagan-era yuppies. A student security enforcement group known as The Sentinels runs the show at an isolated, affluent high school. Populated exclusively by WASPy future leaders of America types who live in mansions and drive Corvettes, outfit ostensibly was organized to check theft, squash graffiti writing on walls and the like, but, due to the members' arrogance, it now has begun to go "too far."

"Too far" means the adoption of Nazi and KKK-type tactics, including beating up, nearly lynching and finally killing those who rebel against them or don't fall in line with their imperious ways.

Impressively, Pyun and writers Scott Fields, John Stockwell (who also stars) and Marty Ross manage to raise this considerably above the level of a mere social tract by making recognizable and sufficiently fleshed out characters out of these kids. Dialog through the first two-thirds proves both believable and efficient.

At the same time, Pyun keeps the action moving and the tension high as the baddies dig themselves ever deeper into their cesspool of rationalized cruelty, dragging others with them as they go. Shots and editing style are fancy, occasionally self-consciously so, but director clearly knows what he's doing and impresses with his confidence.

Almost from one minute to the next, however, pic goes utterly flat. J. Eddie Peck, the good-looking, relatively poor editor of the school paper who stands uncomfortably in the middle between The Sentinels and their victims, finally teams up with the group leader's ex-girlfriend to expose the crimes.

The viewer is so far ahead of the girl, Julie, that one becomes exasperated with how long it takes her to catch on to what's been happening. This slow awakening is coupled with very routine search, chase and fisticuffs sequences, which are laughably concluded by the left-field disclosure that a Vietnam vet was behind all the mayhem.

Resolution leaves a sour taste and the impression that perhaps the buildup wasn't as good as it seemed at the time. Nevertheless, the serious intent, solid performances and nice directorial touches put it well above most other teenpics of the era.

Stockwell, Don Michael Paul, Thom Mathews and Jerry Dinome make a disturbingly convincing bunch of spoiled brats on the rampage. Peck and Carey Lowell, who plays Julie, are very appealing despite the degeneration of their roles toward the end, and Bradford Bancroft excels as the raffish school punk who is unafraid of the budding fascists.

Lensed under the title "Choice Kill," pic shows pleasurable evidence of close attention to detail in such matters as fresh locations, a very attractive cast (all students look like future Vogue or G.Q. cover models) and sensitive lensing (numerous scenes have been caught very effectively in late afternoon light).—*Cart.*

★★★★★★★★★★★★★★★★★★★★★★★★★
★ ★
★ # Cannes: Non-Competing ★
★ ★
★★★★★★★★★★★★★★★★★★★★★★★★★

Short Changed
(AUSTRALIAN-COLOR)

A Greater Union (Australia) release of a New South Wales Film Corp. presentation of a Magpie Films production. Produced by Ross Matthews. Directed by George Ogilvie. Screenplay, Robert J. Merritt, based on a screenplay by Ken Quinnell, Merritt; camera (Eastmancolor), Peter Levy; editor, Richard Francis-Bruce; music, Chris Neal; production design, Kristian Fredrikson; associate producer/production manager, Barbara Gibbs; assistant director, Steve Andrews; sound, Peter Barker; casting, Liz Mullinar. Reviewed at the Cannes Film Festival (market), May 16, 1986. Running time: **104 MINS.**
Stuart Wilkins . . . . David Kennedy
Alison Wilkins . . . . Susan Leith
Tommy Wilkins . . . . Jamie Agius
Marshall . . . . Ray Meagher
Curly . . . . Mark Little
Also with: Ronald Merritt (Uncle), Rhys McConnichie (Headmaster), Ron Haddrick (Garrick), "Lucky" Wikramanayake (Gopowalla), Alan McQueen (Cummings), Daphne Grey (Judge), Denis MacKay (Edwards), Lyndel Rowe (Counsellor), James Robertson (Brian), Michael Gow (Sinclair).

Cannes — "Short Changed" has been completed for at least six months, but held tightly under wraps by the N.S.W. Film Corp., allowing rumors to circulate that it was a dud. It isn't. Legit director George Ogilvie's first solo feature (after codirecting "Mad Max Beyond Thunderdome" with George Miller) is a somber urban drama about a custody case between an aboriginal man and his white ex-wife over their 10-year old son. It's a serious, absorbing, human pic.

It begins as the marriage between Stuart (David Kennedy) and Alison (Susan Leith) is on the rocks, though she still loves him. But, as a Catholic girl from a well to-do family, she finds the pressures of living in an inner city aboriginal ghetto too hard to take. When Stuart is arrested after his father's funeral (the father died in prison), and later goes "walkabout," she ankles and gets a divorce.

Seven years later, Stuart returns to see his son, who attends a Catholic boarding school and can't remember his father. A custody case ensues in which the wealth and power of Alison's ruthless father (Ray Meagher) are pitted against the dogged persistence of the impoverished Stuart.

Within this dramatic structure, the film has more to say about contemporary aboriginal city life and casual, everyday racism, than any Australian film has attempted heretofore. It compares interestingly with Bruce Beresford's "The Fringe Dwellers," which by and large avoids the unpleasant details. This pic tackles them head on.

Early on there's a telling scene in which Stuart, searching for his son (nicely played by young Jamie Agius), comes across a couple of youngsters playing in the street, who reveal chillingly their built-in prejudices not only against aboriginals ("My Dad says blacks are useless") but also against Catholics. Ironic, too, that the only barrister who'll help Stuart in court is a friendly Sri Lankan (a great cameo from "Lucky" Wikramanayake).

The cycle of unemployment leading to boredom, alcoholism and violence is indeed a tragic one, as are the scenes in which Stuart, looking for an apartment when the court gives him temporary access to his son, is continually rebuffed purely on the grounds of his color. "Short Changed" is not a pretty picture, but it's a sincere and one.

Pics centering on aboriginal characters, including Fred Schepisi's trail-blazing "The Chant Of Jimmie Blacksmith," haven't fared well at the local boxoffice, and Greater Union will have to handle "Short Changed" with great finesse to find an audience. Keeping it hidden, as it has been till now, is not the answer. The arthouse route is the way to go.

Technically, pic is okay, with grainy, low-key camerawork by Petèr Levy and somber music by Chris Neal. Richard Francis-Bruce could have edited a bit more tightly. Ogilvie now is in post-production on his second solo feature, "The Bee Eater."—*Strat*.

Sid And Nancy
(BRITISH-COLOR)

An Embassy Home Entertainment presentation of a Zenith production in association with Initial Pictures. Produced by Eric Fellner. Coproduced by Peter McCarthy. Directed by Alex Cox. Screenplay, Cox, Abbe Wool; camera (color), Roger Deakins; editor, David Martin; music, The Pogues, Pray For Rain; sound, Peter Glossop; production design, Andrew McAlpine; casting, Vicki Thomas. Reviewed at the Cannes Film Festival (Directors Fortnight), May 14, 1986. Running time: **111 MINS.**
Sid Vicious . . . . Gary Oldman
Nancy Spungen . . . . Chloe Webb
Malcolm . . . . David Hayman

Cannes — "Sid And Nancy," a sensational new film by Alex Cox ("Repo Man"), is the definitive pic on the punk phenomenon. The sad, sordid story of Sid Vicious, a lead member of the British punk group The Sex Pistols, and his relationship with his American girlfriend, Nancy Spungen, is presented by Cox without flinching. It's a pic for young audiences and not just for punks, but for anyone interested in how these apostles of all that was ugly (musically as well as visually) behaved. Authenticity is the film's major asset.

Cox doesn't attempt to show the background; we don't know *why* a working class English youth became the unsightly, some would say untalented, Sid Vicious. Film opens in New York with the discovery of Nancy's body in a bathroom at the Chelsea hotel and a stunned Vicious, knife in hand, in the bedroom. Flashbacks flesh in their relationship.

It's a world of drugs and booze, with sex lagging behind in interest for the most part. When Sid and Nancy meet, she's much more interested in sex than he is: but for a while they get it together until the drugs and the liquor bring with them a deadening lethargy. The film recreates some concerts given by Vicious, including his memorably bad rendition of "My Way," and the aimless life-style of the couple.

But grim as much of the film is, it's not without humor. Nancy takes Sid home to meet her folks for Thanksgiving, and granddad asks him: "When are you going to make an honest woman of our Nancy?"

With his unwashed hair sticking out at all angles, his pale face and brash British accent, Gary Oldman fits the part like a glove. Chloe Webb doesn't spare her looks as the ravaged, shrill Nancy. Both actors are beyond praise.

As would be expected, the film's

dialog is extremely rough, the settings sordid, the theme of wasted lives (and talent?) depressing. But "Sid And Nancy" is a dynamic piece of work, which brings audiences as close as possible to understanding its wayward heroes.

It should open strongly, and certainly will attract youth audiences around the world. Technically the production is impeccable. —*Strat*.

Invaders From Mars
(U.S.-COLOR)

A Cannon Films release of a Golan-Globus production. Produced by Menahem Golan, Yoram Globus. Directed by Tobe Hooper. Screenplay, Dan O'Bannon, Don Jakoby, based on the 1953 motion picture written by Richard Blake; camera (J-D-C Widescreen, TVC color), Daniel Pearl; editor, Alain Jakubowicz; music, Christopher Young; sound (Dolby), Russell Williams 2d; production design, Leslie Dilley; art direction, Craig Stearns; special visual effects, John Dykstra, Apogee Inc.; invader creatures design, Stan Winston; costume design, Carin Hooper; second unit director, Dykstra; additional editing, Daniel Lowenthal; additional synthesizer music, David Storrs; postproduction coordinator, Michael R. Sloan; casting, Robert MacDonald, Perry Bullington; associate producers, Edward L. Alperson Jr., Wade H. Williams 3d. Reviewed at the Cannes Film Festival (market), May 16, 1986. (MPAA Rating: PG) Running time: **100 MINS.**
Linda . . . . Karen Black
David Gardner . . . . Hunter Carson
George Gardner . . . . Timothy Bottoms
Ellen Gardner . . . . Laraine Newman
Gen. Wilson . . . . James Karen
Mrs. McKeltch . . . . Louise Fletcher
Mark Weinstein . . . . Bud Cort
Police Chief . . . . Jimmy Hunt

Cannes — Tobe Hooper's remake of "Invaders From Mars" is an embarrassing combination of kitsch and boredom. Except for some interesting scenes with some monsters created by Stan Winston, picture marks two wipeouts in a row (after "Lifeforce") for Hooper and his ongoing employer, Cannon Films.

Unlike many remakes, the idea of redoing William Cameron Menzies' 1953 3-D classic was a reasonable one, in that the original has not been seen by most filmgoers but is a familiar milestone title. Unfortunately, Dan O'Bannon and Don Jakoby's inferior screenplay fails to

Original 1953 Version
(COLOR-3-D)

20th Fox release of Edward L. Alperson production. Features Helena Carter, Arthur Franz, Jimmy Hunt. Directed by William Cameron Menzies. Screenplay, Richard Blake; camera (Cinecolor, 3-D), John Seitz; editor, Arthur Roberts; music Raoul Kraushaar. Tradeshown, N.Y., April 6, 1953 Running time: **73 MINS.**
Dr. Pat Blake . . . . Helena Carter
Dr. Stuart Kelston . . . . Arthur Franz
David MacLean . . . . Jimmy Hunt
George MacLean . . . . Leif Erickson
Mary MacLean . . . . Hillary Brooke
Colonel Fielding . . . . Morris Ankrum
Sgt. Rinaldi . . . . Max Wagner

Kathy Wilson . . . . Janine Perreau

bring in new ideas or provide interesting dialog. The story elements here have been done to death in the interim.

First 45 minutes are interminably dull, as story slavishly covers familiar ground at a lugubrious pace. Little David Gardner (Hunter Carson) sees a spaceship land one night in the sandpits at the end of his backyard and soon after, his father George (Timothy Bottoms), biology teacher Mrs. McKeltch (Louise Fletcher) and even the police chief who investigates (Jimmy Hunt, who as a child played the lead role in the 1953 original) begin behaving unemotionally and out of normal character, each with a telltale fresh scar on the back of their neck. David sees his father take mom (Laraine Newman) out to the sandpits and next day she is scarred and zombie-like as well.

David finally gets his school nurse Linda (Karen Black) to believe his tall tale and they whip into action to stop the invasion and spread of controlled people. Film finally comes alive when David wanders into Martian subterranean tunnels and finds nightmarish, ostrich-type toothy mosters controlled by a brain-design Martian supreme intelligence creature.

The two believers get a marine general (James Karen) to verify their story and he brings the military's forces to bear, cueing several battles and the same (now toothless) trick ending used in the original. Black humor accompanies many scènes eliciting mainly groans.

Though played straight, film's emphasis upon cliches and predictable events makes it seem like a spoof. Not helping is some subpar acting. Bottoms as the first victim performs like a zombie both before and after, while, in a major inconsistency, Fletcher is allowed to be flamboyantly mean and hyper, unlike all the other humans that have been taken over. She's occasionally quite scary, but it's cheating and destroys the plot's credibility.

Trick casting of Black, who's Carson's real-life mother, not as his fictional mom but rather his only friend doesn't pay off. Their teaming doesn't generate the expected empathy and both overact. As his screen mom, Newman is far more sympathetic and even gets to do her "Saturday Night Live" tv show Conehead voice as a gag in the final reel.

Best acting is by James Karen as the sterotyped gung-ho marine. As the genre's corny "we must try to communicate with them" naive scientist, Bud Cort has one funny scene.

Technical honors to designer Leslie Dilley, whose subterranean

sets are quite arresting. Winston's monsters and some grisly scenes (such as the method of implanting people in the back of their necks) will probably succeed in generating nightmares for young viewers. Christopher Young's musical score merely amplifies the duller scenes sounding like a drone way in the background. — *Lor*.

Koneko Monogatari
(The Adventures Of Chatran)
(JAPANESE-COLOR)

A Toho release of a Fuji Television Network production. Produced by Masaru Kakutani, Satoru Ogata. Written and directed by Masanori Hata. Associate director, Kon Ichikawa. Camera (color), Hideo Fujii, Shinji Tomita; editor, Chizuko Osada; music, Ryuichi Sakamoto; sound, Minoru Nobuoka, Tetsuya Ohashi; production supervisor, Hisashi Hieda. Reviewed at the Cannes Film Festival (market), May 12, 1986. Running time: **90 MINS.**

Cannes — This extraordinary film may at first blush turn off non-animal fanciers since it's about the adventures of an over-inquisitive, ginger-colored feline who strays from a farm located on the northern Japanese island of Hokkaido. But be advised: "The Adventures Of Chatran" is a stunning achievement, and easily ranks among the genuine sleepers of the 1986 Cannes Festival.

The film is about the title character, a male cat, and the animals and reptiles —- dogs, bears, deer, pigs, snakes, cows, birds — he encounters during extended and risky forays into the Hokkaido countryside, far from the security of the farm. There is not a single human being in the picture.

What places "Chatran" far above the standard National Geographic-type special is the artistry of the pic's director, Masanori Hata, who worked closely with renowned Japanese director, Kon Ichikawa. They whittled down some 400,000 feet of footage originally shot into a crisp, 90-minute narrative with a defined structure that puts "Chatran" somewhere between a docu and drama.

The pic tracks the title character's journeys covering a period of several years. The trips coincide with seasonal changes. Chatran begins his encounters as a tiny kitten and winds the pic as fully grown with a mate and family of his own (five cats of various ages were used to accomplish this maturation).

Of incomparable — even essential — help here is Ryuichi Sakamoto's score and Shuntaro Tanigawa's poetry, which frames each section of the cat's journeys.

Sakamoto, a former member of the Yellow Magic Orchestra and sometimes referred to (not quite accurately; he's more talented) as Japan's David Bowie, has come up with strongly evocative interpolations of a basic melodic base that once heard is hard to forget. Sakamoto, of course, wrote the superb score for Nagisa Oshima's "Merry Christmas, Mr. Lawrence," and costarred in the pic with Bowie.

Director Hata, who also wrote the pic's spare narration (separate from Tanigawa's poems), is a zoologist and novelist, who writes under the pen name of Mutsugoro. He also runs a private animal farm on Hokkaido, an all-important factor in the production of "Chatran."

Hata, as the pic makes obvious, has an unusually strong rapport with animals. He places his charges in situations required by the pic's general structure, and then captures the unpredictable results in eye-popping ways. The cat's survival of a drop over a huge waterfall is one of several scenes that will have audiences applauding.

He treats the animals anthropomorphically — that is, he puts them in situations and shows them acting much like humans. This, however, is done while maintaining a sense of dignity, even reverence, for his charges.

Production values are topnotch especially Hideo Fujii and Shinji Tomita's photography, Chizuko Osada's editing (undoubtedly under Ichikawa's supervision) and Minoru Nobuoka and Tetsuya Ohashi's sound mix. Pic, lensed over a five-year period, is a production of Fuji Television Network, a leading commercial web in Japan, and is being sold abroad by Fuji's Masaru Kakutani working in conjunction with Toho Intl.

Given the subject matter, minimal dialog and overall excellence, "The Adventures Of Chatran" should do well in foreign release. In Japan, Toho is already predicting the pic will break "E.T.'s" record as the market's all-time top b.o. winner.

Fuji is heavily promoting the pic on its network, and will continue the flogging until "Chatran's" Japan bow on July 12, at 200 theaters.

The pic more than deserves every good thing it gets. —*Sege.*

Spookies
(U.S. COLOR)

A Twisted Souls production. World sales, Safir Films. Produced by Eugenie Joseph, Thomas Doran, Brendan Faulkner, Frank M. Farel. Directed by Joseph, Doran, Faulkner. Screenplay, Farel, Doran, Faulkner; additional material, Joseph Burgund; camera (Precision color), Robert Chappell, Ken Kelsch; editor, Joseph; music, Kenneth Higgins, James Calabrese; production manager, C.W. Cressler, Farel; special makeup effects, Arnold Gargiulo 2d, Vincent Guastini; Gabriel Bartalos, Jennifer Aspinal; additional effects, John Dods; special effects camera, Larry Revene, Al Magliochetti; assistant director, Michael

Blundell, Sarah Rivers; stunt coordinator, Tony Guida, David Farkas. Reviewed at the Cannes Film Festival (market) May 14, 1986. (No MPAA Rating.) Running time: **84 MINS.**

Kreon	Felix Ward
Kreon's servant	Dan Scott
Billy	Alec Nemser
Isabelle	Maria Pechukas

Cannes — "Spookies" is a silly horror picture which contains some interesting special makeup effects along with very amateurish ones, presented in the usual package of a group of hapless travelers murdered one by one. It's of interest to undiscriminating horror fans.

Felix Ward, wearing some pretty phony old age makeup, toplines as Kreon, a sorcerer who is bringing back to life his bride (lovely Maria Pechukas), who committed suicide 70 years ago. He needs human sacrifices and fortunately (for him), two carloads of people lost en route to a party stop in at Kreon's mansion that night. Earlier that evening, a young boy named Billy (Alec Nemser) wandered into the mansion, found a grisly birthday party being held there for him and is scared off by Kreon's servant (Dan Scott) and other monsters.

The nine partygoers with no party play with a vintage ouija board and make dumb jokes but one of them, Carol, is suddenly turned into a monster Linda Blair-lookalike from "The Exorcist" by Kreon and all hell breaks loose. Disjointed film never explains why the survivors don't just jump into their cars and head on home. Instead, in time-honored, stupid horror film tradition, they split up in ones and twos and search the mansion repeatedly, making for easy victimization.

Film's novelty is that the entire cast is wiped out (no last-minute rescue) and the final reel even has Pechukas, whose reanimation was after all the purpose of all the killing, running around for dear life as a neighborhood full of ghouls shamble around and paw at her.

Rule of thumb here is that when makeup is applied to a person's face it's strictly amateur night, while several of the from the ground up (no pun intended) monster creations are well done. Among these goodies are a huge spider transformed from an oriental lady, a grim reaper skeleton with illuminated red eyes, a gill man who probably saw Ridley Scott's "Alien" and several green lizard monsters. Low point is when some imitation clay people (out of "Flash Gordon" but poorly designed) terrorize a busty babe and her boyfriend in the basement, while postproduction amplified sounds of flatulence lamely attempt to make the scene humorous.

Three directors are credited for "Spookies:" Brendan Faulkner and Thomas Doran teamed up to shoot the bulk of the N.Y.-lensed picture,

originally titled "Twisted Souls," while editor Eugenie Joseph contemplated the film after there was squabbling with the British-based financial backer. — *Lor.*

Competing At Cannes

The Mission
(BRITISH-COLOR)

A Warner Bros. release (U.S.) of a Goldcrest Films and Television and Kingsmere Prods. presentation of an Enigma production in association with Fernando Ghia. Produced by Fernando Ghia and David Puttnam. Directed by Roland Joffé. Stars Robert De Niro, Jeremy Irons. Screenplay, Robert Bolt; camera (J-D-C Widescreen, Rank color), Chris Menges; editor, Jim Clark; music, Ennio Morricone; production design, Norma Dorme, Francesco Bronzi, George Richardson, John King; costume designer, Enrico Sabbatini; special effects supervisor, Peter Hutchinson; assistant director, Bill Westley; associate producer, Ian Smith; production coordinator, Judi Bunn; production supervisor, Barrie Melrose; location managers, Phil Kohlar, David Nicholls, Pamela Wells; casting, Juliet Taylor, Susie Figgis. Reviewed at the Cannes Film Festival (Official Competition) May 16, 1986. (No MPAA Rating.) Running time: **128 MINS.**

Mendoza	Robert De Niro
Gabriel	Jeremy Irons
Altamirano	Ray McAnally
Fielding	Liam Neeson
Felipe	Aidan Quinn
Hontar	Ronald Pickup
Cabeza	Charles Low
Ibaye	Monirak Sisowath
Indian Chief	Asuncion Ontiveros
Carlotta	Cherie Lunghi
Sebastian	Daniel Berrigan
Father Provincial	Tony Lawn
Spanish Commander	Rafael Camerano
Carlotta's maid	Maria Teresa Ripoll
Nobleman	Enrique Llamas
Nobleman	Antonio Segovia
Secretary	Harlan Venner
Priest	Alberto Borja
Priest	Jacques des Grottes

Cannes — Spectacular scenery and an extraordinarily high degree of production values can't conceal serious flaws in "The Mission," making the $23,000,000 Goldcrest pic a questionable prospect for longterm b.o. success in the U.S. Film won the Golden Palm in competition at Cannes.

Limited initial bookings — which Warners is arranging for its Oct. 31, preem — tagged to promotion of the film as a prestige-laden item with Robert De Niro might well yield solid wicket action at the outset. After that, all bets are off.

The elements here seem surefire, on paper. The director is Roland Joffé whose initial feature, "The Killing Fields," demonstrated an incomparable gift for handling giant-scale physical production without compromising character development and story line. The script by Robert Bolt is based on a little-known but nonetheless intriguing historical incident in mid-18th-century South America pitting avaricious colonialists against the Jesuit

order of priests.

Then there's the picture's coproducer, David Puttnam. An energetic, voluble defender of quality British cinema, he has shown an uncanny knack of linking culture (he's about to teach a seminar at Harvard) to commerce. The fillip is the presence in the leads of De Niro and Jeremy Irons, a nifty combo of British classicism with American box-office appeal.

But, it doesn't come together cohesively. The fundamental problem is that the script is cardboard thin, pinning labels on its characters and arbitrarily shoving them into various stances to make plot points.

Worse yet, key events are either telegraphed in advance or over-explained, thus virtually eliminating suspense. On top of that, the pic's ending is a glumly demoralizing muddle which the filmmakers apparently interpret as "life-may-be-God-awful-but-we-must-have-hope" uplift.

The two principal actors work hard to animate their parts. But there is little to do. "The Mission" is probably the first film in which De Niro gives a bland, uninteresting performance.

The pic is set in 1750. Portugal and Spain are haggling over territorial boundaries along the river of Paraná at Iguazú, which today cover the borders of Brazil, Paraguay and Argentina. Sitting in a rain forest literally above the squabbling is a Jesuit mission established by Father Gabriel (Irons) as a refuge for native Indians. The mission is a sanctuary where the Indians are treated with respect, and kindness; they own the small parcels of land they farm.

At issue between the colonialists are essentially two things: maintenance of a thriving (and, for Spain, illegal) slave trade, and reduction of the power of the Jesuits. Spain would like Portugal to take over mission lands so that it can continue its illicit slave trading unimpeded.

While these points take some explaining — perhaps even the showing of a map or two, which "The Mission" doesn't do — they don't require the over-explication that goes on in this film. Even then, ironically, fine points of the arguments are not made fully clear.

De Niro is cast as a slave trader, who invades what is to become mission territory to ensnare Indians for the Spanish traders. His performance in this capacity seems stiffly perfunctory at odds with the passionate conversion he is about to undertake — he joins the Jesuits — after he murders his brother (Aidan Quinn in an extremely brief appearance) for stealing his fiancée.

Curiously, De Niro's part following the conversion becomes strictly secondary to that of Irons. In all, the American actor finds himself in his first glorified supporting (as opposed to cameo parts) role, since he became a marquee name.

As is often the case in underwritten costumers where the principals are stuck in thin parts, the juicier performances come in "The Mission" from the supporting players. Ray McAnally is fine as the papal emissary sent in to decide whether or not the Jesuits should pull out of their mission.

McAnally has great fun as the all-too-sophisticated Cardinal who pulls the rug from under the missionaries to preserve significant Jesuit presence in Europe. He gets to deliver the pic's narration which frames the film in the form of a report to the Pope — and to deliver some of Bolt's sharpest lines.

Charles Low is crisply forceful as a hypocritical Spanish slave trader. In one of the strangest pic cameos this year, maverick Jesuit Daniel Berrigan shows up in an non-speaking part as one of the missionaries. He looks convincing.

Irons turns in a solid, technically accomplished performance as the mission founder who combines strength, purpose and a canniness at deflecting nonsense from others. That the part is tiresomely benign is not the actor's fault.

Director Joffé has come up with some stunning scenes. He and his crew use the impressive Iguazú waterfall, the Cataratas del Iguazú, to supreme advantage. Footage before the opening credits, showing a martyred missionary strapped to a cross sent down over the falls, is truly eye-popping. Another scene showing the jaded Cardinal visiting the mission for the first time is skillfully and memorably handled.

On the downside, Joffé botches the climactic battle scene when the colonialists take over the mission. An absurd touch is the demise of De Niro's character in a manner qualifying for grand opera.

Overall, however, "The Mission" crew under Joffé has turned in an exemplary job under extremely difficult circumstances. As anyone who followed the making of Werner Herzog's "Fitzcarraldo" can testify, shooting in South America can be grueling. "The Mission" was lensed over a 16-week period largely in Colombia and (for three weeks) at the falls touching Argentina, Paraguay and Brazil.

Besides the expected hazards of shooting in the South American jungles, the production had to cope with "anarchy" (Puttnam's word) among Colombians on the location assigned to work with the crew.

Despite the snafus, pressure — chief among them were the production's hassles with a Goldcrest on the verge of financial collapse — illnesses (director Joffé was felled for a spell), rains, floods, snakes, etc., "The Mission" crew came back with a physically impressive picture. Too bad it didn't more skillfully tell its story.

At the pic's two Cannes screenings, efforts of the crew were implicitly thanked via an extended credit crawl listing those involved right down to the caterers. The crawl was followed by a trick ending showing McAnally as the Cardinal staring playfully, enigmatically at the audience. Since "The Mission" is still in post-production, both the crawl and the ending may or may not make it to prints to be shown theatrically.—Sege.

Otello
(Othello)
(ITALIAN-COLOR)

A Cannon Group release of a Cannon Italia production in collaboration with RAI. Producers, Menahem Golan, Yoram Globus. Executive producers, John Thompson, Fulvio Lucisano. Directed by Franco Zeffirelli. Screenplay, Zeffirelli, adapted from Arrigo Boito's libretto for Giuseppe Verdi's "Otello." Stars Placido Domingo, Justino Diaz, Katia Ricciarelli. Camera (Eastmancolor), Ennio Guarnieri; no editor credited; musical consultant, Rolf Feichtinger; music produced and conducted by Lorin Maazel with the orchestra and chorus of Milan's Teatro alla Scala; costumes, Anna Anni, Maurizio Millenotti; art direction, Gianni Quaranta; sound, Roberto Forrest; production manager, Gianfranco Diotallevi. Reviewed at the Cannes Film Festival (Official Competition), May 15, 1986. Running time: **120 MINS.**
Otello . . . . Placido Domingo
Desdemona . . . . Katia Ricciarelli
Iago . . . . Justino Diaz
Emilia . . . . Petra Malakova
Cassio . . . . Urbano Barberini
Roderigo . . . . Sergio Nicolai
Montano . . . . Edwin Francis
Lodovico . . . . Massimo Foschi

Cannes — Franco Zeffirelli wants his feature film version of Verdi's opera "Otello" spelled without the "h" used in the Moor's name by Shakespeare to stress right from the start that this is, in fact, opera first and foremost, and that he has adhered closely to the original opera libretto by Arrigo Boito. Nevertheless, Zeffirelli puts enough sweeping action and finely shaded psychology along with splendidly rendered music into his work to satisfy ardent Shakespeare fans and sensitive opera buffs alike.

Magnificent camerawork in majestic natural surroundings (a castle in Crete among them) serve this retelling of Venice's Moor governor of Cyprus who has the poison of jealousy infused in his veins by his friend Iago. The latter, by means of manipulating with a handkerchief once given as a love token gift, has Otello kill first his beloved wife Desdemona, then Iago and finally himself. All this, while young Cassio, Desdemona's supposed but innocent lover watches what havoc men may wreak on their own souls and bodies when passion has relieved them of reason.

It is a particular point in Zeffirelli's telling of the story that Iago is as much a victim of his passion as is Otello, Iago recognizing the evil forces within himself but declaring himself unable to be anything but at their beck and call. As clumsy a machination as modern audiences may find the handkerchief plot when they see it on stage, Zeffirelli works cinema magic by making everything seem perfectly logical on the screen (a small one, incidentally, for the Cannes press screening, but general distribution will be widescreen format.

As natural as all the action looks, just as matter-of-fact is the sound of the singing, especially as natural body language goes with every note sung. There is fresh invention of truly dramatic movement in every frame whether it is Otello landing Desdemona alone in their bedchamber, or fight scenes in the castle's armory, or grand merry-making in the royal halls.

It would seem a fairly safe bet that Zeffirelli reaches even wider general audiences with "Otello" than he did with "La Traviata" four years ago. Many factors contribute. First there is nothing short of superior handling of all musical chores from the singing of Placido Domingo in the title role, Puerto Rico's Justino Diaz as Iago and Italy's Katia Ricciarelli as Desdemona to all other singers, and to the La Scala orchestra and chorus performing under Lorin Maazel's direction.

Then there are the great arias, duets and quartets ("Dammi la dolce e lieta parola," "Temete, signor, la gelosia," etc.), and although this particular opera may lack what in Broadway parlance is known as the "11 o'clock song" (to be hummed by audiences on their way home), Verdi's music has rarely come through with greater lucidity.

Domingo is at the very summit of his singing art as the Moor. The role also fits his trunk-like frame better than did his hang-dog army captain in Francesco Rosi's "Carmen." Even more important is the singer's emergence in this film as a first-class natural actor who never stumbles into the pitfalls of bravado or other excess.

As Iago, Justino Diaz has human warmth mixed into his evil cunning. He nearly comes through as likeable, which makes the character more complex and more interesting. Katia Ricciarelli is straight out of Medieval Madonna portraiture but has some obvious physical appeal, too. Her extreme blondness is a dramatic contrast to Domingo's rough, dark looks (his Moor coloring does not seem like a paint job at all).

All production credits are of the very highest order. Every frame has the magnificence of composition as well as the color shadings of Renaissance paintings of the Italian School. There is nothing in this film that does not serve the purpose of high drama, musical, cinematic or otherwise, to ultimate perfection.
— Kell.

Le Lieu du crime
(The Scene Of The Crime)
(FRENCH-COLOR)

AMLF release of a T. Films-Films A-2 coproduction. Produced by Alain Terzian. Stars Catherine Deneuve. Directed by André Téchiné. Screenplay, Téchiné, Pascal Bonitzer, Oliver Assayas; camera (Eastmancolor), Pascal Marti; editor, Martine Giordano; music, Philippe Sarde; art direction, Jean-Pierre Kohut-Svelko; sound, Jean-Louis Ughetto; production managers, Jean-François Pierrard, Françoise Galfré; makeup, Ronaldo Ribeiro de Abreu; assistant director, Michel Bena. Reviewed at the UGC Biarritz theater, Paris, May 16, 1986. (In Official Competition at Cannes Film Festival.) Running time: **90 MINS.**
Lili . . . . Catherine Deneuve
Grandmother . . . . Danièlle Darrieux
Martin . . . . Wadeck Stanczak
Thomas . . . . Nicolas Giraudi
Maurice . . . . Victor Lanoux
Grandfather . . . . Jean Bousquet
Alice . . . . Claire Nebout
Father Sorbier . . . . Jacques Nolot
Also with: Jean-Claude Adelin, Christine Paolini, Philippe Landoulsi, Michel Grimaud.

Paris — After several years of wandering in a commercial desert, director André Téchiné re-emerged impressively last year with "Rendezvous," which revealed actress Juliette Binoche, and won his Cannes laurels as best director. This year Téchiné is back at Cannes with "Le Lieu du crime," another stylishly crafted film, perhaps his best, in which elements of genre melodrama are effectively mixed with an acrid chronicle of provincial family life.

Film also stands out for the role it offers Catherine Deneuve, who has not been implicated so dramatically in a part since François Truffaut's "The Last Metro" in 1980. It's a welcome change from the decorative roles she tends to portray too often.

Here she plays a woman living in the southwest of France who helps, then falls in love with a young escaped convict who has saved the life of her rebellious 14-year-old son, with whom she lives after having separated from her husband.

Her actions trigger a series of personal crises among her family members, who have gathered to celebrate her son's first communion. When the fugitive is shot down by his childhood girlfriend, and her complicity is revealed, Deneuve decides to turn her back on her conventional responsibilities and accept the full implications of her complicity with the criminal.

Téchiné and his coscripters, Olivier Assayas and Pascal Bonitzer (all three nurtured as critics for the Cahiers du Cinéma revue), provide a rich, well-balanced frame in which its numerous characters and incidents are set, with Deneuve and her son (strikingly portrayed by Nicolas Giraudi) sharing center-front attention in their linked destinies.

Téchiné's direction is even better than it was in ''Rendezvous,'' with his masterly sense of mood and sustained dramatic tension most evident in the long climactic chain of events that unfold in a violent, nocturnal storm. Another setpiece is the communion meal that brings together the estranged members of Deneuve's uncomprehending family.

Good as Deneuve is, she inevitably pales in the presence of a grande dame of the screen, Danièlle Darrieux, who brings incandescent simplicity to the role of the nostalgic, tradition-minded grandmother.

Wadeck Stanczak, another young revelation of ''Rendezvous,'' confirms his dramatic presence as the young fugitive who saves Giraudi from his fellow-escapee and captivates his mother; and Victor Lanoux is fine as Deneuve's estranged husband. Jacques Nolot, as a priest exasperated by the insolent Giraudi; Jean Bousquet as the misanthropic granddad; and Claire Nebout, as Stanczak's demonic childhood friend, complete the firstrate cast.

The superb lensing (on location in the Garonne region, where Téchiné grew up) promises a luminous future for cinematographer Pascal Marti. Other credits are equally elegant.—Len.

Max Mon Amour
(Max My Love)
(FRENCH-COLOR)

A Greenwich Film Prod., Greenwich Films (USA), Films A-2 production. Produced by Serge Silberman. Directed by Nagisa Oshima. Stars Charlotte Rampling, Anthony Higgins. Screenplay, Oshima, Jean-Claude Carriere; camera (Panavision, Centralcolor), Raoul Coutard; editor, Helen Plemiannikov; music, Michel Portal; sound, Jean-Phillippe Le Roux; production designer, Pierre Guffroy, production manager, Olly Pickardt. Reviewed at the Cannes Film Festival (Official Competition), May 13, 1986. Running time: **98 MINS.**
Margaret ....Charlotte Rampling
Peter..................Anthony Higgins
Camille ....Diana Quick
Nelson ....Christopher Hovik
Margaret's mother ....Miléna Vukotic

Maria ....Victoria Abril
Detective................Pierre Etaix
Zoologist................Claude Jaeger
Françoise ....Sabine Haudepin
Archibald.....Bernard-Pierre Donnadieu
Hélène ....Nicole Calfan
Nicolas ....Fabrice Luchini
Suzanne ....Anne-Marie Besse
Robert................Bernard Haller
Dr. Mischler ....Laurent Spielvogel

Cannes — With ''Max Mon Amour,'' Japanese director Nagisa Oshima takes a slightly bent excursion into Luis Buñuel territory to decidedly mixed results. Prestige names and a sensational subject matter make the pic a reasonable b.o. bet in European markets, although U.S. action looms lukewarm.

The point of departure here is a romance between a British diplomat's wife (Charlotte Rampling) and a chimpanzee. The liaison is presented, although for obvious reasons not shown, as heartfelt — entirely serious and sexual. There's no stinting on this point.

The script by Oshima and longtime Buñuel colleague Jean-Claude Carriere, based on his ''idea,'' it says here, treats the material in several ways. ''Max'' emerges as a bleary combination of surrealistic comedy and tv-movie earnestness about the resiliency of marital love.

Oshima thrives in handling tough, controversial material (''Merry Christmas, Mr. Lawrence,'' ''In The Realm Of The Senses''), but can't seem to generate the deft touch required here to make the surrealism snap as it should. What's left is a consideration of motivation rather than an appreciation of the ridiculous. ''Max'' sags badly several times before it winds to a bittersweet resolution that manages to satisfy all parties.

Peter (Anthony Higgins) is a cultural attaché at the British Embassy in Paris. He, his svelte wife (garbed in Christian Dior) and genial, young son (Christopher Hovik) live in an expensively furnished flat on what looks to be Paris' Right Bank. He is having a fling with a woman at the embassy (Diana Quick). She disappears for long periods, much to the husband's dismay when the wife's destination is revealed to be a seedy apartment she pays for and not the residence of a friend.

''Max'' moves the exposition quickly with the husband's discovery with the aide of a private detective (played in funny style by Pierre Etaix) of his wife in bed with a former circus chimp.

''Max'' shifts into high gear when, after getting a grip on his emotions, the husband takes the civilized approach and invites the chimp to live together with the couple in a strange menage-a-quatre. Some familiar Buñuelian touches ensue — a dinner party that turns into a petting session between wife and chimp, the subsequent appear-

ances of a dour neurologist (Laurent Spielvogel) and a greedy zoologist (Claude Jaeger) eager for a best-selling book.

The husband becomes obsessed with finding out how his wife actually performs sexual congress with the monkey, and hires a tart to provide a demonstration at home while the wife is out. All this sounds funnier and more titillating than it plays onscreen.

The cast is generally solid. Higgins is excellent as the husband, giving him dignity and sympathetic warmth in an awkward position. Hovik is fine as the couple's son, and Diana Quick displays a winning blend of sexiness and vulnerability as the husband's lover. The chimp appears to be an uncredited performer inside a very realistic get-up designed by special effects maven Rick Baker. The monkey has an anthropomorphic appeal.

A problem is Rampling. As the wife, she turns in little more than a junior Lauren Bacall turn. She looks like, and acts with the passion of, a fashion model. It's hard to envision her character locked in heated romantic embrace of anyone, much less a monkey.

Producer Serge Silberman (Akira Kurosawa's ''Ran'' was last from him; he worked for two decades with Buñuel) hasn't stinted in production values. Despite the fact it was shot mostly in Paris' Billancourt Studios, ''Max'' reportedly cost in the neighborhood of $5,000,000, a high figure for a French production.

A good chunk of cash underwrote production designer Pierre Guffroy's elaborate set, lushly photographed by Raoul Coutard. Director Oshima pursued a simple, unobtrusive photographic style and Coutard's camera and Michel Portal's attractive score compliment the overall approach.

''Max Mon Amour'' is in competition in Cannes this year. The pic's principal cast members are bilingual with subtitles provided in whichever of two languages (French, English) is not spoken onscreen.) —Sege.

Thérèse
(FRENCH-COLOR)

A UGC release of a AFC/Films A-2/CNC coproduction. Produced by Maurice Bernart. Directed by Alain Cavalier. Stars Catherine Mouchet. Screenplay, Cavalier, Camille De Casabianca; camera (Eclair color), Philippe Rousselot; editor, Isabelle Dedieu; sound, Alain Lachassgne, Dominique Dalmasso; art direction, Bernard Evein; costumes, Yvette Bonnay; assistant director, Louis Becker. Reviewed at the Cannes Film Festival (Official Competition), May 16, 1986. Running time: **90 MINS.**
Thérèse ....Catherine Mouchet
Céline................Aurore Pristo
Pauline ....Sylvia Habault
Marie ....Ghislaine Mona

Lucis ....Helène Alexandridis
Prioress ....Clémence Massart
The father ....Jean Pelegri
Also with: Nathalie Bernart (Aimee), Béatice De Vigan (singer), Noële Chantra (old nun).

Cannes — A film as visually beautiful and simple as its heroine, ''Thérèse'' recounts the life and death of teenage St. Thérèse with the calm objectivity of a documentary. Its stripped-down sets, essential staging, and reverent camerawork are reminiscent of the cinema of Robert Bresson, but not as severe. On the other hand, the joyous, outgoing girl who enters the cloister at 15 is a full-bodied, very appealing heroine, and gives film a warmth and immediacy that should make it a favorite of arthouse auds.

Director Alain Cavalier (''Martin at Léa,'' ''Un Étrange Voyage'') has done his homework on the known facts about Thérèse Martin, who became a Carmelite nun (like her three sisters) at the end of the 19th century, died of tuberculosis a few years later, and was canonized in 1925. Much is based on the saint's famous diaries.

He chooses his incidents carefully, building up a portrait of a normal girl with a strong streak of idealism, who was bold enough to journey to Rome to get the Pope's permission to be admitted to the cloister at a tender age. Convent life is harsh; the nuns have a rule of silence that is rarely broken; the prioress believes in the spiritual benefits of chastisement and humiliation. Although more than a few viewers will be dismayed by this picture of walled-in existence and voluntary deprivation, Cavalier avoids the route of easy condemnation or condescension. The tone of the film is so straightforward, so even-handed, it isn't always clear what message viewers are supposed to be taking away from the events that are told. It isn't even clear that Thérèse, whose life ends in intense physical suffering and spiritual doubt, is a ''real'' saint. But film remains respectful of its central character and her choices, preferring to reserve judgment and merely tell her story as simply as possible.

Young lead Catherine Mouchet portrays Thérèse as a starry-eyed adolescent deeply in love (like all the Carmelites) with a man who, as Thérèse says wistfully in one of her frequent moments of doubt, ''may not ever have lived.'' The nuns comfort each other in times of trouble, and there is a great sense of love filling the convent. Enlightened people from the outside world, like the doctor who the prioress grudgingly calls in to examine Thérèse, are of the opinion the place should be burned to the ground. Viewers are left to make up their own minds.

Many members of the cast are non-pros, but blend flawlessly into the web of characters.

Cavalier concentrates less on acting per se than on movements and facial expressions to communicate with the audience. Lensing by Philippe Rousselot is outstanding for its pure simplicity, echoing Bernard Evein's spare, almost abstract art direction. —*Yung.*

Boris Godunov
(SOVIET-COLOR)

A Sovexport presentation of a Mosfilm (Moscow) production, with Studio Barrandov (Prague). Directed by Sergei Bondarchuk. Stars Bondarchuk, Alexander Soloviev. Screenplay, Bondarchuk, based on Alexander Pushkin epic poem; camera (color), Vadim Yusov; art direction, Vadim Aronin; music, Vyacheslav Ovchinnikov. Reviewed at the Cannes Film Festival (Official Competition), May 18, 1986. Running time: **164 MINS.**
With: Sergei Bondarchuk (Boris Godunov), Alexander Soloviev, Anatoli Romachine, Anatoli Vassiliev, Adriana Bierdjinskay, Elena Bondarchuk.

Cannes — Sergei Bondarchuk won an Oscar for best foreign film in 1967 (''War And Peace''), but there will hardly be any kudos nor any kind of commercial future internationally for his latest screen adaptation of a literary masterpiece, in this case Alexander Pushkin's Shakespearean verse play ''Boris Godunov.''

Out of the play's treasure chest of scenic devices, exclamatory dialog and majestic tragedy, Bondarchuk has fashioned an incredibly tame, mammoth-length epic feature that kills just about everything it claims to hold dearest. Seeing the film is like being burdened with an illustrated classics tome that weighs on one's lap and one's mind like a ton of bricks, albeit historically worthy ones.

The real-life Boris Godunov, on whose violent life and death Pushkin's play, then Moussorgsky's opera, and now the film, is based, took power as czar in 1598 at the death of Ivan the Terrible's son. A nephew had been in line for the succession, but this little boy died. Or was he killed?

Godunov, who had proved himself an admirable statesman under Ivan, was popular at first. He had, after all, acted more on behalf of the people than of the landed gentry than any czar before him. But his short reign was to be haunted by the little boy's death.

The common Russian gradually came to believe that Godunov was the killer. A resistance movement of a kind, an unholy alliance of Russians, Poles and German, sprang up. A boyish former monk was claimed to be the crown prince, who had somehow escaped the assassination ordered by Godunov.

Now, armies clashed, and much intrigue was indulged in on all sides. Godunov's soul was tormented by doubts, and he turned to excessive violence in an attempt to escape his inner voices of accusation. When illness felled him after a reign of only six years, he was really a dead man already.

In the title lead, Bondarchuk himself looks most of all like an accountant worried about a client's cashflow. He has all his fellow actors follow his lead with leaden performances. The verse dialog, which may sound like heavenly music in Russian, sparks no fire even as sound, and as read via the subtitles, the words just seem dumb or pretentious.

Narrative development is slow and murky, but film's production dress constitutes riches from Russia's museums and national monuments on gorgeous display. All frames are composed with nods to older Russian film directors, notably Sergei Eisenstein, and they are handsomely lit, too. You will probably never see the point-domed golden towers of Russia as beautifully kissed by the sun or caressed by winter's first snow as in Vadim Yusov's cinematography.

None of all this comes alive, however, in any truly dramatic context. Even the counterpoint stagings of the many big battle scenes fail to come across as anything but juxtposed tableaux. At the end of the film, the sound of a broken bell is heard. This leaves the viewers with a feeling less of tragedy than of sheer mechanical failure.

The fate of Boris Godunov serves to tell us that you cannot build power on criminal acts. It is reassuring that Russians think so, too. But what is the punishment for the crime of high-falutin' dullness?
—*Kell.*

Genesis
(INDIAN-FRENCH-BELGIAN-SWISS-COLOR)

A Scarabée Films presentation of a Mrinal Sen PL R T-Les Films de la Dreve-Cactus Film-Scarabée Films coproduction, with the participation of the French Ministry of Culture, the French Ministry of Foreign Relations, the Belgian Ministry of French Communications, the Swiss Federal Dept. of the Interior, Maran Films (Munich) and Film Four (London). Executive producer, Marie-Pascale Osterrieth. Directed by Sen. Screenplay, Sen., with the collaboration of Mohit Chattopadhya, from a novella by Samaresh Basu; camera (Eastman color), Carlo Varini; editor, Elizabeth Waelchli; music, Ravi Shankar; sound, Henri Morelle, Frank Struys; production design, Nitish Roy; production coordinator, Mukul Chaudhuri; production manager, Jitesh Basu Thakur; assistant director, Amal Sirkar; associate producers, Palaniappan Ramasamy, Eliane Stutterheim, Joan-Jacques Adrien. Reviewed at the Cannes Film Festival (Official Competition), May 13, 1986. Running time: **108 MINS.**

The Woman	Shabana Azmi
The Farmer	Naseeruddin Shah
The Weaver	Om Puri
The Trader	M.K. Raina

Cannes — Backing by three European countries has permitted Indian director Mrinal Sen to make his most technically perfect film to date: beautiful images and rich color greatly enhance this knowing parable of the rise, decline and fall of man, and the repetition of this inevitible cycle.

Setting for this Hindi-language pic is a crumbling, ruined village. Workers in the area have been rounded up and told they'll be given adequate food and water if they conform to the orders of the local bosses. Two men, a farmer (Naseeruddin Shah) and a weaver (Om Puri) opt out. They establish themselves in this eerie, broken-down place and find they can work in peace, the farmer planting crops and the weaver making patterned cloth he sells to a visiting trader.

One day, a lone woman (Shabana Azmi) arrives, lost and frightened. The men take her in, she stays; and she brightens their lives, helps them, cooks for them. Inevitably, both men fall for her, and just as inevitably the seeds of dissension are sown in this little Eden. With the watchful, scheming trader in the background, the two friends begin to fight each other.

Straightforward story and treatment used by Sen makes for a disarmingly simple, yet timeless and timely film. The four thesps are excellent, and the photography of Carlo Varini is a major plus. So, too, is the music score of Ravi Shankar, which is not overused, but which makes an important contribution.

Almost a cautionary fable, ''Genesis'' is a fascinating example of European money aiding a leading Third World director to make (presumably sans interference) an impressively idiosyncratic and uncompromising pic. —*Strat.*

Down By Law
(U.S.-B&W)

An Island Pictures release of a Black Snake-Grokenberger Films production. Produced and directed by Jim Jarmusch. Coproduced by Rudd Simmons. Stars Tom Waits, John Lurie, Roberto Benigni. Screenplay, Jarmusch; camera (b&w), Robby Müller; editor, Franck Kern; music, Jonh Lurie; production design, Roger Knight; sound, Mark Goodermote; assistant director, Guido Chiesa. Reviewed at the Cannes Film Festival (Official Competition), May 16, 1986. (No MPAA Rating.) Running time: **106 MINS.**

Zack	Tom Waits
Jack	John Lurie
Roberto	Roberto Benigni
Nicoletta	Nicoletta Braschi
Laurette	Ellen Barkin

Cannes — With his first feature, ''Stranger Than Paradise,'' Jim Jarmusch scored an international cult success that was unexpected from a slow-moving black and white picture. Reason was undoubtedly the helmer's offbeat, ironic humor, coupled with fine acting; and the formula is repeated in ''Down By Law,'' his second effort.

Set in New Orleans, pic opens with brief, sharply funny scenes establishing the characters of Zack (Tom Waits) and Jack (John Lurie). Zack's a disk jockey who neglects his blond mistress; Jack's a pimp who also has woman trouble. Both men are framed; Zack is caught driving a car with a body in the trunk and Jack is found by the cops in a hotel room with an unquestionably underage girl. They wind up in the slammer, in the same cell.

At this point the pic drags for a few moments as the characters warily find out about each other, but it picks up considerably with the arrival of a third cell mate, Roberto (played by Italian actor-director Roberto Benigni, who speaks fractured English but whose naive friendliness proves contagious. He's in jail because he was caught cheating at cards and brained a man with a billiard ball.

After several funny scenes of the three men in their cell, including a wonderful routine from Benigni when his character is afflicted with hiccups, the Italian proposes they escape, ''just like they do in American movies.'' And so they do, out into the Louisiana swamps (some great photography here by Robby Müller) and eventually stumble on an isolated, unlikely diner where, surprise, surprise, the owner chef is a lonely Italian woman (Nicoletta Braschi) who immediately falls for Benigni.

The Jarmusch penchant for off-the-wall characters and odd situations is very much in evidence in ''Down By Law,'' but audiences attuned to his special brand of comedy will have lots of fun with the picture. Presence of Benigni is an added plus for European audiences, though his Italian dialog should be subtitled in English (it wasn't in the Cannes print).

As noted, the black and white photography is a major plus, and so is John Lurie's score, with songs by Tom Waits. Both men are fine in their respective roles, but Benigni steals the film.

''Down By Law'' (what does the title mean?) will be popular at fests this summer and on the international arthouse circuit. Jarmusch's humor and steadily paced style won't accrue huge returns, but as a genuine original on the American film scene, it's good to welcome ''Down By Law'' as a delightful followup to his first modest hit. — *Strat.*

Le Derniere Image
(The Last Image)
(FRENCH-ALGERIAN-COLOR)

An ENADEC release of an E.M.A. Films, TF-1 Films Prod. (Paris), S.I.A. (Algiers) co-production. Executive producer, Jean Pierre Sammut. Written and directed by Mohamed Lakhdar-Hamina. Stars Véronique Jannot. Camera (Panavision, GTC color), Youcef Sahraoui; editor, Youcef Tobni; art direction, Mohamed Kessai; sound, Catherine D'Houar; music, Philippe Arthuys and Jean Paul Cara; makeup, Phuong Maittret; costumes, Sylviane Combes and Mohamed Bouzit; production manager, Smail Ait Si-Selmi. Reviewed at the Cannes Film Festival (Official Competition), May 10, 1986. Running time: **109 MINS.**
Claire Boyer ....Véronique Jannot
Mouloud ......Merwan Lakhdar-Hamina
Simon Attal ....Michel Boujenah
Touhami ....Hassan El Hassani
Miller ....Jean-Francois Balmer
Bachir ....Malik Lakhdar-Hamina
    Also with: Jean Bouise (Langlois), Mustapha El Anka (Kabrane), Jose Artur (Forestier) Mustapha Preur (Boutaleb), Genevieve Mnich (Mme Lanier), Brigitte Catillon (Mme Leguenne), Radid Fares (Omar).

Cannes — Mohamed Lakhdar-Hamina, the Algerian helmer who already has two Cannes wins for "Le Vent des Aurés" (Camera d'Or, 1965) and "Les années de Braise" (Palme d'Or, 1975), turned up this year with "The Last Image," an atmospheric piece of romantic-sentimental nostalgia.

Laced with Hamina's childhood memories and shot in his hometown, film is laden heavily with atmosphere but lacks the tightness and clarity needed for a gripping story. Though Hamina is unquestionably a talented and poetic director, a collection of lyrical images, funny memories do not a coherent film make.

To further disjoint this tale of an Algerian schoolboy who has a crush on his pretty French teacher, picture shifts between two viewpoints, his and hers. The time is 1940 and little Mouloud (played by the director's talented 14-year-old son Merwan) is coming of age at a difficult period in Algerian history. The sleepy town is under the thumb of French colonialists allied to the Vichy government, and the local boys are being drafted into a foreign war.

When young blond schoolmarm Claire Boyer (Véronique Jannot) appears on the scene, Mouloud attaches himself to her instantly. He's not alone; the whole village falls for her sweet temper and dimpled smiles, including Mouloud's big brother Bachir (Malik Lakhdar-Hamina) and Simon Attal (Michel Boujenah), a Jewish teacher who like Claire is a friend to the Algerians.

Most of the story is wrapped in the lyrical mists of memory, like Claire cycling through town to the accompaniment of a respectful chorus of male sighs, or Mouloud finally spending a rainy night in Claire's room and stealing her garter belt.

By pic's end more dramatic events start occurring, including two murders and Simon's narrow escape from being deported as a Jew, rescued by Claire and his Arab friends. But the tension remains trapped behind Claire's sunny smiles and fails to build to a climax.

Youcef Sahraoui's dazzling widescreen lensing and Philippe Arthuys and Jean Paul Cara's epic score strain towards an "Out Of Northern Africa" magic, which in its very best moments "Last Image" achieves. — *Yung.*

Shadow Play
(U.S.-COLOR)

A New World Pictures release of a Millennium Pictures production. Produced by Dan Biggs, Susan Shadburne and Will Vinton. Directed and written by Shadburne. Camera (color), Ron Orieux; editor, Kenji Yamamoto; music, Jon Newton; production manager, Don Zavin; art director, Steve Karatzas. Reviewed at the Cannes Film Festival (market), May 15, 1986. (No MPAA Rating.) Running time: **95 MINS.**
Morgan Hanna ....Dee Wallace Stone
Millie Crown ....Cloris Leachman
John Crown ....Ron Kuhlman
Jeremy Crown ....Barry Laws
Byron ....Al Strobel
Bette ....Delia Salvi

Cannes — A supernatural thriller about a playwright who's haunted by the death of her lover, "Shadow Play" skimps on suspense and serves up few spooky moments. Expect a short theatrical life for this New World release .

Dee Wallace Stone limns a Manhattan writer who, suffering from writer's block, figures she'll get some inspiration by going back to the island where seven years earlier her fiancé (Barry Laws) plummeted to his death from atop a lighthouse.

In flashbacks, she relives the times they spent together and, staying at his mom's house, she keeps seeing his image in windows and mirrors. That's very disconcerting for her, and maybe that explains why the play she's writing, as workshopped by the local drama group (a real bunch of weirdos), is very, very bad.

Question is: Did Laws fall or was he pushed? Writer-director Susan Shadburne makes it a slow build to the denouement, and the entire exercise is rather uninvolving, not helped any by a breathless, brittle performance by Dee Wallace Stone. Also on hand are Cloris Leachman as Laws' mother, Ron Kuhlman as his brother, and Al Strobel as a one-armed psychic who makes glib pronouncements from his tarot cards. No great acting skills are called for, or delivered.

The location — Orcas Island off the coast of Washington — is a picturesque setting. Maybe someday someone will shoot an interesting picture there.—*Dogo.*

Mr. Vampire
(HONG KONG-COLOR)

A Golden Harvest presentation of a Bo Ho Films Ltd. production. Executive producer, Leonard Ho. Produced by Samo Hung. Directed by Lau Kun Wai. Screenplay, Wong Ying, Szeto Cheuk Hon; camera (color), Peter Ngor; editor, Cheung Yiu Chung; music, Anders Nelson; special effects, Ng Kok Wah; martial arts choreographers, Lam Ching Ying, Yuen Wah; stuntman, Pang Yau Cheung; associate producer, Jacob Cheung; production supervisors, Eric Tsang, Barry Wong. Reviewed at the Cannes Film Festival (market), May 15, 1986. Running time: **95 MINS.**
Man Chor ....Ricky Hui
Ting Ting ....Moon Lee
Chau ....Chin Suit Ho
Master ....Lam Ching Ying
Jade ....Pauline Wong
    Also with: Billy Lau, Anthony Chan, Wu Ma, Wong Ha, Yuen Wah.

Cannes — "Mr. Vampire" is an offbeat, sometimes hilarious, often outrageously silly chopsocky treatment of the vampire myth, given so many new twists and breaking so many of the old rules that this pic is a genuine curiosity that could cross over from the local Chinese to other markets.

Western audiences are accustomed to the classical trappings of Dracula; garlic, mirrors, bloodsucking in the throat; but this film comes up with a whole new litany of rules, often very funny. The living dead here, instead of walking zombielike, move about by short hops; one of the things these creatures hate most is sticky rice; and one can momentarily freeze them in their steps by holding one's breath.

Slapstick acting, chopsocky stunts and droll situations are mixed up with a story about a group of vampires-zombies who menace a Chinese family and repeatedly are turned back by an uncle, a nephew, a pretty niece, a bumbling policeman and others. The stunts are well done, as are the martial arts sequences, but all are subservient to the shenanigans when the "living dead" appear.

Pic may just be strange enough to cull a following, if it is carefully released as an offbeat camp item that is sometimes so bad it is actually refreshing. —*Besa.*

Un Homme et Une Femme: Vingt Ans Déjà
(A Man And A Woman: 20 Years Later)
(FRENCH-COLOR)

A Warner Bros. release of a Films 13 production. Produced and directed by Claude Lelouch. Stars Anouk Aimée, Jean-Louis Trintignant. Screenplay, Lelouch adapted by Lelouch, Pierre Uytterhoeven, Monique Lange, Jerome Tonerre; camera (Eastmancolor), Jean-Yves Le Mener; editor, Hugues Darmois; music, Francis Lai; sound, Harald Maury; art director, Jacques Bufnoir; assistant director, Didier Grousset; production manager, Tania Zazulinsky; car stunts Rémy Julienne; casting, Arlette Gordon. Reviewed at the Cannes Film Festival (Official selection out of competition), May 11, 1986. Running time: **120 MINS.**
Anne Gauthier ....Anouk Aimée
Jean-Louis Duroc .. Jean-Louis Trintignant
Françoise ....Evelyne Bouix
Marie-Sophie ....Marie-Sophie Pochat
Prof. Thevenin ...Philippe Leroy-Beaulieu
Charlot ....Charles Gerard
Antoine ....Antoine Sire
Film Director ....André Engel
    Also with: Richard Berry, Patrick Poivre d'Arvor, Thierry Sabine, Robert Hossein, Tanya Lopert, Nicole Garcia (as themselves).

Cannes — Since no one else has seen fit to pay tribute to Claude Lelouch's prolific career as yet he has decided to take things into his own hands, in a typically energetic manner.

Not only has he chosen for the subject of his new movie a reunion of the two characters in his most famous production, "A Man And A Woman," but he uses it to bow to many of his earlier pictures, from "L'Amour avec des Si" done when he was still an unknown, to his ambitious later superproductions such as "Les Uns Et Les Autres." Naturally he uses extensive footage from the first encounter between his two protagonists 20 years ago and sprinkles all over it pieces of filmic bravura indicating he is still the most earnest advocate of a cinema constantly on the move and exploiting all its technical resources.

The couple from "A Man And A Woman," a race driver and a script girl, played by the same actors, Jean-Louis Trintignant and Anouk Aimée, are 20 years older. He has retired and is organizing races for others, she has become a film producer through marriage. After a boxoffice fiasco similar to some of Lelouch's own (he has conceded a great resemblance to the character of the producer in the film to himself), he has his heroine decide that putting her old romance on the screen must be just what the doctor ordered to recuperate from financial catastrophe. To do so, she contacts her erstwhile flame to ask for his permission and old fires are rekindled, as they are watching the evolution of their own story for the screen.

If such a plot would satisfy a less ambitious filmmaker, it is only the beginning for Lelouch, who throws in for a subplot a mad killer escaping from a hospital, the family problems and complications on each side of the renewed couple, while all through the film, the audience is permanently invited to see movies within movies, learn how they are produced now, what are the secrets behind a video clip and so on. There is also a trip to Africa which almost ends tragically when a car is lost in the desert, a film production which changes course in the middle from romantic musical to hard-boiled thriller (Lelouch uses one of his own experiences for that), and stars look delighted to join in, crossing the screen for a second or two, to show their warm feelings for the director.

To open this extravaganza, there are some 10 minutes of cars racing on French highways, which, it turns out, isn't in earnest but just for the benefit of a commercial, shot by Lelouch himself and continues with a crowd scene, war prisoners being marched by the Resistance, in what soon appears to be a sequence from a new film being produced by the heroine.

Thus, fact and fiction, film and reality are supposed to blend in marvelous unity, the only trouble being that nothing even suggests reality. It is film blending with more film, cinema tricks with the camera, at the editing table, in the laboratory, showing Lelouch to be still smitten with the tools of his trade to the extent they become more important than anything else in his picture.

Following him through the many labyrinths of his script it becomes evident that he tries to manipulate human stories the way he manipulates the camera for the most spectacular results. Such persistence is finally self defeating, for the movies are after all about people, not about cameras, filters and special effects.

A cast packed with faithful who have been around Lelouch for years does its best to cope with the soap-operatic dialog in the best life-like fashion they can muster. Visually, as is normal with Lelouch, the result is impressive. His own handling of the camera allows for flexibility in following the actors. Francis Lai's score using the original best-selling soundtrack adds to the general glamor.

While his fans probably will adore his observations about the nature of the film trade, and the changes in the last 20 years, this picture may well confuse audiences not particularly interested in behind-the-camera secrets and may find some rough seas ahead.—*Edna.*

Heavenly Pursuits
(BRITISH-COLOR)

A Film Four presentation of an Island Film in association with Skreba. Produced by Michael Relph. Executive producer, Ann Skinner. Directed by Charles Gormley. Stars Tom Conti, Helen Mirren. Screenplay, Gormley; camera (color), Michael Coulter; editor, John Gow; production design, Rita McGurn; music, B.A. Robertson; production manager, Liz Kerby; assistant director, Clive Reed; casting, Anne Henderson. Reviewed at the Cannes Film Festival (market), May 14, 1986. Running time: **92 MINS.**
Vic Mathews . . . . .Tom Conti
Ruth Chancellor . . . . .Helen Mirren
Jeff Jeffries . . . . .David Hayman
Father Cobb . . . . .Brian Pettifer
Also with: Jennifer Black (Sister), Dave Anderson (Headmaster), Tom Busby (Brusse), Sam Graham (Doctor), Kara Wilson

(McAllister), Robert Paterson (MacKrimmond), John Mitchell (Gibbons).

Cannes — ''Heavenly Pursuits'' will have to rely a great deal on the charm of Tom Conti to make its way, because there's not much else going for it. Heavy-handed comedy, set in a Catholic school in Glasgow, starts off with an uninteresting screenplay by director Charles Gormley. It's apparently meant to be funny, and to carry a message about present-day miracles, but it's merely dull.

Conti plays a remedial teacher who doesn't believe in miracles. Unknown to him, he has a brain tumor which is mysteriously cured after he falls from the roof of the school trying to help a boy: he's unhurt, and healthy again. Also, pupils at the school start improving their standards. More miracles?

The mystery is why anybody found this lackluster idea amusing in the first place. Conti tries very hard to make his character a relaxed, charming and likeable fellow, and does the best possible job under the circumstances. So, too, does Helen Mirren in the thankless role of a music teacher attracted to Conti.

Gormley's direction is as leaden as his screenplay, and the whole thing quickly becomes a bore. Technical credits are only average.—*Strat.*

Lightning — The White Stallion
(U.S.-COLOR)

A Cannon Group release. Produced by Harry Alan Towers. Directed by William A. Levey. Screenplay, ''Peter Welbeck'' (Towers), camera (TVC color) Steven Shaw; editor, Ken Bornstein; no further credits given. Reviewed at the Cannes Film Festival (market), May 13, 1986. (No MPAA Rating.) Running time: **95 MINS.**
Barney Ingram . . . . .Mickey Rooney
Steff . . . . .Isabel Lorca
Madame Rene . . . . .Susan George
Lucas . . . . .Billy Wesley

Cannes — Forget about ''The Black Stallion'' even if Mickey Rooney is starring in ''Lightning — The White Stallion,'' too. If there is a special niche in the homevideo trade for pictures catering exclusively to very young girls enamored with horses and the riding of them, ''Lightning'' may have an audience, but even here a snort and a whinny in protest may be registered.

Shot in Californian national parks and on various race tracks, pic has gambler-multimillionaire Barney Ingram (Rooney) losing both the horse of the title and his money. Crooks have stolen the animal. Only young Steff, a sweet young thing who is going blind, may ride Lightning to a big money win and thus save the Ingram estate and get enough for herself to pay an

eye surgeon to restore her sight.

Story also has a mean stepfather, an assortment of hoodlums lookin' real menacin' and speaking their dialog with the proper snarl. As Ingram, Rooney is trotted out for some mugging, and he just can't help being endearing. As a stable owner helping Steff in her various predicaments, Susan George does some real lively acting, too. All other performances, including that of helmer William A. Levey, are rather amateurish. Even in show jumping sequences, lame is the only way to describe the proceedings.—*Kell.*

Welcome In Vienna
(AUSTRIAN-B&W)

A Thalia Film (Vienna) production for the ORF, in association with ZDF (West Germany) and the SSR (Switzerland), with the participation of the Austrian Federal Ministry of Education, Arts and Sports. Directed by Axel Corti. Screenplay, Georg Stefan Troller, Corti; camera (b&w), Gernot Roll; editors, Ulrike Pahl, Claudia Rieneck; sound, Rolf Schmidt-Gentner; art direction, Fritz Hollergschwandtner; costumes, Uli Fessler; music, Hans Georg Koch, Schubert's String Quartet C-Major Opus 163; production manager, Matija Barl. Reviewed at the Centre National du Cinéma, Paris, April 30, 1986. (In Un Certain Regard section at Cannes Film Festival). Running time: **126 MINS.**
Freddy Wolff . . . . .Gabriel Barylli
Seg Adler . . . . .Nicolas Brieger
Claudia Schütte . . . . .Claudia Messner
Capt. Karpeles . . . . .Hubert Mann
Treschensky . . . . .Karlheinz Hackl
Russian woman . . . . .Liliana Nelska
Stodola . . . . .Kurt Sowinetz
Lt. Binder . . . . .Joachim Kemmer
Oberst Schütte . . . . .Heinz Trixner

Paris — Purportedly the first film on the subject, ''Welcome In Vienna'' is a forceful dramatization about the shock of homecoming of Austrian and German emigrés to Europe as soldiers in the U.S. Army in 1944. Screenwriter Georg Stefan Troller, himself a former exile who returned to Europe as a G.I., and director Axel Corti draw an unrelieved portrait of Vienna and the Austrians in the last months of the war and the first moments of liberation.

The two protagonists are Jewish: Freddy, a Vienna-born young man, and Adler, a Communist intellectual from Berlin, both part of the liberating American Army en route to Austria as part of an interrogation unit. As war ends and reconstruction begins, both find their youthful dreams mocked and destroyed by the cynicism, moral capitulation and opportunism that engulf them.

Freddy, who learns the ruined property of his family has been ''bought'' by rapacious neighbors, falls in love with a young actress whose father has been a Nazi colonel, and allows himself to be manipulated in order to further her career in the post-war theater. Adler, devoted to the Soviet Union,

makes contact with the Russian army to offer his services, but his ideals crumble in a meeting with a stone-faced Party contact, whose Jewish husband was a victim of Stalinist antisemitism.

Aided by Gernot Roll's apt b&w lensing and Fritz Hollergschwandtner's essential art direction, Troller and Corti have recreated a moment in their country's past with cruel, vivid immediacy, though the story is at times burdened by redundant dialog sequences, which state what already is implicit in the action.

Gabriel Barylli and Nicolas Brieger limn Freddy and Adler with poignant subtlety. Claudia Messner is fine as the young actress who takes advantage of Barylli's devotion to build a career, and Karlheinz Hackl is brilliantly ambiguous as downtrodden a Wehrmacht deserter who becomes an self-confident black market operator.—*Len.*

Ninguen No Yakusoku
(The Promise)
(JAPANESE-COLOR)

A Toho Towa Presentation of a Seibu Saison Group, TV Asahi, Kinema Tokyo production. Directed by Yoshishige Yoshida. Screenplay, Yoshida, Fukiko Miyauchi, from the novel by Shuichi Sae; camera (Fujicolor), Yoshishiro Yamazaki; editor, Akira Suzuki; music, Haruomi Hosono; sound, Toshio Nakano; art director, Yoshie Kikukawa. Reviewed at the Cannes Film Festival (Un Certain Regard), May 14, 1986. Running time: **123 MINS.**
With: Rentaro Mikuni (grandfather), Sachiko Murase (grandmother), Choichiro Kawarazaki (Voshio), Orie Sato (Ritsuko), Tetsuta Sugimoto, Kumiko Takeda, Reiko Tazima, Koichi Sato, Tomisaburo Wakayama.

Cannes — It must have taken a lot of courage for a director who hasn't made a feature film in 13 years to attempt a comeback with such a difficult and uncompromising subject. The plot, which for the first few minutes suggests a mystery thriller, with the police inquiring into the death of an old woman living with her son's family, soon develops into something quite different. The victim's husband (who has been living with her) comes forward and confesses to his wife's murder.

But in a long flashback, introduced without any warning and taking up most of the film, it soon becomes clear he was not the only one who could or who wanted to do this. The real tragedy is that no one really wanted to see the old woman go on living, not her children, nor her husband nor herself.

Yoshida's point is that after a certain age, when body loses control of its functions and the mind starts to wander uncontrollably, there is no real reason to go on living, and it is only the loss of the ancient tradition of the death rites, which taught people to prepare for their death, which makes it so difficult for both the old people and their offspring to accept the end. This could be interpreted as a plea for euthanasia as the only merciful way to treat people on whom time has racked such ravages.

If Yoshida does not display any revolutionary techniques in this picture, he displays a single-minded determination to follow the theme to its bitter end. That is commendable, even if commercially it may put off some of the customers. He does not forgive any of his characters, nor sentimentalize the situations.

This is human tragedy on its most basic level, treated with no concession, the family concerned being a middleclass, unexceptional one, to make the case as representative and universal as possible.

Rentaro Mikuni and Sachiko Murase offer tremendous performances as the old couple. All technical credits are of a superior order, particularly the sober, subdued work of cameraman Yoshishiro Yamazaki, in spite of some repetitiousness which slows down the film.—*Edna*.

Vesnicko ma Strediskova
(My Sweet Little Village)
(CZECH-COLOR)

A Barrandov Studio production. World sales, Czechoslovak Filmexport (Prague). Directed by Jiri Menzel. Screenplay, Zdenek Sverak. Camera (color), Jaromir Sofr; editor, Jiri Brozeck; music, Jiri Sust. Reviewed at the Cannes Film Festival (market), May 13, 1986. Running time: **101 MINS**.
With: Janos Ban, Marian Labuda, Rudolf Hrusinsky, Petr Cedak, Evzen Jegorov.

Cannes — "My Sweet Little Village" finds director Jiri Menzel in the warm winning form of his "Capricious Summer" as well as other more recent of his pictures such as "Cutting It Short." This comedy about smalltown life in Czechoslovakia is a modest but very entertaining opus, and elicited a rarely heard ovation at its conclusion upon screening in one of the smaller salles in the Cannes market.

Simple story emphasizes situation comedy and running gags as bumbling young Otik, thought by his friends and neighbors to be mentally retarded, is rejected by his older workmate, Mr. Pavel, on delivery jobs. Pavel is not the only one tired of Otik, as an influential type is working on getting the boy transferred to a job in Prague so his local house can be lucratively modernized and resold, complete with an "English garden."

There are all sorts of goofy local intrigues, such as the young married woman who is always conspiring to get Otik out of his house (one time he is sent off to catch a "must-see" Rumanian film) so she can dally

there undetected with her young boyfriend. The town doctor (Rudolf Hrusinsky) is forever crashing his car into almost everything in its path, and though he is sympathetic, he is given to talking his patients out of their symptoms rather than prescribing any treatment.

Using a lowkey, simple style that perfectly matches the rural setting and unsophisticated characters, Menzel very warmly coaxes humor out of familiar material. Some of his running gags are priceless and no matter what happens, including inevitable physical violence (as in the cuckolded husband's reaction), there is no hint of malice here. Menzel very gentle pokes fun at the provincialism of his countrymen, in a universal way, as when two guys discuss how the bra-less look has caught on in the West — and how glad they are it has spread as far as their village.

Cast is uniformly excellent as an ensemble, with stalwart Rudolf Hrusinsky particularly delicious as the doctor.—*Lor*.

Qui A Tire Sur Nos Histoires d'Amour?
(A Question Of Loving)
(CANADIAN-COLOR)

A J.A. Lapointe Films release (in Quebec) of a La Maison Des Quatres production with financial participation of Telefilm Canada, Société Générale du Cinéma du Quebec and the Canadian Broadcasting Corp.'s Radio-Canada tv web. Executive producer, Louise Carré. Written and directed by Louise Carré. Camera (color), Jean-Charles Tremblay, Pierre Duceppe, Christiane Guernon, Michel Caron; editor, Louise Coté, Teresa De Luca; sets, Vianney Gauthier, Jean Kazemirchuk, Pierre Gauthier; sound, Michel Charron; music, Marc O'Farrell; assistant directors, René Pothier, Catherine Didelot; associate producer. Suzanne Laverdière. Reviewed at the Cannes Film Festival (market), May 11, 1986. Running time: **91 MINS**.
Madeleine . . . . Monique Mercure
Renee . . . . Guylaine Normandine
Fabien . . . . August Schellenberg
Michel . . . . Claude Gauthier

Cannes — Likable, well-acted, good technical credits, a prod that starts off skillfully and goes round in circles sums up this one.

Heroine, a middle-aged former film scripter back doing a radio talk show is visited for the summer by her college-age daughter. The mother must prove something to herself every day, via gymnastics, talking on world issues on the air to the annoyance of her boss, shedding a lover for another one, and even competing with her daughter.

Some perceptive lines click, as when the new lover remarks metaphorically about his previous affairs that he's slept with Betty Friedan and Germain Greer and failed them.

Lead trio make for good companions on screen but pic is likely to have best playoff at women's fests

where issues might count for more than fully satisfying realization on screen. At the end of the pic, the daughter goes off to school and the mother has another relationship and another hope for permanence.
—*Adil*.

Golden Eighties
(FRENCH-BELGIAN-SWISS-COLOR)

A Pari Films-Gerick Films release (France) of a La Cecilia (Paris)/Paradise Films (Brussels)/Limbo Film (Zurich) coproduction, in association with the French Ministry of Culture and the Ministry of the French Community of Belgium. Produced by Martine Marignac. Directed by Chantal Akerman. Screenplay, Pascal Bonitzer, Henry Bean, Akerman, Jean Gruault, Leora Barish; camera (Fujicolor), Gilberto Azevedo, Luc Benhamou; editor, Francine Sandberg; music, Marc Herouet; lyrics, Chantal Akerman; sound, Henri Morelle, Migual Rejas; art direction, Serge Marzolff; costumes, Pierre Albert. Reviewed at the Cannes Film Festival (Directors Fortnight), May 15, 1986. Running time: **96 MINS**.
Jeanne . . . . Delphine Seyrig
Robert . . . . Nicolas Tronc
Eli . . . . John Berry
Mado . . . . Lio
Lili . . . . Cottençon
M. Schwartz . . . . Charles Denner
M. Jean . . . . Jean-François Balmer
Sylvie . . . . Myriam Boyer
Pascale . . . . Pascale Salkin

Cannes — Chantal Akerman's "Golden Eighties" is an exuberant, witty, tongue-in-cheek musical for the modern age. The inescapable comparison is with the light-opera musicals of Jacques Demy, but Akerman's touch is distinctly more vicious. The theme may be love, but the song lyrics (which she wrote herself) are unblushingly explicit, sometimes tender and sometimes malicious.

Akerman is one of the most prolific and accessible avant-garde directors around, and the film's state financing attests to the respect in which she is held. "Golden Eighties" is fast-moving and amusing enough to garner her a wider audience than before, but still looks headed for the arthouse circuits.

The whole film takes place in a shopping mall, as windowless and claustrophobic as a studio set. In a staid boutique we meet Jeanne (Delphine Seyrig) and her husband M. Schwartz (Charles Denner), whose preoccupation with business and "the shop" amounts to an obsession and crowds live out of their lives. When Eli (John Berry), Jeanne's G.I. lover during the war, turns up after all these years, she sings about her fears of running her predictable life off the rails.

Across the mall is a beauty parlor, which the kittenish Lili (Fanny Cottençon) has been given to run by her married lover M. Jean (Jean-François Balmer). Observed by a gossiping, singing and dancing chorus of shampoo girls and boys in the

mall, Lili cheats on him with the Schwartzes' son Robert (Nicolas Tronc), who in turn is worshipped by one of the shampoo girls (Lio).

Film manages to mix its characters and their stories into a biting critique of love and mores in the 1980s. The devilish lyrics are just the punctuation it needs to keep from wandering into routine sentimentalism. They also provide an amusing reflection on musical conventions, and the possibility of using the genre to talk about unromantic things like sex and business. The cast is perfectly chosen. Special kudos to Delphine Seyrig, who is aging beautifully, for her insight into Jeanne.
—*Yung*.

Population: One
(U.S.-COLOR)

An American Scenes presentation. Executive producers, Greg Farber, Joseph Kaufman. Produced by Bianca Daalder. Directed, written and music produced by Renee Daalder. Camera (color), Jurg Victor Walther; additional camera, Frans Bromet, Daniel Pearl; editor, Woody Wilson, Renee Daalder, Carel Struycken, Bianca Daalder; art direction, set design, Keith (KK) Barrett; animation, Dominic Orlando; music, Daniel Schwartz; assoc. producer, Carel Struycken. Reviewed at the Cannes Film Festival (market), May 14, 1986. Running time: **70 MINS**.
Himself . . . . Tomata DuPlenty
Sheela . . . . Sheela Edwards
Also with: Jane Gaskill, Gorilla Rose, Mike Doud, Beck Campbell, Tommy Gear, Susan Ensley.

Cannes — A frenetically paced montage of multiple-layered images, special effects and musical numbers, linked by a rambling monolog by toplined Tomata Du-Plenty, "Population: One" is an assault on the senses, both visual and aural.

Whether audiences will welcome and appreciate this kind of assault is highly questionable.

Unconventional structure and the abstract, surreal style of Dutch-born director-writer Renee Daalder likely will designate this pic a fringe item. It's a bizarre experience that could alienate, baffle or just plain confuse mainstream audiences.

DuPlenty imagines he's the only survivor of a nuclear holocaust. Holed up in an underground shelter, he conjures up via video screens and dreams a kaleidoscope of scenes and images that go all the way from the Great Depression through World War II to the apocalypse that inters civilization under radioactive rubble.

As a panorama of American history, it's a somewhat jaundiced view; the underlying philosophy seems to be that Yanks are hellbent on self-destruction.

DuPlenty and the love of his life, Sheela (Sheela Edwards) deliver performances that are as demented and abandoned as the Daalders presumably wanted.

The music — both the score and the production numbers that mostly feature the gaptoothed Sheela — is a strong element, a well-integrated blend of rock, jazz, classical and punk.—*Dogo.*

Crawlspace
(U.S.-COLOR)

An Empire Pictures release of a Charles Band production. Produced by Roberto Bessi. Executive producer, Band. Directed by David Schmoeller. Stars Klaus Kinski. Screenplay, Schmoeller; camera (color), Sergio Salvati; editor, Bert Glastein; music, Pino Donoggio; art director, Gianni Cozzo; production design, Giovanni Natalucci; casting, Anthony Barnard; associate producer, Ron Underwood. Reviewed at the Cannes Film Festival (market), May 16, 1986. (MPAA Rating: R.) Running time: **77 MINS.**
Dr. Karl Gunther . . . . Klaus Kinski
Lori Bancroft . . . . Talia Balsam
Harriet . . . . Barbara Whinnery
Martha . . . . Sally Brown
Also with: Carol Francis (Jess), Tané (Sophie), Jack Heller (Alfred), Kenneth Robert Shippy (Joseph Steiner).

Cannes — In terms of production values and technical competence, "Crawlspace" is well up there with the generally top quality Empire Pictures productions. But writer-director David Schmoeller has pulled his punches, and as a result this gothic tale is not as scary as it might have been.

It does have the distinct advantage of Klaus Kinski playing another tormented maniac, this time the son of a Nazi war criminal who has discovered, after a stint as a doctor in Argentina, that he's addicted to killing. He owns an apartment building, and rents out to attractive young women, spying on them from his "crawlspace," a narrow area behind the walls. He keeps a tongue-less woman in a cage in the attic, and is writing his grim memoirs.

The heroine, played by Talia Balsam, rents an apartment but is soon worried by the noises, the rats, and the generally bizarre goings-on. She escapes with her life in the end, but she's about the only one who does.

Trouble is, most of the thrills take place off-screen, or are muted severely. No telling why Schmoeller held back on the kind of shock shlock moments that addicts for this kind of pic like to see.

There are a few creepy moments in "Crawlspace," but not really enough. Still, with Kinski at his manic best, it's never really unenjoyable.—*Strat.*

The Fantasist
(IRISH-COLOR)

An ITC Entertainment release (Almi Pictures in U.S.) of a New Irish Film production. Produced by Mark Forstater. Directed by Robin Hardy. Stars Christopher Cazenove, Timothy Bottoms, Moira Harris. Screenplay, Hardy, from the novel "Goosefoot" by Patrick McGinley; camera (color), Frank Gell; editor, Thomas Schwalm; music, Stanislas Syrewicz; associate producer, Vivien Pottersman. Reviewed at the Cannes Film Festival (market), May 14, 1986. (No MPAA Rating.) Running time: **96 MINS.**
Patricia Teeling . . . . Moira Harris
Inspector McMyler . Christopher Casenove
Danny Sullivan . . . . Timothy Bottoms
Robert Foxley . . . . John Kavanagh
Also with: Mick Lally (Uncle Lar), Dairbre Ni Chaoimh (Monica), James Bartley (Hugh), Deirdre Donnelly (Fionnuala), Liam O'Callaghan (Farrelly).

Cannes — Writer-director Robin Hardy's first feature, "The Wicker Man," became a cult picture in many parts of the world. His second, "The Fantasist," is unlikely to do the same, yet it's a different kind of thriller, imbued with some comedy and a lot of Irish atmosphere. It is also a pretty uneven pic, with a few awfully awkward moments.

There's a killer on the loose, who charms single women by telephone, then comes to their homes, strips them, places them in a pose resembling a famous nude painting, and stabs them. Latest target for death is the delightfully innocent Patricia (Moira Harris) who arrives in the city from her home on a country farm looking for the man of her dreams. In what could surely happen only in Ireland, she finds a place to stay, sharing a bed with another girl. Neither of them seems to think that's an odd way to live.

Two suspects hover around Patricia. Robert (John Kavanagh), a fellow teacher at her school, who gargles wine in a posh restaurant and, on their first date, wants her to rub his tummy. Very odd. Then there's Danny (Timothy Bottoms), who lives in the same building as Patricia with his artist wife. He seems only marginally perturbed when the wife becomes the latest victim of the killer.

Or is the one-legged police inspector in charge of the case more than he seems? As played by Christopher Cazenove, he seems to have his share of neuroses, too. Pic is overburdened with rather corny red-herrings (Bottoms is always making strange phone calls), but the astute thriller addict will spot the murderer early on.

Pic's most bizarre scene comes when a naked Patricia is facing the knife wielding killer and is able to say sweetly, "Do you realize I don't even know your first name?" before seducing him. It's one of the stranger sex scenes in recent memory, but thanks to actress Moira Harris it works very well.

Harris is a major asset to the film. This vibrant newcomer handles a difficult role with skill and charm. The men aren't so memorable, mainly because they have to act "odd" all the time.

There's a fine feel for Dublin and its environs via the top notch cinematography of Frank Gell, and the pic has been pacily edited. On reflection, and even during viewing, it doesn't add up, but it may find its audience via its appealing central character and the bizarre twists to this tale of twisted sex and strange, tormented behavior.—*Strat.*

Dancing In The Dark
(CANADIAN-COLOR)

A Norstar Releasing release (in Canada) of a Brightstar Films-Film Arts-Film House Group production in association with the Canadian Broadcasting Corp. Executive producer, Don Haig. Produced by Anthony Kramreither. Directed by Leon Marr. Stars Martha Henry, Neil Munro, Rosemary Dunsmore and Richard Monette. Screenplay by Leon Marr based on the novel by Joan Barfoot; camera (color), Vic Sarin; editor, Tom Berner; coproducer, John Ryan; art direction, Lillian Sarafinchan; casting, Stuart Aikins Casting. Reviewed at the Cannes Film Festival (Directors Fortnight), May 14, 1986. Running time: **98 MINS.**
Edna . . . . Martha Henry
Harry . . . . Neil Munro
The Nurse . . . . Rosemary Dunsmore
The Doctor . . . . Richard Monette
Edna's roomate . . . . Elena Kudaba
Susan . . . . Brenda Bazinet

Cannes — "Dancing In The Dark," an intense psychological drama, marks an astonishing feature film debut for Toronto director-scripter Leon Marr.

The plot covers previously well-plowed territory. Edna (Martha Henry) is in hospital unwilling to communicate with her doctor and needing nurses to bathe and order her to eat. But her mind is lucid, recalling her marriage which lasted 20 years.

Mainly told by voiceover, the marriage unfolds slowly; she being an overly meticulous housewife and supremely satisfied doing nothing else. Her businessman husband talks incessantly of work and compliments her on being an excellent cook. They are shown eating, making small talk but that is not enough for him, as she learns from a telephone call.

Being told of his offscreen infidelity, she stabs him with a kitchen knife and meticulously cleans the knife. Scenes of her hospitalization are intercut with the years of marriage.

Marr works with admirable economy in building intensity; her scrubbing and taking a few moments every day in private pleasure listening to standard pop tunes and then being the perfect attentive wife and cook.

Vic Sarin's camerawork is always the detached observer, and without calling attention to itself, subtly changes mood from house to drab hospital, from bright colors to dark. It circles the dinner table, as if to get around the banal chatter between husband and wife.

Vet Canadian actress Martha Henry is outstanding as Edna. Neil Munro, the husband, also is terrific. And there is quiet, strong support from Rosemary Dunsmore and Richard Monette, an ever-questioning doctor who gets no answers.

Marr's work bursts with confidence and, except for an unnecessary final scene where Edna puts away the notebook in which she is writing her story, every move he makes fits seamlessly.

No gesture is wasted, neither is one camera shot, neither is a single touch — such as Edna wearing more makeup as she reaches her 40th birthday and her 20th anniversary. All technical credits are first-rate.

Pic should have a vibrant life on the art house and film festival circuit.—*Adil.*

My Little Pony
(U.S.-ANIMATION-COLOR)

A De Laurentiis Entertainment Group release of a Sunbow Prods. Intl. animated feature. Executive producers, Margaret Loesch and Lee Gunther. Supervising producer, Jay Bacal. Produced by Bacal and Tom Griffin. Coproduced and directed by Michael Joens. Screenplay, George Arthur Bloom; story consultant, Roger Slifer; music, Rob Walsh; songs composed by Tommy Goodman; lyrics by Barry Harman. With the voices of Danny DeVito, Madeline Kahn, Cloris Leachman, Rhea Perlman, Tony Randall, Tammy Amerson, Jon Bauman, Alice Playten. Reviewed at the Cannes Film Festival (market), May 12, 1986. (MPAA Rating: G.) Running time: **89 MINS.**

Cannes — Charmingly made fully animated feature is aimed at the moppet market (ages 3-10) as a followup to the Little Pony fad. As such, pic should captivate youngsters as the ponies become embroiled in many adventures. Helping is an intelligent script, some pleasant tunes and imaginative animation.

Opposing the little ponies, after their spring festival, are a phalanx of baddies, the wicked witch Hydia and her nasty daughters Reeka and Draggle. Helping the ponies are the Grundles, ugly but friendly little creatures who have lost their kingdom to the Smooze, a creation of the dreaded phlume, which flows over the countryside like a lava.

After many and sundry adventures, just when the little ponies and their friends are about to be engulfed by the Smooze, the sky fills with Flutter Ponies who create a tremendous wind which forces the Smooze all the way back to the Volcano of Doom, uncovering the Dream Castle and dumping the witch and her daughters back into the volcano.

Good prospects at wickets for moppet audiences, but bound to remain restricted mostly to very young children.—*Besa.*

Dumb Dicks
(U.S.-COLOR)

A Cannon Group release and production Produced by Menaham Golan and Yoram

Globes. Associate producer, John Thompson. Directed by Filippo Ottoni. Stars David Landsberg, Lorin Dreyfuss. Screenplay, Landsberg, Dreyfuss; camera (Telecolor), Giancarlo Ferrando; editor, Cesare d'Amico; music, G. & M. De Angelis; production design, Antonello Geleng. Reviewed at the Cannes Film Festival (market), May 12, 1986. (MPAA Rating: PG.) Running time: **90 MINS.**
Donald Wilson . . . . David Landsberg
Paul Miller . . . . Lorin Dreyfuss
Carlo Lombardi . . . . Christian De Sica
Caterina . . . . Valeria Golino
Also with: Rik Battaglia, Francesco Cinieri.

Cannes — As actors-writers, David Landsberg and Lorin Dreyfuss score with the poorly titled Cannon comedy "Dumb Dicks." There are plenty of laughs in this comedy-thriller, largely set in Italy, which is slated for a May 30 U.S. opening.

A pre-credits sequence establishes nebbish who keeps losing his jobs. A detective story addict, he signs up as a student of private eye Dreyfuss, who can't pay his bills and sees the gullible Landsberg only as a source of easy money.

Before long the pair are involved inadvertently with feuding Italian families, kidnaping and murder. Fleeing from a tough hitman, and trying to get a message to an Italian businessman about to fly home to Rome, they steal boarding passes from a couple of Japanese (the air hostess calls them by Japanese names without blinking an eye) and accidentally wind up in Italy sans passports or money. (There's a particularly good line of dialog here, with Dreyfuss noting that "the people here are still mad at us about all the babies and gum we left after the war.")

Through various and mostly funny misadventures, slapstick and running gangs, some of it almost in the same league as those vintage Bob Hope comedy-thrillers of the 1940s, these unlikely detectives win through. Handsome Italian backdrops add to the fun, though a stopover in Pisa late in the film slows things down a bit just as the pic should be heading fast for a finale.

There's some breezy stunt work, amusing running gags (involving a couple of Yank tourists forever posing for photos at the wrong time) and a general air of freshness and elan that makes for fun viewing. Pic should establish Landsberg and Dreyfuss as a top comedy team.

All technical credits are tops.
—*Strat.*

Giovanni Senzapensieri
(Carefree Giovanni)
(ITALIAN-COLOR)

An Istituto Luce/Italnoleggio release of an ASA Films/RAI-1/Istituto Luce coproduction. Produced by Gabriella Curiel. Directed by Marco Colli. Stars Eleonora Giorgi and Sergio Castellitto. Screenplay, Gianni Di Gregorio and Marco Colli; camera (Eastman-color), Emilio Bestetti; art director, Enrico Colli; editor, Roberto Schiavone; music, Lamberto Macchi; costumes, Clary Mirolo, Valeria Sponsoli; makeup, Franco Rufini; casting, Rita Forzano. Reviewed at the Cannes Film Festival (Directors Fortnight), May 11, 1986. Running time: **97 MINS.**
Giovanni . . . . Sergio Castellitto
Claire . . . . Eleonora Giorgi
Gino . . . . Franco Fabrizi
Armando . . . . Aldo Fabrizi
Teresa . . . . Anita Durante
Also with: Luigi De Filippo (Achille), Gastone Pescucci (Gastone), Rodolfo Bigotti (mechanic), Franca Ballette (Letizia).

Cannes — "Carefree Giovanni," a first feature for young director Marco Colli, is as simple and charming a story as its unpretentious hero, the dreamy, last-of-the-line descendant of a family of Roman aristocrats. Coproduced by RAI-1/ this dignified opener will find its natural audience on the small screen, at least locally.

Curtain rises in the year 1519, on a Renaissance court where the old Duke, patron of the arts, is informed of the death of Leonardo Da Vinci. He promptly has a heart attack and falls out the window.

This inauspicious beginning turns out to be only a playful prolog, however, and the next scene finds us in present-day Rome with the last Duke of the ruined family, Giovanni (Sergio Castellitto). Called "Carefree Giovanni" because of his childlike innocence, our hero lives with two old ladies (one is the great Anita Durante) who tyrannize him and he escapes to sit on the rooftop and dream most of the time.

Director Colli shows a sure touch in guiding his actors through this curious modern-day fable; besides an exceptionally on-key performance by Castellitto, the character roles are filled by some legendary Roman faces like Aldo Fabrizi, who cameos as a grocer. Franco Fabrizi (no relation) makes an appropriately detestable antique dealer who robs Giovanni blind. A good deal less convincing is Eleonora Giorgi as the pretty girl next door Giovanni moons over, and to whom he sends paper airplanes made out of priceless letters written by Leonardo himself.

Film is shot in the old quarter of the Roman ghetto, with its decaying patrician atmosphere and Renaissance ghosts. The appeal of "Carefree Giovanni" comes from the lost spirit of the age, recaptured for a moment in the exhilarating finale, when Giovanni escapes the world and soars through the air in Leonardo's wings.— *Yung.*

San Antoñito
(Little Saint Anthony)
(COLOMBIAN-COLOR-16m)

A Focine production. Executive producer, Interimagen. Directed by Pepe Sánchez. Screenplay, Sánchez, Dunav Kuzmanich; camera (color), Carlos Sánchez; music, Juan Lanz; editor, Gabriel González; sound, Osmar Chávez; costumes, Susana Carrie, Rosario Lozano. Reviewed at the Cannes Film Festival (Critics Week), May 13, 1986. Running time: **80 MINS.**
With: Carlos Jaramillo, Angela Calderón, Nubia Tapia, Margarita María Muñoz, Ana Arango de Mejía.

Cannes — At 40 minutes, "San Antoñito" could have made a tight little story, but at double that length it tends to become repetitive, unraveling its structure. Made on a small budget of approximately $60,000, its best chance of recouping costs will probably be television sales.

Story deals with Damián, a saintly 15-year-old peasant boy. The people of his village organize a bazaar to raise money that will get him to Medellín to enter the seminary and become a priest. Once there, he is helped by the women at the boarding house who look after him, feed him, buy his clothes and enjoy his leading them in their evening prayers. This situation continues over two years and only towards the end, when he starts arriving later and later at night, does something appear to be amiss. It finally turns out that he was neither chaste nor a little saint.

The leisurely pace in a turn-of-the-century provincial city is quite well portrayed and, although director Pepe Sánchez rather neatly adopts the same trusting attitude towards the boy as the characters in the film, he simply makes the same point (Damian's saintliness) too many times. Camera work is adequae but unimpressive and sound, on the print exhibited in Cannes, was poor. —*Amig.*

Tarot
(WEST GERMAN-COLOR)

An AAA Classic Presentation of a Moana Films (Berlin) production with Anthea Films (Munich), Executive producer, Hans Brockman. Directed by Rudolph Thome. Screenplay, Hans Zihlmann, based on Goethe's "Elective Affinities;" camera (color), Martin Schäfer; editor, Dörte Völz; music, Christoph Oliver; art director, Anamarie Michnevich; costumes, Gioia Raspe; assistant director, Petra Seeger; production manager, Dagmar Heuer. Reviewed at the Cannes Film Festival (Directors Fortnight), May 13, 1986. Running time: **115 MINS.**
Charlotte . . . . Vera Tschechowa
Edouard . . . . Hanns Zischler
Otto . . . . Rüdiger Vogler
Ottilie . . . . Katharina Böhm
Mittler . . . . William Berger
Also with: Kerstin Eiblmaier, Martin Kern, Peter Moland, George Tabori.

Cannes — This heavy-handed intellectual drama about the flow of relations between a temporarily unemployed film director, an actress writing her first novel, a scriptwriter going through a dry spell and a young student who leaves school to concentrate on music, does nothing else but talk about emotions, which are drawn into a sea of verbosity.

The entire thing starts in an idyllic manner. The director is about to marry the actress and direct her novel for the screen, so he invites the scriptwriter to live with them for a while until he overcomes his personal crisis. The foursome is completed with the arrival of a pretty blond student.

A game of affinities is being unconsciously played, as the four characters switch sympathies and discuss the meaning of their emotions, the moral aspects of their behavior and their personal responsibilities to the others as well as the distinctions between what they feel they would like to do and what they believe they are allowed to, each reacting to these questions in a different manner.

This could, as far as the subject is concerned, fit very well in one of the series of Moral Tales of French director Eric Rohmer, who is paid a tribute in one of the film's early sequences — a clip from "Full Moon In Paris." The trouble is, Thomé lacks the sensitivity, the perspicacity and the humor that make Rohmer's analyses so easy to watch.

Thomé has his protagonists cue each other into interminable dialogs as they sit around a table, walk through the woods or drive in a car. All the lines are delivered in an earnest, urbane and very cool manner, altogether, as if each one of the persons involved constantly is trying to hide his emotions from the others. There are many speculations on abstract theories, including one sequence in which tarot cards uncannily predict the future, and others in which the possibility of life after death is discussed at length.

The problem is that none of the participants seems to transcend the written text, and Thomé appears quite content to deal with the whole thing mainly on an intellectual level. Hanns Zischler and Rüdiger Vogler, who made such a marvelous pair in Wim Wenders' "Kings Of The Road," are at best awkward, and so is Vera Tschechowa, as the actress. Katharina Böhm seems to be the most affected of all four characters by the events, but even her efforts can't change the overall impression of a serious reading recital being played on a picturesque background.

The setting, a house in the middle of the forest, is the most appealing of pic's features, intended, no doubt, to stress the inner turmoils of the foursome, by putting them in **such peaceful surroundings. All technical credits are above average and it is only a pity they do not serve more lively proceedings.**
—*Edna:*

Osobisty Pamietnik Grzesznika Przez Niego Samego Spisany
(The Memoirs Of A Sinner)
(POLISH-COLOR)

A Film Polski presentation of a Zespoly Filmowe Film Unit "Rondo" Production. Directed by Wojciech Has. Screenplay, Michal Komar, from a novel by James Hogg; camera (color), Grzegorz Kedziersky; editor, Barbara Lewandowska-Cunio; music, Jerzy Maksymiuk; sound, Janusz Rosol; production design, Andrzej Przedworski; production manager, Konstanty Lewkowicz. Reviewed at the Cannes Film Festival (Directors Fortnight), May 13, 1986. Running time: **125 MINS.**
With: Piotr Bajor, Maciej Kozlowski, Janusz Michalowski; Hanna Stankowna, Eva Wisniewska, Franciszek Pieczka.

Cannes — Film has never been a very good vehicle for philosophical speculations, and even a gifted and established director such as Wojciech Has can't make much of it here. Choosing to deal with no lesser subjects than the essence of good and evil, with the dualism of the human soul and with the contradictions between righteousness and purity of heart, the film turns out as a magnificently spectacular piece of visual bravura. But it's so terribly confused and complex that most audiences will stop caring about it long before any serious train of thought can be embarked upon.

The 18th century novel on which the script is based tells the story of a youngster whose memories, recounted after death, are supposed to be a long series of wrong moral choices ending up with his killing his evil alter-ego, which translates into committing suicide.

The script disintegrates in the early stages into a morass of postulations from Goethe to de Sade. The one redeeming feature that gives some substance to the film is its pictorial splendor. Both production design and camera work are most carefully prepared in this period piece, with costumes, backdrops, sets and lighting all blending together sumptuously. The camera constantly moves on dolly tracks, and indeed the technical credits are topnotch from the director on down.

Since such a production as this, which had to cost far more than the average Polish picture, could have only limited appeal to arthouse audiences, it is probably to be commended that the Polish industry would indulge in such adventures for art's sake. —*Edna.*

Fair Game
(AUSTRALIAN-COLOR)

A C.E.L. release (Australia) of a Southern Films Intl. production. Produced by Ron Saunders, Harley Manners. Directed by Mario Andreacchio. Screenplay, Rob George; camera (Eastmancolor), Andrew Lesnie; editor, A. J. Prowse; music, Ashley Irwin; art director, Kimble Hilder; action coordinator, Glenn Boswell; production manager, Gay Dennis; assistant director, Chris Williams, sound, Toivo Lember. Reviewed at the Cannes Film Festival (market), May 12, 1986. Running time: **85 MINS.**
Jessica . . . . Cassandra Delaney
Sunny . . . . Peter Ford
Ringo . . . . David Sandford
Sparks . . . . Garry Who

Cannes — A lone woman in the dusty outback is terrorized by three toughs who first try to run her pickup truck off the road, then take photos of her as she lays, sleeping naked in her bedroom during stifling midday heat, then leave a dead kangaroo on the driver's seat of her car and finally tie her, almost naked, to the front of their truck as they drive wildly through the scrub. After all this her violent retaliation comes as no surprise.

This is a well made, unassuming suspense thriller of no particular distinction. The screenplay by Rob George is at fault in that it completely lacks characterization or motivation: we don't know anything about the beleaguered heroine, except that she seems to have a man who's away somewhere, and we don't know anything about the three marauders, except that they shoot kangaroos illegally on a game reserve. Two of them are manic, scrungy types, while the third is a smooth, handsome fellow, but just as bad as the others.

Women may well be turned off by the mindless attacks on this lone femme, though she does manage to eliminate all three of her tormentors by fadeout. There's a nasty, leering tone to it all.

On the plus side, first-time helmer Mario Andreacchio shows promise as an action director; he handles the suspense well, aided by good camerawork by Andrew Lesnie which emphasizes the isolation and desolation of the remote farm where the heroine lives.

As the woman, Cassandra Delaney gives a spunky performance, and manages to look beautiful even when the going is at its roughest; the three actors are merely cyphers.

Tight editing helps things along, and the pic should do good biz on vidcassette, though it may be a bit lightweight to score as a theatrical proposition.—*Strat.*

Say Yes
(U.S.-COLOR)

A Cinetel Films release of a Faunt Le Roy Prods. production. Executive producer, Rosemary Le Roy Layng. Produced by Larry Yust, Layng. Written and directed by Yust. Camera (United color), Isidore Mankofsky; editor, Margaret Morrison; sound, Michael Moore; production manager-line producer, Bill Hoyt; assistant director, Michael Haynie; set design, John Retsek; casting, Bob Gibson. Reviewed at the Cannes Film Festival (market), May 13, 1986. (MPAA Rating: PG-13.) Running time: **88 MINS.**
Annie . . . . Lissa Layng
Luke . . . . Art Hindle
George . . . . Logan Ramsey
W.D. Westmoreland . . . . Jonathan Winters
Gladys . . . . Maryedith Burrell
Belinda . . . . Jensen Collier
Message taker . . . . Jacque Lynn Colton
Cynthia . . . . Devon Ericson
Ernest . . . . Art La Fleur
First bride . . . . Laurie Prange
Major . . . . Anne Ramsey
Lady on bus . . . . Paula Trueman

Cannes — "Say Yes" is an old-fashioned comedy (have you heard the one about the guy who had to get married before midnight to qualify for a vast inheritance?) that just doesn't pack enough laughs.

Art Hindle portrays Luke, grandson of tycoon W.D. Westmoreland (Jonathan Winters), whose will bequeaths $250,000,000 to Luke if he marries before his 35th birthday. Grandpa has a fatal stroke leaving Luke only half a day to get hitched.

What follows is an unconvincing string of circumstances to prevent Luke from tying the knot, including the interference by his venal father George (Logan Ramsey), who stands to get the dough if Luke remains single. Director Larry Yust extracts humor out of several well-staged setpieces (particularly a disruption of the workforce at an egg-breaking factory), but generally his writing is uninspired.

Though numerous old girlfriends come out of the woodwork to try and snatch Luke and his impending boodle, for some unexplained reason he becomes infatuated with a homely country girl (Lissa Layng) who's left the farm to be free. Guess who ends up with Luke.

Acting is okay, although Jonathan Winters is only intermittently funny as he half improvises (with his patented use of handy props) his way through a corny role. Film was lensed over three years ago in New York City and San Diego and tech credits are fine; Cinetel released it domestically commencing last March.—*Lor.*

Dangerous Orphans
(NEW ZEALAND-COLOR)

A Cinepro Films production, in association with The New Zealand Film Commission. Produced by Don Reynolds, Directed by John Laing. Screenplay, Kevin Smith; camera (Colorfilm N.Z.), Warrick Attewell; production design, Ralph Davies; editor, Michael Horton; music, Jonathan Crayford; associate producer, Robin Laing; executive producer, Campbell Stevenson; production manager, Lyn Galbraith; sound, Mike Westgate. Reviewed at Cannes Film Fest (market), May 14, 1986. Running time: **90 MINS.**
O'Malley . . . . Peter Stephens
Costello . . . . Jennifer Ward-Lealand
Moir . . . . Michael Hurst
Rossi . . . . Ross Girven
Jacobs . . . . Peter Bland
Hanna . . . . Ian Mune
Also with: Zac Wallace (Scanlan), Grant Tilly (Beck), Ann Pacey (Mooney), Peter Vere-Jones (Handesman), Michael Haigh (Dutchman), Des Kelly (O'Malley Sr.), Tim Lee (Krebs), Michala Hanas (Anna Hanna), Toby Laing (Young O'Malley), Alexis Banas (Young Rossi), Edin Cox (Young Moir), Miles Tilly (Pope), Kevin Wilson (Inspector Lucas).

Cannes — John Laing, New Zealand's most prolific director, has come up with a fast-moving, far-fetched, glossy thriller in "Dangerous Orphans." Kevin Smith's screenplay isn't a model of coherence, but pic races along at such a pace that the viewer hardly has time to worry about such things as how or why.

Promise involves three young Robin Hood types, orphaned from an early age, who've been buddies since school. They team up to smash a drug ring, at the same time pocketing lots of ill-gotten loot for themselves. Opening scenes involve the assassination of a Yank drug courier in Auckland, then shift to Geneva where one of the trio poses as the courier to withdraw $5,000,000 from a Swiss bank. Back in New Zealand, the baddies are understandably peeved, and the action goes into high gear.

Matters are complicated because O'Malley (Peter Stephens), one of the trio, is in love with Costello (Jennifer Ward-Lealand), a sultry piano player and the ex-wife of Hanna, one of the gang leaders. Latter is played by Ian Mune, director of such pics as "Came A Hot Friday" and "Bridge To Nowhere."

There are holes aplenty in the plot, but most viewers won't mind. Main thing is that the pic is sufficiently flashy and pacy and contains enough action and mayhem to keep action-oriented customers happy.

Technically it's up to the highest standard of N.Z. films, with nifty camerawork, very tight editing, and good stuntwork. Acting in all roles is fine. The Kiwis should have another winner with this one.—*Strat.*

Going Sane
(AUSTRALIAN-COLOR)

A Sea Change Films production, in association with the New South Wales Film Corp. Executive producer & screenplay, John Sanford. Produced by Tom Jeffrey. Directed by Michael Robertson. Camera (Eastmancolor), Dean Semler; editor, Brian Kavanagh; music, Cameron Allan; production designer, Igor Nay; costume designer, Jan Hurley. Reviewed at the Cannes Film Festival (market), May 14, 1986. Running time: **90 MINS.**
Martin Brown . . . . John Waters
Ainslee Brown . . . . Judy Morris
Irene Carter . . . . Linda Cropper
Nosh . . . . Kate Raison
Sir Colin Grant . . . . Frank Wilson
Irwin Grant . . . . Jim Holt
Also with: Tim Robertson (Owen Owen), Anne Semler (Marta).

Cannes — In the same vogue as "Bliss," here's another Australian comedy-drama dissecting a man's midlife crisis, in this instance an affluent Sydney mining engineer who at age 40 decides he's bored with his job, his wife and his life.

While "Bliss" had a long and profitable run on the Australian circuit and played widely, although not lucratively in the U.S. via New World, prospects for "Going Sane" are nowhere near as bright.

Problem is the central character who for most of the picture is depressingly gloomy and sour, compounded by languid pacing, patchy acting and a script infused with some wit but few memorably funny passages.

Boxoffice outlook Down Under is far at best, relying mostly on the popularity of leading thesps John Waters and Judy Morris, and the chance that segments of the 40-plus audience may identify with Waters' situation, but it will be tv and homevideo fodder elsewhere.

After walking out on both his marriage and job, Waters lurches into an affair with his secretary (Linda Cropper). That comes unstuck after they take a trip to the outback and have an amusing encounter with a raving Welshman (Tim Robertson) and his man-eating German wife (Anne Semler).

Losing the will to continue living, Waters ends up in hospital, where he has the good fortune to meet the alluring Kate Raison, whose zest for life inspires him. They head off for Kate's country retreat only to find that Waters' previous employer, the big, bad mining company, has pegged a claim to the land (a blatant plug here for the conservation cause).

Waters, a talented and resourceful actor, understandably finds it tough to enliven a mostly jaded and morose character. Judy Morris turns in an embarrassingly strained and affected performance as his wife; she's such a pain-in-the-butt it's no wonder he bails out. Raison is a treat and Frank Wilson is excellent as the tyrannical mining boss.

Dean Semler's photography invests the picture with a rich, glossy and warm look that goes some way toward offsetting the grayness of the subject matter.

Director Michael Robertson shows some flair, but cannot elevate what is basically telepic material into a theatrical event. —Dogo.

The Big Bet
(U.S.-COLOR)

A Bert I. Gordon film distributed by Golden Communications, Golden Harvest Group. Directed, written and produced by Bert I. Gordon. Stars Lance Sloane, Kim Evenson, Sylvia Kristel and Ron Thomas. Camera (color), Tom DeNove. Reviewed at the Cannes Film Festival (market), May 13, 1986. (No MPAA Rating.) Running time: **98 MINS.**

Cannes — The name Sylvia Kristel used to mean a lot to the trade and filmgoers alike. However,

with her string of duds and cameo appearances in small-league filmmaking such as "The Big Bet," she will facilitate her anonymity in the art of tasteful serio-comic erotica.

The word "big" is something that can't be attached to this youth-oriented comedy caper that drags with pimply pace. "Big Bet's" thin storyline about an oversexed hero trying to bed the troubled and passive daughter of the minister in a week's time is not enough to make it to the softcore senior league.

Lance Sloane is the blond teenager who thinks of sex all the time, and he deserves to have Kristel for an understanding, worldly lady available to listen and be of practical comfort in restoring the young man's confidence in the field of scoring (American style), to meet his deadline.

The low-budget adolescent appeal of this feature is more suitable for video with youths intending to be initiated to something light first before graduating into harder, steamier stuff. But you can't bet on that really with this dragging high school sexcapade. —Mel.

Valhalla
(DANISH-ANIMATED-COLOR)

A Metronome (Copenhagen) release (world sales: J&M) of a Swan Film (Michael Andreasen) with Interpresse, Metronome, Palle Fogtdal, Danish Film Institute production. Based on Nordic myths and on design and characters from Peter Madsen, Henning Kure, Hans Rancke-Madsen, Per Vadmand and Sören Hakonsson's "Valhalla" comic strip. Directed by Peter Madsen. Screenplay, Peter Madsen, Henning Kure; codirected, Jeffrey James Varab; music, Ron Goodwin; dialog adaption and voice direction, Liane Aukin; art direction, Madsen; editor, Lidia Sablone. Reviewed at the Cannes Film Festival (market), May 12, 1986. Running time: **88 MINS.**

Voices
Thor . . . . .Stephen Thorne
Loke . . . . .Allan Corduner
Roskva . . . . .Suzanne Jones
Chalfe . . . . .Alexander Jones
Udgaardsloki . . . . .Michael Elphick
Hymer . . . . .John Hollis
Odin. . . . . .Mark Jones
Quark . . . . .Thomas Eje
Additional voices: Benny Hansen, Jesper Klein, Claus Ryskjär, Geoffrey Matthews, Percy Edwards, others.

(English soundtrack)

Cannes — "Valhalla" is a Danish-made cartoon feature with an English soundtrack and, obviously, a future on the international exhibition circuit. It is technically a highly accomplished work based on a syndicated cartoon strip dealing with gods, giants and strange beings of Viking and other ancient Nordic lore. Goings-on were violent in those days, and grotesques peopled Heaven and Earth, so Peter Madsen's picture probably will appeal less to smaller children than to youngsters and adults who have tough cartoon strips of the action genre as part of their daily diet.

Story has two kids of humankind following brawny Thor, the god of Thunder, and Loke, an evil demigod, across the rainbow from Valhalla, home of the gods, to Udgaard, the land of wicked sorcery and unholy Giants, where much trickery has to be overcome before the little group can return home. The Giants are a cross between Maurice Sendak uglies and various Ralph Bakshi beasts, and throughout the Bakshi inspiration is more in evidence than any of the Disney persuasion.

Thor is a run-of-the-mill muscleman with very little brains. Loke lacks only green eyes in being undiluted meanness. The human kinds are pretty nondescript, but Quark, a little cannonball of a fellow with fangs and lousy manners joins them, and whenever he has center stage, he works merry mayhem like the old bulldog of the Tom & Jerry shorts.

In one sequence, a set of chessmen are strictly out of "Alice In Wonderland." Otherwise, more traditional patterns of animation are adhered to. Ron Goodwin's score is nice enough. —Kell.

The Vindicator
(Frankenstein '88)
(CANADIAN-COLOR)

A 20th Century Fox release of a Michael T. Levy Enterprises presentation. World sales, Manley Prods. Executive producers, André Link, Pierre David. Produced by Don Carmody, John Dunning. Directed by Jean-Claude Lord. Screenplay, Edith Rey, David Reston; camera (color), René Verzier; supervising editor, Debra Karen; music, Paul Zaza; Frankenstein created by Stan Winston Studio; second unit director, Jim Hanley; stunt coordinator, Jerry Wills. Reviewed at the Cannes Film Festival (market), May 13, 1986. (MPAA Rating: R.) Running time: **88 MINS.**
Lauren Lehman . . . . .Terri Austin
Alex Whyte . . . . .Richard Cox
Burt. . . . . .Maury Chaykin
Hunter . . . . .Pam Grier
Carl/Frankenstein . . . . . .David McIlwraith

Cannes — "The Vindicator" is an extremely strange horror/sci-fi film with too many plot twists for its own good. Filmed in 1984, feature has sat on the shelf for over a year at 20th Century Fox and is, unfortunately, not crazy enough to give Fox a followup to its midnight hit "The Rocky Horror Picture Show."

As its alternate title "Frankenstein '88" implies, pic is yet another update of the Mary Shelley classic. For the space program, scientist Alex Whyte (Richard Cox) is working on creating a nearly indestructible cyborg using a human brain, metal body and special computer hookup with programming from his Primates Lab's "rage reinforcement" experiments on chimpanzees. This hookup causes the cyborg to react violently and lethally to any threatening stimulus, unless ordered

off by a remote control device.

Whyte's colleague Carl Lehman (David McIlwraith) is angry at Whyte for diverting research funds to his own experiments, and Whyte has a henchman kill Lehman in a lab explosion. Using Lehman's corpse, Whyte creates the first of his Frankenstein monsters, but the creature escapes before the remote control unit is attached to it, making it a deadly monster that will attack anything that approaches it.

Although a ruthless killer, the creature still has Lehman's memories, making it a self-divided, rather pathetic being. Lehman's pregnant wife Lauren (Terri Austin) tries to help it while Whyte hires a talented and ruthless female bounty hunter (guest star Pam Grier) to track it down and destroy it.

This familiar story provides the springboard for a dizzying array of mostly unconvincing plot twists, particularly in the final two reels when one is never certain who is going to pop up and get the drop on whom next. Because the artificial (post-synchronized) dialog is so clichéd and silly, the net effect of rather well-staged action sequences is a horror parody.

Earnest cast, especially the pretty but unpersuasive leading lady Terri Austin, is laughable, with even Pam Grier making very little of a patented macha role. Tech credits are okay though the lab facility looks more like a shopping mall than a high-security installation. The Frankenstein monster designed by Stan Winston Studio has a new look, in its tattered state (and backlit) closer to The Mummy than the original Karloff makeup job. —Lor.

Nightmare Weekend
(BRITISH-COLOR)

A Troma Inc. release of a Vision Communications production, in association with English Film Co. G.I.G. Prods. and Les Films des Lions. Produced by Bachoo Sen. Executive producer, Gerald Gottlieb. Associate producer, Andre Feingold. Directed by Henry Sala. Screenplay, George Faget Bernard; camera (Eastmancolor), Bob Baldwin; editor, David Gilbert; music, Martin Kershaw; sound, Arthur Sarkissian; special effects and props, Mike de Silva; special effects make-up, Dan Gates. Reviewed at the Cannes Film Festival (market), May 12, 1986. (MPAA Rating: R.) Running time: **85 MINS.**
Julie Clingstone . . . . .Debbie Laster
Jessica Brake . . . . .Debra Hunter
Edward . . . . .Dale Midkiff
Mary Rose . . . . ,. . . . . .Lori Lewis

Cannes — This is a low-charged softcore horror item in which three nubile and sexually active teens are invited to a weekend at a plush Florida home unaware they're to take part in some devilish experiments involving character transference. Thanks to the interference of the chief scientist's bitchy assistant, the kids are turned into "neuropaths," meaning they go berserk and start spewing nasty liquids.

More for voyeurs than horror freaks, thanks to the low level of special effects and general thrills, pic has ample scenes of pretty young girls disrobing and becoming involved in fevered, but evidently unarousing, petting. It gets dull after a while.

The only nighmare is the fear that this weekend will never end.

— Strat.

Jackals
(U.S.-COLOR)

The Movie Store release of a Hunter/MFG Prod. (World Sales, Skouras). Executive producer, Martin F. Goldman. Produced by Jack Lucarelli and Jameson Parker. Directed by Gary Grillo. Screenplay, Dennis A. Pratt; camera (Panavision, Deluxe color), Steve Yaconelli; editor, Steve Mirkovich; art direction, Bruce Crone; music, Paul Chihars; stunt coordinator, Bill Burton; special effects, Richard Helmer and Grant McCune. Reviewed at the Cannes Film Festival (market), May 13, 1986. (MPAA rating: R.) Running time: 92 MINS.
Joe Cass . . . . Jack Lucarelli
Jake Wheeler . . . . Gerald McRaney
Sheriff Mitchell . . . . Wilford Brimley
Dave Buchanon . . . . Jameson Parker
Jess Buchanon . . . . Jeannie Wilson
Also with: Dennis A. Pratt, Danelle Hand, Rick Hurst, Sherry Adamo, Sharon Hughes, Warner Glenn, David Steen, Rosanna De Soto, Roman Cisneros.

Cannes — This smoothly paced actioner set on the Arizona-Mexican border is competently lensed by helmer Gary Grillo, but offers little in the way of story to excite or intrigue. Alternately titled "American Justice," "Jackals" uses a Western horses-and-pickup truck setting to unwind a pretty routine police story. Good for its kind, but it doesn't reach very far.

Producer/star Jack Lucarelli is Joe, a former L.A. cop whose partner got killed in a messy arrest (flashback). He comes out to relax at friend Dave's (Jameson Parker) ranch, but it's a busman's holiday — first time out on the trail he rides right into a murder. Jake Wheeler (Gerald McRaney), a close-cropped ex-Green Beret type who works on the local police force with Dave, is running a profitable white-slave trade, bringing Mexican girls across the border. When he brutalizes one and she tries to run away, he shoots her in cold blood, not knowing Joe has seen everything from behind a bush. (A far cry from McRaney's tv role as half the brother detective team of "Simon & Simon," with Jameson Parker.)

The amazing thing is how "Jackals" manages to spin out a feature-length yarn, since everything is out in the open and fully known to the legal authorities in the first 15 minutes. Yet to its credit the plot keeps rolling, first with Joe convinc-

ing pal Dave he really saw a girl get killed, then with a tussle with the can't-be-bothered sheriff (Wilford Brimley), finally with Joe and Dave's extended private investigations. A fair amount of foot and truck chases keeps things hopping until the final roundup, where the blood flows freely. It comes as no surprise to learn the sheriff is a silent partner to Jake's evil-doing. The final scene, in which Joe blows Jake off the map, has some nice touches of eerie night-time special effects, all of which looks like practice for a more substantial picture to come. Acting is competent but no more than the action requires, which keeps viewer from becoming very concerned with the characters as people. — Yung.

Unmasking The Idol
(U.S.-COLOR)

A Polo Players presentation. Produced by Betty J. Stephens and Robert P. Eaton. Directed by Worth Keeter. Screenplay, Phil Behrens, Eaton; editor, Matthew Mallinson; music, Dee Barton. Features Ian Hunter, William T. Hicks, Charles K. Bibby. Reviewed at the Cannes Film Festival (market), May 13, 1986. Running time: 90 MINS.

Cannes — This is essentially a morning-type comic strip, such as are seen in kidvid selections, made into a live actioner. The infantile dialog, pastiche plot, and rudimentary sets all are impeccably phony, with not a single human element preserved.

That shouldn't bother audiences that this low-budgeted item is aimed at, who may while away 90 minutes, probably on tv, watching Duncan Jax, "America's first Hero-and-a-half" and his trained baboon going through this high-flying non-stop adventures.

These include a Charlie Chan-type Asian computer wiz Goldtooth, the "crazed emissary of a Third World power," who intends to trade atomic weapons with a baddie called the Scarlet Leader, and our hero, Duncan, who is given the task of seizing a Caribbean fortress. Pic seems tailored to tv outlets and theatrical and homevideo in third-world territories and in those markets pic should rack up what it sets out for.—Besa.

Flying
(CANADIAN-COLOR)

A Columbia Pictures release of a Brightstar Films production, in association with Rawifilm. World sales, Golden Communications. Executive producer, Pierre David. Produced by Tony Kramreither. Directed by Paul Lynch. Stars Olivia D'Abo. Screenplay, John Sheppard; camera (Filmhouse color), Brian Foley; editor, Ernie Rotundo; music, Ollie E. Brown, Joe Curiale; songs, Brown; sound (Dolby), Urmas Rosin; associate

producer, Ousama Rawi; casting, Lucinda Sill, Barbara Claman. Reviewed at the Cannes Film Festival (market), May 14, 1986. (No MPAA Rating.) Running time: 97 MINS.
Robin . . . . Olivia D'Abo
Jean . . . . Rita Tushingham
Tommy . . . . Keanu Reeves
Cindy . . . . Jessica Steen
Leah . . . . Renee Murphy
Jack . . . . Sean McCann

Cannes — If viewers missed the hot boxoffice flashes of "Flashdance," "Fame" and "Footloose," then "Flying" can serve as minor hybrid to temporarily satisfy the creative drought of the youth-oriented market. Olivia D'Abo makes an appealing but plump lonely kid with not much of a future in this film.

She has enemies at school, has a crush on a rich, handsome lad, has a lousy mean stepfather and is haunted by a car accident that left her without a real dad plus a recurring leg injury. But she has a dream, to be a member of an exclusive gymnast club and the chance to represent her school at a championship near Niagara Falls.

Poor Olivia suffers a lot and her only soap-opera consolation is an understanding and sickly mom who encourages her to follow that ambition, to push herself to excel. And she does work hard and in typical underdog approach she wins the hearts of the audience and soars to number one position in the finale. All sound very similar with all the essential unoriginal ingredients, plus 13 supposedly new (but sound old) songs by Ollie E. Brown, responsible for "Flashdance," "Karate Kid," "Breakin'," danceable tie-in soundtrack may help sell the photoplay.

"Flying" is something like a teenage version of "Heavenly Bodies," exploitative and imitative, but works in some parts to inspire the crowd it was made for. Pic doesn't look like it will soar to anything special, though the Canadian shots are visually charming and the presence of Rita Tushingham as the tough coach with the wrong hairdo can attract the nostalgic and oldies crowd for curiosity's sake. Altogether, a minor effort that deserves little attention — Mel.

Jake Speed
(U.S.-COLOR)

A New World Pictures release of a Crawford/Lane Prod. in association with Foster Prods. and Balcor Film Investors. Executive producer, John Roach. Produced by Andrew Lane, Wayne Crawford, William Ivey. Directed by Lane. Stars Crawford, Dennis Christopher, Karen Kopins, John Hurt. Screenplay, Crawford, Lane; camera (color), Bryan Loftus; editor, Fred Stafford; art direction, Norman Baron; music, Mark Snow. Reviewed at the Cannes Film Festival (market), May 13, 1986. (MPAA Rating: PG.) Running time: 100 MINS.
Remo . . . . Dennis Christopher
Margaret . . . . Karen Kopins

Sid . . . . John Hurt
Pop . . . . Leon Ames
Also with: Donna Pescow, Roy London, Barry Primus, Monte Markham, Alan Shearman, Rebecca Ashley.

Cannes — "Jake Speed," a cross between "Romancing The Stone," "Raiders Of The Lost Ark" and a whole lot more in that vein, is fun — deliberately mindless adventure that keeps tongue firmly in cheek.

Pic begins in thriller fashion, with a pair of thugs in Paris chasing an American tourist girl and grabbing her.

Cut to her home back in the U.S. where the family is worried about her disappearance. Pop wanders in, saying they ought to hire Jake Speed to find her. Who's he? The hero of paperback thrillers. Pop gets sent to bed because he's obviously senile.

But daughter number two gets a note to meet Jake Speed at a seedy bar. She goes, meets Speed and his sidekick author Remo. They have her booked on a flight to Africa where, as Speed tells her, the sister has been kidnaped by an international gang of white slavers. Remo says the pair "defeat evil where it exists" and do so for no fee.

Sure enough on all counts.

After a hilarious false start once in Africa, the trio crashes the den of the international white slavers lorded over by a malicious and deliciously evil John Hurt. Against the rescue attempt is a country in the middle of a revolution.

So if chasing baddies isn't enough, the trio has to dodge flame throwers from the guerrillas. But as if by magic, a bulletproof van drops from the sky in the nick of time to effect a getaway to the last plane to safety.

Speed is well played by a heavy-lidded and laconic Wayne Crawford who talks as an old-fashioned paperback hero would — in cliches. Karen Kopins tackles her role with style and Dennis Christopher is a delightful sidekick who, in the middle of the action, takes time to get some chapters off his typewriter.

But the language is too rough for the kiddies and that spoils what otherwise would be a rollicking adventure for all.

Andrew Lane's direction, for the most part, is fast paced right to the "Casablanca"-type penultimate scene. Pic ends back in the U.S. with Kopins getting to the newstand in time for arrival of the Speed book about the story.

Technical credits are all fine, especially the 1940s-type look to the setting in Africa and the revolution action. Film buffs will note dozens of scenes imitating pics of years ago. Much of "Jake Speed" is right out of the 1940s into 1986, as only films would have it.—Adil.

Rih Essed
(Man Of Ashes)
(TUNISIAN-COLOR)

A Satpec/Cinetelefilms coproduction. Executive producers, Ahmed Attia and Radhi Trimech. Written and directed by Nouri Bouzid. Stars Imad Maalal. Camera (Satpec Gammarth color), Youssef Ben Youssef; editor, Mika Ben Miled; music, Salah Mahdi; art direction, Claud Bennys, Mohsen Rais; sound, Faouzi, Riadh Thabet; costumes, Laila B. Mahmoud, Lilia Lakhoua; special effects, Ahmed Bourguiba, Med Choukou; casting, Mounir Baaziz. Reviewed at the Cannes Film Festival (Un Certain Regard), May 12, 1986. Running time: **108 MINS.**

Hachemi . . . . Imad Maalal
Farfat . . . . Khaled Ksouri
Touil . . . . Habib Belhadi
Azaiez . . . . Mohamed Dhrif
Neffisa . . . . Mouna Noureddine
Also with: Mahmoud Belhassen (Mustapha), Mustafa Adouani (Ameur), Yacoub Behiri (Levy), Wassila Chawki (Sejra).

Cannes — "Man Of Ashes" is a remarkable first film from Nouri Bouzid, longtime assistant director who has worked on everything from Tunisian classics like "Aziza" to "Raiders Of The Lost Ark." "Man Of Ashes" springs to life as a fully mature, completely cinematic work. But no less exceptional is the delicate handling of its subject, a boy's coming of age in a society where the values of family and tradition are sacred and unquestionable.

The story takes place in the days before the marriage of Hachemi (Imad Maalal), a sensitive young wood carver living in the old town of Sfax. His fear of women is gradually revealed to have its origins in early boyhood, when he and his friend Farfat (Khaled Ksouri) another apprentice wood carver, were raped by their master. Hachemi's horror of marriage comes up against the rigid expectations of his stern father and superstitious mother, and a social mechanism from which there apparently is no escape.

Hachemi's nightmare coincides with Farfat's public exposure as "not a man" and explusion from his family. While Hachemi reacts with painful inwardness, Farfat rebelliously challenges society's ostracism. After a bachelor party in a brothel, in which both boys have their first experiences with women, Farfat deliriously stabs their rapist in the abdomen, and vanishes, undefeated.

Film is exceptionally well lensed, with a nervous energy that echoes the hero's anxiety and reflects his memories and thoughts. The seaside and shipyards, narrow streets and fascinating interiors build up an intimate, colorful picture of the everyday life of the sympathetic and very human characters.

Though there is little action in the picture, Bouzid uses skillful camerawork and editing to give the jumble of images rhythm and to build emotional tension into a crescendo. Parallel with Hachemi's problems, we get glimpses of other contradic-tions and separations: the separate roles assigned to men and women; the friendship of the Arab boy with Levy, an old Jewish friend of the family, who gives him a wedding present but offers no answers. Acting is topnotch, particularly Imad Maalal's introspective Hachemi and Khaled Ksouri's scornful, untamed Farfat. — Yung.

Sixty-Four Day Hero
(BRITISH-DOCU-COLOR/B&W-16m)

A British Film Institute production, in association with Channel Four. Produced by Franco Rosso and Joanna Smith. Directed by Rosso. Writer, Gordon Williams; camera, (color/b&w, 16m), Chris Morphet; editor, Edward Roberts. Reviewed at the Cannes Film Festival (market), May 14, 1986. Running time: **100 MINS.**

Cannes — According to the screen credits, this absorbing documentary was made in association with the U.K.'s Channel Four, and tv is the natural home for "Sixty-Four Day Hero," the life story of Randolph Turpin, the British middleweight boxing champ who held the world title for just a couple of months.

Meticulously researched by Gordon Williams, who also narrates, it is a detailed story of the half-caste boy from the back streets of Leamington in England, who started boxing at the age of eight and by the time he was 23 had defeated Sugar Ray Robinson to win the world title. Just 64 days later, Robinson got his revenge, and from then on it was a slow journey downhill until at the age of 38 Turpin threw in the sponge, shot his baby daughter (who survived) and then shot himself in the head and heart.

With the aid of a wealth of archive material (all in black and white) plus interviews (in color) with members of his family, his managers, trainer and friends, Williams' research confirms Turpin was a bully from childhood, a fool about money, ignored the advice of his friends, and just threw his money around. His first marriage at the age of 18 ended in divorce, and neither his first wife nor the son of that union agreed to be interviewed. His second wife has plenty to say, and though his investments failed and he went bankrupt, she complains little.

When Turpin won the championship, he was feted in his home town with a civic reception, but as he raced downhill he soon was forgotten by the bigwigs and, as Williams puts it, the only tribute to the city's "favorite son" is a plaque in the town hall presented by an admirer.

Surprisingly, this is at times a moving and emotional tale, and it consistently holds the interest. The library material, mainly newsreels and tv, is superbly edited by Edward Roberts to give the highlights of many of his bouts, particularly when in his prime, contrasting with later contests when he ended on the canvas. Franco Rosso has given the docu straightforward direction and Chris Morphet's camerawork (16m) is okay.—Myro.

Flagrant Desir
(A Certain Desire)
(FRENCH-COLOR)

A UGC Worldwide Distribution release Hemdale in U.S. of a Martel Media Production Sofracima Films A2/Third Eye Prods./Odessa Films coproduction. Executive producer, Kenneth F. Martel. Produced by Catherine Winter; coproducer, Frederic Golchan. Stars Sam Waterston, Marisa Berenson, Lauren Hutton. Written and directed by Claude Feraldo. Camera (color), Willy Kurant; editor, Chris Holmes, Marie Castro; music, Gabriel Yared; sound, Jean Umansky; art direction/costume design, Françoise Deleu; assistant director, Jacques Cluzaud; casting, Evelyne Vidal. Reviewed at the Cannes Film Festival (market), May 15, 1985. Running time: **95 MINS.**

Gerry Morrison . . . . Sam Waterston
Jeanne Barnac . . . . Marisa Berenson
Robert Barnac . . Bernard-Pierre Donnadieu
Marlene Belle-Ferguson . . . . Lauren Hutton
Marguerite Barnac . . . . . . Arielle Dombasle
Eveline Barnac . . . . Anne Roussel
Vittorio . . . . François Dunoyer
Georges Barnac . . . . François Dyrek

Cannes — "A Certain Desire" brings together a classy international cast in a disconnected murder mystery oozing expensive production values like an overly-rich desert. Director Claude Faraldo's vision of how French millionaires live, love and scheme to get their hands on each other's francs is pure fantasy-time. The overall effect is similar to leafing through French Vogue in the doctor's office.

Gerry Morrison (Sam Waterston) is an Interpol cop asked to probe into the death of Marguerite Barnac (Arielle Dombasle), member of one of the big wine dynasties in the Bordeaux area. The family insists the corpse in the lake got there by accident, a theory the local police would be happy to adopt, but Gerry has a thirst for the truth.

While the investigation proceeds, film goes off in all sorts of strange directions designed to uncover all those nasty secrets the filthy rich hide behind their outward respectability. Thus we find murdered Marquerite was a cynical money-grabber, and master of the estate Robert (Bernard-Pierre Donnadieu) a mean-spirited baddie. On the more angelic side of the family is Jeanne (Marisa Berenson), who has a tasteful love relationship with Marlene (Lauren Hutton). Jeanne's major worry in life is her beautiful daughter Eveline (Anne Roussel), whose virginity weighs on mom so heavily she hires her own ex-gigolo (François Dunoyer) to cure the problem. When Eveline and the gigolo abruptly fall in love, question of propriety arises: is it vulgar to pay the man?

Several relationships later, inspector Gerry has cracked the case but keeps mum for Jeanne's sake. (The murderess) gets off with a reprimand: "You can't kill people just because they're not nice!"

Camerawork by Willy Kurant is gorgeously lush, and the fashions, sets and wine goblets most attractive. Cast just walks through their roles, though it's hard to imagine what can be done with dialog the likes of, "So you tasted my mother's wine? Did you savor it?" The women are uniformly beautiful, though for some reason Lauren Hutton is given a huge birthmark that covers half her face. — Yung.

Busted Up
(CANADIAN-COLOR)

A Rose & Ruby presentation of a Damian Lee/David Mitchell Prod. Executive producer, Lawrence Nesis. Produced by Lee, Mitchell. Directed by Conrad E. Palmisano. Stars Irene Cara and Paul Coufos. Screenplay, Lee; camera (color), Ludvik Bogner; editor, Gary Zubek; art direction, Stephen Surjik; costumes, Nancy Kaye; music, Charles Barnett; songs "Dying For Love" by Gordon Groddy and Carlota McKee, "I Can't Help Feeling Empty," by Cara and "Busted Up" by Cara, Groddy; sound, Gary Zubek. Reviewed at the Cannes Film Festival (market), May 14, 1986. Running time: **90 MINS.**

Early Bird . . . . Paul Coufos
Simone . . . . Irene Cara
Angie . . . . Stan Shaw
Irving Drayton . . . . Tony Rosato

Cannes — "Busted Up" is a dull, predictable, slackly directed actioner about a boxer trying one last fight to save his neighborhood from blockbusters.

Win the fight and he also gets back his singer wife who walked out on him and their young child. Risking all, he pits his gym against the meanest fighter the blockbusters can find.

Irene Cara as the wife sings four numbers including the title song she cowrote with Gordon Groddy, but throughout she appears distracted. Understandable, considering her wooden costar Paul Coufos and poor script by Damian Lee. Boxing fight sequences predominate and are the only ones that show some vigor.

Conrad E. Palmisano's direction leaves much to be desired, as do all technical credits.

Mark this one down for homevid at best and Canadian paycable.
— Adil.

Rhosyn a Rhith
(Coming Up Roses)
(BRITISH-COLOR)

A Red Rooster S4C production. Produced by Linda James. Directed by Stephen Bayly. Screenplay, Ruth Carter; camera (Kay color), Dick Pope; editor, Scott Thomas; music, Michael Storey; production design, Hildegard

Bechtler; sound, Simon Fraser. Reviewed at the Cannes Film Festival (Un Certain Regard), May 12, 1986. Running time: **93 MINS.**
Trevor Jones . . . . .Dafydd Hywel
Mona . . . . .Iola Gregory
Gwen . . . . .Olive Michael
June .Mari Emlyn
Eli Davies . . . . .W.J. Phillips
   Also with: Glan Davies (Dino), Gillian Elisa Thomas (Sian), Ifan Huw Dafyyd (Dave), Rowan Griffiths (Pete), Bill Paterson (Mr. Valentine), Clyde Pollitt (Councillor).
(Welsh dialog)

Cannes — Welsh-language films are few and far between, and this is the first to have been selected for an official section at Cannes. It's a gentle, sweet little item about the effect on various characters of the closure of a small town cinema.

The Rex wasn't much of a cinema to begin with: the screen is covered with patches of dirt, the projectors break down, and it has a sadly tatty air (reminiscent of many a provincial British theater). But when it shutters, the projectionist, Trevor (Dafydd Hywel) and ice-cream saleslady, Mona (Iola Gregory) are thrown out of work. Trevor soon finds himself deep in debt, since he has an ex-wife and three sons to support, and, hoping against hope the Rex will reopen, borrows the £700 funeral fund of the ex-manager, Eli (W.J. Phillips) to tide him over. But the cinema doesn't reopen, and when old Eli falls ill, Trevor realizes he has to raise the money quickly. Helped by Mona, he hits upon an unusual idea: growing mushrooms inside the fetid, dark atmosphere of the old picture palace.

There's a touch of the old Ealing comedies in this rather quaint tale of little people pulling together in time of adversity, and though a very small film (the blowup from 16m is fuzzy at times), helmer Stephen Bayly (who made another Welsh-track pic, "And Pigs Might Fly," in 1983) gets the most out of his material.

Dafydd Hywel and Iola Gregory are fine in the lead roles, with all the supporting players expertly cast. The forlorn setting of a town that seems to be dying before our eyes is a major factor (pic was shot in Aberdare, South Wales).

Dedicated to a real-life "cinema manager and showman," "Coming Up Roses" is modest, gentle, unassuming and quite charming.
—*Strat.*

Serpent Warriors
(U.S.-COLOR)

A Frank Wong & Eastern Media Entertainment presentation (world sales, Walter Manley) of an E&C production. Directed by Niels Rasmussen. Stars Clint Walker, Chris Mitchum. Screenplay, Martin Wise; camera (color) Greb von Berblinger; stunts by Stunt Actors of America (Las Vegas); second unit production, Kee Woo Film Co. (Hong Kong). No further credits available. Reviewed at the

Cannes Film Festival (market), May 15, 1986. Running time: **96 MINS.**
Jason King . . . . .Koo Huan
Mrs. King . . . . .Kathleen Lu
Morgan Bates . . . . .Clint Walker
Laura Chase . . . . .Anne Lockhart
Tim Moffet . . . . .Chris Mitchum
Snake Priestess . . . . .Eartha Kitt

Cannes — "Serpent Warriors" must be seen as aimed straight at the homevideo market although there might still be cinema outlets in various backlands of civilization where this kind of animal scare actioner has an audience.

Director Niels Rasmussen, a deft hand with action sequences and at a loss with having anyone speak acceptable dialog, mixes old-fashioned fisticuffs and shoot 'em up tableaux on a southern California desert and mountain locations with the most hideously accomplished orgies of mass snake attacks on humans in Hong Kong and Japanese studios simulating a high-rise condominium.

It seems some old curse issued by a dying snake-worshipping tribe's chieftain works 40 years later on Jason King, an Asian construction company president. If he goes on building, armies of snakes and one particular giant boa constrictor will invade his territory. His wife has dreams about this and warns Jason, but in vain.

The wife goes to California and enlists the help of a trio of zoologists (Clint Walker, Anne Lockhart and Chris Mitchum) who soon join battle with Caucasian roughneck correspondents of the surviving Far Eastern snake voodoo'ers (all led, incidentally, by a wildly grimacing and ferociously growling Eartha Kitt).

With stunt and special effects plus snake farm alumni by the thousands, the Caucasian protagonists of Rasmussen's rawboned, blood-gushing entertainment are lost completely in a 20-minute climax of horror. Here, we witness, in closeups and in totals, the snake army's invasion of the privacy of a high-rise's population of Asians in their offices, in their bubble baths, and on their disco nightclub floors.

"Serpent Warriors" may constitute primitive scare entertainment, but it has bite and clout in a zestily vulgar way on par with the best of its dubious genre.—*Kell.*

Monster In The Closet
(U.S.-COLOR)

A Troma release of a Closet Prods. production (world sales, Manley Prods.). Produced by David Levy, Peter L. Bergquist. Executive producers, Lloyd Kaufman, Michael Herz. Written and directed by Bob Dahlin. Camera (color), Ronald McLeish; editor, Raja Gosnell, Stephanie Palinski; music, Barrie Guard; sound, Don Parker; assistant director, Bergquist; monster design, William Stout; monster crew supervisor, Doug Beswick; second unit camera, Bill Mendenhall; casting Sally Ann

Stiner, Cindy Pierson. Reviewed at the Cannes Film Festival (market), May 15, 1986. (MPAA Rating: PG.) Running time: **87 MINS.**
Richard Clark . . . . .Donald Grant
Diane Bennett . . . . .Denise DuBarry
Sheriff Ketchum . . . . .Claude Akins
Father Martin . . . . .Howard Duff
Prof. Pennyworth . . . . .Henry Gibson
Gen. Turnbull . . . . .Donald Moffat
Roy Crane . . . . .Paul Dooley
Margo Crane . . . . .Stella Stevens
Joe . . . . .John Carradine
Scoop Johnson . . . . .Frank Ashmore
Professor . . . . .Paul Walker
Ben Bernstein . . . . .Jesse White
Monster . . . . .Kevin Peter Hall

Cannes — "Monster In The Closet" is a pleasant, occasionally funny combination of homage and spoof directed at the science fiction monster films popular in the 1950s. It will be appreciated by fans of old B-pictures but is out of step with the tastes of contemporary audiences.

Writer-director Bob Dahlin carefully apes the rigid format of the traditional monster opus (with corny dialog intact): an unknown creature is killing Californians living in the small town of Chestnut Hills in their closets and San Francisco obituary writer Richard Clark (Donald Grant) is sent by his editor to cover the story. He soon teams up with science prof Diane Bennett (Denise DuBarry) and her brilliant child nicknamed Professor (Paul Walker) to follow up clues.

Monster eventually shows up, looking like a brown-skinned, huge-mouthed imitation of Carlo Rambaldi's oft-copied "Alien" creation, and the military, led by no-nonsense Gen. Turnbull (Donald Moffat) steps in to handle the situation. It turns out the monster is impervious to conventional weaponry, leaving the star trio to invent methods of destroying it. In several funny twists, the monster's unexplained affinity for closets turns out to be a key script element.

Despite some dull patches in which parody becomes merely repetition of cliches, "Monster" is cute with lots of guest stars. Stella Stevens does a fine version of Janet Leigh's "Psycho" shower sequence, generating solid laughs opposite Paul Dooley as her husband. As a goofy old scientist, Henry Gibson has his moments, too. Moffatt is perfect as the tough-talking general.

Lead players are fine, particularly Donald Grant, who, in film's well set-up and funniest payoff, turns out to be the object of the monster's affections (once his Clark Kent glasses are taken off) rather than the heroine.

Overproduced in relation to the targets of its parody, "Monster" is well-made (it was shot in 1983 and had postproduction completed more recently). End crawl is unintentionally funny as what seems like a thousand people are individually credited or thanked for working on the picture. Film probably will be best remembered for the inspired

silliness of its tagline solution to the monster problem, when the heroine goes on tv to plea: "Destroy all closets!" — *Lor.*

Whoops Apocalypse
(BRITISH-COLOR)

An ITC Entertainment presentation of a Picture Partnership production. Produced by Brian Eastman. Directed by Tom Bussman. Stars Loretta Swit, Peter Cook. Screenplay, Andrew Marshall, David Renwick; camera (Rank color), Ron Robson; editor, Peter Boyle; music, Patrick Gowers; production design, Tony Noble; sound, Sandy Macrae; assistant director, Gary Gavignon; casting, Mary Selway. Reviewed at the Cannes Film Festival (market), May 15, 1986. Running time: **89 MINS.**
President Barbara Adams . . . .Loretta Swit
Sir Mortimer Chris . . . . .Peter Cook
Lacrobat . . . . .Michael Richards
S.A.S. Sergeant . . . . .Rik Mayall
Rear-Admiral Benish . . . . .Ian Richardson
General Mosquera . . . . .Herbert Lom
Alexei Sayle in a Hawaiian
   Shirt . . . . .Alexei Sayle
   Also with: Joanne Peace, Chris Malcolm, Shane Rimmer, Richard Murdoch.

Cannes — Based on a popular British television series, "Whoops Apocalypse" is a frantic, uneven, mostly funny and very British comedy. It has the tastelessness of Monty Python coupled with a fondness for bizarre characters and irreverence to authority figures that's very English. It's really a series of tv-style sketches loosely based around a theme of power-politics in the Caribbean, and some audiences will respond more to its often outrageous humor than others.

It opens with the death of the U.S. president, a popular former circus clown (Uncle Yuk-Yuk), who dies when he asks a tv reporter to punch him in the stomach to show how strong he is. He's succeeded by the Vice President (Loretta Swit in the film's sanest and least interesting role), who immediately consults a former president, author of a book, "Commie Bastards I Have Known," and now serving a life sentence on a rock pile.

Meanwhile, a powerful Caribbean nation, led by dictator Herbert Lom, invades a tiny British colony. The British prime minister (Peter Cook) reacts by sending a mighty task force, which includes a gay Admiral (cue for a very nice parody of World War II movies and all those domestic leave-taking scenes) and a beautiful, blond Princess, serving as a nurse, who accidentally castrates a sailor while shaving him.

As the pic lurches from one gag to the next, the British win the war, but the Princess is kidnaped by an international terrorist (Michael Richards) known for his clever disguises. Cook threatens to nuke Lom's country if the Princess isn't released by a certain time. Meanwhile, the British P.M. has become convinced that unemployment is caused by pixies, and that the only cure is to have workers jump off a cliff by the thousands, thus making way for the unemployed. Members of his cabinet who disagree are literally crucified.

Two of Britain's most popular "alternative" comics appear in the film. Rik Mayall is a foul-mouthed, gung-ho leader of an anti-terrorist squad, whose shoot-any-thing-that-moves credo manages to get half his men killed while attacking London's wax museum searching for the missing Princess. And Alexei Sayle is a Russian unconvincingly disguised as a Caribbean hotelier on an island filled with Soviet rockets.

Some of the comedy, especially in the Mayall sequence, is raw and violent; most of it is cheerfully vulgar and anti-establishment. It doesn't make for a very coherent picture, and the direction by first timer Tom Bussman is noticeably slapdash, but there'll be an enthusiastic audience for the pic wherever the wilder fringes of British comedy are known and popular.

Technical credits are all pro, and Peter Boyle edited to a commendably tight 89 minutes. —Strat.

Separate Vacations
(CANADIAN-COLOR)

An RSL Entertainment release and production, with Playboy Enterprises. Produced by Robert Lantos and Stephen J. Roth. Associate producers, Andras Hamori and Julian Marks. Directed by Michael Anderson. Stars David Naughton, Jennifer Dale. Screenplay, Robert Kaufman; camera (color), François Protat; editor, Ron Wisman; (no music credit listed); sound, Doug Ganton; production designer, Csaba Kertesz; set decorator, Murray Sumner; costume designer, Laurie Drew; casting, Clare Walker. Reviewed at the Water Tower Theater, Chicago, April 29, 1986. (MPAA Rating: R.) Running time: **82 MINS.**
Richard Moore . . . . David Naughton
Sarah Moore . . . . Jennifer Dale
Jeff Ferguson . . . . Mark Keyloun
Karen . . . . Laurie Holden
Alicia . . . . Blanca Guerra
Helen Gilbert . . . . Suzie Almgren
Shelle . . . . Lally Cadeau
Annie Moore . . . . Jackie Mahon
Donald Moore . . . . Lee-Max Walton
Bobby Moore . . . . Jay Woodcroft
Harry Blender . . . . Tony Rosato
Robyn . . . . Colleen Embree

Chicago — This witless sex comedy takes some 82 minutes of screen time to discover that a married couple occasionally needs times away from the kids to keep the romantic fires stoked. Yawns and listless box-office loom.

Written by Robert Kaufman and directed by Michael Anderson, "Separate Vacations" plays part tv sitcom, part Playboy philosophy. It is wholly uninteresting as a theatrical feature although Playboy, which has a financial interest in the pic, might extract from it some minimal mileage on its cable-tv channel.

Produced on the cheap in Canada, "Separate Vacations" has a 30-ish architect and harried wife (David

Naughton and Jennifer Dale) living in domestic suburban chaos with three obnoxious children. He decides to take off solo to Mexico; she takes off for a nearby ski resort.

Despite several temptations, the husband and wife reunite with marital fidelity vows unviolated. On the wife's side, there's that cute ski instructor, badly played by Mark Keyloun. For the husband's part, there's a series of aborted encounters better handled by Lally Cadeau, Suzie Almgren, Mexican thesp Blanca Guerra, Carolyn Dunn and Laurie Holden.

Scripter Kaufman ("Love At First Bite," among others) invariably takes a puerile approach to the thin material, opting for the most mindless gags — one has the husband vomiting at key moment in his adulterous quest. Nothing here is funny. Even the sex scenes remain on the conservative side of the R spectrum.

Anderson's direction is deficient. Naughton as the husband comes across as an unappetizing mix of Jerry Lewis and Elliott Gould. Dale as the wife shows she has difficulty handling comedy, or at least supposed comedy.

Production values, from set design to photography and scoring, reflect the pic's modest origination. —Sege.

Free Ride
(COLOR)

Amateurish, unfunny sex comedy.

A Galaxy Intl. release of a Trancas production. Produced by Tom Boutross, Bassem Abdallah. Executive producer, Moustapha Akkad. Associate producer, M. Sanousi. Directed by Tom Trbovich. Screenplay, Ronald Z. Wang, Lee Fulkerson, Robert Bell; camera (color), Paul Lohmann; editor, Ron Honthaner; sound, Steve Nelson, Clark King; set decoration, Joe Mirvis; art direction, Daniel Webster; assistant director, Lawrence Lipton; special effects, A&A Special Effects; casting, Dan Guerrero. Reviewed at Coronet Theater, L.A., May 3, 1986 (MPAA Rating: R.) Running time: **82 MINS.**
Dan Garten . . . . Gary Hershberger
Greg . . . . Reed Rudy
Jill Monroe . . . . Dawn Schneider
Carl . . . . Peter DeLuise
Elmer . . . . Brian MacGregor
Dean Stockwell . . . . Warren Berlinger
Debbie Stockwell . . . . . Mamie Van Doren
Kathy . . . . Babette Props
Vinnie Garbagio . . . . . Anthony Charnota
Vito Garbagio . . . . Mario Marcelino
Old Man Garbagio . . . . Frank Campanella

Hollywood — On certain days, videocassettes can be rented for 99¢ a day. If outlets reduce the price of some to 49¢, films like "Free Ride" might do a little business.

Picture doesn't even qualify as sophomoric because even some silly films about teen antics can be amusing at some level — which this never is.

Low-budget work lasting 82 tedious minutes concerns the antics of a couple of spoiled prep school boys, led by the supremo jerk of them all, Dan Garten (Gary Hershberger), who inadvertently takes possession of mob money belonging to old man Garbagio (Frank Campanella) that he found in his son's red Corvette.

Hershberger finds the ideal hiding place for the dough in a hole bored into the lower backside of a nude statue, located on the grounds of the neighboring "finishing school," where he meets the not-too-virtuous daughter of his school's owner, Jill Monroe (Dawn Schneider).

Predictably, the two brats get together to outsmart the stupid mobsters, but not until the audience suffers through one humorless scene after another showing the boys peeping at the girls showering, dropping their drawers for the dean's lascivious nurse wife and an aborted romp with a perky callgirl.

Whole production has the feel of being shot by a home movie camera in someone's backyard using props found in the garage. —Brit.

Routine Pleasures
(FRENCH-BRITISH-DOCU-COLOR)

A ZDF, Institut National de la Communication Audiovisuelle, Channel Four Television, London and Jean-Pierre Gorin production. Directed by Jean-Pierre Gorin. Screenplay, Gorin, Patrick Amos; camera (color), Babette Mangolte; editor, Gorin, Mangolte. Reviewed at Film Forum, N.Y., May 2, 1986. (No MPAA Rating.) Running time: **81 MINS.**

Jean-Pierre Gorin's "Routine Pleasures" is a pleasure and anything but routine. Film is a strangely satisfying study of a group of model railroad enthusiasts who twice weekly meet at an elaborately constructed world of miniature trains, buildings and cities, a miniature train system so large it occupies a portion of a Del Mar, Calif., airplane hangar, intercut with a study of two paintings by film critic Manny Farber and numerous quotes and passages of his writing.

Gorin draws many parallels between the endearing, and often humorous, model world of the train buffs and Farber's far-roaming writings on American culture, but leaves making connections to the viewer.

At times the film has a dream-like quality, as Babette Mangolte's expert camerawork takes us on a meandering tour of the painstakingly detailed lilliputian landscape. Juxtaposed with studies of two Farber oil paintings, "Birthplace: Douglas, Arizona" and "Have A Chew On Me," themselves stylized representations of other worlds,

Gorin manages to create his own intriguing landscape in the synthesis between the two.

Many may find Gorin's question-raising style of filmmaking disconcerting, and it's doubtful that the pic will find an audience beyond the arthouse circuit. However, "Routine Pleasures" stands as a highly unique, and memorable, film. —Roy.

The Dirt Bike Kid
(COLOR)

Teen-bike themer loosely aimed at family trade.

A Concorde/Cinema Group release of a Trinity Pictures film. Produced by Julie Corman. Directed by Hoite C. Caston. Screenplay, David Brandes, Lewis Colick from a story by J. Halloran (Corman); camera (color), Daniel Lacambre; music, Bill Bowersock, Phil Shenale; editor, Jeff Freeman; art director, Becky Block; set director, J. Grey Smith; costumes, Sawnie R. Baldridge; hair/makeup, Jean A. Black; casting, Los Angeles, Eileen Kelton/Patti McCormick, Dallas, Susan Grogg/Shirley Abramson; production coordinator, Robin Fleck; sound editor, Frank Smathers. Reviewed at Crown Center Cinema, Kansas City, May 1, 1986. (MPAA Rating: PG.) Running time: **90 MINS.**
Jack Simmons . . . . Peter Billingsley
Mr. Hodgkins . . . . Stuart Pankin
Janet Simmons . . . . Anne Bloom
Mike . . . . Patrick Collins
Miss Clavell . . . . Sage Parker
Bo . . . . Chad Sheets
Max . . . . Gavin Allen
Flaherty . . . . Danny Breen
Big Slime . . . . (Weasel) Forshaw
Chief . . . . John William Galt
Rocky, the Dog . . . . Himself

Kansas City — Motorcycles being a subject of prime interest to teens, this one sets out to capitalize on that theme for the big screen with a special aim at family trade. It delves into the bike world deeply, but meanders in several directions and never laces it all neatly together. What family trade turns out to see the picture will have to be families that are not too picky.

Concorde/Cinema Group is releasing the picture regionally, having opened it in the Dallas territory and then Kansas City. Denver may be next. Boxoffice record in these stands is mediocre.

The basic fault likely is the story, which pits Peter Billingsley as a young white knight against an adult world, and those are steep odds, indeed, especially for a 14-year-old, however capable and earnest. He takes on the chore of saving the "Doghouse," the hotdog and soft drink stand of his coach and friend Patrick Collins, against the scheming of banker Stuart Pankin, who seeks the site for a new bank building.

Pankin delivers his meanness almost tongue-in-cheek, but shows his nasty is well polished. He would succeed, but for some major help which Peter gets from "the bike," a double spotlighted Yamaha which (shades of "E.T.") can start itself, take Peter for a ride over the city, buck a bulldozer and scatter the viscious adult cycle gang. He also gets some help from Anne Bloom, very good as his understanding young mother (a widow of course), and Sage Parker, as Pankin's straightlaced secretary. Pankin relents after being taken for a hair-raising ride on "the bike," and to no one's surprise the Doghouse is saved. Peter gets the credit, but it's a so-what chevron.

The viewer is taken astray by a variety of incongruities, such as the adult cycle gang, fiercely grimacing throughout, apparently in pic for no other reason than to give "the bike" an opportunity to scatter them pell-mell. There is some redeeming footage of young bikers on the motocross, but generally the film is loosely strung and uninspired. The family appeal is marred slightly by a very few obnoxious words and some extended adult leering by Pankin at comely would-be borrowers, explaining the PG rating.—*Quin.*

Last Resort
(COLOR)

Inane vacation comedy.

A Concorde/Cinema Group release. Produced by Julie Corman. Executive producer, Nessa Cooper. Directed by Zane Buzby. Screenplay, Steve Zacharias, Jeff Buhai; camera (color), Stephen Katz, Alex Nepomniaschy; editor, Gregory Scherick; music, Steve Nelson, Thom Sharp; sound, Walter Martin; production design, Curtis A. Schnell; art director, Colin Irwin; set dresser, Douglas Mowat. Reviewed at SRO's Grand Cinemas Alderwood, Seattle, April 17, 1986. (MPAA Rating: R.) Running time: **84 MINS.**
George Lollar ....Charles Grodin
Sheila Lollar ....Robin Pearson Rose
Phil Cocoran ....John Ashton
Dorothy Cocoran ....Ellen Blake
Jessica Lollar ....Megan Mullally
Brad Lollar ....Christopher Ames
Bobby Lollar ....Scott Nemes
Bartender ....John Lovitz
Curt ....Gerrit Graham
Pino..................Mario Van Peebles
Veroneeka ....Brenda Bakke
Etienne................William Bumiller
Jean-Michel................Phil Hartman
Mimi ....Mimi Lieber
Pierre......................Steve Levitt
Martine ....Zane Buzby

Seattle — "Last Resort" bills itself as a "first-class comedy," but in reality, its dialog is so inane and the tone so crass it's unlikely to draw more than a limited audience or become much of a success.

Film follows the Christmas vacation of a Chicago family at a Caribbean resort called Club Sand. The vacation is the idea of the father, a furniture salesman who believes he's in danger of becoming a failure in his career and family life. He sells his reluctant family on the trip as a "once-in-a-lifetime opportunity." His wife fears it's nothing but a sex club, and her worst fears are con-

firmed when the resort turns out to be a sleazy singles' hangout on an island about to undergo a revolution.

The mother, liberated through various kinds of recreational drugs during the vacation, manages to escape into the emancipated spirit of the resort and has a great time. So do the kids: the teenaged daughter falls in love with a suave French counselor who actually is a rebel; the shy, teenaged son emerges from his shell through the tutoring of a beautiful sexpot, and the adolescent son enjoys it all vicariously — after he escapes from the kids' mini-camp by burning it down.

The husband, unlike his wife, becomes increasingly uptight as he finds himself unable to get into the liberated pace of the place. He finds he can't deal with his daughter going to nude beaches, his son having sex, his wife exposing her breasts or the propositions he receives from camp counselors, straight and gay.

The storyline — if there is one — climaxes when some hairy guerrillas burst onto the scene and the father, who everyone has basically decided is a first-class nerd, saves the day by grabbing a machinegun and herding the guests to safety.

Charles Grodin, despite a near-absence of credible dialog, does an okay job as the over-organized, self-possessed father, and pulls off a few nice scenes, such as one when he realizes a gay counselor is propositioning him. In fact, the cast in general is pretty good.

Written by the team responsible for "Revenge Of The Nerds," the film was directed by first-time director Zane Buzby, who also plays a bit part as the resort's dictatorial babysitter. —*Magg.*

Bloody Birthday
(COLOR)

Predictable horror film about killer kids.

A Judica Prods. release. Produced by Gerald T. Olson. Executive producer, Chris Tufty. Directed by Ed Hunt. Screenplay, Hunt, Barry Pearson; camera (color), Stephen Posey; editor, Ann E. Mills; music, Arlon Ober; art direction, Lynda Burbank, J. Rae Fox; set construction, Alex Hajdu; casting, Judith Holstra; special effects, Roger George. Reviewed at Adams theater, Detroit, April 24, 1986. (MPAA Rating: R.) Running time: **85 MINS.**
Mrs. Davis ....Susan Strasberg
Doctor ....José Ferrer
Joyce Russel ....Lori Lethin
Mrs. Brody ....Melinda Cordell
Beverly Brody ....Julie Brown
Mr. Harding ....Joe Penny
Curtis ....Billy Jacoby
Steven Seaton ....Andy Freeman
Debbie Brody ....Elizabeth Hoy
  Also with: Bert Kramer, K. C. Martel, Ben Marley, Erica Hope, Cyril O'Reilly, Shane Butterworth, Michael Dudikoff, Daniel Currie, Norman Rice, George Paul, Bill Boyett, Ellen Geer, Ward Costello, Ruth Silveira.

Detroit — Although there is

something perversely appealing about a band of ten-year-olds offing unsuspecting townspeople, "Bloody Birthday" is so predictable and suspenseless that by the end it's also unsatisfying and forgettable.

Three children — Debbie, Steven and Curtis — are born earlier than expected in June 1970 during a total eclipse of the sun. Ten years later they are planning a neighborhood 10th birthday party amid a panic-stricken town trying to solve a series of seemingly senseless murders.

Director Ed Hunt doesn't take long to snuff out the first two in a string of killings — two teenagers making love in a cemetery. When Debbie's father, the town sheriff, begins to piece the murders together, he becomes the next victim.

When Timmy, the neighbor boy, sees these suburban satans tugging at the sheriff's body, he becomes target number four, but proves difficult prey. His sister Joyce, a high school student with a fascination for astrology, also catches wind of the band's murderous ways, but no one believes her.

It's Joyce who provides the scientific explanation for this murderous band's ways. Seems the total eclipse blocked out the astrological effects of Saturn, creating a void in this terrible trio's psyche, specifically a lack of conscience.

Joyce is a lot better with astrology than she is with common sense. When Debbie asks her to babysit while her mother is out, Joyce agrees. She and her brother soon discover it's a ruse to kill them, however, as Debbie, Curtis and Steven trap them in their boobytrapped house with bullets, arrows and nooses.

Acting is strong enough in this predictable yarn to have made it an entertaining B flick, but there is never any suspense. Hunt telescopes the murders, which seem to occur with rapid clock-like regularity, usually in broad daylight.

There is no motivation, no sense of terror and with the sheriff snuffed early on, seemingly no competent police force to get on the case.

Although the townsfolk are immobilized by these homicidal daycare escapees, one just wants to grab them by the ears and wash their mouths out.

Susan Strasberg adds little as Mrs. Davis and José Ferrer as the doctor adds even less.

This film was made in 1980 and was to have been released by Analysis Releasing, which has since gone defunct. It was alternately titled "Creeps."—*Advo.*

La Donna del Traghetto
(The Ferrywoman)
(ITALIAN-COLOR)

An Airone Cinematografica release of a Daedalus production. Directed by Amedeo Fago. Stars Alessandro Haber and Teresa Ann Savoy. Screenplay, Fago, Stefano Rulli; camera (Agfa color), Aldo Di Marcantonio; editor, Alfredo Muschietti; music, Franco Piersanti; sound, Graziano Ruzzeddu; art director, Lia Francesca Morandini. Reviewed at the Cannes Film Festival (Critics' Week), May 12, 1986. Running time: **90 MINS.**
Gioli ....Alessandro Haber
Viola.................Teresa Ann Savoy
Libero ....Philippe Leroy
Tommaso ....Paco Fabrini
Funeral driver ....Nicola Di Pinto

Cannes — "The Ferrywoman" is a true rarity on the Italo scene, a low-budget indie production packed with charming simplicity. Film marks the directing debut of Amedeo Fago, who has been best known for his work as an art director and playwright. Local b.o. being what it is, pic's Italo commercial future looks rocky, but the touching tale of a lonely man who longs for a baby is perfect for tv pickups.

Stage thesp Alessandro Haber, who has had a diversified career on film in character roles, is right on target as Gioli, a poor puppeteer living in a picturesque old town in the Po Valley. When his mother dies, simple-hearted Gioli buries her in a riverside grave beside his father. There he meets Viola (Teresa Ann Savoy), a silent young lady who ferries occasional passersby across the river.

Reveling in the awesome peace of the still river, and the strength of character of the people who live beside it (including Viola's blind father, Philippe Leroy), "Ferrywoman" admirably succeeds in placing its unworldly crew in the midst of a moving fairy tale. Gioli's good heart and infantile personality suffer at the hands of the normal people around him. When his innocent friendship with a little boy (Paco Fabrini) is misinterpreted as perversion, he is ostracized totally from society. At this point he becomes obsessed with children and babies, and even carves a puppet-baby with tape-recorded wails to keep him company.

Viola's story is much less original. Her greedy brother wants to sell the family property to land developers, and the sibling battle evolves predictably. Though it's not much of a role, Savoy has never looked more broodingly lovely. She is, of course, the only character who sympathizes with the poor puppeteer. In some magic off-screen moment they come together, allowing her to substitute a real infant for Gioli's puppet by film's end.

Film steers an interesting course between fairy tale and harsh reality, where a hundred years' worth of puppets made by Gioli's family can be cruelly destroyed in an instant. Atmospheric lensing and sets contribute to the unearthly mood.

— *Yung.*

Awesome Lotus
(U.S.-COLOR)

An A.W.O. release of a Dilettante Prods. production. Executive producer, Peter Schuyler. Produced by Donna Davis. Directed by David O'Malley. Stars Peter Schuyler, Loraine Masterson, Joyce Schuyler, Dan Kopper. Screenplay, Anna Blake, Peter Schuyler; camera (color), Arch Bryant; editor, Elmer Armstrong, Rich Roessler; art direction, Paul Conly; music, Paul Syaheli; lyrics by Peter Schuyler and Paul Conly, performed by Kay Orlando; sound, Jim Emerson. Reviewed at the Cannes Film Festival (market), May 14, 1986. Running time: **90 MINS.**

Awesome Lotus	Loraine Masterson
Tofu Caca	Peter Schuyler
Barbara	Joyce Schuyler
Tuna	Dan Kopper

Also with: Dutch Shindler, Shelly Chester, Loren Reyher, Stephanie Small, Meg Thayer, Pat Mahoney.

Cannes — "Awesome Lotus" is silly and ridiculous and just the ticket for cult fave sweepstakes.

Awesome Lotus, a retired karate assassin who can maim with a flick of her finger, is called back into action. The silk fashion industry is being threatened. Their models are being killed by the Federation of Associated Rayon Textiles (the acronym is in keeping with the pic which has one character named Polly Esther).

Awesome calls in her associates, a blind, deaf and dumb karate champ who wields a mean stick, and Tuna, who is equally forceful using a tennis racket as a weapon.

The blind man, named Tofu Caca, wears a bathing cap and when it falls off in battle he can not only see but he sings Wagner arias.

Before she kills, Awesome spouts pontificating Oriental sayings that are accompanied by spoofy Chinese subtitles with English pictographs.

The villain speaks Nazi-ese and is driven to wickedness because the basset hound he loved was killed in the Orient by silkworms.

Awesome and her team are successful and even manage a musical number; throwaway lines abound as do sight gags that are all on the surface. There is even a shot of bloody dead bodies labeled Gratuitous Gore.

The acting ranges from adequate to amateur, and technical credits reflect a low budget. David O'Malley's direction is okay but it's the wacky script by Anna Blake and Peter Schuyler that keeps the pic hopping from one inanity to another.

Pic may not do well in firstrun release but has a life in latenight showings where cult oddities are appreciated. It's also a natural for homevid where those too young to attend midnight screenings will keep it active. — *Adil.*

Blood Tracks
(SWEDISH-COLOR)

A Smart Egg Pictures production. Executive producer, George Zecevic. Produced by Tom Sjoberg, Directed by Mike Jackson (Mats Olsson); associate director, Derek Ford. Stars Jeff Harding, Naomi Kaneda, Michael Fitzpatrick. Screenplay, Jackson (Olsson), Anna Wolf; camera (Widescreen, Fuji color), Hans von Dittmer; editor, David Gilbert; music, Dag Unenge; songs, Easy Action; sound, Lars-Gunnar Anderson, Hans-Eric-Ahrn; production manager, Bruno Johanson; special makeup effects, Dick Ljunggren; stunt coordinator, Tommy Ellgren. Reviewed at the Cannes Film Festival (market), May 18, 1986. Running time: **86 MINS.**

John	Jeff Harding
Suzie	Naomi Kaneda
Bob	Michael Fitzpatrick
Soundman	Brad Powell
Nick	Peter Merrill
Carrie	Harriet Robinson
Sahra	Tina Shaw
Louise	Frances Kelly
Mary	Karina Lee
Linda	Helena Jacks
Solid Gold group	Easy Action

Cannes — "Blood Tracks" is a gory horror film that although it was made last year belongs rightfully in the cycle of teen slasher features from five years ago. Prospects are modest in international markets.

Silly premise has a rock group named Solid Gold (played by Swedish band Easy Action) on location in the Colorado mountains (actually filmed in Sweden) to shoot a music video. A large contingent of attractive femme models is along, to provide the usual scantily clad decoration (even though it's cold and strictly snowsville, with frequent avalanches to boot).

While the troupe is holed up in a snug mountain cabin, workmen disturb the peace of a barbaric clan of savages living underneath an abandoned factory nearby. A prolog sequence shows how an ultraviolent domestic quarrel some 10 years earlier ended up with daddy dead and mom and the kids trekking to the remote spot where they're living and murdering primitively today.

When the rock entourage youngsters aren't engaged in sex they're wandering out in the snow (this being a cornball horror picture after all) to be attacked by the primitives.

"Blood Tracks" emphasizes some grisly makeup effects, particularly one in which a girl suddenly is split in two from head to toe. Several sex and nude scenes are included, the silliest of which has blond Mary (Karina Lee) making love to a musician out in a car when they're buried by an avalanche; when rescued she scrambles across the snow naked much to the merriment of the rescuers.

Cast is hampered by the use of post-synchronized English dialog, but the youngsters are good looking and that apparently is all that is required in this genre. — *Lor.*

Playing For Keeps
(U.S.-COLOR)

A Universal release of a J & M presentation of a Miramax production. Executive producers, Julia Palau, Michael Ryan, Patrick Wachsberger. Produced by Alan Brewer, Bob Weinstein and Harvey Weinstein. Written and directed by Bob and Harvey Weinstein. Camera (color), Eric Van Haren Noman; editor, Gary Karr, Sharyn Ross; musical director, Alan Brewer; production designer, Walderman Kalinowski; associate producer, Ira Halperstadt. Reviewed at the Cannes Film Festival (market), May 16, 1986. (No MPAA Rating.) Running time: **95 MINS.**

Danny D'Angelo	Danny Jordano
Spikes	Matthew Penn
Silk	Leon W. Grant
Chloe	Mary B. Ward
Tracey	Marisa Tomei
Rockerfeller	Harold Gould
Cromwell	Robert Millie

Cannes — A high-spirited, good-natured comedy, "Playing For Keeps" can probably count on doing good business among the youth market in the U.S. for Universal.

Among the pic's aces: It's fast-paced, peopled with attractive characters, loaded with mostly slapstick humor, and peppered with 13 original pop songs by such performers as Phil Collins, Julian Lennon, Sister Sledge and China Crisis.

Priming the pic's stateside release, producers are readying a half-hour music special, using the featured acts, for tv airing, plus an album and two musicvideos.

Plot is a trifle far-fetched, but young audiences and anyone else who enjoys escapist entertainment are not likely to be too picky about that.

Film marks the directorial debut of brothers Bob and Harvey Weinstein, who have had a solid grounding in production (concert films, musicvideos and the Orion release "The Burning") and distribution (they own New York-based Miramax Films).

The Weinsteins' script revolves around attempts by three New York youngsters to convert a dilapidated hotel in the boondocks into a pleasure palace for teenagers, complete with MTV in every room, video arcades and a nightclub.

Their dream runs counter to secret plans by corrupt town council president Robert Millie to use the site as a chemical waste dump. Millie dupes most of the townfolk, who are exceedingly gullible, into trying to make life as difficult as possible for the trio and their helpers, led by Harold Gould as a failed Wall Street type who had taken up residence in the ramshackle hotel, and good-looking farmer's daughter Mary B. Ward.

Through a series of amusing — but highly illegal — maneuvers, the New York entrepreneurs expose Millie, and their dream hotel becomes a reality. In real life the crooked town official and his developer cohorts would probably have had an easy victory, but here it's a feelgood ending to a story that never takes itself too seriously.

The three leading players, Danny Jordano, Matthew Penn and Leon W. Grant imbue the picture with lots of energy and style, and the supporting cast all do their jobs well.

Production values are consistently high, with two fantasy sequences among the standouts. — *Dogo.*

The Girl From Mani
(BRITISH-GREEK-COLOR)

An M.N.K. Prods. presentation of a Manos Noyes-Kyriazis film. Produced by Noyes-Kyriazis. Directed by Paul Annett. Stars Angela Gerekou. Screenplay, Nikos Gatsos, Philip Broadley; camera (Panavision, Rank color), Takis Zervoulakis; editor, Bob Dearberg; art direction, Kes Karapiperis; music, Theodore Antoniou; associate producer, George A. Kyriazis. Reviewed at the Cannes Film Festival (market), May 11, 1986. Running time: **110 MINS.**

Eleni Kaleas	Angela Gerekou
Alan Cooper	Alex Hyde-White
Petros	Andreas Manoslikakis
Calchas	George Katuridis

Also with: George Foundas, Emilia Della Rocca

Cannes — High production values and breathtaking scenery can't make up for the corny plot in "The Girl From Mani." The British-Greek coproduction is obviously targeted for a wide English-speaking market; in the artificial world of this picture, painfully stilted English dialog is the *lingua franca* of the remotest Greek village. It seems unlikely the most indulgent viewer will be able to get over the accent hurdle.

Should some filmgoers succeed in tuning out the dialog, they will have to contend with no less implausible characters, who appear to still be packaged between the leaves of Prof. H.F. Noyes' original story. This amounts to a tragic tale of doomed love between a young Yank music teacher, Alan (Alex Hyde-White), and his beautiful and extremely talented pupil Eleni Kaleas (Angela Gerekou). She has been betrothed since childhood to marry a nasty-tempered boy named Petros (Andreas Manoslikakis), whose rich papa paid for her musical education in Athens and wiped out the family debt. Though Eleni has modernized herself considerably after leaving the village, she can never forget the vendetta of Mani that awaits her if she breaks the ancient customs, etc.

The predictability of this chestnut is matched only by the clichés cast uses in putting across the characters. Gerekou's frozen good looks rule out any vestige of illusion it could really be her voice singing Italian opera so ethereally; Hyde-White's brilliant young professor with glasses awry convinces even less.

Film's strong point is the sheer majesty of the Greek landscape which director Paul Annett wisely puts in front of the camera as often as possible. One shot of Mani's terraced cliffs plummeting into the churning sea has more drama than the story and cast combined. Too bad it couldn't have been worked in more effectively than as the tragic site of the final quarrel between the rivals for Eleni's love, Alan and Petros. If Mani really has a tradition of vendetta for wrongs performed, the producers should be sleeping with one eye open.

— *Yung.*

Dead-End Drive In
(AUSTRALIAN-COLOR)

A New World Pictures release (Greater Union in Australia) of a Springvale Prods./New South Wales Film Corp. production. Produced by Andrew Williams. Directed by Brian Trenchard-Smith. Coproduced by Damien Parer. Stars Ned Manning, Natalie McCurry. Screenplay, Peter Smalley, from the short story "Crabs" by Peter Carey; camera (widescreen, Eastmancolor), Paul Murphy; editor, Lee Smith; music, Frank Strangio; production design, Larry Eastwood; sound, Leo Sullivan; assistant director, Adrian Pickersgill; casting, Guy Norris; casting, Maizels & Associates. Reviewed at the Cannes Film Festival (market), May 13, 1986. Running time: **90 MINS.**

Crabs	Ned Manning
Carmen	Natalie McCurry
Thompson	Peter Whitford
Hazza	Wilbur Wilde
Don	Brett Climo

Also with: Ollie Hall, Sandy Lillingstone, Lyn Collingwood, Nikki McWaters, Melissa Davis, Dave Gibson.

Cannes — New World's latest Aussie pickup is, like their previous acquisition "Bliss," based on a story by Peter Carey, though the two films couldn't be more different. This one's a futuristic thriller which spends most of its running time building up a moody feeling of tension until the violent release of the last 10 minutes.

Set in the 1990s, pic posits a time when the authorities herd unwitting youngsters into makeshift prison camps. Jimmy, nicknamed Crabs (he once thought he had them) borrows his older brother's '56 Chevy for a night out with his girl at the Star drive-in, not knowing it is such a prison camp. While the couple make love, his back wheels are stolen, and he quickly finds himself stranded inside the electrified wall that surrounds the drive-in, with no way out.

The place is full of bored young people, lorded over by a seemingly kindly manager, Thompson, who keeps all their details on a computer. Crabs, a born outsider who refuses to conform, chafes at the bit until he seizes his chance to escape in a breathless final reel.

As crabs, Ned Manning, a playwright turned actor, is a definite find; he brings a dogged, cheerful, tough intensity to the role of one guy who just won't give in. Natalie McCurry as his girl doesn't have much to do, but does it charmingly, while Peter Whitford gives the apparently friendly Thompson just the right degree of malevolence. Rest of the cast are punk types or cops.

Director Brian Trenchard-Smith is at his best with action films, and this is probably his most successful effort to date. Aided by the superb widescreen photography of Paul Murphy (who also shot "Bliss") and the delightfully scrungy production design of Larry Eastwood, film is handsome to look at. Some of the plot machinations are a bit unexplained (we never know for sure exactly why the authorities are incarcerating the youngsters), but there's a welcome sense of humor that ads to the fun. According to a film poster glimpsed in one scene, by 1990 we'll be watching "Rambo Takes Russia."

Pic is not action packed: indeed, until a fight scene 50 minutes in, there's no real action as such. But the stunts at the end, though a bit over-edited, are sensational, with the final image of Crabs literally bursting out of the drive-in, quite something. Pic has something of the feel of the first "Mad Max" film, and doubtless will attract cult audiences as well as action fans. It manages to be an international film, and at the same time still a distinctively Australian effort, which is no mean feat. —*Strat.*

Emma's War
(AUSTRALIAN-COLOR)

A Curzon Film Distributors (U.K.) release of a Belinon Prod. Executive producer. Robin Dalton. Produced by Clytie Jessop, Andrena Finlay. Directed by Jessop. Screenplay, Peter Smalley, Jessop; camera (Kodak color), Tom Cowan; editor, Sonia Hoffman; music, John Williams; production manager/associate producer, David Hannay; sound, Ross McKay; art director, Jane Norris. Reviewed at the Cannes Film Festival (market), May 15, 1986. Running time: **95 MINS.**

Anne Grange	Lee Remick
Emma Grange	Miranda Otto
Laurel Grange	Bridey Lee
Frank Grange	Terence Donovan
John Davidson	Mark Lee
Miss Arnott	Pat Evison
Hank	Donal Gibson

Cannes — A wartime drama about the coming of age of an Australian schoolgirl, "Emma's War" ambles through a four-year period without developing much momentum or energy.

It's acted ably and handsomely shot, but direction (first-timer Clytie Jessop) and script (Jessop and her husband Peter Smalley) are so laid back and gentle, audience will have to be patient to go the distance.

That's if they can be coaxed into the cinema, which is a dubious proposition. In most markets item will play better on television.

Pic opens in 1942 when Emma (Miranda Otto) is 14 and attending a religious boarding school along with her younger sister (Bridey Lee). Their father (Terence Donovan) is attached to the Australian army in New Guinea as official war artist. Mother (Lee Remick) is working in a factory and missing him desperately, while spending time (innocently) with a U.S. sailor (Dobal Gibson).

After Japanese submarines attack Sydney Harbor, Remick takes the family to a safer location, the Blue Mountains. Emma hates her new school, plays hookey and befriends a conscientious objector (Mark Lee) who's hiding out in the bush. That leads to a bitter confrontation with her mother, who is becoming overly fond of alcohol.

It isn't until Donovan returns home that the pic really comes alive, but the family's shock at discovering he's been injured, and his problems in readjusting, are skated over so fast, much of the dramatic potential is lost.

Tyro actress Otto admirably handles the transition from awkward schoolgirl to self-assured young lady, and Remick invites a lot of sympathy as a woman who has a lot to cope with.

Atmosphere of wartime Sydney is expertly recreated through songs and radio broadcasts of the period, costumes and newsreel footage.

—*Dogo.*

The American Way
(BRITISH-COLOR)

A Maurice Phillips film. Executive producers, Maqbool Hameed, Jean Ubaud. Supervising exec producer, Keith Cavele. Produced by Laurie Keller and Paul Cowan. Directed by Phillips. Stars Dennis Hopper, Michael J. Pollard. Screenplay, Scott Roberts; camera (color), John Metcalfe; editor, Tony Lawson; music, Brian Bennett; production designer, Evan Hercules. Reviewed at the Cannes Film Festival (market), May 11, 1986. Running time: **105 MINS.**

Captain	Dennis Hopper
Doc	Michael J. Pollard
Ace	Eugene Lipinski
Claude	James Aubrey
Ben	Al Matthews
Jerry	William Armstrong
Sen. Willa Westinghouse	Nigel Pegram

Cannes — British helmer Maurice Phillips' debut feature is an attempt at manic, off-the-wall comedy about a bunch of Vietnam vets operating an airborne pirate television station; item gets unglued soon after takeoff and never manages to regain control. As an anti-war tract, it's neither subtle nor funny; "Dr. Strangelove" it isn't.

Fans of Dennis Hopper and Michael J. Pollard might be tempted to go see "The American Way," if they ignore word-of-mouth which is bound to be negative. It's difficult to predict any kind of future for this pic, except maybe as a curiosity piece.

Hopper limns the captain of a B-29 crew that flies around the U.S. monitoring regular tv broadcasts for any signs of warmongering, hawkish sentiments or, indeed, anything they fear may herald a return to the Vietnam mentality.

Fighting a war of words, the oddballs behind the self-styled S&M tv jam the offending station and superimpose their own propaganda. Their enemy number one is presidential contender Willa Westinghouse, who looks set to cruise into the White House on a "bomb the Commies" ticket.

Hopper and Co. use every trick in the pirate transmission book to thwart her, while she's prepared to do anything, up to and including ordering them shot out of the skies, to silence them. From the outset, it's clear Westinghouse is not what she appears, and most viewers are likely to guess how she'll be undone way before it happens.

Scott Roberts' script contains few amusing lines, and the effect, if any, is often lost in the cacophony of rock video clips (where director Phillips cut his teeth) and tv broadcasts. It may be organized bedlam up there on screen, but the result is a shambles.—*Dogo.*

The Whistle Blower
(BRITISH-COLOR)

A Reeve Enterprises presentation of a Portreeve Ltd. production. Produced by Geoffrey Reeve. Directed by Simon Langton. Stars Michael Caine, James Fox, Nigel Havers. Screenplay, Julian Bond, from the novel by John Hale; camera (Technicolor), Fred Tammes; editor, Bob Morgan; music, John Scott; production design, Morely Smith; sound, Bob Allen; assistant director, John Watson; production manager, Christine Benton; production executive, James Reeve; associate producer, Peter Dolman; casting, Maude Sepctor. Reviewed at Cannes Film Festival (market), May 17, 1986. Running time: **104 MINS.**

Frank Jones	Michael Caine
Lord	James Fox
Robert Jones	Nigel Havers
Cynthia Goodburn	Felicity Dean
Sir Adrian Chapple	John Gielgud
Bruce	Gordon Jackson
Charles Greig	Barry Foster

Also with: Kenneth Colley (Bill Pickett), Dinah Stabb (Rose), Andrew Hawkins (Allen Goodburn), Trevor Cooper (Inspector Bourne), James Simmons (Mark), Bill Wallis (Dodgson), David Langton (Secretary to the Cabinet), Arturo Venegas (Alex).

Cannes — British secret service films aren't what they were when

Michael Caine was Harry Palmer and James Bond started out on his cheerful career. In the wake of "Defense Of The Realm" comes "The Whistle Blower," another highly charged conspiracy theory drama, which suggests the British security forces are (a) expecting and preparing for a nuclear war and (b) would think nothing of murdering an innocent young man to fool the Americans into thinking he was a Soviet agent and thus prevent the embarrassment of revealling that the real agent is — yet another — pillar of the Establishment.

The murdered man, played by Nigel Havers, works as a Russian translator at the top-secret listening center, GCHQ, in Cheltenham. Early scenes establish Havers' warm relationship with his father, ex-pilot Michael Caine, and his affair married worman (Felicity Dean) whose husband also works at the security center. Gradually Havers begins to lose his faith in the system, and after his death his father is determined to get to the bottom of the matter, rightly suspecting murder, not accident as the police claim.

Caine, who's having a series of good film roles at the present, is excellent as the father, a role rather similar to that played by Jack Lemmon in "Missing" — a non-political, middle-aged man who's driven to radical action as a result of what the government he once trusted has done to his son. When Caine, tears in his eyes, says simply: "I really miss the silly bugger" or "I want to believe in England again," his understatement is immensely moving.

James Fox, Gordon Jackson and Barry Foster play security types involved in a dangerous, devious, ruthless game, while John Gielgud is in for two brief scenes as the Soviet mole who lives a life of privileged luxury; all are in their usual fine form. There's also a fine cameo from Kenneth Colley as a crusading, left-wing journalist who dies in a contrived car crash. Felicity Dean is appealing as Havers' mistress.

After a slow start, pic gains momentum and the central sections, as Caine doggedly insists on finding out who killed his son and why, are tautly handled, creating considerable tension. Unfortunately, the film ends rather lamely, almost as if the writer wasn't sure how to finish it, and the result is something of an anticlimax.

Technical credits are tops, with a special nod to Bob Morgan's precise editing. But the title, which fails to capture the flavor of this well-made thriller, should be changed.
— *Strat.*

Dream Lovers
(HONG KONG-COLOR)

A D&B Films and Pearl City production and release. Produced by Dickson Poon. Executive producer, Vicky Lee Leung. Directed by Tony Au. Stars Chow Yun Fat, Lin Ching Hsia, Cher Yeung and Mandred Wong. Screenplay, Chui Dai An Pin. Production assistant, Jessinta Lin; camera (color), Bill Wong; art direction, William Chang; music, Law Wing Fai. Reviewed at King's theater, Hong Kong, April 21, 1986. Running time: **98 MINS.**
(Cantonese soundtrack with English subtitles.)

Hong Kong — "Dream Lovers" is a dream for romantic escapists, but it sorely lacks the material to sustain an average filmgoer's interest. Chow Yun Fat is most unconvincing (miscasting for box-office reasons) as an orchestral maestro while Lin Ching Hsia looks stunning in her brothel red wardrobe.

Soong Yu (Chow Yun Fat), a homecoming conductor, faints during a concert after some mysterious visions. He visualizes an antique stone figure rising to the surface of a lake and the figure has a striking resemblance to his face. Later on, he and his girlfriend of eight years, Wah Lei (Cher Yeung) look at a high-rise apartment. Soong has yet another visual attack; this time he sees a desirable woman in a period costume, dancing and singing.

Soong is apparently a reincarnation of a man who lived and died violently during the Qin Dynasty, 2,000 years ago. His lover of that time has also been reborn and reunion in Hong Kong in the 1980s is fated. At an exhibition of the Qin Emperor's famous Terracotta army (stone statues buried with the Emperor), Soong is immediately drawn to Cheung Yuet Heung (Li Ching Hsia), daughter of a well-known antique collector. Soong and Cheung come to realize the affinity of their lives and destiny. They explore the tragedy of their past romance and decide to part after a series of flashbacks. —*Mel.*

Smart Alec
(COLOR)

Inventive comedy about indie filmmaking.

An American Twist/Boulevard production. Executive producer, Ashok Amritraj. Produced and directed by Jim Wilson. Screenplay, Rob Sullivan, Wilson; camera (color), John Huneck; editor, James Addison, Brian Lee Ross; music, Stephen Hunter, Jan King, Morgan Cavett, Bruce Langhorne; production manager, Johnine Novosel; casting, Barbara and Ann Remsen; art direction, Nancy Arnold; costumes, Sunny Chayes; co-producer, Richard Strickland; associate producer, Lisa Sonne. Reviewed at the Houston Intl. Film Festival, April 19, 1986. (No MPAA Rating.) Running time: **87 MINS.**

Alec Carroll	Ben Glass
Julie	Natasha Kautsky
Zsa Zsa Gabor	Zsa Zsa Gabor
Arthur Fitzgerald	Orson Bean
Rodney	Antony Alda
Samantha Gibbs	Kerry Remsen
Carla Rochester	Lucinda Crosby
Frank Wheeler	David Hedison
Bert	Bill Henderson

Houston — Much of the material in this low-budget indie production was gathered as producers searched for filming funding: "Smart Alec" is a film about making films, or more precisely, about wooing investors. Alec Carroll crews by day in small Hollywood productions and spends his nights tapping out a screenplay that he intends to direct once he gets the money.

Alec, played competently by newcomer character actor Ben Glass, is a mixture of zealous ambition and childish befuddlement at the way of the rich people he hopes to win over.

With opus in hand, Alec begins an odyssey that brings him in contact with a horde of eccentric investors. Eager to please and ready to play the game, Alec takes up the various pastimes of his would-be financial partners, from duckhunting to sex games. The fact that the film ends with Alec no closer to his dreams than when he started does not diminish the humor and barely tarnishes Alec's enthusiasm.

Orson Bean turns in a good performance as Arthur Fitzgerald, a monied old coot more interested in Alec than his screenplay, though not disinterested enough to set a precondition for his funding: Zsa Zsa Gabor has to have a role in the picture. Gabor does appear in a brief role as herself; real-life fundraisers for "Smart Alec" needed her name for investors just as Alec did. While Gabor lets Alec down gently, Fitzgerald reveals his true intentions and Alec narrowly escapes.

Like the investors, the viewers never find out much about the actual screenplay, although it has something to do with ballet dancers and parachuting over the Dakotas.

The plot is inventive and moves anecdotally from one experience to the next. Since Alec is continually dead-ended in his pursuit of funding, the picture moves circularly around one premise. Two subplots, one involving Alec's reverential pursuit of a leading lady (Natasha Kautsky) for his film and the other involving Alec's sleazy friend Rodney (Antony Alda), are never developed.

The picture has a strong low-budget sheen to it, even in its best segments. While the film maintains a consistently humorous tone, it is an inconsistent picture. Some of the humor fails and the dialog ranges from witty to flat. A dance scene at the end of the film does not work.

Due to its subject matter and some funny segments, the film should get some play on the art house circuit. — *Jole.*

★
★ Cannes Film Reviews ★
★

Saving Grace
(U.S.-COLOR)

A Columbia Pictures release of an Embassy Films Associates production. Produced by Herbert F. Solow. Directed by Robert M. Young. Stars Tom Conti. Screenplay, David S. Ward, based on the novel by Celia Gittelson, adapted by Richard Kramer; camera (Technovision, Technicolor), Reynaldo Villalobos; editor, (uncredited); sound, Peter Sutton; art direction, Giovanni Natalucci; costumes, Vittoria Guaita; casting, Francesco Cinieri; associate producer, Newton Arnold. Reviewed at the Cannes Film Festival (market), May 13, 1986. (MPAA Rating: PG.) Running time: 112 MINS.

Pope Leo XIV	Tom Conti
Cardinal Biondi	Fernando Rey
Msgr. Ghezzi	Erland Josephson
Abalardi	Giancarlo Giannini
Msgr. McGee	Donald Hewlett
Ciolino	Edward James Olmos
Lucia	Patricia Mauceri
Giuliano	Angelo Evans

Cannes — This may be the first comedy ever about a Pope running away from office — for a short, private spree in the country among the real people whose shepherd he is supposed to be, sans the bureaucratic interference of the Vatican hierarchy.

Humorous without being satirical, this is the kind of good-natured romp that could be accepted even by literally minded religious people who do not like taking such things lightly.

A middleaged but sprightly Cardinal (Tom Conti) is elected Pope, anointed as Leo XIV, and soon finds himself submerged by his numerous public activities which rob him of any time for reflection and any chance of initiative. One days he locks himself by mistake out of the Vatican garden while dressed in civvies. On the spur of the moment he decides to make the best of it, and takes a trip to Montepetra, a forsaken village in the South of Italy, which, he has been told, is without a priest.

There he is taken in by an ex-streetwalker whose daughter is mute, and hiding his identity, sets out to relearn his trade — bringing help and solace to the people around him. With the help of some juvenile delinquents and a number of women, he sets out to repair the aqueduct which will bring water back into the village from the valley, in spite of the opposition of the town thug and his acolytes, who prefer to rip the government off instead of working for a living.

The naive spirit of Italian comedies from the '50s is felt all through David Ward's script, which carefully sidesteps any major issue involving faith or religion, concentrating instead on human foibles taken with a smile except for one tragic occurrence near the end, which imparts some weight to the moral of the story. Director Robert M. Young seems satisfied staying on this level, and has a great time with a cast which appears to have enjoyed itself greatly during production.

Tom Conti may be a little young and literally too light on his feet to play a Pope, but he is too good an actor not to make the best of it, eliciting lots of personal sympathy even when not quite convincing as a High Pontiff. Fernando Rey, Erland Josephson and Donald Hewlett are an amusing trio of Cardinals covering for their boss in his absence. Giancarlo Giannini is effective as a mysterious goatherd of few words, and Angelo Evans displays plenty of vitality as a 'ough-acting kid with a good heart.

While both script and direction are too relaxed to be truly compelling, and the subject is peculiar enough not to fit immediately in any particular market niche, the overall result is pleasant enough to find its own audience, if carefully handled.

There is one audience hurdle, however. It is strange that with the entire cast in the film speaking English (in spite of the plot taking place in Italy) Conti uses a heavy Italian accent, which seems a rather obsolete approach. Either dub him or let him use his normal speech, like the rest of the cast.—*Edna.*

A Judgement In Stone
(CANADIAN-COLOR)

A Norstar Releasing release (in Canada) of a Rawifilm and Schulz Prods. production. Executive producers, David Pady, Ousama Rawi, Harve Sherman. Produced by Sherman. Directed by Rawi. Stars Rita Tushingham. Screenplay, Elaine Waisglass, based on the novel "A Judgement In Stone" by Ruth Rendell; camera (color), David Herrington; editor, Stan Cole; art direction, Reuben Freed; music, Patrick Coleman, Robert Murphy; sound, Peter Shewchuk; costumes, Linda Matheson. Reviewed at the Cannes Film Festival (market), May 13, 1986. Running time: 100 MINS.

Eunice Parchman	Rita Tushingham
George Coverdale	Ross Petty
Jackie	Shelley Peterson
Bobby	Jonathan Crombie
Melinda	Jessica Steen
Joan Smith	Jackie Burroughs
Norman Smith	Tom Kneebone
William	Peter MacNeill
Mr. Parchman	Donald Ewer
Aunt	Joyce Gordon
Young Eunice	Aisha Tushingham

Cannes — Potential is nowhere realized in Ousama Rawi's pic of Ruth Rendell's tense offbeat thriller about a plain Jane who kills when people mock her for not being able to read.

Rita Tushingham, as Eunice the housekeeper who emigrates from Britain to the U.S. to work for a doctor's family, approaches her role with care. But Rawi, a vet commercials director in his first feature away from the camera, provides an inadequate supporting cast and gets slack, careless results.

Ross Petty and Shelley Peterson, the actress wife of Ontario Premier David Peterson in her first feature, play the married couple but act as if they've just been introduced. Jonathan Crombie and Jessica Steen, their children from other marriages, trudge through the piece without effect.

Jackie Burroughs as a religious fanatic who befriends Eunice and accompanies her into violence gives a performance that is over the top in hysterics.

Camerawork by David Herrington is more reminiscent of tv commercials, too many closeup shots without reason.

Neither editing nor Rawi's work aids Elaine Waisglass' script which follows Rendell's story closely, except for transfer of the locale to an unnamed U.S. city from England.

Lack of attention to detail includes Eunice slashing her hand and being bandaged one day and the next day no bandage.

Other technical credits including music lack snap. Pic is overlong but even if edited down by maybe 10 minutes won't improve because of the mainly sleepwalking performances by all except Tushingham.

Dim theatrical playoff predicted, but tv for sure in Canada where Canadian content is required no matter what on paycable. Virgin has homevid rights but will have to work hard to overcome. —*Adil.*

Biggles
(BRITISH-COLOR)

A Compact Yellowbill presentation, in association with Tambarle. World sales, NVC. Executive producer, Adrian Scrope. Co-exec producer, Paul Barnes-Taylor. Produced by Pom Oliver and Kent Walwin. Directed by John Hough. Stars Neil Dickson, Alex Hyde-White, Fione Hutchison, Peter Cushing. Screenplay, John Groves, Walwin, based on characters created by Capt. W.E. Johns; camera (Technicolor), Ernest Vincze; editor, Richard Trevor; music, Stanislas; sound (Dolby), Peter Pardoe, Paul Le Mare; production design, Terry Pritchard; costumes, Jim Acheson; associate producer, Peter James; co-associate producer & assistant director, John O'Connor; stunt coordinator, Gerry Crampton; second unit director, Terry Coles. Reviewed at the Cannes Film Festival (market), May 9, 1986. (No MPAA Rating.) Running time: 108 MINS.

Biggles	Neil Dickson
Jim Ferguson	Alex Hyde-White
Debbie	Fiona Hutchison
Col. Raymond	Peter Cushing
Von Stalhein	Marcus Gilbert
Chuck	William Hootkins
Algy	Michael Siberry
Ginger	Daniel Flynn
Bertie	James Saxon
Marie	Francesca Gonshaw
Bill	Alan Polonsky

Cannes — This stylish romp combining World War I heroics and the currently in-vogue plot device of time travel has all the makings of a solid b.o. draw in British Commonwealth countries, where older audiences are familiar with the fictional hero from Captain W.E. Johns' series of "Biggles" books.

Pic looks to be a tougher sell in the U.S., where lack of recognizable talent (save Peter Cushing in a minor role), unfamiliar subject matter and low-tech effects limit theatrical prospects. Pic may draw well here among the pre-teen male set with a thirst for swashbuckling, but paycable playoff is a better bet.

Script by coproducer Kent Walwin and John Groves updates the WWI set piece to 1986 Manhattan via the time travel gimmick, which has food service entrepreneur Jim Ferguson (Alex Hyde-White) inexplicably hurled across the decades. Trouble is, he doesn't know when this phenomenon will recur, which makes for some amusing (and not-so) juxtapositions of past and present. Best bit is his drop in to a French convent under siege, attired only in a bath towel.

Ferguson keeps meeting up with Biggles (Neil Dickson), a dashing, WWI British aviator who's out to stop the Hun from implementing a hi-tech secret weapon which, as they find out later, is akin to a big microwave oven for men and machinery. Ferguson is aided and advised in the present by Col. Raymond (Cushing), who somehow knows what's going on. In one of the pic's best scenes, Raymond, who turns out to be Biggles' former c.o., meets up with the pilot in their first contact since the end of the war.

Amidst all this, Ferguson's co-worker girlfriend Debbie (Fiona Hutchison) has followed him to London to learn why he's behaving so strangely. More window-dressing than anything else (original "Biggles" books forsook dames for male camaraderie), credibility is strained further when Debbie winds up going back with her beau to the trenches, where her full-length fur is anything but practical.

Debbie, of course, must save all their skins at least once, which she does handily, when the Germans have Biggles and his buddies literally against the wall. Climax features Biggles' bunch using a London police helicopter brought back by Biggles and Ferguson, to stymie the Germans and Biggles' arch-enemy, the smoothly sadistic yet aristocratic Von Stalhein (convincingly played by Marcus Gilbert), who's also a flying ace.

Thesping among the supporting

cast, especially Biggles' mates (Michael Siberry, Daniel Flynn and James Saxon) is uniformly lively, but Neil Dickson as Biggles steals the film. A huskier, younger version of Peter O'Toole, he evokes a Biggles who's survived on wits and more than a little luck, with a genteel streak underlined by a viciousness required in war. He's convincing in all aspects, from physically demanding scenes to comic oneliners.

Unfortunately, Hyde-White as the time-jumping American is pic's major drawback. His thesping is as animated as the White Cliffs of Dover. Wooden delivery, combined with poor comic timing dissolves any chance at chemistry between the leads, to the film's detriment. With a proved American comic in the role, ''Biggles'' would have had markedly better chances Stateside.

Technically, pic it topnotch, especially aerial sequences using vintage bi-planes in chase sequences reminiscent of ''The Blue Max.'' Battle in the trenches is depicted with just the right touch of muddy squalor, and costumes are evocative of the period, though the aviators' all-leather gear was hardly standard-issue,. A chintzy blue lightning effect when the hole in time opens up is a drawback, as is the schizophrenic rock soundtrack by Stanislas, which rarely fits in with the on-screen action.

John Hough's direction keeps things moving at just the right pace, offering, for a change, the chance to get familiar with the characters. Ending leaves the pic wide open for a sequel, and with the right actor to light up the screen alongside Dickson's Biggles, series possibility looms. — *Mich.*

Za Kude Putovate
(Where Are You Going)
(BULGARIAN-COLOR)

A Bulgariafilm release and production. Directed by Rangel Vulchanov. Screenplay, Georgi Danailov, Vulchnaov; camera (color), Radoslav Spassov; art director, Georgi Todorov. Music, Kiril Donchev. Reviewed at the Cannes Film Festival (Un Certain Regard), May 17, 1986. Running time: **90 MINS.**
With: Stoyan Alexiev, Georgi Kaloyanchev, Katerina Evro, Yossif Surchadijev.

Cannes — This comedy about a mathematician bored with his own career who decides to drop everything and go back to nature manages to supply a half-hour of amusing inventions and then gradually loses any control, confuses the issues and lacks the necessary imagination to pursue the original tempo.

The young scientist who decides there is no fulfillment in his profession, starts his withdrawal process by retreating under a table during a boring faculty staff meeting. Next

he burns all the medicine in his house, throws the telephone away, locks his wife out of the flat and sets out for new horizons he cannot define.

Soon enough, a mysterious wheel leads him into a remote village escorted by one lonely goatherd with whom he has to cohabitate. But then, it turns out, it is not to nature that the scientist wishes to escape but to the farther domains of imagination, which means that from the realism of pastoral surroundings the film takes one more leap into pure fantasy. All this is managed in a clumsy manner, both visually and stylistically.

The film ends with the oldest copout of all in fantasy pictures, when the script indicates this was just a daydream and nothing more.

Acting is generally on the broad side, and humor is on the heavy side. —*Edna.*

Sorekara
(And Then)
(JAPANESE-COLOR)

A Toei Co. release and production. Produced by Mitsuru Kurosawa, Sadatoshi Fujimine. Executive producer, Shigeru Okada. Directed by Yoshimitsu Morita. Screenplay, Tomomi Tsutsui, based on the novel by Soseki Natsume; camera (color), Yonezo Maeda; editor, Akira Suzuki; art direction, Isutomu Imamura; lighting, Kazuo Yabe; sound, Fumio Hachimoto and Hisoyuki Miyamata; music, Shigaru Umnhoyoshi; costumes, Michiko Kitamura. Reviewed at the Cannes Film Festival (Directors Fortnight), May 13, 1986. Running time: **130 MINS.**
Daisuke . . . . Yusaku Matsuda
Michiyo . . . . Miwako Fujitani
Hiraoka . . . . Kaoru Kobayashi
Father . . . . Chishu Kyu
Sister-in-law . . . . Mitsuko Kusabue
Brother . . . . Katsuo Nakamura

Cannes — This stately film from director Yoshimitsu Morita stacks up as a high-level costume drama that impressively handles with restraint what in Japanese cinema is all-too-often presented with pull-out-the-stops emotionalism. The subject here is a love triangle set in a time when the limits of socially acceptable behavior in Japan were drastically less broad than they are today.

A 30-year-old (Yusaku Matsuda) is driving his family nuts. The time is 1909, when second sons of wealthy Japanese households are expected to get serious, settle down and raise a family. Our idler, jobless and only interested in opera, theater and literature, will have none of it.

The stalemate is moved forward when a college chum of the principal character returns home from Tokyo with the news he's departed his bank job under a cloud resulting form the bookkeeping orders of a subordinate. The chum is rough, sharp tempered and appalled at the

lassitude of the idler.

The chum's wife is pretty, submissive, tired of her marriage. She is also the idler's former girlfriend in university days. When the two meet again, sparks begin to fly.

To ''Sorekara's'' enormous credit, the audience is transported to the first decade of this century, and thus sympathizes with the main character's dilemma. Should he fulfill a deep and passionate love by scandalizing his family and alienating his friend? Should he beg off and destroy what's left of his fragile emotional state?

Such considerations form the basis of ''Sorekara's'' subtle power. Director Morita and scripter Tomomi Tsutsui (working from a novel by Soseki Natsume) approach the material reverently, providing rich roles for an excellent group of actors.

A particular standout is the director's boldness in spicing up with what could have been a visually constricting costumer. Noteworthy is the use of special photographic effects when, for example, the idler rides the local tram or walks through the family garden. Yonezo Maeda's photography is especially impressive in carrying out these effects, as is Kazuo Yabe's lighting.

The cast is particularly strong especially Miwako Fujitani as the chum's wife and Kaoru Kobayashi as the friend. Matsuda does what he can to make the enigmatic principal character, the idler, come alive, facing long olds, he succeeds.

Overall,. ''Sorekara'' runs a bit long, and is a bit too formal in its pacing in spots. But make no mistake: this is work of a high order. Pic should be reviewed by fest directors on the prowl for product, and might well become fodder for specialized commercial distribution. —*Sege.*

Faubourg Saint-Martin
(FRENCH-COLOR)

A Gerick Films release of a Films du Passage production. Produced by Paolo Branco. Written and directed by Jean-Claude Guiguet. Camera (color), Alain Levent; editor, Kadicha Baraha; music, Serge Tomassi, Verdi; sound, Jean-Françoise Chevalier; make-up, Pascale Tisseraud; production manager, Renaud Victor; assistant director, Charles Tible. Reviewed at the Cinémathèque Française, Paris, May 25, 1986. (In International Critics Week at the Cannes Film Festival.) Running time: **87 MINS.**
Marquessa . . . . Françoise Fabian
Marie . . . . Marie Christine Rousseau
Madam Coppercage . . . ., . Patachou
Paul . . . . Stéphane Jobert
Suzanne . . . . Ingrid Bourgoin
François . . . . Emmanuel Lemoine
Also with: Patrick Couet, Chantal Delsaux, Valérie Jeanet, Renaud Victor, Vincent Ducastel, Howard Vernon, Greg Germain.

Paris — Romantic hookers with

hearts of gold again are walking French celluloid streets of late. After Paul Vecchiali's ''Rosa-The-Rose, Public Woman,'' writer-director Jean-Claude Guiguet offers ''Faubourg Saint-Martin,'' which also tells of a beautiful young prostitute's tragic attempts to leave her past behind when she finds true romance.

Like Vecchiali, Guiguet casts a nostalgic eye back to French film classics, notably Marcel Carné's populist drama ''Hotel du Nord,'' which is paraphrased in numerous scenes. Geographic center of the film is a three-star hotel near the Canal Saint-Martin (where Carné's film was set) out of which a young hooker (Marie Christine Rousseau) operates. So too does another flashy callgirl (Françoise Fabian), who is bringing up her 10-year-old son.

Their mother hen is the hotel's bossy owner (played by veteran music hall star Patachou), who hides a solicitous heart behind her tough, no-nonsense manner. She is there to soothe the pain when Rousseau's lover (Stéphane Jobert) is shot to death by her brutal pimp, who earlier had her roughed up to dissuade her from her foolish dreams.

Guiguet, who made a promising debut in 1979 with ''Les Belles Manières,'' falls victim to the clichés he tries to sublimate in this unconvincing melodrama, which leaves one unmoved and irritated. Rousseau, an attractive young newcomer from the theater, is uneasy in a part composed essentially of movieland conventions. Fabian has one lovely scene in which she sings a poem by Louis Aragon at Rousseau's ill-fated engagement banquet. Patachou has obvious dramatic presence but, under Guiguet's direction, lays it on so thick she becomes a caricature.

Among film's pluses is superb nighttime lensing by Alain Levent. Other credits are okay. Pic ran in the Intl. Critics Week sidebar at Cannes.—*Len.*

Beginners' Luck
(U.S.-COLOR)

A New World Pictures release of a Hot Talk Co. production. Produced, written and directed by Frank Mouris, Caroline Ahlfors Mouris. Camera (Fuji color, Du Art prints), Anne S. Coffey; editor, Ray Anne School; music, Richard Lavsky; sound, Charlie Lew; assistant director, Suzie Marshall. Reviewed at the Cannes Film Festival (market), May 17, 1986. (MPAA Rating: R.) Running time: **83 MINS.**
Hunter . . . . Sam Rush
Tech . . . . Riley Steiner
Aris . . . . Charles Humet
Also with: Kate Talbot, Mickey Coburn, Bobbie Steinbach, Rima Miller.

Cannes — Lensed in 1983 on locations at Boothbay, Maine, bearing a 1984 copyright date, and tested earlier this year, ''Beginners'

Luck'' is a New World pickup of staggering banality.

This is the more disappointing since it was made by the husband and wife team of Frank and Caroline Mouris whose short films, including the award winning ''Frank Film,'' were utterly charming and inventive. Their debut feature tries hard to be charming and inventive, too, but fails by miles.

Story concerns a couple on the brink of marraige who bring their lonely neighbor into their home for a ménage à trois. But there's no sex involved (despite the R rating), and precious little humor, though the film seems to be straining for a kind of cute domestic comedy. The three leads (Riley Steiner as the girl, Charles Humet as her fiance and Sam Rush as the neighbor) all have pleasant personalities, and given a decent script might have provided some laughs. But the poor writing and clumsy handling doom the project from the opening scene. It just isn't remotely amusing.

Theatrical release seems slim for the pic, with little joy to be expected from vidcassette or tv sales either. Technical credits are standard.
— *Strat.*

Koibumi
(Love Letter)
(JAPANESE-COLOR)

A Shochiku release of a Shochiku-Fuji, Kosaido Eizo and Kei Enterprise coproduction. Executive producers, Kazuyoshi Okuyama, Jun Nagara. Directed by Tatsumi Kumashiro. Screenplay, Jun Takada, Kumashiro, based on a novel by Mikihiko Renjo; camera (widescreen, color). Yoshihiro Yamazaki; music, Takayuki Inoue. Reviewed at the Cannes Film Festival (market), May 16, 1986. Running time: **109 MINS.**
With: Kenichi Hagiwara, Mitsuko Baisho, Keiko Takahashi, Motoyoshi Wada.

Cannes — Mitsuko Baisho is one of Japan's undiscovered (in the West) cinematic treasures, an actress of warmth, sensuality and range. She's the only solidly positive attribute of this marginally interesting weeper that plays strictly to the femme component of the Japan theatrical audience — it's significant — but looms lackluster in other world territories.

Baisho, who has been comp ᵣred to a younger Sophia Loren, moves with likable assurance in almost any role she takes. In ''Koibumi,'' she plays the role of a working mother of a pre-pubescent son and wife of a ne'er-do-well artist in Tokyo (Kenichi Hagiwara).

He gets a letter from an old girlfriend (Keiko Takahashi) with the unsettling news that she has leukemia and only months to live. The husband decides to leave his wife and son to take an apartment to be near the old flame.

To complicate matters, the hus-

band also decides to conceal his marriage by presenting his wife — who develops an attachment to the dying woman — as his cousin. Finally, husband divorces wife to marry dying woman, much to the dismay of his son (nicely played by Motoyoshi Wada).

Can the first wife win back the husband following the second wife's death? This question is answered in unexpected fashion at pic's conclusion for which the audience has not been prepared fully by scripters Jun Takada and Tatsumi Kumashiro.

The chief problem here is the Hagiwara as the husband is allowed by director Tatsumi Kumashiro to play his part as such a confused wimp the audience is left wondering why the first wife was eager to have him return to home and hearth in the first place. The actor has an unsettling habit of grinning while emoting in heavily — and distinctly unfunny — emotional scenes.

As for Baisho, she can do no wrong. Particularly appealing are her scenes interacting with Wada as her young son.—*Sege.*

Girls School Screamers
(U.S.-COLOR)

A Troma release of a Bandit production. Produced by John P. Finegan, Pierce J. Keating, James W. Finegan Jr. Executive producers, Lloyd Kaufman, Michael Herz. Directed by John P. Finegan. Screenplay, John P. Finegan, from story by John P. Finegan, Katie Keating, Pierce J. Keating; additional dialog, Charles Braun, Robert Fisher; camera (Du Art color), Albert R. Jordan; editor/second unit director, Thomas R. Rondinella; music, John Hodian; sound, Bruce Levin; art direction, Glenn Bookman; assistant director, Rondinella; production manager, Megwin Finegan; special makeup effects, John Mafei; second unit camera, Gerard Hughes. Reviewed at the Cannes Film Festival (market), May 17, 1986. (MPAA Rating: R.) Running time: **85 MINS.**
Jackie/Jennifer . . . . Mollie O'Mara
Liz . . . . Sharon Christopher
Kate . . . . Mari Butler
Karen . . . . Beth O'Malley
Susan . . . . Karen Krevitz
Sister Urban . . . . Vera Gallagher
Rosemary . . . . Monica Antonucci
Paul . . . . Peter Cosimano

Cannes — ''Girls School Screamers,'' originally titled (more appropriately) ''The Portrait,'' is an utterly routine supernatural horror picture. Bearing a 1984 copyright, the just-released Troma pic has little to offer genre fans.

Plot has been done 100 times before: seven girls from Trinity School in Philadelphia are assigned to spend the weekend at the Tyler Estate mansion (which has been willed to the school) to catalog the artworks there anent an impending sale of the joint. They are killed off one by one, with very fake and pointless makeup effects applied.

Familiar gimmick has Jackie (Mollie O'Mara) apparently the re-incarnation (per a matching wall

portrait) of Jennifer Welles (no, not the 1970s porno star, just a fictional character), a young woman killed in 1939 in the Tyler mansion by her uncle when she resisted his lecherous advances. The girls' chaperone Sister Urban (Vera Gallagher) was a mother superior back in Jennifer's time, as shown in junky flashbacks.

A hurried, incomprehensible finale fails to tie up the dangling plot threads, indicating helmer John P. Finegan and his collaborators were anxious to merely wrap this one up. Screening audience was even more anxious to head for the exits.

Mollie O'Mara in the lead role projects a pleasant personality but the supporting cast, particularly male performers, is weak. Technical credits are perfunctory, film delivers none of the genre's expected nudity and scares are absent.—*Lor.*

Working Girls
(U.S.-COLOR)

An Alternate Current presentation of a Lizzie Borden/Alternate Current production. Produced by Borden, Andi Gladstone. Directed by Borden. Stars Louise Smith. Screenplay, Borden, based on story by Borden, Sandra Kay; camera (Eastmancolor), Judy Irola; editor, Borden; sound, J.T. Takagi; art direction, Kurt Ossenfort; music, David Van Tieghem. Reviewed at the Cannes Film Festival (Directors Fortnight), May 17, 1986. (No MPAA Rating.) Running time: **90 MINS.**
Molly . . . . Louise Smith
Susan . . . . Ellen McEldruff
Shawn . . . . Amanda Goodwin
Gina . . . . Marusia Zach
April . . . . Janne Peters
Mary . . . . Helen Nicholas

Cannes — ''Working Girls'' is a simulated docu-style feature that allows audiences to be invisible guests for one day and part of the evening in a Manhattan brothel staffed by about 10 whores working two shifts and charging $50 per half-hour when special services of limited scope (''mild dominance'' is undertaken by some of the girls) are not required. When their shifts are over, the girls go home to private life with or without husbands or boyfriends.

Lizzie Borden did an experimental feature (''Born In Flames'') three years ago, but calls ''Working Girls'' her first work of fiction. Still, she has done sufficient research for her new picture to appear convincingly realistic, and commercially it should find audiences wherever such curiosity items as ''Pumping Iron'' and ''Pumping Iron, 2 — The Women'' made headway.

Centering on Molly (a nice, subdued job by Louise Smith, a professional actress like everybody else in the cast), Borden neither glamorizes, romanticizes nor condemns anything or anybody connected to the brothel. She has chosen film's title to stress how non-committal she is: the girls get up in the morning, go to work, do their chores (a labor of love) and go home again — just like

any typist or factory worker.

Film's advance publicity, supposedly controlled by Borden herself, will also have us believe she describes these prostitutes as neither strung-out nor junkies, and that she sees prostitution as work, not as a moral or psychological problem. The picture she has made differs slightly from such a point of departure.

Molly, a college graduate, is matter-of-fact about her work, but she is obviously sick and tired of it (and quits in the happy ending to this no-plot film). Shawn, a gum-chewing teenager spouting vile language, is obviously just one step above street prositution. Another girl has come back to the brothel after a physical and mental breakdown.

The work these girls perform may be ''an economic alternative'' to other underpaid and undervalued work available to women, but is clearly enough a more demeaning toil. Borden sugars her pill with clean, crisp, often witty recording of brothel action and shop-talk. Most of the time, the girls are seen as being in full control of all proceedings, but it also occurs that they are not, and a little thing like having their customers wash themselves properly on arrival can cause trouble.

All acting is credible, the camerawork is smooth, the non-action a bit on the long-winded side. Film's combined production dress is no more grainy than to smack of proper *cinema verité*.—*Kell.*

Cobra
(COLOR)

Exciting, violent Sylvester Stallone police thriller headed for paydirt.

A Warner Bros. release of a Cannon Group/Golan-Globus production. Produced by Menahem Golan, Yoram Globus. Executive producer, James D. Brubaker. Directed by George Pan Cosmatos. Stars Sylvester Stallone. Screenplay, Stallone, based on the novel ''Fair Game'' by Paula Gosling; camera (Technicolor), Ric Waite; additional photography, Nick McLean; editor, Don Zimmerman, James Symons; music, Sylvester Levay; production design, Bill Kenney; art direction, William Skinner, Adrian H. Gorton; set design, David Klassen; set decoration, Robert Gould; costume design, Tom Bronson; sound (Eagle stereo), Michael Evje; associate producer, Tony Munafo; assistant director, Duncan Henderson; second unit director/stunt coordinator, Terry Leonard; casting, Joy Todd. Reviewed at the RKO Warner Twin, N.Y., May 22, 1986. (MPAA Rating: R.) Running time: **87 MINS.**
Marion Cobretti . . . . Sylvester Stallone
Ingrid . . . . Brigitte Nielsen
Gonzales . . . . Reni Santoni
Detective Monte . . . . Andrew Robinson
Nancy Stalk . . . . Lee Garlington
Cho . . . . John Herzfeld
Captain Sears . . . . Art La Fleur
Night Slasher . . . . Brian Thompson
Dan . . . . David Rasche
Chief Halliwell . . . . Val Avery
Supermarket killer . . . . . . Marco Rodriguez
TV news reporter . . . . Christine Craft
Comm. Reddesdale . . . . Bert Williams

"Cobra" is a sleek, extremely violent and exciting police thriller. Buoyed by a 2,131-print launch by Warner Bros., the widest in industry history, and riding the crest of star Sylvester Stallone's popularity, picture should be a massive hit this summer.

Stallone's screenplay carries many echoes of WB's 1971 hit "Dirty Harry." The star is cast as unconventional cop Marion Cobretti, nickname Cobra, who with partner Gonzales (Reni Santoni, also Clint Eastwood's partner in the earlier film) works the L.A. zombie squad, doing jobs no other cops will do. Against the objections of by-the-book Det. Monte (Andrew Robinson, the psycho killer in "Dirty Harry"), they're called in to track down a serial killer who's claimed 16 victims in a month.

They protect the one surviving witness, a beautiful model (Brigitte Nielsen) and discover that the killer is actually a neo-fascist army of killers, led by angular-featured Brian Thompson and a renegade female cop (Lee Garlington).

Director George Pan Cosmatos (of "Rambo: First Blood Part II") tightens the screws for a very fast ride, punctuated by outstanding stunt set pieces supervised by Terry Leonard, including a hair-raising four-minute car chase midway through the film. Enhanced by an eerie soundtrack by Sylvester Levay, film maintains its tension impressively.

His lowkey personality defined by his souped-up 1950 Mercury coupe and funny throwaway lines of dialog, Stallone's Cobra is a far more ingratiating character than his recent Rocky and Rambo guises. His real-life wife Nielsen makes for a resourceful heroine who is extremely sexy during a music video-styled fashion modeling montage sequence. Santoni is fine and Robinson, though nominally a good guy cop here, is again a powerfully hissable adversary for the hero to oppose. The bad guys, particularly Thompson, are comic strip exaggerations.

Tech credits, especially Ric Waite's flashy lighting, are excellent and a flavorful song score helps lighten up the Sturm und Drang atmosphere.

Film was produced by Cannon toppers Menahem Golan and Yoram Globus for Warner Bros. under a tradeoff arrangement for Stallone's services, as the star was previously committed to make "Over The Top" for Cannon (with WB handling domestic release) and that film's start was pushed back to make way for "Cobra."—Lor.

Killer Party
(COLOR)

Minor splatter opus.

A UA/MGM release from MGM of a Marquis Prods. presentation. Produced by Michael Lepiner. Executive producer, Kenneth Kaufman. Directed by William Fruet. Screenplay, Barney Cohen; camera (Technicolor), John Lindley; editor, Eric Albertson; music, John Beal; production designer, Reuben Freed; assistant art dirctor, Alicia Keywan; set decorator, Enrico Campana; costumes, Gina Keillerman; sound, Bryan Day, Michael Lecroix; coordinating producer, Majorie Kalins; associate producer, Grace Gilroy; assistant director, Gordon Robinson; casting, Peg Halligan (L.A.), Armstrong/-Clysdale (Toronto). Reviewed at MGM/UA screening room, Culver City, Calif., May 8, 1986. (MPAA Rating: R.) Running time: 91 MINS.
Blake....................Martin Hewitt
Martin...................Ralph Seymour
Phoebe...................Elaine Wilkes
Professor Zito...............Paul Bartel
Vivia................Sherry Willis-Burch
Veronica...................Alicia Fleer
Harrison..................Woody Brown
Jennifer................Joanna Johnson
Melanie..................Terri Hawkes

Hollywood — "Killer Party," a.k.a. "Fool's Night," is a cut above standard splatter fare in production values and casting, but sinks to the lower depths in script and execution. Pickup for UA/-MGM is unlikely to generate much heat in regional playoff.

April Fool's Day seems to be becoming as much of an excuse for nefarious doings among teenagers as Halloween these days. "Killer Party" uses the holiday as a setting for springtime bloodletting, although much of the gore is thankfully implied rather than witnessed.

Action revolves around the initiation of three pledges into the fun-loving Sigma Alpha Pi sorority at an unidentified Eastern college. The sadistic sisters, known fittingly as goats, put the three lovelies through trial by fire, but then some weird things start happening for real at the old campus haunted house, where else.

What exactly is going on is anybody's guess, something to do with a murdered student whose spirit is coming back for revenge and possesses young Veronica's body.

Script by Barney Cohen is full of strange characters even without the supernatural happenings. There are also a number of non sequiturs such as two bizarre opening sequences, one a funeral and the other a mock rockvideo, that serve as prologs except they don't have anything to do with the rest of the film.

Direction by William Fruet is strongest when he goes for the camp humor but fails to generate very much suspense or involvement, even for the film's overlong finale at the scene of the crime.

On the camp side, bit part by Paul Bartel as a literature professor, who winds up like all students would like to see their English teach-

er, is the tongue-in-cheek highlight of the pic.

Rest of the cast is attractive but with hardly a character among them. Alica Fleer, a young Cybill Shepherd lookalike, is appealing as the most reticent of the girlfriends. Elaine Wilkes and Sherry Willis-Burch are also likable as the sidekicks and together the trio almost manage to keep the film together.

As for the men,. Martin Hewitt receives top billing for a smallish part, probably due to his previous triumphs in "Endless Love" and others. He suffers through like the others. As the resident crazy, Ralph Seymour has a few good moments when he isn't bludgeoning his part to death.

Tech credits are fine and make the film look better than it has any right to. —Jagr.

Sizzle Beach, U.S.A.
(U.S.-COLOR)

A Troma release. Produced by Eric Louzil. Directed by Richard Brander. Screenplay, Craig Kusaba; camera (color), John Sprang; editor, Howard Heard; music, the Beach Towels, Rick Dunham, Melodye Condos; associate producer, Laurel A. Koernig. Reviewed at the Cannes Film Festival (market), May 15, 1986. (No MPAA Rating.) Running time: 93 MINS.
With: Terry Congie, Leslie Brander, Roselyn Royce, Kevin Costner.

Cannes — "Sizzle Beach, U.S.A." isn't a beach picture Although its trio of heroines live in a house in Malibu, where a few love interests develop, there is less sizzling than slow burning in this film, particularly since it has been on the fire for a long time before Troma decided to release it.

Janice, Sheryl and Dit (Terry Congie, Leslie Brander and Roselyn Royce) meet up on their way to L.A. Sheryl is a blond body-conscious P.E. instructor who soon lands a job at the local high school, with the help of an investment broker she meets jogging on the beach. Dit, who is characterized as having a thing for Bette Davis, wants to be an actress and to that end takes acting lessons. For fresh air she goes riding at a stable owned by a very young, teenage Kevin Costner (only passable performance in the film). Janice, finally, strums the guitar and sings very pretty folk songs. Since the owner of the recording studio is a drooling jerk, her nights are spent with cousin Steve, a well-built hunk the girls share the house with.

Female nudity is plentiful, since every scene is aimed at getting one of the leads to take her clothes off. The girls are quite ordinary looking and embarrassing with their patchy bikini tans, oversize sunglasses, and fashions from the 1970s. To remove any doubt about when "Sizzle Beach" was made, there is an un-

mistakable picture of President Jimmy Carter on the high school principal's desk.

Lensing is strictly home-movie level; dialog reaches its peak in lines like, "Hey, that would be GREAT!" Thesping, apart from Costner, ranges from amateur to atrocious. —Yung.

Yume Miruyoni Nemuritai
(To Sleep So As To Dream)
(JAPANESE-B&W-16m)

A Shibata Organization release of an Eizo Tanteisha production. Produced by Kaizo Hayashi, Takashige Ichiso. Written and directed by Hayashi. Camera (b&w)/editor, Yuichi Nagata; music, Hidehiko Urayama; art director, Takeo Kimura; sound, Akihiko Suzuki. Reviewed at the Cannes Film Festival (market), May 17, 1986. Running time: 80 MINS.
Bellflower.................Moe Kamura
Botsuka....................Shiro Sano
Kobayashi..................Kojji Otake
Also with: Fujiko Fukamizu (Mme. Cherry-Blossom), Yoshio Yoshida (Matsunosuke, the director), Shunsui Matsuda (Akagaki, the Benshi), Kyoko Kusajima (Old Lady), Akira Oizumi, Morio Agata, Kazuikari Ozawa (The Three Magicians), Tsuneo & Tatsuo Nakamoto (The White Masks).

Cannes — A low budget, 16m, black and white first feature that indicates not only an interesting new talent but also an extraordinary love and feeling for the silent cinema. Pic is shot like a Japanese detective film of the 1920s, with inserts in the mold of a samurai film of the mid-teens. Both eras of silent cinema, which were distinctively different, are evoked in an uncannily accurate fashion.

Plot involves a detective and his comic sidekick on the trail of a kidnaped actress, known as The Princess. With no dialog — they "speak" only in captions — they follow up various leads and solve intriguing riddles. Meanwhile, an old lady is viewing and reviewing an old samurai film in which she starred as a girl; but the last reel is tantalizingly missing.

The film is so charming it seems churlish to note it hardly contains enough to sustain its feature length. Maybe this ambitious and inventive new director should have turned it into a short subject on which to cut his teeth.

Nonetheless, it's an immensely affectionate tribute to a bygone style of filmmaking, and silent film buffs will be entranced. It's planned to blow it up to 35m, and hopefully it will unspool at a fest or two this summer to gain this charming oddity the wider exposure it deserves.
— Strat.

Lola
(SPANISH-COLOR)

A Figaro Films presentation. Executive producer, Enrique Viciano. Directed by Bigas Luná. Screenplay, Luis Herce, Luná, Viciano; camera (Eastmancolor), José María Civit; editor, Ernest Blasi; music, José Manuel Pagan; sets, Felipe de Paco; costumes, Consol Tura; sound, Joan Quilis; production manager, Luis Puig. Reviewed at the Cannes Film Festival (market), May 18, 1986. Running time: **100 MINS.**
Lola .... Angela Molina
Robert .... Patrick Bauchau
Mario .... Feodor Atkine
Silvia .... Assumpta Serna
Also with: Angela Gutiérrez, Constantino Romero, Marian Rodes, Pepa López, Maria González, Rosa Gabin, Andrés Salmón, Patrick Honore, Boris Mastramon.

Cannes — Well-paced thriller bears many of the hallmarks associated with Bigas Luná's films, such as a penchant for sexual aberrations, a concern for nasty closeups and an atmosphere of repressed violence, which nonetheless fail to deliver the final punch pic seems to be leading up to.

This sort of story has been often told before, but Bigas pulls it off well enough, partly through fine performances by Angela Molina as the title character and Feodor Atkine, respectively cast as the poor working girl who's a sucker for punishment and the sadistic lover who can make her flesh tingle like no one else.

After being brutally manhandled by her paramour Mario, Lola finally decides to run off to less painful pastures; scene shifts to four years hence, after Lola has set up life with a French businessman in Barcelona, and they have a small daughter.

To no one's surprise, Mario comes to haunt her from the past; he is convinced that he's the father of the child; moreover, he seems determined to ensnare Lola in his s&m clutches again. But just as he's about to succeed in his devilish and drunken design, the husband unexpectedly returns from a trip and finds them together in his apartment.

Here, at the moment of climax, instead of telling the story straight, Bigas suddenly jumps ahead to a courtroom scene; then he provides a flashback to what has actually happened: Mario has stabbed Lola during a squabble about the child. The husband is at first wrongly suspected of being the culprit, but is then cleared. Pic ends rather blandly with the husband watching the young girl, now grown into adolescence, flirting with a boy in a pool.

Pic might chalk up some sales in homevid and theatrical markets, but on a modest scale, passed off essentially on the name of Molina and billed as a suspense thriller, which it only in part is.—*Besa.*

Las Vegas Weekend
(U.S.-COLOR)

A Shaprio Entertainment presentation of Pygmalion production. Executive producer, Charles Black. Written, produced and directed by Dale Trevillion. Stars Barry Hickey. Camera (Eastmancolor), Christopher Tufty; editor, David Kern; music, Scarlet Rivera, Alan St. Jons; sound, Craig Smith; assistant director, Vic Atway. Reviewed at the Cannes Film Festival (market), May 17, 1986. (No MPAA Rating). Running time: **82 MINS.**
With: Barry Hickey, Jace Damon, Macka Foley, Vickie Benson, Kimberlee Kaiser, Dyanne DiRosario, Ray Dennis Steckler.

Cannes — This "Las Vegas Weekend" looms as a loser although writer-producer-director Dale Trevillion has at his disposal all the right ingredients for light farcical comedy fare. There is chubbily handsome Barry Hickey, who can do some fine comedy mugging when given half a chance, and there is the classical plot of an innocent abroad in a wonderland of temptations.

What went wrong then? Simply that Trevillion steers his innocent (Hickey playing a computer whiz with a special talent for figuring out systems for winning at blackjack) through the fleshpots and money-traps of Las Vegas in so bland a way that just about every calculated sight gag or verbal punchline fails to work. Hickey and a couple of supporting actors strive mightily to overcome the handicaps of the lax helming, but to practically no avail.

An excess of footage of Las Vegas' famous scenery of lights serves only to underscore the fact that no other Vegas reality, funny, sad or otherwise, is ever on display. Toward the end, some softcore sex and some sentimental morality is thrown in. Only the music by Scarlet Rivera and Alan St. Jons is vigorous throughout. —*Kell.*

Opera do Malandro
(Malandro)
(BRAZILIAN-FRENCH-COLOR)

An MK2, Austra (Brazil) and TF-1 Films (Paris) production with the participation of the French Ministry of Culture. Produced by Marin Karmitz and Ruy Guerra. Executive producer, Alberto Grana. Directed by Guerra. Screenplay, Chico Buarque, Orlando Senna, Guerra, adapted from Buarque's musical, "Opera de Malandro;" music and lyrics, Buarque; musical direction, Mauro Monteiro and Irenio Maia; costumes, Maria Cecilia Motta; choreography, Regina Miranda; editors, Mair Tavares, Ide Lacreta, Kenout Peltier; sound, Claude Villand, Bernard le Roux. Reviewed at the Cannes Film Festival (Directors Fortnight), May 16, 1986. Running time: **105 MINS.**
Max .... Edson Celulari
Lu .... Claudia Ohana
Margot .... Elba Ramalho
Tigrao .... Ney Latorraca
Otto Strüdell .... Fabio Sabag
Geni .... J.C. Violla
Satiro Bilhar .... Wilson Grey
Victotria Strüdell ..... Maria Silvia
Fiorella .... Claudia Gimenez
Fichinha .... Andreia Dantas
Doris Pelance .... Ilva Niño
Dorinho Tubao .... Zonaide
Shirley Paquete .... Djenane Machado
Mimi Bibeló .... Katia Bronstein
Porfirio .... Luthero Luiz

Cannes — First staged as a musical a decade ago, "Malandro" is a Brazilian style version of the "Three Penny Opera" that could do well at home and, thanks to Chico Buarque's music and songs, get some arthouse exposure abroad.

Max is a happy-go-lucky pimp and smalltime smuggler, while Tigrao, a classmate of his at school has become chief of police, and Otto Strüdell, a German, runs a cabaret and prostitution ring. Margot is the whore with a heart of gold who keeps Max. When the Nazi fires her from his nightclub, Max tries to get his own revenge back by seducing his daughter Lu, who turns to be a tougher nut to crack than he expected. All this takes place in the early 1940s.

Plot outline and characters are derived from the (not credited) Brecht-Weill "Three Penny Opera," but the social background and political context are barely sketched in and far removed from the incisiveness of the German piece of the late 1920s. In fact, "Malandro" rather tries for the light touch of the Hollywood musicals of the period it portrays. One point of interest may well be that there have been practically no musicals in Latin-American cinema the last three decades.

Acting and technical level are good and some of the production numbers quite attractive, particularly the Margot-Lu dance sequence. On the other hand, director Ruy Guerra seems to be more at home with realistic subjects and, just as he failed to recreate the fantastic world of Garcia Marquez's "Erendira," he lacks the light touch required by a musical here.—*Amig.*

Uemura Naomi Monogatari
(Lost In The Wilderness)
(JAPANESE-COLOR)

A Toho release of a Dentsu-Mainichi Hoso production. Executive producers, Juichi Tanaka, Haruyuki Takahashi, Hiroshi Takayama. Directed by Junya Sato. Screenplay, Yoshiki Iwama, Sato, based on books by Naomi Uemura; camera (color), Hiroyuki Namiki, Etsuo Akutsu; music, William Ackerman. Reviewed at the Cannes Film Festival (market), May 13, 1986. Running time: **140 MINS.**
With: Toshiyuki Nishida, Chieko Baisho, Masato Furuoya, Go Wakabayashi, Muga Takewaki, Ryo Ikebe.

Cannes — This pleasant pic tells the story of Naomi Uemura, an actual figure who became the first Japanese mountain climber to scale the world's most formidable peaks: Mont Blanc, the Matterhorn, Kilimanjaro, South America's El Plata and Aconcagua, Alaska's Mount Sanford, and Mount Everest.

A straightforward biopic with few plot twists and turns, "Lost In The Wilderness" comes across as an okay adventure-nature film sparked by a likable klutz as a hero. Moderate foreign sales loom in markets where nature-adventure pics find a niche.

Hewing closely to actual events (scripters Yoshiki Iwama and Junya Sato worked from the climber's own books), "Lost" tracks Uemura's growing obsession with mountain climbing and other types of high-risk ventures — he once traveled across Greenland, alone, by dogsled.

Pic nicely shows that Uemura's obsession is traced to his earlier clumsiness in climbing and his quite justified feelings of being an inferior outsider in a land that prizes collective enterprise. A bit of an eccentric, Uemura valued one thing — taking on near-impossible challenges, almost invariably alone.

"Lost" spends much time scaling peaks with Uemura. This fairly quickly becomes monotonous since, to the viewer, one snow-capped peak looks and plays like the next. The pic runs two hours and 20 minutes, a time impossible to sustain by its slender plot and thematic thread. Some pruning would be welcome.

Balancing all the mountain and Arctic adventuring is the climber's earthbound romance and marriage. These parts of the pic are less interesting than those involving physical action, especially since the climber's wife (winsomely played by Chieko Baisho, a regular in Shochiku's "Tora-San" film series) is a submissive character all too willing to accept her husband's lengthy absences.

Director Junya Sato and cameramen Hiroyuki Iwama and Etsuo Akutsu try most often successfully to give at least a measure of suspense to the mountain climbing, although repeated triumphs against long odds imparts a feeling of repetition. Uemura was lost after scaling Alaska's Mount McKinley on Feb. 13, 1984. His body was never found.

Little emotionally is made of his finale. Toshiyuki Nishida plays the climber-explorer with such zest and verve that the character becomes at times cloyingly eager to please.

Overall, "Lost In The Wilderness" takes few risks and offers modest rewards. —*Sege.*

Field Of Honor
(DUTCH-COLOR)

A Cannon Group release of an Orianda Films production. Executive producer, Henk Bos. Produced by Menahem Golan and Yoram Globus. Directed by Hans Scheepsmaker. Stars Everett McGill. Screenplay, Henk Bos; camera (Fujicolor), Hein Groot; editor, Victorine Habets; music, Roy Budd; sound, Tom Tholen; production manager, Jong Ho Hoo. Reviewed at the Cannes Film Festival (market), May 13, 1986. (No MPAA Rating.) Running time: **95 MINS.**

With: Everett McGill (Sire), Ron Brandsteder, Jun-Kyung Lee, Frank Schaafsma, Hey Young Lee, Min Yoo, Guus Van Der Made, Marc Van Eegham, Dong Hyun Kim.

Cannes — "Field Of Honor" is a Korean War action pic nicely shot on location that has a fatal flaw for an exploitation pic of its type. Largely devoid of action, most of the fatalities incurred with this peculiar Dutch production will occur in the audience, which gets talked to death. That would be okay if pic had something to say, but the Dutch-accented English dialog makes the thin "war is heck" message unintelligible. Domestic playoff prospects for Cannon appear minimal, with foreign playdates a bit less likely.

Pic is replete with clichés of old World War II films that went before it — the harmonica-playing tenderfoot around the campfire, the requisite whorehouse scene, mail call, everyone longing for the girl back home, the rookie lieutenant with the textbook strategy.

Everett McGill plays the hard-bitten squad sergeant Sire as a sadistic, brutal leader of nincompoops who shampoos with cathouse scotch and whose idea of a good time is walking around with his genitals beribboned until he can find his underwear.

Later denouement of McGill as a sensitized soldier with a sense of honor doesn't come off. Better scripter Henk Bos had left him an unsympathetic hero. Not a great leading man, McGill is much more believable and credible as a vicious warmonger, evening up the score with the Chinese who slaughter his unit in a surprise attack while the Dutch volunteers are distracted in sexual revelry with a Korean refugee mother and daughter. In such a situation, it's hard to root for the alleged "good guys."

Lensing by Hein Groot has the look of a solid Hollywood production, but the poorly lit night scenes, substandard pyrotechnics and slack editing push the scenery into the background. A meatier script might have saved this pic that's short on action, too long on McGill. Even the respectable supporting cast can't talk their way out of this one.
— *Silv.*

Taxi Boy
(FRENCH-COLOR)

A UGC release of a Président Films-UGC-TF1-Films-Marie Coline Films-Cinédeal-Coni Prods. coproduction. Executive producer. Jacques-Eric Strauss. Produced by Alain Depardieu. Written and directed by Alain Page. Stars Claude Brasseur, Richard

---

Berry. Camera (Panavision, Fujicolor), Renato Berta; editor, Sophie Schmitt; music, Charlélie Couture; sound, Pierre Lenoir; art direction, Jean-Pierre Kohut-Svelko; assistant director, Renald Calcagni; technical advisor, Luc Besson; casting, Mamade. Reviewed at the UGC Normandie theater, Paris, May 25, 1986. (In market at the Cannes Film Festival.) Running time: **93 MINS.**
Petrus . . . . Claude Brasseur
Manuel . . . . Richard Berry
Corrine . . . . Charlotte Valandrey
Marthe . . . . Evelyne Didi
Touré . . . . Isaach de Bankole
Pascal . . . . Alex Descas
Martine . . . . Marie-Christine Darah
Miguel . . . . Raymond Jourdan
Henri . . . . Alain Floret

Paris — For his first film in the director's chair, novelist-screenwriter Alain Paige has camped out in the nocturnal urban landscape of the *film noir,* which served as backdrop to his novel, "Tchao Pantin," which he co-adapted for Claude Berri's César-winning 1983 film. If the terrain is familiar, so too are the stereotypical characters and platitudinous script.

Page brings together in a chance encounter Richard Berry, a cabbie and taxi dancer who dreams of opening a tango school, and Claude Brasseur, an inveterate gambler who is fleeing some fellow players he has gypped at the card table, and who also entertains hopes of escape from a dreary reality. Writer-helmer also throws in a long-estranged teen daughter for Brasseur played by Charlotte Valandrey, a waitress who also coasts on reveries.

As scripter, Page is unable to bring off anything dramatically engrossing in the meeting of these dreamer-losers, and his action moves limply to an anti-climactic conclusion in which Berry triumphs at a tango competition, while Brasseur escapes with his hide after his pursuers catch up with him (one wonders what took them so long). There are some minor personal epiphanies for each of the leads, but little empathy for the viewer.

Uncertain direction reflects Page's obvious uneasiness with the medium in this first effort, and his work with the actors is equally inconclusive. Berry has some fine moments as the fastidious, vaguely ridiculous "taxi boy," but lacks the guidance for a fully-limned portrait. Brasseur is conventional as the gambler. Valandrey, who made a promising debut in Vera Belmont's "Rouge Baiser," is surprisingly wooden as the daughter who only dreams of selling fried potatoes on the Riviera. — *Len.*

Mambrú Se Fue a la Guerra
(Mambru Went To War)
(SPANISH-COLOR)

An Altair Prods., Filmográficas production. Executive producer, Miguel A. Pérez Campos. Directed by Fernando Fernán-Gómez. Screenplay, Pedro Beltrán; camera (Eastmancolor), José Luis Alcaine; editor,

---

Pablo González del Amo; music, Carmelo Bernaola; sets, Julio Esteban. Reviewed at the Cannes Film Festival (market), May 17, 1986. Running time: **100 MINS.**
Emiliano . . , ... Fernando Fernán-Gómez
Florentine . . . . María Asquerino
Hilario . . . . Agustin González
Encarna . . . . Emma Cohen
With: Jorge Sanz, Nuria Gallardo, Carlos Cabezas, Maria Luisa Ponte, Alfonso del Real, Francisco Vidal.

Cannes — Despite some droll situations, this pic thesped and helmed by Fernando Fernán-Gómez fails to rise above a certain middling level of Spanish films which deal with the political situation in that country. Thesping is okay, but script goes nowhere, as potential plot developments are never followed up.

Yarn concerns a man who has been hiding in a cave in a village for the 40 years of Franco's rule. When the dictator dies in 1975, his "widow" brings him out at last, but upon discovering the widow may be eligible to a pension, the family is determined to conceal that he's alive. In fact, at one point his son-in-law suggests killing off the old man, but pic ends in sudden inconclusiveness after the old Republican has failed to convince some of the old villagers he is really the man whom they once knew when a young man.

A few smiles may be generated by the old man trying to come to grips with the new Spain he finds upon emerging from his cave. González gives his by-now overly familiar performance as a blustering, dominant Spaniard. Fernán-Gómez is excellent in his similarly familiar role. Best, perhaps are Maria Asquerino as the widow and Emma Cohen as the daughter. —*Besa.*

Cabaret
(Left Alone)
(JAPANESE-COLOR)

Toho Intl. release of a Haruki Kadokawa Prod. production. Produced and directed by Haruki Kadokawa. Screenplay, Yozo Tanaka, based on a book by Kaoru Kurimoto; camera (color), Seizo Senmoto; sound, Tetsuo Segawa; art direction, Chikara Imamura. Reviewed at the Cannes Film Festival (market), May 14, 1986. Running time: **104 MINS.**

With: Takeshi Kaga, Hironobu Nomura, Mitsuko Baisho, Junko Mihara, Tetsuro Tamba.

Cannes — This stylish melange of jazz, smoky nightclubs and Japanese gangsters is the latest outing from Japan's pre-eminent indie producer-director, Haruki Kadokawa. A man of nearly unfailing popular touch in Japan — his previous productions rank among the market's all-time b.o. champs — Kadokawa is betting that he is riding current taste trends with "Cabaret."

Whatever, the pic has some glaring deficiencies and despite its glittering studio look, it looks to have

---

at best moderate export potential. It is, meanwhile, doing well in its initial release in Japan.

The chief character is a teenage saxophonist (Hironobu Nomura) who aspires to play as well as American and topflight Japanese jazz musicians. He joins a band — a rather good one — in a Yokohama cabaret frequented by the Yakuza — The Japanese underworld faction. The gangster is drawn to the young musician's rendition of "Left Alone," a tune that the mobster associates with his first murder.

The saxophonist finds himself being adopted by the thug (who sports sunglasses throughout the pic despite the fact he's a genuine lounge lizard) and gradually being drawn towards the fringes of underworld dealings.

The plot, which ambles along at a leisurely pace, introduces several female characters: the young musician's two girlfriends and a world-weary barmaid played with sophistication by one of Japan's premier actresses Mitsuko Baisho.

Action, naturally enough, centers around the gangland doings of the Yakuza figure. The events leading up to the thug's virtual suicide at pic's end (he is dispatched in larger-than-life manner by the bodyguards of a top Yakuza boss) comprise reasonably entertaining crime melodrama.

Less assured are scenes involving the musician's loss of innocence when one of his girlfriends is raped by a minor gang figure.

One problem is that while the jazz heard on the soundtrack is proficient, it hardly measures up to the standards the plot requires to send the pic's characters into swoons. The young musician starts the film as an adept saxophonist, and despite script demands, ends the pic exactly the same way.

Nomura as the young musician is not quite physically up to his part. He looks much too the prepubescent. The cast, otherwise, is generally quite good, especially Takeshi Kaga as the gangster.

Production values are excellent, especially Seizo Senmoto's photography, Chikara Imamura's art direction and Tetsuo Segawa's sound recording. As for Kadokawa, he remains far more authoritative as a producer rather than as a helmer.
— *Sege.*

Mountaintop Motel Massacre
(COLOR)

Unintentional laughs in standard slasher film.

A New World Pictures release of a Jim McCullough production. Produced by Jim McCullough Sr., Jim McCullough Jr. Directed by McCullough Sr. Screenplay, McCullough Jr.; camera (Eastman color), Joe Wilcots; editor, Mindy Daucus; music and sound, Ron Dilulio; special makeup effects, Drew Edward Hunter; makeup, Cathy Glover; wardrobe design, Melinda McKeller. Reviewed at RKO Warner Twin Theater, N.Y., May 17, 1986 (MPAA Rating: R.) Running time: 95 MINS.

Rev. Bill McWilley . . . . Bill Thurman
Evelyn . . . . Anna Chappell
Al . . . . Will Mitchel
Tanya . . . . Virginia Loridans
Crenshaw . . . . Major Brock
Sheriff . . . . James Bradford
Prissy . . . . Amy Hill
Mary . . . . Marian Jones
Vernon . . . . Greg Brazzel
Lori . . . . Jill King

There are vacancies in "Mountaintop Motel Massacre" for suspense, originality and coherence. The usual cast of characters check in to this unintentionally funny and decidedly mild slasher, and checkout at the hands of mad Mountaintop Motel proprietor Evelyn, a pudgy, slow-moving woman with a sickle.

Trouble starts at the motel, little more than several shacks set up on more of a hill than a mountain, when Evelyn finds daughter Lori worshipping Satan in the motel office basement and does what any mother in that situation would do — slashes her to death with a knife. Special effects here, and throughout the film, are so cheesy they can only be shown for the briefest of moments.

An alcoholic preacher conducts a funeral service, Evelyn having explained the incident away as an accident to the local sheriff, and guests start arriving for the night as a downpour drives them off the road.

A journeyman carpenter arrives, as do a newlywed couple, and an exec who has picked up two young woman in wet T-shirts (their car having got stuck in the mud), and the wide-eyed Evelyn sends them to their bungalows for the night's activities.

A seemingly endless system of tunnels runs under the tiny motel, and through it travels Evelyn, climbing up through creaking trap doors and tossing snakes and rats and other animal life into the rooms, all to ridiculously little effect. In one such funny incident, the black carpenter wakes up literally covered with insects, calmly starts brushing them off and says, with weary resignation, "They ought to call this place the Roach Motel."

Well, Evelyn finally hits upon the sickle method of dispatching guests, and one by one they fall against the terrifying blade of this aging and rather harmless-looking woman.

Climax finds the survivors and the sheriff running around the tunnels. It takes all the strength the large policeman can muster to wrestle this little old lady to the ground so that a falling beam can sickle Evelyn to that big motel in the sky and put an end to all this nonsense.
— *Roy.*

Stand Alone
(COLOR)

Geriatric 'Rambo' is a mild entry.

A New World Pictures release of a Texas Star production, presented by George Kondos. Executive producers, George Kondos, Daniel P. Kondos. Produced by Leon Williams; coproducer, David Thomas. Directed by Alan Beattie. Stars Charles Durning. Screenplay, Roy Carlson; camera (color), Tom Richmond, Timothy Suhrstedt; music, David Richard Campbell. Reviewed at 42d St. Lyric theater, N.Y., May 21, 1986. (MPAA Rating: R.) Running time: 90 MINS.

Louis Thibadeau . . . . Charles Durning
Cathryn Bolan . . . . Pam Grier
Det. Isgrow . . . . James Keach
Paddy . . . . Bert Remsen
Meg . . . . Barbara Sammeth
Neighbor . . . . Lu Leonard
Santos . . . . Luis Contreras

"Stand Alone" is a drama which takes its structure directly from an uncountable number of Westerns, updated to urban, crimeridden American society. Extremely mild, low-budget entry is a New World pickup filmed in L.A. in the summer of 1984 and quietly slipped into territorial release beginning last September.

Charles Durning gets a rare starring (above the title) role as Louis Thibadeau, a decorated (by Gen. MacArthur, he's fond of telling everybody) World War II hero living quietly in a sleepy L.A. neighborhood with his daughter and a grandson.

He witnesses a gangland-style murder executed by three Latin youths in a cafe owned by his old buddy Paddy (Bert Remsen) and reluctantly agrees to help police Det. Isgrow (James Keach) identify the suspects and testify against them.

Thibadeau's young lawyer friend Cathryn Bolan (Pam Grier), who as a public defender encounters the chief suspect Santos (Luis Contreras), tries to convince Thibadeau not to get involved, noting that the drug smugglers involved in the killing will probably blow him away if he fingers the killers.

Thibadeau decides to send his family away to stay in Long Beach and make his stand, going up to the attic to get his marine weapons and hold off the villains in his house.

Though played fairly straight, the sight of Durning blacking up his face and making like Rambo is amusing. His acting is solid, though the role is one-dimensional. Cast against type as a nice, professional woman, Grier is engaging, and it comes as no surprise in the final reel when she grabs a gun to protect lone wolf Durning against the killers. Rest of the cast is adequate.

The big showdown could have used some of the suspense and thrills of "Straw Dogs," which it resembles structurally. Director

Alan Beattie did a better job at atmospherics and grabbing the viewer in his previous film, a horror opus featuring Joseph Cotten: "The House Where Death Lives." — *Lor.*

SpaceCamp
(COLOR)

Trite teen comedy in space.

A 20th Century Fox release of an ABC Motion Pictures presentation. Executive producer, Leonard Goldberg. Produced by Patrick Bailey, Walter Coblenz. Directed by Harry Winer. Screenplay, "W.W. Wicket," Casey T. Mitchell, from a story by Patrick Bailey and Larry B. Williams; camera (MGM color, Deluxe prints), William A. Fraker; editor, John W. Wheeler, Timothy Board; music, John Williams; production design, Richard MacDonald; art director, Richard J. Lawrence, Leon Harris; set decorator, Richard C. Goddard; special visual effects supervisor, Barry Nolan; special visual effects, Van Der Veer Photo Effects, sound (Dolby stereo), David MacMillan; special effects coordinator, Chuck Gaspar; assistant director, James B. Simons; associate producer-production manager, David Salven; costumes, Patricia Norris; casting, Mike Fenton, Jane Feinberg. Reviewed at Zanuck Theater, 20th Century Fox, L.A., May 21, 1986. (MPAA Rating: PG.) Running time: 107 MINS.

Andie . . . . Kate Capshaw
Kathryn . . . . Lea Thompson
Tish . . . . Kelly Preston
Rudy . . . . Larry B. Scott
Max . . . . Leaf Phoenix
Kevin . . . . Tate Donovan
Zach . . . . Tom Skerritt
Brennan . . . . Barry Primus
Launch director . . . . Terry O'Quinn

Hollywood — "SpaceCamp" is a youthful view of outer space made more timely and resonant by recent events. Story of a group of youngsters accidentally launched on a shuttle mission could have had enormous emotional impact, but unfortunately pic doesn't tap the built-in curiosity and plays to a much younger audience. Older filmgoers are likely to be left on the ground.

Set at the real-life United States Space Camp in Huntsville, Alabama for aspiring young astronauts, pic never successfully integrates summer camp hijinks with outer space idealism to come up with a dramatically compelling story. Script by "W.W. Wicket" (Clifford and Ellen Green were credited during production) and Casey T. Mitchell fails to achieve the poetic dimensions of "E.T."

Probably weighing the film down more than anything are the thinly-drawn characters. Diverse mix collected at the camp and later taking off in the shuttle is reminiscent of a World War II platoon, and about as subtle. Inability to create working relationships and believable people on the ground undermines the drama once the kids are up in space.

Hampered by cliché-ridden dialog, performances suffer from a weightlessness of their own. Kate Capshaw as the instructor and one trained astronaut to make the flight neither looks nor acts the part of a serious scientist. As for the kids, Tate Donovan as the shuttle commander-in-training is uninteresting and Lea Thompson as his would-be girlfriend is too young and naive for words, even the ones she's given.

Giving the film a hopelessly saccarine flavor is Leaf Phoenix as the moppet in the crowd whose friendship with the too-cute robot Jinx is the reason the kids get launched in the first place, although the scientific explanation for the event is obscure and unsatisfying.

Kelly Preston as a flakey genius disguised as a new-waver has the most personality of the kids but Larry B. Scott's young black with a heart but not a head for science is pat and flat.

Most of the film, in fact, has a processed, programmed feel about it with exposition and editing chugging along with no apparent rhythm or reason, although some scenes manage a modicum of suspense. Movement is hampered rather than heightened by John Williams' brassy, overblown score.

Special visual effects supervised by Barry Nolan and cinematography by William Fraker supply a few soaring vistas, but wonders of space are more of a backdrop to the slight human story.

Ultimately the failure of what must have been a promising premise at the outset has to go to debuting feature director Harry Winer who narrows the focus of the film. Instead of a view of the Earth through young and unspoiled eyes, we get a trite teen comedy set in space.

— *Jagr.*

Moi Drug Ivan Lapshin
(My Friend Ivan Lapshin)
(SOVIET-COLOR/B&W)

A Sovexportfilm release of a Lenfilm production. Directed by Alexei Guerman. Screenplay. Edouard Volodaraki; camera (color), Valeri Fedossov; editor, L. Semionova; music, Arkadi Gagulachvili; costumes, G. Deyeva; art direction, Yuri Pougatch. Reviewed at the Cannes Film Festival (market), May 11, 1986. Running time: **92 MINS.**
Ivan Lapshin ....Andrei Boltnev
Natasha Adashova ......Nina Rouslsnova
Khanin ....Andrei Mironov
Friend ....Alexei Jarkov

Cannes — Alexei Guerman's third feature, "My Friend Ivan Lapshin," is one of the most dazling, original works to appear on the Soviet film scene in the last decade. Though lensed several years ago, film became available for offshore release only last month, after being aired on Soviet tv. Fans of Guerman's "Twenty Days Without War" and "Trial On The Run" will find the same down-to-earth characters and expressive lensing, refined into a moving, rather troubling portrait of the 1930s.

The story is framed by dreamy pans over the interior of a modern apartment, where an aged narrator we never glimpse begins telling about the life of his friend Ivan Lapshin many years ago. In the mid '30s, Lapshin (Andrei Bolthev) was the head of criminal investigations in a small town. A tall, ungainly fellow, tough with criminals but well-liked by his friends, Lapshin lives in a dismal rooming house overcrowded with tenants. One of these is his dashing friend Khanin, whose wife has just died. Ivan is in love with an extroverted actress named Natasha, (Nina Rouslsnova), but when he climbs up her drainpipe to visit her room one night, she tells him she loves Khanin.

Interwoven with the-way-we-were memories are scenes of the police hunting down a dangerous criminal, Soloviev. The murderer and black marketeer finally is cornered in his country hideaway, peopled by whole families living on the fringes of society and even poorer than the police chief and his friends. During the stakeout Khanin is wounded seriously, and Lapshin takes cold blooded revenge on the unarmed Soloviev.

Although the narrator informs us he is about to tell "a sad tale," and the picture of poverty after the civil war is unsettling, the sense of the film is not easy to pin down. The collection of "dear memories" is filmed extremely well. Cameraman Valeri Fedossov alternates dream colors with sharp black and white photography and tinted scenes, as though some memories were sharper, some softer; at other times the image is almost snowed out under haze and fog. Guerman makes expressive use of tracking shots, swish pans, framing, zooms and long takes and fills the picture with amusing details so there's not an empty moment.

The funny, joyful moments of Ivan's life blend into scenes of painful events and terrible longing. This rich film about ordinary people is enhanced by very naturalistic performances from all hands. — *Yung.*

Ferris Bueller's Day Off
(COLOR)

Airheads without a cause.

A Paramount Pictures release. Executive producer, Michael Chinich. Produced by John Hughes, Tom Jacobson. Written and directed by Hughes. Stars Matthew Broderick. Camera (Panavision, Metrocolor), Tak Fujimoto; editor, Paul Hirsch; music, Ira Newborn; sound (Dolby), James Alexander; production design, John W. Corso; set design, Marilyn Vance; additional music, Arthur Baker, John Robie; assistant director, Stephen Lim; second unit directors, Bennie Dobbins, Kenny Ortega; stunt coordinator, Dobbins; choreographer, Ortega; second unit camera, George Kohut; associate producer, Jane Vickerilla; casting, Janet Hirshenson, Jane Jenkins. Reviewed at Paramount Studios, L.A., May 28, 1986. (MPAA Rating: PG-13.) Running time: **103 MINS.**
Ferris Bueller.........Matthew Broderick
Cameron Frye.............Alan Ruck
Sloane Peterson..............Mia Sara
Ed Rooney.................Jeffrey Jones
Jeanie Bueller...........Jennifer Grey
Katie Bueller..............Cindy Pickett
Tom Bueller..............Lyman Ward
School Secretary..........Edie McClurg
Boy In Police Station.......Charlie Sheen
Homeroom Teacher...........Ben Stein
History Teacher...............Del Close
School Nurse...........Virginia Capers
Garage Attendant.........Richard Edson
Attendant's Sidekick ..Larry Flash Jenkins

Hollywood — "Ferris Bueller's Day Off" exhibits John Hughes on an off day. Teenpic maestro seemingly has run out of fresh things to say about his beloved highschoolers, and paucity of invention here lays bare the total absence of plot or involving situations. Irreverent attitude, cast sassiness, tons of rock music and all the other expected ingredients are present to make this a reasonable summer comedy hit for Paramount, but Hughes has gone to this well at least once too often.

. Writer-director has now recycled his notions of adolescent hipness, the rewards of arrogant irresponsibility, the frivolous advantages of modern technology and the irredeemable idiocy of adults so many times that they have become clichés in their own time. For good measure, he also has lifted a central gimmick — the "borrowing" and subsequent destruction of the old man's expensive foreign sportscar — from "Risky Business," one of the most successful North Chicago suburb films Hughes didn't make himself.

In a nutshell, the thin premise demonstrates the great lengths to which the irrepressible Ferris Bueller goes in order to hoodwink his parents and high school principal into thinking he's really sick when, in fact, all he wants to do is play hooky for a day.

Like the kids in the most recent film Hughes directed, "Weird Science," Ferris is something of a technical wiz, and is able to rig recorders so as to fool the dimwitted adults.

Oddly, for a rich kid, Ferris doesn't have his own car, so he shanghais his best friend for the day, appropriates the vintage Ferrari of the buddy's father, spirits his girlfriend out of school and speeds off for downtown Chicago.

Even though pic has hardly been great shakes up to this point, it is here, contrary to expectations, that it just sinks. Instead of a wild adventure, threesome spends what is, for the most part, an utterly conventional day of leisure in the big city.

Trio visits the top of Sears Tower, has lunch at a fine restaurant (even if they have to bully their way in), takes in a game at Wrigley Field and visits the Art Institute. Ferris caps things off by singing along to the Beatles' version of "Twist And Shout" on a float in a downtown parade, but the group does nothing particularly outrageous and not a thing they couldn't have done on any given day at any point in their lives.

Of course, there's the threat of hell to pay if they're caught, but Hughes' endorsement of the kids' shenanigans is so total that the possibility of reprisal seems unreal. As always, Hughes presents his teenagers' feeling of superiority to adults as being totally justified.

At the same time, however, the kids come off as airheads without a cause. Rebelling against nothing and quite willing to subscribe to their parents' bank accounts, they are revealed, unironically, for what they are in a brief scene in which the girl asks the tag-along buddy, "What are you interested in?" "Nothing," he replies. "Me either," she says with a smile.

Matthew Broderick's essential likeability can't replace the loony anarchy of Hughes' previous leading man, Anthony Michael Hall. Alan Ruck can't do much with his underwritten second-banana role, and Mia Sara is fetching as Ferris' g.f.

Picture's one saving grace is the absolutely delicious comic performance of Jeffrey Jones as the high school principal driven nearly out of his mind in his frustrated pursuit of Ferris. With a series of reactions exaggerated to perfection, Jones is pricelessly funny, and his constantly imaginative work stands in vivid contrast to the insipid carrying-on of the would-be protagonists.

— *Cart.*

Can Yue
(Broken Moon)
(CHINESE-COLOR)

A Pearl River Film Studio production. Produced by Tao Yi. Directed by Cao Zheng. Screenplay, He Jiesheng, from the novel "Sacrifice Of The Heart" by Wen Bin; camera (color), Wei Duo, Pang Lei; music, Du Jiang, performed by the Pearl River Studio Orchestra. Leading players: Zheng Zhenyao, Zhao Erkang, Hong Rong, and Huo Xiu. No further credits available. Reviewed at the Ridge Theater, Vancouver Intl. Film Festival, May 22, 1986. Running time: **90 MINS.**

Vancouver — An effective tearjerker, notable for its assured style and sprightly score, Cao Zheng's atmospheric "Broken Moon" details the self-sacrifice of a widow for her five daughters' sake over a period of tumult and social dislocation.

Zheng Zhenyao stoically plays the unnamed mother figure who has carried a torch for family friend Uncle Ah Fu since long before the 1948 Liberation. The couple unjustly earned the opprobrium of malicious villagers and was kept apart by divisive social forces for a dozen years.

When mother is reunited with her grownup daughters she still longs to reencounter her old flame who took away her youngest child Xiulan. But once the entire extended family is brought together, her own children refuse to countenance that she (an old woman) even think for a moment of remarrying. Even supposedly open-minded, sensitive city cadres cling to the past and want to appear truly filial to their neighbors. It's not a quandary that will incite fervor among Western audiences.

Initially consisting of a series of pictuesque vignettes of pre-Communist village life, "Broken Moon" builds a strong emotional drive that is highly dependent upon the lovely face and resigned mien of its leading lady.

All technical credits are firstrate, particularly the svelte camerawork and its apposite lighting. As a prospect for export the pic is handicapped by its old-fashioned theme, more characteristic of 1950 Ross Hunter/Douglas Sirk weepies.
—*Gran.*

Big Trouble
(COLOR)

Orphaned by distrib, amiable screwballer faces uphill b.o. battle.

A Columbia Pictures release of a Columbia-Delphi III production. Produced (uncredited) by Michael Lobell. Directed by John Cassavetes. Screenplay, "Warren Bogle" (Andrew Bergman); camera (Panavision, Metrocolor), Bill Butler; editor, Donn Cambern, Ralph Winters; music, Bill Conti; cosdesigner, Joe I. Tompkins; casting, Mike Fenton, Jane Feinberg, Judy Taylor, production manager, Howard Pine; production designer, Gene Callahan; assistant directors, Duncan Henderson, Chris Ryan; set decorator, Lee Poll; sound Martin Bolger. Reviewed at Cinema I, N.Y., May 30, 1986. (MPAA Rating: R.) Running time: **93 MINS.**

Steve Rickey ....Peter Falk
Leonard Hoffman ....Alan Arkin
Blanche Rickey ....Beverly D'Angelo
O'Mara ....Charles Durning
Noozel ....Paul Dooley
Winslow ....Robert Stack
Arlene Hoffman ....Valerie Curtin
Dr. Lopez ....Richard Libertini
Peter Hoffman...........Steve Alterman
Michael Hoffman ....Jerry Pavlon
Joshua Hoffman ....Paul La Greca
Detective Murphy........John Finnegan
Police Captain ....Karl Lukas
Maid....................Gloria Gifford

As yet another major studio title that almost didn't make it off the shelf because of poor test previews, "Big Trouble" is a small, mild-mannered comedy featuring an ensemble of screen comedians doing what the public is accustomed to seeing them do. It's up to older moviegoers, those disenfranchised from today's broad screen teen comedies, to pack the theaters and prove Columbia wrong. That, however, makes for an unlikely scenario.

Conceived to capitalize on the success of Falk-Arkin's 1979 laughriot "The In-Laws," "Big Trouble" saw trouble during production in early 1984. Original helmer Andrew Bergman ("In-Laws" scripter) withdrew and John Cassavetes took over. Final product omits the names of coproducer/writer Bergman and coproducer Michael Lobell.

Echoing the story line of their earlier collaboration, Falk plays the incorrigible conman, a comic to straight man Arkin's hapless, unwilling accomplice. Pic also borrows from the classic "Double Indemnity," with Arkin as the insurance salesman gone bad and Beverly D'Angelo as the wife who conspires to murder her husband (Falk).

Unlike Fred MacMurray and Barbara Stanwyck, however, it's not love that motivates them to swindle the insurance company but a $5,-000,000 insurance policy. D'Angelo can collect if Falk dies in a fall off a train (sound familiar?). Arkin, under pressure from wife Valerie Curtin to send his three sons to Yale, would also reap the ill-gotten gain.

In the intermittently amusing variation on the "Double Indemnity" theme, it turns out Falk and D'Angelo faked the husband's murder. Arkin finds out he was duped when Falk comes to a meeting with Arkin's superiors (Charles Durning and Robert Stack) "disguised" as the widow's attorney.

Although laboring outside of his narrative element, to say the least, Cassavetes did a creditable job directing his actors, all of whom rise above the thin screenplay. Comedic highlights include initial meeting of the conspiratorial trio and Falk's attempts to act the corpse during the investigation by skeptical claims chief Durning.

Proceedings get out of hand toward the end in a misfired climax involving terrorists out to bomb Stack's insurance offices. But the authorities are all too willingly to embrace more white lies from the lovable, resourceful conmen out to make a dishonest living. That yields an all's-well-that-ends-well conclusion, and even a sequel setup.

Tech credits are fine, although Bill Conti's ceaselessly whimsical score evokes tv sitcoms. Overall tame tone of "Big Trouble," however literate and well-intentioned, might explain preview audience apathy. Barring boffo returns in its exclusive Gotham run, distrib reportedly isn't willing to expend any more energy and money on the film at this juncture. — *Binn.*

Jogo Duro
(Hard Game)
(BRAZILIAN-COLOR)

A Luar release of a Luar Produções Cinematográficas production. Produced by Raul Rocha. Directed by Ugo Giorgetti. Screenplay, Giorgetti; camera (Eastmancolor), Pedro Pablo Lazzarini; editor, Paulo Mattos; music, Mauro Giorgetti; sound, Miguel Angelo Costa; assistant director, George A. Walford; art direction, Maria Isabel Giorgetti; production director, Newton Mello; associate producers, Ugo Giorgetti, Fathom Filmes. Reviewed at Cine Embaixador, Gramado Film Festival, April 10, 1986. Running time: **91 MINS.**

With: Cininha de Paula, Carlos Augusto Carvalho, Jesse James, Valéria de Andrade,

Antonio Fagundes, Cleide Yaconis, Paulo Betti, Eliane Giardini, Luiz Guilherme, Carlos Meceni, Paulo Ivo, Veronica Teijido.

Gramado — The small environment of a luxurious empty house being sold in São Paulo becomes the stage for social conflicts that arise from the relations between a real estate agent, a night watchman, and a young woman living clandestinely in the house with her daughter.

Director Ugo Giorgetti, whose previous credits include a lengthy documentary on world champion boxer Eder Jofre, tries a realistic approach to his screenplay. Aim is partially achieved thanks to fine dialog and good performances by Cininha de Paula, as the woman, and Jesse James as the real estate agent, besides a brief but strong appearance by Antonio Fagundes.

Although Giorgetti's narrative efficiency seems evident, there are problems with his screenplay, despite potential richness of the few characters. Plot lacks action, which makes its 91 minutes seem overlong. Technical credits are fine.
—*Hoin.*

Hong Yi Shao Nu
(The Girl In Red)
(CHINESE-COLOR)

An Emei Studio production. Written and directed by Luxiao Ya, from an original story by Tie Ning. Camera (color), Xie Erxiang; music, Wang Ming, performed by the Central Philharmonic Society. Leading players; Zou Yitian (An Ran), Luo Yan (An Jing), Wang Ping (Mother). No further credits available. Reviewed at the Vancouver Intl. Film Festival, Ridge theater, May 25, 1986. Running time: **102 MINS.**

Vancouver — By contemporary Chinese standards femme helmer's Luxiao Ya's "The Girl In Red" may be risqué. The heroine, a spunky 15-year-old in the first year of senior school, defies her teacher Miss Wei Wan, a would-be poet who curries favor with the heroine's elder sister who is a literary editor.

An Ran (a.k.a. Ran Ran) has inherited a stubborn streak from her artist father, who was excluded in past year from the mainstream due to his lack of politics. Her mother sacrificed her teaching profession to provide her brood with a correct political background. Mom is cynical and burned out. Dad is resigned to his plight.

An Ran's peers are a surly lot, suffering from broken homes and parental oppression. They are also alarmed by her individualism, and herd together to contain such high spirits.

Reputedly an admirable attempt to free some of the shackles imposed upon the portrayal of youth, Ya's pic snapped up the best picture award at the 1985 Golden Rooster ceremony. Regrettably it will need a

rooster or two to keep viewers awake for its prolonged duration.

Stagey and talkative, "The Girl In Red" cannot sustain its frequent efforts after lyricism. Very shaky camerawork, handicapped by dull pastel colors and a hollow postsynch job, hobble any effort to have the bland, trite tale spread its wings and fly above a clutter of domestic detail and pedestrian plotting.

More's the pity since young lead Zou Yitian is a genuine find. With her pageboy hairdo and her frisky physicality she is charming and fits the role like a glove. She is ably supported by Luo Yan as her demure sister, a fount of platitudes who has a clandestine affair with a widower, thus defying society in her own style.

Technical credits are marginal, with a distinct ineptitude in the cutting department. It's unlikely to gain sales overseas.—*Gran.*

14 Numara
(Number 14)
(TURKISH-COLOR)

A Hakan Film production, Istanbul. Written and directed by Sinan Cetin, based on a novel by Irfan Yalcin. Camera (color), Cem Molvan; music, Baris Manco, Kurtalan Ekspres. Reviewed at Istanbul Film Fest (Turkish series), April 15, 1986. Running time: **86 MINS.**

With: Hakan Balamir, Serpil Cakmakli, Keriman Ulusoy, Bulent Bilgic.

Istanbul — Sinan Cetin's "Number 14" scores as a striking piece of fiction documentary about prostitution in Istanbul. Several shots seem to be authentic (perhaps done with secret cameras), while a heavy emphasis is placed on the seamy side and the degradation of having to work in such houses of vulgarity and humiliation.

A young girl has been sent to the "Number 14" address in a rundown neighborhood of Istanbul. Apparently she has nowhere else to go, but further details are omitted. The other girls are friendly enough, but a pimp takes an interest in her — and sets her up to take over her earnings when his other girlfriend dies of a fatal stomach ailment and plenty of beatings on the side.

The young girl has another suitor, a shy lad who can't stand up to violence and rough handling. However, he does his best to win the humiliated girl's hand and succeeds in the end. Meanwhile, the girl's family back in a remote village discover via a newspaper clipping and a photo in it that their girl has disgraced the family name. Her brother heads for Istanbul with a gun in his pocket.

The pimp, too, is a deadly menace now that he's about to lose his free ticket daily to the horseraces. Besides, he has terrible head pains that drive him to acts of fearful violence. At the end he goes on a stabbing rampage just as the girl is about to leave the "Number 14" house in a white wedding gown.

Not consistent in its story line, film's docu scenes are nonetheless notable glances behind the facade of Turkish houses of prostitution.
—*Holl.*

Durruti
(W. GERMAN-DOCU-B&W-16m)

A documentary in the form of a film-novel written and directed by Hans Magnus Enzensberger, in collaboration with Westdeutscher Rundfunk (WDR), Cologne. Camera (b&w, 16m), Carlos Bustamente. Only credits available. Reviewed at Landesbildstelle Berlin, April 1, 1986. Running time: **72 MINS.**

Berlin — There is a lot to be said about a documentary made in 1972 that still stands as a classic of its kind and can be seen at regular intervals. The German poet Hans Magnus Enzensberger was fascinated by a legendary figure in Spanish Civil War history, Buenaventura Durruti (1896-1936), and so he researched his subject thoroughly by tramping across Europe with a camera on his shoulder to make "Durruti," subtitled "Biography Of A Legend."

The docu opens with newsreel footage of 500,000 workers accompanying Durruti, the leader of the Spanish Anarchists, to his grave in November 1936. Then contemporary footage is matched to the newsreel to show how posters and demonstrations and songs have combined to keep the man's legend alive to the present (a decade ago, but things haven't changed much since). After that come the interviews, each serving as a piece in a mosaic to tell the full story — and, at the end, expose the usual hollow core of a legend that's drifted far away from the truth.

Because Enzensberger does not take sides but shows an active curiosity throughout, the viewer is also caught in the flow of history as it unfolds around a leader considered as dynamic in his own way as a Tito in Yugoslavia or a Zapata in Mexico. Durruti, born in northwestern Spain, was 20 when he took part in a general strike and was fired from his job as mechanic. A year later, he joined the CNT anarchist union and rose so quickly in its ranks that he was forced to emigrate to France.

Durruti thereafter lived the life of a union organizer who kept the coffers filled with hold-ups and bank robberies. He was arrested several times and grew tired of long stretches in prison, mostly under trumped-up charges to keep him from organizing city guerrilla fighters to combat government and mercenary troops sent to quell demonstrations by angry workers and hungry strikers. During the mid-1920s he was forced again to leave the country, this time escaping to France and then going to Latin America to try and organize the workers into a striking and fighting force there. Back in Paris, after admitting defeat in the wild adventure, he was arrested again for a suspected assassination attempt on the Spanish king during an official state visit.

The outbreak of the Spanish Civil War proved to be Durruti's hour of glory, for he was having as much trouble acclimating himself to the democratized Republican government as under the Spanish dictatorship. As the head of a bedraggled anarchist corps he won several key battles until his death, apparently killed accidentally by his own gun when it misfired.

Enzensberger's interviews are with schoolfriends, comrades-in-arms, his widow Emilienne Morin in Paris, and the then-head of the still existing CNT union, Federicia Montseny. These collective stories about the man and the legend serve to weave a fictitious account (the legend) as well as a factual one (the man). One has in the end the feeling of having met, and perhaps partially understood, the fate of a guerrilla leader who did somehow bridge the exploits of a Zapata to those of a Tito. Durruti was a complex man, both an outlaw and a man of integrity.

Photographs and newsreels being the backbone of the docu, the film was appropriately made in black and white. Text and narration are by Enzensberger. —*Holl.*

Sunset Strip
(COLOR)

Boring action pic.

A Westwind production. Executive producer, James Kent. Produced and directed by William Webb. Stars Tom Eplin. Screenplay, Webb, Brad Munson; camera (color), Eric Anderson; editor, David Schwartz; music, David Storrs; art direction, Riley Morgan; set decoration, Don Fernandez; assistant director, Ralph Portaco; production manager, Jeff Spelan; coproducer, Monica Webb; casting, Mary Williamson. Reviewed on Vestron Vidcassette, N.Y., May 27, 1986. (No MPAA Rating.) Running time: **82 MINS.**

Mark Jefferson	Tom Eplin
Carol Wyatt	Cheri Cameron Newell
Roger Lucas	John Mayall
Jake	John Smith
John Moran	Danny Williams
Nick	George Brady
Police Lt.	Al Hansen
Martin	Miles Clayton
Mrs. Peters	Rita Rogers

"Sunset Strip" is another lame attempt at a thriller geared to the glamorous sleaziness of Hollywood street life (or at least its reputation). Filmed in the summer of 1984, feature is being released directly to homevideo, bypassing U.S. theatrical (as have filmmaker William Webb's previous efforts).

Opening with some unimpressive and instantly dated breakdancing footage, picture toplines Tom Eplin as Mark Jefferson, a young still photographer with a fancy motorbike who agrees to help pal Roger Lucas (John Mayall), whose music club is being threatened by strongarm men who he thinks want to take it over and use it as a front for prostitution. Ruthless baddie John Moran (Danny Williams) has his goons kill a girl in the opening reel to show they mean business. His real goal is to use the club to front his operations for selling guns to youngsters.

With various chase scenes as filler, film plods along to a happy ending, as Jefferson gets evidence against the bad guys and uncovers a corrupt cop. Along the way, Lucas and others are killed, but Jefferson manages to save his cute ex-girlfriend who sings at the club, Carol (Cheri Cameron Newell).

Minus suspense or interesting detailing, film is limp. Leads Eplin and Newell are attractive in their walk through assignments, while legendary British bluesman John Mayall has little to do in a small role. Tech credits are competent.
—*Lor.*

Birds Of Prey
(CANADIAN-COLOR)

A Trapped Prods. production. Produced and written by Peter Haynes and Jorge Montesi. Directed by Jorge Montesi. Camera (color), Gary Armstrong; music, Paul Zaza. Reviewed at the Cannes Film Festival (market), May 17, 1986. Running time: **90 MINS.**

Detective Carlos Solo	Jorge Montesi
Harry Card	Joseph Patrick Finn
The Woman	Linda Elder
Fence	Maurice Brand

Cannes — Reviewed for the record only, "Birds Of Prey" means to be a moral thriller. A cop trails a series of murders and evidence leads him to his criminal friend. Acting is amateurish, direction spongy, plot has as many holes, lighting is weak and camerawork undecided whether scenes should be day or night.

Good title though. No resemblance to any other pic with the same title. —*Adil.*

The Intruder
(INDONESIAN-COLOR)

A Parkit Films presentation of a Punjabi production (Indonesia). Produced by Dhamoo and Raam Punjabi. Directed by Jopi Burnama. Stars Peter O'Brian, Craig Gavin, Dana Christina, Lia Warokka, Jenny Farida. Screenplay, Debby Armand; camera (color), Sodikin; music, GSD 'Arto. Reviewed at the Cannes Film Festival (market), May 9, 1986. Running time: **90 MINS.**

(English soundtrack)

Cannes — Exploitation and strictly non-intellectual action features for international release are often made in places like the Philippines, Hong Kong, and so why not Indonesia also. "The Intruder" from Indonesia is a direct inspirational lift from "Rambo" (without shame), with male lead unknown and much less muscular bargain basement look-alike Craig Gavin as a foreigner in Asia without a job but no difficulty in getting into trouble.

His name in the film is "Rambu" (rhymes with Dumbo) short for Alex Tarambuan, professional bum. It is very obvious that Gavin had no acting training and looks doped as he fights for justice and decency against the all-powerful criminal mobs and underworld kingpins.

The baddies have beaten and tortured him, then raped and killed the woman who supports him. They made one big mistake: they haven't and will never kill this hybrid of Stallone somewhere in Djakarta, Indonesia. Rambu has to face two strong gangster groups, but the foreign devil John White empire is the strongest in dealing with prostitution, extortion, kidnapping, rape and dope-peddling.

Made for a measly U.S.$500,000, there are the stereotype villains, overweight cheap-looking oriental vixens, violent gangsters (complete with the standard dark glasses). They are either over or underdressed for the series of calculated messes they often find themselves into.

One doesn't take this kind of Asian kitsch seriously, more as a high camp joke comedy that Woody Allen could easily transform into something even funnier with a new soundtrack.

However, there should be some markets available to dump this type of production. "Rambu" ("The Intruder") rates zero for originality, style, presentation and for the seriocomic English dialog that is to embarassing beyond belief. —*Mel.*

Departure
(AUSTRALIAN-COLOR)

A Cineast Prods. presentation of a Rychmond film. Executive producer, William Oswald. Produced by Christing Suli, Brian Kavanagh. Directed by Kavanagh. Stars Patricia Kennedy, Michael Duffield, June Jago and Serge Lazareff. Screenplay, Michael Gurr, based on his play, "A Pair Of Claws;" camera (Eastmancolor), Bob Kohler; editor, Ken Sallows; music, Bruce Smeaton; art director, Paddy Reardon. Reviewed at the Cannes Film Festival (market), May 16, 1986. Running time: **93 MINS.**

Sylvia Swift	Patricia Kennedy
Presley Swift	Michael Duffield
Frances	June Jago
Simon Swift	Serge Lazareff

Alex Rowen................Sean Scully
Joseph......................Jon Sidney

Cannes — Although the stage origins of Michael Gurr's screenplay of "Departure" are fairly obvious, it doesn't detract from the basic plot of a scandal in high places revealed after a lapse of many years. It's an intriguing situation, somewhat verbose in its development, but strong on characterization. B.o. prospects outside Australia are problematical, partly due to the absence of names in the cast.

Filmed on location in Hobart, capital of Tasmania, the central characters are a retired diplomat (Michael Duffield) and his wife, played by Patricia Kennedy. Having returned to their native Australia on retirement, they both get itchy feet and pack up to return to Rome, where he had served as ambassador. Their final weekend is to be spent with their son (Serge Lazareff) an aspiring politician, and their best friend (June Jago).

The serene atmosphere is shattered when they are told the press has got hold of the details of a scandal in which the diplomat was involved way, way back, which ended in the death of a young girl, an incident which was hushed up by the authorities. There is mounting tension as the son fears his political ambitions are threatened, while the friend feels she has been betrayed.

Brian Kavanagh's authoritative direction partly succeeds in glossing over the stage origins of the subject, though there are hints in a measure of padding as when father and son go to a football game, and when the whole family visits a theater. Bob Kohler's color camera handsomely captures some of the scenic attractions of the location, and other credits are up to par.

Good all-round performances by the four principals are a positive feature, with a standout job by Patricia Kennedy as the formidable and domineering wife and mother. Michael Duffield changes from smug contentment to serious concern when the scandal breaks, and Serge Lazareff, not playing a likable character, is forced to denounce his own father to save his own political skin. June Jago, the family's longtime friend, believes herself to have been shamed by the revelation, making the break with an emotional outburst.

Lesser parts are adequately filled.
— *Myro.*

Windrider
(AUSTRALIAN-COLOR)

A Hoyts (Australia) release of a Barron Films production. Produced by Paul Barron. Directed by Vincent Monton. Stars Tom Burlinson, Nicole Kidman. Screenplay, Everett De Roche, Bonnie Harris; camera (Eastmancolor), Joe Pickering; editor, John Scott; mu-

---

sic, Kevin Peak; sound, Mark Lewis; art director, Phil Monaghan; assistant director, Steve Jodrell; production manager, Terri Vincent; associate producer, Bonnie Harris; casting, Michael Lynch. Reviewed at the Cannes Film Festival (market), May 15, 1986. Running time: **92 MINS.**
P.C. Simpson............Tom Burlinson
Jade..................Nicole Kidman
Simpson Sr.............Charles Tingwell
Miss Dodge..............Jill Perryman
Also with: Simon Chilvers, Kim Bullad, Matt Parkinson, Penny Brown.

Cannes — An unpretentious, lightweight offering about a romance between a windsurfer and a rock singer, "Windrider" is a modestly effective debut as director for former cinematographer Vincent Monton (whose credits include "Newsfront" and "Heatwave").

Shot in and around Perth, in Western Australia, pic looks sumptuous. It's pitched at young audiences, but its youthful protagonists live almost impossibly luxurious lives, so there's plenty of wish-fulfillment involved.

Hero Tom Burlinson, son of wealthy businessman Charles Tingwell, lives in a superbly located beach house. His passion is riding the heavy surf, and the film opens with an impressive, even breathtaking, display of windsurfing involving some incredible 360° flips. Heroine Nicole Kidman, graduating from children's roles in such kidpics as "BMX Bandits" and "Bush Christmas," is delightful as a harddriving rock star who falls for Burlinson. Their numerous loves scenes are sexually more explicit than might have been expected from this type of film.

Nothing much actually happens. Burlinson's father disapproves when he neglects his work to design a new surfboard, but secretly admires and respects him. Kidman, after some passionate lovemaking, ankles when Burlinson gets bad tempered after a narrow escape from a man-eating shark (a "Jaws"-type moment that's effectively scary).

On the day of an all-important surf championship, Burlinson's rival tricks him into arriving at the wrong beach at the far side of the city, but despite traffic jams he manages to get to the right place just in time.

Burlinson is effortlessly charming as the wealthy young outdoorsman, while Kidman has the looks and personality for her first adult role which indicates a solid future. Paul Barron's production is tops, with fine technical qualities in all departments.

Monton hasn't over-extended himself first time out, but "Windrider" emerges as a modestly appealing little item which might click with the teen audience given the right marketing approach. It's certainly a great promo for the spectacular scenery of Western Australia. —*Strat.*

Schmutz
(AUSTRIAN-COLOR)

A Paulus Manker production. Produced, written and directed by Manker, with the support of the Austrian Film Promotion Fund and Austrian Television ORF. Camera (color), Walter Kindler; editor, Maria Homolkova; costumes, Erika Navas; music, Yollo; sound, Walter Amann. Reviewed at the Cannes Film Festival (Directors' Fortnight), May 14, 1986. Running time: **100 MINS.**
Joseph Schmutz.........Fritz Schediwy
Chief inspector....Hans Michael Rehberg
Girl.................Siggi Schwientek
Also with: Josefine Platt, Mareile Geisler, Axel Böhmert, Günther Bothur, Constanzia Höchle, Hanno Pöschl.

Cannes — A night watchman goes off his rocker guarding a worthless old factory in "Schmutz," a first feature by young Austrian helmer Paulus Manker. The low-budget indie made with a handful of actors shows a great deal of originality, a keen sense of paradox, and even a symbolic dimension that takes film beyond the case history level. Though Manker still has a way to go before he becomes a sophisticated director, "Schmutz" is a promising start from all points of view.

A key choice was to give the central role to actor Fritz Schediwy, who resembles a latter-day Peter Lorre in his weird mixture of outer meekness and inner ruthlessness. As Joseph Schmutz, long-time employee of a security guard company, he starts slowly and lets the character's obsessions come out a little at a time. At first, when the prim chief inspector assigns Schmutz to guard an abandoned paper mill with a goofy fellow guard, he seems to be the bug-eyed straight man to a comedian's antics. Schmutz' sense of duty makes him want to report this misbehavior to his superiors, but the sudden apparition of a peacock beside the phone booth stops him.

The goofy guard soon gets sacked anyway, and to Schmutz' immense pride and pleasure, the chief inspector entrusts guarding the factory solely to him. Alone with dusty cobwebs and crumbling walls, Schmutz', misanthropy grows. By the time he is relieved of his duties, because the company's client has decided to raze the building, he is so far gone he attacks his boss and holes up in the factory in secret. His burning sense of his "mission" leads him to homicidal attacks first on a pair of innocent lovers, then on a little blond girl he catches breaking windows, and finally on a demolition worker. Schmutz' violence climaxes in a bizarre religious rite somewhere between a sacrifice out of the Old Testament and hari-kari, in the presence of the eagle that is the logo of the security company, and the mysterious peacock.

Though film drags a little at the start and has some trouble avoiding parody when Schmutz deals with other people, it eventually hits its stride and builds effectively into a horrifying, touching conclusion. Technically it does a lot with limited means, managing to turn a few old buildings into a disturbingly symbolic site. —*Yung.*

Class Of Nuke 'Em High
(U.S.-COLOR)

A Troma release of a TNT Co./Troma production. Executive producer, James Treadwell. Produced by Lloyd Kaufman, Michael Herz. Directed by Richard W. Haines, "Samuel Weil" (Lloyd Kaufman). Screenplay, Haines, Mark Rudnitsky, Kaufman, Stuart Strutin, from story by Haines; camera (TVC color), Michael Mayers; associate camera, Jim Grib; editor, Haines; music, Michael Lattanzi; nightmare music, Biohazard; songs, Clive Burr, David Barreto, David Behennah; sound, Marc Pancza; production manager, Sandra Byrd Curry; special makeup effects & special effects, Scott Coulter, Brian Quinn; special matte effects, Théo Pingarelli; associate producer, Strutin. Reviewed at the Cannes Film Festival (market), May 17, 1986. (No MPAA Rating.) Running time: **81 MINS.**
With: Janelle Brady (Chrissy), Gilbert Brenton (Warren), Robert Prichard, R.L. Ryan, James Nugent Vernon, Brad Dunker, Gary Schneider, Théo Cohan, Mary Taylor, Rick Howard.

Cannes — "Class Of Nuke 'Em High," originally titled simply "Nuke 'Em High" (which remains the theme song), is a misguided attempt to extract grossout humor from the very real concerns about nuclear power plants. The Troma filmmakers assume that sadistic behavior, on an exaggerated level, is funny, but the film is punishing rather than fun.

Students at Tromaville High School (the name is one of numerous unfunny in-jokes) are exposed to nuclear waste from a nearby power plant. In the precredits teaser, an Eddie Deezen-lookalike nerd goes through ugly (and phonylooking) makeup contortions after drinking green radioactive liquid out of a water fountain.

Attractive couple Chrissy (Janelle Brady) and Warren (Gilbert Brenton) are exposed to a milder dose of radiation in the form of tainted reefers. First effect is to cause them to make love at a party. Next day, both go through temporary physical transformations (expanding stomachs and necks), with Chrissy emitting a small, lizardlike creature which escapes in the plumbing to end up at the power plant as a grownup monster.

Rest of the film consists of a punk-styled gang called the Cretins (former honor students who have apparently degenerated due to the radioactive weed) terrorizing the entire school. Level of violence is extreme with slapstick overtures that are intended to be funny. Format has lengthy segments of the gang dishing out mayhem, supposedly balanced by a superstrong Warren and later the monster giving them a grisly comeuppance. It's difficult to endure.

Janelle Brady is a well-built, beautiful heroine and it's distasteful to watch her being manhandled here, including a thoroughly irrelevant set of aggressive lesbian gropes applied to her by a female member of the Cretins. Other cast members shout the dialog and overplay.

Makeup effects are variable, ranging from the amateurish to standard expanding bladders and gore effects. The radioactive monster is wisely never shown fully, limited to closeups only.—*Lor.*

The Last Of Philip Banter
(SPANISH-SWISS-COLOR)

A Tesauro S.A. and Banter A.G. coproduction. Executive producers, Clifford W. Lord Jr., Alvaro De La Huerta. Produced and directed by Hervé Hachuel. Screenplay, De La Huerta, adapted by De La Huerta, Hachuel, from novel by John Franklin Bardin; camra (Eastmancolor), Ricardo Chara; editor, Eduardo Biurrun; music, Phil Marshall; songs, Gregg Henry; sound, Chris Munro; art direction, José Maria Tapiador; assistant director, Miguel A. Gil; production manager, Luis Briales; casting, Fenton & Feinberg, Troy Neighbours; associate producer, Tadeo Villalba. Reviewed at the Cannes Film Festival (market), May 15, 1986. Running time: 103 MINS.

Philip Banter . . . . Scott Paulin
Elizabeth Banter . . . . Irene Miracle
Robert Prescott . . . . Gregg Henry
Brent . . . . Kate Vernon
Charles Foster . . . . Tony Curtis
Dr. Monasterio . . . . José Luis Gómez
Alicia . . . . Patty Shepard
Enrique . . . . Fernando Telletxea
Carmen . . . . Lola Bayo

(English language soundtrack)

Cannes — "The Last Of Philip Banter" is a glamorous suspense film that misses the mark. Filmmaker Hervé Hachuel tries hard to create another "Last Year At Marienbad" puzzler but comes up with a hyped-up trifle.

An interesting basic story, taken from a novel by the late John Franklin Bardin, has Philip Banter (Scott Paulin) as a young man going crazy as he is working in Madrid for his father-in-law Charles Foster (Tony Curtis). His marriage ·to beautiful Elizabeth (Irene Miracle) is breaking up and returning to the office he is amazed to find a big chunk of a manuscript typed on his typewriter (presumably by himself) which tells a credible melodramatic tale about people in his life.

In a confusing structure, film presents illustrations of what Banter is reading in the manuscript, interspersed with real scenes he experiences, both types of footage having the same characters and actors. Banter seems paranoid, but it also is quite obvious that he is being manipulated, with the connivance of his best friend Bobby (Gregg Henry) and a pretty blond (Kate Vernon).

There's a decided air of anticlimax by the time all the plot threads are tied up. Finale is not only pat but downright stupid, with the villain falling under a subway train.

Paulin is wholly unsympathetic and a bit tiresome as the nominal hero, while most of the other cast members simply glide through their roles as if involved in a fashion show. In an unsubtle, one-note performance, Tony Curtis telegraphs his nefarious motives and robs the story of its suspense. In a quirky role, Vernon proves far more interesting than lead Miracle. Gregg Henry is unimpressive, but perks things up by singing three of his own jazz-flavored songs on the soundtrack.

Ricardo Chara's visuals of elegant Madrid locations are a bit too distracting for the good of the film overall. English language dialog for this European production is recorded up to U.S. standards. —*Lor.*

Fire In The Night
(U.S.-COLOR)

A Shapiro Entertainment presentation of a Medallion Entertainment production. Executive producer, Reynaldo P. De Leon. Produced by Norbert Buddy Reyef, Simeon Muni Zano. Written and directed by John Steven Soet. Camera (color), Eugene W. Jackson 3d; editor, Gani Pastor; music, Toti Fuentes; sound, Bill Fiege; art direction, Reyef; production manager, Dan Griffith; assistant director, Frank Carlston; fight coordinator, Ted White; martial arts advisor, Graciela Casillas; associate producer, Terry Ballard; casting, Patti Kirkpatrick. Reviewed at the Cannes Film Festival (market), May 16, 1986. (No MPAA Rating.) Running time: 89 MINS.

Jason Williams . . . . John Martin
Terry Collins . . . . Graciela Casillas
Mike Swanson . . . . Patrick St. Esprit
Manolo Catalba . . . . Muni Zano
Paul . . . . Burt Ward
Mary Swanson . . . . E.J. Peaker
Hubert Swanson . . . Peter Henry Schroeder
Kathy . . . . Robin Evans
Bill Collins . . . . Ron Leath
Elaine Collins . . . . Jacquelyn Masche
Fred . . . . Mark Stuart Lane
Blond . . . . Susan Schroder
Sheriff . . . . Terry Ballard

Cannes — "Fire In The Night" (a pointless title) is an amateurish feature that unconvincingly tries to pull a gender switch on "The Karate Kid." Commercial prospects are poor.

Musclebound Graciela Casillas toplines as Terry Collins, a young college girl in a small California town dominated by the rich Swanson family. When not terrorizing people randomly, young Mike Swanson (Patrick St. Esprit) keeps hitting on virginal Terry to bed him and wed him. This culminates in a near-rape, when Terry is saved by a newly arrived old army (former) buddy Jason Williams (topbilled John Martin). Mike also is putting pressure (through his dad) on Terry's father, threatening to foreclose on the mortgage on his business.

Terry hits on the absurd idea of challenging Mike to a martial arts contest: she claims she can throw him in the river in a fair fight (even though Mike is a 6-ft., 3-inch karate expert and she's about five-foot-three-inches and untrained). If she wins, his dad has to donate the business mortgage to her dad; if he wins, he insists on having a night with her in bed.

For some ridiculous reason, both sets of parents agree to this contest. Even less credible is the presence in town of a Filipino cement contractor and folk dance teacher Manolo (Muni Zano), who reluctantly agrees to teach Terry the secrets of Filipino martial arts in the six weeks before the coed contest. He also hires her to work at cementing driveways to toughen her up (unfortunately, actress Casillas is an obvious weightlifter with shoulders like Lyle Alzado and thighs to match, destroying the plot premise of her vulnerability).

Of course Terry wins in a very poorly photographed fight finale, and Manolo even makes her a partner in his business.

Preposterous film is acted poorly to boot, with Casillas having trouble reading dialog. Looking like Wings Hauser, St. Esprit is a hammy villain. It's hard to believe the filmmakers could keep a straight face cranking out this one. —*Lor.*

Raw Deal
(COLOR)

Comic book blood bath won't wash.

A De Laurentiis Entertainment Group release of an Intl. Film Corp. production. Produced by Martha Schumacher. Directed by John Irvin. Stars Arnold Schwarzenegger. Screenplay, Gary M. DeVore, Norman Wexler, from a story by Luciano Vincenzoni, Sergio Donati; camera (J-D-C widescreen, Technicolor), Alex Thomson; editor, Anne V. Coates; music design, Cinemascore; production design, Giorgio Postiglione; art direction, Maher Ahmad; set decoration, Hilton Rosemarin; visual consultant, Tom Cranham; costume design, Clifford Capone; sound (Dolby), David Hildyard; assistant director, Henry Bronchtrin; second unit director/stunt coordinator, Glenn Randall; casting, Mary Colquhoun. Reviewed at the Samuel Goldwyn Theater, Beverly Hills, June 2, 1986. (MPAA Rating: R.) Running time: 106 MINS.

Kaminski . . . . Arnold Schwarzenegger
Monique . . . . Kathryn Harrold
Patrovita . . . . Sam Wanamaker
Rocca . . . . Paul Shenar
Max . . . . Robert Davi
Baker . . . . Ed Lauter
Shannon . . . . Darren McGavin
Baxter . . . . Joe Regalbuto
Marcellino . . . . Mordecai Lawner
Lamanski . . . . Steven Hill
Amy Kaminski . . . . Blanche Baker

Hollywood — Before the carnage really starts in "Raw Deal," Arnold Schwarzenegger reveals to a gangland boss that he's killed three men in his life. By the conclusion, count must be at least 10 times that many, but even big Arnold probably couldn't keep track, so quickly do the bodies fall.

Comic book crime meller suffers from an irredeemably awful script, and even director John Irvin's engaging sense of how absurd the proceedings are can't work an alchemist's magic. Programmed to money-making specifications, first release by the new De Laurentiis Entertainment Group undoubtedly will pull in some hefty coin at first, but after "Cobra" and this one, audiences may have had enough numbing machine gun action for awhile.

Bald exposition sees former FBI man Schwarzenegger, now rather implausibly a southern sheriff, recruited to infiltrate Chicago's biggest mob, which has been rubbing out men scheduled to testify against it.

The big man impresses kingpin Sam Wanamaker with his brain and lieutenant Paul Shenar (as well as tarty Kathryn Harrold) with his brawn, and soon wins himself a job with the gang.

Finally, in two ludicrous shootouts in which a heavily armed Schwarzenegger takes on at least a couple of dozen men, he performs heroic deeds for which the florists of Chicago would undoubtedly be eternally grateful. Scenes are the artillery equivalents of Bruce Lee's successful face-offs with countless opponents, although somehow avoiding the aim of 20 or so gunmen at a time is infinitely more ridiculous than taking out multiple fighters in kung fu.

Director Irvin, whose leap from the subtle intelligence of his last picture, "Turtle Diary," to this was both enormous and ill-advised, does have some fun with the periodically outrageous dialog, and also lightly sends up the slick fetishism surrounding the armaments, costumes and thug attitudes that come with the territory. He's also backed up by some first-class talent in the persons of lenser Alex Thomson and editor Anne V. Coates.

But screenplay by Gary M. DeVore and Norman Wexler is largely a joke, as it casually crams in an action sequence every 10 minutes or so, creates no credibility and generates no genuine concern or tension, so that the climactic slaughter is just a bore.

Cast members do what's necessary, but have all been seen to better advantage on other occasions.

Although in no way related other than by title, this film can't hold a candle to Anthony Mann's 1948 hardboiled meller, "Raw Deal."
—*Cart.*

Breeders
(COLOR)

Effective B-horror picture for cultists.

An Empire Pictures release of an Entertainment Concepts (Tycin Entertainment) production. Produced by Cynthia DePaula. Written and directed by Tim Kincaid. Camera (Precision color), Arthur D. Marks; editor, Barry Zetlin; music, Tom Milano, Don Great; sound, Russell Fager; art direction, Marina Zurkow; set decoration, Ruth Lounsbury; assistant director, Budd Rich; production manager, Rebecca Rothbaum; special effects makeup, Ed French; special effects, Matt Vogel; postproduction coordinator, Juliette Claire. Reviewed on Wizard Video vidcassette, N.Y., May 29, 1986. (No MPAA Rating.) Running time: 77 MINS.
Dr. Gamble Pace . . . . Teresa Farley
Det. Dale Andriotti . . . . Lance Lewman
Karinsa Marshall . . . . Frances Raines
Donna . . . . Natalie O'Connell
Gail . . . . Amy Brentano
Kathleen . . . . Leeanne Baker
Dr. Ira Markum . . . . Ed French
Ted . . . . Matt Mitler
Alec . . . . Adriane Lee
Monster . . . . Owen Flynn

"Breeders" is an interesting, modestly produced film mixing elements of the traditional 1950s monster pic with the explicit sexuality of softcore adult filmmaking. The Empire Pictures pickup was released directly to homevideo (probably avoiding potential rating problems), but would make an effective midnight film entry in theatrical use.

Filmmaker Tim Kincaid's story has five women in as many days raped in New York and found with similar characteristics, including severe acid burns on their bodies and traces of some unknown organic material. Each was a virgin prior to the attack and suffers partial amnesia with widely differing descriptions of the assailants.

Dr. Gamble Pace (Teresa Farley) at Manhattan General Hospital is working on the mysterious case with police detective Dale Andriotti (Lance Lewman) and they trace the source of the attacks to a place underground, below the Empire State Building. It turns out that alien monsters (masquerading in human guise) are the rapists, using Earth women in an attempt to propagate their kind.

The simple story is an excuse to pack "Breeders" with nude scenes of some rather attractive young women, notably local starlet Frances Raines in her sexiest appearance to date, sort of approximating last year's "Lifeforce" nude times five. Ed French, who appears effectively in a support role as a bearded doctor who turns out to be one of the aliens, has created impressive low-budget makeup effects. The monster is black and scaly, with huge insect eyes on the sides of its head.

In addition to the five comely victims, black actress Teresa Farley is another beauty as the doctor heroine, who figures prominently in a trick ending. Kincaid keeps matters simple, avoiding expensive set pieces and thankfully, having his script played straight. Dialog discussing and substantiating the unlikely presence of so many still-virginal beauties in Manhattan is a fun touch.

Tech credits are adequate in a film that reflects an awareness of the potential of B-level sci-fi, even in an era dominated by big-budget versions. —*Lor.*

La Ballata di Eva
(The Ballad Of Eva)
(ITALIAN-COLOR)

An Istituto Luce/Italnoleggio release of an Aura Film production. Produced by Roberto Cicutto and Vincenzo De Leo. Directed by Francesco Longo. Stars Ida Di Benedetto. Screenplay, Manlio Santanelli, Longo; camera (Eastmancolor), Claudio Meloni; editor, Cleofe Conversi; music, Tony Esposito. Reviewed at Quattro Fontane theater, Rome, April 27, 1986. Running time: 86 MINS.
With: Ida Di Benedetto (Eva), Concetta Barra, Nunzia Fumo, Massimo Ghini, Maria Luisa Santella, Lino Troisi.

Rome — Francesco Longo's second feature, "The Ballad Of Eva," inevitably will be compared to Lina Wertmüller's release this season, "Camorra." Both are set in Naples and both involve worried mothers frantically trying to keep their pre-teen offspring out of underworld hands and destruction. In the present case, Ida Di Benedetto has a 15-year-old daughter intent on prostituting herself in a juvenile bordello. Its heart is in the right place, but film just doesn't have enough muscle or story, or actors, to get to the end without faltering.

Di Benedetto often has played a Neapolitan working class heroine (her best go at it was in "Immacolata And Concetta") and has the role down pat. At the center of the picture, she's a sympathetic and tough Eva, although a little too glib and well-coifed to be totally convincing. She has left her young daughter in Naples with her mother while she works in a Turin factory; the girl's disappearance brings her south again and in the eye of the local Camorra. (A likable boss turns out to have been the daughter's father.)

Story proceeds without surprises — Di Benedetto bravely bullies the bullies, gets beaten up, finds allies, and in the end saves the girl against her will. Technically, film is shot well and Tony Esposito's soundtrack is a plus. Though the little girl is miscast, some of the older character actors are wonderful. —*Yung.*

Y.V. Andropov — Stranitzi Zhizni
(Andropov — Pages From His Life)
(SOVIET-DOCU-COLOR)

A Central Studio of Documentary Films production. Written and directed by Oleg Uralov. Camera (color), Sergei Cherkassov; editor, Galina Dukhovskaya. Reviewed at Central Studio of Documentary Films, Moscow, June 3, 1986. Running time: 70 MINS.

Moscow — Oleg Uralov, one of the young talents in the field of Soviet documentaries, made this rare biopic on the late Soviet leader Yuri Andropov (for many, Gorbachev's mentor) just before Uralov took over the direction of Moscow's huge Central Documentary Studio. Film is said to be the only biopic in existence on a party chairman, apart from some lives of Lenin. Made for domestic audiences, film leaves out too much basic background to be of general interest in the West, though researchers and historians could pick up some interesting clues from it.

"Andropov — Pages From His Life" is clearly an authorized biography. Its main interest lies in looking at the public figure from the most human side possible, building up a portrait of what Andropov was like as a child, a young man, "off-duty." The picture that emerges is that of a gentle, mild-mannered soul without pretension, who loved ordinary people and wrote poetry in his spare time.

As for the political dimension, Andropov's career is sketched glancingly without particular emphasis. In 1939 he joined the party; during the war, he won fame as a young party leader. In 1954 he was named ambassador to Hungary, but his role in the events of 1956 is disappointingly left out, and substituted with pleasant reminiscences of old-timers who knew the Soviet ambassador. Similarly unexplored are Andropov's 15 years as chief of the KGB, ending in 1982 when he became party secretary, until his death in 1984.

As a craftsman, Uralov knows how to work with his material, intercutting reportage footage with interviews of old friends and acquaintances, teachers and schoolmates. Best section of the docu is on Andropov's boyhood in Stavropol and Ribinsk, when he dreamed of becoming a steamboat captain. Pic is edited beautifully and subtly scored. —*Yung.*

Dark Night
(TAIWANESE-HONG KONG-COLOR)

A Goodyear Movie Co. production. Produced by Hsu Li-Hwa. Executive producer, Lo Wai. Written and directed by Fred Tan, based on the novel by Sue Li-Eng; camera (color), Yang Wei-Han; editor, Chen Po-Wen; music, Peter Chang; sound design, Duh Duu-Jy; art and costume design, Yu Wei-Yen. Reviewed at Melnitz Theater, UCLA, L.A., June 3, 1986. (No MPAA Rating.) Running time: 115 MINS.
Li Ling . . . . Sue Ming-Ming
Yeh Yuen . . . . .Hsu Ming
Hwong Cheng-teh . . . . . . .Chang Kuo-Chu
Mrs. Niu . . . . Emily Y. Chang
(In Chinese; English subtitles)

Hollywood — A big boxoffice draw and subject of enormous controversy in its native territories due to its comparatively explicit presentation of its heroine's sex life, "Dark Night" is a slickly made melodrama which comes off as tame and conventional by Western standards.

Dramatic devices used here were clichés when Joan Crawford and Lana Turner were in the romantic trenches, and they have not been reinvigorated sufficiently to bring to life this languid tale of a woman's marital and extramarital woes. Sex angle makes this potentially salable for many overseas markets, but U.S. interest would be rather limited.

"Dark Night" is the first feature from Fred Tan, a native of Taiwan who, for several years, has been a film critic and Hollywood correspondent for the China Times, and has an MFA in film production from UCLA. Tan's technique and command of filmmaking grammar is soundly professional, and there is no reason to expect he could not do solid work on either side of the Pacific if he would extricate himself from the grasp of such tired material.

How many times has the story been told, of the beautiful, bored housewife whose husband neglects her and who, while he's off on a business trip, becomes drawn into a passionate but doomed affair with her husband's friend?

Basing his film on a reportedly controversial Taiwanese novel, Tan spikes the picture with sex scenes every 10 or 15 minutes. But what initially promises to become a hot and spicy film eventually proves listless and thoroughly unexciting on a sexual level — nudity is mostly implied rather than shown, and simulated action is shown almost entirely in discreet long shots. Pic easily falls within R rating specifications.

Nevertheless, that such a picture could be made in Taiwan created a media frenzy there, and eight minutes of sex footage had to be cut before it was cleared for exhibition. A smaller number of deletions were made for Hong Kong release, but SRO screening at UCLA represented the first presentation of Tan's original version.

Made on a $300,000 budget, pic was post-synched in the manner of all Chinese films, and as an inadvertent result one doesn't quite know how to read the reactions of the reluctant adultress when she finally succumbs to her suitor. Her face shows painfully mixed emotions, but on the soundtrack are enthusiastic cries, moans and heavy breathing which could have been lifted from a porno wild track.

Tan has set most of the action in sleek, upscale locations all new to U.S. eyes, but film might have profited from placing it more specifically in a Taiwanese context. Both the picture and the characters seem to be without a culture, and films are always richer when they express the time and place from which they come. —Cart.

Back To School
(COLOR)

Funny string of one-liners from Rodney Dangerfield.

An Orion Pictures release of a Paper Clip production. Produced by Chuck Russell. Executive producers, Estelle Endler, Michael Endler, Harold Ramis. Directed by Alan Metter. Stars Rodney Dangerfield. Screenplay, Steven Kampmann, Will Porter, Peter Torokvei, Harold Ramis, from story by Dangerfield, Greg Fields, Dennis Snee; camera (Deluxe color), Thomas E. Ackerman; editor, David Rawlins; music, Danny Elfman; production design, David Snyder; set design, Edmund Silksitis; sound, William Nelson; assistant director, Robert P. Cohen; casting, Caro Jones, Melissa Skoff. Reviewed at Samuel Goldwyn Theatre, Beverly Hills, May 30, 1986. (MPAA Rating: PG-13.) Running time: **96 MINS.**

Thornton Melon .....Rodney Dangerfield
Diane ....Sally Kellerman
Lou ....Burt Young
Jason Melon ....Keith Gordon
Derek ....Robert Downey Jr.
Philip Barbay ....Paxton Whitehead
Valerie ....Terry Farrell
Coach Turnbull ....M. Emmet Walsh
Vanessa ....Adrienne Barbeau
Chas ....William Zabka
Dean Martin ....Ned Beatty
Dr. Barazini.............Severn Darden
Prof. Terguson ....Sam Kinison
Giorgio ....Robert Picardo
Kurt Vonnegut Jr. ....Himself
Marge ....Edie McClurg

Hollywood — For his particular brand of sophomoric humor, Rodney Dangerfield gets a B-plus for "Back To School." The comedian is up to his usual silly and improbable antics that work better here than they did in either "Caddyshack" or "Easy Money," which is sure to please his fans and at least amuse anyone else easily entertained by an unsophisticated comedy that makes light of the pretentiousness of academicians.

In "School," Dangerfield plays the rags to riches owner of a chain of Tall and Fat clothing stores who divorces his insufferable nouveau riche wife and then figures to get a new lease on life by fulfilling a lifelong dream of earning an undergraduate degree.

He decides to enroll in the prestigious lakeside university where his son Jason is a student, believing his son is B.M.O.C. and that the admissions dean will admit him just because he's rich.

Although he's wrong about his son, who turns out to be a wimp, he's right about buying his way into academia by offering to pay for a new business school.

Scripters Steven Kampmann, Will Porter, Peter Torokvei and Harold Ramis have written a 96-minute string of one-liners that only the bug-eyed and goofy comedian could get away with delivering.

"Maybe you can help me straighten out my Longfellow," Dangerfield asks a cute, blond coed.

Dialog hovers at about this level and is complemented with a corresponding number of pseudo-serious gags.

Everyone portrayed in this film is a stereotype, from the tweedy, uptight business professor with an affected English accent (Paxton Whitehead) to the touch-feely literature instructor (Sally Kellerman) who recites Dylan Thomas with breathless perfection and tutors the same seductive way.

Audience is supposed to feel for Dangerfield's too-serious and under-achieving son, Jason (Keith Gordon), who resents his father's Joe Palooka mannerisms and habit of greasing everyone's palms — but we don't.

Eventually, even Jason gets seduced by his father's wily ways, and besides, this is escapist entertainment, not a complex satire. —Brit.

Il Mostro di Firenze
(The Monster Of Florence)
(ITALIAN-COLOR)

A Titanus release of a G.M.P. (Milan) production. Produced by Mario Giacomini, Bruno Noris. Directed by Cesare Ferrario. Stars Leonard Mann. Screenplay, Fulvio Ricciardi, Ferrario, based on the book by Mario Spezi; camera (Cinecittà, Kodak color), Claudio Cirillo; music, Paolo Rustichelli; art director, Mario Ambrosino. Reviewed at Quirinale Cinema, Rome, April 14, 1986. Running time: **92 MINS.**

Andreas Ackermann ......Leonard Mann
Julia ....Bettina Giovinini
Mother ....Lidia Mancinelli
Newsman..................Gabriele Tinti

Rome — The stormy release history of "The Monster Of Florence," a first feature effort by young helmer Cesare Ferrario, may have stirred some initial interest at the b.o. for this curiosity item, but has not been enough to keep audiences coming. Purporting to be a type of docudrama about the infamous Tuscan murderer-mutilator of loving couples, film labors against a built-in defect: the killer is still on the loose and no one has the slightest idea who he is. Getting a screenplay out of a few vague clues and police deductions turns out to be a losing proposition from the start.

Nevertheless, the series of chilling crimes (one a year for the last 16 years), false suspects, and gruesomely butchered bodies undoubtedly has a hold on the public imagination. In spite of outcries about bad taste, film was made, passed the board of censors, and subsequently was cut a bit under pressure from judiciary authorities and the victims' relatives. Release version is fairly unsensational, with little nudity, few love-making scenes, and no post-mortem gore at all.

Story takes a young writer, Andreas (Leonard Mann), as its pivotal point-of-view. In the familiar tradition, he investigates the murders and becomes obsessed with the book he's writing on the monster of Florence. Andreas' much more interesting girlfriend (Bettina Giovinini), a reporter, is dropped unwisely from the proceedings as soon as she is introduced. Interwoven are re-creations of the first and last double murders.

The crazed assassin is a shadowy figure, but to go anywhere at all film invents a young psycho-killer with cropped hair whose problem is his mother (Lidia Mancinelli in film's most original role). Apparently as a tyke he witnessed a ménage à trois version of the primal scene, ergo his later distaste for illicit goings-on in the park.

"Monster" closes with a moralistic flourish, literally a flash-forward into the future when the killer will go on trial and the horror will come to an end. Technical work is uneven. —Yung.

Ein Fliehendes Pferd
(A Runaway Horse)
(WEST GERMAN-COLOR-16m)

A coproduction of Artus Film, Munich and Westdeutscher Rundfunk (WDR), Cologne. Directed by Peter Beauvais. Screenplay, Ulrich Plenzdorf, Beauvais, Martin Walser, based on Walser's novel; camera (color), Gernot Roll; editor, Liesgret Schmitt-Klink; sets, Peter Scharff; costumes, Anastasia Kurz; tv producer, Hartwig Schmidt. Reviewed at SFB Screening Room, Berlin, April 8, 1986. Running time: **105 MINS.**

With: Vadim Glowna (Helmut Halm), Rosel Zech (Sabine, his wife), Dietmar Mues (Klaus Buch), Marita Marschall (Helene, his wife).

Berlin — Peter Beauvais' "A Runaway Horse" is a literary adaptation for theatrical and tv exhibition that is of interest by virtue of its source novella by Martin Walser. The Frankfurter Allgemeine Zeitung published the story in serial form in 1978, which scored such a hit with the reading public that the subsequent book sales soared and a radio-play and legit version followed.

Martin Walser's writings and dramas are imbued with an ironic ring. In this case, the runaway horse is a metaphor for two former school chums who tend to run away from their hopes and dreams rather than confront them. Both are losers and require each other's presence for self-serving dialog tinged with vanity and deception. The setting is Lake Constance in southern Germany near the Swiss border, where the bourgeois middle class spend their summer vacations.

Helmut is a teacher who rose in the ranks to school principal, but he's now content to be left in peace to soak in life and philosophy in the great books. Even his wife Sabine disturbs his regrettable slide towards sexual impotency. Klaus, on the other hand, is a journalist with élan and a quite younger second wife with which to measure the course of success. His conversations are all too often on sexual verve and the general rewards of a playboy existence.

Neither one, it turns out, is what he pretends to be on the surface. The couple meet regularly on the quay in order to test each other, then Helmut retires with his Sabine to reflect on just who won today's subtle game of oneupmanship — and one supposes that the same was true of Klaus as well afterwards. Each meeting, however, pushes the confrontation closer to the brink of an action that spells the final break, and it's to Walser's literary finesse that this takes place in a sailboat in the midst of a dangerous squall. Klaus is washed overboard, and Helmut appears to be at fault for the tragedy — until, at the end, a surprise twist leaves everything open once again.

Film contains finely etched thesp performances, particularly by Vadim Glowna as the ultimate book-worm and stuffy intellectual Helmut. Unfortunately, the uninspired dictates of gearing a project for the dialog-oriented tv screen, instead of the narrative imagery of the theater screen, reduces a promising story to heavy-handed superficiality.—*Holl.*

Balboa
(COLOR)

Dreary soap opera.

An Entertainment Artists presentation of a Production Associates production. Executive producers, Shirley Rothman, Allen Brent. Produced and directed by James Polakof. Stars Tony Curtis, Carol Lynley. Screenplay, Polakof; writing contributions, Gail Willumsen, Nicki Lewis; camera (Deluxe Color), Christopher Lynch; editor, Millie Paul; music, Richard Hieronymus; sound, Anthony Santa Croce; production design, Charles D. Tomlinson; assistant director-production manager, Carol Land; associate producers, John Cannon, Nancy Judd. Reviewed on Vestron Video vidcassette, N.Y., June 4, 1986. (No MPAA Rating.) Running time: **91 MINS.**

Ernie Stoddard ....Tony Curtis
Erin Blakely ....Carol Lynley
Kathy Love ....Jennifer Chase
Alabama Dern ....Chuck Connors
Rita Carlo ....Lupita Ferrer
Terry Carlo ....Sonny Bono
Cindy Dern ....Catherine Campbell
Angie Stoddard ......Cassandra Peterson
Lance Armstrong ....━....David Young
Narrator ....Martine Beswicke
  Also with: Russell Nype (Sen. Highsmith), Henry Jones (Jeffry Duncan), Joy Brent (Joy Eastland), Shirley Rothman (Shirley Sanders), Steve Kanaly (Sam Cole), Jaime Allison (Robin Woodbury), Michael Polakof (Benjie), Linda Kenton (Candy), Kay Parker (Apple), Jennifer Smith (Kathleen Blakely).

"Balboa" is a poor man's version of the popular nighttime soap operas such as "Dallas" and "Dynasty."

Feature had a checkered history: bearing a 1982 copyright date, it was produced in lengthy form as a proposed tv series aimed at cable tv, replete with nudity and four-letter words. In postproduction, project was edited down to feature length, with handsome British actress Martime Beswicke (a.k.a. Beswick) filmed in new shots as on-screen narrator to bridge plot gaps. Item was acquired by Jenson Farley Pictures but never released theatrically when that firm went bankrupt, surfacing instead as a homevideo enry.

Suffering from extremely clichéd dialog, "Balboa" bears a simple-minded plot concerning crass entrepreneur Ernie Stoddard's efforts to bring legalized gambling to California on Goat Island in the chic Balboa district. His foes believe Stoddard had a former partner killed before taking up with the partner's wife Erin Blakely (Carol Lynley), who has since split with Stoddard (though still carrying a torch for him) and become involved romantically with local councilman Sam Cole (guest star Steve Kanaly, a regular from "Dallas").

Cole opposes Stoddard's attempts to get his gambling plan approved by having crony Joy Eastland (Joy Brent), a former brothel madam, appointed to the building commission. Also conspiring against Stoddard are Cindy Dern (Catherine Campbell), whose grandpa (Henry Jones) had his business foreclosed by Stoddard, Angie Stoddard (Cassandra Peterson, a.k.a. tv horror host Elvira), the baddie's ex-wife, and Lance Armstrong (David Young), an opportunist lawyer.

Feature is short on action, concentrating on lots of chatty talk involving threats, blackmail and mucho exposition. Nudity is delivered by various bit players, as well as Stoddard's main squeeze, a vapid but beautiful model type played by Jennifer Chase. One surprise touch has hardcore porn superstar Kay Parker showing up in one scene that has a senator (Russell Nype) dallying with her, suitable for blackmail by Stoddard.

True to format, nasty Stoddard outwits everyone and emerges victorious, but at film's end, Beswicke voices over further adventures in store, featuring Chase with a new cast.

Filmmaker James Polakof directs in perfunctory fashion, with an underwhelming cast. At best, the thesps approach camp level, particularly Lupita Ferrer as a fiery Latin screen star trying to make a comeback in a film produced by the improbably named Alabama Dern (played friskily by Chuck Connors). Acting by Tony Curtis (as Stoddard), Sonny Bono and Cassandra Peterson is mildly embarrassing.

Locations and lovely homes are pretty to look at, but not much is happening within them.—*Lor.*

Naked Vengeance
(COLOR)

Formula rape/revenge exploitationer.

A Concorde Pictures release of a Westbrook/M.P. Films presentation in association with D.S. Pictures of a Santiago/Maharaj production. Executive producer, Anthony Maharaj. Produced by Cirio H. Santiago, Maharaj. Directed by Santiago. Screenplay, Reilly Askew, from story by Maharaj; camera (color), Ricardo Remias; editor, Pacifico Sanchez, Noah Blough; music, Ron Jones; title song, Michael Cruz; sound, George Mahlberg; production manager, Honorato Perez; second unit director, Maharaj; dialog supervisor, Joseph Zuccero; postproduction supervisor, Ernesto Bontigas; casting (Manila), Henry Strzalkowski. Reviewed on Lightning Video vidcassette, N.Y., May 26, 1986. (No MPAA Rating.) Running time: **97 MINS.**
Carla Harris ....Deborah Tranelli
Fletch ....Kaz Garas
Sheriff Cates ....Bill McLaughlin
Burke ....Ed Crick
Sparky...................Nick Nicholson
Arnie ....Don Gordon
Ray ....David Light
Timmy ....Steve Roderick
Det. Russo ....Carmen Argenziano
Mark Harris ....Terence O'Hara
Dr. Fellows ....Joseph Zuccero
Deputy ....Henry Strzalkowski

"Naked Vengeance," alternately titled "Satin Vengeance," is a routine exploitation film, nicely acted but strictly to formula. Feature has gone directly to the homevideo market, with theatrical release still upcoming.

Deborah Tranelli toplines as Carla Harris, a former actress whose husband is killed on their fifth wedding anniversary when he tries to prevent a woman from being assaulted in a parking lot.

She goes to stay with her parents in Silver Lake, Calif., where she grew up. Virtually all the men there, including since-married old high school classmates, hit on her for a date with her increasingly uptight rebuffs angering them. Getting drunk one night, a bunch of the guys decide to visit her parents' home (where Carla has been left alone for the weekend) and get her.

Ensuing gang-rape scene is violent and graphically simulated, with Carla's parents killed by the thugs when they arrive home early. A young handyman Timmy (Steve Roderick) also is shot to death when he threatens to go to the police.

In an unconvincing plot gimmick, Carla is left for dead (though she wasn't shot) and she recovers in a hospital. There follows the genre's standard female on the warpath payoff, including some unnecessarily ultraviolent scenes such as a castration and an exploding head effect.

A stupid epilog has Carla popping up in New York to unbelievably find and kill the murderer of her husband after she runs out of rapists to wipe out.

Story has been limned many times before, notably in Meir Zarchi's 1978 opus "Day Of The Woman" (a.k.a. "I Spit On Your Grave"). Filipino director Cirio H. Santiago directs competently, with a solid performance by Tranelli keeping the picture watchable.

As with several other recent features from Roger Corman's Concorde Pictures banner such as "Streetwalkin' " and "Barbarian Queen," film is being released on vidcassette in both R-rated and unrated versions as a comeon to gullible fans. Ultimately, such a practice will sabotage the theatrical release, since the target audience will want to see the entire film, not the truncated R-rated theatrical edition.
—*Lor.*

Nadia
(ISRAELI-COLOR)

A Nachshon Films presentation of a Abba Films production. Executive producer, Ehud Ben-Shach. Produced by David Lipkind. Directed by Amnon Rubinstein. Screenplay, Rubinstein, Eitan Green, Galila Ron-Feder, from story by Ron-Feder; camera (color), Ilan Rosenberg; editor, David Tur; music, Yoni Rechter; title song by Rechter, Eli Mohar, performed by Giddi Gov. Reviewed at the Esther Cinema, Tel Aviv, April 25, 1986. Running time: **90 MINS.**

With: Hanna Azoulai-Haspari (Nadia), Yuval Banai (Ronen), Meir Banai (Dani), Meir Suissa (Udi), Yussuf Abu-Warda (Ali), Ossi Hillel (Nurith), Ree Rosenfeld (Tami), Salwa Nakkara-Hadad (Dr. Najla).

Tel Aviv — A well intentioned but rather innocent attempt to deal with the Israeli-Arab conflict on a Disney-like level, Amnon Rubinstein's first feature "Nadia" is inoffensive enough not to make anybody angry, but falls short of the goals it set itself.

Based on a story by Galila Ron-Feder, one of the best selling local writers of youth-oriented literature, the plot confronts a teenage Arab girl with the realities of a Jewish boarding school, and manages to come out of this clash almost unblemished. Nadia is a determined young person, who wants to become a doctor and help her people. To do so, she needs the best of education, and for that she has to leave the sheltered environment of her village and the limited tuition she can get there.

She is supported by her father, who believes this is the only way to progress, and by an aunt who had gone the same way before her, while the rest of the adults in the family oppose such a rash initiative.

She goes ahead and indeed has to measure up to different customs, a language she controls only tentatively, and kids her own age who are as suspicious of her as she is of them. However, the minor crises are surmounted easily enough, even the embarrassing moments when she has to fend off the brash courtship of her new male comrades, less single-minded than she is about getting an education, and keener on having a good time. She manages, through her own good sense, to keep all these under control, until the news of a terrorist bomb in a bus station, which has made numerous victims, makes her the black sheep of the entire school. She feels hate and mistrust directed at her, she is desperate when her colleagues do not understand that she should not be blamed for what others have done, and is about to give everything up and go back home to her village, when the script comes in to provide a ray of hope in the last sequence.

As long as it deals with the everyday type of problems encountered in a boarding school, the plot is pretty relaxed, episodic, and a stronger directorial hand might have put a bit more urgency in the proceedings. The problems of identity faced by Israeli Arabs are far more complex than this picture lets on, and the animosity erupting quite often on nationalistic grounds isn't as polite.

As Nadia, Hanna Azoulai-Haspari has all the thespian qualities required, except one, she is older than her part, which make some of her partners mismatched. From the supporting cast, Yussuf Abu-Warda, as Nadia's father, and Salwa Nakkara-Hadad have strong screen personalities which should be exploited further. The presence of two pop star cousins, Yuval and Meir Banai, as Nadia's classmates, will certainly help at the box-office.—*Edna.*

Cesta Kolem Me Hlavy
(Round My Head In 40 Days)
(CZECH-COLOR)

A Ceskoslovensky Filmexport release of a Barrandov Studio production. Directed by Jaroslav Papousek. Screenplay, Papousek, Pavel Hajny; camera (color), Jiri Samal; editor, Jiri Brozek; music, Peter & Pavel Orm; art director, Jaromir Svarc; assistant director, Milan Klacek; production manager, Jaroslav Solnkka. Reviewed on SBS tv, Sydney, May 29, 1986. Running time: **81 MINS.**
With Ondrej Havelka, Miroslav Machalek, Marta Vankurova, Petr Hanicinec, Eva Vidlarova, Jana Andresikova, Eugen Jegorov.

Sydney — Sculptor-turned-filmmaker Jaroslav Papousek was one of the key figures of the Czech new wave of the mid-1960s. He wrote the book on which Milos Forman's first feature, ''Black Peter,'' was based, and coscripted Forman's ''Loves Of A Blonde'' and Ivan Passer's ''Intimate Lighting'' before turning to direction himself with ''The Most Beautiful Age'' (1969). Sadly ''Round My Head In 40 Days,'' made in 1984, turns out to be a lackluster comedy, set in a psychiatric hospital, about a wimpish character who falls for a lady doctor.

Kilian (Ondrej Havelka) is unable to make up his mind about anything, which is why he finds himself in the loosely run hospital in the first place, surrounded by a group of mildly interesting eccentrics. Before long, however, he's besotted with his therapist and pursues her relentlessly, though another patient in turn has the hots for him.

The comedy is not so much understated as nonexistent, and the central character is a pale shadow of earlier indecisive Papousek heroes, such as Peter in the Forman film. It's technically quite acceptable, but instantly forgettable. —*Strat.*

Khoziain
(The Master)
(SOVIET-COLOR)

An Armenfilm Studios production. Directed by Bagrat Oganesyan. Stars Khoren Abramyan. Screenplay, Grant Matevosyan; camera (color), G. Avakyan; editor, N. Oganyan; music, T. Mansuryan; art direction, L. Gevorkyan. Reviewed at Tashkent Film Festival, May 24, 1986. Running time: **97 MINS.**
Rostom Sarkisyan . . . . . Khoren Abramyan
Rostom's wife . . . . A. Gukasyan
Director . . . . O. Galoyan
Senik . . . . K. Dzhanibekyan
Felix . . . . A. Martirosyan

Tashkent — Armenian director Bagrat Oganesyan has no story to tell in ''The Master,'' which accounts for film's dragging pace and trouble holding audience interest. Its strong point is the melancholy atmosphere of things gone by pervading the vast wooded hills and dales of the Armenian countryside, a funereal tone untouched by pic's occasional efforts to inject hope for the future in the form of children and young people.

''The Master'' could be termed an ecology film. Central character Rostom (Khoren Abramyan) is a crotchety old forester nobody likes. The village kids throw stones at him and at one point a neighbor almost beats him to death with a club in a fit of exasperation. Even his wife looks dubious about Rostom's activities, which appear aimed at preventing illegal deforestation by enterprising woodcutters who work at night.

As disgruntled as Rostom is with humankind, he exults in the beauty of nature. Riding through the woods on horseback, he is in his element, while the soundtrack abandons natural noises for the poetry of wind and bird calls. There are memorable shots of apples rolling down a waterfall with a naked girl bathing underneath, and a procession of villagers leaving the land where they were born, in a snowy procession. The old man and his wife just fold their arms and dig in. For Rostom and his undying values, the exiles are ''traitors,'' and to film's credit we can empathize with his despairing point-of-view.
—*Yung.*

Granny General
(SOVIET-COLOR)

An Uzbek Studio production. Executive producer, Sherif Nasimbaiev. Directed by Melo Absalov. Stars Zainob Sadrieva. Screenplay, Resivoi Muhamidjanov; camera (Panavision, color), Najmidin Gulyamov; editor, Rano Hamraeva; music, Mirhalil Makmudov. Reviewed at Tashkent Film Festival, May 27, 1986. Running time: **72 MINS.**
Granny . . . . Zainob Sadrieva
Husband . . . .~. . . . . Hussan Sharipov
Wife . . . . Noila Tashkenbaira

Tashkent — Director Melo Absalov is the young hope of Uzbek cinema; his third feature, ''Granny General,'' is strongly reminiscent of the previous ''The Daughter-in-Law's Rebellion,'' only a little more refined and set in a country village rather than the city. A simple comedy graced with a subtle sense of humor, ''Granny General'' offers quiet laughs and an insider's view into contemporary rural life in the USSR's Central Asian republic.

Judging by Absalov's films, Uzbek women are mighty tough customers. Granny (played by spirited character actress Zainob Sadrieva) arrives in her remote village from the sky, dropping in via a helicopter. By pic's end she will disappear calmly into the breathtaking mountains surrounding the town, preferring a dignified exit to a slow death in the hospital. In the middle, she makes life hell for everyone, beginning with her son (Hussan Sharipov).

Her son is a father of 10 boys and is mad about soccer. He has formed a ''family soccer team'' but needs one more player, who his long-suffering, pregnant wife (Noila Tashkenbaiva) is supposed to supply. Granny takes a hand and after being locked out of his own house he wanders off around the countryside, saying he plans to go to Japan where women obey their husbands.

Meanwhile, Granny looks around for a wife for the eldest boy (who must be 14) and picks the surliest girl in town. She also sticks her nose into public affairs, insisting the regional committee build an unneeded bridge. In the end she is chastised and makes peace with the village.

Film is fast-moving and gay, full of colorful local faces and staggering widescreen landscapes. Lensing is professional, though colors look a bit washed out. A light-hearted music track keeps pace with the film. — *Yung.*

The Sun On A Hazy Day
(SYRIAN-COLOR)

A National Film Organization production. Directed by Mohamed Chahin. Screenplay, Chahin, Mohamed Mouri Farouge, from the novel ''The Sun On A Hazy Day'' by Hana Mina; camera (color), George Houry; editor, Haithan Kouatili; music, Soulhi el Wadi. Reviewed at the Tashkent Film Festival, May 26, 1986. Running time: **90 MINS.**
Old man . . . . Rafik El Soubeil
Adil . . . . Jihad Sahd
Prostitute . . . . Mouna Wasef
Nour . . . . Jada El Charnaa

Tashkent — ''The Sun On A Hazy Day'' is based on a famed novel by Hana Mina describing Syria in the 1930s. Film by director Mohamed Chahin gives a colorful glimpse of the period of French protectorate rule and the growing independence movement, but is made too clumsily to stir much emotion. Though the story is dramatic, film sadly is not.

Hero is Adil (Jihad Sahd), a handsome youth from the upper classes whose modern, clean-cut good looks could pass for Californian. Though engaged to marry a girl of his caste who insipidly plays the piano at evening parties, Adil has a secret life he keeps hidden from his genteel family. Apart from studying music, like sister Nour (Jada El Charnaa), at the conservatory, he has a real passion for dancing, and takes ''lessons'' from old Rafik El Soubeil (one of Syria's great character actors) in a poor but lively section of town. The dance he's learning is called the ''knife dance,'' and it sends shivers down the onlookers' backs (not the viewers') just to watch young Adil waving the glinting blade around. Adil's\performance attracts the attention of a fiery prostitute (Mouna Wasef). She soon has a strong hold over the boy, but his erotic attraction to her is frustrated continually, and seems more symbolic of his flirtation with the lower classes than an actual love affair.

Outdoor lensing captures the beauty of the picturesque waterfront, where the lifeless body of a young partriot is found. Adil's rebellion against his origins and his powerful father becomes more open. It culminates in helpless rage at the death of old Rafik, punished by his father for his friendship with Adil. Conclusion is low-key and more effective than the melodramatic tones meted out to the rest of the film.

Besides Rafik El Soubeil, Mouna Wasef turns in a fine performance as the wise, mysterious woman of the streets, a symbol of her people.
—*Yung.*

Robinsoniada anu Chemi Ingliseli Papa
(Robinsoniad; Or, My English Grandfather)
(SOVIET-COLOR/B&W)

A Georgia Film Studio production. Directed by Nana Dschordschadse. Screenplay, Irakli Kwirikadze; camera (color, b&w), Lewan Paataschwili; editor, Dschordschadse; music, Enri Lolaschwili; art direction, Wachtang Kurna. Reviewed at Tashkent Film Festival, May 29, 1986. Running time: **70 MINS.**
Christopher Hughes . . . . . Janzi Lolaschwili
Anna . . . . Nineli Chankwetadse
Revolutionary . . . . Guram Pirchalawa
Landowner . . . . Gudze Duzduli

Tashkent — ''Robinsoniad; Or, My English Grandfather'' is a delightful Georgian comedy whose experiments with film technique put it in a category by itself. The partly historical, partly tongue-in-cheek tale of a British telegraph operator too stubborn to leave Georgia after the revolution was lensed by young talent Nana Dschordschadse and penned by her husband Irakli Kwirikadze, director of "The Swimmer." Film's lively good humor, and more than a little dialog in English, mark it as a popular export for fests and art house audiences.

Christopher Hughes (Janzi Lolaschwili) is a short, prematurely balding employee of the "Indoeuropean Telegraph — London," who takes his job seriously. As an English gentleman said to be irresistible to women, he comically defends two menaced maidens on a train, thus meeting love interest Ana (Nineli Chankwetadse), sister of the town's revolutionary leader Guram Pirchalawa.

While the Bolsheviks and Mensheviks fight the battle of Georgia, and a villanious feudal landowner (Gudze Duzduli) is driven into hiding, Hughes goes about his business as if nothing's up. But after he interferes at a revolutionary rally, protesting "nobody insults England," he is gently but firmly run out of town. Hughes, however, recalls that 10 feet of ground around each telegraph pole is British soil, and takes up residence underneath one.

Dschordschadse uses a variety of viewpoints to tell her story, from a modern-day orchestra composer who ostensibly recounts the story of his English grandfather, to a wizened old lady with a gray goatee, who we later discover to be Anna.

Lensing by cameraman Lewan Paataschwili is sharp and original; pic randomly alternates sepia-toned black and white with color photography, creating a wild jumble of impressions. As if that wasn't enough, story flits madly back and forth in time, between reminiscences, reportage footage, old stills, and the story set in 1927. Only problem for the Anglo-eared is adjusting to Hughes' Yank accent (though plans are afoot to redub the part.)—*Yung*.

Fulaninha
(BRAZILIAN-COLOR)

An Embrafilme release of an Encontro Produções Cinematográficas/Ipê Artes production, in association with Embrafilme, Skylight Cinema and Nadia Filmes. Produced by Paulo Thiago, Carlos Moletta. Directed by David Neves. Screenplay, Neves, Haroldo Marinho Barbosa, Onezio Paiva, Paulo Thiago; camera (Eastmancolor), Antonio Penido; editor and director assistant, Marco Antonio Cury; music, Sergio G. Saraceni; song "Fulaninha" written and performed by Paulinho da Viola; sets, Paulo Dubois; costumes, Isabel Paranhos; production director, Marcelo França; producers, Paulo Thiago and Carlos Moletta. Reviewed at Cine Exbaixador, Gramado Film Festival, March 10, 1986. Running time: **95 MINS.**

Fulaninha	Mariana de Moraes
Bruno	Claudio Marzo
Rose	Katia D'Angelo
Sulamita	Zaira Zambelli
Canela	Roberto Bonfim
Jardel	José de Abreu
Herminio	Flavio São Thiago
Armando	Paulo Vilaça
Rubinho	Marcos Palmeira
Doorman	Nelson Dantas
Police inspector	Gilson Moura
Officer	Ivan Setta
Sabonete	Mario Petraglia
S. Antonio	Pascoal Vilaboim
Camarão	Mario Tupinambá

Gramado — A charming comedy set entirely in one block of Prado Junior Street, at Copacabana, a traditional meeting point of Bohemians, intellectuals and prostitutes in Rio de Janeiro, "Fulaninha" is the second part of the trilogy of Rio de Janeiro imagined by its author, David Neves. The first, "Muito Brazer," was produced in 1979. The third, filmmaker foresees for 1988.

This is the story of a filmmaker in his 40s who falls in love with an unknown teen he always sees across the street. Filmmaker Bruno (Claudio Marzo), is inseparable from his group of friends: Jardel (José de Abreu), a Bohemian always in trouble with women; Herminio (Flavio São Thiago), obsessed enemy of any kind of work; and Canela (Roberto Bonfim), a producer of porno videos. The meeting between Bruno and his beloved (who the group simply call Fulaninha — a general nickname for everyone) happens through an affair with Fulaninha's mother Rose (Katia D'Angelo), an attractive widow in her 30s.

The fifth feature directed by David Neves, this is probably his most complete film. Essentially autobiographical (even Bruno's home is his own home in real life), "Fulaninha" captures the magic of the carioca spirit due in part to the great deal of creativity the director transfers to his interpreters.

The result is a funny work. Title song by composer Paulinho da Viola helps accomplish an international appeal.—*Hoin*.

O Homem da Capa Preta
(The Man With The Black Coat)
(BRAZILIAN-COLOR)

An Embrafilme release of a Morena Filmes production, in association with Embrafilme, Therezinha Calil Petrus, Lock All and Montevideo. Directed by Sergio Rezende. Screenplay, Rezende, Tairone Feitosa, José Louzeiro, based on "Tenório, o Homem e o Mito," by Maria do Carmo Cavalcanti Fortes, "Meu Pai, Tenório," by Sandra Cavalcanti Freitas Lima, and "Capa Prete e Lurdinha," by Israel Beloch; camera (Eastmancolor), Cesar Charlone; editor, Rafael Valverde; music, David Tygel; sound, Zeze d'Alice; art direction, Rita Murtinho; costumes, Murtinho, Isabel Paranhos; set design, Alexandre Mayer, Pedro Nanni, Barbara Mandonça; production directors, Luiz Carlos Lacerda, Rossy Caetano and Adnor Pitanga. Reviewed at Cine Exbaixador, Gramado Film Festival, April 7, 1986. Running time: **119 MINS.**

Tenorio Cavalcanti	José Wilker
Zina	Marieta Severo
Adolfo	Jonas Bloch
Silas Gonçalves	Carlos Gregório
Inspector Maragato	Paulo Vilaça
Bereco	Tonico Pereira
Cabral	Jackson de Souza
Manezinho	Chico Dias
Tenorio's mother	Isolda Cresta
Venâncio	Jurandir de Oliveira
Flavio Cavalcanti	Guilherme Karan

Gramado — Tenorio Cavalcanti, in his 80s and living in a suburb of Rio de Janeiro, in his time was a representative in the Municipal Chamber and in Congress. Much more, he became a legend of Brazilian politics of the 1940s and 1950s. A blend of politician and gunfighter, Tenorio used to show up in Congress wearing a long beard, a black coat and a machine-gun. That was his own way of solving his problems. His gun even had a nickname, Lurdinha, and reputedly was responsible for killing dozens of political oponents and enemies of what he considered "his people" of Duque de Caxias.

He retired from politics shortly after the revolution of 1964, and three biographies are being published now, two by his daughters Sandra and Maria do Carmo, and one by social scientist Israel Beloch. Filmmaker Sergio Rezende went to these sources to build the screenplay of this film.

The result is a well-researched work — and one of the finest Brazilian films to appear in the last few years.

Rezende took an impressionistic approach. Biographical material was limited to the period between 1945 (when Tenorio joined UDN, the biggest political party in the country) and 1964, year of the military coup that overturned President Joao Goulart.

José Wilker, as Tenorio Cavalcanti, gives his best film performance to date, while Marieta Severo is nearly perfect as his wife. Cinematography by Uruguay-born Cesar Charlone is dense, beautiful, and creates a permanent atmosphere of violence and uncertainty. Editing by veteran Rafael Justo Valverde is concise, as is music by David Tygel.

Rezende lacks a critical vision of his character, often shown as a hero, a viewpoint very few people would endorse. Tenorio's family, in fact, was involved deeply in the production, allowing the crew to shoot at his famous fortress in Duque de Caxias, built by Tenorio in order to protect himself against his enemies, including the police and eventually the army. Yet, "O Homem da Capa Preta" shows a fine profile of this rich character through a technical and artistic standard that makes the film comprehensive and almost always exciting.
—*Hoin*.

Adi Vasfiye
(Her Name Is Vasfiye)
(TURKISH-COLOR)

An Estet Film, Instanbul. Directed by Atif Yilmaz. Stars Müjde Ar. Screenplay, Baris Pirhasan, based on stories by Necati Cumali; camera (color), Orhan Oguz; music, Atilla Özdemiroglu; art director, Sahin Kaygun. Reviewed at Istanbul Film Fest (Turkish series), April 14, 1986. Running time: **88 MINS.** With: Müjde Ar (Vasfiye), Aytac Arman (Emin), Macit Koper (Rüstem), Yilmaz Zafer (Fuat), Levent Yilmaz (Hamza), Erol Durak (the writer).

Istanbul — Winner of the Turkish film competition at Istanbul (fest has two juries, an international one and a domestic one), Atif Yilmaz' "Her Name Is Vasfiye" scores as a delightful "Rashomon"-style comedy.

The setting is Izmir (Smyrna), the second largest city in Turkey on the Aegean seacoast. A young writer wanders through the streets at night in search of a theme and happens upon a wall poster that sets him wondering just who this nightclub singer named Sevim Suna might really be.

A man emerges out of the shadows and addresses himself mysteriously to the writer's thoughts. He just happens to know who the girl is — her real name is Vasfiye — and he was in love with her in his youth. In fact, they eloped, and it was the girl who took matters of running away from home into her own hands. Just when the story begins to get interesting, however, the storyteller disappears.

Along comes another who knew Vasfiye. This time, the gentleman who takes up the thread of the tale says he was formerly a doctor in a town where the girl lived with her jealous husband. Being the lothario type, and she being a sex kitten of sorts herself, they have an affair for the simple reason that the husband keeps her inside the house where only a doctor can be admitted demurely. One day, however, the husband comes home a couple hours earlier than expected.

Once again, the tale is broken off. Next comes a visit to the nightclub and still another encounter with a ruined gentleman who once knew the girl. This time, however, the details about the person are so confused that the young writer is driven to the desire to meet the girl herself.

There she is on the stage: Vasfiye as the dancer-singer Sevim Suna hidden under a blond wig. The writer steals back to her dressing room, and awaits his chance to burst out of his habitual shyness. In walks one of the fellows from the story he's been hearing; it's the nightclub bouncer and hardly the jealous husband.

After getting stabbed for his troubles, the writer finds himself on the street again before the poster and comes to the realization he's not bleeding at all. Did he imagine everything?

Atif Yilmaz is a veteran Turkish director with critical and b.o. winners to his credit since the 1950s. "Her Name Is Vasfiye" is a real delight.—*Holl.*

Die Zwei Gesichter des Januar
(Two Faces Of January)
(WEST GERMAN-COLOR)

A coproduction of Monaco Film, Munich, and Süddeutscher Rundfunk (SDR), Stuttgart. Produced by Georg Althammer. Directed by Wolfgang Storch. Screenplay, Karl Heinz Willschrei, Storch, based on Patricia Highsmith's novel; camera (color), Wolfgang Treu; editor, Inez Regnier; music, Eberhard Schoener; sets, Mike Karapiperis. Reviewed at Lupe 1, Berlin, April 3, 1986. Running time: **100 MINS.**
With: Yolande Gilot (Colette MacFarland), Charles Brauer (Chester MacFarland), Thomas Schücke (Rydal Keener).

Berlin — The latest in an impressive list of 16 film adaptations of Patricia Highsmith novels, Wolfgang Storch's "Two Faces Of January" is surely among the least imaginative of them. The setting this time is Greece, first Athens and then the island of Crete (to visit the cradle of Minoan civilization at Knossos), and finally back to Athens for the wrapup with a twist of the psychological thriller.

According to Storch's version of a book that mystery experts don't rank among Highsmith's best, three oddball types on the run from themselves as well as their pasts team up as an uncomfortable trio to outwit the police after one has unwittingly killed a police detective in a hotel.

It appears that the same Chester MacFarland is also wanted back in the States for bank fraud, so he and his young wife (Colette) have hightailed it first to Switzerland for their stashed away funds, and then it's off with false papers to Athens.

Parallel to this chain of prior events, a young archaelogy student, Rydal Kenner, receives word from his mother that his tyrannical father, a Harvard professor for Greek culture, has died. The unnerving coincidence is that Chester is a dead ringer for Rydal's father at the age of 40. By following the "double" around for a while in the streets of Athens, the student stumbles onto the scene of the crime just as it is being committed in the deluxe tourist hotel.

More falsified passports are needed to make a getaway, which Rydal provides — and then decides to tag along in order to sort out his own destiny. This happenstance leads, naturally enough, to a *ménage à trois* affair and subsequent accidental killing of Colette by the jealous husband.

"Two Faces Of January" suffers principally from stifling a psychological thriller in the straitjacket of a typically stereotyped form of the tv crime series, German-style. All the subtle elements are subverted by ominous music and intrusive camera angles. —*Holl.*

Com Licença, eu vou à Luta
(Sorry, I'll Make It My Way)
(BRAZILIAN-COLOR)

An Embrafilme release of an Embrafilme/R.F. Farias Produções/Time de Cinema production. Directed by Lui Farias. Screenplay, Farias, Alice de Andrade, Marcos Magalhães, Fernanda Torres, Marieta Severo, Roberto Farias, based on the novel "Com Licença eu vou à Luta" by Eliane Maciel; camera (Eastmancolor), Walter Carvalho; sets, Mauricio Sette; costumes, Tetê Amarante; editor, Martha Luz; sound, Heron Alencar and Mauro Duque Estrada; production design and opening cartoon, Marcos Magalhães; song "Já Fui," written by Marina Lima and Antonio Cicero, sung by Lima; assistant director, Alice de Andrade. Reviewed at Cine Embaixador, Gramado Film Festival, April 11, 1986. Running time: **84 MINS.**

Eliane	Fernanda Torres
Mother	Marieta Severo
Otávio	Carlos Augusto Strazzer
Father	Reginaldo Farias
Grandmother	Yolanda Cardoso
Aunt	Tania Boscoli
Neighbour	Duse Nacaracci
Otavio's mother	Ilva Piño
Lawyer	Analu Prestes
Inspector Braulio	Carlos Wilson
Janina	Marise Farias
Daniel	Caio Torres
Judge	Paulo Porto

Gramado — This debut film of Lui Farias, 27, son of filmmaker Roberto Farias (former Embrafilme director-general) is a first work exhibiting a maturity not achieved by many experienced filmmakers.

Starting point is a not very good autobiographical novel written by a young woman, Eliane Maciel, about her family problems and subsequent escape from her parents' home. Farias develops the theme, setting his film mostly in Rio's suburb of Nilopolis and managing to create an inferno out of a family life in which a teen, Eliane, is oppressed continuously by her family. It is a highly intense drama where the weight of an adverse environment is fully transferred to the audience.

It starts in a fine screenplay where the oppressive characters — as well as Eliane's boyfriend, Otávio — gain dramatic power, as does the equally oppressive environment. It is crystalized through remarkable performances by Fernanda Torres, Marieta Severo and Carlos Augusto Strazzer.

Out of the drama of a pregnant 15-year-old girl, driven to madness by her family, arises a universal tragedy.

Technical credits are way above average, though one can feel the absence of a stronger musical reference (the only song, which actually comments on the plot, is not ac-

companied by incidental music). Commercial potential seems very big, not only for the technical standards and intensity of the drama, but also for its universality.—*Hoin.*

Kirlangic Firtinasi
(The Swallow Storm)
(TURKISH-COLOR)

A CFL (Candimir Film) production, Instanbul. Produced by Tulin Candimir. Directed by Atilla Candimir. Stars Halil Ergun. Screenplay, Ergun; camera (color), Selcuk Taylaner; music, Engin Noyan. Reviewed at Istanbul Film Fest (Turkish series), April 14, 1986. Running time: **97 MINS.**
With: Halil Ergun, Perihan Savas, Aytan Kavas, Hüseyin Kutman, Asuman Arsan, Jale Aylanc.

Istanbul — Invited to unspool at the San Remo fest, Atilla Candimir's "The Swallow Storm" was one of the few independently produced features made in Turkey last year.

Story is set in a fishing village, where a young man rebels against becoming a cobbler like his father after finishing school and a training period at a shoemaking factory in Istanbul. The father wants him to stay in the old hometown, but the lad yearns to go back to Istanbul instead. When he meets a young and pretty village teacher, he also falls in love — for she too rebels against traditional customs here by demanding that the children receive an education, rather than being constantly dragged out of the classroom for family and working obligations.

The pair marry and go to Istanbul. The possibilities of a job in a shoe workshop there vanish when the shop has to close due to financial problems. Our hero Kemal then gets into regular squabbles with the more educated Gonul, while Kemal's younger brother becomes an extra burden on the household when he arrives in Istanbul to study at the university. In the end the marriage is on the rocks, and the two part company.

Everything is told in flashback to a reporter. As for the symbolic title, the "swallow storm" refers to sudden storms that not only endanger fishermen and boaters, but can also wipe out young swallows not yet strong enough to combat the winds.

It's a nice debut film, with an extra plus due to fine lensing. —*Holl.*

Tongs — A Chinatown Story
(HONG KONG-COLOR)

A Pan Pacific Prods. production, presented by Peter C.M. Chan. Distributed by D & B Films. Executive producer, Jimmy Yang. Directed by Philip Chan. Stars Simon Yam, Larry Tan, Anthony Gioia, Christopher O'Connor, Ouitan Han and Daisey Yong. Story by Peter C.M. Chan, Neil P. Mainiello, Felipe Luciano. (No other credits provided by producers). Reviewed at Jade theater,

Causeway Bay, Hong Kong, May 24, 1986. Running time: **98 MINS.**
(Cantonese soundtrack with English subtitles. English soundtrack also available.)

Hong Kong — Hong Kong has produced an exploitative triad tale mixed with the American mobster/gangster theme. Documentary-fiction in approach, it is generally shallow.

Story begins with two brothers, Paul and Mickey Lee, illegally leaving China on a fishing boat for Hong Kong. Eighteen years later, they manage to reach New York with the help of relatives.

While staying with relatives who did not benefit from the American dream, Paul gets involved with the notorious Chinatown gang, The Dragons, while Mickey is pressured by the competing gang, The Red Eagles, to join up.

The two gangs fight for attention, committing immature delinquent acts. The unknown cast act out their respective parts with energy and enthusiasm.

Mickey is eventually thrown into the arena of taking sides. He gets the attention of Mr. Chan, the leader of the all-powerful triad group called The Tongs who has in its payroll a police captain. How the Tongs slyly manipulate and intrigue the two factions of Lee and Shanghai Kid serves as the framework for the other half of the film.

This curiosity piece was shot on location in New York. the finale leaves a fascinating but frightening vision about some Chinese residing in America. "The Tongs" is a reminder once again that those who live by the gun die by the gun and that corruption begets evil.

An English version exists which will be better appreciated by foreign viewers and avid fans of exotic Chinatown. The film lacks the cohesiveness and power of "Year Of The Dragon," but the cinematography fully captures the ambience of Hong Kong, U.S.A. Philip Chan is a multi-talented Hong Kong celebrity/singer/director who happens to be an ex-cop of the Royal Hong Kong police force which helped a lot in the realistic presentation of a hot and often controversial subject — gangsters of the triad society both here and abroad. —*Mel.*

Kuyucakli Yusuf
(Yusuf From Kuyucak)
(TURKISH-COLOR)

A Mine Film production, Istanbul. Produced by Kadri Yurdatap. Written and directed by Feyzi Tuna, based on Sabahattin Ali's novel. Camera (color), Cetin Tunca; music, Timur Selcuk; sets, Gürel Yontan. Reviewed at Istanbul Film Fest (competition), April 17, 1986. Running time: **127 MINS.**
With: Talat Bulut, Derya Arbas, Ahmet Mekin, Engin Inal, Sema Ceyrekbasi, Melih Cardak, Nilgun Nazli, Ferda Ferdag, Atilla Yigit, Seda Yildiz, Bülent Oran, Kemal Inci.

Istanbul — Unspooled in the international competition at the Istanbul fest, Feyzi Tuna's "Yusuf From Kuyucak" attracted some attention as a competently made literary adaptation. The book on which it's based is also a classic of sorts: penned in 1937 by Sabahattin Ali, a pioneering exponent of realism in Turkish literature, it describes the struggles of an underdog to right himself against injustice in a decaying Ottoman Empire at the turn of the century.

Pic opens with a young boy in a village returning home to find his parents murdered by bandits. He's taken by the kindly investigating prefect to his residence and raised there, against the wishes of the woman of the house, together with the family's daughter, who's about his age. When they grow up and the prefect dies, they decide to marry — in spite of the lustful gazes showered upon the 16-year-old girl by the son of the richest man in the area.

The rest is pretty much melodrama. Young Yusuf is given a tax-collecting job by town officials to keep him out of the way while attempts are made to win the girl for the rich man's son. One day, however, Yusuf returns home and kills all the intruders. He takes the wounded bride with him on the escape route, only to discover that she's been wounded in the fight. She dies, and he buries her under the open sky next to a protective tree they both loved during courting days.

Pic's stolid pace is the main drawback, along with a lack of drama when it counts the most in the direction. Derya Arbas as the teen-aged maid comes from Los Angeles (Turkish mother, Yank father) and is one of the discoveries of the festival. —Holl.

Lie Chang Zha Sha
(On The Hunting Ground)
(CHINESE-COLOR)

An Inner Mongolia Film Studio production. Directed by Tian Zhuangzhuang. Features Bawaltu, Sewangi Dalgi, Tiegn Yiwal. Screenplay, Jiang Hao; camera (color), Lu He, Hou Yong; music performed by Central Symphony Orchestra. No further credits available. Reviewed at the Ridge Theater, Vancouver, May 14, 1986. Running time: 83 MINS.

Vancouver — Reportedly both the fifth annual Vancouver Intl. Film Festival and the upcoming Montreal fest vied for rights to give this simple, lightly dramatized ethnographic docu its North Amerian preem. Vancouver won (on paper), with its May 26 screening, but the pic will offend and dismay any viewer who cares about animal rights. Definitely not for the squeamish.

Set among the rude hutments of the descendants of Genghis Khan, whose rules about pursuing game the local peasantry seem still to respect, helmer Tian Zhuangzhuang's pic delights in showing the death throes of small quadrupeds cut down in their prime by a posse of callous hunters. A Chinese Western that owes more to the docu tradition of Robert Flaherty than the humanism of John Ford, "On The Hunting Ground" barely can be bothered with plot or character as it follows the seasons as relentlessly as its protagonists savage their own ecology.

Two farmers, Wangzenzabu and Bayasiguleng, develop a feud over a disagreement about the game their respective hounds have brought down. Their antics are photographed lovingly by astute lensers Lu He and Hou Yong. The result is a weird marriage of a Disney true-life adventure with a "Mondo Cane" pseudo docu. Look, Mom, at the lovely little fawn! Ouch! Suddenly it's riddled with buckshot and about to be mauled by two huge German shepherds, who break its spine.

Performances, seemingly by non-professionals recruited from the Mongols portrayed, are never more than rudimentary. A badly post-synchronized soundtrack, which combines native dialect with Cantonese voiceover narration *and* English subtitles in the print under view, proves most distracting. The gruesome pic will have minimal appeal away from its homeland except for hunters who want the wolf population further reduced. —Gran.

Never Too Young To Die
(COLOR)

Tedious low-budget James Bond imitation.

A Paul Entertainment release. Executive producers, Hank Paul, Dorothy Koster-Paul. Produced by Steven Paul. Directed by Gil Bettman. Screenplay, Lorenzo Semple Jr., Steven Paul, Anton Fritz, Bettman, from a story by Stuart Paul, Steven Paul; camera (Metrocolor), David Worth; editor, Bill Anderson, Paul Seydor, Ned Humphreys; music, Chip Taylor, Ralph Lane, Michael Kingsley, Irene Koster; production design, Dale Allen Pelton; art director, Dean Tschetter; Michelle Starbuck; set decorator, Deborah K. Evans, Carol Westcott; sound, Don Parker, Edwin J. Somers; costumes, Fred Long; assistant director, Thom Anable, Fred Wardell; assistant producer, Vikki Hansen; casting, Dorothy Koster-Paul. Reviewed at Hollywood Pacific theater, Hollywood, June 13, 1986. (MPAA Rating: R.) Running time: 92 MINS.

Lance Stargrove	John Stamos
Danja Deering	Vanity
Velvet Von Ragner/Carruthers	
	Gene Simmons
Drew Stargrove	George Lazenby
Cliff	Peter Kwong
Pyramid	Ed Brock
Arliss	John Anderson
Riley	Robert Englund

Hollywood — Featuring some of the most sadistic scenes seen on screen in recent memory, Paul Entertainment's "Never Too Young To Die" belies the company's motto as "Creators Of Loving Entertainment." There are those who may think the contamination of L.A.'s water supply by a leather-dressed hermaphrodite and his creepy band of warriors an act of love and for them this picture was made.

"Never Too Young To Die" is an awkward attempt at a low-budget James Bond picture with a dose of "Road Warrior" thrown in for bad measure. For starters there's the derivative title and a script credit to Lorenzo Semple Jr. who penned "Never Say Never Again," the one recent Bond not produced by Cubby Broccoli.

Also on the scene with Bond pedigree is George Lazenby who played 007 in "On Her Majesty's Secret Service." At times film is more bondage than Bond as Gene Simmons adds a decidedly heavy metal beat to his super-villain role.

Unfortunately, the elements don't work well together. The joy of the "Road Warrior" characters was their total anarchy in the face of a crumbling civilization. Simmons' Velvet Von Ragner is still trying to destroy it with some preposterous plot involving recovery of a floppy disc which will enable him to contaminate the area's water supply.

Search leads him to Lazenby, a Bond-type undercover agent for the U.S. government. After he's disposed of, his son John Stamos must fill his shoes assisted by the lovely Vanity (named Danja Deering in another Bond touch).

Most of the action is silly and tedious when it's not violent and tedious with the script by Semple, producer Steven Paul, Anton Fritz and Gil Bettman supplying some of the limpest dialog this side of a Bond film. Neither the cast nor director Bettman can get the necessary camp laughs out of the material.

Film is best when Simmons is on screen mugging and cavorting shamelessly. His song in the Incinerator Club, "It Takes A Man Like Me To Be A Woman Like Me," pretty much sums up his character. Except for moments like these, he and his herd of followers never really do anything vaguely interesting.

Stamos as the young man trying to save the day and win the girl is so dull as to make one long for Lazenby, who is actually more than credible in his limited turn.

As for Vanity, she could have been a great star of the silent screen. She looks interesting and has a real presence as long as she doesn't ruin it by acting. She is alluring as herself but fails at projecting a character.

Cinematography by David Worth is competent but not helped by choppy and clichéd editing. Production design lacks texture and variety overall but is striking in any given scene. Production often seems too ambitious for its resources.

—Jagr.

Black Mic-Mac
(Black Hanky-Panky)
(FRENCH-COLOR)

A Fechner-Gaumont release of a Chrysalide Films-Films Christian Fechner-FR3 Films coproduction. Produced by Monique Annaud. Directed by Thomas Gilou. Screenplay, Annaud, Patrick Braoude, Cheik Doukoure, Gilou, with the participation of François Favre; camera (Fujicolor), Claude Agostini; editor, Jacqueline Thiédot; music, Ray Lema; sound, Dominique Levert; art direction, Dan Weil; costumes, Corinne Jorry; assistant director, Olivier Peray; production manager, Hugues Nonn. Reviewed at the Gaumont Colisée theater, Paris, May 23, 1986. Running time: 92 MINS.

Michel Le Gorgues	Jacques Villeret
Lemmy	Isaach de Bankole
Anisette	Felicité Wouassi
Amina	Khoudia Seye
Mamadou	Cheik Doukoure
Samba	Mohamed Camara
Ali	Sidy Lamine Diarra
Aida	Lydia Ewande
Rabuteau	Daniel Russo

Paris — "Black Mic-Mac" is a sometimes hilarious, always charming comedy about a group of African immigrants in Paris who send for a witch doctor from back home in order to fix an eviction order a city health official has slapped on their overcrowded squatters site.

Rather than the wizened old sorcerer they expect, they get someone who claims to be his disciple, in fact a long-toothed young African on his way to join relatives in France, who decides to replace the sorcerer when latter tells him on the plane over that his work is to be remunerated nicely.

This creates problems galore for the imposter who has to find ways to keep up his act, yet come through with the desired results from hexing the zealously honest functionary from the Prefecture.

Sympathetically directed by newcomer Thomas Gilou, pic is really a producer's film: Monique Annaud, a former journalist and showbiz revue editor, spent 20 years in Africa and saw in the subject a sort of valentine to the Dark Continent. She chose Gilou (who is white) to direct (on the basis of an excellent prize-winning short, "La Combine de la girafe," he made in 1983), set up her own company to produce, and took part as well in the writing of the script with Gilou, Patrick Braoude and Cheik Doukoure, one of the film's actors. Results are a commercial product full of affection and fun.

The mostly black cast, led by Isaach de Bankole as the brash protagonist, is winning, though best acting laurels go to pudgy Gallic comedian Jacques Villeret, who gives a glowing funny/sad performance as the hoodwinked city health official who in the end falls for the charms of de Bankole's pretty African cousin.

Tech credits are okay. —Len.

Trikal
(Past, Present, Future)
(INDIAN-COLOR)

A Blaze Film Enterprises production. Produced by Freni M. Variava, Lalit M. Bljlani. Written and directed by Shyam Benegal. Camera (color), Ashok Mehta; editor, Bhanudas Divkar; music, Vanraj Bhatia; playback singers, Remo Fernandes, Alisha Chinai; sound, Hitendra Ghosh; production manager, Raj Pius; assistant director, Mandeep Kakkar. Reviewed at Sydney Film Festival, June 8, 1986. Running time: 139 MINS.
Dona Maria Souza-Soares .... Leela Naidu
Ana ....Sushma Prakash
Milagrenia ....Neena Gupta
Leon ....Dalip Tahil
Ruiz Pereira (1985).....Naseeruddin Shah
Ruiz Pereira (1961) ....Nikhil Bhagat
Also with: Makqsoom Alie (Erasmo), Anita Kanwar (Sylvia, Ana's mother), K.K. Raina (Lucio, Ana's father), Soni Razdan (Aurora), Keith Stevenson (Dr. Pereira), Ila Arun (Cook), Kulbhushan Kharbanda (Vijay Singh Rané/Kushtora Ranj.

Sydney — Despite its length, Shyam Benegal's "Trikal" is the most accessible and enjoyable Indian pic seen in many years, and could well find arthouse audiences around the world. The big mystery is why it hasn't been grabbed to compete in a major fest since it was unveiled at the annual Indian meet in January.

The film is set in Goa, once a Portuguese colony on the Indian continent, and opens in the present day when a middle-aged man, Ruiz

(Naseeruddin Shah), returns to the now dilapidated house where he spent much time as a youth. Flashback to 1961, as the Portuguese were about to leave Goa, and the local populace was divided as to whether to stay on or flee to Lisbon.

Story centers around Ana (Sushma Prakash), the beautiful young granddaughter of a wealthy old couple. She's about to become engaged to the wimpish Erasmo (Makqsoom Alie), but is secretly in love with Leon (Dalip Tahil), a freedom fighter on the run from the authorities and hiding in the cellar.

The betrothal ceremonies are interrupted by the sudden death of old Souza-Soares, and his widow, played by Katy Jurado-lookalike Leela Naidu, is so shocked by her bereavement that everything in the grand old house simply grinds to a halt while she spends time fruitlessly trying to contact the spirit of her dead husband but, instead, summoning up the ghosts of long-ago victims of the family.

The most endearing aspect of this sumptuously made family saga is its sense of humor. There are running gags galore, apart from the recurring joke of the unwanted ghosts. Ana's frustrated and furious father keeps losing his dentures at awkward moments, while an ardent suitor of Ana's sister keeps passing out in the lap of his beloved (the result of too much liquor) just as he's about to propose.

When the betrothal between Ana and Erasmo finally takes place, it's a lavish affair interrupted when the girl collapses in a faint and a doctor quickly diagnoses she's pregnant. Her unfortunate fiance, who knows he wasn't responsible, is left out in the cold. These scenes are played beautifully by Alie, son of the famous comedian Mahmood, in a style very similar to that of Harry Langdon: indeed, his is a very Langdonish situation.

"Trikal" is full of pleasures, and ends on a genuinely touching note as Ruiz is unable to find the pretty servant (Neena Gupta) he thoughtlessly impregnated, then abandoned, all those years ago.

Benegal, one of India's most accomplished directors, tells his sweeping story of a society in the middle of radical change without pretension. All his characters are human and likable, making the film, after a slightly confusing opening when all the members of the large family are introed, entertaining from start to finish.

Technically the film is terrific, with lush color photography and a superb music score. Though two hours and 20 minutes in length, time passes quickly. Dialog is in Hindi, though the characters normally would have spoken Portuguese (and the film makes a joke of this).
— Strat.

Democracy
(AUSTRALIAN-DOCU-16m)

A Film Australian production. Executive producer, Tom Haydon. Produced by Macek Rubetzki. Directed by Graham Chase. Camera (color, 16m), Tony Wilson; editor, Chase; sound, Leo Sullivan; animation, Don Ezard; narrator, Jill McKay. Reviewed at Sydney Film Festival, June 10, 1986. Running time: 76 MINS.

Sydney — The first in a series of seven feature-length cinema-verité docus produced by Film Australia, "Democracy" is a stimulating record of a campaign during the December 1984 federal elections which returned the ruling Labor Party and Prime Minister Bob Hawke to power. Director Graham Chase concentrates on a marginal seat in the Sydney beachside electorate of Cook, and follows the (mis)fortunes of the Labor candidate, a hard-working, rather rotund chemist called Peter McIlwain.

Cook, at the time of the election, is held by the opposition Liberal party, but Labor is cautiously confident of winning this time. Film begins as McIlwain, seen to be on the left of the Labor Party, although his beliefs on such key items as nuclear weapons merely reflect the longstanding policies of the party which were overturned by Hawke in a successful effort to capture the middle-of-the-road vote, narrowly wins pre-selection over an urbane rep of the party's right.

From then on, the film suggests, McIlwain is virtually ostracized by the leaders of his own party; he only gets to meet the Prime Minister in an agonizingly embarrassing photo session, and Hawke breaks an appointment to visit the Cook electorate, which would, it's estimated, have helped attract swing voters owing to the Prime Minister's extraordinary popularity. "Democracy" is thus as much an analysis of factions within the Australian Labor Party as it is coverage of an election campaign.

The hard-working McIlwain, and his equally dedicated wife and family, slog away at attracting the voters via fundraising dinners, displays of posters all over the area, meetings with the public at shopping centers, and so on, all minutely observed by Tony Wilson's camera. Chase brings out the humor inherent in this microcosm of grassroots politics at work. There are quarrels among McIlwain's staff, and furstrations galore, before polling day and the sad realization of defeat.

This is bound to be a controversial film in Australia, since it was made by the government film production arm and implicitly criticizes the Prime Minister and his policies, supporting instead the traditional Labor policies which have, the film asserts by implication, become

eroded in recent years.

Overseas, the film should spark interest on its study of a would-be politician's doomed efforts to get himself elected. It's technically fine, though there's an overuse of music, often drowning out an already noisy soundtrack.—Strat.

The Karate Kid Part II
(COLOR)

Overlong, dumb sequel.

A Columbia Pictures release of a Jerry Weintraub production from Columbia-Delphi II Prods. Produced by Weintraub. Executive producer, R.J. Louis. Directed by John G. Avildsen. Stars Ralph Macchio, Noriyuki "Pat" Morita. Screenplay, Robert Mark Kamen, based on characters created by Kamen; camera (Deluxe color), James Crabe; editor, David Garfield, Jane Kurson, Avildsen; music, Bill Conti; production design, William J. Cassidy; art direction, William F. Matthews; set design, Jim Teegarden; set decoration, Lee Poll; costume design, Mary Malin; sound (Dolby), William J. Randall; associate producers, William J. Cassidy, Karen Trudy Rosenfelt, Susan E. Ekins; assistant director, Clifford C. Coleman; casting, Caro Jones. Reviewed at The Burbank Studios, Burbank, June 12, 1986. (MPAA Rating: PG.) Running time: 113 MINS.
Daniel ....Ralph Macchio
Miyagi...........Noriyuki "Pat" Morita
Yukie ....Nobu McCarthy
Sato...................Danny Kamekona
Chozen ....Yuji Okumoto
Kumiko.................Tamlyn Tomita

Hollywood — "The Karate Kid Part II" is a pokey and hokey sequel to the 1984 chop socky kidpic, which pulled in $41,700,000 in domestic rentals. Given the lack of terribly strong b.o. contenders at the moment, familiarity in this case should breed success.

Producer Jerry Weintraub has played it smart by assembling all the major creative talents from the first entry, and played it safe by not tampering at all with the tried-and-true elements.

Film literally picks up where the last one left off, with spunky teen Ralph Macchio winning a karate contest against no-good ruffians. Post-credit scene takes place in the parking lot minutes after the battle, with teach Noriyuki "Pat" Morita giving his unscrupulous opposing coach a final lesson he won't forget.

Informed that his father is gravely ill, Morita heads back to his native Okinawa, with Macchio in tow. His father, who soon dies, turns out to be the least of Morita's concerns.

Morita loved a young woman on the island, but left in deference to her arranged marriage to Sato. Latter, also a karate expert, has never forgiven Morita for backing out of a fight which would have determined who got the girl, and is determined to settle the matter once and for all with Morita back home.

In addition, Sato's nephew takes an instant disliking to Macchio and tries to take him on whenever possible. At such moments, Morita has an uncanny habit of appearing out of thin air to save the day, one of the film's numerous dumb devices.

As in the first installment, Robert Mark Kamen's script delivers any number of wise old Eastern homilies, and these are spoken with such authority and good humor by Morita (who was Oscar-nominated the first time out) that one tends to feel real good when he's around.

By contrast, anyone over the age of 18 is liable to start fidgeting when Macchio dominates the action, but then viewers beyond that advanced age are irrelevant with this film.

Given kids' attention spans, however, it's unimaginable why this simple little film was made to run nearly two hours. John G. Avildsen has directed the dialog scenes at an extremely leisurely pace, and has larded the picture with endless sunset and nature shots, as if he were trying to be David Lean. Ninety minutes would have been just fine.

Just when the film seems headed for the final credits, a major climactic fight scene is concocted to match the conclusion of the first picture. Action is okay until the very end, which is filmed in such tight close-up that viewer can't see the moves that win the bout.—*Cart.*

Legal Eagles
(COLOR)

Well-cast yuppie comedy should hit big.

A Universal Pictures release of a Northern Lights Enterprises production. Executive producers, Joe Medjuck, Michael C. Gross. Produced and directed by Ivan Reitman. Stars Robert Redford, Debra Winger, Daryl Hannah. Screenplay, Jim Cash, Jack Epps, Jr.; camera (Panavision, Technicolor), Laszlo Kovacs; editor, Sheldon Kahn, Pem Herring, William Gordean; music, Elmer Bernstein; production design, John DeCuir; art director, Ron Hobbs (L.A.), David Chapman (N.Y.); set decorator, Thomas L. Roysden (L.A.), Alan Hicks (N.Y.); set design, Peter J. Kelly, Carlos Cerrada, Steve Sardanis; sound (Dolby), Jim Webb, Crew Chamberlain; costumes, Albert Wolsky; assistant director, Peter Giuliano; additional photography, Bill Butler; special affects, Boss Film; casting, Deborah Lucchesi, Howard Feuer; associate producers, Sheldon Kahn, Arnold Glincher. Reviewed at Academy of Motion Pictures Arts & Sciences, Samuel Goldwyn theater, Beverly Hills, June 12, 1986. (MPAA Rating: PG.) Running time: **114 MINS.**

Tom Logan . . . . Robert Redford
Laura Kelly . . . . Debra Winger
Chelsea Deardon . . . . Daryl Hannah
Cavanaugh . . . . Brian Dennehy
Victor Taft . . . . Terence Stamp
Bower . . . . Steven Hill
Blanchard . . . . David Clennon
Forrester . . . . John McMartin
Jennifer Logan . . . . Jennie Dundas
Judge Dawkins . . . . Roscoe Lee Browne
Carol Freeman . . . . Christine Baranski
Barbara . . . . Sara Botsford

Hollywood — Producers bill "Legal Eagles" as a comedy thriller, but it's better described as a yup-

pie comedy. Loss of intrigue with a scattered plot involving art fraud and murder is made up for by an often witty, albeit lightweight dialog led by the ever-boyish star Robert Redford. Combination of his easygoing comedic performance as an astute assistant d.a. and scenes set in some very upscale Manhattan locales should add up to a winning verdict at the b.o.

Lavish production opens with charmer Redford as one of the d.a.'s office's winningest attorneys, Tom Logan, assigned to prosecute the daughter of a famous artist for trying to steal one of her dead father's paintings.

He faces the opposing counsel of Laura Kelly (Debra Winger), a court-appointed defense attorney known for daffy courtroom antics to get her clients off, like putting a dog on the witness stand.

It's when the burglary charges are suddenly dropped against the imbalanced defendant Chelsea Deardon (Daryl Hannah), a spacey performance artist who works out her father's arson death by acting out the horror in her SoHo loft before the uncomfortable Redford, that he becomes intrigued by her peculiar situation and decides to go over to Winger's side to discover why.

With "Legal Eagles," producer/director Ivan Reitman moves away from the genre he perfected in "Ghostbusters" to a more sophisticated level of comedy, though film has its share of gratuitous slapstick episodes (car chase, narrow escapes from deadly traps, a clumsy Redford who tapdances to cure insomnia, etc.).

Scripters Jim Cash and Jack Epps, Jr., whose only previously produced film is the simplistic but slick "Top Gun" (their Michael J. Fox-starrer "The Secret Of My Success" is currently filming), have created some cleverly-written scenes that expose the ironies of our venerated legal system.

They also have worked in, less successfully, almost too many twists in the plot to incorporate the corrupt dealings of a high-brow gallery owner, Victor Taft (Terence Stamp) and his unctuous ways of doing business in the sale of the world's greatest artworks.

Winger and Redford work well as an attorney team, but in true yuppie form, become more friends attracted by each others' professional acumen than by each others' bodies.

That's not to say there's no spark in their bantering or tension created for the audience to want them to get together in the end, but they just don't have the electricity of Katharine Hepburn and Spencer Tracy in "Adam's Rib" or Myrna Loy and William Powell in the "Thin Man" series.

Roles represent a refreshing

departure for Winger in a strong, self-assured part and a perfect choice for Redford playing Redford. Hannah is the self-same vulnerable and stunning beauty that she was in "Splash."

Production notes list that real art by Picasso, Miro, Warhol, deKooning, Dubuffet, Calder, etc., was used in the sets, and not fakes.

Production designer John De-Cuir, art directors Ron Hobbs (in L.A.) and David Chapman (in N.Y.) and set decorators Thomas L. Roysden (in L.A.) and Alan Hicks (in N.Y.) have a feel for the New York art scene, from the tony high-tech East Side galleries to the new-wave, off-beat lower Manhattan artists' world. Credit also to set designers Peter J. Kelly, Carlos Cerrada and Steve Sardanis.

Special note also should be made to terrific pyrotechnics (special effects) by Boss Film which make it look like all those million-dollar works were going up in flames when we know very well they weren't.
—*Brit.*

Applause, Applause ...
(Ovation)
(SOVIET-COLOR)

A Lenfilm Studios production. Directed by Viktor Buturlin. Stars Lyudmila Gurchenko. Screenplay, Viktor Merezhko; camera (Sovcolor), Vladimir Vasilyev; art director, Alexei Rudyakov; music, Alexander Morozov. Reviewed at Mandarin theater, Sydney (Soviet Film Week), April 30, 1986. Running time: **74 MINS.**

Lera Goncharova . . . Lyudmila Gurchenko
Shevtsov . . . . Oleg Tabakov
Vadim . . . . Alexander Filippenko
Polina . . . . Olga Volkova

Sydney — An unalloyed showcase for one of the Soviet cinema's most popular actresses, the versatile Lyudmila Gurchenko, "Applause, Applause ..." is a slight showbiz story about a musical star who longs to be accepted in dramatic roles.

Virtually plotless, the pic manages to include scenes that demonstrate the range and energy of its star, whether belting out a song and dance routine against a spectacularly ugly decor, or, in austere makeup, playing a gritty, dramatic scene in which a middle-aged woman bares her soul. Gurchenko, who's been popular since her debut in the musical, "Carnival Nights," has already been seen in strong dramatic roles in such films as Nikita Mikhalkov's "Five Evenings" and Andrei Konchalovsky's "Siberiade," but this must be a rare instance in Soviet production of a pic created specially for its star.

Nobody else really gets a look in, though Oleg Tabakov makes the director of the dramatic film Gurchenko yearns to appear in an amusingly cornball character, and

Olga Volkova, in the Eve Arden role, is fun as his loyal, cynical girl Friday.

The Sovcolor print caught was below par, but otherwise pic is technically adequate. This is the first feature of director Viktor Buturlin, and won the prize for best first film in the 1985 Soviet Film Awards in Minsk, though it bears a 1984 copyright date.—*Strat.*

Vamp
(COLOR)

Sensational horror comedy has plenty of bite.

A New World Pictures release, in association with Balcor Film Investors, of a Donald P. Borchers production. Produced by Borchers. Directed by Richard Wenk. Screenplay, Wenk, from story by Wenk, Borchers; camera (Metrocolor), Elliot Davis; editor, Marc Grossman; additional editing, Alan Holzman; music, Jonathan Elias; title song, Elias, Grace Jones, sung by Jones; sound, Mark Ulano, Jan Brodin; production design, Alan Roderick-Jones; special makeup effects, Greg Cannom, Pamela Westmore; special visual effects, Apogee Inc.; assistant director, Matia Karrell, Betsy Pollack; production manager, Mario Davis; costumes, Betty Pecha Madden; stunt coordinator, Dar Robinson; casting, Linda Francis. Reviewed at Loews New York Twin theater, N.Y., June 13, 1986. (No MPAA Rating.) Running time: **94 MINS.**

Keith . . . . Chris Makepeace
Vic . . . . Sandy Baron
A.J. Robert Rusler
Amaretto . . . . Dedee Pfeiffer
Duncan . . . . Gedde Watanabe
Katrina . . . . Grace Jones
Snow . . . . Billy Drago
Vlad . . . . Brad Logan
Cimarron . . . . Lisa Lyon

"Vamp" is an extremely imaginative horror film styled as jet black comedy. True test when New World releases the feature July 25 is whether the picture's violent approach will limit it to a loyal horror audience or extend to more faint-of-heart souls seeking comic diversion.

Debuting filmmaker Richard Wenk displays a mature gift for sleight-of-hand, opening the film with the deceptively familiar format of a teenage sex comedy. Fraternity pledges Keith (Chris Makepeace) and A.J. (Robert Rusler) agree to find a stripper for the frat party that night, as part of their initiation duties. They team up with a rich oriental kid on campus, Duncan (Gedde Watanabe), who is desperate for friendship and, more significantly, has the car to transport them to town.

Upon their arrival in the big city, film quickly makes a permanent detour into The Twilight Zone when their car skids and comes out of a lengthy spin with bright daylight suddenly turned to spooky nighttime. Trio heads for the After Dark Club, a sleazy strip joint managed by Vic (Sandy Baron) with an ominous bouncer named Vlad (Brad Logan). Keith is befriended by a cute blond waitress named Amaretto, actually Allison (Dedee Pfeiffer), but both he and A.J.'s real interest is in the smashing black stripper Katrina (Grace Jones).

It turns out that the club is a den of vampires (a cute gag has Vic making like "Dracula" 's Renfield character, eating large cockroaches out of the bowl usually containing after-dinner mints). A.J. literally succumbs to Katrina's wiles and turns into a most unusual, ambivalent vampire still loyal to Keith but with uncontrollable urges that come with the territory. In trying to escape from the series of horrors, Keith and Amaretto also have to deal with a violent punk gang made up of albino-type men and black women, led by the sinister Snow (Billy Drago). Through all the mayhem, Duncan spends the entire evening partying, his eyes glued on the succession of strippers performing at the club.

Like its recent predecessors in the vampire comedy genre ("Love At First Bite," "Nocturna," "Dracula Blows His Cool" and "Once Bitten"), "Vamp" makes the connection between swinging night life and dark terrors lurking beneath the glamorous surface. In this regard, picture benefits immensely from the casting of disco star turned actress Grace Jones as the leader of the vampires. Jones' truly exotic dance number (featuring strange makeup and a male torso prop chair designed by Keith Haring) is an outré showstopper. As a deadly monster she has no dialog in the film, but expresses herself sexily in several scary scenes, resulting in gore effects which will delight horror fans but probably turn off mainstream audiences. Pamela Westmore and Greg Cannom's makeup effects for Jones and the other vampires are effectively frightening.

Beyond Jones' showy appearance, cast is very good, with the picture stolen by Robert Rusler. Maintaining his fast-talking, precocious ability to cope with any situation even after he becomes a vampire, Rusler perfectly mocks the genre's clichés, aided by sharp dialog by writer-director Wenk. Makepeace and Pfeiffer are pleasant leads and Sandy Baron is terrific as the Italianate emcee/night club owner/-vampire whose dream for the past 75 years in the boondocks has been to make it to Las Vegas. Watanabe (costar of "Gung Ho") is immensely likable as the little man on campus who just wants to be one of the guys.

Elliot Davis' lighting, favoring spooky purple and green pastel light sources, serves to stylize the proceedings into the realm of fantasy and Jonathan Elias' rhythmic score is another big plus. —Lor.

Nebyvalshina
(Believe It Or Not)
(SOVIET-COLOR)

A Lenfilm Studios production. Written and directed by Sergei Ovcharov. Camera (color), Valery Fedosov; editor, I. Tarsanova; music, I. Matzievsky; art direction, Victor Amelchekov. Reviewed at Tashkent Film Festival (market), May 23, 1986. Running time: 83 MINS.
Neznam . . . . Aleksandr Kuznetzov
Soldier . . . . Aleksei Buldakov
Bobyl . . . . Sergei Bekhterev

Tashkent — A marvelous children's offering, "Nebyvalshina" (which can be translated "Believe It Or Not" or "Impossible Things") illustrates a series of Russian folk tales, accompanied with folk songs but very little dialog. Lensed well and simply by Sergei Ovcharov, pic is charming and a bit mysterious, often recalling silent comedy.

The story is hard to trace, since a number of folk tales get woven together and the characters are the main source of reference. A country yokel decides to get married to a peasant girl, but he naively thinks kissing her on the cheek is all there is to a roll in the hay. She angrily bars herself in the house, and he takes to the road, where he meets another stock character, a clever old soldier who can solve any probelm that comes up.

They meet an inventor, who is intent on fashioning a flying machine, but his Leonardo-like efforts only stir up the populace and get him beaten up by police and disappointed locals alike. Back at home, meanwhile, a shopkeeper's assistant who styles himself a ladies' man serenades the young hero's wife.

Director Ovcharov is obviously a fan of silent films. Parts of "Believe It Or Not" are pure slapstick; others hark back to masters like Méliès (like the wonderful scene where the simpleton and the soldier get catapulted into an underground hell, replete with naked women boiling in pots whose lids are held down by monsters). There is even a parody of Alexander Nevsky's battle on the ice, in which the local populace wearing white gas masks beats off a foreign invasion. Lensing by Valery Fedosov is imaginative and striking; Victor Amelchekov's art direction often amazing. —Yung.

Reis 222
(Flight 222)
(SOVIET-COLOR)

A Lenfilm Studios production. Written and directed by Sergei Mikaelyan. Stars Larisa Polyakova, Aleksandr Babnov. Camera (color), Sergei Astakhov; music, Sergei Banevitch; art direction, Elizaveta Urlina. Review at Tashkent Film Festival (market), May 23, 1986. Running time: 120 MINS.

Irina . . . . Larisa Polyakova
Strelkov . . . . Aleksandr Babanov
Misha . . . . Aleksandr Kolesnikov
Zhigalin . . . . Aleksandr Ivanov
Kurzanov . . . . Nikolai Alyoshin
Bekkeris . . . . Vilnis Paulovitch

Tashkent — An unabashed commercial offering, this Russian political actioner is chiefly curious in presenting the "other side" of the familar Yank/British thriller in the "White Nights" vein. Here the guys in the black hats are from Immigration, the FBI, and State Department (for film's purposes, no great distinctions are drawn). Though meant to be a tense, taut actioner, "Flight 222" doesn't approach the suspense levels of a tv thriller, making it a curiosity item without punch.

One problem is there are so many potentially leading characters the audience doesn't know for whom to cheer. The obvious choice would be Irina (Larisa Polyakova), young member of an ice dance group on tour in New York, if she wasn't so colorless and unemotional. When Irina hears her husband, an athlete, has defected and wants her to join him, she is given hasty orders by the embassy to get on the next plane for Moscow, and there she sits moping for the rest of the picture.

At this point Immigration officers decide to detain the plane at Kennedy, claiming Irina isn't leaving of her own free will, and gradually a regular diplomatic incident builds, with Russian and American officialdom squaring off in the airport waiting room. Aboard the plane a state of siege reigns; Yank passengers get off, while the Russians melt into a unanimous patriotic front in support of Irina.

Pic's main interest lies in the way it directly confronts the delicate issue of political asylum in the U.S., and surprisingly, it's more broadminded about the business than you might think. The Soviet's concern is to keep a defection from turning into an anti-Russian propaganda campaign. The State Department's concern is to make it do just that. Between the absurd negotiations going on in the waiting room and Yank agitators outside the plane chanting things like, "Man and wife must stay together!" pic takes on an air of unreality that can only be enjoyed as kitsch. — Yung.

Flight Of The Spruce Goose
(COLOR)

Earthbound love story.

A Michael Hausman/Filmhaus release. Produced by Michael Hausman. Directed by Lech Majewski. Screenplay, Majewski, Chris Burdza; camera (color), Jerzy Zielinski; editor, Corky O'Hara; music, Henri Seroka. Reviewed at Egyptian Theater, Seattle Film Festival, June 6, 1986. (No MPAA Rating.) Running time: 97 MINS.
Adam . . . . Dan O'Shea
Terry . . . . Jennifer Runyon
Mother . . . . Karen Black
Friend . . . . Dennis Christopher
Also with: George A. Romero.

Seattle — This is an obsessional love story, filmed in Pittsburgh, that has such believability problems it never quite gets off the ground. The story is an old one: working-class boy falls in love with glamorous rich girl against the advice of parents and friends. It has some original moments on the way to a far-fetched finish.

Producer Michael Hausman ("Amadeus," "Places In The Heart") has assembled a crew of first-timers, including Polish-born director Lech Majewski and star Dan O'Shea and they provide both the charm and problems with "Spruce Goose." Commercial appeal seems limited, given a downbeat second reel.

Adam is a young coal-miner going nowhere in the depressed industry. He meets ambitious model Terry when she comes to the mine to shoot an ad layout. Adam falls for the blond and begins an impossible pursuit. He is given the dustoff by Terry's mother, icily played by Karen Black, and her sleazy agent, who is doing porno videos on the side.

Realizing he can't win, Adam kidnaps Terry and drives across the country to Hollywood, where they tour the Spruce Goose and dream of a ne life. The Spruce Goose, which flew once, works as a metaphor of the love story.

All of this is given a strangely European touch by director Majewski, especially in the bleak work and home scenes. There is a class difference between the doomed lovers that seems just a little too "old world" for America.

Dan O'Shea is a sad-faced newcomer, difficult to like, who struggles to win the audience, Jennifer Runyon is just right as the out-of-reach dream girl and Black seems wasted in a one-note performance as the mother who cold-shoulders Adam.

Location photography makes good use of the Pittsburgh locale, especially the newcomer-downtown sections, contrasted with the dying coal fields. Obnoxious rock score adds nothing but irritation. Ace horror director and Pittsburgh native George A. Romero has a cameo. —Magg.

Ruthless People
(COLOR)

Hilarious black comedy looms as a summer blockbuster.

A Buena Vista Distribution release of a Touchstone Films presentation, in association with Silver Screen Partners II, of a Wagner/-Lancaster production. Produced by Michael Peyser. Executive producers, Richard Wagner, Joanna Lancaster, Walter Yetnikoff. Directed by Jim Abrahams, David Zucker, Jerry Zucker. Screenplay, Dale Launer; camera (Deluxe color), Jan DeBont; editor, Arthur Schmidt; film editor, Gib Jaffe; music, Michel Colombier; art direction, Donald Woodruff, visual consultant, Lilly Kilvert; set design, William Teegarden; set decoration, Anne McCulley; costume design, Rosanna Norton; sound (Dolby), Thomas D. Causey; assistant director, Bill Beasley; animation sequence produced by Sally Cruikshank; casting, Ellen Chenoweth. Reviewed at the Village Theater, W. L.A., June 18, 1986. (MPAA Rating: R.) Running time: **93 MINS.**
Sam Stone . . . . Danny DeVito
Barbara Stone . . . . Bette Midler
Ken Kessler . . . . Judge Reinhold
Sandy Kessler . . . . Helen Slater
Carol . . . . Anita Morris
Earl . . . . Bill Pullman
Police Commissioner . William G. Schilling
Lt. Bender . . . . Art Evans
Lt. Walters . . . . Clarence Felder
Bedroom killer . . . . J.E. Freeman

Hollywood — ''Ruthless People'' is a hilariously venal comedy that promises to be the b.o. smash of the summer. Dazzlingly fresh and modern variation on ''The Ransom Of Red Chief,'' about a kidnaped harridan whose rich husband won't pay for her return, overflows with deliciously black comic treats. Though quite sophisticated, it is pitched just right to include everyone in on the joke. In a way a companion piece to Touchstone's recent hit, ''Down And Out In Beverly Hills,'' new pic is infinitely more corrosive and will make even more money.

Every element in the film works splendidly, beginning with Sally Cruikshank's wacky animated title sequence and Danny DeVito's terrific opening monolog, which deftly establishes the setup and his own crass, heartless personality.

In short, impoverished couple Judge Reinhold and Helen Slater kidnap Bel-Air princess Bette Midler because her mercenary husband, played by DeVito, has ripped off — and made a fortune from — Slater's design for spandex miniskirts.

DeVito, who wanted to get rid of Midler anyway so he could set up shop with his voluptuous mistress (Anita Morris), is thrilled with this turn of events, and steadfastly refuses to pay the ever-decreasing ransom, although he plays the bereft husband act to the hilt for the benefit of the police.

There is much, much more to it than that, as screenwriter Dale Launer cleverly builds twist upon complication to a point where prac-tically everyone in the cast is writhing in frustration and mystification as they wonder whether their latest opportunistic scheme is going to work.

Theme of unbridled greed has, of course, been dealt with countless times in both comedy and drama, but treatment here works so well because the crazed characters are tied so skillfully to the contemporary social scene.

DeVito has built a palace for himself that is the latest in high-priced vulgarity; post-modernist furniture abounds, and the astute art direction by Donald Woodruff, with undoubted input from visual consultant Lilly Kilvert, takes the soft satire of ''Down And Out In Beverly Hills'' to an acid extreme.

For her part, Midler, when first glimpsed, is an absolute fright who looks like a cross between Cyndi Lauper and Divine. After terrorizing her kidnapers, she embarks upon an energetic self-improvement program, and not surprisingly emerges with the upper hand.

It is possible that some viewers might be put off by the unrelenting selfishness of the characters and thereby accuse the film of irredeemable cynicism. But only the truly thick-headed could fail to grasp that the picture is sending up the attitudes of the crazed characters and, once clued in, audiences should revel in the madness.

Actually, film is not uproarious from beginning to end, but it is constantly amusing, and is so satisfying because it is loaded with plot. Launer's script is intricate and beautifully constructed, and in an age when many pictures can't even muster anything deserving of being called a plot, this looks like a major achievement.

The tremendous number of funny, rude bits come as no surprise from the ''Airplane''-''Top Secret'' team of Jim Abrahams and David and Jerry Zucker, but what is new is that the film is very well directed by any standard. In league with ace lenser Jan DeBont, they have come up with a beautiful style of pastel vulgarity, in which the design and lighting conjure up a 1980s equivalent of a Frank Tashlin picture.

Arthur Schmidt and Gib Jaffe's cutting is right on the money, as is the 93-minute running time, and musical score, which features some high-priced talent, including Mick Jagger on the title song, also contributes considerably to the polished, hip tone of the proceedings.

DeVito carries the picture, Midler steals it and a particularly fine supporting turn is delivered by William G. Schilling, as a police commissioner whose little dalliance threatens to topple his standing as a pillar of the community.—*Cart.*

Piaobo Qiyu
(Strange Encounters)
(CHINESE-COLOR)

A China Film Corp. release of a Shanghai Film Studios production. Produced by Zhang Ianmin. Directed by Yu Benzheng. Screenplay, Ai Wu, from the book ''Going To The South;'' camera (Widescreen, color), Peng Enli; music, Yang Shaolin. Reviewed at Sydney Film Festival, June 18, 1986. Running time: **96 MINS.**
The Wanderer . . . . Wang Shihuai
Wildcat . . . . Xue Shujie
Bandit Chief . . . . Li Wei
Knight Errant . . . . :. . . . . . Liu Xinyi
    Also with: Lu Qing (Ghost brother), Wa Ling (Wife,) Yuo (Despot).

Sydney — A handful of excellent, trail-blazing Chinese films has emerged at film fests over the last year, but ''Strange Encounters,'' actually made in 1982, isn't one of them. It's a handsomely produced adventure story, set in 1925 in the south of the country, and tells a familiar tale of bandits in opposition to the rule of a local despot.

Focus of attention is on an itinerant student who stumbles on the bandit gang and is virtually kidnaped by them. He's attracted to the daughter of the gang's leader, but she's also wooed by a lone bandit, a swashbuckling type who always seems to be in the right place at the right time.

Action scenes are either perfunctory or nonexistent (two major plot developments, involving lethal action, take place off-screen), and the morality of the characters is, to say the least, quaint: the student frets that the bandit chief killed his wife years earlier, but it's explained to him (in flashback) that he only killed her after she suffered rape. That fact seems to make it quite all right.

Pic's main asset is the handsome location photography. —*Strat.*

Running Scared
(COLOR)

Rowdy action comedy with topnotch teaming of Hines & Crystal.

A UA/MGM Distribution release from MGM Entertainment Co. of a Turman-Foster Co. production. Produced by David Foster, Lawrence Turman. Executive producer, Peter Hyams. Directed by Hyams. Stars Gregory Hines, Billy Crystal. Screenplay, Gary DeVore, Jimmy Huston; story by DeVore; camera (Panavision, Metrocolor), Hyams; editor, James Mitchell; music, Rod Temperton; production design, Albert Brenner; set decoration, George P. Gaines; sound (Dolby), Gene Cantamessa; associate producer, Jonathan A. Zimbert; stunt coordination, Carey Loftin, Bill Couch Sr.; assistant director, Jim Van Wyck; casting, Penny Perry. Reviewed at the MGM Studios, Culver City, Calif., June 18, 1986. (MPAA Rating: R.) Running time: **106 MINS.**
Ray Hughes . . . . Gregory Hines
Danny Costanzo . . . . Billy Crystal
Frank . . . . Steven Bauer
Anna Costanzo . . . . Darlanne Fluegel
Snake . . . . Joe Pantoliano
Captain Logan . . . . Dan Hedaya
Tony . . . . Jonathan Gries
Maryann . . . . Tracy Reed
Julio Gonzales . . . . Jimmy Smits
Vinnie . . . . John DiSanti
Ace . . . . Larry Hankin

Hollywood — Set in dead of winter in Chicago, ''Running Scared'' is fine, fast-moving summer entertainment. Ultra-hip cop picture, shot in gritty style by Peter Hyams, plays like a combination of ''Beverly Hills Cop'' and ''Hill Street Blues,'' and should rack up some good grosses for UA/MGM (film and press materials mention only MGM as distributor).

Gregory Hines and Billy Crystal are undercover cops too cool for words, guys who risk their necks by the hour without a hint of fear, chase women together at night and feel smugly superior to their cohorts on the force. They goof off and goof up on occasion, but they leave little doubt that they consider themselves top dogs.

As elsewhere, drugs keep flowing into Chicago as through open floodgates, and Hines and Crystal are concerned particularly with aborting the career of aspiring Spanish godfather Jimmy Smits, a ruthless thug whose favorite film undoubtedly would be ''Scarface.''

The good boys and bad boys come close to knocking each other off several times and, after a brief vacation in ''Miami Vice'' land (during which the film loses a fair amount of its tension), the cops return to put the screws to their nemesis.

Plot is no more original or eventful than an average police tv show, so it must sink or swim on the moment-by-moment cleverness of the dialog and the behavioral talents of Hines and Crystal. Fortunately, these elements prove formidable.

Nonstop banter between the two stars is rowdy, intimate, natural and often very funny. Within the contrivance of the buddy-buddy format, the men seem like real soul mates who have been together for years and still manage to maintain mutual respect and competition in equal measure. Pairing of Hines and Crystal works exceedingly well; former has never seemed this engaging and self-confident onscreen, and latter is tremendously likable and energetic in his bigscreen reentry after starring in the 1978 flop ''Rabbit Test.''

Well-paced pic is punctuated with the usual shootouts, confrontations with superiors, street talk and low-life bad guys that come with the territory, as well as the inevitable stops-out climax in which hundreds of rounds of ammo are discharged. Hyams keeps most of it fresh, including the action ending, staged within one of Chicago's latest architectural spectacles, the cavernous, glass-enclosed Illinois State Building.

By contrast, a self-consciously rousing chase scene featuring cars racing for miles on the elevated train tracks comes off as faintly ridiculous, and sometimes sloppily cut to boot.

Bouncing back from "2010," Hyams deserves credit not only for getting his actors into such a sympatico groove, but for his sharp, naturalistic lensing on a strong variety of locations.

All other tech contributions are exellent, and casting is notable down to the smallest parts.—*Cart.*

The Perils Of P.K.
(COLOR)

Old jokes spliced together.

A Joseph Green Pictures release of a P.K. Co. production. Executive producer, Naura Hayden. Produced by Sheila MacRae; coproducer, Marge Cowan. Directed by Joseph Green. Stars Hayden. Screenplay, Hayden; camera (color), Paul Glickman; editor, Hayden; music and lyrics, Hayden; music arranged/conducted by Dunn Pearson; sound, Laszlo Haverland; associate producers, Green, Sam E. Beller. Reviewed at Oak Park Plaza theater, Kansas City, June 6, 1986. (MPAA Rating: R.) Running time: 90 MINS.
With: Naura Hayden, Kaye Ballard, Sheila MacRae, Heather MacRae, Larry Storch, Norma Storch, Dick Shawn, Sammy Davis Jr., Altovise Davis, Louise Lasser, Prof. Irwin Corey, Virginia Graham, Jackie Mason, Joey Heatherton, Anne Meara, Al Nuti, Mike Murphy.

Kansas City — This indie film classes largely as a hobby project of actress and health-book author Naura Hayden, who rounded up enough investors to total a $1,500,000 production fund and a bevy of her showbiz friends to people a "cast." They apparently have some fun visualizing a string of tired jokes, but aside from a smidgeon of insider interest, as an entry for general exhibition it comes up nought.

The faint storyline has Hayden as a faded screen queen, reduced to bumping and grinding at stag smokers, but still yearning to make it back to the big time. She checks out her fantasies with a shrink, Dick Shawn, and each episode segues into a flashback of her once florid career and/or some wacky interludes in the psychiatrist's office. There Larry Storch, Kaye Ballard, Sheila MacRae, Prof. Irwin Corey and the other names at random parade in and out while pictorializing the ancient jokes.

Typical is the one about the man wearing ladies silk panties because his wife found them in the glove compartment, plus a score or more of that ilk. The author, present at the preem, claimed a mixture of old and new jokes, but winnowing out the new is not for the unskilled.

The story veers off to Florida and Argentina for a time, as the film queen must go there to negotiate with the number one male star to play opposite her in her next film. The fantasies take her back to the psychiatrist's office, and a final ironic touch has all going back to the nuthouse whence they had escaped to make this picture.

The rating is barely R, based on a brief incident of Hayden in the partial nude and freer use of naughty language, but no violence or bloodletting. The title refers to the perils of Patricia Kathleen, the screen name of the former star.

A cult status has been mentioned, but even that is a long shot as it is doubtful if the film will get enough screen exposure for any prospective cultists to recognize the potential. Even for the in crowd, the vaudeville-like gags and punch lines do not have the makings of a marketable film. —*Quin.*

Labyrinth
(COLOR)

Disastrous fantasy from Henson & Lucas is a costly bore.

A Tri-Star Pictures release of a Henson Associates and Lucasfilm Ltd. presentation. Produced by Eric Rattray. Executive producer, George Lucas. Executive supervising producer, David Lazer. Directed by Jim Henson. Stars David Bowie, Jennifer Connelly. Screenplay, Terry Jones, from a story by Dennis Lee, Henson; camera (J-D-C Widescreen, Rank Fujicolor), Alex Thomson; editor, John Grover; music, Trevor Jones; songs, David Bowie; production design, Elliot Scott; art direction, Roger Cain, Peter Howitt, Michael White, Terry Ackland-Snow; conceptual design/creature design, Brian Froud; director of choreography and puppet movement, Cheryl McFadden; puppeteer coordinator, Brian Henson; costume design, Froud, Ellis Flyte; sound (Dolby), Peter Sutton; special effects supervisor, George Gibbs; chief animatronic design, Tony Dunsterville; assistant director, Ken Baker; associate producer, Martin Baker. Reviewed at MGM screening room, Culver City, Calif., June 19, 1986. (MPAA Rating: PG.) Running time: 101 MINS.
Jareth . . . . David Bowie
Sarah . . . . Jennifer Connelly
Toby . . . . Toby Froud
Stepmother . . . . Shelley Thompson
Father . . . . Christopher Malcolm
Fairy . . . . Natalie Finland
Hoggle . . . . Shari Weiser, Brian Henson
Henson (voice)
Ludo . . . . Ron Mueck
Rob Mills (voice)
Didymus . . . . . . Dave Goetz, David Barclay
David Shaughnessy (voice)
The worm . . . . Karen Prell
Timothy Bateson (voice)

Hollywood — An array of bizarre creatures and David Bowie can't save "Labyrinth" from being a crashing bore. Directed and conceived by muppeteer Jim Henson, fantasy characters have a sameness that is deadly even for the targeted moppet audience. Filmgoers are bound to get lost in this "Labyrinth."

Characters created by Henson and his team are terminally cute with no real charm or texture to capture the imagination. They become annoying rather than endearing and after a while they all look and sound the same, some are just a little bigger than the others.

What is even more disappointing is the failure of the film on a story level. Pic opens promisingly when young Sarah (Jennifer Connelly) embarks on an adventure to recover her baby stepbrother from the clutches of the Goblin King (David Bowie) who has taken the child for some unknown reason to his kingdom.

From the start, story seems to be shooting for a "Wizard Of Oz" and "Alice In Wonderland" feeling, but soon loses its way and never comes close to archetypal myths and fears of great fairy tales. Instead it's an unconvincing coming of age saga in which the young Sarah tests her own power.

What's seriously lacking here that great tales have is a sense of dread and menace to the ordeal. "Labyrinth" is too cute ever to be dangerous. The result is a silly and flat excursion to a land you can't wait to leave. As it is, film is almost unwatchable and an insult to kids' intelligence and imagination.

Considering the talent involved, the utter failure of "Labyrinth" is surprising. George Lucas acted as executive producer and either didn't have much to do with it or his instincts for cutesiness got the better of him here.

The adaptability of Henson's creatures to film is not really the problem either since he has done credible jobs artistically and commercially with his Muppet pictures. In "Labyrinth," however, the technique seems more limited than ever and locations and production design fail to stir the eye or the mind.

Where things may have gone hopelessly, irrevocably wrong is in the conception which tried to mix live action with puppet characters. As the Goblin King, Bowie seems a fish out of water — too serious to be campy, too dumb to be serious. He looks intriguing in his long shaggy mane and contributes a few interesting, if out of place songs, but, most important, he doesn't seem to be having much fun.

Poor Jennifer Connelly, so lovely in "Once Upon A Time In America," must endure a hundred hardships along the yellow brick road, not the least of which is the script by Terry Jones (of Monty Python) which makes her seem stiff and childish. Unfortunately she must keep going to the end while those in the audience can catch a few winks along the way. —*Jagr.*

Psycho III
(COLOR)

Fear strikes out.

A Universal Pictures release. Produced by Hilton A. Green. Directed by Anthony Perkins. Stars Perkins. Screenplay, Charles Edward Pogue, based on characters created by Robert Bloch; camera (color), Bruce Surtees; editor, David Blewitt; music, Carter Burwell; production design, Henry Bumstead; set decoration, Mickey S. Michaels; sound (Dolby), Jerry Jost; special makeup design and development, Michael Westmore; associate producer, Donald E. Zepfel; assistant director, Gary Daigler; casting, Nancy Taylor. Reviewed at the Writers Guild Theater, Beverly Hills, June 26, 1986. (MPAA Rating: R.) Running time: 96 MINS.
Norman Bates . . . . Anthony Perkins
Maureen . . . . Diana Scarwid
Duane . . . . Jeff Fahey
Tracy . . . . Roberta Maxwell
Sheriff Hunt . . . . Hugh Gillin
Myrna . . . . Lee Garlington
Statler . . . . Robert Alan Browne

Hollywood — A few amusing little notions are stretched to the point of diminishing returns in "Psycho III." Latest installment in the adventures of everybody's favorite psychopath, Norman Bates, has its moments — about 20 minutes' worth — but the rest is filler in which the filmmakers gamely but futilely try to breathe new life into a tired body. "Psycho II" generated $15,800,000 in domestic film rentals in 1983, and this one undoubtedly will fall short of that against heavy competition in midsummer release.

Opening sequence is a full-fledged homage to Alfred Hitchcock's "Vertigo" and helps set the comic, in-joke tone of the rest of the picture. Unhappy novice Diana Scarwid is all set to jump from a church belltower but, in an effort to save her, one of the nuns falls to her death instead.

Scarwid flees in distress, is given a ride through the desert by aspiring musician Jeff Fahey, and where should the unlikely and unsuspecting duo wind up but the Bates Motel, where Norman is trying to mind his own business after, as seen in flashback from the last picture, killing the woman (Claudia Bryar) who was creating mayhem while claiming to be the real Mrs. Bates.

Fahey takes a job as assistant manager of the motel, while Scarwid tries to recover from her traumatic experience, but slowly becomes attracted to Norman, who himself is upsettingly entranced by this young lady. To a great extent, Norman's interest seems to stem from the fact that she's a blond, just like the original film's Janet Leigh, and is staying in room number one. He finally becomes genuinely fond of her and even shares a love scene with her, only to see his mother fixation get the better of him and ruin his big chance at happiness.

The visits of a couple of bimbos

to the motel provide the opportunities for two bloody kitchen knife murders, and the two most famous killings from "Psycho" — those of Leigh and Martin Balsam — are given twists in major scenes here. In one gruesome but amusing sequence, Scarwid is found in the bathtub having just slit her wrists. The next day she apologizes to Norman, saying "I guess I did leave the bathroom a mess," to which Norman drily quips, "I've seen it worse."

This sort of playing around with the "Psycho" legend is fun for awhile, but the whole enterprise is dependent almost entirely upon self-referential incidents and attitudes for its effect, and it eventually becomes wearying. One can take only so much agonizing over the paralyzing effects of mother love and religious hangups, and doing variations on the original "Psycho" murders leaves only so much room to maneuver.

Main pleasure of the picture stems from Anthony Perkins' amusing and clearly self-amused performance in his patented role. Every little quirk, raised eyebrow and hesitation has been considered well and timed for generally comic effect, and the in-crowd looking for a campy time spiked by a few gory thrills could be well satisfied.

In his behind-the-camera debut, Perkins does an adequate job, but his occasional attempts at visual bravado are undercut mildly by the threadbare look of the proceedings; budget was obviously kept to a minimum. Other actors acquit themselves in okay fashion.

Ending once again leaves the door open for another sequel, but Norman Bates clearly needs another rest at this point. Perhaps when Perkins is an old man, he could return and do something really intersting with both Norman and Mrs. Bates, but the Bates Motel will probably remain closed for some time. —*Cart.*

Floodstage
(COLOR-16m)

Interesting indie effort.

A Spring Films release. Produced and directed by David Dawkins. Screenplay, Dawkins; camera (color, 16m); Wade Hanks; editor, Dawkins; sound, Joe Brennan; art direction, Gregory Frank; costume design, Lois Simbach; production supervisor, Avery Crounse. Reviewed at Mango Preview screening room, N.Y., June 19, 1986. (No MPAA Rating.) Running time: **80 MINS.**
Lenny . . . . .David Dawkins
Pinky . . . . .Patience Pierce
Merrit . . . . .Lenard Petit
Cookie . . . . .Gregory Frank
Faye . . . . .Deborah Barham
Mona . . . . .Diane Brown
Red . . . . .David Jaffe
Marty . . . . .Marty Rossip
Maggie . . . . .Joanne Zonis
Narrator . . . . .Roger Rabb

"Floodstage" is a quirky low-budgeter centered on the relationships between members of a struggling show troupe that travels down the Mississippi River each summer by raft. The film is a unique blend of narrative and documentary elements reportedly lensed on a shoestring $33,000. Though technically rough and slow getting started, it succeeds in generating more interest in its story and characters than many pics costing 10 times as much.

Told through the eyes of a narrator who observes the unfolding events as a member of the ragtag revue's small band, tale concerns the arrival of new member Merrit and the growing tension that results from his increasing involvement with Pinky, the sultry longtime girlfriend of Lenny, the show's director.

Much of the footage is performance related as the troupe gamely puts on evening shows in various river towns despite worsening financial straits. Heavy rains keep away crowds and make river travel dangerous, adding to the pressures facing the group as things heat up between Merrit and Pinky.

Abundance of handheld camerawork and use of actual audiences and situations root the film in a docu-like reality. The story is as meandering as the river at times, however, it does build to an effective climax. River scenes provide a pleasant backdrop, and Patience Pierce as Pinky is an alluring presence.

Filmmaker David Dawkins is to be commended for the final product, which, though facing no strong b.o. prospects, stands as an interesting eddy in the currents of fiilmmaking. — *Roy.*

About Last Night
(COLOR)

Okay comedy in surface look at relationships.

A Tri-Star Pictures release of an Arnold Stiefel and Brett/Oken presentation from Tri-Star-Delphi IV & V Prods. Produced by Jason Brett, Stuart Oken. Executive producer, Arnold Stiefel. Directed by Edward Zwick. Stars Rob Lowe. Screenplay, Tim Kazurinsky, Denise DeClue, based on the play "Sexual Perversity In Chicago" by David Mamet; camera (Metrocolor), Andrew Dintenfass; editor, Harry Keramidas; music, Miles Goodman; production design, Ida Random; art director, William Elliott; set decorator, Chris Butler; set designer, Beverli Eagan; costumes, Deborah L. Scott; sound (Dolby), Jacques Nosco; assistant director, Allan Wertheim; associate producer, E. Darrell Hallenbeck; casting, Gail Eisenstadt. Reviewed at Coronet Theater, Westwood, Calif., June 19, 1986. (MPAA Rating: R.) Running time: **113 MINS.**
Danny . . . . .Rob Lowe
Debbie . . . . .Demi Moore
Bernie . . . . .Jim Belushi
Joan . . . . .Elizabeth Perkins
Mr. Favio . . . . .George DiCenzo
Mother Malone . . . . .Michael Alldredge
Steve Carlson . . . . .Robin Thomas

Hollywood — "About Last Night" has little to do with perversity, let alone "Sexual Perversity In Chicago," the David Mamet play on which it ostensibly is based. Film lacks much of Mamet's grittiness, but is likable in its own right. Tri-Star, which timidly changed the name when newspapers and tv threatened not to accept advertising, now is faced with a marketing challenge for this slight but entertaining picture.

Film presents a look at the mating habits of young Americans, the ones who frequent singles bars and regard commitment as a lifelong disease. Given the territory, this could have been a great film, but instead it settles for witty one-liners and a happy ending. It is savvy enough to recognize points of conflict, but not daring enough to look beneath the surface.

In expanding Mamet's one-act play, filmmakers have added material without filling in the holes. Film races along at a brisk pace, really going nowhere emotionally, but it's amusing and diverting along the way.

Focus of the story is on Danny (Rob Lowe) and Debbie (Demi Moore) who meet, move in together, separate and get back together with an ease and casualness that makes it both appealing and disturbing. Ups and downs of the relationship are delivered in a series of montages that look like soft-drink commercials for the now generation.

Luckily in between there is the abrasive influence of friends Bernie (Jim Belushi) and Joan (Elizabeth Perkins). Bernie is a macho man totally at sea in the world of sexual warfare and with a code of behavior that would have made Hemingway blush. Joan is a casualty of the battlefields and carries a deep bitterness and hostility towards men and is not shy about expressing it.

In the midst of this stew, Danny and Debbie try to sort out what it is they like about each other and whether it is anything that can last. At the same time they are scared stiff of what it all means. Anyone who ever has tried to get close to another person should respond to their predicament and screenwriters Tim Kazurinsky and Denise DeClue supply enough key phrases and familiar situations to make the audience groan in recognition.

Beneath the pleasure of witnessing an all-too-common spectacle, there is the nagging sensation of something missing. Beyond the physical, what exactly do these two attractive people see in each other? The Rob Lowe characer in particular is pretty but only skin deep. Guided by his lust, there is barely a clue as to what is going on behind his eyes.

For her part, Moore is a bit more communicative, but equally devoid of an emotional core. She does suggest a longing and honesty that is likely to keep viewers in her corner, but, perhaps, wondering what she sees in Lowe. Reconciliation is a further mystery, not unlike a fairy tale come true, playing on the audience's desire for things to work out but disregarding the realities of a relationship without much range.

As the sour note, Belushi is probably the high point of the film. Performance borrows much from his late brother (John) in its outrageousness and unpredictability. One never knows what he is going to do or say next. His excessiveness is not exactly likable or endearing, but is right on the money in capturing a particular species.

Equally good is Perkins as Moore's roommate. She is able to communicate a state of anger barely under control and one step from total hysteria. It's almost a little cruel to watch her suffer, but generally director Ed Zwick, in his feature directorial debut, keeps the proceedings looking on the lighter side.

Cinematographer Andrew Dintenfass makes a solid contribution with good use of a variety of Chicago locations. Ida Random's production design is tasteful and captures well the physical surroundings of the characters. Music, however, is another story with songs too often serving to bridge scenes and illustrate emotions. —*Jagr.*

Sherman's March
(U.S.-DOCU-16m)

A First Run Features release of a McElwee production. Produced directed, written, edited, recorded and narrated by Ross McElwee. Conarrator, Richard Leacock; assistant editors, Kate Davis, Alyson Denny, Meredith Woods. Reviewed at Sydney film fest, June 9, 1986. Running time: **155 MINS.**

Sydney — A quirky, enjoyable extended home movie in which filmmaker Ross McElwee, who lives in Boston but hails from the South, sets out, ostensibly, to make a film about the effect of Sherman's Civil War campaigns. He uses the project to explore the South himself, to meet up with his family, including his sister (a believer in cosmetic surgery), and former friends.

Most of the film, in fact, is given over to the director's fascination for women, and he emerges as a Woody Allen type who loves women but, at the same time, is rather nervous of them. Eight women are featured prominently during the course of the film, all of them photographed and recorded (we're told) without advance scripting. McElwee falls in and out of love with them, one by one, providing the audience with beaucoup chuckles.

Standouts among the women are an aspiring actress who exercises regularly sans underwear (she smilingly tells the camera and thus the audience), a former flame still hungup on another man, and a singer who heads for New York to further her career. There are also religious types who expound their (sometimes strange) philosophies.

Climax, of a sort, comes when McElwee meets one of the South's great icons, Burt Reynolds, making a film, but Reynolds' bodyguards won't let McElwee close enough to talk to the star, though we meet some of his most ardent (and breathless) fans.

In all, despite its length, "Sherman's March" is a continually enjoyable trip, thanks to the personality of McElwee and the beguiling assortment of characters he meets along the way. —*Strat.*

Big Trouble In Little China
(COLOR)

Tongue-in-cheek misfire from John Carpenter.

A 20th Century Fox release. Executive producers, Paul Monash, Keith Barish. Produced by Larry J. Franco. Directed by John Carpenter. Stars Kurt Russell. Screenplay, Gary Goldman, David Z. Weinstein; camera (Panavision, Deluxe color), Dean Cundey; editor, Mark Warner, Steve Mirkovich, Edward A. Warschilka; special visual effects, Richard Edlund; music, Carpenter; production design, John J. Lloyd; art direction, Les Gobruegge; set direction, George R. Nelson; costumes, April Ferry; sound, Thomas Causey; assistant director, Larry Franco; casting, Joanna Merlin. Reviewed at Little Theater, 20th Century Fox, L.A., June 18, 1986. (MPAA Rating: PG-13.) Running time: **99 MINS.**

Jack Burton . . . . Kurt Russell
Gracie Law . . . . Kim Cattrall
Wang Chi . . . . Dennis Dun
Lo Pan . . . . James Hong
Egg Shen . . . . Victor Wong
Margo . . . . Kate Burton
Miao Yin . . . . Suzee Pai
Eddie Lee . . . . Donald Li
Thunder . . . . Carter Wong
Rain . . . . Peter Kwong
Lightning . . . . James Pax

Hollywood — "Big Trouble In Little China" suffers from production overkill and confused direction by John Carpenter, who did a better job with the musical scoring. It is likely to be a b.o. disappointment for 20th Century Fox.

Story is promising, involving an ancient Chinese magician Lo Pan (James Hong) who controls an evil empire beneath San Francisco's Chinatown and who hasn't had a woman in 2,000 years while he searches to find a green-eyed Chinese beauty to mate with and make him mortal.

Carpenter seems to be trying to make an action-adventure along the lines of "Indiana Jones And The Temple Of Doom." The effect goes painfully awry for he seems to throw in special effects, horrible creatures and kung fu fighting at regular intervals just because they

have worked to make other films more exciting.

Leading the cast is Kurt Russell who looks embarrassed, and should be, playing his CB philosophizing truck driver character as a cross between a swaggering John Wayne, adventurous Harrison Ford and wacky Bill Murray.

He's caught in Hong's supposedly ghostly underworld with restaurateur friend Wang Chi (Dennis Dun) while trying to rescue Chi's green-eyed Chinese fiancee, Miao Yin (Suzee Pai), from Hong's lascivious clutches.

Thrown in for Russell's fancy is a local attorney he meets by chance with a silly name of Gracie Law (Kim Cattrall) who also has green eyes, making her the second object of Hong's desire, but otherwise having little else to do but scream and act frantic trailing Russell and Dun around until the seven-ft. Hong catches her and mercifully zaps her into submission.

Also along for this overwrought excursion through Hong's labyrinth of unhorrifying horrors is a tour bus driver (Victor Wong), a wide-eyed reporter (Kate Burton) and a sizable Chinese cast who probably were under the mistaken impression when they signed to appear in this effort that it could be the vehicle to show off talents of Chinese actors too rarely featured in mass-appeal films.

Script rewritten (uncredited) by W.D. Richter from an original screenplay by Gary Goldman and David Z. Weinstein is thin and lifeless, having little or no twists, virtually no subplots and sorry one-liners badly delivered by Russell.

Maybe by relying on a succession of gags, Carpenter was trying to parody other actioners and produce a comedy, but his attempt misfires.

Costuming, sets, stunts and special visual effects by Richard Edlund are particularly lavish, with the curious exception that certain Chinatown street scenes look as if they were filmed on the flat Fox lot while anyone familiar with San Francisco knows its streets are narrow and steep.—*Brit.*

Secangkir Kopi Pahit
(Bitter Coffee)
(INDONESIAN-COLOR)

A Sanggar Film-Inter Studio production. Produced by Bambang Widitomo, Nyoohansiang. Written and directed by Teguh Karya. Camera (Widescreen, color), Tantra Suryadi; editor, Ed Kamarullah; music, Eros Djarot; art director, Benny Benhardi. Reviewed at Sydney Film Festival, June 15, 1986. Running time: **99 MINS.**
With: Alex Komang (Oleh Togar), Rina Hassim (Lola), Sylvia Widiantono, Ray Sahetapy.

Sydney — A downbeat tale of a young man who leaves his village in north Sumatra to seek work in

Indonesia's capital, Jakarta, "Bitter Coffee" explores the theme of many a Third World picture: migration to overcrowded cities.

In the case of Togar, protagonist of Teguh Karya's film, he seems at first to have more luck than most, collaring a job as reporter on a city newspaper. He finds lodging with Lola, an older woman who runs a small brothel, and soon is having an affair with her, though he has a disconcerting habit of waking up in the night to vomit all over the floor.

His downfall begins when he mishandles a story involving the kidnap/rape of a 16-year-old girl, and soon after, his father dies and he returns to his village, with Lola in tow, to face the wrath of his neglected mother. There's a tragic climax involving a drowning accident, though this is the scene that, in fact, opens the film with the rest told in flashback.

Karya is Indonesia's best known director (his "Mementos" was shown at the Hong Kong fest two months ago) and he usually tackles interesting and important themes. By Western standards, however, he's not an accomplished storyteller. "Bitter Coffee" is overly confusing in its structure and matters aren't helped by the woefully inadequate English subtitles provided.

In the lead role, Alex Komang is more effective than he was in "Mementos," while the other cast members acquite themselves well. Widescreen camerawork is okay and visually the film spares nothing in its depiction of the seedier aspects of the Indonesian capital. —*Strat.*

Liang Jia Funu
(A Girl Of Good Family)
(CHINESE-COLOR)

A China Film release of a Beijing Film Studio production. Directed by Huangjian Zhong. Screenplay, Li Kuanding; camera (color), Yun Wenyao; music, Shi Wanchun; art director, Shao Ruigang. Reviewed at Sydney Film Festival, June 18, 1986. Running time: **102 MINS.**
With: Cong Shan, Zhang Weixin, Zhang Jian, Ma Lin, Liang Yan.

Sydney — "A Girl Of Good Family" (also known as "A Good Woman") is a quality film from China about a bizarre subject: an arranged marriage between an 18-year-old girl and a six-year-old boy. The year is 1948 and the Communist revolution, which will alter forever old customs such as arranged marriages, is on the verge of overwhelming the country. In one little village, however, things go on as before.

Xingxian, the young woman, is faced with living a very strange life, sleeping with little husband Weiwei, but acting as more of a nurse to him, even having to change the sheets after he wets the bed. When

she falls in love with a married man, and starts meeting him secretly, the lives of all the protagonists undergo some drastic changes.

All this is set in another of those remotely beautiful little villages so beloved of Chinese filmmakers, a place where workship of Buddha is still paramount, and where bandits can still raid and loot during the night and escape back to the hills before being captured.

Hard to believe all this was going on less than 40 years ago, but director Huangjian Zhong, who was actually born in Indonesia in 1940 and returned to China with his family while still young, subsequently suffering considerably during the Cultural Revolution, brings complete conviction to the unusual and fascinating story.

Though the print screened in Sydney was a bit on the soft side, camerawork looks to be well up to the standards of current Chinese films.—*Strat.*

Manhattan Baby
(ITALIAN-COLOR)

A Fulvia Film production. Produced by Fabrizio De Angelis. Directed by Lucio Fulci. Screenplay, Elisa Livia Briganti, Dardano Sachetti; camera (Telecolor), Guglielmo Mancori; editor, Vincenzo Tomassi; music, Fabio Frizzi; production design & costumes, Massimo Lentini; assistant director, Roberto Giandalia; production manager, Palmira De Negri; makeup, Maruizio Trani. Reviewed on Lightning Video vidcassette, N.Y., June 26, 1986. (No MPAA Rating.) Running time: **89 MINS.**
With: Christopher Connelly (Prof. George Hacker), Martha Taylor, Brigitta Boccoli, Giovanni Frezza, Cinzia De Ponti, Laurence Welles, Andrea Bosic, Carlo De Mejo, Vincenzo Bellanich, Mario Moretti, Lucio Fulci, Antonio Pulci.

"Manhattan Baby" is an incoherent Italian horror film, shot on N.Y. and Egyptian locations (with studio work back in Rome) in 1982. Pic, with alternate titles "The Evil Eye" and "Eye Of The Dead," was acquired by 21st Century Distribution with a 1984 release targeted but has debuted instead via vidcassette.

Christopher Connelly portrays an archaeologist who digs up the blue "evil eye" stone in Egypt and is zapped by it, rendering him blind (doctors say his sight will come back in six months). His young daughter Suzy is presented with a matching eye-amulet by a mysterious black woman and returns to New York suddenly possessing telekinetic powers.

A parapsychology expert figures out that an ancient Egyptian cult that worshiped the forces of evil is at work again using Suzy. The expert manages to substitute himself for Suzy and gets wiped out in a very gory finish. Corny tag scene has another talisman presented to another little girl back in Egypt.

Fulci is hampered here with a rotten screenplay which cribs interesting elements from other films but fails to resolve them. An early in-joke has Suzy's younger brother asking her if Egyptian mummies are as scary as zombies, referring to Fulci's earlier zombie epics. Except for the butcher-shop makup effects climax, "Baby" is free of the director's usual gore. — *Lor.*

American Anthem
(COLOR)

Poorly directed clunker about gymnastics competitors.

A Columbia Pictures release of a Lorimar Motion Pictures presentation. Produced by Robert Schaffel, Doug Chapin. Executive producer, Freddie Fields. Directed by Albert Magnoli. Screenplay, Evan Archerd, Jeff Benjamin, from a story by Archerd, Benjamin, Susan Williams; camera (MGM color), Donald E. Thorin; editor, James Oliver; music, Alan Silvestri; production design, Ward Preston; set decorator, Chris Westlund, Jo-Ann Chorney; set dresser, Randy Gunter, Billy Jett; sound (Dolby), Chuck Wilborn; costumes, Jodie Tillen; assistant director, Jerry Ballew; technical adviser, Kathy Johnson; casting, Barbara Miller, Irene Mariano, Darlene Wyatt. Reviewed at Samuel Goldwyn Theater, Beverly Hills, Calif., June 25, 1986. (MPAA Rating: PG-13.) Running time: **100 MINS.**

Steve Tevere	Mitch Gaylord
Julie Lloyd	Janet Jones
Linda Tevere	Michelle Phillips
Mikey Tevere	R.J. Williams
Coach Soranhoff	Michael Pataki
Danielle	Patrice Donnelly
Kirk Baker	Stacey Maloney
Becky	Maria Anz
Arthur	Andrew White

Hollywood — There may have been a good idea for a film behind "American Anthem," but it certainly is not on the screen. Romantic melodrama set in the world of gymnastics and featuring Olympic star Mitch Gaylord is a cluttered, misdirected mess. Athletic performances may attract an initial audience, but pic won't be in competition for long.

Director Albert Magnoli's fast-cutting, glossy style may have worked in "Purple Rain," but is totally inappropriate here and misses all the emotional beats. Characters are stranded in a cartoon land of lurid colors and overwrought emotions. Scenes don't last long enough to bring out their meaning and viewers are left with nothing to hold on to.

Further obscuring the impact of a complicated web of relationships is an overbearing soundtrack which often creeps into the foreground over the action on the screen. Not only is the music nonstop and too loud, but it often doesn't fit the scene, as when choral, almost religious music is used inside the training gym.

Story, too, is a muddled affair with some of the blame having to go to scripters Evan Archerd and Jeff Benjamin. Steve Tevere (Mitch Gaylord) is a former high school star and gymnastics champ who had his glory days yanked from under him when his father broke his arm in a family scuffle. Things went from bad to worse and now father (John Aprea) and son just fight constantly while mother (Michelle Phillips) and younger brother (R.J. Williams) helplessly watch the family come apart.

If this isn't enough, fresh-faced gymnast Julie Lloyd (Janet Jones) arrives from New York to train at the prestigious Tops Gym somewhere in Arizona where she encounters a rigorous schedule and stiff competition. She also takes up with Gaylord in a baffling romance that has the emotional resonance of a tv commercial. Adding even more shlock sentimentality to the mix is Julie's crippled cousin (Andrew White) who composes a controversial score for her routine.

There's plenty of sound and fury here, but it doesn't signify much. Performances aren't given a chance to breathe and strike only one note. Gaylord pouts, Jones smiles gamely, the mother smiles stoically and the father grimaces. Michael Pataki as the demanding coach has a bit more texture, but his assistant Patrice Donnelly, a former runner herself, is given little to do but frown and look severe.

Last 20-minute segment of the picture featuring the gymnastics competition mysteriously drops many of the film's mannerisms and almost seems like a different picture. Magnoli curbs his impatience and stays with a scene long enough to build up some dramatic tension. Spotlighting an assortment of professional gymnasts in the heat of competition is far more compelling than anything that has come before and Gaylord finally gets a chance to shine.

With a body that could well belong to a professional athlete, Jones is also believable in this section. Adding credibility are Maria Anz as a game competitor in the face of injury and Stacey Maloney as Gaylord's supportive teammate. —*Jagr.*

Bar 51
(ISRAELI-COLOR)

A Shapira Films presentation of a Sadar production. Executive producer, Enrique Rottenberg. Produced by David Lipkind. Directed by Amos Guttman. Screenplay, Guttman and Edna Mazia, camera (color), Yossi Wein; editor, Tova Asher; music, Erich Rudich, art director, Ariel Roshko. Reviewed in Tel Aviv, June 16, 1986. Running time: **95 MINS.**

With: Giuliano Mer (Thomas), Semadar Kilchinsky (Mariana), Irith Shelag (Zara), David Patrick Wilson (Nicholas), Ada Valeria Tal (Appolonia), Alon Aboutboul (Aranjuez), Moscu Alkalay (Karl).

Tel Aviv — Amos Guttman's second feature confirms his position as the most marginal of Israeli filmmakers, whose obsessions with sexual and social fringes limits the appeal of an otherwise considerable talent.

After describing in his first opus the sad lot of a film director at throes with his homosexuality, he focuses now on the incestuous relationship between a brother and his slightly younger sister. Both have to leave their hometown, in the provinces, after the death of their mother. They arrive penniless in Tel Aviv and find their way into the sleazier nightlife of the city.

He becomes the gigolo of an aging, overweight nightclub entraineuse, moonlights as the lover of an exotic dancer, all the while hoping to make enough money to keep his sister next to him, yearning to unveil his passion for her but not daring to. His fierce jealousy is too much for her to bear and she finally realizes she has to find some way out of his grip.

Visually, the film is inventive and rich, the decadent background being remarkably colorful and imaginative, considering the limitations of a small budget, and both cameraman Yossi Wein and art director Ariel Roshko should be praised for their efforts. However, the script is full of arbitrary lapses and it seems at times that Guttman refuses to pick characters that are not either weird, desolate or both.

The most serious obstacle to the film's success is the wooden performance of Giuliano Mer in the lead, as the brother damned by his love. He wears one single, gloomy expression from beginning to end, and since his credibility is supposed to carry most of the story, his failure is crucial for the entire picture.

Semadar Kilchinsky, as his sister, is far more sensitive, in her own introvert way, and there are a couple of nice cameos from the Fellinies-aque Ada Valeria Tal as the older entertainer, and Alon Aboutboul, one of the most versatile actors of the young Israeli generation, who plays a gay transvestite attracted by the macho charms of Giuliano Mer.

Strictly for specialized markets, this film indicates Guttman has the talent but hasn't found yet the right story to exploit it.—*Edna.*

Pimeys odotta
(Waiting For Darkness)
(FINNISH-COLOR)

A Finnkino release of Villealfa production (foreign sales via Finnish Film Foundation). Produced and directed by Pauli Pentti. Screenplay, Antti Lindquist, Pauli Pentti; camera (Kodakcolor), Heikki Katajisto; editor, Anne Lakanen; music, Rauol Björkenheim; sound, Juuso Hirvinkangas. Reviewed at Midnight Sun Film Festival, Lapinsuu Cinema, Sodenkylä, Finland, June 15, 1986. Running time: **78 MINS.**

Mack	Pekka Valkeejärvi
The singer	Riita Havukainen
The blond girlfriend	Ritva Sorvali
Police lieutenant	Arno Virtanen
Mack's friend	Turo Pajala

Sodenkylä, Finland — If, at this time, another parody tribute to the film noir genre is really called for, Finland's Pauli Pentti has supplied one with "Waiting For Darkness." He serves up a neat stew with plenty of tongue-in-cheek existentialist dialog hokum thrown in to make sure he is not caught intellectually unawares by the genre cognoscenti. He also keeps things going at a lively clip with a fleet narrative style so his plot's many inconsistencies are readily forgiven and forgotten.

While waiting for the darkness of the title, Mack, a young drifter of morose good looks, is employed by a big city police lieutenant to shadow latter's wife and to take, if possible, incriminating photos of her with a lover. The shots are meant to help the policeman's cause in an upcoming divorce trial.

The dark-haired wife is a night-club singer of the sultry-torchy cast. Her alleged lover is a swarthy hotel owner. The young man soon is to find out nobody and nothing are what they seem. Mack is set up as the fall guy in some obscure big bucks swindle, and fall he does in a final shootout.

The drifter (Pekka Valkeejärvi) and the seedy-looking policeman (Arno Virtanen) give their roles a just-right dash of absurd realism. Unfortunately, Riita Havukainen and Ritva Sorvali, as the bad girl brunet and the good girl blond, are as rigid as store window mannequins and exude as little emotion, let alone sex. The whole thing is adrift in a sea of red herrings, but that does not keep helmer Pentti from steering his course with knowledgeable skill. Film has fine production credits belying an extremely low budget. — *Kell.*

Spiker
(COLOR)

Volleyball drama packs no punch.

A Seymour Borde and Associates release of a Roger Tilton Films production. Executive producers, Clarkson Higgins, Mary Lee Coleman. Produced and directed by Tilton. Screenplay, Marlene Matthews, from story by Tilton, Matthews; camera (color), Robert A Sherry; editor, Richard S. Brummer; music, Jeff Barry; casting, Hank McCann; associate producers, Dusty Dvorak, Wendi Dvorak. Reviewed at Chouteau theater, Kansas City, Mo., June 10, 1986. (MPAA Rating: R.) Running time: **104 MINS.**

With: Patrick Houser, Kristi Ferrell, Jo McDonnel, Natasha Shneider, Stephan Burns, Christopher Allport, Michael Parks, Ken Michelman, Eric Matthew, Philip Mogul, Jan Ivan Dorin, Tim R. Ryan, Mark

Hesse, Sandy-Alexander Champion, U.S. Men's National Volleyball Team, Doug Beal.

Kansas City — "Spiker" tackles a subject seldom, if ever, seen on the motion picture screen, volleyball, structured as a feature film and not as a documentary where it might have succeeded. It is a story about how the members of the U.S. Men's Olympic team are chosen. That is the basic downfall, that it is not about how the team goes out and wins one for the good ol' U.S.A., but how the college athletes slave and struggle and perspire to make it to the team roster. Filmed in 1984, pic was released territorially commencing last November.

A handful of prize college athletes are invited to try out for the team, under the drill-sergeant methods of Michael Parks as the hard-as-nails U.S. coach. That brings in such plot angles as the talented athlete who won't go for the coach's hazings and ankles the team, the married athlete whose young wife doesn't like being alone while hubby is off on training tours, the injury to the star server, etc.

Filmmaker Roger Tilton has peopled the cast with attractive male and female college types who give the film something of a gloss. The film gets its R rating from a few sleeping-around instances and very few four-letter words.

"Spiker" is almost airborne when it does get around to real volleyball action, one sequence of the U.S. team versus Japan, another versus Poland. These present front-line action, championship-level volleyball at its best, enough to intrigue most sports fans, but are midway in the film and when it comes to the clincher it is not how the Americans won or lost (they lose both games), but how they tried and tried and made the team.

Tilton and writer Marlene Matthews took on a monumental task in trying to find drama in volleyball. They have given the film adequate production values (albeit the running time is overlong by 15 minutes) and the action sequences are good. —*Quin.*

As Sete Vampiras
(The Seven Female Vampires)
(BRAZILIAN-COLOR)

An Embrafilme release of an Embrafilme/Superoito production. Produced by Ivan Cardoso, Mauro Taubman, Claudio Klabin, Antonio Avilez, Flavio Holanda and Skylight. Directed by Ivan Cardoso. Screenplay, R.F. Lucchetti; camera (Eastmancolor), Carlos Egberto Silveira; editor, Gilberto Santeiro; makeup and special effects, Antonio Pacheco; art direction, Oscar Ramos; choreography, Carlos Wilson; music, Julio Medaglia; song "As Sete Vampiras" written and performed by Leo Jaime. Reviewed at Cine Embaixador, Gramado Film Festival, April 7, 1986. Running time: **100 MINS.**
With: Alvamar Tadei, Andrea Beltrão, Ariel Coelho, Bené Nunes, Colé, Carlo Mos-

si, Danielle Daumerri, Dedina Bernardelli, Felipe Falcão, Ivon Curi, John Herbert, Leo Jaime, Lucélia Santos, Nicole Puzzi, Nuno Leal Maia, Pedro Cardoso, Simone Carvalho, Suzana Matos, Tania Boscoli, Wilson Grey, Zezé Macedo.

Gramado — One of the top names of Brazilian experimental cinema of the 1970s, Ivan Cardoso made his debut in feature films four years ago with "O Segredo da Mumia," which got several prizes at the 1982 Gramado Film Festival. "As Sete Vampiras" is a followup. It keeps two of the author's most important trademarks: the concern with a horror atmosphere and with the 1950s.

The elements chosen by Cardoso to recreate his roots are, as usual, top performers of the 1950s, here represented by follies actor Colé, comedian Zezé Macedo, singer Ivon Curi, actor Wilson Grey, musician Bené Nunes; all are artists who have strongly influenced the Brazilian generation now in its 30s. They mostly resume roles they have played before, now serving a plot in which a killer vegetable transforms a scientist into a vampire, who brings horror to the chorus girls of the night club at traditional Quitandinha Hotel, who are performing the show "The Seven Female Vampires."

Cardoso's universe is laced with humor, though one can feel the absence of the originality and intuition of his first feature. "As Sete Vampiras" finds itself somewhere between a cult picture and a commercially oriented product, in which the subtle touch of the author is replaced by a determination to provide all keys (including the inner codes of the author's world) quickly to the audience.

As a result, pic does not work as well as "O Segredo da Mumia," despite the presence of a fine female team (Andrea Beltrão, Lucélia Santos, Nicole Puzzi, Suzana Matos) and a young singer very much identified with Cardoso's purposes (Leo Jaime).

Pic can be enjoyed by filmgoers determined to laugh with those not too original but always attractive and sometimes funny female vampires.—*Hoin.*

The Throne Of Fire
(ITALIAN-COLOR)

A Cannon Group presentation of a Visione Cinematografica production. Produced by Ettore Spagnuolo. Directed by Franco Prosperi. Screenplay, Nino Marino, from story by Marino, Giuseppe Buricchi; camera (Technicolor), Guglielmo Mancori; editor, Alessandro Lucidi; music, Carlo Rustichelli, Paolo Rustichelli; art direction, Franco Cuppini; costumes, Silvio Laurenzi; special effects, Paolo Ricci; associate producer, Umberto Innocenzi. Reviewed on MGM/UA Home Video vidcassette, N.Y., June 5, 1986. (No MPAA Rating.) Running time: **89 MINS.**
Princess Valkari . . . . Sabrina Siani

Siegfried . . . . Peter McCoy
Morak . . . . Harrison Muller
Also with: Benny Carduso, Peter Caine, Dan Collins, Stefano Abbati.

"The Throne Of Fire" is a very ordinary Italian fantasy adventure cranked out in 1982 with the same cast and virtually same plotline as a dozen other pictures at that time. Cannon pickup bypassed U.S. theatrical release to debut on vidcassette instead.

Peter McCoy (real name: Pietro Torrisi) toplines as Siegfried, a muscleman destined to save the world from evil, latter personified by Morak (Harrison Muller), the son of the devil's messenger Belial (also played by Muller) and the witch Azira.

For evil to continue to exist in the world, Morak must take the title throne "on the day of the night in the day" (another cornball eclipse coming up). To qualify, he must marry beautiful blond princess Valkari (Sabrina Siani), daughter of King Egon who recently died. To sit on the throne without qualifying means instant death as it magically generates flames.

Imbued by his sorcerer father with invulnerability (except for a susceptibility to fire), Siegfried also gets the temporary use of invisibility, just like his legendary namesake of "The Nibelungen" saga.

Sluggishly paced low-budgeter has okay swordfight action but little else. The uncrowned queen of the genre, Siani (who made at least seven such films in 1982) is an athletic, intense beauty who deserved to graduate to better roles. She costarred with the wooden McCoy in "The Sword Of The Barbarians," which Cannon released theatrically in 1983 and the much sexier "The Invincible Barbarian" (released here on vidcassette only). Costar Muller (of "2020 Texas Gladiators") is funny with his rapidfire (self-dubbed) dialog delivery. —*Lor.*

No Time To Die
(W. GERMAN-INDONESIAN-COLOR)

An Atlas Intl. presentation of a Rapid Film-Lisa Film (Munich) production, in joint venture with Rapi Films (Jakarta). Executive producer, Peer J. Oppenheimer. Produced by Wolf C. Hartwig, Gope T. Samtani. Directed by Helmuth Ashley; codirectors, Has Manan, E.G. Bakker. Stars John Phillip Law, Horst Janson, Grazyna Dylong, Barry Prima. Screenplay, Heinz Werner John, Günther Heller, Ashley; camera (color), Wolfgang Grasshoff, Asmawi; editor, Norbert Herzner; music, Hans Hammerschmid; dialog director, Joseph Ellison; production manager, Eric Moss; assistant director, Andrea Buttenstedt; stunt coordinator, Kerry Rossall; special effects, Nuryadi. Reviewed on Trans World Entertainment vidcassette, N.Y., June 20, 1986. (No MPAA Rating.) Running time: **87 MINS.**
Ted Barner . . . . John Phillip Law

Martin Forster . . . . Horst Janson
Judy Staufer . . . . Grazyna Dylong
Pat Lesmany . . . . Barry Prima
Jan Van Cleef . . . . Francis Glutton
Jack Gull . . . . Christopher Mitchum

"No Time To Die" is a low-energy, instantly disposable action film, one of the endless flow of European features shot in the Far East. Made in Indonesia under the title "Hijacked To Hell" in July 1984, pic managaes to be even duller than a Filipino-lensed actioner shot four months later with the same U.S. stars, "American Commandos." Latter pic achieved a theatrical release recently while "No Time" went directly to homevideo.

John Phillip Law (the only cast member here who does not sleepwalk) toplines as Ted Barner, a soldier of fortune and a womanizer currently working as a flunkie in Indonesia for Multi Industrial Corp. MIC is planning to test a new laser cannon in a remote mine with Barner, engineer Forster (Horst Janson) and Barner's local pal Lesmany assigned to drive it there.

A rival industrialist from Texas, Jack Gull (Christopher Mitchum, as animated as a zombie), is out to steal the cannon. After a very talky first half, film segues to endlessly boring footage of bad guys chasing the truck. Improbably, a beautiful news agency reporter Judy (Grazyna Dylong) joins up with the truck driving heroes for the trip. A dumb plot twist has miners and scientists trapped in the mine, with the cannon needed pronto to save them.

Poor dubbing helps make this one a deadly experience. —*Lor.*

Moments Of Play
(DANISH-DOCU-COLOR)

A Cinnamon Film release (international sales: The Danish Film Institute) of a Leth & Uldal production. Produced by Hanne Uldal. Written and directed by Jörgen Leth. Camera (Eastmancolor), Dan Holmberg; editor, Kristian Levring, Camilla Skousen; original music, Antonio Carlos Jobim; additional music, Christian Uldal-Leth; music performers, Antonio Carlos Jobim, Paulo Jobim, Uldal-Leth, others; sound, Niels Arnt Torp, production managers, Wayan Korda (Bali), Bill Fogtman (Brazil), Tom Grady (California), Brent Owens (N.Y.), Johnny Sandaire, Jane McRae (Haiti), Ebbe Traberg (Spain). Reviewed at the Dagmar, Copenhagen, June 25, 1986. Running time: **82 MINS.**
(English soundtrack)

Copenhagen — Jörgen Leth continues his illustrious international career as a poet-filmmaker ("A Sunday In Hell" documentary of the Paris-Roubaix bicycle race) with "Moments Of Play," which is, ultimately, a tribute to *homo ludens*, Latin for such members of the human race who have, regardless of age, race or social standing, retained the spirit of play in their various endeavors. This long docu is also a tribute to Leth himself, since he, once more, is playing at the game of documentary filmmaking while at the same time being deadly serious about it.

Undoubtedly, Leth did extensive research and interviewing ahead of shooting "Moments Of Play" in New York, California, Bali, Haiti, Brazil, Denmark and China, but his film comes through as sheer poetry-in-motion. He does his own narration in brief poetic statements that emulate the feelings of each player caught by the camera, the players being masked dancers in Bali; pick-up basketball players in Harlem; former tennis champ Torben Ulrich who is now bashing his tennis ball, dipped in paint, towards Chinese paper to create works of visual art; a six-year old boy improvising with flawless technique and original invention at a piano; a bullfighter rehearsing with a decoy *toro,* and kids fishing with bow and arrow on the Amazon.

Nowhere does a hectoring lecturer's voice intrude, and Antonio Carlos Jobim's score serves only to enhance the general joy of the games being played. These games are all repetitive in character even when most finely nuanced in execution, and they thus emerge as instances from real life of what is currently in fashion as various expressions of minimalistic art. "Moments Of Play" toured the U.S. art museum and minor fest circuit earlier this year and would seem assured of a future in similar situations for years to come, the game it plays with gamesters at play being unrestricted by time and place. —*Kell.*

Screamtime
(BRITISH-COLOR)

A Rugged Films release of a Manson Intl. presentation. Produced and directed by Al Beresford. Screenplay, Michael Armstrong; camera (Rank color), Don Lord, Alan Pudney, Mike Spera; editor, uncredited; music, KPM, sound, Gene Defever, Stan Phillips, David Stevenson; art direction, Adrian Atkinson, Martin Atkinson, Brian Savegar; assistant director, Tony Dyer, Rex Piano, Paul Tivers; production manager, Brian Bilgorri, Hugh O'Donnell; special makeup effects, Nick Maley. Reviewed on Lightning Video vidcassette, N.Y., June 15, 1986. (MPAA Rating: R.) Running time: **89 MINS.**
Jack Grimshaw . . . . Robin Bailey
Lena . . . . Ann Lynn
Tony . . . . Ian Saynor
Susan . . . . Yvonne Nicholson
Gavin . . . . David Van Day
Emma . . . . Dora Bryan
Mildred . . . . Jean Anderson
Also with: Vincent Russo, Michael Gordon, Marie Scinto (video watchers); Jonathan Morris, Dione Inman, Bosco Hogan, Lally Bowers, Veronica Doran, Matthew Peters, Phillip Bloomfield, Gary Linley.

"Screamtime" is a low-grade, three-part anthology horror film. British-made (circa 1983) picture was released regionally commencing February 1985, subsequently available in the homevideo market.

Three desultory stories, lensed in England, are bookended by flimsy wraparound sequence in which two guys steal three videocassettes from a Times Square store and go to a girl's apartment to watch them.

The three cassettes they watch are the British stories: one about a mad Punch 'n' Judy Show puppeteer (Robin Bailey) who uses the puppet to take vengeance on his nasty stepson; a dull tale of a young couple (Ian Saynor and Yvonne Nicholson) who move into a new house wherein she has violent hallucinations which turn out to be flash-forwards of what will happen to the next family that moves in there; and lastly, three young robbers who are killed by ghouls and fairies (the fantasy kind) that guard an old mansion.

Makeup effects by the usually reliable Nick Maley are unimpressive and execution of stories (credited to "Al Beresford" as director) is on the cheap. Writer is Michael Armstrong, most famous for directing the 1970 exploitation hit "Mark Of The Devil."

Some excellent thesps (e.g., Ann Lynn and Dora Bryan) are wasted in nothing roles.—*Lor.*

Odinotchnoye Plavaniye
(The Detached Mission)
(SOVIET-COLOR)

A Mosfilm Studios production. Directed by Mikhail Tumanishvili. Screenplay, Evgeny Mesiatzev; camera (color), Boris Bondarenko; editor, I. Tzinin; music, Victor Babushkin; art direction, Tatyana Lapshina, Aleksandr Myagkov. Reviewed at Tashkent Film Festival (market), May 23, 1986. Running time: **93 MINS.**
Shatokhin . . . . Mikhail Nozhkin
Kruglov . . . . Aleksandr Fatiushin
Danilov . . . . Sergei Nosibov
Parshin . . . . Nartai Begalin
Harrison . . . . Vitaly Zikora
Hassolt . . . . Arnis Litzitis

Tashkent — The U.S. military-industrial complex hatches a nefarious plot to spoil Soviet-U.S. relations in "The Detached Mission," a technically top-of-the-line Russian actioner with a higher than usual suspense quotient. The special effects aren't much and the storyline, with its Russian sailors defusing a CIA rocket base, is as implausible as any Western spy pictures but made from the other point-of-view. Its ferocious mixture of action, politics, and anti-war message is the chief novelty of "Detached Mission."

Story begins with the Russians holding their annual maneuvers in the Pacific, while a Yank tv reporter on an American observation vessel notes, "It's a dangerous situation, but these are dangerous times we live in." At the same time, CIA agents are on a deserted atoll, preparing to launch a winged nuclear rocket at the Soviet navy. Their goal, naturally, is to provoke World War III.

Heroes are two Soviet marines, who unluckily never get very clearly identified to the audience. The anti-hero is a CIA agent down on his luck, who messed up his last mission in Vietnam and this is his last chance. A misfired U.S. rocket sinks a small pleasure cruiser, shipwrecking the crew, a young Yank couple, on a desert isle.

To cover up their mistake, CIA agents in masks raid the island and ice the wife, but the husband escapes. Eventually he joins the Russian navy detachment which, in bargain-basement James Bond fashion, penetrates into the CIA rocket base and destroys it.

In the Soviet screen tradition, violence (which is frequent) is bloodless and goreless. The offhanded way boats and subs sink off-screen, however, seems more a failure of the director and special effects department than anything else. Curious, but no cigar. —*Yung.*

Aliens
(COLOR)

Solid followup should hit big.

A 20th Century Fox release of a Brandywine production. Produced by Gale Anne Hurd. Executive producers, Gordon Carroll, David Giler, Walter Hill. Directed by James Cameron. Stars Sigourney Weaver. Screenplay, Cameron, from a story by Cameron, Giler, Hill, based on characters created by Dan O'Bannon, Ronald Shusett; camera (Rank color, Deluxe prints), Adrian Biddle; editor, Ray Lovejoy; music, James Horner; production design, Peter Lamont; supervising art direction, Terence Ackland-Snow; art direction, Bert Davey, Fred Hole, Michael Lamont, Ken Court; set decoration, Crispian Sallis; costume design, Emma Porteous; alien effects created by Stan Winston; second unit director, Winston; certain special visual effects created by The L.A. Effects Group; visual effects supervision, Robert Skotak, Dennis Skotak; visual effects supervision-postproduction, Brian Johnson; original alien design, H.R. Giger; conceptual designer, Ron Cobb; conceptual artist, Syd Mead; special effects supervision, John Richardson; sound (Dolby), Roy Charman; assistant director, Derek Cracknell; casting, Mike Fenton, Jane Feinberg, Judy Taylor (U.S.), Mary Selway (U.K.). Reviewed at the 20th Century Fox Studios, W. L.A., June 25, 1986. (MPAA Rating: R.) Running time: **137 MINS.**
Ripley . . . . Sigourney Weaver
Newt . . . . Carrie Henn
Corporal Hicks . . . . Michael Biehn
Burke . . . . Paul Reiser
Bishop . . . . Lance Henriksen
Private Hudson . . . . Bill Paxton
Lieutenant Gorman . . . . William Hope
Private Vasquez . . . . Jenette Goldstein
Sergeant Apone . . . . Al Matthews

Hollywood — "Aliens" proves a very worthy followup to Ridley Scott's 1979 sci-fi shocker, "Alien." James Cameron's vault into the big time after scoring with the exploitation actioner "The Terminator" makes up for lack of surprise with sheer volume of thrills and chills — emphasis here is decidedly on the plural aspect of the title. Original pic earned $40,300,000 in domestic rentals, and new entry could well top that.

First film closed by showing Sigourney Weaver and her tabby cat as the sole survivors of a death struggle Weaver's crew waged with an ungodly monster picked up on a very distant planet. Beast was so terrifying for two reasons — H.R. Giger designed it to be as gruesome and ugly a thing as ever stalked this world or any other, and it needed to be fed by preying on the innards of living human beings.

Cameron picks up the thread 57 years later, when Weaver and the cat (who have been in hibernation) are rescued by a deep space salvage team. In the interim, the far-off planet has been colonized and, although authorities tend to dismiss her horror stories as extreme and insist that nothing untoward has occurred there, they nevertheless ask her to accompany a team of Marines back to the planet to investigate why all contact with the colony has suddenly been lost.

It does take a moment to swallow

the notion that the extremely sane Weaver would agree to return to hell's core under any circumstances, but Cameron's gung-ho, no-nonsense handling of the material easily brushes past any objections or gaps in logic. Group sent this time consists of a bunch of tough grunts with a sour attitude about having been sent on such a dippy mission.

That's when the audience can start rubbing together its collective hands in anticipation of the big surprise these tough guys and girls are in for when they try to slug it out in hand-to-hand combat with the monsters, which are more than happy to welcome them to their planet. From this point on, Cameron & Co. tighten the screws mercilessly, as the multitude of possibilities for alien attacks are explored in gross and imaginative detail.

Weaver finds one human survivor — a cute, tough, terrified little girl played by Carrie Henn — on the planet, but otherwise, there's a potential monster out there for every one of the 157 colonists known to have inhabited the place.

The odds against the crew are, in a word, monstrous, and unsurprisingly, its members are dispatched one by one until it once again comes down to a battle royal between Weaver, who still wears sexy underwear, and one last monster. Final sequence has been very well conceived and beautifully realized for maximum suspense and action impact.

Because the nature of the alien creature was already revealed in the first film, sequel doesn't possess the potential to shock and scare the viewer to quite the same extent, and original had more visceral impact. Despite the lengthy 137-minute running time, Cameron maintains the tension at a very high level throughout, and audiences will be rivetted to their seats with drooling dread in anticipation of the next attack.

Although film accomplishes everything it aims to do, Cameron suffers just a bit by comparison to Ridley Scott in that his eye for visuals isn't nearly as fine. In addition, a rather mechanical orientation prevades the picture, not so much in the execution, but in Cameron's obvious addiction to guns, tank-like vehicles, military gear of all kinds, exposed piping and the like. Overall impression is of a film made by an expert craftsman, while Scott clearly has something of an artist in him.

Another curiosity is that very contemporary behavioral and language patterns have been applied to these futuristic warriors. No attempt has been made to imagine how attitudes and looks will have changed in this future; these Marines could be plunked down in a Rambo film and look right at home.

Weaver, who was an unknown

when she debuted in the role seven years ago, does a smashing job here as Ripley, one of the great female screen roles of recent years. Strength with which she invests the part is invigorating, and the actress really gets down and dirty with tremendous flair.

Carrie Henn is very appealing as the little girl and Jenette Goldstein makes a striking impression as a body-building recruit who is tougher than any of the guys in the outfit. Other than Lance Henriksen, as an android on the mission, and Paul Reiser, as a venal corporate rep along for the ride, men in the cast are relatively anonymous and unexciting.

Technically, film is superior in all respects. Special effects are varied and always convincing, and behind-the-scenes artisans have helped sustain the effective mood and tension all the way.—*Cart.*

Under The Cherry Moon
(B&W)

Embarrassing mixed-combo ego trip from Prince.

A Warner Bros. release of a Cavallo, Ruffalo & Fargnoli production. Executive producers & produced by Bob Cavallo, Joe Ruffalo, Steve Fargnoli. Directed by Prince. Stars Prince. Screenplay, Becky Johnston; camera (Rank b&w, Technicolor prints), Michael Ballhaus; editor, Eva Gardos; film editor, Rebecca Ross; production design, Richard Sylbert; art director, Damien Lafranchi; set decorator, Ian Whittaker; sound (Dolby), Daniel Brisseau; costumes, Marie France; music, Prince & the Revolution; orchestral music, Clare Fischer; associate producer-production supervisor, Graham Cottle; assistant director, Michel Cheyko; creative consultant, Mary Lambert; casting, Jose Villaverde; casting (France), Caroline Mazaurie. Reviewed at the Burbank Studios, screening room 12, Burbank, Calif., July 2, 1986. (MPAA Rating: PG-13.) Running time: 98 MINS.
Christopher Tracy . . . . Prince
Tricky . . . . Jerome Benton
Mary Sharon . . . . Kristin Scott-Thomas
Mr. Sharon . . . . Steven Berkoff
Mrs. Wellington . . . . Francesca Annis
Katy . . . . Emmanuelle Sallet
Mrs. Sharon . . . . Alexandra Stewart
Also with: Victor Spinetti, Pamela Ludwig.

Hollywood — "Cherry Moon" is an example of ego gone amuck — Prince's ego. Even the rock star's adoring fans have some standards. Pic will open well and quickly die, destined for the vanity graveyard.

The rock star charmed his way through first acting effort in "Purple Rain," punctuating his performance with lots of on-stage musical numbers and interplay with other colorful Revolution band members.

In "Under The Cherry Moon," Prince tries to direct too, giving himself a lot of closeups kissing but hardly any of him singing. What is left is a trite story about a rich girl and a poor musician (Prince) that's set on the Riviera and shot in, of all things, black and white.

Before a shooting began, Prince reportedly fired director Mary Lambert (who has retained the dubious distinction of having credit as creative consultant) and took over the set.

What he does with this power is feature himself in 95% of the film, which would have been okay if he brought some of his animated singing persona to the screen.

Story has less plot than the average music video, featuring Prince as a pianist at a Nice hotel and Revolution back-up singer, Jerome Benton, as his friend Tricky.

After a half-hearted rendezvous with a wealthy woman (Francesca Annis), Prince sets his sights on meeting a young, wealthy woman. Through the newspaper, he finds out that young, beautiful Mary Sharon (Kristin Scott-Thomas) is about to turn 21 and come into her $50,000,000 trust fund. He meets her, they fall in love, and Dad (Steven Berkoff) gets his thugs to rid his sheltered daughter of Prince.

Prince takes himself too seriously as the poor lover boy — so seriously that Benton's jive-talkin' one-liners fall flat with no one there against which to play them off.

When Prince gets together with Thomas, he forces the little chemistry there is between them by first having them shout at each other, then with long looks into each others' (mostly Prince's) eyes and finally with a lot of hard-driving kissing that neither looks to be enjoying.

Before ennui sets in, the rock star throws in a ridiculous ending that is sure to solicit groans of incredulity in the theaters.

Film was shot in color (at the insistence of Warner Bros.) with prints in black and white (at the insistence of Prince) on location in Nice, one of the jewel cities of the Mediterranean, and comes out looking about as flat and uninteresting as a newsreel from the 1930s about vacationing in the south of France.

Costumes by Marie France are firstrate. —*Brit.*

A Fine Mess
(U.S.-COLOR)

Laurel & Hardy, RIP.

A Columbia Pictures release of a B.E.E. production from Columbia-Delphi V. Prods. Executive producer, Jon D. Krane. Produced by Tony Adams. Directed by Blake Edwards. Stars Ted Danson, Howie Mandel. Screenplay, Edwards; camera (Panavision, DeLuxe color), Harry Stradling; editor, John F. Burnett; music, Henry Mancini; production design, Rodger Maus; sound, William Stevenson; costumes, Patricia Norris; stunts & 2d unit director, Joe Dunne; production manager, Alan Levine; assistant director, Mickey McCardie; casting, Nancy Klopper. Reviewed at Hoyts screening room, Sydney, May 26, 1986. (MPAA Rating: PG.) Running time: 88 MINS.
Spence Holden . . . . Ted Danson
Dennis Powell . . . . Howie Mandel
Turnip . . . . Richard Mulligan
Binky . . . . Stuart Margolin
Claudia Pazzo . . . . Maria Conchita Alonso
Ellen . . . . Jennifer Edwards
Tony Pazzo . . . . Paul Sorvino

Sydney — Blake Edwards' obsession with the slapstick comedy genre has, over the years, produced some all-time comedy classics and some best-forgotten clinkers. "A Fine Mess" belongs in the latter category.

The writer-director, acknowledging his debt to the immortal Laurel & Hardy, has come up with not one, but two comedy teams in his latest effort, but has forgotten, or ignored, a cardinal principle of the Stan and Ollie pics: the fact that the team shared an extraordinary complicity with audiences, via their lovable characters and their innate innocence and helplessness. Neither Ted Danson and Howie Mandel nor Richard Mulligan and Stuart Margolin offer audiences such affection, or are likely to receive affection in turn. Without such empathy, there's only a series of mechanically contrived funny business, most of which falls pretty flat.

Danson plays a small-time actor who, during location filming at a racing stable, overhears two crooks (Mulligan and Margolin) as they dope a horse on the instructions of their boss (Paul Sorvino). Before long, Danson and his buddy, Mandel, who works as a roller-skating carhop at a drive-in restaurant, are being chased all over L.A. by the incompetent villains, cueing in plenty of over-familiar car chases.

Pic segues into equally hackneyed bedroom farce when Danson takes up with lovely Maria Conchita Alonso, the all-too-available wife of gang-boss Sorvino. Sorvino has a few bright moments as "The Singing Godfather," a big-time criminal as fond of his own voice as he is of his hideously decorated apartment.

Mandel's love interest is lissome Jennifer Edwards, essaying the role of clerk at an auction where Danson and his pal accidentally purchase a valuable antique player piano coveted by Sorvino.

"A Fine Mess" is light on plot and instead concentrates on strenuous, familiar comedy routines. Trouble is, the principal players are all quite charmless, though Richard Mulligan enters into the spirit of the thing as he usually does, with a typically no-holds-barred performance.

Audiences looking for comedy in late summer, when "A Fine Mess" is set to open, may turn out initially on Edwards' considerable reputation for bringing off this kind of film successfully in the past. But word of mouth is unlikely to be favorable, and Columbia may expect a quick dropoff of business. (Film was rated PG last year and originally scheduled as a Christmas 1985 release, later postponed till May and then August. —Ed.)

Production credits are superior, with sharp lensing by Harry Stradling, very tight editing by John F. Burnett, clever production design by Rodger Maus and catchy music by Henry Mancini. Edwards' direction is far better than his screenplay and his choice of comedy players. What the film lacks, above all, is heart. —Strat.

The Great Mouse Detective
(ANIMATED-COLOR)

Disney delight.

A Buena Vista release of a Walt Disney Pictures presentation, in association with Silver Screen Partners II. Produced by Burny Mattinson. Directed by John Musker, Ron Clements, Dave Michener, Mattinson. Story adaptation by Clements. Mattinson, Michener, Musker, Pete Young, Vance Gerry, Steve Hulett, Bruce M. Morris, Matthew O'Callaghan, Melvin Shaw from the book, "Basil Of Baker Street" by Eve Titus. Supervising animators, Mark Henn, Glen Keane, Robert Minkoff, Hendel Butoy; art direction, Guy Vasilovich; music, Henry Mancini; editor, Roy M. Brewer Jr.; animation camera, Ed Austin; special photographic effects, Philip L. Meador; assistant director, Timothy J. O'Donnell, Mark A. Hester. Reviewed at Walt Disney Studios, Burbank, June 28, 1986. (MPAA Rating: G.) Running time: 80 MINS.
Voices of:
Professor Ratigan . . . . Vincent Price
Basil . . . . Barrie Ingham
Dawson . . . . Val Bettin
Olivia . . . . Susanne Pollatschek
Fidget . . . . Candy Candido
Mrs. Judson . . . . Diana Chesney
The Mouse Queen . . . . Eve Brenner
Flaversham . . . . Alan Young

Hollywood — At least one solution to solving the summertime blues for kids five and over will be to see Disney's latest animated feature, "The Great Mouse Detective." The animation is rich, the characters memorable and the story equally as entertaining for adults as for children. Boxoffice should be healthy.

In "Great Mouse Detective," supersleuth Basil (Barrie Ingham) and bumbling partner Dawson (Val Bettin) are the Sherlock Holmes and Dr. Watson of Victorian London's mouse scene.

Basil gets involved in a case where a master toymaker is kidnaped and the villain turns out to be none other than Basil's longtime adversary, the evil Prof. Ratigan (Vincent Price).

Directors John Musker, Ron Clements, Dave Michener and veteran Disney animator Burny Mattinson have pulled together many of the elements of a classic Disney animated feature, which they have updated for the current generation of moppets by holding back on the sentimentality while building up the story through imaginative new forms of animation.

The story of the clever mouse detective determined to outwit Ratigan's plan to dethrone the Mouse Queen (Eve Brenner) lends itself to inventive gags, including the expected run-ins with a menacing oversized cat and wonderfully creative scenes where benign-looking toys seem to come alive to trap poor Basil and Dawson and foil their attempts to save the Empire.

Price's enjoyment of playing the rat comes through in his voice, although he is perhaps too convincing and might scare very small children.

Vocal work of others is also fine, and especially Ingham as the urbane and witty Basil and Candy Candido 'as Ratigan's Bronx-accented nasty peglegged bat, Fidget.

Other animation houses should take note of Disney's latest offering. Characters are drawn to stand out against beautifully detailed backgrounds that, in and of themselves, add depth and humor to the story.

Henry Mancini's scoring is adequate, but one wonders why there are only four songs and those written are not the kind children could, or would, learn to sing.

Even so, "The Great Mouse Detective" puts Disney back on top of G-rated entertainment for kids. —Brit.

Le Débutant
(The Debutant)
(FRENCH-COLOR)

An AMLF release of a T. Films/Films A2 coproduction. Produced by Alain Terzian. Stars Francis Perrin. Directed by Daniel Janneau. Screenplay, Janneau, Perrin, from an original story by Perrin; camera (Agfa color), Robert Fraisse; editor, Ghislaine Desjonquères; music, Yves Gilbert; sound, Michel Desrois; art direction, Dominique André; assistant director, Michel Thibaud; production manager, Françoise Galfré, Philippe Lièvre. Reviewed at the Marignan-Concorde theater, Paris, June 28, 1986. Running time: 88 MINS.
François Veber . . . . Francis Perrin
Valérie Michel . . . . Christiane Jean
Lucien Berger . . . . Julien Guiomar
Marguerite . . . . Dominique Lavanant
Willy . . . . Jean-Claude Brialy
Jean Rex . . . . François Perrot
Also with: Philippe Lelièvre, Christian Charmetant, Cécile Magnet, Valérie Rojan, Angela Torossian, Patricia Elig, Philippe Brizard, Henri-Jacques Huet, Xavier Saint-Macary, Maurice Baquet, Roger Dumas, Bertrand Lacy, Pierre-Yves Pruvost, Charlotte Walior.

Paris — "Le Débutant," a dull, stodgy comedy about a timid provincial electrician who finds fame as a legit actor in Paris, is based largely on the success story of its star and coauthor, Francis Perrin, a popular comic who alternates between films and one-man legit shows.

To judge from what Perrin and director Daniel Janneau put on the screen, the comic didn't find too many imposing obstacles to vault on his obstinate course, and his paral-

lel romantic entanglements did not seem very traumatizing, since he beds just about every skirt he sets his eyes on and wins the heart of the attractive young actress who seems to elude him for most of the picture.

Perrin himself began as a stage manager, and studied acting at the Paris Conservatoire, with the venerable Louis Seigner (here called Lucien Berger and portrayed by Julien Guiomar). Landing a first prize in acting, he was accepted into the Comédie-Française, where despite the reticence of its skeptical administrator (apparently Pierre Dux, here enacted by François Perrot), he triumphed as a comic actor in the role of Molière's Scapin.

Despite a few farcical incidents (which purportedly did happen to Perrin) the film attempts to remain realistic in its depiction of characterization and milieu, but the scenes of backstage and conservatory life are re-enacted poorly.

Perrin self-consciously bridles his usual comic high spirits for the purposes of dramatic composition, but ironically deserves low grades for his most boring screen role to date. He comes to life briefly in a monolog from Beaumarchais' "The Marriage Of Figaro," with which he wins the conservatory's first prize.

Dominique Lavanant and Jean-Claude Brialy are a little better as the heads of a traveling company who offer Perrin a job as stage manager. Christiane Jean has poise and good looks as Perrin's dream lady, though she still awaits a decent film role that will put her talent to the test.—Len.

Sno-Line
(COLOR)

Modest actioner loaded with too many subplots.

A Vandom Intl. Pictures production and release. Produced by Robert Burge. Directed by Douglas F. O'Neons. Screenplay, Robert Hilliard; camera (United color), Gary Thieltges; editor, Beth Conwell; music, Richard Bellis; sound, Tim Himes; production design, Chuck Stewart; assistant director-associate producer, Lou Wills; casting, Bob Burge Prods. Reviewed on Lightning Video vidcassette, N.Y., June 15, 1986. (MPAA Rating: R.) Running time: 89 MINS.
Steve King . . . . Vince Edwards
Duval . . . . Paul Smith
Audrey . . . . June Wilkinson
Ralph Salerno . . . . Phil Foster
Gus . . . . Louis Guss
Michael . . . . Carey Clark
Tina . . . . Charity Ann Zachary
Also with: Gary Lee Love, Edward Talbot Matthews 3d, Scott Strozer, Maggie Egan, Dominic Barto, Roy Morgan, Kelly Nichols, Gary Angelle, Michele Ewing, Fredrika Duke, Cassandra Edwards, Kay Elrod, Billy J. Holman.

"Sno-Line" (filmed in 1984 under the title "Texas Sno-Line") is a competently handled Texas-style action film which suffers from too many subplots. Feature was re-

leased in June 1985 on its home turf in Beaumont and Corpus Christi; it became a homevideo title early this year.

Vince Edwards stars as Steve King, an upwardly mobile gangster who uses a dairy business as his front. Using money borrowed from N.Y. gangster Ralph Salerno (the late Phil Foster), he's making a multi-million dollar cocaine buy from Duval (Paul Smith) with which to create a "sno-line" across Texas in terms of his coverage of drug users.

King is at war with good ole boy gangster Bedford (Billy J. Holman) and a group of young punks led by Michael (Carey Clark) and Eddie (Gary Lee Love). All hell breaks loose when the punks rob King's casino, run by beautiful Audrey (June Wilkinson) and accidentally steal King's drug buy money in the bargain. Bedford's men waylay Duval and hold him prisoner. King and his minions go on the warpath for a bloody finale loaded with silly plot twists and a most unconvincing happy ending for several survivors.

Picture is watchable, but its constant cutting back and forth between stories involving various members of an overly abundant cast diffuses one's interest. In addition to the various gangsters and their machinations, there is a dull love story involving wayward young Michael and his girlfriend Tina (Charity Ann Zachary). A simplifying rewrite on Robert Hilliard's script would have helped.

Edwards is fun as a bad guy for a change while massive Paul Smith obviously relishes the opportunity to take on half a dozen opponents at a time. Veteran sex symbol June Wilkinson is looking good, but her role is underwritten and, alas, she keeps her clothes on throughout. Supporting cast is sprinkled with locals, some sporting thick accents. Much of the production team and cast recently encored to film the comedy "Vasectomy, A Delicate Matter." —Lor.

Stoogemania
(COLOR/B&W)

Embarrassingly inept homage.

An Atlantic Releasing release of a Thomas Coleman and Michael Rosenblatt presentation. Executive producer, Scott Rosenfelt. Producer by Chuck Workman, James Ruxin, Directed by Workman. Screenplay, Jim Geoghan, Workman; camera (United color, b&w), Christopher Tufty; editor, Ruxin; music, Hummie Mann, Gary Tigerman; sound, Jan Brodin; assistant director-production manager, Ronald Colby; art direction, Charles D. Tomlinson; set decoration, Tom Talbert; optical & video effects, Workman; special color effects, Color Systems Technology; additional photography, Steve Posey; casting, Paul Ventura. Reviewed on Paramount Video vidcassette, N.Y., June 29, 1986. (MPAA Rating: PG.) Running time: 83 MINS.

Howard F. Howard . . . . Josh Mostel
Beverly . . . . Melanie Chartoff
Son of Curly . . . . Mark Holton
Dr. Flxyer Minder . . . . Sid Caesar
Also with: Patrick De Santis, Armin Shimerman, Thom Sharp, Josh Miller, Victoria Jackson, Ron House, Diz White; The Three Stooges (in compilation footage).

Take a faulty concept and execute it ineptly and you have "Stoogemania," feature-length filler intended as homage to The Three Stooges. Understandably never trade-screened, Atlantic release had a few regional playdates in October and is now available on vidcassette.

Filmmaker Chuck Workman, better known as a director of coming attractions trailers as well as the poor B-picture "Kill Castro," attempts here to cash in on the ongoing craze among young folks for the Stooges, which recently has pushed the late lowbrow comedians to the top of the heap in terms of screen team popularity.

Poor Josh Mostel is cast as a stoogemaniac, a young man whose life is falling apart due to his obsession with the Stooges. He wants to marry girlfriend Beverly (Melanie Chartoff) but is afraid her parents will object to him. Oddly enough, they approve but he gets cold feet and ultimately ends up in a mental home for stoogemaniacs. Sappy happy ending has them get married with the puerile message that it's okay to love the Stooges.

Film makes all the wrong moves, starting with the unforgivable boner of including mainly Shemp Howard 1940s editions of the Stooges in the film clips. Shemp certainly is okay and had an interesting solo career, but "Stoogemania" should be primarily about original stooge Jerry (Curly) Howard. Curly does appear in a few clips, but fans are bound to be bewildered and disappointed. Quality of the film clips chosen is quite variable as is the mode of presentation. Essentially, Mostel keeps dreaming or hallucinating about the Stooges, cueing poorly selected excerpts. Centerpieces here are Shemp plus Larry Fine and Moe Howard in a marriage sketch and Curly & teammates in a courtroom skit.

At one point, Workman incompetently attempts a "Dead Men Don't Wear Plaid" gambit of matching old and new footage. Sloppily added color (credited to Color Systems Technology) to the Stooges' original material is drab and smeared, as well as failing to fill the whole frame (walls and a couch occasionally are left gray & white). Use of colorization in several sequences is pointless in context; original 1932 MGM Stooges shorts exist that were filmed in color as well as the 1961 feature "Snow White And The Three Stooges" featuring Joe de Rita as third Stooge, but none of this material is used.

For no good reason, several segments of the new Mostel scenes (or Josh Miller as Young Mostel) are presented in black & white to match the original Stooges' work in this mishmash. When all else fails, Workman adds inappropriate rock songs to drown out the action. True to his trailermaker roots, he has a filler montage at the end, not of additional material but merely a recap of Stooges' scenes already used earlier.

Mostel tries hard but his slapstick routines aren't funny. Best bit is by Mark Holton (effective as the villain last year in "Pee-wee's Big Adventure") doing a nice Curly impression as a fellow stoogemaniac. Sid Caesar guest stars doing his mittle-European professor shtick as a shrink who diagnoses Mostel's problem. Hopefully no one will do a fan's tribute to Caesar's "Your Show Of Shows" that's as shoddy as this feature. —Lor.

Buta To Gunkan
(Pigs And Battleships)
(JAPANESE-B&W)

An East-West Classics release. Produced by Nikkatsu Corp. Executive producer, Kazu Otsuka. Directed by Shohei Imamura. Screenplay. Hisashi Yamuchi; camera (Nikkatsu-Scope, b&w), Shinsaku Himeda; art director, Kimihiko Nakamura; music, Toshiro Mayuzumi; assistant director, Kiriro Urayama. Reviewed at Film Forum 1, N.Y., July 1, 1986. (No MPAA Rating). Running time: 108 MINS.

Kinta . . . . Hiroyuki Nagato
Haruko . . . . Jitsuko Yoshimura
Tetsu . . . . Tetsuro Tamba
Himori . . . . : . . . . Masao Mishima
Also with: Shiro Osaka, Takeshi Kato, Shoichi Ozawa, Yoko Minamida, Hideo Sato, Eijiro Tono, Akira Yamauchi, Sanae Nakahara, Kin Sugai and Taiji Tonoyama.

Made in 1961, Shohei Imamura's "Pigs And Battleships" is a raucous, unsentimental study of the yakuza (Japanese mafia) subculture, young love and grinding poverty in the Japanese port city of Yokosuka circa 1960. Its long-delayed U.S. theatrical premiere at Gotham's Film Forum 1 will illuminate for the limited circle of Japanese film buffs the evolution of the anthropological propensity Imamura displayed in his 1979 murder classic, "Vengeance Is Mine" and his 1983 Cannes Golden Palm winning "The Ballad Of Narayama."

It's unfortunate that the audience here for "Pigs And Battleships" is likely to be so limited, because Imamura unfolds his sardonic, emotionally searing tale with the rapid-fire pacing and sordid grit that could appeal to a broader spectrum of film noir cultists.

Kinta (Hiroyuki Nagato) is a dull-witted but scrappy junkman's son who wants a better life and seizes the opportunity to work for a yaku-za gang. He participates in sadistic protection racket shakedowns, pimping and drug dealing, and ultimately becomes an accessory to the murder of a rival mobster. He's also assigned to a job in the gang's legit front business — pigtender for the porkers that gang boss Himori is raising on leftover slop from the local military base. Kinta's girlfriend, Haruko, wants him to quit the gang and get a factory job, but the lad is mesmerized by the "gangster's fate" and its lure of easy money.

Imamura portrays the gangsters unromantically as shiftless brutes whose one ethic is "to get a cut" of any action within their reach. Much of the action comes from the large U.S. Navy fleet docked in Yugosuka, and the director depicts the Yank sailors and their U.S. dollars as a corrupting and degrading presence inflicted upon a suffering nation as the price of defeat.

This moral and spiritual corruption is epitomized in Haruko's struggle against her mother and sister's campaign to turn here into a kept mistress for an American — any American — as a way out of their hovel-dwelling existence Imamura captures the tawdry port city and life in its brackish slums with a jarring naturalism that convincingly evokes the bitter struggle for day-to-day survival.

The film's portrayal of the futility of slum life and the swaggering enterprise of the yakuza viciously lampoons post-war Japan's move toward modernization and the new corporate state. The penultimate shoot-out scene in which Kinta and the double-crossing mobsters settle their differences in streets overrun with a stampeding juggernaut of pigs is memorable cinema and, as it turned out, was Imamura's calling card of things to come. —Rich.

Club Paradise
(COLOR)

Not quite boffo.

A Warner Bros. release of a Michael Shamberg production. Produced by Shamberg. Executive producer, Alan Greisman. Directed by Harold Ramis. Stars Robin Williams, Peter O'Toole, Rick Moranis. Screenplay. Ramis, Brian Doyle-Murray; story, Ed Roboto, Tom Leopold, Chris Miller, David Standish; camera (Technicolor), Peter Hannan; editor, Marion Rothman; music, David Mansfield, Van Dyke Parks; production design, John Graysmark; art director, Tony Reading; set decorator, Peter Young; sound (Dolby), Roy Charman; associate producer, Trevor Albert; assistant director, Pat Clayton; casting, Wally Nicita. Reviewed at The Burbank Studios, July 7, 1986. (MPAA Rating: PG-13). Running time: 104 MINS.

Jack Moniker . . . . Robin Williams
Gov. Anthony C. Hayes . . . . Peter O'Toole
Barry Nye . . . . Rick Moranis
Ernest Reed . . . . Jimmy Cliff
Phillipa Lloyd . . . . Twiggy
Prime Minister Gundy . . . . . Adolph Caesar
Barry Steinberg . . . . Eugene Levy
Terry Hamlin . . . . Joanna Cassidy
Linda White . . . . Andrea Martin
Voit Zerbe . . . . Brian Doyle-Murray
Randy White . . . . Steve Kampmann

Hollywood — There are enough funny skits in "Club Paradise" to make for a good hour of SCTV, where most of the cast is from, but too few to keep this Club Med satire afloat for 104 minutes. With the boxoffice already overbooked with comedies this summer, "Club Paradise" is bound to sink fast.

Screenplay by Harold Ramis ("Ghostbusters") and Brian Doyle-Murray originally was written with Doyle-Murray's comedian brother, Bill Murray, in mind as the lead — possibly with the idea of making an adult version of "Meatballs" at the beach.

Murray reportedly was unavailable and Robin Williams was signed to head the cast as a disabled Chicago fireman who uses his insurance settlement to become partners with a reggae musician (Jimmy Cliff) in a seedy Caribbean club they hope to turn into a first-class resort à la Club Med.

Williams can be a terrific actor/comedian, but the spark isn't here between him and the other Second City veterans as it might have been with Murray, another SCTV and "Saturday Night Live" chum.

Somehow, former "Meatballs" camp counselor Murray might have come up with cleverer ways of getting back at complaining guests (Andrea Martin, Steven Kampmann), nerdy, sex-crazed 100-pound and 165-pound weaklings (Rick Moranis and Eugene Levy, respectively) and the other expected amalgam of folks that equate resort living with nirvana.

Film lags with several extraneous subplots that appear to be filmmakers' attempt at serious satire and instead turn out to be just serious and tedious. Cliff's talents are misused as the laid-back club owner who leads an insurgency to overthrow Adolph Caesar as the island's corrupt prime minister before he sells the island to a multinational corporation.

Taken in three-minute tv bites, there are some hilarious scenes that stand out on their own, most notably with Moranis and Levy as two wild and crazy guys out to score some pot and a couple of chicks.

Former supermodel Twiggy looks great, but doesn't add anything as Williams' girlfriend, nor does Peter O'Toole as Her Majesty's emissary to the island, the pompous leech Gov. Anthony Croyden Hayes.
—Brit.

Sloane
(COLOR)

Uneventful action film.

A Skouras Pictures presentation of a Venture Intl. Pictures production. Executive producers, Peter Wilson, Clifford Wilson; co-executive producer, Douglas Rastello. Produced by Daniel Rosenthal, David Feder. Directed by Rosenthal; codirector, Richard Belding. Screenplay, Aubrey K. Rattan; camera (Metrocolor), John Hart; editor, 3-D Editorial, Andrew Horvitch; music, Phil Marshall; sound (L.A.), George Mahlberg; production manager, Glen Parian, Bert Asuncion; assistant director, Joel Apuyan, Soc Jose; production design, Robert Lee; associate producer, Pamela Resnik Rosenthal. Reviewed on Vestron Video vidcassette, N.Y., June 13, 1986. (No MPAA Rating.) Running time: 95 MINS.
Philip Sloane . . . . Robert Resnik
Cynthia Thursby . . . . Debra Blee
Pete Saimi . . . . Raul Aragon
Sal . . . . Victor Ordoñez
Naili Saimi . . . . Carissa Carlos
Chan Se . . . . Jonee Gamboa
Janice Thursby . . . . Ann Milhench
Arthur Margolis . . . . Charles Black
Richard Thursby . . . . George Mahlberg

"Sloane" is an example of how a film is doomed to failure if it doesn't begin with a workable script. Dull actioner was filmed in 1984 in the Philippines and Los Angeles, but was released directly to vidcassette domestically this year.

Handsome Robert Resnik portrays Sloane (his name is repeated constantly by the supporting cast as a reminder), a former L.A. cop sent to Manila (where he lived for many years) to find kidnaped Janice Thursby (Ann Milhench). He's been hired by Janice's dad, whose son-in-law Richard Thursby (George Mahlberg) was murdered during the kidnaping.

In Manila, Sloane reluctantly teams up with Richard's sister Cynthia (Debra Blee) to try and find Janice. They're aided by Sloane's Filipino pal Pete (Raul Aragon), whose pretty sister Naili (Carissa Carlos) quickly becomes Sloane's bedmate. Uneventful search is padded by okay car chases and violent shootouts. Entire plot, concerning some money supposedly stolen by Richard from an international religious cult, is sloughed off in a quick speech by Pete near the end of the picture.

Cast becomes increasingly bored with the pointless exercise and any audience is likely to join in the sentiment. For a good guy, Resnik's character of Sloane is distastefully ruthless and clashes horribly with the actor's niceguy personality. When he's called upon to laugh maniacally while mowing down bad guys in the final reel, Resnik really has egg on his face. Costar Blee (who starred in Crown's "The Beach Girls") is styled as a tomboy but delivers one requisite topless scene for her fans. Supporting cast is weak, with several thesps doubling (as usual in a low-budgeter) as soundman, location coordinator, etc. —Lor.

Deathmask
(COLOR)

Overly morbid suspense drama.

An Art Theater Guild presentation. Executive producer, Gloria Hope Sher. Produced by Louis K. Sher. Directed by Richard Friedman. Screenplay, Jeffrey Goldenberg, Friedman; camera (Movielab color), Yuri Denysenko; editor, Ian Maitland; music, Robert Ruggieri; sound, Jack Higgins; art direction, James Sherman; assistant director, Tommy Burns; casting, Sylvia Fay; associate producer, Goldenberg. Reviewed on Prism Entertainment vidcassette, N.Y., June 20, 1986. (No MPAA Rating.) Running time: 103 MINS.
Doug Andrews . . . . Farley Granger
Jane Andrews . . . . Lee Bryant
Jim O'Brien . . . . John McCurry
Dr. Riordan . . . . Arch Johnson
Suzy Andrews . . . . Barbara Bingham
Beatrice Van den Berg . . . . . Ruth Warrick
Capt. Mike Gress . . . . Danny Aiello
Victoria Howe . . . . Veronica Hart
Also with: John Calonius, Erika Katz, Kelly Nichols, R. Bolla.

"Deathmask" (a.k.a. "Unknown") is a well-acted, brooding suspense film too morbid to engage audience sympathies. Reviewed here for the record, feature was lensed in New York in 1983 and self-distributed via a four-wall booking in Phoenix in December 1984 ahead of its current homevideo availability.

Farley Granger toplines as Doug Andrews, a chief medical investigator who becomes obsessed with the case of a four-year-old boy whose corpse is found in a cardboard box in the woods in 1970. He is reminded of the tragic death of his young daughter Jennifer a year earlier in his swimming pool, an incident for which he feels guilty as well as blaming daughter Suzy who was watching her sister.

Not helped by resistance from incompetent chief medical examiner Dr. Riordan (Arch Johnson), Andrews and cop Mike Gress (Danny Aiello) are unable to identify the boy and solve the case. His family relationships are coming unglued, as Andrews crazily carries around with him the deathmask made of the boy's face.

Some 10 years later Andrews still is working on the case, even consulting a psychic (Ruth Warrick in a campy guest appearance). He finally tracks down the cause, as the boy was killed accidentally as a result of a violent love triangle involving jealous Victoria Howe (Veronica Hart). Film's end is extremely melancholy, as Andrews' wife has died of a stroke and his life force seems gone with the resolution of his single-minded quest. After a sad scene in which Victoria confesses but doesn't reveal her son's name to Andrews, pic ends with him tossing the deathmask in the ocean.

Granger is extremely effective in the driven role (claimed on screen to be a true story), which recalls the extremely downbeat pictures he starred in circa 1950: "Side Street" and "Edge Of Doom." Supporting cast is solid, with an excellent contribution by former porn star Veronica Hart in the pivotal role of the child's mystery mom. As an odd touch, Hart is joined in the love triangle in flashback by her frequent porn costars Kelly Nichols and R. Bolla. —Lor.

L'Amant Magnifique
(The Magnificent Lover)
(FRENCH-COLOR)

An AAA Classic release of a G.P.F.I./Soprofilms coproduction, with participation of the C.N.C. Executive producer, Jean-Claude Fleury. Produced by Patrick Denauneux (France), Antonio Cunha Telles (Portugal). Written and directed by Aline Issermann. Script collaborator, Michel Dufresne; camera (Eastmancolor), Dominique Le Rigoleur; sound, François de Morant, Dominique Hennequin; editor, Dominique Auvray; art director, Danka Semenovicz; production manger, Alain Mayor. Reviewed at the Marignan-Concorde theater, Paris, June 20, 1986. Running time: 100 MINS.
With: Isabelle Otero (Viviane), Hippolyte Girardot (Vincent), Robin Renucci (Antoine), Didier Agostini (Luc), Daniel Jegou (Marc), Michel Fortin, Corinne Cosson, Anna Azevedo, Patrick Perez, Renaud Isaac, Marie Guyonnet, Gregory Cosson.

Paris — Aline Issermann, a former cartoonist and journalist who made a fine feature writing-helming debut in 1983 with "Le Destin de Juliette," disappoints with her second film, which tells of a passion between a horse-breeder's wife and the handsome young groom in her husband's employ.

Isabelle Otero is a lovely screen newcomer though she doesn't muster much dramatic interest as the wayward wife whose senses suddenly come awake after three years of marriage to Robin Renucci, and who decides to flee with Hippolyte Girardot, with whom she experiences extraordinary carnal pleasures.

They find temporary refuge in the beachside cabin of Otero's brother, though their intense idyll is disturbed by a wound incurred by Girardot's beloved horse, with which the groom refuses to separate. He finally decides he must take the animal to find a vet and the two take leave of one another. So much for romance.

Where the narrative style of "Le Destin de Juliette" was naturalistic and simple, the direction of "L'Amant Magnifique" is larded with symbolism and emphatic effects, and the two principals spend so much time coupling (usually against superb natural backdrops) that little time is left for any essential characterization and empathy.

Shot mostly in Portugal, film's chief assets are the technical contributions of Dominique Le Rigoleur (one of the few femme cinematographers around, and a first-rate lenser) and sound specialists François de Morant and Dominique Hennequin, who together create the sensuous environment in which the lovers entwine ecstatically. —Len.

Notebook From China
(U.S.-DANISH-DOCU-COLOR)

A Burlington Northern (Seattle) presentation of a World Pacific Pictures (Portland, Ore.) with the Danish Film Institute production. Produced by David Talbott. Executive producer, Hanne Uldal. Written and directed by Jörgen Leth. Camera (Eastmancolor), Dan Holmberg; editor, Janus Billeskov Jansen, Rumle Hammerich, Vinca Wiedemann; music, folk music excerpts and quotes from Mozart. Reviewed at Dagmar theater, Copenhagen, June 30, 1986. Running time: 75 MINS.

Copenhagen — "Notebook From China" is hardly what it set out to be, when World Pacific Pictures of Oregon two years ago sent Danish poet-filmmaker Jörgen Leth to China to record in a docu whatever impressed his mind during a 6,000-mile trip by rail. Economically troubled en route, production later was salvaged by Burlington Northern of Seattle and the Danish Film Institute, while its present title was changed from the original "China By Rail."

There is plenty of railroad and rail travel footage left in Leth's film, and audiences will get an impression of quite romantic travel — for Chinese and foreigner alike — through verdant and often dramatic landscapes.

We get precious few facts, if any, about travel by rail in China, while Leth as narrator waxes poetic on the nicety of everything. Soon, however, the railroad footage is reduced to serving as intermission play between prolonged visits with Chinese at work in various fields, most of them either artistic or seen as very arty. This way, the making of noodles, the cutting up of a fish, etc., are seen as just as individually creative endeavors as the work of a calligraphic painter and that of a juggler keeping a giant jar up in the air.

Leth also meets students at Peking's conservatory prepping the first-ever Chinese staging of Mozart's "The Marriage Of Figaro" and a team of woman bicycle racers training to approach world standards. Wherever Leth takes us and whoever he introduces to us, he leaves us dangling with plenty of questions about whats, whys and wherefores. Everything is recorded and later edited in a rather haphazard way.

The method — or lack of method — may intrigue special situation audiences, but it probably will annoy most others. Leth never gets coy or cute with his material, but he does let it run on too long and dulls the effect of repetition as a pictorial rhythm device. Dan Holmberg's cinematography is sometimes stunning and original, and other times flat in its intended unobtrusiveness. —*Kell.*

Muzskoe Vospitanie
(Manly Education)
(SOVIET-COLOR)

A Turkmenfilm production. Directed by Usman Saparov, Jazgeldy Seidov. Screenplay, Cary Japan, Saparov; camera (color), Nurjagdy Shamuchammedov; art direction, Aleksandr Mitta; sound, Nellja Bazarov; music, Nury Chalmamedov. Reviewed at Pesaro Film Festival, June 17, 1986. Running time: **77 MINS.**

Caman . . . . Bengene Kurbandurdyev
Mergenaka . . . . Ata Dovletov
Sejli . . . . Dyrdgmamet Oraev
Dzeren . . . . Gulja Kerimova

Pesaro —.Finely constructed kid-pic ''Manly Education'' shows a timid little boy forcibly learning the lessons of manhood in the desert with his father and grandfather, nomadic shepherds.

Directors Usman Saparov and Jazgeldy Seidov have an ax to grind with mothers who over-protect their male offspring and keep them from growing up tough.

Fortunately, film goes beyond its title and presents a more complicated picture of childhood sensitivity clashing with adult reality, through contact with harsh and marvelous nature.

When his father sees young Caman (Bengene Kurbandurdyev) called a coward because he's scared to cross a narrow mountain bridge, he decides to make him spend a few months herding sheep in the desert. It isn't hard to understand the boy's terror at suddenly being made to assume responsibility like a grownup, being lowered into a deep well to retrieve a rope, or his horror on learning the fate that awaits his flock of lambs when they are taken to the central farm (and skinned to make coats).

True, the pint-sized hero is exasperatingly slow at shedding his fears of the desert, but by pic's end he also has won a small victory of his own over his scowling, tough-as-nails père: he saves his lambs, and earns parental respect for not jumping ship when the going gets rough.

Film is well lensed and paced tightly enough to hold interest from beginning to end. — *Yung.*

Er Woo Dong
(The Entertainer)
(KOREAN-COLOR)

A Tae Hung Film Co. production (Seoul). Produced by Lee Tae-won. Directed by Lee Jang-ho. Screenplay, Lee Hyon-hwa, based on a story by Bang Gi-hwan; camera (color), Park Sung-bae; editor, Hyung Dong-choon;

music, Lee Chong-ku; production design, Yun Geong-hwan; costumes, Lee Hon-gung. Reviewed at Vancouver Intl. Film Festival, June 17, 1986. Running time: **115 MINS.**
Er Yoon Chang/Hyanjgi . . . Ahn Sung-ghi
Assassin . . . . Lee Bo-hee

Vancouver — The official Korean entry for 1985 Academy Award consideration, Lee Jang-ho's perfervid period meller ''Er Woo Dong'' is a sadomasochistic erotic action programmer masquerading as a dignified women's lib protest pic. Touted by the Vancouver festival as a breakthrough for women's rights in Korea, the glossy epic revels in both gore and tititlation. There is no full frontal nudity, other than a longshot of a nude young boy, but the pic boasts a plethora of suggestive scenes. In the first reel alone three rapes occur.

It is 1379 A.D. and in the 10th year of the reign of King Sung-jong, during the 500-year Chosun Dynasty, unfolds the tale of Prince Taesan's ex-wife, stage name Hyanjgi, a wandering courtesan disowned by her stern father and settled briefly in Deer Valley. Father has hired an assasin to put an end to Hyanjgi's life and to his shame. The killer, emasculated in his youth, stalks his prey who is protected by deaf-mute Chonga, a boyhood friend of the assassin. Both were mutilated the same night by noblemen.

The courtesan is well connected, being the niece of Prime Minister Chung and the daughter of Minister of the Left Park. After her bodyguard Chonga murders her rapist (Ho), a silversmith (Mr. Kang of the Criminal Investigation Office) maneuvers the proclivities of her ex and her father to arrange her execution. Hyanjgi simply asserted her iron will too often and too indiscriminately for a stern patriarchal society to countenance.

Leading lady Ahn Sung-ghi swoons on cue, making the most of her porcelain frailty. Her costars mug in the background, with hero Lee Bo-hee doing a nifty impersonation of Henry Silva, circa 1957. Lenser Park Sung-bae uses every trick in the book with versatility: freeze-frame, rack-focus, zoom; and cutter Hyun Dong-choon contributes some dandy dissolves and montages. Technical credits are to be reckoned with, but ''Er Woo Dong'' is simply an exploitation film, a smooth and silly slice of exotica that arouses mild prurience in the viewer.—*Gran.*

Fear
(Unconscious)
(ITALIAN-FRENCH-COLOR)

A Dionysio Cinematografica (Rome)/Societe Nouvelle Cinevox (Paris) coproduction, presented by Enzo Boetani, Giuseppe Collura, Simon Mizrahi. Directed by Riccardo Freda. Screenplay, Antonio Cesare Corti, Fabio Piccioni, Freda; adaptation dialog, Miz-

rahi; camera (Telecolor), Cristiano Pogany; editor, uncredited; music, Franco Mannino; sets & costumes, Giorgio Desideri; assistant director, Corti, Bernard Cohn. Reviewed on Wizard Video vidcassette, N.Y., June 26, 1986. (No MPAA Rating.) Running time: **90 MINS.**
Michael Stanford . . . . Stefano Patrizi
Shirley . . . . Martine Brochard
Hans . . . . Henri Garcin
Beryl . . . . Laura Gemser
Oliver . . . . John Richardson
Glenda . . . . Anita Strindberg
Deborah . . . . Silvia Dionisio

Riccardo Freda, doyen of Italian horror film directors, attempts to modernize his approach (with mixed results) in ''Fear.'' Reviewed here for the record, feature was made in 1980 with various alternate titles including ''Unconscious'' and ''Murder Syndrome;'' it is now available domestically on vidcassette.

Stefano Patrizi portrays a film actor who is haunted by nightmares and daydreams relating to having witnessed in childhood the murder of his dad. When he and a film crew visit his mother's home in the country as part of a location-hunting trip a series of grisly murders occurs.

Freda includes hints of various fantasy elements here, ranging from black magic to an invisible kirlian-effect killer, but essentially this is a gothic murder mystery dressed up with modern sex & violence. Key plot element emphasizes the too-close relationship of Patrizi and his mother, played by former sex symbol Anita Strindberg. More recent sex stars Laura Gemser and Silvia Dionisio are on hand in various stages of undress as Patrizi's leading lady and girl friend, respectively.

Tech credits other than the subpar dubbing are fine and Franco Mannino provides a pleasant musical score emphasizing classical themes. Even for the horror genre, Freda's gloomy ending is a bit much.—*Lor.*

One Night Only
(CANADIAN-COLOR)

An RSL Entertainment presentation of a Robert Lantos/Stephen J. Roth production. Produced by Lantos, Roth. Directed by Timothy Bond. Screenplay, P.Y. Haines; camera (Medallion color), René Verzier; editor, Michael Karen, Jaki Carmody; music, Lawrence Shragge; sound, Don Cohen; production design, Csaba Kertesz; production manager, Julian Marks; assistant director, Michael Zenon; costume design, Laurie Drew; postproduction supervisor, Jennifer Black; casting, Deirdre Bowen, Ginette D'Amico. Reviewed on Key Video vidcassette, N.Y., June 19, 1986. (No MPAA Rating.) Running time: **86 MINS.**
Anne . . . . Lenore Zann
Suzanne . . . . Helene Udy
Louella . . . . Taborah Johnson
Elizabeth . . . . Judy Foster
Winkeau . . . . Hrant Alianak
Wes . . . . Ken James
Mack . . . . Jeff Braunstein
Jean . . . . Wendy Lands
Johnny . . . . Martin Neufeld
Jamie . . . . Geoffrey MacKay

''One Night Only'' is one of four Canadian features that rolled in November 1983 with financial backing from The Playboy Channel. Of interest only to voyeurs, feature, originally titled more appropriately ''New Year's Eve,'' is an embarrassing example of what is euphemistically called Canadian content. It is currently available on vidcassette.

Girls at a Montreal sorority house suddenly decide they want to go to bed with the players on the pro hockey team (apparently the Canadiens). Led by busty young blond Anne (Lenore Zann) they maneuver to take over the annual New Year's Eve sex party traditionally organized by gangster Winkeau (Hrant Alianak) and borrow the posh mansion of the parents of sorority sister Elizabeth (Judy Foster) for the occasion. When there aren't enough college girls to service the pucksters, Anne recruits local prostitutes to join the party, led by beautiful Louella (Taborah Johnson),who also coaches the coeds in lovemaking techniques.

Exercise in dumb puns and vulgarity is designed mainly to show off some pretty girls sans clothing, okay for Playboy viewers, but a bore as a feature film. Pic's lame concept of satire is evident when team owner Mack (Jeff Braunstein) has to force his hotshot star Johnny (Martin Neufeld) to engage in drinking and sex when all the youngster wants to do is play hockey, do endorsements and appear on tv.

For a basically tame softcore outing, scripter P.Y. Haines oddly emphasizes incest, with several of the couples imagining they're father & daughter or mother & son during sex, and the romantic payoff occurring when young Anne beds down with her even younger cousin Jamie (Geoffrey MacKay). Cast does a good job and is worthy of much better material.—*Lor.*

The Lunatics
(HONG KONG-COLOR)

Produced and presented by D&B Films. Executive producer, Dickson Poon. Directed by Yee Tung Sing. Stars Fung Sui Fan, Deanie Yip, Chow Yun Fat, John Sham, Chun Pui, Lai Huen, Dennis Chan, Leung Chieu Wai. Screenplay, Yee Tung Sing; theme song performed by Deanie Yip. (No other credits provided by the producer.) Reviewed at Jade Cinema, Hong Kong, June 19, 1986. Running time: **95 MINS.**
(Cantonese soundtrack with English subtitles)

Hong Kong — Mental or emotional illness is a luxury in the success/money/status-oriented city of Hong Kong. The competition is grave and survival in the hectic urban jungle is good if a person maintains his or her regular work output. Thus, there's no time to go crazy or have a nervous breakdown in the demanding pressure cooker environment.

"The Lunatics" wax jinx-stricken from the first day the company exhibited its teaser poster campaign warning Hong Kong people about the imminent presence of many suicidal, depressed and murderous madmen, running free in society. The company was met with public ire from local politicians and the Television and Entertainment Licensing Authority which claimed it did not issue an advertising permit.

"The Lunatics" seemed bound for commercial disaster with its serious subject matter and negative publicity, but there was a complete turnaround as the film now will likely be a commercial and artistic success. The fuss created a lot of publicity. The outcome is that the HK$3,000,000-budgeted production which took 15 months to finish (according to the filmmaker) is now the hot film to see in Hong Kong.

The film is actually a realistic, compassionate and well-balanced presentation as directed by Yee Tung Sing, younger brother of ex-Shaw Bros. kung fu star, David Chiang.

Deanie Yip is believable as the newspaper columnist while actor Fung Sui Fan as the concerned social worker deserves an award.

There are many wonderful perfomances by matinee idols like Chow Yun Fat, John Sham and Leung Chieu Wai who crashed their glamorous images to play stunning cameo roles of emotionally unstable vagrants who live in a world of their own on the streets of Hong Kong.

The pacing, screenplay, photography and other technical production credits are of high quality. The finale actually points the finger at the "normal" people, rather than thsoe who have been victimized by fate, society, humans and plain bad luck. It points to the fact that street vagrants are harmless, unless provoked. —Mel.

Zazzennyj Fonar
(The Lit Lantern)
(SOVIET-COLOR)

An Armenfilm production. Written and directed by Agasi Ajvazjan. Camera (color), Levon Atojano; art direction, Grigor Torosjan; sound, Eduard Vanuno; music, Tigran Mansurjan. Reviewed at Pesaro Film Festival, June 18, 1986. Running time: **87 MINS.**
Vano .... Valdimir Kocarjan
Vera .... Violeta Gevorkjan
Mkrtum .... Abesalom Loria
Gasparelli .... Leonid Sarkisov
Also with: Genrich Alaverdjan (Bankutuzjan), Karpos Martirosjan (Pakule).

Pesaro — As simple and imaginative as its hero, "The Lit Lantern" sketches the life of folk artist Vano Khodzhabekov around the turn of the century. Veteran scriptwriter Agasi Ajvazjan imparts a feeling of tenderness and melancholy to the struggles of the impoverished artist in his second feature.

Nagged by his wife Vera (Violeta Gevorkjan) and with two small kids to feed, Vano (Vladimir Kocarjan) sells pots and pans for a rich merchant. Or better, he sits in the dark store scribbling and drawing. When he loses his job, he trudges around the countryside with coal makers and lamp sellers, hiding his joblessness from fearsome Vera.

"Lantern" owes much of its poignancy to Kocarjan's humble, unassuming doodler, unaware of his own great talent and stymied when confronted with oil paints and canvas from the first time. Character actors are excellent, like Abesalom Loria the lampmaker, who consoles Vano with the thought everyone must follow the light inside him.

Camerawork is fresh and colors nuanced in this very visual film. As though echoing the style of a naif painter, Ajvazjan repeats some of his best shots — a man diving off a building into a lake — several times in a row. Also striking is the recurrent use of a band of sober-faced folk musicians, who appear out of nowhere to musically comment on Vano's trials and tribulations.

Amusing, philosophical and touching, "Lit Lantern" shows the Armenian cinema reaching out beyond standard models to get at the heart of its folk traditions. — Yung.

Pulsebeat
(SPANISH-COLOR)

A Calepas Intl. presentation. Produced by José Frade. Directed by Marice Tobias. Screenplay, Steven Siebert; camera (color), George Herrero; editor, Matt Cope; music, Walter Murphy; sound (Dolby), Phil Pearl; art direction, Alfonso L. Barajas; production manager, Josi Konski; assistant director, Don Moody; costume design, Frank Carretti; choreographer, Bill Williams. Reviewed on Lightning Video vidcassette, N.Y., June 21, 1986. (No MPAA Rating.) Running time: 92 MINS.
Roger .... Daniel Greene
Annie .... Lee Taylor Allan
Alvin .... Bob Small
The Bat .... Alice Moore
Marlene .... Helga Line
Adrian .... Alex Intriago
Cyndi .... Carole James
Vincent .... Miguel De Grandy
Leyna .... Earleen Carey
Greg Adonis .... Peter Lupus

"Pulsebeat" is an embarrassingly inept film that attempts to capitalize on the current interest in fitness and, specifically, aerobic workouts. Shot in Florida in May 1984 by a Spanish production outfit, picture is being released domestically on vidcassette.

Steven Siebert's wafer-thin screenplay posits a battle between two Florida healthclubs: Roger's Gym, run by hunk Roger (Daniel Greene) and the Rejuvenarium owned by Marlene (Spanish star Helga Line). Marlene is stealing away Roger's best aerobics instructors as well as employing a spy in his camp, Latin hunk Adrian (Alex Intriago).

Feature is all padding designed to build to an extremely tedious annual Aerobithon contest. Halfway through it's revealed that Marlene is Roger's mother (quite a joke considering their obvious differing nationalities), removing any tension or interest from the competition. Among boring "sporting" events, it would be harder to find competition duller than watching people do jumping jacks or ride stationary exercise bicycles, exactly what constitutes the big finish here.

In attempting to make an imitation-U.S. film, producer José Frade trips up by having some scenes dubbed, some using direct-sound dialog and others a mixture as some actors require dubbing. End credits manage to several times misspell a function as "coreography."

Cast is weak, with topliner Greene wooden in the extreme. Novelty of giving equal time to male beefcake as well as the usual femme cheesecake is initially intriguing but goes nowhere. Former "Mission Impossible" tv regular Peter Lupus has a guest role as a Steve Reeves-type muscleman star who serves as the hero's inspiration. —Lor.

The Manhunt
(ITALIAN-COLOR)

A Samuel Goldwyn Co. presentation of a Fulvia Film production. Written, produced and directed by "Larry Ludman" (Fabrizio De Angelis). Camera (Luciano Vittori color), "Joseph Mercury" (Guglielmo Mancori); editor, "Vincent P. Thomas" (Vincenzo Tomassi); music, Francesco De Masi; sound, Steve Connely; car stunt coordinator, Alan Petit. Reviewed on Media Home Entertainment vidcassette, N.Y., June 29, 1986. (No MPAA Rating.) Running time: 89 MINS.
Stranger .... John Ethan Wayne
Guard .... Raymund Harmstorf
Prison boss .... Henry Silva
Sheriff .... Bo Svenson
Ben Robeson .... Ernest Borgnine
Also with: Terry Lynch, Don Taylor, Randy Mulkey, Farris Castleberry, Susan Wilson.

"The Manhunt" is a competently made but uninteresting drama of a man wrongfully sent to jail who stubbornly tries to settle accounts. Italian production filmed in April 1984 in Arizona laughingly tries to palm itself off as all-American with anglicized credits, except (as usual) for the musical composer billed correctly as Francesco De Masi, since soundtrack collectors love and respect Italian cleffers.

Following in the family footsteps, John Ethan Wayne toplines as a never-named stranger who buys two horses at a Tucson racetrack and heads home. On the way, he stops off on land owned by a rancher played by Ernest Borgnine to water them and is accosted by Borgnine for trespassing. Borgnine nastily pretends the horses are his and, with no receipt for sale, Wayne is sent packing without them. Borgnine scoffs at future efforts to regain the horses and has Wayne sent to jail on a three-year rap when he tries to steal them back.

Resembling innumerable earlier and much better rustic prison films such as "Cool Hand Luke" and "Mean Dog Blues," "Manhunt" degenerates into a routine series of escape and chase scenes. Filmmaker Fabrizio De Angelis' gutless approach is evident in a sappy conclusion. After starting off effectively as a nasty villain (like he used to play early in his career), Borgnine improbably turns into Mr. Nice Guy to help Wayne out in the final reel.

Wayne is okay in action scenes, but evokes little personality here. Technical credits are good, with sound recording virtually up to U.S. standards, but De Angelis overuses slow motion at every opportunity.—Lor.

Heartburn
(COLOR)

Flawed but funny look at modern marriage. Streep & Nicholson should draw the customers.

A Paramount Pictures release. Produced by Mike Nichols, Robert Greenhut. Directed by Nichols. Stars Meryl Streep, Jack Nicholson. Screenplay, Nora Ephron, based on her novel; camera (Technicolor), Nestor Almedros; editor, Sam O'Steen; music, Carly Simon; sound, James Sabat; production design, Tony Walton; art director, John Kasarda; set decorator, Susan Bode; costumes, Ann Roth; assistant director, Joel Tuber; associate producer, Tuber; casting, Juliet Taylor. Reviewed at Paramount screening room, Hollywood, June 24, 1986. (MPAA Rating: R.) Running time: **108 MINS.**

Rachel	Meryl Streep
Mark	Jack Nicholson
Richard	Jeff Daniels
Vera	Maureen Stapleton
Julie	Stockard Channing
Arthur	Richard Masur
Betty	Catherine O'Hara
Harry	Steven Hill
Dmitri	Milos Forman
Annie	Natalie Stern
Thelma Rice	Karen Akers

Hollywood — "Heartburn" is a beautifully crafted film with flawless performances and many splendid moments, yet the overall effect is a bit disappointing. Perhaps it is because Jack Nicholson and Meryl Streep as husband and wife end up pretty much where they started out and reveal little of themselves along the way. Nonetheless, pic has plenty of laughs and as one of the few serious summer entries should perform respectably at the boxoffice.

From the start Streep and Nicholson are never quite a couple. Mark's a Washington political columnist and Rachel's a New York food writer. They meet at a wedding and he overpowers her. Soon they're having their own wedding.

Nora Ephron has adapted her own novel for the screen which in turn borrowed heavily from her marriage with Watergate reporter Carl Bernstein. Oddly enough she has virtually left out the couples' professional life which is treated merely as an extension of their personal affairs.

While the day-to-day details are drawn with a striking clarity, Ephron's script never goes much beyond the mannerisms of middle class life. Even with the sketchy background information revealing that this is a second marriage for Rachel and Mark's been around the block, it's hard to tell what these people are feeling or what they want. It is abundantly clear, however, what they eat, where they live and how they dress. Woes of renovating an old townhouse in Georgetown are, in fact, rather old hat by now.

Where the film does excel is in creating the surface and texture of their life. Director Mike Nichols knows the territory well enough to throw in some subtle but biting satire and Nicholson and Streep fill in the canvas.

Film is played from Rachel's perspective and Mark may be a little shortchanged in the process. Streep breaks some new ground in playing the lighter side of a highstrung modern woman. Rachel is the kind of person who lives to eat and can say with a straight face that "rice pudding is a very personal thing."

Streep handles urban neurotic comedy without missing a beat. As a mother she has some priceless scenes with her young daughter reciting nursery rhymes.

Nicholson is equally impressive but more within his recognizable range. He has at least one smashing scene when, learning that his wife is pregnant, proceeds to serenade her with a selection of old standards with "baby" in the title.

As good and as charming as he is, casting Nicholson, who is inherently untrustworthy, instantly puts the marriage in question right from the start. He has a history of philandering and when he does it here it comes as no surprise. (Mandy Patinkin was originally set to play the role, with Nicholson replacing him during production.—*Ed.)*

·The inevitability of the relationship's failure is like a cloud hanging over the marriage as the film plays out old patterns of behavior for Mark and Rachel. "Heartburn" answers how the marriage breaks up, not why. Ephron's script seems to suggest it can all happen again.

Nichols shoots modern marriage as if under a magnifying glass with constant use of closeups. Staging is impeccable and Nestor Almendros' moody photography is rich and evocative. Other tech credits are firstrate including Tony Walton's precise production design.

Characters on the edge of the canvas deftly enhance the tone of the picture. Jeff Daniels as an editor with a crush on Rachel is perfect in suggesting a man whom she could like but not love. Stockard Channing and Richard Masur are just catty enough as friends of the family but not nearly as much as tv newswoman Catherine O'Hara who seems better suited to a career as a gossip columnist.

Also fine is Steven Hill as Rachel's father. He has one special scene in his bedroom with his daughter after her marriage has broken up. He's as sympathetic as he can be but is busy making his own mistakes.

In fact, there are enough good touches throughout the film to make its lightness and shortcomings more glaring.—*Jagr.*

Ocean Drive Weekend
(COLOR)

Stillborn nostalgia exercise.

A Troma release of an L.A. Prods. production. Executive producer, Dwight D. South. Produced by Marvin Almeas. Directed by Bryan Jones. Screenplay, Jones, from story by Jones, Charles Redmond; camera (color) & editor, John Godwin; music, Alan Kaufman; sound, Robert Landau; dialog director, Pat Hurley; costume design, Ann Jones; casting, Carol Jones. Reviewed on Vestron Video vidcassette, N.Y., June 27, 1986. (MPAA Rating: PG-13.) Running time: **98 MINS.**

With: Charles Redmond (Miller), Robert Peacock, P.J. Grethe, Konya Dee, Jon Kohler, Tony Freeman, John Aschenbrenner, Sharon Brewer, Kay McCelland, Will Redmond, Dan Byrd, Wallace Eastland, Grant Elliot, Smitty Flynn & The Rivieras.

"Ocean Drive Weekend" is a tame, uneventful teen comedy aimed at the 1960s nostalgia market. Picture was released in South Carolina (where it was shot) in July 1985 sans trade screenings and has just entered homevideo release.

Talkathon concerns overage boys and girls from a southern university in the early 1960s who head out to Ocean Drive for a weekend of boozing and, hopefully, romancing. Abbreviated, mainly cover versions of several 1960s hits plays on the soundtrack as well as numbers performed on camera by the inimitable Smitty Flynn & The Rivieras.

Filmmaker Bryan Jones (may the late Rolling Stones guitarist rest in peace) tries meekly for some humor but picture is hardly competitive in these post-"Porky's" grossout times. An audience could be forgiven for chanting "more plot, more plot" by the end of the aimless exercise.

Tech credits are weak and cast not very attractive. Filmed in Georgetown and Myrtle Beach, S. C., picture obviously features local talent with drawls to match.—*Lor.*

Le Bonheur a encore frappé
(Happiness Strikes Again)
(FRENCH-COLOR)

A Visa Film Distribution release of a Harvert Prods./Chloé Prods. coproduction, with the participation of the CNC. Executive producer, Marc André Grynbaum. Produced by Patricia Fauron. Written and directed by Jean-Luc Trotignon. Script collaborators, Sylvie Chauvet, Gérard Krawczyk; camera (Eastmancolor), Michel Abramowicz; editor, Thierry Rouden; sound, Jean-Paul Bernard; art direction, Laurence Vendroux; music, Jean-Claude Deblais; assistant director, Pascale Thirode; production manager, Dominique Szpindel. Reviewed at the AMLF screening room, Paris, July 2, 1986. Running time: **80 MINS.**

Achille Pinglard	Jean-Luc Bideau
Ginette Pinglard	Michèle Brousse
Adolf Pinglard	Jean-Noël Brouté
Josette Pinglard	Caroline Apperé
Grandma Pinglard	Denise Péron
Ingrid Bermouthe	Marie-Christine Orry
Charles Delacroix	Raymond Aquilon
Marie-Eve Etrecy	Valérie Schoeller

Paris — "Le Bonheur a encore frappé" is a "bad taste" comedy in which 27-year newcomer Jean-Luc Trotignon skewers traditional values with a portrait of a family wallowing in its own vulgar nullity. The comic mode of outgrossing the public is not new, and has been done better by others. Trotignon, who wrote and directed, has occasional ideas and some effectively crass dialog, but doesn't show much skill at constructing a fluid screenplay and bringing it to life as a filmmaker.

Script is essentially a series of vignettes about the Pinglard family, whose head, Jean-Luc Bideau, is a mediocre foreman in a munitions factory. His wife, Michèle Brousse, works in a porno cinema. Their daughter, Caroline Apperé, the family scapegoat, is partially immobilized by a neck brace and channels her boredom and frustration into a diary, later exploited by her parents to become a bestselling memoir. There is also a son, who returns from military service to find his room rented out, and a cackling, boozing grandmother in a wheelchair.

The performances are aptly cartoonish, but Trotignon doesn't have a style with which to animate his gallery of foul grotesques. Bideau, a past master at incarnating lowlifes and lecherous types, is in his element here but fails to lift the film out of its own grubby indigence. —*Len.*

Dragon Rapide
(SPANISH-COLOR)

A Televisión Española and Tibidabo Films production, in collaboration with Rete 1 (Italy). Produced and directed by Jaime Camino. Screenplay, Román Gubern, Camino; camera (Eastmancolor), Juan Amorós; editor, Teresa Alcocer; music, Xavier Montsalvatje; sets, Félix Murcia; historical consultant, Ian Gibson. Reviewed at Cinearte Studios, Madrid, July 4, 1986. Running time: **105 MINS.**

General Franco	Juan Diego
Carmen Polo de Franco	Victoria Peña
General Mola	Manuel de Blas
General Kindelan	Saturno Cerra

Also with: Eduardo McGregor, Francisco Casares, Pedro D. del Corral, Santiago Ramos, Laura Garcia Lorca, Miguel Molina, Iosé L. Pellicena, Pedro del Rio.

Madrid — "Dragon Rapide" was the name of the small airplane, rented in London in July 1936, which carried General Francisco Franco from the Canary Islands to Morocco from where the Spanish Civil War began. Jaime Camino's film meticulously traces the political and military events of the two weeks leading to the uprising. Day by day the spectator is privy to the plottings, uncertainties and differences of the generals involved in the overthrow of the Republican government.

Presumably due to a small budget for this sort of sweeping historical film, Camino has been obliged to limit the on-scene action to interiors.

A replica of the original plane has been built and appears constantly throughout the film, but the few key outdoor scenes could have used a few hundred extras. Instead, we *hear* the shouts in the streets and the clang of the trolley cars, imagining the turmoil, but it is never shown.

Thesping is excellent throughout, especially by Juan Diego as Franco, first time the Generalissimo has been portrayed in a Spanish film. Diego mimics the movements, mannerisms and poses of Franco to perfection. Victoria Peña is a believable Doña Carmen, the general's wife and supporting cast is fine. Franco, however, was never a dramatic or exciting figure, the way Hitler and Mussolini were, and this detracts from the film's interest.

Camino and cowriter Román Gubern choose to hop swiftly about from one scene of conspiracy to another: Madrid, London, Canaries, Morocco, Navarre, Biarritz. Occasionally the spectator may get lost; ditto for the dozen or more generals thrown at us, many of whom will remain only a blur to those not students of the period.

Pic ends with the landing of the "Dragón Rapide" in Morocco. The plane pulls up to the camera and goes out of focus. It is the beginning of three years of civil war and ultimately the victroy of the Fascists. As a historical document, Camino's pic is not without interest, but somehow it fails to convey the excitement of one of the most dramatic episodes in Spanish history.

Despite the well-known left-wing affiliations of many involved in making the film, treatment of Franco and of others involved in the rebellion is always respectful and factual. Perhaps that is one of the film's shortcomings: Camino has reconstructed in a virtually documentary manner the events of those weeks, rather than playing up the dramatic elements involved.
—*Besa*.

Roller Blade
(COLOR)

Demented science fiction.

A New World Pictures presentation. Produced and directed by Donald G. Jackson. Screenplay, Jackson, Randall Frakes, from story by Jackson; camera (color), Jackson; editor, Ron Amick; music, Robert Garrett; production manager, Elaine Edford; assistant director-stunt coordinator, Clifford Davidson; set design, Jackson, Amick; special visual effects, Tony Tremblay, Amick; associate producer, Amick. Reviewed on New World Videocassette, N.Y., July 12, 1986. (No MPAA Rating.) Running time: **97 MINS.**
Sister Sharon Cross . . . . Suzanne Solari
Marshall Goodman . . . . . . Jeff Hutchinson
Hunter/Sister Fortune . . . . Shaun Michelle
Mother Speed . . . . Katina Garner
Waco . . . . Sam Mann
The Deputy/Dr. Saticoy . . . . Robby Taylor
Chris Goodman . . Chris Douglas-Olen Ray
Also with: Michelle Bauer, Barbara Peckinpaugh, Lisa Marie.

The fad of low-budget science fiction films inspired by the Aussie hit "The Road Warrior" reaches its nadir with New World's "Roller Blade," an amateurish junker released directly to the homevideo market.

Set in the "City of Lost Angels" during an unspecified post-W.W. III period of barbarism, pic has a female religious order controlled by Mother Speed (Katina Garner) battling with Dr. Saticoy (Robby Taylor dressed like a "Road Warrior" bad guy) and his evil henchmen. The novelty of everyone performing on roller skates (except Mother Speed, who's in a wheelchair and young punkers called spikers who use skateboards) soon wears off and film becomes interminable.

Saticoy sends a foxy blond girl (Shaun Michelle) to infiltrate Mother Speed's order and steal her power crystal, which has the ability to heal and even bring the dead back to life (it only works one time per customer, however, on stiffs). She ultimately rebels and joins the good guys, who, led by Sister Sharon (Suzanne Solari) and a local cop (Marshall Goodman) destroy Saticoy.

Filmmaker Donald G. Jackson apparently shot this mess silent and poorly dubbed new voices for the characters, which only makes it seem inferior to the numerous post-synched Italian films in the genre. Special effects (some of which appear to be executed by video techniques) are poor and there is no evidence of a futuristic society in the west coast locations and familiar looking freaks. Inane dialog fails to be funny and Saticoy's hand puppet/doll "baby" sidekick (at one point it does a Froggy the Gremlin impression from Andy Devine's 1950s tv show) is too silly for a pro feature.

Obviously aware of the video marketplace, Jackson features a great deal of female nudity, including several porn actresses in minor roles.

End credits promise a sequel, subtitled "Holy Thunder."—*Lor*.

The Girl In The Picture
(BRITISH-COLOR)

A Samuel Goldwyn Co. presentation of a coproduction of the National Film Finance Corp. and Rank Film Distributors. Produced by Paddy Higson. Directed by Cary Parker. Screenplay, Parker; camera (color), Dick Pope; editor, Bert Eeles; sount, Louis Kramer; designer, Gemma Jackson; production supervisor, Alan J. Wands; costumes,
Mary-Jane Reyner; production coordinator, Alison Campbell. Reviewed at Magno Preview 4 screening room, N.Y., July 8, 1986. (MPAA Rating: PG-13.) Running time: **90 MINS.**
Alan . . . . John Gordon-Sinclair
Mary . . . . Irina Brook
Ken . . . . David McKay
Bill . . . . Gregor Fisher
Annie . . . . Caroline Guthrie
Smiley . . . . Paul Young
The Minister . . . . Rikki Fulton
The Girl . . . . Simone Lahbib
Susannah . . . . Helen Pike
Stephanie . . . . Joyce Deans

A flat, inoffensive comedy about the breakup and reconciliation of live-in lovers, "The Girl In The Picture" stars John Gordon-Sinclair, the young Scottish actor whose understated charm infused Bill Forsyth's 1981 comedy of adolescent ups and downs, "Gregory's Girl." Tyro director-writer Cary Parker, an American working in Scotland, strives to emulate Forsyth in this mildly engaging effort but fails on the most elementary level to elicit involvement in the fate of the relationship between a mild-manered photographer and his student girlfriend. Firstrun theatrical prospects are slim, although "The Girl In The Picture" might enjoy a pleasant, if limited afterlife on video shelves.

Alan (John Gordon-Sinclair), who works in the Smile, Please photo shop ("weddings, passports, children, pets"), wants to break off with his most attractive girlfriend-roomate Mary (Irina Brook) for vague reasons having to do with general restlessness and over-familiarity. He's trying to get a portfolio together, she's trying to get a job and they don't seem to be communicating very well. Alan
can't cope with the prospect of hurting Mary, but she makes things easy for him by deciding to move out before he can muster up the nerve to ask her to leave.

Most of the picture follows Alan at work and ambling about Glasgow while trying to come to terms with his transition to the single life. He gets advice from his happily married boss, Smiley (Paul Young) and gives some to his photo shop sidekick and perpetually lovelorn pal, Ken (David McKay). He watches with jealousy as Mary takes up with a new beau, notches a one-night stand with an oddball customer and, since Glasgow is obviously a pretty small town, keeps crossing paths with an alluring mystery lady who turns out to be a hooker. Soon Alan realizes that if he couldn't live with Mary, he certainly can't live without her.

Mary doesn't make things easy for him, but their reunion is a foregone conclusion that's effected with nearly the same offhanded resignation that attended their breakup.

Although Gordon-Sinclair is an appealing presence on screen, the unflappable persona that worked so well in Forsyth's "That Sinking Feeling" and "Gregory's Girl" seems so detached from the emotional crisis at hand that Alan's plight elicits more indifference than empathy. Parker's dialog does feature some Forsyth-style deadpan ironies, but there's no comic resonance or new territory covered in this harmless film. — *Rich*.

★★★★★★★★★★★★★★★★★★★★★★★★★★
★   ★
★ **Cartagena Festival** ★
★   ★
★★★★★★★★★★★★★★★★★★★★★★★★★★

Terror y Encajes Negros
(Terror And Black Lace)
(MEXICAN-COLOR)

A Conacite II production. Directed by Luis Alcoriza. Screenplay, Alcoriza; camera (color), Xavier Cruz; editor, Federico Landero; music, Pedro Placencia. Reviewed at Cartagena Film Festival (competition), June 19, 1986. Running time: **90 MINS.**
With: Gonzalo Vega, Maribel Guardia, Jaime Moreno, Olivia Collins, Claudia Guzmán, Martha Ortiz, Roberto Cobo.

Cartagena — Luis Alcoriza coscripted many of Luis Buñuel's films of the 1950s, and, although this past association can be detected in "Terror And Black Lace," the results are quite different. Quite unintentionally, this pic became the Cartagena fest's most hilarious event.

On one floor of an apartment building lives a meek gentleman who plays clarinet with a chamber
music ensemble at a nearby church. He also happens to be a hair fetishist with a closet full of pigtails and strands of hair he has collected personally from a succession of terrified women who fear his razos is intended for their throats.

In the penthouse of the same building lives a married couple. The husband is a possessive type who, in true macho style, tries to keep his wife under virtual house arrest. Inevitably, she rebels and finds a lover. By the time she returns home after her first tryst, the hair collector has become an assassin trying to dispose of a corpse. When the unfaithful wife accidentally stumbles upon them, he does his best to turn her into corpse number two, with a series of chases up and down the building which are intended to become ever more terrifying, but only become funnier and funnier.

Acting is on the leve of a second-rate tv situation comedy and the pic's camerawork also makes an unwitting contribution to its humor. —*Amig.*

Visa U.S.A.
(COLOMBIAN-CUBAN-COLOR)

A Focine (Colombia) production in association with ICAIC (Cuba). Executive producer, Guillermo Calle Delgado. Directed by Lisandro Duque. Screenplay, Duque; camera (color), Raúl Pérez Ureta; editor, Nelson Rodriguez; music, Leo Brouwer. Reviewed at Cartagena Film Festival (competition), June 20, 1986. Running time: **90 MINS.**

Adolfo	Armando Gutierrez
Patricia	Marcela Agudelo
Papá Adolfo	Raúl Eguron Cuesta
Mamá Adolfo	Lucy Martinez Tello
Papá Patricia	Elios Fernandez
Mamá Patriaia	Vicky Hernandez
Pedro Guillermo	Diego Alvarez
Adriana	María Lucla Castrillión
Moncho	Gellver de Currea Lugo
Felmo	Gerardo Calero

Cartagena — Although certainly one of the better Colombian films, "Visa U.S.A." is unlikely to obtain commercial distribution abroad, although it deserves to reappear on the festival circuit. At Cartagena it won the best film award.

Adolfo is the 20-year-old son of a not particularly welloff chicken farmer in provincial Sevilla del Valle and his overwhelming ambition is to make it as a radio/tv announcer in the U.S. Meanwhile, he hypes the merchandise at a local record store and falls in love with Patricia, one of the two high school seniors to whom he gives English lessons. Her middle-class parents disapprove, because they feel he is not good enough for their girl.

When Adolfo requests a tourist visa, his application is rejected because his older brother had earlier entered the U.S. the same way, obtained a job and remained. The youngster does not want to lose face and spends his savings on a false passport and visa. The film implies there is considerable trade in those commodities.

Patricia's father discovers Adolfo's visa was rejected and decides to send her to New York on a holiday in the hope that will make her forget him. This, of course, would have enabled them to travel together, were it not for the fact that the fake documents don't pass muster at the airport, where Adolfo barely escapes arrest.

She decides to stay behind with him and gives up her trip to N.Y. Implication is that the youngsters give up their naive dream of success and happiness in the U.S. and decide to make it at home.

This is the second feature made by Lisandro Duque, a 42-year-old anthropologist, and throughout most of the film he tells his story well, with believable characters and relationships, well-etched in local background and a valid theme.

The film's flaw lies in its denouement. Duque's screenplay wants to make the point of the protagonists giving up the alienation implicit in their Latin version of the American dream, but fails to convey this as convincingly as the rest of the film. The airport chase, after Adolfo's false documents are discovered, is poorly shot and the basic film's basic point not too clearly made after that.

Otherwise, technical credits are good and Marcela Agudelo (Patricia) is a promising young actress. The Cuban share of the coproduction consisted of the camera team, music, sound, postproduction and to actors in supporting roles. —*Amig.*

La Banda de los Panchitos
(The Panchito Gang)
(MEXICAN-COLOR)

A Roberto Leycegui production. Directed by Arturo Velazco. Screenplay, Velazco, Roberto Madrigal; camera (color), Donald Bryant; editor, Carlos Savage; music, Federico Alvarez del Toro and El Tri. Reviewed at Cartagena Film Festival (competition), June 17, 1986. Running time: **85 MINS.**
With: Oscar Velásquez, Mario de Jesús Morales, Oscar Medina, Claudia Sánchez and the groups of Los Panchitos, Los Musgos, Los Pitufos and Z.R.

Cartagena — Well meaning, but rather amateurish, this attempt to show Mexico City youth gangs in action and insinuate some explanation for their behavior is unlikely to be of international interest.

Actors are handled poorly and director Arturo Velazco makes the adults appear stiff and stilted. Pic's main merit may well be his convincing the members of several youth gangs to cooperate by playing themselves. This they do with a certain amount of lusty spontaneity.

The screenplay fails to establish relationships between the characters or provide some other form of dramatic progression. The final result is a film that cannot be taken seriously, either as a documentary or as a fictional drama.

Technical credits are, at best, uneven, but the José Luis Cuevas drawings used with the initial credits are outstanding and make one expect a different and better film.—*Amig.*

Manon
(VENEZUELAN-COLOR)

A Gente de Cine production. Executive producer, Miguelangel Landa. Directed by Roman Chalbaud. Screenplay, Emilio Carballido, Chalbaud, based on the Abbé Prévost's novel; camera (color), Javier Aguirresarobe; editor, José Alcalde; music, Federico Ruiz. Reviewed at Cartagena Film Festival (market), June 20, 1986. Running time: **112 MINS.**

Manon	Mayra Alejandra
Roberto	Victor Mallarino
Lescaut	Miguelangel Landa
Obsidiana	Eva Moreno
Díaz Lopez	Gonzalo J. Camacho

Cartagena — Adapted to a Venezuelan background, this latest remake of "Manon" (dating back to several silent era versions) is a lush melodrama that lays no claim to greatness but works pretty well on its own level. It is already doing well in Caracas, has been sold to Mexico, and will compete at the upcoming San Sebastián fest.

Manon, as ever a sexy wench, attracts Roberto, a seminarist and son of a rich landowner. His plans for a life of chastity soon are dispelled as he runs off with Manon and a suit-

1949 Version
(FRENCH-B&W)

A Corona release of a Paul-Edmond Decharme production. Directed by Henri-Georges Clouzot. Stars Serge Reggiani, Cecile Aubry, Michel Auclair, Gabrielle Dorziat. Screenplay, Clouzot, Jean Ferry, from novel by Abbé Prévost; camera (b&w), Armand Thirard; music, Paul Misraki. At the Marivaux, Paris, March 13, 1949. Running time: **105 MINS.**

Manon Lescaut	Cecile Aubry
Robert Desgrieux	Michel Auclair
Leon Lescaut	Serge Reggiani
Captain	Henry Gilbert
The Madame	Gabrielle Dorziat
Monsieur Paul	Raymond Souplex

case full of his father's money. The couple live quite happily while it lasts, but as they build their love nest at the Caracas Hilton's presidential suite, bliss is not forever.

When the money runs out, Roberto obtains a job as a salesman, which hardly suffices. Manon does a lot better with D'López, a middle-aged businessman who can afford to keep her in the style she considers her due. In the end, after more than once betraying both her lovers, Manon receives her comeuppance.

Roman Chalbaud is a thoroughly professional director who milks the same sort of mechanisms and emotional range that have made Latin telenovelas so popular, but does so more soberly and with greater production values. The casting of Mayra Alejandra, a telenovela star, as Manon reinforces this transfer of a genre from one medium to another.

Her scheming brother Lescaut is played well by Miguelangel Landa and, although Alejandra is by no means a full-fledged film actress, she does convey Manon's sexy magnetism.

There are some scenes with strong local backgrounds and technical credits are good. —*Amig.*

Malabrigo
(PERUVIAN-COLOR)

A Perfo Studio production in association with ICAIC (Cuba) Channel Four (U.K.) and ZDF (W. Germany). produced by Andrés Malatesta, Emilio Salomón. Directed by Alberto Durant. Screenplay, Jorge Guerra, Durant; camera (color), Mario García Joya; editor, Justo Vega; sound, Guillermo Palacios. Reviewed at Cartagena Film Festival (information section). Running time: **84 MINS.**
With: Charo Verástegui, Luis Alvarez, Ricardo Blume.

Cartagena — "Malbrigo" unravels with considerable atmosphere, but this Peruvian film makes the mistake of a talky finale which, instead of becoming a welcome explanation of the ongoing mystery, turns into something of an anticlimax.

Sonia travels to Malabrigo, a fishing village, to meet her husband, only to discover he has not been seen or heard of for two days. She receives little help on making inquiries at the small hotel where he had been living, the police station and with other villagers. An explosion at the fish flour factory where the husband worked as accountant preceded his disappearances and an insurance adjuster arrives to investigate.

In the buildup, there is suspense plus a sense of deepening mystery and the feeling something is rotten at the core of this environment. Where the film fails is in its manner of solving the conundrum, explained in a longwinded and static conversation between the factory owner and insurance adjuster. Even a final bout of action does not recover the lost impetus. The weak ending hurts the development of the film's social background and the ideas it tries to convey.

Otherwise, 34-year-old director Alberto Durant shows visual flair in this, his second feature. Technical credits are all right, although acting is somewhat uneven. —*Amig.*

Shadows Run Black
(COLOR)

Formula slasher film.

A Media Gallery presentation of a Mesa Films production. Executive producer, Laurel A. Koernig. Produced by Eric Louzil. Directed by Howard Heard. Screenplay, Craig Kusaba, Duke Howard, from story by Kusaba; camera (United color), John Sprung; editor, Raul Davalos, Davide Ganzino; music supervisor, Steve Mann; sound, Ann Krupa; additional photography, Chris Tufty, Ron Charman; second unit camera, Ron Halpern; associate producers, William J. Kulzer, Julius Metoyer, Charles Domokos; stunt coordinator, Kulzer. Reviewed on Lightning Video vidcassette, N.Y., July 4, 1986. (No MPAA Rating.) Running time: **89 MINS.**

Rydell King	William J. Kulzer
Judy Cole	Elizabeth Trosper
Morgan Cole	Shea Porter
Priest	George J. Engelson
Helen Cole	Dianne Hinkler

Billy . . . . Julius Metoyer
Lee Faulkner . . . . Terry Congie
Jimmy Scott . . . . Kevin Costner
  Also with: Lee Bishop, Rhonda Selesnow, Ann Hull, Barbara Peckinpaugh, Wendy Tolkin, Ron Halpern.

Though bearing a 1984 copyright, "Shadows Run Black" is a very ordinary slasher film shot in spring 1981, heyday of the unlamented genre. Announced as a 1983 release by CineWorld, pic went directly to vidcassette.

Episodic presentation (with little continuity evident) has a serial killer, dubbed "The Black Angel" by the press, offing pretty young coeds. Cop on the case, Sgt. Rydell King (William J. Kulzer), is coming off a leave of absence that followed the unsolved kidnaping of his daughter (hint, hint).

Prime suspect is Jimmy Scott (Kevin Costner, uncredited), who knew the girls. However, after Scott is arrested the murders continue. Dumb ending is telegraphed in the second reel.

Apart from an early role by star-of-the-future Costner (whose character is omitted from the otherwise complete end credits), "Shadows" is notable only for its unusually capacious amount of full nudity featuring well-built young women, an obvious draw in the cassette market. Tech credits are weak and acting, apart from Costner, only semi-pro. Derek Stratten was listed as director when film was in production while one "Howard Heard" is credited on screen.

Many of the filmmakers and cast members reunited last year to make "Georgia County Lockup," a women's prison film notable for casting wrestling/roller derby star Dee Booher (a.k.a. Queen Kong).
                       —*Lor.*

A Blade In The Dark
(ITALIAN-COLOR)

A National Cinematografica and Nuovo Dania Cinematografica production. Directed by Lamberto Bava. Screenplay, Dardano Sacchetti, Elisa Briganti; camera (Luciano Vittori color), Gianlorenzo Battaglia; editor, Bava; music, Guido & Maurizio De Angelis; set design & costumes, Stefano Paltrinieri; makeup, Giovanni Amadei; production manager, Roberto De Laurentiis; assistant director, Michele Soavi; special effects, Giovanni Corridori. Reviewed on Lightning Video vidcassette, N.Y., June 25, 1986. (No MPAA Rating.) Running time: **96 MINS.**
With: Andrea Occhipinti (Bruno), Anny Papa, Fabiola Toledo, Michele Soavi, Valeria Cavalli, Stanko Molnar, Lara Naszinski.

Lamberto Bava, currently riding high with his horror hit "Demons" (and lensing a sequel) made "A Blade In The Dark" in 1983, but it already shows the heavy influence of his "Demons" producer Dario Argento. Italian feature went directly to the homevideo market Stateside.

Andrea Occhipinti (best known as male lead in Bo Derek's "Bolero") portrays a composer who is at an isolated villa scoring a horror film. Typically, the film he is working on provides clues as to the identity of a murderer slashing girls for real in the vicinity. For the umpteenth time in this genre, the killer turns out to be a transvestite.

Picture is mainly padding between the killings, which (à la Argento) stress physical violence in a tactile, grisly fashion. Prefiguring the insider's point-of-view of "Demons," Bava jokingly has the femme film director choked to death by having 35m film tightened around her neck.

Unlike most Italo horror films of late, "Blade" is not articulated in English, so the lip movements of the dubbing don't match. Unidentified cast of interchangeable victims includes Lara Naszinski, Nastassja Kinski's cousin, in an inauspicious screen debut. —*Lor.*

Wild Beasts
(ITALIAN-COLOR)

A Euramco Intl. presentation of a Shumba Intl. production. Produced by Federico Prosperi. Written and directed by Franco E. Prosperi. Dialog adaptation and direction, Lewis E. Ciannelli; camera (Luciano Vittori color), Guglielmo Mancori; editor, Mario Morra; music, Daniele Patucchi; assistant director, Ignazio Dolce; animal trainers, Pasquale Martino, Giancarlo Triberti; special makeup effects, Maurizio Trani; special effects, Cataldo Galiano; special effects with animals, Alvaro Passeri. Reviewed on Lightning Video vidcassette, N.Y., June 28, 1986. (No MPAA Rating.) Running time: 92 **MINS.**
Laura Schwarz . . . . Lorraine de Selle
Dr. Rupert Berner . . . . John Aldrich
Nat . . . . Ugo Bologna
Suzy . . . . Louisa Lloyd

"Wild Beasts" is an Italian horror feature that underscores the ongoing dilemma between fantasy and realism in the shriek genre. Filmmaker Franco Prosperi applies his experience in the "Mondo Cane" school of shock tactics to a science fiction theme with technically good results but an audience turnoff and counter-productive to the film's socially conscious theme. Pic was made in West Germany in 1982 with alternate title "Savage Beasts" and has been released domestically to the homevideo trade.

Premise is that PCP (angel dust) has seeped into the water supply of a German city as a result of industrial waste, with the immediate result that animals in the local zoo freak out, break out (aided by a power outage) and go on the rampage. Along with a horde of sewer rats, the revenge of abused Mother Nature in the form of zoo beasts quickly turns the feature into a disaster film mode. Zoo scientist Rupert Berner (John Aldrich), police inspector Nat (Ugo Bologna)

and reporter Laura (Lorraine de Selle) lead the fight to save humanity.

Prosperi's talented special effects and animal experts crew provide the utmost realism to even absurd stagings, such as a polar bear attacking the dance class that Laura's daughter Suzy (Louisa Lloyd) attends. Some footage, such as flamethrowers applied to the horde of rats, looks real rather than faked. Mixed with the usual, overdone makeup effects of gorily mangled human victims, the thrills are gruesome rather than entertaining. Just as in so many Italian-made cannibal films, the message alerting us to stop raping the environment gets lost in the urge to maximize the titillation value of the horror scenes.
                       — *Lor.*

Angkor-Cambodia Express
(THAI-ITALIAN-COLOR)

A Monarex Hollywood presentation of a Network Film/Spectacular Trading coproduction. Executive producer, Chari Amartyakul. Produced by Lek Kitiparaporn, Richard Randall. Directed by Kitiparaporn. Screenplay, Roger Crutchley, Kailan; camera (Technicolor Rome), Roberto Forges Davanzati; editor, Morris Goodyear; music, Stelvio Cipriani; production manager, Vegraphan Lohsowan; art direction, U-Rai Sirisombat; second unit director-production supervisor, Walter Licastro; special effects, Eduardo Torrente, Bung Sarasuk. Reviewed on Vestron Video vidcassette, N.Y. July 6, 1986. (No MPAA Rating.) Running time: 92 MINS.
Andy Cameron . . . . Robert Walker
MacArthur . . . . Christopher George
Woody . . . . Woody Strode
Sue . . . . Nancy Kwan
Mitr Saren . . . . Lui Leung Wai
Porn Pen . . . . Sorapong Chatri
Mieng . . . . Nit Alisa

It's reassuring to know that for every world crisis or momentous happening there's an exploitation film in the offing. "Angkor-Cambodia Express" (a.k.a. "Kampuchea Express") comes from Dick Randall, the Rome-based Yank producer who brought us "The Wild, Wild World Of Jayne Mansfield" and more recently "Pieces." Filmed in 1981, it was released Stateside on vidcassette.

Robert Walker toplines as Andy Cameron, a magazine journalist returning to Kampuchea to get his girlfriend out of the country before she's massacred along with a big chunk of the rest of the population.

Walker tries to team up with a gung-ho American (court-martialed during the Vietnam War) calling himself Gen. MacArthur (the late Christopher George), who has a private army in the hills of Thailand. MacArthur gives him a hard time but his righthand man Woody (Woody Strode) agrees to help Walker. Also aided by a local helper Porn Pen (Sorapong Chatri), Walker gets into Kampuchea, defeats arch villain Mitr (Lui Leung

Wai), but his girl Mieng (Nit Alisa) dies on the way out.

Walker and Strode turn in good performances in a rather dull film, rendered remote by the usual subpar dubbing. Massacre footage is kept to a minimum and special effects are okay. Opening reels are needlessly confusing as to proper time frame in presenting Walker in earlier trips to Kampuchea. —*Lor.*

Uphill All The Way
(COLOR)

Buddy Western goes nowhere.

A New World Pictures release of a Melroy production, in association with Guardian Films. Executive producers, Renée Valente, Mel Tillis, Roy Clark. Produced by Burr Smidt, David L. Ford. Written and directed by Frank Q. Dobbs. Camera (Deluxe color), Roland (Ozzie) Smith; editor, Chuck Weiss; music, Dennis M. Pratt; sound, Wayne Bell; production design, Hal Matheny; set decoration, Pat O'Neal; assistant director, Tad Devlin; production manager, Walt Gilmore; second unit director-stunt coordinator, Dave Cass; second unit camera, Scott Smith; casting, Rachelle Farberman; associate producer, Bob Younts. Reviewed on New World Video vidcassette, N.Y., July 5, 1986. (MPAA Rating: PG.) Running time: 86 MINS.
Ben . . . . Roy Clark
Booger Skaggs . . . . Mel Tillis
Sheriff . . . . Burl Ives
Capt. Hazleton . . . . Glen Campbell
Widow Quinn . . . . Trish Van Devere
Dillman . . . . Richard Paul
Poker player . . . . Burt Reynolds
Jesse . . . . Elaine Joyce
Lucinda . . . . Jacque Lynn Colton
  Also with: Frank Gorshin, Sheb Wooley, Burton Gilliam, Gailard Sartain, Rockne Tarkington, Christopher Weeks, Pedro Gonzalez-Gonzalez.

"Uphill All The Way" is a flop Western self-tailored to expose the nonmusical talents of singers Roy Clark and Mel Tillis. Pic was made in Texas in 1984 during the brief resurgence in Western production (New World vidcassette opens with a trailer for "Lust In The Dust," another Western dud made at that time) and received a few theatrical playdates in the South and Southwest commencing in January 1986.

Set in the early 1900s, picture has Clark and Tillis as incompetent conmen, so stupid they go into a bank seeking a loan but brandishing a shotgun, causing them to be mistaken for bank robbers. Stealing a car, they are the subject of a manhunt (which takes up the rest of the picture) led, reluctantly, by local sheriff Burl Ives. Joining the chase later is an army captain played by Glen Campbell (a kindred singer whose own Western screen career remained stillborn after "True Grit").

Writer-director Frank Q. Dobbs (no relation to Bogey's Fred C. Dobbs) seems to be aiming here for a bawdy comedy similar to Sam Peckinpah's "The Ballad Of Cable Hogue," but film is tame, unfunny and meaningless. The would-be Laurel & Hardy team has slapstick misadventures that amount to mere filler and supporting cast is wasted.

Of the stars, Clark makes the best screen impression, delivering witless lines as if they meant something, while Tillis is a blank, downplaying his stuttering routine. Elaine Joyce is fun in the Stella Stevens role from Peckinpah's picture. Burt Reynolds contributes an effective cameo as a poker player who skins the heroes early on.

Tech credits are fine and film has several unmemorable songs sung over by Tillis, Clark, Campbell and Waylon Jennings. —*Lor.*

Thunder Warrior
(ITALIAN-COLOR)

A Trans World Entertainment presentation of a European Intl. Film production. Produced by Fabrizio De Angelis. Directed by "Larry Ludman" (Fabrizio De Angelis). Screenplay, David Parker Jr., "Ludman" (De Angelis), from story by Parker; camera (Telecolor), Sergio Salvati; editor, Eugenio Alabiso; music, Francesco De Masi; assistant director, Goffredo Unger; art direction-costumes, Massimo Lentini; stunt coordinator, Alan Petit; special effects, Giovanni Corridori. Reviewed on TWE vidcassette, N.Y., June 14, 1986. (MPAA Rating: R.) Running time: **84 MINS.**
Sheriff Bill Cook . . . . Bo Svenson
Thunder . . . . Mark Gregory
Barry . . . . Raymund Harmstorf
Sheila . . . . Valeria Ross
Thomas . . . . Antonio Sabato
Also with: Giovanni Vettorazzo, Paolo Malco, Richard Harley, Slim Smith.

"Thunder Warrior" (a.k.a. "Thunder") is an okay Italian action picture, benefiting immensely from gorgeous Arizona locations in Monument Valley, the Grand Canyon and environs. Released theatrically overseas, the shot-in-1983 opus debuted on vidcassette domestically, with a sequel, "Thunder 2," currently in production.

Mark Gregory portrays Thunder, a young Navajo indian who returns home to find that the tribal burial ground is being destroyed to become the site of an observatory, breaking a treaty signed 100 years ago by his grandfather. After starting a fight on the construction site with a worker named Thomas (Antonio Sabato), Thunder sits in at the office of Sheriff Cook (Bo Svenson). Brushed off by Cook, he shifts his sit-in to the local bank that is financing the project and is promptly escorted out of the county by the cops.

Subsequently beaten by Thomas and his coworkers, and then treated to police brutality by Deputy Barry (Raymund Harmstorf), Thunder arms himself and becomes a mini-Rambo out of "First·Blood." He survives, hence the sequel, and is established as a local folk hero after numerous encounters with the police and rednecks who try to hunt him down.

Filmmaker Fabrizio De Angelis (who likes to use the pseudonym "Larry Ludman" when directing) delivers fine stunts and chases, but overuses slow motion·to stylize violent scenes. Western-flavored music by Francesco De Masi is a plus, though film's main draw is its beautiful locations. Typically for an Italian visiting production, interiors were lensed back in Rome.

Star Gregory is good as the sullen Indian, a big improvement on his campy thesping in De Angelis' production of "1990: The Bronx Warriors." — *Lor.*

The Sea Serpent
(SPANISH-COLOR)

A Calepas Intl. production. Produced by José Frade. Directed by Gregory Greens. Screenplay, Gordon A. Osburn; camera (Photofilm Madrid color), Raul Cutler; editor, Anthony Red; music, Robin Davis; sound, Joseph Cherry; art direction, Joseph Galic; assistant director, John Freeman. Reviewed on Lightning Video vidcassette, N.Y., May 21, 1986. (No MPAA Rating.) Running time: **92 MINS.**
Capt. Pedro Barrios . . . . Timothy Bottoms
Margaret Roberts . . . . Taryn Power
Lenares . . . . Jared Martin
Prof. Timothy Wallace . . . . . . Ray Milland
Also with: Gerard Tichy, Carole James, Jack Taylor, Leon Klimovsky, Paul Benson.

"The Sea Serpent" is a lowgrade Spanish monster picture shot in 1984 in Portugal and Spain. Entry is aimed at youngsters who like watching miniatures (here in the form of boats, train, helicopter, lighthouse, bridge and monster) and went directly to vidcassette release Stateside.

Timothy Bottoms portrays Capt. Barrios, a seafarer given a second chance after accused of being drunk on a disastrous earlier voyage wherein the brother of Lenares (Jared Martin) was lost at sea.

In a prolog, a U.S. bomber in trouble drops an A-bomb in the sea, exploding it (stock footage of a mushroom cloud) so as to avoid the sophisticated weapon being retrieved by a nearby Russian boat. The explosion awakens a sea monster on the ocean bottom, and said monster proceeds to destroy Barrios' ship.

At a naval hearing, disgruntled Lenares testifies that Barrios was drunk at watch again, and no one believes the captain's tale about a sea serpent. Stripped of his captain's license and subject to criminal proceedings, Barrios leaves Spain and heads for Lisbon after reading a newspaper story about a woman who reported seeing a sea monster there.

He finds her (Taryn Power) in a hospital and breaks her out, the two of them traveling to a university to consult Prof. Wallace (Ray Milland, in his final feature film) about the monster's legend.

After having seen the monster-himself, Lenares turns over a new leaf and joins up with the heroes, the four of them going hunting. They singe the beastie when an oil car of a passing train falls on it and explodes, with the monster swimming away towards Africa, setting up (horror of horrors) the prospects of a sequel.

Since the monster is alternately a silly handpuppet or a full-size Venus Flytrap-styled mouth for chewing hapless cast members, picture is obviously for smallfry only. Articulating in English but crudely dubbed, cast is bland and tech credits are weak. —*Lor.*

The Ark Of The Sun God
(ITALIAN-TURKISH-COLOR)

A Trans World Entertainment presentation of a Flora Film (Rome)/U.F.M. (Istanbul), production. Executive producers, Renata Cevinini, Maria Martino, Sedat Akdemir, Ugur Terzioglu. Directed by Anthony M. Dawson (Antonio Margheriti). Screenplay, Giovanni Simonelli, from story by Giovanni Paolucci; camera (Luciano Vittori color), Sandro Mancori; editor, Alberto Moriani; music, Aldo Tamborrelli; assistant director, Edoardo Margheriti, Bulent Engin; art direction, Ylmaz Zenger; special effects, Augusto Salvati, Roberto Ricci. Reviewed on TWE vidcassette, N.Y., July 9, 1986. (No MPAA Rating.) Running time: **89 MINS.**
Rick Spear . . . . David Warbeck
Dean . . . . John Steiner
Carol . . . . Susie Sudlow
Rupert . . . . Anthony Berner
Mohammet . . . . Ricardo Palacios
Beetle . . . . Alan Collins
Also with: Aytekin Akkaya, Suleyman Turhan.

After filming the fantasy "Yor, The Hunter From The Future" there, Italian filmmaker Antonio Margheriti returned to Turkey in 1983 to shoot "The Ark Of The Sun God," a subpar entry in his series of imitative adventure films. Pic debuted domestically on vidcassette.

British thesp David Warbeck (veteran of 10 Italian films to date) gets to play a British character for a change, as Rick Spear, a London cracksman sent to Istanbul on a cockeyed mission: he's to find the temple of the Sun God which is the resting place of Gilgamesh. A legendary jeweled scepter of the king is inside and can be used as a limitless source of power to the bearer. Because the golden door is booby-trapped (with the entire temple set to self-destruct), a master burglar like Spear is needed for the job.

If this sounds a bit like "Raiders Of The Lost Ark," it's because Margheriti earlier raided that hit with an interesting variation, "The Hunters Of The Golden Cobra." This time there's too much padding, as Spear is tested and then goes hunting for the site, aided by survivor of a mission over 40 years earlier, Beetle (Alan Collins).

The Turkish locations are again impressive, but this "Ark" doesn't pick up steam until the final reels containing cliff-hanger derring-do in the temple and caverns surrounding it.

Soundtrack features a lovely romantic theme but elsewhere pointlessly includes the main theme from "Battlestar Galactica." —*Lor.*

El Tren de los Pioneros
(The Train Of The Pioneers)
(COLOMBIAN-COLOR)

A Maya TV, Institute for the Development of Antioqula production. Produced by Focine. Directed by Leonel Gallego. Screenplay, Gallego; camera (color), Carlos Sánchez; editor, Patricia Bruggisser; music, Mauricio Mejla; costumes, Ana María Gallón; décor, Yolanda Botero. Reviewed at Cartagena Film Festival, June 18, 1986. Running time: **72 MINS.**
With: Manuel Restrepo, Ana María Ochoa, Fabio Ríos, Alvaro Guerrero, Pablo Agudel, Raúl Emilio Correa, Donald Esguerra, Ernesto Aguilar and Rubén Darlo Trejos.

Cartagena — The construction during the 19th century of a railway from Medellín to the river Magdalena is the subject of a film unlikely to find an audience on any level, although it may obtain a slot on local tv.

There is plenty of potential drama in the exploration of the train's route through swamp and jungle and in the actual construction, often held up by coups and civil wars. Unfortunately, none of this comes to life in a film which, although obviously made on a small budget, is unimaginatively shot, poorly acted and, on all counts, the sort of item that should not be found at a film festival.—*Amig.*

Out Of Bounds
(COLOR)

Disappointing teen thriller overloaded with clichés.

A Columbia Pictures release of a Fries Entertainment production from Columbia-Delphi V Prods. Produced by Charles Fries, Mike Rosenfeld. Executive producers, John Tarnoff, Ray Hartwick. Directed by Richard Tuggle. Stars Anthony Michael Hall. Screenplay, Tony Kayden; camera (Deluxe color), Bruce Surtees; editor, Kent Beyda; additional film editor, Larry Bock; music, Stewart Copeland; production design, Norman Newberry; set design, Joseph Pacelli Jr.; set decoration, Cloudia; costume design, Donna Linson; sound (Dolby), James Tannenbaum; assistant director, Bill Scott; second unit director, M. James Arnett; casting, Janet Hirshenson, Jane Jenkins. Reviewed at the Samuel Goldwyn Theater, Beverly Hills, July 18, 1986. (MPAA Rating: R.) Running time: **93 MINS.**

Daryl Cage	Anthony Michael Hall
Dizz	Jenny Wright
Roy Gaddis	Jeff Kober
Lt. Delgado	Glynn Turman
Hurley	Raymond J. Barry
Murano	Pepe Serna
Crystal	Michelle Little
Marshall	Jerry Levine
Lemar	Ji-Tu Cumbuka
Tommy Cage	Kevin McCorkle
Chris Cage	Linda Shayne
Mrs. Cage	Maggie Gwinn
Mr. Cage	Ted Gehring
Gil	Meatloaf
Biker	Allan Graf

Hollywood — Clichés, of both the old and new varieties, abound in "Out Of Bounds." Filmmakers have tried to dress up yet another tale of a hapless individual caught between the law and criminals with the latest in hip garb and throbbing musical accompaniment, but the outrageous plot contrivances can't be disguised by the application of heavy doses of "attitude." Moderate b.o. would appear to be the limit for this disappointing outing.

Richard Tuggle did impressive work on the scripts of "Escape From Alcatraz" and "Tightrope," and in his direction of the latter film, but here has made the mistakes of directing someone else's (lame) material, and of succumbing to the temptation of aspiring to become the latest high-powered stylist in town.

Set-up has Iowa farmboy Anthony Michael Hall escaping the stultifying atmosphere at home by taking off for Los Angeles to stay with his adored brother and latter's wife. Hall picks up the wrong duffel bag at baggage claim which turns into the family misfortune since this one is loaded with 10 keys of heroin.

The next morning, Hall finds his hosts murdered. When he tries to make contact with the police, they shoot at him, so, with the help of a punky bimbette he met on the plane, he goes underground to try to ferret out the murderer from among the denizens of L.A.'s street culture.

First stop on the tour is Melrose Avenue, where Hall can become suitably wardrobed and trans-

formed from a hayseed into a suitably cool new wave teen. Hot on his trail is bad boy drug dealer Jeff Kober, a creepy James Remar type who's a tortured sadist just waiting to be put out of his misery, but will give plenty to others while he's waiting.

Many colorful L.A. locations, from Silver Lake to Venice, from Barney's Beanery to several obligatory punk clubs, backdrop the action, which is so studded with holes and impossibilities as to disengage belief. Due to the relentless pace and very hot score by Stewart Copeland, pic is not exactly unentertaining, but it is dispiriting.

Disappointing as well is Hall, so energetic and fresh in his films for John Hughes, but so sullen and uncommunicative here that one suspects he might have become the latest in a long line of method acting imitators. His transformation from despondent hick to mightily able street fighter is unconvincing, and his personality is far from lively.

Film needs a pick-me-up, and what might have been very interesting — or at least amusing — would have been for Hall to play essentially his same goofy character from "Sixteen Candles," but in this context. Results would have provided some intriguing dynamics in any event, and added a comic edge to an overly self-serious enterprise.

— *Cart.*

Las Noches del Califas
(Caliph's Nights)
(MEXICAN-COLOR)

An American General Films release of a Producciones Filmica Intl. production. Produced by Morau Montes. Directed by José Luis García Agráz. Stars Héctor Suárez. Camera (color), Enrique Murillo; editor, Martín Luis; music, Son de Merengue. Reviewed at Big Apple Cine 1, N.Y., July 8, 1986. Running time: **92 MINS.**

Macho Prieto	Héctor Suárez
Marda	Sasha Montenegro
Hugo (El Conde)	Manuel Capetillo
Rengo	Pedro Weber
Muñeca	Sergio Ramos

Mexican filmmaker José Luis García Agráz made his feature film debut with the 1983 critically acclaimed national boxoffice hit "Nocaut" (Knockout), dealing with the sordid underbelly of professional boxing.

His new film continues this exploration of Mexico's seedy nightlife and the characters who inhabit it centering on the activities of a cabaret named "Noches del Califas," based on the novel of the same name by Armando Ramírez. The name (Caliph's Nights) also refers to the nighttime world of the bar owner, Macho Prieto (whose name translates as "dark macho"), shown as an autocratic caliph who needs to

own all those he allows to enter his life.

Headlining the cast is Mexico's most versatile actor, Héctor Suárez, a longtime veteran of films, legit and host of the popular national tv series "Que Nos Pasa?" He became Mexico's leading actor by playing the title role in "El Milusos," the top domestic boxoffice draw for 1984, repeating the role of the sympathetic bumpkin in the 1985 sequel "El Milusos II." Playing opposite is the popular Mexican sex star Sasha Montenegro, in the role of Marda.

The storyline concerns the development and destruction of a father-son relationship between Macho and Hugo (Manuel Capetillo), later known as El Conde (The Count). Macho meets Hugo and invites him to the cabaret. Hugo meets Eva and invites her to the cabaret. Macho steals Eva while Marda amuses herself with Hugo.

Hugo and Eva enter Macho's world thinking they can withdraw at any time, yet his love (paternal and romantic) demands control and ownership. When they attempt to assert their independence, they receive the consequences.

In the long run, the consequences also affect Macho: he loses control not only over Hugo and Eva, but also over himself.

García Agráz has a good sense of pacing and he carries the narration well. However, some of the sideplots could have been simplified with time better spent to develop further the changes in the principal characters. Cinematographer Enrique Murillo's lensing is topnotch and imaginative.

Although film will pick up coin on the Hispanic circuit, its melodramatic themes and clichéd characters are too harsh to find any real success in the Anglo market.

—*Lent.*

Nothing In Common
(COLOR)

Misguided mixture of comedy and drama.

A Tri-Star Pictures release of a Rastar production. Produced by Alexandra Rose. Executive producer, Roger M. Rothstein. Directed by Garry Marshall. Stars Tom Hanks, Jackie Gleason. Screenplay, Rick Podell, Michael Preminger; camera (Metrocolor), John A. Alonzo; editor, Glenn Farr; music, Patrick Leonard; sound, Bruce Bisenz; production design, Charles Rosen; set decorator, Jane Bogart; set design, William L. Skinner, Roland E. Hill Jr.; costumes, Rosanna Norton; assistant director, Katy Emde; associate producer, Nick Abdo; casting, Jane Alderman, Shelley Andreas. Reviewed at Plitt Century Plaza theater, July 17, 1986. (MPAA Rating: PG.) Running time: **118 MINS.**

David Basner	Tom Hanks
Max Basner	Jackie Gleason
Lorraine Basner	Eva Marie Saint
Charlie Gargas	Hector Elizondo
Andrew Woolridge	Barry Corbin
Donna Mildred Martin	Bess Armstrong
Cheryl Ann Wayne	Sela Ward
Roger	John Kapelos
David's secretary	Carol Messing

Hollywood — "Nothing In Common" is the kind of film that tries to be all things to all people and as a result succeeds at none of them. Part youth comedy, part sappy family drama, pic continually seems to be tripping over itself. Only consistent element is the manic and entertaining performance of Tom Hanks as an ad exec on the way up, but even he is not likely to charm much of an audience into seeing this misdirected production.

Director Garry Marshall and writing team Rick Podell and Michael Preminger have relied on too many calculated touches to move the story along. After setting up Hanks as a wild and crazy guy they introduce a series of family calamities to spice up the stew. Unfortunately it tastes like a tv dinner.

The father (Jackie Gleason) clearly has seen better days and when his wife of 36 years (Eva Marie Saint) walks out on him things go melodramatically downhill. To complicate matters, Gleason's health is deteriorating and the film climaxes around his operation.

While Hanks is off in his own world everything is supposed to come together under the heading of filial devotion, but it never really works out that way. Main problem is that the thinness of the characters doesn't allow believable relationships to develop.

The Hanks character never successfully shifts gears between a superficial and a sensitive man. Furthermore, he's far more entertaining as a man about town. Basically the two tracks are on a collision course.

With the exception of Hanks none of the leading players is convincing or compelling. Gleason's performance is sound technically but fails to transcend his own deeply etched comic persona. The mother is a weakly drawn figure with Saint only emphasizing that weakness.

On the supporting side, Hector Elizondo turns in his usual fine job as Hanks' boss. Sela Ward is right on the money as a client's drop-dead beautiful and colder than ice daughter who becomes Hanks' sex interest. Bess Armstrong is a bit too cloying as an old friend who could still be a love interest.

Early part of the film given over to the office politics of Hanks' high-powered ad firm and his flirtations with women breezes along painlessly and is full of witty one-liners and sight gags. It is only when the film hits the serious stuff that it comes to a screeching halt and one realizes that there is just too much going on here for one picture.

Technically film is undistinguished with a gloomy kind of lighting infecting the whole effort. John Alonzo's photography appeared to be fuzzy around the edges, at least at the review screening. Production design is rather uninspired as well and sheds little light on the characters. —*Jagr.*

A la Salida nos Vemos
(See You After School)
(COLOMBIAN-VENEZUELAN-COLOR)

A Focine production in association with Cinematográficas Macuto (Venezuela), Hangar Films and Producciones Solsticio (Colombia). Executive producers, Esperanza Palau, María Teresa Bonilla. Directed by Carlos Palau. Screenplay, Palau, Sandro Romero; camera (color), José Medeiros; editor, Armando Valero; art director, Pedro Alcántara; sound, Stefano Gramito; music, Alejandro Blanco Uribe. Reviewed at Cartagena Film Festival (competition), June 17, 1986. Running time: **85 MINS.**

With: Santiago Madriñán, Alejandro Madriñán, John Klonis, Johnny Price, José Luis Botero, July Pedraza, Bacheba Agula, Krisnaiza Castro, Angela María Ortegón, Abril Mendez, Luis Miguel González.

Cartagena — Pleasant enough with its nostalgia and rose-tinted look at adolescence in the 1960s, "See You After School" is a promising first feature likely to do well on its home ground, but not yet ripe for international exposure.

The 14 and 15-year-old youngsters go to strict Catholic schools run by religious congregations and director Carlos Palau pokes gentle fun at padres and nuns, although he avoids the scathing irony and satire this subject so often provokes in film and literature.

The kids' spontaneity and freshness come across in a series of funny pranks and situations, but tighter editing and a more solid screenplay were in order. As it stands, film is basically a succession of anecdotes which amuse in varying degrees, but don't add up to a point-of-view or provide the film with an adequate rhythmic pattern.

The youngsters' acting is fine, but the adults (priests and nuns) tend to be stereotypes. Technical credits are okay.—*Amig.*

Avanti Popolo
(ISRAELI-COLOR-16m)

A Raphi Bukaee-Kastel Films release. Produced, written and directed by Raphi Bukaee. Stars Suheil Hadad, Salim Daou. Camera (Agfacolor, 16m), Yoav Kosh; editor, Zohar Sela; music, Uri Ofir; sound, Itamar Ben-Yaakov, Dani Matalon, Ronny Berger, Shmuel Ettinger; art director, Ariel Glazer; makeup, Irith Elazar. Reviewed at the Jerusalem Film Festival, June 28, 1986. Running time: **84 MINS.**

With: Suheil Hadad, Salim Daou, Danny Roth, Danny Segev, Tuvia Gelber, Michael Koresh, Shalom Shmuelov, Barry Langford, Dan Turgeman, Mukhammad Manadre.

Jerusalem — Appearing without previous publicity, Raphi Bukaee's first film is a pleasant surprise. A student featurette extended through several grants and a lot of private sacrifice into a feature-length picture, it has a most unexpected theme for an Isareli film. Its protagonists are two Egyptian soldiers caught in the middle of the Sinai desert at the end of the Six Days War, trying to find their way back to the Suez Canal, through the dunes and around the Israeli patrols.

In a series of incidents and encounters, Bukaee's picture shows the absurdity of war and offers a series of intelligent personal profiles along the way. The tone is understated, there is no attempt at preaching or reaching any political conclusions, only the melodramatic last sequence departing from this admirable restraint.

The script does not try avoid the usual patterns suggested by this kind of story but manages to solve dramatic situations in an unexpected and usually humorous manner. Thus, the moment when the two Egyptian soldiers stumble upon a stranded jeep with a dead Scandinavian UN soldier in it develops into a comic scene. Likewise, the encounter with a bloodthirsty tv reporter ends up in slapstick and the suspicions of an Israeli patrol are allayed by one of the Egyptians, an actor by profession, when he give them a soulful rendition (in English) of Shakespeare's Shylock monolog about all humans being flesh and blood, whatever their race or color.

The film's title uses a line from the anthem of the Italian Socialists, a universal tune picked by both the Egyptian tandem and the Israeli patrol they meet in the second part of the film, and exploited for a Taviani Bros.-style scene of fraternity.

While not all sequences are equally successful and script could stand some corrections as to rhythm and credibility, the film comes through as a simple, human, warm and modest story, effective because of its unpretentiousness.

Salim Daou, playing the frustrated actor in uniform, walks away with most of the scenes, both funny and touching in a natural way, but he has strong support from a cast whose rough-edged performances fit in well with the movie's unadorned style. Considering the shoestring budget and the lack of experience on the part of some of the technical crew, the results are more than satisfactory. Kastel Films, getting a coproduction credit, came in at the last moment to salvage the project which was stuck with most of the material in the can and no money to wrap it up.

No distribution has been secured as yet, neither for home nor international release, but there is no doubt that this anonymous entry turned out to be one of the favorites of the Jerusalem Film Festival.—*Edna.*

Choke Canyon
(COLOR)

Unintentially hilarious sci-fier with terrific action footage.

A United Film Distribution Co. (UFDC) release of an Ovidio G. Assonitis production for Brouwersgracht Investments. Produced by Assonitis. Directed by Chuck Bail. Stars Stephen Collins, Janet Julian, Lance Henriksen, Bo Svenson. Screenplay, Sheila Goldberg, Assonitis, Alfonso Brescia; additional dialog, Steve Luotto, Victor Beard; camera (Widescreen, color), Dante Spinotti; editor, Robert Silvi; music, Sylvester Levay; sound, Tony Testa; production design, Frank Vanorio; assistant director, Stuart Fleming; aerial coordinator, Richard R. Holley; stunt coordinator, Phil Adams; associate producer, Peter Shepherd. Reviewed at Magno Preview 9 screening room, N.Y., July 9, 1986. (MPAA Rating: PG). Running time: 94 **MINS.**

David Lowell	Stephen Collins
Vanessa Pilgrim	Janet Julian
Brook Alistair	Lance Henriksen
Captain	Bo Svenson
Rachel	Victoria Racimo
John Pilgrim	Nicholas Pryor

"Choke Canyon" (a.k.a. "On Dangerous Ground") is an entertaining action picture in the sic-fi genre which has too silly a script to be an outright success. Yeoman work by a talented film crew cannot overcome frequent dialog howlers and other unintentional wackiness.

Stephen Collins, dressing as if he were auditioning for a role in "Silverado," plays obstinate physicist David Lowell, experimenting on converting sound waves into usable energy, hopefully to solve the Earth's energy problems. He's calculated that the passing of Halley's Comet in April 1986 will create the maximum distortion of sound waves in Choke Canyon in Utah, at which time he will test his prototype machine there.

Though Lowell has a 99-year lease on the site, its owner Pilgrim Corp. is shipping nuclear waste to be dumped there. Fearing that Lowell, as a physicist, will make public its scheme, Pilgrim president John Pilgrim (Nicholas Pryor) orders him bought off. Lowell turns down the offer so Pilgrim sends for a hitman, the Captain (Bo Svenson, very funny in an exaggeration of the laconic tough-guy type). In a series of standoffs worthy of The Road Runner vs. Wile E. Coyote, Lowell keeps outwitting the Captain and sticking to his demands that Pilgrim replace his ruined equipment and remove the "black ball" (a huge container of nuclear waste plopped down in the canyon which makes the sound wave experiments too dangerous to conduct).

Picture becomes truly nutty when Lowell doffs his Western garb, puts on a tux and crashes a party given by Pilgrim. He kidnaps Pilgrim's beautiful daughter (Janet Julian), insisting his demands be met before she is released. She's quickly won over to his cause and before the comet arrives and experiment succeeds, they're chased all over the place by the Captain in a barnstorming biplane.

With Svenson reportedly doing all his own dangerous flying stunts, Bail (a stunt director in his own right) stages spectacular aerial craziness that exploits the beautiful locations near Moab, Utah (film is dedicated to its helicopter pilot and aerial coordinator, Richard R. Holley).

Cast plays it straight, but "Choke Canyon" nearly chokes on its dialog. Early on, a security guard gets slapped down by Svenson for examining latter's high-powered rifle, and Bo mutters "Never touch my things." This kind of double entendre pushes the film into campy territory instead of the suspenseful nail-biter it tries to be. Tech credits are all pro. —*Lor.*

Karlovy Vary Festival

Siesta Veta
(The Sixth Sentence)
(CZECHOSLOVAKIAN-COLOR)

A Slovak Film Studios-Bratislava-Koliba production. Directed by Stefan Uher. Screenplay, Zuzana Tatarova, Hana Cielova, Stefan Uher; camera (color), Stanislav Szomolanyi; art direction, Roman Rjachovsky. Reviewed at Karlovy Vary Film Festival, July 4, 1986. Running time: **87 MINS.**

Bozena	Erika Ozada
Slancik	Elo Romancik
Slancikova	Brigita Bobulova
Irena	Tana Radeva

Also with: Matus Olha, Miroslav, Hesek, Stefan Kozka, Ivan Romancik, Jirina Jiraskova.

Karlovy Vary — "The Sixth Sentence" is an engrossing biopic of Bozena Slancikova-Timrava, one of the most important figures in Slovak literature. Concentrating on the forces shaping Bozena during her childhood and youth, film puts across a strong feeling for personality, period (late 19th century), and place (Slovak villages life). It is directed with tender, Chekhov-like affection by veteran Stefan Uher.

Film is divided into six "sentences" or episodes (Timrava said any life can be explained in five).

The daughter of a poor vicar, Bozena lives as a member of the impoverished gentry, fascinated and militantly supportive of the peasants who live around her. Though dubious about the value of her maiden aunt Irena (Tana Radeva), who drags her around distributing books to the illiterate, young Bozena soaks up every detail of the villagers. A few episodes later, she publishes her first book, whose characters are so true-to-life their real-live models threaten to kill her.

Hungarian actress Erika Ozada gives the heroine a plain face but uncommon perception and moral backbone. She never marries, and her loneliness and unrequited love are all the more touching for being unsentimentally presented. In one scene, aunt Irena and Bozena (a wallflower at local balls) dress up in peasant costumes and go to a rowdy country wedding incognito. The evening ends with Bozena being raped outside the door, but the aunt shrugs it off as of little importance. And so it is, in comparison to the murder of a young patriot fighting, like Bozena, for the Slovak National Uprising. The two women find his body in a well.

Despite its realistic portrayal of an imperfect life, "Sixth Sentence" avoids coming across as downbeat. It is aided by an especially charming musical score and lensing by cameraman Stanislav Szomolanyi. — *Yung.*

Zimni vecher v Gagrakh
(A Winter Night In Gagra)
(SOVIET-COLOR)

A Mosfilm Studios production. Directed by Karen Shaknazarov. Screenplay, Aleksandr Borodyansky, Vladimir Shevtzik; music, Anatoly Kroll; art direction, Valery Filipov. Reviewed at Karlovy Vary Film Festival, July 4, 1986. Running time: 87 MINS.
With: Evgeny Evstigneev, Aleksandr Pankratov-Chyorny, Natalya Gundareva, Sergei Nikonenko, Pyort Scherbakov.

Karlovy Vary — This slight but off-beat Soviet film by director Karen Shaknazarov made at Mosfilm Studios bears a rather somber title, which belies the fact that it is actually a light human comedy, laced with music and tap dancing no less.

The winter night of the title took place in the 1950s, when the hero, Aleksei Beglov, was a popular tap dancer and had performed in a show with his five-year-old daughter. This and other flashbacks are delightfully stylized, with the moppet bearing some resemblance to a sort of Russian Shirley Temple as she hoofs it with dad.

Aleksei is now a coach with a modern dance troupe and is also trying to teach tap dance to Arkady Romanov, who has come to Moscow in the hope of breaking into showbiz. It is only when a tv show screens a film Aleksei appear- ed in during his youth that he again becomes feted. This discovery of his famous past provides the opportunity for the most extended musical number in the film, with all the principals joining in.

Evgeny Evstigneev has a lugubrious face which he uses well to convey the memory of his past pain and pleasures. He also makes some unforced excursions onto the dance floor and into song.

The film moves along at a crisp pace and has a nice sense of humor, even gently satirizing the earlier days of Soviet filmmaking.—*Cain.*

Lel Hab kessa akhira
(Broken Images)
(EGYPTIAN-COLOR)

An El Alamia production for T.V. and Cinema A.T.V. Directed by Rafaat El Mihi. Screenplay, El Mihi; camera (color), Mahmoud Abdel Sameii; editor, Said El Sheik; music, Mohamed Hilal; sound, Ibrahim Abdel Gayed; set decoration, Maher Abdel Mour. Reviewed at Karlovy Vary Film Festival (competition), July 5, 1986. Running time: 129 MINS.
Rifat . . . . Yehia El Fakharani
Salva . . . . Maali Zayed
Rifat's mother . . . . Tahia Karioka
Also with: Ahmed Rateb, Rohia Khalid, Abdel Aziz Makhiou, Abdel Hafiz El Tatawi, Abla Kamel, Fatma Mahmoud.

Karlovy Vary — Working from his own script, director Rafaat El Mihi portrays life on an island on the Nile, focusing in particular on one couple, Salva and her husband Rifat. The island is underdeveloped and the people poor and still influenced by local superstitions.

Rifat's mother came to the island when half the population was either criminals or fishermen. She and her husband have built up a good business and now own several brick kilns, as well as apartment houses, but have been unwilling to accept Rifat's wife as she came to the marriage without a dowry.

Rifat, who works happily as a teacher, tries to heal the rift between mother and wife, especially as he knows that he is seriously ill. Salva is very much in love with him and desperately wants a child, but she is shielded from the real truth about her husband's state of health by the local doctor.

Director Mihi does not pander to much local exotica, presenting a realistic picture of life among the people on the island. His central characters, the husband and wife, have a naive yet touching relationship, but some of the subsidiary characters tend to fall into clichés — the unyielding mother, the local scoundrel, and the local doctor.

The lives of these supporting characters, while being picaresque in their own way, tend to distract from what was presumably the director's main theme, the conflict between the modern generation and the older superstition-ridden one, exemplified by the local "saint" which is so revered by the locals.

Heroine Maali Zayed, a local girl, acquits herself well, and Yehia El Fakharani is a cuddly bear of a hero who suffers nobly. Music is used sparingly and other technical credits, notably some good color photography, are well up to standard.—*Cain.*

Mirza Nowrouz' Shoes
(IRANIAN-COLOR)

A Novin Film release of a Novin production. Produced by Houchang Nourollahi. Directed by Mohammad Motevasselani. Stars Ali Nassirian. Screenplay, Dariouch Farhang; camera (Widescreen, color), Maziar Parto; editor, Mehdi Radjaian; music, Freydoun Nasseri; art direction, Valiollah Khakdan. Reviewed at Karlovy Vary Film Festival, July 8, 1986. Running time: 106 MINS.
Mirza Nowrouz . . . . Ali Nassirian
Governor . . . . . Mohammad-Ali Kechavarz
Wife . . . . Zahra Boroumand
Merchant . . . . Said Amir Soleimani

Karlovy Vary — A colorful folk tale springs to life in "Mirza Nowrouz' Shoes," directed by veteran Mohammad Motevasselani, who has been absent from the film scene for some time. Set in long-ago times of despotic kings and Ali Baba, picture presents itself as an entertaining, imaginative kidpic with authentic atmosphere and Western-style production values.

Stage thesp Ali Nassirian plays the sympathetic miser Mirza Nowrouz, a rich man who brews essences in his backyard and sells them as perfume and medicine. His overworked wife leaves him because his worn-out old shoes have made him the laughingstock of the city. Since his family provides free labor for his business, Mirza is forced to buy a new pair of shoes. He finds the old shoes won't leave him in peace, and boomerang back at him wherever he throws them, landing him in hot water with the tyrannical governor (Mohammad-Ali Kechavarz).

Film is professionally lensed and boasts sumptuous interiors in the governor's palace, a bathhouse and Mirza's own lavish residence, as well as picturesque costumes on a large cast of extras and even a glimpse of Ali Baba's Forty Thieves plotting amid some ruins. Underlining the fairytale atmosphere are camera tricks with disappearing objects, fast-motion guards, and of course Mirza's shoes walking after him by themselves when he tries to throw them away.

Pic opens with a short cartoon credit sequence that summarizes the story. —*Yung.*

Pomnalui Nunsogi
(Thaw)
(NORTH KOREAN-COLOR)

A Korfilm production (Pyongyang). Directed by Rim Chang Bom and Ko Hak Rim. Screenplay, Lin Chun Gu; camera (Widescreen, color), Kwak Chol Sam, Liu Hui Song. Reviewed at Karlovy Vary Film Festival (competition), July 10, 1986. Running time: 100 MINS.
With: Cho Ji Sun, An Su Bok, Kim Ryong Rin, Kum Jun Sik, So Gyong Sop.

Karlovy Vary — Korean cinema has a long tradition stretching back to the 1920s but it has, of course suffered two blows, first the domination of the country by the Japanese, with consequently very tough censorship in the '30s, and then after World War II the country became divided. The reunificaton of the country is the overriding concern of the north. Both these themes are dealt with in this film from North Korea.

The story has an interesting setting in that it takes place in Japan, where a considerable number of Koreans now live. It enables the script to bring together representatives of all factions of Korea, north, south, those living in Japan as well as some who fled to America after the end of the Korean war.

The occasion is the forthcoming wedding between two young Koreans who were born in Japan. The girl's parents are rich and support South Korea, with the father something of a weak man and drunkard, being in the hands of his wife who owns his company and whose brother only lives for money.

The boy's parents are poor, the father a cripple, losing his legs at the hands of the Japanese. It is not surprising that things take a turn for the worse for the young couple, as the uncle persuades the girl's mother to call off the wedding — he has a more suitable South Korean bride.

Plot complications flow thick and fast. For once it is not the Yanks who are the prime targets, the role of the heavies going mainly to the Japanese, who did of course have a pretty terrible record with the Koreans. We are presented with a plotted history of Korea in the form of flashbacks every so often and it is here that the color and widescreen photography comes to the fore most effectively. Interiors tend to be overlit, and too many location scenes tend to be accompanied by gawking crowds. Music and songs are used to good effect.

The two young leads, subject to innumerable plots convolutions, make an attractive couple when given the chance, but the other characters, ranging from the money-mad uncle to the girl's mother, are in the old theatrical style. — *Cain.*

Dahan
(Affliction)
(BANGLADESH-B&W)

A Nasco Movies release of a Snap Films production. Written and directed by Sheikh Niamat Ali. Camera (b&w), Anwar Hossain; editor, Saidul Anam; music, Amanul Haque; sound, Mohamed Hanif; art direction, Mashooq Helal. Reviewed at Karlovy Vary Film Festival, July 4, 1986. Running time: **120 MINS.**
Munir .... Humayun Faridee
Ivy .... Babita
Mustaq .... Buibul Ahmed
Lina .... Dolly Anwar

Karlovy Vary — "Affliction" refers to the sufferings of just about everybody in Bangladesh society. Director Sheikh Niamat Ali piles up a towering inferno of social ills that end up canceling themselves out in a film with some well-handled moments.

Shot in b&w and partially financed by a government grant for young talent, "Affliction" is a crusader's picture on the borderline of naivete that crushes itself under the sheer weight of trying to portray too many problems at once.

Hero Munir (Humayun Faridee) is a young sociologist who has trouble getting magazines to publish his think pieces: all readers want is sex, violence and crime stories. To support his family, he is forced to tutor a dull-witted rich girl (Babita), who prefers making eyes at the teacher to studying about social stratification. Though not an appealing character, by pic's end she, too, falls victim, making a loveless marriage with a businessman.

Main storyline follows Munir's naive attempts to become a businessman himself, by investing a friend's cash in an obviously doomed venture. Parallel to this, and far more interesting, is the disintegration of Munir's family. His aged uncle, once a respected politician, loses his reason and disappears one day, never to return. His sister Lina (a fine performance by Dolly Anwar) is driven to despair by an unhappy love affair and her mother's indifference.

Film abounds in cripples, murderers, and hungry children eating out of garbage cans, but the images are too forced to carry much weight. —*Yung.*

Loi ré trái tren duong mon
(Return To The Right Path)
(VIETNAMESE-COLOR)

A Famin (Hanoi) release. Produced by Ho Chi Minh City Studios. Directed by Huy Thanh. Screenplay, Nguyen Manh Tuan; camera (color), Le Dinh An; music, Hong Dang. Reviewed at Karlovy Vary Film Festival (competition), July 8, 1986. Running time: **96 MINS.**
With: Lam Toi, Kim Thanh, Kim Thi, Kung Bac.

Karlovy Vary — Title of "Return To The Right Path" gives away the ending in this tale of a factory boss' struggle with his conscience. In spite of its obvious moral, film manages to stay engrossing for most of its run, thanks to well-rounded characters, tight pacing, and an insider's glimpse into daily life in Vietnam today. To its credit, "Return" doesn't try to pull punches, and everything from alcoholism in the factory to bureaucratic corruption is splashed on the screen without reserve.

The moral pivot of the film is Hung, a man on the verge of being promoted to Deputy Minister who is tormented by a guilty conscience. He alone knows he is responsible for a factory accident that sent a security woman into a coma. The investigating committee prefers to label the accident sabotage and avoid a blot on the plant's record. Hung's wife, a calculating social climber, bribes everyone to keep quiet, while even his comically spoiled teenage son champions "being practical" over "ideals." Only his little daughter is incorrupted enough to expect Dad to set a moral example — which he eventually does. It costs him his job, family, and home.

Director Huy Thanh shows a talent for deftly sketching characters and the environment that produced them. The division of Vietnamese society into classes is shown by the Hung family's affluent lifestyle (including the son belonging to a nightly motorcycle gang). They are contrasted to the poor relations of the girl in a coma.

Film is professionally made and action moves on smoothly, until a slowdown at the end. Acting is high-quality across the board. —*Yung.*

Proka
(YUGOSLAVIAN-COLOR)

A Jugoslavija Film (Belgrade) release of a Kosovafilm Studio production. Directed by Isa Qosja. Screenplay, Eqrem Basha, camera (color), Arim Spashu; editor, Agron Vula; music, Krist Lekaj; costumes, Violeta Xhaferi. Reviewed at Karlovy Vary Film Festival (competition), July 8, 1986. Running time: **100 MINS.**
Proka .... Xhevat Qorra
Girl neighbor .... Ahdrijana Videnovic
Mayor .... Abdurrahan Shala
Proka's sister .... Dorota Kaminska
Sotka, Mayor's aide .... Faruk Negolli

Karlovy Vary — "Proka" is the feature debut from Isa Qosja, who graduated from the Belgrade film school after directing two shorts. The film is basically a fable concerning Proka, who is treated by the rest of his villagers as a crazy fool. However, he works his fields successfully, causing the jealousy of the local gendarme who covets the field. The corrupt local mayor also has his eyes for Proka's sister, who has lost her husband and now looks after both Proka and her son.

At the start of the film the village is attempting to induce a spell to bring much needed rain, and force Proka to join in. They later conspire, falsely accusing him of causing trouble, which is eagerly seized upon by the mayor and gendarme who lock him up.

After a brief spell of freedom, Proka is again arrested and taken off to the local monastery, where he is incarcerated and tortured.

The main problem with the film is that one has difficulty gaining any sympathy for Proka. Apart from the girl neighbor and one of the fathers in the convent, the cast is made up of heavies, who go over the top in their roles. The director's penchant for arranging striking visuals is fine but often upsets the sense and rhythm of the film.

Xhevat Qorra is given little opportunity by the script to even speak, as Proka, while Belgrade stage actress Ahdrijana Videnovic as the kindly neighbor looks appropriately touching and pious.

The lack of any contrast in the color photography becomes tiring after a while, with other technical credits being adequate. —*Cain.*

El Narco — Duelo Rojo
(The Narc — Red Duel)
(MEXICAN-COLOR)

A Peliculas Mexicanas release of a Corporativa Cinematográfica Astro, S.A. de C.V. production. Produced by Leonel González. Written and directed by Alfonso de Alva. Stars González. Camera (color), Xavier Cruz; editor, Enrique Murillo; music, Héctor Sánchez, featuring the groups Los Rurales del Bravo, N.L. and Trío Raíces. Reviewed at Big Apple Cine 1, N.Y. July 2, 1986. Running time: **94 MINS.**
Leonel (El Narco) Rojas .. Leonel González
Frank .... Víctor Junco
Ramón Solis .... Arturo Martínez
Octavio Loyo .... Antonio Zunbiaga
Also with: Jorge Fegan, Mario Cid, Armando Duarte, Douglas Sandoval, Braulio Zertuche, Tammy González, Lisa Willer, Oscar Treviño.

As illegal drugs continue to pour into the United States via Mexico, Mexico continues to produce low-budget adventure pics such as "El Narco" about the problems related to drug trafficking.

Compared to other pics in this genre, "El Narco" is both technically and structurally superior, but the film still fails to be interesting. Alfonso de Alva's script is full of humor and quirks in an attempt to create believable and memorable characters, yet it fails curiously to generate any interest in the hero Leonel (The Narc) Rojas, a wooden puppet played as such by Leonel González.

Film's action begins abruptly with the violent deaths by crossbow of a popular political candidate, his caretaker and dog somewhere in the U.S.-Mexican border region. The day before, the candidate had promised to clean the state of all drug trafficking.

Police detective Ramón Solis (Arturo Martínez) is sent to handle the case all by himself. He makes no headway and realizes that only one person can do it: his best friend and former partner "El Narco," who dropped from sight two years earlier.

The film wastes a lot of time in an overlong search for the former narcotics officer replete with flashbacks. It seems that El Narco's young daughter drowned, his wife went crazy and he has been living in squalor and drunkenness. At last, Ramón finds him in a run-down tenement and convinces him to clean up his act and save the day.

Lensing by Xavier Cruz makes the film look more lush than it deserves, especially in the scenes with El Narco in training. Here the pic tries to copy the Rocky formula with closeups of pectorals flexing and calves pumping into shape complemented by Héctor Sánchez's brash music. Within two minutes of screen time, El Narco becomes an expert marksman on the crossbow.

There are few surprises. Unlike Rocky, El Narco is not an underdog. González gives El Narco all the humanity of Pac Man and we respond accordingly, with a stifled yawn. —*Lent.*

Se Sufre Pero Se Goza
(It Hurts But It Feels Good)
(MEXICAN-COLOR)

A Peliculas Mexicanas release of a Producciones Films Seneca production. Produced and directed by Julio Ruiz Llaneza. Screenplay, René Cardona Sr., Fernando Oses; camera (color), Rúben Mendoza; editor, Raúl Domínguez. Reviewed at Big Apple Cine 1, N.Y., July 7, 1986. Running time: **87 MINS.**
Perioache Echevarría .... Rafael Inclán
Rene .... Evita Muñoz
Matuta .... Guillermo Rivas
Dona Luz .... Carmelita González
Don Juliano .... Manuel Ibañez
Rosita .... Rosella

The super low-budget Mexican sex comedy "Se Sufre Pero Se Goza" (It Hurts But It Feels Good) is little more than a string of sophomoric jokes from beginning to end.

Originally lensed in 1984 under the more apt title "Mascara Vs. Bikini" (Mask Vs. Bikini), pic's action revolves around sports enthusiast Perioache Echevarría (Rafael Inclán) and his buddy/chauffeur Matuta (Guillermo Rivas), who decide to make big bucks by changing their management from male to female wrestlers. One of the wrestlers is masked and the other sports a bikini. The catch: whoever loses must surrender the object of her title and is either unmasked or dis-bikinied.

Inclán plays the same shrill characterization throughout the film as if life were a continual party that demands constant drunkenness and a roving eye. This wears thin after the first five minutes.

Almost the entire film is handled from only one or two camera angles, with extras mugging during crowd scenes. If this isn't enough, the wrestlers' choreography is so lax that it makes tv wrestling look real.

The weak script, reading like a compendium of dirty jokes, is touted to be by veteran Mexican filmmaker René Cardona Sr. in collaboration with Fernando Oses. —*Lent.*

What Waits Below
(COLOR)

Stillborn spelunking saga.

A Blossom Pictures release of an Adams Apple Film presentation of a Sandy Howard production. Executive producers, Mel Pearl, Don Levin. Produced by Howard, Robert D. Bailey. Directed by Don Sharp. Screenplay, Christy Marx, Robert Vincent O'Neil, from story by Ken Barnett; camera (Bellevue Pathé Quebec color), Virgil Harper; editor, John R. Bowey; music, Michel Rubini, Denny Jaeger; sound (Dolby), Craig Feldberg, David Lee; art director, Stephen Marsh; special photographic effects design, Bailey; assistant director, Oliver Manton; special makeup, William Munns; prosthetic corpse design, Greg Cannom; casting, Victoria Plummer; technical advisor, Roy Davis. Reviewed on Lightning Video vidcassette, N.Y., June 11, 1986. (MPAA Rating: PG.) Running time: 88 MINS.
Wolfson ....Robert Powell
Major Stevens ....Timothy Bottoms
Leslie Peterson ....Lisa Blount
Ben Gannon ....Richard Johnson
Frida Shelley ....Anne Heywood
Lt. George Barwell ..........A.C. Weary
Lemurian elder ....Liam Sullivan
Hunter ....Jackson Bostwick
Santos Arias........Richard Beauchamp

"What Waits Below" is a dull rendering of a lost race fantasy yarn. Filmed in 1983 under the title "Secrets Of The Phantom Caverns," picture received only a test release in November 1984, subsequently appearing in vidcassette stores.

Robert Powell toplines as Wolfson ("call me Wolf"), a soldier of fortune first encountered being chased around Nicaragua by enemy troops. He's recruited by military pal George (A.C. Weary) to go to Belize and help U.S. Army Major Stevens (Timothy Bottoms) make the Omega Station there operational (transmitting signals to aid submarines in navigation).

Near the Omega base, a team of anthropologists is exploring caves and being bossed around by Major Stevens. Seismic tests by the army force an opening in the rocks and soon thereafter, army guards are killed and the Omega transmitter is stolen.

Stevens, Wolfson and the scientists search the new cave and find a lost race of fabled Lemurians, styled here as albinos. The Lemurians stole the transmitter because

its high frequency signal was bothering their sensitive hearing. In warring with this lost race, many casualties occur until Wolfson finally escapes and orders the caves sealed off permanently, to leave the Lemurians in peace.

Extremely tame, "What Waits Below" meanders around below ground without the expected action-adventure excitement. Except for a huge snake head that attacks in one scene, it is minus the monsters that could have made this a fun picture for kids.

An impressive cast is wasted, with most of the attention resting on vast caverns (filmed on Alabama and Tennessee locations), augmented by okay mattework and miniatures.
—*Lor.*

Da ebichash na inat
(All For Love)
(BULGARIAN-COLOR)

A Bulgariafilm production. Directed by Nikolai Volev. Screenplay, Volev from short story by Chavdar Shinov; camera (color), Krassimir Kostov; art direction, Konstantin Roussakov. Reviewed at Karlovy Vary Film Festival (competition), July 13, 1986. Running time: 87 MINS.
Rado ....Velko Kunev
Rado's wife............Maria Statoulova
Plamen, Rado's son ....Ivan Velko
Stefka, the controller ....Leda Tasseva
Headmaster ....Yordan Spirov
Teacher...............Yulia Kozhinkova

Karlovy Vary — This third feature film from Bulgarian director Nikolai Volev takes a fairly critical look at some aspects of the society in that country today and has caused a certain amount of debate.

The crisis in the relationship of father Rado and his 14-year-old son Plamen is brought about through an incident at school, where Plamen laughs at an elderly teacher, explaining that the teacher, supposedly instructing them in singing, is actually out of tune. When told to apologize by the headmaster he refuses. Rado's father is brought into the conflict and when he eventually learns the real story supports his son.

In the meantime, however, the son has found out that his father is involved in black marketing, and runs away.

It is through the boy's strong moral attitude of refusing to accept advice from his father, a thief, that the latter begins to change and try to redeem himself by renouncing his former way of life.

Young Ivan Velko catches the strength and innocence of the young boy well. Velko Kunev, known up to now as a comedian, imparts a driving force to the role of the father who has to chose between his son's love and a continuing corrupt life. With the exception of the overly distraught Maria Statoulova as

the wife, other roles are sensitively filled.—*Cain.*

Bi chamd khayrtay
(I Adore You)
(MONGOLIAN-COLOR)

A Mongolkino production. Produced and directed by B. Baljinnyam. Screenplay, N Nyamgawaa, B. Baljinnyam; camera (color), G. Tseren, B. Baljinnyam. Reviewed at Karlovy Vary Film Festival (competition), July 9, 1986. Running time: 91 MINS.
Delger ....D. Erdenbayer
Urlei ....D. Purevmaa
Sambuu ....Z. Jarantau
Bayaras.....................N. Badral

Karlovy Vary — It seems that teenagers are the same the world over — at least on the evidence of "I Adore You" by the Mongolian director B. Baljinnyam.

The story concerns three pupils at high school, Delger, Urlei and Bayaras, who are in the final grade and have to decide, together with the rest of the class, whether to go on to college or find a job. Bayaras comes from a well-off family and he rejects the collective ideas of manual work. Delger's father is an invalid and he welcomes the chance to work in a shoe factory during school holidays.

While the film upholds the basic premise of the virtue of collective work, it is made universal and human through the use of the classic teenage triangle situation, with both boys falling in love with the same girl, Urlei. She of course initially chooses the wrong boy, who is quickly scared off when she starts talking seriously about babies.

There is quite a bit of teenage partying, with pop music and even a schmaltzy song at the finale which could have been a Mongolian entry in the Eurovision song contest.

Producer/director Baljinnyam, who also had a hand in the script and photography, has presented a cautionary tale with all the right values emphasized but coated in terms which youngsters in all countries who are not too sophisticated would appreciate.

The director seems happier on locations, making something of the austere surroundings, while interiors are occasionally awkwardly composed. Otherwise the technical credits are good.—*Cain.*

Chrzesniak
(The Godson)
(POLISH-COLOR)

A Film Polski release of Zespoly Filmowe Film Unit, Iluziion production. Directed by Henryk Bielski. Screenplay, Jerzy Janicki; camera (color), Boguslaw Lambach; editor, Ewa Smal; music; Waldemar Kazanecki; sound; Andrzej Lewandowski; set decorations, Jerzy Karol Zielinski, Edward Papierski; production manager, Jacek Moczydlow-

ski. Reviewed at Karlovy Vary Film Festival (competition), July 9, 1986. Running time: 96 MINS.
Gregori Purowski ....Maciej Goraj
Strzykalski ....Franciszek Pieczka
Wacek, the minister ....Leon Nieczyk
Blicharski ....Gustaw Lutkiewicz
Chaladaj ....Jerzy Michotek
Gregory's lover ....Emilia Krakowska

Karlovy Vary — "The Godson" is a basically unexceptional Polish film with only slight interest for Western audiences. The rather parochial storyline shows how unwise it is to step out of line by taking a personal decision, because not even an influential godfather will be able to help you.

The film depicts three days in the life of state farm director, Gregori Purowski, during which he celebrates his 40th birthday, steps out of line, loses his job, but regains the affection of his son.

Although he is professionally successful, Gregori is basically a lonely man, separated from his wife who went to Canada some years before, and with a son who is distant from him and wants to visit his mother as soon as his exams are finished. Gregori only finds some shallow sexual pleasure with the female superintendant of the local cinema.

His birthday is a time for reflection, for he was born at the end of the war, his mother died after giving birth to him. He was adopted by four godfathers who have helped him throughout his life and have themselves all reached positions of some influence; one has even become a Government Minister.

After his birthday celebration, which brings together all his godfathers, Gregori makes a mistake at work in turning away from the farm some Austrian businessmen. In sending them away Gregori is not only held responsible for a previously-signed contract but also has to personally pay the cost of the helicopter ride which brought them. Even his godfathers are unable to help him and his career seems to be in ruins, in addition to his personal life.

The small town atmosphere is nicely created and the scenes on the farm captured in the generally attractive photography by Boguslaw Lambach. Maciej Goraj as Gregori makes an effective stab at the lonely hero, but as his relationship with his son is only sketchy and that with the godfathers basically reminiscences, he does not have much to work on. —*Cain.*

Stand By Me
(COLOR)

Well-acted memoir of Summer of '59 presents a difficult marketing challenge.

A Columbia Pictures release of an Act III production. Produced by Bruce A. Evans, Raynold Gideon, Andrew Scheinman. Directed by Rob Reiner. Screenplay, Gideon, Evans, from the novella "The Body," by Stephen King; camera (Technicolor, Deluxe prints), Thomas Del Ruth; editor, Robert Leighton; music, Jack Nitzsche; production design, Dennis Washington; set design, Richard Mackenzie; costumes, Sue Moore; assistant director, Irby Smith; casting, Jane Jankins, Janet Hirshenson. Reviewed at the Samuel Goldwyn theater, Beverly Hills, July 22, 1986. (MPAA Rating: R.) Running time: **87 MINS.**

Gordie Lachance	Wil Wheaton
Chris Chambers	River Phoenix
Teddy Dechamp	Corey Feldman
Vern Tessio	Jerry O'Connell
The Writer	Richard Dreyfuss
Ace Merrill	Kiefer Sutherland

Hollywood — "Stand By Me" falls somewhat short of being a firstrate "small" picture about adventurous small-town adolescent boys, although director Rob Reiner is to be lauded for coming close. Pic is sure to generate strong word-of-mouth, but Columbia has a formidable job attracting business considering current b.o. competition and film's undeserved R rating that effectively locks out a sizable chunk of its target audience.

Formerly titled "The Body" based on a novella of the same name by Stephen King, "Stand By Me" is the experiences of four youths on a two-day trek through the woods around their hometown of Castle Rock, Ore. to find the yet-undiscovered body of a dead teenager reported missing for several days.

Film opens very slowly with the extraneous narration of grownup writer Richard Dreyfuss reminiscing on that certain summer of 1959 between sixth and seventh grades that he spent with three close buddies as they sought to become heroes in each others' and the town's eyes.

Scripters Raynold Gideon and Bruce A. Evans have written inspired dialog for this quartet of plucky boys at that hard-to-capture age when they're still young enough to get scared and cry and yet old enough to want to sneak smokes and cuss 'cause that's what's cool.

Each is a particular personality type drawn together in friendship because each seems to have the characteristics the others find endearing and amusing, not unlike the makeup of other ensemble films that up to now have been made mostly about teenagers or adults.

Leading the cast is the introspective, sensitive "brain" of the bunch, Gordie Lachance (Wil Wheaton), whose natural storytelling talent provide him an escape from an alienating homelife that's gone sour because of his brother's untimely death.

He turns to his friends for affection and admiration which he gets in the form of complete rapture as he tells tall tales, including the film's highlight as he wards off the evil spirits around the campfire by sketching a hilarious scene of a fat boy's revenge on the cruel townsfolk during a pie eating contest.

His somber personality is matched by best friend Chris Chambers (River Phoenix), a toughie who is an abused child; Teddy Dechamp (Corey Feldman), the loony kid of an institutionalized father; and the perfectly named wimp, Vern Tessie, the chubby kid who everyone else enjoys poking fun at.

Despite the rough language, including 11 uses of the "F" word that qualified this pic for an R rating, "Stand By Me" has an underlying moral tone that is brought forth through these kids' actions as they relate to each other during times of crisis and especially during the ultimate trauma when they face off against the town's rough boys lead by big bully Ace Merrill (Kiefer Sutherland) when they finally find the dead body.

While Reiner succeeds in building the story around Wheaton's convincing vulnerability, he also has achieved a rare feat of getting equally empathetic and outstanding performances from everyone else in the cast.

Unfortunately, pic falls flat at the end with a quick wrapup by Dreyfuss of what happened to his pals and a parting shot of him sitting at a word processor typing the last, rather banal, words to his story.

The beginning and end do not detract from the overall rich core of the film that is enhanced by the lush cinematic treatment by Thomas Del Ruth of the verdant Oregon countryside.

Overall look of the effort seems oddly contemporary since 1950s tunes, buzzcuts and clothing styles are now back in vogue. —*Brit.*

HaKrav al HaVa'ad
(House Committee Rivalry)
(ISRAELI-COLOR)

A Noah Films presentation of a Kayitz Films production. Produced by Avraham Deshe (Pashanel). Executive producer, Shlomo Orbach, Directed by Avi Cohen. Screenplay, Assi Dayan, camera (color), Gad Danzig, Benny Carmeli; editor, Anath Lubarsky; music, Erich Rudich; lyrics, Eli Mohar; costumes, Ruth Dar. Reviewed at the Ben Yehuda theater, Tel Aviv, July 13, 1986. Running time: **90 MINS.**

Khalfon	Shayke Levy
Dr. Shemesh	Israel Poliakoff
Jimbo	Gavri Banai

Also with: Tamar Gingold, Shula Khen, Dori Ben-Ze'ev, Moshe Ivgi, Eyal Geffen, Alon Aboutboul.

Tel Aviv — Levy, Poliakoff and Banai, better known in Israel as HaGashash HaKhiver, are the top local entertainment group, longstanding favorites who have had no competition on the light stage for the past 20 years. Sharp wit, polished performances and excellent timing have made them an object of admiration and respect for the entire trade.

While videos of their stage shows have been tremendously popular on the local market, their charm has never made it, somehow, on film. This is their third feature and by far the least funny.

Assi Dayan, the helmer of their previous film efforts, has supplied a sort of rickety, unfocused script, directed with a heavy hand and very little sense of timing by Avi Cohen. Once control is taken out of the hands of the trio, they go through the motions, but not much more.

The plot, concerning the feud between two condo tenants, uses references of topical issues, from anti-terror defense to Rambomania, from ethnic conflicts to religious wars, including a parody of an election campaign, but it is all pretty tame, compared to the potential of the three leads.

Name value obviously will rustle business at home, the summer season being the obvious timing for it to find its audience. Not much chance, however, of its traveling out of the country. — *Edna.*

Flight Of The Navigator
(COLOR)

Unremarkable fantasy exploring Special Relativity theory.

A Buena Vista Distribution release of a Walt Disney Pictures presentation of a Producers Sales Organization picture. Produced by Robby Wald, Dimitri Villard. Executive producers, Jonathan Sanger, Mark Damon, John Hyde. Directed by Randal Kleiser. Screenplay, Michael Burton, Matt MacManus, based on a story by Mark H. Baker; camera (Technicolor), James Glennon; editor, Jeff Gourson; music, Alan Silvestri; production design, William J. Creber; art director, Michael Novotny; set decorator, Scott Jacobson; visual effects supervisor, Peter Donen; creatures performed by Tony Urbano, Tim Blaney; sound, Robert Wald; assistant director, Peter Bogart; coproducer David Joseph; co-executive producer, Malcolm Harding; casting, Mike Fenton, Jane Feinberg, Valerie Massalas. Reviewed at Monica Theater, Santa Monica, Calif., July 26, 1986. (MPAA Rating: PG.) Running time: **90 MINS.**

David Freeman	Joey Cramer
Helen Freeman	Veronica Cartwright
Bill Freeman	Cliff De Young
Carolyn McAdams	Sarah Jessica Parker
Jeff (16 years)	Matt Adler
Dr. Faraday	Howard Hesseman
Voice of Max	Paul Mall (Reubens)
Troy	Robert Small
Jeff (8 years)	Albie Whitaker

Hollywood — Ever since Steven Spielberg created a sense of otherworldly wonder for a whole generation, filmmakers have been trying to duplicate the magic. "Flight Of The Navigator" explores some of the same territory, but instead of creating an eye-opening panorama it looks through the small end of the telescope. Life on Earth is magnified but without an expansive vision. Results make for an entertaining if tame time for a young audience and should yield modest b.o. returns.

Film does not really get rolling until the second half after spending a good deal of time setting up, exploring and explaining some extraordinary goings on. Young David Freeman (Joey Cramer) vanishes from his Fort Lauderdale home only to return to the identical spot unchanged eight years later, though he has experienced being away for only a couple of hours.

When a sleek silver flying saucer turns up on the scene NASA gets into the act and all roads lead to David. It seems his head has been filled with star charts and he's been serving as navigator for an exploratory ship from a distant planet.

Film finally gets on track when 12-year-old David is reunited with the spacecraft for a trip which ultimately will deposit him right back where he started. Along the way the journey is imaginative and fun but earthbound. Rather than revealing the ordinary world from a new perspective, in this case a robotic flight commander (voiced by an uncredited Paul Reubens, a.k.a. Pee-wee Herman) who becomes fascinated with American pop culture, and also becomes David's endearing playmate.

As is often the problem with extraterrestrial adventures, all life forms are anthropomorphized with a selection of cute and cuddly creatures. Earthlings are all recognizable with Veronica Cartwright and Cliff De Young playing the role of the loving but baffled parents and Matt Adler the younger brother who becomes the older brother. (Albie Whitaker plays him when he's younger.)

Center of the universe created by scripters Michael Burton and Matt MacManus, from a story by Mark Baker, is the family and most of the tension of the film revolves around whether David can get back to where he belongs. While there is some mild danger and film deals gently with fear of abandonment, it is nothing too disturbing for moppets despite the PG rating.

Kids should also be attracted by the visuals and some nifty special effects in the space craft sequences. Performances are all workmanlike with Cramer doing a believable job as the ordinary kid in extraordinary circumstances. Howard Hesseman as the head NASA scientist on the case is an odd bit of casting but performances are not really what make this film move.

Director Randal Kleiser is strongest at creating a mood, a sense of place and time when the ordinary rules don't apply and in its best moments, this is where the film comes sporadically to life. —*Jagr.*

★★★★★★★★★★★★★★★★★★★★★★★★★★
★   Pula Festival Reviews   ★
★★★★★★★★★★★★★★★★★★★★★★★★★★

Srecna Nova '49
(Happy New Year — 1949)
(YUGOSLAVIAN-COLOR)

A Vardar Film (Skopje), Union Film (Belgrade), Makedonija Film (Skopje), Gradski Kina (Skopje) coproduction. Directed by Stole Popov. Screenplay, Gordan Mihic; camera (Widescreen, color), Miso Samoilovski; editor, Laki Cemcev; music, Ljupco Konstantinov; sound, Jordan Janevski; art direction, Nikola Lazarevski; costumes, Jasminka Jesic. Reviewed at Pula Film Festival (competition), July 24, 1986. Running time: **130 MINS.**
Dragoslav............Svetozar Cvetkovic
Kosta.................Meto Jovanovski
Girl ....Vladica Milosavljevic
Inspector ....Kusko Kostovski
Also with: Aco Djorcev, Petar Arsovski, Goce Todorovski, Milica Stojanova, Mite Grozdanov, Ivan Bekjarev.

Pula — Prize-winning documentarist Stole Popov carries skill at depicting believable, human characters into his second feature, "Happy New Year — 1949." Picture was voted best Yugoslav film of the year at Pula.

Setting is Macedonia, just after the war. On a train carrying festive soldiers home from the USSR, some opt to stay behind in Russia. Dragoslav (Svetozar Cvetkovic) talks another young man out of his idea, but the depressed youth blows his brains out in the train. When he testifies to the local police, Dragoslav inexplicably comes under suspicion of being a Russian spy. Although eventually arrested, imprisoned, and released for lack of evidence, he never loses his primitive loyalty to the Party.

Just the opposite is his brother Kosta (Meto Jovanovski), a happy-go-lucky black marketeer addicted to American-style clothes and Bing Crosby. Though run out of the house by his brother and father, Kosta never loses his courage for living, and is the one character to survive till New Year, 1949.

Third pole of the film is the brothers' common love interest, Vladica Milosavljevic. Her faithfulness to Dragoslav is tried severely when he is jailed for an indefinite period of time, and she moves in with Kosta, precipitating the final tragedy. Well paced and convincing up to this point, "New Year" unfortunately falters as it comes down the homestretch, with a string of easy-out suicides.

Popov creates period atmosphere without forcing, and slides effortlessly from gentle comedy and tongue-in-cheek action sequences (involving the likable local gangsters, who seem to model themselves on American movie types) to human and historical betrayals. Living with the threat of "Russian tanks on the border" and the West just a forged passport away, pic's characters fight out their personal problems against the larger historical backdrop. —*Yung.*

Bal na vodi
(Dancing On Water)
(YUGOSLAVIAN-COLOR)

A Smart Egg Pictures release of an Avala Film/Inex Film (Belgrade) coproduction. Produced by George Zecevic. Written and directed by Jovan Acin. Camera (color), Tomislav Pinter; editor, Snezana Ivanovic; music, Zoran Simjanovic; art director, Sava Acin. Reviewed at Pula Film Festival (competition), July 19, 1986. Running time: **112 MINS.**
Esther ....Gala Videnovic
Rile......................Milan Strljic
Sasha.................Dragan Bjelogrlic
Also with: Goran Radakovic, Nebojsa Bakocevic, Srdan Todorovic, Relja Basio, Marko Todorovic.

Pula — "Dancing On Water" is an openly nostalgic trip in time back to Belgrade of the 1950s, where a group of clean-cut teens, four boys and a girl, clown around, play in a band and have their first romantic stirrings. Though shot through Yugoslav companies, pic was lensed by Paris-based tv director Jovan Acin and financed by London-based George Zecevic, which goes some way toward accounting for its Westernized look and concerns.

Linking the five friends is the fact they all belong to the middle-class, dispossessed after the revolution. "Dancing" has nothing very profound to say about these characters, except they were badly treated during the 1950s at the hands of presumptuous party members, like young Rile (Milan Strljic). Rile, who comes from the provinces and is slightly older than the band of friends, quickly makes inroads to the heart of pretty Esther (Gala Videnovic), nicknamed after her idol Esther Williams. He wins a sensually lensed scene with her, beating out her four admirers. When she gets pregnant, he ungallantly disappears.

Pic is framed by Esther's funeral many years later. The boys have grown into heavy-set middle age. All live abroad — London, New York, Milan — and some have achieved chauffered-limo status. Rile, too, returns to pay his last respects — he typically has switched hats and now spouts off against the party interfering in his business ventures.

The key scene to which film returns is Esther's escape to Italy, where her father is waiting for her. The boys row her across the Adriatic in a crew boat, and are arrested for their trouble. We know it also will be their fortune, as they start new lives in the West.

Gala Videnovic and the rest of the young cast are adequate, but bland, and a bit hard to single out in a crowd. Strljic, in the role of the comical villain Rile, is at least a distinguishable face. Behind the camera, Acin knows how to keep the film moving and he shows a flair for comedy that peeps through here and there. Tomislav Pinter's cinematography gives film a sunny cast. Less distinguished is the art direction, which fails to give any but a rudimentary feeling for the period. —*Yung.*

Vecernja Zvona
(Evening Bells)
(YUGOSLAVIAN-COLOR)

A Jadran Film (Zagreb), Jugoart (Zagreb), Montenegroexport (Niksic) coproduction. Executive producer, Sulejman Kapic. Directed by Lordan Zafranovic. Stars Rade Serbedzija. Screenplay, Mirko Kovac, from his novel "Entrance To The Womb;" camera (Widescreen, Agfa Gevaert color), Andrija Pivcevic; editor, Andrija Zafranovic; music, Vladimir Kraus-Rajteric; art direction, Ivica Sporcic; costumes, Ruta Knezevic. Reviewed at Pula Film Festival (competition), July 25, 1986. Running time: **127 MINS.**
Tomislav ....Rade Serbedzija
Also with: Petar Bozovic, Neda Arneric, Tatjana Blagojevic, Miodrag Krivokapic, Mustafa Nadarevic.

Pula — Prolific director Lordan Zafranovic attempts to cover too much ground and too much history in "Evening Bells." Based on a book by Mirko Kovac (the scriptwriter) that was voted novel of the year, pic breathlessly flips through 22 years in the life of its hero Tomislav K., including the Nazi rise to power in Germany, Communist resistance to fascism in Yugoslavia, the war, the revolution, and its aftermath. Though Zafranovic was awarded best director kudos at Pula this year, and star Rade Serbedzija best actor ribbons, characters certainly had more chance to develop on paper than they do in this two-hour film.

As the pivot of "Bells," Tomislav stays just the other side of a sympathetic character. We first glimpse him as a mischievous boy playing tricks on the nuns in his fancy school and spying on the bedchamber of his brother Stjepan and his beautiful country bride Rosa. Later in life, Tomislav's secret love affair with Rosa doesn't keep him from marrying a rich Zagreb girl he meets in Germany.

During the war she saves him from a concentration camp by becoming the mistress of a fascist officer, but with his typical hard-nosed principles Tomislav, unaware of her sacrifice, upbraids her as a collaborator and goads her to suicide.

In politics as in love, Tomislav coldly follows his own path. His charisma as a leader is more stated than demonstrated in the film. After the war he gets into all sorts of trouble as national politics veer left and right of Stalin, and his accidental death in prison carries little weight either symbolically or dramatically. To be appreciated as a victim of history, he needed to be a little more likeable a character.

Lensing is professional throughout, and director now and then takes time out for a few moments of real cinema — notably, fleeting romantic trysts charged with considerable eroticism, and some joyful moments of colorful country idylls. —*Yung.*

Haunted Honeymoon
(COLOR)

Mild sendup of thunderstorm mystery pics.

An Orion Pictures release. Produced by Susan Ruskin. Directed by Gene Wilder. Screenplay, Wilder, Terence Marsh. Stars Wilder, Gilda Radner, Dom DeLuise. Camera (Rank color, Deluxe prints), Fred Schuler; editor, Christopher Greenbury; music, John Morris; production design, Terence Marsh; art direction, Alan Tomkins; set decoration, Michael Seirton; costume design, Ruth Myers; sound (Dolby), Tommy Staples; stunt coordintor, Colin Skeaping; special effects consultant, John Stears; associate producers, Basil Rayburn, Emile Buyse; makeup supervision, Stuart Freeborn; assistant director, Roy Button; casting, Irene Lamb. Reviewed at the Hollywood Pacific, L.A., July 25, 1986. (MPAA Rating: PG.) Running time: **82 MINS.**
Larry Abbot ....Gene Wilder
Vickie Pearle ....Gilda Radner
Aunt Kate ....Dom DeLuise
Charles ....Jonathan Pryce
Dr. Paul Abbot ....Paul L. Smith
Francis Sr................Peter Vaughan
Pfister ....Bryan Pringle
Francis Jr. ....Roger Ashton-Griffiths
Montego ....Jim Carter
Sylvia ....Eve Ferret
Nora Abbot ....Julann Griffin
Susan ....Jo Ross
Rachel ....Ann Way

Hollywood — Gene Wilder is back in the rut of sending up old film conventions in "Haunted Honeymoon," a mild farce due for mild b.o.

Title is a misnomer, since set-up has radio actor Wilder taking his fiancee **Gilda** Radner out to his family's **gloom**y country estate to meet the **kin**folk just before tying the knot. **Clan** is presided over by the tubby, **genial** Aunt Kate, played by Dom **DeL**uise, who maintains that a **werewolf** is on the loose in the vicinity.

At **the same** time, Wilder's sinister **uncle and** shrink, the glowering Paul **L.** Smith, determines to cure **Wilder of** his irrational fears by scaring **him** to death, while Smith's son, **Jonathan** Pryce, is destitute and **may** have jealous reasons for **wanting** to knock off his sweet-natured **cousin.** Again, maybe the butler **intends** to do it.

In **any** event, Wilder is obliged to **contend with** numerous assaults on his **health, and** much of the blessedly **brief running** time is devoted to frantic **running** among different rooms **in** the mansion for reasons that **occasionally** prove faintly amusing **but** are singularly uncompelling. **Pic** provokes a few chuckles along **the** way, but no guffaws.

Wilder and Radner perform with **enthusiasm,** while DeLuise, in a role he has **been** working toward during his **entire** career, sports an odd, halting delivery that sometimes comes off as funny but is mostly just odd. Best in the supporting cast are Bryan Pringle and Ann Way as the old, eccentric butler and maid.

Set in the U.S. but lensed in Britain, pic has a strange mid-Atlantic quality to it, since most of the thesps except the leads are British and the mythology upon which it draws is distinctly English. Production values are on the economical side, while John Morris' score keeps things spirited.— *Cart.*

Jungle Raiders
(ITALIAN-COLOR)

A Cannon Group presentation of a L'Immagine production. Produced by Luciano Appignani. Directed by Anthony M. Dawson (Antonio Margheriti). Stars Christopher Connelly, Marina Costa, Lee Van Cleef. Screenplay, Giovanni Simonelli; camera (Luciano Vittori color), Guglielmo Mancori; editor, Alberto Moriani; music, Cal Taormina; set design, Walter Patriarca; assistant director, Edoardo Margheriti; production manager, Ignazio Dolce; special effects, Cataldo Galiano. Reviewed on MGM/UA Home Video vidcassette, N.Y., July 26, 1986. (MPAA Rating: PG-13.) Running time: **102 MINS.**
Capt. Yankee . . . . Christopher Connelly
Yanez . . . . Marina Costa
Insp. Warren . . . . Lee Van Cleef
Gin Fizz . . . . Alan Collins
Also with: Dario Pontonutti, Mike Monty, Rene Abadeza, Cirillo Vitali, Francesco Arcuri.

Italian filmmaker Antonio Margheriti went to his favorite Indiana Jones clone well once too often and came up with "Jungle Raiders," a lowercase adventure pic filmed in the Far East in fall 1984, with "Captain Yankee" as an alternate

title. Cannon ultimately decided to send this pickup directly to the vidcassette market, as part of its deal with MGM/UA Home Video.

Film begins promisingly with a lengthy sequence directly aping the opening of "Raiders Of The Lost Ark," as soldier of fortune Duke Howard (Christopher Connelly), a.k.a. Capt. Yankee, leads a dude through a rain forest to hunt in a boobytrapped cave for a golden idol, pursued all the while by natives shooting arrows. The dude even escapes in a seaplane Indy might use, all before it's revealed that Duke and the natives have staged the whole incident to fleece another gullible tourist seeking high adventure.

Set per opening credit card in "Malaysia, 1938" (too bad the filmmakers didn't realize the British colony was still called Malaya for decades to come), tongue-in-cheek story deals with Duke guiding a museum curator Yanez (Marina Costa) from Colombia on her quest for the fabled Ruby of Gloom. Repetitive incidents in caves containing lakes on fire and jousting with the local firebrand Borneo pirates pad out the dull running time until an obligatory cynical ending.

Although there is a requisite amount of chasing around, pyrotechnics and stuntwork, "Jungle Raiders" is singularly unexciting and pointless. Even the expected supernatural content is absent, with the ruby turning out to be just a big stone suitable for chopping up in Amsterdam.

Cast is merely okay, with Connelly a colorless hero, Van Cleef a minor guest star who dresses alternately in all-white or all-black outfits, Collins the chummy sidekick for the nth time in a Margheriti film and Costa simply along for the ride. Tech credits are acceptable, though the often jaunty musical score occasionally lapses into the same library music already used in Margheriti's earlier pic, "The Ark Of The Sun God." —*Lor.*

Maximum Overdrive
(COLOR)

Unconvincing mechanical thriller from Stephen King.

⚠ De Laurentiis Entertainment Group release. Produced by Martha Schumacher; coproducer, Milton Subotsky. Executive producers, Mel Pearl, Don Levin. Written and directed by Stephen King. Camera (J-D-C Widescreen, Technicolor), Armando Nannuzzi; editor, Evan Lottman; music, AC/DC; production design, Giorgio Postiglione; set designer, Hilton Rosemarin; art director, Rod Schumacher; special effects coordinator, Steve Galick; special visual effects supervisor, Barry Nolan; special optical effects, Van Der Veer Photo Effects; sound (Dolby), Ed White; special effects makeup, Dean Gates; costumes, Clifford Capone; stunt coordinator, Glenn Randall Jr.; assistant director, Tony Lucibello; casting, Mary Colquohon.

Reviewed at Hollywood Pacific theater, July 25, 1986. (MPAA Rating: R.) Running time: **97 MINS.**
Bill Robinson . . . . Emilio Estevez
Hendershot . . . . Pat Hingle
Brett . . . . Laura Harrington
Connie . . . . Yeardley Smith
Curt . . . . John Short
Wanda June . . . . Ellen McElduff
Duncan . . . . J.C. Quinn
Camp Loman . . . . Christopher Murney
Deke . . . . Holter Graham

Hollywood — "Maximum Overdrive" is the kind of film audiences want to talk back to, the kind that throws credibility out the window in favor of crass manipulation. Unfortunately, master manipulator Stephen King, making his directorial debut from his own script, fails to create a convincing enough environment to make the kind of nonsense he's offering here believable or fun. The devout may turn out for an initial spurt but not too many others.

As a director, King must fancy himself a blue-collar Steven Spielberg starting out with a small-town idyll soon disrupted by a mindless revolt of trucks. It's one part "Duel" and one part "Christine" and altogether lame.

When in doubt King seems to revert to the supernatural or the extraterrestrial as an explanation for almost any pyrotechnics he wants to stage. In this case it's the passage near the Earth of a "rogue comet" which makes some, but not all mechanical devices go haywire. (Why, for instance, trucks do and not cars, is probably a function more of visuals than any internal logic.)

King collects a typical mix of rednecks, good old boys, restless youth, drifters and the decent folk in a small corner of North Carolina where they hold up at a truck stop as the trucks stampede. There's really not much more to it than that and in between explosions a network of relationships develop.

Truck stop is run as if it were a feudal fiefdom, complete with arsenal, by redneck despot Pat Hingle who gives an amusing performance as a true screen swine. Also on hand is Emilio Estevez as a cook in bondage to Hingle by virtue of his probation from the pen, but he's gone to college and is really a good kid.

Estevez, in his usual sullen performance, is pouty enough to attract Laura Harrington, a hitchhiker who packs a switchblade in her boot but would rather make love. It's a thankless role for her and she adds little to make the goings-on more believable, but she does dress the film up a bit.

Surprisingly, the weakest ingredient in the picture is the script by King, who has had more best sellers than half a dozen writers combined. Screenplay is full of unintentional howlers such as when Harrington warns Estevez that giving more fuel to the rampaging trucks is "like

Neville Chamberlain giving in to the Nazis."

King, as well, shows little flair in handling actors. Where he does display considerable talent is in staging the action sequences. Repetitious and routine though they may be, there certainly are enough of them and technically they look fine. In fact, entire film looks good, highlighted by Armando Nannuzzi's crisp cinematography. Heavy metal score by AC/DC fits like a glove.

Where the film falls flat is in human values despite a sprinkling of pop philosophy and heavy symbolism about the purity of man corrupted by his mechanical society.—*Jagr.*

Good To Go
(COLOR)

Go-go music linked to weak storyline.

An Island Pictures release of an Island Alive production presented by Island Visual Arts. Produced by Doug Dilge, Sean Ferrer. Executive producers, Chris Blackwell, Jeremy Thomas. Written and directed by Blaine Novak. Stars Art Garfunkel. Camera (Technicolor), Peter Sinclair; editor, Gib Jaffe, Kimberly Logan, D.C. Stringer; music producers, Rob Fraboni; art director, Ron Downing; sound editor, John Dunn; associate producer, Maxx Kidd; some music sequences directed by Don Letts. Reviewed at the West End theater, Washington, D.C., July 16, 1986 (MPAA Rating: R.) Running time: **87 MINS.**
S.D. Blass . . . . Art Garfunkel
Max . . . . Robert Doqui
Harrigan . . . . Harris Yulin
Little Beats . . . . Reginald Daughtry
Chemist . . . . Richard Brooks
Evette . . . . Paula Davis
Editor . . . . Richard Bauer
Gil Colton . . . . Michael White
Mother . . . . Hattie Winston

Washington, D.C. — The faded fad of "go-go" music from the heart of Washington, D.C. ghettos provides a lively backdrop for a not-so-lively story of journalism exploited by the police in a classic pattern of racist corruption. "Good To Go" is what the hipsters say to reinforce their faith in their music, apparently, as said by an addict in the opening scenes after he steals his little brother's money.

Lurching into this scene is Art Garfunkel, toplining as a boozing journalist desperate for a story, so desperate he lets himself be framed by a maniacally racist cop to blame a PCP-inspired gang rape and murder of a nurse on the go-go music, so the cops can close down the go-go clubs.

Played off in stark contrast are the blacks with faith in the music and the blacks who have given up and taken to drugs, particularly "love boat" or PCP. The tension within the community is what the film wants to explore, but instead, a watery-eyed Garfunkel upstages story as an impotent investigator in unfortunately stark contrast with the powerful, rhythm-and-blues rapping of the go-go concert footage. Featuring the hopping D.C. groups Trouble Funk, Chuck Brown & the Soul Searchers, Redds & the Boys, and the local music mogul Maxx Kidd, who has promoted and produced this scene, the music goes way beyond the plot in terms of appeal and even message.

The worst development is the rabbit-out-of-the-hat ending, in which an anchor lady explains what has happened and her report effectively sterilizes the plot's implications of police persecution of blacks, journalistic exploitation of the black ghetto scene, and all the social-working consciousness of the script.

The spare storyline is padded out with a visual montage of the despair and dead-end lives on the streets of Washington's Southeast district, but is also replete with didactic dialog full of philosophical clichés about racism. The two major failings of pic reside in the writing and direction. Thesps leave teethmarks all over the scenery, but the concert footage recurs often enough to work as the engine to keep pic humming. A flashy, hip editing job welds together the social commentary footage, concert footage, and the dramatic scenes as best it can, providing a pace worthy of the music behind it.

When the production was launched, the first film to be shot in its entirety in Washington, D.C., Don Letts was at the helm. Somewhere along the way, Blaine Novak replaced him, and Letts is credited with some musical sequences, possibly the best thing in pic. Because last summer's publicity push for the go-go scene failed to gain a hold on the nation's imagination or money, the b.o. potential will depend upon the ability to awaken the public's musical memory. Off-shore art-house audiences, with their unflagging interest in American racism, may find the location shooting in Washington revealing of an aspect of the nation's capital never shown in politico-pics. — *Kaja.*

Delivery Boys
(COLOR)

Unappealing breakdancing pic.

A New World Pictures presentation of a Pegasus Pictures production. Executive producer, Chuck Vincent. Produced by Per Sjostedt, Craig Horrall. Written and directed by Ken Handler. Camera (TVC color), Larry Revene; editor, uncredited; songs, Handler; additional songs, Charlie (Rock) Jimenez, others; sound (Dolby), Dale Whitman; assistant director, Sjostedt; art direction, George Brown; production manager, David Larkin; choreography, Nelson Vasquez ; second unit camera, Arthur Marx; animal trainer,

Capt. Haggerty; casting, Horrall. Reviewed on New World Video vidcassette, N.Y., June 28, 1986. (MPAA Rating: R.) Running time: **91 MINS.**

Max .... Joss Marcano
Joey .... Tom Sierchio
Conrad .... Jim Soriero
Izzie .... Nelson Vasquez
Scandal .... Yayo Gonzalez
Sike .... Sammy Luquis
Spider................ Mario van Peebles
Angelina .... Jody Oliver
Sir Fresh .... Richie Pineiro
Sailor.................... George Ovalle
Fast Action .... Rodney Harvey
Paulie .... Deckard Fontanes
Elizabeth .... Kelly Nichols
Art snob .... Veronica Hart
Also with: Carolyn Green, Lisa Vidal, Taija Rae, Suzanne Remey Lawrence, Samantha Fox, John De Bello.

''Delivery Boys'' is a lesser entry in the spate of breakdancing films made during the short-lived fad in 1984. Low-budgeter was acquired by New World but sent directly to homevideo with no theatrical release.

Films dealing with breakin' are as rigidly circumscribed as kung fu pictures: lots of preliminaries building to an inevitable showdown between opposing crews. This pic focuses on the comical misadventures of three dancers who work literally as pizza delivery boys. Bad guy Spider (Mario van Peebles) orders their boss at work Angelina (Jody Oliver) to keep the boys from showing up that night as part of the seven-man Delivery Boys crew so his team, The Devil Dogs, will win the annual $10,000 prize. To frighten her, he shows the shrunken heads and shrunken other key body parts (first of many vulgar bits) belonging to last year's winners.

She sends Max (Joss Marcano) to deliver a pizza to Elizabeth (porn star Kelly Nichols), who seduces the Puerto Rican lad and won't let him go. Eventually Max escapes in drag. Conrad (Jim Soriero) is sent to a Brooklyn hospital where scientists test an experimental drug on him that results in an embarrassing permanent erection. Joey (Tom Sierchio) is sent to an art gallery where he accidentally breaks a statue and is forced by the sculptor to pose as the statue (with fig leaf) at an exhibit that night.

Filmmaker Ken Handler's approach to ''Porky's''-style grossout humor is uninspired, as are the performances by a cast of mainly nonactor dancers. Marcano does his drag routine well and nominal villain Mario van Peebles has fun with a West Indies accent. Music is weak and dance choreography repetitive.—*Lor.*

Le Paltoquet
(The Nonentity)
(FRENCH-COLOR)

An A.A.A. release of an Eléfilm/Erato Films/Soprofilms/TF1 Films/Sofia/Sofima coproduction, with the participation of the

C.N.C. Executive producers, Michel Deville, Daniel Toscan du Plantier. Produced by Rosalinde Damamme. Directed by Michel Deville. Screenplay, Deville, based on the novel, ''On a tué pendant l'escale,'' by Franz-Rudolf Falk; camera (widescreen, Eastmancolor), André Diot; editor, Raymonde Guyot; music, Dvorak, Janacek; art direction, Thierry Leproust; sound, Philippe Lioret, Claude Villand; costumes, Cécile Balme; makeup, Ronaldo Ribeiro de Abreu; production manager, Franz Damamme. Reviewed at the Club 13, Paris, July 21, 1986. Running time: **92 MINS.**

Lotte .... Fanny Ardant
Journalist .... Daniel Auteuil
Doctor .... Richard Bohringer
Honorable Tradesman ... Philippe Léotard
Proprietress .... Jeanne Moreau
Nonentity .... Michel Piccoli
Professor.............. Claude Piéplu
Commissioner .... Jean Yanne

Paris — Michel Deville, who won a César award for his direction of ''Péril en la demeure,'' rounds up an all-star cast for this prankish whodunit bristling with gags, puns and other forms of humor. Impeccably made, designed and acted, it is nonetheless a stylistic conceit that outstays its welcome long before the final, trite solution. Pic, first indie production by former Gaumont general manager Daniel Toscan du Plantier, who championed Deville during his years at the major, will need imaginative subtitling or dubbing to crack foreign-language markets.

Deville sets the unrealistic tone of the story by shooting it entirely in the studio, where theater designer Thierry Leproust has imagined the principal setting: a vast, sinister, warehouse-like cafe in some undefined port city, run by a weird couple, played by Jeanne Moreau and Michel Piccoli. Latter has the title role of the *paltoquet,* which might be translated as a nonentity.

Action revolves around these barkeeps and their regular nightly clientele: four town notables who gather for a hand of cards. They are identified generically as the Journalist (Daniel Auteuil), the Doctor (Richard Bohringer), the Honorable Tradesman (Philippe Léotard) and the Professor (Claude Piéplu). There is also Lotte, a mysterious woman in white (Fanny Ardant), who lies languorously in a hammock strung up between two pillars, and fires the sexual fantasies of the men.

When a murder is committed in a neighboring hotel, the notables wind up chief suspects for the investigating police commissioner (Jean Yanne) who cracks the case after a series of various murder attempts and apparent accidents involving the bar habitués.

Apart from the pictorial stylization, film's singularity lies in the dialog, which often adopts the rhythms of music-hall repartee. Characters tend to wisecrack, make puns, automatic word associations and the like, and the general effect is of an Agatha Christie plot whose parlance seems drawn from Samuel

Beckett or Tom Stoppard. It's all cleverly done, but has little point in the long run.

Deville also has fun with film conventions, beginning with the seedily ominous Piccoli impatiently shoving the opening credits offscreen. Seen regularly reading the very novel from which the story is adapted, Piccoli looms over the action like an enigmatic puppeteer, guiding the action and even providing the mood and theme music with a portable record player.

Superbly moody lighting by lenser André Diot accentuates the eerie qualities of Leproust's settings (which also include some hotel rooms and street locations). Editing by Raymonde Guyot (who also won a César for "Péril") has deceptive crackle. Other credits are fine.
—*Len.*

Alex Khole Ahava
(Lovesick Alex)
(ISRAELI-COLOR)

A Noah Films presentation of a Berkey-Pathe-Humphries production. Produced by Itzhak Shani, Yosef Diamant. Executive producer, Mark Rosenbaum. Directed by Boaz Davidson. Screenplay, Davidson, Eli Tavor, camera (color), Amnon Salomon, editor, Bruria Davidson; music, original recordings of 1950s hits; costumes, Ron Salomon; assistant director, Shaul Dishi. Reviewed at the Lev theater, Tel Aviv, July 9, 1986. Running time: **94 MINS.**

With: Yosef Shiloach, Hana Roth, Avraham Mor, Sharon Hacohen, Eitan Anshel, Avi Kushnir, Uri Cabiri, Shmuel Rodensky, Yael Wasserman, Gad Keinar.

Tel Aviv — Boaz Davidson is once again digging into his past, hoping to come up with another ''Lemon Popsicle,'' but by now it seems he has milked this cow quite dry. What is supposed to be a tender, tentative infatuation of a 13-year-old boy for his aunt, visiting the family and looking for her long-lost boyfriend, becomes a series of unconnected incidents, mixing sex and pathos, throwing in a rather uncomfortable twinge of Holocaust memories, and messing up completely the time element, as the story could take place anywhere from the late 1940s to the early 1960s.

Even the geographical location isn't too well defined, any visual references to identifiable places being avoided, to give the picture a sort of universal flavor.

This is yet another portrait of sexually obsessed young Peeping Toms who do not seem to think or worry about anything else. Technical credits and performances are on the whole undistinguished except for a very broad, lowbrow parody by Yosef Shiloach of a Persian immigrant, which, in a different context, would have been deemed literally offensive. As summer fare for the domestic market, this is bound

to find a receptive audience, but it is limited to local consumption.
—*Edna.*

Beau temps, mais orageux en fin de journée
(Fine Weather, But Storms Due Towards Evening)
(FRENCH-COLOR)

A Gérick Film release of a Diagonale/JM Prods./Films A2 coproduction. Directed by Gérard Frot-Coutaz. Stars Micheline Presle, Claude Piéplu. Screenplay, Frot-Coutaz, Jacques Davila; camera (Agfa color), Jean-Jacques Bouhon; sound, Yves Zlotnicka; editor, Paul Vecchiali, Frank Mathieu; music, Roland Vincent. Reviewed at the French-American Film Workshop, Avignon, July 7, 1986. Running time: **83 MINS.**
With: Micheline Presle, Claude Piéplu, Xavier Deluc, Tonie Marshall.

Avignon — Two usually fine actors, Micheline Presle and Claude Piéplu, fail to provide a needed lift to this threadbare domestic drama, first feature by Gérard Frot-Coutaz, who scripted with Jacques Davila, himself helmer of a current feature, "Qui trop embrasse." Producer-filmmaker Paul Vecchiali, known for his laudable efforts to promote young talent, produced this picture, and edited both films.

Story, which unfolds on a single day, concerns an aging couple, both retired teachers, whose daily habits are interrupted by a phone call from their rarely seen son, who's in town and wants to present them with his fiancée.

Old hurts and neuroses arise predictably during the hastily prepared lunch, in which Presle fusses and flaps about her boy, who has trouble getting around to announcing his upcoming marriage. The young couple finally take their leave and have an argument in the street.

The banal events turn to tragedy when Piéplu, returning from a nearby park where he's been Sunday painting with Presle, takes a fatal fall in a neighbor's apartment.

The arbitrary climax apart, this is stale slice-of-life realism cut with a rusty knife. Presle, usually more subtle, overacts ineffectually the role of a neurotically insecure wife and mother, and Piéplu is little more than a straight man to her hysterical effusions.

Son is played by the appealing Xavier Deluc, and his girlfriend is Tonie Marshall, Presle's real-life daughter.

Tech credits are mediocre.—*Len.*

Etats d'ame
(Moods)
(FRENCH-COLOR)

An AMLF release of a Films 7/FR3 Films coproduction. Produced by Marie-Dominique Girodet. Written and directed by Jacques Fansten. Stars Robin Renucci, Jean-Pierre Bacri, François Cluzet, Tcheky Karyo, Xavier Delluc. Camera (Widescreen, Fujicolor), Dominique Chapuis; editor, Nicole Saulnier; art direction, Jean-Louis Poveda; sound, Pierre Gamet; music, Jean-Marie Senia; production manager, Pierre Gauchet; assistant director, Francis de Gueltzl. Reviewed at the Gaumont Ambassade theater, Paris, July 10, 1986. Running time: **100 MINS.**

Maurice	Robin Renucci
Romain	Jean-Pierre Bacri
Pierrot	François Cluzet
Bertrand	Tcheky Karyo
Michel	Xavier Delluc
Marie	Sandrine Dumas
Martine	Nathalie Nell
Hélène	Zabou

Also with: Pascal Bardet, Martine Sarcey, Guillaume Le Guellec, Jean-Paul Roussilon, Evelyne Didi.

Paris — French films are traditionally shy on topical subject matter and Jacques Fansten's "Etats d'ame" has not really shaken off that timidity in an overly lightweight chronicle of five leftist buddies and their gradual disillusionment during the recent five years of socialist government.

Fansten's basic good idea, insufficiently probed, was to interweave the lives of his sympathetic, idealistic protagonists, former high school militants of the post-1968 generation, beginning with the street celebration of the Socialist victory in the May 1981 elections, and following them in their professional and personal paths.

Latter course tends to circle around a young pregnant girl whom they meet on that intoxicating May fête, and who gives birth the same night. Each of the men tries and fails to link up with the elusive young lady, who partly represents a new generation and a more down-to-earth outlook on life.

Fansten, a talented, prize-winning tv helmer who made one previous theatrical feature in 1976, has an obvious skill and sensibility in the bittersweet mode of French intimate comedy-drama, but fails to limn a more perceptive picture of mentalities of the socialist '80s.

He at least gets mileage from an appealing cast composed of five of the French screen's brightest young male talents: Robin Renucci, as a sociologist who lands an important ministerial post; Jean-Pierre Bacri, as a naive teacher promoted to academic inspector; François Cluzet, a tax inspector; Tcheky Karyo, a culture center director; and Xavier Delluc, a tv journalist.—*Len.*

Panther Squad
(BELGIAN-FRENCH-COLOR)

A Dan Simon presentation from Eurocine of a Brux Inter Film/Greenwich Intl. coproduction. Produced by Daniel Lesoeur; coproducers, Sybil Danning, Ken Johnston. Executive producer, A.L. Mariaux. Directed by Peter Knight. Stars Sybil Danning. Screenplay, George Freedland, from story idea by Ilona Koch; camera (GTC color), Phil Uyuer; editor, Barry Lensky, Peter Marks; music, Douglas Cooper Getschal, Jeffrey G. Gusman; sound, John Comon; assistant director, John Goby, Peter Markess; stunt coordinator, Johnny Polck; costume design, Ann Laynn; second unit camera, Roy Fellous; associate producer, Bob van Eesbeke; casting, Sylvia Perrot. Reviewed on Lightning Video vidcassette, N.Y., July 14, 1986. (No MPAA Rating.) Running time: **77 MINS.**

With: Sybil Danning (Ilona), Karin Schubert (Barbara), Jack Taylor, J.R. Gossar, Joan Virly, Franca Bocci, Donna Cross, Karin Brussels, Virginia Svenson, Donald O'Brien, Arch Taylor, Roger Darton, John Rounds, Robert Foster.

"Panther Squad" is bound to be a disappointment for Sybil Danning fans as, in stepping into a coproducer role in addition to starring, the statuesque actress has deleted the sexy elements of her earlier work. Feature, filmed last year in Spain and Belgium, is a direct-to-vidcassette release.

A dumb sci-fi storyline has an anti-pollution group called Clean Space terrorizing the space program of New Organization of Nations (a followup to the UN). Clean Space sabotages a launch of NOON's futuristic Space Jeep and kidnaps the female backup astronaut in order to prevent a second mission.

NOON calls in female commando Ilona (Sybil Danning) who brings in her six femme assistants to free the astronaut and put Clean Space out of business.

Not only is there no nudity and no sex in the picture, the action scenes are poorly photographed and edited. Sight of Danning and her minions in campy, bare-midriff leather outfits easily disposing of male cast members is silly wish fulfillment executed on a G-rated level. Sci-fi content is limited to Danning using a disintegrator gun in the final reel.

Actors speak English slowly and clearly, allowing for acceptable post-synched dialog, but the lines are stupid, such as Danning confronting a megalomaniac general's soldiers, yelling: "Surrender or I'll blow your Nikes off." It's sobering to find out that the political climate has swung so far to the right of late that the environmentalists are portrayed as the bad guys. —*Lor.*

I Own The Racecourse
(AUSTRALIAN-COLOR)

A Barron Films production. Executive producer, Paul Barron. Produced by John Edwards, Timothy Read. Directed by Stephen Ramsey. Screenplay, Edwards, Ramsey, from the book "I Own the Racecourse," by Patricia Wrightson; camera (Eastmancolor), Geoff Burton; editor, Denise Haslem; music, Red Symons, Martin Armiger; sound, Kevin Kearney; production design, Richard Roberts; production manager, Adrienne Read; assistant director, Corrie Soeterbeck; casting, Jenni Kubler. Reviewed at Film Australia screening room, Sydney, July 20, 1986. Running time: **77 MINS.**

Andy Hoddel	Gully Coote
Bert Hammond	Tony Barry
Drunken Old Man	Norman Kaye
Joe	Rodney Burke
Connelly	Paul Bertram
Terry	Safier Redseposki

Also with: Anthony Mangan (Mike), Brett Adlard (Matt), Bob Noble (Sgt. Willis), Brett Climo (Const. Eadie), Gillian Jones (Mrs. Hoddel), Les Murray (Creevy), Bob Ellis (Renehan), Tim Elston (Keogh), Rob Steele (Evangelist).

Sydney — A modestly charming kidpic, "I Own The Racecourse" so far has failed to find theatrical distribution in Australia and goes out on vidcassette shortly. It's an engaging piece of wish-fulfillment about a not-too-bright youngster (Gully Coote) who's fooled into believing he purchased a racecourse for $20 from the alleged owner, actually a drunken bum (an offbeat role for the usually urbane Norman Kaye).

Staff at the racecourse go along with the gag, and young Coote is given the run of the place. Meanwhile, the law is looking for a supposed gang of vandals, and a couple of inefficient crooks are involved in a doping scam (these roles are played, with offhand dexterity, by Les Murray and Bob Ellis, latter better known as a writer and, more recently, a director).

Pic was made in association with the Australian Foundation for Children's Films and Television, and probably will achieve popularity on video once the word gets out. Young Coote is fine as the gullible youngster, and Tony Barry gives his usual amiably relaxed performance as the caretaker of the racecourse who encourages the kid's fantasies.

Modestly budgeted item has a nice feel for the inner suburbs of Sydney, and cowriter-director Stephen Ramsey shows promise.
—*Strat.*

Prunelle Blues
(FRENCH-COLOR)

A UGC release of a Sara Films production, in association with Cinérgie. Produced by Alain Sarde. Stars Michel Boujenah. Written and directed by Jacques Otmezguine, based on his novel. Camera (Eastmancolor), Yves Dahan; editor, Yves Deschamps; art direction, Katia Vischkof; sound, Claude Bertrand, Jean-Claude Loublier; music, Hubert Rostaing, Yvan Julian; production manager, Christine Gozlan; assistant director, Philippe Guez; associate producer, Christian Spillemaecker. Reviewed at the UGC Biarritz theater, Paris, July 21, 1986. Running time: **82 MINS.**

Freddy	Michel Boujenah
Florence	Valérie Steffen
Fernand	Vincent Lindon
Albert	Karim Allaoui
Cade	Michel Aumont

Also with: Jean-Claude Bourbault, Geneviève Brunel, Robert Bahr, Gilette Barbier, Jean-Pierre Laurent, Alain Floret, Guy Guerri, Alain-Jacques Adiba, Christian Duval, Bruno Moynot.

Paris — Michel Boujenah, the voluble Tunisian Jewish comic who won a César award for his performance in the smash "Three Men And A Cradle," toplines in this unsuccessful first feature by Jacques Otmezguine, which latter adapted from his own novel. Production is also the first in a long while from indie Alain Sarde, who withdrew temporarily after the failure of his megabuck "Harem."

Story is essentially a routine thriller in which Boujenah, the manager of a flea-pit porno theater, has a secret crush on the young stripper who performs there between films. Hospitalized after being shot by robbers who make off with the cinema receipts, Boujenah finds himself menaced by a gang of drug dealers who are after a filched shipment and think he is the culprit.

In fact, it's the stripper (Valérie Steffen) who has the dope, but Boujenah nevertheless goes blindly to her aid when the gang, led by the cinema's pseudo-maternal cashier, lay siege to the suburban house they are holed up in.

Otmezguine's script and direction suffer from his apparent non-familiarity with film, but there are enough good moments here (notably in the injection of comic details) to indicate potential.

As the nebbish emboldened by love and crisis, Boujenah is ingratiating in early scenes, though he fails to make his transformation convincing. Steffen does adequate service in a basically decorative part. Vincent Lindon, another recent newcomer to film, steals the show hilariously as a bumbling rookie detective assigned to investigate Boujenah's shooting. —*Len.*

Howard The Duck
(COLOR)

Overstuffed special effects duckumentary is an embarrassment for George Lucas.

A Universal Pictures release of a Lucasfilm Ltd. production, presented by George Lucas. Produced by Gloria Katz. Coproducer, Robert Latham Brown. Executive producer, George Lucas. Directed by Willard Huyck. Stars Lea Thompson, Jeffrey Jones, Tim Robbins. Screenplay, Huyck, Katz, based on the Marvel Comics character "Howard The Duck" created by Steve Gerber; camera (Deluxe color), Richard H. Kline; editor, Michael Chandler, Sidney Wolinsky; music, John Barry; additional music, Sylvester Levay; songs, Thomas Dolby, others; production design, Peter Jamison; art direction, Blake Russell, Mark Billerman; set design, Jim Pohl, Pamela Marcotte; set decoration, Philip Abramson; costume design, Joe Tompkins; sound (Dolby), Agamemnon Adrianos; sound design, Randy Thom; visual effects, Industrial Light & Magic; visual effects supervisor, Micheal J. McAlister; visual effects art director, Phillip Norwood; alien monster design, Phil Tippett; Dr. Jenning's makeup design, Tom Burman, Bari Dreiband-Burman; associate producer, Ian Bryce; assistant director, Dan Kolsrud; special effects supervisor, Bob MacDonald Jr., second unit director, Thomas J. Wright; second unit camera, Bobby Byrne; casting, Dianne Crittenden. Reviewed at the Directors' Guild theater, L.A., July 30, 1986. (MPAA Rating: PG.) Running time: **111 MINS.**

Beverly Switzler	Lea Thompson
Dr. Jenning	Jeffrey Jones
Phil Blumbrutt	Tim Robbins
Howard T. Duck	Ed Gale, Chip Zien, Tim Rose, Steve Sleap, Peter Baird, Mary Wells, Lisa Sturz, Jordan Prentice
Lt. Welker	Paul Guilfoyle
Ginger Moss	Tommy Swerdlow

Hollywood — Daffy Duck will be pleased to hear he didn't miss any career opportunities when he wasn't chosen to star in "Howard The Duck," although producers certainly could have benefitted from his talents.

Scripters Gloria Katz and Willard Huyck have taken the cigar chompin', beer drinkin' comic book character and turned him into a wide-eyed, cutesy, midget-sized extraterrestrial accidentally blown to Cleveland from a misdirected laser beam.

Howard encounters rock singer Beverly Switzler (Lea Thompson) after a few harrowing minutes on Earth and they become instant friends after he defends her from a couple of menacing punkers following his landing outside the rock club where she has just finished performing with the band Cherry Bomb.

Thompson has been given too sweet and innocent a personality to be a lead singer in a punk band, which may be the fault of director Huyck in only allowing her such a one-dimensional character.

Film just about dies in the first 15 minutes when she takes Howard home and brings him into bed with her — teasing that she wants to make love to him because he's so cute and she feels sorry for him. Even if pic is undeniably fiction,

there is no way they have enough time together to develop this kind of sappy rapport.

Fortunately, the two are interrupted with the unexpected arrival of Thompson's hapless science lab assistant friend, Phil Blumbrutt (Tim Robbins) and the physicist Dr. Jenning (Jeffrey Jones) who bungled the laser experiment bringing Howard to Earth and hopes to reverse the process and beam him home.

In the meantime, there are several amusing sequences as Howard tries to fit into human society, notably his encounter with an overpowering, no-nonsense unemployment counselor determined that he remain off the welfare rolls no matter how strange he looks to prospective employers.

Pic then lapses into formulaic predictibility with nearly an hour of frenetic chase scenes and technically perfect explosions from Industrial Light & Magic as Thompson and Robbins try to thwart the authorities' attempts to capture the duck before he gets a chance to be beamed

Action comes sporadically alive in scenes with scientist Jones, who becomes possessed by the spirit of an evil Dark Warlord that entered his body during the same fateful mishap that brought Howard to Earth.

There is an abundant amount of special effects widardry that emanates mostly from Jones as he transforms into a monster, but it is not spectacularly unique enough to distinguish this film from other, more entertaining, sci-fi thrillers.

While John Barry's scoring just adds noise to the already clamorous scenes, Thomas Dolby's songs written for Cherry Bomb's club sets are catchy. —*Brit.*

Hot Chili
(COLOR)

Drivel.

A Cannon Group presentation of a Golan-Globus production. Produced by Menahem Golan, Yoram Globus. Directed by William Sachs. Screenplay, Joseph Goldman, Sachs; camera (TVC color), Jorge Senyal; editor, Michael J. Duthie; production design, Alberto Negron; assistant director, Richard Whiting; casting, Bob MacDonald; sound, Manuel Rincon; costume design, Laura Santi; post-production supervisor, Michael R. Sloan; associate producer, Jonathan Debin. Reviewed on MGM/UA Home Video vidcassette, N.Y., July 25, 1986. (MPAA Rating: R.) Running time: **91 MINS.**

With: Charles Schillaci, Allan J. Kayser, Joe Rubbo, Chuck Hemingway, Taaffe O'Connell, Victoria Barrett, Louisa Moritz, Flo Gerrish, Bea Fiedler, Robert Riesel, Jerry Lazarus, Peter Bromilow, Ferdy Mayne.

Theatrically released regionally in the summer of 1985, "Hot Chili" is an unintentionally surreal mishmash concerning four sex-starved teenage boys and their employment at Tropicana Cabana, a Mexican va-

cation resort with an exclusive, oversexed clientele. Total absence of plot and abundance of kinky activities combine to give the film, reviewed for the record, a hard-edged, porno-like quality.

The four teens, Ricky (Charles Schillaci), Stan (Chuck Hemingway), Arney (Joe Rubbo) and Jason (Allan Kayers), arrive at the spa and are harangued immediately by Señor Rodriguez, their boss, who lays down the one law — no fraternizing with guests.

At this point you need a scorecard to differentiate between the buxom blonds, who seem to lurk behind every door, nook and cranny of the picturesque resort. Tame opening quickly takes an odd turn, however, as the inexperienced boys are introduced to bondage, S&M and a lot of random face slapping.

There is no time frame or connection between these brief episodes, as the guest list at the resort grows to include a Nazi, a Russian playboy and a geriatric Texas couple, among others. A homosexual tryst towards pic's end further darkens the mood of what could have been a light and mildly diverting comedy.

Dialog is mind-numbing, production values poor. The only extraordinary thing about "Hot Chili" is that it took two writers, Joseph Goldman and William Sachs (who also helmed), to come up with it. — *Roy.*

Loving Walter
(BRITISH-COLOR-16m)

A Central Television production. Produced by Richard Creasey. Directed by Stephen Frears. Screenplay, David Cook, based on his novel "Winter Doves;" camera (color, 16m), Chris Menges; editor, Mick Audsley; music, George Fenton; sound, Tony Jackson; art director, Michael Minas. Reviewed at Film Forum 1, N.Y., July 25, 1986. (No MPAA Rating.) Running time: **110 MINS.**

Walter	Ian McKellen
June	Sarah Miles
Walter's Mother	Barbara Jefford
Walter's Father	Arthur Whybrow
Mrs. Ashby	Paula Tilbrook
Social Worker	Marjorie Yeats
Graham	John Gordon-Sinclair
Young Walter	Frankie Connolly

"Loving Walter," a depressing but masterfully acted drama about the life struggles of a retarded man, is a theatrical film compilation of two tv programs originally aired by Britain's Channel 4 (which co-financed production) in 1983 and shown here as part of the Film Forum Channel 4 Festival.

The overlong film's static pacing makes its unflinching portrayal of Walter's journeys between a state institution and the remorseless outside world particularly difficult to endure. Nevertheless, director Stephen Frears has fashioned a cumulatively powerful study of the fringe world of the handicapped as viewed by one of its own, and "Loving Walter" is most likely to appeal to British film buffs who are familiar with the harsh, unsparing perspective Frears has taken in films like "The Hit" and "My Beautiful Laundrette."

Unlike standard American tv and film fare about the handicapped, "Loving Walter" is totally devoid of sentimental contrivance. Walter (Ian McKellen) is the son of a stern, high-strung mother (Barbara Jefford) who considers her retarded offspring a punishment from God, and a remote father who raises pigeons. As a young man he works as a janitor in the stock room of a factory where more often than not the earnest Walter is the butt of cruel jokes and sadistic pranks by his bitter, dead-ended coworkers.

McKellen, in a difficult, physically demanding performance, quickly established Walter's lifelong desire to help and please others. This inclination soon takes on deeply tragic dimensions given the indifference of his family and coworkers to the barely articulate Walter's desperate emotional need for self-expression and communication. Written off by everyone as a lost case ("You must be the ugliest person in this town and you spent nine months inside of me," his mother laments) Walter's only true companions are his pigeons.

Director Frears depicts Walter's England as a shabby, mean-spirited world ruled by unfeeling bureaucracy and conditioned by narrow, superstitious thinking that's embodied by Walter's bible-surfeited mother. When his parents die within 24 hours of one another, Walter brings the pigeons into the home he knows he's about to lose. The image of him weeping over his dead mother, her face caked with pigeon droppings, is an especially harrowing visual tableau in a film packed with brutal imagery.

The brutal whims of nature are evident everywhere in the state institution to which Walter's consigned. There, where he is made to work with deformed cripples and brain-damaged souls far more helpless than he, Walter slowly develops a sense of self-worth and grudgingly earns the respect of the calloused hospital attendants who jokingly call their wards "Brussels sprouts."

Almost 20 years pass and Walter the handyman becomes a fixture at the institution, where a ward for mentally disturbed mothers has been created. Walter, who has had little contact with women, meets June (Sarah Miles), an attractive schizophrenic who shuttles between states of self-confident lucidity and delusionary madness. June makes a determined effort to communicate with Walter, improbably schemes with him for their joint escape from the institution and, in one of the film's many overtly symbolic scenes, seduces him in a church.

Their tenuous relationship living in an abandoned building provides the film's few grains of lightness and hope, but its fragile foundation obviously dooms the couple's love from the outset.

Technical credits are all firstrate, particularly Chris Menges' photography which chillingly evokes the shadowy grimness and incoherent suffering in the other world of institutional life. —*Rich.*

Lies
(COLOR)

___

Unconvincing thriller.

___

An Intl. Film Marketing release, presented by James Hart in association with Wescom Prods., of a Midnight Prods. picture. Executive producers, James Hart, Lawrence Taylor-Mortorff. Produced by Jim Wheat, Ken Wheat, Shelley Herman. Written and directed by Ken Wheat, Jim Wheat. Camera (Deluxe color), Robert Ebinger; editor, Michael Ornstein; music, Marc Donahue; sound, Ron Curfman; production design, Christopher Henry; art direction, Deborah Moreland; set decoration, Escott Norton; assistant director, Peter Manoogian; production manager-associate producer, Michael Bennett; costume design, Brad Loman; visual consultant, Paul Chadwick; stunt coordinator, B.J. Davis; casting, Barbara Remsen & Associates, Theodora Parker, Ann Remsen. Reviewed on Hollywood Video vidcassette, N.Y., July 19, 1986. (MPAA Rating: R.) Running time: **98 MINS.**

Robyn Wallace . . . . Ann Dusenberry
Jessica Brenner . . . . Gail Strickland
Stuart Russell . . . . Bruce Davison
Dr. Bartlett . . . . Clu Gulager
Eric Macklin . . . . Terence Knox
Murray. . . . . Bert Remsen
Uncle Charles . . . . Stacy Keach Sr.
Dr. Ted Whitmyer . . . . . . Douglas Leonard
Aunt Louise . . . . Patience Cleveland
Elizabeth . . . . Julie Philips
Nurse. Ann Gibbs
Producer . . . . Dick Miller

___

"Lies" is a convoluted thriller overloaded with tons of exposition and unbelievable twists, making it collapse early on like a house of cards. Filmed in 1983, it resembles virtually all of the pictures backed by Wescom Prods. in not having any definable audience in mind, aimed apparently at the since dried-up pay-cable market. Pic played regional test bookings in March 1985 ahead of its vidcassette release.

Hapless Ann Dusenberry portrays Robyn, a struggling actress conned into an eleborate scheme to dupe heiress Elizabeth (Julie Philips, who looks a bit like Dusenberry) out of her $20,000,000 inheritance. A transparent set of baddies led by Elizabeth's husband Stuart (Bruce Davison) and two psychiatrists (Gail Strickland and Clu Gulager) trick the gullible Robyn into making a rehearsal videotape for a projected film about Elizabeth's life story and then use the tape in various ways to confuse the two girls' identities and have each one in turn branded as loony.

Until the film devolves into corny shootouts and chases, filmmakers

Ken & Jim Wheat (who later helmed one of George Lucas' telefilms about the Ewoks) keep the pot boiling in unconvincing fashion with twists and coincidences. Since the story often refers to the perils of being a gullible actress, one feels sorry for the real-life actors who appear herein, all of whom acquit themselves well while clearly resisting the impulse to ask the tandem directors "What's my motivation?"—*Lor.*

Sex Appeal
(COLOR)

___

Limp farce.

___

A Platinum Pictures release of a Vestron Entertainment presentation, national distribution by Seymour Borde & Associates. Produced and directed by Chuck Vincent. Screenplay, Chuck Vincent, Craig Horrall, based on the film "Fascination," written by Chuck Vincent, Jimmy James; camera (color), Larry Revene; editor, Marc Ubell (Chuck Vincent); music, Ian Shaw, Kai Joffee; sound, Peter Penguin; assistant director, Bill Slobodian; art director-production manager, Philip Goetz; costumes, Robert Pusilo Studio. Reviewed at Magno Preview 4 screening room, N.Y., July 31, 1986. (MPAA Rating: R.) Running time: **84 MINS.**

Tony Cannelloni . . . . Louie Bonanno
Corrine . . . . Tally Brittany
Christina Cannelloni . . . . Marcia Karr
Joseph Cannelloni . . . . Jerome Brenner
Louise Cannelloni . . . . Marie Sawyer
Ralph . . . . Philip Campanaro
Donald Cromronic . . . . Jeff Eagle
Also with: Gloria Leonard, Molly Morgan (a.k.a. Merle Michaels), Veronica Hart, Candida Royalle, Taija Rae, Stasia Micula (a.k.a. Samantha Fox), Kim Kafkaloff (a.k.a. Sheri St. Claire), Jill Kumer, Norris O'Neil, Stephen Raymond, Edwina Thorne, Cindy Joy, Terry Powers, Ron Chalon, Robin Leonard, Janice Doskey, Johnny Nineteen, Larry Catanzano, Ann Tylar, Suzanne Vale.

___

"Sex Appeal" is a farcical comedy let down by its script. Yet another opus about a young man trying anything to get laid, picture went into regional release in May but is best suited to the less demanding ancillary markets.

Filmmaker Chuck Vincent has remade here his 1980 hardcore porn production "Fascination" (which was directed by Larry Revene, who returns as cinematographer this time) that starred Ron Jeremy as a Jewish kid consulting a how-to-book on getting dates. This time around Louie Bonanno toplines as Tony Cannelloni, an Italian kid from New Jersey who buys the book "Sex Appeal" as a guide to sexual conquests. Key element of the strategy is to move out of his parents' home to a bachelor pad in Manhattan, where his landlord/neighbor Donald (Jeff Eagle) eavesdrops and uses Tony's misadventures as the basis for writing a lucrative series of articles for Playhouse magazine about the New Jersey Casanova.

Film briefly moves into the territory of Billy Wilder's "The Apart-

ment" as Tony's father and sister separately try to use his pad for their own secret trysts, but essentially it's bedroom farce without enough laughs. Early scenes at home around the dinner table are particularly flat, in the vein of "Saturday Night Fever" ethnicity.

A supporting cast loaded with talent familiar from adult films turns in good performances, particularly two actresses who also appeared in "Fascination:" Merle Michaels, cute as a nonstop talker with a Judy Holliday accent, and Vernonica Hart ("Fascination" was her screen debut), hilariously spoofing the false passion of erotic scenes as she squeals loudly and endlessly at the slightest touch. Lead actor Bonanno is not very interesting and his terrifically-built leading lady Tally Brittany is unfortunately consigned to a small role that is more tease than necessary.

Cast employs a variety of pseudonyms, real names and alternate stage names arising from each thesp's attitude to the demarcation between adult and mainstream filmmaking. Fans will easily sort it all out by recognizing familiar faces. —*Lor.*

Le Rayon vert
(Summer)
(FRENCH-COLOR)

___

A.A.A. Classic release (Orion Classics in U.S.), of a Films du Losange production. Produced by Margaret Menegoz. Written and directed by Eric Rohmer. Stars Marie Rivière. Camera (color), Sophie Maintigneux; editor, Marie-Luisa Garcia; music, Jean-Louise Valero; sound, Claudine Nougaret, Dominique Hennequin. Reviewed at Ponthieu screening room, Paris, July 25, 1986. Running time: **98 MINS.**

With Marie Rivière (Delphine), Amira Chemakhi, Sylvia Richez, Lisa Heredia, Basile Gervaise, Virginie Gervaise, René Hernandez, Doninique Rivière, Isabelle Rivière, Béa-Jullien, Laetitia Rivière, Isabelle Rivière, Béatrice Romand, Rosette, Marcello Pezzutto, Irène Skobline, Eric Hamm, Gérard Quéré, Brigitte Poulain, Gérard Leleu, Liliane Leleu, Vanessa Leleu, Huger Foote, Maria Couto-Palos, Isa Bonnet, Yves Doyhambourg, Dr. Friedrich Gunther Christlein, Paulette Christlein, Carita, Marc Vivas, Joel Comarlot, Vincent Gauthier.

___

Paris — "Le Rayon vert," Eric Rohmer's first film in two years and fifth episode in his "Comedies and Proverbs" cycle, probably will delight his usual art house following, but may leave others with the feeling that this exceptionally literate and literary filmmaker is running out of steam. Though it has its moments of finesse and humor, this is among the flimsiest and least satisfying of his efforts. It's competing at Venice Aug. 31, just after its Gotham opening by Orion Classics (under the title, "Summer") and before its French bow Sept. 3.

Rohmer, whose screenplays are among the most *written* in film history, has modified his working methods here by opening the door to dialog improvisation from his actors, notably his lead, Marie Rivière. Rivière, like many of the others in the cast, is part of the director's regulars, intimately versed in his style and mannerisms, so there is no real tonal rupture with previous pictures, though it probably explains why some scenes here are less polished and even downright banal.

Film's dramatic problem is its young protagonist — aptly portrayed without a shred of personality by Rivière — who is such a drip that one's patience is sorely tried. Rohmer has put us in the company of insipid folks before, but never so limp a noodle as this languid Paris secretary who can't for the life of her decide how to spend her summer vacation.

The nerd doesn't have a boyfriend, has no apparent interest in anything and now finds the friend she was to spend her holiday with has changed her plans. What to do?

Another friend invites her to her country place in Normandy, but after three days of listless boredom (which the filmgoer somewhat shares) she returns to Paris. Then she heads out for the mountains where her former flame has offered her use of an apartment. No sooner there, she does an about-face and returns home.

Drooping away, she jumps at an offer of a pad in Biarritz, where she is exasperated by a fun-loving Swedish girl and importuning males. As she sits in the station waiting for a train back to Paris, a good-looking young fellow sidles up to her and strikes up a conversation, in which — miracle! — she seems to take some interest.

Film's original title comes up in this last part, when the impressionable Rivière overhears a conversation about "Le Rayon vert," a Jules Verne novel in which characters acquire mind-reading powers if they should glimpse the usually invisible green ray of the setting sun.

So when the young man in the station invites Rivière to spend a few days with him, she stalls for an answer, her eyes riveted to the sunset. She lets out a screech of joy: she's seen it: And then ... the film ends. Looks like Rohmer got tired of this dopey girl as well.

An apparent newcomer, Sophie Maintigneux, has lensed adaquately (pic was shot in 16m and blown up to 35m). An amusing end-credit has somebody listed for "the sunset." — Len.

Friday The 13th, Part VI: Jason Lives
(COLOR)

Kill and be bored.

A Paramount Pictures release of A Terror Inc. production. Produced by Don Behrns.

Written and directed by Tom McLoughlin. Camera (Metrocolor), Jon R. Kranhouse; editor, Bruce Green; music, Harry Manfredini; songs, Alice Cooper; production design, Joseph T. Garrity; art direction, Pat Tagliaferro; set decoration, Jerie Kelter; costume design, Maria Mancuso; sound (Ultra-Stereo), James Thornton; assistant director, Martin Walters; additional photography, J. Patrick Daily; special effects, Martin Becker; casting, Fern Champion, Pamela Basker. Reviewed at the Paramount Studios, L.A., July 31, 1986. (MPAA Rating: R.) Running time: **87 MINS.**

Tommy	Thom Mathews
Megan	Jennifer Cooke
Sheriff Garris	David Kagen
Paula	Kerry Noonan
Sissy	Renee Jones
Cort	Tom Fridley
Jason	C.J. Graham
Nikki	Darcy Demoss
Deputy Rick Cologne	Vincent Guastaferro
Darren	Tony Goldwyn
Lizbeth	Nancy McLoughlin
Allen Hawes	Ron Palillo

Hollywood — Jason lives, but 18 other people die in this sixth entry in "Friday The 13th" series. Body count works out to an average of one corpse every 4.83 minutes, which should be enough to satisfy the die-hard horror fanatics who are ensuring that 13 remains a lucky number for Paramount. Nevertheless, domestic rentals for Part V dropped to $10,000,000 from the $16,000,000 level maintained by III and IV, and if b.o. sinks much further, Jason probably will be buried once and for all.

Vivid and vigorous opening sequence has two dopey kids digging up the grave of the Masked One on a dark and stormy night to make sure he's dead. He looks like a stiff when the coffin is opened, but a bolt of lightning brings the insatiable killer back to life, and one of the boys becomes this year's first victim.

Believing old Jason croaked for good in Part V, the powers-that-be in Crystal Lake refuse to believe Tommy, the survivor, when he insists a new rampage has begun. The local sheriff thinks Tommy's gone loco and is committing the murders himself to emulate the community's most famous product.

But the sheriff's pert teenage daughter thinks Tommy's cute, so she gets him out of jail and they head back to the summer camp where it all began to try to head off Jason before he starts playing with all the little kids there.

Writer-director Tom McLoughlin, who a few years ago made the scare entry "One Dark Night," puts comic spin on some of the predictable material and turns in a reasonably slick performance under the circumstances. But there's only so much anyone can do when you're locked into such a rigorously regimented format, when the death alarm clock rings every 4.83 minutes.—Cart.

Deadly Impact
(ITALIAN-COLOR)

A European Intl. Films production. Executive producer-production manager, Richard Garrett. Produced and directed by "Larry Ludman" (Fabrizio De Angelis). Stars Bo Svenson, Fred Williamson. Screenplay, "Ludman" (De Angelis), David Parker Jr., from story by Parker; camera (Telecolor), "Robert D. Forges" (Sergio Salvati); editor, "Vincent P. Thomas" (Vincenzo Tomassi); music, Frank Penteary; sound, Steve Connelly; art direction, Alexander M. Colby; car stunt coordinator, Alan Petit. Reviewed on Vestron Video vidcassette, N.Y., July 18, 1986. (No MPAA Rating.) Running time: **91 MINS.**

With: Bo Svenson (cop), Fred Williamson (Lou), Marcia Clingan (Kathy), John Morghen (thug), Vincent Conte (thug), Alain Blondeau, Norma Thyssen, Karen De Witt, Rik Wallace, Bill Dunun, Genie Thompson, Wanita Brown, Don Champlin, Alan Sylvia, Jeanne Marie, Janet Francis.

"Deadly Impact" is a caper film with one of the silliest premises yet. Italian-made production was lensed in Las Vegas and Phoenix in November 1983 with such pointless working titles as "The Believer" and "Giant Killer," finally debuting on vidcassette a year ago.

A young computer expert named Harry from Phoenix has come up with a system to break the bank in Vegas: he ties in his computer terminal via secret codes with all the casino computers to monitor when each of their slot machines is ready to pay off. Then he sends his girl friend Kathy around to play the winning slots, generating a take of about $30,000 per weekend in Vegas.

Two thugs noticing the winnings track down Harry and torture him for his secret but accidentally kill him, later kidnaping Kathy. Phoenix cop Bo Svenson and his helicopter tour pilot pal Fred Williamson get on the case and predictably end up with the system and its spoils for their own corrupt use.

Assuming the viewer buys the unlikely premise that slot machines are computerized and go off like clockwork rather than according to the laws of probability, "Impact" is boring anyway with its series of cornball chases and car stunts. Filmmaker Fabrizio De Angelis (a.k.a. "Larry Ludman") is interested in just killing time with the type of mindless saga that used to keep 42d St. grindhouses purring but is now just a random title to take up space on a video store's shelf.

Bo Svenson is tiresome in another of his stereotyped cop roles and his sidekick Fred Williamson (previously teamed in the Italian war pic "Inglorious Bastards") merely makes wisecracks and chomps on his trademark stogie. —Lor.

Dolce Assenza
(Sweet Absence)
(ITALIAN-COLOR)

A Sacis release of a RAI TV-Channel 3 production. Directed by Claudio Sestieri. Stars Jo Champa. Screenplay, Sandro Petraglia, Sestieri; camera (color), Charles Rose; editor, Gennaro Oliveti; music, Mauro Pagani; art direction, Ada Legori; costumes, Ester Marcovecchio. Reviewed at RAI-TV, Rome, July 28, 1986. Running time: **100 MINS.**

Gloria	Jo Champa
Sara	Fabienne Babe
Vittorio	Sergio Castellito

Also with: Pierluigi Crespi (Paolo), Stavros Tornes (Grandfather), Franca Marchesi (Truka), Alessandro Balducci (Giancarlo).

Rome — One of the pair of Italo entries in competition at Locarno, "Sweet Absence" marks young helmer Claudio Sestieri's directorial bow. Though set in contemporary swinging Milan, pic's story recalls Michelangelo Antonioni's southern classic "L'Avventura" in its triangular love relationship. Here again one woman searches for another, who's missing for most of screentime. In Sestieri's version, a downplayed love affair between the female leads triumphs in the end, over the likable but unprepossessing hero (Sergio Castellito) who loves, and loses them both.

Attractively lensed and cast, "Absence" should have some market appeal with young audiences. Emotionally it is simply not very involving, and the mystery surrounding the missing girl's absence becomes smaller and less dramatic the more it unfolds.

Response to the film will depend on how much the viewer feels drawn to the minimal acting style of Jo Champa (recent title star of "Salomé"), a model playing a model named Gloria. Initially a pushy, conceited, jealous lover, she evolves to reveal a shred of humanity in the course of the film.

Missing girl is a babysitter, Sara (Fabienne Babe), shy, introverted, and strangely given to making video-diaries of herself speaking into a remote-controlled tv camera. Thanks to the video gimmick, Babe is able to return to the screen long after she has vanished, when Jo and Sara's would-be boyfriend Vittorio (Castellito) are hot on her trail.

The search proceeds predictably. Gloria visits Sara's Jewish grandfather, who tells of a traumatic episode in her past, Vittorio, the ultimate nice guy, turns up an unexpected trail through the gaudy world of Milan modeling agenices and hangouts, which Gloria knew nothing about. The searchers spend a night in bed together, which leads to nothing, and finally Sara reappears safe and sound. Pic concludes with a tactful implication that Gloria and Sara will stay together happily.

Though it stumbles in exploring the hidden recesses of psychology,

"Absence" remains watchable thanks to super-colorful lensing by cameraman Charles Rose and fun sets from Ada Legori. Pic has the commercial savvy to concentrate on glamor locales (a photo modeling session, a screen test, sprawling country villas and Italian design apartments). Cast looks the part, but can't overcome wave upon wave of banal dialog. Still, helmer Sestieri shows many signs of talent to be developed in other, better scripts.—*Yung*.

Pula Film Festival

Za Srecu Je Potrebno Troje
(Three's Happiness)
(YUGOSLAVIAN-COLOR)

A Jadran Film (Zagreb), Centar Film (Belgrade) coproduction. Directed by Rajko Grlic. Screenplay, Grlic, Dubravka Ugresic; camera (Widescreen, Eastman color), Zivko Zalar; music, Vlatko Stefanovski, Bogdan Arsovski; sound, Marijan Loncar; art direction, Dinka Jericevic; production manager, Milan Samec. Reviewed at Pula Film Festival, (competition), July 21, 1986. Running time: **102 MINS.**

Drago ....Miki Manojlovic
Zdenka ....Mira Furlan
Nina ....Dubravka Ostojic
Jozo......................Bogdan Diklic
Ivan ....Vanja Drach
Joagoda ....Ksenija Pajic

Pula — Rajko Grlic crafts a subtle, witty film around three overlapping love triangles. The characters' busy efforts to escape their life and times through love are doomed to failure, and gradually wry comedy turns into ashes in the mouth. Scripted by Grlic and Dubravka Ugresic, "Three's Happiness" is a sophisticated look into human relations and strivings, entertaining and on-target at the same time.

Drago (Miki Manojlovic) has just been released from jail. His crime — trying to rob a village bank with a toy gun. He spends the night on a sofa offered by a shy working girl, Zdenka (Mira Furlan), and waits for the morrow when he can look up his sophisticated girlfriend Nina (Dubravka Ostojic).

In the meantime, Nina's become the manager of a flourishing art gallery, thanks to the patronage of her married lover. Drago's return puts her comfortable relationship into crisis, but in the end the lure of money and security proves greater than going abroad with a penniless tramp.

Drago, who looks like a young Walter Matthau and assumes a wry detachment toward life to mask his vulnerable side, goes on living at Zdenka's place. She falls hard for him, abandons her dull boyfriend at the factory, and even steals shoes off the assembly line for the ungrateful rake. The three relationships go back and forth until a bittersweet ending brings the right people together in the wrong way.

Manojlovic and Furlan deliver exceptional performances in the main roles, backed by a fine supporting cast. Comedy comes mainly from the witty dialog and Drago's sardonic repartee. Lensing by Zivko Zalar is top-flight and music by Vlatko Stefanovski, a rock composer, is mellow and varied.

—*Yung*.

Lepota Poroka
(The Beauty Of Vice)
(YUGOSLAVIAN-COLOR)

A Centar Film (Belgrade) production. Written and directed by Zivko Nikolic. Stars Mira Furlan, Miodrag Karadzic. Camera (color), Radoslav Vladic; editor, Zoltan Vaghen; music, Zoran Simjanovic; art direction, Miodrag Miric. Reviewed at Pula Film Festival (competition), July 20, 1986. Running time: **113 MINS.**

Jaglika ....Mira Furlan
Luka ....Miodrag Karadzic
George..................Petar Bozovic
Also with: Mira Banjac, Alain Nouny (nudist), Ines Kotman (nudist).

Pula — From bedroom comedy to high tragedy, from backwoods puritanism and misogyny to the fleshly overabundance in a nudist colony, "The Beauty Of Vice" fearlessly tackles the contradictions of modern Yugoslavia. Zivko Nikolic attractively dramatizes these contradictions in a light, airy comedy with dark underpinnings.

Bread and honor are said to be the roots of Montenegro traditions. "Beauty" begins with a savage ritual killing: an adulterous woman places a loaf of bread on her head and passively waits for her husband to bludgeon her to death, while she asks forgiveness for not being worthy of the bread he feeds her with. Meanwhile, Luka (Miodrag Karadzic) and Jaglika (Mira Furlan) are united in matrimony under the protection of godfather George (Petar Bozovic), an Americanized businessman from the hills who makes his money running a nudist colony for tourists on the coast. When the newlyweds come to live with him in search of jobs, he puts Jaglika to work as a maid in the nudist colony, to the couple's shocked horror.

Though essentially a one-joke film, "Beauty Of Vice" milks the situation of the prudish maid who makes love to her husband fully clothed and with a handkerchief over her face, cast forcibly into the decadent world of Western hedonism and vacation-paradise values. Her charges, a beautiful young English couple, dazzle her like gods descended from the sky, and by pic's end she gives in to the sensuality of her surroundings in a lyrical, extended scene of liberation. Shedding her long black uniform, Jaglika joyfully becomes part of a modern threesome — followed by bitter disappointment and a reprise of pic's opening scene, when she confesses to her husband. The appropriate variation is that it's not his wife he kills, but himself. Times have changed.

Much of the charm film has comes from Furlan, its leading lady, a rising star of Yugoslav cinema and one of its most versatile players. Abundant nudity should make picture a popular hit — along with amusingly hammy performances from Karadzic and Bozovic in the comic roles of husband and godfather. —*Yung*.

The Wild Wind
(YUGOSLAVIAN-SOVIET-U.S.-COLOR)

A Film Danas (Belgrade), Moldava Film (USSR) and Noble Prods. (Los Angeles) coproduction. Directed by Aleksandar Petkovic. Screenplay, Zivojin Pavlovic from his novel "The Wild Wind;" camera (Eastmancolor), Vadim Jakovljev; music, Evgenij Doga; art director, Nemanja Petrovic, Nikolai Apostolidi; assistant director, Veleri Zeregi; production manager, Dusan Djokovic; costume design, Emilija Kovacevic. Reviewed at Pula Film Festival, July 24, 1986. (No MPAA Rating.) Running time: **100 MINS.**

Svetozar ....Svetozar Cvetkovic
Major Mestrovic.....George Montgomery
Soviet Officer ....Victor Proskurin
Also with: Milan Puric, Ljuba Poliscuk, Dusan Janicijevic.
(English subtitles)

Pula — A rare East-West coproduction combining U.S. as well as Soviet and East European partners, "The Wild Wind" is an actioner which indicates that Yugoslav cinematographer Aleksandar Petkovic is a lesser director than he is a cameraman. However, it serves as a competent war spectacular though it's short on requisite ticket-selling pyrotechnics.

Ideologically naïve screenplay by Yugoslav Zivojin Pavlovic is too long-winded exposing dastardly deeds between communist Partisans and local fascists. Though the build-up to the final battle has tension the end is an anti-climax being short on blood, guts and mass destruction. In the context of the screenwriter's track record this soft antiwar film should be taken with the pinch of salt that director Petkovic omitted.

Emphasis on epic landscapes and weaponry dwarfs solid performances. Noteworthy are American George Montgomery, Yugoslav Svetozar Cvetkovic and Russian Viktor Proskurin whose talents Petkovic could have further exploited.

Evgenij Doga, who was responsible for the music in the excellent "The Gypsy Camp Vanishes Into The Blue," has come up with a fine score that fits with Petkovic's vast canvasses.

Pic may be a boxoffice winner in East Europe and the Third World, but Western export chances are limited. Ika Panajotovic's L.A.-based Noble Prods. was involved in production.—*Down*.

Dobrovoljci
(Volunteers)
(YUGOSLAVIAN-COLOR)

A Zeta Film (Budva), Dunav Film (Belgrade), Televizija (Titograd) coproduction. Directed by Predrag Golubovic. Screenplay, Golubovic, Vlatko Gilic, Ratko Durovic; camera (color), Milivoje Milivojevic; music, Kornelije Kovac; art direction, Milenko Jeremic. Reviewed at Pula Film Festival (competition), July 24, 1986. Running time: **96 MINS.**

With: Velimir Bata Zivojinovic, Ljubisa Samardzic, Boro Begovic, Mustafa Nadarevic, Bogdan Kiklic, Radko Polic, Ljuba Tadic, Zarko Lausevic, Biljana Ristic.

Pula — An anonymous, campy satire on war, "Volunteers" sets seven inexperienced Gomer Pyles down on a desert island, where they bumble their way through some trumped-up misadventures, such as capturing the crew of an enemy submarine. As commercial fare "Volunteers" may have some local takers, particularly fans of the cast. For other purposes it is forgettable.

Though presumably out to make a point about how mindless war is, pic fails to reach beyond well-oiled variety sketches. In one scene the straggling band of reluctant soldiers, parachuted onto a gorgeous island beach (where whole film takes place) and united under an improvised commander, notices some helicopters setting down. Out jump a team of beautiful girls, sent to entertain the troops and keep morale high. A few dances later they leave, and pic trips on to the enemy sub sequence.

It's technically adequate, with undistinguished and indistinguishable performances from the cast.

— *Yung*.

Lijepe Zene Prolaze Kroz Grad
(Beautiful Women Walking About Town)
(YUGOSLAVIAN-COLOR)

An Art Film '80 (Belgrade) release. Produced by Zvezda Film, in association with Croatia Film, Forum and Art Film. Executive producer, Aleksandar Stojanovic. Directed by Zelmir Zilnik. Screenplay, Zilnik, Miroslav Mandic; camera (color), Ljubomir Becejski; music, Koja; costume design, Bjanka Andzic-Ursulov; production manager, Bosko Ivkovic; art director, Slobodan Djosic. Reviewed at

Pula Film Festival (competition), July 21, 1986. Running time: **95 MINS.**
With: Ljuba Tadzic, Svetolik Mikacevic, Hahela Ferari, Nikola Milic, Milena Dravic, Rade Markovic, Ljubisa Ristic, Tom Gottowac.

Pula — One-hundred years after the revolution, Belgrade in 2041 is the setting for this very low-budget Yugoslavian sci-fier, by Zelmer Zilnik. Though southern Europe is overrun by 21st century thought police, a retired journalist (Ljuba Tadzic) meets a surviving politician and a retired policeman in charge of a boarding school housing eight girls being brought up in old (meaning 1980s) Yugoslavian traditions, prohibited by the ruling gang. Their wish is to revive the once-lively old Belgrade, now in semi-ruins with no electricity and little drinking water.

Population is scattered among wild settlements in the countryside. With the help of a 150-year-old tramp, veteran of the uprising, going by the name of Vladimir Dedijer (theoretician for Tito), the survivors finally prevent liquidations by leather-jacketed 1984-style police and bring the city back to life.

Zilnik combines situations and images from favorite directors, in homages to Buster Keaton's "The General" and to Charles Chaplin. Shot on an unbelievable budget of around $9,000, claims Zilnik, the film was part of a jont docu-drama project for Novi Sad tv.

The comedy is sure to become a *cause celebre* when it opens this fall on home grounds, probably for the wrong reasons. Half the audience in Pula's Arena were walkouts, however, which may indicate a current mood of political weariness. —*Milg.*

Kormoran
(Cormorant)
(YUGOSLAVIAN-COLOR)

A Viba Film production (Ljubljana). Executive producer, Stane Malcic. Directed by Anton Tomasic. Screenplay, Boris Cavazza; camera (Eastman color), Jure Pervanje; editor, Andrija Zafranovic; music, Zoran Predin; sound, Matjaz Janezic; art direction, Janez Kovic; costume design, Irena Felicijan. Reviewed at Pula Film Festival, July 21, 1986. Running time: **88 MINS.**
Maks Cok . . . . Boris Cavazza
Lenka Cok . . . . Milena Zupancic
Zoran . . . . Igor Samobor
Mother . . . . Mila Kacic

Pula — "Cormorant" is a hard-on-the-nerves psychological drama from debuting Slovenian director Anton Tomasic. Its potential outside East Europe is limited.

The film takes as its theme the alcoholic demise of a wayward sailor and the consequent suffering of his family. It comes off as a photographically dark and generally depressing, sometimes sinister look at contemporary life in Slovenia, Yugoslavia's most affluent republic. For the most part pic is dismally dull until it picks up steam in the final reel with a seat-edge surprise finish.

Maks, well played by Boris Cavazza (also the screenwriter), comes home from a voyage and picks up an amourous one night stand. With Maks impotent and unconscious through booze, the girl makes away with his cash but not before sating her sexual appetite with Maks' son (Igor Sambor). Remainder of plotline deals with resultant money problems.

Looking at Maks' family though, it's not surprising he's hooked on the demon drink. At home he is superfluous and loathed by his neurotic hairdresser sister (Milena Zupancic), profligate boxing-mad son, and wheelchair-bound mother (Mila Kacic). The only commmunication he has is with his illegitimate nephew Jani, through their habitual games of chess.

The cormorant of the title is actually a caged seagull but the bird's presence is irrelevant.

Cavazza convinces in the tricky main role simultaneously inspiring sympathy and loathing though his turgid dialog doesn't match his performance. Other actors are mostly up to scratch. Technical credits are adequate. — *Down.*

Obecana Zemlja
(The Promised Land)
(YUGOSLAVIAN-COLOR)

A Croatia Film (Zagreb) release of a Jadran Film (Zagreb) production. Directed by Veljko Bulajic. Screenplay, Ivo Bresan; camera (Widescreen, Eastman color), Goran Trbuljak; music, Alfi Kabiljo; art director, Milenko Jeremic; costumes, Jasna Novak. reviewed at Pula Film Festival (competition), July 23, 1986. Running time: **117 MINS.**
Markan . . . . Bata Zivojinovic
Marta . . . . Mirjana Karanovic
Stana . . . . Dara Dzokic
Milisa . . . . Vjenceslav Kapural
Judge . . . . Vanja Drach
Zec . . . . Dragan Nikolic

Pula — "The Promised Land" continues the colonist saga director Veljko Bulajic began in 1959 with his first film, "The Train Without A Timetable." The sweeping cast of characters are again poor peasants who were resettled to cooperative farmlands in 1946 in vast migration movements.

Bulajic shows his flair for drawing audiences into a story, astutely modeling film around a comic-dramatic trial and a series of flashbacks leading up to the climactic crime.

Markan (Bata Zivojinovic) is the honest, stalwart leader of the collective, who guides the farmers to their new land and tries to administer the new socialist system, occasionally resorting to strong-arm tactics. His principal nemesis is a stubborn old peasant named Milisa (Vjenceslav Kapural), who holds out for private property to his last breath. In a dispute with Markan, partly private and partly ideological, he is shot to death by the *kolkhoz* leader.

During the trial the whole collective has its say. Simple, clearly drawn characters intertwine in stories of love and greed like in any respectable soap opera, accounting for pic's audience appeal. Melodramatic flourishes, like the sudden death of Markan's aged mother in the middle of the trial, are corny but in keeping with the spirit of the film.

Yet despite its drop in taste, "The Promised Land" paints a detailed fresco of the period and conflicting interests, while remaining entertaining.

Actors are well cast and come across strongly in their roles. Most subtle performance is by Mirjana Karanovic as the sister-in-law of the slain farmer, who is in love with Markan and functions as the purveyor of balanced, moral values in the film. Also of note is Dara Dzokic, the inflamed widow, fighting against the kolkhoz at her husband's side, hiding cows and hoarding grain. At trial's end justice is meted out by a people's jury as befits the crime.

In a final ironic touch, news arrives that the collective farms are being abolished as failures, and the farmers gather to demand their land back. —*Yung.*

San o Ruzi
(The Dream Of A Rose)
(YUGOSLAVIAN-COLOR)

A Centar Film/Kinematografi Zagreb release, of a Zagreb Film, Centar Film coproduction. Directed by Zoran Tadic. Stars Rade Serbedzija. Screenplay, Pavao Pavlicic; camera (color), Goran Trbuljak; editor, Vesna Kreber; music, Alfi Kabiljo; art direction, Ante Nola; costumes, Lada Gamulin. Reviewed at Pula Film Festival (competition), July 23, 1986. Running time: **96 MINS.**
With: Rade Serbedzija, Fabijan Sovagovic, Iva Marjanovic, Ljubo Zecevic, Anja Sovagovic, Vlatko Dulic.

Pula — The third feature by Zoran Tadic, "The Dream Of A Rose" is a wistful crime story, halfway between a foggy backstreets thriller and a tormented search for values. Strong on atmosphere, pic runs dry somewhere in the middle and falls into repetition, until a final payoff in the closing minutes. Though story stumbles, "Rose" is an exceptional mood piece.

Returning home from work one night (he is on a late shift at a foundry), a man (Rade Serbedzija) stumbles across the scene of a crime — two murders in a corner of the market square. He impulsively grabs a sack full of money and a gun, and hurries home. From that moment he struggles with his conscience, his wife who wants to spend the booty, suspicious cops, tough gangsters, and a butcher who has seen him make off with the stash.

As the net tightens slowly around the hero, "Rose" builds to a bloody but unexpected climax a step at a time. Unfortunately the steps are quite small. The butcher and his shop become an obsession for the glum hero, who can't make up his mind whether to spend the money, and stares fixedly at huge pieces of meat (called "roses") which are the symbol of a better life for his poverty-stricken family.

Cameraman Goran Trbuljak creates a mysterious night universe of foggy streets and expressionist shadows, dreamlike scenes where the only recognizing signs belong to a cocktail bar and the butcher shop. Acting is kept appropriately low-key across the board. — *Yung.*

Karlovy Vary Film Festival

Pavucina
(Cobweb)
(CZECH-COLOR/B&W)

A Czechoslovak Filmexport release of a Gottwaldov Film Studios production. Written and directed by Zdenek Zaoral. Stars Eva Kulichová. Camera (color, b&w), Michal Kulic; music, Václav Hálek. Reviewed at Karlovy Vary (market), July 11, 1986. Running time: **96 MINS.**
Radka . . . . Eva Kulichová
Marie . . . . Jirina Trebická
Helena . . . . Milena Svobodová
Father . . . . Jiri Zahájský
Mother . . . . Radka Fiedlerová
Also with: Miroslav Machácek (psychiatrist), Jana Kremanová (head doctor), Frantisek Husák (psychologist), Zdenek Dusek (Karel), Yvetta Kornová (Marcela).

Karlovy Vary — An off-beat and courageous pioneer effort to bring Czechoslovakia's drug problem out into the open, "Cobweb" is also a very well-made picture that can rival Western films on the same subject. Debuting helmer Zdenek Zaoral avoids facile moralism directed either against addicts or society, and instead builds up a dense world echoing the drug user's nightmare abode. Pic's difficult production history shows how the subject was not an easy one to film, though Gottwaldov Studios (specialized in children's films) eventually picked up the project once it was started, to their credit.

Focusing on a strongly drawn young heroine, Radka (convincingly limned by Eva Kulichová), "Cob-web" explores both life in a drug treatment institute that resembles a cross between an Army barracks and a prison, and Radka's unhappy family life and love affair, leading up to her problem. Camerawork contributes enormously to the power of the picture, switching freely between color, black and white, and sepia-tones, while film flutters dreamily between Radka in the institute and out of it.

She lives with her mother, as much of a psychological mess as she is. One of the mother's casual boyfriends drugs and seduces her. The romantic story she tells the shrinks — all depicted as cold and unsympathetic — about her boyfriend dying tragically in Sweden is gradually revealed to be pure fabrication. Meanwhile, some hair-raising therapy sessions are shown. For example, one involves the fragile patients in macabre acting-out with death-masks and the like.

Parts of the film are shot in a documentary style so convincing it looks like repertory footage. Other scenes go in for hallucination-type lensing. The soundtrack is also experimental, adding to pic's interest from the technical side. The strongest point of "Cobweb" is its theme, unfortunately universal, and easily understandable for foreign audiences. —*Yung.*

Chicherin
(SOVIET-COLOR)

A Mosfilm Studios production. Directed by Alexander Zarkhi. Stars Leonid Filatov. Screenplay, Zarkhi, Vladen Loginov; camera (color), Anatoli Moukassei; music, Irakly Gabeli; art direction, David Vinitzki. Reviewed at Karlovy Vary Festival (competition), July 14, 1986. Running time: **148 MINS.**
Georgi V. Chicherin . . . . . . .Leonid Filatov
Gabriele D'Annunzio . . . . . . .Rolan Bykov
Also with: Leonid Bronievoy, Oleg Golubitski, Ruben Simonov, Vera Venczel, Valeri Zolotukhin, Algimantas Masyulis, Natalia Saiko.

Karlovy Vary — In commemoration of the 50th anniversary of the death of Russian statesman Georgi Chicherin, Mosfilm has brought out a sumptuous production under the skilled hand of veteran director Alexander Zarkhi ("Anna Karenina"), a long-time codirector with partner Josef Heifits.

"Chicherin" is quite a history lesson, tackling the tough years of diplomacy that eventually led to foreign recognition of the new Soviet state. This crash course is divided into two lengthy episodes and seems destined for small screen scholars.

Despite the pedantry of the subject, Zarkhi's professional skills lead him back into more watchable scenes by the second episode, when a trip to Italy brings his hero into contact with D'Annunzio (amusingly limned by director-thesp Rolan Bykov), Lloyd George, and the King of Italy. Pic's biggest boon is casting popular thesp Leonid Filatov in the title role, where his twinkling-eyed intelligence cuts through the ponderousness of recreated history and adds an appealing human dimension.

Film opens with Chicherin in a London prison, being visited by love interest Vera Venczel, an attractive British newswoman who pops up for the rest of the film every time a treaty is signed. Lenin gets the ex-aristocrat Chicherin out of jail and appoints him People's Commissar in charge of foreign relations. First assignment is the Brest-Litevsk peace accord with the Germans, which he underwrites with a heavy heart as a weaker-stomached general shoots himself off-screen. Pic's pacifist message is first heard in Lenin's line, "Everything but not war."

After some hokey scenes of the statesman holding a banquet for London street urchins when a full guest list of ambassadors snubs him and a tearful reunion with his old nanny to the strains of the Internationale, pic gets back in stride in time for the Genoa conference with Lloyd George in 1922. In its most sustained and well-staged scene, Chicherin practices some clever nighttime diplomacy in the corridors of the Imperial Hotel, leading to a peace accord with Germany that first broke the diplomatic blockade against the Soviets.

Admittedly, authentic events of this kind are hard to bring to life on the screen. "Chicherin" is intermittently successful and casts light on the period without the dubious aid of a lot of silly subplots, or going off the deep end of patriotism. Though one wonders about some of the details, like Victor Emanuel speaking fluent Russian, pic mostly looks genuine. Sets are sumptuous, lensing notable. Pic is being massively released (1,500 prints) in the USSR in September.—*Yung.*

New Delhi Times
(INDIAN-COLOR)

A P.K. Communication Private release. Produced by P.K. Tewari. Directed by Ramesh Sharma. Screenplay, Gulzar; camera (color), Subrata Mitra; editor, Rene Saluja; music, Louis Banks; art director, Nitish Roy, Samir Chandra. Reviewed at Karlovy Vary Film Festival (competition), July 7, 1986. Running time: **123 MINS.**
With: Shashi Kapoor, Sharmila Tagore, Om Puri, Kulbhushan Kharbanda, Manohar Singh, A.K. Hangal.

Karlovy Vary — In the maturing Indian cinema of the mid-'80s, so-called hard-hitting stories of corruption in high places are becoming more frequent, with occasional box-office success (Govind Nihalani's 1984 "Half Truth") but "New Delhi Times," a National Fest prizewinner, has been too hot a potato for Indian commercial distribution Sharma has been persona-non-grata on Indian tv also, where film was withdrawn at the last minute recently just before the evening screening.

For a first feature by young, Montreal-trained, ex-journalist Sharma, film is a smooth piece of work, highly aided by thesps Shashi Kapoor and Sharmila Tagore, playing loyal lawyer-wife to eponymous New Delhi Times editor-in-chief Kapoor, whose first-person story ties underworld boss (Om Puri), and parliament member, to his role in the murder of a rival politician.

The investigation leads to the chief minister of the state, who attempts to suppress the story. In the process, everything from drug peddling, the racket in dowries and gold smuggling gets dredged up for criticism.

Best scene in the film is the realistically staged riot in regional center Ghazipur, in which the town goes up in flames, touched off by the court probe of the exposé.

Although film ends without vindication for its idealistic editor, in face of current cynicism about Indian state politics, audience is left to believe that the national game of toppling ministers will go another round. The film, which goes on a bit long about First Amendment-type freedoms, is seen as an explosive one for India. —*Milg.*

Tommaso Blu
(ITALIAN-GERMAN-COLOR)

A FFF (Florian Furtwängler Filmproductions) production. Directed by Florian Furtwängler. Screenplay, Tommaso Di Ciaula, Peter Kammerer, Furtwängler from the novel "Tuta Blue" by Di Ciaula; camera (color) James Jacobs; music, Peer Raben. Reviewed at Taormina Film Festival (competition), July 20, 1986. Running time: **90 MINS.**
With: Alessandro Haber, Antonella Porfido, Marina Eugeni.

Taormina — In the competition at the Taormina fest as the entry from the Federal Republic of Germany, "Tommaso Blue" was hot in the region of Bari, in southern Italy and performed in Italian. It proved to be one of the strongest films in the festival, boasting a tremendously effective title performance by Alessandro Haber who enacted a factory worker at the end of his emotional tether.

As Tommaso, he embodied the lost dreams and frustrations of assembly-liners everywhere who, after more than a decade at their machines, might suddenly turn inward in despair, visualizing family, children and urban environment as symbolically indifferent and stultifying as the machines at hand.

The film shows, in steadily mounting episodes moving from satire to high melodrama, the rebellious hysteria that overcomes Tommaso. He runs away. from his job and family and tries to restructure his entire personality. As a young farm boy, he had been forcibly apprenticed to a metalworker in a factory, when he had actually longed to remain close to nature and his fellow man.

Now middle-aged and balding, he tries to regain contact with his youthful past that was thwarted. His efforts to establish rapport with a Saturday-night crowd of youngsters and their fresh, amorous dalliances in a local park are tragically dramatized, and he winds up a total misfit and outcast from the industrialized order around him.

It is during the final episodes of the film that the director and co-scripters (including Tommaso Di Ciaula, an outspoken worker-novelist) bring a symbolic tone to the story. Sprinkled through the narrative are sharp gibes at the platitudes spoken by the President, and the hypocrisies of contemporary Italian morality. The world of apartment complexes and industrial terrain are impressively photographed in memorable images by James Jacobs, often with a twilight glow that complements the hero's dreamy impulses.

Underlying the story is a bitter thread of social comment about the casual destruction of man's nobler instincts. Tommaso, full of the swarthy, hirsute machismo of a working-class Everyman, cannot be accepted by society as a potential poet.

The film is expertly directed and Haber's acting is incomparable. He appears in just about every scene and gives a definitive portrayal.

"Tommaso Blu" received a special prize given by the city of Taormina, but the festival jury's decision not to give Haber the major acting award was a controversial issue.
—*Aljo.*

Malayunta
(ARGENTINE-COLOR)

An Instituto Nacional De Cinematografía Argentina production. Directed by José Santiso. Screenplay, José Santiso, Jacobo Langsner; camera (color), Eduardo Legaria; editor, Valencia-Blanco; music, Litto Nebbia; art direction, Ponchi Morpugo. Reviewed at Taormina Film Festival (competition), July 24, 1986. Running time: **90 MINS.**
Bernardo . . . . .Federico Luppi
Amalia . . . . .Barbara Mujica
Nestor . . . . .Miguel Angel Solà
Angelita . . . . .Silvia Millet
Also with: Jorge Petraglia, Edgardo Moreira.

Taormina — Winner of the Silver Cariddi at the Taormina Film Festival, "Malayunta" is one of those gripping, darkly-provocative dramas reminiscent of Luis Buñuel, and indicative of a growing renaissance of Argentine film talents.

Aided by an excellent trio of players, director José ̦Santiso proves able to provide many levels of sociological and political interpretation to what amounts to a dramatized battle-of-wills.

An elderly couple, obviously used to better times, rents a room from a young sculptor, Nestor, who lives alone in a large, cluttered apartment in the center of Buenos Aires. Bernardo and Amalia courteously attempt to share the amenities of the place, but find Nestor to be by turns insolent and contemptuous toward them.

Resentful of this behavior, they decide to assert themselves when Nestor reveals unusual sexual alliances and a defiant belligerence. Since there seems to be no possibility of compromise, the *ménage à trois* becomes a violent clash of youth vs. fanatic intolerance. There are also strong intimations that Bernardo is one of the guilt-ridden individuals who assisted in the regime of the "disappeared ones" when he is accosted by a street entertainer who recognizes and chases him.

Throughout the film, one observes the janitor's young grandchild, Angelita, who acts as a silent witness to the struggles of the three protagonists.

Federico Luppi's portrayal of Bernardo has all of the subtleties of respectable menace. He provides the character with levels of interpretation without revealing all of his secrets. Barbara Mujica, in the difficult role of his wife, makes the most of some powerful moments as she shifts personalities midway through the film.

Perhaps the most difficult and absorbing character is Nestor, the ambivalent, arrogant artist, played brilliantly by Miguel Angel Solà. He deliberately camouflages the softer side of Nestor, so that one is never certain where intelligence becomes pretension, or sympathy becomes villainy. Solà manages to hold the tensions of the film intact with his unusual physical presence.

José Santiso, in his directorial debut here, reveals a strong sense of theater.

"Malayunta" is a triumphant contender for international distribution and festival exposure, and should fascinate audiences everywhere.—*Aljo.*

Zastihla me noc
(I Was Caught In The Night)
(CZECH-COLOR)

A Czechoslovak Filmexport release of a Barrandov Film Studios/Slovak Feature Film Studio production. Directed by Juraj Herz. Stars Jana Rihakova. Screenplay, Jaromira Kolarova, Juraj Herz; camera (color), Viktor Ruzicka; music, Michael Kocab. Reviewed at Karlovy Vary Film Festival (competition), July 3, 1986. Running time: **129 MINS.**
Jozka Jaburkova ....Jana Rihakova
Mother ....Jana Brejchova
Zdena ....Andrea Bogusovska
Bozka ....Jana Paulova
Also with: Jana Svobodova, Sylvie Turbova, Jiri Stepnicka, Radoslav Brzobohaty, Rudolf Hrusinsky.

Karlovy Vary — Based on the life of militant Communist journalist Jozka Jaburkova, "I Was Caught In The Night" reviews events in its heroine's life as she dies a slow, tortured death in the Nazi concentration camp of Ravensbrück. Helmer Juraj Herz portrays Jaburkova as an unfaltering and selfless idealist, easy to admire but hard to identify with. Ditto the picture as a whole, finely lensed but too familiar in the way it presents Nazi horrors to be deeply affecting.

For many years editor of a political paper for women, "The Disseminator," and a fiery member of the Prague City Council, Jaburkova was arrested as part of the anti-Nazi resistance movement. The camp sequences are chillingly shot, though not as graphically horrific as some. Cinematographer Viktor Ruzicka adopts brutal gray-blues for these scenes. When the heroine escapes into her memories, colors turn to warm golden hues. Pic's high professional standards are a plus throughout.

The problem is, the script never really gets under the skin of its subject. As a child, Jozka is shown the unhappy victim of a crazed mother, who tries to atone with religious fanaticism for having a child out of wedlock. As a student in a girls' school, Jozka gets into trouble for nobly defending the underdog. Her later jobs as governess, nurse, and foundry worker all get entangled with her uncompromising principles.

Stage thesp Jana Rihakova takes Jozka from adolescence to her mature 40's like a woman destined for martyrdom from the start. When she finally succumbs, as a group of Russian prisoners join in a heroic national anthem outside her death cell, it is a saint's end, and the dominant emotion is relief.

"Caught" is finely edited, and moves back and forth from the grueling camp sequences to flashback memories with admirable smoothness. — *Yung.*

Vakvilàgban
(Blind Endeavor)
(HUNGARIAN-COLOR)

A Hungarofilm release. Produced by Hungarian Television and Mafilm — Dialóg Studio (Budapest). Directed by Livia Gyarmathy. Screenplay, Gyula Marosi, Ildikó Kórody, Pál Belohorszky; camera (Fujicolor), Ferenc Pap; editor, Eva Kármentó, Eva Palotai; music, Ferenc Balázs, art direction, Gábor Balló; costumes, Erzsébat Mialkovszky. Reviewed at Karlovy Vary Festival (competition), July 10 1986. Running time: **87 MINS.**
Sándor ....Andor Lukáts
Károly ....György Dörner
Eva ....Kati Sir
Károly's mother ....Hédi Temessy
Sándor's wife.............Judit Meszléry
Also with: Cecilia Esztergályos (secretary), Lajos Szabó, János Dégi, and György Kölgyessi (brigade members).

Karlovy Vary — "Blind Endeavor" is an unflinching portrayal of ordinary people's frustrations and the difficulty of human relations in general. With fine dramatic savvy, helmer Livia Gyarmathy alternates two seemingly unconnected stories, only to bring the threads together in a shocking final scene of senseless tragedy. Though it entered production as a tv film, pic was finished by Mafilm's Dialóg Studio as a regular theatrical feature.

Sándor (Andor Lukáts) and his factory team receive a bonus for an invention of theirs. At a festive restaurant dinner, Sándor gets bombed and his inner tension and bitterness come to a head. Staggering off to a nightclub, he has a humiliating encounter with an arrogant youth that culminates in tragedy.

Second story: Károly (György Dörner) is the psychological victim of an overprotective mother (Hédi Temessy). He takes his girlfriend Eva (Kati Sir) on a ski trip to the mountains and they almost break up. Instead they decide to get married. For the first time Károly stands up to his mother, but on his way to work the next morning, he's accidentally killed.

Brought to life by a fine cast of thesps, a wide range of characters portray all their weaknesses and problems. Gyarmathy is a sophisticated observer of the human comedy and injects moments of grotesque irony into her canvas. It ends on the tragic note of multiple lives lying in total ruin, but pic is full of real feeling for its characters that keeps it absorbing. Technical work is good. Though lensed quickly on a shoestring budget, pic gains in speed and lightness anything it might have lost in more costly finesse. — *Yung.*

The Fly
(COLOR)

Gory remake short on believability; b.o. looks good.

A 20th Century Fox release of a Brooksfilms production. Produced by Stuart Cornfeld. Coproducers Marc-Ami Boyman, Kip Ohman. Directed by David Cronenberg. Screenplay, Charles Edward Pogue, Cronenberg, from a story by George Langelaan; camera (Deluxe color), Mark Irwin; editor, Ronald Sanders; music, Howard Shore; production design, Carol Spier; art director, Rolf Harvey; set decorator, Elinor Rose Galbraith; set designer, James Mc Ateer; sound (Dolby stereo), Gerry Humphreys; costumes, Denise Cronenberg; the Fly created and designed by Chris Walas Inc.; assistant director, John Board; casting, Deirdre Bowen. Reviewed at 20th Century Fox screening room, Century City, Calif., Aug. 4, 1986. (MPAA Rating: R.) Running time: **100 MINS.**
Seth Brundle ....Jeff Goldblum
Veronica Quaife ....Geena Davis
Stathis Borans ....John Getz
Tawny ....Joy Boushel
Dr. Cheevers ....Les Carlson

Hollywood — David Cronenberg's remake of the 1958 horror classic "The Fly" is not for the squeamish, faint-hearted or those prone to motion sickness. All others may find it suitable entertainment.

One does not have to be totally warped to appreciate the film, but it does take a particular sensibility to embrace it. This "Fly" actually has much to recommend it but it is the gory and grotesque that leave a lasting impression. Audience could extend beyond the thrill-seekers and turn out in respectable numbers.

Cronenberg has long made a career out of dissecting the medically deformed, and "The Fly" proves an ideal vehicle. But while he is expertly able to create some shocking scenes, the film lacks a vision that would give them weight and importance. Instead they tend to rise and then fall with a thud until the next one comes along.

It is to Cronenberg's credit that he can still stir an audience that has presumably seen everything. Not only does he pull out all the stops, part of the experience is getting your nose rubbed in it.

First half of the film, before things start going irrevocably, hopelessly wrong for scientist Seth Brundle (Jeff Goldblum), actually is stronger, with screenwriters Charles Edward Pogue and Cronenberg setting up a solid human context for the fantastic story to come. Casting Goldblum here was a good choice as he brings a quirky, common touch to the spacey scientist role.

Cronenberg gives him a nice girlfriend (Geena Davis), too. She's a reporter who soon falls under Goldblum's spell. But there's trouble in paradise. Goldblum's got a set of teleporters that he promises will "change the world as we know it," and indeed, it does change his world.

Even though the machinery is not

yet perfected (a baboon is transported inside-out), Goldblum, in a moment of drunken jealousy, throws himself in the works. Although he seems to come out better than ever, unbeknownst to him a fly accompanies him on the journey and he starts to go through a slow metamorphosis.

Unlike the original "Fly" where Al (David) Hedison gets the head and arm of the insect and becomes a figure of sympathy trying to recover his original identity for the rest of the film, Cronenberg's version centers on a slow disintegration with little energy spent on trying to undo the deed. Consequently the sympathy from the early going is squandered on sensationalism later on.

It really does become difficult to take this romance seriously when Goldblum loses an ear and Davis reaches out to hug him anyway. Other scenes to look forward to include an abortion played for pure sensationalism, almost devoid of human dimensions.

There is no denying, however, that all this is handsomely staged with Chris Walas' design for the Fly never less than visually intriguing. Production design by Carol Spier, particularly for Goldblum's warehouse lab, is original and appropriate to the hothouse drama.

Cronenberg contains the action well in a limited space with a small cast. Goldblum carries the action until the action starts carrying him, and Davis is a charming presence until she too becomes secondary to the spectacle. John Getz as an ex-boyfriend is a curious character who never really comes off, due more to the writing than any lapse in his performance.

Finally, "The Fly" is too trapped by its desire to shock to be truly affecting. — *Jagr.*

The Transformers
(ANIMATED-COLOR)

Loud, unintelligible cartoon exercise.

A De Laurentiis Entertainment Group release. Produced by Joe Bacal, Tom Griffin. Executive producers, Margaret Loesch, Lee Gunther. Supervising producer, Jay Bacal. Directed and coproduced by Nelson Shin. Screenplay, Ron Friedman, based on the Hasbro toy, "The Transformers;" story consultant, Flint Dille; editor, David Hankins; music, Vince DeCola; sound, R. William A. Thiederman, W. Howard Wilmarth, Peter S. Reale; animation, Toei Animation Co. Ltd.; supervising animation director, Kozo Morishita; special effects, Masayuki Kawachi, Shoji Sato; casting, Reuben Cannon & Associates, Carol Dudley. Reviewed at DEG screening room, Beverly Hills, Aug. 7, 1986. (MPAA Rating: PG.) Running time: **86 MINS.**
Voices Of:
Planet Unicron . . . . .Orson Welles
Ultra Magnus . . . . .Robert Stack
Megatron . . . . .Leonard Nimoy
Wreck Gar . . . . .Eric Idle
Hot Rod Rodimus Prime . . . . .Judd Nelson
Kup .Lionel Stander

Hollywood — "The Transformers," in which Orson Welles plays a planet, is pure headache material. Target audience of cartoon-watchers also will probably find the film unintelligible, noisy and unoriginal. Boxoffice prospects are dismal.

This film begs the question: Why pay for a lengthy version of a cartoon that can be seen on commercial television every afternoon?

Celebrity voices of Welles, Leonard Nimoy, Robert Stack and Judd Nelson presumably were added to enhance appeal, but little tykes wouldn't know who they were anyway and besides, the actors' voices have been synthesized to the extent they are nearly unrecognizable.

Then there is the question of even being able to hear the dialog. A heavy metal rock score hammers on in 99% of the film.

As far as plot goes, story takes place in 2005 when the Transformers led by good guy Ultra Magnus (Stack) uses his special powers provided by the Matrix of Leadership to save the universe from the evil Planet Unicron (Welles) and his troops of nasty Decepticons led by captive leader, Megatron (Nimoy).

Action basically is one continuous series of fighting and battle scenes as the Transformers transform into high-performance cars, dinosaurs, jets, etc., to destory Junkions, Sharkicons and other blackhearted beasts.

(The key is that anything whose name ends in the letters "on" is evil.)

Animation by Toei Animation of Japan is flat and cluttered with so many indistinctive images, it's often difficult to separate the characters from their background. —*Brit.*

Manhunter
(COLOR)

Pretentious, pounding thriller has some good performances.

A De Laurentiis Entertainment Group release of a Dino De Laurentiis presentation of a Richard Roth production. Produced by Roth. Executive producer, Bernard Williams. Written and directed by Michael Mann, based on the novel "Red Dragon" by Thomas Harris. Camera (Technicolor, Joe Dunton Cameras widescreen), Dante Spinotti; editor, Dov Hoenig; music, the Reds & Michel Rubini; production design, Mel Bourne; art direction, Jack Blackman; costume design, Colleen Atwood; sound (Dolby), John Mitchell; associate producer, second unit director, Gusmano Cesaretti; assistant director, Herb Gaines; casting, Bonnie Timmerman. Reviewed at the Samuel Goldwyn theater, Beverly Hills, Aug. 4, 1986. (MPAA Rating: R.) Running time: **119 MINS.**
Will Graham . . . . .William L. Petersen
Molly Graham . . . . .Kim Greist
Reba .Joan Allen
Doctor Lektor . . . . .Brian Cox
Jack Crawford . . . . .Dennis Farina
Freddie Lounds . . . . .Stephen Lang
Francis Dollarhyde . . . . .Tom Noonan

Hollywood — "Manhunter" is an unpleasantly gripping thriller that rubs one's nose in a sick criminal mentality for two hours. Michael Mann's nerve-jangling style builds up an unhealthy head of dread, result of which is that the viewer is kept constantly on edge. Audiences may be impressed by the picture without really enjoying it, and b.o. won't be helped by the exploitation-type title and no-name, albeit very good, cast. General outlook is moderate.

Pic is based upon Thomas Harris' well-received novel "Red Dragon," which was the original shooting title but was changed, probably so that people wouldn't think they were going to see a sequel to "Red Sonja" or "Year Of The Dragon."

Like the recent De Laurentiis production "Raw Deal," this one deals with a southern former FBI agent who is summoned from retirement to work on a particularly perplexing case, that of a mass murderer who appears to stalk and select his victims with particular care.

Agent William L. Petersen leaves his wife and son to take on the assignment, and it soon becomes apparent he left the investigative field for good reason — his excellent deductive talents are due, in large measure, to his tendency to deeply enter the minds of killers, to begin thinking like them to such a degree that he can ultimately figure out when and where they will strike next.

This trick has left Petersen with unfortunate psychic scars he doesn't wish to add to, and also takes the film into interesting Hitchcockian guilt transference territory. For too long, however, telling concentrates on familiar police procedural detail, and Mann's stylistic gambits and constant use of rock music sometimes push to the adjacent borders of the pretentious and the ludicrous.

Once his attention turns to the murderer, tale takes an unexpected and satisfying left turn. The killer is clearly as mad as he is dangerous, and every moment the film spends with him is tension-filled, since he is capable of anything.

Although the opening hour could have stood a bit of pruning, Mann's grip on his material is tight and sure. Director is at all times preoccupied by visual chic, but this reaches ridiculous extremes, as he endows everyone from cops to criminals with dramatic high-tech surroundings. Even inmates inhabit designer prisons, as the mental hospital here, with its exposed, wall-hugging ramps, resembles a Guggenheim Institute for the Insane (scene was, in fact, shot in an Atlanta art museum).

Similarly, Mann overdoes the musical overlay, most notably in a critical scene in which the killer imagines his girlfriend kissing another man. Sequence clearly calls out for silence, but Mann apparently doesn't know the meaning of the word and pounds this psychologically important moment into the ground with yet another rock song.

In the end, Mann's virtues and excesses more or less balance each other out, and the cast helps out. Petersen, looking scruffy, again registers a strong, essentially sympathetic presence, although, as in "To Live And Die In L.A.," his character goes way beyond what a normal viewer can hope to identify with.

Tom Noonan cuts a massive swath as the killer, who late in the game is surprisingly humanized by a blind girl, played in enormously touching fashion by Joan Allen. Brian Cox has some delicious moments as a brilliant, depraved criminal successfully hunted by Petersen before the latter's retirement, and Stephen Lang is outrageously despicable as a scandal sheet writer. Kim Greist, as the hero's wife, has little to do but worry and wait around.

Technical contributions are all of the slickest order. —*Cart.*

The Boy Who Could Fly
(COLOR)

Well-intentioned but somber drama.

A 20th Century Fox release of a Gary Adelson production. Produced by Adelson. Coproducer, Richard Vane. Written and directed by Nick Castle. Camera (Deluxe color), Steven Poster, Adam Holender; editor, Patrick Kennedy; music, Bruce Broughton; production design, Jim Bissell; art direction, Graeme Murray; set design, Jim Teegarden; costumes, Trish Keaton; sound (Dolby), Rob Young; visual effects, Boss Film Corp.; visual effects supervisor, Richard Edlund; visual effects art director, George Jensen; associate producer, Brian Frankish; assistant director, Michael Steele; casting Barbara Miller. Reviewed at Lorimar-Telepictures screening room 21, Culver City, Calif., Aug. 5, 1986. (MPAA Rating: PG.) Running time: **114 MINS.**
Milly . . . . .Lucy Deakins
Eric . . . . .Jay Underwood
Charlene . . . . .Bonnie Bedelia
Louis .Fred Savage
Mrs. Sherman . . . . .Colleen Dewhurst
Uncle Hugo . . . . .Fred Gwynne
Psychiatrist . . . . .Louise Fletcher

Hollywood — "The Boy Who Could Fly" is a well-intentioned film that deals with mental illness, suicide and other weighty subjects and their effects on children in a general and understanding way. Even with an upbeat ending it still may be too intense to capture enough of an audience to take off at the b.o.

Story involves the special relationship between a sweet, patient teenage girl named Milly (Lucy Deakins) and the autistic neighbor Eric (Jay Underwood), who sits for hours on his roof directly across from her bedroom window with his arms outstretched as if ready to take off and fly.

Milly has just moved in with her recently widowed mother (Bonnie Bedelia) and precocious little brother (Fred Savage) following the suicide of their father who killed himself instead of having his family watch him die slowly from cancer.

Unlike nearly everyone else around who dismisses Underwood simply as a nut case, Deakins is super-sensitive and understands how lonely and misunderstood the troubled boy must be, considering how she feels following her father's untimely death.

Tone of the pic is evenly somber throughout — perhaps too somber.

Under Nick Castle's careful direction, scenes never become maudlin, which is remarkable considering the potential of the subject matter.

Deakins as the sympathetic girl and Underwood as the mute boy handle their difficult roles with amazing grace. If only their bittersweet moments together could have been broken up by a few more lighthearted ones.

The few comic scenes are rationed out to kid brother Louis (Savage) who trains in his G.I. Joe outfit to take on the neighborhood toughies and outwit them at their own evil games.

Otherwise, it's heavy going as we watch Deakins and Underwood challenge the odds: she gets him to open up and talk; he takes her flying. It's an arduous process for them and only a slightly less difficult one to watch.

Near the end of the film comes the breather as the twosome finally become airborne — soaring over the city at night in beautifully crafted scenes by special effects wizard Richard Edlund and Boss Film Corp.

Supporting cast of pros all turn in terrific performances, counting in Colleen Dewhurst as a sympathetic high school teacher, Fred Gwynne as the boy's alcoholic, but benign, uncle, Louise Fletcher as a soft-spoken psychiatrist and Bedelia as the understanding mom. —*Brit.*

One Crazy Summer
(COLOR)

Unpolished, scattershot teen comedy.

A Warner Bros. Pictures release on an A&M Films production. Produced by Michael Jaffe. Executive producers, Gil Friesen, Andrew Meyer. Written and directed by Savage Steve Holland. Camera (CFI Color), Isidore Mankofsky; editor, Alan Balsam; music, Cory Lerios; production design, Herman Zimmerman; set decorator, Gary Moreno; sound, David Roonie; costumes, Brad R. Loman; animation, Bill Kopp; assistant director, Albert Shapiro; associate producer, William Strom; casting, Judith Holstra, Marcia Ross. Reviewed at UA Egyptian theater, Westwood, Calif., Aug. 8, 1986. (MPAA Rating: PG.) Running Time: **93 MINS.**
Hoops McCann . . . . .John Cusack
Cassandra . . . . .Demi Moore
George Calamari. . . . . .Joel Murray
Ack Ack Raymond . . . . .Curtis Armstrong
Egg Stork . . . . .Bobcat Goldthwait
Clay Stork . . . . .Tom Villard
Teddy Beckersted. . . . . .Matt Mulhern
Aguilla Beckersted . . . . .Mark Metcalf
Old Man Beckersted . . . . . .William Hickey
General Raymond. . . . . .Joe Flaherty
Squid Calamari . . . . .Kristen Goelz

Hollywood — Savage Steve Holland, the writer and director of "One Crazy Summer," probably is the kind of guy who would be great fun to hang out with at a party where he could tell stories and clown around and be as outrageous as he wants. These, however, are not necessarily qualities that make a director, though he continues to stuff his films with a nonstop barrage of sight gags and non sequiturs. "One Crazy Summer" (filmed under the titles "My Summer Vacation" and "Greetings From Nantucket") has a few laughs but the real joke is that it got made.

This is a film with a story so lame it needs crutches. Script is a comic book of exaggerated characters and ludicrous situations. It does not, however, have the inspired lunacy and anarchist touch that a great comic director would elicit from it.

Holland has improved since his first feature last year, "Better Off Dead," and might even make an entertaining picture if he could focus his obvious talents for scattershot humor and broaden his targets.

Once again story is about the travails of teen love with young Hoops McCann (John Cusack) trying to figure it all out. He (like Holland) is a cartoonist trying to draw his way into art school by submitting an illustrated love story. Trouble is he's never been in love.

As luck would have it he stumbles on to Demi Moore, a young girl in all sorts of trouble. Hoops save the day and saves her Nantucket house from, what else, a ruthless land developer (Mark Metcalf) and solves the riddle of his cartoon.

Along the way, story is accompanied by a running animation sequence commenting on his progress and an assortment of characters who look like they stepped out of the cartoon. Chief among them is Bobcat Goldthwait whose brand of humor must be an acquired taste.

Others along to help are Joel Murray (Bill's brother) who makes an outstanding debut as Hoops' unreliable but well-meaning good buddy. SCTV's Joe Flaherty is moderately amusing in an obnoxious bit as a militaristic boy scout leader.

Holland manages to squander most of the talents of a generally fine cast by not giving them better characters. Cusack's hound dog looks and expressive face make him fun to watch, if only it were worth the trouble. Moore proves once again she is one of the most alluring young female actresses working today but her role here is thankless, thanks to Holland.

Tech credits also display a certain sloppy thinking. Editing is jumpy, photography is grainy and overall look is unpolished. —*Jagr.*

Der Pendler
(The Informer)
(SWISS-B&W)

An Inter Team Films release (Metropolis Films, Zurich, outside Switzerland) of a Limbo Film production. Executive producer, Theres Scherer. Directed by Bernhard Giger. Screenplay, Giger, Martin Hennig; camera (Kodak black & white, Schwarz Filmtechnik Laboratories), Pio Corradi; editor, Daniela Roderer; music, Benedikt Jeger, song "Wenn i hei chume" by Markus Kühne and Polo Hofer, performed by Hofer; sound, Hans Künzi; art direction, Marianne Milani; production manager, Theres Scherer, Rose-Marie Schneider. Reviewed on the Piazza Grande, Locarno Film Festival (out of competition), Aug. 9, 1986. Running time: **100 MINS.**
With: Andreas Loeffel (Tom), Elisabeth Seiler (Su), Anne-Marie Blanc (Aunt Martha), Bruno Ganz (Steiner), Tiziana Jelmini (Elsbeth), Beat Sieber (Sander).

Locarno — Journalist turned filmmaker Bernhard Giger describes his third film as the final part of a trilogy on man's search for his identity. This is a crime story of sorts, about a former drug peddler who becomes police informer to save his own skin. All through the film he oscillates between his old world and friends and his new occupation, imposed on him by a ruthless police inspector who threatens to put him back in jail if he does not comply.

The informer, Tom, lives with a girl who knows nothing of his record or his police connections; he acts as if all this doesn't burden his conscience too much, as long as he can manage to keep his freedom and enjoy the loot he makes both for and against the law.

The insouciance of the main character is the film's main stumbling block. He certainly doesn't look as if he is capable of going through an identity crisis at all, being far too concerned with his own comfort and oblivious, most of the time, of other people's feelings or safety, including that of his girlfriend, whom he sends to serve as his go-between in a drug deal he engineers with the blessing of the police.

The fault may be with the performance of Andreas Loeffel who suggests a shallow character with whom it is difficult to sympathize and thus deprives the film of its most important ingredient. The rest of the cast fits in better (albeit in easier jobs), and Bruno Ganz, probably the best-known Swiss actor today, handles the police inspector with the kind of rich ambivalence one would have liked to see in the lead.

Giger's other problem is his concern with mood at the expense of plot. His image of Bern's lowlife is credible all through, often humorous and with some nice human touches, particularly in scenes between Tom and his aunt. Technical credits are superior but the story itself lacks the careful attention dedicated to image or sound, and it is often left stranded, as if not important enough to elaborate upon, and leading to an inconclusive ending.

Giger's local reputation as well as the authentic flavor of his film may help it at home, but outside Switzerland it may be more difficult to handle.—*Edna.*

The Liberation Of Auschwitz
(GERMAN-DOCU-B&W)

A National Center for Jewish Film release of a Chronos-Film production. Produced by Bengt von zur Mühlen. Directed by Irmgard von zur Mühlen. Camera (b&w), Alexander Irmgard Vorontsov. Reviewed at Film Forum 1, N.Y., Aug. 6, 1986. Running time: **60 MINS.**

It was on the afternoon of Jan. 27, 1945, remembers Russian cameraman Alexander Vorontsov, when the Red Army overran the sprawling Auschwitz-Monowitz industrial complex. Vorontsov was there to film the joyous liberation of a labor camp, but the unexpected horror waiting within the camp's electrified confines soon redefined his role.

Vorontsov's footage is a thorough documentation of the atrocities that took place within the Nazis' largest, and deadliest, concentration camp. A portion of the film was shown as evidence during the Nuremberg trials, while the remainder has been stored for some 40 years in a Russian film vault.

Bengt and Irmgard von zur Mühlen (whose past films include the Oscar-nommed 1973 "The Battle Of Berlin" and 1981 "The Yellow Star" docus) have compiled the unearthed footage into a stark, shocking and unflinching testament to the countless millions who were murdered there.

The pair have not embellished the soundless footage with music, opting instead for a straightforward recital of the factual information gathered by the Soviets at the time of the camp's liberation. The camera pans over a mountain of private property confiscated by the Nazis from their victims — 348,000 men's suits, 158,000 dresses, tens of thousands of eyeglasses — and these are only a fraction, representing what could not be taken during a hasty retreat from the Soviet army.

Other images — a warehouse of bagged human hair intended to be made into felt for socks, huge gas chambers made to look like showers, survivors of medical experiments, a portable gallows, the uncomprehending gaze of freed prisoners — are indelible. The film stands as a powerful tool in efforts to never let the world forget what happened during Nazi rule. — *Roy.*

Royal Warriors
(HONG KONG-COLOR)

A D&B Films production and release. Executive producer, Dickson Poon. Produced by John Sham. Written and directed by Chung Chi Man. Camera (color), Chung Chi Man. (No other credits provided by producers.) Reviewed at Jade theater, Hong Kong, July 19, 1986. Running time: 93 MINS.
(Cantonese soundtrack with English subtitles)

Hong Kong — This latest D&B Films laugh-a-minute presentation has nothing royal about it. "Royal Warriors" is yet another expensive (supposedly $HK15,000,000) excursion into a mélange of cars, cops, rotten to the core criminals against charming people from the Royal Hong Kong Police Force. There is really no storyline and 95% of the performers must have graduated with honor from the Stone Age School of Performing Arts.

Michelle Kheng (a former Miss Malaysia beauty contest winner) is no better than costar Michael Wong, a handsome, American-born body beautiful, devoid of emotional depth or acting ability.

The screenwriter does not even give fictitious names to Michelle and Michael.

The film did well (grossed $HK13,000,000) at the Hong Kong boxoffice. The cinematography is erratic, from grainy or hazy to out-of-focus and the continuity is plain careless.—*Mel.*

Die Walsche
(The False One)
(GERMAN-AUSTRIAN-SWISS-COLOR-16m)

A ZDF/ORF/SRG presentation of a Peter Voiss (Munich) production. Produced by Peter Voiss. Directed by Werner Masten. Screenplay, Masten, Joseph Zoderer from Zoderer's novel "Die Walsche," camera (color), Klaus Eichhamer; editor, Michael Breining; music, Muzzi Loffredo; sound, Dieter Laske; art direction, Peter Kaser; production manager, Jörg Schifferer; costumes, Karin Gulberlet. Reviewed at the Morettina Film Center, Locarno Film Festival (in competition), Aug. 9, 1986. Running time: 95 MINS.
Olga ....Marie Colbin
Silvano ....Lino Capolicchio
Also with: Johannes Thanheiser (the fa-

ther), Martin Abram (Florian), Michele Remo Remotti, Anni Pircher, Siegelinde Müller, Otto Donner, Raimund Marini.

Locarno — The title's literal translation is "The False One," but the meaning in this case is something like "the tramp." It is a derogatory nickname used by the German-speaking minority in Northern Italy for anyone denying his roots and fraternizing with the southerners.

Name is applied to Olga, a young woman who has left the village in which she was born, and gone to live with an Italian in Bolzano. The ensuing conflict, while clearly localized in the Dolomites, easily could be transported to any similar socio-political background anywhere in the world.

The plot is condensed into a period of three days, from the moment Olga is told her father has just died back home, until she leaves the village after his burial. In between, she has to face the animosity of her own people, for whom she was traitor, but also her own alienation from her man and his friends, leading a train of life she can't get used to. All through the film, she persists in her stubborn decision to speak only German, both to her own people and to the Italians, who accept her mania good-humoredly, and she finds herself in the uncomfortable position of feeling a stranger on both sides.

While the theme is both valid and relevant, helmer Werner Masten walks into several pitfalls, complicating his life needlessly. By going back and forth in time, transposing events that happened in the past into the present, he often confuses his audience and distracts it from the thrust of the story.

In spite of his belonging to the German minority, his sympathy clearly is on the Italian side, portrayed as rambunctious, noisy, over-familiar in their relations, but finally positive in their attitude, while the German lot, in the village, is a threatening, backward, even slightly degenerated community, sometimes reminiscent of the villagers in Sam Peckinpah's "Straw Dogs."

Austrian actress Marie Colbin, who has a sound reputation in German-speaking countries due to "The Bachmeier Affair," gives another one of her highstrung performances, nicely balanced by a more relaxed Lino Capolicchio as her Italian partner.

Technical credits are satisfactory except for some empty spots on the soundtrack, left there for no evident purpose in the mixing.—*Edna.*

Jour et Nuit
(Day And Night)
(SWISS-FRENCH-COLOR)

A Challenger Films release (Metropolis Films, Zürich outside Switzerland) of a Strada Films (Geneva), Flach Films (Paris) production. Directed by Jean-Pierre Menoud. Screenplay, Menoud, Hubert Selby Jr.; camera (color), Patrick Blossier; editor, Christine Benoit; music, Dmitri Shostakovich (selections from orchestral works); sound, François Musy. Reviewed at the Morettina Center, Locarno Film Festival (in competition), Aug. 10, 1986. Running time: 90 MINS.
With: Peter Bonke (Harry), Mireille Perrier (Anna), Patrick Fierry (John), Lisbeth Koutchoumow (Ingrid).

Locarno — Jean-Pierre Menoud's first feature film is a moody piece taking his protagonists exactly nowhere. Hubert Selby's script, said to have been inspired by Dostoevsky's "Notes From The Underground," follows four characters in their doomed search for happiness, doomed, so it seems, because the scripter couldn't find it in himself to grant them more than that.

Harry is a Danish diplomat stationed in Switzerland, divorced and living with his teenage daughter, Ingrid. John drives a limousine and serves as go-between from time to time in other kinds of business to improve his income. Anna supplies pleasant company to rich tourists at high rates, while Ingrid is going through her first sexual explorations.

Harry is in a black mood from the very first moment, but he seems to lighten up when he meets the lively driver and goes hunting with him. He almost comes alive when an affair with Anna seems to blossom, but finally he doesn't have the courage to face a chance at happiness and destroys it all with his own hands.

All this may sound great in theory, the man who is afraid to give himself a break, but on screen it doesn't move, neither emotionally nor physically. It is difficult to identify with a handsome man with a solid economic situation, nice friends and a great daughter who adores him, who puts himself through hell for reasons he does not care to elaborate.

All of which is a pity because the actors do a nice job, particularly Lisbeth Koutchoumow as the bewildered girl facing sex for the first time with no help from her father, and Mireille Perrier as the call girl tempted for a minute to believe in true romance. Menoud, a former cameraman who has worked for Jean-Luc Godard, manages to get some fascinating images from his cameraman, and several sequences, taken separately, indicate promise that does not materialize the rest of the time. —*Edna.*

El Mercado De Humildes
(Market Of The Humble)
(MEXICAN-COLOR)

A Videocine release of a Televicine production. Directed by René Cardona Jr. Stars Rafael Inclán. Screenplay, Alfonso Torres Portillo, Fernando Galiana; camera (color), Raúl Domínguez; editor, Sergio Soto; music, H. Baltazar. Reviewed at Big Apple Cine 2, N.Y., July 29, 1986. Running time: 87 MINS.
El Multiple ....Rafael Inclán
Lupe .Maribel (La Pelongocha) Fernández
Rita ....Leticia Perdigón
Concepción (Conchita) ....Lilia Prado
Don Próculo ..Pedro Weber (Chatanooga)
Pistón..........Manuel (El Flaco) Ibañez
Maid ....Lupita Sandoval
Mariela ....Edith González
Also with: Mario Cid, Carlos East, Lyn May.

In recent years, Mexico's most internationally recognized director of low-budget schlock dramas, René Cardona Jr. (best known in the Anglo market for terrors such as "Guyana, The Cult Of The Damned," "Alive" and last year's "Treasure Of The Amazon"), has turned his attentions back to the domestic market, making films in Spanish and exploiting national themes.

Working with Televicine, motion picture production arm of the Mexican tv conglomerate Televisa, Cardona has directed feature film versions of Televisa small-screen properties "Siempre En Domingo" and "Cachún Cachún, Ra-Ra." His latest Televicine undertaking unsuccessfully tries to mix humor with social statement and emerges with the uneven comedy "El Mercado De Humildes" (Market Of The Humble), originally filmed in 1984 under the moniker "Lagunilla 3."

The low-budget "El Mercado De Humildes" does not possess the charm of some earlier comedies. The plot concerns the misadventures of Multiple (played by character actor Rafael Inclán) and his family and friends who inhabit the Lagunilla-Tepito market areas of Mexico City, a combination flea market, thieves market and center for contraband electronics items.

All of the male characters strive for a better life but no one besides antique shop owner Don Próculo (Pedro Weber) wants to earn it. They all just want to have fun and at the same time blame Mexico's economic problems and their own lowly birth as the reason for not having big cars, fancy homes and other bourgeois niceties.

In order to achieve a better life, Multiple sneaks his family across the border into the U.S., where he plans to be rolling in bucks by selling stolen merchandise. Don Próculo, however, is punished for his kindness and hard work by having his shop ransacked while he is away on vacation.

Multiple brings his family back to Mexico and they all use the money he has earned abroad to open up a modest family restaurant in Don Próculo's empty store front and they all live happily ever after.

The message of the pic is that even though the characters don't have a lot of money, their true riches are to be found in their family and friends.

This is all well and good, but Cardona approaches the material with little imagination and most of the humor and interest lie in the script's one-liner sense of comedy. Lensing by Raúl Domínguez is purely functional.

It seems that after years of making second-rate horror movies and cheapo shock dramas, Cardona doesn't really have a feel for comedy. — *Lent.*

Extremities
(COLOR)

Intense drama stands to stir up emotions, controversy and respectable b.o.

An Atlantic Releasing Corp. release. Produced by Burt Sugarman. Executive producers, Thomas Coleman, Michael Rosenblatt. Directed by Robert M. Young. Line producers, George W. Perkins, Scott Rosenfelt. Screenplay, William Mastrosimone, from his play; camera (color), Curtis Clark; editor, Arthur Coburn; music, J.A.C. Redford; production design, Chester Kaczenski; assistant directors, Sharon Mann, Victoria E. Rhodes; casting, Richard Pagano. Reviewed at the Mark Goodson Theater, N.Y., Aug. 8, 1986. (MPAA Rating: R.) Running time: **90 MINS.**
Marjorie ....Farrah Fawcett
Joe ....James Russo
Terry....................Diana Scarwid
Patricia ....Alfre Woodard
    Also with: Sandy Martin, Eddie Velez, Tom Everett, Donna Lynn Leavy, Enid Kent.

Benefiting from steadfast direction and true performances, pic version of "Extremities" is a taut and powerful drama that will probably rattle audiences more than entertain them. Sure-handed, fair treatment of grave subject matter should generate b.o.-abetting word-of-mouth.

Since its off-Broadway premiere in late 1982, "Extremities" has been performed several times in the U.S. and abroad. Playwright Mastrosimone adapted his personal work for the screen, but it seems to be director Robert M. Young who is responsible for virtually exploiting cinema's power to propel the viewer into the on-screen action.

Pic starts off from the point-of-view of a motorcyclist who is stalking a number of women at a shop-

Original Play

Frank Gero, Mark Gero, Chris Gero, Jason Gero & Della Koenig presentation of a drama in two acts by William Mastrosimone. Staged by Robert Allan Ackerman; setting, Marjorie Bradley Kellogg; lighting, Arden Fingerhut; costumes, Robert Wojewodski; fight staging, B.H. Barry; sound, Scott Lehrer; general manager, Randy Finch; company manager, Kim Sellon; stage managers, Louis Pietig, Jonathan Gero; publicity, Solters, Roskin & Friedman. Opened Dec. 22, '82, at the Westside Arts Center, N.Y.; $18 top weeknights, $20 weekends.
Cast: Susan Sarandon, James Russo, Ellen Barkin, Deborah Hedwall.

ping center. Settling on Marjorie (Farrah Fawcett), a museum employee on her way home from work and a workout, the ski-masked assailant imprisons and terrorizes her in her own car.

Marjorie manages to escape but the attacker knows her identity and address. Successive events document the trials of any woman in a similar predicament: essentially unsympathetic police and friends, insomnia, fear of things that go bump in the night, yen to own a gun, suspicion of men.

Finally, Marjorie's worst night-

mare comes true. She is visited at her secluded home by the man who attacked her (James Russo). Taunting and tyrannical, Joe graphically humiliates and brutalizes Marjorie. At the point where rape and murder look inevitable, Marjorie blinds her assailant with bug spray, starting a startling reversal of roles that must be a catharsis for anyone who is familiar with the experience.

Pic could have turned into another kind of "Death Wish," but Marjorie's roommates (Diana Scarwid and Alfre Woodard) gradually convince her killing him is not the answer. She settles for a confession, which Joe emotionally provides after Marjorie gives him a harsh taste of his own medicine.

Young keeps his direction as controlled as the relatively brief running time. In order to involve the viewer, he effectively favors tight closeups of each character, and at the start of their followup encounter, Fawcett and Russo speak their lines to each other right into the camera.

Fawcett, who acquainted herself with the role of Marjorie on stage following Susan Sarandon and Karen Allen, acts with a confidence and control not often seen in her screen work.

Adapting his stage role to film, Russo draws a sharp portrait of a hissable maniac at the outset, ultimately developing into a pathetic victim himself toward the end. In between, he's even a source of comic relief as he squints and snarls demands for his attorney as he's crouched in the hearth bound by an electrical cord.

Initially, Scarwid also adds a comic dimension to her role as the roommate who is as shocked by Marjorie's vengeful plans as much by the would-be rapist. Later, her big moment emerges when she reveals she was raped as a child, but kept quiet about it.

Representing the unpopular voice of modern justice, Woodard gives as much, if not more, sympathy to the perpetrator than the victim.

Technical contributions are all pretty much first-rate, especially J.A.C. Redford's music, fitting background to the dire events.
— *Binn.*

One More Saturday Night
(COLOR)

Messed up comedy of the Midwest.

A Columbia Pictures release of a AAR/Tova Laiter production. Produced by Laiter, Robert Kosberg, Jonathan Bernstein. Executive producer, Dan Aykroyd. Directed by Dennis Klein. Screenplay, Al Franken, Tom Davis; camera (Astro Color Labs (Chicago) color, prints by DeLuxe), James Glennon; editor, Gregory Prange; music,

David McHugh; sound, Wayne Artman, Tom Beckert, Tom E. Dahl; set decoration, Karen O'Hara; costume designs, Mickey Antonetti, Jay Hurley; second unit director, Gregory Prange; assistant director, William Hassell; casting, Jane Alderman, Glenn Williams. Reviewed at the Directors Guild, L.A., Aug. 14, 1986. (MPAA Rating: R.) Running time: **95 MINS.**
Larry.....................Tom Davis
Paul ....Al Franken
Peggy ....Moira Harris
Eddie ....Frank Howard
Tobi ....Bess Meyer
Russ Cadwell ....Dave Reynolds
Dad Lundahl...............Chelcie Ross
Doug ....Eric Saiet
Traci ....Jessica Schwartz

Hollywood — Weekends in a small Minnesota town may get awfully tedious, but who'd want to pay to sit through "One More Saturday Night" to find out? Even the most bored midwesterner can find something better to do. Pic deserves to be deep-sixed in Lake Superior.

The good reputations that co-scripters Tom Davis and Al Franken made in their association with "Saturday Night Live" have been effectively sullied with this effort.

Film has virtually no redeeming moments, not even ones featuring these two as horny band members panting after a couple of naive local high school girls.

For what it's worth, action revolves around activities of several groups on a Saturday night in St. Cloud, Minn.: a babysitter and her boyfriend, a couple of hapless teenage cat burglars, a nervous middle-aged widow on a first date, a pubescent nosy kid brother and a scorned boyfriend.

Script contains few one-liners, presumably because filmmakers hoped to make up for the absence of funny dialog in scenes where the action creates humor.

Setups aren't conducive to creating original comedy.

It's amateur hour before the cameras, too. Actors would be better cast in a student film. —*Brit.*

Touch And Go
(COLOR)

Unsure drama needs a push.

A Tri-Star release. Produced by Stephen Friedman. Executive producer, Harry Colomby. Directed by Robert Mandel. Screenplay, Alan Ormsby, Bob Sand, Harry Colomby; camera, Astro Labs (Chicago), Movielab (Los Angeles) color; prints by Technicolor), Richard H. Kline; editor, Walt Mulconery; music, Sylvester Levay; production design, Charles Rosen; set decoration, James Payne, Jean Akan; costume design, Bernie Pollack; sound, Arthur Rochester, Glenn Williams; assistant directors, Paul Deason, Gary Daigler; second unit director, Jack Grossberg; second unit camera, Gregory Lundsgaard; casting, Penny Perry, Deborah Brown. Reviewed at Lorimar-Telepictures, Culver City, Calif., Aug. 8, 1986. (MPAA Rating: R.) Running time: **101 MINS.**
Bobby Barbato ....Michael Keaton
Denise DeLeon ...Maria Conchita Alonso
Louis DeLeon ....Ajay Naidu

Dee Dee	Maria Tucci
Lester	Max Wright
Courtney	Lara Jill Miller
Lupo	D.V. de Vincentis

Hollywood — "Touch And Go" mixes humor, heart and considerable hokum in an engaging story matching an unusually serious Michael Keaton and zesty Latin star Maria Conchita Alonso as lovers in spite of themselves brought together by her juvenile delinquent son. Pic has been on the shelf for over a year and needs a big campaign to attract an audience, considering it's now being released against more highly commercial summer fare. Film has the potential to be a sleeper, more likely will be in vid stores first.

Pic features Keaton as a hot-shot hockey jock with the Chicago Eagles, spending his time off the ice either training or watching himself in replays on the VCR sitting alone in his high-tech, high-rise lakefront apartment. Relationships with females take the form of one-night stands with women who come on to him in bars.

His regimen gets disrupted one night when a punk kid (Ajay Naidu) acts as the innocent front for his thug friends as they try to mug the sports star as he gets into his Jaguar outside the deserted Eagles arena after a game. Keaton fends the rascals off, they split and he's left throttling the 11-year-old.

But the kid's a charmer and talks his way out of being taken to the police, and Keaton gives in, returning him home to his slummy neighborhood and to Mom (Alonso) for discipline — putting a quick end to Keaton's isolated life and opening the way for romance.

While certainly typecast, Alonso is very engaging as the hot-headed Latina, partially blaming her son's bad behavior on her own irresponsibility (she never married his father) and on his crummy environment. Her feelings are clear, wanting to get something going with the steely Keaton — even if he insists he's not interested.

Rapport between the disrespectful kid and Keaton unfolds immediately, which is less true of the athlete's relationship with Alonso.

Naidu plays the pivotal role, never too much the smart alec or the vulnerable lost soul in search of a father figure. He prevents scenes from becoming too sappy, and they would if Keaton weren't always so cool and wasn't given so many caustic lines.

Keaton more easily can dismiss the flaky Mom's disruption into his life than he can the impressionable kid. Alonso seems to irritate Keaton at the outset. It's when he finally relaxes and takes on some added character other than a macho man that the story begins to work.

Unfortunately, this all happens well into the pic and after stops and starts playing the crusty Keaton off against the kid, the mom, the relatives, etc. — until finally he finds himself inextricably head of a family.

It all comes together a little too succinctly in the end and it may not be a stand-up-and-cheer kind of film, but it still leaves one with a warm feeling with a lot more to say about commitment than so many other, more pretentious pics.

Prints by Technicolor were grainy.
—*Brit.*

Armed And Dangerous
(COLOR)

Funny bits don't add up to much; b.o. chances slim.

A Columbia Pictures release. Produced by Brian Grazer, James Keach. Directed by Mark L. Lester. Screenplay, by Harold Ramis, Peter Torokvei, from a story by Grazer, Ramis, Keach; camera (Deluxe color), Fred Schuler; editors, Michael Hill, Daniel Hanley, George Pedugo; music, Bill Meyers; production design, David L. Snyder; set decorator, Tom Pedigo; sound (Dolby stereo), Richard Raguse; assistant director, Robert P. Cohen; associate producer, Christopher Mankiewicz, Jerry Baerwitz; costumes, Deborah L. Scott; casting, Jane Jenkins, Janet Hirshenson. Reviewed at Samuel Goldwyn theater, Beverly Hills, Aug. 7, 1986. (MPAA Rating: PG-13.) Running time: **88 MINS.**

Frank Dooley	John Candy
Norman Kane	Eugene Levy
Michael Carlino	Robert Loggia
Clarence O'Connell	Kenneth McMillan
Maggie Cavanaugh	Meg Ryan
Anthony Lazarus	Brion James
Clyde Klepper	Jonathan Banks
Sergeant Rizzo	Don Stroud
The Cowboy	Steve Railsback

Hollywood — "Armed And Dangerous" is a broad farce slightly elevated by the presence of John Candy and Eugene Levy. Material is ordinary at best, but the two SCTV veterans are able to milk laughs out of even the weakest setups. After some initial firepower, pic is likely to run out of ammunition at the boxoffice.

Somewhere, deep inside development, this project may have had a good idea behind it, but as executed here it's painfully thin. Script by Harold Ramis and Peter Torokvei is a perfunctory effort without much to keep it going. Luckily Candy and Levy are on hand.

Story functions as little more than a fashion show for Candy, as a cop, then a security officer and later in motorcycle garb. But the pièce de résistance is Candy in a blue tuxedo with a ruffled shirt that makes his enormous bulk look like a wrapped Christmas present.

Candy plays one of L.A.'s finest until he's wrongfully kicked off the force for corruption. He winds up at Guard Dog Security where he teams with shyster lawyer Levy on a new career. Company, it turns out, is under the thumb of the mob headed by union honcho Robert Loggia. Also on hand is Kenneth McMillan as the exploited owner and Meg Ryan as his daughter and Levy's would-be love interest.

It's all pretty basic stuff delivered with a minimum of imagination. Characters and their problems are strictly two-dimensional. Ryan is likable as the boss' lovely daughter and Levy is endearing, in an offbeat way, as the romantic hero, but what their attraction is based on remains a mystery. Things have a way of just happening in this film.

Director Mark Lester allows Candy free rein and in isolated scenes — fully clothed in a steam room or chased by guard dogs — he recalls the inspired lunacy of SCTV. Unfortunately script doesn't supply enough context to make the physical humor more effective than a five-minute skit.

Production values are fine, with kudos to costume designer Deborah L. Scott. —*Jagr.*

The Whoopee Boys
(COLOR)

Would-be comedy takes the low road to nowhere.

A Paramount release of an Adam Fields-David Obst production. Produced by Fields, Peter Macgregor-Scott. Executive producers, Steve Zacharias, Jeff Buhai, Obst. Directed by John Byrum. Screenplay, Zacharias, Buhai, Obst; camera (Continental Film Labs color; Technicolor prints), Ralf D. Bode; editor, Eric Jenkins; music, Jack Nitsche; production design, Charles Rosen; set decoration, Don Ivey; costume design, Patricia Norris; sound, Bill Kaplan; assistant director, Richard Espinoza; casting, Sally Dennison, Julie Selzer, Risa Bramon, Billy Hopkins. Reviewed at the Paramount Studios, L.A., Aug. 14, 1986. (MPAA Rating: R.) Running time: **88 MINS.**

Jake Bateman	Michael O'Keefe
Barney	Paul Rodriguez
Colonel Phelps	Denholm Elliott
Henrietta Phelps	Carole Shelley
Roy Raja	Andy Bumatai
Eddie	Eddie Deezen
Officer White	Marsha Warfield
Shelley	Elizabeth Arlen
Clorinda Antonucci	Karen A. Smythe
Guido Antonucci	Joe Spinell
Humping the Butler	Robert Gwaltney
Olivia	Lucinda Jenney
Judge Sternhill	Dan O'Herlihy
Strobe	Stephen Davies
Whitey	Taylor Negron
Tipper	Greg Germann

Hollywood — A very late, redundant entry in the bad taste sweepstakes, "The Whoopee Boys" is an equal opportunity picture — every ethnic group is represented, and thereby equally insulted. Crude sex jokes on parade here sound like rejects from the "Porky's" catalog, and scriptwriting technique employed resembles painting-by-numbers with a limited palette —

blue, bluer and bluest. Commericial prospects for this low-flying fowl appear equally limited, and first results will be known from regional openings currently underway in the South and Southwest.

As in a tacky, domestic variation on Prince's "Under The Cherry Moon," pic takes New York City street hustlers Michael O'Keefe and Paul Rodriquez to cushy Palm Beach, where they attempt to crash high society. Even though they are not instantly installed on the A-list for parties, the lewdsome twosome end up helping out at the delapidated mansion of a blond heiress, who runs a school there and quickly needs to marry an acceptable young fellow in order to receive her inheritance and thereby save the estate from being turned into condos.

O'Keefe decides to win the lady's hand, so he and his Latino buddy enroll in a Florida swampland charm school, which is run by Denholm Elliott and Carole Shelley and attended by apparent Police Academy delinquents.

No one seems to learn anything, but back to Palm Beach they go to, inevitably, disrupt a major social function and show up the rich folks for the pompous fools they undoubtedly sometimes are.

Rodriquez, the irreverent East Los Angeles comedian, here specializes in anatomical jokes of every possible persuasion, and does a number of perverted things with fruits, vegetables and cooked animals. One hopes he's now explored all the possibilities in this area and sees clear to moving on to more fertile comic terrain next time.

As his straightman, O'Keefe doesn't look good in a Don Johnson shave. Eddie Deezen and Marsha Warfield have a couple of moments as hopeless students at the charm school but, otherwise, director John Byrum does absolutely nothing with the numerous character actors who were assembled and, presumably, ready and eager to work. —*Cart.*

Hands Of Steel
(ITALIAN-COLOR)

An Almi Pictures release of a National Cinematografica/Dania Film/Medusa Distribuzione production. Directed by "Martin Dolman" (Sergio Martino). Stars Daniel Greene, Janet Agren. Screenplay, "Dolman," Elisabeth Parker, Saul Sasha, John Crowther, from story by "Dolman;" additional dialog, Lewis Clanelli; camera (Luciano Vittori color), "John McFerrand" (Giancarlo Ferrando); music, Claudio Simonetti; special makeup effects, Sergio Stivaletti; special effects, Robert Callmard, Paul Callmard; explosion effects, Elio Terry. Reviewed at Delray Drive-In 1 theater, Delray Beach, Fla., Aug. 9, 1986. (MPAA Rating: R.) Running time: **94 MINS.**

Paco Querak	Daniel Greene
Linda	Janet Agren
Francis Turner	John Saxon
Raoul Fernandez	George Eastman

Dr. Peckinpaugh . . . . Amy Werba
Also with: Claudio Cassinelli, Robert Ben, Pat Monti, Andrew Louis Coppola, Donald O'Brien.

Delray Beach — "Hands Of Steel" is a derivative, often silly Italian sci-fi action pic that entered regional domestic release in April. Film is second title (following "After The Fall Of New York") from filmmaker Sergio Martino (who again uses the pseudonym "Martin Dolman") to be distributed by Almi.

Beefy American tv actor Daniel Greene (previously seen in the Spanish production "Pulsebeat") toplines as Paco Querak, whom we find out is a cyborg with 70% of his body mechanically remade after an accident by scientists working for evil Francis Turner (John Saxon). Film is set in the near future, with Turner having Paco programmed to assassinate Rev. Arthur Mosely, a blind ecologist who heads up a national movement whose environmental goals threaten Turner's industrial interests.

Paco's vestige of humanity prevents him from coldbloodedly killing Mosely with a deadly judo chop from one of his bionic hands, but a lesser blow puts Mosely into the hospital and sets off a chase for Paco, led by FBI forensic expert Dr. Peckinpaugh (Amy Werba).

Paco heads for Arizona, where he was born, in an attempt to regain his memories and thereby his humanity. He is befriended by the beautiful owner of a truckstop cafe/motel, Linda (Janet Agren), and film promptly detours into sublime territory. Prefiguring (and beating to the marketplace) the long-in-the-works Sylvester Stallone vehicle "Over The Top," Paco repeatedly becomes involved in Western genre-style confrontations with truckers in which the payoff is not a shootout or fist fight but an arm wrestling match.

Our bionic ringer of a hero naturally dusts off all the local champions but almost meets his match when Turner sends a blond girl (slavishly styled to imitate Daryl Hannah in "Blade Runner"), who is actually a cyborg, to kill him. Ultimately Turner shows up to do the job himself, wielding a laser cannon, but Paco survives and pic ends on an unconvincing "am I at all human?" note.

Greene is well-cast as an imitation of Arnold Schwarzenegger's "The Terminator" character thanks to his muscular physique, but his stiff acting fails to arouse sympathy in the man vs. machine self-questioning scenes. His funniest line comes during an incipient romantic scene with Scandinavian beauty Agren, as Greene declares: "Linda, I want to show you something,"

and instead of reaching to his button fly jeans he exposes his mechanical arm to her. Agren and the supporting cast (including Claudio Cassinelli, who died during filming) are okay, speaking in a mixture of direct-sound and dubbed dialog.

Tech credits emphasize scenic Arizona locations and Claudio Simonetti comes up with his usual high standard of energetic electronic keyboards for the musical score.—*Lor.*

Diapason
(ARGENTINE-COLOR)

A P.K.H. (Buenos Aires) production. Executive producer, Pedro Passarini. Written and directed by Jorge Polaco. Camera (color), Carlos Torlaschi; editor, José del Peón; music, Lito Vitale; sound, Abelardo Kuschnir; art director, Rodolfo Hermida; sets and costumes, Norma Romano; production manager, Javier Szerman. Reviewed at the Morettina Center, Locarno Film Festival (in competition), Aug. 10, 1986. Running time: **94 MINS.**
With: Harry Havilio (Ignacio), Marta Frydman (Boncha), Margot Moreyra (Margarita), Carlos Kaufman (Franz)

Locarno — In the tradition of the Spanish-speaking surrealist cinema established by Luis Buñuel, Jorge Polaco's first feature film is a harsh, uncompromising and unusually cruel criticism of middle-class morality, combined with snipes at the political climate in the recent past of his country, Argentina. Probably because of the helmer's relative lack of experience, he tends to indulge in sometimes gratuitous flights of fancy, but he drives his message home unerringly.

The message is that the forcible attempt of one person to mold another into what he imagines to be an ideal shape can only result in total destruction of both parties. In this case, a 50-ish man with blueblood illusions picks up a woman his own age, a lively and endearing slob, and tries to make a lady out of her, to fit his own pretty grotesque ideas of that definition.

This Pygmalion situation develops quickly into a satire of the values represented by the man, whose sexual hangups, combined with countless other manias, leave no doubt he is intended as a caricature of the degenerate bourgeois mentality, his behavior being sufficiently despotical to suggest political significance as well. Point is that Ignacio's efforts to impose his rules on the hapless Boncha are in no way different from the measures employed by regimes to tell their subjects what is good for them, whether they like it or not.

A considerable amount of nudity by actors who are well past their physical prime may shock some of the audience, intentionally so since Polaco's dispassionate look at his characters and the imperfections of

their bodies as well as their minds displays a brutal irony but also anger and despair.

The script, which up to a certain point is focused clearly on the Ignacio-Boncha relationship, tends to veer at a certain point to more general aspects, tries to use a film-within-a-film climax and gets stuck inconclusively as it can't find a satisfactory solution for the narrative line. Some of the sequences in the second part of the film, dedicated to the decadence of the two servants observing their masters' conduct and aping it, go overboard in their effort to reinforce things that already have been said.

Harry Havilio and particularly Marta Frydman appear to be totally devoted to their parts, Frydman essaying with a lot of courage the character of Boncha, the true explosive, magnetic Jewish dynamo, hopelessly trying to fit into what she believes for a time to be the better world.

While this is hardly the kind of film to please large audiences who may be both bewildered and offended by some of the sights, it is an item art circuits could go for willingly.
—*Edna.*

Il Camorrista
(The Professor)
(ITALIAN-COLOR)

A Titanus release (Intra Films world sales) of a Titanus and Reteitalia coproduction. Executive producer, Arlac Film. Line producer, Enzo Silvestri. Directed by Giuseppe Tornatore. Stars Ben Gazzara, Laura Del Sol. Screenplay, Massimo De Rita, Tornatore, based on the novel "Il Camorrista" by Giuseppe Marrazzo; camera (Eastmancolor; prints by Telecolor), Blasco Giurato; editor, Mario Morra; art direction, Osvaldo Desideri, Antonio Visone; costumes, Luciana Marinucci; music, Nicola Piovani; sound, Gianfranco Cabiddu. Reviewed at Telecolor screening room, Rome, Aug. 11, 1986. Running time: **140 MINS.**
The Professor . . . . Ben Gazzara
Rosaria . . . . Laura Del Sol
Chief Jervolino . . . . Leo Gullotta

Rome — The recent boom in Mafia and Camorra films has included several b.o. hits (Squitieri's "The Repented," Wertmüller's "Camorra"), suggesting that newspaper stories are more violent, exciting and dramatic than most scriptwriters' imaginations.

Titanus' classy big-budget entry "The Professor" should cash in on the fashion, both as an overly long theatrical film and five-episode tv series. Based on a book by newsman Giuseppe Marrazzo, it is the thinly veiled story of one of the bloodiest criminals ever to organize the Neapolitan underworld, Raffaele Cutolo. The inherent repulsiveness of its central character — here monikered simply "The Professor" — sorely tries the skills of Yank lead Ben Gazzara, who slowly builds

momentum through pic's two-and-a-half-hour running time until finally breaking through to the audience somewhere near the end. Meanwhile, with nary a sympathetic character in sight, pic plows ruthlessly ahead through a chronicle of infamies that have to be enjoyed for themselves, as it were.

Stylishly lensed with a professional feeling for action directing by Giuseppe Tornatore, one of the season's most striking debut helmers, "Professor" shows Gazzara's cold-blooded rise to power within the walls of a prison. He has been sentenced for his half-crazed murder of a stranger who made overtures to his sister Rosaria (a subdued Laura Del Sol). The semi-incestuous gangster-sister rapport, with its echoes of "Scarface," provides the only undercurrent of human warmth in the professor's life. While he recruits a private army of desperados inside, sis pays off their needy families outside, thus commandeering their indestructible loyalty as her brother moves up the ladder.

After butchering the head of the old crime syndicate, Gazzara takes his place and, from his cell, wages a war to gain control of Naples' thriving rackets. Bodies swing from every meat-hook, until the Professor stages a flamboyant prison bust and heads for New York to connive with the Cosa Nostra.

It is long into the film before anyone turns up to challenge his authority; by the time modest but honest police chief Jervolino (well-limned by Leo Gullotta, who gets more beaten up and mangled with every scene) begins meting out law and order, auds have given up hoping the prof's demonic power can be tamed. Not only does he have American gangster Frank Titas' entrails ripped out, barely offscreen, and his best friend's eyes gouged out for supposed betrayal, he also is shown with the country's top politicians under his thumb. Even terrorists from the Red Brigades come to him for help. Miraculously, Jervolino finally renders him innocuous in a maximum security prison, at which point film ends.

Though pic abounds with well-staged incident atmospherically filmed by cameraman Blasco Giurato and plaintively scored by Italo soundtrack king Nicola Piovani, its first half is sadly lacking in dramatic impetus. Tighter editing and sacrifice of footage in the tv version would be a great help, because newcomer Tornatore demonstrates a talent for classy lensing and exciting action sequences.—*Yung.*

Noir et Blanc
(Black And White)
(FRENCH-B&W)

A Forum Distribution presentation of a Films du Volcan production with the assistance of the Ministry of Culture. Written and directed by Claire Devers. Camera (black & white, Delta Print Laboratories), Daniel Desbois, Christophe Doyle, Alain Lasfargues, Jean Paul Da Costa; editors, Fabienne Alvarez, Yves Sarda; sound, Pierry Donnadieu; art director, Anne Isabelle Estrada. Reviewed at the Morettina Center, Locarno Film Festival (out of competition), Aug. 12, 1986. Running time: **80 MINS**.
With: Francis Frappat (Antoine), Jacques Martial (Dominique), Josephine Fresson, Marc Berman, Benoit Regent, Christophe Galland, the Rhapsodes Choir.

Locarno — Recipient of the Camera d'Or award in Cannes as the best first film, Claire Devers' effort shows considerable subtlety leading to a blood-curling climax that is logical but totally unexpected.

Pic traces the strange relationship between an anonymous young accountant sent to check the books of a health club and a black masseur working there. To begin with, the typical, cultured, white middle-class pen-pusher, a timid person whose hobby consists of singing classical music in an amateur choir, thinks it would be a good idea to get back in shape as a fringe benefit of his job. However, without anything being said, a sadomasochistic dependence develops between these two, the first discovering the sensual pleasure of being manhandled and even maimed while his partner cooperates tacitly in this dangerous game.

Soon enough, the physical evidence of this obsession cannot be dissimulated any more. The accountant, his body all black and blue, tries to lie his way out of it, until the couple is caught in action by the health club's owner and are thrown out in disgust. The victim has to be hospitalized with broken bones, he escapes with the assistance of the masseur, they spend a desperate night in a fleabag hotel and when they leave the next day, it is to prepare ritualistically the gruesome end the accountant has prepared for himself, which could be interpreted as both the ultimate punishment for his crime against the morality he was brought up in, or as the ultimate consummation of his obsession.

Devers uses a minimum of means to tell her story. There is practically no dialog, and what there is of it is intentionally irrelevant except for the last dialog between the two protagonists, in which everything is implied.

The title refers to the relations between a white and a black man, but also is relevant to the stock used, and to the accountant's world.

Careful, well-framed photography and two actors who fit it physically with their roles and are asked to keep emotions undercover to the bitter end, help Devers achieve her goal. She certainly goes to extremes to make her point, and does it with a disturbing persistence, which may offend part of the audience.
— *Edna.*

Full Moon High
(COLOR)

Promising werewolf spoof goes flat.

An Orion Pictures release of a Filmways/Larco production. Produced, written and directed by Larry Cohen. Camera (color), Daniel Pearl; music, Gary W. Friedman; art direction, Robert Burns; makeup, Steve Neill. Reviewed at The Public Theater, N.Y., Aug. 8, 1986. (MPAA Rating: PG.) Running time: **93 MINS**.
With: Adam Arkin, Roz Kelly, Elizabeth Hartman, Ed McMahon, Kenneth Mars, Joanne Nail, Pat Morita, Alan Arkin, Louis Nye, John Blythe Barrymore.

"Full Moon High," Larry Cohen film that enjoyed a brief regional release in 1981 but just now receiving Gotham theatrical exposure, begins as a promising tongue-in-cheek remake of the 1957 science-fictioner "I Was A Teenage Werewolf," but soon transforms into a plodding, toothless yarn (or yawn). Pic, which leaves few shticks unturned, has resurfaced in a Cohen retro and is reviewed here for the record.

Film opens in the 1950s setting of Full Moon High School, where student Tony Walker (Adam Arkin) is the big man on campus as the captain of the football team. Before he can lead his team to victory in the big game against a rival school, Tony is sidetracked by his CIA dad (humorously limned by Ed McMahon) to Rumania, where he is bitten by a werewolf.

Campy mix of wordplay and slapstick is effective here and for several reels afterward, as Tony loses the ability to play football (he keeps hearing Rumanian violin music) and starts turning into a werewolf who nips, rather than bites, his victims. Headline of the local newspaper reading "Werewolf Annoys Community" captures the breezy mood perfectly.

The center does not hold, unfortunately, when Tony leaves the town for 20 years to wander the earth as one of the living dead. One wonders if Cohen had a script that continued past this point, as the remaining scenes follow a disjointed and convoluted course that has something to do with Tony returning to the present day high school so he can win the big football game he never had the chance to play in.

Parodies of the hand-from-the-grave scene in "Carrie" and shower scene in "Psycho" provide some laughs, and Kenneth Mars, Alan Arkin, Louis Nye and Pat Morita are strong in bit parts that provide momentary lifts to the otherwise flat second half of the film.—*Roy.*

Cocaine Wars
(COLOR)

Dull and derivative blast-'em-up.

A Concorde Pictures release of an Aries/Roger Corman production. Produced by Alex Sessa and Roger Corman. Directed by Hector Olivera. Screenplay, Steven M. Krauzer, based on a story by David Vinas, Olivera; camera (color), Victor Kaulen; editor, Edward Lowe; sound, Norman Newcastle; makeup, Laura Lowe; production manager, Alex Plowing; stunts, Arthur Chestnut. Reviewed at the UA Twin Cinema, N.Y., Aug. 12, 1986. (MPAA Rating: R.) Running time: **83 MINS**.
With: John Schneider, Kathryn Witt, Federico Lupi, Royal Dano, Rodolfo Ranni, Miguel Angel Sola.

"Cocaine Wars" is a poorly written, acted and directed action pic with low-budget production values and an amazing lack of suspense considering its South American drug war theme. John Schneider, best known for his work on the now-syndicated "Dukes Of Hazzard" skein, has the thankless job of starring in this poor man's "Rambo," for which b.o. prospects look dim.

Shot in Mexico, film is set in an unspecified South American country where coke kingpin Regis (Federico Lupi) runs a ruthless drug camp with the help of the country's army head, Mario. Schneider portrays Cliff, a boozing rough-guy pilot who says things like "I don't like people pointing guns at me — it makes me crazy."

Well, Regis owes Cliff money, and Cliff has a cache of documents that can put Regis away, and there's a candidate running for some kind of office in this generic Latin American land who wants to run Regis and Mario out of town, and let's not forget the jet-setting photojournalist love interest of Janet (Kathryn Witt), to whom Cliff confides he is in fact an agent with the Drug Enforcement Agency.

Most of the film is taken up with badly directed and edited chase scenes — jumbles of rapidfire images that give no sense of the action and soon become a strain for the eyes. The hired killers themselves are slow-moving and stupid, even falling before the boozy blows of Royal Dano, who limns a piano player in a local brothel.

Climax finds Schneider suiting up with armament and ammo (getting to be a common scene these days) and blasting Regis' coke factory back to the Stone Age. One line of dialog in this final skirmish is lifted directly from "Commando," underlining the filmmakers' failed intention of cashing in on the success of recent megabuck actioners.
— *Roy.*

Jean de Florette
(FRENCH-COLOR)

An AMLF release of a Renn Prods./Films A2/RAI 2/D.D. Prods. coproduction. Produced by Pierre Grunstein. Directed by Claude Berri. Stars Yves Montand, Daniel Auteuil, Gérard Depardieu. Screenplay, Berri, Gérard Brach, based on the novel by Marcel Pagnol; camera (Eastmancolor, Technovision), Bruno Nuytten; editors, Arlette Langmann, Hervé de Luze, Noëlle Boisson; sound (Dolby), Pierre Gamet, Dominique Hennequin; production design, Bernard Vezat; costumes, Sylvie Gautrelet; makeup, Michel Deruelle, Jean-Pierre Eychenne; music, Jean-Claude Petit; production administrator, Colette Suder; assistant director, Xavier Castano; casting, Marie-Christine Lafosse; associate producer, Alain Poiré. Reviewed at the AMLF screening room, Paris, Aug. 5, 1986. Running time: **120 MINS**.
César Soubeyran
"Le Papet" .... Yves Montand
Ugolin .... Daniel Auteuil
Jean Cadoret .... Gérard Depardieu
Aimée Cadoret ...... Elisabeth Depardieu
Manon Cadoret ... Ernestine Mazurowna
Pique-Bouffique .... Marcel Champel
Baptistine .... Margarita Lozano
Guiseppe .... Bertino Benedetto

Paris — "Jean de Florette" probably is the most uncharacteristic film of Claude Berri's career, and certainly one of the least modish commercial pictures from France in years. It's also one of this risk-taking producer-director's affecting and unaffected best.

This is the first of two related, and simultaneously lensed, films — at a global cost of 120,000,000 francs (about $17,000,000), the most expensive production in French film history — that Berri adapted from a two-part novel by Marcel Pagnol, who died in 1974. Since the books and films of this beloved Provencal author, dramatist and filmmaker continue to bring in handsome royalties annually, both here and abroad, Berri's big gamble should find a ready audience.

The casting helps. Berri doesn't have the great Pagnol regulars like Jules Raimu, Fernandel or Pierre Fresnay to animate the author's evergreen peasant universe, but he has contemporary international stars like Yves Montand and Gérard Depardieu, and Daniel Auteuil, a young actor whose popularity is still local, who slip with professional ease into their vivid personages.

Pagnol drafted his novel "L'Eau des collines" years after making his penultimate feature film, "Manon des sources" in 1952, to which "Jean de Florette" is a "prequel." The picture, typically long and talky (four hours in its original release, subsequently cut by distributor Gaumont), supposedly left Pagnol dissatisfied, prompting him to recast and expand his tale in literary form.

It's a marvelous yarn, which Pagnol carried in him all his life (he had heard of its tragic real-life counterparts as a child). It also reveals a darker side to Pagnol's talent, though there still are doses of humor and farcical peasant asides, as in a scene in which a funeral cortege scatters when its members realize the hair-trigger shotgun the deceased asked to be buried with has been put loaded in the coffin.

Montand and Auteuil play a proud, self-centered village elder and his rat-faced sub-intelligent nephew who covet a local piece of fertile land which seems to be the perfect site for their planned carnation-growing operation, it's chief asset being a subterranean spring whose existence is known only to the locals.

When the farm's owner kicks off providentially (with a little help from the still vigorous Montand), the greedy pair suddenly find themselves confronted with an heir: a hunchbacked young city slicker (Depardieu), who has brought his wife (played by Elisabeth Depardieu, the thesp's real-life mate) and young daughter, Manon, to settle and live off the land in Rousseauist simplicity.

Depardieu doesn't know about the spring, which Montand and Auteuil have blocked up in the hope the bookish, gentle but tenacious hunchback will get discouraged and sell the property. Drought, the sirocco winds and the long desperate treks to fetch water from another spring in the mountains wear down Depardieu's optimism. Auteuil befriends him and feeds him hypocritical advice, while Montand watches with patient scorn from the sidelines.

Berri's sympathetic work with his small cast, and his subservience to Pagnol's story and dialog are key factors in the film's robust dramatic appeal. He and co-scripter Gérard Brach have resisted any temptations to revamp or update the story (set in a Provencal village of the 1920s) for that vague entity called the modern-day audience. The script is a model of deferential adaptation, curbing only Pagnol's habitual prolixity in order to bring situation, environment and character into sharper cinematic relief.

Berri has directed with tact and feeling, and brings to the material a classy production (with luminous lensing by Bruno Nuytten), and technical savoir-faire.

"Jean de Florette" opens in France Aug. 27. Part two, "Manon des sources," which relates the vengeance Depardieu's daughter exacts on the village, will be released Nov. 19.—*Len.*

Hijo del Palenque
(Child Of The Palenque)
(MEXICAN-COLOR)

A Películas Mexicanas release of a Producciones Chapultepec production. Written and directed by Rúben Galindo. Stars Valentín Trujillo. Music, Gustavo Carrión, with an appearance by Los Cadetes de Linar. Reviewed at Big Apple Cine 1, N.Y., Aug. 7, 1986. Running time: **88 MINS.**
Damian Corona . . . . Valentín Trujillo
Flor Corona . . . . Patricia María
Anatasio . . . . Pedro Infante Jr.

The low-budget "Child Of The Palenque" is a Mexican genre picture as unrelenting and humorless as it is manipulative. Director Rúben Galindo covers no new ground either in his straightfoward script or his plodding direction, and the results are as uninteresting as other Mexican films following the revenge motif in such a 1-2-3 fashion.

The skimpy chronological plot concerns the plans of Damian Corona (Valentín Trujillo) to avenge the brutal and senseless murder of his parents, who operated an illegal "palenque" (cock-fight arena) in a small Texas border town.

Since two of the killers have been sent to prison on other charges, Corona manages to end up behind the bars of Brownsville Prison and as Prisoner No. 136, he manages to waste a lot of film time looking sullen and observing shockingly harsh prison life. Finally the chance arrives and he manages to kill his adversaries (who don't even have speaking lines, much less characterizations) and then escapes to finish the job in slap-dash style.

The predictable ending is so shopworn one wonders why such films continue to be made in Mexico, and can only serve to be used as a boring second feature on a double-bill featuring a more substantial draw.
—*Lent.*

Jako Jed
(Like Poison)
(CZECHOSLOVAKIAN-COLOR)

A Barrandov Film Studios, Prague, production. Executive producer, Jaromir Lukas. Directed by Vit Olmer. Screenplay, Jiri Just, Vit Olmer, Karel Zidek, based on Zidek's novel "Like Poison;" camera (color), Otocar Kopriva; editor, Ivan Kacirkova; music, Jiri Stivin; art director, Boris Halmi; sound, Jiri Moudry; costume design, Ivana Sislerova. Reviewed at Czechfilmexport screening room, Prague, July 25, 1986. Running time: **76 MINS.**
Pavel Hnyk . . . . Zdenek Sverak
Julka . . . . Ivona Krajcovicova
Alice Hnykova . . . . Libuse Svormova
Vlasta . . . . Ladka Kozderkova
Also with: Vaclav Svorc, Frantisek Rehak, Vlado Durdik, Jaromira Milova, Dana Balounova, Vera Tichankova.

Prague — The middle-aged male and the charming, uninhibited young female relationship takes on a Czech twist in this bitter comedy, a Czech specialty, about a fast-paced office romance in Prague, whose wit recalls the famous '60s Forman/Passer styles, but lacks the pointed political overtones of the latter. Nonetheless, director Vit Olmer's waggish look at a kind of East European mid-life male crisis in an architect's office is droll enough to translate well into any contemporary social language.

Playwright and screenwriter Zdenek Sverak, who has teamed up with stage and film director Ladislav Smoljak in numerous Prague shaggy dog stories about the fictitious scientist Jara Cimrman, plays the disappointed Romeo, Pavel, who falls for the new colleague, Julka, nicknamed the "Czardas Queen" by office mates as a putdown because the seductive brunet hails from Slovakia. (Never intending to become an actor, Sverak has found himself now in more than 20 roles in recent Czech films.)

The affair develops fast, like a poison, however, since Pavel's routine marriage to wife Alice, a lawyer, already has been complicated by another mistress and it doesn't take long for office gossipers to notice that Pavel's designs for rebuilding the old quarter in Prague (the "Mala Strana") suffer because of his infatuous designs on Julka.

When Julka drops him and returns to her Slovakian home base, Pavel finds himself faced with a set of serious charges wife Alice could nail him on, clearly not the resolution the audience was hoping for him. Sverak coolly underplays the role, which draws him more sympathy than he probably deserves, since he is outnumbered by everyone who is out to make him fail in his romantic quest.

Entire cast shows all-around excellence and veteran director Olmer (FAMU film school grad, 1966; last feature 1970). displays a deft wand for comedy pace. Handsome Prague locale is a plus, but script's one-liners about Czech-Slovakian culture differences weren't appreciated in Bratislava.

Film, which was shown at the Karlovy Vary fest, should be a sure bet for Czech film weeks and festivals and could see arthouse playoff. — *Milg.*

Jezioro Bodenskie
(The Lake Of Constance)
(POLISH-COLOR)

A Film Polski presentation of a Zespoli Filmowe, Perspektiwa Unit production. Directed by Janusz Zaorski. Screenplay, Allan Starski; camera (color), Witold Adamek; editor, Halina Prugal-Ketling; music, Jerzy Satanowski. Reviewed at the Morettina Center, Locarno Film Festival (in competition), Aug. 13, 1986. Running time: **90 MINS.**
With: Krzysztof Pieczynski, Malgorzata Pieczynska, Joanna Szczepkowska, Maria Pakulnis, Gustaw Holoubek, Andrzej Szczep-kowski, Henryk Borowski, Krzysztof Zalewski.

Locarno — A remarkably smooth and professional production, well shot and adroitly directed, this is Janusz Zaorski's first theatrical effort. It is, however, a hard nut to crack for anyone not directly interested in the essence of the Polish nature, for this is the film's main goal throughout.

Of course there is a plot of sorts, all traced through a movie-length flashback. A Pole who spent time in an internment camp during the war on the Swiss-German border, visits the site many years later and reminisces about the days gone by. What the audience is offered is a static series of encounters of the young protagonists with other Poles confined in the same camp, including several women with whom there are tentative stabs at romance which never quite materialize.

Through the hero himself as well as the other Poles he meets, Zaorski attempts to reach the profound meaning of the Polish existence, its destructive nature, its presumptions of glory and its fits of gloom, the tragedy of its history and the cosmopolitanism of its intellectuals. In short, it is a film to be taken mostly on a symbolic level, since the plot itself is hardly meaningful by itself.

Naturally, such an approach can only create problems for an average audience out for a night on the town, and the polished photography, the highly extroverted acting and the long, meaningful monologs don't really compensate for the lack of real characters or authentic drama. It relies too often on myths, some suggested by the film itself; by wishing to establish all-embracing truth it ignores the basic veracity which would make the elementary ingredients believable.

As an exercise in filmmaking and a decoding test for film students or historians, Zaorski's effort may be justified. —*Edna.*

Doktor
(The Doctor)
(YUGOSLAV-COLOR)

A Viba Film (Ljubljana) production. Written and directed by Vojko Duletic. Camera (color), Karpo Godina; editor, Toni Ziherle; art director, Mirko Lipuzic; costumes, Milena Kumar; sound, Matjaz Janezic. Reviewed at Pula Film Festival, July 22, 1986. Running time: **95 MINS.**
With: Slavko Cerjak (Dr. Vladimir Kantet), Tea Glazar, Zvone Hribar, Ivan Rupnik, Demeter Bitenc, Dare Valio, Andrej Kurent.

Pula — As an attempt to bring to life the true story of a doctor involved in the underground resistance movement during the occupation of Ljubljana, "Doktor" fails dismally. As a string of scenes showing goose-stepping Nazis, terrified locals being beaten up for no reason, complacent bourgeois attending the opera next to German officers, and secret messengers slipping in and out of apartments under surveillance, it is excruciatingly familiar, but could prove marketable to fans of the genre, as long as they don't demand expressive acting.

Slavko Cerjak, in the role of Dr. Vladimir Kantet, must qualify as one of the most stony-faced thesps in Slovenian cinema. Psychologically, Kantet remains less an enigma than an impenetrable wall, incapable of arousing empathy, sympathy or even plain liking.

As a Resistance actioner "Doktor" tiredly hits all the tired cliches. From his key position in the ranks of the political police, Kantet is above suspicion, which is why it takes first the Italians, then the Germans, so long to catch on to him as an informer for the Liberation Front. His death at the hands of torturers, while he hallucinates about a restful sea, is the one touching scene in the picture. — *Yung.*

In 'n' Out
(Gringo Mojado)
(U.S.-MEXICAN-COLOR)

A Peliculas Mexicanas release of an Instituto Mexicano de Cinematográfica (Imcine)/Conacite Dos/Camrose production. Produced by Michael James Egan. Directed by Ricardo Franco. Stars Sam Bottoms. Screenplay, Eleen Kesend, Franco; camera (color), Juan Ruiz Anchias; music, T-Bone Burnett. Reviewed at Big Apple Cine 1, N.Y., Aug. 7, 1986. Running time: **106 MINS.**
Murray Lewis Jr. . . . . .Sam Bottoms
Nieves Blanco . . . . .Rafael Inclán
Lupita Blanco . . . . .Rebecca Jones
Mona Mur . . . . .Isela Vega

Filmed in English in 1984, "In 'n' Out" has yet to be released on the Anglo market, but the comedy's Mexican point of view will limit its success at the U.S. boxoffice. A dubbed Spanish-language version released in Mexico and abroad finds its ideal audience to be either Mexican or those of Mexican descent.

This U.S.-Mexican coproduction, whose Spanish-language distribution rights are held by the Mexican federal film institute Imcine, stars U.S. actor Sam Bottoms and Mexican thesp Rafael Inclán. They join up as a wacky comedy team with Bottoms as the straight man. Duo is offset by the inclusion of Rebecca Jones as Inclán's sister who, although she disapproves of her brother's crazy stunts, wants to go along for the ride.

The complicated storyline has Bottoms receiving an announcement to attend his father's funeral in Mexico 30 years after his supposed death. When he drives down from California to discover the answer to this mystery, he only discovers more confusion. And the sit-

uation gets complicated. He gets kicked out of Mexico several times only to come back for more.

Obviously the notion here is that Mexico has the corner on eccentricities, especially when it confronts an innocent American. The other message is that once an American penetrates the surface of this chaos, it is impossible to return to the dull normal life he had before.

Granted, the characterizations of the principals have their charms and there are many amusing scenes. But the humor is dependent on many situations and crazy circumstances that seem to arise from a particularly Mexican standpoint. Anglos who have not had much contact with Mexico will find the situations forced and the message having all the subtlety of a cannon blast.

Production values rate high, especially lensing by Juan Ruiz Anchia. Bottoms play the wide-eyed innocent with verve and Inclán has toned down his usual shrillness to emerge as a truly comic character.

Although all of the Mexican actors in the dubbed version speak with their own voices, Bottoms' character loses believability because he's dubbed in flawless unaccented Spanish and yet tells us this is his first trip to Mexico. —*Len.*

François Simon — La Présence
(François Simon — The Presence)
(SWISS-FRENCH-DOCU-COLOR - 16m)

A CSS Geneva presentation of a CSS/Television Suisse Romande Institut Audiovisual (INA) (Paris) coproduction. Executive producer, Axel Naccache. Directed by Ana Simon, Louis Mouchet. Camera (color, 16m, Cinigram Labs), Jan Neuman; editor, Najet Ben Slimane; sound, Marek Jezienicki; production manager, Louis Mouchet; interviewer, George Bratschi. Reviewed at the Morettina Center, Locarno Film Festival (out of competition), Aug. 11, 1986. Running time: **90 MINS.**

Locarno — This is a detailed in-depth documentary on the life and work of François Simon, probably the best known Swiss actor of his generation, who died our years ago.

Simon, who was the son of the great French film star Michel Simon, had a rich and varied career which started before World War II in Paris, where he was associated with some of the greatest luminaries of that period, including Copeau, Dullin, Barrault and the Pitoeff company, and later became a leading figure in film but even more so on stage in Switzerland.

His widow, Ana, a writer and short-films director in her own right, has collected an incredible wealth of documents with the help of Louis Mouchet, and put together an impressive selection of visual testimonies, showing Simon in a great

variety of parts, from classical and modern stage roles and traditional films to some of the best known Swiss New Wave productions, to which he contributed abundantly. He accepted both leading parts, in films like Alain Tanner's "Charles, Dead Or Alive" and secondary roles of particular significance, such as the hired butler in Claude Goretta's "The Invitation."

In later years he had the opportunity to play French philosopher Jean-Jacques Rousseau in a tv series dedicated to him, and to play opposite the character of Rousseau as the cynical Voltaire, in Thomas Koerfer's film "Alzire."

A lot of time is dedicated to Simon's stage performances, particularly his work with his own company, a truly non-profit organization known as the Theatre de Carouge, as well as to his tv work. Jeanne Moreau, the French actress who featured him in the first film she directed, pays tribute to his talent, and so do two other film directors, Koerfer and Tanner.

With Ana Simon behind the camera, this is first and foremost a homage, sometimes too rich for those unfamiliar with Simon and who won't be able to assess the full impact of his talent only from the snippets included in the film. However, as an accompaniment to the tribute paid by Locarno this year to the late actor, it is an impressive document, which may well interest French-speaking audiences. —*Edna.*

Ghame Afghan
(The Tragedy Of The Afghan)
(SWISS-COLOR)

A Europa Films (Locarno) presentation of a Mark M. Rissi production. Directed by Zmarai Kasi, Rissi. Screenplay, Kasi; camera (color), Werner Schneider; editor, Evelyne von Rabenau; music, Malek Salam, Rissi. Reviewed at the Morettina Center, Locarno Film Festival (in competition), Aug. 14, 1986. Running time: **90 MINS.**
With: Aamir Farid, Jawed Babur, Bushra Ejaz, Hukun Jana Abai, Anita Gul, Zar Khan, Muhamad Asam, Muhamad Yuesuf, Besmilla, Silvia Silva.

Locarno — This is a typical evolvement of the type of film developed by Swiss documentarists, partly ethnic and partly fictional, the fiction being based always on facts and intended to make the document itself easier for consumption.

Indeed, at least half the film is dedicated to the way of life and the traditions of Afghan villagers. The first shot warns that the film intends to be more than that, as the camera follows a police patrol breaking into a house and dragging out the man of the house for no obvious reason.

The matter is left to rest for almost half the film as the story follows the man's family, the prepara-

tion for the second son's marriage, and the general conditions of the folks there. Only after the marriage does the groom's brother stumble upon a wounded resistance fighter, and because of his willingness to extend help to the dying man, the whole family is plunged into an irreversible tragic process. They have to leave the village and attempt to cross the border into Pakistan, on the way they are swindled and robbed, and when they manage finally to join one of the miserable refugee camps in Pakistan, all the final miseries and insults they have to submit to there destroy what is left of the family.

The plot is schematic, the acting, mostly by people who have never seen a camera but have experienced firsthand most of the things referred to in the picture, is amateurish but authentic. The film's main purpose is to focus attention on the tragedy of a people over a six-year period in which nobody raises his voice about the inhuman conditions. Avoiding any political reference that could antagonize directly one of the interested parties, but speaking clearly about graft, corruption, abject poverty and primitive customs that chain this nation to its miseries, the film could be considered as a kind of stylized documentary supplying considerable information and leaving a bitter taste.

While it may have difficulty finding theatrical distribution, television could find a worthy cause here to dedicate an hour and a half of its time.—*Edna.*

Memoires d'un Juif Tropical
(Memories Of A Tropical Jew)
(FRENCH-COLOR)

A Boites A Images presentation and production. Produced, written, directed and narrated by Joseph Morder. Editors, Yves Abreys, Arnaud Boland, Sophie Revault d'Allones. Reviewed at the Morettina Center, Locarno Film Festival (in competition), Aug. 13, 1986. Running time: **75 MINS.**
With: François Michaud, Vincent Toledano, Nicole Tufelli.

Locarno — This is a home movie by definition, using the cinema language of a Jonas Mekas or Chantal Akerman to evoke Joseph Morder's own childhood as the son of Jewish refugees from Poland living in Guayaquil, Ecuador. The entire film is shot, however, in Paris, Morder's present base, depicting his moods as a grown-up going through a love affair and the sights of Paris emptied of its inhabitants in the month of August, triggering the train of memories on which he embarks.

The entire sense of the picture is contained in the narration, the visuals offering no real added value or insight to the spoken text. Sometimes they are obliquely connected to the process of past recollections, sometimes they just create moods and here and there they suggest, in a pretty obvious fashion, a forced illustration of the text. When Morder refers to the birth of his younger sister Judith, he shows a poster of Judy Garland, and when he talks about a full moon, he uses the poster for Rohmer's "Full Moon In Paris." In any case, there is no attempt to use the images at any time to tell a story.

The most remarkable feature here is the fact that Morder has shot the entire film in 8m, with the blow-up supplied by the Telcipro laboratories unusually clear. There is nothing amateurish about the technical aspects, almost all of them handled by Morder himself, which should be no surprise since he has made a voluminous number of films, over 250, in Super 8 in the last few years.

Finally, in spite of the title which suggests possible ethnical, religious or even geographical exploration, this item is mostly for avant-garde aficionados with all the aspects taking a secondary place.—*Edna.*

Corps et biens
(With All Hands)
(FRENCH-COLOR)

A Films du Semaphore release of a Lyric Intl./FR3 Films coproduction, with the participation of the Ministry of Culture (CNC). Executive producers, Humbert Balsan, Jean-Pierre Mahot. Stars Dominique Sanda, Lambert Wilson, Danielle Darrieux, Jean-Pierre Leaud. Written and directed by Benoit Jacquot, based on the novel "Deadlier Than The Male" by James Gunn. Camera (Eastmancolor), Renato Berta; sound, Michel Bionnet; editor, Dominique Auvray; music, Eric Lelann; art direction, Dominique Dalmasso; costumes, Christian Gasc; makeup, Jacques Clémente; assistant director, Jérôme Jeannet. Reviewed at Club 13, Paris, Aug. 12, 1986. Running time: **100 MINS.**

Hélène	Dominique Sanda
Michel Sauvage	Lambert Wilson
Madam Krantz	Danielle Darrieux
Marcel	Jean-Pierre Leaud
Paule Krantz	Sabine Haudepin
Laurie	Laura Betti
Ariane	Ingrid Held
Dr. Loscure	Roland Bertin
Filasse	Jérôme Zucca
François	Siener
Simone	Marie Wiart

Paris — Writer-director Benoît Jacquot, who trashed Henry James in a pointless modern-day film version of "The Wings Of The Dove" back in 1980, lowers his cultural sights to an American mystery novel by James Gunn. But, like many an auteur revamp of Anglo-Saxon thrillers, "Corps et biens" squeezes the pulp appeal out of the material as it tries to intellectualize theme and narrative.

In his usual icy, style-concious manner, Jacquot plots a tale of greed, lust and perversion in swank settings as tormented gigolo Lambert Wilson weds a rich Parisian heiress (Ingrid Held) after murdering a former client (Laura Betti) at her seaside house.

Unfortunately for Wilson, his spouse has a beautiful film actress half-sister (Dominique Sanda), who's also eyeing her fortune and is drawn ambiguously to the gigolo, whose crime she learns about when his victim's neighbor (Danielle Darrieux) arrives in town to track down her friend's murderer.

This would be just another handsome (lensing by Renato Berta) but vain stylistic exercise if it were not for the welcome doses of humor injected by Darrieux, hilarious as the hard-drinking provincial proprietress turned amateur detective, and the reliably weird Jean-Pierre Leaud, as Lambert's henchman, who keeps a bead on Darrieux's investigation, and then tries to murder her (inexplicably Wilson intervenes and kills him instead).

A number of other minor characters walk in and out of the convoluted action, with little or no influence on the central complications.

Wilson and Sanda are right at home in Jacquot's coldly inscrutable world, peopled with murkily motivated marionettes. Laura Betti and Roland Bertin, as a mysterious psychoanalyst, limn brief but helpful comic portraits.

Other tech credits and a brassy score by Eric Lelann are good.
—*Len.*

Le Môme
(The Kid)
(FRENCH-COLOR)

An AMLF release of an Orly Films/Sara Films coproduction. Produced by Jean-José Richer. Directed by Alain Corneau. Stars Richard Anconina, Ambre. Screenplay, Corneau, Christian Clavier; camera (Fujicolor), Jean-Francis Gondre; editor, Marie-Josephe Yoyotte; sound, Dominique Levert; music, Otis Redding; stunts adviser, Philippe Guégan; car stunts, Michel Julienne; production managers, Fathia Zmouli, Jean-Claude Bourlat; assistant director, Frédéric Blum; casting, Romain Brémond. Reviewed at the AMLF screening room, Paris, Aug. 12, 1986. Running time: **100 MINS.**

Willie	Richard Anconina
Jo	Ambre
Darmines	Michel Duchaussoy
René	Georges Montillier
Michel Charki	Yan Epstein
Jean Pierre Charki	Thierry de Carbonnières
The Tunisian	Kamel Cherif

Paris — Director Alain Corneau has shaken off the sand after his odd foray into the colonial heroics of "Fort Saganne" (1983) and is back on the urban pavements in "Le Môme," a minor, routine thriller and his first genre effort (in which he has made his reputation) since his glossy 1981 melodrama "Choice Of Weapons." After experiencing the relentless Sahara sun, Corneau has gone to the other extreme by shooting the entire film at night.

Richard Anconina stars as a young marginal cop who works as a loner and is as much attached to his tape deck of Otis Redding blues as he is to his revolver. During the investigation of a drug link, he comes across a mulatto hooker in the employ of a pair of shady Lebanese brothers involved in arms trafficking, falls for her and tries to pull her from their clutches at the risk of his own life.

The girl is wary and indifferent, and keeps running back to her brutal protectors and her former activities. But the stubborn cop retrieves her and in the course of lying low in suburban motels and passionate lovemaking sessions, manages to draw her out of her protective shell. He then succeeds in disposing of the hoods during a climactic car chase.

Despite Anconina's homely tender-tough presence, and Corneau's whiplash efficiency in the action scenes, "Le Môme" cruises predictably through the rutted mean streets of convention and trendiness (the hero turns into an asphalt Rambo by blowing his antagonists away with a bazooka).

The script, by Corneau and Christian Clavier, strains for psychological depth with fragmented flashbacks explaining Anconina's traumatic loneliness (gangsters murdered his parents when he was a kid), and in the peripheral figure of an aging police veteran, a surrogate father who nonetheless betrays Anconina at the end of his extralegal odyssey.

A Senegalese-born model named Ambre makes a photogenic but dramatically unsure debut as the jaded prostitute whose rootless solitude strikes a corresponding chord in Anconina.

Tech credits are solid, with fine rubber-burning car stunt coordination by Michel Julienne. —*Len.*

Op hoop van zegen
(The Good Hope)
(DUTCH-COLOR)

A Concorde Film release of a Sigma Film production, in association with Elsevier-Vendex Film and TROS. Executive producer, Matthijs van Heijningen. Directed by Guido Pieters. Screenplay, Karin Loomans, based on play by Herman Heijermans; camera (color) Frans Bromet; editor, Ton Ruys; music, Rogier van Otterloo; sound, Georges Bossaers, Marc Nolens, Hans Treffers; art direction, Dick Schillemans; set decoration, Peter Jansen; assistant director, Wilfried Depeweg; production manager, Kees Groenewegen; costume design, Jany van Hellenberg Hubar; sea sequences, Peter Brugman; camera, Pinewood Studios, Roy Field; special effects, Martin Gutteridge; casting, Frank Krom. Reviewed at Cinema International, Amsterdam, Aug. 6, 1986. Running time: **102 MINS.**

Kniertje	Kitty Courbois
Barend	Danny de Munk
Jo	Renée Soutendijk
Geert	Huub Stapel
Clemens Bos	Rijk de Gooyer
Mathilde Bos	Willeke van Ammelrooy
Simon	Ramses Shaffy
Kaps	Leen Jongewaard

Also with: Dorijn Curvers, Luc Lutz, Tamar van den Dop, Lex Goudsmith, Albert Mol.

Amsterdam — Following their successful "Ciske De Rat," producing-directing-writing team Matthijs van Heijningen, Guido Peters and Karin Loomans have collaborated on the fourth film version of Herman Heijerman's legit play "The Good Hope" (previous versions: 1918, 1924 and 1934).

With a big (for Holland) budget of $2,500,000, an excellent crew, a choice of good actors and British special effects work, on paper it must have looked a cert. The result, however, is iffy.

The noted and well-traveled 1900 legit melodrama, frequently revived, has lost something in this latest screen adaptation.

"The Good Hope" is set in a fishing village peopled with vivid characters — including self-made, conniving ship owner Bos and widow Kniertje whose husband and two elder sons drowned and who loses her remaining sons in a storm at sea.

Heijerman, perhaps the most important Dutch dramatist of the past two centuries, penned a moving and well structured play that offered actors "dream" roles. But because Danny de Monk scored with his coltish charm, vivacity and brash singing as "Ciske," this film restructures the play to expand the character of the youngest son (70 lines in the play) into the star role.

Lame devices such as a love affair with the shipowner's schoolgirl daughter have been trotted out. And gone is much of Heijerman's telling dialog. Characters and scenes have been added to make the plot clearer for less discerning audiences. The melodrama has thinned under such treatment.

There's a waxen air about the film. The ill-fated boat, the house, even the people appear to come from Madame Tussaud's. Dirt-poor and hungry, the villagers don't have a scratch or a hair out of place. Far from inhabiting "dream" parts, the actors have to fight to inject life into characterizations under some deadening direction.

The storm and shipwreck scenes technically are well done, but the actors appear not to drown but seem instead somehow stranded by the special effects.

Danny de Monk gets little chance to prove any acting ability. Kitty Courbois, Rijk de Gooyer and Huub Stapel try hard to get the film off the ground. Ramses Shaffy does best while Renée Soutendijk and Willeke van Ammelrooy go bravely under.

Tech credits are above average. TROS-TV connection with film indicates it may also surface as a miniseries. —*Wall.*

Kuningas lähtee Ranskaan
(The King Goes Forth To France)
(FINNISH-B&W)

A Kinosto release (international sales contact, the Finnish Film Foundation) of a Reppufilmi production. Executive producer, directed by Anssi Mänttäri. Screenplay, Paavo Haavikko, Mänttäri, Heikki Katajisto, based on Haavikko's original radio play and on his libretto for Aulis Sallinen's opera "The King Goes Forth To France;" camera (black & white), Heikki Katajisto; editors, Irma Taina, Marjo Valve; production design, Pertti Hilkamo, Tuula Hilkamo; sound, Timo Linnasalo, Jouko Lumme; lighting, Kari Kekkonen, Aki Kaurismäki; assistant director, Pauli Pentti. Reviewed at the Finnish Film Foundation, Helsinki, Aug. 12, 1986. Running time: **85 MINS.**
The King ....Paavo Piskonen
Caroline the Cheerful ...Susanna Haavisto
The Prime Minister ......Harri Nikkonen
Anne the Stripper ......Riitta Havukainen
Caroline Mare's Mane ......Kati Outinen
The Stablemaster ....Lasse Pöysti
King of Bohemia ....Kalevi Kahra
Also with: Heikki Paavilainen, Matti Pellonpää, Markku Toikka, Pertti Sveholm, Heikki Ortamo, Timo Toikka, Tupuna Vaissi.

Helsinki — Paavo Haavikko wrote a radio play making allegorical fun of certain real or imagined events from the One Hundred Years War between France and England. Haavikko went on to supply composer Aulis Sallinen with the title — "The King Goes Forth To France" — and the libretto for an opera that over the past two years has had several international performances, one at the Santa Fe Festival last year. Now Anssi Mänttäri, a film director with a reputation for tongue-in-cheek works, has collaborated with the playwright-librettist to do the same story as a seriocomic film fairytale.

Mänttäri's "The King" has a bunch of good actors performing as if they were playing at amateur theatricals, either reading their lines solemnly or singing them in a troubadourish way. Story has the English King, his Prime Minister and an entourage including three young women trying to reach Paris and a milder climate. The Royal party never makes it to Paris. It sees battle, though, against France and her ally, the Blind King of Bavaria, and joins in the Siege of Calais where gruesome deeds are in evidence.

En route, everybody spouts enigmatic *bon mots* and indulge in all kinds of action that is obviously allegorical. The three women, whether demure, exhibitionistic or introverted, possibly are meant to represent the gamut of female behavior patterns, while the men either symbolize dilly-dallying or self-defeating scheming at the executive level.

With black & white views of starkness and beauty, including references to classical works by Dreyer and Eisenstein, helmer Mänttäri often defeats his designs on being taken seriously by having his characters appear, in action and speech, just too plain silly. Still, fun and games are played out with verve to the enjoyment of the more indulgent genre explorer. Anachronisms are, of course, added as visual spice throughout (a VW being dragged by oxen and pushed by hooded men). But never mind, since this story really takes place in the never never land of cinematic fancy anyway. The enthusiast may even imagine the Marx Bros. lurking somewhere in the background.—*Kell.*

Una Casa In Bilico
(A House Poised On The Edge)
(ITALIAN-COLOR)

An Angio Film production. Directed by Antonietta De Lillo and Giorgio Magliulo. Stars Marina Vlady. Screenplay, Giuditta Rinaldi, De Lillo, Magliulo; camera (color, 16m), Magliulo; editor, Mirko Garrone; art director, Paola Bizzarri; costumes, Sandra Montagna; music, Franco Piersanti; sound, Uberto Nijhuis; director of production, Roberta Fainello. Reviewed at Fonorete Studios, Rome, Aug. 5, 1986. (Shown at Locarno Film Festival in competition.) Running time: **83 MINS.**
Maria ....Marina Vlady
Teo ....Riccardo Cucciolla
Giovanni ....Luigi Pistilli

Rome — Codirecting their first feature, Antonietta De Lillo and Giorgio Magliulo (both with a background in cinematography) show talent at depicting the quiet lives of three nice people over 60, co-residents in an old Roman apartment. Shot on a shoestring, "A House Poised On The Edge" is well lensed, barely noticeable as a blowup from a 16m original. It assembles a trio of fine thesps, from the ever-fascinating Marina Vlady in the role of a spirited Russian emigrée, to Italo veterans Riccardo Cucciolla and Luigi Pistilli. All that is lacking is a story.

Basically a situation film, "House" establishes its characters early on and has trouble deciding what to do with them. Giovanni (Pistilli) is the generous, *bon vivant* Don Juan of the household; an old flame left him her apartment when she died, and he impulsively invites the introverted clock-collector Teo (Cucciolla) and idealistic Maria (Vlady) to share his fortune. After a little adjusting they all get on civilly enough, until Maria decides to help a young Russian girl join her parents in the States. All she needs to do is acquire Italian citizenship by marrying a very reluctant Teo. Finally he gives in.

Some legal problems threaten their apartment-sharing, and a car accident whittles their number down to two, but the survivors hang on. The point seems to be that even oldsters can bloom with *joie de vivre* in the right, loving surroundings. Pic is commendably unsentimental in getting this across. It also is a rather banal point.

The spirit of the film is gentle in the extreme, maybe too soft to say anything incisive, or face its characters head-on. Good fare for rest homes.

Pic was one of the two Italo entries competing at Locarno.—*Yung.*

Passion
(HONG KONG-COLOR)

A D&B Films production and release. Executive producer, Dickson Poon. Produced by John Sham. Written and directed by Silvia Chang. Stars Silvia Chang, George Lam, Cora Miao. Camera (color), Ma; production supervisor, Winnie Yu; art direction, William Chang; music, Lowell Lo; editor, Cheong Kwok Kuen. Reviewed at Pearl theater, Hong Kong, July 29, 1986. Running time: **98 MINS.**
(Cantonese soundtrack with English subtitles)

Hong Kong — "Passion" is Taiwanese actress turned director Silvia Chang's answer to Ingmar Bergman, starring herself and an equally talented costar, Cora Miao, in a comprehensible, non-sensational human drama that is most convincing.

It has a touching story told in jagged flashback laden with implications rather than strong statements. On a sunny Saturday afternoon, two close friends (Silvia Chang and Cora Miao), both widowed and well-off, gather their respective families in an exclusive country club. While the children play, the two ladies chat, recollect and question each other about their past and present lives.

There is a fascinating buildup that leads to the climactic emotional surprise twist as the two women confess their true love for the same man (George Lam).

The film is a concentration of sorrow, pain, nostalgia and close friendship shaded with subtle humor. The decor, clothes, hairdos, makeup and style of the 1950s and 1960s have been lovingly captured.

Chang suffers in silence and in love with the studied distance of a traditional Chinese lady. Miao delivers a bravura performance that evokes her effective fight for the love of the man she wants to marry. Both leads show engagingly tough but vulnerable feminine heroines.
—*Mel.*

Noche De Juerga
(A Night On The Town)
(MEXICAN-COLOR)

A Videocine release of a Televicine production. Directed by Manuel M. Delgado. Screenplay, José María Fernández Unsain; camera (color), Miguel Arena; music, Nacho Méndez. Reviewed at Big Apple Cine 2, N.Y., July 29, 1986. Running time: **91 MINS.**
Ricardo Bermudes ....Juan Ferrara
Dolores Vertiz................Helena Rojo
Police Lieutenant ....Víctor Junco
Alicia Bermudes ....Norma Herrera

When his wife and kids leave to visit relatives at Christmas, a young office worker named Ricardo Bermudes (Juan Ferrara) decides to go to a nightclub where, quite by chance, he happens to meet Dolores Vertiz (Helena Rojo). Since her car won't start, he offers to drive her home and she invites him inside for a drink, saying that her husband (a powerful political figure) is out of town. When she disappears to slip into something more comfortable, Bermudes discovers the murdered body of her husband on the living room floor and the sound of police sirens en route.

So runs the storyline of the Mexican drama "A Night On The Town," directed by Manuel M. Delgado. This Hitchcock-style murder mystery, penned by José María Fernández Unsain (head of Mexico's writers society Sogem), successfully builds tension during the events that follow.

A strong case is constructed against Bermudes during his flight and subsequent capture. His cigaret lighter — a recurring image — is found at the scene of the crime, the murder weapon bears his bloodied fingerprints and his own shirt is smeared with the victim's blood. Even the murdered man's wife swears she witnessed the accused drive the knife home. Despite his pleas to the contrary, Bermudes cannot convince his wife and lawyer of his innocence.

The pic works best when focusing on the plight of Bermudes and showing his frustration and futility in the face of such overwhelming evidence, presented by the able police lieutenant (Víctor Junco).

This tension, however, often is diffused through unimaginative overuse of merely functional medium shots and a brash and distracting score by Nacho Méndez, which would be better suited for a comedy.

Actors Ferrara and Rojo present arresting and believable characters, and the script attempts to give life to a handful of bit parts such as the maid, Bermudes' best friend Julio and also his pickpocket cellmate. But routine direction does little to raise the storyline above that of a run-of-the-mill cop show. — *Lent.*

Monster Dog
(COLOR)

Surprisingly tame.

A Trans World Entertainment release of a Continental Motion Pictures presentation. Executive producers, Helen Sarlui, Eduard Sarlui. Produced by Carlos Auréd. Written and directed by Clyde Anderson. Stars Alice Cooper, Victoria Vera. Camera (Technicolor), Jose Garcia Galisteo; editor, Antonio Jose Ochoa; additional editing, Gabrio Astori, Peter Teschner; music, Grupo Dichotomy; songs, Alice Cooper; art direction, Gumersindo Andres; production manager, Roberto Bessi; assistant director, Michael Gutierez; costume design, Eugenia Escriva; special effects, Carlo De Marchis. Reviewed on TWE vidcassette, N.Y., July 22, 1986. (No MPAA Rating.).Running time: **84 MINS.**
Vincent .Alice Cooper
Sandra . . . . .Victoria Vera
Frank . . . . .Carlos Sanurio
Angela . . . . .Pepita James
Jordan . . . . .Emilo Linder
Marilou .Jose Sarsa
Deputy . . . . .Luis Maluenda
Sheriff . . . . .Ricardo Palacios
Old man . . . . .B. Barta Barri

A lesser entry in the screen annals of lycanthropy, "Monster Dog" is an old-fashioned horror pic notable only for the presence of rock star Alice Cooper in the lead role. It was shot in Spain in 1984 and planned for theatrical release that year by since-defunct distributor Film Ventures Intl. but has debuted on vidcassette instead.

Story premise resembles a more recent horror opus, "Blood Tracks," in having rock star Vincent (Alice Cooper) visiting his ancestral home to shoot a music video there, directed by his girlfriend Sandra (Victoria Vera). It turns out that 20 years earlier, Vincent's dad was murdered by a mob of torch-carrying townsfolk, accusing him of being a werewolf responsible for a string of murders.

Another set of murders is occurring, blamed on a pack of wild dogs until Vincent shows up and makes for a convenient scapegoat. Ultimately, Vincent is cleared when a real monster dog attacks him, but since such afflictions are communicable he becomes the new king of the wild dogs and it's up to Sandra to put him out of his misery and save the day. She's probably not the first music video director to be put in such a situation.

Instead of a campy offering, "Dog" is a brooding, relatively serious affair. Biggest surprise is Cooper, who looks uncannily like character actor Timothy Carey (circa "Poor White Trash") and plays the role straight. He also contributes two interesting songs filmed as music videos. Spanish supporting cast is adequate with okay dubbing.

The inevitable monster transformation effect (into dog rather than wolf) is done poorly. — *Lor.*

Los Ases De Contrabando
(Contraband Aces)
(MEXICAN-COLOR)

A Peliculas Mexicanas release of a Hermanos Tamez S.A. de C.V. production. Produced by Orlando Tamez G. & Guadalupe E. Viuda de Tamez. Executive producer, Hugo Tamez C. Stars Sergio Goyri. Directed by Fernando Durán. Screenplay, Carlos Valdemar, based on a story by Matilde Rivera and Felipe Morales; camera (color), Agustín Lara; editor, Enrique Murrillo; music, Diego Herrera, with appearances by the groups Los Líricos de Terán and Hermanos Mier; special effects, Jorge Farfen. Reviewed at Big Apple Cine 1, N.Y., July 30, 1986. Running time: **92 MINS.**
Ernesto Castro . . . . .Sergio Goyri
Elizabeth Calvo . . . . .Rebeca Silva
Commandant Rodolfo
  Benavitas . . . . .Gregorio Casals
Marcos . . . . .Juan Valentin
Jesús Castro . . . . .Humberto Herrera
Also with: Diana Ferreti, Carlos East, Manolo Cárdenas, Armando Araiza and Nena Delgado.

"Contraband Aces" is a Mexican action pic that gets its priorities confused by making illegal drug traffickers more likable than the law enforcement officers, and yet tries to preach that illegal drugs and drug trafficking is inherently bad. But director Fernando Durán is not attempting to make another "Bonnie And Clyde."

What he has produced is a boring collection of scenes based around a group of barely sketched characterizations set against an equally impoverished action-packed plot that goes from car chase to violent showdown every few minutes.

If this isn't bad enough, antidrug sermons emerge throughout the pic only to be topped by the old cliché that crime doesn't pay.

The majority of the production budget appears to have been spent on automobiles that get smashed up in each new scene with little left over to pay for quality shooting.

The amateurish acting, despite the likable characterization of national action star Sergio Goyri, cannot bring life to the sketchy script. The routine camera work makes it appear the pic was as boring to make as it is to watch.—*Lent.*

The Texas Chainsaw Massacre Part 2
(COLOR)

Satisfying followup.

A Cannon Films release. Produced by Menahem Golan, Yoram Globus. Executive producers, Henry Holmes, James Jorgensen. Directed by Tobe Hooper. Stars Dennis Hopper. Screenplay, L.M. Kit Carson; camera (TVC color), Richard Kooris; editor, Alain Jakubowicz; music, Hooper, Jerry Lambert; production design, Cary White; art director, Daniel Miller; set decorator, Pat Welsome; special makeup effects, Tom Savini; costumes, Carin Hooper; sound, Wayne Bell; assistant director, Richard Espinoza; co-producer, Hooper; associate producer, Carson. Reviewed at Mann Chinese Theater, Hollywood, Calif., Aug. 22, 1986. (No MPAA Rating.) Running time: **95 MINS.**
Lt. "Lefty" Enright . . . . . .Dennis Hopper
Vanita "Stretch"
  Brock . . . . .Caroline Williams
Leatherface . . . . .Bill Johnson
Cook (Draytor Sawyer) . . . . . . .Jim Siedow
Chop-Top . . . . .Bill Moseley
L.G. McPeters . . . . .Lou Perry
Mercedes Driver . . . . .Barry Kinyon
Gunner . . . . .Chris Douridas

Hollywood — "The Texas Chainsaw Massacre Part 2" plays like a warped American Gothic. Mainstream values are pushed beyond the lunatic fringe to reveal a vision at once ghastly and hilarious. Fans of the genre may find the sociological musings an unnecessary distraction, but there's still enough blood let to satisfy their wildest dreams.

Success of the lowbudget "Chainsaw" in 1974 spawned a generation of splatter films which largely have lost the power to shock and entertain. Not so "Chainsaw 2." Director Tobe Hooper is back on the Texas turf he knows best and proves there still a few thrills and chills left to be found.

Also a big help is L.M. Kit Carson's tongue-in-cheek script which supplies the mandatory ingredients, but also has the humor and self-awareness to play as a parody of the genre it helped start.

In truth the story doesn't amount to much and is basically a setup for a series of gory confrontations, but undercurrent of humor keeps one interested while the action scenes are too perverse to turn away from. The underlying pathology of the attraction is not lost on the filmmakers and in fact, they make it the subject of the film.

The family is just an ordinary American hard luck story — butchers who have fallen on hard times and take their resentment out on the human race. Back from the original "Saw" is Jim Siedow as the cook who delights Dallas gourmets with his chili made with 100% grade "A" U.S. prime people meat.

This is clearly a family with an ax to grind and throughout their abandoned Alamo theme park are lockers of curing limbs and human hamhocks. Not a sight for the squeamish.

Also at the butcher block are Leatherface (Bill Johnson) and Chop-Top (Bill Moseley), a Vietnam vet who literally left the better part of his skull over 'here.

On the other side is Dennis Hopper, a retired Texas Ranger out to revenge the killing of his family back in the original "Saw." Packing chainsaw sixguns in a holster at his side, Hopper has the zeal of a fundamentalist preacher setting out to clean up the filth. It's a classic good guys-bad guys confrontation, but by this time both sides have become extreme crazed cases.

Caught between the two poles are an array of "normal" people and good old American fun — parades, football games, eating, drinking and working. Innocent caught in the middle is young radio deejay Caroline Williams who accidently steps over the line of sanity and winds up as bait for Hopper's revenge scheme. Her performance consists mostly of screaming at a variety of human atrocities.

Although Hopper gets top billing his role is surprisingly limited, climaxing in a chainsaw duel to the death with Leatherface. Performances of the family are fine, especially Siedow and a crazed Moseley, but the real star here is carnage, highlighted through Cary White's production design and Tom Savini's makeup.

And if ever a film called for a heavy metal score this is it, supplied here by Hooper, Lambert and a selection of rock tunes.—*Jagr.*

Jonas, Dejme Tomu Ve Stredu
(Jonas Say, For Instance, On Wednesday)
(CZECH-COLOR)

A Barrandov Studios Prague, production Directed by Vladimir Sis. Stars Jiri Suchy and Jitka Molavcova. Screenplay, Suchy; camera (color), Ota Kopriva. Reviewed at Karlovy Vary Film Festival (market), July 16, 1986. Running time: **86 MINS.**

Karlovy Vary — Prague's famous "Semafor" theater, which influenced the whole '60s Czech filmmaking generation with its intellectual-political-musical cabaret, is remembered lovingly in this touching tribute to the theater (still going strong), to its lyricist, singer Jiri Suchy and its late composer-songwriter Jiri Slitr. (Czech film directors Jiri Menzel and Milos Forman were members of the socalled "S&S" Semafor "family.")

Suchy still works the Semafor, along with popular Czech songstress Jitka Molavcova. The pair play Jonas and Char, fictitious entertainers, who re-do many of the

Semafor routines and songs that bring back to life the art and atmosphere of the '60s Prague jazz scene. Directed by veteran Czech film and tv specialist in musicals Vladimir Sis, the film is a screen version of the longrunning Semafor production, with story by Magdalena Dietl, collaborator with the late Jaroslav Dietl, leading Czech tv playwright.

Archive sequences including excerpts from Forman's 1963 semi-documentary "Competition" (Forman's 1971 U.S. debut "Taking Off" borrows from it) and Menzel's satiric 1968 "Crime In The Night Club," with Semafor locales, recall the revolutionary Prague '60s.

The music is irresistible, and if there are Prague in-jokes, it won't matter to an international audience, for the words, though heavy with nostalgia if not political double meanings, have a universal appeal to "life in the night club shut away in the closet of your heart," as one lyric phrases it. Suchy has lost none of his acting charm and voice and Molavcova, doing her own musical routines, reveals a talent that deserves wider recognition.

Both are still drawing lines at the popular Semafor in downtown Prague, though Suchy, in disfavor at the time, had a few lean years in the '70s. Technical credits are strong and film would be a "find" for Czech film weeks, festivals and specialized arthouse runs. —*Milg.*

Hud
(Skin)
(NORWEGIAN-COLOR)

A Synchron Film release of an As Film production with Norway Film Development. Producers, Vibeke Lökkeberg, Terje Kristiansen. Executive producer, Kristiansen. Directed by Lökkeberg. Screenplay, Kristiansen, Lökkeberg; camera (Technicolor), Paul Roestad; editor, Terje Kristiansen; music, Arne Nordheim; production design, Grethe Heier; costumes, Tull Engö; sound (Dolby stereo), Erik Ryr, Jacob Trier; production management, Ole Björn Salvesen, Hans Lundgren. Reviewed as official entry in 14th Norwegian Film Festival at the Fönix Cinema, Kristiansand, Aug. 19, 1986. Running time: **186 MINS.**
Vilde . . . . Vibeke Lökkeberg
Sigurd, her stepfather . . . . Keve Hjelm
The Vicar . . . . Per Oscarsson
Vilde's mother . . . . . Elizabeth Granneman
Edward, an artist . . . . Terence Stamp
Edward's wife . . . . Patricia Hodge
Malene . . . . Tonje Kamilla Kristiansen
Also with: Per Janssen, Reine Torleifsson, Tage Svenneby.

Kristiansand — "Skin," a second feature by writer-helmer Vibeke Lökkeberg, clearly is a victim of "Heaven's Gate" syndrome. First, Lökkeberg was lauded internationally for her low-budget "Kamilla." Then, she and Terje Kristiansen, her producer-husband, who took over as helmer, saw "The Chieftain," their rough-hewn takeoff on male

chauvinism mellers, top Norwegian boxoffice several months running. And now, with "Skin," a top-coin production by local standards ($2,000,000), Lökkeberg, who stars, directed and co-wrote and co-produced with Kristiansen (who did nearly everything else except perform), has indulged to an excess in stylistic mannerisms and narrative repetition amounting to a quagmire.

As far as boxoffice goes, item (if so flimsy a word can be applied to a picture running well over three hours) seems destined to sink without a trace both at home and abroad. But "Skin" has a lot going for it and may well end up as an important footnote when the century's history of European filmmaking is written.

"Skin" is, in concept and looks, akin to David Lean's "Ryan's Daughter" and Karel Reisz' "The French Lieutenant's Woman." It has stunning production values: each frame moves fluently, gracefully, into its successor, and they amount cumulatively to the experience of a slow walk through London's National Gallery. There is nothing wrong with the acting, either, although sustained looks of silent torment severely challenge even talents like Terence Stamp and Lökkeberg herself.

The story is High Gothic with additions of present-day sexual psychodrama. On an island off Norway's rocky North Sea coast in 1895, Lökkeberg is seen as Vilde, stepdaughter of economically troubled Sigurd, who incestuously abused her when she was still a good deal below her teens. She has a small daughter, Malene, who is seemingly mute. Is she the product of her mother's affair with an English sculptor (Stamp), who once came to the island to use Vilde as model for a ship's figurehead? Or is Sigurd her father? At any rate, the child is present throughout the film to watch while her mother submits, more or

less voluntarily, to Sigurd's sexual abuse again and again.

Very often, Vilde goes off to wander along the storm-whipped coast in search of an escape from life in general or from the rough approaches of either Sigurd or a rich suitor. There also is a fat, elderly and invalid mother well worth getting away from. Whatever happens, the stepfather, seen mostly as abject and glassy-eyed or moaning in raw passion, keeps insisting it is all Vilde's fault anyway, probably for just being there and for being of the feminine gender.

When the family finally succeeds in getting Vilde married off to the local bigwig, latter obviously considers rape the only way to reach her sexually. Breaking out finally of her torpor, Vilde goes into action and pierces more than the skin of the man's back with a kitchen knife. Whatever skin symbolism may be gleaned from this may find support in the fact that the guy ran a tannery.

By murdering the wrong man, so to speak, Vilde must see Sigurd, the real culprit, go free, while her small daughter, who defiantly has smeared herself with her mother's lipstick and who now mouths the word "Mama" for the first time, may be left to a fate even worse than Vilde's own. Everybody is a victim in some way or another, in this story. The males are doomed to be beasts, the women to sexual slavery. There is no hope.

When Ibsen's Nora slammed the door behind her, she did not mean to come back. With helmer Lökkeberg's grand-scale technical mastery and artistic originality applied to stories not so strictly out of her private family workshop, she is sure to return as a major European filmmaker. Meanwhile, her "Skin" may be salvaged only via severe application of scissors, cutting film by at least one hour. —*Kell.*

★★★★★★★★★★★★★★★★★★★★★★★
★ **Venice Film Festival Reviews** ★
★★★★★★★★★★★★★★★★★★★★★★★

Mélo
(FRENCH-COLOR)

An MK2 production and release. Co-produced by Films A2, with the participation of the C.N.C. (Ministry of Culture). Produced by Marin Karmitz. Directed by Alain Resnais. Screenplay, Resnais, based on Henry Bernstein's play, "Mélo" (1929); camera (Agfa-Gevaert color), Charlie Van Damme; editor, Albert Jurgenson; production design, Jacques Saulnier; sound, Henri Morelle, Jacques Maumont; music, Brahms, Bach, Philippe Gérard; costumes, Catherine Leterrier; makeup, Doninique De Vorges; assistant director, Florence Malraux; production manager, Catherine Lapoujade. Reviewed at Club 13, Paris, Aug. 18, 1986. (Showing at Venice Film Festival out of competition.) Running time: **110 MINS.**
Romaine Belcroix . . . . Sabine Azéma
Pierre Belcroix . . . . Pierre Arditi
Marcel Blanc . . . . André Dussollier
Christiane Levesque . . . . Fanny Ardant
Also with: Jacques Dacqmine (Dr. Rémy), Hubert Gignoux (a priest), Catherine Arditi (Yvonne).

Paris — "Mélo" is canned theater, with a quality label applied by producer Marin Karmitz, director Alain Resnais, lenser Charlie Van Damme, production designer Jac-

ques Saulnier and players Sabine Azéma, Pierre Arditi and André Dussollier.

Resnais, who until now has worked only from original screenplays, has been scrupulously faithful to this 1929 legit melodrama by Henry Bernstein, and has given his stage-to-screen transfer a tasteful and finely tuned production. But the question that lingers is: Why?

Bernstein dominated the French theater of the inter-war years with his cruel high society dramas of sex, money and power, and film producers of the period avidly snatched up screen rights to prolong their theatrical lucrativeness. "Mélo" was filmed five times, most notably in a 1932 French production by Paul Czinner, with Gaby Morlay and Pierre Blanchar, recreating their parts in the original stage production, and Victor Francen, in the role created by Charles Boyer (who was in Hollywood when the picture was made).

Bernstein's plays no longer are performed today, the best known of them being chiefly remembered via their screen versions. Even if it has conserved its well-oiled dramatic efficiency, "Mélo" is still a hackneyed ménage à trois piece, and its exhumation by Resnais is perplexing. Film's commercial value will be limited to the art circuit.

Arditi and Dussollier play two violinists, old friends from Conservatory days, who are in love with the same woman, Azéma, the former's wife. Dussollier, now a famed soloist with a reputation of a ladies' man, conquers Azéma and makes her his mistress.

Their passion becomes so intense and exclusive that Azéma tries to poison her husband, but her nerve fails and she commits suicide instead. Before throwing herself in the Seine she writes Arditi a farewell letter, in which she confirms her love, but reveals nothing of her affair with Dussollier.

Some years later, Arditi, who has built something of a morbid cult around his dead wife (whose letter he keeps locked away in a shrine-like bank deposit box), comes across Azéma's old address book with a telltale hint of her passionate fling. In a superb final scene, Arditi confronts Dussollier and tries to extract the truth, but latter holds out and preserves Arditi's illusion about Azéma's fidelity.

Under Resnais' meticulously controlled direction, Azéma, Arditi and Dussollier perform their cruel sonata with evident dramatic relish, even if the tone of restrained emotion sometimes does a disservice to the melodramatic gist of a scene.

A fourth role, that of an adoring woman friend who marries Arditi after Azéma's death, is played by Fanny Ardant, who is bland in a thankless part. Ironically it was Ardant who first suggested "Mélo" to Resnais, who was looking for a vehicle in which to cast the quartet of players of his previous film, "L'Amour à mort."

With the exception of the brief scene of Azéma's suicide, the entire film, respecting Bernstein's stage instructions, was shot in the studio, and Saulnier's sets — notably the garden patio decor of the long opening act, and Dussollier's art deco apartment (furnished with work by painter Juan Gris, architect Robert Mallet-Stevens and others) — are elegantly evocative of the drama's sense of entrapment and frustration.

Resnais makes some nostalgic winks to old films with the opening credit gimmick of a hand turning the pages of a program, and shots of a stage curtain to denote act changes.

"Mélo" is screening out of competition at Venice. —*Len.*

X
(NORWEGIAN-COLOR)

A Norena release (foreign sales via Norsk Film/Frieda Ohrvik) of Elinor Film/Filmgruppe 84/Christiania Film Compagnie production. Executive producers, Laila Mikkelsen, Ola Solum, Odvar Einarson. Written and directed by Odvar Einarson. Stars Jon Gabriel Svendsen, Bettina Banoun. Camera (Eastmancolor), Svein Krövel; production design, Torun Müller; editor, Inger-Lise Langfeldt; sound (Dolby stereo), Ragnar Samuelsson; music, Andrej Nebb, Holy Toy; production manager, Ole Björn Salvesen. Reviewed in official program of 14th Norwegian Film Festival at the Fönix, Kristiansand (in competition at Venice Film Festival), Aug. 17, 1986. Running time: **93 MINS.**
Jon . . . . Jörn Christiansen
Flora . . . . Bettina Banoun
Also with: Atle Mostad, Sigrid Huun, Hege Schöyen, Are Storstein, Caspar Evensen, Sven Henriksen, Trond Lybekk, Ola Solum and rock groups Holy Toy, Garden Of Delight, Backstreet Girls.

Kristiansand, Norway — For his feature film debut — after successful short subject excursions into a variety of film styles and genres — writer-helmer Odvar Einarson, 27, is adamant that the title "X" must suffice. What is really more important than any symbolism, which would tend to be trite anyway, is Einarson's obvious display of an extraordinary cinematic talent. He, himself, will hardly remain an unknown factor after this one.

Einarson uses soft-focus cinematography, clean-cut narrative, sharply edged vignette, open-ended episodes plus many asides of expressionistic strength to offer as a plot the short run of an impossible love affair. The lovers are 19-year-old Jon, a gangly, awkward loner, who also is a photographer of obdurate artistic convictions and obvious talent, and Flora, a runaway girl of 14 who moves in with Jon without really being asked.

Having the child-woman around to be taken care of, to have fun with, to sleep with (mostly like a boy with a puppy) distracts Jon from work on a gallery show he is preparing, but the work gets done somehow, while Flora, a demure little brunet beauty, either tags along, pouting, joyful, bewildered or remarkably self-assured, or absconds temporarily. She may return to her messy home (a drunken father, a dope-addict sister, the dreary works, although not seen without some warmth and empathy) or she may rejoin squatter friends in a condemned house. When with Jon, she sees (in a beautifully dizzying sequence) a rock group at work in a film studio or she hunts junk treasurers in the cobwebbed nooks of the huge basement of an abandoned factory.

As long as the two youngsters are together, their love lives like a flickering candle. Flora is the one to finally snuff out the feeble flame, admitting to being really too young not to go on exploring the world on her own. All this comes across without a single touch of the maudlin. On the other hand, the couple serve mostly as devices to allow the director to roam at will through a mental cityscape of eerie attraction.

The X of the title, scrawled across one of many backyard walls, may be allusion to Big City anonymity. It could also mark the spot where fates met and somehow left their anonymous imprint on the larger scheme of things. Visual pleasures serve to make the matter unimportant.

The flame, the candle and fire in general are, along with water, among picture's many obvious tributes to Andrei Tarkovsky trademarks. Einarson and cinematographer Svein Krövel's pictorial flow in general is pure Tarkovsky in its interchanging of stark, still frames and gently moving nocturnal views. With a larger psychological theme and a less filmsy story to tell, Einarson would appear to command enough fresh imagery and keen insight to soon move beyond what some undoubtedly will see as a merely derivative exercise.—*Kell.*

Directed By William Wyler
(U.S.-DOCU-COLOR)

A Tatge production. Produced by Catherine Tatge. Executive producer, Catherine Wyler. Directed and edited by Aviva Slesin. Narration, interviews, A. Scott Berg; camera (color), Richard Leacock, others. Reviewed at World Film Festival, Montreal, Aug. 22, 1986. Running time: **60 MINS.**
With: William Wyler, Bette Davis, Laurence Olivier, Lillian Hellman, Gregory Peck, Billy Wilder, Audrey Hepburn, John Huston, Greer Garson, Terence Stamp, Samantha Eggar, Charlton Heston, Barbra Streisand, Ralph Richardson, Talli Wyler.

Montreal — A compact, exemplary study of one of Hollywood's premier directors, Aviva Slesin's affectionate portrait is built around an interview with William Wyler filmed in July 1981, three days before his death.

Wyler talks with candor and great good humor about his career and his collaborators as Slesin lucidly fills in biographical details and incorporates judiciously chosen excerpts from pics spanning "Crook Buster," a 1925 shoot-'em-up, to "Funny Lady."

Wyler comes across as an immensely likeable man, and an instinctive, rather than intellectual, talent. As John Huston wryly remarks, "It's an utter mystery to me where Willie got it!" and several actors testify that Wyler found it hard to communicate with them. Charlton Heston notes that, on "Ben-Hur," Wyler would say only, "You just gotta be better," and Terence Stamp even says he doubted the director could speak good English.

But when Wyler found material that engaged him, he was able to bring emotion to the screen like few others before or since, and scenes from "The Best Years Of Our Lives" are as moving today, even in excerpt form, as they always were: Billy Wilder notes, sardonically, that he cried all through that picture — "And I laughed at Hamlet!"

Other fascinating comments include Lillian Hellman's that she thought "Mrs. Miniver" was "a piece of junk" and Laurence Olivier explaining how, on "Wuthering Heights," Wyler taught him how to act for the cinema. Bulk of the interview footage, apart from Wyler himself, goes to Bette Davis, in fine form and still quibbling about the right way to play the famous line from "The Letter."

Color home movie footage includes coverage of the filming of "Wuthering Heights" and Wyler with his wife, Talli, on vacation in Europe and at home. Other film excerpts include "These Three," "Counsellor-at-Law," "Jezebel," "The Heiress," "Roman Holiday," "The Friendly Persuasion," "The Big Country," "Ben-Hur" and "Funny Girl."

This is an excellent, though too brief, study of Wyler and deserves to be widely seen: it's already been nabbed by the New York, Venice, Deauville, Nyon, Chicago and Berlin fests.—*Strat.*

Pong
(The Mulberry Tree)
(SOUTH KOREAN-COLOR)

A Tac Hung production. Produced by Lee Tae-won. Directed by Lee Doo-yong. Screenplay, Yoon Sam-yook; camera (color), Son Hyunchae; music, Choi Chang-kwon; assistant director, Kim Hy-ok. Reviewed at World Film Fest, Montreal, Aug. 24, 1986. Running time: **107 MINS.**
With: Lee Mee-sook, Lee Tae-gun, Lee Moo-jung, Han Tai-il, Kim Jung-Ha.

Montreal — Set during the Japanese occupation of Korea in the '20s, "The Mulberry Tree" is a comedy-drama whose abrupt shifts of mood are disconcerting. Located in a small village, story centers on An Hy-op, an attractive woman whose husband, Sam-bo, is away for long periods on business. In order to survive, Hy-op starts sleeping with the men in the village who give her rice and other necessities, thus she attracts the wrath of the village women, who demand she be ousted.

Comedy comes from the presence of Sam-tol, a plump village idiot, who's played by an actor very much in the Buddy Hackett mold. Hy-op refuses to sleep with Sam-tol, who gets mad and stirs trouble for her. A climax, of sorts, comes when the villagers bring in a wise old man to instruct Hy-op to leave town, but she seduces him by showing her scars, obtained as a result of a beating from the village women.

Combination of low comedy and drama makes for an odd little item, with over-the-top acting and camerawork that relies far too much on the zoom lens to be very attractive. Technical credits are otherwise fine. —*Strat.*

Ein Virus Kennt Keine Moral
(A Virus Knows No Morals)
(WEST GERMAN-COLOR)

A Rosa Von Praunheim production. Produced, directed, scripted by Rosa Von Praunheim. Camera (color), Elfi Mikesch; editors, Michael Schaeffer, Von Praunheim; music,

Maran Gosov, The Bermudas; sound, Michael Schaefer, Reinhard Sterger. Reviewed at World Film Fest, Montreal, Aug. 22, 1986. Running time: **82 MINS.**

Rudiger (club owner)	Rosa Von Praunheim
Christian	Dieter Dicken
Dr. Blut	Maria Hasenaecker
Student	Christian Kesten
Carola	Eva Kurz
Therapist	Regina Rudnick
Mother	Thilo von Trotha

Montreal — The films of Berlin-based Rosa Von Praunheim (real name, Holger Mischwitzki) are undoubtedly an acquired taste, but his latest is, in some ways, his most interesting. It's an irreverent, yet deadly serious, comedy about the spread of the AIDS virus among the gay community, and, via a series of often bizarre characters and caricatures, it manages to touch on many of the probelms facing the community as a result of the disease.

Von Praunheim himself plays the insensitive owner of a gay sauna for whom the disease is merely an annoying intrusion on his business. Other characters are more directly affected, including a man whose mother refuses to help him, though he's dying. A variety of establishment figures are energetically lampooned, including a voracious woman scientist. Dr. Blut (Blood), who goes to Africa to find the source of the virus and gets AIDS from an ape, a woman journalist, working for a scandal sheet; and a government minister whose solution to the problem is to have all gays incarcerated in a kind of modern concentration camp on an island.

Among all these crazy scenes and characters, Von Praunheim covers just about every aspect of AIDS and its effects, as well as the rumors surrounding it. The film's frivolous tone is in marked contrast to other, serious AIDS pics, and at first it's hard to accept such a subject handled in such a comic way; yet ultimately the points are made, via humor, with as much, if not more, effect.

Technically the pic is pretty sloppy, with grainy camerawork and choppy editing, but the overall effect is quite powerful. —*Strat.*

Aghaat
(Blood Of Brothers)
(INDIAN-COLOR)

A Neo Films Associates production. Produced by Manmohan Shetty. Pradeep Uppoor. Directed by Govind Nihalani. Screenplay, Nijay Tendulkar; camera (color), Nihalani; editor, Sutanu Gupta; art director, Nitish Roy; music, Ajit Varman; assistant director, R. Parsekar; consultant, Sandeep Pense. Reviewed at World Film Festival, Montreal (in competition), Aug. 22, 1986. Running time: **148 MINS.**

Madhav Verma	Om Puri
Krishnan Raju	Gopi
Chotelal	Pankaj Kapoor
Rustom Patel	Naseeruddin Shah

Also with: Deepa Sahi, Amrish Puri, Sadashiv Amrapurkar, Rohini Hattangadi, K.K. Raina, M.K. Raina, Harish Payel.

Montreal — India's competing entry in Montreal is the latest political drama of director/cinematographer Govind Nihalani, who could be described as the Costa-Gavras of India in that his films usually deal in dramatic terms with a political situation. This time the theme is the bitter rivalry between unions in a large factory.

The film's hero, Verma (Om Puri) is organizer for the long-established Communist (pro-Lenin) union. He's presented as a decent man, genuinely concerned about the welfare of his members, and willing to work on good terms with management to ensure things at the plant run smoothly.

Trouble starts when a new, more militant union is formed (sans political allegiances). The militant union's organizer (Naseeruddin Shah), who isn't seen until the penultimate scene, uses a muscleman and strong-arm tactics to bully and menace his way into the factory, also making far higher demands than Verma and his colleagues. The dilemma Verma faces is whether to stoop to the same low tactics of intimidation as his rivals, while meanwhile the factory management holds back to see who'll win the conflict.

A subplot involves a factory accident in which a worker is paralyzed and, eventually, dies. The factory's response, when he's first hospitalized, is to present him with a bedpan. But the film does present in a sympathetic light a young p.r. officer at the factory who's seen as caring more than others for the plight of the injured man.

The film is overlong and slowly paced, and overly emphatic at times. For instance, early sequences involving the muscleman (Gopi) have him always shot from behind, giving him the kind of menace found in old B-features. Despite flaws, it's an interesting and dramatically satisfying film. —*Strat.*

Mammame
(FRENCH-COLOR)

A Maison de la Culture du Havre production. Produced by Jean-Luc Larguier. Written and directed by Raul Ruiz. Camera (color), Jacques Bouquin; editor, Martine Bouquin; production design, Ruiz; music, Henry Torque, Serge Houppin; choreography, Jean-Claude Gallota; costumes, Francoise Chanas, Patricia Goudinoux. Reviewed at the Parisien 3, Montreal, Aug. 22, 1986 (Montreal World Film Festival out of competition). Running time: **65 MINS.**

With: Eric Alfieri, Mathilde Altaraz, Muriel Boulay, Christophe Delachau, Jean-Claude Gallota, Pascal Gravat, Priscilla Newell, Viviane Serry, Robert Seyfried.

Montreal — The surrealist sensibilities of expatriate Chilean film-maker Raul Ruiz are married with avant-garde dance in this intriguing, elliptical short film which examines the inextricable bond between the sexes on a metaphoric battleground of primal emotions. The dance motif renders "Mammame" more accessible than much of Ruiz' determinedly oblique work and could fit the bill for arthouse programmers seeking a short second film to complement an esoteric feature.

A company of five male and four female dancers engage one another in a series of stylized, demi-pantomimic routines in which the women's touch reduces the men to a state of babbling semi-paralysis. States of being are transitory here, however, and the men rebound in short order, driven by the engine of sexual-emotional desires that are both reciprocated and rejected by the women, who vacillate between aggression, tenderness and tense caution.

These dance encounters unfold in ever-changing patterns against an antiseptic backdrop of metallic gray-green corridors and an empty stage upon which simple props such as a telephone and mattress appear and disappear. The dancers are garbed in institutional blue-gray denim, suggesting either that humans are all prisoners of their most repressed emotions or simply reduced to insanity by their inability to express them.

Ruiz depicts the hidden personality, stripped of the usual social defenses, through dialog that is a fragmentary linguistic melange of feverish, infantile psychobabble, and reinforces the sense of personality disassociation through shifting, vertiginous camera angles.

Suddenly the nine dancers (an odd man out is pushed and pulled by homosexual impulses) are transported to a rugged promontory overlooking a spectacular sunrise and the sea. On this windswept landscape they finally appear reconciled to their existence as human animals elevated through spiritual love.

The dancers effectively execute the athletic choreography and convincingly evoke a state of emotional nakedness that's heightened by an impressionistic, jazz-influenced musical score. —*Rich.*

Exit-Exil
(Exit-Exile)
(FRENCH-BELGIAN-COLOR)

An MBC Prods.-Cinété coproduction, in association with the French and Belgian Ministries of Culture. Produced by Willum Thijssen. Written and directed by Luc Monheim. Camera (Fujicolor), Mario Barroso, Frederic Variot; art director, Pierre Cadiou; editor, Yves Deschamps; sound, Miguel Rejas; assistant director, Albert Sales; production manager, Catherine Staub. Reviewed at World Film Festival, Montreal, Aug. 23, 1986. Running time: **110 MINS.**

Dutch	Philippe Léotard
Olivia	Frederique Hender
Solange	Magali Noël

Also with: Georges Geret, Jean-Pierre Sentier, Fabrice Eberhard, Jean Lescot, Jean de Coninck, Brigitte Audrey.

Montreal — A brash, noisy fantasy of little distinction. "Exit-Exile" is an infuriating film. First section is set in a sleazy nightclub where Olivia (Frederique Hender) works as a stripper. Her alcoholic lover, Duke (Philippe Léotard) wants her out of there, and when she's not involved in endlessly long and unerotic dance routines, they shriek at each other.

After this audience-alienating opening, the action shifts to a giant garbage dump where Olivia's apparent parents (it's not too clear) live with other bums. She's gone home. Duke follows her. More yelling. At the end, a religious theme enters the picture, but as unconvincingly as the rest of it.

Maybe director Luc Monheim knew what he was doing, but he kept his ideas to himself. The unfortunate actors are left to flay around in some of the worst over-acting in a long while, and although there's some inventive and fluid camerawork, it doesn't save this obscure, pretentious effort. —*Strat.*

Last Song
(SWISS-FRENCH-COLOR)

A La Cécilia production. Produced by Martine Marignac. Directed by Denis Berry. Screenplay, Berry, Anna Karina; camera (color), Armand Marco; editor, Jennifer Auge; production design, Laurent Allaire; music, Stephane Vilar; sound, Alix Comte; costumes, Eve Marie Arnaul. Reviewed at the Parisiene 2, Montreal, Aug. 23, 1986 (Montreal World Film Festival out of competition). Running time: **90 MINS.**

With: Gabrielle Lazure, Scott Renderer, Anna Karina, Anouk Grinberg, Geoffrey Carey, Remy Kolpa, Michel Didym, Laurent Allaire, Steve Baes, Jimi Dragotta, Peter Smith.

Montreal — A psychological murder-mystery love story with a rock 'n' roll motif, "Last Song" is laced with flaws but of some interest as an English-language feature made by an American director in Europe with French-speaking filmmakers. Like the clearly superior French film "High Speed," also debuting at the Montreal World Film Festival, "Last Song" may signal a trend by continental indies to storm the lucrative (but foreign-language resistant) U.S. market with hip contempo films in the native tongue. A scrappy U.S. distributor willing to gamble on a loss-leader with limited run potential might opt for this botched continental tale.

An opening setup in "Hoboken,

New Jersey, U.S.A.," finds Tommy (Scott Renderer) working in a dead-end gasoline alley job on the waterfront. Suddenly a radio announces the death by suicide in Paris of the great rock star Billy Steel, who happens to be his older brother. Voila, Tommy's in Paris in search of reasons for his brother's death. Tom soon discovers his brother knew some very nasty people who enjoy things like pushing pretty girls' faces through plate glass windows. In the best tradition of do-it-yourself amateur detective pics, Tom begins to wonder if Billy wasn't murdered.

His search leads him to Billy's widow, a blowzy French rock singer who says things like "everything he left behind he wanted to collapse," and advises him not to go looking for trouble. Naturally, he goes looking for trouble in Billy's old warehouse digs, where he finds tapes of songs the two brothers wrote together before Billy reached stardom and Tommy oblivion.

The songs are maudlin Springsteen ripoffs, rendered in a depressing, barely melodic croak. However, Billy's old associates need to finish the superstar's last LP and they want Tom (who's got a Huey Lewis look and a Don Johnson beard) to stop his sobbing, pick up a guitar and play in a band that looks as if it were recruited at a halfway house.

Indeed, Tom's investigation of Billy's past leads to a drug clinic and also to a rock club where he meets his brother's old flame Julie (Gabrielle Lazure) a gorgeous aspiring rock chanteuse. She's powerfully drawn to this mirror image of her dead lover, and the mutual attraction is so strong they usually have sex without taking the time to disrobe entirely or find a bed. Julie, however, is a mixed up American rich kid with secrets to hide, and she knows a lot more about Billy's death than she wants to admit.

A couple of murders later, Tom discovers Julie's father is a U.S. senator and that her dead transvestite brother also was Billy's lover. All of these rock 'n' roll expatriate gumshoe adventures are unfolded with agonizingly overwrought acting and a script rife with unintentionally funny melodramatic overkill. The film's forced hip mannerisms are not made any easier to bear by an undistinguished rock soundtrack, choppy editing and scratchy sound during key musical scenes. —Rich.

Reform School Girls
(COLOR)

Tame titillation.

A New World Pictures release. Produced by Jack Cummins. Executive producers, Gregory Hinton, Leo Angelos. Written and directed by Tom deSimone. Camera (Foto-Kem color; Technicolor prints), Howard Wexler; editor, Michael Spence; music, Tedra Gabriel; production design, Becky Block; set decoration, Tom Talbert; sound, Steve Nelson; associate producers, Charles Skouras 3d, Kathy Lee Kennedy; assistant director, Kristine Peterson; casting, Dan Siegal. Reviewed at the Hollywood Pacific Theater, L.A., Aug. 18, 1986. (MPAA Rating: R.) Running time: 94 MINS.
Jenny . . . . Linda Carol
Charlie . . . . Wendy O. Williams
Edna . . . . Pat Ast
Sutter . . . . Sybil Danning
Dr. Norton . . . . Charlotte McGinnis
Lisa . . . . Sherri Stoner
Claudia . . . . Denise Gordy
Nicky . . . . Laurie Schwartz
Fish . . . . Tiffany Helm
Knox . . . . Darcy DeMoss

Hollywood — "Reform School Girls" don't have it so bad. For one thing, they don't have to wear uniforms — or much else for that matter. They talk dirty, play dirty and are allowed to take long, long showers. They can even earn special privileges from the head matron for consenting to various requests. Film has a certain, limited b.o. appeal.

Wendy O. Williams doesn't exactly qualify as a girl, but she has the lead role here anyway as the gravelly voiced, hardened delinquent, Charlie.

The busty actress, who made a name for herself as the head-banging lead singer of the rock group, The Plasmatics, continues her trashy theatrics here as a leather-clad lesbian who reigns terror over the other girls serving time at Pridemore Juvenile Facilities.

Supported by her gang of "death rockers," Williams intimidates each new arrival into submission until she encounters fresh-faced Jenny (Linda Carol), who is bent on countering corruption at Pridemore.

Except for a couple of moments where Charlie and head matron Edna (Pat Ast) make a few gestures to establish their sexual preferences, there are no scenes of same gender sex, just a lot of harsh words and several contrived confrontations where the girls thrash around in their undies.

"Girls" manages at times to be funny in its baseness.

Every character is a caricature, from the rifle-toting, Bible-quoting warden (Sybil Danning) to the lineup of lovelies who parade as reform school girls.

Ast looks like a man dressed like a woman and is described in the production notes as cantankerous and corpulent, which she certainly is.

She and Williams play their rotten roles to the hilt and get most of the juicy lines, but they — nor anyone else — don't deliver all that much in the way of action that could be considered offensive or perverted enough that teenage boys wouldn't be able to giggle at.

Low-budget pic is simply a thinly-veiled excuse to tamely titi-late, which it manages to do quite well. —Brit.

Yiddish Connection
(FRENCH-COLOR)

A UGC release of an AFC/FR 3 Films/UGC/TOP 1 coproduction, in association with Cinérgie. Produced by Maurice Bernart. Directed by Paul Boujenah. Stars Charles Aznavour, Ugo Tognazzi, André Dussollier. Screenplay, Didier Kaminka, from an original story by Aznavour; camera (Eastmancolor), Yves Dahan; editor, Eva Zora; sound, Roger Di Ponio; music, George Garvarentz; art director Michèle Abbé-Vannier; production manager, Marcel Godot; assistant director, Philippe Guez. Reviewed at the UGC screening room, Neuilly, France, Aug. 20, 1986. Running time: 84 MINS.
Aaron Rapoport . . . . Charles Aznavour
Moshe di Cremona . . . . Ugo Tognazzi
The Seminarian . . . . André Dussollier
Zvi . . . . Vincent Lindon
Samy . . . . Charlie Chemouny
Also with: Geneviève Mnich, Roland Blanche, Jean-Claude Dauphin, Bill Dunn, Caroline Chaniolleau, Alain Sarde, Jean-François Perrier, Alicia Alonso, Anne Berger.

Neuilly — In "Yiddish Connection," Charles Aznavour and Ugo Tognazzi are Jewish merchants in Paris who unceasingly roll their eyes Heavenward as they plot, with the help of God and a safecracking clergyman, the heist that will solve their financial headaches.

Audiences may do likewise (after looking down at their watches), if only to ask the Good Lord (who didn't make movies during those first Six Days), how talented professionals can sin so dopily against their metier by taking part in such amateurish nonsense.

For Aznavour the answer is obvious: he's the author of the lamentable original story, adapted witlessly by Didier Kaminka, who has written some good comedies ("My New Partner") and some bad ones.

As for Tognazzi and André Dussollier, who plays the drawling outlaw cleric, one can only surmise that, like their roles, they needed the gelt.

The director is 28-year-old Paul Boujenah, brother of the engaging comedian Michel Boujenah, which may be the only notable thing about him. "Big Deal On Yiddishe Mamma Street," his film isn't. — Len.

Night Of The Creeps
(COLOR/BLACK & WHITE)

Derivative horror comedy.

A Tri-Star Pictures production and release. Produced by Charles Gordon. Executive producer, William Finnegan. Written and directed by Fred Dekker. Stars Jason Lively, Steve Marshall, Jill Whitlow. Camera (CFI color/black & white), Robert C. New; editor, Michael N. Knue; music, Barry DeVorzon; production design, George Costello; art director/decorator, Maria Caso; costumes, Eileen Kennedy; makeup effects/creeps design, David B. Miller; associate producer production manager, Donna Smith; production supervisor, Vahan Moosekian; assistant director, Mark Allan; special visual effects, David Stripes Prods.; creeps supervisor, Dimensional Animation Effects, Ted Rae; casting, Ilene Starger. Reviewed at Rae Twin Cinema, Staten Island, N.Y., Aug. 23, 1986. (MPAA Rating: R.) Running time: 85 MINS.
Chris . . . . Jason Lively
J.C. . . . . Steve Marshall
Cynthia . . . . Jill Whitlow
Ray Cameron . . . . Tom Atkins
Det. Landis . . . . Wally Taylor
Sgt. Raimi . . . . Bruce Solomon
Coroner . . . . Vic Polizos
Brad . . . . Allan J. Kayser
Also with: Ken Heron, Alice Cadogan, June Harris, David Paymer, David Oliver, Evelyne Smith, Ivan E. Roth.

Borrowing freely from such films as "Alien" and "Night Of The Living Dead," with elements of "Animal House," "Night Of The Creeps" is a moderately entertaining horror comedy from first-time director Fred Dekker. Teen audiences expecting a mix of laughs and gruesome effects should be amused, but the mix is uneven at best. Commercial life should be spirited but brief.

Pic, which sports two prologs, takes too long to get to the main action, in which a pair of college freshmen (Jason Lively and Steve Marshall) are trying futilely to pledge a snobby fraternity, led by Allan J. Kayser (whose hair obviously has been bleached blond, as filmmakers apparently think all preppy frat brothers are blond).

For the umpteenth time in films, the incoming pair are told they must place a dead body in some conspicuous place in order to be accepted. Their search turns up a body cryogenically frozen in a lab, and when they let it out they also let out the creeps, large slug-like creatures that enter their victims through the mouth, incubate in the brain and turn the unlucky ones into zombies.

Bulk of the picture deals with how the icky things discreetly infiltrate the college campus, while the two heroes and Lively's would-be girlfriend (Jill Whitlow) try to battle the things off with the aid of the local police detective (Tom Atkins). The detective, it turns out, was on the beat when the creatures first landed in the community in 1959 — he thought he'd never have to deal with them again, and Atkins' cynical remarks throughout the pic are the only comic relief.

Acknowledging his mentors, Dekker has given his characters such last names as Romero, Hooper, Cronenberg, Landis, Raimi, Cameron and Craven, but the indiscriminate kids that turn out for this film probably won't catch the jokes. Technically, pic is sound enough.
—Gerz.

Double Messieurs
(Double Gentlemen)
(FRENCH-COLOR)

A BAC Films (Paris) presentation of a Sagamore Cinema production. Produced, written and directed by Jean François Stevenin. Camera (color), Pascal Marti; editor, Yann Dodet; sound, Dominique Hennequin. Reviewed at the Morettina Center, Locarno Film Festival, Aug. 16. Running time 90 MINS.
François . . . . Jean François Stevenin
Leo . . . . Yves Alonso
Helene . . . . Carole Bouquet

Locarno — Jean Paul Belmondo isn't going to like this picture which quite intentionally sends up the image of boyish charm and insouciance which have become the trademark of the French actor and the loving image he has been known to project for many years now.

Belmondo doesn't play in this picture, but one of the two male protagonists, Yves Alonso, pretends to be doing Belmondo's stunts for him, and bears from certain angles, an uncanny resemblance with the star himself.

This doesn't have to be taken on a personal level, however, since Stevenin is concerned with the difficulty of certain persons to grow out of their adolescence. His story concerns two such friends, one played by Alonso, the other by Stevenin himself, who are trying to recapture the spirit of their youth by going out to find a friend of theirs, of whom they used to make fun of 25 years ago in summer camp.

Their little joke, intended to put their friend in a spot, just like in the good old days, turns sour when instead of him they stumble on his wife, and through her into a whole new aspect of human relationships which have nothing to do with boisterous joviality.

Stevenin uses once again the close, intimate style of his first directorial effort, "Passe Montagne." Live sound puts strong accent on background noises, and indeed, unless the audience is very familiar with French and its slang, it might have difficulty following the dialog. Stevenin argues this is of secondary importance, but the Locarno audience didn't seem to agree with him.

There isn't much plot to follow, most of the film being based on situations and moods mostly implied by the camera, the background scenery of the mountains becoming increasingly important in the last part. The acting is remarkably effective and Pascal Marti's unusually flexible camera work indicates there is a close relationship in establishing the visual concept for this picture.

The absence of a clearcut, definite story as well as the language barrier, no doubt will constitute obstacles in the commercial career of the film, but Stevenin seems to possess the kind of personal style and is sufficiently determined not to compromise, to establish his own niche in the French cinema of the '80s.
— Edna.

Linna
(The Castle)
(FINNISH-COLOR)

A Kinosto release (international sales contact, the Finnish Film Foundation) of a Kaj Holmberg/Skandia Filmi production. Executive producer, Kaj Holmberg. Written and directed by Jaakko Pakkasvirta, based on Franz Kafka's novel. Camera (Fujicolor), Esa Vuorinen; editor, Pipsa Valavaara; sound (Dolby stereo), Johan Hake; music, Otto Donner; production design, Pentti Valkeasuo. Reviewed at the Finnish Film Foundation, Helsinki (in competition at Venice Film Festival), Aug. 12, 1986. Running time: 99 MINS.
With: Carl-Kristian Rundman (Josef K.), Titta Karakorpi (Frieda), Pirkka-Pekka Petelius, Vesa Vierikko, Risto Autio, Sari Mällinen, Anna-Leena Härkönen, Ulla Koivuranta.

Helsinki — While Jiri Menzel is prepping a Czech film version of "The Castle" (his countryman Franz Kafka's 1926 novel, previously filmed by Maximilian Schell and next to "The Trial" Kafka's most widely published work), Jaakko Pakkasvirta has been quietly at work on his own version of the book and has come up with a strikingly handsome, big-scale retelling of the story of land-surveyor Josef K. who loses his way in the alienation byways supposed to lead him to The Castle's owner. En route, he suffers abuse from villagers and castle officials, but seeks consolation in a few sexual encounters and in the idea of being in love with Frieda, a waitress and ex-mistress of Herr Klamm, the never-to-be-seen ruler of the story's claustrophobic realm.

A couple of viciously clownish assistants serve only to make Josef K. more miserable as he gets gradually more and more ensnared in the doubletalk employed by virtually everyone around him. When fighting to get out of the morass, Josef K. sinks deeper and deeper and finally dies from suffering what is — in the film — spelled out to be the total incomprehension of all the misfortune that befalls the faultlessly brought-up child.

The ending's moralistic point does not come through very convincingly — if of any interest at all — as spoken by a voice-over narrator. Otherwise, Pakkasvirta's picture turns the trick of making lively pictorial matter out of Kafka's essentially empty universe. The eeriness of the novel and all its alienation are rendered in a spirited way. The production values are of the highest order, and the acting in all roles combines menace with abject victimization in a mutely terrifying way. As Josef K., Carl-Kristian Rundman has some of the dark, good looks and nervy manners of a young Dirk Bogarde. As a film, "The Castle" succeeds far better than Orson Welles' 1962 version of "The Trial" in being truly Kafkaesque.—Kell.

Shanghai Surprise
(COLOR)

Silly, old-fashioned vehicle for Mr. & Mrs. Penn.

A UA/MGM release from MGM of a Handmade Films presentation produced in association with The Vista Organization. Produced by John Kohn. Coproducer, Robin Douet. Executive producers, George Harrison, Denis O'Brien. Directed by Jim Goddard. Stars Sean Penn, Madonna. Screenplay, Kohn, Robert Bentley, based on the novel "Faraday's Flowers" by Tony Kenrick; camera (Technicolor), Ernie Vincze; editor, Ralph Sheldon; music, George Harrison, Michael Kamen; songs, Harrison; production design, Peter Mullins; art direction, John Siddall, David Minty; costumes design, Judy Moorcroft; sound (Dolby), Andrew Boulton; associate producer, Sara Romilly; assistant director, Gino Marotta, Patty Chan (Hong Kong); casting, Ann Fielden, Judy Dennis, Pat Pao. Reviewed at the MGM Studios, Culver City, Aug. 29, 1986. (MPAA Rating: PG-13). Running time: 97 MINS.
Glendon Wasey . . . . Sean Penn
Gloria Tatlock . . . . Madonna
Walter Faraday . . . . Paul Freeman
Willie Tuttle . . . . Richard Griffiths
Justin Kronk . . . . Philip Sayer
Joe Go . . . . Clyde Kusatsu
Mei Gan . . . . Kay Tong Lim
China Doll . . . . Sonserai Lee
Ho Chong . . . . Victor Wong
Yamagani San . . . . Professor Toru Tanaka
Mr. Burns . . . . Michael Aldridge
China Doll's maid . . . . Sarah Lam

Hollywood — If "Shanghai Surprise" was the best project Sean Penn and Madonna could find to star in together, the screenplays floating around the industry these days must comprise a sorry lot indeed. Pic is a silly little trifle that wouldn't even have passed muster as a 1930s programmer, which is what it resembles in all ways except for its location lensing. Despite the potent names above the title, MGM is opening this one in the boonies before hitting the big cities but it won't make any difference, because this firecracker is a dud.

Tale is a phony, thoroughgoing concoction. For some reason that remains just as unclear and uninteresting at the end as it is at the beginning, a missionary, played at a stretch by Madonna, enlists the services of a down-and-out, would-be adventurer, none other than Mr. Penn, to help her track down a substantial supply of opium that has disappeared under mysterious circumstances a year before, in 1937, during the Japanese occupation of China.

The blood-stirring premise provides the excuse for any number of encounters with exotic and shady characters who would have been right at home in Warner Bros. foreign intrigue mellers 45 years ago. The actors playing most of these roles — notably Paul Freeman, Richard Griffiths, Philip Sayer, Kay Tong Lim, Sonserai Lee and especially Clyde Kusatsu as a baseball crazy underworld type — are pretty amusing in their own right and sustain the viewer through the nonsense, much as old-style supporting actors used to do.

But centerstage is the completely illogical relationship between the hustler and missionary. Penn seems game and has energy, but even he would have seemed somnambulant next to the fast-talking Warners stars of the 1930s. For her part, Madonna, with blond locks longer than those she currently sports, can't for a moment disguise that her character makes no sense at all. After starring as the latest thing in hip in ''Desperately Seeking Susan,'' playing a missionary next was not the way to go.

Maurice Binder's Bond-like credit sequence gets things off to an attractive start, the local color contributed by Hong Kong and Macao provide plenty of relief from what's in the foreground, and George Harrison's songs, as well as his score composed with Michael Kamen, prove moderately catchy at times (Madonna chirps not on this soundtrack). —*Cart.*

Sauve-toi, Lola
(Run For Your Life, Lola)
(FRENCH-CANADIAN-COLOR)

An AAA Classic release of an Onyx Prod./Cinépix/Films A2 coproduction, with the participation of Téléfilm Canada, the C.N.C (Ministry of Culture), Sofimage, Sofica Conseil and Gestimage. Executive producers, Gabriel Boustani, André Link. Associate producer, Nader Attassi. Directed by Michel Drach. Screenplay, Jacques Kirsner, from the novel by Ania Francos; camera (Fujicolor), Robert Alazraki; editor, Henri Lanoë; art director, Nicole Rachline; sound, Claude Hazanavicius; music, Lewis Furey; makeup, Daniéle Vuarin, Arlette Pipart; production manager, Jean Lara; assistant director, Xavier de Cassan. Reviewed at the Club de l'Etoile, Paris, Aug. 19, 1986. Running time: 105 MINS.
Lola Friedlander . . . . .Carole Laure
Marie-Aude . . . . .Jeanne Moreau
Cathy . . . . .Dominique Labourier
Dr. Tobman . . . . .Sami Frey
Ferdinand . . . . .Robert Charlebois
Charles . . . . .Jacques François
Bertrand Benoît . . . . . .Jean-Yves Gauthier
Tsoukolvsky . . . . .Guy Bedos
Marielle . . . . .Isabelle Pasco
Maurice . . . . .Philippe Khorsand

Paris — Laughter through tears, tears through laughter — that's the desired emotional texture of Michel Drach's ''Suave-toi, Lola,'' set in a cancer ward. Unfortunately, Drach and screenwriter Jacques Kirsner mismanage the tragi-comic mode in this dramatization of an autobiographical novel by Ania Francos.

Central personage is Lola Friedlander (Carole Laure), a successful young lawyer who enters the clinic of a media-star oncologist (Sami Frey) to undergo a long treatment. There her life overlaps with those of several other women of different walks of life, including the terminally ill wife of a diplomat (Jeanne

Moreau), and a financially troubled young woman (Dominique Labourier) who becomes her closest friend.

Rather than construct the narrative from Laure's point of view, Kirsner's script too often leaves her for anecdotal seriocomic scenes involving subsidiary characters. Particularly poor are those involving Laure's clownish Canadian boyfriend (singer Robert Charlebois), her young politically minded son and her stereotypical Jewish family.

Drach applies a heavy hand to the comedy and not enough delicacy to the pathos, foundering most when the two intermingle to sometimes grotesque effect, as in the scene in which Moreau bequeaths her personal belongings to guests at a reception before retiring to her deathbed.

Uncertainty of direction also affects the cast, with Laure notably failing to communicate the character's fierce inner strength and will to live. Moreau's now puffy features give her performance some added poignancy, but otherwise it's not a high point of her career. Frey is okay as the matinee idol doctor. The other patients in the clinic are portrayed adequately.

Technically, film is satisfactory. —*Len.*

Lethal
(KGB — The Secret War)
(COLOR)

Deadly dull.

A Cinema Group release, in association with Sandy Howard. Produced by Sandy Howard, Keith Rubinstein. Executive producers, Peter Collister, Grahame Jennings. Directed by Dwight Little. Screenplay, Sandra K. Bailey, from story by Little, Bailey; camera (Bellevue Pathé Quebec color), Collister; editor, Stanley Sheff, John Peterson; music, Misha Segal; sound, Jonathan Stein: art direction, Phillip Duffin; set decoration, Farnouche Kamran; assistant director, Martin Walters; production manager, William Fay; costume design, Gail Viola; stunt coordinator, Dan Bradley; associate producers, Michael Murphey, Joel Soisson; casting, Mary Gail Artz. Reviewed at 42d St. Cine Rialto 1 theater, N.Y., Aug. 30, 1986. (MPAA Rating: PG-13.) Running time: 89 MINS.
Peter Hubbard . . . . .Michael Billington
Adelle Martin . . . . .Denise DuBarry
Taylor . . . . .Michael Ansara
Viktor/Nickolai . . . . .Walter Gotell
Fran Simpson . . . . .Sally Kellerman
Alex . . . . .Christopher Cary
Ryder . . . . .Philip Levien
Ilya . . . . .Julian Barnes
Yuri . . . . .Clement St. George

''Lethal'' is an extremely boring espionage film lensed in L.A. in 1984. Picture was released regionally last November as ''KGB — The Secret War'' (its original title, which is retained in the end credits) and recently surfaced in Manhattan on the lower half of a double bill.

Michael Billington toplines as Peter Hubbard (supposedly a fic-

tionalized version of a true story), a KGB spy in Los Angeles targeted to become a double agent by U.S. counter-intelligence.

With the unwitting help of his girl friend Adelle (Denise DuBarry), Hubbard breaks into an aerospace installation and steals scientific secrets for the Russians, but he narrowly escapes being killed by the unscrupulous KGB when he tries to deliver. He is ripe for recruitment by CIA operative Fran Simpson (Sally Kellerman), who wants the names of spies in Hubbard's network.

Overloaded with dull exposition, pic founders in familiar cat and mouse chases with very cheap, uneventful action scenes. Hokey finale involving Hubbard and his thought-to-be dead young son (who the KGB has turned against him) is ridiculous.

Billington, who was featured in the Bond film ''The Spy Who Loved Me,'' is an acceptably virile, cool secret agent but remains unsympathetic here. Walter Gotell is well-cast as the nasty villain while other roles are perfunctory. Helmer Dwight Little did a much better job creating interest and sustaining suspense in his other recent release ''Hostage: Dallas.'' —*Lor.*

Motten im Licht
(Flies In The Light)
(SWISS-COLOR)

A Metropolis Film presentation of a Xanadu Films (Zurich) Swiss-German (DRS) TV/George Reinhart production. Directed by Urs Egger. Screenplay, Egger, Martin Henning, Michael Zochow; camera (color), Hugues Ryffel; editor, Georg Janett; music, Stephane Wittwer. Reviewed on the Piazza Grande, Locarno Film Festival, Aug. 14, 1986. Running time: 90 MINS.

With: Patrick Bauchau, Renée Soutendijk, Ivan Desny, Kurt Raab, Sibylle Courvoisier, Therese Affolter, Sven-Erich Bechtoff, Norbert Schwientek.

Locarno — A polished thriller about a gentleman thief who is asked to remove a valuable painting, first from an art gallery, and later from the home of an obscure religious sect, this picture's plot wanders in enough directions to fill up a couple of films. Instead of pursuing one clear plot and furnishing plausible solutions to develop it further, there is a feeling the scriptwriting trio preferred to continuously bring new elements into the picture instead of resolving the existing ones.

The tribute paid to the American B picture is evident all through, and it is indeed true that some of those pictures managed at the time to prevail in spite of similar shortcomings. However, what those films had, and this one doesn't, are strong affective characters, with whom one identifies come hell or high water. Nothing like that happens here. The camera, the sets, the moods, are all there, but neither Patrick Bauchau nor Renée Soutendijk are forceful enough by themselves, or sufficiently aided by the script, to create any kind of affinity with them.

Because of this, the film's main task is to condition its audience to care or worry about the characters on the screen. As this practically never happens, the picture becomes a kind of exercise in style, a tribute to ''The Big Sleep'' and ''The Maltese Falcon.'' And in such cases, the original is preferable to the imitation, as adroit and clever as this may be. —*Edna.*

★ ★ ★ ★ ★ ★ ★ ★ ★ ★ ★ ★ ★ ★ ★ ★ ★ ★ ★
Toronto Festival Reviews
★ ★ ★ ★ ★ ★ ★ ★ ★ ★ ★ ★ ★ ★ ★ ★ ★ ★ ★

That's Life!
(COLOR)

Heartfelt Blake Edwards drama.

A Columbia Pictures release of a Paradise Cove-Ubilam production. Produced by Tony Adams. Executive producer, Jonathan D. Krane. Directed by Blake Edwards. Stars Jack Lemmon, Julie Andrews. Screenplay, Milton Wexler, Edwards; camera (Panavision, Deluxe color), Anthony Richmond; editor, Lee Rhoads; music, Henry Mancini; set decoration, Tony Marando; costume design; Tracy Tynan; sound, Don Summer; associate producers, Trish Caroselli, Connie McCauley, assistant director, Alan Levine. Reviewed at The Burbank Studios, Burbank, Aug. 21, 1986. (In Toronto Festival of Festivals.) (MPAA Rating: PG-13.) Running time: 102 MINS.
Harvey Fairchild . . . . .Jack Lemmon
Gillian Fairchild . . . . .Julie Andrews
Holly Parrish . . . . .Sally Kellerman
Father Baragone . . . . .Robert Loggia
Megan Fairchild Bartlet .Jennifer Edwards
Steve Larwin . . . . .Rob Knepper
Larry Bartlet . . . . .Matt Lattanzi
Josh Fairchild . . . . .Chris Lemmon
Janice Kern . . . . .Cynthia Sikes
Fanny Ward . . . . .Dana Sparks
Kate Fairchild . . . . .Emma Walton
Madame Carrie . . . . .Felicia Farr
Corey . . . . .Theodore Wilson
Andre . . . . .Nicky Blair
Dr. Keith Romanis . . . .Jordan Christopher

Hollywood — If ''10'' was Blake Edwards' comic spasm of anxiety about mid-life crisis, then ''That's Life!'' represents his barely controlled freak-out over the prospect of entering old age. Personal virtually to the point of being a home movie, film proves thoroughly absorbing and entertaining except for a few dud scenes that are curiously bunched together, and benefits enormously from a terrific lead performance by Jack Lemmon. Produced independently on a very low budget under the title "Crisis" and picked up by Columbia, this looks like a decent, if not stellar, b.o. draw. World premiere is set for Sept. 9 at the Toronto Festival of Festivals.

After misfiring with most of his recent comedies, Edwards turns reflective and inward here but, showman that he is, still remains ever-conscious of his responsibilities to the mass audience. Despite its having been shot at his own home in Malibu with family members deeply populating the cast, pic is as slick as one expects an Edwards film to be, and enough laughs are sprinkled around to keep things fizzy most of the time.

Nevertheless, the vet director, working here from a script by himself and his shrink, Milton Wexler, has very serious concerns on his mind, most notably mortality and growing old. Story opens with Lemmon's wife, played by Edwards' wife, Julie Andrews, leaving a hospital and knowing she'll have to wait all weekend to learn the results of a biopsy.

For his part, Lemmon is not taking the arrival of his 60th birthday at all well. He doesn't know if he can face the big party planned for him over the weekend, is fretting because he can't perform sexually these days and can't stand the idea that he is soon to become a grandfather.

Undoubtedly the film's best scene comes early on, as Lemmon, in bed with his wife, pours out his life's worth of frustrations and directly addresses his severe disappointment over what he has, and hasn't accomplished in his career. He's a successful architect with wealthy clients and a lovely family, but since he didn't manage to become Frank Lloyd Wright, he considers himself a hack and a flop.

One doesn't know if this is Edwards speaking from the heart or not, but Lemmon's release of anguish — even while admitting his love for his wife — hits home with great force, and represents one of the actor's finest moments.

Gradually, the kids — played by Lemmon's son Chris, Edwards' daughter Jennifer and Andrews' daughter Emma Walton — all turn up, some with mates, and Lemmon runs manically around looking for comfort and counsel. He goes to confession for the first time in decades, consults his doctor, tries to let himself be seduced by a sexy client and even visits a local fortune teller.

Film's major problems stem from Edwards' natural impulse to graft physical comedy even onto the most serious material, a tactic that can sometimes work but often doesn't here. The gags frequently seem gratuitous and desperately thrown in, most embarrassingly when Lemmon is asked to squirm in agony while speaking in front of a church congregation. Scene and its followup don't play because the audience doesn't know what's wrong with him — does he have to go to the bathroom, does he have gas, is he all of a sudden sexually excited? All of this material could be profitably removed.

Unfortunately, a couple of other flat scenes, involving the fortune teller, played by Lemmon's wife, Felicia Farr, and one between Andrews and Walton, immediately surround it, and the film is brought so far down during this 10 to 15 minute stretch that it never recovers entirely.

Andrews responds beautifully to Lemmon's sweaty, nerve-wracked state, betraying years of love and understanding of her mate, but doesn't receive equal dramatic opportunities because her character chooses to keep her own problems a secret.

Sally Kellerman literally runs in and out of the picture as a warm, fast-talking neighbor, Robert Loggia is a very unlikely priest who must have gotten that great tan walking to all of his parishioners' beachfront homes, and the family members, with few heavy demands placed upon them, aren't too memorable. And what is that Oscar doing in Loggia's office?

Despite all the flaws, pic sticks to the ribs because it is obviously deeply felt and, unlike most Hollywood product these days, is actually *about* something. As Lemmon says, maybe one can't live up to all of one's aspirations, and Edwards doesn't fulfill all of his ambitions here, but his partial success with lofty aims is preferable to many others' total, but empty, triumphs.
— *Cart.*

My Life For Zarah Leander
(U.S.-DOCU-COLOR)

A Christian Blackwood production. Produced, written, and edited by Christian Blackwood. Camera (color), Blackwood; sound, Fritz Berg, Isolde Kaiser, Michael Eiler. Reviewed at Bloor Cinema, Toronto, Aug. 28, 1986. (In Toronto Festival of Festivals.) Running time: 90 MINS.
With: Zarah Leander, Paul Seiler, Margot Hielscher, Douglas Sirk, Michael Jary, Bruno Blaz, Harold Prince.

Toronto — Part career biopic, part fan confessional, Christian Blackwood's "My Life For Zarah Leander" is an intriguing docu that explores the fascinating psychology of the film fan as well as the enigmatic style of chanteuse-thesp Leander. German-born Blackwood, whose film was shot in German with English subtitles, is also repped by "Nik And Murray" at the Toronto fest.

Zarah Leander was a Swedish-born singer who was extremely popular in Germany during the Third Reich and became the premiere star of Ufa. Her deep, dark voice, great beauty, and tailor-made roles made her the darling of the big directors, including Douglas Sirk and Carl Frolich, and she was said to be one of Hitler's favorite actresses. She retired to Stockholm in 1943 despite a promise by Goebbels of a villa and citizenship.

Unfortunately Blackwood was turned on to Leander's vocal talents after she died in 1981 and didn't have the advantage of interviewing her personally.

Blackwood, however, discovered Paul Seiler, a homosexual fan whose life was devoted to Zarah. The director then chose to weave Seiler's obsession with a bio of Zarah, the results of which are powerful. Blackwood bought a television interview that Leander made before she died and has cut that footage with original interviews he conducted to create a "pseudo" tv docu that Seiler watches from his living room throughout the pic.

Much of the film consists of judiciously selected archival footage from Leander's pics, including "New Shores," "La Habanera," "Ave Maria" and her comeback film "Gabriella." There's also b&w footage of her singing "Don't Cry For Love" and "Wunderbar" and clips of her crooning on her 60th birthday in Berlin.

In the snippets from her tv interview Leander asks the camera as she lights one cigaret after another, "Doesn't an actress have the right to grow old?" She recalls she became an "egomaniac" after two pics Sirk directed. She remembers doing a screen test for Carl Frolich, who said, "What a big snout she has."

Leander admits she was never a great actress, that the roles were written for her type. And she also sniffs, "Goebbels didn't like me at all."

Seiler's confessions to the camera are as striking as Leander's. He shares, "Her voice haunted me. It left me no peace. She always came back and let me love her." He collected every article ever printed about her, wrote her scores of letters which said, "Miss Leander, I would die for you," and ultimately formed a friendship with her. He went to recording sessions and openings and consoled her when she got bad reviews. "I was addicted to Zarah, to her style, her emotional outbursts," he confesses. He's at ease in front of the camea, willing to spill all.

Directors and actors who worked with Leander recall her extraordinary beauty and her "remarkable fascinating voice." Harold Prince remembers how she fell down drunk from her wheelchair at a premiere in her later years, and Douglas Sirk describes her as an "undaunted worker."

The fan psychology is riveting as Paul admits, "She was mother — and something erotic." But he also has trouble with Leander's politics, not understanding her silence during the Nazi era. He claims she was very ambitious and didn't get involved in the Jewish issues, and this hurts him. Docu touches on what it was like to be a studio star for Ufa during the Nazi era.

The least successful aspect of the pic intercuts a dream sequence in which Paul walks through city streets with a transvestite dressed like Zarah, wearing a white and gold brocade caftan that we find out he bought at a final auction of Zarah's personal effects. The duo go to a niteclub to watch a Zarah impersonator (Armand) strut her stuff, which is another opportunity to hear her unique voice.

Another minor quibble is some poor subtitling, with the screen staying blank during some director's anecdotes. It would also help if the occasional name of the speaker were flashed on the screen.

"My Life For Zarah Leander" may open up a new wave of fans for Leander's talents. It's another strong entry for Blackwood and certainly will zip around the fest circuit with style. With proper handling it could also fare quite well in specialized theatrical situations.
—*Devo.*

****
Montreal Festival Reviews
****

Blue Velvet
(COLOR)

———

Weird David Lynch drama hits the bullseye.

———

A De Laurentiis Entertainment Group release. Produced by Fred Caruso. Executive producer, Richard Roth. Written and directed by David Lynch. Camera (J-D-C Widescreen, color), Frederick Elmes; editor, Duwayne Dunham; music, Angelo Badalamenti; production design, Patricia Norris; sound (Dolby), Ann Kroeber; sound design, Alan Splet; assistant director, Ellen Rauch. Reviewed at the DEG Screen Room, Beverly Hills, Aug.

14, 1986. (In Montreal Film Festival, competing.) (MPAA Rating: R.) Running time: **120 MINS.**

Jeffrey Beaumont ......Kyle MacLachlan
Dorothy Vallens ....Isabella Rossellini
Frank Booth ....Dennis Hopper
Sandy Williams ....Laura Dern
Mrs. Williams ....Hope Lange
Ben ....Dean Stockwell
Paul ....Jack Nance
Raymond ....Brad Dourif
Aunt Barbara...............Frances Bay
Detective Williams .....George Dickerson
Mr. Beaumont ....Jack Harvey
Mrs. Beaumont..........Priscilla Pointer
Mike......................Ken Stovitz

Hollywood — "Blue Velvet" finds David Lynch, after "Dune," back on familiar territory, which is very strange territory indeed. New picture, long a pet project and shot on a relatively low budget, takes a disturbing and at times devastating look at the ugly underside of Middle American life. Result is compelling and sure to generate strong critical support in many corners, which, along with the Lynch name, will make it a must for buffs and seekers of the latest hot thing. Mainstream viewers will likely find it unpleasant, which would indicate crossover potential from the specialized market is only moderate.

Lynch built a major cult with his bizarre student feature, "Eraserhead," and won widespread acclaim with "The Elephant Man." "Dune" might well have defeated anyone, but here the modest proportions of the film are just right for the writer-director's desire to investigate the inexplicable demons that drive people to deviate from expected norms of behavior and thought.

Like Lynch himself and his virtual lookalike leading man, Kyle MacLachlan, the setting, a small town called Lumberton, seems on the surface to be utterly conventional, placid, comforting and serene. A wonderful opening sequence presents the community as an ideal white bread burg lifted intact from a 1950s Sunday magazine supplement, all to the accompaniment of Bobby Vinton crooning the title tune.

The bland perfection is disrupted when a man collapses in his yard and is further upset when, in a superbly Buñuelian touch, MacLachlan discovers a disembodied, ant-covered human ear in an empty lot.

The earnest, wholesome MacLachlan is told to keep a lid on things by the neighborhood detective, whose sweet daughter, Laura Dern, the young man begins to see. Defiantly, and with Dern's initial help, he begins investigating whose ear he might have found, and ends up spying on local roadhouse chanteuse and prostie Isabella Rossellini.

Peeping through a closet keyhole, what he sees violent client Dennis Hopper do to her lunches MacLachlan into another world, into an unfamiliar, dangerously provocative state of mind concerning notions of sex, love, pain and obsession.

Rossellini, dressed in lingerie or less much of the time, throws herself into this mad role with complete abandon, but the character behaves so oddly, is so tense and intense, and so readily accepts abuse, that she is difficult to take at times.

Drawn to the unknown, MacLachlan becomes involved with this desperate woman, which places him in the clutches of druggie and all-around maniac Hopper, who creates a flabbergasting portrait of unrepentent, irredeemable evil. Hopper savors putting everyone through the wringer, and while his crimes inevitably require a bit of conventional action and melodrama to wrap things up, he and the film remain sufficiently off-kilter to keep matters from becoming predictable.

More directly, and graphically, than any commercial Hollywood film in memory, "Blue Velvet" explores the connections between sexuality and torture, suspense and death. The would-be innocent, MacLachlan has no particular need to become immersed in the cesspool surrounding the small-time mystery, but floats into it by nature. Good, it would seem, is much more attracted to evil than vice versa.

Dealing with basic material that could provide a field day for moralists and exposé-minded sensationalists, Lynch proves himself to be neither. Rather, like the surrealists of yore, he would seem to be in very close touch with his dreams, nightmares and fantasies, and here has managed to put them to quite striking creative use. Lynch's motto, uttered in the film, would surely be, "It's a strange world, isn't it?"

As before, the director's pacing leaves something to be desired at times, and some of the widescreen framing in Frederick Elmes' otherwise impeccable cinematography leaves too much room around the edges. Patricia Norris' production design helps create a 1950s feel without the film being set then, and Rossellini's grim apartment could easily exist in the same building with the one in "Eraserhead." Music and sound work are superior.
—*Cart.*

Welcome To The Parade
(CANADIAN-COLOR)

A Northern Outlaw production. Produced by Peter Gentile. Written and directed by Stuart Clarfield. Camera (color), Jon Joffin; editor, Clarfield; music, Robb Wright, Mark Lalama, Paul James; sound, John Gadjecki; art director, Frank Gentile. Reviewed at World Film Fest, Montreal, Aug. 29, 1986. Running time: **82 MINS.**
With: Paul James.

Montreal — "Welcome To The Parade" is a modest low-budget student pic about a spoiled rich kid who, at 22, still lives at home, though he abuses his well-meaning family. When he's caught with dope, there's an argument and he walks out and checks into a sleazy downtown hotel inhabited by hookers and pushers. He unwisely tries to rip off a cocaine dealer and is almost killed.

With a central character who's by turn arrogant and almost wilfully dumb, pic is something of a turnoff. Writer-director-editor Stuart Clarfield apparently is attempting a cautionary tale for the sons of the wealthy, but his boorish hero seems to deserve everything he gets, and more.

Handling is static and tentative, with acting stiff and camerawork lacking in vitality. Commercial chances are poor.—*Strat.*

River's Edge
(U.S.-COLOR)

A Hemdale release and production. Executive producers, John Daly, Derek Gibson. Produced by Sarah Pillsbury, Midge Sanford. Directed by Tim Hunter. Screenplay, Neal Jimenez; camera (Metrocolor), Frederick Elmes; editor, Howard Smith, Sonya Sones; music, Jurgen Knieper; art director, John Muto; sound, David Brownlow; production manager, David Street; assistant director, Richard Hanley; casting, Carrie Frazier-Reinhold. Reviewed at World Film Festival, Montreal, Aug. 27, 1986. (MPAA Rating: R.) Running time: **99 MINS.**

Layne ....Crispin Glover
Matt ....Keanu Reaves
Clarissa ....Ione Skye Leitch
Samson ....David Roebuck
Feck ....Dennis Hopper
  Also with: Joshua Miller (Tim), Josh Richman (Tony), Tom Bower (Mike), Roxana Zal, Constance Forslund, Leo Rossi, Phil Brock.

Montreal — Tim Hunter's "River's Edge" is an unusually downbeat and depressing youth pic. It's peopled with a bunch of thoroughly unlovely characters, and it seems doubtful that many people will fork out money to spend time in their company.

The setting is a small town, presumably in Oregon. Pic opens with 12-year-old Tim destroying his kid sister's doll and then spotting high-schooler Samson sitting on the river bank with the naked body of a girl he's just murdered. Tim's reaction is to steal a couple of cans of beer for the killer. Samson isn't hiding his crime; he tells his friends all about it, even though the victim was one of their group. Group leader Layne wants to help and protect Samson, while the rest seem indifferent. Actually, Tim's older brother, Matt, does call the cops, but secretly so that his friends won't know he's a stoolie. This is some gang of kids.

But they're really nice at heart, the film seems to be saying. They have to cope with broken homes and the threat of the Bomb and teachers who used to be hippies, otherwise they wouldn't be so hopeless.

Layne hides Samson out at the dilapidated home of Feck, a character which offers Dennis Hopper yet another opportunity to play a doped-up eccentric. Feck is a one-legged former biker who feels sentimental about the gun with which he once killed the girl he loved and who is currently enamoured with a plastic sex doll he calls Ellen.

At this point it almost seems as though Hunter is turning the film into a loony, paranoid comedy, since audiences are surely not meant to take these people seriously. But the tone, unfortunately, remains deadly serious. Even the moderately sympathetic Matt and his sex-obsessed girlfriend Clarissa aren't terribly endearing types. There's no-one in "River's Edge" for the audience to identify with; just about every character borders on the repulsive.

As Layne, Crispin Glover could have used more restraint: he gives a busy, fussy performance. Others in the cast are more effective, with young Joshua Miller particularly striking as the awful child, Tim.

Oddly enough, many elements in the film — the young people, the small town setting, the body — evoke Col's current "Stand By Me," but the two films could not be more different in mood and level of audience identification.

"River's Edge" was produced by Midge Sanford and Sarah Pillsbury, who previously had a hit on their hands with "Desperately Seeking Susan"; this is a step backward for them. Technically, pic is first-rate starting with the well-designed credit titles and continuing via the superior photography of Frederick Elmes and the fine music score of Jurgen Knieper. Nothing wrong with the way Hunter handles his directing chores either. The trouble here is in the basic concept, and the viewer is left wondering why on earth they ever made this one in the first place.—*Strat.*

The Good Father
(BRITISH-COLOR)

A Film Four Intl. presentation of a Greenpoint Films production. Produced by Ann Scott. Directed by Mike Newell. Stars Anthony Hopkins. Screenplay, Christopher Hampton, from the book by Peter Prince; camera (color), Gabriel Beristain; editor, Peter Hollywood; sound, David Stephenson; art director, Alison Stewart-Richardson; production manager, Ann Wingate; assistant director, Tony Hopkins. Reviewed at World Film Fest, Mon-

treal, Aug. 29, 1986. Running time: **90 MINS.**
Bill Hooper . . . . .Anthony Hopkins
Roger Miles . . . . .Jim Broadbent
Emmy Hooper . . . . .Harriet Walter
Cheryl Miles . . . . .Fanny Viner
Mark Varner . . . . .Simon Callow
Mary . . . . .Joanne Whalley
Jane Powell . . . . .Miriam Margolyes
Leonard Scruby . . . . .Michael Byrne

Montreal — The effect of the women's movement on marriage and families has been the subject of a handful of films involving fathers attempting to win custody of their children, most notably "Kramer Vs. Kramer." "The Good Father," latest quality offering from Britain's Film Four Intl., is the best on this theme, though its uncompromising attitudes and gritty look may limit theatrical audience appeal.

Anthony Hopkins plays Bill Hooper, a magazine designer distraught over the breakup of his marriage (his wife is living in their apartment with another man) and loss of contact with his six-year-old son. At a party, he meets Roger Miles (Jim Broadbent), a pleasant, rather weak schoolteacher, who's lost his son too: his wife left him to go and live with her lesbian lover, and plans to relocate, with the child, to Australia.

Hooper decides to vent his anger and frustration at his own situation vicariously by helping his friend. He pushes him into taking legal action against his wife, and much of the film is taken up with trenchant sequences involving Britain's legal profession, including a woman lawyer who won't accept men clients in custody cases on principle, and a male lawyer whose way of manipulating the law is as clever as it is expensive. There's also an unctuous barrister, played with suave style by Simon Callow, actor best known for his role as the reverend in "A Room With A View."

"The Good Father," tightly adapted by Christopher Hampton from a book by Peter Prince, is a fascinating experience because the character of Hooper, brilliantly limned by Hopkins, is so multilayered. Barely suppressing his anger, Hooper can be touching with his new, much younger, girlfriend (Joanne Whalley) and obviously still cares for his ex-wife (Harriet Walter). Only late in the film do we come to realize that, for Hooper, his marriage came to an end not directly because of his wife's infidelity — which has proved to be a short-term arrangement — but because the arrival of their son drastically changed the relationship. Thus the pic makes the interesting point that the birth of a baby can destroy a marriage as well as give it new meaning.

Scenes of legal maneuverings are fascinating as Callow brings to court evidence of past illegal activities of Miles' wife (an incident with drugs when she was a student, loss of a driving license) while craftily working on the sitting judge's known and deep-seated prejudice against a lesbian relationship.

The background for this sad little tale of broken homes and relationships is a grimly unappealing London in winter. A garbage strike has filled the streets with rotting plastic bags of rubbish, which visually emphasize the decaying society we're witnessing, while violent riots seen on television only add to the feeling that established values are irredeemably breaking down.

Director, Mike Newell, always very good with actors, has made a modest but most impressive film. In the lead role, Hopkins has a part somewhat akin to that played by Jack Thompson in Newell's finest film to date, the sadly little-seen New Zealand item "Bad Blood" (1980): that of a man barely able to control his anger at the world and the people around him. This is one of those British pics in which every role, down to the smallest bit part, is played to perfection.

Photography is very grainy, which may mitigate against successful theatrical release, but this is a pic which should garner fine reviews and find a limited, but most appreciate, audience. —*Strat.*

Knights And Emeralds
(BRITISH-COLOR)

A Warner Bros. release of an Enigma production. Produced by Susan Richards and Raymond Day. Executive producer, David Puttnam. Written and directed by Ian Emes. Camera (color), Richard Greatrex; editor, John Victor-Smith; sound, John Midgley; costumes, Ann Hollowood. Reviewed at the Montreal World Film Festival - British Cinema of Today, Aug. 27, 1986. (No MPAA Rating.) Running time: **94 MINS.**

Kevin . . . . .Christopher Wild
Melissa . . . . .Beverley Hills
Also with: Warren Mitchell, Bill Leadbitter, Rachel Davies, Tracie Bennett, Nadim Sawalha, Tonu Milner, Ptrick Field, Maurice Dee, David Keys, Andrew Goodman.

Montreal — "Knights And Emeralds" is an endearing small film that places the serious theme of race and class conflicts among English workingclass youth in an upbeat comedic context. Warner Bros. could have a real specialty sleeper here, given the pic's attractive interracial cast, musical ambience, involving screenplay and happy ending. Hopefully, WB will increase the film's U.S. chances of success by having the British actors redub the small proportion of dialect dialog that's virtually foreign to the American ear.

Kevin (Christopher Wild) is a talented drummer from a poor rowhouse district in Birmingham, who also plays in Mr. Kilpatrick's awful-sounding Windyvale brass marching band, the Knights. Kevin's beaten-down dad is a virulent racist, but Kevin has many friends among the black youths at his tough "people factory" high school.

Due to budget problems, the Knights are compelled to join forces with the Emeralds, a razzle-dazzle majorette troupe of incredibly nubile local girls who are aiming for the championship at an upcoming tourney. The irrepressible Kevin immediately falls for the sexiest Emerald, Tina, but she prefers the tough, racist "national front" types with whom Kevin has grown up.

The black youths have a marching band and majorette troupe of their own, the Crusaders, and it's obvious to all but prejudiced eyes (which abound) that they're the most talented bunch around. Their white bandleader, Enoch, takes abuse with the patience of a saint as he tries to discipline the Crusaders in a conventional competitive routine. After hours the Crusaders jam on hot contempo-tropical rock, and their spirited, beautiful conga drummer Melissa, urges him to drop in.

When the Knights and Emeralds are knocked out of the opening competition by the Crusaders, Kevin risks ostracism at home and in the neighborhood to join the black kids. A romance blossoms but it's spiked with the thorny pressures and problems unique to these musically ambitious workingclass teens.

Filmmaker Ian Emes in his first feature uses this situation for a serio-comic look at an England in difficult transition to a multiracial society. The film's musical pulse and fresh youth appeal prevent things from ever getting preachy, but the director assiduously avoids the fluff that plagues so many Hollywood teen pics. There are wonderful subthemes on the passing of the old Britannia, the middle-aging of the '50s rocker generation and the curious place of assimilated Anglo-Indians in modern England.

Performances by Christopher Wild as Kevin and Beverley Hills as Melissa are thoroughly winning and supported by a fine cast of players. —*Rich.*

Venice Festival Reviews

O Melissokomos
(The Bee Keeper)
(GREEK-FRENCH-ITALIAN-COLOR)

A Greek Film Center, Theo Angelopoulos production, with Marin Karmitz Productions (Paris), I.C.C. (Rome), RAI, RAITRE, ERT-1. Executive producer, Nikos Angelopoulos. Coproduced by Enzo Rispoli, Giuseppe Colombo. Written and directed by Theo Angelopoulos, with the screenplay collaboration of Dimitris Nollas, Tonino Guerra. Camera (color), Giorgos Arvanitis; editor, Takis Yannopoulos; music, Helen Karaindrou; art director, Mikes Karapiperis; sound, Nikos Achladis; songs, Giorgos Dalaras, Julie Massino; production manager, Emilios Konitsiotis. Reviewed at Venice Film Festival (In Competition), Sept. 2, 1986. Running time: **142 MINS.**

Spyros . . . . .Marcello Mastroianni
The Girl . . . . .Nadia Mourouzi
Sick man . . . . .Serge Reggiani
Anna .Jenny Roussea
Friend . . . . .Dinos Iliopoulos
Also with: Vassia Panagopoulou. Dimitris Poulikakos, Nikos Kouros, Yannis Zavradinos, Chris Nezer.

Venice — The political themes that have dominated the films of Theo Angelopoulos thus far are shunted aside in "The Bee Keeper," a haunting, demanding, impressive picture about the last days in the life of a broken, disappointed man.

Almost entirely absent, too, are the intricate, lengthy shots composed by the director and his brilliant cinematographer Giorgos Arvanitis. There are certainly plenty of long takes in the film, but the camera mostly stays still, observing the characters with a calmness and serenity that adds to the quiet, mournful mood. The screenplay is extremely spare, and the viewer has to pay careful attention throughout the lengthy running time, because this is a film in which what's *said* is not as important as what's left unsaid.

Marcello Mastroianni is Spyros, a middle-aged man whose stooped shoulders and dejected look reflect a lifetime of disappointments; his passion, as the title suggests, is beekeeping. We first meet him at the rain-soaked wedding of his daughter, an uneasy family gathering with little joy evident; after the wedding party departs, he quietly weeps.

Later, he sets out in his truck to inspect his bee hives, scattered all over the barren, bleak countryside. He picks up a young hitchhiker, a sensual girl who makes a play for him that he at first rejects. But when she brings a soldier back to their hotel room, he's evidently jealous and frustrated.

He visits various people from his past. He tells Anna, his ex-wife, that he's come to take her away, but leaves abruptly when she tells him their son is about to arrive. He sees an old friend (Serge Reggiani) in hospital, and they walk together on a chilly beach. He goes to see his daughter, who works at a gas station, but again departs abruptly leaving whatever it was he had to say to her unsaid.

He makes a pilgrimage to the house where he'd lived as a child, and finds the mask once worn by his father when he'd tended bees. Throughout, he keeps meeting the frustrating young hitchhiker, even furiously driving his truck through the window of a cafe where he sees her drinking with anther man. Eventually, they camp out in a deserted, closed-down `cinema, where her desperate attempts to seduce him end in some pathetic grappling that gets nowhere and paves the way for the tragic final sequence.

With its steady pace and enigmatic storyline, "The Bee Keeper" will need sympathetic audiences to make its mark.

Mastroianni is in every scene of the film, and submits himself entirely to Angelopoulos' vision. The actor gives a beautiful performance, clearly indicating the despair and loneliness of the character not through dialog but through looks and body language.

The images of Arvanitis are quite beautiful, and the film is technically first-rate in every department. Some might wish for tighter editing, but for Angelopoulos the pacing is all important. In all, an impressive film which could make its mark on the art house circuit and will certainly be much in demand by fests over the coming months. —*Strat.*

La Seconda Notte
(The Second Night)
(ITALIAN-COLOR)

A Futura Films release of a BOA Cinematografica (Rome) production. Producers, Emilio Bolles, Enzo Bruno. Directed by Nino Bizzarri. Screenplay, Bizzarri, Andrea Ferreri, Lucio Gaudino; camera (Telecolor, Fujicolor), Franco Lecca; editor, Alberto Benotti; music, Luigi Cinque; art direction, Massimo Corevi; costumes, Simonetta Leoncini. Reviewed at CDS screening room, Rome, Aug. 27, 1986. (In Venice Film Fest, Italian Showcase.) Running time: **95 MINS.**

Fabris . . . . Maurice Garrel
Lea . . . . Margherita Buy
Mother . . . . Kara Donati
Singer . . . . Katia Rupé
Also with: Luigi Mezzanotte (hotel guest), Mauro Caruso (Walter), Ernesto Massi (friend).

Rome — A refined old gentleman sends admiring notes to a girl in his hotel. It's hard to classify "The Second Night," a meandering, turgid first feature by Nino Bizzarri, screened in the Italian Showcase at Venice. Tyro helmer's attempt to make a film without a story behind it is doomed from the start. Small Italo art-film distribbery Futura Films has taken its courage in both hands to release pic nationally, but

off-shore interest would be surprising.

Film takes its time moving hero Fabris (Maurice Garrel) from one set to another, via a buildup of mostly meaningless details and prolonged memories. Given the fact Fabris is a refined gentleman of means who doesn't need to hurry, and well into retirement age to boot, the dirge-like pace may have some function in characterizing the man. It is not the best way to captivate viewers.

After an extended train sequence climaxes in his arrival at a deluxe spa hotel, Fabris settles into his exceedingly staid yearly vacation. The atmosphere is so soporific we're relieved when he starts penning childish secret notes to the hotel's youngest guest, Lea (Margherita Buy), who seems to be taking lessons from mom Kara Donati in how to become a vapid dowager. The notes spark her interest, but the secret admirer never materializes, and she settles for the young desk clerk instead.

Liveliest performance is provided by German thesp Katia Rupé as a rich, indolent singer not above collecting a check for her afternoons spent entertaining Fabris. Garrel, a French stage thesp, is so understated he fades into the surroundings. Even the final moment of embarrassing tenderness between man and girl is too glancingly sketched to have an impact. Technically, pic relies heavily on gorgeous interiors to make up for some inexperienced lensing. — *Yung.*

The Wolf At The Door
(FRENCH-DANISH-COLOR)

A Kärne Film (Copenhagen) release of Dagmar Film Prod., Henning Dam Kärgaard (Denmark), Cameras Continentales, Famous French Films, TF-1 Film Prod. (France) production, in association with the Danish Film Institute and the French Cultural Affairs Ministry. Directed by Henning Carlsen. Stars Donald Sutherland. Screenplay, Christopher Hampton, based on script by Carlsen, Jean-Claude Carrière; camera (Eastmancolor), Mikael Salomon; editor, Janus Billeskov Jansen; music, Ole Schmidt; sound, René Levert; production design, André Guérin, Karl-Otto Hedal; costumes, Charlotte Clason; assistant director, Gert Fredholm, Else Heidary, Terje Dragseth; production management, Bo Christensen, Didier Gyuard; production associates, Jean-Pierre Cottet, Alain Moreau, Léon Zuratas, Henning Dam Kärgaard. Reviewed at the Grand, Copenhagen, Sept. 1, 1986. (In official competition, Venice Film Festival.) Running time: **140 MINS.**

Paul Gauguin . . . . Donald Sutherland
Annah . . . . Valerie Glandut
August Strindberg . . . . Max von Sydow
Judith . . . . Sofie Graböl
Mette, Gauguin's wife Merete Voldstedlund
Edward Brandes . . . . Jörgen Reenberg
Degas . . . . Yves Barsack
Jourdan . . . . Thomas Antoni
Also with: Bill Dunn, Fanny Bastien, Morten Grunwald, Hans Henrik Lehrfeldt, Jean-Claude Flamant, Solbjörg Höjfeldt, Jesper

Bruun Rasmussen, Anthony Michael, Chili Turell.

Copenhagen — "The Wolf At The Door," into which Donald Sutherland in the lead role as painter Paul Gauguin (1848-1903) has put much heart as well as personal money, will appear in some territories under the title "Oviri," the Tahitan word for The Wild One. Danish director Henning Carlsen, working from an English-dialog screenplay by Christopher Hampton as well as from an original script by Carlsen himself with Jean-Claude Carrière, surely will be accused of being too tame in his factual-cum-a-little-fancy retelling of a few years in the early 1890s of the artist's Montmartre, Paris, life.

Still, Carlsen's picture looks beautiful and Donald Sutherland portrays enough of the wolf, refusing to be collared by bourgeois society, to make his classic artist's struggle come through in a convincing, sometimes moving, always interesting way.

Gauguin has left a Danish wife and four children in Copenhagen to try his luck in Polynesia for the first time, and "The Wolf At The Door" finds him back in Paris. Here, he finds few buyers for his art as critics dislike his "lack of perspective" technique. From up north, his abandoned wife nags him about money. He finds models for further South Seas paintings. He beds some of them, but he is a kind man with the women and not the lecher some biographers would have him.

Gauguin feels his best in the company of fellow artists and writers and thinks he has enlisted a bunch of them to go back with him to Tahiti. August Strindberg is one casual acquaintance who would not dream of any such venture. Strindberg is repelled by the luscious females of Gauguin's paintings and quite happy with his own hatred of Europe's "civilized women." He recognizes the Frenchman's talent, however, and lends a writing hand towards the painter's getting the money to return to his paradise.

Most of Carlsen's film has Gauguin at work with models and canvas or at talk with male friends. A prolonged fight sequence and a few sexual trysts are conventionally and clumsily handled. Only as the artist at work and struggling for the survival of his artistic integrity is Gauguin seen rising above the humdrum confines of the conventional Life Of The Artist biopic.

Max von Sydow and Danish actor Jörgen Reenberg (as an early but reluctant buyer of Gauguin's work) shine in thier small supporting roles. Actresses of a child-women appearance have been chosen as Gauguin's models and would-be or actual lovers, and of these, only Sofie Graböl as a failed composer's teen-

age daughter who substitutes forlornly as a model for Polynesian Annah (Valerie Glandut) radiates anything beyond teen freshness and/or sulkiness. Most everybody else in the picture appears as a cliché.

More luck is had with a music score by noted Danish composer Ole Schmidt, which has a dramatic subtlety and depth to match Sutherland's finely tuned minimalistic acting. The rest of the pic is mostly polite genre painting and ditto portrayal. Mikael Salomon's expert cinematography too rarely gets a chance to cut loose, but when it does, as in its superbly lighted renditions of Gauguin originals and in an art gallery sequence that has Sutherland rolling out a carpet with his feet, it is a match to the true subject matter at hand: the exposure and survival of the artistic nerve.
—*Kell.*

Regalo di Natale
(Christmas Present)
(ITALIAN-COLOR)

A Sacis release of a Due A Film/DMV Distribuzione coproduction, in association with RAI-1. Produced by Antonio Avati. Directed by Pupi Avati. Stars Diego Abatantuono. Screenplay, Pupi Avati; camera (Telecolor), Pasquale Rachini; editor, Amedeo Salfa; music, Riz Ortolani; art direction, Giuseppe Pirrotta. Reviewed at Venice Film Festival (In Competition), Aug. 31, 1986. Running time: **100 MINS.**

Franco . . . . Diego Abatantuono
Ugo . . . . Gianni Cavina
Lele . . . . Alessandro Haber
Santelia . . . . Carlo Delle Piane
Stefano . . . . George Eastman
Martina . . . . Kristina Sevieri

Rome — In "Christmas Present," director Pupi Avati takes a significant step forward from the off-beat light comedies that are his trademark, to venture into shadier and more resonant psychological realms. One of the few directors to rely on a cast of stock players in his films, Avati deals out weightier roles for this homespun drama of the card table, without abandoning the comic touches that have earned him a regular Italian audience. Offshore art houses could develop a new following among audiences turned off by the cloying cuteness of some earlier pics.

The only remnant here of Avati's wacky Bologna-based humor is Carlo Delle Piane, a lascivious eccentric with a weakness for cards and apparently the means to be a big loser. Roped into spending Christmas eve in an empty villa with four friends intent on taking him for all he's worth, the supposed industrialist catalyzes relationships among the conspirators gathered around the felt-top table.

In the tradition of male-bonding films, women are drooled over in fantasy, married in flashback, and lied to on the phone, but love, hate and longing are exchanged between men only.

Lynchpin of the group (and an acting revelation for Diego Abatantuono, previously known only for comic roles) is Franco, owner of a film theater who is secretly on the verge of bankruptcy. His feud with Ugo (Gianni Cavina), a goofy tv host who was once his best friend, goes back to when Ugo seduced his young wife (Kristina Sevieri). The holiday card game is supposed to be the occasion for a reconciliation between them, and is, until in a clever but improbable turnaround finale the players are shown lined up on very different sides. Friendship is indeed no deeper than the wallet.

Rounding out the offbeat crew is Alessandro Haber as a second-string film critic whose own editor won't read his pieces, and George Eastman as a controlled host who emcees the unholy night. This strange type of ensemble acting, in which every character is limned with a different degree of comedy and believability, is pic's main limitation, along with stop-action flashbacks of deadening triteness. Nevertheless, cast succeeds in building up tension to the climactic round — without much help from Lady Luck, it may be added, who seems to deal flushes and full houses much too often. Technical credits are undistinguished but adequate. — *Yung.*

La Storia
(History)
(ITALIAN-COLOR)

A Sacis release of a RAI-2/Ypsilon Cinematografica coproduction, in collaboration with Antenne 2/Maran Film/TVE. Produced by Paolo Infascelli. Directed by Luigi Comencini. Stars Claudia Cardinale. Screenplay, Suso Cecchi D'Amico, Cristina Comencini, Luigi Comencini, from the novel by Elsa Morante; camera (color), Franco Di Giacomo; editor, Nino Baragli; music, Fiorenzo Carpi; art direction, Paola Comencini; costumes, Carolina Ferrara; assistant director, Maurizio Sciarra. Reviewed at Telecolor screening room, Rome, Aug. 27, 1986. (In Venice Film Festival, noncompeting.) Running time: 251 MINS.
Ida .... Claudia Cardinale
Carlo/Davide .... Lambert Wilson
Bartender .... Francisco Rabal
Useppe .... Andrea Spada
Nino .... Antonio Degli Schiavi
Cucchiarelli .... Fiorenzo Fiorentini

Rome — Following star Claudia Cardinale's public outcry against the Venice Film Fest's posting "La Storia" in a tv sidebar rather than regular competition (a flap director Luigi Comencini politely but firmly declined to enter into), classification looks destined to remain problematic. French and other viewers will have a chance to screen the two-hour theatrical release version now in preparation. Given the stature of novelist Elsa Morante, to whose work film is faithful, Venice evidently found the four-hour-plus version a must-show. Comencini and editor Nino Baragli have given it a comfortable, classic pace without dead-weight, and with time to explore character psychology at leisure.

Set in the years 1941-1947, "La Storia" shows the war and its aftermath through the eyes of a small child and his mother. Ida (Cardinale) already has a 15-year-old son when she is raped by a young German soldier. The widowed, half-Jewish schoolteacher, inclined to passively accept all the sorrows life and the war dole out to her, can't bring herself to give the child up for adoption, and keeps little Useppe at home, much to the joy of her other son, Nino (Antonio Degli Schiavi).

When a bomb destroys their home, Ida and Useppe move to a community shelter. Nino returns from the Russian front and joins the partisans, but mainly for the thrill of adventure. After the war he becomes a black marketeer and his tragic death breaks Ida's heart. Shortly thereafter Useppe, unable to find a place in a world tormented by great historic events, follows him.

The director's legendary proficiency in directing child actors is here used to excellent effect, with little Andrea Spada playing a child of six like a veteran. Even better is Degli Schiavi as the carefree, doomed older son, and Cardinale's performance as the downtrodden, beaten mother is mature and moving, one of her finest roles to date. The one serious quibble, which won't bother foreign audiences, can be made with the dubbing of Useppe and especially Lambert Wilson in the more abstract and consequently less convincing role of Davide, a Jewish intellectual who falls to pieces, all too symbolically, with the decay in civilization's values.

Technically film is professional all the way, from lighting to art direction and music. A high-quality production for tv or cinema, though in the last analysis its informative qualities as a history of the common people during the war in Italy may make the small screen its most natural home. — *Yung.*

Demoner
(Demons)
(SWEDISH-COLOR)

A Swedish Film Institute release of a Viking Film with the Swedish Film Institute production. World sales, Swedish Film Institute. Produced by Bo Jonsson. Directed by Carsten Brandt. Screenplay, Brandt from the play "Demons" by Lars Norén; camera (Fuji-Color), Göran Nilsson; editor, Kaspar Schyberg, Lars Hagström; production design and costumes, Mona Theresia Forsén; sound, Björn Gunnarsson, Stefan Ljungberg; line producer, Britt Ohlsson; production management, Rune Hjelm, Bamse Ulfung. Reviewed at Sandrews screening room, Stockholm, Aug. 25, 1986 as simultaneous official competition entry in Montreal Film Festival. Running time: 125 MINS.
Katarina .... Ewa Fröling
Frank .... Lars Green
Thomas .... Björn Granath
Jenna .... Pia Oscarsson

Stockholm — Denmark's Carsten Brandt, long familiar with handling the stage works of Sweden's Lars Norén, was brought to the Swedish capital to turn, as screenwriter and director, Norén's "Demons," another look at "Marriage As Living Hell," into a feature film. Brandt has done so and succeeded in matching the blackest and best of August Stringberg, Ingmar Bergman and Edward Albee.

"Demons" surely will find audiences on the international art house circuit willing to sit through this latest dissection of the marriage institution's most sinister potential, while they will also feel themselves grandly entertained. Brandt has added plenty of outright comedy relief to his acid brew. Even at 125 minutes running time, picture seems tightly paced and not a second overlong.

"Demons" has one married couple in a near-empty, but still elegant apartment yield center stage occasionally to another married couple. The second couple is invited up mostly to serve as sparring partners in the first couple's running (for 10 years, it seems) fight to obtain supremacy and, perhaps, a little love on the side. Very soon, the hell within the first couple proves contagious.

Moving with grace like tigers in a cage, Frank (screen newcomer Lars Green) and Katarina (Ewa Fröling, the young mother of Bergman's "Fanny & Alexander") make love and show claws with the same urgency. She breaks into occasional hysterics and smashes a variety of glassware. He remains outwardly cool while radiating inner hatred. In the early evening, Frank has brought home a square package, carefully wrapped and sealed. It contains his mother's ashes. The funeral is set for the next day, and Katarina declares herself happy: "At last, we shall meet some people."

To relieve the immediate tension, Frank brings up the couple from downstairs. While Frank and Katarina fight over Frank's possibly imaginary, onetime affair with an Italian singer and over his ensuing passion for Italian clothes, cologne and everything else from Italy, Thomas (Björn Granath) and Jenna (Pia Oscarsson) are bogged down in more ordinary worries about small kids who keep them from living a fun life.

Frank and Katarina have, of course, no children. Soon, however, the original twosome's confrontations are turned in quadruple free-for-alls, most of the time with Frank as the instigator. Everybody gets his sexual identities brought into doubt, nobody's dignity is left unsoiled.

But amidst the wildest hysterics, a certain control is exercised all around, including by the writer-director. High physical drama comes as needed relief after the most diabolic statements in dialog.

Superior acting in all four roles helps, too. If anybody shines in particular, it is Ewa Fröling, who far surpasses her previous screen efforts. She literally breathes fresh air into the claustrophobic confines of her role without ever diluting it with the sugary or maudlin. — *Kell.*

Evixion
(CANADIAN-COLOR)

A Chbib production. Produced, directed and edited by Bachar Chbib. Screenplay, Chbib, Claire Nadon, Dafna Kastner, Stephen Reizes; camera (color), David Wellington, Sylvain Gingras; sound, Doug Taylor, Marie-Claude Cagne. Reviewed at World Film Fest, Montreal, Aug. 26, 1986. Running time: 78 MINS.
With: Roland Smith, Claire Nadon, Kennon Raines, Pierre Curzi, Piotr Lysak, Jean-Claude Gingras, Suzanne Stark.

Montreal — "Evixion" (the misspelling is deliberate) is an infuriating experimental film about the denizens of a rundown Montreal apartment block.

Despite the mind-boggling presence of no less than four writers on the film, Syrian-born director Bachar Chbib has either been unwilling, or unable, to tell a comprehensible narrative about these people. Instead he's made a non-narrative film about caricatured cyphers for which most audiences will care nothing.

They include a slogan-spouting femme revolutionary, a gay couple, a heroin dealer, a woman forever taking polaroid pics, a couple forever exercising, a transvestite who adores Jayne Mansfield, and others.

There's little dialog, and what there is, is banal. Camerawork is so murky it's often impossible to tell who's doing what to whom, but few will care.

This one's only for seekers after esoteric filmmaking. It's also a good example of a government-funded pic that's basically a waste of taxpayers' money. If the funding bodies were looking for some cinematic pioneering, they've come away empty-handed. — *Strat.*

La Guêpe
(The Wasp)
(CANADIAN-COLOR)

A Via Le Monde François Floquet production. Directed by Gilles Carle. Screenplay, Carle, Camille Coudari, Catherine Hermary-Vieille; camera (color), Guy Dufaux; editor, Michel Arcand; music, Osvaldo Montes; sound, Patrick Rousseau. Reviewed at Montreal World Film Festival, Aug. 27, 1986. Running time: **93 MINS.**
With: Chloé Sainte-Marie, Warren Peace, Donald Pilon, Ethné Grimes, Claude Gauthier, Gilbert Turp.

Montreal — Gilles Carle, one of Quebec's directing legends, was apprehensive about attending and presenting his latest, "La Guêpe," at pic's world preem, in conjunction with the World Film fest. And for good reason.

Critics and spectators shook their heads in utter disbelief exiting the theater. Film wasn't billed as a comedy, but guffaws were all that could be discerned during and after the screening.

A ludicrous, bordering on imbecilic, melodrama, the film marks the acting debut of Carle's latest prodigy, Chloé Sainte-Marie (Carole Laure was another). Saint-Marie may be pleasing to the eye, but she can't cut it as the pistol-toting fashion-plate and airline pilot, a former aerial acrobat.

The heroine's two young children are callously run down and killed by the drunken wife of a wealthy anglo industrialist, who practices voodoo. Sainte-Marie, dressed in chic combat fatigues, seeks revenge by launching a one-woman aerial blitzkrieg. Enough said.

Production values are acceptable, but pic doesn't have a chance on domestic screens, let alone abroad.—*Bro.*

Grandeur Et Décadence D'Un Petit Commerce De Cinéma
(The Grandeur And Decadence Of A Small-Time Filmmaker)
(FRENCH-COLOR-16m)

A Hamster Prods. production. Produced by Pierre Grimblat. Directed by Jean-Luc Godard. Screenplay, Godard, based on the novel by James Hadley Chase; camera (color, 16m), Caroline Champetier. Reviewed at the Montreal Film Festival, Cinema of Today and Tomorrow, Aug. 28, 1986. Running time: **90 MINS.**
With: Jean-Pierre Leaud, Jean-Pierre Mocky, Marie Valéra.

Montreal — In this made-for-French telefilm, Jean-Luc Godard brings his abstract drollery to bear upon the story of a faded film producer and his high-strung director as they try to mount — what else — a low-budget public television movie. Film buffs and Godard fans willing to put up with the type of arcane and desultory detours that have

marked Godard's recent work should find some moments to savor in "Grandeur And Decadence." Given Godard's U.S. following, the film could find its way into art houses if English subtitles are provided together with a cleaned-up 35m print, advertised but not delivered for its showing at the Montreal World Film Festival.

Working under hectic, ulcer-inducing pressures, the two filmmakers (Jean-Pierre Leaud and Jean-Claude Mocky) are auditioning actors in hilariously assembly-line fashion, while they literally count their coins and scheme for ways to come up with some German coproduction funds. When they're not in their cramped little office, these small-time filmmakers hold court in a café of the absurd, where they thresh-out philosophy and interview ingénues with one eye on a seduction.

These frazzled film hustlers, however, are walled-off from real emotions, so exhausted are they by this desperate effort to resurrect a reputation whose faded grandeur is symbolized by a Mercedes Benz. In their dark nights of the soul they reflect on great cinema, theater and renaissance art, alone, together with their assistants or an actress (Marie Valéra), whose charms merit multiple call-backs for consideration as the lead. All of this is presented by Godard with a purposefully out-of-kilter perspective and a soundtrack mixing mournful orchestrations and old Janis Joplin recordings such as "Mercedes Benz" and "Me And Bobby McGee."

Godard has some fun with the conventions of tv such as using color bar test patterns for "artistic" effect in his film on film. Perhaps the high point of "Grandeur And Decadence," however, is a cameo appearance by Godard himself, in which he commiserates with the producer (who's gambling everything he's got on this whacky venture) about the difficulty of raising funds and the sheer impossibility of cracking the U.S. film establishment (taking a quick sideswipe at Roman Polanski in the process) but doesn't offer to help this pathetic loser. In typically Godardian fashion, the producer and an assistant are later murdered in the Mercedes, but the show goes on.

Print reviewed here had a candy-like look of artificial colorization which may have been intentional, and a bothersomely jumpy sound level.—*Rich.*

Chopper
(INDIAN-COLOR)

A Zoom Enterprises production. Written and directed by Nabyendu Chatterjee, from

a story by Ajoy Bhattacharya. Camera (color), Pantu Nag; editor, Bulu Ghosh; music, Nikhil Chattopadhyay; art director, Prasad Mitra; sound, Durga Mitra. Reviewed at World Film Fest, Montreal, Aug. 31, 1986. Running time: **105 MINS.**
Rajat Ray ....Joy Bannerjee
Reena ....Sreela Mazumder
Shubhra Ray ....Pradip Mukherjee
Father ....Karunakanta Bhattacharya
Mother ....Sova Sen
Also with: Niranjan Roy, Goutam Chakraborty, Santana Basu, Mrinal Basu, Chowdhury, Bidyut Chatterjee, Ajoy Bhattacharya, Bidyut Nag.

Montreal — A grim picture of Calcutta in the mid-1980s is presented in "Chopper," a technically and cinematically ragged, but quite fascinating film.

Story centers on the Ray family. The eldest brother, Shubhra, is a union activist shot dead during a rally outside a factory. He was the breadwinner, and now it's up to his rather dreamy younger brother Rajat, who is unequipped for his role. An almost painfully moral man, he won't accept a job that would mean keeping two sets of books, nor will he sleep with his willing, lonely girlfriend. He also suspects his sister may be drifting into prostitution, and takes stern action to prevent this. Even his parents are dismayed by his apparent rigidity, but it seems the only way the family can avoid starvation is to go along with Rajat.

Background to all this is Calcutta itself, choked with people, with streets that flood when it rains, crowded public transport, and constant parades, processions, demonstrations and political rallies. Pic was lensed when Indira Gandhi was prime minister.

"Chopper" is technically very rough indeed, with poor camerawork, even poorer processing, ragged editing and sometimes awkward acting. Its international chances thus are nil, yet it presents, in a rather primitive way, a truly frightening picture of a great city in death throes. —*Strat.*

La Femme secrète
(The Secret Wife)
(FRENCH-COLOR)

An AAA release of a Flach Films/FR3 Films/Séléna coproduction. Produced by Jean-François Lepetit, Pascal Hommais. Directed by Sébastien Grall. Screenplay, Grall, Sylvain Saada; camera (color), Robert Alazraki; editor, Jacques Comets; music, Bruno Coulais; art direction, Valérie Grall; sound, Bernard Aubouy; production manager, Farid Chaouche. Reviewed at the Club de L'Etoile, Paris, Aug. 28, 1986. (In Montreal Film Festival — noncompeting.) Running time: **95 MINS.**
Antoine Béraud ....Jacques Bonnafé
Camille Alligheri ......Clémentine Célarié
Pierre Franchin ....Philippe Noiret
Zaccharia Pasdeloup ...François Berleand
Marc Alligheri ......Wladimir Yordanoff
Marie ....Claire Nebout
Stirner ....Jean-Louis Richard

Paris — Newcomer Sébastien Grall shows a smart directorial hand but a convoluted sense of scripting in this psychological thriller about a young man who investigates the death of his wife and stumbles upon her secret life.

Jacques Bonnafé is an experimental submarine diver working on a North Sea platform when an urgent telegram calls him back to Paris. His wife, to whom he's been married six years (during which he has spent most of the time abroad) has been fished out of the Seine, an apparent suicide.

Suspecting foul play, Bonnafé starts conducting his own inquiry with his wife's friends and acquaintances and unwittingly opens up a Pandora's Box of ambiguous relationships and illegal activities.

The trail leads him notably to a morbid, institutionalized painter (Philippe Noiret) who has used the wife as a model, a stamp-collecting bank messenger anxious to recover a stolen computer accounting code stashed in Bonnafé's apartment, and an attractive banking agent (Clémentine Célarié) who has had a lesbian affair with the wife and was her accomplice in a banking swindle.

Bonnafé's suspicions that his wife was murdered become near certainties when he finds himself involved with Célarié in the consequences of the two women's dangerous embezzlements.

Grall and co-scripter Sylvain Saada plot out their involved and often murky tale skillfully, but one never warms up to the characters who, though adequately portrayed, remain remote and somewhat cold. Still, it's a promising debut for Grall, who has been an assistant director and cut his helming teeth on some short subjects.

Pic is first released production from Flach Films since its smash comedy, "Three Men And A Cradle," and contains an in-joke: the bank in the story is named after producers Pascal Hommais and Jean-François Lepetit.—*Len.*

Tampopo
(Dandelion)
(JAPANESE-COLOR)

An Itami production. Produced by Yasushi Tamaoki, Seigo Hosogoe. Written and directed by Juzo Itami. Camera (color), Masaki Tamura; editor, Akira Suzuki; art director, Takeo Kimura; sound, Fumio Hashimoto. Reviewed at World Film Fest, Montreal, Aug. 28, 1986. Running time: **114 MINS.**
With: Ken Watanabe, Tsutomu Yamazaki, Nobuko Miyamoto, Koji Yakusho, Rikiya Yasuoka, Kinzo Sakura, Shuji Otaki.

Montreal — Former actor Juzo Itami's second feature, after the success of "The Funeral" (1985), is a thoroughly offbeat but most enjoyable comedy on the subject of food. Indeed, no film in memory, save "La Grande Bouffe," has been so obsessed with culinary delicacies.

Main plotline is pretty slight: a truck-driver and his friend take pity on a pretty widow who operates a rundown noodle shop. They undertake to teach her how to make a success of her business, and through the course of the film she learns how to make the best noodles and the best soup as well as how to give the best service to her customers in the best surroundings.

Along the way, Itami takes dozens of sidetracks, all of them on the theme of food. Pic actually opens with a gangster addressing the cinema audience and warning them not to eat noisy food during the screening. Later on, the gangster and his moll do some pretty erotic things with food, especially the yolk of an egg. At the end the gangster is gunned down but still talks about rare food delicacies before he expires.

The viewer learns how to make noodle soup in three minutes flat, and how to make the best turtle soup. This is a film that's as informative as it is funny.

Some may find the whole concept a bit precious, and pic is certainly a bit too long. It had mostly downbeat reviews in Japan, and only modest business. But it richly deserves international attention on its superb filmcraft (with great lensing by Masaki Tamura) and cheerfully loony obsession with all things gastronomical.

Pic's title is the name of its heroine, and also the name given to her restaurant, which is completely transformed by fadeout. Pic should not be seen on an empty stomach, as its loving images of food are truly mouth-watering. It confirms Itami as a genuinely original comic talent. — *Strat.*

The Champions Part 3 — The Final Battle
(CANADIAN-DOCU-COLOR)

A National Film Board of Canada and Canadian Broadcasting Corp. production. Produced by Donald Brittain, Adam Symansky. Written, directed and narrated by Donald Brittain. Camera (color), Andreas Poulsson; editor, Richard Bujold; story consultant, Graham Fraser; music, Eldon Rathburn; sound, Hans Oomers. Reviewed at Montreal World Film Festival, Aug. 30, 1986. Running time: **90 MINS.**

Montreal — Donald Brittain's followup to his two-part "The Champions" (1978) may be classified as a docu, but its drama is as taut as the best fictional political thriller.

If anyone ever wanted to give an outsider a 90-minute crash course on Canada, Brittain's "The Final

Battle" would suffice in explaining all about the complexities and eccentricities of the "two solitudes" — Anglos and Francos — who comprise the country to the north of the U.S.

As was the case in Brittain's original two-parter, he traces the careers — this time, in their latter stages — of two of Canada's most influential politicos and arch-adversaries. On the one hand, there's Pierre Elliott Trudeau, the former Canadian Prime Minister and intellectual federalist whose great political wish was to unite Canada's two solitudes, repatriate the Canadian constitution and create the ultimate "just society."

Trudeau's career-long sparring partner is René Lévesque, the former, equally dynamic and cagey Premiere of Quebec who sought an independent — albeit watered-down compared to the platform of some francophone nationalists — status for Quebec and an eventual separation from the rest of Canada.

In this last chapter, Brittain focuses on Lévesque's famous referendum of 1980 on the issue of Quebec separation and Trudeau's quest to stifle Lévesque on this issue as well as on the matter of repatriating the Canadian constitution in 1982 behind Lévesque's back. Through some fascinating archival tv and original interview footage with foot-soldiers close to both opposing camps, Brittain is able to convey the power and charisma, the ups and downs of these two most unforgettable Quebec-born politicos — even without their tacit approval of the project.

Brittain also catches with a great deal of poignancy the ultimate downfalls of both gents as their iron wills eventually get the best of them.

Production values are sharp, and interest shouldn't just be limited to Canadiana buffs, but to anyone in search of a revealing, behind-the-scenes look at political power-brokering. Not that there was much doubt, but Brittain, Canada's foremost documentarist, reaffirms his position here. —*Bro.*

Merci Monsieur Robertson
(Thank You Mr. Robertson)
(BELGIAN-COLOR-16m)

A SODEP S.P.R.L. production. Produced, written and directed by Pierre Lévie; camera (color, 16m), Paul Vercheval, Michel Baudour, Raymond Fromont, Désiré Berckmans; editor, Rosanne Van Haesbrouck; sound, D. Warnier, Vvo Geeraert; design, Claire Lise Leisegang; costumes, Leisegang; special effects, Etienne De Bruyne, Daniel Schelfthout. Reviewed at the Montreal Film Festival (Cinema of Today and Tomorrow), Aug. 26, 1986. Running time: **77 MINS.**

With: Suzy Falk, Catherine Ferriere, Pierre Laroche, Jean Marie Petiniot, Robert Roanne, Félix Simtaine, Nicholas Talalaeff, Jean Marc Turine.

Montreal — "Merci Monsieur Robertson" is an affectionate tribute to the history of the moving image that uses the true story of 18th century French projectionist Etienne Gaspard Robert (a.k.a. Robertson) as a framework for a whimsical reflection on the century-long international effort to create motion pictures. If English subtitles are provided it could find a place at some festivals and on the film society circuit.

Rather than opt for a conventional docu-history on the subject of movies, filmmaker Pierre Lévie takes the inventive approach of recreating the milieu of Paris during the French revolution, when the enterprising pioneer showbiz nomad, Mr. Robertson, staged elaborate moving image shows in a darkened auditorium. To the delight and terror of his astounded audiences, Robertson put on displays of moving skulls and other ghoulish images using a screen, mirrors, synchronized sound effects and music, as well as theatrical props and live actors to create a three-dimensional theatrical experience. He also used a socalled "magic lantern" to conjure phantasmagoria on a screen of smoke.

Robertson's adventures in early cinema, including his friendship with one of film history's first aspiring ingenues, are intercut with dramatic and historical narrative accounts of 19th century explorers in photography and animation up through Edison and the Lumière brothers. The film's extensive sequences of exotic antique animation will be of particular interest to buffs of the genre.—*Rich.*

Angel River
(U.S.-MEXICAN-COLOR)

A Robert Renfield-Dasa Films coproduction, in association with Estudios Churubusco. Produced by Robert Renfield. Directed by Sergio Olhovich Greene. Screenplay Renfield; camera (color), Rosalio Solano; art director, Teresa Pecanins; editor, Victor Petrashevich, Suzanne Fenn; music, El Garcia Campos; casting, Pat Edden. Reviewed at World Film Fest, Montreal, Aug. 23, 1986. Running time: **92 MINS.**

Jensie . . . . Lynn-Holly Johnson
Toral . . . . Salvador Sanchez
Hannah . . . . Janet Sunderland
Zach . . . . Peter Matthey
Dee . . . . Joey Shea

Montreal — Producer of this low-budget indie coproduction Robert Renfield was responsible for the screenplay (based on the novel "Rockspring" by Vilet), and thus must shoulder the blame for an incredibly old-fashioned pic. Indeed story and dialog could have been used without change for an early silent.

Pic opens with beautiful, virginal

blond Jensie (Lynn-Holly Johnson) unwisely bathing in a picturesque river. She's spied by a cheerful, bearded Mexican bandit (Salvador Sanchez) who practically twirls his mustache in evil anticipation. He kidnaps and rapes her.

Later on, she manages to shoot him, but he cries out for help, and instead of ankling back to her beloved parents (hard-working sons of the soil) she stays to tend his wound and, yes, falls in love with him. He has a cave (a very obvious studio set) full of stolen treasure, including clothes and jewelry and candelabras and so on, so although their source of food isn't always clear, they're living high until our heroine, now a Woman, wants to go home.

"You'll meet my folks and they'll understand," she says, and that gives some idea of the level of the dialog. Whether they do or not, we never discover. She's left, as she started out, by the river, sadder but (maybe) wiser.

"Angel River" is without distinction on any level, least of all the wan acting, though admittedly even the best actors would find trouble with this plot. —*Strat.*

Declaratie de Dragoste
(Declaration Of Love)
(RUMANIAN-COLOR)

A Studio 3, Romaniafilm, production. Directed by Nicolae Corjos. Screenplay, George Sovu; camera (Orwocolor), Doru Mitran; editor, Elena Pantazica; art director, Ion Nedelcu; assistant director, Daniel Barbilescu. Reviewed at World Film Fest, Montreal, Aug. 31, 1986. Running time: 99 MINS.
Ioana Popa . . . . Teodora Mares
Alexander Birsan . . . . Adrian Paduraru
Mihaela . . . . Tamara Buciuceanu
Also with: Ion Caramitru, Cristina Deleanu, Carmen Enea, Dorel Visan, Florin Chiriac, Adela Marculescu, Constantin Diplan.

Montreal — "Declaration Of Love" is a rather trite teenage romance which sheds no new light on a very familiar subject.

Ioana and Alexander are high schoolers in love, but a variety of incidents keep them apart, including Alexander's temporary relationship with Mihaela. When Alexander gets into a fight at school he's disciplined by having his university entrance exam postponed. He goes to work in a mine, but eventually is reunited with the faithful Ioana on a beach by the sea as a syrupy music score floods the soundtrack.

Backing these tired goings-on are scenes involving rivalry between conservatives and progressives among teachers at the school, and it's this element of the pic that may have made it more interesting on home territory. Internationally, it has little going for it.—*Strat.*

●●●●●●●●●●●●●●●●●●●●●●●●●●●●●●●●●●●●●●●

Venice Festival Reviews

●●●●●●●●●●●●●●●●●●●●●●●●●●●●●●●●●●●●●●●

Miss Mary
(ARGENTINE-COLOR)

A New World Pictures release of a GEA Cinematografica production. Produced by Lita Stantic. Directed by Maria Luisa Bemberg. Screenplay, Bemberg, Jorge Goldemberg; camera (Eastmancolor), Miguel Rodriguez; editor, Cesar D'Angiolillo; music, Luis Maria Serra; sound, Jorge Stavropoulos; costumes, Garciela Galan; art director, Esmeralda Almonacid. Reviewed at Venice Film Fest, Sept. 3, 1986. (No MPAA Rating.) Running time: **102 MINS.**
Miss Mary Mulligan . . . . .Julie Christie
Caroline . . . . .Sofia Viruboff
Johnny . . . . .Donald McIntire
Teresa . . . . .Barbara Bunge
Mecha (mother) . . . . .Nacha Guevara
Alfredo (father) . . . . . .Eduardo Pavlovsky
    Also with: Guillermo Battaglia (Uncle Ernesto), Iris Marga (aunt), Luisina Brando (prostitute).

Venice — Following her international fest success, "Camila" (1984), Maria Luisa Bemberg's new film is a handsomely produced, intelligent drama about a repressed English governess hired to supervise the upbringing of three youngsters living on an immensely prosperous cattle station in the Argentine hinterlands just before the start of World War II. It offers Julie Christie another fine role to add to her already impressive collection.

Pic unfolds in flashback as, in 1945, Miss Mary prepares to return to England (the same year, in fact, that Juan Peron's assumption of power brought radical changes to Argentina). The Englishwoman recalls that in 1938 she arrived at the estate in Verano to take responsibility for Johnny and Caroline, both in their early teens, and the younger Teresa. The immensely wealthy family lives in splendid isolation from the rest of the country. They speak English most of the time, but otherwise the views of Alfredo, the head of the house, are ultra-conservative. He believes a strict religious upbringing is essential, because "religion keeps women out of trouble" and, significantly, his wife has a small room she refers to as "my little crying room."

Bulk of the film chronicles the elegant lives of these privileged people, the kind of people who, in fact, virtually ran Argentina during this period. Miss Mary fits well into this background; she tells her charges, when asked what a socialist is that "In England, we call them robbers," and also remarks that at least in India "it's clear who the natives are."

There are a few minor upsets, as Caroline attains puberty and the girls shock their governess with some of their immature fantasies, but all the while Johnny is obviously infatuated with the Englishwoman,

and matters come to a head one stormy night when, after being initiated into sex with a prostitute (a present from his uncle), he comes to Miss Mary's room and they make love, a sin which results in her dismissal, Caroline's madness and Teresa's eventual marriage to a man she doesn't love.

As noted, Julie Christie is fine as the outwardly cool and respectable but inwardly frustrated and lonely governess, while she gets topnotch support from the rest of the cast, especially Donald McIntire as the lovelorn Johnny. Pic's only flaw is its sometimes confusing continuity: it begins with a redundant prolog, set in 1930, involving an earlier governess to the children, and towards the end the flash-forwards employed are sometimes irritating. Despite these relatively minor problems, "Miss Mary" is a superior effort which should make its mark on the international art house circuit, helped, of course, by Julie Christie's name. Almost all the dialog is spoken in English, ironic given the strained relations between England and Argentina these days following the Falklands conflict.

All production credits are tops, with some lovely photography of the wide open spaces around the ranch by Miguel Rodriguez.—*Strat.*

Sembra Morto ... Ma è Solo Svenuto
(He Looks Dead ... But He Just Fainted)
(ITALIAN-COLOR)

A Tecno Image production. Produced by Alessandro Verdecchi. Directed by Felice Farina. Stars Sergio Castellitto, Marina Confalone. Screenplay, Gianni Di Gregorio, Sergio Castellitto, Felice Farina; camera (Luciano Vittori, Eastmancolor, 16m), Renato Tafuri; editor, Roberto Schiavone; art director, Valentino Salvati; music, Lamberto Macchi. Reviewed at RAI-TV screening room, Rome, Aug. 9, 1986. (Showing at Venice Film Festival out of competition.) Running time: **91 MINS.**
Romano Duranti . . . . . . .Sergio Castellitto
Marina Duranti . . . . . . .Marina Confalone
Alfio . . . . .Mario Prosperi
    Also with: Anita Zagaria, Claudio Spadaro (police agent), Marco Giardina (commissioner), Susanne Rust (Jasmine).

Rome — Repping Italy in Venice's Intl. Critics' Week, "He Looks Dead ... But He Just Fainted" is a touching, tender comedy about ordinary folk living on the outskirts of Rome. Devoid of pretension, and faultlessly limned by a cast as low-key as the direction, pic runs short of the dramatic tension needed to bring out the darker side of its story. It is nonetheless a

noteworthy directorial bow for Felice Farina, former stage thesp and special effects whiz.

Film gets off to a leisurely start introducing Romano and Marina Duranti, siblings who have rounded 30 and lead an aimless existence in the family apartment. While the plain sister (Marina Confalone) types school papers to support them, her indolent but likable brother (Sergio Castellitto) lounges around the house and secretly picks up some pocket money as a part-time dognapper.

The arrival of new neighbor Alfio (Mario Prosperi) turns their life upside down. Not only is he the first love in Marina's life, he also stashes a kilo of pure cocaine under their fridge, source of a long string of gags. He eventually is chased away by the narcs (with Marina at his heels), and Romano, almost accidentally, gets rich overnight.

Much of the credit for hitting the right, light tone is due to Castellitto and Confalone, as unglamorous as they come, but able to make the most impulsive actions believable and sympathetic. The change that comes over Romano in the several-years-later epilog, when he has become a tough bookie on the dog track, is more poignant for being underplayed. Final pages of the script — Marina inconveniently turn up nine months pregnant, just in time to make Romano botch the dognaping of his career — are meant to end story with a bang and bring home the sadness of the siblings' estrangement. It's just a little too tall an order for a first film, and "He Looks Dead" misses that final punch.

Music by Lamberto Macchi ranges pleasantly from humorous to plaintive, as needed. A grainy blowup from the original 16m tempers enjoyment of Renato Tafuri's normally fine camerawork.—*Yung.*

Franza
(AUSTRIAN-COLOR)

A Heinz Scheiderbauer Filmproduktion. Directed by Xaver Schwarzenberger. Screenplay, Rolf Basedow, Consuleo Garcia, from the novel "The Franza Case" by Ingeborg Bachmann; camera (color), Schwarzenberger; editor, Ulrike Schwarzenberger; art director, Egon; music, Bert Breit; assistant director, Gabriela Bacher. Reviewed at Venice Film Fest, Sept. 4, 1986. Running time: **100 MINS.**
Franza . . . . .Elisabeth Trissenaar
Martin . . . . .Gabriel Barilly
Dr. Jordan/
   Dr. Korener . . . . . . .Armin Müller-Stahl
British officer . . . . ,Gottfried John
    Also with: Hilde Krahl, Jan Niklas.

Venice — "Franza" is an overwrought drama in which a young man (Gabriel Barilly) tries to help his older sister who, as a result of a painful marriage to a sadistic doctor, is broken in spirit and has a

death wish. Latter half of the film takes place in Egypt, as the woman, an effective performance from Elisabeth Trissenaar, gradually reveals to her brother the details of her sad life.

The story, adapted from a novel, is not in itself especially original or interesting. There are flashbacks to 1945 (calling the ages of the protagonist very much into question, since the film apparently takes place in the present day, but they don't look nearly as old as they should) when young Franza had an affair with a British officer, and also flashbacks to her marriage to the remote and unfeeling Dr. Jordan. She goes to see another doctor in Cairo, but he reminds her of her hated husband — both roles are played, with his customary authority, by Armin Müller-Stahl.

The main point of interest in the film is the luminous photography, whether of the Austrian mountains, where the story begins, or the haunting landscapes of Egypt. Xaver Schwarzenberger, the director, was himself a camerman, so the pristine visuals come as no surprise. Best sequences take place on a houseboat in Cairo where Franza meets the disbarred Dr. Koerner, and the gentle rocking of the boat adds to the feeling of unease and disorientation.

On balance this is rather cold and hollow drama, whose surface beauty can't compensate for its familiar dramatic excesses. It's technically quite superb. — *Strat.*

Innocenza
(Innocence)
(SWISS-COLOR)

An Imago Film/SSR/RTSI (Lugano) production. Executive producer, Anres Pfäffli. Produced and directed by Villi Hermann. Screenplay, Hermann, Angelo Gregorio from a short story by Francesco Chiesa; camera (Eastmancolor), Hugues Ryffel; editor, Claudio Cormio; music, Graziano Mandozzi; sound, Felix Singer, Giovanni Doffini; art direction, Raffaella Leggeri; costumes, Sylvia de Stoutz. Reviewed at Venice Film Festival, Sept. 1, 1986. Running time: **90 MINS.**
Schoolteacher . . . . .Enrica Maria Modugno
Mayor . . . . .Alessandro Haber
Luca . . . . .Patrick Tacchella
    Also with: Teco Celio, Sonia Gessner, Marino Campanaro, Franco Serena.

Venice — In a little Swiss town in the 1950s, a pretty new schoolteacher stirs up the dormant sexuality of her young pupils. Unlike most portrayals of older woman-inexperienced boy relations, Villi Hermann's "Innocence" has nothing to do with delicate romance in soft focus.

Here the schoolmarm is an outright seductress with a bent for boys in short pants. Without vulgarity or false moralism, film sets out a premise about the limits of adult-child sexuality worth pondering.

Unfortunately, it doesn't develop beyond setting up the basic situation. Simply but watchably lensed on a budget, "Innocence" needs to find inventive programmers — possibly for tv — to reach its audience.

Enrica Maria Modugno's long black tresses and scarlet lipstick immediately establish the irrepressible carnality of the young woman who crosses the lake on a ferryboat every week to teach in a picturesque village. Italo thesp Alessandro Haber (somewhat improbable as a lecherous Swiss mayor) has his eye on her, but her eyes are elsewhere, dreaming, to a passionate Spanish-sounding song she plays over and over. In class she's strict, but after hours turns kittenish and provocative when she gives private lessons to her favorites. First Luca (Patrick Tacchella), then his rival Titta, are called on to do special sessions.

There is some uncertainty as to whether the teacher or Luca is the center of the film. The boy's infatuation is handled with delicacy and realism, his feelings develop step by step as he senses the teacher's sensual response, but doesn't know how to proceed. His family finds him so moody they call in a priest to talk to him. Then just as the teacher's teasing seems on the point of becoming concrete, Luca is judged no longer in need of extra help and another boy chosen for the special lessons — much to his impotent fury.

The schoolmarm is a mysterious, impenetrable character, and film leaves one wondering how conscious she is of what she's doing to her pupils' precocious psyches. Modugno's Botticelli-faced vamp is left so ambiguous it's impossible to know whether her ultimate persecution at the hands of the town is merited or unjustified — at which point "Innocence" closes rather unemotionally. Based on a short story by scribe Francesco Chiesa, film might have benefited from some psychological retuning at the end.
— *Yung.*

Tramp At The Door
(CANADIAN-COLOR)

A CanWest-Burbank production. Executive producer, Don Brinton. Produced by Stan Thomas. Written, directed by Allan Krocker, from a story by Gabrielle Roy. Camera (color), Ron Orieux; editor, Lara Mazur; music, Randolph Peters; sound, Leon Johnston; art director, Bonnie von Elmont; assistant director, Nives Lever. Reviewed at Venice Film Fest, Sept. 6, 1986. Running time: **80 MINS.**
Gustave . . . . Ed McNamara
Albert . . . . August Schellenberg
Madeleine . . . . Monique Mercure
Gabrielle . . . . Joanna Schellenberg
Lemieux . . . . Eric Peterson
Hebert . . . . Jean Louis Hébert

Venice — Set in Manitoba in 1936, "Tramp At The Door" is a slight, quite charming low-budgeter about a stranger who arrives at the home of a hard-working farming family and claims to be a relative.

Ed McNamara plays the tale-telling stranger with considerable charm, and this mysteriously endearing figure is viewed nostalgically through the eyes of the daughter of the house (Joanna Schellenberg). It adds up to a modest piece of drama, based entirely on dialog and interrelations, but in essence a bit lightweight to attract much attention.

Period feeling is attractively captured, and performances all add to the enjoyment of the piece, especially that of Monique Mercure as the young girl's hard-working mother.
— *Strat.*

Storia D'Amore
(Love Story)
(ITALIAN-COLOR)

A Pont Royal Film TV/Istituto Luce/Italnoleggio Cinematografico/RAI-3 coproduction. Produced by Carlo Tuzii. Written and directed by Francesco Maselli. Stars Valeria Golino. Camera (Luciano Vittori color), Maurizio Dell'Orco; editor, Carla Simoncelli; music, Giovanna Salviucci Marini; art direction, Marco Dentici; costumes, Lina Nerli Taviani. Reviewed at Venice Film Festival (Competition), Sept. 4, 1986. Running time: **109 MINS.**
Bruna . . . . Valeria Golino
Sergio . . . . Bals Roca-Rey
Mario . . . . Livio Panieri
Father . . . . Luigi Diberti
Sergio's mother . . . . Gabriella Giorgelli
Also with: Teresa Ricci (Amalia), Franca Scognetti (Soro Assunta), Pierpaolo Benigni (Giovanni), Massimiliano Martoriati (Marco).

Venice — "Love Story" marks the big screen return of Francesco Maselli — one of the cornerstones of political documentary filmmaking in Italy — with his first feature since "Il Sospetto" (The Suspect) of 1975. This portrait of 1980s have-nots in the person of a spunky girl of the slums is painted with the brush of good intentions, but ultimately fails to bring the viewer face to face with the anguish of living in poverty, the way the post-war neorealists or directors like Pasolini have done. Maselli's honest working folk who clean offices at night, collect garbage, and work on the assembly line are sympathetic in principle, but don't come across emotionally because they're just too good to be true.

"Love Story" is a misleading title: although heroine Bruna (Valeria Golino in a credibly limned role) has not one but two affairs in quick succession, the focus remains entirely on her.

Since she was 13 she's been getting up at 3 a.m. to clean offices, and her life is an interminable round of buses, hard work, and caring for her motherless brothers and father.

Opening sequences describing her average day are handled with the finesse of a classic neorealist scene, and skillfully build solidarity for Bruna. In spite of her exhausting existence, she is the epitome of freshness, vitality and affection.

Taught by père Luigi Diberti to think for herself and act on her convictions, Bruna nonetheless shocks the family by having her boyfriend move into their crowded apartment. Sergio (Bals Roca-Rey) is her first love, 18 like her, a loader at the general markets with dreams of becoming a mechanic. Following her heart, Bruna regretfully drops him for a gorgeous, taciturn 16-year-old (Livio Panieri) up from the south and minimally employed. The three eventually move in together (Sergio just as a friend) in a building slated for demolition.

In this apparently well-balanced moment, when everything seems to be running smoothly on the emotional plane, film ends with Bruna's inexplicable gesture of self-destruction. The meaning of this gratuitous finale is not obvious; maybe the prospect of a lifetime of work is enough to do in the hardiest sort. But in a film too full of sensitive, caring people strangely short on anger, jealousy and aggression, its violence rings hollow.

As though unwilling to vulgarize the poor but noble heroes, film sidesteps a lot of realities, which gives it the feeling of being bleached for public view. Avoiding drugs and prostitution (mentioned only in passing) might be justifiable as worn slum clichés, but why scratch the color out of Roman street slang? Hearing themselves talk the way they really do has always appealed to Italian audiences, who will be the film's main public. — *Yung.*

'38
(AUSTRIAN-WEST GERMAN-COLOR)

A Satel Film (Vienna)-Almaro Film coproduction. Produced by Otto-Boris Dworak, Jan Syrovy. Written and directed by Wolfgang Glück, from the novel "What Else Vienna Was" by Friedrich Torberg. Camera (color), Gerard Vandenberg; editor, Heidi Handorf; music, Bert Grund; sound, Werner Böhn; art direction, Herwig Libowitzky; assistant director, Harald Eberhard. Reviewed at Venice Film Fest, Sept. 4, 1986. Running time: **103 MINS.**
Martin Hoffman . . . . Tobias Engel
Carola Hell . . . . Sunnyi Melles
Toni Drechsler . . . . Heinz Trixner
Mother . . . . Lotte Ledl
Frau Schostal . . . . Ingrid Burkhard
Also with: Josef Frölich (Kemetter), David Camerum (Col. Jovanic), Romuald Pekny (Sovary), Maria Singer (Frau Pekarek), Miguel Hertz-Kestranek (Ferry), Michael Kehlmann (Hebenstein), Walter Starz (Sollnau), Ulf Dieter Kusdas (Andi).

Venice — There have been dozens of films about the way ordinary citizens in central Europe reacted to the rise of Nazism, probably the best of the recent crop being Istvan Szabo's "Mephisto." Simply titled "'38" is adapted from a novel, "What Else Vienna Was," by Friedrich Torberg, and is a handsome, quite gripping story of a young Viennese journalist (Tobias Engel) who happens to be a Jew, and his relationship with an up-and-coming actress (Sunnyi Melles).

Familiar filmic territory, perhaps, but writer-director Wolfgang Glück brings a certain intensity to the proceedings, as the encroaching disaster is foreshadowed by such casual remarks as the fact that theater director Max Reinhardt is, after all, a Jew.

There are solid performances from the leads, with Melles especially good, and authentic-looking, as the young actress. She already made her mark in Josef Roedl's "The Wild Clown," which competed for West Germany in Montreal.

Above all is the look of the film, with rich photography by Gerard Vandenberg and great care and attention given to the art direction. Despite its basically familiar theme, pic could get some attention on its study of the gradual erosion of civil rights as the annexation of Austria by Hitler draws closer. In a lighter vein, there's an amusing sequence in which Melles plays a Ginger Rogers-type song-and-dance role in a black and white musical being made at Wien Film.—*Strat.*

Blood Ties
(Il Cugino Americano)
(ITALIAN-COLOR)

A Sacis and Viacom release of a Racing Pictures/RAI-1 coproduction. Produced by Alessandro Fracassi. Directed by Giacomo Battiato. Stars Brad Davis. Screenplay, Corrado Augias, Battiato; camera (Panavision, color), Romano Albani; editor, Mario Morra; music, Celso Valli; production manager, Maurizio Anticoli. Art direction, Paolo Biagetti; costumes, Francesca Panicali. Reviewed at Cannes Film Festival (market), May 20, 1986. (In Venice Film Festival.) Running time: **120 MINS.**
Julian Salina . . . . Brad Davis
Giuliano Salina . . . . Tony LoBianco
Mark Ciuni . . . . Vincent Spano
Luisa Masseria . . . . Barbara De Rossi
Also with: Arnoldo Foà (Vincenzo Ammirati), Delia Boccardo (Sara Salina), Ricky Tognazzi (Riccardo), Michel Gazzo (Joe Salina), Maria Conchita Alonso (Caterina Ammirati).

(English language soundtrack)

Rome — "Blood Ties" is a rare example of a made-in-Italy production with the story interest and technical sophistication to garner an international audience. On the rebound from "Hearts In Armour," director Giacomo Battiato puts aside all pretensions towards arty filmmaking to demonstrate solid, almost anonymous prowess as an action director. The genre is straight Mafia, the locations New York and

Sicily, and the script (penned by Battiato and Corrado Augias) plausible and exciting. Both big screen and four-hour tv versions should sell well on action markets.

Pic's simple premise is to have the Cosa Nostra force an honest, unsuspecting young American, Julian Salina (Brad Davis), to murder a cousin he has never met in Sicily. The leverage is they've kidnaped Julian's aged father, Michel Gazzo, who once had dealings with the underworld but who long ago went straight. The Sicilian cousin, coincidentally named Giuliano Salina (Tony LoBianco), is a courageous young magistate forced to live behind steel-lined doors while he investigates Mafia doings. Only Julian can break through his barricades and bodyguards.

Nemesis of both cousins is Vincent Spano as Mark Ciuni, a sadistic, coke-sniffing punk who has become one of the top Mafia managers and financial whizzes. Ciuni is easily the most interesting character in the film, and Spano achieves a striking balance between flamboyance and credibility, whether he's mistreating his mistress Maria Conchita Alonso or egging on his horse in a dangerous clandestine race held inside a barn (one of pic's set pieces).

Aided by realistic dialog, rest of cast turns in convincing performances all around, even down to the accents. As the all-American boy catapulted into a survival situation, Brad Davis is suitably bewildered. Violent but not too gory, "Ties" portrays the Mafia as a nasty sickness it's a relief to win out over. — *Yung.*

Al Bedaya
(Satan's Empire/The Beginning)
(EGYPTIAN-COLOR)

An Al Alamiya for Cinema and Tv production and release. Produced by Hussein Kalla. Executive producer, Adel El Mihi. Directed by Salah Abou Seif. Screenplay, Seif, Lenine El Ramli; camera (Hungarofilm color), Mohsen Ahmed; editor, Hussein Afifi; music, Ammar El Cherii, Sayed Hegab; art direction, Mahmoud Mohsen. Reviewed at Venice Film Festival, Sept. 6, 1986. Running time: **123 MINS.**
Painter .... Ahmed Zaki
Hostess .... Yousra
Journalist .... Safiya El Omari
Businessman .... Gamil Ratib
Peasant .... Hamdi Ahmed
Also with: Soad Nasr (belly dancer), Sabri Abdel Moneim (boxer), Medhat Morsi (pilot), Nagat Ali (metallurgist), Hussain El Hakim (steward), Samir Wahid (copilot), Wissam Hamdi (boy).

Venice — Shown at the Venice Festival as a special tribute to its maker, Salah Abou Seif (the Egyptian director has made 40 films in as many years) "The Beginning," or "Satan's Empire," as it is alternately titled in English, marks one of Seif's rare excursions into comedy. Designed as the first part of a trilogy on democratic socialism, it is disappointingly simplistic and predictable as an allegory about the creation of society, when a plane crashes in the desert and the survivors take over a tiny oasis.

Traces of the master's hand are there to enjoy, but despite the presence of a cast rich in Arab stars, film only works to a certain extent. It has done middling business in Egypt.

Idea for "Al Bedaya" dates back to the early 1960s, when socialism appeared in Egypt, but film is so schematic it could be set in any period. The dozen survivors of the crash represent various groups. Thus we have the businessman who wastes no time in becoming the oasis' dictator — pasha, ensconced in a house he forces the others to build; a handsome painter (matinee idol Ahmed Zaki), progressive voice of the people urging the oppressed colony to throw off its shackles; the uneducated peasant and boxer, gullible victims of the tyrant's lies, etc.

On this politicized Gilligan's Isle, not a date is eaten without a social point behind it. In fact, once the capitalist has grabbed power through a combination of gambling, force, and insidious persuasion, he pays his workers in starvation date wages, likely to be reduced at the first sign of slackness on the job or a slowdown in production. Naturally, he's overthrown by pic's end, when the group is rescued.

More than in the conventional comic acting and dialog, pic's humor lies in continually rolling out the far-fetched analogies between the oasis-microcosm and society at large. These are intermittently funny, particularly when they're understated, which is not always the case.

Lensed entirely in the desert without any scenery to speak of, film is deliberately stripped down and propless, the better to underline the purity of its parable. A few more frills on the story might have let Seif's message emerge more naturally. — *Yung.*

La Puritaine
(The Prude)
(FRENCH-BELGIAN-COLOR)

An MK2 release of a Philippe Dussart/Man's Film, Brussels/La Sept coproduction, with the participation of the CNC (Ministry of Culture), the Belgian Ministry of Francophone Culture, and Cinérgie and Investimage. Produced by Philippe Dussart. Directed by Jacques Doillon. Screenplay, Doillon, Jean-François Goyet; camera (color), William Lubtchansky; editor, Marie Robert; music, Philippe Sarde; sound, Jean-Claude Laureux; art direction, Jean-Claude de Bemels; production manager, Michelle Tronçon; assistant director, Guy Chalaud. Reviewed at the Celtec screening room, Paris, Aug. 28, 1986. (In Venice Film Fest, competing.) Running time: **86 MINS.**
Pierre .... Michel Piccoli
Manon .... Sandrine Bonnaire
Ariane .... Sabine Azéma
François .... Laurent Malet
Also with: Brigitte Coscas, Anne Coesens, Corinne Dacla, Jessica Forde, Vinciane Le-Men, Kitty Kortes-Lynch, Nicole Persy, Pascale Salkin, Pascale Tison.

Paris — Director Jacques Doillon, who tends to blow hot and cold, is in a warmer register with his new intimate opus, "La Puritaine," which dramatizes the reconciliation between a father and daughter in an empty legit theater. Doillon treated a similar psychologically fraught rapport in his 1980 feature, "The Prodigal Daughter," which was complicated by incest.

The situation here is less extreme but still full of psychic hurts and perverse angers. Michel Piccoli (who played the father in "Prodigal Daughter") is the artistic manager of an Antwerp playhouse trying to prepare himself for the homecoming of his daughter (Sandrine Bonnaire), who ran away a year earlier without explanation and has sent dad a laconic message announcing her return.

While waiting for Bonnaire to show, Piccoli, accompanied by his current girl friend (Sabine Azéma), gathers the young actresses of his troupe and has them impersonate various aspects of his daughter in an attempt to come to terms with the imminent confrontation.

Bonnaire arrives, but after a sexually explosive run-in with her old boy friend (Laurent Malet), prefers to play hide-and-seek with dad before making her entrance. At last they meet in a long, wrenching coming-to-terms mediated by Azéma.

Unlike some of Doillon's early audience-turnoffs like "La Pirate" and "The Temptations Of Isabelle," where characters tended to vent their neuroses in the noisiest, most obnoxious way possible, the characters of "La Puritaine" usually speak in hushed, but no less intense, tones, which allows the spectators less abrasive access to the film's emotional concerns.

Doillon's scripting (with Jean-François Goyet, the collaborator of his two previous pictures) is still nagged by occasional bathos and precious dialog, but the stylization here is usually successful because the legit setting and the theater games aspect nicely contain the psychodramatic content and give it a metaphorical richness.

Bonnaire and Piccoli are riveting as the inflexible daughter and the exhibitionist father who are separated then united in the same loss of purity. However, Azéma is somewhat sacrificed in a more passive and vaguely limned role of catalyst and go-between. A special word for William Lubtchansky's hypnotically burnished photography, especially the sublime closeups of Bonnaire.

A competing selection at the Venice Festival, "La Puritaine" is the first completed film to be coproduced by La Sept, the projected French-directed European culture web. It's an auspicious debut. — *Len.*

✱✱✱✱✱✱✱✱✱✱✱✱✱✱✱✱✱✱✱✱✱✱✱✱✱✱✱✱✱✱✱
Montreal Festival Reviews
✱✱✱✱✱✱✱✱✱✱✱✱✱✱✱✱✱✱✱✱✱✱✱✱✱✱✱✱✱✱✱

Karma
(SWISS-B&W)

A Ho Quang Minh (Lausanne) production. Produced and directed by Ho Quang Minh. Screenplay, Nguy Ngu, Ho Quang Minh, from the novel by Nugy; camera (b&w), Tran Dinh Muu, Tran Ngoc Huynh; editor, Trinh Cong Son; art direction, Le Troung Tieu, Ngo Huu Phuoc; sound, Ngo Anh Giang. Reviewed at World Film Fest, Montreal, Aug. 29, 1986. Running time: **103 MINS.**
Binh .... Tran Quang
Nga .... Phuong Dung
Tri .... Le Cung Bac

Montreal — Though technically Swiss (the production company is based in Lausanne, and the Swiss government helped with finance), "Karma" is in every other way a Vietnamese film. It was shot entirely on Vietnamese locations with a Vietnamese cast and crew, and is thus something of a curiosity on the fest circuit: an unofficial film from Vietnam.

Story is told in an extended flashback and opens in 1972 as a young woman, Nga, and her friend, Tri, a South Vietnamese soldier, wait by a river in a small village for the arrival of a Buddhist priest to perform the funeral rights over Binh, Nga's dead husband.

Story then shifts to 1968 when Binh (the name, ironically, means peace) is missing in action. To survive, Nga becomes a Saigon bargirl after her village is forcibly evacuated by the army. When Binh, who's been horribly wounded, returns, he rejects Nga. She follows him to the battlefield, but he dies during a Communist attack.

As will be evident from the above, the film is set entirely in *South* Vietnam, and presents the two South Vietnamese soldiers involved as decent, honorable men, though fighting for a lost cause and a corrupt regime.

Pic is rather slow moving, and could stand some tightening, but otherwise should be heard from on the fest circuit, especially where Third World or Asian films are programmed: it was world-preemed in Montreal. Black and white lensing is sharp and quite beautiful, and the principal actors all acquit themselves well.

Result is a very worthy effort which will find the going tough commercially, but which deserves to be seen by connoisseurs. —Strat.

High Speed
(FRENCH-COLOR)

An Orca Prods./Avida Films/Frankfurter Filmwerkstatt production. Produced by Jean-Luc Ormieres. Directed by Monique Dartonne and Michel Kaptur. Screenplay, Olivier Douyere, Dartonne, Kaptur; camera (color), Alain Lasfargues; editor, Dartonne; music, Olivier Hutman; sound, Jean Pierre Duret. Reviewed at the Montreal World Film Festival (out of competition), Aug. 22, 1986. Running time: **86 MINS.**
With: Mireille Perrier, Bruce Thurman, Reinhardt Kolldehoff, Peter Schlesinger.

Montreal — "High Speed" is an absorbing, well-made example of a new type of hybrid film, shot in three languages and focusing on the mobile community of international free spirits in Europe. Although exploring familiar themes of paranoia and existential rootlessness, "High Speed" unfolds with a gritty brio, and the film's high proportion of English-language dialog makes it an excellent pickup prospect for U.S. indie distributors seeking an offbeat pic with drawing potential.

Edith (Mireille Perrier) is a stunning film editor from Paris who journeys to Frankfurt to take a job with a German colleague and friend who's prominent in h er own country. Upon arrival, Edith's friend tells her she must go to Berlin on urgent business, but will return shortly. Edith heads for the house her friend shares with another German girl of Turkish extraction.

Unbeknownst to her, Edith soon catches the eye of Gordon (Bruce Thurman) an American expatriate photographer with a checkered past. He's nicknamed "Pulitzer" because he once won U.S. journalism's highest prize only to have it revoked for an unstated ethical transgression so severe he's persona non grata in the land of the free. Gordon spends a lot of time hanging around a lowlife bar in Frankfurt, works as a freelance blackmail photographer specializing in philanderers, and photographs pretty girls and plays chess for hobbies.

Gordon's hired by a wealthy German trucking magnate to photograph some pesky video journalists who are prying into his business. One of these snoops is Edith's friend. In his spare time, Gordon

tails Edith and photographs her, unaware of the connection to his job assignment. One night he rescues Edith from an attacker, and they develop an open, but non-romantic friendship, which begins to intensify before it's shattered by an escalating web of suspicion and intrigue.

The film succeeds admirably in using its somewhat contrived plot as a vehicle for dissecting the cultural affinities and barriers between its cast of nomadic, international individualists. While suspense is sustained through the question of just what is being smuggled into Germany on those trucks and why Edith's friend is so obsessed with the dangerous search for the answer, these self-interested young adults are made increasingly aware of their vulnerabilities in a fast-moving modern world where there are no easy answers.

Perrier and Thurman give sturdy, believable performances, Alain Lasfargues' photography is appropriately sharp-surfaced, and Monique Dartonne's editing reveals the mark of experience that makes for a natural sub-theme in a first-rate first feature. — Rich.

My Little Girl
(U.S.-COLOR)

A Black Swan Prod. production in association with Merchant Ivory Prods. Produced and directed by Connie Kaiserman. Screenplay, Kaiserman, Nan Mason; camera (color), Pierre Lhomme; editor, Katherine Wenning; music, Richard Robbins; sound, Robert A. Hein; design, Dan Leigh; costumes, Susan Gammie. Reviewed at the Montreal World Film Festival, Aug. 31, 1986. (No MPAA Rating.) Running time: **120 MINS.**
Franny Bettinger . .Mary Stuart Masterson
Ike Bailey . . . . .James Earl Jones
Grandmother . . . . .Geraldine Page
Mrs. Bettinger . . . . . .Pamela Payton Wright
Mr. Bettinger . . . . .Peter Michael Goetz
Alice. . . . . .Traci Lin
Joan .Erika Alexander
Mrs. Chopper . . . . .Anne Meara
Kai .Peter Gallagher
Also with: Jordan Charney, Page Hannah, Jennifer Lopez, Naeemah Wilmore, George Newberth, Bill O'Connell.

Montreal — "My Little Girl" is a well-intentioned but flatly written story about an affluent teenage girl's summer of awakening, working with emotionally troubled youths at an institution for homeless kids. The film is redeemed from ordinariness, however, by several fine performances and the cut of some seven minutes planned by the producers for its U.S. release should get "My Little Girl" a crack at **theatrical exposure prior to cable and videocassette playoff.**
Franny Bettinger (Mary Stuart Masterson) is the 16-year-old daughter of a bigshot lawyer (Peter Michael Goetz) and an insufferably self-centered and dense mother (Pamela Payton Wright) who, with

her parents' reluctant approval takes a summer job at a halfway house for homeless kids run by a tough but caring administrator, Ike Bailey (James Earl Jones). The only person at her suburban dream home who's genuinely supportive of Franny's new endeavor is her improbably liberal grandmother (Geraldine Page).

In stark contrast to her pampered world of lawn parties and yachting daytrips, Franny is confronted with grim institutional reality at the halfway house, which serves as a sort of holding shelter and school for impoverished homeless kids until they're placed in permanent institutions. Mr. Bailey assigns Franny to work with Joan and her younger sister Camilla whose mother attempted suicide and is emotionally unable to care for them. Joan is very withdrawn, Camilla speaks not at all, and the earnest Franny is determined to help them. Franny also becomes involved in the mixed-up life of the brassy, sullen laundry room girl, Alice (Traci Lin) who's having a bitter confrontation with Bailey

over her determination to leave the shelter on her upcoming 18th birthday.

Although she's very naive about what she can and cannot accomplish for her charges, Franny, played with convincing sensitivity by the appealing Masterson, is determined to effect a change in their lives. She convinces Bailey (whose character Jones fits with tailor-made authority) to take her on as a fulltime worker and sets about to organize a talent show to give the shelter's restless girls an outlet for their pent-up emotions and a means of discovering their latent talents.

Although she's cautioned by Bailey about over-involvement with her job, Franny's zeal and naiveté lead her and the picture's plot line into some not wholly credible developments until all is made well by a predictable conclusion that borders on the lachrymose. Technical aspects of the production show polish, particularly for a low-budget first feature. — Rich.

★★★★★★★★★★★★★★★★★★★★★★★★★★★★★
★   ★
★   **Toronto Festival Reviews**   ★
★   ★
★★★★★★★★★★★★★★★★★★★★★★★★★★★★★

'night, Mother
(COLOR)

Well-acted drama is a questionable audience attraction.

A Universal Pictures release. Produced by Aaron Spelling, Alan Greisman. Executive producers, Dann Byck, David Lancaster. Directed by Tom Moore. Stars Sissy Spacek, Anne Bancroft. Screenplay, Marsha Norman, based on her play; camera (Deluxe color), Stephen M. Katz; editor, Suzanne Pettit; music, David Shire; sound, Bruce Smith; production design, Jack De Govia; art director, John R. Jensen; set design, Beverli Eagan; costumes, Bob Blackman; assistant director, Cheryl Downey; associate producers, Cheryl Downey, Wallace Worsley; casting, Tony Shepherd. Reviewed at Universal Studios screening room, Universal City, Calif., Sept. 3, 1986. (In Toronto Festival of Festivals.) (MPAA Rating: PG-13.) Running time: **96 MINS.**
Jessie Cates . . . . .Sissy Spacek
Thelma Cates . . . . .Anne Bancroft
Dawson Cates . . . . .Ed Berke
Loretta Cates . . . . .Carol Robbins
Melodie Cates . . . . .Jennifer Rosendahl
Kenny Cates . . . . .Michael Kenworthy
Agnes Fletcher . . . . .Sari Walker

Hollywood — " 'night, Mother" is an excruciating exploration of failed family relationships and a life gone to seed. Not exactly the stuff for a cheery night out, but as adapted from Marsha Norman's Pulitzer Prize-winning play there is a razor sharp edge to the film that cuts through to basic human concerns. Whether people want to pay to see

this is questionable since they usual-

Original Play

A Dann Byck, Wendell Cherry, The Shubert Organization and Frederick M. Zollo presentation of a drama in one act by Marsha Norman. Staged by Tom Moore. Setting and costumes, Heidi Landesman; lighting, James F. Ingalls; associate producer, William P. Suter; stage manager, Steven Beckler; general managers, McCann & Nugent; company manager, Sam Pagliaro; publicity, Hunt/Pucci. Opened March 31, 1983 at the John Golden Theatre, N.Y. $27.50 top weeknights, $29 weekend nights.
Thelma Cates . . . . .Anne Pitoniak
Jessie Cates . . . . .Kathy Bates

ly go to the pictures to get away from this kind of drama.

On its own terms, " 'night, Mother" is a triumph. Still somewhat stagebound, it's a production pared down to its basic elements — script, actors, stage, director. Set in anywhere U.S.A., it's a chamber drama limited to a small house where things seem normal at first and then heat to an almost unbearable intensity.

Jessie Cates (Sissy Spacek), the daughter, is a character given to observing life from the distance and remaining in the background. Now it is her turn to seize center stage, before she carries out her deliberate plan to take her own life.

Mother Thelma Cates (Anne Bancroft) goes through a series of predictable responses: rejection, confrontation, anger — until she can no longer argue or refute her daughter's logic and all that's left for her is to grieve.

At the heart of this primal action, and absolutely essential if it is to have any impact, are the incandescent performances of Spacek and Bancroft. Together they create a symbiotic relationship with a chain of actions that play perfectly off of each other. With her blank stare and vague country accent, Bancroft is a fully realized and disturbing character.

Although as the mother and the one who must carry the responsibility for her daughter's actions ("Everything you do has to to with me," she says), Bancroft has most of the juicy parts, Spacek also gets a chance to spill her guts as well. It's a remarkably peaceful, though terribly sad parting and Norman, who adapted her play for the screen, treats her characters honestly and without a drop of condescension.

Director Tom Moore, who handled the chores on Broadway, does well with the translation to the screen. He keeps his direction simple with limited camera movement, often only closing in and moving back when appropriate. Lensing by Stephen M. Katz is sharp and David Shire's soundtrack is kept to a bare minimum, supplying a rueful guitar score at the beginning and ending.

All this is in service of Norman's vision. She successfully weaves together philosophical issues and the emotional history of the characters into a seamless, mostly unlabored family drama.

For Jessica, her suicide is the last chance for her to claim possession of a life that has somehow gotten away from her. Although Norman's existential reading of the situation is a bit dated, it is nonetheless provocative. The details that lead up to it — epilepsy shamefully neglected by her parents, a broken marriage and a juvenile delinquent son — supply a background verging on the bathetic.

Spacek's level-headed and matter-of-fact performance has a logic to it that makes her decision more heroic than pitiful.

Norman's play reaches for a level of understanding that was denied her characters until it was too late. It's a plea for communication.
— *Jagr.*

Confidential
(CANADIAN-COLOR)

A Cineplex Odeon Films release (in Canada) of a Brightstar Films production. Produced by Anthony Kramreither. Written, directed and edited by Bruce Pittman. Camera (color), John Herzog; music, Bruce Ley; sound, Urmos Rosin. No other credits available. Reviewed at the Toronto Festival of

Festivals, Sept. 7, 1986. Running time: 95 MINS.

Hugh Jameson .... Neil Munro
Charles Ripley .... August Schellenberg
Amelio .... Chapelle Jaffe
Edmund Eislin .... Tom Butler
Rufus .... Antony Parr
Mrs. McAlister .... Doris Petrie
Doris .... Kay Hawtrey

Toronto — "Confidential" is a well-acted, intended *film noir* whose plot doesn't make sense.

A newspaper reporter is shown living with a stripper, but engrossed in an ax murder trial that took place 30 years previously in 1917. He sets out to find the current whereabouts of the murdered man's wife, whom it later appears got off scot-free.

He finds her son's house, sneaks in and disappears. Reporter's wife, whom the audience didn't know he had, hires a private eye. He, in turn, finds the trail, but doesn't know the son's wife is a psychotic.

She kills her husband and the private eye, who also sneaks into the house, while her small children hear what's going on.

Why does she do that? What does it have to do with her now-dead mother-in-law? Director-scripter Bruce Pittman keeps all that confidential.

Neil Munro and a roguish-looking August Schellenberg score as the reporter and private eye respectively. Chapelle Jaffe looks ominous as the son's wife.

Low-budget pic was shot in Toronto in two weeks; seems Pittman took far less than that with the script. Other credits are okay.

Theatrical or tv potential is very dim. — *Adil.*

Where The River Runs Black
(COLOR)

Beautifully lensed tale of nature and innocence.

An MGM/UA release from MGM of an Ufland/Roth production. Produced by Roth, Harry Ufland. Executive producer, James G. Robinson. Coproducer, Dan Farrell. Directed by Christopher Cain. Screenplay, Peter Silverman, Neal Jimenez based on the novel "Lazaro," by David Kendall; camera (Metrocolor), Juan Ruiz-Anchia; editor, Richard Chew; music, James Horner; sound (Dolby), Romeu Quinto; production design, Marcos Flaksman; art direction, Paulo Flaksman; Amazon animal effects, Donald Pennington; associate producer-assistant director, James Ragan; casting, Penny Perry (U.S.), Flavio Tambellini (Rio de Janerio), Tuinho Schwartz (Belem). Reviewed at MGM Studios, Culver City, Calif. Sept. 3, 1986. (In Toronto Festival of Festivals.) (MPAA Rating: PG.) Running time: **100 MINS.**

Father O'Reilly .... Charles Durning
Lazaro .... Alessandro Rabelo
Segundo .... Ajay Naidu
Father Mahoney .... Peter Horton
Mother Marta .... Conchata Ferrell

Hollywood — "Where The River Runs Black" is a beautifully simple film that celebrates an innocent

boy's peaceful coexistence with nature while subtly despairing man's abuse of it. Story is lusciously photographed and scored and is as wondrous a trip down river as film audiences ever get.

Theme closely parallels that of John Boorman's "The Emerald Forest," but is less complicated and far less extravagantly made.

Both films revolve around a boy with roots in modern civilization being raised by Amazon tribespeople without the knowledge he is the child of two, very distinct worlds.

Scripters Peter Silverman and Neal Jimenez have taken David Kendall's novel, "Lazaro," and crafted a screenplay where the few words of dialog spoken speak worlds of meaning.

Supported by Juan Ruiz-Anchia's stunning camerawork, director Christopher Cain leisurely opens the story as Father O'Reilly (Charles Durning) makes one of his infrequent visits to Father Mahoney (Peter Horton), a wayward missionary assigned to a jungle outpost at the mouth of the Rio Negro.

While not a rebel priest, Horton is enough of an iconoclast to differ with Durning's beliefs in salvation and after an unpleasant meeting that ends badly, the jungle missionary seeks solace by boating down river.

When he comes to the place "where the river runs black," the priest encounters a stunning Indian maiden swimming with dolphin — finding himself instantly enchanted and powerless to resist making love to her.

Not unexpectedly, Horton is killed on his return up river, but he leaves behind the legacy of a son (Alessandro Rabelo). Legend soon spreads among the Indians that the boy born among the dolphins is a spiritual being because he is the offspring of a sorceress and a holy man.

It is years later when the legend finally reaches Durning. In that time, the dolphin boy has survived through the violent death of his mother by the brutal hands of gold prospectors to swim and thrive protected by his mammal friends.

Durning, however, is intent on saving the boy's soul and brings him to live in a Catholic orphanage, baptizing him "Lazaro" (raised from the dead). Even though the child readily adapts to his new, strange surroundings and makes at least one close friend (Ajay Naidu), we learn through the dolphin boy's huge brown expressive eyes that he finds "civilization" ugly and evil.

As compared to the more adventurous "Emerald Forest," and to most other boisterous pics geared for the PG crowd, this film may seem slow and, at times, in love with its own quiet mood.

Minutes go by where there is no dialog — only the beat of James

Horner's music that oftentimes obscures what normally would be background noises like the sound of water lapping or of baby Lazaro crying.

Still, much is said in silence and most effectively told through the movements of 10-year-old Rabelo, a waif-like Brazilian swimmer perfectly cast to portray the physically and emotionally confused dolphin boy traumatized by competing forces.

Durning is a natural as the fatherly Irish priest, letting his heart — not the fact that he wears a collar — determine the ultimate fate of the orphan boy.

In the end, the film finds just as much goodness in Durning's spirituality as it does in the dolphin boy's, which is why the story works and is so compelling.

Supporting cast is all fine, except for Conchata Ferrell, who is much too severe as the orphanage's Reverend Mother.

Special note goes to Donald Pennington and his animal effects crew in making dolphins out to be saintly and, to an equal degree, snakes to be sinister. — *Brit.*

Place Of Weeping
(SOUTH AFRICAN-COLOR)

A New World Pictures release of an Anant Singh production. Written and directed by Darrell Roodt. Camera (color), Paul Witte; editor, David Heitner; art direction, Dave Barkham; sound, Craig Walmsley, Chris Pieterse. Reviewed at Festival of Festivals, Toronto, Sept. 5, 1986. (MPAA Rating: PG.) Running time: **90 MINS.**

Philip Seago .... James Whylie
Grace .... Gcina Mhlophe
Tokkie .... Charles Comyn
Father Eagen .... Norman Coombes
Also with: Michelle du Toit, Ramolao Makhene, Patrick Shai.

Toronto — "Place Of Weeping," subtitled "A Film About South Africa," is a vivid statement on black oppression by young, independent filmmaker Darrell Roodt. Its leisurely pace and spare struggle may not send off big commercial sparks, but it's an assured fest and art house entry, acquired for domestic distribution by New World.

The story is simple but all too common. A black farm laborer in Weenen, South Africa, complains to his boss that his wages are not sufficient to support his family. When he tries to steal a chicken later, he is beaten to death by the farmer. The black community is horrified yet impotent, but the worker's sister Gracie, who's the Norma Rae of the group, insists they bring the farmer to justice.

A journalist, Philip Seago, is transferred from Johannesburg on assignment to Weenen to cover the factional fighting and stumbles upon Gracie's plight while visiting the local parish priest. Father Eagen does not support Seago's involvement, warning him that journalists are not welcome in Weenen because they cause trouble. The priest insists the only thing on their side is time.

The reporter aligns with the blacks and is beaten by the white farmers. The final confrontation is done on an individual level — the black workers can't change the system, but they can mete out revenge on a one-to-one basis.

Roodt deals openly with the abhorrent treatment of blacks by their oppressors, and while pic is clearly on the side of the afflicted it's not a heavy-handed political treatise. The director is well served by a solid cast, especially Gcina Mhlophe as Gracie, the feisty, responsible black girl, and James Whylie as the hard-pressed reporter. Charles Comyn is all one note as the autocratic farm boss.

Lensing is lovely, as Roodt's camera pans the countryside of South Africa, but he uses too many aerial shots of cars heading for their destinations, which slackens the stride a bit too much.

The potency in "Place Of Weeping" comes from the forthright dramatic tension in a screenplay that is unfortunately timely. — *Devo.*

Close To Home
(CANADIAN-COLOR)

A Hy Perspectives Media Group production, with the participation of Telefilm Canada. Produced by Harvey Crossland. Directed by Rick Beairsto. Screenplay, Beairsto, Crossland; camera (color), Tobias Schleissler; editor, Crossland; art director, Anne O'Donoghue; music, Ken Ilemmerick, Richard Baker. Reviewed at Bloor Cinema, Toronto, Aug. 27, 1986. (In Toronto Festival of Festivals.) Running time: **95 MINS.**
Flynn . . . . Daniel Allman
Michelle Fontaine . . . . Jillian Fargey
Donna Pedlar . . . . Anne Petrie

Toronto — In his feature debut, Vancouver filmmaker Ric Beairsto aims to dramatize the underworld of runaway teens who flee to the urban cores, continuing the spiral of abuse and neglect they often experienced at home. But the helmer chooses to combine a dramatic storyline with a companion tv debut filmed on the subject, enervating the effectiveness of either form.

The drama comes off as weak and artificial, the docu stilted and unconvincing. Boxoffice prospects are dim, but pic may fare better with paycable sales or on the educational circuit.

Not that Beairsto's efforts aren't well intentioned, but his agenda is up there in neon. He uses the stories of three runaways who flock to Vancouver's Davey Street, a known hotbed of prostitution where sex is for sale on every corner.

Michelle (Jillian Fargey) escapes from her home in Calgary, where she was sexually abused by her father. She hooks up with some dope-peddling street kids, gets counseling assistance, confides in a social worker that her father abused her after he tries to lure her off the streets, and goes to a trial hearing. She's put in a foster home, runs off to Seattle with a girlfriend, starts hooking and is sent back to a youth residence in Vancouver, where she attempts suicide and winds up splitting with an older man for Reno.

Flynn is a vet teen male hooker who freely offers his body to older men on Davey Street until he is stabbed by one of his tricks. Randy is a novice runaway who befriends Flynn and moves in with him to learn the ropes.

Interspersed throughout the teen drama is the ongoing making of a tv docu by aggressive newswoman Donna Pedlar (Anne Petrie), who brings her camera to the streets and cross-examines the hookers in a process that comes off as intrusive. Beairsto uses Donna's docu as a forum for real social workers, police officers, judges and johns to reveal the process of teens accusing parents of abuse and to unfold statistics. The q. & a. format here is often pedantic.

It's when the documaker and teen stories are intercut that "Close To Home" wears down and the encounters are unintentionally laughable.

When Michelle escapes to Seattle and is turning tricks on the street, Pedlar mysteriously turns up and announces, "Hi, Michelle, you're from Vancouver. I'm Donna Pedlar, making a docu ..." And when Flynn winds up in the hospital after being assaulted, she pulls the same "Hi, remember me?" line.

The thesps are mired in an unstimulating script and offer little to the overall impact. Night photography is fine and the cruising shots on Davey Street are convincing, but Beairsto resorts to theatrical freeze frames too often to emphasize controversial confrontations.

Had Beairsto gone the straight docu route his feature would have had more momentum. This is a misfired effort that scores higher on intention than on achievement.
— *Devo.*

Super Citizen
(TAIWANESE-COLOR)

A Cinema City production. Produced by Karl Maka, Dean Shek, Raymond Wong, Wang Ying Hsiang. Directed by Wan Jen. Screenplay, Wan Jen, Lio Cheng Song; camera (color), Lin Horng Jong; editor, Liao Cheng Song; music, Li Show Chaun; art direction, Tsai Jen Bin. Reviewed at the Toronto Festival of Festivals, Sept. 5, 1986. Running time: **97 MINS.**
With: Li Chih Chyi (Li Shicheong), Chen Bor Jeng (Rolly), Wang Yeu, Su Ming Ming, Lin Shou Ling.

Toronto — A study of a country bumpkin who finds himself way in over his head in the big city, "Super Citizen" works most effectively as a travelog against Taipei. The city appears so congested, corrupt, unattractive and vulgar that propagandists for China scarcely could have done a better job of discouraging anyone from ever wanting to have anything to do with the place. This one is of conceivable interest only to Asian cinema specialists.

Clever opening presents a picture postcard impression of Taipei, an image quickly shattered by the overbearing reality of the place. Earnest young Li Shicheong has come to the metropolis to search for his sister, who has not been heard from in at least a year.

Since he has no leads whatsoever, this quest is a joke, although the kid makes perfunctory checks in such establishments as night clubs, beauty parlors and massage emporiums, often in the company of a two-bit hustler who takes to looking out for the youth.

Despite the marginally criminal elements seen around the edges, there is little incident or drama to enliven matters here. Most of the diversion stems from the odd assortment of characters who inhabit the cramped neighborhood from which the aspiring hood operates, but this is hardly enough to sustain the film.

Director Wan Jen shows solid technical competence, and there is no doubt of his serious intentions, but screenplay is woefully dull and pacing is lethargic. —*Cart.*

Shoot For The Sun
(BRITISH-COLOR-16m)

A BBC production. Produced by Andree Molyneaux. Directed by Ian Knox. Screenplay, Peter McDougall; camera (color, 16m), Remi Adefarasin; editor, Robin Sales; music, Michael Kamen, Ray Cooper; production design, Stuart Walker; costume design, Rita Reekie; sound, Terry Elmes. Reviewed at the Toronto Festival of Festivals. Sept. 5, 1986. Running time: **81 MINS.**
With: Jimmy Nail (Geordie), Brian Cox (Duffy), Sara Clee (Sadie), Billy McColl, Bill Simpson.

Toronto — Shoot For The Sun" marks the descent of English drama from the kitchen sink to the toilet bowl. Dull look at the sordid underbelly of Edinburgh's drug culture, and the little lives of the little people who inhabit it, is unvaryingly grim and offputting, no matter how authentic it may happen to be. Commercial prospects would be nil, even without the barrier presented by the extraordinarily thick Scottish accents, which would require English subtitles for American comprehension.

Peter McDougall's gritty, massively colloquial script delineates several strata of the scum lining the bottom of the barrel in the most forbidding rendition of the Scottish capital ever put on the screen. At the bottom are the simple drug users, the trash whose entire lives are consumed by the basest form of obsession. Just above them are the petty criminals who make a living wage from victimizing the helpless ones, while above them is the smalltime boss who's carved out a turf for himself, and above him are the real pros who can put the pinch on anytime it best suits them.

Only scenes of any interest whatsoever are those centering upon the neighborhood thug, a tough customer who lives with his mother, hoards his cash and has a ready answer for any situation. At times reminding of Bob Hoskins, Brian Cox (recently seen as the criminal genius in "Manhunter") plays the role with impressive authority, and has a couple of standout scenes, one in which he irrationally attacks a potted palm in a nightclub, another in which he memorably conducts a conversation while swinging from a rope in a cemetery.

Otherwise, it's all drudgery, as the smaller fish progressively get eaten by the bigger fish, to little apparent artistic or sociological effect. Tech contributions, while professional, are on the rough side.—*Cart.*

Qui Trop Embrasse
(FRENCH-COLOR)

A Les Films de l'Atalante production. Produced by Gerard Vaugeois. Directed by Jacques Davila. Screenplay, Davila, Michel Gautier; camera (color), Jean-Marie Dreujou; editor, Paul Vecchiali; music, Bruno Coulais. Reviewed at Bloor Cinema, Toronto, Sept. 1, 1986. (In Toronto Festival of Festivals.) Running time: **84 MINS.**
With: Anne Wiazemsky, Tonie Marshall, Andrzej Seweryn, Michel Gautier.

Toronto — A lumbering, quirky commentary on contempo romantic relationships, "Qui Trop Embrasse" will have a bit of a battle commercially. Jacques Davila's second feature will probably do healthier business on his home turf, as Paris night scenes and lifestyles are keenly featured.

While not nightmarish in Martin Scorsese's "After Hours" fashion, pic is a hip, downtown Paris stab at male-female bonding. A series of couples break up and regroup, while various individual partners exchange war wounds. English subtitles are often amateurish.

Christian and Nathalie work as information officers at the Pompidou Center. Christian has returned home to his city flat to discover that his lover, Françoise, is having an affair with someone she works with. Christian is distraught and shares his exasperation with Nathalie; she tells him broken hearts last two years.

Cut to Nathalie in bed in early morning with her lover Mark. Her ex-lover René phones, leading to a jealous fit by Mark, who's obsessively curious about Nathalie's past. He's comfortable seeing her every other day, which infuriates her. She teases him with kinky sexual anecdotes about her old flames.

Next encounter is Françoise in her flat with her new lover, the compulsive Jean-Pierre, who announces that he thinks he loves her less. End of affair, much to Françoise's bewilderment and anger. Next night she arrives at J-P's house to retrieve a gift she gave him, only to discover he's got company.

Christian returns home to mom and asks her if she loved her second husband. Seems mom had tough luck with men, too. Finale finds the spirit of Christian's mom's dead husband rising from a painting and coming to whisk her heavenward.

Much of the lensing is static but crisp, with the camera standing stationary as the characters walk in and out of the frame. This works well in light of the formality and tension of some of the relationships.

Davila takes his time here, but the pacing is often slow to the point of boredom. There's glorious attention to detail, though, as every eccentric nuance of behavior of these Parisians is magnified.

The set designs crystallize the urban scene and the Paris street scenes are quite topical. Thesping is marked by ennui, reflecting the mood of the screenplay. A little more humor and a little less aridity would have snapped this tedious effort along.—*Devo.*

The Adventure Of Faustus Bidgood
(CANADIAN-COLOR/B&W-16m)

A Faustus Bidgood Production, with assistance of National Film Board of Canada, Atlantic Region Production Studio. Written, produced and directed by Michael Jones and Andy Jones. Camera (color, b&w) and editing, Michael Jones; music director, Robert Joy; original music, Paul Steffer, Robert Joy, Pamela Morgan; lighting, Derek Butt, Jim Maynard; set decoration, Michael Kearney, Bawnie Oulton, Susan Hickey. Reviewed at Festival of Festivals, Toronto, Sept. 4, 1986. Running time: **110 MINS.**
Faustus Bidgood ....Andy Jones
Vasily Bogdanovich Shagoff .Greg Malone
Eddy Peddle ....Robert Joy
Fred Bonia-Coombs ....Brian Downey
Phyllis Meaney ....Maisie Rillie
Heady Nolan ....Mary Walsh
Henry Harry ....Beni Malone
Frank Dollar...............Tommy Sexton
Premier Jonathan Moon ....Nelson Porter

Toronto — Chaos reigns in "The Adventure Of Faustus Bidgood," the 10-years-in-the-making Newfoundland feature that's long on satire as well as confusion. There are some inspired comic moments, but much of the plot and script makes this outing a touch inaccessible. It should score well on the home turf since it's mounted by members of the Newfoundland Comedy Collective (Codco) and will appeal to devotees of Monty Pythonesque humor.

Faustus Bidgood (Andy Jones) is a nerdy clerk and "closet human being" in the Dept. of Education in St. John's. He has a Walter Mitty persona and envisions doing violent and gory things to his superiors who mock him. In his mind (sequences shot in black and white), he is made premier of the revolutionary Republic of Newfoundland that secedes from Canada, and on the first anni of his government's formation, he must decide whether or not to resign while being cheered on by the people.

In reality, shot in color, Bidgood is involved in a myriad of evil subplots. Nefarious Minister of Education Eddy Peddle (Robert Joy) is trying to infiltrate the masses with a cult philosophy called Total Education, based on the geometry of the grid. Fred Bonia-Coombs (Brian Downey) has the goods on Peddle's secet past as flamenco dancer from Vancouver.

Faustus is accompanied on his manic illusions by an angel/demon (Greg Malone), who provides confusing advice. The teetering line between reality and illusion is getting too thin for Faustus to negotiate, and his dreamworld becomes more horrific.

Michael and Andy Jones oversee some manic moments here and the film goes beyond the outline of a psychotic's downward spiral to a statement about Newfoundland's reduction from a self-sufficient country to a self-deprecating Canadian province.

Acting is appropriately outlandish and deadpan, especially Andy Jones' Faustus and Robert Joy's Peddle. Lensing is stronger in the grainy black and white newsreel look of the dream sequences.

"Faustus Bidgood" took a decade to complete, used practically every working thesp in the province, and proves that Newfoundland comedy goes beyond the one-shot Newfie joke.—*Devo.*

Sarraounia
(BURKINA FASOAN-COLOR)

A Soleil O production. Produced and directed by Med Hondo. Screenplay, Hondo, Abdul War, based on a Nigerian book by Abdoulaye Mamani; music, Pierre Akendengue. Reviewed at the Montreal Film Festival (In Competition), Aug. 27, 1986. Running time: **130 MINS.**
With: Lynn Watts, Jean Roger Milo, Jean-Pierre Sentier, Feodor Atkin, Jean-Pierre Casteldi.

Montreal — Said to be based on real events that occurred in central Africa in 1898-99, "Sarraounia" is an ambitiously mounted, handsomely lensed, sprawling tale about an eponymous African warrior-sorceress queen and her victory over a French colonial expedition. "Sarraounia" is noteworthy as evidence of an emerging international-quality filmmaking capability in Africa (it was made in Burkina Faso, formerly Upper Volta) and, if edited down and supplied with English subtitles, could qualify for specialty release in major U.S. cities.

In the film's beautiful and engrossing opening sequences, Sarraounia is given over to a wise and kindly surrogate father who initiates the tall and supple girl in the arts of archery, swordsmanship, herbal medicine — and sorcery. Early on she proves her mettle by leading her villagers in repelling an invasion by the Foulanis, a neighboring central African tribe.

Director Med Hondo then flashes forward to the last years of the 19th century, when Africa was overrun by French, English and German colonial invaders. By this time, Sarraounia has become queen of the Aznas, respected and feared far and wide for her prowess in battle and her magical powers. In a totally male-dominated society, Sarraounia is an untamed, independent woman and her warrior lover leaves in a huff when she informs him she'll bow to no man's will.

The filmmaker then takes leave of Sarraounia in an overlong and overdone midsection that follows the rapine colonial expedition of two maverick French army officers, Captains Voulet and Chanoine. Sent on a mission from their base in the Sudan to repel the forces of a black sultan, Rabah, the French officers, like a pair of latterday Herzogian Aguierres, become intoxicated with power and bloodlust far from the "bureaucrats of Paris." Leading a large army of black mercenaries, the French and their eager African accomplices, murder, rape, burn and loot everything in their path.

Hondo displays impressive production skills in executing the long march and battle sequences. The scenario is also stiletto-sharp in its satirical slicing of the cruel French colonial personality and the craveness of the invaders' African lackeys. With their insufferably pompous superiority and bestial indifference to the human suffering they trail in their path, the French officers are quintessential villains.

As they plunge deeper into the African heartland, the French captains become insanely obsessed with their desire to conquer a territory larger than France itself. Their mad conduct is not appreciated in Paris, however, and when the officers ignore dispatches ordering them to return to the Sudan, a French colonel and troops are sent to retrieve them. The captains, however, have one goal above all — the conquest of the legendary Sarraounia and her fortress city. With the help of Africans who will betray Sarraounia for their own gain, the bloodthirsty captains close in. When Sarraounia conjures up a firestorm that destroys much of their camp, the French soldiers become even more enraged.

They finally get their comeuppance, but not before destroying Sarraounia's fortress and killing the colonel who was sent to bring them back. Sarraounia, however, triumphs with the help of the sultan king and her former warrior-lover, to live on, as the closing song sings, in immortal legend — a prophecy nicely fulfilled by this film. Indeed, the sub-theme of Africans putting aside tribal differences for the sake of unity has relevance today.

Performances are effective, if mannered due to the extreme personalities of the characters. The musical score is wonderful, and a sound-soundtrack LP could help sell "Sarraounia" abroad. — *Rich.*

★★★★★★★★★★★★★★★★★★★★★★★★★★★★★★★
★
★ # Toronto Festival Reviews
★
★★★★★★★★★★★★★★★★★★★★★★★★★★★★★★★

Fatherland
(BRITISH-WEST GERMAN-COLOR)

A Film Four Intl./MK2/Classart presentation of a Kestrel II production with the participation of the Ministry of Culture. Produced by Raymond Day. Executive producer, Irving Teitelbaum. Directed by Kenneth Loach. Screenplay, Trevor Griffiths; camera (color), Chris Menges; editor, Jonathan Morris; music, Christian Kunert, Gerulf Pannach; production design, Martin Johnson; costume design, Antji Peterson; sound, Karl Laabs. Reviewed at the Toronto Festival of Festivals, Sept. 13, 1986. Running time: **110 MINS.**
With: Gerulf Pannach (Klaus Dritteman), Fabienne Babe (Emma de Baen), Sighert Steiner (Father), Christine Rose (Lucy Bernstein).

Toronto — "Fatherland" is a major film from Ken Loach, one of the crucial, if difficult, figures in British cinema since the 1960s. A rigorous examination of the impulses behind, and results of, an East German artist's defection to the West, it is strictly fare for serious, intellectual audiences. It will prove a hard sell even on the domestic art market, but its quality earns it a shot.

Loach's fastidious, analytical approach and deliberate, documentary-like style have prevented him from enjoying anything resembling a significant commercial success, but he has always been a director to watch and has proved influential to other filmmakers.

Working here from a fascinating script by Trevor Griffiths ("Reds"), he has created an ambiguous yet penetrating work about two opposing cultures and the way they both manipulate and control artistic expression, and about the response of two generations to those cultures.

Focus of the drama is Klaus Dritteman, a dissident folk singer first silenced by the East Germans, then allowed to leave quietly. He is greeted in West Berlin with a major recording contract, lavish treatment from the label and a big press conference, but he remains curiously diffident and unmoved by his new position.

Unwilling to play ball with Western governments and press by overtly criticizing communism, he is profoundly uncomfortable being treated as a commodity in the West and, having been deprived of his own country and set of references, doesn't know if he can be creative in his new environment.

Even more pressing than his work, however, is his preoccupation with tracking down his father, a classical musician who defected in 1953, when Klaus was six (his sister also crossed the wall). This search puts him in league with an attractive female journalist who has her own reasons for pursuing the old man, but ultimately it is Klaus who alone must face some exceedingly painful and ironic political and personal truths when he finally finds his father in Cambridge.

Conventional filmmakers would be expected to make a thriller out of such fare, one in which the evils of communism would be neatly laid out while the conveniently linked couple develops a romance while effecting a reunion with old dad. To top it off, the guy becomes the latest pop music rage.

Loach and Griffiths deliberately undercut all these expectations, the better to zero in on potent observations about how the West reflexively tries to absorb and systematize all comers, political paranoia, and the sad historical shortcomings to be found on both sides.

While not designed to satisfy lookers for adventure and romance, film is very tightly constructed and will certainly prove gripping to anyone interested in politics or history. Filmmakers are concerned here particularly with the subject of collaboration, whether it be political, artistic or personal, and it is treated with considerable complexity and nuance.

As usual with Loach, performers are not encouraged to "act" in the expected emotive way, and everyone, notably singer Gerulf Pannach, who plays Klaus, is quietly thoughtful and low-key. The limitations of Pannach and femme lead Fabienne Babe are to be seen in a crucial revelatory scene between them in which they both have trouble with their English, but this is immediately forgotten with the arrival of the stunning confrontation between father and son. —*Cart.*

The PPPerformer
(DUTCH-COLOR)

A Cannon Group release of a De Roje He/Added Films production. Produced by Dirk Schreiner. Directed by Casper Verbrugge. Screenplay, Verbrugge, Freek de Jonge, based on "De Bedevaart" (A Dutch Theater Show by de Jonge); camera (color), Jules V.D. Steenhoven; editor, Ot Louw; music, William Breuker, Hennie Vrienten; art director, Hella de Jonge; sound, Piotr Van Dijk. Reviewed at Toronto Festival of Festivals, Sept. 7, 1986. Running time: **87 MINS.**
With: Freek de Jonge, Rosita Tamara, Johnny Van Elk, Jan Raub, Jugo Van Den Berge, Jelle de Jonge.

Toronto — The comedy of Freek de Jonge is certainly an acquired taste, the key to whether "The PPPerformer" (formerly "The C-C-Comedian"), will cross over for mainstream audiences. It's a double Dutch treat, irreverent and acerbic as well as confounding.

In director Casper Verbrugge's ("The Manbird") first feature, a young boy asks his circus clown father (de Jonge) why he stutters. It's a l-l-long story, says Dad, so the boy asks if he can make a movie about it.

What follows is a wild, labyrinthine explanation that includes a fortuneteller, a dream about a lion, a street comedy, stage work, and circus buffoonery. The main thrust is de Jonge's stage act, which is frenetic and madcap, highlighted by a miracle curing of wheelchair-ridden Luke at Lourdes.

Verbrugge juggles the surrealism of de Jonge's recounting his personal history with his attempt to grasp his own identity. The director has de Jonge visit a gypsy while casting his past performance life on a backdrop. De Jonge starts out as a street performer, imitating a U.S. journalist interviewing a deaf and dumb dictator in a banana republic. He goes on to become a music hall comic, a circus clown and a touring jester. His childhood stutter resurfaces along the way.

Amid de Jonge's antics there's a sympathetic character who appears vulnerable and searching throughout his searing attacks.

The young boy narrates the film while the director cleverly combines dreams, religious visions, and performance footage. A few on-stage bits could become popular rock video clips themselves, especially one in which a batallion of perky young maids tidy up de Jonge's room.

"The PPPerformer" is not to everyone's taste, but it's one way to see the famed Dutch comic's stage piece. Martin Cleaver gets special credit for translating a Dutch stutter into English subtitles. —*Devo.*

Nanou
(BRITISH-FRENCH-COLOR)

An Umbrella Films/Arion production. Produced by Simon Perry. Written and directed by Conny Templeman. Stars Imogen Stubbs, Jean-Philippe Eccoffey. Camera (Kay-MGM color), Martin Fuhrer; editor, Tom Priestley; music, John Kean; production design, Andrew Mollo; sound, Pierre Donnadieu; assistant director, Charles Lusseyran. Reviewed at the Toronto Festival of Festivals, Sept. 7, 1986. Running time: **110 MINS.**
With: Imogen Stubbs (Manou), Jean-Philippe Ecoffey (Luc), Christophe Lidon (Jacques), Daniel Day Lewis (Max), Valentine Pelca, Roger Ibanez.

Toronto — After a bright beginning, "Nanou" gradually becomes as static and stagnant as its heroine. A rare English-French coproduction played in both languages, this first feature by Conny Templeman exhibits some modest, appealing talent on her part, as well as from newcomer Imogen Stubbs, but drama is too muted and uneventful to hold much domestic b.o. potential.

Director shows a deft, understated comic touch in the virtually silent early scenes detailing the young English woman's misadventures while bumming around Europe. After failing as a waitress in Geneva, she decides, on a whim, to look up an eye-catching Frenchman she passingly met on a train, and before long is living with him in a drab flat in a dull provincial town.

Nanou is so unformed and maleable that she's willing to put up with considerable abuse from Luc, who has no visible means of support and spouts stock 1960s radical ideas about everything from politics to women's place in the scheme of things.

Luc steals Nanou's passport, apparently to help out an Italian terrorist on the run, enlists her aide in painting political slogans on walls in the strike-ridden city, and finally includes her in a group plotting to blow up a train track in the cause of the workers. But specific causes are kept carefully in the background, the better to concentrate specifically on the position into which Nanou has placed herself.

Blond, softly attractive and open to life, Imogen Stubbs quietly manages to hold the interest even with her strictly reactive character. Unfortunately, the character of Luc, played by Jean-Philippe Ecoffey, is meant to be dangerously fascinating, but is quickly revealed as a slob, a male chauvinist pig and two-bit anarchist posing in the quise of a romantic revolutionary. He's just a loser, and the downfall of the film is that it takes Nanou about five times as long to figure this out than it does the audience.

Even with the dramatic faults that are part and parcel of the picture, matters could be remedied by the removal of 10 or 15 minutes in the second hour, when it becomes only a matter of time as to Nanou's leaving Luc and his banal existence.

Daniel Day Lewis makes a perfunctory appearance as an old friend of Nanou's who pays her a brief visit. Tech contributions are good.—*Cart.*

Are We Winning, Mommy? America And The Cold War
(U.S.-DOCU-COLOR/B&W)

A Cine Information production in association with the NFB/Channel Four/Swedish Television. Produced and directed by Barbara Margolis. Written by L.S. Block, John Crowley; narrated by Anne Jackson; Camera (color), Tom Hurwitz; editor, Kathryn Taverna, Peter Kinoy; music, Wendy Blackstone;

sound, Juliet Weber. Reviewed at Toronto Festival of Festivals, Sept. 7, 1986. Running time: **85 MINS.**

Toronto — Five years in the making, "Are We Winning, Mommy? America And The Cold War" reflects the extensive research and editing Barbara Margolis devoted to her first feature film. The director concentrates more on the historical perspective of America's involvement in the cold war, with only a peripheral peep into today's issues, but has mounted a crisp, assured docu on the subject. It should find a vital niche in international fest slots as well as public broadcasting.

Starting from the grand alliance of the U.S. and the Soviet Union in World War II, Margolis traces the history of the cold war from a time when its existence couldn't be imagined. Army promotional films, General Motors Victory clips, newsreel footage of U.S. post-war prosperity and men reenlisting, and looks at ravaged post-war Europe, the 1945 Potsdam conference and the Hiroshima bomb are all enlightening.

Clips of Bing Crosby singing "Freedom Train" and school children ducking for cover in air raid drills give the docu a comic edge in "Atomic Cafe" style, but these bits are interspersed in a more serious agenda. U.S. government films about the "Red Nightmare" are truly frightening, as well as the requisite clips of the McCarthy era and "Dr. Strangelove."

Talking heads include a Moscow director of the U.S.A. and Canada Institute, who said the first murder weapon used against the Japanese was the beginning of the cold war. Former Truman adviser Clark Clifford remembers the Truman policy of containment told the world the U.S. intends to confront communism from now on anywhere in the world.

Noam Chomsky and Jerome Weisner are most articulate about the origins of the cold war. Fred Friendly recalls that many of his friends at CBS lost their jobs in the '50s for Communist affiliations they may have had in the '30s.

Margolis also includes absorbing interviews with a lawyer who was one of the legal consultants called in to get a stay of execution for Ethel and Julius Rosenberg, and with a New York woman who was tried during the McCarthy hearings on no charges.

The director also outlines the history of the Communist party in the U.S. from its formation in 1919 and gives an overview of the 1948 Henry Wallace campaign for president based on an anti-cold war platform.

One flaw is the glossing over of the U.S. civil rights movement as the impetus for more public involvement and the revival of activism, including an anti-cold war sentiment.

Docu runs quickly through the space race and Star Wars policy.

The film stresses that in the 1950s all distinctions were erased — you were either a loyal American or a Communist — and it's clear Reagan's current stance is enmeshed in the historical routes Margolis has assembled.

It's a well-researched, handsomely edited feature, with informative narration by Anne Jackson. Although it may be preaching to the converted, it can also prove enlightening to those who subscribe to the current administration's rampant anti-Red point of view. —*Devo.*

Seize The Day
(U.S.-COLOR-16m)

A Miramax Films release of a Robert Geller presentation of a Learning In Focus production, in association with Great Performances. Produced by Chiz Schultz. Executive producer, Geller. Directed by Fielder Cook. Stars Robin Williams. Screenplay, Ronald Ribman, based on the novel by Saul Bellow, camera (color, 16m), Eric Van Haren Noman; editor, Sidney Katz; music, Elizabeth Swados; art direction, John Robert Lloyd; costume design, Peggy Farrel Salten; sound, Leslie Shatz, Tom Johnson, Gary Alper; associate producer, Brian Benlifer; assistant director, Dwight Williams. Reviewed at the Toronto Festival of Festivals, Sept. 9, 1986. (No MPAA Rating.) Running time: **93 MINS.**

Tony Wilhelm	Robin Williams
Doc	Jerry Stiller
Dr. Adler	Joseph Wiseman
Girlfriend	Clenne Headly
Peris	William Hickey
Bernie	Tony Roberts

Toronto — The first film ever made based upon a Saul Bellow novel, "Seize The Day" can boast of earnest performances and intent, but is swamped in obviousness and the broadness of its brush strokes. Robin Williams will receive plenty of attention for his "serious" starring role as a victimized little man, and perhaps this overwrought piece will play better on television, for which it was made, rather than on the big screen.

Set in 1956, around the time the book was written, "Seize The Day" does seem particularly applicable in theme to the current day: in the world under examination here, big business is sacred, profit is the holiest of rewards, and decency and human kindness are considered things of the past.

Having lost his job as a salesman, disappointed his girl friend and allowed himself to be bled dry by his estranged wife, Tommy, who's pushing 40, returns to New York City to call in old favors and appeal to his father in an attempt at a new start.

As eager to please as a puppy, Tommy finds heartlessness everywhere he turns. His father, a successful doctor forever disappointed that his son didn't follow in his footsteps, can rank second only to

Nicholas Nickleby's uncle in filial meanness. All of his old buddies have big smiles and plenty of excuses for Tommy, who persists, in the face of the evidence, to believe it's right to aspire to goodness.

The only one to take a positive interest in poor Tommy is Doc, a physician of great alleged healing powers who in fact spends most of his time playing the commodities market. Doc talks a great game, and Jerry Stiller is quite amusing in the role, but when Tommy finally decides to trust him with what's left of his savings, it's just one more disaster for the hapless fellow.

Story's concerns are of interest, but the fact that nearly every scene is the same, with Tommy beating his head into an unrelenting wall of callousness, makes for a dull, repetitive, offputting film. The world of power here is made up exclusively of crusty old Jewish men who play cards and hang out at the steam bath, and it is not a pretty picture.

Talking as quickly as he does in comedy roles, Williams throws himself entirely into his character, and one can become slightly physically ill watching him incessantly smoke, sweat and suffer. His desperation is palpable, but it is at times difficult to believe someone with Williams' amount of energy would have trouble succeeding at something.

Fielder Cook's direction is extremely literal, and lack of modulation is a major problem. Joseph Wiseman is chilling as the father, but everyone else is in for only brief appearances. Technically, pic fully betrays its 16m format. —*Cart.*

Les Vidangeurs
(Garbagemen)
(CANADIAN-DOCU-COLOR-16m)

An ACPAV production. Produced by René Gueissaz. Screenplay, Camille Coudari; camera (color, 16m), Jean-Claude Labreque; editor, Michel Juliani; msuic, Yves Godin, Lady Luck; sound, Michel Charron, Claude Beauregard, Diane Carrière. Reviewed at the Toronto Festival of Festival, Sept. 8, 1986. Running time: **75 MINS.**

Toronto — An intelligent, articulate doc, "Les Vidangeurs" profiles Montreal garbagemen but is overblown at current running length. All the material is there for a reedit to fit a one-hour tv timeslot, its most appropriate market.

The garbagemen talk well about their lowly state in society and amusingly but pointedly about not being pigs but having to "clean up after pigs." A garbage truck is shown mashing a large chesterfield and swipes are taken at the upper middle class and rich throwing out enough food to feed starving nations.

Jean-Claude Labreque's camerawork is excellent, particularly of city streets lined with green garbage bags waiting to be taken away.

Original songs, as pointed as the garbagemen's comments work for a while, but are repeated too much as are the intended poetic scenes of a garbage dump.—*Adil.*

Nik And Murray
(U.S.-DOCU-COLOR)

A Christian Blackwood production. Produced and directed by Blackwood. Camera (color), Blackwood; editor, Blackwood, Elizabeth Rich; sound, Pam Katz, John Murphy, Michael Penland. Reviewed at Toronto Festival of Frestivals, Sept. 9, 1986. Running time: **82 MINS.**
With: Alwin Nikolais, Murray Louis, Nikolais Dance Co., Murray Louis Dance Co.

Toronto — Alwin Nikolais and Murray Louis are two very influential choreographers in modern dance, and Christian Blackwood chooses to explore their personal and artistic kinship in this occasionally enlightening docu.

The director presupposes a prior knowledge of the subject by his viewers: one doesn't find out who Nik and Murray are until near the end of the film when you catch a glimpse of the dance companies' names on a marquee.

With no voice-over narration, Blackwood lets Nik and Murray chat about their art and their friendship. The director crosscuts between the two and follows their individual companies in rehearsal and on tour, Nik's company in Japan and Aix-en-Provence, Murray's in Paris.

Murray Louis met Alwin Nikolais in the summer of 1949 when he was a dancer in Nik's class. Clips of both their early works from the 1950s are shown. Nik wanted to make "motional architecture," as displayed in his "Tensile Involvement" (1959); Murray, who is still dancing, has always been guided by an intuitive judgment in his physical movement, as shown in "Harmonica Suite" (1955).

Docu is strongest when each talks about their art. Blackwood carefully weaves footage of the rehearsal process of the key works through their final performances. Nik's Japanese show uses his definitive blend of color, lights, sound and movement on a stage set up only with mirrors. Nik opines that leaping high does not guarantee artistry in dance. He prefers the interior movement of a dancer like Murray.

Other high points include the Murray Louis company performing in Paris with the Dave Brubeck quartet and Nik's company hiring young French gymnasts to climb ropes up tall trees in "The Bird Dance" in Aix.

Nik and Murray are clearly a mutual admiration society. Nik thinks Murray is an effervescent spirit; Murray considers Nik "sagacious." But there are lots of gaps in what we learn about their relationship. How long have they lived with each other? Does their setup interfere in their creative process?

Nik comes off as the solid paternal figure, while Murray giggles, "Unfortunately, Nik still thinks I'm 22." Dance binds them but there's not enough about their life together to flesh out the docu. There's also no placement of Nik and Murray in the history of 20th-century dance. We don't find out what influences surrounded them, who were their role models, and what do other dancers think of their work.

"Nik And Murray" is a specialized pic which will find an audience in art house and film-dance festival venues. Maybe Nik is correct when he says "choreography isn't verbalizable." —*Devo.*

Lily Tomlin
(U.S.-DOCU-COLOR-16m)

A Churchill Films production. Produced, directed by Nicholas Broomfield, Joan Churchill. Camera (Duart color), Churchill; editor, sound, Broomfield. Reviewed at the Toronto Festival of Festivals, Sept. 6, 1986. (No MPAA Rating.) Running time: **91 MINS.**
With: Lily Tomlin, Jane Wagner, Peggy Feury.

Toronto —The subject of an ongoing legal dispute between the filmmakers and their subject, "Lily Tomlin" proves as amusing as the comedienne herself happens to be at any given moment, but sheds a disappointing amount of light on the creative process under investigation.

Docu has a substantial built-in audience due to the star presence at its center, and fans probably will come away more satisfied than the casually interested, for the film offers no controversy or privileged insights into anything beyond how her one-woman show was assembled.

Formidable team of Nicholas Broomfield and Joan Churchill spent 20 months with Tomlin as the comedienne, along with writer Jane Wagner, built up what was to become the hit show, "The Search For Signs Of Intelligent Life In The Universe."

Starting with public workshop presentations in Austin, Texas, it follows the trail from similar work-in-progress showcases in Atlanta and San Diego to previews in Boston and, finally, opening night on Broadway in September 1985. Although, as Tomlin has protested, a great deal of material from the show (and its embryonic versions) is on display here, it is virtually impossi-

ble for one who has not seen it to get a sense of the entire work, or to figure out how the assorted monologs fit into an overall context.

Additionally frustrating is a lack of a sense of the driving creative force behind the piece. Wagner is prominently credited as the writer of the show, but all one sees is Tomlin herself addressing her audiences with various versions of similar material. It would have been undramatic to show Wagner working at a typewriter, but more than helpful to reveal where the ideas came from, and to what extent collaboration was implemented in the early stages.

In fact, a striking aspect of the docu is that there is never, ever a display of temperament, surely a unique occurrence in the annals of joint creativity. Film reveals nothing but complete artistic and personal accord, all highs and no lows, which is enough to make one suspect the complete picture is not being presented.

Filmmakers work in some background on Tomlin's career, and are able to document earlier stages of her comic development, through the use of some tv clips, most notable of which is a very early one from "The Merv Griffin Show." Tomlin, Wagner and acting teacher Peggy Feury, to whose memory the film is dedicated, gave some only moderately revelatory interviews in an attempt to round out this portrait, but the film shies away from any exploration of the principals' personal lives.

Fundamentally, however, pic fails to achieve what it clearly set out to do, to lay out and analyze Tomlin's creative process. Amusing and amiable due to the performer's comic gifts, it is nonetheless a considerable disappointment.—*Cart.*

Hombre Mirando Al Sudeste
(Man Looking Southeast)
(ARGENTINE-COLOR)

A Cinequanon production. Executive producer, Lujan Pflaum. Written and directed by Eliseo Subiela. Camera (color), Ricardo de Angelis; editor, Luis Cesar D'Angiolillo; music, Pedro Aznar; art direction, Abel Facello; set design, Marta Albertinazzi; sound, Carlos Abbate. Reviewed at the Toronto Festival of Festivals, Sept. 10, 1986. Running time: **108 MINS.**
Dr. Dennis . . . . Lorenzo Quinteros
Rantes . . . . Hugo Soto
Beatriz . . . . Ines Vernengo

Toronto — The revelation of this year's Toronto Festival of Festivals, "Hombre Mirando Al Sudeste" is a gripping, piercingly intelligent fable about an alien whose story deals significantly with faith, madness and medicine. Not at all what audiences are conditioned to expect from the new Latin American cinema, this mysterious and disturbing drama

bears all the earmarks of an international art circuit hit.

This supremely confident second feature by Eliseo Subiela takes place in large measure in a mental hospital, where divorced, world-weary Dr. Dennis is confronted with yet another weirdo, one who claims he has come to Earth from another planet.

Very quickly, however, the doctor discovers this new patient, called Rantes, is different. A brilliant musician and a natural leader to whom the loonies surrounding him are drawn like disciples, he possesses an extraordinarily penetrating intelligence, has no apparent past, and claims he, and others like him, have been placed on this planet to save victims of its terror. He also stands by the hour in the hospital courtyard gazing to the southeast.

Of course, reason says Rantes is merely insane, but Dr. Dennis is not terribly anxious to make that pronouncement. The physician would dearly like to solve the mystery posed by Rantes' case, but increasingly he wants to believe his subject could be the genuine article, someone in whom faith can be placed.

Along the way, many other points are made deftly and dramatically, one of the most salient being society's need to repress exceptional, disturbing brilliance when it threatens the status quo.

Constructed like a mystery, with the doctor as the plausible investigator, film flirts with becoming a Christ story allegory, but fortunately knows just how far to go in that direction. Subiela also could have succumbed to the temptation of trying to explain too much in his wrap-up, but satisfyingly doesn't attempt to "solve" the mystery of Rantes.

Director's dialog is of a particularly high order, and Subiela knows exactly how and when to move the camera for maximum impact. His control over all aspects of this ambitious work is utterly rigorous and precise, and all technical contributions are immaculate.

Critical to the film's success is Hugo Soto's sternly charismatic performance as the visitor. Calm and implacable, his unblinking black eyes seem to see through everything, his talk is measured and perfect, his spiritual qualities ever manifest. Lorenzo Quinteros is rumpled and quizzical as the doctor trying to puzzle it all out.

As the latest in the long recent line of "alien" pictures, this stops short of being outright science-fiction, but should still succeed in developing a sizable cult among fans of the unusual as well as film lovers.
—*Cart.*

The Patriot
(COLOR)

Clumsy actioner about nuclear arms thieves.

A Crown Intl. Pictures release. Produced by Michael Bennett. Executive producer, Mark Tenser. Directed by Frank Harris. Screenplay, Andy Ruben, Katt Shea Ruben; camera (Fotokem color), Harris; editor, Richard E. Westover; music, Jay Ferguson; art director, Brad Einhorn; set decorator, Tori Nourafchan; costumes, Robin Lewis; sound, Glenn Berkovitz; assistant director, Scott Javine; associate producer, Diane Harris; casting, Paul Bengston, David Cohn. Reviewed at Beverly Hills screening room, Sept. 12, 1986. (MPAA Rating: R.) Running time: **88 MINS.**
Lt. Matt Ryder . . . . Gregg Henry
Sean . . . . Simone Griffeth
Howard . . . . Michael J. Pollard
Mitchell . . . . Jeff Conaway
Atkins . . . . Stack Pierce
Admiral Frazer . . . . Leslie Nielsen
Pink . . . . Glenn Withrow
Bite . . . . Larry Mintz

Hollywood — Disjointed story development, tiresome conventions of violence and mostly empty dialog overwhelm the kernel of a good premise in a clumsy attempt to make "The Patriot" a plausible hero fighting nuclear arms thieves. Released regionally in July, pic may well deep-six at the b.o. before many have seen whether an atomic bomb can be recovered from underwater on time.

There is little consistency in pacing or unfolding of plot here — just an effort to quickly manufacture tension over stealing and arming of a nuclear warhead. It's not clear right off who's doing the taking and why. There's certainly no indication of an international terrorist ring or foreign power — just some hired thugs who could as easily have heisted a crate of tv sets.

Of course, the Navy is upset one of its nukes is gone.

So, Lt. Matt Ryder (Gregg Henry) is summoned from his post-dishonorable discharge life to take up his former skills as a SEAL (Sea, Air, Land) commando since it appears the nuke has been smuggled undersea to an offshore rig area. Portrayed as an aimless biker and "Easy Rider" anti-hero type, Ryder is given a chance to clear his unsavory military record by tackling this tough assignment of recovering the weapon.

In perhaps the only scene reflecting any substantive characterization, Leslie Nielsen (as Admiral Frazer) provides crucial plot details and credible authority reflecting the government's concern over an AWOL bomb that could blow up three cities.

Nielsen's screen time is all too short, however, as he returns just once more a few minutes later before disappearing to a meeting with the top brass in Washington. It must have been a handsome day's work for Nielsen, but his swift departure leaves us stuck with two unseemly new characters he's introduced.

Sean (Simone Griffeth) and Mitchell (Jeff Conaway) fill out Ryder's love triangle. Sean's his former g.f. and Mitchell her current flame. Ryder and Sean get it on again soon enough after some jumbled exposition about his Vietnam experiences — only to find Mitchell stalking her residence.

His angry entry after the Sean-Ryder tumble deteriorates into the plot's lamest twist as Mitchell, a Navy commander, reveals it is he who has stolen the nuke. His recitation of a gobbledygook rationale is the film's nadir.

It's now clear who all the goodies and baddies are and the race is on to see whether nuclear holocaust can be prevented. Film now further descends into a low-grade, hackneyed chase — with machine guns frequently ablaze.

Acting is generally flat and tech work is spotty, with some fine aerials, but underwater shots are often murky. Sound occasionally was muffled in screening caught.

Offbeat touches were added on screen by Glenn Withrow (as Pink) and Larry Mintz (as Bite), low-life simps who do the dirty work of stealing the bomb while still boogeying the the Boulevard beat.

—*Tege.*

Avenging Force
(COLOR)

Routine action pic.

A Cannon release of a Golan-Globus production. Produced by Menahem Golan, Yoram Globus. Directed by Sam Firstenberg. Stars Michael Dudikoff. Screenplay, James Booth; camera (TVC color), Gideon Porath; editor, Michael J. Duthie; music, George S. Clinton; production design, Marcia Hinds; art direction, Bo Johnson; set decoration, Michele Starbuck; costume design, Audrey Bansmer; sound (Ultra-Stereo), Jacob Holdstein; stunt coordinator, B.J. Davis; second unit director, Michael Schroder; casting, Wilma Francis. Reviewed at Paramount Theater, Hollywood, Calif., September 12, 1986. (MPAA Rating: R.) Running time: **103 MINS.**

Matt Hunter...........Michael Dudikoff
Larry Richards..............Steve James
Admiral Brown ....James Booth
Glastebury.................John P. Ryan
Delaney....................Bill Wallace
Wallace....................Karl Johnson
Lavall ....Mark Alaimo
Sarah Hunter ....Allison Gereighty
Parker ....Loren Farmer
Grandpa Jimmy...........Richard Boyle

Hollywood — The shoe is on the other foot in "Avenging Force" and the Rambos of the world are the bad guys, not that it matters very much. Politics is far from the issue here and as the body count mounts it makes no difference if they're left or right. Genre junkies should get their fill but few others will care.

Beneath its liberal politics, "Avenging Force" is a routine actioner with characters too thinly drawn to make the battles anything more than monotonous. In the end it's still the bad guys against the good guys in a bloody, brutal fight to the finish.

Hero here is ex-secret service man Matt Hunter (Michael Dudikoff) who quit to protect his kid sister after their parents are accidently murdered.

He's soon drawn back into the struggle when buddy Larry Richards (Steve James) becomes the target of a lunatic fringe right wing terrorist organization called Pentangle.

You can tell this is serious stuff by the way Dudikoff grimaces. James is running for the U.S. Senate, but Pentangle will have nothing of a liberal black man running the country.

Led by sinister businessman John P. Ryan, Pentangle is actually unintentionally quite humorous as it spews venom at the human race. Other members are weathly white trash bent on their own survival in a crumbling society. To this end they practice a deadly hunt of their victims as sport and it is here that the final confrontation takes place.

Lensed in New Orleans and environs, scenery is often more interesting to watch then the action. Final chase is through the bayou swamps with an artificial rainstorm wetting the front of the scene. Despite an array of weapons and battle garb and varied setups, fight scenes just become a non-stop blur.

Director Sam Firstenberg fails to vary the intensity or pace of the film or provide a reason to care. Human dimension is superficial at best. James Booth's script makes as much of a cartoon out of these right wing villians as "Rambo" did of its evil reds.

Performances don't supply the missing link either. Dudikoff is likable at best but hardly believable. Villains fare a bit better with Mark Alaimo as a striking martial arts Kojak. Best of all is Ryan's smooth-edged industrialist with sharp teeth and a jaw-line that makes him more beast than man.

Although almost everyone is wiped out, filmmakers have concocted an ingenious way into the sequel. If only they had taken such care with the original.—*Jagr.*

✻✻✻✻✻✻✻✻✻✻✻✻✻✻✻✻✻✻✻✻✻✻✻✻✻✻✻✻
✻   ✻
✻ Montreal Festival Reviews ✻
✻   ✻
✻✻✻✻✻✻✻✻✻✻✻✻✻✻✻✻✻✻✻✻✻✻✻✻✻✻✻✻

Der Wilde Clown
(The Wild Clown)
(WEST GERMAN-COLOR)

A Bavaria Filmverleih Prods./Joseph Roedl Filmproduktion/ZDF production. Produced by Helmut Krapp, Tilman Taube. Written and directed by Josef Roedl. Camera (color), Karlheinz Gschwind; editor, Juliane Lorenz; music, Eberhard Schoener; sound, Guenther Berthold; design, Gert B. Venzky; costumes, Barbara Grupp; special effects, Heinz Ludwig. Reviewed at the Montreal World Film Festival — In Competition, Aug. 29, 1986. Running time: **107 MINS.**
Jacob ....Sigi Zimmerschied
Janis ....Sunnyi Melles
The Boss ....Peter Kern
Also with: Ivo Vrzal-Wiegand, Ursula Straetz, Jack Luceno, Elisabeth Bertram, Renate Muhri, Erich Kleiber, Otto E. Fuhrmann.

Montreal — A black comedy of haunting originality, "The Wild Clown" pits an untamed, humanist-rogue against unfettered capitalism and the U.S. military in Germany in a bittersweet fable about the battle for individual freedom in an oppressively ordered modern world.

A memorable performance by Sigi Zimmerschied as the clown-rebel, Jacob together with fine supporting acting, lyrical cinematography and excellent English subtitles should make "The Wild Clown" difficult to ignore for a determined specialty distributor up to the challenge of marketing a unique film.

Jacob (Sigi Zimmerschied) is a good-natured, boisterous spirit trying to survive in "the world of bosses and bigshots." He takes a job as chauffeur to The Boss (Peter Kern), an obese bigshot in their provincial Bavarian town whose appetites for money and power are insatiable. The Boss is a land speculator and nitery owner eager to do business with the local American military base. He hires Jacob (whom he rechristens "Jack" out of love for "big America") in order to get title to his house (owned by Jack's aunt in the loony-bin) to complete a land parcel. When Jack refuses to cooperate, The Boss pressures his beautiful assistant Janis (Sunnyi Melles) to lure him into a blackmail trap.

Betrayed by the amoral Boss and the girl he loves, Jack reverts with determined madness to a life of primal independence in an abandoned barn on a U.S. Army firing range, in what was his ancestral village before its absorption into a sprawling military reservation.

Rededicating his life to "freedom and anarchy," Jack dons army fatigues and shaves himself bald, which with his bulging proboscis and savage grin makes the brawny

ex-chauffeur look like a jester-warrior. He's joined occasionally by a wise old woman who knew his grandfather, a rollicking local wino and, finally, Janis, who couldn't bear to leave this nonconforming primitive for a Boss-supplied trip to America.

To Jack's way of thinking, living on the military reservation is as good as living in the U.S., and he uses his little piece of America as a base for guerrilla strikes against The Boss. He also settles down into a surreal "married" existence with Janis, their two companions and his mute aunt, whom they liberate from the asylum. Jack is in heaven, but Janis eventually breaks down from the stress imposed by living in the midst of dive-bomber runs and artillery practice. Then her long-lost American officer husband shows up with another offer to cross the sea to the promised land, and Janis must choose between anarchy and security.

Director Josef Roedl's screenplay veers at times into hectoring the obvious, but on the whole, "The Wild Clown," through its improbably philosopher hero, makes his rebellion seem urgently believable.

—*Rich.*

Auf Immer und Ewig
(Now Or Never)
(WEST GERMAN-COLOR)

A Rocco Film production, in association with ZDF (World sales: Oko Film). Produced, written and directed by Christel Buschmann. Camera (color), Frank Brühne; editor, Jane Seitz; music and title song, Chris Rea; art directors, Georg von Kieseritzky, Heidrum Brandt; sound, Chris Price; associate producer, Christoph Holch; assistant director, Peter Carpentier; production manager, Hans-Christian Hess. Reviewed at World Film Festival, Montreal, Aug. 26, 1986. Running time: **91 MINS.**
With: Eva Mattes, Werner Stocker, Teo Gostischa, Silke Wülfing, August Zirner, Hans Kremer, Ulrich Wildgruber, Hans Wyprächtiger, Eva Zlonitzky, Barbara Ossenkopp.

Montreal — Christel Buschmann's latest, world preemed in Montreal out of competition, is a sometimes wrenching drama about love and death. It opens and closes with exceptionally fine, strong sequences, and maintains interest throughout, though occasionally stretches credulity in the middle sections.

Eva Mattes has one of her best screen roles as a woman who, at the beginning of the film, discovers she's dying of a brain tumor. She doesn't tell her 9-year-old son (she's unmarried) or her current lover, but sets off from Frankfurt to Hamburg to meet with the love of her life (Werner Stocker) who's also the boy's father.

She leaves the boy in a hotel while meeting with Stocker for passionate lovemaking in another hotel. Stocker has his own life (a cute live-in girlfriend), and doesn't know why Mattes has so unexpectedly returned: she doesn't tell him, either, about her imminent death.

The powerful climax has Mattes die in hospital, leaving for her son the name and address of the father he never knew. The boy goes to find Stocker, who's been away on a survival trip in Tunisia (a quite redundant sidetrip as far as the film's concerned) and there's an emotional ending.

What constitutes the center of the film isn't as strong as the first and last sections, partly because Mattes' refusal to tell any of the people in her life about her condition comes across as rather foolish under the circumstances. These central scenes are, as a result, more conventional than the riveting moments already mentioned.

Pic is expertly shot by Frank Brühne and skilfully enacted by all the principals. Buschmann handles the direction with skill, but tends to overuse the music score, and especially the theme song which is reintroduced at the end at just the wrong moment (the meeting between father and son is a strong enough scene without a rather banal pop song to accompany it).

There's enough intensity of emotion in "Now Or Never" (the original German title literally translates as "For Ever And Always"), to make audiences sit up when the pic opens in Germany in October, and it could attract attention at international fests on its fine playing and emotional intensity.—*Strat.*

Le Sixième Jour
(The Sixth Day)
(EGYPTIAN-COLOR)

A MISR Intl. Films/Lyric Intl. production. Directed by Youssef Chahine. Screenplay, Chahine, based on the book by Andrée Chédid; camera (color), Moshen Nasr; music, Omar Khairat; sound, Tierry Sabatier; costumes, Yvonne Sassinot, Nahed Nasrallah. Reviewed at the Montreal World Film Festival — out of competition, Aug. 28, 1986. Running time: **110 MINS.**
With: Dalida Moshen, Moheidine Chouikar, Hamdy Ahmad, Salal Saadani, Sanaa Younes, Mohamad Mounir, Youssef El Ani.

Montreal — A tale of repressed love and thwarted fantasy set in the cholera-stricken Egypt of 1947, "Le Sixième Jour" is a convoluted melodrama that's only partly redeemed by dedicated performances.

While this handsomely lensed film should find an audience in France and other western locales with large Arab emigré populations, its commercial prospects on the U.S. market seem dismal, although festival programmers seeking some third world flavor might safely add it to their programs if English subtitles are provided.

After burying her sister who's died of cholera, Saddika (Dalida Moshen) returns to her village in a "sanitary zone" where she works as a washerwoman and lives with her paralyzed husband. Saddika is a comely, strong-willed grandmother at 40 whose only escape from a life of hardship is the movies. She does laundry for an actress whom she worships in spite of the star's indifference to her daydreams.

Another movie-struck daydreamer is Okka (Moheidine Chouikar), a peripatetic young organ grinder whose singing and dancing talent leads him to fantasizing about becoming an Egyptian Gene Kelly. The handsome Okka also constantly fantasizes about blond European women, and goes to the extraordinary length of dying his hair and dressing in a British army uniform in the hope of being abducted by a strange Parisienne who's been kidnapping and seducing Brit soldiers with the Suez forces. Instead, the hapless Okka is beaten by local nationalist youths, then taken along with his marvelous monkey by Saddika's grandson, Hassan to recover at her house.

The taciturn Saddika and the gregarious street-entertainer who's half her age clash immediately and she tosses him out of her house, which onlys tokes his suddenly kindled desire for this nobly remote washerwoman. Soon the cholera advances into their village, and Saddika's husband comits suicide by starting a fire which burns down their entire house. Saddika and Okka are drawn close together. He introduces her to hashish ("to forget your troubles") and declares his love, stressing their common affinity for the silver screen. In the film's best scene, director Youssef Chahine stages a musical fantasy production number in which Okka puts on an amazing display of Kelly-like hoofing and singing. Saddika, however, is not won over and suggests that Okka should stick to girls his own age.

Nevertheless, when the homeless Saddika and Hassan board a Nile boat for Alexandria, Okka is along. Finally, Saddika's grandson contracts cholera, the outcome of which, it is believed, is only known on the sixth day of the illness. Journey's end is bittersweet, but Okka has learned something new of life and Saddika — in character — is a survivor.

Dalida Moshen in the lead role anchors the entire film, which the talented Moheidine Chouikar tries his best to steal with a wide-eyed hamminess that may be appreciated in Egypt. The musical score is one of the film's assets, although there's not quite enough of it. —*Rich.*

Blue Snake
(CANADIAN-DOCU-
COLOR-16m)

A Rhombus Media production. Produced by Niv Fichman, Louise Clark. Directed by Niv Fichman; camera (color, 16m), John Walker; editor, Bruce Lange; sound, Aerlyn Weissman. Reviewed at the Montreal World Film Festival — Cinema of Today and Tomorrow, Aug. 24, 1986. Running time: **60 MINS.**
With: Robert Desrosiers.

Montreal — Canadian choreographer and dancer Robert Desrosiers provides a focus of understated charm and charisma for this behind-the-scenes documentary on the creation of his fantastical totemic ballet, "Blue Snake." Although the rehearsal and backstage interview footage is routine stuff, the filmed record here of the dance's opening night at the National Ballet of Canada makes for spellbinding viewing. It's an ideal short film for public television, paycable and nontheatrical outlets.

After a notable career with the National Ballet of Canada, Desrosiers formed his own troupe and was later commissioned by the national company to choreograph an original work. As the National Ballet officials note with wry bemusement, Desrosiers leaped at the chance to give rein to his imagination and let them worry about the budget. Regarded by the dancers as a one-of-a-kind balletic maverick, Desrosiers conceived a dance influence by Brazilian *macumba,* Caribbean voodoo and other Afrotropical animistic cultures. With the help of highly creative costume and set designers plus musicians, what evolved was an enthralling, polychromatic spectacle of perpetual motion.

Filmmaker Niv Fichman dutifully follows Desrosiers and his dancers through rehearsals of the demanding routines, and records comments such as "the creation of the dynamics starts to come to life," as the tall, long-haired choreographer uses gentle persuasion and forceful exhortation to bring the best out of his charges. The dancers are pleasing to watch in rehearsal, if rather bland interview subjects. When the curtain rises, however, they deliver an hypnotically kinetic realization of Desroisers' vision. Costumed like mummers in a dream-like carnival, the dancers are subject to the whims of gigantic anthropomorphic puppets that swallow and smash them in contemptuous indifference to their otherworldly freedom of motion.

The lighting limitations imposed by lensing a live performance make for a darker than desired print, but this doesn't obscure the ballet's uniqueness. The sound is quite good given the 16m format. —*Rich.*

Vyiti Zamuzh Za Kapitana
(To Marry The Captain)
(SOVIET-COLOR)

A Lenfilm production. Directed by Vitaly Melnikov. Screenplay, Valentin Tchernykh; camera (Sovcolor), Boris Liznev; art director, Bedla Manevitch; music, Isaak Schwarz; sound, Assia Zvereva. Reviewed at World Film Festival, Montreal, Aug. 26, 1986. Running time: **88 MINS.**
Capt. Blinov . . . . Viktor Proskourine
Elena Juravilova . . . . Vera Glagoleva
Liadov . . . . Nikolai Rybnikov
Woman friend . . . . Vera Vassilieva

Montreal — "To Marry The Captain" is a disarming romantic comedy featuring an endearingly odd couple. He is Captain Blinov, an officer in the Soviet Security Forces (KGB, no less) and in charge of a frontier post. She is Elena, a pretty, wilful divorcee who's a very independent young lady indeed.

They meet when he's on leave to visit his mother in the country and delivers Elena some books. She immediately seeks his help with an obnoxious neighbor with whom she shares a bathroom. Blinov reluctantly agrees to pose as her lover. Soon he's really in love, and tags along with her as she goes to work in a tv studio or on a photographic assignment. They even swim in a river, and, being a bit prudish, he's alarmed to discover she's naked. But all remains platonic until they fight over another man in her life, a smooth tv producer, and the captain leaves for the frontier again. As the title indicates, there's a pleasantly sentimental happy ending.

It's slight material, but it works thanks to the relaxed and charming playing of the two leads, the deftness of the direction, the attractive camerawork, and the very unexpectedness of some of the situations. It's certainly an entertaining pic, breaking no fresh ground, but fun to experience for an hour and a half. — *Strat.*

Ora Tokyo Sa Yukuda
(I Go To Tokyo)
(JAPANESE-COLOR)

A Shochiku Co. production. Produced by Yoshihide Konda. Directed by Tomio Kuriyama. Screenplay, Masakuni Takahashi, Toshio Sekine; camera (Widescreen, color), Kosuke Yasuda; editor, Masuichi Tsuruta; music, Hiroshi Wada; sound, Yukio Obi; art director, Mamoru Narusawa. Reviewed at World

Film Festival, Montreal, Aug. 27, 1986. Running time: **93 MINS.**
With: Eisaku Shindo, Yoshie Kashiwabara, Hitoshi Ueki, Michiko Hayashi, Ikuzo Yoshi.

Montreal — This Japanese variation on "The Out-of-Towners" is a modest little comedy about a middle-aged couple from the country who come to Tokyo to visit their son, a photographer.

Pic extracts a few mild jokes about the old-fashioned pair's reaction to the aggressively modern city, but is essentially only for the domestic market with little chance of export. The husband is a farmer, and the wife, who wears a kimono throughout, thinks she has to make the beds in their motel room. Their son isn't too pleased to see them, but they find their way to his tiny apartment and while the mother starts to clean the place up, father goes to greet the neighbors, who include a transvestite.

Eventually the couple meet up with a girl who works at the same studio as the son. She takes them in hand, showing them around, and they return home happily.

Pic is technically top-notch, with fine location widescreen lensing in the crowded Tokyo streets and parks. Most of the humor is derived from the farmer's horror at the things he sees, including kids breakdancing in a city park. It adds up to a pleasant, but very minor, local item.—*Strat.*

La Femme de ma vie
(The Woman Of My Life)
(FRENCH-COLOR)

A UGC release of an Odessa Films/TF-1 Films coproduction, with the participation of Investimage, and the collaboration of the Regional Council for l'Ile de France. Executive producer, Yannick Bernard. Directed by Régis Wargnier. Stars Jane Birkin, Christophe Malavoy, Jean-Louis Trintignant. Screenplay, Wargnier, Alain Le Henry, Catherine Cohen, Alain Wermus; camera (Eastmancolor) François Catonné; editor, Noëlle Boisson; music, Romano Musumarra; art direction, Jean-Jacques Caziet; sound, Paul Lainé, Jean-Paul Leublier; costumes, Corinne Jerry, Cristine Guégan; assistant director, Alain Wermus; production manager, Ilya Claisse; casting, Françoise Menidrey. Reviewed at the UGC screening room, Neuilly, France, Aug. 27, 1986. (In Montreal Film Festival, noncompeting.) Running time: **102 MINS.**
Simon . . . . .Christophe Malavoy
Laura . . . . .Jane Birkin
Pierre . . . . .Jean-Louis Trintignant
Marion . . . . .Béatrice Agenin
Bernard . . . . .Andrzej Seweryn
Xavier . . . . .Didier Sandre
Sylvia . . . . .Dominique Blanc
Jacques . . . . .Jacques Mercier

Paris — A first film of considerable dramatic force and cinematic skill, "La Femme de ma vie" relates the psychological torments of an alcoholic musician's struggle to get back on the wagon without the help of his wife, whose exclusive sense of love is an abiding threat to his equilibrium.

Director Régis Wargnier, working with a solidly carpentered script co-written with Alain Le Henry, Catherine Cohen and Alain Wermus, takes his film beyond the "Lost Weekend" mode to a more subtle and complex melodrama about the limits of passion and the transcendence of egotistical ambition. Wargnier's control of the material and his direction of the actors make this one of the more impressive French directorial debuts in recent years.

Christophe Malavoy, seen last year in Michel Deville's thriller "Péril en la demeure," gives the full measure of his talent as the film's besotted hero, a gifted solo violinist in an orchestra created and managed by his wife (Jane Birkin). Driven to drink by his own professional anxieties and lack of confidence, he seems at the end of his tether when, in the opening sequence, he collapses onstage during a televised provincial concert.

His fellow musicians (who include Birkin's first husband) think he's a lost cause and unfit to participate in the orchestra's upcoming seventh anniversary recital. Birkin is determined to help him, but her proprietarial nature, which make no allowance for Malavoy's giving up his career, only increases his d.t.'s.

Help and hope comes unexpectedly from a stranger, Jean-Louis Trintignant, a boat manufacturer who has been to alcoholic hell and back, and has created with others a small AA group, which Malavoy begins to attend at his insistence. The growing friendship between the two men, and Malavoy's concern for an even more desperate young woman in the group, gradually restore the musician's sense of dignity and purpose, though ironically at the possible price of his relationship with Birkin. She cannot accept Malavoy being beholden to others, and is not above jealous attempts to short-circuit their aid.

Birkin gives a strong, understated performance as the passionate, but odiously inflexible wife, who cannot dissociate the personal and the professional, and Trintignant provides dimension to the role of the Good Samaritan industrialist who shows Malavoy the way.

Dominique Blanc, a new screen face, is heart-rending as the alcoholic woman Malavoy cannot save from suicide. There are good supporting characterizations from Andrzej Seweryn as the orchestra leader and Didier Sandre as Birkin's first mate.

François Catonné's crisp lensing is complemented by first-rate work in other tech departments and Romano Musumarra's musical scoring enhances the drama.—*Len.*

Zakonny Brak
(Marriage Of Convenience)
(SOVIET-COLOR)

A Mosfilm Studios production. Directed by Albert Mkrtchyan. Screenplay, Afanasy Belov; camera (color), Mikhail Koroptsov; music, Isaak Schwarz; design, Valentin Poliakov. Reviewed at the Montreal World Film Festival — In Competition, Aug. 31, 1986. Running time: **93 MINS.**
Olga . . . . .Natalia Belokhvostikova
Igor . . . . .Igor Kostolevsky

Montreal — Using the Great Patriotic War — the staple theme of Soviet cinema — as its backdrop, "Marriage Of Convenience" is a simply plotted love story which has its small charms but is basically a classy tear-jerker. At best, the film's U.S. theatrical prospects are for scattered locked runs, although it seems a nice item for specialty cable services.

In the early days of World War II (Igor Kostolevsky), a popular young actor, is sent with his Moscow theatrical troupe to the wilds of central Asia. There he meets Olga (Natalia Belokhvostikova) a comely, demure young lady who was a music professor in Moscow but is working as a nurse in the boondock town's clinic. Olga is ill with malaria and the good-hearted Igor, solicitous of her health, strikes up a friendship. Although most women are mad about the tall, handsome thespian, Olga keeps her distance.

Igor and Olga are mutually homesick for Moscow and returning to the capital's cooler climate seems the only hope for curing her malaria. Access to Moscow is strictly limited, but when Igor discovers that married couples are being allowed to return there he proposes a "marriage of convenience" to Olga, who, after much persuading, accepts on the condition that they will divorce as soon as they arrive.

Predictably, the newlyweds' friendship deepens on the long train ride home, especially during an episode in which they become separated from the train virtually in the middle of nowhere. When they finally reach Moscow, Olga learns her parents are dead and their beautiful town house has been destroyed by German bombs. With the marriage still unconsummated and his ardor growing, Igor magnanimously gives Olga his small apartment and moves in with his sister. Although fond of him, Olga continues to press Igor for a divorce while he procrastinates. One day Igor's sister shows up to browbeat Olga for the way she's been treating him. On that same day, the heartbroken Igor finally persuades the military to release him from entertainment duties for combat at the front.

Melodramatic logic dictates Olga will realize her love for Igor just as her husband has 24 hours to report for service and she has the same 24 hours of mandatory hospital duty.

Their morning-misted last farewell is also nothing new. The two lead performers, however, are undeniably appealing and the film does have quick flashes of humor and engaging moments. There are also a number of nice folksy turns by the supporting cast, and the Central Asian locations are effective. —*Rich.*

Chidambaram
(INDIAN-COLOR)

A Suryakanthi Filmmakers production. Written and directed by G. Aravindan. Camera (color), Shaji; music, Devarajan; sound, Harikumar. No additional credits supplied. Reviewed at World Film Fest, Montreal, Aug. 30, 1986. Running time: **103 MINS.**
Shankaran . . . . .Gopi
Sivakami . . . . .Smita Patil
Muniyandi . . . . .Sreenivasan
Jacob .Mohan Das

Montreal — Made in Kerala, Southern India, and based on a short story, this is a beautiful, sometimes touching, but over-extended drama. The setting is a lush dairy farm where a Tamil, Muniyandi (Sreenivasan) does menial work. The farm supervisor, Shankaran (Gopi) is a kindly, educated man, though Muniyandi's immediate superior, Jacob (Mohan Das) is a bully and a snob.

Miniyandi marries Sivakami (Smita Patil), a woman from his village, and brings her to live with him on the farm. Her beauty has many of the men there, including Jacob, making lewd remarks, but the gentle authority of Shankaran always protects her.

Until this point in the film, everything has been shown in minute detail, accounting for the pic's relative length given the slightness of the story. Then, unaccountably, writer-director G. Aravindan omits a crucial sequence, which leaves the audience wondering if perhaps the reels have been projected out of order. What we *don't* see is Shankaran's seduction of Sivakami, Muniyandi's discovery of this, his beating of his wife, and his suicide. We next see him, like Burt Lancaster in "1900," hanging in the cowshed.

Last part of the film deals with the decline and fall of the guilt-wracked Shankaran, who quits his job and wanders the country seeking oblivion in alcohol. Gopi, one of India's finest actors, is most impressive in this final third of the film, and the last scene, where he gives money to a beggar woman and then recognizes her as Sivakami, prematurely old and scarred, is very powerful.

The film is handsome, with clear, sharp color photography, and the verdant farm background makes for an unusually lush setting for the drama. One image, of an approaching storm, is so striking it deserves framing.

Despite the film's many significant qualities, however, it will need tolerant Western audiences to accept the stately first two-thirds.
—*Strat.*

Der Rosenkonig
(The Rose King)
(W. GERMAN-PORTUGUESE-COLOR)

A Udo Heiland Filmproduktion production. Produced by Paolo Branco. Directed by Werner Schroeter. Screenplay, Schroeter, Magdalena Montezuma; camera (color), Elfi Mikesch; editor, Juliane Lorenz; sound, Joaquim Pinto, Vasco Pimentel. Reviewed at the Montreal World Film Festival - Cinema of Today and Tomorrow, Aug. 24, 1986. Running time: **103 MINS.**
With: Magdalena Montezuma, Mostefa Djadjam, Antonio Orlando.

Montreal — With its stunningly photographed, lavish imagery and its evocation of an hermetic, dreamlike world, "The Rose King" could serve as a true example of the overworked term "art film." Werner Schroeter's hallucinatory tale of Oedipal and homosexual passion, played out against an otherworldly Mediterranean landscape, is both entrancing and excessive. It deserves theatrical exposure in carefully selected specialty release.

Anna (Magdalena Montezuma), an extremely eccentric and beautiful German woman, lives on a rose farm off the Italian coast with her son Albert (Mostefa Djadjam). Albert's father was an Arab whom they've left behind in some desert nation but cannot forget. Albert, a young man who mirrors his mother's beauty, is in love with an equally Apollonian farmhand, Arnold (Antonio Orlando). They are all obsessed with one another and with the roses that grow in wild profusion on the crumbling estate. The flowers serve as a symbolist metaphor for their passionate fixations and for Schroeter's concern with life, death and regeneration.

The haunting mood of the film is enhanced by a fevered operatic soundtrack and spoken and stream-of-consciousness dialog in German, Italian, English, Portuguese and Arabic. Stunningly composed and brilliantly lit frames provide a feast of visual imagery evoking the flowering and decay of life and the human spirit. Things get somewhat out of hand during the leisurely resolution (scenes of a cat being crucified and the strong suggestion of Antonio's castration push to the limits of artistic tolerance) but "The Rose King" is an experience that's testimony to Schroeter's undeniable talents. —*Rich.*

●●●●●●●●●●●●●●●●●●●●●●●●●●●●●●●●
Venice Festival Reviews
●●●●●●●●●●●●●●●●●●●●●●●●●●●●●●●●

Die Reise
(The Journey)
(W. GERMAN-SWISS-COLOR)

A Regina Ziegler Filmproduktion (Berlin)/Limbo Film (Zurich)/Westdeutscher Rundfunk/Schweizerische Radio un Fernsehgesellschaft coproduction. Produced by George Reinhart, Regina Ziegler. Directed by Markus Imhoof. Screenplay, Imhoof, Martin Wiebel, based on a novel by Bernhard Vesper; camera (color), Hans Liechti; editor, Ursula West; music, Franco Ambrosetti; sound, Luc Yersin; art direction, Götz Heymann; assistant director, Götz Hermann. Reviewed at Venice Film Festival (In Competition), Sept. 4, 1986. Running time: **110 MINS.**
Bertram Voss ....Markus Boysen
Dagmar ....Corinna Kirchhoff
Schröder ....Claude Oliver Rudolph
Bertram as a child ....Gero Preen
Mrs. Voss.................Christa Berndl
Mr. Voss ....Will Quadflieg
Florian ....Alexander Mehner

Venice — If "The Boat is Full" dealt with Jewish refugees seeking asylum in Switzerland from Hitler's Germany, Markus Imhoof's new feature "The Journey" is in some way a continuation, examining the Nazi heritage on the succeeding generation. Film's originality lies in the unerring line it traces between the intolerable, unhidable, public guilt of the fathers, and the end some of the sons have made in terrorism. In addition to intelligence and clarity, film is blessed with excellent lensing and skillful storytelling that makes it absorbing up to the end.

Its flaw is structural — the lack of a powerful finale that seems to be building, but never arrives.

Even without a hard-hitting conclusion to consolidate its points, "Journey" remains a film of great interest, and one of the most serious attempts to deal in depth with the theme of terrorism. It will have an art house and festival play far beyond the Swiss mountains.

Based on an autobiographical novel by Bernhard Vesper — like film's Bertram Voss, the son of a Nazi poet, who made a painful break with the terrorist movement in Germany — "Journey" tells of a young father who kidnaps his 5-year-old son Florian, rather than let the child's mother take him to a PLO camp. As Bertram, German thesp Markus Boysen embodies the disappointment of the war-born generation who took to the barricades in '68, only to see their utopias come crashing down. While his girlfriend Dagmar (Corinna Kirchhoff) turns to the blind hatred of terrorism as the only way to respond, Bertram has too troubled a conscience to be a hard-liner. In a key scene, he proposes they burn down the police stables in protest for the killing of a student during a demonstration, but at the last moment is overcome with pity for the suffering horses and risks exposure to free them. When Dagmar breaks with him and joins the terrorist underground, he makes up his mind to save his young son from growing up, like he did, with the burden of his parents' actions.

A dazzling "kidnaping" operation in Sicily opens the film and sets its tone of fast-moving action and unexpected turnarounds (the rough, heartless kidnaper pulls off his wig and turns into gentle, loving Bertram).

Pio's main point is made over the course of a series of flashbacks that show Bertram as a child, cruelly mistreated at the hands of his sadistic, distant father. The shock of seeing him stripped of his privileges at war's end leaves as deep a scar, and neatly represents the gulf between generations, ultimate source, according to the film, of the sons' rebellion against the fathers.

Acting by principals and supporting players (notably Will Quadflieg as Bertram's father) is sensitive and rounded, allowing us to see the characters from many points of view. Though film ends almost quietly, compared to what seems to be coming, the sense of tragedy is there. Instead of ending with a cathartic bang, Imhoof is content to let little Florian symbolize the continuation of a tragedy with deep roots. — *Yung.*

Acta general de Chile
(General Document On Chile)
(CUBAN-DOCU-COLOR/B&W)

An Alfil Uno Cinematografica/TVE coproduction, in collaboration with the Comision Organizadora para el quinto centenario de descubrimento de America. Produced by Bernadette Cid, Luciano Balducci. Written and directed by Miguel Littin. Camera (color, b&w), Ugo Adilardi, Jean Ives, Tristán Bahuer, Pablo Martinez; editor, Carmen Frias; music, Angel Parra; songs by Violeta and Isabel Parra. Reviewed at Venice Film Festival, Sept. 6, 1986. Running time: **215 MINS.**

Venice — In exile from his country for the last 12 years, Chilean filmmaker Miguel Littin secretly returned at the beginning of 1985 and spent six weeks filming around the country. Disguising himself and his intentions, Littin managed to direct three European camera crews and six more local teams belonging to the resistance movement. The result is a unique eyewitness report made to be shown as four tv hours (the version screened in Venice's Open Space for Filmmakers) or a reduced 2-hour theatrical version. Of great interest to anyone concerned with Latin America, "Acta general de Chile" could also find an audience on college film circuits.

An impassioned outcry against Augusto Pinochet's military dictatorship, the Cuban-produced documentary chooses subjectivity as the only possible way to view the changes that have occured since the military regime was installed on Sept. 11, 1973. Littin's emotional journey, through cities, ports and countryside, talking to people he meets in head-on interviews, is intercut with nostalgic walks through familiar places, a visit to Pablo Neruda's house by the sea, brief talks with government officials and personages like Castro and Gabriel Garcia Marquez (who wrote a book on the making of the film). Integrating the current information is a proud if pained account of Chile's stormy history, giving film a sense of poignancy and historical breadth.

Each of the four tv segments is a self-contained unit revolving around a theme. The first, a type of introduction, opens with a montage of official interviews, juxtaposing the regime's supporters with its opponents. It then takes a look at the poverty of Valparaiso, interviews relatives of missing *despareceidos* abducted by the regime, shows families banding together to buy food wholesale, etc., in a disorganized grabbag of miscellaneous footage. Better structured is the next episode of the north of the country, which skillfully weaves a deeply felt history lesson into current images of harsh life in barren land. Visuals are not particularly inspired, but the sentiment behind the quickly shot footage carries the weight of sincerity.

Third part deals with the political opposition and its leaders, from the late poet Neruda (the government has forbidden visits to his house) to a long interview with two guerrilla leaders, their faces protected by black shadow. Docu reaches its emotional peak in the fourth segment, an exciting, moving reconstruction of the death of Salvatore Allende, under attack in the presidential palace. Only flaw is that the tightly edited Allende sequences end before the tv hour is up, and like much of the rest Littin is forced to pad it with extra material that lessens its impact. The theatrical version presumably will eliminate a lot of the dead weight.—*Yung.*

Mon Cas
(My Case)
(FRENCH-PORTUGUESE-COLOR)

A Les Films du Passage/La Sept (Paris)/Filmargen (Lisbon) coproduction. Produced by Paulo Branco. Directed by Manoel de Oliveira. stars Bulle Ogier, Luis Miguel Cintra. Screenplay, De Oliveira, based on "O Meu Caso" by José Regio, "Pour finir encore et autres foirades" by Samuel Beckett, and The Book of Job; camera (color), Mario Barroso; music, Joao Pais; art direction, Maria José Branco, Luis Monteiro; costumes, Jasmin. Reviewed at Venice Film Festival, Aug. 30, 1986. Running time: 90 MINS.
With Bulle Ogier, Luis Miguel Cintra, Axel Bougousslavsky, Fred Personne, Wladimir Ivanovski, Heloise Mignot, Gregoire Oestermann.

Venice — Portugal's premiere filmer Manoel de Oliveira has never been known for light entertainment; in "Mon Cas" he tosses his viewers an even tougher steak than usual. Like last year's 7-hour opus "The Satin Slipper," current offering (screened out of competition on Venice's opening night) is interested in exploring the possibilities of filmed theater. Unlike "Slipper," the audience's patience is tried not by running time but by the difficulty of relating various parts of the film, a cerebral exercise some may find rewarding, but most won't stick around to puzzle out.

The first, and most amusing, segment of "Mon Cas" is inspired by a one-act play written by famed Portuguese poet José Regio. Bulle Ogier's sophisticated, meticulously rehearsed role as a flapper in a frivolous play is unexpectedly interrupted when a tormented young man (the fine Luis Miguel Cintra) bursts onstage and insists, in spite of the theater custodian's frantic protests, on airing his grievances to the play's audience. Ironically, we already have seen how this audience is composed of director Oliveira and his camera crew occupying the theater seats, and lensing with an immobile camera from fifth row center. The lamenter, who gets to be quite a bore before long, is offset by the delightful Ogier and her dead-serious threats to make him leave the stage, while the custodian and playwright expound their own "cases."

When this part of the film has run its course, Oliveira plays it back in several variations; once in speeded up black and white, silent but commented on by Samuel Beckett's enigmatic text, "Pour finir encore et autres foirades;" once with the soundtrack speeded up to match the racing image, until someone puts a screen up onstage and world disasters appear on it, ending with Picasso's Guernica.

Last third of "Mon Cas," still using fixed frame and long takes, lacks the bizarre fascination of the first part. Cintra, dressed in clown-like rags, his faced plastered with makeup boils, recites the complaints of that most woebegone Biblical figure, Job, and argues his "case" with wife Ogier and friends. The laments behind the laments are Oliveira's, a creative filmmaker struggling to make films of severely limited commercial interest. The laments behind his are from the audience.
•— *Yung.*

Khrani Menio, Moi Talisman
(Protect Me, My Talisman)
(SOVIET-COLOR)

A Douzhenko Studios (Kiev) production. Directed by Roman Balajan. Stars Oleg Yankovski. Screenplay, Roustam Ibragimbékov; camera (color), Vilène Kaliuta; music, Vadim Khrasatchev; art direction, Alexei Levtchenko. Reviewed at Venice Films Festival (Competition), Aug. 30, 1986. Running time: 70 MINS.
Liosha Dmitriev . . . . Oleg Yankovski
Tania . . . . Tatiana Droubitch
Klimov . . . . Alexandra Abdoulov
Mitia . . . . Alexandre Zbrouev

Venice — The real hero of "Protect Me, My Talisman," an off-beat offering from the Ukraine competing at Venice, is the long-gone poet Pushkin. Director Roman Balajan's contemporary tale of jealousy unwinds during the Pushkin Poetry Festival in Boldino, and for those viewers not up on their Russian classics, the film's edge of fascination will be considerably dulled.

What does come through the cultural gap is a glimpse into the enviably cozy, relaxed attitude toward a towering literary figure shared by common folk and specialists alike. It's a curiosity item, stronger in atmosphere than drama.

Film begins as a lovers' duet between the journalist-husband Liosha and his pretty young wife Tania. At their arrival in the spring-green woods of Pushkin's town, all is playfulness and romance. Soon, however, a sinister figure appears lurking behind a tree, a kind of trouble-making minor devil named Klimov (Alexandre Abdoulov), whose sudden appearances and disappearances are truly diabolical.

The handsome stranger insinuates himself into the couple via a query on a fine point of Pushkin scholarship. By the time he comes over to borrow a book Liosha has offered him, the stage has been set for Tania's seduction. The heretofore reasonable husband, obviously intoxicated from too much Pushkin reading, challenges the intruder to a shotgun duel in a marsh, and destiny takes its course.

Balajan, an Armenian-born filmmaker working in Kiev, now on his fourth feature, enlivens the tale with unexpected touches and plot turns somewhere between art, magic, and the realm of possibility. As background, there are the various activities of the poetry festival, which include a sort of Pushkin in the Park played in mask, locals singing folksongs, and—most curious for Western viewers — heated literary debates between friends and strangers at every occasion.

Oleg Yankovski (seen in Andrei Tarkovsky's "Nostalghia") is a riveting but amiable journalist busy with his tape recorder, and able to offset Tatiana Droubitch's irritating role as the childish wife, silly to the point of hysteria.

Supporting thesps, like Alexandre Zbrouev's young museum caretaker, add a touch of realism to the atmosphere of literary sorcery. Vilène Kaliuta's camerawork is a plus: lack of lip-synch a distracting minus.— *Yung.*

The Death Of The Heart
(BRITISH-COLOR)

A Granada production. Produced by June Wyndham-Davies. Directed by Peter Hammond; Screenplay, Derek Mahon, from the novel by Elizabeth Bowen; camera (color), Ray Goode; editor, David Reece; music, Geoffrey Burgon; sound, Ken Reynolds; art director, Peter Phillips; production manager, Don Bell; costumes, Anne Salisbury; casting, Carolyn Barrett. Reviewed at Venice Film Fest, Sept. 8, 1986. Running time: 109 MINS.
Portia Quayne . . . . Jojo Cole
Anna Quayne . . . . Patricia Hodge
Thomas Quayne . . . . Nigel Havers
Matchett . . . . Wendy Hiller
Daphne . . . . Miranda Richardson
Eddie . . . . Daniel Chatto
Major Brutt . . . . Robert Hardy
St. Quentin Miller . . . . Jonathan Hyde
Mrs. Heccomb . . . . Phyllis Calvert
Also with: Samantha Gates (Lilian), Damaris Hayman (Miss Paullie), Meryl Hampton (Phyllis), Sophie Thompson (Doris).

Venice — A fine adaptation of Elizabeth Bowen's novel , "The Death Of The Heart" is a beautifully scripted, directed and acted picture. Its chief discovery is young Jojo Cole as 16-year-old Portia Quayne, an orphan who, in 1937, is sent to live with uncaring relatives in London.

These are the spoiled, selfish and amoral Anna (the superbly waspish Patricia Hodge) and her diffident, bemused husband, Thomas (Nigel Havers). In their company, the naive, totally innocent Portia meets Eddie (Daniel Chatto), secretly one of Anna's many admirers, a philandering young upper class layabout who dallies with the girl's affections while deliberately humiliating her in front of her friends.

When, eventually, Portia runs away and appeals for help from the impoverished, slightly needy Major Brutt (Robert Hardy), the Quayne household is thrown into complete confusion. The film's funniest sequence is a dinner for three in which the Quaynes and their guest, the insufferable St. Quentin (Jonathan Hyde), discuss the problem without ever coming to grips with it. This scene is a small masterpiece of humor mixed with pain.

With its fine cast of British players, including veterans Wendy Hiller and Phyllis Calvert, plus its elegant recreation of upper-class British life in the pre-war years, "The Death Of The Heart" is a sophisticated, appealing film. Although aimed primarily at television, theatrical possibilities are not out of the question and video release is definitely indicated. The director, Peter Hammond, who's had a long career as a television director, previously made one cinema feature, "Spring And Port Wine" (1970).
—*Strat.*

Werther
(SPANISH-COLOR)

A Pilar Miró P.C. production. Produced and directed by Miró. Screenplay, Miró, Mario Camus, from the novel by Johann Wolfgang Goethe; camera (color), Hans Burmann; editor, Jose Luis Matesanz; music, Jules Massenet; art directors, Gil Parrondo, Fernando Saez; production manager, Carlos Orengo. Reviewed at Venice Film Fest (In Competition), Sept. 7, 1986. Running time: 110 MINS.
Werther . . . . Eusebio Poncela
Carlota . . . . Mercedes Sampiètro
Alberto . . . . Feodor Atkine
Beatriz . . . . Vicky Peña
Federico . . . . Emilio Gutierrez Caba
Jerusalen . . . . Luis Hostalot

Venice — Pilar Miró's return to film directing, after a three-year stint as Spain's Director-General of Cinema, is a modernization of Goethe's "The Sorrows Of Young Werther" (written in 1773, when the author was 24). Miro has updated the story, setting it in contemporary Spain, and her Werther is some 10 years older than the character in the book. The result is a respectable, literary and ultimately rather bland film.

Werther is a teacher of Greek who's come from southern Spain to a northern city. He takes the additional job of tutoring the son of a separated couple: a well-off, rather remote man and his more sensitive wife, a surgeon whose specialty is with children.

A romance develops between the tutor and the child's mother, though it's a romance singularly lacking in passion. This makes the film's tragic ending, as presented here, inexplicable: Werther commits suicide when he thinks the woman he loves has returned to her husband.

It's frankly hard to understand what attraction there could have been for Miró in this particular project, which is a perfect decent film, but a curiously uninvolving one. There's a remoteness about the characters that prevents audience sympathy or identification to the extent that the film becomes nothing more than a rather cold exercise.

Camerawork by Hans Burmann evocatively captures the damp beauty of this northern city, and in every technical respect the film is exemplary. The music used is taken from Jules Massenet's opera, "Werther" (sung by José Carreras and Federica von Stade with Colin Davis conducting the Symphony Orchestra of the Royal Opera House, Covent Garden); the artificial music only adds to the remote feeling of the project, though it, like the film, is coldly beautiful. —*Strat*.

Romance
(ITALIAN-COLOR)

An M.V.M. Films production. Produced by Paolo Pagnoni, Camilla Nesbitt. Directed by Massimo Mazzucco. Screenplay, Mazzucco, Lucia Zei; camera (color), Fabio Cianchetti; editor, René Condoluci; music, Andrea Centazzo. Reviewed at Venice Film Festival (In Competition), Sept. 6, 1986. Running time: **88 MINS.**
Father....................Walter Chiari
Andrea................Luca Barbareschi
Young girl......Julia Hiebaum Colombo
Andrea's wife...........Patrizia Fachini
German tourist............Regina Nitsch

Venice — In "Romance," father-son relations are explored with the same painstaking delicacy evident in helmer Massimo Mazzucco's first feature, "Summertime" (winner of the Venice Italian Showcase in its day). However, painstaking turns to painful over time, in a film where the characters are too slight to keep film going for a long-drawn-out hour and a half. Despite its moments of offhanded verité and shy charm, "Romance" remains a disembodied relationship in search of a story.

"Summertime" lead Luca Barbareschi reprises in the role of Andrea, a 30-year-old Milanese yuppie who has smugly settled into a perfect family and designer apartment, yet feels something is missing in his life. Summoned by père Walter Chiari to a lonely mountain refuge, son and father meet for the first time in 20 years and, in the course of the next few days, get a little reacquainted.

In comparison to Andrea's complacent Brooks Brothers existence, the haggard father has weathered many storms in his life. In this screen comeback, Chiari is a magnificently doomed individualist at grips with his own demons, conscious he's aging and that his attraction to a 14-year-old beauty calls for more control than perhaps he can muster. His talk seems beside the point to his sophisticate son, who wants manly assurance it's all right to cheat on his wife and a general salve for his own anxieties.

The father, however, has no easy answers to offer for either of them. His ambiguous relationship to the young girl is disturbing, but all told

seems preferable to Andrea's ridiculous lies to get a pretty German tourist (Regina Nitsch) into bed.

If there's doubt about who the more appealing character is, it's settled when we compare their taste in movies — Chiari whiles away his loneliness watching a sensational 1960s porn film he surely filmed himself; Andrea proudly unspools lethal home movies of his wedding and the kids.

Tiptoeing through the picture on padded feet, helmer Mazzucco (who also works as a fashion photographer in Milan) shoots sensitively, with great attention to the acting. Though Chiari overshadows his young costars, every performance is credible. Fabio Cianchetti's lensing and Andrea Centazzo's musical score are further pluses, and there is some breathtaking mountain scenery to be enjoyed.
— *Yung*.

La Pelicula del Rey
(A King And His Movie)
(ARGENTINE-COLOR)

A Carlos Sorin Cine production. Produced by Axel Harding. Directed by Carlos Sorin. Screenplay, Jorge Goldenberg, Sorin; camera (Eastmancolor), Esteban Courtalon; editor, Alberto Yaccelini; music, Carlos Franzetti; associate producers, Perla Lichtenstein, Gustavo Sierra, Ezequiel Abalos. Reviewed at Venice Film Fest (In Competition), Sept. 7, 1986. Running time: **104 MINS.**
David Vass...............Julio Chaves
Arturo..................Ulises Dumont
Desfontaines.........Villanueva Cosse
Madama..............Ana Maria Giunta
Oso....................Miguel Dedovich
Also with: David Llewellyn (Lachaise), Roxana Berco (Lucia), Marilia Paranhos (Lula), Ruben Szuchmacher (German translator), Cesar Garcia (Bonnano), Eduardo Hernandez (Rosales), Ruben Patagonia (Quillapan), Ricardo Hamlin (Maxi).

Venice — Carlos Sorin's first feature is a cheerful, well-made in-joke about the making of an historical feature film that quickly turns into a disaster. The inspiration here seems to be the Latin American projects of Werner Herzog, but the entire process of making films is lampooned in Sorin's film.

David Vass, a young director, is planning a film about an obscure Frenchman, Orellie Antoine de Tounenes, who, in 1860, declared himself King of Araucania and Patagonia. Unable to find a professional actor to play the wild-eyed, bearded madman he's envisaged, Vass spies a street vendor he thinks would be just right for the part. When this non-actor realizes someone is looking for him, he fears the police are after him and shaves off all his hair as a disguise. The next problem is the abrupt departure of the film's producer, with the production funds, for Europe, forcing the crew to head south with reduced numbers and an entirely

non-professional cast that includes a hugely fat prostie and a gay dancing instructor.

Sorin has fun with just about every aspect of the filmmaking process, from the tv interview program that opens the film, to the impact of a noisy, self-absorbed crew on a small, conservative community. They all stay at an orphanage, until the disgraceful behavior of the dance instructor gets them into trouble. As the money runs out, Vass is forced to improvise until, without the hundreds of Indian extras he'd counted on, his film takes on the style of a surrealist epic, with dummies standing in for people (the excellent music score underlines the strangeness of it all by evoking the theme of Alexandro Jodorowsky's "El Topo").

Anyone who's ever worked with a film crew will appreciate the humor in Sorin's film, especially scenes like the one in which the director retires from the chaos all around him to quietly sneak yet another look at John Ford's "Stagecoach." Problems with a leading actor who can't ride a horse, or a capricious leading lady ("The new Sonia Braga!"), or lack of accommodation and proper catering all are amusingly presented.

For a first feature, "A King And His Movie" is an impressive achievement. Sorin's background as a cinematographer shows in the attractive visuals (such as a shot in which the film crew huddles at a windy bus stop miles from anywhere), but he knows about pacing, structure and narrative, too. There are plenty of good performances, including Julio Chaves as the obsessed director, Ulises Dumont as his loyal but despairing assistant and, in a small but perfect cameo, Cesar Garcia as the disapproving boss of the orphanage.

All technical credits are first-rate.—*Strat*.

Vendetta
(COLOR)

Subpar women's prison exercise.

A Concorde Pictures release. Produced by Jeff Begun, Ken Solomon, Ken Dalton. Directed by Bruce Logan. Screenplay, Emil Farkas, Simon Maskell, Laura Cavestani, John Adams; camera (Filmhouse color), Robert New; editor, Glenn Morgan; music, David Newman; sound, Dennis Carr; art direction, Chris Clarens; set decoration, Timothy Ford; costume design, Meg Mayer; associate producers, Richard Harrison, Greg Hinton; assistant director, Elliot Rosenblatt; second unit camera, Bryan Greenberg; casting, Brown & Livingston. Reviewed at Mann Westwood, L.A., Sept. 5, 1986. (MPAA Rating: R.) Running time: **88 MINS.**
Laurie....................Karen Chase
Bobo.....................Lisa Clarson
China....................Lisa Hullana

Wanda................Linda Lightfoot
Kay.......................Sandy Martin
Bonnie...............Michelle Newkirk
Star....................Marianne Taylor
Paul...................Marshall Teague

Hollywood — "Vendetta" is too violent and humorless to qualify as the usual woman-behind-bars pic. Film, alternately titled "Angels Behind Bars," will disappoint audiences who have come to expect a little tongue and a lot of cheek when they pass through the turnstile. Pic opened regionally beginning last March.

Considering the genre, most of the cast turn in very credible performances, even if they don't look much like prisoners.

That includes starrer Karen Chase as inmate Laurie Collins, a wholesome, karate-chopping professional stunt woman who intentionally gets herself incarcerated at the Duran Correctional Institute to seek revenge on some prison nasties who killed her sister.

Film opens with one brutal slaying and 88 minutes later, closes with the umpteenth one as Chase finally witnesses her number one adversary, Kay (Sandy Martin), fall dead from a bloody gunshot wound to the chest.

In the intervening hour, Chase eliminated one-by-one all the girls who had a hand in her sister Bonnie's death. She pushes Wanda (Linda Lightfoot) to her death, drowns China (Lisa Hullana), strangles Bobo (Lisa Clarson) and then throws Martin into some machinery before she's picked off by one of the prison security guards in the final scene.

There are no food or pillow fights in "Vendetta" but there are the requisite shower and wrestling scenes plus a couple of group fighting scenes where an untold number of women die.

There is also a lot less flesh exposed here than in most other woman-prisoner films, but that which is shown looks seamy, not sexy.

The only light moments — not to be confused with humorous ones — are those with Martin, the lesbian who plays the butch bit to the hilt. As the prison's chief bully and main supplier of heroin, when she walks into a scene, she takes over.

Production values are better than average for a B pic. — *Brit*.

Codename: Wildgeese
(WEST GERMAN-ITALIAN-COLOR)

A New World Pictures release of an Ascot Film/Gico Cinematografica coproduction. Produced by Erwin C. Dietrich. Directed by Anthony M. Dawson (Antonio Margheriti). Stars Lewis Collins, Lee Van Cleef, Ernest Borgnine, Mimsy Farmer, Klaus Kinski. Screenplay, Michael Lester; camera (Widescreen, color), Peter Baumgartner; editor, uncredited; music, Jan Nemec, played by Eloy. In Dolby stereo. Reviewed at Loews State 1 theater, N.Y., Sept. 12, 1986. (MPAA Rating: R.) Running time: **101 MINS.**

Capt. Wesley . . . . Lewis Collins
China . . . . Lee Van Cleef
Fletcher . . . . Ernest Borgnine
Kathy Robson . . . . Mimsy Farmer
Charlton . . . . Klaus Kinski
Priest . . . . Alan Collins

———

"Codename: Wildgeese" is a routine commando action film boasting an interesting (though poorly used) cast of international talent. Pic was shot in the Far East in spring 1984 with working titles such as "Wild Geese Five" and "Wild Rainbow," followed shortly by an uppercase British production "Wild Geese II" which ironically did not receive as wide a domestic release (via Universal last year) as this New World pickup.

Lewis Collins (who toplined "Who Dares Wins" for the "Wild Geese" and "Wild Geese II" producer Euan Lloyd) stars as Capt. Wesley, a mercenary who brings his international team to carry out a daring raid against drug depots in Thailand. Very predictably, the businessmen who are working with his boss, drug enforcement official Fletcher (Ernest Borgnine), turn out to be the bad guys.

Trekking through the jungle and endless machine gun battles are just the excuse for prolific Italian director Antonio Margheriti to display his usual topnotch explosions, both full scale and miniatures. For gung ho action and interesting storylines, he did a far better job recently with "The Last Hunter" (1980) and "Tornado" (1983).

Inadequate post-synching of dialog hurts the picture, with Klaus Kinski not even showing up to loop his own lines (he is given an inappropriate British voicing). Collins fits the part as a cool commando, but his grumpy acting looks as if he's just received a call from UA telling him the James Bond role went to Timothy Dalton, so he's stuck in this Continental B-pic. Mimsy Farmer is properly shrill as a freed prisoner who's been forcibly turned into a drug addict, while Lee Van Cleef and Ernest Borgnine lend their formidable personalities to nothing roles. Margheriti's favorite actor, Alan Collins (real name: Luciano Pigozzi) shows up uncredited as a Swiss priest who is literally crucified by the baddies.

Margheriti has since completed a followup film "Commando Leopard," starring Collins and Kinski. —*Lor.*

———

The Armour Of God
(HONG KONG-COLOR)

A Toho-Towa release of a Golden Harvest production. Produced by Chua Lum. Executive producer, Raymond Chow. Directed by Jackie Chan. Stars Chan. Screenplay, Edward Tang, based on an original story by Barry Wong, based on an original idea by Eric Tsang; camera (Technicolor), Bob Tompson and Peter Nakaguro Ngor; music, Michael Rai; editor, Cheung Yiu Chung; art direction, William Cheung. Reviewed at Nippon Gekijo theater, Tokyo, Aug. 29, 1986. Running time: **98 MINS.**

Jackie, Hawk of Asia . . . . Jackie Chan
Alan . . . . Alan Tam
Loralie . . . . Rosamund Kwan
May . . . . Lola Forner
Count . . . . Bosidale Sumiljanik
Conjurer . . . . : . . . . Ken Boyle
Also with: Mars, Brackie Fong, Alicia Shawnte, Marcia Chizam, Vivian Wickliff, Linda Denly.

———

Tokyo — This ineptly-made actioner's sole source of interest to all but resolute Jackie Chan fans is fact that the Hong Kong chop-socky star's career was nearly ended during its production. Boxoffice in the U.S. appears virtually zilch.

Pic is a mélange of bad writing worse acting and atrocious dubbing. Customers don't expect art with a capital A from Chan. "Armour Of God" is beyond the pale, however, even considering the minimal standards of the genre.

One problem is that Chan, who at 32 is easily Asia's dominant marquee name, directs himself. So apparently taken is he with his own modestly appealing brand of wholesome prankishness that director Chan emphasizes plot complications involving his character and stints on the action. When the action does come, largely at pic's end, it is superbly choreographed — by "Jackie's Action Team" — and executed. However eyecatching, it's too little too late.

"Armour" is not a total loss. There's a fine, wordless opening sequence showing Chan outwitting an African tribe in the midst of a worship ceremony, and stealing a precious sword — one part of the medieval suit of armour that is the pic's title subject. Despite unfortunate racial overtones, the bits are funny. Then there is a 007-style nonsense with Chan eluding an imminent, explosive death by propelling himself from his souped-up Mitsubishi on a motorized seat with wheels. Martial arts action at pic's end, with Chan besting hordes of villains, is genuinely impressive since he performs most of his own stunts. An amusing turn has a muscular group of black women karate experts attacking Chan. He gallantly declines to return the aggression until he's kicked in the groin.

The plot has two groups pursuing all five pieces of the priceless suit of armour used in the Crusades. There's a rich, young woman (Spanish thesp Lola Forner, 1980's Miss Spain), the daughter of a decadent Count (Bosidale Sumiljanik). Then there is a mean bunch of villains who dress up as monks, reside in the Yugoslavian hills (pic was lensed largely in Yugoslavia) and throw orgies. Chan is somewhere in between.

Hong Kong pop singer Alan Tam is cast as Chan's sidekick who joins in the search for a kidnapped fashion designer (Rosamund Kwan), the object of both their affections. Those amazing Amazons who beset Chan at pic's end are identified collectively as the All-American Ladies Karate Champions.

Multilingual cast is dubbed in the worst manner possible. Sychronization is obviously off and voices heard stylistically conflict with what's seen onscreen. Chan and Tam sound in this pic like two refined Cockneys.

Despite his on-the-set injury, Chan finished the film, and even included over closing credits an outtake showing him being carried off the set on a stretcher, bloodied but unbowed. A curious bit of self-exploitation. —*Sege.*

———

Shin Yorokobimo Kanashimimo Ikutoshitsuki
(Big Joys, Small Sorrows)
(JAPANESE-COLOR)

A Shochiku Co. presentation of a Shochiku/Tokyo Broadcasting System/Hakuhodo production. Produced by Nobuyoshi Ohtani, Soya Hikida, Kazuo Watanabe, Masatake Wakita. Written and directed by Keisuke Kinoshito. Camera (Vistavision, color), Kozo Okazaki; editor, Yoshi Sugihara; music, Chuji Kinoshita. Reviewed at the Morettina Center, Locarno Film Festival, Aug. 17, 1986. Running time: **129 MINS.**

With: Go Kato (Yoshiaki), Reiko Ohara (Asako), Hayao Okamoto (Eisuke), Kuni Konishi (Kenso), Hitoshi Ueki (Kunio), Misako Konno (Yukiko), Kiichi Nakai (Daimon), Ken Tanaka (Nagao), Yoko Shinoyama (Masako).

———

Locarno — Coming at the end of the Locarno retrospective dedicated to Kinoshita, this picture seems to sum up the director's world and his cinematic scope, insofar as it deals with subjects which always have been close to his heart, such as family life and relations, unabashed sentimentality combined with a considerable sense of humor, respect for traditions juxtaposed with modern life, all of this laced with anti-militaristic remarks.

This, however, is evident only after early impressions are digested. For at first glance pic looks very much like a travelog commissioned by the Maritime Safety Authority in Japan, with the Muzak-like accompaniment breaking once or twice into martial marches enforcing this suspicion. After a while, this becomes irrelevant, as a second, stronger feeling prevails, that the film is the veteran director's tribute to his own country, and to an entire plethora of characters who have been parading through his films, in one disguise or another, for the last 40 years.

Picture is a family saga centered around a lighthouse guardian (Go Kato), his wife (Reiko Ohara), their three children, and his father who drops in to visit him every time he is moved from one lighthouse to another, all over the map of Japan. Through the years, the relations between the members of the family and some close friends who all are in the same line of business, develop in a peaceful, idyllic manner, only the elements of nature daring to disturb momentarily this process of unification.

Sympathetic acting by Kato and Ohara as the leading couple gets a strong boost from Hitoshi Ueki as the father, whose nagging mannerisms and egotism mellow with time, until he becomes the most endearing character in the whole picture. Camera work is lush and colorful, as would befit a travelog. Kinoshita, who already has used the same basic situation in a previous film by the same name made in 1957, considers this a sequel, rather than a remake, a further elaboration on the life of a lighthouse guardian first explored in the earlier picture, which is referred to lovingly, in one of the early scenes.

As the final item in a Kinoshita retrospective, it is a fascinating opportunity to observe how one of the great Japanese filmmakers is coping with the cinema of the '80s while trying to preserve the themes and the values of his younger days.

— *Edna.*

———

Peking Opera Blues
(HONG KONG-COLOR)

A Cinema City production, released by Golden Princess. Coproduced and directed by Tsui Hark. Executive producer, Claudie Chung. Stars Lin Ching Hsia, Sally Yeh, Cherie Chung, Mark Cheng. Screenplay, To Kwok Wai; camera (color), Poon Hung Seng; martial arts director, Ching Sui Tung, art direction, Vicent Wai, Ho Kim Sing, Leung Chi Hing; costume design, Ng Po Ling; music and theme song, James Wong; editor, David Wu; special effects, Cinefex Workshop. Reviewed at President theater, Hong Kong, Aug. 27, 1986. Running time: **98 MINS.**
(Cantonese soundtrack with English subtitles)

———

Hong Kong — Cinema City, true to its domestic leadership reputation as a pacesetter, has successfully devised a showbiz gimmick known as The Triple Treat — casting three popular "name" stars together in one film.

"Peking Opera Blues" stars three of the most photogenic '80s domestic actresses around — Lin Ching Hsia, Cherie Chung and Sally Yeh.

Together, they draw people to the cinema. The simplistic storyline has the very alluring Lin attired in chic Oscar Wilde costumes and gelled hair as the comedy daughter of an influential military man in

Peking at the turn of the century. She finds herself caught up in a guerrilla movement, and is sent on a mission to steal a valuable document from the vaults of her amorous papa.

Chung turns up and does her dizzy dumb-blonde routine. Meanwhile, Yeh is the daughter of the manager of an all-male Peking opera troupe. She is stagestruck but being a woman those days was an impediment.

Somehow, the three ladies are brought together by a series of unexpected happenings that always end up in the public opera house.

Tsui Hark's film is generally good fun, with many well-executed zany slapstick sequences. —*Mel.*

El Juego de la Muerte
(The Death Game)
(MEXICAN-COLOR)

A Peliculas Mexicanas release of a Cinematográfica Rodríguez production. Directed by Alfredo Gurrola. Stars Blanca Guerra. Screenplay, Roberto Rodríguez, Jorge Patiño; camera (color), Javier Cruz Osorio; editor, Federico Laneros; music, Suzy Rodríguez. Reviewed at Big Apple Cine 1, N.Y., Aug. 26, 1986. Running time: **93 MINS.**
Yolanda . . . . Blanca Guerra
Lorenzo Rojas . . . . Valentín Trujillo
Don Rafael . . . . Victor Junco

"El Juego de la Muerte" (The Death Game) is a corny treatment of an overdone subject. Storyline concerns poor little rich girl Yolanda (Blanca Guerra), who becomes bored with the idle good life and angry with the hypocrisy that separates Mexico's rich and poor. She is also outraged by her inability to communicate with her parents, who are both involved in extramarital affairs.

One night when Yolanda is out with her boyfriend, they are robbed by a motorcycle gang. Later, when she happens to meet the gangleader (Valentín Trujillo), she notes the attractiveness of his outlaw life as a means of expressing her discontentment while wreaking havoc on small shop keepers.

When her father's thugs kill her lover, she dons a wig, takes up a gun and becomes the leader of "The Blond Yolanda Gang."

Guerra is one of Mexico's best talents and the production credits are certainly adequate, but why bother? There is absolutely nothing new in this storyline of a good girl gone bad in her protest and the pic only acts as a platform to deliver a confused denunciation of bourgeois hypocrisy. —*Lent.*

Dans Un Miroir
(In A Mirror)
(FRENCH-COLOR/B&W-16m)

A Maison de la Culture de Grenoble production. Directed by Raul Ruiz. Screenplay (uncredited) based on the novel by Louis René Des Forêts; camera (color/black & white), Acacio de Almeida; editor, Rodolpho Wedeles; production design, Alain Hecquard; sound, Francis Bonfanti. Reviewed at the Montreal World Film Festival (out of competition), Aug. 22, 1986. Running time: **65 MINS.**
With: Anne Alvara, Jean-Claude Wino, Melvil Popaud.

Montreal — During his 12-year exile from his native Chile, Raul Ruiz has enjoyed the support of French producers who have permitted him to indulge a penchant for baffling, excruciatingly arty exercises in cinematic ennui such as this static, passingly arch little film. Judging by the steady walkout traffic during a public screening at the Montreal World Film Festival, "Dans Un Miroir" has no prospects of surfacing anywhere but at esoteric fests or in a complete retrospective of the director's oeuvre.

Louise (Anne Alvara) and Leonard (Jean-Claude Wino) inhabit a gothic house in whose parlor they incessantly plan an act of aggression against someone who may or may not be Louise's brother. Louise is a manipulative woman with an insistent, hectoring manner and the cold, elegantly beautiful features of an ancient Egyptian queen. Leonard is an indecisive wimp whose need of Louise, however dispassionately expressed makes him subject to her will.

During an interminable discourse covering themes such as the impulse to action and the need for self-expression, Ruiz shifts gears to a smudgy, nightmarish black and white. Gaining the upper hand, Leonard holds Louise spellbound with a long-winded rundown on his views of existence. Louise's full-lipped, mesmerizing mouth swells and glistens black as she registers emotion, then strives to regain her position of psychological dominance.

Fearing they may be overheard by their intended victim, they open the door of the parlor (a prominent feature of which is a mirror that reflects these goings on) and are blown away by a cleansing wind. With this welcome breeze the film comes back to focus and to color, revealing that what's been seen may or may not be the precocious literary exercises of a young boy (Melvil Popaud) who may or may not be Louise's son or brother, may or may not be Leonard. In a housewife's dressing gown, Louise takes on a more human dimension as she attempts to come to an understanding with this gifted youth. Surrealistic literature and Oedipal fantasies should not be the concerns of young

boys, Louise advises, lovingly and triumphantly casting his manuscript pages to the obliterating wind.

While the actors convincingly inhabit Ruiz' dreamworld, "Dans Un Miroir" is fatally undermined by tortuously stagy pacing, and dialog as windy as the breeze that resolves this affair. — *Rich.*

Equinoxe
(Equinox)
(CANADIAN-COLOR)

An Ateliers Audio-Visuel du Quebec production. Produced by Nicole Lamothe. Directed by Arthur Lamothe. Screenplay, Arthur Lamothe, Gilles Carle, Pierre-Yves Pepin; camera (color), Guy Dufaux; editor, François Gill; music, Jean Sauvageau; director, François Lamontagne; sound, Yvon Benoit; assistant director, Alain Chartrand. Reviewed at World Film Fest, Montreal (In Competition), Aug. 25, 1986. Running time: **83 MINS.**
Guillaume . . . . Jacques Godin
Nathalie . . . . Ariane Frederique
Rita . . . . : . . . . . . Marthe Mercure
Rosario . . . . Michel Sabourin
Also with: Andre Melançon (Bert), Luc Proulx (Arthur), Jerry Snell (Joe).

Montreal — Arthur Lamothe's return to feature filmmaking after 13 years is an extraordinarily slight and unconvincing little drama. Tale centers on Guillaume (Jacques Godin), a man in late middle-age, who years before served a prison sentence as a result of the perjury of the man he thought was his best friend. Now, after many years overseas, he returns to the picturesque lakeside community where he grew up to confront the man who ruined his life.

Accompanied by his 12-year-old granddaughter (why take a child on such a mission of revenge?), Guillaume's crazy, macho driving on narrow roads understandably upsets three local toughs who swear revenge. Lamothe attempts to build up suspense as Guillaume, a dogged performance from Godin, tracks down his enemy (Michel Sabourin) and is in turn hunted by the crazy trio. Both confrontations, despite menacing buildup, quickly peter out to nothing.

The audience is left with some beautiful river and lake scenery, lovingly shot by Guy Dufaux, and some minimal characterization, but little else. Marthe Mercure is in for a tiny role as the hero's former girlfriend. Holes in the plot are legion (what happened to Guillaume's wife? How come he served a 10-year prison sentence solely on the word of his buddy, who'd actually committed the crime in question?) and despite the presence of top Quebec director Gilles Carle as cowriter, the thin screenplay is the pic's main problem.

It's technically good in every department, but rated a major disappointment as the locally-made film competing in the Montreal fest.

Commercial chances don't look promising outside home ground, and doubtful even there. — *Strat.*

Dulce Patria
(Sweet Country)
(CHILEAN-DOCU-COLOR-16m)

A Ciné Libre, Latin American Film Project production. Produced by Barbara Margolis, Juan Andres Racz. Written and directed by Juan Andres Racz. Camera (color, 16m), Juan Forch, Jaime Reyes, Leonardo De Labarra; editor, Marcello Navarro. Reviewed at the Montreal World Film Festival - Latin American Cinema, Aug. 24, 1986. Running time: **59 MINS.**

Montreal — The brutally oppressive military dictatorship of Chilean general Augusto Pinochet is indicted here in a documentary that reveals the despair and courage of the country's people under a regime that's contemptuous of its subjects. Although unabashedly one-sided, "Dulce Patria" makes its case convincingly with newsstyle footage, interviews with representatives from all classes of Chilean society and by letting Pinochet hang himself with his own words.

Pinochet sees himself (and Chile) as the one leader and nation that's successfully defeated "Soviet communism" in this century. Most Chileans, however, regarded the violently overthrown, legally elected president Salvador Allende as a non-ideological politician with their interests at heart. The testimony of a former Pinochet state security agent and the mother of a "disappeared" girl provide grim testimony to the military regime's legacy of torture and rule by murder.

People in the street, who are confronting hopeless unemployment and hunger in the day-to-day struggle for survival, scoff at the notion that foreign (communist) governments are behind the resurgent opposition to the military dictatorship.

While a coalition of students, the poor and middle class professionals risk their lives in violent street battles with the police and military, a small and privileged class leads a life of relative comfort and ease. This "American-style" life, say opposition economists, political scientists and union leaders, has been bought by "looting" the country of its wealth in return for loans that subsidize the import of luxury goods. With so many suffering and so few flourishing under the regime, it seems inevitable that the opposition — with the essential support of the Chilean clergy — will triumph but that the victory of democracy will have to be won with blood. —*Rich.*

El Hermano Bastardo De Dios
(The Bastard Brother Of God)
(SPANISH-COLOR)

An Almadraba Producciones production, in collaboration with Television Española and the Ministry of Culture. Executive producer, Jesus Palacios. Produced by Ricardo Garcia Arrojo. Directed by Benito Rabal. Screenplay, Rabal, Agustin Cerezales Laforet, from the novel by José Luis Coll; camera (color), Paco Femenia; editor, José Maria Biurrun; music, Juan Pablo Muñoz Zielinski; sound, Carlos Faruolo; art director, Felix Murcia; costumes, Javier Artiñano; assistant director, Walter Prieto; casting, Carlos Ladron de Guellara. Reviewed at Venice Film Fest (in competition), Sept. 9, 1986. Running time: **110 MINS.**
Pepe Luis (7-8 years) . . . . . . .Lucas Martin
Pepe Luis (10-11 years)...Paco Rabal Cerezales
Grandfather . . . . .Francisco Rabal
Grandmother . . . . .Asuncion Balaguer
Alejandra . . . . .Maria Luisa Ponte
Uncle Julio . . . . .Mario Pardo
Also with: Agustun Gonzales (Don Enrique), Terele Pavez (Ramona), Miguel Angel Rellan (Commissario), Manolo Zarzo (Doctor), Juan Diego (Omar Hazim).

Venice — This first feature from the son of actor Francisco Rabal covers familiar territory for Spanish cinema: the Civil War and the beginning of the Franco period as seen via the alert eyes of a child living in a provincial city (Cuenca). Earlier films such as Victor Erice's ''The Spirit Of The Beehive'' or Carlos Saura's ''Cria,'' latter dealing with a later period, had little girls as protagonists; the new film features a little boy, but otherwise the mixture is much the same.

Story is told by Pepe Luis as an old man (voiced by José Luis Coll) looking back to events of 50 years earlier. The boy lived with his grandparents (his parents were leftists who eventually fled to Argentina) and shared a bedroom with his uncle. He spends most of his time doing the things little boys like to do, exploring a dangerous deserted mineshaft, mooning over a pretty little girl, fighting with friends and enemies, assisting the priest at a funeral service and, in a particularly nasty pre-credit sequence, stoning a stray cat to death.

As the Civil War occupies the thoughts of everyone, even young Pepe Luis can't avoid it. His uncle loses a leg in a less than glorious military encounter, while the house is searched by Leftists looking for secret radios (they find, instead, an old home movie projector). While visiting his uncle in hospital, the boy befriends a Moroccan who has also been caught up in the war.

This is an anecdotal film whose title comes from the boy's childish contention that all the terrible things that are happening can't be the responsibility of God but of a deviant sibling. Benito Rabal handles the material with a relaxed confidence, and the images of Paco Femenia are impressive, but it all goes on too long and some fantasy sequences are as irrelevant as they are ugly. On the strength of this first feature, Rabal will bear watching in the future, but this derivative effort won't arouse much international interest outside Spanish-lingo territories. It was a rather thin competing entry in Venice.—*Strat.*

Ein Blick — und die Liebe bricht aus
(One Look — And Love Begins)
(WEST GERMAN-COLOR)

A Von Vietinghoff Filmproduktion (Berlin). Produced by Joachim von Vietinghoff. Written and directed by Jutta Brückner. Camera (color), Marcelo Camorino; editor, Ursula Höf, Jutta Brückner; music, Brynmore Jones; art direction, Guillermo Kuitka; costumes, Marion and Britta Vollmer; sound, Lothar Mankewitz, Martin Steyer. Reviewed at Venice Film Festival, Sept. 3, 1985. Running time: **85 MINS.**
With: Elda Araoz, Rosario Blefari, Regina Lamm, Margarita Munoz, Maria Elena Rivera, Norberto Serra, Daniela Trojanovsky.

Venice — ''One Look — And Love Begins'' is a plotless, almost formless, and definitely disappointing feature from Jutta Brückner, prized for her conscientiously crafted ''Hungerjahre'' and ''Air Roots.'' Attempting to present various female attitudes toward love and men, film lines up a loosely joined series of surrealist scenes of little emotional or cerebral import. Commercial chances are slim.

The project of ''One Look'' is to depict women's raw feelings about love without a story structure. Though it was lensed in Argentina for color, oddly enough, only interiors are used — huge empty slaughterhouses littered with debris, unidentifiable ruins of the modern age. The imaginary setting is made even more abstract by mirrors dissolving space, sparse props that look like they came out of a junk shop, and theatrical costumes mixed as wildly as possible.

In this symbolic land of the feelings, a tango is heard, an odd couple dance. A strapping young bride poses at her husband's side for the camera. Comically grimacing through her wedding night, she runs into the bathroom space and obsessively starts scrubbing herself, to the accompaniment of comically exaggerated sounds.

This is ''Ein Blick's'' most enjoyable scene. It is followed by abstract but uninspired scenes of domestic slavery, rape, abortion, woman-to-woman exploitation, violent couplings and actresses' joyless sexual relations with interchangeable macho males. Film lacks the inventiveness that could bring its symbolic tableaux off, while the point behind the sequences is either too obvious, or obscure.

Brückner performs some interesting tricks with the soundtrack, interrupting the predominant silence with snatches of poetry, music, and semi-intelligible language. In general, film feels like a mental exercise preparing the raw material to be woven into a more engaging narrative film, next time.— *Yung.*

Peggy Sue Got Married
(COLOR)

Smashing return to form by Francis Coppola.

A Tri-Star Pictures release from Rastar of a Tri-Star/Delphi IV and V Prods. production. Produced by Paul R. Gurian. Executive producer, Barrie M. Osborne. Directed by Francis Coppola. Stars Kathleen Turner. Screenplay, Jerry Leichtling, Arlene Sarner; camera (Deluxe color), Jordan Cronenweth; editor, Barry Malkin; music, John Barry; production design, Dean Tavoularis; art direction, Alex Tavoularis; set decoration, Marvin March; sound, Richard Bryce Goodman; costume design, Theodora Van Runkle; assistant director, Douglas Claybourne; casting Pennie duPont. Reviewed at MGM Studios, Culver City, Calif. Sept. 11, 1986. (MPAA Rating: PG-13.) Running time: **104 MINS.**
Peggy Sue . . . . .Kathleen Turner
Charlie Bodell . . . . .Nicolas Cage
Richard Norvik . . . . .Barry Miller
Carol Heath . . . . .Catherine Hicks
Maddy Nagle . . . . .Joan Allen
Michael Fitzsimmons . .Kevin J. O'Connor
Evelyn Kelcher . . . . .Barbara Harris
Jack Kelcher . . . . .Don Murray
Elizabeth Alvorg . . . . .Maureen O'Sullivan
Barney Alvorg. . . . . .Leon Ames
Beth Bodell . . . . .Helen Hunt
Also with: Jim Carrey, Lisa Jane Persky, Lucinda Jenney, Wil Shriner, Sofia Coppola, John Carradine.

Hollywood — Who would have thought that Francis Coppola could make a sentimental, lighthearted, adult version of ''Back To The Future?'' Well, he has and it's called ''Peggie Sue Got Married.'' Film has the director's mark of distinction. It is provocative, well-acted, stylish and uneven. Pic is a marked improvement over anything else he's done lately and is sure to bring many disenchanted Coppola fans back to the theater.

''Peggy Sue'' may seem to be a ripoff of ''Back To The Future,'' but it was originally in production at the same time. When the pic was announced in October of 1984, Debra Winger was set to star and Penny Marshall to direct, but they left in a script dispute and the production was halted. The project was in limbo until Coppola took over last year with Kathleen Turner in the lead and the result is one terrific matchup.

Coppola doesn't overdirect Turner, a natural for playing Peggy Sue, the grown up all-American girl with a rebellious streak.

First-time scriptwriters Jerry Leichtling and Arlene Sarner have written a nice mix of sap and sass for Peggy Sue's character, a melancholy mother of two facing divorce who gets all dolled up in her 1950s-style ballgown to make a splash at her 25th high school reunion.

We get a clue that something special is going to happen to her just by the way cinematographer Jordan Cronenweth frames her face — backlit and dreamy-like — a technique he returns to at pivotal parts of the film.

Sure enough, she's selected Prom Queen. In all the excitement, she collapses on stage while accepting her crown — finding herself revived as an 18-year-old high school senior of the class of 1960.

Almost immediately, she realizes she's returned to her youth with all the knowledge and experience learned as an adult, quickly figuring out that she can alter the course of her future life by changing certain crucial decisions she made as a teenager.

Will she, or would we if we had to do it all again? This is the provocative question that is raised, and only superficially answered in "Peggy Sue."

The most important relationship for her is with steady boyfriend Charlie (Nicolas Cage), who she eventually marries, has two children by and only later seeks to divorce because of his infidelity.

Cage is almost a caricature of the primping, self-centered, immature high school jerk who is really insecure deep down. His character becomes exaggerated as the film progresses, giving a good clue to his future notoriety as an obnoxious tv appliance pitchman. He is strangely unintelligible at times but the dialog isn't missed.

Turner seems so in control of her feelings throughout most of the film and he remains fairly static, which leaves one wondering why, with all her new found perspective, she goes for him all over again.

Film stereotypifies the other people important in her teenage years (adoring parents, wise grandparents, gawky sister), but it does heighten the amusement factor when their one-dimensional personalities are played off against hers.

What makes this treatment unique is that the jokes aren't so much derivative of pop culture, as they were in "Back To The Future," but are instead found in the learned wisdom of a middle-aged woman reacting to her own teenage dilemmas.

At one point, she makes a play for the outcast beatnik Michael Fitzsimmons (Kevin J. O'Connor), who she always believed to be a lot more sensitive and sexy than her boyfriend. O'Connor plays the part to the hilt — taking her to some moonlit area where he very seriously recites some of his drekky poetry. It's a hoot.

Film also manages to tug on the old heartstrings without being maudlin as Turner revisits with her parents (Barbara Harris, Don Murray) and grandparents (Maureen O'Sullivan, Leon Ames), realizing she's taken them for granted and now has a chance to make up for past ingratitudes.

Sometimes Coppola doesn't know how to end his pics, and "Peggy Sue" is another example.

Contrived scene at the men-only club is silly and breaks the flow of the film.

Tech credits, as in all of Coppola's efforts, are terrific.

Soundtrack of 1950s tunes, including the Buddy Holly classic from which the film's title is taken, are integrated well into the story. —Brit.

Foreign Body
(COLOR)

Clever social comedy is a showcase for Victor Banerjee.

An Orion Pictures release of a Christopher Neame-Colin M. Brewer production. Produced by Brewer. Executive producer, Christopher Neame. Directed by Ronald Neame. Stars Victor Banerjee. Screenplay, Celine La Freniere based on the novel by Roderick Mann; camera (Rank color, prints by Deluxe), Ronnie Taylor; editor, Andrew Nelson; music, Ken Howard; production design, Roy Stannard; production manager, Donald Toms; assistant director, Patrick Clayton; casting, Sharon Howard Field. Reviewed at the Ziegfeld theater, N.Y., Sept. 15, 1986. (MPAA Rating: PG-13.) Running time: 108 MINS.

Ram Das	Victor Banerjee
I.Q.	Warren Mitchell
Lady Ammanford	Geraldine McEwan
Prime Minister	Denis Quilley
Susan	Amanda Donohoe
Norah	Eve Ferret
Miss Furze	Anna Massey
Mr. Plumb	Stratford Johns
Dr. Stirrup	Trevor Howard
Jo Masters	Jane Laurie

If "Foreign Body" doesn't have quite the comic and narrative richness of Ronald Neame's Ealing Studios classics, this variation on the "great impostor" plot device is still an unalloyed pleasure to watch, particularly in an era of brassy, slapdash "high concept" releases. Built solidly upon a fluid, comic virtuoso performance by Victor Banerjee, the picaresque fable of an impoverished refugee from Calcutta faking it as a doctor to London's upper crust makes some jaunty points about racism, gullibility and pluck.

Banerjee's multi-faceted performance in David Lean's "A Passage To India" had its comic moments, but it was essentially a dramatic role drawn with the gentle sincerity he also brought to Satyajit Ray's 1985 masterpiece, "The Home And The World." Even though he's a deceiver, sincerity is a bedrock trait of the "Foreign Body" hero, Ram Das, but here Banerjee is free to romp with bug-eyed zaniness through the improbable adventures of this Asian naif abroad.

After a typically hapless misunderstanding with a stark naked beauty and her brute boyfriend, Ram Das loses his job as a flophouse desk clerk in Calcutta where he's cast adrift among the unemployed masses. As a last resort, this well-meaning blunderer "borrows"

money from his father's strongbox and ships out with fake seaman's papers for jolly England, where his one distant relative, I.Q. Patel (Warren Mitchell), mops a loo at Heathrow Airport. However, indomitable cousin I.Q. is also a keen student of human nature who takes the culture-shocked immigrant under his wing and initiates him in the art of survival in the strange and cold new world of England.

Ram Das shares the sexual innocence common to many poor young Indian men, and the hero's nervousness over his virginity and his eagerness to shed it colors the plot with comic poignancy. Pragmatic and virile older cousin I.Q., who "services" their shrewish landlady for supplemental income, advises Ram Das to forget about girls and get a bus conductor's job. In Neame's cinematic world there's never a need to demonstrate just how Ram Das makes experiential leaps. His situation simply changes with the swiftness of a quick cut while Banerjee's "and then I tried ..." voiceover narrative provides the assurance that all things are possible in Ram Das' life.

Aboard his double decker one rainy night, Ram Das is picked up by a lusty, buxom secretary, Norah Plumb (played with broad sassiness by Eve Ferret), who eventually invites him home to dinner. He gets into an absurd argument with her racist dad over the Hindu derivation of words like "bungalow" and the history of British colonialism in India, and when Nora's seduction of Ram Das goes totally awry, her dad sees to it that he loses his job with London Transit.

Having traded the Darwinist jungle of Calcutta for that of London, Ram Das is at the end of his rope when he comes upon the aftermath of a bus accident which has left a beautiful model supine in the street. Without thinking, the well-spoken Indian volunteers his services as a doctor, revives the beauty with mouth-to-mouth resuscitation and sees the grateful model Susan (Amanda Donohoe) safely home. Susan is so impressed with this gentle "M.D." that she promises to stock his practice with her fashion and high society contacts.

Cousin I.Q. regards Ram Das' new medical career as a stroke of genius and offers to invest his gigolo earnings in spiffy offices for his protege. Blessed with a photographic memory, Ram Das reads up on books like "Your Patient And You" and leans for supplemental advice on an old alcoholic sawbones friend of I.Q., one Dr. Stirrup (Trevor Howard).

This sets the stage for a series of comic misadventures in which Ram Das charms his way through treatments of Susan's wealthy aunt Lady Ammanford (Geraldine McEwan)

and upon her recommendation the Prime Minister himself (Denis Quilley). Naturally the hero falls in love with Susan (who's betrothed to an insufferable snob) and his suffering is magnified when Nora turns up to blackmail him. In keeping with the film's upbeat positivism, Neame wraps things up with an all's well that ends well resolution in which good intentions find their just reward.

Production and tech credits are expert, and Ken Howard's musical score enhances the comic resonance of this enjoyable fantasy. —Rich.

Children Of A Lesser God
(COLOR)

Touching, superbly acted romance.

A Paramount Pictures release. Produced by Burt Sugarman, Patrick Palmer. Directed by Randa Haines. Stars William Hurt, Marlee Matlin. Screenplay, Hesper Anderson, Mark Medoff, based on the play by Medoff; camera (Medallion color), John Seale; editor, Lisa Fruchtman; music, Michael Convertino; production designer, Gene Callahan; art director, Barbara Matis; set decorator, Rose Marie McSherry; sound, Richard Lightstone; costumes, Renee April; associate producer, Candace Koethe; assistant director, Jim Kaufman; casting, Gretchen Rennell. Reviewed at Paramount Studio theater, Hollywood, Calif., September 16, 1986. (MPAA Rating: R.) Running time: 110 MINS.

James	William Hurt
Sarah	Marlee Matlin
Mrs. Norman	Piper Laurie
Dr. Curtis Franklin	Philip Bosco
Lydia	Alison Gompf
Johnny	John F. Cleary
Glen	Philip Holmes
Cheryl	Georgia Ann Cline
Danny	William D. Byrd
Tony	Frank Carter Jr.

Hollywood — "Children Of A Lesser God" is the kind of good intentioned material that often gets weighed down with sentimentality on the screen. Fortunately, the translation of Mark Medoff's Tony Award-winning play to film avoids many of those traps by focusing on a touching and universal love story between a deaf woman and a hearing man. Subject matter may be a little offputting but film is likely to pick up favorable word-of-mouth thanks to its upbeat treatment.

In an age of fashionable cynicism it has become nearly impossible to present a truly moving love story without it either coming off as old

Original Play

An Emanuel Azenberg, the Shubert Organization, Dasha Epstein & Ron Dante presentation of a Mark Taper Forum production of a play in two acts, by Mark Medoff. Staged by Gordon Davidson; setting, Thomas A. Walsh; costumes, Nancy Potts; lighting, Tharon Musser; associate producers, William P. Wingate, Kenneth Brecher. Features John Rubinstein, Phyllis Frelich. General manager, Jose Vega; company manager, Lilli Afan; publicity, Bill Evans, Howard Atlee; stage managers, Mark Wright, Jonathan Barlow

Lee, Richard Kendall. Opened March 20 (reviewed March 28), 1980 at the Longacre Theatre, N.Y.; $20 top weeknights, $22.50 weekend nights.

Sarah Norman .... Phyllis Frelich
James Leeds .... John Rubinstein
Orin Dennis .... Lewis Merkin
Mr. Franklin .... William Frankfather
Mrs. Norman .... Scotty Bloch
Lydia .... Julianne Gold
Edna Klein .... Lucy Martin

fashioned or totally false. Using the extreme circumstances of a deaf woman locked in her own private world and a man desperate to be a part of it, her condition functions almost as a metaphor for the difficulties of communication between people.

At 110 minutes, film definitely has its slow moments and much of the material is thin, but the story is emotionally anchored by the couple's shifting feelings and is superbly played by William Hurt and Marlee Matlin.

Hurt is a teacher who arrives at Governor Kittridge School for the Deaf on the Maine coast where he encounters Sarah (Matlin), a bitter and withdrawn person who has become the cleaning woman at the school where she was a student. One look is enough to attract him, not only to her radiant beauty, but to her prideful refusal to speak or lip read.

For the most part, Sarah is an intriguing and complex character full of unexplored pools of emotion which she is afraid to expose to Hurt or anyone else. Much of her reticence comes from a troubled childhood when her mother (Piper Laurie) failed to accept her condition. She has been deeply wounded and Hurt's work is to coax her back into the world.

Turning this all into a dramatic structure presents a daunting challenge as much of the action takes place internally, in a space between sound and silence. At least half the film's dialog is delivered in sign language while the hearing character speaks both sides of the conversation.

To her credit, director Randa Haines gives the mercurial territory a sense of movement and cinematographer John Seale actually creates a visual look neither like everyday reality nor pure fantasy.

At the heart of the picture is the attraction of Hurt and Matlin, to each other and to the audience. Their need and feeling for each other is so palpable that it is almost impossible not to share the experience and recognize it in one's own life.

It's another seamless performance for Hurt, who plays the quirky teacher with an effortless and totally believable charm. Matlin, who makes her professional acting debut here and is in real life hearing impaired, as is much of the cast, is simply fresh and alive with fine shadings of expression.

Philip Bosco is entertaining as the school's superintendent and a cast of hearing-impaired non-pros who are Hurt's students are likable but lack a fullness that would fill in the film's slower passages.

That Hesper Anderson and Medoff's script is a bit weak in developing the relationship and supplying supportive business is finally secondary to the strength of the feelings at the film's center.—*Jagr.*

Overnight
(CANADIAN-COLOR)

An Exile production. Producer by Jack Darcus, John Board. Executive producer, Don Haig. Directed by Jack Darcus. Screenplay, Darcus; camera (color), Brian Hebb; editor, Sally Paterson; music, Glenn Morley, Michael Conway Baker; sound, Bryan Day, Michael Lacroix; art director, Andrew Deskin; production manager, Bob Wertheimer; assistant director, John Board; casting, Melissa Bell. Reviewed at World Film Fest, Montreal, Aug. 22, 1986. Running time: **98 MINS.**
Scott .... Victor Ertmanis
Del .... Gail Garnett
Alison .... Barbara Gordon
Vladimir Jezda .... Alan Scarfe
Arthur .... Duncan Fraser
Livingstone .... Ian White

Montreal — A modest, talky comedy about an out-of-work actor who gets the lead in a sleazy porn film being directed by a Czech emigré and former Cannes prizewinner, "Overnight" appears to be trying for a statement about the oft-beleaguered Canadian film industry.

Writer-director Jack Darcus, who's been directing feature films in Canada since the early 1970s, doubtless knows all about the problems of filming north of the border, but his message fails to come across with much humor or astringency here. The film's producer is presented (and played by Duncan Fraser) as a no-talent bum, while the director (amusingly limned by Alan Scarfe) is a sad figure of a talent gone to seed. The visit of a Hollywood producer scouting talent only sparks envious recriminations ("We may be a little dirty, but we're Canadian!") and the climax of the pic (an experienced porno star, played by Ian White, expires on set) is banal.

Pic has some ideas and might have worked with lighter treatment and a pruned screenplay. It sounds more like a stageplay than a film. Sex scenes are extremely coy.
—*Strat.*

Radioactive Dreams
(COLOR)

Raymond Chandler meets Mad Max.

A De Laurentiis Entertainment Group release. Produced by Thomas Karnowski, Moc-

tesuma Esparza. Executive producer, H. Frank Dominquez. Directed by Albert Pyun. Screenplay, Pyun; camera (Deluxe color), Charles Minsky; editor, Dennis O'Connor; music, Pete Robinson; production designer, Chester Kaczenski; set designer, Kaczenski; costumes, Christine Boyar; sound, Don Sanders; assistant director, Roger Holzberg; associate producer, Holzberg; casting, Janet Hirschenson. Reviewed at the DEG screening room, Beverly Hills, Sept. 18, 1986. (MPAA Rating: R.) Running time: **98 MINS.**
Phillip .... John Stockwell
Marlowe .... Michael Dudikoff
Miles .... Lisa Blount
Spade Chandler .... George Kennedy
Dash Hammer .... Don Murray
Rusty Mars .... Michele Little
Sternwood .... Norbert Weisser
Harold .... Paul Keller Galan
Chester .... Demian Slade
Brick Bardo .... Chris Andrew

Hollywood — This richly stylized depiction of post-nuclear life winds up largely as a series of grotesque images and impressions rather than a compelling story. "Radioactive Dreams" may find little more than a small niche among those curious about a black humor treatment of life after the bomb.

Comedic undercurrents are immediately evident as we join Phillip (John Stockwell) and Marlowe (Michael Dudikoff) inside their nuclear bomb shelter. Growing up inside over 15 years, they've taken on the joint personality of Raymond Chandler's private eye after untold hours reading his detective novels.

Employing periodic narration characteristic of the original Marlowe films, Phillip sets up the parody as the duo emerges from the shelter in the year 2010 with all the cadence and confidence of Bogie's Marlowe. Story teeters on the brink of absurdity but avoids actually falling into that abyss.

Straining to make the ploy seem engaging, writer-director Albert Pyun arranges for Phillip-Marlowe's first encounter with a woman via the tough and new-worldly Miles (Lisa Blount). Contact leads to calamity as she accidentally leaves behind keys for launching the only MX Warhead not exploded in the earlier holocaust.

With P-M now possessing the keys, a bizarre series of assaults unfolds as post-nuke factions attempt to retrieve the keys and control the world. Mutant Surfers, Biker Women and Disco Mutants provide some action and twisted humor as P-M nears the treacherous urban area.

Edge City is populated by a conglomeration of 20th Century period devotees, such as Greasers and Hippies, who have become embittered survivors. Chester Kaczenski's production design takes over here as sensational environs such as the punk and video districts give Edge City a vivid, if haunting, reality.

Direction, lighting and music score combine for intense buildups to the climactic shootout and surprise revelation as chieftains of the

city districts each try to get the keys.

Throughout it all, Phillip maintains his rap with the audience. The technique alternately comes off as silly and daringly ingenious as a humorous device offsetting some of the bleakness of this profound subject.

Stockwell and Dudikoff manage to breathe some plausible life into their characters and most performances are tops. Blount and George Kennedy (as Spade Chandler) are lackluster. Look and feel of the sets merit kudos for all involved.
— *Tege.*

A Better Tomorrow
(HONG KONG-COLOR)

A Golden Princess release of a Cinema City presentation. Executive producer, Tsui Hark. Written and directed by John Woo. Stars Chow Yun Fat, Ti Lung, Leslie Cheung and Young Pao I. Camera (color), Wong Wing Hang; editor, Kam Ma; music, Joseph Koo; art director, Bennie Liu; action director, Tung Wai; production supervisor, Paul Lai; post-production manager, Tony Chow. Reviewed at President theater, Hong Kong, Aug. 9, 1986. Running time: **98 MINS.**
(Cantonese soundtrack with English subtitles)

Hong Kong — A contemporary cop and gangster action drama burdened with an excess of practically everything except sex, "A Better Tomorrow" nevertheless should be a very potent boxoffice property for Cinema City.

Chow Yun Fat, the glamor boy who's no longer afraid of being ugly, and perennial teenager Leslie Cheung, who at 30 looks like an overaged spoiled youth imprisoned in a mature body, both overact in this one. But Ti Lung shines in his comeback role as he maintains a silent masculine presence and believably underplays his portrayal of a reformed ex-gangster. He has laced his portrayal with inner strength and vulnerability, despite his overdressed look. The trio make a formidable team of urban misfits.

Pic is a contrived bang-bang thriller with overdone violence and bloodshed.

It's a fine vehicle for the return from Taiwan of ex-Golden Harvest contract director John Woo ("Money Crazy," "Princess Cheung-ping") who evidently has changed his style from light comedy to the "macho" genre.

Based on the '60s storyline of an old Lung Kong (story of a discharged prisoner), film is about two brothers in conflicting roles, the outlaw and the cop. Leslie Cheung is a dedicated policeman who blames his elder brother (Ti Lung) for their father's death and for obstructing his career in the police force.

Chow Yun Fat is Ti Lung's ex-associate also betrayed by jealous subordinate Lee Tse Ho in the counterfeit syndicate. After serving a jail term in Taiwan, repentant Ti Lung returns to Hong Kong to lead a new life. He realizes soon enough a man with a past will have difficulties adjusting to a normal life.

For addicts of razzle-dazzle action and Cantonese dramatics, this summer entry is more than acceptable in popular cinemas showing local pulp. —*Mel.*

The Name Of The Rose
(WEST GERMAN-ITALIAN-FRENCH-COLOR)

A 20th Century Fox release of a Bernd Eichinger/Bernd Schaefers-Neue Constantin/Cristaldifilm/Fioms Ariane coproduction in association with ZDF. Produced by Bernd Eichinger. Executive producers, Thomas Schuehly, Jake Eberts. Coproducers, Franco Cristaldi, Alexandre Mnouchkine. Directed by Jean-Jacques Annaud. Stars Sean Connery, F. Murray Abraham. Screenplay, Andrew Birkin, Gerard Brach, Howard Franklin, Alain Godard, based on the novel by Umberto Eco; camera (color), Tonino Delli Colli; editor, Jane Seitz; music, James Horner; production design, Dante Ferretti; art direction, Giorgio Giovannini, Rainer Schaper; set decoration, Francesca Lo Schiavo; costume design, Gabriella Pescucci; sound (Dolby), Frank Jahn; special effects supervisor, Andriano Pischiutta; supervising makeup artist, Hasso Von Hugo; production executive, Anna Gross; associate producers, Pierre Hebey, Herman Weigel; assistant directors, Gianni Arduini, Victor Tourjansky; casting, Lynn Stalmaster and Associates, David Rubin, Gianni Arduini, Dominique Besnehard, Celestia Fox, Sabine Schroth. Reviewed at the 20th Century Fox Studios, L.A., Sept. 16, 1986. (MPAA Rating: R.) Running time: **130 MINS.**
William of Baskerville......Sean Connery
Bernardo Gui....... F. Murray Abraham
Adso of Melk............Christian Slater
Severinus..................Elya Baskin
Jorge de Burgos.....Feodor Chaliapin Jr.
Ubertino de Casale.......William Hickey
The Abbot...............Michaël Lonsdale
Salvatore ....Ron Perlman
Malachia.................Volker Prechtel
Remigio de Varagine...Helmut Qualtinger
The Girl...............Valentina Vargas

Hollywood — "The Name Of The Rose" is a sorrowfully mediocre screen version of Umberto Eco's surprise international best-selling novel. Confusingly written and sluggishly staged, this telling of a murder mystery in a 14th century abbey will certainly disappoint the book's readers and prove uninviting to uninitiated general audiences. Commerical prospects look soft.

Despite the remote setting and arcane aspects of the material, there is no reason why Eco's fastidiously researched 500-page novel couldn't have been made into an absorbing popular film — the essential mystery is as provocative as it is peculiar, and the characters comprise a lively and eccentric bunch of principal players.

The opportunity has been completely flubbed by director Jean-Jacques Annaud and his team of four (credited) screenwriters, as they struggle even to get the basics of the

story up on the screen, never mind the religious, historical and personal nuances, and niceties of cinematic style.

Tale has English Franciscan monk Sean Connery and his novice Christian Slater arriving at an Italian abbey in preparation for a conclave at which the future direction of the Catholic Church will be determined.

A series of murders at the massive edifice sours the atmosphere for the conference, and Connery, in the style of an aspiring Sherlock Holmes, undertakes an investigation of the deaths while more delegates continue to arrive.

One of the latecomers is F. Murray Abraham, an inquisitor who sees Satan behind every foul deed and who threatens to condemn his old rival Connery due to the latter's insistence on seeking a rational solution to the crimes.

Basic story, with its accompanying subplots and intellectual adornments, is meaty stuff, but Annaud, even with a striking medieval backdrop to work with, has staged it indifferently and with very little coherence.

Film is not a pleasure to watch. Tonino Delli Colli's lensing often appears distractingly dark, but much worse is the virtually haphazard, terribly jarring editing style. Frequency of cuts results in perhaps three times more shots than necessary or desirable to tell the story lucidly, and their random nature prevents pic from ever achieving any sort of rhythm.

At times, during an interior dialog scene, an exterior overview shot of the monastery will be inserted for no reason making one wonder what on earth the filmmakers are trying to convey. It's impossible to know in these cases whether responsibility for such awful editing rests with the cutter or the director for not covering himself properly, but result is aesthetically disastrous.

Also, the question occurs as to why nearly everyone in the film is made up to look like Klaus Kinski in "Nosferatu," or at least a close relation. Except for Connery and his charge, all the men, with their shaved heads, decaying teeth, creepy eyes and sickly skin, look like candidates for a chamber of horrors in a wax museum.

Connery lends dignity, intelligence and his lovely voice to the proceedings. His performance, however, along with some tantalizing E.M. Escher-style labyrinths in the interior of the abbey, are about the only blessings to be found in this plodding misfire. —*Cart.*

Me Hace Falta Un Bigote
(I Need A Mustache)
(SPANISH-COLOR/B&W)

An M. Summers-M2 Films-Bermúdez de Castro production. Executive producer, Paco Lara Polop. Written and directed by Manuel Summers. Camera (color, b&w), Tote Trenas; editor, Maria Elena Sainz de Rozas; music, Carlos Vizziello, David Summers; production manager, Helena Matas; sets, Gumersindo Andrés; makeup, Fernando Pérez. Reviewed at Cine Velázquez, Madrid, Sept. 4, 1986. Running time: **90 MINS.**
With: Jacob Echeverria, Paloma San Millan, Gregorio Garcia Morcillo, Manuel Summers, Paco Lara Polop, Pedro Civera.

Madrid — Opening scenes of this new pic by Manuel Summers are taken from his own highly acclaimed 1963 film "Del Rosa al Amarillo," which got him started on his career. After his more recent three candid camera features and some infelicitious earlier pics about love among adolescents, Summers here limns a film about the making of the film we are seeing.

The results are sometimes tinged with nostalgia (about 80% of pic is shot in black and white simulating the post-war era), occasionally droll and sometimes tenderly moving. Summers, as always, has a way with directing moppets, and these new youngsters are a pleasure to watch. The story within the story is kept easy to follow.

On a tv talk show, where Summers' first film has been shown, the panelists, which include the director, are asked to recall their first love affair. A few days later, Summers receives a letter from his first flame of 30 or 40 years ago. The wheels in his head start to spin, and he begins writing a script about a young boy from a rightwing family who has a crush on the grocer's daughter.

The pretty girl, in turn, has lost her heart to the matinee idol of the day, Mexican actor Jorge Negrete. Summers deftly leads us through the amusing puppy love affair, well documented against the reconstructed Spain of the times, occasionally bringing us back to the modern-day quest by the producer and director to find the moppet thesps who are to do the roles.

Item has a winning, simple charm to it, reminiscent of that captured in Summers' first film 23 years ago. Sadly, however, the expectations raised by that first film never have been fulfilled. This pic is largely a rehash of the first part of that fine film Summers made as a young man. —*Besa.*

Dead End Kids
(U.S.-DOCU-COLOR/B&W-16m)

A Mabou Mines production in association with Ikon Films. Produced by Marian Godfrey and Monty Diamond. Written and directed by JoAnne Akalaitis. Camera (color), Judy Irola; editor, Darren Kloomok; music, David Byrne, Philip Glass; production designer, John Arnone; sound editor, Margie Crimmins; costumes, Kristi Zea. Reviewed at the Toronto Festival of Festivals, Sept. 13, 1986. Running time: **87 MINS.**
With: Ellen McElduff, Ruth Malaczech, George Bartenieff, David Brisbin, B-St. John Schofield, Terry O'Reilly, Frederick Newmann.

Toronto — "Dead End Kids" serves up the ever-gnawing presence of nuclear holocaust in a compelling, inventive and caustically witty screen adaptation of the Mabou Mines play that ran at New York's Public Theater in 1980. Written and directed by Mabou Mines cofounder JoAnne Akalaitis, pic marks a red-hot film debut for the avant-garde director, who uses the best devices from her theatrical bag of tricks to make an accessible and disturbing docu without being preachy.

Although seemingly disjointed at the outset, the threads of the drama do blend into the thesis that in some ways the bomb already has transcended our collective unconscious and resulted in social fallout.

Akalaitis begins with a history of alchemy, tracing the medieval scientists' search for the philosopher's stone and then cuts to a cheapo 1950s tv show, "The Wonderful World Of Alchemy." The telling of the Faust story is transformed into a press conference headed by Gen. Groves of the Manhattan Project in 1945, rattling off details of the victorious New Mexico atomic bomb explosion. Then there's a hilarious black and white 1940s musical number, "Hubba Hubba," which reduces the atomic bomb detonation to song while musing "It's Mighty Smoky Over Tokyo."

The story of Marie Curie is also told, as an actress reenacts her discovery of radium intercut with archival photos of the Curies in their lab. A teacher reads to a few students about the horrific effects of nuclear explosions. A 1950s high school exhibit on "Atoms For Peace" displays wares made from nuclear power, while a tv hostess explains the "fission, fusion, fission" formula for making a homemade hydrogen bomb. A family points out nifty survival techniques in their homemade bomb shelter, capping the nuclear madness in our society.

A sleazy nightclub performer's shtick is crosscut throughout until in the finale, the comic calls on a naive audience member to manipulate a dead chicken while reading a government document on the "Effects of Radioactive Fallout on Livestock in the Event of Nuclear War." Sprinkled throughout are archival footage, pithy quotes from Jung and Bacon on knowledge and power, black and white pics of Hiroshima, and various presidential press conferences.

The Mabou Mines cast is a first-rate ensemble and each thesp glides deftly into a number of roles. Exceptional performances are extracted from Ellen McElduff as the singer, audience slouch, and bomb builder, David Brisbin as the lowlife lounge lizard, and Ruth Malaczech as Marie Curie.

The director uses all forms of theater here to propel her message about nuclear insanity. What it loses in the immediacy of a live presentation is gained in the tight editing of the information and performances.

The film was made for $500,000, but production values belie the low budget. Lighting and lensing are fine, as are the rich, medieval costumes in the simple sets. David Byrne and Philip Glass' score punctuates the fast pace toward nuclear destruction.

"Dead End Kids" already has a distribution deal with PBS, but it would benefit by a theatrical run in art houses as well. It's a palatable, worrisome, and entertaining film that tackles a tough subject with positive provocation. —Devo.

The Men's Club
(COLOR)

Distasteful portrait of male faults has limited audience appeal.

An Atlantic Releasing release. Produced by Howard Gottfried. Executive producers, Thomas Coleman, Michael Rosenblatt, John Harada. Directed by Peter Medak. Screenplay, Leonard Michaels, based on his novel; camera (CFI color), John Fleckenstein; editor, Cynthia Scheider, David Dresher, Bill Butler; music, Lee Holdridge; production design, Ken Davis; art director, Laurence Bennett; set decorator, Thomas Lee Roysden; costumes, Marianna Elliot, Peter Mitchell; sound, Jim Tannenbaum; assistant director, Roger Joseph Pugliese; associate producer, Jimsie Eason; casting, Barbra Claman. Reviewed at Atlantic screening room, L.A., Sept. 19, 1986. (MPAA Rating: R.) Running time: **100 MINS.**
Cavanaugh . . . . Roy Scheider
Harold Canterbury . . . . Frank Langella
Solly Berliner . . . . Harvey Keitel
Terry . . . . Treat Williams
Kramer . . . . Richard Jordan
Phillip . . . . David Dukes
Paul . . . . Craig Wasson
Nancy . . . . Stockard Channing
Jo . . . . Ann Wedgeworth
Teensy . . . . Jennifer Jason Leigh
Hannah . . . . Cindy Pickett
Page . . . . Ann Dusenberry
Lake . . . . Penny Baker
Felicia . . . . Gina Gallegos
Stacey . . . . Claudia Cron
Stella . . . . Rebecca Bush
Redhead . . . . Gwen Welles

Hollywood — Those who think men are immature, destructive, insensitive and basically animals may find "The Men's Club" great fun. Others are likely to balk at the film's contrived and dated treatment of the battle between the sexes. This is a club few will want to join.

Film is a distasteful piece of work that displays the worst in men. Leonard Michaels' screenplay is all warts and no insight, full of self-loathing for the gender.

In addition, filmmaking is as tired as the material. Pic plays like a stageplay, so static is Peter Medak's direction. Group of friends nearing age 40 get together and for most of the film's 100 minutes the camera is on their heads talking.

And in the background, contributing to the film's 1970s encounter group mentality, is a trite and bouncy score that would be more appropriate in an Arthur Murray dance hall. Filmmakers have tried to create a group of swinging men but wound up with a bunch of creeps.

Talents of the large cast are squandered on lines like "I feel in love with a woman I couldn't find the next day," and other such platitudes. Mix of friends is also unlikely with thinly drawn charcters.

Leader of the group is Cavanaugh (Roy Scheider), supposedly a retired baseball star who looks too unhealthy to have ever played anything more strenuous than cards. He's a hopeless philanderer who is spoon-fed a lesson in life.

Totally weird is Richard Jordan as a therapist who seems in need of one. He has a maniacal gaze and proves he's capable of anything when he tries out a set of throwing knives in his dining room. Harvey Keitel adds a bit of class to the proceedings as a working class tough guy with a soft center.

Others along for the ride include Treat Williams as a nondescript doctor. Most grating of the bunch is David Dukes as an insufferably stiff college prof. Gathering takes a turn for the worse when lawyer Frank Langella takes the boys to a "house of affection" where they can wallow in their own self-pity and failure.

Fortunately the woman are the proverbial whores with a heart of gold. Without much characterization to work with, Ann Dusenberry is particularly lovely.

What, it turns out, men want is love, but they don't know where to find it. All the noise is just soul bearing without any soul. —Jagr.

Star Crystal
(COLOR)

Copout space opera.

A New World Pictures release from Star Crystal Prods. of an Eric Woster production. Produced by Woster. Executive producers, Charles Linza, Frank Rhodes. Directed by Lance Lindsay. Screenplay, Lindsay, from story by Woster, Lindsay; camera (color), Robert Caramico; editor, Woster; music, Doug Katsaros; sound, Clyde Sorensen; production design, Steve Sardanis; set decoration, Jay Burkhart; assistant director, Eric Weston; production manager, Edwin Oliver; special visual effects, Lewis Abernathy; visual effects consultant, Chuck Comisky; second unit director, Woster; model construction supervisor, John Coats; special makeup effects, Ken Diaz, Woster; costume design, Mary Ann Bozer; associate producers, Thomas Frantz, Don E. Porter, Robert Badger; mattes, Dave Goetz. Reviewed on NW Video vidcassette, N.Y., Aug. 30, 1986. (MPAA Rating: R.) Running time: **92 MINS.**
With: C. Jutson Campbell, Faye Bolt, John Smith, Taylor Kingsley, Marcia Linn, Eric Moseng, Lance Bruckner, Thomas William, Don Kingsley, Robert Allen, Emily Longstreth, Lisa Goulian, Charles Linza, Frank Alexander.

"Star Crystal" is another imitation of "Alien," which, as sci-fi fans know, was itself highly derivative of both earlier fiction (A.E. van Vogt's "Voyage Of The Space Beagle") and cinema ("It! The Terror From Beyond Space"). Filmed in 1983 and regionally released last April, "Crystal" is wimpier than most "Alien" clones and rendered redundant by the current availability of the real thing in the form of the hit sequel "Aliens."

Unidentified cast of male and female space jockeys escapes from an exploding space station in a shuttlecraft which two months earlier had become infested by an alien creature picked up during a routine Mars expedition. The creature, which possesses a crystal that it uses as a power supply and computer, grows and kills the crew off one by one until communication is established. Disappointing payoff has the alien turning into Mr. Nice Guy and selflessly sacrificing its own future to help the surviving humans get back towards Earth.

Weak story material and subpar acting sink this film, wasting some rather impressive model work. Makeup effects are variable, with phony looking corpses but an interesting design for the sorrowful-eyed monster. Silly end credit states "Filmed entirely in Space." A clever suspense gimmick has all the chambers in the shuttlecraft connected by narrow tunnels, a realistic design element which makes for scary chases on all-fours when the monster is lethal. —Lor.

And The Pursuit Of Happiness
(U.S.-DOCU-COLOR)

A Pretty Mouse Films production. Produced, directed and narrated by Louis Malle. Camera (color), Malle; editor, Nancy Baker; sound, Danny Michael, Neelan Crawford. Reviewed at Toronto Festival of Festivals, Sept. 11, 1986. Running time: 90 MINS.

Toronto — From Russian Jews in Brooklyn to Vietnamese settlers in Houston, Louis Malle took his camera across the U.S. on a three-month sojourn to explore the breadth of experiences of immigrants to this country. The French director returns to the docu form in an assured, sincere way with "And The Pursuit Of Happiness," with mixed results.

From the outset, as he interviews a Rumanian emigré doing a marathon walk to celebrate Texas' sesquicentennial, Malle introduces himself through voiceover narration and opines, "We immigrants come with a lot of dreams and work as hard as we can to achieve them."

His theory is that the immigrant experience runs the gamut from elation at freedom to a nostalgic longing for the homeland. Immigrants alternately are accepted as part of the community, as in the case of Dr. Diem, a Vietnamese physician practicing in a small town in Nebraska, or discriminated against with a passion, as are the Indochinese occupants of a city housing development for blacks in Houston.

Most of Malle's subjects are unknowns, which works well as a technique of getting real people to bare their souls. Malle has established an extraordinarily comfortable rapport with the speakers, and they are completely at ease as they face the camera, share their goals, and invite the helmer into their homes.

He visits a West Ghana immigrant who started his own cab company in Dallas, a stage actor from the Soviet Union starting his "second life" in the U.S., as well as a Cuban boat person who came to Miami in 1980 and never looked back. He chats with the first NASA astronaut not born in the U.S. and with a Korean immigrant who's applying to Ivy League universities while helping out his parents in their vegetable store. One immigrant sums it up: "I don't like the freedom without direction in the U.S., but to get the worldly things is better."

Malle includes an unbelievably problem-free immigration encounter at New York's Kennedy Airport, where a cheery immigration officer welcomes with ease a family of Cambodian refugees. He also pays an unintentionally hilarious visit to General Somoza's manse in Miami in which Somoza's son shows off all the costly "movables" they took with them when they fled Nicaragua. The general is becoming a "typical suburban American," observes Malle.

While West Indian poet Derek Walcott's intelligent opinions that the U.S. is an aggressive democracy are sharp, somehow they seem misplaced among the other interviewees.

Malle peppers his narration with occasional statistics about certain immigrant populations, but is not consistent with providing facts throughout. There is also not enough of an historical overview. Curiously, he only included one Washington immigration official's view.

. The narration is often witty here. When Malle's camera pans Cambodian refugees bringing rice into the country he states, "For them food is survival; for the U.S. government it is microbes." He also captures Southeast Asian refugees in an English-language class repeating in unison, "Let's go to Wendy's and have a hamburger."

In spite of its gaps, "And The Pursuit Of Happiness" should score well with art house audiences across the country, as it is an earnest, well-edited, and entertaining panorama of opinions and slices of life of new wave settlers. The cozy home-movie initmacy is a plus.
—*Devo.*

Il 45mo Parallelo
(45th Parallel)
(ITALIAN-B&W)

An MVM Film production. Produced by Paolo Pagnoni. Directed by Attilio Concari. Screenplay, Concari, Davide Ferrario; camera (b&w, Ilford, Technicolor lab), Renato Tafuri; editor, Michael Hesser; music, Manuel De Sica; art direction, Francy Bertagnolli. Reviewed at Luciano Vittori screening room, Rome, Aug. 25, 1986. (In Venice Film Fest, Italian Showcase.) Running time: **85 MINS.**
Tom . . . . Thom Hoffman
Anna . . . . Valeria D'Obici
Andrea . . . . Andrea Puglisi
Salati . . . . Enzo Robutti

Rome — To describe the countryside around Parma as halfway between the North Pole and the Equator may seem whimsical in the extreme; original, but a little pretentious. "The 45th Parallel" is all those things, with the balance coming out on the positive side. This year's esthete's entry in Venice's Italian Showcase, pic is a first feature directed by Attilio Concari, a Milan fashion photographer.

Not by chance, the way "Parallel" is lensed is the most striking thing about it. Renato Tafuri's black and white camerawork is a knockout and takes center stage in a film without much story. Unjustly, the choice to go b&w will penalize pic at the national b.o.; it deserves art-circuit playoff to find its appreciators.

In line with the photography angle, hero Thom Hoffman is a professional shutterbug, taking documentary-style pictures of the local Parma-Gothic farmers while he's between assignments. Anna (Valeria D'Obici) is a wide-eyed, seasonal waitress curious about everything, especially the good-looking foreigner Thom. Fun but no beauty, she makes more progress with a little boy (Andrea Puglisi),

another out-of-towner spending the summer with his aunts, who run the friendly local trattoria. Between fishing for catfish in the river, rolling down hills, and slaloming around in Thom's dusty jeep, the summer passes.

"45th Parallel" is an unabashed atmosphere film, and whether it's the location or the filmmaker's native sensibility, that atmosphere often harks back to early Bernardo Bertolucci (also Parma-bred). Fostering this impression is the hip, off-beat trio of characters and a pervasive use of opera on the soundtrack.

If Anna objects that Thom's posed peasants look unnatural, what are we to make of pic's unashamed folklore at mealtimes stuffed with prosciutto, tortellini, and a waiter who bursts into highlights from Verdi? Like its hero Thom, film can't resist the urge to document the eccentric locals and their half-mad preoccupations, such as building a speed-boat engine that "sings like Callas." When a mad fisherman (Enzo Robutti) is inserted into the fiction, however, pathos and humor both fall flat. Innovative editing and a well-chosen collection of pop tunes and modern music concord with the spirit of the rest. — *Yung.*

My Man Adam
(COLOR)

Unimpressive daydreaming comedy.

A Tri-Star Pictures release from Tri-Star-Delphi III Prods. of a Mount Co. production. Produced by Renée Missel, Gail Stayden and Paul Aratow. Executive producer, Thom Mount. Directed by Roger L. Simon. Screenplay, Simon, Missel; camera, (color), Donald McAlpine; editor, Don Zimmerman; music, Sylvester Levay; production design, Ferdinando Scarfiotti; production supervisor, Richard Hashimoto; costume design, Robert Weiner; casting, Judith Holstra, Marcia Ross. Reviewed on Key Video cassette, Aug. 26, 1986. (MPAA Rating: R.) Running time: **84 MINS.**

Adam Swit . . . .Raphael Sbarge
Sabrina . . . . .Page Hannah
Elaine Swit . . . . .Veronica Cartwright
Jerry Swit . . . . .Dave Thomas
Leroy .Charlie Barnett
Tina Swit . . . . .Kelly Wolf

The makers of "My Man Adam" took a good cast, a few interesting characters and some pleasant scenery and stuck them all into a film with no story. Slapdash plot development turns what could have been a diverting comedy into a hopeless muddle. Regionally released in October 1985, pic (reviewed here for the record) will best be remembered as an early vehicle for lead thesp Raphael Sbarge, who shows real potential despite the circumstances.

Adam Swit is a lad who dreams of being an anchorman but in fact is

a 17-year-old constantly nagged by his money-hungry parents (finely portrayed by Veronica Cartwright and Dave Thomas) and sex-starved sis. Their nouveau riche L.A. home, and sets throughout, are a testament to Ferdinando Scarfiotti's strong production design.

When Adam isn't being attacked at home he's attacked at school, a strange cross between a paramilitary camp and a liberal playground where courses such as designer jean design comprise the curriculum.

To escape the realities of his existence, Adam dreams of exotic and dangerous situations in which he winds up with a beautiful girl. The femme in these fantasies appears at Adam's school one day as a transfer student (Page Hannah). Their first date ends when they come upon a teacher beaten up in the parking lot, plunging them into a conspiracy with all the danger of "Who Squeezed The Charmin?"

At this point she warns Adam, "I want you to be careful with those guys because this could get stupid," truer words never uttered in a film. Reality falls by the wayside, along with logic and commonsense, and this bad pic finally runs free.

One of the stranger loose ends of note turns out to be the narrator, jive-talking Leroy (Charlie Barnett), who says things like, "Now this situation be looking bad for Adam," and is finally a peripheral character at best.—*Roy.*

Bandera Negra
(Black Flag)
(SPANISH-COLOR)

An Altube production. Executive producer, Joseba Prieto Atxa. Directed by Pedro Olea. Screenplay, Olea, Rafael Castellano; camera (Fujicolor), Carlos Suárez; editor, José Salcedo; music, Carmelo Bernaola; sets, Ramiro Gómez; production manager, Daniel Vega; make-up, Manuel Martin. Reviewed at Cine Tivoli, Madrid, Sept. 11, 1986. Running time: **88 MINS.**
Patxi . . . . .Alfredo Landa
Esteban . . . . .Imanol Arias
Begoña . . . . .Virginia Mataix
Don Javier . . . . .Carlos Lucena
Also with: Luis Ostalot, Juan Jesús Valverde, Alito Rodgers Jr.

Madrid — Subsidized by the Basque regional government and ETB, the Basque tv, this pic nonetheless steers clear of grinding any apparent political axe, as have some Basque films of the past. Pedro Olea, who has made a score of "serious" films over the last two decades, here turns his talents to an adventure yarn in a minor key which holds one's interest throughout but lacks punch.

. Yarn revolves about an out-of-work skipper, recently become a widower; his pretty waitress daughter, a petty ex-con rip-off artist who's a ship's machinist, and the rather tamely unscrupulous owner of a shipping line doing illegal arms

business with a corrupt African country. (Pic was partly shot in Guinea, the other part in Bilbao.)

While the elderly ship owner is making advances to the waitress, her father and the machinist, who have become pals, get embroiled in local African intrigues and land in the clink. The daughter flies down to try to help, but shortly after her arrival the father is killed. Balance of pic, back in the Basquelands, shows how the machinist and the waitress, now lovers, reap their revenge on the ship owner, who was behind the whole plot. Pic ends on an almost humorous note, rather out of keeping with the rest of the film.

Fine thesping by Imanol Arias as the tough machinist, who livens up the screen each time he's in a frame, and Alfredo Landa, as the rather too lachrymose papa. Technical credits up to crack, with Olea keeping the pacing lively, though lacking are some more spectacular scenes that would enhance the action.
—*Besa.*

De Wisselwachter
(The Pointsman)
(DUTCH-COLOR)

A Concorde Film release of a Jos Stelling Filmprodukties production. Executive producer, Stanley Hillebrandt. Directed by Stelling. Stars Jim Van Der Woude. Screenplay, George Brugmans, Hans De Wolf, Stelling, based on the novel by Jean-Paul Franssens; camera (color), Frans Bromet, Theo Van de Sande, Paul Van Den Bos, Goert Giltaij; editor, Rimko Haanstra; music, Michel Mulders; art direction, Gert Brinkers. Reviewed at Venice Film Festival, Aug. 30, 1986. Running time: **95 MINS.**
Pointsman . . . . .Jim Van Der Woude
Woman . . . . .Stéphane Excoffier
Engineer . . . . .John Kraaykamp
Postman . . . . .Josse De Pauw
Asst. engineer . . . . .Ton Van Dort

Venice — Fans of Jos Stelling's previous feature, the stops-out surrealist comedy "De Illusionist," will have no trouble getting into the way-out, wordless representation of "The Pointsman." If anything, Stelling has taken great strides in the direction of narrative coherency, and even emotion. This new work could garner him an audience in foreign art houses willing to handle experimental films.

The pointsman of the title (Jim Van Der Woude) is a dull simpleton living in some undefined Highlands, far from the nearest city. He is slavishly devoted to his job, which is switching the rare train that passes by his railway lodge from one track to another. He never talks — but speech is quite rare among the rest of the cast, too.

One day something happens to interrupt the unnoticed monotony of the pointsman's life: a mysterious femme fatale (Stéphane Excoffier) gets off a train by accident, and ends up staying in the railway lodge for the rest of the film. In this introductory section, the duet of glances, gestures, and costume (the woman is lavishly dressed and made up, the pointsman is in scratchy leather bumpkin's attire) is impeccably handled, and the actors subtly manipulate their characters like puppets, giving the old boy-meets-girl situation a refreshingly original twist. The appearance of the villain, a fascistic postman (Josse De Pauw) intent on getting his hands on the woman, eventually sets off an act of violence that brutally terminates the couple's idyll, and leads the pointsman to a sad, frozen death.

Despite its promising beginning, film slacks off the farther it goes. The characters' burgeoning feelings of attraction to each other develop into drama, too tenuous to keep from running out of steam. For this simple story, which could have been told in many ways, Stelling chooses the most difficult. Except for a few words of French from the lady, story unfolds via camerawork and pantomime only, which is very hard to sustain at feature length. It is an interesting failure anyway, and points to a director in the process of development. — *Yung.*

Mix-Up
(Meli-Melo)
(FRENCH-DOCU-COLOR-16m)

An Antenne-2 production with the participation of the Ministry of Culture. Produced by Pascale Brougnot. Directed by Françoise Romand. Camera (color), Emile Navarro; editor, Maguy Alziari; music, Nicolas Frize; sound, Philippe Places. Reviewed at the Toronto Festival of Festivals, Sept. 12, 1986. Running time: **65 MINS.**
Interviewer: Claire Moreau Shirbon.
(English soundtrack)

Toronto — Made last year for French television, this is a thorough, curiously arch documentary about a freak case of two babies having been mixed up at birth and raised by the wrong parents. Okay for fests and special exhibition formats with a sociological slant, pic might also fit on tv and cable where esoteric fare is welcome.

Employing extremely self-conscious "staging" devices which sometimes involve mirrors, transparent screens and different planes of lighting, first-time director Françoise Romand relates, with great deliberation, the story of the Wheelers and the Rylatts. Mothers of both families entered a nursing home in Nottingham, England, to deliver children at virtually the same time in 1936. Due to a paperwork foulup, they took home the wrong daughters, something Mrs. Wheeler always strongly suspected, but a possibility entirely discounted by Mrs. Rylatt.

Girls finally met their real parents when they were 20, and docu both tells the tale in perhaps excessive detail, considering its limited ramifications, and explores the feelings of all those concerned, particularly the mothers and daughters.

Blood tests and other attempts to resolve the question over the years proved inconclusive, and the problem with this particular case is that, unlike the occasional celebrated experiments with twins raised in diverse societies, it doesn't illustrate any particular sociological point.

Therefore, the only pressing interest lies in discovering how the mixup was accepted by the two potential "victims," the daughters themselves. One, who still seems somewhat insecure, admits that "it's left its mark," while the mother of the other one insists that "it brought a great enrichment to all our experiences" by enlarging their sphere of relations and people close to them. Pic itself takes an upbeat attitude about the result. — *Cart.*

The Aurora Encounter
(COLOR)

Mild sci-fi Western.

A New World Pictures release of a Jim McCullough Prods. production. Executive producers, Fred Kuehnert, M. Sanousi. Produced and directed by Jim McCullough Sr. Screenplay/coproduced by Jim McCullough Jr.; camera (Allied & WBS color), Joseph Wilcots; editor, Sheri Galloway; music, Ron F. Diulio; sound, Paul Taylor; production design, Drew E. Hunter; assistant director, Chuck Comisky; visual effects, Ken Jones, Cinevisual Consultants; stunt coordinator, Gary Paul; associate producer, Phil Flora. Reviewed on NW Video vidcassette, N.Y., Aug. 27, 1986. (MPAA Rating: PG.) Running time: **90 MINS.**
Charlie Hawkins . . . . Jack Elam
Sheriff . . . . Peter Brown
Alain . . . . Carol Bagdasarian
Irene . . . . Dottie West
Spaceman . . . . Mickey Hays
Preacher . . . . Charles B. Pierce
Governor . . . . Spanky McFarland
Texas ranger . . . . Will Mitchell
Sue Beth . . . . Mindy Smith
Ginger . . . . Carly McCullough

"The Aurora Encounter" is a pleasant, very mild entry in the unusual genre of sci-fi Westerns. Second recent New World release from the filmmaking McCulloughs, who earlier made "Mountaintop Motel Massacre," opened regionally in March and quickly moved to its proper home, the video stores.

With full white beard and ample girth, Jack Elam has fun as the teller of this tall tale concerning a spaceman visiting the small town of Aurora, Texas in the 1800s. Amidst antics by the friendly little guy who brings a magic crystal with him, there is a minor plotline of school marm Alain, pronounced "Elaine" (Carol Bagdasarian), inheriting her dad's newspaper and using it to play

up the spaceman's visit while championing women's rights on the side.

A corny, melodramatic climax (plus sentimental denouement) spoils the otherwise acceptable picture which boasts okay visual effects. Diminutive Mickey Hays, a bald youngster with genuinely bizarre features made up here to resemble a pint-sized Max Schreck of "Nosferatu," adds to the sci-fi premise. Rest of the cast is interesting, with Bagdasarian a feisty heroine, country singer Dottie West adding sex appeal and former Our Gang comedies star Spanky McFarland popping in as Texas' very short governor. — *Lor.*

Debshishu
(The Child God)
(INDIAN-COLOR/B&W)

A National Film Development presentation and production. Written and directed by Uptlendu Chakraborty. Camera (color, b&w), Soumendu Roy; music, Chakraborty. Reviewed at the Morettina Center, Locarno Film Fest, Aug. 14, 1986. Running time: **100 MINS.**
With: Smita Patil, Sadhu Meher, Rohini Hattangady, Om Puri.

Locarno — The subject of "Debshishu" would fit quite nicely into a folk comedy. A peasant who can't get rid of his monstrous three-headed baby soon enough, discovers him later enthroned as a sort of deity by a fast-talking con man, making a fortune from the gifts brought over to the freak by the ignorant peasants who believe he possesses supernatural powers. The peasant goes back home to his wife, beats her up and demands that she give birth to another baby like this, for he wants to get rich too.

Director Uptalendu Chakraborty opts, however, for the tragic aspects of this tale. The parents are poor, destitute farmers, all their possessions are swept away by the flood, their rich relatives won't help, and it is misery and despair which drives the hapless father to act as he does. There are references galore to political corruption ruling in all the parties, the poor are good, the rich are bad and traditions chain them all to their destiny. No hope is possible as long as the heavy load of religion and age-old superstitions isn't removed.

Well intentioned, but rather naive in its approach, the film is better when it deals with the details of daily life, but fails to make any character, except that of the long-suffering mother, Sita, come alive.

The film employs flashbacks several times in order to tell its story, the flood memories being in black and white, all the rest in color. In spite of these niceties, the main appeal of the film lies in its folkloric

nature, and in its sincere compassion for its characters. — *Edna.*

Chuzhaja, Belaja i Rjaboj
(The Wild Dove)
(SOVIET-COLOR/B&W)

Produced by Kazach Film Studios. Written and directed by Sergei Soloviev. Camera (color, b&w), Youri Klimenko; art direction, Marxen Gaukman-Sverdlov; music, Isaak Schvartz. Reviewed at Venice Film Festival, Aug. 31, 1986. Running time: **98 MINS.**
With: Slava Iliutschenko, Sergei Garmache, Soultan Banov, Vladimi Steklov, Ludmila Savelieva.

Venice — Venerable Russian helmer Sergei Soloviev ("100 Days After Childhood") sets his tale of a boy struggling for manhood in Kazakhstan, 1946, the time and place of exiles in the Stalinist period.

Camera pyrotechnics and the latest editing crazes give "The Wild Dove" a modern, up-to-the-minute look, but have little to add to the story, too fragile to fight its way through walls of alternating color and black and white. Tantalizingly, submerged under the surface, potentially involving characters fail to spring to life and imbue film with some human warmth.

Distancing itself from the audience seems to be the film's intention. Opening and closing it is a mysterious frame — newsreel footage of an astronaut in outer space looking back at the Earth, while a subdued voice that seems to come from the other side of the Apocalypse leads us into the Kazach story.

Using deliberately grainy airplane film stock alternated with blurry soft-focus lensing and a wild gamut of randomly changing color tints, Soloviev introduces the inhabitants of a small provincial town, who were evacuated during the war and now are filtering back, laden with their pain and losses. Vania, the young hero of the tale, is a natural leader, son of a painter who has come back from the war with one arm and a serious brain injury. Despite his handicap he is a sensitive, morally upright man, tragically unable to help the woman he loves, an exiled actress whose husband has deserted her. Like some fragile character in a play, unable to adjust to lonely poverty, she kills herself.

Vania's story is told next. In a town whose inhabitants' only recreation and joy seems to be collecting pigeons (and selling them to each other for high prices), Vania captures a legendary white dove. Almost immediately it's stolen by a gang of hoodlums, who seem to be in league with the town's new authorities. In a final twist, Vania's father debunks all his son's fantasies and shows the "conspiracy" to be nothing more than poor, broken old men with a passion for pigeons. Son frees dove.

Though the results may be questionable, camera technique is masterful and much of film is visually a delight. In its best moments, "Dove" gets across the bitter taste of a victory that means only desolation.— *Yung.*

Mord i mörket
(Murder In The Dark)
(DANISH-COLOR)

A Nordisk Film release of Nordisk Film with Danish Film Institute (Peter Poulsen) production. Directed by Sune Lund-Sörensen. Stars Michael Falch, Ole Ernst. Screenplay, Erik Balling, Henning Bahs, Sune Lund-Sörensen, based on novel by Dan Turéll; camera (Eastmancolor), Claus Loof; editor, Leif Axel Kjeldsen; production design and special effects, Peter Höimark; music, Michael Falck (theme), Pete Repete; sound, Michael Dela, others; costumes, Annelise Hauberg; assistant director, Tom Hedegaard. Reviewed at the Palads, Copenhagen, Sept. 17, 1986. Running time: 96 MINS.

The Reporter . . . . Michael Falch
Bille . . . . Ove Sprogöe
Police lieutenant . . . . Ole Ernst
Editor-in-chief . . . . Morten Grunwald
Ole Kok . . . . Tommy Kentner
Hanne . . . . Kine Knutzon
Barbara . . . . Lise-Lotte Norup
Bartender . . . . Peter Schröder
Cabbie . . . . Ahmed Rahmani
Transvestite . . . . John Martinus
Kaspersen . . . . Hans Henrik Voetman
   Also with: Bent Warburg, Gorm Valentin, Martin Spang Olsen, Benny Bundgaard, Jörn Budolfsen, Arne Hansen, Benny Juhlin, William Kisum, Kit Eichler.

Copenhagen — "Murder In The Dark" is a tribute picture based on a tribute novel. Object of the adulatin is the combined oeuvre of Raymond Chandler and Dashiell Hammett as they have been established in both popular and intellectual minds via books and films. Dan Turéll, with tongue in cheek; wrote the original novel about a tough, hard-drinking, womanizing but ever-so-straight hombre, this time a freelance crime reporter, walking down Copenhagen's mean streets and cleaning them up with nary a helping hand from the police.

A teenage girl is forced into prostitution and heroin addiction. Her good friend, a cook and occasional jazz pianist, gets shot. An elderly second-hand book store owner shakes his head in commiseration with the noble poor who have to live in this red light district. He is also owner of two old-fashioned Smith & Wessons and hands one of them to the crime reporter. This at a time when the reporter is himself being chased by the cops as a murder suspect.

When he isn't too drunk, the reporter plays a mean blues on tenor sax. A tape of the music he made with the late cook also contains evidence against The Thin One, the shadowy organizer of dope traffic and crime in general, living in splen-

did isolation from the squalor he causes. Now, who gets the tape? Who gets to The Thin One first? Certainly not the fumbling cops, and maybe not the reporter either who is apt to get beaten up at crucial moments.

Story has a nice, off-beat and reasonably sentimental denouement. It is also good on blue note moods and is handsomely produced. Director Sune Lund-Sörensen has a deft hand with the setting up of action scenes. He also knows how to make his actors handle clichés to come off with a fresh shine. What bogs him down is a screenplay with too many loose ends and a lack of the essential abstract mystery and absurd lyricism of the genre.

All the plots are driven home with ham-fisted glee, but Michael Falch has tough guy good looks to convince as a son of Bogart. The women of the plot are given remarkably little to work with. While item obviously is headed for rich rewards locally, it hardly matches the standard of the general U.S. tv crime meller fare. It is an added irritant that it is literally seen through a lens darkly to an extent where long stretches are to be discerned as shadow boxing only. —*Kell.*

Half Moon Street
(COLOR)

Unbelievable melodrama.

A 20th Century Fox release of an RKO/Edward R. Pressman presentation in association with Showtime-The Movie Channel. Produced by Geoffrey Reeve. Executive producers, Edward R. Pressman, David Korda. Directed by Bob Swaim. Stars Sigourney Weaver, Michael Caine. Screenplay, Swaim, Edward Behr, based on novel "Dr. Slaughter" by Paul Theroux; camera (Technicolor), Peter Hannan; editor, Richard Marden; music, Richard Harvey; production design, Anthony Curtis; art direction, Peter Williams; set decorator, Peter Young; costumes, Louise Frogley; sound, Robin Gregory; assistant director, Michael Zimbrich; associate producer, John Davis; casting, Nancy Klopper. Reviewed at 20 Century Fox studio, L.A., Sept. 18, 1986. (MPAA Rating: R.) Running time: 90 MINS.

Lauren Slaughter . . . . . . Sigourney Weaver
Lord Bulbeck . . . . Michael Caine
General Newhouse . . . . . Patrick Kavanagh
Hugo Van Arkady . . . . Keith Buckley
Karim Hatami . . . . Nadim Sawalha
Bill Rafferty . . . . Angus MacInnes
Tom Haldane . . . . Michael Elwyn
Rex Lanham . . . . Jasper Jacob

Hollywood — "Half Moon Street" is a half-baked excuse for a film that is redeemed not a whit by having Sigourney Weaver and Michael Caine in the starring roles. B.o. prospects look dim.

Script, based on Paul Theroux' thriller "Dr. Slaughter," has been rendered nonsensical and incoherent by screenwriters Edward Behr and Bob Swaim.

Swaim also directed, or rather misdirected "Half Moon Street," his first film in English and a far fall from "La Balance," which earned him the prestigious César (France's equivalent of the Oscar).

Pic has a plot that borders on incredulity to begin with and, unlike most other thrillers that somehow neatly explain the inexplicable, this one ends up a complete morass.

Weaver plays Dr. Slaughter, a scholar at the Middle East Institute in London who turns to working as an escort to supplement her paltry income.

Escort translates to whoring and mostly with well-paying Mideastern customers, one of whom (Nadim Sawalha) likes her as much for her brain as her body and sets her up at his swanky apartment on Half Moon Street.

Weaver plays one tough cookie with no soft edges, insisting to the escort service she use her real name because she's not ashamed to let her "dates" know she's also a Ph.D, and not just a pretty plaything.

Weaver was supposed to portray an intelligent, independent woman with no hangups about sex and nudity, but only scenes showing the latter two remain in the film.

She manages to avoid any emotional attachments with her clients until she arrives one rainy night to be the paid guest of Lord Bulbeck, played competently if uninvolving-

ly by Caine.

Caine is somehow mixed up with Arabs in a convoluted scheme involving a wealthy British banker (Keith Buckley), a senior official with the British Foreign Office (Michael Elwyn), his nephew (Jasper Jacob), a high-ranking American diplomat (Angus MacInnes) and a few other turncoats all taking meetings on the q.t. where their expository dialog must have been left on the cutting room floor.

That leaves Weaver high and dry wondering what happened to lover boy Caine at the same time she's managing to keep up a full schedule of nightly rounds on the Arab party circuit and elsewhere.

Somehow she becomes inextricably and unwittingly wound up in his dealings, although it's never adequately revealed to the audience just how.

Of course, there's the burning question of whether she and Caine can be together in the end.

After sitting through all that's gone before, who cares?—*Brit.*

Das Schweigen des Dichters
(The Silence Of The Poets)
(WEST GERMAN-COLOR)

A Filmverlag der Autoren release of an Edgar Reitz Filmproduktions, in coproduction with Westdeutscher Rundfunkt. Produced by Edgar Reitz. Executive producer, Inge Richter. Written and directed by Peter Lilienthal, from a story by Abraham B. Yohoshua. Camera (color), Justus Pankau; editor, Siegrun Jäger; music, Claus Bantzer; art direction, Charlie Leon, Franz Bauer; costumes, Rina Doron; sound, Manfred Arbter, Uli Winkler. Reviewed at Vence Film Festival (In Competition), Sept. 2, 1986. Running time: 98 MINS.

Jacob . . . . Jakov Lind
Gideon . . . . Len Ramras
Gideon as a child . . . . Daniel Kedem
   Also with: Towje Kleiner, Vladimir Weigl, Barbara Lass, Gudrun Weichenhanh, Roberto Polac, Jacob Ben-Sira, Peter Freistadt, Mischa Natan.

Venice — A gentle, atmospheric film content to describe the relations between an aging poet who won't write and his mentally retarded son, based on Abraham B. Yehoshua's short story, "The Silence Of The Poets" was shot in Israel by director Peter Lilienthal and his German crew. This sensitive, compassionate view of an odd couple living out the years in rainy Tel Aviv should be a natural pickup for tv, and with the right handling could play in art house situations.

Jacob (Jakov Lind) is a graying poet of some renown. Why he has put down his pen is never explained, though it has something to do with the tension of the period following the Yom Kippur War with its enervating cycle of battles and truces. Without directly talking about war, Lilienthal charges the whole film with the devastation of the times.

This provides the background for a moving relationship between father and son Gideon (played with winning instinctiveness by Yank newcomer Len Ramras). Born by accident when Jacob and his wife were already old, Gideon is, in the eyes of most, a troublesome child who should be put in an insititution; for Jacob, he's "a borderline case," and he refuses to let him go. After the death of the wife, and his daughter's marriage, Jacob lives to take care of the backward boy. As time goes by, it's Jacob who grows feebler, and Gideon — unable to carry on at school, but taught to cook and keep house — looks after the old man.

First half of film is in perfect balance with its respectfully observed characters, who are understated and convincing. In the second half, tone slips a notch toward forced comedy, when 17-year-old Gideon learns his father was a poet and strains to make him start writing again. Naively thinking his presence is what blocks the creative process, the boy takes to disappearing during the day, after setting out sharpened pencils and writing paper. All this unfamiliar activity and decisiveness jars with the delicate portrait that has been built up of Gideon, when he suddenly starts traveling places on buses, working, carousing, and taking his father's unpublished work to a vanity press.

Jacob's response is to sell the old house they live in, retire from his job, and make plans to end his days travelling, without his constant burden. By this point film is on its way to a happy ending.

A lively editing style and pro lensing keep the pic watchable and swift-moving. Actors are so natural they seem to be playing themselves (and indeed Jakov Lind, an Austrian writer conscripted for the father role, is). — Yung.

Vasectomy: A Delicate Matter
(COLOR)

Moronic attempt at comedy.

A Seymour Borde & Associates release of a Vandom Intl. Pictures production. Produced by Robert Burge, Lou Wills. Executive producers, Glen Guilett, Clint Hendricks. Directed by Burge. Screenplay, Robert Hilliard, Burge; camera (United color), Gary Thieltges; editor, Beth Conwell; music, Fred Karlin; art director, Terry Welden, Bruce Cameron; assistant director, Wills; associate producer, Beverly Dixon. Reviewed at Mann Westwood Theater, Westwood, Calif., Sept. 27, 1986. (MPAA Rating: PG-13.) Running time: **90 MINS.**
Gino ....Paul Sorvino
Det. Edwards ....Abe Vigoda
Anna ....Cassandra Edwards
Theo Marshall..............Lorne Greene
George ....Gary Raff
Regine ....Ina Balin
Mr. Cromwell ....Frank Aletter

Mrs. Ellison ....Catherine Battistone
Mildred .:.............Suzanne Charney
Francis ....John Moskoff
Marie ....Janet Wood

Hollywood — The odd thing about "Vasectomy: A Delicate Matter" is that the dreaded operation takes a backseat to an idiotic "Dynasty"-like family power play, but not far enough back. It is hard to imagine a film with less wit or commercial appeal.

Why coproducer Robert Burge (with Lou Wills), who also wrote (with Robert Hillard) and directed this travesty, would think the subject of a vasectomy fertile material for a bawdy comedy is perhaps the biggest joke here.

Film fails to go far enough with either the vasectomy or family plot to be entertaining, but does not stop short of being moronic. The characters are an insult to the intelligence of third graders.

Leading the pack is Paul Sorvino, roly-poly bank exec who brays with wounded Italian pride when his wife (Cassandra Edwards) lays down the law — vasectomy or no bedroom privileges. That other methods of birth control are dismissed with barely a shrug of the shoulders hardly adds to the credibility.

At the same time some incomprehensible plot is gong on involving the philandering young owner of the bank (Gary Raff) and attempts by his family to get their fair share of the loot.

Burge's writing and directing fails to deliver anything in the least bit interesting to watch despite valiant efforts by the cast in the face of some of the worst material imaginable. Treatment of women and sex is bound to be offensive to anyone with the least bit of sensitivity.

In the case of this film, an abortion would have been preferable to a vasectomy. —Jagr.

Fouetté
(SOVIET-COLOR)

A Lenfilm Studios production. Directed by Vladimir Vasilyev and Boris Yermolayev. Screenplay, Yermolayev, Savra Kulish; camera (color), Valery Mironov; art direction, Mikahail Sheglov, Yelizaveta Urlina; music, Anatoly Balchev, Oleg Karavaichuk. Features Ekaterina Maximova, Vladimir Vasiliev, Natalia Bolshakova, Valentin Graft, Aristarkh Livanov. Reviewed at Cine Victoria Eugenia, San Sebastian Film Fest, Sept. 20, 1986. Running time: **100 MINS.**

San Sebastian — "Fouetté" is a confused and tedious exercise in dance and ballet in which the slim story gets lost in the midst of dance sequences and rehearsals ranging from "Swan Lake" to an experimental "Mephisto." One of the Bolshoi's leading lights, Ekaterina Maximova, is topcast, but she's given little opportunity to dance or act,

as directors hop about from one setup to the next.

The little story there is concerns the prima donna's being elbowed out of the limelight because of her age. Touched upon sketchily are her relations with her husband, the company choreographer and an aspiring newcomer. Pic has a washed-out look to it and direction and editing are erratic and confused. It's difficult to sit through to the end.—Besa.

Kinema No Tenchi
(Final Take: The Golden Days Of Movies)
(JAPANESE-COLOR)

A Shochiku Co. production. Executive producer, Toru Okuyama. Produced by Yoshitaro Nomura, Shigemi Sugisaki, Nobutoshi Masmuoto, Kiyoshi Shimazu. Directed by Yoji Yamada. Screenplay, Hisashi Inoue, Taichi Yamada, Yoshitaka Asama, Yoji Yamada; camera (color), Tetsuo Takaba; music, Naozumi Yamamoto; art director, Mitsuo Dekawa. Reviewed at Venice Film Fest, Sept. 6, 1986. Running time: **125 MINS.**
Koharu Tanaka ....Narimi Arimori
Kihachi, her father ......Kiyoshi Atsumi
Kenjiro Shimada ....Kiichi Nakai
Yuki ....Chieko Baisho
Kida (studio head)....Koshiro Matsumoto
Sumie Kawahima ....Keiko Matsuzaka
Ogura ....Kei Suma
Ogata ....Ittoku Kishibe
Tomo.....................Chishu Ryu

Venice — Made to celebrate the 50th anniversary of the opening of Shochiku's Ofuna Studios, "Final Take: The Golden Days Of Movies" is a nostalgic romantic comedy which is almost all fiction but which tantalizingly uses the background of filmmaking in Japan in the early 1930s. Buffs will be intrigued by scenes like the ones in which Ittoku Kishibe plays a director evidently modeled on the great Yasujiro Ozu who squats on the floor as he directs his celebrated low-angle shots.

Pic tells a familiar tale of a young woman plucked from obscurity as a candy seller in one of the company's theaters to become a bit-player and, when the studio's No. 1 female star is embroiled in a scandal, a leading actress and an overnight sensation. Narimi Arimori is charming in this role as a shy, inexperienced young girl who initially has trouble coping with the demands of the studio's perfectionist directors.

Great trouble has been taken to depict the atmosphere at the studio during this period (1933-34), with wooden huts serving as sound stages and behind-the-scenes debates going on vis-à-vis the necessity for art films, like those of Ozu, alongside the entertainments. Eventually, the inexperienced leading lady is given the lead role in a production of the perennially popular "Floating Weeds," but is unable to play the key climactic scene to the satisfac-

tion of her director. However, back at home, her father (a touching performance by Kiyoshi Atsumi) tells his daughter about her late mother's sad life, giving the girl a new emotional experience and enabling her to play her part, next day, to the acclaim of all.

The first half of "Final Take" is rather sluggish, with director Yoji Yamada (best known for his hugely popular "Tora-San" series) making heavy weather of what should have been light-hearted material. The second half of the film is a major improvement, and by the end the combination of nostalgia and emotion weaves its spell. Some tightening of the first hour might well improve the pic's prospects.

Production is technically tops in every department. Scenes of the actual process of filmmaking, and of the heroine at home with her father, are the best. A rather dull romance with an ambitious young assistant director only serves to slow things down. Performances are all good, with a charming cameo by Ozu's favorite actor, Chishu Ryu, as the studio janitor whose canny wisdom is seriously sought by everyone from the studio head on down.

Disconcerting for Western audiences is the use, as a main music theme, of a famous number from Rudolf Friml's "The Vagabond King," which sounds very out of place. —Strat.

Tough Guys
(COLOR)

Hokey caper for the over-the-hill gang.

A Buena Vista release of a Touchstone presentation in association with Silver Screen Partners II and Bryna Prods. of a Joe Wizan production. Produced by Joe Wizan. Coproducers, Richard Hashimoto, Jana Sue Memel. Directed by Jeff Kanew. Stars Burt Lancaster, Kirk Douglas. Screenplay, James Orr, Jim Cruickshank; camera (Panavision, Deluxe color), King Baggot; editor, Kaja Fehr; music, James Newton Howard; production design, Todd Hallowell; set decoration, Jeff Haley; costume design, Erica Phillips; sound (Dolby), C. Darin Knight; assistant director, Ed Milkovich; casting, Jane Jenkins, Janet Hirshenson. Reviewed at the Walt Disney Studios, Burbank, Sept. 22, 1986. (MPAA Rating: PG.) Running time: **104 MINS.**
Harry Doyle ....Burt Lancaster
Archie Long...............Kirk Douglas
Deke Yablonski ....Charles Durning
Belle ....Alexis Smith
Richie Evans................Dana Carvey
Skye Foster ....Darlanne Fluegel
Leon B. Little ....Eli Wallach
Vince ....Monty Ash
Philly......................Billy Barty

Hollywood — "Tough Guys" is unalloyed hokum that proves a sad waste of talent on the parts of costars Burt Lancaster and Kirk Douglas. Dimwitted concoction would have had difficulty passing muster as a made-for-tv feature, and looks even thinner as a theatrical release. A quick cash-in on whatever interest can be generated in the actors' seventh teaming stands as the only b.o. hope.

The two venerable thesps, both 70-ish and looking fit and alert, turn up here as Harry Doyle and Archie Long, two gentleman crooks celebrated in the annals of American crime for having been the last outlaws to rob a train.

Film opens as the pair is released from prison after a 30-year hitch. Their yuppie parole officer idolizes them, but passes along the bad news that they'll have to go their separate ways, Lancaster into an old folks' home and Douglas into a seedy hotel and, because he's a bit younger, on the rounds to seek employment.

A little boozing and womanizing is more on the fellows' minds, however. Lancaster happens upon old flame Alexis Smith (looking very sharp) at the retirement home, while Douglas wanders into a gym and is picked up by aerobics hotshot Darlanne Fluegel (looking very sharp indeed), with whom he makes up for three decades of presumed abstinence in a couple of nights.

Pic pokes along with Lancaster provoking havoc at the home and Douglas quitting a series of jobs in disgust until scripters decide that perhaps a plot would be nice, so the guys get together and — surprise — decide to rob the train again.

Undeterrred by the fact that, on its upcoming anniversary run, the Gold Coast Flyer will be carrying nothing worth stealing, the irrepressible duo carry on and end up hijacking the locomotive all the way to Mexico, even though the tracks don't stretch quite that far.

It's all silly, meaningless and vaguely depressing, since the awareness lingers throughout that both actors are capable of much, much more than is demanded of them here. Douglas' character is forced to endure numerous small humiliations, which are not terribly enjoyable, while Lancaster's graver, more meditative mien merely serves to remind one of the great reserves he possesses that are not being profitably mined.

Supporting turns are uniformly broad, lending proof to the view that director Jeff Kanew hasn't taken any lessons in subtlety since "Revenge Of The Nerds." — *Cart.*

Rockin' Road Trip
(COLOR)

Diffuse comedy.

A Troma release from Triad Entertainment Group of a William Olsen production. Produced by William Olsen, Michael Rothschild. Directed by Olsen. Screenplay, Olsen, Nancy Sterling, from story by Olsen; camera (TVC color), Austin McKinney; editor, David H. Lloyd; music, Ricky Keller; sound, Lee Strosnider; production design, James Eric; assistant director, Jeff Leighton; production manager, Amy McGary; second unit director, Phil Smoot; casting, Kim DeCoste. Reviewed on Key Video vidcassette, N.Y., Aug. 30, 1986. (MPAA Rating: PG-13.) Running time: **101 MINS.**
Martin . . . . .Garth McLean
Nicole . . . . .Margaret Currie
Samantha . . . . .Katherine Harrison
Wally . . . . .Steve Boles
Lenny .Marty Tucker
Ivan .Graham Smith
Curtis Little . . . . .LeLand Gantt

"Rockin' Road Trip" is a youth comedy laden with music that fails to find a strong storyline and stick to it. North Carolina filmmaker William Olsen displays the same quirky sene of humor as in his 1983 feature "Getting It On," but to weaker cumulative effect. Pic was filmed in fall 1984 as "Summertime Blues," the title song of which is repeated three times, and was released regionally in May.

Margaret Currie stars as Nicole, lead singer of the rock group Cherry Suicide. Group is a hit in Boston, where Nicole's sister Samantha (Katherine Harrison) is visiting her, up from their home in North Carolina. Suddenly, everyone, including Samantha's new boy friend Martin (Garth McLean) and his blind buddy Wally (Steve Boles) jump into a taxicab and drive south on a lark.

Road movie features various slapstick incidents en route to North Carolina, where it becomes mired in some rather trite spoofing of local religious revivalists. The oddball booking of Cherry Suicide as an entertainment act at a televised tent meeting is merely silly rather than the intended satire of clashing cultures.

An energetic cast puts across the material well, aided by a good musical score featuring music performed by the Cheryl Wilson Band (lip-synched on screen by Cherry Suicide) and the group Guadalcanal Diary. Tech credits are okay.
—*Lor.*

Hashigaon Hagadol
(Funny Farm)
(ISRAELI-COLOR)

A Cannon Group presentation of a Menahem Golan and Yoram Globus production. Associate producer, Itzhak Kol. Directed by Naftali Alter. Screenplay, Golan based on story by Yossi Savaya; camera (color), Ilan Rosenberg; editor, Moshe Avni; music, Alter; sound (Dolby), Shabtai Sarig; costume design, Debbie Leon. Reviewed in Tel Aviv, Aug. 6, 1986. Running time: **105 MINS.**
With: Seffi Rivlin, Arik Lavie, Yehuda Efroni, Dina Doron, Anath Waxman, Louis Rosenberg, Shmuel Vilozhni.

Tel Aviv — Naftali Alter's second film dispels any promises his first one, "Irith, Irith," might have held. Once gain it is a comedy, this time of the broadest manner, in which the helmer's hand is hardly felt.

The script, for which Cannon chairman Menahem Golan takes full credit, attempts to present Israel's chaotic economy in a satirical light, using the old principle that a mental institution is the sanest and safest place to be in, when the world itself has gone crazy.

The protagonist is a bank manager who accidentally stumbles upon a plant for the production of counterfeit dollars, operated by certified mental patients, in the cellar of their hospital. The script spreads itself wide and thin in all sorts of directions from this point, relying far too much on the grotesque mimicry that the actors, some of them entertainers with a reputation for it, would supply. Since director Alter can't really keep his cast under control, the story, the characters and the audience's interest, disintegrate after the first few minutes.

While production proudly mentions it is the first in Israel to use Dolby sound, it has very little to show for its efforts. Other technical credits are acceptable but far from spectacular. Promoted as a big summer comedy with the name of Seffi Rivlin, a highly popular stage and tv entertainer, in the foreground, the film has generated very little business at home. Abroad, chances are iffy, at best. —*Edna.*

Hombre Mirando al Sudeste
(Man Looking Southeast)
(ARGENTINE-COLOR)

A Cinequanon production. Executive producer, Luján Pflaum. Written and directed by Eliseo Súbiela. Camera (color), Ricardo de Angelis; editor, Luis Cesar d'Angiolillo; sets, Abel Facello; music, Pedro Aznar; sound, Carlos Abbate; production manager, Hugo Lauria. Features Lorenzo Quinteros, Hugo Soto, Inés Vernengo. Reviewed at Cine Victoria Eugenia, San Sebastián Film Fest, Sept. 20, 1986. Running time: **105 MINS.**

San Sebastian — This is an often absorbing psychological puzzler, at times a little reminiscent of "One Flew Over The Cuckoo's Nest," mostly set in an Argentine insane asylum, anent relationship between a weary psychiatrist and a high I.Q. patient who claims to be an extraterrestrial.

Helmer-writer Eliseo Subiela probes not only into the shifting contest between the two men, but goes off on many a philosophical tangent about what, ultimately, is sanity. He never makes it quite clear whether we are to really believe the patient is an alien, or just imagines himself to be one. In a few of the scenes we see him performing Christ-like minor miracles, such as moving plates on the counter of a restaurant to feed a needy family. The air of mystery, at first intriguing, gets a bit tedious, as the long dialogs proceed and the E.T.'s ultimate reality is left hanging in the air.

The enigma is compounded when a young girl pays the patient a visit, and later also claims to be one of "them." Near the end of the film, Subiela adds a sequence in which the patient, the girlfriend and the doctor go to a performance of Beethoven's Ninth, and the supposed E.T. walks up to the conductor, takes his baton, and finishes conducting the "Ode To Joy;" simultaneously the asylum's inmates indulge in an orgy of joy and march about the halls of the madhouse.

Pic ends on a downbeat note, with the death of the patient; the psychiatrist sinks into a mire of hopelessness. Good thesping, okay direction, some interesting parts but it's not a subject that will have them lining up at the wickets. —*Besa.*

Henri
(CANADIAN-COLOR)

A Les Vision 4 production. Produced by Claude Bonin. Directed by François Labonté. Screenplay, Jacques Jacob; camera (color), Michel Caron; editor, André Corriveau; music, Denis Larochelle; sound, Alain Corneau; art director, Jean-Baptiste Tard; associate producers, Jacques Bonin, Suzanne Hénaut. Reviewed at the Toronto Festival of Festivals, Sept. 11, 1986. Running time: **92 MINS.**
Henri .Eric Brisebois
Joseph . . . . .Jacques Godin
Jeanne Painchaud . . . . . . .Marthe Turgeon
Roch Chabot . . . . .Claude Gauthier
Raoul Martineau . . . . .Yvan Ponton
Lilianne . . . . .Lucie Laurier
Bégin . . . . .Julien Poulin
Dr. Lamarre . . . . .Kim Yaroshevskaya

Toronto — "Henri," a beautifully shot family pic, languishes for sufficient plot action to satisfy young teens for whom it is apparently most aimed.

Story somewhat parallels last year's Canadian pic, "Toby McTeague," with a teenage boy's struggling both against his father, now tormented because he let his wife die in a boating accident to rescue a young daughter, and in a village cross-country race that pits the youth against an arch school principal.

A twist here is that the saved 11-year-old daughter happily remains in hospital, apparently suffering from apparent mental after-effects of losing her mother. Her brother secretly brings her food and comfort and she rightly accuses the shoemaker father of wishing he saved her mother instead.

The youth is the butt of schoolmate pranks; he is expelled and moves out of the house. All is resolved when he wins the race as a reunited father and sister cheer him on from the sidelines.

Michel Caron's camerawork of a Quebec village in autumn is first class. There's good acting from handsome Eric Brisebois who, for young female teen audiences, should have been allowed at least to go bare chested, father Jacques Godin, sister Lucie Laurier and the youth's adult supporters, teacher Marthe Turgeon and garage owner Claude Gauthier.

Direction and pacing are slow and the plot plays even softer than it reads.

Pic has limited theatrical chance, but suitable for family hours on tv.
—*Adil.*

27 Horas
(27 Hours)
(SPANISH-COLOR)

An Elías Querejeta production. Executive producer, Elias Querejeta. Directed by Montxo Armendariz. Screenplay, Armendariz, Querejeta; camera (color), Javier Aguirresarobe; editor, Juan I. San Mateo; sets, Iñigo Altolaguirre; sound, Pierre Lorrain; music, Angel Illarramendi, Imanol Larzabal, Carol Jimenez, Luis Mendo; production manager, Primitivo Alvaro; production chief, Gregorio Hebrero. Reviewed at Cine Victoria Eugenia, San Sebastian Film Festival, Sept. 19, 1986. Running time: **77 MINS.**
Jon . . . . Martxelo Rubio
Maite . . . . , ... Maribel Verdu
Patxi . . . . Jon San Sebastián
Also with: Antonio Banderas, Michel Duperrer, André Falcón, Josu Balbuena, Silvia Arrese-Igor.

San Sebastian — The problem of drugs among the youth of San Sebastian is tackled obliquely in this sincere, occasionally touching film by Elias Querejeta and Montxo Armendariz; but rather than point the way to solution, they merely chronicle the ill. A finger seems to be pointed at the national police, fleetingly and rather gratuitously depicted as intrusive ogres. Otherwise pic is void of any overt political references.

Downbeat plot revolves around three kids. One is a high school dropout who scrapes along with petty thefts, handouts from his estranged family and odd jobs. He and his girlfriend are hooked on hard drugs. Third of the trio urges them to kick the habit, to no avail.

Matters veer sharply for the worse when the girl takes an overdose, which turns out to be lethal. The boy, despite urgings from his friend, voluntarily follows her on the road to perdition, 27 hours after the beginning of the action.

Besides the digs at the police, there are passing references to the unemployment and exploitation of dock workers in the Basque area. Direction is good, and the kids are fine, though sometimes expressionless. However, the story is so unrelievedly downbeat that its appeal is apt to be very limited. —*Besa.*

Et skud fra hjertet
(A Shot From The Heart)
(DANISH-COLOR)

A Metronome release of Grönlykke, Levring & Magnusson production. Produced by Tivi Magnusson. Directed by Kristian Levring. Stars Claus Flygare, Lars Oluf Larsen. Screenplay by Leif Magnusson, based on an idea by Kristian Levring; camera (Eastmancolor), Steen Veileborg; editor, Leif Magnusson; music, Lars Hug; sound, Henrik Langkilde; production design, Claus Bjerre; production management, Jacob Grönylkke, Janne Find; costumes, Stine Marott. Reviewed at the Palads, Copenhagen, Sept. 8, 1986. Running time: **80 MINS.**
Captive gangleader . . . . Claus Flygare
Rookie soldier . . . . Lars Oluf Larsen
Brok, older soldier . . . . Niels Skousen
Roaming girl . . . . Susanne Voldmester
Army Captain . . . . Frank Schaufuss
Yellow, rival gangleader . . . . Steen
⠀⠀⠀⠀⠀⠀⠀⠀⠀⠀⠀⠀⠀⠀⠀⠀⠀⠀⠀⠀Birger Jörgensen
Also with: Lizzie Corfixen, Pouel Kern, Lars Sidenius, Ejner Jensen, Claus Lembeck, Morten Suurballe, Henrik Birk.

Copenhagen — It is the conceit of director Kristian Levring, a recent Danish Film School graduate, that the feature film with which he debuts is "just an attempt at following in the footsteps of the classical, lowbudget and visceral B-picture."

"A Shot From The Heart" also follows very much in the footsteps of the "Mad Max" trio of visions of a near-future world as a wasteland where the forces of evil, in a comic book medieval way, are also the protagonists of some kind of moralistic, psychological power play.

A clumsily and often outright naively fashioned screenplay often has helmer bogged down in narrative dead ends, but most of the time Levring and cinematographer Steen Veileborg deliver the promised visceral goods and prove themselves possessors of obvious cinematic talent. While "Shot" will hardly be heard around the world, a nice apprentice markmanship and a good aim have been put on display.

Story has a rookie soldier left alone with the assignment of getting a captive gangland boss (or is he a freedom fighter?) across the desert to a stockade where he will be interrogated (presumably before being shot) for information deemed vital for a green & black clad army representing law & order.

Although the rookie is considered a crack shot, he recoils from having to kill anybody. It is the captive who at one point has to grab the gun and blaze away at a rival bandit and his gaudily costumed marauders. Soldier and prisoner are united in some kind of mute, reluctant fellowship. At the end, the soldier gets up his nerve to shoot only when he does so to kill his prisoner so as to save latter from his interrogators.

A young woman in erotically chic tatters pops up now and again, and built-in action and moralistic intent ooze freely from every carefully composed frame. Visually, "Shot" rates higher than it does in the acting department, where things work best when sans dialog. Blowup from 16m to 35m has been done expertly.
—*Kell.*

La Mitad del Cielo
(Half Of The Sky)
(SPANISH-COLOR)

A Luis Megino production. Directed by Manuel Gutiérrez Aragón. Screenplay, Gutiérrez Aragón, Luis Megino; camera (color), José Luis Alcaine; editor, José Salcedo; music, Milladoiro; direct sound, D. Goldstein, R. Steinberg; sets, Gerardo Vera; production manager, José G. Jacoste; costumes, Marina Rodriguez. Reviewed at Cine Victoria Eugenia, San Sebastian Film Festival, Sept. 21, 1986. Running time: **127 MINS.**
Rosa . . . . Angela Molina
Don Pedro . . . . . . Fernando Fernán Gómez
Grandma . . . . Margarita Lozano
Juan . . . . Antonio V. Valero
Delgado . . . . Nacho Martinez
Antonio . . . . Santiago Ramos
Also with: Francisco Merino, Mónica Molina, Carolina Silva, Enriqueta Carballeira, Julia Martínez, Mercedes Lezcano, Concha Leza.

San Sebastian — The life of a well-known Madrid distaff restaurant operator, whose rise from obscure origins to owner of the capital's poshest restaurants in the postwar era, a hangout for Franco politicos, could have all the ingredients for a fascinating film. One imagines either an ironic or a scathing and incisive treatment of the behind-the-scenes intrigues, amours and scandals witnessed and shared by the restaurant owner and her often presumably unsavory big-shot clientele.

Luis Megino and Manuel Gutiérrez Aragón have instead opted for a fanciful and ultimately undramatic story to which the writer-director has added his customary allegorical touches.

The poetic license and imagery are beautifully limned, but detract from what might have been an effective, straightforward plot. Helmer weaves into plot an inscrutable daughter who has a friendship going with her grandmother's ghost while the politicians and restaurant intrigues are relegated to an inconsequential backdrop. Outcome is the story of three women in postwar Spain, the relationships among them, mixed with a heavy dose of symbolism.

First half of pic tracing Rosa's early years in a pueblo and her arrival in Madrid are somewhat drawn out, but nonetheless effective. Rosa lands a job nursing the infant of a widower with political connections, then manages to get coin to set up a small stand in a meat market. So far it's all believable.

Then, in a move never adequately explained, we suddenly see the bumpkin lady transmogrified into the doyenne of a fancy restaurant. No explanation how she got the money, what political strings were pulled, whose beds she had to warm. Gutiérrez Aragón prefers parable.

Only relationships dwelled upon are those between Rosa and her benefactor, touchingly played by Fernán-Gómez, and with a young admirer. There is some symbolic foreboding of death to the young man should she marry him. Pic ends inconclusively with the young man's wedding to another, held in Rosa's restaurant, as the grandmother's ghost re-appears. The specter is followed out the door by Rosa's daughter, lyrical metaphors the meanings of which may be lost on audiences not of a transcendental bent.

Item is well directed and well acted, with occasional touches of wry humor. But Gutiérrez Aragón's obsession for lyrical symbols while it may please some gets in his way for telling what might have been a fine straightforward story. —*Besa.*

True Stories
(COLOR)

Tongue-in-cheek celebration of small-town Americana is only half-realized.

A Warner Bros. release of a True Stories Ventures production. Produced by Gary Kurfirst. Executive producer, Edward R. Pressman; coproducer, Karen Murphy. Directed by David Byrne. Screenplay, Byrne, Beth Henley, Stephen Tobolowsky; camera (color), Ed Lachman; editor, Caroline Biggerstaff; music, Byrne and the Talking Heads; production design, Barbara Ling; costumes, Elizabeth McBride; choreography, Meredith Monk, Dee McCandless, Gene Menger. Reviewed at Alice Tully Hall, N.Y. (in 24th New York Film Festival), Oct. 1, 1986. (MPAA Rating: PG.) Running time: **90 MINS.**

Narrator .... David Byrne
Louis Fyne .... John Goodman
Miss Rollings .... Swoosie Kurtz
Earl Culver .... Spalding Gray
The Cute Woman .... Alix Elias
Kay Culver .... Annie McEnroe
Mr. Tucker ..... Roebuck ''Pops'' Staples
Ramon .... Umberto ''Tito'' Larriva
The Preacher .... John Ingle
The Lying Woman .... Jo Harvey Allen
The Computer Guy .... Matthew Posey

In more than 10 years with the Talking Heads, David Byrne has received well-earned if often slavishly uncritical praise for his distinctive marriage of polyrhythmic pop-rock with an archly skewed perspective on mechanistic modern life. ''True Stories'' is a natural progression into film for Byrne, but represents neither a musical advance nor a significant artistic flowering for the thinking person's rock 'n' roller.

In his feature directorial debut, Byrne takes a bemused and benevolent view of provincial America's essential goodness in a loosely connected string of vignettes that amount to sophisticated music video concepts dressed up as filmmaking. Ed Lachman's stunning picture-postcard cinematography doesn't entirely compensate for Byrne's fixation with stock images of mainstreet Americana, while his wry sense of comic detachment and scattershot use of the soundtrack songs (only three of which are sung by the Heads) may prove unsatisfying to the pop masses and artsy intelligensia alike.

Consequently, Warner Bros. will be hard pressed to duplicate the boxoffice success of the Cinecom/Island Alive-distributed 1984 Talking Heads concert film, ''Stop Making Sense,'' which was directed with compelling momentum by Jonathan Demme.

Byrne uses the surreal, cartoonish conceit of examining life in the hypothetical town of Virgil, Texas (how many Heads fans will grab the reference to the Roman poet-storyteller?), with the human interest perspective of a supermarket tabloid feature. Affecting a trusting innocence as easily as he slips into natty Western duds, Byrne drives into Virgil during its sesquicentenni-

al ''celebration of specialness'' for a series of close encounters with the town's peculiar denizens.

These include Louis Fyne, (John Goodman), a lovelorn and loveable ''dancing bear'' of a man, Miss Rollings (Swoozie Kurtz), ''the laziest woman in the world'' and Earl Culver (Spalding Gray), owner of the town's microprocessor plant who has not spoken directly with his wife for 30 years. These actors turn in affecting and funny turns that help to distract from the film's lack of narrative depth. Byrne seems more intent on making obvious and unremarkable observations on the nature of change in America while indulging in a fondly romantic, overstated celebration of the virtues of small town life. He also tries to get away with tossing off didactic one-liners like ''some people say freeways are the cathedrals of our time — not me.''

Along with freeways, Byrne tosses darts at the homogenizing cultural forces at work in shopping malls, pre-fab housing, the computer revolution and, of course, television. Underlying everything is a poignant sense of sympathy with decent folk who don't quite have the narrator's refined perspective on the inexorability of change. Byrne is at his best, however, in celebrating the unique humanity of his characters and, by extension, everybody. This joyously affirmative populism is best expressed in a marvelous nightclub scene in which various Virgilians take to the stage to lip-synch lines from the Heads' irresistible tune ''Wild, Wild Life.'' There are other good moments in the film as well, but more frequently, as in a prairie-kitsch ''fashion show,'' Byrne is a mite too self-absorbed with his own sense of the absurd. Ultimately, ''True Stories'' emerges as a stylishly designed, occasionally amusing concoction of snappy songs, half-realized concepts and scattered, dry-witted jokes. —*Rich.*

The Color Of Money
(COLOR)

Arresting, terrifically performed followup to 'The Hustler.'

A Buena Vista release of a Touchstone Pictures presentation. Produced by Irving Axelrad, Barbara De Fina. Directed by Martin Scorsese. Stars Paul Newman, Tom Cruise. Screenplay, Richard Price, based on novel by Walter Tevis; camera (DuArt color), Michael Ballhaus; editor, Thelma Schoonmaker; music, Robbie Robertson; production design, Boris Leven; set decorator, Karen A. O'Hara; sound (Dolby), Glenn Williams; assistant director, Joseph Reidy; associate producer, Dodie Foster; casting, Grethchen Rennell. Reviewed at Disney Studios screening room, Burbank, Calif., Oct. 2, 1986. (MPAA Rating: R.) Running time: **119 MINS.**

Eddie .... Paul Newman
Vincent .... Tom Cruise
Carmen ..... Mary Elizabeth Mastrantonio
Janelle .... Helen Shaver
Julian .... John Turturro
Orvis .... Bill Cobbs
Earl .... Robert Agins
Grady Seasons .... Keith McCready
Band singer .... Carol Messing
Duke .... Steve Mizerak
Moselle .... Bruce A. Young

Hollywood — ''The Color Of Money'' is another inside look at society's outsiders from director Martin Scorsese. This time out it's the subculture of professional pool hustlers that consumes the screen with a keenly observed and immaculately crafted vision of the raw side of life. Although lacking some of the intensity of Scorsese's earlier work, pic has a distinctive pulse of its own with exceptional performances by Paul Newman and Tom Cruise insuring healthy boxoffice.

Based on a reworking of Walter Tevis' novel by scripter Richard Price, ''The Color Of Money'' is a continuation of the 1961 film, ''The Hustler,'' 25 years later. It's perfect Scorsese territory — men revealed through what they do.

These are not men with an ordinary connection to their work, it's their religion. Back as Fast Eddie Felson, Paul Newman is a self-proclaimed ''student of human moves'' — a hustler. When he happens on Vincent Lauria (Tom Cruise) in a nondescript midwest pool hall, Eddie's juices start flowing and the endless cycle starts again.

Somewhat lax in the story department, what interests Scorsese is what these people are in the process of becoming. Fans of the director's previous films may find the characters a bit less extreme than Jake La Motta (''Raging Bull'') or Jimmy Doyle (''New York, New York''), but it is the distillation of what makes them tick that gives the film its arresting form.

There is nothing predictable about ''The Color Of Money.'' It is impossible to tell what Vincent will do next as Eddie courts him almost like a lover. There is always the irrationality of relationships propelling the film and, with the introduction of Vincent's girlfriend Carmen (Mary Elizabeth Mastrantonio), a triangle of constantly shifting dimensions is created.

On a plot level the film is fairly simple and even routine. Newman is the teacher who becomes jealous of his pupil. After a stormy week on the road in preparation for his first tournament in Atlantic City, Vincent and Carmen decide they can make it on their own.

For his part, Eddie returns to the pool table for the first time in years and when he loses, it is the necessary fall before his resurrection. Unfortunately, at this point Price's script fails to deal with what has happened to Eddie since George C. Scott issued a warning to him at the

end of ''The Hustler'' never to shoot again or he'd kill him.

Scorsese is less interested in explaining Eddie's psychology than in showing his actions. Watching Vincent, Eddie says, is like ''watching a home movie'' of the way he used to be. The hunger for money and power and sex are all things Eddie recognizes and while he may thirst for that himself initially, in the end he is left with something more important.

Much of this is only suggested and what is going on beneath the surface is only revealed in bits and pieces. Some viewers may find this treatment incomplete while others willing to roll with the punches will find these characters getting under their skin. The story is not tightly structured to draw conclusions and tie up loose ends, but these characters move with a sense of being alive in the world.

On a filmmaking level, it is refreshing to see a film in which every shot serves a function and is there for a reason. Cinematographer Michael Ballhaus has given the film a richly colored and seedy texture. Actual pool shooting scenes may be too numerous for most viewers but Scorsese has attempted to keep them dramatically interesting by introducing an array of shoots and angles.

There is never just flash for its own sake overshadowing the characters. Newman's performance is as much a comment on the actor's maturity as the characters. He is quietly commanding without overstating. Indeed one of the undercurrents of the film deals with the process of aging itself.

As the young buck, Cruise is necessarily more flamboyant and his work here is proof, for those who may have been wondering, that he really can act given the right direction. He embodies the explosive street smarts of a kid who has a lot to learn but who isn't afraid of making mistakes.

As Carmen, Mastrantonio is working on her own short fuse and is learning how to use her main talent too — her sexuality. It's a hot and disturbing performance as her actions contradict her choirgirl good looks.

In the background, however, Robbie Robertson's score, particularly an abundant selection of obscure rock and rhythm 'n' blues tunes, is too insistent and occasionally seems to be forcing the mood of the picture. Songs will probably make better listening on the soundtrack record. —*Jagr.*

Armed Response
(COLOR)

Okay action fodder.

A Cinetel Films production and release. Produced by Paul Hertzberg. Executive producer, Lisa Hansen. Coproduced and directed by Fred Olen Ray. Stars David Carradine, Lee Van Cleef. Screenplay, T.L. Lankford, from story by Lankford, Hertzberg, Ray; camera (United color), Paul Elliott; editor, Miriam L. Preissel; music, Tom Chase, Steve Rucker; sound, Rob Janiger; art director, Maxine Shepard; assistant director, Bruce Fritzberg; special makeup effects, Makeup & Effects lab; second unit camera, Scott Ressler. Reviewed at UA Twin 2 theater, N.Y., Oct. 4, 1986. (MPAA Rating: R.) Running time: **85 MINS.**
Jim Roth..............David Carradine
Burt Roth...............Lee Van Cleef
Akira Tanaka.....................Mako
Sara Roth................Lois Hamilton
Cory Thorton...............Ross Hagen
Tommy Roth................Brent Huff
Deborah Silverstein......Laurene Landon
Steve.......................Dick Miller
F.C.................Michael Berryman
Clay Roth..................David Goss
Also with: Sam Hione, Dah've Seigler, Conan Lee, Burr DeBenning, Susan Stokey, Bob Hvilon, Kai Baker, Bobbie Bresee, Michelle Bauer, Dawn Wildsmith, Fred Olen Ray.

"Armed Response" punches up a mundane action-revenge film plotline with above-par casting and enough style to make the formula work for genre fans. L.A.-lensed opus was filmed early this year under the better title "Jade Jungle."

Instead of his real-life acting clan, David Carradine here is surrounded by a dissimilar dad (Lee Van Cleef) and brothers (Brent Huff, David Goss) in a simple tale out of the "Maltese Falcon" bag. Youngest sibling Goss is a private eye hired with his partner Ross Hagen to retrieve a stolen jade antique for Japanese gangster Mako, who must get the object and save face before a war with the Chinese Tongs breaks out. Greedy Hagen executes several double crosses, with Goss ending up dead and his family now at odds with Mako, who kidnaps Carradine's wife and daughter.

Papa Van Cleef is an ex-cop and Carradine a war vet plagued with recurring nightmares (weak flashback footage) of Vietnam, so both grab their weaponry and lurch into action. Helped by some effective car stunts and pyrotechnics, plus several allusions for film buffs to catch, pic delivers the action goods.

For his sixth feature film, director Fred Olen Ray steps up to a bigger budget with some stylish compositions and a few elaborate setpieces. Cast is adequate, overcoming some very corny dialog, with Ross Hagen as the double-dealing bad guy making a strong impression resembling the late Gig Young. — *Lor.*

Blue Paradise
(Adam And Eve)
(ITALIAN-SPANISH-COLOR)

A Trans World Entertainment release, presented by Enzo Doria, of an Alex Film Intl. (Rome)/Arco Film (Madrid) coproduction. Directed by "John Wilder" (Luigi Russo). Stars Mark Gregory, Andrea Goldman. Screenplay, Domenico Rafele, Russo, Donald Forrest, Eugenio Benito, from story by Gisella Longo, Russo; camera (Telecolor), Russo; editor, Alan O'Neal; music, Guido & Maurizio De Angelis; art direction, Xavier Fernandez; set decoration, Longo; production manager, Mario Pedrazza; assistant director, Annamaria Liguori; special visual effects, Mario Bernardo; costume design, Rossana Romanini. Reviewed on TWE vidcassette, N.Y., Aug. 29, 1986. (No MPAA Rating.) Running time: **90 MINS.**
With: "Mark Gregory" (Massimo Spattini) (Adam); Andrea Goldman (Eve); Angel Alcazar, Pierangelo Pozzato, Liliana Gerace, Costantino Rossi, Vito Fornari, Maurizio Margutti, Leda Simonetti, Antonio Andolfi, Andrea Aureli.

"Blue Paradise" is an interesting though highly derivative 1982 Italian feature from producer Enzo Doria, his second genre followup to the hit "The Blue Lagoon" (the first was "Blue Island," starring Sabrina Siani).

Originally titled "Adam And Eve," pic combines biblical material with science fiction in an off-beat tale of primitive man. Opening reel is in the vein of the 1972 Mexican film "The Sin Of Adam And Eve" (which stars Jorge Rivero), limning familiar story of the first couple in the Garden of Eden and their expulsion. In this version, Adam (Massimo Spattini, a.k.a. Mark Gregory) is born full-grown out of a large sac in the ground and Eve (lovely young blond Andrea Goldman) comes to life in a storm out of a body fashioned by Adam out of sand (rib removal is not featured here). Duo romps in a nearby blue lagoon, natch.

After the snake and apple incident, duo flees from the Garden in another storm through a cave in which a poorly back-projected stop-motion animation rock chases them à la "Raiders Of The Lost Ark." She's ashamed of her nudity so loincloths are put on for the remainder of the film.

Bulk of picture is devoted to their wanderings, derived from another hit, "Quest For Fire." They argue, split and come back together, after capture and fights with primitive tribes and even Eve's satisfying infidelity with a handsome young tribesman. Finale has reunited couple on a glacier which thaws and allows Eve to give birth to their child in the sea.

Pic is nicely photographed by director Luigi Russo (using "John Wilder" as his anglicized *nom de film*) and benefits from the casting of two attractive lead players.
—*Lor.*

Cool Runnings: The Reggae Movie
(U.S.—JAMAICIAN-DOCU-COLOR)

An R5/S8 release of a Sunsplash Filmworks-Synergy Prods. production. Executive producer, Tony Johnson. Produced and directed by Robert Mugge. Camera (color), Lawrence McConkey; editor, Mugge; sound (Dolby), William Barth. Reviewed at the Mill Valley Film Festival, Sept. 28, 1986. (No MPAA Rating.) Running time: **105 MINS.**
With: Third World, Rita Marley, Musical Youth, Gregory Isaacs, Gil Scott-Heron.

Mill Valley — "Cool Runnings" was shot at the 1983 Reggae Sunsplash Festival at Montego Bay, Jamaica, and wrapped in time for play at that year's London filmfest. But according to producer-director Robert Mugge, theatrical distribution was delayed until now "because it took all this time to get music clearances in Jamaica." The distrib, R5/S8, is helmed by Michael Jeck in Washington, D.C.

Docu should have vast appeal to reggae fans and may draw a few curious to a music genre which leading performer Gil Scott-Heron describes as "having a different beat that took some time to get used to. It's like inside-out music."

Footage itself is straightforward as Mugge's four cameras follow the Sunsplash fest action both on stage and in the audience with some side trips for background commentary. The music, even for the non-buff, is quite fetching, and Scott-Heron scores well with a number called "The Bottle." The only technical flaw is an occasional jump cut between performers, but sound is rich and compelling.

"Cool Runnings" is set to open at a Frisco house Oct. 15, with a Boston booking to follow. On a limited-play basis in selected bookings pic figures to perform decently at the b.o. —*Herb.*

Ratboy
(COLOR)

Gentle fable has little impact.

A Warner Bros. release of a Malpaso production. Produced by Fritz Manes. Directed by Sondra Locke. Screenplay, Rob Thompson; camera (Technicolor), Bruce Surtees; editor, Joel Cox; music, Lennie Niehaus; production design, Edward Carfagno; set design, Bob Sessa; set decoration, Cloudia; Ratboy design, Rick Baker; sound, C. Darin Knight; associate producers, David Valdes, Rob Thompson; assistant director, Valdes; casting, Phyllis Huffman. Reviewed at The Burbank Studios, Sept. 30, 1986. (MPAA Rating: PG-13.) Running time: **104 MINS.**
Nikki Morrison ....Sondra Locke
Manny....................Robert Townsend
Acting coach.........Christopher Hewett
Jewell....................Larry Hankin
Dial-A-Prayer...........Sydney Lassick
Billy Morrison..........Gerrit Graham
Omer Morrison..........Louie Anderson
Ratboy....................S.L. Baird
Psychic..................Billie Bird
Ratboy's voice........Gordon Anderson

Hollywood — Yet another picture about how a semi-human, quasi-alien being just can't fit in among earthlings, "Ratboy" can boast of some modest virtues, but is simply too mild on all counts to carry much impact. Oddball first feature from Sondra Locke, who also stars, deals with eccentric, desperate individuals but in a rather straightforward, unobsessed manner. Pic's gentleness and lack of big names will require Warner Bros. to work hard to cultivate an audience for this one, advisedly through exclusive openings in carefully selected theaters in key cities.

From "E.T." to "The Elephant Man" and dozens of others, recent pictures have almost relentlessly focused upon the plight of an alien, or outsider, in society. In the case of "Ratboy," the origins of the title character are never investigated or explained. Indeed, after the terrified little bugger is trapped by some transients, he is just blithely manipulated and used by a succession of hustlers who can't put their greed and self-interests on hold long enough to even inquire where the tiny one came from or how he got that way.

First and foremost of these careerists is Locke, an out-of-work journalist whose natural talent for promotion revealed once she's found Ratboy would indicate she missed her calling by not going into p.r. Within hours of taking charge of the half-rodent, she has a meeting with a big producer, makes the scene at a power party, appears on "The Merv Griffin Show" (before it went off the air) and garners banner headlines due to a crazed press conference from which Ratboy makes his dash for freedom.

Also looking for a piece of the action is Robert Townsend, a good-natured black hipster who takes Ratboy off Locke's hands for awhile but ultimately proves too distracted to be an effective protector.

One problem is that Ratboy can hardly speak. He does manage to squeak out a few words from time to time, mainly to the effect that he likes and wants Locke, but most of the time he is simply running around in a panic because he (correctly) views everyone he meets as predatory.

Played by actress S.L. Baird in effective makeup devised by Rick Baker that makes the character look disconcertingly like Roman Polanski at certain moments, a distressed little creature such as this should be an easy bet for audience sympathy, but Locke the director doesn't particularly tilt the film that way. Instead, she concentrates more on the inability of any of the characters to behave in either a rational or productive way in the face of making contact with this unique being.

Despite the appealing touch in evidence in numerous scenes, Rob Thompson's script offers little in the way of fresh insights into a familiar subject. Some quick pacing can't compensate for an overall feel of slowness, which is due to some aimless scenes and a puzzling stretch when Ratboy becomes inexplicably separated from Locke for a long period.

An amusing continuity problem that will be apparent to Hollywoodsters has Townsend driving Ratboy west through town; hitch is that shots of Townsend in the front seat position him on Hollywood Blvd., while glimpses of Ratboy reveal Sunset Blvd. in the background.

Locals might also get a laugh out of Locke staging her lavish press conference at the Million Dollar Theater, which is actually a downtown Spanish-language grind house.

Acting tends to the broad side, and Ratboy's nose twitching is cute. Tech contributions are pro.—*Cart.*

Isaac In America
(DOCU-COLOR-16m)

An Amram Nowak Associates production. Produced by Kirk Simon. Executive producer, Manya Starr. Directed by Amram Nowak. Camera (color, 16m), Jerry Pantzer; editor, Riva Freifeld; music, Ross Levinson; sound Dan Kinoy, Larry Lowinger; art director, Marlene Marta. Reviewed at Alice Tully Hall, N.Y. (in 24th New York Film Festival), Sept. 26, 1986. Running time: **58 MINS.**
With: Isaac Bashevis Singer, readings by Judd Hirsch.

For writers in America honor is hard to come by, usually won by bestsellers and rewarded with cash, talk show celebrity and Hollywood options. In rare cases a serious author wins renown when a lifetime of artistic labor is rewarded with a major prize, particularly a Pulitzer or, in the case of Isaac Bashevis Singer, a Nobel Prize for literature. As Singer points out in this engaging documentary on his life and work, he is not really an American writer but a Jewish writer in permanent exile from a vanished way of life working in Yiddish, a language that's "been dying for the last 200 years — since it was born."

Amram Nowak captures the wry, self-deprecating charm of his avuncular subject in cozy visits with Singer and his wife at their Upper West Side apartment, and tours of the sidewalks and cafeterias of Manhattan and Coney Island, where he sought refuge in 1935 from the impending Nazi holocaust. The theme of Singer's uprooting from the Warsaw of his youth, "the center of the universe" and the supernatural folklore of cabalistic spirits and demons that inspired his writings, lends the documentary a deeper poignance than a simple autobiographical look

back. "Every writer loses in translation, but especially a fiction writer and one who believes in the supernatural," observes the author who told the staid audience at the Nobel laureate ceremonies that he was a writer of "ghost stories."

Singer believes that "memory is the most important thing to a writer," and the documentary blends his memories of life in the talmudic *shtetl* culture of pre-war Poland with his days in New York, adjusting to a new land, and struggling to survive by contributing short fiction to the Daily Forward and other Jewish newspapers. Singer notes he was attacked by Jewish critics for abandoning what he called the "sentimental" tendencies of Yiddish writing in order to focus on "the great comedy and tragedy of the Jewish people." Nevertheless, the documentary does have its share of sentimental moments, particularly a visit by the author to Coney Island, where he spent his first years in America, and a reunion with a 102-year-old friend from those days.

Sympathetic readings by Judd Hirsch from Singer's demi-autobiographical writings enhance the intimacy of a documentary ideally suited for PBS and nontheatrical showcases. —*Rich.*

Link
(BRITISH-COLOR)

A Cannon release of a Thorn EMI Screen Entertainment production. Executive producer, Verity Lambert. Co-producer, Rick McCallum. Produced and directed by Richard Franklin. Screenplay, Everett DeRoche, based on story by Lee Zlotoff, Tom Ackerman; camera (Technicolor, Rank prints), Mike Molloy; editor, Andrew London; music, Jerry Goldsmith; production design, Norman Garwood; art direction, Keith Pain; costume design, Terry Smith; sound (Dolby), David Stephenson; assistant director, Chris Rose; ape trainer, Ray Berwick; second unit camera, Gale Tattersall (England), Mike Proudfoot (Scotland); casting, Priscilla John (London), Jackie Burch (Los Angeles). Reviewed at the Hollywood Pacific, L.A., Oct. 3, 1986. (MPAA Rating: R). Running time: **103 MINS.**
Dr. Steven Phillip . . . . Terence Stamp
Jane Chase . . . . Elisabeth Shue
David . . . . Steven Pinner
Dennis . . . . Richard Garnett
Tom . . . . David O'Hara
Bailey . . . . Kevin Lloyd
Link . . . . Locke

Hollywood — What is missing from "Link" is a reason to see it. When Cannon acquired Thorn EMI Screen Entertainment this was part of the package — and a worthless one at the B.o. prospects look bleak, even in the vidcassette market.

You know right off the film is in trouble when the chimpanzees outperform their human counterparts.

Credit here goes to animal trainer Ray Berwick for getting a full range of expressions out of the primates that director Richard Frank-

lin couldn't get out of the actors. However, he didn't have much material in the story to work with.

Film takes nearly one entire evolutionary phase to get started, plodding along for almost an hour at an isolated English coastal manor house where preeminent primatologist Dr. Steven Phillip (Terence Stamp) conducts rudimentary experiments on a handful of chimps with the help of his fresh-faced student assistant, Jane Chase (Elisabeth Shue).

The chimps' malevolent ringleader, Link (Locke), takes over the lead from the first time he is seen as the tuxedoed butler — even though he never utters a word.

Stamp is so wooden, he appears somnambulent. No wonder that when he disappears, it takes a while to even miss him.

Presumably, it's when we find out that Link is not the dutiful cigar-smoking house servant that things are supposed to get scary. "Link" is being billed as a horror film, after all.

Alas, the chimps are too cute and cuddly and Shue too unfazed and unscared by the deaths that are occurring around her that when she finally finds herself trapped in the house along with Link even the thunderstorms and heavy drum scoring by Jerry Goldsmith can't make things spooky.—*Brit.*

Hardbodies 2
(COLOR)

Limp attempt at sexploitation.

A Cinetel Films release of a Lee Fry presentation of a Chroma III/First American Capital production. Produced by Jeff Begun, Ken Solomon, Dimitri Logothetis, Joseph Medawar. Executive producer, Lee Fry. Directed by Mark Griffiths. Screenplay, Griffiths, Curtis Scott Wilmot, based on characters created by Steve Greene, Eric Alter; camera (color), Tom Richmond; editor, Andy Blumenthal; music, Jay Levy, Eddie Arkin; art direction, Theodosis Davlos. Reviewed at the UA Movies, Granada Hills, Calif., Oct. 3, 1986. (MPAA Rating: R.) Running time: **88 MINS.**
Scott . . . . Brad Zutaut
Rags . . . . Sam Temeles
Sean . . . . Curtis Scott Wilmot
Morgan . . . . Brenda Bakke
Cleo . . . . Fabiana Udenio
Cookie . . . . Louise Baker
Logan . . . . James Karen
Zacherly . . . . Alba Francesca
Carlton Ashby . . . . Sorrells Pickard
Lana Logan . . . . Roberta Collins
Ms. Rollins . . . . Julie Rhodes
Brucie . . . . Alexi Mylones
Cleo's father . . . . George Tzifos
Kidnaper's wife . . . . Ula Gavala
Kidnaper . . . . George Kotandis

Hollywood — With "Hardbodies 2," the sexploitation film comes almost full circle back to its 1950s origins in the nudist camp picture. Even if the Greek isle of Rhodes is not officially a nudist camp, it func-

tions very much like one for the film's sole purpose, which is to expose as much sun-drenched female flesh as possible. This would have been fine for the raincoat brigade 25 years ago, but there's no conceivable audience for this limp dirty-old men's farce except for diehard fans of the modestly successful 1984 original.

Two randy Yanks arrive in Greece to work on a low-budget picture along with a third fellow, Scott, who is saddled with a drip of a fiancee. With time for a side trip on a floating classroom which all students attend topless, the cheeky threesome get through the chaotic film shoot, while Scott transfers the engagement ring to the finger of his native leading lady, whom he discovers waiting tables on the island.

Crude and stupefyingly unimaginative attempts at comedy abound, and only the scenery — both human and natural — keeps one from dwelling for 88 minutes on the fact that life is too short to fill it with this sort of thing.

Only bright spot is Fabiana Udenio, who somewhat resembles Michelle Johnson physically and comes off very sweetly as the local girl upon whom the sleaziness of those surrounding her has not yet rubbed off. —*Cart.*

Sitting In Limbo
(CANADIAN-COLOR)

A National Film Board of Canada production. Produced by David Wilson, John N. Smith. Directed by Smith. Screenplay, Wilson, Smith; camera (color), Barry Perles, Andreas Poulsson; editor, David Wilson; sound, Richard Nichol, Hans Oomes; associate producer, Elizabeth Klinck; production manager, Carol Jarry. Reviewed at World Film Fest, Montreal, Aug. 28, 1986. Running time: **96 MINS.**
With: Pat Dillon, Fabian Gibbs, Sylvie Clarke, Debbie Grant.

Montreal — The National Film Board of Canada's alternative drama program has so far come up with such worthwhile items as "The Masculine Mystique," "90 Days" and now "Sitting In Limbo." The style of these pics, seemingly derived from the school of dramatized documentary popular in Hungary, is to take non-professional actors and have them play roles very close to their own experiences. In "Sitting In Limbo," the characters are teenage blacks who speak only English though they live in the predominantly French-speaking city of Montreal.

Pat (Pat Dillon) is a lively youngster who shares an apartment with her friends Sylvie and Debbie, both unwed mothers living on welfare. When she finds herself pregnant by her boyfriend, Fabian (Fabian Gibbs) who's just been expelled from high school for chronic lateness and laziness, Pat accepts the situation philosophically. She and Fabian move into a chilly, bare apartment, they both find jobs, and they buy furniture on credit.

Before long Fabian has been fired, again for his idleness. He doesn't tell Pat he's out of work, and one day returns to find the furniture has all been removed. Later, Pat miscarries, and returns, sadder but wiser, to live with her old girlfriends.

There's nothing especially original about the plotline, which tells a sadly familiar story of immature teens trying to cope with the realities of adult life. But these non-pros, especially the endearing Dillon, breathe life into their roles and pull the audience along with them.

Filmmaking side of things, led by director John N. Smith, is unobtrusively fine, and was probably more difficult to handle than it appears to be. An upbeat reggae music score, by Jimmy Cliff and others, helps things along.

Commercial chances look doubtful, but "Sitting In Limbo" should have a life on television among stations that are willing to book something a bit closer to actuality than the tv norm.—*Strat.*

Reporter X
(PORTUGUESE-COLOR)

Produced and directed by Jose Nascimento. Screenplay, Nascimento, Manuel Joao Gomes, Edgar Pera; camera (color), Manuel Costa e Silva; editor, Ana Luisa Guimares, Nascimineto; music, Antonio Emiliano; sound, Carlos Alberto Lopez. Reviewed at San Sebastian Film Festival (Open Section), Sept. 26, 1986. Running time: **100 MINS.**
With: Joaquim Almeida, Paula Guedes, Fernando Heitor, Eunice Munoz, Susana Borges, Anamar, Mario Vieges, Jorge Silva, Filipe Ferrer.

San Sebastian — This first feature from a young director who has worked as a professor of editing at the National Conservatory of Cinema appears to be a deliberate pastiche of a 1940s spy thriller.

The film is heavy on mood, atmosphere and mystery, but tediously complicated, sometimes hilarious in its lack of professionalism and certainly a strange effort if meant to be taken at face value.

The hero, always referred to as Reporter X, has returned from abroad, ill, full of morphine. A headless body appears in Lisbon, later the head appears in a hat box, but it turns out to be only a mask. Our intrepid reporter is carried off to meet a mysterious Moroccan woman, a sort of Mata Hari. Then he becomes involved with Hannah, a mysterious Jewish refugee and meets her mother, who knows a secret formula for a disease which could wipe out the world.

Various plot complications pile up, characters wear their hats nicely and Manuel Costa e Silva's night time photography of Lisbon is very evocative of *film noir,* but there seems little rhyme or reason for the spectator to become involved in a collection of clichéd characters. Certainly the central one remains as mysterious as his name, giving no central substance to the film.

This will have only curiosity value in festivals looking for Portuguese representation or those specializing in mysteries. The rest will probably ask not who did it, but why did he do it? —*Cain.*

Womens Prison Massacre
(ITALIAN-FRENCH-COLOR)

A Flor Films release of a Unistar film. Executive producer, Jean Lefait. Directed by Gilbert Roussel. Screenplay, Claudio Fragasso, Olivier Lefait; camera (Telecolor), Henry Froger; editor, Gilbert Kikoine; music, Luigi Ceccarelli; assistant director, Gerard Olivier; second unit director, Fragasso. Reviewed at UA Twin 1 theater, N.Y. Sept. 26, 1986. (MPAA Rating: R.) Running time: **89 MINS.**
Emanuelle ....Laura Gemser
Crazy Boy Henderson ......Gabriele Tinti
Warden................Lorraine de Selle
Also with: Ursula Flores, Maria Romano, Antonella Giacomini, Raul Cabrera, Roberto Mura, Michael Laurant, Francoise Perrot, Franca Stoppi, Flo Astaire.

"Womens Prison Massacre" (sic) is a substandard Continental exploitation film first released domestically in May 1985. Originally titled "Emanuelle's Escape From Hell," picture was filmed back-to-back in Rome in 1982 with the 1984 release "Caged Women," featuring mainly the same cast.

Laura Gemser is Emanuelle, an undercover reporter in "Caged Women," but here unjustly incarcerated as a result of a frameup by the corrupt district attorney. Lorraine de Selle again plays the beautiful warden, but a low budget provides fewer than a dozen femme prisoners and only a couple of guards.

While Emanuelle and her two lesbian cellmates are warring with a feisty prisoner named Albina, four male prisoners led by Crazy Boy Henderson (Gabriele Tinti, Gemser's real-life husband) are delivered to the coed facility, and immediately take the warden as hostage and start a siege. The d.a. shows up with lots of police leading to a hokey bloodbath and an unhappy, pointless ending of Emanuelle back in stir.

Though director Gilbert Roussel occasionally provides an interesting composition or lighting effect, film is the usual mixture of sadism and titillation. Its best element is grotesque humor provided by the over-acting, poorly dubbed thesps, especially one of Tinti's henchmen, who resembles comedian Mark Blankfield in rolling his eyes and pulling faces. —*Lor.*

Passiflora
(CANADIAN-DOCU-COLOR-16m)

A National Film Board of Canada production. Produced by Jacques Vallée. Directed by Fernand Bélanger, Dagmar Gueissaz Teufel. Camera (color), Serge Giguere; sound, Yves Gendron; music, René Lussier, Jen Dérome, Andre Duchesne. Reviewed at the Toronto Festival of Festivals, Sept. 13, 1986. Running time: **90 MINS.**

Toronto — Imaginatively fashioned and shot, "Passiflora" focuses on visits to Montreal of Pope John Paul II and Michael Jackson the same day in 1984, with both appearing at Olympic Stadium at different times of the day.

No wonder execs of the government-run National Film Board withheld release for a while and remain queasy about playoffs.

Directors Fernand Bélanger and Dagmar Gueissaz Teufel intercut news footage of both events with a dramatized transvestite club procession mocking Pope's appearance, homosexuals kissing and pawing each other in the street and footage of an actual street demonstration against his visit.

While live tv coverage airs of his rally in a cafe, a couple discusses an unwanted pregnancy and a planned abortion.

Wall grafitti against the Pope is shown, along with scenes of the faithful at his rally.

Pic features only setup of the Jackson concert, throwing overall balance out of whack. Masses of harried police are shown at both events handling crowd and tv camera control.

Direction and Serge Giguere's camerawork are good. Pic was released on a limited basis in Quebec and so far is not subtitled in English.

Theatrical and tv possibilities are minimal but pic is emminently suitable for specialized programs at film fests. —*Adil.*

Dernier Cri
(The Last Word)
(FRENCH-COLOR)

A Harvert production. Produced by Marc André Grynbaum. Directed, edited by Bernard Dubois. Screenplay, Dubois, Baynac Bieglanci; camera (color), Marc André Batigne; music, Chopin, Beethoven; art director, Berthelemy Fougea; assistant director Agathe Vannier. Reviewed at Montreal Film Festival, Aug. 28, 1986. Running time: **87 MINS.**
With: Hubert Lucot (Henri), Christine Laurent, Catherine Bonin, Julien Dubois, Eric Mitchell, Anne Gautier, Jean-Claude Vannier.

Montreal — An improbable thriller about a gang of urban terrorists, "The Last Word" is slick, has a high body count and an even higher quotient of sex scenes, but adds up to a very little.

It opens literally with a bang as a bike rider makes a suicide attack on the car carrying American military advisers in downtown Paris. He did so without authorization from his superiors, and they fear that, when he's identified, his sister, Catherine, will give them away. Vet terrorist Henri (Hubert Lucot) is sent to assassinate Catherine, but refuses and goes on the run himself. The other members of the gang set out to track him down.

There was, potentially, a moving story in the character of Henri, a man still dedicated to the principles of the terrorist gang but frightened at the mindless violence they're now employing. Though Lucot seems more than capable of bringing the role to life, the surface screenplay gives him few chances.

There are an unusually large number of sex scenes involving full nudity, and all the women in the film are attractive. But things get rather silly before the end as the incompetent killers fight among themselves in the home of Henri's former wife.

Pic could have some commercial chances via its sex and violence theme, but won't appeal at all to the kind of cinemagoer who seeks out quality French product in the world's art houses.—*Strat.*

Ina Laska
(Another Love)
(CZECH-COLOR)

Produced by Slovak Film Studios, Bratislava-Koliba. Directed by Dusan Trancik. Screenplay, Jiri Krizan; camera (color), Alojz Hanusek; art director, Juraj Fabry; music, Marian Varga. Reviewed at Karlovy Vary Film Festival (market), July 15, 1986. Running time: **77 MINS.**
With: Maros Kramar, Georgy Czerhalmi, Zlata Adamovska, Vilhelm Perhac, Milos Cernousek, Rudolf Hrusinsky Jr., Thomas Zilincik.

Karlovy Vary — A dark picture of manners and morals in the mountain provinces of Slovakia emerges in this story of a young medical student from the city who, unable to get his diploma because he once illegally terminated a pregnancy, comes to work with a gang of tough loggers. In the same mountain village is the woman whose pregnancy he aborted, who advises the newcomer to leave. When word gets out about his medical experience, the cocksure foreman of the woodcutters (played by Hungarian actor Georgy Czerhalmi), who is selling illegal lumber on the side, wants young doc to perform an abortion on his mistress in exchange for political contacts that will restore his diploma.

He refuses, which brings him into further moral and physical conflict. Bloody but unbowed, he is undecided whether to remain in the village.

Director Dusan Trancik employs

rising young Slovakian actor Maros Kramar as the inexperienced and overly sensitive medic going toe-to-toe against the corrupt and chilly wintery village. Technical credits are satisfactory; story with social implications considered important for homegrounds is too downbeat for international commercial prospects and weighed down by unresolved subplot threads.—*Milg.*

Congo Express
(BELGIAN-COLOR)

A Cinete Production. Executive producer, Willem Thijssen. Directed by Armand de Hesselle and Luk Gubbles. Screenplay, Bob Goossens, based on his original script, "Everything Remains, Nothing Changes;" camera (color), Willy Stassen; editor, Chris Verbiest; music, Kreuners Group; production manager, Dirk Impens; sound, Jules Goris; art director, Hubert Pouille; costumes, Frieda Dauphin; assistant director, Stijn Conin. Reviewed at San Sebastian Film Fest (Open Section), Sept. 19, 1986. Running time: **85 MINS.**

Jean the mercenary . Francoise Beuckelaers
Nadia . . . . Caroline Rottier
Jean . . . . Mark Verstraete
Roger . . . . Mark Peeters
Lucienna . . . . Christine Bosmans
Gilberte . . . . Chris Cauwenberghs
Louis . . . . Mark van Eeghem
Louisette . . . . Veronique Waumans
Theo . . . . Filip van Luchene
Also with: Dries Wieme, Elie Aerts.

San Sebastian — A first feature effort from two youngish Belgian directors, who have worked on shorts together for over 10 years, "Congo Express" is an effective, economical statement about relationships and life today as seen in the microscope of the wastelands of city life in current day Belgium. Although made by two people the film has a style and consistency of tone which belies that fact. This contemporary story carries echoes of the past both in the range of individual characters and in the country's recent history.

The film is centered around a bar, the Congo Express of the title, on the outskirts of the city, which a number of the film's characters have occasion to visit from time to time. The bar owner is a former mercenary in the Belgian Congo and still carries macho and fascist attitudes with him. He was at one time in love with a young girl, who has now returned with her current lover, a rich but weak man.

The film is built on three couples of different generations. With flashbacks to past moments in their lives and relationships it also cleverly links the characters through events, as a disillusioned ex-missionary provides something of a central observing role. The film has a nice sense of black humor, bitter about life, yet not without feeling for the way people have to live. Pic does not preach and makes its points sharply and well. Fine photography from Willy Stassen, who shot "Brussels By Night" and a vibrant and lively music score from a pop group Kreuners carry the story along well. —*Cain.*

Laghi Profondi
(Deep Lakes)
(SWISS-COLOR-16m)

An RTSI (Italian Switzerland Radiotelevision) production. Written and directed by Bruno Soldini. Camera (color), Renato Volger; editor, Sonia Bertini; music, Daniele Mainardi; sound, Alberto Buletti. Reviewed at the Venice Film Festival (Venice TV), Sept. 9, 1986. Running time: **80 MINS.**
Romeo . . . . Antonio Ballerio
Manuela . . . . Manuela Beillard
Policeman . . . . Giampaolo Rossi
Also with: Lidia Costanzo, Germano Diverio, Enrico Maggi, Giovanni Battezzato, Giuseppe Troccoli.

Venice — Set between northern Italy and Switzerland, this way-out tale of a young industrialist who stages his own disappearance has little to recommend it, apart from its dogged determination to deviate from conventional filmmaking. Results are amateurish, despite helmer Bruno Soldini's florid career as a documentarist for Swiss tv, the producer of "Deep Lakes."

Anti-hero is a bankrupt Italian named Romeo. As pic opens he is presumed dead, having jumped into the deepest part of an icy lake with a stone around his neck (police reconstruction). However, we soon find him hiding out in a fancy spa, in a disguise the Marx Bros. couldn't get away with. Small wonder the room service boy recognizes him as an enemy of the people and begins stuffing threatening tapes into his shoes.

After a daring escape from the hotel through the swimming pool, the unlucky man has his suitcase of money (his last) snatched and is forced to sneak into Switzerland in total penury with some Turkish wetbacks. In an abandoned hotel where he takes refuge, he slowly goes crazy, until a reporter miraculously locates him. With him is the rich couple who ruined Romeo by inducing him to smuggle his fortune into tax-less Switzerland.

In a first climax, Romeo takes his revenge by locking the cheaters in a fallout shelter, then jumping in the lake for real. In a second, he wakes up from a prolonged nightmare — the film was just a dream — and gets ready to make the same mistakes over again.

Soldini gives us little insight into Romeo's mind, and it's far into the film before we feel an inkling of sympathy for his riches-to-rags woes. In the main role, Antonio Ballerio ranges from belligerent and snooty to shriekingly in pain. At one point, script has him crawl on the floor screaming "I'm a worm." Other characters have little chance to emerge.— *Yung.*

Sonho Sem Fim
(Endless Dream)
(BRAZILIAN-COLOR)

A Cinefilmes Ltda./Embrafilme production. Produced by Luciola Villela. Directed by Lauro Escorel Filho. Screenplay, Walter Lima Jr., Nelson Nadotti, Escorel Filho; camera (color), Jose Tadeu Ribeiro; editor, Gilberto Santeiro; music, Antonio Adolfo; design, Adrian Cooper; sound, Jose Luis Sasso; costumes, Rita Murtinho. Reviewed at Montreal World Film Festival (Latin American Cinema), Aug. 30, 1986. Running time: **112 MINS.**
With: Carlos Alberto Riccelli, Debora Bloch, Fernanda Torres, Marieta Severo, Imara Reis, Emmanoel Cavalcanti.

Montreal — Brazilian cinematographer Lauro Escorel Filho makes his directional debut with a charming picaresque film based on the life of an early 20th century "stuntman" from southern Brazil who became one of that country's moviemaking pioneers. Escorel Filho's affection for his subject is enhanced by lovely period design, camerawork and appealing performances, but the film's leisure pace and inconclusive midstream ending won't help its chances with U.S. distributors.

Eduardo Abelim (Carlos Alberto Riccelli), a handsome, self-assured yokel who drives a cab in the backwater town of Porto Alegre, fakes tuberculosis to get discharged from Army duty and launches an entertainment career putting on stunt driving shows. Growing restless in the sticks he heads for Rio de Janeiro where he's sure he'll quickly become a star in the nascent Brazilian movie studio. Naturally, Edu falls flat on his face and heads back home with his tail between his legs.

On the boat voyage back, fate intervenes in the form of a lonely wealthy woman with whom he has a shipboard affair and who gives him a goodly sum of money as an "investment" in his own filmmaking career. Edu's friends in Porto Alegre, played with a broad humor by enthusiastic character actors, initially scoff at his dream of making films about Brazil by and for Brazilians, but they're won over when he mail-orders a German camera and casts his buddies as crew and cast in his first starring vehicle, a hilariously inept Brazilian "Western."

Edu and his retinue barnstorm the hinterlands persuading local exhibitors to show the film, but the people want Hollywood pics and hoot his amateurish efforts out of town. Undeterred, the budding auteur recruits an established stage actress with his considerable charm, persuading her that film is the true art form of the modern age and that Brazil should have its own cinema. Edu's next film, a lachrymose tale about a cast-off wife, features an on-screen kiss which so scandalizes his audiences (who can only tolerate imported celluloid passion) that the filmmaker's career is shattered in disgrace. In desperation, he and his troupe turn to a gypsy life of nomadic fortune telling. However, when the revolution of the 1930s breaks out Edu grabs his girlfriend and his camera and rides a troop train off into the sunset becoming, as a postscript crawl says, a trailblazing documentarist.

Perhaps Edu's story reached its peak at this point, but Escorel Filho seems to have ended it just as things really begin to get interesting.
—*Rich.*

Aizlicgta zona
(The Forbidden Zone)
(SOVIET-DOCU-B&W)

A Riga Film Studio production. Written and directed by Herz Frank. Camera (b&w), Juris Podniek, Sergei Nikolaev; editor, Maia Selecka; music, Ivar Vigner; sound, Alfred Vishnewski. Reviewed at Repino Domkino (USSR), Sept. 13, 1986. Running time: **66 MINS.**

Repino — Made in 1975 by Latvian documentary master Herz Frank, "The Forbidden Zone" is a timeless look into the hidden world behind bars of juvenile delinquents. As horrifying as it is fascinating. "Zone" is cinéma verité at its very best, and of top festival quality.

Lensed over a one-year period in a Latvian boys' reformatory, film mainly follows 16-year-old inmate Misha, arrested for robbery. Instead of the usual psychological probe, Frank prefers to let his camera capture the bleak emptiness of Misha's haunted face and shaved head, one among many.

The boys, who have been sentenced for theft, misconduct or car accidents, are surprisingly passive, cooperative, apparently penitent for having wronged society; sadly resigned to their fate. Maybe their parents were partly to blame, but "Zone" has more to say about their life now and uncertain prospects for the future. —*Yung.*

A Composer's Notes
(DOCU-COLOR)

A Michael Blackwood Prods. production. Produced and directed by Michael Blackwood. Camera (color), Mead Hunt; editor, Peter Geismar. Reviewed at the Mill Valley Film Festival, Oct. 2, 1986. (No MPAA Rating.) Running time: **87 MINS.**

Mill Valley — "A Composer's Notes: Philip Glass And The Making Of An Opera" is a fascinating docu, albeit with limited general public appeal, glimpsing the work and personality of avant garde composer Philip Glass. It concentrates on the research, writing and production preparation for his opera "Akhnaten," and perhaps a third of the pic is devoted to footage of the opera being performed in Houston and Stuttgart.

Most striking, and of most general interest, are Glass' confabs with directors in both cities. Anybody involved in legit will find these sessions stimulating fodder, although one has the feeling there's a bit of playing to the camera. Glass himself becomes a full figure as pic progresses. Early on, as his ensemble begins a tour, he comes off as arrogant. But as he begins to discuss his background, and his operas, Glass emerges as engagingly informative and, every now and then, churlish. If only his music had similar variations.

As one of the conductors interviewed in the pic observes, "The notes are repeated so often, you tend to glaze over. And sometimes it's a problem keeping the musicians awake."

Save for "ghosts" in some of the opera performance scenes (blown up off video, one suspects) technical credits are seamless. —Herb.

El Imperio de la Fortuna
(The Realm Of Fortune)
(MEXICAN-COLOR)

Produced by Instituto Mexicano de Cinematografia. Distribution by Direccion General de Cinematografia. Executive producer, Hector Lopez. Directed by Arturo Ripstein. Screenplay, Paz Alicia Garaciadiego, from an original story by Juan Rulfo; camera (color), Angel Goded; editor, Carlos Savage; music, Lucia Alvarez; sound, Daniel Garcia; art direction, Anna Sanchez. Reviewed at San Sebastian Film Festival, Sept. 18, 1986. Running time: **155 MINS.**
Dionisio Pinzo . . . . . . Ernesto Gomez Cruz
La Caponera . . . . Blanca Guerra
Benavides . . . . Alejandro Parodi
La Pinzona . . . . Zaide Silvia Gutierrez
Canary Face . . . . Margarita Sanz
Patilludo . . . . Ernesto Yanez

San Sebastian — "The Realm Of Fortune" is a classic drama depicting the rise to fame and fortune, through the world of cock-fighting and gambling, of a poor peasant with a withered hand. Initially, he achieves minor fame through a fighting cock he has rescued back to full strength and subsequently and more importantly, through meeting with a bewitching singer, La Caponera, who becomes his talisman, bringing him good luck.

The film covers a long narrative time, provides plenty of strong dramatic action, about passionate people always living on the edge, through fighting, gambling or sex. Based on a story, "El Gallo de Oro," by the Mexican writer Juan Rulfo, it had already been filmed once before in the early 1960s by Roberto Gavaldon. Before he died Rulfo approved the script by Paz Alicia Garciadiego, which was a first-time work for the writer.

Arturo Ripstein had long wanted to make this film and has successfully created a powerful, if overlong drama. There is much symbolism and although individual scenes are skillfully mounted, film bear per-

haps too much faithfulness to the original for its own good. As the tragedy is, even for those not knowing the story, pretty obvious, a sharper attitude could have been beneficial.

Angel Goded's photography captures the dusty atmosphere of the Mexican villages, the oppressive heat and the astonishing blackness of the nights.

Ernesto Gomez Cruz, after a slightly crude portrayal of the poor man at the start, very effectively assumes his demanding role, and becomes a convincing man of power, eventually to be broken by the loss of his talisman, La Caponera. In this role, Blanca Guerra gives an uninhibited performance, although whether everyone will be captivated by her singing as the poor peasants were supposed to be is doubtful.
—Cain.

Les Clowns de Dieu
(The Clowns Of God)
(FRENCH-COLOR)

A L'Atelier 8-Gazan Films production. Produced by Dolly Schmidt. Written and directed by Jean Schmidt. Camera (color), Pierre Boffety; editor, Noun Serra; music, Mikis Theodorakis, Teddy Lasry; sound, Philippe Lioret; art director, Emmanuel Maintifneux. Reviewed at World Film Fest, Montreal, Sept. 1, 1986. Running time: **100 MINS.**
With: Daniel Kenigsberg (Méliès), Jean-Paul Roussillon, Jean-Roger Milo, Nathalie Schmidt.

Montreal — A quirky tale about a modern-day Ship of Fools, "The Clowns Of God" takes place among the tramps and bums of Paris. It's a tragi-comedy that's uneven in tone but ultimately quite affecting, though its odd, crazed characters won't appeal to many.

Story is built around Méliès, a survivor of 1968, who is almost always drunk, but who still sometimes dreams of the films he'd like to make. He falls hopelessly in love with a bruised young girl, Absinthe, an escapee from a hospital for the insane, but he loses sight of her and later she's viciously gang-raped by a gang of drunken youths.

Other characters include Garnicks, an old man who is vainly searching for God in the sewers and bars of the city, and who gets savagely beaten for his pains; Carcass, who gives shelter to the catatonic Absinthe; Biglewander, a kind of modern Wandering Jew, who drives around in a garishly painted van; and a mysterious angelic character who roller-skates silently around the streets wearing a black cape and a skull on his chest.

The film is a frenzied vision of a society without reason, with fascism on the rise again and love harder than ever to find. It's technically fine, with excellent location lensing by Pierre Boffety and knowing di-

rection. Unfortunately, the alienating mood of much of the pic and many of the scrungy characters may prove an audience turnoff. Commercial chances are therefore iffy.
—Strat.

Dirt Cheap
(AUSTRALIAN-DOCU-COLOR-16m)

Produced, written and edited by David Hay, Marg Clancy, Ned Lander. Directed by Hay. Camera (color), 16m), Lander, James Grant; sound, Anne-Marie Chandler; music, The Early Kookas. Sponsored by 38 Australian trade unions; Doctors Against Uranium Mining; Friends of The Earth; Australian Council of Churches. Reviewed at Margaret Mead Film Festival, N.Y., Sept. 13, 1986. Running time: **110 MINS.**

The title of this documenta.y is a bitterly ironic pun, because digging up uranium ore is not dirt cheap. Instead, it's destructively expensive to Australia's economy, displacing manufacturing workers from the populous industrialized south to the barren north, where Aboriginals scratch out a marginal living and where the uranium mines are the world's biggest.

"Since the mining has come, everything has changed — the land, the people, everything" are the first words of the film, setting its tone, expressing its theme, words spoken by an Aboriginal elder. The film plainly opposes uranium and bauxite mining by multi-national corporations, motivated solely by profit and with no concern with Australia's welfare. Further, the U.S. Nuclear Regulatory Commission is a heavy, as the N.R.C. is a partner of these mining groups, and AEC siets on the boards of directors.

Aboriginals, primarily the older people, fear the incoming billion-dollar mineral exploitation will shatter the fragile ecosystem of the north, destroying fishing, pearl-shell farming, subsistence agriculture and hunting of birds and small game. "We must make sure our culture lives on," they say, "despite the mining and the white people passing through."

As quickie mining communities spring up in their midst, the Aboriginals set up regional councils or collectives in self-protection, aided by liberal whites opposed to multi-nationals, opposed to nuclear proliferation and concerned with ecology and the disposal of hazardous waste materials. As a counter-measure, the uranium companies offer money to the Aboriginals, comparatively small sums, as compensation for what is, in effect, a kind of genocide. Under great pressure to conform, some Aboriginal councils sign the documents yielding up their lands and rights, as the Australian media cry out — "Stone Age Millionaires."

After the signing ceremony, the elders curiously examine the ballpoint pens and other small gifts given to them by the white executives. "Our grandparents died here, so that makes it our country," the Aboriginals say, hoping things somehow will soon return to normal, but the productive span of the north's mineral deposits is estimated variously at 25 years to a century.

Elsewhere, other Aboriginal councils hold off signing over their lands. Australian labor unions support their resistance. The film ends with a standoff.

Although overlong, "Dirt Cheap" seems a natural for public tv. Also, it perhaps can join that small company of documentaries that circulate among anti-nuke, peace and ecology organizations.
—Hitch.

Land Of Doom
(COLOR)

Weak 'Mad Max' imitation.

A Matterhorn Group presentation. Produced by Sunny Vest, Peter Maris. Executive producer, Ken Kimura. Directed by Maris. Stars Deborah Rennard, Garrick Dowhen. Screenplay, Craig Rand, from story by Peter Kotis; camera (Getty and United color), Orhan Kapai; editor, Richard Casey; music, Mark Governor; sound, Gerald Wolfe; set design, Christopher Watson; production manager, Yelmas Kanat; assistant director, Richard Bontrager; costume design, Oya Vest. Reviewed on Lightning Video vidcassette, N.Y., Aug. 30, 1986. (No MPAA Rating.) Running time: **87 MINS.**
Harmony . . . . Deborah Rennard
Anderson . . . . Garrick Dowhen
Demister/Slater . . . . Daniel Radell
Purvis . . . . Frank Garret
Halsey/Alfred . . . . Richard Allen
Orland . . . . Akut Duz

"Land Of Doom" is an uneventful U.S. imitation of the popular Aussie hit "The Road Warrior," second of the Mad Max adventures. Film was shot in 1984 and recently released (sans a theatrical run) on vidcassette.

Set typically after a "final war," picture is one long trek by tough girl Harmony (Deborah Rennard) and idealistic Anderson (Garrick Dowhen) who is trying to get the nihilistic bands of raiders to get serious and start rebuilding the world. Leader of the marauding raiders, Slater (Daniel Radell), has a grudge against Anderson and has his henchmen trying to kill him.

Though duo is vaguely searching for a fabled, faraway place where people already have banded together to recreate civilization, they accomplish nothing during this trek and are left at film's end with a bad case of sequelitis, ready to trek on.

Lacking special effects or any science fiction content, "Doom" is just an excuse to watch guys dressed up like "Mad Max" villains, riding around on motorcycles and souped-up vehicles. Absence of any nudity makes it of little interest to exploitation film fans. Stark locations are atmospheric, looking as if it were filmed in Turkey or some other exotic locale.—*Lor.*

Macaroni Blues
(NORWEGIAN-B&W)

A Norena Film release (foreign sales via Norsk Film/Frieda Ohrvik) of an A/S Elan Film (Kirsten Bryhni) production in association with Norsk Film. Produced by Kirsten Bryhni. Directed by Bela Csepcsanyi. Codirector, Fred Sassebo. Screenplay, Odd Börretzen; editor, Fred Sassebo; sound, Tom Sassebo; production design, Frode Krogh; production manager, Arve Figenschow. Reviewed as official entry at Norwegian Film Festival, at the Fönix Cinema, Kristiansand, Norway, Aug. 18, 1986. Running time: **78 MINS.**
With: Riccardo de Torrebruna, Anne Marie Ottesen, Patrizio Caracchi, Odd Börretzen, Arild Nyquist, Knut Andersen, Harald Krogtoft, Hot Club of Norway, Eddie Constantine.

Kristiansand — "Macaroni Blues" has great story potential but fails to deliver on its comedy-satire goals. Director Bela Csepcsanyi works smoothly and in a classical Italian (he is an Italian resident of Hungarian origin who also has worked in Norway for several years) Neorealism tradition, using black & white photography in a lyrical way and giving much attention to details of his characters' facial and other physical traits. It is Odd Börretzen's screenplay that lets him down badly.

The satire of 'Macaroni Blues" is directed at Norwegian welfare state's lack of confidence in the citizens' individual ability to run their own lives in an orderly way — as expressed especially through the country's rigidly enforced liquor laws and its state monopoly on wine and liquor import, distribution and retailing.

When Vincenzo (Riccardo de Torrebruna) lose his life in frustration over authorities forcing him to turn his Italian restaurant in Oslo into a speakeasy, his brother (Patrizio Caracchi) comes up from Italy to take proper revenge. He does so in the second half of the film, where gentle comedy satire is abandoned for attempts at Runyonesque farce. The brother and Vincenzo's Norwegian friends take advantage of a strike among Wine & Liquor Monopoly workers, break into setup's main warehouse and get away with thousands of crates of alcoholic beverages, which they promptly arrange to have infused in the capital city's milk supply.

The mechanics of the heist, an essential part of such fun on film, are not shown at all, and how the alcohol gets transferred to millions of milk cartons is not indicated. A drunken population is hinted at, but a hint or two is all. Having had his revenge, the brother quietly leaves

the country with a polite word about authorities probably being as bad everywhere, although in different ways. Not much of a climax for either comedy or satire. Eddie Constantine, in a super-brief cameo as a rum-runner, is left with a useless non sequitur reference to his Lemmy Caution fame. In short, what "Macaroni Blues" could have used was a good shot of something with a kick to it. —*Kell.*

Gavilán o Paloma
(Hawk Or Dove)
(MEXICAN-COLOR)

A Películas Mexicanas release of a Prods. Carlos Amador, production. Produced by Carlos Amador. Directed by Alfredo Gurrola. Stars José José. Screenplay, Fernando Gaiano, based on the life of José José; camera (color), Javier Cruz; editor, Francisco Chiu. Reviewed at Big Apple Cine 2, N.Y., Sept. 7, 1986. Running time: **106 MINS.**
José José ....Himself
First wife.................Gina Romand
Anel ....Cristian Bach
Jorge ....Jorge Ortíz de Pineda

The biopic "Gavilán o Paloma" (Hawk Or Dove) brings Mexican producer Carlos Amador back to feature production after a hiatus of 16 years.

The film is based on the life of romantic singer José Sosa, better known to his fans as "The Prince Of Song," José José.

The full title of this pic is a question that the singer poses to the audience: "What Was I ... Hawk Or Dove?" The pic never gives the audience an objective story and the question lies mute.

The story of José's life is common knowledge in Mexico: coming from poverty, he achieved fame through his singing. He then met Anel, they fell in love and lived together. Fame exacted a heavy toll and the singer took to drink, drugs and women. He married a party girl and soon his career was on the skids. Later, abandoned and in the hospital with liver problems, he was visited by Anel. She reinspired him and everything fell back into place: love, fame and happiness.

In the trailer, José says this is the true story of his life. Yet the film's depiction doesn't ring true. The singer is shown only as a victim. Was he a hawk or dove? We never know. Other people ply him with drink, false friends give him drugs and the film presents such a horrendous picture of his first wife (played by Gina Romand) that it is hard to see why he married her in the first place. She is never even referred to by name.

On the other hand, Anel (played by Argentine actress Cristian Bach) is so selfless and caring that she is unreal.

Rather than answer the question, the film is a testimonial to Anel (the real Anel is given a brief cameo, as

are other real-life persons Manolo Noreña, Anel's brother and José's manager, and Ariola Records chief Fernando Hernández).

The pic features 15 songs, both old and new, and yet they are performed anachronistically, which tends to confuse viewers familiar with José's work. In fact, the title track, which was his comeback song, makes an appearance early in his career.

Most of the photography is routine, except for performance footage, which uses star filters, dramatic closeups and other devices effectively.

On the whole, the acting is strong, but the weak script doesn't give the actors much to work with. The writer and director have decided to pursue the cliché inherent in the material and the result is uninspiring. —*Lent.*

Dot And The Whale
(AUSTRALIAN-ANIMATED-COLOR)

A Yoram Gross Film Studio production. Produced and directed by Yoram Gross. Screenplay, John Palmer; camera (color) Graham Sharpe; editor, Rod Hay; music, Guy Gross; director of animation, Ray Nowland; production coordinator, Greg Flynn; associate producer, Sandra Gross. Reviewed at Gross Studio screening room, Sydney, Sept. 12, 1986. (Commonwealth Film Censor rating: G). Running time: **75 MINS.**
With: Robyn Moore, Keith Scott.

Sydney — Sydney-based producer-director Yoram Gross perfected the art of matching animation and live footage some years back, and it's been a winning formula.

Although generally not strong enough to merit theatrical playoff outside Australia, his films have generated tidy sums around the world from television and home-video exploitation.

"Dot And The Whale," sixth in the seemingly never-ending series of "Dot" adventures, already has been sold to the Disney Channel where it no doubt will delight the targeted under age-10 audience. A noticeable improvement in animation standards in the last few "Dot" pics is further evident in the latest offering. The simple, somewhat crude drawing that characterized early works has matured into a much more elaborate, detailed and imaginative style. Likewise, the storylines have become a touch more sophisticated and thoughtful.

There's a moral subtlety tucked away in each Gross picture, and here the message is a plea for protecting that endangered species, the whale.

Dot and her dolphin friend Nelson discover a distressed whale, Tonga, marooned on an Australian beach. To save the mammal from the whale-hunters and an opportu-

nisitic fish shop proprietor, Dot comes up with an ingenious plan.

Underwater scenes filmed by Ben Cropp, a specialist in marine photography, are a real plus, as is Guy Gross' lilting score.

All the character voices are provided as usual by just two actors — Robyn Moore and Keith Scott, both blessed with an amazing versatility. —*Dogo.*

El Bronco
(MEXICAN-COLOR)

A Películas Mexicanas release of a Producciones Egan production. Stars Valentín Trujillo and Maribel Guardia. Produced and directed by Edgardo Gazcón. Screenplay, Gazcón, Rene Retes; camera (color), Agustín Lara; editor, Sergio Soto; music, Ernesto Cortazar. Review at Big Apple Cine 1, N.Y., Aug. 14, 1986. Running time: **92 MINS.**
Ulises Vargas ....Valentín Trujillo
Gabriela Meneses ....Maribel Guardia
Burro.........Alberto Rojas (El Caballo)
Ernesto ....Tony Bravo
Beatriz ....Ana Luisa Peluffo
Also with: Jorge Patiño, Armando Silvestre.

· The Mexican pic "El Bronco" is an improbable tale of the love between beautiful, American-educated and rich Gabriela (Maribel Guardia) and high school dropout washerwoman's-son Ulises (Valentín Trujillo). To attain her love, he aspires to become a championship boxer, fighting under the name El Bronco.

The only problem with their romance is that her family wants her to marry rich kid Ernesto (Tony Bravo), who has El Bronco beaten up by a couple of thugs. Things complicate further when Gabriela discovers her family is suffering financial problems which a marriage to Ernesto could alleviate.

Guardia (Miss Costa Rica before emigrating to Mexico to become a sex star) looks good in a bikini and the director makes sure we see her in lots of different styles — she soon has the pugilist bucking like a bronco. But it is when she suffers a cramp while waterskiing and requires mouth-to-mouth resuscitation that the wall between their disparate worlds crumbles.

The action takes place in Mazatlán and is full of local color. But director Edgardo Gazcón wishes to clutter the pic with lots of parallel cuts contrasting the action, driving viewers to grit their teeth.

Another hokey device overused in the film is the abundance of voice-overs as the lovers remember touching moments. At one grueling moment, Gabriela's face is superimposed on the screen four times telling El Bronco she loves him. Ernesto Cortázar's dreadful score only manages to take the corny love scenes into realm of pure camp. —*Lent.*

Amor a la Vuelta de la Esquina
(Love Around The Corner)
(MEXICAN-COLOR)

An Azteca Films release of a Producciones Emyil production. Produced by Miguel Camacho. Written and directed by Alberto Cortés Calderón, based on Albertine Sarrazin's novel "El Astrálago." Stars Gabriela Roel. Camera (color), Guillermo Navarro; editor, Juan Manuel Vargas; music, José Elorza. Reviewed as part of 10th Latino Festival, Public Theater, N.Y., Aug. 30, 1986. Running time: 95 MINS.
María . . . . Gabriela Roel
Julián . . . . Alonso Echanove

Mexican director Alberto Cortés Calderón's debut pic "Love Around The Corner" was originally lensed to participate in the III Experimental Film Competition, sponsored by the Mexican Film Institute (Imcine).

A more fitting title would be "Love On A Street Corner," since the film deals with the travails of a prostitute, María (Gabriela Roel), who conducts a large part of her business from Mexico City street corners.

Although the pic's theme is generic in Mexico, publicity for the film says it exposes "the hitherto unrevealed seamy underworld of Mexico City." Obviously, the copywriter hasn't seen many Mexican films.

What is different is the coldness of the pic's tone. The narration unravels in a series of disparate scenes showing María pursuing her career, along with robbing her customers, with a seeming indifference to everything. Guillermo Navarro's able camera is but an eye, and the audience never penetrates into her thoughts or motivations.

At the beginning of the film, María breaks her ankle escaping over a wall. Where is she escaping from? A prison? A mental institution? Either place would explain her subsequent actions.

She comes to the capital looking for a friend, but when she finds her, the friend is forgotten quickly. She also has continuing relationships with two different men. She apparently feels something for one of them and the other she robs and humiliates numerous times, although he never mentions it.

Even though the pic is based on Albertine Sarrazin's novel "El Astrálago" (The Anklebone), (previously filmed in France in 1968 as "L'Astragale"), the tone is closer to the 1982 German film "A Woman In Flames," by Robert Van Ackeren, a debt that is acknowledged in the film.

The lensing is provocative and lean, complemented by José Elorza's jazzy score.

Overall, the pic is disturbing more for what is not said than for what we see. The almost scientific approach leaves the audience asking why does María behave the way she does? What does she want? Who is she? Unfortunately, the director never tells us fully.—*Lent.*

El Maleficio II
(The Spell II)
(MEXICAN-COLOR)

A Videocine release of a Televicine production. Produced by Gabriel Figueroa. Directed by Raúl Araiza. Stars Ernesto Alonso, Lucía Méndez. Screenplay, Araiza, based on characters from the Televisa telenovela "El Malficio;" camera (color), José Ortiz Ramos; editor, Jesús Paredes; music, Guillermo Méndez; special effects, Juan Carlos Muñoz. Reviewed at Big Apple Cine 1, N.Y., Sept. 11, 1986. Running time: 105 MINS.
Enrique de Martino . . . . Ernesto Alonso
Marcela . . . . Lucía Méndez
Gabriel . . . . Antonio Monsell
David . . . . Alejandro Camacho
Guillermo . . . . Juan Carlos Ruiz
Prof. Andrés . . . . Eduardo Yañez
Abel Romo . . . . Manuel Ojeda
Aunt . . . . María Teresa Rivas

Due to high ratings of its 1983 soap "El Maleficio" (The Spell), Mexican tv conglomerate Televisa, through its feature film production company Televicine, has produced a big-screen venture. Acknowledging the soap as part one, the pic begins where the soap left off and offers an entirely new storyline.

The feature version is directed by Raúl Araiza, helmer of the small-screen venture. Also, pic brings back actor Ernesto Alonso, star and also producer of the first version.

Story begins with Alonso (who had formerly been killed but his body never recovered) searching two continents for a boy who had posed for a painting titled "Portrait Of Gabriel." Alonso's master — personified in another painting — wants him to find the boy and develop his potential psychic powers. The boy, we find out, is eventually to take Alonso's place as the devil's emissary.

Meantime, the boy has been discovering his supernatural abilities on his own. He has a bad temper and every time it flares up, the boy busts windows and cracks plaster, much to the consternation of his aunt.

He also has incestuous feelings for his beautiful sister, played by Lucía Méndez.

When Alonso also falls for Méndez, he and the boy have a falling out, with fatal results.

Lensing by José Ortiz Ramos is on target, crisp and compelling. Special effects are also believable and technically effective. Yet, as they pile up in one scene after another, they lose power through sheer quantity.

The main flaw of the film is that in transferring it from soap to big screen, there is still a lingering soap opera feel. Situations and character confrontations are too melodramatic, even when dealing with the conventions of the genre.

The opening half of the film is the most effective. Also the perverse brother-sister scenes are disturbing. However, everything stumbles in the Méndez-Alonso pairing. Its predictability is as corny as it is distracting from the drama.

The acting is good, especially Alonso. Unfortunately, many times Méndez' costumes are out of place. For example, she wears a formal cocktail dress to her art class. Secondary characters Ojeda, Ruiz and Yañez also provide some good moments. —*Lent.*

Contacto Chicano
(The Chicano Connection)
(MEXICAN-COLOR)

A Películas Mexicanas release of a Producciones de Rey production. Produced by Arnufo Delgado. Directed by Luis Quintanilla. Stars Gerardo Reyes, Rosa Gloria Chagoyán. Screenplay, Augusto Novaro, Laura H. de Marchetti; camera (color), Antonio Ruiz; editor, Angel Camacho; music, Rafael Elizondo, with appearances by Los Diablos, Federico Villa, Rosenda Bernal and Víctor Manuel Sosa. Reviewed at Big Apple Cine 1, N.Y., Aug. 14, 1986. Running time: 98 MINS.
Tony Andrade . . . . Gerardo Reyes
Linda Lince . . . . Rosa Gloria Chagoyán
Gino Valetti . . . . Armando Silvestre
Ivonne . . . . Livia Michel
Also with: Alvaro Zermeño, Carlos León, Lilian Gonzales, Olivia Roival.

Taking his cue from "The French Connection," Mexican filmmaker Luis Quintanilla has concocted an improbable tale of diamond smuggling into the U.S. via frogmen from Mexico. The governments of both countries are determined to stop this venture at all costs. Unfortunately, the costs don't include good production values for this cheapo pic, inappropriately titled "The Chicano Connection."

Because the U.S. doesn't want to risk problems in its "delicate relations with Mexico," the case is handled in San Francisco by two unlikely Mexican detectives (Gerardo Reyes and Rosa Gloria Chagoyán), who are hot on the trail of the smugglers and their Italian boss (Armando Silvestre).

The director has decided to chop up the action throughout the pic by throwing in performances by popular ranchero singers. Even this does not distract us from the gaping holes in the plot.

The background music also seems like a hodge-podge of whatever was lying around (at one point while our heroes are riding horses, "God Rest Ye Merry Gentlemen" actually plays accompaniment!).

Neither Reyes nor Chagoyán are convincing in the leads. Also, the mediocre photography tends to distance the audience in scenes that need to be gripping and suspenseful.

In any case, "The Chicano Connection" doesn't connect with the audience lured in by the promise of adventure, a promise that is never kept. — *Lent.*

The Generals
(BRITISH-DUTCH-GREEK-EAST GERMAN-COLOR)

A coproduction of ETV Films (London)/Euro-Television Prods. (Amsterdam)/Acropolis Films & TV (Athens)/Taller Cinematografico H & S (Berlin) for "Generals For Peace And Disarmament" (London). Directed by Watler Henowski and Gerhard Scheumann with Peter Hellmich, Horst Donth, Graphic Art Studio, Vienna, Neithardt Willerding, Franz Endlicher, TV-Film-Photo-Service Vienna, Traute Wischnewski, Armand Meppiel, Walter Martsch, Harry Landis, Wolfgang v. Polentz, Georgis Samiotis, Menios Nikolaidis, Eberhard Schwarz, Sarah Blum, Ilse Radtke, Renate Heckman, Jorge Honig, Carment Barwaldt, Marie-Claude Reverdin, Stanley Forman, Mathias Remmert, Georgis Tsiokos, Gerardo Barolo. Assessor, Prof. Gerhard Kade; music, Udo Zimmermann. Reviewed at San Sebastian Film Festival (Open Zone Section), Sept. 24, 1986. Running time (Part II): 100 MINS.
With the participation of Marshall Francisco da Costa Gomes, General Nino Pasti, Admiral Antoine Sanguinetti, General Georgios Koumanakos, General Gert Bastian, General John Christie, General Michael Harbottle, General Micheil H. von Meyenfeldt.

San Sebastian — "The Generals" is a two-part film made as a coproduction between four companies in Europe for the Year of Peace to promote nuclear disarmament. The second part only was screened at San Sebastian, the first part (80 minutes in length) deals apparently with the role of the participating officers in the second World War, while the second concentrates on post-war activities of the same men, in particular their work with NATO.

The film is a propaganda documentary, for it was made in connection with the signing of a declaration against the siting of missiles in Europe by eight distinguished former high ranking officers from different European countries. It is a sober, powerful film dealing with a subject of immense importance, the peace of the world in the face of the escalating nuclear arms race. It is of course lent considerable weight by the high office the generals all attained while in service.

These men bring a breadth of experience to the subject of nuclear warfare, and all had experience with NATO in some form or other, but became opponents of the siting of nuclear bases in Europe. The film sketches in their military background with liberal use of film photos and archive footage, and each man is allowed to make his own points in his own manner and his reason for coming to sign the public declaration, "Europe Says No

To Nuclear Bases.''

Each is interviewed in the same style, seated on a chair with black background and responding to questions. The weight of opinion of such a wide range of former distinguished officers is formidable and raises the level of the argument about nuclear war to a high moral level. (Some of the generals emphasize the fact that they are not pacifists, and also that they are anti-communist.) Only a slightly sentimental ending, complete with freeze-frame on children, mars the admirably straightforward tone of this film. —*Cain.*

Kali Patritha Syntrophe
(Happy Homecoming, Comrade)
(GREEK-COLOR)

A Greek Film Center presentation of a GFC, Lefteris Xanthopoulos production. Directed by Lefteris Xanthopoulos. Screenplay, Xanthopoulos, George Bramos, Thanassis Scroumbelos, assisted by Fekete Obolya; camera (color), Andreas Sinanos; editor, Antonis Tempos; music, Eleni Karaindrou; sound, Dinos Kittou; art director, Panos Papadopoulos; production manager, Yannis Latsios. Reviewed at the Morettina Center, Locarno Film Fest, Aug. 16, 1986. Running time: **85 MINS.**

With: Athena Papadimitriou, Peter Trokan and the inhabitants of Beloiannisz, Hungary.

Locarno — A handsome, slow-moving first feature by a director with considerable experience in tv documentaries, ''Happy Homecoming, Comrade'' evokes the tragedy of post-war Greece.

From 1945 to 1949, Greece was torn apart by civil war, pitting leftist resistance against the regular army supported by the West. After the army crushed the opposition, over 100,000 members of the Leftist Democratic Forces crossed the border into neighboring socialist countries, settled there and only now are they, or their children, being allowed to return back home.

Lefteris Xanthopoulos shot the entire film in Beloiannisz, a village in Hungary, some 30 miles outside Budapest, built by the Greek refugees some 35 years ago, and now being abandoned as many of them are going back to Greece.

Whatever fiction there is in this story, is only an excuse to lead into an almost entirely documentary portrait of a human tragedy of major proportions. The villagers living in Hungary have kept intact not only their identity, but also their language and their customs. They have established new homes and new families. Now they are tormented between the longing for the old country and their strong affinity with their new home. —*Edna.*

Hoosiers
(COLOR)

Powerful character study in the world of Middle American athletics.

An Orion Pictures release of a Hemdale presentation of a Carter De Haven production. Produced by De Haven, Angelo Pizzo. Executive producers, John Daly, Derek Gibson. Directed by David Anspaugh. Stars Gene Hackman. Screenplay, Pizzo; camera (CFI color), Fred Murphy; editor, C. Timothy O'-Meara; music, Jerry Goldsmith; production design, David Nichols; art direction, David Lubin; set decoration, Janis Lubin, Brendan Smith; costume design, Jane Anderson; sound (Dolby), David Brownlow; assistant director, Herb Adelman; second unit director, Pizzo; second unit camera, Oliver Wood; associate producer, Graham Henderson; casting, Ken Carlson. Reviewed at the Directors Guild Theater, L.A., Oct. 6, 1986. (MPAA Rating: PG.) Running time: **114 MINS.**

Coach Norman Dale	Gene Hackman
Myra Fleener	Barbara Hershey
Shooter	Dennis Hopper
Cletus	Sheb Wooley
Opal Fleener	Fern Persons
Whit	Brad Boyle
Rade	Steve Hollar
Buddy	Brad Long
Everett	David Neidorf
Merle	Kent Poole
Ollie	Wade Schenck
Strap	Scott Summers
Jimmy	Maris Valainis

Hollywood — ''Hoosiers'' is an involving tale about the unlikely success of a smalltown Indiana high school basketball team that paradoxically proves both rousing and too conventional. Centered around a fine performance by Gene Hackman as the coach, Orion release will have to be groomed carefully, but there is likely an audience in Middle America for this solid, upbeat fare. Pic will open for a week's Oscar-qualifying run in Los Angeles in December, and will bow nationally early next year.

Opening stretch is highly promising, as Hackman, a former college coach, arrives in Hickory, Ind., in 1951 after a 10-year Navy stint. Althought tough and proud, Hackman is clearly being given a last chance here by an old friend and, despite his bravura, he lives under something of a cloud.

The locals, who take basketball as seriously as they do God and corn, are slow to accept this newcomer, particularly when his unusual coaching methods turn a winning team into a loser early in the new season. Just when he's about to be booted out, a former star player returns, Hackman's lessons begin to pay off and the team starts winning.

And winning and winning. Hickory High, a farmland school with only 64 boys to draw upon for a team, soon finds itself heading for the qualifying rounds for the state championship. At this point, what had been a carefully calibrated, closely observed character study of a driven man and his charges becomes a well-made but standard-issue sports yarn about the triumph of an underdog.

First half offers Hackman many special moments, as he superbly delineates the determination of a man to teach and, in the process, build character in his own way regardless of the negative consequences this might have for himself. In fact, the most intriguing aspect of the character is his invariable compulsion to help others and bring out their best, even at this own expense.

This tendency is seen not only in his relationships with the kids on the team, but in his unnecessary but valiant effort to resurrect the life of town drunk Dennis Hopper, a former basketball star and father of one of the team's current players, and in his partially successful effort to draw out school official Barbara Hershey, an emotional closet case.

During the opening reels, first-time feature director David Anspaugh, an award-winner for his tv work on ''Hill Street Blues'' and ''St. Elsewhere,'' paints a richly textured portrait of rural American life, both visually and through glimpses of the guarded reticence of the people. Dialog by Angelo Pizzo, like Anspaugh a native Hoosier, rings true, and the characters are neither sentimentalized nor caricatured.

Tension is built nicely as the farmboys advance through the playoffs, but it nearly becomes a different picture, one devoted almost exclusively to the matter of winning or losing games. The sport, as played in early 20th century gymnasiums, is covered extremely well, but the feeling persists that we're now in ''Rocky'' country; that we've seen this same routine many times over.

By the time the games accumulate, one has come to care about the characters sufficiently to root them on, but one also regrets losing the concentration on them that brightened the earlier parts of the film.

Pic belongs to Hackman, but Hopper, after ''Blue Velvet'' and ''River's Edge,'' gets another opportunity to put in a showy turn as a local misfit. Hershey's role is perfunctory, and one of the great virtues here is the authentic feel stemming from all-Indiana shooting and the extensive use of local actors.

Fred Murphy's lensing is excellent, Jerry Goldsmith's score is engaging and uncharacteristically throbbing in a disco way, and David Nichols' production design and Jane Anderson's costumes contribute heavily to the verisimilitude.
—*Cart.*

Burial Ground
(Le notti dei terrore)
(ITALIAN-COLOR)

A Film Concept Group release of an Esteban Cinematografica production. Produced by Gabriele Crisanti. Directed by Andrea Bianchi. Screenplay, Piero Regnoli; camera (La Microstampa Fujicolor), Gianfranco Maioletti; editor, uncredited; music, Elsio Mancuso, Burt Rexon; set design, Giovanni Fratalocchi; masks & special makeup effects, Rosario Prestopino; special effects, Gino De Rossi. Reviewed on Vestron Video vidcassette, N.Y., Aug. 26, 1986. (No MPAA Rating.) Running time: **85 MINS.**

With: Maria Angela Giordano (Evelyn), Karin Well, Gian Luigi Chirizzi, Simone Mattioli, Antonietta Antinori, Roberto Caporali, Peter Bark, Claudio Cucchett, Anna Valente, Renato Barbieri.

''Burial Ground'' is a subpar Italian horror film, shot in 1983 with the original title ''The Nights Of Terror.'' Pic was released domestically last year with no rating, capitalizing on its heavy gore.

Filmmaker Andrea Bianchi is hardly the first Italian helmer to copy George A. Romero's successful ''Living Dead'' formula, but unlike predecessors Lucio Fulci and Umberto Lenzi he adds little to the mythos. Weak storyline has a group of visitors (i.e., victims) visiting the mansion of Prof. Ayres, who has been studying the magic practices of the ancient Etruscans, dealing with the survival of the dead. Skeletal ghouls attack everyone and eat their innards, with the usual butcher-shop makeup effects applied.

A sick subplot flirts with incest as Evelyn (Maria Angela Giordano) has to fend off the sudden sexual advances of her weird-looking young son, who eventually turns on her and kills her after he's been attacked and turned into a ghoul.

As usual, the only way to kill these ghouls is to blow their heads off. Also typical for the genre is the stress on maggots covering the ghouls' decayed faces. Monster masks used here are convincing enough, but the format's power to shock has worn off via frequent repetition.—*Lor.*

Jumpin' Jack Flash
(COLOR)

Boring solo vehicle for Whoopi Goldberg.

A 20th Century Fox release of a Lawrence Gordon/Silver Pictures production. Produced by Lawrence Gordon, Joel Silver. Directed by Penny Marshall. Stars Whoopi Goldberg. Screenplay, David H. Franzoni, J.W. Melville & Patricia Irving, Christopher Thompson, from story by Franzoni; camera (DeLuxe color), Matthew F. Leonetti; editor, Mark Goldblatt; music, Thomas Newman; production design, Robert Boyle; art director, Frank Richwood; set decorator, Donald Remacle; sound (Dolby), Jerry Jost; assistant director, Beau E.L. Marks; associate producers, Richard Marks, George Bowers, Elaine K. Thompson; casting, Nancy Klopper. Reviewed at Zanuck Theater, 20th Century Fox, Century City, Calif., Oct. 7, 1986. (MPAA Rating: R.) Running time: **100 MINS.**

Terry Doolittle	Whoopi Goldberg
Marty Phillips	Stephen Collins
Jeremy Talbot	John Wood
Cynthia	Carol Kane
Liz Carlson	Annie Potts
Mr. Page	Peter Michael Goetz
Archer Lincoln	Roscoe Lee Browne
Lady Sarah Billings	Sara Botsford

Mark Van Meter . . . . Jeroen Krabbé
Carl . . . . Vyto Ruginis
Jack . . . . Jonathan Pryce
Repairman . . . . Jim Belushi
Hunter . . . . Tony Hendra
Doug . . . . Jon Lovitz
Gillian . . . . June Chadwick
Fiona . . . . Tracey Ullman
Detective . . . . Garry K. Marshall

Hollywood — "Jumpin' Jack Flash" is not a gas, it's a bore. A weak idea and muddled plot poorly executed not surprisingly results in a tedious film with only a few brief comic interludes from Whoopi Goldberg to redeem it. Pic may open on its title and star but won't stick around very long.

Anyone who has been longing for a film in which a black office worker talks dirty to a computer terminal (and almost anyone else in earshot) should find "Jumpin' Jack Flash" just what they've been waiting for.

Goldberg is Terry Doolittle, sort of a second-rate Pee-wee Herman with toy animals on her desk and funky clothes on her back and an apartment that looks like a novelty shop showroom. Working alongside bimbo Carol Kane and hounded by boss Peter Michael Goetz, it's a setup worthy of any good sitcom.

Just when her life is looking most bleak along comes Jack. He's a British spy trapped somewhere behind the Iron Curtain who somehow, someway, taps into Goldberg's terminal and asks for help to escape. Goldberg is plunged into a web of intrigue involving a sinister repairman (Jim Belushi) who conveniently disappears, a crippled diplomat (Roscoe Lee Browne) and another spy (Jeroen Krabbé) who winds up floating face down in the East River.

It really doesn't make much sense and is never sufficiently explained. Even more deadly, it never succeeds in hooking the audience. There is about as much menace to these goings on as a soft drink commercial. Director Penny Marshall fails to generate the least bit of suspense, partially because the screenplay, credited to no fewer than four writers, is trying to do too many things at once.

Goldberg may be cute but she's not dangerous and talking to Jack through the computer is hardly involving. A number of supporting players pass in and out of the action, but even an actor the caliber of John Wood as a KGB mole in the British consulate can't do anything to save the day.

It is also questionable whether Goldberg can carry a film on her own. Occasionally there are amusing bits and pieces such as when she attends a dress ball at the consulate disguised as Diana Ross or is dancing around her apartment to the Rolling Stones' title song. More often the humor is too self-conscious and seems to be missing only a laugh track.

Other scenes are equally overstated for effect as when a slow moving cab is totally upended when it taps another car or when a phone booth with Goldberg in it is picked up by a tow truck and dragged down the avenue.

Tech credits are fine but the film's a mess.—*Jagr.*

Hullumeelsus
(Madness)
(SOVIET-B&W)

A Tallinnfilm production (Estonia). Directed by Kaljo Kiisk. Screenplay, Victor Lorencs; camera (Widescreen, b&w), Anatoli Zabolotski. Reviewed at Repino Domkino (USSR), Sept. 20, 1986. Running time: 90 MINS.
Doctor . . . . Valdemar Panso
Gestapo man . . . . Jüri Järvet
Girl . . . . Mare Garsnek-Hellat
Also with: Bronius Babkauskas (Willy), Valeri Nosik (the writer), Vaclavas Bledis (the "Führer").

Repino — At the time it was made, Kaljo Kiisk's "Madness" (1968) was screened only in the director's native Estonia and banned in the rest of the country. Viewed today, the censor's reasoning is unfathomable, for the film is a gem of black humor with all the freshness and dazzle of a genuine classic.

Anatoli Zabolotski's classy black and white camerawork sets "Madness" in its time, but film's slightly dated look shouldn't prevent it from being seen in special situations.

Scene is set at the end of the war, in a little town where, we are told, the Fascists killed millions. An SS squadron marches past a "Judenfrei" sign (absurdly, posted in the middle of a field) and enters a huge, Marienbad-like mental asylum to the music of a toy band, while inmates shout "Long live our liberators!"

Actually, the intent is to liquidate all "5,083" patients, but first a pompous gym teacher-turned-Gestapo chief (Jüri Järvet) has to catch an English spy supposed to be hiding inside. Taking the director of the institute (the kindly Valdemar Panso) into his confidence, he announces he will postpone shooting the patients while he masquerades as a new doctor and ferrets out his man.

Using minimalist sets and wide stretches of white walls that recall 1960s' pop style, Kiisk strips down his story to its most grotesque bones. Many patients may be lodged in the asylum, however, and as the good doctor gives us to understand, more than a few are spurious madmen — we only meet five "suspects," each a symbolic case. A paranoid young writer is obsessed with the little devil in his head who writes for him; a pudgy gentleman clad like Caesar thinks he's the Führer; a pretty girl (Mare Garsnek-Hellat) who looks like an Estonian Anna Karina is a wistful romantic, the mistress of a high-ranking Nazi. What ensues between these likable crazies and the Gestapo doctor is a terribly logical/illogical dialog between madmen, where questions like "Who set fire to the Reichstag?" are just as sensible as "How many years have you been in the British Secret Service?"

Music is an ironic medley of out-of-place tunes. — *Yung.*

Soul Man
(COLOR)

Hilarious farce on race relations spells big b.o.

A New World Pictures release in association with Balcor Film Investors of a Steve Tisch production. Produced by Steve Tisch. Coproducers, Carol Black, Neal Marlens. Directed by Steve Miner. Screenplay, Carol Black; camera (CFI color, Technicolor prints), Jeffrey Jur; editor, David Finfer; music, Tom Scott; production design, Gregg Fonseca; art direction, Don Diers, John Rienhart; set design, Larry Fulton; set decoration, Dorree Cooper; costume design, Sharon Simonaire; makeup, Devorah Fischa; sound, Donald Summer; assistant director, Betsy Magruder; production manager-line producer, Donna Smith; associate producers, Bernhard Goldmann, Stephen Vaughan; casting, Melissa Skoff. Reviewed at the Samuel Goldwyn theater, Beverly Hills, Oct. 8, 1986. (MPAA Rating: PG-13.) Running time: **101 MINS.**
Mark Watson . . . . C. Thomas Howell
Gordon Bloomfeld . . . . Arye Gross
Sarah Walker . . . . Rae Dawn Chong
Professor Banks . . . . James Earl Jones
Whitney Dunbar . . . . Melora Hardin
Mr. Dunbar . . . . Leslie Nielsen
Bill Watson . . . . James B. Sikking
Dr. Aronson . . . . Max Wright
Ray McGrady . . . . Jeff Altman
George Walker . Jonathan (Fudge) Leonard
Lisa Stimson . . . . Julia Louis-Dreyfus
Brad Small . . . . Mark Neely

Hollywood — This social farce is excellently written, fast paced and intelligently directed. "Soul Man" is arguably the best comedic review of the state of America's racist attitudes during an era one character calls "the Cosby decade." New World's reward for success with such provocative material should be substantial business.

Film is hilarious throughout as initial screenplay by Carol Black consistently engages via fable-like tale of a white man (C. Thomas Howell) darkening his skin in order to win a law-school scholarship intended for a black.

If there is a paradox here, it is that this soul man's transformation may be initially unconvincing, but is so propelled by swift story movement and complementary performances that the preposterous becomes plausible.

Director Steve Miner skillfully guides pic through visually compelling scenes, including one of a pickup basketball game revolving around Howell's desirability due to presumed prowess at the hoop.

Ron Reagan shows up as one of the team's captains vying for the supposedly skilled "black" player. The presidential progeny returns later with some ably delivered punchlines.

The racist-oriented humor escalates from here on as two fellow students periodically unload jokes slurring blacks.

Perhaps the zaniest turn of events comes at a dinner during which fantasies of the uppercrust white hosts are mentally conjured in extreme racial stereotypes.

In boldly — if not brazenly — tackling this subject matter, filmmakers could be perceived as edging toward racism themselves. They verge the closest in shots of Howell mimicking Stevie Wonder as not only blind but hearing-impaired. Ultimately, the depiction may have risked bad taste more than personal or racial slight.

Such scenes appear neither destructive nor maliciously-intended. Indeed, the entire film's point of view strikes a chord for racial harmony, enlightened evolution of one white man and a 1980s sensibility to address these topics with ease and good humor.

Black, Miner, et al., are able to empathize with the black perspective without pandering. Their plot intricacies also understate, rather than overblow, antiblack sentiments by several characters.

Howell as the white-turned-black law student is just effective enough to be believable. His portrayal does require, and is substantially enhanced by, at least three other cast members.

As Howell's close buddy, Arye Gross delivers gifted and energized screen humor. This is not just a second banana. This is a sidekick who gets most of the guffaws and absolutely shines in a climactic classroom monolog.

Rae Dawn Chong is wholly natural and intellectually appealing. Her reluctant romantic involvement with Howell focuses his ultimate moral dilemma over the skin deception. Jonathan (Fudge) Leonard, as her young son, is so charming that he nearly steals the entire picture.

And then there is James Earl Jones. As a criminal law prof, Jones' imposing voice and stern demeanor result in a hybrid of his Darth Vader and John Houseman's Prof. Kingsfield of "The Paper Chase." Jones' representation of authority, with occasional glimpses of human warmth, are critical to the film's denouement.

Long before the story's resolution, however, it is clear that this film is going to provide audiences with a cascade of visual and verbal humor.

Early on, when one college prepster declares that "it's never too soon to start networking," the biting social insights begin flowing.

In some sense, the picture's overall thrust is aimed as much at this country's absurd preoccupation with lawyering as it is at race.

Story winds up delivering both an uplifting and entertaining tone — proving that the combination is compatible. —*Tege.*

Les Territoires De La Défonce
(Dope Territory)
(BELGIAN-DOCU-COLOR/ B&W-16m)

A S.A. F3 production. Produced by Godefroid Courtmans. Directed by Joao Correa. Camera (color, 16m), Michael Sander, Alessandro Usai; editor, Yves Van Herstraeten; sound, Alain Sironval. Reviewed at the Montreal World Film Festival-Cinema of Today and Tomorrow, Aug. 28, 1986. Running time: **95 MINS.**

Montreal — "Dope Territory" is a didactic, talking heads documentary about the evils of heroin addiction amongst Belgian youth, intercut with a superficial overview of drug use through the ages and a pretentious effort to relate the social problems that have spawned addiction to an interpretation of world history.

This type of film is old hat in the U.S. where such docus as "Streetwise" have examined the problems of modern youth adrift with far superior documentary technique and execution. It scarcely seems worth the trouble to subtitle in English for the minimal exposure it might get at documentary fests.

Interviews with various former and still-addicted heroin users tell much the same sad tale of teenage involvement with hashish and psychedelics followed by peer pressure to try heroin. Once hooked, these children of bourgeois Europe engaged in various types of prostitution and degradation to feed the drug craving that ruled, or still rules, their lives. A sense of extreme boredom and alienation led to their experimentation with drugs, it is suggested.

Using stills and stock footage, the docu also gives a quick once over to the history of the English opium trade in China, cocoa-chewing South American indians, and the place of drugs in various epochs including the time of ancient Rome, the renaissance, the industrial revolution WWI, the jazz age, WWII and the modern era. It also runs down the familiar roster of famous druggies: Baudelaire, Racine, de Maupassant, Freud, Gauthier, Cocteau, etc.

The docu unsuccessfully tries to dramatize this tired subject with a narrative tone of grave urgency and a jittery jazz soundtrack.—*Rich.*

L'Ultima Mazurka
(The Last Mazurka)
(ITALIAN-COLOR)

An Italnoleggio release of a RAI-1 production. Directed by Gianfranco Bettetini. Stars Erland Josephson, Senta Berger. Screenplay, Bettetini, Luigi Lunari, with the collaboration of Alberto Farassino, Aldo Grasso, Tatti Sanguineti; camera (color), Giulio Albonico; editor, Gianni Lari; music, Gino Negri; art direction, Enrico Tovaglieri; costumes, Franca Zucchelli; choreography, Mario Pistoni. Reviewed at Sacis screening room, Rome, Aug. 28, 1986. (In Venice Film Fest, non-competing). Running time: **120 MINS.**
Serra . . . . Erland Josephson
Grete . . . . Senta Berger
Reiger . . . . Mario Scaccia
Lanza . . . . Paolo Bonacelli
Also with: Marina Berti, Adele Cossi (soprano), Giuseppe Fallisi (tenor), Claudio Lobbia (porter).

Rome — Though appearing in Venice's tv sidebar, "The Last Mazurka" will first be seen locally on the big screen, courtesy of Italnoleggio distribution. Its chances off-shore look mostly limited to television (length is a convenient two hours).

Based on real events, film recounts the tragic bombing of the Diana Theater in Milan in 1921, on the eve of Mussolini's rise to power. As reconstructed in "Mazurka," the bombing was masterminded by the right and made to look like a terrorist act by left-wing/Communist extremists, thus giving the authorities an excuse to let the fascists move in.

Though the historical background comes across clearly (even simplistically), real heart of pic is the story of a flighty, light opera company, inadvertently involved in the tragedy. Directed by clownish Mario Scaccia, always on the verge of hysteria, the company's light is its leading lady, Grete. Senta Berger never emerges from the frivolous affectations of the soubrette role, though her dubbed singing is divine. Film is generous to a fault in showing long excerpts of Franz Lehar's "Mazurka Blu" in rehearsal after rehearsal.

Meanwhile, in the hotel where Grete is lodged, Milan's Chief of Police Erland Josephson takes up residence, both to be near his mistress and to meet with the town's rich burghers, who are holding a convention. Josephson's dignified, grave official is several notches above the rest of the cast, and the film as a whole, which, given all its intrigues, relationships and rehearsals, should be more entertaining than it actually is.

Director Gianfranco Bettetini's main profession is that of professor of semiotics and mass communication, which doesn't automatically translate into communication with the masses. A plus for the small screen are costumes and sets, afflicted with too much gaudy Art Deco madness for big screen space.
—*Yung.*

You Must Be Joking
(SOUTH AFRICAN-COLOR)

A Ster-Kinekor release of an Elmo de Witt Films/Kavalier Films/Koukus Prods. film. Directed by Elmo de Witt. Stars Leon Schuster. Screenplay, Schuster, Fanus Rautenbach; camera (color), Gerry Lotter; editors, Gerrie van Wyk, Mac Errington; art director, Andrew Whitlock; set decoration, Hein Schaap; sound, John Bergman; special effects, Max Poolman; associate producers, Ami Wright, Andre Scholtz, Hermann Visser; makeup supervision, Anni Taylor; assistant director, Schuster; continuity, Judi Lottant director, Schuster. Reviewed at Sterland, Pretoria, Aug. 14, 1986. Running time: **95 MINS.**
With: Leon Schuster, Golda Raff, Jannie Pretorius, Johann Stemmet, Carike Keuzenkamp, Rina Hugo, Trevor Nasser, Ed van Wyk, Buddy Vaughn, Joanna Field, Lukas Maree, Kallie Knoetze, Mike Schutte, Daan Smuts and Fanus Rautenbach.

Pretoria — South African filmmakers' obsession with candid camera pics continues with the latest offering from radio funnyman Leon Schuster. With little foreign potential due to constant crossover between English and Afrikaans in dialog, pic was a smash winner at the local b.o., a sad statement about the depth of local audiences.

Schuster plays various roles trapping gullible members of the public, leaving good taste and style behind. Particularly disturbing is the extent to which he plays with susceptible blacks, obviously taking advantage of those lesser educated and adding, in a sickly comic way, to the polarization of the two race groups in a troubled society.

Length of the various skits is hopelessly long, losing much appeal in the process, and comments provided by two narratives are plain corny.

This pic follows previous candid camera-type offerings from Jamie Uys ("Funny People" I and II) and Emil Nofal's "You're In The Movies." Idea for pic sprung from Schuster's success as a radio comedian with fellow scriptwriter Fanus Rautenbach, and both visited U.S. for an extended period to gather material.

Tech credits are okay, with special effects meriting a mention as does lenser Gerry Lotter. —*Glee.*

Toomas Nipernaadi
(Nipernaadi)
(SOVIET-COLOR)

A Tallinnfilm production (Estonia). Directed by Kaljo Kiisk. Stars Tõnu Kark. Screenplay, Juhan Viiding, from a novel by August Gailit; camera (color), Jüri Sillart; music, Raimo Kangro, Andres Valkonen; verses, Ernst Enno; songs, Anne Maasik; art direction, Tonu Virve. Reviewed at Repino Domkino (USSR), Sept. 20, 1986. Running time: **90 MINS.**
Toomas Nipernaadi . . . . Tõnu Kark
Also with: Viire Valdma, Paul Poom, Egon Nuter, Margus Oopkaup, Karin Kohv, Aire Johanson, Vilma Luik, Ilmar Tammur, Ain Lutsepp, Oskar Liigand, Rita Raave, Kaie Mihkelson, Jaan Rekkor.

Repino — Kaljo Kiisk again demonstrates he is one of the most original filmmakers working in Estonia with his latest (1983) offering, "Nipernaadi." These cheerfully disconnected adventures of a picaresque folk hero (based on August Gailit's novel from the late 1920s) won't be to the taste of all, but contain a wealth of original filmic folklore that points film in the direction of anyone interested in the spirit and imagination of this republic. It can also be recommended for junior viewers.

Toomas Nipernaadi, played with winsome earnestness by Tõnu Kark, wanders around the countryside from village to village all summer long, seeking his Queen of Hearts. His white suit is dirty but his pockets are full of money, when he needs to buy a farmstead or pay for his night's lodgings. He tells tall tales about himself to everyone he meets, especially the pretty girls he longs for, and conquers hearts with a mixture of comical con stores and an almost supernatural talent for making people dream.

Only at pic's end do we learn Nipernaadi's true story, when his rich wife suddenly appears in a car and explains he's an eccentric writer who travels in the summer and writes books in the winter. The gentle humor and impossible events of the folk tale abruptly change to a melancholy tone, as the wild hero is put in a three-piece suit and brought back to a realm of relative normality.

Among the pleasures of this unpretentious film are its dreamy landscapes of the Estonian countryside, shot in the hazy colors and blurred forms of a naif watercolor (lensing by Jüri Sillart). —*Yung.*

Behind The Dam
(AUSTRALIAN-DOCU-COLOR)

A Haydon production. Produced and directed by Tom Haydon. Camera (color), Ray Henman, Kevin Anderson, Gert Kirchner, Haydon; editor, Haydon; sound, Bob Clayton, Bob Haynes, Ned Dawson, Nick Armstrong, Laurie Robinson; associate producer, Hilary Burt; production manager, Roz Berrystone. Reviewed on SBS television, Sept. 24, 1986. Running time: **91 MINS.**

Sydney — Tom Haydon, one of Australia's most distinguished documentary filmmakers, has come up with a fascinating film record of the long-running battle against government plans to construct a huge dam on the scenic Franklin River in Tasmania. Though "Behind The Dam" gives the impression of being even-handed in its account of the struggle between environmentalists and the Tasmanian government, the film's heart seems clearly on the side of the greenies, and this was a battle the greenies won.

Disputed area consisted of cool-temperate rain forest, one of the last surviving in the world, and the proposed dam was located right in the heart of the forest. In addition, ancient caves containing priceless prehistoric treasures were discovered in the area due to be flooded by the dam. World-famous botanists and environmentalists, including British tv personality David Bellamy, protested when succeeding Tasmanian state governments, urged on by the powerful Hydro-Electric Commission, seemed determined to go ahead with the dam. Already, during an earlier dispute, another part of the Tasmanian wilderness had been destroyed by the creation of a dam and resulting lake.

Film's opposing view comes from Russell Ashton, electrical commissioner at the HEC, who claims to be an environmentalist himself. He feels it's essential for future generations of Tasmanians to have cheap electricity to enable them to compete both with mainland Australian states and overseas markets. Succeeding Tasmanian governments of different political persuasions back the HEC, and a rather loaded referendum seems to endorse majority opinion in the state behind the dam construction.

The battle crossed over into mainland Australia and became a nationwide issue, sparking the largest environmental demonstration in the country's history in downtown Melbourne. Even after the rain forest was listed by the World Heritage Organization, the (Liberal) Federal government refused to intervene, and clearing of the forest began, with 1,272 greenies — including a millionaire businessman — arrested by police at the dam site. Resolution came only at the March, 1983, federal elections when Labor, under Bob Hawke, won power and, amid controversy, ordered the Tasmanian government to abandon work on the dam.

All of this is vividly presented via newsreel footage, interviews and on-the-spot filming shot over many months. Haydon has skillfully edited a wealth of material down to a tight 91 minutes, and the result is a powerful docu of considerable interest. —*Strat.*

Desiderando Giulia
(Desiring Giulia)
(ITALIAN-COLOR)

A Medusa release. Produced by Monica Venturini for Filmes Intl., Dania Film, National Cinematografica, and Medusa Distribution. Directed by Andrea Barzini. Stars Serena Grandi. Screenplay, Gianfranco Clerici, Domenico Matteucci, Barzini based on a novel "Senility" by Italo Svevo; camera (Kodak color; Telecolor), Mario Vulpiani; editor, Sergio Montanari; music, Antonio Sechi; art direction, Gianfranco Clerici. Reviewed at Quirinale Cinema, Rome, Oct. 9, 1986. Running time: 104 MINS.
Giulia . . . . Serena Grandi
Emilio . . . . John Leysen
Amalia . . . . Valeria D'Obici
Stefano . . . . Sergio Rubini
Also with: Giuliana Calandra.

Rome — "Desiring Giulia" belongs to that popular Italo combo genre, half-art, half-softcore sex. More schizophrenic than most of its cousins, this Medusa entry fervidly insists on having it both ways, with the result half the audience comes out cringing in embarrassment, the other half wondering what hit them between sex scenes.

The embarrassed patrons are the ones who wandered in looking for a new screen version of Italo Svevo's classic novel, "Senility." Young helmer Andrea Barzini, on his second feature, strained to keep the spirit of the tale, recounting the tragic infatuation of Emilio (John Leysen), a young man from a good

Original Film: Senilita
(ITALIAN-B&W)

A Columbia-Ceiad release of a Moris Ergas (Zebra) production. Stars Claudia Cardinale, Anthony Franciosa; features Betsy Blair, Philipe Leroy, Marcella Valeri, Nando Angelini, Ersilia Di Marco, Raimondo Magni. Directed by Mauro Bolognini. Screenplay, Bolognini, Tullio Pinelli; Goffredo Parise, based on novel by Italo Svevo; camera (b&w), Armando Nannuzzi; music, Piero Piccioni; editor, Nino Baragli. At Quattro Fontane, Rome, May 8, 1962. Running time: 97 MINS.
Emilio . . . . Anthony Franciosa
Angiolina . . . . Claudia Cardinale
Amalia . . . . Betsy Blair
Balli . . . . Philipe Leroy
Sorrani . . . . Nando Angelini

family in decline, with Giulia, a girl of humble origins who betrays him practically under his nose.

For the sake of the second half of the audience, the puzzled ones, Barzini thoughtfully dispenses with the practical and unleashes the mighty sex appeal of Serena Grandi (immortalized by Giovanni Tinto Brass in "Miranda"). Rewarming her previous roles of fleshy coarseness (Grandi is an actress of Titian-like proportions), she stimulates a number of partners to perform a variety of simulated acts, to the accompaniment of full orchestration.

The graphic but hasty groping and coupling scenes, featuring both male and female frontal nudity, are intercut at regular intervals, interrupting the main story like tv commercials (or vice versa, depending on one's point-of-view).

John Leysen is a duly obsessed intellectual on the skids, as unhealthily attached to Giulia as an alcoholic to a bottle. He has a hard time matching the formidable screen presence of Grandi, however, who plays Svevo's ambiguous Trieste heroine with all the subtlety of a comic book parody. The performance that makes pic worth watching is Valeria D'Obici's as Emilio's spinster sister Amalia, a character so sensitively rendered she gives the whole film a boot upstairs. Also convincing is Sergio Rubini as Emilio's best friend. Director Barzini evinces talent in search of a better vehicle. —*Yung.*

Slane Cukriky
(Salty Sweets)
(CZECH-COLOR)

Produced by Slovak Film Studio, Bratislava-Koliba. Directed by Eva Stefankovicova. Screenplay, Zuzana Suchanova; camera (color), Stacho Machata; music, Andrej Seban; art director, Juraj Cervik. Reviewed at Karlovy Vary Film Festival (market), July 16, 1986. Running time: 93 MINS.
With: Monika Horakova, Zuzana Krupicova, Jaroslav Rostinsky, Jonas Kirasek, Jakub Kohl.

Karlovy Vary — A school for apprentice hairdressers is the setting for this deft and amusing look at Czechoslovak teenagers who dream big dreams but may have to settle for small beer. Helena (Zuzana Krupicova) wants to compete for a hairdresser's prize in top competition in Slovakian capital Bratislava, while sister Vlasta (Monika Horakova) has her heart set on becoming a top model. Her hair becomes the tryout lab for Helena's newest experiments (which range from punk fads to Paris couture). The seamstress sisterhood at the apprentice boarding school also use Vlasta to launch stylish concoctions.

Both sisters are in great demand as well by the guys in the local rock band (the group is Pedal), who follow the girls to the regionals in Toplice, where Helena's last-minute crazy hairdo, which Vlasta sports, cops first place. Model Vlasta, lacking radiance because of a late night out, still takes a prize herself. They now train for the nationals in Bratislava. Dreams of glory fade, however, with only a fourth prize this time for Helena and zip for Vlasta.

Back to sobering reality, they buckle down to school and practical experience, including ditching boyfriends only interested in their glamorous aspirations.

This small and unpretentious film offers a good look at how teenagers in a socialist society fit into the adult world. Director Eva Stefankovicova, the first woman director in Slovak cinema, in her second feature after tv and documentary stints, handles departments well, and has a sure touch with her teenage, non-professional cast, with whom she developed the script.

Lack of a strong denouement, however, leaves one wishing there was more to the story. —*Milg.*

Pasodoble Pre Troch
(Paso Doble For Three)
(CZECH-COLOR)

Produced by Slovak Studios, Bratislava-Koliba. Directed by Vladimir Balco. Screenplay, Ivan Stadtrucker, Balco; camera (color), Vincent Rosinec; music, Angelo Michajlov, Ladislav Jezek; art director, Jan Svoboda. Reviewed at Karlovy Vary Film Festival (market), July 16, 1986. Running time: 74 MINS.
With: Ladislav Jezek, Rena Neudorflova, Milan Jankovic, Jana Calabkova.

Karlovy Vary — The ballroom dance floor is the field of battle in this unexpected treat from Slovakia about two miners, rivals for the favor of a sultry young specialist in Spanish dance. Both finally lose out, however, to a new dancing partner in this apolitical contemporary fairytale proving a paso doble (two-step) was intended for two partners, not three.

Miner Blazej Antal's (Ladislav Jezek) infatuation with dancer Iris (Rena Neudorflova) at a workers celebration leads to his becoming a ballroom groupie and finally love and marriage, acing out his buddy, Roman. Daughter's career, however, is main interest of Iris' mother, who prefers a third party, Oscar, as partner. Their respective jobs separate Iris and Antal commanders a forklift to invade the big ballroom competiton, scattering judges, audience and diaphanous dancers, before he finally realizes his absurd action only proves that respective words and values of miner and dancer don't mix and that he and Iris are unsuited for each other.

Aside from the improbable premise of the film about worlds of art and of work (which may have worked for "Flashdance" but not here), story is a well-scripted and directed second feature by former documentarist Vladimir Balco. Film supports notion of Slovakian filmmaking seeking an offbeat international style that can win points for overseas and pan-national European markets. Light touch with actors and Neudorflova's eye-catching dance silhouette are pluses, overlooking unstable mixture of dancing and mining milieux.—*Milg.*

Ideaalmaastik
(Ideal Landscape)
(SOVIET-COLOR)

A Tallinnfilm production (Estonia). Directed by Peeter Simm. Screenplay, Karl Helemäe; camera (color), Arvo Iho; music, Jaanus Nogisto, Erkki-Sven Tüür; art direction, Priit Vaher. Reviewed at Repino Domkino (USSR), Sept. 18, 1986. Running time: 90 MINS.
Kukumägi . . . . Arvo Kukumägi
Trunike . . . . Tönu Kark

Repino — "Ideal Landscape" is an unpretentious, likable little film about a young Komsomol organizer from the C.P. sent to a backward Estonian village in the 1950s. At times gently involving, at times too slow, film shows director Peeter Simm's talent at sensitive character sketching with comic overtones.

Greenhorn Arvo Kukumägi's first impact with the village where he is sent to double the harvest is disconcerting. He is looked upon with disinterest by the farmers, and when his no-nonsense committee boss turns up, he is overruled inconsiderately and marched out to start plowing fields with the locals. Finally some friendly villagers take pity on him and show him some shortcuts, with the aid of a few white lies to his superiors. In the end he miraculously collects the grain he needs and succeeds in his mission — all too well, because instead of letting him start a university in the fall, they give him a promotion and another assignment.

As gentle and laid-back as the characters are the rolling hills of the first hostile, then accommodating countryside over which the young hero pedals his oft-damaged bike (work of a mischievous schoolboy). This lovely portrait of the "ideal landscape" has just a touch of melancholy about it. —Yung.

Formula For Murder
(ITALIAN-COLOR)

A Fulvia Intl. Films production. Directed by "Martin Herbert" (Alberto De Martino). Screenplay, Hank Walker, "Herbert" (De Martino); camera (Luciano Vittori color), Lawrence Barkey; editor, "Vincent P. Thomas" (Vincenzo Tomassi); music, Francesco De Masi; sound, Steve Connely; art direction, Julian Wilson; stunt coordinator, Arthur Mulkey; dubbing editor, Nick Alexander. Reviewed at 42d St. Selwyn theater, N.Y., Oct. 4, 1986. (No MPAA Rating.) Running time: **88 MINS.**
Joanna . . . . .Christina Nagy
Craig . . . . .David Warbeck
Ruth . . . . .Carroll Blumenberg
Dr. Sernich . . . . .Rossano Brazzi
Also with: Andrea Bosic, Loris Loddi, Adriana Giuffre, Daniela De Carolis, Arthur Webber Jr.

"Formula For Murder" is an above-average Italian thriller. Concurrent with its U.S. theatrical release, pic is available on vidcassette under the slightly different title "Formula For A Murder" from Lightning Video.

Set in Boston, where most of the film was shot, pic falls loosely into the "Gaslight" genre, as Craig (British thesp David Warbeck, dubbed with an American accent) trains paraplegic Joanna (Christina Nagy) for special athletics events to be held in New York City. They fall in love and plan to marry, which makes Joanna's lovely live-in companion Ruth (Carroll Blumenberg) very jealous.

Confined to a wheel chair, Joanna's paralysis dates back to a childhood trauma (shown in film's opening footage) when she fell down the stairs while being attacked by a rapist posing as a priest. Craig, who it

turns out is in cahoots with Ruth to get Joanna's fortune, dresses up like a priest and repeatedly scares Joanna.

Carried by fine acting by Christina Nagy, pic drags a bit halfway through as Warbeck procrastinates while Blumenberg urges him to kill Nagy, but it picks up again with okay twists. Tech credits are okay and, except for the post-synchronized dialog, pic adequately passes for a U.S.-style production. —Lor.

Naves Ena
(In The Shadow Of Death)
(SOVIET-B&W)

A Riga Film Studio production (Latvia). Directed by Gunars Piesis. Screenplay, Ian Kalnine, Piesis, from the novel by Rudolf Blauman; camera (Widescreen, b&w), Martin Kleins; editor, Piesis; music, Marger Zarinche; art director, Herbert Likums. Reviewed at the Repino Domkino (USSR), Sept. 13, 1986. Running time: **80 MINS.**
Grintal . . . . .Edward Pavul
Birkenbaum . . . . .Gunar Tsilinsky
Karlen . . . . .Peter Chogolov
Old Dalda . . . . .Arnold Videnieks
Young Dalda . . . . .Giert Yakovlev
Also with: Karl Sebris (Zalga), Yuris Plaivine (Gourloum).

Repino — Never screened outside the USSR, Gunars Piesis' "In The Shadow Of Death" (1971) is one of the milestones in Latvian cinema. Still a harsh, gripping classic, it could well be revived for retrospectives, and is reviewed here for the record.

Story, based on a novel by Rudolf Blauman, has the stark simplicity of a timeless thriller. A group of men out fishing on an icy embankment find themselves suddenly stranded when a huge ice floe breaks off and starts drifting around the Baltic. In a dramatic opening, the men race for the broken edge, but the first to jump into the icy water and swim for the mainland goes under after a few strokes.

Apart from a few unsettling jumps in the story, Piesis (who has worked steadily at Riga Studios for the last 25 years) succeeds in bringing his handful of characters to life and putting them through a gripping battle with cold, hunger and desperation, as they face the prospect of their own death.

Main characters are a young boy (Peter Chogolov) and his older friend and protector (Gunar Tsilinsky), an old fisherman (Arnold Videnieks) and his son, and the village's selfish "rich" man who owns the nets and pair of horses stranded with them on the floe. As the ice keeps breaking up, the group gets separated. Their numbers dwindle, morale dives, the lowest human instincts come out — until, miraculously, a small boat appears out of nowhere, but able to rescue only five of the eight survivors.

Ending is grim, to say the least, but Piesis sticks to his guns and

closes film with a steady, unblinking gaze at the harshest realities of life in an inhospitable clime. —Yung.

Calacán
(MEXICAN-COLOR)

A Pelic Mexicanas release of an Emulsión y Gelatina-Dasa Films production. Produced by Luis Kelly Ramírez, Mauro Mendoza, Fernando Fuentes. Written and directed by Luis Kelly Ramírez. Starr David Gonzáles, Humberto León, Camera (color) Fuentes; editor and art director, Kelly Ramírez; music, Luis Guzmán. Reviews as part of the 10th Latino Festival, Public Theater, N.Y., Aug. 31, 1986. Running time: **80 MINS.**
Ernesto . . . . .David González
Felipe . . . . .Humberto León
Also with: Silvia Güevara, Mauro Mendoza, Emilio Ebergenyi and members of La Trouppe theater group.

The Mexican pic "Calacán," labeled as a "nonfiction" film, concerns the efforts of a small boy to help a village of living skeletons save Mexico's "Day Of The Dead" traditions against a devil and his crew, who want to replace traditional sugar skulls with plastic jack-o'-lanterns. Obviously, our ideas of "nonfiction" are not the same.

The pic's short length (80 minutes) seems to indicate that this children's film was made for eventual tv sales as a holiday special, although it was one of the participants in Mexico's III Experimental Film Competition, sponsored by the Mexican Film Institute (Imcine).

The story, as related by two anthropologists, concerns a young boy (David González), who stumbles upon a midnight meeting called by a menancing red devil. The devil has ordered two henchmen, Max and Metz, to journey to Calacán, village of the dead. They are to sabotage the annual manufacture of handmade decorated sugar skulls and replace them with two U.S. imports: Halloween and plastic jack-o'-lanterns.

The boy and his father go to head off the attack while in Calacán, a young skeleton boy (Humberto León) also learns of Max and Metz' plans. The two boys, one living and one dead, join forces and save the day.

The pic concentrates on Mexican folklore with characters made up to resemble traditional Day Of The Dead figures, all played by members of La Trouppe theater group.

The message here is that tradition should not be abandoned easily just to make way for progress.

There are opportunities for some cute visual and verbal jokes, especially when using reversed clichés: "It could scare the death out of you," "So dangerous you could lose your death," etc. And, although there are many ingenious bits of business and nice songs and dances, the film suffers at times

from being a bit too self-consciously cute.

Mexican youngsters should enjoy it, but tots not familiar with Mexico's death traditions might need a bit of exposition first to avoid the risk of confusion. —Lent.

Deadly Friend
(COLOR)

Special effects dominate a tongue-in-cheek horror pic.

A Warner Bros. release of a Pan Arts/Layton production. Produced by Robert M. Sherman. Coproduced by Robert L. Crawford. Executive producer, Patrick Kelley. Directed by Wes Craven. Screenplay, Bruce Joel Rubin based on novel "Friend" by Diana Henstell; camera (Technicolor), Philip Lathrop; editor, Michael Eliot; music, Charles Bernstein; production design, Daniel Lomino; set design, Roy Barnes; set decoration, Edward J. McDonald; "BB" robot, Robotics 21; Ray Raymond; sound, Don Cahn, Allan Stone, Jim Williams; assistant director, Nicholas Batchelor; casting, Marian Dogherty. Reviewed at the Vogue theater, L.A. Oct. 10, 1986. (MPAA Rating: R.) Running time: **99 MINS.**
Paul . . . . .Matthew Laborteaux
Samantha . . . . .Kristy Swanson
Tom . . . . .Michael Sharrett
Jeannie . . . . .Anne Twomey
Elvira . . . . .Anne Ramsey
Harry . . . . .Richard Marcus

Hollywood — Hardcore Wes Craven fans might find "Deadly Friend" a bit on the tame side as compared to the director's "A Nightmare On Elm Street," but pic has enough gore, suspense and requisite number of shocks to keep most hearts pounding through to the closing credits.

Elm Street has a different name, but it's still a cluster of dilapidated homes occupied by a handful of crazies — that is until an apparently normal teenager named Paul (Matthew Laborteaux) takes up residency with his mom (Anne Twomey).

Paul is a bit accelerated for his age, having built a semi-intelligent robot named BB that is programmed to talk simple sentences and most importantly, defend his master. BB is a big hit with the neighborhood kids, Samantha (Kristy Swanson) and Tom (Michael Sharrett), since he helps them successfully fend off the local nasties.

It doesn't take a genius to figure out that the nastiest of the bunch is Swanson's dad (Richard Marcus), a drunk who beats up on his innocent daughter with some regularity (actions duly recorded in BB's memory chip of a brain as he watches from next door).

One night, Marcus goes a bit too far slapping his daughter around and she ends up having to be hospitalized. Just when the doctors determine she's brain-dead, Laborteaux steals her body and transplants BB's "brain" into her gray matter.

That's when the fun begins.

Viewers can just as easily scream as laugh through "Deadly Friend" watching the obviously made-up Swanson come back to life and walk around like a robot, crushing her enemies one by one.

Unlike psychological thrillers that have some threads of possibility and really play on the viewers' emotions, this kind of pic is really more an homage to special effects wizards who create the most startling and bloodiest scenarios possible and pace them out fairly evenly.

Craven succeeds on that level in "Deadly Friend," contrasting the transformed wholesome Swanson with her benevolent Dr. Frankenstein as he tries to control her as best he can in between rampages.

While this isn't a vehicle to showcase fine acting talents, cast members assembled here are all terrific, most notably Anne Ramsey as the paranoid recluse and too much of a busybody for her own good.—*Brit.*

Puika
(The Boy)
(SOVIET-COLOR)

A Riga Film Studios production (Latvia). Directed by Aivars Freimanis. Screenplay, Imants Ziedonis, Freimanis, from the works of Ianis Iaunsudrabine; camera (Widescreen, color), Davis Simanis; music, Martins Brauns; art direction, Inara Antone. Reviewed at Repino Domkino (USSR), Sept. 15, 1986. Running time: **94 MINS.**

Iantsis . . . . Indars Lacis
Grandmother . . . . Zigrida Lorentse
Woodsman . . . . Edgars Liepinche
Grandfather . . . . Peters Martinson

Repino — This poetic, exceptionally beautiful film was one of the undisputed gems turned up in the Baltic republics' show in Repino. Shot by Latvian director Aivars Freimanis in 1980, "The Boy" is a joyful, unsentimental celebration of childhood needing no story to keep an audience engrossed from beginning to end. In its straightforward depiction of how a little child experiences nature through one winter and summer of his life, film could almost be classified a kind of nature documentary, whose subject is a tiny human.

Starting with a picturesque view of an old-style farmhouse covered with snow, Freimanis introduces first the season, then a row of faces, inhabitants of the house. Only as film ends do we discover they are a family of migrant workers, forced to move from house to house at season's end. A tow-headed 5-year-old, played with candor by Indars Lacis, looks out the frosted windowpane at a snowy wonderland. Davis Simanis' camera contrasts the frozen black and white outdoors world with warm red and yellows inside, where a cat may snooze by the

hearth, or a noisy crowd of masked merry-makers bursts in the door. Everything follows natural rhythms — the boy's mother gives birth and the summer equinox is greeted with a joyful collective, half-Christian, half-pagan celebration.

A spirit of playfulness and discovery predominates, making "Boy" an ideal film for children (as well as adults). The only hint of the hard life around the corner is a sequence of milling hay at night, where the boy is called on to do the small but essential job of riding a miniature cart, pulled by the horse that turns the stone. With typical sensuality, film makes viewer feel personally dragged out of a warm bed and put to work in a freezing barn. —*Yung.*

Sunus Palaidunas
(The Prodigal Son)
(SOVIET-COLOR)

A Lietuvos Film Studio production (Lithuania). Written and directed by Marijonas Giedrys. Camera (color), Jonas Tomasevicius; music, Jusras Sirvimoskas; art direction, Algimantas Sirigzda. Reviewed at Repino Domkino (USSR), Sept. 16, 1986. Running time: **80 MINS.**

Vilius . . . . Markunas Rimas
Petras . . . . Petras Vazdiks
Liuda . . . . Brone Braskyte

Repino — Lithuanian cinema is said to be famous for the theme of the struggle between brothers. In "The Prodigal Son," this favorite story line is given a contemporary twist, morally comparing a sensitive, artistic and unemployed hero with the bearish older brother he goes to live with, a "success" in that he has become rich.

Basically, the characters could come from small town America and film's values and concerns are surprisingly universal. Yet its main value for offshore audiences will be the rich, detailed picture of local life it builds up.

Set in a village, "Son" contains the full complement of cows, dogs, kids and pregnant women that are a hallmark of Lithuanian cinema, plus a direct window on the familiar angst of moving through your 20's "without a job and without owning anything," outside the rules of a hard-working, industrious society. "Son" would make a good representative film in specialized showings and Marijonas Giedrys is a director worth knowing.

Vilius (Markunas Rimas) is a young stonecarver recuperating from an accident without much help from his mellow, hippie friends. Leaving his squalid city quarters behind, he decides to visit brother Petras (Petras Vazdiks) in the country, where he lives with his neglected wife and two kids.

In contrast to Vilius' dreamy, childish innocence and professional aimlessness, Petras is a smug home-

owner with a big car and rough ways of treating the workers under his supervision. These include his mistress, Liuda (Brone Braskyte), a widow with a daughter, who decides to leave the village when she learns she's pregnant.

Vilius moves through this universe of normal unhappiness like a visitor to a planet he would like to belong to, but can't. Unable to connect with his aged parents — the father wants him to get a job and settle down — he hesitatingly makes an approach to Liuda, but without results.

Incidentally, "Son" offers glimpses of such rarely seen species as Lithuanian punks, complete with blaring radios, butch haircuts and shirtless jackets. —*Yung.*

The Sons Of Eboshi
(JAPANESE-DOCU-COLOR-16m)

Produced by the National Museum of Ethnology, Osaka. Directed by Yasuhiro Omori. Camera (color, 16m), Omori, Masayuki Watari; editor, Kiumo Sudiyama; sound, Zyunkiti Watari. Reviewed at Margaret Mead Film Festival, N.Y., Sept. 13, 1986. Running time: **75 MINS.**

Besieged by modernity, Japan tries to preserve its ancient traditions. In a mountain village north of Kyoto, holy city and Japan's ancient capital, and not far from big bustling Osaka, 700 villagers act out an annual mystic rite — the initiation of its young men into adult responsibility. Founded in the 7th century, the village is transformed for a few days every spring as the eldest teenage son of each qualifying family is ceremoniously inducted into the village's association of young men, sworn to keep old customs alive, follow Shinto law and promote the village welfare.

Film documents how in April, the four chosen boys undergo the rite of Eboshigi, transition to mature status. They thereafter can be called Eboshigo, or sons of Eboshi. Their membership fees, dues and duties are discussed minutely. Family honor, protocol and hierarchy are strictly observed.

At the all-night banquet — incredibly expensive for such a small village — dignitaries, guests, families engage in prolonged eating and drinking, alternating with prayers for health and safety, and recitations of scriptures and Noh verses of good fortune. As sacred sake flows, older guests pass out quietly, nap a while, then awaken to rejoin the festivities.

In the morning, the initiated four young men bathe in the river, are purified, and don white linen kimonos with black sashes. Scriptures complete the Eboshigi rite. The spiritual continuity of the village is affirmed. The sons of Eboshi now

become symbols of community identity, unity and purpose, keeping faith with the traditions of their ancestors. —*Hitch.*

Naerata Ometi
(Keep Smiling, Baby!)
(SOVIET-COLOR)

A Tallinnfilm production (Estonia). Directed by Leida Laius. Screenplay, Marina Sheptunova, from the novel "Stepmother" by Silvia Ranama; camera (color), Arvo Iho; music, Lepo Sumera; art direction, Tõnu Virve; co-director, Arvo Iho. Reviewed at Repino Domkino (USSR), Sept. 19, 1986. Running time: **90 MINS.**

Mari . . . . Monika Kärv
Robi . . . . Hendrik Toompers
Tauri . . . . Touri Tallermaa

Repino — Under the unpropitious title "Keep Smiling, Baby!" lies a compassionate story of lonely kids making the best of life in an orphanage. Actually, few are real orphans; they're the offspring of alcoholic, jailed and delinquent parents, whose sporadic reappearance causes more anguish than good.

Shot by Estonian director Leida Laius (co-direction credit goes to cameraman Arvo Iho), pic is surprisingly smooth and absorbing. Low-key and believable, banking on its sympathetic cast of young nonpro actors, "Baby" chooses to avoid hardcore documentary realism for more conventional scripting.

Center of story is Mari (Monika Järv), a young teen thrown out of her home by her beloved drunkard father. As pic opens she has run away from the institute, after her first day, but, attacked by a gang of toughs, she is jailed and sent back.

Being a newcomer, Mari goes through a hard time at the beginning, especially when she finds out one of the boys who jumped her, Robi (Hendrik Toompers), lives in the orphanage and is something of a local hero for his swaggering defiance of the teachers. In reality he's as sensitive as the vulnerable Mari, who he rescues when the other kids torment her by reading her diary out loud. Their burgeoning feelings for each other are cut short, however, when Robi is transferred to a reformatory after getting into a fight.

Though the institute is shown as clean, comfortable and progressive, film doesn't shirk from depicting the inner hell of these abandoned kids struggling to get through adolescence with the additional burden of knowing they're unwanted at home. Cast is made up entirely of schoolkids, since real orphans were found too traumatized to play themselves on the screen. Even pacing and good dialog add to pic's watchability. —*Yung.*

Svesas kaislibas
(Other People's Passions)
(SOVIET-COLOR)

A Riga Film Studio production (Latvia). Written and directed by Ianas Streitch. Camera (Widescreen, color), Hari Kukels; editor, Streitch; music, Uldis Stabulnieks; art direction, Gunars Balodis. Reviewed at Repino Domkino (USSR), Sept. 13, 1986. Running time: 93 MINS.
Marite ....Zane Ianchevska
Antanas ....Alguirdas Paulavitchus
Anna ....Via Artmane
Ausma ....Vizme Ozolinia
Old man ....Leonid Obolensky

Repino — A simple peasant girl goes to work for rich farmers after the war and finds herself disgusted by their convoluted love affairs and dramas. "Other People's Passions" is a beautifully lensed Latvian period piece that stops just a little short of bringing its ends together. What it lacks in emotional power, however, it makes up for in a generous point-of-view able to encompass both the honest working folk on the side of the new Soviet government, and those better-off who resented their loss of privileges, without schematizing either group.

Story is told through the eyes of 17-year-old Marite (Zane Ianchevska), sent by her last surviving relative to work for a family of kulaks. The family consists of a senile old farmer, speechless but still arrogant, and his attractive blond wife Anna (Via Artmane), who hates him, his simple-minded son and beautiful, proud daughter Ausma (Vizme Ozolinia). A farmhand, Antanas (Alguirdas Paulavitchus), has all but usurped the old man's place as head of the household, and is Anna's lover. But he wants to marry Ausma, and when she gets pregnant, he thinks his dreams of becoming the new patriarch are about to come true. Instead the girl has an abortion, precipitating tragedy.

This complicated cast of characters is convincingly limned as hard-living, hard-loving types, all except for little Marite, who is too timid to ask for wages until the last reel. She shows spunk when it's a question of defending her deeply-felt sense of morality, and film is behind her all the way. Helmer Ianas Streitch (who also penned the story) keeps pic running along smoothly, without villainizing the human failings of the rich farmers, or turning the other, pro-Soviet farmers into paper saints. Everyone, film seems to say, has his reasons for acting the way he does, though it is clear whose side history is on. — *Yung.*

K'Fafoth
(Gloves)
(ISRAELI-COLOR)

A Cannon Group presentation of an Emil Prods. & Cannon (Israel) production. Produced by Ami Amir. Directed by Rafi Adar. Screenplay, Adar, Judith Sole-Adar," based on novel by Dan Tzapka; camera (color), Yossi Wein; editor, David Tur; music, Shalom Hanoch; sound, Shabtal Sarig; art director, Yoram Shayer; costumes, Mika Saban; associate producer, Itzhak Kol. Reviewed at the Orly Cinema, Tel Aviv, Sept. 15, 1986. Running time: 92 MINS.
With: Ika Zohar, Sharon Hacohen, Ezra Kafri, Danny Muggia, Amnon Meskim, Antonio Mersina, Shlomo Tzafrir.

Tel Aviv — Rafi Adar, who has been working in films for many years but here makes his first directorial effort, has managed to produce a handsome picture but one which never takes a firm grasp on its own plot.

Based on a novel highly regarded at home, this is the story of a young, good-looking, introvert proletarian with a gift for boxing. He dislikes the nature of this sport, but inner conflicts as well as social pressures not only push him into the ring, but even convince him to take on an American pro.

Since all this is supposed to take place in 1937, in British-occupied Palestine, much effort is invested in bringing back that period, and if the results aren't always accurate, they are very pleasant to look at, a credit both to art direction and costume department.

If the background is satisfying, however, the foreground is much less so. The script is loosely built, it doesn't give characters credible and evident motivations, the atmosphere doesn't generate any real tension and the boxing scenes, quite often reminiscent of many films of the genre, from "Rocky" to "Raging Bull," fall short of the models.

Ika Zohar, playing the reluctant champion Tolek, is supposed to carry most of the film on his shoulders, but he lacks the experience or the guidance to fill such a complex job. Sharon Hacohen, as his Hebrew teacher and love interest, is pretty and soulful, but doesn't seem able to figure much better than her partner what the film is really about.

Technical credits are above average, particularly Yossi Wein's camerawork. Initial reception of film was cool and indicates it will have an uphill struggle to find its audience. — *Edna.*

America
(COLOR)

Satirical misfire from Robert (He's A Prince) Downey.

An ASA Communications release of a Moonbeam Associates production. Produced by Paul A. Leeman. Executive producer, Paul E. Cohen. Directed by Robert Downey. Screenplay, Downey; additional dialog, Sidney Davis; camera (Movielab, Guffanti color), Richard Price; editor, C. Vaughn Hazell; music, Leon Pendarvis; sound, Lawrence Hoff, Ron Harris, Frank Stettner; creative consultant, Ralph Rosenblum; art direction, C. J. Strawn; assistant director, Forrest Murray; production manager-associate producer, Ron Nealy; additional camera, Michael Sullivan, Terry Kosher, Michael Davis; post-production supervisor, Elliott Schwartz. Reviewed at 8th St. Playhouse, N.Y., Oct. 11, 1986. (MPAA Rating: R.) Running time: 83 MINS.
Terrence Hackley ....Zack Norman
Joy Hackley ....Tammy Grimes
Bob Jolly.............Michael J. Pollard
Gypsy Beam ....Richard Belzer
Floyd Praeger ....Monroe Arnold
Dolores Frantico ....Liz Torres
Hector Frantico ....Pablo Ferro
Mr. Management ....David Kerman
Earl Justice......Howard Thomashefsky
Martin Lang ....Michael Bahr
Tina Lyle.................Laura Ashton
Also with: Robert Downey Jr., Corinne Alphen, Minnie Gentry, Chuck Griffin, Ron Nealy, Forrest Murray, Melvin Van Peebles, Michael Rubenstein, Rudy Wurlitzer.

"America" is an unfunny social satire from filmmaker Robert Downey. It's a hard-to-watch misfire representing a severe decline from the creator of "Putney Swope" and "Greaser's Palace" some 15 years ago.

Though produced in 1982 and on the shelf till now, picture seems a decade or more older than that, in its counterculture sensibility, washed-out color and grainy photography.

Zack Norman toplines as a reporter for the 9 o'clock news for New York cable tv channel 92, an amateur operation which features a black anchorman (Howard Thomashefsky) who shouts as if his microphone wasn't close enough.

Episodic mishmash has Norman deciding to wear a plaid skirt (a la wrestling's Rowdy Roddy Piper) while interviewing people on the street and on the air, because his wife (Tammy Grimes) found the incriminating apparel in his suitcase. Inexplicably, Norman becomes a big hit in this new guise; later the station becomes a huge success after Grimes and the weatherman (Michael J. Pollard) fiddle with the equipment and accidentally beam its signal off the moon, broadcasting briefly all over the world (film's original shooting title was "Moonbeam").

Various running gags and subplots include a tiresome routine about a big lottery winner (Monroe Arnold) who decides to have a homosexual marriage with a millionaire investment adviser (Michael Bahr) and then buys Channel 92.

Closest the film gets to actual laughs is a ridiculous homage to Martin Scorsese in the final reel: standup comic Richard Belzer portrays a looney taxi driver who accosts Norman and literally drives his cab onto the set in order to do his comedy routine on the cable news show. He becomes a hit and a regular on the news, which is literally turned into a circus.

Acting is quite loose, with Norman, once funny in the semi-improvisational atmosphere of Henry Jaglom's "Sitting Ducks," merely grim in the lead role. Name talent such as Grimes and Pollard gives embarrassing performances, especially with poor lighting and makeup proving quite unflattering. Most technical credits are a shambles.—*Lor.*

The Good Wife
(AUSTRALIAN-COLOR)

An Atlantic Releasing (in U.S.) release of a Laughing Kookaburra production. Produced by Jan Sharp. Directed by Ken Cameron. Stars Rachel Ward, Bryan Brown, Sam Neill. Screenplay, Peter Kenna; camera (Eastmancolor), James Bartle; editor, John Scott; music, Cameron Allan; production design, Sally Campbell; costumes, Jennie Tate; sound, Ben Osmo; production manager-associate producer, Helen Watts; assistant director, Phil Rich; casting, Liz Mullinar; production consultant, Greg Ricketson. Reviewed at Colorfilm laboratory screening room, Sydney, Oct. 8, 1986. Running time: **92 MINS.**

Marge Hills . . . . Rachel Ward
Sonny Hills . . . . Bryan Brown
Neville Gifford . . . . Sam Neill
Sugar Hills . . . . Steven Vidler
Daisy . . . . Jennifer Claire
Archie . . . . Bruce Barry
Mrs. Jackson . . . . Clarissa Kaye-Mason
Also with: Peter Cummins (Ned Hopper), Carole Skinner (Mrs. Gibson), Barry Hill (Mr. Fielding), Susan Lyons (Mrs. Fielding), Helen Jones (Rosie), Lisa Hensley (Sylvia) May Howlett (Mrs. Carmichael), Maureen Green (Sal Day), Garry Cook (Gerry Day).

Sydney — Ken Cameron's third feature, "The Good Wife" (filmed earlier this year as "The Umbrella Woman") is a classy romantic drama set in the small Australian country town of Corrimandel in 1939. Rachel Ward toplines in her best role since "Dead Men Don't Wear Plaid" as the eponymous wife who's bored with her unexciting life in this rural backwater. She's married to a burly, well-intentioned logger (real-life hubby Bryan Brown) and spends her time cooking, cleaning and helping other women in childbirth; part of her problem is that she's childless herself.

Sonny, her husband, and his younger brother, Sugar (Steven Vidler), who comes to stay with them, are immature, unknowingly insensitive young men who can't understand Marge's loneliness and isolation. When Sugar unexpectedly asks if he may sleep with her too, Marge's reaction is to suppose "one man's like another," and to approach her husband for permission — permission reluctantly given. But sex with Sugar is even duller than sex with Sonny, and Marge remains frustrated and unsatisfied until, 30 minutes into the film, Neville Gifford (Sam Neill) arrives in town. He's the new hotel barman and instantly (and somewhat unbelievably) makes a play for her in broad daylight in the main street. Understandably, Marge refuses, though she's obviously attracted. Gifford warns her "you only get one chance with me," and he apparently means it.

Before long he has more women than he can handle — married women as well as naive shopgirls and hotel chambermaids — while Marge becomes more and more obsessed with the handsome stranger, eventually openly chasing after him, bringing about scandal and shame on herself and her uncomprehending spouse.

"The Good Wife" is the story of an obsession; the obsession of a woman for a man who cares nothing for her. With fine performances from Ward, Brown, Neill and Vidler, plus exquisite recreation of a close-knit rural community just before the outbreak of World War II, it's an impressive new Aussie production, though its downbeat theme and serious tone will confine it to art houses in most territories.

Ken Cameron has already proved, in "Monkey Grip" and "Fast Talking," that he's excellent with actors, and for his first period film he's been ably assisted by the glowing cinematography of New Zealander James Bartle ("The Quiet Earth") and production designer Sally Campbell. John Scott did a tight job of editing. Jan Sharp has marshalled a classy team for her first production, and "The Good Wife" should do modest-to-good business worldwide.—*Strat.*

The Tomb
(COLOR)

Okay supernatural adventure with tongue firmly in cheek.

A Trans World Entertainment presentation and production. Produced by Fred Olen Ray, Ronnie Hadar. Executive producers, Richard Kaye, Paul Hertzberg; coproducer, Miriam L. Preissel. Directed by Fred Olen Ray. Screenplay, Kenneth J. Hall; additional dialog & material, T.L. Lankford; camera (color), Paul Elliott; editor, Preissel, music, Drew Neumann; sound, Stephan Von Hase; art direction, Maxine Shepard; production manager, Robert Tinnell; assistant director, Tony Brewster; special effects animation, Bret Mixon; special makeup effects, Makeup & Effects Lab; costume design, Elizabeth A. Reid; stunt coordinator, John Stewart, second unit camera, Scott Ressler. Reviewed on TWE vidcassette, N.Y., Oct. 12, 1986. (No MPAA Rating.) Running time: **84 MINS.**

Prof. Howard Phillips . . Cameron Mitchell
Mr. Androheb . . . . John Carradine
Jade . . . . Sybil Danning
Helen . . . . Susan Stokey
David Manners . . . . . . Richard Alan Hench
Nefratis . . . . Michelle Bauer
John Banning . . . . David Pearson
Dr. Stewart . . . . George Hoth
Also with: Stu Weltman, Frank McDonald, Victor Von Wright, Jack Frankel, Peter Conway, Brad Arrington, Emanuel Shipow, Craig Hamann, Kitten Natividad, Dawn Wildsmith.

"The Tomb" is a goofy but entertaining low-budget thriller made last year by the same team that more recently produced the actioner "Armed Response." Tongue-in-cheek exercise in the supernatural was at one time planned for theatrical release by Cardinal Entertainment, which later went out of business and pic debuted recently on vidcassette instead.

Story structure closely resembles the Bram Stoker novel "Jewel Of The Seven Stars" (twice filmed), with an Egyptian princess Nefratis (Michelle Bauer) coming to life and heading for California to obtain ancient amulets necessary in the human sacrifice rituals that keep her alive, as well as on a mission to kill the desecrators of her tomb.

After his professor father is killed by Nefratis, David Manners (Richard Alan Hench) and a student of Egyptian dynasties, Helen (Susan Stokey) set out to solve the mystery, with Helen almost getting sacrificed in the process.

Lowbudgeter is aided by effective animation to simulate Nefratis' laser-like powers, as well as good makeup illusions (a fake chest effect also used in "Armed Response").

Filmmaker Fred Olen Ray includes many knowing references to previous films, with plenty of in-jokes in Kenneth J. Hall's script: guest star Cameron Mitchell, as an unscrupulous prof and art collector, is named Howard Phillips after H.P. Lovecraft (though film bears no relationship to Lovecraft's 1917 story "The Tomb"); the hero is named David Manners after the 1930s actor in "Dracula" and "The Mummy," etc.

Cast is effective, with Michelle Bauer, previously seen in softcore sex pics, smashing as the seductive, fanged villainess. Sybil Danning makes a pointless cameo appearance in a precredits sequence and does not reappear in the film proper. Mamie Van Doren was originally announced in the cast but does not appear. —*Lor.*

The Revenge Of The Teenage Vixens From Outer Space
(COLOR)

Innocuous sci-fi spoof.

A Malamute Prods. production. Produced and written by Michelle Lichter, Jeff Farrell. Directed by Farrell. Camera (color), Farrell; editor, Lichter; music, Louis X. Erlanger, Lane James, Gary Schmidt; sound, Eric Lichter; makeup, Michelle Lichter. Reviewed on Continental Video vidcassette, N.Y.; Sept. 21,1986. (No MPAA Rating.) Running time: **84 MINS.**

Carla . . . . Lisa Schwedop
Paul Morelli . . . . Howard Scott
Stephanie . . . . Amy Crumpacker
Danny . . . . Sterling Ramberg
Jack Morelli . . . . Julian Schembri
John . . . . Peter Guss
Mary Jo . . . . Anne Lilly
Also with (as the vixens): Lisa McGregor, Kim Wickenburg, Susanne Dailey, Sarah Barnes.

This cleverly titled feature is a contemporary salute to the 1950s teen sci-fi films. More childish than titillating, pic is an okay video timekiller, made in the Seattle area last year.

Laidback hero Paul (Howard Scott) finds out from his dad that mom was an alien from Outer Space who visited here 16 years ago. A foursome of new vixens, plus mom (played by tall Anne Lilly) have come to Earth, attracted by a teen magazine that somehow arrived on their planet.

Although the lusty females are looking for sex with Earthlings, film is extremely tame in its presentation of the havoc they wreak among the local teen population.

Film's special effects are chintzy and downright silly when some of the kids are turned into large size human vegetables.

Feature runs 84 mins., though the cassette packaging lists it at only 74.
—*Lor.*

Sapore del Grano
(The Flavor Of Corn)
(ITALIAN-COLOR)

An Antea production, in collaboration with RAI-3, Veneto. Produced by Chantal Bergamo, Enzo Porcelli. Written and directed by Gianni Da Campo. Camera (Eastmancolor), Emilio Bestetti; editor, Fernanda Indoni; music, Franco Piersanti; art direction, Stefano Nicolao; assistant director, Guido Cerasuolo. Reviewed at the Venice Film Festival (Open Space for Directors), Sept. 9, 1986. Running time: **100 MINS.**

Lorenzo . . . . Lorenzo Lena
Duilio . . . . Marco Mestriner
Cecilia . . . . Alba Mottura
Grandpa . . . . Mattia Pinoli
Bruno . . . . Egidio Termine
Stepmother . . . . Marina Vlady
Father . . . . Paolo Garlato
Also with: Elisabetta Barbini (grandma), Elena Barbalich, Efisio Coletti, Maria Baldo, Michele Pastres.

Venice — The love of a 12-year-old country boy for his young (male) teacher is the delicate theme of "A Taste Of Corn." Filmer Gianni Da Campo handles a difficult subject with maximum delicacy and understanding. Going solo on the script, however, Da Campo takes a bad fall on the dialog, which ranges from stiff, flat and banal to risible.

A few other wrong turns on the sex scenes (not between boy and teacher, but teacher and girlfriend) are enough to cut the tenuous thread binding viewer to film. As it now stands, "Corn" won't make it beyond local tv airwaves, though a number of its ills might be doctored by a good editor and dubbing director.

Certainly leads Lorenzo Lena (the student teacher) and Marco Mestriner (little Duilio) are magnetic faces onscreen, full of understated personality.. Tyro educator Lorenzo, on his first job and lonely in the small town, has an unhappy off-and-on affair with a sensual girl (Alba Mottura) he meets, and beds, on a train. The problem is she already has a boyfriend, who she insists on introducing in an embarrassingly off-target party sequence.

When Duilio begins to invite him over to the farm where he lives with his father, stepmother (a cameo role for Marina Vlady), and grandparents, Lorenzo is happy to find himself part of a cozy family atmosphere. Almost unconsciously he lets his relationship with the boy develop, but Vlady senses danger and has her husband put an end to Lorenzo's after-school visits.

While film handles the boys' relationship sensitively, it tips into bathos when the father begins reciting a litany of poor man's woes, and generally everything to do with the girlfriend rings false. By the end, not even the principals' intensity and a romantic Sunday in the country score can salvage the picture. Technical credits are adequate.
—*Yung.*

Strangers In Paradise
(COLOR/B&W)

Failed attempt at music video-style feature.

A New West Films production, presented by David DuBay. Executive producer, DuBay. Produced and directed by Ulli Lommel. Line producers, Bruce Starr, Ron Norman. Screenplay, Lommel, Suzanna Love; created by Lommel, DuBay; additional dialog, Thom Jones; camera (color and b&w), Jurg V. Walther; editor, Ron Norman; music, Moonlight Drive; sound, William Wang; art director, Priscilla van Gorder; costume design, Leslie Levin; choreography, Sarah Elgart; assistant director, Steve Brill; dialog coach, Paul Willson; associate producers, David Garland, Gary Gillingham, Jochen Breitenstein, Clay Weiler. Reviewed on Vestron Video vidcassette, N.Y., Sept. 24, 1986. (No MPAA Rating.) Running time: **81 MINS.**
Jonathan Sage/Hitler . . . . Ulli Lommel
Staggers . . . . Ken Letner
Larry Larkin Jr. & Sr. . . . . Thom Jones
Strickman . . . . Geoffrey Barker
Irma. . . . . Gloria McCord
Ratcliffe . . . . Cliff Brisbois
Anita . . . . Ann Price
Also with: Gayln Gorg, Paul Murray, Bette Chapel, Evakay Favia, Richard Green, Ula Hedwig, Rick Chaff, Steve Adore, Moonlight Drive, Nicholas Love.

German actor-director Ulli Lommel has made a name for himself Stateside with a series of lowbudget horror and fantasy features (notably "Boogey Man"), but comes a cropper with the music video-styled misfire "Strangers In Paradise." Filmed in 1983, incoherent picture tries hard to enter the cult territory of a "Rocky Horror Picture Show" but fails.

Opening reel is in black & white, with Lommel cameoing as Hitler in 1939 Berlin, while also playing stage mentalist Jonathan Sage, who escapes in 1940 to London where he is frozen. Decades later, a scientist (Geoffrey Barker) unfreezes Sage to help his right wing group of Californians in their quest to modify young people's aberrant behavior. For the umpteenth time, rock 'n' roll music is treated by the straw man bad guys as a symbol of moral decay that must be wiped out.

Everyone in sight keeps belting out songs, while expository dialog is poorly recorded in what sounds like an echo chamber, and crudely post-synchronized with the action. Fantasy musical numbers aren't very in-

teresting to watch here, while the eclectic music track by Moonlight Drive includes material sounding like everyone from The Doors to Devo.

Running time is padded by a boring highlights sequence that repeats mucho footage already seen and pic then ends abruptly with no resolution of the storyline. —*Lor.*

Rocktober Blood
(COLOR)

Formula horror-on-tour pic.

A Sebastian Intl. Pictures Distribution production. Produced and written by Ferd Sebastian, Beverly Sebastian. Directed by Beverly Sebastian. Camera (color), Ferd Sebastian; editor, uncredited; music, Nigel Benjamin, Richard Onori, Patrick Regan; songs, Perry Morris, Richard Taylor, Lon Cohen, Rich King; sound, Walter Martin; production design, Beverly Sebastian; special effects, Ben Sebastian; wardrobe, Renee Hubbard. Reviewed on Vestron Video vidcassette, N.Y., Oct. 4, 1986. (MPAA Rating: R.) Running time: **88 MINS.**
Billy Eye/John . . . . Tray Loren
Lynn Starling . . . . Donna Scoggins
Honey . . . . Cana Cockrell
Donna. . . . . Renee Hubbard
Head of security . . . . Ben Sebastian
Chris . . . . Nigel Benjamin
Tony . . . . Tony Rista

"Rocktober Blood" is a 1984 horror picture, now available in homevideo stores, that fits into the unsuccessful genre of films that tried to combine this genre with rock music (e.g., "Terror On Tour," "Blood Tracks").

Tray Loren portrays Billy Eye, a rock star in the KISS vein, who goes on a bloody rampage one night at the recording studio and is executed for his murderous crimes. Two years later, his protege Lynn (Donna Scoggins), who testified against him in the murder case, is a successful rock star with the group Rocktober Blood. She is terrorized repeatedly by a mysterious figure who she thinks is Billy Eye back from the grave. Mystery is resolved on stage at the climax of the group's tour.

Pic is standard slasher fare, with a diverting music track, the usual steady flow of blood and little in the way of originality. Made by the filmmaking team of Ferd and Beverly Sebastian, "Rocktober" has Beverly taking a solo directing credit, which they usually share. —*Lor.*

The Sex O'Clock News
(COLOR)

Weak spoof of tv newscasts.

A Chase films release. Produced and directed by Romano Vanderbes. Written by Vanderbes, Sherry Cloth, Paul Laikin, Cary Bayer, Victor Zimet, Linda Haas; camera (Technicolor), Oliver Wood; editor, Zimet; sound, John Sutton; assistant director, Carl Clifford;

production manager, Robin Grey; casting, Bill Williams; associate producer, Haas. Reviewed on Prism vidcassette, N.Y., Sept. 24, 1986. (MPAA Rating: R.) Running time: **86 MINS.**
With: Doug Ballard, Lydia Mahan, Wayne Knight, Kate Weiman, Rob Bartlett, Joy Bond, Jerry Winsett, Philip McKinley, Bruce Brown, Judith Drake, Veronica Hart, Vanessa Del Rio.

Romano Vanderbes' "The Sex O'Clock News" arrives very late in the cycle of tv skit comedies, popularized a decade or so ago by "The Groove Tube" and "Tunnelvision." Pic achieved a regional theatrical release in August 1985 and is now available in homevideo stores.

While including the usual acted-out parodies of familiar tv commercials and newscast banter, Vanderbes differs from previous films in this genre by emphasizing the use of newsreel and other existing footage, redubbed and rendered comical by being taken out of context. Unfortunately, the laugh quotient is rather low. For example, a supposed wrestling match between Joan Rivers and Liz Taylor unflatteringly has footage of the Magnificent Moolah as Taylor. Footage from the feature "Hell's Angels Forever" is used to present a Hell's Angels comedy hour, programmed against Johnny Carson in "The Tonight Show."

Doug Ballard and Lydia Mahan rise above the vulgar material as the anchors for KSEX Evening News. Although most of the feature revolves around sex jokes, there are a few segments of reasonably effective social satire, including a game show involving capital punishment for the losers. —*Lor.*

To Dendro pou Pligoname
(The Tree We Were Hurting)
(GREEK-COLOR)

A Demos Avdeliodis production. Produced and directed by Avdeliodis. Screenplay, Avdeliodis; camera (color), Philippos Koutsaftis; editor, Costas Foundas; music, Demetris Papademetriou; costumes, Maria Avdeliodis; sound, Dinos Kittou. Reviewed at the Thessaloniki Film Fest, Sept. 30, 1986. Running time: **76 MINS.**
With: Yannis Avdeliodis, Nicos Mioteris, Marina Delivoria, Takis Agoris, Demos Avdeliodis.

Thessaloniki — This film created a scandal at this year's Thessaloniki festival because it was not included in the official program. It is an enchanting and sensitive film made by a young and talented filmmaker.

The story narrates the adventures of two boys during their summer vacations in 1960 on the island of Chios where they hurt the gum tree to extract the gum. Film is reminiscent of some classic French films ("The 400 Blows," and "The War Of the Buttons") though it is entirely Greek in conception and spirit. Demos Avdeliodis handles it with

directorial know-how, enriches it with humor, poetic sequences and convincing characters.

There are some other minor flaws, but they do not harm the film's captivating beauty. Camerawork by Philippos Koutsaftis is excellent. Other technical credits are above standard. —*Rena.*

Father Balweg, Rebel Priest
(FILIPINO-DOCU-Color-16m)

A Moving Pictures presentation. Executive producers, Mark Roces Jr., Amable R. (Tikoy) Aguiluz Jr. Directed by Aguiluz. Camera (color), Boy Yniguez; editor, Mirana Median-Bhunjun; sound, Orly de los Reyes. Reviewed at the Toronto Festival of Festivals, Sept. 12, 1986. Running time: **68 MINS.**

Toronto — This docu about a castoff priest whose fight against the Filipino government began in 1979 under the Marcos regime and continues today under Aquino proves both infuriating and vividly expressive. Considerable tightening in the first half and addition of subtitles would be necessary if the film is to be positioned for international consumption, but interest in the ongoing political struggle in the Philippines creates a certain market where documentaries and politically-oriented pictures are welcome.

Father Conrado Balweg was ordered to stop his ministry in 1980, a year after he joined the New People's Army among the Cordillera people, mountain dwellers who have traditionally resisted attempts at co-option by rules and under Marcos became entrenched against the ruler's grabs at their land. Autonomy for their region is their ultimate goal.

Unfortunately, prior knowledge of the domestic situation is a necessity, since director Amable (Tikoy) Aguiluz, who made the 1985 feature "Boatman," and was an assistant to Lino Brocka, provides no historical background. Futhermore, Father Balweg is a disappointingly inarticulate spokesman for the cause, as he spouts tired Third World liberationist rhetoric in both his native (untranslated) tongue and pidgin English, and speaks in general, rather than specific, terms about the state of affairs in question.

Even if one tunes completely off of all the mumbo-jumbo, latter section of the film turns absorbing. In response to natives' demands, a representative of the new government, none other than the brother-in-law of President Aquino, comes to attend a public meeting at which all the Cordillera's grievances are aired. he, in turn, discusses them and promises to take them back to Manila for an official response.

This segment represents a vibrant, almost moving portrait of elemental democracy in action, and will provide a valuable document down the line as an example of how Aquino's government tried to reach out to various groups disenfranchised under Marcos, especially so since it was filmed from the rebel point-of-view.

Ultimately, the technically crude picture offers a singularly unimpressive portrait of its ostensible subject, but almost off-handedly provides a bracing insight into the workings of politics in the Philippines. —*Cart.*

Perros de la Noche
(Dogs Of The Night)
(ARGENTINE-COLOR)

Produced and directed by Teo Kofman. Screenplay, Pedro Espinosa, Enrique Medina, Kofman from a book by Enrique Medina; camera (color), Julio Lencina; editor, Norbert Rapado; music, Tarrago Ros, Leion Gieco; set design, Miguel Angel Lumaldo, Enrique Bordolini; costumes, Angelica Fuentos. Reviewed at Miramar theater, San Sebastian Film Festival (Open Section), Sept. 21, 1986. Running time: **85 MINS.**
With: Emilio Bardi, Gabriela Flores, Hector Bidone, Gustavo Belatti, Enrique Alonso, Mario Alarcon, Neomi Morelli, Raquel Albeniz.

San Sebastian — Firsttime feature from Argentine director Teo Kofman has echoes of Luis Buñuel's early critical films about social conditions, dealing as it does with the struggle of a brother and sister to make their way out of the slums and poverty of a shanty town in current day Argentina.

The young man, Mingo, engages in petty crime, while sister Mecha struggles through ill-paid menial jobs to keep them both going. When Mingo is finally caught on one of his thefts, being none too bright, he is sent to jail where, because of his pretty looks, he becomes a victim of macho gangsters.

He is given the idea of using his sister as a singer in the provinces, in reality a prostitute. Mingo starts using her, first with an honest local who has fallen for her, but he soon takes her off to earn more from customers of the cheap sing-and-strip joints on the road. It is here that Mecha finally meets someone, bar owner Ferreira, considerably older than she, who honestly feels for her and gives her the courage to make a stand against the corrupting influence of her brother.

Kofman is effective in capturing the life and time of people living on the edge of society. Pic was shot in actual locations and is marked by some fine playing from Gabriela Flores as the initially innocent and pliable sister, who although younger than her brother, grows and matures so that by the end of the film she considers him her younger brother. Emilio Bardi portrays the rootless, uneducated brother who sees the only way to exist is through others, even his sister.

Film has something of a double-edged approach to its subject, and some may find it exploitive. Certainly some scenes in the cheap nightclubs are pretty raunchy and the film, unlike the book on which it was based, has an upbeat ending which seems a bit forced. Director maintains events have changed in his country since the book was written, to give some cause for hope.

Julio Lencina's camera captures the dust and sweat of the shantytowns and the countryside. Other credits are good.—*Cain.*

Knock Out
(GREEK-COLOR)

A Pavlos Tassiosepe and the Greek Film Center coproduction. Produced and directed by Pavlos Tassios. Screenplay, Tassios; camera (color), Philippos Koutsaftis; editor, Yannis Tsitsopoulos; music, George Hatzinassios; sound, Marinos Athanassopoulos; costumes, Demetris Kakridas. Reviewed at the Thessaloniki Film Festival, Oct. 1, 1986. Running time: **100 MINS.**
George ....George Kimoulis
Costas ....Costas Arzoglou
Fanis ....Fanis Henas

Thessaloniki — "Knock Out" won four prizes at the Thessaloniki fest including a shared prize for the best picture, best direction, best actor and supporting actor. It is a modern philosophical suspenser, an interplay of human nature, with very good prospects at local b.o. and an equal chance abroad if well placed and presented.

The central characters are two young men who are close friends. George (George Kimoulis) is always desperate about his miserable life and his love affairs, attempting suicide many times. Costas (Costas Arzoglou) is always present and saves his friend. George's desire to die becomes an obsession, torturing himself and his friend. Finally Costas, with the help of Fanis (Fanis Henas) a serious middle-aged man, notify George that a society helping desperate men will kill him. From that moment George, fearing he really will die, lives a nightmare of fear which cures him of his crazy ideas. There is a certain naiveté in the screenplay and other major flaws in the film's construction, but it unfolds forcefully with suspense.

George Kimoulis, though sometimes overdoing it, won the best actor prize for his performance. Costas Arzoglou is good and Fanis Henas gives a memorable interpretation and won the best supporting actor award. All technical credits are tops. —*Rena.*

Springen
(Jumping)
(BELGIAN-COLOR)

A Visie Film production. Produced by Roland Verhavert. Directed by Jean-Pierre de Decker. Screenplay, Decker, Stijn Coninx, Fernand Auwera, based on a novel by Auwera. Camera (color), Michel van Laer; editor, Ludo Troch; music, Dirk Brosse; sound, Henri Morello; assistant director, Fors Faeyerts. Reviewed at the Toronto Festival of Festivals, Sept. 10, 1986. Running time: **96 MINS.**
With: Mark Verstaete (Pieter Paul), Herbert Flack (Axel), Ingrid de Vos, Maja van den Broccke, Emy Starr.

Toronto — An eccentric first feature from Belgian legit director Jean-Pierre de Decker, "Jumping" erratically mixes goofy flights of fancy with more conventional elements of sex farce. Pic is of some interest to festivalgoers as a sign of life in the Belgian cinema, but is not consistent or substantial enough to spark commercial interest.

Opening sequence emerges as the most captivating in the entire film, as the advent of doomsday, observed on tv monitors and in the vicinity of a chateau full of elderly aristocrats, apparently has arrived.

In due course, one discovers this elaborate event merely has been staged for the benefit of the members of this unique old folks' home; in exchange for hefty fees, occupants have real-life memories or desires played out by an ingenious, dedicated staff. It's a sort of "Fantasy Island" for the moneyed geriatric set.

In this line, actual court cases lost by attorneys are reenacted on the premises with a different verdict to the satisfaction of the lawyer, operatic triumphs are produced, successful safaris completed and, as in the opening sequence, nuclear wars fought.

All this proves fitfully, if forgettably, amusing, but the sexcapades of the home's director and his activities organizer, are rather routine, exhaustingly frantic and somehow besides the point of the rest of the picture. The two men responsible for the extraordinary nature of their institution are initially presented as brilliant men, but they are increasingly revealed, as the narrative lurches forward, as thoroughgoing nincompoops who can't manage their own lives, much less those of their demanding guests.

Performed in Flemish, pic benefits for a generally talented cast and an aboslutely stunning setting. But matters get out of hand to such an extent that result finally seems silly and more than a bit pointless. —*Cart.*

Hard Asfalt
(Hard Asphalt)
(NORWEGIAN-COLOR)

A Syncron release (foreign sales, Norsk Film/Frieda Ohrvik) of a Filmkammeraterne production with Norway Film Development, Team Film, Skagen-Wadman Film. Produced by John M. Jacobsen. Written and directed by Sölve Skagen. Based on book by Ida Halvorsen with Liv Finstad, Cecilie Höigard. Camera (Eastmancolor), Erling Thurmann Andersen; editor, Malte Wadman; music, Marius Müller; production design, Anne Siri Bryhni. Reviewed at Oslo Municipal Cinemas screening room, Sept. 30, 1986. Running time: **97 MINS.**
Ida ....Krisin Kajander
Knut.......................Frank Krog
Ase..................Marianne Nilsen
Ida's mother ....Tone Schwarzott
Ida's father...............Tom Tellefsen

Oslo — Asphalt is, of course, harder to walk upon when you are on dope, a parttime prostitute, a mother of a small kid and the wife of an alcoholic. This is what "Hard Asphalt," a feature film debut by documentarist Sölve Skagen based on a best-selling autobiography, is all about. It's without too many frills and excuses and filmed with crude efficiency.

There are lots of flashbacks to the lead character Ida's sorrowful childhood with an amiable alcoholic father and her at first happy, then increasingly unhappy years with her nice, charming, also alcoholic husband and their baby daughter.

Most of this is dull stuff, but it's meant to be. There are flashes of robust humor and, to relieve the intended monotony, doors occasionally are opened to have (following the Raymond Chandler dictum) men come in with a blazing gun — or to push Ida out of a third floor window.

Ida is a survivor. At film's end, she is seen propositioning a man with a rough-tough listing of her prices and services. Local audiences will know the poor woman actually got out of her sorry predicament. Foreign audiences will be left with a no-issue ending that once again emulates the freeze-frame with which François Truffaut closed "400 Blows."

Director-writer Skagen turns maudlin, but most of the time she avoids sentimentality, and she has her two lead characters (Kristen Kajander and Frank Krog) perform with perfect control in moments of quiet as well as of violent turmoil. The soundtrack music is trite and imposing, while the cinematography suffers from garish lighting. —*Kell.*

Schetika me ton Vassili
(In Relation With Vassilis)
(GREEK-COLOR)

A Stavros Tsiolis production. Produced and directed by Stavros Tsiolis. Screenplay, Tsiolis, Constantine Tzoumas and Christos Vacalopoulos; camera (color), Vassilis Kapsouros; editor, Costas Jordanides; sound, Thanassis Gueorguiades, George Michaloudis. Reviewed at the Thessaloniki Film Festival, Sept. 30, 1986. Running time: **75 MINS.**
Professor ....Tassos Den gris
Also with: Constantinos Tzoumas, Katerina Tsioli, Loukia Pistiola, Eva Vlahkou, Maria Argyraki, Costas Stavropoulos, Christos Vacalopoulos, Christos Hatzakis.

Thessaloniki — Though this picture did not win a prize at Thessaloniki fest, it is not inferior to the winners. It's a psychological item excellently made by Stavros Tsiolis, but due to a lack of dramatic tension its b.o. possibilities appear slim.

The central character is a sociology professor who resigns from a university and from life as well. He lives alone, not willing to see anyone except his daughter. His final isolation is a kind of indictment against the lack of human communication.

Director Stavros Tsiolis tries to present the problems of modern men who live in an unfriendly and alien environment. He does it without emphasis but with pretty images.

Tassos Denegris is convincing as the peculiar professor. Pic is nicely lensed by Vassilis Kapsouros and all other technical credits are up to standard. —*Rena.*

Whodunit?
(COLOR)

Who cares?

An SRN production in association with Creative Film Makers. Produced by Tom Spalding, Sally Roddy, Bill Naud. Directed by Naud. Screenplay, Naud; camera (United color), Spaldin; editor, Hari Ryatt; music, Joel Goldsmith; sound, Dan Oldman, George Hose; assistant director, Alex Daniels; line producer, Roddy; special effects, Makeup Effects Lab, Image Engr.; associate producer, Pamela Scrape; casting, Lorene Cummins. Reviewed on Vestron Video videcassette, N.Y., Oct. 10, 1986. (No MPAA Rating.) Running time: **82 MINS.**
With: Marie Alise (Donna), Bari Suber (BJ), Rick Dean (Jim), Ron Gardner (Franklin Phlem), Terry Goodman (Steve Faith), Richard Helm (Rick), Jeanine Marie (Lyn), Red McVay (Bert), Gary Phillips (Taylor), Jim Piper (John), Michael Stroka (Mayor), Steven Tash (Phil), Jim Williams (Cop).

"Whodunit?" is a very trite slasher film shot in 1981 and finally surfacing for homevideo fans. Pic's alternate title "Island Of Blood" is more appropriate.

Dated horror formula is rigidly adhered to: a group of youngsters arrives at a remote island on the California coast where they expect to act in or provide music for a feature film. Pic's director Franklin Phlem (Ron Gardner) and fast-talking producer Steve Faith (Terry Goodman) arrive for a weekend of rehearsals, during which the cast members are gorily killed off one by one, with a portable cassette player blaring a rock song each time that describes the method of each murder.

Despite its title, film offers little suspense and the final twist (involving the making of a snuff film) is disappointing. Acting and tech credits are weak. Irony is that the awful feature being rehearsed, namely a goody-goody up with people message pic, is subjected to satirical barbs, yet is no worse than the actual feature "Whodunit?"
—*Lor.*

Alligoria
(Allegory)
(GREEK-COLOR)

A Costas Sfecas and Greek Film Center coproduction. Produced and directed by Sfecas. Screenplay, Sfecas; camera (color), George Kanayas; editor, Vaguelis Goussias; costumes, Dora Lelouda Papaeliopoulou; carved images, Natalia Mela; engravings, Rassos Abatzis; sound, Thanassis Georgiades. Reviewed at the Thessaloniki Film Festival, Oct. 4, 1986. Running time: **120 MINS.**
With: 12 actors appearing as certain symbols.

Thessaloniki — "Allegory" is a semi-documentary film which droops with symbolism. It is a rare piece of cinematography at home and internationally. With symbols and images carved and engraved, filmmaker Costas Sfecas presents the fall of paganism followed by mythology and other religions.

It was shown to the accompaniment of audiences catcalls, indicating it is a difficult film.

The film starts with the eye of the Almighty, which moves slowly from one corner of the frame to the other. Then several carved and/or engraved symbols parade on the screen, endlessly traveling, which takes two hours. Film ends with the eye of the Almighty on screen.

Sfecas had made two other films, "Modello" and "Metropoles," in a similar style. Due to his unique way of expression and his insistence on making films knowing they will never recoup, The Panhellenic Union of Film Critics awarded him with a special citation.

Technically and in concept the film is adequate. —*Rena.*

Anemia
(ITALIAN-COLOR)

A RAI-TV Channel 3 production. Written and directed by Alberto Abruzzese and Achille Pisanti, based on a novel by Abruzzese. Camera (color), Angelo Sciarra; editor, Mirella Mencio; music, Lorenzo Ferrero; art direction, Nicola Rubertelli; costumes, Giovanna La Placa Wolmsley. Reviewed at the Venice Film Festival, Sept. 7, 1986. Running time: **87 MINS.**
Umberto . . . . Hanns Zischler
Marcella . . . . Gioia Maria Scola
Grandfather . . . . Gérard Landry

Venice — The most off-beat Italo title at Venice, screened in the Open Space for Directors, "Anemia" is a cerebral in-joke without the punchline, conceived by Alberto Abruzzese, a professor of mass communications, and Achille Pisanti, who has directed for television. Though filled with potentially amusing ideas, film is of doubtful comprehension outside Italy, and there only appreciable by a narrow circle of souls on the same wavelength. Produced by RAI-TV's Channel 3, film is most probably slated for a fast trip through local airwaves.

Anemia (title seems coy, but is mainly symbolic) is the complaint of Umberto, a tightly controlled suit-and-tie leader in Italy's Communist Party. Played expressionlessly in a dubbed monotone by German thesp Hanns Zischler, Umberto is not an easy person to like. Even his dazzling grilfriend Marcella (Gioia Maria Scola), who shares several sensual bedroom scenes with him, wishes he'd be more open.

Actually Umberto is obsessed with blood. His natural morbidity is heightened when he spends a few days alone in the abandoned family manor, a classic haunted house, reading his dead grandfather's diary. After soaking up a lot of spooky atmosphere and realizing weirdness runs in the family, he returns to normal life, until on vacation near Naples Marcella is bitten on the breast by a bat. Film concludes with Umberto's new-found pleasure in sucking blood.

If all this sounds like fun, it sometimes is. Filmmakers know their films and how to use the camera to create a comic-book retro style, that recalls everything from cheap thrillers to schlock horror with garish reds and yellows plus lots of clumsy point-of-view shots. Though not intended as parody, "Anemia" often cashes in on that level of entertainment. Well-paced, well-scored, and blessed with fine art direction, its nonsensical denouement is a great disappointment. Whatever the tenuous political symbolism intended, if any, "Anemia" runs bloodless quite a while before the vampires appear. — *Yung.*

I Photographia
(The Photograph)
(GREEK-COLOR)

An Ikones EPE and Greek Film Center coproduction. Produced, written and directed by Nicos Papatakis. Stars Aris Retsos, Christos Tsamgas. Camera (color), Aria Stavrou; editor, Delphine Desfons; music, Christodoulos Halaris; costumes, Nicos Meletopoulos; sound, Alexis Pezas. Reviewed at the Thessaloniki Film Fest, Oct. 1, 1986. Running time: **92 MINS.**
Elias . . . . Aris Retsos
George . . . . Christos Tsangas
Also with: Zozo Zarpa, Despina Tomazzani and Cristos Valavanides.

Thessaloniki — Though awarded the best picture prize by the Panhellenic Union of Film Critics, this film got only a festival prize for best screenplay which its maker Nicos Papatakis did not accept. It is a powerful picture, based on an original story and showing in every shot the eye of a craftsman. It has tremendous commercial potential and should have no problem picking up a major distribution.

The story follows the adventure of Elias, who, persecuted by the junta in 1971 as a son of a communist, goes to Paris to stay and work with his distant relative George. A photograph of a popular singer which he had accidentally with him is the cause of a frivolous lie at first which, however, has dramatic consequences later.

George falls in love with the women in the photograph, believing she is the sister of Elias. Meanwhile a strong bond develops between the two men which lead finally to a dramatic denouement.

The lie and truth are connecting both men, Elias desiring a comfortable life and George looking for love and affection.

The film has technical polish, rounded characters but it is loaded by an overdose of dialog, the only flaw in the picture.

Aris Retsos and Christos Tsangas lend outstanding performances and the rest of the cast is adequate.
—*Rena.*

Enas Isichos Thanatos
(A Quiet Death)
(GREEK-COLOR)

A Greek Film Center and Negative D.E. coproduction. Produced and directed by Frieda Liappa. Stars Eleonora Stathopoulou, Pemi Zouni Yakis Moschos. Screenplay, Liappa, Kyriacos Amgelacos, Christos Anuelacos, George Bramos; camera (Fujicolor), Nicos Smaragdis; editor, Takis Yannopoulos; costumes, Panos Papadopoulos; sound, Nicos Achladis. Reviewed at the Thessaloniki Film Fest, Oct. 2, 1986. Running time: **88 MINS.**
Martha . . . . Eleonora Stathopoulou
Anna . . . . Pemi Zouni
Mercos . . . . Takis Moschos
Also with: Georges Moschos (Truck driver) Electra Alexandropoulou (a woman) Christos Nikitaides (boy) Raame Soukouli (Martha as a child).

Thessaloniki — "A Quiet Death" won a prize at the San Sebastian Festival and five prizes at the Thessaloniki fest. It is a psychological suspenser with a believable plot, good lensing and acting that might attract international attention besides doing well at home.

The central heroine is Martha (Eleonore Stathopoulou), a writer who refuses to write anymore. Running away from her husband Marcos (Takis Moschos) and her psychiatrist Anna (Pemi Zouni) she wanders through a storm in a strange and deserted city, wishing to rediscover a lost world of unity. Wandering here and there she ends up in the arms of a truck driver.

Director Frieda Liappa, in order to paint the inner conflict of the heroine, makes a great use of flashbacks by which the love, desire, the pain and fear of this sensitive woman are brought out into the open. These flashbacks mark the film with a quality that reflects the suspenseful mood of the story. There is a little nudity but not explicit lesbian coupling between the writer and her psychiatrist, handled with delicate care.

Acting is good, particularly the key performance of Eleonora Stathopoulou, for which she won the best actress prize at the fest.

Visually the film is a treat featuring outstanding camerawork by Nicos Smaragdis who was awarded the best photography prize. All other technical credits are good.

— *Rena.*

Ballerup Boulevard
(Pinky's Gang)
(DANISH-COLOR)

A Metronome release of a Metronome production with the Danish Film Institute (consultant-producer Ida Zeruneith). Produced by Tivi Mahnusson. Directed by Linda Wendel. Screenplay, Wendel (with Kirsten Thorup, Synne Rifbjerg; camera (Eastmancolor), Anja Dalhoff; production design, Poul Dubienko; editor, Stefan Henszelman; music, Elizabeth Gjerluff Nielsen plus recorded works by Jim Messina, Herreys, etc.; production management, Marianne Moritzen. Reviewed at the Dagmar, Copenhagen, Sept. 29, 1986. Running time: **83 MINS.**
Pinky . . . . Stine Bierlich
Janni . . . . Anja Kempinski
Eva . . . . Anja Toft
Pinky's father . . . . Morton Grunwald
Pinky's mother . . . . Helle Hertz
Pinky's brother . . . . Pelle Koppel
Also with: Allen Olsen, Otto Brandenburg, Edward Fleming, Ole Ernst, Mika Heilmann.

Copenhagen — "Ballerup Boulevard," State Film School graduate Linda Wendel's first feature, was granted a government subsidy in the children's film category. To be marketed abroad as "Pinky's Gang," this small and well-intentioned item may have an offshore tv future in youth programming since it has an abundance of young, fresh teenage faces radiating young moods and feelings nicely. Film's theatrical appeal would appear slim even on home turf.

Pinky, 13, is ambitious at school sports and with her little rock band, Ballerup Boulevard. She suffers defeat all around when her mother has to serve a short jail sentence for bookkeeping trickery meant to save her high-roller father's moving van business. Her girl friends desert her. Somehow, the little family sticks together anyway, and Pinky's little rock group triumphs as a duo at a school concert. Still, Pinky sees her world as shattered.

Film is a composite of vignettes of family and school life. The vignettes are cut short before they are allowed to develop cohesively in any larger dramatic context. There is nice, natural non-acting coached from several of the young players. Some of the adult actors (Morten Grunwald, Helle Hertz, Ole Ernst) strive mightily to rise above the bombastic lines they are given; others look like refugees from Madame Tussaud's only tentatively come to life.

Film's production dress is glaring

as if neon-lit throughout. The editing is jerky (or has nothing to work from), the music is insipid and far too tame to be convincing in the context of seeing youngsters inspired by it to shriek happily and jump around the dance floor. Only Stine Bierlich as Pinky and Anja Kempinski and Anja Toft as her friends seem to be truly alive among the dummies surrounding them.

—*Kell.*

Danilo Treles, o Fimismenos Andalousianos Mousikos
(Danilo Treles, The Famous Andalusian Musician)
(GREEK-COLOR)

A Stavros Tornes, Greek Film Center and George Emirzas coproduction. Produced and directed by Tornes. Screenplay, Charlotte van Gelder, Tornes; camera (color), Yannis Daskalothanassis; editor, Spyros Provis; music, Pepe de la Matrona, Aren Bee, Deedee Mafdul; costumes, Anastassia Arseni; sound, Marinos Athanassopoulos, Yannis Eliopoulos. Reviewed at the Thessaloniki Film Fest; Sept. 30, 1986. Running time: **82 MINS.**
Sotiria . . . . Sotiria Leonardou
The Fox Man . . . . . . Stelios Anastassiades
British Musician . . . . Aren Bee
African Man . . . . Deedee Mafdul
Also with: Roberto de Angelis, Francesco Calimera, Yannis Eliopoulos, François Stephanou, Elias Kanellis, Helen Staphanou, Danayota Lattas, Christos Marcopoulos and Yannis Kostoglou.

Thessaloniki — This is a pretentious art film which lacks the narrative thrust to assure audience appeal, even in art houses.

The central hero is an Andalusian musician who was lost in the Greek mountains and never found. Some crazy people are looking for him in vain, all presented from a comic angle: An African, two Italians, a Frenchman and an Englishman. A girl wandering with them on the mountains is perhaps the lost musician's friend.

The point director Stavros Tornes is trying to make is that the only thing understood by all people is music. It is an unusual sort of picture, sometimes folkloric, sometimes erratic yet imaginative with a lot of humor, symbolism and poetic images, meaning madness is man's only way of escape from the routine of life.

Thesping and technical credits are above average. —*Rena.*

Caravan Sarai
(Caravan Palace)
(GREEK-COLOR)

A Tassos Psarras- Greek Film Center and ERT I coproduction. Produced and directed by Psarras. Screenplay, Psarras, based on the novel by Lazaros Pavlides; camera (color), Stavros Hassapis; editor, Panos Papakyriacopoulos; music, George Tsanguaris; set decoration, Antonis Halkias; costumes, Anastassia Arseni; sound, Arguyris Laza-

rides. Reviewed at the Thessaloniki Film Festival, Sept. 29, 1986. Running time: **115 MINS.**
Marguaritis . . . . Thymios Karakatsanis
Irene . . . . Demetra Hatoupi
Whore . . . . Mirca Kalatzopoulou
Antonis . . . . Vassilis Kolovos
Invalid . . . . Tassos Palatzides
Also with: Lazaros Andreou, Zafiris Katramados, Melina Botelli, Costas Itsios, Alexandros Revidis.

Thessaloniki — "Caravan Palace" won five prizes at the Thessaloniki Festival. It is a realistic reconstruction of one of the most disturbed periods of Greek history. The film can easily make its way into foreign markets if handled and presented well.

In the unrest and turmoil that swept Greece during the civil war, a villager is forced to leave his house and property and go to Thessaloniki with his daughter and son. They find refuge in a taken-over old building with hundreds of others. Without money or work they live a miserable and humiliating life during which the innocent daughter becomes a whore and the son a worker. When the fighting is over Marguaritis returns home alone.

This story was more ambitious than director Tassos Psarras could handle, especially burdened with a script from which he failed to weed out a lot of political propaganda. The film is somewhat slow in the first part, but it picks up in the second half.

There is excellent thesping by Thymios Karakatsanis as the villager struck by misfortune who can not understand the real cause. Mirca Kalatzopoulou is very good as the whore who introduces the farmer's innocent girl to work in a bar. She rightly won the supporting actress prize. A special citation awarded by the jury went to Tassos Palatzides as the invalid crawling in the corridors of a ruined building. Credits are tops especially lenser Stavros Hassapis and sets by prize winner, Antonis Halkias. —*Rena.*

Erdsegen
(Blessings Of The Earth)
(WEST GERMAN-AUSTRIAN-COLOR)

An MR production, with ORF and ZDF. Produced and directed by Karin Brandauer. Screenplay, Felix Mitterer, from the novel by Peter Rosegger; camera (color), Hans Liechti, Helmut Pirnat; editor, Marie Homolka. Reviewed at Venice Film Fest, Sept. 7, 1986. Running time: **110 MINS.**
Hans Trautendorffer . . . . Dietrich Siegl
Herr Adamshäuser . . . . Alexander Wagner
Frau Adamshäuser . . . . . Barbara Petritsch
Micheline . . . . Cilli Wang
Barbel . . . . Gudrun Trummer
Also with: Sepp Trummer (Michel), Karl Pongratz (Rocherl), Christian Spatzek (Guido Winter), Heinrich Schweiger (Dr. von Stein).

Venice — The novels of scholarly Peter Rosseger were compulsory reading for years for Austrian

schoolchildren: now Karin Brandauer (wife of actor Klaus-Maria Brandauer) has brought a major work by this "poet of the fatherland" to the screen with results that indicate the gentle beauty of the text.

The story is set in 1910, and deals with a Viennese journalist (Dietrich Siegl) who decides to live for 12 months working as a laborer with farmers in the rugged Stiria region. Pic opens beautifully as the well-dressed man emerges from the mist and arrives at a small community with the surprising news that he's looking for manual work. He gets a job with a farming family, and after initial difficulties more than proves his worth.

It's much to the credit of director Brandauer that she carries the viewer with her into this remote corner of Europe with such conviction. We find, initially, that many of the local customs such as sipping the blood of a freshly slaughtered pig are alien, but gradually, like the protagonist, come to accept and even admire and enjoy this traditional, peaceful life.

Pic may be too slight to merit theatrical exposure, but should play very successfully on television. Acting is fine down the line, with Gudrun Trummer especially effective as the farm girl who comes to like and admire the stranger from the city who's arrived in their small community.—*Strat.*

Torpidonostci
(Torpedo Bombers)
(SOVIET-COLOR)

A Lenfilm production. Directed by Simon Aronovitch. Screenplay, Svetlana Karmelita, based on a novel by Yuri Gherman; camera (color), Vladimir Ilyin; art direction, Isa Kaplan. Reviewed at Repino Domkino (USSR), Sept. 18, 1986. Running time: **92 MINS.**
With: Rodion Nakhapietov, Alexei Zharkov.

Repino — This cozy, home-grown action picture from Lenfilm Studio is dedicated to the heroes of the air who lost their lives in fighter plane battles during World War II. Storyline is weak and characters barely present, but "Torpedo Bombers" has one extended action sequence which demonstrates what kind of exciting effects can be obtained from machine-gun cutting. It's unlikely a single sequence will be enough to get "Bombers" widely screened offshore, but helmer Simon Aronovitch evinces ingenuity that could pay off in future films.

A classic script, penned by Svetlana Karmelita, shows the fearless young pilots grinning goodbye to their wives and kids before bravely going off on quasi-suicidal missions. A pilot goes down in flames;

another who knows he's a goner kamikazes his plane into a German ship and blows it up. A buddy of one of the downed pilots timidly courts his grieving widow. Another pilot has his motherless son delivered to the air force base, but when the boy arrives he doubts whether the child is really his — it's been so long, neither remembers the other. All is told with a slight detachment that clouds the emotional impact of the scenes, until a final roll-call of heroes brings a long gallery of faces in uniform before us in a touching silent homage.

Actors are kept largely in the background, although cast reprises many thesps from Alexei Gherman's "My Friend Ivan Lapshin," banned shortly before. Gherman's actors from the provinces had been stranded in Leningrad without much chance of working, until Aronovitch took them over.

— *Yung.*

Sapirhurin
(The Step)
(SOVIET-COLOR)

A Georgia Film Studio production. Directed by Alexander Rekhviascwili. Screenplay, Dato Chubiniswili, Rekhviascwili; camera (color), Archil Filipaswili; editor, Rekhviascwili. Reviewed at Moscow Domkino (USSR), Sept. 23, 1986. Running time: **84 MINS.**
Alexei . . . . .Mirab Ninidze
Woman . . . . .Ira Chichinadze
Mito . . . . .Levan Abashidze
Girl . . . . .Nino Tarhaniswili

Moscow — Director Alexander Rekhviascwili ("The Georgian Chronicles Of The 19th Century," "The Road Home") has crafted a deliciously offbeat comedy in "The Steps." Though the films are unrelated in theme, the Western viewer will find "Step" 's evanescent, mocking sense of humor strongly reminiscent of Eldar Shengalaya's "Blue Mountains," and any audience who enjoyed the first bout of Georgian wit should cotton to this picture, too.

Entire film is set in claustrophobic but totally undefined and anarchic interiors, where youthful hero Alexei (Mirab Ninidze) rents a room from a landlady (Ira Chichinadze) as spacy as she is beautiful. Somewhere else lie the eccentric, corridor-like offices of Alexei's botany profs, who spend their apparently unlimited time blowing up balloons and making paper dolls. Alexei wants them to find him a job, but with typical laziness, everybody tries to help him by finding someone else to help him, all the while showing exasperating interest in his business.

In the artful chaos of Alexei's quarters, meanwhile, a bizarre procession of friends and visitors begins casually dropping in and out. The landlady and her daughter, who spy on him through a peephole, take it all with great calm, even when Alexei begins to grow more introverted, then sick, and finally decides to move out altogether and take to the hills, back to nature.

Boredom, nosiness, and extreme lethargy characterize everybody in the film but the hero. Somehow, Rekhviascwili turns it all into hilarious comedy so understated you're not always sure a joke just flew by. The absurd situations have a repetitiveness that is positively pleasing, and film rolls along with the leisurely monotony of a wheel set in motion, easier to keep turning than to stop. This comedy of the absurd — or, better, of the faintly ridiculous — may not be everybody's cup of tea, but should find fest and art house appreciation. —*Yung.*

Plovec
(The Swimmer)
(SOVIET-COLOR)

A Georgia Film Studio production. Written and directed by Irakli Kwirikadze. Camera (color), Guram Tugushi; music, Temo Bakuzadze; art direction, Aleksandr Dshanshieu. Reviewed at Moscow Domkino (USSR), Sept. 23, 1986. Running time: **105 MINS.**
Durishhan Dumbadze . . . . .Gudea Buzduli
Dometi . . . . .Ruslan Mikabezidze
Anton . . . . .Badur Zuladze

Moscow — Made in 1981, released in a cut version in 1984, Irakli Kwirikadze's offbeat, comic family chronicle "The Swimmer" has only now become available in its full version. Though pic's deliberately naïf style sometimes falters on the shoals of technical difficulties and turns into naive scripting, on the whole it is an imaginative exercise with many fetching glimpses of local folklore and a critique of the Stalinist purges that is staggeringly direct. Film was shot in Russian and postproduction halted before a Georgian version could be dubbed.

Film humorously describes the lives of three swimmers, father, son and grandson. By far the most arresting is the 1913 tale of Durishhan, played with great silent screen presence by bearish muscleman Gudea Buzduli. A local phenomenon in Batumi, where he developed his long-distance technique by swimming after his sheep, Durishhan is able to accomplish such feats as holding his breath underwater for six minutes; once he out-distances a famous English swimming champ. No great genius, he forgets to document his feat and is laughed out of town, after which he turns into a lush. When a Communist Commissar tries to make him "our first Red champion," he staggers into a dark tunnel and is run over by a train.

The story is narrated like a folk tale, to the accompaniment of rinky-tink piano music, weird American songs, and abstract sounds and noises.

Durishhan's son, Dometi (Ruslan Mikabezidze), seems to have mostly inherited dad's foolishness. In 1947, Marx's portrait has been replaced by Stalin's, riding atop every trolley. In the glorious 1940s, we are told, mass swim meets were very popular, and Dometi helps organize events like a formation of powerful swimmers floating Stalin's portrait out to sea on a raft. Disaster strikes unexpectedly, when his kids innocently drop a porcelain figurine of Uncle Joe into a fishtank during a party; Papa disappears the next day, and his face is snipped out of the family album.

This brings pic up to the present day, where Durishhan's overweight grandson Anton (who turns out to be the narrator) talks over the family's unhappy past with his sister. By profession he's a travel agent, but "looking for his roots in the sea," he plunges into the water in a gesture of solidarity with his ancestors, and starts dog-paddling toward a raft. On it, we can see director and crew shooting the film.

Story is consistently amusing, even if the way it is told doesn't always manage to bring out its full bouquet. Kwirikadze has a tendency to overreach himself technically, and ideas often outstrip craft. What comes through very impressively is a love of Georgia and pride in her history, as it dovetails not without pain into the Soviet period. — *Yung.*

Massey Sahib
(INDIAN-COLOR)

A National Film Development Corp. production. Executive producer, Ravi Malik. Written and directed by Pradip Krishen. Camera (color), R.K. Bose; editor, Mohan Kaul; music, Banraj Bhatia; art direction, Sanjay Parkash. Reviewed at Venice Film Festival (Critics' Week), Sept. 1, 1986. Running time: **124 MINS.**
Francis Massey . . . . .Raghuvir Yadav
Charles Adam . . . . .Barry John
Saila . . . . .Arundhati Roy
Ruby . . . . .Jacqueline Grewal
Also with: Virendra Saxena (Saila's brother), Sudhir Kulkarni (storekeeper).

Venice — "Massey Sahib" is "A Passage To India" told from the Indian point of view. It isn't as magically plotted as E.M. Forster, it isn't well-shot or dialoged à la David Lean (on a technical level, "Massey Sahib" is always teetering on the brink of disaster, exactly like its hapless hero). Yet despite its basic failings, Pradip Krishen's first feature film has a great deal to say about Indians and Englishmen living on the uncertain crossroads of two different cultures, and says it more forcefully because it comes from the inside.

Francis Massey (Raghuvir Yadav) is pic's comical hero, a typist-secretary for a British Deputy Commissioner in Central India at the end of the 1920s. His dubious command of English has won him what seems a gentleman's position, but without the sympathy of boss Charles Adam (Barry John) his freehanded way with the office financing would soon land him on the street again.

Yadav is a believably exasperating social-climber, ridiculous at aping Brit dressing, church-going, even his wedding with a silent tribal beauty (Arundhati Roy). At the same time he's endowed with many contradictory traits from courageous to cringing, naive to brilliantly intuitive. Like the good commissioner and his wife, he lives in an impossible zone between two conflicting cultures, which brings about his downfall. Ending is all the more tragically poignant for pitting reasonable English law against Massey's total vulnerability before what he believed in.

Unlike the ending of Forster's tale the kindly Sahib is powerless to get his Indian friend off the hook, precisely because Massey is Massey, a victim of the times. — *Yung.*

Proverka Na Dorogach
(Trial On The Road)
(SOVIET-B&W)

A Lenfilm production. Directed by Alexei Gherman. Stars Rolan Bykov, Vladislav Zamansky. Screenplay, Edward Volodarsky, from a novel by Yuri Gherman; camera (widescreen b&w); credit unavailable; music, Isaac Schwartz; art direction, Valeri Yurkvitch. Reviewed at Repino Domkino (USSR), Sept. 18, 1986. Running time: **95 MINS.**
Lazarev . . . . .Vladislav Zamansky
The Captain . . . . .Rolan Bykov
The Major . . . . .Anatoli Solonitzin
Also with: Oleg Borisov, Arda Zaitzs.

Repino — Alexei Gherman's feature film debut, "Trial On The Road" (also called "Road Check" and "Checkpoint"), has survived 15 years on the blacklist with amazing vitality. Not only was the 1971 production refused commercial distribution at the time it was made; Lenfilm Studios was even made to pay compensation to the state for the money it had "misspent" on the project.

What Goskino took most exception to was apparently the problematic central character, Lazarev, a former Red Army sergeant who becomes a Nazi collaborator, then switches back to fighting Germans with a partisan division and finally dies a hero's death. Overturning the role of the classic screen traitor, Gherman strikes an early and important blow against the cardboard heroes and straw villains populating Soviet cinema at the time. Apart from this nuance, "Trial" is a watchable, human-scale war picture of striking visual beauty, steady pacing, and enlivened by Rolan Bykov's top-drawer performance as a warm-hearted captain. Pic is one of the most interesting items on Sovexportfilm's list for art house programmers.

Vladislav Zamansky plays the handsome, square-jawed Lazarev with laconic stoicism. As film opens, he lets himself be arrested by a raw recruit from the partisans' unit. The stiff-backed Major in charge (Anatoli Solonitzin) is in favor of shooting him straight off, but the simple wiser Captain (Bykov) gives him a chance to show whose side he's really on. Lazarev manages to trick some German officers into stopping on the road, where overpowers them without much help from his buddies. Despite his success in this difficult mission, the Major isn't convinced. The compassionate Captain gives him one last, near-impossible mission — hijacking a train — which ends in a wild, one-man machine gun battle in a railroad depot.

Story, scripted by Eduard Volodarsky and based on a novel by Gherman's father, Yuri, spaces out the action sequences with scenes showing Lazarev's painful re-entry into the Red camp, where many can't help but look on him as a hateful traitor. A host of characters is convincingly, effortlessly limned, while the black and white widescreen camera paints a cold portrait of the snowy Russian landscape. In a moving postscript, the victorious Red Army enters Berlin. The authoritarian major has been promoted; the little captain is good-naturedly pushing a broken truck.

Original title, now abandoned, was "Operation Happy New Year." — *Yung.*

Kan
(Blood)
(TURKISH-COLOR)

A Film Pop production. Executive producer, Ismet Kazancioglu. Directed and edited by Serif Gören. Screenplay, Osman Sahin, from a story by Gören; camera (color), Aytekin Çakmakçi; art director, Aysegul Gökçe; music, Zuifu Livaneli; sound. Necip Saricioglu; assistant director, Muzaffer Hiçdurmaz. Reviewed at Venice Film Fest, Sept. 8, 1986. Running time: **90 MINS.**
With: Tarik Akan, Makan Balamir, Serpil Çakmakli, Alev Sayin, Necmettin Çobanoglu, Muazzez Kurtoglu, Filiz Kügüktepe, Mustafa Yavuz.

Venice — This is a lurid tale of a tribal feud which is so clumsily executed it's hard to believe the same director, Serif Gören, directed Yilmaz Güney's screenplay in the magnificent prize-winner "Yol" a few years back.

Trouble begins when the leader of one tribe is insulted while visiting a rival tribe: the tail of his horse is cut. He reacts by killing first the unfortunate horse and then his host. The resulting feud lasts the rest of the picture.

"Blood" is handled in such a perfunctory, offhand way that it works neither as a Turkish Western nor as an exploration of tribal customs in the Turkish hinterlands. Action scenes are directed indifferently, and the occasional striking shot doesn't help to make the film as a whole the least bit appealing.

Another problem for potential audiences in the West is the male chauvinism; there's usually a certain amount of this in Turkish films, but here it's all-pervading with the unpleasant hero finally instructing his last living friend to wait until his son is born and then kill his wife. The friend concurs, without hesitation. It could be argued that Gören is condemning all this, but there's little suggestion of condemnation in the film as presented.

At first it seems all this bloodshed is taking place in the distant past, but the arrival of a squad of modern police in one scene abruptly makes the viewer realize it's all happening today.

Technically, the film is poor, with offhand editing by the director and pale color processing. Acting is by the numbers. — *Strat.*

Nemesio
(CHILEAN-COLOR)

A Compañia Cinematográfica Nacional release of a Cristián Lorca B. Prods.-Cinematográficas production. Executive producer, Alberto Celery. Directed by Cristián Lorca. Screenplay, Lorca; camera (color), Humberto Castagnola; editor, Jorge Valenzuela; music, Payo Grondona. Reviewed at CCN screening room, Santiago, Chile, Oct. 7, 1986. Running time: **80 MINS.**
With: Andres del Bosque, Marcela Medel, Hugo Medina, Ana Victoria Mourgues, Ignacio Agüero, Douglas Hübner, Luz Jiménez, Winzlia Sepúlveda, Javier Maldonado, Faruko Abdalah, Manuel Velasco, M. Eugenia Lorca, Roberto Roth, Joaquin Eyzaguirre.

Santiago — Shot in 16m and blown up to 35m, Cristián Lorca's first film shows promise although, barring the possibility of festivals, it is unlikely to gain exposure abroad.

Nemesio heads a department at a downtown office in Santiago until he is called into the manager's office, told his section will be eliminated though he may stay on, working in a subordinate position in another department.

Although humiliated and angry, Nemesio is too much of an introvert to explode. He tries to work it out of his system through a date with an attractive secretary from his office, but she stands him up. A few drinks later, he tries a prostitute but fails to perform. His home life, with a bedridden invalid mother, does not help and only in the privacy of his room does he feel relatively free, indulging in a fantasy life, inspired by movies and tv with the likes of Clint Eastwood and "Shogun's" Richard Chamberlain.

Nemesio is basically a grey character who seldom expresses his feelings. Although there is a stream of minor incidents before he settles down in his new, more lowly job, the film tends to lack rhythm and, in spite of its short running time, could have done with tighter editing to strengthen its emotional atmosphere.

Andrés del Bosque's acting is commendable and there are several solid secondary characters and significant short incidents which, in different ways, suggest the background of life in Santiago. The film cost $50,000 which is low, even by local standards. — *Amig.*

Malabrigo
(PERUVIAN-COLOR)

Produced by Perfio Studio in coproduction with Instituto del Arte e Industria Cinematograficos de Cuba, Channel 4, ZDF, Kleine Fernsehspiel. Directed by Alberto Durant. Screenplay, Durant, Jorge Guerra; camera (color), Mario García Joya; editor, Justo Vega; sound, Guillermo Palacios. Reviewed at Miramar theater, San Sebastian Film Festival (Open Section), Sept. 19, 1986. Running time: **85 MINS.**
With: Charo Verastegui, Luis Alvarez, Ricardo Blume, Ramon Garcis, Gianfranco Breto, Felix Alvarez.

San Sebastian — A second feature from director Alberto Durant uses a mystery format to show something of life and corruption in a small fishing port, the Malabrigo of the title. It is thus a critique of the region, although in an abstract way it doubtless could apply to many Third World countries where money and power politics still hold sway.

The film does not seem to make up its mind quite what it wants to be, hedging its bets and using its central character in a way that does not give her any chance to communicate with the audience. It thus becomes something of a well-shot, but formal exercise, with an unsatisfactory resolution of a symbolic nature which will leave most audiences puzzled.

Sonia (Charo Verastegui) is traveling to Malabrigo, where her husband is working in a fish processing factory. On the way, the bus is held up by two masked men who remove a man and shoot him. On arrival at Malabrigo, Sonia finds her husband disappeared a couple of days previously. She is hardly made welcome at the local hotel and has trouble in making any headway in discovering where her husband might be, or indeed if he is still alive. She learns there was a mysterious explosion at the processing factory and, with the help of a local reporter and a sympathetic old man, begins to unravel a mystery of corruption among the locals, who want to hush up matters.

Charo Verastegui appears suitably bemused by all that goes on around her, while most other roles are clichéd or too mysterious to make much dramatic impact.

The dusty and hot atmosphere is well conveyed through Mario Garcia Joya's camerawork, but script seems to run into as many dead-ends as the heroine.

TV investment in production from Channel 4 and ZDF indicates its natural home, although even here it will have difficulty holding its audience. — *Cain.*

Den frusna leoparden
(The Frozen Leopard)
(SWEDISH-COLOR)

A Svensk Film (SF) release of a Viking Film for SF, the Swedish Film Institute, Sonet Film production. Produced by Peter Hald. Associate producer, Bo Jonsson. Directed by Lárus Oskarsson. Screenplay, Lars Lundholm; camera (Eastmancolor), Göran Nilsson; production management, Susanne Ruben, Ruben, Marianne Persson; sound, Anders Ingermarsson; production design, Mona Theresia Forsén; costumes, Elisabeth Hamfelt; editor, Lárus Oskarsson; music, Leifur Thorarensson. Reviewed at SF screening room, Stockholm, Aug. 28, 1986. Running time: **98 MINS.**

Kiljan	Joakim Thaström
Jerry	Peter Stormare
Morrig	Christian Falk
Rita	Maria Granlund
Stella	Jacqueline Ramel
Bess	Agneta Ekmanner
The Father	Keve Hjelm
Insurance agent	Björn Granath

Also with: Gösta Bredefeldt, Tuncel Kurtiz, Hjalti Rognvaldsson, Tord Petterson, Fanny Hulten Aulin, Mikaela Steen.

Stockholm — "The Frozen Leopard" is a subculture meller that plods heavily through the Swedish October slush of a story about an older brother (Peter Stormare) who has gone straight as a used-car repair mechanic and who now tries to save his still errant kid brother (Joakim Thaström) from a life of car thefts and other crime.

To save the youngster, the big brother accidentally kills an insurance detective. At the end, the kid may go free, while the brother is taken away by the cops, but the kid seems to have lost what was most important to him anyway, a dream of roaming East Africa in a big American car with the freedom of a giraffe. Animal and other symbolism abounds. Film's title alludes to Ernest Hemingway's telling of a leopard that strayed to the top of Kilimanjaro.

Icelandic writer-helmer Lárus Oskarsson had some luck on the secondary film fest circuit five years ago with another made-in-Sweden feature, "The Second Dance," an unpretentious road movie. "The Frozen Leopard" is all pretense, laden with aforementioned murky symbolism, badly-lit sequences shot in shady or pitch-dark interiors, and acting that is either non-descript (Joakim Thaström is a moodily handsome rock singer of local superstar status) or mannered.

Lars Lundholm's screenplay is devoid of narrative rhythm and is full of characters out of a 1960s museum of film grotesques. Only Björn Granath comes through with lively menace as the man who gets killed. This happens early in a film that goes on to lose its way entirely with boredom and darkness reigning supreme. — *Kell.*

Drömmeslotter
(The Dream Castle)
(NORWEGIAN-COLOR)

A Kommunernes Filmcentral release (foreign sales, Norsk Film/Frieda Ohrvik) of a Norsk Film production. Norsk Film consultant producer, Lasse Glomm. Produced. written and directed by Svend Wam and Petter Venneröd; camera (Eastmancolor), Philip Oegard; editor, Inge Lise Langfeldt; music, Svein Gundersen; sound, Ragge Samuelsson; production design, Tone Skjelfjord; costumes, Eirin Olsen; production management, Erik Disch. Reviewed at the Klingenberg, Oslo, Sept. 30, 1986. Running time: 92 MINS.
```
Thomas ................. Öyvin Berven
Trine-Lise ...... Birgitte Victoria Svendsen
Anders ................. Lasse Lindtner
Kjersti ................. Mari Maurstad
Arild ................. Petter Venneröd
Mona ................. Hilde Grythe
Lars ................. Torstein Hölmebak
Else ................. Jorunn Kjelsby
```
Also with: Nikolai Kolstad, Runa Grandlund, Yvonne Fosso, Hans Krövel, Dag Richard Badendyck, Richard Egede Nissen, Anders Hatlo, Mette Wesenlund.

Oslo — "The Dream Castle" is actually number two in a trilogy, the final part of which, "Farewell, Illusions," was released locally two years ago (and will go into U.S. distribution via Intl. Home Cinema in mid-November). Trilogy deals with the noble idealists of 1968 readying for total revolt, and with what happened to them later.

While "Farewell, Illusions" is a cataclysmic look at the final sellout of ideals and collapse of the idealists-turned-bourgeois, "The Dream Castle" finds everybody still hopeful in the mid-1970s, when three couples and six kids move into an old white frame house to give communal life a try. Communal life soon turns out not to mean absolute interdependence, let alone solidarity.

The couples maintain separate sleeping quarters. They drive to town in separate cars to jobs that classify them among the affluent: one is a psychiatrist in private practice, another a lawyer, two are school teachers, one a social counselor, etc.

There is a young brother in the house, too, an emerging punker who makes vile gestures and rude remarks to set off the swelling complacency of the grownups. Only the small kids seem to really enjoy sharing a home. Soon their parents have brawls either in the privacy of their beds or in the sauna. At a big party to celebrate their first year in the new house, now looking like something out of "Better Homes & Gardens," mental and physical

stripping is done, and an ax as well as pistol are put to bloody use.

There is never a dull moment in "The Dream Castle." As usual, the filmmaking team of Svend Wam & Petter Venneröd come out swinging wildly, and they stay loud and emphatic about the points they want to make throughout.

Before they wind up drowning their film in bombast, Wam & Venneröd provide grand cinematic entertainment. Action moves gracefully and naturally through well-composed frames, and everything is clad in a handsome and inventive production dress. All actors perform with conviction, gusto and much charm (including Venneröd himself as the meek school teacher who ends up doing a fatal Russian Roulette with a gun).

If "Farewell, Illusions" makes headway in the U.S., there is good reason to expect "The Dream Castle" to come across even better.
— *Kell.*

La Noche de los Lápices
(The Night Of The Pencils)
(ARGENTINE-COLOR)

An Aries release and production. Produced by Fernando Ayala. Directed by Héctor Olivera. Screenplay, Olivera, Daniel Kon, based on a story by María Seoane, Héctor Ruiz Nuñez; adviser, Pablo Diaz; camera (Eastmancolor), Leonardo Rodriguez Solis; music, José Luis Castiñeira de Dios. Reviewed at the Broadway theater, Buenos Aires, Sept. 30, 1986. Running time: 95 MINS.
With: Alejo Garcia Pintos, Vita Escardó, Pablo Novarro, Adriana Salonia, Pablo Machado, José Monje Berbel, Leonardo Sbaraglia, Tina Serrano, Héctor Bidonde, Lorenzo Quinteros, Alfonso De Grazia.

Buenos Aires — With this gripping, disturbing account of the kidnaping, torture and ultimate disappearance of six highschool students in the early times (1976) of the military regime's "dirty war" against subversion, Héctor Olivera resumes the historical-political line of his two best films: "La Patagonia Rebelde" (The Rebel Patagonia) (1975) and "No Habrá Mas Penas Ni Olvido" (Funny, Dirty Little War) (1983), both winners of Silver Bears at Berlin fests.

Olivera and Daniel Kon's script focuses on seven youngsters (five boys and two girls) who led a noisy campaign to attain a discount for students in the bus fares of La Plata, capital of the province of Buenos Aires. The discount was granted during the presidency of Isabel Perón. After she was ousted by the military and when strict rules were enforced to curb students' unrest, the same youths conducted another campaign — mostly by painting slogans and distributing leaflets — against the restrictions to freedom imposed in the schools.

They were followed by security

agents and one night police forces — disguised as hooded civilians — struck simultaneously at their homes, carrying them to secret detention sites where they were tied, blindfolded, tortured and abused both to punish them for their actions and to extract "confessions" about their nonexistent links with the guerrillas.

The ordeal of the youths is depicted with impressive realism although short of gory details. Except for a brief scene showing a boy tied naked to a metal bed and being tortured with an electrical rod, Olivera has avoided visualizing the most degrading physical brutalities inflicted on the prisoners, chosing instead to register the merciless ways employed to humiliate them and break their dignity and morale as human beings, wipe out their courage and reduce them to cornered animals. All face their fate with fear, but no cowardice, helpless but not surrendered. This spirit excites the admiration of the audience, beyond the compassion for their suffering, giving the film a tremendous emotional impact. The desperate, fruitless search of their relatives, as well as the shamelessness of the authorities pretending to know nothing about them, adds dramatic charge.

Based on facts told by the only survivor of the group, Pablo Diaz, hired by Olivera as adviser, and lensed in La Plata locations where most of it took place, pic has a ring of truth enhanced by the able acting of the newcomers chosen for the main roles — notably Vita Escardó and Alejo Garcia Pintos — and the vivid handling of the action. Olivera has succeeded in attaining the chronicle of a tragedy without fathoming the political and psychological motivations of the characters involved in it.

Technical credits are good.
— *Nubi.*

Burys
(The Detachment)
(SOVIET-COLOR/B&W)

A Lietuvos Film Studio production (Lithuania). Directed by Alexei Simonov. Screenplay, Yevgeny Grigoriev; camera (color, b&w), Yonas Gritzus; editor, Simonov; music, Vladimir Kamolikov; art direction, Algis Nithus. Reviewed at Repino Domkino (USSR), Sept. 18, 1986. Running time: 99 MINS.
With: Aleksandr Feklistov (Doronin), Sergei Sarmas (Urin), Dimitri Brusnikin (Nikitin), Mikhail Morozov (Petrov), Yakov Stepanov (Kuzmin), Aleksandr Peskov (Okunev), Viktor Nesterov (Stiopa).

Repino — The reason why it took director Alexei Simonov four years to get a green light from Goskino on the script of "The Detachment" is not immediately apparent in this war film about a patrol of new recruits that finds itself cut off from

its regiment. True, the time is June-July of 1941, and the quick Soviet victory that was prophesized is nowhere in sight at pic's end. On the other hand, film follows a fairly standard scenario and virtually the entire cast dies a hero's death.

A coproduction between the Lithuanian and Russian republics, "Detachment" lacks the pronounced local vision that gives many Baltic films cultural interest. It is well-made, contains some good action sequences, and won the 1985 Soviet national festival prize.

Most original part of film is its first half, where a band of young Red Army soldiers taking up arms for the first time is shown — quite realistically — as rambunctious teenagers thrilled with the virility of the machine guns and grenades they're going to use. In their first brush with Germans in the Lithuanian woods, however, they are caught without weapons, and are mockingly chased by a German soldier on a motorcycle. Their instinctive reaction is to run away screaming, but soon they realize they have to fight, and turn into fearless soldiers.

When they find themselves cut off from camp, they capture guns, hijack a German Army truck, lose some of their number in guerrilla actions and pick up others along the way. A Bielorussian teacher who deserted because he found himself fighting against tanks with only a gun is shamed into joining them. Only one of the group will survive, seriously wounded in action.

Film freely cuts in authentic newsreels when Nazi planes are needed; a little more mysterious is the deliberate, unmotivated alternation of color with black and white photography. Technical credits are good. — *Yung.*

Yako — Cazador de Malditos
(Yako — Hunter Of The Damned)
(MEXICAN-COLOR)

A Peliculas Mexicanas release of a Producciones Galubi/Producciones Torrente/Dinamic Films production. Produced by Raúl Galindo. Directed by Rubén Galindo. Stars Eduardo Yañez. Screenplay, Rubén Galindo, adapted by Carlos Valdemar; camera (color), Víctor Manuel Herrera; editor, Enrique Murillo; music, Pedro Galarra. Reviewed at Big Apple Cine 2, N.Y., Aug. 24, 1986. Running time: 101 MINS.
```
José Luis (Yako) ......... Eduardo Yañez
Diana ................. Diane Ferretti
Texas ................. Gregorio Casals
```
Also with: Pedro Weber (Chatanooga), Roberto Montiel, Gabriela Goldshmied, Humberto Elzondo, Bob Nelson.

The feature "Deliverance" manifested the fear that plagues many urban dwellers when confronted with the untamed wilds. Terror, in the form of crazed hillbillies, lurked in the woods away from major thoroughfares.

This same premise is the basis of the Mexican pic "Yako — Cazador de Malditos" (Yako — Hunter Of The Damned), directed by Rubén Galindo.

José Luis (Eduardo Yañez), better known as Yako, and his wife Diana (Diane Ferretti), decide to spend their honeymoon camping out in the woods. Little do they know that they are observed by a band of mountain men with evil intent. The hillbillies attack the unsuspecting couple: Diana is gang raped and murdered while Yako watches, helplessly tied to a tree. The rest of the pic concerns Yako's revenge.

Once again, Galindo has taken a shopworn idea and produced a serviceable vehicle through able direction, strong leads and a cameraman who knows how different lensing techniques can affect tones necessary to relating an engaging tale.

But, there are some tremendous holes in the script and many unanswered questions: When Yako loses his rifle at the beginning of the film, he does not seem particularly bothered to take on the remaining armed hicks with his bare hands. After disarming and killing them, it never occurs to him to take their guns. His city-bred ingenuity also manages to create a whole arsenal of primitive weapons salvaged from the forest floor.

Yañez brings a humanity to his role, yet his early macho stance is called into question by the pain that accompanies his vengeance.

Despite its many flaws, "Yako — Cazador de Malditos" manages to be effective and offer the viewers a few thrills.—Lent.

Igreja Dos Oprimidos
(Church Of The Oppressed)
(BRAZILIAN-FRENCH-DOCU-COLOR-16m)

A Prods. Cinemat. L.C. Barreto/Société Franc. de Production Audiovisuelles production. Produced by Luciola Villela. Directed by Jorge Bodanzky. Screenplay, Hélèna Salem based on her book "Argument;" camera, (color, 16m), Serge Guitton, Lucien Msika; editor, Yves Charoy; sound, Wiliam Fogtman, Michel Olany. Reviewed at the Montreal World Film Festival — Latin American Cinema, Aug. 28, 1986. Running time: 75 MINS.
With: Father Ricardo Rezende, Father François Gouriou, Father Aristides Camio. Don Alano Pena, Friar Leonard Boff, Sister Irene.

Montreal — Far from the beaches of Rio de Janeiro and the bustle of São Paolo in the south Brazilian state of Para, desperately poor land squatters are struggling against powerful land barons for a system of agrarian reform that would give them some control over their destinies. They are being aided by progressive Catholic priests, social workers and union organizers, some of whom have been murdered by hired gunmen or arrested by the soldiers that police the sprawling, dusty region of forests and rivers when they are called in by the distant landlords.

For those unfamiliar with these events or curious to learn more, "Church Of The Oppressed" provides a sympathetic inside view of the plight of these dirt poor landworkers and fisherman, and the "people's priests" who provide them with activist spiritual leadership. Interviews with principals involved document the intractable resistance to agrarian reform and the brutality with which it's been implemented. Happily, there are signs of hope and determination reflected in the beautiful folk music that's essential to the masses and political rallies of the region. On the uglier side is an interview with a suspected gunman who denies everything on camera and who was released from a month-long jail stint for lack of evidence.

This otherwise well-done docu is seriously undermined by a histrionic French voiceover that obliterates the voices of the film's subjects with an abrasive interpretation of testimony that would be better rendered in their native tongue, accompanied by subtitles. —Rich.

El Vecindario — Los Mexicanos Calientes
(The Neighborhood — Oh, Those Hot Mexicans)
(MEXICAN-COLOR)

A Peliculas Mexicanas release of a Frontera Films production. Produced by Alfonso Martínez Solares. Directed by Gilberto Martínez Solares. Screenplay, Gilberto and Alfonso Martínez Solares; camera (color), Armando Castillón; editor, José Monguía; music, Ernesto Cortázar. Reviewed at Big Apple Cine 1, N.Y., Sept. 10, 1986. Running time: 92 MINS.
Roberto . . . . Alfonso Zayas
Irma . . . . Angélica Aragón
Rubén . . . . Rafael Inclán
Julieta . . . . Angélica Chaín
Hilda . . . . Ana Luisa Peluffo
Sofia . . . . Rossy Mendoza
Edmundo . . . . Gilberto Trujillo
Anita . . . . Anaís de Melo
El Compadre . . . . Rene Ruiz (Tun Tun)

Mexico's Martínez Solares brothers, Alfonso and Gilberto, have managed to produce a truly distasteful film under the aegis of comedy.

"El Vecindario," subtitled proudly "Oh, Those Hot Mexicans," tries to milk comedy out of rape, incest, homosexuality, adultery, religion, blackmail and corruption of adolescents. These themes can be fit subjects for comedy, but the attitude expressed here is distasteful.

The convoluted plot concerns the exploits of three philanderers, played by Alfonso Zayas, Rafael Inclán and Gilberto Trujillo.

A few points of contention in the plot concern the character of Roberto (Zayas), who abducts women off the street and rapes them. Pic says he is such an adroit lover that none of the women will press charges. In fact, he becomes the envy of other males.

The script's one-liner sense of comedy is little more than a series of comic sketches developed around a single-minded desire for self satisfaction. Not one character in the film is faithful much less expresses any affection beyond immediate gratification.

Surprisingly, the cast reads like a "Who's Who" of Mexican comedians. None of them is allowed to develop his character beyond that of stereotype.

The camerawork and editing are functional only in keeping the narrative moving. It's just that it doesn't move very far.—Lent.

Es Mi Vida — El Noa Noa 2
(It's My Life — El Noa Noa 2)
(MEXICAN-COLOR)

A Pelínez Mexicanas release of a Producciones del Rey/Producciones Alarca production. Produced by arnulfo Delgado and Alberto Aguilera (Juan Gabriel). Directed by Gonzalo Martínez Ortega. Stars Juan Gabriel. Screenplay, Martínez Ortega; camera (color), Feberón Tepoztle; editor, Angel Camacho; music, Gabriel and Eduardo Malallemo. Reviewed at Big Apple Cine 1, N.Y., Aug. 26, 1986. Running time: 106 MINS.
Alberto Aguilera (Juan Gabriel) . . Himself
Daniel . . . . Narciso Busquets
Don Alfredo Moras . . . . Guillermo Murray
Also with: Fernando Balzaretti, Marcela Rubiales, Leonor Llausás, César Bono, Edgar Wald, Lilian González.
Special guest stars: Meche Carreño, Federico Villa, Dacia González, Tito Junco, La Prieta Linda, Bruno Rey.

The Mexican pic "Es Mi Vida" (It's My Life) is the second big-screen bio of popular national ballad singer-songwriter Alberto Aguilera, known to his fans as Juan Gabriel.

The first installment, "El Noa Noa," was made by director Martínez Ortega in 1979. It depicted the musician's early years in his hometown, Juárez, and his initial fame working at a local cabaret named "El Noa Noa."

The second Martínez Ortega-Gabriel team-up begins with young Aguilera arriving in Mexico City loaded with ambition and talent with nary a penny in his pockets.

Early in the film, he is framed for robbery and is sent to Mexico City's Lecumberri Prison where he stays for almost the remainder of the pic. His suffering and brooding is broken up two ways: he sings to his fellow prisoners, and, he has lots of dream sequences. Of course, these sequences allow the filmmaker to explore a variety of sets and also delve into what will come later: recording his first LP, singing in public, etc. They also serve to showcase appearances by a bevy of invited national guest stars.

Gabriel plays an idealized self, too likeable, too sincere and too innocent. He has poetic justice on his side and the whole audience knows well in advance that the singer will be vindicated by his later fame.

Not wanting his mother to be aware of his incarceration, he writes her fictitious letters about his success in the capital. These letters are augmented by fantasies bordering on Oedipal.

Although fans will find this bio satisfying, the rest of the public will find its portrait of Gabriel too good to be true and any further interest in the star's life is strictly ho-hum.
— Lent.

Something Wild
(COLOR)

Overlong road movie shifts from quirky comedy to a bold thriller.

An Orion Pictures release of a Religioso Primitiva presentation. Produced by Jonathan Demme, Kenneth Utt. Executive producer, Edward Saxon. Directed by Demme. Stars Jeff Daniels, Melanie Griffith. Screenplay, E. Max Frye; camera (Du Art color, Deluxe prints), Tak Fujimoto; editor, Craig McKay; music, John Cale, Laurie Anderson; opening song, David Byrne; production design, Norma Moriceau; art direction, Steve Lineweaver; set decoration, Billy Reynolds; sound (Dolby), Les Lazarowitz; associate producers, Bill Miller, Ron Bozman; assistant director, Bozman; casting, Risa Bramon, Billy Hopkins. Reviewed at the Samuel Goldwyn Theater, Beverly Hills, Oct. 22, 1986. (MPAA Rating: R.) Running time: **113 MINS.**

Charles Driggs . . . . Jeff Daniels
Audrey Hankel . . . . Melanie Griffith
Ray Sinclair . . . . Ray Liotta
Irene . . . . Margaret Colin
The Country Squire . . . . Tracey Walter
"Peaches" . . . . Dana Preu
Larry Dillman . . . . Jack Gilpin
Peggy Dillman . . . . Su Tissue
Tracy . . . . Kristin Olsen
Also with: John Sayles, John Waters, Charles Napier, The Feelies, Kenneth Utt.

Hollywood — "Something Wild" gets better the wilder and bolder it becomes, but it does take awhile. Conceptually and stylistically compelling under Jonathan Demme's sometimes striking direction, offbeat thriller about an unlikely couple on the run begins conventionally but finally generates strong tension after jettisoning the many accumulated clichés close to the midway point. Heavily trendy musical trappings encumber the film as much as they enhance it, and positioning this hybrid creation commercially will be a tricky task for Orion.

With elements of "After Hours" and "Blue Velvet" reverberating not far from the surface, first-time screenwriter E. Max Frye's story sees superyuppie Jeff Daniels being picked up by hot number Melanie Griffith at a luncheonette, driven out to New Jersey and, before he knows what's happening, being handcuffed to a bed and ravished by this crazy lady, all as he protests he really should be getting back to the office that afternoon, and shouldn't be doing this because he's got a wife and kids.

A stolen car or two later, Mr. Nice Guy tags along with Griffith to meet her mother, to whom he is introduced instantly as the young woman's husband. Not wanting to appear slow on his feet, he accepts the guise, and continues it when he unwittingly accompanies her to her 10th highschool reunion.

All the above is overelaborated unnecessarily as the same territory could have been covered in 15 minutes with no loss of character or dramatic value. The viewer, like Daniels, is being set up by Griffith, to whom there clearly is more than meets the eye, but the fascination she inspires fails to warrant the extended display of her wiles.

All changes at the reunion, however, as Griffith's ex-con husband makes an unexpected appearance and proceeds to change the couple's joyride into a nightmare. From this point on, Demme and Frye adroitly tighten the screws as the focus shifts from Griffith to the showdown between the two utterly different men vying for her attentions.

Part of the reason for the film's sudden transformation for the better lies with Ray Liotta's mesmerizingly menacing performance as the sadistic cast-off lover, but it is equally due to the energy derived structurally from his character's role in the drama. What had been a cute but hopelessly contrived little anecdote becomes a story of twin obsessions and, finally, a life-or-death struggle.

Demme brilliantly handles some of the set-pieces, notably the reunion, a low-key, high-stakes restaurant confrontation, a convenience store robbery and the final battle between the men, in which he displays a hitherto unrevealed flair for violent action. The film develops considerable force during the second half, only to end on a disappointingly trite and conventional note.

At the same time, there are some odd choices in evidence. For a story about three white misfits, the telling is oddly backdropped by a preponderance of black culture — rappers, hitchhikers, Baptist church members, musicians and countless others are floating constantly on the periphery of the images, interestingly, but for no apparent reason. Most absurd is the instance of Griffith, whose character may have street smarts but no book-learned intelligence, suddenly turning up reading a biography of Winnie Mandela.

Daniels does a good job in transforming himself from straightlaced good boy to loosened up, wised-up man. Griffith is provocative enough, but falls a little short in putting across all the aspects of this complicated woman (when she repeatedly calls out to Daniels' character, "Charlie," she sounds very much like Dorothy Comingore addressing "Charlie" Foster Kane).

Supporting roles are all beautifully filled, with Margaret Colin making a strong impression as Liotta's punky, aggressive prom date, and Jack Gilpin and Su Tissue projecting a hilariously accurate image of self-satisfied, well-to-do young successes. Directors John Waters and John Sayles are in for brief cameos.

There may be a lot of good music on the track, but Demme lays it on a bit thick here, and some of the music distracts as the suspense mounts. Tak Fujimoto's lensing and Norma Moriceau's production design are tops, while Craig McKay's editing is excellent within scenes, even if entire pic could have been considerably shorter.—*Cart.*

Saxophone Colossus
(DOCU-COLOR)

An ASA Communications release of a Mug-Shot production. Produced, written and directed by Robert Mugge. Coproducers, David Mazor, Michael Phillips. Camera (color), Lawrence McConkey. Reviewed at Denver Intl. Film Festival, Oct. 19, 1986. (No MPAA Rating.) Running time: **101 MINS.**
With: Sonny Rollins, Lucille Rollins, Heikki Sarmanto, Gary Giddins, Ira Gitler, Frances Davis, and Yomiuri Nippon Symphony.

Denver — In a scheduled "sneak preview," Robert Mugge's "Saxophone Colossus," named for a Sonny Rollins album, was shown on the final night of the Denver Intl. Film Festival. Its official world premiere has been set for Nov. 14 at the London Film Festival. It is subject to very minor alterations in film titles prior to that event.

As documentary of a supreme jazz artist and man of artistic integrity, "Saxophone Colossus" is an electrifying record of an artist at work. Scenes at Opus 40 festival near Saugerties in upstate New York, New York City, and in Tokyo present the musicmaking against varied, vivid backgrounds.

Central event in the film is the premiere of a concerto for tenor sax, product of a collaboration between Rollins and Finnish musician Heikki Sarmanto, for a Tokyo concert. Twelve previous concert tours in Japan by Rollins proved he had an audience that would attend.

Rollins' intelligence and relaxed conversational manner make him an ideal subject, both lucid and knowledgable. In performance he plays with inexhuastible power matched by a vivid musical imagination. Rollins tells how "I learn the material then blot out my mind, then try to relax, and let it come by itself."

The concerto is a remarkable work of seven movements of which five are done intact. Cocomposer and conductor Sarmanto is shown as intense and creative. For each of the used movements director Mugge devised specific visual motifs, taking the camera outside the hall for shots of Tokyo streets, spectacular neon lights, and views of the people. In all, Rollins remains the center of interest, and the wonder of the concerto is that despite the huge orchestra with its many musicians fiddling away, Rollins never loses his position at the center of the work.

Rollins is heard in his lengthy "G-Man" composition at the start of the film, and subsequently plays a great set of improvisations on "Over The Rainbow," "How Are Things In Glocca Morra" and "Peer Gynt. He also plays a portion of the extended work, "Don't Stop The Carnival."

It is in the set of improvisations that Rollins suddenly jumps from the 7-ft.-high stage to the ground, chipping his heel as he lands, then lies on his back to play for 30 minutes, though not all of this is filmed.

Observations by three critics, Gary Giddins, Ira Gitler and Frances Davis, put Rollins in perspective through their incisively expressed thoughts. Throughout, the taste, judgment and appreciation of writer-director-producer Robert Mugge is shown as keen and sensitive. —*Alyo.*

Sky Bandits
(BRITISH-COLOR)

A Galaxy Intl. Releasing release of a London Front Ltd. production. Produced by Richard Herland. Directed by Zoran Perisic. Screenplay, Thom Keyes; camera (Rank color), David Watkin; editor, Peter Tanner; music, Alfie Kabiljo; sound, David Hildyard; production design, Tony Woollard; supervising art director, Charles Bishop; art direction, Malcolm Stone, John Siddall (U.K.), Jose Maria Taprador (Spain); set decoration, Hugh Scaife; assistant director, Michael Murray; costume design, Betsy Hermann; stunt coordinator, Marc Boyle; visual effects supervisor, Perisic; special effects supervisor, Ian Wingrove; model effects supervisor, Brian Smithies; second unit director, Terry Marcel; aerial unit director, Terry Cole; casting, Mary Selway. Reviewed at Magno Preview 9 screening room, N.Y., Oct. 22, 1986. (MPAA Rating: PG). Running time: **93 MINS.**

Barney . . . . Scott McGinnis
Luke . . . . Jeff Osterhage
Fritz . . . . Ronald Lacey
Bannock . . . . Miles Anderson
Yvette . . . . Valerie Steffen
Mitsou . . . . Ingrid Held
Von Schlussel . . . . Keith Buckley
Col. Canning . . . . Terrence Harvey

"Sky Bandits" misfires on all cylinders. Meant as a rollicking World War I adventure, mishmash of a feature is missing a plotline. Touted as the most expensive (production budget pegged at $18,-000,000) indie British film ever, pic doesn't deliver the expected values on screen and has a no-name cast that won't help it attract attention domestically or overseas. Distrib Galaxy Intl. has unwisely opted for a national saturation release.

Originally titled "Gunbus" (after the small fighter planes featured), Thom Keyes' unsatisfactory screenplay opens with a reel of two young heroes (Scott McGinnis and Jeff Osterhage) making like Butch Cassidy & Sundance (the early days, that is) in montages of bank robberies. With this pointless material headed nowhere the boys are suddenly sent to France to fight in the Great War against the dreaded hun.

Misadventures for the duo include a game of one upsmanship with haughty British flyers, a little sack time with two pretty mademoiselles (Valerie Steffen, Ingrid Held) and a mission to destroy a vast Graf Zeppelin the Germans are using for bombing runs. With dogfighter prowess picked up instantly (heroes decide to try piloting biplanes on a dare), they save the day and are subsequently back in the west blowing up banks quicker than you can say "Blue Max."

Film plods along episodically with no forward momentum to the story: every once in a while there is a dissolve and a new scene has begun. Since Keyes' script lacks humor, the boring repartee between the two wooden heroes is downright deadly. What producer Richard Herland and director Zoran Perisic deliver is a succession of pretty but very fake-looking model plane shots or process shots. The excitement of aerial dogfights, which have entertained audiences in hundreds of war films and served as the inspiration for "Star Wars," is missing.

Cast is truly awful, with the only familiar actor, Ronald Lacey, hamming it up and American leads McGinnis and Osterhage lacking the charisma this sort of yarn calls for. Production, including David Watkin's photography, is technically adequate but wholly lacking in verisimilitude. For all the money spent, it would have been more convincing to use stock footage left over from "Hell's Angels." The comic book approach doesn't work.

With Rank, ITC and Thorn EMI as recent examples, experienced British producers have learned how difficult it is to try and compete with the Americans via big-budget projects; modest efforts like "Gregory's Girl" and "My Beautiful Laundrette" have been more successful. "Sky Bandits" will undoubtedly reinforce this conventional wisdom. —*Lor.*

Weekend Warriors
(COLOR)

Cornball service comedy.

The Movie Store release. Produced by Hannah Hempstead. Executive producers, Bert Convy, Stanley Fimberg. Directed by Convy. Screenplay, Bruce Belland, Roy M. Rogosin; camera (color), Charles Minsky; editor, Raja Gosnell; music, Perry Botkin; sound, John Brasher; production design, Chester Kaczenski; costume design, Susie Desanto; assistant director, Dean Stevens; stunt coordinator, Wally Crowder; casting, Junie Lowry. Reviewed at the Hollywood Pacific theater, L.A., Oct. 17, 1986. (MPAA Rating: R.) Running time: **85 MINS.**
Vince Tucker.............Chris Lemmon
Sergeant Burge.............Vic Tayback
Colonel Archer............Lloyd Bridges
Congressman Balljoy......Graham Jarvis
Phil McCracken..........Daniel Greene
Decola...................Marty Cohen
Cory Seacomb...........Brian Bradley
Ames.................Matt McCoy
Duckworth..............Alan Campbell
Mort Seblinsky.............Tom Villard
Tom Dawson................Jeff Meyer
Captain Cabot............Mark Taylor
Nurse Nancy................Gail Barle
Betty Beep.............Camille Saviola

Hollywood — "Weekend Warriors" is another low-budget comedy release, originally shot as "Hollywood Air Force Base," that throws in ribald hijinks, a little nudity and not much of a story in order to lure a teenage audience with nothing better to do. The pic may very soon grace the shelves of video stores.

It's Hollywood 1961 and the boys are doing anything to avoid active military duty. So they join the National Guard. Obviously, since it's Hollywood, where nothing or no one is taken seriously, the crew of this guard spend their duty time gambling and conducting flatulence contests.

It's only when the brass come to visit and threaten to put these would-be actors on active duty that they decide to shape up their act.

Of course, since it is Hollywood, shaping up their act means putting on a show, hiring people who look like good soldiers, stocking the place with sexy nurses and wowing the often-clichéd dirty old colonel.

As in all B films, the plan works and the men are free to pursue their slovenly ways.

The film, Bert Convy's directorial debut, obviously was put together quickly and somewhat haphazardly, with scenes that sometimes look like they're from a home movie and camera angles that leave one wondering what's happening with the film while one watches someone's back.

Chris Lemmon, son of Jack, plays Vince Tucker, the lead crony of this band, who comes up with the star-spangled plan to save the men. Lemmon has a good screen persona and even in this inane release, it's obvious he will endure.

Brian Bradley puts in a good performance as a bisexual gossip columnist who gets out of active duty by declaring he is homosexual.

Others in the film, including veteran actors Lloyd Bridges and Vic Tayback, are mildly amusing.

The best part of the film comes when Lemmon's character and the boys host their own Hollywood extravaganza to wow the brass. This includes some pretty talented marching bands, dancing drill teams and a rather spectacular baton twirler. Now that's entertainment, or at least it's the only kind found in this pic. —*Teen.*

Trick Or Treat
(COLOR)

Silly rock/horror opus for youngsters.

A De Laurentiis Entertainment Group release. Produced by Michael S. Murphey, Joel Soisson. Directed by Charles Martin Smith. Screenplay, Murphey, Soisson, Rhet Topham, from a story by Topham; camera (Technicolor), Robert Elswit; editor, Jane Schwartz Jaffe; music, Christopher Young; original songs, Fastway; production design, Curt Schnell; art direction, Colin D. Irwin; set decoration, Doug Mowat; special makeup effects, Kevin Yahger; sound (Ultra-Stereo), Ed Paul Bengston, David Cohn. Reviewed at DEG, Beverly Hills, Oct. 21, 1986. MPAA Rating: R.) Running time: **97 MINS.**
Eddie Weinbauer............Marc Price
Sammi Curr................Tony Fields
Leslie Graham.............Lisa Orgolini
Tim Hainey................Doug Savant
Angie Weinbauer...........Elaine Joyce
Roger Mockus.............Glen Morgan
Nuke..................Gene Simmons
Rev. Aaron Gilstrom.....Ozzy Osbourne

Hollywood — Like a relatively dark street on Halloween night, "Trick Or Treat" is ripe for howls and hoots, but only manages to deliver a choice handful of them when the festivities are just about over. Last half-hour has some first-rate scenes for a B picture with a C theme (horrors of heavy metal rock) that is only likely to appeal to adolescents.

Film doesn't quite parody bad musicians as well as "Spinal Tap," despite a story with an equally hilarious premise.

A recently killed rock star named Sammi Curr (Tony Fields, made up like a member of KISS), comes back to life when his last, awful unreleased record is played backwards. He's determined to seek revenge on his most ardent critics, among them Ozzy Osbourne in a real role reversal as a bilious tv preacher on an anti-rock crusade.

The thing is, the satanic rocker takes himself seriously in reincarnation and ends up acting out all those evil acts he's been singing about for years — drawing his power from the megawatts that surge through his guitar.

There's a geeky highschool kid, Eddie (Marc Price), who idolizes the rocker and is responsible for his appearances. Every time he puts the record on the stereo or the cassette in the deck, everything that's electrically charged starts to heat up and the singer materializes — at first to help his fresh-faced fan revenge the jocks at school who taunt him (which the little punker appreciates) but later he turns against Eddie. The kid begins to fret over Fields' excessive guitar playing.

Fortunately, filmmakers went light on the music (by the group Fastway) that is awful and presumably supposed to be, making the film a lot more endurable for those who can't stomach a minute of heavy metal.

Scoring is only intense when Fields is on one of his rampages electrifying people, who beautifully disintegrate, or throttling them — as he does with Osbourne by reaching into a tv and zapping the blithering fool to death with his super-charged fingers (one of the film's highlights, such as they are).

Price is cast perfectly as the dismayed rock worshipper, as is most of the cast. Gene Simmons gets top billing for appearing as the disk jockey who hands over the rock star's unreleased song to his number one fan, but is only on the screen for a few opening minutes.

Technical credits are superb and possibly unintentionally too absurd to be horrifying, especially in one scene when Price's amour Leslie (Lisa Orgolini) tries to electrocute the frazzled rocker by flushing the toilet with the star's strummin' hand writhing in it. —*Brit.*

Rage
(ITALIAN-SPANISH-COLOR)

A Tiber Intl. (Rome)/Arco Film (Madrid coproduction. World sales, Gel Intl. Produced by Paolo Ferrara. Directed by "Anthony Richmond" (Tonino Ricci). Stars Conrad Nichols. Screenplay, Jaime Comas Gil, Eugenio Benito; camera (Luciano Vittori color), Gianni Bergamini; editor, Vincenzo Tomassi; music, Stelvio Cipriani; production manager, Maurizio Mattei; assistant director, Giancarlo Bastianoni; stunt coordinator, Roland Zamperla; set design, Javier Fernandez. Reviewed at 42d St. Liberty theater, N.Y., Oct. 25, 1986. (No MPAA Rating.) Running time: **91 MINS.**
With: Conrad Nichols (Rage), Stelio Candelli, Werner Pochat, Taida Urruzola, Chris Huerta.

"Rage" is a tedious 1984 follow-up film to the modest sci-fi opus "Rush," featuring the same director and star. As with the original, pic is a cheap mishmash of leftover costumes and vehicles from a World War II actioner.

Opening montage of nuclear explosions stock footage sets tale after World War III. Star Conrad Nichols, a beefy Sylvester Stallone type, is assigned to head a mission to find Alpha Base, from which a persistent radio signal has alerted the holocaust survivors that the base still exists, with a treasure trove there of technical info and needed uranium reserves.

Nichols (known by the nickname "Rage") takes along an old army chum (Werner Pochat), a beautiful girl (who insists on wearing short shorts and a revealing top during the dangerous mission) and an electronics/weapons expert. They visit an evil warlord named Slash (though his facial scar is a victim of continuity sloppiness) to get a map to Alpha Base and spend the rest of the film playing cat and mouse with Slash's violent henchmen and women. Boring pic climaxes with a lengthy battle chase involving a locomotive.

Plot ends up like "On The Beach," with the base found to be deserted, its signal being automatic. There's no uranium, but the heroes bring back an elegant edition of the Bible, just the ticket to rebuild Western Civilization.

Dubbing is poor, as are technical credits. —Lor.

Je hais les acteurs
(I Hate Actors)
(FRENCH-B&W/COLOR)

A Gaumont release of a Septembre Films/-Gaumont/Films A2 coproduction. Executive producer, Jean Nainchrik. Associate producer, Alain Poiré. Directed by Gérard Krawczyk. Screenplay, Krawczyk, based on novel, "I Hate Actors," by Ben Hecht; camera (b&w, Kodak color), Michel Cenet; editor, Marie-Joseph Yoyotte; music, Roland Vincent; sound, Pierre Befve; art direction, Jacques Dugied; costumes, Rosine Lan; makeup, Irène Ottavis; assistant director, Gérard Pujolar; production manager, Guy Azzi. Reviewed at the UGC Biarritz, Paris, Oct. 18, 1986. Running time: **90 MINS.**

Orlando . . . . Jean Poiret
Mr. Albert . . . . Michel Blanc
J.B. Cobb . . . . Bernard Blier
Korman . . . . Patrick Floersheim
Bison . . . . Michel Galabru
Elvina . . . . Pauline Lafont
Miss Davis . . . . Dominique Lavanant
Egelhofer . . . . Guy Marchand
Potnik . . . . Vojtek Pszoniak
Devlin . . . . Jean-François Stevenin
Also with: Sophie Duez, Patrick Braoude, Jezabel Carpi, Claude Chabrol, Lionel Rocheman, Alexandre Mnouchkine, Yann Epstein, Mike Marshall, Michel Such, Jean-Paul Comart, Allan Wenger.

Paris — Gérard Krawczyk, an IDHEC film school graduate who won several fest honors for his student short, "The Subtle Concept," a *film noir*-styled visualization in English of Woody Allen's print lampoon, "Mr. Big," flunks the test of a first theatrical feature film in this awkward adaptation of Ben Hecht's novel, "I Hate Actors."

Even Hecht admirers are cool about this rather dour satire of Hollywood, cast in the form of a whodunit in which a top talent agent becomes prime suspect in the murder of several male stars during the production of a studio spectacular.

Krawczyk, who also scripted, remains faithful to the book, but his 1940s Hollywood is a meek French Riviera stand-in peopled by an all-Gallic troupe who neither correspond to any models or legends nor pass auditions of dramatic plausibility. In the central role of the harassed impresario, Jean Poiret has all the urbanity but none of the aggressive drive the personage suggests. And by no stretch of the imagination can one swallow Michel Galabru as a former silent screen matinee idol trying to make a comeback in the sound remake of his earlier success.

The miscasting is corollary to Kawczyk's misconceived direction, which replaces Hecht's often mean-spirited barbs and observations with a broad, unconvincing caricature style.

Apart from the book-ending modern-day color sequences (which set up a closing gag Hecht never could have imagined), "Actors" was shot in b&w, but Michel Cenet's clean lensing is evocative of no particular studio style.

Given the circumstances Jacques Dugied's art direction was doomed to inadequacy from the start — the corner of a sound stage at Billancourt studios is a paltry understudy for what is meant to suggest a tumultuous 1940s Hollywood dream factory. —Len.

From Beyond
(COLOR)

Solid followup to 'Re-Animator.'

An Empire Pictures release of a Brian Yuzna production. Produced by Yuzna. Executive producer, Charles Band. Line producer, Roberto Bessi. Directed by Stuart Gordon. Screenplay, Dennis Paoli, adapted from the story by H.P. Lovecraft by Yuzna, Paoli, Gordon; camera (Technicolor), Mac Ahlberg; editor, Lee Percy; music, Richard Band; production design, Giovanni Natalucci; set decoration (U.S.), Robert Burns; special effects, John Buechler, Anthony Doublin, John Naulin, Mark Shostrom; costume design, Angee Beckett; sound (Ultra-Stereo), Mario Bramonti, associate producer, Bruce Curtis; assistant director, Mauro Sacripanti. Reviewed at the Empire screening room, L.A., Oct. 7, 1986. (MPAA Rating: R.) Running time: **85 MINS.**
Crawford Tillinghast . . . . . . Jeffrey Combs
Dr. Katherine
McMichaels . . . . Barbara Crampton
Dr. Edward Pretorious . . . . Ted Sorel
Bubba Brownlee . . . . Ken Foree
Dr. Roberta Bloch . . . . Carolyn Purdy-Gordon
Hester Gilman . . . . Bunny Summers
Jordan Fields . . . . Bruce McGuire

Hollywood — Less wigged-out and somewhat more conventional than his wild debut feature, "Re-Animator," Stuart Gordon's H.P. Lovecraft followup, "From Beyond," still stands as an effectively gruesome horror entry that should please fans of the genre. R rating will help this one penetrate the marketplace further than its unrated predecesor was able to do, so this rates as a solid fall exploitationer for Empire.

"Re-Animator," a cult fave, was one of the most graphically gory blood feasts since the heyday of Herschell Gordon Lewis. While not quite up to that level, "From Beyond" still has its share of enjoyably gross scenes, and works some nifty variations on the haunted house genre.

When the brilliantly mad Dr. Pretorious is found headdless in his laboratory after conducting an experiment, a beautiful shrink under-takes to interrogate the scientist's assistant to discover what happened (these two are played by Barbara Crampton and Jeffrey Combs, in a reunion from "Re-Animator").

Upon visiting Pretorious' mansion, however, Crampton begins taking an unusual interest in the doctor's invention, the Resonator, a device designed to stimulate the pineal gland, a sixth sensory organ that allows one to see "beyond."

Intense usage of the Resonator can produce results both ecstatic and horrible, and here the emphasis is on the latter, as victims tend to become crazed and then have the asparagus-like gland itself grow out of a hole in their foreheads.

Determined to get to the bottom of what the Resonator did to Pretorious, and intrigued by the machine's capacity for sexual stimulation, Crampton goes all the way in her investigation. This brings back Pretorious in a new, horrendous, tremendously lecherous form, and the ooze only stops flowing after a grand battle to the death.

The special effects team had a field day with all the transformations, monsterish getups and horrible deaths, and connoisseurs of such things will delight in the artisans' many accomplishments.

Director Stuart Gordon, too, and his cowriters clearly enjoyed wallowing in the gruesome possibilities, and he and lenser Mac Ahlberg have brought a fair degree of style and flourish to the visual approach.

But the greatest pleasure the film offers is afforded by Barbara Crampton, who is centerstage most of the time and proves a constant delight to watch. Striking at first glimpse as the serious, bespectacled psychiatrist, she gradually exposes the inquisitive, sexual and resourceful sides of her character, and is a terrific screamer to boot.

Shot in Rome at no loss of verisimilitude, pic is actually the third film to be directed by Gordon, after "Dolls," but second to be released. —Cart.

Vacation Nicaragua
(DOCU-COLOR-16m)

A Rock Solid production. Produced and directed by Anita Clearfield. Executive producer, David A. Griffin. Camera (color) & editor, Geoffrey Leighton; sound, John Luck; additional camera & lighting, Cathy Zheutlin. Reviewed at the Fox Intl., Venice, Calif. Oct. 10, 1986. (No MPAA Rating.) Running time: **77 MINS.**

Hollywood — "Vacation Nicaragua" takes a fresh approach to the political documentary form, as filmmaker Anita Clearfield accompanied a group of 25 middle-class American tourists on a trip to the embattled Central American country, saw what they saw, and recorded their responses. Pic sags in spots and lacks the fervor to be found in successful "committed" docus, but is unavoidably interesting to anyone concerned with ongoing events in the region. Film opened Oct. 17 at the Fox Intl. in Venice, Calif., and has a place at fests and specialized venues, as well as on public television outlets.

Clearfield announces no-political agenda at the outset, and is at pains to present the travelers as resolutely normal types who are not already converted to the Sandinistas' cause, but instead simply individuals with a curiosity about what's going on and a taste for adventurous excursions.

Although their trip was organized by the government tourist agency, the Americans were free to roam about on their own, and early on visited with U.S. Congressman Richard Cheney and others who had less than complimentary things to say about the Sandinistas.

Gradually, however, the effect of the person-to-person contact with the natives and their struggle to build a new society created a strong sympathy among the visitors, who by the end uniformly expressed the view that the U.S. is utterly wrong to continue its age-old policy of meddling in the destiny of Central American people.

Seen along the way are portions of a speech and q&a with President Daniel Ortega, a private conversation with the Minister of Culture, Father Ernesto Cardenal, and a trip to the Managua McDonald's, where the only items available were hamburgers and tamarind juice.

Most unusual, however, is a glimpse of the odd, imporverished community of Bluefields. Isolated on the Atlantic coast, far from the political hotbed of Managua, and reachable only by boat, Bluefields is more Caribbean than Latin in nature, boasts an English-speaking population and is full of mistrustful people who are skeptical about, if not openly opposed to, the course of the revolution.

Pics tries to deal with both the pros and cons of what has happened in Nicaragua since 1979 by talking about the preservation of culture and advances in education and health care on the one hand, and censorship and repression on the other. Because Clearfield locks herself into the tourist's point-of-view, however, only a superficial look at such issues as possible, and this robs the film of any possibility of incisive analysis.

Technically, effort is okay, and it does give one a good look at the country and its people. —Cart.

Recruits
(COLOR)

Cheap carbon of 'Police Academy.'

A Concorde Pictures release of a Concorde/Maurice Smith production. Produced by Smith. Directed by Rafal Zielinski. Screenplay, Charles Wiener, B.K. Roderick; camera (color), Peter Czerski; editor, Stephan Fanfara; music, Steve Parsons; art direction, Craig Richards; set decoration, Nick White; costume design, Eva Gord; sound, Urmas John Rosin; assistant director, Rob Malensant; second unit director, Randy Bradshaw. Reviewed at the Egyptian Theater, L.A., Oct. 17, 1986. (MPAA Rating: R.) Running time: **82 MINS.**

Steve	Steve Osmond
Mike	Doug Annear
Howie	Alan Deveau
Winston	John Terrell
Susan	Lolita David
Brazil	Tracey Tanner
Tanya	Annie McAuley
Stonewall	Tony Travis
Magruder	Mike McDonald
Sgt. S	Colleen Karney
Mayor Bagley	Jason Logan
Mrs. Bagley	Caroline Tweedle
Clint	Mark Blutman
Thunderhead	Thor

Hollywood — "Recruits" is a non-name brand "Police Academy." Only marginally sillier and less funny than the real thing, pic was even shot near Toronto, where most of the successful Warner Bros. series entries were lensed. Sole differences are that "Recruits" looks a lot cheaper and will make a tiny fraction of the amount at the b.o.

Produced by Maurice Smith and directed by Rafal Zielinski, same team responsible for last year's "Loose Screws,' this concoction reeks of familiarity from the outset, as a group of goofballs is put together by a scheming police department in order to discredit the local mayor and get him booted out of office.

About an hour is taken up with the familiar shenanigans stemming from training camp mishaps, confrontations with local thugs and the occasional comic sex scenes, in which women's tops come flying off as if connected to wires.

Having stumbled through one mud puddle after another, affable gang finally shapes up and redeems itself, although final reel feels like padding added to stretch matters out to feature length.

Performances and staging assume cartoon-like proportions in this harmless but profoundly frivolous farce. One debit is the unattractive lensing, which makes everyone look pasty. —Cart.

Red-Headed Stranger
(COLOR)

Feeble Willie Nelson vehicle.

An Alive Films release. Produced by Willie Nelson and William Wittliff. Written and directed by Wittliff. Camera (color), Neil Roach: Reviewed at Denver Intl. Film Festival, Oct. 18, 1986. (MPAA Rating: R.) Running time: **105 MINS.**

With: Willie Nelson, Morgan Fairchild, Katharine Ross, Royal Dano.

Denver — Willie Nelson made "Red-Headed Stranger" two years ago, but only now has its first public screening occurred. Chances for subsequent showings are doubtful because of excessively clichéd and unconvincing characters. More than Nelson's vast popularity would be required to lift this melodrama into acceptance.

Nelson plays a parson who travels from Philadelphia to Driscoll, Mont., to take over a church, taking with him his glittery bride Raysha, played by Morgan Fairchild in plastic fashion. The town turns out to be in thralldom to Larn Claver, played by Royal Dano, and his four roughneck bully sons, who have closed down the town well and forced citizens to get their water at the town bar.

Parson Shay decides to contest these water controls, but it is a long winter before he succeeds. Meantime, Raysha runs away with her Philadelphia lover, and in his fury, Shay finds them in the next town and shoots them.

On a rampage after this, he leaves the church, and shoots anyone who gets in his way, until he meets Laurie, played by Katharine Ross, who ranches with her son after she has sent her lazy husband packing. Shay works the ranch and finds the peace of mind to enable him to return to put down the Claver klan.

Nelson sings frequently but not enough to alter the dull tone of the action. There is an effort to frame the narrative in a ballad but it does not work. The film is an outgrowth of Nelson's 1975 album of the same name.

Nelson has taken on a character of great intensity, but the direction by William Wittliff and his acting fail to measure up to the challenge. His brooding manner doesn't help the film along.

Morgan Fairchild seems here the classic Hollywood heroine in the wilds, lavishly gowned and made up to perfection, and always unbelievable.

Of interest to Denver residents is the name of Barry Fey, listed both as coproducer and "Friend." Fey's Feyline Presents, applied last May for a Chapter 11 reorganization. —Alyo.

Demoni 2 — L'Incubo Ritorna
(Demons 2 — The Nightmare Is Back)
(ITALIAN-COLOR)

A Titanus release. Produced by Dario Argento for DAC Film Productions. Directed by Lamberto Bava. Screenplay, Argento, Bava, Franco Ferrini, Dardano Sacchetti; camera (color), Lorenzo Battaglia; editor, Pietro Bozza; art direction, David Bassan; makeup, Rosario Prestopino; special effects, Sergio Stivaletti; music, Simon Boswell. Reviewed at Quirinale Cinema, Rome, Oct. 11, 1986. Running time: **94 MINS.**

With: David Knight, Nancy Brilli, Coralina Cataldi Tassoni, Bobby Rhodes.

Rome — Grisly, gory, and effectively scary, Lamberto Bava's latest addition to the Italo horror genre is a new, improved version of last year's "Demons." In "Demons 2 — The Nightmare is Back," Halloween-style zombies run amok in an apartment building. Once they get going, the bleeding, throbbing, melting-faced uglies keep up a merciless pace, and only complaint of patrons should be that they're kept sitting on the edge of their seats too long. It's a good bet for the teen drive-in crowd.

Source of these resurrected dead is the innocent tv set, where an enterprising zombie decides to pop out of the late movie and possess a teen viewer. Her birthday party happens to be going on in the next room, and quicker than you can say Dario Argento (producer of the film), a roomful of gloppy, howling monsters is ready to contaminate the world.

Although shot in Bavaria, locale is quite beside the point. Most action takes place in the rooms, halls and garage of the apartment building. The acid blood of the grislies flows freely, seeps through floors and ceilings and contaminates everything it touches. It also short-circuits the wiring, sealing the unfortunate tenants in an impregnable, no-exit fortress.

In the nothing sacred Argento-Bava tradition, no one is safe from their rage. Not a gym-full of body builders, which turns into a mini-army captained by the black muscleman. Not a wide-eyed tyke left alone by mom and pop, who tries to defend himself with a toy ray gun. Not even a cute little dog, turned into a ferocious canine zombie to its mistress' dismay. In this kind of pic, the stars of the show are the ones who remain human the longest.

Scary makeup and Sergio Stivaletti's special effects (featuring an almost endearing zombie version of E.T.) contribute to the chills. —Yung.

Räven
(The Fox)
(SWEDISH-COLOR)

An SF (Svensk Filmindustri) release of a Moviemakers production for SF, the Swedish Film Institute, Clas Lindberg Film, Tonservice Läthner & Löthner, Movie Makers Sweden. Produced by Lasse Lundberg, Bert Sundberg. Written and directed by Clas Lindberg. Stars Licka Sjöman, Göran Dyhrssen. Camera (Eastmancolor), Old Frederik Haug; sound, Lars Liljeholm; editor, Lasse Lundberg; music, Bo Anders Persson; production management, Ray Jones. Reviewed at the Palladium, Malmö, Sweden, Oct. 23, 1986. Running time: **78 MINS.**

Monika	Licka Sjöman
Kaare	Göran Dyhrssen
Monica's father	Willie Andreasson
Police sergeant	Allan Svensson
The hunter	Gustav Kling

Malmo — "The Fox," a first-time effort by Dramatic Academy graduate Clas Lindberg, was unanimously savaged by Swedish critics and sank from view almost immediately after release via an outlet that had been reluctant to touch the item at all. Still, Lindberg has proven himself a cinematic talent.

What is irretrievably wrong with "The Fox" is its dialog. It is stilted, artificial, comical and downright phony, and it drags down with it a screenplay that is otherwise bubbling with slick ideas and which might easily have been salvaged by any professional film writer to work as the groundwork for the intended small-scale, Gothic chillerthriller comedy, both gaudily colorful and decidedly black.

Monika (sturdily handsome Licka Sjöman) runs away from her village cop father to join Kaare, her boyfriend, who is an arsonist just out on probation. The boy hides at his parents' farm in a remote forest area and tells Monika that he is alone since Mom & Dad have just been killed in an automobile accident. Lurking about on the premises is a tame fox. Actually, Kaare may be innocent of the arson he had been sentenced for, but he does play around with matches a lot and tries to set most of the farm's furniture on fire.

The trusting girl beds down with skinny Kaare whose eyes are never at rest. One moment he is busy burning selected pieces of furniture (we glimpse blood stains), the next he is in a fight with a party of wedding party guests in a nearby village. There are also creaking of doors and ghoulish discoveries made via extraordinary camera angles.

All of this silliness is handled with deft camera movement and within inventive frame compositions. The acting is neat, the editing swift and to the point. Given a sterner producer and a re-worked screenplay, Lindberg's fun & chills would have worked. As it is, the dialog and the script serve to put out all the story's fire like a wet blanket. — Kell.

I Nichta Me ti Silena
(The Night With Silena)
(GREEK-COLOR)

A Demetris Panayotatos and Greek Film Center coproduction. Produced and directed by Demetris Panayotatos. Screenplay, Panayotatos, Antonis Kafetzopoulos based on an idea from the novel "Silena" by Vassilis Vassilicos; camera (color), Tassos Alexakis; edi-

tor, Yannis Tsitsopoulos; music, Kyriacos Sfetsas; sets, Maria Kaltsas; costumes, Spyros Karayannis; sound, Marinos Athanassopoulos. Reviewed at the Thessaloniki Film Festival, Oct. 2, 1986. Running time: **80 MINS.**
Christos . . . . Antonis Kafetzopoulos
Silena . . . . Eva Vlahakou
Also with: Loukia Sterguiou, Magda Mavroyanni, Michalis Gounaris, Fotis Mestheneos, Alexis Pezas, Maria Peza, Constantinos Maguioros.

Thessaloniki — This is a featherweight festival entry. The story centers around Christos (Antonis Kafetzopoulos) who is obsessed by a desire to sleep with Silena (Eva Vlahakou), a whore working in the bar opposite his house. He is looking for her believing that she is the girl of his dreams.

Acting by Antonis Kafetzopoulos and Eva Vlahakou is adequate as well as the rest of the cast.

All technical credits are average.
— *Rena.*

Enas Melissokomos Petheni — O Alles Mythos
(A Beekeeper Dies — The Other Tale)
(GREEK-COLOR)

A Maria Hatzimichali Papaliou production. Written, produced and directed by Maria Hatzimichali Papliou. Camera (color), Yannis Daskalothanassis; editor, George Triantafyllou; sound, Christos Acelestos. Reviewed at the Thessaloniki Film Festival, Oct. 3, 1986. Running time: **80 MINS.**
With: Theo Angelopoulos, Marcello Mastroianni, Serge Reggiani, Nadia Mourouzi.

Thessaloniki — This is a well-made documentary film on the shooting of the picture "The Beekeeper" by Theo Angelopoulos. Maria Hatzimichali Papaliou followed the production unit of "The Beekeeper" from Florina of Northern Greece to Nafplion in Peloponnese, showing Angelopoulos directing his actors and teaching Marcello Mastroianni to speak Greek.

She also interviews Angelopoulos, Mastroianni, Serge Reggiani and Nadia Mourouzi concerning the film. The music of "Beekeeper" by Heleni Karaendrou serves as a background to this documentary film.

There is only one objection: how did this slight documentary get included in the official program of the festival, even if it is well-made.
— *Rena.*

Més Enllà de la Passió
(Beyond Passion)
(SPANISH-COLOR)

A Manderley S.C.C.L., Cyrk S.A., I.C.C. production. Executive producer, Antonio Chavarrias. Written and directed by Jesús Garay. Camera (Agfacolor), Carles Gusi; editor, Ernest Blasi; music, Leo Mariño. Reviewed at Cine Retiro, Sitges Film Festival, Oct. 9, 1986. Running time: **98 MINS.**
With: Patricia Adriani, Junajo Puigcorbé,

Angel Jové, Rosa Novell, Remei Barrio, Arnau Vilardebó.
(Catalan Soundtrack)

Sitges — This narcissistic exercise in self-indulgence consists of a string of non-events and scenes none of which seem to have a point or are ever explained to the viewers. Slow, artsy camerawork dwells on a trio of characters, but no story, not even an elemental one, emerges from this murky, confused film.

Involved are a pop singer who loses her voice just before a performance, and her quasi-mystical relationship to an expressionless journalist and an amateur filmmaker. The girl suffers from stigmata, seems to yearn for crucifixion, but none of the symbolisms are intelligible, even within the context of the film. What director-writer Jesús Garay had in mind is hard to divine. But the outcome on celluloid is amateursville. — *Besa.*

Rue du départ
(Street Of Departures)
(FRENCH-COLOR)

An AAA release of a Films Plain Chant/-Films Ariane/Soprofilms/TF 1 Films co-production. Produced by Philippe Diaz. Directed by Tony Gatlif. Screenplay, Gatlif, Marie-Hélène Rudel; camera (Eastmancolor), Bernard Zitzermann; editor, Claudine Bouché; music, Charles Benarroch; theme song composed and performed by Sapho; sound, Bernard Ortion and Jean-Paul Loublier; art direction, Denis Champenois; make-up, Maite Alonso; costumes, Rose-Marie Nelka; assistant director, Yvon Rouve; casting, Marie-Hélène Rudel; production manager, Nicole Flipo; associate producer, Films Merry Lines. Reviewed at the Marignan-Concorde theater, Paris, Oct. 20, 1986. Running time: **95 MINS.**
With: Ann-Gisel Glass (Clara Lombart), Christine Boisson (Mimi), François Cluzet (Paul Triana), Roger Coggio (Cedonazzi), Jean-Pierre Sentier (Boris), Gérard Depardieu (Dr. Lombart), Hugues Quester, Jean-Pierre Bacri, Maurice Barrier, Gérard Darmon, Henri Deus, Daniel Laloux, Jean-Claude Lecas, Roger Mirmont, Chantal Neuwirth, Bruno Pradal, Marie-Hélène Rudel.

Paris — "Rue du départ" is a sharp disappointment from Tony Gatlif, whose 1983 feature, "The Princes," was a powerful, naturalistic vision of gypsy life, which heralded a singular new directing talent. Gatlif, an Algerian-born gypsy, ostensibly drew on autobiographical elements in making "Princes," but this new film, a modish tale of misery on the fringes of society, recruits its antiheroes from the Central Casting of movieland and literary cliché.

Though Gatlif's script (cowritten and Marie-Hélène Rudel) is an original one, it falls into the same family of sordidly baroque street romances characterized especially by two recent Gallic adaptations of David Goodis novels, Gilles Béhat's "Street Of The Lost" ("Rue Barbare") and Jean-Jacques Beineix' "The Moon In The Gutter." On

Gatlif's streets there are plenty of lost folk mooning about, surrounded by sex, violence, blood and urine. Pic was shot around the docks of Le Havre and on the highway-choked outskirts of Paris, which have become a popular decor for melodramas of this sort.

Plot brings Ann-Gisel Glass, a young runaway from a troubled bourgeois family, into the lower depths of the city where she befriends Christine Boisson, a local denizen trying to rise above her condition despite the clutches of a local pimp. She also becomes pals with François Cluzet, an escaped convict who plans to avenge the death of his father before shipping out for the poetic elsewhere, a little like Jean Gabin in the 1938 classic, "Quai des brumes," also set in Le Havre (which means, ironically, "the haven").

Cluzet has his revenge but gets involved with Glass, who brings her estranged doctor father (Gérard Depardieu in a small, but well-filled, role) to treat his wounds. Cluzet returns the favor by saving Glass from the pimp (Jean-Pierre Sentier) who tries to press her into service. Boisson is shot down by Sentier for betrayal, while Cluzet and Glass head out together for other climes.

Despite the evident talent of the cast, the characters remain artificial marionettes in an over-familiar shadowplay of the pseudopoetic. Gatlif's direction has its moments of fire, but is bloated by the sentimentality and penchant for caricature that married certain parts of "The Princes."

Lensing by Bernard Zitzermann, however, is outstanding. — *Len.*

Via je a Ninguna Parte
(Voyage To Nowhere)
(SPANISH-COLOR)

A Ganesh Prods. Cinematográficas film. Produced by Maribel Martin and Julián Mateos. Written and directed by Fernando Fernán Gómez. Camera (color), José Luis Alcaine; editor, Pablo G. del Amo; music, Pedro Iturralde; production manager, Andrés Santana; assistant producer, Franciso Villar; sets and costumes, Julio Esteban. Reviewed at Cine Gran Via, Madrid, Oct. 16, 1986. Running time: **135 MINS.**

Carlos Galván . . . . José Sacristán
Juanita Plaza . . . . Laura del Sol
Sergio Maldonado . . . . Juan Diego
Julia Iniesta . . . . Maria Luisa Ponte
Also with: Gabino Diego, Nuria Gallardo, Fernando Fernán Gómez, Queta Claver, Agustín González, Miguel Rellán, Emma Cohen, Carlos Lemos, Simón Andreu.

Madrid — The subject of itinerant thesps scraping together a living on the road is certainly not a new one, but the multi-faceted Fernando Fernán Gómez here manages to give it a few new twists in what to date is the most distinguished and

poignant Spanish film of the year.

Fernán Gómez, highly visible on the Spanish scene for decades, seems to have an inexhaustible fund of talent, not only as an actor but as a director and writer as well. In this pic, he brilliantly portrays the minor adventures of a troupe of thesps in the 1950s tramping from one pueblo to another putting on farces and grandiloquent mummery.

Writer-helmer chooses to tell the story in a long flashback, as former actor Carlos Galván, being treated in an old age home in 1973 by a psychiatrist, narrates the highlights of his life. What would have been a murky rural drama is given delightful touches of wry humor by Fernán Gómez, though the pathos of the players' situations is never lost sight of. Pic also has some nice twists at the end which make it even more believable and heighten its poignancy.

Story concentrates on the pitiful struggles of a middle-aged actor, Carlos Galván, brilliantly played by José Sacristán, his father (Fernán Gómez) and other members of the family of thesps. Sacristán has a pretty lover who's also in the troupe (Laura del Sol), as well as an illegitimate son, aged 17, who unexpectedly shows up to join the players. He is ugly and useless, but is told to tag along, a nice piece of comic relief.

The story takes us through some of the hardships the players endure in the villages, still hunger-ridden in those years of misery; but tale is lightened by the humor and the romantic entanglements of Carlos. Finally, the troupe breaks up and some of its members wend their way to Madrid to work as film extras. Carlos tells the psychiatrist of his seven years as a successful film star, but fame is evanescent, and he has wound up in an old age home for the impecunious. Even the brief period of fame and glory turns out to be a self-deceiving fabrication.

Though pic could do with a little editing to shorten its running time (especially out of character is a scene where three of the actors cruelly harass a couple making love in an entranceway), as it stands it is nonetheless a memorable, touching and sensitive tribute to travelling players which should appeal to select audiences anywhere, even if some of the linguistic subtleties and references to Spanish theater will be lost to non-Spaniards.

Superb performances, especially by Sacristán, Fernán Gómez and Juan Diego, are enhanced by skillful direction, crisp lensing by José Luis Alcaine and an offbeat but highly effective soundtrack by jazz musician Pedro Iturralde. — *Besa.*

Nobody's Fool
(COLOR)

Rustic romance falls flat.

An Island Pictures release of an Island production in association with Katz/Denny Prods. Produced by James C. Katz, Jon S. Denny. Executive producer, Cary Brokaw. Directed by Evelyn Purcell. Stars Rosanna Arquette, Eric Roberts. Screenplay, Beth Henley; camera (CFI color), Mikhail Suslov; editor, Dennis Virkler; music, James Newton Howard; production design, Jackson DeGovia; art direction, John R. Jensen; set decoration, Laurie Scott; costume design, Ellen Mirojnick; sound, James Tannenbaum; assistant director, Marty Ewing; second unit camera, James Carter; casting, Sally Dennison, Julie Selzer. Reviewed at the Century Plaza, L.A., Oct. 24, 1986. (MPAA Rating: PG-13.) Running time: **107 MINS.**

Cassie	Rosanna Arquette
Riley	Eric Roberts
Pat	Mare Winningham
Billy	Jim Youngs
Pearl	Louise Fletcher
Shirley	Gwen Welles
Kirk	Stephen Tobolowsky
Nick	Charlie Barnett
Ralphy	J.J. Hardy
Mr. Fry	Lewis Arquette

Hollywood — More appealing in premise and promise than accomplished in execution, "Nobody's Fool" features kookiness without real comedy, romance without magic. First original screenplay by playwright Beth Henley and directorial debut of Evelyn Purcell veers dramatically between good and bad, with modest pleasures barely holding their own against serious lapses in storytelling and tone. This is the first Island release to be going out in a relatively wide break, which might be a good thing since critical reaction may be less enthusiastic than with most of the distrib's carefully nurtured pictures.

Basic thrust of the story is engaging, with Rosanna Arquette gamely playing a smalltown Western girl whose life has come to a premature end before ever really beginning. Working as a cocktail waitress in a saloon, she attends dutifully to her burned-out mother and bratty younger brother as she tries to forget the public shame and ridicule she endured when she impulsively stabbed her old beau in a restaurant.

Her boyfriend survived the incident, but their relationship and baby, whom she gave away, did not, and she is as insecure as can be when Eric Roberts, the lighting technician with a visiting theatrical troupe, begins quietly noticing her.

Too ashamed of her past to have any self-worth, Arquette keeps Roberts at bay but joins an acting workshop and continues playing footsie with her former lover, who is now married but not disinclined toward a little outside activity with his voluptuous ex.

Convincing Arquette he's just as "bad" as she is, Roberts finally breaks the ice romantically, and his looming departure stands as a threshhold for her as to whether she will leave the past behind or remain burdened with it.

Familiarity and predictability of the plot's progress handicap matters considerably, particularly when Purcell attempts to milk "suspense" out of the question of Arquette's leaving or not. Numerous scenes designed to emphasize the character's alternating indecisiveness and impetuousness are more exasperating than charmingly illuminating, and numerous effects undoubtedly don't come off as intended.

Nevertheless, certain sequences, notably a car ride in which the two leads first connect with one another, and a visit by Arquette to the depressing suburban home of a mentally sick friend, stand out for the precision of their writing and performance, and lead one to realize the full potential of the material has not been fulfilled.

Arquette's performance, like the film, features hits and misses, yet there is something frequently moving about the character's scattershot approach to emotional salvation that is highly unusual and memorable. Roberts, more subdued than usual, effectively registers the impulses of a young man who tries to subdue the rough edges of his personality and thinks he can save Arquette from her prospective dismal fate.

Well-chosen supporting players make sharp impressions with relatively brief opportunities, and the Prescott, Ariz., area has provided backdrops both beautiful and depresingly bland. Lensing is unaccountably on the plain side. —*Cart.*

Jönssonligan dyker upp igen
(The Return of the Jönsson League)
(SWEDISH—COLOR)

An SF (Svensk Filmindustri) release of SF (Sweden), Nordisk Film (Denmark) production. Produced by Waldemar Bergendahl, Ingemar Ejve. Directed by Mikael Ekman. Stars Gösta Ekman, Ulf Brunneberg, Björn Gustafson. Screenplay, Rolf Börjlind with Gösta Ekman, Mikael Ekman; camera (Eastmancolor), Gunnar Källström; production design, Bengt Peters; costumes, Inger Pehrsson, Mona Theresia Forsén; editor, Jan Persson; music, Ragnar Grippe, production management, Jan Marnell. Reviewed at the Palladium, Malmö (Sweden), Oct. 23, 1986. Running time: **90 MINS.**

Sickan Jönsson	Gösta Eckman
Ragnar Ignoble	Ulf Brunnberg
Dynamite Harry	Björn Gustafson
Doris	Birgitta Andersson
Tycoon	Per Grunden
Police chief	Kent Andersson
Police lieutenant	Dan Ekborg
Iron-Arm	Johannes Brost
The Ham	Lars Dejert

Also with: Jarl Borssen, John Harryson, Jan Dolata, Jacob Dahlin, Sten Johan Hedman, Frederich Offrein.

Malmö — After Denmark's string of undiluted boxoffice toppers with 13 instalments in Henning Bahs & Erik Balling's "Olsen Gang" comedy series (a Nordisk Film property), Sweden did three cover version features to similar fine business.

Now, with "The Return Of The Jönsson League," SF (Svensk Filmindustri) (with Nordisk as a silent partner) has turned out a fourth title that is not a cover version. It has an original screenplay and the producers want it judged on its purely Swedish merits. Alas, the merits are modest.

Without the almost uncanny percision of Henning Bahs' personal handling of humorous special effects and without Bahs & Balling to maneuver the gang's or league's loveable trio of petty crooks through a plot's and character gallery's mix of Runyonesque and Mack Sennett-inspired fun with the added salt of truly humanist touches, director Mikael Ekman and his coscripters deliver flat and uninspired farce mechanics and a muddled storyline above which the otherwise fine comedy actors with one exception fail to rise.

The exception is slim, distraught-looking Gösta Ekman as Jönsson, who tries to steer his two lunkhead fellow thieves through a plot to, among other things, outwit both a business tycoon who has a multi-million-worth piece of electronic merchandise to sell to the USSR.

The fun of this particular game, as it was invented and perfected by the Danes, was the pitting of wits between the petty crooks and the mighty powers of clumsy police and big business hoods along with many a satirical blow at various local and international political and social phenomena. Apart from the presence of a Soviet sub in Swedish territorial waters, nothing here reflects the shattered image of real life so necessary for true farce to work. — *Kell.*

Mesmerized
(BRITISH-NEW ZEALAND/-AUSTRALIAN-COLOR)

A Thorn EMI (Vidcassette) release of an RKO-Challenge presentation of an Orinward Ltd-Camperdown production. Produced by Antony I. Ginnane. Executive producers, Mark Seiler, Christopher Kirkham. Directed by Michael Laughlin. Screenplay, Laughlin, from an original work by Jerzy Skolimowski; camera (Panavision, Eastmancolor), Louis Horvath; editor, Petra von Oelffen; music, Georges Delerue; visual consultant, Susanna Moore; art director, John Wingrove; sound, Tim Lloyd; costumes, Patricia Norris; production manager, Howard Grigsby; assistant director, Terry Needham; coproducer, Jodie Foster; associate producers, Howard Grigsby, Richard Moore. Reviewed on Thorn EMI vidcassette, Sydney, Oct. 13, 1986. Running time: **97 MINS.**

Victoria	Jodie Foster
Oliver Thompson	John Lithgow
Rev. Wilson	Michael Murphy
Old Thompson	Harry Andrews
George Thompson	Dan Shor

Also with: Philip Holder (Dr. Finch), Reg Evans (Mr. Simmons), Beryl Te Wiata (Mrs. Simmons), Jonathan Hardy (Burley), Don Selwyn (Joseph), Derek Hardwick (Longwood.

Sydney — Michael Laughlin's third feature as director, after "Dead Kids" (a.k.a. "Strange Behavior") in 1981 and "Strange Invaders" in 1983, was made in New Zealand for Australian-based producer Antony I. Ginnane and bears a 1984 date. Having failed to find theatrical playoff, it's gone straight to the Aussie vidcassette market, and is reviewed here for the record.

As with Laughlin's earlier pics, this one is neither a traditional horror film nor a straight romantic drama. It falls between two stools, making it a doubtful proposition for the mass audience, though buffs could be intrigued with this strange, gothic, turn-of-the-century melodrama. Jodie Foster, who coproduced, toplines as a naive young orphan girl who is unexpectedly courted by a middle-aged businessman (John Lithgow) who marries her, then leaves her at school to complete her studies before sending for her. "How did he even know I existed?" asks Foster at one point, but the question is never answered and the audience, like the heroine, remains in the dark.

Lithgow turns out to be a pennypinching voyeur, who spies on his virgin bride, via a "Psycho"-like hole in the wall, as she prepares for bed. The marriage remains unconsummated, and Lithgow seems more worried about the rats that infest his food warehouse than about his marital problems. For a while, Foster endures the stifling atmosphere of Lithgow's house, and the occasional visits of his strange old father (Harry Andrews), but eventually she persuades her young brother-in-law, George (Dan Shor) to help her run off and board a ship for America. Before the ship sails, however, husband and father-in-law appear on the scene and in the ensuing fray Foster wrongly believes she's killed Shor.

Back in the marital house, she finally allows Lithgow to sleep with her and quickly becomes pregnant, though the baby is born dead. She decides the only way out is to murder her husband, and starts slowly poisoning him, while cultivating an American preacher (Michael Murphy), new to the neighborhood.

Pic climaxes with Lithgow's death and the subsequent trial in which Foster is charged with his murder.

Foster, looking relaxed and pretty, doesn't convince as a cold-blooded murderess. Lithgow, who makes a brave stab at a Kiwi accent, is more successful as the doomed businessman, but too many questions about his motivations remain floating in the air. Murphy has little to do as the sympathetic reverend.

Main problem here is Laughlin's own screenplay, based on an original treatment by Jerzy Skolimowski; there are just too many loose ends and red herrings. It's safe to say that Skolimowski would have invested the project with far more bizarre detail and black humor had he directed himself.

Technically, pic is first-rate, with a fine Georges Delerue score and notable camerawork from Louis Horvath. A scene in which Lithgow's teeth are pulled out is gruesome, but overall the film, being billed as a horror item, is notably lacking in horror, suspense or tension. It remains frustratingly bland and, ultimately, rather pointless. —*Strat.*

Le Complexe du kangourou
(The Kangaroo Complex)
(FRENCH-COLOR)

An AMLF release of a Fildebroc-CAPAC coproduction, with the participation of Investimage. Produced by Michelle de Broca, Paul Claudon. Directed by Pierre Jolivet. Stars Roland Giraud, Clémentine Célarié, Zabou. Screenplay, Jolivet, Olivier Schatzky, with collaboration of Henry Béhar; camera (Fujicolor), Christian Lamarque; editor, Jean-François Naudon; music, Serge Perathoner; art direction, Eric Simon; production manager, Hubert Mérial; assistant director, Jean-Claude Marchant. Reviewed at the Gaumont Ambassade theater, Paris, Oct. 14, 1986. Running time: **84 MINS.**

Loic . . . . Roland Giraud
Claire . . . .'. . . . . Clémentine Célarié
Odile . . . . Zabou
Bob . . . . Stéphane Freiss
Brother-in-law . . . . François Berleand
Polish neighbor . . . . Maaike Jansen
Arthur . . . . Maka Kotto
Eric . . . . Stéphane Duchemin
Jeanne . . . . Caroline Chaniolleau
Bank manager . . . . Robert Rimbaud
Fabrice . . . . ▴ . . . . Marc Jolivet

Paris — The runaway success of "Three Men And A Cradle" no doubt catalyzed this new domestic comedy about latent paternalism — the parentage is underlined by the casting of one of the "Three Men," Roland Giraud, whose wry performance is one of the chief attractions in this sympathetic feature by Pierre Jolivet.

Giraud is an aspiring painter who is nagged by a yearning for fatherhood after a belated and badly treated case of the mumps — at age 26 — renders him sterile. A doctor friend analyzes his case as a "kangaroo complex," since male kangaroos don't have pouches to carry their young.

The complex takes a serious turn when Giraud runs into an old girl friend (Clémentine Célarié), accompanied by her six-year-old son. Not-

ing latter's resemblance to him, and putting two and two together, he gradually acquires the conviction he is the boy's father.

Attempts to see the boy are complicated by the fact that Célarié is still in love with Giraud and is using the child to lure him back into her life. Giraud, who has a girl friend (Zabou), wants the boy but not his mother.

Jolivet and coscripter Olivier Schatzky orchestrate the increasingly problematic sentimental snafus with adequate distance and a fine sense of irony, strengthened by the understated performances by Giraud and Célarié, and an appealing supporting cast.

Direction is a noticeable improvement on Jolivet's debut feature last year, "Strictement personnel," in which Pierre Arditi played a cop investigating his own family. The labored dramatic tone of that effort is here replaced by brisk, light touch and a sense of rhythm that don't preclude an emotional pinch beneath the comic complications.

Tech credits are smart. —*Len.*

Alkistis
(GREEK-COLOR)

A Toni Lycouressis and Greek Film Center coproduction. Produced and directed by Toni Lycouressis. Stars Antonis Theodoracopoulos, Olia Lazaridou. Screenplay, Lycouressis, Demetris Nollas; camera (color), Andreas Bellis; editor, George Triantafyllou; costumes, Julia Stavridou; sound, Nicos Achladis. Reviewed at the Thessaloniki Film Fest, Oct. 3, 1986. Running time: **94 MINS.**
Aithor . . . . Antonis Theodoracopoulos
Anna . . . . Olia Lazaridou
Also with: Maria Zafiraki.

Thessaloniki — "Alkistis" is the third picture by Toni Lycouressis and less ambitious than the previous ones. It is an underplayed love story brought off effectively which should do very well at home. Up against stronger competition outside the country the film's chances may be moderate.

The plot introduces a 41-year-old writer, just returnd from an unsuccessful lecture. Disappointed he goes to his home island to see his mother and hears that Alkistis, his first love, is on the island. Trying desperately to meet her he visits remote little islands and places of his youth. He did not meet her but he finds little by little his inner peace with the help of Anna, a young woman and his companion.

Lycouressis turns out a wellmeaning but uninspired tale about the problem of a critical turn in a man's life. He presents it with a tenderness and understanding. His direction is neat, unpretentiously poetic, but lacks the deeper insight to give his story a dramatic bite.

Acing is outstanding. An asset of the picture is the photography by

Andreas Bellis who captures the sunlit landscapes of the Ionian islands sharply.

All other technical credits are above standard. —*Rena.*

Malkat Hakita
(Prom Queen)
(ISRAELI-COLOR)

A Cannon Films presentation of a Menahem Golan & Yoram Globus production. Produced, written and directed by Itzhak (Zeppel) Yeshurun. Camera (color), Avi Karpik; editor, Tova Asher; music, Alex Kagan; sound, Itamar Ben Yaakov; art direction, Zmira Hershkovitz; costumes, Anath Messner; associate producer, Itzik Kol. Reviewed at the Lev 3 theatre, Tel Aviv, Oct. 15, 1986. Running time: **89 MINS.**
With: Alon Aboutboul, Itzhak Ben-Ner, Avital Beer, Ranan Hefetz, Doron Avrahami, Shmuel Shilo, Ronnie Arditi, Rami Baruch, Anath Sanderovitch.

Tel Aviv — This extremely painful and disenchanted allegory of Israel's acute social crisis, as reflected in a boarding school, is writerdirector Itzhak Yeshurun's latest and loudest warning to his fellow countrymen to come to their senses. He has been profoundly concerned with the quality of human relations around him for a long time now, but never has he expressed himself in such a violent and uncompromising fashion. As a matter of fact, the panic and despair which seem to have taken control over him, wreak havoc on the film itself, which comes out disjointed, a series of brief and anguished episodes which establish a climate more than telling a story.

The action evolves around a moody and mercurial student, jilted by his girlfriend, who takes it out on everybody around him, friend and foe alike, supplying the spark that once ignited, blows up the entire school. His involvement in a project to build a home-made airplane with some of his fellow students, the attraction of his former girlfriend for one of the teachers, and the animosity against some of the Arabs enrolled in school (who automatically become scapegoats for anything that goes wrong), are brought very quickly to a boil, with the social nucleus completely disintegrating once the hoodlum brother of the "Prom Queen" appears and establish clearly that violence and brutality are the only rules by which all involved abide.

Yeshurun seems to not really care about telling the story, and he goes about it in such a frustrating fashion that audiences at home have vociferously reacted to it, while some of the critics give him credit for establishing an esthetic system which fits the requirements of his theme. The actors, a mixed bag of pros and amateurs, never get a chance to develop real characters, most looking simply bewildered by

the proceedings. The quality of technical standards varies widely, from satisfactory to clear mismatches between shots, as if they had not been intended to follow each other, originally, while sound has a difficult time catching the lines of untrained actors.

As a social statement, this is surely an important contribution, the problem will be only with that párt of the audience which does not patronize cinemas for such statements. —*Edna.*

Matter Of Heart
(DOCU-COLOR/B&W)

A Kino Intl. release of a production by the C.G. Jung Institute. Executive producer, George Wagner. Produced by Michael Whitney. Directed by Mark Whitney. Conceived and written by Suzanne Wagner; camera (color) & editor, Mark Whitney; special consultant, Sam Francis; original music, John Adams. Reviewed at Quad theater, N.Y., Oct. 26, 1986. Running time: **104 MINS.**

"Matter Of Heart" is not an objective, unbiased career-portrait of the famed Swiss psychologist-philosopher, Carl Gustav Jung, who died at age 26 in 1961, the year his autobiographical "Memories, Dreams, Reflections" was published. Instead, this documentary comes to praise Jung, not to examine him or to debate his legacy by giving equal time to his critics.

Instead, "Matter Of Heart" is warm and personal, is frankly proJung, as befits a film emanating from the Jung Institute. The film calls as expert witnesses Jung's family, friends, colleagues, exstudents, even neighboring farmers. They remember Jung fondly, his wisdom and humane tolerance and serenity. They recall his impact on their careers and personal lives. Of the dozen Jungian analysts in the film, all testify to the strength of Jung's personality, his deep faith that was religious but free of cant and supernatural dogma.

One wishes that these fascinating testimonials were uniformly audible, or rather intelligible. All are lipsynched in English, but most speak heavily accented English as their second language. In addition, several are very elderly, their voices unclear. One Swiss lady speaking English is given English subtitles, an option that the producers perhaps should have considered for some other speakers. Interviews, cut from 40 hours, are rich with complex ideas about Jung.

But the accents are a quibble, as the film is to be commended for daring to give us Jung, a giant intellect and a great spirit of our age. Jung on Jung — in old b&w interviews, speaking clearly in English, an informal and witty and charming old party, always with his pipe, puttering around his chateau on a Swiss mountain lake — these scenes are the best parts of the film. We get Jung directly and immediately, not second-hand. Intercut are old b&w stills showing his family, boyhood, medical schooling, and his years as a disciple of Freud, with whom Jung later broke.

"Matter Of Heart" concludes with and emphasizes Jung's alarm at the world arms race and prospects of nuclear extermination. Jung saw this threat, not simply as global politics gone mad, but as expressions of man's need for psychic health. Man's inner wars must be healed by reconciliation and balance. "Not nature but the genius of mankind," observes Jung, "has knotted the hangman's noose, with which it can execute itself at any moment."—*Hitch.*

Islands
(U.S.-DOCU-COLOR-16m)

A Carl Flach Jeanne-Claude presentation of a Maysles Films, C. Zwerin production. Directed by Albert Maysles, Charlotte Zwerin, David Maysles. Camera (color), Albert Maysles; sound, David Maysles; editor, Kate Hirson; music, Scott Cossu; Producers (Miami Installation), Susan Froenke, Joe Hinman. Reviewed at Nyon Intl. Film Festival, Oct. 11, 1986. Running time: **60 MINS.**

Nyon — "Islands" is the most recent episode in the continuing film series on Bulgarian expatriate artist Christo (Javacheff). A slight but intensely strong-willed architect-engineer-sculptor who has (so far) wrapped or enshrouded the Rocky Mountains, California, Miami, the Pont Neuf in Paris ... Set soon for Christo gift-wrapping is the Reichstag in Berlin. What's next?

"Islands" challenges and disturbs our notions of art and perhaps also our notions of film reviewing. These Christo works are community construction efforts, collective creativity involving hundreds of workers. These are *objets d'art* outdoors in God's grand natural museum, where beauty originated, but re-fashioned by man who is now outside nature.

Christo has hung a quarter-mile orange "Valley Curtain" between two mountain peaks in Colorado, the first film on Christo, 1974, by the Maysles Brothers and Ellen Hovde. Christo followed with a 24-mile white nylon wrap of the California coastline, in "Running Fence," 1978, by the Maysles and Charlotte Zwerin. "Pont Neuf" is nearing completion, and the Reichstag is recently approved for wrapping and filming.

"Islands" documents Christo's conversion of 11 uninhabited scrub-pine Biscayne Bay islands in Miami, with a total coastline of seven miles, into huge pink water-lilies. Why not?

Christo surrounded the islands with enormous floating pink platforms. This daily work is shown in detail.

"Islands" is funny and ironical in its depiction of Christo's confrontations with suspicious city fathers in Miami's Metro Commission, jealously guarding the city's coffers and image. Christo charms with Willy Brandt and his German colleagues, in regard to final approval of the Reichstag wrap-up. Jacques Chirac, then mayor of Paris, now prime minister, yields cautiously in regard to the Pont Neuf. Thus the film is a paradigm of artist vs. government/patron, talking different languages, motivated by different values, somehow co-existing and creating/permitting art to happen sometimes.
—*Hitch.*

Nuit d'ivresse
(Drunken Night)
(FRENCH-COLOR)

A Fechner/Gaumont release of an I.C.E. Films/Films Flam/La Cinq Prod. coproduction, with the participation of Cofimage. Produced by Trinacra Films. Directed by Bernard Nauer. Stars Josiane Balasko, Thierry Lhermitte. Screenplay, Lhermitte, Balasko, from latter's play; camera (Eastmancolor), Carlo Varini; editor, Olivier Morel; music, Jacques Delaporte; theme song, les Rita Mitsouko; art direction, Ivan Maussion; sound, Alain Lachassagne; assistant director, Etienne Dhaene; production manager, Louis Becker. Reviewed at the Gaumont Ambassade theater, Paris, Oct. 20, 1986. Running time: **85 MINS.**
With: Thierry Lhermitte (Jacques Belin), Josiane Balasko (Fréde), France Roche, Jean-Michel Dupuis, Marc Dudicourt, Jean-Claude Dauphin.

Paris — Josiane Balasko and Thierry Lhermitte, two stars of the Parisian café-theatre scene who also have found screen popularity, coproduced and star in this adaptation of Balasko's own 1985 play, in which she was billed with Michel Blanc. Lhermitte aided her in elaborating the piece for the cinema, with more complicated farcical interludes, though its stage origins remain obvious in this essentially two-character romantic comedy, reminiscent of the classic Hollywood screwball formula.

The plump Balasko plays a young woman just released from prison who has a chance run-in in a train station bistro with Lhermitte, a handsome tv personality who's had one drink too many after receiving an award as most courteous Frenchman of the year.

Lhermitte's manners with Balasko leave something to be desired, however, though a series of incidents throw them together for a heavily alcoholic evening in which the dapper home-screen star wrecks his public image and ends up proposing to Balasko.

The next morning Lhermitte awakens with a whopping hangover

and no memory of the previous evening's events, but Balasko has forgotten nothing and already is making plans for the future. They quarrel violently but fall into each other's arms in a predictable sentimental wrapup.

Newcomer Bernard Nauer packages the piece adequately with polished aid from lenser Carlo Varini and art director Ivan Maussion. This is basically a vehicle for its sharply contrasted duo, who play off one another with engaging comic facility, though the material itself is mostly mechanical stuff.—*Len.*

Desperate Moves
(COLOR)

Romance on roller skates.

A Chesham production. Executive producer, Peter Sheperd. Produced by Ovidio G. Assonitis; line producer, Jacques Goyard. Directed by "Oliver Hellman" (Ovidio G. Assonitis). Screenplay, Allan Berger, Kathy Gori, from story by Robert J. Gandus; camera (Deluxe color; Technicolor prints), Roberto D'Ettore Piazzoli; editor, Robert Curi; music, Steve Power; sound (Dolby), Tony Testa; assistant director-choreography, Fred Curt; production manager, Roger Salvadori; set decoration, Frank Vetrano. Reviewed on TWE vidcassette, N.Y., Oct. 14, 1986. (No MPAA Rating.) Running time: **98 MINS.**

Andy Steigler	Steve Tracy
Olivia	Dana Handler
Red	Eddie Deezen
Dottie Butz	Isabel Sanford
Cosmo	Paul Benedict
Dr. Boxer	Christopher Lee
Ernie Steigler	Dan Leggant
Earl	Michael Phenicle
Beefy	Donald McLean
Mrs. Evinson	Linda Hoy
Hooker	Sallee Young

"Desperate Moves" is a truly oddball motion picture, unreleased domestically since its 1980 filming until recently surfacing in homevideo stores. Pic is an all-American picture made by Italian filmmakers in San Francisco, headed by Ovidio G. Assonitis, who previously made the horror hit "Beyond The Door" there.

Pic's alternate titles were "Steigler And Steigler," "Save The Last Dance For Me" and "Rollerboy," last of which suggests its goofy storyline of a young man (Steve Tracy) addicted to roller skating who leaves his small hometown to venture to the big city (Frisco) with dreams of glory. He meets a beautiful but nasty girl (Dana Handler) who alternately teases him and romances him.

Landing a flunky job at the local rollerama, Tracy is befriended by fellow employee Eddie Deezen, local gay deejay Paul Benedict and worldwise landlady Isabel Sanford. Sanford even gives his $50 from her "Billy Dee Williams fund" to buy a whore's services, but is dismayed to find the young hero has blown the cash on an unproductive date at a posh restaurant with Handler.

Picture's best subplot has Tracy sent by Benedict to a psychiatrist who's an expert in ways of dominating people: enter Christopher Lee, deliciously cool as the master of viciousness.

Its age betrayed by frequent outbursts of dated disco music, "Desperate" is an enjoyable rites of passage opus. A conventionally happy ending fails to resolve the mystery of the leading lady's behavior. Tech credits are fine, with sound recording up to U.S. standards (none of that artificial post-synching favored by Italian helmers). —*Lor.*

Paradies
(Paradise)
(WEST GERMAN-COLOR)

A Delta (Berlin) release of a Delta Film, Berlin, production. Produced by Chris Sievernich, Richard Claus. Written and directed by Doris Dörrie. Stars Heiner Lauterbach, Katharina Thalbach, Sunnyi Melles. Camera (color), Helge Weindler; editor, Raimund Barthelmes; music, Claus Bantzer; Combo Cocktail; sound, Michael Etz; art direction, Jörg Neumann; light and set direction, Jürgen Bauer, Gofi Höhn, Däni Händl; assistant director and dramaturg; Michael Juncker; production managers, Danny Krausz, Gerd Huber; associate producer, Martin Wiebel. Reviewed at Central-Theater, Hof, West Germany, Oct. 24, 1986. Running time: **100 MINS.**

Victor Ptyza	Heiner Lauterbach
Lotte Kovacz	Katharina Thalbach
Angelica Ptyza	Sunnyi Melles

Also with: Hanne Wieder (Angelica's mother), Ernst-Erich Buder (Lotte's customer), Ulrike Kriener (prostitute), Brigitte Janner (private detective).

Hof — Just as the phenomenal success of Doris Dörrie's "Männer" (Men) does not prove she is the greatest German helmer to come along since Fritz Lang, so the flaws of "Paradise" do not imply that "Men" was just a happy accident of fate. Dörrie is still a fine dialog writer who knows how to put together a well-made picture and get the best out of her actors even though she has not succeeded in getting her intentions across to the audience in "Paradise."

"I just want to warn you: this film is poisoned," she said cryptically as a word of introduction to the world premiere at the Hof Film Days. Presumably she means the sweet comedy turns bitter, provokes tears. Unfortunately, the wonderful comic approach of the first half not only turns serious, it begins to drag and to transmute into melodrama.

If "Men" is the battle of two men for one of their wives, "Paradise" turns into the struggle of two women for the husband of one of them. Here the more obvious similarity ends.

Angelica (Sunnyi Melles) is convinced her husband Victor (Heiner Lauterbach) must be having an affair, because he no longer pays attention to her, especially in bed.

When this proves false, she seeks refuge in attack by introducing him to childhood friend Lotte (Katharina Thalbach), an undersized, oversexed country lass, according to the theory that a bite of spicy salami will whet his appetite for delicate chocolates. Well, chocolates she ain't, and hubby Victor delves into the salami as if he'd been starving for it all his life. Lotte, who was happy being alone, takes off to Hamburg to become a whore, hotly pursued by an obsessed Victor.

Here pic threatens to fall apart, with unnecessary repetitions, unattained depth and a lack of logic, culminating in a kind of tragic grotesque.

Katharina Thalbach, who before coming to the West in 1976 was voted best actress of East Germany at the age of 15 by theater critics, steals the show as the hot-blooded Lotte struggling against love up to the very end. Sunnyi Melles' prim, would-be seductress is a strong second, with frightfully red-haired Lauterbach bringing up the rear.

As could be expected of a production (the budget is purported to be $3,500,000) by Wim Wenders' producers Chris Sievernich and Richard Claus, all credits are first-rate for a German film. Riding on the crest of the "Männer"-wave and, despite flaws, on its own merits, "Paradise" can be expected to have good b.o. results at home and abroad as well as an active festival career.

—*Loc.*

Streets Of Gold
(COLOR)

Thin imitation of the 'Rocky' formula.

A 20th Century Fox release presented by James G. Robinson, of an Ufland/Roth production. Produced by Joe Roth, Harry Ufland. Coproduced by Patrick McCormick, Dezso Magyar. Directed by Roth. Stars Klaus Maria Brandauer. Screenplay, Heywood Gould, Richard Price, Tom Cole based on a story by Magyar; camera (Deluxe color), Arthur Albert; editor, Richard Chew; music, Jack Nitzsche; production design, Marcos Flaksman; art direction, Bill Pollock; set decoration, Victor Kempster; costume designer, Jeffrey Kurland; sound, Frank Stettner (N.Y.), Peter Hliddal (L.A.); assistant director, James Chory; fight choreographer, Jimmy Nickerson; casting, Margery Simkin, Todd Thaler. Reviewed at CBS Studios, Studio City, Calif., Oct. 29, 1986. (MPAA Rating: R.) Running time: **95 MINS.**
Alek Neuman . . . . . Klaus Maria Brandauer
Timmy Boyle . . . . Adrian Pasdar
Roland Jenkins . . . . Wesley Snipes
Elena Gitman . . . . Angela Molina
Klebanov . . . . Elya Baskin
Brenda . . . . Rainbow Harvest

Hollywood — How many versions of "Rocky" do film audiences want to see? How many boxing pictures can be sold to the public? Not too many if the tale doesn't have a protagonist with the charm of a Rocky Balboa or unique variation of his melodramatic rise from street fighter to champion.

"Streets Of Gold" tries and fails on both accounts. It's a likable, but hardly compelling story of not one, but two kids trying to box their way out of the slums. B.o. should be lightweight.

Klaus Maria Brandauer is at the center of the ring, playing a Russian Jew and former boxing champion who was banned from competing for the Soviet team because of his religion — so he emigrated to the U.S. and now lives in Brighton Beach, works as a dishwasher and gets drunk a lot.

Brandauer has a chip on his shoulder as big as the borough of Brooklyn, making him a belligerent drunk with a failed image of himself and of his new homeland, that he laments ain't the land of promise it was cracked up to be.

One night in a stupor, he picks a fight with a young, streetwise black kid, Roland Jenkins (Wesley Snipes), and starts to whip on him — telling the youth he couldn't box his way out of a bag if he tried.

While the kid's a bit ruffled, it isn't he, but his chief rival at the neighborhood boxing club, a brash Irish tough named Timmy Doyle (Adrian Pasdar) who's so impressed that this middle-aged and seemingly out-of-shape lunk can so easily humiliate an athlete half his age, he seeks him out the next day, and asks him to be his coach.

A little too neatly, Snipes and Pasdar become pals and work together training with Brandauer.

Snipes turns out to be the better boxer, but illogically is denied his big chance to compete, a plot move that undermines the story's value.

Needless to say, when the Ruskies come to town to go up against the local boys, Brandauer's veins practically pop out with the chance to wage a vendetta against the Soviet coach (and his team) who did him wrong those many years before by putting his two hungry proteges into the ring.

"Streets Of Gold" is paved with credibly gritty scenes shot in and around a dingy local boxing club and the grimy environs of Brighton Beach, but the end result comes off as a highbrow boxing training film.

There are just too many rounds watching Brandauer instructing his pupils on how to dodge hits to the head than scenes of dialog to get a feel for what's really rolling behind all those punches.

The characters aren't developed enough to be enthusiastic about getting behind their struggle to achieve beyond their misfortunate lot in life.

It's not that these three aren't worth rooting for, it's just that they don't encounter the kind of roadblocks along the way to make the trip seem worthwhile.

Snipes and Pasdar are basically affable, good-hearted kids with the requisite number of muscles to play boxers and Brandauer has that beefy, authoritarian demeanor to be at once intimidating and the next moment, sternly compassionate.

But the three scripters credited for the dialog (Heywood Gould, Richard Price and Tom Cole) should have put more meat on the material.

The only other person who figures ever so slightly here is Brandauer's love interest and fellow emigre, Elena Gitman (Spanish star Angela Molina). She appears perhaps too earnest in explaining very succinctly to the boxers at dinner one night the whys and wherefores for their coach's detached personality. There is a certain sweetness, but no fire, in her love for him.

On a technical level, film is stunning — from Arthur Albert's photography to Jack Nitzsche's scoring, as was Ufland/Roth's previous feature, "Where The River Runs Black."—*Brit.*

El Secuestro de Camarena
(Camarena Taken Hostage)
(MEXICAN-COLOR)

A Peliculas Mexicanas release of a Prods. A.D. Agrasánchez-Filmadora Dal production. Produced by J. David Agrasánchez. Directed by Alfredo B. Crevenna. Stars Armando Silvestre. Screenplay, José Loza; camera (color), Antonio Ruis; editor, Fernando Landero; music, Marco Flores, with appearance of the group Los Invaciones de Nuevo León. Reviewed at Big Apple Cine 2, N.Y., Oct. 30, 1986. Running time: **90 MINS.**
George Camarena . . . . . Armando Silvestre
Criston Caro
Quintero . . . . Fernando Casanova
Alejandra . . . . Sasha Montenegro
Also with: Rebeca Silva, Jorge Vargas, Arlette Pacheco, Estela Inda.

The Mexican exploitation pic "El Secuestro de Camarena" (Camarena Taken Hostage) is an attempt to cop a few fast bucks from the 1984 disappearance and subsequent alleged murder of U.S. narcotics agent Enrique Camarena Salizar by drug kingpin Rafael Caro Quintero.

Besides changing the first names of those involved, this low-budget pic carries a disclaimer at both the beginning and end of the film noting any relation to real persons living or dead is purely coincidental. It's funny how manay coincidences pop up in this film that deals with a U.S. narcotics agent seeking to expose the drug dealings of one Caro Quintero and later is tortured and murdered. The plot details are about the only thing not related to coincidence.

All the atrocities and alleged crimes of the villain are handled with wanton abandon. Sex interest is supplied by Sasha Montenegro. Yet, despite the exploitation of the theme, the individual scenes do not hold together. As a film, the storyline does not jell.

The American actor playing Camarena's boss obviously knows no Spanish and simply has memorized lines that are stiffly delivered with one of the worst accents imaginable. But he is not out of place in this film where everything is uniformly bad: the dialog is laughable, the acting wooden and the movements stagey.

The shoddy production and script make this film a sad legacy to Enrique Camarena's memory. His sacrifice surely deserves better. —*Lent.*

52 Pick-Up
(COLOR)

Unexciting thriller in the hard-boiled school.

A Cannon Films release. Produced by Menahem Golan, Yoram Globus. Executive producer, Henry T. Weinstein. Directed by John Frankenheimer. Stars Roy Scheider, Ann-Margret. Screenplay, Elmore Leonard, John Steppling, based on the novel by Leonard; camera (TVC color), Jost Vacano; editor, Robert F. Shugrue; music, Gary Chang; production design, Philip Harrison; art director, Russell Christian; set decorator, Max Whitehouse; sound (Ultra-Stereo), Ed Novick; assistant director, Bradley Gross; casting, Lou DiGiaimo. Reviewed at Cannon screening room, L.A., Calif., Oct. 31, 1986. (MPAA Rating: R.) Running time: **114 MINS.**
Harry Mitchell . . . . Roy Scheider
Barbara Mitchell . . . . Ann-Margret
Doreen . . . . Vanity

Alan Raimy . . . . John Glover
Leo Franks . . . . Robert Trebor
Jim O'Boyle . . . . Lonny Chapman
Cini . . . . Kelly Preston
Bobby Shy . . . . Clarence Williams 3d
Averson . . . . Doug McClure

Hollywood — "52 Pick-Up" is a thriller without any thrills. Although director John Frankenheimer stuffs as much action as he can into the screen adaptation of Elmore Leonard's novel (previously filmed by Cannon in Israel in 1984 as "The Ambassador"), he can't hide the ridiculous plot and lifeless characters. Boxoffice outlook is modest at best.

Genre efforts like "52 Pick-Up" should move like a wave — sweeping up viewers and not letting them go until the film settles down 90 minutes later. But in this case there

Original Film:
The Ambassador
(U.S.-COLOR)

A Cannon Films release of a Golan-Globus-Northbrook Film production. Executive producers, Menahem Golan, Yoram Globus. Associate producer, Isaac Kol. Directed by J. Lee-Thompson. Stars Robert Mitchum, Ellen Burstyn, Rock Hudson. Screenplay, Max Jack, based on Elmore Leonard's novel, "52 Pick-Up;" camera (TVC color), Adam Greenberg; editor, Mark Goldblatt; music, Dov Seltzer; production design Yoram Barzilai. Reviewed at Cannes Festival (Market), May 17, 1984. Running time: **90 MINS.**
Peter Hacker . . . . Robert Mitchum
His wife Alex . . . . Ellen Burstyn
Frank Stevenson . . . . Rock Hudson
Mustapha Hashimi . . . . Fabio Testi
Defense Minister Eretz . . Donald Pleasence
Rachel . . . . Heli Goldenberg
Tova . . . . Michal Bat-Adam
Abe . . . . Ori Levy
Assad . . . . Uri Gavriel

is no rush of energy to propel the film past its improbability.

Failure of the film to fly can be traced directly to boring characters and blame must be spread around to the actors, Roy Scheider and Ann-Margret, the screenplay by Leonard and John Steppling and the direction by Frankenheimer. Characters are never given a chance at winning the audience's sympathies.

Scheider is an all-American hero who has worked his way up by his bootstraps and after many lean years now owns a successful business and a luxurious home in the Hollywood hills. He's supposedly a working class kid who's made good, but hasn't forgotten his roots.

Unfortunately the original story, set in Detroit in the novel, has been transposed to L.A. with much of the grittiness of the character and his surroundings being sacrificed for a sunnier view. Despite a number of low-life locations, cinematographer Jost Vacano fails to create a menacing environment.

Caught in a blackmail scheme by an unlikely trio of porno operators who film him in bed with a cute young thing (Kelly Preston), Scheider balks at giving up his hard-earned

wealth, but even more at being told what to do.

When blackmailers start playing hardball and film the murder of the girl carried out with Scheider's stolen gun, they soon learn they are not in his league. He craftily tears their plans apart by sowing doubt and playing each against the other until they destroy themselves.

Since he is clearly caught with his pants down and maintains a controlled and cold center Scheider is just a man in trouble, not a man who needs anyone's help, even his wife's. Married for 23 years to the still attractive Ann-Margret, she seems more disturbed that her husband's problems will destroy her political aspirations than her marriage. Declarations aside, there isn't much emotion holding these people together.

Against a backdrop of sordid relationships and distasteful people, the bond between husband and wife should be what keeps the film going, but as the picture opens it's already a marriage that has gone astray. Chemistry between Scheider and Ann-Margret is minimal and undermines the film's foundation.

More lively (and likable, in a perverse sort of way) are the three thugs who are fingering Scheider. Ringleader of the group is John Glover as porno filmmaker and proved psychopath. Glover gives the role such a decadently sinister turn that he's far more interesting and lively to watch than Scheider.

Robert Trebor is a quivering tub of jelly who somehow should have been in the garment business but wound up in porn. He's hardly a contest for Scheider, but amusing nonetheless. Last of the bad guys is black hitman Clarence Williams 3d, a time bomb waiting to explode. As his girlfriend stripper, Vanity seems born to play the role.

Tech credits are individually fine but overall production fails to find a groove to give the unlikely events a measure of power. —*Jagr.*

Al Asheke
(The Lover)
(IRAQI-COLOR)

A Babel Films production and release. Directed by Mohamed Mournir Fanari. Screenplay, Tamer Mahdi, from a novel by Abdulkhalek Al Rakabi; camera (color), William Daniel; editor, Tarek Abdulkarim; music, Helmi Al Wadi; art direction, Najem. Reviewed at the Carthage Film Days (in competition), Oct. 19, 1986. Running time: **110 MINS.**
Abdullah . . . . Jawad Al Choukrgi
Nerjis . . . . Layla Mohamed
Mullah . . . . Khalil Chawki

Tunis — Iraq makes a pair of features a year, almost all dealing with the war. "The Lover" 's problem is it wasn't one of them. No matter: though set in the past, during the

English colonial period, pic tacks on an opening and closing frame that makes explicit the story's relevance to the present-day conflict.

The Lover is a bit of a misnomer, since Abdullah (Jawad Al Choukrgi) never has a chance to get the girl during the film. Anyway, his attraction to Nerjis (Layla Mohamed), the village beauty, takes a back seat to two more important problems — the haughty, stupid British Army, determined to humiliate the populace any way it can, and the tyrranical sheik who'd sooner see the village die of thirst and hunger than divert water from his rice paddy. When his bestial overseer rapes Nerjis, and the villagers find her dying, Abdullah castrates the rapist and takes off on his Arabian stallion.

Many years later, he miraculously rides back with a gray beard, ready to lead the populace against Iranian bombs, uniting them in their common love for the fatherland.

Pic is technically passable.
—*Yung.*

50 Years Of Action!
(DOCU-COLOR-16m)

A Directors Guild of America Golden Jubilee Committee presentation of a DMS Prod. Services production. Produced, written and directed by Douglass M. Stewart Jr. Camera (CFI color), John A. Alonzo, Caleb Deschanel, Chuck Clifton; additional camera, James Mathers; editors, John Soh, Stewart; music, Bill Conti; art direction, Jim Clayter; associate producer, Soh; assistant directors, Walter Gilmore, Steven Tramz (West Coast), Joe Napolitano, Dwight Williams (East Coast); sound, Fred Ginsburg, John Lifavi, Mike Lonsdale; narrator, Richard Crenna. Reviewed at the Directors Guild of America Theater, W. Hollywood, Nov. 1, 1986. (No MPAA Rating.) Running time: **60 MINS.**
With: Morris R. Abrams, Stanley Ackerman, Woody Allen, John A. Alonzo, Warren Beatty, Steve Besner, Richard Brooks, Himan Brown, Gilbert Cates, Michael Cimino, Martha Coolidge, Norman Corwin, William Crain, Chico Day, Tom Donovan, Edward Dmytryk, Milos Forman, Arthur Forrest, Michael H. Franklin, George L. George, Alan Gordon, John Huston, Elia Kazan, Kim Kurumada, Sheldon Leonard, Dan Lew, Lynne Littman, Sidney Lumet, Rouben Mamoulian, Joseph L. Mankiewicz, Fletcher Markle, Patricia McBrearty, Adam Merims, Richard Mutschler, Gordon Parks, Ernest Ricca, Martin Ritt, John Rich, John Schlesinger, Gene Searchinger, Susan Seidelman, George Sidney, Joan Micklin Silver, Elliot Silverstein, James E. Wall, Robert Wise, Joseph C. Youngerman.

Hollywood — To mark its golden anniversary, the Directors Guild of America has sponsored this hour-long documentary covering its history, from its turbulent formation to the ongoing struggle for creative rights in a commercial industry. Necessarily telescoped, film nevertheless covers a lot of territory in a short time.

With Milos Forman leading the way in describing the guild as "one

of the noble institutions," and Richard Brooks affirming that "the guild really stands behind the directors and the studios know it," nearly 50 directors and assistants, veterans and comparative youngsters, fill in the highlights of the DGA's five decades, and in a general sense give the impression of an organization composed of strong individuals with character and serious purpose.

Rouben Mamoulian, the only survivor among the guild's original dozen organizers, narrates the guild's lean beginnings and battle with the studios for recognition. Rare film clips and photographs help bring the key players to life, and producer-director-writer Douglass M. Stewart Jr. adroitly mixes straightforward history with colorful anecdotes and personal angles.

Key moment in guild history and, rightly, of the film, is the internal struggle prompted by the Red Scare. Legendary guild meeting in 1950 in which the forces of the right, led by Cecil B. DeMille, attempted to oust guild president Joseph L. Mankiewicz but ultimately were thwarted by George Stevens, John Ford and others, is recounted excitingly by Mankiewicz and some fellow participants.

This episode represented the DGA's finest hour, but interest is maintained as docu covers such significant occurences as the merging of radio and television directors' guilds into the DGA, and the passage of a "Bill of Rights," which is still being evolved.

Although he is not interviewed on camera, Frank Capra emerges as an ongoing guild hero through the decades. Pic admirably spotlights the important role of the assistant director, and points up the growing frequency of women occupying the director's chair after years of nearly total male domination.

Pic is very professionally done, although video transfers do betray themselves. Many top names participated here both before and behind the camera, and result is a worthy self-tribute by an impressive organization. —*Cart.*

Tai-Pan
(COLOR)

Soap opera adaptation misfires.

A De Laurentiis Entertainment Group release. Produced by Raffaella De Laurentiis. Directed by Daryl Duke. Screenplay, John Briley, Stanley Mann, based on the novel by James Clavell; camera (J-D-C Widescreen, Technicolor), Jack Cardiff; music, Maurice Jarre; production design, Tony Masters, art director, Benjamin Fernandez, Pierluigi Basile; set dresser, Giorgio Desideri; sound (Dolby), Nelson Stoll, John Haptas; special effects, Kit West; associate producer, Jose Lopez Rodero; casting, Rose Tobias Shaw. Reviewed at De Laurentiis screening room, Beverly Hills, Calif., Nov. 5, 1986. (MPAA Rating: R.) Running time: **127 MINS.**

Tai-Pan	Bryan Brown
May-May	Joan Chen
Brock	John Stanton
Culum	Tom Guinee
Gorth	Bill Leadbitter
Gordon	Russell Wong
Mary	Katy Behan
Tess	Kyra Sedgwick
Shevaun	Janine Turner
Quance	Norman Rodway
Orlov	John Bennett
Vargas	Derrick Branche

Hollywood — "Tai-Pan" is a big, sprawling foolish film — a historical epic lost somewhere between 19th century Hong Kong and 20th century Hollywood. Despite flashes of brilliance and color, "Tai-Pan" fails to evoke a mysterious and moving world as a backdrop to its romantic drama. In the end it's pretty humdrum stuff and is unlikely to provoke much of groundswell or must-see quality, even among fans of the novel.

Over a decade in the works on paper, perhaps that's where this film should have remained. After numerous false starts by filmmakers including Carl Foreman and Richard Fleischer and stars Patrick McGoohan, Steve McQueen and Sean Connery, Dino De Laurentiis, with producer/daughter Raffealla De Laurentiis, was the one to actually make it, but he didn't solve the multitude of problems inherent in a production of this scope and complexity.

For all of its bravado "Tai-Pan" is sorely lacking in human qualities. Director Daryl Duke and his team have made an attractive shell but failed to put in any heart. The delicate balance between large-scale action and the lives going on within is never achieved. Characters are drawn only in broad strokes without revealing what was particular to life at that time and place.

Story is so dense and complex with numerous threads that it is impossible to tell exactly what is going on at any given moment or who is doing what to whom. Script by John Briley and Stanley Mann based on James Clavell's bestseller sadly plays like a period soap-opera. Film is surprisingly lacking in the resonance and richness that the material should generate. One learns little about the period other than that characters fight a lot and are blessed with an abundance or cursed with a paucity of "joss," a quality akin to cosmic luck.

No one has more joss than the Tai-Pan, or trade leader of the European community first in Canton and then later in Hong Kong. As the Tai-Pan, Aussie thesp Bryan Brown looks the part well enough, but lacks some of the charisma and authority Connery, for instance, might have brought to the role.

Within the exotic setting the story is actually rather conventional. Brown is opposed by arch villains Brock (John Stanton) and his son Gorth (Bill Leadbitter) for the control of the trading rights. At the same time there is considerable politicking going on with the Chinese over the opium trade and the British over trade regulations, although unfortunately not much of that intrigue is seen on screen.

Instead film presents a good deal of romancing, between Brown and his lovely Chinese concubine May-May (Joan Chen) and several other women who seem to have a bottomless supply of revealing costumes. Lovemaking alternates with bitter power struggles between the Tai-Pan and his enemies who are portrayed as little more than animals in human dress. At one point Gorth is even seen whipping a prostitute for no other reason than the sport of it.

With the sides so blatantly drawn there is little room for subtlety and yet it is difficult to root for Brown in a way that would make the silliness of the film emotionally rewarding. The impact remains little more than looking in a shop window at some beautiful costumes.

Although the film went to great lengths to shoot in China, scenery is surprisingly limited and unexceptional. Much of the action takes place indoors and could just as easily have been filmed on a backlot closer to home.

Lensing by Jack Cardiff does take in a few scenic vistas, but generally is hampered by Duke's stuffy and contrived staging. Script also contributes a stilted quality to the dialog as when a doomed ship captain confesses to his would-be lady that "I love thee."

Music by Maurice Jarre is appropriately lush and tech credits are fine. But underneath all the gloss this film isn't really about anything. —*Jagr.*

What Happened Next Year
(SYRIAN-COLOR)

A National Film Organization production and release. Written and directed by Samir Zikra. Camera (color), Hanna Warde; editor, Zouheir Dayé; music, Ziad Rabbani; art direction, L. Arslan, R. Hoshos. Reviewed at the Carthage Film Days (in competition), Oct. 20, 1986. Running time: **140 MINS.**

Mounir	Najah Safkouni
Lamia	Naila El Atrache
Haifa	Hala Al Faucal

Tunis — "What Happened Next Year" is a serious Syrian effort by Samir Zikra, director of the prize-winning "The Half-Meter Incident." Its portrait of modern Damascus and life among Arab intellectuals presents a rare glimpse into upper-class Syrian life.

Story revolves around a sympathetic young orchestra conductor and composer, Mounir (played with understated assurance by Najah Safkouni), back in Syria after music studies around the world. While he struggles to carry on a frustrating love affair with Haifa (Hala Al Faucal), he takes proposal after proposal for a national symphony orchestra to a deaf cultural ministry. He considers emigrating, but in the end achieves some creative satisfaction by organizing an Arab musical ensemble, mixing classical and modern sounds.

Zikra's portrait gallery of characters concentrates on their everyday business in the city. Balancing Mounir's frustration are Haifa's anxieties; with an abortion, failed marriage, and failed suicide attempt behind her, she's understandably leery of tying herself down in a country she may soon decide to leave. Tragicomic relief is provided by Lamia (Naila El Atrache), a 33-year-old maid, obsessed with sex in general and good-looking Mounir in particular.

Film's main fault is that it meanders. Thesps are well directed and lensing first-rate. Action unfolds in some splendid historical surroundings. —*Yung.*

Quiet Cool
(COLOR)

Superficial thriller on the war with marijuana growers.

A New Line Cinema release of a Robert Shaye production. Executive producers, Pierre David, Arthur Sarkissian, Larry Thompson. Produced by Shaye, Gerald T. Olson. Directed by Clay Borris. Screenplay, Borris, Susan Vercellino; camera (Deluxe color), Jacques Haitkin; film editor, Bob Brady; music score, Jay Ferguson; associate producer, Sara Risher; casting, Annette Benson. Reviewed at Mann's Hollywood, Hollywood, Calif., Oct. 7, 1986. (MPAA Rating: R.) Running time: **80 MINS.**

Joe Dillon	James Remar
Joshua Greer	Adam Coleman Howard
Katy Greer	Daphne Ashbrook
Mike Prior	Jared Martin
Valence	Nick Cassavetes
Ma	Fran Ryan

Hollywood — "Quiet Cool" is a brutal, sensationalistic story about a two-man war waged against a band of ruthless marijuana growers that often is predictable, yet manages to hold a good amount of tension throughout. It probably will draw its fair share of "Rambo" lovers to the boxoffice.

The story opens in New York with police officer Joe Dillon, played with an offbeat type of cool macho by James Remar. Dillon is the type of cop who obviously does not play by the rules as he throws a purse-snatcher into the Hudson River. Yet he is a dedicated policeman, so when a former girlfriend living in Northern California calls for help, he drops everything and goes.

The former girlfriend, a forgettable performance by Daphne Ashbrook, is an environmentalist who lives in a tiny town in the heart of the Emerald Triangle, the mountainous northwestern areas of California nicknamed for its large percentage of marijuana fields. Her brother's family also lives in this remote town and they have disappeared.

The audience at this point already knows the brother and his wife have been killed viciously by the marijuana growers and their son, Joshua Greer (admirable performance by Adam Coleman Howard) has been thrown off a cliff and left to die.

As the story progresses, the New York cop and the son team up to fight the savage marijuana growers, using guerrilla-type warfare that ultimately ends with a Western-style shoot-out on the main street of this tiny town.

Obviously the last person to get his comeuppance is the mysterious person who masterminds the whole operation. That is supposed to be the surprise ending, but it was obvious who "Mr. Big" was within the first 10 minutes of the film.

The story is nothing new, it just substitutes marijuana growers as the bad, bad guys. Yet the performances by leads Remar and Howard are unusual and captivating enough to carry the film.

The bad guys are mostly forgettable except for Nick Cassavetes as the black-haired Valence. He doesn't have much to say, yet he brings a cold, scary element to the character.

The one big problem with this film is that it is trying to ride on the coattails of recent news stories about drug enforcement activities in Northern California, more specifically the activities of CAMP, Campaign Against Marijuana Planting. Last year, CAMP confiscated 800,-000 lbs. of high-grade marijuana.

CAMP even has published a warning guide for tourists and hikers who may accidentally happen upon a marijuana farm.

Yet from this, the producers of this pic have put together a sensationalist film that really does little to reveal the actual problem. Other than the bad guys getting high a few times, the subject of marijuana is hardly ever brought up. In fact, these guys are not bad because they are growers, they are bad because they are killers. The true nature of the Emerald Triangle never comes into play.

Director Clay Borris (who also cowrote the script with Susan Vercellino) in his first major screen feature in the United States has done a good job of creating a fast-paced action film with a lot of tension. The story and dialog are minimal, yet for the type of film it is, it is entertaining. —*Teen.*

Pisma Mertvogo Cheloveka
(Letters From A Dead Man)
(SOVIET-COLOR/B&W)

A Sovexportfilm release. Produced by Lenfilm Studio. Directed by Konstantin Lopushanski. Stars Rolan Bykov. Screenplay, Lopushanski, Vjacheslav Rybakov, with Boris Strugacki; camera (color/b&w), Nikolai Prokopcev; music, Alexander Zhurbin; art direction, Elena Amshinskaya, Viktor Ivanov; sound, Leonid Gavrichenko. Reviewed at Italia-URSS screening room, Rome, Oct. 29, 1986. Running time: **86 MINS.**
The Professor . . . . Rolan Bykov
Also with: I. Ryklin, V. Michailov, A. Sabinin, V. Lobanov, N. Griakalova, V. Maiorova, V. Dvorzhecki, S. Smirnova, N. Alkanov.

Rome — "Letters From A Dead Man," quickly dubbed the Soviet "Day After" because of its post-nuclear holocaust theme, has had patrons standing in line to see it since it opened in Moscow. Not only is this feature debut of Konstantin Lopushanski topical (it was in production before the Chernobyl tragedy, but released just afterwards), it's also well-made and involving.

Initial interest may be aroused for pic as a curiosity item, but "Letters" has more going for it than a gimmick plot. Its bleak view of the end of humanity is marked by a desolating sense of prophecy, or at least warning, and its sincerity is unquestionable. It already has been picked up by Western distribs.

Though as intense as "The Day After," "Letters" is a much more cerebral effort than its emotionally involving Yank counterpart. It begins after the fatal button has been pushed, presumably (rumor goes) by accident, from the Soviet side, because a technician choking on coffee couldn't give a counter-order fast enough. Film alternates between an underground bunker which used to be a museum, strewn with now useless cultural artifacts, and the apocalyptic upper world, a place of perpetual twilight, rubble and mud. Pic is shot almost entirely in sepia tones and blue tints drained of color. Lopushanski was once Andrei Tarkovsky's assistant, and visually pic recalls the desolation of "Stalker."

The central survivor is an aged Nobel Prizewinner, played with touching restraint by Rolan Bykov. Holed up in the museum basement with his dying wife and a handful of co-workers, the Professor writes mental letters to his son Erik, missing since the explosion. In his forays outside, where gas-masked black marketeers barter medicine and play roulette among the ruins, the professor aids a group of mute orphans living in the remains of a Protestant church. Eventually he chooses to join them instead of seeking shelter in the Central Bunker, and they celebrate a heart-rending Christmas together before he dies. Last shot has kids marching off through the snow to an unknown future.

Despite the grim horror of its theme, and a tendency to clutter its eloquent images with a lot of banal speeches proclaiming the poignancy of mankind's demise, "Letters" is a compulsive watch, and a sobering parable from the other side.— *Yung.*

Monster Shark
(Red Ocean)
(ITALIAN-FRENCH-COLOR)

A Cinema Shares release of a Filmes Intl.-Nuovo Dania-National Cinematografica (Rome)/Les Filmes du Griffon coproduction. Produced by Mino Loy (uncredited). Directed by "John Old Jr." (Lamberto Bava). Screenplay, Gianfranco Clerici, others, from story by "Lewis Coates" (Luigi Cozzi), Don Lewis, "Martin Dolman" (Sergio Martino); camera (Telecolor), "John McFerrand" (Giancarlo Ferrando); editor, Bob Wheeler; music, Antony Barrymore; assistant directors, Gilbert Roussel, Fredy Unger; special effects, Germano Natali; production design, A.M. Geleng; monster shark creator, Ovidio Taito. Reviewed at 42d St. Liberty theater, Nov. 2, 1986. (No MPAA Rating.) Running time: **92 MINS.**
With: Michael Sopkiw (Peter), Valentine Monnier, "John" (Gianni) Garko (Sheriff Gordon), William Berger (Dr. West), Iris Peynard, Lawrence Morgant, Dagmar Lassander (Sonja).

"Monster Shark," previously titled "Red Ocean," is a poor science fiction/horror film from Europe. Since Universal is planning a fourth "Jaws" epic, there's apparently some life left in this lame material.

Yank actor Michael Sopkiw gets involved in a hunt for a giant underwater killer off the Florida Coast when he's hired to rig up some electronic equipment for scientists studying the series of gory attacks on humans. Eventually they discover that the culprit is a 15,000,-000-year-old ancestor of the shark, 40 ft. long and hungry. Worse yet, the critter's individual cells are capable of reproduction, meaning that if it isn't found and destroyed soon the ocean will be filled with the beasties.

Cornball film relies once again for the usual conflict between gung ho scientists (led by William Berger) who want to save the creature for study, and practical types like the local sheriff (Gianni Garko) who want to kill it. Monster itself is a very fake-looking cross between shark and octopus, wisely shown in its entirety only briefly on screen. Cast is peppered with pretty women, but the acting is miserable, becoming downright funny during some exaggerated death scenes or shrieking bouts.

Surprisingly for such a routine picture, five well-known Continental helmers are credited in various capacities, with the Italian contingent (Lamberto Bava, the film's director, as well as Luigi Cozzi and Sergio Martino) hiding behind pseudonyms, while their French confreres, Max Pecas and Gilbert Roussel, are less shy. —*Lor.*

Al-Kas
(The Cup)
(TUNISIAN-COLOR)

A SATPEC production and release. Directed by Mohamed Damak. Screenplay, Mohamed Mahfoudh; camera (color), Belgacem Jelliti; editor, Sabiha El Haj Slimane. Reviewed at the Carthage Film Days, Oct. 21, 1986. Running time: **76 MINS.**
Mustapha . . . . Slim Mahfoudh
Mustapha's wife . . . . Fatma Larbi
Rached . . . . Kamel Touati
Hedi . . . . Hassen Hermes
Also with: Nabil Kaaniche (Hassan), Jamila Ourabi (Lamine), Mohamed Lassoued, Fathi Haddoi (Malabar).

Tunis — Mohamed Damak's first feature comedy, "The Cup," has the distinction of being SATPEC's last release before the state distribbery was dismantled, and one of its more popular Tunisian releases. The subject — soccer mania — is as universal as the game, and could pass easily to other markets where the Sunday soccer match is the obsession and despair of every household. The tone is right, the humor accessible, and the picture quite enjoyable.

A group of friends gets together for dinner one Saturay, on the eve of the Tunisian cup match. Both teams are from the city, and loyalties are divided. Mustapha roots for one team, but bets on the other. His wife, left alone the next day, has a tryst with Mustapha's cousin. Meanwhile, in the stadium, fights hospitalize a number of agitated spectators. When the doctor gazes into injured fans' eyes, he can still see the match going on. The worst is facing the rest of the week, after their team loses the game; the tortured fans are mad with grief. Only Mustapha has the consolation of collecting on his bet.

The skits are well lensed and fast moving. Script could have been shot in Europe; only the actors — and a picturesque Tunisian wedding — give away film's origins. —*Yung.*

Star Trek IV:
The Voyage Home
(COLOR)

Excellent time-travel entry in the series.

A Paramount Pictures release of a Harve Bennett production. Executive producer, Ralph Winter. Produced by Bennett. Coproduced by Industrial Light & Magic. Directed by Leonard Nimoy. Screenplay, Bennett, Steve Meerson, Peter Krikes, Nicholas Meyer from a story by Nimoy, Bennett, based on "Star Trek" tv series created by Gene Roddenberry; camera (Panavision, Technicolor), Don Peterman; editor, Peter E. Berger; music, Leonard Rosenman; sound (Dolby), Gene S. Cantamessa; production design, Jack T. Collis; art direction, Joe Aubel, Pete Smith; set design, Dan Gluck, James Bayliss, Richard Berger; set decorator, John Dwyer; visual effects supervisor, Ken Ralston; visual effects, Industrial Light & Magic; special effects supervisor, Michael Lanteri; costume design, Robert Fletcher; assistant directors, Patrick Kehoe, Douglas E. Wise; casting, Amanda Mackey. Reviewed at Paramount Studios, Hollywood, Nov. 12, 1986. (MPAA Rating: PG.) Running time: **119 MINS.**
Kirk . . . . William Shatner
Spock . . . . Leonard Nimoy
McCoy . . . . DeForest Kelley
Scotty . . . . James Doohan
Sulu . . . . George Takei
Chekov . . . . Walter Koenig
Uhura . . . . Nichelle Nichols
Amanda . . . . Jane Wyatt
Gillian . . . . Catherine Hicks
Sarek . . . . Mark Lenard
Lt. Saavik . . . . Robin Curtis
Fed. Council
President . . . . Robert Ellenstein
Klingon Ambassador . . . . John Schuck

Hollywood — Kirk and company may be without a USS Enterprise and grounded temporarily in earthly predicaments, but their adventure in "Star Trek IV: The Voyage Home" is no less entertaining than in the previous filmed missions.

Latest excursion is warmer, wittier, more socially relevant and truer to its tv origins than prior odysseys, which will satisfy the legions of trekkies while conquering a galaxy of new admirers with its more commercial treatment.

Already this year's b.o. leader, Paramount should load its coffers even more with this entry.

This voyage finds the crew earthbound to face trial for stealing the Enterprise and journeying to a restricted planet to battle the Klingons — and seeing their beloved starship destroyed in the process.

Forced to travel homeward on a Klingon klunker, they find the galaxy dark and messages from Earth distorted, triggering a bit of worrying on the ship's deck.

In his inimitable, calculated, reasoning mind, Spock locates the source of the trouble in the bleeting, eerie sounds of an unidentified probe and links them to a cry from the Earth's past that has long been silenced.

Scripters employ successful use of time travel, found in many sci-fi stories and a certain number of celebrated "Star Trek" tv episodes, to take Kirk et al. back to where they stand a chance to save the Earth of the 23d Century — the San Francisco Bay of the 20th Century.

Opening scenes don't give off the feeling that this will be a particularly precarious mission for the crew, they seem to be having too much fun exchanging lighthearted barbs to be worried if the Klingon klunker can survive warp speed in one piece.

Spock (Leonard Nimoy), resurrected in "Star Trek III" and not fully himself yet, is the foil for most of the jokes, being the quintessential straight man still suffering from rebirth trauma that resulted in some lapses in memory.

He and Kirk (William Shatner) play off each other in a sort of deadpan futuristic version of Hope and Crosby with Nimoy, surprisingly, as the awkward one relying on Shatner's smooth talking to win the help of a zealous save-the-whales biologist (Catherine Hicks) in capturing a couple of specimens readily available for the taking upon their arrival on Earth.

Audiences may find the save-the-whales message overwrought and a bit heavy-handed for what is ostensibly a space fantasy film. Theme might have been received better in the ecologically more aware 1970s than mid-1980s, although principle is no less valid today.

Nice that filmmakers have moved away from reliance on special effects wizardry and series of inter-gallactic confrontations to carry the story, instead developing drama and suspense through a strong narrative.

Nevertheless, some of the more ardent trekkies may find the dialog a bit too cute at times and derivative of the kind of slick one-liners so well employed in "Back To The Future." They may also object to the violation of the cardinal science fiction rule not to tamper with the past.

Characters' situations and banterings are certainly enjoyable to watch, but there are a handful of gratuitous scenes that only contribute to the overall frenetic pacing of the picture without furthering the story. One notable cut could have been made of Chekov's (Walter Koenig) contrived emergency surgery scene. Presumably, each of the crewmates are guaranteed a certain amount of screen time for each film appearance, even if their moments might not integrate well into the plot.

Technical credits are terrific, as should be expected in such a high-budget film, though strangely not much is made of the geographic San Francisco setting.—*Brit.*

Chams
(MOROCCAN-COLOR)

A Caméra 3 production and release. Written and directed by Najib Sefrioui. Camera (color), Mohamed Affane, Thierry Lebigre; editor, Anne Leconidec, Maria Lebbar, Sefrioui. Reviewed at the Carthage Film Days (in competition), Oct. 20, 1986. Running time: **81 MINS.**
Chams....................Aicha Sefrioui
Aicha ....Khadija Bouderba
El Haj ....Bousalem Guennoun
Salim...................Abdou Sefrioui

Tunis — "Chams," name of the young heroine, is a murky, rather incoherent feature from Moroccan helmer Najib Sefrioui. Its images, linked by a theory of montage hard to fathom, are often suggestive and settings raise some interest, but a unifying vision is lacking. Underneath pic's inconclusiveness, one senses the director had some original observations to make, which adds to the frustration rather than otherwise. Pic seems unlikely to travel outside its borders.

In a film where little is concretely described, the clearest character is El Haj the politician. Played with middle-aged sympathy and nuance by Bousalem Guennoun, El Haj is a millionaire businessmen in a permanent race to meet his wife and demanding mistresses. When son Abdou Sefrioui comes back from a Swiss medical school with the intention of running against him in the upcoming elections — to his dismay and the voters' confusion — El Haj starts drinking too much. Then he finds solace in the arms of pretty young Chams (Aicha Sefrioui), the modern, free-thinking daughter of one of his ex-mistresses. In one sense, the girl reminds him of the woman he loved and wronged; in another, she is meant to incarnate an abstract idea of freedom. Viewers are likely to find her insignificant and hard to trace from scene to scene.

"Chams" is partially redeemed by fine lensing from Mohamed Affane and Thierry Lebigre. — *Yung.*

The Mosquito Coast
(COLOR)

Harrison Ford is great, but bleak film self-destructs.

A Warner Bros. release. Produced by Jerome Hellman. Executive producer, Saul Zaentz. Directed by Peter Weir. Stars Harrison Ford. Screenplay, Paul Schrader, based on novel by Paul Theroux; camera (Technicolor), John Seale; editor, Thom Noble; music, Maurice Jarre; production design, John Stoddart; art director, John Wingrove, Brian Nickless; set decorator, John Anderson; costumes, Gary Jones; sound (Dolby stereo), Mark Berger; assistant director, Mark Egerton; casting, Dianne Crittenden. Reviewed at Warner Bros. screening room, Burbank, Calif., Nov. 5, 1986. (MPAA Rating: PG.) Running time: 117 MINS.
Allie Fox..................Harrison Ford
Mother ....Helen Mirren
Charlie ....River Phoenix
Jerry.....................Jadrien Steele
April......................Hilary Gordon
Clover ....Rebecca Gordon
Rev. Spellgood ....André Gregory
Mr. Haddy ....Conrad Roberts
Mr. Polski................Dick O'Neill
Emily Spellgood ....Martha Plimpton
Mrs. Spellgood ....Melanie Boland
Francis Lungley ....Michael Rogers

Hollywood — It is hard to believe that a film as beautiful as "The Mosquito Coast" can also be so bleak, but therein lies its power and undoing. A modern variation of "Swiss Family Robinson," it starts out as a film about idealism and possibilities, but takes a dark turn and winds up questioning the very values it so powerfully presents. Stunning performance by Harrison Ford and firstrate filmmaking by Peter Weir should induce some interest but boxoffice will be hampered by downbeat conclusion.

Ford's Allie Fox is one of those great screen characters that immediately captures an audience's imagination by sheer force of will. Described by his neighbor as the worst kind of trouble-maker, "a know-it-all who's sometimes right," Fox is a world-class visionary with the power to realize his vision.

He rants and raves against pre-packaged, mass consumed American culture and when he invents what he considers a major breakthrough and no one is interested, he packs up his wife and four kids and moves them lock, stock and barrel to a remote Carribean island — the Mosquito Coast.

Clearly a man of rare brilliance and talent, Fox is the kind of person other people are attracted to, his family no exception. He has the charisma to lead and his family follows unquestioningly on his mission. Wife (Helen Mirren), younger son (Jadrien Steele), twin daughters (Hilary and Rebecca Gordon) and especially his eldest son (River Phoenix), who serves as the narrator of the story, are all caught up in his glorious experiment.

Fox transforms a remote outpost on the island into a thriving community equipped with numerous Rube Goldberg-like gadgets to harness the forces of nature and make life better for the inhabitants.

For a while it's an idyllic little utopian community, but the seeds of its downfall are present even as it thrives. Indeed there have been enemies, both internal and external, present along the way, but with the completion of his great invention, a machine that turns fire to ice, the inherent contradictions literally explode.

Fox' nemesis is the populist polyester missionary Reverend Spellgood (André Gregory), a man with a world view totally antithetical to his own. More immediately responsible for the settlement's failure is the arrival of three degenerate criminal types who unleash the destructive side of Fox' imagination. It is obviously a thin line between inspiration and insanity and here Fox starts tipping over into madness and obsession.

As Fox starts to unravel so does the film. None of the outside antagonists supplied by Paul Schrader's screenplay (based on Paul Theroux' novel) are fitting adversaries for Fox' genius. He carries his own downfall within him and his self-destructiveness ultimately outshines his creativity.

Fox is a fascinating character until his ranting takes on a bitter tinge and turns back on itself. The film stops going anywhere about two-thirds of the way through. In the end there is barely a thread of hope to take home, other than some strikingly beautiful and sad images of a man grasping for something just beyond his reach.

John Seale's photography once again illuminates Weir's vision of unfriendly cultures caught in a moment of decision. Other tech credits are equally in service of the material including Maurice Jarre's moody score and John Stoddart's production design. Locations filmed in Belize are engaging without being uniformly lush.

As for the rest of the cast, River Phoenix is both likable and believable as the eldest son who must carry the burden of having such a strong and contradictory personality as his father. Mirren, as the mother, is forced to maintain an unquestioning loyalty to her husband, and while that weakens her character, it is through her unwavering love and admiration that Fox is most clearly seen.—*Jagr.*

The Boss' Wife
(COLOR)

One-note comedy fails to deliver.

A Tri-Star Picture release. Produced by Thomas H. Brodek. Written and directed by Ziggy Steinberg. Camera (Metrocolor), Gary P. Thieltges; editor, John A. Martinelli; music, Bill Conti; production design, Brenton Swift; casting, Karen Rea; art direction, Albert J. Locatelli; sound, Stephan von Hase. Reviewed at the USA Cinemas Charles theater, Boston, Nov. 8, 1986. (MPAA Rating: R.) Running time: 83 MINS.
Joel Keefer................Daniel Stern
Louise Roalvang........Arielle Dombasle
Carlos Delgado ....Fisher Stevens
Janet Keefer ....Melanie Mayron
Harry Taphorn............Lou Jacobi
Tony Dugdale ....Martin Mull
Mr. Roalvang ......Christopher Plummer
Suzy Dugdale ....Diane Stilwell
Eddie ....Robert Costanzo
Barney ....Thalmus Rasulala

Boston — "The Boss' Wife" plays like a dirty joke without a punchline. Daniel Stern is a stockbroker in the bullpen of Roalvang & Co., looking for his first big break. His presentation to Roalvang (Christopher Plummer) gets him invited to an exclusive company weekend where he and Martin Mull will battle it out for a new opening higher in the company.

While her husband remains oblivious, Louise Roalvang (Arielle Dombasle) starts coming on to Stern. Her method typifies the problem with the film: it's all tease and no payoff. Sitting at the dinner table with Stern and Plummer, she slips a pat of butter into her decolletage. Before you can say Grauman's Chinese, she has left a deep impression on both Stern and the butter.

Yet when the moment of truth for Stern finally comes (will he foresake his own marital vows to bed the boss' wife?) nothing happens except some pointless running around. The story ends with Stern apparently ready to spurn both the Roalvangs.

Firsttimer Ziggy Steinberg tries to pep up his script with additional farcical elements, but they fail to deliver. Melanie Mayron is Stern's wife, in one of the most sympathetic portrayals in the film, who Stern is trying (and failing) to find the time to impregnate. (An opening gag, that goes on far to long, involves Stern having to give a sperm sample while the doctor's messenger impatiently waits.)

Fisher Stevens plays the obnoxious Carlos, a photographer whose book Mayron is editing. He insults everyone he meets so that he can take their picture for his book on the faces of anger. Stevens' shtick quickly wears thin, especially when Steinberg's script requires the audience to believe that everyone thinks that Stern and Stevens are lovers.

While Plummer, Mayron, Mull and Lou Jacobi (as Stern's mentor) can more than handle their barely sketched-in roles, Stevens and Dombasle are constrained by them, playing the same note over and over. Stern is an odd choice for the lead role, coming across as a doormat for the other characters for most of the film.

This is the sort of picture where you go out humming the sets, which are much sturdier than the plot conventions. This is especially so of Roalvang's office, which comes complete with a miniature train that delivers lunch, and a luxury private railroad car that transports private vang and his guests to their weekend destination.

The chief flaw here is that "The Boss' Wife" has no point to it. The changes in the characters' lives seem unearned, and the trip to get us from here to there is only intermittently funny. It will probably play a lot better on cable. —*Kimm.*

Days Of Hell
(ITALIAN-COLOR)

A Mary Film production. World sales, Gel Intl. Produced by Eugenio Startari. Directed by "Anthony Richmond" (Tonino Ricci). Stars Conrad Nichols. Screenplay, Tito Carpi, Tonino Ricci; camera (Luciano Vittori color), Giacomo Testa; editor, Vincenzo Tomassi; music, Francesco De Masi; assistant director, Riccardo Petrassi; stunt supervisor, Neno Zamperla; special effects, Paolo Ricci. Reviewed on Mogul vidcassette, N.Y., Nov. 16, 1986. (No MPAA Rating.) Running time: **88 MINS.**

Capt. Williams . . . . Conrad Nichols
Samantha . . . . Kiwako Harada
Prof. Sanders . . . . Werner Pochath
Russ . . . . Richard Raymond
Gen. Smith . . . . Stelio Candelli
Amin . . . . Lawrence Richmond
Grayson . . . . Howard Ross

Occasionally life mirrors film art (e.g., "The China Syndrome"), but "Days Of Hell" is an unusual surprise among the dross of B-action pictures. Routine Italian pic was made 18 months ago, but is right on the money with plot elements seemingly torn from today's headlines. Its domestic release is direct to the homevideo stores.

Conrad Nichols again stars for his "Rush" and "Rage" director Tonino Ricci (who uses the pseudonym Anthony Richmond, not the British helmer-lenser by that name) as a commando sent with a four-man team to Afghanistan by American General Smith (Stelio Candelli, who uses pseudonymn Steve Eliot). Far-fetched plot has the Russian ambassador asking Gen. Smith to have the U.S. clean up a problem that is vexing to both superpowers: two journalists in Afghanistan, Hunter and his beautiful oriental daughter Samantha (Kiwako Harada), have evidence of Russians using nerve gas and chemical weapons against the Afghans. Both Russia and the U.S. agree that the journalists *must be silenced* before they contact Amnesty Intl.; the U.S. is involved because of evidence of its own chemical weapons experiments in North Dakota which already were violently covered up by the authorities.

Williams and his men enter Afghanistan through Iran, *bringing spare parts for Iranian fighter planes* in exchange for safe passage. Their skirmishes with Russian troops and warring locals go so smoothly that Williams figures they're being set up; changing their plans they succeed in rescuing Samantha (her father has died from the nerve gas) and her Afghan pal Amin (Lawrence Richmond, presumably the director's son), and escape to Pakistan where they're granted political asylum. Samantha dies of her own nerve gas exposure but in a happy ending Amin flies off with the four soldiers of fortune in their stolen Russian helicopter for new adventures.

Picture conforms with the tradition of Italian actioners (dating back to the often political Spaghetti Westerns of the 1960s) of siding with Third World interests against the dastardly superpowers. With all the jingoistic films being made today, it's refreshing to see the U.S. getting its lumps along with the Russkies, while the heroes are either daring soldiers of fortune not tied to U.S. government policy or stalwart freedom fighters of Afghanistan, Iran and Pakistan. Most of the characters, regardless of nationality, are played by Italians, adding to the parallel world nature of the whole affair.

Tech credits for the action scenes are fine with okay English dubbing. Pic manages to steal some thunder from Sylvester Stallone; lead Nichols is one of the many Rambo imitations on the market and "Rambo III" is supposed to also concern a mission to Afghanistan. —*Lor.*

Every Time We Say Goodbye
(COLOR)

Warm romance provides change of pace for Tom Hanks.

A Tri-Star Pictures release. Produced by Jacob Kotzky, Sharon Harel. Directed by Moshe Mizrahi. Stars Tom Hanks. Screenplay, Mizrahi, Rachel Fabien, Leah Appet, from story by Mizrahi; camera (color), Giuseppe Lanci; editor, Mark Burns; music, Philippe Sarde; sound, Daniel Brisseau; art director, Micky Zahar; production manager, Avner Peled. Reviewed at Preview 4 screening room, N.Y., Nov. 13, 1986. (MPAA Rating: PG-13.) Running time: **95 MINS.**

David . . . . Tom Hanks
Sarah . . . . Cristina Marsillach
Peter . . . . Benedict Taylor
Victoria . . . . Anat Atzmon
Lea . . . . Gila Almagor
Nessin . . . . Monny Moshanov
Raphael . . . . Avner Hizkiyahu
Sally . . . . Caroline Goodall

"Every Time We Say Goodbye" is a tale of star-crossed lovers played out against a backdrop of Jerusalem in 1942. Tom Hanks is featured as an American pilot recovering from an injury who falls in love with a girl from a traditional Sephardic Jewish family. Draw will be watching an effective Hanks in this warm, though sometimes slow-paced, film.

David (Hanks) and Sarah (Cristina Marsillach) meet through the impending marriage of David's squadron leader to Sarah's best friend. Though attracted to David, Sarah is particularly conscious of their vastly different backgrounds and the fact that a relationship with an American pilot would not be tolerated by her family.

The film is not devoid of humor. Early scenes when Hanks is accepted to dinner by the family as a friend and not yet a suitor are funny and believable. Culturally rich story is aided throughout by the pic's all-Israel shoot, nicely highlighting the different worlds these two lovers come from.

The power of tradition and family turns against David when Sarah's brothers step in to stop their romance. A scene when Sarah is dragged from David's apartment back to her home to be confronted by her hysterical mother and disapproving family is memorable.

As the film's title suggests, David and Sarah's love is one of fits and starts. David must go back to the war, Sarah decides to uphold her heritage and marry a man she doesn't love and things look bleak for the pair indeed. A leave from the front for David and a last minute change of heart by Sarah, however, make for a happy ending.

Cristina Marsillach is alluring in her American film debut and supporting cast is strong, particularly Benedict Taylor as Peter.—*Roy.*

Scuola di Ladri
(Thief Academy)
(ITALIAN-COLOR)

A C.D.I. release of a C. G. Silver production. Produced by Mario and Vittorio Cecchi Gori. Associate producers, Bruno Altissimi and Claudio Saraceni for Maura Intl. Films. Directed by Neri Parenti. Stars Paolo Villaggio, Lino Banfi, Massimo Boldi. Screenplay, Castellano and Pipolo; editor, Sergio Montanari; art direction, Mario Ambrosino; music, Bruno Zambrini. Reviewed at Quattro Fontane cinema, Rome, Nov. 4, 1986. Running time: **84 MINS.**

With: Paolo Villaggio, Lino Banfi, Massimo Boldi (the three nephews), Enrico Maria Salerno (uncle), Barbara Scoppa.

Rome — Three short, fat, middle-aged Italo comics join forces in "Thief Academy," a featherweight collection of gags that were old in the Stone Age. The merry trio play the bumbling, over age nephews of a millionaire who gets them a job as self-employed crooks. The setup seems inspired more by Disney's Uncle Scrooge and Huey, Dewey and Louie than by the Three Stooges, who are sophisticated comedians compared to this triumvirate.

Pic has started off as one of the leaders of the Italo film season thanks to the comic book audience, from tykes to teens. With nothing especially Italian about it, pic could move on to related markets offshore.

Funnymen Paolo Villaggio (long associated with director Neri Parenti in the "Fantozzi" series), Lino Banfi and Massimo Boldi, all the same height and rotundity and dressed in identical prep school jackets, appear in the palatial mansion of uncle Enrico Maria Salerno. Bald as Daddy Warbucks and in a motorized leather wheelchair, Salerno offers to train the boys as expert thieves, provided they split the take with him. An athletic black trainer puts them through a grueling course, where naturally they make everything backfire — including a bazooka they shoot backwards. People fall out of third-floor windows, get electrocuted and knocked out by boomerangs. Occasionally animation techniques are used to heighten the impression of the film being a kind of photographed comic strip.

The jokes are old as the hills, but Parenti smartly caters to his audience's minimal attention span and keeps them rolling out thick and fast. Disappointingly, none of the thesps is given an individual personality, so even work by veteran gagman Villaggio is totally anonymous. Pic was obviously lensed quickly, but technical credits are adequate.
— *Yung.*

Notte d'Estate con Profilo Greco, Occhi a Mandorla e Odore di Basilico
(Summer Night With Greek Profile, Almond Eyes And Scent Of Basil)
(ITALIAN-COLOR)

A Medusa release of an A.M.A./Leone Films/Medusa Distribuzione coproduction, in collaboration with Reteitalia. Produced by Gianni Minervini. Written and directed by Lina Wertmüller. Stars Mariangela Melato, Michele Placido. Camera (Cinecittà color), Camillo Bazzoni; editor, Luigi Zitta; music, Dangiò-Greco; art direction, Enrico Job; costumes, Valentino; associate producer, Elio Scardamaglia. Reviewed at Ariston Cinema, Rome, Nov. 10, 1986. Running time: 95 MINS.
The Signora .... Mariangela Melato
Giuseppe Catania .... Michele Placido
Salvatore Cantalamessa . Roberto Herlitzka
His assistant .... Massimo Wertmüller

Rome — A paradisiacal Sardinian island is once more the setting for the battle between the sexes and classes in Lina Wertmüller's "Summer Night With Greek Profile, Almond Eyes And Scent Of Basil." All resemblance to the director's "Swept Away By A Strange Destiny In The Blue August Sea" (1974) is purely intentional, down to casting "Swept Away" star Mariangela Melato as a terrible Milanese capitalist and pairing her off against Sicilian brute Michele Placido, repping the have-nots.

It's obviously a subject the Wertmüller never tires of finding twists to, and to pic's credit the femme industrialist verbally clobbers the bandit in some of pic's wittiest dialog, on a par with anything the director has written. But once the basic situation is set up, "Summer Night" proves a disappointment. It wafts away on the breeze with no place to go, leaving even the director's fans with a feeling they've heard the melody, performed better, before.

In this update of the class war, the super-rich from Northern Italy, tired of being kidnaped by Sardinian bandits and held for extravagant ransoms, charge the imperious Signora (Melato) with turning the tables on bandit leader Giuseppe Catania (Placido). Once rounded up by unmarked helicopters on a barren island, the good-looking young bandit is trussed in designer chains and transported to the lady's fabulous island villa. With the assistance of one-eyed, one-armed Roberto Herlitzka and Massimo Wertmüller, Melato heckles and torments her victim, then proposes to release him for $100,000,000. After an escape attempt, numerous verbal parleys, and an endless night at the side of the Signora, he agrees to pay up — but only to turn the tables once more in a forgettable finale.

Melato is in top form here and steals the show with paradoxes worthy of Oscar Wilde, beginning with the irony that this degraded rep of the undernourished classes is richer than she is and wears Valentino leather jackets. There is really no contest between the two, as the hogtied and blinkered Placido (who only gets a look at his captor in the final scene) can't hold a candle to Melato's glamorous, articulate, cocky millionairess. Next to her stock brokers and managers, his ruthless kidnapers are primitive stuff. The idea of the crook as failed capitalist may go back to Bertolt Brecht, but Wertmüller dishes it up wittily and, irony of ironies, has audiences walk away from "Summer Night" firmly on Melato's side.

In this pic, where violence is limited to drawing room insults prefaced by "Excuse me, but...," feminists may be pleased to find all the cards stacked in the Signora's favor. It just doesn't make for a very dramatic film, and the lack of tension takes its toll as "Summer Night" winds down to a predictable, ho-hum conclusion.

Visually pic is superb publicity for Sardinia as a Blue Lagoon resort, with special mention owing to Enrico Job's fantasy sets lifted from 1,001 Nights. Melato's Valentino gowns could have done with a little less self-sponsorship in the dialog.
— *Yung.*

Chopping Mall
(Killbots)
(COLOR)

Unappealing mixture of in-jokes and horror.

A Concorde Pictures release of a Concorde/Trinity Pictures production. Produced by Julie Corman. Directed by Jim Wynorski. Screenplay, Wynorski, Steve Mitchell; camera (Deluxe color; Foto-Kem processing; Filmhouse prints), Tom Richmond; editor, Leslie Rosenthal; music, Chuck Cirino; sound, Walt Martin; art direction, Carol Clements; Killbots created by Robert Short; production manager-associate producer, Charles Skouras 3d; assistant director, Kristen Peterson; second unit director, Mitchell; associate producer, Ginny Nugent; optical effects, Motion Opticals; special makeup effects, Anthony Showe. Reviewed at RKO Warner 1 theater, N.Y., Nov. 14, 1986. (MPAA Rating: R.) Running time: 76 MINS.
Allison .... Kelli Maroney
Ferdy .... Tony O'Dell
Michael .... John Terlesky
Boyfriend .... Russell Todd
Paul Bland .... Paul Bartel
Mary Bland .... Mary Woronov
Walter Paisley .... Dick Miller
Linda .... Karrie Emerson
Suzy .... Barbara Crampton
Leslie .... Suzee Slater
Greg .... Nick Segal
Also with: Gerrit Graham, Mel Welles, Angela Aames.

"Chopping Mall" is a wafer-thin horror picture which relies overmuch on the current trend towards cameos and in-jokes in place of substance. Its 76 minutes length is mainly padding rather than trim. Alternately titled "R.O.B.O.T.," pic was released in March as "Killbots" and subsequently given its silly "Chopping Mall" moniker.

Premise is an inferior update of Frank De Felitta's well-done 1973 telefilm "Trapped" that featured James Brolin trapped overnight in a department store with six Doberman guard dogs. This time around, eight teens are caught in a shopping mall overnight with three malfunctioning guard robots.

Opening reels include many unfunny, knowing references for film buffs, with guest stars Paul Bartel and Mary Woronov in their "Eating Raoul" characterizations and even Dick Miller supposedly in his "A Bucket Of Blood" role. When the teens search for weapons to defend themselves, they break into Peckinpah's Sporting Goods store.

Such attempts at humor peter out as film slides quickly into the regimented horror format of the robots killing off the youngsters gruesomely one by one. Highlight in the gore department is when ultra-busty Suzee Slater's head is blown to smithereens, a scene the filmmakers liked enough to reprise during the end credits.

While Slater handily wins the big bosoms contest this time around for director Jim Wynorski (who rivals Frank Tashlin and Russ Meyer in this fetish), Barbara Crampton of "Re-Animator" and "From Beyond" is the best screamer. Lead player Kelli Maroney has lost the freshness and cuteness of her similar role in "Night Of The Comet" and is awkwardly poised between teen and adult parts.

Robert Short's "killbots" and other technical credits are functional. Pic briefly segues into the territory of George A. Romero's "Dawn Of The Dead" midway through, but lacks that film's social satire. — *Lor.*

An American Tail
(ANIMATED-COLOR)

Corny feature for kids only.

A Universal Pictures release of a Steven Spielberg presentation from Amblin Entertainment. Produced by Don Bluth, John Pomeroy, Gary Goldman. Executive producers, Spielberg, David Kirschner, Kathleen Kennedy, Frank Marshall. Directed by Bluth. Screenplay, Judy Freudberg, Tony Geiss, from a story by Kirschner, Freudberg, Geiss; created by Kirschner; designed and storyboarded by Bluth; Deluxe color; music, James Horner; original songs, Cynthia Weil, Horner, Barry Mann; associate producers, Kate Barker, Deborah Jelin; assistant directors, G. Sue Shakespeare, David Steinberg. Reviewed at the Samuel Goldwyn Theater, Beverly Hills, Nov. 12, 1986. (MPAA Rating: G.) Running time: 80 MINS.
Voices: Cathianne Blore (Bridget), Dom DeLuise (Tiger), John Finnegan (Warren T. Rat), Phillip Glasser (Fievel Mousekewitz), Amy Green (Tanya Mousekewitz), Madeline Kahn (Gussie Mausheimer), Pat Musick (Tony Toponi), Nehemiah Persoff (Papa Mousekewitz), Christopher Plummer (Henri), Neil Ross (Honest John), Will Ryan (Digit), Erica Yohn (Mama Mousekewitz).

Hollywood — "An American Tail" represents one of the rare attempts these days to do serious, richly textured, old-fashioned animation in a feature film format. Unfortunately, the quality of the drawing and visual design merely emphasize the gaping distance between those artistic elements and the script, which stands as a model of yawn-inducing predictability. Steven Spielberg's name as presenter and "quality" aura surrounding the production make this an automatic b.o. magnet for the holiday kiddie trade, but anyone over the age of 12 will likely experience more boredom than pleasure.

Director-designer Don Bluth is clearly devoted to maintaining classical standards of animation in these days of pervasive blandness and computerization in the field; his characters are expressive, the backgrounds are vividly colorful and often strikingly imagined and executed, and the entire venture bespeaks an artist's care.

Even the premise seems ambitious on paper, as the film endeavors to tell the story of Russian immigrants, who happen in this case to be mice of the Mousekewitz clan, and their flight in the late 1800s to the United States, where Papa Mousekewitz insists, "There are no cats."

Cartoons with ambitions even this noble are as rare as Spielberg films that lose money, but every character and every situation presented herein have been seen a thousand times before.

The mouse-vs.-cat stand-off is as old as animation itself, Dom DeLuise's friendly feline is uncomfortably close to the Cowardly Lion in concept, a little bug smacks directly of Jiminy Cricket, and assorted villains are straight out of Dickens by way of Damon Runyon.

Using every cliché in the book, tale is told of how little Fievel Mousekewitz becomes separated from his family during a storm at sea, then makes his way through the cat-ridden, treachery-filled jungles of Manhattan before inevitably being reunited with his kin. By-the-numbers plotting is enough to drive an adult to utter distraction.

If one didn't have to sit through the inane musical numbers and insipid dialog, there would be plentiful delight to be derived from gazing at any number of Bluth's drawings, which often employ bold use of color and imaginative renderings of New York City before the turn of the century.

Bottom line is that an album of full-color frame enlargements from the film would be more edifying than the picture itself.—*Cart.*

Il Caso Moro
(The Moro Affair)
(ITALIAN-COLOR)

A Columbia (Italy) release of a Yarno Cinematografica production. Produced by Mauro Berardi. Directed by Giuseppe Ferrara. Stars Gian Maria Volonté. Screenplay, Robert Katz, Armenia Balducci, Ferrara, from Katz' book "Days Of Wrath;" camera (color), Camillo Bassoni; editor, Roberto Perpignani; art direction, Francesco Frigeri; costumes, Laura Vaccari; music, Pino Donaggio. Reviewed at Archimede Cinema, Rome, Nov. 18, 1986. Running time: **110 MINS.**

With: Gian Maria Volonté (Aldo Moro), Margarita Lozano (Eleanora Moro), Mattia Sbragia, Bruno Zanin, Consuelo Ferrara, Enrica Maria Modugno, Enrica Rosso, Maurizio Donadoni (terrorists); Daniele Dublino, Piero Vida, Bruno Corazzari, Gabriele Villa, Francesco Carnelutti, Paolo M. Scalondro, Dante Biagioni (politicians).

Rome — Giuseppe Ferrara's fast-paced political thriller "The Moro Affair" shows once more how real events in Italy seem to make better stories than invented ones. This screen version of Robert Katz' "Days Of Wrath," a documented investigation of the 1978 kidnaping and murder of Christian Democrat leader Aldo Moro, sparked violent controversy around the country even before it began playing to packed houses in Milan. Daily frontpage headlines have something to do with pic's fast start, but local auds obviously are intrigued by the case, many details of which have never been cleared up. Pic looks headed for major b.o. onshore, and its subject is fascinating enough to carry over into other markets, particularly in light of current concern with terrorism.

The terrorists responsible for the Moro kidnaping were members of the then numerous Red Brigades. The authors of the crime are now behind bars, but film's reach is much wider. In addition to reconstructing the mechanics of the kidnaping, "Moro" turns a critical eye on reactions in the political world of the time, painting a gamut of characters ranging from some cynical, self-serving Christian Democrats who view the kidnaping only in terms of party politics, to the split in Parliament between those who insisted on keeping a hard line with the terrorists (practically everybody) and a few, like Craxi's Socialist party, willing to bargain out an exchange to save Moro's life.

The real dialog, or lack of it, isn't between the Red Brigades and the Italian state, but between Moro and members of his party, most of whom are shown to have abandoned their leader in his hour of need without too much ado.

Although scripters Ferrara, Katz and Armenia Balducci have done their painstaking best to reconstruct all this objectively, total impartiality is impossible and the issues are loaded. Part of the controversy it has stirred regards pic's tendency to favor the policy not chosen; i.e., dealing with the terrorists. This comes out in the sympathy with which Moro is depicted. In Gian Maria Volonté's sensitive performance, his second shot at the role (the first was a grotesque caricature of Moro in Elio Petri's "Todo Modo"), the aging politician is a humble, pious man dedicated to service of his country, and found martyrdom for it. This saintly figure is pitted against stupid, repugnant politicians and generals who decide his fate between ministerial offices and the Masonic lodge of the P2.

Ferrara skillfully balances characters and forces to build up a complex global impression of power politics, emotional stress (Margarita Lozano as Moro's strongwilled wife is especially good), and the basic helplessness of the self-convinced, sloganeering terrorists, who are murderous cogs in the wheel of the embroiled Italian state, but in some ways also its victims. Pic's point of view and occasional speculation obviously will have their detractors, but its bulldog determination to bring one of the country's messiest political tragedies out of comfortable oblivion makes it hard to ignore.

Technically, film is well-lensed and briskly paced. — *Yung.*

Modern Girls
(COLOR)

Teen gabfest is way boring.

An Atlantic Releasing Corp. release. Produced by Gary Goetzman. Executive producers, Thomas Coleman, Michael Rosenblatt. Directed by Jerry Kramer. Screenplay, Laurie Craig; camera (United Color Labs), Karen Grossman; editor, Mitchell Sinoway; music, Jay Levy, Ed Arkin; production design, Laurence Bennett; art direction, Joel Lang; set decorator, Jill Ungar; sound, Steve Nelson; costumes, Beverly Klein; choreographer, Sarah Elgart; assistant director, Mary Ellen Woods; casting, Paul Ventura. Reviewed at Atlantic screening room, L.A., Nov. 18, 1986. (MPAA Rating: PG-13.) Running time: **84 MINS.**

Margo	Daphne Zuniga
Kelly	Virginia Madsen
Cece	Cynthia Gibb
Clifford/Bruno X	Clayton Rohner
Ray	Chris Nash

Hollywood — Teen pics can be amusing, clever, cute, endearing, lively, sappy and, occasionally, memorable. Alas, none such qualities can be found in 84 minutes of "Modern Girls," a picture so innocuous, even its target audience will find it dull. B.o. looks weak.

Drawn-out story revolves around a one-night adventure of three comely teenage girls out for a good time in the downtown L.A. club scene.

There's vulnerable Kelly (Virginia Madsen), starry-eyed Cece (Cynthia Gibb) and pragmatic Margo (Daphne Zuniga), roommates whose collective credo is: "We never pay for parking. We never carry cash. We never pay for drinks. We never stand in line."

With standards like these, why do mothers worry?

Dialog doesn't rise much above this kind of idiom and most of the time is considerably less alliterative.

One evening while Madsen's out panting after a disk jockey who will pant after anything, along comes Clifford (Clayton Rohner), the date she's stood up. The perennial nice guy, Rohner gets suckered into chauffeuring her two buddies around to their favorite hotspots — finding himself listening to Zuniga's woes about men and Gibb's obsession with a British punker, Bruno X (also played by Rohner).

"Modern Girls" works against its purpose of entertaining teenagers by depicting how truly boring those years can be.

The girls fill our, and Rohner's, ears, with silly talk about nothing meaningful, surrounded by other dull teenagers on the prowl for more empty experiences in successive scenes.

Story reaches bottom when Madsen, the kind of milky-skinned, blond beauty boys dream about, is sprawled on a pool table and drugged out talking about the parents she never knew to a dozen lecherous middle-aged men who are itching to pounce on her bones.

Despite the winsomeness of the cast, none of the actors is particularly distinguishable, although Rohner does a credible job in a dual role as the pushover, smitten suitor and as a low-class British rocker with a most unique accent.

On the plus side, the rock 'n' roll score is kept under control. The music is constant, but it doesn't overpower the action — a rarity for such films. — *Brit.*

Solarbabies
(COLOR)

Futuristic tale is a derivative dud.

An MGM Entertainment Co. release of a Brooksfilms production. Produced by Irene Walzer, Jack Frost Sanders. Directed by Alan Johnson. Screenplay, Walon Green, Douglas Anthony Metrov; camera (Metrocolor), Peter MacDonald; editor, Conrad Buff; music, Maurice Jarre; production design, Anthony Pratt; art director, Don Dossett; set decorator, Graham Sumner; costumes, Bob Ringwood; sound mixer (Dolby), Jim Willis; visual effects, Richard Edlund; assistant director, Juan Carlos L. Rodero; casting, Pennie Du Pont, Meg Simon/Fran Kumin. Reviewed at Lorimar-Telepictures, L.A., Nov. 20, 1986. (MPAA Rating: PG-13). Running time: **94 MINS.**

Grock	Richard Jordan
Terra	Jami Gertz
Jason	Jason Patric
Daniel	Lukas Haas

Metron . . . . James Le Gros
Rabbit . . . . Claude Brooks
Tug . . . . Peter DeLuise
Gavial . . . . Peter Kowanko
Darstar . . . . Adrian Pasdar
Shandray . . . . Sarah Douglas
The Warden . . . . Charles Durning

———

Hollywood — This futuristic teenage morality tale pitting good against evil plods along unconvincingly as it swiftly becomes more laughable than plausible. Stillborn concept barely makes the slightest pretension of originality while conjuring key aspects of some of the biggest hits of the past few years. It's a dud.

The force is back — this time in the shape of a magical sphere named Bodhi. The orb has come to earth during a gloomy period in which a parched planet suffers from both the absence of abundant water and gestapo rule of the Protectorate.

Bodhi turns up near a bleak orphanage on a barren terrain in the midst of nowhere. While youngsters housed in the facility are manipulated towards ultimate obedience and service to the state, some honorably rebel in an attempt to maintain free-spirited humanness while others capitulate to their darker sides.

Discovered after an unauthorized confrontation between these two groups in a roller skateball contest, the sphere assumes a guiding persona role that inevitably recalls youthful responses to a lovable extraterrestrial of another pic. About the size of a bowling ball — but dressed up visually with postproduction special effects — Bodhi even makes electronic sounds that only the nice kids understand.

Dubbed the Solarbabies for team skating purposes, these five teens and young Lukas Haas are propelled into action when one Darstar steals the orb and heads for the outside world. Tyrannical police chieftain Richard Jordan sends his men in pursuit in ridiculously styled vehicles that make one wonder for a moment if this Brooksfilms outing was actually a "Springtime Hitler" spoof.

However, it's readily apparent that the pic takes itself seriously but can't find a way out of the dramatic desert. Story is virtually abandoned — save for its most simplistic right versus wrong framework — as production design dominates once chase is underway.

As film takes on even more of a "Mad Max" quality, characters enter the Tiretown village. Inventive construction of this haunting post-industrial factory captures eerie moods of the dismal period filmmakers are depicting.

Pursuit of the Bodhi leads to a climactic confrontation between an octopus-like robot and the sphere. Orb triumphs; baddies are felled; and the universe's ultimate authority is reinstated. A pic that easily keeps one on the edge of his watch finally concludes.

Maurice Jarre's score exceeds the material here. Alan Johnson's direction seems weakest with the teen thesps. Charles Durning's nominal part as orphanage warden is forgettable. —*Tege.*

———

Firewalker
(COLOR)

———

Clumsy comic adventure.

———

A Cannon Group release of a Golan-Globus production. Produced by Menahem Golan and Yoram Globus. Executive producers, Norman Aladjem, Jeffrey M. Rosenbaum. Directed by J. Lee-Thompson. Screenplay, Robert Gosnell from a story by Gosnell, Rosenbaum, Aladjem; camera (TVC color), Alex Phillips; editor, Richard Marx; music, Gary Chang; production design, Jose Rodriguez Granada; sound (Ultrastereo), Barney Cabral, Bruce Stambler, Michael Wilhoit; set decorator, Poppy Cannon; assistant costume designer, Poppy Cannon; assistant directors, Russ Harling, Javier Carreno; associate producer, Carlos Gil; casting, Robert MacDonald. Reviewed at the Cannon screening room, L.A. Nov. 19, 1986. (MPAA Rating: PG.) Running time: **104 MINS.**
MINS.
Max Donigan . . . . Chuck Norris
Leo Porter . . . . Lou Gossett
Patricia Goodwyn . . . . . . Melody Anderson
Tall Eagle . . . . Will Sampson
El Coyote . . . . Sonny Landham
Corky Taylor . . . . John Rhys-Davies
Boggs . . . . Ian Abercrombie
   Also with: Richard Lee-Sung, Zaide S. Gutierrez, Alvaro Carcano, John Hazelwood.

Hollywood — Chuck Norris' latest outing for Cannon suffers from boilerplate scripting that sabotages whatever hope there may have been that a buddy pic with the estimable Lou Gossett would be compelling. Duo moves predictably through a search-for-the-gold yarn that is devoid of suspense. Pic should move swiftly through the b.o. turnstile.

Adventuring team is joined early on by Melody Anderson in basic setup for the search to find an Aztec temple. Her involvement all too quickly degenerates into a clumsy vehicle for a series of Pauline's perils intended to validate basically meaningless action scenes.

Anderson takes the two guys along into Indian country where they encounter one Will Sampson. He provides the magical protection and warning of dangers that lie ahead. His involvement, however, is all to brief as trio moves toward the jungle once the villainous El Coyote (Sonny Landham) is introduced.

Not unexpectedly, story pauses long enough for a lengthy barroom brawl that gives Norris time to dispatch at least a dozen locals with karate kicks. It could be a high point — if Norris devotees go looking for martial arts action.

Disconnected scenes continue unfolding as a train ride to the back country — with the three disguised as members of the clergy — brings them closer to the temple. Strange detour, however, finds them in the hands of natives bent on beheading Norris and Gossett.

With the blade hovering above Norris' head, an old Marine sidekick (John Rhys-Davis) appears to save the day. Tale bogs down in a boring bit of drunken reminiscing before action resumes.

Back in the countryside, Gossett disappears as Norris whines, "This whole idea was stupid, stupid." He might have been talking about the entire picture.

Pressing on nonetheless, everybody inevitably ends up inside the temple where the gold is. The evil El Coyote seems at first to have the upper hand as he prepares to sacrifice Anderson in a bloody slaying, but alas Norris and Gossett emerge just in time to prevent the dagger from being plunged into her chest — or was it to untie her before the railroad train ran over her?

In any case, inner temple action provides unconvincing resolution to a strained tale. Overstaging is especially in evidence here, as it often is throughout.

Temple scenes and early ones inside a cave especially are marred by fakish environments that do nothing to enhance the credibility of the story. —*Tege.*

———

The Wraith
(COLOR)

———

Hotrod actioner for boys.

———

A New Century/Vista Film Co. release. Produced by John Kemeny. Executive producer, Buck Houghton. Written and directed by Mike Marvin. Camera (Metrocolor), Reed Smoot; editors, Scott Conrad, Gary Rocklin; art director, Dean Tschetter; set decorator, Michele Starbuck; costumes, Elinor Bardach, Glenn Ralston; sound, Richard Portman, Robert Glass, Bob Minkler; music, Michael Hoenig, J. Peter Robinson; visual effects, VCE Inc./Peter Kuran; assistant director, Leon Dudevoir; second unit camera, Chuck Colwell; associate producer, Jeffrey Sudzin; casting, Ilene Starger. Reviewed at the Hollywood Pacific, L.A., Nov. 21, 1986. (MPAA Rating: PG-13.) Running time: **92 MINS.**
The Wraith/Jake . . . . Charlie Sheen
Packard . . . . Nick Cassavetes
Loomis . . . . Randy Quaid
Keri . . . . Sherilyn Fenn
Oggie . . . . Griffin O'Neal
Skank . . . . David Sherrill
Gutterboy . . . . Jamie Bozian
Rughead . . . . Clint Howard
Billy . . . . Matthew Barry
Minty . . . . Chris Nash

———

Hollywood — "The Wraith" features the relatives of several famous actors and as many as three times the number of stuntmen, most of whom drive their souped-up cars into oblivion for the duration of this epic.

But as long as the producers are willing to indulge the American male's fascination with fast cars and car chases, there will be American males willing to pay the price to be indulged. Filmmakers should expect to break even.

It doesn't take long to figure out that "The Wraith" is the ominous-looking Turbo Interceptor (a Dodge PPG pace car) that mysteriously materializes one day on the roads outside a small Arizona town to challenge a gang of local car thieves, led by chief thug Packard (Nick Cassavetes).

The gang's idea of amusement is to force other hotrodders to race and then when the suckers lose, Cassavetes and company take possession of the loser's car.

Being a bully in the worst way, and it seems also the biggest guy around, Cassavetes easily runs roughshod over his band of grease monkeys. Among them is an amusing pair of mush brains, Skank (David Sherrill) and Gutterboy (Jamie Bozian), who drink lubricating oil to get their jollies and also have the only funny lines of dialog.

There's also Cassavetes' girl, Keri (Sherilyn Fenn), the cutest thing on skates at the local hamburger stand whose affections for a new guy raise Cassavetes' ire to an abnormal level.

He and his merry band of punks run up against the Turbo one night — and lose. The sacrificial member is Oggie (Griffin O'Neal), who crashes over a cliff in a fiery ball only to be found minutes later with his dead body completely intact and unscarred.

This scenario is repeated several times throughout the film, whereby gang members are mercifully eliminated and Cassavetes' power over the highways diminished.

Lending a sort of tongue-in-cheek authoritative air to the proceedings is Randy Quaid as the town's lieutenant, giving filmmakers more cause to have more cars do more chasing.

The action is not suspenseful nor the story particularly original, but pictures like this always manage to entertain on the simplest level since the pyrotechnics are usually fun to watch.

For the girls, there's a saccharine love story that revolves around Fenn and Charlie Sheen, who smacks more of his parentage than do the other actors.—*Brit.*

———

Impure Thoughts
(COLOR)

———

Perceptive fantasy comedy about Catholic schooldays.

———

An ASA Communications release. Executive producers, Kirk K. Smith, Stan M. Wakefield. Produced by William VanDerKloot, Michael A. Simpson, Michael J. Malloy. Directed by Simpson. Screenplay, Malloy, Simpson; camera (Eastmancolor), VanDerKloot; editor, VanDerKloot, Wade Watkins; music, James Oliverio; production design; Guy Tuttle; sound design, David Terry; Sister of Purgatory narration by Dame Judith Anderson. Reviewed at USA Cinemas Copley Place, Boston, Nov. 12, 1986. (No MPAA Rating.) Running time: **83 MINS.**

Danny Stubbs ....John Putch
William Miller ....Terry Beaver
Kevin Harrington ....Brad Dourif
Steve Barrett ....Lane Davies
Young Bill ....Benji Wilhoite
Young Danny ....J. J. Sacha
Young Kevin ....Sam McPhaul
Young Steve ....Jason Jones
Sister Juliet ....Mary McDonough
Father Minnelli ....Joe Conley
Also with: Mary Nell Santacroce (Sister Gertrude), Charlie Hill (Bill Miller Sr.), Carmen Thomas (Marie Borkowsky), Sandra Dorsey, Randi Layne, Muriel Moore, Carol Haynes, Dennis Harrington, Bob, Bost, Shirlene Foss.

Boston — "Impure Thoughts" plays like a Catholic version of "The Twilight Zone." An opening bit of dialog has Dame Judith Anderson defining purgatory followed by a grey, virtually featureless room. This is the waiting room to the afterlife where the four main characters bide their time waiting to be cleansed of their sins.

There's Danny (John Putch) who was killed in Vietnam, Steve (Lane Davies) who's become a gay atheist, Bill (Terry Beaver) the businessman and Kevin (Brad Dourif) the good husband and father. Since they are different ages and were never all close friends, they try to figure out what they have in common, other than having attended St. Jude's parochial school in West Virginia in the early '60s.

In flashback we get to see a series of blackouts of what life was like for students of a Catholic school in that time and place. The jokes are somewhat predictable and many will be lost on non-Catholic audiences.

As for Catholics, many may well be amused, and will appreciate that in spite of the jokes and complaints, the positive side of church life is stressed as well.   •

Davies' character does much of the carping, having authored "The Catholic Church: From Latin To Lunacy." Dourif argues for the benefits of their shared education, but the flashbacks also show him to be the nerd of the group. Whether Dourif's remaining the only practicing Catholic of the four is a comment on the result of a parochial school education is left for the viewer to judge.

Most of the film is spent either at the school or in purgatory, which prove to be rather unappealing locations, particularly with the low whine heard throughout the purgatory scenes. It is those few flashbacks outside the school that are the highlights of the film.

The Springfield, Mass., distribu-

tor of "Impure Thoughts" is attempting to tap into Boston's large Catholic audience. Without a strong word-of-mouth campaign, this is a picture that may have a difficult time reaching the audience that would most appreciate it. —*Kimm.*

Descente aux enfers
(Descent Into Hell)
(FRENCH-COLOR)

An AAA release of a Partner's Prod./La Cinq Prod. coproduction. Produced by Ariel Zeitoun. Directed by Francis Girod. Stars Sophie Marceau, Claude Brasseur. Screenplay, Girod, Jean-Loup Dabadie, based on the novel "The Wounded And The Slain," by David Goodis; camera (Eastmancolor), Charlie Van Damme; editor, Geneviève Winding; music, Georges Delerue; sound, André Hervée, Claude Villand; art direction, Jacques Bufnoir; assistant director, Olivier Horlait; production manager, Daniel Deschamps. Reviewed at the Marignan-Concorde theater, Paris, Nov. 7, 1986. Running time: **90 MINS.**

Alan Kolber ....Claude Brasseur
Lola Kolber ....Sophie Marceau
Theophile Bijou ....Sidiki Bakaba
Philippe Devignat ....Hyppolyte Girardot
Elvis ....Gérard Rinaldi
Lucette Beulemans ....Marie Dubois
Mrs. Burns ....Betsy Blair
Commissioner Redoux .....Umban U'kset

Paris — Third local adaptation in as many years of a tale by Yank pulp novelist David Goodis, who is something of a cult figure here, Francis Girod's "Descent Into Hell" never lives up to its title. Colorful Haitian locations and glossy production tend to work texturally against this description of an apparently ill-matched couple's struggle to deal with personal obsessions, their marital gulf and the threats of blackmail that ironically unite them.

Claude Brasseur and Sophie Marceau are the couple, separated as much by age as experience, who take a sort of second honeymoon in Haiti with vague hopes of defrosting the chill that separates them.

Brasseur's a blocked mystery novelist who starts boozing again when he realizes that the distant and somewhat frigid Marceau is not ready to thaw out. Sullen and secretive, she kills her boredom in a quick fling with another hotel guest.

One heavily alcoholic night, Brasseur cuts the throat of a mugger in self-defense and subsequently finds himself being blackmailed by a bizarre couple (Sidiki Bakaba and Marie Dubois), who have evidence of Brasseur's "crime."

Jolted from their mutual torpor, Brasseur and Marceau, who herself harbors the traumatic memory of an act of violence in self-defense (against a would-be rapist), find common ground for a new relationship in their attempts to undo the blackmail scheme.

Scripter Jean-Loup Dabadie dis-

plays his usual penchant for slick gab and colorful secondary characters, but not much understanding for the subterranean workings of *film noir* nightmare and psychology. Girod's direction is never more than blandly proficient, unable to exteriorize the hellish states of mind of its personages.

Brasseur and Marceau (who played father and daughter in the smash Gaumont "La Boum" features) are not very credible as a tortured couple. Some of the supporting parts are amusing, but largely expendable. —*Len.*

Kamikaze Hearts
(COLOR)

Tiresome docudrama about porn performers.

A Legler/Bashore production. Produced by Heinz Legler. Directed by Juliet Bashore. Features Tigr Mennett, Sharon Mitchell. Written and conceived by Bashore and Mennett; camera (color), david Golia; editor, John Knoop; art-set direction, Hans Fuss, Miriam Tinguely; music, Paul M. Young, Walt Fowler; sound, Leslie Schatz; coproducers, Sharon Hennessey, Bob Rivkin. Reviewed at San Francisco Film Arts Festival, Roxie theater, Nov. 8, 1986. Running time: **87 MINS.**

San Francisco — "Kamikaze Hearts" sold out two performances at the second annual S.F. Film Arts Festival. Picture, a story of lesbian lovers working in the porn industry in Frisco, was billed as a "conceptualized" docudrama based on real life experiences of performers involved.

The film-within-a-film yarn, much of it with verité dialog and plenty of frontal nudity, quickly grows tiresome because neither of the principals, Sharon Mitchell as the porn star and Tigr Mennett as her lover, is particularly interesting or has much to say worth noting.

Occasionally, some of the fringe characters have some insightful comments to make about their line of work; an overview of pornpic production might have made for a revealing docu, but "Hearts" lacks the soul for that chore.

Much of the effort smacks of conceit, a trait rendering picture unlikely fodder for wide pornhouse distribution and overall a bit too harsh for any other kind of playoff.

Technical credits are acceptable for a low-budgeter. —*Herb.*

Neon Maniacs
(COLOR)

Idiotic horror filler.

A Bedford Entertainment release of a Cimmaron production. Produced by Steven Mackler, Chris Arnold. Executive producers, H. Frank Dominguez, Bernard E. Goldberg.

Directed by Joseph Mangine. Screenplay, Mark Patrick Carducci; camera (Cinema color), Mangine, Oliver Wood; editor, Timothy Snell; music, Kendall Schmidt; sound, Peter Bentley, Ed White; art direction, Katherine Vallin; special makeup effects, Makeup Effects Labs, Allan A. Apone, Douglas J. White; special effects, Image Engr.; assistant director, Linda Graeme; costume design, Joseph Porro; casting, Paul Bengston, David Cohn; associate producer-production manager, Herb Linsey; associate producers, Bran Arandjelovich, Edwin Picker, Brian Leonard. Reviewed at RKO Warner 2 theater, N.Y., Nov. 14, 1986. (MPAA Rating: R.) Running time: **91 MINS.**

Steven ....Allan Hayes
Nathalie ....Leilani Sarelle
Paula ....Donna Locke
Devin ....Victor Elliot Brandt

Even as standards for plausibility and coherent storytelling in horror films continue to degenerate, "Neon Maniacs" represents another low in the genre. Idiotic monster film is an overlong timekiller with no redeeming features.

Nonstory concerns a polyglot group of armed monsters who kill a bunch of high schoolers out on a date one night in San Francisco. Nathalie (Leilani Sarelle) improbably survives, but the police don't believe her tale of monsters. She teams up with boyfriend Steven (Allan Hayes) and a precocious student videomaker Paula (Donna Locke) to hunt down and destroy the creatures.

Monsters here look like amateur participants in a best costume contest at a comic book convention, ranging from a Neanderthal man to a humanoid lizard. Where they came from or why they're hanging out together is never questioned or explained. Film presents them as real, though the only logical explanation might be that the heroine had eaten a pepperoni pizza just before bedtime and dreamed them up.

It turns out that water destroys the monsters and film's only true laughs are generated by kids and cops going after them with water pistols. An anachronistic cop (Victor Elliot Brandt) who looks like he escaped from the 1940s also provides a laugh as he holds up the final assault on the monsters' lair when he takes time out to light up his stogie.

Acting is generally poor and cinematographer-turned-director Joseph Mangine has trouble maintaining any interest in the narrative. Lead actress Leilani Sarelle goes through hell but fails miserably at portraying the least bit of being afraid. Audience also goes through hell, being forced to listen to several rotten musical numbers at a costume party's battle of the bands staged at the local high school.
—*Lor.*

Matador
(SPANISH-COLOR)

An Andres Vicente Gomez production. Executive producer, Vicente Gomez. Directed by

Pedro Almodovar. Screenplay, Almodovar, Jesus Ferrere; camera (color), Angel Luis Fernandez; editor, Jose Salcedo; sound, Bernard Orthion; music, Bernardo Bonezzi. Reviewed in competition at Rio Intl. Film Festival, Nov. 21, 1986. Running time: **102 MINS.**

Maria . . . . .Assumpta Serna
Angel . . . . .Antonio Banderas
Diego . . . . .Nacho Martinez
Eva . . . . .Eva Cobo
    Also with: Julieta Serrano, Chus Lampreave, Carmen Maura, Eusebio Poncela and Bibi Andersson.

Rio de Janeiro — In his raw 1985 black comedy, "What Have I Done To Deserve This!" Pedro Almodovar brought a radical, sexually anarchic perspective to bear upon working class life in Madrid. In "Matador," Almodovar displays more polished filmmaking technique, but moves away from social commentary for a frenzied feeding on themes of carnal and blood obsession. The film's pulsing sexuality and mock mystery structure could hook specialty audiences, but those unfamiliar with Spanish society may not fully appreciate some of "Matador's" corrosive, satirical subtexts.

Angel (Antonio Banderas) an emotionally repressed 21-year-old who lives with his conservative harridan of a mother, secretly attends the bullfighting school of Diego (Nacho Martinez), a gored-into-retirement ex-champion matador with the sexual appetite of a lusty bull. Diego supplements his relationship with the gorgeous but vacuous fashion model Eva (Eva Cobo) with diversionary flings, hardcore bondage porn and "snuff" videos and, as it transpires, the occasional murder of pretty girls whom he buries on the grounds of his opulent estate in suburban Madrid.

Eva, as it happens, is Angel's next-door neighbor. Frustrated in his attempt to win the respect of his hero maestro, Angel one night attempts to rape the matador's girlfriend, but fails in humiliating fashion. Nevertheless, the troubled youth confesses to the police and, in spite of Eva's unwillingness to press the case, their mutual obsession with Diego binds them. When young girls are reported missing Angel confesses to their murders and is taken into custody while the police search for evidence. Angel is assigned a feminist lawyer, Maria (Assumpta Serna), who, it turns out, has the greatest obsession of all for the fallen matador.

On the suface, Maria is a woman liberated from the machismo domination of Spanish men. Steely and confident, she takes no nonsense from cops and fights to protect the rights of Angel, who's been shifted to a mental clinic. Secretly, however, Maria has a morbid sexual fascination with the matador Diego, whom she has worshipped for years. Inexorably, the elegant attorney and the matador are swept into a maelstrom of orgasmic and suicidal passion.

Almodovar unfolds this convoluted plot with zig-zagging surrealism and a careening, sordidly erotic energy that effectively undermines the culturally institutionalized repression targeted by the filmmaker. Serna and Martinez stand out as victims of psycho-sexual passion gone amok, while supporting performances are very effective.
　　　　　　　　　　　　　—*Rich.*

The Nutcracker:
The Motion Picture
(COLOR)

Magical adaptation destined to be a holiday classic.

An Atlantic Releasing Corp. release of a Thomas Coleman and Michael Rosenblatt presentation of a Hyperion/Kushner-Locke production. Produced by Willard Carroll, Donald Kushner, Peter Locke, Thomas L. Wilhite. Executive producers, Coleman, Rosenblatt. Directed by Carroll Ballard. Conceived by Kent Stowell, Maurice Sendak from the story by E.T.A. Hoffman. Camera (MGM color), Stephen M. Burum; production, costume design, Maurice Sendak; choreography, staging, Kent Stowell; music, Peter Ilyich Tchaikovsky; editors, John Mutt, Michael Silvers; first assistant director, Eugene Mazzola; art director, Peter Horne; visual film adaptation, Henry Selick; models and miniatures, Rick Heinrichs; additional photography, Hiro Narita; sound, Ben Burtt. Reviewed at Laird Studios, Culver City, Calif., Nov. 21, 1986. (MPAA Rating: G.) Running time: **84 MINS.**

Herr Drosselmeier . . . . .Hugh Bigney
Young Clara . . . . .Vanessa Sharp
Dream Clara . . . . .Patricia Barker
Nutcracker . . . . .Wade Walthall
    Also with: Dancers from the Pacific Northwest Ballet Co.

Hollywood — Despite some moments of disarray, "The Nutcracker: The Motion Picture" is a wonderfully expressive and fanciful film that surely will become a holiday classic for children and adults.

This production of the timeless ballet is not only a beautiful version of the dance, but also incorporates much of the dark-natured story of E.T.A. Hoffman's original fairytale, "The Nutcracker And The Mouse King" — that of a young girl on the threshold of maturity who confronts many of her fears and hopes through a dream about a sinister controller of the universe, Pasha, and her nutcracker prince.

Whereas live performances often have underplayed the sensitive storyline in preference to the dance, the film intricately and subtly delves into the story. The whimsical tale then becomes an outpouring of the young girl's confusion and at the same time exuberance of what is yet to be.

The ballet was first created in Russia in 1890. It was performed by the Imperial Ballet to the newly written score by Tchaikovsky and has become a holiday favorite with many ballet companies.

Bringing it to film obviously had some drawbacks, yet director Carroll Ballard ("The Black Stallion," "Never Cry Wolf") has incorporated special effects adeptly within the staged piece to bring about a finely tuned creation. There are no heavy-handed film effects nor is there just a standard dance production.

This version of "The Nutcracker" ballet was presented first by the Pacific Northwest Ballet in 1983. The company's artistic director, Kent Stowell, his wife, Francia Russell, and Maurice Sendak decided to veer from the often-pat sugarplum ballets to a more darkly intense version that was more true to the Hoffman fairytale. This film version also is very much their creation, with Stowell as choreographer and Sendak credited with production and costume designs.

The filmmakers obviously were intent on bringing out the undertones of the story in this magical setting and they have accomplished it. The only time when this film begins to lose its adept handling of the dance is during the fight scene between the toy soldiers and the mice. In the erupting chaos, the beauty of the dance is lost in a blur of images.

Yet, without a doubt, the movie is an enchanting adventure that will delight audiences for years to come.
　　　　　　　　　　　　　—*Teen.*

Violated
(COLOR)

Inept sexploitation treatment of a serious topic.

A Cinematronics production. Produced and directed by Richard Cannistraro. Screenplay, Cannistraro, Bennet Sims, from story by Cannistraro; camera (TVC color), Skip Roessel; editor, Michael R. Miller; music, Lee Shapiro; sound, Dorielle Rogers, Steven Rogers; production design, Karen Morse; art direction, Howard Kling; production manager, Chris Ingvordsen; additonal photography, Barry Sonnenfeld; casting, Jack Kelly, Ronnie Yeskel; associate producer, Robert Maier. Reviewed on Vestron Video vidcassette, N.Y., Nov. 14, 1986. (No MPAA Rating.) Running time: **88 MINS.**

Kevin McBane . . . . .J.C. Quinn
Lisa Robb . . . . .April Daisy White
Skipper . . . . .John Heard
Jack Diamond . . . . .D. Balin
Shirley Robb . . . . .Kaye Dowd
Judy Engels . . . . .Lisanne Falk
Liz Grant . . . . .Elizabeth Kaitan
Katy Carson . . . . .Carol Francis
    Also with: Samantha Fox, Jonathan Ward, Carl Gordon, Alec Massey, Charles Gilbert, Claude Vincent, Richard Cannistraro, Bill Galarno, Randy Jurgensen.

In "Violated," filmmaker Richard Cannistraro can't seem to make up his mind whether he is making a sexploitation film for grindhouses or a serious treatment of the off-filmed rape topic. Resulting hodgepodge, like so many other unreleased features that surface on vidcassette, plays like an unfinished film bailed out of a lab. Two distinct rape-themed films with this title were made in 1984, the other one acquired by New Line Cinema and renamed "The Ladies Club."

Storyline, which resembles a telefilm but features loads of extraneous nude scenes, has gangsters Jack Diamond (D. Balin) and Frank Lyon (Alec Massey) throwing parties to which young girls are invited and raped. Focus is narrowed here on a young victim, Lisa (April Daisy White), a soap opera actress in New York. Though she doesn't report the incident, her aunt and guardian Shirley (Kaye Dowd) does and it's spread all over the front page when a N.Y. Post reporter badgers the family for info.

Lisa quickly falls in love with the cop on the case, McBane (J.C. Quinn), but the gangsters buy off testimony and ridicule her in front of a grand jury. Film's credibility falls apart completely when gangster boss Zimmerman (Charles Gilbert) hires a hitman to kill the gangster-rapists and cop McBane turns out to be moonlighting as the pro hitman. Film ends abruptly midstream with a fadeout after one of the hits and none of its plot threads resolved.

Actors perform capably in a losing cause, with April Daisy White lending panache to her central role. Picture is not likely to be listed in the resume of John Heard, who is nonetheless excellent in a brief role as a fidgety lowlife who acts as intermediary in hiring the cop-hitman and dreams of someday becoming a hitman himself. —*Lor.*

Rai
(The Opinion)
(ALGERIAN-COLOR)

An ENAPROC production. Written and directed by Said Ali Fettar. Camera (color), Ali Yahyaoui; editor, Rachid Ben Allal; music, Farid Balkhirrat. Reviewed at Carthage Film Days (in competition), Oct. 17, 1986. Running time: **94 MINS.**

Rachid . . . . .Abdelkader Tadjer
Mother . . . . .Salima
Friend . . . . .Hamid Lourari

Tunis — "Rai," a fairly routine Algerian drama about a small-time gangster with a mother complex, has the kind of characters and plotting that might appeal to Arab audiences, but its fest outings look destined to finish with Carthage. Director Said Ali Fettar, who also penned the tale, has two colors in his pallette: black and white, corrupt and innocent, only the hero can't tell them apart. When he realizes the obvious, that his mother is a selfish, greedy shrew who led him down the path of vice, he soon reforms.

Abdelkader Tadjer plays Rachid,

the neighborhood crook, as an un-pleasant, swaggering cock of the walk. Since he has a sympathy quotient of zero, it's hard to be very concerned about his shattering post-prison discovery that his parents are divorced. His kindly old father sadly fills him in on the details of Mom's real nature. After constantly reproaching him for not bringing home enough money, she got a job and spent after-hours in the back room with her employer. Rachid has a number of traumatic flash-backs to the scene. All these repressed memories lead him to drink, but the good offices of honest friends get him back on the right path. — *Yung.*

Argentina, The Broken Silence
(DOCU-COLOR)

A Victor Fridman Prods. release. Produced, directed, edited and camera (color) by Fridman. Narrator, Butch Engle; written by William Winans, Elaine Vergelin, Fridman; associate producer, Luis Cousillas. Reviewed at Film Arts Festival, Roxie theater, San Francisco, Nov. 8, 1986. Running time: 60 MINS.

San Francisco — Two documentaries based on the military terrorism in Argentina in the years 1976-83 have come from San Francisco area independents in the past two years. The first, "Las Madres del Plaza de Mayo," earned an Academy Award nomination in the docu feature category and tells the story with far more compelling impact and lucidity than "Argentina, The Broken Silence."

Victor Fridman is an Argentine who has lived in the Bay area since 1981. With this docu he has tried to cover Argentine history dating back a half century and reflecting the current tone of the people and government. Those latter segs are covered with, in effect, musical photographic poetry.

Picture opens with quick capsulized history and eventually returns to elaborate on several of those eras, including death squad operations and the Falklands war. In effect, there's a doubling-up of some information. Too much ground is covered, and then re-covered, in too short a time. — *Herb.*

Final Mission
(COLOR)

Standard revenge picture.

A Westbrook and M.P. Film presentation; in association with D.S. Pictures, of a Santiago/Maharaj production. Executive producer, Anthony Maharaj; line producer, Tamar Glaeser. Produced and directed by Cirio H. Santiago. Screenplay, Joseph Zucchero, J.M. Avelcana, from story by Maharaj; camera

(Technicolor), Ricardo Remias; editor, Bass Santos; music, George Garvarentz; art direction, Fiel Zabat; second unit director, Maharaj; casting, J.M.G. & Associates. Reviewed on Thorn EMI/HBO vidcassette, N.Y., Sept. 29, 1986. (No MPAA Rating.) Running time: 84 MINS.
With: Richard Young (Vince Deacon), John Ericson (Col. Joshua Cain), Christine L. Tudor, Jason Ross, John Dresden, Karen Ericson, Kaz Garas, E. Danny Murphy, Jack Daniels.

"Final Mission" is a routine action drama about a war vet out for revenge. Filmed by prolific Filipino helmer Cirio H. Santiago at the beginning of 1984, pic bypassed theatrical release for the homevideo market.

Richard Young portrays Vince Deacon, a Vietnam vet living with his family in California, who is suspended from the police force for being ultra-violent with thieves. The punks later boobytrap his boat on a family outing, blowing up his wife and kid. It's revenge time.

A key subplot involves a turncoat who was at odds with Vince back in Laos in 1972 and turns out to be involved with the punks who killed his family. Final reel is a manhunt in a forest with Vince as the prey, heavily influenced by "First Blood."

As usual with a Santiago film (he cranks out about two a year like clockwork), technical credits are good. Acting is okay, with a guest appearance by John Ericson as a military expert who helps Vince figure out who had the explosives expertise to help the punks blow up his boat. — *Lor.*

Play Dead
(COLOR)

Not so nice doggie.

A Troma release of a United Construction production of a Rudine-Wittman film. Executive producer, F.L. Rudine. Directed by Peter Wittman. Screenplay, Lothrop W. Jordan; camera (TVC color), Robert E. Bethard; editor, Eugenie Nicoloff; music, Bob Farrar; sound, John Pritchett; assistant director, Robert Elkins; production manager, Michael Phillips; art direction, Robert A. Burns. Reviewed on Academy Home Ent. vidcassette, N.Y., Oct. 30, 1986. (MPAA Rating: R.) Running time: 86 MINS.
Hester . . . . Yvonne De Carlo
Audrey . . . . Stephanie Dunnam
Jeff . . . . David Cullinane
Det. Otis . . . . Glenn Kezer
Richard . . . . Ron Jackson
Stephen . . . . David Ellzey
Greta the dog . . . . Itself

"Play Dead" is an old-fashioned horror film about a killer dog. Though filmed in Texas in 1981, picture was not released until early this year.

Yvonne De Carlo toplines as Aunt Hester, a rich woman who decides to kill off her relatives. Her sister just died after years in a mental home and Hester was always jealous of her, and in love with sis'

husband who also died. Bringing a rottweiler dog named Greta home from Europe, Hester gives the animal as a gift to her niece Audrey (Stephanie Dunnam) and via supernatural incantations orders the dog to kill Audrey and other family members or innocent bystanders.

Silly film unfolds leisurely as a police investigation with folksy Det. Otis (Glenn Kezer) padding out the running time with his slow-witted tracking down of clues until the dog slips a dose of lye into Otis' Alka-Seltzer. Pic's finale of Hester ironically getting her just desserts is not very exciting but is played twice, once as a flash-forward during the opening credits and later in its proper sequence.

Director Peter Wittman (who later made the comedy "Ellie") uses stop-motion slow motion footage of the dog during each attack, but Greta remains unscary, as does the film itself. Acting is okay, with De Carlo a campy highlight. Oddly, Earl Owensby produced his much-publicized but little-seen 3-D horror opus "Rottweiler" (a.k.a. "Dogs Of Hell") in 1981 also, but neither production was able to extract horror from the noble breed. — *Lor.*

Inside Out
(COLOR)

Unsuccessful portrait of an agoraphobic.

A Sidney Beckerman production. Produced by Beckerman. Directed by Robert Taicher. Screenplay, Taicher, Kevin Bartelme; camera (color), Jack Wallner; editor, David Finfer; music, Peer Raben; sound, Steve Nelson; art direction, Jack Wright 3d; costume design, Arlene Ansel. Reviewed at Chicago Intl. Film Festival, Nov. 1, 1986. (No MPAA Rating.) Running time: 87 MINS.
With: Elliott Gould (Jimmy Morgan), Howard Hesseman, Jennifer Tilly, Beah Richards, Nicole Norman, John Bleifer, Dana Elcar.

Chicago — An interesting idea — psychological study of an agoraphobic in present-day New York City — is brought down by a stilted script and heavy-handed direction.

Elliott Gould plays the hermit, Jimmy Morgan, who hasn't ventured out of his high-rise apartment in several years. He leaves the running of the business to the partner of his late father, spends his time with his daughter (from an earlier divorce) in the apartment, relies on an escort service to supply him with his sexual conquests and even has a drug dealer who makes housecalls.

Surrounded by the luxuries of life, including what seems like a remote control for everything but the toilet, Gould protects himself, screening his calls and checking out guests on his tv screen with a closed-circuit picture from the building's vestibule.

The danger of this lazy existence begins to dawn on Gould when, in rapid succession, he realizes he's blown all his money-market funds on losing sports bets, senses some impropriety in the business and learns from his ex-wife that she and their daughter are moving to Chicago.

Meanwhile, Gould is having trouble hiding his problem from old friend Howard Hesseman, who is on vacation from California. Hesseman keeps asking Gould to go out with him and finally becomes suspicious after a series of rejections.

The other major supporting performer is Jennifer Tilly (Meg's sister), the woman sent over by the escort service. In a pleasant, affecting performance, Tilly's Amy is a California girl oblivious to Jimmy's problems and her unquestioning affection brings him out of his doldrums until, finally, even she can't help.

The film winds up with Jimmy facing up to his illness — and this disaster that his life has become because of it.

But before it progresses that far, the pace of the picture is ruined by terrible dialog (a stereotyped black drug dealer leaves a message that "a heavy snow storm's blowing into town," scenes in which Gould discusses sports events are totally antiseptic, because the dialog is generic) and the romantic scenes with Gould and Tilly never really take off because they're not given anything credible to say to one another.

Helmer Robert Taicher has another, more peculiar problem: he can't seem to find enough interesting things with which to fill the screen. There are far too many tv shots (including a few seconds from a football game with a voiceover that, if meant to be an approximation of Howard Cosell, is a poor one; the millionth picture of tv's sign-off with the playing of the national anthem. By the end of the film, Taicher's extended blackouts — some lasting two to three seconds — become annoying.

Gould, for the first time in a long time, is interesting. He's been phoning in his performances in recent years, but here makes an effort to create a fully rounded character. Ultimately, though, he can't decide exactly how he wants to play Jimmy; in most of the scenes he's the same kind of cynical off-the-cuff character he played in "Mash" or "California Split," but in other, more sober scenes, he becomes almost a manic depressive, physically shaken by the idea of venturing outside. The only warning the viewer has to these mood swings are Taicher's melodramatic excesses — violins rising to crescendo as Gould opens a patio door — so that any tension one might have felt is sabotaged long before the film's climax.—*Camb.*

Zoning
(WEST GERMAN-COLOR)

A Cine Intl. release of a Scala Z film, Munich. Directed by Ulrich Krenkler. Screenplay, Krenkler, Angelika Hacker; camera (color), Nikolaus Starkmeth; editor, Ute Albrecht-Lovell; music, Tangerine Dream; sound, Christian Baudisson; art direction, Thomas V. Klier, P. Ranody. Reviewed at the Chicago Intl. Film Festival, Oct. 30, 1986. Running time: **89 MINS.**
With: Norbert Lamla, Hubertus Gertzen, Vernika Wolff, Rainer Frieb, Dieter Meier, Eleonore Weisgerber.

Chicago — "Zoning" is a German adventure film that works on the same kind of silly logic as American World War II films in which the Japanese and Germans spoke English. The action here involves two men, Ozzy and Düe, who go on a crime spree in a 78-story skyscraper that operates as shopping center and office building. One should not be bothered by the fact that the building is Chicago's State of Illinois Center (16 stories) or that everyone speaks German even though the signs to all the stores are in English. This is not the sort of film in which logic ever gets in the way of plot development.

If you buy that you might also believe that Ozzy and Düe (who want revenge for being fired by the building operator during the construction of the building) can go on a four-day binge in which they make a couple dozen robberies, wear no disguises, never change clothes and still can walk throughout the building without being stopped by the security force. They hide out in an abandoned duct on a basement floor that was forgotten when the building had to reduce its dimensions to conform with local zoning ordinances.

Story follows the pair through four days of escapades, accompanied by fight scenes right out of a junior high school production of "Guys And Dolls." The most ludicrous of those has a security guard karate chopping a shoplifter so hard his fall breaks off half a porcelain bathroom sink, which lands with a decidedly metallic clink.

During the third day, the brooding Ozzy (Hubertus Gertzen) decides the two would make more money by tapping into the building's computer system. With the help of some unopened crates in a storeroom and the world's longest extension cord, he brings a personal computer down to their hideout. This leads the pair to holding up a software company for "vital information," but a window cleaner sees the holdup in progress and Düe (Norbert Lamla) give chase to the roof to apprehend the witness. This is the silliest plot development of all

since the hundred or so people who have been robbed in the previous three days are also witnesses, so why is Düe so worried about the window cleaner?

At this point, the head of security makes the observation that "we've overlooked something." Meanwhile, Ozzy has run into a cleaning lady (Veronika Wolff) who has discovered the hideout and demands a bribe to keep quiet. Eventually, she tries to help them escape, but only one of the robbers makes it out.

Technical credits are below average, with lighting a problem in several scenes. Screenplay, by the aptly named Hacker and director Krenkler, is written at about the third-grade level and, as mentioned, even third-graders won't buy the bogus fight scenes. Tangerine Dream provides the soundtrack, with its usual bit of bloodlessly annoying synth-pop.

"Zoning" has no snap, no sense of humor, trivial character development and a plot that wouldn't even make good crime show fodder.
—*Camb.*

Lisi und der General
(Lisi And The General)
SWISS-COLOR)

A Europa Film Locarno release of a Mark M. Rissi production. Directed by Rissi, Screenplay, Steve Burckhardt, based on the novel "Lisi" by Alexander Heimann; camera (color), Edwin Horak; editor, Evelyne von Rabenau; music, Renato Anselmi; title song, Peter E. Mueller, Pia Emmenegger; production manager, Käthi Hug; stunts, Markus Scharowsky, Verkehrs-Sicherheitszentrum Veltheim, Skischule Lenk. Reviewed at the Frosch Cinema, Zurich, Nov. 6, 1986. Running time: **118 MINS.**
General .... Walo Lüönd
Lisi .... Silvia Silva
Commissar .... Franz Matter
Rosa .... Eva Bendig-Lüönd
Max .... Peter Schneider
Edi .... Manfred Liechti
Katrin .... Sabine Stutzmann
Soldier .... Daniel Ludwig

Zurich — Swiss helmer Mark M. Rissi was represented in competition at this year's Locarno Festival with his partly ethnic, partly fictional documentary, "Ghame Afghan" (The Tragedy Of The Afghan). "Lisi und der General" is a comedy based on a Swiss novel, "Lisi," by Alexander Heimann. It concerns a middle-aged higher-echelon clerk fed up with his routine work and dull family life, who sneaks out of the house during a New Year's Eve party with a whisky bottle and some money, and drives off with no special destination in mind. After sleeping off his hangover in the car, he suddenly meets an attractive redhead the next day who insists on riding with him.

As he happens to have his colonel's cap and coat in the car, she nicknames him "general." It later

turns out the girl was involved in a bank robbery with two accomplices and is on the run, with almost 500,-000 Swiss francs in her bag.

The pair drives to a deserted mountain region almost completely snowed in. They settle in a cabin where they find some provisions. They become lovers. From a nearby Swiss army depot, they steal weapons and ammunition. When they are discovered, they shoot at the police surrounding the cabin, but the adventure takes some unexpected turns, and all ends happily.

Credibility is strained almost through the entire storyline. There are loose ends galore, and the film wavers between realistic action, satire and romantic comedy. Finally, none of these possibilities is realized satisfactorily.

The film's chief asset is the cast — the two leads, to be exact, as there are hardly any other roles of consequence. Walo Lüönd is a seasoned actor who even manages to generate some sparks out of the unconvincing role of the midlife crisis-stuck "general." Swiss stage actress Silvia Silva in her first film role is a looker with a refreshing pertness. Technical credits are okay. —*Mezo.*

Picardia Mexicana Numero Dos
(Mexican Picaresque, Part II)
(MEXICAN-COLOR)

A Peliculas Mexicanas release of a Cima Films production. Directed by Rafael Villaseñor Kuri. Stars Vicente Fernández. Screenplay, Pedro Urdimulas, based on book by Armando Jiménez; camera (color), José Luis Lemus; editor, Max Sánchez. Reviewed at Big Apple Cine 1, N.Y., Nov. 1, 1986. Running time: **95 MINS.**
Nicho .... Vicente Fernández
Rosita .... Marcela Delgado
Macaco .... Héctor Suárez
Sireno .... Lalo (El Mimo)
Don Tilo Aguilar...Pedro Weber (Chatanooga)

The sequel fever that hit Hollywood has run amok in Mexico. Very few pics — no matter how they do at the boxoffice — escape the ignominy of being sequel-less.

The first "Picardia Mexicana" film, directed by Abel Salazar, was based on the book of the same name by Armando Jiménez, a compendium of idiosyncratic Mexican double-entendres called "albures," which can best be translated as locker-room humor. The book's high national sales provoked over 100 editions and the first film version, starring popular ranchero singer Vicente Fernández, registered high ticket sales.

The sequel is directed by Rafael Villaseñor Kuri, who has helmed several Fernández vehicles ("Como México No Hay Dos," "Todo un Hombre," "El Sinvergüenza"). Also in the cast are comedians Héctor Suárez and Lalo (El Mimo),

whose characterizations are sketchy at best.

Whereas the first feature was at times funny, serious and even charming, the sequel is a thrown-together mish-mash based on a confused plot and disagreeable characters. It has nothing to do with the book, but rather continues with variations on the characters from the first pic.

The plot concerns three picaros who, besides working with produce delivery, raise hell and chase women. Although the first half of the film has a few picaresquely humorous moments, the film runs out of steam, takes a serious turn and then it's downhill all the way.

As soon as the love interest develops between Nicho (Fernández) and Rosita (Marcela Delgado), problems threaten the script with notions of machismo, honor and philandering.

Perhaps the main problem is that Fernández' character, upon which the entire story rests, is disagreeable and pedantic. There is no room for his usual charm and flair. As a result, the film bogs down and never finds its way back to solid footing. Even loyal Fernández fans will find this film hard to take.—*Lent.*

Hadda
(MOROCCAN-COLOR)

An Ohra release. Produced by Chkili Farrad/Izza Gennini for Prodar Films (Casablanca)/Ohra-Film (Paris). Directed by Mohamed Aboulouakar. Screenplay, Aboulouakar, Tijani Chrigui; poems, Mohamed Mechaal; camera (color), Mustapha Stitou; editor, Marie Josef Yoyotte, Chrigui, Aboulouakar; costumes, Mosaique; art direction, Aboulouakar, Chrigui. Reviewed at Carthage Film Days (in competition), Oct. 16, 1986. Running time: **110 MINS.**
Hadda .... Zohra Obaha
Hamid .... Hamid
The poet .... Mohamed Mechaal
Aouicha .... Thourayah

Tunis — Mohamed Aboulouakar's "Hadda" is poetic Maghreb cinema at its most exasperating. In a proliferation of visual metaphors and unexplained folk traditions "Hadda" (name of the young heroine) stretches viewer patience well past the breaking point. In return, it offers some beautiful visuals. It's strictly for those who like puzzles with no guaranteed solution.

Pic's basic metaphor is an arid, infertile desert village where in some unspecified past time a handful of inhabitants wait for rain. In the end it arrives, but not before a series of symbolic disasters occurs. Picture unfolds lethargically, and reconstruction of any story at all is an iffy process.

Young Hamid, heir to land in the village and aided by his rich, crafty mother, is at odds with the wealthy Hadj Omar. At one point, Hadda is raped, an act which engenders an epidemic. Hadda and her sister Aouicha, also an outcast, go to live together in the desert. Finally, the rain falls.

At times film can be hypnotic viewing, but it lacks the enormous control and intuition needed to make a folk poem. Director Aboulouakar has a knack for striking images, but ought to tackle more tightly structured material.
—*Yung.*

The Emperor Caligula: The Untold Story
(COLOR)

Actually more of the same sex & gore.

A Metaxa Corp. presentation. Executive producer, Alexander Sussman. Directed by David Hills. Screenplay, Richard Franks, Hills; camera (Telecolor), Federico Slonisco; editor, George Morley; music, Carlo Maria Cordi; production design, Linda Mann; art direction, Lucius Pearl; costumes, Helen Zinnerman; casting, Frank Steiner. Reviewed on TWE vidcassette, N.Y., Oct. 30, 1986. (No MPAA Rating.) Running time: **91 MINS.**
Caligula . . . . David Cain Haughton
Miriam . . . . Laura Gemser
Messala . . . . Oliver Finch
Petreio . . . . Charles Borromel
Livia . . . . Fabiola Toledo
Ulmar . . . . Sasha D'Arc
Marcellus Agrippa . . . . Gabriele Tinti
Clizia . . . . Ulla Luna

This exploitation film, made in 1981 in Rome for Helen Sarlui by the director of the "Ator" epics, delivers the same basic goods as the Giovanni Tinto Brass hit, but without the hardcore porn inserts Bob Guccione added to "Caligula." Surprisingly serious in tone, pic is an adequate homevideo entry for strong stomachs.

David Cain Haughton has a tour de force in the title role, resembling French star Pierre Clementi, as he revels in power, decadence and general craziness until coming to his senses in an ironic finale. Much of the incidental material here is reminiscent of the Tinto Brass version, but without the lavish sets.

Main storyline has Miriam (sex superstar **Laura Gemser**) on a mission to kill Caligula after he rapes her girlfriend, who kills herself. In dreamily romantic footage (at odds with the yucky violence of the rest of the film), Miriam gradually falls in love with the evil emperor and even gets him to change his ways, just before he is assassinated in the final reel.

Sex is strong stuff here, but just inexplicit enough to escape the hardcore porn tag that was "Caligula's" selling point. Violence is extremely rough, especially in an impaling scene in which senator Marcellus at odds with Caligula (and played by Gemser's real-life husband

an inevitable costar Gabriele Tinti) gets caught from behind.

Haughton's acting carries the show. —*Lor.*

I lagens namn
(In The Name Of The Law) (SWEDISH-COLOR)

A Sandrews release of Sprice Filmproduktion production with the Swedish Film Institute, Sandrew Film, SR/TV-2. Produced by Hans Iveberg. Directed by Kjell Sundvall. Stars Sven Wollter. Screenplay, Hans Iveberg, Leif GW Persson, based on Leif GW Persson's novel "Samhällsbärarna" (Pillars Of Society); camera (Panavision, Eastmancolor), Peter Mokrosinski; sound, Klaes Engström, Björn Gunnarsson; production design, Eric Lison Johnson; editor, Ulla Lennman; music, Ulf Dageby; production management, Peter Hald. Reviewed at the Sandrews 1-2-3, Malmö, Sweden, Nov. 4, 1986. Running time: **87 MINS.**
Police Captain Jarnebring . . . Sven Wollter
Patrolman Häll . . . . Stefan Sauk
Patrolwoman Pilstam . . . . Pia Green
Patrolman Mikkelsson . . . . . Marvin Yxner
Patrolman Berg . . . . Sven Holm
Narcotics Chief . . . . Ernst Günther
Djurgevic . . . . Carlo Barsotti
The Greek . . . . Micke Klöver
The Yugoslav . . . . Gustav Bartfay
Näbben . . . . Rolf Skoglund
Puma . . . . Jonas Granström
Secretary . . . . Anita Wall
Also with: Johan Ulvesson, Asko Kivistö, Sten Johan Hedman, Lennart Hjulström, Mathias Henrikson, Margreth Weivers-Norström, Niels Dybeck, Anne Petrén, Jans-Erick Lindquist.

Malmö — Whether eventually pigeonholed as entertainment or art fare, Kjell Sundvall's "In The Name Of The Law" comes through with flying colors to stand up to police thriller competition from Hollywood at its best or from anywhere else. Item has raw excitement, suspense, credible characters, a plot as muddy as the genre permits, superior acting and top-notch production dress and will attract audiences wherever there is a venue for subtitled pictures.

Based on novel "The Pillars Of Society" by sociologist and police behavior researcher Leif GW Persson (who supplied the basic prose for Bo Widerberg's "The Man From Mallorca"), "In The Name Of The Law" looks through a Panavision lens darkly at a robust slice of life in a Stockholm police precinct headquarters and in the back alleys and occasional nicer neighborhoods surrounding it.

Seen in action are a quartet of young patrolmen (one is a woman, but she yields a night stick as expertly as her male colleagues), who like to beat up drunks and dope addicts and to march (literally to their walkman's strains of a popular Swedish martial song) into battle in private vendettas against anybody they imagine to be threats to society's nobler strata.

Trying to rein in this Wild Bunch is Jarnebring (played with irony and

covert humor by Sven Wollter), the precinct captain, who is being pressured by rookie cop and top brass alike, while fumbling manfully (and with the aid of pretty, 40-ish secretary Anita Wall in the dark of a plot that has a narcotics division chief (Ernst Günther) imagining every tax-evading citizen to be a big-league Mafia chieftain pitted against assorted mugs, hoods and drug addicts plus, of course, the Cop Quartet.

In the film, the four vicious, uniform-defiling youngsters wind up in a jail cell, but we are given no reason to think they won't soon be covering their regular beat again. If one real criminal is caught, he probably is caught for the wrong reasons because of the manipulations of the narcotics chief. The police captain may take another night off with his lady friend or with his trombone, which he plays mournfully in his home, but he will, of course, soon be walking those mean streets again — unprotected by anybody but his own conscience.

All this is partly Raymond Chandler territory, but it is also thoroughly modern filmmaking (Peter Mokrosinski's cinematography is inventive, but it never interferes to stem the flow of the action nor does Ulf Dageby's quietly menacing music), based on and inspired by these facts (as given by author-researcher Persson):

Out of 100 cases of police brutality filed in Stockholm last year, 95 were dismissed, filed and forgotten. Nationwide, the prosperous Swedish welfare state has 1,000 such cases reported annually against a like number of its 17,000 member police force. The escalation in police brutality is seen by Persson as directly proportional with the rise in drug addiction among the socially bereft. —*Kell.*

El Secuestro de Lola — Lola la Trailera 2
(Lola's Kidnaping - Lola The Trucker 2) (MEXICAN-COLOR)

A Películas Mexicanas release of a Scope Films production. Executive producer, Xavier Rizzo. Produced by Rolando Fernández López. Directed by Raúl Fernández. Stars Rosa Gloria Chagoyán. Screenplay, Carlos Valdemar, Rolando Fernández camera (color), Laura Ferlo; editor, Jorge Rivera; music, Tino Geisar, with appearance of groups Los João, Conjunto Michoacán and Grupo Audáz. Reviewed at Big Apple Cine 1, N.Y., Oct. 15, 1986. Running time: **103 MINS.**
Lola Cuevas . . . . Rosa Gloria Chagoyán
Jorge . . . . Rolando Fernández López
Federal Police Capt. . . . . Isela Vega
Police Chief . . . . Emilio (Indio) Fernández
Comandante . . . . Wolf Rubinskys
Maestro . . . . Frank Moro
Also with: María Cardinal, Isaura Espinoza, Edna Bolkan, Borolas and Xavier Rizzo.

If Mexican producer-actor

Rolando Fernández López has learned anything from the U.S. film industry, he has learned how to make a truckful of money — as seen by the national and international (among U.S. Hispanics) success of "Lola la Trailera" (Lola The Trucker). Although good filmmaking is not one of his salient points, his knowledge of strong marketing through a publicity blitz has more than made up for his on-camera faults, as seen in massive boxoffice returns. Fernández credits his publicity coup for hoisting this homegrown turkey to the position of Mexico's No. 2 b.o. national grosser of 1985.

The sequel, "El Secuestro de Lola" (Lola's Kidnaping), helmed by Fernández' relative Raúl, also is receiving its ample share of publicity. If the first pic didn't make much sense, a bigger budget has not aided the patchwork script of its sequel.

It would have been nice if Fernández knew exactly what type of film he wanted to produce. Here a high-tech James Bond adventure pic is unhappily wed to a sex comedy full of prostitutes and effeminate homosexuals. Add to this a routine cop show and the resulting mish-mash spells confusion, such that its plot defies easy synopsis.

A basic logic is lacking. Consider this: in the film, Lola is shot several times in the chest at close range with a machinegun, yet in a matter of days she is out of the hospital wearing a low-cut blouse without so much as a bandaid, fighting drug-smugglers and gun-runners.

Stretching the audience's imagination beyond its limits is not as disgusting as the pic's use (or misuse) of some of Mexico's best talents, including Isela Vega and actor-director Emilio (Endio) Fernández, who died in August.

The gaudy-glitzy costumes sported by all of the actresses look as if they had been supplied by Frederick's of Hollywood.

Rolando Fernández' wife, Laura Ferlo (an acronym for Fernández López) is one of Mexico's few women cinematographers. Her work here is uneven, but overall it is imaginative, lush and exciting. Her labors alone cannot carry the confused script. The merely functional acting by leads Fernández López and Rosa Gloria Chagoyán does nothing to bring life to the sketchy characterizations.

Spanish-speaking audiences, unaccustomed to such hype over Hispanic films, undoubtedly will flock to the sequel as they did to part one.

More able Hispanic filmmakers should learn something from Fernández' marketing lessons. If they matched promotion with the quality of their product, boxoffice tallies would vindicate their efforts.
—*Lent.*

La Tierra Prometida
(The Promised Land)
(MEXICAN-COLOR)

A Películas Mexicanas release of a Producciones Roberto Ge. Rivera production. Produced and directed by Roberto G. Rivera. Stars Roberto (Flaco) Guzmán. Screenplay, Ricardo Gariby; camera (color), Raúl Dominguez; editor, Enrique Puente Portillo; music, Rafael Carrión. Reviewed at Big Apple Cine 2, N.Y., Sept. 29, 1986. Running time: **101 MINS.**
Serafín . . . . Roberto (Flaco) Guzmán
Pascual . . . . Manuel (Flaco) Ibañéz
Con man . . . . . Pedro Weber (Chatanooga)
Serviana . . . . Claudia Guzmán
Tolín . . . . Alejandro Guce
Mother . . . . Alejandra Meyer
The Madame . . . . Lilia Prado

In recent years Mexican filmmaker Roberto G. Rivera has earned a reputation for his social realistic hard-hitting pics. This began with the short 1972 docu ''Los Marginados,'' which reported the poverty of those living marginal lives in Monterrey. Joining with writer Ricardo Gariby, he made two national box-office hits: ''El Milusos'' (The Jack-Of-All-Trades) and its sequel. These films concerned the difficulties of poor country folk who migrate to Mexico City in search of a better life.

In no way connected with the 1972 Miguel Littin pic of the same name, ''La Tierra Prometida'' (The Promised Land) is another venture dealing with the problems of Mexico's poor farmers. Lacking the charm of the ''Milusos'' pics, this latest Rivera-Gariby collaboration was made with a pedantic earnestness and the message is as blatant as a new car commercial.

The film was originally titled ''Jodidos pero Contentos'' (Screwed Over But Content) and its storyline, replete with clichés, relates the trials of Serafín (Roberto Guzmán) and his family. Unable to eke out a living on their small farm, they go to the capital where, illiterate and unskilled, they are corrupted and taken advantage of at every step. One son is claimed by disease, another by the temptation of drugs and armed crime, while the eldest daughter takes to entertaining gentlemen in bars. Instead of watching his family completely destroyed, Serafín gathers what's left of his kin and they return to the simple life.

At this point, the pic turns into a commercial for the national agrarian reform commission.

Serafín discovers that the formerly arid wasteland he left behind now boasts abundant crops, homes have been fixed up and the quality of life has improved. How did this happen? Easy. Too easy. Instead of despairing, the farmers banded together. They formed a cooperative and received low-interest government loans and everything smacks of official propaganda.

Whereas Rivera's cinema-verité style worked in his ''Milusos'' films, in this pic it looks like sloppy, low-budget filmmaking.

The film is saved only by the skills of the two ''flacos'' (skinnies), Roberto (Flaco) Guzmán and Manuel (Flaco) Ibñéz, whose strong acting carry the script's dead weight and bring a few minutes of light to a dark venture. —Lent.

Ese Loco Loco Hospital
(That Mad Mad Hospital)
(MEXICAN-COLOR)

A Películas Nacionales release of a Prods. Esme Films-Seneca Films-Alianza Cinematográfica Mexicana production. Produced by Carlos Vasallo. Directed by Julio Ruiz Llaneza. Screenplay, Ramón Obón; camera (color), Xavier Cruz; editor, Jorge Peña; music, Carlos Torres. Reviewed at Cine Agustin Lara, Mexico City, Oct. 26, 1986. Running time: **90 MINS.**
Doctor Matilda . . . . . . Susana Dosamantes
Doctor Chivago . . . . Fernando Luján
Gino Beruggi . . . . Guillermo Rivas
Nurse Bigotes . . . . Lucila Mariscal
Edipo Peres . . . . Sergio Ramos
Lucy . . . . Rebeca Silva
Dr. Luis Rubio . . . . José Magaña
    Also with: Charly Valentino, Polo Ortín, Raúl Padilla, Gina Leal, Yirán Aparicio, José Natera, Juan Pelaez, Paco Sañudo, Alejandra Peniche, Julio Ruiz Llaneza.

Mexico City — For several years Mexican filmmaker Julio Ruiz Llaneza produced what he called ''quality films,'' such as the 1984 ''Luna de Sangre,'' starring Alma Muriel and Humberto Zurita. These films were unappreciated by critics and brought in modest returns.

Ruiz Llaneza declared his dissatisfaction and said in the future he planned to produce low-budget trash comedies and make some quick cash. He has kept his promise.

In 1985, he directed the unfunny comedy ''Al Garote Limpio.'' This was followed immediately by this year's ''Ese Loco Loco Hospital'' (That Mad Mad Hospital), a collection of shopworn comedy sketches based on nurses in tight mini-uniforms.

The plot, which vaguely concerns the imminent expiration of the hospital's lease, is merely tacked onto the film and only accounts for a few minutes of screentime. It offers no sense of momentum to this corpse of a film.

The rest of the pic is composed of skits about inept doctors, nurses, interns, ambulance drivers, unfaithful husbands, gangsters, police and unfortunate patients. Director Ruiz Llaneza even jumps into the act in a bit part as the police chief. His acting talents rank slightly better than his plodding abilities as a director.

There is not one original gag in the entire film and the bargain-base-ment production values give a slapdash look to the proceedings. The pic can best be recommended as a remedy for insomnia. —Lent.

Just Like The Weather
(HONG KONG-COLOR)

A Feng Huang Motion Picture production, released by Sil-Metropole Organization Ltd. Directed by Allen Fong. Features Christine Li, Chan Hung-Lin, Fong. (No other credits provided.) Reviewed at Astor theater, Hong Kong, Nov. 5, 1986. Running time: **98 MINS.** *(Cantonese, Mandarin, English dialog with English subtitles)*

Hong Kong — ''Just Like The Weather'' is an uncommercial and uncommon Hong Kong production by once upon a time new wave Hong Kong director Allen Fong, now part of the ''old wave,'' clutching on to his established image as innovative filmmaker. This film likely will flop on any commercial theatrical run, but will surely make the rounds of film festivals; it has been invited to the 1986 Hawaii Intl. Film Festival.

Fong's 1982 effort, ''Father And Son,'' was a heartwarming surprise debut followed by the realistic ''Ah Ying'' in 1983. ''Weather'' was shot on location in America in 16m to provide an improvisational quality, then blown up to 35m in Tokyo with a surprisingly good visual end result.

''Just Like The Weather'' tells the story of a young Hong Kong couple who dream of emigrating to the U.S. with great expectations of moving away from their rags to develop riches in another country. The storyline supposedly emerged from interviews with the couple and their verbal discussions about whether to go to the land of milk and honey. But the best sequence happens in China, dealing with abortion as it reflects their indecision about raising a child, making a complete Asian family.

In the study of this boring Canto-marriage, the audience experiences prolonged sequences of the husband ironing a shirt, frying an egg for breakfast and the wife singing off-key when not pouting or eating her noodles early in the morning. Some may find some significant hidden meanings to these daily trivialities, but they seem to be a series of masturbatory cinematic exercises at the expense of the viewer.

On the plus side is the natural acting ability of Christine Li who physically resembles dramatic actress Cecilia Yip in acting and even vocal mannerisms.—Mel.

El Disputado Voto del Sr. Cayo
(The Disputed Vote Of Mr. Cayo)
(SPANISH-COLOR)

A Prods. Cinematográficas Penelope production. Executive producer, José María Calleja. Produced by José G. Blanco Sola. Directed by Antonio Giménez-Rico. Screenplay, Manuel Matji, Giménez-Rico, based on novel by Miguel Delibes; camera (color), Alejandro Ulloa; editor, Miguel González Sinde; sets, Rafael Palmero; sound, Miguel Angel Polo. Reviewed at Cine Calderón, Valladolid, Oct. 31, 1986. Running time: **98 MINS.**
Cayo . . . . Francisco Rabal
Victor . . . . Juan Luis Galiardo
Rafael . . . . Iñaki Miramón
Laly . . . . Lydia Bosch
    Also with: Eusebio Lázaro, Mari Paz Molinero, Abel Vitón, Gabriel Renom, Paco Casares, Juan Jesús Valverde.

Valladolid — If the poster announcing this film, of Paco Rabal dressed as a peasant, is strongly reminiscent of that used in ''The Holy Innocents'' it is perhaps because both are based on books by Miguel Delibes, a back-to-nature proponent cherishing the homely basics of the man who lives close to the earth over the sophisticated philosophies of intellectuals and politicians.

Antonio Giménez-Rico and Manuel Matji have deftly limned a script that rivets the audience's attention throughout, even though the story is a simple one. Though this, too, like so many Spanish films, is downbeat in its story and its message, item comes across effectively in portraying modern man's alienation from nature and as a plea to shun the sophistries of modern dialectics and get down to basics.

Most of the pic is told as a flashback after the death of a former socialist politico, who dropped out of the political rat race in 1977, the year Spain's first free elections were held. Politico's widow has lunch with a former friend of her husband's, now a bigshot congressman, and reminisces about an incident in 1977, when the three of them went to an obscure pueblo north of Burgos as part of their campaign tour.

When the three get to the village, they find it virtually deserted. Only ones remaining are the hick mayor, Sr. Cayo, his wife, their dog and a neighbor Cayo hasn't talked to for years. The campaigners try to explain the importance of the coming election, brandishing arguments germane to the country's political condition. But Cayo's answers and comments, profound in their simplicity, cause the politico, Victor, to realize the superficiality of his views and life.

A run-in with a group of campaigning fascists ends the memorable day. Back in the present, the widow urges the congressman to return to the pueblo to see what has become of Sr. Cayo. Reluctantly he does so, and discovers the old man alone and in ill health. As Sr. Cayo is taken away in an ambulance, only living thing left in the pueblo is his whining dog.

Pic, well directed and acted, with good technical credits, could be of interest in select art houses and on the festival circuit. —Besa.

Revenge
(COLOR)

Oklahoma crude.

A United Entertainment Pictures production and release. Produced by Linda Lewis. Executive producer, Bill F. Blair. Written and directed by Christopher Lewis. Stars Patrick Wayne, John Carradine, Bennie Lee McGowan. Camera (color), Steve McWilliams; editor, James Lenertz; music, Rod Slane; production manager, Scott Clark; assistant director-associate producer, Jill Clark; makeup effects, DFX Studio; sound effects, Musipak; stunt coordinator, David Stice. Reviewed on United Entertainment Pictures vidcassette, N.Y., Nov. 6, 1986. (No MPAA Rating.) Running time: 100 MINS.
Michael Hogan . . . . Patrick Wayne
Sen. Bradford . . . . John Carradine
Gracie Moore . . . . . . Bennie Lee McGowan
Doctor White . . . . Josef Hanet
Liz . . . . Stephanie Kropke
Dean Bayley . . . . Fred Graves
Ron . . . . Charles Ellis
Deputy . . . . David Stice
Psychiatrist . . . . John Bliss
Reporter . . . . Andrea Adams

Shot on film as a sequel to the shot-on-video "Blood Cult," "Revenge" is a dreary horror item that wastes some decent actors in a confused story about a cult of dog worshipers who are harassing a widow to sell her farm, which they want as a location for their sacred rite.

Pic's Oklahoma setting provides the only redeeming aspect, with its clear views of blue skies and open terrain. After a clumsy, studio-shot opening scene in which a young femme reporter is knifed by a cop while interviewing a doctor about the latest in a series of murders, action moves outdoors and, with a few exceptions, stays there. It seems the doctor being interviewed is part of the insidious Cult of Caninus, which includes other prominent members of the small community. The murder of the reporter is the cult's first attempt at silencing those who might suspect they're not altogether solid citizens.

Patrick Wayne wanders on the scene to attend a funeral and soon is teamed with poor old widow Bennie Lee McGowan (who gives the only real performance) in her battle against those who would terrorize her into leaving home. John Carradine appears in a couple of scenes as a senator and head of the cult, and in at least one of his scenes it's more than apparent that he's reading his lines from cue cards. Other actors of lesser stature stumble over their lines as well.

Main purpose of the film is to showcase some gory mutilations and effects, notably in a scene (totally removed from the rest of the picture) in which a female camper is getting her leg chopped off with a knife, while her buddy remains in the camper chopping sausage for breakfast. The obvious intercutting of the two scenes is something that would be laughed out of most high school Super 8m film clubs.

Twist ending, in which one of the main characters, whom we've been led to believe is on the side of right, suddenly switches allegiance, seems to have been thought of at last minute and renders all that has come before as pointless. —Gerz.

Mort un dimanche de pluie
(Died On A Rainy Sunday)
(FRENCH-SWISS-COLOR)

An AAA Classic release of an Incite/Soprofilms/FR3 Films/Slotint/Radio Télévision Suisse Romande coproduction, with the participation of the Centre National de Cinématographie. Executive producers, Daniel Messère, Joel Santoni. Produced by Yves Perrot. Associate producers, Jacques Tronel, Raymond Vouillamoz. Directed by Santoni. Screenplay, Santoni, Philippe Setbon, based on the novel, "Died On A Rainy Sunday" by Joan Aiken, camera (Eastmancolor), Jean Boffety; editor, Martine Barraqué; music and songs, Vladimir Cosma; songs performed by Marshall Titus; art direction, Max Berto; special effects, Coyote; makeup, Joel Lavau; sound, Jean-Pierre Ruh; assistant director, Raphael Blanc; production managers, Daniel Messère, Henri Lacombe. Reviewed at the Paramount Opera theater, Paris, Oct. 14, 1986. Running time: 109 MINS.
Elaine Briand . . . . Nicole Garcia
David Briand . . . . Jean-Pierre Bacri
"Cappy" Bronsky . . . . . Jean-Pierre Bisson
Hazel Bronsky . . . . . Dominique Lavanant
Cric Briand . . . . Cérise Leclerc
Christian . . . . Etienne Chicot
Diane . . . . Christine Laurent
Betty Bronsky . . . . Céline Vaugé
Singer . . . . Marshall Titus
Alain Miller . . . . Jean-Pierre Malo

Paris — "Mort un dimanche de pluie" is a psycho thriller with a French accent, though drawn from an Anglo-Saxon novel by Joan Aiken. Director Joel Santoni and coscripter Philippe Setbon try to give more psychological density to the main characters, though the manipulation of suspense and the horrific climax are as unsubtle and obvious as in innumerable Yank products of this sort.

Jean-Pierre Bacri and Nicole Garcia play a striving architect and his wife who are vampirized by a disquieting cripple (Jean-Pierre Bisson) and his no less freaky wife (Dominique Lavanant), whom Bacri employs respectively as gardener and babysitter at their lonely residence — a modern architectural monstrosity designed by him — in the rain-drenched Swiss countryside.

Bisson turns out to be an ex-construction worker who had lost an arm and had his leg crushed in a building site accident for which Bacri was in good part morally, if not legally, responsible. Now, years later, Bisson turns up with wife, kid and trailer, begging for a handout, but in fact plotting revenge by moving his family into the Bacri-Garcia residence.

Santoni attempts to instill a degree of subtlety in his description of the victimized couple, their shaky marriage, his guilt-ridden ambitions, and her boredom and frustration in this cold, godforsaken environment. But these efforts are continually undercut by the Grand Guignol limning of Bisson and Lavanant. As in too many second-rate chillers, the viewer is left to rage at the blindness and stupidity of the main characters before such glaringly evident monsters.

Director still manages to play on audience nerves in a crudely effective manner, though the final payoff misses on even the most elementary level, with Bacri getting his moral comeuppance (a kitchen knife in the back) while Garcia flees into the rain. Bisson turns out to be a hard man to keep down since he keeps coming after Garcia hacks at his artificial arm with a meat cleaver and unloads a shotgun blast into him. It takes the collapse of a garage (echoing the accident that first maimed him) to do away with the creep — maybe.

Jean Boffety's ominous images and Max Berto's sinister production design perfectly serve the tale's pseudo-Hitchcockian conception.
—Len.

Heartbreak Ridge
(COLOR)

Predictable drama of maverick marine will satisfy Clint Eastwood fans.

A Warner Bros. release of a Malpaso production in association with Jay Weston Prods. Produced and directed by Clint Eastwood. Stars Eastwood. Executive producer, Fritz Manes. Screenplay, James Carabatsos; camera (Technicolor), Jack N. Green; editor, Joel Cox; music, Lennie Niehaus; production design, Edward Carfagno; set decoration, Robert Benton; costume supervision, Glenn Wright; sound (Dolby), William Nelson; assistant director, Paul Moen; casting, Phyllis Huffman. Reviewed at The Burbank Studios, Dec. 1, 1986. (MPAA Rating: R.) Running time: 130 MINS.
Highway . . . . Clint Eastwood
Aggie . . . . Marsha Mason
Major Powers . . . . Everett McGill
Sgt. Webster . . . . Moses Gunn
Little Mary . . . . Eileen Heckart
Roy Jennings . . . . Bo Svenson
Lieutenant Ring . . . . Boyd Gaines
Stitch . . . . Mario Van Peebles
Choozoo . . . . Arlen Dean Snyder
Fragetti . . . . Vincent Irizarry
Aponte . . . . Ramon Franco
Profile . . . . Tom Villard
Quinones . . . . Mike Gomez
Collins . . . . Rodney Hill
"Swede" Johanson . . . . Peter Koch

Hollywood — "Heartbreak Ridge" offers another vintage Clint Eastwood performance — this time within a flat and predictable story. There are enough mumbled half-liners in this contemporary war pic to satisfy those die-hards eager to see just how he portrays the consummate marine veteran, which should translate into bountiful box-office.

Eastwood is Gunnery Sergeant Tom Highway — a man determined to teach some of today's young leathernecks how to behave like a few good men. Decorated for action in Korea and Vietnam, the aging Eastwood confronts a ragtag bunch of feisty lads in a plodding series of drills that often look more like an unauthorized training film.

While relishing his chance to give these grunts some old-style values, Eastwood is challenged by a modern major (Everett McGill) bent on driving him out of the corps because of his fisticuffs, hard-drinking and officer-challenging ways.

Audience is thus assured that he's going to punch out a few more and even tangle with the major himself. This Eastwood character, however, is supposed to represent more than brawn and have some added dimensions. Enter Marsha Mason.

She's cast as his foul-mouthed ex-wife struggling to survive by pushing drinks at a town bar. She just happens to have returned to the area right before he did and there's no doubt they'll be struggling to sort out previous troubles.

Effort to revisit that past prompts Eastwood to begin reading various femme publications in search of knowledge about such matters as nurturing a relationship — a comical touch that fails to give him much of the depth that was apparently intended.

Meantime, he is indeed shaping up his troops — who are destined, of course, to give the sarge their grudging respect. As one of that group, Mario Van Peebles delivers perhaps the film's finest performance as a soldier who initially cares mostly about rock guitar-playing gigs and boisterous invective.

Eastwood's stern ways inevitably prevail as his platoon is called up for emergency overseas combat. Since this is a 1980s tale, there were few actual choices and presumably the Marine's calamitous Beirut experience was not a viable one. Grenada got the nod.

Guns are blazing as Clint's cadre faces its first real action after hitting the beaches. For good measure, he leads off the combat by blowing away a handful of Cuban regulars and swiping one of their renowned cigars for later pleasures.

As film moves towards its jingoistic peak in these sequences, Eastwood's insubordinate bent culminates in a final conflict with the major — whose orders he had blatantly ignored. No matter. A general conveniently shows up and absolves him of any wrongdoing.

Events are proceeding so assuredly by now that one nearly forgets that Eastwood has once more left behind Mason — just as the duo was possibly getting together. Earlier pretense of a genuine rapport — including one fine scene in which Mason recalls her side of his Vietnam experience — collapses upon his return from the Grenada battle when not a word is spoken as the credits roll. So much for an evolving man who can love, think, articulate and still go to war.

Notwithstanding the unsatisfying storyline, Eastwood's direction stands out in sure pacing through the latter two-thirds of the pic. —*Tege.*

Cyoei No Mure
(The Catch)
(JAPANESE-COLOR)

A Shochiku production and release. Produced by Akira Oda. Directed by Shinji Somai. Screenplay, Yozo Tanaka, from the novel by Akira Yoshimura; camera (color), Mitsuo Naganuma; music, S. Saegusa. Reviewed at Chauvel theater, Sydney, Nov. 23, 1986. Running time: **140 MINS.**
Fusajiro Kohama . . . . Ken Ogata
Tokiko . . . . Masako Natsume
Shunichi . . . . Koichi Sato
Aya . . . . Yukiyo Toake

Sydney — Shinji Somai's "Typhoon Club" won the main prize at the first Tokyo fest last year; now he's come up with a more conventional yarn, backed by a major studio, about a family of tuna fishermen.

Fusajiro (Ken Ogata) was abandoned by his wife 20 years earlier and now lives with his daughter, Tokiko (Masako Natsume). She's fallen for Shunichi (Koichi Sato), a young shopkeeper who wants to be a fisherman, too; Fusajiro reluctantly agrees to teach his prospective son-in-law, who's terribly seasick on their first outing.

Next time out, there's an accident and the younger man is nearly killed when the fishing line wraps round his forehead. Fusajiro seems more interested in saving the tuna than the life of his daughter's beau, but the lad survives. One year later, the couple has married and moved away. Fusajiro goes to find his ex-wife, but a reconciliation seems impossible. He tracks down his now pregnant daughter and son-in-law just in time to be present at another accident which, this time, proves fatal.

It's not much of a plot to fill a 2-hour 20-minute film, and the pacing is decidedly slow. Though the principal actors are all good, especially Ogata who gives a very solid, physical performance, characterization is minimal. The background of small fishing communities, rough weather and achingly hard work is all presented adequately, but the personal drama never really comes to life.

Visually, Somai and his cameraman, Mitsuo Naganuma, have opted for long, sometimes intricate takes, usually using a hand-held camera judging by the frequent jerkiness of the images. The many scenes shot on the tuna boats are filmed excitingly, but when the same visual pyrotechnics are used back on shore, it looks unnecessarily fussy. Almost complete lack of closeups prevents much audience identification. —*Strat.*

Platoon
(COLOR)

Flawed study of men in war.

An Orion Pictures release of a Hemdale Film Corp. presentation of an Arnold Kopelson production. Produced by Kopelson. Coproducer, A. Kitman Ho. Executive producers, John Daly, Derek Gibson. Production executive, Pierre David. Written and directed by Oliver Stone. Stars Tom Berenger, Willem Dafoe, Charlie Sheen. Camera (CFI color), Robert Richardson; editor, Claire Simpson; music, Georges Delerue; production design, Bruno Rubeo; art direction, Rodel Cruz, Doris Sherman Williams; special effects supervisor, Yves de Bono; special makeup effects, visual continuity, Gordon J. Smith; sound (Dolby), Simon Kaye; assistant director, H. Gordon Boos; second unit camera, Tom Sigel; casting, Pat Golden, Bob Morones, Warren McLean. Reviewed at the Samuel Goldwyn Theater, Beverly Hills, Nov. 18, 1986. (MPAA Rating: R.) Running time: **120 MINS.**

Sergeant Barnes . . . . Tom Berenger
Sergeant Elias . . . . Willem Dafoe
Chris . . . . Charlie Sheen
Big Harold . . . . Forest Whitaker
Rhah . . . . Francesco Quinn
Sergeant O'Neill . . . . John C. McGinley
Sal . . . . Richard Edson
Bunny . . . . Kevin Dillon
Junior . . . . Reggie Johnson
King . . . . Keith David
Lerner . . . . Johnny Depp
Tex . . . . David Neidorf

Hollywood — "Platoon" is an intense but artistically distanced study of infantry life during the Vietnam War. Writer-director Oliver Stone seeks to immerse the audience totally in the nightmare of the United States' misguided adventure, and manages to do so in a number of very effective scenes. But his set of dual impulses — to stun the viewer with a brutal immediacy on the one hand, and to assert a reflective sense of artistic hindsight on the other —dilutes whatever the film was meant to say, and takes the edge off its power. Commercial prospects look okay, better than that if it reaps some strong critical notices.

A Vietnam vet himself, Stone obviously had urgent personal reasons for making this picture, a fact that emerges instantly as green volunteer Charlie Sheen is plunged into the thick of action along the Cambodian border in late 1967.

Unit with which he's placed is broken down into three rough categories of men: the macho, might-is-right tough guys led by heavily scarred Sergeant Tom Berenger, the marginally more intelligent potheads whose ostensible figurehead is doubting war veteran Willem Dafoe, and assorted loners who just hope to get by watching out for their own skins.

Sheen soon is adopted by the dopers, and the long periods of waiting for action are fraught with dissension among the groups, a conflict epitomized by the rivalry between Berenger, the unreflective man of action, and Dafoe, a man of conscience who learns from experience.

Most traumatic sequence, which will shock many viewers through its exposé of shameful and unprovoked American brutality, has the unit taking a tiny village where local farmers are suspected of hiding and aiding the Vietcong. The G.I.s mercilessly murder a young man, terrorize the entire populace, and gang rape a young girl, among other atrocities, treatment that provokes a complete split between the group's two main factions and paves the way for further senselessness and tragedy.

Also striking is a long scene of the men at play, drinking, getting high and dancing, that nicely points up the unnatural aspects of this enforced all-male society, as well as the climactic, nocturnal battle which becomes a hideous slaughter.

Where Stone's previous effort, "Salvador," was hot and explosive, however, despite its flaws, "Platoon" is cool and never goes quite as far as one imagines it will. All the images in the earlier film seemed caught on the run under extreme pressure, while all the beautiful and undoubtedly difficult moving camera shots here express a sense of grace and precision that removes the visceral quality from the violence.

One is forcibly reminded of "Apocalypse Now" throughout because of the presence centerscreen of Charlie Sheen, who bears a remarkable resemblance here to his father, star of Francis Coppola's epic.

Otherwise, however, "Platoon" in form resembles the taut, close-up army unit films of the 1950s such as Anthony Mann's "Men In War," Robert Aldrich's "Attack!" and Samuel Fuller's "The Steel Helmet" and "Fixed Bayonets." Despite its violence and barrage of realistically dirty language, "Platoon" could have used some of these films' ferociousness, starkness and unpretentiousness. The artistic veneer Stone applies, along with the simpy narration provided for Sheen in the way of letters to his grandmother, detract significantly from the work's immediacy.

Nevertheless, there is plenty of good work to be found here, and pic certainly grabs the viewer by the collar in a way not found everyday in contemporary films. Working on an undoubtedly modest budget in the Philippines (lensing started just as President Aquino was replacing Marcos), team has mounted an impressive-looking production in all respects, although cinematographer Robert Richardson overdoes the filters at times. Georges Delerue's plaintive score consists largely of a new arrangement of Samuel Barber's "Adagio For Strings."

Willem Dafoe comes close to stealing the picture as the sympathetic sergeant whose drugged state may even heighten his sensitivity to the insanity around him, and each of the members of the young cast all have their moments to shine.

Stone implicitly suggests the U.S. lost the war because of divisions within its own ranks and an unwillingness to go all the way, which leaves one with the tragic result that all the suffering and trauma was for nothing. Unfortunately, the analysis here goes no further than that; better if Stone had stuck to combat basic.—*Cart.*

Wired To Kill
(COLOR)

Okay 'Mad Max' Carbon.

An American Distribution Group release. Produced by Jim Buchfuehrer. Executive producer, Paul McGuire. Coproduced by Peter Chesney. Written and directed by Franky Schaeffer. Camera (Foto-Kem color), Tom Fraser; editor, Daniel Agulian, Schaeffer; music, Russell Ferrante; art director, Diana Williams, Gay Redinger; set decorator, Ainslee Colt DeWolf; costumes, Dorothy Bulac; special effects, Bruce Hayes; assistant director, Guy Louthan; sound (Dolby stereo), Ken Ross; casting, Pamela Seaman. Reviewed at Hollywood Pacific Theater, Nov. 14, 1986. (MPAA Rating: R.) Running time: **96 MINS.**

Rebecca	Emily Longstreth
Steve	Devin Hoelscher
Reegus	Merritt Butrick
Sly	Frank Collison
Loady	Garth Gardner
Sleet	Tom Lister Jr.
Rooster	Kim Milford
Zero	Michael Wollet
Mother	Kristina David
Sergeant	Don Blakely
Grandmother	Dorothy Patterson

Hollywood — "Wired To Kill," originally titled "Booby Trap," is another post-apocalyptic "Mad Max" rip-off with flashes of its own style and some evidence of talent lurking in there somewhere. But it is unlikely that very many people will be intrigued enough by the premise to check it out.

On a story level "Wired To Kill" is totally routine and verges on the moronic. Franky Schaeffer seems to have more going as a director than a writer and manages to create a modicum of suspense and interest despite the nonsensical plot.

Set in 1998 following a massive plague a few years earlier, packs of renegades roam free in rundown quarantine areas. Working with a shoestring budget, Schaeffer and art directors Diana Williams and Gay Redinger have succeeded in creating an environment that is at once familiar and bizarre, where garbage trucks are the main source of transportation.

For no apparent reason a gang breaks into a ramshackle house and terrorizes one of the few remaining families. Rest of the film is a revenge tale for young Steve (Devin Hoelscher) and his girlfriend (Emily Longstreth). Story could have taken on some added depth if Longstreth had been a more forceful heroine instead of just a victim.

Only unusual twist is that Hoelscher conducts his vendetta by remote control from his wheelchair after being maimed by the attackers. With unlikely robot named Winston doing most of the dirty work, the film turns highly implausible.

Acting is not particularly distinguished but the leads are earnest and fresh enough to be likable and win the crowd's sympathy. As the leader of the goons, Merritt Butrick appears to be the only gang member with a triple digit I.Q.

Only real rewards of the film are visual with Tom Fraser's camerawork seemingly casting a shadow over everything in this nether world.
— *Jagr.*

Billy Galvin
(COLOR)

Family drama with tv rather than theatrical future.

A Vestron Pictures release of an American Playhouse presentation. Produced by Sue Jett, Tony Mark. Executive producers, Stuart Benjamin, Howard L. Baldwin, William Minot, Lindsay Law. Written and directed by John Gray. Camera (color), Eugene Shlugleit; editor, Lou Kleinman; production design, Shay Austin; production manager, Eva Fryer; art design, Cecilia Rodarte; costume design, Oleska; casting, Judy Courtney, D.L. Newton. Reviewed at Main Library, Fort Lauderdale (Greater Fort Lauderdale Intl. Film Festival), Nov. 26, 1986. (MPAA Rating: PG.) Running time: **94 MINS.**

Jack Galvin	Karl Malden
Billy Galvin	Lenny Von Dohlen
Mae	Joyce Van Patten
Nora	Toni Kalem
Donny	Keith Szarabajka
Georgie	Alan North
Nolan	Paul Guilfoyle
Kennedy	Barton Heyman
Margaret the Bingo Queen	Lynne Charnay

Fort Lauderdale — "Billy Galvin" is a tale about the friction between a father and his grown son in blue collar Boston. Produced with funding from the PBS' American Playhouse, it is family drama which will play well on television and vidcassette thanks to headliner Karl Malden and a strong supporting cast.

Malden plays Jack Galvin, a lovably crusty union ironworker nearing retirement. Since he was young, Jack dreamed of being an architect, but his working class father was unable to send him to school. Jack hopes his son Billy (Lenny Von Dohlen) will go to college and fulfull his father's dreams.

Billy has other plans, though. He wants to follow in his father's footsteps and doggedly tries to secure a union construction job. But Jack blocks him, conspiring with his union cronies to keep the boy off the job.

Writer-director John Gray presents a realistic picture of his working class characters and their male-dominated culture. There's much about male friendship here. Billy's two friends Donny (Keith Szabarajka) and George (Alan North) help him out when his own father won't, forming a rival family for the kid.

There's also a lot about traditional male-female roles. When Jack's wife and Billy's mom Mae (Joyce Van Patten) is not trying to patch up the split in her family, she's off playing bingo with her best buddy Margaret (Lynne Charnay). Billy's tough-speaking bartender girlfriend Nora (Toni Kalem) is from a younger, more liberated generation. She nevertheless spends much of her time adapting to her boyfriend's stubborn moods and problems.

This is Gray's first feature length film. Previously he directed several shorts and an episode of the televi-

sion series "Powerhouse." In "Billy Galvin" he sustains the action well, despite a plot that too often takes the characters back and forth over the same ground — Billy and Jack bickering, then making up, then fighting again.

Eugene Shlugleit broadens the story with some nice camerawork. He photographs the Galvins' world from its best vantage point, from the buildings they help assemble and from within their blue collar homes and bars.

Unlike the recent Playhouse offering "Smooth Talk," "Billy Galvin" does not promise a strong art house or regular theatrical run. It has a lot of heart, but it lacks polish to make it on the art circuit and action to please regular audiences.
— *Bux.*

The Big Easy
(U.S.-COLOR)

A Kings Road Entertainment presentation. Produced by Stephen Friedman. Executive producer, Mort Engelberg. Directed by Jim McBride. Stars Dennis Quaid, Ellen Barkin, Ned Beatty. Screenplay, Dan Petrie Jr.; camera (Deluxe color), Afonso Beato; editor, Mia Goldman; music, Brad Feidel; production design, Jeannine Claudia Oppewall; set decoration, Lisa Fischer; costume design, Tracy Tynan; sound, Mark Ulano; assistant director, Michael Schroeder. Reviewed at the Rio de Janeiro Film Festival, Nov. 27, 1986. Running time: **108 MINS.**

Remy McSwain	Dennis Quaid
Anne Osborne	Ellen Barkin
Jack	Ned Beatty

With: John Goodman, Ebbe Roe Smith, Lisa Jane Persky, Charles Ludlam, Tom O'Brien, Marc Lawrence, Solomon Burke, Jim Garrison.

Rio de Janeiro — Until conventional plot contrivances begin to spoil the fun, "The Big Easy" is a snappy, sassy battle of the sexes in the guise of a melodrama about police corruption. World premiered at the Rio de Janeiro Film Festival, stylish Jim McBride pic figures to be the first release from the new distribution arm of Kings Road Entertainment, sometime early next year. Selling this one will be a challenge, however, as film's quirky quality will have trouble prevailing over cop story clichés and lack of star power at the b.o.

This marks McBride's first outing since "Breathless" and reappearance of scenarist Dan Petrie Jr. after "Beverly Hills Cop." Most of the time, the director is in strong form, but he is finally undone by the script's insistence on a final act that would look at home on any formulaic tv show.

Buildup is quite engaging. In the classic screwball comedy tradition of opposites irresistibly attracting, brash New Orleans homicide detective Dennis Quaid puts the make on Ellen Barkin, a northern import assigned by the D.A.'s office to investigate possible illegal activities in the

department.

Opening reels possess a breezy freshness, as Quaid overcomes Barkin's personal anxiety and professional reservations about becoming involved with a member of the force she's supposed to check out. Couple's nights on the town include some visits to scenes of apparent gangland murders as well as to colorful, Cajun-flavored restaurants and clubs, and the inevitable sex scene, while not tremendously explicit, still manages to be provocatively frank in regard to the specifics of what's going on and how Quaid finally turns Barkin on.

Despite his conquest, the cocky cop quickly finds himself holding the short end of the stick, as he's set up and prosecuted by Barkin personally for being on the take.

Although clever and resourceful enough to wiggle out of trouble, Quaid gradually realizes the rules of the game he's been playing for years are irredeemably corrupt. Convinced the drug-related murders are really the work of crooked cops rather than mobsters, Quaid cleans up his act and goes to the root of the problem on the road to an unbelievably rosy-hued resolution.

Not necessarily the likeliest of couples, Quaid and Barkin bring great energy and an offbeat wired quality to their roles. A bit like Richard Gere in McBride's "Breathless," Quaid's character is always "on," always performing for effect, during most of the action, and actor's natural charm easily counterbalances character's overbearing tendencies. Barkin is sexy and convincing as the initially uptight target of Quaid's attentions, his provocation to shape up and, finally, his enthusiastic partner in crime-busting.

Ned Beatty projects an appealing paternalism as the homicide chief, while top supporting turn comes from the Ridiculous Theater Co.'s Charles Ludlam as a very Tennessee Williams-ish defense attorney. Offbeat cameos are contributed by veteran baddie Marc Lawrence, singer-preacher Solomon Burke and one-time Kennedy assassination conspiracy theorist Jim Garrison.

New Orleans' local color is fully exploited by McBride and Brazilian lenser Afonso Beato, as camerawork beautifully brings out the bold, rich hues without looking either gaudy or overly stylized. Jeannine Claudia Oppewall's production design and Tracy Tynan's costume design artfully add to the snazzy look, while Mia Goldman's editing keeps things zipping along. Brad Feidel's evocative score is abetted by a host of mostly Cajun tunes.

Overall, the cooks here did the best they could with ingredients that tasted good but were a little tough to chew. — *Cart.*

Eye Of The Tiger
(COLOR)

Corny revenge pic.

A Scotti Bros. release. Produced by Tony Scotti. Executive producers, Herb Nanas, Ben Scotti. Directed by Richard Sarafian. Screenplay, Michael Montgomery; camera (United color), Peter Collister; sound, Dennis Carr; editor, Greg Prange; first assistant directors, Scott Maitland, Leo Zisman; production coordinator, Pilar Stallwort; art director, Wayne Springfield; set director, Kurt Gauger. Reviewed at the Mann's Hollywood, Nov. 22, 1986. (MPAA Rating: R.) Running time: **90 MINS.**
Buck Matthews . . . . Gary Busey
J.B. Deveraux . . . . Yaphet Kotto
Sheriff . . . . Seymour Cassel
Father Healey . . . . Bert Remsen
Blade . . . . William Smith
Dawn . . . . Kimberlin Ann Brown
Christie . . . . Denise Galik
Jennifer . . . . Judith Barsi
Doctor . . . . Eric Bolles
Jake . . . . Joe Brooks

Hollywood — Gary Busey is yet another lone vigilante out to avenge his wife's brutal murder in this new pic, "Eye Of The Tiger." Yet even Busey's name and some high-action sequences will not save this one from an early arrival on the video store shelves.

In this first release (other than pickups) by Scotti Bros., producers have opted for a very predictable story and a lot of one-dimensional characters that end up stagnating the film.

The pic opens with Buck Matthews' (Busey) release from prison, where he apparently was serving time for murder (that is not made too clear). He comes back to the small town where he grew up, to his loving wife Christie (Denise Galik), and his eight-year-old daughter, Jennifer (Judith Barsi).

There is some bad blood between Matthews and the hick sheriff (Seymour Cassel) in this town who apparently helped to set Matthews up on the murder charge (although this is not made clear either).

Matthews' hometown is being terrorized by a gang of motorcycle-riding drug peddlers, all of whom wear black with black helmets and ride in packs.

One night when the pack attempts to rape a nurse, Matthews comes to the rescue, thus raising the wrath of the gang's leader, Blade (William Smith—remember Falconetti from "Rich Man, Poor Man"?).

And so the motorcycle gang makes a visit to Matthews' house, killing his wife, beating him up and sending their daughter into a catatonic state.

The rest of the film is about Matthews' one-man quest for vengeance, most of which is set to the pounding beat of rock music. Of course the townfolk are reluctant to get involved, the hick sheriff is in cahoots with Blade, and Matthews is pretty much left to his own in-

genuity.

The best character in the film is J.B. Deveraux (Yaphet Kotto), one of the sheriff's lackeys.

Deveraux is a black man who has had to live in a white man's town. He is beaten down by prejudice and corruption, and has become afraid to stand up for what is right because he just wants to get his pension and leave. His friendship with Matthews finally intercedes and he comes to his aid in the end. This is obviously the most fleshed out character in this film.

Busey's character supposedly has a whole history of hard times (he fought in Vietnam, he was framed for murder), but this is only brought out in passing, never delved into as to how it affected him.

Directing by Richard Sarafian often is sluggish as scenes in between the action slow considerably. Pic starts out slowly, only gaining momentum after the rape attempt.

Busey, who has brought in his share of memorable film moments (an Oscar nomination for "The Buddy Holly Story") obviously did not have his heart in this one. He's as forgettable as the rest.

There are some good action moments with a lot of fine stunt work, but it's not enough to save the picture.—*Teen.*

Geronima
(ARGENTINE-COLOR)

A Cooperativa de Arte Cinematográfico Avellaneda Ltda. production. Executive producer, Luis Barberis. Directed by Raúl Tosso. Screenplay, Carlos Paola, Tosso, based on the book by Jorge Pellegrini; camera (color), Carlos Torlaschi; music, Arnaldo di Pace, Aimé Paine (Mapuche themes); editor, Fernando Guariniello, Ulises Francezon, Juan José Arhancet; sound, Daniel Otobre. Reviewed at Rio de Janeiro Film Festival (competition), Nov. 25, 1986. Running time: **96 MINS.**
Geronima . . . . Luisa Calcumil
Morales . . . . Patricio Contreras
El Turco . . . . Mario Luciani
El Huinca . . . . Ernesto Michel
Eliseo . . . . Rufino Muŏz

Rio de Janeiro — First shot as 40-minute short that combined 16m and video, the next step for "Geronima" was a 16m feature, finally blown up to 35m. Although anything but a commercial project, the film — aided by festival exposure — could recover its modest $70,000 cost through tv sales and it also has some art house possibilites.

Geronima is a Mapuche indian who lives with her four small children in Trapalco, Argentine Patagonia. Until a snowstorm killed their animals, they managed reasonably well; afterwards they barely subsist. Their real troubles start when a well-meaning official from the Health Ministry decides to help them and transfers Geronima and her family to the hospital in a nearby town. The

crossover into civilization (sleeping in a bed, using a toilet, etc.) is a failure, but what makes Geronima ever more desperate is the seperation from her children, a situation that increases progressively in intensity and drives her into mental illness. Faced with this, the doctors decide the hospital is not able to give this case the attention it deserves and that she would be better off in her tiny one-room shack.

Unfortunetly it is too late. Soon after, all four children fall sick with whooping cough, contracted during their stay at the hospital. Due to their lack of defenses, two of the children die. Geronima herself also has no defenses against the immersion in an entirely different way of life in the hospital; she becomes psychotic and soon dies.

The film alternates the off-screen questioning of the real Geronima by Doctor Pellegrini (from tapes during her stay at the hospital in the mid '70s), with the reenactment of her story. Director Raúl Tosso, 33, avoids many of the pitfalls inherent in this kind of subject. He does not grind an ideological axe, nor does he attempt to sentimentalize his material, nor is there an attempt to establish a villain as responsible for the fate of Geronima and her children.

Luisa Calcumil provides an outstanding performance as Geronima; of Mapuche descent herself, she makes the character entirely credible. Although in a way this is almost an anthropological film, largely thanks to the actress, it also packs an emotional wallop that is far from usual with this type of cinema.

Technically the film has its rough edges, which fortunately do not detract from its feeling of authenticity.

—*Amig.*

Welcome To 18
(COLOR)

Meek approach to girls' rites of passage.

An American Distribution Group release of a Summer Release production. Executive producer, Bruce W. Brown. Produced by David C. Thomas. Directed by Terry Carr. Screenplay, Carr, Judith Sherman Wolin; camera (Metrocolor), Stephen L. Posey; editor, Lois Freeman-Fox; music, Tony Berg; sound (Dolby), Ron Judkins; production design, Steven Legler; set design, Don Ferguson; associate producers, Cheryl Downey, Kathleen Lawrence; assistant director, Cheryl Downey; aerial camera, Rex Metz; casting, Junie Lowry, Marcy Carriker. Reviewed at Movies At Town Center, Boca Raton, Fla., Nov. 20, 1986. (MPAA Rating: PG-13.) Running time: **89 MINS.**
Lindsey . . . . Courtney Thorne-Smith
Joey . . . . Mariska Hargitay
Robin . . . . Jo Ann Willette
Talia . . . . Cristen Kauffman
Roscoe . . . . E. Erich Anderson
Corey . . . . John Putch
Also with: Jeff MacGregor, Brian Bradley,

Michael MacRae, Eli Cummins, Graham Ludlow, Micole Mercurio, Brandis Kemp, Cletus Young, Clay Stone, Michael Greene, Max Trumpower, Mickey Jones, Deanna Booher, Bob Gould.

Boca Raton — "Welcome To 18," originally titled "Summer Release," is a ho-hum approach to the usual teenage comedy-drama about youngsters (in this case 18-year-old girls) finding out about the cold, cruel world and adults who inhabit it. The format worked as drive-in fodder about 15 years ago, but this watered-down version lacks even titillation value.

An attractive cast is headed by striking blond Courtney Thorne-Smith as Lindsey, who hops in her convertible with redhead pal Robin (Jo Ann Willette) and brunet Joey (Mariska Hargitay) to spend the post-high school graduation summer working at a dude ranch in Nevada.

Overly busy and unconvincing plotline has the trio splitting quickly from the ranch after they are cheated in the first payroll and forbidden to fraternize with the hunks there. They go to the mansion of a girl they've met, Talia (Cristen Kauffman), at Lake Tahoe where her young gangster-lover Roscoe (E. Erich Anderson) gets the girls phony IDs and jobs working at a casino.

The girls end up at a rundown motel in the mountains where they make new friends including a goofy entomologist and a sympathetic transvestite neighbor. After a party involving prostitution and drugs, the three girls end up in jail and are bailed out for $5,000 by Roscoe, who steals Lindsey's car as collateral until he is repaid.

While trying to protect Talia from this young brute, the girls devise a scheme in which Lindsey ends up winning about $35,000 in a poker game for local highrollers (it's never explained how Lindsey is so proficient at poker). After two of the girls succeed in having sex with their new boyfriends, a happy ending is contrived of them spiriting Talia away from Roscoe and all four heading for San Francisco before the fall college term begins.

Aided by an appealing set of players, picture tries to give young girls various lectures on the false lures of the fast life (living high, wild parties, gambling, prostitution, etc.) but sends out the same old messages of the genre, especially re: sex as fulfillment of the transition to womanhood.

Director Terry Carr displays the dreaded influence of music videos, with feature having more silent-plus-music montages than most films have had even at the height of romantic filler interludes in the 1960s. Four lead actresses all deserve better vehicles in future.

—*Lor.*

Crimes Of The Heart
(COLOR)

Warm and winning Beth Henley adaptation benefits from star power.

A De Laurentiis Entertainment Group release of a Freddie Fields/Burt Sugarman production. Produced by Fields. Executive producer, Sugarman. Directed by Bruce Beresford. Stars Diane Keaton, Jessica Lange, Sissy Spacek. Screenplay, Beth Henley, based on her play; camera (Technicolor), Dante Spinotti; editor, Anne Goursaud; music, Georges Delerue; sound, Bruce Bizenz; production design, Ken Adam; art direction, Ferdinando Giovannoni; set decorator, Garrett Lewis; costume design, Albert Wolsky; production manager, Don Heitzer; assistant director, Richard Luke Rothschild; production supervisor, Lucio Trentini; coproducers, Arlyne Rothberg, Bill Gerber; associate producer, P.K. Fields Zimmerman; casting, Susan Bluestein. Reviewed at MGM screening room, N.Y., Nov. 21, 1986. (MPAA Rating: PG-13.) Running time: **105 MINS.**

Lenny Magrath	Diane Keaton
Meg Magrath	Jessica Lange
Babe Magrath	Sissy Spacek
Doc Porter	Sam Shepard
Chick Boyle	Tess Harper
Barnette Lloyd	David Carpenter
Old Granddaddy	Hurd Hatfield
Zackery Botrelle	Beeson Carroll
Lucille Botrelle	Jean Willard
Uncle Watson	Tom Mason
Willie Jay	Gregory Travis

Thoughtfully cast, superbly acted and masterfully written and directed, ''Crimes Of The Heart'' is a winner. Diane Keaton, Jessica Lange and Sissy Spacek are a delight in their roles as southern sisters attempting to come to grips with the world, themselves and the past. Hu-

Original Play

Manhattan Theater Club (Lynne Meadow, artistic director; Barry Grove, managing director) presentation of a comedy-drama in three acts by Beth Henley. Staged by Melvin Bernhardt; setting, John Lee Beatty; costumes, Patricia McGourty; lighting, Dennis Parichy; stage manager, Connie Alexis; publicity, Susan Schulman Assocs. Opened Dec. 21, 1980, at the Manhattan Theater Club Upstage Theater, N.Y.

Cast: Lizbeth MacKay, Julie Nesbitt, Stephen Burleigh, Mary Beth Hurt, Mia Dillon, Peter MacNicol.

morous and moving, the film should generate enough critical praise and word-of-mouth for a healthy b.o. run, and looks to be a shoo-in for Oscar nominations in a number of categories.

Based on Beth Henley's 1980 play, Lenny (Keaton) is the eldest of three sisters and the only one still living in the large North Carolina home of their youth. It is Lenny's birthday, a day marked by youngest sister Babe's (Spacek) jailing for shooting her husband and the arrival of middle sister Meg (Lange), visiting from L.A. where she pursues a singing career.

Far from being downbeat, the interplay between Keaton's nervously frantic Lenny, Spacek's unpredictable Babe and Lange as the hard-living Meg is as funny as it is riveting.

Freed on bail, the somewhat unstable Babe joins Lenny and Meg in living in the house, bringing back a flood of memories both good and bad. We learn their father abandoned the family long ago, and that their mother committed suicide. Childhood jealousies resurface, and in the midst of it all their grandfather (Hurd Hatfield) is dying at a nearby hospital.

Yet even at its darkest, Henley's finely crafted screenplay never loses its sharp, comic edge. In the midst of a truly touching scene in which the three sisters reminisce while looking through Babe's scrapbook (chronicling all the bad events of her life), we learn their mother hung herself with the family cat via the surreal use of a newspaper photo clipping showing a sheet-covered body beside the small, sheet-covered feline.

Bruce Beresford's direction within the house is graceful, effortlessly following the action from room to room. Henley has taken the story outside with wonderful results, and Beresford makes the most of using the exterior locations.

Sam Shepard notches a strong performance in the relatively small part of Doc, and Tess Harper shows her ability as a comic actress in the role of neighbor/relative Chick. Supporting cast is strong throughout, particularly newcomer David Carpenter, and tech credits are uniformly firstrate.

Kudos go to producer Freddie Fields for bringing material that must have been a tough sale to the studios to the screen: —*Roy.*

Scorpion
(COLOR)

Dull actioner.

A Crown Intl. Pictures release of a Summons Ltd.-William Riead production. Executive producer, John R. Burrows Jr. Produced, written and directed by Riead. Stars Tonny Tulleners. Camera (color), Bill Philbin; editor, Gigi Coello; music, Sean Murray; sound, Stan Gordon; art direction, Heather Cameron; assistant director, Wendy West; associate producer, Peter Martineau; casting, Lisa Pontrelli. Reviewed at the Paramount theater, L.A., Dec. 5, 1986. (MPAA Rating: R.) Running time: **98 MINS.**

Steve Woods	Tonny Tulleners
Gifford Leese	Don Murray
Gordon Thomas	Robert Logan
Phil Keller	Allen Williams
Jackie Wielmon	Kathryn Daley
Sam Douglas	Ross Elliott
Noel Koch	John Anderson
Mehdi	Bart Braverman
Lt. Woodman	Thom McFadden
Wolfgang Stoltz	Bill Hayes
Jack Devlin	Adam Pearson

Hollywood — ''Scorpion'' (a.k.a. ''The Summons'') is an actioner with virtually no action, and what there is of it is almost laughably unconvincing. In his film debut, former karate champ Tonny

Tulleners makes Chuck Norris look like Laurence Olivier, or at least Clint Eastwood. This Crown Intl. pickup will be history before Xmas.

With its diverse international locations (Spain, Amsterdam, L.A., Hawaii) lensed on lousy stock with countless random zoom shots and mediocre sound to match, pic has the physical feel of those late, unlamented German-Italian-Yugoslavian coproductions of the mid-1960s that boasted no-name casts shooting it out over mysterious stakes on glamorous settings.

Here, the determinedly inexpressive Tulleners is supposed to be a top ''DIA'' agent with a major in anti-terrorist work. Early on, he single-handedly dispatches four armed airplane hijackers with his martial arts trickery.

Then, however, he's assigned the dull job of protecting a terrorist-turned-informant, which means the film settles down to bedroom and hospital settings for roughly half its running time, something Chuck or Clint would never sit still for.

Naturally, there are a few shootings, but more often than not the guns are tossed away so Tulleners can take on his adversaries in hand-to-hand combat. Amazingly, these fight set pieces are over within a matter of seconds, so action fans will feel enormously cheated. Indeed, the opening day Hollywood Boulevard crowd was talking back to the screen with noticeable regularity.—*Cart.*

Little Shop Of Horrors
(COLOR)

Weird adaptation of the hit musical is funny but uninvolving.

A Geffen Co. release through Warner Bros. of a Geffen Co. production. Produced by David Geffen. Directed by Frank Oz. Screenplay, Howard Ashman, based on the musical stage play, book and lyrics by Ashman, music by Alan Menken; camera (Technicolor), Robert Paynter; editor, John Jympson; music, Menken; lyrics, Ashman; score, Miles Goodman; production design, Roy Walker, art director, Stephen Spence; set decorator, Tessa Davies; costumes, Marit Allen; special effects, Bran Ferren; ''Audrey II'' created by Lyle Conway; assistant director, Dusty Symonds; associate producers, David Orton, Denis Holt; casting, Margery Simkin. Reviewed at Disney Screening Room, Burbank, Calif., Dec. 2, 1986. (MPAA Rating: PG-13.) Running time: **88 MINS.**

Seymour Krelborn	Rick Moranis
Audrey	Ellen Greene
Mushnik	Vincent Gardenia
Orin Scrivello	Steve Martin
Crystal	Tichina Arnold
Chiffon	Tisha Campbell
Ronette	Michelle Weeks
Patrick Martin	Jim Belushi
Wink Wilkinson	John Candy
First customer	Christopher Guest
Arthur Denton	Bill Murray
Voice of Audrey	Levi Stubbs

Hollywood — ''Little Shop Of

Horrors'' is a fractured, funny production transported rather reluctantly from the stage to the screen. Kooky songs about a boy, a girl and a man-eating plant may have been swell entertainment in the theater, but come up a bit soft in the cinema. Nonetheless, production is offbeat enough to win a cult audience and perhaps a bit of crossover from the mainstream.

Almost nothing is left besides the

Original Film
(B&W)

A Filmgroup release of a Roger Corman production. With Jonathan Haze, Jackie Joseph, Mel Welles, Myrtle Vail, Leola Wendorff, Dick Miller, Jack Nicholson. (No character names given). Directed by Corman. Screenplay, Charles B. Griffith; camera (b&w), Archie Dalzell; editor, Marshall Neilan Jr.; art director, Daniel Haller; music, Fred Katz; assistant director, Richard Dixon. Reviewed at Pic theater, N.Y., April 20, 1961. Running time: **70 MINS.**

setting and story outline from the 1961 Roger Corman film that inspired the stage musical. Tone, intent and execution are miles apart. Where the original was sinister, low budget and shot in a flash, the musical is lush, lovable and elaborate with shooting dragging on some seven months. The comparison is really one of apples and oranges.

While some musicals have made the jump effectively to film, book here by Howard Ashman, who also wrote the film's screenplay, is a narrow bridge between the show's amusing songs by Alan Menken. On film the numbers are impressive

Original Play

WPA Theater, David Geffen, Cameron Mackintosh and Shubert Organization presentation of a musical in two acts based on the film of the same name by Roger Corman, originally presented by the WPA Theater (Kyle Renick, producing director), with book and lyrics by Howard Ashman; music by Alan Menken. Staged by Howard Ashman. Musical staging, Edie Cowan; scenery, Edward T. Gianfrancesco; lighting, Craig Evans; costumes, Sally Lesser; sound, Otts Munderloh; puppets, Martin P. Robinson; vocal arrangements, musical supervision and musical direction, Robert Billig; orchestrations, Robby Merkin; general manager, Albert Poland; stage manager, Paul Mills Holmes; publicity, Solters & Roskin, Millie Schoenbaum. Opened July 28, 1982 at the Orpheum Theater, N.Y.; $18.95 Tues.-Thurs. nights, $19.95 Fri. nights, $22.95 Sat. nights.

Cast: Marlene Danielle, Jennifer Leigh Warren, Sheila Kay Davis, Hy Anzell, Ellen Greene, Lee Wilkof, Martin P. Robinson, Franc Luz, Ron Taylor.

set pieces, imaginatively staged with wonderful sets, but a film's requirements are not the same as a play's.

In musical theater one is accustomed to show-stopping numbers and the more the better. In film, story and character development are the key ingredients of a cinematic experience. Too many set pieces only slow down the pace and that's what happens here.

Individually, ''Little Shop Of Horrors'' is filled with many memorable moments. It is the cumulative effect that is rather slight.

Film opens splendidly on Roy Walker's skid row set as the three-woman Greek chorus named after 1960s girl groups, Crystal (Tichina Arnold), Chiffon (Tisha Campbell) and Ronette (Michelle Weeks), introduce the down and out denizens of this part of town. Walker's street includes a grand elevated subway as artificial as anything in 1950s musicals.

Living a rather mundane life, working in Mushnik's flower shop are Seymour (Rick Moranis) and Audrey (Ellen Greene), that is until lightning strikes and the natural order of things is turned upside down. Through a chain of events just silly enough to be fun, Seymour becomes the proud owner of Audrey II, a rare breed of plant that makes him famous and his boss (Vincent Gardenia) prosperous.

Audrey II develops an insatiable appetite for human flesh and as Seymour recognizes the plant as his meal ticket, he scurries about to keep it happy. As morbid as this might sound, director Frank Oz has a light enough touch to realize the absurd comedy inherent in the material.

When characters like Steve Martin's sadistic dentist get swallowed alive, it's unlikely anyone will feel sorry for them. People are not really people here, but broad caricatures, and Martin's is one of the best. Riding a motorcycle, wearing black leather with hair dyed black, Martin was born to play the role of Audrey's bullying boyfriend and his number about the pleasures of delivering pain is one of the film's most delicious.

Film is full of oddball cameos like Bill Murray (in the role Jack Nicholson handled in the original) as Martin's masochistic patient and John Candy as a Wolfman Jack-type d.j. on Skid Row radio.

And Moranis and Greene are no less weird. Greene is as dipsy as they come and Moranis is a nerd to reckon with. Nothing here is stranger than the plant itself. Designed by Lyle Conway with the voice of Levi Stubbs, Audrey II is a hip, soul brother disguised as a "mean green mother from outer space," in the words of its big number.

As the plant grows and makes life miserable for Seymour and nonexistent for some others, special effects by Bran Ferren give the film a "Ghostbusters" look as it threatens to explode beyond the screen.

Other tech credits are excellent and Robert Paynter's camerawork suggests a world like no other. That's one of the film's problems. It's too weird to be involving.
—*Jagr.*

Joe Polowsky — ein amerikanischer Träumer
(Joe Polowsky — An American Dreamer)
(W. GERMAN-DOCU-COLOR)

A Con Film release of a Wolfgang Pfeiffer Filmproduktion. Written and directed by Wolfgang Pfeiffer. Camera (color), Johann Feindt, Claus Deubel; editor, Klaus Volkenborn. Reviewed at Leipzig Docu and Short Film Festival, Nov. 26, 1986. Running time: **82 MINS.**

Leipzig — Winner of this year's Golden Dove award at the Leipzig Docu Festival, "Joe Polowsky — An American Dreamer" is an excellent example of how a documaker can create a complex, engrossing portrait of a man (and an era) without turning his subject into a saint.

This touching, witty, at times hilarious story of a Chicago cabbie who as a G.I. was present at the Elbe River when Yank and Russian allies joined forces on April 25, 1945, and his lifelong obsession with that historic meeting — fated to shortly be swept aside by the Cold War — marks the diretorial debut of Wolfgang Pfeiffer.

With special handling it could hold its own at an art house venue, as well as fest outings. Soundtrack is mostly in down-home American English, with some undisturbing sections in Russian. It is probably one of the few pics that could play equally well East or West.

The basic message of "Polowsky" is a plea for peace, but it makes its point via a multi-faceted personality constructed, à la "Citizen Kane," post-mortem. Pic opens with Joe's funeral — which is in a way the crowning achievement of his life, since his dream of being buried at Torgau in a big memorial service has, miraculously, come true.

Pfeiffer and his German crew travel from Chicago and North Carolina to the USSR, interviewing people who knew the dead man. Many of the G.I.'s with Joe at Torgau provide testimony, hovering between the touching and the bizarre, about the reunion of Yank and Russian soldiers in Moscow, engineered by Joe in 1955 at the height of the Cold War. Highlight is an excerpt from the "Strike It Rich" tv show, where the group of 10 Americans found money for their plane tickets at the eleventh hour, and a poolside interview with show's host Walt Framer.

With suprising intuition, Pfeiffer captures a flavor of America, in all its naiveté and good heartedness. It is this image of grass root America, more than an old Soviet soldier's long speech about peace in the world, that gives "Joe Polowsky" a sense of hope. As Studs Terkel sums it up, Joe was just an ordinary guy with passion, who showed you can

fight City Hall and the big guys.

Though his decades-long campaign to get the U.N. to officially hail April 25 as a special day came to nought (and was, according to his endearingly money-minded son, a financial disaster for the whole family), Joe's eccentricity and dreams are inseparable from hopes for peaceful coexistence between the superpowers, and that gives food for thought.

Only criticism to be leveled is that pic has too many finales, after its emotional climax has come and gone. One also leaves curious to know more about the opposition Joe's efforts must have encountered, during and after the 1950s, which is glossed as his being censured by the Senate during the McCarthy period.— *Yung.*

Three Amigos
(COLOR)

Western spoof fails to set any saddles ablaze.

An Orion Pictures release. Produced by Lorne Michaels, George Folsey Jr. Executive producer, Steve Martin. Directed by John Landis. Stars Chevy Chase, Steve Martin, Martin Short. Screenplay, Martin, Michaels, Randy Newman; camera (Technicolor, prints by DeLuxe), Ronald W. Browne; editor, Malcolm Campbell; music, Elmer Bernstein; songs, Newman; production design, Richard Sawyer; set decorator, Richard Goddard; set designers, Mark Faybus, Stan Tropp; costumes, Deborah Nadoolman; sound, William Kaplan; second unit director, Folsey; second unit camera, John Stephens; assistant director, David Sosna; casting, Jackie Burch. Reviewed at the Samuel Goldwyn theater, Beverly Hills, Nov. 24, 1986. (MPAA Rating: PG.) Running time: **105 MINS.**
Dusty Bottoms . . . . .Chevy Chase
Lucky Day . . . . .Steve Martin
Ned Nederlander . . . . .Martin Short
Carmen . . . . .Patrice Martinez
El Guapo . . . . .Alfonso Arau
Jefe . . . . .Tony Plana
Harry Flugelman . . . . .Joe Mantegna

Hollywood — A few choice morsels of brilliant humor can't save the "Three Amigos" from missing the whole enchilada.

Film is a reheated mish-mash of old oaters that teases one's buds with familiarity without enough new flavoring to make it a completely satisfying concoction.

With stellar comedic cast, b.o. prospects should be hearty, which is to say, there's no accounting for taste.

Film is a takeoff of "The Magnificent Seven," but also tries perhaps too hard to parody the style of a number of other classic westerns. It has a stunning desert setting captured beautifully by cinematographer Ronald Browne, luscious scoring by the old pro Elmer Bernstein (who scored "The Magnificent Seven") and clever original songs by Randy Newman that Gene Autry or Roy Rogers could have sung easily.

It also has three funny guys, Steve

Martin, Chevy Chase and Martin Short, playing the three wimpy matinee idols known as the "Three Amigos," each doing his particular brand of shtick that is priceless in some scenes but not at all amusing in others.

Martin does clever slapstick, Chase does goofy slapstick and Short doesn't do slapstick, but plays off the other two with a certain wide-eyed innocence.

These singing cowboy stars of the silent screen have just been fired by the flamboyant Goldsmith Studios mogul Harry Flugelman (a throwaway performance for Joe Mantegna) when they get a cryptic telegram from a Mexican woman (Patrice Martinez) offering them 100,000 pesos to come to her dusty desert town of Santa Poco.

It turns out she's hired them under the mistaken belief that they are as macho in real life as on screen and will be able to stop the notorious bandito El Guapo (Alfonso Arau) from terrorizing the poor Santa Poco people. Well, the "Three Amigos" think they're traveling south of the border to put on a show.

Much of the humor is derived from gags where these three hapless gringos make fools of themselves trying to uphold their images as valiant screen heroes, when in fact they are really singing sissies scared out of their britches by the irascible Arau.

Some of the gags work when taken in two-minute bites, not unlike the kind scripters Martin and Michaels perfected for "Saturday Night Live," but they don't make for a cohesive comedic romp when strung together into a feature film.

Cardboard characters, such as these guys, can only perform a certain number of silly antics before they become redundant.

The writers have come up with some hilarious one-liners. Unfortunately, a few too many are beaten to death as when Arau is teasing his sidekick Jefe (Tony Plana) on the meaning of plethora.

It's also hard to figure out what the scripters were thinking putting a medieval dungeon under a dinky adobe house and a German fighter pilot zooming in from overhead, elements that are ludicrous without adding any chuckles.

And what about the depiction of Mexicans as mostly dirty, unattractive, ignorant peasant people (who in this picture have exaggerated accents to say "peeeeeeeple"), unable to solve the bandito problem by themselves while three dumb Americans can. Filmmakers have treated the story, whether a spoof of old Westerns or not, with little regard for another people's culture, especially considering the heightened awareness of contemporary society.

There are moments in the film, however, that just shine with all the inventiveness these comedians can muster.

Martin doing bird calls atop the studio gate is a real treat as is the obviously staged scene where the Three Amigos are sitting around a campfire in front of a matte drawing of Monument Valley singing a corny cowboy bedtime song where they are joined in the chorus by a mountain lion, a turtle, a coyote, an owl and other desert creatures.

—*Brit.*

Sensi
(Evil Senses)
(ITALIAN-COLOR)

A D.M.V. release of a Dania/National/-Filmes/Globe coproduction. Produced by Pietro Innocenzi. Directed by Gabriele Lavia. Stars Lavia, Monica Guerritore. Screenplay, Lavia, Dardano Sacchetti, Vincenzo Manino, Gianfranco Clerici; camera (Kodak color, prints by Luciano Vittori), Mario Vulpiani; editor, Daniele Alabiso; music, Fabio Frizzi; art direction, Giovanni Agostinucci. Reviewed at Quirinale Cinema, Rome, Nov.

7, 1986. Running time: **101 MINS.**
Manuel . . . . .Gabriele Lavia
Vittoria . . . . .Monica Guerritore
Micol . . . . .Mimsy Farmer
   Also with: Lewis Eduard Ciannelli, Dario Mazzoli, Gioia Maria Scola.

Rome — Latest softcore effort by slumming stage thesps Gabriele Lavia (who also directs) and Monica Guerritore is a hackneyed thriller called "Evil Senses." Despite advertising, however, there is little explicit sex in "Evil Senses." In respect to last year's "Scandalous Gilda" by the same uninhibited duo, this is a far tamer offering, which accounts for its Italo rating of being off-limits to 14-year-olds and under (rather than a more restrictive rating) and the exasperated sighs of disappointed patrons expecting fewer fadeouts when the sex scenes begin. Pic has gotten off to a slow start at local wickets. Offshore chances appear limited by a blah script.

In London, professional killer Manuel (Lavia) gets a threatening phone call, flushes a list of names down the john, and blows out the brains of a hit man during the credit

sequence. Mr. Cool then lights a cigaret and takes a plane to Italy, where he takes shelter in a swanky Belle de Jour brothel run by old flame Mimsy Farmer.

While he hides from the baddies who want to rub him out after getting their hands on the list, Manuel has time to fall for one of the bored housewives working in the Art Deco brothel. Vittoria (Guerritore), beautiful, refined and insatiable, soon has the heartless killer wrapped around her little finger. No one will be surprised to find out she's working for the bad guys, neither Manuel, who knew it all along, nor the audience who has seen it all before. Story proceeds with numbing predictability until a gratuitous final twist.

Lensing is serviceable, concentrating on closeups of him and her and on glorifying Giovanni Agostinucci's arty sets. Pic contains no frontal nudity, and no acting to speak of. — *Yung.*

London Festival Reviews

Castaway
(BRITISH-COLOR)

A Cannon Films release of a Cannon Screen Entertainment production in association with United British Artists. Produced by Rick McCallum. Executive producers, Peter Shaw, Richard Johnson. Directed by Nicolas Roeg. Stars Oliver Reed, Amanda Donohoe. Screenplay, Allan Scott, based on the book by Lucy Irvine; camera (Fujicolor), Harvey Harrison; editor, Tony Lawson; music, Stanley Myers; sound, Paul le Mare; production design, Andrew Sanders; assistant director, Michael Zimbrich, Waldo Roeg, Lee Cleary; costumes, Nic Ede. Reviewed at the London Film Festival, Nov. 13, 1986. Running time: **118 MINS.**
Gerald Kingsland . . . . .Oliver Reed
Lucy Irvine . . . . .Amanda Donohoe
Nun .Georgina Hale
Young Nun . . . . .Frances Barber
Jason . . . . .Tony Richards
Rod .Todd Rippon
Ronald . . . . .Len Peihopa
Janice . . . . .Virginia Hey
Schoolteacher . . . . .Sarah Harper
Shop Manager . . . . .Stephen Jenn
Lara . . . . .Sorrel Johnson
Man in pub . . . . .John Sessions
Mike Kingsland . . . . .Paul Reynoids
Geoffrey Kingsland . . . . . . .Sean Hamilton
Manager . . . . .Arthur Cox

London — For a film so rich in cinematic style and shot in glorious locations, Nicolas Roeg's most accessible film to date is remarkably lacking in a storyline, despite towering performances by the two topliners.

"Castaway" looks unscathed despite many changes of production

companies since project's inception almost two years ago—first United British Artists, then Thorn EMI and finally Cannon—and admirably demonstrates how boring desert island life must be. Prospects are good for those interested in beautiful scenery and naked bodies.

Newcomer Amanda Donohoe (previously in "Foreign Body") spends most of the pic displaying the absence of bikini marks on her body (palm trees always seem to obscure the vital parts of Oliver Reed as Gerald Kingsland), and she copes well with a character whose motives and methods for going to the tiny desert island remain dubious.

Picture this: London is cold, wet and miserable, and the tv and newspapers are full of doom, gloom and despondency. What else does a girl do but answer an ad from a man looking for a wife to take to a tropical island for a year?

She works in a boring tax office while he spends a lot of time in swimming pools and looking wistfully at goldfish. As she says when they decide to go to the island, "It's amazing this . . . it's the ultimate blind date."

The unlikely pair—she takes him to bed but isn't really interested in him—are dropped off on the tiny island of Tuin, in the Torres Strait between Papua New Guinea and

Australia, with great intentions of creating an idyllic life. Of course they have managed to forget vital medical supplies.

The sea is deep blue, the sand clean and white, and the atmosphere undeniably romantic, and as they settle down to their first night in the small tent, Reed makes a move towards her, only to receive a slap. That sets the scene for the rest of the film—sexual tension on a desert island.

"Castaway" is based on two nonfiction books—Lucy Irvine's version, also called "Castaway," and Gerald Kingsland's "The Islander"—and tries to tread a path between the two conflicting versions of their sojourn. Pic was shot in sequence, and Roeg's problem is telling an essentially straight story.

His previous pics, like "Don't Look Now" and "Bad Timing," were complex narratives with flashbacks cleverly interwoven. With "Castaway," the story is straightforward and creates a feeling that he is restraining his directorial talents and relying more on the locations (shot in the Seychelles) and the actors.

Reed gives the performance of his career as a sexually frustrated middle-aged man in search of sun and sex, and is admirably complemented by Amanda Donohoe as the determined but fickle object of

his lust.

Photography is excellent (especially underwater scenes by Mike Valentine that Jacques Cousteau would have been proud of), and as the couple's supplies dwindle and the insects start biting, impressive special effects show horribly swollen ankles, undernourished bodies, and open wounds.

Sexual tension is the center and catalyst of the film, but at a running time of almost two hours you feel there should be a bit more to the story. Roeg is an overcriticized talent, but though "Castaway" is a great ad for the tropical Seychelles, it won't be remembered as a classic.

—*Adam.*

Slum "Zum Paradies"/ Deim Dar El-Naemi
(Paradise Slum)
(WEST GERMAN/SUDANESE-DOCU-COLOR)

An Eikon-Film production. Written and directed by Cornelia Schlede. Camera (color) Henning Stegmüller, Jan Betke; editor, Sylvia Regelin; sound, Heike Pilleman. Reviewed at the London Film Festival, Nov. 23, 1986. Running time: **115 MINS.**
   With: Roghia Hamza Osman, Haregu Ghebre Micael, Judith Schulz.

London — While most recent docus on the Sudan have focused on the effects of the famine there, director Cornelia Schlede has chosen otherwise for her film debut. She spotlights the work of three women in Port Sudan helping African women set up small business enterprises. It's an enterprise worth airing, but Schlede lets down both her subjects and herself by leaving the splicer on "Off." With a running time of close to two hours, only the most committed students of women's struggle for self-improvement in Africa are going to appreciate this documentary.

Camera follows a native Sudanese, an Eritrean refugee and a German relief worker over the course of a day's work. There is no obstrusive commentary and the subjects are allowed to speak directly the the camera as they visit clients and talk among themselves.

All three communicate with each other and the camera in English and although they speak eloquently of their hopes and disappointments, the quality of the soundtrack makes it difficult frequently to decipher what they are saying. Whole chunks of conversations are lost in background rumble, or because their accents are difficult to decode.

One can't help but admire the spirit and dedication of these women as they battle prejudices in their communities, the grandiose plans of foreign relief projects and lack of resources, but it's a dedicated viewer who won't want 30 minutes lopped off this docu. —*Coop.*

Gothic
(BRITISH-COLOR)

A Virgin Films release of a Virgin Vision production. Produced by Penny Corke. Executive producers, Al Clark, Robert Devereaux. Directed by Ken Russell. Screenplay, Stephen Volk; camera (Eastmancolor), Mike Southon; editor, Michael Bradsell; music, Thomas Dolby; sound, Bruce White; production design, Christopher Hobbs; assistant director, Iain Patrick; art director, Michael Buchanan; costumes, Victoria Russell. Reviewed at the London Film Festival, Nov. 30, 1986. Running time: **90 MINS.**
Byron . . . . Gabriel Byrne
Shelley . . . . Julian Sands
Mary . . . . Natasha Richardson
Claire . . . . Myriam Cyr
Dr. Polidori . . . . Timothy Spall
Fletcher . . . . Andreas Wisniewski
Murray . . . . Alec Mango
Rushton . . . . Dexter Fletcher
Justine . . . . Pascal King
Tour guide . . . . Tom Hickey
Turkish automaton . . . . Lynda Coggin
Mechanical woman . . . . . . Kristine Landon

London — The thinking man's "A Nightmare On Elm Street," or a poetic masterpiece capturing the drug-ridden inspiration for a literary event? Ken Russell's "Gothic" in many ways defies classification.

Russell's films always have been very much an acquired taste, but with "Gothic" he is back to his theatrically extravagant best in a similar style to "Mahler" and "The Music Lovers." B.o. potential may be limited, but for unrelenting terror and style the pic could gain cult impact.

Set on a stormy June night in 1816 at the Villa Diodati in Switzerland, the drug-induced excesses of the poet Byron (Gabriel Byrne) and his four guests inspired both Mary Shelley to write "Frankenstein" and Dr. Polidori "The Vampyre," two gothic horror classics.

Pic starts as Shelley (Julian Sands), his lover Mary (Natasha Richardson) and her half-sister Claire (Myriam Cyr) arrive at the sprawling villa. Shelley is chased by poetry-mad groupies avid for his body, and runs to the building to be met by Byron and his lover/guest Dr. Polidori.

Being established poets and artistic types, they soon get down to some serious drug taking, and after a short orgy in which they decide "it is the age of dreams and nightmares," they hold a seance round an ancient skull to conjure up their deepest fears.

By all accounts it is just a quiet night in for Byron, but while Dr. Polidori tucks himself away in his room to dream of vampires, Shelley and his two women become convinced there is something lurking outside.

As the storm grows so does the terror in the villa, and Shelley, wandering into a ramshackle barn, comments "the smell of the grave is here." As the group becomes more drug-soaked and terrified, the villa with its darkened passages, spiral staircases, shuttered rooms, and menacing candlelight, becomes a labyrinth of horror.

They eventually manage to conquer their "monster" by smashing that pesky skull, the storm abates, and next thing you know it is morning, and everything was—surprise, surprise—drug-induced dreams.

Ken Russell has made an unrelenting nightmare that is both uncomfortable and compulsive to watch. Photography, by Mike Southon, and lighting are exceptional, and Stephen Volk's screenplay amply displays the power of imagination on minds wracked with opium.

Gabriel Byrne and Natasha Richardson (daughter of Vanessa Redgrave and Tony Richardson) are powerful and hold the film together, while Julian Sands is as wooden as in "A Room With A View" and his only saving graces are that he runs about well and looks poetic. Timothy Spall, previously seen in the tv series "Auf Wiedersehen Pet," is an unexpected delight as the foppish Dr. Polidori, and brings needed touches of humor to the pic.
—*Adam.*

Coast To Coast
(BRITISH-COLOR)

A BBC Television Britannia-Dean-Clough production. Produced by Graham Benson. Executive producer, David N. Wilkinson. Associate producer, Martyn Auty. Directed by Sandy Johnson. Screenplay, Stan Hey; camera (color), Colin Munn; editor, Ken Pearce; music, various Tamla-Motown artists; sound, Roger Long; production design, Christopher Robbilliard; costumes, Paula Bruce. Reviewed at the London Film Festival, Nov. 24, 1986. Running time: **96 MINS.**
Ritchie Lee . . . . Lenny Henry
John Carloff . . . . John Shea
Kecks McGuinness . . . . . . Peter Postlewaite
Greaves . . . . George Baker
Chiropodist . . . . Peter Vaughan
Susan . . . . Cherie Lunghi
Curtis Duchamps . . . . Al Matthews
Garage owner . . . . Bobby Knutt

London — "Coast To Coast" is probably one of the best arguments for the BBC changing its policy of denying tv features a theatrical release. It is stylish and amusing and would have a good chance of traveling well to the U.S.

Film draws heavily on American themes and influences, has a compulsive soundtrack of 1960s Tamla-Motown music, and leading performances one would be hard-pressed to fault. In all, a gem of a smallscale feature which will probably have the U.K. lifespan of a couple of tv screenngs.

Pic opens with John Carloff — cue the jokes "I bet everyone calls you Boris" — returning to the Liverpool he knew as a youngster in those musically halcyon days of the 1960s. Carloff (John Shea) has a collection of classic Motown singles, while Richie Lee (Lenny Henry) owns an old ice-cream van that doubles as a mobile disco. So they do the obvious and team up.

After two abortive gigs, the first at an old folks home — "they said they wanted '60s music" — their van acts up, so they take it back to the shady dealer who sold it to Lee, con man Kecks McGuinness.

He, though, has stolen some forgery plates from a gang of London East End villains, and stashes them in the dynamic duo's van. Here starts the road movie aspect, as Carloff and Lee are chased across England by the two cockney killers — marvelous performances by Peter Vaughan and George Baker who are suitably malevolent and funny at the same time.

The boys decide an ice-cream van is a bit too obvious in the Lake District in midwinter, so they trade it in for the nearest thing England had to offer for a U.S. style car, a 16-year-old Zodiac.

It transpires that Carloff is AWOL from an English USAF base, so he is not best pleased when Richie decides an American air base is a good place for them to hide out and play a disco, before their final showdown with the villains.

The teaming of Shea and Henry is inspirational, and similarly to "Gregory's Girl" (also directed by a Scot) the pic is packed with wonderful asides and comic irrelevancies — they stop at a lonely country inn on the moors where the landlady (Cherie Lunghi) for reasons totally unexplained keeps a llama.

Lenny Henry is a well-known black comedian/mimic in the U.K., and excels as the fast-talking Liverpudlian who wishes he was American. He's nicely complemented by Shea, who underplays the slightly enigmatic Yank who wishes he was born black.

Director Sandy Johnson has structured the feature perfectly, with all segments linked with classic Motown hits, though some of the Liverpudlian accents may prove a bit bemusing for overseas viewers. All technical credits are fine. Pic ends with Lee, complete with gleaming white Cadillac, meeting Carloff as he is released from an air base in Boston, Mass., ready for the planned sequel. —*Adam.*

The Passion Of Remembrance
(BRITISH-COLOR)

A Sankofa Film/Video Collective release. Produced by Martina Attille. Written and directed by Maureen Blackwood and Issac Julien. Camera (Technicolor), Steven Bernstein, Nina Kellgren; editor, Nadine Marsh-Edwards; music, Tony Remy; sound, Diana Ruston. Reviewed at the London Film Festival, Nov. 22, 1986. Running time: **80 MINS.**
Female speaker . . . . Anni Domingo
Male speaker . . . . Joseph Charles
Maggie Baptiste . . . . Antonia Thomas
Gary . . . . Carlton Chance
Tony Baptiste . . . . Jim Findley
Benjy Baptiste . . . . Ram John Holder
Glory Baptiste . . . . Shiela Mitchell
Tonia . . . . Tania Morgan
Michael . . . . Gary McDonald
Louise . . . . Janet Palmer

London — "The Passion Of Remembrance" is a very worthy film that covers homosexuality, racism, sexism, and the generation gap, and their effects on a black British family. That, though, is the problem—pic tries to do too much.

With a $100,000 budget, pic is plainly a small-scale production, but the makers seem to have got carried away with a sense of the project's importance, spending too much time on lingering shots of swimming pools and cityscapes.

There are two aspects to the story: the first features a black man and woman in a desert landscape discussing the plight of blacks in the U.K., with aggression from the man, and restrained passion from the woman. The second shows life for the Baptiste family where conflicts over culture and sex have reared their ugly heads.

Also featured are numerous blurred scenes of the inner-city riots that swept Britain in 1981, which are linked with frames from gay demonstrations, to portray the government's attitude to the minorities.

However well intentioned the film may be, acting, sound and cinematography are only adequate, and the passion of the dialog does not cover up the technical deficiencies.

Soundtrack is too muted and garbled to have full impact, and the film tends to raise far too many questions and not enough answers. There is a great deal of passion in the first 20 minutes, but after that pic tends to lose its way and tries to be too stylized.

Antonia Thomas as Maggie is the only actor to stand out, doing more than posing in front of the camera reciting lines. Importantly, though, the film is directing itself mainly to Britain's black community rather than preaching at whites,
—*Adam.*

Blunt
(BRITISH-COLOR-16m)

A BBC-TV production. Executive producer, Graham Massey. Produced by Martin Thompson. Directed by John Glenister. Stars Ian Richardson, Anthony Hopkins. Screenplay, Robin Chapman; camera (color), John McGlashan; editor, Jim Latham; music, Hector Berlioz; production design, Colin Shaw; set decoration, Stuart Moser; assistant director, Jacinta Peel; costume design, Colin Lavers. Reviewed at London Film Festival, Nov. 12, 1986. Running time: **85 MINS.**

With: Ian Richardson, Anthony Hopkins, Michael Williams, Rosie Kerslake, Geoffrey Chater, Albert Welling, Michael McStay, Emma Cottrell, Casey Doy.

London — "Blunt" is an extremely well-acted, fictionalized account of a crucial moment in the lives of two of Brtiain's most celebrated spies, Anthony Blunt and Guy Burgess. However, it is not a traditional spy story, but rather an exploration of friendship and betrayal, an analysis of the heart rather than the mind of a spy.

It focuses on Anthony Blunt, a respected art historian who worked for military intelligence until 1964 when he confessed to spying for the Russians. During a few short suspenseful days n 1951, Blunt is obliged to engineer the escape of a fellow spy to the Russians. Unbeknownst to him, Burgess, his lover since student days at Cambridge, decides in those few days to defect too.

In a series of highly charged if low-key vignettes, the characters of the two men are admirably contrasted: Blunt, slightly fastidious even haughty (played consummately by Ian Richardson) and the blustering, extroverted but exasperating Burgess (a brilliant effort by Anthony Hopkins) demonstrate how apparently easy it was to accommodate spying into their lives.

Providing an outside view of the two and a measure of normalcy is their journalist friend Goronwy Rees, who knows about his friends but doesn't wish to betray them. His anguish and that of his wife puts the dictum about betraying one's country before one's friends to its severest test.

In a final *coup de théâtre* Rees tries to denounce Burgess as a spy, but Blunt deflects the blow, succeeding in protecting himself for another decade from suspicion.

Although the film lacks the resonance and charm of the award-winning BBC drama, "An Englishman Abroad" (which focused on actress Coral Browne's encounter with Burgess in the Soviet Union), it is subtle and illuminating, unobtrusively directed. —*Guid.*

Karsh: The Searching Eye
(CANADIAN-DOCU-COLOR)

A Canadian Broadcasting Corp. production. Produced, written, directed and narrated by Harry Rasky. Camera (color), Kenneth Gregg; editor, Paul Nikolich; music, Louis Applebaum; set decoration, Erik Hoppe, Joe Grimaldi; Karsh photo sequences, Geoff Cheesbrough. Reviewed at London Film Festival, Nov. 29, 1986. Running time: **82 MINS.**

London — A good many more people will want to be karshed after seeing this film. And if they can't afford karshing, they'll at least know what it is.

For the camera of well-known still photographer Yousef Karsh regularly captures the spirit as well as the face of those celebrities who sit for him. This docu lets us see from behind and alongside the camera how he does it.

Unobtrusively and entertainingly, it traces Karsh's professional career from poor Armenian emigrant to Canada, to his breakthrough in the 1940s photographing wartime generals and politicians, to his highly successful life today.

Karsh himself is constantly on camera, explaining his artistic predilections, commenting on people he's worked with, responding to the director's questions.

While some 500 photos are flashed on-screen during the film, a dozen are singled out for special comment — Winston Churchill, Pablo Casals, Helen Keller, Ernest Hemingway. Karsh's anecdotes about them are rounded out with pertinent historical footage and music.

An interesting, highly charged encounter takes place between Karsh and Leonard Bernstein, who was asked to pose for the photographer and the docu camera in one unrehearsed session. Result: it is far from simple or easy to photograph the famous. Bernstein concludes the ordeal by saying, half jokingly, "there are too many egos in the room."

Only irritating element in the docu are the overt compliments paid to Canada, whose pubservice broadcaster commissioned the film. —*Guid.*

Playing Away
(BRITISH-COLOR)

A Film Four Intl. release of an Insight production. Executive producer, Brian Skilton. Produced by Vijay Amarnani. Directed by Horace Ové. Screenplay, Caryl Phillips; camera (color), Nic Knowland; editor, Graham Whitlock; music, Simon Webb; sound, Christian Wangler; assistant director, Simon Hinkly; associate producer, Christopher Sutton; art direction, Pip Gardner. Reviewed at London Film Festival, Nov. 25, 1986. Running time: **100 MINS.**

Willie-Boy	Norman Beaton
Godfrey	Robert Urquhart
Marjorie	Helen Lindsay
Derek	Nicholas Farrel
Stuart	Brian Bovell
Errol	Gary Beadle

London — "Playing Away" takes a lighthearted look at what happens when a West Indian team from a black London neighborhood plays a "friendly" game of cricket against a local village team in the idyllic English countryside. Director Horace Ové chose to play this one in a lowkey style, gunning for laughs to show the chasm that divides these two cultures, but despite a strong opening the uneven script loses its way and the pic doesn't jell.

The film undoubtedly will invite comparisons with "My Beautiful Laundrette," which, like "Playing Away," was funded by Channel 4 tv and also deals with the clash of black and white cultures in modern Britain. "Playing Away" should appeal to the same audiences as "Laundrette" in the U.K. arthouse circuit but it might leave viewers in non-cricketing territories a little bewildered.

The film darts busily between characters on the two teams as they prepare for the match, organized by the village as the climax to "Third World Week." Although the sporting fixture serves as good structure in which to air mutual prejudices of the two cultures, it's also a limiting factor as pic tries to cover too many characters too briefly. Also, as with many "sporting" films, the actual contest in the last quarter serves as an anticlimax to the previous buildup.

Areas of racial conflict which might have upset the rural setting discreetly are swept under the carpet, ironically in the time-honored English tradition. Plot lines are left dangling in the air giving a jerky and unsatisfactory feel to the film.

Norman Beaton as the captain of the West Indian team gives a realistic performance of a man caught between two cultures, countries and generations, while hiding most of his fears in the bottom of a whiskey bottle. —*Coop.*

Comrades
(BRITISH-COLOR)

A Film Four Intl. release of a Skreba, Curzon Film, National Film Finance Corp., Film Four Intl. coproduction. Produced by Simon Relph. Written and directed by Bill Douglas. Camera (color), Gale Tattersall; editor, Mick Audsley; music, Hans Werner Henze, David Graham; production design, Michael Pickwoad; art direction, Derrick Chetwyn; set decoration, Clive Winter; assistant director, Redmond Morris; costumes, Doreen Watkinson, Bruce Finlayson. Reviewed at London Film Festival, Nov. 15, 1986. Running time: **160 MINS.**

With: Robin Soans, William Gaminara, Stephen Bateman, Philip Davis, Jeremy Flynn, Keith Allen, Alex Norton, Michael Clark, Arthur Dignam, James Fox, John Hargreaves, Michael Hordern, Freddie Jones, Vanessa Redgrave, Robert Stephens, Imelda Staunton.

London — Bill Douglas' long-awaited first, full-length feature is hypnotically engaging in parts, but disappointing in its final effect.

If it remains at its current running time, it is not likely to have much of a boxoffice future, at least not outside Britain.

The problems, however, don't involve simply length. There is no dramatic center, no clear-cut conflict, no precise focus which satisfies sufficiently. For example, the viewer is well into the second half of the film before he has actually clear in his mind the relationships among the principal characters.

But that said, film is bound to have avid fans who'll appreciate its worthiness and its magical qualities, Douglas, who made a trilogy of short features in the '70s about his Scottish childhood, has an eye for fresh detail, the rituals of rural life, and the dignity of countryfolk which remind one of Ermanno Olmi's approach to similar material. Rarely before have the poverty, the pains and the pleasures, the oppressiveness of the work routine, even of the weather, been so well conveyed on film.

However, because so much time is spent on building up this rich tapestry of rural England in the 1830s, the focus is lost. Just what all the fuss was over the so-called Tolpuddle Martyrs, the subject of the film, is somewhat obscured.

Eventually one pieces together that they were a small group of peasant craftsmen who dared to form a union and ask for higher wages. They were singled out for their subversion by the British authorities, though never apparently having perpetrated any violence themselves, and deported to Australia. After a public outcry they were subsequently recalled to England.

Douglas did have the bright idea of framing the action from the point-of-view of a magic lantern entertainer. Many scenes have the stylized, naive quality of shadow play, with flat characters and the circular, evenly spaced narrative movement associated with events depicted in the then popular diorama shows.

The device not only distances the viewer, but reinforces the naive, wonder-filled attitude of mind of the chief character, George Loveless, who is the instigator and moral leader of the Tolpuddle martyrs. Unfortunately, this character is lost sight of once the story moves to Australia.

If the film devotes too much attention to recreating the feel of the times in the first half, it loses its way in too many rivulets, trying to track too many characters, in the latter half, set in Australia.

Although there is a unique vision at work in "Comrades" — technical credits are excellent and the performances, mostly from virtual unknowns, dignified — it's a pity that more ruthlessness in scripting and editing was not exercised. —*Guid.*

Yes, det er far!
(Yes, It's Your Dad)
(DANISH-COLOR)

A Regnar Grasten Film release of Nordisk Film/Regnar Grasten Film production with Per Holst Filmproduktion and the Danish Film Institute. Produced by Bo Christensen. Directed by John Hilbard. Screenplay, Jarl Friis-Mikkelsen, Ole Stephensen, John Hilbard; camera (Eastmancolor), Claus Loof; production design, special effects, Henning Bahs; editor, Edda Urup; sound, Leif Jensen; costumes, Pia Myhrdal; music, Jan Gläsel; production manager, Michael Obel. Reviewed at the Palads, Copenhagen, Nov. 27, 1986. Running time: **81 MINS.**

Carlo . . . . .Jarl Friis-Mikkelsen
Walter .Ole Stephensen
Viola van Heimweh . . . . . . .Kirsten Rolffes
Charlotta . . . . .Ewa Carlsson
Barbara . . . . .Linda Lauersen
Ewald . . . . . . .Flemming (Bamse) Jörgensen
Crook No. 1 . . . . .Erik Paaske
Crook No. 2 . . . . .Jess Ingerslev
The bodyguard . . . . .Claus Nissen
Also with: Kirsten Lehfeldt, Preben Kristensen, Thomas Eje, Erik Stephensen, Olaf Nielsen, Gerda Gilbo, Jörn Hjorting.

Copenhagen — In scripting, acting, helming and general execution, "Yes, It's Your Dad" is probably the most inept piece of motion picture making in the entire history of Danish film. With one possible exception being item's immediate predecessor, "Walter & Carlo: Up At Dad's Hat," which made it into the history books in spades last year by also doing better at the boxoffice than any other Danish feature title ever.

Released in a locally record-breaking 40 prints, the producers of "Yes" obviously are opting for a fast playoff this time around, believing, most likely, in the old dictum that you cannot fool all of the people all of the time.

The maybe/maybe not foolproof formula, which in "Dad's Hat" had Jarl Friis-Mikkelsen and Ole Stephensen, Danish pubcaster television's beloved Saturday Night cohosts and (only intermittently) light comedy muggers, plunging themselves as writers and performers into outright farce, is repeated mercilessly in "Yes."

Emulating the old Jerry Lewis-Dean Martin teamwork, Friis-Mikkelsen and Stephensen now have themselves involved in a plot of smuggling coffee from Sweden to Denmark's suddenly coffee-bereft old-age pensioners and in another one of Danes and Swedes trying to cheat each other out of their ill-gotten loot.

Friis-Mikkelsen, who is a disaster as an actor (he is stiff as a board and has only two facial expressions) plays Carlo, a shrill and choleric male chauvinist halfwit who wriggles out of whatever predicament he lands in by his cement-head perseverance and in spite of his constant boozing and grabbing at nubile women passing by in an endless parade. He does his Jerry Lewis bit without one iota of redeeming deep-er humanity being indicated anywhere along the line.

Ole Stephensen, a handsome hulk, plays Carlo's straight man and patsy Walter and has latter down to the Dean Martin prototype by also breaking into romantic vocalizing in improbable situations now and again. Even with Stephensen, the amateurishness shows through, however, and what is worse, it has rubbed off on everybody else involved in the making of "Yes."

The camera fails to keep up with the frantic demands of the script; the script has no natural structure; and the editing just throws everything to the winds.

Yes, "Yes" does have a helmer, but veteran John Hilbard (of the "Bedside" porno spoofs of the '60s and early '70s) hardly makes his professional presence felt, having most likely preferred to duck the barrage of sputtering, stuttering or otherwise unintelligible monologs issuing from the Carlo character and to have been content to transfer willy-nilly to the big screen every underdeveloped twist, turn or contortion offered by the screenplay devised by the two stars of the tube.

So overwhelming is Friis-Mikkelsen's and Ole Stephensen's local television fame that, as suggested by one Copenhagen critic, "you could put the guys in a coffin and nail down the lid, and people would still flock to see them." Well, since that coffin is unlikely to travel an inch beyond any borders, the eventual fate of "Yes" will be strictly a down home phenomenon and maybe a matter of what is ripe or rotten as cinema fare in the State of Denmark. —*Kell.*

La Alacrana
(The Scorpion)
(MEXICAN-COLOR)

A Peliculas Mexicanas release of a Cinematográfica Rodríguez, production. Executive producer, Eddie Rodriguez. Produced by Roberto Rodríguez E. Directed by José Luis Urquieta. Stars Maribel Guardia, Carlos Ancira. Screenplay, Jorge Patino, based on an argument by Roberto Rodríguez R.; camera (color), Alberto Arellanos; editor, Rogelio Zúñiga. Reviewed at Big Apple Cine 1, N.Y., Nov. 21, 1986. Running time: **86 MINS.**

Eugenia (La Alacrana) . . .Maribel Guardia
Don Eliseo Mendieta . . . . . . .Carlos Ancira
Fernando . . . . .Juan Delaez
Colonel . . . . .Naciso Busquets
Raquel . . . . .Claudia Guzmán
Irene . . . . .Susy Rodriguez
Also with: Barbara Gil, Gina Morett, Sandra Boyd, Maria Luisa Alcala, Carlos Pouliot, Rojo Grau.

The Mexican pic "La Alacrana" (The Scorpion), directed by José Luis Urquieta, is a suspenseful cop show starring former Miss Costa Rica Maribel Guardia as the no-nonsense detective "Alacrana" hot on the pursuit of a psychotic killer in Mexico City.

The killer (Carlos Ancira) is a gentle antique dealer by day and by night is a raving religious fanatic intent on inflicting seven identical mortal wounds to his wife and five other participants in a homemade porno video.

Detective Alacrana, whose cop husband was killed years earlier in the line of duty, tracks down all leads to find the murderer — exploring the *demimonde* and its practitioners of kinky sex en route.

Guardia, usually known only for her physical talents, puts in a believable job as the serious cop married to her duty. The side characters are also engaging, albeit some are little more than simplified clichés.

Urquieta has wisely decided not to dwell on the gruesome murders by keeping the story focused on the principals and the script generates enough suspense to keep the viewer interested. The pic should do well at Hispanic boxoffices. —*Lent.*

Manon des sources
(Manon Of The Springs)
(FRENCH-COLOR)

An AMLF release of a Renn Production/Films A2/RAI 2/DD Prods. coproduction. Executive producer, Claude Berri. Produced by Pierre Grunstein. Associate producer, Alain Poiré. Directed by Berri. Stars Yves Montand, Daniel Auteuil. Screenplay, Berri, Gérard Brach, based on the novel by Marcel Pagnol; camera (Technovision, Eastmancolor), Bruno Nuytten; editor, Geneviève Louveau, Hervé de Luze; music, Jean-Claude Lepit (theme adapted from Verdi's "The Force Of Destiny"); sound (Dolby), Pierre Gamet, Dominique Hennequin; art direction, Bernard Vezat; costumes, Sylvie Gautrelet; makeup, Michèle Deruelle, Jean-Pierre Eychenne; production administrator, Colette Suder; assistant director, Xavier Castano; casting, Marie-Christine Lafosse. Reviewed at the Marignan Concorde-Pathé cinema, Paris, Dec. 4, 1986. Running time: **113 MINS.**

César "Le Papet" . . . . .Yves Montand
Ugolin . . . . .Daniel Auteuil
Manon Cadoret . . . . . . .Emmanuelle Béart
Bernard Olivier . . . . . . .Hippolyte Girardot

Paris — "Manon des sources" is the poignant, but more dramatically wobbly followup to "Jean de Florette," producer-director Claude Berri's risky two-film adaptation of a novel by Marcel Pagnol, who, unsatisfied with his own next-to-last feature in 1952, expanded it as a two-part novel.

When Pagnol filmed his own "Manon des sources" nearly a quarter of a century ago, he came up with a picture running just under four hours. As producer-writer-director with his own home-spun "repertory" acting troupe, he could indulge his digressively prolix theory of cinema (though his distrib, Gau-

Original Film
(FRENCH-B&W)

A Gaumont release of a Marcel Pagnol film. Stars Jacqueline Pagnol, Rellys, Ray-mond Pellegrin; features Robert Vattier, Henri Poupon, Henri Vilbert, Roger Sardou, Rene Sarvil. Written and directed by Marcel Pagnol; camera (b&w), Willy; editor, Jacques Bianchi; music, Roger Legrand. At Colisee, Paris, Feb. 5, 1953. Running time: **109 MINS.**

Manon . . . . .Jacqueline Pagnol
Maurice . . . . .Raymond Pellegrin
Ugolin . . . . .Rellys
Professor . . . . .Robert Vattier
Uncle . . . . .Henri Poupon
Mayor .Roger Sardou
Gendarme . . . . .Rene Sarvil
Priest . . . . .Henri Vilbert

mont, obliged him to cut the film, destroying some of the rhythms Pagnol instinctively built into his superb peasant yarn).

Berri and his coscripter, Gérard Brach, had only a relatively compact novel to tackle when they prepared "Jean de Florette," which recounts the events leading up to "Manon des sources," both film and book (*Variety,* Aug. 20).

But with "Manon," Berri met the more complex challenge of a casually-paced motion picture transferred into a literary work with a more tragic dimension. Berri had the obligation of squeezing this more diffuse material into a conventional feature length span — hence the feeling of haste and cut corners of this new "Manon des sources," which, though based on the print reworking, cannot escape the inevitable remake comparisons.

"Manon" takes place some 10 years after the action of "Jean de Florette," which dealt with the plot of an arrogant village elder and his nephew (Yves Montand and Daniel Auteuil) to buy up the land of a hunchbacked city slicker (Gérard Depardieu), who, kept deliberately ignorant of the secret spring on his property, accidentally killed himself in his vain efforts to water his land.

In Film Two, Manon, the hunchback's daughter, grown into a beautiful young woman who now lives in the hills as a reclusive shepherdess, learns of the treachery that brought about her father's death and exacts vengeance on Montand, Auteuil and the village by blocking up the subterranean spring that provides water to the area.

The resulting crisis brings about a public reckoning and the open accusation of Montand and Auteuil. Latter's guilt is deepened because he has fallen in love with Manon, and hangs himself when he realizes there is no hope for forgiveness. Montand, grieved by his nephew's death, soon follows him to the grave when he learns Depardieu was in fact his own illegitimate son.

That final revelation is what Pagnol added in his novel and Berri rushes the action along to get to these scenes, which provide Montand with some fine moments of pathos.

Auteuil is again superb as the ratty unmalicious nephew, Ugolin, and triumphs over the sometimes cramped dramaturgy, notably in his declaration of love to Manon in the hills and the scene of the latter's public denunciation, two set pieces that made Pagnol's film memorable (thanks especially to the performance of an obscure Marseilles comic named Rellys, as Ugolin).

Berri has been forced to substantially reduce the collective role of the villagers — for Pagnol an essential serio-comic choral element — and is unable to overcome the inherent feebleness of Manon character, here played ineffectually by the lovely and talented Emmanuelle Béart. In Pagnol's film the part was no better, but enjoyed more screen time (and was incarnated by the charming Jacqueline Bouvier, later to become Madame Pagnol). Another dull, unconvincing personage was that of the schoolmaster who marries Manon, here played by Hippolyte Girardot (succeeding Raymond Pellegrin in the original).

As with "Florette," tech credits are smart. All told, Berri has rendered, despite its faults and later patchiness, Pagnol's splendid yarn to the screen with the requisite emotion and psychological texture.

—Len.

Plácido
(CUBAN-COLOR)

An ICAIC production. Directed by Sergio Giral. Screenplay, Giral, Sergio Fulled; camera (color), Raul Rodriguez; music, Sergio Vittier; editor, Nelson Rodriguez. Reviewed at Rio de Janeiro Film Festival (competition) Nov. 26, 1986. Running time: **92 MINS.**
With: Jorge Villalón, Mirta Ibarra, Rosita Fornés, Miguel Benavides, Ramoncito Veloz, Miguel Gutierrez, Orlando Casín.

Rio de Janeiro — Plácido is a mid-19th century Cuban mulatto poet who becomes aware of the injustices of slavist Cuban colonial society. At first he feels he should keep his poetry in a world of its own, but before long he becomes a committed artist. Accused of heading a conspiracy of black slaves against their white masters, he is tortured and executed in the trial known as "La Escalera" (The Staircase). Many others share his fate, while thousands are imprisoned.

An interesting film certainly could have come out of this historical context of Cuban society over a century ago, when it was a Spanish colony, but except for isolated moments, the characters and period don't come to life. Acting is poor and Sergio Giral's direction is quite unimpressive.

Given the limited budget on which the film obviously was shot, he certainly should not have attempted full-scale set pieces like a cavalry charge and slave massacre. Period style is nonexistent beyond costumes. The film is far too pre-

dictable and within the context of Cuban cinema, it is old fashioned and even a little amateurish.

—Amig.

Alter Ego
(Letters From A Doctor In Africa)
(DUTCH-DOCU-16m)

A NIS/filmdistribution release of a Molenwiek and Joop de Jong production. Produced by Hillie Molenaar, De Jong. Directed by Molenaar, Joop van Wijk. Screenplay, Van Wijk; camera (ECN II color), Eugene van den Bosch, Sana Na N'Hada; editor, Hens van Rooy; music, Daniel Smith; sound, Van Rooy, Dabana Piqui. Reviewed at Desmet theater, Amsterdam, Nov. 17, 1986. Running time: **87 MINS.**

Amsterdam — As part of its Third World aid program, the Dutch government lent a young psychiatrist to the authorities of the West African state of Guinea-Bissau from 1982-85. As head of the Dept. of Mental Health of the Ministry of Health, he was supposed to organize psychiatry in the whole country, build a new psychiatric hospital, train staff and find and register mental patients in the countryside. He insisted the new hospital be open to all, and he tried to cooperate with the traditional healers.

Hillie Molenaar and Joop van Wijk made this outstanding docu in four shooting periods (from '83 to '85), using Dutchmen and Guineans alternately for photography and sound recording.

Center of interest is the psychiatrist, Joop de Jong, "Dr. Joop" to everyone. He has a daunting task. It's difficult to build a hospital out of shortages (nails, water, electricity, cement, money, food, beds, linen, etc.). It's difficult to get patients from the villages to town without transport; to talk to patients (partly through interpreters, because there are many languages); to diagnose complaints about "the wind in the head which the witches have planted;" to ensure treatment after hospitalization when the villagers refuse to re-admit the patients before a goat or a pig has been sacrificed (three-fifths of the population are animists) and the patient has no money.

After two years the hospital is finished and functioning, an occasion for a big party with the minister, people from the World Health Organization, lots of food, music and sacrificial ceremonies. There is a trained staff; the organization creaks, but it works. Dr. Joop still travels everywhere on his red motorbike, provided he can get gasoline and the budget allows it.

There is growing contact with the native healers, mutual respect and curiosity. Local healer Augusto works without mumbo jumbo. When he finally visits the hospital

after many days' walking, he's not so much interested in the building and the instruments, but in pills and powers. Augusto and Dr. Joop both remain puzzled and skeptical about the strange practices of the other.

Pic takes no sides, but just reports, and it easily keeps the viewer's attention. We recognize some patients, but as types — the one who always complains, the one who always tries to get something extra, the one who always lies. But what are their illnesses, do they get better, is anyone definitely cured? We're not told.

The filmmakers, very much involved in the problems of the Third World, probably wanted to prevent their own feelings from getting in the way of judicious reporting. But unfortunately they overdid this a bit. Pic is a great success with the Dutch public, surprising for a documentary without frills. Technical credits are all good. —Wall.

No Mercy
(COLOR)

Stylish cop thriller with strong lead performances.

A Tri-Star Pictures release of a Tri-Star-Delphi IV and V production. Produced by D. Constantine Conte. Executive producer, Michael Hausman. Directed by Richard Pearce. Stars Richard Gere, Kim Basinger. Screenplay, Jim Carabatsos; camera (Metrocolor), Michael Brault; editor, Jerry Greenberg, Bill Yahraus; music, Alan Silvestri; art direction, Doug Kraner; sound (Dolby), Lon E. Bender, Wylie Stateman; assistant director, Ned Dowd; casting, Howard Feuer. Reviewed at the Lorimar theater, Culver City, Calif., Dec. 9, 1986. (MPAA Rating: R.) Running time: **105 MINS.**

Eddie Jillette	Richard Gere
Michel Duval	Kim Basinger
Losado	Jeroen Krabbé
Captain Stemkowski	George Dzundza
Joe Collins	Gary Basaraba
Allan Deveneux	William Atherton
Paul Deveneux	Terry Kinney
Lt. Hall	Bruce McGill
Angles Ryan	Ray Sharkey
Alice Collins	Marita Geraghty
Cara	Aleta Mitchell

Hollywood — Despite some graphically brutal violence and a fair bit of "too-cool" police jargon, "No Mercy" turns out to be a step above most other films in this blooming genre of lone-cop-turned-vigilante stories. Considering the big name leads and stylish directing, film should see a good life in the theaters.

Eddie Jillette (Richard Gere) and his partner, Joe Collins (Gary Basaraba) get wind of a contract to kill a Louisiana crime overlord. They go undercover as the hit men, but find they are dealing with a much bigger, much deadlier fish as Collins is murdered brutally along with the man who had attempted to hire them, Paul Deveneux (Terry Kinney).

Jillette, who barely escapes, has only one lead in tracking his partner's murder, a mysterious blond (Kim Basinger) who had accompanied Deveneux. This lead takes Jillette down to New Orleans where tough tactics and an uncanny ability to dodge bullets enable him to find the blond, Michel Duval (Basinger).

He subsequently abducts her from beneath the nose of the evil kingpin, Losado (Jeroen Krabbé) and hauls her through the Louisiana swamplands, intent on taking her in for arrest. Of course Losado is hot in pursuit.

Through two-thirds of the film, the story remains unpredictable and the picture maintains a highly charged atmosphere. Unfortunately, when Gere's character returns to finish off Losado, the film quickly falls into predictability.

Director Richard Pearce ("Heartland," "Country") and cinematographer Michael Brault, who previously worked with Pearce on "Threshold," get credit for making "No Mercy" work. From the native, wild beauty of the Louisiana swamplands to the steamy, colorful French quarter of New Orleans, the film is a tightly woven piece, also thanks to editors Jerry Greenberg and Bill Yahraus, that is a delight to watch.

Credit also goes to Gere, now sporting a noticeably older, grayer look, who manages to bring that maturity to his often typecast roles of the angry young man. Despite some gray hairs, he is still a sexy screen persona.

Basinger, too, has something about her that probably best could be described as a mysterious, enigmatic screen presence.

The bad guy, played by Krabbé, might have stolen the best acting honors in this trio though, for he manages to bring depth to an otherwise one-dimensional role. One of Holland's leading actors, Krabbé is a magnetic leading man type who nonetheless does a good job playing second fiddle to Gere.

"No Mercy," while falling into a much-worn genre, does turn out to have some surprises thanks to screenwriter Jim Carabatsos, whose previous films include "Heroes" and the recently released "Heartbreak Ridge."

Carabatsos shows a knack for going for the unobvious and building to exciting climaxes. He needs to leave behind a lot of the hip jargon though, especially by these cops, from whose mouths it comes off as stilted and silly.—*Teen.*

New Kid 21
(The New Morning Of Billy The Kid)
(JAPANESE-COLOR)

A Parco-VAP production. Produced by Akira Morishige. Directed by Naoto Yamakawa. Screenplay, Yamakawa, Genichiro Takahashi; camera (color), Kenji Takama; editor, Kan Suzuki; music, Shuichi Chino. Reviewed at Chauvel theater, Sydney, Nov. 24, 1986. Running time: **109 MINS.**
Billy The Kid . . . . Hiroshi Mikami
Sharlotte Rampling . . . . . . Kimie Shingyoji
Nakajima Miyuki . . . . Shigeru Muroi
Master . . . . Renji Ishibashi

Sydney — "The New Morning Of Billy The Kid," which preemed in August at the Edinburgh Film Fest, is a delirious concoction in which youthful director Naoto Yamakawa flings together a variety of cinematic icons from east and west in one glorious mish-mash.

The setting for this comical convocation is a Tokyo bar called "Schlachtenhaus" (Slaughterhouse), a watering hole where one wall is filled with a large black-and-white photo of Monument Valley. The pic begins as Billy The Kid, in color, emerges from this monochrome background and gets an un-

paid job working as a waiter. It seems the bar is a safe haven from the ruthless gangsters who rule the streets outside, and among the bar staff are a samurai warrior; a roller-skating waitress and part-time poetess; a G.I. from World War II (played by a Japanese actor); a genius called 104 (the enquiries number in the Tokyo phone book); and a suave type who's a combination of Marx and Engels.

Billy, who seems to have a Lolita complex, is attracted to the bar-owner's young daughter, Tatum — though she already has a boyfriend her own age, Ryan. Then he takes to the mysterious Sharlotte Rampling, who always eats alone and is accompanied by gusts of wind wherever she goes. She turns out to be one of the gangsters, as is Hurry Carahan, a police inspector who moonlights as a gangster in his spare time.

Other characters include an old lady who's spent most of her life with a monster; an unkempt type who claims to be Jesus Christ; and a bike rider called Bluce Springsteen.

Eventually, the gangsters break into the bar and there's a furious gun battle from which only three characters survive.

It may all sound a bit precious, but it works thanks to Yamakawa's boundless energy and ideas, and his sure visual touches (he started out making experimental films). This effort could achieve cult status on the college circuit, thanks to its engaging spoofing of familiar film, music and political characters well known just about everywhere.

There also are moments of poetry among all the comic-strip anarchy, giving this unusual and disarming film additional impetus. Lovers of traditional Japanese cinema may be startled, but Yamakawa definitely is a talent to be reckoned with.—*Strat.*

Brighton Beach Memoirs
(COLOR)

Mild but effective Neil Simon adaptation.

A Universal Pictures release of a Rastar production. Produced by Ray Stark. Executive producer, David Chasman. Directed by Gene Saks. Screenplay, Neil Simon, based on his play; camera (color), John Bailey; editor, Carol Littleton; music, Michael Small; production design, Stuart Wurtzel; art direction, Paul Eads; set decoration, George DeTitta Jr., Gary Jones; costume design, Joseph G. Aulisi; sound, Chris Newman; associate producer, Joseph M. Caracciolo; assistant director, Robert Girolami; casting, Howard Feuer. Reviewed at the Samuel Goldwyn theater, Beverly Hills, Dec. 11, 1986. (MPAA Rating: PG-13.) Running time: **108 MINS.**
Kate . . . . Blythe Danner
Jack . . . . Bob Dishy
Stanley . . . . Brian Drillinger
Laurie . . . . Stacey Glick

Blanche . . . . Judith Ivey
Nora . . . . Lisa Waltz
Eugene . . . . Jonathan Silverman
Frank Murphy . . . . James Handy
Mrs. Murphy . . . . Bette Henritze
Mr. Stroheim . . . . Steven Hill

Hollywood — "Brighton Beach memoirs" emerges as one of the more successful transfers of a Neil Simon play to the screen. Admittedly, the track record on this score has not been too favorable over the years, as what had been funny and tightly played onstage often ended up as overly broad and limply directed on film. But the result here is surprisingly satisfactory on most counts, and domestic b.o. should follow suit into the new year.

The first of Simon's now-com-

Original Play

An Emanuel Azenberg, Wayne M. Rogers, Radio City Music Hall Prods., in association with Center Theater Group-Ahmanson, presentation of a play in two acts by Neil Simon. Staged by Gene Saks; setting, David Mitchell; costumes, Patricia Zipprodt; lighting, Tharon Musser. Features Matthew Broderick, Elizabeth Franz, Peter Michael Goetz, Mandy Ingber, Zeljko Ivanek, Jodi Thelen, Joyce Van Patten. General manager, Jose Vega; publicity, Bill Evans, Sandra Manley; company manager, Maria Anderson; technical supervision, Arthur Siccardi, Pete Feller; stage managers, Martin Herzer, Barbara-Mae Phillips. Opened March 27, 1983 at the Alvin Theater, N.Y.
Eugene . . . . Matthew Broderick
Blanche . . . . Joyce Van Patten
Kate . . . . Elizabeth Franz
Laurie . . . . Mindy Ingber
Nora . . . . Jodi Thelen
Stanley . . . . Zeljko Ivanek
Jack . . . . Peter Michael Goetz

pleted semi-autobiographical trilogy ("Broadway Bound," the final installment, is Broadway's latest smash), "Brighton Beach" bowed in Los Angeles in late 1982 and opened in New York in March, 1983. None of the original cast members, which included Matthew Broderick and Zeljko Ivanek as the young brothers, have returned for the screen edition, although stage director Gene Saks has repeated his chores with a solid but non-star-name lineup of thesps here.

Set in 1937 in a lower-middle class section of Brooklyn, story details assorted life crises of members of the Jerome family, hard-working moral Jews whose problems are all taken to heart by Mama Kate, played by Blythe Danner.

Kate's sister Blanche (Judith Ivey) is a widow with two girls, one a frail bookworm (Stacey Glick), the other a burgeoning hot number (Lisa Waltz) with an offer to become a hoofer on Broadway. This clan is on a long temporary stay in the apartment, and there's no telling when more relatives may be on the way if some of them get out of Poland in time.

Older brother Stanley (Brian Drillinger) is under the greatest pres-

sure, as he's on the point of being fired from his menial job, has lost money gambling and is thinking of joining the Army as an escape from his problems.

The main focus is on teenage Eugene, an aspiring writer who thinks almost exclusively of sex, of which he knows very little, and baseball, of which he probably knows a great deal. In contrast to the uncontrolled libidos on display in the raunchy teen films of recent years, the extreme innocence and naivete of Eugene come off as archaic, but beguilingly so, reminders of a more protected family-oriented age.

Despite the assurance of verbal reprisals, all family members are expected to speak their minds and share their difficulties (there can be no secrets anyway, since nothing can escape Mama's notice).

Emotions are fully felt, responsibilities accepted and decisions taken, not avoided; presence of all these traditional elements will make the film particularly satisfying for older audiences.

On the other hand, this rendition of the play isn't all that funny. Amusing and sprinkled with chuckles, yes, but there are few outright laughs.

Performances are skilled all the way through, with familiar pros Danner, Bob Dishy (as the preoccupied but very decent father) and Ivey all delivering strongly. Newcomers Silverman, Drillinger, Waltz and Glick (who, in her hornrimmed glasses, quite resembles Neil Simon) make fine impressions as well.

Gene Saks, always much more successful in his stage work than in films, has a good handle on matters this time out, and pic has a pleasant, gentle feel. But the hero of the picture has to be cinematographer John Bailey, a top emergent lenser who succeeds where many others over the years have failed, i.e., in giving a Neil Simon stage transfer a lovely look.

Production designer Stuart Wurtzel and costume designer Joseph G. Aulisi have kept to muted, brownish hues, which could have combined for a muddy, depressing result, but Bailey's lighting gives everything an airy, luminous quality that makes the largely studio-bound piece come to life. It's nothing at all flashy, but it makes all the difference.

Carol Littleton's editing keeps things moving along, and Michael Small's score is spritely. Overall impact is mild, but very pleasantly so.
—*Cart.*

The Pink Chiquitas
(CANADIAN-COLOR)

A Shapiro Entertainment release of a Mt. Pleasant production. Executive producer, Syd Cappe. Produced by Nicolas Stiliadis. Written and directed by Anthony Currie. Camera (color), Stiliadis; editor, Stephen F. Withrow; music, Paul J. Zaza; art director, Danny Addario; visual effects, Films Effects/David Stipes Prods.; associate producers, George Flak, Carl Zittrer. Reviewed at Mt. Pleasant Theater, Toronto, Dec. 2, 1986. (MPAA Rating: PG-13.) Running time: **86 MINS.**

Tony Mareda Jr. . . . . Frank Stallone
Mayor Ernie . . . . John Hemphill
Barney . . . . Don Lake
Clip Bacardi . . . . Bruce Pirrie
Marianne . . . . Elizabeth Edwards
Nurse . . . . Claudia Udy
Trudy Jones . . . . McKinlay Robinson
Sheila . . . . Cindy Valentine
Dwight Wright . . . . Gerald Isaac
Voice of meteorite . . . . Eartha Kitt

Toronto — Frank Stallone bows in his first feature role as slick-suited Tony Mareda Jr., America's toughest private eye, in "The Pink Chiquitas," a Canadian-made 1950s sci-fi spoof. While there's titillation value and some goofy situations, the giggles are too sporadic for a full one-two punch at the b.o. Big brother Sly doesn't have to sweat out the cinematic rivalry here, as pic would fit in much more comfortably as drive-in fare or a homevideo offering.

After Mareda attends the funeral service of his famous detective dad, he hops into his flashy white convertible, complete with giant tusk on the hood, and picks up a nubile hitchhiker in a tight yellow tube top on a bleak midwestern highway. She's going to Beansville, U.S.A., and off they drive to a "Peter Gunn" soundtrack, all the while being attacked by a Mafia-type gang who keep shooting at Mareda.

They arrive at a drive-in, where "Zombie Beach Party III" is playing, and the pursuit is still on. Stallone, still impeccable in his white suit, kills his two adversaries. Meanwhile, at the drive-in local tv meteorologist Clip (Second City's Bruce Pirrie) is on a date with his librarian g.f. Marianne (Liz Edwards), who had decided to run for mayor of the town. As soon as she asks him if he believes there's life in outer space, a flaming pink meteor falls to earth.

The town abandons the movie to hunt for the meteor. The girls run to the site and mysteriously start disrobing and rubbing their bodies, oohing and aahing about the need to be satisfied. The pink meteorite transforms the women into sexual nymphs, the pink chiquitas.

Rest of plot revolves around the chiquitas capturing Mareda in an all-out effort to entrap and enslave the men of the world through their new erotic powers.

The girls walk around like zombies from "Night Of The Living Dead" until they become the militant gun-toting Amazonian sex masters.

Ernie, the current mayor of Beansville, played with wild abandon by John Hemphill, is trying to keep a lid on this disaster until after the election. Mareda is on the case,

and often recalls the words of his famous dad in gauzy "Godfather" flashbacks. He's given a number of daredevil tricks to display his inherited gumshoe talents, notably firing a gun while water-skiing.

There are some classic dialog sendups that do work, but many of the other supposedly ridiculous setups are just that. On the plus side, writer-director Anthony Currie has fun with a lot of the plot elements and allows the cast to exploit the cardboard parameters of their absurd characters.

But too much is watered down. The special effects are so-so, and even the molten lava love meteorite Betty (voice of Eartha Kitt) is silly. Of course, the ending finds Stallone saving the day by pushing the meteor into the water, causing the girls to lose their power.

But the pink chiquitas in the underground cave gyrating in bras and panties in front of the pink mamma meteorite, the running gag of a transvestite chiquita, and a host of other sci-fi in-jokes might be campy enough to make this a cult item.

—*Devo.*

Alla vi barn i Bullerby
(The Children Of Bullerby Village)
(SWEDISH-COLOR)

A Svensk Filmindustri release and production. Produced by Waldemarr Bergendahl. Directed by Lasse Hallström. Screenplay, Astrid Lindgren, based on her own novel; camera (Fujicolor), Jens Fischer; editor, Susanne Linnman; music, George Riedel; casting, Catti Edfeldt; sound, Gran Carmback, Eddie Axberg; production design, Lasse Westfelt; costumes, Inger Pehrsson, Susanne Falck; production management, Anita Tesler, Erik Spangenberg, Göran Lindberg, Thomas Allercrantz. Reviewed at the Palladium, Malmö, Sweden, Dec. 9, 1986. Running time: **90 MINS.**

Lisa . . . . Linda Bergström
Lasse . . . . Crispin Dickson Wendenius
Bosse . . . . Henrik Larsson
Britta . . . . Ellen Demerus
Anna . . . . Anna Sahlin
Olle . . . . Harald Lönnbro
Kerstin . . . . Tove Edfeldt
The shoemaker . . . . Olof Sjögren
Country store owner . . . . Lasse Stahl
Also with: Sören Petersson, Ann-Sofi Knape, Ingwar Svensson, Elizabeth Nordquist, Bill Jonsson, Catti Edfeldt (Elin of South Farm), Louise Raeder, Peter Dywik, Britt Sterneland, Nina Englund, Sigfred Eriksson (Granddad).

Malmö — "The Children Of Bullerby Village" is about all the little events that make up the summer holidays for six kids, age seven to nine, in the rural idyll of their remote Swedish province in the late 1920s. Film, based on an Astrid Lindgren novella and directed from Lindgren's own screenplay by Lasse Hallström, will be available soon in an English-dubbed version. Anticipating its arrival in the U.S., Viking/Penguin is already out with a reprint of the book.

Undoubtedly, kids under seven and their parents will have a fine time with "Bullerby," but picture's fate with all the in-between audiences is more doubtful. Lindgren's "Bullerby" stories are the least controversial in an *oeuvre* that describes children — and talks to them — in very adult terms.

"The Children Of Bullerby" comes closer to the never-never land of eternal sunshine as the three girls and three boys romp merrily through a landscape caught in tender nuance (fittingly, Fujicolor is used) with nary a conflict to face or faze them.

The boys sneak up on the girls and cry "Boo!" when they all have decided to spend the night in a hayloft. The boys even snitch the sandwiches given to girls for their outing by their parents. There is a hunt for a treasure they themselves have hidden, but the girls get the best of the boys here, having substituted the coins of the original "chest" (a tin can) with goat droppings.

Nothing more exciting happens. The kids all come from neat, well-kept farms. The adults are all seen as nice and easy going. There are no older boys or girls to threaten or challenge the six friends. No wonder they all wind up longing to go back to school.

Film, shot back-to-back with a sequel, "More About The Children Of Bullerby," which will come out by next Christmas, is decked out in a just plain lovely production dress, and Hallström, whose own childhood memoir film "My Life As A Dog" is now doing the international rounds, can not only make one kid act natural, he can make six of them act natural at the same time. There is nary a false or phony note in his film, but there is precious little salt, spice or suspense either.

In their evocation of a summer of innocence in a time of idyll, Hallström and Lindgren have stuck close to the famous Keats observation that "Heaven lies about us in our infancy," but they also have abandoned their usual awareness of the Hell without which Heaven is a pretty vapid affair.—*Kell.*

Memorias de una Guerra Cotidiana
(Images Of An Everyday War)
(CHILEAN-CANADIAN-DOCU-COLOR)

A Cinemateca Chilena production. Written and directed by Gaston Ancelovici, Jaime Barrios, Rene Davilla. Camera (color, 16m), Jaime Rojas; editor. Hugo Molina; music, Rodrigo Villaseka; songs, Lilia Santos. Reviewed at Leipzig Docu and Short Film Festival, Nov. 24, 1986. Running time: **60 MINS.**

Leipzig — "Images Of An Everyday War" is a militant, committee-type docu on the repression suffered by people under Pinochet's government in Chile. The joint Chilean-Canadian coprod, filmed by the directing trio Gaston Ancelovici, Jaime Barrios and Rene Davilla, limits itself to showing scenes from everyday life, and has little to add to larger-scope works like Miguel Littin's recent "Acta General de Chile." Main playoff will be for militant groups interested in Latin American politics.

Using a simple, direct camera style, filmers concentrate on submerged efforts to fight the dictatorship in small ways. While Army tanks rumble menacingly through the barrios, boys throw stones at them and run away. Songs of struggle are sung in small groups and in larger concerts. A commentator reels off statistics about how Pinochet's Army has cost the country $10-billion in the last six years, while camera shows the streets full of starving faces.—*Yung.*

Positive I.D.
(COLOR)

Effective low-budget thriller.

An A.C. Anderson/Anderson Film, Positive I.D. Prods. film. Written, produced and directed by Andy Anderson. Camera (color), Paul Barton; editor, Robert J. Castaldo, Anderson. editors. Reviewed at the Greater Fort Lauderdale Intl. Film Festival, Nov. 28, 1986. (No MPAA Rating.) Running time: **104 MINS.**
With: Stephanie Rascoe, John Davies, Steve Fromholz, Gail Cronauer.

Ft. Lauderdale — Gorgeous Bobbie King, whose real identity is a languid, troubled Fort Worth housewife, goes to a gun shop to buy a weapon. The store clerk asks her matter-of-factly if the gun is "for protection or sport."

"Both," she replies. "I want to kill a golfer."

Moments of wit like this make the suspense film "Positive I.D.," despite its low-budget feel, a fine mystery. It comes from Andy Anderson, who takes the setting and pace from Fort Worth, where he now lives. Raised in Miami and having started the film as a Florida State U. undergraduate, Anderson saw the work become one of the darlings of the recent Greater Fort Lauderdale Intl. Film Festival.

Stephanie Rasco is fascinating in the lead role as the brooding housewife. After being brutally raped by a stranger, she reawakens from a trance-like state into a person obsessed with changing her identity.

The slow reawakening is sparked by a random news report she hears about a man caught after establishing multiple identities. True to the nature of many emotionally disturbed persons, she shows an amazing faculty and energy to pursue her new-found obsession. A trip to get a birth certificate begins an odyssey that results in the emergence of an entirely new personality.

The immensity of the physical transformation will initially leave many viewers baffled. As time goes by, the woman's aim of revenge begins to emerge.

John Davies is convincing as the woman's husband, with similar results from Steve Fromholz as the "new" woman's bartender friend.

The opening pace is on the slow side for most audiences, but the bizarre and devastating ending climaxes a series of engrossing scenes. Cinematography and sound could be much better, though Anderson as writer/director has provided realism throughout.—*Dole.*

Native Son
(COLOR)

Weak adaptation of Richard Wright's novel.

A Cinecom release of a Diane Silver production, presented in association with American Playhouse and Cinétudes Films. Produced by Silver. Executive producer, Lindsay Law. Directed by Jerrold Freedman. Screenplay, Richard Wesley, based on novel by Richard Wright; camera (color), Thomas Burstyn; editor, Aaron Stell; music, James Mtume; song, "Jones Comes Down," lyrics by Mtume, Silver, performed by Stephanie Mills, orchestrated and arranged by Dunn Pearson; production design, Stephen Marsh; casting, Hank McCann. Reviewed at Apollo Theater, N.Y., Dec. 8, 1986. (MPAA Rating: PG.) Running time: **112 MINS.**

Mrs. Dalton	Carroll Baker
Bessie	Akousua Busia
Jan	Matt Dillon
Doc	Art Evans
Max	John Karlen
Bigger Thomas	Victor Love
Mary Dalton	Elizabeth McGovern
Mr. Dalton	John McMartin
Peggy	Geraldine Page
Gus	Willard E. Pugh
Buckley	David Rasche
Britton	Lane Smith
Mrs. Thomas	Oprah Winfrey

"Native Son" is a corny adaptation of Richard Wright's chilling 1940 bestseller about the life of a poor black teenager who commits a horrible murder.

Set in Chicago in the late 1930s, focus of the story is on Bigger Tho-

---

Original Play

Melodrama presented without intermission, presented at the St. James, N.Y., March 24, 1941, by Orson Welles and John Houseman; dramatized by Paul Green and Richard Wright from latter's novel of same title; Bern Bernard, associate producer; staged by Welles; settings, James Morcom; $3.30 top.

Bigger Thomas	Canada Lee
Hannah Thomas	Evelyn Ellis
Vera Thomas	Helen Martin
Buddy Thomas	Lloyd Warren
A Neighbor	Jacqueline Ghant André

Miss Emmett	Eileen Burns
Jack	J. Flashe Riley
Clara	Rena Mitchell
G.H. Rankin	Rodester Timmons
Gus Mitchell	Wardell Saunders
Ernie Jones	C.M. Bootsie Davis
Mr. Dalton	Erskine Sanford
Mrs. Dalton	Nell Harrison
Britten	Everett Sloane
Peggy	Frances Bavier
Mary Dalton	Anne Burr
Jan Erlone	Joseph Pevney
Buckley	Philip Bourneuf
Paul Max	Ray Collins
A Reporter	Paul Stewart
Judge	William Malone
Newspaper Men — John Berry, Stephen Roberts, George Zorn, Don Roberts.	

---

mas (Victor Love), a morose, sullen black teenager, brimming with hate and confusion, who'd rather rob and steal than work for white folks. Bigger reluctantly takes a job working as a chauffeur for the wealthy white liberal Dalton family. On his first night on the job, he is instructed to take the Daltons' 19-year-old daughter Mary (Elizabeth McGovern) to school.

Once away from the house, Mary decides she's not going to school and tells Bigger to drive to a Communist Party headquarters where she picks up her boyfriend Jan (Matt Dillon). The couple attempt to treat the confused boy as an equal and they question him about his background and life and force him to take them where he eats dinner. At the smoky, after-hours restaurant Bigger is humiliated by the reactions of the black patrons and the condescending remarks by Jan and Mary, who proceed to get drunk.

Bigger drops Jan off at the train station. He hands Bigger a bunch of Communist pamphlets and says he'll be in touch. Bigger then drives Mary home but she's too drunk to walk so he carries her into the house and eventually up to her bedroom. When he places her on the bed, she appears to flirt and just as he attempts to respond, Mrs. Dalton (Carroll Baker), who is blind, enters the room. Bigger panics and in a flash tries to quiet Mary by placing a pillow over her face until Mrs. Dalton exits the room. He accidentally suffocates Mary. Bigger sweats it out for a second or two and within a minute, stuffs Mary in a trunk, carries it down to the basement and shoves her body, feet first, into the huge burning furnace. He flees to his home on the South Side and returns the next morning as though nothing has happened. His actions are so stupid and unbelievable, the audience actually begins to snicker from this point on.

The police get involved, Bigger and Jan are both questioned about Mary's whereabouts, the remains of the body are discovered by a bunch of newspapermen who happen to be in the basement as the ashes are be-

---

Original Film
(ARGENTINE-B&W)

An Argentina Sono Film release of the Jaime Prades production. Stars Richard Wright. Directed by Pierre Chenal. Original novel by Richard Wright. Screenplay, Wright and Chenal; camera (b&w), Antonio Merayo; music, Juan Ehlert. At Gran Rex, Buenos Aires, April 10, 1951. Running time: **105 MINS.**

Bigger Thomas	Richard Wright
Mary Dalton	Jean Wallace
Bessie Mears	Gloria Madison
Mr. Dalton	Nicholas Joy
Mrs. Dalton	Ruth Roberts
Detective Britten	Charles Cane
Farley	Georges Riguad
Jan Erlone	Jim Michael
Panama	George Green
Hannah Thomas	Willa Pearl Curtiss
Lawyer Max	Don Dean
Housekeeper	Cecile Lazard
(English soundtrack)	

---

ing taken out of the furnace, and Bigger flees and goes into hiding. He's later captured and sentenced to death. If the pic had ended with his capture, the audience would be spared the worst, a scene where Mrs. Thomas (Oprah Winfrey) comes to the D.A.'s office, looks at Bigger, who is bewildered, and covered with scars and bruises, and asks, "Are they treating you all right son?" She then falls to her knees and begs Mrs. Dalton, without an ounce of conviction or a single tear, to spare her son's life.

What could have been a compelling psychodrama turns out to be a boring collection of caricatures of stereotypes that nobody cares about. Wright's message never reaches the viewer and the audience is never drawn into the pic. The true talent of these gifted actors is never realized. Victor Love is passable as Wright's hero but by the time he begins to generate the least bit of pathos, the pic ends.

In the novel, Wright points out that he doesn't expect anyone to weep for Bigger Thomas. But surely he didn't intend for anyone to snicker either.

Shot on the South Side of Chicago and in Los Angeles, the abject poverty of the blacks is aptly captured, as well as the wealth and opulence of the Daltons. —*Mur.*

The Golden Child
(COLOR)

Idiotic fantasy featuring a watered-down Eddie Murphy.

A Paramount Pictures release of a Feldman/Meeker production in association with Eddie Murphy Prods. Produced by Edward S. Feldman, Robert D. Wachs. Executive producers, Richard Tienken, Charles R. Meeker. Directed by Michael Ritchie. Stars Eddie Murphy. Screenplay, coproducer, Dennis Feldman; camera (Metrocolor), Donald E. Thorin; editor, Richard A. Harris; music, Michel Colombier; production design, J. Michael Riva; art direction, Lynda Paradise; set design, Virginia Randolph; set decoration, Marvin March; costume design, Wayne Finkelman; sound (Dolby), Jim Alexander; visual effects produced at Industrial Light & Magic; visual effects supervisor, Ken Ralston; visual effects coordinator, Pamela Easley;

makeup designed and created by, Ken Chase; associate producer, Gordon A. Webb; second unit director, Peter Norman; second unit camera (L.A.), Robert Thomas. Reviewed at the National theater, L.A., Dec. 10, 1986. (MPAA Rating: PG-13.) Running time: **93 MINS.**

Chandler Jarrell	Eddie Murphy
Sardo Numspa	Charles Dance
Kee Nang	Charlotte Lewis
The Old Man	Victor Wong
The Golden Child	J.L. Reate
Til	Randall (Tex) Cobb
Doctor Hong	James Hong
Kala	Shakti
Yu	Tau Logo
Khan	Tiger Chung Lee
Fu	Pons Maar
Tommy Tong	Peter Kwong

Hollywood — "The Golden Child" is a golden turkey, which in this case means that a lousy film will make a nice piece of change. Eddie Murphy represents the one and only draw, which will be quite enough to get the pic profitably through the holiday season. But the superstar, while still likeable, is operating here at reduced levels of energy, sass and humor, which should prevent the Paramount release from reaching blockbuster status.

Aside from the negligible "Best Defense," in which the comedian had a glorified cameo role, "The Golden Child" is by far the weakest and silliest film to date in which Murphy has appeared. A strange hybrid of Far Eastern mysticism, treacly sentimentality, diluted reworkings of Murphy's patented confrontation scenes across racial and cultural boundaries, and dragged-in ILM special effects monsters, film makes no sense on any level, which sometimes matters to mass audiences and sometimes doesn't.

Concoction dreamed up by Dennis Feldman has Murphy as a social worker specializing in tracking down missing children who is recruited to rescue the virtually divine Golden Child. Eponymous character, a socalled perfect child with magical powers of good, has been kidnapped in an overblown opening sequence by an unmitigated villain portrayed by a bearded Charles Dance, who wears a long leather coat à la a Sergio Leone baddie.

Much nonsense ensues involving assorted bikers, chop-socky-happy Orientals, a serpentine sorceress and Charlotte Lewis, the dark beauty from Roman Polanski's "Pirates" who is sent to inform Murphy that he is the Chosen One, i.e., the one who must save the Golden Child and thus rescue the world from the forces of evil.

The second unit, but not Murphy and Lewis, travels to Nepal at this point, which enables Murphy to produce a large knife which Dance says he will accept in trade for the kid. Going back on his word, the dapper Dance promptly transforms himself into a winged dragon, but the outcome of the climactic battle is as predictable as the ending of a Republic Western.

As in "Beverly Hills Cop," the villain is an imperious, jaded Englishman whose mansion Murphy must penetrate in order to save the day. Instead of taking on a bunch of rednecks, as in "48 HRS.," the master of jive and profanity here lets a pack of bikers know who's boss. Only precedent set by this film is the presence of Murphy in a PG-13-rated release, an indication of the performer's watered-down material here.

Michael Ritchie, who used to make films that were about something, directs in a visually busy and cluttered manner, and employs such baffling strategies as cutting away to a heavy metal music video while a major fight sequence is in progress.

Michel Colombier's score is brain-poundingly idiotic, but other contributions, including J. Michael Riva's production design, the gentler special effects involving birds and a dancing Pepsi can, and the presence of the beatific J.L. Reate (actually a girl) in the title role, represent fleeting grace notes in an otherwise mindless enterprise.

— Cart.

Kamikaze
(FRENCH-COLOR)

A Gaumont release of a Films du Loup/Gaumont/ARP coproduction. Executive producer, Luc Besson. Produced by Louis Duchesne. Directed by Didier Grousset. Stars Richard Bohringer, Dominique Lavanant, Michel Galabru. Screenplay, Michèle Halberstadt, Besson, Grousset; camera (Eastmancolor), Jean-François Robin; editor, Olivier Mauffroy; music, Eric Serra; art director, Dan Weil; sound, Paul Laine; costumes, Création Express; special effects, Georges Demetreau, Pierre Foury, Jacky Dufour; assistant director, Hubert Engammare; production manager, Gisèle Thenaisie. Reviewed at the Gaumont Ambassade cinema, Paris, Dec. 10, 1986. Running time: **87 MINS.**
With: Michel Galabru (Albert), Richard Bohringer (Romain), Dominique Lavanant (Laure), Riton Liebman (Olive), Kim Massée (Léa), Harry Cleven (Patrick), Romane Bohringer (Julie), Etienne Chicot (Samrat).

Paris — Luc Besson, who became the current mainsteam wonderboy with his 1985 success, "Subway," imagined, coauthored and produced this half-baked thriller, about a lunatic who invents a death ray that can kill people on television, but he did not direct. Even if he had, he most likely would have failed to pump much more life into its lame script, zapped by strained plotting and feeble characterizations.

Didier Grousset, previously Besson's assistant, takes his first crack at directing, trying frantically to prove himself on a technical level with complicated dolly and sequence shots. Unfortunately, the human element slips from his grasp

almost as soon as the actors open their mouths to utter the poor dialog he penned with Besson.

Michel Galabru is a mad electronics genius who is pinkslipped from his company and withdraws into his attic to brood in front of the boob tube. Further enraged by the idiocies of tv announcers, he concocts a ray gun that can blast them through screen and tv camera.

Enter a clever detective (Richard Bohringer), who figures out how the murders are being committed and brings in an army of specialists to figure out how to shoot back from the tv studios. In an on-camera showdown, Bohringer neutralizes Galabru but fails to kill him, and engages in additional snooping to flush him out.

Story's credibility is definitively impaired by Galabru's undisciplined overacting, especially as he dons a kamikaze pilot headband and kimono in preparation for a broadcast battle with Bohringer, seated behind a weapon that looks like a leftover prop from a Buck Rogers serial. Bohringer's typically low-keyed performance saves him from the embarrassment that attends most of the cast, including Dominique Lavanant, in a dramatically pointless role. —Len.

Mauvais sang
(Bad Blood)
(FRENCH-COLOR)

An AAA Classic release of a Films Plain Chant/Soprofilms/FR3 Films coproduction. Executive producer, Philippe Diaz. Produced by Alain Dahan. Written and directed by Léos Carax. Stars Juliette Binoche, Michel Piccoli, Denis Lavant. Camera (Fujicolor), Jean-Yves Escoffier; editor, Nelly Quettier; music, Benjamin Britten, Serge Prokofiev, Charlie Chaplin; songs, David Bowie, Charles Aznavour, Serge Reggiani; sound, Harrick Maury; makeup, Chantal Houdoy; assistant director, Antoine Beau; production manager, Michèle Arnould. Reviewed at the UGC Champs-Elysées theater, Paris, Nov. 26, 1986. Running time: **128 MINS.**
Alex .Denis Lavant
Anna . . . . .Juliette Binoche
Marc . . . . .Michel Piccoli
Hans .Hans Meyer
Lise . . . . .Julie Delpy
The American . . . . .Carroll Brooks
Boris . . . . .Hugo Pratt
Also with: Serge Reggiani (Charlie), Mireille Perrier (the young mother), Jérôme Zucca, Charles Schmitt, Philippe Fretin, Ralph Brown.

Paris — Léos Carax, then only 24, was spotted at Cannes two years ago for his weirdly appealing b&w debut feature, "Boy Meets Girl," for which he was hailed in some quarters as France's new whiz kid. His second feature demonstrates he is indeed a whiz, but one also wonders whom he thinks he's kidding. "Mauvais sang" is all pyrotechnic flash and self-indulgence, finally unbearable at its uncalled-for two-hour-plus running time. But pic has the playful undis-

ciplined dazzle that can make a cult favorite.

Production attracted early attention when Carax reportedly brought the film in 18 weeks late and nearly 40% over budget.

Numerous scenes attest to Carax' talent, as well as that of his equally dazzling lenser Jean-Yves Escoffier, who also shot "Boy Meets Girl," but helmer's personal vision is still immaturely limited to stylistic cribbing (notably of his mentor, Jean-Luc Godard) and a deluge of buff references, with everybody from Charlie Chaplin to Jean Cocteau and Mel Brooks getting a big pointless wink.

Plot, or what little there is, falls into a *film noir* mold. A young ex-con (Denis Lavant, the plug-ugly protagonist of "Boy Meets Girl") sides with an aging gangster (Michel Piccoli) for a special burglary and ends up falling in love with his much younger mistress (Juliette Binoche), who rejects his advances because she is still in love with Piccoli.

Though the ostensible chief interest of the story is Lavant's offbeat courtship of Binoche (who is photographed with extra-loving care in what is a superior screen test but not much of a performance), viewer interest is constantly deflected by Carax' show-off direction and Escoffier's frequently virtuoso camerawork. Piccoli's sheer professionalism and presence carries him through a poorly developed part.

Question remains if Carax will grow from a clever wunderkind into a mature filmmaker with something to say and a style not cultivated at the Cinémathèque. —Len.

Dogs In Space
(AUSTRALIAN-COLOR)

A Hoyts/Ronin release (in Australia) of an Entertainment Media/Burrowes Film Group presentation of a Central Park Films production. Produced by Glenys Rowe. Executive producers, Robert Le Tet, Dennis Wright. Written and directed by Richard Lowenstein. Camera (Widescreen, color), Andrew de Groot; editor, Jill Bilcock; musical director Ollie Olsen; sound, Dean Gawen, Stephen Vaughan; art director, Jody Borland; executive in charge of production, John Kearney; production manager, Lynda House; assistant director, Ross Hamilton; casting, Forcast. Reviewed at Hoyts screening room, Sydney, Nov. 25, 1986. Running time: **105 MINS.**
Sam . . . . .Michael Hutchence
Anna .Saskia Post
Tim . . . . .Nique Needles
The Girl . . . . .Deanna Bond
Luchio . . . . .Tony Helou
Chainsaw man . . . . .Chris Haywood
Also with: Peter Walsh (Anthony), Laura Swanson (Clare), Adam Briscomb (Grant), Sharon Jessop (Leanne), Edward Clayton-Jones (Nick), Martii Coles (Mark), Chuck Meo (Charles), Caroline Lee (Jenny), Fiona Latham (Barbara), Stephanie Johnson (Erica), Gary Foley (Barry), Glenys Osborne (Lisa), Helen Phillips (Stacey), Barbara Jung-

wirth (Sam's mother), Joe Camilleri (terry towelling man).

Sydney — "Dogs In Space" isn't a sci-fi pic about canines of the future. It's a film about a generation of young people and their lifestyle, specifically centering around the inhabitants and hangers-on at a house in the Melbourne inner-city suburb of Richmond during 1978. Writer-director Richard Lowenstein, in a complete change of pace from his gritty "Strikebound" (story of a 1930s coal miners' strike) has eschewed a formal storyline and instead presented a kaleidoscope of characters and incidents. It's immensely impressive.

Though some of these young people work, and one (Tony Helou) is studying rather vainly for his exams most spend their days sleeping off the party of the night before. Their house is cluttered with empty bottles and beer cans and other junk, and the eight or so regular residents invariably are augmented by overnight visitors or just people passing through.

Among the regulars is Sam, played by local rock star Michael Hutchence, very effective in his first acting job; he has a regular girlfriend, Anna (Saskia Post), who has a certain amount of ambition (she'd like to be an air hostess), but no hope for the future as long as she stays with Sam. Her tragic fate provides the impetus of the film's final scenes.

Another key character is a runaway girl (Deanna Bond) who looks to be about 15. No one asks her name, or where she comes from — she just drifts into the house and becomes a resident, eventually losing her virginity to Tim (Nique Needles), an amiable layabout.

As noted, there's no formal narrative as such in the film. The structure is very loose, with Andrew de Groot's very classy camerawork a major asset. The pristine soundtrack, which picks up all kinds of overlapping conversations as the camera roves through the house, is another plus. Indeed, technically "Dogs In Space" is just about faultless.

The large cast is filled with interesting characters, including the always reliable Chris Haywood as a visitor with a strange fetish for chainsaws and Fiona Latham as an attractive, very radical girl who drops by to mouth the latest slogans, though without much success.

The local police, often called in by irate neighbors because of the noise, seem extremely tolerant of the goings-on, even when the youngsters move their furniture out into the narrow street and set fire to their tv set (during a transmission of "His Girl Friday").

With its deafening soundtrack of rock numbers, its apparently aimless structure, and its forthright depiction of a neo-hippie lifestyle, "Dogs In Space" is not a film for everyone. It should have great appeal for youngsters, however, and the tragic ending could serve as a dire warning against the taking of harder drugs such as heroin. With this in mind, the controversial decision of Australia's film censorship board to rate the picture "R," thus legally preventing anyone under the age of 18 attending, is inexplicable. Unfortunately, this misguided decision may well affect the film's commercial chances Down Under, unless a reversal is possible.

Overseas, pic should spark interest among young audiences, since it shapes up as akin to an antipodean "Sid And Nancy," though without some of the excesses of Alex Cox' film. It certainly confirms Lowenstein as a versatile and accomplished talent. —*Strat.*

Mikhail Romm: Ispoved Kinorezhisera
(Mikhail Romm: Confessions Of A Director)
(SOVIET-DOCU-B&W)

A Zentrnautchfilm production (Moscow). Directed by Arcady Zinemann. Written by Semion Freilich; camera (b&w), Oleg Sguridi; editor, S. Kudrjawzewoi. Reviewed at Leipzig Docu and Short Film Festival, Nov. 24, 1986. Running time: 77 MINS.

Leipzig — Mikhail Romm (1901-1971), one of the most venerated Russian directors (he received five Stalin prizes during his 30-year career), is the subject of a lively, well-made biopic likely to be of interest to archivists and buffs.

Helmer Arcady Zinemann intercut homey personal notes and interviews with Romm's famous co-workers, plus generous excerpts from the director's best-known films. More introductory than in-depth, pic paints an entertaining portrait of a warm, witty, intelligent man with a gift for self-irony.

Penned by film scholar Semion Freilich, "Mikhail Romm: Confessions Of A Director" is shot a great deal in Romm's own voice. His early, ill-fated ambition was to be a sculptor, and he describes his studies under the tutelage of a lady who he says taught him nothing about sculpture, but gave him an approach to art. He landed his first film jobs in the 1930s as assistant and scripter, before a chance to direct landed in his lap. Declaring himself unprepared at the time, Romm nevertheless made a 14-day shoestringer, "Boule de Suif," which is still considered one of the best screen versions of Guy de Maupassant.

Romm's first-person anecdotes flavor pic's account of the making of his famous Lenin biopic, "Lenin in October" (1937) with lionized actor Boris Shchukin in the title role. Though Romm's film was originally ordered by Stalin himself to commemorate the 20th anni of the revolution, documakers have carefully excised all reference to Stalin here, preferring to stick to the safe territory of pure cinema. Pic ventures into politics only briefly towards the end, to tack on a bafflingly gratuitous peace message and to underline Romm's horror at Hitler's death camps.

More appreciable are current interviews with thesps like Innokenti Smoktunovsky and director Grigori Chukhrai; souvenirs of Romm's meetings with Eisenstein; and pic's homage to a stout-hearted veteran of Soviet film history. The 35m b&w film clips have an enivably well-preserved clarity that are a joy to watch. —*Yung.*

Kojak Budapesten
(Kojak In Budapest)
(HUNGARIAN-B&W)

A Mafilm production and release. Directed by Sandor Szalkai. Screenplay, Szalkai, Istvan Kallai; camera (b&w), Ivan Lakatos; editor, Andrea Gellert; assistant director, Adam Csillag. Reviewed on SBS television, Sydney, Nov. 28, 1986. Running time: 96 MINS.

With: Laszlo Inke (Kojak), Cecilia Esztergalyos, Gabor Harsanyi, Lajos Oze, Klari Tolnay, Adam Szirtes, Hilda Gobbi, Ildiko Pecsi.

Sydney — Telly Savalas lookalike Laszlo Inke steps into the shoes of Kojak in this amiable comedy, made in 1980 but not reviewed hitherto. The bald-headed cop wings into Budapest to attend an International Crime Writers' Conference (he's been invited by the Communist Youth Council and the Hungarian Women's Assn.), but it turns out that he's Hungarian by birth ("Most famous people are of Hungarian origin," he notes), and actually served on the Budapest police force before emigrating.

During his stay in Hungary, he's romanced by a beauteous blond and threatened by a mysterious type in dark glasses. He also becomes involved in an investigation into the death of a famous scientist. It's during these scenes that director Sandor Szalkai and his co-scripter Istvan Kallai have fun with lampooning local targets, such as cruising taxi-drivers who won't pick up fares, postmen in such a hurry to get home they deliver urgent mail to any old address, bosses who spend their highly paid time on pursuits other than those they're supposed to be doing, workers who have to be cajoled into getting things done and

sex-starved beauties on the make for foreigners or influential locals.

It's a minor pic, aimed at local audiences, but some of the jokes included in the screenplay are quite pointed and funny, in a bitter kind of way. As for Inke, he's got the Kojak dress style and mannerisms down to a fine art. —*Strat.*

The Happy Valley
(BRITISH-COLOR-16m)

A BBC-TV production. Produced by Cedric Messina. Directed by Ross Devenish. Screenplay, David Reid; camera (Eastmancolor), John Baker; editor, Clare Douglas; music, Geoffrey Burgon; production design, Don Taylor; set decoration, Martyn Clift; costumes, Odile Dicks-Mireaux; consultant, Juanita Carberry; associate producer, Chris Cherry. Reviewed at London Film Festival, Nov. 26, 1986. Running time: 90 MINS.

Juanita Carberry	Holly Aird
Sir Henry Broughton	Denholm Elliott
June Carberry	Kathryn Pogson
John Carberry	Michael Byrne
Helen Tapsell	Cathryn Harrison
Diana Broughton	Amanda Hillwood
Superintendent Poppy	Richard Heffer
Lord Erroll	Peter Sands

Also with: Ka Vundla (Gatimu), Mawa Makondo (Waiganjo), Fiona Walker (Miss Tanner), Frank Lazarus (doctor), Jon Cartwright (police inspector).

London — Entertaining and moving as it is, "The Happy Valley" unreservedly indicts the British colonials who caroused and philandered their way through Kenya before that African colony gained independence. Its effectiveness lies in its oblique, elliptical style, which never allows for the heavyhanded.

Seen from the point-of-view of a young adolescent girl, Juanita Carberry, on whose diaries it is based, the film recreates one of the most sensational crimes to ever shake the colonial community in Africa. The murder victim, Lord Erroll, openly flaunted his love affair with the beautiful young wife of another peer, Lord Broughton, who apparently condoned the affair. The husband was accused and tried, however, but eventually acquitted of the slaying. Europeans were too busy fighting World War II to pay much attention to goings-on out in Africa.

Through Juanita's eyes we are witness to the cruelty and superficiality of the privileged clique into which she was born and against which by the end of the film she rebels.

In fact, the film is really Juanita's story, about her loneliness and growing awareness of the shallowness of the adults she observes so sharply. Sadistically treated by her father, she finds refuge and solace in the animals around her and the natives, with whom she converses in Swahili. The scenes of frivolous parties and callous conversations, which Juanita regularly finds herself on the edge of, alternate effec-

tively with scenes of her riding a favorite horse or talking to the servants.

Juanita's innocence and self-containment, mistaken for stupidity by her elders, prompts Broughton to entrust to her his secret: he did in fact kill his rival Lord Erroll in cold blood. The scenes between Juanita (played with restraint and aplomb by Holly Aird) and the world-weary Broughton (Denholm Elliott), are especially powerful.

When Broughton is eventually acquitted and even his suspecting wife has closed ranks around him to reinforce class solidarity, Juanita tries to set things right by letting the truth out. She is savagely beaten for her pains and runs away from home.

Although there are some confusing moments in the early part of the film trying to identify characters, overall it is well-constructed and well-acted. Technical credits are excellent. —*Guid.*

Der Schone Augenblick
(SWISS-DOCU-COLOR/B&W-16m)

A production of the Swiss Assn. for Folk Crafts, with Filmcooperative Zurich, Switzerland. Produced by Friedrich Kappeler, Pio Carradi. Directed by Kappeler. Camera (color, 16m), Corradi; editor, George Janett; music, Bruno Spoerri; sound, Felix Singer, Martin Wirz; commentary, Kappeler, Dieter Bachmann; narrator, Getrud Leutenegger. Reviewed at Nyon Intl. Film Festival (Switzerland), Oct. 18, 1986. Running time: 83 MINS.

(German soundtrack)

Nyon — The Aschwanden family has produced three generations of still photographers. Along with two other families of photographers, seen in this film, the Aschwandens have produced a vast collection of pictures, a miniature pictorial history of German-speaking eastern Switzerland spanning the last century.

We see the customs and manner of dress, the hairstyles, the suppressed excitement of the stiffly posed wedding couple, the over-dressed dandy, the proud young motorcyclist displaying his new machine, the peasant girls, the hunter and his rifle, also the mountains and pastoral landscapes and village street scenes. All this is caught in the camera's click, in a beautiful blink of the eye — hence the title of the film.

The film is also a history of a changing vocation, with changing technology, as cameras became smaller, lenses sharper. The old street photographer, with his "little bird" atop a heavy box-like camera, itself atop a clumsy tripod — all that has faded away like an old photograph. Some wonderful old pictures survive to tell us of a simpler time.

Old photographers also appear in the film, describing what had been and what now was changed.

This charming film joins some others about the history of photography. We owe them a debt for having preserved who we were long ago — in the blink of an eye. —*Hitch.*

Un Hombre Violento
(A Violent Man)
(MEXICAN-COLOR)

A Películas Mexicanas release of a Cinematográfica Sol production. Produced by Gilberto de Anda. Directed by and starring Valentín Trujillo. Screenplay, De Anda, camera (color), Antonio de Anda; editor, Sergio Soto; music, Ernesto Cortázar, with appearance of groups Los Cadetes de Linar, Los Humildes. Reviewed at Big Apple Cine 2, N.Y., Nov. 22, 1986. Running time: **91 MINS.**
Julián Carrera .... Valentín Trujillo
Don Emilio .... Mario Almada
Charly................... Rafael Inclán
Lucía Castillano .... Maribel Guardia
Carlos .... Gilberto Trujillo
Susana .... Victoria Ruffo
Also with: Chelo, Gilberto de Anda, Victor Alcocer, Humberto Elizondo, Juan Gallardo.

On his latest venture "Un Hombre Violento" (A Violent Man), Mexican action star Valentín Trujillo has decided to man both sides of the camera. Bloody to an excess, the genre pic combines many elements surprisingly to create a satisfying whole.

As an actor, Trujillo has learned the value of strong, well-developed characters, roles he filled here with top national boxoffice draws such as Mario Almada, Rafael Inclán and Maribel Guardia. The personalities and appeal add texture to the film, keeping it from being merely a senseless exploitation of carnage. The blood flows, but always for a reason.

Storyline involves revenge. Julián Carrera (Trujillo) was not always a violent man. At the beginning of the film he is quite happy running the family auto repair shop with his brother Carlos (played by Trujillo's real-life brother Gilberto). When their father is robbed and brutally murdered, honor is at stake and Julián must wreak vengence. But the matter does not drop here. The killer's family also wants their revenge, and the bodies stack up ... 14 in all.

Although the film has its share of corny moments, production values rate high with imaginative camerawork by Antonio de Anda, fast pacing and an upbeat score by Ernesto Cortázar consisting mostly of quick bluegrass guitar picking with harmonica accompaniment. Also appearing in the pic are the *norteño* groups Los Humildes and Los Cadetes de Linar.

The film's overuse of flashbacks is hokey and impedes the forward thrust of the pic while adding little to the storyline.

Trujillo's acting is often bogged down by a brooding sincerity. Here his character is balanced by his irreverent friend Charly (Rafael Inclán), who brings wit and humor to the proceedings and allows Trujillo to develop other facets to his own role.

In all, despite its many flaws, Trujillo manages to make a satisfying action pic that unites believable characters with such b.o. pluses as realistic violence, car chases, top national guest stars, musical groups and a bit of sex within a strong storyline. "Un Hombre Violento" should pick up a fair amount of coin among Hispanic action fans. —*Lent.*

Soldier's Revenge
(COLOR)

War is heck.

A Continental Motion Pictures presentation. Executive producers, Helen Sarlui, Eduard Sarlui. Produced by J.C. Crespo. Directed by David Worth. Stars John Savage. Screenplay, Lee Stull, Worth, from story by Eduard Sarlui; camera (color), Leonard Solis; Stephen Sealy (L.A.); editor-2d unit director, Raja Gosnell; music, Don Great, Gary Rist; production design, George March; art direction, Robert Summer; costume design, Gloria von Hartenstein; additional editing, Cesare D'Amico; assistant director, George Gundin; production supervisor, Richard Vacas; associate producer, Tony Brandt. Reviewed on TWE vidcassette, N.Y., Nov. 8, 1986. (No MPAA Rating.) Running time: **88 MINS.**
Frank Morgan.............. John Savage
Baetriz .... Maria Socas
Ricardo .... Edgardo Moreira
Gomez .... Frank Cane
Gen. Burns .... Paul Lambert
Tiny .... Sebastian Larrie

Just when you thought you were safe from another disgruntled Vietnam war vet picture, along comes "Soldier's Revenge" (a.k.a. "Vengeance Of A Soldier''), an unreleased 1984 production just hitting the homevideo stores.

John Savage toplines, doing a James Dean turn (that comes off more like Michael Parks) as a war vet who returns home to Freemont, Texas (pic was lensed in L.A. and Argentina) after the death of his mother. Local folk hate him and call him a traitor because he spilled the beans to a magazine about a secret mission he was on that massacred innocent villagers.

Between hokey fights in a pool hall with local toughs led by Tiny (Sebastian Larrie), Savage gets a job piloting a cargo plane containing munitions headed for the wartorn Latin American nation of San Florian. Beauteous Maria Socas hires him, but upon arrival both are arrested. After daring escapes and chases, Savage has a final confrontation with Ricardo (Edgardo Mor-

eira), a rebel leader, and believe it or not, Savage talks Ricardo into a mutual laying down of weapons "to set an example for the world." Savage, Socas and a little girl escape in a boat into the sunrise.

With overwritten narration (delivered by Savage) hammering home the peacenik message, picture is a bit silly. Director David Worth does all right by the action scenes; postsynched dialog material is poor. —*Lor.*

Zahrat El Kindoul
(Women From South Lebanon)
(LEBANESE-DOCU-COLOR)

A Jean Chamoun production. Written and directed by Chamoun and Mai Masri. Camera (color, 16m), and editing, Masri; music, Jawed Berri and Ali Jihad Rassi. Reviewed at the Carthage Film Days (in competition), Oct. 16, 1986. Running time: **70 MINS.**

Tunis — "Women From South Lebanon" (also called "Fleur d'Ajone") is a militant documentary on the role of ordinary civilian women in resisting the Israeli occupation of their villages in southern Lebanon. In a series of head-on interviews, women talk about their sons and daughters who have been arrested, their own stay in Israeli terrorist prisons, how to make a bomb and how to plant mines in the paths of tanks. This is a document rather than a persuasive message picture. It's noteworthy as one of the rare films of its type showing female perceptions, attitudes and — especially — actions, and as such could interest feminist groups.

Filmmakers Jean Chamoun and Mai Masri produced, directed and lensed the film by themselves on a shoestring. Their point of view belongs to Lebanon's Christian faction, though film has no religious message. Instead, it celebrates the ironclad determination of the village women — some Palestinian, some Lebanese — to fight for their land to the last breath, even at the risk of their lives and those of their families. Some of the women's stories are impressive, others chilling.

Filming the precarious life of people in a village where a foreign army periodically advances and retreats, "Women" has the immediacy of a behind-the-scenes newsreel. It is essentially a one-note film, and attention flags over the course of its 70 minutes. Nevertheless, it succeeds in getting across a portrait of people with the strength to resist forever, which is its ultimate message. The female p.o.v. lends disturbing power to the harsh reality depicted; one example: a cooking lesson in which the recipe is for bombs. It is a film with little weeping and much determination. —*Yung.*

El Año de las Luces
(The Year Of Awakening)
(SPANISH-COLOR)

An Iberoamericana de TV production. Executive producer, Andrés Vicente Gómez. Directed by Fernando Trueba. Screenplay, Rafael Azcona, Trueba; camera (Eastmancolor), Juan Amorós; editor, Carmen Frias; music, Francisco Guerrero; sets, Josep Rosell; production manager, Cristina Huete; sound, Jean Claude Laureux, Gilles Orthion. Reviewed at Cine Proyecciones, Madrid, Dec. 5, 1986. Running time: **120 MINS.**
Manolo .... Jorge Sanz
María Jesús .... Maribel Verdú
Emilio .... Manuel Alexandre
Rafaela .... Rafaela Aparicio
Jesús .... Lucas Martin
Irene .... Veronica Forqué
Also with: Santiago Ramos, Chus Lampreave, José Sazatornil, Pedro Reyes, Violeta Cela, Miguel Angel Rellán.

Madrid — If not innovative, "The Year Of Awakening" is at least a touching, well-acted and well-directed story of a 16-year-old boy's first sexual awakening during a summer spent in 1940 in a children's sanitorium for TB patients located near the Portuguese border. Throughout, the ironic hand of co-scripter Rafael Azcona (best known for his association with Luis Garcia Berlanga in many films) lends touches of irreverent humor to the story, converting what in those dreary days was in fact oppressive tyranny into a droll mockery of set moral, political and religious values in post-war Franco Spain.

Under the skillful direction of Fernando Trueba, pic is a lighthearted romance; characters that could have been heavies are in fact only foolish anachronisms. Yarn concerns three brothers, two sent to a sanatorium. Manolo, budding forth sexually, is attracted to several of the pretty nurses and helpers working in an institution designed for smaller children.

The adolescent first tries to take up with one pretty nurse, who chides him on his advances and nightly masturbation. She is sent back, or requests transfer, to her hometown, and Manolo latches onto a pretty second helper, with whom he falls madly in love. After demurring, she too requites his advances and they live a short, secret idyll before their "scandalous" romance is discovered.

The girl is punished by her father for her waywardness and the boy is picked up by his elder brother to be taken back to Madrid. Some typically Azconian touches of humor are provided by such excellent supporting players as José Sazatornil, as the local priest who shoots bothersome pigeons fluttering about the rafters of his church, Rafaela Aparicio as the querulous, nagging kitchen maid and Chus Lampreave as the straitlaced, inept headmistress. —*Besa.*

Rocinante
(BRITISH-COLOR)

A Cinema Action production with Channel 4 Television. Produced by Gustav Lamche. Directed by Ann Guedes, Eduardo Guedes. Screenplay, Ann and Eduardo Guedes; camera (Eastmancolor), Thaddeus O'Sullivan; editor, Cinema Action; music, Jurgen Knieper; sound, Stan Philips; art director, Caroline Amies; assistant director, Andrew Warren; design development, Max Gottlieb; costume design, Jo Thompson. Reviewed at London Film Festival, Nov. 15, 1986. Running time: **93 MINS.**

Bill . . . . .John Hurt
Jess . . . . .Maureen Douglass
The Jester . . . . .Ian Dury
The Projectionist . . . . .Jimmy Jewel
Molly . . . . .Carol Gillies
Gillian . . . . .Gillian Heasman
Joe .David Travena
Stan . . . . .Tony Rohr
Charlie . . . . .Nicky Bee
Estate Manager . . . . .Richard Worthy
Mrs. Matheson . . . . .Jill Lamede
Charles Matheson . . . . .Adam Daye

London — Early in this film, a character makes the meaningful comment that the life he prefers has "no story, no plots, just a landscape and perhaps a few faces." That can stand as the verdict on the pic.

Then again, perhaps that was what he was supposed to be doing because "Rocinante" tries to be just too deep and meaningful for its own good, and offshore prospects must be dim.

The directors started out with good intentions of depicting the problems of Britain during the miners' strike of 1984, but their pretensions got the better of them, and they got lost in their efforts to create an up-to-date mystical version of Emeric Pressburger and Michael Powell's "A Canterbury Tale."

Pic opens with Bill (John Hurt) stealing a Christmas tree from a truck and taking it to his home, a derelict cinema. There he projects onto the screen tranquil landscape scenes and is happy in his false environment. He comments to the old projectionist that he "doesn't like plots, the world's full of them."

The bad news is that the cinema is about to be pulled down, so off goes Bill, humming "Jerusalem," hunting for a fresh place to squat where he can sit around looking at views ... real or false. On his travels he gets picked up by Jess (Maureen Douglass), an enigmatic woman with a mission — along with a computer and oddly annotated maps in the back of her van.

It transpires that she is involved in a plot to disrupt the computer security systems of some coalmines, and the police are after her (cue the obligatory van crashing through the roadblock scene). She dumps Bill who promptly ambles off in search of her, only taking time out to get back to his roots by staying overnight in a ramshackle old cottage.

The story rambles on but never seems to get anywhere, and though "Rocinante" proclaims to be about the miners' dispute it spends more time dwelling on England as a secret state in a vague way rather than ever touching on the hardships of the strikers.

Writer-directors Ann and Eduardo Guedes try to pack too much into the film, whether it be cinematic styles, literary analogies or political comment. John Hurt performs manfully, and is well complemented by newcomer Maureen Douglass, herself a miner's wife who was on the picket line. Ian Dury, though, is wasted in the narrating role of The Jester, which is a shame as he has real screen presence.

Rocinante was, in fact, Don Quixote's horse, but the filmmakers have not really managed to tilt at reality, let alone windmills.
—*Adam.*

El-Gooa
(Hunger)
(EGYPTIAN-COLOR)

An Egypt Video Cassette production and release. Produced by Mamdo Youssef. Directed by Ali Badrakhan. Screenplay, Mustapha Moharram, Badrakhan; camera (color), Mahmoud Abdessamieh; editor, Adel Mounir; music, George Kaza Zayani; art direction, Salah Mari. Reviewed at the Carthage Film Days (in competition), Oct. 20, 1986. Running time: **121 MINS.**
Zebeda .Souâd Hosni
Farag . . . . .Mahmoud Abdelaziz
Malak . . . . .Yosra
Gaber . . . . .Abdul-Aziz Makoun

Tunis — "Hunger," Egypt's big-budget film of the year, is something of a national landmark; first of all, for the elaborate political metaphor painstakingly planted under an apparently conventional story; second for Cleopatra-size sets of 19th-century Cairo that provide story's backdrop. In spite of its merits, "Hunger" retains a very Egyptian style of acting and storytelling which the uninitiated won't automatically appreciate. It is quality local product, however, and despite the title (which put some distribs off), it should do well in Arab markets. At the time it appeared at the Carthage Film Days, it already was available in the hotels on video.

In the poor section of old Cairo, two brothers dream of social justice and equality. Farag (burly Mahmoud Abdelaziz) thinks he will be the people's defender when he becomes the neighborhood "foutua," a cross between a local cop and Mafia boss. Once he achieves this powerful position, though, he gradually leaves the side of the people and goes over to the monied set. He marries a pretty, rich second wife (Yosra), abandoning his first wife and mother.

Gaber, the other brother (mild-mannered Abdul-Aziz Makoun), meanwhile makes the radical choice to marry a fallen woman (Souâd Hosni) who is pregnant by another man, and so defies the morality of the time to follow his heart. It is he who eventually becomes the focal point of a popular uprising, but in an impressive closing scene, with the people cutting tree branches to fight the merchants, he tells them not to wait for a leader but to take the revolution into their own hands.

Pic's historical setting got it past the censors, but also dulls its cutting edge — clearly, director Ali Badrakhan means now is the time for revolt. The melodramatic love-story, a dying mother, and a good deal of comic relief make pic an easy watch. Lensing is good; Salah Mari's much-publicized sets a little overwhelming. Dreamy score by George Kaza Zayani is a plus.
— *Yung.*

Italian Fast Food
(ITALIAN-COLOR)

A Columbia release of a C. G. Silver Films/Reteitalia/Video 80 coproduction. Produced by Mario and Vittorio Cecchi Gori. Associate producers, Carlo and Enrico Vanzina. Directed by Lodovico Gasparini. Screenplay, Gasparini, Ezio Greggio, Lorenzo Beccati, Carlo and Enrico Vanzina; camera (Luciano Vittori color), Luigi Kuveiller; editor, Raimondo Crociani; music, Detto Mariano; art direction, Ennio Michettoni. Reviewed at Quattro Fontane cinema, Rome, Dec. 3, 1986. Running time: **84 MINS.**
With: The Trettré, Sergio Vastano, Enzo Braschi, Carlo Pistarino, Susanna Messaggio.

Rome — "Italian Fast Food" is above-average entertainment for the burger generation. Director Lodovico Gasparini performs the tricky feat of transferring the catchy beat of pop tunes into teen imagery. The scene is universally familiar, but offshore markets will, paradoxically, be limited by pic's strong point — its fast and easy dialog that ranges from Italo teen *patois* to Calabrian slang. This low-budgeter without stars in the cast has achieved good b.o. locally.

Fast-rapping characters with a sense of jive are the key to the gastronomic experience, which delights in blending flavors. Thus we have a Yank-inspired fast food joint in Milan run by Calabrians, catering to everyone from millionaire industrialists to imitation punks. When the manager loses his African and Arab cooks, he hires his lazy brother-in-law and the bathroom attendant. A pretty waitress who aspires to being the Marilyn Monroe of the 1980s has tough luck with casting directors, but ends up marrying a Southerner who gate-crashes VIP cocktail parties in his doomed efforts at social climbing.

A gang of would-be toughs clashes with a rival band of mean punks. Then there is the delivery boy who spends an afternoon photographing

fashion models, via a case of mistaken identity. It's a tribute to helmer, scripters, and a cast of unknowns that out of this flimsy material a lively film has been lensed.

Technically, pic aims at, and achieves, a bright-colored bubblegum look. — *Yung.*

The Magic Toyshop
(BRITISH-COLOR)

A Granada Television production. Produced by Steve Morrison. Directed by David Wheatley. Screenplay, Angela Carter, from her novel; camera (color), Ken Morgan; editor, Anthony Ham; music, Bill Connor; sound, Nick Steer; production design, Stephen Fineren; costumes, Hilary Buckley. Reviewed at London Film Festival, Nov. 15, 1986. Running time: **104 MINS.**
With: Tom Bell, Patricia Kerrigan, Caroline Milmoe, Kilian McKenna, Lorcan Granitch, Marlene Sidaway, Gareth Bushill, Georgina Hulme, Marguerite Porter, Lloyd Newson.

London — Despite the title, this is no film for children but, as the producers insist, "an adult fairytale." It is both haunting and disturbing in its mixture of the realistic and the surreal, dreaminess and down-to-earth harshness. The feature was made for tv but may get a theatrical release in the U.K. It is not likely, however, to appeal to a wide general audience.

Setting for this fantasy is a London toyshop, where three recently orphaned children take up abode with their uncle and his family. Clearly this is no ordinary family. Uncle Philip is sadistic and authoritarian; his wife is mute; her two live-in brothers alternately pugnacious and puckish.

Conflict centers around Uncle Philip's improvised plays in which huge, lifelike mannequins which he builds perform increasingly violent and sexually suggestive acts in front of the captive family audience.

Amelia, the 15-year-old orphan, is caught up in her uncle's obsession and also tenderly involved with Finn, the more extrovert of the two brothers.

Finally there is rebellion against the tyranny of the uncle. Havoc is wreaked. Uncle Philip's wife throws off her shackles and regains her voice. Amelia's little brother, a lover of model boats, is dispatched to sea in a dream sequence, Finn destroys his brother-in-law's stage props, including an ungainly swan, and the older brother copulates with his sister. To climax these increasingly preposterous events, the uncle is killed and his body thrown onto a bonfire.

As the distinctions between animate and inanimate are broken down in the film, the nature of fantasy is caught, at least intermittently. Helping to do it are some sophisticated special effects and suitably haunting music. —*Guid.*

Im Jahr 1932 — Der rote Kandidat
(In 1932 — The Red Candidate)
(EAST GERMAN-DOCU-B&W)

A Defa Film production. Directed by Kurt Tetzlaff. Written by Tetzlaff, Jochen Niebelschütz; camera (b&w), Jürgen Greunig; editor, Christa Bramann; director of production, Ulrich Kling. Reviewed at Leipzig Docu and Short Film Festival, Nov. 23, 1986. Running time: **90 MINS.**

Leipzig — "In 1932 — The Red Candidate," about German Communist leader Ernst Thälmann and working class opposition to Hitler in the 1920s, is an authentic historical time-trip, an excellent example of how history can be recreated through the skillful use of period photos, newsreels, and music. Director Kurt Tetzlaff doesn't restrict himself to the tragic career of his subject, who died in Buchenwald in 1944, but lets pic range over the whole period.

Though some historical figures will be more familiar than others to non-German viewers, "Candidate" creates a feeling of atmosphere that can be appreciated without special expertise. Its subject will keep sales to Socialist-leaning countries, but pic could find some fest play in the West.

The curtain rises in 1925, when Thälmann, leader of the German working class movement, ran against Hindenburg in the national elections. The election atmosphere is recreated lovingly with historical footage of parades and voting booths, newspaper headlines and rephotographed newsreels (film is shot in 35mm). While SS troops murder Communists before the elections, the rival Social Democrats try to equate Communists and Nazis in the minds of voters. Hindenburg becomes president of the Republic from 1925-34, and "Candidate" shows the consequences of his politics.

History rolls on, with the rearming of Germany and Hitler's rise. Even in 1932, when the Nazis have become the strongest party, the opposition to Hitler is surprisingly strong, Communist and Socialist parties are still in existence. In her last, opening address to Parliament, 75-year-old Communist leader Clara Zetkin even calls for a united front against fascism. While crowds swoon before the Führer, pic insists on a strong base of working class resistance, which would be dissipated only by murder and force.

Technically, "Candidate" is unusually well lensed.—*Yung.*

Nyamanton
(The Garbage Boys)
(MALI-COLOR)

A Centre National de Prod. Cinematographique du Mali production. Written and directed by Cheik Omar Sissoko; camera (color), Cheik Hamala Keita; editor, Vojislav Korijenac; music, Sidiki Diabate, Moriba Keita, Mamadou Diallo, Marouna Barry. Reviewed at the Carthage Film Days (in competition), Oct. 18, 1986. Running time: **90 MINS.**
Mother ....Diarrah Sanogo
Kalifa ....Maciré Kante
Fanta ....Ada Thiocary
Karim ....Alikaou Kante

Tunis — This outcry against the substandard living conditions of Mali's poor won a gold medal at the Mannheim festival, and is skedded for Edinburgh after Carthage's Bronze Tanit. A highly watchable film tinged with moments of humor, and crowned with one of the most effective child casts since Vittorio de Sica's "Shoeshine," it deserves exposure on specialized circuits, repping the best of this year's black African product.

"The Garbage Boys" is a first feature from director Cheik Omar Sissoko, who studied film in Paris and with Jean Rouch. Opening shows little Kalifa (Maciré Kante) being thrown out of school on the first day, because his family is too poor to give him a wooden desk to sit in. Kalifa, a spunky, streetwise eight-year-old who looks 80, watches more fortunate tykes stumbling with the effort of dragging their desks to and from school each day, and realizes his future is already sealed.

In order to earn money for school, he starts collecting garbage in a little wagon. Sissoko's pint-sized star is full of four-letter words and witty observations about life, which saves him from the mawkish sentimentality that would seem endemic to this kind of picture. "Garbage" is meant to be viewed without any veil of tears, only indignation at the injustice of a society polarized between rich and poor. The children's plight in the middle of this no-exit misery is summed up by Kalifa's little sister, when she says "we should have died young." Equally chilling is the story of Kalifa's aunt, who dies in childbirth when the hospital sends her penniless husband out to buy medicine he can't afford. By the time he borrows enough money to buy it, it's too late to save her.

"Garbage Boys" was shot on a shoestring, but suffers little from it. The stripped down, real-life sets bring audiences closer to the characters, simply limned by nonpros.
— *Yung.*

Tahounet Al Sayed Fabre
(Mr. Fabre's Mill)
(ALGERIAN-COLOR)

An ENAPROC production. Directed by Ahmed Rachedi. Screenplay, Commandant Azzeddine, Rachedi, Boukalfa Hamza; camera (color), Rachid Merabtine; editor, Rachid Mazouza; music, Noutil Fadel. Reviewed at Carthage Film Days (in competition), Oct. 12, 1986. Running time: **124 MINS.**
Fabre ....Jacques Dufilho
Ali ....Ezzat El Allaili
Captain..............Sid-Ahmed Agouni
Party man ....Abdelmoneim Madbouli

Tunis — Veteran filmer Ahmed Rachedi sets his critique of an authoritarian government betraying the ideals of the Algerian revolution (the country gained independence from the French in 1962) in the past, during the time of Pres. Ahmed Ben Bella. The message is presented so forcefully, however, it's hard not to give the tale a more topical reference. This intelligent, well-crafted film (Silver Tanited at Carthage) relies on humor to make its points, and in spite of a variable pace it would make a watchable Algerian entry for fest and special screenings.

Cast of skilled thesps is led by Egyptian actor Ezzat El Allaili as Ali, idealistic mayor of an east Algerian village. With his friends, who make up an informal city council, he does his best for a poor town lacking the basics — work, bread, hospitals. Instead of help, two government officials arrive bringing news of a upcoming visit from the "Leader." This initiates a series of fights between the good locals, who have the people's welfare at heart, and the bad feds, who order a wall built to hide the town slum instead of constructing new houses. In the end all the city fathers are arrested by secret police. A perfunctory epilog informs us they were honorably reinstated after a coup d'etat brought the current government to power.

Lightening up the story is a crew of eccentric townsfolk, especially an old Frenchman named Fabre (comic Jacques Dufilho) who owns the town's only "industry," a flour mill with exactly one employee. For the Leader's visit, it is ordered "nationalized," to everyone's scorn but Fabre's.

Pic suffers from an uneven rhythm and is very talky. The ingenious/absurd solutions the mayor and his men find to problems are entertaining, but some jokes are so protracted they lose their glow. Technical credits are adequate.
— *Yung.*

Barndommens gade
(Street Of My Childhood)
(DANISH-COLOR)

A Metronome Film release of Metronome Film production with the Danish Film Insti-
tute and Danmark's Radio/TV. DFI consultant producer, Peter Poulsen. Produced by Tivi Magnusson. Written and directed by Astrid Henning-Jensen, from an original script by Erik Thygesen, based on novel "Barndommens Gade" and autobiography "The Early Spring" by Tove Ditlevsen. Stars Sofie Graböl. Camera (Eastmancolor), Mikael Salomon; production design, Sören Krag Sörensen; sound, Stig Sparre-Ulrich; lighting, Sörensen; costumes, Manon Rasmussen; editor, Ghita Beckendorff; music, Ann Linnet; production management, Marianne Moritzen, Marianne Christensen. Reviewed at the Dagmar, Copenhagen, Nov. 3, 1986. Running time: **90 MINS.**
Esther ....Sofie Graböl
Her mother ....Vigga Bro
Her father ....Torben Jensen
Her brother ....Carl Quist Möller
Lisa ....Louise Fribo
Also with: Claus Nissen, Kirsten Lehfeldt, Daimi Gentle, Lene Vasegard, Benny Poulsen, John Hahn-Petersen, Litten Hansen, Peter Schröder, Margrethe Koytu, Eva Madsen.

Copenhagen — Tove Ditlevsen (1918-76) wrote finely honed prose and poetry often based on her recollections of growing up in a respectable working-class home in a Copenhagen near-slum, where she dreamed herself away from the miseries of no privacy and the general harassments of well-meaning but mostly boorish relatives, neighbors, teachers, et al.

Ditlevsen's bestselling "Street Of My Childhood" and her book of memoirs, "The Early Spring," have not been strayed from noticeably in director Astrid Henning-Jensen's feature film carrying the same title as the novel. Where Ditlevsen's written lines evoke sweetness and sadness in a mutedly dramatic way, the film comes out deadly dull even if it pictorially follows closely in the footsteps of the original narrative texts.

The deadweight of Erik Thygesen's spineless and anemic basic script, to which Henning-Jensen was committed contractually, has been impossible to overcome. It serves as quicksand to the helmer's noble efforts, which include a sensitive way with actors and neatly cinematic stagings of moods and conflicts never resolved with anything but vague hints at true drama.

No new depths of subject matter are explored, no new viewpoints are in evidence. Everything is insipid and trite from period (circa 1935) backdrops to characters, latter mostly seen as essentially well-intentioned victims of social circumstances.

Sofie Graböl, skinny and big-eyed (and recently seen opposite Donald Sutherland as one of Paul Gauguin's models in Henning Carlsen's "The Wolf At The Door"), is well cast in the lead role of the teenager who dreams her way to the stars via the poetry she hides under her pillow. But even she looks bored most of the way. —*Kell.*

Flaming Borders
(IRAQI-COLOR)

An Iraqi Cinema release. Produced by the General Establishment for Film and Theater. Directed by Sahib Haddad. Screenplay, Kacem Mohamed; camera (color), Nihad Ali; music, Solhi El Wadi. Reviewed at the Carthage Film Days (in competition), Oct. 21, 1986. Running time: **93 MINS.**

Sana	Hind Kamel
Mother	Saadia Ezzidi
Soldier Faycel	Hamded
Mansour Majiid	Sami Khaftan

Tunis — "Flaming Borders" is the prototypical Iraqi film of our day, an all-action war pic, designed as patriotic progaganda for local auds. Its entertainment quotient is strictly for fans of interminable battle scenes, and sales to foreign markets appear unlikely.

Nevertheless, "Borders" has a curiosity value in presenting a frontline view of the Iran-Iraq war, more or less an official call to martyrdom from government to populace. Pic opens with the stern tag-line from Pres. Saddem Hussein, "All attempts to violate our borders will be repressed," and proceeds to introduce a cast of soldiers who are mostly blown to smithereens by the end credits. One survivor of the climactic battle scene is Mansour (Sami Khaftan), an archaeology prof in love with his pretty student Hind Kamel. The relative normality of Baghdad life, where only an air raid recalls the war, contrasts with chillingly realistic battles, reconnaissance missions behind enemy lines, and hand-to-hand combat at the front.

This government-financed pic employs an enviable array of real tanks and weapons, and director Sahib Haddad's grenade stunts are so realistic they look like hidden-camera documentaries, complete with mutilated corpses dangling from barbed wire fences after each explosion. One only wonders how the Iraqi army could blow up so much equipment. Before the big battle, entrenched soldiers nervously wait to mow down a pitiful wave of Khomeini's ragged shock troops, some mere boys in t-shirts. But this is a rare human moment in a film meant to exalt the war as a just, noble and excitingly virile activity.

Not neglected is the role of mothers in supporting the war effort with their sons, proudly called "martyrs and combatants."
— *Yung.*

Ntturudu
(GUINEA-BISSAU/ FRENCH-COLOR)

A Republic of Guinea-Bissau/Wac Prods. (France)/S.F.C. (France) coproduction. Executive producer, Florence Trouillard. Directed by Umban U'Kset. Screenplay, U'Kset, Benjamin Legrand; camera (color, 16m), Jean Michel Humeau; editor, Mireille Abramovici; music, Wazis Diop, Ze Manel, Loy Ehrlich; sound, Dominique Lever. Reviewed at Carthage Film Days, Oct. 16, 1986. Running time: **75 MINS.**

Mario	Mario Acqlino
N'Bedjo	Joao Bento
Faustino	Faustino Gomes

Also with: Adalgiza Vaz (Giza), Bya Gomez (Mario's wife).

Tunis — "Ntturudu" is the first feature length film shot in Guinea-Bissau by a local filmmaker. Simple tale of a boy who runs away to see Carnival aims to show a little bit of everyday rural life, and to proudly put some of the country's traditions on the screen. In this it succeeds, without breaking any speed records. Although pace lags, "Ntturudu" has moments of engaging freshness, particularly the last part regarding little N'Bedjo's dreams of Carnival masks. This curiosity item will mainly attract those who already have a special interest in the region.

First half of pic describes life in a sleepy Guinean village, where people work hard at farming. The only sign of the times is a friendly soccer game. When 12-year-old N'Bedjo hears about the Carnival in Bissau, he runs away without saying anything to brother Mario Acqlino, with whom he lives. Mario and friend Faustino Gomes set out on a 30-mile trek to find him, having a few adventures on the way.

Film's setpiece is, of course, the Carnival, an inspiring parade of grotesquely masked dancers. There are no lavish floats, but the huge clay masks coupled with native music are astounding and, as the little boy dreams, closely connected to native traditions and rites.

Lensed by a French crew, pic has acceptable technical credits. Director Umban U'Kset, a Paris-based actor on his first trial behind the camera, shows relaxed skill at directing a cast of mainly non pro thesps, who improvise dialog.
— *Yung.*

La Mansión de Araucaima
(The Araucaima Mansion)
(COLOMBIAN-COLOR)

A Focine production. Executive producer, Bertha de Carvajal. Directed by Carlos Mayolo. Screenplay, Julio Olaciregui, based on a story by Alvaro Mutis; camera (color), Rodrigo Lalinde; editor, Luis Ospina, Karen Lamassone; art direction, Miguel González; music, German Arrieta; sound, Gustavo de la Hoz. Reviewed at Rio de Janeiro Film Festival (competition), Nov. 24, 1986. Running time: **86 MINS.**

Girl	Adriana Herran
Machiche	Vicky Hernandez
Servant	Antonio Luis Sampaio
Pilot	Luis Fernando Montoya
Landowner	José Lewgoy
Priest	Alejandro Buenaventura
Guardian	Carlos Mayolo
Boyfriend	David Guerrero
Director	Luis Ospina

Rio de Janeiro — Time has stood still for the inhabitants of the mansion located in the middle of nowhere, until an innocent young girl accidentally finds her way there and upsets longstanding equations. Atmosphere is the strong point of Carlos Mayolo's second feature, but, beyond festivals, it is unlikely to gain much international exposure.

"The Araucaima Mansion" is based on a story by Alvaro Mutis, a Colombian writer who has lived in Mexico for many years. It originally had been intended for Luis Buñuel, who died before he could shoot the film. Among the characters there is a landowner, a priest, a soldier, a servant and a pilot, all of whom are serviced by Machiche, a sort of earthmother. They are all quite set in their ways and relationships, until the young girl enters their midst, leading to violence and the end of this self-enclosed society. The presence of two Brazilian actors (José Lewgoy and Antonio Luis Sampaio) tends to emphasize the non-specificity of the mansion's location.

Director Mayolo, who also acts the soldier, describes his work as "tropical gothic" and, stylistically, he may have a point. But the film's decisive flaw lies not in its style but in the screenplay (and probably the original Mutis story) inasmuch as it plays around with symbol for symbolism's sake. The atmosphere is created, but it all leads nowhere and fails to acquire a consistent meaning.

Acting is good, as is the film's technical level, which is superior to most of the current crop of Colombian pictures. —*Amig.*

The Morning After
(COLOR)

Implausible thriller fails despite Fonda-Bridges teaming.

A 20th Century Fox release of a Lorimar Motion Pictures presentation of an American Filmworks production. Produced by Bruce Gilbert. Executive producer, Faye Schwab. Directed by Sidney Lumet. Stars Jane Fonda, Jeff Bridges, Raul Julia. Screenplay, James Hicks; camera (Deluxe color), Andrzej Bartkowiak; editor, Joel Goodman; music, Paul Chihara; production design, Albert Brenner; art direction, Kandy Stern; set decoration, Lee Poll; costume design, Ann Roth; sound, David Ronne; associate producers, Wolfgang Glattes, Lois Bonfiglio; assistant director, Glattes; casting, Nancy Klopper. Reviewed at the Samuel Goldwyn Theater, Beverly Hills, Dec. 12, 1986. (MPAA Rating: R.) Running time: **103 MINS.**

Alex Sternbergen	Jane Fonda
Turner Kendall	Jeff Bridges
Joaquin Manero	Raul Julia
Isabel Harding	Diane Salinger
Sgt. Greenbaum	Richard Foronjy
Bobby Korshack	Geoffrey Scott
Frankie	James (Gypsy) Haake
Red	Kathleen Wilhoite
Hurley	Don Hood

Hollywood — Overwrought and implausible, "The Morning After" is a dramatic situation in search of a thriller plot. Jane Fonda stars as a boozy, washed-up actress who wakes up one morning next to a man with a dagger in his heart, and her efforts to cope with the dilemma are neither terribly suspenseful nor entertaining. This Fox release won't prove to be too many filmgoers' idea of what to rush out and see over the holidays.

When Fonda awakens to find the bloody remains of her sleazy one-night stand cold and stiff in bed, she honestly can't remember how she ended up there, and is not even entirely certain that she didn't kill the man.

She therefore removes any trace that she was ever present at the fellow's place, doesn't call the cops and heads for the airport, where, instead of catching a plane, she hooks up with friendly redneck Jeff Bridges, who begins by driving her around and gradually insinuates himself into her life.

Along the way, Fonda battles the bottle, succumbs to Bridges' charms and is forced into a divorce by estranged hubby but good chum Raul Julia, an outrageously successful Beverly Hills hairdresser who now wants to marry a Bel-Air heiress.

While attempting to build up tension, Fonda and director Sidney Lumet more often succeed in creating hysteria. Brittle, suspicious and high-strung, Fonda's former small time star is a potentially interesting character, a woman with her prime well past her who must aggressively pick herself up by the bootstraps if she's not going to spend the rest of her days just wasting away.

Unfortunately, unlike Fonda's Oscar-winning "Klute," to which this bears certain superficial resemblances, ''The Morning After'' doesn't reveal the hearts of its characters, and therefore emerges as both a failed character study and a failed thriller. Fonda never revealingly explores or confronts her drinking problem, and the interesting age difference between her and Bridges is never commented upon; there are ways to make light of this humorously, or in passing, without making a big deal out of it, but not mentioning it seems like an unrealistic avoidance and detracts from the dramatic urgency of the ending.

A handful of the scenes between Fonda and Bridges legitimately engage the interest, and things pick up a bit whenever the actor is on the scene. But this one won't go down as either of their major credits.

Pic will also deserve the status of no more than a footnote in Lumet's career, and that only because it marks the first of the New-York based director's 33 films to be shot on location in Los Angeles. He and lenser Andrzej Bartkowiak have made use of some boldly colorful backdrops to try to jazz up the bland material, but to little avail. —Cart.

Prison Mother, Prison Daughter
(CANADIAN-DOCU-COLOR- 16m)

Produced by the Canadian Broadcasting Corp., Toronto, Ontario. Directed by John Kastner. Camera (color, 16m), Edmund Long; editor, Leslie Borden Brown; sound, John Crawford. Reviewed at Nyon Intl. Film Festival (Switzerland), Oct. 17, 1986. Running time: 87 MINS.

Nyon — The last of three long CBC-TV documentaries by John Kastner on the Canadian penal system, this film examines two lives, a mother and a daughter (not related), who enter prison for long sentences. The women, both in their 20s, struggle desperately for parole. Their separate ordeals are intercut so that viewers see alternately the privileged treatment accorded the daughter, the harsher treatment accorded the mother.

The daughter is 23, blond and attractive, caught in a drug bust, a first offense, and given seven years. She is supported strongly by an educated, comfortably well-off family that organizes the press shrewdly and clergy to endorse an early parole. She is alternated in the editing with the other prisoner, the mother, who has a long history of petty offenses, many arrests, an alcoholic and recidivist. At age 29, looking much older, she has given away her four children, and now, as the film begins, she has just given birth to a fifth child, born in jail.

As the mother now enters prison for repeatedly passing bad checks, the newborn baby is dumped into the custody of her alcoholic common-law husband. In contrast to the speedy parole being organized for the daughter, the mother faces bureaucratic suspicion of her capacity to keep straight if paroled.

The film parallels these two convicts, their two stories side by side in one film, as they are side by side in the same tier of cells. All these people are authentic, of course, as this is a documentary, but the drama and emotions of their predicaments could hardly have been improved upon if scripted, directed and acted by professionals.

Many months pass within the film, demonstrating how the two women-prisoners are totally different in their origins and in their destinies. In time, the young first-offender is paroled and restored to her family. Meanwhile, the older woman, inarticulate and uneducated and most in need of social services and therapy, is broken and doomed. At the film's end, her baby is given up for adoption by strangers, her common-law husband is hospitalized for alcoholism, and she is resentenced for new crimes committed during her brief probation.

The film does more than merely report and observe. Instead, it seems determined to illustrate a thesis, jeopardizing its journalistic neutrality. The parole system plays favorites, the film says, allowing the daughter of an educated, wealthy family of connections to find easy, quick parole. In contrast, the working-class woman is a victim of class bias. One suspects that this thesis is unproved and that the lives depicted are more complex.

Still, this film of prison/punishment/parole should succeed in specialized screenings and for public tv. — Hitch.

King Kong Lives
(COLOR)

Superfluous sequel.

A De Laurentiis Entertainment Group release. Produced by Martha Schumacher. Executive producer, Ronald Shusett. Directed by John Guillermin. Screenplay, Shusett, Steven Pressfield, based on a character created by Merian C. Cooper, Edgar Wallace; camera (J-D-C Widescreen, Technicolor), Alec Mills; editor, Malcolm Cooke; music, John Scott; production designer, Peter Murton; art direction, Fred Carter, Tony Reading, John Wood; set decoration, Hugh Scaife, Tantar LeViseur; costume design, Clifford Capone; sound (Dolby), Peter Stephenson; creatures' creation and construction, Carlo Rambaldi; special visual effects supervisor, Barry Nolan; assistant director, Brian Cook; casting, Donna Isaacson, John Lyons; Reviewed at the Hollywood Pacific theater, Dec. 19, 1986. (MPAA Rating: PG-13.) Running time: 105 MINS.

King Kong ....Peter Elliot
Lady Kong ....George Yiasomi
Hank Mitchell ....Brian Kerwin
Amy Franklin ....Linda Hamilton
Colonel Nevitt ....John Ashton
Dr. Ingersoll ....Peter Michael Goetz
Dr. Benson Hughes.......Frank Maraden

Hollywood — King Kong's revival after a decade serves as little more than a sequel in service to a possible sequel. Story and acting are too weak to outdo the 1976 remake and it will take more than curiosity over updated mechanics and special effects to deliver anything but modest business.

Film leads off with the previous pic's closing footage of Kong being slain atop the World Trade Center in New York as Jessica Lange weeps. Advancing to the present, we learn the giant ape has been kept alive by the marvels of recent medical technology.

Kong is stunningly revealed to be breathing via life support systems, with Linda Hamilton heading a surgical team preparing to give him an artificial heart. The visual scope of this oversized medical environment — with cranes delivering a seven-foot artificial heart — provides an early high point that is never quite matched.

While Hamilton declares it will take nothing short of a miracle to save Kong, Brian Kerwin enters from far-off Borneo, where he has stumbled onto a female Kong. He strikes a purely mercenary deal to deliver her to the Hamilton group so her blood can be used for the heart transplant operation.

In portraying an Indiana Jones-type figure — there's even a direct on-screen comment about the likeness — Kerwin strains for plausibility and film swiftly begins to lose some early credibility. His tough jungle ways are unconvincingly transformed into sensitive concern for both animals — apparently, and presumably insincerely, because of his attraction to Hamilton.

Meantime, the proximity of the two Kongs prompts these primates to seek what comes naturally. The pyrotechnics, machine gun barrages and stomping of cars begins in earnest as Kong frees the female from her entrapment before the pair escape together into the woods. This would prove to be the moment when director John Guillermin loses all control of the pic.

Mindless chase then proceeds pell mell for the rest of the film, with the army in hot pursuit. While John Ashton turns in a fine performance as a crazed colonel (à la Capt. Ahab's pursuit), his seeming carte blanche to slaughter Kong is devoid of rationale. All other authority — military, civilian and scientific — by now has been banished from the script.

The Kongs do manage one night together on ''Honeymoon Ridge,''

with Hamilton and Kerwin paralleling the coupling as supposedly the only two people alive who care for the apes. What fails here and throughout is creation of empathy for them or the Kongs as was the case when Lange and Fay Wray provided the vital connecting emotional links between ape and audience.

Action sequences do serve to highlight excellent Kong torso movements thanks to latest work by Academy Award winner Carlo Rambaldi. Facial gestures are wonderfully precise here as they are when the Kongs are exchanging affections.

However intriguing such elements may be, story by now has so deteriorated that there's really no logic to its progression at all.

Before the bloody ordeal of the inevitable kill, however, it's revealed that Lady Kong is pregnant. In a shamelessly melodramatic bit of climactic hokum, Kong is brought down just as his mate is delivering the offspring.

As Kong slumps to his death after touching his youngster, one finally understands that his 10-year medical trauma and this film update may have been little more than a setup for a ''Son Of Kong'' sequel. Otherwise, why resurrect the big guy and then so brutally ravage him again? The King is dead. Long live the King.—Tege.

Solo Trubui
(Trumpet Solo)
(SOVIET-DOCU-COLOR/B&W)

A Moscow Documentary Film Studios production. Directed by Alexander Ivankin. Written by Lev Roschal; camera (color/b&w), Vladimir Nikonow; editor, E. Agadschanjan; music, R. Ledenew. Reviewed at Leipzig Docu and Short Film Festival, Nov. 25, 1986. Running time: 60 MINS.

Leipzig — Alexander Ivankin (''Pyramid'') continues to develop as one of the most talented young Soviet documakers, with a unique ability to bring out the human dimension of his subjects through skillful technical work.

''Trumpet Solo'' is a moving, sometimes humorous, portrait of a 92-year-old working woman who lived through the turbulent events of her century. It is told partly in her voice, and partly through the fiery diaries of her son, killed in action in 1944. Pic should be a natural pickup for festivals and specialized audiences.

We meet Rosa Fedotova as a lonely old lady, living in an apartment with mementos of her dead son. Grief over her loss would have pushed her to suicide, she says, had she not remembered her life as a Bolshevik. Film contrasts these two poles — the emotional emptiness of the present, the richness of the past — in a tense balancing act.

Born at the turn of the century, Rosa Fedotova went abroad looking for work as a girl, first to Paris, then to New York. Both are memories filled with the energy and good humor of youth. Even when she was arrested as a Communist in New York, she ironically remembers the fine view she and her friends had of the Statute of Liberty from their jail cell on Staten Island.

Rosa returns to Moscow in 1918, after the Soviets have taken power, and when warned by a sailor on her boat she's walking into misery, she retorts she'd rather eat black bread in her country than white bread abroad. The bitter future that awaits her is the war, when her son, also a committed Communist, dies in combat. His war diaries make up a good part of the picture, turning attention away from the heroine for a while. Only at pic's end does Rosa take center stage once more, finishing this portrait of Soviet history with her own voice, a lonely but brave "trumpet solo." —*Yung.*

Hyper Sapien: People From Another Star
(U.S.-COLOR)

Inept sci-fi.

A Tri-Star Pictures release of a Jack Schwartzman presentation of a Taliafilm II production. Produced by Schwartzman, Ariel Levy. Directed by Peter Hunt. Screenplay, Christopher Adcock, Christopher Blue, Marnie Paige, from story by Blue; camera (Technicolor), John Coquillon; editor, Robert Benrich; music, Arthur B. Rubenstein; production design, Harold Lange; costumes, Kathy Marshall; sound, Frank Griffiths; special effects, David Harris; "Kirbi" animatronics, Rodger Shaw; casting, Mike Fenton Associates. Reviewed at the Cineplex Royal Center, Vancouver, Dec. 14, 1986. (MPAA Rating: PG.) Running time: **93 MINS.**
Robyn .Sydney Penny
"Dirt" (Robert Edward
  McAlpin) . . . . .Ricky Paull Goldin
Jasper McAlpin . . . . .Keenan Wynn
Tavy . . . . .Rosie Marcel
Sen. Myrna King . . . . .Gail Strickland
Uncle Aric . . . . .Dennis Holahen
Les .Chuck Shamata

Vancouver — Juvenile sci-fi in the 1950s utopian style, revamped ineptly for the Spielberg era, "Hyper Sapien" fails to deliver more than indulgent Saturday matinee chuckles and groans. Colorless leads hampered by leaden dialog, fail to strike any sparks from a Johnny-Come-Lately fantasy featuring a woozily executed comic alien, and a horse-opera setting that reeks of pastiche.

Unlikely to ring bells among homo sapiens, the listless pic is hardly a contender in the Yuletide stakes nor will it prove much more to the point during its wider U.S. re-

lease next February, except for the undemanding family audience.

Written originally by its initial director Michael Wadleigh ("Wolfen") this second of two films lensed in Western Canada in 1985 (the first was "RAD") was initially also a Canada-U.K. coproduction.

It intros a trio of ETs from the planet Taros who flee from their mothership moored on our moon. Robyn, a young woman, Tavy, a girl-child, and Kirbi, a three-eyed, three limbed baby sloth are taken under the wing of rancher's son Dirt in Aladdin, Wyo. The quartet finds refuge at the homestead of feisty Granpa Jasper (Keenan Wynn in his 211th pic, and final screen appearance).

Meantime, Robyn's Uncle Aric, commander of the mothership, sets out in desultory pursuit, tracked in turn by a suspicious cop, Les, who fears an assassination attempt on the life of Senator King, who is stumping the boondocks for re-election. King is a friend of the McAlpin family and at a barbecue-hoedown at the ranch the aliens let the cat out of the bag.

Sluggishly directed by British veteran Peter Hunt, "Hyper Sapien" is floored by reliance on sub-par special effects that will not deceive the average six-year old. The Tri-Lat Kirbi is a gas-guzzling non-starter that feeds on hot coals and drains off gas tanks to aid its growth. Cute it ain't.

Kirbi's human protectors are no more appealing, and his alien companions proffer no real competition when it comes to winning characterizations. Seldom, even in the annals of moppet sci-fi, has there been so much ado about so little.

Technical credits are passable, with veteran British cameraman John Coquillon's lensing a severe disappointment for those acquainted with his Sam Peckinpah days. Arthur B. Rubinstein's score is more robust than the occasion merits.—*Gran.*

Les Fugitifs
(The Fugitives)
(FRENCH-COLOR)

A Gaumont release of a Fideline Films/D.D. Prods./Efve Films/Orly Films coproduction. Produced by Jean-José Richer. Written and directed by Francis Veber. Stars Gérard Depardieu, Pierre Richard. Camera (Eastmancolor), Luciano Tovoli; editor, Marie-Sophie Dubus; music, Vladimir Cosma; art director, Gérard Daoudal; sound, Jean-Pierre Ruh; assistant director, Xavier Castano; Françoise Menidrey; production manager, Jean-Claude Bourlat. Reviewed at the Gaumont Ambassade cinema, Paris, Dec. 19, 1986. Running time: **87 MINS.**
Jean Lucas . . . . .Gérard Depardieu
François Pignon . . . . .Pierre Richard
Mr. Martin . . . . .Jean Carmet
Dr. Bourdarias . . . . .Michel Blanc

Commissioner Duroc . . . . . .Maurice Barrier
Labib . . . . .Jean Benguigui
Idriss . . . . .Roland Blanche
Jeanne .Anaïs Bret

Paris — Comedy writer-director Francis Veber hits the funnybone with his usual blithe invention in "The Fugitives," his third picture with the "odd couple" of Gérard Depardieu and Pierre Richard, who were delightfully combustible companions in Veber's "La Chèvre" and "Les Compères," both box-office smashes here, as this new one certainly will be, too.

Veber, France's most versatile screen gagsmith, has mined the vein of male-bonding farce with surprising freshness and variety since his first success in this mode: the 1973 Edouard Molinaro comedy "L'Emmerdeur." Since then becoming his own director, Veber has polished his manner, succeeding in giving his well-oiled laugh machines a pleasing human hum, thanks especially to the Depardieu-Richard tandem. Once again cast as the virile (but vulnerable) pro and the neurotic booby, thrown together by wild circumstance and forced to see it through in each other's unwanted company, they transcend artifice and routine, becoming old friends one is always happy to see again.

In "Fugitives," Depardieu is a professional bank robber who wants to go straight, and Richard an unemployed man who desperately attempts a holdup as a solution to his woes.

The bank where Depardieu decides to open an account on his first day out of prison is the same one Richard ineptly tries to rob. As police surround the premises, the neophyte wrongdoer grabs a hostage: Depardieu. "Can't you take somebody else?" the ex-con growls.

Unable to convince the cops he's been taken hostage by the puny Richard, Depardieu is forced to flee with him and lie low until he can clear himself. But their lives are inextricably cemented by Richard's autistic six-year old daughter, who becomes attached to the hulking outlaw and recovers her speech to ask him to stay. Unsuccessfully fighting his own feelings, Depardieu helps Richard regain custody of the child and escapes with them across the border.

Veber's comic imagination is in high gear as he whips along his cleverly assembled gag vehicle, loaded with snappy dialog and droll scenes of role-reversal and farcical mishaps. Among instances that would figure in any Veber anthology are the bungled bank robbery and a sequence in which Depardieu is treated for a bullet wound by a senile veterinarian, played to hilarious perfection by Jean Carmet.

Veber's use of overt sentiment as a pilot device (employed previously

in "Les Compères," with its theme of disputed paternity) is taken much farther here in the scenes with the child. Veber tugs at the heart strings with relative tact, misjudging only his use of Vladimir Cosma's slightly saccharine musical theme. The new tone of seriousness also is reflected in Richard's more realistically nuanced portrayal of the hapless chump.

Fine supporting cast includes Michel Blanc (Depardieu's Cannes-laureled costar in "Ménage") in a cameo as a drunken doctor. Tech credits, which include lensing by Italo ace Luciano Tovoli, are firstrate.
—*Len.*

New World
(BRITISH-COLOR-16m)

A BBC-TV and Lella Prods. coproduction. Produced by David Thompson. Directed by Norman Stone. Screenplay, William Nicholson; camera (color), Russ Walker; music, Stanley Myers; production design, Gerald Murphy. Reviewed at London Film Festival, Nov. 27, 1986. Running time: **125 MINS.**
William Bradford . . . . .James Fox
John Billington . . . . .Bernard Hill
Alice Southwark . . . . .Betsy Brantley
Miles Standish . . . . .Frederick Jaeger
Christopher Martin . . . . . . .John Ringham
Lyford . . . . .Joss Ackland
Squanto . . . . .Eloy Casados
Also with: Jack Watson (Brewster), Robert Bathurst (Newcomen), Andrew Keir (Carver), Rosalind Ayres (Dorothy Bradford), Robert Duncan (Winslow), Philip Raymond (Salter).

London — What exactly went on when the pilgrims weren't eating Thanksgiving dinner is the subject of this overlong, far too stagey drama.

It centers on the conflict, historically sound, between the Puritan idealist William Bradford and the adventurer John Billington for control of the fledgling colony at Plymouth Rock in the 1620s.

Unfortunately, film gets too carried away with its own theme, so that dramatic confrontation appears stilted and unmotivated, and speeches are mouthed unconvincingly as set pieces. In other words, it never quite comes alive.

It is interesting, however, to see a film focus on what happened after the Mayflower dropped anchor. The award-winning production team (recipients of an Emmy for "Shadowlands") has upturned fascinating material, a positive addition to the generally limited and iconographic view of the first settlers.

In this version, the founding fathers are not just the dour Puritans but also adventurer soldiers, rapacious and self-willed, who crossed the Atlantic to exploit whatever riches they could lay their hands on. Point apparently being made by the filmmakers is that the two groups closely mirror the dual nature of the American character.

Naturally, there had to be some Indians around to heat up the action and, to be fair, "New World" has dug up from the historical documents an interesting specimen to focus on. The white settlers' first encounter with Squanto is superb: before guns can be fired, the apparent savage disarms them with his almost perfect British English. As interpreter between the local Indian chief and governor Bradford, he ends up being the most multi-faceted character in the film.

There are several other strands to the plot, including love interest in the form of a young Puritan widow torn between Bradford and Billington and a false minister who foments trouble by preaching against Bradford's policy of common property. Neither adds much to the general effect.

While the performances and technical credits are all adequate, Bradford, one would think, was a more charismatic figure than James Fox makes him out to be. —*Guid.*

Crazy Moon
(CANADIAN-COLOR)

A Cinegem Canada release of an Allegro Films production in coproduction with the National Film Board. Produced and written by Tom Berry, Stefan Wodoslawky. Directed by Allan Eastman. Camera (color), Savas Kalogeras; sound, Andre Galbrand; art director, Guy Lalande; production manager, Michel Martin; assistant director, John Rainey. Reviewed at Cineplex Odeon screening room, Toronto, Dec. 16, 1986. Running time: 87 MINS.
Brooks . . . . Kiefer Sutherland
Cleveland . . . . Peter Spence
Anne. . . . . Vanessa Vaughan
Alec . . . . Ken Pogue
Mimi . . . . Eve Napier
Dr. Bruno . . . . Harry Hill
Anne's father . . . . Sean McCann
Anne's mother . . . . Bronwen Mantel

Toronto — "Crazy Moon" is a loopy love story between an oddball rich kid and a feisty deaf girl. If warning bells are going off, not to worry. Allan Eastman's directorial effort, originally titled "Huggers," is done with good humor and an offbeat p.o.v., but it never really develops its potential quirkiness. The interaction between the two leads is too contrived to pull off a major boxoffice coup either. It should go straight to tv or paycable as a small screen smile.

Kiefer Sutherland, in another weirdo role as Brooks, the bizarre teen who's a throwback to the 1930s, is celebrating his birthday with his autocratic daddy (Ken Pogue), his irresponsible brother Cleveland (Peter Spence), and dad's bimbo mistress. Brooks slicks back his hair, dresses in bowties and baggy pants, listens to Tommy Dorsey on his Walkman, and inhabits a room steeped in memorabilia.

Later that day he steals a mannequin from a sporting goods store, dresses her up as a female lawyer, puts her in the jump seat of his motorcycle and he drives around. He photographs feces on the street and hangs the results on his walls as art.

During the robbery Brooks eyes a cute salesgirl, follows her to her house and finds out she's deaf. Romance blooms: Anne (newcomer Vanessa Vaughan) reads lips; Brooks memorizes "The Joy Of Signing." Pic is a chronicle of their courtship. As she feels more comfy with him, she starts to "speak." She plans to go off to Europe by herself soon, too.

Clichés come quickly, as Anne spray paints "What is music like?" on the sidewalk on St. Helen's Island in Montreal, where pic was shot, and the duo dance together under a full moon with dueling Walkmen.

Anne tries to teach Brooks to swim but he's petrified, only to come to the fore during his final confrontation with his brother at their father's pool. Brooks and Anne attend their first rock concert together, after Cleveland tricks Brooks into waiting on line all night for tickets to a Rational Youth concert for himself.

Funny bits with Brooks on a blind date with a young lawyer as he simultaneously puts the moves around his mannequin-lawyer, and Brooks hanging of a model of his dad's g.f. while she arrives in his room are too few here.

Set design of Brooks' room is a perfect period piece, and soundtrack is a memory-laden mélange of Glenn Miller, Russ Morgan, Guy Lombardo and Jo Stafford, mixed with Rational Youth's contempo offerings.

A couple of insights into Anne's deaf life — how to type out a message on a deaf telephone, practicing "speaking" with a therapist — are instructional, but almost too serious for tone of the pic.

Sutherland is a sickie here, affectless and mired in his family's pathology, but opens up in an affectionate way to Vaughan. She's likable and capable, so what's she doing with such a nut? Other characters are one-dimensional. Eastman directs largely for the laughs but manages to make the leads' romance goofy and warm.

if the cast of "Children Of A Lesser God" watched "Harold And Maude," they'd end up in "Crazy Moon." — *Devo.*

Cairo Festival Reviews

Awdat Mowatin
(Return Of A Citizen)
(EGYPTIAN-COLOR)

A Misr Co. release of an Actor Films Prods. production. Produced by Yehia El Fakharani. Directed by Mohamed Khan. Screenplay, Assem Tawfik; camera (color), Ali El Ghazuli; editor, Nadia Chukri; music, Kamal Bakir. Reviewed at the Cairo Film Festival, Dec. 9, 1986. Running time: 116 MINS.
Chaker . . . . Yehia El Fakharani
Fawzia . . . . Marvet Amin
Younger sister . . . . Magda Zakhi
Ibrahim . . . . Sherif Mounir

Cairo — Mohamed Khan again shows he's one of Egypt's most original directors in "Return Of A Citizen." Pic's topliner, Yehia El Fakharani, also produced this melancholy study of a family falling apart at the seams in contemporary Cairo, where new values and Western-style individualism have destroyed traditional family life. Pic could be a festival choice offshore.

"Return" opens with Chaker (Fakharani) flying back home from the Gulf a comfortably rich man, after working abroad for years. There's nobody to meet him at the airport. Back home, Chaker finds his two sisters and brothers still living under one roof, but hardly united. He moves into his old room and spends most of the day sleeping. Little sister Magda Zakhi is getting married, to the others' complete indifference; big sister Marvet Amin uses Chaker's money to get her "Marie Antoinette Sweet Shop" (let them eat cake ...) started, but moves into her own apartment when business booms.

Even sadder are the fates of his younger brothers. One, unemployed too long, retreats into solitary chess games and eventually into drugs; the other, a cheerful boy whose passion is raising homing pigeons, winds up in jail — he belonged to an outlawed political group that was using the pigeons to send messages. Chaker is left with the dilemma, to go or to stay? As he says at one point, there are two types of people, those who take from their country, and those who pay for it. He makes the harder choice.

Story is told simply, without exaggeration. Khan sets his action in real-life locales, ordinary homes and streets. An accomplished cast turns in natural performances; the fat and puffy Fakharani may be no matinee idol, but he commands attention and sympathy whenever he's on the screen. Pic is technically superior. —*Yung.*

Sikat Safar
(A Way To Go)
(EGYPTIAN-COLOR)

Produced by Abdel Malik El Khamisi. Written and directed by Bashir El Deek. Camera (color), Tarak El Telmisani; editor, Adel Mounir; art direction, Rogdi Hamed. Reviewed at the Cairo Film Festival, Dec. 6, 1986. Running time: 114 MINS.
Zarlu . . . . Nour El Sherif
Noemi . . . . Noura
Old man . . . . Abdel Salam Mohamed
  Also with: Hasam Mustapha, Aida Abdelaziz.

Cairo — In "A Way To Go" (literally, "The Travel Path") a hayseed returns to his village a rich man after working abroad, but loses his money for the girl he loves in a bittersweet finale.

This second feature by scripter Bashir El Deek shows its social theme underpinnings a little too blatantly, as the drama of having too little money merges with the family-splitting tragedy of emigration to find work. Pic's seriousness is fortunately enlivened by good performances from Nour El Sherif and Noura, who give their characters a comic edge.

Pic opens with Zarlu (Sherif) staging a grand return to his country town. Outfitted worse than a Jim Jarmusch hick from New Jersey, he has brought back a comical wealth of tvs, tape players, electric fans. In his purple patterned pants and dapper moustache he's the village hero, and soon is brought together with the local tycoon in a business venture. As it turns out, both Zarlu and his partner love the same spunky girl (Noura), but bad counselors get Zarlu married to the partner's daughter instead. The crossed loves are eventually rectified, but Zarlu loses his "fortune" in the process. In a poignant postscript, he gets the girl but has to leave her to find a job, in a journey that reverses pic's start.

El Deek is particularly good at sketching full-bodied, believable characters, and even the baddies have a human side. Money is the obsession of the whole village, and their poverty isn't glossed over. Many people are graphically shown to be so hungry they steal bits of food when their friends' backs are turned. College grads wait despondently for a job; shoemakers turn to smuggling, or break their backs working in the salt lakes. It's an ugly picture painted realistically.

Technical credits are adequate.

—*Yung.*

Kahir Elzaman
(Time Stops)
(EGYPTIAN-COLOR)

A Tamido release of an El Rania Prod. Directed by Kamal El Cheik. Screenplay, Ahmed Abdel Wahab, from a novel by Nihad Sherif; camera (color), Ramses Marzouk; editor, Hassan Helmi; music, Georges Kazazian; art direction, Mokhtar Abdel Gawad. Reviewed at the Cairo Film Festival, Dec. 8, 1986. Running time: **115 MINS.**

Kamal . . . . Nour El Sherif
Zein . . . . Athar El Hakim
Dr. Halim . . . . Gamil Ratap
Cousin . . . . Khalid Zaki

Cairo — Kamal El Cheik is a respected Egyptian director who's lensed over 50 features in his long career. "Time Stops" (literally, "Conquerors Of Time") is his latest offering, a film with ambitions to being a pioneer sci-fi work in a country where the genre doesn't exist. To Western eyes it is much closer in spirit to a standard Hardy Boys mystery, with b.o. star Nour El Sherif playing both Hardy boys. As sci-fi it's a talky pic that travels in the slow lane. Boxoffice looks iffy onshore and off.

Yet the basic idea, linking the modern possibility of deep-freezing terminally ill patients for resuscitation in the future, when their diseases can be cured, with the ancient Egyptian practice of mummification, is a promising one. Unfortunately, film doesn't develop the parallel.

A science writer, Kamal (Sherif), and his cousin Khalid Zaki begin investigating the mysterious disappearances of patients from a provincial hospital. Soon Khalid himself is missing, and the search for him leads Nour to the isolated villa of a brilliant scientist, Dr. Halim (Gamil Ratap). Halim and his sinister bodyguard-assistants holds Nour prisoner in the house, where Halim's Koran-reading daughter Athar El Hakim provides a bit of love interest.

Long dialogs later, after preserving corpses through refrigeration has been discussed and rediscussed, Nour stumbles onto Halim's secret lab. The frozen cousin is brought back to life, but Halim and his underground lab (decorated with hieroglyphics) perish in an earthquake which the special effects department is barely able to suggest.

Film is lensed professionally, but in many respects Cheik's practiced technique works against him, turning scenes in predictable, old-hat formulas. Cast runs through the stereotypes with a straight face.

Pic's one brilliant shot is its last, where in some future hospital a deep-frozen patient is wheeled by in a glass case, decorated with a life-size image of King Tut. — *Yung.*

Flamberede hjerter
(Coeurs Flambés)
(DANISH-COLOR)

A Kärne Film release of Per Holst Film production with the Danish Film Institute. Produced by Holst. Film Institute consultant producer, Peter Poulsen. Written and directed by Helle Ryslinge. Stars Kirsten Lehfeldt, Torben Jensen. Camera (Eastmancolor), Dirk Brüel; editor, Birger Möller-Jensen; music, Peer Raben; sound, Mikkel Bo; costumes, Malin Birch-Jensen; production management, Michael Christensen, Janne Find; assistant director, Lone Scherfig, Ilse Haugaard. Reviewed at the Grand, Copenhagen, Dec. 11, 1986. Running time: **112 MINS.**

Henriette . . . . Kirsten Lehfeldt
Loewe . . . . Torben Jensen
Bent . . . . Sören Oestergaard
Ole . . . . Peter Hesse Overgaard
Finn . . . . Anders Hove
Mr. Holm . . . . Ingolf David
Mrs. Holm . . . . Lillian Tillegren
Lisbeth Castillo . . . . Kirsten Peuliche
Woodroof . . . . Aage Haugland
Also with: Yrsa Gullaksen, Arne Siemsen, Else Petersen, Pernille Höjmark, Margrethe Koytu, Knud Dietmer, Morten Suurballe.

Copenhagen — "Coeurs Flambés" is the funny-sad saga of a young Danish nurse, pert, pretty and a kook, who knows the solution to everybody's troubled affairs of the heart but her own. Directed expertly by first-timer Helle Ryslinge and produced by veteran Per Holst, it should be a shoo-in for international art house exposure.

The nurse with the burning heart is Henriette, a.k.a. Henry, who called it quits when her musician-lover was too ambiguous about the married-life-with-kids she herself so openly covets. She now has an unconvincing affair going with a nice, nondescript man, but she soon abandons herself totally to Loewe, a mildly macho hospital surgeon, who doesn't mean business, at least not marriage business, either.

Henry's kooky front is, of course, a self-protective measure, and when the surgeon proves too deceitful, it helps her take a revenge that comes out as a piece of gorgeous burlesque theater: expected to act as dinner-at-home hostess to the surgeon's famous foreign colleague (a cameo performance of controlled ebullience by international Grand Opera's Aage Haugland), Henry dresses up with eels in woolen stockings, dishwater hair and her teeth tainted with black, while she serves sausages stuck upright into a dish of mashed potatoes along with vintage wine in crystal goblets.

Will Henry ever achieve the goal she has set? Not if she insists on keeping company mostly with social outcasts, general misfits and romantic dwellers on the big city fringe. What, one might ask, is a nice nurse doing there, anyway? One suspects the director's personal empathy with the milieu (she is a graduate of basement, loft and political activist theater) of having written this low-life nostalgia rather too forcefully into the Henry character.

Acting in this comedy is buoyant throughout, with Kirsten Lehfeldt in the lead and Torben Jensen as the surgeon shining in particular. Cinematographer Dirk Brüel works the fringes as well as the busy hospital corridors with natural ease, while the writer-helmer has peppered her film with a string of background vignettes that come close to clamoring for too much attention. The fun of the filmmaking is more convincing than the heartbreak of the story, but the genuine comedy goods have been delivered with style and flourish. —*Kell.*

Milwr Bychan
(Boy Soldier)
(BRITISH-COLOR)

A Cine Cymru production for S4C (Channel 4 Wales). Produced by Karl Francis, Hayden Pierce. Coproducer, Ruth Kenley. Written and directed by Francis. Camera (Rank color), Roger Pugh Evans; editor, Aled Evans; music, Graham Williams; sound, Pat Graham; production design, Pierce; assistant director, Sergio Leon Alarcon; costumes, katie Pegg. Reviewed at the London Film Festival, Nov. 25, 1986. Running time: **98 MINS.**

Wil Thomas . . . . Richard Lynch
Sgt. Crane . . . . Dafydd Hywel
Lt. Col. Truscott Jones . . . . Janes Donnelly
Officer . . . . Bernard Hill
Deirdre . . . . Emer Gillespie
Roberts . . . . Bernard Latham

London — Though set in the troubled streets of Northern Ireland, "Boy Soldier" is about the Welsh not the Irish, specifically the young lads from the valleys whose only alternative to the jobless dole queue is the army.

The "squaddies" from the Welsh unit use their language as a weapon against the military hierarchy, but when one makes the mistake of shooting an important civilian in the line of duty and falling in love with an Irish girl, it seems only his birthright can keep him sane. Though compelling the pic must have limited overseas b.o. potential.

Wil Thomas (Richard Lynch) loves the army and is a good soldier but events get the better of him, and when the army needs a scapegoat for the man he shot Wil is imprisoned and bullied by the brutal Red Bands, the army prison officers.

In a series of flashbacks we see the events leading up to the killing, and of Wil's shortlived romance with an Irish girl Deirdre (Emer Gillespie), who ends up being tarred-and-feathered when locals discover she is seeing a soldier.

Wil refuses to plead guilty to murder, and with the help of his unit sergeant (Dafydd Hywel) eventually gets the charge lessened, and the pic ends with him sentenced to two years in jail and dishonorably discharged.

Pic solidly shows the cruelty and duplicity of the army's situation and attitude in Northern Ireland, and according to director Karl Francis is based on actual incidents. "Boy Soldier" has subtitles for the Welsh language sections.

Francis uses a complex series of flashbacks to tell what is essentially a very straight "tale of injustice" type story, though his Welsh locations double well for Northern Ireland, and newcomer Richard Lynch (not the American actor by that name) as Wil, and Dafydd Hywel as Sgt. Crane have the character and screen presence to make what could have been an ordinary film a bit more special. There is a lingering feeling, though, that the romance sequence is unnecessary addition to what is really a traditional prison drama. —*Adam.*

The Best Man
(BRITISH-COLOR)

A Northlands production and release. Produced by Denis Bradley. Written and directed by Joe Mahon. Camera (color), Terry McDonald; editor, McDonald; music, Eamon Friel; songs sung by Friel; sound, Billy Gallagher; production design and assistant director, Bradley. Reviewed at the London Film Festival, Nov. 23, 1986. Running time: **85 MINS.**

Billy Maguire . . . . Seamus Ball
Jamsie McDaid . . . . Denis McGowan
Maureen McDaid . . . . Mairead Mullan
Mrs. Maguire . . . . Jean Flagherty
Joe McLaughlin . . . . Mickey McGowan
Pat McIntyre . . . . Aiden Heaney
"Professor" . . . . Hugh McIntyre

London — "The Best Man" is a rarity, a comedy from Northern Ireland that never mentions the conflict there and only briefly touches on religion. Its focus is totally on a hard-drinking bachelor charmer.

Pic was obviously made on a shoestring, and the thick Irish accents and poor sound quality make it impossible to understand at times. But the performance of Seamus Ball as the boozy Billy Maguire is a joy. Prospects, though, must be limited anywhere outside N. Ireland (even if subtitles were added).

Billy wakes up with a can of beer in his hand (purely medicinal he tells his long-suffering mother) and just about manages to fall out of bed. He is to be best man at a pal's wedding, but sees his main purpose in life as extoling the values of alcohol and arguing against marriage.

His mother tells him he should go to confession before the wedding, and as an afterthought asks him if he even knows where the church is. "Of course," he says, "I pass it every day on my way to the bookies."

Gambling and pontificating in the bar are Billy's strengths, and with his gang of drinking chums he taunts Jamsie, his friend who has given up the bottle to try and save his marriage.

Being best man is not Billy's favorite role — as he says: "It's like asking the undertaker to give someone the kiss of life" — but he performs his duties well, and leads the drinking at the reception. The day ends in drama, though, when Jamsie reverts back to the booze, and his wife Maureen (Mairead Mullan) blames Billy.

The storyline is thin but all the characters have a rough charm and wit, and importantly the pic shows another side to life in Northern Ireland. Some of director Joe Mahon's camera angles are amateurish, but he directs with gusto, and his cast members give their all. —Adam.

The Devastator
(COLOR)

Typical revenge pic.

A Concorde Pictures release of a Rodeo Prods. production. Produced and directed by Cirio H. Santiago. Screenplay, Joseph Sugarman; camera (Metrocolor, prints by Film House Group), Richard Remington; editor, George Saint, Margaret Carlton; music, Matthew Ender, Mark Governor; sound, Vic Donna; production design, Joe Mari Avallon; art direction, Ronnie Cross; production manager, Eugene Navarro; second unit director, Joseph Anderson; casting, Stan Shaffer. Reviewed on MGM/UA Home Video vidcassette, N.Y., Dec. 14, 1986. (MPAA Rating: R.) Running time: 78 MINS.
Deke Porter . . . . Richard Hill
Audrey King . . . . Katt Shea
Carey . . . . Crofton Hardester
Sheriff . . . . Kaz Garas
Spencer . . . . Terrence O'Hara
Bartlett . . . . Bill McLaughlin
Ox . . . . Jack S. Daniels
Reese . . . . Steve Rogers
Elaine . . . . Debbie Brooks

"The Devastator" once again brings the Vietnam war back to the homefront as a vet uses military tactics to clean up bad guys in California. Originally titled "Kings Ransom" (after the town where it is set) and alternately "The Destroyers," pic is similar to "Final Mission," a 1984 Cirio Santiago opus as well. "Devastator" opened regionally in September 1985.

Wracked by nightmares about his stint in Vietnam, Richard Hill visits the small town of Kings Ransom after Debbie Brooks, the widow of his pal Marty, calls from there telling him her husband has been killed in a car wreck. Befriended by gas jockey Katt Shea, Hill is terrorized by locals for being an outsider. It seems that local growers have taken over the valley for their marijuana business and corrupted the local sheriff (Kaz Garas).

Hill barely escapes when the thugs burn down Brooks' house (where he is staying), but comes back in force with other war vets armed to the teeth. With the sheriff won over to their side they burn up the pot fields, rescue Shea from the villains and set things straight.

Action scenes are acceptable and both Hill and Shea make for sympathetic protagonists. Crude editing job has the picture ending very abruptly, perhaps acceptable to antsy homevideo consumers but a definite irritation for a theatrical film. Several credits seem to have been anglicized, e.g. Richard Remington for Santiago's regular cinematographer Ricardo Remias. — Lor.

Hob Fee Baghdad
(Love In Baghdad)
(IRAQI-COLOR)

A General Establishment for Cinema and Theater production and release. Written and directed by Abdul Hadi Al Rawi. Camera (color), Hatam Hoosein; editor, Al Rawi; music, Abdul Amtr Alcarraf; art direction, May Dawood. Reviewed at the Cairo Film Festival, Dec. 11, 1986. Running time: 102 MINS.
Hamadi . . . . Kasim Al Mallak
Fitna . . . . Ikbal Naaim
Jemil . . . . Sanaa Abdul Rahman

Cairo — Using a cast of topflight stage comedians, young Iraqi helmer Abdul Hadi Al Rawi constructs an unpretentious, mild-mannered comedy. "Love In Baghdad" has no trouble standing out in Iraq's minimal film production, since it's unique in not once mentioning the war with Iran. This passes for refreshingly escapist entertainment locally, and audiences have shown their appreciation. Mideast sales unfortunately will be limited by its Iraqi dialect.

Hamadi (popular young thesp Kasim Al Mallak) plays a clumsy simpleton who, one day, falls out of a palm tree in front of his country wife Fitna (Ikbal Naaim). They take him to the hospital, while in a confusing series of flashbacks we see how he met his wife and future brother-in-law. A man with no past, Hamadi is revealed in more flashbacks to have lost his memory following a blow on the head. Now he resumes his old personality as Cassam, a Baghdad carpenter.

He escapes from the hospital, pursued by his country relatives in a pickup truck, and hotfoots it back to Baghdad, where he discovers he's rich and marries his childhood sweetheart Jemil (Sanaa Abdul Rahman). The tangled plot is straightened out in the end, just in the nick of time.

A lack of continuity makes it tough to follow the storyline, but the cast is good in any language and Al Rawi's camera technique above average. One would like to see him at work on more promising material. —Yung.

Al Dahiya
(The Victim)
(EGYPTIAN-COLOR)

Produced by Mohamed Muktar Pictures. Directed by Atif Salim. Screenplay, Bashir El Deek, from a story by Hosam Shah; camera (color), Mohesen Nasr; music, Gamal Salama. Reviewed at the Cairo Film Festival, Dec. 12, 1986. Running time: 117 MINS.
Zinip . . . . Nadia El Gindi

Cairo — In "The Victim" Nadia El Gindi, one of Egypt's leading sex symbols, steps daringly out of the glamor roles that have made her famous. This is about the extent of the film's interest. An overlong melodrama divided into two stories that barely fit together, it may be too atypical to go far even in local markets.

In the first half of the picture, an average housewife's world collapses when the apartment building the family lives in caves in. With her unemployed husband and two small kids, Zinip (Gindi) moves into a crowded tent shelter. Her job as a nurse isn't enough to get them a new apartment, so she reluctantly kisses the family goodbye and takes off for a job in a rich Gulf hospital. Her selfless intention is to come back in a few months with enough cash to get them going again.

A year and a half passes, and the family is able to buy a new apartment with the money she sends them. Just as she's on the verge of leaving for home, a spiteful co-worker accuses her of stealing morphine and gets her fired.

Once back in Cairo, Zinip has the shock of finding her husband has divorced her and remarried. A messy court battle almost wins her custody of the kids, but then the morphine story comes out. In her despair at losing her children, husband, apartment, money and reputation, she becomes a real morphine addict, at which point pic turns into a lurid illustration of the zombifying effects of drugs.

Helmer Atif Salim takes sadistic pleasure in turning his rosy-cheeked matron into a sniffing, scratching green hag and Gindi throws herself into the role wholeheartedly. Neatly divided into two films in one, "The Victim" fails twice to get a spark of significance out of either of its scandal-sheet stories. — Yung.

El-Sada El-Rigal
(The Gentleman)
(EGYPTIAN-COLOR)

A Studio 13 production. Written, produced and directed by Rafaat El Mihi. Camera (color), Samir Farag; editor, Sayed El Sheikh; music, Mohamed Hellal. Reviewed at the Cairo Film Festival, Dec. 12, 1986. Running time: 113 MINS.
Fawzia/Fawzi . . . . Mali Zayed
Also with: Mahmoud Abdelaziz; Hala Foad; Ibrahim Yousri.

Cairo — "The Gentleman" is an Egyptian "Victor/Victoria" minus Julie Andrews, plus sex-change operation. This is an off-beat comedy indeed for its Mideast market, but local audiences have responded favorably to its daring irony. However curious the premise, its look is too primitive to pass far offshore.

Fawzia (Mali Zayed) is a plump, average-looking bank employee who's fed up with her male co-workers and too-busy husband (Mahmoud Abdelaziz). It strikes her she'd be under less pressure if she were a man, so she slips into the hospital and emerges in a pin-striped suit and tie.

The funniest thing about pic is the way helmer Rafaat El Mihi shows the dead-pan solidarity of friends, relatives, and co-workers, who are perfectly pleased with the new "Fawzi." Only her husband protests, but is curtly silenced by the well-wishers and a few karate chops form his newly male wife. In the end he wonders if he wouldn't be better off as a lady.

Lest El Mihi be accused of radical feminism, story has masculinized Fawzi turn against women, although he forms a liaison with a pretty bank teller. A sick baby brings things back to normal in the end. —Yung.

Tokimedi ni shisu
(Deaths In Tokimeki)
(JAPANESE-COLOR)

A Nikkatsu release of a Nikkatsu (Tokyo) production. Produced by Hiroshi Okada, Shogo Hosokoshi, Shin Omori. Directed by Yoshimitsu Morita. Screenplay, Morita, from a novel by Kenji Maruyama; camera (color), Yonezo Maeda; music, Osamu Shiomura; production design, Katsumi Nakazawa. Reviewed at London Film Festival, Nov. 13, 1986. Running time: 105 MINS.
Kudo, the man . . . . Kenji Sawada
Kozue . . . . Kanako Higuchi
Okura . . . . Naoki Sugiura

London — The eclectic young Japanese director Yoshimitsu Morita has concocted a taut, stylish thriller that should widen his following.

While some may be put off by the coldness of the exercise, the extremely slow, controlled direction allows viewers to solve the film's puzzle, jigsaw piece by jigsaw piece.

What is puzzled together is the last days in the life of a hitman, holed up in a remote villa in the Japanese countryside, waiting to be called into action. He is kept company by an overly garrulous, sexually obsessed minder and a young girl, dispatched to the villa to "entertain" the protagonist.

Normal routine actions like eating, drinking, exercising and riding in a car acquire ritualistic overtones and become charged with meaning, fraught with tension in this preparation. Only slowly does it dawn on the viewer, through intercutting of computer printouts from a mysterious controlling organization, that the protagonist is practicing for an "elimination."

The viewer is made to feel the unbearable weight and tension which must lead up to a terrorist act. Aside from consummate pacing, the performance from Kenji Sawada as the hitman is wonderfully controlled. He projects underlying menace behind an imperturbable exterior. His loyalty to his calling is almost a religious devotion; it is an irony that he is tapped to eliminate a religious leader.

When the showdown, staged with great panache, finally comes, the hitman's attack backfires and in frustrated rage he kills himself. It is suggested that he too has been set up.

The film is highly circumscribed, even impersonal. No noticeable political comment, it would appear, is being made, but it is a perfect matching of form to content.

Set design must be singled out as contributing effectively to the subtly shifting mood of the piece.

One can only hope that Morita will develop his talent to tackle larger themes.—*Guid.*

Pékin-Central
(Peking Central)
(FRENCH-COLOR)

A Forum Distribution release of a Melody Movies production. Produced by Bernard Verley. Written and directed by Camille de Casabianca. Camera (color), Raymond Depardon; editor, Denise de Casabianca; music, Michel Hardy; title song lyrics, Camille de Casabianca; sound, Luc Perini; production manager, Hubert Watrinet. Reviewed at the Georges V cinema, Paris, Oct. 21, 1986. Running time: **95 MINS.**
With: Yves Rénier (Yves), Christine Citti (Valérie), Marco Bisson (Bruno), Sophie Deschamps, Béatrice Lord, Jacques Pibarot, Françoise Taguet, Hubert Watrinet, Pascale Bailly, Alain Tasma, Cai Xinming, Camille de Casabianca.

Paris — For her helming debut, Camille de Casabianca, 29, who began her screen career in 1980 as actress and coscripter with her director dad Alain Cavalier (most recently cowrote his highly-praised "Thérèse"), beat out more heavyweight competition as the first Western filmmaker to shoot in China. Casabianca slipped behind the Bamboo Curtain with a compact cast and crew — and a lensing permit granted on a fake scenario — to make this wry comedy-drama about a young woman's romantic upheavals during a voyage to the East.

Using as her lenser veteran photojournalist and docu filmmaker Raymond Depardon (who recently directed a Citroën commercial on the Great Wall of China!), Casabianca fashions a casual, reportage-styled road movie about a nonchalant miss (Christine Citti) who joins her journalist boyfriend (Yves Rénier) on an assignment to cover Western tourism in China.

Since he's married, Citti thinks the journey as part of a typical group tour will enhance and deepen their rapport, though in fact their relationship falls apart. Gradually Citti drifts into an affair with Rénier's photographer associate (Marco Bisson). He too is married and proves unwilling to make any sacrifices for her. Citti returns home to Paris no more advanced in her emotional life than before, though perhaps a bit wiser about her own sentimental propensities.

Casabianca and Depardon follow the ill-matched trio, and their often comically self-absorbed fellow voyagers, across the officially beaten tracks of China with breezy detachment and irony. Aptly Casabianca doesn't spoil the viewer with long-held vistas of Oriental splendor precisely because we are meant to see as much as her central personages see — not all that much.

"Peking Central" remains modest in its probings, and performances are only passable (with caricatural limning from Rénier as the fatuous first lover), but Casabianca suggests more than a merely touristy new film eye and refreshing sense of family continuity. Her mom, veteran editor Denise de Casabianca, cut the pic.—*Len.*

Le Passage
(The Passage)
(FRENCH-COLOR)

A UGC release of an Adel Prod./LM Prod. coproduction. Produced by Alain Delon, Francis Lalanne. Written and directed by René Manzor. Stars Delon. Camera (Eastmancolor), André Diot; editor, Roland Baubeau; music, Jean-Félix Lalanne; art direction, Emmanuel de Chauvigny; sound, Jean-Paul Mugel; special effects makeup, Christopher Tucker; animation, René Manzor. Reviewed at the UGC Normandie cinema, Paris, Dec. 16, 1986. Running time: 79 MINS.
Jean Diaz . . . . Alain Delon
Catherine Diaz . . . . Christine Boisson
David Diaz . . . . Alain Musy
Patrick . . . . Jean-Luc Moreau

Paris — Alain Delon, who has mercilessly gunned down innumerable adversaries in sundry thrillers, goes pacifist in his latest vehicle, "Le Passage," a puerile pseudo-mystical fantasy imagined and directed by newcomer René Manzor.

Delon is Jean Diaz, a humanitarian filmmaker planning a cartoon that would stand as a plea against hate and violence. Before he can execute his project he is snatched from this world by Death itself in a car accident.

Diaz wakes up on a mortuary slab for a conversation with the Grim Reaper in person, who demands that he make his film under its auspices as a blueprint for the universal destruction it's planning. If Diaz doesn't comply, his young son, who has survived the accident but is in a coma, will join him in death.

Manzor's inanely pretentious script pictures the Grim Reaper in its traditional guise, but with a voice like E.T.'s and a hi-tech control room from which it monitors activities.

Film's only mystery surrounds Delon's reason for choosing to produce and star in such cinematic infantilism. The star's confused quest or renewal is one of the saddest sights on the domestic filmmaking scene. —*Len.*

Cours privé
(Private Classes)
(FRENCH-COLOR)

A Sara/CDF release of a Sara Films/La Cinq coproduction. Executive producer, Christine Gozlan. Produced by Louis Grau. Directed by Pierre Granier-Deferre. Screenplay, Jean-Marc Roberts, Pierre Granier-Deferre, Christopher Frank, from Roberts' novel, "Portait craché;" camera (color), Robert Fraisse; editor, Jean Ravel; music, Philippe Sarde; art director, Dominique André; sound, Pierre Lenoir, Claude Villand; assistant director, Dominique Brunner; casting, Romain Brémond. Reviewed at the Marignan-Concorde theater, Paris, Dec. 1, 1986. Running time: 95 MINS.
Jeanne Kern . . . . Elizabeth Bourgine
Bruno Ketti . . . . Michael Aumont
Laurent . . . . Xavier Deluc
Patricia . . . . Sylvia Zerbib
Zanon . . . . Emmanuelle Seigner
Mme. Ketti . . . . Lucienne Hamon

Paris — "Cours privé," a murky but melodramatically predictable tale of poison pen letters in a private prep school, is the third collaboration between director Pierre Granier-Deferre and novelist-scripter Jean-Marc Roberts, whose work often revolves around sociosexual games people play in professional milieus. Their 1982 film, "Un Etrange affair," was among the helmer's best, but Roberts' scripts since them (including this one, co-adapted by fellow writer-filmmaker Christopher Frank) have not kept the promise of his debut.

Roberts dramatizes the persecution of an attractive young history teacher (Elizabeth Bourgine) whose out-of-class morals and private life are viciously denounced by a series of anonymous letters addressed to the establishment's director (Michael Aumont), who has vainly been courting her.

The campaign against Bourgine escalates when the entire faculty begins receiving photos of an orgy with the face of one particular participant — Bourgine? — cut out.

The questions that arise from this premise are all easy to answer and the script's refusal to analyze its characters prevents much involvement for the viewer.

It's clear early on that Bourgine is a sexually inhibited lady whose sterile personal life is limited mostly to roaming around her sparsely furnished apartment in nothing but a red corset listening ad nauseum to a single record (Marianne Faithfull's "The Ballad Of Lucy Jordan"). It's no less obvious that Aumont is the author of the poison pen missives and photos, acting out sexual frustration and jealousy (since Bourgine did have a brief lesbian fling with one of her students — her partner in the photo, who sent the first anonymous letters).

Granier-Deferre manages to sustain a certain amount of tension, thanks notably to the performance of Aumont, who distills in his role the ambiguity lacking elsewhere, through Bourgine can't provide the same for her inscrutably two-dimensional part.

Tech credits are okay. —*Len.*

Grandi Magazzini
(Department Store)
(ITALIAN-COLOR)

A Columbia Pictures Italia release of a C.G. Silver Film production. Produced by Mario and Vittorio Cecchi Gori. Written and directed by Castellano & Pipolo. Camera (color), Nino Celeste; editor, Antonio Siciliano; music, Detto Mariano. Reviewed at Adriano Cinema, Rome, Nov. 15, 1986. Running time: 100 MINS.
Umberto Anzellotti . . . . . Alessandro Haber
Elena Anzellotti . . . . Laura Antonelli
Alvise . . . . Enrico Montesano
Robot . . . . Paolo Villaggio
Salvietti . . . . Nino Manfredi
Store manager . . . . Michele Placido

Also with: Renato Pozzetto (Fausto), Massimo Civilotti (young Kruger), Heather Parisi (girl with contacts), Lino Banfi (street singer), Ornella Muti (herself), Christian De Sica (prize winner), Massimo Boldi (guard).

Rome — In a season bereft of Italo product, veteran comedy team Castellano & Pipolo have tallied good b.o. with their latest quickie, "Department Store." The idea is to throw 13 popular film and tv stars into the offices, selling floors and delivery trucks of a bustling store and cut back and forth between a number of little stories, most involving old variety show gags. Main aud is drawn from mature women's lingerie and the preteen departments.

Most sustained tale is a case of mistaken identity when Laura Antonelli, married to personnel director Alessandro Haber, convinces her husband that an incompetent young salesman in bathroom fixtures actually is the store owner's son, incognito. They wine, dine and even seduce him, but Enrico Montesano, as any Italo filmgoer knows, is just a hopelessly Roman street kid.

Nino Manfredi appears in a cameo as a tippling thesp called on to do a commercial; Ornella Muti as herself delights a shy salesman-fan with an unexpected appearance in the midst of men's sportswear; and Paolo Villaggio tries to sell himself to the store as a robot.

Those who remember Mario Camerini's charming 1939 comedy of the same title will find it a sign of the times to see star Vittorio De Sica's lookalike offspring Christian turning up as a macho greaser who wins a night in bed with an attractive employee-prostitute, in a skit so tasteless it can only be a deliberate knock at the refined comedy of yore. —Yung.

Charlotte For Ever
(FRENCH-COLOR)

An AMLF release of a GPFI/Constellation coproduction. Produced by Jean-Claude Fleury, Claudie Ossard. Written, directed and scored by Serge Gainsbourg. Stars Charlotte and Serge Gainsbourg. Camera (Fujicolor), Willy Kurant; editor, Babeth Si Ramdane; sound, Michel Brethez; art director, Raoul Albert; production manager, Charlotte Fraisse; assistant director, Jean Couturier. Reviewed at the Marignan-Concorde cinema, Paris, Dec. 10, 1986. Running time: 94 MINS.
With: Serge Gainsbourg (Stan), Charlotte Gainsbourg (Charlotte), Roland Bertin (Léon), Roland Dubillard (Herman), Anne Zamberlan (Lola), Anne Le Guernec (Adelaide), Sabeline Campo (Thérèse).

Paris — "Charlotte For Ever" is Serge Gainsbourg's neurotic motion picture valentine to his daughter Charlotte, who won critical kudos and a César award for her performance of a troubled adolescent in Claude Miller's film, "L'Effrontée" (Charlotte And Lulu).

It's also the portrait of the artist as a dirty old man. Papa Gainsbourg, one of France's most talented pop performing songwriters, has earned equal notoriety as a raunchy provocateur. He has carefully groomed a media image as a sort of Gallic Charles Bukowski, whose sex-obsessed parlance and grungy hungover face have abraded many while enchanting young followers.

Even his fans are not likely to think much of his third effort as filmmaker, in which he indulges his unhealthy fixation with his gangly offspring, who looks embarrassed to be involved in daddy's psychodramatic display of self-disgust.

Gainsbourg's flimsy one-set script dramatizes an ambiguous father-daughter relationship. He plays a washed-up screenwriter torn by the disaffection of his daughter, who holds him responsible for the death of her mother in a road accident. His tortured musings with a

sleazy film producer (Roland Dubillard), a depressed homosexual friend (Roland Bertin), and flings with an incredibly gross prostitute he brings home, and two young nymphets of Charlotte's age, don't help matters.

A last-minute reconciliation, as sudden as it is unjustified, brings the two together. Her heart belongs to daddy. And what else?... An overhead camera pulls up and away to reveal the decor as a studio set, suggesting all this has been just for play. But it hasn't been any fun.

Gainsbourg showed genuine filmmaking ability in his two previous films. None of that here, except the virtuoso feat of simultaneously contemplating one's navel and gaping at a daughter in ways that evoke more than simple paternal affection.—Len.

A Kind Of English
(BRITISH-COLOR)

A Silver Films production for Film Four Intl. Produced by Richard Taylor. Directed by Amin. Screenplay, Paul Hallam, from an idea by Amin; camera (Technicolor), Jonathan Collinson; editor, Richard Taylor; music, Fire House, songs sung by Lucy Rahman; sound, Albert Bailey, Andrew Parker; art direction, Jock Scott; assistant director, Jonathan Ripley; costumes, Leslie Gilda. Reviewed at the London Film Festival, Nov. 27, 1986. Running time: 75 MINS.
Mariom, mother . . . . Lalita Ahmed
Tariq, uncle . . . . Andrew Johnson
Chan, father . . . . Badsha Haq
Shahanara, grandmother . . . Afroza Bulbul
Samir, boy . . . . Jamil Ali

London — The problems of a Bengali household in London are well outlined in "A Kind Of English," which relies on the complex relationships within the family to carry the story rather than incident.

Tariq (Andrew Johnson) has adapted to life in Britain and works as a taxi driver, but his brother Chan (Badsha Haq) can't adjust and his frustrations and anger affect the family unit. Pic is very much limited to only an interested audience, and b.o. potential is probably nil.

Mariom, the mother, copes as best she can with both new life and her moody husband, while her son Samir and his grandmother spend the film making a model of their village in Bangladesh.

Their own culture and its adaption to England affects them all in different ways, and as the film develops all characters give vent to their own different attitudes to their Bangladesh past and their new life in England.

It takes a parental row to bring the family together, as nine-year-old Samir runs off into London and the family members take to the streets to hunt for him.

The small cast performs well,

especially Andrew Johnson as Tariq who has adapted to his new life, but is constantly reminded of his roots, and Afroza Bulbul as the grandmother who is at her happiest when remembering what life was like back in their village in Bangladesh. Jamil Ali as the boy Samir acts functionally, but has an irritating squarky voice.

Ruhul Amin has constructed the film well, and sensibly not relied on obvious scenes of racial attack to portray the problems of the immigrant community, instead giving all the characters a dignity which presents itself in varying ways. Technical credits are fine. —Adam.

Dünki-Schott
(SWISS-GERMAN-COLOR)

A Rex Film Zollikon (Zurich) release of a Bernard Lang, Zurich-Maran-Film/SDR, Stuttgart-Alfred Richterich, Laufen-Walter Schoch, Zurich coproduction. Directed by Tobias Wyss, Hans Liechti. Screenplay, Franz Hohler, Wyss; camera (Eastmancolor), Liechti; editor, Fee Liechti; music, Ruedi Haeusermann; sound, Hans Kuenzi; art direction, Fritz Huser, Chrigi Seiler; costumes, Monika Schmid; lighting, Hans Meier. Reviewed at the Alba Cinema, Zurich, Dec. 12, 1986. Running time: 90 MINS.
Dünki-Schott . . . . Franz Hohler
Santschi . . . . René Quellet
Döltschi Bea . . . . Dodo Hug
Frau Rüegg . . . . . . Elisabeth Müller-Hirsch
Pia . . . . Christel Förstsch
Dr. Indermühle . . . . Jodoc Seidel
Lt. Witschi . . . . Herbert Leiser
Herr Schnyder . . . . Walter Hess

Zurich — Swiss cabaretist and writer, Franz Hohler, adds his own version of Cervantes' "Don Quixote" in the form of a modern-day Swiss comedy about an eccentric history professor riding an attack against the evils and "monsters" of our time. As everyone knows, today's dragons and windmills bear such names as pollution, nuclear energy and highway speeding.

It must have seemed a good idea on paper, especially since Hohler is an undauntedly engaged, acerbic author with a satirical bite. He wrote the script of "Dünki-Schott" (a fictitious Swiss name sounding similar to the German pronunciation of "Don Quixote") together with Tobias Wyss, who codirected with Swiss cameraman, Hans Liechti.

Hohler's and Wyss' lack of experience in theatrical films is written all over "Dünki-Schott." It's one of those films where good intentions alone just aren't enough. Hohler plays the professor about to write a book, on a scholarship, about the influence of crusaders on early Swiss history. Wanting to experience the "Crusader feeling" himself, he buys a horse and ends up riding attacks, as a modern-day Don Quixote, against cars on a national highway, detergents causing pollution

and the cooling-tower of an atomic plant. He narrowly escapes the authorities and is celebrated as a hero by the village where he has retired to write his scientific work.

His companion is a scrap-dealer named Santschi (Sancho Panza), and his Dulcinea (named Döltschi Bea here) is the secretary of the trust sponsoring his book.

It all adds up to little more than a rather helpless and amateurish attempt and the feeling that Hohler tried to bite off more than he could chew. His stilted and declamatory performance is no help, either. Hans Liechti's pastel-colored, delicate lensing is one of the picture's few assets. — Mezo.

Eat And Run
(COLOR)

Lame spoof.

A New World Pictures release of a BFD Prods. production. Produced by Jack Briggs. Directed by Christopher Hart. Stars Ron Silver. Screenplay, Stan Hart, Christopher Hart; camera (DuArt color), Dyanna Taylor; editor, Pamela S. Arnold; music, Donald Pippin; sound, Felipe Borrero; art direction, Mark Selemon; production manager, Briggs; assistant director, Gary Marcus; associate producer, Tom Field. Reviewed at Magno Preview 9 screening room, N.Y., Dec. 22, 1986. (MPAA Rating: R). Running time: 90 MINS.
Mickey McSorely . . . . Ron Silver
Judge Cheryl Cohen . . . . . Sharon Schlarth
Murray Creature . . . . R.L. Ryan
Police captain . . . . John F. Fleming
Sorely McSorely . . . . Derek Murcott
Also with: Robert Silver, Mimi Cecchini, Tony Moundroukas, Frank Nastasi, Peter Waldren, Gabriel Barre, Ruth Jaroslow, George Peter Ryan, Lou Criscuolo, Tim Mardirosian, Louis Turenne.

"Eat And Run" is a one-joke horror spoof that plays like a "Saturday Night Live" tv sketch stretched out to 90 minutes duration. Filmed as "Mangia" two summers ago in Manhattan, New World pickup opened in Chicago in October and is headed mainly for midnight bookings.

Ron Silver toplines as a police detective given to narrating out loud his misadventures in 1940s tough guy fashion, a habit picked up from his dad (Derek Murcott). He's on a missing persons case, the result of a tubby alien (R.L. Ryan) landing in New Jersey and eating up Italian Americans because the first person he meets (and eats) is Italian, making him addicted to "Italian food."

Silver links up romantically with a judge (Sharon Schlarth) who despite being named Cohen turns out to be Italian. She improbably falls in love with the alien, but Silver saves the day, only to end up in hot water himself in a ridiculous, unsatisfying ending.

Chatty film is directed by newcomer Christopher Hart (who scripted with his dad Stan Hart) in the manner of a radio play; static visuals present a pleasant but unatmospheric background to verbal humor. High points are two well-delivered (by Silver and cohorts) variations on Danny Kaye's patented, fast-paced alliteration routines, though without Kaye's rhythm or singing attributes. Otherwise, pic is deadly dull, hammering its gag firmly into the ground via repetition.

With no special effects, gore or sexploitation, film seems like a G-rated approach with dirty words inserted to get an R rating. —Lor.

Twist Again à Moscou
(Twist Again In Moscow)
(FRENCH-COLOR)

An AMLF release of a Gaumont Intl./Renn Prods./Films A2/Caméra One coproduction. Executive producer, Alain Poiré. Directed by Jean-Marie Poiré. Screenplay, Jean-Marie Poiré, Martin Lamotte, Christian Clavier; camera (Panavision, Eastmancolor), Pascal Lebegue; editor, Catherine Kelber; music, Michel Goglat; art director, Pierre Guffroy; costumes, Catherine Leterrier; sound, Alain Sempe; stunt coordinator, Rémy Julienne; second unit director, Jacques Monnet; assistant director, Jean Couturier; casting, Marie-Christine Lafosse; production manager, Jean-Pierre Spiri-Mercanton. Reviewed at the Gaumont Ambassade theater, Paris, Nov. 10, 1986. Running time: **103 MINS.**
Igor Tatiatev ....Philippe Noiret
Youri ....Christian Clavier
Natasha Tatiatev ....Marina Vlady
Pikov ....Martin Lamotte
Tatiana ....Agnès Soral
Minister ....Bernard Blier

Paris — "Twist Again In Moscow" is the latest in a long line of local comedies that suffers from commercial gigantism: megabuck production lavished on a flimsy script. Director Jean-Marie Poiré and his co-writers Martin Lamotte and Christian Clavier, café-theater talents who've moved with more or less success into cinema, got some yocks out of their previous topheavy screen farce, "Papy fait de la Résistance," but drown in the borscht-belt humor of this labored sendup of Soviet life.

"Twist" was shot largely on location in Yugoslavia, a suitable stand-in for the principal Russian settings, but the costly concern for outward realism jars with the chosen vein of broad farce and lampooning and the unmistakably Gallic cast who make no effort to sound Russian. On the stage this would get by, but on the screen it undermines the basic credibility all good comedy requires to function.

Poiré and his cohorts poke facile fun at communist lifestyles and attitudes in a plot centered at a luxury hotel in Moscow, whose director (Philippe Noiret) lives lavishly off his Black Market connections. His world goes haywire when Party inspectors and KGB agents descend on his establishment hunting for administrative irregularities and fugitive Jewish dissidents whom Noiret is obliged to smuggle to the West to save his own hide.

Noiret and his costars, including scripters Clavier and Lamotte as Noiret's rock show organizer brother and the no-nonsense inspector, are capable tongue-in-cheek farceurs, but their concerted efforts cannot lift an iron curtain of mechanical contrivance that weighs on the frenetically unfunny proceedings, which constantly remind one that Billy Wilder did it funnier and faster in "One, Two, Three." —Len.

Impressions de L'Ile des Morts
(FRENCH-DOCU-COLOR-16m)

A coproduction or Arcanal, (H) Enoch and Metatron. Icav, Paris. Directed by Richard Leacock, Hans-Peter Litscher. Screenplay (from Strindberg), Litscher; camera (color, 16m), Richard Leacock, Robert Leacock; editor & sound, Gloriana Davenport. Reviewed at Nyon Intl. Film Festival (Switzerland), Oct. 17, 1986. Running time: **85 MINS.**
With: Alain Cuny, Hans-Peter Litscher.

Nyon — Veteran French actor Alain Cuny, star of theater and cinema for decades, is the center of this documentary reconstruction of his stage performance of an August Strindberg work at the Theatre de la Bastille.

Included are Cuny's rehearsals, press conferences and backstage encounters with adoring fans. The young Swiss theater director, Hans-Peter Litscher, presides over these rehearsals, and he codirected this film record of the performance. These backstage preparations have a nervous excitement that is oddly contradicted by Cuny's slow manner and hesitant speech. His performance largely takes place while he is seated alone at a table in the center of a bare stage, reading aloud from his character's memoirs of his strange experience while passing from life to death.

In the background are a painted diorama or moving settings by Arnold Boeckin. Silent figures occasionally enter and dance or move about stylistically. Beside Cuny, two screens receive projected b&w images.

This work dramatizes Strindberg's impressions of a man who has ceased to live, who has been to the island of the dead, posing mysterious questions. The film may have value to advanced graduate students and faculty and historians of modern theater, but it is too esoteric for public theatrical and tv purposes. —Hitch.

Cinema Falado
(Talking Pictures)
(BRAZILIAN-COLOR)

An Embrafilme release of a Caetano Veloso/Guilherme Araujo production. Produced by Veloso, Araujo. Executive producer, Rodolfo Dodo Brandao. Written and directed by Veloso.Camera (Eastmancolor), Pedro Farkas; editor, Mair Tavares; sound, Jorge Saldanha; musical director, Veloso; assistant director, Bruno Wainer, Sky Light. Reviewed at Sala Glauber Rocha, Hotel Nacional, Rio Intl. Film Festival, Nov. 11, 1986. Running time: **110 MINS.**
With: Caetano Veloso, Regina Case, Antonio Cicero, Paula Lavigne, Elza Soares, Chico Diaz, Hamilton Vaz Pereira, Rogerio Duarte, Felipe Murray, Dede Veloso, Dadi, Dorival Caymmi, Mauricio Mattar, Julio Bressane, Dona Cano Veloso.

Rio de Janeiro — First film directed by outstanding singer-composer Caetano Veloso, "Talking Pictures" has slight commitment to traditional film narrative. It's a free panel of Caetano's ideas at one particular time. There is no dialog as such, but mostly literary clippings read by Caetano's friends. Audience hears a long segment of "Grande Sertao Veredas" by Brazilian writer Guimaraes Rosa, as well as parts of Thomas Mann's "Death In Venice" read in German, and excerpts from Heidegger and Sartre. In addition, long dialogs featuring Caetano's own impressions on Wim Wenders' "Paris, Texas," on Fidel Castro and on the current situation of Brazilian cinema.

It is an "essay of essays," says the author, and mostly a beautiful and involving essay. Caetano aims to get the same freedom he has accomplished in his music, and dramatically challenges the medium to reach that. It is sometimes a violent fight, in which author and medium seem to be trying to prove which is stronger. When they get in harmony, magnificent moments are born. One of the most beautiful sequences of modern Brazilian cinema is a salute to Fellini when Caetano recreates "I Vitelloni" square at Santo Amaro da Purificacao, Bahia. Beside a church, resembling the big ship in "Amarcord," Caetano just whistles Nino Rota's themes and searches for his past with an old-time friend.

Reminiscences, though, are not the basic raw material of the film. The uncommitted space the author fights for becomes a stage for a discussion on art, expression, sexuality. Those who take this difficult trip will find themselves in an enchanted search for the freedom to express their own values in their own way. —Hoin.

Il Ragazzo del Pony Express
(The Pony Express Boy)
(ITALIAN-COLOR)

A CIDIF release of a Numero Uno/Reteitalia coproduction. Produced by Claudio Bonivento. Directed by Franco Amurri. Stars Jerry Calà. Screenplay, Amurri, Cesare Frugoni, Calà, Stefano Sandrie, Marco Cavaliere; camera (Fujicolor), Giuseppe Berardini; editor, Raimondo Crociani; music, Umberto Smaila; art direction, Egidio Spagnini. Reviewed at Ariston Cinema, Rome, Dec. 2, 1986. Running time: **108 MINS.**
The Beast..................Jerry Calà
Claudia ....Isabella Ferrari
Accountant ....Alessandro Benvenuti

Rome — "The Pony Express Boy," feature debut of helmer Franco Amurri, aims for the tried and true formulas of Italo teen comedy. Milanese comic Jerry Calà, who also had an input into the script, is the decisive element here. Fans of Calà and his popular costar Isabella Ferrari may be interested in his location switch to Rome, but it makes little difference to the story. Once more he is an aspiring young exec temporarily at odds with obstacles that will vanish by pic's happy ending. It's strictly local fare.

After Calà's festive graduation party at home amid his beaming relatives, the hard realities of the job market find him turned down for entry-level managerial posts time and again. At last roommate Alessandro Benvenuti gets him into a porn film, but hero flees when he learns the part will put him on the receiving end. He swipes a girl's handbag and buys a broken-down motor scooter to work as a delivery boy for the "Pony Express," a door-to-door mail service that has become booming business, thanks to the legendary irregularities of the national post office.

While he zooms around town handing out letters, he crosses paths with the snobbish rich girl (Ferrari) whose favorite attire, a red riding habit, is the extent of her characterization.

In a grand finale, the two switch roles, and Calà on horseback organizes the entire Pony Express crew into corralling Isabella on scooter-back in Piazza Navona.

Technical credits don't disguise the shoestring pic was made on. —Yung.

Silk
(FILIPINO-COLOR)

A Concorde Pictures presentation of a Premiere Intl. production. Produced and directed by Cirio H. Santiago. Screenplay, Frederick Bailey, from story by Santiago, Bailey, based on a character created by Claudine St. James; camera (color), Ricardo Remias; editor, Pacifico Sanchez Jr.; music, Willie Cruz; sound, Rolly Rota; production design, Joe Mari Avellana; assistant director, Jose Torres; production manager, Aurello Navarro; associate producers, Leonard Hermes, Jose F. Buenaventura; casting, Enrique

Reyes. Reviewed on MGM/UA Home Video vidcassette, N.Y., Dec. 12, 1986. (MPAA Rating: R.) Running time: **83 MINS.**

Jennie (Silk) . . . . Cec Verrell
Tom Stevens . . . . Bill McLaughlin
Yashi . . . . Joe Mari Avellana
Brown . . . . Frederick Bailey
Tyler . . . . Nick Nicholson
Carnahan . . . . David Light
Walker . . . . Rex Cutter

Also with: Ronnie Patterson, Peter Shilton, Henry Strzalkowski, Leo Martinez, Joonie Gamboa, Vicky Suba, Zenaida Amador, Vic Diaz.

"Silk" is a 1985 Filipino action pic set in Honolulu, which recently bypassed theatrical release to debut as a vidcassette as part of Concorde Pictures' deal with MGM/UA Home Video.

Tough babe Cec Verrell, previously seen as a cop in "Hollywood Vice Squad," title roles as a one-woman Swat team for the Honolulu police. Episodic screenplay, resembling a tv episode of a cops show, has the police investigating a series of murders, ultimately resolved as drug-related. A corrupt cop teammate of Silk's is involved and the key element is a racket whereby the identities (papers, etc.) of dead people are sold to gangsters for reuse.

Action helmer Cirio H. Santiago does an okay job of staging stunts and shootouts, featuring a combination of American and familiar Filipino thesps. English-language dialog, much of it recorded in direct sound format, is effectively done.

Verrell sports an unusual hairdo: greased-back short haircut which is not punk nor butch. Fortunately, for social occasions her character goes glamorous with curls and dresses instead of the otherwise unbecoming macho look.—*Lor.*

Leonora
(AUSTRALIAN-COLOR)

A Revolve Party production. Produced by Geoffrey Brown. Written and directed by Derek Strahan. Camera (Eastmancolor), music, Strahan; editor, Anthony Egan; sound, Peter Morton; associate producers, Paul Watson, Ruth Redmond. Reviewed on Showcase vidcassette, Sydney, Nov. 21, 1986. Running time: **85 MINS.**

Leonora . . . . Mandi Miller
Mark . . . . Leon Marvell
Simon . . . . David Evans
Helena . . . . Angela Menzies-Wills
Dogon . . . . Ron Beck

Sydney — A low-budget softcore sex pic produced in Sydney last year and released on vidcassette sans theatrical release, "Leonora" is a mundane effort.

Attractive Mandi Miller is the eponymous heroine, married to an unpleasant ex-racing driver and current car salesman (David Evans). When he suggests an open marriage, she starts an affair with Leon Marvell, the film director who makes her husband's tv commercials. His hobby is painting, and before long she's posing for him in the altogether.

All the standard ingredients of this kind of film are here, including lots of simulated sex, a little (female) masturbation, and some brief lesbian coupling. The added ingredient is witchcraft, as one of the characters (Angela Menzies-Wills) claims to be a sorceress ("You should have been burned at the stake," mutters one of her unhappy lovers. "I was," is her reply.)

With its mix of attractive naked femmes and the most scenic Sydney landmarks as a background, "Leonora" probably will pass with fans of the genre. Dialog is awful, acting soporific, lensing frustratingly misty, and music often melodramatic. The audience will be limited to the Playboy set. —*Strat.*

The Last Day's Work
(AUSTRALIAN-DOCU-COLOR-16m)

Produced by Brian McKenzie Film Production, South Malvern, Victoria, Australia. Directed, camera (color, 16m), and edited by Brian McKenzie. Reviewed at Nyon Intl. Film Festival (Switzerland), Oct. 16, 1986. Running time: **100 MINS.**

Nyon — Increasingly, work in modern society is oriented toward providing and receiving services. Much of this work is monotonous, repetitive, numbing to the sensibilities.

Structured like a week of work, of seven parts, this film examines various work-occupations. One segment concerns a junkyard of spare parts from used automobiles, the kind of place you seek out if you need obscure or out-of-date valves and carburetors. Arthur Miller wrote about such a marginal enterprise in his "A Memory Of Two Mondays," a bypassed leftover of the industrial age, but Miller's workers had dignity, even in their sadness and defeat.

In McKenzie's film, a half-naked old man of prodigious memory squeaks out a living by rummaging around for parts to sell, in his warehouse of junk under the superhighway ramp. He is dissipirited. His work seems useless. He picks up a broom now and then, makes a pass at the dirty wooden floor, but quickly loses interest.

Other vocations are similarly examined — a clinic; an ambulance driver; a ticket vendor; etc.

"The Last Day's Work" is shot in cinema verité style, as was McKenzie's 1982 "I'll Be Home For Christmas," a study in futility amid alcoholic derelicts who live in a public park. Both films are painfully slow, minutely detailed, although ultimately providing a thesis: society needs to restructure itself by redirecting its energies and resources.
—*Hitch.*

School For Vandals
(BRITISH-COLOR)

A Children's Film Unit production for Film Four Intl. Produced by Joanie Blaikie. Directed by Colin Finbow. Screenplay, Finbow and children; camera (Kodak color), Titus Bicknell, Will Grove-White, Orlando Wells, Leigh Melrose; editor, Finbow; music, David Hewson; production design, Griselda Wallace; sound, Sharon Nokes, Charles Robertson, Matthew Landauer; assistant director, David Weeks. Reviewed at London Film Festival, Nov. 30, 1986. Running time: **80 MINS.**

Sharon . . . . Jennifer Barrand
Rupert . . . . Jeremy Coster
Tiger Lily . . . . Samantha McMillan
Bill . . . . Nicholas Mott
Deakin . . . . Deakin Glynn
Miss Duff . . . . Anne Dyson
Neil . . . . Charles Kay
Sir Oswald Kane . . . . Peter Bayliss

London — The Children's Film Unit, set up in 1981, puts out its sixth production, "School For Vandals," a witty, well-told yarn that scarcely betrays its adolescent authorship. It justifies continuation of the project.

Middle-class parents have bought a run-down school in the country, but they can't raise enough money for the opening term. Their two kids, plus assorted friends and visitors staying in the rambling mansion for the summer, make their contribution by grannynapping an old lady who strays into the school one night. She claims she used to work there and has returned to reclaim some belongings.

The old lady, played endearingly by Anne Dyson, is locked in a crumbling chapel while the children call up the police to inform them of the event and to demand a ransom.

Luckily for the kids, she seems to enjoy the experience of being a prisoner more than they do of being guards. Unluckily, nobody seems bothered about putting up the ransom money. Even worse, the local tv station doesn't carry the story in its news coverage.

Script, by director Colin Finbow aided by the children, wittily shows up the childishness of the parents and the adventurousness of the kids.

There is hardly a shake in the camera movements to admit that the crew members were all 12 to 14.

Finbow has paced the film well, holding interest to the end (when the chapel burns down) and shows a deft hand at creating moments of genuine spookiness that bodes well for future forays into adventure pics. —*Coop.*

Les Frères Pétard
(The Joint Brothers)
(FRENCH-COLOR)

A Fechner/Gaumont release of a Films Christian Fechner/Films Optimistes/Films A2 coproduction. Executive producer, Bernard Artigues. Directed by Hervé Palud. Stars Gérard Lanvin, Jacques Villeret. Screenplay, Palud, Igor Aptekman; camera (Eastmancolor), Jean-Jacques Tarbès; editor, Roland Baubeau; music, Jacques Delaporte; songs, Jesse Garon; art direction, Ivan Maussion; sound, Jean-Charles Ruault; costumes, Martine Rapin; makeup, Eric Muller; assistant director, Alain Nauroy; production manager, Henri Brichetti; casting, Gérard Moulevrier; technical advisor, Jean-Paul Meurisse. Reviewed at the UGC Normandie theater, Paris, Nov. 18, 1986. Running time: **90 MINS.**

With: Gérard Lanvin (Manu), Jacques Villeret (Momo), Michel Galabru (Mr. Javert), Josiane Balasko (Aline), Valérie Mairesse (Brigitte), Daniel Russo, Bruce Johnson, Philippe Khorsand, Raymond Aquilon, Jean-Paul Bonnaire, Dominique Lavanant, Alain Pacadis, Cheik Doukouré.

Paris — Local heartthrob Gérard Lanvin and roly-poly funnyman Jacques Villeret form the new comedy tandem of Christian Fechner, the green-thumbed commercial producer who recently celebrated 15 years of enviable boxoffice success. "Les Frères Pétard" is, like many of Fechner's pics, for domestic consumption mainly.

Lanvin and Villeret are two ne'er-do-well buddies who — at first ignorantly, then reluctantly, finally determinedly — become soft drug peddlers on the make, in search of the big haul that will have them sitting pretty the rest of their days.

Script by Igor Aptekman and Hervé Palud (whose previous directing credit was a docu on French gangster Jacques Mesrine) piles up incident in helter-skelter fashion, without any genuine farcical invention or picaresque exuberance.

Since Fechner tolled up over 5,-000,000 admissions for his 1985 caper comedy-adventure, "The Specialists," it's no surprise to find another burglary set piece here in which the pair loot the dope squad of police headquarters dressed as cleaning ladies and suck up a seized load of heroin in a vacuum cleaner. Palud's flat-footed direction blows the sequence, as it does most of the rest of the film.

Lanvin and Villeret have both seen better days (and films), and the guest roles for Michel Galabru and Josiane Balasko don't help.

Film stirred some controversy before release because it deals sympathetically with its drug-pusher protagonists at a time when the French government has been running an intense anti-drug campaign.
—*Len.*

El-Touk Wa El-Esswera
(Fetters)
(EGYPTIAN-COLOR)

An El Alamia for TV and Cinema production and release. Produced by Hussein Kalla. Directed by Khairy Bishara. Stars Ezzat El Alaily, Fardos Abdelhamid. Screenplay, Yahia Azmi, Bishara; camera (color), Tarek El

Telmissany; editor, Adel Moneir; music, Intisar Abdul-Fatah. Reviewed at the Carthage Film Days (in competition), Oct. 22, 1986. Running time: **116 MINS.**

Behet/Mustapha..........Ezzat El Alaily
Fahima/Farhana................Sherihan
Hazina..............Fardos Abdelhamid
Also with: Mohamed Mounir.

Tunis — Khairy Bishara's "Fetters" describes the tragic lives of three women — grandmother, mother and daughter — in Upper Egypt, victims of an interlocking system of patriarchal traditions that binds men and women like unbreakable chains. With a feeling of authenticity — local and psychological — rare for Egyptian cinema, film unfolds its drama with great naturalness, and lets the story make its own point. Already prized in Valencia, it should have a future on the fest circuit and for art house audiences.

"Fetters" (original title is the more graceful "The Necklace And The Bracelet") begins in the 1930s, in a village near the ruins of Luxor. Hazina (Fardos Abdelhamid) lives with her crippled husband (Ezzat El Alaily) and their beautiful, joyous daughter Fahima (Sherihan), while son Mustapha is away working. Following the father's death, Fahima marries a youthful smithy, but their happiness is ruined when she finds he's impotent. Mother Hazina counsels a trip to the temple, where according to an old custom an obliging stranger impregnates her. The smithy drives her out when he learns what she has done. After giving birth to a baby girl, she falls ill, and not even one of the most grisly cures ever depicted on the screen can save her.

Twenty years later, son Mustapha returns to the village, a modern man of the 1950s. As though to emphasize that the more things change, the more they remain the same, he also is limned by El Alaily. Similarly, his pretty niece Farhana is another incarnation of Sherihan, doomed to an even worse fate when she gets pregnant out of wedlock. The supposedly modern uncle buries her up to her neck in the backyard and with grandma waits for her to die. She is rescued by a village boy in love with her, but only so he can revenge himself personally.

Pic is lensed professionally and manages to keep a decent face for its two-hour running time. Bishara is a sensitive director of actors who prefers naturalness to caricature, and who has a knack for lacing gentle comedy through the drama. He's aided by a strong cast of Egyptian stars playing against glamor. Particular praise is owing Intisar Abdul-Fatah's soundtrack, which brings motifs of folk music into the score.
—*Yung.*

La Grande Allure
(CANADIAN-DOCU-COLOR-16m)

Produced by the National Film Board of Canada, Montreal, Quebec. Executive producer, Jacques Vallee. Produced by Louisette Neil, Helene Verrier. Directed by Pierre Perrault. Camera (color, 16m), Martin Leclerc; editor, Monique Portier, Claire Boyer; narration, Christine Prud'homme. Reviewed at Nyon Intl. Film Festival (Switzerland), Oct. 14, 1986. Running time: **60 MINS.**
(French soundtrack)

Nyon — The allure of the sea, the thrill of sail and muscle in contest with nature, the grand experience of crossing a mighty ocean — these are among the themes of this film, which recreates the 17th century trans-Atlantic voyage of French explorer Jacques Cartier, a historical hero in French Canada.

Under canvas from St. Malo, Brittany, to the St. Lawrence in Canada, fueled only by a seemingly inexhaustible cargo of Pernod, this sailing vessel and its crew encounter icebergs, storms and squalls of verse from the resident shipboard poet and playwright, Michel Garneu, popular figure in French-Canadian academic and cultural worlds.

Garneau's meditations, his discoveries and enthusiasms during the crossing, his daily new poem like a skipper's entry into a logbook, these are in effect the narration and spine of this film. Garneau makes us hear it all, including a few quatrains on the mutual sexual attraction of his wife and himself. As the film ends, Garneau is at a college lectern before an appreciative audience, reciting and reliving his epic odyssey. His adventure has a second life in his poetry. Perhaps the appeal of this film is limited to patriotic French-Canadians. —*Hitch.*

Astérix chez les Bretons
(Asterix In Britain)
(FRENCH-DANISH ANIMATED-COLOR)

A Gaumont/Dargaud/Gutenberghus co-production. Produced by Yannick Piel. Directed by Pino Van Lamsweerde. Screenplay, Pierre Tchernia, based on the cartoon album by René Goscinny, Alberto Uderzo (Dargaud press); camera (Eastmancolor), Philippe Laine; editor, Robert and Monique Isnardon; music, Vladimir Cosma; lyrics, Jeff Jordan; theme song performed by Cook Da Book; animation director, Keith Ingham; layouts, Andrew Knight; art direction, Michel Guérin; production manager, Philippe Grimond. Reviewed at the Gaumont Ambassade theater, Paris, Dec. 10, 1986. Running time: **78 MINS.**
Voices of: Roger Carel (Astérix), Pierre Tornade (Obélix), Pierre Mondy (Cétinlapsus), Serge Sauvion (Caesar), Nicolas Silberg (Motus), Graham Bushnell (Jolitorax).

Paris — Second of Gaumont's adaptations of the popular French comic strip by René Goscinny and Alberto Uderzo is another pleasant if unexceptional cartoon feature that should function best as a kidpic holiday item, notably in territories where the Asterix albums sell like hotcakes.

Like "Asterix vs. Caesar," released last December, this new adventure was produced in the special studios Gaumont created and staffed in Paris with international animators and artists. Succeeding Paul and Gaetan Brizzi, director Pino Van Lamsweerde gives brisk and charming motion to the beloved cartoon figures and their anachronistic exploits under the Roman Empire.

This time Asterix, the plucky little Gaul, his brawny dimwitted sidekick Obelix, and their canine Idefix, answer a call for help from Asterix' cousin in Britain, whose village is threatened with imminent invasion of Caesar's juggernaut legions.

They can provide the secret weapon — a strength-endowing Druid potion that has saved Asterix' village from Latin domination — but there is still the practical challenge of transporting a conspicuously large barrel through occupied territory, notably the city of Londinium.

Our heroes eventually lose the barrel and come up with an even more potent liquid for the Britons: tea. — *Len.*

White Slave
(Amazonia — The Catherine Miles Story)
(ITALIAN-COLOR)

A Cinevega (Rome) presentation. Directed by Roy Garrett. Screenplay, Franco Prosperi; camera (Staco color), Silvano Ippoliti; editor, Gianfranco Amicucci; music, Franco Campanino; assistant director, Giuseppe Giglietti; production manager, Antonio Almeida; special effects, Aldo Gasparri. Reviewed on Force Video vidcassette, N.Y., Sept. 5, 1986. (No MPAA Rating.) Running time: **89 MINS.**
With: Elvire Audray (Cathy Miles), Will (Alvaro) Gonzales, Dick Marshall, Andrew Louis Coppola, Dick Campbell, Alma Vernon, Grace Williams.

"Amazonia — The Catherine Miles Story" (released Stateside on vidcassette as "White Slave") is an interesting Italian exploitation film, shot in South America in 1984, which takes a different approach to the traditional "captured by natives" tale. Helped by a solid central performance by blond star Elvire Audray, pic is watchable genre fodder.

Pic, written by action pic and "Mondo Cane" vet Franco Prosperi, is framed as a true story related by Miles (Audray) years later as a housewife in London. For her 18th birthday vacationing at her parents' plantation on the Amazon River, she went on a river trip with her family, during which an attack by Indian darts resulted in her parents' death and her capture by the natives.

Amidst several gory scenes, pic details Cathy's life as a novelty in the Indians' camp, being both blond and very tall. She is befriended and protected by young warrior Umu Kai (Alvaro Gonzales) and finally becomes accepted as one of the tribe. Corny climax has Cathy returning to civilization to kill her young aunt and uncle who were the actual killers of her parents, framing the Indians by using their blowdart modus operandi.

Cathy commits an act of sadistic revenge on the duo, is tried for murder and sent to a mental institution and finally freed with a happy ending of marriage and a child in London.

Native rituals hold a fascination here, though the emphasis is on sensationalism. Technical credits are good. —*Lor.*

Les Traces du Reve
(CANADIAN-DOCU-COLOR-16m)

A production of the National Film Board of Canada, Montreal, Quebec. Written and directed by Jean-Daniel Lafond. Camera (color, 16m), Martin Leclerc; editor, Babalou Hamelin; sound, Yves Gendron, Claude Beaugrand. Reviewed at Nyon Intl. Film Festival (Switzerland), Oct. 13, 1986. Running time: **95 MINS.**

Nyon — Tracing or tracking down a dream, as in a hunt, is a conceit or metaphor used by Quebecois film director Pierre Perrault to describe his creative process for 25 years. When you make a film, you search as in a forest, and either you come upon the beast, or you have nothing.

In this career-sketch film (with French soundtrack) by Jean-Daniel Lafond about Perrault, Lafond similarly is tracking down his prey, Perrault, trying to make this film a discovery about Perrault, to bag him. Accordingly, the film tracks or follows Perrault through typical events — his visits with prominent French-Canadian artists; tabletalk with family and friends; a press conference at the Cannes Film Festival, where his integrity and purposeful manner seem out of place; and yes, a hunt with rifle through snow-covered woods. Perrault the hunter has become the hunted, the chaser chased, in Lafond's film about him.

Excerpts from Perrault's many films complete Lafond's portrait of the director. Prospects for distribution of this film in the U.S. seem dubious, as it is specialized and presupposes a viewer's familiarity with Perrault's career. —*Hitch.*

Hiroshima — Erinnern und Verdrängen

(Hiroshima — Remembering And Repressing)

(SWISS-DOCU-COLOR)

An Erwin Leiser Filmproduktion. Written and directed by Erwin Leiser. Camera (color, 16m), Peter Warneke; editor, Thea Eymesz; sound, Birgit Terrill. Reviewed at Leipzig Docu and Short Film Festival, Nov. 25, 1986. Running time: **60 MINS.**

Leipzig — Swiss documaker Erwin Leiser returns to Hiroshima, where he made a film about the A-bomb survivors in 1962, to examine the continuing effects on the second and third generations.

What he shows is not a pretty picture, but it's a worthy attempt to rescue the *hibakshas* as the bomb victims are called, and their children and grandchildren from the ghetto of oblivion where they've been put by a society eager to close its eyes.

The bombs dropped on Hiroshima on Aug. 6, 1945 and on Nagasaki a few days later killed 250,000; Leiser's thesis, quietly stated at film's beginning, is that it was unnecessary as the Japanese were ready to capitulate anyhow.

Hiroshima today is, almost eerily, a rebuilt city of sports marathons. The only outward traces of the bomb's devastation is a single skeleton of a building, left standing as a type of grim souvenir, and a monument to the dead..The *hibakshas,* who once lived together in slums, are now dead or dispersed in hospitals and homes for the aged: they account for only 6% of the population.

But "Hiroshima — Remembering And Repressing" insistently points out the continuing suffering of the survivors' offspring, who live with constant fear of developing latent diseases related to radiation. They live at the margins of an uncaring society, forced to marry each other or remain celibate. Even sadder is the fate of the many thousands of Koreans living in Hiroshima at the time of the blast, who took a long time being recognized as victims by the Japanese government; even now they are shown as segregated in hospitals.

Only in the last part of the film does Leiser show horrifying photos and medical footage of the victims, made by Japanese and Americans shortly after the bomb fell.

— *Yung.*

Odd Balls

(CANADIAN-U.S.-COLOR)

A New Horizons Picture Corp. presentation of a Maurice Smith Prods./Rodeo Prods. production. Produced by Smith. Executive producer, Peter McQuillan. Directed by Miklos Lente. Screenplay, Ed Naha; camera (Film House color), Fred Guthe; editor & 2d unit director, Marcus Manten; music, Ron & Dave Harrison; sound, Terry Cooke; production design, Sandy Kybartas; assistant director, Peter Saunders; production manager, Colin Brunton; casting, Lucinda Sill. Reviewed on Lightning Video vidcassette, N.Y., Dec. 9, 1986. (MPAA Rating: PG.) Running time: **92 MINS.**

With: Foster Brooks, Mike MacDonald, Konnie Krom, Milan Cheylon, Donnie Bowe, Terrea Foster.

Reviewed for the record, "Odd Balls" is a weak imitation of the Bill Murray hit from Canada, "Meatballs." Shot in 1983 and released regionally the following year, trite pic has comedian Foster Brooks going for it and little else.

Brooks plays the owner of decrepit boys' camp Bottomout, across the lake from a posh girls camp, whose owner is a corrupt land developer trying to get control of Brooks' camp. The baddie even sends his son to try and seduce Brooks' pretty daughter as part of his plan.

Lame script by Ed Naha has a heavy emphasis (within restrictions of a PG-rating) on the young boys angling to see the girl campers nude, while including idiotic spoofs of other film genres, such as an unfunny routine involving subtitles as inadequate translating or purposely bad synchronization on a dubbed karate wiz. Even incorporated is a dated spoof of "E.T.," which was also present in the Tri-Star pickup "Meatballs II."

Brooks does a nice job while the youngsters make little impression. Dumb sound effects are used to try to generate laughs much in the manner of a tv laughtrack. — *Lor.*

Duet For One

(COLOR)

Drama loses its way despite winning Julie Andrews performance.

A Cannon Films release of a Golan-Globus production. Produced by Menahem Golan, Yoram Globus. Directed by Andrei Konchalovsky. Stars Julie Andrews, Alan Bates, Max Von Sydow. Screenplay, Tom Kempinski, Jeremy Lipp, Konchalovsky, based on the play by Kempinski; camera (Rank color), Alex Thomson; editor, Henry Richardson; orchestration, Michael Linn; soloist, Nigel Kennedy; production design, John Graysmark; set decoration, Peter Young; art director, Reg Bream, Steve Cooper; sound (Dolby), David Crozier; costumes, Evangeline Harrison; assistant director, David Tringham; associate producer, Michael J. Kagan; casting, Noel Davis, Jeremy Zimmerman. Reviewed at Cannon screening room, L.A., Dec. 18, 1986. (MPAA Rating: R.) Running time: **107 MINS.**

Stephanie Anderson	Julie Andrews
David Cornwallis	Alan Bates
Dr. Louis Feldman	Max Von Sydow
Constantine Kassanis	Rupert Everett
Sonia Randvich	Margaret Courtenay
Penny Smallwood	Cathryn Harrison
Leonid Lefimov	Sigfrit Steiner
Totter	Liam Neeson
Anya	Macha Meril

Hollywood — The story of a world-class violinist who contracts multiple sclerosis and is forced to abandon her career does not seem like the most promising material for the big screen, but as long as "Duet For One" stays personal and specific it is a moving portrait of a life in turmoil. Unfortunately, when director Andrei Konchalovsky shoots for big statements the film degenerates into saccharine platitudes and even Julie Andrews' gritty performance as the stricken artist can't save it. Still, Cannon could have some luck selling this one as a quality item.

First half of film is clearly stronger as Konchalovsky draws the

Original Play

Ray Cooney presentation, in association with Ian B. Albery and Herbert Jay, of a play in two acts (six scenes) by Tom Kempinski. Staged by Roger Smith; setting, Caroline Beaver; lighting, Mick Hughes. Stars Frances de la Tour, David de Keyser. Opened Sept. 23, 1980, at the Duke of York's Theater, London; $15.60 top.

Stephanie Abrahams	Frances de la Tour
Dr. Alfred Feldman	David de Keyser

viewer into the richly textured and fascinating world of major league music. At the top of her craft and heralded as one of the greats, it's no wonder that Andrews' Stephanie Anderson doesn't want to give it up.

She has studied since childhood to get where she is and music defines her life. Married to conductor/composer David Cornwallis (Alan Bates), the couple have a comfortably elegant house in London that just reeks with culture thanks to John Graysmark's inviting production design and Alex Thomson's warm cinematography.

When Andrews leaves her dressing room for a performance at the Royal Albert Hall, it's a glamorous look at a life that's hard to resist. It's also a life that's coming to an end and she must adjust to the reality of her illness, which she learns about in the first five minutes of the film.

Initially the film is not really about illness but the relationship of an artist to her art. What it means to perform is intensified because it's something that's ending. Film is full of lovely musical interludes, both in concert and practice, and Andrews actually looks credible stroking her violin. (Nigel Kennedy plays the solos, Michael Linn arranged the music.) At the same time Andrews approaches her predicament in a pragmatic, overly rational manner as she plans out her recording schedule and the remaining days of her career.

In addition to the suggestion of a story, first half of the film offers an array of eccentric characters swirling around Andrews' life. As the philandering husband, Bates is a complex and restless soul afraid to face his own failings. Until he callously runs off with his secretary, Bates' vulnerability and physical deterioration brings an added and welcome dimension to the film.

Also filling out the picture is Sigfrit Steiner as Andrews' old and venerable accompanist and friend. He's a warming old world presence in the center of stormy scene. Rupert Everett plays Constantine Kassanis, a punk prima donna of a violinist who is Andrews' best student. As a character he's a bit hard to swallow, but amusing to watch nonetheless.

Bates leaves, Steiner dies and Everett goes to Las Vegas to make money. Now with the people and music that have anchored her life gone, both Andrews and the film haven't a clue where to go and the film gets into philosophical deep water. Stripped down to the bare essentials, film focuses on the "big questions" of life and death and becomes about the illness itself.

To confront her demise, Andrews goes into analysis and it is here the film becomes most static and inflated. As her analyst Max Von Sydow is a cold Freudian with a soft heart who seems to have just stepped off the bus from Vienna. Add "Duet To One" to the long list of films that present therapy with the solemnity of a summit conference.

Probably by accident, one of the real life fears that people have about analysis occurs here. Andrews, so winning and likable in the early going despite her adversity, loses her personality. She is no longer in control of what she's doing, takes up with a local junk dealer (Liam Neeson) and tries to kill herself. Things just seem to happen to her and the final coda, one year later, is a feeble attempt at tying it all together.

Screenplay was adapted from Tom Kempinski's two-person stage play by Kempinski, Jeremy Lipp and Konchalovsky and, in the end, it stretches too far for metaphor and meaning.—*Jagr.*

Another Side
(JAPANESE-B&W/COLOR)

A Bungei-za production. Produced by Yudai Yamashita. Written and directed by Naoto Yamakawa, from the novel "A Bottle Of Whiskey" by Yoshiteru Aoki. Camera (b&w/color), Wataru Hayashi; sound, Yasushi Kondo, Hidenori Sugimori. Reviewed at Chauvel theater, Sydney, Nov. 24, 1986. Running time: **112 MINS.**

Tadashu Fujii	Akihiro Sato
Ryo Tachibana	Shigeru Muroi
Yabe	Takeshi Naito
Maki	Akifumi Yamaguchi

Sydney — Made in 1980 by 22-year-old Naoto Yamakawa, this fascinating example of Japanese youth cinema is touring Australia in a Japanese season and is reviewed here for the record.

At first, pic is hard to follow, as various strands, seemingly unconnected, are presented for the viewer. Gradually, however, plot develops into a tale of a group of students involved both in an experimental theater company and with a rugby club. A young girl, steeped in theoretical knowledge about dramas, joins the theater group and two of the students fall for her. One dies on the railway tracks, a probable suicide.

"Another Side" (the original title of the film, even in Japan) includes a good many apparently improvised arguments among the young people. Yamakawa has a good visual sense, though, and inserts some dramatic images of bleak seascapes or urban blight. He switches to color for the final sequences.—*Strat.*

Footrot Flats
(NEW ZEALAND-ANIMATED-COLOR)

A Magpie Prods. Ltd. presentation. Produced by John Barnett, Pat Cox. Directed by Murray Ball. Screenplay, Ball, Tom Scott, based on characters by Ball. Animation director, Robbert Smit; music, Dave Dobbyn; backgrounds, Richard Zaloudek; editor, Michael Horton, Denis Jones; sound design, John McKay. Reviewed at Embassy theater, Wellington, N.Z., Dec. 8, 1986. Running time: **70 MINS.**

Voices: Peter Rowley (Dog); John Clarke (Wal); Rawiri Paratene (Rangi); Fiona Samuel (Cheeky Hobson and Pongo); Peter Hayden (Cooch and Irish Murphy); Dorothy McKegg (Aunt Dolly); Billy T. James (Pawai); Brian Sargent (Spit Murphy) Marshall Napier (Hank Murphy).

Wellington — Footrot Flats, the cartoon strip, is a New Zealand institution. The creation of Murray Ball, it features humans and animals (notably Wal and his oversensitive, ever-loyal Dog) in an archetypal backwoods farming community that could exist anywhere. Some 70% of adult New Zealanders read it and an equivalent proportion of Australians are familiar with it. It appears translated in a number of publications in Scandinavia and books of the strip are published in Japanese.

Now, "Footrot Flats," emerges as film — the first full-length animated feature to come out of the New Zealand film industry. With the well-known characters marvelously drawn (on the meticulous say-so of Ball) by Dutch-born Australian Robbert Smit, and backgrounds etched by Richard Zaloudek from the Sydney studios of Hanna Barbera, it is certain to be absorbed with pleasure by the strip's addicts everywhere.

For the uninitiated, it could be that a lexicon of New Zealand sayings and folklore will be useful in distilling the detail of the Kiwi magic of the piece. However, the copious action and sly raunchiness should knock down most cultural barriers.

Like the strip, "Footrot Flats," the film, is for adults, while being accessible to children — rather than vice versa. The tale chronicles Dog's life and loves on the small farm of Wal Footrot and his entanglement with the forces of evil that emanate from the Murphy property across the river. Uppermost in Dog's gentle, less-than-macho-meat-eating mind, is protection of Wal, his lumbering mate, and his passion for Jess, a neighboring bitch.

Guarding Wal means diverting his attention from the wiles of buxom Cheeky Hobson, hairdresser of La Parisienne in the nearby town of Raupo (pop. 406). Winning Jess means saving her from the hellhounds, croco-pigs and villainous vermin that guard the Murphy clan and its wicked ways.

Throughout there is a blend of whimsy, warm irony and observation of human — and animal — frailty that delights. What is lacking is a drive in the screenplay to shock and set one on the edge of the seat. The high action sequences lack a feral tension of the kind that the medium of film animation is particularly adept at achieving. They are a trifle too frenetic with cliff-hanging moments inadequately manipulated.

Even so, by creating an animated feature in structure more akin to printed cartoon form than film, director Ball is unlikely to lose those aficionados of the strip. Indeed, he may well win many thousands more. It seems a safe and profitable marketing choice in Australia, Scandinavia and possibly Japan.

Elsewhere it will have to be handled carefully. Although now indoctrinated in Down Under colloquialisms and symbols, following the huge success of "Crocodile Dundee," North American audiences may have difficulty with such expressions as "rattle your dags" and "dash to the dunny for a quick slash."

Equally, the mythologies that surround the hillbillies of the Appalachians are closer to the denizens of Footrot Flats, in the remote reaches of remote New Zealand, than the expense of the Pacific Ocean and the American continent might initially suggest. — *Nic.*

Dahalo Dahalo
(Once Upon A Time In The Midwest)
(MADAGASCAR-COLOR)

A Sorex Intl. Engineering production. Directed by Benoit Ramampy. Camera (color), Justin Limby Maharavo; sound, Guy Rasamoelina (no other credits available.) Reviewed at the Carthage Film Days (in competition), Oct. 15, 1986. Running time: **93 MINS.**

With: Masy Fonteno, Eugene Randrianarison, Thomas Rakotoyao.

Tunis — Madagascar has a serious problem with bandits, called the Dahalos. This local product will principally interest ethnographers of the region, though helmer Benoit Ramampy is quick to hit on the story's similarity to Wild West tales of cattle rustlers and posses; hence the alternate title; "Once Upon A Time In The Midwest."

Here the cattle are hump-backed zebos, prey of the murderous outlaws. From a cinematographic p.o.v., Ramampy's best scene in the opening. The idyllic peace of the African countryside — as dry and authentically sun-broiled as "Out Of Africa" was lush — is abruptly broken when two hunters are speared to death by savage jungle warriors.

A cast of wooden thesps then reenacts the fictionalized but obviously real difficulties of tracking down the dangerous bandits. An overworked police chief is the voice of reason: he wants to catch the rustlers, but not get killed doing it. The Dahalo chief has been captured by some villagers, who intend to execute him. The policeman has nothing against this solution (even the Christian minister absolves his flock from wrongdoing when they defend themselves against bandits).

But a hysterical functionary (who later turns out to be in bad faith) insists they rescue the captive and bring him to justice to avoid tribal warfare. The sheriff reluctantly forms a posse, but he and the film are on the side of simpler methods. In a trial sequence before a judge, pic demonstrates how easy it is for villains to get off on legalities. Pic concludes by urging authorities to give the populace more Army help. —*Yung.*

---

10 Jours...48 Heures
(CANADIAN-DOCU-COLOR-16m)

A coproduction of the National Film Board of Canada and Atlantic Studio/English Prod. Directed and camera (color, 16m), by Georges Dufaux. Editor, Dufaux, Catherine Martin; sound, Jim Rillie. Reviewed at Nyon Intl. Film Festival (Switzerland), Oct. 17, 1986. Running time: **90 MINS.**

Nyon — An award-winning veteran of 30 years with the National Film Board, French-born director Georges Dufaux works in the cinéma vérité style, emphasizing the recording of unstructured spontaneous activity, using an unobtrusive observant camera, as in his "Candid Eye" series on Canadian tv.

As director-cinematographer, Dufaux has grown more personal and intimate in style in recent years, as illustrated by this affectionate study of hardworking Canadian fishermen engaged in a perilous profession. Perils include the fear of being cut off incommunicado by sudden Arctic storms.

Dufaux does not passively record the lives of these seamen and their families but instead contemplates them philosophically, selecting and shooting to document their lifestyle at work, risks, returning home for rest. It is man's fate. Thus the title of this film: 10 days of work at sea, followed by 48 hours ashore with the family. Then the cycle repeats, a simple process, work and rest, again and again.

Using a six-month strike as his starting-point, Dufaux shows the big trawlers moving out for Newfoundland. They're after the cod that abound off the icy Labrador coast. In their spare moments, the fishermen are never idle, as they must mend nets. Their catches of cod are fated to become fish nuggets in the big new fish-processing plants of Massachusetts. To persuade children to eat fish, you must package it as nuggets to look and taste like chicken.

Doubtlessly this fascinating Canadian film will surface on American public tv before long. —*Hitch.*

Ráfaga de Plomo
(Burst Of Lead)
(MEXICAN-COLOR)

A Videocine release of a Casablanca Prods.-Televicine production. Executive producer, Jesús Galindo. Produced by Eduardo Galindo. Directed by Pedro Galindo 3d. Stars Fernando and Mario Almada. Screenplay,

Pedro Galindo, Carlos Valdemar; camera (color), Miguel Arana; editor, Carlos Savage; music, Ricardo Carrión. Reviewed at Big Apple Cine 1, N.Y., Oct. 28, 1986. Running time: 87 MINS.

Fernando Treviño......Fernando Almada
Mateo Treviño..........Mario Almada
Tony Snake ....Jorge Reynosa
Rene ....Javier Garcia
Diana :..................Hilda Aguirre
Elsa.............Marta Elena Cervantes
    Also with: Eleazar Garcia Jr., Carlos Cardán, Adelindo Arvizu, Ricardo Noriega, Gabriela de León and Jorge Guerra.

————

Mexico's Almada brothers, Mario and Fernando, are the stars of yet another action-packed adventure pic guaranteed to deliver excitement to fans.

Titled "Ráfaga de Plomo" (Burst Of Lead), the film centers on a long-time feud between smalltown Texas sheriff Rene (Javier Garcia) and Mateo (Mario Almada) over the love and paternity of Rene's wife and daughter. The situation comes to a head when Mateo is accused of massacring all the patrons of the local Texas Bar and winds up in prison.

The slaughter actually was masterminded by drug smuggler and gang leader Tony Snake (Jorge Reynosa), who besides entertaining a house full of live rattlesnakes, pulls the police chief's strings.

There is an exciting break from prison and then, watch out! The two Almada brothers join forces to exculpate Mateo by finding the real culprits. From then on, the pic is full of gratuitous violence and it virtually oozes with fake blood.

Even though parts of the plot are rather hard to swallow and the Almada brothers are getting too old to tackle some of the stunts believably, there is something attractive about their teamwork and good-natured characters that works.

Technical credits are uneven and the cutaways, when showing threatening live rattlesnakes for example, are awkward at best. —Lent.

————

Broken Arrow 29
(BRITISH-DOCU-COLOR-16m)

An Intl. Broadcasting Trust Prod. for Channel Four. Executive producer, David Tereshchuk. Produced, written and directed by Dina Hecht. Camera (Technicolor), Gabriel Beristain; editor, Monica Henriquez; music, Los Iberos; production design, Kennedy Bradley; set decoration, Bob Doyle. Reviewed at London Film Festival, Nov. 25, 1986. Running time: 72 MINS.
    With: Fernando Benavidez, Pedro Pinilla, Amendino Armada, the Duchess of Medina Sidonia, Los Iberos, and the people of Palomares and Villaricos.

————

London — This well-made docu describes the individual and collective plight of the people of two Spanish villages which were "dumped on" by the U.S. military and alternately lied to and neglected by their own government.

Docu is well-researched, easy to follow and not overly simplistic in it conclusions — in the solid tradition of good investigative reporting. While the situation it deplores has been generally known about in outline for some time, the film should contribute to a wider understanding of this kind of mishap.

The facts are these: in 1966 a B-52 collided with a refueling tank, crashing to the ground in Almeria scattering deadly plutonium over an extended area. Film details how the U.S. hushed up the affair, with the connivance of the Franco regime, and how even now, under a socialist regime, little has changed. There is still no adequate compensation for the people living in the affected area — just a si vote from the country to remain in NATO.

Film makes the effort to interview government, legal and medical figures who pooh-pooh the claims of the victims, but the testimony of the villagers, as usual in such cases, is more convincing. One villager describes movingly the death of her son, at 24, from leukemia, a few years after the tragedy.

As in many other such accidents, it is still unclear just how future ailments caused by radiation can be dealt with or compensated for. This docu helps at least point up the problem. —Guid.

————

Naar Kerk en Werk
Was Hunne Gang
(To Church And Work You Go)
(DUTCH-DOCU-COLOR)

A Stichting Zuidenwind production. Written and directed by Joost Seelen, Arnold Vogel. Camera (color, 16m), Willem Heshusius; editor, Seelen, Vogel; music, Pieter de Bruin. Reviewed at Leipzig Docu and Short Film Festival, Nov. 24, 1986. Running time: 60 MINS.

————

Leipzig — This unusual docu by Joost Seelen and Arnold Vogel traces several generations of working folk in the Dutch town of Rijen, a tanners' village since the turn of the century. While the tanning industry has changed radically during this period, so have people's traditional beliefs in the Catholic church, which was once the cornerstone of village life.

Clearly, logically, and a little prosaically, filmers carry their twin threads of church and work forward into the present day, leaving viewers with mixed emotions about the changing times. "To Church And Work You Go" is a hard subject to place outside its home territory, but should get more fest play.

Beautifully recapturing the atmosphere of old Rijen through period photographs, "Church" tells the story of the town through interviews with old-timers, who began plying the difficult trade of tanning leather as boys. It was a trade passed on from father to son, and workmen took satisfaction in seeing their small tanneries grow into real factories when leather demand boomed during World War II. Skillfully intercut is a young tanner today, who says he enjoys the work but doesn't know if there's a future in it, and money is the main incentive.

Running parallel to the rise and fall of the tanneries is the church theme. Once the Church had a tyrannical hold on private and public life (if you didn't go to Mass the boss could fire you, one oldster recalls). To illustrate the contemporary indifference, film stages a silly scene of kids smashing old religious icons for fun.

Mostly, though, pic lets people speak for themselves, and the end of a churchgoing tradition that was once part of the fabric of life comes across as a sad loss of identity.

It's technically well lensed.

—Yung.

————

Rao Saheb
(INDIAN-COLOR)

————

A PBC release and production (Bombay). Executive producer, Satish Rajmachikar. Produced by Vinay Welling. Directed by Vijaya Mehta. Screenplay, Mehta, Aneel Chaudhari, from a novel by Jaywant Dalvi; camera (color), Adeep Tandon; editor, Suresh Avdhoot; music, Bhaskar Chandavarkar; production design, Shyam Bhutkar, Pramod Pawar; set decoration, Ravindra Sathe, Vijay Shinde; assistant director, Harish Bhonsale. Reviewed at London Film Festival, Nov. 19, 1986. Running time: 130 MINS.
    With: Anupam Kher, Tanvi, Vijaya Mehta, Mangesh Kulharni, Chandrakant Gokhale, Nilu Phule, Tatoba Wellingkar, Vasant Ingale, Arvind Gadgil.

London — While apparently about the emancipation of women in rural turn of-the-century India, this film develops into a study of the limits and shams of progress. Based on a well-known Indian novel, and subsequent play, pic betrays both its past incarnations.

Helmer Vijaya Mehta, who runs her own theater company, directed and starred in the play before deciding to refashion the material into a feature. In the cinema version she plays the wizened but witty old aunt, who has passed most of her life as a shaven-headed widow.

Although slow paced and theatrical, film is dignified, delicate and rewarding for the patient. For arthouse audiences who appreciate Indian cinema, "Rao Saheb" is a welcome, if minor addition.

Story centers on a rich, giddy Indian who has soaked up Western liberal reformist ideas and is bent on testing them out on those around him. He listens to Mozart on the gramophone and bursts into English whenever he gets overexcited.

While the material has obvious comic potential, overall the treatment is more somber than lighthearted. What really exercises Rao Saheb's reformist urge is the plight of a young woman (Radhakka) who is married to one of his retainers. He scandalizes everyone by trying to treat her equally.

What the film captures particularly well is the rhythm of life as lived in a rambling old house of a good family at the turn of the century. The well-modulated interaction among the four main characters all takes place within that shaping environment of bedroom, veranda, reception room and passageway.

Although not an easily accessible film, it is a worthy first feature. The performances are well-honed and thoughtful, but technical credits somewhat compromised by lack of money. —Guid.

————

Jubiaba
(BRAZILIAN-FRENCH-COLOR)

An Embrafilme release of a Regina Films (Brazil), Societé Française de Prods., Antenne-2 (France) coproduction. Directed by Nelson Pereira dos Santos. Screenplay, dos Santos, from a novel by Jorge Amado; camera (color), Jose Medeiros; music, Gilberto Gil. Reviewed at London Film Festival, Nov. 19, 1986. Running time: 101 MINS.
    With: Charles Balano, Françoise Goussard, Grande Otelo, Raymond Pellegrin, Zeze Motta, Betty Faria, Ruth DeSouza, Alayr Bigori, Ylmara Rodrigues, Tatiana Issa, Catherine Rouvel, Luiz Santana.

————

London — Although based on a 1935 novel of no small pretenses by Jorge Amado, this film manages to be trite, inconsistent and awkwardly constructed. It is not well acted either, a serious defect because it is about psychological obsession.

Only devotees of the songs, dance and scenery of Bahia will be able to respond to this film. There is plenty of atmosphere but not much else to rivet the attention. Boxoffice outlook is modest at best.

Plot centers upon a poor black from the favelas, Baldo, who as a youngster falls in love with a rich blond from the other side of the tracks. Their obsession with each other is never consummated, but is suggested by the superimposition of the other's image everytime either makes love to anyone else.

In keeping with the clichés of this type of fiction, the rich blond is reduced to penury, prostitution and drugs by the end of the film. Baldo goes through a bewildering series of ups and downs, from servant, petty thief, smalltime boxer, circus performer, loafer and strike organizer.

Too many transformations, unexplained and unmotivated, make it impossible to really explore any of these episodes properly.

The role of Jubiaba is also mystifying and unsatisfyting. Although apparently the local sage or witch-doctor, he doesn't seem central to the goings-on of the plot.

And there are simply too many smiling, rumba playing Bahians and lascivious, unhappy rich people to be credible. Amado and the viewers deserve better. —*Guid.*

Al Kettar
(The Train)
(EGYPTIAN-COLOR)

An Ahab El Leassy release. Produced by Hussein Yahout, El Leassy. Directed by Ahmed Fouad. Screenplay, Sayed Mohamed Marzuk, Fouad; camera (color), Ramses Marzuk; editor and art direction, Fouad; music, Tarak Sarara. Reviewed at the Cairo Film Festival, Dec. 12, 1986. Running time: **95 MINS.**

Khalid	Nour El Sherif
Farida	Marvat Amin
Train engineer	Fouad Ahmed
Asst. engineer	Abou Bak Ezzat

Also with: Amin El Henidi (drunk), Nabila El Sayed (drunk's wife).

Cairo — Ahmed Fouad's "The Train," an Egyptian actioner describing the dramatic situation of a passenger train careening down the tracks without a driver, was made five years ago; its release got held up in a distributor's rights wrangle. All resemblance to Cannon's Konchalovsky-Kurosawa picture is purely coincidental, but the similarities are striking, even in this low-budget version forced to rely on back projection and to keep stunts and special effects to a minimum. Obviously the runaway train was an idea whose time had come.

Actioners are rare birds in the Egyptian cinema, but this one looks like a local winner. Beyond the Mideast, it has only curiosity value.

Pic opens with the train's engineer murdering his unfaithful wife; he's then left to seethe and plan mayhem on her lover, who happens to be his copilot. Their mortal struggle behind the controls on the Cairo-Assiut line leave the train rudderless on a single track. Naturally, the Assiut-Cairo train is fast approaching from the opposite direction.

Only witness to the fatal quarrel is a drunk (Amin El Henidi) nobody believes. Star Nour El Sherif has barely got an acquaintanceship started with pretty Marvat Amin before the train begins passing stations and general panic ensues. A quickie action scene is staged on top of the speeding cars. With the aid of a helicopter, Nour gets into the engine room and averts disaster, braking just feet away from the oncoming train.

Though a number of distracting minor characters disrupt the main story, Fouad keeps tension decently high in film's finale. It's technically passable. —*Yung.*

Riisuminen
(The Undressing)
(FINNISH-COLOR)

A Jörn Donner Prods. Oy production. Produced by Donner. Directed by Lauri Törhönen. Screenplay, Törhönen, Raija Oranen; camera (Fujicolor), Esa Vuorinen; sound, Olli Soinio; editor, Tuula Mehtonen. Reviewed at Mosman screening room, Sydney, Nov. 13, 1986. Running time: **88 MINS.**

With: Eeva Eloranta, Erkki Saarela, Aarno Laitinen, Alpo Suhonen.

Sydney — "The Undressing," a recent release from Finland's Jörn Donner Prods., is a gripping drama played out between two players (it's virtually a two-hander) almost entirely within the confines of a Helsinki hotel room. Despite these limitations, the film is never dull and director Lauri Törhönen keeps it from seeming theatrical or looking like small-screen fodder.

The man in question (Erkki Saarela) is a minister in the government, member of a leftwing party who's gone stale over the years and softened his principles. He's about to leave on a brief trip to Denmark when he accidentally meets a woman (Eeva Eloranta) he hasn't seen in 10 years. Though he's married and an important man in the community, he unhesitatingly takes her to a hotel.

The rest of the film consists of a post-coital slinging match between the couple, as he accuses her of being an unrelenting communist and she accuses him of betraying his formerly held beliefs. She also accuses him of male chauvinism, hypocrisy and, ultimately, desertion as she reveals something he never knew: that she had a daughter by him. Both thesps are fine, with Eeva Eloranta giving a quite remarkable performance ranging from the sexually aroused woman of the early scenes to the bitterly accusatory feminist of the latter part of the film.

Title is apt, because both players are fully naked almost throughout; rarely these days does one see so much full frontal, male and female, nudity in a film. But it adds to the authenticity of the drama, and is never prurient.

Several potent political issues are touched on in the screenplay, including the question as to whether, in Finland today, there's an anticommunist blacklist, and also whether the police would allow a politico to get away with something a member of the public would be arrested for.

This is an impressive battle of the sexes, a small-scale film with plenty of power and potency. It should be viewed by fest directors on the look-out for original, exciting material. —*Strat.*

Ex Voto
(SWISS-DOCU-COLOR-16m)

A presentation of Filmcooperative Zurich, Switzerland. Produced, written, directed, camera (color, 16m), edited and sound by Erich Langjahr. Reviewed at Nyon Intl. Film Festival (Switzerland), Oct. 15, 1986. Running time: **106 MINS.**
(German soundtrack)

Nyon — "Ex Voto" means a votive offering, a gift to a saint, in gratitude for fulfillment of a need. Young Swiss director Erich Langjahr, who prodigiously performed all the principal creative functions in the making of this excellent film, offers his "Ex Voto" as a holy duty. He is keeping his pledge to himself to film his beloved mountainous homeland in eastern Switzerland, to capture its beauty and to sound the alarm as industrialization threatens that beauty.

"Ex Voto" is a deeply personal film, poetic and lyrical, shot over a period of six years. For Langjahr, the film is a pilgrimage, a coming-home-again, his attempt "to touch the essentials of life, and of survival."

Langjahr shot in all seasons, in all extremes of weather, filming the cycle of life — plowing, planting, harvesting, time to milk the cows, time to slaughter the goat, time to worship. But it is always time to worship, even as you pass a small shrine beside a narrow mountain path, the pause that refreshes, then you resume trudging down to the village market deep in the valley. Langjahr's point is that these mountain folk find joy in their work and in being close to nature, living with animals. They have a spontaneous spirituality about their lives. The Church works, too. The young nuns of the neighboring monastery sing as they thresh grain. These scenes from a one-man documentary could not be bettered by Robert Wise in "The Sound Of Music."

What a shame that these idyllic mountain villages and steep pastures are being menaced by the big caterpillar tractors. Their way of life is being excavated, because under their earth are deposits of gravel and hard stone needed to build the expanding cities, the factories, the superhighways. So the proud old mountains are being gutted, their innards trucked out to the construction sites.

A recurrent figure or motif or "Ex Voto" is a strong, fat, elderly farm woman, who embodies indestructible Swiss optimism. She sings, recites and chatters to herself continuously, as she works tirelessly at a thousand farm chores, often seen carrying heavy burdens uphill without panting. The camera at first seems unkind to her, emphasizing her grotesquely thick legs, but we soon admire her Earth Mother quality, and we hope her faith in Swit-zerland prevails.

"Ex Voto" was perhaps the best film at the Nyon festival. —*Hitch.*

Heimkinder
(WEST GERMAN-DOCU-COLOR-16m)

Coproduction by Common Film Prod. and Nord Deutscher Rundfunk, Hamburg. Directed, camera (color, 16m), and edited by Gisela Tuchtenhagen; sound, Alf Olhrisch, Klaus Rosentreter. Reviewed at Nyon Intl. Film Festival (Switzerland), Oct. 13, 1986. Running time: **290 MINS.**

Nyon — Tough kids, that's what they are. "Heimkinder" can be translated as juvenile delinquents, but that's sociologist jargon. These are simply tough kids. They are from the streets of Hamburg, boys who got in trouble with the law, dropped out of school or were expelled, kicked out of the house by their parents, or abandoned, or fled broken homes.

A thousand titles come to mind of films about tough kids, both documentaries and fiction works. "Heimkinder" differs because of its length and cumulative impact, almost five hours. Also, it comes from a prosperous nation with strong family and law-and-order traditions. Germany seems an uncongenial environment in which to grow young criminals.

Yet here they are: Christian, Andreas, Tarkan, Wolfgang, a dozen others, ages 12-15, packed into two vans for a five-day drive to Portugal, for a work-holiday of three months. These tough kids are fated for rehabilitation, maybe, by four teachers and social workers who live with them in tents. Goal is to train and inspire the boys to pass certain strict school exams that can bring a positive redirecting of their misdirected young lives.

The trip by van to Portugal, and the months there, are an intense dramatic enclosure for knocking feelings and heads together. Will they pass these exams? Can these school certificates instill a new pride and self-respect? Or are the patterns of personality, even in the early teens, already fixed and unchangeable? The film offers no easy answers. The distrust and cynicism in these boys are hard to eradicate. The film ends, just like life, in ambiguity. The fates of tough kids always remain uncertain even when the last scene seems encouraging.
— *Hitch.*

INDEX

A

A. K. 5-22-85
A la Salida Nos Vemos 7-23-86
A Marvada Carne 5-22-85
A Me Mi Piace 1-1-86
Aanslag, De 2-12-86
Ab Heute Erwachsen 2-12-86
Abandon (See: Afzien)
Abducted 5-14-86
Abel 4-9-86
Ablakon 9-11-85
Abortion: Stories from North and South 6-12-85
About Argentina (See: De l'Argentine)
About Last Night 7-2-86
Absentee, The (See: Rejtozkodo, A)
Absolute Beginners 3-26-86
Accomplished Fact, An (See: Hechos Consumados)
Aces Go Places IV 3-26-86
Achalgazrda Kompozitoris Mogzauroba 2-26-86
Acta General de Chile 9-17-86
Ad Soff Halayla 4-24-85
Adam and Eve (See: Blue Paradise)
Adela 9-11-85
Adeus Portugues, Um 11-27-85
Adi Vasfiye 6-11-86
Adieu, Bonaparte 5-15-85
Adios, Roberto 5-29-85
Adjo, Solidaritet 4-24-85
Adolescent Sugar of Love, The (See: Gazl el Banat)
Adventure of Faustus Bidgood, The 9-10-86
Adventures of Chatran, The (See: Koneko Monogatari)
Adventures of Hercules (See: Hercules II)
Adventures of the American Rabbit, The 1-29-86
Affair, The (See: Relasyon)
Affaire des Divisions Morituri, L' 5-15-85
Affliction (See: Dahan)
After Darkness 2-27-85
After Hours 9-11-85
After the Fall of New York 2-6-85
Afternoon Breezes (See: Kazetachi no Gogo)
Afzien 2-19-86
Agada 11-27-85
Again Forever (See: Roman Behemshechim)
Agatha (See: Agada)
Agent on Ice 5-7-86
Aghaat 8-27-86
Agitatorok 3-5-86
Agitators (See: Agitatorok)
Agnes of God 8-21-85
Agonia 9-4-85
Agony (See: Agonia)
Ah-Fei 8-14-85
AIDS - A Danger for Love (See: AIDS - Gefahr fur die Liebe)
AIDS - Gefahr fur die Liebe 12-11-85
Aizlicgta Zona 10-8-86
Akropolis Now 1-9-85
Al-Kas 11-12-86
Alacrana, La 12-10-86
Alamo Bay 4-3-85
Alchemist, The 1-15-86
Alcova, L' 10-23-85
Alcove, The (See: Alcova, L')
Alem da Paixao 9-4-85
Alex Khole Ahava 7-30-86
Alexina Mystery, The (See: Mystere Alexina)
Alien Dead, The 7-31-85
Aliens 7-9-86
Alkistis 11-5-86
All Because of a Wedding Dress (See: Por un Vestido de Novia)
All Benigni (See: Tuttobenigni)
All for Love (See: Da Ebichash na Inat)
All Mixed Up (See: Sac de Noeuds)
Alla vi Barn i Bullerby 12-17-86
Alle Geister Kreisen 7-17-85
Allegory (See: Alligoria)
Alley Cat, The (See: Matou, Le)
Alligoria 10-22-86
Almacita di Desolata 4-2-86
Almanya Aci Vatan 4-3-85
Alone Among His Own (See: Sam Posrod Swoich)
Alpine Fire (See: Hoehenfeuer)
Alska Mig 2-26-86
Alter Ego 12-10-86

Always 3-27-85
Am Nachesten Morgen Kehrte der Minister Nicht an Seinen Arbeitsplatz Zuruck 2-19-86
Amansiz Yol 4-23-86
Amant Magnifique, L' 7-9-86
Amants Terribles, Les 4-10-85
Amara Scienza, L' 9-18-85
Amargo Mar 8-28-85
Amarosa 3-26-86
Amateur Hour 12-11-85
Amazonia - The Catherine Miles Story (See: White Slave)
Amerasia 4-23-86
America 10-15-86
America 3000 5-14-86
American Anthem 7-2-86
American Commandos 3-19-86
American Drive-In 5-15-85
American Flyers 8-14-85
American Ninja 9-4-85
American Rebel 10-30-85
American Tail, An 11-12-86
American Way, The 5-21-86
Amigos 1-1-86
Among the Shadows (See: En Penumbra)
Amor a la Vuelta de la Esquina 10-8-86
Amor Brujo, El 4-2-86
Amor Estranho Amor 9-4-85
Amour Braque, L' 3-13-85
Amour en Douce, L' 4-10-85
Amour Propre Ne le Reste Tres Longtemps, L' 11-13-85
Ana 10-9-85
And End to the War (See: Ein Kriegsende)
And Never the Twain Shall Meet (See: Het Land Van Mijn Ouders)
And the Pursuit of Happiness 9-24-86
And Then (See: Sorekara)
...And When They Shall Ask 1-23-85
Andropov - Pages from His Life (See: Y.V. Andropov - Stranitzi Zhizni)
Anemia 10-22-86
Angel of Fire (See: Osnisty Anoil)
Angel River 9-3-86
Angel Skin (See: Peau d'Ange)
Angelic Conversations 4-3-85
Angels, The (See: Anges, Les)
Angels in Love (See: Naar Engle Elsker)
Anges, Les 5-22-85
Angkor-Cambodia Express 7-16-86
Angriff der Gengenwart au die Ubrige Zeit, Der 11-13-85
Ankaemaul 1-9-85
Anne Trister 2-26-86
Annihilators, The 1-15-86
Ano de las Luces, El 12-17-86
Another Love (See: Ina Laska)
Another Side 12-31-86
Antonio Gaudi 9-18-85
Applause, Applause ... 6-18-86
Apple of Our Eye (See: Eszterlanc)
Appointment with Fear 10-30-85
April Fool's Day 5-22-85
April Fool's Day 3-26-86
Aqueles Dois 10-16-85
Araignee de Satin, L' 9-4-85
Araucaima Mansion, The (See: Mansion de Araucaima, La)
Arbre sous la Mer, L' 3-6-85
Architecture of Frank Lloyd Wright, The 5-29-85
Are We Winning, Mommy? America and the Cold War 9-17-86
Argentina, The Broken Silence 11-26-86
Arhats in Fury 6-19-85
Ark of the Sun God, The 7-16-86
Armed and Dangerous 8-20-86
Armed Response 10-8-86
Armour of God, The 9-17-86
Aroma Tis Violetas, To 10-30-85
Around the World in Eighty Ways 5-14-86
Arriving Tuesday 5-14-86
Arthur's Hallowed Ground 2-5-86
Artie Shaw: Time Is All You've Got 3-20-85
Arunata Pera 1-1-86
Ases de Contrabando, Los 8-20-86
Asheke, Al 11-12-86
Assam Garden, The 7-24-85
Assault, The (See: Aanslag, De)
Assault of the Present upon the Rest of Time, The (See: Angriff der Gengenwart au die ubrige Zeit, Der)
Assisi Underground, The 8-28-85
Asterix Chez les Bretons 12-24-86
Asterix et la Surprise de Cesar 12-25-85
Asterix in Britain (See: Asterix Cehz les Bretons)
Asterix vs. Caesar (See: Asterix et la Surprise de Cesar)

D

E

F

G

House 1-22-86
House Committee Rivalry (See: HaKrav al HaVa'ad)
House for Swap (See: Se Permuta)
House on the Edge of the Park 2-6-85
House on the River, The (See: Haus am Fluss, Das)
House Poised on the Edge, A (See: Casa in Bilico, Una)
How Young We Were Then (See: Kak Molody My Byli)
Howard the Duck 8-6-86
Howling II ... Your Sister Is a Werewolf 6-12-85
Huang Shan Lai de gu Niang 7-31-85
Huang Tudi 8-21-85
Hud 8-27-86
Huey Long 10-2-85
Hullumeelsus 10-15-86
Hulyeseg nem Akadaly 5-14-86
Hunger (See: El-Gooa)
Hungry for Profit 7-3-85
Huomenna 5-14-86
Hurlevant 8-28-85
Hussy, The (See: Effrontee, L')
Hustruer, 2 - Ti ar Eetter 11-13-85
Hyinch Ha'gdi 2-12-86
Hyper Sapien: People from Another Star 12-24-86

I

I Adore You (See: Bi Chamd Khayrtay)
I Am Not Afraid Anymore (See: Uz Se Nebojim)
I Go to Tokyo (See: Ora Tokyo sa Yukuda)
I Hate Actors (See: Je Hais les Acteurs)
I Jizn, i Slezy, i Liubov 8-28-85
I Lagens Namn 11-26-86
I Like Her (See: A Me Mi Piace)
I Live, But ... (See: Ikite Wa Mita Keredo ...)
I Love Dollars 2-19-86
I Love You 4-16-86
I Need a Mustache (See: Me Hace Falta un Bigote)
I Own the Racecourse 7-30-86
I Played It for You 10-30-85
I Soliti Ignoti ... Vent'Anni Dopo 1-29-86
I Was Caught in the Night (See: Zastihla me Noc)
Ice-Cream Parlor, The (See: Ijssalon, De)
Ideaalmaastik 10-15-86
Ideal Landscape (See: Ideaalmaastik)
Idi I Smotri 7-17-85
Idiots May Apply (See: Hulyeseg Nem Akadaly)
Ido Van 3-5-86
Idol 4-3-85
Idol, The (See: Idol)
Igor and the Lunatics 5-22-85
Igreja de Libertacao 1-1-86
Igreja dos Oprimidos 10-22-86
Ijssalon, De 2-13-85
Ikite Wa Mita Keredo ... 3-6-85
Ikiteru Uchiga Hanananoyo Shindara Soremadeyo to Sengen 6-19-85
Illegal Immigrant, The 5-29-85
Illustres Inconnus 8-28-85
Im Himmel Ist die Holle Los 7-17-85
Im Innern des Wals 3-27-85
Im Jahr 1932 - Der Rote Kandidat 12-17-86
Imagemaker, The 1-29-86
Images of an Everyday War (See: Memorias de una Guerra Cotidiana)
Imperio de la Fortuna, El 10-8-86
Impieati 4-3-85
Impressions de l'Lle des Morts 12-24-86
Impure Thoughts 11-26-86
In a Glass Cage (See: Tras el Cristal)
In a Mirror (See: Dans un Miroir)
In de Schaduw van de Overwinning 2-19-86
In Heaven All Hell Is Breaking Loose (See: Im Himmel Ist die Holle Los)
In Her Own Time 12-11-85
In Memory of 450,000 Hungarian Peasant Jews (See: Let Ye Inherit)
In 'n' Out 8-20-86
In 1932 - The Red Candidate (See: Im Jahr 1932 - der Rote Kandidat)
In Relation with Vassilis (See: Schetika me ton Vassili)
In the Name of the Law (See: I Lagens Namn)
In the Name of the People 4-3-85
In the Shadow of Death (See: Naves Ena)
In the Shadow of Kilimanjaro 5-7-86
In the Shadow of Victory (See: In de Schaduw van de Overwinning)
Ina Laska 10-8-86

Indebted to Death (See: Dluznicy Smierci)
Indecent Exposure (See: Tosha 1/250 Byo)
Indecent Obsession, An 6-12-85
Indomitable Teddy Roosevelt, The 4-10-85
Infatuation 7-17-85
Informer, The (See: Pendler, Der)
Inganni 1-1-86
Ingrid 6-12-85
Innocence (See: Innocenza)
Innocent, The 5-22-85
Innocenza 9-10-86
Inside Out 11-26-86
Inside the Whale (See: Im Innern des Wals)
Insignificance 5-15-85
Insomnes, Los 3-5-86
Insomniac on the Bridge, The (See: Eveille du Pont d' Alma, L')
Insomniacs, The (See: Insomnes, Los)
Inspector Lavardin 3-19-86
Insurance Man, The 11-27-85
Interdits du Monde, Les 2-19-86
Interno Berlinese 11-6-85
Into the Night 2-20-85
Intruder, The 6-4-86
Inughuit - Folket vid Jordens Navel 3-5-86
Inughuit - The People at Earth's Navel (See: Inughuit - Folket vid Jordens Navel)
Invaders from Mars 5-21-86
Invasion U.S.A. 9-25-85
Invincible, The (See: Unbesiegbare, Der)
Invitation to Dance (See: Aufforderung zum Tanz)
Invitation to the Wedding 3-13-85
Io e Il Duce 5-22-85
Irith, Irith 10-30-85
Iron Eagle 1-22-86
Ironmaster 8-28-85
Irrsee 3-6-85
Is That It? 12-4-85
Isaac in America 10-8-86
Island (Life and Death), The 10-30-85
Islands 11-5-86
Isle of Fantasy 1-29-86
It Don't Pay to Be an Honest Citizen 2-27-85
It Hurts But It Feels Good (See: Se Sufre Pero se Goza)
It Only Happens to Me (See: Ca N'Arrive Qu'a Moi)
Italian Fast Food 12-17-86
It's My Life - El Noa Noa 2 (See: Es Mi Vida - El Noa Noa 2)
It's Up to Us to Keep This Spirit Alive (See: Es Liegt an Uns, Diesen Geist Lebendig Zu Erhalten)

J

Jack-of-All-Trades, Part II, The (See: Milusos II, El)
Jackals 5-21-86
Jacques and November (See: Jacques et Novembre)
Jacques et Novembre 6-12-85
Jade Love (See: Yu Qing Sao)
Jagged Edge 9-11-85
Jagode u Grlu 9-4-85
J'ai Recontre le Pere Noel 1-23-85
Jake Speed 5-21-86
Jako Jed 8-20-86
James Joyce's Women 3-20-85
Jangnam 11-27-85
Janyo-nok 10-2-85
Jardin Secreto, El 5-15-85
Jatszani Kell 2-27-85
Je Hais les Acteurs 10-29-86
Je Vous Salue, Marie 2-6-85
Jean de Florette 8-20-86
Jenny Kissed Me 8-28-85
Jeune Fille et l'Enfer, La 2-19-86
Jewel of the Nile, The 12-11-85
Jezioro Bodenskie 8-20-86
Jibaro 1-1-86
Jo Jo Dancer, Your Life Is Calling 4-30-86
Joan Lui: But One Day in the Country I Come on Monday (See: Joan Lui: Ma un Giorno nel Paese Arrivo Io di Lunedi)
Joan Lui: Ma un Giorno nel Paese Arrivo Io di Lunedi 1-15-86
Job, The (See: Fucha)
Joe Polowsky - An American Dreamer (See: Joe Polowsky - Ein Amerikanischer Traumer)
Joe Polowsky - Ein Amerikanischer Traumer 12-10-86
Joey 12-25-85

M

O

O-Bi, O-Ba — Koniec Cywilizacji 9-11-85
O-Bi, O-Ba — The End of Civilization (See: O-Bi, O-Ba — Koniec Cywilizacji)
Obecana Zemlja 8-6-86
Oberst Redl 2-20-85
Obituary for a Beast (See: Nachruf auf eine Bestie)
Objection 10-2-85
Ocean Drive Weekend 7-16-86
October Won't Return (See: Bao Gio Cho Toi Thang Muoi)
Odd Balls 12-24-86
Odd Birds 10-30-85
Odinotchnoye Plavaniye 7-2-86
Ofelia Kommer Til Byen 11-13-85
Off Beat 4-16-86
Official History, The (See: Historia Oficial, La)
Offret 5-14-86
Ohan 6-12-85
Old Forest, The 10-30-85
Old Henry (See: Olle Henry)
Old Music, The (See: Vieja Musica, La)
Olle Henry 3-6-85
Omega, Omega ... 2-20-85
On a Narrow Bridge (See: Gesher Tzar Me'od)
On Course (See: En Plo)
On Ne Meurt Que 2 Fois 9-4-85
On the Edge 5-22-85
On the Hunting Ground (See: Lie Chang Zha Sha)
On the Loose 6-19-85
On the Next Morning the Minister Didn't Return to His Post (See: Am Nachesten Morgen Kehrte der Minister Nicht an Seinen Arbeitsplatz Zuruck)
On the Tracks of the Killers (See: Zahn um Zahn)
On Valentine's Day 1-29-86
Once Bitten 11-6-85
Once upon a Time in the Midwest (See: Dahalo Dahalo)
Once upon a Time There Was Television (See: Etait une Fois la Tele, Il)
One and Only, The (See: Unique, L')
One Crazy Summer 8-13-86
One Look — And Love Begins (See: Ein Blick — und die Liebe Bricht Aus)
One Magic Christmas 11-20-85
One More Saturday Night 8-20-86
One Night Only 7-9-86
One Woman or Two (See: Une Femme ou Deux)
Op Hoop van Zegen 8-20-86
Opera do Malandro 5-28-86
Operation Judas (See: Bras de Fer)
Operation Violin Case (See: Untermehmen Geigenkasten)
Ophelia Hits Town (See: Ofelia Kommer Til Byen)
Opinion, The (See: Rai)
Ora Tokyo Sa Yukuda 9-17-86
Oragens Fange/I na Kamnjakh Rastut Derevja 8-28-85
Orchestre Noir, L' 9-4-85
Orfeo 9-11-85
Orfeus es Eurydike 9-11-85
Oriana 5-15-85
Oriane (See: Oriana)
Orion's Belt (See: Orions Belte)
Orions Belte 2-27-85
Orissia 2-19-86
Ornette: Made in America 5-8-85
Orpheus (See: Orfeo)
Orpheus and Eurydice (See: Orfeus es Eurydike)
Osa 10-23-85
Osnisty Anoil 10-2-85
Osobisty Pamietnik Grzesznika Przez Niego Samego Spisany 5-21-86
Ososhiki 5-15-85
Osslinaja Schkura 3-6-85
Otac na Sluzbenoh Putu 5-8-85
Otello 5-21-86
Othello (See: Otello)
Other, The (See: Otro, El)
Other Cuba, The 2-20-85
Other Halves 1-9-85
Other People's Passions (See: Svesas Kaislibas)
Other Side of the Moon, The (See: Ruckseite des Mondes, Die)
Otoko Wa Tsurai Yo: Torajiro Yuyake Koyake 6-12-85
Otra Vuelta de Tuerca 10-9-85
Otro, El 5-8-85

Otryad 10-2-85
Otto — Der Film 8-7-85
Otto Klemperers Lange Reise Durch Seine Zeit 3-13-85
Otto Klemperer's Long Journey Through His Times (See: Otto Klemperers Lange Reise Durch Seine Zeit)
Otto — The Film (See: Otto — Der Film)
Our Father (See: Padre Nuestro)
Our Lady of the Paints (See: Dame en Couleurs, La)
Our Marriage (See: Notre Mariage)
Out of Africa 12-11-85
Out of Bounds 7-23-86
Out of Control 5-29-85
Out of the Darkness 12-11-85
Outlaws (See: Hors-la-loi)
Ovation (See: Applause, Applause ...)
Over the Summer 2-27-85
Overnight 9-24-86
Oye for Oye 4-24-85

P

P.O.W. The Escape 4-9-86
P.P. Rider (See: Shonben Raidaa)
Pacific Inferno 3-6-85
Package Tour (See: Tarasutazas)
Package Tour II — Snowroller, The (See: Saliskapsresan II — Snow Roller)
Pactole, Le 5-8-85
Padre Nuestro 5-8-85
Paidia Tou Kronou, Ta 10-23-85
Pajaros Tirandole a la Escopeta, Los 3-6-85
Palace 3-27-85
Pale Face (See: Visage Pale)
Pale Rider 5-8-85
Paltoquet, Le 7-30-86
Panchito Gang, The (See: Banda de los Panchitos, La)
Pandit Nehru 4-24-85
Panther Squad 7-30-86
Parad Planet 7-17-85
Parade of the Planets (See: Parad Planet)
Paradies 11-5-86
Paradise (See: Paradies)
Paradise Is Not for Sale (See: Paradiset Er Ikke til Salg)
Paradise Motel 5-22-85
Paradise Slum (See: Slum "Zum Paradies"/Deim Dar El-Naemi)
Paradise View 8-21-85
Paradiset Er Ikke til Salg 4-3-85
Paraises Perdidos, Los 7-31-85
Parfait Armour 2-13-85
Paris Midnight (See: Paris Minuit)
Paris Minuit 3-5-86
Parker 2-27-85
Parking 7-3-85
Parole de Flic 8-28-85
Partenaires 2-20-85
Parting Games 1-29-86
Parting of the Ways, The (See: Lejania)
Partir Revenir 5-8-85
Partisans of Vilna 10-23-85
Partners (See: Partenaires)
Party Animal, The 1-23-85
Pas in Doi 2-26--86
Paso Doble (See: Pas in Doi)
Paso Doble for Three (See: Pasodoble pre Troch)
Pasodoble pre Troch 10-15-86
Passage, Le 12-24-86
Passage, The (See: Passage, Le)
Passage Secret 5-22-85
Passiflora 10-8-86
Passing, The 6-12-85
Passion 8-20-86
Passion of Remembrance, The 12-10-86
Past Caring 11-27-85
Past, Present, Future (See: Trikal)
Patakin 4-24-85
Patriot, The 9-17-86
Paul Chevrolet and the Ultimate Hallucination (See: Paul Chevrolet en de Ultieme Hallucinatie)
Paul Chevrolet en de Ultieme Hallucinatie 11-13-85
Paulette 3-5-86
Paul's Awakening (See: Risveglio di Paul, Il)
Pavucina 8-6-86
Peanut Butter Solution, The 12-4-85

Q

R

S

T

Texaco Hour, The (See: Hora Texaco, La)
Texas Chainsaw Massacre Part 2, The 8-27-86
Thank You Mr. Robertson (See: Merci Monsieur Robertson)
That Couple (See: Aqueles Dois)
That Damned Meat (See: A Marvada Carne)
That Mad Mad Hospital (See: Ese Loco Loco Hospital)
That Was Then ... This Is Now 10-23-85
That's Dancing! 1-23-85
That's Life! 9-3-86
That's My Baby 5-15-85
Thaw (See: Pomnalui Nunsogi)
The au Harem d'Archimede, Le 5-8-85
Their Own Faces (See: Tasveer Apni Apni))
There Are Some Guys Downstairs (See: Hay Unos Tipos Abajo)
There Were Times, Dear 11-6-85
Therese 5-21-86
Thermokipio 10-30-85
Thief Academy (See: Scuola di Ladri)
Third Dragon, The (See: Tret i Sarkan)
'38 9-10-86
37°2 le Matin 4-2-86
This Folly of the Russian People (See: Ce Fou de Peuple Russe)
Thomas and Senior on the Track of Barend the Brute (See: Thomas
    en Senior op het spoor van brute Barend)
Thomas en Senior op het Spoor van Brute Barend 2-19-86
Thousand and One Daisies, A (See: Mille et une Marguerites)
Thrashin' 5-14-86
Three Against Three (See: Drei Gegen Drei)
Three Amigos 12-10-86
Three Feet Above the Ground (See: Trzy Stopy Nad Ziemia)
3:15 4-2-86
Three Men and a Basket (See: Trois Homme et un Couffin)
Three Sisters - A Film Novel (See: Harom Nover - Filmregeny)
Three's Happiness (See: Za Srecu Je Potrebno Troje)
Thrill of Genius, The (See: Hitchcock, Il Brivido del Genio)
Throne of Fire, The 7-2-86
Thunder Alley 5-15-85
Thunder Run 5-14-86
Thunder Warrior 7-16-86
Tiempo de Morir 12-11-85
Tiempo de Silencio 4-2-86
Tierra Prometida, La 11-26-86
Tigers in Lipstick 2-20-85
Tigipio 10-30-85
Tigress, The 1-23-85
Time (See: Ido Van)
Time After Time 12-11-85
Time Destroyed: Letters from a War, 1939-40 (See: Temps Detruit:
    Lettres d'une Guerre 1939-40, Le)
Time Interval (See: Zwischenzeit)
Time of Leopards, The (See: Tempo dos Leopardos, O)
Time of Silence (See: Tiempo de Silencio)
Time of the Star, The (See: Hora da Estrela, A)
Time Stops (See: Kahir Elzaman)
Time That Remains, The (See: Zeit die Bleibt, Die)
Time to Die, A (See: Tiempo de Morir)
Time to Live and a Time to Die, A (See: Tong Nien Wang Shi)
Timing 9-4-85
Titan Serambut Dibelah Tujuh 1-15-86
To Church and Work You Go (See: Naar Kerk en Werk Was Hunne Gang)
To Kill a Stranger 10-2-85
To Live and Die in L.A. 10-30-85
To Live and Die in Westallgau (See: Daheim Sterben die Leut)
To Marry the Captain (See: Vyiti Zamuzh za Kapitana)
To See the Light (See: Eszmejes)
To Sleep So As to Dream (See: Yume Miruyoni Nemuritai)
Toby McTeague 2-26-86
Tod des Weissen Pferdes, Der 3-6-85
Todesspringer, Der 2-13-85
Tokimedi ni Shisu 12-24-86
Tokyo-Ga 4-24-85
Tokyo Melody, A Film about Ryuichi Sakamoto 4-24-85
Tokyo Saiban 2-27-85
Tokyo Trial, The (See: Tokyo Saiban)
Tomb, The 10-22-86
Tomboy 1-30-85
Tommaso Blu 8-6-86
Tomorrow (See: Houmenna)
Tong Nien Wang Shi 2-26-86
Tongs - A Chinatown Story 6-11-86
Too Scared to Scream 1-30-85
Toomas Nipernaadi 10-15-86
Top Gun 5-14-86
Topos 10-23-85
Tora's Sunrise and Sunset (See: Otoko Wa Tsurai Yo: Torajiro
    Yuyake Koyake)
Torachianhun Milsa 1-9-85
Torakku Yaro: Goiken Muyo 6-12-85
Torment 4-23-86

Tornado 11-20-85
Torpedo Bombers (See: Torpidonostci)
Torpedo Planes (See: Torpedonosszy)
Torpedonosszy 3-6-85
Torpidonostci 10-22-86
Tosha 1/250 Byo 9-11-85
Touch and Go 8-20-86
Tough Guys 10-1-86
Toxic Avenger, The 5-22-85
Traces du Reve, Les 12-24-86
Tracks in the Snow (See: Pervola)
Tragedy of the Afghan, The (See: Ghame Afghan)
Train, The (See: Kettar, A1)
Train of the Pioneers, The (See: Tren de los Pioneros, El)
Tramp at the Door 9-10-86
Tranches de Vie 2-27-85
Tranen in Florenz 2-13-85
Transformers, The 8-13-86
Transfuge, Le 1-1-86
Transit Dreams (See: Transittraume)
Transittraume 2-19-86
Transplantados, Los 7-31-85
Transplanted, The (See: Transplantados, Los)
Transylvania 6-5000 11-13-85
Traps 6-26-85
Tras el Cristal 3-5-86
Treasure of the Amazon, The 6-19-85
Tree Under the Sea, The (See: Arbre sous la Mer, L')
Tree We Were Hurting, The (See: Dendro Pou Pligoname, To)
Treffpunkt Leipzig 10-16-85
Tren de los Pioneros, El 7-16-86
Tret i Sarkan 3-5-86
Trial on the Road (See: Proverka na Dorogach)
Trick or Treat 10-29-86
Trikal 6-18-86
Trip to Bountiful, The 12-4-85
Tristesse et Beaute 8-28-85
Trois Homme et un Couffin 10-16-85
Troll 1-22-86
Troppo Forte 2-19-86
Trottoirs de Saturne, Les 10-9-85
Trouble in Mind 12-18-85
Troupers 9-25-85
True Stories 10-8-86
Trumpet Solo (See: Solo Trubui)
Trzy Stopy Nad Ziemia 10-2-85
Tschechow in Meinem Leben 4-10-85
Tsui Tai-Chi 8-21-85
Tuff Turf 1-9-85
Tuntematon Sotilas 2-5-86
Tupac Amaru 8-28-85
Turk 182 2-6-85
Turn of the Screw, The (See: Otra Vuelta de Tuerca)
Turn-On (See: Declic, Le)
Turncoat, The (See: Transfuge, Le)
Turtle Diary 9-11-85
Tutta Colpa del Paradiso 1-15-86
Tuttobenigni 3-26-86
TV and the Hotel, The (See: Telo y la Tele, El)
Twelfth Night 4-30-86
28 Up 3-20-85
27 Horas 10-1-86
27 Hours (See: 27 Horas)
Twice in a Lifetime 9-18-85
Twist Again a Moscou 12-24-86
Twist Again in Moscow (See: Twist Again a Moscou)
Twisted Passion 10-23-85
Two Cops, The (See: Due Carabinieri, I)
Two Faces of January (See: Zwei Gesichter des Januar, Die)
Two Friends 5-14-86
Two Lives of Mattia Pascal, The (See: Due Vite di Mattia
    Pascal, Le)
2020 Texas Gladiators 11-13-85
Two Valentianos (See: Tuo Valentianos)
Typhoon Club 6-12-85

U

Uemura Naomi Monogatari 5-28-86
Ultima Mazurka, L' 10-15-86
Umi-Tori 3-20-85
Una 3-6-85
Unbesiegbare, Der 10-2-85

V

W

Z

X

Y